The Future of Peace

in the Twenty-First Century

A Reader and Sourcebook

Then went Samson...to Timnath...and, behold,
a young lion came roaring against him.
And the spirit of the Lord came mightily upon Samson...
and he had nothing in his hand...
and Samson tore the lion apart...
And after a time Samson returned...and he turned
aside to see the carcase of the lion: and behold, there was
a swarm of bees and honey in the carcase of the lion...
And Samson said:
And out of the fierce came forth sweetness.
—Judges 14:6-14

Cover illustration: *Samson and the Lion* by P.P. Rubens. Reprinted by permission of the National Museum of Fine Arts, Stockholm, Sweden

To Mitigate Domestic Discontents and Harmonize Global Diversity

The Future of Peace in the Twenty-First Century

Edited by
Dr. Nicholas N. Kittrie, KStJ
H.E. Rodrigo Carazo
H.E. James R. Mancham, KBE

Carolina Academic Press
Durham, North Carolina

Published in the United States by
Carolina Academic Press
700 Kent Street
Durham, NC 27701
Phone: 919-489-7486
Fax: 919-493-5668
Email: cap@cap-press.com
Web: www.cap-press.com
for
The Eleanor Roosevelt Institute for Justice and Peace
2023 Q Street, NW
Washington, DC 20009-1009

Cover Illustration, *Samson and the Lion,* by P.P. Rubens courtesy of The National Museum of Fine Arts, Stockholm, Sweden.

ISBN: 0-89089-211-3
LCCN: 2002117086

In Celebration
of the One Hundredth Anniversary
of the
Nobel Peace Prize

and as

A Multicultural and Multidisciplinary
Reader and Sourcebook
for the
Second Centenary
of the
Nobel Peace Prize
2002–2101

Peace, Peace,
and there is no Peace
—Jeremiah 8:11

Credits, Acknowledgments, and Editor's Notes

Credits:

Associate Editors:
Gordon Anderson, Cameron Hudson
Editorial Associates:
Laureen Enright, Katherine Newell, Nancy Schapiro

Executive Editor:
Georgette Sobel
Assistants to the Executive Editor:
Justin Pimenta, Fred Pirone

Cover design:
Larry Orman

Administration:
Tawana Warren

Editors Note:
The papers included in this volume are from authors in a variety of disciplines. No effort was made to edit these papers for consistency of style; thus, individual styles of the authors remain intact.

Every effort has been made to contact all rights holders of reprinted material in this printing of *The Future of Peace in the Twenty-First Century.* The editors promise to correct any omissions or mistakes in acknowledgments if there are future editions.

Acknowledgments:
The Editors of this volume and The Eleanor Roosevelt Institute for Justice and Peace wish to thank the following individuals for their support and efforts, assisting our quest toward peace in the twenty-first century to become a reality: Gregory Breland, Allan Gerson, Norge Jerome, Patrick Kirkbride, Arthur Kobrine, Chung Hwan Kwak, Frank LaGrotteria, Eugene Miknowski, Frank Moscarillo, Neil A. Salonen, Betty Sitka, Adrienne Smith, Frederick Swarts, Lourdes Swarts, Megumi Ueda, Thomas Walsh, Paul Williams, Rosemary Yokoi, Shunichiro Yoshida, and Andrezj Werner, President and Director of the Jean de Bloch Society in Warsaw, Poland.

Contents

PART SIX

Confronting the Universal Quest for Identity: Family, Religion, and Culture

PART SEVEN

Pluralism and Its Discontents: Harmonizing Domestic and Global Diversity

PART EIGHT

Arts, Science and Technology in the Service of Peace

Foreword

H. E. Oscar Arias
Former President of Costa Rica and 1987 Nobel Peace Laureate

Now that the twentieth century is behind us, we may allow ourselves some moments of retrospection before turning our gaze towards the future. As we look back upon the century just ended, we see two major world wars; two totalitarian doctrines which, after wreaking havoc on the earth, by the end of the century were buried; we see the holocaust; and we see countless conflicts that have taken millions of lives, not only of soldiers, but increasingly of civilians, especially women and children. One shudders at the continued barbarity of the human species.

Today we are at the threshold of a new century; perhaps we can forge something different. Over the past fifty years the world has grown more selfish, and we have seen this selfishness manifest itself in many ways: as a lack of leadership, a lack of wisdom, a lack of compassion, a lack of love. The new century must be one in which these qualities we have been lacking begin to predominate in governments, in organizations, in businesses, in academics, and in our daily lives. We must revive the best in the human spirit in order to combat the worst manifestations of selfish violence that we have ever seen.

The most essential action the world must take to eliminate conflict in the coming decades is to work to alleviate poverty. Not only are conflicts most likely to occur in poor countries, as a quick glance at current events will show, but poverty itself is a form of violence. In a world with so much wealth, the extreme social inequality and poverty that we see today are morally unacceptable.

Through all their suffering, the poor have been weary witnesses to history. They have seen the rise of dictators who promised law and order, and the triumph of revolutions that called for a new sharing of wealth. They were there to see these ideologies exposed as empty promises. They have seen government funds enrich both self-appointed and democratically elected leaders, while their lot has remained unchanged. They have seen aid flow into their countries from Cold War superpowers anxious to garner strategic support, only to see that aid dry up when armed conflicts ended. They have learned the bitter lesson that the wealthy and powerful nations of the world are more interested in investing in war than in peace. They have paid with their blood.

Many governments continue to give aid based on their own strategic interests rather than on the needs of the world's poor. Some countries give the bulk of their foreign aid in the form of weapons, something which is absolutely contrary to the principles of development and peace. Delivering weapons to poor countries always has the effect of putting a spark to a powder keg. Where desperate poverty and social injustice meet weapons proliferation, the only result is violence, and further postponement of the hopes for rebuilding economies and societies.

Powerful nations are not only committing an immoral act by selling and giving weapons to countries too poor to afford them and too beaten down to bear their consequences. They are also damaging their own long-term interests. The growth of global trade and interdependence demonstrates, today more than ever, that the developed countries stand to benefit more from stable, well-fed and well-educated populations in the developing world than from continued poverty and prolonged conflict.

It is widely recognized that the best way to help poor countries is through freer trade, but the reality is that the markets of wealthy countries remain effectively closed to the exports of poor countries, in particular their agricultural products. Debt relief programs have begun, but the relief that has so far been offered to the poorest countries is a mere token. Not only should the poorest countries receive more debt relief, but such relief should also be extended to those countries that are not the poorest in absolute terms, but that have healthy priorities: that is, those that spend more on health and education than on their militaries.

Eliminating poverty is not only the task of the leaders of wealthy nations. The governments of the developing world also have their part to play. In some countries, half of the population lives in slums, while members of the military ride air-conditioned jeeps in parades that are offensive to human dignity. As long as the leaders of some countries spend more on their military establishments than they spend on the health care and education of their citizens, they are condemning their people to poverty.

It will be a long road to ensure the security of those billions of people who live in the developing world. By security I mean not only the lack of conflict and violence, but also the security of food, the security of having work and a livelihood, and the security of medical care and education. Until these needs are taken care of, the world will not have lasting peace.

Everyone has a role to play in bringing this security about. The business sector must contribute to economic growth in the developing world that brings benefits to all involved, and not only a lucky few. This will entail foreign investment that incorporates principles of fairness and respect, as well as truly free trade, in which the wealthy countries open their markets to the exports of developing countries. At the same time, the people of developing countries must work to strengthen their democracies, fight corruption, and support actions for a better future. The leaders of developing countries must place a high priority on the education and health of their citizens. Civil society must continue to raise its cry against the madness of arms build-up and officially sanctioned violence as means of resolving conflicts. It should be clear to the world by now that, as Martin Luther King once wrote, "violence merely increases hate.... Darkness cannot drive out darkness, only light can do that. Hatred cannot drive out hatred, only love can do that."

The bottom line is that we must all do our part to create a world in which the values that predominate are generosity, tolerance, and respect, rather than greed, hatred and cynicism. The transformation of values is a change that spreads slowly and silently, but surely, around the world. There are encouraging signs: much of the barbarity that was considered "normal" a hundred years ago is no longer tolerated, in most places. If we can continue to bring to light violations of the most basic standards of humanity, and at the same time work to change people's hearts, then the struggle for peace will continue to gain ground, until the world is ever so gently wrapped in its embrace.

Preface

Dr. Jehan Sadat
Former First Lady of Egypt

The future belongs to those who believe in the beauty of their dreams. —Eleanor Roosevelt

If the future is guided only by the failures of the past, then the twenty-first century is doomed to the devastation of war, the pain of poverty, and the marginalization of illiteracy. On the other hand, if the future can be shaped by people of good will, by those who dream of a better life for their countries and their people, then peace will prevail in the twenty-first century, prosperity and development will be possible for all nations and individuals, and the tragedies of the past will never again repeat themselves. A just, comprehensive, and lasting peace in the Middle East was my husband's dream; his dream is still mine.

At the dawn of the Third Millennium, most people thought of terrorism as something happening to a particular people in a faraway land. Then came September 11. Suddenly the fists of terrorism were beating at the doors of the most powerful nation in the world, crumbling two of the world's largest buildings, splitting apart one of the world's largest military headquarters, and destroying the future for thousands of innocent victims from nearly a hundred different nations. In a matter of hours, terrorism was no longer isolated incidences but rather a worldwide issue, a global blight threatening the safety and security of peace-loving people throughout the world.

I was glued to the television screen, but in my mind, I was in Cairo and it was October 6, 1981. The Sixth of October is a day all Egypt celebrates our victory in the 1973 War, a victory that opened the road to peace between Egypt and Israel. With my grandchildren by my side, I could see my husband proudly reviewing the troops, and I could see him when he turned to smile at me. Then, in an instant and without warning, I was watching terrorists robbing him of his life. Although I tried with all the power in me, I could do nothing to help my husband, nothing to stop those angry, misguided men who were determined to take him from me.

The memory of that day like the memory of September 11, 2001 will be with me forever. I will not, however, allow memories of inexplicable hatred and violence, as vivid as they are, dictate the course of my life. Nor can the memories and anger felt by the civilized world concerning the tragedy of September 11 and its subsequent events dictate the course of theirs. If this were so, then there would be no hope for peace, now or in the future. Mahatma Gandhi, one of my husband's heroes, wrote that if man continues to seek an eye for an eye, then eventually the whole world will be blind. It is time for the peacemakers to step forward and be heard despite any objections and threats hurled at them just as Anwar Sadat did in November, 1977 when he took his message of peace directly to the Israeli people. My husband and I both knew the risks he would be taking if he recognized the right of Israel to exist and to live with us as neighbors. But my husband had the courage, the foresight, and the boldness to do what no other leader of the region was prepared to do: propose peace between Arabs and Israelis. All that he did to bring us peace and the way he did it prove that honest, sincere, and direct dialogue among leaders, not revenge and retaliation, is the gateway to peace. Sadat's method worked then, and it will work now.

My husband knew that without peace no society or nation can truly advance and develop. This is as true now as it has always been. But development can only be accomplished in an environment of peace. Providing for education and health care, improving the standard of living, and creating jobs —especially for the young people—require huge financial commitments by governments with the support from intense and prolonged human dedication, determination, and energy. What then can any single human being do within the broad scope of the problems facing the world today? Perhaps nothing. On the other hand, we can choose to follow the examples given by gentle, unassuming men and women who dreamed of a better way and whose lives echo the eternal message of peace on earth. Together, we can build a future of peace in the twenty-first century.

Realistically, I know the future will not be free of conflict, but surely the solutions to our conflicts can exact a less catastrophic toll if our hearts were to embrace and our hands were to practice the tenets of peace. Mahatma Gandhi, Nelson Mandela, and Anwar Sadat were ordinary men with extraordinary courage. Each possessed a dream of peace for his people. Each was willing to make the personal sacrifices to make these dreams come true. My husband's dream of peace changed the course of history for Egypt, Israel, and the world. Peace filled his heart, and peace became the reality of his actions.

Although each of us will not be the President of a country or the leader of a people, each of us can be an example of peace. And we can start the quest for peace in the confines of our homes. We can talk and listen to each other even when we disagree. We can possess a spirit of hope and reconciliation, proving that only in giving to others do we receive ourselves. We can teach our children how to love not hate, accept not reject, wage peace not war. We can practice forgiveness in our daily lives, for forgiveness forms the foundation of peace. When we do not forgive the evil done to us, then we are turning that same evil against ourselves and those we love.

In light of recent events and the spread of conflict throughout the world, I can understand why people find it difficult to talk about, even imagine, a world of peace, a way of life in which love ultimately defeats the forces of evil. Yet as I write this, I can see my husband and President Carter and Prime Minister Begin—the Muslim, the Christian, and the Jew—signing the document that ended decades of war between Egypt and Israel. With that day so vividly in my memory, how could I forsake the possibility of peace? How could I dismiss the fact that my husband gave his life for peace? How could I, the widow of this great statesman, abandon his dream? Despite the tragedies and suffering in my own life, despite the animosity I see existing between nations and peoples today, I still believe in peace. I believe a just, comprehensive, and lasting peace will come to the Middle East. Furthermore, I believe a path to peace can be found in the heart of Europe, in Indonesia, the Korean Peninsula, anywhere on the face of this earth when leaders truly want peace and are willing to do all in their power to make peace.

As you read the essays of the learned professors, scientists, politicians, philosophers, and journalists, men and women searching for peace; remember the words and deeds of the world's great peacemakers. Be inspired by them, and dream of peace, pray for peace, work for peace, long for the day in which peace will prevail. And remember these words written by Anwar Sadat, "When the bells of peace ring, there can be no hands to beat the drums of war."

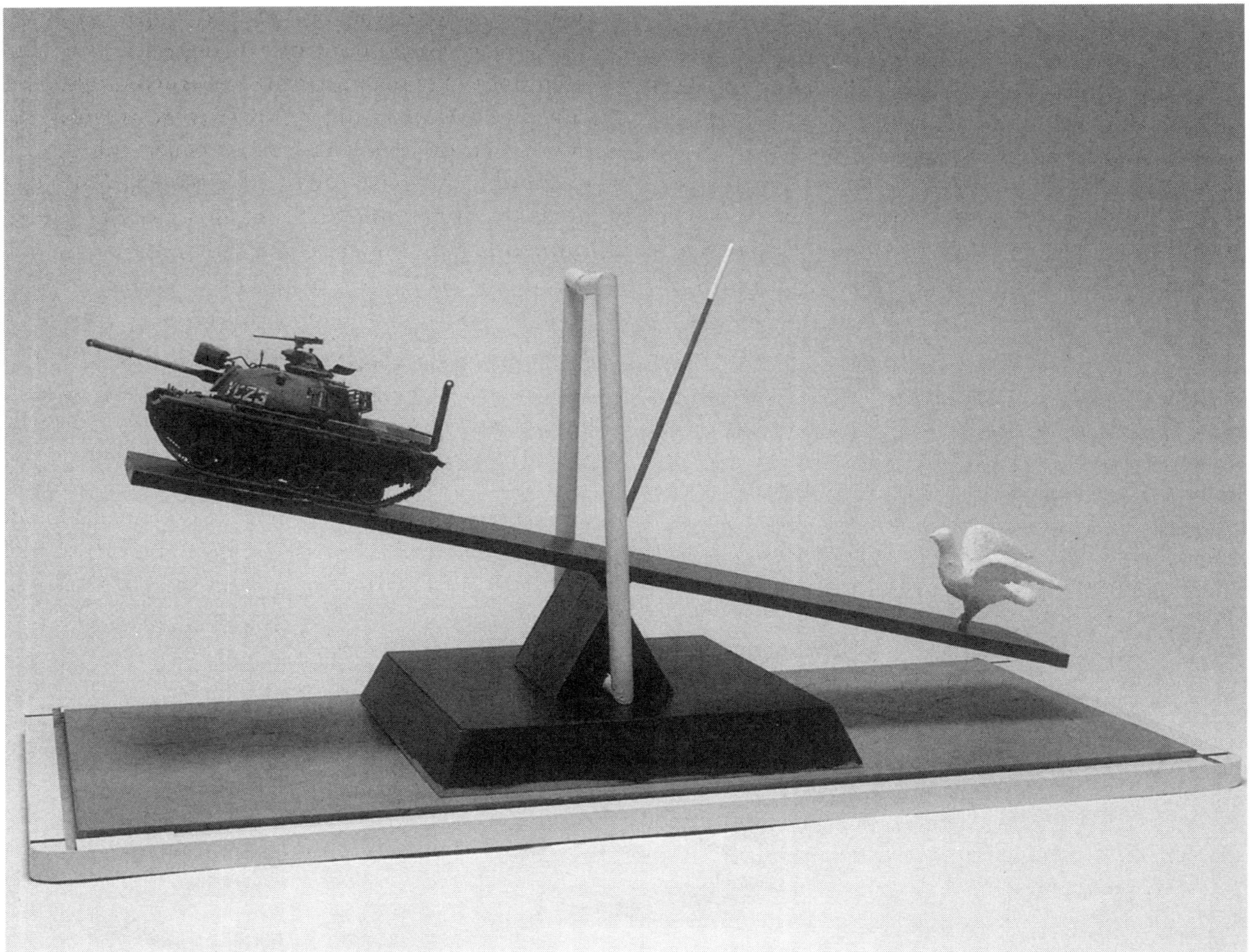

Courtesy of the artist.

The Weight of Peace by Baruch Wind

Prologue

War is on its last legs; and a universal Peace is as sure as is the prevalence of civilization over barbarism, of liberal governments over feudal forms. The question for us is only how soon?

—Ralph Waldo Emerson (1803-1882)

From the War of the Future to the Future of Peace

Dr. Nicholas N. Kittrie, KStJ
American University Washington College of Law

Perpetual Peace is no empty idea...

—Immanuel Kant

When Alfred Nobel, an entrepreneurial scientist and the inventor of dynamite, who was described as a man with "astounding antitheses—dynamite and pacifism, socialistic beliefs and a vast fortune," provided in his 1895 will for the creation of a world prize for peace—which assumed the form of a diploma, a gold medal and 150,000 Norwegian kroner—to be awarded each year to "champions of peace," his beneficence did not spring forth in a political and scholarly vacuum. A growing interest in reducing the ravages of war, and in pursuing avenues for peace, was long on its way, at least on the European continent.

Many historians, politicians, students of war and peace activists, have pointed to numerous earlier signs of humanity's striving for more pacific communities of peoples, clans, tribes and nations. Admonitions against the extreme war-time destruction of the environment or the particularly cruel and inhuman treatment of war captives, have been noted not only in biblical texts ranging from Genesis through Kings, but also in earlier scriptures of various other cultures: East and West, North and South. Yet, century after century, the rise and fall of civilizations and empires, the massive and constant population shifts, the invasions of indigenous communities (in Africa, Asia, the Americas, Australia, as well as Europe) by both so-called "barbarians" and "civilizers," and the unquestioning recognition of the sovereign right of chieftains, kings, princes and others in power to wage war, produced nearly a total disregard for the refinements of warfare and the stirings for peace.

Still, the centuries beginning with the Crusaders incursions into the Orient through the Age of Enlightenment, and then on from the convulsive post-French Revolutionary era to the European drive for pan-national unifications, particularly in Italy and Germany, gave rise to many changes in the conduct of war and to earnest considerations of the possibilities of peace. Beginning especially at the end of the eighteenth century and continuing through the late nineteenth century's rational, liberal and pacificist individuals and organizations, both church-connected and secular, were much in evidence, particularly in Europe and later in the United States. However, they mostly had limited appeal or success. Several noted exceptions must be recognized, however. These included the efforts of Dutch scholar and diplomat Hugo Grotius, who in his 1625 treatise, *De Jure Belli ac Pacis*, articulated that era's customary rules of war and peace. Important also was the systematic compilation of legal military standards, carried out by Austrian immigrant scholar Francis Lieber upon the request of President Abraham Lincoln, for the conduct of the Union Army in America's Civil War.

There were however, many other earlier and later attempts in the pursuit of peace that need to be recognized. Particularly outstanding was William Penn's nearly utopian program in 1672 for the peaceful resolution of conflicts between Pennsylvania's European settlers and the displaced local Native Americans. Attention must be drawn, furthermore, to the numerous proposals, resolutions, congresses, conferences, institutions, conventions and a persistent stream of scholarly and popular writings pleading for, or intended to serve, the world community's commitment to peace. But it was not until the very last decades of the nineteenth century that the interest in the prevention or curtailment of warfare gained major momentum.

In 1898, Jean de Bloch, a wealthy Russian-Polish industrialist who made his fortune in railroad construction and in international trade, published his voluminous six-part text on *The War of the Future* (*La Guerre*). Concerned about the economic as well as human costs of war, de Bloch assembled detailed data about the national costs of armaments and warfare. His analysis concluded that the economic and social well-being of Russia, as well as of the other countries of Europe, would be most adversely affected by both the weapons races and the actual conduct of hostilities. His carefully compiled evidence offered the proof "that war would ultimately become impossible through sheer expense and deadliness." To Jean de Bloch, war, evidently, was much less a moral question than an unbearable economic burden.

Due in part to de Bloch's compelling arguments and evidence, and, furthermore, in response to his own and to some of his counselors economic as well as humanitarian considerations, Czar Nicholas II authorized the issuance on August 24, 1898 of an unexpected Rescript. The document called for an international conference, to be convened in the Hague, in order to address the dangers posed by war, both as a destroyer of civilization and as an imposer of intolerable armament burdens. To be discussed also was the gradual displacement of warfare by the pacific settlement of disputes.

Throughout the world the peace movements and their leaders seized the opportunity to declare war on war. Twenty-six countries were present at the 1899 Hague Conference. The work was carried out through three committees: one on armament, another on the laws of war, and a third on international arbitration and conciliation. While calling for the codification of the laws of war and doing the groundwork for the establishment of a Court of International arbitration, the 1899 Conference was described, nevertheless, as securing not disarmament but only "the disarmament spirit." It was this new surge of energy that led the subsequent Hague Conference of 1907 to produce what remains to this day the most fundamental international code for the conduct of military hostilities. But much like before, the 1907 Conference concentrated on war and its regulation rather than on the pursuit and establishment of peace.

It is significant, and worth reiterating at this point, that the interests, concerns, benevolence, and charity of Swedish inventor and philanthropist Alfred Nobel were addressed primarily to the realms of the sciences and literature. Yet he was also drawn into the arena which has, since the days of Biblical Cain and Abel, posed the greatest threat to humanity and its well-being: the taking of human life—whether individually as in murder, or en masse by means of war.

While the granting of the other Nobel Prizes was delegated to the Swedish Academy of Sciences, and the Caroline Institute of Stockholm, responsibility for the Nobel Peace Prize was vested in a committee to be elected by the Norwegian Storting (parliament). No authoritative explanation for this diversion was ever advanced. Some attributed the Norwegian gesture to the fact that in Nobel's time Norway and Sweden constituted a unitary kingdom.

Accordingly, the benefactor of the prizes, that were soon to become world benchmarks, wanted both countries of his heritage to share in his bounty. Whatever the reason, Alfred Nobel's will failed to specify the objectives and standards that were to apply to the granting of his Peace Prizes. The most specific instruction given was that the Prize was to recognize the person who shall have done the most or the best work for *"fraternity between nations"* (emphasis supplied).

Nobel's sketchy and vague instructions would prove to become a burden upon the Norwegian Prize Committee in decades to come. What was the scope of the "peace" envisioned by Alfred Nobel? Was his concern exclusively for peace among states or nations, or did he also consider peace between governments and the governed, as well as peace among diverse segments of the population? What "doings" or "work" referred to by Nobel—whether communicative or physical—were intended, by the benefactor, to qualify one for candidacy? Were the candidacy ranks to include only, or mostly, statesmen, politicians, and those engaged in the signing or ratification of treaties, peace agreements and armistices? Were scholars and researchers, seeking innovative explanations for the causes of war and offering creative approaches to the institution of peace, to be encouraged in their efforts by means of the prizes? Were scientific, economic, social, political, cultural and religious workers, contributing to the enrichment of the quality of human life and to global harmony, to be equally eligible? Were human rights watchers, anti-war protestors, environmental militants, and genocide resisters to be high on the list of candidates for Nobel laureates?

As one reviews and studies carefully the list of Nobel Peace Prize honorees during the Prize's first century, many questions seem inescapable. Have the prizes much too often been given to persons of notoriety, known for a single, and not always sufficiently significant, act, event or accomplishment? Have some prizes been given prematurely, for accomplishments which at the very end resulted in fiascos (i.e., the 1973 award to Viet Cong's Le Duc Tho and United States' Henry Kissinger; the 1994 award to Palestinian Authority's Yasser Arafat and Israel's Shimon Peres and Yitzhak Rabin)? Have some prizes been deliberately, unreasonably or thoughtlessly denied to other highly deserving candidates?

The absence, except one, of Nobel Peace laureates from the religious services category, in light of the tremendous role religion has and can play in the furtherance of peace, is inexplicable. The absence of international jurists from the list of prize winners since 1919 is similarly puzzling, for it appears to the common mind that in most societies law has served as one of the more important alternatives to conflict and violence. No behavioral scientists appear anytime in the list of honorees. Nor have economists, sociologists, and other social scientists ever graced the company of recipients. Significant also is the fact that prize winners in the human rights category go back only to 1960. Accordingly, many of the former 107 recipients have faded, deservedly, into oblivion, and some of the others have failed to make long lasting contributions. In consequence, the names and achievements of many Nobel Peace Prize laureates are unknown, and often unworthy of notice, a century, a decade or even a year later.

This volume on "The Future of Peace" consists of recently assembled and mostly specially commissioned essays, enriched by the inclusion of some earlier classical or otherwise worthy contributions. The editors have sought, through this carefully constructed collection to portray and reflect in depth upon the numerous issues involved in and the requisites necessary for the establishment of a sustainable peace. In the first place, unlike Jean de Bloch's six-volume treatise, our emphasis in upon *"The Future of Peace,"* not *"The War of the Future."* The objective of these multi-disciplinary and broad-ranging essays is to reflect on past approaches and proposals and to explore, address and suggest such fitting remedies as are sufficient not merely to reduce the underlying causes of conflict, but are likely, moreover, to enhance the chances and opportunities for peace. Unlike de Bloch and his generation, and most writers and activists of the past century, we can no longer be satisfied with mere "humanitarian warfare"—which primarily seeks to reduce the ravages of war. Unless the underlying causes of conflict and war, whether material, emotional, or spiritual, whether rational or irrational, are addressed and alleviated; unless newer and more effective problem-solving and conflict resolution methods and institutions are advanced and are firmly established; unless effective mediating and conciliating means are instituted and implemented, a widespread and lasting peace is not likely in the foreseeable future, if ever in our lifetime.

Moreover, in light of the realities of the contemporary world, Alfred Nobel's fundamental premise about the required partners for the effective carrying out of the peace mission, appears considerably lacking. One can understand that being a product of the nineteenth century, a century which saw the growth of nationalism, which dwelled on the nation as the primary and legitimate unit of governing authority, and which was committed to the proposition that peace and war are primarily the instruments of nations, Nobel believed, quite expectedly, that emphasis upon furthering the fraternity of *nations* was the key to viable peace. His was an era in which it was believed that Pan-Germanism and Pan-Italianism—which called for the bringing together in one single state all members of a dispersed or fragmented nation—were the first steps towards peace. Beyond that, he quite reasonably believed that we must see to it that all nations, the German nation, the Italian nation, the French nation and the United Kingdom nation, were to be made increasingly aware of their fraternity. What that era's concept of the fraternity of nations ignored is today's compelling reality of the need for a greater recognition of the fraternity of all *humankind:* men and women, old and young, rich and poor, urban and rural, religious and secular.

Individuals, men and women, are not islands unto themselves. They belong not only to nations, but also to clans, tribes, religions, ideologies, castes and economic classes. The recent disturbances in Ireland, Corsica, the former Yugoslavia, Rwanda, Cambodia, Sri Lanka, Spain, and Turkey testify to this reality. No approach to peace and no peace formula which ignores the reality that most contemporary states are not made up of one homogenous nation—that most nation-states usually consist of diverse national, ethnic, religious, linguistic, or economic communities—will be capable of producing a sustainable peace. The eras following World War II, and particularly the Cold War, clearly demonstrate that the greatest number of conflicts and war-like conduct involved intra national rather than international discontents. The quest for peace must, therefore, search out and seek to overcome not merely the discontent of nations, but the discontents of people, and the various categories, organizations, classes and groups to which these people belong.

A realistic, meaningful and contemporary concept of peace must apply, therefore, not only to traditional international warfare but also to domestic, or communal, violence and war. Peace, furthermore, cannot be completely satisfied and maintained, even if measures dealing with intra national conflicts are added to the agenda for controlling traditional international warfare. The evidence is compelling that not only conflicts between nations, or between sub-national communities, have been disturbing the peace of the globe. Possibly the greatest disturbance of peace and the toll of human life and suffering can be attributed, unfortunately, to wars waged by governments against their citizenries.

The thrust of this volume, therefore, is not merely peace between nations. Peace cannot be partial, applicable to only one human community, the nation, while overlooking such sub-national communities as family, ethnic, religious, cultural and class affiliations. It is, moreover, to a broader concept of peace, to the remedying of the underlying causes preventing fuller peace, to achieving not merely the absence of war, but the attainment of mutual, cooperative, and constructive peace, that this volume is committed. It is such comprehensive peace, its requisites and implications, that have been inadequately addressed to date by existing international political and financial organizations, and by the scholarly and peace-advocacy communities.

The quest for the outlining and implementation of such peace, and possibly its diverse variations, need not be viewed as an unattainable utopian. Particularly relevant to such quest are the myriad avenues for cooperation between international and national entities and organizations, between the public and private sectors, between government bureaucracies and civil society, between the sciences and arts of governance and the economic, social and behavioral disciplines. Peace, as we have noted, must be recognized as a much more complex institution than the end of the nineteenth century peace advocates realized. The time has come for all of us, and particularly the Nobel Peace Prize Committee, to go beyond bestowing recognitions upon a few worthy, and at time lesser, people and events known for their visibility. The Nobel Peace Prize Committee, admittedly, is not a research and grant making agency. Yet, by its very acts of recognition, it has the prestige and capacity to impact, to encourage and to stimulate the work of peace researchers and implementers worldwide. This prestige and capacity need be exercised vigorously.

This volume, in summary, not only presents a carefully constructed worldwide panorama of the peace quest to date, but advocates and invites the Nobel Peace Prize Committee, as well as the wider community of scholars and activists, to endorse and explore the broadest scope and objectives in the pursuit of peace. We, further, call for more concerted efforts to explore, demonstrate and perfect the *character* and *makeup* of peace as a central principle—indeed a lynch-pin—in the agendas of students, scholars, peace workers, and peace promoting and recognizing agencies throughout the world.

War, by Pablo Picasso

Part One

Confronting the Prophets of War

In war, whichever side may call itself the victor,
there are no winners…

—Neville Chamberlain (1938)

Peace is better than a place in history.

—Justo Pastor Benitez (1935)

A COMPREHENSIVE EXAMINATION of the future of peace must necessarily address, however briefly, the primary causes of its natural corollary: war. The five essays in Part One are intended to fill this need. The reader is presented, essentially, with two conflicting hypotheses regarding the roots of warfare: the first argues that evil, conflict and war are inherent in the human makeup. The second urges that war is an inescapable product of man's socio-economic and cultural environment. The essays in Part One cast different lights on this fundamental question and bring considerable diversity to the arguments regarding the symbiotic relationship between man and warfare.

The very nature and causes of war have been a long-queried area of scholarship, stretching across manifold academic disciplines. Beginning with Freud's pre-eminent psychoanalytical analysis of man's proclivity to war, this collection is ultimately framed by a nature vs. nurture dichotomy. Are the discontents, hostilities and evils that exist in the world, and the wars they engender, the result of the fundamental human nature or are they instead the behavioral manifestations of the inherently conflictual environment we inhabit? Though both arguments might be viewed as putting forward a pessimistic view of the future of peace, their divergence is worthy of study.

The future, indeed, is not all that unpromising. The first school of thought, as we noted, seeks to demonstrate that man simply succumbs to the violence which is apart of him. An appropriate response to this school is thus likely to point out the imperative need for institutions and sanctions that will harness, control, manipulate or rehabilitate this inherent evil nature. The response to the second school which sees violence and war as products of the physical and social environment, will dwell more heavily on the need to reform man's physical and social environment: by eliminating or reducing poverty, ignorance, broken families, and other deprivations. Regardless of which school one favors, and even if one chooses a combination of both approaches, the reforming tasks will be demanding and lengthy. In the final analysis, society will not for long be able to escape the ravages of evil, conflict and war.

Why War?—A Letter to Albert Einstein

Sigmund Freud
Psychoanalyst (1856-1937)

You begin with the relation between Right and Might. There can be no doubt that that is the correct starting point for our investigation. But may I replace the word 'might' by the bolder and harsher word 'violence'? Today right and violence appear to us as antithesis. It can easily be shown, however, that the one has developed out of the other; and, if we go back to the earliest beginnings and see how that first came about, the problem is easily solved.

It is a general principle that conflicts of interest between men are settled by the use of violence. This is true of the whole animal kingdom, from which men have no business to exclude themselves. To begin with, in a small human group, it was superior muscular strength which decided who owned things or whose will should prevail. Muscular strength was soon supplemented and replaced by the use of tools; the winner was the one who had the better weapons or who used them more skillfully. From the moment at which weapons were introduced, intellectual superiority already began to replace brute muscular strength; but the final purpose of the fight remained the same—one side or the other was to be compelled to abandon his claim or his objection by the damage inflicted on him and by the crippling of his strength. That purpose was most completely achieved if the victor's violence eliminated his opponent permanently—that is to say, killed him. Such, then, was the original state of things: domination by whoever had the greater might—domination by brute violence or by violence supported by intellect. As we know, this regime was altered in the course of evolution. There was a path that led from violence to right or law. What was that path? It is my belief that there was only one: the path which led by way of the fact that the superior strength of a single individual could be rivalled by the union of several weak ones. *'L'union fait la force.* Violence could be broken by union, and the power of those who were united now represented law in contrast to the violence of the single individual. Thus we see that right is the might of a community. It is still violence, ready to be directed against any individual who resists it; it works by the same methods and follows the same purposes. The only real difference lies in the fact that what prevails is no longer the violence of an individual but that of a community. But in order that the transition from violence to this new right or justice may be effected, one psychological condition must be fulfilled. The union of the majority must be a stable and lasting one. If it were only brought about for the purpose of combating a single dominant individual and were dissolved after his defeat, nothing would have been accomplished. The community must be maintained permanently, must be organized, must draw up regulations to anticipate the risk of rebellion and must institute authorities to see that those regulations—the laws—are respected and to superintend the execution of legal acts of violence. The recognition of a community of interests such as these leads to the growth of emotional ties between the members of a united group of people—communal feelings which are the true source of its strength.

From that time forward there are two factors at work in the community which are sources of unrest over matters of law but tend at the same time to a further growth of law. First, attempts are made by certain of the rulers to set themselves above the prohibitions which apply to everyone—they seek, that is, to go back from a dominion of law to a dominion of violence. Secondly, the oppressed members of the group make constant efforts to obtain more power and to have any changes that are brought about in that direction recognized in the laws—they press forward that is from unequal justice to equal justice for all. This second tendency becomes especially important if a real shift of power occurs within a community, as may happen as a result of a number of historical factors. In that case right may gradually adapt itself to the new distribution of power; or, as is more frequent, the ruling class is unwilling to recognize the change, and rebellion and civil war follow, with a temporary suspension of law and new attempts at a solution by violence, ending in the establishment of a fresh rule of law. There is yet another source from which modifications of law may arise, and one of which expression is invariably peaceful: it lies in the cultural transformation of the members of the community. This, however, belongs properly in another connection and must be considered later.

Thus we see that the violent solution of conflicts is not avoided even inside a community. However, the everyday necessities and common concerns of a community will tend to bring such struggles to a swift conclusion and create an increasing probability that peaceful solutions will be found. Yet a glance at the history of the human race reveals an endless series of conflicts between one community and another or several others, between larger and smaller units—between cities, provinces, races, nations, empires—which have always been settled by force of arms. Wars of this kind end either in the spoliation or in the complete overthrow and conquest of one of the parties. It is impossible to make any sweeping judgement upon wars of conquest. Some have brought nothing but evil. Others, on the contrary, have contributed to the transformation of violence into law by establishing larger units within which the use of violence was made impossible and in which a fresh system of law led to the solution of conflicts. In this way the conquests of the Romans gave the countries round the Mediterranean the priceless Pax Romana. Paradoxical as it may sound, it must he admitted that war might be a far from inappropriate means of establishing the eagerly desired reign of 'everlasting peace' since it is in a position to create the large units within which a powerful central government makes further wars impossible. Nevertheless it fails in this purpose, for the results of conquest are as a rule short-lived: the newly created units fall apart once again, usually owing to a lack of cohesion between the portions that have been united by violence. Hitherto, moreover, such unifications have only been partial, and the conflicts between these have called out more than ever for a violent solution. Thus the result of all these warlike efforts has only been that the human race has exchanged numerous, and indeed unending, minor wars for wars on a grand scale that are rare but all the more destructive.

If we turn to our own times, we arrive at the following conclusion. Wars will only be prevented if mankind unites in setting up a central authority to which the right of giving judgement upon all conflicts of interest shall be handed over. There are clearly two separate requirements involved in this: the creation of a supreme agency and its endowment with the necessary power. One without the other would be quite useless. The League of Nations is designed as an agency of this kind, but the second condition has not been fulfilled: the League of Nations has no power of its own and can only acquire it if the members of the new union, the separate States, are ready to resign it. And at the moment there seems very little prospect of this.

I can now proceed to discuss another of your remarks. You express astonishment at the fact that it is so easy to make men enthusiastic about a war and add your suspicions that there is something at work in them—an instinct for hatred and destruction—which goes halfway to meet the efforts of the warmongers. Once again, I can only express my entire agreement.

According to our hypothesis human instincts are of only two kinds: those which seek to preserve and unite—which we call 'erotic' exactly in the same sense in which Plato uses the word 'Eros' in his *Symposium* or 'sexual', with a deliberate extension of the popular conception of sexuality—and those which seek to destroy and kill and which we group together as the aggressive or destructive instinct. Neither of these instincts is any less essential than the other; the phenomena of life arise from the mutually opposing actions of both. Now it seems as though an instinct of the one sort can scarcely ever operate in isolation; it is always accompanied—or, as we say, alloyed—with a certain quota from the other side, which modifies its aim or is, in some cases, what enables it to achieve that aim. It is very rarely that an action is the work of a single instinctual impulse. In order to make an action possible there must be as a rule a combination of compounded motives.

I should like to linger for a moment over our destructive instinct whose popularity is by no means equal to its importance. As a result of a little speculation, we have come to suppose that this instinct is at work in every living creature and is striving to bring it to ruin and to reduce life to its original condition of inanimate matter. Thus it quite seriously deserves to be called a death instinct, while the erotic instincts represent the effort to live. The death instinct turns into the destructive instinct when it is directed outwards on to objects. Some portion of the death instinct, however, remains operative within the organism, and we have sought to trace quite a number of phenomena to this internalization of the destructive instinct. You will notice that it is by no means a trivial matter if this process is carried too far: it is positively unhealthy. On the other hand if these forces are turned to destruction in the external world, the organism will be relieved and the effect must be beneficial. This would serve as a biological justification for all the ugly and dangerous impulses against which we are struggling.

For our immediate purposes, then, this much follows from what has been said: there is no use in trying to get rid of men's aggressive inclination. We are told that in certain happy regions of the earth, where nature provides in abundance everything that man requires, there are races whose life is passed in tranquility and who know neither coercion nor aggression. I can scarcely believe it and I should be glad to know more of these fortunate beings. In any case, as you yourself have remarked, there is no question of getting rid entirely of human aggressive impulses; it is enough to try to divert them to such an extent that they need not find expression in war.

Our mythological theory of instincts makes it easy for us to find a formula for indirect methods of combating war. If willingness to engage in war is an effect of the destructive instinct, the most obvious plan will be to bring Eros, its antagonist, into play against it. Anything that encourages the growth of emotional ties between men must operate against war. These ties may be of two kinds. In the first place they may be relations resembling those towards a loved object, though without having a sexual aim. There is no need for psycho-analysis to be ashamed to speak of love in this connection, for religion itself uses the same words: 'thou shalt love thy neighbour as thyself'. This, however is more easily said than done. The second kind of emotional tie is by means of identification. Whatever leads men to share important interests produces this community of feeling, these identifications. And the structure of human society is to a large extent based on them.

I should like to offer another suggestion for the indirect combating of the propensity to war. One instance of the innate and ineradicable inequality of men is their tendency to fall into the two classes of leaders and followers. The latter constitute the vast majority; they stand in need of an authority which will make decisions for them and to which for the most part they offer an unqualified submission. This suggests that more care should be taken than hitherto to educate an upper stratum of men with independent minds, not open to intimidation and eager in the pursuit of truth, whose business it would be to give direction to the dependent masses. It goes without saying that the encroachments made by the executive power of the State and the prohibition laid by the Church upon freedom of thought are far from propitious for the production of a class of this kind. The ideal condition of things would of course be a community of men who had subordinated their instinctual life to the dictatorship of reason. Nothing else could unite men so completely and so tenaciously, even if there were no emotional ties between them. But in all probability that is a Utopian expectation. No doubt the other indirect methods of preventing war are more practicable, though they promise no rapid success. An unpleasant picture comes to one's mind of mills that grind so slowly that people may starve before they get their flour.

I should like, finally, to discuss one more question which specially interests me. Why do you and I and so many other people rebel so violently against war? Why do we not accept it as another of the many painful calamities of life? After all, it seems to he quite a natural thing, to have a good biological basis and in practice to be scarcely avoidable. There is no need to be shocked at my raising this question. For the purpose of an investigation such as this, one may perhaps be allowed to wear a mask of assumed detachment. The answer to my question will be that we react to war in this way because everyone has a right to his own life, because war puts an end to human lives that are full of hope, because it destroys precious material objects which have been produced by the labours of humanity. It is my opinion that the main reason why we rebel against war is that we cannot help doing so. We are pacifists because we are obliged to be so for organic reasons. And we find no difficulty in producing arguments to justify our attitude.

No doubt this requires some explanation. My belief is this. For incalculable ages mankind has been passing through a process of evolution of culture. We owe to that process the best of what we have become, as well as a good part of what we suffer from. Though its causes and beginnings are obscure and its outcome uncertain, some of its characteristics are easy to perceive. The psychical modifications that go along with the process of civilization are striking and unambiguous. They consist in a progressive displacement of instinctual aims and a restriction of instinctual impulses. Sensations which were pleasurable to our ancestors have become indifferent or even intolerable to ourselves; there are organic grounds for the changes in our ethical and aesthetic ideals. Of the psychological characteristics of civilization two appear to be the most important: a strengthening of the intellect, which is beginning to govern instinctual life, and an internalization of the aggressive impulses, with all its consequent advantages and perils. Now war is in the crassest opposition to the psychical attitude imposed on us by the process of civilization, and for that reason we are bound to rebel against it; we simply cannot any longer put up with it. This is not merely an intellectual and emotional repudiation; we pacifists have a constitutional intolerance of war, an idiosyncrasy magnified, as it were, to the highest degree. It seems indeed as though the lowering of aesthetic standards in war plays a scarcely smaller part in our rebellion than do its cruelties.

And how long shall we have to wait before the rest of mankind become pacifists too? There is no telling. But it may not be Utopian to hope that these two factors, the cultural attitude and the justified dread of the consequences of a future war, may result within a measurable time in putting an end to the waging of war. By what paths or by what side tracks this will come about we cannot guess. But one thing we can say: whatever fosters the growth of civilization works at the same time against war.

Why IS There Evil?

Roy F. Baumeister
Case Western Reserve University

Why *is there* evil: [war], crime, violence, oppression, cruelty, and the rest? As we have seen, there is no single or simple answer. Evil does not exist in terms of solitary actions by solitary individuals. Perpetrators and victims—and in many cases, bystanders or observers, too—are necessary to the vast majority of evil acts. Evil is socially enacted and constructed. It does not reside in our genes or in our soul, but in the way we relate to other people.

Evil requires the deliberate actions of one person, the suffering of another, and the perception or judgment of either the second person or an observer. Very few people see their own actions as evil, and hardly any acts are regarded as evil if they do not bring harm, pain, or suffering to someone. Occasionally, masturbation, intoxication, or blasphemy may be considered evil even though no one is hurt, but victimless evil is a marginal, derivative category. Victimization is generally essential to evil. Victims are the first persons to spot evil.

Because evil depends so heavily on the perceptions of the victim (along with those of observers who identify with the victim), it is disturbing to the social scientist to realize how many biases and distortions shape the victim's perceptions. I have called these stereotypes collectively the *myth of pure evil.* Social scientists are fully prepared for whitewashing rationalizations on the part of perpetrators, but to recognize the extent to which everyone else's perceptions are also biased discourages one about the prospects of seeing through to the essential nature of evil. People tend to adapt real events to their expectations, based on the myth of pure evil. The result is a scenario involving wholly innocent, well-meaning victims attacked for no valid reason by arrogant, sadistic, out-of-control evildoers who hate peace and beauty and get pleasure from making people suffer.

There are four major root causes of evil, or reasons that people act in ways that others will perceive as evil. Ordinary, well-intentioned people may perform evil acts when under the influence of these factors, singly or in combination. Combinations are harder to defeat.

The first root cause of evil is the simple desire for material gain, such as money or power. These ends are not universally regarded as wrong, although occasionally a religious group or other authority has condemned the desire itself. What distinguishes evil in these cases is not the ends, however, but the means. Everyone wants money, but only criminals use violence to get it. Violent or evil means are chosen because the individual does not think that more legitimate means will be successful. Violent and evil means often do furnish short-term, limited success, but in the long run they do not reliably furnish the material benefits they were intended to bring. At best, violence seems to be an effective tool for creating and sustaining power relationships.

The second root of evil is threatened egotism. Villains, bullies, criminals, killers, and other evildoers have high self-esteem, contrary to the comfortable fiction that has recently spread through American culture. Violence results when a person's favorable image of self is questioned or impugned by someone else. Showing disrespect, attacking someone's honor, insulting or humiliating someone, or in some other way causing a person to lose face will often elicit an aggressive response. The people (or groups or countries) most prone to violence are the ones who are most susceptible to ego threats, especially those who have inflated, exalted opinions of themselves or whose normally high self-esteem does occasionally take a nosedive. Moreover, violence is usually directed toward the source of the ego threat (or occasionally, a meaningful substitute). Such violence may often fall short of providing proof of the disputed self-worth, but it does intimidate, silence, and punish the critic, and it boosts the ego by establishing dominance over the critic.

The third root of evil is idealism. When people believe firmly that they are on the side of the good and are working to make the world a better place, they often feel justified in using strong measures against the seemingly evil forces that oppose them. Noble ends are often seen as justifying violent means. In reality, such means often discredit and contaminate the noble goals, but this outcome is rarely anticipated. Human nature inclines people to align themselves in groups that square off against each other, each group seeing itself as good and the other as bad. Group competition can evolve into brutal conflict in which each side sincerely sees itself as the good guys who need to take strong measures to defeat the forces of evil that oppose them. When the perpetrators are driven by idealism, the victims do not get much mercy.

The fourth root of evil is the pursuit of sadistic pleasure. This root is responsible for a much smaller proportion of the world's evil than the others, and indeed most observations of killers, torturers, rapists, and similar evildoers indicate that only about 5 or 6 percent of perpetrators actually get enjoyment out of inflicting harm. Moreover, sadism appears to be an acquired taste. Possibly, it emerges from body's natural pattern of compensating for unpleasant emotional reactions with positive feelings, so that people might learn to enjoy torturing or killing in much the same way as they learn to enjoy skydiving despite the innate fear of falling. Still, most people do not seem to learn to enjoy hurting others (possibly because they refuse to let themselves do so, out of guilt or empathy). What looks to victims like sadism, such as when perpetrators laugh among themselves, may be simply insensitivity or camaraderie.

All told, the four root causes of evil are pervasive, which leads one to wonder why violence and oppression are not even more common than they are. The answer is that violent impulses are typically restrained by inner inhibitions; people exercise self-control to avoid lashing out others every time they might feel like it. The four root causes of evil must therefore be augmented by an understanding of the proximal cause, which is the breakdown of these internal restraints. Self-control may fail because upbringing and socialization have not made it strong enough, because the capacity for self-control is depleted by stress, because being emotionally upset makes people cease to care, or because the culture tells people that it is appropriate to lose self-control under some circumstances. Many instances of profound evil begin with a small, ambiguous act that crosses a fuzzy line and then escalates gradually into ever-greater levels of violence. In groups, especially, evil escalates as the group members bring out one another's worst impulses, lose track of individual responsibility, and reinforce one another's wavering faith in the broad justifications for what they are doing.

Harming another person typically makes one feel bad, although this feeling often takes the form of physical disgust rather than pangs of conscience. Many evildoers work out elaborate justifications by which they convince themselves that what they are doing is acceptable and that they should ignore their own unpleasant feelings. Victims and observers often find these justifications to be feeble and absurdly inadequate. But perpetrators make them work by building them around some palpable grains of truth and by refusing to subject them to critical scrutiny. When they want to believe that their actions are justified, they can often manage to do so. The justifications look weak to victims and outsiders because victims and outsiders are far less motivated to accept them.

The myth of pure evil may portray cohesive, dedicated groups of evil-doers preying on homogeneous ranks of innocent victims, but in actual cases of evil there tends to be division on both sides. Some members of the victim group collaborate with and accept the perpetrators, and some members of the perpetrator group object to the violence and try to help the victims. In addition, there is often a large group of uninvolved bystanders who may have far more power than they realize.

Nature and Culture

Many centuries of human thought and religious dogma have explained evil as a supernatural phenomenon, but the present approach of treating evil as a human, interpersonal phenomenon raises the question of whether one should look to nature or culture to explain evil. Psychology has certainly witnessed strong and powerful statements on both sides, with some wise and profound observers proposing that human beings are naturally, instinctively aggressive, while laboratory researchers have scrupulously insisted that learning and socialization explain a great deal point and perhaps all of aggression.

The deeper questions here are more than a matter of fashion and parsimony in scientific explanation. The deeper questions are ones that are familiar to most thoughtful people: Are human beings basically good evil? Are certain human beings basically evil? Should parents blame their own mistakes when their children grow up to become killers, rapists, or swindlers? Do genes dictate violent, criminal behavior, and if so, is the liberal ideal of rehabilitation merely a foolish, idle fantasy? Can society be redesigned so that everyone will live together in peace and harmony?

We are past the point at which an explanation in terms of either innate nature or socializing culture can completely explain what is known about human aggression. Both extreme views are untenable. Violence and aggression cannot be fully explained by pointing simply to instincts or heredity. It is clear that much aggression is learned and that most is specific to particular situations. Nature does not program most mammals to kill one another, and the awesome carnage of the twentieth century suggests that the process of civilizing the human animal has, if anything increased rather than decreased the violence. The cultural and historical variation in rates of violent crime and similar indices of evil also suggests that culture plays a powerful role.

A sobering look at some other facts also makes it implausible to chalk all human violence up to culture and socialization. Social structures can increase or decrease violence and other evils within certain limits, but no one has come close to eliminating it. Contrary to some idealistic fantasies, children do not need to be taught hate and prejudice: They are all too ready to pick on the one kid who is different or to reject the children in the other group. Physiological processes such as testosterone levels have a significant effect on aggressive behavior. And all over the world, regardless of culture or background, the same biological group is responsible for the bulk of the violence: young males from puberty through the prime age of reproductive potency.

A satisfactory understanding of human aggression is likely to invoke both culture and nature. It is unlikely that researchers will ever be able to trace specific violent actions directly to specific genes or other inherited physiological properties, but it is clear that nature has programmed people with some tendencies that can lead toward aggressive responses. Rage appears very early in life and is expressed in lashing out at the source of frustration. The tendency to align with one's fellows and feel hostile toward potential opponents and rivals seems almost ineradicable. Yet culture can exert a great deal of influence in teaching people how to express and control their aggressive impulses. Culture also shapes the situations that form the context for those impulses, including the opportunities or response, the importance of proper response, and the norms of what is proper. And culture articulates the beliefs and myths about evil.

The causes of evil have roots that are deep in human nature as well as in human culture, and it does not seem likely that culture can be changed to eliminate them. Culture can make them better or worse, however. Equalizing opportunity can perhaps reduce the tendency to resort to violent means as a way of achieving material gain, although there is no very convincing proof of this. Decreasing the emphasis on pride, self-esteem, and public respect, or providing multiple and clear criteria for proving oneself, may work against the tendency to use violence to maintain one's face. A strong cultural belief in the rights of individuals and in the inability of noble ends to justify violent means can help prevent idealism from fostering brutality.

Individuals have far less control over broad cultural patterns than over one another, however. Individuals can do far less about the root causes of evil than about the immediate causes. The internal restraints that prevent violent impulses from turning into action are probably the most important and promising place for people to make a difference. The question of whether parents should blame themselves because their child grew up to kill someone has a two-part answer. They should probably not blame themselves for the fact that their child had such murderous or violent impulses. But they may blame themselves for failing to teach their child enough self-control to stifle those urges. In some cases, however, they probably had no chance.

The Future of Evil

Is the world getting better or worse? The enlightened intellectuals of nineteenth century understood history as a gradual evolution toward more perfect societies filled with more perfect individuals. The twentieth century, in contrast, was marked by pessimism about history and a growing sense that the future might be a nasty, evil place. The century's wars and massacres far outclassed anything the less civilized past came up with. By one careful count, the four decades after the end of World War II saw 150 wars and only 26 days of world peace—and that's not even counting internal wars and police actions. The Nazis set the historical standard for efficient mass killing, yet even their records have been broken. Their body count has been surpassed by the Chinese Cultural Revolution of the 1960s. The Cambodians of the 1970s destroyed a larger percentage of the population. The Rwandese genocide of the 1990s killed people at five times the rate of the Nazi death camps, even though the country was much smaller. Meanwhile, even in peaceful countries like the United States, rates of violent crime continue to rise.

Yet toward the end of the century, the totalitarian regimes that kept much of the world's population enslaved changed or were overthrown. Eastern Europe and South America have shifted almost completely to democratic governments in place of the Fascist and Communist ones that ruled for decades. Even Asia and Asia have made huge steps toward freedom and human rights. The progress of democracy is especially welcome because historical surveys suggest that democracies hardly ever choose to go to war against one another. If the world's governments continue to become more democratic, and democracies remain nonviolent toward one another, the world might actually be able to sustain peace.

Thus, both optimists and pessimists can find

plenty of current trends to support their predictions of humanity's future. Let us consider the issue from the perspective of what has been covered in this book as the major sources of human evil.

The perceived need to use violence as a means of securing material gain is probably going to diminish, although slowly. The spread of opportunity and freedom gives people more access to legitimate, nonviolent means of getting what they want, and in the long run these work far better than violent ones. On the other hand, the planet's population may be approaching the limit of what the resources can support, in which case wars over arable land or drinking water may arise.

Egotism is unfortunately on the rise, especially now that modern morality has abandoned its religious commitment to humility and the condemnation of selfishness. At the international level, one has to worry about Russia, whose rapid loss of global prominence and prestige is reminiscent of the humiliations that pushed Germany toward World War II. The rising appeal of strong nationalist and Communist parties in Russia does not bode well for international harmony.

Idealistic violence is difficult to forecast. Christianity no longer seems to have the force to set off holy wars, but Islam does. The Soviet Union is no longer actively committed to fostering world socialist revolution, and indeed there is no longer any Soviet Union as such. On the other hand, the main reason that the United States never seriously flirted with Communist revolution was that social reforms improved the lot of the poor and narrowed the gap between the haves and the have-nots, and recent economic commentators seem to agree that this gap is widening again. Extreme differences between wealth and poverty increase the potential for violent political movements that promise leveling in the name of fairness. It is difficult to imagine that the United States would actually have an internal war based on political idealism, but the possibility of such conflicts (especially if one extends the argument to include all countries with vast inequalities of wealth) cannot be dismissed.

I have hardly mentioned China, which is ironic because in my own lifetime China has certainly done more evil than any other country in the world. China's record is remarkable. The body count of the Cultural Revolution, as already mentioned, is currently estimated at around 20 million, which is unsurpassed in world history. China also played a major role in helping the Khmer Rouge, whose mass murder campaign in Cambodia nearly destroyed the country in a few years and showed a ferocity that has rarely been matched. In 1989, when other Communist countries abandoned their repressive ways and let freedom begin, the Chinese brutally put down demonstrators, most famously in the massacre at Tiananmen Square. China has consistently been one of the most unscrupulous members of the international community. They have abused human rights without even pretending remorse, they violate international copyright laws and flagrantly steal the property of other nations, and they show minimal concern for the environment. Worst of all, they destroyed the Tibetan culture, with its priceless knowledge of the human mind and spirituality. China marches on unreformed and unrepentant, and any attempt to make optimistic forecasts about the twenty-first century must reckon with it.

Future generations are likely to look back on people living now as evil, because of the profligate use of the planet's limited and dwindling resources. When future centuries say that the twentieth was the age of supreme evil, they will be referring not only to death camps and world wars, but also to the selfish, reckless consumption of energy and the destructive pollution of the air and water. Projections vary as to how long the planet's precious resources will last, but inevitably they will start to become scarce. Technological advances will probably postpone the crisis—but not forever.

Citizens of the future will look back on us much the way people today look back on the slave traders or warmongers of past eras, with one twist: Future populations will be our victims, whereas relatively little of today's suffering is directly caused by the actions of our nefarious ancestors. When the oil really runs out, or when the water supply is fatally contaminated, or even when the national debt forces a major drop in everyone's standard of living, people will look back on our era as the culprits responsible for their suffering. Moreover, as we have seen, victims' perceptions tend to be especially stark and unforgiving. The future will have its own version of Satan, and it is likely to be you and me (and our governments). But, like most perpetrators, we do not see ourselves as doing evil.

After Understanding, What?

It is customary for psychology or social science books on evil to insist that understanding does not mean forgiving. Unfortunately, there is ample reason to fear that understanding can promote forgiving. Seeing deeds from the perpetrator's point of view does change things in many this ways. To perpetrators, their apparently voluntary acts appear to be driven or mitigated by external circumstances. To perpetrators, starkly evil motives lie in moral gray areas. To perpetrators, the scope and power of events seem much less extensive than to victims. Even when perpetrators recognize that what they did was wrong, it seems much smaller to them than to the victims.

This book has tried to understand violent, cruel, and oppressive actions as an extraordinary human phenomenon. The effort to understand has required some suppression of moral judgment. Few social scientists today really believe that their work can be totally value-free, but still the ideal of being value-free is important because values prevent one from seeing the facts. For students of torture, of rape, of the Holocaust, and of countless other forms of cruelty, the dilemma is unavoidable, because the interest in these topics is driven by values. Mass murder is not just another interesting human phenomenon comparable to wearing blue jeans or forgetting someone's name. Yet one can learn about evil most effectively by studying it as if it were. It is difficult and perhaps impossible to understand any human phenomenon at the same time that one is condemning it. Setting aside one's moral values, however risky that may be, is helpful when one attempts to understand the perpetrators of evil.

Yet, after making a long and strenuous effort to set aside one's values and look objectively and dispassionately at the causes of human violence—a look that itself requires a complex understanding of a daunting mass of information—it is all too easy to stop with that understanding. It is too easy to forget that we had to take a one-sided view of things in order to understand them, and to escape the intuitive tyranny of the victim's view. Understanding how people commit evil acts is one important key to appreciating the human condition, and it may even hold some helpful clues on how to control human violence. But knowledge about evil ultimately can be fully useful only if it is used with the moral sense that had to be silenced for the sake of gaining that knowledge.

The Nature of Aggression and Hatred

Gordon W. Allport
Psychologist (1897-1967)

Nature of Aggression—Problem of "Drainage"—Social Patterning of Aggression—Nature of Hatred

...[Previously] we considered aggression in its relation to frustration and to displacement. But more needs to be said, for aggression is often held to be central in explaining the origin of most social ills. In a century of unparalleled bloodshed, the attention of social scientists has been riveted upon aggression. It is frequently used as a basic explanatory principle.

Nature of Aggression

The tendency in Freud's own writing, and in that of many other psychodynamicists, is to consider aggression as a global, instinctive, steam boiler-like force. It is regarded as one of a small number of prime movers in life. It is ubiquitous, urgent, basically unavoidable. Freud writes:

> Men clearly do not find it easy to do without satisfaction of this tendency to aggression that is in them.... It is always possible to unite considerable numbers of men in love towards one another, so long as there are still some remaining as objects of aggressive manifestations.[1]

He equates the instinct with the desire to kill or destroy the object of the aggression. In the last analysis, it makes even for self-destruction. *Thantos* is no less of a blind urge in our natures than is *Eros*, with which it sharply contrasts. But aggression and love often get mixed up in the course of living, so that even our affiliative needs are contaminated by destructive impulses.

Following this line of thought, some psychoanalysts have seen in infant behavior a predominance of aggressiveness. The act of feeding is considered one of destructive devouring. Sucking is a form of attack. Our primordial ancestors, writes Simmel, were cannibals.

> We all enter life with the instinctive impulse to devour not only food, but also all frustrating objects. Before the infantile individual acquires the capacity to love, it is governed by primitive hate-relationship to its environment.[2]

Now the consequence of such a theory of aggression is to make war, vandalism, criminality, personal and group conflict seem entirely natural—even unavoidable. The best that could happen would be a sublimating, a draining, a shifting of the ubiquitous aggressive impulse into acceptable or less damaging channels. Everyone would *need* a scapegoat. We would have to discover or invent victims for our aggression.

We do well to reject this monolithic conception of aggression. It is not a single devouring force. The term covers several different kinds of acts carried on for several different reasons.[3]

The reader should note that while we are here repudiating one aspect of the Freudian theory of aggression, we are accepting another. Aggression is not a grandiose instinct that demands an outlet. Reactive aggression is, however, a capacity most people seem to have, and this capacity sometimes leads to displacement. The frustration-aggression-displacement theory is a part of the total Freudian theory. And this part...is valid, provided several important qualifications are held in mind.

The difference between an "instinct" and a "capacity" is crucial. An instinct demands an outlet. A capacity is only latent—and may never be brought into play. This distinction is obviously vital for our outlook upon prejudice. If an instinct is involved—always seeking satisfaction—the prospects for restraining or eliminating prejudice are dim. If a mere reactive capacity is involved it is probable that inner and outer conditions can be created that will avoid arousing this capacity altogether. Theoretically at least, we can create conditions in the family and in the community that are less frustrating; we can train children to meet such frustrations as occur without extropunitive aggression; or we can train them to direct such aggression as remains upon the true source of their frustration rather than upon a scapegoat.

The Problem of "Drainage"

We sometimes encounter the term "free-floating aggression." Thus the anthropologist Kluckhohn writes, "In every known human society there appears to exist a varying amount of free-floating aggression."[4] Kluckhohn goes on to explain, by the reactive hypothesis, that in most cultures restraints are placed upon children in the process of socialization, and that severe deprivations and frustrations occur throughout the adult stage of life in all societies. There must be an accumulation and a merging of aggressive impulses. Sometimes chronic irritation builds up a vast amount of vague unattached protest; sometimes, when life is smoother, there may be relatively little of such free-floating aggression.

Up to this point we may accept the concept. It seems to make sense, both for whole societies of people and for individuals. When we meet an individual who is full of complaints, resentment, and has many out-group prejudices, we can safely assume he has much unresolved reactive aggression, undoubtedly built up through a long series of chronic frustrations which he has not known how to handle.

But we cannot accept the steam-boiler and safety-valve image which Kluckhohn next offers to account for the course of this aggression:

> In many societies this "free-floating aggression" has been mainly drained off by periodic (or almost continual) wars. Some cultures, at their flowering, seem to have been able to channel most of it into socially creative channels (literature and the arts, public works, invention, geographical exploration, and the like). In most societies, most of the time, the greater part of this energy is diffused into various streams: into the small angry outbursts of daily living; into constructive activities; into occasional wars. But history shows that at epochs in the careers of most nations much of this aggressive energy has been, for longer or shorter periods, concentrated against segmental or distributive minorities within the society.[5]

To say that free-floating aggression may be channeled into creative work in literature, art, public works, is too far-fetched. Normally there is no aggression in painting a picture or drafting a blueprint. This passage seems to return full force to the Freudian view that a certain quantum of aggression exists. It may "float" anywhere. It may even be sublimated into non-aggression (peaceful pursuits). In other words it may exist even when it doesn't exist.

To deny "drainage" is not to deny "displacement."

In two respects the concepts are utterly unlike: (1) Displacement refers only to a specific tendency sometimes found in reactive aggression. It can be demonstrated experimentally to occur. A limited impulse acquires a substitute object. "Free-floating" aggression with drainage, on the other hand, suggests vague channels of possible sublimation—even in nonaggressive ways. Displacement does not in the least imply that the "release" of aggression in one channel lessens the likelihood of "release" in another. It is compatible with the finding that the more aggression is expressed the more of it there will be. The drainage theory holds the opposite.

Social Patterning of Aggression

The competitive way of life in the United States puts a premium on certain kinds of aggressiveness. The little boy is expected to stand up for himself and engage in fist fights, if necessary. In certain regions, custom sanctions verbal and physical hostility against selected minority groups. But culture not only provides norms for the development of aggressive behavior, it also supplies the source of many of the characteristic frustrations individuals suffer.

Take the case of western culture. Parsons has pointed out certain features of social structure that have a marked bearing upon the evolution of aggressive traits, and thus predispose the individual to prejudice.[6] In the western home (perhaps particularly in the United States) the father is absent most of the day. The child is thrown with the mother so continuously that she alone provides the model and mentor for his conduct. An early identification with the mother usually sets in. Since the daughter in the family early learns that she too will be a housewife and mother, the identification gives her little or no trouble—at least for several years. The young son, however, is early placed in conflict. Womanish ways are not for him. While he is accustomed to them, he early senses a different set of expectations for himself. He learns that males have power, freedom of movement and strength. Women are weaker. Yet his tie to his mother is close. The love she gives him fulfills his deepest needs. This love, however, may be contingent upon his being brave, being a little man, and thus, in a sense, repudiating the very femininity with which he identifies. A large number of neurotic difficulties in older males stem from "mother fixation" and a "sissy complex" which the son is trying to escape.

As a kind of overcompensation, boys may later identify vigorously with the father, aping particularly his masculine *ways*. The rough, tough, and nasty behavior in boyhood culture can be explained, at least in part, as an over-reaction to mother domination. While most males make the transition somehow, and finally contrive to balance filial love toward the mother with requisite adult masculinity, there are cases that continue an over-dependence on the mother, along with over-aggressiveness toward the outer world. There is some evidence that among these cases will be found a large proportion of anti-Semitic males. The sufferer conceives himself to be masculine, aggressive, and tough, but underlying he has not mastered his passive and dependent attitude. The consequence is a compensatory hostility—displaced upon a socially sanctioned scapegoat.[7]

The father too often plays his part in inducing a compulsive masculinity in the son. He is a carrier of the competitive culture with its frontier tradition. He encourages the son, often beyond his age, to exploits of prowess. The standard is set higher than the youth can attain. One common response is to confuse sheer aggression with masculinity. The boy can at least talk tough, criticize loudly, and berate out-groups. This pattern of sham ferocity may in time turn into genuine hostility. The gang pattern and the "bad boy" pattern in our culture are basically signs of compulsive masculinity. So, too, to a degree, is ethnic prejudice. German culture is in many respects unlike ours, but it seems likely that the cult of compulsive masculinity among the Nazis, accompanied by ferocious persecution of the Jews, was also related to prevailing family patterns.

Turning to the occupational situation in America, it too seems to invite both reactive aggression and displacement. Standards of achievement are so high (every son is ordinarily expected to surpass his father in wealth and prestige) that failure and frustration frequently result. Yet the occupational situation that instigates aggression fails to provide any legitimate outlets at all.

One might say of Western society in general that aggression is sharply inhibited from direct expression within the very groups which generate it. There is, as a result, an immense amount of irritation ready for displacement. When we consider the commonness of frustration within family and occupation, and the amount of repression required to prevent inconvenient expression of hostility, we may wonder that so many people escape developing out-group prejudice.

The type of sociological analysis here presented helps account for the uniformity in prejudice patterns within a society. It does not, however, account for the enormous range of individual differences encountered. To do so requires us to turn our attention back to the development of the personality as a selective agent.

The Nature of Hatred

Anger is a transitory emotional state, aroused by thwarting some on-going activity. Since it is aroused at a given time by an identifiable stimulus, it leads to impulses to attack the source of the frustration directly and to inflict injury upon this source.

Long ago Aristotle pointed out that anger differed from hatred in that anger is customarily felt toward individuals only, whereas hatred may be felt toward whole classes of people. He observed, too, that a person who gives way to anger is often sorry for his outburst and pities the object of his attack, but in expressing hatred, repentance seldom follows. Hatred is more deep-rooted, and constantly "desires the extinction of the object of hate."[8]

To put the matter another way, we may say that anger is an emotion, whereas hatred must be classified as a sentiment—an enduring organization of aggressive impulses toward a person or toward a class of persons. Since it is composed of habitual bitter feeling and accusatory thought, it constitutes a stubborn structure in the mental-emotional life of the individual. By its very nature hatred is extropunitive, which means that the hater is sure that the fault lies in the object of his hate. So long as he believes this he will not feel guilty for his uncharitable state of mind.

There is a good reason why out-groups are often chosen as the object of hate and aggression rather than individuals. One human being is, after all, pretty much like another—like oneself. One can scarcely help but sympathize with the victim. To attack him would be to arouse some pain in ourselves. Our own "body image" would be involved, for his body is like our own body. But there is no body image of a group. It is more abstract, more impersonal. It is especially so if there is some visibly distinguishing characteristic. A different-colored skin removes the person to some extent from our own circle. We are less likely to consider him an individual, and more likely to think of him only as an out-group member. But even so, he remains at least partially like ourselves.

This sympathizing tendency seems to explain a phenomenon we have frequently noted: people who hate groups in the abstract will, in actual conduct, often act fairly and even kindly toward individual members of the group.

There is another reason why it is easier to hate groups than individuals. We do not need to test our unfavorable stereotype of a group against reality. In fact, we can hold it all the more easily if we make "exceptions" for the individual members we know.

Fromm points out that it is essential to distinguish between two kinds of hate: one might be called "rational," the other, "character conditioned."[9] The former kind serves an important biological function. It arises when fundamental natural rights of persons are violated. One hates whatever threatens his own freedom; life, and values. Also, if well socialized, he hates whatever threatens the freedom, lives, and values of other human beings.

Rational hatred does not concern us so much as "character-conditioned" hatred. Here we have, as Fromm points out, a continuing readiness to hate. The sentiment has little relation to reality, although it may be the product of a long series of bitter disappointments in life. These frustrations become fused into a kind of "free-floating hatred"—the subjective counterpart of free-floating aggression. The person carries a vague, temperamental sense of wrong which he wishes to polarize. He must hate something. The real roots of the hatred may baffle him, but he thinks up some convenient victim and some good reason. The Jews are conspiring against him, or the politicians are set on making things worse. Thwarted lives have the most character-conditioned hate.

Neither kind of hate can exist unless something one values has been violated. Love is a precondition of hate. Always some affiliative relationship is interrupted before the agent thought to be responsible for the interruption can be hated.

What governs an individual at the beginning of his life is a dependent, affiliative relationship with the mother. There is little, if any, evidence of destructive instincts. After birth, the affiliative attachment of the child to his environment still remains dominant while nursing, resting, playing. The social smile early symbolizes contentment with people. Toward his entire environment the baby is positive, approaching nearly every type of stimulus, every type of person. His life is marked by eager outgoingness and, normally, by positive social relationships.

The initial affiliative tendencies, when threatened or frustrated, may give way to alarm and defense. Ian Suttie puts the matter picturesquely, "Earth hath no hate but love to hatred turned, and hell no fury but a baby scorned."[10] Thus, the genesis of hatred is secondary, contingent, and relatively late in the development process. It is always a matter of frustrated affiliative desire and the attendant humiliation to one's self-esteem or to one's values.

Perhaps the most perplexing problem in the entire field of human relations is this: why do so relatively few of our contacts with other people fit in with, and satisfy, our predominating affiliative needs, and why do so many find their way into sentiments of hatred and hostility? Why are loyalties and loves so few and restricted, when at bottom human beings feel that they can never love or be loved enough?

The answer to this riddle seems to lie in three directions. One concerns the amount of frustration and the hardness of living that beset people. Because of severe frustration it is easy to fuse one's recurring anger into rationalized hatreds. In order to avoid hurt and achieve at least an island of security it is safer to exclude than to include.

A second explanation has to do with the learning process. . . . Children brought up in a rejective home, exposed to ready-made prejudices, will scarcely be in a position to develop a trustful or affiliative outlook upon social relationship. Having received little affection, they are not in a position to give it.

Finally, there is a kind, of economy in adopting an exclusionist approach to human relations. By taking a negative view of great groups of mankind, we somehow make life simpler. For example, if I reject all foreigners as a category, I don't have to bother with them—except to keep them out of my country. If I can ticket, then, all Negroes as comprising an inferior and objectionable race, I conveniently dispose of a tenth of my fellow citizens. If I can put the Catholics into another category and reject them, my life is still further simplified. I then pare again and slice off the Jews. . . so it goes.

Thus the prejudiced pattern, involving various degrees and kinds of hatred and aggression, takes its place in the individual's world-view. It has an economy about it that we cannot deny. Still it falls considerably short of the dreams men have for themselves. At bottom they still long for affiliation with life and peaceful and friendly relations with their fellow men.

Notes

1. S. Freud. *Civilization and Its Discontents.* London: Hogarth Press, (Translated) 1949, 90.

2. E. Simmel (Ed.). *Anti-Semitism: A Social Disease.* New York: International Universities Press, 1948, 41.

3. Franziska Baumgarten, Zur Psychologie der Aggression. *Gesundheit und Wohlfahrt,* 1947, 3, 1-7.

4. C.M. Kluckhohn. "Group tensions: analysis of a case history." In L. Bryson, L. Finkelstein, and R. Maciver (Eds.), *Approaches to National Unity.* New York: Harper, 1945, 224.

5. *Ibid.*

6. T. Parsons. "Certain primary sources and patterns of aggression in the social structure of the western world." *Psychiatry,* 1947, 10, 167-181.

7. Else Frenkel-Brunswik and R.N. Sanford. "Some personality factors in anti-Semitism." *Journal of Psychology,* 1945, 20, 271-291.

8. Aristotle. *Rhetoric.* Book II.

9. E. Fromm. *Man for Himself.* New York: Rinehart, 1947, 214 ff.

10. I.D. Suttie. *The Origins of Love and Hate.* London: Kegan Paul, 1935, 23.

War And Aggressiveness

H.J. Eysenck
Psychologist (1916-1997)

Aggressiveness

Discussions of the contributions which psychology can make to the understanding of war almost invariably centre around the problem of aggressiveness. Writers of the psycho-analytic school, like Hopkins (39), Glover (36), and Durbin and Bowlby (19), take the view that the ultimate origin of the aggression which finds expression in war and other types of social conflict is to be found in childhood experiences of the individual; much play is made with such concepts as the 'unresolved Oedipus conflict'. Followers of the frustration-aggression hypothesis, like Dollard, Miller and Hovland (14), take a somewhat wider view and believe that frustration in any field serves as a source of aggressiveness, a view adumbrated by McDougall and Drever. They also, however, recognize that conflict in the family may have a powerful part to play in the creation of frustration and aggression.

Isolated attempts have been made by Lasswell (50), and by Krout and Stagner (48), to discover if emotional experiences of childhood influence adult attitudes towards a variety of issues. Thus it was shown that attitudes favourable to revolt against established institutions were found more frequently in subjects who had repressed aggression against the father, a parent-child relation not so frequently found in conservatives. Similarly, radicals[1] were found to show more frequent feelings of rejection by their parents, and more unhappiness in childhood. Other studies also show significant correlations between radicalism and antagonism to the father (66). Respect for law and education were found to be more marked in subjects whose home life had been satisfactory (79).

Another study deserves mention. As part of a general investigation carried out for the Society for the Psychological Study of Social Issues Committee on the "Psychology of War and Peace," Stagner (98, 99, 100) gave to various groups of students, scales measuring attitudes towards war, force, nationalism, fascism, intolerance, capital punishment, as well as towards father antagonism and childhood satisfaction. The results showed that in general, antagonism to parents correlated *negatively* with all the social-aggressive attitudes mentioned. A more detailed breakdown of results showed that the subjects who liked the father and did not like the mother scored highest on many of the aggressive scales; this result is, of course, well in line with our cultural stereotype of the stern, aggressive father and the gentle, yielding mother. Preference for mother, dislike for father, showed an anti-aggressive pattern, as might have been expected.

It was also found that on contrasting students satisfied and dissatisfied with their childhood, those who were satisfied tended to be much more nationalistic/capitalistic than the other group.

Interpretation of these results is difficult because they are all derived from a single culture-pattern; that of American capitalism. Thus it might be inviting to speculate that radical attitudes towards social issues are founded on parent antagonism, but it must be remembered that the correlations apparently supporting such a belief were obtained in a society in which radical beliefs are ostracized, where even mildly liberal attitudes are considered 'subversive', and where organizations such as the Dies Committee flourish. Where the great majority of parents of all classes, and particularly of college students, share a capitalistic outlook, the rising generation's disagreement with their parents on emotional grounds may easily make them critical of social and political beliefs held by the parents, thus inevitably leading them to the only alternative social and political outlook. (Republican and Democratic partisanship, of course, does not provide such alternatives, being merely a game of Box and Cox with political patronage as its basis.) The crucial test would be a repetition of the experiment in a socialist country; would children of socialist parents, who are antagonistic to these parents, develop a conservative outlook? If so, the alleged affinity between childhood antagonism and radical attitudes would be shown to be merely an instance of a more embracing generalization of the linking up of emotional antagonisms with cognitive disagreements, a generalization which in other circumstances would lead to a correlation between childhood antagonisms to parents and conservative political attitudes.

We have spoken hitherto as if 'aggressiveness' constituted a general factor, i.e. as if there were a marked tendency for a person who was aggressive in one set of circumstances to be aggressive in others also. This belief is by no means universal. Beginning with William James, psychologists in search of a 'moral equivalent for war' have thought that aggressive impulses might be sublimated through sport, physical exercise, the conquest of disease, etc. Writers of the psycho-analytic school in particular have made much of this concept of sublimation, and have often added the view that persons who express aggressiveness freely in personal relationships have less hostility which can be 'displaced' on to 'out-groups'. This belief, indeed, lies at the basis of some modern therapeutic tendencies of the 'group therapy' kind.

Evidence regarding this important point is furnished by Stagner (98), who showed that students who evinced aggressive attitudes in one direction also tended to show them in other directions, the average intercorrelation being as high as +0.4 for various groups. This work is particularly convincing because extensive questionnaire studies were supplemented by personal interviews and other special observations, such as thematic apperception tests, free association, reaction time and galvanic measures. Stagner also inquired into certain alleged 'sublimating' activities, such as playing football, expressing annoyances openly, and so forth. If the 'sublimation' theory were correct, we should expect that students who had 'sublimated' their aggressive impulses would be less aggressive on the various scales (capital punishment, war, fascism, etc.) than those who had failed to 'sublimate'. In actual fact, exactly the opposite was observed; all instances and expressions of aggressiveness showed positive correlations. While we must recognize that only verbal behaviour is involved in these tests, the onus of proof would seem to lie definitely on the proponents of the 'sublimation' theory; the results quoted are plainly incompatible with that theory. The same might be said of correlations reported by Eysenck (24, 25) and by Ferguson (31) in a series of articles, in which a consistent tendency was found for persons aggressive in one context to be aggressive in another context.

We may conclude this brief review by saying that it has been established that aggressive attitudes tend to be general, extending over large areas of belief and conduct; that evidence has been found in favour, and much evidence against, the 'sublimation' type of theory; and that work on the genesis of aggressive attitudes is inconclusive in virtue of being restricted to a single culture-pattern.

Primary Social Attitudes

In a recent Gallup Poll in this country, the question was asked: "Do you think that another world war is likely during the next twenty-five years?" Forty-eight per cent of the respondents thought it likely, 31 per cent unlikely, with 21 per cent undecided. Great differences were found between the well-to-do, 61 per cent of whom thought war likely, and the poorer classes, only 39 per cent of whom thought so. Conservatives and Liberals were more convinced of the likelihood of war than were Labour voters.

These results show that attitudes towards certain aspects of the problem of war are related to social class, or to political affiliation. The question inevitably arises: Are there certain persistent, all-embracing groupings of attitudes, to which isolated opinion statements such as the above can be related? What light has social psychology to throw on the organization of social attitudes, with particular reference to the place of attitudes towards war and peace in this scheme? Much evidence is available in this connection through the work of Thurstone, Ferguson, Carlson, Eysenck, and others, and it is believed that an understanding of the underlying issues will throw some light on the general problem.

Attitude structure may be conceived as having four distinct levels. At the lowest level we have haphazard, isolated statements of opinion which may or may not represent accurately a person's views on a given subject. When the same statement is made repeatedly, we may say that there is evidence that it represents more than a passing fancy, without deep roots in the general matrix of the person's mind. Statements such as: "War is often the only means of preserving the national honour," or "War is a futile struggle resulting in self-destruction" were shown by Stagner (95), to have repeat reliabilities of between +0.85 and +0.96; we may take this fact as evidence that over a period of several months opinion statements of this kind remain remarkably steady.

So far we are still on the level of opinion measurement. When it can be shown that a number of statements dealing with one and the same issue—war, or anti-Semitism, or religion—tend to correlate highly together, so that they can be arranged on a unidimensional scale for the measurement of attitude toward that particular issue, then we can claim to have isolated an *attitude.* Below is given a brief scale of this kind measuring the relative favourableness towards war of the respondents. The statements were derived from a larger number by means of the Thurstone technique; the scoring is based on the Likert method, however, as in our experience this combination of techniques gives a higher reliability than either alone (Eysenck and Crown, 27).

The score on the scale is simply the sum of the numbers printed against each answer underlined by the subject; these numbers were derived by multiplying an item's scale position by the numerical value of the chosen answer, dividing by a constant, and rounding off.

Detailed results regarding the reliability and validity of this questionnaire are given in a paper by Eysenck and Crown (28); here we may just note certain points. A factorial study of the inter-correlations between the eight items disclosed the existence of a strong factor of militarism or war-mindedness, which accounted for 38 per cent of the variance. Question 1 had the highest saturation with this factor (.94), followed by Question 4 (.80). The index of reliability for the scale was found to be .83. Further points from this study will be noted later, particularly the correlation between militarism and conservatism, and the correlation between militarism and neuroticism; here our main insistence is on the demonstration that different statements dealing with attitudes towards war display a certain amount of functional unity.

Questionnaire Used in Measuring Attitude Towards War

Underline the answer which in each case agrees most with your own opinion on the issue in question; underline the '?' only when you find it impossible either to agree or disagree with the proposition. Disregard the numbers written against the answers.

1. Certain issues are so vital for a nation that war is preferable to submission.

Strongly agree	Agree	?	Disagree	Strongly disagree
-2	-1	0	+1	+2

2. In war, even the winner loses more than he can hope to gain.

Strongly agree	Agree	?	Disagree	Strongly disagree
+4	+2	0	-2	-4

3. War is an important factor in progress, eliminating the unfit.

Strongly agree	Agree	?	Disagree	Strongly disagree
-6	-3	0	+3	+6

4. Under no circumstances can war ever be justified.

Strongly agree	Agree	?	Disagree	Strongly disagree
+8	+4	0	-4	-8

5. War brings out virtues in people which in peace lie undetected.

Strongly agree	Agree	?	Disagree	Strongly disagree
-4	-2	0	+2	+4

6. There is no such thing as a 'righteous war'.

Strongly agree	Agree	?	Disagree	Strongly disagree
+2	+1	0	-1	-2

7. War is a glorious adventure.

Strongly agree	Agree	?	Disagree	Strongly disagree
-8	-4	0	+4	+8

8. War never settles the problems at issue between the nations involved.

Strongly agree	Agree	?	Disagree	Strongly disagree
+6	+3	0	-3	-6

When the existence of a definite attitude has been demonstrated, the question arises whether concepts of a higher order may not exist which are based on the intercorrelation of several attitudes. For instance, may not militarism, anti-Semitism, nationalism, religionism, and pro-capitalism intercorrelate and define an attitude of 'conservatism'? This type of higher-order concept constitutes the fourth and highest level in the hierarchy of attitude structure, and may justly be called a 'primary social attitude'.

Large-scale correlational studies, involving widely differing groups of students, middle-class adults, Liberals, Conservatives, Socialists, Englishmen, Americans, men and women, old and young, Eugenicists, Fabians, and various others, have given us a picture of these Primary Social Attitudes which is presented diagrammatically in Figure 1 (next page). It will be seen that two orthogonal (uncorrelated) factors are involved, and that a large number of different social issues are shown in their relation to these two primary social attitude factors. The nature of the factors can easily be determined by inspection of the issues which define them. The first factor is clearly a radicalism-conservatism one, as has been proved independently by showing that the items which define this factor also show large differences in endorsement between Conservative and Socialist groups equated for age, sex, and education (24, 25).

The second factor is perhaps less easy to label. It has been variously called 'practical-theoretical' and 'tough-minded *v.* tender-minded'. That it is more than a statistical artefact, and has a very real existence, has been shown elsewhere (25). These two, the 'R' and 'T' factors, as they have been called, will be seen to influence and determine the attitude to about an equal extent; when correction is made for the unreliability of the scale used for measuring this attitude we find that over 50 per cent of its variance is accounted for in terms of R and T, leaving some 40 per cent to be accounted for in terms of more specific factors.

We can now see that the items in the conservative-tough-minded quadrant are essentially similar to the items which were used by Stagner to define

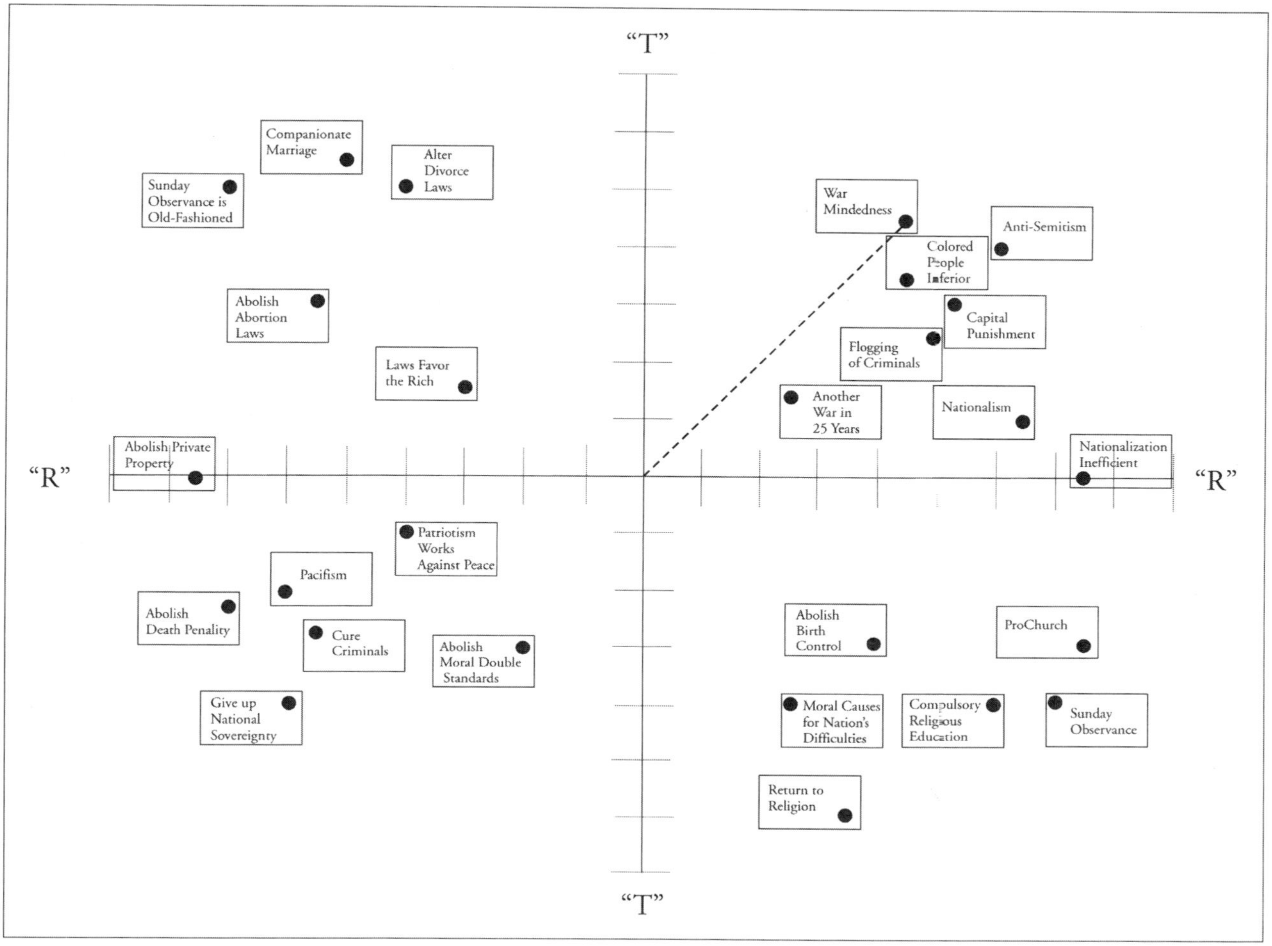

Figure 1

his 'aggressiveness' factor; our analysis shows that this is not a simple factor but a composite one which may be reduced to a combination of the two primary social attitudes. This is an important discovery, because we know a great deal about the distribution and the correlates of these two factors, while our information about 'aggressiveness' is very meagre; thus we can bring a much wider range of knowledge and information to bear on our topic. It is also important because the correlation between 'war-mindedness' and 'conservatism' is apparently not conditioned by the specific American or British culture-pattern, but comes out quite clearly in samples of various kinds drawn from both nations. Again, it would be most desirable to repeat investigations of this kind in culture-patterns even more unlike each other than American capitalism and British social-democracy; it may be predicted that much might be learned regarding the nature and structure of attitudes from comparative studies in Germany, Italy, Poland, Russia, India, Mexico, etc.[2]

Correlates of War-Mindedness

We may study the correlates of war-mindedness either directly, or by reference to the two primary social attitudes which give rise, in combination, to this quality. In one study of the 'direct' type (95), a questionnaire somewhat similar to the one printed in the previous section was used with various adult and college groups in the southern states of America, during the academic year 1937-8. Age was not found to be of great importance, but women tended to give less militaristic replies; this difference, however, was much smaller than might have been expected. Republicans were significantly more militaristic than Democrats, but again the difference was slight. Jews were considerably less militaristic than Protestants or Catholics; there was no significant difference between these two religious groups. Men having had fighting experience, and/or some military training, or who were members of a veterans' society, scored significantly more militaristic than people without any military training, and members of a labour union.

As regards occupational differences, professional and labour groups were less militaristic than the average, while clericals and business men were more militaristic. Children of business men and of labourers have shown a similar difference, according to a report by Porterfield (73). These results all fit into the radical-pacifist *v.* conservative-militaristic pattern discussed in previous sections.

Militaristic and pacifist groups, as measured by the questionnaire, also differed profoundly with respect to beliefs about methods of keeping out of war. Organizations approving of 'complete military preparedness' often claim that this policy is intended to keep the peace; yet persons holding this view were found much more militaristic than the other groups. On the other hand, those who believed in 'united action of workers, farmers, and consumers', in 'taking profits out of war', in 'socialism', and in the 'League of Nations' tended to be less militaristic than the average. These results again appear to fit in well with our general picture. Lastly, it may be noted that personal willingness to fight (as verbally asserted, at least) is related to militaristic attitudes.

Other studies by Pintner (72), Turteltaub (109), Lundberg (56), Smith (89), Droba (15, 16, 17, 18), Pihlblad (71), Farnsworth (29), Jones (41), Stump and Lewis (105), Page (68) and many others give results similar to those quoted above. There is a general tendency for respondents to be pacifistic rather than militaristic; parents tend to be more militaristic than their children; males tend to be more militaristic than females; the influence of college education tends to be in the direction of lessened militarism, except for students at military academies. Jews, Christian Scientists, and Methodists tend to be more pacifistic than Lutherans, Catholics, and Congregationalists; Republicans are more militaristic than Democrats, while Socialists are much less militaristic than either group. *Mutatis mutandis,* these results would appear to be broadly true of British respondents also.

Parent-child correlations in attitude toward war tend to be roughly similar to correlations found for other social attitudes (cf. below). In one of the best controlled studies, Newcomb and Svehla found that mothers and sons, mothers and daughters, fathers and sons, fathers and daughters, and mothers and fathers all agreed in their war attitudes to about the same extent; coefficients of correlation varied from .43 to .46 for these different pairs (cf. 50). The same investigators also found that parent-child relationships varied more definitely and more consistently with socio-economic status than with age, correlations being higher for the lowest occupational levels, and lower for the highest occupational levels. This generalization was derived from studies of different attitudes; the figures for attitudes toward war read as follows:

Parent-child Correlation in Attitude Towards War

	Occupational Level		
Age of child	High	Medium	Low
19 and under	.24	.45	.66
20-23	.26	.25	.54
24 and over	.27	.40	.32

These figures are of absorbing interest; they also point up the importance of further research into the reasons why parent-child correlations are higher in the working-class than in the middle-class groups, and into the relation between attitude-formation and the dynamics of the family situation. They also suggest national comparisons—does a similar law hold true in England, for instance? And are there systematic differences in the size of parent-child correlations between different nations—are correlations higher in Germany, for instance, than they are in less autocratic countries? These are questions which urgently call for an answer if we are to understand the genesis of war-minded attitudes.

We have shown that parental influences determine to some extent the individual attitudes which children exhibit; does parental influence also condition the patterning of attitudes in children? If certain children resemble their parents with respect to one set of attitudes, will they also resemble them with respect to other attitudes? A group of 220 parents was selected whose attitude toward the church correlated very highly with that of their children; another group of 227 parents was selected who correlated very highly with their children on attitude toward communism. For these two groups, the parent-child attitude correlation of war-mindedness was .41 and .35, as compared to a correlation of .44 for an unselected group of 1,090 parents and children. This suggests that the attitude correlations between parents and children are relatively specific to the issue involved, and that there is no tendency for certain children to agree or disagree in general with their parents.

Again, if parents are selected in such a way that they show high agreement between two attitudes, say towards communism and towards the Church, will the children also show unusually high agreement on these two issues? For unselected parents, this particular correlation was found to be .48; the selected group showed a correlation of .96. Unselected children showed a correlation of .43; the children of the selected parents showed a correlation of .60. As Murphy (66) points out "what might be called a cluster effect is thus passed from parents to children to the extent of the difference between coefficients .600 and .430." But this patterning does not seem to be particularly strong in its influence, and it does not seem to extend to other issues: the unselected group showed a correlation of .26 between attitudes towards church and war, while the selected group of children showed a correlation of .31....

'War-mindedness' and Stereotypes. A militaristic or aggressive attitude seldom exists *in vacuo;* it is likely to be related closely to some object or class of objects. In thus becoming attached to a nation, or a race, our adient or abient reactions tend to become rationalized into consistent and meaningful systems of ideas regarding the object in question; such systems are called 'stereotypes'.[3] They have their origin in feeling, emotions, and 'intuition' rather than in fact. The individual who holds stereotyped views is often entirely unaware of the part played in their creation by preferences or aversions, rationalizing and emotional reactions. Such views are evidence of uncritical acceptance of unanalysed circumstances; they may be true in isolated cases, they may apply to a limited number of members of the group to which they are referred, but on the whole they confuse thinking by always introducing the 'class-error',[4] and by failing to stress the importance of individual differences.

Stereotypes are legion—spinsters and Bolsheviks, Irishmen and professors, lords and cockneys, gangsters and senators, capitalists and journalists, actors and Jews, each word conjures up a caricature of a whole group of people, each a libel on the uniqueness of man. Experimental work shows these weeds in rich profusion—Rice (77), Farnsworth (30), Katz and Braly (43), Hartmann (38), Menefee (61), Fink and Cantril (32), Sherif (84) and others have demonstrated the wide-spread nature and the growth of stereotyped opinion. Eysenck (22) has shown in one particular example both the existence and the falseness of a well-known stereotype, viz, that of national differences in sense of humour. Using humorous pictures with captions culled from such journals as *Punch*, the *New Yorker*, *Berliner Illustrierte*, *Lilliput*, the *Saturday Evening Post*, etc., he showed that not only did British people find it impossible to discriminate which were American, which British, which German, but they liked the products of all three nations equally well. They also tended, however, to ascribe German nationality to pictures which they did not like, on the basis of the false stereotype that Germans have no sense of humour. Other experimental approaches to this problem gave similar results.

While there is little doubt that stereotyped attitudes play a part in the opinions of people, social psychology is in danger of developing stereotyped views about the nature of this concept of 'stereotype'. Much of what is accepted as experimental evidence is in reality artefact produced by inadequate methodology. As an example of this danger, we may quote the investigation of Katz and Braly (43), in which 100 students were presented with eighty-four adjectives, with the request that they should pick out those characteristic of various nationalities. Considerable agreement was found among the answers—Germans are scientifically minded, methodical; Italians are artistic, musical; Negroes are superstitious, lazy; Americans are industrious, sophisticated; Turks are cruel, sensual. Attitudes were most stereotyped about Negroes, Germans, and Jews; least about Japanese, Chinese, and Turks.

Doubtful about interpretations of such data, Eysenck and Crown (26), repeated the investigations with slight modifications on an adult, middle-class, non-student population in this country. Results of the experiment were identical; much agreement was found in the adjectives used, and those most frequently employed with respect to the various nations were similar to those reported by Katz and Braly. Table 1 shows the results in an abbreviated form.

Table 1

Five adjectives most characteristic of each race.

GERMAN Science-minded Industrious Arrogant Aggressive Over-nationalistic

ITALIAN Musical Lazy Artistic Religious Unreliable

NEGRO Superstitious Religious Lazy Faithful Happy-go-lucky

IRISH Religious Quick temp. Happy-go-lucky Witty Superstitious

ENGLISH Sportsmanlike Reserved Tradition loving Conventional Intelligent

JEW Shrewd Mercenary Industrious Intelligent Loyal to family

AMERICAN Boastful Pleas. Loving Generous Materialistic Talkative

CHINESE Industrious Courteous Meditative Loyal to family Intelligent

JAPANESE Cruel Fanatic Treacherous Imitative Industrious

FRENCH Sophisticated Talkative Artistic Passionate Witty

RUSSIAN Industrious Tough Suspicious Brave Progressive

* * *

While the existence of stereotypes is undoubted, the tendency in social psychology to look for unconscious processes and 'rationalizations' in relation to all social thinking is open to criticism. Many people are rational in their views, and know full well how little they are qualified to judge such difficult questions as 'national character'; in a number of cases, no doubt, emotional and unconscious processes obscure this natural attitude, and lead to vehement anti-semitic or anti-negro attitudes (cf. Eysenck and Crown (28) for experimental proof). But such cases may only constitute a small percentage of the total population and it is dangerous to generalize from the exception to the rule. Experimental design will have to be much improved before we can claim to be fully informed on the subject of 'stereotypes'. In the absence of such knowledge, little can be said usefully about the relation of stereotypes to war-minded attitudes; the hypothesis frequently put forward that a positive correlation obtains between war-mindedness and stereotypy of attitude remains to be proved.

In thus stressing the fact that many recent writers have rather tended to over-emphasize unconscious, unreasonable and emotional factors, it has not been our desire to gainsay the existence of such motives, tendencies, and determinants. There is too much strictly experimental evidence regarding the importance of autistic factors for a generally negative attitude to be possible; our intention has been merely to plead for a less one-sided outlook. In their excitement about the discovery of the powers of 'emotion' over 'intellect', many psychologists have gone to extremes, portraying the 'man in the street' as the mere plaything of uncontrollable unconscious forces which cannot in any way be influenced by reason. Such a view is no less contrary to fact than the previous over-estimation of rationalistic influences; what is needed is a more realistic appraisal of the relative importance of these two factors in each individual case.

Much of the more impressive work along these lines has been in the interpretation of ambiguous perceptual stimuli, in which a conflict is precipitated between realistic and autistic tendencies (Sanford, 80, 81; Levine, 51, 52). Thus, for instance, a larger number of food interpretations were made of certain ambiguous pictures by hungry than by satiated subjects. Murray (67) found similarly that the induction of fear in his subjects made them attribute 'maliciousness' to faces in photographs. Sherif (85, 86) in his well-known work on the autokinetic phenomenon, showed the influence of the desire to conform, on judgments of the position of a point of light in a dark room. Proshansky and Murphy (75), and Haggard and Rose succeeded in influencing perceptual experiences through arbitrary rewards and punishments; Schafter and Murphy (82), showed that the control of the figure-ground relation played an important part in the process....

It should be noted that in this discussion we have treated 'stereotypes' as unconsciously determined, emotionally toned caricatures of really existing objects or classes of objects; this is the original meaning of the term as used in social psychology. More recently, it has become fashionable to extend this meaning to cover all that is general in social attitudes. Thus Britt (7), quoting Vetter's (110) finding that people who endorse one radical opinion tend also to endorse other radical opinions, comments that "such studies demonstrate the psychological advantages of stereotyping. To know an individual's attitudes in certain situations may tell you a great deal about what attitudes to expect from him in other situations."

Changing War-minded Attitudes

If attitudes arise through social learning, presumably they can be changed through the provision of novel educational or propaganda influences. The work of Arnett et al. (3), Barry (4), Knower (45), Kulp (49), Marple (58), Moore (63), Sorokin and Boldyreff (91), Wheeler and Jordan (111), as well as studies summarized below, go to show that this assumption is in fact true, and that the effects of oral and written argument, of film shows, of expert and majority opinion can be traced experimentally in the changing attitudes of the subjects taking part in these experiments.

Longstreet (53), gave a series of lectures on the facts of war to a class of schoolboys, changing their views (at least temporarily) in the direction of opposition to war. Kirkendall (44), showed that a class of seventy-five students, listening to a talk on "Investigations of War Profits and Munitions Manufacturing," became more strongly pacifist in their views. Charrington and Miller (12), showed the effectiveness on a group of 170 college students of a pacifist lecture; not only was their attitude at the time shifted strongly toward the pacifist end of the scale, but on re-testing after six months the group still showed a statistically significant shift from its original position, although a certain amount of regression had occurred....

One other feature of propaganda may be briefly noted, as it has good experimental backing. The propagandist attempts to convert his victims to a general viewpoint; he inevitably does so by specific instruction and examples. Thus in attempting to convert people to socialism in general, he may discuss the iniquities of capitalist management of the coal mines, or the responsibility of capitalism for war, etc. Now Rosenthal (78) has shown that so far as his results are concerned the effects of specific stimulation are largely specific; no generalization of learning or 'transfer of training' takes place from the specific instance to the general principle. He showed the film *Capitalist World* to 1000 students, measuring their opinions on forty-seven radical-conservative statements. Eight of these statements were closely related to the theme of the film, which is a socialist propaganda device, while ten had no particular counterpart in the film. On retesting the group after viewing the film, changes were significant on the 'related', but not on the 'unrelated' statements. As Bird (6) points out, "this study suggests that motion-picture propaganda exerts effects which are specific to their content. Whatever transfer occurs from related to remote attitudes is slight and seems due to identical elements in the movements and in the statements in the test." The application of this principle to propaganda against militarism is obvious.

We noted the fact of 'opinion regression' in connection with the Cherrington-Miller (12) study. Similar effects were noted by Peterson (69), and Thurstone (107) in following up the observations on the children whose attitudes had been changed by the films used in the various studies mentioned; after periods of delay varying from two to eight months, opinion had regressed toward the original point of view, but not all the way. Propaganda, even of so moderate a form, was still effective after this lapse of time. In these studies, counter-influences to the original propaganda film or talk were haphazard and unsystematic, and consequently not very effective over the period investigated. Regression, however, may be almost simultaneous, as when a 'pro' talk is immediately followed by a 'con' talk (88); in such a case cancellation of effects takes place in the majority of cases.

Such simultaneous regression is also reported by Cherrington (11) in his study of the effects of participation in conferences dealing with the causes of war and the cures for war. While participation tended to lead to well-structured, consistent attitudes, it did not lead to any changes on the Thurstone scales of attitude towards war.

The studies summarized in this section show that attitudes towards war are easily modified by various propaganda devices; recent history gives melancholy emphasis to this finding. As Bird (6) points out, "these results constitute a challenge to our educational procedures. Only as students are trained to relate fields of knowledge, to think critically in terms of facts rather than opinions and fictions, to question their own gullibility, and to have a fine regard for opposed points of view held by intelligent people will our educational system fulfil its function in the social sciences."

Opinions on the Prevention of War

Attitude studies do not extend only to the measurement of opinion of certain issues, they may also legitimately cover views on the methods which ought to be adopted in order to change existing malpractices, or to prevent contingencies such as war from arising. Much important material has been collected in this sphere by Fletcher (33), Stagner (97), and others....

The finding that social scientists in general tended to advocate relatively *radical* policies for the preservation of peace seems to indicate that the view of those who advocate an instinctive basis for war is widely rejected nowadays. Certainly few psychologists believe in such a genetic basis of aggressiveness; of several hundred American psychologists polled by Fletcher in 1932 well over 90 per cent rejected the view that human nature made war inevitable. As will be seen from Fig. 1, the view that war is inherent in human nature forms part of the conservative-tough-minded group of 'aggressive' beliefs and attitudes of which war-mindedness is one. This general view is not in accordance with scientific belief, and policies based on it are, therefore, hardly likely to find favour with social scientists.

What then are the policies which according to expert social psychologists would be likely to make a recurrence of war less likely?[5] A sample of fifty-two American social psychologists was queried in considerable detail by Stagner (97); these men represented an authoritative cross-section of the whole group. "They were unanimous on the need for both political and economic nationalism. They endorsed a democraticaly organized League with sovereignty above that of nations on specified issues. They advocated a 'reasonable' rather than a 'vengeful' peace. They favoured an end to 'white imperialism'." "The chief obstacles to durable peace (on the American scene) were perceived as: economic nationalism; absence of loyalty to an international government; and facist indoctrination of the Axis peoples." "A long-range programme was based on the assumption that uncontrolled aggression anywhere is a menace to the peace of the world. Some frustrations are socially necessary, but many frustrations of biological needs and of ego-values could be ended by the extension of political and economic democracy. Further, the aggression which results from unavoidable frustration can be handled realistically if we improve our mental hygiene practices, reduce scapegoating, and develop a scientific attitude towards human relationships."

Retrospect and Prospect

Social psychology as a whole has charted for itself a dangerous course, threatened by the Scylla of nebulous Freudian generalizing, and by the Charybdis of pointlessly amassing unrelated 'facts'. Thus we have two great groups of workers whose efforts bring extraordinarily little return for the labour expended: On the one hand the Neo-Freudian, Crypto-Jungian group of 'intuitionists' who scorn the pedestrian methods of scientific verification, who base their conclusions on very small, biased samples, and whose alleged 'facts' are themselves only interpretations according to very dubious canons of evidence; on the other, the mole-like calculators of innumerable correlations between measures taken without any theory or hypothesis capable of proof or disproof, who mistake the collection of a thousand unrelated 'facts' for science, who seek to atone for the scientific barrenness of their results by stressing the mathematical beauty and purity of the methods used, and who seem incapable of seeing the wood for the trees....

[I]t should be stressed again that to be successful such research must get away from the all-too-frequent pattern of asking large numbers of people large numbers of questions in the vague hope of arriving at scientifically and socially important conclusions. The need is for single, clearly stated, verifiable hypotheses, supplemented by suitable, methodologically adequate investigations. Research to date has suggested many worth-while hypotheses, and has succeeded in clarifying the problem of methodology; it is doubtful if in the circumstances it could have done much more.

References*

1. Allport, G.W. "The Composition of Political Attitudes." *Amer. J. Sociol.*, 1929, 35, 220-238.
3. Arnett, C.S., Davidson, H.H., and Lewis, H.G. "Prestige as a Factor in Attitude Change." *J. Sociol. Soc. Res.*, 1931, 25, 373-81.
4. Barry, H. "A Test for Negativism and Compliance." *J. Abn. Psychol.*, 1931, 25, 373-81.
6. Bird, C. *Social Psychology.* New York: Appleton-Century, 1946.
7. Britt, S.H. *Social Psychology of Modern Life.* New York: Farrar and Rinehart, 1941.
11. Cherrington, B.M. "Methods of Education in International Attitudes." *Teach. Coll. Contrib. Educ.*, 1934, No. 595.
12. Cherrington, B.M., and Miller, L.W. "Changcs in Attitude as a Result of a Lecture and/or Reading Similar Material." *J. Soc. Psychol.*, 1933, 4, 479-84.
14. Dollard, J., et al. *Frustration and Aggression.* New Haven: Yale University Press, 1939.

*Numbers refer to reference numbers in the original article.

15. Droba, D.D. "A Scale of Militarism-Pacifism." *J. Educ. Psychol.*, 1931, 22, 96-111.

16. Droba, D.D. "Effect of Various Factors on Militarism-Pacifism." *J. Abn. Soc. Psychol.*, 1931-2, 26, 141-53.

17. Droba, D.D. "Churches and War Attitude." *J. Sociol. Soc. Res.*, 1932, 16, 547-52.

18. Droba, D.D. "Political Parties and War Attitudes." *J. Abn. Soc. Psychol.*, 1933-4, 28, 468-72.

19. Durbin, J., and Bowlby, E. *Personal Aggressiveness and War.* New York: Columbia Univ. Press, 1939.

22. Eysenck, H.J. "National Differences in 'Sense of Humour': Three Experimental and Statistical Studies." *Char. and Person.*, 1944, 13, 37-54.

24. Eysenck, H.J. "General Social Attitudes." *J. Soc. Psychol.*, 1944, 19, 207-227.

25. Eysenck, H.J. "Primary Social Attitudes: 1. The Organization and Measurement of Social Attitudes." *Internat. J. of Opin. and Attit. Res.*, 1947, 1, 49-84.

26. Eysenck, H.J. and Crown, S. "National Stereotypes: An Experimental and Methodological Study." *Ibid.*, 1948, 2, 1-14.

27. Eysenck, H.J. "An Experimental Study in Opinion Attitude Methodology." *Int. J. Opin. and Att. Res.*, 1948.

28. Eysenck, H.J. "The Psychology of Anti-Semitism." *Nineteenth Century*, 1948, 164, 277-284.

29. Farnsworth, P.R. "Changes in 'Attitude Toward War' During the College Years." *J. Soc. Psychol.*, 1937, 8, 274-9.

30. Farnsworth, P.R., and Misumi. "1. Further Data on Suggestion in Pictures." *Amer. J. Psychol.*, 1931, 43, 632.

31. Ferguson, L.W. "Primary Social Attitudes." *J. Psychol.*, 1939, 8, 217-223.

32. Fink, K., and Cantril, H. "The Collegiate Stereotypes as a Frame of Reference." *J. Abn. Soc. Psychol.*, 1937, 32, 352-6.

33. Fletcher, J.M. "Verdict of Psychologists on War Instincts." *Sci. Mon.*, 1932, 35, 142-5.

34. Gardiner, H.N., Metcalf, R.C., and Neene-Center, J. G. *Feeling and Emotion: A History of Theories.* New York: American Book Co., 1937.

36. Glover, E. *War, Sadism, and Pacifism.* London: G. Allen and Unwin, 1935.

37. Haggard, E., and Rose, G.S. "Some Effects of Mental Set and Active Participation in the Conditioning of the Autokinetic Phenomenon." *J. Exp. Psychol.*, 1944, 34, 45-59.

38. Hartmann, G.W. "The Contradiction Between the Feeling-Tone of Political Party Names and Public Response to Their Platforms." *J. Soc. Psychol.*, 1936, 7, 336-55.

39. Hopkins, P. *Psychology of Social Movements.* London: Allen and Unwin, 1938.

41. Jones, E.S. "The Opinions of College Students." *J. Appl. Psychol.*, 1926, 10, 427-36.

43. Katz, D., and Braly, K. "Racial Stereotypes of One Hundred College Students." *J. Abn. Soc. Psychol.*, 1933, 28, 280-90.

44. Kirkendall, L.A. "A Study of the Changes, Formation, and Persistence of Attitudes of Pacifism." *J. Educ. Sociol.*, 1937, 1, 222-8.

45. Knower, F.H. "Experimental Studies of Changes of Attitudes. I. A Study of the Effects of Oral Argument on Changes of Attitudes." *J. Soc. Psychol.*, 1935, 6, 315-47.

48. Krout, M.H., and Stagner, R. "Personality Development in Radicals." *Sociometry*, 1939, 2, 31-46.

49. Kulp, D.H. "Prestige, as Measured by Single-Experience Changes and Their Permancy." *J. Educ. Res.*, 1934, 27, 663-72.

50. Lasswell, H.D. *Psychopathology and Politics.* Chicago: Univ. of Chicago Press, 1930.

51. Levine, J.M., and Murphy, G. "The Learning and Forgetting of Controversial Material." *J. Abn. Soc. Psychol.*, 1943, 38, 507-17.

52. Levine, R., Chein, I., and Murphy, G. "The Relation of the Intensity of a Need to the Amount of Perceptual Distortion: A Preliminary Report." *J. Psychol.*,

1942, 13, 283-93.

53. Longstreet, R.J. "An Experiment with the Thurstone Attitude Scales." *Sch. Rev.,* 1935, 43, 202-8.

56. Lundberg, G.A. "Sex Differences on Social Questions." *Sch. and Soc.,* 1926, 23, 595-600.

58. Marple, C.H. "The Comparative Susceptibility of Three Age Levels to the Suggestion of Group Versus Expert Opinion." *J. Soc. Psychol.,* 1933, 4, 176-86.

63. Moore, H.T. "The Comparative Influence of Majority and Expert Opinion." *Amer. J. Psychol.,* 1931, 32, 16-20.

61. Menefee, S.C. "The Effect of Stereotyped Words on Political Judgments." *Amer. Sociol. Rev.,* 1936, 1, 614-21.

66. Murphy, G., Murphy, L. B., and Newcomb, T. M. *Experimental Social Psychology.* New York: Harpers, 1937.

67. Murray, H.A. "The Effect of Fear Upon Estimates of the Maliciousness of Other Personalities." *J. Soc. Psychol.,* 1933, 4, 310-29.

68. Page, K. "19,000 Clergymen on War and Peace." *World Tomorrow.* 1931, 14, 138-54.

69. Peters, H.N. "The Judgmental Theory of Pleasantness and Unpleasantness." *Psychol. Rev.,* 1935, 42, 354-86.

71. Pihlblad, C.T. "Student Attitudes Towards War." *J. Sociol. Soc. Rev.,* 1936, 20, 248-54.

72. Pintner, R.A. "A Comparison of Interests, Abilities, and Attitudes." *J. Abn. Soc. Psychol.,* 1933, 27, 351-7.

73. Porterfield, A.L. "Opinions About War." *Sociol. Soc. Res.,* 1937-38, 22, 252-64.

75. Proshansky, H.M., and Murphy, G. "The Effects of Reward and Punishment on Perception." *J. Psychol.,* 1942, 13, 295-305.

77. Rice, S.A. "Stereotypes: A source of error in judging human character." *J. Person. Res.,* 1926, 5, 267-76.

78. Rosenthal, S.R. "Change of Socio-Economic Attitudes Under Radical Motion Picture Propaganda." *Arch. Psychol.,* New York: 1934, No. 166.

79. Rundquist, A., and Shelto, D. *Personality in the Depression.* Minnesota: Univ. of Minn. Press, 1933.

80. Sanford, R.N. "The Effects of Abstinence from Food Upon Imaginal Processes: A Preliminary Experiment." *J. Psychol.,* 1936, 2, 129-36.

81. Sanford, R.N. A Further Experiment." *Ibid.,* 1937, 3, 145-59.

82. Schaffer, R., and Murphy, G. "The Role of Autism in a Visual Figureground Relationship." *J. Exp. Psychol.,* 1943, 32, 335-43.

84. Sherif, M. "An Experimental Study of Stereotypes." *J. Abn. Soc. Psychol.,* 1935, 29, 371-75.

85. Sherif, M. *The Psychology of Social Norms.* 1936.

86. Sherif, M. "A Study of Some Social Factors in Perception." *Arch. Psychol.,* 1935, No. 187.

88. Sims, V.M. "Factors Influencing Attitude Toward the T.V.A." *J. Abn. Soc. Psychol.,* 1938, 33, 34-56.

89. Smith, J.J. "What One College Thinks of War and Peace?" *J. Appl. Psychol.,* 1933, 17, 17-28.

91. Sorokin, P.G., and Goldgreff, J.W. "An Experimental Study of the Influence of Suggestion on the Discrimination and the Valuation of People." *Amer. J. Social.,* 1932, 37, 720-37.

94. Stagner, R. "Fascist Attitudes: Their Determining Conditions." *J. Soc. Psychol.,* 1936, 7, 438-54.

95. Stagner, R. "Some Factors Related to Attitude Toward War." 1938. *J. Soc. Psychol.,* 1942, 16, 131-42.

97. Stagner, R. "Opinions of Psychologists on Peace Planning." *J. Psychol.,* 1945, 19, 3-16.

98. Stagner, R. "Studies of Aggressive Social Attitudes: 1. Measurement and Interrelation of Selected Attitudes." *J. Soc. Psychol.,* 1944, 20, 109-20.

99. Stagner, R. II. "Changes from Peace to War." *J. Soc. Psychol.,* 1944, 20, 121-28.

100. Stagner, R. III. "The Role of Personal and Family Scores." *J. Soc. Psychol.,* 1944, 20, 129-40.

105. Stump, N.F., and Lewis, A. "What Some Ministers Think About War." *Rel. Educ.,* 1935, 70, 135-57.

107. Thurstone, L.L. "Influence of Motion Pictures on Children's Attitudes." *J. Soc. Psychol.*, 1931, 2, 291-305.

109. Turteltaub, D. *The Influence of Suggested Majority Opinion Upon Attitude Toward Prohibition and Militarism.* Minneapolis: Univ. Minn. Ph.D. Thesis, 1932. Quoted by Bird, C., q.v.

110. Vetter, G.B. "The Measurement of Social and Political Attitudes and the Repeated Personality Factors." *J. Abn. Soc. Psychol.*, 1930, 25, 149-89.

111. Wheller, D., and Jordan, H. "Change of Individual Opinion to Accord With Group Opinion." *J. Abn. Soc. Psychol.*, 1930, 25, 149-89.

Notes

1. The term 'radical' in psychological literature denotes the person occupying the Opposite pole of an attitude continuum to the 'conservative'; it is roughly synonymous with 'progressive', signifying 'advanced' opinions.

2. Such studies are in progress at the moment.

3. In classifying stereotypes in terms of pleasant (adient) and unpleasant (abient) reactions, the writer wishes to bring the whole concept of 'stereotyped' attitudes into relation with the judgmental theory of affectivity as stated by Carr (1925) and elaborated by Peters (1935). According to this theory, Affection is a meaning; the meaning P (pleasantness) is a function of a normal reaction tendency to approach the object (ad-ire), the meaning U (unpleasantness) of a reaction tendency to avoid it (ab-ire). This way of looking at stereotypes is useful because it brings to bear on the discussion a whole mass of experimental and theoretical work done in connection with affective states generally. Summaries of this work, as well as a treatment of the judgmental theory of affectivity, will be found in McGeoch (1942), Rapaport (1942), Beebe-Center (1932), Young (1943), Gardiner et al. (1937), and Hunt (1939).

4. Class error-judging the individual not in terms of his personal unique characteristic but only as a member of some class or group, i.e. a Jew, a Communist, an old maid, or a Negro.

5. In addition to the papers here discussed, the reader may wish to consult a symposium, "Psychological Considerations in Making the Peace," *J. Abnorm. Soc. Psychol.* 38, 131-224.

The Disparity Between Biological and Cultural Evolution in the Pursuit of Peace

David P. Barash
University of Washington

The pursuit of peace is, to put it mildly, an enormous undertaking. As such, it ironically calls for both arrogance and humility: Arrogance because its goal is so vast and one that has withstood intense, well-meaning efforts on the part of wonderfully competent people for hundreds of generations; humility because the issue is simply too large, too complex, too multifactorial, to be easily pigeonholed or encompassed by any single theory, or book chapter. In the pages to come, I shall nonetheless seek to describe a way of thinking about why human beings find themselves in such dire straits and why the pursuit of peace is so difficult. I shall also suggest how the general theory I am about to propose might contribute toward creating a more peaceful world.

The Case for Humility

The arrogance implicit in suggesting a single general theory along these lines is likely to be painfully obvious. Hence, before going on, I must gesture toward humility. Any attempt to include such enormous issues within a single theory brings to mind the famous story of the blind men and the elephant, as told by the nineteenth-century American poet, John Saxe:

> "It was six men from Industan, to learning much inclined,
> Who went to see the elephant (though all of them were blind),
> That each by observation might satisfy his mind..."

Not surprisingly, each blind man felt a different part of the elephant, so that the one touching its legs thought they were tree trunks, the one touching its tail thought it was a snake, and so on. At the end, they

> "Disputed loud and long, each in his opinion stiff and strong,
> Though each was partly in the right, and all of them were wrong."

War is a bit like an elephant: too complex to be easily tamed, or readily understood, maybe even too large to be perceived accurately. (And also, of course, too big and too potentially dangerous to ignore!) But at the same time, because it is so large and so dangerous, we need all the help we can get when it comes to understanding, and perhaps, even controlling it. (And although peace is assuredly more than the avoidance of war, the latter is a necessary precondition for the former.)

The conflict between biological and cultural evolution—for that is what I shall be discussing—does not hold *the* key to all issues of peace and war, nor will it unlock all human distress generally…but I think it is a useful intellectual instrument, one of many tools that should be of help. I propose it, therefore, not as the only explanation for war, somehow carrying within it *the* key to peace, but as one of many ways to help clarify and understand the human dilemma encompassed in this volume's inspiring yet tantalizing title.

The Argument in a Nutshell

Human beings are intelligent creatures, intelligent enough to have developed many concepts, including that of intelligence itself. We are by our own accounts the smartest inhabitants of this planet. How can such very clever beasts be in danger of exterminating themselves? How can we be so smart and yet so suicidal? How can we allow ourselves to drift toward the unparalleled catastrophe of war? How is it that peace has long been so tantalizing, so difficult to achieve?

In one of the opening scenes of Stanley Kubrick's masterpiece movie, "2001: A Space Odyssey," viewers witnessed what might have been the world's first murder. The ape-man exultantly threw his club (actually, the leg-bone of a zebra) into the air, and as it spun, it morphed into an orbiting space station. In this stunning image, millions of movie-goers saw the human dilemma in microcosm: We are unmistakably animals, yet we also behave in ways that transcend the merely organic. Ape-men all, we are the products of biological evolution—a Darwinian process that is both slow and altogether organic—yet at the same time we are enmeshed in our own cultural evolution, which, by contrast, is blindingly fast and which proceeds under its own rules.

We are on Mr. Toad's wild ride…yet at the same time, we are *all* toads. Therein lies the rub, and also the argument I am about to make: Much of the human dilemma, and our problems with violence and war in particular, derives from our peculiar existence, simultaneously, in two worlds, the often inconsistent realms of biology and of culture. While the cinematic ape-man's club traveled through air and ultimately, into outer space, millions of years of biological and cultural evolution were collapsed into five seconds. My point, however, is that this isn't simply a camera trick: We are all time-travelers, with one foot thrust into the cultural present and the other stuck in the biological past. Athough it seems arrogant to propose anything as *the* primary root of our human difficulty—and despite my earlier protestations!—I am about to do just that.

"It is dangerous," wrote Pascal,

> to show man too clearly how much he resembles the beast without at the same time showing him his greatness. It is also dangerous to allow him too clear a vision of his greatness without his baseness. It is even more dangerous to leave him in ignorance of both. But it is very profitable to show him both.

As purely biological creatures, we are neither more nor less "great" than our fellow organic beings. As cultural creatures, however, we are extraordinary indeed. We compose symphonies, travel to the moon, and explore the world of subatomic particles. But at the same time we are unique among living things in being genuinely uncomfortable in our situation. This should not be surprising, because even though our cultural greatness must have somehow derived from our organic beastliness, the two processes (organic and cultural) have become largely disconnected; and as a result, so have we: from ourselves, each other, our environment.

The little hyphen in ape-man is the longest line imaginable, connecting two radically different worlds, one biological and one cultural. Imagine two people chained together; one a world-class sprinter, the other barely able to hobble. Now, imagine that they are both expected to run as quickly as possible: the likely outcome includes more than a bit of tension all around.

To understand why biological and cultural evolution can experience such conflict (despite the fact that they both emanate from the same creature), consider the extraordinarily different rates at which they proceed. Biological evolution is unavoidably slow. An individual, after all, cannot evolve. Only populations or lineages do so. And they are shackled to the realities of genetics and reproduction, since organic evolution is neither more nor less than a process whereby gene frequencies change over time. It is an unfolding Darwinian event in which new genes and gene combinations are evaluated against existing options, with the most favorable making a statistically greater contribution in succeeding generations. Accordingly, many generations are required for even the smallest evolutionary step.

By contrast, cultural evolution is essentially Lamarckian, and astoundingly rapid. Acquired characteristics can be "inherited" in hours or days, before being passed along to other individuals, then modified yet again and passed along yet more—or dropped altogether—everything proceeding in much less time than a single generation. Take the computer revolution. In just a decade or so (less than an instant in biological evolutionary time), personal computers were developed and proliferated (also modified, many times over), such that they are now part of the repertoire of all technologically literate people. If, instead, computers had "evolved" by biological means, as a favorable mutation to be possibly selected in one, or even a handful, of individuals, there would currently be only a dozen or so computer-users instead of a billion or more.

Just a superficial glance at human history shows that the pace of cultural change has been not only rapid—compared with the rate of biological change—but if anything the *rate of increase* in that change seems itself to be increasing, generating a kind of logarithmic curve. Today's world is vastly different from that of a century ago, which is almost unimaginably different from 50,000 years ago…not because the world itself has changed, or the biological nature of human beings, but because such cultural creations as fire, the wheel, metals, writing, printing, electricity, internal combustion engines, television and nuclear energy have been generated at blinding speed.

Try the following *Gedanken*-experiment. Imagine that you could exchange a newborn baby from the mid-Pleistocene—say, 50,000 years ago—with a twenty-first century newborn. Both children—the one fast-forwarded no less than the other brought back in time—would doubtless grow up to be normal members of their society, essentially indistinguishable from their colleagues who had been naturally born into it. A Cro-Magnon infant, having grown up in twenty-first century America, could very well end up contributing an essay to a volume published by the Eleanor Roosevelt Institute for Justice and Peace, while the offspring of today's peace activists and scholars would fit perfectly into a world of mastodon skins and chipped stone axes. But switch a modern human adult and an adult from the late Ice Age, and there would be Big Trouble either way. Human biology has scarcely changed in tens of thousands of years, whereas our culture has changed radically, presenting us with opportunities and challenges for which our biology has not prepared us, or, in some crucial cases, has positively misled us.

Admittedly, our capacity for culture is itself a product of our biological evolution, and yet, this is no guarantee that the two must proceed in synchrony. If anything, the opposite is more likely, since culture, like an errant and headstrong child—or Frankenstein's monster—has become disconnected from its biological moorings, and has pretty much developed a momentum of its own, proceeding nearly independently of the biological process that originally spawned it. This is because cultural evolution has the capacity to take off on its own, to mutate, reproduce, and spread with such speed as to leave its biological parent far behind in the dust. In theory, the two might still be pointed toward the same ends, but biological evolution remains shackled by genetics—and thus, it lumbers along at the pace of a tortoise, never faster than one generation at a time, and nearly always much slower than that—while cultural evolution plays by its own rules, which often means a mad dash, like a hare. There isn't even much reason to expect the two to be headed in the same direction.

In Aesop's fable, the tortoise eventually wins, because the hare is foolish, over-confident and easily distracted, whereas the tortoise (although slow) is persistent. In the real world, culture and biology differ in speed but they are equally foolish and equally stubborn. Most important, they will both cross the finish-line together because despite their differences they are inextricably tied to each other. It is a strange spectacle, a cosmic sack-race featuring two mismatched Siamese twins. Except that we are part of the show.

Don't misunderstand: Cultural evolution isn't altogether foreign to certain animal species (doubters might want to consult Frans de Waal's recent book, *The Ape and the Sushi Master*[1]) and biological evolution leaves a definite imprint on human behavior (much of my own writing and research, such as *Revolutionary Biology*[2] and *The Myth of Monogamy*[3] seeks to make precisely this point). But it remains true that in the case of human beings, culture provides the dominant context whereas biology lurks in the background, with the two intersecting and interacting in ways that suggest few generalizations except this: the outcome is likely to be troublesome.

Fortunately, there can also be considerable harmony between our culture and our biology, in part because our biology is flexible, like a "one size fits all" garment, able to conform to many different shapes, and in part because culture isn't so stupid as to attempt to force our biology to conform to patterns that are "inhuman," such as a society in which people are expected to sleep 23 hours a day, or not at all. Whereas all human behavior derives from both biology and culture, both nature and nurture, it does not necessarily follow that biology and culture are always comfortably adjusted to each other. On balance, just as we must look to the interaction between nature and nurture for the sources of our behavior, we can look to the conflict between nature and nurture for the sources of most of our difficulties. A useful rule in murder mysteries has long been "cherchez la femme"; when *Homo sapiens* is having trouble, a useful rule—although not yet a cliché—would be to look for possible conflict between the hare and the tortoise, between our culture and our biology.

To change the metaphor: two huge continents have drifted apart and now these great tectonic plates, culture and biology, grind together. The results range from nearly trivial squeaks and wriggles, such as our troublesome sweet tooth or some of our sexual peccadilloes, to the most portentous quakes, including nuclear war, environmental abuse and overpopulation, while in between lie a host of middle-sized tremors such as personal alienation and family dysfunction. And violence. The conflict between culture and biology, the Siamese sack-race between hare and tortoise, is an event of paradoxical proportions, ranging from the seismic to the microscopic, from whole societies (indeed, the whole planet and its past, present, and future) to individual people and their likes and dislikes.

We might think of war as representing, at least in part, a kind of evolutionary hangover, fully aware that the phrase is something of a *double entendre*. On the one hand, it refers to hangovers in the common usage; that is, a bad, unpleasant, painful consequence of earlier indulgence...perhaps our species-wide indulgence in rapid cultural evolution. But at the same time, it refers to something hanging over us all, like a dangerous rockfall, or potential avalanche, threatening to cause great distress to its victims. I suggest that we all suffer from hangovers of both these types, and that in the disparity between our biological inclinations and our cultural reality lies much of the difficulty that bedevils the human species, including—but not limited to—the problem of war, and constituting one of the major obstacles encountered by people pursuing peace.

Violence and Aggression as Evolutionary Hangovers

With this admittedly long preface, let us turn specifically to violence and aggression. After all, this is what our cinematic ape-man was doing when so adroitly captured on film. It is also something that many people do. The history of "civilization" is, in large part, one of ever-greater efficiency in killing: with increasing ease, at longer distance, and in larger numbers. Just consider the "progression" from club, knife and spear, to bow and arrow, musket, rifle, cannon, machine gun, battleship, bomber, and nuclear-tipped ICBM. At the same time, the human being who creates and manipulates these marvelous devices has not changed at all. Considered as a biological creature, in fact, *Homo sapiens* is poorly adapted to kill: The reality is that with our puny nails, non-prognathic jaws and laughably tiny teeth, a human being armed only with his biology is hard-pressed to kill just one fellow human, not to mention hundreds or millions. But culture has made this not only possible but easy.

Animals whose biological equipment make them capable of killing each other are generally disinclined to do so. Eagles, wolves, lions, and crocodiles have been outfitted by organic evolution with lethal weaponry and not coincidentally, they have also been provided with inhibitions to their use against fellow species-members. (This generalization was exaggerated in the past.[4] Today, we know that lethal disputes, infanticide, and so forth do occur, but the basic pattern still holds: Rattlesnakes, for example, are not immune to each other's venom, yet when they fight, they strive to push each other over backwards, not to kill.) Since human beings have not been equipped, by biological evolution, with lethal weaponry, there was little pressure to balance our nonexistent organic armamentarium with behavioral inhibitions concerning its use. And so, we find ourselves outfitted via cultural evolution with a truly awesome and terrifying capacity for killing and destruction, while at the same time bereft of any biologically mediated inhibitions against doing so. No competent engineer would allow such a souped-up model to leave the assembly line without a good set of brakes, but that is precisely what has happened to the human species as a result of the disconnect between our biology and our culture.

One reason why guns are so dangerous is that the lethal consequence of a very small movement—curling a finger around a trigger, with barely a few ounces of pressure—are magnified, by superb technology, into violent acts of dreadful consequence. If, by contrast, we had to live—and die—by the application of direct, biological force alone, there would be far more living and less dying. For another, and terrifyingly recent example of the multiplier effect of technology upon a biological creature, consider the paradox that on September 11, 2001, a handful of people armed only with the lowest-tech weapons—box-cutters—were able to commandeer high-tech devices, civilian airliners, and turn them into effective devices of mass destruction.

The dreadful history of human-human slaughter leaves little doubt that our species is not automatically prone to respect the subordination gestures of potential victims. Moreover, even if he possessed such instinctive inhibitions on his own lethal violence (and usually it is *his* violence), the bombardier, flying 20,000 feet above his victim—or the military leader on a distant continent with his finger on The Button—couldn't even perceive such gestures.

Nuclear Weapons in Particular

The disconnect between culture and biology is especially acute in the realm of nuclear weapons. At the one-year anniversary of the bombing of Hiroshima, Albert Einstein famously noted that "the splitting of the atom has changed everything but our way of thinking; hence we drift toward unparalleled catastrophe."

To clarify Einstein's point, and connect it to my own, consider animals known as musk-oxen. These great beasts, which look like shaggy bison and occupy the Arctic tundra, have long employed a very effective strategy when confronted by their ancient biological enemies: wolves. Musk-oxen respond to a wolf-attack by herding the juveniles into the center, while the adults face outward, arrayed like the spokes of a wheel. Even the hungriest wolf finds it intimidating to confront a wall of sharp horns and bony foreheads, backed by a thousand pounds of angry adult musk-oxen. For countless generations, their anti-predator response served the musk-oxen well. But now, the primary danger to musk-oxen is not wolves, but human hunters, riding snowmobiles and carrying high-powered hunting rifles. Under this circumstance, musk-oxen would be best served if they spread out and ran for the horizon, but instead they respond as previous generations have always done: they form their trusted defensive circle, and are easily slaughtered.

The invention of the snowmobile and the rifle have changed everything but the musk-oxen way of thinking; hence they drift toward unparalleled catastrophe. (Musk-oxen are currently a threatened species.) They cling to their biology, even though culture—our culture—has changed the payoffs. Human beings also cling to—or remain unconsciously influenced by—their biology, even as our own culture has dramatically revised the payoffs for ourselves as well. That musk ox-like stubbornness is especially evident when it comes to thinking—or not thinking—about nuclear weapons.

For millenia, violence and war have been effective ways of solving human disputes. This is not to claim that they have been good, or ethically acceptable, simply that they have been effective, at least in that the victors have often—although not always—achieved their ends. And so people have grown accustomed to thinking of war as achieving potential success; they are ill-prepared to consider that nuclear war, or other conflicts involving weapons of mass destruction, are unlikely to generate victory, even for the side nominally "victorious."

Similarly, success has typically gone in the past to the side with more weapons: more warriors, more bows and arrows, more spears, more muskets, more artillery generally translates into victory. As a result, people have been mesmerized into thinking that more nuclear weapons, too, will mean more success and that conversely, having fewer than one's opponent will necessarily result in failure. The result has been a frustrating and perhaps tragic refusal to accept reductions and even limitations on these weapons. The ancient tendency to equate numerical superiority with security and lower numbers with insecurity has long blocked potential arms-control agreements.

For another example of the dangerous disparity between our cultural creations and our biological inclinations, consider the widespread difficulty so many people have when it comes to conceiving nuclear effects. When told something is "hot," human beings readily think in terms of boiling water, burning wood, or perhaps molten lava. The biological creature that is *Homo sapiens* literally cannot conceive of temperatures in the millions of degrees. Before the artificial splitting of uranium and plutonium atoms (a cultural/technological innovation if ever there was one), nuclear energy had never been released on earth. No wonder we are unprepared to "wrap our minds" around it. Similarly with the vast scale of nuclear destruction: We can imagine a small number of deaths—so long as none of them include our own!—but are literally unable to grasp the meaning of deaths in the millions, all potentially occurring within minutes. And so, the conflict between our biological natures and our cultural products has cloaked nuclear weapons in a kind of psychological untouchability.

By the same token, the "cave man" within us has long prospered by paying attention to threats that are discernible—a stampeding mastodon, a Neanderthal with an upraised club, a nearby volcano—while remaining at the same time less concerned about what cannot be readily perceived. Since nuclear weapons generally cannot be seen, touched, heard or smelled, they tend to evade our radar, allowing the "nuclear Neanderthal" to function as though these threats to his and her existence don't exist at all. (Not surprisingly, national policies that "refuse to confirm or deny" the presence of such weapons add further yet to their aura of invisibility, and hence, non-existence.) If a homicidal lunatic were to stalk one's workplace, or if a fire suddenly broke out at home, most people would doubtless respond, and quickly. But although we are all stalked by a far more dangerous menace, the Neanderthal within us remains relatively complacent.

Consider, as well, the phenomenon of pain. Pain is an important biological attribute of living things, and although it is—by definition—uncomfortable, pain is a crucial sensation, insofar as it warns us that we are being injured, and at risk of further damage. Not surprisingly, pain is something that living creatures take seriously; they also go to great lengths to avoid it. Indeed, it is doubtless adaptive to do so: Our ancestors were unlikely to enhance their biological success if they stuck their hands in a fire, or banged their heads against rocks. And so, like other creatures, we are deeply imbued with a healthy tendency to avoid pain. To this common-sense observation must be added the fact that pain can be emotional no less than physical. The result is a strangely dangerous combination, especially in the twenty-first century.

Thus, the great majority of Americans—and in all likelihood, human beings in general—are strongly disposed to go about their lives following ancient evolutionary instructions to minimize their pain, which, in the case of war (including but not limited to nuclear weapons) typically involves minimizing their emotional and intellectual contact with the topic. Even thinking about nuclear war is painful; indeed, I can attest from personal experience that it can lead to nightmares and a variety of unpleasant anxiety reactions.

People are therefore inclined to think about other things. I would venture to suggest that even people who are professionally called to immerse themselves in the likely effects of various war-fighting modalities tend to insulate themselves from the horror of what they are supposed to be contemplating, leaving the field pretty much to those who are dangerously insulated from the "healthy pain" that they ought to be feeling, and which would likely diminish their commitment and enthusiasm for their own work. Ironically, therefore, an otherwise adaptive trait—avoidance of pain—further contributes to our species-wide reluctance to face the danger of war, thereby making us all *less* safe.

According to Greek mythology, the gods punished Prometheus—who had impudently given fire to human beings—by chaining him to a great mountain, whereupon he was visited daily by a vulture, who chewed on his liver. Modern human beings, biological creatures acting not in deliberate evolutionary time but in a cultural frenzy, have unleashed a much more dangerous fire than Prometheus could ever have imagined, a fire made all the more lethal by the fact that, deep inside, we really aren't very modern ourselves. In "Prometheus Bound," Aeschylus asks:

> "Prometheus, Prometheus, hanging upon Caucasus,
> Look upon the visage of yonder vulture:
> Is it not thy face, Prometheus?"

Two-thousand years later, Pogo said it more simply:

> "We have met the enemy and it is us."

Nationalism

There are numerous other arenas in which the conflict between cultural and biological evolution plays itself out, with the outcome being an intensification of violence and a propensity for war that must somehow be overcome if we are not only to pursue peace, but to obtain it. One of the most prominent is nationalism, a force that has generated extraordinary devotion as well as horrendous suffering and death. Nationalism makes no biological sense in its current form, but I suggest that if we inquire into its evolutionary roots—both biological and cultural—a familiar pattern emerges. Thus, it is consistent with evolutionary wisdom that individuals feel themselves closely associated with others in order to survive and eventually, to achieve personal success. Initially, the number of crucial "others" is small, notably one's parents, then it enlarges to include immediate family members, with the circle of concern, dependence and affiliation gradually expanding as each person grows older. The evolutionary concept of "kin selection" is directly relevant here, whereby individuals are selected to be responsible for and to seek safety within the protective embrace of close relatives.

This circle of concern continues to grow, including lineages and small tribal groups, reflecting the social organization that doubtless characterized human ancestors for more than 99 percent of their evolutionary history. In recent historical times, however, the circle of concern has expanded at an extraordinary rate, such that it currently encompasses nation-states consisting of literally millions or hundreds of millions of individuals. Such national affiliations make no biological sense, but they nonetheless continue to tug at our deeper emotions, probably because they reflect a basic biological wisdom: When in doubt, affiliate with a group, and the larger the group the better. (After all, solitary individuals were typically at the mercy of groups, and when prehistoric groups came into conflict, the larger group was likely to win.) In short, it seems plausible that human beings today are left with a biologically generated fondness for groups, the larger the better, such that even though cultural evolution has rendered these affiliations biologically meaningless—and even downright dangerous—we are nonetheless attracted to them, like moths to a flame.

Here, too, an animal model may be helpful. There exists a crow-sized bird known as the American oystercatcher, which incubates its eggs like any other species. However, when researchers make an artificially enlarged egg—including one as big as a watermelon, and thus weighing more than ten times the largest adult—American oystercatchers will abandon their real eggs and sit, absurdly yet determinedly, atop these grotesque devices. Specialists in animal behavior refer to "supernormal releasers," exaggerated stimuli that—like the artificially enlarged oystercatcher "eggs"—generate an exaggerated and biologically inappropriate response.[5]

My suggestion is that when it comes to nationalism, human beings have provided themselves with supernormal releasers that are equivalent to the oystercatcher's watermelon/egg. Taking advantage of our species–wide susceptibility to the appeal of large social units, we have provided ourselves through modern culture with compelling stimuli in the form of nation–states, which, ironically, are divorced from biological reality but nonetheless exert a powerful influence on the human psyche. There is evolutionary meaning to small social groups consisting of genetic relatives and reciprocating friends, just as there is to the largest social unit: the human species. But there is virtually no biological payoff that human beings derive from affiliating with countries whose population is both too large and too small to be meaningful. Cultural evolution created these entities, and biological evolution renders them attractive, even as they are not only nonfunctional, but downright dysfunctional.

Pursuing Peace with the Environment

The pursuit of peace must include the prevention of war (plus the termination of wars that are ongoing, as well as peacekeeping in situations in which war is imminent, or has only recently been interrupted). At the same time, it is important to note that anti-war policies—aimed at producing what practitioners in the rapidly growing field of Peace Studies call "negative peace"—is not enough. In the long run, we must orient ourselves toward "positive peace," a clear-eyed acknowledgment of what we are *for*, not just what we are *against*. In this regard, positive peace must include (but not be limited to) peace with our environment. And here, once again, the conflict between our cultural and our biological evolution appears to loom large.

In a sense, it can be argued that nothing human

beings do can ever be "unnatural," since after all, *Homo sapiens* is a biological organism. But since we are also creators and creatures of cultural evolution, our actions have tended, increasingly, to transcend the organic realm. In a sense, we destroy our environment because we are able to. No other species of animal or plant poses a threat to the integrity of the earth, because none has the means to to so; any that made their environment uninhabitable for themselves are—not surprisingly!—not around today, and none ever had the capacity to destroy more than their immediate niche or limited ecosystem. But as with our weapons, our destructive capacity does not derive solely from our biological characteristics. As animals we make only a small dent in natural communities, and, except for our extraordinary numbers, from the neck down we are interesting but unremarkable animals. However, with the addition of tools, division of labor, language, and higher rational and technological capabilities, we have been exploiting nature in a way never seen before. Without cultural evolution, this would not be possible. With it, we have accomplished most of the things we prize as making us particularly human. And with it, like unruly Samsons, we threaten to bring the earthly temple crashing down upon our heads.

Whenever animals and plants went extinct in the course of geological time, they did so because they could not adapt to a changing environment, not because they evolved themselves into extinction. Species suicide is unknown in nature, simply because the characteristics of living things are the result of biological evolution. Any genetically influenced tendencies that lead to decreased reproductive success would necessarily be selected against in the course of evolution, to be replaced by more benign traits. In the course of biological evolution, extinction occurs only as a result of happenings beyond the species control, or possibly when individuals, pursuing their selfish benefit, temporarily undercut the benefit of the larger whole.

By contrast, human environmental abuse—whether indirectly as a result of population growth, or directly as a result of destructive and polluting technology—is not subject to the typical biological controls. It is mediated by our culture, not by our genes. Furthermore, even if the tendency for environmental destruction were under genetic control, as it would be in animals subject only to biological evolution, the pace of our culturally induced environmental destruction is much too fast for differential reproduction to have any hope of restoring an equilibrium. Cultural evolution has provided us, almost overnight, with the tools to destroy the earth, while once more (as in the case of violence and war) denying us the kinds of inhibitions needed to restrict their use. Biology, acting alone, would never have granted us this awesome capability without also including protective controls; at least, not for long.

In general, biological evoluton proceeds by relatively small steps, rather than large, discontinuous leaps. The consequences of a particular trait—whether anatomical such as venomous fangs, or behavioral, such as threatening postures...or their absence—can therefore be evaluated by natural selection as it develops incrementally. By contrast, the enormous advances of human cultural evolution have provided us with great chunks of new characteristics, upon which evolution has not had opportunity to ruminate, and which in many cases must be either accepted or rejected as momentous technologic quantum leaps: the steam-powered locomotive, electronics, nuclear power, long-lasting pesticides, strip mining, acid rain, genetic engineering. If some Paleolithic forebear had evolved a propensity to do something that was ultimately harmful to itself or its genes, natural selection would have nipped it in the bud. But if the trait was beneficial to itself, even if harmful to others, it would have spread. Moreover, if it had the capacity of destroying the world, then it could hardly be selected against, since natural selection could only act upon it after it had its effect.

As in the case of weaponry and war, our failure to make peace with our environment has been stimulated, at least in part, by the ironic fact that we have been equipped with *fewer* biological inhibitions upon environmentally destructive behavior than have most animals. Once again, we are threatened more by the instincts that we lack than by those we possess.

"Man's chief difference from the brutes," wrote William James in *The Will to Believe*,[6]

> lies in the exuberant excess of his subjective propensities—his pre-eminence over them simply and solely in the number and in the fantastic and unnecessary character of his wants: physical, moral, aesthetic, and intellectual. Had his whole life not been a quest for the superlfuous, he would never have established himself as inexpungably as he has done...

As James saw it, this was a cause for celebration, not regret: "And from the consciousness of this he should draw the lesson that his wants are to be trusted; that even when their gratification seems furthest off, the uneasiness they occasion is still the best guide of his life, and will lead him to issues entirely beyond his present power of reckoning. Prune down his extravagance, sober him, and you undo him." It remains to be seen, however, whether human beings will undo themselves first, as a result of this extravagance, combined with the force-multiplying power of technology, in a context devoid of biologically mandated inhibitions.

Among the most pressing environmental dangers facing our planet must be numbered global warming and the rapid destruction of the world's tropical forests. Both are due to the "extravagance" of human need and greed. Both are clearly anthropogenic, and have been going on for thousands of years. But human beings, outfitted only with biological equipment, had limited negative impact in both cases: The occasional fire, or the tiny patch cleared for small-scale plantings, had minimal effect on a very large atmosphere and on forests of which people were only a small component, especially when slash–and–burn agriculturists would leave an area fallow for many years before returning.

A small—or even a moderate—quantity of something may be inocuous or even healthy. Excessive amounts, however, readily go beyond diminishing returns and often become troublesome, or dangerous. In small doses, such elements as zinc, cadmium, or nickel are necessary for life; in excess, they are poisons. Food is also necessary for life; in excess, it produces obesity. We would all die without oxygen; we would also die if forced to breathe 100 percent oxygen. A smokestack may be a sign of jobs and economic vitality; a forest of smokestacks may be a sign of air pollution and an environment rendered toxic. Agriculture is a marvelous way of providing food for people; unrestrained agriculture—complete with wholesale deforestation, water table depletion, and excessive use of fertilizers, pesticides, and herbicides—could sterilize the planet. There is, in short, much to be said for the Platonic "golden mean," but human cultural evolution seems to lead eventually not to moderation but rather, to excess.

Our environmental crisis has been fueled by three fundamental factors: First, the capability of producing enviornmental destruction (technology in a broad sense); second, the lack of inhibitions and integrated control regarding the exercise of this capability; and third, a particular attitude toward nature. Animals probably have no "attitude" toward nature, and it would make little difference if they did. Their mental abilities are too poorly developed for such abstract considerations and in any case, their lack of culture prevents them from acting effecively upon any "world view." By contrast, human beings typically do have an attitude toward nature and furthermore, they act on it, often very effectively.

This attitude is generally antagonistic and exploitative, at least in the Western world. Our capacity to exploit may even have directly diminished our need—and hence, our ability—to live peacefully with other *Homo sapiens.* Since we have the ability to "defeat" nonhuman nature even as we may be defeated by other human beings, we may have taken the path of least resistance during much of our experience as a species. After a conflict, if the loser leaves and succeeds elsewhere, his and her descendants may eventually have inherited the earth, but part of that inheritance would include relatively little capacity or inclination for working things out with our fellow human beings. It is therefore at least possible that our success in subduing nonhuman nature, and thereby colonizing new areas, has empowered us to be (at least for the short term) the masters of our planet, while at the same time depriving us of the much needed ability to live more harmoniously with each other.

Many people see the earth as something to be conquered rather than to be appreciated, as challenging and threatening rather than nourishing and protecting. Wilderness is to be tamed, not savored. Wildlife is a "resource," rather than fellow inhabitatants of our shared planet. And once you have seen one redwood tree, you have seen them all. Caught in a fundamantally schizophrenic division between culture and biology, we also tend to dichotomize the world, seeing it in arbitrarily dualistic terms: subject versus object, good guy versus bad guy, man versus nature. We live in two worlds, the biological and the cultural, and we therefore feel somehow separated from ourselves. And from nature as well.

Although this isolation of human beings from their natural environments may be largely unavoidable, a natural result of our capacity for cultural development, to some extent such attitudes are also encouraged by our peculiar cultural systems. Thus, the Western world view is strongly colored by Judeo-Christian religious concepts, which are themselves dualistic. Strict alternatives are at the core of Western religion: God vs His creation, sin vs redemption, heaven vs hell. We are only rarely sensitive to the unity of organism and environment. Nor are we readily inclined to act so as to preserve the integrity of the system as a whole. Under the traditional view, we were given "dominion" over all the earth, with explicit instructions to multiply and subdue it. We face life with a chip on our shoulder.[7]

Not only do we feel isolated from and antagonistic toward nature, we also "use" our environment to provide various complex gratifications: leisure, recreation, the experience of speed, of overblown material abundance, and of control. An animal asks only for the necessities, in return for which it provides necessities to others. The primitive Stone Age human being and the enlightened Eastern mystic are alike in taking from nature only the basic necessities while refraining from grossly destructive pursuits. The latter does so because of his greater understanding, the former because he is unable to do anything different. The rest of us lean on cultural levers of great power to pry from nature our various personal and collective needs and wants.

As Max Weber pointed out,[8] to the Easterner, rationalism means rational adjustment *to* nature; to most Westerners, by contrast, it means rational mastery *over* nature, a mastery that would be impossible without the levers of culture...and that may well be ultimately impossible in any event. Seeking to "win" in our self-proclaimed battle against our environment, to wrest satisfactions from a biological world that is equally intense—but often less successful—in seeking to retain its own structural integrity, we may yet defeat our environment. But if so, we shall also lose ourselves.

Comforts and luxuries become "necessities" because they are accessible through technology and because our colleagues have them. In addition, the simple facts of economic survival often require environmentally destructive behavior; the modern world "makes a living" by mining the environment, sometimes literally. Doing so, we are committing an economic sin, if not a theological one: dipping into our capital rather than living off the interest.

In our violent treatment of the earth we often reflect our own aggressiveness. Ethologists identify something called "redirected behavior," as when an angry man pounds a table or slams a door because he is inhibited from attacking the real object of his aggression.[9] We may similarly redirect much of our frustrated interpersonal aggressiveness toward our environment. It may be no coincidence that some of the world's most aggressive people, notably

Americans and Europeans, are also among the most environmentally destructive. In the process, we do violence to each other, and to ourselves.

Nobel Prize-winning physicist Murray Gell-Mann[10] pointed out

> [I]t used to be true that most things that were technologically possible were done but that certainly in the future this cannot and must not be so. As our ability to do all kinds of things, and the scale of them, increases—for the scale is planetary for so many things today—we must try to realize a smaller and smaller fraction of all the things that we can do. Therefore an essential element of engineering from now on must be the element of choice.

And here, there is some good news. Human beings can exercise choice. Increasingly, environmentally sensitive religious groups are seeking to redefine the human relationship to nature as one of stewardship rather than exploitation.[11] And increasingly—one hopes—a level of environmental sensitivity has seeped into daily thinking and even political discourse. As with the problem of violence and war, it remains to be seen whether such new culturally inspired ways of thinking will effectively counteract the lack of thinking, and—as important—the lack of inhibitory instincts—with which our species has been saddled.

Implications for Obtaining Peace

If you are "with me" at this point, you might be eager for some proposed solutions, but alas, the thrust of my message is more a way of thinking about our problem than a source of policy proposals. One thing, however, seems clear: Biology will not ride to our rescue. Evolution by natural selection is simply too slow, too short-sighted and stupid, too unresponsive to the challenges generated by our concurrent cultural evolution. Insofar as our difficulties derive from the disconnect between human biology and culture, we must look, therefore, to the latter, and to our large and multi-competent brains, for ways out of our current mess. After all, the remarkable flexibility of our cognitive capacities is itself a biological trait, by which evolution has endowed us, paradoxically, with the ability to transcend our own proclivities. We, alone among all living things, can say no to many of our inclinations, shed light on our blind spots, and maybe even help reconcile our ancient biology with our modern culture, to the ultimate benefit of ourselves, our fellow creatures, and our shared planet.

I worry, however, that readers might be feeling discouraged and pessimistic about whether humanity could ever overcome the disabling consequences of its biology/culture misfit. After all, we are not about to change our biological evolution…at least, not for many thousands of years. But this is to ignore the other side of the biology/culture divide: the role of culture. Although we would indeed be ill-advised to wait for biological evolution to ride to our rescue, there is every reason to think cultural evolution up to the task. After all, it was, in a sense, our rampaging culture that got us into our current mess; it seems only appropriate for culture to get us out of it! Moreover, although we assuredly are biological creatures, we are cultural creatures, too. Not only that, but our species has already shown itself to be extraordinary—indeed, unique—in the degree to which it can say no to our own biologically mediated inclinations. We, perhaps alone among all living things on earth, can do this.

After all, we engage in all sorts of activities that do not come naturally, but can be achieved once their desirability is apparent and sufficient social pressure is applied. For a homey example, take toilet-training. It is almost certainly unnatural, as evidenced by the fact that all people, all over the planet, take literally years to develop the skill. Moreover, an evolutionary perspective suggests an answer to this paradox: Whereas children have great difficulty with toilet-training, dogs and cats—creatures that are certainly stupider than *Homo sapiens*—can generally be house-broken in just a few days. As primates, we evolved in the trees, where tidy latrine habits were not a concern. (They are more an issue for those poor unfortunates down below!) But dogs and cats evolved in a two-dimensional world, in which it was adaptive to avoid fouling their dens. And so, they have developed a readiness to learn where—and where not—to relieve themselves. This is almost certainly the reason why other primates, such as chimpanzees or monkeys, also resist toilet-training. It goes against a deep-seated inclination.

But is it hopeless? Not at all. The likelihood is that virtually everyone reading this book has been successfully toilet-trained, his or her genetic predispositions notwithstanding. The point is this: Whatever our biological tendencies, there is reason for optimism about our capacity to rise above such inclinations, especially if we recognize the wisdom of doing so, once cultural forces are engaged. A primate that can learn to control its bowels can do almost anything. Certainly, it can learn to control its itchy trigger-finger, not to mention its inappropriate penchant for violence, along with its new-found capacity to destroy the earth.

But let there be no illusions: it will not be easy. In fact, the perspective espoused in this essay sheds some light on one of the most frustrating problems confronted by those of us attempting to teach peace, and by others wishing to generate peace-related activism. I believe that this problem—like so many others—also derives from the conflict between biological and cultural evolution. It has to do with people's tendency to become involved or not, the basis by which human beings decide where and how to expend their time, energy, and resources. Just as it has long been adaptive for human beings to attend only to threats that are apparent, to attempt to win, to avoid pain, and to affiliate with large groups, it was also appropriate—biologically as well as culturally—for them to select problems that are human-sized. It availed little, and was likely costly as well, to try to cap a volcano, to wrestle with a hurricane, or, for that matter, to struggle single-handedly against a mastodon. There are very few Don Quixotes...at least, among people who are in their right minds! Those who tilt against windmills, or battle oversized opponents, are likely to have been defeated. Biologically, their genes will not have prospered, and culturally, they will not have been emulated.

The sad reality is that war and environmental destruction are two of the largest and most intimidating of opponents. This discouraging asymmetry—between would-be peace and environmental activists and the forces of war and destruction—is enhanced by the fact that the "war establishments" and the forces promoting resource exploitation within all countries are immensely larger than any corresponding peace establishment. As a result, the great majority of people are disinclined to engage themselves in a struggle that seems so unlikely to be successful. Most human beings are far more likely to focus on day-to-day efforts, which promise day-to-day gratifications.

Peace Studies—a discipline in which I feel myself very much at home—has been analogized to medicine in that both fields, in contrast to most others, are not reluctant to identify a goal as "good," and thus, worth striving for. Thus, medicine unapologetically strives for health, just as Peace Studies unequivocally acknoweldges peace as a normative goal. However, one of the fundamental rules of medicine is that in order to prescribe effectively, one must first diagnose. I hope that the present essay has at least been helpful in this regard, in suggesting a partial diagnosis for the human predicament.

As to specific suggestions, I would point especially to interventions that might break up the dangerous incongruence between our biological inclinations and our cultural situation. Thus, anything that de-emphasizes national identity and focuses instead on world-wide similarities and shared interests should be encouraged. International exchange programs, which facilitate person-to-person interactions, would seem to merit special attention and resources, along with support for shared goals that cross traditional state boundaries.

I also believe that a form of planet-wide cognitive therapy would pay significant dividends.

Thus, primitive biologically mediated tendencies have been able to survive and prosper in part because they have largely gone unrecognized. There might therefore be great merit in identifying and criticizing dangerously outmoded ways of thought (or avoidance of thought), of the sort described in this essay. Most importantly, perhaps, is that the problems I have outlined are problems of human thinking or—all too often—not thinking. In many cases, they can, I believe, be rectified by appealing to that remarkable trait of *Homo sapiens*, the one that above all distinguishes us from other animals: our large cerebral hemispheres and our ability to behave with enlightened self-interest, once the issues are made clear. Thus, my experience is that it often helps if people are encouraged to understand the primitive nature of some of their automatic reactions—toward war, weapons, groups, the planet. It can also be beneficial to label these inclinations, in suitably pejorative terms. In the United States, for example, littering was greatly reduced by public-education campaigns labelling people who toss garbage onto the landscape as "litterbugs." No one wants to be a litterbug.

Similarly, it can be helpful to label those of us in the thrall of primitive thinking patterns as being captive of a "Neanderthal mentality," more suitable for the Pleistocene savanna than the twenty-first-century. (Some anthropologists may be incensed by this suggestion, pointing out, for example, that Neanderthalers had large brains, and evidently buried their dead with flowers; they may have been very fine, upstanding citizens in their own right. Nonetheless, the concept is metaphoric, and no one wants to be called a Neanderthal.)

Accordingly, there might be advantages to identifying such mental habits and labeling them invidiously, as they deserve. A bit of creative and well-meaning name-calling would not be amiss. As a result, I believe that some human misbehavior could be forestalled or redirected if people could be encouraged to rethink their premises, including their current inclinations to be cavalier and downright wrong when it comes to the dangers of nuclear weapons, to deal with increasingly lethal technology as though it is simply a bow-and-arrow writ large, to destroy their natural environment (the only one they have).

We would generally be well advised, as well, to be on guard against technologies that offer the prospect of killing with increased efficiency, at longer range, and with minimal personal impact upon the perpetrator. Similarly, we need to go beyond primitive inclinations to derive a sense a security from the accumulation of ever larger quantities of weapons, to divide the world into simple "with us or against us" dichotomies, to dehumanize our apparent opponents, to ignore the fact that the world has become vastly more interdependent than ever before.

Finally, a biologically informed peace strategy would suggest that the peace community may have been a bit unrealistic in assuming that people would willingly partake of agreements designed to foster the general welfare without obvious and direct personal benefits. Evolution is nothing if not selfish—at the level of individuals and even more so, that of genes. Accordingly, it may be that traditional *realpolitik* must be supplemented with what we might call *realbiology*, a recognition that the pursuit of peace, if it is to be successful, ought to take the biological nature of human beings more directly into account. Given that peace is not only patriotic, but—in a world bristling with weapons of mass destruction—in the biological interest of everyone, this should not be unrealistic, or even terribly difficult.

The argument of this essay does not disparage traditional interpretations as to the causes of war and other forms of organized violence and environmental abuse, such as the frustrations of those ill-served by current economic, social and political systems, failures of communication among elites in competing countries, the violence-generating components of ideologies, ethnic intolerance and religious fundamentalism, competition over resources, historical grievances, the manipulation of imagery by media, short-sighted greed, even the possible existence of plain, old-fashioned human evil. Ditto for the struggle to achieve a peaceful relationship with the nonhuman environment: it, too, involves many factors. The problems that bedevil any pursuit of peace are—as the psychoanalysts put it—"overdetermined," influenced by numerous considerations, most of them acting at the same time. Of these, the conflict between biological and cultural evolution is but a single consideration, although I believe that it is an important one, and that it suggests possible courses of therapy.

My point is that the pursuit of peace, to be successful, must take account of the unique situation in which *Homo sapiens* finds itself: the only species that lives simultaneously in two worlds, the cultural and the biological, and whose penchant for war and planetary destruction seems due, at least in part, to the dangerous discrepancy between them.

Any effort to pursue peace taking account of our own human nature must unavoidably grapple with certain fundamental uncertainties. (And any effort that ignores these issues will likely fail.) At minimum, we seem doomed to a kind of existential agnosticism, never knowing—and perhaps, never able to know—ourselves. What, then, should we do? It would be foolhardy if not irresponsible to let "nature" take its course, either our own biological nature, or the nature of human culture as currently constituted, because nature isn't necessarily good,[12] and moreover, nature at this point has no course independent of the one we plot. We are also deeply ignorant both of our limitations and our capabilities.

For a useful recommendation, we might turn to the philosopher Hans Vaihinger, who developed the philosophy of "Als Ob": As If.[13] Vaihinger emphasized that we make the world meaningful—indeed, tolerable—by living with certain fundamental fictions. We believe As If we are not personally going to die; As If the sensory-impressions that we receive are accurate reflections of an underlying reality; As If a just and benevolent god will reward virtue. (Or, for some of us, As If virtue carries its own reward... while for others, As If such worries can be ignored altogether.) We might also want to consider behaving As If we are free to say "no" or "yes" to our biology and our culture, as we choose, depending on the values we embrace. Wishful thinking cannot hold off personal death, or manipulate the insensate world, or create god from indifferent chaos. But when applied to human action on our human-dominated planet, behaving As If can become a self-fulfilling prophecy, something that empowers us in proportion as we believe it.

It remains to be seen whether *Homo sapiens* really does want to seize the future, and to do so in a uniquely human way, not just as the agents of natural selection acting around us and through us. "One of the most striking things about the struggle for freedom from intentional control is how often it has been lacking," wrote B. F. Skinner, in *Beyond Freedom and Dignity*.[14] "Many people have submitted to the most odious religious, governmental, and economic controls for centuries." I submit that this is due, at least in part, to the fact that our biology is, if anything, remarkably permissive, compared with that of most other animals. As a result, whereas zoologists can specify the typical living arrangements of honeybees, lions, or chimpanzees, it is remarkably difficult to identify the "normal" human social system. Our genes do very little to specify how we should live, and as a result, our institutions generally lack the validating infrastructure found in most animals; the result is an instability that may be truly human. Whether this is seen as distressing or exhilirating, however, is up to us.

In "The Grand Inquisitor" chapter of Dostoyevsky *The Brothers Karamazov*, for example, Christ returns to earth during the Spanish Inquisition and is informed that "nothing has ever been more insupportable for a man and a human society than freedom."[15] And in describing the effects of the Inquisition, we are told that "men rejoiced that they were again led like sheep, and that the terrible gift that had brought them such suffering was, at last, lifted from their hearts." At least, according to the Inquisitor.

Our challenge—as peacemakers and as human beings more generally—is to use this "terrible gift," our unique freedom as human beings, to humanize culture, technology, science, and society; in doing so, our reward is that we shall have humanized ourselves. The struggle to maintain selfhood, peace, and sustainability in the face of such dangers is extraordinary, but not altogether new. After all, the effort to avoid being dehumanized in the twenty-first-century is not all that different from the earlier effort to avoid being dehumanized by a saber-tooth. We won that battle; we can also win this one.[16]

Notes

1. De Waal, Frans. *The Ape and the Sushi Master.* New York: Basic Books, 2001.

2. Barash, David. *Revolutionary Biology: the new, gene-centered view of life.* New Brunswick, NJ: Transaction Publishers, 2001.

3. Barash, David, and Judith Eve Lipton. *The Myth of Monogamy: fidelity and infidelity in animals and people.* New York: W.H. Freeman, 2001.

4. E.g., Lorenz, Konrad. *King Solomon's Ring.* New York: Thomas Y. Crowell, 1952

5. Alcock, John. *Animal Behavior: an evolutionary approach.* Sunderland, MA: Sinauer Associates, 1998.

6. James, William. *The Will to Believe and Other Essays in Popular Philosophy.* Cambridge, MA: Harvard University Press, 1979.

7. White, Lynn. "The historical roots of our ecological crisis." *Science* 155 (1967): 1203-1207.

8. Weber, Max. *Collected Essays in the Sociology of Religion.* Leiden: E.J. Brill, 1985.

9. Eibl-Eibesfeldt, Irenaus. *Ethology the Biology of Behavior.* New York: Holt, Rinehart and Winston, 1975

10. Gell-Mann, Murray. *The Quark and the Jaguar.* New York: W.H. Freeman, 1994.

11. E.g., Wilkinson, L. (ed.) *Earthkeeping.* Grand Rapids, MI: Eerdmans, 1980

12. Barash, David. "The tyranny of the natural." *The Chronicle of Higher Education.* November 2 B (2001): 16-17.

13. Vaihinger, Hans. *The Philosophy of "As If."* New York: Harcourt, 1935

14. Skinner, B.F. *Beyond Freedom and Dignity.* New York: Alfred A. Knopf, 1971.

15. Dostoyevsky, Fyodor. *The Brothers Karamazov.* (transl, C. Garnett) New York: The Modern Library, 1937.

16. Barash, David and Charles Webel. *Peace and Conflict Studies.* Thousand Oaks, CA: Sage Publications, 2002.

Alfred Nobel circa 1885

Part Two

Peace Theories and Research:

From Restraining War to Planting Seeds of Peace

Peace becomes mankind;
fury is for beasts.

—Ovid (c. 2 B.C.)

Recognizing that conflict is endemic to human existence, man has sought to understand and explore the means for tempering both the impulses produced by man's "nature" and the "nurturing" pressures resulting from humanity's environment in an often vain attempt to create a durable peace. This section introduces the reader to the field of peace research. The wide survey of both classical and modern research efforts for the cause of peace seeks to demonstrate the range of theories on the subject. Peace research, in the words of one of the authors, is intended "to reduce the immense variety and complexity of the real world to simpler patterns and components which the mind can grasp." Through such pioneering researchers as Kenneth Boulding and Johan Galtung, the reader is introduced to the scientific foundations of peace research; and to the theoretical hypotheses that will form the basis of empirical studies in later essays. What needs to be added is that despite the blossoming of this field in the post-World War II era, the attention of most peace research scholars almost exclusively has tended towards the international rather than intranational conflicts. This deficiency in the scope of the peace research might be one of the reasons for the contemporary decline or at least the lack of progress in this field. Ironically, what is most in evidence through this survey is the fact that man's quest to secure an analytical understanding of the means for attaining peace goes farther back into history than any known period of consecutive peace.

Peace Theory

Kenneth E. Boulding
Economist (1910-1993)

Theories are attempts by the human mind to reduce the immense variety and complexity of the real world to simpler patterns and components which the mind can grasp. A theory has somewhat the relationship to the real world that a map has to the landscape. Thus, chemical theory describes how the world is organized by elements of different valency into compounds of varying complexity. Economic theory studies how the world of human beings and their artifacts is organized by exchange, production, prices, and so on. In the last few decades a new discipline has developed, in English usually called 'peace and conflict studies' (the French call it *polernologie,* from polemics), which studies how the world is organized through conflict, war, violence, nonviolence, and peace. A British meteorologist, Lewis F. Richardson, whose major works were not even published during his lifetime (Richardson, 1960a and 1960b), may well be regarded as the father of this new discipline, although there were precursors and Contemporaries (Wright, 1942; Lentz, 1955). There is now an extensive bibliography and a number of journals in this field, and an increasing number of universities are offering programs in it.

The beginning of good theory is the identification of significant classifications of things in the real world. Alchemy never got very far because its elements—earth, air, fire, and water—were hopelessly heterogeneous. Until the chemical elements were discovered—like oxygen, hydrogen, and so on—chemistry did not get very far. Similarly, peace theory begins with the identification of significant classifications of human behavior and organizations. This can begin with the division of human activity into war and 'notwar,' which might be called 'inclusive peace.' Five billion human beings spend about 120 billion hours a day, one-third in sleep, mostly peaceful; two-thirds in waking-time activities: working, conversing, travelling, partying, and so on. Some of these hours can clearly be related to war, which involves producing and using the means of destruction of life and of things that at least some humans value.

A rough measure of the 'war industry' is given by the size of military budgets, which on a world scale run something on the order of five percent of economic activity. Something like half the human race is in the labor force, which occupies something like a third of our time. So about a sixth of human time is devoted to economic activity; five percent of this would mean something less than one percent of human time devoted to war. To this we might add non-war conflict activity: police, the legal pro-

Kenneth E. Boulding, "Peace Theory." Reprinted by permission of the editors of *A Reader in Peace Studies*, edited by Paul Smoker, Ruth Davies, and Barbara Munske. Published in UK by Pergamon Press, plc.

fession, quarrelling, and so on, which might bring up the total conflict activity to something like one percent of the 120 billion hours a day which we spend. It is, however, a very visible and dramatic one percent. Conflict gets in the newspapers, is the subject of drama and novels, so it is not surprising that we pay a good deal of attention to it. Nevertheless, as we look at the arts as they reflect human life, at least ninety percent of paintings are of peaceful landscapes and portraits, music is mainly concerned with harmony and the resolution of discord, fortifications are a very small part of architecture, and so on.

The distinction between war and inclusive peace is fairly sharp. Most historians can say whether two countries were at war or not on a given date, though there are a few ambiguous cases. Within this area of conflict we have violent and nonviolent conflict. Within the area of peace we have a great variety of human conditions. One of the pioneers of peace theory, Johan Galtung, identified what he called 'structural violence,' which can be most clearly defined as social structures leading to an expectation of life less than the biological potential, now approaching 75 to 80 years. Where the expectation of life is lower than this as a result of oppression, poverty, nutritional deficiencies, pollution, dangerous work, human ignorance, and so on, structural violence may be said to exist. Inclusive peace includes a great variety of human conditions, some of which may be judged much better than others.

Good theory has to be 'dynamic' in the sense that it must portray not only a flashlight photograph, as it were, of the world at a given moment of time, but also the succession of these photographs, like the frames of a movie, as we move from the past into the future. These patterns in time may include equilibrium systems, like a ball rolling down to the bottom of a bowl, a forest recovering its original state after a forest fire, or a system of peace emerging after it has been interrupted by war. We have to recognize, however, that the world is in constant evolutionary change, that all equilibria are temporary. Nevertheless, there are situations in which a disturbance from some temporary equilibrium results in a movement back towards it: disputes are resolved, a loving couple makes up after a quarrel, and so on. On the other hand, we also have to recognize the long-run evolutionary, irreversible changes. The totality of human knowledge, for instance, has grown almost continuously, even at an accelerating pace, from the first human beings, and this profoundly affects the history of human society and behavior. Both biological and societal evolution seem to have a 'time's arrow' in terms of complexity which seems to be almost irreversible.

An example of peace theory involving a dynamic movement towards a possible equilibrium is the theory of arms races, first developed by Lewis F. Richardson. This is expressed in Figure 1.

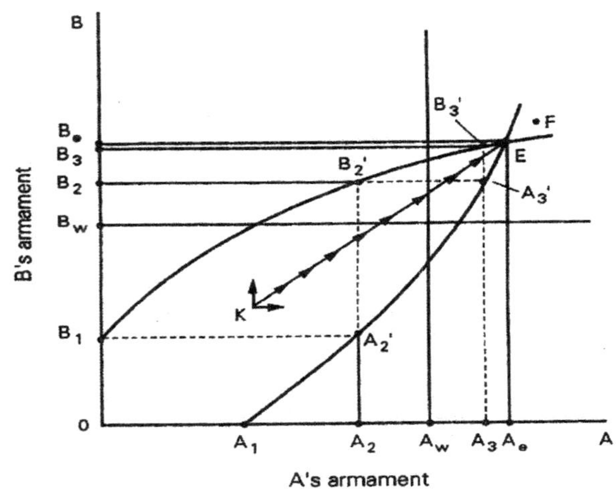

Figure 1

Here we suppose two countries, **A** and **B**, each of which sees the other as something of a threat to it. We measure **A**'s level of armament horizontally (Axis 0A), **B**'s level of armament vertically (Axis 0B). Then we suppose two 'reaction curves.' A_1E, which shows the level of armament that **A** wants to achieve for each level of **B**'s armament; B_1E, which shows the level of **B**'s armament that **B** wants to achieve for each level of A's armament. We suppose that even if **B**'s armament level is zero, **A** will have some armament, 0A if **A**'s is zero, **B** will have some armament, $0B_1$. If we were to start off with both countries' armaments at zero, let us suppose that **B** goes to $0B_1$, which would make **A** feel insecure. **A** would then go to $0A_2$, represented by the point A'_2 on its reaction curve. This would make **B** feel insecure and he would go to B'_2 on his reaction curve, with a level of armament $0B_2$. **A** would then go to A'_3, **B** to B'_3, and so on.

In Figure 1, the two reaction curves intersect at E, which would be the point of equilibrium of the 'arms race.' If we had a level of arms in the interval between the curves above E, say at F, we would have a disarmament race, back to E. This is a little reminiscent of the old 'balance of power' theory of international relations. We do not have to assume that the dotted line B_1, A'_2, B'_2, A'_3, and so on, is necessarily the dynamic process. If we were to start from some point such as K within the two reaction curves, both parties would increase their armaments, **A** to A_k, **B** to B_k, ending up as they move towards a reaction line so we might get a dynamic path somewhat like the line KE (marked with arrows).

In Figure 1 we have drawn the reaction lines A_1E and B_1E as curves. The slope of each line at any point shows how much each country reacts to a unit increase in the armaments of the other. This might be called a 'reaction coefficient.' If an increase of 1 unit in **A**'s armament level increases **B**'s by .5 unit, then **B**'s reaction coefficient is .5. An important conclusion is that in order to have an equilibrium such as point E, the reaction coefficients, no matter what level they start at, must fall below 1. If the reaction coefficients are both 1 or greater, the reaction curves will either be parallel or will diverge and will not intersect at all. The arms race will go on until the system breaks down, usually into war. This indeed is why so many arms races have in fact led to war, and why deterrence is fundamentally unstable in the long run. A decline in the reaction coefficient may be a result of economic forces. As armaments increase they become more and more of an economic burden, and one country or the other or both may simply not be able to afford to continue the arms race at a high reaction coefficient. On the other hand, there may also be some level of armaments at which one nation or the other decides that a further increase is intolerable and this frequently breaks down into war. If this level were, say $0A_w$ for **A** and $0B_w$ for **B**, and if the dynamic process were represented by the line KE, then war would begin at the point B_w, since **B** would reach the breakdown point first. This, incidentally, suggests why it is so difficult to define an 'aggressor' in the origins of a war. Which of the two parties starts the war depends on which reaches the breakdown point first. This may be quite arbitrary. When the dynamics of the arms race goes outside the limits of the rectangle $0B_wWA_w$, war starts.

In this model the 'causes' of war are almost irrelevant. The pattern of economic conflict, for instance, has very little to do with the pattern of war. War emerges because of the existence of government-financed 'unilateral national defense organizations,' which specialize in fighting wars and in preparing for them. These unilateral national defense organizations can only justify their existence and their budgets if they have an enemy or a potential enemy. They tend to create enemies even where there are no severe conflicts. The situation becomes much more complex when we have more than two parties and it can be shown that for an equilibrium of an arms race to exist under these circumstances, the reaction coefficients must be considerably less than 1, and the more parties, the lower the reaction coefficients have to be in order to ensure an equilibrium. This is why unilateral national defense has rarely produced more than an unstable peace, but has always tended to break down into war, quite regardless of the structure of real conflicts.

Another aspect of peace theory which can only be mentioned briefly here is the study of the impact of the different kinds and destructive powers of weaponry on the consequence of using them. An important distinction is between offensive weapons, which are designed to destroy either the opponent's weapons or the opponent and the opponent's properties; and defensive structures, like suits of armor, castle walls, city walls, and so on, which are designed to reduce the destructiveness of the other party's weapons. A change in the capacity of offensive weapons to overcome defensive structures will have a profound effect on social institutions. Thus the development of the effective cannon in the sixteenth century destroyed the feudal system, made the city-state very unstable, and helped to create the national state. As long as the weapons were spears and arrows, the castle wall and the city wall made some sense. With the development of the effective cannon, they made no sense at all. The baron who stayed in his castle got blown up with it. A national state, however, of the size of France or England, Sweden or Russia, could be defended at the borders with cannon. A very important question now is whether the development of the long-range missile and the nuclear weapon has done for the national state precisely what the cannon did for the feudal baron, in that it is no longer defensible by war.

We have seen in the last 150 years a new phenomenon, the development of stable peace between independent national states, in which neither of two countries has any plans to go to war with the other. This begins in Scandinavia in the mid-nineteenth century, spreads to North America by about 1870, and to Western Europe after the Second World War. With the nuclear weapon, this may be the only way in which the national state can achieve security. The conditions of stable peace are fairly simple: both parties must take national boundaries off their agendas, except by mutual agreement; both parties have to have a minimum amount of intervention in each other's affairs. The fact that military conquests and imperialism have not paid off economically on the whole for aggressive powers suggests that a learning process is going on which will expand the area of stable peace.

Peace theory is illuminated and tested by peace history, which is very undeveloped. There are very few historical studies of peace (Melko, 1973), fewer studies of the economic costs of military victory, and still fewer of the benefits of military defeat, which has often in history produced both a cultural expansion and an economic expansion for the defeated. In one sense Germany and Japan, the defeated powers, won the Second World War economically, as they were able to devote a larger proportion of their resources to getting rich rather than being powerful in the military sense. There are also many examples in history, like the defeat of France by Germany in 1870-71, which was followed in France by a great upsurge in art, literature, and music, as well as in economic life. It is peace history that has to provide the data for peace theory, and much of this still remains to be written.

References

Axelrod, Robert. *The Evolution of Cooperation.* New York: Basic Books, 1984.

Boulding, Kenneth. *The Economics of Peace.* New York: Prentice-Hall, 1945 (reissued, New York: Books for Libraries Press, 1972).

Boulding, Kenneth. *Conflict and Defense.* New York: Harper and Brothers, 1962.

Boulding, Kenneth. *Ecodynamics: A New Theory of Societal Evolution.* London: Sage, 1978.

Boulding, Kenneth. *Stable Peace.* Austin: University of Texas Press, 1978.

Boulding, Kenneth. *The World as a Total System.* London: Sage, 1985.

Lentz, Theodore. *Towards a Science of Peace: Turning Point in Human Destiny.* New York: Bookman Associates, 1955.

Melko, Matthew. *52 Peaceful Societies.* Ontario: Canadian Peace Research Institute Press, 1973.

von Neumann, John, and Oskar Morgenstern. *The Theory of Games and Economic Behaviour,* 2nd ed. Princeton, NJ: Princeton University Press, 1947 (originally published 1944).

Rapoport, Anatol. *Fights, Games, and Debates.* Ann Arbor: University of Michigan Press, 1960.

Rapoport, Anatol, and Albert Chammah. *The Prisoner's Dilemma: A Study in Conflict and Cooperation.* Ann Arbor: University of Michigan Press, 1965.

Richardson, Lewis F. *Arms and Insecurity: A Mathematical Study of the Causes and Origins of War.* Chicago: Quadrangle Books, 1960a.

Richardson, Lewis F. *Statistics of Deadly Quarrels.* Chicago: Quadrangle Books, 1960b.

Singell, Larry D. (ed.). *Collected Papers, Vol. V: International Systems: Peace, Conflict Resolution, and Politics.* Colorado: Colorado Associated University Press, 1975.

Singell, Larry D. (ed.). *Collected Papers, Vol. VI: Toward the 21st Century: Political Economy, Social Systems, and World Peace.* Colorado: Colorado Associated University Press, 1985.

The Evolution of Theories on War and Peace

A.C.F. Beales
Historian (1905-1974)

About the middle of the nineteenth century there began to be expounded by western philosophers the theorem that all wars in the future would tend to become world wars. Before the century was out a Russian strategist added a rider to the effect that wars in the future would threaten civilisation itself.[1] Within the next twenty years the world demonstrated both propositions and accepted them as sufficiently proved. In the meantime a counter-proposition had been developed which endeavoured to show that the days were gone in which war, as an institution was necessary, and that in the modern world no nation was compelled to go to war. As the theory and practice of settling international disputes otherwise than by resort to arms progressed this belief gained in appeal. The creation of alternative machinery destroyed "the sole juridical and ethical excuse" which was still being advanced by those who believed that war could never be eradicated. Whereupon it was but a single logical step to the Pact of Paris, whereby, though only the most sanguine believed that it would be possible in practice to make armed conflict impossible, war was formally abjured and outlawed. The future of international relations lay thereafter with the machinery of world organisation, which alone could allow the renunciation to be kept, by welding together a living International Community with a personality of its own.

The history of the efforts which produced the present ordering of world politics hardly oversteps a century. Disarmament proposals can be traced as far back as B.C. 546 in China; universal brotherhood has been the keynote of all organised religion from the earliest days; the Middle Ages abounded in schemes for world peace and cosmopolitan unity. But the first organised and coherent movements towards these ends were born of the Napoleonic Wars, when world politics had already long been international in the strict sense of the word, and when it was at last possible to appreciate the problem of patriotism *versus* internationalism.

These first movements were not altogether mushroom growths. Though the founders of organised pacificism emerged suddenly and were long in earning respect or even tolerance, and though the economists who became their first allies were prone to harp on contemporary evils as insistently as on eternal principles, they had behind them at least fifteen centuries of thought. They themselves were but disciples: their Bible and their Prophets extended far back in the past—from Augustine to Wyclif, and from Pierre Dubois to Kant. For this reason it is necessary that an account of organised Peace should be prefaced by a summary sketch of the older efforts—articulate but inchoate—to fashion a better world. The prophets furnished not only ideas and catchwords, principles and formula, but elaborate and complicated schemes, and laboured arguments on their practical and everlasting potency. Much of the argument, and all the plans, survive largely as academic curiosities. But the nineteenth century extracted from them a measure of permanent truth and a fund of maxims for practical guidance.

There emerges from a study of medieval philosophy one theory of war and peace. In the centuries that followed the collapse of medieval universality, schemes of world organisation were evolved to accommodate the new system of national Sovereign States. Arguments were launched for and against arbitration; a beginning was made at establishing and codifying International Law; and—supreme achievement—an experiment among the American Indians was placed on record as an earnest that ideals may sometimes be realised.

To 1500

(i) Pacifism

The earliest thoughts of universal peace were religious and sentimental; they envisaged the unity of mankind and preached humanitarianism as a means thereto. Among the Israelite Fathers, Micah and Isaiah formulated texts which are still the most favourite heirlooms of the Peace Movement, measuring the future in terms of swords and ploughshares, spears and pruning-hooks.[2] Paganism contributed to the same end in the writings of Zeno, Seneca, Epictetus, and Marcus Aurelius; and the birth of Christianity consecrated the whole of ancient pacifist thought in the name of a God who was the Father of all. But Christianity had to condone the principle of military service within the Roman Empire. A decree of A.D. 314 rendered deserters from the imperial armies liable to excommunication, on the argument of Christ's "Render unto Cesar..." The unqualified protests against warfare which had been raised by Justin the Martyr, by Tertullian, and by St. Martin of Tours, ceased on the recognition of Christianity by Constantine, and it became a common practice for priests to accompany the armies.

In time there developed a body of Christian theory which explained and vindicated the change, and which can be regarded as representing the attitude of the Medieval Church towards war. The argument is built up from Augustine, Thomas Aquinas, and Francis de Victoria. It emphasises the horrors of war and all the attendant moral crimes, but stops short of a categorical denunciation of all war. In certain conditions war is "just"; though the conditions prescribed are strict enough to condemn every war that has ever been fought. When there has been an injustice committed on one side only, amounting to moral and not merely material guilt; and when this injustice is known for certain; and when all peaceful methods of settlement have been tried in vain, the aggrieved nation might with justice, says Augustine, resort to arms. But in doing so that nation must intend to further good and relieve evil by war, must be certain of victory beforehand, must conduct the war "rightly and without excesses of any kind, must make the punishment of the enemy strictly proportionate to the offence, and must scrupulously avoid all unnecessary upheaval among neutrals." Failing any one of these conditions, the war would be unjust.[3]

Such was the medieval theory. Suarez contrived centuries later to conjure with it, balancing degrees of guilt and equating the moral cases put forward by contending princes. He served only to weaken a doctrine that was already diffuse and obscure. Long disputations were held as to who was to make the declaration of war. Augustine's ruling vested the power to do so in "lawful authorised authority exercised in the name of God." In the light of this it was asked further whether the whole of the aggressor nation was to be held morally responsible for the misdeeds of its prince; and further still, whether any aggressive act could be other than immoral.

In this wise, because it empowered the Prince to plunge his people into war, and because it seemed to be using war as a means to its ideal of Peace, the theory of the Just War provoked protests which crystallised into the first true pacifist doctrines. The medieval sects which broke away—Albigenses, Vaudois, Lollards, Paulicians, Manicheans, Waldenses, Mennonites—took their stand firmly on the sanctity of human life, stood out uncompromisingly against all war, and took the whole world for their country. They were pacifist and cosmopolitan. The counterbias to Augustine's *Civitas Dei* is to be found in Wyclif's *Trialogus*. But here again there is a limitation. The sects, having no frontiers, were not interested in the State. Thus they have a survival value for pacifism but not for internationalism.[4]

Translated into action, the medieval theory produced on the one hand the Crusades and the Truce of God, and on the other hand Chivalry. Irrespective of the setting of a Holy War, the conception of Chivalry embodied a lofty Christian ideal. Its four corners were honour, the pledged word, defence of the innocent and weak, and idealised womanhood. It created an ethic and an aristocracy; it helped to humanise warfare and exalt the middle class; and it knew no geographical boundaries. It typifies medieval universality. When that universality had at last collapsed, the fall echoed throughout Europe in the Decree of Eternal Pacification (1495), by which private war among the descendants of the Age of Chivalry was abolished.

(ii) Organisation

At a lower level, that of mere political expediency, efforts had been made to regulate intercourse between nations—partly to promote defence, partly to diminish friction. The earliest recorded experiment in interstatal organisation is the Amphictyonic Council of the second century B.C. The twelve tribes of ancient Greece banded themselves together in 1497 B.C., naming their League after Amphictyon, the son of Deucalion....

The League is last heard of about A.D. 200.[5]

Its importance in history is apt to be overstressed. Undoubtedly the principles of federation and interstatal obligation which it involved were of immense significance for the future. The idea of federation among city States bore fruit in the Confederation of Delos during the age of Pericles, and in the Athenian League. Peaceful settlement of disputes within the League, moreover, due to a community of interests produced by the regular assemblies, gave the Council a reputation as a peace organisation.

* * *

The Romans allowed the custom of arbitration to persist where they found it prevalent in Greek colonies; but no Roman dispute was ever submitted to outside judgment. Rome was the arbiter of the world. Similarly, the conditions under which imperial Rome expanded did not allow the development of a code of international law. In no sense were the Greeks or Romans internationalist; for in place of the two fundamentals of internationalism—equality and unity—they postulated slavery and absorption, and a world-empire administered under the *Pax Romana*. The legacy of Rome was thus the struggle in the Middle Ages between Empire and Papacy.

The great work of the medieval Church was to attack the problem of mitigating warfare and organising perpetual peace from another angle. By the Truce of God, proclaimed in 989 at the Council of Charroux (in Poitou) and extended in 1027, fighting among the feudal nobles was prohibited from sunset every Wednesday till dawn on the following Monday, and on certain festivals. Fantastic as it sounds to modern ears, the prohibition was tolerably well respected for close on two centuries, and it serves as an index of the influence exerted by the Papacy. Early in the thirteenth century it waned, owing to the needs of the Popes themselves in the struggle against the Hohenstaufen. But as an attempt to organise war its significance remains.

The Crusades, spread over three centuries, exemplified the same ideal of unity. They girded up the whole of Christendom into an array of warriors, priests, cities, and kings, to conquer and convert Islam. De Quincey saw in them an ecstacy of chivalry and martyrdom, and a triumphant manifestation of Augustine's just war. Modern scholarship emphasises the commercial and æsthetic contact between East and West which they achieved rather than their religious aspirations. Judged by the canons of Augustine and Aquinas, the Crusades do not satisfy the contemporary test of a just war, despite their ostensible motive. They were not the only means available to achieve the end in view; the tide of Islam had been steadily ebbing since before 1095. Nor was there any reasonable certitude that they would be successful. The canonists, however, accepted and glorified them; for their aim transcended everything.

About the time of the Third Crusade the first definite plan was formulated for abolishing war. It was as simple as it was logical. The author, one Gerohus of Regensberg, proposed that the Pope should forbid all war, that differences between princes should be referred to Rome for decision, and that any party who rejected the Pope's award should be excommunicated and deposed. His deposition would be accelerated by the priests in his dominions, who would stir up a popular revolt against him. What is chiefly remarkable in the scheme is the complete assumption of a united Christendom which underlies it. Had it been carried into effect, its insistence on the political power of the Papacy could only have exacerbated an already perennial feud. Nonetheless it was not an isolated piece of extravagance. Contemporary schemes of a similar purport were being aired in both France and Italy.[6]

From the imperial side, [several] treatises on the organisation of the world were written during the fourteenth century. The first, *On the Recovery of the Holy Land*, by Pierre Dubois of Normandy, an adviser of Philip le Bel of France, is significant in so far as it advocated for the first time a federation of Christian Sovereign States. Dubois held that peace was the *summum bonum* among Christian nations, and that therefore a Council of the Nations should be established, ministering to the needs of the federated member States in their dealings one with another, and deciding quarrels among them by means of arbitration. The appearance of this new principle of federation, however, is discounted by two other features on which Dubois was equally insistent—that France (his own country) was to become dominant in Europe, and that the Council of the Nations should make its first and pre-eminent duty the subjugation of the Turk. The first of these two features alone would have enabled growing national feeling in the emergent modern kingdoms to wreck his scheme for organisation.

[Another] scheme is that of Dante's *De Monarchia,* written in 1310-14 but not published until 1559. Dante wrote at a time when the whole question of the true nature of law had been opened by the imperial struggle against the Papacy, and when Boniface VIII had lately fortified the papal claim to temporal power in the Bull *Uram Sanctam* of 1302. Dante's refutation vindicated the claim of an Empire which, he argued, had existed before the Church and independently of the Church, and which was divinely sanctioned. The Emperor was absolute; the Pope's authority was spiritual only. But by the rule of the Emperor Dante meant the rule of Law. His word monarch connoted government. The actual personal sovereign was an official, removable if he proved unfaithful to the sovereign people (as in Marsiglio). Law was "the rule which directs life." There should be one Law and one Prince, whose principles and conduct should secure that state of "peace and calm" in which alone the human race could live a fullest life. The organisation of the world, in a word, should be a universal Empire based on a universal Law.

Only one other plan of importance was propounded before 1500—by George Podiebrad, King of Hungary. It echoed Dubois in its insistence on a Holy War against the infidel (Constantinople had fallen seven years before the work appeared); and it adopted Dubois' plan for a Parliament or "Consistory" of Nations. What Podiebrad preached was, in essence, the realisation of peace in the Christian world by means of warfare outside its religious frontiers.

Meanwhile the federative principle had been put to the test in two practical interstate compacts. One of them, the Hanseatic League, founded by Lubeck and Hamburg about 1239 among fourteen Baltic cities, on a basis of "peaceful umpirage" sanctioned by force, did not long survive the Reformation. The other, the Swiss Confederation, constituted by the Treaty of Sempach in 1393 on a roughly similar defensive foundation, persisted and flourished—partly because of its geographical homogeneity. One other interesting phenomenon is on record during the same period, of an attempt in 1429 to intercept the advance of the Turks and to compose the rivalry between Slavs and Germans by means of concerted effort on the part of all Europe. An amazing Congress for the purpose was held at Loutsk in Russia. Eight rulers, including the Emperor and the Pope, attended either in person or by delegates. But no common basis of agreement could be found, and the enterprise collapsed.[7] Nevertheless, for all its freakishness, it is worthy of note as a rehearsal of the first Hague Conference nearly five hundred years later.

A trend parallel to that of small federations can be found in the growing resort to arbitration and mediation by contending princes during the later Middle Ages.[8] The number of authentic settlements by these means is enormous. In the thirteenth century there were a hundred cases in Italy alone. Usually the Pope was chosen as arbiter in virtue of Europe's spiritual affinities. When this was impossible one of his representatives (often an archbishop) served instead. The Emperor rarely acted in an arbitral capacity, for princes were jealous of their own temporal sovereignty. Edward I of England, Philip le Bel of France, the Emperors Henry III, Sigismund, and Maximilian, the Doge of Venice, the Republics of Venice and Switzerland, all submitted minor disputes and differences to the decision of disinterested third parties. In 1291 the Swiss Confederation even recognised the principle of obligatory arbitration. On one occasion the Parlement of Paris composed a dispute between an Emperor and a Pope (1244). Thus a growing federative sentiment can be traced, resulting, perhaps, not so much from the Church as from the Crusades, which Guizot hailed as "the first European Movement."

By 1500, then, there were in existence a number of articulate pronouncements regarding the future of the world; theories of war, doctrines of extreme pacifism, projects of world organisation from both the Papal and the Imperial standpoint, and arguments in praise of arbitration, federation, and popular sovereignty. There had been as yet, however, no mention of a specific High Court of Nations, and no attempts to frame a code of interstate law. The conception underlying most of this medieval thought was that of Unity and Universality. When, therefore, the sixteenth century ushered in the era of individual Sovereign States and all hope of universality was dispelled, the prophets took a new turn. Their aim after 1500 had to be to seek for unity in diversity. And this is true internationalism.

To 1815

(i) The New Modern Conditions

The sixteenth century opened a long period of chronic warfare, produced by a welter of conflicting causes. The discovery of the New World revealed vast fields for enterprise which sharpened the rivalry of European monarchies already sundered by the loss of a common language and by the concentrated ambitions of their ruling classes. Columbus was to leave as legacy the African slave-trade and the American colour question. The Renaissance and the Reformation proved disruptive forces. While Catholicism continued universal, Protestantism, for lack of a "single authoritative religious centre," created State churches and aggravated sectarianism, with Calvin as a lineal descendant of the medieval sects. At the same time the Renaissance in Italy carried across the Alps a new diplomacy based on balance of power, and spread it throughout Christendom, where it had barely reached its geographical limits when the Peace of Westphalia put an end to wars of religion and set the stage for wars of commerce and conquest, justified by considerations of "vital interests."[9]

The nation States of post-Renaissance Europe throve and developed in an atmosphere of war. Their conception of state-craft turned on national sovereignty and a meticulous balance of power, in the light of which the only justification for war was *raison d'etat.* The new state-craft had its apologists in Machiavelli, Bodin, Hobbes, and Spinoza. Theorising on war and peace had reference no longer to a Universal Unity, manifested in the Church and co-extensive with Christendom itself, but to the individual national State. Cosmopolitan unity was lost, even as a dream. Carried to their logical conclusion, Machiavellism and Hobbism led straight to Hegel and the conception of the State as an end in itself.

(ii) The Sixteenth and Seventeenth Centuries

Therefore, though pacifism remained permanent, being (as will be shown later) a dogmatic principle based on a fixed state of mind, international thought underwent a series of modifications after 1500 to meet changing conditions. Its bulk increased, with contributions from humanists, sovereigns, and statesmen, arguing variously from humanitarian, philosophical, and legal viewpoints. Many of their passages have become classics in literature and landmarks in history.

Among the Renaissance humanists Erasmus, the "greatest single influence north of the Alps," contributed most to the philosophy of war. More's *Utopia* furnishes occasional homilies on the vanity of war and the moral baseness of the spirit of conquest; Sebastian Franck taught the same lesson in his *Kriegbüchlin des Frides,* Rabelais and Montaigne noisily scoffed at warfare as an unintelligent extravagance; but Erasmus, in his *Laus Stultitiæ* (1510), elaborately condemned the whole concept of violence. War was wholesale homicide, albeit the Church condoned it. It was completely devoid of benefits; and it was morally unjustifiable. Even the Turk should be converted by persuasion and not by violence; for force could plead no certainty of success. Erasmus developed no plans for perpetual peace; but his *Praise of Folly* and his *Complaint of Peace* were both called forth by contemporary events. An endeavour had been made to induce universal peace by means of a conference at Cambrai between the Emperor Maximilian, Francis I of France, and Henry VIII of England. Its authors, William of Ciervia and John Sylvagius, worked out the details of the meeting; but the project came to nothing. In its place there came the "Universal Peace" of 1518, a landmark in that it was a diplomatic instrument ratified by the same three powerful monarchs—though the peace it proclaimed lasted barely four years.

The most famous of all the world's international projects is the *Grand Dessein* of 1603, conceived and drafted by Henry IV and his minister Sully. Inspired by the need for eradicating the Wars of Religion, the French King fashioned a panacea which he would have put into operation had he lived. Elizabeth was informed of it in a personal visit from Sully, and it even secured written approval in a treaty of 1596.[10] Its primary object was to overthrow the House of Austria and so remove the chief obstacle to lasting peace. This achieved, Europe was to be divided in equal proportions among fifteen Powers in order to extinguish any future uneven balance of power. The fifteen Powers were to be represented in a Great Council, whose members would be subject to reelection every three years: four representatives from each major and two from each minor Power—in all, about seventy members. The Council's expenses were to be furnished by proportional contributions from the member States, and its duty was to consist in dealing with common affairs as they arose and settling disputes between the States. No definitive provisions for the arbitration of disputes were formulated,[11] but precaution was taken against any flouting of a Council award by prescribing (the first proposal of its kind) an international army and navy to enforce compliance.

It is easy to exaggerate the merits of the *Great Design* by emphasising the earnestness and the political wisdom of its author, but the later significance of the plan can hardly be overestimated. Henry IV's conception offered the raw materials for every subsequent internationalist project; and in many cases his structure was adopted completely, with only trifling modifications. Its historical value lies in its conception of a federal partnership among Sovereign States, in its provision of machinery whereby different national influences could function in harmony, and in its resort to combined sanctions of force to execute awards when good faith failed. The modern problem of sanctions has its first tentative solution here.

Twenty years later two further advances of tremendous significance were made with the publication of Emeric Crucé's *Nouveau Cynée*. The central theme was the same as that of Henry and Sully—a federation rather than a sovereign authority of the medieval type. A city was to be chosen (preferably Venice) to which all sovereigns were to send resident ambassadors who would form an assembly for the purpose of settling disputes.)

* * *

His plan...laid down rules for safeguarding free transit and exterminating piracy. Its two innovations, however, were, first, that the League of States should comprise non-Christian as well as Christian States (the invitations being issued by the King of France and the Pope respectively); and, secondly, that war should be entirely superseded by a regulated system of arbitration. This is the first distinct proposal for substituting organised international arbitration for war, and the first daring suggestion of a world federation.

* * *

Grotius' work, *De Jure Belli ac Pacis*, published in 1625, sought to supersede contemporary canons of self-interest by an ethical principle of right. He was not a pacifist: indeed his thesis rests in part on the theory that war was both ineradicable and on occasion just. What he essayed to prove, starting from the "licentiousness in regard to war" which he observed everywhere around him, was that, just as each State enjoyed a system of law which served its own interests, so there was a higher law, divine in origin, established in the interests of all nations. It is unnecessary here to follow the argument in its analysis of *jus naturæ* and *jus gentium*. What matters for the present purpose is that, in addition to providing for a "Congress of Christian Powers" in which international disputes would be resolved by impartial outsiders, Grotius sketched a code of rules which were to be ratified by the Powers as laws determining their several relations, and so founded the modern science of international law; or, more precisely, he "divides the lay science of international law from the Church's tradition."[12]

Extreme pacifism, meanwhile, had developed with the sects which had renounced violence. While the organised Churches, Catholic and Protestant, found it vitally necessary to allow and even to use war as a means of self-preservation, and while Bellarmin and Calvin and Luther sanctioned war by their writings, the various Anabaptist sects uncompromisingly condemned resort[ing] to force in any circumstances. Their spokesmen, Memno Simons in Holland and Sozzini in Switzerland, extended the arguments of Erasmus and recognised resistance to oppression as purely subjective—a matter of conscience alone. Their cardinal rule was that of obedience and outward submission. How far they and their brethren obeyed it can be seen in the long list of martyrs—Mennonites, Simonians, Socinians, Moravians, Brownists—handed down from the sixteenth century. Most of the sects expired. Their anti-militarist tradition was continued however, by the Society of Friends.

* * *

William Penn, the son of the founder of Jamaica, was the Quaker apologist on war and peace as conclusively as Barclay was the exponent of the Friends' general position. Penn advanced, in his *Plan for the Permanent Peace of Europe* (1694), a scheme for the future organising of the world which he claimed would create untold benefits. By averting wars he hoped to secure a saving of blood, a saving of money by princes and peoples, a strengthening of Christianity's threatened reputation, an increase in trade and commerce, a period of security from the nightmare of Turkish inroads, and—ironically—a possibility that princes might in future marry for love and not for power. The scheme propounded was a revival of the "Grand Design." A permanent International Tribunal was to be set up by the sovereigns of Europe. It was to consist of ninety representatives, chosen by a system of proportional representation, and meeting every year to discuss and settle all international differences which had not been successfully composed by diplomatic means. The tribunal was to give its decisions by means of a ballot, with a minimum majority of three-quarters of the votes. All business was to be done in Latin or French; records were to be kept and circulated to each sovereign; and quarrels over precedence were to be obviated by holding the annual assembly in a circular room containing many doors, through which at a given signal the delegates could enter simultaneously.

The scheme presents problems. Penn's tribunal had as one of its functions the establishment of "rules of justice" which would endow it with judicial powers, and therefore seem to limit the sovereignty of the member States. Penn denied that national sovereignty would be thus restricted, since all the obligations undertaken were mutual compacts; the effect would be not to limit sovereignty, but to forge a situation in which "the great fish can no longer eat up the little ones." Again, he gave no decision as to the employment of force to constrain a recalcitrant State to abide by an arbitral award—which seems incompatible with Quaker principles. Here, indeed, was a sharp dilemma. To have provided sanctions would have been to forsake his faith; to forbid sanctions would have rendered his whole scheme futile—for every government that has ever existed, except one, has cherished the inalienable right to employ force.[13]

The exception was his own government. Penn's famous treaty with the Indians, concluded in 1682 in terms of complete fellowship, enabled him to set up the first and only unarmed government in the world. "We meet," he said, "on the broad pathway of good faith and good will. No advantage shall be taken on either side, but all shall be openness and love.... The friendship between me and you I will not compare to a chain, for that the rains may rust, or the falling tree may break. We are the same as if one man's body were to be divided into two parts; we are all one flesh and blood."[14] In pursuance of this he paid the Indians for the land his people settled, and settled all disputes with amazing success by an arbitral tribunal of six colonists and six Indians.

(iii) The Eighteenth Century

A rough distinction can be drawn between the sixteenth and seventeenth centuries—the age of ethical theories of war—and the eighteenth century—the age of national theories of peace. While Addison and Swift, Pascal and La Bruyère, continued the Rabelaisian attack in a vein of ridicule, a more reasoned condemnation of war became apparent, particularly in Montesquieu, as a necessary evil. The French Encyclopédistes, led by Diderot, even foresaw clearly the modern interdependence of the whole world. At all times the opposition to war was based on reason.

The work of Grotius was expanded by Emerich Vattel in Switzerland. Vattel's *Law of Nations* (1758) conceived the Society of Nations as a *natural* fact, and as functioning according to certain laws which ought to be codified. Arbitration was declared to be "a very reasonable mode...of deciding every dispute which does not concern the safety of the nation," though the national sovereignty of the members remained intact and force was permissible in cases of extreme necessity. But neither Grotius or Vattel actually furnished a Code of International Law. What they produced was rather a collection of precedents and opinions—the work "not of legislators, but of scholars."[15] The fund of maxims was steadily enlarged as the century wore on—from Alberoni's scheme for a European Parliament (1735) to Chateaubriand's *Genie du Christianisme* (1802).

Four monumental works tower high above the rest, published (in order of time) by Saint-Pierre, Rousseau, Bentham, and Kant.

The Abbé de Saint-Pierre's *Project for Settling Perpetual Peace in Europe* (1713), prompted by the peace negotiations at Utrecht at the close of the War of the Spanish Succession, ranks as the greatest exposition of its kind up to that time. The sordid bargaining that went on at Utrecht convinced the Abbé of the need for an International Tribunal, to the discussion of which he devoted eleven "fundamental" and eight "important" articles. His work shows the inspiration of Henry IV. There was to be a League of Sovereign States enshrined in a permanent Congress of Representatives; a code of Articles of Commerce; provisions for arbitration of disputes by the permanent Senate; combined military sanctions against any State which flouted an arbitral award. Peace-time armies were to be reduced in all States to 6000; weights and measures and coinage were to be standardised throughout Europe; and efforts were to be made to create a similar self-contained Asiatic League. All these features were described in the most comprehensive manner, and the whole essay was rounded off with answers (in advance) to sixty-two objections. But despite its minuteness and its circumspection, there are two criticisms which could not be adequately met. First, it was too patently a scheme for a coalition of kings—"wolves to guard the sheep," as Comte put it. Secondly, it was too deeply rooted in, and dependent on, the contemporary *status quo*.[16]

Rousseau made Saint-Pierre's project the text of the *Judgment on a Plan for Perpetual Peace* which he published in 1761. He endorsed its principle, believing with the Abbé that war was a matter not between nations, but between princes and cabinets; and he endeavoured to succeed (where Saint-Pierre had failed) in making it possible to set the international machine in motion by guaranteeing the existing *status quo* and rendering it subject to modification by arbitration only. He provided, further, for the drafting of a Code of International Law, and for its amendment by the unanimous vote of the Diet or Congress of Representatives. But his finished plan had two serious defects. The first—that the interests of princes would effectively postpone its realisation—he admitted. The other was more insidious, and left a legacy of dissension and bloodshed which endured far into the next century. This was the principle that sovereigns should be guaranteed against rebellions among their subjects—the principle that was made the cornerstone of the Holy Alliance in 1815.

At the same time the rationalistic conception of a world united by common ties was being vindicated on more concrete grounds—by economists like Adam Smith and David Hume, and the French Physiocrats under Quesnay and Turgot, and from the legal standpoint by Jeremy Bentham. The *Fragment of an Essay on International Law* occupied Bentham during the years 1786-89. He was completely cosmopolitan in sentiment. His view of the future, never quite explicit in his writings, resolved itself, among later thinkers, into the idea of a United States of Europe. He insisted on reciprocal rights and duties among civilised nations—the duty of abstaining from injury to others, and the right of expecting from them a like consideration. To avert war for the future he devised a plan which comprised four fundamentals: the reduction of armaments;[17] the establishment of a "Permanent Court of Judicature" with powers of arbitration backed by sanctions of force; the codification of International Law; and—a sidelight on the wars of the eighteenth century—the emancipation of all colonies.

But there had already occurred, through the revolt of one group of colonies, a shock to the prevailing conception of the State, to which the French Revolution was to administer a death-blow. The French and American Revolutions together changed the connotation of the word State. International relations were to be the affairs no longer of dynastic princes but of whole nations. So apparent was the transformation and so strong the realisation of the growing interdependence of the nations that as early as 1793 a World State was being trumpeted by one Anacharsis Klootz.

The last of the eighteenth-century philosophers, Immanuel Kant, accepted the new theory of the nation State but rejected the headstrong logic that would enlarge the nation into a Cosmopolis. Kant's *Perpetual Peace (Zum Ewigen Frieden)* won him the reproach of being a Jacobin (1795). The book falls into two parts—an examination of certain reforms to be undertaken while war still existed, in order to create a public opinion favourable to the abolition of war, and a body of suggestions for the final organisation of perpetual peace. Kant firmly believed eternal peace to be an unrealisable ideal; therefore his suggestions were more properly concerned with seeking the right road and following it as far as was humanly possible. He agreed with Hobbes that man was by nature selfish and base, but he drew from history the lesson that mankind had risen to a high state of civilisation through the competition and "mutual antagonism" of individuals "in society," which not only had produced social chaos but also had brought out all man's latent powers, until the chaos had been resolved by the formation of the State. This argument he employed similarly to foreshadow an analogous development among States themselves, culminating in a "federation of free republics." By republic he meant any form of government which embodied the liberty and equality of its subjects; and he favoured federation in preference to a World State, for the psychological reason that "law weakens as territory expands." Federation would involve "the surrender of a portion of power in return for participation in a wider, richer, and more secure life." In order to hasten this federation, and in order thereby to essay the path towards everlasting peace, Kant prescribed his series of "preliminary articles," concentrating on nonintervention and the gradual abolition of standing armies. He made no detailed provisions for an International Tribunal. What struck him most in the institution of war was the use of methods so diabolical and revolting to secure the ends of justice.

The criticism that is most usually offered as a retort to Kant's philosophy of Peace is that his analogy between individual and social evolution is not altogether true; that individuals have, and that States have not, the power to curtail an acute dispute by literally retreating out of the way; and that, therefore, disputes between States are "likely to reduce to questions of existence."[18] But Kant's enduring contribution to the theory and literature of his problem was not so much the foundations of his plan as the fact that he lifted the discussion of war and peace far above the level of politics—at which it had lain since the days of Pierre Dubois—and exalted it into a question of ethics and social conscience. Wherefore it was Kant alone who could do battle on their own plane with the high-priests of ethical war—Hegel, Schiller, and Treitschke.

(iv) The Settlement of 1815

The theories and projects that have been outlined in the preceding pages may be regarded as the body of scientific speculation from which the physicians of the first organised Peace Movements of the nineteenth century, when once they had realised that the abolition of war was a question of analysis and diagnosis as well as mere empirical awareness, drew their formula for nourishing a better world. But by 1815 the old world of Henry IV and Rousseau had undergone a serious operation, and during the recovery it became evident, by several ominous and characteristic symptoms, that its malady had not been cured. One symptom—"balance of power"—reappeared in a more chronic form than before; another—"legitimacy"—returned vigorously, though not for long; a third—"dynastic marriages"—showed itself occasionally, but rarely with the strength of an outbreak. On the whole, Europe was only patched, though the patch held for forty years.

It is still fashionable to praise the Treaty of Vienna and the Concert of Europe because they kept Europe at peace till 1854. An equally attractive case might be made out for the thesis that Europe contrived to stay tranquil in spite of the Treaty and the Concert. Certainly the Vienna Settlement accentuated dangers and aggravated problems that were foreseen at the time, and ignored warnings that had long ago been borne across the Atlantic from the New World.

* * *

Nevertheless the Vienna Settlement shows evidences that the phrase "international government" was already beginning to have significance. The Vienna Final Act has indeed been called the first example of "deliberate international legislation." It contained provisions regarding the navigation of certain rivers, which led to the establishment of the first International Executive—the Danube Commission. It provided, further, a prohibition of the Slave Trade which ultimately rendered necessary the creation of some form of control (by right of search) to prevent infringements of the prohibition. In both decisions statesmen and diplomats had met expressly to regulate the vital interests of all nations. The whole settlement, moreover, can be regarded as a rudimentary form of international organisation rather than an alliance of the customary dimensions. Even intervention can be made to postulate (in theory) a conception of a society of nations. Actually the truth was far otherwise; diplomacy vacillated between desires of union and dominion. The Concert degenerated into a series of reunions, and very soon waned, to revive later in an altered form.

Finally, the Vienna Treaties formally annexed the principle of arbitration and made it an orthodox means of adjusting disputes among the nations—by resorting to it to settle four vexed questions of the time. These were the problems of the Rhine transit dues, the Netherlands public debt, the customs dues between Uri and Tessin (Swiss Cantons), and the succession to the Duchy of Bouillon.[19]

But besides the Concert of Europe, which became a six-Power responsibility when France was admitted in 1818, there existed the Holy Alliance of the three autocrats, conceived by the Tsar Alexander I in 1815 and enshrined in a tripartite declaration (issued on 26th September) which was thrown open to the whole of Christian Europe for adherence.[20] All sovereigns signed except two—the Pope and the British Prince Regent. Castlereagh dubbed the Alliance a "loud-sounding nothing." Its inspiration, in so far as it emanated from the Tsar, was partly Christian and partly mystical. Its text, embodied in the declaration, was "a fixed resolution" on the part of all three monarchs "to take for their sole guide the precepts of...Justice, Christian Charity, and Peace...as being the only means of consolidating human institutions and remedying their imperfections."

Notes

1. Jean de Bloch, *The War of the Future* (1898).
2. Micah iv. 3; Isaiah ii. 4.
3. *See* F. Stratmann, *The Church and War,* p. 79 *seq.*
4. *See* M.E. Hirst, *Quakers in Peace and War,* chap. i; and C.L. Lange, *La Doctrine Pacifique,* chap. i.
5. *See* Eliz. York, *Leagues of Nations,* p. 25 *seq.*
6. *See* R.L. Jones, *International Arbitration,* pp. 85-6.
7. R.L. Jones, *International Arbitration,* pp. 107-9.
8. M. Novakovich, *L'Arbitrage International du 12ᵉ au 15ᵉ Siècle* (1905).
9. *Cf.* Luigi Sturzo, *The International Community, p.* 31; and C.L. Lange, *La Doctrine Pacifique,* pp. 216-17.
10. See *Grand Design,* ed. E.D. Mead (1909).
11. *Cf.* W.E. Darby, *International Tribunals* (1904), p. 18.
12. *See* W. Barry, in *Dublin Review,* vol. 160 (1917); and F.M. Stawell, *Growth of International Thought* (1929), p. 121 *seq.*
13. For an admirable discussion of this problem see F.M. Stawell, *Growth of International Thought* (1929), pp. 138-9.
14. Cited at Frankfort Peace Congress (1850); see *Report,* p. 15.
15. *Cf.* Elihu Burritt at Brussels Peace Congress (1848); Report, p. 24.
16. Spain, for instance, was to remain in the hands of the Bourbons.
17. In 1787 he projected a Franco-British treaty for the limitation of naval armaments. *Cf.* C.L. Lange, *Doctrine Pacifique* (1926), p. 335.
18. *See* particularly Mary C. Smith's edition of Kant.
19. J. Gennadius, *International Arbitration,* p. 56.
20. Text in Eliz. York, *Leagues of Nations,* pp. 319-21.

Violence and Peace

Johan Galtung
University of Hawaii

To discuss the idea of peace we shall start from three simple principles: (1) The term 'peace' shall be used for social goals at least verbally agreed to by many, if not necessarily most; (2) These social goals may be complex and difficult, but not impossible, to attain; and (3) The statement "peace is absence of violence" shall be retained as valid.

What we intend is only that the terms 'peace' and 'violence' be linked to each other such that 'peace' can be regarded as 'absence of violence'. Everything now hinges on making a definition of 'violence'.

On the Definition and Dimensions of Violence

As a point of departure, let us say that violence is present when human beings are being influenced so that their actual somatic and mental realizations are below their potential realizations. This statement may lead to more problems than it solves. However, it will soon be clear why we are rejecting the narrow concept of violence—according to which violence is somatic incapacitation, or deprivation of health alone (with killing as the extreme form), at the hands of an actor who intends this to be the consequence. If this were all violence is about, and peace were seen as its negation, then too little is rejected when peace is held up as an ideal. Highly unacceptable social orders would still be compatible with peace. Hence, an extended concept of violence is indispensable but that concept should be a logical extension, not merely a list of undesirables.

The definition points to at least six important dimensions of violence. But first some remarks about the use of key words above: 'actual' and 'potential'. Violence is here defined as the cause of the difference between the potential and the actual, between what could have been and what is. Violence is that which increases the distance between the potential and the actual, and that which impedes the decrease of this distance. Thus, if a person died from tuberculosis in the eighteenth century it would be hard to conceive of this as violence since it might have been quite unavoidable, but if he dies from it today, despite all the medical resources in the world, then violence is present according to our definition. Correspondingly, the case of people dying from earthquakes today would not warrant an analysis in terms of violence, but the day after tomorrow, when earthquakes may become avoidable, such deaths may then be seen as the result of violence. In

Johan Galtung, "Violence and Peace." Reprinted with permission from the editors of *Essays on Peace: Paradigms for Global Order* edited by Michael Salla, Walter Tenetto, & Enrique Martínez.

other words, when the potential is higher then the actual is, by definition, avoidable and when it occurs when it is avoidable, then violence is present.

When the actual is unavoidable, then violence is not present even if the actual is at a very low level. A life expectancy of only thirty years during the neolithic period was not an expression of violence, but the same life expectancy today (whether due to wars, or social injustice, or both) would be seen as violence according to our definition.

The meaning of 'potential realization' is highly problematic, especially when we move from somatic aspects of human life, where consensus is more readily obtained, to mental aspects. Our guide here would probably often have to be whether the value to be realized is fairly consensual or not, although this is by no means satisfactory. For example, literacy is held in high regard almost everywhere, whereas the value of being Christian is highly controversial. Hence, we would talk about violence if the level of literacy is lower than what it could have been, not if the level of Christianity is lower than what it could have been. We shall not try to explore this difficult point further in this context, but turn to the dimensions of violence.

The first distinction to be made is between physical and psychological violence. The distinction is trite but important mainly because the narrow concept of violence mentioned above concentrates on physical violence only. Under physical violence human beings are hurt somatically to the point of killing. Psychological violence includes lies, brainwashing, indoctrination of various kinds, threats, etc. that serve to decrease mental potentialities.

The second distinction is between the negative and the positive approach to influence. Thus a person can be influenced not only by punishing him when he does what the influencer considers wrong, but also by rewarding him when he does what the influencer considers right.

The third distinction to be made is on the object side: whether or not there is an object that is hurt. Can we talk about violence when no physical or biological object is hurt? When a person, a group, or a nation is displaying the means of physical violence, whether by throwing stones around or testing nuclear arms, there may not be violence present in the sense that anyone is hit or hurt, but there is nevertheless the threat of physical violence and the indirect effect of mental violence that may even be characterized as some type of psychological violence since it constrains human action. Indeed, this is also the intention: the famous balance of power doctrine is based on efforts to obtain precisely this effect.

The fourth distinction to be made, and the most important one, is on the subject side: whether or not there is a subject (person) who acts. Again it may be asked can we talk about violence when nobody is committing direct violence, i.e., is acting? We shall refer to the type of violence where there is an actor that commits the violence as personal or direct, and to violence where there is no such actor as structural or indirect. In both cases individuals may be killed or mutilated, hit or hurt in both senses of these words, and manipulated by means of 'stick-or-carrot' strategies.

The important point here is that if people are starving when this is objectively avoidable, then violence is committed, regardless of whether there is a clear subject-action-object relation, as during a siege yesterday, or no such clear relation, as in the way world economic relations are organized today. We have baptized the distinction in two different ways, using the word-pairs 'personal-structural' and 'direct-indirect' respectively. Violence with a clear subject-object relation is manifest because it is visible as action. It corresponds to our ideas of what drama is, and it is personal because there are persons committing the violence. It is easily captured and expressed verbally since it has the same structure as elementary sentences in (at least Indo-European) languages: subject-verb-object, with both subject and object being persons. Violence without this relation is structural, i.e., built into structures. Thus, when one husband beats his wife there is a clear case of personal violence, but when one million husbands keep one million wives in ignorance there is structural violence. Correspondingly, in a society where life expectancy is twice as high in the upper as in the lower classes, violence is exercised even if there are no concrete actors one can point to as directly attacking others, as when one person kills another.

The fifth distinction to be made is between violence that is intended or unintended. This distinction is important when guilt is to be decided, since the concept of guilt has been tied more to intention, both in Judaeo-Christian ethics and in Roman jurisprudence, than to consequence (whereas the present definition of violence is entirely located on the consequence side). This connection is important because it brings into focus a bias present in so much thinking about violence, peace and related concepts: ethical systems directed against intended violence will easily fail to capture structural violence in their nets—and may hence be catching the small fry and letting the big fish loose. From this fallacy it does not follow, in our mind, that the opposite fallacy of directing all attention against structural violence is elevated into wisdom. If the concern is with peace, and peace is the absence of violence, then action should be directed against personal as well as structural violence.

Sixth, there is the traditional distinction between two levels of violence, the manifest and the latent. Manifest violence, whether personal or structural, is observable; latent violence is something which is not there, yet might easily come about. For personal violence this would mean a situation where a little challenge would trigger considerable killing and atrocity, as is often the case in connection with racial confrontations. It indicates a situation of unstable equilibrium. Similarly with structural violence; we could imagine a relatively egalitarian structure insufficiently protected against sudden feudalization, against crystallization into a much more stable, even petrified, hierarchical structure.

If peace is now regarded as absence of violence, then thinking about peace (and consequently peace research and peace action) will be structured the same way as thinking about violence. And the violence cake can evidently be cut a number of ways. It has been traditional to think about violence as personal violence only, with one important subdivision in terms of 'violence vs. the threat of violence', another in terms of physical vs. psychological war', still another (important in ethical and legal thinking) about 'intended vs. unintended', and so on. The choice here is to make the distinction between personal and structural violence the basic one; justification has been presented firstly in terms of a unifying perspective (the cause of the difference between potential and actual realization) and secondly by indicating that there is no reason to assume that structural violence amounts to less suffering than personal violence.

On the other hand, it is not strange that attention has been focused more on personal than structural violence. Personal violence shows. The object of personal violence perceives the violence, usually, and may complain—the object of structural violence may be persuaded not to perceive this at all. Personal violence represents change and dynamism—not only ripples on waves, but waves on otherwise tranquil waters. Structural violence is silent, it does not show—it is essentially static, it is the tranquil waters. In a static society, personal violence will be registered, whereas structural violence may be seen as about as natural as the air around us. Conversely, in a highly dynamic society, personal violence may be seen as wrong and harmful and still somehow congruent with the order of things, whereas structural violence becomes apparent because it stands out like an enormous rock in a creek, impeding the free flow, creating all kinds of eddies and turbulences. Thus, perhaps it is not so strange that the thinking about personal violence (in the Judaeo-Christian-Roman tradition) took on much of its present form in what we today would regard as essentially static social orders, whereas thinking about structural violence (in the Marxist tradition) was formulated in highly dynamic northwest-European societies.

In other words, we conceive of structural violence as something that shows a certain stability, whereas personal violence (e.g., as measured by the tolls caused by group conflict in general and war in particular) shows tremendous fluctuations over time.

On the Definition of "Peace" and "Peace Research"

With the distinction between personal and structural violence as basic, violence becomes two-sided, and so does peace conceived of as the absence of violence. An extended concept of violence leads to an extended concept of peace. Just as a coin has two sides, one side alone being only one aspect of the coin, peace also has two sides: absence of personal violence and absence of structural violence. We shall refer to them as 'negative peace' and 'positive peace' respectively.

For the sake of brevity the formulations 'absence of violence' and 'social justice' may perhaps be preferred, using one negative and one positive formulation. The reason for the use of the terms 'negative' and 'positive' is easily seen: the absence of personal violence does not lead to a positively defined condition, whereas the absence of structural violence is what we have referred to as social justice, which is a positively defined condition (i.e., the egalitarian distribution of power and resources). Peace conceived of in this way is not only a matter of control and reduction of the overt use of violence, but of what we have elsewhere referred to as 'vertical development'. And this means that peace theory is intimately connected not only with conflict theory, but equally with development theory. And peace research, defined of as 'research into the conditions —past, present and future—of realizing peace', will be equally intimately connected with conflict research and development research; the former often more relevant for negative peace and the latter more relevant for positive peace, but with highly important overlaps.

To justify this way of looking at peace and peace research, let us see where the many efforts to conceive of peace in terms of only one of these 'sides' or aspects leads us. Such efforts are likely to bring into focus, in theory and indeed in practice, the onesidedness on which they are based.

Thus a research emphasis on the reduction of personal violence at the expense of a tacit or open neglect of research on structural violence leads, very easily, to acceptance of 'law and order' societies. Personal violence is built into the system as work is built into a compressed spring in a mattress: it only shows when the mattress is disintegrating. And on the other hand there may be a research emphasis on righting social wrongs, on obtaining social justice, at the expense of a tacit or open acceptance and use of personal violence. The short-term costs of personal violence appear as small relative to the costs of continued structural violence. But personal violence tends to breed manifest physical violence, not only from the opponent but also inside one's own group—and the aftermath of violent revolutions generally seems to testify to this.

We may summarize by saying that too much research emphasis on one aspect of peace tends to rationalize extremism to the right or extremism to the left, depending on whether one-sided emphasis is put on 'absence of personal violence' or on 'social justice'.

Both values, both goals are significant, and it is probably a disservice to try, in any abstract way, to say that one is more important than the other. To realize one of them is no mean achievement either, particularly if we consider the number of social orders and regimes that realize neither.

But the view that one cannot meaningfully work for both absence of personal violence and for social justice can also be seen as essentially pessimistic, as some sort of intellectual and moral capitulation. First of all there are many forms of social action available today that combine both in a highly meaningful way. Secondly, once the double goal has been stated—that peace research is concerned with the conditions for promoting both aspects of peace—there is no reason to believe that the future will not bring us richer concepts and more forms of social action that combine absence of personal violence with the light against social injustice once sufficient effort is put into research and practice. There are more than enough people willing to sacrifice one aspect of peace for the other—it is by aiming for both that peace research can make a real contribution.

The Reduction of War and the Creation of Peace

Frances A. Beer
University of Colorado

Theories of Peace

Peace theory focuses on a particular opportunity and problem—peace. Peace theory draws strength from the fact that we probably enjoy greater peace today than we have at any time in past history. There appears to be a long-run general historical trend toward the diffusion of peace. Wars have become less frequent and the periods of tranquillity between them are longer today than in earlier times. Peace theory draws urgency from the contradictory fact that today's wars are more concentrated and severe than before. When wars occur, they are shorter; but casualties have increased both in absolute terms and relative to population (see Beer, 1983, 1974).

Many theorists deal with peace, but peace theory is not a unified whole. It does not begin from abstract axioms, follow through a set of rigorously deduced and exhaustively validated principles, and end with a coherent and consistent set of action recommendations. Rather it is a family of discourse that comes from many diverse traditions, seeing the world in various ways. Space prevents us from considering all of its manifold aspects. We shall focus here on action dimensions of peace theories, on different ways that theorists suggest we may enhance peace.

War Reduction

Two major branches of peace theory, defined in this normative way, concentrate in turn on war reduction and peace creation. The first branch, war reduction, accepts the international system as given and tries to alleviate its most extreme dangers by reducing and limiting war.

Some theorists of war reduction concentrate directly on limiting international violence. These emphasize the rational management of international crises that might lead to war, and of wars themselves once they occur. Crises management implies special vigilance and control in situations that have a high probability of resulting in war (see Allison, Carnesale, and Nye, 1985). When war does occur, a conscious, organized effort at war management may help prevent smaller incidents of violence from turning into larger ones, keep limited wars limited, and preclude substantial wars from becoming total.

Self restraint and the development of nonviolent techniques may also be important. The future benefits of violence are problematic; the immediate costs—casualties and physical damage—are very real. People are killed and injured; limited 'bushfire' wars sometimes spread out of control, expanding dramatically in space, time, and weapons. It seems more prudent to shy away from using violence as a tool and, instead, to try and prevent it from breaking out or, once it has occurred, to attempt to limit it. Nonviolence is as old as the history of religious leaders and movements. Traditions embodied by Buddha and Christ have inspired successful modern political movements and leaders—the Indian struggle for independence under the leadership of Gandhi and the struggle of the American Blacks for greater equality under the leadership of Martin Luther King, Jr., are but two modern examples (see Sharp, 1973).

Other war reduction theorists aim at military aspects of the international system that are preconditions for violence. Strategic deterrence and arms control are policies with this focus. Strategic deterrence is 'the threat to use force in response as a way of preventing the first use of force by someone else' (Morgan, 1977: p. 9). Such deterrence has been quite popular through history (see Naroll, Bullough, and Naroll, 1974), but the advent of nuclear weapons has given it a whole new dimension. Arms control, on the other hand, aims to keep violence in check by putting a cap on forces available to all parties.

Peace Creation

War reduction theories appeal to most people because they deal directly with the use of force and weapons. They are, however, limited because they focus on immediately observable symptoms rather than on deeper underlying causes. Theories of peace creation go beyond buffering existing international relations. They focus on balancing and restructuring of the world system.

Balancing

International balancing is an attempt to rearrange the importance of, and relations between, the different levels of the system. The traditional view of international relations has been very state-centered. Historically the international system has consisted of states with sovereignty; and only states could be subjects of international law. Balancing begins from the premise that the national level is overdeveloped and might usefully be constrained or even diminished. The international, transnational, group, and individual levels might be enhanced through strategies of world order, international functionalism, softening and shrinking the nation-state, and human rights.

World order theories have a strong 'top-down' emphasis. One strand of world order—world federalism—implies that the most desirable approach would be the creation of a single effective world government, perhaps modeled along the lines of modern federal polities, with lawmaking authority. If total unification is not possible, then a partial core union might serve as a growth center for the larger global enterprise (see Clark and Sohn, 1966; and Streit, 1949).

Failing such an ambitious solution, world order approaches the globe as a developing country and aims to forge strong strands of cohesion. World order implies support for continued international legal codification; signature and ratification of, and compliance with, multilateral treaties, agreements, and declarations; international courts and other attempts at adjudication, arbitration, mediation, and conciliation of conflicts and disputes; participation in, contributions to, and compliance with international organizations and the collective decisions reached in them; development of and participation in international transactions, including trade; the establishment of substantial global reserves of commodities in short supply such as money, food, and energy; increased international communication through such means as diplomacy, travel, media, and education (see Falk, 1975; and Mendlovitz, 1975).

International functionalism comes to the world system with less sweeping ambitions. International functionalists tend not to believe in grand solutions to world problems. Instead they take a more piecemeal approach. Following functionalist logic, nations and groups can best build international peace by cooperating on specific projects, one at a time. Such cooperation implies different regimes in different sectors. For example, one set of international cooperative arrangements may exist with regard to the law of the sea, another for trade in oil, and a third for nuclear weapons (see Keohane, 1984; Krasner, 1982; and Haas, 1964).

The most controversial aspect of balancing involves softening and shrinking the nation-state, which has been the basic building block of the modern international system. The nation-state and nationalism have been, and will continue to be, central elements of the global system. They combine subordinate groups, with diverse identities and interests, into political communities with shared territory and aspirations. Yet the sharp edges of nations, like those of international blocs, increase the structural tendencies to violence. National aggrandizement is an important force leading to war.

Expanding states exert lateral pressure on others that, feeling threatened, attempt to defend themselves (see Choucri and North, 1975; and Organski and Kugler, 1980).

Balancing at the lowest level of the world system includes human rights, the protection and development of individual human beings. Peace creation includes a premise that a strong and healthy system grows through the growth of its component parts, rather than at their expense (see Clark, 1977).

Restructuring

We have seen that peace creation involves balancing relations *between* levels of the international system. A second major task of peace creation is to restructure processes and activities *within* different levels of the international system. International restructuring includes demilitarization, as well as the enhancement of equality and stability.

Peace creation implies demilitarization at the international, domestic, and individual levels. This means less emphasis on the law of war, international military peacekeeping, international military alliances, domestic military regimes, military expenditure, and military themes in media and culture.

Restructuring the international system also means moving towards greater equality, a more equal sharing of power, wealth, and knowledge. More groups and actors can participate actively in various dimensions of the world environment. As they articulate and defend their own particular concerns, they will also contribute their resources to the development of a shared human community.

International balancing finally carries a stabilizing logic. Rapid change benefits some, but not all. Changes cannot be implemented all at once through a sudden, apocalyptic global revolution. Rather they must take place gradually over time, through evolution. Revolutionary change is dramatic; but, by historical definition, it often carries with it a good deal of violence. The great revolutions of the modern world—France, the United States, China, the Third World—have been associated with important changes. Nevertheless, many beneficial developments might well have taken place without violent revolution. It is not clear, in any event, that violent revolution necessarily improves international peace.

Constructive actions can and should be undertaken incrementally, in small pieces, as experiments. Policy makers should define their expected impacts in advance and then monitor the results to see if they achieve the anticipated results. If so, additional steps can be taken; if not, little will be lost. Whether the actions succeed or fail, policy makers will have a systematic basis for learning and innovation. They can subsequently try new and better policies aiming at the same end.

Paths to International Peace

Our discussion has suggested a number of possible paths towards the reduction of international war and the creation of greater international peace.

Violence limitation includes various strands some of which, like crisis management and war management, are easily applicable to specific situations. Others, restraint and nonviolence, are more difficult in the current context of international politics. Strategic deterrence and arms control are minimalist, narrowly defined, specific, short-term approaches. Balancing the levels of the international system through world order, functionalism, denationalization, human rights—and restructuring it by demilitarization, equalization, stabilization—are obviously maximalist, difficult, and distant goals.

It is often assumed that many of the paths presented here are mutually exclusive. National peace vs. international peace, strategic deterrence vs. arms control, short-term vs. long-term, practical vs. visionary. There certainly are trade-offs between them; yet some of the trade-offs may be more apparent than real. For example, we usually believe that advances in deterrence will set back arms control, or that progress in arms control or demilitarization will hinder deterrence. This is not necessarily true; indeed deterrence and arms control may, to some extent, be preconditions for each other. If deterrence were completely assured, arms control might become easier in areas which were not deemed essential to national peace. If arms control existed to a greater degree, deterrence might be more effective or less important. The Strategic Defense Initiative offers a striking example of this complementarity. Space-based strategic technology will be deployed primarily to provide deterrence (see Jastrow, 1985). Yet much of it will also provide the ability to monitor and enforce arms control. And its vulnerability to attack will, in turn, require arms control measures to ensure its safety.

The short-term and the long-term, the practical and the visionary, are not always at odds. Short-term practical considerations are necessary for us to navigate the shoals and narrows of our present day world; but a longer range vision provides a more stable direction for policy. Even if several of the approaches were mutually exclusive at the present time, they must not necessarily be opposed in the future. Present contradictions may be resolved through subsequent deconstruction, recombination, and synthesis. Survival and reform are not enemies. Both are important components of a comprehensive, coherent, and constructive international peace theory.

References

Allison, G.T., A. Carnesale and J.S. Nye, Jr. *Hawks, Owls, and Doves: An Agenda for Avoiding Nuclear War.* New York: Norton, 1985.

Beer, F.A. *Peace Against War: The Ecology of International Violence.* San Francisco: W. H. Freeman, 1981.

Choucri, N., and R. North. *Nations in Conflict: National Growth and International Violence.* San Francisco: W. H. Freeman, 1975.

Clark, J.R. *The Great Living System.* Pacific Grove: Boxwood, 1977.

Clark, G., and L.B. Sohn. *World Peace through World Law: Two Alternative Plans,* 3rd ed. Cambridge: Harvard University Press, 1966.

Falk, R. *A Study of Future Worlds.* New York: Free Press, 1975.

Haas, E.B. *Beyond the Nation-State.* Stanford: Stanford University Press. 1964.

Jastrow, R. *How to Make Nuclear Weapons Obsolete.* Boston: Little, Brown, 1985.

Keohane, R.O. *After Hegemony: Cooperation and Discord in the World Political Economy.* Princeton University Press, 1984.

Krasner, S.D. (ed.). "International Regimes," special issue of *International Organization* 36:2. Cambridge: M.I.T. Press, 1982.

Mendlovitz, S. *On the Creation of a Just World Order: Preferred Worlds for the 1990s.* New York: Free Press, 1975.

Morgan, P.M. *Deterrence: A conceptual Analysis.* Beverly Hills: Sage, 1977.

Naroll, R., V.L. Bullough and F. Naroll. *Military Deterrence in History: A Pilot Cross-Historical Survey.* Albany: State University of New York Press, 1974.

Organski, A.F.K. and J. Kugler. *The War Ledger.* Chicago: University of Chicago Press, 1980.

Roberts, A. (ed.). *Civilian Resistance as a National Defence: Non-Violent Action Against Aggression.* Baltimore: Penguin, 1969.

Sharp, G. *The Politics of Nonviolent Action.* Boston: Porter Sargent, 1973.

Streit, C. *Union Now: A Proposal for an Atlantic Federal Union of the Free.* New York: Harper, 1949.

Peace Education and Peace Research: East-West and North-South Confrontation in Theory and Practice

Amalendu Guha
Institute for Alternative Development Research

While the East-West difference and confrontation are based on the ideology of collective well-being versus individual welfare and growth, the conflict of North-South lies in the diverging ideology of (a) affluence versus satisfaction of fundamental human needs, (b) individual development based on economic growth versus human development based on social development and social self-reliance, (c) material value (to be acquired through technology and monetary power) versus human value (combined with social and ethical value and to be obtained without the needs or "wants" beyond capacity to have as well as at the deprivation of other or others in the society) and family, (d) egocentric "i" versus social "i" (an integral part of collective "We"). The Developed North consists of both the capitalist West and socialist East while the Peripheral South is composed of the vast majority of the underdeveloped countries. This development and underdevelopment is to be understood purely from the economic standpoint as it has no connection with the cultural, social and moral aspects. From the territorial standpoint, the difference is between the "Haves" and "Have-nots" i.e., between the 24 industrial countries of the O.E.C.D. (Organisation for Economic Cooperation and Development) and six East European Socialist countries (with the exception of Rumania which has accepted the membership of the "Group of 77" in 1977) and the 112 developing countries, popularly known as the countries of the "Group of 77." While the gap between the East and the West is mostly of ideological and political nature, the same between the North and the South is of the nature of affluence or over-consumerism and deprivation or under-consumption.

On the question of overall development, they have, perhaps, some commonness. Most of the countries and not all, belonging to all these three worlds, generate development from "above" or from the centre. If a development is generated from the centre, and the localities or the peripheries become only instruments of implemention without any participatory function, it is a maldevelopment. The degree of this maldevelopment varies from country, depending on the strength, power and role of the ruling class, elite and technobureaucracy, which form the very core decision-making. All the maldevelopments are of vertical structure and this vertical structure implies both dominance and exploitation. To the contrary, the decentralised development at localities level, on horizontal basis of both of mobilisation and participation, is the uniform development. The Post-Liu Shao-chi and

Amalendu Guha, "Peace Education and Peace Research." This chapter is reprinted from Proceedings of the International Peace Research Association Seventh General Conference by permission of the International Peace Research Association.

Pre-Hua Kuo-feng China applied this model. The Soviet or the East European model of development, on the other hand, conceives that a proper and balanced correlation between both the horizontal and vertical structures or the centre and the calities, can generate the balanced and optimum development. In peace research and peace education, these conceptual divergences will constitute some basic points of departure.

While the general education, in its formal form, develops the reproductive educational capacity of a man, peace education and peace research...try to impart learning and knowledge, both informal and non-reproductive, in all the system-divided worlds.

The West is formulating the conceptual framework of peace and conflict theory. The East believes in peace action while the South embraces the both, though for theoretical concepts depends much on the West.

This paper, apart from dealing with the concepts on peace education and peace research on East-West and North-South level, also discusses the values in peace education and peace research as well as their future trends, without trying to draw any conclusion.

Concepts of Peace, Peace Research, Peace Education, Peace Action, Peacelessness, etc.

What is peace? It is only the absence of violence, both armed and social? It is naturally inclusive of the above but not conclusive. The need for peace arises from the existence of peacelessness and disorderly behavioural trends in social life. Negation of negation is affirmation and hence negation of violence is peace. But this in an escapist definition. Popular definition of peace is (a) absence or freedom from war, (b) cessation of war, or (c) the stage in which there does not exist armed conflict or war between and among states. But it leaves out a vast arena completely uncovered—the arena of social life which deals with the day-to-day activities of the society. The broad definition of peace should, therefore, include (a) the existence of social situation free from exploiting classes and strata, (b) absence of dominance-dependence or centre-periphery relationship or presence of autonomy, (c) absence of deprivation on one hand and wastage on the other hand (or negation of overdevelopment, underdevelopment and maldevolopment), (d) establishment of optimum and equitable correlation between human needs and human rights, social rights and social duties, social production and social consumption, production and distribution, needs and distribution etc., (e) absence of the tension of peacelessness in social life, (f) existence of harmony in the values (i.e, equilibrium correlation) of: Material Man and Sacrificing Man, Outer Man and Inner Man, and Self-Man and Social Man, etc. These conditions are valid and so applicable at inter-nation and intra-nation as well as inter-territory and intra-territory levels.

Peace research is to analyse and theoretise the above aspects and peace education is to verify them through applied peace action. Peace education is the intermediary linkage between peace research and peace action, with enriching and contributory functions, on both the ways. This message is valid for both of East-West and North-South.

Peacelessness is the stage, just before and after a war or crisis, both of social and nonsocial nature, which sickens the social and human life and mind within a stage of tension, agony and sufferings. Sometimes, this situation is worse than the period and stage of war or crisis. The study of their action and phenomena is no less important than the study of direct peace and conflict as well as crisis studies. Their appeal and validity is the same whether in the East or West, or, North or South. Sometimes, its effects are very negative on the individual as well as social nerves and hinders the course of normal development.

East-West and North-South as Regards to Peace Research and Peace Education

There is one similarity between the Western part of the North, or simply the West and the South as regards to peace research and peace education: it was never and has not yet become a working class and the peasantry movement. Its origin lies in the urban middle class intellectuals, who need solidarity with the urban and semi-urban working class and rural agricultural population, for establishing the intellectual leadership. Unless it attains the very aspirations of the working class and the peasantry with their embodiment into it, it will naturally remain an elite hobby or activity, purely alienated from the masses.

In order to liquidate the economic underdevelopment in the underdeveloped countries there has appeared a concept of bridging the gap between the rich and the poor countries, [a] concept advocated by the exponents of growth economics, which, naturally, has given birth to conflict, confrontation and contradiction between the developed and developing nations. These confrontation, conflict and contradiction constit[ut]ed the basic fields of peace studies and peace research on the pattern as the North-South dominance-dependence relationship studies. There are peace educators and peace researchers who believe in the stage theory of peace-making or peace-realisation. The stage theory or process, because of its timekilling nature, becomes conformist and destroys some of the very basic essences of peace realisation.

The North, more or less, has solved the problem of material needs of her people and so can divert attention towards discussion and solution of humanistic needs (or non-material needs). The South has not yet been able to solve the problem of basic material needs of the greater portion of her people (which is lying at the under-sufficiency level) and so the discussion on the solution of non-material needs (or humanistic needs) does not represent anything rather than mere talks. It is universal truth that nobody, with empty or half-full stomach can struggle for freedom of expression and impression, freedom to travel, freedom to alternative choices, freedom of association and dissociation etc. Once, when the material needs are satisfied then starts the problem of satisfaction of non-material or humanistic needs. Non-material or humanistic needs are succession to the material needs. Again, though they are complementary to each other, being essential parts of the total human realisation, yet their stages of satisfaction are successive. The northern peace-researchers may ask: why these stages are successive and not simultaneous? Isn't it a type of East European argument of submission of demands for non-material or non-fundamental needs to those of material or very fundamental needs, which never return back or conditions for whose fulfilment are never created even though the material or fundamental needs are satisfied? The underdeveloped South has...two basic points of reply to the above arguments: a) in order of priority it is to meet the material needs which are essential as well as fundamental in nature, because they affect the life of 80% of its population, and b) in social mobilisation and participation process for development some individual desires, aspirations and measures are to be sacrificed, to reach to the commonness or collectivity of goals and means and the demands for non-material needs are those which are to be sacrificed for a certain period of time. Again, they are the masses of the people of the South to decide and simultaneously fix the policy of when and how to achieve or fulfil the nonmaterial or non-fundamental needs.

Concepts on Peace Research and Peace Education

There appeared, in recent years, two clearly distinct concepts on peace research and peace education: the structural concept and the class concept. The structural concept deals with the study and analysis of linkage and inter-connections of parts of a system or whole and affirms that changes take place only when all parts undergo a qualitative leap. All the constituents of a system or elements of the whole are necessarily dependent on their respective structures and, they do, at the same time, play distinctive role on the mode, system and organisation, depending on the specific particularity, organic unity and importance. The distinctive of the structural school of thought is that it puts stress on the organic integrity of the whole, in its cognitive analysis, in which parts contain the essentials of the whole. The structural theory of imperialism, sub-imperialism and studies on multi-national corporations, dominance-dependence theory etc. have clearly revealed this aspect. Most of, and not all, the peace-researchers and educators belong to this structural school.

The class concept of peace research and peace education is based on the Marxist class ideology. To start with Lenin's definition, social classes "are large groups of people differing from each other by the place they occupy in a historically determined system of social production, by their relation (in most cases fixed and formulated in law) to the means of production, by their role in the social organisation of labour, and, consequently, by the mode and dimensions of acquiring the share of social wealth of which they dispose. Classes are groups of people one of which can appropriate the labour of another owing to the different places they occupy in a system of social economy." The appearance of social division of labour and private ownership is the root of emergence of class and social strata. The class concept of peace outlines that social peace may arrive only when the stage of classlessness will emerge. Hence it does not exclude class struggle, of any finding out solution of social problems, as the interests between and among classes are incompatible and contradictory. The East European peace-researchers and some radicals of the Third World belong to this school of thought.

There are some inter- and counter-distinctions in theoretical approach and practice between both of these concepts. In respect of social change, the structural school prefers non-violent structural change which is nothing but reform, while reform can never produce the needed change. In this respect the school of class concept demands social revolution, in any form, in order to effect the desired social change. So class struggle remains the central concept here. The peace-researchers and peace educators of both the North-West and South have centred their studies around the following domains:

- North-Western (of structural concept)
- Paying more attention on the analysis of, and obtaining knowledge of superstructure.
- Problem of satisfaction of non-fundamental non-material needs occupy the main issue.
- Problem of reduction of affluence, super-saturation and overdevelopment also stands at the base of study and education.
- Research and activities are more theoretical (of conditional nature) and education-oriented.
- Overdevelopment makes the researchers and educators to find out alternative life-style on the basis of reduction of wastage.
- Believes that the social, political, economic and overall power-structure is unbreakable and so suggests for negotiated reforms.

Southern (of class concept)

- Devoting more attention on acquiring knowledge of structure.
- Problem of satisfaction of fundamental material needs constitute the basic point of study.
- Problem of basic needs and their means of satisfaction, de-underdevelopment is the central theme of investigation.
- Research and activities are more action oriented.
- Underdevelopment, under-nourishment and under-sufficiency in the basic material needs induce the researchers and educators to find out basic needs-satisfaction based alternative life style.
- Believes in class struggle and consequently in the breaking up of power structure.

In inter- and intra-nation social and spatial relation, while explaining and elaborating the dominance-dependence relationship,

a) the peace-researchers and peace-educators belonging to the class-concept school find its root in the existing class structure,

b) while those belonging to the structure-concept find its root in the existing centre-subcentre-periphery structure.

In analysing the inter-action and counter-action processes of the inter- and intra-national, organizational, class and strata relationship as well as consequences, the proponents of class-concept adopt the concept and action of Marxian dialectics, and those of structural concept follow the Hegelian dialectics. Existence of different social classes is the cause of exploitation and subjugation, as the Marxists think. Emergence of upper and lower strata within all the social classes (even within the East European social sturure) is the root of creation of priviligentsia and deprivation, as the structuralists believe. The Marxists, theoretically, believe in classlessness or in a classless society which can solve the problems of social differences, antagonism and confrontation. But they have not, yet, been able to find out any means as how to solve the antagonistic and non-antagonistic problems among the existing privileged bureau- and technocratic social strata (but not class as it does not posses any ownership over the means of production, possesses only the right to distribute the ends of production), working class and the peasantry. The people belonging to the bureau- and techno-cracy are top-dogs, those belonging to the working class are mid-dogs while the peasants are the under-dogs. Mao, who developed Marxism-Leninism further, could, perhaps, give a theoretical and practical solution to this problem, when he introduced the method of:

i) horizontal cycling and recycling among different professions (industrial, agricultural and national as well as local administrative) and,

ii) vertical cycling and recycling of professionals (of different types; workers, technical cardres and management) within the same production unit,

at regular periodical intervals, within Chinese structure during the Cultural Revolution period.

The structuralists believe in a stateless society and think that it is an improvement over the Marxian concept of classless society.

Since the Marxists believe in the class concept, they believe in class struggle and class revolution for social changes. Both as strategy and tactics, the Marxists keep both the means of revolution open: armed and non-violent. The structuralists are, either, afraid of armed revolution (and it is also not possible within the present framework of the Western societies where the state-elite possesses enormous military power and mechanism to suppress any revolutionary effort), or, opt for a negotiable social order (negotiable among different classes on the one hand and between the state bureaucracy and the people belonging to different classes). So, the conformist Gandhian model of non-violent revolution or the peaceful method of negotiated social change constitute the very foundation of the ideology and methodology of the structural conceptualists. The basic reason behind promoting this type of ideology and methodology by the structuralists, in peace research and peace education, is that they belong to a over-developed society and, as a result, are afraid of parting with the material and immaterial privileges they enjoy in a society of this type. Social origin and social environment, in which they live, influence the moulding of their social outlook, and so, in order not to sacrifice the existing privileges, they had to be conformist and are always [trying] to find...newer arguments to strengthen their approach.

The structural theory of peace research and peace education is, directly or indirectly, indebted to the class concept for its origin. Besides this origin there are also two other factors which contributed to its further development:

a) the East European dogmatic (and hence non-dynamic) and static (hence non-creative) application of Marxist theory, and

b) emergence of newer trends, complexities and contradictions in the approach and behaviour of the West European and North American imperialism.

The class concept of peace research and peace education is not outdated, it is rather very strong in the non-West European and non-North American countries.

There is one basic difference between the Marxists and the structuralists as regards to social progress, social process and social change. The Marxists believe in the spiral and ascendent development, in which the forthcoming is an improvement over the former. The structuralists believe in the cyclical development, in which each process and system finds birth, growth and death within a historical period of time. Hence, the Marxists believe in the process of continuity while the structuralists believe in the process of discontinuity. Therefore, the Marxists are revolutionaries while the structuralists are evolutionaries. The evolutionaries are pacifists, but, unfortunately, the mass-oriented social changes do not take place in the peaceful or continued evolutionary process. Had it taken place so, the whole world could be a good society, free from class and structural violence. The pacifist peace-doyens of the Western world believe in the moral value of peaceful action, but in these societies of ever-increasing multilateral exploitation, the faith in the moral value of action does not strengthen the moral value of cause and hence the course of change.

A section of peace-researchers and educators of both the West and the East believe in the establishment of a global soci[ety] based on an international framework of law or legal system. Here, peace is valued as "equity" or "modelled order." In ultimate analysis, it shows the tendency of negation of dialecties, and in action, the affirmation or imposition of modelled order in which "big power" or "great nation" hegemonism have got more chance to dominate.

As regards to approaches to peace research we can find three basic schools, namely,

a) Marginal or Limited Sense School: Its basic approach and stands are absence and avoidance of international and national war, threat, and violence; reduction of militarisation and destruction of destructive weapons with a view to obtain a "stable peace" or stabilise peace.
b) Structural School: Its basic approach is the absence or prevention of direct and structural violence as well as harmonization of interests at all levels in the broader or realistic society.
c) Action School: Its basic approach is the elimination of dominance-dependence relation, promotion of self-reliance and self-realisation by appropriate means. It accepts and recognises both types of antagonistic and non-antagonistic contradictions [are] the society and proposes for adoption of proper measures to remove them.

But absence of war is not peace and prevention of war by balancing huge military forces is also not peace. Because, prevention of war assumes unlimited build-up of arms with diversion of vast, material resources from human needs-satisfaction. To be objective we are to realise that economic oppression, inequality, hunger, ignorance etc. do not and cannot constitute the very fundamentals of lasting and guaranteed peace. To the contrary, these will be the very elements of anti-peace. Active involvement of the people in removing social disparities; combating poverty and ignorance; fighting for rights of women, children and social minorities; overcoming racial and social prejudices and strikes etc. are to be the main tasks of peace activists, peace researchers and peace educators. Therefore, peace research, peace education and peace action are to constitute the inter-linked triangle of the whole system of peace order.

There always arises a basic question: Peace for whom? It is not naturally for the upper class or social elite, it is the common masses. In the human society, there will always be struggle between "haves" and "have nots," between the consumer strata and the deprived strata; between the more privileged strata and the suffering strata: between the dominant class and the dominated class and between the combined ruling class and bureaucracy and ruled classes. Therefore, classlessness only can generate peacefulness. The dialectics of peace is that it should, by no means, mean static or passive action, it is rather, dynamic and active force. Its dialectical relation is as such:

Thesis:	Peacelessness
Antithesis:	Negation to peacelessness
Synthesis:	Peacefulness

Is peace research and peace education meant only for the specialists, or for the masses? This is the question we are very often asked. There are complaints that, for the last 15 years, the arm-chair peace researchers of the West are dealing mainly with the peripheral theories and subjects on abstract models. Some of them are making theories and models without sufficient analysis. There are also some others, who do make very good empirical analysis, though only up to the situation of the fifties and not beyond that, but fail to give any theoretical approach.

While peace research and peace education, in the broader sense, is to generate the feeling of internationalism and raise the consciousness of the masses beyond prejudice, it has not yet been able to cross the level of prejudiced feeling of nationalism, whether in the East or the West, the North or the South. It misses the very effective correlation of deduction and induction in treatment of the problems.

Values in Peace Education and Peace Research

Right to live humanly is the most important value of human life and this value forms the essential aspect of peace education and peace research. But there is difference in approach and ideology as well as in action between the East and the West. The deprived South, which is still in the economic orbit of the West, is trying to find out the meaning of right of life and so to live. Right to work and right of economic security are the two essential prerequisites and values of life, and both East and the West accept these two terms as goals of human life and realisation. But the difference lies in how they are interpreted and implemented. Work is the precondition and condition of life and hence necessary for human maintenance and survival. The East, in its socialistic approach, has successfully been able to [include] both the functions of work: right to work and duty to work. The duty to work does not constitute an important part of work the current political ideologies of the West, and instead, right not to work, as a symbol of individual freedom, is gaining momentum. The right to live and right not to work are self-contradictory, since the means of the life and survival can only be fulfilled and guaranted by only the right to work. Right to live on the basis of right not to work means survival or maintenance either by exploitation of others' work or by dependence on others' work. Simple birth does not solve the problem of survival, it is economics which does it.

In the socialist societies, the economic security of the citizens is guaranteed by the state through allocation of jobs to each member of workable age of the society. In the West, the right to work for members of its working force is not guaranteed, while in exchange, in certain circumstances and cases a portion of the unemployed working forces are given unemployment or social assistance for a certain of time. So, while the solution of the East is to guarantee incomes for its citizens, the West tries to solve it through expansion of personal consumption and hence creation of more jobs in the consumption sector of the economy. The paradox, here, is that if the purchasing through full social employment is not guaranted first, there cannot be enough purchasing power to absorb the increased production of the consumers' goods, thus to ensure ultimately stimulation and expansion of this sector of economy. The exponents of the efficient or growth economy in the West therefore conclude that unemployment is the essential condition of ensuring a rational economy, which results in lowering the labour-cost of production. Reduction of labour-cost means umemployment and unemployment means reduction of purchasing power for the working forces. Then, for whom is this efficient or rational economy? The Western ideologists, again the East European socialist economy as an economy of "overemployment" because of the fact that it guarantees job and economic security to each of the labour forces even at stages when an additional input of labour is not economically necessary for a certain economic sector. But, economic development for whom? It is for the society and to satisfy the economic right and needs of every citizen.

The economy of the South is an underemployed economy, not only because of the fact that it suffers from the lack of economic means, but, mostly because of the fact that its economic structure on the Western capitalist pattern and social structure is maintained at [feudal]-primitive bourgeois level. So, two important values of life, right to work and right of economic security, are not being fulfilled there. The third value, i.e., duty to work, is not either being sufficiently explained (since it may give birth to its complementary part—the right to work, which may result in class struggle with the feudo-bourgeoisie) or not being explained at all. Duty is creative and right is distributive, while both are the two integral parts of the whole equitable social process. The correlated use of these values is the action which the South is to adopt, which, ultimately, can guarantee the economic right, the other value, to its age-long deprived nationals.

A very well-manifested phenomenon of the South is that the under-dogs of yesterday have become or are trying to become top-dogs of today, completely just forgetting their origin and class background as well as duty to their oppressed class members. Peace education and peace research is to promote both the idea and action that they become equal halves tomorrow.

Peace and Human Values

Like the North-South dominance-dependence relationship there exists a very visible trend of North's domination over the South in the basic fields of peace research and peace education and hence conflict in approach, attitude, treatment, analysis and solution of the problems. For example, we can see two different "Man" in the Capitalist-North and Underdeveloped-South: in the first case he is a "Material Man" while in the second case he is a "Sacrificing or Deprived Man." The social education and social philosophy in the Capitalist North teaches its man to be self-reliant, self-sufficient and self-dependent which grows in the direction of developing an ego-centric and isolated man. To the countrary, the social ethics of the underdeveloped periphery teaches its man to be family and kinship-conscious and, consequently, does not induce the idea of alienation from the family, kinship and the social collectivity. Social relation is a relation of interdependence, of interexchange of feelings and thoughts, of impressions and expressions etc. between and among the members of the society, of the locality. There is a growing tendency of monetisation of a good part human and social relations like services and duties in side and within the family, kinship, neighbours and locality in the North American as well as Northern, Central and Western parts of the Capitalist Europe. This "pay and take" and "take when can pay" it's a mechanistic self-centric approach in human relation in the society which, gradually and in course of time, alienates an individual from the virtues and qualities of happy and co-functional life. Perhaps, this is the outcome of advanced capitalism. To the contrary, the overdependence of a section of people on the family, kinship and social collectivity in the poverty-stricken South, caused mainly by structural violence and class-domination, hinders the development of self-confidence, self-dignity and self-motion. It is the outcome of backward feudalism and tribal-bondage system. This contradiction and solution-seeking study on this, is becoming a topic of vital importance in the Southern and Eastern countries.

Now, if we come to the case of the East European socialist countries we find that some sub-sections of social sciences, irregularly, devote some time to peace research, specially, on the eve of participating in some international and regional peace conferences of vital importance. Of course, there are official peace organisations affiliated to the action-oriented World Peace Council, whose activities lie mainly in the organisation of some conferences or meetings of national or regional character which discuss the problems of imperialism, neo-colonialism, exploitation and dominance, national liberation movement, ways of economic development etc. covering the capitalist and developing economies. They never discuss the problems of their own societies as they believe that they have reached the stage of classless or one-class society where there is no class-exploitation and exists both equality and equity. They also believe that their social contradictions belong to the category of non-antagonistic contradictions, which, we cannot yet accept clearly. Strata differentiation, wage-differentiation (with existence of about 40 grades and 10-fold difference between the highest-paid and lowest-paid wage earners), apparatus and hence power-consciousness, socio-economic privilege-differentiation etc. cannot, simply, be attributed as the result of non-antagonistic social contradictions. Again, the distinction between the bureaucrat and the working class and the peasantry and the bureaucrats and the peasantry is wide—which does not prove the arrival to the stage classlessness yet. When the dictatorship of the proletariat changes hands and is vested in the bureaucrat-intellectual professionals (whose provenance is, of course, the working class and the peasantry, unfortunately) there is doubt that the stage of classless society without social contradictions can be arrived at so easily. The analysis of only other societies and social problems, the problems of armaments and disarmaments etc. constitute only the partial objects of peace research and peace activities. What is good with them is that they put more accent on the practical and soluble aspects of the present and emerging socio-economic problems, of social mobilisation and participation, of creation of action-oriented class-consciousness, etc., as against the abstract theory-creative efforts in the West.

Now, about the South. The South has her mixed trends of activities. The West-educated peace-researchers are more theory-oriented and that also of structural-type. The Marxists and the grass-root researchers are mostly engaged in empirical analysis of the current problems affecting the social life and trying to seek immediate solution. For applying the theory into practice they have started also some permanent as well as periodical peace action centres. For example, there are some centres of this type in Gujrat, Maharastra, Delhi and Varanasi in India. Their activities differ, basically, from the peace study schools or peace courses of the West (mostly organised during the summer or autumn, for short period) which is theoretical-input oriented. These action-centers mobilise the people of the villages or the communities, or the others to come from other places or localities, in the activities of collective (at village or community level self-reliance on the basis of Gandhian non-violent non-aggressive principles and neo-Gandhian approach of peaceful social pressure. Their non-greedy and "self reliance with the minimum" approach is directed towards voluntary structural change or reform. Their negation of class struggle and change of hearts through voluntary action and examples are also very near to the Buddhist and Christian ideas and also suit those belonging to the structural school, but the success is yet to be seen. Peace researchers in Japan so also mobilise the people not only in the gatherings like the political parties, but also in peace-actions. In North Ireland, the peace activists are deeply engaged in mobilising the masses in marches for peace, and we are yet to see their effectiveness. Anyhow, in consciousness-raising of the public as well as public opinion building these types of action have got more practical values.

Peace Research, Peace Action and Peace Education

On peace-research and peace-action, there exist three distinctive characteristics in three different worlds of socio-economic systems:

a) The East European countries of the socialist system concentrate more efforts on peace-action than peace-theory. Hence, its characteristic is more mobilisational and participatory:

(i) mobilisational in the sense that the masses mobilised on different national and international social, economic, political and cultural issues, resulting in raising their consciousness and adopting adequate measures towards their remedies, and (ii) participatory in the sense that the masses, voluntarily, participate in constructive solution of the above types of problems. The World Peace Council promotes these sort of peace actions.

b) In the Western countries, theory-making occupies the primordial activity in peace research and peace education. A senior group of them is engaged in making abstract theory without giving due consideration to the empirical finding and analysis. A younger group is engaged in the empirical analysis with contributory progressive solution, lacking much in the conceptual contribution.

c) Peace activities in the South are a combination of the both. The peace-activists and the organisations which are affiliated to the World Peace Council do engage themselves in the peace-actions consisting of socio-economic and political-cultural issues, both of national and international character. There are also groups of intellectuals, mostly educated in the West, who are engaged in the abstract and structural theory-making. So, the South experiences both trends. Practically, there is no peace research and peace education in the socialist countries on East Europe and Asia. Their occasional studies explain and elaborate only the very centrally-decided messages of the party leadership, without any notable contribution. They believe that all the problems, whether of antagonistic or nonantagonistic nature, inside the socialist societies, are solved, while the problems are accumulating in both the developed capitalist and the underdeveloped countries. Again, they minimise the role of social problems and inequalities in peace research and peace education, at the same time giving priority only to the problems and aspects of armament and disarmament. So, it is one-sided. Occasionally, in the internal spheres, the socialist countries try to awaken their people only with the tasks of duties, omitting the same of rights, even though more than three decades have passed since their liberation. Denial or negligence of participatory might and mobilisation only from above contravene the very essence of peace research and peace education. It is not an anti-socialist propaganda, but the contemporary social reality of the socialist countries.

To the contrary, the non-action oriented peace research and peace education in the Western part of the Northern globe is also not at all rosy. Apart from its being an armchair hobby, it occupies only with the studies and preachings of inter-system inter-action models; models of peaceful change without disturbing the existing social and economic order, mechanism or decision-making; social change through press media, etc.

In spite of the existence of very occasional compromising attitude, peace research and peace education in the underdeveloped South, contain the elements of class struggle, struggle for national and local rights, human rights in the sense of right to live and life as normal human being, struggle for normal human needs-satisfaction, social change in the sense of common good for all the members of the society. Since these principles demand direct action without they cannot be realised, peace research and peace education, in this part of the world, though not so developed, yet is much action-oriented.

What is to educated and why, are two essential questions which can be asked to a peace-researcher and educator. If we start from the second question: why peace research and peace education, we can put forward the answer as such: to establish a classless, structureless and stateless horizontal social, economic, political and cultural order at local, national and global levels, in which human life, its security and maintenance as well as development is best assured. In order to attain such a type of society or social order, we, the peace-researchers, educators or the activists are to study and analyse the very roots of social and non-social conflicts, their behaviours, and attitudes, their trends and complexities etc. in order to find out solution in the common human interest. The theories of violence, simultaneously, with the theories of non-violence [are] also to be studied [as] well. Otherwise, we can never find out real solutions. For example, if the national of the colonies cannot be materialised under the conditions of peaceful negotiation or non-violent manner, with the metropoles or the internal minority ruling class, an overall struggle, both at the armed and social levels, is to be staged. For smooth running of the structural function of the state, the state bureaucracy and the ruling elite always demand peaceful order. But, why peaceful order? If it is for peaceful exploitation, then there cannot be peaceful coexistence of the exploited masses with it.

Peace education is to based on the analysis of the socially objective situation, motivated towards removing the obstacles standing on the way of uniform human development. For self-realisation of a human being, peace education is to have the inclusions and exclusions below.

But the success of both the peace research and peace education, depends much on:

(i) how far the permanent dialogue or mutual communication between the new and the old (on dialectical process) can be established;

(ii) to what extent the correlation between social mobilisation and participation, implementors and decision-makers etc. can be established;

(iii) to what extent horizontal and action can break the vertical structure; and

(iv) to what extent tolerance, consensus and democracy can function, etc.

There is not, until now, attitudial homogeneity in peace research, peace education and peace action. And we even cannot say that there exists any harmony among there diverse attitudes. There are peace researchers and educators, who opt for violence preventive research and education. There are others who prefer struggle-inducive research and action, for acquiring self-determination and sufficiency. They can be called as acquisitive researcher, educators and activists. As the values of one nation or the society cannot be internationalised or intersocialised because of existence of non-homogeneous values and characteristics between and among nations, such also is the case the heterogeneous character in peace research and peace education, existent in different schools. But there is one common point among all the schools of thoughts representing their own national and territorial problems, and that is: Basic Human Needs-Satisfaction and Realisation of Basic Human Right. This is the transnational value of peace research, peace education and peace action.

Inclusions	**Exclusions**
a) Common principles of collective self-reliance and self-determination.	a) Elements of passivity and dominance, ignorance and fear, structure-imposed fatalism, etc.
b) Principles of educating the masses to avoid greeds, and not to have more than the basic needs-satisfaction.	b) Elements of both the social and individual over-development.
c) The principle that man is an integral part of the whole social collectivity.	c) Individual egoism.
d) The principle of man's right from the society with that of duty to the society. In other words, both the functions of distribution and production are to be organically and harmonically inter-linked.	d) The excesses and absence of both the duties and rights, which generates imbalance between the production and the distribution and thus causes social disorders manifested in revolutions, counter-revolutions etc.

Where is Peace Research Headed?

Joseph D. Ben-Dak
University of São Paulo

Systematic thinking and research regarding the objectives as well as the means for the implementation of international peace first unfolded on the world stage in April, 1974, when the Asia-based International Conference on World Peace was held. The case can be made for attributing the origins of serious world-wide peace research to the Consortium on Peace Research, Education and Development which formulated priorities for its members in 1974. It is regrettable that scholarly work on the issue of war prevention and the institution of peace is not truly satisfactory. The principal problems are quite simple. However, while this essay is intended to put forward some corrective measures in future approaches to peace studies, it does not attempt to change the present direction or orientation of the field. Rather, our interest here is not in the meticulous documentation of the current state of peace studies, but to offer a brief glimpse at some of the big challenges to the discipline and what some of its future manifestations might be.

It should first be noted that there has not been a substantial change in the topical concentration of peace research since 1964. Subjects like: the effects of war; the limits of action in foreign policy; crisis management; and global effects of international organizations are all perennial topics of scholarly research in the field. Moreover, these approaches have limited their scope of questioning to the notion of achieving what theorists call "negative peace", i.e., the absence of physical violence or war. I contend that at the dawn of the twenty-first century, there is a much needed time and place in peace research to search for ways of achieving a "positive peace," i.e. the proactive measures intended to create ties of solidarity and cooperation between people, groups and states. As Lester Pearson once put it, "We are all prepared for war like precocious giants and for peace like retarded pygmies."

As a truly multidisciplinary field, peace research continues to prove to be one of the most vibrant and dynamic fields of study; drawing upon elements of psychology, behavioral science, religion, philosophy, culture and of course, international relations and political science. It is a great benefit to those researchers to be able to present their findings and to seek contributions of colleagues in such a wide variety of fields. However, some serious questions arise precisely as a result of this arrangement. Have these various fields of thought properly sought out and included contributions from peace researchers into their own courses of study? Or perhaps more succinctly, has peace research, by not subscribing to any single, overarching discipline missed its opportunity to gain greater recognition in the academic world? Clearly, if this very necessary field intends to generate new thinkers and new theories, it must work harder to define itself in both the public and academic realms.

Schools of Peace Research

It is worth examining how the various schools of peace research have organized themselves over the last half century in order to ascertain where the future of research might lie. One could argue that a "Narrow school" of peace research evolved out of such quantitative academic journals as *The Journal of Conflict Resolution* and *Sage's Yearbook of Foreign Policy Research.* These researchers showed a preference for experimentation, testing and mathematically presentable peace research and operated under the narrow assumption that the absence of war between nations was the ultimate goal of any academic pursuits in the field.

Perhaps as a result of the aforementioned narrowness of peace studies to that point, a "broad" school of thought developed which tended to be more inclusive of the cultural and sociological environments in which war and peace occurred. Whereas the narrow school perceived peace research as a pure scientific discipline ("peace science"), this later, broad school projected a demonstrably different value orientation, namely the promotion of anti-violent acts.

Another, formal area of thought in the school of peace research is attributable to the "Radicals", who saw their heyday of scholarly work come during and as a direct result of the fervent anti-war movements of the 1960s and 70s. Today, scholars in this area of thought are no longer as adamant or anti-establishment as they once were, but their focus on societal strife, across national, ethnic, religious and class lines remains the same. The end of the Vietnam War served as an initial chink in the armor of the radical school. Later, as the Berlin Wall fell researchers wondered if their fight to free the minds and the spirits of oppressed people around the world was over. However, if the events of September 11 are any indication, it is that there is a renewed and dire need for the examination of the causes of societal strife and oppressive ideologies.

A last and closely related group of peace activists have contributed significantly to the body of research in this area as well. Though not truly scholarly, but committed to peace nonetheless, groups associated with Muslim, Jewish and Christian religions and their churches have provided dynamic contributions to the field in the last quarter century. One example of their work is that of the Christian Fellowship of Reconciliation, a religious-based organization which "recognizes the essential unity of all humanity and who have joined together to explore the power of love and truth for resolving human conflict." However, in light of these sometimes competing activities and organizations, one can begin to determine several impediments that cut across the peace research field, regardless of school.

Challenges to Current Peace Research

For a discipline such as peace research to lend leadership in the making of policy, most notably foreign policy, it must align itself to the study of real world problems of policymaking. For example, peace research may have had a profound impact on a policy outcome as it relates to the general notion of arms control vs. complete disarmament. At a time when disarmament was not a workable political option, it was the predominant theory emanating from peace research groups. Even today, virtually nothing has been contributed to the modern debate of abrogating the 1972 Anti-Ballistic Missile Treaty and the development of a system of national missile defense. Ultimately, if the field hopes to regain its standing on college campuses and revitalize itself as a dynamic and relevant discipline, then it must begin to recognize the underlying assumptions and processes of policymakers so that future fields of thought contribute concretely to the debates of our time.

The simple fact that peace researchers have largely stopped searching for a definition of peace outside the realm that it could be something more than the mere lack of organized and collective violence further limits the field to the much narrower concepts of war and militarism. Again, for rejuvenation in this field of study to occur, new and daring methodologies are needed which break from the staid and accepted notions of peace and war. Research which leads to a discovery of conditions that facilitate or inhibit the establishment of a certain kind of "positive peace", not only opens new areas of thought, but creates a direct bearing on the formation of new policies in the avoidance of war.

What we would like to suggest is that the survivability of peace thinking is in the final analysis dependent upon its testing of new types of relations among individuals and groups, specifically as they relate to current topics of debate. After all, the science behind peace theory involves one of testing and revision. It favors no specific theory, but rather depends upon a scientific methodology. Clearly, the further away any research-derived knowledge is from direct translation to policy, the less useful the discipline will be on college campuses and within the public at large.

Therefore, what is being advocated here is not a less sophisticated methodology, since quantitative analysis and cross-disciplinary investigation are the cornerstones of modern scientific work, but rather a new cross-methodology that puts equal weight on the policy prescriptive results of peace research as it does on the nature of the research itself.

Taking Peace Research out of the Western World

The geographic progress of peace research in the past half century roughly correlates to the path of modern social sciences, which is to say that the major schools of thought have centered on academic centers and research institutions in the United States, Europe and Japan. Unlike many other disciplines in social science, peace studies have preoccupied themselves with the study of conflict outside this geographic framework. Therefore, I assert that there is significant need among academics to involve and enlist the support of their colleagues from the developing world to contribute to the discipline of peace studies.

First, essential to any credible or useful study on peace are valid and reliable first-person sources of information regarding the subject being studied. Looking at peace studies over the last decade, one finds that conclusions extended regarding the actions of foreign governments or groups fall well short of convincing as a result of a basic lack of direct knowledge. Ironically, as the present war on terrorism shines a light on the cultures and governments of South and Central Asia, the media and the public are being exposed to never before seen or understood conflicts that could have profound consequences for the potential for peace and war in the years ahead. Additionally related is the notion that valid and reliable research should be pursued first and foremost by the people whose lives will be most affected by it. Clearly, the impetus to resolve conflict and reduce war is most apparent among those people who risk being affected by conflict. For this reason, it is important for future peace researchers to not only increase their own regional focus, but also to empower those academics at the grassroots level to carry out their own research on the world around them. This could be done through the establishment of cooperative exchanges and joint programs or through the creation of specialized regional centers for the study of conflict.

Perhaps most importantly, though, peace research needs to move away from the form of questioning where the nation-state serves as the primary unit of conflict analysis. In the modern age, peace research must remain open to the never-ending evaluation of varying social, economic, cultural and religious influences that can constitute and contribute to the notion of positive peace. One of the major advantages of this conceptualization is that it allows for new answers to old questions. It is entirely possible that a solution to a given international conflict, or inter-societal conflict, could lie in an altogether different unit of analysis. Departing from this historical perspective, it is worthwhile revisiting analyses of old and examining them through the prism of time and unencumbered research freedom.

Lastly, future peace research must allow for a dynamic interpretation of its prescriptive process. In assessing the conflicting relations between or within states, peace researches roughly define four categories that allow for the characterization of both violent and peaceful relations. If the conflict is not governed by any type of normative order and is allowed to escalate, unchecked, over time, it can be interpreted as "rancorous conflict". In this type of conflict, all manner of weapons can be utilized while little can be done to predict outcomes or behaviors. Presently, perhaps the best available example for this type of violence is terrorism, where the means, methods and even the perpetrators are unknown to us.

If a conflict develops along a more normative order, along recognizable lines that limit or sanction the full application of aggressive behavior, we can term these disputes "conventional conflicts." If however, the conflicting parties respect the authority or some existing law or institution, allowing for example for the presence of third party mediation, we can label this a "conflict settlement." And lastly, when parties to a dispute allow for the eventual promoting and perpetuating of positive ties through a program of self-perpetuating and reinforcing positive interactions, this process is known as "conflict resolution."

Labeling the behaviors of nation-states and its actors has served peace researchers in helping to reconceptualize the idea of social justice as the end result of conflict resolution behaviors. The focus then, inasmuch as peace research is concerned, is on the testing of behavioral interactions leading to and from the solutions offered.

The future of peace research is today still in question. As this volume discusses, while the number of conflicts in the world is most assuredly increasing, so to are the kinds of conflicts in the world. In order to offer any meaningful solutions to the groups affected by these conflicts, or to the policymakers grappling with them, peace researchers must begin to think outside the early and rigid intellectual confines of their discipline. They must hold forward new hope that allows for more creative and practical answers.

Russian Poster.

Artist: Erhard Grutner, Moscow, 1980

Part Three

Historical and Multicultural Perspectives of Peace:

Global Survey

Men make their own history but they don't make it just as they please; they do not make it under circumstances chosen by themselves, but under circumstances directly encountered, given, and transmitted from the past.

—Karl Marx (1852)

I don't know whether war is an interlude during peace, or peace is an interlude during war.

—Georges Clemenceau (1841-1929)

A STRONG INTEREST IN the meaning and the possibilities of peace has served as a common thread in the history of man and most recorded cultures. This section includes such diverse and well-known philosophers, historians, political scientists and anthropologists as Immanuel Kant, Majid Khadduri, and Margaret Mead to illustrate how differing cultures, their leaders and governments concerned themselves with the notions of peace and war from antiquity to modernity. Kant's optimistic assertion that peace is indeed possible through tolerant and inclusive governance is juxtaposed with Khadduri's examination of classic Islam as a defining doctrine of war, peace, law and religion. Gerardo Zampaglione provides further historical depth through his portrayal of the vibrant Greek and Roman societies and the classic debates which struggled to determine whether violence and conflict held appropriate places in civilized society.

The modern examination of this topic would not be complete without a survey of American and European views on force and conflict. Michael Hunt and Nigel Young help to establish the stark differences in approach between these two modern societies, the first calling for a judicious use of American force, coupled with a greater acceptance of the notion of collective responsibility in America; while the latter continued, to be a war-fatigued and fractious European assembly of nations.

While the resulting analysis presents a significant first step towards understanding the varying multiethnic and multicultural views on war and peace, as held by some of times most powerful societies, it is by no means complete. As has been advocated previously in this volume, until a fuller understanding of African, Latin American and Eastern approaches to these concepts is studied there will be no truly global understanding of the causes of conflict.

Perpetual Peace

Immanuel Kant
German Philosopher (1724-1804)

No state having an independent existence—whether it be great or small—shall be acquired by another through inheritance, exchange, purchase or denotation.

For a state is not a property *(patrimonium)*, as may be grounded on which it[s] people are settled. It is a society of human beings over whom no one but itself has the right to rule and to dispose. Like the trunk of a tree, it has it own roots, and to graft it on to another state is to do away with its existence as a moral person, and to make of it a thing. Hence it is in contradiction to the idea of the original contract without which no right over a people is thinkable…

Standing armies (miles perpetuus) *shall be abolished in course of time.*

For they are always threatening other states with war by appearing to be in constant readiness to fight. They incite the various states to outrival one another in the number of their soldiers, and to this number no limit can be set. Now, since owing to the sums devoted to this purpose, peace at last becomes even more oppressive than a short war, these standing armies are themselves the cause of wars of aggression, undertaken in order to get rid of this burden. To which we must add that the practice of hiring men to kill or to be killed seems to imply a use of them as mere machines and instruments in the hand of another (namely, the state) which cannot easily be reconciled with the right of humanity in our own person…

No state shall violently interfere with the constitution and administration of another.

For what can justify it in so doing? The scandal which is here presented to the subjects of another state? The erring state can much more serve as a warning by exemplifying the great evils which a nation draws down on itself through its own lawlessness. Moreover, the bad example which one free person gives another, (as *scandalum acceptum)* does no injury to the latter. In this connection, it is true, we cannot count the case of a state which has become split up through internal corruption into two parts, each of them representing by itself an individual state which lays claim to the whole. Here the yielding of assistance to one faction could not be reckoned as interference on the part of a foreign state with the constitution of another, for here anarchy prevails. So long, however, as the inner strife has not yet reached this stage the interference of other powers would be a violation of the rights

Immanuel Kant, "Perpetual Peace." *From Perpetual Peace*, by Immanuel Kant. 1795. Translated by Mary Campbell Smith, 1917. London: Allen and Unwin.

of an independent nation which is only struggling with internal disease. It would therefore itself cause a scandal, and make the autonomy of all states insecure…

A state of peace among men who live side by side is not the natural state, which is rather to be described as a state of war: that is to say, although there is not perhaps always actual open hostility, yet there is a constant threatening that an outbreak may occur. Thus the state of peace must be *established*. For the mere cessation of hostilities is no guarantee of continued peaceful relations, and unless this guarantee is given by every individual to his neighbour—which can only be done in a state of society regulated by law—one man is at liberty to challenge another and treat him as an enemy.

The civil constitution of each state shall be republican.

The only constitution which has its origin in the idea of the original contract, upon which the lawful legislation of every nation must be based, is the republican. It is a constitution, in the first place, founded in accordance with the principle of the freedom of the members of society as human beings; secondly, in accordance with the principle of the dependence of all, as subjects, on a common legislation; and, thirdly, in accordance with the law of the equality of the members as citizens. It is then, looking at the question of right, the only constitution whose fundamental principles lie at the basis of every form of civil constitution. And the only question for us now is, whether it is also the one constitution which can lead to perpetual peace.

Now the republican constitution apart from the soundness of its origin, since it arose from the pure source of the concept of right, has also the prospect of attaining the desired result, namely, perpetual peace. And the reason is this. If, as must be so under this constitution, the consent of the subjects is required to determine whether there shall be war or not, nothing is more natural than that they should weigh the matter well, before undertaking such a bad business. For in decreeing war, they would of necessity be resolving to bring down the miseries of war upon their country. This implies: they must fight themselves; they must hand over the costs of the war out of their own property; they must do their poor best to make good the devastation which it leaves behind; and finally, as a crowning ill, they have to accept a burden of debt which will embitter even peace itself, and which they can never pay off on account of the new wars which are always impending. On the other hand, in a government where the subject is not a citizen holding a vote, (i.e., in a constitution which is not republican), the plunging into war is the least serious thing in the world. For the ruler is not a citizen, but the owner of the state, and does not lose a whit by the war, while he goes on enjoying the delights of his table or sport, or of his pleasure palaces and gala days. He can therefore decide on war for the most trifling reasons, as if it were a kind of pleasure party.

The law of nations shall be founded on a federation of free states.

Nations, as states, may be judged like individuals who, living in the natural state of society—that is to say, uncontrolled by external law—injure one another through their very proximity. Every state, for the sake of its own security, may—and ought to—demand that its neighbour should submit itself to conditions, similar to those of the civil society where the right of every individual is guaranteed. This would give rise to a federation of nations which, however, would not have to be a State of nations. That would involve a contradiction. For the term "state" implies the relation of one who rules to those who obey—that is to say, of lawgiver to the subject people: and many nations in one state would constitute only one nation, which contradicts our hypothesis, since here we have to consider the right of one nation against another, in so far as they are so many separate states and are not to be fused into one....

The depravity of human nature shows itself without disguise in the unrestrained relations of nations to each other, while in the law-governed civil state much of this is hidden by the check of government. This being so, it is astonishing that the word "right" has not yet been entirely banished from the politics of war as pedantic, and that no state has yet ventured to publicly advocate this point of view. For Hugo Grotius, Puffendorf, Vattel and others—Job's comforters, all of them—are always quoted in good faith to justify an attack, although their codes, whether couched in philosophical or diplomatic terms, have not—nor can have—the slightest legal force, because states, as such, are under no common external authority; and there is no instance of a state having ever been moved by argument to desist from its purpose, even when this was backed up by the testimony of such great men. This homage which every state renders—in words at least—to the idea of right, proves that, although it may be slumbering, there is, notwithstanding, to be found in man a still higher natural moral capacity by the aid of which he will in time gain the mastery over the evil principle in his nature, the existence of which he is unable to deny. And he hopes the same of others; for otherwise the word "right" would never be uttered by states who wish to wage war, unless to deride it like the Gallic Prince who declared: "The privilege which nature gives the strong is that the weak must obey them."

A treaty of peace makes, it may be, an end to the war of the moment, but not to the conditions of war which at any time may afford a new pretext for opening hostilities; and this we cannot exactly condemn as unjust, because under these conditions everyone is his own judge. Notwithstanding, not quite the same rule applies to states according to the law of nations as holds [the] good of individuals in a lawless condition according to the law of nature, namely, "that they ought to advance out of this condition." This is so, because, as states, they have already within themselves a legal constitution, and have therefore advanced beyond the stage at which others, in accordance with their ideas of right, can force them to come under a wider legal constitution. Meanwhile, however, reason, from her throne of the supreme law-giving moral power, absolutely condemns war as a morally lawful proceeding.

For states, in their relation to one another, there can be, according to reason, no other way of advancing from that lawless condition which unceasing war implies, than by giving up their savage lawless freedom, just as individual men have done, and yielding to the coercion of public laws. Thus they can form a State of nations *(civitas gentiurn)*, one, too, which will be ever increasing and would finally embrace all the peoples of the earth. States, however, in accordance with their understanding of the law of nations, by no means desire this, and therefore reject *in hypothesi* what is correct *in thesi.* Hence, instead of the positive idea of a world-republic, if all is not to be lost, only the negative substitute for it, a federation averting war, maintaining its ground and ever extending over the world may stop the current of this tendency to war and shrinking from the control of law. But even then there will be a constant danger that this propensity may break out.

Third Definitive Article of Perpetual Peace

The rights of men, as citizens of the world, shall be limited to the conditions of universal hospitality.

We are speaking here, as in the previous articles, not of philanthropy, but of right; and in this sphere hospitality signifies the claim of a stranger entering foreign territory to be treated by its owner without hostility. The latter may send him away again, if this can be done without causing his death; but, so long as he conducts himself peaceably, he must not be treated as an enemy. It is not a right to be treated as a guest to which the stranger can lay claim—a special friendly compact on his behalf would be required to make him for a given time an actual inmate—but he has a right of visitation. This right to present themselves to society belongs to all mankind in virtue of our common right of possession on the surface of the earth on which, as it is a globe, we cannot be infinitely scattered, and must in the end reconcile ourselves to existence side by side: at the same time, originally no one individual had more right than another to live in any one particular spot....

The intercourse, more or less close, which has been everywhere steadily increasing between the nations of the earth, has now extended so enormously that a violation of right in one part of the world is felt all over it. Hence the idea of a cosmopolitan right is no fantastical, high-flown notion of right, but a complement of the unwritten code of law—constitutional as well as international law—necessary for the public rights of mankind in general and thus for the realisation of perpetual peace. For only by endeavouring to fulfill the conditions laid down by this cosmopolitan law can we flatter ourselves that we are gradually approaching that ideal.

The idea of international law presupposes the separate existence of a number of neighbouring and independent states; and, although such a condition of things is in itself already a state of war, (if a federative union of these nations does not prevent the outbreak of hostilities) yet, according to the Idea of reason, this is better than that all the states should be merged into one under a power which has gained the ascendency over its neighbours and gradually become a universal monarchy. For the wider the sphere of their jurisdiction, the more laws lose in force; and soulless despotism, when it has choked the seeds of good, at last sinks into anarchy. Nevertheless it is the desire of every state, or of its ruler, to attain to a permanent condition of peace in this very way; that is to say, by subjecting the whole world as far as possible to its sway. But nature wills it otherwise. She employs two means to separate nations, and prevent them from inter-mixing: namely, the differences of language and of religion. These differences bring with them a tendency to mutual hatred, and furnish pretexts for waging war. But, none the less, with the growth of culture and the gradual advance of men to greater unanimity of principle, they lead to concord in a state of peace which, unlike the despotism we have spoken of, (the churchyard of freedom) does not arise from the weakening of all forces, but is brought into being and secured through the equilibrium of these forces in their most active rivalry.

As nature wisely separates nations which the will of each state, sanctioned even by the principles of international law, would gladly unite under its own sway by stratagem or force; in the same way, on the other hand, she unites nations whom the principle of a cosmopolitan right would not have secured against violence and war. And this union she brings about through an appeal to their mutual interests. The commercial spirit cannot co-exist with war, and sooner or later it takes possession of every nation. For, of all the forces which lie at the command of a state, the power of money is probably the most reliable. Hence states find themselves compelled—not, it is true, exactly from motives of morality—to further the noble end of peace and to avert war, by means of mediation, wherever it threatens to break out, just as if they had made a permanent league for this purpose. For great alliances with a view to war can, from the nature of things, only very rarely occur, and still more seldom succeed.

In this way nature guarantees the coming of perpetual peace, through the natural course of human propensities: not indeed with sufficient certainty to enable us to prophesy the future of this ideal theoretically, but yet clearly enough for practical purposes. And thus this guarantee of nature makes it a duty that we should labour for this end, an end which is no mere chimera.

Warfare as an Invention

Margaret Mead
American Anthropologist (1901-1978)

Is war a biological necessity, a sociological inevitability, or just a bad invention? Those who argue for the first view endow man with such pugnacious instincts that some outlet in aggressive behaviour is necessary if man is to reach full human stature. It was this point of view, which lay behind William James's famous essay, 'The Moral Equivalent of War', in which he tried to retain the warlike virtues and channel them in new directions. A similar point of view has lain behind the Soviet Union's attempt to make competition between groups rather than between individuals. A basic, competitive, aggressive, warring human nature is assumed, and those who wish to outlaw war or outlaw competitiveness merely try to find new and less socially destructive ways in which these biologically given aspects of man's nature can find expression. Then there are those who take the second view: warfare is the inevitable concomitant of the development of the state, the struggle for land and natural resources, of class societies springing not from the nature of man, but, from the nature of history. War is nevertheless inevitable unless we change our social system and outlaw classes, the struggle for power, and possessions; and in the event of our success warfare would disappear, as a symptom vanishes when the disease is cured.

One may hold a sort of compromise position between these two extremes; one may claim that all aggression springs from the frustration of man's biologically determined drives and that, since all forms of culture are frustrating, it is certain each new generation will be aggressive and the aggression will find its natural and inevitable expression in race war, class war, nationalistic war, and so on. All three of these positions are very popular today among those who think seriously about the problems of war and its possible prevention, but I wish to urge another point of view, less defeatist, perhaps, than the first and third and more accurate than the second: that is, that warfare, by which I mean recognised conflict between two groups as groups, in which each group puts an army (even if the army is only fifteen pygmies) into the field to fight and kill, if possible, some of the members of the army of the other group—that warfare of this sort is an invention like any other of the inventions in terms of which we order our lives, such as writing, marriage, cooking our food instead of eating it raw, trial by jury, or burial of the dead, and so on. Some of this list anyone will grant are inventions: trial by jury is confined to very limited portions of the globe; we know that there are tribes that do not bury their dead but instead expose or cremate them; and we know that only part of the human race has had the knowledge of writing as its

Margaret Mead, "Warfare as an Invention." From *Warfare is Only an Invention—Not a Biological Necessity,* by Margaret Mead. 1940. Asia, XL: 402-5.

cultural inheritance. But, whenever a way of doing things is found universally, such as the use of fire or the practice of some form of marriage, we tend to think at once that it is not an invention at all but an attribute of humanity itself. And yet even such universals as marriage and the use of fire are inventions like the rest, very basic ones, inventions which were, perhaps, necessary if human history was to take the turn that it has taken, but nevertheless inventions. At some point in his social development man was undoubtedly without the institution of marriage or the knowledge of the use of fire.

The case for warfare is much clearer because there are peoples even today who have no warfare. Of these the Eskimos are perhaps the most conspicuous examples, but the Lepchas of Sikkim described by Geoffrey Gorer in Himalayan Village are as good. Neither of these peoples understands war, not even defensive warfare. The idea of warfare is lacking, and this idea is as essential to really carrying on war as an alphabet or a syllabary is to writing. But, whereas the Lepchas are a gentle, unquarrelsome people, and the advocates of other points of view might argue that they are not full human beings or that they had never been frustrated and so had no aggression to expand in warfare, the Eskimo case gives no such possibility of interpretation. The Eskimos are not a mild and meek people; many of them are turbulent and troublesome. Fights, theft of wives, murder, cannibalism, occur among them all outbursts of passionate men goaded by desire or intolerable circumstance. Here are men faced with hunger, men faced with loss of their wives, men faced with the threat of extermination by other men, and here are orphan children, growing up miserably with no one to care for them, mocked and neglected by those about them. The personality necessary for war, the circumstances necessary to goad men to desperation are present, but there is no war. When a travelling Eskimo entered a settlement, he might have to fight the strongest man in the settlement to establish his position among them, but this was a test of strength and bravery, not war. The idea of warfare, of one group organising against another group to maim and wound and kill them was absent. And, without that idea, passions might rage but there was no war.

But, it may be argued, is not this because the Eskimos have such a low and undeveloped form of social organisation? They own no land, they move from place to place, camping, it is true, season after season on the same site, but this is not something to fight for as the modern nations of the world fight for land and raw materials. They have no permanent possessions that can be looted, no towns that can be burned. They have no social classes to produce stress and strains within the society, which might force it to go to war outside. Does not the absence of war among the Eskimos, while disproving the biological necessity of war, just go to confirm the point that it is the state of development of the society, which accounts for war and nothing else?

We find the answer among the pygmy peoples of the Andaman Islands in the Bay of Bengal. The Andamans also represent an exceedingly low level of society; they are a hunting and food gathering people; they live in tiny hordes without any class stratification; their houses are simpler than the snow houses of the Eskimo. But they knew about warfare. The army might contain only fifteen determined pygmies marching in a straight line, but it was the real thing nonetheless. Tiny army met tiny army in open battle, blows were exchanged, casualties suffered, and the state of warfare could only be concluded by a peacemaking ceremony.

Similarly, among the Australian aborigines, who built no permanent dwellings but wandered from water hole to water hole over their almost desert country, warfare—and rules of 'international law'—were highly developed. The student of social evolution will seek in vain for his obvious causes of war, struggle for lands, struggle for power of one group over another, expansion of population, need to divert the minds of a populace restive under tyranny, or even the ambition of a successful leader to enhance his own prestige. All are absent, but warfare as a practice remained, and men engaged in it and killed one another in the course of a war because killing is what is done in wars.

From instances like these it becomes apparent that an inquiry into the causes of war misses the fundamental point as completely as does an insistence upon the biological necessity of war. If a people have an idea of going to war and the idea that war is the way in which certain situations, defined within their society, are to be handled, they will sometimes go to war. If they are a mild and unaggressive people, like the Pueblo Indians, they may limit themselves to defensive warfare, but they will be forced to think in terms of war because there are peoples near them who have warfare as a pattern, and offensive, raiding, pillaging warfare at that. When the pattern of warfare is known, people like the Pueblo Indians will defend themselves, taking advantage of their natural defences, the mesa village site, and people like the Lepchas, having no natural defences and no idea of warfare, will merely submit to the invader. But the essential point remains the same. There is a way of behaving which is known to a given people and labelled as an appropriate form of behaviour; a bold and warlike people like the Sioux or the Maori may label warfare as desirable as well as possible, a mild people like the Pueblo Indians may label warfare as undesirable, but to the minds of both peoples the possibility of warfare is present. Their thoughts, their hopes, their plans are oriented about this idea that warfare may be selected as the way to meet some situation.

So simple peoples and civilised peoples, mild peoples and violent, assertive peoples, will all go to war if they have the invention, just as those peoples who have the custom of duelling will have duels and peoples who have the pattern of vendetta will indulge in vendetta. And, conversely, peoples who do not know of duelling will not fight duels, even though their wives are seduced and their daughters ravished; they may on occasion commit murder but they will not fight duels. Cultures, which lack the idea of the vendetta, will not meet every quarrel in this way. A people can use only the forms it has. So the Balinese have their special way of dealing with a quarrel between two individuals: if the two feel that the causes of quarrel are heavy, they may go and register their quarrel in the temple before the gods, and, making offerings, they may swear never to have anything to do with each other again.... But in other societies, although individuals might feel as full of animosity and as unwilling to have any further contact as do the Balinese, they cannot register their quarrel with the gods and go on quietly about their business because registering quarrels with the gods is not an invention of which they know.

Yet, if it be granted that warfare is, after all, an invention, it may nevertheless be an invention that lends itself to certain types of personality, to the exigent needs of autocrats, to the expansionist desires of crowded peoples, to the desire for plunder and rape and loot which is engendered by a dull and frustrating life. What, then, can we say of this congruence between warfare and its uses? If it is a form, which fits so well, is not this congruence the essential point? But even here the primitive material causes us to wonder, because there are tribes who go to war merely for glory, having no quarrel with the enemy, suffering from no tyrant within their boundaries, anxious neither for land nor loot nor women, but merely anxious to win prestige which within that tribe has been declared obtainable only by war and without which no young man can hope to win his sweetheart's smile of approval. But if, as was the case with the Bush Negroes of Dutch Guiana, it is artistic ability, which is necessary to win a girl's approval, the same young man would have to be carving rather than going out on a war party.

In many parts of the world, war is a game in which the individual can win counters—counters which bring him prestige in the eyes of his own sex or of the opposite sex; he plays for these counters as he might, in our society, strive for a tennis championship. Warfare is a frame for such prestige seeking merely because it calls for the display of certain skills and certain virtues; all of these skills—riding straight, shooting straight, dodging the missiles of the enemy and sending one's own straight to the mark—can be equally well exercised in some other framework and, equally, the virtues endurance, bravery, loyalty, steadfastness—can be displayed in other contexts. The tie-up between proving oneself a man and proving this by a success in organised killing is due to a definition, which many societies have made of manliness. And often, even in those societies which counted success in warfare a proof of human worth, strange turns were given to the idea, as when the Plains Indians gave their highest awards to the man who touched a live enemy rather than to the man who brought in a scalp from a dead enemy—because the latter was less risky. Warfare is just an invention known to the majority of human societies by which they permit their young men either to accumulate prestige or avenge their honour or acquire loot or wives or slaves or sago lands or cattle or appease the blood lust of their gods or the restless souls of the recently dead. It is just an invention, older and more widespread than the jury system, but nonetheless an invention.

But, once we have said this, have we said anything at all? Despite a few stances, dear to the instances of controversialist, of the loss of the useful arts, once an invention is made which proves congruent with human needs or social forms, it tends to persist. Grant that war is an invention that it is not a biological necessity nor the outcome of certain special types of social forms, still once the invention is made, what are we to do about it? The Indian who had been subsisting on the buffalo for generations because with his primitive weapons he could slaughter only a limited number of buffalo did not return to his primitive weapons when he saw that the white man's more efficient weapons were exterminating the buffalo. A desire for the white man's cloth may mortgage the South Sea Islander to the white man's plantation, but he does not return to making bark clothe, which would have left him free. Once an invention is known and accepted, men do not easily relinquish it. The skilled workers may smash the first steam looms which they feel are to be their undoing, but they accept them in the end, and no movement which has insisted upon the mere abandonment of usable inventions has ever had much success. Warfare is here, as part of our thought; the deeds of warriors are immortalised in the words of our poets, the toys of our children are modelled upon the weapons of the soldier, the frame of reference within which our statesmen and our diplomats work always contains war. If we know that it is not inevitable, that it is due to historical accident that warfare is one of the ways in which we think of behaving, are we given any hope by that? What hope is there of persuading nations to abandon war, nations so thoroughly imbued with the idea that resort to war is, if not actually desirable and noble, at least inevitable whenever certain defined circumstances arise?

In answer to this question I think we might turn to the history of other social inventions, and inventions, which must once have seemed as finally entrenched as warfare. Take the methods of trial, which preceded the jury system: ordeal and trial by combat. Unfair, capricious, alien as they are to our feeling today, they were once the only methods open to individuals' accused of some offense. The invention of trial by jury gradually replaced these methods until only witches, and finally not even witches, had to resort to the ordeal. And for a long time the jury system seemed the best and finest method of settling legal disputes, but today new inventions, trial before judges only or before commissions, are replacing the jury system. In each case the old method was replaced by a new social invention. The ordeal did not go out because people thought it unjust or wrong; it went out because a method more congruent with the institutions and feelings of the period was invented. And, if we despair over the way in which war seems such an ingrained habit of most of the human race, we can take comfort from the fact that a poor invention will usually give place to a better invention.

For this, two conditions, at least, are necessary. The people must recognise the defects of the old invention, and someone must make a new one. Propaganda against warfare, documentation of its terrible cost in human suffering and social waste, these prepare the ground by teaching people to feel that warfare is a defective social institution. There is further needed a belief that social invention is possible and the invention of new methods which will render warfare as out of date as the tractor is making the plough, or the motor car the horse and buggy. A form of behaviour becomes out of date only when something else takes its place, and, in order to invent forms of behaviour, which will make war obsolete, it is a first requirement to believe that an invention is possible.

Peace in Classical Greece

Gerardo Zampaglione
Italian Ambassador (1917–1996)

Fool, sacking towns, laying temples waste, desecrating tombs, the sanctuaries of the dead! He who sows destruction shall reap destruction.

—The Daughters of Troy

The Idea of Peace in Greek Civilization

Certain values regarded as essential and unchallengeable in our civilization, even though they may be thought ephemeral if they are cherished at all in other cultures, owe their very existence to the Hellenic genius. The idea of justice sustained by respect for the law, progress understood and the propulsive force of existence, acknowledgment of the individual's faculty for penetrating reality beyond any limits set by what is clearly demonstrable (on all of which we base our moral system and our methods of scientific research) link up with principles which asserted themselves in the Hellenic world and with the thinking of its most eager and vigilant minds. It is mainly to the credit of the Greeks—and here they broke completely new ground in the history of civilization—that the individual was deemed personally responsible for his acts and thoughts and that freedom and authority were reconciled through institutions which defined the rights and duties of the citizen and of the community, surrounding these rights and duties with clear guarantees and limits. The human framework in which this stupendous germination of ideas took place unfortunately developed a tendency to break up into a large number of separate states, from which the natural inventive and reflective capacities of the individual received a further stimulus.

This is particularly true in the *Odyssey* where the change of psychology was expressed in another manner: by emphasis on the ills engendered by war and its intrinsic absurdity. One passage discusses the brevity of human life: "Man's life is short enough. A churlish fellow with no idea of hospitality earns the whole world's ill-will while he is alive and its contempt when he is dead." In the composite structure of the *Odyssey*, however, it is possible to distinguish the more recent sources of inspiration from the older ones. As we have sought to show, the *Odyssey* is instinctively inclined to consider violence as the yardstick of human conduct; it shows a desire to resist this blind exaltation and to approve a pattern of behavior informed with a certain respect for justice, moderation, and peace.

Even the earliest Greek literature, then, was sensitive to man's longing for a greater degree of tolerance in mutual relations and evidenced a timid desire to achieve forms of cooperation and understanding between peoples of varying origins. Thus peace was anchored in economic prosperity, the bearer of serenity if it was acquired through work, whilst it was the cause of misfortune if it was obtained by violence. This is an opinion of which modern man can only approve.

Later on, religion began by inspiring a new and more mature interpretation of the concept of peace, fitting it into a context in which the emphasis was not on material benefits but on the certainty that divine protection was concentrated on a given community, ensuring peace for it, peace being first and foremost the certainty of enjoying the favor of the gods and the grace dispensed by them. This did not mean that peace should not also procure material advantages (such as prosperity), but these were lesser achievements compared with the main one, associated with peace of mind. No longer interpreted in the narrow terms of Homer and Hesiod, the word was identified with a specific condition of divine goodwill, bringing spiritual and material advantages stemming from the gods, whose love men should strive to deserve.

The feeling of peace and solidarity, for which Plato was later to provide a theoretical basis, led to the conclusion that war between Greek cities should be waged according to different rules from those governing war against the barbarian. It engendered a number of customary principles and rules recognized by all the Greeks as binding, so that any violation of them was regarded as a crime. War began to be accepted by all as the right instrument for regulating interstate controversies, a weapon of pressure to resolve major problems when agreement could be reached in no other way. It became almost a necessity, surrounded by legal and religious safeguards. As their scope widened, the rules derived to protect the sanctuaries during these violent struggles matured into laws consistently complied with. Thus war tended to be distinguished from the confused alarms and disorders of the Homeric poems and changed gradually into an activity governed by known principles. For example, the declaration of war had to be announced by heralds, almost in the form of the modern ultimatum; aggression without warning was condemned.

Military customs, even tactics and strategy, became more standardized. Even the behavior of the victors gradually adapted to certain standards. After the battle the opposing forces would grant each other a truce so that the dead could be buried and the wounded cared for. Every violation of this rule was regarded as a sacrilege and a crime. The acts of violence and brutality described in Homer's poems were tempered because of the great value the Greeks attached to human life and their desire to mitigate the sufferings caused by war. A beginning was made in disciplining actual combat by rules intended to curb its cruelty and to transform war itself from a form of collective bestiality into a legitimate instrument of pressure.

Despite the unifying forces at work in the polis, Greece was torn by violent aggressive impulses which from time to time dragged its people into sharp and bitter conflicts. A paradoxical situation emerged: On the one hand, the city-states were the expression of one of the most splendid experiments in civilization of all time; on the other hand their citizens utterly failed to discern the tragic implications of their quarrelsomeness and of the political divisions. The two phenomena were by no means as incompatible as might appear at first sight. Necessity being the mother of invention, war was often an incentive to progress and to a deeper, more thorough examination of problems and techniques which would otherwise have been neglected. In spite of the endemic strife and the endless conflicts, the civilization of the polis reached unsurpassed heights in artistic creation and intellectual activity. In the long pageant of human endeavor probably nothing was as important for the future of civilization as this period of Greek history.

The Decline of the Fatherland as Ideal

Under the pressure of historical and environmental

circumstances, the panorama of Greek life was soon to change. A gradual refinement of creative activity in the fields of culture, philosophy, art, and politics was largely due to the conclusions reached by the pre-Socratics as to the nature of the world. They had overthrown many beliefs which had for centuries been treated as matters of faith and therefore as an ultimate frontier beyond which the probing mind of man might not venture. Precisely because of these beliefs, all research relating to peace and the need to ban war and violence from human relations had been carried out principally in terms of a re-evocation of the Golden Age, just as all speculation was presented as an effort to understand more fully religious truths enjoying common acceptance. The idea of peace was therefore being rediscovered, not invented.

The Teaching of the Sophists

The moral and political program of Protagoras was a direct attack on the concept of the polis. It is probable that in one of his works, called "Refutatory Arguments," he struck at the traditional ideas of the state and of war and urged his contemporaries to seek activities other than those pursued within the circle of the city's walls. Such a dislike of war and the development of a viewpoint wider than the narrow small-town interests were, in the last analysis, worthwhile attitudes if men forsook parish patriotism in favor of a loyalty to mankind. But this approach does not seem in accordance with the fragmentation of the cognitive process taught by Protagoras. Perhaps, then, the traditional interpretation of Protagorean thought is wrong. Perhaps it was not the individual who, in the opinion of Protagoras, was the measure of all things, but mankind as a whole. According to Plato, Protagoras believed that the gods were the origin of the principles of justice and of duty, which controlled moral conduct. His subjectivism therefore allowed of an exception in the field of politics, the aim of which might ultimately be the elimination of war.

Gorgias believed that only between the Greeks could a condition of peace be achieved, war with the barbarians being unavoidable. Peace in the Greek world he saw as a precondition for stability and the basis for any resistance to aggression from outside. To attain this very objective, he urged that his compatriots put an end to their ancient and ill-starred feuding and reach concord, within and without the cities. This argument lay behind a speech made by Gorgias at Olympia and now lost, but of which Philostratus has left us a record. The position of Gorgias was perhaps close to that assumed in the Renaissance by thinkers who advocated that European sovereigns end their secular wars to prepare themselves for a crusade against the Turks.

Despite its seeming anarchic approach, the teaching of the Sophists fit into the evolution of contemporary morality. The abolition of war because of the recognition of the natural common identity of peoples and of their single origin was a necessary corollary to this approach.

A challenge to Callicles and Thrasymachus came from the anonymous author of the Sophistic work which has been discovered in an essay called "Protrepticus" [Exhortation to philosophy], by Iamblichus, the fourth-century Neoplatonist. Scholars have argued about the identity and the work of this anonymous writer for decades. He seems to have disapproved of the anarchical approach of the two Sophists and thought that the weak had a mission to fulfill in the effort to abolish war, as is evidenced in the following passage:

"War, producer of the greatest evils, bringing disaster and slavery, is undertaken rather by the lawless than by the law-abiding."

War therefore was caused, or at least encouraged, by illegality and other ills like social inequality. This was seen against the background of a plan for regenerating society in the name of tolerance. According to the unknown author, it was not necessary to let oneself be guided by violence, nor to believe that the defeat of one's neighbor was a form of virtue or compliance with the laws a sign of cowardice.

In respect to the problem of peace, the dangers

inherent in this position are obvious. Every doctrine based on an awareness of the relativity of things and of human relationships and on a presumption that no single criterion of knowledge can be pre-established is liable to lead to aberrant and conflicting conclusions. In view of this, attitudes hostile to war and cosmopolitan conceptions of community life were evidence of a general and vague feeling, not of hard conviction. From a pessimistic vision of life which took man as the yardstick of reality and the common denominator of all things, the Sophists inferred a distaste for war. But they were all too ready to retreat from this point of view as soon as the interests of man were threatened or seen in a different light: The points made by Gorgias in the Olympic oration and in the speech paying tribute to the Athenian citizens who had fallen in battle show that there was no plough to which Sophistic relativism could not be harnessed, no axe it could not grind—and that of the warrior was no exception.

Socrates and Virtue as Knowledge

With all its paradoxes and facile cleverness, Sophistic speculation was nevertheless a bold attempt to emancipate man from the state of intellectual serfdom in which he had languished for so long. Following the road mapped out by the Sophists and drawing together the jagged edges of a fabric which, in an orgy of destructive fury, the Sophists had torn in two, Socrates (470-399 B.C.) made it his task to free thought from the fetters which had so long held it down, pressing it forward in the speculative adventure, guided not by the immediate and vulgar suggestions of the senses, but by rational abstractions. This was the real achievement of the great philosopher, to whom Western thought is still in debt.

Enlightened in this way, human behavior would escape the trap of the passions and serenity could be achieved. A state of happiness and tranquility was therefore the ultimate objective. It stands to reason that a thinker basing his teaching on the identification of knowledge with virtue should come out against war, emphasizing its absurdity. But no direct condemnation seems to emerge from Socratic doctrine, as handed down to us in the writings of Plato and Xenophon. The reason for this is perhaps that the problem of war, no less than that of the cult of the gods, constituted a limit beyond which—despite the ample freedom of teaching accorded the philosophers in Athens—it was not permitted to go.

By his tragic death, Socrates was to show how serious were the risks run by those who assumed unconventional attitudes toward problems on which either public opinion or the authorities were still intransigent: The participation of the citizens in military campaigns imposed by the state constituted an obligation sanctioned by the law, and those who failed to comply could be severely punished. For the very reasons to which we have referred, Socrates system, too, was to induce an aversion to war, the tragic consequence of an explosion of worldly passions.

In his speculative activity Socrates tried to get closer to his fellow human being, guiding him along the road to truth and supplying him with the necessary enlightenment. He spent his whole life educating his fellow citizens through personal contacts and conversation. The problem of participation in wars would naturally be stated in terms other than the traditional ones. What could be more irrational than the behavior of a state which had taken the field merely out of greed for dominion or thirst for vengeance? The only campaigns meeting the Socratic ideal of virtuous action were defensive ones, such as the wars fought against the Persians.

Now that ethical values had been given a universal setting, man's ambitions, hopes, and opportunities could no longer be realized within the polis. For all philosophic thought, by the very fact of posing human problems on a universal basis, distinguishing them from instincts and elemental appetites, was to help to bring individuals closer together and to make evident the vanity of their strife. Hence, Socratic doctrine was colored with a cosmopolitan light, essentially pacifist. A general love for fellow human beings and a natural propensity toward compromise and moderation flowed from his discoveries. And this is true although Xenophon points out that on at least two occasions the master showed that he could be tough with opponents. However, not all the ancient sources were in agreement on this point. Plato, for example, although he gives the news of Socrates participation in the battles of Pontidaea, Delium, and Amphipolis, reports that he showed great humanity toward the enemy. Cicero, too, in a controversial passage of the Tusculan Disputations, attributed to him cosmopolitan leanings and the feeling of being a "citizen of the world." This was confirmed by other authors, such as Diogenes Laertius and Arrian.

Despite the lack of direct evidence, then, it may be inferred that peace within and between the Greek cities was, in Socrates view, the catalyzing element of unity and of Hellenic civilization. It would be bound to lead—and on this Socrates invited his listeners to meditate—to a renaissance of the Greek world and the reestablishment of a genuine and peaceful community life. Let us follow him in an argument preserved for us by Xenophon. Shorn of the literary ornamentation which is Xenophon's own, it reveals an attitude informed with humility, serenity, and love for orderly equilibrium, unfailing attributes of any system well disposed toward the quest for peace:

> Among rulers in cities, are you not aware that those who do most to make the citizens obey the laws are the best, and that the city in which the citizens are most obedient to the laws has the best time in peace and is irresistible in war? And again, agreement is deemed the greatest blessing for cities: their senates and their best men constantly exhort the citizens to agree, and everywhere in Greece there is a law that the citizens shall promise under oath to agree, and everywhere they take this oath.

The passage proves that in the Socratic system the usual claim of Sophistic ethics—which began by praising man and ended by denying that moral precepts were of any value—underwent a radical transformation, based on real human needs. Civil law was no longer an expedient always opposed to the natural law but the instrument of a process of moral betterment designed to regenerate mankind and to eliminate all conditions of anarchy harmful to his peace of mind.

Socrates' view of the state was wholly new and quite different from that of the Sophists. The state and politics, factors of the greatest importance, should serve—and this was Socrates innovation—the well-being and the happiness of citizens. The duties of the men engaged in government, as Xenophon recalled, were comparable to those of a shepherd protecting his flock. This was the first formulation of a line of thought destined to influence the development of subsequent systems (for example those of the Cynics and the Stoics), based on the conviction that men, being brothers, must act in accordance with feelings of humanity and concord.

A number of factors peculiar to the Greek, indeed to the Athenian, mentality also affected the thinking and attitudes of the philosopher. For Socrates, the individual's membership in a given polis was the premise governing, and the yardstick for assessing, all political and civil behavior. This explains his conduct during the famous trial, when prosecuted by the Athenian authorities. Here he proclaimed his faith in the supremacy of the spirit and in the freedom of the individual. Although he could not stoop to compromise or meet the hostile judges halfway, he confirmed his submission to the state, whose rulings he accepted, even though he knew them to be unjust. His death would serve to teach posterity a lesson in internal discipline and to prove, through personal example and sacrifice, the vanity of intolerance. War and violence could not escape this condemnation, as is shown in these words attributed to him by Xenophon:

> But I hold that they who cultivate wisdom and think they will be able to guide the people in pru-

> dent policy never lapse into violence: they know that enmities and dangers are inseparable from violence, but persuasion produces the same results safely and amicably.... It is not, then, cultivation of wisdom that leads to violent methods, but the possession of power without prudence. Besides, many supporters are necessary to him who ventures to use force: but he who can persuade needs no confederate, having confidence in his own unaided power of persuasion. And such a man has no occasion to shed blood; for who would rather take a man' s life than have a live and willing follower?

Plato on Peace

Protest against a civilization in thrall to war was implicit in Cynic teaching, but we shall seek in vain for attitudes as precise as this in the work of Plato (ca. 428-ca. 348 B.C.), the leading disciple of Socrates and his spiritual heir. It is no easy matter to condense his thinking, in this any more than in other fields: His ideas are spread over a considerable number of dialogues, the legacy of a literary career extending into his extreme old age, containing many inconsistencies, restatements of particular ideas, and actual changes of opinion. Thus it has been possible to argue that there is no genuine Platonic system. Efforts to give unity to his scattered intuitions and reflections are no more than so many attempts to straitjacket them in fixed patterns. Plato must be judged above all on his devotion to things of the spirit, his untiring quest for the essence of problems through persistent research: In his dialogues thesis balances antithesis, each viewpoint put forward by a different person, one of whom always predominates but can never make headway in the discussion without the critical cooperation of the others. The speculative enterprise therefore develops through a series of attitudes of mind emerging from a succession of comments on a specific subject, and no firm conclusion is necessarily arrived at.

This sort of pendular movement through which Platonic thought advances and gains in complexity does not facilitate full understanding and his thought on peace is no exception. It must be emphasized, first, that politics was for Plato an essential field of inquiry. Plato's man was a social being whose personality and behavior were determined by identifiable community instincts. As a result the state was idealized and with it that part of the individual soul which is expressed through the state. While the problem of war and peace—that is, of the relations between human societies—was well to the fore, the use of the dialogue form precluded any clear-cut statement of attitude by Plato himself. At certain moments he discerned the conflict between war and a harmonious development of the collective soul, of which the state was the practical expression; at others, war was seen as a fact on which life and the development of the community depended. Hence he defined the art of war as part of the art of government.

These ideas, insofar as they were linked to the political situation of Greece, had probably already lost their actuality when Plato was discussing them. His vision of the state was by no means new. Despite the brilliant presentation and the imaginative impetus which informs his writing, the ancient polis was always his model of a perfect organization. Neither the advent of the democratic regimes, nor the continuing struggles for hegemony, nor the Peloponnesian War seem to have affected the thinking of the great Athenian. He remained attached to conventional patterns and perhaps failed to understand the changes made by the new generations, longing to move outside the confines of the small but ferocious cities to scan wider horizons. Nor could he resolve the conflict between the position thus assumed and the reality of the times by formulating his ideas in utopian terms.

The exercise of justice, which is the source of concord and agreement, can tend toward a unifying objective only if an overall vision of it is sought and if this vision is derived from immutable moral and legal premises. But experience taught, then as now, that there is room for diametrically opposed opinions as to the nature of justice. In a state governed by a military caste (Sparta, for example), the definition of justice differed from that accepted in an environment informed by feelings of humanity and tolerance. In Sparta anything serving the purpose of war was deemed "just." Elsewhere, justice was seen as a means of facilitating peaceful agreements, of bringing together divergent points of view and making compromise possible. The practice of this virtue was a state of mind as well as a rule of conduct and it enabled man to overcome his passions and curb his appetites. Plato failed to discern the conflict between points of view and assumed a wait-and-see position hardly reconcilable with the principles of equity and harmony on which he based his idea of the state and of good government.

By arguing that the reasoning part of man was divine in origin, Plato offered man a route for his earthly journey which would lead him to a perfection having two components. The first, which derived from a vision—in some respects a mystic vision—recognizing in the soul-body duality the poles of a permanent conflict, urged man to adopt superior models of life inspired above all by love, the quality which led men to perform good acts. To this element, which some writers felt foreshadowed the Christian message, there was added a second one, based on the ideal of Hellenic life and therefore centering on the body, whose instincts were not considered as the origin of all guilt. This second element represented part of the cult of physical beauty and of the aesthetic ideal of the classical world. Through the continual interweaving of the two lines of thought, Plato proposed in *The Republic,* a plan for the organization of community life and of the perfect state.

There is no clear statement of hostility to war in this famous treatise. The ideal state was, in fact, capable of waging war, and was required to train soldiers for external defense. The fifth book of *The Republic* advocated the Severest sanctions for deserters and for those who fell, even through no fault of their own, into the hands of the enemy. Again, since the brave must be rewarded if they were to give their best, they should be welcomed with special tributes; they should be crowned with garlands, and no one whom they "had a mind to kiss should refuse to be kissed" by them. This paradoxical line of thought concealed the desire—apparently in no way prompted by a love of peace—of ensuring privileges for the warrior caste.

But perhaps with the intention of balancing such excesses, in Plato's state it was not the soldiers but the wise men who bore the highest responsibility of government. The "guardians," as they were called, must obey only the dictates of reason and moderation and shun temptations contrary to equity and justice. The warriors thus came under an authority determined to safeguard the governance of the commonweal from the precarious fluctuation of all things human. Here, clearly, Plato had no illusions as to the harmful nature and origins of war, though he had described it as a "fine thing" in the Protagoras. In a famous passage of *The Republic* he wrote: "Then, without determining as yet whether war does good or harm, this much we may affirm, that now we have discovered war to be derived from causes which are also the causes of almost all the evils in states, private as well as public." A passage in the Phaedo shows war as a harmful exercise: "Whence come wars, and fightings and factions? Whence but from the body and the lusts of the body?" For peace is not for the sake of war, but war for the sake of peace. "And therefore, as we say, every one of us should live the life of peace as long and well as he can."

Being recruited among the wise men, the guardians were required to pursue harmony and equilibrium at all times. This could be done only through the exercise of self-control, and thus their behavior was bound to be moderate. The discipline the guardian imposed on himself was, as it were, the link between the social and the political world, and at the same time it enabled man's instincts to be tempered. This had been considered in *The Republic* but in *The Laws,* the political study written late in Plato' s life, it was treated as a decisive factor for all public action. Here Plato asserts that wisdom should condition the work of the ruler but points out that wisdom can be of benefit and can aid equilibrium only in the serenity provided by harmony. Self-discipline was seen as the fundament not only of political virtues, but of virtues in general, like courage, temperance, and justice.

Exercised unreservedly, self-control would generate order and harmony, making a free organism of the state, harmonious and open to an understanding of the world. Its function was not only internal to the polis but essential, too, in relations with the outside. If it prevailed, together with moderation and brotherly understanding, peace and not war would be fostered. Starting from this premise, Plato regarded constitutions modeled on that of Sparta, designed for the preparation and conduct of war, as mistaken and unnatural.

In working out and describing the ideal state, to illustrate it to rulers and founders of constitutions and to promote harmonization of the citizens' rights and duties with those of the community, Plato, as we have seen, was guided by the actual situations existing in his own time. This aggravated the inconsistencies, for alongside moderate and calm statements are to be found passages of bewildering intransigence and severity. What are we to make, for example, of Plato's refusal to allow the citizen to follow a calling other than that allocated by fate, leaving it to the state to deal with any attempt to escape the law of destiny? How are we to judge the principles which the warriors were required to teach their sons? Besides keeping fit at all times, they were asked to train their children in handling arms, taking them to the battlefields so that they could acquire direct experience of combat. The poor pedagogic value of the spectacle, intended to increase the natural bellicosity of youth, did not seem to worry Plato, who was apparently concerned only with the dangers these practices might entail for the physical safety of the young? Nor, indeed, were women exempt from military training, which was to be carried out even in time of peace.

And yet even these rules should not be examined separately but should be seen in a wider context. Despite certain harsh and paradoxical passages, Platonic thought is based on the awareness that war is always a source of grief. This is inferred from *The Laws,* in which many earlier exaggerations were tempered by Plato's more mellow understanding of reality, suggesting that experience and the years had taught the author prudence and understanding for the changes which had taken place in Greek thought. The problem of peace and war is treated more humanely in *The Laws* than in *The Republic.* The myth of the Golden Age reemerges, a myth which had inspired Greek civilization from the earliest times. The legend, which in Hesiod's story was given the status of a religious allegory, is treated by Plato as historical certainty. Whereas Hesiod was concerned with moral considerations and used the myth as an instrument of edification and warning, Plato revives the allegory to plot the course of an ideological journey by appealing to past realities.

However, the story would be incomplete if the philosopher had not examined whether propensity to violence was an essential trait of human nature. This subject was also tackled in *The Laws.* Here, Plato, having accounted for the Cretan custom of eating meals together by the need to practice, even in time of peace, habits likely to facilitate the conduct of warlike operations, then put the following words into the mouth of one of his speakers: "For what men in general term peace is in fact only a name; in reality every city is in a natural state of war with every other, not indeed proclaimed by heralds, but everlasting." In a most famous passage of *The Republic,* Plato had stressed the supremacy of the intellect, likening mankind to a group of prisoners chained in a cave or den, to whose eyes light came glimmering through an opening. They could achieve knowledge only after a difficult process of adaptation to incoming light. It is amazing that he should express himself so differently in the case of war, for here he offers man no comparable means for overcoming darkness. Plainly the bonds which bind the individual to the authority of the state, operating in an atmosphere of underlying conflict or open war, seemed to him of such importance as to preclude man's shaking himself free from them, substituting concord for the old habits and primitive fatalism of the warrior.

A passage in *The Republic* already foreshadows this attitude. It examines the relations of the Greeks among themselves and with the barbarians. The Greeks had traditionally placed themselves above other peoples, seeing themselves as a privileged race to whom the gods had vouchsafed talent and critical capacity in a measure superior to the average. The barbarians were relegated to the status of inferiors. The current ideas on war and on the relations among peoples accepted the "race-gap" which nothing, it was felt, could bridge. Plato endorsed these ideas when he explained the difference between "discord" and "war": The first term stood for a controversy between peoples belonging to the same race (for example, between Greeks), the second between peoples of different races. In the case of a contest between Greeks, the adversaries, although using armed force, should concentrate not on the enemy citizenry, but on "only [the] few at any time [who] are their foes, those, namely, who are to blame for the quarrel." Military pressure was to be used until it provoked a civil uprising sufficient to force those governing the opposing city to withdraw from the fight. In the case of non-Greeks, however, they were to have recourse to total war.

The distinction between the ways of waging war showed that although Plato regarded the fragmentation of Greek civilization in small states as necessary, he eventually conceded the existence of an underlying solidarity among people of Hellenic stock. In this way he formulated implicitly a moral judgment on war. Thus, in the Gorgias, the dialogue on rhetoric, Plato described with compassion the human predicament, for man is a prey to violence and recklessness, condemned ever to wander from the path mapped out for him by those having his best interests at heart. What was important, he warned, was not external serenity but peace of mind, which could be won by those whose conduct was balanced and honest and who preferred to suffer an injustice rather than to commit one. He pitied Archelaus, who had become the sovereign of Macedonia after a long series of crimes: He was wrongly thought fortunate and happy by his contemporaries, whilst in fact he was the most miserable of men because he had despised the fundamental rule of honesty.

Plato's output was large, and he was not always consistent. Yet his dialogue must be examined and judged as a whole. A passage in *The Laws* relating to the harmful consequences of soldiering for the education of the citizen is exactly counterbalanced in *The Republic* by a passage in which warriors are advised to use the battlefield as a stage on which to educate the young in their atrocious trade. However they should be judged, these passages bring us to consider what is the most genuine and inspired source of Platonic thought and thus to move more rapidly through the contradictions between the objectives of the philosopher and those of the legislator. And this is true although it is difficult to distinguish how much of his system is an effort to overcome the traditional concept of war along bold idealistic lines and how much is the consequence of his acceptance of certain aspects of community life. Plato was prepared to condemn war as the cause of many disasters, but he did not delude himself that it was in his power to transform the entire Hellenic conception of power. His aim was not submission, the destruction of traditional modes of life, nor did he wish to be seen as a visionary lost on the paths of utopia. To escape the tragic dilemma, he would have needed a faith or a mystic impetus sufficient to regenerate the political and military tradition of Greek society and to guide it toward completely new ethical and religious attitudes.

His attempt to persuade the Greeks that war should not be the supreme care of the state was by itself a bold enterprise. He advocates in *The Laws* that rulers should be most concerned with peaceful activities. Peace was not only the final aim of human existence but also the reward for virtuous conduct. Men lived happily if they abstained from all unjust conduct and if they sheltered themselves from that of others. The same could be said of the state. "And cities are like individuals in this, for a city, if good, has a life of peace, but if evil, a life of war within and without." An underlying harmony was what gave the behavior of men and of groups a noble completeness. Plato thus sought to achieve the unity of a world torn by discord, corroded by the lust for power, tormented by primeval appetites and urges, for he believed that man must bend, despite everything, to the imperatives of reason.

Aristotle and the Choice between Peace and War

The works of Aristotle (384-322 B.C.)—in particular, *The Politics,* in which he set down his thoughts on the organization of the state—contain no precise statement on the problem of peace. In his system, the behavior of man and society was the basis of community morality, the function of which was to show man the right behavior in personal relations and in those maintained with society and its institutions.

In his system the state was the framework within which man must find fulfillment and in which his aspirations must become specific actions and choices. According to his famous definition, man is a political animal, naturally inclined to associate with his own kind, abhorring isolation. Community life is not only a response to the dictates of nature, but it enables the individual to give of his best, since it creates a context of legality and justice, outside which man's savagery knows no bounds.

Aristotle's approach to the problems of community organization is more realistic than Plato's: He is more respectful of institutions and acquired experience, less anxious to change the whole world in obedience to abstract principles worked out without warmth and perhaps originating in a certain distrust of the group instinct. It was precisely the warnings of experience which led him to challenge some of Plato's proposals for solving community problems: sharing of women and of goods, the rigid separation between social classes, the imposition by the state of heavy burdens on the citizens. He was bound to find these objectives unattainable and in conflict with the nature of man, a political animal, it is true, but also a creature endowed with a sensitivity and a critical capacity could not be neutralized or silenced. There is nothing rigid or burdensome, then, in his vision of the state, but a tendency to idealize it, while assigning it a specific function with regard to its basic and indispensable unit: the individual. The ultimate objective of the state was the happiness of the citizens. In this, too, he deviated from Plato. He replaced the just state, founded on immutable, abstract principles, by a more elastic concept, with a doctrine more sensitive to historical realities.

However, Aristotle's vision of the state did not go beyond the Greek polis, which he saw as the ultimate form of political organization. But the polis, given its limited geographical and environmental scope, offered no soil suitable for the germination of the ideas on peace then fermenting in the Greek world. These ideas needed much wider horizons. While conceding that peace was the ideal condition for the progress of any community and advising statesmen to encourage its consolidation, he was incapable of establishing a systematic approach to the problem without denying some postulates of his political thought. Among these we may recall his claim, scarcely credible for a thinker of his caliber, that the rights of the Greeks were fundamentally different from those of the barbarians, since between them there could not exist relations based on equality but only on the subjection of the latter to the former. From this he derived his famous justification of slavery. And in a society permanently fragmented into so many states, war was sure to survive.

Hence even the art of war will by nature be in a manner an art of acquisition (for the art of hunting is part of it) that is properly employed both against wild animals and against those of mankind who, though designed by nature for subjection, refuse to submit to it, inasmuch as this warfare is by nature just.

Since he advocated a constitution modeled on the historic experience of Greece, Aristotle saw war as a legitimate instrument for settling disputes. In his opinion, it was right to be prepared for war, although this did not make fighting praiseworthy in itself, much less the ultimate goal of community life: Peace is the ideal condition toward which mankind must work. "War," he said, "must be for the sake of peace, business for the sake of leisure, things necessary and useful for the sake of things noble...." This led him to condemn the deformed habits of mind of the professional soldier: "...a man should be capable of engaging in business and war, but still more capable of living in peace and leisure; and he should do what is necessary and useful, but still more what is noble." Therefore those constitutions which made conquest and military activity in general the fundamental aim of the state were erroneous. Peoples governed in this way would live in misery. The final goal of the state was in fact to ensure happiness for its inhabitants and to see that the army was trained not to enslave neighbors nor to throw into bondage those who were free:

> For we do business in order that we may have leisure, and carry on war in order that we may have peace. Now the practical virtues are exercised in politics or in warfare; but the pursuits of politics and war seem to be unleisured—those of war indeed entirely so, for no one desires to be at war for the sake of being at war, nor deliberately takes steps to cause a war: a man would be thought an utterly bloodthirsty character if he declared war on a friendly state for the sake of causing battles and massacres.

These words illustrate Aristotle's aim of distilling his experiences into lessons for the holders of power. They also reveal his feeling that it is important to plan ahead against the dangers and unexpected developments that issue from conflict. He felt that every type of state must comply with its own rules, and within the elaborate nexus of international relations the needs and problems of each community and the choices of its rulers must meet, though they were not bound to clash. That war was to be undertaken only with the aim of peace implied that if peace was obtainable by other means, war should no longer be the final arbiter.

Nor was military activity to be regarded as a valuable means of training, as Plato had argued. Day-to-day experience showed that communities devoted to the preparation of war, being too busy in the practice of military training, were severely handicapped when it came to organizing a peaceful existence. "Most military states remain safe while at war but perish when they have won their empire; in peacetime they lose their temper like iron. The lawgiver is to blame, because he did not educate them to be able to employ leisure." These words derive from a careful observation of history and attachment to moral principles, the indispensable guides of any society. The idea that the legislator and the statesman should concern themselves with the instruction of the citizens shows the maturity of Aristotle's thinking. The education rule applied to all the constitutions, among which he judged that of Sparta the worst, since that state's authorities were constantly engaged in waging or making ready for war. He felt there could be no weaker or more one-sided approach than this, since it caused dangerous disequilibria and left unbridgeable gaps in time of transition from war to peace:

> In Sparta the entire system of the laws is directed toward one part of virtue only, military valor, because this is serviceable for conquest. Owing to this [the Spartans] remained secure while at war, but began to decline when they had won an empire, because they did not know how to live a life of leisure, and had been trained in no other form of training more important than the art of war. And another error no less serious than that one is this: They think that the coveted prized of life are won by valor more than cowardice, and in this they are right, yet they imagine wrongly that these prizes are worth more than the valor that wins them.

The general bias of Aristotle's thinking is unmistakable in these passages and is manifestly colored by a preference for peace. They stress man's natural inclination toward moderation and tolerance, toward the liberal arts and the activities that only peace can favor and which war, if possible. The philosopher was to serve as guide in the state, his job being, so to speak, that of throwing light on the work of the rulers, especially in the sectors related to the spiritual life and the training of the individual. This responsibility should be discharged on the basis of principles of humanity and the aim of a kind of moral improvement which would concern not only one state and one community, but should embrace them all, since it referred to an attitude of mind. The question was not one of a choice between violence and tolerance; Aristotle argued that one should reject the first, as contrary to the nature of man, or because it was unlikely to ensure serenity for those who desired it. A universalist bias was therefore implicit in his teaching, which started with an approach much more widely based than that traditionally circumscribed by the polis and was extended to embrace the entire Greek world and perhaps, by implication, other peoples.

Peace In Roman Thinking

Gerardo Zampaglione
Italian Ambassador (1917–1996)

The formation of the Roman empire led to political unity of a geographical area achieved by force of arms and the subsequent total submission of the conquered peoples; in the eyes of the Romans, the Roman state had a different status from that of the foreign nations, for the latter were required to relinquish all claims to independence and sovereignty and to throw themselves on the clemency of the victor. The Romans were convinced of the impossibility of maintaining relations with other countries on bases other than that of subjection to their own power.

We must, however, distinguish the period of expansion—with the gradual formation of the empire—from that during which, once past her prime, Rome was held at bay and finally vanquished by the peoples living on her borders. When we speak of the warlike ambitions of the Romans, we are referring to the first period, which may be dated roughly from the earliest time to the end of the century A.D. The psychological, political, and institutional outlook of the Roman people was at that time essentially military. The etymology of a number of words may help us here. Thus, virtues stood for military valor and only later acquired the meaning of moral virtue: hostis was at one and the same time the enemy and the foreigner, enjoying no civil rights but subject to the discretionary powers of the Roman state as laid down in a rule contained in the twelve tables. Roman citizenship was closely identified with military service, and the sovereign power was referred to by a term of military origin: imperium. The exercise of imperium over the provinces was equivalent to a consolidated occupation, which imposed on provincials the payment of a stipendium, a tribute.

Economically, the Roman state in the first centuries was kept permanently on a war footing. It was ready at any moment to embark upon wars of aggression. The wars were used partly as a means of solving the economic crises and neutralizing the recurrent discontent of the ordinary people by diverting attention to happenings abroad.

The consequences of peace—if the concept were not limited to individual preoccupations, affections, and interests were of course reflected in community life, especially in that of the state: To maintain the mind free of disturbances and passion, free to aspire to the joys of the contemplative life, political and social stability must be secured. It will be understood, therefore, why the peace imposed by Rome became the principal ideological justification for the empire when it took the place of the Roman Republic, which had fallen prey to civil strife. The word pax gradually assumed the meaning of security based on a centralized system in which authority occupied a position of primacy over liberty. In the celebration of the order and stability assured by the empire there was a sense of legitimate satisfaction for the tranquility achieved, from which every citizen benefited, whether brought up on philosophy or not. We may cite, in this connection, Vellcius Paterculus (9 B.C.-ca. 32 A.D.), a court writer who praises time benefits deriving from the pacification of the state and then adds: "The pax augusta, which has spread to the regions of the east and of the west and to the bounds of the north and of the south, preserves every corner of the world safe from the fear of brigandage."

Pax Romana

The various shades of meaning which the word pax embraced were to lead to the formulation of a wider concept: that of the pax romana, which embodied the idea of external relations based on the great power achieved by the Roman Empire, that of the liberation of the body politic from the shadow of civil war, amid the idea of the formation of an atmosphere favorable to the activities of the mind, but the background remained the formalized set of atitudes centered around the Romans proud conviction that they had been vested with the mission of imposing their laws and way of life on the rest of the world. The expression was given currency by Seneca, who used it in his *De providnetia* (IV 14).

Almost all Roman writers agreed that spreading peace among mankind meant subjecting other peoples to Roman dominion. It was implicit in the reasoning that the nonsubject peoples could not enjoy conditions of peace and tranquility. [This feeling was an aspect of the conviction among the Romans that they were the sole artificers of history and were free to ignore completely the reactions of the nations over which their dominion was exercised.] None took the trouble to question the subject peoples, of whose views very little is now known, mainly because, even when expressed, nobody thought them worth writing down. A pertinent example is in the words of Florus: "Thus the civil wars came to an end; the other wars were waged against foreign nations and broke out in different quarters of the world while the empire was distracted by its own troubles. Peace was a new state of affairs, and the proud and haughty necks of the nations, not yet accustomed to the reins of servitude, revolted against the yoke recently imposed upon them."

The pax romana thus became associated with good administration keeping the peace between peoples subject to the same authority, amid, after Constantine, even a single religion. This explains why its memory was often evoked nostalgically when the empire warmed and the benefits of the pax romana had been lost as a result of religious upheaval, economic crisis, or barbarian invasion.

Virgil and the Prophecies of the Sibylline Books

The end of the civil wars and the restoration of authority in the person of a prince, in fact an absolute monarch although outwardly complying with the ancient republican formalities, and the pacification, now complete, of the entire imperial territory—incursions from outside and the occasional internal rebellion were becoming steadily easier to handle—strengthened the conviction felt by many that mankind was really on the threshold of an age in which society would be governed by the love of peace. Wars would disappear and prosperity would reign supreme. This would, of course, be due to the pax romana and to the superiority it ensured for the Roman state.

This notion underlies the famous prophecy which Virgil (70-19 B.C.) puts in the mouth of Jupiter, referring to the closing of the Temple of Janus by Augustus: "Then shall wars cease and the rough ages soften; hoary Faith and Vesta, Quirinus with his brother Remus, shall give laws. The gates of war, grim with iron and close-fitting bars, shall be closed; within, impious Rage, sitting on savage arms, his hands fast bound behind with a hundred brazen knots, shall roar in the ghastliness of blood-stained lips." Thus the disappearance of "impious Rage" would herald the return of the Golden Age, described by poets like Hesiod and philosophers like Plato.

Imperial Society: The Longing for Peace

The problem of the best system of government became the key political issue in Rome. Having imposed unity over a wide area of the world, it was now troubled more by internal difficulties than by any desire to pursue expansion. Ideologically the Romans saw themselves at the center of society, according themselves primacy deriving from their superiority in relations with all peoples, whether they were subject peoples or not. The evolution of the system was therefore studied closely, both by those belonging to the old republican governing class, for whom the ideal constitution was still that for which Pulybius had supplied a theory, and by those who were aware of the scale of the changes which had taken place in the body politic and thought it right to accept their implications. Roman imperial society, in the last analysis, sought two types of peace: the internal peace of the state, for so long torn by civil strife, and that of the spirit, desired particularly by the philosophers.

A change was very soon to occur in the general view of the old republican constitution. With the passing of generations its memory faded until it became hard to distinguish myth from reality. The respect showed by some writers of the imperial time toward the virtues which, it was claimed, had prevailed during the first centuries of Rome was partly a matter of literary convention and reflected no real desire to revert to a past constitutional system associated in many minds with administrative anarchy and the civil war of the last decades of the Republic. Later Stoic speculation, however, could accept the new reality, under the illusion that it was an anticipation of universal order, which mankind appeared to be approaching and which would be achieved through the empire. True freedom was internal freedom, which allowed men, particularly wise men, to achieve superiority over their environment, to withdraw into themselves and to abandon life itself, if the surroundings in which they worked proved too different from those cherished in their ideals.

Stoic training thus helped the old governing class to find its place in the new imperial order. Internationalism, which Zeno and his disciples had done so much to foster, was achieved de facto in the Roman state, for within its frontiers peoples having nothing in common, historically and ethnically, were governed by a single authority. And yet, war, as a brutal means of expansion and subjugation of other nations, was not subjected to adequate criticism by the new governing classes, who failed, perhaps, to discern its true nature.

However, it would have been a mistake to tackle the problem too directly, not only because this might annoy the emperor and his entourage; but also because outspoken views on this subject might appear to reflect on the origin of the Roman state itself. The Stoics of the imperial age preferred to skirt the question and avoid the dangers of certain opinions by emphasizing the individual's membership in a community in which each was committed to contributing to the edification of his neighbor. The very existence of the empire confirmed Zeno's doctrine that the age old struggles between cities and between countries must be ended so that man could become the free citizen of one state, governed by a single law and subject to a single authority. Zeno had stated the case for subjecting every man to the government of reason, so that disturbances engendered by lack of logic and discipline could be properly contained. This objective, with its natural implications—the first being the condemnation of war—seemed largely to have been achieved in the Roman Empire

Plutarch and the Origins of War

The unification of the known world within one state, guided by a single will instead of the old senatorial class, made it easier for the schools to overcome the contradictions between the various traditional teachings, using, if necessary, religious feeling for the purpose. Plato, Aristotle, Pythagoras were regarded as the forerunners and prophets, through whom the divine spirit had made itself known to the world. Aristotelian doctrine tended to merge into that of Plato, which became in its turn Neoplatonism, a leading school of thought in the later era of classical speculation. Neoplatonism also contained mystical elements drawn from Eastern religions and philosophies.

This is where we find Plutarch of Chaeronea (45-125), famous as the author of the *Parallel Lines* and of a number of discourses on moral subjects. Plutarch was convinced that philosophy was man' s only hope of betterment and salvation. God existed and was identical with the good. This was all that could be known about him. Nonetheless this was a truth accessible to the human intellect, despite the views of the Neoplatonists, for whom God was a being so far removed from corporeal life as to be perceptible only through forms of ecstasy or mysterious metaphysical forms of communication.

The problem of identifying God with goodness posed the problem of evil, which Plutarch solved by treating its essence as the malevolent soul of the universe. In the framework of this antithesis—which has a dualistic undertone—he sets his judgments on the phenomenon of war, the worst calamity that man could be called upon to bear. Those who claimed otherwise showed little love for the truth and precious little sensitivity. Here was the nub of his quarrel with the Stoic Chrysippus, who had observed that warfare had the merit of lightening the pressure of population in the overcrowded cities. Devoid of any attribute of nobility, warfare, in Plutarch's view, derived from profound defects of character: "for no war springs up among men without vice but one breaks out from lust for pleasure, another from greed, and still another from a lust for glory or for power. Well then, if god induces wars, he induces vices too by inciting and perverting human beings."

Plutarch based his system on these premises, relating his judgment on war and on the behavior of politicians to them. Although he opposed Stoicism, on which he had written an essay pointing out its inherent contradictions, he was sympathetic to the humanitarian and universalistic aspects of Stoic doctrine. His criticism was that they failed to match up to a noble vocation which should have led them to dedicate themselves solely to achieving Zeno's objectives. His interpretation of the personality of Alexander the Great makes this attitude clear. Although he narrated heroic deeds, he was impressed not by the captain-at-arms as much as by the unifier of peoples and the precursor of the Stoic cosmopolis. He related that because Alexander believed that he came as a heaven-sent governor to all, and as a mediator for the whole world, those whom he could not persuade to unite with him, he conquered by force of arms, and he brought together into one body all men everywhere, uniting and mixing in one great loving-cup, as it were, men's lives, their characters, their marriages, their very habits of life. He bade them all consider as their fatherland the whole inhabited earth, as their stronghold and protection his camp, as akin to them all good men, and as foreigners only the wicked.

Everyone should feel part of and partly responsible for community life, the aim being to work toward higher objectives of pacification. War, on the other hand, whether in the form of a campaign for the conquest of new territories or whether as civil war, the most painful kind, was an appeal to the past. The Roman Empire was in a position to ensure serenity and prosperity to the human race under a single sovereign. It was therefore the task of the moralist to promote peace in the family and civil interests. In the last analysis Plutarch's plan was the same as that of Pliny the Elder, but it was developed along more consistent lines:

For observe that of the greatest blessings which States can enjoy—peace, liberty, plenty, abundance of men, and concord—so far as peace is concerned the peoples have no need of statesmanship at present; for all war, both Greek and foreign, has been banished from among us and has disappeared; and of liberty the peoples have as great a share as our rulers grant them, and perhaps more would not be better for them; there remains, then, for the statesman, of those activities which fall within his province, only this—and it is the equal of any of the other blessings—always to instill concord and friendship in those who dwell together with him and to remove strifes, discords and all enmity.

These words show a sense of satisfaction generated by condition of the Roman citizen, living in a happy age, under the guidance of enlightened sovereigns in disciplined order, where all disorders such as war were resolved in general harmony. Here were the premises for a more complete and systematic doctrine of peace, but this was something that Plutarch's eclecticism was not able to provide.

Philo Judaeus: The Revision of the Biblical Message

Philo's explanation of the actual genesis of war differed from the traditional one given both in pagan and in Jewish literature. Some mystical aspects of his thinking, in which scholars have even thought they discerned Christian influences, could not be reconciled with the opinions then held on the nature of war. It would be useless to seek a doctrine like Philo's in Jewish tradition, for he believed that war often derives from circumstances outside man's will—for example, from "poverty and ill fame." At other times it was connected with the evils of the soul. Here is a clear attempt to probe the nature of the phenomenon more deeply. War is considered not as an instrument for achieving domination, but as a consequence of the corruption of the human soul, which would be kept pure if people would not "even admit any heinous thoughts, but live with our fellow-citizens in peace and law-observance, that order of which justice is the guiding influence."

The Ends of Classical Speculation

Efforts to define the nature of peace were confined to rational descriptions, generally referring to activities of the mind and often presented in a context spoiled by literary preciousness. Together with classical philosophy, the pacifist and humanitarian ideas spread by the Hellenistic-Roman schools also faded away.

Contrary to current opinion, as we have sought to show, classical civilization was not wholly on the side of armed violence but in some, not negligible, instances extolled peaceful community life. Wars, as such, were often regarded as abominable catastrophes. The societies that had succeeded one another from the times of the Greek polis to Alexandrian times, the time of the Rome of the kings and the empire had, it is true, waged war almost continuously and had glorified valor, regarded as the supreme expression of human virtue, but they had also encouraged intellectuals and mystics who argued that brotherly love was superior to violence. During this long era, a considerable number of writers, thinkers, historians, orators, essayists, and statesmen had denied that war was the normal situation of peoples and the only appropriate instrument for controlling human relations.

Adulation of heroism in the field, characteristic of the early centuries of Greek history, was already outmoded by the time of Pericles. Because it lasted so long, because it was a burden on the economy and sapped the strength of the cities, because of the more sophisticated military techniques it encouraged, the Peloponnesian War did much to rob war in general of its literary glamour. Pressing their destructive criticism of traditional values, the Sophists had spared neither the braggadocios and the warmongers nor war itself. They publicized the idea of a common origin of man, stressing the existence among citizens and cities of Greece of a common heritage. This meant that military valor was no more than a talent for liquidating fellow-men, whose only fault was that they had been born in an alien city. Since war escaped the control of the intellect, they rejected it, believing it to be dominated by irrational impulses and by a purely physical and almost muscular concept of the duties of man. They saw all praise of war as the deplorable consequence of that ignorance fraught with conceit which was a peculiar quality of men trained to the trade of arms. In the fifth century B.C. the Sophist Gorgias had already reflected on all this, concluding that peace was health for the mind of the individual as well as for the entire human society. War, conversely, was illness.

Stoicism was to take these premises further, including in a single embrace all men—whether Greeks or barbarians—giving them a single citizenship and laying the moral and rational fundaments for a leveling process that Alexander the Great had already implemented. Thus was born that humanitarian line of thinking which was to penetrate by various roads into the Hellenistic courts and then into Roman circles, becoming a feature of the ideology prevailing among the imperial bureaucracy and even the senate class. It was a constructive and concrete view which brought men closer by seeing them as members of a universal community.

Cynic teaching was different. Developing the corrosive criticism of the Sophists, the Cynics appealed to a superior idea of virtue, concluding that worldly values were without substance and the opinions of others of no consequence, since the only good was virtue and the only evil, vice. Military glory and love of the fatherland, incidental and precarious concepts bound up with the individuals membership in a body politic, were definitely second-rate ideas in the eyes of the Cynics, for they had no time for states or nations and believed that the wise man and the enlightened should reject them. The Cynics were therefore among the supporters of the idea of a cosmopolis, though there was more than a hint of anarchism in an attitude which abhorred all kinds of dependence. The Cynic cosmopolis had no hierarchies and, unlike that of the Stoics, there was no subjection to a single authority.

The position of the Epicureans, though starting from different premises, was similar. The Cynics were driven by an extraordinary faith in the independent virtue of the spirit, which enabled them to ignore community life, to yield to a deep longing for personal freedom, while the Epicureans argued that utilitarian considerations had led to the decay of the customs and moral rules inherited from the old Hellenic tradition. The need to escape all disturbance led them to loosen the bonds with society. In their eyes the wise man should abstain from all public activities and not merely show indifference to them, as Stoicism taught. In this effort to free himself from the trammels of life in society, the Epicurean despised war, which added the sufferings of the body to those of the mind. Epicurean cosmopolitanism, like that of the Cynics but for different reasons, became an all-out individualism, a single-minded pursuit of serenity. Thus all moral substance and all importance was denied to community life, for the Epicurean believed that the happiness of the individual depends on his independence of society.

These three schools influenced the later ones, though to varying extents and with the adjustments entailed by historical situations and current circumstances. Where the social factor gained the upper hand, Stoic thinking prevailed; otherwise it was Cynic and Epicurean individualism which led to a more or less marked detachment from old warlike tradition. Equilibrium seemed to be achieved in the Roman Empire with the Mediterranean world under a single state and the internal pacification of that state after long periods of savage civil wars. This apparently justified the view that the Stoic cosmopolis had finally been attained. But it was a dangerous illusion and those who cherished it ignored the fact that world peace had been won at the price of the violent subjugation of many peoples. After the Antonines, war reemerged as the means by which succession was determined and as an instrument needed to defend the empire against outsiders. In both forms it was evidence of decadence.

The attempt made by Hellenistic-Roman philosophers to revive the old themes, were it only in mystic terms and in such indirect forms as were lowed by the times and by the political order, was doomed to failure. These themes had, as we have seen, lost their edge and power of penetration. In their weakened presentation, they could not prevail over the formidable moral force embodied in Christianity.

Peace and Jihâd in Muslim History

Majid Khadduri
Johns Hopkins University

The state, which is regarded as the instrument for universalizing a certain religion, must perforce be an ever-expanding state. The Islamic state, whose principal function was to put God's law into practice, sought to establish Islam as the dominant reigning ideology over the entire world. It refused to recognize the coexistence of non-Muslim communities, except perhaps as subordinate entities, because by its very nature a universal state tolerates the existence of no other state than itself. Although it was not a consciously formulated policy, Mohammed's early successors, after Islam became supreme in Arabia, were determined to embark on a ceaseless war of conquest in the name of Islam. The jihâd was therefore employed as an instrument for both the universalization of religion and the establishment of an imperial world state.[1] The mission of Islam was rapidly and successfully carried out during the first century of the Slavic era—although the peaceful penetration of Islam continued—and the empire extended over a large portion of the Old World and became as large as the Roman Empire.

But the expanding Muslim state, not unlike other universal states, could not extend *ad infinitum*. The hitherto victorious Muslim warriors were defeated in the West at Tours (A.D. 732) and in the East found they could not proceed further than the Indian borders.[2] Thus the wave of Muslim expansion, strong as it was, could not complete the Sun's circle; it imperceptibly subsided where it reached its utmost limits at the Pyrenees and the Indus.[3] The Muslim (world) state consequently did not correspond to the then known world. Outside it there remained communities which the Muslim authorities had to deal with, though in theory only temporarily, throughout all the subsequent history of Islam.

The world accordingly was sharply divided in Muslim law into the dâr al-Islam (abode or territory of Islam) and the dâr al-harb (abode or territory of war). These terms may be rendered in less poetic words as the "world of Islam" and the "world of war." The first corresponded to the territory under Muslim rule. Its inhabitants were Muslims, by birth or conversion, and the communities of the tolerated religions (the dhimmîs) who preferred to hold fast to their own cult, at the price of paying the jizya (poll tax). The Muslims enjoyed full rights of citizenship; the subjects of the tolerated religions enjoyed only partial rights, and submitted to Muslim rule in accordance with special charters regulating their relations with the Muslims.[4] The dâr al-harb consisted of all the states and communities outside the world of Islam. Its inhabitants were often called

Majid Khadduri, "Peace and Jihad in Moslem History." Khadduri, Majid. *War and Peace in the Law of Islam.* pp. 51-58, 62-64.

infidels, or, better, unbelievers.

On the assumption that the ultimate aim of Islam was worldwide, the dâr al-Islam was always, in theory, at war with the dâr al-harb. The Muslims were required to preach Islam by persuasion, and the caliph or his commanders in the field to offer Islam as an alternative to paying the poll tax or fighting; but the Islamic state was under legal obligation to enforce Islamic law and to recognize no authority other than its own, superseding other authorities even when non-Muslim communities had willingly accepted the faith of Islam without fighting. Failure by non-Muslims to accept Islam or pay the poll tax made it incumbent on the Muslim state to declare a jihâd (commonly called "holy war") upon the recalcitrant individuals and communities. Thus the jihâd, reflecting the normal war relations existing between Muslims and non-Muslims, was the state's instrument for transforming the dâr al-harb into the dâr al-Islam. It was the product of a warlike people who had embarked on a large-scale movement of expansion. Islam could not abolish the warlike character of the Arabs who were constantly at war with each other[5]; it indeed reaffirmed the war basis of intergroup relationship by institutionalizing war as part of the Muslim legal system and made use of it by transforming war into holy war designed to be ceaselessly declared against those who failed to become Muslims. The short intervals which are not war—and these in theory would not exceed ten years—are periods of peace.[6] But the jihâd was not the only legal means of dealing with non-Muslims since peaceful methods (negotiations, arbitration, and treaty making) were applied in regulating the relations of the believers with unbelievers when actual fighting ceased.

The Muslim law of nations was, accordingly, the product of the intercourse of an ever-expanding state with its neighbors, which inevitably led to the development of a body of rules and practices followed by Muslims in war and peace. The practices followed by the Arabs before Islam in their intertribal warfare were regarded as too ungodly and brutal, because they were motivated by narrow tribal interests. Islam abolished all war except jihâd and the jurist-theologians consciously formulated its law subordinating all personal considerations to *raison d'état,* based on religious sanction.

The Doctrine of Jihâd

The Meaning of Jihâd

The term jihâd is derived from the verb jahâda (abstract noun, juhd) which means "exerted";[7] its juridical-theological meaning is exertion of ones power in Allah's path, that is, the spread of the belief in Allah and in making His word supreme over this world. The individual's recompense would be the achievement of salvation, since the jihâd is Allah's direct way to paradise. This definition is based on a Qur'ânic injunction, which runs as follows:

> O ye who believe! Shall I guide you to a gainful trade, which will save you from painful punishment? Believe in Allah and His Apostle and carry on warfare (jihâd) in the path of Allah with your possessions and your persons. That is better for you. If ye have knowledge, He will forgive your sins, and will place you in the Gardens beneath which the streams flow, and fin houses in the Gardens of Eden: that is the great gain. [8]

The jihâd, in the broad sense of exertion, does not necessarily mean war or fighting, since exertion in Allah's path may be achieved by peaceful as well as violent means. The jihâd may be regarded as a form of religious propaganda that can be carried on by persuasion or by the sword. In the early Makkan revelations, the emphasis was in the main on persuasion. Muhammad, in the discharge of his prophetic functions, seemed to have been satisfied by warning his people against idolatry and inviting them to worship Allah. This is evidenced by such a verse as the following: "He who exerts himself (jâhada), exerts only for his own soul,"[9] which expresses the jihâd in terms of the salvation of the soul rather than a struggle for proselytization.[10]

In the Madînan revelations, the jihâd is often expressed in terms of strife, and there is no doubt that in certain verses he conception of jihâd is synonymous with the words war and fighting.[11]

The jurists, however, have distinguished four different ways in which the believer may fulfill his jihâd obligation: by his heart; his tongue; his hands; and by the sword.[12] The first is concerned with combatting the devil and in the attempt to escape his persuasion to evil. This type of jihâd, so significant in the eyes of the Prophet Muhammad, was regarded as the greater jihâd.[13] The second and third are mainly fulfilled in supporting the right and correcting the wrong. The fourth is precisely equivalent to the meaning of war, and is concerned with fighting the unbelievers and the enemies of the faith.[14] The believers are under the obligation of sacrificing their "wealth and lives" (Q. LXI, 11) in the prosecution of war...[15]

The Jihâd as *Bellum Justum*

The idea that wars, when institutionalized as part of the mores of society, are just may be traced back to antiquity. It was implied in the concept of vendetta as an act of retaliation by one group against another. In the *Politics*, Arustitke refers to certain wars as just by nature.[16] The Romans instituted the *jus fetiale*, administered by a *collegium fetialium* (consisting of twenty members, presided over by *magister fetialium*), embodying the proper rules of waging war in order to be just.[17] In medieval Christendom, both St. Augustine and Isodore do Seville were influenced in their theory of just war by Cicero. St. Thomas Aquinas, who was acquainted with Muslim writings, formulated his theory of just war along lines similar to the Islamic doctrine of the jihâd.[18] St. Thomas and other medieval writers influenced in their turn the natural law theories of the sixteenth, seventeenth, and eighteenth centuries. Grotius, the father of the modern law of nations, developed his system under the impact of the natural law theory of just war, and his ideas remained predominant until the end of the eighteenth century.[19] Although the doctrine of war during the nineteenth century was far less influenced by natural law than in previous centuries, the concept of just war reappeared after the first World War in the form of a doctrine of outlawing war, save that against an aggressor....

The Jihâd as Permanent War

War, however, was not introduced into Arabia by Islam. It was already in existence among the Arabs; but it was essentially a tribal war. Its nature was peculiar to the existing social order and its rules and procedure were thoroughly integrated as part of the sunna. Since the tribe (in certain instances the clan) was the basic political unit, wars took the form of raids; mainly for robbery or vendetta (tha'r). This state of affairs had, as observed by Ibn Khaldûn, developed among the Arabs a spirit of self-reliance, courage, and co-operation among the members of the single tribe.[20] But these very traits intensified the character of warfare and rivalry among the tribes and created a state of instability and unrest.

The importance of the jihâd in Islam lay in shifting the focus of attention of the tribes from their intertribal warfare to the outside world; Islam outlawed all forms of war except the jihâd, that is, the war in Allah's path. It would, indeed, have been very difficult for the Islamic state to survive had it not been for the doctrine of the jihâd, replacing tribal raids, and directing that enormous energy of the tribes from an inevitable internal conflict to unite and fight against the outside world in the name of the new faith.

The jihâd as such was not a casual phenomenon of violence; it was rather a product of complex factors while Islam worked out its jural-doctrinal character. Some writers have emphasized the economic changes within Arabia which produced dissatisfaction and unrest and inevitably led the Arabs to seek more fertile lands outside Arabia.[21] Yet this theory—plausible as it is in explaining the outburst of the Arabs from within their peninsula—is not enough to interpret the character of a war permanently declared against the unbelievers even after the Muslims had established themselves outside Arabia. There were other factors, which created in the minds of the Muslims a politico-religious mission and conditioned their attitude as a conquering nation.

* * *

Thus the jihâd may be regarded as Islam's instrument for carrying out its ultimate objective by turning all people into believers, if not in the prophethood of Muhammad (as in the case of the dhimmîs), at least in the belief in God. The Prophet Muhammad is reported to have declared "some of my people will continue to fight victoriously for the sake of the *truth* until the last one of them will combat the anti-Christ."[22] Until that moment is reached the jihâd, in one form or another, will remain as a permanent obligation upon the entire Muslim community. It follows that the existence of a dâr al-harb is ultimately outlawed under the Islamic jural order; that the dâr al-Islam is permanently under jihâd obligation until the dâr al-harb is reduced to nonexistence; and that any community which prefers to remain non-Islamic—in the status of a tolerated religious community accepting certain disabilities—must submit to Islamic rule and reside in the dâr al-Islam or be bound as clients to the Muslim community. The universalism of Islam, in its all-embracing creed, is imposed on the believers as a continuous process of warfare, psychological and political if not strictly military....

The Jihâd and Secular War

Islam, it will be recalled, abolished all kinds of warfare except the jihâd. Only a war, which has an ultimate religious purpose, that is, to enforce God's law or to check transgression against it, is a just war. No other form of fighting is permitted within or without the Muslim brotherhood.

Throughout the history of Islam, however, fighting between Muslim rulers and contending parties was as continuous as between Islam and its external enemies. The *casus foederis* of a jihâd was frequently invoked on the grounds of suppressing innovations and punishing the leaders of secession from the faith. Not infrequently the naked ambition of opposition leaders who resorted to war for the sake of a throne or high political offices was too apparent to be ignored. When the caliph's prestige and power declined, lack of respect for and opposition to the central authority became fashionable among local rulers. This state of affairs accentuated the struggle for power and created instability and anarchy in the world of Islam. Ignoring existing realities, the jurists continued to argue—following the example of al-Mâwardî—that ultimate authority belonged to the caliph and that no one else had the right to renounce it even if the caliph proved to be unjust and oppressive, since tyranny, it was then contended, was preferable to anarchy[23]—a sad comment on existing conditions.

A few publicists, in their reflections on the state of affairs as they then existed, have said that wars, in forms other than the jihâd, had often recurred in the Islamic society. Paying lip service to the jihâd as a religious duty, they looked upon wars as dangers, which Muslim rulers should avoid. Al-Turtûshî (died A.H. 520) described "war crises" as social anomalies[24] and al-Ilasan ibn 'Abd-Allah compared them to diseases of society.[25] Both of these writers, who expatiated on the ways and means of conducting fighting, advised their rulers that the best way to win wars, if they found it impossible to avert them, was to be adequately prepared militarily. Thus Muslim publicists, like their Roman predecessors, seemed to have been convinced that *si vis pacem, para bellum.*

It was, perhaps, Ibn Khaldûn (A.D. 1332-1406) who for the first time recognized that wars were not, as his Muslim predecessors thought, casual social calamities. He maintained that war has existed in society ever since "Creation." Its real cause, which accounts for its persistence in society, is man's will-to-revenge. Man, in other words, is by nature warlike. He is forever moved to fight either for his own selfish interests or by such emotional motives as jealousy, anger, or a feeling of divine guilt. Thus the members of one group or nation, in order to attain their objectives, combined against others and the inevitable result was war.

Wars, according to Ibn Khaldûn, are of four kinds. First is the tribal warfare, such as that which existed among the Arabian tribes; second, feuds and raids which are characteristic of primitive people; third, the wars prescribed by the sharî'a, i.e., the jihâd; fourth, wars against rebels and dissenters. Ibn Khaldûn contends that the first two are unjustified, because they are wars of disobedience; the other two are just wars ('adl).

Notes

1. See The Doctrine of Jihâd, below.

2. The Muslims suffered another defeat before the battle of Tours at Constantinople (A.D. 717-18).

3. Edward Gibbon maintains that had the Muslims been successful at Tours the Qu'rân would have been taught at Oxford and Cambridge instead of the Bible (Gibbon, *History of the Decline and Fall of the Roman Empire,* ed. Bury [London, 1898], Vol. VI, p. 15); but in fact the Muslim Empire, due to internal forces, reached its utmost limits.

4. See chap. 17, below.

5. "The primitive nomad of the desert and steppes," says Quincy Wright, "has a hard environment to conquer....His terrain, adapted to distant raids and without natural defenses, leads him to institutionalize war for aggression and defense" (Q. Wright, *A Study of War* [Chicago, 1942], Vol. I, p. 64.

6. The idea that intergroup relationships were normally unpeaceful goes back to Antiquity (Plato, *The Laws,* Bk. I, 2) and it recurred in the writings of Medieval and modern thinkers. See Ibn Khaldûun, *al-Muqaddima,* ed. Quatremère (Paris, 1858), Vol. II, pp. 65-79; Hobbes, *Leviathan,* Chap. 13; "Elements of Law," Pt. I, chap. 14, 2. See also Q. Wright, *op.cit.,* Vol I, chaps. 6 and 7.

7. For the literal meaning of jihâd, see Fayrûzâbadî, *Qâmîs al-Muhit* (Ciiro, 1938) Vol. I, p. 286. For the Quar'ânic use of jihâd in the sense of exertion see Q. VI, 108; XXII, 77.

8. Q. LXI, 10.13. Se also Jurjânî, *Kitâb al-ta'rîfât,* ed. Gustavus Flügel (Leipzig, 1845), p. 84.

9. Q. XXIX. 5.

10. See Shâfî, *Kitâb al-Umrn* (Cairo, A.H.1321), Vol. IV, pp. 84-85; 'Abd al-Qâhir al-Baghdâdî, *Kitâb Usûl al-Dîn* (Istanbul 1928) Vol. I, p. 193; Shaybânî, *al-Siyar al-Kabîr,* with Sarakhsi's Commentary (Hyderabad, A.H. 1335), Vol. I, p. 126.

11. See Q. II 215; IX, 41; XLIX, 15; LXI, II; LXVI, 9.

12. See Ibn Hasm, *Kitâb al-Fasl fî al-Milal wa'l-Ahwâ' wa'l-Nihal* (Cairo, A.H. 1321), Vol. IV, p. 135; Ibn Rushd, *Kitâb al-Muqaddimat al-Mumahhidât* (Cairo, A.H. 1325), Vol. 1 p. 259; Buhûtî, *Kashshâf al-Qinâ' 'An Matn al-Iqnâ'* (Cairo, A.H. 1366), Vol. III, p 28.

13. Ibn al-Humâm, *Sharh Fath al-Qadîr* (Cairo, A.H. 1316), Vol IV, p. 277.

14. Ibn Hazm distinguishes between the jihâd by the tongue and the jihâd by ra'y and tadbîr (i.e., reason) and he maintains that the Prophet Muhammad showed preference for reason over the sword. lbn Hazm, Vol. IV, p. 135.

15. Bukhârî, *Kitab al-Jâmi' al-Sahîh,* ed. Krehl (Leiden, 1864), Vol. II, p. 199; Abû Dâ'ûd *Sunan* (Cairo, 1935), Vol. III, P. 5; Dârimî *Sunan* (Damascus, A.H. 1349), Vol. II, p. 213.

16. *Politics,* Bk. I, chap. VIII.

17. In the *Offices,* Cicero, who may be regarded as the representative legal philosopher of ancient Rome, has discussed the rules and formalities, which constitute the *bellum justum.* See Cicero, *Offices, Essays and Letters* (Everyman's edition), Bk. I, § 11-12.

18. See A.P. D'Entreves, *Aquinas: Selected Political Writings* (Oxford, 1948) pp. 59-61; John Epstein, *The Catholic Tradition of the Law of Nations* (London, 1935); William Ballis, *The Legal Position of War: Changes in its Practice and Theory* (The Hague, 1937), pp. 32-60.

19. Hugo Grotius, *De Jure Belli ac Pacis,* first published in 1625 (Oxford, 1925).

20. Ibn Khaldûn, *al-Muqaddima,* ed. Quatremère (Paris, 1858), Vol. II, pp. 220-1.

21. The economic factors are discussed by Carl H. Becker in *The Cambridge Medieval History* (Cambridge, 1913), Vol. II, pp. 329 ff; Henri Lammens, *Le Berceau*

de l'Islam (Rome, 1914), Vol. 1, Pp. 114 ff; the Semitic migratory theory is discussed in Prince Caetani, *Annali dell'Islam* (Milan, 1907) Vol. II, 831-61.

22. Abu Dâ'ûd, Sunan (Cairo, 1935), Vol. III, p.4.

23. Badr al-Dîn Ibn Jamâ'a, *Tahrîr al-Ahkâm fîTadbîr Ahl al-Islâm,* ed. H. Koefler in *Islamica,* Vol. VI (1934), p. 365.

24. Turtûshî, *Sirâj al-Mulûk,* pp. 150-153.

25. Ibn 'Abd-Allah, who wrote his book in A.H. 708, gives seven reasons for the recurrence of war in society: First, for the establishment of a new state (dawla) or dynasty; second, for the consolidation of an already established state or dynasty; third, the wars of a just state (dawla 'âdila) against rebels and dissenters; fourth, wars between two nations or tribes in the form of raids; fifth, the annexation of one state by another, regardless of whether the latter was just or unjust; sixth, wars for the purpose of mere robbery, not for any political purpose; seventh, intertribal warfare as those existed in pre-Islamic Arabia. Al-Hasan ibn 'Abd-AIlah, *Âthâr al-Uwal fi Tartîb al-Duwal* (Cairo, A.H. 1295), pp. 167-8.

The American Dream and the Pursuit of Peace

Michael H. Hunt
University of North Carolina

We would do well to accept the young Marx's promptings. In foreign policy as in other spheres of human activity, the past is important to our understanding of the present in a paradoxical fashion. It instructs us in the special ways we are compromised by circumstances not of our own making, and at the same time it equips us to rise above those circumstances. A familiarity with the history of those ideas that led Americans into the thicket of international politics may, as Geertz in turn suggests, prove helpful in getting us through the perils that lie ahead.

We have previously made the case for the existence of an American foreign-policy ideology. Its origins are inextricably tied up with the emergence of an American nation. Its main features reflected from the start the class and ethnic preferences of those most intimately concerned with questions of foreign policy. Under the sway of that ideology, American policy-makers measured the worth of other peoples and nations against a racial hierarchy. They displayed hostility toward revolutions that diverged from the American norm, especially those on the left. Finally, they were convinced that national greatness depended on making the world safe for liberty.

The general direction American policies have taken is inexplicable, perhaps even inconceivable, without taking account of the influence of this constellation of ideas. It was not inevitable that the United States would become dominant in the Americas and the hegemon in Central America and the Caribbean. Some mysterious fate did not decree the ambivalent relationship with China and Japan, which translated into three decades of hostility with one country, followed after a Pacific war by three decades of hostility with the other. Nor was it preordained that the United States would emerge as a crucial player in the European balance of power, twice throwing itself into the bloody wars of that continent and finally seeking to fill the vacuum created by the collapse of empires after 1945. In historical perspective, however, these developments should not seem surprising or accidental. An ideology that had been tested, refined, and woven into the fabric of the national consciousness had helped propel twentieth-century U.S. foreign policy ever deeper into the thicket of international politics and warfare.

***

Ideology has set Americans at odds with the assumptions and practices of traditional power politics. As Walter Lippmann once observed, "The history of diplomacy is the history of relations among rival

Reprinted by permission from "The Contemporary Dilemma," by Michael H. Hunt, pp. 171-198 (ch. 6) from the book *Ideology and U.S. Foreign Policy,* Yale University Press, New Haven, CT., 1988.

powers, which did not enjoy political intimacy, and did not respond to appeals to common purposes."[1] Yet Americans have indeed assumed that intimacy and friendship among peoples of the world was the norm and have ascribed evil intentions to those whose exercise of power or pursuit of self-interest ran athwart American expectations. At the heart of this American aversion to traditional forms of great-power rivalry has been a hostility to spheres of influence. Though such spheres were the product of time-honored security calculations, American leaders have with few exceptions condemned them as illegitimate, an affront to the principles of liberty and self-determination.

Ironically, the more actively Americans have devoted themselves to destroying spheres of influence, the farther we have gone toward creating our own. To an incredulous world Americans have time and again explained that our benevolent intentions and selfless treatment of the countries of Central America, the Caribbean, and the Pacific clearly distinguish the extension of American influence from traditional practice. Where others seek to exploit and repress, so the argument goes, Americans seek only to protect and guide.

This American position on spheres of influence—denying them to others while carving them out for ourselves—has from the foreign perspective made the United States seem hypocritical and aggressive rather than enlightened and peace-loving. Not surprisingly, then, that position has been a prime source of international misunderstanding and conflict. The collisions with Japan over Northeast Asia in the 1930s, with the Soviet Union over Eastern Europe at the end of World War II, and with China over North Korea in late 1950 demonstrate dramatically how a principled American rejection of one of the constants of international life has led to redoubled and unexpected resistance on the part of the indicted party.

Ideology has also set the nature and force of revolutionary change beyond the bounds of American comprehension. Revolutions that failed to conform to the standards of America's own moderate, constitutional beginnings inspired hostility and, with increasing frequency, active opposition. Vietnam was part of a pattern going back to the late eighteenth century. That pattern was confirmed in response to the two major twentieth-century revolutions—in Russia and China—and carried forward more recently in Nicaragua, El Salvador, and Iran.

Accommodation to revolution has, if anything, become more difficult in the twentieth century. Peasant economies, where problems of commercialization and land tenure have helped set the stage for the most dramatic social revolutions of recent times, lay well beyond the experience of contemporary Americans. Leaders in Washington responded with development policy, an ethnocentric exercise in fitting a diverse world on the procrustean bed of the American experience. They expected to find a neat, unilinear advance from traditional to modern ways in countries whose course of development in fact bore little if any resemblance to the American pattern. Moreover, the tendency to see a conspiracy by the Soviet Union and international communism behind every outbreak of disorder has intensified the old allergy to revolution. By denying the social roots and historical legitimacy of radical revolutions, the United States arrays itself on the side of an unpopular and often oppressive status quo (as in China), sets itself against the nationalist impulses that have swept much of the world in recent times (as in Vietnam), and exposes itself to feelings of frustration and humiliation after each counterrevolutionary failure (as in Cuba).

***

Paradoxically, the counterrevolutionary stance taken by the United States must be regarded as a failure even where it has seemingly succeeded. Each American victory has served notice on aspiring revolutionary leaders that their strategies must anticipate and prepare for an American policy of active hostility. Leaders such as Fidel Castro have as a result become more determined, as well as more formidable, foes intent on mobilizing the popular, military, and international support essential to holding at bay the counter-revolutionary forces that the past teaches the United States will sponsor.

Successful campaigns against the left have, moreover, repeatedly created time bombs. Repressive rightist regimes favored by the United States have neglected or exacerbated serious social and economic problems, creating preconditions for an explosion against the established order and against Americans implicated in the creation and maintenance of that order. Counter-revolutionary victories followed after a time by still-greater defeats has been the story of the American experience in Nicaragua, Cuba, South Vietnam, and Iran. Seemingly cost effective in promoting a semblance of order, collaborative arrangements with the Somoza family for fifty years, Batista for over twenty-five years, Ngo Dinh Diem for nearly a decade, and the Shah in Iran for a quarter century each proved in the end costly beyond imagination. By continuing this practice, Americans will have more of these bills to pay with the names of other countries marked on them.

U.S. foreign-policy ideology has also proven disabling by cutting Americans off from an understanding of, not to mention sympathy for, distant from our own. The sense of national superiority central to that ideology has given rise to stereotypes that diminish other people by exaggerating the seemingly negative aspects of their lives and by constricting the perceived range of their skills, accomplishments, and emotions. By denigrating other cultures as backward or malleable, these stereotypes raise in Americans false expectations that it is an easy enterprise to induce and direct political change and economic development. On encountering obstinacy or resistance, Americans understandably feel frustrated and resentful and in extremity may indulge dehumanizing stereotypes that make possible the resort to forms of coercion or violence otherwise unthinkable. This pattern, first fully apparent in relations with blacks and native Americans, continues to govern American dealings with "Third World" peoples.

***

The paternalism and contempt evident in the Vietnam "adventure" testifies to the continuing influence of a culture-bound, color-conscious world view that still positions nations and peoples in a hierarchy defined at the extremes by civilization and barbarism, modernity and tradition. It renders us sympathetic to forward-looking Israelis, seen largely as European, at loggerheads with swarthy, bearded, polygamous, fanatical Arabs. It supports empathy for civilized white South Africans rather than a black underclass barely removed from their "primitive" tribal origins. We wring our hands over repression of Soviet-dominated Eastern Europe, while the continuing plight of the native peoples of the Americas—of dark skin and peculiar habits—could for all the attention it gets in the United States be a problem on some yet undiscovered planet.[2]

The American refusal to accept the legitimacy of spheres of influence, to tolerate social revolutions, and to respect cultural patterns fundamentally divergent from our own has carried a price tag. One part of the bill must be calculated in terms of the collapse of American reform movements. In the competition for limited national resources and psychic energy, the protagonists of global greatness promising a better ordered, more liberal, and hence more secure world have repeatedly prevailed over their domestic-oriented opponents. Progressivism, whether defined as a political outlook, a national movement, or a political program, was quickly eclipsed once the United States entered World War I. In the late 1930s Mr. New Deal made way for Mr. Win-the-War as a growing preoccupation with international crises sealed the fate of Roosevelt's already floundering reform program. Lyndon Johnson launched his Great Society in 1964 in response to a pent-up demand for change, only to have Vietnam steal the money and erode the public and Congressional support needed to keep reform a going concern.

The lesson is clear: by attempting to honor the claims the world ostensibly makes on us, an activist foreign policy diminishes our capacity for domestic renewal. Such a foreign policy diverts us from the public issues raised by rapid technological, economic, and social change. It also devours the funds essential to improving the quality of our lives, whether measured in terms of health, education, environment, or the arts. Currently more than half of the federal budget is committed to international programs and military operations past, present, and future. The pursuit of greatness reflected in those figures severely compromises the stewardship of our domestic affairs and imposes costs in socially inequitable and politically irresponsible ways. To serve their ideological vision policymakers, comfortable in their affluence, have channeled national resources abroad to the detriment of both their less comfortable countrymen and future generations....

***

In evaluating the costs of particular foreign policies the public in a democracy serves as the ultimate arbiter. The role of arbiter is, however, one the public is seemingly ill equipped to fill. Polling data has long suggested that the mass public is ignorant of international affairs....

The concomitant to this ignorance on major international questions is, the polls reveal, an intolerance of ambiguous policy, an impatience with complicated, long-term solutions to difficult policy problems, and deep divisions over how to handle major commitments that run into serious, unexpected difficulties.

Precisely because of these traits and the suspicion that many Americans are at heart isolationist, policymakers have been reluctant to make the public a genuine partner in policymaking or to risk open and vigorous debate. Dean Acheson revealed the underlying mistrust felt by other post-World War II influentials when he observed in a fit of candor, "If you truly had a democracy and did what the people wanted, you'd go wrong every time."[3] Policymakers have instead preferred to exploit the tendency of the electorate to take at face value official estimates of the world scene and to withhold information likely to excite popular isolationism or diminish the likelihood of getting the national resources essential to realizing their vision of national security.

***

Much of the power that foreign-policy ideology retains—as well as much of the difficulty reformers will encounter in combatting it—can be traced to the intimate connection between that ideology and American nationalism. Core foreign-policy ideas emerged and gained focus in the context of a prolonged struggle to identify and promote a single, coherent notion of American purpose and character. Viewed in this light those ideas are expressions of a civic religion formulated to hold an ethnically, racially, regionally, and religiously diverse country together.

***

Domestic trends over the [nineteenth] century have accentuated this nationalist function of foreign policy. In contrast to domestic issues, which have an inherent tendency to be divisive, foreign policy has the potential to promote solidarity in the face of a common external problem or danger. As politics at home has become increasingly dominated by the seemingly petty, at times even sordid, squabbling among competing interest groups, foreign affairs has retained a nobility and grandeur appropriate for the expression of national purpose. Consequently, a single-minded foreign policy has provided a symbolic counterweight to a pluralistic domestic political system that, in the exasperated words of one recent president, seems to involve nothing more than "handing out goodies."[4] Moreover, foreign-policy ideas have offered a sense of continuity for a nation apparently in constant flux, a steady set of reference points for nationalists hard pressed to find a solid, unchanging, inspiring core of Americanism at home. Little wonder, then, that the enunciation of a nationalist foreign policy has proven irresistible to leaders wishing to rally the electorate while simultaneously appearing to stand "above politics."

***

The tendency for policy to assimilate nationalist ideas and then to deal with the world in terms of those ideas is by no means a monopoly of Americans. Indeed, it is a commonplace, perhaps even universal, phenomenon in international relations. The parallels between the late nineteenth-century British conception of imperial mission and the American views treated in this volume are so obvious as to need no elaboration....

The impulse to deny our own deeply nationalist ideological outlook and, even more, to fail to see the parallels with other nationalisms can itself be traced to one of the more pronounced features of American nationalism itself: its strong millennial strain. That strain has cast and kept the nation in the role of a redeemer bearing an extraordinary obligation to all humanity. Thomas Paine, in placing within the grasp of Americans the prospect of creating the world anew, and John Adams, in making the United States no ordinary nation but one "destined in future history to form the brightest or the blackest page," gave voice to this view that was to prevail in nationalist thinking.[5]

Americans increasingly understood their redemptive role in active, missionary terms rather than merely passive and exemplary ones. They were saviors with a duty to reach out to enslaved and backward peoples. By the early twentieth century Wilson was not alone in seeing the national duty in terms of creating a just international order, altogether new and morally superior to the corrupt system it would displace. The dream of global renovation, sustained by the time-tested jeremiad and appropriately adorned by occasional references to Paine, continued to move twentieth-century Americans. Their duty was clear. Mankind groaning in bondage cried for liberation. The forces of evil were on the march. World peace hung in the balance. Time for action was short.

A foreign policy whose costs are high yet whose guiding ideas are intertwined with American nationalism confronts us with the contemporary dilemma that the critics have thus far played down. How do we reconcile our sense of nationhood with an enlightened foreign policy? We are thrust toward one horn of the dilemma if we take as our first principle that nationalism is a force for ill, so pernicious in its effects on humanity that a sane policy must work to shake free of its influence. Thorstein Veblen spoke eloquently for those who take this first position. "Born in iniquity and conceived in sin, the spirit of nationalism has never ceased to bend human institutions to the service of dissension and distress. In its material effects it is altogether the most sinister as well as the most imbecile of all institutional encumbrances that have come down out of the old order."[6] A foreign policy no longer chained to our current tribal misconceptions and vaulting ambition might well be a better policy. However—and this is the crux of the matter—it would also be policy without any supporting ideological base....

***

Refashioning the nationalist base so that it will support a new, more prudent and restrained American policy would require a twin effort. The less daunting half of that effort would involve cross-cultural education. By exposing Americans to the yawning gap between our own national experience and ideals and those of most of the other inhabitants of the globe, we might curb the arrogant and ethnocentric impulses evident in our long-standing views on international affairs. While it must be conceded that exposure to other cultures might stimulate an ugly intolerance rather than greater empathy or understanding, that risk is easy to accept when the alternative is to acquiesce in the current state of popular ignorance about the world. A more cosmopolitan view might help dampen our nationalist fervor and promote tolerance for ways of life markedly different from our own. An America alive both to the universal quest for community, security, and purpose and to the many different roads others might take in pursuit of these goals might feel more at ease in the world and with itself.[7]

***

If education can serve on one side as a check on the old foreign-policy ideology and its recent accretions, republicanism offers a source of inspiration for the other, more formidable task of creating a base of support for a new orientation in foreign policy. The crucial step here involves resuscitating a strain of republican thinking strong early in American history but since the late nineteenth century fallen into eclipse, ignored or rejected for its insistence on defining American greatness in terms of perfecting liberty at home rather than promoting it abroad.

Central to any new republicanism would have to be the notion that American greatness should be measured against domestic conditions. The question always to ask is how free Americans are and how closely their welfare is attended to. In relation to the world, republicanism places the United States in the role of a model, not a molder. By better arranging our own affairs Americans can serve as an inspiration to others to win and preserve freedom. Not all nations will respond, and among those who do some will lack the resolve or internal circumstances essential to success. Americans cannot be indifferent witnesses to the fate of freedom abroad, but neither can we impose liberty without doing harm to ourselves and without violating the right of others to make their own choices, whether for good or ill.

...John Quincy Adams eloquently stressed the limits historical experience set for a republican foreign policy. While proclaiming the cause of freedom and cheering on those who struggled for it, America should not go roaming overseas "in search of monsters to destroy." His warning against the United States violating that rule still deserves a respectful hearing.

> By once enlisting under other banners than her own, were they even the banners of foreign independence, she would involve herself beyond the power of extrication, in all the wars of interest and intrigue, of individual avarice, envy, and ambition, which assume the colors and usurp the standard of freedom. The fundamental maxims of her policy would insensibly change from *liberty to force....* She might become the dictatress of the world. She would he no longer the ruler of her own spirit.[8]

Much in our recent experience bears out the insights of the early republicans and the repeated warnings of their disciples as they fought unsuccessfully against an activist foreign policy. Abroad the United States has assumed a position of imperial dimensions. There is no other adjective to apply to a nation that has come to hold substantial control over the fate of a great number of other nations. As with any empire, our intentions are benevolent; our interests are far-flung and interdependent; and our mechanisms of control are as diverse as the nations that we have brought within our sway. One student of the Roman Empire has written of it thus:

> There was no corner of the known world where some interest was not alleged to be in danger or under actual attack. If the interests were not Roman, they were those of Rome's allies; and if Rome had no allies, then allies would be invented. When it was utterly impossible to contrive such an interest—why, then it was the national honor that had been insulted.... Rome was always being attacked by evil-minded neighbors....[9]

It is easy to recognize in this portrait more than a faint resemblance of ourselves.

Americans have long fancied themselves unique on precisely this point, that other, less enlightened nations might embrace the goals and tools of empire, but not the United States. To accept the republican contention that we have evolved into precisely what we thought we were the antithesis of should arm us with a degree of historical perspective. Only thus armed can we hope to reverse the drift from our early national vision and undo the serious self-deception we have, in the process, worked on ourselves.

Pericles, addressing downhearted Athenians in the midst of the Peloponnesian War, observed, "You cannot decline the burdens of empire and still expect to share its honors."[10] Americans still stalking greatness would well to ponder the converse: with the glories of empire come its costs. Those doleful symptoms of empire anticipated by republicans are evident in the rise of an imperial presidency; the economic distortions, drains, and long-term indebtedness associated with preparing for and fighting our wars; the rise of bureaucratic and industrial fiefdoms resistant to policy change and popular control; the encroachment on civil liberties; and the increase in government secrecy....

***

A foreign policy informed by republican values would not be a vehicle for the pursuit of national greatness abroad but a buffer against outside shocks and threats to our pursuit of greatness at home. It would have to be guided above all by the recognition that Americans can work toward a just, equitable society only by restraining the impulse toward global reform. A world that is resistant to our ministrations is also infinitely capable of consuming resources desperately needed at home.

Fashioning a new policy will prove a formidable task. It will mean tailoring our list of regional commitments and expensive client states to conform to demonstrable security needs.[11] It will mean accepting the limits of our ability as a nation to transform a world prone to violence, chaos, exploitation, brutality, and oppression. It will mean breaking out of the vicious cycle of suspicion with the Soviet Union and, under the compelling threat of mutual annihilation, finding ground for mutual accommodation. It will mean perhaps above all fashioning a fresh conceptual basis, a new ideology, for American foreign policy that is both acceptable to the public and comprehensible to our allies. It will *not* mean—and this deserves emphasis—the triumph of isolationism, if that term is taken to mean a refusal to take an interest in the workings of the wider world. Even though embarked on a more prudent international course, the United States will still have political friends and foes, will continue as an important player in the global economy, and will remain in the mainstream of the transnational flow of technology, ideas, and people.

Those who embrace this...republican alternative are launched on an experiment whose success is far from assured and indeed whose consequences, it must in candor be admitted, cannot be entirely or clearly foreseen. Once again we would do well to listen to Pericles, who warned his countrymen as they wavered on the edge of retreat from empire, "to recede is no longer possible....For what you hold is, to speak somewhat plainly, a tyranny; to take it perhaps was wrong, but to let it go is unsafe."[12] Retreat to safer ground will not be easy. Even a narrowed definition of American policy objectives will leave ample room for disagreement from moment to moment over the course of action that best serves American interests. A fresh approach can supply a general policy orientation biased toward a calculated restraint, but it cannot supply, any more than the old verities could, detailed solutions to a host of ever-present problems. The collision of opinion that is inescapably a part of making policy will be compounded by the need, initially at least, to reappraise inherited commitments. In some cases unwanted or unjustified responsibilities will have to be balanced against the possible harm extrication may do to the consensus at home or to the countries directly involved.

Notes

1. Walter Lippmann, *The Cold War: A Study in U.S. Foreign Policy* (New York, 1972), p. 50.

2. Gallup polls asking for approval ratings of various countries, attitudes toward marriage between whites and nonwhites, and even the nationality of the most beautiful women provide evidence for the hardihood of the old racial hierarchy from the late 1930s down to the beginning of the 1980s. See George H. Gallup, *The Gallup Poll: Public Opinion, 1935–1971* (New York, 1972), 1:54, 126, 167, 2:1464–65, 3:2168, 2304; Gallup, *The Gallup Poll: Public Opinion, 1972–1977* (Wilmington, Del., 1978), 1: 39–40, 128–29; Gallup, *The Gallup Poll: Public Opinion, 1978* (Wilmington, Del., 1979), p. 218; Gallup, *The Gallup Poll: Public Opinion, 1980* (Wilmington, Del., 1981), pp. 47–49.

3. Dean Acheson quoted in Walter LaFeber, "American Policy-makers, Public Opinion, and the Outbreak of the Cold War, 1945–50," in Yônosuke Nagai and Akira Iriye, eds., *The Origins of the Cold War in Asia* (New York, 1977), p. 60.

4. Carter quoted in Brzezinski, *Power and Principle,* p. 522.

5. Charles Francis Adams, ed., *The Works of John Adams* (Boston, 1850–56), 10:417–18. Anthony D. Smith, *Theories of Nationalism,* 2d ed. (London, 1983), pp. xxv–xxviii, makes the case—contrary to my own position here and that of Ernest Lee Tuveson, *Redeemer Nation: The Idea of America's Millennial Role* (Chicago, 1968), and of Sacvan Bercovitch, *The American Jeremiad* (Madison, Wis., 1978)—that nationalism and millennialism can be related only incidentally.

6. Thorstein Veblen, *Absentee Ownership and Business Enterprise in Recent Times* (New York, 1923), pp. 38–39. Elie Kedourie, *Nationalism* (London, 1960), provides a powerful elaboration of Veblen's indictment.

7. Serious and systematic academic study of foreign cultures developed haltingly in the United States in the 1920s and 1930s and more vigorously since the 1950s, but specialists have, so Robert A. McCaughey contends in his critical *International Studies and Academic Enterprise: A Chapter in the Enclosure of American Learning* (New York, 1984), failed to reach the broader public.

8. John Quincy Adams, address of 4 July 1821, in Walter LaFeber, ed., *John Quincy Adams and American Continental Empire* (Chicago, 1965), pp. 44–46.

9. Joseph Shumpeter, *Imperialism and Social Classes,* trans. Heinz Norden (Cleveland, 1955), p. 51.

10. Thucydides, *The Peloponnesian War,* ii.7.63.

11. Earl C. Ravenal has argued that retrenchment of regional commitments offers the greatest potential for savings. Europe, which will claim $129 billion in the projected 1985 defense budget, can and should do more to defend itself against conventional attack. The defense of Middle East oil, estimated by Ravenal at $47 billion, is another candidate for cuts, since those outlays exceed the possible cost if that oil, constituting less than 2.5 percent of total U.S. energy needs, were to be lost. Still further cuts might be made on the $47 billion allocated to Asia. Ravenal has estimated on the basis of the 1985 budget that $154 billion in savings could be [a]ffected chiefly through scaling back our forward defense in these areas. Ravenal, "The Case for a Withdrawal of Our Forces," *New York Times Magazine,* 6 March 1983; Ravenal, "On Scaling Down Defense Ambitions, *New York Times,* 16 Feb. 1984, p. A27.

12. Thucydides, *The Peloponnesian War,* ii.7.63.

Violence and the Western Political Tradition

Sheldon S. Wolin
Princeton University

In the history of Western political philosophy, several writers have taken the view that the state represents nothing but organized force, a theory whereby the history of Western political institutions is but a chronicle of the several ingenious ways that coercion has been disguised by laws, constitutions, judicial guarantees and civil rights. This conception of the state is at least as old as Thrasymacus's assertion of it in Plato's *Republic*. It reappears in Bodin in the sixteenth century, Marx in the nineteenth, and in the works of the greatest sociologist of our century, Max Weber. We cannot pause to criticize this view, but only to point out that force and violence are not always identical, although the two may share certain common attributes. As does force, violence implies the application of power over unwilling objects, but, once this has been stated, the differences between the two begin to crowd in on our attention.

* * *

Historical development has not always taken counsel from philosophers, and is not surprising that the relationship between the state and violence has owed rather less to theories than to the steady and unrelenting effort of rulers, or their agents, to establish a monopoly over the instruments of violence. Following the slow breakdown of the Roman Empire after the fifth century A.D., a complex and infinite fragmentation of power occurred. This condition persisted into the Middle Ages; everywhere in Europe the primary concern of political authorities was to maintain and, if possible, extend the precarious reign of law and order. This required an incessant campaign to eliminate the pockets of violence throughout Western-Europe. The construction of the national, centralized state was the result an unrelenting war, carried on over centuries, to divest local and parochial magnates of their authority to apply violence in their own bailiwicks. Feudalism had been not only a system of land tenure and a status structure of rights and duties but also a decentralized system for maintaining order. Feudal lords were expected to enforce law, allot punishment, levy taxes and maintain their own fighting forces....

The next important phase in the development of the theory and practice of violence was the attempt to delimit the exercise of force within the boundaries of national societies and, simultaneously, to eliminate the unpredictable element that seemed stubbornly to cling to all political power. For convenience, this phase may be called the Age of Liberal (or Constitutional) Democracy. It begins approximately in 1640, when the forces of parliamentarism and Puritanism first challenged the monarchy in England.

* * *

The theory and practice of constitutional democracy have signified a concerted effort to restrict the application of violence by setting defined limits to power, by insisting on the observance of regularized procedures and by establishing strict methods for rendering those in power accountable for their actions. The paraphernalia of constitutionalism—the rule of law, due process, the separation of powers, checks and balances and the system of individual rights, with its significant emphasis on privileges and "immunities"—have not eliminated power, but they have contributed to its regularization, to eradicating that unpredictable, sheerly destructive quality that epitomizes all violence.

Despite the success of constitutionalism in delimiting the role of violence in political life, the twentieth century has witnessed unprecedented experiments with violence. The number of victims, the magnitude of destruction and the ingenuity of the instruments are without historical parallel. This is the century of secret police, concentration camps, gas chambers, labor camps and the calculated "liquidation" of specified classes, races and whole populations.

* * *

Classical thought of the fifth and fourth century B.C. abhorred any act that exceeded customary standards of moderation, or the mean. Accordingly, an act of violence was considered a breach of those natural and moral limits that the good man was duty-bound to observe. The finest expression of this position was the work of the political philosopher Aristotle, who had tutored Alexander the Great. Few military conquerors could equal Alexander's record of devastation or match his genius for the organization of force and violence. Aristotle pondered long about this new breed of man who went about destroying old societies and creating new ones, who somehow combined a genius for smashing with an uncommon skill at uniting diverse peoples. What was the relation, Aristotle wondered, between the impulse for destruction and the traditional political impulse toward order. Beneath Alexander's restless urge for domination Aristotle perceived an unnatural passion that perverted the noble calling of the *politikos* or statesman. Mastery, Aristotle insisted in his *Politics* (VII. ii. 1324b 32), must never be confused with true statesmanship; there is something deeply wrong when a profession such as statesmanship is so practiced as to countenance deliberate killing and needless destruction as the legitimate measures of a skilled art. The unprecedented success of a conqueror does not place his acts beyond the limits set by nature and morality (VII. ii. 1324b 26). It is fundamentally wrong and unnatural that the conqueror employs violence to degrade a particular species, the political animal, which nature had not intended for domination or subjection. "One does not hunt men to furnish a banquet or a festival: one hunts what is meant to be hunted for that purpose…" (VI. ii. 1324b 38–41).

The conviction that natural limits to violence existed and that violence was inherently wrong[1] persisted to the sixteenth century. The same cultural and historical forces that shattered the Aristotelian-Thomistic view of the cosmos and turned to reconstructing it in the name of mathematics and science were simultaneously at work in the field of political theory. Machiavelli was to political theory what Galileo was to modern physics, a dispeller of illusions who passionately wished to confront things "as they really were." Once Machiavelli's *Prince* achieved notoriety, the whole course of political theory was changed. For our purposes the most important change affected the outlook of the political theorists, who ceased to view violence as an expression of passion. They sought instead to treat it as a measured application of force, the study of which should aspire to be a precise science and the actual exercise of which should be in the hands of men of cool and calculating temperaments. Machiavelli had hoped that a true "economy of violence" could be achieved—a system of maxims and rules of action that would assist rulers in adjusting the application of violence to the precise requirements of a situation. If the exercise of violence could be invested with truly surgical precision, it might be possible to confine injury, death and destruction to an absolute minimum. As envisaged by Machiavelli, the science of violence presupposed an extraordinary detachment on the part of both the theoretician and the political actor, a detachment insulating them from contact with the pain of those who were the objects of violence. This outlook was present in Machiavelli's *The Prince,*—chapter VIII; there he distinguishes between "good" and "bad" forms of cruelty, counseling that a ruler should prepare an inventory of necessary injuries before he seizes power and then quickly commit them so that his subjects "may taste their bitterness but a short time." Benefits, on the other hand, should be doled out slowly so that subjects will live in constant hope of future enjoyments and hence be submissive.

These changing attitudes toward violence were accompanied by still another, albeit quieter and less spectacular revolution in thought, namely a drastic reduction in the estimate of what force and compulsion could achieve. Although there were exceptions,[2] the major political theorists of the seventeenth and eighteenth century, those who left the strongest imprint on later thinking, believed unanimously that mankind could not be improved by force. Citizens could not be terrorized into virtue or saintliness, nor could societies be forcibly transformed into prosperous and benevolent utopias. Although such theorists as Harrington, Locke, Montesquieu, Rousseau and Jefferson disagreed on a large number of political matters, they all agreed that violence could not regenerate man or society. This conclusion may seem a considerable advance over the position maintained by religious fanatics of the sixteenth and seventeenth century who had proclaimed the purifying effects of violence on the soul.

A more revealing contrast is provided by comparing the older views of Augustine or Plato with those of the modern writers mentioned above. Both the great Bishop of Hippo and the Greek philosopher justified the application of force to induce correct belief, yet a careful examination of both arguments shows that, however deplorable the policy they advocated, neither writer believed that force could actually create belief. Each believed that man was endowed with a nature, and that that nature ought to be perfected. And because each believed so profoundly in the perfectibility of man or, in Christian terms, his salvation, each was prepared to countenance what each had plainly and publicly rejected on numerous occasions, the use of force to correct belief. Both vacillated on the issue because they were firmly convinced that any exercise of violence constituted a threat to the inherent structure of man and that any sustained program of violence risked reducing man to a dehumanized and brutalized condition.[3]

But, beginning with Hobbes in the seventeenth century, the assumption that man had a structure and that this structure was known began to weaken. . . .

Modern political thought has largely surrendered the conception of society informed by a natural structure. Beginning with Machiavelli and extending through Hobbes and Locke, gaining additional momentum from the French Revolution and the revolutionary movement of the nineteenth and twentieth century, the conviction has grown that society is an artifact, a pragmatic creation that men can design to meet their needs or wishes; there is no inherent structural principle in society standing in the way of what men want.[4]

* * *

Finally, the whole notion of limit as a restraint on the violence of international conflicts has been all but destroyed. As has already been noted, the Greeks had rejected the notion that a conqueror could utilize any means of force against the enemy. The early Christians expressed the notion of limit by trying to establish a distinction between the just and unjust war. Our own age has obliterated all of these distinctions, first, by ignoring the distinction between civilians and soldiers, home front and battle front, and, second, by tacitly abolishing all limits to the amount of force allowable in gaining victory. If Hiroshima is the symbol of limitless violence, it is not the *ultima Thule* beyond which no state will press its claim of justifiable violence.

Today little vitality remains in the idea that force is justifiable only to the extent that it is used to protect the common interest or well-being of society. This norm has ceased to operate as a limit because the "interest of society" no longer coincides with either the geographic boundaries of society or the foreign commitments of a society. Today the claim to use violence to protect society has been extended far beyond the borders of national society and far beyond the traditional meaning of foreign commitments. Those claims now literally approach infinity. President Kennedy proclaimed that the space program of the nation was "firmly based upon the awareness that space competence is as essential for national security as it is for national growth."[5] The redefinition of national interest to include outer space inevitably includes the claim that violence in interstellar regions is justifiable in defending and advancing that interest. And, in the same way that national or even international boundaries no longer set limits to the justifiable province of violence, so the older belief that the application of force ought to be directed at lawbreakers or at an easily definable "enemy" has also been replaced by a notion that is limitless.

In the past, the idea of force was based on the assumption that those who should be punished or even destroyed could be isolated—singled out from the rest of humanity. It is now accepted as rational political thinking to contemplate the possible destruction of all, or most, of the inhabitants of the globe and to project violence in a way unparalleled in human thought except in theological terms. It has often given sceptics wry amusement that the God of the Calvinists and the Augustinians should have been so omnipotent as to be able to punish Adam's original sin by transmitting it as an inherited and ineradicable taint to all his progeny from generation to generation. Yet the genetic destruction potentially present in modern instruments of violence makes today's political man as omnipotent as the God of Christian theology. Man, too, can inflict a taint on generations yet unborn; he, too, can create an apocalypse that will render the earth uninhabitable. It remains to be seen whether he can match God's promise that the Day of Judgment will find the earth uninhabitable for the sinners alone.

Notes

1. This is in contrast to the superficial view often encountered in contemporary discussions; this claims that power itself is not bad, it all depends on how it is used. The difficulty is that this assertion presupposes a moral judgment, namely, that power is neutral. This cannot be allowed, for, as soon as one abandons high abstractions and deals with concrete instances, it becomes obvious that power always means the ability to coerce or to apply control over others. In technical language, the concept of power "contains" the element of compulsion; we may disagree about its value or use, but it is not neutral.

2. These exceptions were almost wholly religious fanatics, such as the Fifth Monarchy Men in England. After 1650 they had ceased to be a significant factor in European politics.

3. Augustine's views were most carefully worked out in his *Epistles,* 87, 93, 97, 185. See also J. N. Figgis, *Political Aspects of Augustine's A City of God,* London, 1921, Lectures III, IV; *La doctrine politique d'Augustin,* Paris, 1927, pp. 330 ff., views see *Laws X.* 907DC912D.

4. The clearest expression of this viewpoint is to be found in Hobbes' *Leviathan,* especially the Introduction.

5. *New York Times.* Feb. 1, 1962, p. 3.

War and Peace in European Consciousness: Images of Past Conflict in Forging a Transnational Identity

Nigel Young[1]
Colgate University

The themes discussed in this essay derive in part from a reaction to feelings of frustration engendered by the spate of recent articles, mainly by political scientists in the USA[2]—and widely discussed there, speculating on the future of Europe after the cold war—and in particular the prospects for peace, and the role of war preparation in 'keeping' that peace. I must confess at the outset to some feeling of dismay at the predominance in these pieces of arid postulations about systemic interactions of states in which, even in the events of 1989, people, culture, social movements (not least the role of the artist) have little, or no, place.

For example, in the formulations of John Mearsheimer ('Back to the Future') and John Mueller ('Retreat from Doomsday')[3] as well as Robert Jervis and John Gaddis[4] (and their critics), there is little place for creativity or social action in their paradigm; social concerns are subservient to military considerations, the keys to war and peace lie more in the structure of the international system than in the nature of the individual states. Domestic factors are less important than the character and application of military power.

Yet we live in a time when the possibilities of the emergence of a major new state are being analysed, and when the collapse of other states are occurring or indeed recurring. Most discussions, for example, of the emergence of a new European state are couched in the language of political economy, interstate political relations or at best the culture of national identity. In the USA the idea of a role for longer term historical developments, for example the growth of a European identity, are not taken very seriously; some recent European work on nationalism, like A.D. Smith's recent work in Britain, does confront these issues, although still within a I real-political paradigm.[5]

I will in the following, be more concerned with shared symbols and collective representations, especially of war and peace in the common European memory, of how these are expressed culturally, and what these may signify for our future in terms of inter-state or intra-European, conflict and the role of cross boundary interactions.

Many, if not all, states have emerged through war, many state boundaries exist because that is where armies stopped or wars ended. Indeed I share a view of the state as founded on force and largely maintained by force. Nevertheless, I want to suggest here that if we are witnessing the creation of a European state, it too is related to the experience of war—to the *memory* of European 'civil-wars', which have been waged for more than 500 years. In other words, in this case the relationship of state and war, and indeed peace, is a mediated one. This time it

Nigel Young, "War and Peace in European Consciousness." Reprinted with permission from the editors of *Essays on Peace: Paradigms for Global Order* edited by Michael Salla, Walter Tenetto, & Enrique Martínez.

is through the shared representation or imagery of war, past, present and future, and it is through memories and mutual experiences that we can begin to envisage a common Continental consciousness, which is of import as part of a revival of a supra-national, cultural identity.

Before pursuing this argument further, it is important to make two points: first, as A.J.P. Taylor observed in his famous essay which introduces *From Sarajevo to Potsdam*,[6] Europe, in 1914, was one 'single civilised community,' one could travel freely, its boundaries had become less and less important (no passports were required) and despite linguistic differences it had a common culture, and common political forums. The boundaries of Europe were the frontiers of the Russian and Ottoman Empires. Hence, the visions of Liberal and Socialist internationalists could appear realistic.

Second, between the 1880s and 1914, peace and anti-war movements, internationalist in orientation, were stronger than at any time before (and arguably since);[7] a whole range of peace related institutions, ideas and projects were flourishing up to the outbreak of war; they were drawn from different traditions and sectors of society.

Thus my thesis is not so much that the new European state is being, or will be, created by war directly, but that, as a result of war, and the threat of war, (e.g. deterrence) there exists an underlying anti-militarism largely latent or subconscious—which contributes to an integrating impulse. Some of this is new, and some dates from pre-1914 traditions, but a sentiment exists nevertheless, that can be tapped both by social movements and by the creative arts.

This peace sentiment rooted in the complex and often ambiguous imagination and ambivalent symbolism of war and peace in the European mind, is one which draws especially on twentieth-century experience and has, with the rise of nuclear weapons, become once more significant.

This anti-war attitude, coupled with the fear of, and (at times) fascinated obsession with war in the past eighty years, has crystallised culturally. It is a flower that has grown alongside the continuing glorification of war (militarism) which marked the Fascist era in particular. Despite the resurgent nationalism and militarist particularism that is still to be seen virulently alive on the margins of Europe, this emergent consciousness, if harnessed creatively, has become both a potential and actual unifying factor for Europeans tired of internecine strife.

Given that of almost 106 million people who are estimated to have so far died *directly* as a consequence of war in the 20th century (i.e., combat-deaths or victims of bombing), at least an estimated 67 million have been *Europeans*,[8] the prominence of war as a theme in the European subconscious would be hardly surprising; and given furthermore, that in each of the three preceding centuries it is estimated that less than 6 million Europeans died (3.3m, 5.2m, and 5.5m) as direct victims of war, the European experience of the twentieth century is unique. Death and suffering, while it cannot be quantified as a single experience (arguing for the use of the singular here), inhabit the soil and culture of a nation in unfathomable ways.

In the 1980s, despite the rapid militarisation of the Third World, more than 70% of the world's armaments were still on European soil. The *Disasters of War*, as Goya called them, in his images of the Guerilla struggle in Spain, have been to modem Europe what famine or disease (as well as political repression) have been (and still are) to the developing world, both a scourge and an ever-present threat.

For a long time *peace* in Europe was the punctuation of war by various state centred, multi lateral treaties, Westphalia, Vienna, Versailles, Potsdam, each one with a gesture towards internationalism, international law, the League, the UN, or towards European integration. But none of these treaties was sustained by a 'peace culture'.

The European experience, especially in the twentieth century has to be judged as novel. It was, as Modris Ecksteins argues in *Rites of Spring*,[9] fundamentally altered by the 'Great War'. This European consciousness, in other words, is reshaped by a modern experience that is different, in kind and degree, both from its own past and the experience of other continents.

The most obvious contrast is with that of the United States whose population, last experienced war of any scale on its own soil, including the destruction of one or two cities, in the 1860s. Since then, its citizens have not been bombed or their country occupied; they have been insulated from the direct effects of war unless they were in the armed services.

It is notable how American students who visit the sites and venues of the disasters mentioned before or look at the war monuments of European cities, remark consistently, 'so many memorials to war, so many museums about war; Europe is obsessed with war'. (There are now even more such venues, at places like Caen, Remagem, Berlin, Verdun where we see the revival of 'peace museums' in recent years.[10]

One other way in which at least Western Europe is different from other continents is that so-called 'nations' fitted into their bounded, territorial states more or less, with a few significantly, uncomfortable minorities who can at other times and places be 'ethnically cleansed.' Partly as result of this, Nationalism came to be seen as a vehicle of progress and liberation, giving an ideological framework for the advance of citizenship rights and legal protection as well as welfare, education and an ordered society. Threats to the nation were a threat to all the advances made in the name of that unit, whether real or imaginary.

Perception of the problematic character of nationalism—whether in Sarajevo in 1914, or Sarajevo in 1993 often had to wait for the killing to begin. Settling old scores in the name of the patrie, a contemporary version of the blood feud is collectivised blood sacrifice. To non-state nationalisms, whether in Ireland or the Balkans it is these mythologised memorie of old wrongs which often serve to keep the struggle alive. It is also true that from Wales to (currently) Kosovo—as well as in Eastern Europe in the 1980s, one can find nationalist struggles which are or have been nonviolent.[11] But the view that war (or the memory of war) is itself both a cause of social injustice, and further war—and that as an institution, war is itself a form of social injustice, is a less widespread realisation.

In what follows I shall argue that the transcendence of this inflated *nationalism* has been made more often by poets, filmmakers, writers and artists, than politicians—or political scientists. Rosenberg's poems, Picasso's outraged scream against the bombing of a city in 1936 his painting, *Guernica;* E.M. Remarque's novel *All Quiet on the Western Front,* Pabst's film *Kameradschaft*[12] (Comradeship), are all illustrations of the kind of transcendence I have in mind, as are examples, I shall mention of film and creative works on the holocaust, such as C. Lanzman's *Shoah* or A. Resnais's *Night and Fog.*

The creation of a common European culture has to be, and to some extent has been, built from consciously transnational elements beyond nationalist historiography, as a peace culture arising from below. Even when drawn from high culture these elements are firm expressions of civil society, not of the state. This must be the cultural or human dimension; for the Helsinki process 'part two' was not by governmental anschluss but by allowing 'all power to the imagination' and to the language of the artists and poets or careerists.

A British television channel gave major programming time in 1992 to a series of broadcasts on war (and peace) ranging from interviews with veterans to the screening of anti-war classics, and included art, music, poetry and literature of war—as a lead up to the Armistice Day commemorations in November. I doubt this would have been possible twenty or even ten years ago and is symptomatic of the shift I am describing.

It is arguable that this development is part of an identification not so much of a European consciousness beyond frontiers, but of a human one. However, the experience from which it draws, is largely a European one (even if nuclear holocaust would hardly respect continental boundaries). Alain Resnais links such themes in memories of place in World War in his film *Hiroshima mon amour*. The final words of the two main characters, a Japanese architect and a woman who had an affair with a German soldier in Nevers, her hometown, are: 'you are Hiroshima', … 'you are Nevers'.

This theme of a common humanity achieves some wonderful moments in European Film, Art and Literature: In Otto Dix's picture 'Flanders 1917' we seem to be looking at the same men depicted in Wilfred Owen's poem, *Dulce et decorum est*—the 'universal soldiers!' 'Old beggars under sacks, knock-kneed, coughing like hags.'[13] So far from the heroic idols of military presentation.

The ability to look beyond both the hero and the enemy image is articulated in Virginia Woolf's essay, *Thoughts on Peace in an Air Raid*,[14] as she considers a young German pilot, trapped in his machine (the man and the machine above London during the Blitz of 1940). The relationship is, even with the threat of death, a warm and sharing one, a thing of unity.

In his 1917 poem 'Break of Day in the Trenches', Isaac Rosenberg depicts his dawn encounter with the sardonic, transnational Rat:

> Droll Rat... They would shoot you if they knew
> your cosmopolitan sympathies.[15]

The Rat is not trapped like the poet, he can travel from trench to trench feeding across the 'sleeping green' of no man's land on British and German, French and Belgian corpses without national distinction.

> Now you have touched this English hand
> You will do the same to a German.

This experience of 'the other' is also dramatically symbolised in Wilfred Owen's poem 'Strange meeting'[16] with the enemy, 'the subterranean shadow in a dugout':

> I am the enemy you killed, my friend (As Jon Silkin points out Owen's original lines were ... 'I am a German conscript and your friend.' More sharply political but less universal).[17]

In film, the famous and wonderfully filmed mine sequence, in Pabst's expressionist masterpiece of the late twenties, *Kameradschaft*, depicts German miners who form a team to rescue trapped French miners from a deep shaft after an explosion under the Franco-German border, an analogue of the trenches of course. When the Germans break through the old escape shaft to rescue the French, the exhausted miners see their saviours in full rescue gear as attacking soldiers, and Pabst introduces the imagery of a German attack seen from a French trench in the recent war.

There is a moment in Remarque's novel[18] when the German, Paul, finds himself sheltering alone in a shell crater with Gerard Duval, the French printer, who is badly wounded but not yet dead. Paul stabs him but then alternates between impatience with his long death and pleading with him not to die. Paul's identification, having tried to kill him, and then promises to the dying Duval are a moving indictment of such confrontation between ordinary men (civilians in uniform). Like 'the other' in Wilfred Owen's 'Strange meeting,' Duval is the enemy that Paul has killed, and he becomes in death a friend.

Such liberal, pacifist or bourgeois sympathies, the pity, the empathy, the cosmopolitanism, all were anathema to the Nazis (and indeed to some of the literary figures who were close to Fascism at the time). In 1930, Goebbels and a gang of cronies went to a Berlin Cinema to break up a showing of *All Quiet on the Western Front*, because it was seen as a pacifist and internationalist work. When they came to power, the Nazis closed down the peace museum in Berlin with its anti-war displays for the same reason—it has recently been reestablished.

Hitler's NeuEuropa was to be created through the barrel of a gun; ironically the vision of our New European Peace order has been made possible in part, I believe, by the tips of Nuclear Missiles, concentrating our minds from the late 50's to the 80's on what unites us: Europeans as peoples living on a potential atomic battlefield; anti-militarist symbolism became an essential part of the response to such a holocaust. One of the first major Nuclear Disarmament posters in the Europe of the 1950s was a Kathe Kollwitz poster of a mother sheltering two children.[19] Kollwitz lost her son and grandson in the two wars.

The *Common European Home,* first promoted by the peace movement, a continent free of nuclear missiles, was a vision that encompassed the larger Europe Atlantic to the Urals, not NATO Europe. That vision, more populist than earlier Peace plans (such as Unden or Rapacki), still needed a peace culture that crossed boundaries. The persistent power of the 1914-18 imagery of the trenches, like the Cold War "Iron Curtain," the Berlin Wall, was an affront to European society, another militarised scar across European civilisation. Both were in part a caricature of national borders, stretching for hundreds of miles from the Channel to Switzerland.

"All Quiet on the Western Front" was in fact the phrase frequently used in dispatches from the front and often denotes the tacit truce observed between the occupants of the lines of trenches[20] from the sea, through Flanders and Picardy, through Artois and the Champagne; and to the mountains.

Like critics such as Paul Fussell before him,[21] Ecksteins argues that along this line an old chivalry died in 1914-15. Ecksteins even argues that the *Christmas Truce* was only still possible in 1914, but 'Never could there be such innocence'—about war and the state—'again'. However *chivalry* and *fraternisation* are two different things; the latter can be linked to self-interest and survival as much as to 'honour' and 'duty'. Moreover, fraternisation certainly became more difficult on the Western front in 1915-17, but has occurred in other, difficult situations since, and so have acts of war-resistance and refusal of orders (which did occur in the years after 1914), and refusal of military service. Indeed these are a part of many conflicts including the Yugoslav war, which has produced its own crop of draft resisters and draft emigres of various kinds, largely ignored by Western commentators.[22]

What *did* disappear from the stage, with this "advance" of technology, was the type of chivalry associated with the equestrian military icon, the "man-on-horseback." Until the Great War, an aristocratic rider synthesised political, military, class and gender dominance, and symbolised social status for centuries—indeed, perhaps over two millennia, even in periods when it was irrelevant militarily. From the statue of Marcus Aurelius, through Donatello's archetypal warrior, the mounted mercenary (Colleoni in *Venice)* to the French painter, to David's romantic image of 'Napoleon crossing the Alps'—this symbol survives up to the equestrian idols of the late nineteenth and early twentieth century. But deployed in 1914 often as farce, and in 1939 in Poland, as tragedy, the useless cavalry became permanently irrelevant; as war became mass war, it became mechanised and civilianised and thus finally, total. The man on horseback was dismounted, replaced by the Battle Tank.

The Nazis, creating their own codes of military 'honour', and believing that war as an assertion of spirit had to continue, carried the conviction that the internationalism and Pacifism which had also flourished again (in new forms) after 1918, with the growth of new peace organisations were pure anathema to the new Europe which Germany would build.

The Nazis drew very different lessons from the Western Front experience, they agreed that trench warfare had been "decadent" but Germany could become strong again through the continuation of struggle and the brotherhood of the front-soldier, expressing itself eventually in the Blitzkrieg. Here our comic stereotyped image of Hitler, the buffoon is misleading and inadequate. It serves us better to understand that he was not the little coward and bully of the cartoons, but, as Ecksteins emphasises, a lonely man who must have had extraordinary courage, a man who was wounded and gassed, blinded, and won two iron crosses. As a courier from the front trenches he had one of the most dangerous jobs at the front and survived.

At Langemarck in Flanders, where in 1914 the British army (the B.E.F.) butchered the German student battalions—the place where Remarque set 'All

Quiet' (the 'massacre of the innocents'); and, near where Adolf Hitler was gassed, one sees the real result of 'Fruhlungsfeuer' taking place. This moment, in the late Summer of 1914, recurs in Ecksteins' *Rite of Spring*. This is the true birth of modernism; the synthesis of technics and irrationalism. As a result, European culture was quickly derailed into a second war, when one had been quite enough. One should also note here, as Ecksteins points out, how Hitler's own experience of gas warfare was directly linked in his mind after Ypres, to ethnic cleansing. As early as 1922, in *Mein Kampf* he wrote of Gas as an appropriate dose for vermin, and for Hebrews.[23]

Here too at Ypres the twentieth-century M.I.A's were born vast lists of 'missing-in-action' on the Menin gate, at the cemeteries at Paschendele and at Langemarck. Indeed, Hitler portrayed himself as that 'unknown soldier.'

Here one also has to confront the problematic difference of each 'national' memory. The neat white rows of the crosses at Tyne Cot (the large British cemetery at Paschendaele): the stars of David and other insignia for Commonwealth troops sit amongst the crowd, with the Crucifix still dominant. The British cemeteries are antiseptic, almost celebratory—a way of forgetting.

In many ways far more impressive and haunting are the dark and sombre German memorials, these are also above mass graves, of often 40 or more unknown German soldiers in one pit. In the ominous and severe German cemetery at Langemarck, near Ypres, built in Weimar times. Is it the difference between victory and defeat or between two approaches to military death that we are witnessing? The Nazis were able to co-opt that memory of 'sacrifice' in a way that no one else did. They refused to collaborate with the war-graves enterprise of other countries (an international anti-war memorial) using it instead, to kindle the urge to wreak vengeance and retribution.

If there is one factor that should unite Europeans, it is the Holocaust.[24] The destruction was of a whole European people in their midst; while little was done to stop it. Unlike the trench experience of the First World War, the concentration camps represented the military bureaucratic machine turning on civilians—as indeed did the mass bombing raids on Europe (105 tons of TNT dropped on Europe, mostly Germany, for every 1 ton dropped on Britain) in the 1940s.

Memories of the Eastern front, (nearly two million dead at Stalingrad) made nuclear weapons especially terrifying in Europe, yet it is arguable that war had been made to appear obsolescent on a large scale even before the two superpowers occupied Europe with their nuclear missiles after 1945. John Mearsheimer's 'Back to the Future,' written after the Cold War, draws the conclusion (from 40 years of nuclear terror) that a controlled proliferation of nuclear weapons in Europe, rather than their rapid removal, is the way to a stable peace. Clearly the language and the logic of nuclear discourse is one of the challenges to the new image-makers and the cultural creators, whether at Greenham Common or anywhere else; but its paradigm cannot be shared.

Did most of Europe become indeed 'peaceful' because of nuclear weapons, or were they the emblematic seal on the unacceptability of war between the major European states, which the peace movement constantly re-emphasized? John Mueller in 'Retreat from Doomsday' argues that, by 1916, when the war became total, Europe had already seen war as "obsolescent", but still the two wars occurred, and pacifist propaganda of the horrors of war was quite insufficient, even irrelevant. The railway lines that ran into Treblinka and Auschwitz performed a different function from those that had rushed the young student battalions of Remarque's novel to the killing fields around Ypres. But they are all *linked*, and the results were the same: the nameless mechanised slaughter of millions.

If we turn to the memories captured by the British "Imperial War Museum" in London, we find that it too is deeply ambivalent about war and weapons; huge naval guns erupt from the former mental hospital (Bedlam)—inside in the foyer the military bric-a-brac is combined with paintings and displays; the casualty clock downstairs, the 'trench' and 'blitz' experience, and art and displays of an altogether more serious kind, (small displays on Belsen and Hiroshima).[25]

In summary: repossessing the memories and histories that I have touched on here is part of the cultural creation that should inform our work as philosophers and critics, as sociologists and peace researchers; it is no more selective or manipulative than any work of the imagination that is founded on half-obscured truths. It is a critical (peaceful) counter weight to the predominance of Security myths.

For in the very act of creative resistance, including the "mental fight" which Orwell and Woolf (both following William Blake) recommended, we deny passivity and collaboration. We identify with "the other," across inhuman (national) barriers; as Woolf did with that young German airman, or Owen with the enemy in "Strange meeting," or Rosenberg and the rat; like the French and German coal miners in Pabst's film, like Paul and Gerard Duval. One recalls the art of Kathe Kollwitz, ever haunted by the deaths of her son in war, yet universalising her grief and compassion. There is a danger that all this sounds Eurocentric; but Europe and its colonised world has been the great armory and the great "seat of Mars"; the model I have described is an exportable one (and where does anyone agree about Europe's frontiers?)

What I have sketched out is both a transnational and communal memory of resistance and cooperation that is in process,[26] and it involves this identification with our "other," a cultural analog of the socialist internationalism preached before 1914. It is particularly vital for this perspective that the links across frontiers have a rootedness in particular communities and places of belonging, other than the nation state (the great pseudo Community). It presages a Europe of Regions and Communities, rather than nations or states where civilians are no longer victims, and where peace is both real and possible, and where the boundaries of Europe fade away.

The Supreme HQ Allied Powers Europe (SHAPE) used to give away postcards entitled 'the SHAPE of Peace.' Wondering what the shape of Peace was, I was fascinated to learn that it took the form of a row of military honour guards, from the member nations, marching with their standards held aloft.

A First World War buff (also at SHAPE) confided that almost opposite SHAPE HQ—just up the road at Mons, are two plaques, one each side of the road. The first commemorates the first British shots fired in the war by the B.E.F., before its famous retreat in 1914; on the other side (on the wall of a hotel) is a plaque recording the last shots by the allied armies when they reached there again, on Armistice Day, 1918. Four years of internecine slaughter to cross the road!

Whilst it may be true that war in that almost ludicrous 1914 sense is unimaginable, there are few who would contend that major war in Europe was impossible, after all, only a few years ago the idea of Serbians, Croatians and others getting into a real war seemed unthinkable, even to those who visited Yugoslavia regularly. But it may be true that war in the old sense is impossible, at least for Western Europe.

The choice between war and peace, for many Europeans has to some extent come to represent the choice between civilisation and barbarism (as Rosa Luxemburg observed in 1918) as well as life or death, creation and destruction. And to have the choice is dependent on imagining the possibility of a European peace; as I have suggested, creative artists have transcended the mere recording of the horrors of war. It is a matter of will, and of the conscious construction of peace, the sustaining of visions and memories. What we share in that consciousness is the disaster that is, war; we can remember this as fighting the good fight, or as sacrifice and renewal, and as vengeance and assertion, as the Nazis did, or we can draw from these great European traumas a common memory of loss, of destruction, of futile self-inflicted holocausts that destroyed our best Jew and Gentile alike, of an irrational mechanised bloodletting, which the language of political scientists cannot sanitise OR mystify.

Notes

1. This is an edited version of a paper delivered at the Interdisciplinary Forum of Human Studies at the University of Bradford, Jan 1993.

2. Sean M. Lynn-Jones, ed., *The Cold War and After: Prospects for Peace* (Cambridge, Mass: MIT Press, 1991).

3. Both articles appear in Lynn-Jones, *The Cold War and After.*

4. Both articles, Gaddis, 'The Long Peace" & Jervis, "Priorities for Peace: Europe after the Cold War," appear in Lynn-Jones, *The Cold War and After.*

5. Anthony D. Smith, "National identity and the idea of European Unity," *International Affairs* 68:1 (1992) 55-76.

6. 1966.

7. Nigel Young, "Peace Movements in Industrial Societies," *The Quest for Peace,* ed. R. Varynen (London: Sage, 1987).

8. Ruth L. Sivard, *World Military and Social Expenditures* (Washington, DC: World Priorities, 1991).

9. Modris Ecksteins, *Rites of Spring: The Great War and the Birth of Modernism* (Boston 1989).

10. Peter van den Dungen, "Peace Museums," *The World Encyclopedia of Peace,* 4 vols, ed. L. Pauling (Pergamon Press, 1986). Several more such museums are planned in Europe.

11. For an account of the struggles in Kosovo, see Misha Glenny, *The Rebirth of History, Eastern Europe in the Age of Democracy* (London: Penguin, 1990).

12. G. W. Pabst, "Kameradschaft" Nero film, Germany 1931.

13. Reprinted in Brian Gardner, ed., *Up the Line to Death* (Methuen, 1976) p.141.

14. "Thoughts on Peace in an Air Raid," *In Death of a Moth* (Harvest, 1966).

15. Rosenberg, "Break of Day in the Trenches," *Penguin Book of First World War Poetry,* ed. Jon Silkin (Penguin, 1979).

16. Anthologised and discussed in Silkin, *Penguin Book of First World War Poetry,* pp. 34-35, 62-63, 196-98.

17. *Ibid.*

18. *All Quiet on the Western Front.*

19. Catalogue (Berlin: Kathe Kollwitz Collection, 1990).

20. K. Ashworth, "The sociology of trench warfare," *British Journal of Sociology,* 1962.

21. P. Fussell, *The Great War and Modern Memory* (New York: Oxford University Press, 1975).

22. Nigel Young, "War Resistance, State and Society," *War, State and Society* (London: MacMillan, 1984).

23. Claude Lanzmann, "Shoah—An Oral History of the Holocaust", in Eckstein, *Rites of Spring.*

24. *Handbook* (London: Imperial War Museum).

25. *Ibid.*

26. Nigel Young, "War Resistance, State and Society," *War, State and Society* (London: MacMillan, 1984).

On the Causes of War and The Efforts that Failed

Nicholas N. Kittrie
American University, Washington College of Law

The Efforts that have Failed: Lessons of the Twentieth Century

"In ancient times, people were few but wealthy and without strife," claimed Chinese philosopher Han Fei-Tzo in approximately 500 B.C. A contrary view was voiced by English philosopher Thomas Hobbes in 1651 A.D. "The natural condition of mankind," Hobbes wrote in the *Leviathan,* "was one where every man is Enemy to every man…." Despite the many subsequent discoveries and advances in history, archeology and anthropology, we will probably still never know which of the two philosophers—writing two thousand years apart—was right. Yet strife, as all records and other evidence seem to demonstrate, has been man's fate for at least the past four and a half millennia.

Peace's eventual coming of peace had been likewise forecasted, nevertheless, in several writings far back in antiquity, and the hope of peace has never vanished. No classical advocate surpassed the fifth century B.C.'s Biblical Isaiah, who in foretelling "the end of times", painted one of the most renowned of all prophetic visions: "The wolf…shall dwell with the lamb and the leopard shall lie down with the kid; and the calf and the young lion…together; and a little child shall lead them." Possibly still better known is Isaiah's other vivid picture of peace: "They shall beat their swords into plowshares, and their spears into pruning hooks; nation shall not lift up sword against nation, neither shall they learn war any more." Unfortunately, however, the scriptures failed to specify when that blessed era of peace was to commence.

Nevertheless, Europe's Age of Reason brought forth the expectation that reason would provide the appropriate climate for the blossoming of peace. Germany's Immanuel Kant assured his eighteenth century audience that "[p]erpetual peace is no empty idea" and that "the commercial spirit cannot co-exist with war." In the second half of the nineteenth century England's Herbert Spencer, the father of the so designated "social Darwinism," likewise concluded that war had become obsolete in an industrial society. In America, the country's leading nineteenth century moralist, Ralph Waldo Emerson, similarly promised his generation that "[w]ar was on its last legs."

With time, science and economics, rather than philosophy, began to be looked to as holding the keys to peace. Concluding his exhaustive eight year research study on *The War of the Future* (St. Petersburg, 1898), Jan de Bloch posed the ultimate question: "We constantly hear the argument that there always have been wars and always will be, and if in the course of all the centuries recorded in history international disputes were settled only by means of war, how can it be possible to get along without it in the future?" Responding to this persistent query, de Bloch relied on his own massive statistical and scientific data: "To this we might reply that not only the numbers, equipment, training, and technical methods of armies, but the very elements from which they are constructed have essentially changed."

De Bloch's forecast of warfare's demise was thus based on the intolerable increase in the economic and social costs of war, brought about by the modern age's technological and economic advances. But like most of his contemporaries, de Bloch had evidently failed to consider the broader panoply of causes of war: xenophobia, nationalism, mass hysteria, religious zeal, racial and ethnic intolerance, greed, and propaganda, along with militarism and irresponsible and fanatic leaderships.

Despite the many compelling hopes, expectations and preventive measures, the twentieth century turned out to be one of the most bellicose, bloody and brutal in human history. The twentieth century's two world wars accounted for nearly ten years of armed conflict. Twelve nations participated on the Allied side in World War I (1914–1918), while four others chose the Central Powers. Altogether, over 8.5 million soldiers were killed or died from diseases in that war. An additional 7.7 million military personnel were reported missing or imprisoned, and more than 21 million were listed as wounded.

Less than two decades later, fifty-seven nations took up arms in World War II (1939–1945). That war, between the Allied and the Axis, produced a total of 15 million military dead, far exceeding those of the previous war, considered in its time to be the "war to end all wars." The Allied cost in World War II exceeded 10.7 million battle dead. The Soviet Union suffered the largest number of casualties of all Allied nations, with approximately 7.5 million members of its military killed. China, with 2.2 million battle losses, had the Allied's second largest number of casualties. The Axis price of aggression and defeat was over 4.6 million military lives, including Germany's 2.85 million military casualties and Japan's over 1.5 million military dead or missing.

World War I and World War II's listed casualties did not include the many millions of civilians who died, were injured or displaced by the two wars. Some forty million civilians lost their lives during World War II. From 1943 to 1945 alone some eight million civilians—Jews, Poles, Russians and others—were exterminated in Nazi camps and gas chambers, and over 350,000 Japanese civilians perished in the unleashing of the atomic bombs over Hiroshima and Nagasaki. In the words of the Catholic League's reader on *Pius XII and the Holocaust*: "The final year and a half of World War II was the most destructive era in the history of the West."

It could be viewed as ironic that as an era combining incomparable advances in both culture and science, the twentieth century failed to provide even the most minimal landing spot for the dove of peace. The reasons for the twentieth century's terrible incidence of international destruction have been sought by many historians and peace workers. Are there any lessons that might be learned from that devastating record? What insights can be retrieved from the ashes that might aid future generations in their continuing search for the instruments and institutions necessary for building a world of peace?

In the ongoing quest for new means of achieving a more peaceful future, one must not overlook nor deny, however, the significant effort made and the steps taken for the advancement and securing of peace during the last century of the Second Millennium. A brief summary of the diverse twentieth century peace projects and undertakings might serve therefore not only to highlight accomplishments but also to point to pitfalls and deficiencies calling for future detouring and correction.

Law instead of Force: The Establishment of Arbitration and Adjudication Tribunals

Many throughout the world perceived the nineteenth century's *fín de siécle* as a grave moment in the history of peace. In advance of the new century, the entrepreneurial Alfred Nobel undertook in his 1895 will to encourage and reward future "champions of peace." Two international conferences held subsequently in The Hague in 1899 and again in 1907, produced the Convention for the Pacific Settlements of International Disputes. The Permanent Court of International Arbitration was created by these conventions as an aid to the peaceful settlement of disputes between nations. Consisting of an assemblage of jurists, including four nominees from each member state, from which conflicting governments could choose an arbitration panel, the Court was more an arbitrators' listing agency than a judicial tribunal. To further encourage the stalled resort to arbitration for the resolution of conflicts new efforts were soon undertaken to transform this agency into an actual tribunal.

By the second Hague conference, in 1907, United States Secretary of State Elihu Root urged that in order to overcome the reluctance of governments to submit controversies to *ad hoc* and possibly partial panels of arbitrators, a permanent tribunal of independent judges be established. The reformation of the Court of International Arbitration was not to materialize, however, until the conclusion of World War I. In 1920 the League of Nations in pursuance of Article 14 of its covenant, moved to establish a Permanent Court of International Justice. By September 1921, the requisite number of national adherents turned the court into a reality. The new Court continued to function, albeit not all that effectively, from January 30, 1922 until its interruption by World War II. It rendered a total of 23 judgments and 27 advisory opinions.

Despite America's central role in the permanent tribunal's creation and the constant presence of United States jurists on the Court's panel of judges, the Court's functioning and prestige suffered from the United States absence from its membership rolls. Overall, the world community was not yet prepared to deal with its disputes through legal means. The availability of the Court hardly affected the eruption of aggression and violence against Ethiopia, China, Austria, Czechoslovakia, and finally Poland. Neither could the Court affect the civil war in Spain or restrain its international outfall.

The Permanent Court was dissolved following World War II, but not before a new International Court of Justice was constituted. Recognizing the central role that a court of justice could play in the maintenance of peace, Article 92 of the United Nations Charter provided for the creation of a 15-member court as the UN's judicial branch. All United Nations members, including the United States, became *ipso facto* members of court, but not necessarily subject to its compulsory jurisdiction. The Court held its first session in The Hague in April 1946. The limitations of the court's jurisdiction by a requirement that conflicting parties had the right to decline to be bound by the tribunal's outcome meant, however, that some of the most urgent and difficult conflicts among nations in the turbulent thirties and forties of the twentieth century were left to resolution by the force of arms. Still, by 2001 the International Court had dealt with nearly 100 cases, rendered over 61 judgments and more than 200 orders, and issued some 33 advisory opinions in over 22 cases. None of the cases heard by the Court presented, however, issues which constituted direct and substantial threats to global peace. Despite the enlightened effort to provide legal mechanisms for addressing and resolving disputes, the nations which served as the primary architects of these institutions refrained from resorting to them in instances of greatest danger.

The Restraint of Violence: Imposing Humanitarian Rules on Warfare

Rules applicable to the conduct of warfare go far back into antiquity. Most ancient customs permitted high degrees of brutality. Through much of the ancient times and even in the pre-modern eras, looting of an enemy's wealth was considered not only lawful but a primary objective of war, and captured warriors were either ransomed or subjected to enslavement. Not until 1863 did the first comprehensive modern law of warfare emerge on the world stage. In that year a code was drafted by Professor Francis Lieber of Columbia College, at the request of President Abraham Lincoln, for use by the Union forces in the United States Civil War. The Lieber instrument, although limited to the conduct of America's army of the North, has had great impact upon the development of the law of war worldwide.

Only later in 1899 and 1907 did The Hague Peace Conferences finally produce the first comprehensive international laws of war (later to be known as the humanitarian code). The Hague Rules' primary purpose was to protect combating parties, prisoners of war and neutral parties against indiscriminate and inhuman conduct during military hostilities.

Not until four decades later were the Hague Rules greatly expanded by new international conventions, formulated in Geneva, which were designed to accord further protections to belligerents, prisoners of war and civilians not only in international wars but also in lesser instances of armed conflict. The four 1947 Geneva Conventions were subsequently expanded and enhanced by two 1949 Protocols, I and II, which, *inter alia*, extended humanitarian law protections to the growing instances of civil wars and other non-international armed conflicts.

Creating Governing Institutions for a Global Community: The League of Nations and the UN

The participants in The Hague Peace Conferences sought to advance primarily two peace-related objectives. The first was to prevent and restrain the cruelties of armed conflicts, once they occurred. The second sought to reduce the initial outbreak of war through the use of tribunals for the peaceful resolution of international conflicts. However, the partial accomplishment of these objectives did not suffice to prevent World War I and its ravages. Not until that terrible war was over did the community of nations actually go beyond the two relatively narrow, earlier undertakings to establish more permanent and comprehensive institutions for the overall fostering of worldwide political and economic cooperation and development as fundamental alternatives to the historical practices of unrestrained international political and economic competition, conflict and war.

To further good will and the fraternal spirit among nations, the new League of Nations, created in 1920, was vested with significant duties and powers not only for the maintenance of peace among nations but also for the fostering of the material, social and cultural well-being of nations, and their citizens. No such comprehensive organization had ever existed or been seriously attempted until United States President Woodrow Wilson first espoused the League's cause in 1916. The later leadership for implementing that idea soon fell to him. The final covenant of the organization, denominated the League of Nations to avoid suggestions of a superstate, was the outcome of a merger between a United States draft plan and a parallel British proposal. Consisting of some 4,000 words, the League's covenant was described as creating a "loose federation" with representatives and administrative organs, but with limited executive authority.

By and large the League covenant "proved to be relatively static." The rigidity of the founding document and the strong opposition to League reforms on the grounds of their likely interference with the sovereignty of nations, had been blamed for the organization's ultimate failure. The weak League, despite its considerable consultative and legislative powers, could not deal with the economic problems produced by the Great Depression of 1929–31. Neither could it prevent the Italian invasion and conquest of Ethiopia in 1936, the Spanish Civil War of 1936–38 and the Great Powers' intervention in it, the Japanese invasion of China in 1937 (accompanied by the execution of 200,000 civilians in Nanking), the Nazi aggressions against Austria and Czechoslovakia in 1938, and the commencement of World War II in 1939 with the German invasion of Poland.

Reformed and reconstituted in 1945 as the United Nations Organization at the post-World War II San Francisco Conference, the former League of Nations rose anew with 50 nations signing its founding charter. The reborn organization reflected a tremendous growth in duties, powers and resources in a deliberate effort to reform past weaknesses. Of the United Nations' six principal organs (the general assembly, the security council, the social and economic council, the trustee department, the International Court of Justice, and the secretariat) the first two proved to be particularly central to the maintenance of peace.

Most important among the UN's innovations was the creation of a "security council," whose decisions were to be binding upon all members of the organization. With time this Council exercised not only the power to render authoritative decisions on matters concerning international security but also assumed the right to authorize international peacekeeping functions and to raise military forces for carrying out the necessary policing in politically and militarily troubled areas. The Korean War, the Gulf War, the Balkan conflict, and most recently, the Afghanistan war all exemplify this increasingly emerging role of the United Nations Security Council.

Global Well-being: Advancing Economic, Social and Cultural Cooperation

It was Immanuel Kant who first urged the creation of "pacific alliances" as instruments of lasting peace. Recognizing that the pursuit of peace and of international cooperation cannot be attained merely by political undertakings, the pursuit of the world population's socio-economic well-being has been increasingly gaining international prominence. Created in 1919, the International Labor Organization (ILO), had in the mid-1930s an international membership exceeding that of the League of Nations, and its staff was about two-thirds the size of the League's secretariat. Although it had declined to join the League of Nations, the United States nevertheless became a member of the ILO in 1934.

Increasingly aware that cooperative and lasting international peace could not flourish in a social, economic and cultural vacuum, the UN's political-military responsibilities were supplemented from the very beginning with an extensive network of duties carried out through the Economic and Social Council (ECOSOC). Unlike the General Assembly, which is the organization's deliberative body and the Security Council, which serves as its executive branch, ECOSOC and its committees have been charged not only with directing and coordinating the UN's complex system of economic and social activities, but have also functioned to monitor freedom of communications and the protection of minorities throughout the world.

New power to carry out innovative economic development programs for the benefit of needy countries and regions was vested in the United Nations Development Programme, a quasi-independent agency. To further address both the immediate and long-term material and cultural needs of all people, and particularly of the rapidly growing populations of the underdeveloped countries, several pre-existing as well as new subsidiary or independent international agencies have been revitalized or newly created. The Food and Agriculture Organization (FAO), the United Nations Educational, Scientific and Cultural Organization (UNESCO), the International Bank for Reconstruction and Development, the International Monetary Fund (IMF), the World Health Organization (WHO), the International Telecommunications Union, the International Civil Aviation Organization, the International Refugee Organization and the Commission on Narcotic Drugs all serve particularized international tasks.

Regionalism and Populism: Regional Cooperation and the Voice of Civil Society

The rich efforts initiated and carried out by several international regional organizations have in recent years become of growing importance to the pursuit of peace, economic development and cooperation, and to the protection of human rights.

Several of these regional organizations have created their own legislative and executive organs, judicial tribunals and other needed instruments for advancing the common interests of the nations and peoples of their regions. Increasingly, some regional organizations have been moving forward not only toward greater economic cooperation and even peacekeeping, but also toward various forms of confederation and federalization, including common currencies, immigration and custom laws.

At the most local level of peace advocacy have been the contributions of the dramatically growing number of Non-governmental Organizations (NGOs), serving the world communities internationally, nationally and locally. NGOs have mostly been effective in enlisting the goodwill and the financial, material, human, organizational, and consulting resources of the private sector—the "civil society"—for the deeper understanding and the more appropriate responses to the needs of the global community. The NGOs have effectively channeled the contributions of the various components of the private sector—secular and religious, not-for-profit and for-profit—into the service of global health, education, welfare and security.

In recent years, NGO organizations have increasingly and more independently set out not only to assist in the running or the energizing of UN and other officially structured programs, but also to address on their own different and overlooked international needs and agendas. These have included the outlawing of land mines and the establishment of the International Criminal Court, dedicated, among its several other missions, to the prosecution of war criminals.

Swords into Ploughshares: Arms Control and Reduction

Since the early part of the twentieth century great emphasis has been placed by both governments and the anti-war movements on reducing the role of "militarism" in domestic and international affairs. Anti-militarism, ranging from peaceful calls for arms reduction and orderly agitation against military conscription to the practice of "general strikes" and even engagement in sabotage, had been much in evidence in the late nineteenth and early twentieth centuries. Beginning in the nineteenth century and continuing through the early part of the twentieth century the syndicalist and anarchist movements were the major leaders of the anti-militarist campaigns. Before, during and after World War I, the socialists took over. Subsequently, anti-militarism continued to be vigorously leftist and advocated in communist circles and publications to the end of the Cold War.

During the second half of the twentieth century, the anti-militarist forces often played an important role in the new and fashionable campaigns against poverty, environmental abuse and globalization. Although civil disobedience and other forms of anti-militarist protests, often commencing with street theatre and concluding with violence, continued to be highly disruptive to contemporary global economic and financial conferences, they appear to have had only a limited impact upon the reduction of tensions, violence and warfare, locally, nationally or internationally.

The efforts by governments have been more constant and more widely supported than those of citizen groups to reduce or even to abolish existing military arsenals, particularly those containing mass destruction capabilities. Over the years many noted binational and multinational treaties and agreements have attempted to regulate the sizes and contents of the military forces—ground, naval or air—not only within hostile but also within friendly and cooperative nations.

Arms limitations and even total disarmament, often imposed compulsorily upon defeated nations as part of peace treaty terms, have been much in evidence throughout history. As early as 1817, the Rush-Bagot Agreement between Great Britain and the United States limited the naval armament on the Great Lakes to three vessels for each power. The Washington Naval Treaty of 1922 similarly prohibited the construction of new fortifications and bases in certain Pacific area possessions of the United States, the British Empire and Japan. The Treaty of Versailles, in 1918, also required the dismantling of all German fortifications in the Rhine and Saar regions.

In the post World War II era, particularly nuclear, chemical and other weapons of mass destruction were subjected to regulation through various and often very sophisticated formulas. Nuclear anti-proliferation agreements have sought to limit access to these weapons. The basic premise of these systems of disarmament, arms limitations, and controls has been that the maintenance of certain balances of destructive capabilities, or even suicidal equality, would have a deterring effect upon the military adventurism of hostile nations (hence the Mutual Assured Destruction or MAD modality).

"Few nations will resort to the use of arms unless reasonably satisfied of their victorious potential," observed an ancient Carthaginian historian. In the absence of binding arms limitations, it is feared that nations seeking to advance the potentials for their victory, as well as their deterrence capabilities, would engage in ever more expensive and ever more hazardous arms races. But the policy incorporated long ago in the Roman *si vis pacem para bellum* (if you wish peace, prepare for war) is still in evidence today among nations, small and great.

Pacific Alliances: Treaties of Friendship, Commerce and Navigation

A particularly growing category of war-prevention or war-diffusing "medicines" has been the voluntary contractual undertakings, in the form of bilateral or multi-lateral "Friendship, Commerce and Navigation" (FC&N) treaties, among various nations. Although many of these treaties have dealt primarily with such mundane topics as commerce, investments, the status of alien persons, and the protection of foreign properties and enterprises, other agreements set out more directly to advance the causes of peace. These treaties often serve to better cement peaceful relations as well as to outline the means for resolving unexpected commercial or other frictions, particularly among nations that are inherently friendly, similarly situated and of like ideological persuasion. No less than 5,000 such bilateral treaties have been concluded by various European and other countries since the 1920s. Yet the primary value of these treaties, much like the value of most commercial and other private contracts, depends ultimately on the intentions, characters, and stability of the signatories.

A major function performed by these FC&N treaties has been the articulation of the signatories' common undertakings to submit claims and complaints to agree upon institutions for arbitration or adjudication. These undertakings have frequently institutionalized the process of conflict-resolution and have served to reduce the escalation of international tensions and prevent preemptory resorts to arms.

Being aware of the diffusing and reassuring impacts of peace treaties, the democratic leaders of the era preceding the rise of Nazi and Fascist powers considered with satisfaction the August 27, 1928 entry into force of what was to become a landmark twentieth century anti-war measure. Known commonly as the Pact of Paris, or the Kellogg-Briand agreement, the pact was intended to denounce the traditional power and perceived *right* of sovereign nations to engage in armed conduct any time they considered it necessary for "reasons of state."

Determined to strip war of its historical standing as a respectable institution, Aristide Briand, the French Minister of Foreign Affairs, proposed in 1927 to United States Secretary of State Frank B. Kellogg the conclusion of a French–United States treaty providing for the "outlawry of war." Responding favorably to the proposal, Secretary Kellogg suggested that instead of contenting themselves "with a bilateral declaration, the two governments might make a more significant contribution to world peace by joining an effort to obtain the concurrence of all powers."

The multilateral treaty, drafted and presented

in Paris on behalf of the United States on June 23, 1928, specified, in part, as follows:

> **Article I**
>
> The High Contracting Parties solemnly declare in the names of their respective peoples that they condemn recourse to war for the solution of international controversies, and renounce it as an instrument of national policy in their relations with one another.
>
> **Article II**
>
> The High Contracting Parties agree that the settlement or solution of all disputes or conflicts of whatever nature or whatever origin they may be, which may arise among them, shall never be sought except by pacific means.

The American draft was accepted and signed in Paris on June 27, 1928 by both countries, as well as by 14 other governments. Signed and ratified later by 63 nations, the Pact of Paris was to serve, unexpectedly, as a historical death warrant for the Nazi aggressors of World War II some twenty-eight years later.

Ending Impunity: Punishing Offenders Against Peace and War

By the end of World War II the victorious Allies, for the first time in the world's history of war, set out not to execute, enslave or recklessly release the captured leaders of their vanquished adversary, but to bring them before courts of justice. Despite British Prime Minster Winston Churchill's initial inclination to have Germany's offending Nazi leaders summarily executed, these Nazi leaders were brought to trial before the newly created Nuremberg International Military Tribunal.

In the face of similar failed attempts to have the German Kaiser tried for war crimes at the conclusion of World War I, the Nuremberg Tribunal, for the first time in history, served notice to governments, the military, political leaders and the broader public that aggressive wars and violations of the laws of war (later labeled humanitarian laws) would not go unpunished. One of the prime motives for punishment was evidently the desire to deter potential wrongdoers from engaging in such despicable international crimes in the future.

The criminal charges against the Nazi leadership, as specified in the London Agreement of August 8, 1945, which set up the tribunal, consisted of four distinct crimes: (1) offenses against peace—being aggression and other violations of international law and customs, including the 1928 Kellogg-Brian pact which had earlier condemned resort to war; (2) War crimes—consisting of wartime misconduct, such as the execution of prisoners of war, the shelling of civilian targets, and the starving of occupied populations, thereby contravening the Hague and Geneva Conventions; (3) Crimes against humanity—being abuses, deportations, slave labor impositions, and massacres not only of alien civilians but also of Germany's own populations; and (4) conspiracies to carry out the offenses enumerated above.

Critics argued at the time, and later, that the London Agreement had little basis in international law. But the Nuremberg Court's legitimacy was founded on a worldwide public outrage derived from the heinous crimes committed by the Nazis not only against six million perished Jews (including some 4.2 million murdered in extermination camps by Zyklon-B gas), but also against communists, the mentally ill and retarded, homosexuals, blacks, and Christian clergy.

With Hitler, Himmler, and Goebbels, the minister of propaganda, dead, the highest-ranking Nazi defendants at Nuremberg were Reichsmarshall Herman Goering and former deputy Nazi party leader Rudolf Hess. The sitting tribunal consisted of eight judges, two each from the United States, Britain, the Soviet Union, and France. There were 23 men on trial in Nuremberg, with 22 sitting in the court except Martin Bormann, who was tried in absentia. Opening on November 20, 1945, the trial continued through July 1946. By July 26, the prosecution began to present its final arguments, and then the court adjourned for a month while the judges weighed the evidence.

Nuremberg's historical verdict was delivered on October 1, 1946. Three of the 22 accused were acquitted. Nine were found guilty of lesser heinous crimes and were sentenced to long terms of imprisonment. The remaining eleven were found guilty of all four criminal counts and were sentenced to death. Goering, one of those sentenced to death, escaped execution by swallowing a concealed cyanide capsule a few hours before the execution of his sentence. The ten other condemned men, dressed in civilian clothes, were hanged in the middle of the night on October 17, 1946. Hitler's foreign minister Joaching Von Ribbentrop led the way to the scaffold, followed by Nazi ideologue Alfred Rosenberg, the Nazi propagandist Julius Streicher, and former governor-general of occupied Poland, Hans Frank. The bodies of those executed were taken to the former concentration camp Dachau to be cremated. The ashes were never identified or delivered to the families, to prevent their becoming worshiped relics for Nazi sympathizers.

Carried out in order to satisfy the widely held need to call the Nazi leadership to account and to accord it its just deserts, the Nuremberg trials gave rise, nevertheless, to many arguments—legal, ethical and policy-oriented—that continue to this day. What mostly remains in doubt, however, is the tribunal's decree establishing that aggressive war was outlawed, and demonstrating that those responsible for aggressive wars, war crimes, and crimes against humanity can and will be tried and punished by the international community.

Reviewing the record of the post-Nuremberg era, one is troubled by the unpunished massacres, genocides and holocausts that followed the imposition and execution of the severe sentences meted out by the Nuremberg tribunal and its Asian companion, the International Tribunal for the Far East set up by United States General Douglas MacArthur. Millions of victims perished through the crimes against humanity committed in Cambodia's subsequent internal strife. Hundreds of thousands, and, indeed, millions of others—men, women and children—were massacred in the domestic wars in the Congo, Rwanda, Sierra Leone, and the former Yugoslavia. In retrospect, the Nuremberg judgments appear to have been awfully ineffective. Some observers, moreover, entertain a troubling suspicion that the publicity given to the terrible Nazi exploits might have later supplied some added stimulus to those bent on human debasement, mass murder and democide.

The Causes of International Wars: From Antiquity to the Third Millennium

The twentieth century's experience confirms that the key to global peace has consistently kept eluding us. Neither the hope for a natural decline of war in an age of reason and science, nor the improvement of humanity's quality of life worldwide have sufficed to eliminate warfare. Neither the creation of international or regional conflict-management, peacekeeping and peace-building organs (legislative, administrative or judicial; political, economic, or military), nor even the reduction of armaments, the creation of peace treaty networks and the criminal punishment of offender against peace have proven effective in creating a lasting peace. Not one and not even a combination of these curative measures have supplied the appropriate remedies for the prevention of war.

In the absence of a thorough and critical review of the diverse forces which have and still continue to fuel international as well as regional and domestic disputes and armed conflicts, no previously tested nor newly proposed remedies can be expected to produce the hoped for era of peace. Unless a clearer understanding is gained of the causes underlying past, present and potential violence, all attempted precautions, preventive or mitigating measures, or prescribed curative remedies are likely to amount to nothing more than a blind man's stabs in the dark.

Concerned thinkers and writers had addressed

the subject of war's causations generations and centuries ago. English philosopher Thomas Hobbes wrote in 1651:

> In the nature of man, we find three principal causes of quarrel. First, competition; secondly, diffidence; thirdly, glory. The first maketh man invade for gain; the second, for safety; the third, for reputation. (*Leviathan*)

Two millennia earlier, Plato concluded in *The Republic* that "we have discovered war [between nations] to be derived from causes which are also the causes of evils within countries...."

What are these causes? And has the modern knowledge of history, psychology, sociology, law, the arts and the sciences given the contemporary community of peace and war scholars and practitioners a better and more accurate understanding, than previously available, of the causes of wars and the necessary means for their prevention or mitigation?

Much anecdotal, descriptive, and occasionally analytical materials exist regarding the eruption of international warfare as well as the breakout of lesser human hostilities and conflicts. This material includes domestic rebellions and revolutions, ethnic and religious violence, tribal and neighborhood feuds. But despite the long existing interest in the study and understanding of war, its causation and prevention, and the more recent development of peace studies and conflict-resolution programs, few broadly applicable and scientific findings, whether political, economic, socio-psychological or military, have emerged.

One modern approach to the classification of the causes of war distinguishes between four distinct casual categories. The first of these dwells on war as the unavoidable outcome of man's *innate* makeup and unalterable needs—whether labeled genetic, instinctive, physical, psychological or otherwise—but recognizes the possibility of some modification of man and his needs by prevailing physical, environmental or social factors. The second approach to the causes of war sees conflict as the outcome of *diverse*, yet *observable*, and often *avoidable*, political, economic, religious, social, and psychological forces, which differ from one community to another and from era to era. The third approach views war as the outcome of *unpredictable* and *uncontrollable* consequences of the *congruences* of political, social, economic and psychological factors and tensions. The fourth proposed casual category sees in war primarily an application in the social-political realms of the forces of natural selection originally identified in the biological arena. This approach belongs to the school of social Darwinism. Each of these categories might often be manipulated by charismatic leaders.

Humanity's Innate Bellicosity

One portrayal of warfare emphasizes man's underlying bellicose proclivities was offered by Chicago University's Quincy Wright. Wright pointed out that "[w]ar has been a variable phenomena in human history." These variations, he explained, suggest that the causes of war were not to be found in any constant characteristics of human nature but rather in varying social institutions and relations. Nevertheless, he stressed it was men who waged war. It was reasonable, therefore, to assume that there must be qualities of human nature that enable men to initiate and participate in war under appropriate circumstances. Lending qualified support to the innate approach to war causation was Wright's further observation that among animals and primitive peoples, wars had consisted of brief attacks by groups or individuals upon others, with such conduct being "only one step removed from the hunt." Wright saw, however, the underlying causes for human attacks upon each other as not so much associated with the drive for food, but as more directly derived from the psychological drives for dominance, sex, territory and revenge.

The proponents of the *innate* or human *proclivity* approach to warfare have tended, quite expectedly, to picture early man as seeking to survive in the Hobbesian "natural state," in which life consisted of incessant and fierce wild-beast warfare. But this bestial portrayal of mankind has not fared well in recent times. Considering the implications of an *innate* doctrine of human warfare for a peace-seeking humanity, it is not surprising that the claims of mankind's war-like proclivities would come increasingly under attack (i.e., the accompanying Appendix: The Seville Statement on Violence, 1986 which undertakes to debunk such claims).

War as the Outcome of Observable and Avoidable Forces

The second camp of war cause theorists consists of those who see human warfare as the *rational* outcome of varying but *observable* and *foreseeable* categories of existing social, economic and political maladies requiring resolution. This camp is inclined to support its doctrinal perspective by reference to historical examples.

These "rationalists," or more accurately "rationalizers," begin by pointing to bellicose tribal, communal, or clannish forays, mostly in ancient eras but some also in comparatively recent times, for the purpose of looting the wealth of neighboring communities. Plunder and continuing tribute, these students of war suggest, have long been major objectives of warring parties. Alvin Johnson cites as examples of such warfare the raiding of the Eastern Mediterranean civilizations by the Bedouin from the Arabian deserts and grasslands, and attacks upon the Chinese centers of culture by the primitive horsemen of Mongolia. This exploitative motive for warfare was said to have reached its zenith in the invasions of Europe by the Vandals and Huns (led by Attila), during the fourth and fifth centuries, and Genghis Khan's Asian campaigns in the fifteenth century.

An even greater place in human history was occupied by wars driven by the objective of displacing an existing indigenous population with a new conquering people. Many such mass invasions, conquests and occupations had indeed become wars of extermination against long-settled populations. Thus, the third millennium B.C. was identified by scholars as marking the westward surge of the Semitic peoples, the second millennium B.C. as recording the expansion of the so-called Aryans from India and Persia into southern and western Europe, the centuries from 300 B.C. to 700 A.D. as reflecting the westward and southward migrations of the German and Scandinavian tribes, the centuries from 700 A.D. to 1300 A.D. as representing the eastward and westward Arab-Muslim expansion, the period from the thirteenth into the seventeenth century as marking the movement of the Turkish tribes into Asia Minor and southeastern Europe, and the fifteenth to the nineteenth centuries as recording the conquest, and sometimes displacement, of the colonial populations of Africa, the Americas, Asia and Australia by Europe's Spanish, Portuguese, Dutch, Swedish, French, German and English conquistadors and settlers.

Most experts have "assumed that this class of war has disappeared for all time," wrote Alvin Johnson in the mid-twentieth century. But recent developments, including Turkey's post-World War I expulsion of Armenians and Greeks, the post World War II expulsion of Germans from East Prussia and Poland, the Serbian nationalists' ethnic "cleansing" of former Yugoslavia, the Zambabian government's opening estates cultivated by white settlers to Black war veterans, and the hundred year Palestinian-Israeli contest over the lands and historic sites of the Holy Land, readily argue for an opposite conclusion.

Although the displacements of people—but certainly not the pressures of growing populations—have greatly declined in the modern era, due in part to technological advancements which have often dispensed with the need for territorial acquisitions, a different form of expansionism has characterized the twentieth century. It might thus be correctly observed that "in contrast to the wars arising out of the expansive power of populations, are those arising out of the expansive power of political ideologies and political systems." These different grounds for expansive warfare may be noted not only in the empire-building campaigns of the ancient Assyrians, Egyptians, Persians and Greeks, but also in the short-lived German and Italian World War II conquests and the Soviet Union's expansion into Poland, East Prussia and the Eastern Bloc countries at the commencement of the Cold War era. This quest for the expansion of empires and political systems has supplied the motive for a long series of military conflicts, stretching from antiquity to modernity, which readily fall within the second, or the allegedly *observable* and *rational* category of the proposed classification of war causes.

Wars for the expansion of empires were mostly conducted in antiquity for strategic reasons, as a means for fortifying an empire's frontiers against so-called "marauding barbarians." Less frequently these wars served to secure the empire's economic hegemony over highly productive economic territories. The Roman wars were mostly driven by these objectives. Rome's expansion of its frontiers westward as far as England, Rome's war against Carthage, its powerful Mediterranean competitor, fell within this strategic fortification and economic hegemony category of warfare. Modern imperialism's wars, on the other hand, have been attributed exclusively to the desire for economic exploitation. Some scholars have also attributed part of the expansionist drive to Europe's feudal institution of primogeniture, which provided a large supply of relatively impoverished but adventurous younger members of the aristocracy, bent on colonial pursuits. The Dutch, Spanish, Portuguese, English, French, German and Italian colonial expansions provide illustrations of rich and sparsely populated territories being "discovered" by so called pioneers whose unmet expectations in their home lands gave vent to great ambitions overseas.

The Christian crusades, from the eleventh to the thirteenth centuries similarly illustrate the contribution of an impoverished knighthood to aggressive warfare. The crusades served also as examples of a new class of wars—those based on religious zeal. Equally noted must be the crusades' role in reintroducing the ancient yet ever-present drive for seizing and looting accumulations of wealth. "The Eastern treasuries were, according to medieval standards—enormous," report the crusade historians. According to these historians, many Christian principalities, including Venice and Genoa, "rose to wealth and power on the basis of the plunder won not only from the Moslem Levant but [also] from the helpless [fraternal Christian] Byzantine Empire." Even after the conclusion of the crusades, the maritime powers of Europe continued during the thirteenth to the seventeenth centuries to exhibit a similar "inclination to fight for a share of the Levantine loot." It was this inclination which contributed to the discovery, exploration and conquest of Africa, the America's, and the Indies.

Religious wars, initiated by Islam's seventh century thrusts eastward and westward and late rekindled by the Christian Crusades in the eleventh century, were continued not only by the Spain's "reconquest" of its lands from the Moors in the fifteenth century, but also in the subsequent sixteenth century calls for the defense of Christendom against the advances of the infidel Turks. Only a combined Christian naval force, supported by the heroic ground resistance of the knights of Malta (an order of knights hospitalizers dating back to the Crusades) managed to break the Turkish armada in the battle of Leparto (1571). The naval loss was followed a century later by the German and Polish infantry cavalry's defeat of the Ottoman armies before the walls of Vienna in 1683. From that date through the fall of the Ottoman Empire in World War I, the opposition to the Turkish presence in Europe and in the Eastern Mediterranean resulted in one war after another. This new interplay of two causes, religious zeal and a growing call for national self-determination and liberation from the Turkish yoke, was to characterize the subsequent "history of war from the latter part of the fifteenth century to the beginning of the eighteenth century."

Yet the ongoing Muslim-Christian conflict, as manifested in the Crusades, in the Spanish mainland battles and in the expansion and retreat of the Ottoman Empire, did not prevent the eruption of long and deadly intra-Christian conflicts. These were due in part to dynastic competitions rather than to scriptural controversies. Still, the doctrinal and social contests between the Catholic Church and its Protestant challengers had for several centuries contributed in their own right too much fraternal bloodshed in Europe. Particularly illustrative of the capacity of Europe's Christianity to mix territorial, dynastic and religious causes was the Thirty Years War (1618-48) which left Germany in ruins, turned the Holy Roman Empire into a shell and elevated France to become the chief power on the continent.

Subsequent centuries saw other admixtures of various war motives and objectives. These included struggles for the looting of "centers of accumulated treasures," for colonial resources and trade, for relieving population pressures, for meeting strategic objectives and for attaining local, regional or international dominance. Alvin Johnson provided an interesting illustration of these later and complex causes of warfare when he wrote: "Thus the long struggle of the Netherlands against Spain (1572-1579) arose primarily from the resistance to religious oppression, but in the course of its development became more importantly a struggle for the control of the seas and the subsequent control of colonial plunder and commerce."

New wartime pursuits in the coming years often combined nationalistic ambitions with dynastic competitions and the historical pursuit of looting and plunder. Large European communities of exiled nationalists, including thousands of Polish expatriates, gave rise to growing armies of mercenaries, also noted for supplying military volunteers for America's War of Independence. Among the freebooting leaders of these armies was Austrian-Swedish Albrecht von Wallenstein (1583-1634), one of the world's most renowned mercenaries to whom war was merely a commercial enterprise, with "political, social and religious objectives [being] irrelevant."

From the end of the seventeenth century until the middle of the twentieth century, historians increasingly began considering religion as having become "a virtually negligent factor [among] the objectives of war." Dynastic ambitions continued, however, to figure heavily among the causes of war, commercial and strategic motives seeming to predominate. Soon enough, however, the British and French revolutions, reflecting in part the growing domestic conflicts between a rising bourgeoisie and a declining aristocratic order, ushered in a new era of internal rather than international war motives. For a time it appeared that colonial commercial motives were declining and the stirrings of national unification and independence were assuming primary importance. The revolt of the Spanish colonies in the Americas, the wars for German and Italian unification, and the Greek and Balkan struggles for independence from Turkey, were all driven by nationalistic impulses. World War I and the resultant breakup of the Austro-Hungarian, the German, the Czarist and the Ottoman empires, and the creation of numerous new nation states were likewise viewed largely as evidence of the growing modern force of nationalistic motivated modern warfare.

Still the early part of the twentieth century, following the pattern established in the second half of the nineteenth century, continued to reflect constant changes in the admixture of motives underlying the resort to war. Departing from the earlier interplay between religious struggles and wars of national unification, the highly merchanistic countries of Europe once again went on to seek colonial domination as a means for both securing the supply of natural resources and gaining exclusive markets for their products. The further partition of Africa went on as a consequence with great zeal and urgency and the Indo-Chinese region was divided into spheres of influence. It was the same admixture of causes and objectives, which led to the Russo-Japanese war (as a means of blocking Japan's imperialistic ambitions in China), England's expansion of its South Africa dominions through the Boer War, and the United States' gaining, as a consequence of the Spanish-American War, extensive colonial territories beyond its continental borders. It was the conflict among the competing forces of nationalism, capitalism and imperialism, which finally played a critical role in bringing about World War I.

The community of nations, which evolved from the first world conflict, bore within it many of the very tensions, which accounted for the wars of the earlier epochs. The pressures produced by population growth (in countries like Italy, Germany and Japan) gave rise to calls for territorial expansion and population displacements. Fierce nationalism replaced religion as a cause for conflict in the European theatre, and the Soviet Union's insistence on a global revolutionary quest created growing tensions and a worldwide contest between communism and capitalism. It was the combination of a national "hurt" and pride, coupled with expansionist pressures, the worldwide economic instability produced by the Great Depression, the continuing competition for world markets, the fear of class struggle and the overriding ideological fever—accentuated by the Soviet Union, Japan, and later Nazi Germany and fascist Italy—that supplied the kindling for the fires of World War II. Yet that terrible conflagration might possibly have never occurred but for the particular social and economic realities within the Axis camp, the innate aggressiveness of their movements, their fanatic leaderships, including the prominence of a psychopathic Fuhrer—confronting a totally unimaginable passivity on the part of the forces of peace in Europe and the United States.

What does our historical or developmental survey of some two and a half millennia of warfare disclose? The many examples of historical diversity and complex intermingling of causal components, for the violence and military conflicts of previous centuries make it practically impossible to construct a unified theory of the causes of war. Can war, therefore, ever be forecasted, and thereby can it ever be prevented?

Many analysts of the causation of war point to World War II as compelling evidence for the conclusion that no uni-faceted or even multi-faceted theory of war causation can be advanced and supported. They argue that neither humanity's capacity for violence, nor the theory of chaos and natural selection, or any other single cause, not even a combination of the various factors identified through history (including population pressures and displacements, religion, nationalism, economic unrest, competition and exploitation, ideological conflicts and racial or cultural antipathies), can be counted on to explain the sparks which turn into flames sufficient to engulf whole communities, tribes, countries, alliances of nations, and indeed the whole world, in warfare.

Wars as "Acts of God" or "Social Darwinism"

The attempted categorization of the causes of war still needs to be elaborated. The hypothesis of the adherents of the third alternative of the origins of warfare—contrasting with the first's portrayal of human warfare as a social atavism, and the second school's attribution of war to foreseeable and rational combinations of motives—asserts that the eruption of violence and war is frequently, if not always, unpredictable. Wars, this school posits, are much like "acts of God": forest fires, floods, tornadoes, train collisions, aircraft accidents and other mostly natural, and only partially humanly-originated catastrophes. Warfare is thus perceived as primarily part and parcel of the chaos which underlies man's, precarious global existence. This chaos is not usually predicable and might be only partially subject to human prevention, control or modification.

Following in the footsteps of Charles Darwin (1809-1882), the father of "natural selection," Herbert Spencer had set out to advance his claim that not only in the natural but also in the social realms there prevails a competition or a war for the "survival of the fittest." Departing from this fundamental premise, "social Darwinism" has argued that the major forces, which give rise to or escalate the occurrence of warfare in various societies and during diverse historical epochs, are in great part derived from an ongoing and general competition for the survival of the fittest. This competition is usually said to be observed within and between the different species. But this competition is also represented in the human quest for space, food, and other necessities. In the case of humans, however, the contest extends beyond survival to social and psychological needs—whether material or spiritual, ideological or emotional, actual or imagined. War, in sum, is an extreme manifestation of the struggle for material or spiritual commodities among different communities kept apart by real or perceived walls of competing identities.

At the dawn of the Third Millennium, one finds it extremely difficult, if not impossible, to offer a single and unified hypothesis, or even a composite which encompasses the wide range of causes for the outbreak of violence and war. So many causal forces, visible and hidden, predictable and unpredictable, rational and otherwise, are active in the contemporary world to make it extremely difficult for political scholars as well as for activists to marshal the means for the understanding and prevention of future wars. No one adequately forecasted either the causes for or the coming of World Wars I or II or the wars that followed. No one could forecast the outcome of these conflicts. Still less can the causes of future world wars be foretold, until the patterns of human behavior, in peace and war, rational or otherwise, are better understood?

Yet, in the interim, the quest for peace must go on, not only unhindered but with greater energy.

Appendix I: The New State of Conflict: Some Facts*

Deep-rooted conflict: Conflict, originating largely within states, which combine two powerful elements: potent identity-based factors, based on differences in race, religion, culture, language and so on, with perceived imbalance in the distribution of economic, political and social resources.

Characteristics: complex persistent, and intractable; much less amenable to comprise, negotiation or trade-off; rapidly diffuses beyond the boundaries of the particular state.

Intra-state, not inter-state. In the last three years, every major armed conflict originated at the domestic level within a state (intra-state), rather than between states (inter-state).

Of the 101 armed conflicts during 1989-1996, only six were inter-state. The remaining 95 took place within existing states.

Identify-based. Of the 27 conflicts in 1996 classified as "major armed conflicts" (more than 1000 dead per year), 22 had a clear identity component to them.

New weapons of war. Since World War II, cheap, mass-produced, small-caliber weapons have killed far more people than the heavier more traditional battlefield weaponry.

Civilian causalities. During World War I, five per cent of causalities were civilian; by World War II the figure had risen to 50 per cent. In the 1990s the proportion of civilian causalities has soared to 80 per cent.

Refugees. By 1992, there were about 17 million refugees, and a further 20 million people who were internally displaced.

Examples. Deep-rooted conflicts include Russia (Chechnya), Northern Ireland, Iran & Iraq (with the Kurds), Israel, Afghanistan, Bangladesh (Chittagong Hill Tribes), Indonesia (East Timor), Sri Lanka, Burma, Algeria and elsewhere.

Source: Sipri Yearbook 1997: "Armaments, Disarmament and International Security. Oxford: Oxford University Press Four Sipri."

*Permission granted to use Factsheet 1 [p. 14], "The New State of Conflict: Some Facts" from the book *Democracy and Deep-Rooted Conflict: Options for Negotiations,* edited by Peter Harris and Ben Reilly, International Institute for Democracy and Electoral Assistance, Stockholm, Sweden, 1998.

Appendix II: The Seville Statement on Violence (1986)*

Believing that it is our responsibility to address from our particular disciplines the most dangerous and destructive activities of our species, violence and war; recognizing that science is a human cultural product which cannot be definitive or all-encompassing; and gratefully acknowledging the support of the authorities of Seville and representatives of the Spanish UNESCO; we, the undersigned scholars from around the world and from relevant sciences, have met and arrived at the following Statement on Violence. In it, we challenge a number of alleged biological findings that have been used, even by some in our disciplines, to justify violence and war. Because the alleged findings have contributed to an atmosphere of pessimism in our time, we submit that the open, considered rejection of these misstatements can contribute significantly to the International Year of Peace.

Misuse of scientific theories and data to justify violence and war is not new but has been made since the advent of modern science. For example, the theory of evolution has been used to justify not only war, but also genocide, colonialism, and suppression of the weak.

We state our position in the form of five propositions. We are aware that there are many other issues about violence and war that could be fruitfully addressed from the standpoint of our disciplines, but we restrict ourselves here to what we consider a most important first step.

IT IS SCIENTIFICALLY INCORRECT to say that we have inherited a tendency to make war from our animal ancestors. Although fighting occurs widely throughout animal species, only a few cases of destructive intraspecies fighting between organized groups have ever been reported among naturally living species, and none of these involve the use of tools designed to be weapons. Normal predatory feeding upon other species cannot be equated with intra-species violence. Warfare is a peculiarly human phenomenon and does not occur in other animals.

The fact that warfare has changed so radically over time indicates that it is a product of culture. Its biological connection is primarily through language which makes possible the coordination of groups, the transmission of technology, and the use of tools. War is biologically possible, but it is not inevitable, as evidenced by its variation in occurrence and nature over time and space. There are cultures which have not engaged in war for centuries, and there are cultures which have engaged in war frequently at some times and not at others.

IT IS SCIENTIFICALLY INCORRECT to say that war or any violent behavior is genetically programmed into our human nature. While genes are involved at all levels of nervous system function, they provide a developmental potential that can be actualized only in conjunction with the ecological and social environment. While individuals vary in their predispositions to be affected by their experience, it is the interaction between their genetic endowment and conditions of nurturance that determines their personalities. Except for rare pathologies, the genes do not produce individuals necessarily predisposed to violence. Neither do they determine the opposite. While genes are co-involved in establishing our behavioral capacities, they do not by themselves specify the outcome.

IT IS SCIENTIFICALLY INCORRECT to say that in the course of human evolution there has been a selection for aggressive behavior more than for other kinds of behavior. In all well-studied species, status within the group is achieved by the ability to cooperate and to fulfill social functions relevant to the structure of that group. 'Dominance' involves social bondings and affiliations; it is not simply a matter of the possession and use of superior physical power, although it does involve aggressive behaviors. Where genetic selection for aggressive behavior has been artificially instituted in animals, it has rapidly succeeded in producing hyper-aggressive individuals; this indicates that aggression was not maximally selected under natural

*Reprinted by permission of the editors of *A Reader in Peace Studies,* edited by Paul Smoker, Ruth Davies and Barbara Munske. Published in the UK by Pergamon Press, plc.

conditions. When such experimentally-created hyper-aggressive animals are present in a social group, they either disrupt its social structure or are driven out. Violence is neither in our evolutionary legacy nor in our genes.

IT IS SCIENTIFICALLY INCORRECT to say that humans have 'violent brain.' While we do have the neural apparatus to act violently, it is not automatically activated by internal or external stimuli. Like higher primates and unlike other animals, our higher neural processes filter such stimuli before they can be acted upon. How we act is shaped by how we have been conditioned and socialized. There is nothing in our neurophysiology that compels us to react violently.

IT IS SCIENTIFICALLY INCORRECT to say that war is caused by 'instinct' or any single motivation. The emergence of modern warfare has been a journey from the primacy of emotional and motivational factors, sometimes called 'instincts,' to the primacy of cognitive factors. Modern war involves institutional use of personal characteristics such as obedience, suggestibility, and idealism, social skills such as language, and rational considerations such as cost-calculation, planning, and information processing. The technology of modern war has exaggerated traits associated with violence both in the training of actual combatants and in the preparation of support for war in the general population. As a result of this exaggeration, such traits are often mistaken to be the causes rather than the consequences of the process.

We conclude that biology does not condemn humanity to war, and that humanity can be freed from the bondage of biological pessimism and empowered with confidence to undertake the transformative tasks needed in this International Year of Peace and in the years to come. Although these tasks are mainly institutional and collective, they also rest upon the consciousness of individual participants for whom pessimism and optimism are crucial factors. Just as 'wars begin in the minds of men,' peace also begins in our minds. The same species who invented war is capable of inventing peace. The responsibility lies with each of us.

Seville, May 16, 1986

David Adams, Psychology, Wesleyan University, Middletown, CT, USA

S. A. Barnett, Ethology, The Australian National University, Canberra, Australia

N. P. Bechtereva, Neurophysiology, Institute for Experimental Medicine of Academy of Medical Sciences of USSR, Leningrad, USSR

Bonnie Frank Carter, Psychology, Albert Einstein Medical Center, Philadelphia, PA, USA

José M. Rodriguez Delgado, Neurophysiology, Centro de Estudios Neurobiológicos, Madrid, Spain

José Luis Diaz, Ethology, Instituto Mexicano de Psiquiatrla, Mexico D.F., Mexico

Andrzej Eliasz, Individual Differences Psychology, Polish Academy of Sciences, Warsaw, Poland

Santiago Genovés, Biological Anthropology, Instituto de Estudios Antropoloqicos, Mexico D.F., Mexico

Benson E. Ginsburg, Behavior Genetics, University of Connecticut, Storrs, CT, USA

Jo Groebel, Social Psychology, Erziehungswissenschaftliche Hochschule, Landau, Federal Republic of Germany

Samir-Kumar Ghosh, Sociology, Indian Institute of Human Sciences, Calcutta, India

Robert Hinde, Animal Behavior, Cambridge University, UK

Richard E. Leakey, Physical Anthropology, National Museums of Kenya, Nairobi, Kenya

Taha H. Malasi, Psychiatry, Kuwait University, Kuwait

J. Martin Ramirez, Psychobiology, Universidad de Sevilla, Spain

Federico Mayor Zaragoza, Biochemistry, Universidad Autónoma, Madrid, Spain

Diana L. Mendoza, Ethology, Universidad de Sevilla, Spain

Ashis Nandy, Political Psychology, Center for the Study of Developing Societies, Delhi, India

John Paul Scott, Animal Behavior, Bowling Green State University, Bowling Green, OH, USA

Riitta Wahlström, Psychology, University of Jyvaskyla, Finland

Deported to Flossenbürg by Karl Stojka.

Reprinted by permission of the artist.

Part Four

Militarism, the Military, and Deterrence in the Quest for Peace

Not by speechifying and counting majorities are the great questions of the times to be resolved, but by iron and blood.

—Otto von Bismark (1850)

God will see to it that war shall always recur, as a drastic remedy for ailing humanity

—Heinrich von Treitschke (1834-1896)

There can never be too many guns, there are never enough of them.

—Ferdinand Foch (1919)

Again and again we have owed peace to the fact that we were prepared for war.

—Theodore Roosevelt (1897)

Central to the issue of peace in most contemporary cultures are the special interests represented by the military class and by the so-called "military-industrial" complex. While Part Four examines the broad conceptualization of militarism and its implications, one must also take notice of the central role played by the military in maintaining stability in many countries, on one hand, and in propping up tyrannical regimes, on the other hand.

History illustrates that the role of a military class has been a constant throughout organized society. However, how that class is used and the primacy it is given has varied according to the government in place and the level of perceived threat at a given time....

This Part applies a critical analysis to the armaments, costs and military build-ups throughout the world, usually justified in the name of deterrence or self-defense. The constant escalation in the costs of keeping up with the deterrence efforts of a perceived opponent can be compared to the competing bidders in a public auction, constantly raising the price of the desired item. Furthermore, the onset of new types of warfare has dramatically changed the military calculus in this new century. Though scholars and ethicists have long-debated the role of nuclear weapons, as Daniel Deudney does for us here, such analyses have always been calculated within the framework of the nation state. The risk of rogue states, "super-empowered madmen" or rogue warheads have brought the entire question of deterrence into question. Can a state, group or person operating outside the norms of the international system be deterred in a conventional way? The juxtaposition of scholarly conclusions regarding the ineffectiveness of deterrence with the actual conduct of the contemporary United States government gives this Part a particular timeliness.

The Realities of War

Carl von Clausewitz
Prussian Military Thinker (1780-1831)

We propose to consider first the single elements of our subject, then each branch or part, and, last of all, the whole, in all its relations—therefore to advance from the simple to the complex. But it is necessary for us to commence with a glance at the nature of the whole, because it is particularly necessary that in the consideration of any of the parts their relation to the whole should be kept constantly in view.

Definition

We shall not enter into any of the abstruse definitions of War used by publicists. We shall keep to the element of the thing itself, to a duel. War is nothing but a duel on an extensive scale. If we would conceive as a unit the countless number of duels which make up a War, we shall do so best by supposing to ourselves two wrestlers. Each strives by physical force to compel the other to submit to his will: each endeavours to throw his adversary, and thus render him incapable of further resistance.

War therefore is an ad of violence intended to compel our opponent to fulfill our will.

Violence arms itself with the inventions of Art and Science in order to contend against violence. Self-imposed restrictions, almost imperceptible and hardly worth mentioning, termed messages of International Law, accompany it without essentially impairing its power. Violence, that is to say, physical force (for there is no moral force without the conception of States and Law), is therefore the means; the compulsory submission of enemy to our will is the ultimate object. In order to attain this object fully, the enemy must be disarmed, and disarmament becomes therefore the immediate object of hostilities in theory. It takes the place of the final object, and puts it aside as something we can eliminate from our calculations.

Utmost Use of force

Now philanthropists may easily imagine there is a skillful method of disarming and overcoming an enemy without causing great bloodshed, and that this is the proper tendency of the Art of War. However plausible this may appear, still it is an error, which must be extirpated; for in such dangerous things as War, the errors which proceed from a spirit of benevolence errors, which proceed from a spirit of benevolence, are the worst. As the use of physical power to the utmost extent by no means excludes the cooperation of the intelligence, it follows that he, who uses force unsparingly, without reference to the bloodshed involved, must obtain a

Carl von Clausewitz, "The Realities of War." From the book *On War*, by Carl von Clausewitz, as translated by Colonel J.J. Grahams, 1873.

superiority if his adversary uses less vigour in its application. The former then dictates the law to the latter, and both proceed to extremities to which the only limitations are those imposed by the amount of counteracting force on each side.

This is the way, in which the matter must be viewed, and it is to no purpose, it is even against one's own interest, to turn away from the consideration of the real nature of the affair because the horror of its elements excites repugnance.

If the Wars of civilized people are less cruel and destructive than those of savages, the difference arises from the social condition both of States in themselves and in their relations to each other. Out of this social condition and its relations War arises, and by it War is subjected to conditions, is controlled and modified. But these things do not belong to War itself; they are only given conditions; and to introduce into the philosophy of War itself a principle of moderation would be an absurdity.

Two motives lead men to War: instinctive hostility and hostile intention. In our definition of War, we have chosen as its characteristic the latter of these elements, because it is the most general. It is impossible to conceive the passion of hatred of the wildest description, bordering on mere instinct without combining with it the idea of a hostile intention. On the other hand, hostile intentions may often exist without being accompanied by any, or at all events by any extreme, hostility of feeling. Amongst savages views emanating from the feelings, amongst civilized nations those emanating from the understanding, have the predominance; but this difference arises from attendant circumstances, existing institutions, etc., and, therefore, is not to be found necessarily in all cases, although it prevails in the majority. In short, even the most civilized nations may burn with passionate hatred of each other.

We may see from this what a fallacy it would be to refer the War of a civilized nation entirely to an intelligent act on the part of the Government, and to imagine it as continually freeing itself more and more from all feeling of passion in such a way that at last the physical masses of combatants would no longer be required; in reality, their mere relations would suffice—a kind of algebraic action.

Theory was beginning to drift in this direction until the facts of the last War taught it better. If War is an act of force, it belongs necessarily also to the feelings. If it does not originate in the feelings, it reacts, more or less, upon them, and the extent of this reaction depends not on the degree of civilization, but upon the importance and duration of the interests involved.

Therefore, if we find civilized nations do not put their prisoners to death, do not devastate towns and countries, this is because their intelligence exercises greater influence on their mode of carrying on War, and has taught them more effectual means of applying force than these rude acts of mere instinct. The invention of gunpowder, the constant progress of improvements in the construction of firearms, are sufficient proofs that the tendency to destroy the adversary which lies at the bottom of the conception of War is in no way changed or modified through the progress of civilization.

We therefore repeat our proposition, that War is an act of violence pushed to its utmost bounds; as one side dictates the law to the other, there arises a sort of reciprocal action, which logically must lead to an extreme. This is the first reciprocal action, and the first extreme with which we meet (first reciprocal action).

The aim is to disarm the enemy

We have already said that the aim of all action in War is to disarm the enemy, and we shall now show that this, theoretically at least, is indispensable.

If our opponent is to be made to comply with our will, we must place him in a situation which is more oppressive to him than the sacrifice which we demand; but the disadvantages of this position must naturally not be of a transitory nature, at least in appearance, otherwise the enemy, instead of yielding, will hold out, in the prospect of a change for the better. Every change in this position which is produced by a continuation of the War, should therefore be a change for the worse. The worst condition in which a belligerent can be placed is that of being completely disarmed. If, therefore, the enemy is to be reduced to submission by an act of War, he must either be positively disarmed or placed in such a position that he is threatened with it. From this it follows that the disarming or overthrow of the enemy, whichever we call it, must always be the aim of Warfare. Now War is always the shock of two hostile bodies in collision, not the action of a living power upon an inanimate mass, because an absolute state of endurance would not be making War; therefore, what we have just said as to the aim of action in War applies to both parties. Here, then, is another case of reciprocal action. As long as the enemy is not defeated, he may defeat me; then I shall be no longer my own master; he will dictate the law to me as I did to him. This is the second reciprocal action, and leads to a second extreme (second reciprocal action).

Utmost exertion of powers

If we desire to defeat the enemy, we must proportion our efforts to his powers of resistance. This is expressed by the product of two factors, which cannot be separated, namely, the sum of available means and the strength of the Will. The sum of the available means may be estimated in a measure, as it depends (although not entirely) upon numbers; but the strength of volition is more difficult to determine, and can only be estimated to a certain extent by the strength of the motives. Granted we have obtained in this way an approximation to the strength of the power to be contended with, we can then take a review of our own means, and either increase them so as to obtain a preponderance, or, in case we have not the resources to effect this, then do our best by increasing our means as far as possible. But the adversary does the same; therefore, there is a new mutual enhancement, which, in pure conception, must create a fresh effort towards an extreme. This is the third case of reciprocal action, and a third extreme with which we meet (third reciprocal action).

Modification in the reality

Thus reasoning in the abstract, the mind cannot stop short of an extreme, because it has to deal with an extreme, with a conflict of forces left to themselves, and obeying no other but their own inner laws. If we should seek to deduce from the pure conception of War an absolute point for the aim which we shall propose and for the means which we shall apply, this constant reciprocal action would involve us in extremes, which would be nothing but a play of ideas produced by an almost invisible train of logical subtleties. If, adhering closely to the absolute, we try to avoid all difficulties by a stroke of the pen, and insist with logical strictness that in every case the extreme must be the object, and the utmost effort must be exerted in that direction, such a stroke of the pen would be a mere paper law, not by any means adapted to the real world.

Even supposing this extreme tension of forces was an absolute which could easily be ascertained, still we must admit that the human mind would hardly submit itself to this kind of logical chimera. There would be in many cases an unnecessary waste of power, which would be in opposition to other principles of statecraft; an effort of Will would be required disproportioned to the proposed object which therefore it would be impossible to realize, for the human will does not derive its impulse from logical subtleties.

But everything takes a different shape when we pass from abstractions to reality. In the former, everything must be subject to optimism, and we must imagine the one side as well as the other striving after perfection and even attaining it. Will this ever take place in reality? It will if,

(I) War becomes a completely isolated act, which arises suddenly, and is in no way connected with the previous history of the combatant States.

(2) If it is limited to a single solution, or to several simultaneous solutions.

(3) *If* it contains within itself the solution perfect and complete, free from any reaction upon it, through a calculation beforehand of the political situation which will follow from it.

War is never an isolated act

With regard to the first point, neither of the two opponents is an abstract person to the other, not even as regards that factor in the sum of resistance which does not depend on objective things, viz. the Will. This Will is not an entirely unknown quantity; it indicates what it will be tomorrow by what it is today. War does not spring up quite suddenly, it does not spread to the full in a moment; each of the two opponents can, therefore, form an opinion of the other, in a great measure, from what he is and what he does, instead of judging of him according to what he, strictly speaking, should be or should do. But, now, man with his incomplete organization is always below the line of absolute perfection, and, thus these deficiencies, having an influence on both sides, become a modifying principle.

War does not consist of a single instantaneous blow

The second point gives rise to the following considerations:

If War ended in a single solution, or a number of simultaneous ones, then naturally all the preparations for the same would have a tendency to the extreme, for an omission could not in any way be repaired; the utmost, then, that the world of reality could furnish as a guide for us would be the preparations *of* the enemy, as far as they are known to us; all the rest would fall into the domain of the abstract. But if the result is made up from several, successive acts, then naturally that which precedes with all its phases may be taken as a measure for that which will follow, and in this manner the world of reality again takes the place of the abstract, and thus modifies the effort towards the extreme.

Yet every War would necessarily resolve itself into a single solution, or a sum of simultaneous results, if all the means required for the struggle were raised at once, or could be at once raised; for as one adverse result necessarily diminishes the means, then if all the means have been applied in the first, a second cannot properly be supposed. *All* hostile acts, which might follow, would belong essentially to the first, and form in reality only its duration.

But we have already seen that even in the preparation for War the real world steps into the place of mere abstract conception—a material standard into the place of the hypotheses of an extreme: that therefore in that way both parties, by the influence of the mutual reaction, remain below the line of extreme effort, and therefore all forces are not at once brought forward.

It lies also in the nature of these forces and their application that they cannot all be brought into activity at the same time. These forces are *the armies actually on foot, the country,* with its superficial extent and its population, *and the allies.*

In point of fact, the country, with its superficial area and the population, besides being the source of all military force, constitutes in itself an integral part of the efficient quantities in War, providing either the theatre of war or exercising a considerable influence on the same.

Now, it is possible to bring all the movable military forces of a country into operation at once, but not all fortresses, rivers, mountains, people, etc.,—in short, not the whole country, unless it is so small that it may be completely embraced by the first act of the War. Further, the cooperation of allies does not depend on the Will of the belligerents; and from the nature of the political relations of states to each other, this cooperation is frequently not afforded until after the War has commenced, or it, may be increased to restore the balance of power.

That this part of the means of resistance, which cannot at once be brought into activity, in many cases, is a much greater part of the whole than might at first be supposed, and that it often restores the balance of power, seriously affected by the great force of the first decision, will be more *fully* shown hereafter. Here it is sufficient to show that a complete concentration of all available means in a moment of time is contradictory to the nature of War.

Now this, in itself, furnishes no ground for relaxing our efforts to accumulate strength to gain the first result, because an unfavourable issue is always a disadvantage to which no one would purposely expose himself, and also because the first decision, although not the only one, still will have the more influence on subsequent events, the greater it is in itself.

But the possibility of gaining a later result causes men to take refuge in that expectation owing to the repugnance in the human mind to making excessive efforts; and therefore forces are not concentrated and measures are not taken for the first decision with that energy which would otherwise be used. Whatever one belligerent omits from weakness becomes to the other a real objective ground for limiting his own efforts, and thus again, through this reciprocal action, extreme tendencies are brought down to efforts on a limited scale.

The result in war is never absolute

Lastly, even the final decision of a whole War is not always to be regarded as absolute. The conquered State often sees in it only a passing evil, which may be repaired in after times by means *of* political combinations. How much this must modify the degree of tension, and the vigour of the efforts made, is evident in itself.

The probabilities of real life take the place of the conceptions of the extreme and the absolute

In this manner, the whole act of War is removed from the rigorous law of forces exerted to the utmost. If the extreme is no *longer* to be apprehend, and no longer to be sought for, it is left to the judgment to determine the limits for the efforts to be made in place of it, and this can only be done on the data furnished by the facts of the real world by the laws of probability. Once the belligerents are no longer mere conceptions, but individual States and Governments, once the War is no longer an ideal, but a definite substantial procedure, then the reality will furnish the data to compute the unknown quantities which are required to be found.

From the character, the measures, the situation of the adversary, and the relations with which he is surrounded, each side will draw conclusions by the law of probability as to the designs of the other, and act accordingly.

The political object now reappears

Here the question, which we had laid aside, forces itself again into consideration (see No. 2), *viz, the political object of the War*. The law of the extreme, the view to disarm the adversary, to overthrow him, has hitherto to a certain extent usurped the place of this end or object. Just as this law loses its forces the political object must again come forward. If the whole consideration is a calculation of probability based on definite persons and relations, then the political object, being the original motive, must be an essential factor in the product. The smaller the sacrifice we demand from our opponent, the smaller, it may be expected, will be the means of resistance which he will employ; but the smaller his preparation, the smaller will ours require to be. Further, the smaller our political object, the less value shall we set upon it, and the more easily shall we be induced to give it up altogether.

Thus, therefore, the political object, as the original motive of the War, will be the standard for determining both the aim of the military force and also the amount of effort to be made. This it cannot be in itself, but it is so in relation to both the belligerent States, because we are concerned with realities, not with mere abstractions. One and the same political object may produce totally different effects upon different people, or even upon the same people at different times; we can, therefore, only admit the political object as the measure, by considering it in its effects upon those masses which it is to move, and consequently the nature of those masses also comes into consideration. It is easy to see that thus the result may be very different according as these masses are animated with a spirit which will infuse vigour into the action or otherwise. It is quite possible for such a state of feeling to exist between two States that a very trifling political motive for War may produce an effect quite disproportionate—in fact, a perfect explosion.

This applies to the efforts which the political object will call forth in the two States, and to the aim which the military action shall prescribe for itself. At times it may itself be that aim, as, for example, the conquest of a province. At other times the political object itself is not suitable for the aim of military action; then such a one must be chosen as will be an equivalent for it, and stand in its place as regards the conclusion of peace. But also, in this, due attention to the peculiar character of the States concerned is always supposed. There are circumstances in which the equivalent must be much greater than the political object, in order to secure the latter. The political object will be so much the more the standard of aim and effort, and have more influence in itself, the more the masses are indifferent, the less that any mutual feeling of hostility prevails in the two States from other causes, and therefore there are cases where the political object almost alone will be decisive.

If the aim of the military action is an equivalent for the political object, that action will in general diminish as the political object diminishes, and in a greater degree the more the political object dominates. Thus it is explained how, without any contradiction in itself, there may be Wars of all degrees of importance and energy, from a War of extermination down to the mere use of an army of observation. This, however, leads to a question of another kind, which we have hereafter to develop and answer.

A suspension in the action of war unexplained by anything said as yet

However insignificant the political claims mutually advanced, however weak the means put forth, however small the aim to which military action is directed, can this action be suspended even for a moment? This is a question which penetrates deeply into the nature of the subject.

Every transaction requires for its accomplishment a certain time which we can its duration. This may be longer or shorter, according as the person acting throws more or less dispatch into his movements.

About this more or less we shall not trouble ourselves here. Each person acts in his own fashion; but the slow person does not protract the thing because he wishes to spend more time about it, but because by his nature he requires more time and if he made more haste would not do the thing so well. This time, therefore, depends on subjective causes, and belongs to the length so called, of the action.

If we allow now to every action in War this, its length, then we must assume, at first sight at least that any expenditure of time beyond this length, that is, every suspension of hostile action, appears an absurdity; with respect to this it must not be forgotten that we now speak not of the progress of one or other of the two opponents, but of the general progress of the whole action of the War.

There is only one cause which can suspend the action, and this seems to be only possible on one side in any case

If two parties have armed themselves for strife, then a feeling of animosity must have moved them to it; as long now as they continue armed, that is, do not come to terms of peace, this feeling must exist; and it can only be brought to a standstill by either side by one single motive alone, which is, *that he waits for a more favourable moment for action.* Now, at first sight, it appears that this motive can never exist except on one side, because it, *eo ipso,* must be prejudicial to the other. If the one has an interest in acting, then the other must have an interest in waiting.

A complete equilibrium of forces can never produce a suspension of action, for during this suspension he who has the positive object (that is, the assailant) must continue progressing; for if we should imagine an equilibrium in this way, that he who has the positive object, therefore the strongest motive, can at the same time only command the lesser means, so that the equation is made up by the product of the motive and the power, then we must say, if no alteration in this condition of equilibrium is to be expected, the two parties must make peace; but if an alteration is to be expected, then it can only be favourable to one side, and therefore the other has a manifest interest to act without delay. We see that the conception of equilibrium cannot explain a suspension of arms but that it ends in the question of the *expectation of a more favourable moment.*

Let us suppose, therefore, that one of two States has a positive object, as, for instance, the conquest of one of the enemy's provinces—which is to be utilized in the settlement of peace. After this conquest, his political object is accomplished, the necessity for action ceases, and for him a pause ensues. If the adversary is also contented with this solution, he will make peace, if not, he must act. Now, if we suppose that in four weeks he will be in a better condition to act, then he has sufficient grounds for putting off the time of action.

But from that moment the logical course for the enemy appears to be to act that he may not give the conquered party *the desired* time. Of course, in this mode of reasoning a complete insight into the state of circumstances on both sides is supposed.

Thus a continuance of action will ensue which will advance towards a climax

If this unbroken continuity of hostile operations really existed, the effect would be that everything would again be driven towards the extreme; for, irrespective of the effect of such incessant activity in inflaming the feelings, and infusing into the whole a greater degree of passion, a greater elementary force, there would also follow from this continuance of action a stricter continuity, a closer connexion between cause and effect, and thus every single action would become of more importance, and consequently more replete with danger.

But we know that the course of action in War has seldom or never this unbroken continuity, and that there have been many Wars in which action occupied by far the smallest portion of time employed, the whole of the rest being consumed in inaction. It is impossible that this should be always an anomaly; suspension of action in War must therefore be possible that is no contradiction in itself. We now proceed to show how this is.

Here, therefore, the principle of polarity is brought into requisition

As we have supposed the interests of one Commander to be always antagonistic to those of the other, we have assumed a true *polarity.*

The principle of polarity is only valid when it can be conceived in one and the same thing, where the positive and its opposite the negative completely destroy each other. In a battle, both sides strive to conquer; that is true polarity, for the victory of the one side destroys that of the other. But when we speak of two different things which have a common relation external to themselves, then it is not the things but their relations which have the polarity.

Attack and defence are things differing in kind and of unequal force. Polarity is, therefore, not applicable to them.

If there was only one form of War, to wit, the attack of the enemy, therefore no defence; or, in other words, if the attack was distinguished from the defence merely by the positive motive, which the one has and the other has not, but the methods of each were precisely one and the same; then in this sort of fight every advantage gained on the one side would be a corresponding disadvantage on the other, and true polarity would exist.

But action in War is divided into two forms, attack and defence, which, as we shall hereafter explain more particularly, are very different and of unequal strength. Polarity therefore lies in that to which both bear a relation, in the decision, but not in the attack or defence itself.

If the one Commander wishes the solution put off, the other must wish to hasten it, but only by the same form of action. If it is A's interest not to attack his enemy at present, but four weeks hence, then it is B's interest to be attacked, not four weeks hence, but at the present moment. This is the direct antagonism of interests, but it by no means follows that it would be for B's interest to attack A at once. That is plainly something totally different.

The effect of polarity is often destroyed by the superiority of the defence over the attack, and thus the suspension of action in war is explained

If the form of defence is stronger than that of offence, as we shall hereafter show, the question arises, is the advantage of a deferred decision as great on the one side as the advantage of the defensive form on the other? If it is not, then it cannot by its counter-weight overbalance the latter, and thus influence the progress of the action of the War. We see, therefore, that the impulsive force existing in the polarity of interests may be lost in the difference between the strength of the offensive and the defensive, and thereby become ineffectual.

If, therefore, that side for which the present is favourable, is too weak to be able to dispense with the advantage of the defensive, he must put up with the unfavourable prospects which the future holds out; for it may still be better to fight a defensive battle in the unpromising future than to assume the offensive or make peace at present. Now, being convinced that the superiority of the defensive (rightly understood) is very great, and much greater than may appear at first sight, we conceive that the greater number of those periods of inaction which occur in war are thus explained without involving any contradiction. The weaker the motives to action are, the more will those motives be absorbed and neutralized by this difference between attack and defence, the more frequently, therefore, will action in warfare be stopped, as indeed experience teaches.

A second ground consists in the imperfect knowledge of circumstances

But there is still another cause which may stop action in War, viz. an incomplete view of the situation. Each Commander can only fully know his own position; that of his opponent can only be known to him by reports, which are uncertain; he may, therefore form a wrong judgment with respect to it upon data of this description, and, in consequence of that error, he may suppose that the power of taking the initiative rests with his adversary when it lies really with himself. This want of perfect insight might certainly just as often occasion an untimely action, as untimely inaction, and hence it would in itself no more contribute to delay than to accelerate action in War. Still, it must always be regarded as one of the natural causes which may bring action in War to a standstill without involving a contradiction. But if we reflect how much more we are inclined and induced to estimate the power of our opponents too high than too low, because it lies in human nature to do so, we shall admit that our imperfect insight into facts in general must contribute very much to delay action in War, and to modify the application of the principles pending our conduct.

The possibility of a standstill brings into the action of War a new modification, inasmuch as it dilutes that action with the element of time, checks the influence or sense of danger in its course, and increases the means of reinstating a lost balance of force. The greater the tension of feelings from which the War springs, the greater therefore the energy with which it is carried on, so much the shorter will be the periods of inaction; on the other hand, the weaker the principle of warlike activity, the longer will be these periods: for powerful motives increase the force of the will, and this, as we know is always a factor in the product of force.

Frequent periods of inaction in war remove it further from the absolute, and make it still more a calculation of probabilities

But the slower the action proceeds in War, the more frequent and longer the periods of inaction, so much the more easily can an error be repaired; therefore, so much the bolder a General will be in his calculations, so much the more readily will he keep the them below the line of the absolute, and build everything upon probabilities and conjecture. Thus, according as the course of the War is more or less slow, more or less time will be allowed for that which the nature of a concrete case particularly requires, calculation of probability based on given circumstances.

Therefore the element of chance only is wanting to make of war a game, and in that element it is least of all deficient

We see from the foregoing how much the objective nature of War makes it a calculation of probabilities; now there is only one single element still wanting to make it a game, and that element it certainly is not without: it is chance. There is no human affair which stands so constantly and so generally in close connexion with chance as War. But together with chance, the accidental, and along with it good luck, occupy a great place in War.

War is a game both objectively and subjectively

If we now take a look at the *subjective nature* of War, that is to say, at those conditions under which it is carried on, it will appear to us still more like a game. Primarily the element in which the operations of War are carried on is danger; but which of all the moral qualities is the first in danger? *Courage.* Now certainly courage is quite compatible with prudent calculation, but still they are things of quite a different kind, essentially different qualities of the mind; on the other hand, daring reliance on good fortune, boldness, rashness, are only expressions of courage, and all these propensities of the mind look for the fortuitous (*or* accidental), because it is their element.

We see, therefore, how, from the commencement, the absolute, the mathematical as it is called, nowhere finds any sure basis in the calculations in the Art of War; and that from the outset there is a play of possibilities, probabilities, good and bad luck, which spreads about with all the coarse and fine threads of its web, and makes War of all branches of human activity the most like a gambling game.

How this accords best with the human mind in general

Although our intellect always feels itself urged towards clearness and certainty, still our mind often feels itself attracted by uncertainty, instead of threading its way with the understanding along the narrow path of philosophical investigations and logical conclusions, in order, almost unconscious of itself, to arrive in spaces where it feels itself a stranger, and where it seems to part from all well-known objects, it prefers to remain with the imagination in the realms of chance and luck. Instead of living yonder on poor necessity, it revels here in the wealth of possibilities; animated thereby, courage then takes wings to itself, and daring and danger make the element into which it launches itself as a fearless swimmer plunges into the stream.

Shall theory leave it here, and move on, self-satisfied with absolute conclusions and roles? Then it is of no practical use. Theory must also take into account the human element; it must accord a place to courage, to boldness, even to rashness. The Art of War has to deal with living and with moral forces, the consequence of which is that it can never attain the absolute and positive. There is therefore everywhere a margin for the accidental, and just as much in the greatest things as in the smallest. As there is room for this accidental on the one hand, so on the other there must be courage and self-reliance in proportion to the room available. If these qualities are forthcoming in a high degree, the margin left may likewise be great. Courage and self-reliance are, therefore, principles quite essential to War; consequently, theory must only set up such rules as allow ample scope for all degrees and varieties of these necessary and noblest of military virtues. In daring there may still be wisdom, and prudence as well, only they are estimated by a different standard of value.[11]

War is always a serious means for a serious object. Its more particular definition

Such is War; such the Commander who conducts it; such the theory which rules it. But War is no pastime; no mere passion for venturing and winning; no work of a free enthusiasm: it is a serious means for a serious object. All that appearance which it wears from the varying hues of fortune, all that it assimilates into itself of the oscillations *of* passion, of courage, of imagination, of enthusiasm, are only particular properties of this means.

The War of a community—of whole Nations, and particularly of civilized Nations—always starts from apolitical condition, and is called forth by a political motive. It is, therefore, a political act. Now if it was a perfect, unrestrained, and absolute expression of force, as we had to deduce it from its mere conception, then the moment it is called forth by policy it would step into the place of policy, and as something quite independent of it would set *it* aside, and only follow its own laws, just as a mine at the moment of explosion cannot be guided into any other direction than that which has been given to it by preparatory arrangements. This is how the thing has really been viewed

Hitherto, whenever a want of harmony between policy and the conduct of a War has led to theoretical distinctions of the kind. But it is not so, and the idea is radically false. War in the real world, as we have already seen, is not an extreme thing which expends itself at one single discharge; it is the operation of powers which do not develop themselves completely in the same manner and in the same measure, but which at one time expand sufficiently to overcome the resistance opposed by inertia or friction, while at another they are too weak to produce an effect; it is therefore, in a certain measure, a pulsation of violent force more or less vehement, consequently making its discharges and exhausting its powers more or less quickly—in other words, conducting more or less quickly to the aim, but always lasting long enough to admit of influence being exerted on it in its course, so as to give it this or that direction, in short, to be subject to the will of a guiding intelligence. Now, if we reflect that War has its root in a political object, then naturally this original motive, which called it into existence, should also continue the first and highest consideration in its conduct. Still, the political object is no despotic lawgiver on that account; it must accommodate itself to the nature of the means, and though changes in these means may involve modification in the political objective, the latter always retains a prior right to consideration. Policy, therefore, is interwoven with the whole action of War, and must exercise a continuous influence upon it, as far as the nature of the forces liberated by it will permit.

War is a mere continuation of policy by other means

We see, therefore, that War is not merely a political act, but also a real political instrument, a continuation of political commerce, a carrying out of the same by other means. All beyond this, which is strictly peculiar to War, relates merely to the peculiar nature of the means which it uses. That the tendencies and views of policy shall not be incompatible with these means, the Art of War in general and the Commander in each particular case may demand, and this claim is truly not a trifling one. But however powerfully this may react on political views in particular cases, still it must always be regarded as only a modification of them; for the political view is the object. War is the means, and the means must always include the object in our conception.

Diversity in the nature of wars

The greater and the more powerful the motives of a War, the more it affects the whole existence of a people. The more violent the excitement which precedes the War, by so much the nearer will the War approach to its abstract form, so much the more will it be directed to the destruction of the enemy, so much the nearer will the military and political ends coincide, so much the more purely military and less political the War appears to be; but the weaker the motives and the tensions, so much the less will the natural direction of the military element—that is, force—be coincident with the direction which the political element indicates; so much the more must, therefore, the War become diverted from its natural direction, the political object diverge from the aim of an ideal War, and the War appear to become political.

But, that the reader may not form any false conceptions, we must here observe that by this natural tendency of War we only mean the philosophical, the strictly logical, and by no means the tendency of forces actually engaged in conflict, by which would be supposed to be included all the emotions and passions of the combatants. No doubt in some cases these also might be excited to such a degree as to be with difficulty restrained and confined to the political road; but in most cases such a contradiction will not arise, because by the existence of such strenuous exertions a great plan in harmony therewith would be implied. If the plan is directed only upon a small object, then the impulses of feeling amongst the masses will be also so weak that these masses will require being stimulated rather than repressed.

They may all be regarded as political acts

Returning now to the main subject, although it is true that in one kind of War the political element seems almost to disappear whilst in another kind it occupies a very prominent place, we may still affirm that the one is as political as the other; for if we regard the State policy as the intelligence of the personified State, then amongst all the constellations in the political sky whose movements it has to compute, those must be, included which arise when the nature of its relations imposes the necessity of a great War. It is only if we understand by policy not a true appreciation of affairs in general, but the conventional conception of a cautious, subtle, also dishonest craftiness, averse from violence, that the latter kind of War may belong more to policy than the first.

Influence of this view on the right understanding of military history, and on the foundations of theory

We see, therefore, in the first place, that under all circumstances War is to be regarded not as an independent thing, but as a political instrument; and it is only by taking this point of view that we can avoid finding ourselves in opposition to all military history. This is the only means of unlocking the great book and making it intelligible. Secondly, this view shows us how Wars must differ in character according to the nature of the motives, and circumstances from which they precede.

Now, the first, the grandest, and most decisive act of judgment which the Statesman and General exercises is rightly to understand in this respect the War in which he engages, not to take it for something, or to wish to make of it something, which by the nature of its relations it is impossible for it to be. This is, therefore, the first, the most comprehensive, of all strategical questions. We shall enter into this more fully in treating of the plan of a War.

For the present we content ourselves with having brought the subject up to this point, and having thereby fixed the chief point of view from which War and its theory are to be studied.

Result for theory

War is, therefore, not only chameleon-like in character, because it changes its colour in some degree in each particular case, but it is also, as a whole, in relation to the predominant tendencies which are in it, a wonderful trinity, composed of the original violence of its elements, hatred and animosity, which may be looked upon as blind instinct; of the play of probabilities and chance, which make it a free activity of the soul; and of the subordinate nature of a political instrument, by which it belongs purely to the reason.

The first of these three phases concerns more the people; me second, more the General and his Army; the third, more the Government. The passions, which break forth in War, must already have a latent existence in the peoples. The range, which the display of courage and talents shall get in the realm of probabilities and of chance, depends on the particular characteristics of the General and his Army, but the political objects belong to the Government alone.

These three tendencies, which appear like so many different lawgivers, are deeply rooted in the nature of the subject, and at the same time variable in degree. A theory which would leave anyone of them out of account, or set up any arbitrary relation between them, would immediately become involved in such a contradiction with the reality, that it might be regarded as destroyed at once by that alone.

The problem is, therefore, that theory shall keep itself poised in a manner between these three tendencies, as between three points of attraction.

The way in which alone this difficult problem can be solved we shall examine in the book on the 'Theory of War.' In every case the conception of War, as here defined, will be the first ray of light which shows us the true foundation of theory, and which first separates the great masses and allows us to distinguish them from one another.

The Art of War

Sun Tzu

Chinese Philosopher and General (circa. 500 B.C.)

1. Sun Tzu said: The art of war is of vital importance to the State.
2. It is a matter of life and death, a road either to safety or to ruin. Hence it is a subject of inquiry which can on no account be neglected.
3. The art of war, then, is governed by five constant factors, to be taken into account in one's deliberations, when seeking to determine the conditions obtaining in the field.
4. These are:

   (1) The Moral Law;

   (2) Heaven;

   (3) Earth;

   (4) The Commander;

   (5) Method and discipline.

5,6. The Moral Law causes the people to be in complete accord with their ruler, so that they will follow him regardless of their lives, undismayed by any danger.

7. Heaven signifies night and day, cold and heat, times and seasons.
8. Earth comprises distances, great and small; danger and security; open ground and narrow passes; the chances of life and death.
9. The Commander stands for the virtues of wisdom, sincerely, benevolence, courage and strictness.
10. By method and discipline are to be understood the marshaling of the army in its proper subdivisions, the graduations of rank among the officers, the maintenance of roads by which supplies may reach the army, and the control of military expenditure.
11. These five heads should be familiar to every general: he who knows them will be victorious; he who knows them not will fail.
12. Therefore, in your deliberations, when seeking to determine the military conditions, let them be made the basis of a comparison, in this wise:
13. (1) Which of the two sovereigns is imbued with the Moral law?

    (2) Which of the two generals has most ability?

    (3) With whom lie the advantages derived from Heaven and Earth?

    (4) On which side is discipline most rigorously enforced?

    (5) Which army is stronger?

(6) On which side are officers and men more highly trained?

(7) In which army is there the greater constancy both in reward and punishment?

14. By means of these seven considerations I can forecast victory or defeat.
15. The general that hearkens to my counsel and acts upon it, will conquer: let such a one be retained in command! The general that hearkens not to my counsel nor acts upon it, will suffer defeat:—let such a one be dismissed!
16. While heeding the profit of my counsel, avail yourself also of any helpful circumstances over and beyond the ordinary rules.
17. According as circumstances are favorable, one should modify one's plans.
18. All warfare is based on deception.
19. Hence, when able to attack, we must seem unable; when using our forces, we must seem inactive; when we are near, we must make the enemy believe we are far away; when far away, we must make him believe we are near.
20. Hold out baits to entice the enemy. Feign disorder, and crush him.
21. If he is secure at all points, be prepared for him. If he is in superior strength, evade him.
22. If your opponent is of choleric temper, seek to irritate him. Pretend to be weak, that he may grow arrogant.
23. If he is taking his ease, give him no rest. If his forces are united, separate them.
24. Attack him where he is unprepared, appear where you are not expected.
25. These military devices, leading to victory, must not be divulged beforehand.
26. Now the general who wins a battle makes many calculations in his temple ere the battle is fought. The general who loses a battle makes but few calculations beforehand. Thus do many calculations lead to victory, and few calculations to defeat: how much more no calculation at all! It is by attention to this point that I can foresee who is likely to win or lose.

An End to Militarism

Jean de Bloch

Entrepreneur and Pacifist (1836-1902)

We constantly hear the argument adduced, that there always have been wars and always will be, and if in the course of all the centuries recorded in history, international disputes were settled only by means of war, how can it be possible to get along without it in the future? To this we might reply that not only the number, equipment, training, and technical methods of armies, but the very elements front which they are constructed have essentially changed.

The relations of the strength of armies in time of war to their strength in time of peace in former times was very different. Wars formerly were carried on by standing armies consisting mainly of long service soldiers. The armies employed in future wars will be composed mainly of soldiers taken directly from peaceful occupations. Among the older soldiers will be vast numbers of heads of families torn from their homes, their families and their work. The economic life of whole peoples will stand still, communications will be cut, and if war be prolonged over the greater part of a year, general bankruptcy, with famine and all its worst consequences, will ensue....

Consideration of the question is made all the more difficult by the fact that the direction of military affairs belongs to the privileged ranks of society. The opinions expressed by non-specialists as to the improbability of great wars in the future, are refuted by authorities simply by the declaration that lay-men are ignorant of the subject. Military men cannot admit to be unnecessary that which forms the object of their activity in time of peace. They have been educated on the history of warfare, and practical work develops in them energy and capacity for self-sacrifice. Nevertheless, such authorities are not in a position to paint a complete picture of the disasters of a future war. Those radical changes which have taken place in the military art, in the composition of armies, and in international economy, are so vast that a powerful imagination would be required adequately to depict the consequences of war, both on the field of battle and in the lives of peoples.

Yet it cannot be denied that popular discontent with the present condition of affairs is becoming more and more keenly noticeable. Formerly only solitary voices were raised against militarism, and their protests were platonic. But since the adoption of conscription the interests of the army have been more closely bound with the interests of society, and the disasters which must be expected under modern conditions have been better appreciated by the people.

It is impossible, therefore, not to foresee the constant growth of the anti-military propaganda,

Jean de Bloch, "An End to Militarism." From *The Future of War in its Technical, Political and Economic Relations*, 1898. Reprinted by permission of the Jean de Bloch Society on War and Peace.

the moral foundations of which were not so indisputable in the past as they are today. To this moral sentiment has lately been added a consciousness of the complexity of the business relations threatened by war, of the immense increase of means of destruction, and of the deficiency of experienced leadership and the ignorance and cloudiness now prevailing on the subject of war.

***

It is true that the advocates of the settlement of international disputes by peaceful means have not attained any tangible success. But success, it must he admitted, they have had if the fact is taken into account that the necessity of maintaining peace has been recognised by governments, and that dread of the terrible disasters of war has been openly expressed by statesmen, and emphasised even from the height of thrones.

***

But changes which have taken place in political and social conditions, the increased importance of knowledge, industry, capital, and finally, the immense numbers of the military class, considerably reduced its privileges in society. Rivalry in the acquisition of means for the satisfaction of more complex requirements has caused the majority of educated people to see in military service an ungrateful career. And, indeed, there is no other form of exacting activity which pays so badly as the military profession. Owing to the immense growth of armies, governments cannot find the means for improving the position of officers and their families, and a deficiency in officers is everywhere felt.

...The movement against militarism leads to views diametrically opposite. Modern ideals every day see less to sympathise with in the old ideals of distinction in battle, and glory of conquest. Everywhere the idea spreads that the efforts of all ought to be devoted to the lessening of the sum of physical and moral suffering. The immense expenditure on the maintenance of armies and fleets and the building and equipment of fortresses, acts powerfully in the spreading of such sentiments. Everywhere we hear complaints that militarism sucks the blood of all—as it has been expressed, "in place of ears of corn the fields produce bayonets and sabres, and shells instead of fruit grow on the trees." Those who adopt the military career are, of course, not responsible for these conditions, which they did not create and which react injuriously on themselves.

***

The times are passed when officers rushing on in advance led their men in a bold charge against the enemy, or when squadrons seeing an ill-defended battery galloped up to it, sabred the gunners, and spiked the guns or flung them into ditches. Courage now is required no less than before, but this is the courage of restraint and sell-sacrifice and no longer scenic heroism. War has taken a character more mechanical than knightly. Personal initiative is required not less than before, but it is no longer visible to all.

***

As the popularity of war decreases on all sides, it is impossible not to foresee that a time will approach when...governments can no longer rely on the regular payment of taxes for the covering of military expenditure.

***

A detailed examination of the vexed questions of Europe would lead to the conclusion that not one is of such a nature to cause a great war. France has no ally in an offensive war for the recovery of her lost provinces, and single-handed she cannot be assured of success. From an offensive war over the Eastern question neither Russia nor Austria could draw compensatory advantages, and such a war, which in all probability would involve the participation of England, France, Germany and Italy, would lead only to exhaustion of forces. Germany cannot think of attacking France, while out of an offensive war with Russia she could draw no profit.

Of new territory in the West, Russia also has no need, and a war with Germany would involve such immense expenditure as could hardly be covered by an indemnity, all the more so because, exhausted as she would be by a struggle with Russia, Germany could not pay an indemnity corresponding to the case. Generally, the political question for Russia lies in the Far East and not in the West.

As concerns other possible pretexts for war, examination would show that, in the present conditions of Europe, none are of sufficient gravity to cause a war threatening the combatants with mutual annihilation or complete exhaustion, nor need those moral misunderstandings and rivalries which exist between European states be seriously considered. It cannot be supposed that nations would determine to exterminate one another merely to show their superiority, or to avenge offences committed by individuals belonging to one nation against individuals belonging to another. Thus a consideration of all the reasonable causes of war would show that not one was probable.

***

In our time both military and political affairs have ceased to be high mysteries accessible only to the few. General military service, the spread of education, and wide publicity have made the elements of the polities of states accessible to all. All who have passed through the ranks of an army have recognised that with modem weapons whole corps and squadrons may be destroyed in the first battle, and that in this respect the conquerors will suffer little less than the conquered.

Can it be possible that the growth of expenditure on armaments will continue for ever? To the inventiveness of the human mind and the rivalry between states no limits exist. It is not surprising therefore that the immense expenditure on military aims and the consequent growth of taxation are the favourite arguments of agitators, who declare that the institutions of the Middle Ages—when from thousands of castles armed knights pounced upon passing merchants—were less burdensome than modern preparations for war.

The exact disposition of the masses in relation to armaments is shown by the increase in the number of opponents of militarism and preachers of the Socialist propaganda....

The question is naturally asked: What will be given to the people after war as compensation for their immense losses? The conquered certainly will be too exhausted to pay any money indemnity, and compensation must be taken by the retention of frontier territories which will be so impoverished by war that their acquisition will be a loss rather than a gain....

The longer the present position of affairs continues the greater is the probability of...convulsions after the close of a great war.... Thus side by side with the growth of military burdens rise waves of popular discontent threatening a social revolution.

Such are the consequences of the so-called armed peace [of Europe]—slow destruction in consequence of expenditure on preparations for war, or swift destruction in the event of war—in both events convulsions in the social order.

Militarism

C. Delisle Burns (1879-1942)
British Historian and Philosopher

Militarism in its broadest sense may be defined as an attitude toward public affairs which conceives war and the preparation for war as the chief instruments of foreign policy and the highest form of public service. Regarding military service as ennobling both the person who serves and his community, it glorifies personal courage, the adventurous spirit, loyalty to a person or cause and bodily strength and endurance. Militarism of this type, rigidly disciplinarian and hierarchic in its methods, thrives in simple or traditionalist groups where only the more primitive forms of excellence and the least developed kinds of authority are understood. It represents the outlook of an "upper" social class which is unaware of its economic dependence and therefore normally implies a disdain of industry, trade and commerce as occupations. It is mythological and religious in its expressions—using ceremonies, decorations, titles and symbols—and is weakest [when] it is constrained to explain itself. It exists in armed forces, for it is an essential feature of preparation for war. Defined in such terms militarism is not widely prevalent at the present day, being found only in limited groups or at moments of national crisis. But the traditional idea that war is in "the nature of things" still survives, especially at periods of diplomatic tension, when the masses of the population fall easy victims to the warnings of professional militarist groups. In this more limited sense militarism may be conceived as the spark which sets off the tinder of accumulated ignorance.

The psychological origins of militarism are explained by the survival of types of reaction natural to primitive social conditions. I[n] simple forms of society the frontier of civilized life is the wilderness, the desert or the forest. The civilized community faces inward, but it fears what may be at its back. Against unknown dangers outside, two movements are reasonable—first, defense and, second, adventure pressing forward the gains of civilization over the wilderness. Nearly all the older governments have come into existence as isolated oases of order in a surrounding chaos of emptiness; and therefore the traditional attitude toward what is alien, foreign or outside the frontier is that of defense against barbarism. Anyone who does not speak one's own language or follow one's own customs is regarded as a barbarian; and each of two civilized groups can therefore regard the other as barbaric. Such groups, however, are scarcely in contact so long as the intervening wilderness remains. The ancient Roman Empire and the ancient Chinese Empire were coexistent, but almost in separate worlds. In early times, when the frontier was a limit to civilized order, military virtues developed—personal courage in

C. Delisle Burns, "Militarism, pp. 446-451." From *Encyclopedia of Social Sciences*, Vol. 10, edited by Edwin R.A. Seligman, Macmillan Library Reference, Copyright © 1961. Reprinted by permission of the Gale Group.

defense of a community, obedience to authority and adventurousness in the face of danger.

The primitive attitude toward what lies beyond the frontier survives even in our own time. As civilization advances, however, the frontiers of all of its centers are pushed back until they meet; there is then no more wilderness dividing the jurisdictions of separate governments. But the forms of language, of custom and of social institutions continue to differ, because they have grown outward from diverse centers; and what is really another kind of "order" outside the frontier is treated, by those within it, as barbarism. Defense is then no longer defense of civilization itself but defense of one kind of civilization against another; and the hostile attitude toward what is foreign becomes fiercer, not more reasonable, when what is foreign is no longer obviously weaker. The Germans and the French fear each other much more than the Romans or the Chinese feared the outer barbarians of the past. Militarism emerges when the original source of the military virtues no longer exists. The defense of civilization, instead of dying down when frontiers touch, blazes up higher, as it becomes more artificial. It is assumed that the frontier is still endangered by outer barbarians who are "aggressive," although these so-called barbarians are likewise "civilized" and are armed also chiefly in "self-defense."

War is planned far in advance and many years are spent in preparation for a contest. Under a highly professionalized system of this kind the conception that war is ennobling tends inevitably to give way to the conception that it is inevitable; and the modern militarist usually maintains that his activities are entirely for the sake of peace. The ancient habits are maintained when the original reasons for their existence have disappeared; but a new rhetoric and a new mythology are quickly evolved to rationalize vestigial instincts. As personal loyalty to a sovereign decays, defense of the nation takes its place; the "will of God" is replaced by the hypothesis of natural selection through war.

But as war comes to be organized by skillfully prepared professional opponents, it becomes progressively more expensive. Industry and science are drawn into the preparation program. Munitions industries take the place of the armorers' guilds of the Middle Ages, but the scale on which they supply the needs of armed forces gives them a much greater influence.... As the armaments trade is partly international, whichever side wins the race, shareholders on both sides gain money....

The influence of militarist groups on foreign policy is also secured through naval and military attachés, some of whom assist the sale of armaments abroad, search out military secrets and communicate with the war departments independently of the ambassadors to whom they are nominally subordinate. In most systems of government there is also a small general staff which has much more influence upon cabinets than any non-military group. Thus the admiration for war or at least the assumption that it is inevitable or likely—the spirit of militarism—exerts a continuous pressure upon public policy behind the scenes.

The timeworn rhetoric of militarism—punctuated with unrealistic presuppositions regarding the ineradicable pugnacity of man, the biological value of natural selection through war, the responsibilities of citizenship, the nobility of self-sacrifice in defense of fatherland, the cultivation of Spartan virtues—has lost much of its effectiveness in concealing the deeper lying vested interests in whose behalf it is employed. The military caste in every nation is part of the social class in control of public affairs; and nearly all existing communities today are traditionalist in their social standards. Those in control are honored. The desire to control other men, as instruments or inferiors, is much stronger and more widespread than the desire to attack "enemies" or foreigners; and the authoritarian military structure serves to canalize this desire for domination. The sense of superiority is enjoyed by all ranks in armed forces above the rank and file; and the actual exercise of domination is shared by a whole officer class. This gives a social prestige to what might otherwise be a merely individual tyranny over the instruments of a commander's will. Even in "democratic" armed forces preparation for war, like war itself, makes it essential that the majority shall give up all individuality and become passive instruments of another's will. Again, the military caste preserves the self-confidence of those who feel the simpler kind of self-importance. Many who lack qualifications by birth or wealth can gain social prestige by their physical prowess or cunning in a militaristic society; while, on the other hand, a considerable section of the leisure class finds in military activity its only outlet and source of influence. Small groups therefore desire to cure or maintain prestige for themselves or their "nation" by the only means they can conceive as giving prestige—superior force and cunning. War itself is for them a sort of glorified sport, alluring both in its savageness and in its hazards.

But militarism does not survive only upon the desire for domination and violence in "upper" classes. It depends also upon the existence of the type of person in every community who enjoys being ordered about and prefers to have no moral responsibility for his actions. As unconscious supporters of militarism there must be added all who cannot find relief for themselves from the routine or monotony of an industrial civilization. The desire for adventure merges with the desire for being "important." The bank clerk or the grocer can be treated as a "hero" when he wears a military uniform. Wherever a community is rigidly controlled by traditional tabus, the younger and more vigorous are attracted to what promises relief, even at the risk of death for themselves or disaster for all. The drums, flags, medals and signs of rank in connection with war have a great appeal, and all the customs and beliefs they express connect men with a past which they have learned to admire.

The whole moral tradition in the West is affected by the way in which history is written and taught so as to exalt the military virtues and justify past violence. Each nation learns that in past wars it has been victorious; that its most important contacts with other nations have been military conflicts; and that its "heroes" are those who have won victories over foreigners. Naturally all these wars are believed to have been for the maintenance of "right"; and war is conceived as the situation in which one serves the nation, while in peace each man is supposed to pursue his own advantage. In non-republican countries kings and princes wear military uniforms. In all countries national pageantry is military. The past dominates the present and the future, through the unconscious reception of moral standards drawn from early chroniclers and poets. Militarism survives more strongly upon feeling as the reasoning upon which it once rested becomes more obviously inapplicable.

The history of this attitude toward war begins, at least in western civilization, with the primitive adventure described in the Homeric poems, which expressed admiration for bodily strength, cunning, courage and good fellowship. The incidental evils caused by these virtues when employed in war are not remembered, if the vanquished are slain or enslaved. Next comes the admiration for resistance to alien force, as expressed in Greek poetry of the sixth and fifth centuries, which survives in Plato as a tradition of valor. In his *Republic,* war against outsiders is assumed to be inevitable; and the criticism of war in the work of Aristophanes and Euripides seems to have had very little effect. The Spartans appear to have been militaristic in the crudest sense; but the majority of the Greeks were too sensitive to excuse the brutality of war on the ground that it promoted certain virtues.

In China there developed at a very early date a strong antimilitarist sentiment, which is expressed in the conception that the warrior ranks lower than the scholar and the trader. In India Buddhism had enough influence to undermine the primitive admiration for violence and the military virtues. But in Japan, on the contrary, in spite of Chinese and Buddhist influences, the moral ideal implied in bushidô supported an extreme form of militarism in the governing class. Both the good and the bad elements inherent in blind loyalty and disdain of death are still explicitly emphasized in the Japanese tradition.

In the West the Roman tradition has been the most powerful influence in the development of militarism. *Virtus,* or valor, constituted the highest

Roman ideal. The great men of Rome were warriors. The Roman Empire was the result of successful war; it was maintained by military efficiency; and only when Roman citizens began to be civilized enough to desire to avoid service in the armies did Roman civilization decay. In the fourth century it became difficult for the Roman authorities to raise troops except by recruiting "barbarians"; but troops had become the only basis of governmental authority since the later years of the republic. The Christians, who were unwilling to serve in the army, seem to have been influenced by objections to the traditional ritual rather than to war; the educated assumed that they could hire soldiers. There was no conception that war itself was futile or objectionable. The "just" war was always one in which one's own side was involved. The simple enthusiasm of the early Roman attitude, which alone implied "militarism," had died down. Literature and history, however, still preserved the more obsolete primitive admiration for the adventurous warrior, with the simpler virtues of endurance, courage and loyalty to a leader. The names of Alexander and Caesar gave prestige to military virtue.

In the Middle Ages the conception of service combined with the admiration for adventure to create "chivalry"—a source from which modern militarism draws not a few of its tendencies. But no armed forces comparable to a modern army existed between Roman times and the fifteenth century; and at the latter date soldiers were mercenaries, who had only the virtue of loyalty to an employer or leader, if that. They were not regarded as ennobled by their activities. In the Reformation, however, the influence of the warriors of the Old Testament and of certain bellicose sentiments expressed therein gave a new fillip to the admiration for military virtues. War became God's instrument.

In the seventeenth and eighteenth centuries service in arms was one of the recognized careers for a "gentleman." The divine will in war was combined with ideas drawn from an earlier chivalry. War was service of a king or lord and at the same time an opportunity for seeing the world. By the seventeenth century the old feudal levies had already proved useless and mercenaries hired for a particular job were expensive or unreliable. A "standing army" became a necessity for the ambitious sovereign. In England the power of the army during the civil war and the Commonwealth and the fear of an armed force in the king's control led to the section in the Bill of Rights of 1689 forbidding the raising of a standing army except by leave of Parliament. The fear lest the civil power be overcome by an armed force survives in the English practise of making the Army Act dependent upon an annual acceptance by Parliament. Although in a sense this may be taken as an indication of the fear of militarism, it was tyranny which was the real object of attack.

The conception, however, that the civil power should be supreme over the armed forces became a tradition among democratic and liberal circles in England and France. The French Revolution introduced the conception of a citizen army, presumably immune from militarism; but Napoleon showed how easily the two could be connected. Despite the attempts of Benjamin Constant and his liberal successors in France to prove that the older technique of war was being rendered obsolete by the new commercial civilization, the tradition of militarism continued to persist. The most startling revelation of French militarism occurred in connection with the Dreyfus case, when "the word of an officer" was assumed by the spokesmen of the army to be beyond criticism. It seems clear that, even in a citizen army, the officer caste tends toward militarism. In 1911 Jaurès, echoing the antimilitarist sentiments of the parliamentary socialists, sought in *L'Armee nouvelle* to establish the fact that it was possible to have a citizen army without militarism; but even he proposed the training of boys from ten years of age for possible war service in the future; and he accepted the traditional admiration for Napoleon and other military leaders whose intelligence he admired.

Meanwhile Germany was developing a new form of militarism. Prussia had defeated Napoleon by using the same appeal to the nation for raising armed forces which in the French Revolution had given Napoleon himself his first opportunity. The expulsion of alien conquerors by enthusiasts in arms, combined with the traditional Prussian admiration for valor and stern living, gave prestige to the leaders of the army. By an accident of history Bismarck, who had all the traditional admirations and an exceptional ability for putting them into practise, was able to use the results of the earlier resistance to Napoleon, which had saved Prussia, as a basis for uniting the German states in a new empire. The army became the symbol of imperial prestige, setting the standard of service and honor. The emperor was war lord. The feudal aristocracy took the lead in the armed forces and improved its own position by using the glamour of arms. The perfection of militarism, in its good as well as in its bad sense, was attained among the upper classes in Germany in the years immediately before the World War. The German comic papers of the period, especially *Simplicissimus,* provide abundant evidence of the attitude of "outsiders" who were close enough to feel the social atmosphere. The militarism of Germany before the war was felt to be dangerous even by some Germans.

Although during the World War "militarism" came to acquire derogatory connotations as a result of anti-German propaganda, military virtues continued of necessity to be preached and a certain blindness to the actual realities of warfare was cultivated on both sides. At the end of the war there was for a time a violent reaction against militarism. In Fascist Italy, however, militarism soon reappeared disguised as a "national" gospel, and it has been intensively cultivated by Fascist or chauvinistic groups in other nations. Among such groups war is openly championed; a mythology of the nation supplies the place of "the will of God"; and control by an officer class is identified with social order. A less open form of militarism has likewise survived among certain small groups in almost every nation. Such militarism has been fostered to an unprecedented extent in the new systems of military training for boys in schools and colleges. The contention that preparation for service in the armed forces in a future war is useful "educationally," although it is a more or less honest camouflage, is a confession of the necessity in democratic nations of justifying in more rational terms the cultivation of the military spirit.

It is difficult to say whether the philosophers and social theorists have merely reflected contemporary attitudes toward militarism or have actually molded such attitudes. From the outset Christian theology has compromised with the warrior. It was assumed by theologians that war was inevitable; the only problem was how to be on the right side and, in a world whose "plan" was divine, the right side meant the winning side. Many protests were made against excessive cruelty, but few against the military spirit. With the Renaissance, however, Erasmus and others began to suspect the validity of the old arguments which excused war. Cornelius Agrippa in the *De incertitudine et vanitate scientiarum et artium* (Antwerp 1531) has a very pointed analysis of the ruffianism which is disguised as military honor. But philosophers likewise could find excuses as the church had done. In modern times the most systematic rationalization of militarism is to be found in Hegel's *Philosophie des Rechts,* where he says that war promotes unselfishness (sect. 338) and that in modern time's enmity is not directed against individuals. In England the Oxford Hegelian T. H. Green, repudiating Hegel, delivered...an attack upon war as contrary to the nature of the state. Herbert Spencer, impressed by the rapid growth of militarism in Germany, set out to analyze what he called the "militant type of society" and traced the origins of militarism to the strivings of an "upper" class for social control. But on the whole the theorists of the later nineteenth century seem to have disregarded the importance of war as an institution. The wild metaphors of Nietzsche can scarcely be regarded as implying militarism; and Treitschke only repeats Hegel. Since the World War the popular movement which aimed at undermining the militarist admiration for war caused the "outlawry of war" in the Kellogg, or Paris, Pact of 1927; but no philosophical treatise either advocating or repudiating militarism has appeared.

Cultural Dimensions of Militarism: A Marxist Perspective

Malvern Lumsden
UNESCO

Structure and Superstructure

Within social sciences a number of traditions have emphasised the importance of social structure in determining or at least influencing other social phenomena. The notion of social structure has also proved fruitful in peace research and many of the ideas developed within this field will be built upon in this paper.

"Structuralism" within social sciences, however, has come to mean many things to many people. While hitherto peace researchers have mainly focused their attention on social structures—conceived as a set of objective and material social relations—much less attention has been paid to the structure and dynamics of "superstructures". "Superstructure" is a Marxist theoretical term which closely approximates to the Western anthropological term "culture", particularly nonmaterial or subjective culture. That is to say, while structure refers to patterns of economic, social and political relations, superstructure (or culture, which will be used here synonymously) refers to patterns of values, beliefs, ideologies, norms, symbols and so on.[1]

In the materialist conception of history, the superstructure of subjective ideas (which may be shared by a collectivity) is seen as largely determined by the underlying social structure, or base.[2] This view continues to be disputed by others who argue for the primacy of culture over material conditions.[3] In this context, therefore, it may be useful to recall that Engels wrote:

> Political, juridical, religious, literary, artistic, etc. development is based upon economic development. But all these react upon one another and also upon the economic basis. It is not that the economic situation is cause, solely active, while everything else is only passive effect. There is, rather, interaction on the basis of economic necessity, which ultimately always asserts itself.[4]

For his part, Marx wrote that

> What distinguishes the worst architect from the best of bees is this, that the architect raises his structure in imagination before he erects it in reality.[5]

To which George Thomson adds:

> This preconceived image has two aspects. On the one hand, it embodies the knowledge, acquired from previous practice in production, which enables the producer to conduct the process in such a way as to achieve his purpose. This is its objective or cognitive aspect. On the other, it embodies the desire, derived from previous practice in

Malvern Lumsden, "Cultural Dimensions of Militarism: A Marxist Perspective." This chapter is reprinted from Proceedings of the International Peace Research Association Seventh General Conference by permission of the International Peace Research Association.

> consumption, which provides the will to produce. This is its subjective or affective aspect. In these two aspects of the labour process—the purpose and the will—we may recognise the germ of the distinction between science and art.[6]

In passing, it may be added that these notions are quite compatible with much of modern Western psychology and social science, where, for example, the term "cultural ecology" has been introduced to cover much the same idea.[7]

In this paper, the focus is upon such aspects as the imagination, arts and science—or more generally, culture—rather than upon the material conditions which are seen as "conditioning" them rather than absolutely determining them. Conversely, it is assumed that the way ahead must be conceived in the imagination before we can embark upon the journey.

In the present paper it is assumed that, a) a useful distinction can be made between society/structure/base on the one hand and culture/superstructure on the other hand and, b) that there is a dynamic relationship between the two aspects.

The further assumption is made that militarisation is primarily a problem at the level of social structure whereas militarism is a problem at the level of superstructure. Militarisation is part of, and must be seen in relation to, other aspects of socio-economic and political structures, and can be measured by objective criteria, whereas militarism is part of, and must be seen in relation to, other aspects of culture. Just as there is a dynamic relationship between social structure and culture, so there is between militarisation and militarism:

Superstructure	militarism
Structure	militarisation

Militarisation and Social Structure

A considerable amount of work has been done on the study of militarisation and it is only necessary to refer briefly to it here.[8] Most studies have analysed the role of the military in particular societies[9] or, for example, the impact of military expenditures (or conversely, disarmament) on the economy.[10] More recently a number of studies have examined the global role of the military in the world economic order.[11]

In a previous paper it was argued that a primary role of the military is to maintain the present world economic order (structure), an order which is characterised, on the one hand, by a global competition between competing industrial systems, and on the other by vast discrepancies in the utilisation of resources, both within individual countries and between the centre and peripheral elements of the global systems of nations. It was concluded that militarisation (measured in terms of increasing military budgets in the Third World as well as in industrialised countries, the arms trade, military coups, and so on) was due to several related aspects of the present world order: the competition between great powers; attempts by great powers to maintain control of their subsystems by means of direct or covert intervention or by recruiting and building up loyal local military elites; conflicts within and between local military elites as they gain in power; and attempts to overthrow repressive regimes and, conversely, efforts by these regimes to keep in power.

In brief, militarisation is an important element in the dynamic development of social structures at the national and international levels and can be measured by objective indicators.

The Role of the Military in Society

Before discussing the relationship between militarism and culture it is necessary to examine the role of the military in society. This role has both legitimate and illegitimate aspects. The legitimate aspect is to defend society from external military attack; and in so doing provide the security necessary for normal social life.

The fundamental paradox with this legitimate aspect is that strong defence forces in one country may be perceived as a threat by another country which is thereby motivated to increase its forces—in turn provoking increases in the forces in the first country. The danger is that this paradox will be exploited for illegitimate reasons.

Military forces belong to the category of social groups which do not themselves produce for their own material requirements (food, etc.). Like rulers, administrators, priests, artists and scientists they are dependent upon expropriating the surplus produce of others. This expropriation may either take place by force—which military forces are well equipped to do—or by "legitimising" the expropriation either by providing security in the event of a real attack or by inventing an appropriate mythology.

All too often in history, rulers, administrators and the military form a coalition with priests, artists and scientists in order to "legitimise" the expropriation of surplus produce by a combination of force and mythology, becoming "macroparasites" rather than protectors of the people. All too often, too, this pernicious coalition has been able to mobilise support for attempts to expropriate the surplus (or means of production, whether land or labour) of other societies—the phenomenon known as imperialism. Because of the legitimacy paradox referred to above, imperialism generates external hostility which "legitimises" the further build-up of "defensive" forces which are in fact essentially parasitical.

Militarism and Culture

History abounds with examples of relatively small armies controlling large populations and enabling their surplus produce to be expropriated with surprisingly little opposition. In effect, as tribal societies gave way to settled, agrarian societies a dual society, with two cultures ("high" and "low" or folk culture) emerged, the former parasitic upon the latter.[12] Folk culture includes beliefs and values appropriate to a peasant economy, with a world view bounded by the range between the peasant's plot of land and the market. High culture is shared by an elite which may be widely dispersed geographically throughout an empire but is usually focused on a central point, the court of the emperor. The emperor is often seen as an earthly incarnation of god and this religious myth serves as a moral justification for the exploitation of the peasants.

Of the original main high culture (Incan, Mayan, Aztecan, Mesopotamian, Egyptian, Harappan and Chinese) only that of China survived until the twentieth century.[13] The emergence of bourgeois capitalist states and colonial dependencies was also brought about by a combination of military force and ideological transformation, with missionaries in many cases taking care of the latter aspect. This period differs from the classical cultures in that explicit attempts were made to penetrate folk cultures with new religious myths. Christianity was particularly successful in this respect, probably because its original ideology was essentially that of the underdog in an occupied colony. However, under the edict "Render to Caesar that which is Caesar's" it could be readily adapted to serve the aims of imperial exploitation.

In this way, during the colonial period, elements of high culture penetrated folk culture, though almost always blending with older cultural elements. The transformation of culture parallels the transformation of the relationship between man and land from one economic/ecological system to another.

In a third, and current phase, we see the emergence of "mass culture" which consists of degenerate elements of both high culture and folk culture and which is diffused on an industrial scale to the far corners of the world.

Each of these phases is faced with internal contradictions. In the classical and colonial periods, there was a basic contradiction between the producer/consumers and the nonproducer/consumers which could be overcome as long as the producers were able to produce sufficient for the needs of both classes.

The contemporary period is qualitatively different in that the wealth of the ruling classes depends not simply on extracting surplus produce from primary producers but also on selling more industrial products to an ever-increasing market of consumers. The role of mass culture is intended to increase mass consumption, not to decrease it, or maintain it at a minimum level. There are obviously contradictions in offering the masses a vision of conspicuous consumption and at the same time controlling their demands for better living standards.

And in practice, what often happens is that increased consumption is only possible for a portion of the masses and a middle class emerges, jealous of aristocratic privileges and frightened of the impoverished underclass, emotions which create a fertile climate for militarism. This contradiction is heightened by the problem of ecological imbalance. In the classical systems there had to be ecological balance at the local level in order for the system to survive. In the contemporary period, the drive towards excessive consumption in a global economy leads to local ecological imbalances and serious social disturbances which can easily threaten the more visible holders of power.

In the classical systems where there was ecological balance, relatively limited inputs of mythology and military force were sufficient to maintain the allegiance of the masses. In the present period, it seems possible that ecological imbalances and other contradictions require much greater inputs of mythology and military force in order to maintain social control and this may be the explanation of the trend towards militarism and militarisation.

It may be that "mythological force" is more effective than military force:

> A considerable amount of thought control is achieved not by frightening the masses but rather by inviting them to identify with the governing elite and to enjoy vicariously the pomp of state occasions. Public spectacles such as religious processions, coronations, and victory parades work against the alienating effects of poverty and exploitation...during Roman times, the hostility of the masses was kept under control by letting them watch gladiatorial contests and other circus spectaculars...entertainment delivered through the air directly into the shantytown house or tenement apartment is perhaps the most effective form of Roman circus yet devised.[14]

The tenacity of mythological remnants from bygone periods testifies to the force of mythology in human history and there is much evidence that cultural revolution may be much more problematic than social revolution. If reactionary armed forces can be overthrown by revolutionary armed force (which is a difficult enough task), there is still the task of overthrowing or displacing reactionary mythologies with the true consciousness of the social structure which is needed to generate activity to transform the pattern of social relations into one which prevents further oppression.

Conversely, if mythologies can be disposed of, reactionary armed forces may no longer be strong enough to go on expropriating surplus produce, and the task for revolutionary forces will be much easier.

We are now in a position to define more clearly what we mean by militarism:

> Militarism is the military exploitation of "mythology" in order to "legitimise" the expropriation of surplus produce for illegitimate macroparasitic purposes.

In the rest of this paper some examples of what is meant by the military exploitation of mythology are given.

The Social Functions of Mythology

Before examining more specifically military applications of mythology it is as well to point out some of the general social functions of mythology. Man is more than an adaptive creature, passively responding to environmental stimuli. He is able to produce a surplus of energy which can either be used for transformation of the environment or maladaptively for destruction. Man's ability to go beyond mere adaptation is due to several features, in particular the ability to use tools, to communicate by means of language and thereby to form complex social organisations and to transmit culture from one generation to another.

In order to act upon the environment it is necessary to have some understanding of the way the environment works. Observation of regularities in the environment provides empirical data which forms the basis of understanding, but this new data must be organised into causal explanations. One function of mythology is to provide causal explanations of natural phenomena.

But human beings do not only act upon the environment as individuals. Myths perform important functions in developing group solidarity and in "explaining" why certain group activities are done the way they are. More theoretically, in order to act, human beings must cognitively reduce the uncertainty due to their natural and social environment. Myths, like science, are a means of reducing uncertainty, thereby enabling human beings to act in circumstances in which they would otherwise be helpless and passive.

However, human beings do not only act on the basis of what they believe is probable (cognitive aspect) but also on the basis of what is believed to be desirable (affective aspect). This is of particular importance where the source of uncertainty is other, autonomous human beings because other human beings or groups are not bound to act according to "observed regularities."[15]

As a result, in strategic interactions, the affective component (e. g. X is bad, therefore he will attack me) is dominating. In social interactions, therefore, the main function of mythology is not so much to explain why things are as they are but rather to reinforce in-group identification (group solidarity) and out-group rejection. The same applies to public manifestations such as military parades and organised sport.

Let me give an example of a modern myth, for which I am grateful to the late Professor Svale Solheim of Oslo University: Shortly after the German occupation of Norway on 9 April 1940, it was reported that a bus-driver who had been ordered to drive German troops had deliberately driven his bus over a cliff so that he and the enemy soldiers perished. The story aroused a great deal of attention and a collection was held for his family. Subsequently it appeared that the incident had never occurred.

In the Soviet Union, a story appeared during World War II in which an old man, forced to act as a guide to German troops, deliberately led them into an ambush, in which he himself was killed. In this case, the story was based on fact. These stories from recent history have the same structure as many tales in Scandinavian and Russian folklore. They may or not be based on fact—but they have the important social function of boosting the morale of an occupied people and mobilising activity to drive out the enemy. In these examples it will be noted that the myths were generated by the weaker part in a situation of aggression, domination and oppression, with the positive social function of mobilising resistance. But mythology can also be used as a vital tool in the maintenance of oppression. It is this problem that we are more concerned with in the study of militarism.

To summarise, two social functions of mythology are particularly important in the study of militarism:

1. The manipulation of uncertainty and associated anxiety; and
2. The reinforcement of group solidarity.

The Manipulation of Uncertainty

A consequence of the necessity of reducing uncertainty and associated anxiety in order to act is that human beings are willing to "pay" those who can reduce uncertainty for them. Those who are in a position to increase uncertainty—and then offer to reduce it—are in a good position to create themselves an expanding market.

This is a basic principle of the capitalist press. The headlines, which glare at you from the newsstands, create uncertainty which you are invited to reduce by buying the newspaper. This, I believe, is the main explanation of the well-known emphasis on "negative" news.

This principle is also a fundamental one in psychological warfare: on the one hand it aims to create anxiety and on the other to offer the victim a means of reducing that anxiety. This applies just as much to psychological warfare on the home front and in peace-time as to operations directed against an enemy in war.

Thus, in order to legitimise the maintenance of vast military establishments in peace-time, great efforts are made to exploit news items which create public anxiety about the intentions of a possible enemy. The public is then invited to contribute more tax money to buy more military equipment as a means of reducing their anxiety. The creation of the myth of the "missile gap" is a classic example but we are continually subjected to massive efforts of the same kind.

Control of information has, of course, long been used as a basic tool of domination:

> For at least 400 years control of the presses was one of the most powerful instruments in the hands of authority, molding the fate of nations...[16]

Conversely, concientization campaigns which seek to explode dominate mythologies are a powerful force for social change.

The Reinforcement of Group Solidarity

Myths and the manipulation of information can be skillfully used to reinforce in-group solidarity and out-group rejection. The World War II and folklore myths referred to earlier are examples. A drastic example of a different kind is related by Fletcher Prouty in his book on the CIA.[17] He relates the manner in which support for local military commanders in a developing country could be artificially built up. In the course of a counterinsurgency exercise, one group of soldiers is dressed up as "guerrillas" and sent to attack a village; the local commander and his men then arrive on the scene and successfully drive out the "guerrillas". The local people are not told that it is an "exercise". In the course of time, the local commander may have sufficient local support to be able to launch a bid for power at the national level.

The use, of agents provocateurs in this way serves both for manipulation of uncertainty and to reinforce in-group out-group identifications. This dual function is obvious in the way the issue of "terrorism" is handled. Very little is said about governmental terrorism. But when after years of suffering a few persons try to draw attention to the plight of their people by planting a bomb or hijacking a plane, the incident is used (a) to create massive anxiety in the general population (in order to sell newspapers as well as to legitimise further militarisation of the police) and (b) to create further rejection of the outgroup. Little is written of the link between the history and conditions of, for example, the Moluccans in Holland, the Palestinians or the Northern Irish Catholics. Nor is anything written about the fact that, for example, hijacking has long been condemned by the PLO or bombing by the Official IRA: all Palestinians and all IRA are subject to the same rejection. In this way, the authorities are able to reinforce their own position of power and prevent the political ideas of radical organisations—even those which reject terrorism—from "infecting" the general population.

The Functions and Dysfunctions of Militarism in Mass Culture

The purpose of militarism in mass culture is, of course, to promote the militarisation of society and thereby to maintain the power of the élite to expropriate the surplus value of mass society and use it for consumption or investment in overseas military or commercial adventures.

The manipulation of uncertainty and out-group rejection may have dangerous and destabilising consequences, particularly in societies subject to rapid change or which for other reasons harbour powerful emotional forces. In some countries, for example, the opportunity for war has been greeted with great popular enthusiasm. The old élite may lose control of events and find itself swept along on a tide which may eventually smash it.

Myths, symbols, even totems, play a considerable role in the military subculture in the time of the new recruit's induction into the "tribe" and the ensuing rites de passage. Indeed, the military, along with religious sects, are the main bearers of tribal cultural remnants in modern society. The main function of military ritual and symbolism is the strengthening of group solidarity which is often at the expense of solidarity with the civilian population, and should not therefore be underestimated.

Combating Militarism and Militarisation

If, as has been persuasively argued, military force is at the very core of the nation state, then combating militarism requires fundamental changes in the nation-state system of the world. But leaving aside this difficult problem, the conclusion of the present analysis is that combating militarism requires action at the cultural, or subjective, level, in addition to action at the political and economic, or objective level, to restrain the militarisation of society.

> To deny the importance of subjectivity in the process of transforming the world and history is naive and simplistic. It is to admit the impossible: a world without men.... If men produce social reality...then transforming that reality is an historical task, a task for men.[18]

More specifically, combating militarism requires a transformation of militaristic culture and an attack on all the forces which promote militaristic culture, in the mass media, in religion, in the arts and in the sciences. It requires an attack not only on "arms control" (as distinct from disarmament) but an attack on thought control for militaristic ends.

This attack requires an analysis of the cultural dynamics of particular societies, the forces at work in each culture, the role of science, arts, religion, the mass media, and so on, and in particular of the way in which uncertainty is manipulated and out-group rejection artificially reinforced (arms control negotiations being a good case in point). The analysis must then form the basis of action at the cultural level, action which has been very appropriately termed cultural action or The Pedagogy of the Oppressed:

> The pedagogy of the oppressed, as a humanist and libertarian pedagogy, has two distinct phases. In the first, the oppressed unveil the world of oppression and through the praxis commit themselves to its transformation.... In the second stage...this pedagogy...becomes a pedagogy of all men in the process of permanent liberation. In both stages, it is always through action in depth that the culture of domination is culturally confronted.[19]

Notes

1. Thus E.B. Taylor in his book *Primitive Culture* (1871) describes culture as "that complex whole which includes knowledge, belief, art, morals, law, custom, and any other capability and habits acquired by man as a member of society" (1958 ed., p. 1). Marx in his Preface to *A Contribution to the Critique of Political Economy* uses the term superstructure to refer to "the social, political and intellectual life in process in general..." and "the legal, political, religious, aesthetic or philosophic—in short, ideological forms" which should be clearly distinguished from "the material transformation of the economic conditions of production." In Western social science a distinction has recently been made between material culture (meaning, in particular, physical arte-

facts) and "subjective culture" referring to values, feelings, and, most generally meanings; see C.E. Osgood, Probing subjective culture, *Journal of Communication*, 1974 (Winter), pp. 21-34.

2. Marx (op. cit.) writes, "The mode of production of material life conditions the social, political and intellectual life process in general. It is not the consciousness of men that determines their being, but, on the contrary, their social being that determines their consciousness." With regard to social change, he goes on: "With the change of the economic foundation the entire immense superstructure is more or less rapidly transformed." There is a strong tendency to interpret these words mechanistically: first change the ownership of the means of production and people's world views will change accordingly. Paolo Freire, 1972, *The Pedagogy of the Oppressed* (Penguin, Harmondsworth) however, criticises this mechanistic interpretation.

3. See e.g. M. Sahlins, 1976, *Culture and Practical Reason* (University of Chicago Press) for a recent example of this argument.

4. Letter to H. Starkenberg, 25 January 1894.

5. *Capital*, vol. 1, p. 178.

6. G. Thomson, 1974, *The Human Essence* (China Policy Study Group, London), p.7.

7. L.E. Stover, 1974, *The Cultural Ecology of Chinese Civilization* (Mentor, New York), following the ideas of Professor Julian H. Steward of Columbia University, defines cultural ecology as "the functional interrelationships between the basic spheres of life as this pattern is worked out in the course of man's cultural adaptation to the environment." For an introduction to general anthropology based on this approach see M. Harris, 1971, *Culture, Man and Nature* (Crowell, New York).

8. Examples of this literature and some criticisms of it include: H. Bienen, (ed.) *The Military Intervenes* (New York, 1968); *The Military and Modernization* (Chicago, 1971); S.E. Finer, *The Man on Horseback* (Pall Mall, London, 1962); W.F. Gutteridge, *Military Institutions and Power in the New States* (London, 1965); *The Military in African Politics* (London, 1969); S.P. Huntingdon, *Political Order in Changing Societies* (New Haven, 1969); J.J. Johnson (ed.), *The Role of the Military in Underdeveloped Countries* (Princeton, 1962); M. Janowitz, *The Military in the Political Development of New Nations* (Chicago, 1964); J.M. Lee, *African Armies and Civil Order* (London, 1969); C.E. Welch, *Soldier and State in Africa* (Evanston, 1970). Details of actual arms transfers are provided in Stockholm International Peace Research Institute, *Arms Trade Registers: The Arms Trade with the Third World* (Almqvist & Wiksell, Stockholm, 1975) and US Arms Control and Disarmament Agency, *World Military Expenditures and Arms Transfers, 1966-1975* (Washington, DC, 1976). A special issue of the *Bulletin of Peace Proposals* (1977, no. 2) is devoted to the problem of the arms trade and the transfer of military technology. See also M. Kaldor, The significance of military technology, *Bulletin of Peace Proposals*, 1977 (2), pp. 121-123; P. Lock & H. Wulf, Consequences of the transfer of military-oriented technology on the development process; M.D. Wolpin, Military dependency versus development in the Third World, all in the *Bulletin of Peace Proposals*, 1977 (2).

9. There are an increasing number of studies of the role of the military in the development of particular countries, among them: R.M. Fields, *The Portuguese Revolution and the Armed Forces Movement* (Praeger, New York, 1975); A.R. Luckham, *The Nigerian Military: A Sociological Analysis of Authority and Revolt, 1960-1967* (Cambridge, 1971); A.A. Mazrui, *Soldiers and Kinsmen in Uganda: The Making of a Military Ethnocracy* (Sage, Beverly Hills, California, 1975); N.J. Miners, *The Nigerian Army, 1956-1966* (London, 1971); R. Pinkney, *Ghana Under Military Rule, 1966-1969* (London, 1972); A. Stepan, *The Military in Politics: Changing Patterns in Brazil* (Princeton University Press, Princeton, New Jersey, 1971), W.J. Stover, "The armed forces and Nationbuilding: Revolutionary socialist theory and praxis in China," *Journal of Contemporary Asia* 6 (3), pp. 323-333; A. Abdel-Malek, *Egypt: Military Society* (trans. C. L. Markmann) (Random House-Vintage Books, New York, 1968). See also L. Hamon (ed.), *Le Role Extra-militaire de l'Armee dans le Tiers Monde* (Paris, 1966); E. A. Nordlinger, "Soldiers in mufti: The impact of military rule upon economic and social change in the non-Western states," *American Journal of Political Science* (LXIV (2), December 1979, pp. 1131-1148; R.M. Price, A theoretical approach to military rule in the new states: Reference group theory and the Ghanaian case, *World Politics*

(XXIII (3), April 1971, pp. 399-430.

10. Studies of the more specifically economic aspects of military investments are E. Benoit, *Defense and Economic Growth in Developing Countries* (Lexington, 1973) and G. Kennedy, *The Military in the Third World* (Duckworth, London, 1974). The role of military and economic aid as a "Trojan Horse" has been pointed out by S. Weissman et al., *The Trojan Horse: A Radical Look at Foreign Aid* (Ramparts Press, San Francisco, 1974). See also N. Stein, "The Pentagon's protégés: U. S. training programs for foreign military personnel," *Latin America and Empire Report* (North American Congress on Latin America), X (no. 1), January 1976, pp. 1-32; W.R. Kintner, The role of military assistance, *Proceedings of the US Naval Institute*, March 1961, pp. 76-83.

11. J. Oberg, "The new economic and military orders as problems to peace research," *Bulletin of Peace Proposals* (1977 (2); M. Lumsden, "The role of the military in the world economic order," paper presented at the 7th Nordic Peace Research Conference, 1976 and revised for the use of UNESCO, 1977 (a short version will appear in the *Bulletin of Peace Proposals* (1978 (1).

12. See Stover op. cit. for an account of the phenomenon in China.

13. Stover op. cit.

14. Harris op. cit., p. 407.

15. If the interaction between the two groups is one of competition, or contains mixed elements of cooperation and competition, it becomes *strategic*. By strategic interaction is meant one in which what one party does is determined by what he thinks the other party thinks he will do, and so on. Reasoning in a strategic interaction is recursive so that, formally speaking, it is impossible to assign probabilities to the opponent's (or partner's) expected acts. (See M. Lumsden, 1966, "Perception and information in strategic thinking," *Journal of Peace Research*, pp. 257-277).

16. T.K. Derry & T.I. Williams, 1960, *A Short History of Technology* (Clarendon Press, Oxford), p. 707.

17. *The Secret Team* (Prentice-Hall, Englewood Cliffs, 1973).

18. Paolo Freire, 1972, *The Pedagogy of the Oppressed* (Penguin, Harmondsworth), p. 27.

19. Ibid., p. 31.

Militarism and the Pursuit of Peace

William Felice
Royal Institute of International Affairs

Military Spending and Subsistence Rights

The former Secretary-General of the United Nations, Boutros Boutros-Ghali, asserted that 'development cannot proceed easily in societies where military concerns are at or near the centre of life. Societies whose economic effort is given in substantial part to military production inevitably diminish the prospects of their people for development. Preparation for war absorbs inordinate resources and impedes the development of social institutions.'[1] Jack Matlock, a former United States ambassador to Moscow, makes a similar point in relation to the required weapons spending for new members joining NATO: 'It's extraordinarily unwise for these countries to shoulder these costs when they must pay the costs of meeting their social needs.'[2]

Webster's Dictionary defines militarism as a 'policy of maintaining a strong military organization in aggressive preparedness for war'.[3] Militarism thus includes the disposition to maintain national power by means of strong military forces projecting menacing arms potency capable of deterring or compelling enemy nations. The Secretary-General and the ambassador argue that militarism represents a structural choice that accords military priorities and arms spending a higher priority than meeting basic human needs. Are these distinguished diplomats right? Are there dire economic consequences to high levels of military spending? And if so, what are the human rights implications of militarization?

The negative effects of militarism on society overall are often dramatically shown through analysis of the policies of repressive governments in the less developed world from Myanmar (Burma) to Iraq to Syria. These dictatorial regimes clearly choose militarism over human rights. In this article, however, I will undertake a tougher task. My hypothesis is that there is a global tradeoff between militarism and economic growth which impacts on the protection of rights. High levels of military spending in less developed and developed countries prevent all of these from fulfilling the basic economic and social rights articulated in the International Bill of Human Rights.

* * *

Academic studies from the 1980s to the mid-1990s confirm the negative relationships between militarism and economic growth. Steve Chan, for example,

William Felice, "Militarism and the Pursuit of Peace." This article first appeared in *International Affairs* (London), vol. 74: 1, January 1998 and is reproduced with permission.

concludes that the evidence is clear for advanced Western economies: military spending does not encourage or facilitate sustained economic growth. In the long run, 'these expenditures are more apt to have a negative than a positive impact on investment, inflation, employment, balance of payments, industrial productivity, and economic growth. The evidence on the United States...indicates especially significant costs in these regards.' Heavy defense spending 'seems to have a particularly important impact in dampening capital formation and investment, which in turn reduces economic growth in the long run'. Chan also notes the 'customary preference of officials to finance defense and war by running budget deficits rather than by cutting other programs or raising taxes, [with] much of the cost of this spending shifted to future generations'.[4] These conclusions were confirmed in a 1995 study by Alex Mintz and Randolph Stevenson that was grounded solidly in neoclassical economic theory. Using longitudinal data from 103 countries, they demonstrated that increases in nonmilitary spending contribute to growth significantly more than increases in military expenditures. Military expenditures had either a negative effect or no effect on growth in about 90 per cent of the cases. Mintz and Stevenson demonstrated that a shift away from military spending significantly contributes to economic growth in the long run....[5]

In summary, there are at least three different ways in which military spending restricts economic growth in the United States. First, it leads to a decrease in investment and thus retards the expansion of civilian industry; second, it leads to lower employment and an inefficient use of labour resources; and third, it takes resources away from civilian research and development, impeding nonmilitary innovation and growth and siphoning off highly qualified engineers and labour from the civilian sector. The result is a diversion of resources away from the collective human rights of education, health care and subsistence. The implementation of basic economic and social rights depends upon a shift in scarce resources away from militarism and towards these areas of human need.

Militarization, of course, is a global phenomenon. Expensive and sophisticated weapons are sought and purchased everywhere in the name of security and self-determination. Worldwide military spending of $815 billion in 1992 equalled the income of nearly half the world's people. Military expenditures in developing countries rose three times as fast as those of the industrialized countries between 1960 and 1987; from $24 billion to $145 billion, an increase of 7.5 per cent a year, compared with 2.8 per cent for the industrialized countries. In 1990-91 the ratio of military to social spending (calculated as military expenditures as a percentage of the combined education and health expenditures) was an astounding 373 per cent in Syria, 222 per cent in Myanmar and 190 per cent in Ethiopia. Some of the poorest countries are among those which spend more on their military than on education and health: Angola, Mozambique, Pakistan, Somalia and Yemen, as well as Ethiopia and Myanmar.[6] Did these expenditures provide security? Unfortunately not. In developing countries, the chances of dying from social neglect (from malnutrition and preventable diseases) are 33 times greater than the chances of dying in a war from external aggression.[7] Yet U.S. arms and military aid continue to flow to countries that face no significant external enemy. As a consequence, the function of the military in these countries often becomes internal repression (as was heinously demonstrated in Guatemala throughout the 1980s). The human cost of military spending in developing nations is enormous. The statistics are numbing. Twelve per cent of military spending in developing countries could provide funds for primary health care for all, including immunization of all children, elimination of severe malnutrition and reduction of moderate malnutrition by half, and provision of safe drinking water for all. Four per cent could reduce adult illiteracy by half, provide universal primary education and educate women to the same level as men. Eight per cent could provide basic family planning to all and stabilize world population by 2015.[8]

The Enduring Tension between Militarism and Human Rights

Militarism describes one type of society and world vision; international human rights describe a very different world. The two visions are incompatible. To implement a human rights agenda means sacrificing the fixation with military growth and military spending.

Human rights claims evolve over time. There is a strong link between the growth of new human rights and social development. As modern global society has matured, accompanied by deep ecological interdependence, new threats to the individual and the group have surfaced. To combat these threats, governments and nongovernmental organizations (NGOs) have raised issues of environmental balance, economic growth, social equality, refugee relocation, drug interdiction and disease eradication. Global cooperation between state and nonstate actors is seen as critical to addressing this perplexing new agenda of world politics. Accordingly, the list of human rights claims keeps growing. Complex social relations give rise to these demands as new claims are made to alleviate suffering. What appears fundamental in one historical era may not be in another. Human rights claims today have no relation to a primitive state of nature where people's lives were dominated by a few essential needs. As Norberto Bobbio points out, there are no current charters of rights which do not recognize the right to education, which broadens as society develops to include secondary and university as well as primary education. Yet none of the better-known descriptions of the state of nature mentions such a right....[9]

It is now commonly accepted that it is not possible to achieve significant progress on human rights without subsistence needs (food, sanitation, education, etc.) being met. It is also impossible to achieve human rights progress and development in societies controlled by repressive and corrupt regimes. The government can be the main obstacle to achieving either economic or political rights. Most United Nations scholars and human rights activists promote an interdependence between the two sets of rights (civil/political and economic/social/cultural), and criticize those who make too sharp a distinction between them. Economic and social rights are complementary to libertarian principles found within civil and political rights. They are both symbiotic and mutually dependent. Civil and political rights can be enacted only if everyone has a minimum of economic security.

This human rights agenda can also only be implemented within a framework of peace. Militarism has neither created a world of peace and stability, nor protected the human right to physical security. Overemphasis on military superiority undermines the ability to build regimes of trust and harmony. The arsenals of the war system are symptoms of deep conflict. Arms control and disarmament and the demobilization of armed forces are prerequisites to providing the institutional framework within which nations may pursue implementation of the corpus of international human rights law.

International security and stability are dependent on domestic security and stability. The roots of conflict within domestic societies are often the result of economic, social and environmental pressures which cause poverty and unemployment and pit one community, class, sex or ethnic group against another. Human rights as the core of domestic and foreign public policy can provide a route for the achievement of peace and stability. Preoccupations with 'balance of power' and military prowess can only continue to produce a world of insecurity and war. Policies based on outmoded notions of realpolitik exacerbate insecurities. The irony is that human rights policies provide the clearest road to achieve the 'realist' objectives of security and stability. Long-term interests in international stability should compel governments to explore human security and positive peace.

It is commonly accepted that totalitarianism and human rights are incompatible. The negative impact of militarism on basic human rights must also be understood. A militarized society exists in contradiction to basic human rights and negates the opportunities for human freedom.

Inhibiting Militarism

The collective human right to self-determination and the individual human right to personal security are fundamental needs of every human community. For this reason, proposals for immediate and unilateral disarmament consistently fail. As long as societies and individuals feel threatened, the need will be felt to possess armaments to keep aggressors at bay. But could security be achieved without militarism?

Three clear areas in which a beginning could be made in inhibiting militarism while protecting personal security rights are curbing arms sales; initiating steps towards common security and basic deterrence; and launching institutions of war prevention and preventive diplomacy.

Limiting Arms Sales

Global military spending since the Second World War totals at least $30–$35 trillion. Enormous resources are needed every year just to maintain superfluous military equipment. Converting military industries is the first step to the release of resources needed to implement international human rights....

From Thucydides to present-day political scientists, it has been noted that the influx of new weapons into a region sets off arms races and rekindles traditional rivalries. Nations either acquire arms or form alliances with distant states to balance out the perceived military power of their neighbours. The Clinton administration, however, in an Orwellian twist, asserts the opposite: its spokesperson claims that lifting the ban will stabilize the region and promote democracy. Selling F-16s and other high-powered weaponry to Latin America will have, in fact, the opposite effect.

For the United States, a programme of positive peace would be based on converting a military based economic system to a civilian based system. The conversion process can begin with a restriction on arms exports. No longer can such weapons sales be justified as a means of preserving jobs and stemming economic decline. According to the annual arms survey of the Congressional Research Service, the U.S. share of the international weapons trade grew by nearly 23 per cent in 1996, to $11.3 billion in orders, representing 35.5 per cent of the global market.[10] Conversion must begin by transforming these military industries to civilian enterprises. Clearly, cooperative security, positive peace and Third World development are not enhanced by the sale of high-tech weapons systems. The defence technologies developed during the Cold War can be redirected towards productive civilian ends.[11] A compulsory registration of arms sales and transfers should be established under U.N. auspices. World conflicts and the fires of war are fanned by these sales. The NGO community can play a key role in publicizing illegal and surreptitious sales of arms.

Institutions for Peace

To implement this ambitious agenda, it will be necessary to develop new institutions specifically committed to demilitarization and human rights. Since the end of the Cold War, a plethora of proposals for the restructuring of the U.N. has been produced.[12] The following ideas could be useful first steps in the construction of global institutions dedicated to overcoming militarism and establishing a framework of common security.

1. The creation of a new International Verification Agency. This could help create confidence that disarmament enhances rather than undermines security. Reagan's quip to Gorbachev, 'trust but verify', holds true internationally. Effective inspections and monitoring arrangements are essential to verify compliance with disarmament agreements. This new agency could be charged with inspection responsibilities for nuclear, chemical and conventional disarmament. The Chemical Weapons Convention established the

Organization for the Prohibition of Chemical Weapons to verify global adherence to the treaty. The new International Verification Agency could draw on this experience and expand the verification function to cover other armaments.[13]

2. The creation of a Global Demilitarization Fund as proposed by Nobel Peace Prize winner Oscar Arias. Arias calls on the nations of the world, both rich and poor, to 'commit themselves to at least a 3 percent a year reduction in their military spending levels over the next five years'. The rich would be asked to earmark only one fifth of these savings towards the demilitarization fund, and the developing countries would contribute perhaps one tenth. The money raised could address other human security needs, such as those arising from famines, natural disasters and resource depletion.[14]

3. The establishment of a 'crisis management centre' at the U.N. to enable proactive mediation and dispute resolution measures to be taken effectively. The centre would undertake an international monitoring function to ensure compliance with demilitarization and human rights norms. The U.N. will need an independent capacity to verify information and gather data on its own. Such monitoring could help end illegal shipments of arms and technology across borders and deter illegal tests of missiles or warheads.[15]

Notes

1. Boutros Boutros-Ghali, *An agenda for development* (New York: United Nations, 1995), p. 20.

2. *New York Times,* 29 June 1997.

3. David B. Guralnik, ed., *Webster's New World Dictionary of the American Language* (New York: World Publishing Company, 1972), p. 901.

4. Steve Chan, 'The impact of defense spending on economic performance: a survey of evidence and problems', *Orbis,* Summer 1985, pp. 413–14.

5. Alex Mintz and Randolph T. Stevenson, 'Defense expenditures, economic growth, and the peace dividend: a longitudinal analysis of 103 countries', *Journal of Conflict Resolution* 39: 2, 1995, pp. 283–305.

6. United Nations Development Programme (UNDP), *Human development report 1994* (New York: Oxford University Press, 1994), pp. 34, 47–51.

7. *Ibid.,* p. 50.

8. *Ibid.*

9. Norberto Bobbio, *The age of rights* (Cambridge: Polity Press, 1996), p. 53.

10. *New York Times,* 16 Aug. 1997.

11. See Domenick Bertelli, 'Military contractor conversion in the United States', in Lloyd J. Dumas, ed., *The socioeconomic of conversion from war to peace* (Armonk, NY: M. E. Sharpe, 1995).

12. See Boutros Boutros-Ghali, *An agenda for peace 1995*, 2nd ed. (New York: United Nations, 1995); Richard Falk, *On humane governance: toward a new global politics* (University Park, PA: Pennsylvania State University Press, 1995), pp. 207–40; Saul H. Mendlovitz and Burns H. Weston, eds., 'Symposium: preferred futures for the United Nations', *Transnational Law and Contemporary Problems* 4: 2, Fall 1994.

13. Michael Renner, 'Budgeting for disarmament: the costs of war and peace', *Worldwatch Paper 122,* November 1994, p. 44.

14. UNDP, *Human development report 1994,* p. 59.

15. Robert C. Johansen, 'Reforming the United Nations to eliminate war', *Transnational Law and Contemporary Problems* 4: 2, Fall 1994, pp. 471–2.

Deterrence and Provocation

Mary Midgley
University of Newcastle-upon-Tyne

Understanding deterrence is a complex skill, not at all like falling off a log. This emerges from every discussion of the arms problem today, and it is one faintly cheering feature of such discussions that they do not admit this complexity. Professor Laurence Martin's Reith Lectures were doubly cheering in this respect. Firstly, Professor Martin took the problem very seriously, admitting freely that he thought its difficulties crushing, and that it scared him still—a prime qualification, surely, for discussing the subject at all. Secondly, he pointed out how much of this difficulty was political and psychological, yet how crudely those aspects of it had been handled by the earlier architects of modern weaponry. He shows how casually, in the early years, it was assumed that atomic weapons should be designed for 'city busting', merely because no other use for them had yet occurred to anybody. 'There was', he remarks, 'certainly no psycho-political analysis of what it takes to deter.'[1] Larger and larger bombs were therefore provided, and this fairly unconsidered habit of mind was rationalized into the explicit policy of 'mutually assured destruction' (MAD), to be provided by building up the superpowers' capacity to demolish each other's cities instantly. This policy was cheerfully accepted as making a positive virtue of the weapons' destructiveness, and, as he explains, the West made deliberate efforts to convert the Russians to that idea, which they viewed with some alarm.

Inevitably, however, attempts were soon made to refine this hopelessly crude deterrence arrangement by technological advances. 'Flexible response' was developed and the supposedly simple, reliable deterrent was lost for ever. 'The early architects of deterrence, remarks Professor Martin, 'seem to have been so much preoccupied with staving off massive nuclear attack that they gave little thought to why it might occur.'[2] That is, they neglected the whole political context and in particular the fact that most disputes are small. They provided no means of nutcracking except a steam-hammer. When the mass of nut-sized disputes on hand became obvious, they supplemented this with a variety of steam-powered nutcrackers, certain to smash crockery and likely to set the steam-hammer itself going as well. Hence we have, at present, problems of appalling intricacy for which Professor Martin provided an impressive set of very subtle, but by no means confident, diagnoses. (His refusal to dogmatize is another of his virtues.) He concludes that, while it is a great pity that we ever got into this mess, and while we should do all we can to bring about arms control, we probably need for deterrence most of the weapons currently on hand or on offer, and a good few more conventional ones as well. If we say we don't much like this,

Mary Midgley, "Deterrence and Provocation." Reprinted by permission of the author.

he replies (not offensively but sympathetically) in the words of Bruce Bairnsfather's Old Bill, "Well, if you knows of a better 'ole, then go to it."[3]

To say that I find this approach relatively cheering, and an improvement on some earlier ones, is obviously to start from a fairly depressed position. I have in mind two ways in particular in which reliance on weapons used to be defended. The first is the mindless, all-purpose Empire-day patriotism which prevailed in my childhood, and which was recently revived under the name of the Falklands Spirit. The second is the complacent certainty that—given the right aims—the current policy for implementing them must be right, the extraordinary confidence in military judgement about means which prevailed for some time after the Second World War. (It prevailed, in fact, at the very time when the mistakes which Professor Martin now nails were being made.) This is what has brought us to what he justly calls our present "miserably dangerous situation." That kind of complacency is scarcely possible now because the solid simple orthodoxy of belief in MAD has given way. In its place, those who are most expert and professional in these matters are now deeply divided, propounding a range of different ideas on how to deter. Among them are quite a few very distinguished people (such as ex-ambassador George Kennan and Field Marshal Lord Carver), who say that one thing we need badly is fewer nuclear weapons. Professor Martin himself makes an interesting point in noting that George Kennan himself, when he gave the Reith Lectures in 1957, poured scorn on this way of thinking. But the crucial thing is the direction of change. That was in the age of complacency.

Certainly we have to face realistically the problems of how to attempt reduction. If the Angel Gabriel were to persuade all existing governments tomorrow that they had better get rid of the things, there would still be grave problems about how to do it. But that does not mean that these ideas should be swept away. Professor Martin, when he considers them, is discouraged to the point of despair by the difficulty of getting reliable agreements and inspection procedures. That is a psychological problem, concerning the motivation of all concerned. And to this general type of problem I now return, asking in a general way, firstly, what is deterrence?

The Psychology of Deterrence and Provocation

The motivation of deterrence links the threatener's hardware to the motivation of the person threatened in a very simple way. It treats the threat merely as producing fear, and so discouraging action. Threats, however, do not only frighten; they can also provoke. The proportion of discouragement to provocation varies greatly in different situations, and always needs attention. This snag is well-known over deterrent punishment, which is the main sphere in which the idea of deterrence has so far been used outside warfare. The case of penal deterrence compares interestingly with international deterrence.

Someone who has been punished for one offence and is contemplating another does not necessarily see his former punishment, and the threat of a further one, simply as natural phenomena. He can see them also as hostile acts. He does not have to respond in a prudential manner, assessing the warning and the danger as he might when predicting renewed attacks of gout or indigestion. If he resents the punishment and the threat, he may see them instead as expressive gestures by which the punishing authority rejects him, and shows him that it is idle to try to come to terms with it—he will never be fully accepted by that authority. In this case, threats of stronger action will only intensify his defiance. The effectiveness of penal deterrence is limited by this tendency of punishment to turn many people into 'hardened criminals'—even if they have no particular views beforehand about the punishing authority. If they do—if they belong already to a group which feels alien to the authorities—it is even less effective. It is less so still where (as in Northern Ireland) long-standing political feuds underlie the rejection. In that sort of situation, even very heavy penalties fail to deter. This continually surprises judges, who often respond by giving heavier and heavier sentences in the hope that they can somehow get through to the next lot of offenders. But deterrence does not seem to work like this, in a way proportional to the expected penalty. It apparently depends far more on the community with which one identifies. It can even be counterproductive, causing bystanders to join the threatened community and reject the threatening one. Those of us who are thoroughly integrated into the communities which do the punishing are indeed easy to deter, because we mind about the disgrace of offending that community. Such disgrace seems to be far more feared than the mere pain or nuisance of punishment. (The fact that judges and legislators are usually members of this group, and offenders often are not, accounts for a good deal of mutual misunderstanding.) But for people who have no reputation to lose, or who belong to a distinct community in which punishment won't affect their reputation, this danger is removed. In this situation, the mere basic prudence which is adjusted to the size of the penalty is often extraordinarily weak. And judicial reproofs commonly cut no ice at all.

Without Fellowship, Communication Fails

Penal deterrence depends, then, far more than seems to have been noticed on the inclusion of deterrer and deterred within the same moral and emotional community. Where this fails, not only is the motivation presupposed by deterrence undermined, but its credibility also becomes much harder to establish. A normal law-abiding citizen tends to think that, if he offended, he would not get away with it. He expects on the whole that his fellow citizens would catch him and punish him, because on the whole he thinks they ought to, and thinks they will share his view. He sees them as an externalized extension of his own conscience. But to someone who feels detached from that community, things look quite different. For him, the question is one of objective probabilities, as it would be over dangers from disease or weather. And this calculation is often quite uncertain, because the data are scanty. It tends to appear as a gamble. He may well get away with it. And the less he grasps the reasoning of those who may punish him, the less certain it will seem whether they will actually do what they threaten. If he cannot see why they would be strong-willed, he will have less reason to be sure that they will be strong-willed. Even heavy punishments, in such circumstances, tend to have little effect against a strong immediate motive for offending.

This is what made it possible for even quite prosperous eighteenth-century thieves to continue their business in spite of regularly seeing large numbers of their colleagues hanged for doing it. They took the physical risk, as fishermen risk drowning and car-drivers risk accidents, because it was occupational and they had indeed become hardened to it. They were not taking any emotional risk, because thieving was their tribal business, and they would have been despised for leaving it. All this is doubtless very imprudent. What it shows is that the human imagination is rather an unreliable device for producing prudence, because it has innumerable other functions to fulfill as well. And it is particularly unreliable in dealings with alien tribes. This is something which needs to be thought about whenever we are planning to rely on penal deterrence.

Now of course the penal situation is very different from the international one, and I am not trying to draw any simple parallel between them. But I think that the comparison can give us some light—the interesting thing is to see how far it will shine. In the first place I think there is real reason to suppose that between nations too intelligible and useful deterrence can only work within the context of some sense of fellowship resting on shared basic aims, which—in spite of very wide local differences—makes it possible to understand and sympathize with the motives of one's opponent. Without it, effective deterrence becomes impossible, because the basis of reliable communication is undermined. We will understand what others say if we fail to grasp why they are saying it. Complete aliens are in principle unintelligible, and therefore unpredictable. Consequently their threats lack credibility. In saying this, I am not being utopian about what a sense of shared aims can achieve. I am not ignoring the endless cases of successful international blackmail and oppression. Athens wiped out Melos. The Holy Roman Empire bullied its client states into suppressing the Protestant Reformation. And so on. But these are transactions between a dominant state and a much weaker one which is already well within its power. They do not help us to a model of deterrence between independent sovereign states of approximately equal standing.

Pursuing for a moment the case of equal and independent nations, we can put the question why, when they disagree, wars do not continually break out between them? (The question is an odd one, and I put it in this form only because it seems to be the question implicitly addressed by people who say that peace has been produced over the last few decades simply by the presence of nuclear weapons.) The most obvious way to answer this does not begin by listing the armies and the hardware, but by asking why it should. Nations have other ways of settling their disputes, and those disputes do not take place in a social vacuum. Nations are not sealed boxes, isolated from each other except for the conduct of disputes. Their boundaries are often arbitrary and inconvenient for current purposes; all sorts of activities go on across them. Unless deliberately prevented, citizens of different states tend strongly to travel and trade together, and to engage in all sorts of activities, ranging from sport to religion, which ignore political frontiers. Both personally and economically, much advantage is drawn from these habits. When therefore a cause of dispute arises, it has to be weighed against the drawbacks of breaking them. Even to threaten violently is something of a gamble; one may drive lasting friendship away elsewhere. Accordingly, though armed forces and the power of using them are a regular element in such disputes, the threat of using them forms only one part in a whole complex web of bonds, propositions, offers, half-offers, threats and promises, out of which, as a rule, some sort of tolerable understanding emerges. Other sorts of threat, for instance concerned with trade, are of a much commoner coin.

Notes

1. Martin, Lawrence. *The Listener,* 15 November 1981, p. 597.

2. *Ibid.*, p. *598.*

3. Martin, Lawrence. *The Listener,* 12 November 1981, p. *565.*

References

Prins, Gwyn (ed.). *Defended to Death: A Study of the Nuclear Arms Race.* Harmondsworth: Penguin, 1983.

Lifton, Robert Jay, and Richark Falk. *Indefensible Weapons: The Political and Psychological Case against Nuclearism.* New York: Basic Books, 1982.

Miall, Hugh. *Nuclear Weapons: Who's in Charge.* London: Macmillan, 1987.

From Strategic Deterrence to Problem Solving

John Burton[1]
United States Institute of Peace

The Problem: Universal Violence

Contemporary events are characterised by uncontrollable violence and conflict on the streets of cities, among communities, and between nation-states. We read and hear daily about violence at all social levels. We have acquired a sense of resignation because we accept that we can do little, if anything, to eliminate what we assume to be its source: human nature.

Traditional political philosophies of power rest on the assumption, to quote Hans Morgenthau,[2] that 'man is aggressive, therefore the State is aggressive' implying the need for social control of behaviour, nationally and internationally, by power. Breakdown in law and order, such as revolution and war, become the accepted and inevitable means of change. They are the price that is exacted for periods of continuing national and international stability. In this view the best that can be hoped for in human relations is improved means of control by power, for example, improved means of policing, and community and international peacekeeping forces. The use of power as the dominant means of control in social and political organizations has been termed, therefore, 'political realism'.

A great deal of our law-and-order and strategic thinking has rested, and still rests, on these traditional power theories and philosophies. Most members of the world society have institutionalized the traditional power and adversarial means of settling disputes, such as legal processes, arbitration, and forms of power bargaining. We have 'peace-keeping' exercises designed to separate warring factions.

The new reality is, however, that the general availability of means of violence, and communications between like-minded groups, are making possible defiance of political and military power. The traditional so-called 'political realism' becomes wholly unrealistic in contemporary conditions of universal communications and possession of the means of violent protest.

Furthermore, once there are the means of violent protest, the less powerful militarily seem in some circumstances to have a more effective political power that gives an added dimension to their military power. Vietnam and Korea were evidence of this.

We are today faced with many situations, domestic and international, in which neither threat nor force can achieve deterrence, no matter how overwhelming it may be. At the domestic level protracted ethnic conflict is now almost universal, and police are being defeated in the streets of major

John Burton, "From Strategic Deterrence to Problem Solving." Reprinted with permission from the editors of *Essays on Peace: Paradigms for Global Order* edited by Michael Salla, Walter Tenetto, & Enrique Martínez.

cities in many developed and developing countries. The U.S. threat of overwhelming force did coerce Iraq into submission.

Why do individuals, communities and nations employ whatever means of violence are currently available? Human behaviour seems to be more complicated than *real politicians* ever imagined. Modern communications are making possible recalcitrant expression of long-standing personal, social and international grievances. We must assume that throughout history human aspirations have been largely repressed within this power frame, and that we have now entered a new phase in the development of civilizations in which the individual, the ethnic identity group, the community, the nation, will seek opportunities for development, and will no longer be socialized into the norms and patterns of behaviour set down by the more powerful. Empirical evidence suggests, in short, that aggression is not used for its own sake. It is not a part of human nature, as has been assumed all along. Indeed, we perceive the possibility that violence exists not as the preferred means by which to remedy unacceptable conditions, but as the only one available option within social institutions and frameworks that are irremediably based on power. Despite these altered realities, however, the elite of nation-states, and the corrupt United Nations through which they sometimes operate, continue to try to preserve a world order based on coercion by the powerful.

The Task: Conflict Avoidance and Resolution

If military and economic power is no longer effective as a means of control, the societies of the world have no rational option but deliberately to move from deterrence strategies, from the goal of 'control', to solving problems by getting at their roots. There can be few if any societal goals more pressing than substituting interactive problem-solving decision making, for adversarial confrontation.

As a result of recent insights, studies are emerging that challenge traditional power philosophies, and seek to identify the real sources of conflict so that they can be foreseen and prevented, or resolved to the satisfaction of all parties if it has already occurred, even though this means questioning traditional beliefs and institutional frames.

There is a problem of communication when talking about conflict resolution. It still means to many a form of deterrence, arms control or police intervention, because most of us have no conceptual frame other than the traditional deterrence frame in which to deal with conflict. Furthermore, when conflict resolution is put forward as an alternative to deterrence there is for many an impractical and idealistic connotation.

Conflict resolution is a subject now widely researched and taught in many universities. It is not about strategic deterrence, nor is it the product of idealism and personal values. It is a practical response to failures in power political decision making. It is about solving problems that will lead to conflict. It is about using predictive decision making to avoid conflict. 'Conflict resolution' as the term is now being used, could be defined as 'Analytical Problem-Solving Decision Making'.

False Assumptions

In order to predict accurately, a holistic and realistic theory of human behaviour is required. The 'Man is aggressive' theory has misled us. The theories of separate disciplines, and their constructs such as 'economic man', do not provide an adequate alternative. Traditional sociologists seemed to assume that the person and group were wholly malleable, or could be socialized into required behaviours. The premise of conflict resolution is that there are certain fundamental human aspirations and needs that will be pursued, and which cannot be contained in the longer term by socialization processes and the use of power. It is the pursuit of needs of recognition and group identity that explain police defeats in the Street, and military defeats in Vietnam, Korea and elsewhere. This has been captured in the title of a book by Jerel Rosati and Rodger Coates, *The Power of Human Needs,*[3] implying a human power greater than any possible coercive power.

In trying to determine what kind of regional arrangement we should seek and what we should avoid, we must start by rethinking our philosophies and assumptions. We have inherited, and we maintain, an authoritative political environment in which, to use Lord Lloyd's terms, there are those who have a right to expect obedience, and those who have an obligation to obey.[4] This has been justified over the ages by power elites. The institutions we defend are held to be required for purposes of law and order. But when there is enforced law and little order it is time to start questioning. Why are prisons full, why is it not safe to walk the streets of a city, why do we adopt more and more security measures, why do we employ major force to contain the behaviour of small countries, why are there ethnic conflicts globally, and why can we not solve problems such as have emerged in South Africa, Sri Lanka, Cyprus, Northern Ireland, Fiji, Yugoslavia and elsewhere? May we not be defending traditions that are based on principles that seek to preserve outmoded institutions, rather than promoting the needs of peoples?

Let us note in passing that these power political institutions which we have inherited are not just police and military. They include the power-structure adversarial institutions that are an integral part of what we term 'democracy'. There can be nothing more destructive of harmonious and fruitful relationships than the relations of any kind, including party parliamentary systems, adversarial legal systems, exploitative industrial systems and others, which seek short-term interests within a power bargaining frame, and lead societies away from solving their longer-term problems.

Unfortunately, the newly independent nations of Asia and the Pacific have inherited the power political institution of the former colonial powers. In many cases disagreements over territory, autonomy and ethnicity have led, not to attempts to get to the source of the problem but to coercion and violent responses.

We need to rethink quite basic notions. The dictionary tells us that by 'democracy' is meant 'government by the people'. In the past there were probably some societies in which the people formed a homogeneous society, and if all had a vote there could have been a democracy according to this definition. The institutional notion is, however, applied to situations in which there is no such homogeneity. Imperialist aggressions have resulted in boundaries being drawn by the outcome of wars, not by population concentrations. In these circumstances, so-called 'democracy' becomes rule by one national ethnic or tribal group over others.

The world society is backing one-person-one-vote in South Africa as 'democratic', despite evidence throughout the world that this form of franchise creates just the situation of majority rule over minorities that leads to violent and protracted conflict. Separate ethnic and tribal entities are required, probably requiring separate autonomies of a constitutional kind that we have not even started to think about. Tamils as well as Singhalese in Sri Lanka, Turks as well as Greeks in Cyprus, Europeans as well as Blacks in South Africa, have needs to be fulfilled, and these needs are so basic that they must fight for them. There is a human need for identity and recognition, for its own sake and for reasons of security. Institutions must reflect human needs if conflict is to be avoided. We cannot expect human beings to adjust to institutions that frustrate their human needs.

Associated with the assumption that majority rule is democratic is a reluctance to accept separation as a desirable solution. It is assumed that 'integration' of peoples is the desirable goal. We are loath to accept breakaways from the nation-state, or separate autonomies. We were not able to accept a peacefully divided Cyprus as a desirable solution to the majority-minority problem there, and cannot accept a forced separation as the basis for a functional relationship. It is hard for the international community, and the great powers especially, to accept separation in Yugoslavia, together with readjustment of boundaries to cater to ethnicity needs, as something that should be supported.

To deal with problems, to anticipate problems, we must have an adequate predictive capacity, which means an adequate theory of behaviour and sense of the future. It is now clear that the nation-state world order, of which the United Nations is part, has had its day. The future will be a world order comprising identity communities, separate autonomies, seemingly based on religion, ethnicity or tribes, but in practice based on the need for identity and recognition, a need that increases in intensity as living conditions become more threatening. The Soviet Union will not be the last major nation-state to break up into separate autonomies. In the Asia-Pacific region there are demands for autonomy, too frequently resisted by existing nation-states.

The assumptions we must question include many that have been legitimized by special studies, such as Economics, but which have no validity when applied outside the Western region in which Economics was founded. Take, for example, the now current issue of subsidies and tariffs. The great powers, the US in particular, have become great economically as the result of subsidies and tariffs, and opportunities of no competition, such as wars. Now they want underdeveloped countries to forego the processes by [which] they themselves became economically developed. If I prefer to cultivate my own vegetables at a higher price, including my labor, than I can buy them in the supermarket, this is a decision for me to make. If a people decides that its cultural diversity and development are promoted by having industries that are not competitive with foreign ones, this is for it to decide. If Japan or Europe wish to maintain their rural sectors by procuring their own agricultural products at costs higher than exists elsewhere, this is for them to decide. Why should they be required to move populations to cities, creating or adding to social problems that grew out of control? The economics argument that we must exploit resource in the most productive way does not take into account quality of life. It is quality of life that we must seek not resource exploitation. Avoiding conditions that create conflict and violence may require foregoing economic benefits. There are many, many such consensus assumptions that need to be challenged, and will be challenged as the effective coercion of the Greater Powers declines in effectiveness.

Problems-Solving Decision Making

Problems in human relationships require solution, not suppression. Creative solutions are possible when there is recognition by all concerned of the inherent human needs of peoples, and insights into the longer-term costs and consequences of frustrating these needs. We require in this region a fresh approach, in domestic politics no less than in international politics, avoiding power politics and opting for institutions that deal with problems at their source. Problems of cultural identity and its recognition are especially sensitive.

Such an approach challenges many of our preconceived notions. For example, right and wrong are irrelevant notions in a conflict situation: there are problems to be solved. Finding fault with the policies of some Asian-Pacific country faced now with pressing domestic problems, is a superficial approach to the problems being experienced. For some of us who are greatly influenced by European traditions it is not easy to stand back and appreciate the points of view of those who seem not to conform with Western norms.

A no-fault approach is particularly relevant to regional concerns. When considering Asia-Pacific regional problems we must remember that they are very much a carry-over from the past. We must constantly have in mind the way in which the peoples and resources of Asia and the Pacific have been exploited by European colonial powers, and the long-term consequences that remain with us. Forced migrations of cheap labor, and resource exploitation at the cost of denying local development, have left devastating consequences. Current conflicts in the region, both domestic and foreign, are a direct consequence of the past, for example, migrations that now threaten original autonomies, and the colonial boundaries that may divide identity groups, or, on the other hand, enforce diversity.

Exploitation is, of course, what colonialism was and is all about. It has taken many forms in addition to direct resource exploitation. Recall that the depression policies of the European powers were to reserve colonies for their exclusive exploitation of resources and markets. This made quite inevitable Japan's entry into World War II on the side of Germany. It had to have access to markets and raw materials to survive. Recall that after World War II there was, on the party of colonial powers, intensive resistance to Asian and Pacific movements toward independence, supported strongly by the United States. There is very little more concern today for the separate identity and welfare of the peoples of this heavily populated and extensive region. The harsh realities of market mechanisms and Western defence policies persist as though colonial conditions still remain.

This is not necessarily a condemnation of the former colonial powers and of the United States of America. We have to accept that such exploitation of others was and is part of the global system. The question we have to ask and answer is, how in these circumstances can the Asian-Pacific countries, especially the smaller and less affluent ones, promote their security, independence and development?

There are many approaches to dealing with conflicts, and conflict resolution is easily confused with mediation, negotiation and alternatives to courts. What we have to appreciate is that with all possible good-will, including attentive listening and skilled mediation, deep-rooted conflict is not likely to be resolved. The answers are not in the heads of the parties concerned. The answers usually are not within the traditional knowledge frame of a third party. Ethnicity problems cannot be resolved, even with good will, if demands for autonomy challenge the traditional right of states to preserve territorial boundaries, and to exercise control of inhabitants with those boundaries. In the absence of an understanding of ethnicity, which means an understanding of human needs and motivations, it is unlikely that the dominant party will be able to assess the longer-term costs of their coercive policies. It is the same with male-female relations, work-place relations, and any relationships where recognition and identity become key issues.

The role of the third party in conflict resolution must be, therefore, a positive one, drawing attention to human aspirations, questioning the assumptions made by the parties, inducing consideration of issues that do not emerge in mediation and bargaining situations. Such a third party must be informed by intensive studies in human behaviour and relationships, that is, holistic studies that go beyond the fields covered by specialists such as psychology, and by social scientists generally.

When we refer to conflict resolution, therefore, we are implying changed notions about the nature of conflict, greater understanding of attitudes, and furthermore, the availability of persons with special skills that go far beyond those associated with diplomacy and negotiation.

International and Domestic

In making this analysis it is important to note a movement away from the international as a special case, toward perspectives that treat conflict as generic. Separating international from domestic, which is still usual in universities and in scholarship generally, has had serious consequences. Relations between states are essentially no different from relations between groups and persons. Conflict and violence are no less of a problem at these levels, and have the same fundamental sources.

Furthermore, the separation of international and domestic, implying international causes of international conflicts, has diverted attention from the reality that international conflict is usually, if not always, a carry-over from domestic, that is, nation-state problems. US intervention in Vietnam was occasioned by a special American definition of the situation there, influenced by current ideological conflicts within the US. Vietnam was not analysed in the context of post-colonial independence movements. As previously mentioned, war with Japan, a Western ally in World War I, was brought about directly as a result of UK domestic unemployment policies which shut off colonial markets in Asia from this island country which for survival required access to resources and markets. Many current ethnic conflicts are due to national boundaries being drawn as the result of colonial conquest that ignored population distributions. National attempts to maintain such boundaries are a major source of international conflict.

The United Nations

I wish to insert here some comments on the United Nations because the UN was based on some of the notions which we must now question. The domestic jurisdiction clause in the UN Charter totally ignores the link between domestic and international conflict, and thus excludes the United Nations from tackling the sources of international conflict. This is not to suggest that the UN, or a regional body, should have the right to intervene in the affairs of a nation. But interventions are not a difficulty if we move from coercive treatments of problems to attempts to resolve them. Nations welcome help in resolving their problems by interactive and consultative means.

I would go further and suggest that the basic assumptions of the Western-sponsored United Nations have to be questioned, for they remain within the power-political frame and rarely adopt approaches that challenge Western nation-state norms. Peace-keeping forces do not solve problems. Diplomatic representatives of nation-states do not reflect the frustrations and needs of ethnic and cultural minorities within them.

The United Nations was founded on the domestic law-and-order model, it being assumed at the time that this was closest to the ideal conflict-free model: a central authority with coercive powers by which to control deviants. This model, an elitist power model, is now revealed as the prime source of global violence. The most industrially developed, prosperous and so-called democratic states are amongst the most violent as measured by murders and other forms of internal violence. A central coercive authority is not the answer to serious conflict. Fortunately the United Nations has not had at its disposal a standing international force as was intended. Unfortunately the majority of members, most experiencing dissent at home, have allowed the Security Council Permanent Members to use their position to provide a UN sanctioned force in cases in which their interests are involved, leaving unresolved the problems that invite their intervention.

The United Nations is becoming an irrelevant, and even a repressive institution. The future is a global society that comprises autonomies, and it is these autonomies that member states try to suppress within their own boundaries. Conflict in Yugoslavia will be repeated in many African and European states, and the state authorities which are the members of the UN will seek to prevent this happening.

The United Nations has no potential for problem solving conflict resolution. It operates within the traditional power frame, and peace-keeping is its doubtful contribution. The concept of conflict resolution does not come into the Charter. At a recent conference held in Singapore on the changing role of the United Nations there was one session on conflict resolution. It was defined as having three aspects: prevention and persuasion; non-coercive pressure: "otherwise known as sanctions;" and the use of collective force. A new start that reflects experience and increased knowledge since 1945 seems to be required.

A Regional Organisation

An approach to problems of conflict such as I have

been discussing would suggest the need for a regional organisation designed to promote policies that would avoid conflict, and to deal with conflicts in a problem-solving mode if they occur.

Such a regional organisation would necessarily be non-governmental, for governments generally do not take a longer-term perspective, and are too involved in a particular situation to be able to analyse it. They can respond to an invitation to meet with others to discuss in an informal atmosphere and off the record, but it is difficult for them to take an initiative and invite the opposing party, or to respond to an initiative by an opposing party.

If we are seeking a regional organisation, therefore, it will ideally be one that has the backing and support of governments, but one which remains a functional organisation at a non-government level. It would be desirable to have centres throughout the region that provided relevant training in conflict resolution, so that there would be trained persons available to deal with problems within countries and between them. There are now available at various universities many course outlines that could become a shared asset. To begin with there would probably be needed a centre in the region that would train persons from the regions so that they could train others in their own countries.

A Region in the Global Society

Of course, such an independent approach by the countries of Asia and the Pacific is not a simple matter of policy. When the independence movement of the post-war period commenced, the tendency was for newly independent states to be nonaligned, that is, free to pursue their own foreign policies outside power alliances. Nehru took the lead, and was backed by Tito of Yugoslavia and Nasser of Egypt. The Bandung conference was a significant attempt by newly independent states to remain independent. But in due course many nations in the region had no option but to seek financial and commercial support from former colonial powers. They did not, and still do not, feel that they have freedom of choice in determining their domestic and foreign policies.

So we must ask ourselves, can a regional organisation, one that is outside the power-political frame, achieve what was once sought within the wider global system? Perhaps regional cooperation could lead to greater regional independence, and opportunities to resolve problems in more constructive and problem-solving ways than have been attempted in the past. Indeed, perhaps a region such as the Asian-Pacific region could become an experimental model for other regions and for the global society.

There are many pressing problems in relationships in different regions, but we should not, must not, assume that they should or can be dealt with within the coercive frame of great power political interests, or by applying the assumptions that are associated with that feudal frame. If there are peoples in existing post-colonial nation-states who seek separate autonomies, enforced integration is not a practical response. Peoples whose identity and traditional role are submerged as a consequence of past colonial migrations cannot be coerced into behaviour dictated by Western norms.

We have, for example, the serious problem currently being experienced in Fiji. This is not a situation calling for external threat of sanctions on the grounds that Western so-called democratic norms are not being observed. When we stand back from particular situations and think about them, we must conclude that there is nothing less democratic than majority rule in multi-ethnic communities. The traditional one-person-one-vote, relevant in an homogenous society, is not the answer to this now almost universal ethnicity problem. Multi-ethnic conflict is deep-rooted. Repression of minorities is of no avail, as we know from many, many cases in the global society today. So called democratic majorities threaten the cultures and identities of minorities, their future security and development. A solution to the problem calls for an innovative resolution that satisfies the legitimate needs of all in the given circumstances. Such resolutions can emerge only if there is movement out of the traditional Western power frame, and a consideration of the human need for recognition which, being human, is shared by both majorities and minorities. This is but one of many examples of problems to be resolved in the Asia-Pacific region. There are others in Sri Lanka, India, Cambodia, Papua-New Guinea, Indonesia and elsewhere.

Conclusion

It is my hope that a new and questioning approach to the vital issues of human relationships in the global society, and in Asia and the Pacific in particular, can be established. By this I do not mean an approach based on idealism, or humanitarianism, or on a set of ethnic values. I mean an approach that is realistic and practical because it is holistic and takes into account, not just power elite interests, economic and commercial interests, and the cultural values of dominant powers, but also the pursuit of basic human needs that have led to independence movements, that do not promote ethnic conflicts, and that can now help to explain why even within developed societies there is widespread deviance and violence beyond the capacities of authorities to control.

Let us try to face the fact that there are many approaches to security, peace, and conflict resolution, some of which are false and should be abandoned, some of which are justified only by selected empirical support and need to be critically re-examined, many of which have their own specific relevance, and that in determining what approach is relevant to a particular situation threat and coercion, arbitration, mediation or some problem-solving intervention—we must first define the situation. Having done so we must always be prepared to change the approach as more information comes to the surface. What at first appears to be some unconstitutional leadership challenge can turn out be a major ethnic conflict. Let us promote a total rethinking of existing knowledge and practices in our particular areas of interest before any specific proposals are made in relation to the Asian-Pacific region, and in the light of this come up with some firm proposals for cooperation in the future.

Notes

1. This paper was originally presented to a Conference convened by the Asian Peace Research Association, Christchurch, NZ, January, 1992.
2. Morgenthau, Hans. *Politics Among Nations: The Struggle for Power and Peace.* 3rd Ed. 1960.
3. *The Power of Human Needs in World Society* (Reiner, 1988).
4. Dennis Lloyd, *The Idea of Law* (Pelican 1964).

Confronting Arms Races

Alexander Pikayev
Carnegie Endowment for International Peace

Progress in science, together with gradual globalization of the world, led humankind towards a situation when, after the end of World War II, two superpowers emerged, which were able to establish a unique bipolar global security structure, although it had never existed in a pure bilateral form. Simultaneously, the superpowers obtained an absolute weapon—nuclear arsenals. If they were used, the direct large-scale war between them could produce the overall annihilation of the whole human civilization.

The arms race is not a recent phenomenon, and to a considerable magnitude determined relations between great powers since the late nineteenth century. In the nuclear age, the role of the arms race has enormously increased. In principle, both sides realized that the large-scale war between the superpowers should be avoided by all possible means. Therefore, they had to shift their rivalry into lower intensity regional conflicts, economic and ideological competition, and the arms race. The arms race not only forced them to build up massive overkill capabilities—it enabled them to destroy the whole world multiple times. It also exhausted their economic resources. But, most important, the arms race continuously reproduced feelings of insecurity for both competitors, and raised mutual suspicions in bilateral relations. In times of confrontation, the bilateral relationship was very fragile and forced the superpowers to balance on the brink of a chain of hostilities, which could automatically, perhaps, against their will, bring them closer to a catastrophe—for themselves and the remaining world. Understanding that, since the late 1960s, both sides attempted to limit their arms race by concluding a series of arms-control agreements—bilateral and multilateral. However, those efforts failed to halt the arms race, although in some cases they helped to make it slower and more manageable.

The end of the Cold War has marked an end for that type of arms race. Collapse of one of the two superpowers deglobalized the arms race, and made it more multilateral and less traditional. Its post-Cold War pattern was characterized by the following components:

- The failed superpower became unable to compete with the victorious one, and because of economic difficulties it had to reduce significantly its military modernization programs. In a response, the winning power also decreased its deployments and modernization of its weapons of mass destruction (WMD). As a result, in some areas the superpowers' arms race was replaced by their "disarmament race."
- In the 1990s the winning superpower emerged

in a very comfortable environment. Even by maintaining or even relatively reducing levels of its defense expenditures, it has successfully increased the gap with other nations in the area of high-tech conventional military hardware. It has happened because some other nations, like the European countries and Russia, have decreased their military efforts. The others, like China and India, attempted to increase them from levels so low that it prevented them from challenging the supremacy of the sole surviving superpower.

- Although after the Cold War the traditional arms race has not played any visible role in relations between the superpower and other countries, it has shifted to a regional level. During the Cold War, the superpowers often limited the regional arms race. They did it through bringing some regional powers into their systems of alliances or quasi-alliances. That increased feeling of security for some regional states and discouraged them from the regional arms race. In other cases, the superpowers coordinated their efforts in order to convince regional powers not to cross certain red lines in their military build-up—for instance, not going nuclear. The end of the bipolar world often released regional controversies earlier frozen by the superpowers' competition, and consequently, provoked a new round of the arms race on regional levels.
- Finally, in relations with the sole superpower some nations could probably be ready to launch asymmetrical arms race. Given differences in readiness of various societies to absorb war damages, certain third-world nations—and even non-state actors—could be stimulated to acquire modest WMD, missile or other capabilities with the goal to pose an unacceptable risk for valuable assets of the superpower and deterring it by that threat from interfering into vital security interests of those state or non-state actors.

Multilateral Agreements

Positive Developments in Early 1990s

The final days and years immediately after the end of the Cold War probably represented the best period in history when the nations combined their efforts with an aim to consolidate international legal regimes limiting arms race and even reversing it. In 1993 the international community successfully concluded an unprecedented Chemical Weapons Convention (CWC), which for the first time called for unequivocal verifiable global elimination of the whole class of WMD. In 1997, after a long and painful campaign, the international community convinced both CW superpowers—the United States and Russia—to ratify, albeit unwillingly, the document.

In May 1995 the states parties of the Nuclear Non-Proliferation Treaty (NPT) decided to prolong its duration indefinitely. That decision raised hopes that progress, which had been achieved by that time in the area of reversing vertical nuclear arms race, would be accompanied by preventing horizontal nuclear proliferation. The indefinite duration of the NPT was strengthened by establishing more restrictive guidelines of the Nuclear Suppliers Group (NSG), aimed at convincing nuclear exporters to take into account non-proliferation priorities. Besides that, the International Atomic Energy Agency (IAEA) elaborated a new 93+2 Program for its nuclear safeguards, which created more intrusive regime of the IAEA inspections with a goal to monitor compliance with the NPT by the state parties.

Besides the NSG, other multilateral export control regimes were expanded and strengthened. They were created by developed nations in order to limit transfers of sensitive technologies to potential proliferators, mainly located in the Third World. The Missiles Technology Control Regime (MTCR) is most frequently mentioned among them. It was established in 1987 by G7—a group of the seven most developed powers with an aim to restrict export of missiles and missiles technologies to problematic hands, and thus, preventing or restricting missile arms race in the Third World. In the 1990s, the guidelines of the Regime were clarified and strengthened, and the MTCR membership had gradually increased to more than 30 countries. It included some former Eastern block states, like Russia and Ukraine, and a couple of developing countries, among them, Brazil and Turkey. Some other missile powers, like China and Israel, voluntarily accepted self-restraining pledges in the area of missile export on an ad hoc basis, albeit formally remained outside the Regime.

In September 1996 another historic multilateral treaty was opened for signing. The Comprehensive Test Ban Treaty (CTBT) would codify *de facto* nuclear test bans gradually joined by all five legal nuclear powers in the course of the late 1980s to the early to mid-1990s. If implemented, the Treaty might pose new significant barrier for qualitative modernization of nuclear warheads, and, thus, seriously limit qualitative nuclear arms race.

It order to keep the momentum, two more important multilateral consultations started. During one of them, the multilateral Convention for Fissile Materials Cut-Off was discussed. If concluded, the agreement could prohibit production of weapon grade nuclear materials, needed for making nuclear warheads. After a certain period of time, the Cut-Off Convention might effectively install quantitative upper ceiling for nuclear arms race: no new warheads might be produced above the number provided by already accumulated amounts of weapon grade fissile materials.

The second set of consultations was devoted to negotiating the Verification Protocol for the Biological Weapons Convention (BWC). The BWC was concluded in 1972 and, on paper, prohibited that class of WMD. However, the Convention was negotiated during hey day of the Cold War, and contained no verification provisions enabling secure compliance with the document. When the Cold War was over, a decision had been made to fill the gap, and the UN Conference on Disarmament in Geneva hosted multilateral consultations on that problem.

In a manifestation of democratizing international relations in the early 1990s, various nongovernmental organizations (NGOs) successfully promoted an international Convention prohibiting landmines. If implemented, the document could prohibit a class of conventional weapons, which left so many people handicapped, especially civilians in developing countries. Although three major powers (the United States, Russia, and China) refused to join the Landmine Convention, it pressed the states to pay more attention to de-mining.

In Europe, the changes were especially promising. The 1990 Treaty on Conventional Forces in Europe (CFE Treaty) limited deployments of five major types of conventional equipment, as well as imposed ceilings on manpower. In fact, the Treaty limits proved to be too high, and the majority of European countries maintain some conventional deployments below the ceilings. As a result, conventional arms race in the continent was halted.

European nuclear powers, France and Britain, made certain unilateral steps in limiting their nuclear modernization programs. Paris refused the land-based leg of its nuclear triad and decommissioned intermediate-range ballistic missiles (IRBM) deployed on Plateau Albion. The United Kingdom de-alerted its tactical nuclear weapons; only four Trident II nuclear submarines remain on alert status. In that way those "third" nuclear powers also contributed to the general trend of limiting nuclear arms race in the post-Cold War period.

End of Positive Momentum?

Regrettably, in the second half of the 1990s the positive momentum slowed, if not halted or even reversed. Several major factors contributed to that. First, some leading and mighty powers preferred to act unilaterally in order to preserve wider political and military field for maneuvering. Secondly, in the eyes of several key countries the existing and prospective regimes failed to meet their security objectives, or prevented their political status from increasing. Finally, many nations pointed at the discriminatory nature of those regimes, and accused them in dividing countries of the world for those who have and those who have not.

The year 1998 initiated a chain of events, which could lead to the erosion of the regimes limiting or halting the arms race. In May, India and Pakistan conducted nuclear tests and declared themselves *de facto* nuclear states. Although they have never been members of the NPT, a decision to go nuclear was made so openly that it has eroded incentives for some countries to remain inside the Treaty. The fact that two states could remain outside the NPT and do what they wanted without receiving punishment from the global community, produced an attractive precedent for leaving the Treaty and going nuclear.

Also, India, Pakistan, North Korea, and Iran successfully tested missiles they have developed and produced by themselves. That marked a significant development: four states with indigenous missile capabilities emerged outside the MTCR and possessed no obligations to limit their missile export. An alternative source of supply by missiles and missiles technologies has appeared. That demonstrated a failure to prevent arms race outside of the MTCR framework and posed under risk the whole system of supply side export control in the missile field.

Like a landslide, the nuclear and missiles tests undermined credibility of multilateral regimes confronting proliferation of WMD and means of their delivery. It triggered negative developments. In 1999 the U.S. Senate refused to ratify the CTBT. That decision produced another serious strike against the non-proliferation regimes. The leading nation, generally considered the main promoter of non-proliferation values, became unable to convince its own legislature to support them. The move of the U.S. Senate effectively prevented the Chinese, Indian and Pakistani from accession to the Treaty by easing pressure on them. It was a pity, since signing the CTBT by India and Pakistan might prevent their new nuclear tests and contain the nuclear arms race in the South Asia.

The 1998 North Korean missile test revived debates in the United States about a need to deploy a national missile defense, and has considerably, if not decisively, changed the attitude of policy-makers towards the defenses into much more favorable direction. That caused a new round of disagreements between the United States and other key nations in Asia and Europe, which negatively affected relations between them in the following years.

Both consultations in the Conference on Disarmament in Geneva also went into deadlock. China blocked progress in the Cut Off consultations by linking it with launching another consultation on the non-weaponization of Outer Space. After several years of painful talks, by 2001 it seemed that the consultations on concluding the BWC Verification Protocol finally moved ahead. However, in 2001 talks were thrown into disarray by a decision made by the Bush administration not to seek completion of the Protocol anymore.

By early 2002 the situation with confronting arms races by international legal regimes appeared controversial. If recent negative trends continue, further erosion of multilateral arms control regimes might be inevitable. It could result in the crash of important existing barriers confronting both proliferation and vertical arms race in nuclear, missile and biological areas.

Arms Race in the U.S.-Russian Context

End of the Bilateral Strategic Nuclear Arms Race

By the 2000s Russia and the United States had made a significant progress in reducing speed and halting and reversing nuclear arms race between them. Just slightly more than a decade ago the United States simultaneously deployed five new systems of strategic ballistic and cruise missiles *(MX Peacekeeper, Trident I, Trident II, ALCM, and SLCM)*, one new SSBN *(Ohio)*, and one new strategic bomber *(B-1B)*. Washington also developed and tested three more missile systems (*Midgetman, ACM,* and *SRAM-2*) and one new strategic bomber (*B-2*).

In its turn, the Soviet Union deployed six new nuclear ballistic and cruise missiles *(SS-24, SS-25, SS-N-20, SS-N-23,* and sea-launched and air-launched cruise missiles), two new types of SSBNs *(Typhoon and Delta IV)*, and one new heavy bomber (*Blackjack*). It also implemented R&D, at least, on four other new ballistic and cruise missiles (*SS-27*, new SLBM, SLCM, and ALCM). Each side maintained approximately 10,000 to 12,000 deployed strategic nuclear warheads and 15,000 to 20,000 deployed tactical nuclear weapons.

By the 2000s the situation had radically changed. The United States completed construction of the eighteenth—the last—*Ohio* SSBN and slowly fulfilled the deployment of small series of *B-2* strategic bombers. In 1998 and 1999 Russia annually deployed only ten new SS-27 *Topol M* strategic ballistic missiles which can carry only one warhead per missile. In 2000 the rate of deployment further decreased to six *Topol M* ICBMs. Neither Russia nor the United States implemented any other well-financed nuclear modernization program. Moscow slowly developed a new partially universal ballistic missile for the Navy and Strategic Rocket Forces. Only one new *Yuri Dolgoruky*-class Project 955 SSBN was under construction since 1996. Due to financial shortages, its completion was delayed for several years. In the 1990s Moscow halted production of new strategic bombers, and later decided to complete those, which were partially built by the time of the Soviet collapse.

By December 2001 Russia and the United States completed implementation of strategic nuclear reductions stipulated by the START I Treaty. According to the agreement, the level of their deployed strategic nuclear forces had to be decreased to a level of 6,000 accountable strategic nuclear warheads each. Due to economic reasons, the Russians had to decommission their strategic nuclear submarines ahead of schedule. As a result, the level of Russian forces declined below the START I ceiling. Because of differences between the Treaty counting rules and real loading of strategic systems, in practice the United States continued to deploy between 7,000 and 8,000 strategic warheads. But even that figure is still considerably lower than the ceilings Washington maintained 10 years ago.

Besides the START I, in the 1990s the United States and Russia concluded a series of other agreements on further strategic nuclear reductions. Under the 1993 START II Treaty and the 1997 START II Extension Protocol, by 2008 ceilings of Russian and the U.S. strategic nuclear forces should be further reduced to 3,000 to 3,500 warheads. In March 1997 in Helsinki, Moscow and Washington agreed on reducing their strategic nuclear arsenals further down to a level of 2,000 to 2,500 warheads. In August 1999 at the bilateral START III talks, Moscow officially tabled a proposal to decrease the Treaty ceiling down to 1,500 deployed warheads. In November 2000 the Russians hinted on their willingness to go even further down—to a 1,000 ceiling. Although the United States originally expressed its readiness to shrink its strategic arsenals only to 2,000 to 2,500 warheads, in November 2001 during the U.S.-Russian summit the government accepted an idea of somewhat lower limits—from 1,700 to 2,200.

However, a decade since the end of the Cold War, the United States and Russia were unable to implement agreed strategic nuclear reductions beyond the START I provisions. In Moscow, ratification of START II became a hostage of painful and protracted debates. It was finally ratified in Spring 2000—more than 7 years after it was concluded. The United States linked formal negotiations on START III with Russia's ratification of the 1993 agreement. Although the sides finally entered informal START III consultations in late 1997, no progress was demonstrated there because of limbo in the START II ratification process and political disagreements, like eastward enlargement of NATO. In early 1999 the situation became more complicated due to disagreements around the ABM Treaty. Russia opposed an emerging U.S. idea of the Treaty—its limited modification to permit the U.S. national missile defense deployments (NMD) to protect the United States against limited missile attack potentially launched by a rogue state. Moscow suspected that, in fact, the U.S. NMD plans were aimed at gaining disarming strike capability vis-à-vis Russia's strategic deterrent.

To an extent, these disagreements around the ABM Treaty reflected the controversy emerged when issues linked with relations with third nations were involved in traditional U.S.-Russian bilateral interaction. The United States decided to respond by military means to a perceived risk of a missile attack from the Third World country, which might be willing to hit the U.S. national territory in order to deter U.S. involvement overseas. But that attempt produced a reaction from Russia. The Russians were concerned that, in the face of the country's conventional superiority and likely future radical shrinking of Russia's strategic nuclear deployments, even limited NMD would be capable of intercepting a retaliatory Russian strike by a small number of weapons that had potentially survived the U.S.'s first disarming attack. Although at that time the concerns did not provoke Russia's immediate reaction in the area of strategic nuclear forces modernization, the bilateral strategic nuclear arms control was significantly affected.

In 2000 the dialogue between Russia and the United States appeared in a very deep deadlock. In its START II ratification resolution, the Russian Parliament linked the START II Treaty entering into force with the U.S. ratification of the demarcation agreements to the ABM Treaty. The agreements were concluded between Russia and the United States in September 1997 in New York, and were aimed at drawing a line between missile defense tests, restricted and non-restricted by the ABM Treaty. The U.S. Senate consistently refused ratifying those agreements on the grounds that such approval could implicitly legitimize the document, which viability has been questioned by the Republicans for years.

With the advent of the new administration in the United States, the deadlock was further deepened by the administration's vision, that the U.S. nuclear deployments should not depend anymore on Russia's willingness to accept some of their elements. The administration decided to halt the thirty-years long U.S.-Russian formal strategic arms control negotiations mechanism resulting by concluding legally binding agreements. It seems that the idea of formal START III was aborted. This new approach could be partially explained by a disappointment that existed both in Washington and Moscow by failures of formal bilateral strategic nuclear arms control in the 1990s. Another factor was Russia's weakness. Due to economic hardships the Russians could not keep their strategic nuclear ceilings high, and most likely they would go down from recent levels anyway, irrespective to the fate of arms control agreements. If that was true, why should the United States accept complications in its military planning and deployments because of a need to accommodate Russia?

Indeed, since the Soviet times Russia has radically reduced its defense budget and military procurement. If the Soviet Union spent an equivalent of, at least, $100 billion for its military, in FY 2002 the defense budget of the Russian Federation will not exceed $9 billion—compared with more than $300 billion to be spent by the United States. Furthermore, well before the Russian Parliament ratified the START II Treaty, Moscow transformed its nuclear modernization programs in accordance with the Treaty provisions. The new *Topol M* ICBM was developed, tested and currently is under deployment in a single-warhead mode—as the START II requires it.

Thirdly, despite concerns over the U.S. missile defenses and the fate of strategic arms control, Moscow decided to cut further its nuclear modernization programs. For instance, in August 2000 Russia's Security Council considered a draft plan of modernizing national armed forces. According to media leakages, it considered the further downsizing of strategic nuclear weapons. Reportedly, the rate of procuring new ICBMs would be further reduced from the minuscule ten per year procured in 1998-99. Previous plans required an annual production of 20 to 30 missiles in the early 2000s.

As it was mentioned above, in 2000 only six new ICBMs were procured. If present trends continue for the next 10 to 15 years, Russian strategic nuclear deployments might dramatically shrink not only to low thousands, but even to several hundreds.

One has to recognize that strategic nuclear arms control agreements *per se*, especially in a post-Cold War environment, do not necessarily contribute to halting arms race. It could be argued that the major incentive for the United States and Russia to reduce their strategic nuclear modernization programs was an end of political confrontation and Russia's weakness caused by economic difficulties. In times of historically low defense budgets and growing instability along its southern periphery, it was certainly not a priority for Moscow to continue nuclear arms race with the United States, which was not an enemy anymore. Similarly, a desire to secure post-confrontational peace dividends, together with a task to restructure defense spending in order to address more pressing post-Cold War needs, created a real motivation in the U.S. to move away from large-scale nuclear modernization and deployment.

However, the START II Treaty literally forced Russia to continue its strategic nuclear modernization, albeit on a much more limited scale, despite a strong motivation to reduce the modernization rate even more. First, a new single warhead ICBM was urgently needed in order to fulfill the Treaty provisions banning MIRVed[1] land-based strategic missiles. Secondly, the Treaty has invited the Russians to a nuclear build-up of considerable magnitude. Because of prohibiting MIRVed ICBMs, Moscow had to dismantle a bulk of its land-based forces, which constituted a cornerstone of its strategic triad. After the dismantlement, the level of forces would become much lower than the ceilings of 3,000 to 3,500 warheads imposed by the Treaty. Under some estimates, up to 1,000 new single warhead ICBMs should be produced within a decade in order to fulfill the gap.

Because of the strategic arms control, the United States stuck to higher forces levels than required by the post-Cold War military priorities. In order to keep pressure on the Russians to ratify the START II, in 1996 the U.S. Senate amended its START II ratification resolution by a provision prohibiting the U.S. government from going below 6,000 START I ceilings until the 1993 agreement would enter into force. As a result, the U.S. military had to spend extra funds for maintaining artificial deployments of *MX Peacekeeper* ICBMs and the few submarines.

Non-Strategic Nuclear Developments

Developments in the tactical nuclear area demonstrate that the formal arms control does not represent a necessary condition for forces reductions. Although tactical nuclear weapons remain outside any formal arms control regime, both Russia and the United States have significantly reduced their deployments compared to the Cold War levels. On September 27 and October 6, 1991, President Bush and President Gorbachev, respectively, announced their intentions to make reciprocal parallel withdrawals of tactical nuclear warheads from military units to storage sites. In January 1992 Russian President Boris Yeltsin further expanded Gorbachev initiatives.

According to the Bush initiative, the United States decided to withdraw to its territory major parts of its tactical nuclear weapons located abroad—artillery shells, short-range missiles, gravity bombs and nuclear weapons aboard U.S. surface naval vessels. A significant part of them were slated for dismantlement. Only an unspecified number of the U.S. gravity bombs remained stored in the U.S. military bases located in Europe.[2]

In response, the Soviet Union and later Russia agreed to implement a set of measures, which were expected to be complete by the end of 2000. Among them:

- To withdraw all nuclear weapons to Russian territory.
- To withdraw all non-strategic nuclear warheads

from naval vessels.

- To completely eliminate warheads designated for tactical land-based missiles, artillery shells and landmines.
- To partially eliminate warheads for naval aviation.
- To eliminate half of warheads for tactical aircraft.
- To eliminate one-third of the warheads removed from naval vessels.
- To eliminate one-half of the warheads designated for air-defense missiles.
- To store in central storage sites: two-thirds of warheads removed from naval vessels; one-half of the warheads removed from anti-aircraft missiles; and all non-eliminated warheads removed from naval aviation.

If the measures were to be fully implemented, only one-half of warheads designated for tactical aircraft would remain in military bases; all others would be either eliminated or moved to central storage sites.

However, those initiatives lacked data exchange and transparency measures, which make status of their implementation a subject of speculations. What is known is that, according to official statements, withdrawal of tactical nuclear warheads to Russian territory was completed by May 1992, and that of strategic warheads by November 1996. In April 2000 at the NPT Review Conference held in New York the Russian Minister of Foreign Affairs Igor Ivanov stated that by that time Moscow eliminated one-third of the warheads removed from naval vessels and one-half of the warheads removed from air defense missiles and gravity bombs, and was close to complete elimination of all warheads from tactical land-based missiles, artillery shells and landmines.[3] For comparing the 1991-92 pledges with Mr. Ivanov's report, see Table 1.

Under unofficial estimates, by the 2000s each side keeps deployed only 1,000 to 3,000 tactical warheads—an order of magnitude less than during the Cold War. In the 1990s the United States and Russia unilaterally destroyed a considerable part of their tactical nuclear arsenals. According to U.S. estimates, during certain periods the Russian destruction rate reached as much as 2,000 warheads per year.

Therefore, in the tactical nuclear area the absence of formal arms control did not prevent the halting and reversing of the U.S.-Russian arms race. The weapons were eliminated on probably a wider scale than in the strategic nuclear field, as required by START I. However, lack of formal regimes made that trend more uncertain and less transparent. The sides also remain unassured on results of ongoing reductions—what would be their final ceiling. This uncertainty keeps the relations less confident. The risk still exists, that if political relations deteriorate, the initiatives might be reversed towards, at least, increasing the alert status of remaining tactical weapons.

Certain measures were aimed at reducing Russia's nuclear infrastructure. In 1996 Moscow pledged to shut down its weapon grade plutonium-production reactors in Seversk and Zheleznogorsk and, before that, not to use the accumulated plutonium for military purposes. The reactors were not shut down earlier, because they represented the only source of energy for neighboring residential settlements. The shutdown was linked with the U.S. assistance aimed at building alternative-energy producing capacities. Initially, the Russian Ministry on Atomic Energy—Minatom, which supervised the facilities—sought to convert the reactors' core to enable them to continue their operations as commercial. In 2000, however, Minatom changed its earlier plans and reportedly sought U.S. support for building alternative non-nuclear energy sources. Together with some other U.S.-Russian disagreements, the reactors were not shut down, as was expected, in 2000, and their operation might continue until 2004.

In the near future more far-reaching steps aimed at reducing Russian nuclear infrastructure are expected. For instance, plans are being debated to close important facilities, related to nuclear weapons production, and located in Sarov (Arzamas-16) and Zarechny (Penza-19).

Future Risks

Developments in the 1990s show that despite political disagreements, Russia and the United States have abandoned bilateral nuclear arms race in the form that existed during the Cold War. Contrary to the Cold War period, the arms race was confronted by economic and political factors, while the arms control agreements played a rather controversial role by motivating both sides to maintain higher forces levels and nuclear modernization programs, which might be unnecessary otherwise. At the same time, developments in the tactical nuclear field showed that the formal agreements were still needed. Their absence makes political relations more fragile, and military assessment less certain, and risk of reversibility of disarmament trends quite high.

In the future, the risk of a return to the Cold War-type massive nuclear arms race between Russia and the United States is highly unlikely. In the environment of huge asymmetry in economic capabilities, Russia would face significant obstacles if it decided to return to a massive build-up of its nuclear forces. However, the risk still exists. If U.S.-Russian relations deteriorate, the arms race might return in more relative rather than absolute forms. The disarmament efforts of the both sides could be not too significant as they would be otherwise. Both powers might prefer maintaining higher forces levels and more ambitious modernization programs than they recently plan. The weaker side could be also pressed to find asymmetric responses. This would prevent the United States and Russia from benefiting from the reversed arms race, so painfully achieved during the last decade. The relations would be kept unstable, and the environment for global arms race more fertile.

China Factor?

U.S.-Chinese Interaction

The U.S.-Russian debates around the ABM Treaty suddenly demonstrated that with the end of the bipolar world, the arms race obtained a much greater multilateral dimension. During the Cold War, arms efforts of third parties only marginally affected the forces planning of two superpowers. For instance, in the early 1980s the Chinese developed ICBMs capable of hitting targets in North America. That represented a major change in the U.S. strategic environment since the Soviet Union gained similar capabilities in the late 1950s. But that did not affect the U.S. forces allocations. Oppositely, at that time the United States preferred to concentrate its forces on targeting against the Soviets. This influenced deployments and targeting plans of U.S. strategic submarines patrolling in the Pacific, where missiles were traditionally aimed at Chinese targets. As a result, the U.S. government has ignored that new Chinese challenge, and instead of increasing, temporarily reduced a number of its forces targeted against China.

To a degree, the U.S.'s refusal to respond to the Chinese ICBM deployments by an arms race stimulated Beijing to maintain reciprocal restraint. So far China has pursued very self-restrained nuclear policy. Since the early-1980s when it obtained technological feasibility to hit targets located in North America, Beijing reportedly deployed two or three dozen missiles capable to fulfill that mission. In fact, during the last two decades of the twentieth century, the Chinese sent a clear message to Washington on their reluctance to move beyond minimum deterrence relationship with the United States, and thus their desire to avoid a nuclear arms race with them.

Since the mid-1990s with a gradual decline of the Communist ideology, Chinese nationalism was on the rise. Consequently, the Taiwan reunification issue became an increasingly important factor for the new Chinese *raison d'etre.* In the mid-1990s Beijing tested muscles in attempts to convince Taipei to move closer to the mainland by military coercion. In 1995 and 1996 the People's Liberation Army (PLA) launched missile strikes across the Straight of Taiwan. Later the PLA initiated a massive build-up of short-range missiles along the Straight coast. Their number reportedly reached the upper hundreds.

The 1990s crisis around Taiwan drew attention

in the United States to vulnerabilities of U.S.-led security systems created to protect its East Asian allies. Those perceived vulnerabilities became a visible factor in U.S. debates, initially devoted to a need to deploy theater missile defense with an aim to protect the American allies in the region, and then on national missile defense. Although China has never been directly mentioned as an official rationale for potential U.S. missile defense deployments, a considerable segment of the Republican Party believeed that Beijing should be a real target for that.

Under certain circumstances, even initially limited U.S. missile defense might intercept all the Chinese missiles. As a result, if China maintains its intercontinental nuclear deployments at its recent levels, Washington could effectively deprive Beijing with keeping its minimum deterrence option. Consequently, already in the next decade China might strategically find itself in the situation it faced in the 1970s, when it was unable to deliver warheads to the U.S. national territory. However, the geostrategic environment could be very different: since the Cold War Washington clearly indicated that it was not willing anymore to adjust its regional interests to Beijing's sensitivities, especially on Taiwan issues. Due to that, some Chinese analysts might perceive that maintaining minimum nuclear deterrence in relations with the United States could be a vital element guaranteeing American restraint if something happens around the Taiwan Straight.

Until now, the Chinese abstained from publicly announcing their military reaction on possible U.S. missile defense deployments. However, it is not inconceivable that they would try to maintain their recent minimum deterrence capabilities in their relationship with the United States, which they achieved two decades ago. If Beijing develops MIRV technology, it might be assured from negative impact on its deterrence forces, which could be inflicted by the American anti-missile deployments, by initiating relatively modest missile production program already in coming years. By producing, say, 10 to 15 ballistic missiles per year, each capable to carry 4 to 6 warheads, the Chinese would be able to increase the size of their intercontinental nuclear forces up to around 1,000 warheads within the next twenty years. In other words, one could imagine a realistic scenario when Chinese strategic nuclear capabilities would increase by two orders of magnitude already in the foreseeable future, probably before the United States could deploy effective anti-missile defense system.

This policy does not mean initiation of the U.S.-Chinese arms race of a type took place between the Soviet Union and the United States during the Cold War. Contrary to the Moscow position at that time, Beijing evidently does not seek numerical strategic nuclear parity with Washington. The U.S. missile defense deployments could force it to start significant nuclear build-up in order to preserve recent minimum deterrence *status quo*. Given uncertain technological prospects of missile defenses, Beijing might calculate, that in the near future, time would work for its offense rather than for the U.S. defense.

The impact of possible Chinese reaction on the U.S. missile defense deployments could proliferate well beyond the U.S.-China bilateral nuclear interaction. It would affect several other key countries, which security is dependent on Beijing's foreign and defense policy decisions: Russia, Japan, India, Pakistan, South Korea, and Taiwan.

Possible Impact on Russia

Despite recent positive Sino-Russian relations, Moscow might face difficult choices if the Chinese start their nuclear build-up. Recently, the Chinese conventional predominance *vis-à-vis* vast but under-populated Russian Far East is balanced by Moscow's superiority in nuclear weapons. Along with China's nuclear buildup, this superiority might be considerably eroded, and Russia's positions in the Far East would further weaken. Furthermore, so far Beijing does not possess a capability to inflict assured destruction over Russian targets located in the European part of the country. That maintains credibility for an option of responding by nuclear weapons in a case of a large-scale conventional aggression. With the Chinese nuclear build-up, the situation would qualitatively change.

These developments could be contained by additional Russian non-strategic deployments and could create a motivation to abandon the INF Treaty. Due to shrinking strategic forces, Moscow would need a substitute for maintaining its nuclear leverage in the Far East, which might be very difficult to achieve by remaining inside the existing INF restrictions. Beijing is not a party of the INF Treaty and deploying dozens, if not hundreds, of delivery vehicles with a range between 500 to 5,000 kilometers, would enable the hitting of the significant part of populated Russian territory behind the Urals.

In other words, in quite unpredictable ways the U.S.-Chinese disagreements over the missile defense deployment might pose a threat to another important bilateral U.S.-Russian arms control regime containing arms race—the INF Treaty. Given Russia's position in both Europe and Asia, possible Moscow withdrawal from that agreement might affect nuclear developments to the west from its borders and revive debates on continuing U.S. nuclear presence in the European continent.

Possible Impact on Japan

Japan could be considered a country which found itself amidst negative developments without provoking them. The developments directly affect its security, but Japan has few tools in its disposal for dealing with them, since they take place largely beyond its control. Tokyo clearly faces unpleasant choices, and might have to use all its diplomatic skill in order to avoid further complications.

Among powers in the region, Japan probably pursues the most pacifist foreign and security policies. Despite all debates and external pressures, Tokyo still avoids any detectable remilitarization, and its prospects, at least for the time being, remain slim. It seems that the country enjoys strong domestic commitment for continuing that policy. Under those circumstances, Japan is vitally interested in and strongly dependent on the U.S. security guarantees. If so, it also has to support everything, which would help to maintain American presence in the Western Pacific, including the potential U.S. missile defense.

Simultaneously, Tokyo is much closer to Beijing than Washington—in both geographic and cultural terms. From the Japanese Isles it is better seen that large-scale TMD deployments might provoke the Chinese, at least, to retarget dozens if not hundreds of their medium range missiles to the northeast. It faces the same risks by hosting elements of the potential U.S. strategic missile defense on its territory, especially such future weapons systems, as boost phase and early mid-course interceptors. If tensions further grow, Japan might find it increasingly difficult to accommodate its allied obligations and loyalty with a desire not provoking emergence of more militarized regional environment.

Furthermore, to the contrary, say, to South Korea, Japan has more political reasons to pursue less self-restrained attitude towards TMD. The 1998 North Korean missile launch looked clearly offensive *vis-à-vis* Japan, although Pyongyang geographically lacked alternative azimuths for launching its Taepodong (maybe, except a politically much riskier option to fire it towards Russia's Sakhalin). This provides Japan with perceived legitimate security rationale to develop a limited TMD designed exclusively for intercepting few North Korean missiles.

In a case of the Chinese nuclear build-up, the Japanese position could further become even more delicate. Enlarging Pacific Ocean between China and the United States would create more difficulties for Tokyo to accommodate both the U.S. and Chinese centrifugal priorities. Therefore, Tokyo might face increasing motivations to find its own responses to emerging security threats, including military ones. Besides TMD that option could involve increasing naval build-up—both in terms of numbers and deployments. That might be perceived as an insurance policy in case the U.S. security guarantees provided that regional allies, including Taiwan, would be neutralized by Chinese nuclear blackmail and naval activities.

Developments with North Korean nuclear and missile capabilities would play a greater role for the Japanese security calculations than the Chinese nuclear and conventional build-up. But the latter would affect Japan's position indirectly, through potential erosion of credibility of the U.S. security guarantees. An attempt to maintain that credibility through the TMD could trigger additional Chinese military response, directed at TMD targets in Japan. This might stimulate Tokyo to finally give up its traditional military self-restraint, and get involved in regional arms race.

Nuclear Chain?

Possible Chinese nuclear build-up might provoke the whole nuclear chain. Right or wrong, India clearly links its own nuclear capabilities with China, and increase of Beijing's forces could stimulate New Delhi to accelerate and expand its own nuclear weapons programs. If that happens, Pakistan—India's regional archrival—would unlikely stay indifferent, and would proceed forward with its nuclear modernization as well. In its turn, Islamabad possesses delicate relations with its western neighbor, Iran, which also might find it difficult to abstain from that arms race indefinitely.[4]

The Chinese nuclear build-up, especially if accompanied by Japan's remilitarization, could increase pressure on Taiwan and South Korea to rethink their non-nuclear posture. For Taipei the primary factor here would be the Chinese aggressiveness and perspectives of further erosion of reliable U.S. security guarantees. For Seoul, like for Tokyo, developments in North Korea could be more important. Due to historical concerns, the Japanese behavior would play its own role, and might become a sort of critical mass changing a delicate balance of motivations in both capitals into the better, or worse, direction.

Future Risks

The Chinese factor illustrates to what extent modern arms races became multilateralized and interdependent. Beijing's nuclear build-up should be considered as a more realistic option than the Russian one. Given the central role that the Chinese play in Asia, the choice could considerably affect security calculations in other major nations, like Russia, Japan, India, Pakistan, South Korea, and Taiwan. A high risk exists that some of them would have to start their own nuclear build-up; the others would decide to remilitarize or even nuclearize.

Those developments could occur within already unstable background. After the end of the Cold War, the East and South Asia became leaders in arms race. In the 1990s both regions demonstrated one of the most rapid increases in defense expenditures among key world regions. From 1990 to 1999 in the world total, the defense spending decreased by 28 percent. At the same time, in 1999 combined defense expenditures of Eastern and Southern Asian countries exceeded the 1990 level by 25 percent. In ASEAN alone, the expenditures increased by more than 70 percent for the same period, and in China by approximately 80 percent.[5] As a result, if Beijing decides to launch nuclear buildup, the situation in the most populated regions on the Earth could further destabilize and move beyond control.

Regional Conflicts

The U.S. involvement in the dispute between China and Taiwan indicates how easily regional disputes could affect globally important relationships between major powers. After the Cold War, regional disputes, together with the engagement of outside powers into them, probably became the most significant source of the arms race. While in Western Europe the defense expenditures have reduced from $229 billion in 1990 to $194 billion in 1999, in Northern Africa this indicator increased for the same period by more than 50 percent, and in Asia by more than 20 percent.[6] This represents a regrettable trend, since those continents host the poorest part of the world population. Increasing military expenditures divert scarce available resources from much needed economic development and social programs in those countries.

The end of the Cold War produced a mixed effect on developments in the Third World. On the one hand, cooperation between leading nations helped to convince South Africa to give up its existing nuclear capabilities—the phenomenon unprecedented in history. Other countries, like Argentina and Brazil, refused further implementation of their programs aimed at developing nuclear weapons. Belarus, Kazakhstan, and Ukraine agreed to transfer nuclear weapons, which they inherited from the Soviet Union, to Russia. On the other hand, in many cases the international community paid significantly less attention to peace settlement in the Third World. In some regions, political vacuum has emerged, and it created a favorable climate to new regional hostilities, between the states, or within them. In some cases, internal conflicts were accompanied by unprecedented brutality, like in Rwanda.

Conflicts involving the poorest nations probably remain the most brutal. On the first look, the brutality is not necessarily a consequence of the arms race. The most brutal are internal conflicts, like in Rwanda, Burundi, or Sierra Leone, and massacres there were generally made by the use of the most primitive weapons. Nevertheless, one can find a certain correlation between the arms build-up and internal conflicts. It was the civil wars which often caused the largest increases of defense spending after the end of the Cold War. In Algeria, for instance, the domestic conflict became a primary reason for unprecedented increase of defense budget by three times during 1990 to 1999. Probably, the Algerians were absolute champions in the world by growth of that indicator. Similar trends could be found in Liberia and Sierra Leone in the early 1990s, and in the course of the decade, in Nepal.[7]

An embryonic arms race also seriously affected inter-state conflicts in Africa, like those between Ethiopia and Eritrea. Although it is often difficult to detect the arms race there statistically,[8] purchases of aircraft and tanks by warring sides has undoubtedly increased a number of casualties—both civilian and military.

The most developed traditional arms races take place in the oldest regional conflicts inherited from times of the Cold War—in the Middle East, Hindustani, and the Korean Peninsulas. All three emerged soon after World War II and still remain unsettled. Three states there (India, Pakistan, and Israel) have already become nuclear, and there is evidence that two others (Iraq and North Korea) were engaged in conducting illegal nuclear weapons programs in the past. There are realistic prospects, that an arms race there could lead to further nuclearization, and even nuclear war.

There are two sets of concerns in the *Indian-Pakistani conflict.* After acquiring nuclear capabilities in 1998, both of the powers entered the most delicate period of their nuclear status. They are still inexperienced enough to manage nuclear relations, but possession of nuclear arsenals is giving them feelings of new mightiness enabling them to finally solve old disputes. The 1998 crisis in Kargill was among the most serious and direct armed clashes between nuclear powers. Perhaps, it has not escalated into nuclear war between them because, at that time, the sides had not completed weaponization of their nuclear charges.

So far, a risk of nuclear war in the Middle East remains not as high as that in India-Pakistan. However, it is the most complicated region. One can find several pairs of overlapping conflicting sides, which created a very sophisticated picture of motivations and criteria for arms race. Israeli-Arab conflict had already forced the Israelis to develop undeclared nuclear capabilities, which created dangerous arms race instability. Some Arab nations have already decided to maintain freedom of hands in order to compensate the asymmetry by developing their own chemical and biological weapons (CBW). The existing arms race instability also stimulates them to develop secret nuclear weapons programs and conduct open missile development activities. For instance, for Iran and Iraq Tel Aviv criterion might represent a target for increasing the ranges of their missiles.

The Arab-Israeli confrontation is not the only one in the region. After the bloody wars of the 1980s, Iran and Iraq still look at each other suspiciously. Reportedly, the trauma, inflicted for the Iranians by the Iraqi missile launches against Tehran during that war, was a primary motivation for launching Iranians' own missile program. Both Iran and Iraq, together with Syria, maintain uneasy relationships with their northern neighbor, Turkey. Thus, even if anti-Israeli considerations would not play their recent role for new regimes, which hypothetically could come into power in Tehran and Baghdad, the Ankara criterion could still likely keep its relevance for their missile programs. The same might be true within the Iranian-Iraqi-Saudi triangle, due to competition between these three nations over dominance in the Gulf area.

In the 1990s developments in the *Korean peninsula* were also characterized by increasing arms race instability. Much wealthier South Korea has considerably increased its defense budget—from $11.7 billion in 1990 up to $15 billion in 1999. In political terms, Seoul maintained its alliance with the United States, and established direct relations with China and, especially, Russia. The Russians even provided South Koreans with their weaponry. At the same time, North Korea suffered unprecedented economic hardships, which affected its capability to withstand the arms race with the South. From 1990 to 1994 Seoul increased its military expenditures by 16.8 percent, while Pyongyang was able to do so by only 11.7 percent.[3] Politically, by the 1990s North Korea lost support from the Soviet Union, and became a pariah state on the world stage. This feeling of vulnerability feeds Pyongyang WMD and missile ambitions. These weapons could be considered a relatively cheap equalizer, permitting the compensation of huge military and economic asymmetry the North faces *vis-à-vis* the South.

Risks Ahead

In the 1990s major human losses were associated with internal conflicts in Africa. Unfortunately, all prerequisites for resumptions of those conflicts, like poverty, corruption, and tribalism, still remain in force. The civil wars often caused foreign intervention from the neighbors. It makes it difficult to mark a clear line between inter-state and domestic conflicts there. Thus, risk of new brutal conflicts in Africa remains high.

The same should be said about a risk of nuclear war between India and Pakistan. The war in Afghanistan contributed to instability in neighboring Pakistan. In the aim to consolidate the nation, Islamabad could be even more willing to launch foreign policy adventures, particularly in Kashmir. If the Pakistani survive recent difficult periods, they might find themselves more comfortable with the nuclear capabilities they have acquired. However, the trilateral arms race in South Asia (India-China-Pakistan) contains generic instability. The Indians would try to level their forces with more sizable Chinese capabilities. And this might constantly stimulate much more vulnerable Pakistan to continue its arms race with New Delhi.

Contrary to South Asia, the arms race in the Middle East still has not reached a point when nuclear war is possible. However, existing arms race instability in the region, together with its multilateral nature, creates a fertile soil for developing WMD and missile capabilities. If the worst happens, managing nuclear relationships in the Middle East would be a much more difficult task than between India and Pakistan simply because bilateral hostilities might be easier to solve. Thus, in a longer term the arms race in that region could bring even more dangerous consequences than in South Asia.

The future developments in the Korean peninsula depend on progress in the stable reforming of the DPRK, and its gradual removal from an international isolation. Under a pessimistic scenario, the existing arms race asymmetry would only grow, and would stimulate Pyongyang to further accelerate its WMD and missile efforts. The U.S. dimension of that is especially worrisome. The DPRK might continue to calculate that the U.S. soil represents an important criterion for developing ranges of its missiles. In reciprocity, Washington would have to respond by various missile defense developments and deployments. That might trigger an overreaction from China and, as a result, a chain reaction in the East and South Asia.

Problem Solving

Six Challenges

The analysis of arms races after the end of the Cold War has shown that the recent arms races challenges could be summarized into six larger categories. The first challenge is represented by the fact that in the late 1990s increasing *unilateralist trends* in policy of some major powers led to a deadlock, if not gradual erosion, of a process of building and consolidating multilateral regimes aimed at containing, preventing, and reversing arms races. This negative background has added a significant complication to arms races developments—and searching for cooperative preventing means—in many key regions and relationships.

East Asia has become a region where the arms race has one of the highest rates after the end of the Cold War, and where it might have the most considerable political impact on global developments. Recent U.S.-Chinese disagreements about missile defenses might trigger Beijing's nuclear build-up, which would affect security calculations of major countries situated inside huge Eurasian landmass and North America. Among the regional conflicts, the closest attention should be paid to the Korean peninsula and Taiwan. The latter might make more complicated the U.S.-Chinese dialogue aimed at managing the arms race in the region, and has its own arms race dynamics driven by Taiwan inferiorities. The former represents another example on how hostilities, rooted purely in regional controversies and inherited from the Cold War, affect security relationships between major powers and have a much wider impact on regional and global arms races.

South Asia is a region where arms race made nuclear war a quite realistic scenario already in recent days. Perspectives of trilateral arms race between China, India and Pakistan, together with unsettled crisis in Kashmir and other Pakistani vulnerabilities, would maintain the risk of war for the foreseeable future.

The arms race instability in the Middle East and its multilateral nature is difficult to manage. It also produces incentives for acquiring WMD and missile capabilities and, in the long run, could create a risk of nuclear war. The Israeli vulnerabilities pose the most immediate challenge.

Paradoxically, at least in the short term, recent *U.S.-Russian disagreements* around missile defenses might have only a marginal effect on downsizing Russia's nuclear arsenals. They would have a more important impact on arms race in Asia—both between the Asian nations and related to Moscow's responses to challenges of its security coming from such regions like East and South Asia, and the Middle East.

Addressing potential conflicts in the *failed states* of Africa and Asia should probably be the most urgent task, since they cause the greatest numbers of human casualties. Arms build-up in those states—or potentially failed states—with an aim to address domestic threats represents an indispensable part of the problem.

Potential Responses

Multilateral regimes confronting arms races represent by far most important tool for preventing undesirable trends in global developments. This is why a strategy of preserving what could be maintained and, where possible, moving ahead, should be a priority. The CTBT is a key settled agreement, unable to enter into force. However, so far all eight nuclear powers commit to unilateral bans on conducting nuclear testing. The CTBT Technical Secretariat operates; it *de facto* monitors compliance to the Treaty, while accumulating technical and organizational knowledge needed for possible future full-scale activity.

The United States is still affiliated with the Secretariat, which might be interpreted as its remaining interest to the Treaty. Although in coming years prospects for the U.S. Senate ratification of the CTBT are close to zero, maintaining U.S. activity in the CTBT Technical Secretariat might help to secure Washington's commitment to and *de facto* implementation of the document.

At the same time, four nuclear powers—China, India, Pakistan, and Israel—should be pressed to ratify or sign the Treaty irrespectively to the U.S. decision. Two states—China and India—really matter. If New Delhi decides to sign, Pakistan would most likely follow suit. Israel has nowhere to test, and probably does not need to do that in the foreseeable future. As long as their neighbors remain non-nuclear, for the Israelis it would be very risky to abandon recent no-approval-no-denial policy regarding possession of nuclear weapons: such steps would inevitably provoke rapid nuclearization in the region.

Due to self-imposed limited space for maneuvering, the U.S. leading role here could be substituted by the European Union, Japan, and Russia. The Indians could be convinced to sign the Treaty by economic carrots, promises to enter some prestigious clubs, like probably MTCR, and through reconsidering NSG restrictions on supplying nuclear power technologies and materials to India. Removing the above-mentioned restriction would hardly affect non-proliferation. The Indians produce weapon-grade fissile materials not in commercial nuclear power reactors, and softening restriction on such technological transfers could unlikely add anything substantial to technology and know how New Delhi has already possessed. Similar incentives might apply for Pakistan as well.

The Chinese case could be more complicated, since Beijing might keep reservations partially due to a potential need to conduct more tests in order to complete development of MIRV technology for penetrating through potential U.S. missile defense shield. But this option would be kept open, if the ratification is accompanied by an amendment stating that the CTBT approval could be reversed if the United States decides to deploy missile defenses. Also, since China signed the CTBT and observes a unilateral ban on testing, gaining Beijing's ratification seems a less urgent task than India's. Very unlikely China would be the first to leave the ban, as long as relations with the United States would not seriously be chilled.

The European Union, Japan, and Russia could strike a deal with China by linking issues of the Chinese CTBT ratification and opening up Outer Space demilitarization talks in Geneva. In exchange for approving the CTBT, they might offer Beijing a concerted effort aimed at convincing the United States to accommodate the idea of Outer Space consultations. Above all, it could be argued that the U.S., with its unparallel dependence upon orbital assets like nobody else, is interested to keep Outer Space as a sanctuary free from the arms race. If this strategy succeeded, it would also help to reopen the Cut Off talks.

Recent terror in the United States involving mail containing Anthrax spores would inevitably keep the BW-related issue in the focus of the U.S. public opinion. Thus, the administration would be under constant pressure from the voters, who would ask to adequately address the threat. That maintains some prospects for launching cooperative international efforts aimed at enhancing BWC mandated ban on biological weapons.

Viable strategy addressing multiple arms races challenges in *East Asia* requires the significant rethinking of political and military approaches to developments there. The U.S. missile defense plans represent an excellent bargaining chip, which could be used in order to convince the Chinese to refuse from many destabilizing elements of their policy. For instance, Washington might offer China some limits on its future missile defense deployments so that it could meet Chinese concerns about future credibility of their minimum deterrent. In exchange it could demand Beijing to reduce its missile deployments along the Taiwan straight, and halt intimidation campaigns against Taipei. In their turn, the Taiwanese should be approached with strong advice to refrain from provoking the mainland by pro-independence rhetoric.

The arms race in the Korean peninsula could be most effectively addressed by political and economic means as well. In a longer run, Seoul should be helped with elaborating sound strategy aimed at gradual and stable reunification with North Korea. Given challenges, which Pyongyang could create for all neighbors and the United States, along with further deterioration of domestic situation, all four big powers—the United States, China, Japan and Russia—need to elaborate 4+2 (both Koreas) mechanism in order to coordinate their policy towards the Peninsula. For that, Beijing would have to drop its objections towards expanding the recent 2+2 framework by involving Japan and Russia. Tokyo also needs to give up its second thoughts regarding the Korean reunification.

In the near term, it would be very important if the United States resumes dialogue with North Korea on possible rewards for its refuse from the missile program and opening its nuclear facilities for IAEA inspectors. This dialogue should be accompanied by concerted pressure from four other nations, including China and Russia, in order to force Pyongyang to occupy reasonable position during such consultations. So far, the DPRK demonstrated relative flexibility and hinted on its possible willingness to accommodate to international demands. Involvement into a dialogue could also alleviate Pyongyang's feeling of insecurity, and therefore, reduce its motivation to acquire WMD and long-range missile capabilities. That might be a relief for both the United States and Japan, assuming that they are really concerned by those DPRK programs.

Trilateral arms race instability in *South Asia* could be addressed from both ends—China and Pakistan. The China's end was discussed above. The Pakistani challenge could be addressed through better understanding of its security motivations. After the end of the Cold War that country with a 140 million population emerged isolated in the shadow of a neighboring Indian giant. Traditional alliance with the United States was weakened by disagreements over nuclear tests and Washington's lack of interest in the region after the Soviets left Afghanistan in 1989. China also distanced itself a bit from Islamabad due to improved relations with Russia and Central Asian newly independent states, which consider Pakistan as some sort of regional opponent.

Therefore, the outside powers should be more sensitive to Pakistanis' vulnerabilities, and have to compensate a narrow framework of the South Asian politics characterized by undisputable Indian dominance. Islamabad's role in the recent U.S.-led operation in Afghanistan opens hopes that the United States is becoming more cooperative. But other nations should contribute to de-isolation of Pakistan as well. Particularly, Russia needs to see Islamabad as an important partner in the post-war Afghan settlement, rather than an obstacle to its relations with New Delhi. Moscow must carefully establish a more balanced relationship with South Asian countries, which traditionally have been grossly dominated by India.

At the same time, possible Western assistance to Pakistan should be conditioned by its commitment to observe *status quo* in Kashmir. The outside powers also need to keep constant monitoring over Pakistani nuclear assets, and be ready to react if the country falls into hands of the Islamists, or collapses.

The multilateral arms race instability in *the Middle East* would be especially difficult to correct. Fortunately, there might be some period of time until further nuclearization in the region happens. A constant outside patient involvement is required in efforts aimed at settling the Palestinian problem. Beyond other things, an attentive ear of major powers to Palestinians' aspirations will help the international community to maintain responsive partners in the Arab world, which would be the single best containment strategy against acquiring WMD capabilities by them. Besides that, the outside powers, especially Russia and China, should be extremely careful in delivering WMD and missile-related technologies to the region. They must make more efforts to prevent a situation while recent asymmetry in WMD capabilities in the Middle East would transform into real WMD build-up.

Iran could be a potential target for a more cooperative approach. The European Union might take a lead in offering Tehran economic benefits in exchange for self-imposed limits on Iranian nuclear and missile programs. The Iranians have legitimate grounds to be concerned by neighboring Iraq, which launched a war against Iran in 1980s. As a justification for maximum range of Iranian missiles, the Baghdad criterion could be a base for a reasonable deal, which might help to slow the rate of missile arms race in the region.

In the short term more redundant international coalition is needed to persuade another problem state, Iraq, to accept UN inspections in its territory. At the same time, the international community has to realize that it would be hardly possible to maintain sanctions against that country indefinitely. The choice here is tough enough. Either by demonstrating light at the end of the tunnel Baghdad could be appeased, or—if there is consensus that the regime is not transformable—discussions on establishing international protectorate over that country could be considered. Given almost universal reluctance to follow the second option, the first one might become the only realistic political strategy for the moment.

U.S.-Russian disagreements over missile defenses and nuclear reductions could be solved in the best way if the recent cooperation in a campaign against international terrorism would lead to considerable improvement of political relations between Moscow and Washington. Indeed, both powers still maintain deterrence in their bilateral relationship not because they possess the ABM Treaty. They were not able to retreat from deterrence relationship, because mutual mistrust inherited from the Cold War prevents them from overcoming residual political disagreements. Under those circumstances, the bilateral arms control regulates deterrence relations, which exist due to very different political reasons. As long as deterrence is maintained, arms control will play its regulatory and stabilizing role, and abandoning it ahead of deterrence might be destabilizing. Therefore, the deterrence should be addressed first, if one wants to scrap key elements of bilateral arms control.

If Russia and the United States come to an agreement on their recent disputes, Moscow should not ignore concerns it could cause in Beijing. In a dialogue with the United States, Russia has to always bear in mind the fact that Chinese overreaction on the U.S. missile defense plans might potentially pose a serious security challenge for the Russians themselves. This is why Moscow should use every opportunity to convince the Americans and Chinese to establish substantive bilateral dialogue on matters of future concerns.

Finally, addressing an issue of arms build-up in states balancing on *the brink of civil war* would hardly be possible unless an effective mechanism of rapid reaction force is established. Ideally, that mechanism should be under the UN umbrella—in order to avoid concerns in the developing world that the prosperous West is returning back to colonialism.

* * *

The different shape of arms races nowadays, its multilateralization, and the growing interdependence of security developments in very different regions require truly multilateral and cooperative approaches. Here, few universal principles might be suggested. The priority should be given to cooperative political responses, rather than military ones. The military means might address some issues in a more rapid way, and sometimes it might prove impossible to avoid them. However, they often produce many long-term challenges, which might be much more difficult to solve in the end. Security concerns of problematic states should be taken into account whenever possible. Without revealing deep motivations of a nation's behavior, it might be difficult to elaborate a sound strategy to discourage it from certain actions. It is also vital to concentrate international efforts on resolving a few of the most dangerous crises, which continuously reconstitute stimulus for arms races in their most challenging forms. Finally, there is no universal prescription to confront the arms races. Each situation contains its own unique characteristics, and every one of them should be dealt with individually.

Notes

1. MIRV—Multiple Independently Targeted Re-Entry Vehicle

2. It is widely believed, that the United States is keeping more than 100 gravity bombs located not far from the airfields located in the Netherlands, Germany, Belgium, Turkey, and Italy.

3. Statement by Russian Minister for Foreign Affairs Igor Ivanov before the Non-Proliferation Treaty Review Conference, New York, April 25, 2000.

4. For more details about possible reaction in Asia on the U.S. NMD deployment see: Joseph Cirincione, "Asian Nuclear Chain Reaction," *Foreign Policy*, Washington, DC, Spring 2000.

5. *World Armaments, Disarmament, and International Security.* SIPRI Yearbook 2000. Table 5A.1. Military Spending 1990-99. pp. 281-282 (Russian Edition: Moscow, Nauka, 2001). Here and below the estimates are given in constant 1995 U.S. dollars, unless specified otherwise.

6. Ibid.

7. Ibid., pp. 291-294.

8. In Eritrea, for instance, in 1995-97 defense spending has considerably reduced; by 26 percent (Ibidem, p. 291.)

9. Ibid., p. 293.

Nuclear Warfare: Dynamics and Dilemmas of Policymaking

Daniel Deudney
Johns Hopkins University

During the last half century the unlimited destructive capacity of nuclear weapons has put the question of the "fate of the earth" onto the political agenda for the first time in history. This has forced publics, leaders, and theorists to grapple with the nuclear political question: what kinds of policies, practices, and institutions are best suited to providing security in the nuclear era? Because the state and state system are currently the dominant forms of political institutions concerned with security and violence, the nuclear political question is first about the fit between the nuclear forces of destruction and static institutions and practices. Do these capabilities pose a revolutionary challenge to the state and its role as provider of security? Or can these new realities be accommodated with relatively insignificant institutional adjustment?

Realism, the ancient, diverse, and forceful tradition concerned with the relationships between power, security, and political order offers a rich set of theories and practices relevant to answering the nuclear political question. There are, however, fundamental disagreements among Realists on this question. Realist views on this relationship fall into three broad groups, which I call war strategism, deterrence statism, and nuclear one worldism. Each of these interpretations were articulated at the beginning of the nuclear era, and each is based upon the application of a powerful Realist theoretical insight. Definitive resolution of these disputes is difficult but intimately connected with security practice in the nuclear age. The recent end of the Cold War casts these disputes in a new light, and can in turn be better understood by the disputes within Realism.

The first school of Nuclear Realism argues the war strategist view that the advent of nuclear weapons marks no decisive break in world politics and observes the behavior of states to be largely the same before and after their arrival. Interstate conflict is seen as endemic, and the quintessential state activity of preparing for and making war continues to define world politics. This view has been articulated by William Borden, Paul Nitze, Albert Wohlstetter, Herman Kahn, and Colin Gray.[1] It postulates that states seeking security in a nuclear world will and should prepare themselves to exercise a full range of nuclear use options and seek to gain political advantage from relatively small differences in nuclear force levels. Although this view of the nuclear political question has been heavily attacked for a variety of important shortcomings, the actual force structures and military doctrines of the United States and the Soviet Union during the Cold War embodied this view, to a first approximation and with significant anomalies.

A second Realist view, deterrence statism, holds that nuclear weapons have significantly altered, perhaps even revolutionized, interstate life by making war between nuclear armed states prohibitively costly. In this view the states have created a strongly stable perhaps the best of all possible nuclear order by maintaining extensive nuclear forces in order to deter nuclear use. Such Realists take the state as a given, but hold that states can solve the nuclear security problem by changing their behavior and avoiding war. Deterrence statistic commonly holds that nuclear weapons demand revolutionary changes in interstate relations, but not in states or in the state system. Security is found in the deterrence relationship, and arms control is seen either as irrelevant or a modest enhancement of deterrence.

* * *

The third school of nuclear Realism is nuclear one worldism, which holds that nuclear explosives pose a radical challenge to the core security providing function of the state and that only major institutional changes in the state centric world order can meet the challenge posed by nuclear capability. This revolutionary challenge cannot be met solely with changes in interstate relations; rather survival imperatives require polities to achieve political reconciliation in order to practice and institutionalize new forms of nonstate arms control. Most early nuclear one worlders held that the inevitable trajectory of nuclear politics was either a catastrophe or a world government of some sort. Nuclear one worldism reached its theoretical apogee around 1960 in the works of John Herz and Kenneth Boulding,[2] and was also forcefully stated by Hans Morgenthau. Nuclear one world theory has nearly disappeared with the rise in popularity of various deterrence statistic theories.[3] Such ideas have continued to enjoy a strong but indistinct presence in the academic field of peace studies and in the citizen peace movement, where typically they are mixed and linked with ethical critiques of war, militarism and oppression that go far beyond the simple nuclear one world argument.

Is nuclear one worldism really Realist? This argument posits that the state system is obsolete and likely to be replaced with either a world state or complemented with a nonstate system level security institution, but most Realists today hold that the state is the ontological given of Realism. Nuclear one worldism is the application to the nuclear era of the most primitive form of Realism, geopolitics (or what for purposes of clarity I call "security materialism") that analyzes the relationship between material forces of destruction and security providing practices and institutions. The essence of this paleo-Realist argument can be captured by analogy to Marxian historical production materialism: the forces of destruction, understood as the interaction of geography and technology, constitute the "base" which roughly determines the institutional "superstructure" constituted by security providing units and systems, one form of which has been the state. Security materialism posits that states and state systems emerge, persist, and are replaced according to whether they are, in the long term, viable or functional as providers of security. Neo-Realisms that take the state as a given and then examine its interaction with other states are inherently limited in their ability to theorize about the consequences of changes in the deep structure of material forces, such as the development of nuclear weapons.

Conclusions

Three conclusions are suggested. First, the "black box" of the units has been opened, and light has been shed light on the dynamics and dilemmas of nuclear security politics within nuclear possessed polities. The advent of nuclear explosives has fundamentally altered the relationship between the state apparatus and civil society, creating a nuclear legitimacy deficit. Nuclear weapons are revolutionary in their implications for the viability of states as security providers and, thus, of state civil society relations, but this fact has not yet registered in a fundamental or revolutionary restructuring of polities. Rather than a revolution, there is a revolutionary challenge—a set of unresolved contradictions between the security imperatives of the nuclear world, the security approaches of states, and the security requirements of civil society. One important political consequence of this unresolved tension is the reduced legitimacy of states, particularly when they apply statistic approaches to nuclear security issues. Because state apparatuses derive their legitimacy, at least in part, from their viability as providers of security, the unmet nuclear security challenge produces a chronic "legitimacy deficit" for states. How legitimacy deficits are politically expressed depends on the internal structure of the polity. This legitimacy deficiency is generated by the contradiction between statistic approaches to security and the security imperatives of the nuclear world, and it cannot be eliminated or fully resolved except through a displacement of statistic approaches to nuclear security a change that no one polity can unilaterally achieve. It is possible, however, for this nuclear legitimacy deficit to be evaded and cloaked by a variety of stratagems, even if not actually resolved or permanently avoided by them. But such evasion and displacement cannot be achieved in all circumstances, and chronic nuclear legitimacy deficiencies can erupt periodically into full-fledged crises. On these crisis occasions, the public becomes highly aroused and the politics of nuclear weapons become supercharged with potential for far-reaching institutional change.

The ability of states to evade at least for a while the domestic political consequences of nuclear possession helps to solve an important theoretical puzzle in the nuclear one world model. If the state mode of providing security and protection has been rendered obsolete by the advent of nuclear weapons, then it could be expected that alternative institutional forms would emerge to take its place. States with realpolitik orientations might persist after the demise of the real state mode, but if they persist long enough, then doubt must be cast upon the basic proposition that they have been rendered unviable. Contradiction, while a vital analytic tool for understanding change in institutions, can degenerate into a convenient means of avoiding discomfirming evidence. However, if states have a menu of mechanisms for evading and managing the domestic political consequences of the obsolescence of the real state mode, then an explanation is available for the persistence of the contradiction.

Second, Ronald Reagan and his administration are cast in a new light. The odd and unprecedented gyrations of the Reagan Administration on nuclear matters provides initial support for the proposition that nuclear weapons pose fundamental legitimacy problems for the states that possess them. Attacked from both the political Right and Left for deviations from orthodoxy, Reagan ultimately may have served as a better bellwether for the American polity's genuine security interests than either his political friends or enemies are prepared to recognize. His friends on the Right have yet to grasp that his radical anti-nuclearism was profoundly consistent with his general anti-statism. His enemies on the Left, highly critical of the imperialistic tendencies of American foreign policy, have yet to grasp that his radical anti-nuclearism, not the statism of realpolitkers Nixon and Kissinger, is the most consistent application of the core American tradition of republican anti-statism.

Third, and finally, the relationship between Realism and popular anti-nuclearism has been recast, and a new understanding has been achieved about the weaknesses and strengths of its security practices in the nuclear era and their interaction with domestic political structures. The insistence that the real state be transformed into a component of a more general nuclear control system is based in Realism, but is significantly dependent for its realization upon popular mobilization. The political consequences of nuclear illegitimacy may not be so consistently felt as to constitute a major barrier to acquisition and possession of nuclear weapons by states, and even states embedded in polities with relatively strong traditions of civil society supremacy. The strategies available to states to evade the legitimacy burdens of nuclear weapons, rooted in the ease with which nuclear weapons lend themselves to reclusion, suggest that the nuclear revolution is unlikely to generate a political revolution within nuclear polities. Furthermore, the structurally rooted difficulties in sustaining a critical mass of organic intellectuals focused upon genuine nuclear security alternatives provides another hurdle to revolutionary institutional change.

Given that the effectiveness of nuclear reclusion and of popular peace movements are inversely proportional, new avenues for peace movement strategy to combat reclusion deserve consideration. Nuclear reclusion can be countered by institutionalizing public symbolic representations of nuclear reality, so that both the public and its leaders will never be able to forget that they sit eternally perched at the edge of a bottomless well of nuclear destructive energies. Such an agenda has lengthy precedents. States have long sought to instill the requisite patriotism and obedience in their subjects. And republics, unlike the purely liberal polities in which individual preferences are taken as given, have long sought to form civic personalities consistent with their institutional machinery, particularly the virtues of self-restraint and a suspicion of centralized power.

Notes

1. Colin Gray, *The Geopolitics of the Nuclear Era: Heartlands, Rimlands, and the Technological Revolution* (New York: Crane Russak, 1977); and Colin Gray, *House of Cards: Why Arms Control Must Fail* (Ithaca: Cornell University Press, 1992)

2. John Herz, *International Politics in the Atomic Era* (New York: Columbia University, 1959); Kenneth Boulding, *Conflict and Defense: A General Theory* (New York: Harper & Row, 1962).

3. A good index of this disappearance is that no "nuclear one world" arguments appear in recent synoptic overviews of "security studies." See Joseph Nye Jr., and Sean M. Lynn Jones, "International Security Studies: A Report of a Conference on the State of the Field," *International Security* 12, no. 4 (Spring 1988); and Stephen M. Walt, "The Renaissance of Security Studies," *International Studies Quarterly* 35, no. 2 (June 1991): 211–39.

The Best Antidote to War is a Better Defense

George W. Bush
43rd President of the United States of America

This afternoon, I want us to think back some 30 years to a far different time in a far different world. The United States and the Soviet Union were locked in a hostile rivalry. The Soviet Union was our unquestioned enemy; a highly armed threat to freedom and democracy. Far more than that wall in Berlin divided us.

Our highest ideal was—and remains—individual liberty. Theirs was the construction of a vast communist empire. Their totalitarian regime held much of Europe captive behind an iron curtain.

We didn't trust them, and for good reason. Our deep differences were expressed in a dangerous military confrontation that resulted in thousands of nuclear weapons pointed at each other on hair-trigger alert. Security of both the United States and the Soviet Union was based on a grim premise: that neither side would fire nuclear weapons at each other, because doing so would mean the end of both nations.

We even went so far as to codify this relationship in a 1972 ABM Treaty, based on the doctrine that our very survival would best be insured by leaving both sides completely open and vulnerable to nuclear attack. The threat was real and vivid. The Strategic Air Command had an airborne command post called the Looking Glass, aloft 24 hours a day, ready in case the President ordered our strategic forces to move toward their targets and release their nuclear ordnance.

The Soviet Union had almost 1.5 million troops deep in the heart of Europe, in Poland and Czechoslovakia, Hungary and East Germany. We used our nuclear weapons not just to prevent the Soviet Union from using their nuclear weapons, but also to contain their conventional military forces, to prevent them from extending the Iron Curtain into parts of Europe and Asia that were still free.

In that world, few other nations had nuclear weapons and most of those who did were responsible allies, such as Britain and France. We worried about the proliferation of nuclear weapons to other countries, but it was mostly a distant threat, not yet a reality.

Today, the sun comes up on a vastly different world. The Wall is gone, and so is the Soviet Union. Today's Russia is not yesterday's Soviet Union. Its government is no longer Communist. Its president is elected. Today's Russia is not our enemy, but a country in transition with an opportunity to emerge as a great nation, democratic, at peace with itself and its neighbors. The Iron Curtain no longer exists. Poland, Hungary and the Czech Republic are free nations, and they are now our allies in NATO, together with a reunited Germany.

Yet, this is still a dangerous world, a less certain,

George W. Bush, "The Best Antidote to War is a Better Defense." Text from remarks to Students and Faculty at the National Defense University in May, 2001. See http://www.state.gov, January 5, 2002.

a less predictable one. More nations have nuclear weapons and still more have nuclear aspirations. Many have chemical and biological weapons. Some already have developed the ballistic missile technology that would allow them to deliver weapons of mass destruction at long distances and at incredible speeds. And a number of these countries are spreading these technologies around the world.

Most troubling of all, the list of these countries includes some of the world's least responsible states. Unlike the Cold War, today's most urgent threat stems not from thousands of ballistic missiles in the Soviet hands, but from a small number of missiles in the hands of these states, states for whom terror and blackmail are a way of life. They seek weapons of mass destruction to intimidate their neighbors, and to keep the United States and other responsible nations from helping allies and friends in strategic parts of the world.

When Saddam Hussein invaded Kuwait in 1990, the world joined forces to turn him back. But the international community would have faced a very different situation had Hussein been able to blackmail with nuclear weapons. Like Saddam Hussein, some of today's tyrants are gripped by an implacable hatred of the United States of America. They hate our friends, they hate our values, they hate democracy and freedom and individual liberty. Many care little for the lives of their own people. In such a world, Cold War deterrence is no longer enough.

To maintain peace, to protect our own citizens and our own allies and friends, we must seek security based on more than the grim premise that we can destroy those who seek to destroy us. This is an important opportunity for the world to rethink the unthinkable, and to find new ways to keep the peace.

Today's world requires a new policy, a broad strategy of active nonproliferation, counterproliferation and defenses. We must work together with other like-minded nations to deny weapons of terror from those seeking to acquire them. We must work with allies and friends who wish to join with us to defend against the harm they can inflict. And together we must deter anyone who would contemplate their use.

We need new concepts of deterrence that rely on both offensive and defensive forces. Deterrence can no longer be based solely on the threat of nuclear retaliation. Defenses can strengthen deterrence by reducing the incentive for proliferation.

We need a new framework that allows us to build missile defenses to counter the different threats of today's world. To do so, we must move beyond the constraints of the 30 year old ABM Treaty. This treaty does not recognize the present, or point us to the future. It enshrines the past. No treaty that prevents us from addressing today's threats, that prohibits us from pursuing promising technology to defend ourselves, our friends and our allies is in our interests or in the interests of world peace.

This new framework must encourage still further cuts in nuclear weapons. Nuclear weapons still have a vital role to play in our security and that of our allies. We can, and will, change the size, the composition, the character of our nuclear forces in a way that reflects the reality that the Cold War is over.

I am committed to achieving a credible deterrent with the lowest possible number of nuclear weapons consistent with our national security needs, including our obligations to our allies. My goal is to move quickly to reduce nuclear forces. The United States will lead by example to achieve our interests and the interests for peace in the world.

Several months ago, I asked Secretary of Defense Rumsfeld to examine all available technologies and basing modes for effective missile defenses that could protect the United States, our deployed forces, our friends and our allies. The Secretary has explored a number of complementary and innovative approaches.

The Secretary has identified near term options that could allow us to deploy an initial capability against limited threats. In some cases, we can draw on already established technologies that might involve land based and sea based capabilities to intercept missiles in midcourse or after they reenter the atmosphere. We also recognize the substantial advantages of intercepting missiles early in their flight, especially in the boost phase.

The preliminary work has produced some promising options for advanced sensors and interceptors that may provide this capability. If based at sea or on aircraft, such approaches could provide limited, but effective, defenses.

We have more work to do to determine the final form the defenses might take. We will explore all these options further. We recognize the technological difficulties we face and we look forward to the challenge. Our nation will assign the best people to this critical task.

We will evaluate what works and what does not. We know that some approaches will not work. We also know that we will be able to build on our successes. When ready, and working with Congress, we will deploy missile defenses to strengthen global security and stability.

I've made it clear from the very beginning that I would consult closely on the important subject with our friends and allies who are also threatened by missiles and weapons of mass destruction.

Today, I'm announcing the dispatch of high level representatives to Allied capitals in Europe, Asia, Australia and Canada to discuss our common responsibility to create a new framework for security and stability that reflects the world of today.

* * *

These will be real consultations. We are not presenting our friends and allies with unilateral decisions already made. We look forward to hearing their views, the views of our friends, and to take them into account.

We will seek their input on all the issues surrounding the new strategic environment. We'll also need to reach out to other interested states, including China and Russia. Russia and the United States should work together to develop a new foundation for world peace and security in the 21st century. We should leave behind the constraints of an ABM Treaty that perpetuates a relationship based on distrust and mutual vulnerability. This Treaty ignores the fundamental breakthroughs in technology during the last 30 years. It prohibits us from exploring all options for defending against the threats that face us, our allies and other countries.

That's why we should work together to replace this Treaty with a new framework that reflects a clear and clean break from the past, and especially from the adversarial legacy of the Cold War. This new cooperative relationship should look to the future, not to the past. It should be reassuring, rather than threatening. It should be premised on openness, mutual confidence and real opportunities for cooperation, including the area of missile defense. It should allow us to share information so that each nation can improve its early warning capability, and its capability to defend its people and territory. And perhaps one day, we can even cooperate in a joint defense.

I want to complete the work of changing our relationship from one based on a nuclear balance of terror, to one based on common responsibilities and common interests. We may have areas of difference with Russia, but we are not and must not be strategic adversaries. Russia and America both face new threats to security. Together, we can address today's threats and pursue today's opportunities. We can explore technologies that have the potential to make us all safer.

This is a time for vision; a time for a new way of thinking; a time for bold leadership. The Looking Glass no longer stands its 24-hour-day vigil. We must all look at the world in a new, realistic way, to preserve peace for generations to come.

(For the benefit of our readers attached is ancillary government statements on the U.S. national missile defense initiative.)

Text of Diplomatic Notes Sent to Russia, Belarus, Kazakhstan and Ukraine on December 13, 2001

The Embassy of the United States of America has the honor to refer to the Treaty between the United States of America and the Union of Soviet Socialist Republics (USSR) on the Limitation of Antiballistic Missile Systems signed at Moscow May 26, 1972.

Article XV, paragraph 2, gives each Party the right to withdraw from the Treaty if it decides that extraordinary events related to the subject matter of the treaty have jeopardized its supreme interests.

The United States recognizes that the Treaty was entered into with the USSR, which ceased to exist in 1991. Since then, we have entered into a new strategic relationship with Russia that is cooperative rather than adversarial, and are building strong relationships with most states of the former USSR.

Since the Treaty entered into force in 1972, a number of state and nonstate entities have acquired or are actively seeking to acquire weapons of mass destruction. It is clear, and has recently been demonstrated, that some of these entities are prepared to employ these weapons against the United States. Moreover, a number of states are developing ballistic missiles, including long-range ballistic missiles, as a means of delivering weapons of mass destruction. These events pose a direct threat to the territory and security of the United States and jeopardize its supreme interests. As a result, the United States has concluded that it must develop, test, and deploy antiballistic missile systems for the defense of its national territory, of its forces outside the United States, and of its friends and allies.

Pursuant to Article XV, paragraph 2, the United States has decided that extraordinary events related to the subject matter of the Treaty have jeopardized its supreme interests. Therefore, in the exercise of the right to withdraw from the Treaty provided in Article XV, paragraph 2, the United States hereby gives notice of its withdrawal from the Treaty. In accordance with the terms of the Treaty, withdrawal will be effective six months from the date of this notice.

U.S. State Department Bureau of Nonproliferation Statement on Nonproliferation and Missile Defense

September 1, 2001

Weapons of mass destruction (WMD) and their missile delivery systems pose a direct and serious threat to the national security of the United States, our friends, forces, and allies. President Bush has made clear that we must have a comprehensive strategy to counter this complex and dangerous challenge. This strategy must include strengthening nonproliferation measures (prevention), more robust counterproliferation capabilities (protection), and a new concept for deterring contemporary threats, relying more on defenses and less on offensive nuclear forces.

U.S. Nonproliferation Efforts

Our nonproliferation efforts seek to prevent or slow the spread of nuclear, biological, and chemical weapons and their missile delivery systems. We are working to impede WMD and missile development programs existing in key countries and regions of concern such as Iran, Iraq, Libya, North Korea, and South Asia and to halt transfers of missiles and missile related items from countries such as Russia, China, and North Korea. There are four elements of our nonproliferation strategy:

Persuade or induce proliferating governments to change course.

- Engage directly and indirectly with countries of concern to urge them to constrain, halt or reverse proliferation. This includes renewed engagement with North Korea on its nuclear and missile programs, working through the UN to induce Iraq to accept international inspections, and efforts to persuade India and Pakistan to constrain their nuclear and missile competition.

- Use positive and negative incentives to demonstrate to proliferators there are benefits to observing nonproliferation norms and costs for disregarding them.

Deny proliferators the supply of equipment, material, or technology from abroad.

- Work with other governments to monitor and stop foreign shipments of sensitive WMD and missile related technologies to countries and programs of concern.
- Press countries like North Korea, Russia and China to behave more responsibly, and assist others to upgrade their export controls.
- Craft a United Nations control mechanism to deny Iraq sensitive goods while permitting the Iraqi people to receive the civilian goods they need.
- Cut off outside assistance to Iran's nuclear and missile programs.
- Reinforce the Missile Technology Control Regime and other suppliers' nonproliferation arrangements, to create rules that member countries and others use to guide their export behavior.
- Impose sanctions, when warranted, on countries and specific entities that assist proliferators, to deter would-be suppliers.

Use U.S. threat reduction programs to secure or eliminate WMD and missile capabilities left over from the Cold War.

- Pursue programs in the New Independent States (NIS)—especially Russia—to help them meet their arms control obligations, and to control and dispose of the massive quantities of WMD and missile materials there.
- Ensure former Soviet WMD and missile expertise does not leak out of Russia and the NIS to rogue states.

Strengthen existing international nonproliferation treaties, promote new ones that meet U.S. interests, and upgrade the means of verifying them.

- Support formal treaties such as the Nuclear Nonproliferation Treaty (NPT), the Chemical Weapons Convention (CWC), and the Biological Weapons Convention (BWC) that set the international "rules of the road" on possession, deployment or transfer of nuclear, chemical and biological weapons.
- Strengthen the International Atomic Energy Agency's (IAEA) nuclear inspection system.
- Press others to bring into force upgraded IAEA safeguards designed to detect Iraq style clandestine nuclear activities.
- Seek to break the international logjam that is blocking negotiation of a treaty to end the production of unsafeguarded nuclear weapons material.

Nonproliferation Missile Defense

Nonproliferation, deterrence, and missile defense are complementary parts of our overall strategy:

Nonproliferation reduces the threat missile defenses are designed to counter.

- The threat posed by WMD and missile proliferation is the driving force behind our desire for missile defense. To the extent this threat is reduced by other means, the magnitude of the threat that must be dealt with by missile defenses also declines.

Missile defense weakens the incentive to develop, test, produce, and deploy missiles.

- Rogue states such as Iran, Iraq, Libya and North Korea are less likely to invest in missiles as a weapon of choice if they know they will face effective defenses.

Missile defense does not mean that we are giving up on deterrence.

- Missile defense strengthens deterrence and keeps rogue states from being able to blackmail the United States, its friends or allies by threatening a missile attack.

U.S. State Department Bureau of Arms Control Statement on Missile Defense and Deterrence

Deterrence must and will remain a critical component of our security posture. Yet, many of the conditions and assumptions that long guided the way we thought about deterrence and its supporting strategic force posture have changed fundamentally. Deterrence can involve more than just the threat to retaliate in the event of an attack. It can also be based on the ability to prevent potential adversaries from achieving their objectives thereby deterring them from pursuing such objectives in the first place. The United States is developing a forward looking strategy that takes into account the changing nature of the threats we face, as well as the full range of capabilities that we can marshal to protect our nation and its vital interests, as well as meet our commitments to friends and allies.

Deterrence is Our Highest Priority

Maintaining a reliable deterrent against attacks on the U.S. and our allies is a critical objective of our national security strategy. Our nation always prefers peaceful means to maintain its own security and prosperity, and that of its friends and allies, but maintains the military capabilities needed to deter and defend against the threat or potential use of force by prospective adversaries.

Our deterrence strategy to date has largely relied on our ability to respond to attack with a variety of options, ranging from a devastating retaliation through more selective strikes, and our offensive nuclear forces are and will remain a key component of that capability. No group or nation should doubt that the U.S. will continue to depend on the certainty of a devastating response to any attack on the U.S. or its allies to deter attacks by ballistic missiles or other weapons.

Emerging Threats and the Need to Diversify our Approach to Deterrence

However, given the new threats we all face—especially from weapons of mass destruction and increasingly sophisticated ballistic missiles in the hands of rogue states—our deterrence posture can no longer rely exclusively on the threat of retaliation. We now need a strategy based on an appropriate mix of offensive and defensive capabilities to deny potential adversaries the opportunities and benefits they might hope to realize from the threat or use of weapons of mass destruction against our homeland and forces deployed abroad, as well as those of our allies and friends.

Today, we are confronted with a more diverse, less predictable, and less risk averse group of hostile states that are aggressively seeking to develop or acquire weapons of mass destruction and longer range missiles as a means of their delivery. They see such weapons both as operational weapons of war and as coercive tools of diplomacy to preclude us and our partners from assisting friends and allies in regions of vital interest. For such threats, deterrence must take advantage of the contribution of both offensive and defensive forces, working together.

Ballistic missile defenses enhance the traditional deterrence of offensive capabilities by denying rogue states the ability to reliably and predictably inflict mass destruction on other nations. By complicating his calculation of success, these defenses add to a potential aggressor's uncertainty and weaken his confidence. Effective missile defenses may also serve to undercut the value potential aggressor's place on missiles as a means of delivery, thereby advancing our nonproliferation goals.

With these considerations in mind, missile defenses can be a force for stability and security.

Moreover, some potential threats, such as accidental or unauthorized launches of ballistic missiles, cannot be deterred by their very nature. They can only be defended against. To counter such contingencies, missile defenses provide an element of insurance that supplements and enhances their deterrent value.

Summary

Finally, it is worth emphasizing that missile defenses are only one tool among many in maintaining peace, security, and stability, and must be considered within the context of our entire strategic framework. This framework includes offensive nuclear arms as well as our broader diplomatic and security activities, including arms control and nonproliferation efforts. This diversified approach to deterrence is appropriate for the complex and less predictable world in which we live.

Unorthodox Warfare: Does Terrorism Work?

Richard Clutterbuck
Soldier and Academic (1918-1998)

Terrorism was best defined by Sun Tzu over two thousand years ago: "Kill one, frighten ten thousand." Guerrillas and freedom fighters may or may not use terrorism as a technique. A resistance fighter who kills a soldier who invades his country, moral reasons aside, is not a terrorist, because he does not frighten ten thousand other soldiers—indeed he galvanizes them. If, however, he takes innocent hostages from his own village and shoots them to deter others from collaborating with the enemy, then he is a terrorist—just as much as the occupying soldier who shoots hostages to deter support for the resistance. By these criteria, the Palestinians, the *Shia,* the Irish Republican Army, Irish National Liberation Army, Ulster Volunteer Force and the Ulster Freedom Fighters are terrorists, regardless of their cause.

In fact, the efficacy of terrorism is largely a myth. It achieves dramatic short-term dividends but seldom advances the long-term aim. The terrorism of Begin's underground organization *Irgun* did not advance the independence of Israel, which was achieved by Ben Gurion's officially recognized Jewish Agency and the militia organization *Haganah.* Begin embarrassed them as much as the IRA embarrasses the Dublin government in seeking reunification. Begin's terrorism ensured violent Arab hostility, just as 35 years later his terror bombing of refugee camps and his actions in Lebanon ensured that it will continue. Similarly, PLO terrorism has not recovered one acre of Palestine for the Arabs and has ensured that the Israelis will fight to the death rather than accept terrorist bases in the hills of Judea. The short-term dividends, however—publicity, release of prisoners, ransoms—are so spectacular that more and more political and religious groups, frustrated by their inability to get their way, turn to terrorism, above all for publicity. It is because totalitarian state-controlled media can deny such publicity that the Soviet Union suffered only 62 of the 6700 terrorist incidents recorded between 1968 and 1980.

Can the liberal democracies deny the terrorists this "oxygen of publicity" (to use Mrs. Thatcher's phrase) without so restricting freedom of the press as to do more harm than good?

In June 1985 a TWA airliner carrying many American passengers was hijacked by the *Shia* demanding the release of Arab prisoners by Israel. There is no doubt that the highly emotive publicity on America's competing television networks enormously strengthened the hand of the TWA hijackers. To abandon the gallant Captain Trestrake or to fail to save the husband of the weeping wife linked to him live on television was unthinkable and the terrorists knew it. True, a platoon of soldiers, cut off

Richard Clutterbuck, "Unorthodox Warfare: Does Terrorism Work?" Reprinted with the permission of *The Tablet,* 3 August 1985.

in battle, could expect no similar political sacrifices to save it; nor could a kidnapped ambassador—but soldiers, diplomats and policemen accept that their lives are on the line.

In the long run, America's concern for individual lives is one of the things which makes her so much stronger and more resilient than the Soviet Union. Nevertheless, the media should recognize that they did help the terrorists. The answer must lie, not in censorship or government control, but in a voluntary code—which may be a vain hope because the scoops will go to those who break it.

A glimmer of hope lies in the success of the British police in negotiating a media blackout in four kidnap cases since 1975, saving all the hostages and capturing all the kidnappers. The art lay in briefing all the media together, convincing them that life was at risk, that publicity would increase that risk—and woe betide any journalist who broke faith.

It is more difficult if the story itself has already got out—as it inevitably will in the case of a hijack through the foreign press. However, Chancellor Schmidt achieved media silence in the later weeks of the Schleyer case in 1977 when the head of the West German employers' organization was kidnapped and then killed by the Red Army Faction. Again in 1980, after an appalling start, the whole world's press respected the parents' plea for a blackout of the closing stages of the Schild family kidnap in Sardinia.

In the case of the TWA hijack, had President Reagan at the outset briefed all the editors and journalists, he might have got them to agree on a common degree of restraint.

In other respects, the President's handling of the crisis was good. Regardless of the media, fanatical terrorists with lives in their hands hold almost all the cards in dealing with a humane society. A rescue attempt in Algiers would have destroyed a useful working relationship. A rescue attempt in Beirut—with the airport held by *Shia* militia—could only have recovered dead bodies. Bombing *Shia* bases in populated areas would have been a form of terrorism itself, as counterproductive as Begin's own terrorism in Lebanon. So President Reagan courageously swallowed his pride and sought help from the only people who would bring any pressure to bear on the terrorists—Assad and Berri (the President and Justice Minister of Lebanon)—counting on the fact that neither wished to see Lebanon relapse into even greater chaos. They did not want to alienate the Americans too far. The President's ability to apply pressure by economic boycott and destabilization will have counted more with them than military action, and in the long-term these are by far the West's strongest cards.

Nevertheless, joint action by liberal societies—like that by journalists—is too often nullified by greed and self-interest. Are we in a Third World War? In one sense, yes. The Soviet Union set out to extend its power by fair means or foul in 1945—unsuccessfully in Western Europe and East Asia, successfully in Eastern Europe, Cuba, parts of Africa and the Arab world and Afghanistan. One of the most effective methods used by the Soviets has been to exploit internal conflicts and to support any terrorist groups which destabilize Western democracy, almost regardless of the political beliefs of the terrorists. They exploit and support rather than sponsor. They did not (and did not need to) create the IRA, the Red Brigades, the PLO or the Islamic fundamentalists. There is little or no evidence of causes of tactical direction by the Kremlin, though there is of help with weapons (usually through an intermediary state), money, training, propaganda and intelligence, through the ubiquitous KGB under cover of embassies, trade delegations and so forth.

How should we fight it? Not so much by international conventions as by bilateral cooperation at working level between police, intelligence services, soldiers and rescue squads. Such bilateral cooperation is already excellent between such services in, for example, Australia, Britain, Canada, the Netherlands, the United States and West Germany. We must extend this to others, including friendly Third World countries. The West has a lot to offer and can make their cooperation worthwhile.

Where the actions of police, military and the judiciary are concerned, we must always act within our own laws, no matter how great the temptation to do otherwise. Preemptive terror and clandestine assassinations, as well as undermining our whole moral case, will rebound, as the widely documented use of terrorism and torture by the French against the Algerian independence movement rebounded against them.

If the terrorists make our liberal judicial procedure unworkable, by intimidating witnesses and juries, for example, then we must pass emergency laws to make procedures that are workable. The West Germans did it, the Italians did it and we did it in Northern Ireland—all with success. The killings in Northern Ireland in 1972 were 467. In 1973 we passed the Northern Ireland (Emergency Provisions) Bill introducing trial without jury for terrorist offences. In that year, killings fell to 250, where they remained on average for the next four years. From 1977 to 1984 they averaged 90, and only 64 in 1984. The saving of life in Italy after the package of laws was introduced in 1979 was even more dramatic.

The IRA, the UVF, the Palestinians and the *Shia* terrorists all believe fervently in their cause. So do some of their own people, but this does not give them the right to murder those who do not. The right of a minority to kill must never override the right of the majority to live in peace.

The words of the Pope, spoken in the heart of Ireland, cannot be quoted too often: 'We must not call murder by any other word than murder.'

Media in the Service of Terrorism

Harold J. Vetter
Portland State University and

Gary R. Perlstein
Portland State University

> *"We want to shock people, everywhere.... It is our only way of communication with the people."*
>
> —Member of the Japanese United Red Army quoted in Gerard McKnight, *The Mind of the Terrorist*

In the past, when incidents of violence were reported by word of mouth, town crier, correspondence, or newspapers, the impact of a given incident was deadened by the sheer inertia of communications processes as they existed in a primitive form. All of that has changed. Within hours or even minutes, the seizure of an airplane with its passengers as hostages, the car bombing of a crowded market, an attack on a government official—all are subjected to immediate saturation by the broadcast media. The details are dished up for consumption on the televised evening news....

...Terrorist groups since the early anarchists have realized the importance of the media to their goals. In the late 1880s, John Most expressed the anarchist sentiment of "propaganda by the deed":

> We have said a hundred times or more that when modern revolutionaries carry out actions, what is important is not solely these actions themselves but also the propagandistic effect they are able to achieve. Hence we preach not only action in and for itself, but also action as propaganda. (Laqueur, 1978, 105)

Technological advances in communications, such as satellites, microwave relays, and portable cameras and recorders, have made the media an even more important weapon in the terrorist arsenal. The terrorist act is not meant to be a battle that will win the war, but simply a method of getting the media to publicize a group's objectives. Jenkins also observed this phenomenon:

> Terrorism is violence for effect—not primarily, and sometimes not at all for the physical effect on the actual target, but rather for its dramatic impact on an audience. Developments in world communications, particularly the news media, potential audience to national and, more recently, to international proportions. (1978, 101)

Laqueur has claimed that "The media are the terrorist's best friend" (1976, 104). This position is surely an oversimplification. Schmid and De Graaf offer the more balanced appraisal that the media are unwitting allies of the terrorist. Both terrorists and the media have a common interest in reaching a large audience; both want attention, and it is on this basis that collaboration occurs.

Does media portrayal of violence produce more

of the same? This is an easy question to pose, but extremely difficult to answer and fraught with controversy. Jenkins claims that "the news media are responsible for terrorism to about the same extent that commercial aviation is responsible for airline hijackings" (1978, 4). Schmid and De Graaf (1982), on the other hand, explore evidence of the contagion or imitation effects of media coverage as a potential direct cause of subsequent acts of terrorism.

It is already apparent that much of the voluminous literature dealing with mass media and terrorism is polemical, with adversaries confronting one another over various issues from well-polarized viewpoints and perspectives. One can expect public officials (including law enforcement executives, representatives of various agencies, and elected members of local, state, and federal government) to differ sharply with media representatives on nearly every specific issue. There are some interesting exceptions; for example, Patrick Murphy, a law enforcement official, who argues for a generally unrestricted press, and journalist and editor John O'Sullivan favors certain prohibitions on media coverage of terrorists and terrorism (Murphy, 1977; Koppel et al., 1986).

Inevitably, before discussions of terrorism and the mass media have gone very far, the question of censorship is raised. Terrorism, as Laqueur (1987) has observed, is almost entirely a problem for permissive democratic societies and ineffective authoritarian regimes; there is no future in challenging effective dictatorships. But this is precisely where we encounter the ineluctable dilemma of controls: there is an inherent contradiction in restricting a society's civil liberties in the interest or hope of preserving the liberal basis of that society.

We do not believe that a plausible argument can be made at present for imposing official controls (i.e., censorship) on media coverage of domestic terrorist events. On the other hand, case law decisions have placed constraints on unrestricted media coverage, despite well-intentioned and pious invocations of the public's "need to know" and real or imagined threats to First Amendment freedoms by some media representatives. It seems more than probable that the only kinds of controls we are likely to see on media coverage of international terrorist incidents are those that the media themselves impose in the form of voluntary "guidelines."

Presentation of the Event

A terrorist incident is obviously a newsworthy event and deserves media coverage. There is a constant risk, however, that instead of an objective presentation of the news, media representatives may be manipulated into merely presenting propaganda. Fitzpatrick points out the danger:

> The media must not be the dupes of the radical scriptwriters, nor should they be the mouthpiece of government. There is a mean. Law enforcement and the media cannot be locked in combat. Law enforcement has to realize the function of the media is to report the news, and hopefully, not alter it. The media must be cognizant of the very real danger of glorifying the terrorist. (1974, 23)

The Hanafi Muslim Siege

The media coverage of the Hanafi Muslim siege in Washington, DC, is a good example of how the media can be used to make a big story out of a relatively minor terrorist incident. On March 9, 1977, twelve members of a Muslim sect took 134 hostages. A reporter was shot, and other hostages were injured. Their leader, Hamaas Abdul Khaalis, wanted the murderers of his family handed over to him so that he could personally administer justice. He also demanded that a movie, *Mohammad, Messenger of God,* be banned from American movie screens because it was blasphemous. Television reporters began to broadcast live from the scene, and journalists tied up telephone lines by interviewing the terrorists. During the three days that the hostage situation lasted, NBC spent over 53 percent of its evening news time on the story, CBS spent over 31 percent, and ABC spent 40 percent (Schmid &

De Graaf, 1982, 77). One reporter, seeing the police bringing food to the terrorists, broadcast that this was the preparation for an assault. The police were able to convince the Hanafis that the reporter was incorrect, and the situation was calmed (Miller, 1980, 87). In another instance, a reporter called Khaalis and suggested that the police were trying to trick him. The terrorist leader picked ten older hostages to execute, and the police withdrew some of their sharpshooters to put the Hanafis at ease (Schmid & De Graaf, 1982, 77).

A great deal of criticism was directed toward the media because of the intensity of their reporting and their interference with the hostage negotiation process. One of the hostages, a reporter, made the following observation:

> As hostages, many of us felt that the Hanafi takeover was a happening, a guerrilla theater, a high impact propaganda exercise programmed for the TV screen, and secondarily for the front pages of newspapers around the world....Beneath the resentment and the anger of my fellow hostages toward the press is a conviction gained...that the news media and terrorism feed on each other, that the news media and particularly TV, create a thirst for fame and recognition. Reporters do not simply report the news. They help create it. They are not objective observers, but subjective participants—actors, scriptwriters and idea men. (Schmid & De Graaf, 1982,42)

TWA Flight 847

The hijacking of TWA flight 847 in June 1985 by Shiite terrorists is another extremely disturbing example of how media representatives may cross the line from *portrayal* into *advocacy* when covering acts of terrorist violence. Beginning with the exclusive focus of the networks on only one of the terrorists' demands—the release of more than 700 Lebanese detainees in Israel—to the total exclusion of all others, and culminating in the depiction of Amal chief Nabih Bern as a moderate negotiator and impartial go-between striving to save the lives of both the American hostages in Beirut and the Arab "hostages" in Israel, media involvement was intensive, detailed, and thoroughly distorted in its partisan interpretations of the meaning of events for the American television public.

The hijackers had begun by making a number of demands that included (in addition to the release of the more than 700 Lebanese held by the Israelis): the release of seventeen Shiite prisoners held in Kuwait; the release of prisoners held in Greece; the release of two Shiite terrorists held by the Spanish; the overthrow of King Hussein of Jordan and Mubarak of Egypt; an end to American aid to Israel; and the reversal of American policies in the Middle East, that is, a switch in support from Israel to support for the Arab states.

When it became apparent to the hijackers that the television networks were interested only in the quid pro quo transaction of swapping 700 Lebanese for thirty-nine Americans, excluding American Navy diver Robert Dean Stethem, who was brutally murdered by the Shiite terrorists, the hijackers dropped the other demands. Said Israeli journalist Bar-Illan:

> So the familiar scene was set: on one side persecuted Arabs, "understandably enraged" by horrible injustices, making "reasonable demands"...and on the other side, intransigent Israelis cold-bloodedly disregarding the fate of innocent people....Over and over again, television commentators, anchormen, and reporters, alternating hints with accusations, and assuming the roles of negotiators, arbiters, and moralizers, portrayed Israel as an ungrateful ally which had freed 1,150 convicted murderers in return for three Israeli soldiers, but would not free over 700 innocent Lebanese ("not charged with any crime") to save the lives of 39 American tourists. (1986, 111)

Throughout the seventeen-day ordeal, the media uncritically adopted the Shiite interpretations of events. The TWA plane had been hijacked by men desperate to free their "relatives" held captive in Israel, thus creating a parallel with the families of the American hostages. Allyn Conwell, who became the spokesman for the hostages, said: "If my wife and children were abducted and taken illegally across the border, I guess I, too, would have resorted to anything at all to free them."

As Bar-Illan observes, there were no "wives and children" in Israeli custody—only young men of military age, a piece of information that should have been known to even the most ignorant reporter in Lebanon. This is the kind of "moral symmetry" all too similar to that invoked by the media in speaking of the U.S. and the Soviet Union: the Soviets invaded Afghanistan, we invaded Grenada; the Red Air Force shot down KAL Flight 007, we shot down a civilian aircraft from Iran in the Persian Gulf.

In addition to the correspondents on the scene, anchormen and talk-show hosts in the U.S. provided nearly unlimited coverage of the hijackers and their apologists. When asked why they had been given so much air-time, the answer was that the American population needed the education and that it was only fair to give the hijackers an opportunity to present their point of view. On July 10, *New York Times* columnist Tom Wicker wrote: "Was television 'used' by Amal? Of course, just as it is being used all the time by the Reagan administration for its own purposes."

Here, said Bar-Illan, we have ultimate evenhandedness: a "godfather" of cutthroats, kidnappers, and assassins linked with the democratically elected President of the U.S. Given the kind of philosophical orientation and political ideology that supports and makes possible this kind of "moral symmetry," it is not difficult to account for the smugness, complacency, and self-adulation that characterized a post-hijacking program on "Nightline," on which all the senior... correspondents in Beirut agreed that they had advanced the cause of peace and justice in the Middle East by exposing the defects of American policy! Barbara Rosen, the wife of a man who had been held hostage, told of the education she received in how the news is produced at CBS. She draws a sharp picture of the ways technological expertise is employed...

***

Finally, I understood why I could never remember what I saw on TV. Unlike reading, it does not let the viewer reflect, reread, underline, and develop comprehension. I said I thought that there should be a balance between the visual and the auditory, a balance that furthers understanding rather than confusion.

I learned how editing and splicing can destroy an interview.... TV anchormen and journalists... all seem afflicted by historical amnesia (possibly induced by staring at their ever-changing monitors).... Without an understanding of the area's history, and political and social fabric, reporters consistently fail in reporting the whole story....

Everyone knew that terrorists want publicity for their cause, yet no less do they want to inflate their personal status in their communities. They don't care that they look like barbarians to us when among their friends they are heroes. Therefore, each time the media afford terrorists the right to speak, they award them a victory. Giving in to violent extremists who engage in the most deviant behavior reduces the ability of moderates to pursue other, more acceptable avenues to reach their goals....

Media-Induced Contagion of Terrorist Violence

One of the longest-running controversies among social scientists, nearly ranking in longevity with the nature-nurture controversy or the deterrence effects of capital punishment, is the effect of media presentations on aggressive or violent behavior. If one were to include the arguments pro and con about the consumption of pornography (i.e., the effects of literary or graphic presentations of sexually provocative material on sexual behavior), the controversy could be viewed as preceding the advent of movies and television. But it is primarily with the broadcast media, especially television, that most researchers have been concerned.

Modeling and Aggressive Behavior

We are obviously affected by what we see others do; by observing others, one may form ideas of how to perform various acts, including aggressive and violent acts. Bandura points out that one can learn general strategies that provide guides for action beyond those associated with a particular model. The observer must be able to pick out the essentials of a model's behavior and remember them:

> When an observer witnesses a model exhibit a sequence of responses the observer acquires, through contiguous association of the sensory events, perceptual and symbolic responses possessing cue properties that are capable of eliciting, at some time after a demonstration, overt responses corresponding to those that had been modeled. (1971, 14)

In the most widely publicized phase of Bandura's work, groups of children were exposed to adult models who either exhibited aggressive or nonaggressive behavior toward a large Bobo doll. The children were then subjected to a mildly frustrating experience, then a record was made of their actions. Children who had been exposed to the aggressive model showed a greater number of imitative aggressive responses than did the children who were exposed to the nonaggressive model. These same results occurred when children were exposed to the aggressive and nonaggressive models by means of television. In view of the amount of time the average American child spends in front of the television set, the implications of these experimental findings were quickly recognized.

Protests by concerned parents and educators prompted a series of Congressional hearings, in which representatives of NBC, ABC, and CBS gave conflicting testimony regarding the effects of television on behavior in general and in particular. The network executives, under sharp questioning by legislators, appeared to be agreeing to diametrically opposite propositions: "Yes, television affects people in a variety of ways, including their purchasing habits, appetites, product preferences, and brand-name recognition; no, television does not influence people to emulate aggressive or violent behavior portrayed on televised programs." Said Schmid and De Graaf,

> A strange kind of schizophrenia seems to affect television producers. On the one hand, they suggest to the sponsors of advertisements that television has massive effects, that the public copies consuming behavior suggested in alluring commercials. On the other hand, they tend to discard the possibility that the public learns the lessons of television violence which they use to attract large audiences. (1982, 121)

There is overwhelming anecdotal evidence that various types of media portrayals are immediately followed by "copycat" commission of the events portrayed. When a television crime show depicted the sadistic murder of a skid-row derelict by several young thugs who drenched the victim with gasoline and set him afire, the grisly act was emulated by youths in areas as widely separated as Boston and Los Angeles. Heller and Polsky (1971) found that sixty-three of the one hundred institutionalized delinquents they examined reported having imitated characters they had seen on television; twenty-two said they had tried criminal techniques they had seen on television; another twenty-two stated that they had contemplated committing crimes they had seen on television.

Schmid and De Graaf reviewed twenty-six parachute hijackings and concluded that the media "must have played a decisive role" in fostering copycat emulations: "Had the media not reported the detail about the parachutes, most of these imitations would not in all likelihood have taken place" (1982, 136).

Media and Terrorism Motivation

Although researchers agree that the media might encourage violence by providing models of violent behavior and even specific know-how necessary for committing particular acts of violence, there tends to be less agreement on whether the media can provide the motivation for commission of violent acts. Schmid and De Graaf suggest six ways in which the media can motivate potential terrorists.

1. The mass media extend experience, present models, stimulate aspirations, and indicate goals.
2. The media-fostered overestimation of great personalities has given rise to the star cult, which implies that history can be changed by the elimination of "big people"—that is, political assassination.
3. Akin to the above, visibility provided by the mass media has created a new category of people—the celebrities, people who are known to be known.
4. The media can motivate terrorists by inciting them, wittingly or unwittingly, to a terroristic deed.
5. There is a "built-in escalation imperative" that requires that terrorists must commit more and more bizarre and cruel acts to gain media attention.
6. The high news value that violence has in the Western media is, for some people, motivation enough to engage in the kind of violence to which the media are highly responsive. (1982, 137-142)

With regard to the last item, which the authors consider the most important, Schmid and De Graaf emphasize the competitive pressures that drive journalists to report such news and note that "there is something paradoxical and perverse in this relationship."

Summary

Progress in communications technology has greatly increased the importance of the media for terrorists. Whether the media are the terrorist's "best friend" or "unwitting ally" is a matter for debate, but there is little doubt that many, if not most, terrorist incidents are committed with a view to their dramatic impact on a target audience.

A number of incidents—the Hanafi Muslim siege, the hijacking of TWA Flight 847, the Iran hostage crisis—have demonstrated how easily media representatives may cross the line from portrayer of terrorism events to advocate for the terrorists.

One area of sharpest controversy in media/terrorism relations is the extent to which coverage of terrorist incidents such as skyjackings produces "copycat" emulations. Research on the effects of televised violence on the behavior of child viewers indicates that aggressive behavior can be learned (modeled); anecdotal evidence also suggests that violent behavior depicted on television can lead to emulation by delinquent youths.

Another controversial topic is the unrestricted access of media representatives to coverage of terrorist incidents. The U.S. Supreme Court under Chief Justice Burger refused to assign special status to the media and chose to view media access as a privilege granted at the discretion of law enforcement authorities rather than a right guaranteed under the First Amendment. Still another area of controversy involves imposition of government censorship on media coverage of terrorist incidents. Terrorist news reporting is censored in a number of countries, including the Irish Republic and the United Kingdom.

Government imposition of censorship restrictions in the U.S. on media coverage of terrorist events is remote enough to verge upon the improbable. On the other hand, guidelines of some kind seem desirable; the question is who should formulate such guidelines.

> If the media do it themselves, they might be too self-serving, steering in the direction that they still want to use the exciting news terrorists provide without allowing themselves to be used by the terrorists. If the government establishes such guidelines they will tend to serve the government first and this might be even more harmful. (Schmid & De Graaf, 1982, 174)

Schmid and De Graaf propose, as a possible alternative, a council with members drawn from both the government and the media to formulate joint guidelines in matters of media coverage of terrorism.

Let War Bring Peace

Edward S. Luttwak
Center for Strategic and International Studies

War is the great evil but does have one great virtue: by consuming and destroying the material and moral resources needed to continue fighting, warfare itself is the most compelling force for peace-making. The paradoxical logic of strategy may accomplish that reversal by sufficient exhaustion or by decisive victory, but either way warfare can set the stage for peace—if it is allowed to continue till that point is reached. Just as a victorious advance leads to defeat by over-extension after exceeding its culminating point of success, war begins its transformation into the strongest impetus for peace only after passing its culminating phase of violence. Hopes of military success must fade before the path of accommodation is more attractive than further combat.

But ever since the establishment of the United Nations and the formalization of Great Power politics in its Security Council, wars among lesser powers have rarely been allowed to follow their natural course. Instead, they have typically been interrupted very early, long before they could establish the pre-conditions of peace.

It became routine to abruptly stop the combat operations of lesser powers by cease-fires imposed under the aegis of the UN Security Council. Unless further diplomatic interventions ensue to impose peace negotiations as well, cease-fires in themselves relieve war-induced exhaustion and favor the reconstitution and re-arming of the belligerents, thus intensifying and prolonging the fighting once the cease-fire comes to an end. That was true for example of the Arab-Israeli war of 1948-49, which might have ended in a matter of weeks by sheer exhaustion, if two cease-fires ordained by the UN Security Council had not allowed the belligerents to recuperate till they were ready to resume fighting.

After the breakdown of Yugoslavia, imposed cease-fires frequently interrupted the fighting between Serbs and Croats in the Krajina borderlands, between the forces of the rump Serb-Montenegrin federation and the Croat army, and between the Serbs, Croats and Muslims of Bosnia. Each time, the belligerents used the pause to recruit, train and equip additional forces for further combat. Indeed it was under the protection of successive cease-fires that both the Croats and the Bosnian Muslims were able to build up their own armed forces to confront the well-armed Serbs. That is an outcome that many found desirable, but the overall effect greatly prolonged the war and widened the scope of its killings and destructions.

It also became a routine practice to interrupt wars in more lasting fashion by imposing armistices. Again, unless followed by peace accords, armistices artificially freeze the situation, perpetuating the state of war indefinitely because they shield the weaker side from the consequences of refusing the concessions needed for peace, ie., further defeats, territorial losses, etc. Armistices without peace create the strongest possible incentive to endlessly prolonged competitive arms races, as in the case of India and Pakistan and the two Koreas till this day.

Nevertheless, so long as the Cold War persisted, cease-fires and armistices imposed by the United States and the Soviet Union acting in concert had a compelling justification. At a time when both were greatly inclined to intervene in the wars of lesser powers to avert the defeat of their respective clients, US and Soviet leaders often prudently preferred to act jointly stop the fighting. That made competitive interventions unnecessary, avoiding the danger of a direct clash between American and Soviet forces that could escalate to the nuclear level. While imposed cease-fires ultimately increased the sum total of warfare among the lesser powers themselves, and armistices did perpetuate the state of war among them, both were clearly the lesser evil from a global point of view, as compared to the possibility of a catastrophic Soviet-American war caused by reciprocal interventions.

In present conditions by contrast, neither Americans nor Russians are at all inclined to intervene competitively in the wars of lesser powers. The United States acted with many allies to reverse Iraq's conquest of Kuwait of August 1990. The Russian Federation for its part has sent combat forces as well as weapons in support of one side or the other in both Caucasian and Central Asian wars and insurgencies. Neither, however has acted, or would now act, specifically to thwart the other, neither would contemplate armed interventions against the other. And the same is true of such other Great Powers as can still said to exist. It follows that the evil consequences of interrupting war still persist in full, while no greater danger is being averted.

Multi-lateral Interventions

In the absence of anything resembling a classic Great Power competition, cease-fires and armistices are now generally imposed on lesser powers multi-laterally, for essentially disinterested motives—often indeed for no better reason than the revulsion of television audiences exposed to harrowing scenes of war. Of course the result is to ensure that there will be many more such scenes.

It is well known that disinterested behavior, not guided by self-interested calculations, randomizes outcomes. What is now happening, however, is typically much worse than that, for cease fires and armistices imposed on warring lesser powers systematically prevent the transformation of war into peace. The Dayton accords are typical of the genre: they condemn Bosnia to remain divided into three rival armed camps, with combat suspended between them for now at least, but with the state of war indefinitely prolonged. Because no side is threatened by defeat and loss, no side has a sufficient incentive to negotiate peace; because no path to peace is even visible, the dominant priority is to prepare for war rather than reconstruct devastated economies and ravaged societies. The outcome of uninterrupted war would certainly have been unjust from one perspective or another, but would have imposed some sort of peace allowing people to rebuild their lives, and communities to rebuild their economies.

There is now a proliferation of multi-lateral organizations that make it their business to intervene in other peoples' wars. Their common, inherent, characteristic is that they insert themselves in war-situations while refusing to engage in combat. That greatly adds to the damage.

Thus the dominant priority of United Nations' "peace-keeping" contingents is to avoid casualties to their own personnel. Their unit commanders therefore habitually appease the locally stronger belligerent, accepting its dictates, tolerating its abuses. Now it is true that if the totality of UN peace-keeping forces in a given context would appease the stronger side, for example the Bosno-Serbs in the early stages of the Bosnia fighting, the result would be very conducive to peace. For in that case, the UN presence would actually enhance the peace-making potential of war, by helping the strong to defeat the weak that much faster and more decisively.

Unfortunately, the appeasement that is inevitable when forces that do not want to fight are thrust into war situations, is not homogeneous nor strategically purposeful. Instead, it merely reflects the determination of each UN unit to avoid confrontations and casualties. As each one appeases the locally stronger side, the total result is to prevent the emergence of a coherent outcome, of an overall imbalance of strength capable of ending the fighting.

Nor can UN contingents whose dominant priority is to avoid combat effectively protect civilians caught up in the fighting, or deliberately attacked. At best, UN peace-keeping forces remain the passive spectators of outrages and even massacres, as in Bosnia and Rwanda; at worst they collaborate in massacre, as Dutch UN troops did in the Srebenica enclave, where they helped the Bosno-Serbs to separate the men of military age (very broadly defined) from women and children.

At the same time, the very presence of UN forces inhibits the normal remedy of endangered civilians, which is to escape from the combat zone. Deluded into thinking that they will be protected, civilians in danger remain in place until it is too late to flee. Moreover, prospective host countries deny war-refugee status to civilians coming from conflict zones where the UN troops have supposedly intervened to stop the war—even if they entirely fail to shield civilians under attack. In the specific case of the siege of Sarajevo in 1992-1994, appeasement interacted with the pretense of protection in a manner especially perverse: UN personnel strictly inspected outgoing flights to prevent the escape of Sarajevo civilians, in obedience to a cease-fire agreement negotiated with the locally dominant Bosno-Serbs...who habitually violated that cease-fire.

Institutions such as the European Union, the Western European Union, and the Organization of Security and Cooperation in Europe, lack even the UN's rudimentary command structure, and have no assigned let alone organic forces of their own. Yet they too now seek to intervene in warlike situations, with predictable consequences. Bereft of forces even theoretically capable of combat, they satisfy interventionist urges mandated by member states, or even motivated by their own institutional ambitions, by sending lightly-armed or unarmed policemen, gendarmes or simply "observers." All of the latter must necessarily act as UN peace-keeping troops habitually do, only more so, by accommodating the wishes of the locally stronger side. And of course they cannot even try to protect endangered civilians, while their presence again inhibits the private remedy of flight.

Warlike organizations such as NATO and the West African ECOMOG force lately seen at work in Sierra Leone, are potentially capable of stopping warfare. Their interventions too has destructive consequences by prolonging the state of war, but should protect civilians from the consequences of the wars they are prolonging.

Even that fails to happen, however. Multi-national military commands engaged in disinterested interventions that do not justify national casualties, tend to adopt risk-avoiding postures. Thus US troops in Bosnia—acting under orders—repeatedly failed to arrest known war criminals passing through their check-points. And because no differences in troop performance can be admitted, multinational commands are institutionally incapable of exercising quality control over the and troops offered by member-states, and neither can they impose standards of tactical and operational conduct. Deliberately risk-minimizing strategies aside, the conjoined deployment of both potentially combat-capable and irremediably ineffectual troops tends to reduce the performance of all troops involved to the lowest common denominator. That was true of otherwise fine British troops in Bosnia at various times, and of the Nigerian Marines in Sierra Leone. Soon even quasi elite troops adopt passive self-protective tactics that prevent them from keeping the peace or protecting civilians.

The phenomenon of "multi-nationally-induced troop degradation" can rarely be detected by external observers, though its consequences have been abundantly visible in the litter of the dead, mutilated, raped and tortured that attends such interventions. But sometimes the true state of affairs is powerfully illuminated by the rare exception, such as the vigorous Danish tank battalion in Bosnia which promptly replied to each episode of firing against it, quickly stopping all attacks against it. If the pattern of degradation into ineffectual passivity were not so normal, such a case of combat troops acting as combat troops would not attract attention. The record of the ECOMOG troops in Sierra Leone has by contrast included over the years frequent routs at the hands of small bands of rebel child soldiers, many episodes of organized looting directed by unit commanders, countless rapes and some summary executions.

But all prior examples of disinterested warfare and its crippling limitations have been cast in the shade by NATO's Kossovo intervention. Relying on air power alone to minimize the risk of casualties, during the first thirty days of operations US, British, French, German and Italian aircraft bombed targets in Serbia, Montenegro and Kossovo itself without losing a single pilot; only one aircraft was shot down, a US "stealth" F–117 light bomber, and its pilot was successfully rescued.

This miracle of immunity from the large number of Yugoslav anti-aircraft guns and missiles was achieved by layer upon layer of precautions. In the first place, for all the great noise and imagery suggestive of a massive operation, accentuated by the dramatic introduction of both the B-1 heavy bomber and the B-2 stealth super-bomber, very few strike sorties were actually flown, less than 2,700 in thirty days—just about the number that could have been flown by a mere three squadrons.

That certainly reduced the risks—aircraft on the ground are not in danger of being shot down—but it also set a very low limit on the overall scope of the bombing (in the 1991 Gulf War the daily average of strike sorties was 1,250 per day). Actually the destructive impact was even more restricted, because almost half of all the strike sorties were aimed at air-defense targets to further reduce the risks, often nothing more than isolated antenna relays on remote mountaintops.

An even more effective precaution was the outright avoidance of most anti-aircraft weapons by releasing weapons not at optimal altitudes but from an ultra-safe 15,000 feet or more. Royal Air Force Tornado crews expensively trained to drop bombs a mere 300 feet off the ground, stayed above 15,000 feet, and so did the pilots of US fighter-bombers whose laser-guided bombs cannot be aimed at moving targets much above 5,000 feet.

NATO spokesmen constantly complained that dense clouds were impeding the bombing campaign, often restricting operations to cruise missiles aimed at fixed targets of known location. Actually the cloud ceiling was high enough at most times to allow very effective low-altitude bombing. What it did not allow was perfectly safe bombing, with pilots no more endangered on average than passengers on some Third World airlines.

When it was realized that small groups of 80-120 Serb soldiers and police could overawe and terrorize thousands of Albanians because they were backed by armored vehicles, NATO had a ready panoply of aircraft specialized for the very task of finding and destroying armored vehicles. All its major members have anti-tank helicopters, some in expeditionary units equipped to operate without base support. But no country offered to send any of them into action when the ethnic cleansing of Kossovo began, even though the hilly terrain would have been ideal for pop-up attacks against Serbian armor. But of course anti-tank helicopters cannot operate at 15,000 feet; they could have stopped the ethnic cleansing of the rural areas at least, but some might have been shot down.

When US Apaches in Germany were finally ordered to Albania, it seemed that all the vast expenditure devoted to their instantaneous "readiness" over the years had been utterly wasted, because they required more than three weeks of "pre-deployment preparations" to make the journey. On the thirtieth day of the war, the Apaches had yet to fly their first mission amidst complaints that there was "too much mud." More than mere bureaucratic foot-dragging achieved this inordinate delay: the US Army insisted that the Apaches could not operate on their own, but would need the support of MRLS rocket barrages to suppress Serb anti-aircraft weapons, creating a much larger logistic load than the helicopters themselves, and an additional delay that was evidently welcome. Their coupling with protective rocket barrages would ensure the ineffectiveness of the Apaches in most situations, because they could hardly operate anywhere near civilian populations without killing many more of them than their Serb tormentors.

Actually even before the Apache saga began, NATO had aircraft already deployed on Italian bases that could have done the job just as well: US A-10s built around their powerful 30mm anti-tank guns with huge magazines, and Royal Air Force Harriers ideal for low-altitude bombing at the closest ranges. Neither was employed, because again it could not be done in perfect safety.

Obviously in the calculus of the NATO democracies, the immediate possibility of saving thousands of Albanians from massacre, tens of thousands from deportation to uncertain fates, was not worth the lives of a few pilots. That may reflect unavoidable political reality, but it does mean that this disinterested intervention too conspicuously failed to achieve its ostensibly humanitarian aim, while starting a dangerous conflict whose wider strategic repercussions may yet be disastrous.

The Destructive Role of Non-Government Organizations

However the most disinterested of all interventions in warlike settings are humanitarian relief activities. They are also the most destructive.

The largest and most protracted, and still continuing, humanitarian intervention in all of human history is the United Nations Relief and Works Agency (UNRWA). On the model of its predecessor, the United Nations Relief and Rehabilitation Agency (UNRRA), which was then still operating rapidly dwindling Displaced Persons' camps in Europe, UNRWA was originally established during the 1948/49 Arab-Israeli war to feed, shelter, educate and provide health services for Arab refugees who had fled from Israeli zones in the former territory of Palestine to its Egyptian- and Jordanian-controlled parts (the Gaza strip and the West Bank) as well as Lebanon, Syria and Trans-Jordan as it then was.

By keeping refugees alive in spartan conditions that encouraged their rapid emigration or local resettlement, UNRRA's camps in Europe served to assuage post-war resentments and helped to disperse revanchist concentrations of national groups. Not truly because of any Arab policies let alone any ideological patriotism, but simply because UNRWA camps provided on the whole a higher standard of living than most Arab villagers had previously enjoyed, with an assured and more varied diet, organized schooling, infinitely superior medical care and no backbreaking labor in stony fields, they instantly became desirable homes rather than eagerly abandoned transit camps. They turned escaping civilians into life-long refugees who gave birth to refugee children who grew up in turn to have refugee children of their own.

During the half century of its operation UNRWA has thus perpetuated a Palestinian refugee nation, perfectly preserving its resentments in as fresh a condition as they were in 1948, keeping the first bloom of revanchist emotion intact. By its very existence, UNRWA dissuades integration into local societies and inhibits emigration. Moreover, the mere concentration of Palestinians in the camps has always facilitated the voluntary or forced enlistment of refugee youths by armed organizations that fight both Israel and each other. In these different ways, UNWRA greatly contributed to half a century of Arab-Israeli violence, and still powerfully retards the advent of peace.

Had each European war been attended by its own post-war UNWRA equipped to provide a higher-than-average standard of living, today's Europe would be filled with giant camps for millions of descendants of uprooted Gallo-Romans, abandoned Vandals, defeated Burgundians and misplaced Visigoths—not to speak of more recent refugee nations such as post-1945 Sudeten Germans. Such a Europe would have remained a purely geographic expression, a mosaic of warring tribes undigested and unreconciled in their separate feeding camps. And the number of unresolved conflicts would roughly correspond to the total number of wars ever fought.

UNWRA is not unique, having had various counterparts elsewhere, such as the Cambodian camps along the Thai border which incidentally provided safe bases for the mass-murdering Khmer Rouge. But because such United Nations activities are mercifully limited by ungenerous national contributions, their sabotage of peace is at least localized. That is not true of the proliferation of feverishly competitive Non-Government Organizations (NGOs) that aid war refugees.

Their absolute, existential priority is to keep attracting charitable contributions. Their principal means of doing so is to be seen to be as active as possible in high-visibility situations. Only the most dramatic natural disasters attract any significant mass-media attention, and that too only briefly; after the first days after an earthquake or flood, the cameras depart. War refugees by contrast can attract sustained mass-media attention if kept conveniently concentrated in reasonably accessible camps. Because regular forms of warfare among well-organized belligerents in more developed areas offer few opportunities for NGOs, they naturally focus their efforts elsewhere, aiding war refugees in the poorest parts of the world.

That ensures that the feeding, shelter and health care offered, while perhaps abysmal by global standards, exceeds what is locally available to non-refugees. The consequences are entirely predictable. Among many lesser examples, the huge refugee camps along the Congo/Zaire border with Rwanda stand out. They sustain a Hutu nation in exile that would otherwise have been dispersed, which makes the consolidation of Rwanda impossible, and whose activists continually raid across the border to kill more Tutsis.

To keep refugee nations in being forever, to fuel unending conflict by artificially preserved resentments, is bad enough. But to insert material aid into on-going combat situations is even worse. Many NGOs which operate in odor of sanctity routinely enrich the logistics of war. Themselves defenseless, they cannot exclude active warriors from their feeding stations, clinics and such shelter as they provide.

Refugees are presumptively on the losing side, the warriors among them in retreat. By intervening to help them, NGOs systematically impede the progress of their enemies towards a decisive victory that can bring war to an end. Impartial to a fault, NGOs sometimes help both sides, thus also sabotaging the transformation of war into peace by mutual exhaustion.

There is worse. When especially threatened, as in Somalia but less visibly in other places too, NGOs purchase security from local war-bands, often the very same bands that threaten them. No recondite strategic calculation is needed to uncover the result: unless the totality of their payments are insignificantly small—definitely not true of Somalia or Sudan—NGOs themselves prolong the warfare whose consequences they seek to mitigate. This circularity is not just ironical, it is criminally irresponsible.

Almost all wars nowadays become endemic conflicts that need never end, because the transformative effects of both decisive victories and exhaustion are blocked by outside interventions of one kind or another. But unlike the ancient predicament of war, the compounding of its evils by disinterested interventions is a very new malpractice that could be curtailed. In the United States, now the most active of interventionists, policy elites could do more to apply strategic prudence against the emotional impulse to intervene in other peoples' wars—not because of any indifference to human suffering but for the very opposite reason. If cured itself, the United States could exercise its leadership to dissuade multi-lateral interventionism, instead of promoting it as is now the case. New rules could be established for UN refugee-relief activities, to ensure that the immediate succor that humane feelings cannot deny is quicky followed by repatriation, local absorption or emigration, ruling out the establishment of permanent camps (in Cyprus, UN funds paid for town-house complexes for Greek refugees, who bitterly complain of the shortage of parking slots).

No rules can possibly constrain interventionist NGOs, but at least they should not be officially encouraged in any way, nor aided with public funds. War should be allowed to lead to peace.

9/11

Towers of Light.

Cut Military Spending, Meet Human Needs

Reprinted courtesy of the Center for the Study of Political Graphics, Los Angeles.

Part Five

The Global Striving for Social and Economic Justice:

Population, Health, and Livelihood

There are only two families in the world…
the haves and have-nots

—Miguel de Cervantes (1547-1616)

The impact of social and economic factors, such as poverty, population growth and globalization, upon the potentials for both internal and international peace is explored from a variety of perspectives in this section. An understanding of the economic and social forces that drive man is viewed by some philosophers, scientists and political thinkers as the central component in the quest for peace. More recently, however, a growing body of experts has been exploring the growing impact of global economic forces upon the social and economic well-being of local communities throughout the world.

What can clearly be concluded as a result of these inquiries is that no single theory, no scientific formula has been advanced for determining what the true causes of war and peace are. As Lord Bauer suggests in his essay, the role of population growth as a cause of conflict can be mitigated if there is a substantial economic base available to support the well-being of greater numbers. An in-depth discussion about the impact of globalization is carried forward by the contribution of P.J. Simmons and James Mittelman. They address such questions as: In an increasingly inter-connected world, will the liberalizing and democratizing technologies that have brought humans closer together contribute to the future causes of conflict? Is a greater degree of socio-economic justice primarily a humanitarian goal? How important is it to the reduction of domestic frictions between the have's and the have-nots? Is international socio-economic inequality a factor in international war? Do the mounting socio-economic differences inherent in any vibrant society doom man to ongoing conflict? If the adage that good fences make good neighbors holds true, then what will be the result as the forces of globalization remove the social, linguistic, economic, religious and political borders that have historically represented the primary causes of war?

Population Growth: Disaster or Blessing?

Peter T. Bauer
London School of Economics

The twenty-third General Population Conference of the International Union for the Scientific Study of Population, which met in Beijing in October 1997, focused on overpopulation as a serious threat to human survival and a major cause of poverty. Warren Buffet, Bill Gates, corporations, governments, and international organizations are dedicating and promising to dedicate enormous resources to reverse the threat of overpopulation. But population density and poverty are not actually correlated.

Poverty in the Third World is not caused by population growth or pressure. Economic achievement and progress depend on people's conduct, not on their numbers. Population growth in the Third World is not a major threat to prosperity. The crisis is invented. The central policy issue is whether the number of children should be determined by the parents or by agents of the state.

Since the Second World War it has been widely argued that population growth is a major, perhaps decisive obstacle to the economic progress and social betterment of the underdeveloped world, where the majority of mankind lives. Thus Robert S. McNamara, former president of the World Bank, wrote: "To put it simply: the greatest single obstacle to the economic and social advancement of the majority of peoples in the underdeveloped world is rampant population growth.... The threat of unmanageable population pressures is very much like the threat of nuclear war." And many others have made similar statements.

The Apprehensions Rest on False Assumptions

These apprehensions rest primarily on three assumptions. First, national income per head measures economic well-being. Second, economic performance and progress depend critically on land and capital per head. Third, people in the Third World are ignorant of birth control or careless about family size; they procreate regardless of consequences. A subsidiary assumption is that population trends in the Third World can be forecast with accuracy for decades ahead.

Behind these assumptions and, indeed, behind the debates on population are conflicting views of mankind. One view envisages people as deliberate decision makers in matters of family size. The other view treats people as being under the sway of uncontrollable sexual urges, their numbers limited only by forces outside themselves, either Malthusian checks of nature or the power of superior authority. Proponents of both views agree that the

Peter T. Bauer, "Population Growth: Disaster or Blessing?" From *The Independent Review: A Journal of Political Economy* (Summer 1998, vol. III, no. 1).

governments of less developed countries (LDCs), urged by the West, should encourage or, if necessary, force people to have smaller families. National income per head is usually regarded as an index of economic welfare, even of welfare as such. However, the use of this index raises major problems, such as demarcation between inputs and outputs in both production and consumption. Even if an increase in population reduced income per head, a matter to which I shall return later, such a reduction would not necessarily mean that the well-being either of families or of the wider community had been reduced.

In the economics of population, national income per head founders completely as a measure of welfare. It ignores the satisfaction people derive from having children or from living longer. The birth of a child immediately reduces income per head for the family and for the country as a whole. The death of the same child has the opposite effect. Yet for most people, the first event is a blessing, the second a tragedy. Ironically, the birth of a child is registered as a reduction in national income per head, while the birth of a calf shows up as an improvement.

The wish of the great majority of mankind to have children has extended across centuries, cultures, and classes. The survival of the human race evinces that most people have been willing to bear the cost of rearing two or more children to the age of puberty. Widely held ideas and common attitudes reflect and recognize the benefits parents expect from having children. The biblical injunction is to be fruitful and multiply.

Less well known in the West is the traditional greeting addressed to brides in India, "May you be the mother of eight sons." The uniformly unfavorable connotation of the term barren reflects the same sentiment. The practice of adoption in some countries also indicates the desire for children. All this refutes the notion that children are simply a cost or burden.

Some have argued that high birth rates in the LDCs, especially among the poorest people, result in lives so wretched that they are not worth living, that over a person's lifetime, suffering or disutility may exceed utility; hence, fewer such lives would increase the sum total of happiness. The implication is that external observers are qualified to assess the joys and sorrows of others; that life and survival have no value to the people involved. This outlook raises far-reaching ethical issues and is unlikely to be morally acceptable to most people, least of all as a basis for forcible action to restrict people's reproductive behavior, especially when one recalls how widely it was applied to the poor in the West only a few generations ago.

Nor is this opinion consistent with simple observation, which suggests that even very poor people prefer to continue living, as shown, for instance, by their seeking medical treatment of injuries and illnesses. Clearly, the much-deplored population explosion of recent decades should be seen as a blessing rather than a disaster, because it stems from a fall in mortality, a prima facie improvement in people's welfare, not deterioration.

Much of the advocacy of state-sponsored birth control is predicated on the implicit assumption that people in high-fertility Third World countries do not know about contraceptives and that, in any case, they do not take into account the long-term consequences of their actions. But most people in the Third World do know about birth control, and practice it. In the Third World, fertility is well below fecundity; that is, the number of actual births is well below the biologically possible number. Traditional methods of birth control have been widely practiced in societies much more backward than contemporary Third World countries. Throughout most of the Third World, cheap Western-style consumer goods have been conspicuous for decades, whereas condoms, intrauterine devices, and the Pill have so far spread only very slowly. This disparity suggests that the demand for modern contraceptives has been small, either because people do not want to restrict their family size or because they prefer other ways of doing so.

It follows that the children are generally wanted by their parents. Of course, a woman who does not want many children may have to bow to the wishes of her husband, especially in Catholic or Muslim societies. Attempting to enforce changes in mores in such societies raises issues that I cannot pursue here. In any event, this matter does not affect my argument. Children are certainly avoidable. Nor are people in LDCs generally are ignorant of the long-term consequences of their actions. Indeed, young women often say that they want more children and grandchildren to provide for them in their old age. The readiness to take the long view is evident also in other decisions, such as planting slow-maturing trees or embarking on long-distance migration.

Externalities

Under this heading, the first question is whether parents bear the full costs of having and rearing their children. If they do not bear those costs fully, they will have more children than they would otherwise. Then, according to the usual assumptions of welfare economics, the satisfaction the parents gain from the additional children would be less than the additional burden, some of which others must bear. It is often assumed that parents in the Third World do not bear the full costs of having children, in particular the costs of health care and education, and that in fact taxpayers bear a substantial part of those costs. These particular costs, however, are unlikely to be heavy in LDCs. They are likely to be lower relative to the national income than in the West. For instance, schools are often simple, inexpensive structures. For social and institutional reasons, basic health services are extensively performed by medical auxiliaries and nurses rather than fully qualified doctors. In any event, if the adverse externalities warrant remedial action, such action should take the form of changes in the volume, direction, and financing of the relevant public expenditures rather than imposed reductions in family size.

The extended family provides a further example of the same negative externality.... Parents may have more children if they know that other members of their extended family will bear part of the cost. However, as just noted, the burden falling on others is likely to be small. Moreover, the extended family is embodied in the mores of much of the less developed world. Any effect of the operation of the extended family in this context will diminish or disappear if the extended family system gives way with modernization, a prospect to which I shall return.

Congestion in cities is sometimes instanced as an adverse externality resulting from population growth. But the rapid growth of the cities, especially the capitals, derives from their pull. This in turn reflects the limitations of rural life to many people and the higher incomes and other benefits available or expected in the cities. The income differences increase when policies benefitting the urban population, such as have been widely adopted, depress rural earnings. That the growth of large cities results from these influences is evidenced by the large conurbations in sparsely populated LDCs such as Brazil and Zaire and by the rapid urbanization of LDCs. In any case, undesirable crowding in large cities is not a function of their size or growth, much less of the growth of the national population: it is the inevitable consequence of fixing the prices of housing and transport without regard to their true scarcity. Similar considerations apply to the supposed adverse external effects of population growth on the environment, including deforestation, soil erosion, and depletion of fish stocks. The assignment of property rights and free-market pricing can optimize the rate of use of forests, soils, fisheries, and other presently open-access resources. Altogether, it is highly unlikely that population growth would cause major adverse externalities, let alone externalities warranting the placing of pressure on people to have fewer children.

Despite the practically exclusive preoccupation with purported adverse externalities of population growth, population growth often has favorable external effects. It can facilitate the more effective division of labor and thereby increase real incomes. In fact, in much of Southeast Asia, Africa, and

Latin America, sparseness of population inhibits economic advance. It retards the development of transport facilities and communications, and thus inhibits the movement of people and goods and the spread of new ideas and methods. These obstacles to enterprise and economic advance are particularly difficult to overcome. At the more advanced stages of development, significant positive externalities arise from greater scope for the division of labor in economic activity in science, technology, and research.

I shall argue later that even if it were shown that adverse externalities are significant and outweigh the positive externalities, that condition would call for policies quite different from placing pressure on parents to have fewer children.

Does Population Growth Reduce Income per Head?

Even if population growth is unlikely to reduce welfare, is it likely to reduce conventionally measured income per head? It seems commonsensical that prosperity depends on natural resources, namely, land and mineral resources, and on capital and that population growth reduces the per capita supply of these determinants of income. Indeed, if nothing else changes, an increase in population must reduce income per head in the very short run.

This truism, however, reveals nothing about developments over a longer period. Then, productivity depends on other influences, which can be elicited or reinforced by an increase in population. Such influences include the spread of knowledge, division of labor, changes in attitudes and habits, redeployment of resources, and technical change. In short, economic analysis cannot demonstrate that an increase in population must entail a reduction of income per head over a longer period. There is ample evidence that rapid population growth has certainly not inhibited economic progress either in the West or in the contemporary Third World. The population of the Western world has more than quadrupled since the middle of the eighteenth century, yet real income per head is estimated to have increased at least fivefold. Much of this increase in incomes took place when population was increasing as fast as or even faster than it is currently in most of the less developed world. Similarly, population growth in the Third World has often gone hand in hand with rapid material advance. In the 1890s, Malaya was a sparsely populated area of hamlets and fishing villages. By the 1930s it had become a country with large cities, active commerce, and extensive plantation and mining operations. The total population rose through natural increase and immigration from about 1.5 million to about 6 million, and the number of Malays from about 1.0 million to about 2.5 million. The much larger population enjoyed much higher material standards and lived longer than the small numbers of the 1890s. Since the Second World War a number of LDCs have combined rapid population increase with rapid, even spectacular economic growth for decades on end, including Taiwan, Hong Kong, Malaysia, Kenya, the Ivory Coast, Mexico, Colombia, and Brazil.

Conventional views on population growth assume that endowments of land and other natural resources are critical for economic performance. This assumption is refuted by experience in both the distant and the more recent past. Amid abundant land, the American Indians before Columbus were extremely backward while most of Europe, with far less land, was already advanced. Europe in the sixteenth and seventeenth centuries included prosperous Holland, much of it reclaimed from the sea, and Venice, a wealthy world power built on a few mud flats. At present, many millions of poor people in the Third World live amid ample cultivable land. Indeed, in much of South-east Asia, Central Africa, and interior of Latin America, land is a free good. Conversely, land is now very expensive in both Hong Kong and Singapore, probably the most densely populated countries in the world, originally with very poor land. For example, Hong Kong in the 1840s consisted largely of eroded hillsides, and much of Singapore in the nineteenth century was empty marsh. Both places are now highly industrialized and prosperous. The experience of other countries, both in the East and in the West, teaches the same lesson. Poor countries differ in density. For example, India's population density is some 750 people per square mile whereas Zaire's density is approximately 40 people per square mile. And prosperous countries differ in density. Japan's density is some 850 people per square mile whereas U.S. density is approximately 70 people per square mile. All these instances suggest the obvious: the importance of people's economic qualities and the policies of governments. It is pertinent also that in both prosperous and poor countries the productivity of the soil owes very little to the "original and indestructible powers of the soil," that is, to land as a factor in totally inelastic supply. The productivity of land results largely from human activity: labor, investment, science, and technology. The wide differences in economic performance and prosperity between individuals and groups in the same country, with access to the same natural resources, also make clear that the availability of natural resources cannot be critical to economic achievement. Such differences have been, and still are, conspicuous the world over. Salient examples of group differences in the same country include those among Chinese, Indians, and Malays in Malaysia; Chinese and others elsewhere in Southeast Asia; Parsees, Jains, Marwaris, and others in India; Greeks and Turks in Cyprus; Asians and Africans in East and Central Africa; Ibo and others in Nigeria; and Chinese, Lebanese, and West Indians in the Caribbean. The experience of Huguenots, Jews, and Nonconformists in the West also makes clear that natural resources are not critical for economic achievement. For long periods, these prosperous groups were not allowed to own land or had their access to it severely restricted.

Mineral resources have often yielded substantial windfalls to those who discovered erred or developed them or expropriated their owners. Latin American gold and silver in the sixteenth century and the riches of contemporary oil-producing states illustrate the prosperity conferred by natural resources. But the precious metals of the Americas did not promote economic progress in pre-Columbian America, nor did their capture ensure substantial development in Spain. The oil reserves of the Middle East and elsewhere were worthless until discovered and developed by Westerners, and it remains a matter of conjecture whether they will lead to sustained economic advance in the producing countries.

Population growth as such can induce changes in economic behavior favorable to capital formation. The parents of enlarged families may work harder and save more in order to provide for the future of their families. In LDCs as in the West, poor people save and invest. They can sacrifice leisure for work or transfer their labor and land to more productive use, perhaps by switching from subsistence production to cash crops. Poor and illiterate traders have often accumulated capital by working harder and opening up local markets.

Famine and Unemployment

Despite the repeated warnings of doomsayers, there is no danger that population growth will cause a shortage of land and hence malnutrition or starvation. Contemporary famines and food shortages occur mostly in sparsely populated subsistence economies such as Ethiopia, the Sahel, Tanzania, Uganda, and Zaire. In these countries, land is abundant and, in places, even a free good. Recurrent food shortages or famines in these and other LDCs reflect features of subsistence and near-subsistence economies such as nomadic style of life, shifting cultivation, and inadequate communications and storage facilities. Those conditions are exacerbated by lack of public security, official restrictions on the activities of traders, restrictions on the movement of food, and restrictions on imports of both consumer goods and farm supplies. Unproductive forms of land tenure such as tribal systems of land rights can also bring about shortages. No famines are reported in such densely populated regions of the less developed world as Taiwan, Hong Kong, Singapore, western Malaysia, and the cash-crop-producing areas of West Africa. Indeed, where a greater density of population in sparsely populated countries brings about improved transport facilities and greater public security, it promotes emergence from subsistence production.

Nor should population growth lead to unemployment. A large population means more consumers as well as more producers. The large increase of population in the West over the last two centuries has not brought about persistent unemployment. Substantial unemployment emerged when population growth had become much slower in the twentieth century. And when, in the 1930s, an early decline of population was widely envisaged, that development was generally thought to portend more unemployment because it would reduce the mobility and adaptability of the labor force and diminish the incentive to invest.

The experience of the contemporary less developed world confirms that rapid increase of population does not result in unemployment and also that the issue cannot be discussed simply on the basis of numbers and physical resources. Until recently, population grew very rapidly in densely populated Hong Kong and Singapore without resulting in unemployment. Singapore has far less land per head than neighboring Malaysia, yet many people move from Malaysia to Singapore in search of employment and higher wages, both as short-term and long-term migrants and as permanent settlers. The idea that population growth results in unemployment implies that labor cannot be substituted for land or capital in particular activities and also that resources cannot be moved from less labor-intensive to more labor-intensive activities. The idea implies that the elasticity of substitution between labor and other resources is zero in both production and consumption. But the development of more intensive forms of agriculture in many LDCs, including the development of double and treble cropping, refutes such notions, as do frequent changes in patterns of consumption.

What Does the Future Hold?

Dramatic long-term population forecasts are often put forward with much confidence. Such confidence is unwarranted. It is useful to recall the population forecasts of the 1930s, predicting a substantial decline of population, primarily in the West but to some extent worldwide. Articles by prominent academics appeared under such headings as "The End of the Human Experiment" and "The Suicide of the Human Race." Yet within less than one human generation, the population problem had taken on exactly the opposite meaning. The scare remained, but its algebraic sign was changed from minus to plus.

Today, only the roughest forecasts of population trends in the Third World are warranted. The basis for confident predictions for the Third World, or even for individual LDCs, is far more tenuous than it was for the spectacularly unsuccessful forecasts of long-term population trends in the West in the 1930s. In much of the Third World there is either no registration of births and deaths or a very incomplete one. Estimates of the population of African countries differ by as much as a third or more; for populous countries such as Nigeria, this discrepancy means tens of millions of people. Estimates of the population of the People's Republic of China, the most populous country in the world, also differ substantially.

In the coming decades, major political, cultural, and economic changes will occur in much of the Third World. These changes are unpredictable, and so are people's responses. For instance, contrary to expectations, the economic improvement in recent decades in some Third World countries has resulted in higher fertility. Similarly, a decline of mortality in many LDCs has not been accompanied by the decline of fertility that had been widely expected in the belief that people had many children to replace those who died young. Moreover, in some of these countries urban and rural fertility rates are about the same, whereas in others the rates differ widely. The relationship of fertility to social class and occupation also varies much more in the Third World than in the West. The foregoing considerations should put into perspective such widely canvassed and officially endorsed practices as forecasting to the nearest million the population of the world for the year 2000 or beyond. One demographic relationship of considerable generality does bear upon population trends in LDCs. Professor Caldwell, a leading Australian demographer, has found that systematic restriction of family size in the Third World is practiced primarily by women who have adopted Western attitudes toward childbearing and child rearing, as a result of exposure to Western education, media, and contacts. Their attitude toward fertility control does not depend on income, status, or urbanization but on Westernization. In this context, Westernization means the readiness of parents to forgo additions to family income from the work of young children and also to make increased expenditure on education, reflecting greater concern with the material welfare of their children.

Caldwell's conclusion is more plausible and more solidly based than the widely held view that higher incomes lead to reduced fertility. It is true that in the West and the Westernized parts of the Third World, higher incomes and lower fertility are often, though by no means always, associated. But it is not the case that higher incomes and smaller families reflect greater ambition for material welfare for oneself and one's family. Rather, both the higher incomes and the reduced fertility reflect a change of preferences. By contrast, when parental incomes are increased as a result of subsidies or windfalls, without a change in attitudes, the parents are likely to have more children, not fewer. This last point pertains to the proposals of many Western observers who, without recognizing the contradiction, urge both population control and also more aid to poor people with large families.

Some broad, unambitious predictions of Third World population prospects may be in order. Although the speed and extent of Westernization are uncertain, the process is likely to make some headway. Some decline in fertility will result. But the large proportion of young people and the prevailing reproductive rates will ensure significant increases in population in the principal regions of the Third World over the next few decades. The population growth rate for the Third World as a whole is unlikely to fall much below 2 percent per year and may for some years continue around 2.5 percent, the rough estimate for the 1980s. It is therefore likely to remain considerably higher than the rate of growth in the West, Japan, and Australasia. Therefore, over the years, the population of the West, Japan, and Australasia will shrink considerably relative to that of Asia, Africa, and Latin America.

It is unlikely that Third World population growth will jeopardize the well being of families and societies. But if their well-being were for any reason to be seriously impaired by population growth, reproductive behavior would change without official pressure. There is, therefore, no reason to force people to have fewer children than they would like. When such pressure emanates from outside the local culture, it is especially objectionable. It is also likely to provoke resistance to modernization generally.

Conclusion

The central issue of population policy is whether individuals and families or politicians and national and international civil servants should decide how many children people may have.

Advocates of officially sponsored population policies often argue that they do not propose compulsion but intend only to extend the options of people by assisting the spread of knowledge about contraceptive methods. But people in LDCs usually know about both traditional and more modern methods of birth control. Moreover, in many Third World countries, especially in Asia and Africa, official information, advice, and persuasion in practice often shade into coercion. In most of these societies, people are more subject to authority than in the West. And especially in recent years, the incomes and prospects of many people have come to depend heavily on official favors. In India, for example, promotion in the civil service, allocation of driving and vehicle licenses, and access to subsidized credit, official housing, and other facilities have all been linked at times to restriction of family size. Forcible mass sterilization, which took place in India in the 1970s, and the extensive coercion in the People's Republic of China are only extreme cases in a spectrum of measures extending from publicity to compulsion. Policies and measures pressing people to have fewer children can provoke acute anxiety and conflict, and they raise serious moral and political problems. Implementation of such policies may leave people dejected and inert, uninterested in social and economic advance or incapable of achieving it. Such outcomes have often been observed when people have been forced to change their mores and conduct. It is widely agreed that the West should not impose its standards, mores, and attitudes on Third World governments and peoples. Yet, ironically, the most influential voices call for the exact opposite with regard to population control.

There is one type of official policy that would tend to reduce population growth, extend the range of personal choice, and promote attitudes and mores that foster economic advance and improvement of the well-being of the population. That policy is the promotion of external commercial contacts, especially contacts with the West, by the people of LDCs. Such contacts have been powerful agents of voluntary change in attitudes and habits, particularly by eroding those harmful to economic improvement. Throughout the less developed world, the most prosperous groups and areas are those with the most external commercial contacts. And such contacts also encourage voluntary reduction of family size. Thus, extension of such contacts and the widening of people's range of choice promote both economic advance and reduction in fertility. In these circumstances, a reduction of family size is achieved without the damaging effects of placing official pressure on people with regard to their most private and vital concerns. Yet policies of this kind are not on the agenda of those who advocate reducing population growth in LDCs.

Beyond National Boundaries: Immigration and the Flow of Labor

Marcelo M. Suárez-Orozco
Harvard Graduate School of Education

Over the last decade globalization has intensified worldwide economic, social, and cultural transformations. Globalization is structured by three powerful, interrelated formations: 1) the post-nationalization of production and distribution of goods and services—fueled by growing levels of international trade, foreign-direct investment, and capital—market flows; 2) the emergence of new information and communication technologies that place a premium on knowledge-intensive work, and 3) unprecedented levels of world-wide migration. Globalization's puzzle is that while many applaud it as the royal road for development (see, for example, Micklethwait & Wooldrige, 2000; Friedman, 2000) it is nevertheless generating strong currents of discontent that can be ignored only at our peril. It is now obvious that in large regions of the world, globalization has been a deeply disorienting and threatening process of change (Bauman, 1998). Globalization has generated the most hostilities where it has placed local cultural identities, including local meaning systems, local religious identities, and local systems of livelihood, under siege.

Globalization is first and foremost about movement. Its emerging regime—mobile capital, mobile production and distribution, mobile populations, and mobile cultures—is generating deep paradoxes. Some regions of the world, *inter alia* East Asia, have prospered immensely under globalization's regime (see Table 1). Yet in other regions the forces of globalization seem to have conspired to intensify patterns of inequality and human suffering (see Dussel, 2000; Mittelman, 2000; see also Nader, 1993). The last decade has witnessed vast economic growth in the rich nations, especially the United States, while roughly twenty-five percent of the population of the developing world lives in desperate poverty—with less than a dollar a day (see Table 1). China's meteoric integration into the global economy has both significantly reduced poverty *and* increased inequality (World Bank 2001: 1). On the other hand, throughout much of Latin America, globalization has simply increased income inequality (World Bank 2001: 1).

There is a new, somewhat amorphous and eclectic, anti-globalization ethos—ubiquitously named, articulated, and performed in varied contexts from Seattle, to Genoa, to Buenos Aires. Its message seems structured by a common grammar: the global project is de-stabilizing, disorienting, and threatening to large numbers of people the world over.

Yet, just as many hate what they see in globalization, others are seduced by its promise. Here is another paradox of globalization: As it continues to penetrate the local cultural imaginaries of poor

Table 1: Population living below US$1 per day in developing countries 1990 and 1998

	Poverty Rate (%)			
	1990	1998 (estimate)	1990	1998 (estimate)
East Asia	452.4	278.3	27.6	15.3
Excluding China	92.0	65.1	18.5	11.3
South Asia	495.1	522.0	44.0	40.0
Sub-Saharan Africa	242.3	290.9	47.7	46.3
Latin America	73.8	78.2	16.8	15.6
Middle East/N.Africa	5.7	5.5	2.4	1.9
Europe & Cent. Asia	7.1	24.0	1.6	5.1
Total	1276.4	1198.9	29.0	24.0

Source: World Bank. *Global Economic Prospects and the Developing Countries 2000.* (2000).

developing countries, even as it de-stabilizes local economies and livelihoods, it generates structures of desire and consumption fantasies that simply cannot be met by local economies. *It is my claim that these twin factors, globalization's uneven effects on the world economy and the emergence of a global imaginary of consumption, are behind the largest wave of immigration in human history.* Globalization's paradoxical power is in that at once it manufactures both despair and hope. But for millions of people, globalization's hope is to be realized elsewhere, as migrants.

Globalization's discontent visits the "other half," the wealthy advanced post-industrial democracies that have arguably benefited the most under its reign, symmetrically. In the advanced post-industrial democracies, the unprecedented, growing, and seemingly uncontainable migratory flows generated by globalization over the last decade are, alas, experienced as threatening and disorienting to local cultural identities and sensibilities. This is the case in most of Western Europe, the United States, and Australia where anti-immigrant sentiment and xenophobia have emerged as potentially explosive political and social concerns. Item: Somewhat monomaniacal anti-immigrant parties in Western Europe have gained momentum over the last decade—*the Vlams Bloc* in Belgium, *the Freedom Party* in Austria, *the Front National* in France, and the *People's Party* in Denmark. Item: Voters in California overwhelmingly approved Proposition 187, a new law that would deny illegal immigrants a host of publicly funded services—including schooling for children. Item: In mid-2001 Australia denied a ship in distress carrying hundreds of asylum-seekers entry to its ports. To paraphrase Tolstoy, globalization is making all the families of the world unhappy in the same way.

In this essay, I examine large-scale immigration and the flow of labor within the paradigm of globalization. First, I explore the parameters of the phenomena called globalization. Then I turn to the topic of large-scale immigration. Lastly, I examine some of the cultural processes of change facing those who pursue their fortunes beyond their national boundaries.

Global Anxieties

The study of globalization is generating considerable academic interest in a variety of disciplines, including anthropology, economics, sociology, political science, law, and education (see for example, Appadurai, 1996; Baylis & Smith, 1997; Bauman, 1998; Castles & Davidson, 2000; Giddens, 2000; Hardt and Negri, 2000; Jameson & Miyoshi, 1998; King, 1997; Lechner & Boli, 1999; O'Meara, Mehlinger, & Krain, 2000; Sassen, 1988). As I have argued elsewhere (Suárez-Orozco 2001), one of the challenges in the study of globalization is that it is conceptualized, defined, and operationalized differently by different disciplines and by different researchers.[1]

For the purposes of this essay, I define globalization as processes of change, generating at once centrifugal (qua the borders of the nation state) and centripetal (qua post-national nodes) forces that result in the deterritorialization of basic economic, social, and cultural practices from their traditional moorings in the nation state. Because globalization involves a kind of "post-geography"

(Bauman, 1998), it is futile to attempt to map it. Indeed, different regions of the world are, at once, implicated in multiple, overlapping globalization processes. While globalization by definition refers to economic, social, and cultural processes that are post-national, I do not mean to suggest that it augurs the demise of the state apparatus. It is, I think, subtler than that.[2]

What, if anything, is *new* about globalization? Is globalization simply "modernization" on steroids? Is it "Westernization" in fast-forward? Is it "imperialism" now driven by the extraordinarily high octane of American hyper-power? Alternatively, is it a phenomenon or a set of phenomena of a completely different order? A number of prominent scholars have claimed that globalization is best conceptualized as part of a long process of change—arguably centuries in the making (see, for example, Mignolo, 1998; Sen, 2000).

Yet three new formations suggest that globalization in some important respects represents a break with previous processes of economic, social, and cultural change. First, as mentioned earlier, new powerful market forces are bypassing nation-state boundaries. Under the regime of global capitalism, financial markets and the production and distribution of goods and services are completely globalized.[3]

Second, globalization is the product of new information and communication technologies that instantaneously connect people, organizations, and systems across vast distances. In addition to creating and circulating vast amounts of information and data, these technologies have the promise of freeing people from the tyranny of space and time. These new technologies are rapidly and irrevocably changing the nature of work, thought, and the interpersonal patterning of social relations (Turkle, 1997).[4]

The third novel feature of globalization is new patterns of large-scale immigration. Globalization is about deterritorialization not only of markets, information, symbols, and tastes but also of large and growing numbers of people. Large-scale immigration is a world phenomenon that is transforming Africa, Asia, Europe, and the Americas. Roughly 30 percent of Frankfurt's population is immigrant. Amsterdam by the year 2015 will be 50 percent immigrant. Leicester, England, is about to become the first city in Europe where "Whites" will no longer be the majority. Japan, long held as the exception to the North American and European rule that immigrant workers are needed to maintain economic vitality, is now facing a future where immigrants will play a significant role (Tsuda, 1996). Africa has by far the largest number of refugees in the world.

Globalization is the general backdrop for any understanding of the new immigration. At the turn of the Millennium there are an estimated 100 million transnational immigrants plus some 30 million refugees displaced from their homelands. Globalization has increased immigration in a variety of ways. First, transnational capital flows tend to stimulate migration because where capital flows immigrants tend to follow.[5] Second, the new information and communication technologies that are at the heart of globalization tend to stimulate migration because they encourage new tastes, new standards of consumption and life-style choices. Would-be immigrants imagine better opportunities elsewhere and mobilize to achieve them. Third, the affordability of mass transportation has put the migration option within the reach of millions who heretofore could not do so—last year approximately 1.5 billion airline tickets were sold. Fourth, globalization has stimulated new migration because it has produced uneven results.[6]

Globalization pains have been felt in some regions of the developing world—perpetuating unemployment and further depressing wages.[7] On the winning side of the new globalization game, there has been a growth of jobs in some regions of world. These jobs include the knowledge-intensive sector of the new economy as well as more traditional jobs in service and agriculture. The growth in jobs in globalization's winning zones have acted an unstoppable vacuum sending millions of immigrants—skilled and unskilled, legal and illegal—from the developing world into the wealthier centers of the northern hemisphere.

Lives Beyond National Boundaries

In recent years, there has been a renewed interest in the study of human migration (Suárez-Orozco, Suárez-Orozco and Qin-Hilliard, 2001, vol. 1). During the last decades of the twentieth century, most major nation-states have seen the topic of immigration emerge as a significant issue with important public opinion, policy, and research implications. Migration, for the Latin *migrare* meaning to "change residence," has been a defining feature in the making of humanity from our very emergence as a species in the African savanna. Social scientists have traditionally defined migration as the more or less permanent movement of people across space (Petersen, 1968). In the language of the social sciences people 'emigrate' out of one location and become 'immigrants' in a new setting.

The definition of migration as the more or less permanent movement of people across space suggests a number of important concerns. First is the matter of the relative permanence of immigrants in a new setting. For many, perhaps most, immigration represents a permanent move; for others it is a temporary state before eventually returning "home." A central feature of the great transatlantic immigration that took place between Europe, and North America and South America from the 1890s until the 1910s was the high proportion of people who returned to Europe. By some accounts, well over a third of all the Europeans who came to the Americas went back "home" (Moya, 1998).

'Sojourners' represent yet another pattern of labor flow where temporality defines immigration. They are the large numbers of immigrants who move for well-defined periods of time, often following a seasonal cycle to eventually return home. Large numbers of migrant workers have followed this pattern—from African workers in the Sub-Saharan region to Mexican agricultural workers in California (Cornelius, 1992).

A third type is the constant shuttling back-and-forth that seems to define the lives of many new immigrants world-wide. In recent years, some scholars of immigration have argued that new transnational and global forces structure the journeys of immigrants in more complex ways than was previously seen (Basch et al. 1994). This research suggests that many immigrants remained engaged (economically, politically and culturally) both in their newly adopted lands *and* in their communities of origin—moving "back and forth" in ways seldom seen in previous eras of large-scale immigration (Suárez-Orozco, 1998).

The idea of immigration as movement across space also requires some elaboration. Immigration, at a minimum, involves a change in residency and a change in community. Over the years, scholars have concentrated on two major types of large-scale migration: 'internal migration' (within the confines of a nation-state) and 'international migration' (across international borders). While many scholars would argue that the large-scale movement of people *within* a nation-state is a phenomenon of a different order than the large-scale movement of people *across* international borders, the differences between these two broad types of migration are often quite blurred.

Internal migrants often share many characteristics with international migrants: many move from rural villages to urban centers, many experience linguistic and cultural discontinuities, and many face the same bureaucratic and legal restrictions and discriminations international migrants do. While much attention has been focused on international migration, most immigrants today are internal migrants staying within the confines of their nation-states—China, Egypt, and Brazil are countries that have experienced high levels of internal migration. Indeed, *contra* the impression that the majority of international migrants are heading to the developed world (i.e., Europe and North America), most immigration today is an intra-continental (i.e., within Asia, within Africa, etc.) phenomenon.

China alone has an estimated 100 million internal migrants who, in many ways, experience similar circumstances as transnational migrants face when they move across countries (Eckholm 2001: 10).

The Causes and Consequences of Labor Immigration

Scholars of immigration have generally theorized patterns of migration flows in terms of economic forces, social processes, and cultural practices (Suárez-Orozco, Suárez-Orozco and Qin-Hilliard, 2001, vol. 1). Social scientists who study the economic causes of immigration have examined how such variables as unemployment, underemployment, lack of access to credit, and especially, wage differentials are implicated in labor migration (Suárez-Orozco, Suárez-Orozco and Qin-Hilliard, 2001 vol. 2; Dussel, 2000). Immigration has also been framed as a risk-management and diversifying strategy deployed by families and communities hoping to place their eggs in various territorial baskets (Massey, Durand and Malone, 2002). Changing cultural models about social standards and economic expectations have also been implicated in why people migrate (Moya, 1998). In many cases people migrate to actualize new consumption and life-style standards.

In nearly all advanced post-industrial economies, bifurcated labor markets have worked as a powerful "pull" factor attracting large numbers of immigrants to work in the low-wage, low-status, and low-skilled secondary sector. In Japan, for example, immigrant workers are sometimes called "3 k workers" for the Japanese words for "dirty, demanding, and dangerous" jobs (Tsuda, 1996). When certain sectors of the opportunity structure are culturally coded as "immigrant jobs," they become stigmatized and native workers tend to shun them almost regardless of wage dynamics. What would it take, in terms of wages, to make back-breaking work, like strawberry-picking in California, not an immigrant occupation?

Scholars of immigration have long maintained that cultural and social practices can generate—and sustain—substantial migratory flows. In many regions of the world, such as Ireland and Mexico, migration has been an adulthood-defining *rite de passage*. In some cases, people migrate because others—relatives, friends, and friends of friends—migrated before them. Indeed, the best predictor of who will migrate is who migrated before. Transnational family re-unification continues to be a critical vector in immigration today. In the year 1996, 915,900 immigrants were formally admitted in the U.S. Among them, 594,604 were family-sponsored immigrants (Suárez-Orozco, 1999). Since the early 1970's family reunification is one of the few formal ways to migrate into Europe (Suárez-Orozco, 1994).

A number of studies have examined how transnational migratory social-chains, once established, can generate a powerful momentum of their own. Each immigrant lowers the costs associated with migration for those coming after her. Established immigrants lower the costs of subsequent immigration because they ease the transition of new arrivals by sharing crucial economic, linguistic and cultural knowledge—about job openings, good wages, fair bosses, and dignified working conditions. Roger Waldinger (1997) for example, has explored the sociocultural dynamics of transnational immigrant labor-recruiting networks. Immigrants, he concluded, find their kin and kith jobs. Waldinger's research in immigrant-rich Southern California suggests that immigrant social networks provide employers with a nearly unlimited supply of workers with little or no outlay. Transnational social networks provide connections to people able to fill jobs, at times even before the jobs are vacant. The social networks function optimally when they efficiently and economically generate quality information—about jobs, about applicants, about bosses (Waldinger, 1997).

Few topics generate as much controversy as the economic consequences of large-scale labor migration. Do immigrants help or hurt the economies of their new countries? Do immigrants carry their own weight or do they represent a burden to citizens and other established residents? Do complex post-industrial economies need low-skilled immigrant workers or have they become redundant? Much of the recent scholarship on immigration and the economy has tended to focus on such concerns as the fiscal implications of immigration, the issue of immigrant competition with native workers, and the related issue of immigration and wages. Another important theme has been the economic integration and progress of immigrants over time (Suárez-Orozco, Suárez-Orozco and Qin-Hilliard, 2001 vol. 2; Borjas, 1999; Espenshade, 1997; National Research Council, 1997).

The research findings on the economic consequences of immigration are somewhat contradictory—some economists claiming that immigrants are a burden to tax-payers and an overall negative influence especially on advanced post-industrial economies (Huddle, 1993) and others suggesting that they continue to be an important asset (Simon, 1989).

A recent study on the economic, demographic, and fiscal effects of immigration by the U.S. National Research Council (NRC) concludes that in the American setting "immigration produces net economic gains for domestic residents" (NRC, 1997: 3). Not only do immigrants "increase the supply of labor and help produce new goods and services" but their presence also "allows domestic workers to be used more productively, specializing in producing goods at which they are relatively more efficient. Specialization in consumption also yields a gain" (NRC, 1997: 3-4). The NRC estimates that the immigration-related "domestic gain may run on the order of $1 billion to $10 billion a year" (NRC, 1997: 5). Given the size of the U.S. economy (about 7 trillion dollars) it is clear that immigrants will neither "make it" nor "break it."

In fiscal terms the NRC data suggest, "Immigrants receive more in services than they pay in taxes." (NRC, 1997: 7). The panel estimates that "if the net fiscal impact of all U.S. immigrant-headed households were averaged across all native households the burden would be...on the order of $166 to $226 per native household."

The NRC study and other studies conclude that while immigration is a plus in overall economic terms, low-skilled new immigrants have contributed to a modest drop in the minimum wage of low-skilled workers. They found that a 5 percent drop in wages since 1980 among high-school dropouts could be attributed to the new immigrants. There is, however, no evidence to suggest that new immigration has "hurt" the economic condition of native minority workers such as African-Americans (NRC, 1997: 5).

Other recent research engages the theoretical debate over the role of immigrant workers in the global, post-industrial economy. In the context of the increasingly advanced knowledge-intensive economies of today, are low-skilled immigrant workers simply anachronistic? Are immigrant workers a leftover from an earlier era of production?

Wayne Cornelius' comparative research of the use of immigrant labor in two paradigmatic post-industrial economic settings, San Diego County, California, USA; and Hamamatzu, Japan; suggests a remarkable convergence in patterns of growing reliance on immigrant labor—in spite of rather marked differences in national context (Cornelius, 1998). Cornelius' data reveal a pattern of enduring, indeed voracious, post-industrial demand for immigrant labor. Cornelius concludes "As immigrants become a preferred labor force, employers do more to retain them, even in a recessionary economy" (Cornelius, 1998: 128).

Cornelius argues that immigrant workers are desirable to a wide variety of employers for three basic reasons. First, immigrants are willing to do low-pay work that is boring, dirty, or dangerous with little or no prospects for upward mobility and that even in firms involving highly advanced technologies such work is critical. Second, employers perceive them quite favorably—as reliable, flexible, punctual, and willing to work overtime. Indeed, employers often prefer them to native-born workers. And third, immigrant transnational labor-recruiting networks are a powerful method for "delivering eager new recruits to the employer's doorstep with little or no effort on his part" (Ibid.)

Other studies examine the issue of the socioeconomic progress made by immigrant workers. The research of Dowell Myers tracks, over time and across generations, various dimensions of the economic adaptations of immigrant-origin men in a region of the world heavily impacted by immigration: the state of California. His work explores three sequential outcomes: educational attainment, occupational mobility, and earnings. In some fundamental ways, the recent Mexican-immigrant experience in Southern California seems to replicate earlier patterns of immigrant adaptation. Yet in other ways, Myers' findings suggest new—and disturbing—patterns.

Myers' research reveals that upon arrival Mexican-immigrant men tend to be poorly educated, work in low-skilled occupations, and earn low incomes. Myers finds that over time immigrant men make modest improvements in their economic condition. However, he also suggests that important changes occur across younger cohorts within the first generation. These changes, according to Myers, are strongly related to the much higher educational attainment of immigrant children. In other words, Myers finds an old story with a new set of characters: poorly educated immigrant men make modest gains over time but their children are able to attain more education in the new country.

Still, Myers' data reveal a disturbing new pattern: among the children of immigrants higher education "does not appear to fully convert into higher occupational status or earnings; and higher occupational status translates even less well into higher earnings. These under-returns are most pronounced for the more recent arrivals from Mexico and for young cohorts, including native-born, both of whom newly entered the labor market in the 1970s and 1980s." Myers concludes "The social implications of these falling returns to education and occupation are regrettable, because the declining reward system may discourage other" immigrant children from investing in schooling as the route for status mobility (Myers, 1998: 188).

We have a reasonable understanding of how "love" (family-reunification) and "work" drive immigration. On the other hand, the role of war and its relations to large-scale migratory flows has been generally neglected. Yet throughout history war and international migration have been closely linked. The threat of labor shortages during World War II led to the creation of temporary labor-recruiting efforts to attract much needed immigrant workers to the United States (Calavita, 1992). The resultant "bracero" program became a powerful force in building—alas, via family reunification—a Mexican migration momentum that eventually turned into the largest and most powerful immigration flow into the United States this century (Suárez-Orozco, 1998).

In the aftermath of WWII, many of the major Northwestern European democracies, such as Germany and Belgium, developed "guest worker programs" to recruit foreign workers—initially in southern Europe, and subsequently in the Maghreb region of North Africa and in Turkey (Suárez-Orozco, 1994). These programs came to an end in the early 1970s. Yet family-reunification and chain migration continued to bring immigrants from North Africa into Europe for years.

The Cold War both deterred immigration—because of strict Iron Curtain controls—and generated large-population displacements. The robust Cuban diaspora in the United States can be traced more or less directly to the Cold War (Molyneux, 1999). The low-intensity warfare in Central America during the 1980s generated the largest wave of emigration in the region's history. As a result, there are now well over a million Central American immigrants in the United States (Suárez-Orozco, 1989). In the 1990s, the ongoing conflicts in Zimbabwe and Angola have generated large-scale migratory flows, especially into South Africa. The recent war in Afghanistan has resulted in major population displacements—perhaps up to two million Afghans have been displaced from their homes.

Natural disasters have also displaced populations and started new migratory flows. The 1999 hurricanes, which devastated much of Central America, initiated significant flows of emigrants into North America.

The Flow of Labor and the State

Whether social scientists examine the case of internal or international migrants, there is a consensus that the apparatus of the nation-state is decidedly implicated in migratory processes: by both what the state does and by what it cannot do. States are, *inter alia,* in the business of regulating the movement of people—both internally and internationally. The right to leave a country, that is the right to emigrate, is a relatively recent phenomenon (Moya, 1998).

Nation-states regulate, and carefully police, the inflow of international immigrants across borders. Large-scale international immigration is in significant ways the product of nation-building—Argentina, Australia, and Israel come to mind as archetypal examples. Likewise, the reconfigurations of national boundaries have historically and contemporaneously generated large-scale migratory flows. The partition of British India into Pakistan and India was accompanied by one of the "largest migrations in human history" (Petersen, 1968: 290). More recently, the disintegration of the former Yugoslavia led to massive, mostly involuntary, migratory movements.

In the area of international migration, nation-states generate policies designed to establish who is a "legal" or "illegal" immigrant, who is an "asylum seeker," a "refugee" and a "temporary guest worker." States regulate how many immigrants are legally admitted every year. In the U.S., for example, since 1990 an average of about a million legal immigrants have been admitted annually. On the other hand, legal immigration into Northwestern Europe was greatly curbed following the oil crisis of the early 1970s (Cornelius et al. 1994).

States also regulate the flows of asylum seekers—those escaping a country due to a well-founded fear of persecution. Agents of the state decide who is formally admitted as a refugee. In the post-Cold War era, there has been an explosive growth in the numbers of asylum seekers world-wide. For example, some 369,000 foreigners requested asylum in Europe during the year 1998. Only a small portion of those seeking asylum are eventually granted formal refugee status.

In recent years, many post-industrial democracies—including the United States and throughout Northwestern Europe—have developed new strategies to deal with increasing numbers of asylum seekers (Suárez-Orozco, 1994). For example, the 13,000 Kosovars that arrived in Germany in mid-1999 were given a three-month renewable "Temporary Protective Status" on the condition that they not apply for refugee status—in effect, forfeiting all the rights and entitlements that come with formal refugee status. Similar arrangements were made for asylum seekers from Bosnia.

In the face of growing numbers of asylum seekers, and a widespread public concern that many of them are "economic refugees" in search of a better life in wealthier countries, new formal and informal strategies have been put into place in varied countries. Many of these new strategies seem to be designed to prevent asylum seekers from accessing "safe countries"—where, under Geneva Convention agreements, they would have the right to a "fair hearing."

The high-seas interdiction program put into effect in the United States in the early 1990s is an example. The strategy was conceived to prevent large numbers of Caribbean (especially Haitian) asylum seekers from arriving in U.S. territory—or even within its territorial waters—where they could establish certain legal protections. Apprehending them in international waters, and returning them to Haiti, leaves asylum seekers with little practical recourse under international law. In Europe, a similar strategy has been to deem certain areas in international airports not part of the national territory—for example parts of Zaventem airport are not technically Belgian territory but are considered to be international territory. Asylum seekers entering such airports have been turned back because they are said to remain in international territory, and hence not come under the jurisprudence of the Geneva Convention (Suárez-Orozco, 1994).

While advanced post-industrial democracies are likely to continue to face significant numbers of asylum seekers, the greatest numbers of asylum seekers are in the developing world. For example, at the beginning of the Millennium there are over 3 million asylum seekers in the African continent.

While the state wields substantial power—both in regard to internal and international migration—there are nevertheless areas where it faces strict limitations in the management of human migratory flows. Nowhere are the limitations of state power more obvious than in its inability to control illegal immigration. In many parts of the world, undocumented or illegal immigration has become a more or less permanent problem, which periodically emerges as an unsettling political issue.

In the United States, for example, it is estimated that there are some 8 million illegal immigrants. In Europe, the number of illegal immigrants is a more carefully guarded secret because of its dangerous political connotations. Most hard-core, right-wing political parties in Europe, including France's *Front National,* Belgium's *Vlams Bloc,* and Austria's *Freedom Party* revolve around anti- (illegal) immigration platforms. In the decade of the 1990s, these once-marginal parties have made substantial gains with electorates quite concerned with the problem of undocumented immigration.

The enduring problem of illegal immigration in many parts of the world suggests that immigration is now structured by powerful global economic factors, social forces, and cultural practices that seem impervious to state actions such as controls of international borders (Cornelius et al. 1994; Andreas, 2000). Transnational labor recruiting networks, enduring wage differentials between nation-states, changing standards of consumption, family reunification, and war generate a powerful migratory momentum that is not easily contained by unilateral, or even multilateral, state interventions to curb it.

The Varieties of the Immigrant Experience: The Best of Times and the Worst of Times

Once settled in a new country, how do immigrants fare? The United States as the *ür* country of immigration provides an interesting case study. It is the only advanced post-industrial democracy where immigration is at once history and destiny. The intensification of globalization in the last decade—arguably responsible for the greatest peacetime expansion of the U.S. economy ever—coincided with the largest number of immigrants in history.[8] By the year 2000 the "foreign-stock" (foreign-born plus the U.S.-born second-generation) population of the United States was nearly 55 million people—roughly 30 million of them are foreign-born.[9] Two dominant features characterize this most recent wave of immigration: Its intensity (the immigrant population grew by over 30 percent in the 1990s) and the somewhat radical shift in the sources of new immigration (up to 1950, nearly 90 percent of all immigrants were Europeans or Canadians). Today over 50 percent of all immigrants are from Latin America and over 25 percent are from Asia—the regions of the world where globalization has generated especially uneven results (see Chart 1 next page).

Immigrants to the United States today are a heterogeneous population—defying easy generalizations (Suárez-Orozco and Suárez-Orozco, 2001). They include highly educated, highly skilled individuals drawn by the explosive growth in the knowledge-intensive sectors of the economy. They are more likely to have advanced degrees than the native born population (see Chart 2).

These immigrants come to the United States

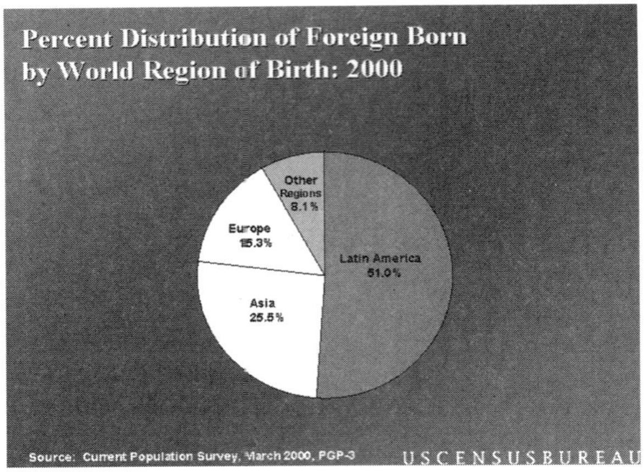

Chart 1

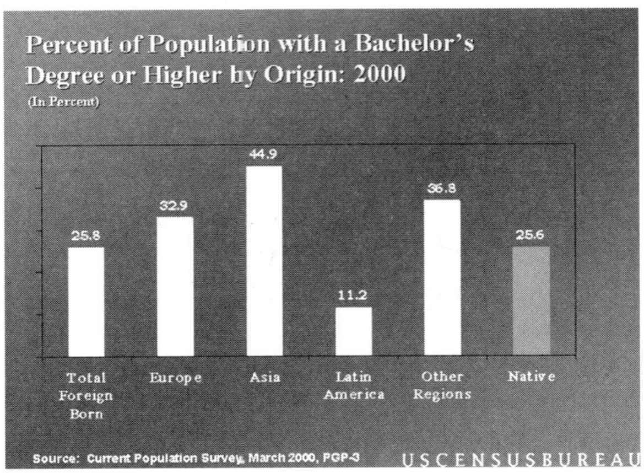

Chart 2

to thrive. Immigrants now, especially those originating in Asia, are among the best-educated and skilled folk in the United States. They are over-represented in the category of people with doctorates. Fully half of all entering physics graduate students in 1998 were foreign-born.[10] Thirty-two percent of all scientists and engineers working in California's Silicon Valley are immigrants (Saxenian, 1999). Roughly a third of all Nobel Prize winners in the United States have been immigrants. In 1999, all (100 percent!) U.S. winners of the Nobel Prize were immigrants. Perhaps with the exception of the highly educated immigrants and refugees escaping Nazi Europe, immigrants in the past tended to be more uniformly poorly educated and relatively unskilled than they are today.[11] Never in the history of U.S. immigration have so many immigrants done so well so fast. Indeed, these immigrants are bypassing the traditional transgenerational modes of status mobility, establishing themselves in the well remunerated sectors of the U.S. economy within a generation.

At the same time, the new immigration contains large numbers of poorly schooled, semi-skilled or unskilled workers—many of them in the U.S. without proper documentation (i.e., as illegal immigrants). In the year 2000, over 22 percent of all immigrants in the U.S. had less than a ninth-grade education (see Chart 3).

These are workers, many of them from Latin America, drawn by the service sector of the U. S. economy where there seems to be an insatiable appetite for foreign folk. They typically end up in poorly paid jobs lacking insurance and basic safeties. Unlike the low-skilled factory jobs of yesterday, the kinds of jobs typically available to low-skilled immigrants today do not hold much realistic promise for upward mobility.[12] These immigrants tend to settle in areas of deep poverty and racial segregation.[13] Concentrated poverty is associated with the "disappearance of meaningful work opportunities."[14] When poverty is combined with racial segregation, the outcomes can be dim (Massey & Denton, 1993: 3).

Immigration and the Discontents of a Global Community

In all countries facing immigration there have been major debates surrounding the socioeconomic and cultural consequences of large-scale population movements. In the U.S. there is a palpable concern, not always fully articulated, relating to how the new immigrants, the majority of whom are non-English speaking, non-European, people of color migrating in large numbers from the developing world will culturally adapt—and, indeed, transform their new country. In Western Europe, there

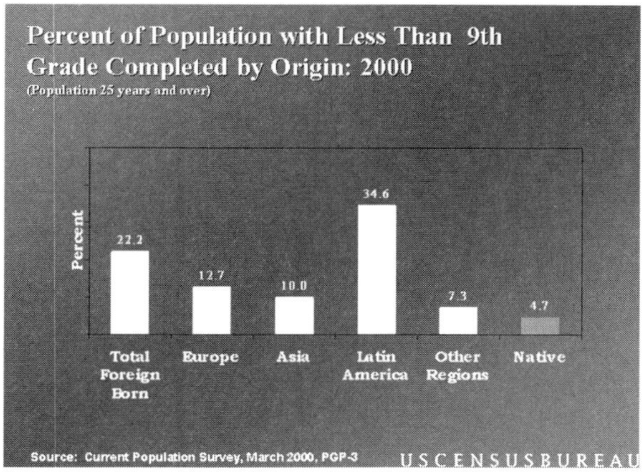

Chart 3

are similar concerns about the cultural adaptations of large numbers of immigrants coming into the Judeo-Christian continent from the Islamic world (Suárez-Orozco, 1991). The anxieties about the long-term vicissitudes of Islam in Europe have probably been greatly accentuated since September 11, 2001. Likewise in Japan, a country where mythologies of racial and cultural homogeneity are deeply implicated in the construction of cultural identity, there are questions about the long-term consequences of increasing migration from Thailand, Korea, China, the Philippines, and South America (Tsuda, 1996).

Some critics of immigration worry about its economic dimensions, while many others have focused on its cultural implications. Analytically, it is sometimes useful to differentiate between two broad spheres of culture: "instrumental culture" and "expressive culture." By instrumental culture, I refer to the skills, competencies, and social behaviors that are required to successfully make a living and contribute to society. By expressive culture, I mean the realm of values, world-views, and the patterning of interpersonal relations that give meaning and sustain the sense of self. Taken together, these qualities of culture generate shared meanings and understandings, and a sense of belonging. In sum, the sense of who we are and where we belong is deeply patterned by these qualities of culture.

In the instrumental realm, globalization is stimulating a world-wide convergence in the skills that are needed to function in today's economy. Whether in Los Angeles, Lima, or Lagos, the skills required to thrive in the global economy are in fundamental respects the same. These include communication; higher-order symbolic and cognitive skills, as well as habits of work, and interpersonal talents that are common in any cosmopolitan setting. Working with the culturally 'other' today is also a skill that will, thanks to globalization, be increasingly remunerated.

Immigrant parents world-wide are very much aware that if their children are to thrive they must acquire these skills. In math, children the world over will need the higher-order skills to at a minimum master fractions, decimals, line graphs, probabilities and other basic statistics. In literacy, they will need, in some cases in more than one language, the ability to read and understand complex instructions and manuals as well as the ability to convey ideas in writing. In logic, they will need problem-solving skills to address given certain antecedent conditions various possible outcomes by formulating and testing hypotheses. Nearly everywhere, working with computers and with people from different linguistic, ethnic, and racial backgrounds, will be the essential new skills required to thrive in the workplace (see Murnane and Levy 1996, especially Chapter 2). Immigration for many parents represents nothing more, and nothing less, than the opportunity to offer children access to these skills.

While immigrant parents encourage their children to cultivate the "instrumental" aspects of culture in the new setting, many are decidedly more ambivalent about their children's exposure to some of the "expressive" elements of culture in the new land. During the course of our research with immigrant families in the United States, it has not been difficult to detect that many immigrant parents strongly resist a whole array of cultural models and social practices in American-youth culture that they consider undesirable. These include cultural attitudes and behaviors that are deemed by immigrant parents to be anti-schooling, anti-authority, and anti-family, and also include the glorification of violence, and sexually precocious behaviors. Many immigrant parents reject and resist this form of acculturation (Suárez-Orozco and Suárez-Orozco 2001).

If acculturation is superficially defined as acquiring linguistic skills, job skills, and participation in the political process, then there is a universal consensus on these shared goals. If, on the other hand, we chose a broader and more ambitious definition of assimilation and acculturation as also including the realm of values, worldviews and interpersonal relations, then a worthy debate ensues.

The first issue that needs airing is the basic question of "acculturating to what?" Taking the U.S. as a point of reference we can observe that American society is no longer, if it ever was, a uniform or coherent system.[15] Given their diverse origins, financial resources, and social networks, immigrants end up gravitating to very different sectors of American society. While some are able to join integrated well-to-do neighborhoods, the majority of today's immigrants come to experience American culture from the vantage-point of poor urban settings. Limited economic opportunities, toxic schools, ethnic tensions, violence, drugs, and gangs characterize many of these settings. The structural inequalities found in what some social theorists have called "American Apartheid" are implicated in the creation of a cultural ethos of ambivalence, pessimism, and despair.[16] Asking immigrant youth to give up their values, world-views, and interpersonal relations to join this ethos is a formula for disaster.

For those immigrants who come into intimate contact with middle-class mainstream culture, other trade-offs will be required. Indeed, new data suggest many immigrant children perceive that mainstream Americans do not welcome them and, indeed, disparage them as not deserving to partake in the American dream.[17] Identifying wholeheartedly with a culture that rejects you has its psychological costs, usually paid with the currency of shame, doubt, and even self-hatred.

But even if the new immigrants were unambivalently embraced by middle-class mainstream Americans, it is far from clear that mimicking their behaviors would prove to be in the long-term an adaptive strategy for immigrants of color. Mainstream-middle class children are protected by webs of social safety-nets that give them leeway to experiment with an array of dystopic behaviors including drugs, sex, and alcohol. On the other hand, for many immigrant youth, without robust socio-economic and cultural safety nets, engaging in such behaviors is a high-stakes proposition where one mistake can have life-long consequences. While a white middle-class youth that is caught in possession of drugs is likely to be referred to counseling and rehabilitation, an immigrant youth convicted of the same offense is likely to be deported.

The current wave of immigration involves people from fantastically diverse and heterogeneous cultural backgrounds. Beneath surface differences, a common grammar can be identified among groups as culturally distinct from each other as Chinese, Haitian, and Mexican immigrants. The importance of family ties, the importance of hard work, and optimism about the future are examples of shared immigrant values.[18]

These three realms are aspects of culture that become highlighted and come to the fore in the process of immigration. Consider, for example, the case of strong family-ties among immigrants. Many immigrants come from cultures where the family system is an integral part of the person's sense of self. These family ties play a critical role in family re-unification—an important force driving the new immigration. Furthermore, once immigrants settle, family ties are accentuated because immigration poses many emotional and practical challenges forcing immigrants to turn to one another for support.[19]

Hard work and optimism about the future are likewise central to the immigrant's *raison d'être*.[20] The immigrant's most fundamental motivation is to find a better life. Immigrants tend to view hard work as essential to this project. The fact that many immigrants will do the impossible jobs that native workers simply refuse to consider is an indication of just how hard they are willing to work. Immigrant family-ties, work ethic, and optimism about the future are unique assets that should be celebrated as adding to the total cultural stock of the nation.

Immigration generates change. The immigrants themselves undergo a variety of transformations. Likewise, the immigration process inevitably changes the members of the dominant culture. Countries unable or unwilling to tolerate or, indeed, thrive in the context of immigration-related changes need to carefully reconsider their dependence on immigrant labor. The one fundamental law of immigration is that it will change everyone involved: the immigrants and those among whom they settle alike. In the U.S. and in Europe today we eat, speak, and dance differently than we did thirty years ago, in part because of large-scale immigration. But change is never easy. The changes brought about by the new immigration require mutual calibrations and negotiations.

Rather than advocating that immigrants, and especially their children, abandon all elements of their culture as they embark on their uncertain assimilation journey, a more promising path is to cultivate and nurture the emergence of new hybrid identities and transcultural competencies.[21] These hybrid cultural styles creatively blend elements of the old culture with that of the new, unleashing new energies and potentials.[22]

The skills and work habits that are required to thrive in the new century are essential elements of assimilation. Immigrant children, like all children, must develop this repertoire of instrumental skills. At the same time, maintaining a sense of belonging and social cohesion with their immigrant roots is equally important. When immigrant children, be they Algerians in France, Mexicans in California, or Thais in Japan, loose their expressive culture, social cohesion is weakened, parental authority is undermined, and interpersonal relations suffer. The unthinking call for immigrant children to abandon their culture can only result in loss, anomie, and social disruption.

In the archetypical country of immigration, the United States, the model of unilineal assimilation—where the bargain was straightforward: please check all your cultural baggage before you pass through the Golden Gate, emerged in another era. The young nation, then, was eager to turn large numbers of European immigrants into loyal citizen workers and consumers. It was an era of nation-building and bounded national projects.

But even then, accounts of immigrants rushing in unison to trade their culture for American culture were greatly exaggerated. German-Americans, Italian-Americans, and Irish-Americans have all left deep cultural imprints in the molding of American culture. Even among fifth-generation descendants of the previous great wave of immigration, symbolic culture, and ethnicity remain an emotional gravitational field.[23]

But beyond the argument that maintaining the expressive elements of culture is symbolically important and strategic from the point-of-view of social cohesion, there is another argument worth considering. In the global era, the tenets of unilineal assimilation are no longer relevant. Today there are clear and unequivocal advantages to being able to operate in multiple cultural codes—as anyone working in a major corporation knows. There are social, economic, cognitive and aesthetic advantages to being able to transverse cultural spaces. Dual consciousness has instrumental and expressive advantages. Immigrant children are posed to maximize that unique advantage. While many view their cultural—including linguistic—skills as a threat, I see them as precious assets to be cultivated.

Large-scale immigration is both the cause and consequence of important global transformations. Immigration, I emphasize, inevitably leads to cultural changes and accommodations among both new arrivals and native citizens (Ainslie, 1998). Immigration can be said to be the consequence of cultural change in that new cultural tastes and changing cultural conceptions of what is an acceptable standard of living have been implicated in large-scale migratory flows (Sassen, 1988). Culturally, immigrants not only significantly reshape the ethos of their new communities (Ainslie, 1998; Gutierrez, 1998) but they are also responsible for significant cultural transformations "back home" (Durand, 1998). As a number of immigration researchers have argued, in many settings, immigrant "social remittances" profoundly affect the values, cultural models, and social practices of those left behind (see, *inter alia,* Levitt 2001). Because of a new ease of mass transportation and because of new communication technologies, it seems that immigration is no longer structured around the "sharp break" with the country of origin that once characterized the trans-oceanic experience (Ainslie 1998). Immigrants today are more likely to be at once "here" and "there"—bridging increasingly unbounded national spaces (Basch et al. 1994) and in the process transform both home and host countries.

Increasingly, transnational immigration will need to be framed in the context of powerful—and as of yet little understood—global formations. New patterns of capital flows, new information technologies, new patterns of communication, changing cultural expectations, and the ease and affordability of mass transportation are generating dynamics that transverse the traditional boundaries of the nation-state. Global capitalism is increasingly characterized by "borderless" economies predicated on transnational capital flows, newly opened markets, and immigrant-dependent economic niches. All of these factors would suggest that immigration is certain to remain a vital social phenomenon in the new Millennium.

References

Ainslie, R. "Cultural Mourning, Immigration, and Engagement: Vignettes from the Mexican Experience" in Suárez-Orozco, M., ed., *Crossings: Mexican Immigration in Interdisciplinary Perspectives* (Cambridge MA: David Rockefeller Center for Latin American Studies and Harvard University Press, 1998).

Andreas, P. *Border Games: Policing the U.S.-Mexico Divide* (Ithaca, NY: Cornell University Press, 2000).

Appadurai, A. *Modernity at large: Cultural dimensions of globalization* (Minneapolis: University of Minnesota Press, 1996).

Basch, L., Schiller, N. & Blanc, C. *Nations Unbound: Transnational Projects, Postcolonial Predicaments and Deterritorialized Nation-States* (Basel, Switzerland: Gordon and Breach Science Publishers, 1994).

Bauman, Z. *Globalization: The human consequences* (New York: Columbia University Press, 1998).

Baylis, J., & Smith, S. *The globalization of world politics* (New York: Oxford University Press, 1997).

Borjas, G. "Assimilation in Cohort Quality Revisited: What Happened to Immigrant Earnings in the 1980s?" *Journal of Labor Economics* 13, no. 2: 211-245.

Borjas, G. *Heaven's Door: Immigration Policy and the American Economy* (Princeton, NJ: Princeton University Press, 1999).

Calavita, K. *Inside the State: The Bracero Program, Immigration and the INS* (New York: Routledge, 1992).

Canclini, N. *Hybrid cultures: Strategies for entering and leaving modernity* Chippari, C. & López, S., Trans. (Minneapolis: University of Minnesota Press, 1995). Original work published 1989.

Castles, S., & Davidson, A. *Citizenship and migration: Globalization and the politics of belonging* (New York: Routledge, 2000).

Chavez, L. *Shadowed lives: Undocumented immigrants in American society* (Fort Worth, TX: Harcourt Brace, 1992).

Cornelius, W. "From soujourners to settlers: The Changing Profile of Mexican Immigration in the United States," in Bustamante, J., Reynolds, C. & Hinojosa Ojeda, R., (Eds.), *U.S.-Mexico Relations: Labor Market Interdependence* (Stanford, CA: Stanford University Press, 1992).

Cornelius, W. "The Structural Embeddedness of Demand for Mexican Immigrant Labor: New Evidence From California," in Suárez-Orozco, M., ed., *Crossings: Mexican Immigration in Interdisciplinary Perspectives* (Cambridge, MA: David Rockefeller Center for Latin American Studies and Harvard University Press, 1998).

Cornelius, W., Martin, P. & Hollifield, J., (Eds.), *Controlling Immigration: A Global Perspective* (Stanford, CA: Stanford University Press, 1994).

Durand, J. "Migration and Integration," in Marcelo M. Suárez-Orozco, ed., *Crossings: Mexican Immigration in Interdisciplinary Perspectives,* (Cambridge, MA: David Rockefeller Center for Latin American Studies, Harvard University Press, 1998).

Dussel, E.P. *Polarizing Mexico: The impact of liberalization* (New York: Lynne Rienner, 2000).

Eckholm, E. "District in Beijing to Shut Schools for Migrants." *The New York Times.* October 31, p. 10.

Espenshade, T., ed., *Keys to Successful Immigration: Implications of the New Jersey Experience* (Washington, DC: The Urban Institute Press, 1997).

Falicov, C. *Latino Families in Therapy: A Guide to Multicultural Practice* (New York: Guilford, 1998).

Friedman, T. *The Lexus and the olive tress: Understanding globalization* (New York: Anchor Books, 2000).

Giddens, A. *Runaway world: How globalization is reshaping our lives* (New York: Routledge, 2000).

Gibson, M. *Accommodation without Assimilation: Sikh Immigrants in an American High School* (Ithaca, NY: Cornell University Press, 1988).

Nathan Glazer and D.P. Moynahan, *Beyond the Melting Pot* (Cambridge, MA: MIT Press, 1970).

Gutierrez, D. "Ethnic Mexicans and the Transformation of 'American' Social Space: Relfections on Recent History", in Suárez-Orozco M., (Ed.), *Crossings: Mexican Immigration in Interdisciplinary Perspectives* (Cambridge MA: David Rockefeller Center for Latin American Studies and Harvard University Press, 1998).

Gupta, A., & Ferguson, J., "Beyond 'culture': Space, identity, and the politics of difference," *Cultural Anthropology,* volume 7, 6-23, 1992.

Michael Hardt and Antonio Negri. *Empire* (Cambridge, MA: Harvard University Press, 2000).

Huddle, D. "The Costs of Immigration" (Released by Carrying Capacity Network, July, 1993).

Jameson, F., & Miyoshi, M., (Eds.), *The cultures of globalization* (Durham, NC: Duke University Press, 1998).

Kao, G. & Tienda, M. "Optimism and Achievement: The Educational Performance of Immigrant Youth." *Social Science Quarterly* 96 (1995): 1-19.

King, A., ed. *Culture, globalization, the world system: Contemporary conditions for the representation of identity* (New York: Cambridge University Press, 1997).

LaFromboise, F., et al., "Psychological Impact of Biculturalism: Evidence and Theory" in Organista, P., Chun, K. & Martin, G., (Eds.), *Readings in Ethnic Psychology* (New York: Routledge, 1998).

Lechner, F., & Boli, J., (Eds.), *The globalization reader* (New York: Bladwell, 1999).

Levitt, P. "Commentary" in Suárez-Orozco, M. (Ed.) *Crossings: Mexican Immigration in Interdisciplinary Perspectives* (Cambridge, MA: David Rockefeller Center for Latin American Studies and Harvard University Press, 1998).

Levitt, P. *The Transnational Villagers* (Berkeley and Los Angeles: University of California Press, 2001).

Mahler, S. *American dreaming: Immigrant life on the margins* (Princeton, NJ: Princeton University Press, 1995).

Massey, D., & Denton, N. *American apartheid* (Cambridge, MA: Harvard University Press, 1993).

Massey, D., Durand, J. & Malone, N. *Smoke and Mirrors: Mexican Immigration in an Era of Free Trade* (New York, NY: Russell Sage Foundation, 2002).

Micklethwait, J., & Wooldrige, A. *A future perfect: The challenge and hidden promise of globalization* (New York: Times Books, 2000).

Mignolo, W. "Globalization, civilization processes, and

the relocation of languages and cultures." In Jameson, F. & Miyoshi, M. (Eds.), *The cultures of globalization*, pp. 32-53 (Durham, NC: Duke University Press, 1998).

Mittelman, J. *The globalization syndrome* (Princeton, NJ: Princeton University Press 2000).

Molyneux, M. "The Politics of the Cuban Diaspora in the United States" in Bulmer-Thomas, J. & Dunkerley, J., (Eds.), *The United States & Latin America: The New Agenda* (Cambridge, MA: DRCLAS & Harvard University Press, 1999).

Moya, J. *Cousins and Strangers : Spanish Immigrants in Buenos Aires, 1850-1930* (Berkeley, CA: University of California Press, 1998).

Murnane, Richard and Frank Levy, *Teaching the New Basic Skills* (New York, NY: Martin Kessler Books, 1996).

Myers, D. "Dimensions of Economic Adaptation by Mexican-Origin Men" in Suárez-Orozco, M., (Ed.), *Crossings: Mexican Immigration in Interdisciplinary Perspectives* (Cambridge, MA: David Rockefeller Center for Latin American Studies and Harvard University Press, 1998).

Nader, R., (Ed.), *The case against free trade: GATT, NAFTA, and the globalization of corporate power* (New York: North Atlantic Books, 1993).

National Research Council, *The New Americans: Economic, Demographic and Fiscal Effects of Immigration* (Washington, DC: National Academy Press, 1997).

National Research Council, *From Generation to Generation: The Health and Well-Being of Children in Immigrant Families* (Washington, DC: National Academy Press, 1998).

New York Times, "Wanted: American Physicists," July 23, 1999, p. A27.

O'Meara, P., Mehlinger H., & Krain, M. (Eds.). *Globalization and the challenges of the new century: A reader* (Bloomington: Indiana University Press, 2000).

Orfield, G. "Commentary," in Suárez-Orozco, M., (Ed.), *Crossings: Mexican Immigration in Interdisciplinary Perspectives* (Cambridge, MA: David Rockefeller Center for Latin American Studies and Harvard University Press, 1998).

Orfield, G. "Commentary." in Suarez-Orozco, M. and Mariela Páez, (Eds.), *Latinos: Remaking America* (Berkeley and London: University of California Press, 2002).

Pessar, P. *A visa for a dream: Dominicans in the United States* (Boston: Allyn & Bacon, 1995).

William Petersen "Migration" in International Encyclopedia of the Social Sciences (New York: Macmillan, 1968).

Phinney, J. "Ethnic Identity in Adolescents and Adults: Review of Research" in P. B. Organista, K. Chun and G. Martin, (Eds.), *Readings in Ethnic Psychology* (New York: Routledge, 1998).

Portes, A. *The New Second Generation.* Special Issue of *International Migration Review* Vol. 28, Winter, 1994.

Portes, A. & Rumbaut, R. *Legacies: The Story of the Immigrant Second Generation* (Berkeley and London: University of California Press. 2001).

Robben, A. *Hitting where it hurts most: The traumatization of Argentine society* (Berkeley: University of California Press, in press).

Roosens, E. *Creating ethnicity: The process of ethnogenesis* (Newbury Park, CA: Sage, 1989).

Rumbaut, R. "Ties that Bind: Immigration and Immigrant Families in the United States." In Booth, A., Crouter, A. & Landale, N., (Ed.), *Immigration and the Family: Research and Policy on U.S. Immigrants* (New Jersey: Lawrence Erlbaum, 1996).

Rumbaut, R. "The New Californians: Comparative Research Findings on the Educational Progress of Immigrant Children," in Rúmbaut, R. & Cornelius, W., (Eds.), *California's Immigrant Children* (La Jolla, CA: Center for US-Mexican Studies, 1995).

Sassen, S. *The Mobility of Labor and Capital* (New York: Cambridge University Press, 1988).

Saxenian, A. *Silicon Valley's New Immigrant Entrepre-*

neurs (San Francisco, CA: Public Policy Institute of California, 1999).

Schlosser, E. *Fast food nation* (Boston: Houghton Miffin, 2001).

Sen, A. "Global doubts." Commencement Address, Harvard University, June 8, 2000.

Simon, J. *The Economic Consequences of Immigration* (Oxford: Basil Blackwell, 1989).

Shweder, R., "What about 'female genital mutilation'?" Daedalus, volume 129, 209-232, 2000.

Steinberg, L., Bradford Brown, B. & Dornbusch, S. *Beyond the Classroom: Why School Reform Has Failed & What Parents Need to Do* (New York: Simon & Schuster, 1996).

Suárez-Orozco, C. "Identities Under Siege" in Robben, A. & Suárez-Orozco, M., (Eds.), *Cultures Under Siege: Collective Violence and Trauma* (New York: Cambridge University Press, 2000).

Suárez-Orozco, M. & Suárez-Orozco, C. *Transformations: Immigration, Family Life and Achievement Motivation Among Latino Adolescents* (Stanford, CA: Stanford University Press, 1995).

Suárez-Orozco, M. & Suárez-Orozco, C. *Children of Immigration* (Cambridge, MA: Harvard University Press, 2001).

Suárez-Orozco, M. *Central American Refugees and U.S. High Schools: A Psychosocial Study of Motivation and Achievement* (Stanford, CA: Stanford University Press, 1989).

Suárez-Orozco, M., (Ed.), *Migration, Minority Status, and Education: European Dilemmas and Responses in the 1990s.* Theme Issue of the *Anthropology and Education Quarterly,* Vol. 22 (2), 1991.

Suárez-Orozco, M. "Anxious Neighbors: Belgium and Its Immigrant Minorities" in Cornelius, W., Martin, P. & Hollifield, J., (Eds.), *Controlling Immigration: A Global Perspective* (Stanford, CA: Stanford University Press, 1994).

Suárez-Orozco, M. "Unwelcome Mats," *Harvard Magazine,* July-August, 1996.

Suárez-Orozco, M. (Ed.) *Crossings: Mexican Immigration in Interdisciplinary Perspectives* (Cambridge MA: David Rockefeller Center for Latin American Studies and Harvard University Press, 1998).

Marcelo M. Suárez-Orozco, "Latin American Immigration to the United States," in Bulmer-Thomas, V. and Dunkerley, J., (Eds.), *The United States & Latin America: The New Agenda* (Cambridge, MA: David Rockefeller Center for Latin American Studies, Harvard University Press, 1999).

Suárez-Orozco, M., Suárez-Orozco, C. & Qin-Hilliard, D., (Eds.), *The New Immigration: Interdisciplinary Perspectives Vol. 1* (New York: Routledge, 2001).

Suárez-Orozco, M., Suárez-Orozco, C. & Qin-Hilliard, D., (Eds.), *The New Immigration: Interdisciplinary Perspectives Vol. 2* (New York: Routledge, 2001).

Suárez-Orozco, M., Suárez-Orozco, C. & Qin-Hilliard, D., (Eds.), *The New Immigration: Interdisciplinary Perspectives Vol. 4.* (New York: Routledge, 2001).

Tsuda, T. "Strangers in the Ethnic Homeland" (Ph.D. diss., University of California at Berkeley, 1996).

Turkle, S. *Life on line: Identity in the age of the internet* (New York: Touchstone, 1997).

U.S. Bureau of the Census, *Profile of the Foreign-Born Population in the United States: 1997* (Washington, DC: Current Population Reports, 1999).

Waldinger, R. "Social Capital or Social Closures?-Immigrant Networks in the Labor Market," (Los Angeles: Lewis Center for Regional Policy Studies, University of California, Los Angeles, Working Paper Series, 26, 1997).

Wikan, U., "Citizenship on trial: Nadia's Case," Daedalus, volume 129, 55-76, 2000.

William Wilson, *When Work Disappears: The World of the New Urban Poor* (New York: Vintage Books, 1997).

World Bank, "Assessing Globalization" http://www.worldbank.org/html/extdr/pb/globalization/paper1.htm.

Zentella, A. "'Latin' languages and identities." In Suárez-

Orozco, M. & Páez, M., (Eds.), *Latinos: Remaking America* (Berkeley: University of California Press, in press).

Zhou, M., & Gatewood, J. "Introduction." In M. Zhou & J. Gatewood, (Eds.), *Contemporary Asian America: A multidisciplinary reader* (pp. 1-46). (New York: New York University Press, 2000).

Notes

1. The term globalization in its current usage is quite broad and lacks well-defined epistemological, theoretical, and empirical boundaries. While the idea of globalization has gained increased circulation in the social sciences and is pregnant with potential—especially for theorizing broad processes of social change from Detroit to Delhi—before its analytic use can be fully mined it is necessary to attend to basic definitional and theoretical matters. Anthropologists, for example, tend to approach the problem of globalization in relation to their long-term interest in culture. Globalization detaches social practices and cultural formations from their traditional moorings in national territories. Globalization decisively undermines the once imagined neat fit between language, culture, and the nation. One hundred years ago European and Euro-American anthropologists took long journeys to remote locations to study exotic social institutions and cultural beliefs. Globalization now delivers the "exotic" to the anthropologist's own back yard. It is in plain sight that Turkish cultural formations—language, marriage, kinship, ritual practices, and so on—are as ubiquitous in parts of Frankfurt as they are in Istanbul. Likewise, Mexican culture is now alive and well in New York City. It can also be suggested that "New York culture" is alive in Puebla, Mexico, via the cash and "social remittances"—that is, the social practices and cultural models immigrants acquire in the new setting and back home. For more on the idea of social remittances see Levitt (2001). Hence we have witnessed over the last decade the emergence of an anthropological taste for such topics as immigration (see Chavez, 1992; Pessar, 1995; Roosens, 1989), transnationalism (see Basch, Schiller, & Blanc, 1994; Gupta & Ferguson, 1992; Mahler, 1995), cultural hybrids (Canclini, 1995 [1989]), delicious dualities (Zentella, in press), and unsettling cultural conflicts (Shweder, 2000; Wikan, 2000), all brought about by globalization. There is a long history to the anthropological involvement with the study of cultural forms and dispersal across time and space. Much of the early literature privileged the study of "culture contact" and "cultural borrowing" via trading, invasions, or conquest. Franz Boas's early efforts, which resulted in the firm establishment of American anthropology as a major scholarly discipline in the early decades of the twentieth century, centered around theoretical debates over the "diffusion" (vs. "multiple invention") of cultural forms (such as a fishing hook, a folk-tale motif, or a kinship term) across distinct "culture areas." This work was critical to the dismantling of earlier extravagant and racist theories of stages in the cultural evolution of societies. Other scholars seem to use the term *globalization* interchangeably with such terms as *transnationalism* or *post-nationality.* Others use globalization to examine themes that in earlier scholarship came under the rubric of "development" or "world systems" theory. Still others use the term as proxy for "*imperialism*" (see Bauman, 1998). Political scientists for their part are focusing on the emergence of international systems (such as human and civil rights) reaching well beyond the confines of individual nation-states. An Argentine torturer who is accused of committing crimes against humanity in his own country can now be arrested in Mexico and tried for crimes against humanity in Spain, as happened in February 2001 (see Robben, in press). Political scientists have also noticed that new deterritorializing processes shape the course of political fortunes in many parts of the world. Peoples in the diaspora—Mexicans in Los Angeles or Dominicans in New York, for example—are emerging as extraordinarily powerful actors across national boundaries. Dual-citizenship agreements—the ability to maintain citizenship rights in more than one nation-state—are complicating and making more interesting the politics of belonging (see Castles & Davidson, 2000). For example, Dominican politicos have long been fully cognizant that election campaigns in their country need to be waged in New York—where Dominicans are now the largest immigrant group—as much as in Santo

Domingo. Mexican politicians have taken longer to wake up to the new global game, but in late December 2000 newly elected President Vicente Fox spent a day at Mexico's busy northern border personally welcoming some of the immigrants returning home for Christmas, performing and telecasting a new strategic approach to *paisanos* living in the United States. Under the Fox administration the nearly eight million Mexicans living in the United States are no longer an afterthought, or worse, an embarrassment, to Mexican national pride. A rough formula: a million people in the diaspora translates to about a billion dollars in remittances sent home every year. This helps explain the new-found interest among Mexican politicians in cultivating ties with their brothers and sisters living in the United States. The old adage "all politics is local" is now somewhat anachronistic.

2. My claim is that nation-states are responding to processes of globalization by displaying new forms of hyper-presence and hyper-absence. Much has been written about how globalization undermines the workings of the nation-state—from national economies, to traditional ideas of citizenship and cultural production (see Castles & Davidson, 2000; Sassen, 1988). In some important ways, states indeed appear hyper-absent *qua* the forces of globalization—as, for example, when billions of dollars enter and exit national boundaries with the agents of the state having little say over the course of this cash flow. On the other hand, states are responding to globalization by hyper-displays of power and theatrics. Arguably the most globalized spot in the world today, which is also, alas, the most heavily trafficked international border in the world, is the vast region that at once unites and separates the United States and Mexico. It is also the most heavily guarded border in history (Andreas, 2000). The militarization of the border at a time of record border crossings suggests a process more complex than the simple erosion or demise of the nation-state. In the places that matter, i.e., where states bump into each other, hyper-presence is the name of the game. This is the case in the United States, in post-Schengen Europe and in Japan. (As per the Schengen agreement, there are no longer internal border-controls among European Union member states. Hence, a French citizen needs no passport or visa to travel to Spain and vice-versa). While internally, Europe has become borderless, external controls—i.e., keeping would-be migrants from outside Europe have intensified. To claim that the state is waning is to miss one of the more delicious paradoxes of state performance.

3. According to the World Bank, a "growing share of what countries produce is sold to other foreigners as exports. Among rich or developed countries the share of international trade in total output (exports plus imports of goods relative to GDP) rose from 27 to 39 percent between 1987 and 1997. For the developing countries it rose from 10 to 17 percent." (World Bank 2001: 1). Likewise, foreign direct investment, that is firms making investments in other countries, overall "more than tripled between 1988 and 1998 from US$ 192 billion to US$ 610 billion"(ibid). From the time the reader woke up this morning to the time she goes to bed tonight, over a trillion dollars will have crossed national boundaries (Friedman, 2000). The archetypical American car, the Chevrolet Camaro, is now a thoroughly globalized product. It is built nowhere and everywhere—with capital, labor, and parts literally originating in multiple continents. It is a car "on the move," so to speak, from its very conception. The global market is also generating global tastes. McDonald's now is Brazil's largest employer (Schlosser, 2001). Market forces seduce and manipulate in even the most remote parts of the world with stunning results.

4. Yet another paradox of globalization is that as it unites it deeply divides the world between those who can access and manipulate the new technologies and those who are left behind; "stuck," so to speak, in local contexts (Bauman, 1998).

5. See, *inter alia*, Sassen, Saskia, *The Mobility of Labor and Capital.* (New York: Cambridge University Press, 1988).

6. In Zhou and Gatewood's (2000) excellent summary,

> Globalization perpetuates emigration from developing countries in two significant ways. First,... capital investments into developing countries transform the economic and occupational structures in these countries by disproportionately targeting production for export and taking advantage of raw material and cheap labor.

7. See, for example, Bauman, Z. (1998). *Globalization: The Human Consequences.* New York: Columbia University Press; Dussel, E. P. (2000). *Polarizing Mexico: The*

impact of liberalization. New York: Lynne Rienner.

8. See for example *Profile of the Foreign-Born Population in the United States: 1997* (Washington, DC: U.S. Bureau of the Census, Current Population Reports, 1999).

9. See Portes, A. and R. Rumbaut, *Legacies: The Story of the Immigrant Second Generation.* (Berkeley and London: University of California Press. 2001).

10. See "Wanted: American Physicists," *New York Times*, July 23, 1999, p. A27. Of course not all of these foreign-born physics graduate students are immigrants—some will indeed return to their countries of birth while others will surely go on to have productive scientific careers in the U.S.

11. See for example, George Borjas, "Assimilation in Cohort Quality Revisited: What Happened to Immigrant Earnings in the 1980s?" *Journal of Labor Economics* 13, no. 2: 211-245.

12. See for example Alejandro Portes, *The New Second Generation,* especially pp. 1-15.

13. See Gary Orfield, "Commentary." in Marcelo M. Suarez-Orozco and Mariela Paez, eds. *Latinos: Remaking America* (Berkeley and London: University of California Press, 2002).

14. See William Wilson, *When Work Disappears: The World of the New Urban Poor* (New York: Vintage Books, 1997).

15. I concur with Alejandro Portes when he argues that we can no longer assume that new immigrants will assimilate into a coherent mainstream. He articulates a critical question that is now in the minds of many observers of immigration:

> The question today is to what sector of American society will a particular immigrant group assimilate? Instead of a relatively uniform 'mainstream' whose mores and prejudices dictate a common path of integration, we observe today several distinct forms of adaptation. One of them replicates the time-honored portrayal of growing acculturation and parallel integration into the white middle class. A second leads straight in the opposite direction to permanent poverty and assimilation to the underclass. Still a third associates rapid economic advancement with deliberate preservation of the immigrant community's values and tight solidarity (Alejandro Portes, *The New Second Generation*).

16. See Douglas Massey & Nancy Denton, *American Apartheid* (Cambridge, MA: Harvard University Press, 1993).

17. See Carola Suárez-Orozco, "Identities Under Siege" in A. Robben and M. M. Suárez-Orozco, eds., *Cultures Under Siege: Collective Violence and Trauma* (New York: Cambridge University Press, 2000).

18. For an overview of recent research on immigration and family ties see Suárez-Orozco, Suárez-Orozco and Qin-Hilliard vol. 4. 2001; see also Ruben Rumbaut, "Ties that Bind: Immigration and Immigrant Families in the United States." In A. Booth, A.C. Crouter, and N. Landale, eds., *Immigration and the Family: Research and Policy on U.S. Immigrants* (New Jersey: Lawrence Erlbaum, 1996). See also Carola and Marcelo Suárez-Orozco, *Transformations: Immigration, Family Life and Achievement Motivation Among Latino Adolescents* (Stanford, CA: Stanford University Press, 1995) and Celia Falicov, *Latino Families in Therapy: A Guide to Multicultural Practice* (New York: Guilford, 1998). For overview of immigrant optimism and achievement orientation, see Grace Kao and M. Tienda, "Optimism and Achievement: The Educational Performance of Immigrant Youth." *Social Science Quarterly,* 96 (1995): 1-19.

19. See Carola Suárez-Orozco and Marcelo M. Suárez-Orozco, *Children of Immigration.*

20. See G. Kao and M. Tienda "Optimism and Achievement: The Educational Performance of Immigrant Youth." *Social Science Quarterly*, 76, No. 1 (1995): 1-19; National Research Council, *From Generation to Generation: The Health and Well-Being of Children in Immigrant Families* (Washington, DC: National Academy Press, 1998); R. Rúmbaut, "The New Californians: Comparative Research Findings on the Educational Progress of Immigrant Children," in R. Rúmbaut and W. Cornelius, eds., *California's Immigrant Children* (La Jolla, CA: Center for US-Mexican Studies, 1995); Steinberg, L., B. Bradford Brown and Sanford Dornbusch, *Beyond the Classroom: Why School Reform Has Failed & What Parents Need to Do* (New York: Simon & Schuster, 1996); and Carola and Marcelo Suárez-Orozco, *Transformations: Immigration, Family Life and Achievement Motivation Among Latino Adolescents* (Stanford, CA: Stanford University Press, 1995).

21. I concur with the Teresa LaFromboise and her colleagues on the need to reconceptualize what they call the "linear model of cultural acquisition." See LaFromboise et al., "Psychological Impact of Biculturalism: Evidence and Theory" in P. B. Organista, K. Chun and G. Martin, eds., *Readings in Ethnic Psychology* (New York: Routledge, 1998).

22. Margaret Gibson articulates a theoretical argument on immigrant transculturation and a calculated strategy of "accommodation without assimilation" in her study of highly successful Sikh immigrants in California. See Margaret Gibson, *Accommodation without Assimilation: Sikh Immigrants in an American High School* (Ithaca, N.Y.: Cornell University Press, 1988). For a theoretical statement on the psychology of ethnic identity and cultural pluralism, see Jean S. Phinney, "Ethnic Identity in Adolescents and Adults: Review of Research" in P.B. Organista, K. Chun and G. Martin, eds., *Readings in Ethnic Psychology* (New York: Routledge, 1998).

23. See for example Nathan Glazer and D.P. Moynahan, *Beyond the Melting Pot* (Cambridge, MA: MIT Press, 1970).

Improving the Health of the Poor

World Health Organization
Commission on Macroeconomics and Health

Technology and politics have thrust the world more closely together than ever before. The benefits of globalization are potentially enormous, as a result of the increased sharing of ideas, cultures, life-saving technologies, and efficient production processes. Yet globalization is under trial, partly because these benefits are not yet reaching hundreds of millions of the world's poor, and partly because globalization introduces new kinds of international challenges as turmoil in one part of the world can spread rapidly to others, through terrorism, armed conflict, environmental degradation, or disease, as demonstrated by the dramatic spread of AIDS around the globe in a single generation.

The world's political leaders have recognized this global interdependence in solemn commitments to improve the lives of the world's poor by the year 2015. The Millennium Development Goals (MDGs) adopted at the Millennium Summit of the United Nations in September 2000, call for a dramatic reduction in poverty and marked improvements in the health of the poor. Meeting these goals is feasible but far from automatic. Indeed, on our current trajectory, those goals will not be met for a significant proportion of the world's poor. Success in achieving the MDGs will require a seriousness of purpose, a political resolve, and an adequate flow of resources from high-income to low-income countries on a sustained and well-targeted basis.

The importance of the MDGs in health is, in one sense, self-evident. Improving the health and longevity of the poor is an end in itself, a fundamental goal of economic development. But it is also a *means* to achieving the other development goals relating to poverty reduction. The linkages of health to poverty reduction and to long-term economic growth are powerful, much stronger than is generally understood. The burden of disease in some low-income regions, especially sub-Saharan Africa, stands as a stark barrier to economic growth and therefore must be addressed frontally and centrally in any comprehensive development strategy. The AIDS pandemic represents a unique challenge of unprecedented urgency and intensity. This single epidemic can undermine Africa's development over the next generation, and may cause tens of millions of deaths in India, China, and other developing countries unless addressed by greatly increased efforts.

Our Report focuses mainly on the low-income countries and on the poor in middle-income countries.[1] The low-income countries, with 2.5 billion people—and especially the countries in sub-Saharan Africa, with 650 million people—have far lower

World Health Organization, "Improving the Health of the Poor." Originally titled "The Executive Summary of the Report, Macroeconomics and Health: Investing in Health for Economic Development," produced by the Commission on Macroeconomics and Health.

Table 1. **Life Expectancy and Mortality Rates, by Country Development Category, (1995-2000)**

Development Category	Population (1999 millions)	Annual Average Income (US Dollars)	Life Expectancy at Birth (years)	Infant Mortality (deaths before age 1 per 1,000 live births)	Under Five Mortality (deaths before age 5 per 1,000 live births)
Least-Developed Countries	643	296	51	100	159
Other Low-Income Countries	1,777	538	59	80	120
Lower-Middle Income Countries	2,094	1,200	70	35	39
Upper-Middle Income Countries	573	4,900	71	26	35
High-Income Countries	891	25,730	78	6	6
Memo: sub-Saharan Africa	642	500	51	92	151

Source: *Human Development Report 2001 Table 8 and CMH calculations using World Development Indicators of the World Bank 2001.*

life expectancies and far higher age-adjusted mortality rates than the rest of the world, as shown in the accompanying Table 1. The same is true for the poor in middle-income countries, such as China. To reduce these staggeringly high mortality rates, the control of communicable diseases and improved maternal and child health remain the highest public health priorities. The main causes of avoidable deaths in the low-income countries are HIV/AIDS, malaria, tuberculosis (TB), childhood infectious diseases, maternal and perinatal conditions, micronutrient deficiencies, and tobacco-related illnesses. If these conditions were controlled in conjunction with enhanced programs of family planning, impoverished families could not only enjoy lives that are longer, healthier, and more productive, but they would also choose to have fewer children, secure in the knowledge that their children would survive, and could thereby invest more in the education and health of each child. Given the special burdens of some of these conditions on women, the well-being of women would especially be improved. The improvements in health would translate into higher incomes, higher economic growth, and reduced population growth.

***

The feasibility of meeting the MDGs in the low-income countries is widely misjudged. On the one side of the debate are those optimists who believe that the health goals will take care of themselves, as a fairly automatic byproduct of economic growth. With the mortality rates of children under 5 in the least-developed countries standing at 159 per 1,000 births, compared with 6 per 1,000 births in the high-income countries,[2] these blithe optimists assume that it's just a matter of time before the mortality rates in the low-income world will converge with those of the rich countries. This is false for two reasons. First, the disease burden itself will slow the economic growth that is presumed to solve the health problems; second, economic growth is indeed important, but is very far from enough....

On the other side of the debate are the pessimists, who underestimate the considerable progress that has been made in health (with the notable exception of HIV/AIDS) by most low-income countries and believe that their remaining high disease burden is a byproduct of corrupt and broken health systems beyond repair in poorly governed low-income countries....

The key recommendation of the Commission is that the world's low- and middle-income countries, in partnership with high-income countries, should scale up the access of the world's poor to essential health services, including a focus on specific interventions. The low- and middle-income countries would commit additional domestic financial resources, political leadership, transparency, and systems for community involvement and accountability, to ensure that adequately financed health systems can operate effectively and are dedicated to the key health problems. The high-income countries would simultaneously commit vastly increased financial assistance, in the form of grants, especially to the countries that need help most urgently, which are concentrated in sub-Saharan Africa. *They would resolve that lack of donor funds should not be the factor that limits the capacity to provide health services to the world's poorest peoples.*

***

Success will require strong political leadership and commitment on the part of countries that can afford to contribute resources as well as from developing countries—in the private and public sectors and in civil society as well. It requires the evolution of an atmosphere of honesty, trust, and respect in donor-recipient interactions. Success requires special efforts precisely in those settings in which health conditions are most troubling and where public sectors are weak. Donor support should be readily forthcoming to help overcome these constraints. Where countries are not willing to make a serious effort, though, or where funding is misused, prudence and credibility require that large-scale funding should not be provided. Even here, though, the record shows that donor assistance can do much to help, by building local capacity and through the involvement of civil society and NGOs. This is a daunting challenge, yet one that is more than ever a strategically relevant objective. Governments and leaders who help stimulate and nurture these actions will be providing a specific antidote to the despair and hatred that poverty can breed.

***

In most middle-income countries, average health spending per person is already adequate to ensure universal coverage for essential interventions. Yet such coverage does not reach many of the poor. Exclusion is often concentrated by region (e.g., rural western China and rural north-east Brazil), or among ethnic and racial minorities. For whatever reason, public-sector spending on health does not attend sufficiently to the needs of the poor....

The Commission examined the evidence relating to organizational requirements for scaling up and some of the key constraints that will have to be overcome. Fortunately, the essential interventions highlighted here are generally not technically exacting. Few require hospitals. Most can be delivered at health centers, at smaller facilities that we refer to as health posts, or through outreach services from these facilities. We call these collectively the *close-to-client (CTC)* system, and this system should be given priority to make these interventions widely accessible....

***

Some recent global initiatives for disease control, including those for TB, leprosy, guinea-worm disease, and Chagas disease, have proved highly successful in delivering quality interventions and, in some cases, changing attitudes and behaviors in some very difficult situations over large geographical areas. An important feature of these initiatives is the inclusion of rigorous systems of monitoring, evaluation, reporting, and financial control as mechanisms for ensuring that objectives are met, problems are detected and corrected, and resources are fully accountable. The result is a growing body of evidence concerning both the degree of progress achieved and the operational and managerial strategies that contribute to success. Lessons from these experiences can provide useful operational guidance, especially for the delivery of interventions at the close-to-client level.

***

A sound global strategy for health will also invest in new knowledge. One critical area of knowledge investment is operational research regarding treatment protocols in low-income countries.[3] There is still much to be learned about what actually works, and why or why not, in many low-income settings, especially where interventions have not been used or documented to date. Even when the basic technologies of disease control are clear and universally applicable, each local setting poses special problems of logistics, adherence, dosage, delivery, and drug formulation that must be uncovered through operational research at the local level....

***

There is also an urgent need for investments in new and improved technologies to fight the killer diseases. Recent advances in genomics, for example, bring us much closer to the long-sought vaccines for malaria and HIV/AIDS, and lifetime protection against TB. The science remains complex, however, and the outcomes unsure. The evidence suggests high social returns to investments in research that are far beyond current levels. Whether or not effective vaccines are produced, new drugs will certainly be needed, given the relentless increase of drug-resistant strains of disease agents. The Commission therefore calls for a significant scaling up of financing for global Research and Development on the heavy disease burdens of the poor....

We need increased investments in other areas of knowledge as well. Basic and applied scientific research in the biomedical and health sciences in the low-income countries needs to be augmented, in conjunction with increased Research and Development aimed at specific diseases. The state of epidemiological knowledge—who suffers and dies and of which diseases—must be greatly enhanced, through improved surveillance and reporting systems.[4] ...Finally, we need a greatly enhanced system of advising and training throughout the low-income countries, so that the lessons of experience in one country can be mobilized elsewhere. The international diffusion of new knowledge and "best practices" is one of the key forces of scaling up, a central responsibility of organizations such as the World Health Organization and the World Bank, and a goal now more readily achieved through low-cost methods available through the internet.

A war against disease requires not only financial resources, sufficient technology, and political commitment, but also a strategy, operational lines of responsibility, and the capacity to learn along the way. The Commission therefore devoted substantial effort to analyzing the organizational practicalities of a massive, donor-supported scaling up of health interventions in the low-income world....

Since scaling up will require a significant increase in international financing, an effective partnership of donors and recipient countries, based on mutual trust and performance, is essential. In this context, the mechanisms of donor financing must change, a point that has been recognized in the international system in the past three years by the creative introduction of a new framework for poverty reduction, often termed the *Poverty Reduction Strategy Paper (PRSP) framework.*[5] ...The strengths of the PRSP include: (1) deeper debt cancellation, (2) country leadership in the preparation of the national strategy, (3) explicit incorporation of civil society at each step of the process, (4) a comprehensive approach to poverty reduction, and (5) more donor coordination in support of country goals. All of these are applicable—indeed vital—to the success of the health initiative proposed here. To achieve the potential benefits of the PRSP framework, donor and recipient countries must specify a sustainable financing scheme and investment plan for the health sector as an integral part of the PRSP scheme for health.

Though we advocate a greatly increased investment in the health sector itself, we stress the need for complementary additional investments in areas with an important impact on poverty alleviation (including effects on health). These include education, water and sanitation, and agricultural improvement....

***

We recommend that each country will need to define an overall program of "essential interventions" to be guaranteed universal coverage through public (plus donor) financing. We suggest four main criteria in choosing these essential interventions: (1) they should be technically efficacious and can be delivered successfully; (2) the targeted diseases should impose a heavy burden on society, taking into account individual illness as well as social spillovers (such as epidemics and adverse economic effects); (3) social benefits should exceed costs of the interventions (with benefits including life-years saved and spillovers such as fewer orphans or faster economic growth); and (4) the needs of the poor should be stressed.

We estimate that by 2010 around 8 million lives *per year,* in principle, could be saved—mainly in the low-income countries—by the essential interventions against infectious diseases and nutritional deficiencies recommended here.[6]

***

It is important to put the total donor assistance into perspective. Although the required assistance is large relative to current donor assistance in health, it would be only around 0.1 percent of donor GNP, and would leave ample room for significant increases in other areas of donor assistance as needed. We stress that the increased aid for health must be additional to current aid flows, since indeed increased aid will be needed not only in health but also in education, sanitation, water supply, and other areas....

This program would yield economic benefits vastly greater than its costs. Eight million lives saved from infectious diseases and nutritional deficiencies would translate into a far larger number of *years* of life saved for those affected, as well as a higher quality of life.... Assuming, conservatively, that each disability-adjusted life years (DALY) saved gives an economic benefit of one year's per capita income of a projected $563 in 2015, the direct economic benefit of saving 330 million DALYs would be $186 billion per year, and plausibly several times that.[7] Economic growth would also accelerate, and thereby the saved DALYs would help to break the poverty trap that has blocked economic growth in high-mortality low-income countries. This would add tens or hundreds of billions of dollars more per year through increased per capita incomes.

***

These financial targets are a vision of what should be done, rather than a prediction of what will happen. We are all too aware of donor countries that neglect their international obligations despite vast wealth, and of recipient countries that abjure the governance needed to save their own people. Maybe little increased funding will take place; donors might give millions when billions are needed, and impoverished countries will fight wars against people rather than disease, making it impossible for the world community to help. We are not naïve: it is no accident that millions of people—voiceless, powerless, unnoticed by the media—die unnecessarily every year.[8]

***

To help channel the increased Research and Development outlays, we endorse the establishment of a new Global Health Research Fund (GHRF), with disbursements of around $1.5 billion per year. This fund would support basic and applied biomedical and health sciences research on the health problems affecting the world's poor and on the health systems and policies needed to address them. Another $1.5 billion per year of Research and Development support should be funded through existing channels....

The public sector cannot bear this burden on its own. The pharmaceutical industry must be a partner in this effort. The corporate principles that have spurred recent and highly laudable programs of drug donations and price discounts need to be generalized to support the scaling up of health interventions in the poor countries. The pharmaceutical industry needs to ensure that low-income countries (and the donors on their behalf) have access to essential medicines at near-production cost (sometimes termed the *lowest viable commercial price*) rather than the much higher prices that are typical of high-income markets. Industry is ready, in our estimation, for such a commitment, enabling access of the poor to essential medicines, both through differential pricing and licensing their products to generics producers.[9] If industry cooperation is not enough or not forthcoming on a general and reliable basis, the rules of international trade involving access to essential medicines should be applied in a manner that ensures the same results....

With globalization on trial as never before, the world must succeed in achieving its solemn commitments to reduce poverty and improve health. The resources—human, scientific, and financial—exist to succeed, but now must be mobilized. As the world embarks on a heightened struggle against the evils of terrorism, it is all the more important that the world simultaneously commit itself to sustaining millions of lives through peaceful means as well, using the best of our modern science and technology and the enormous wealth of the rich countries. This would be an effort that would inspire and unite peoples all over the world. We call upon the leaders of the international community—in donor and recipient nations, in international institutions such as the World Bank, the World Health Organization, the World Trade Organization, the Organisation for Economic Co-operation and Development, and the International Monetary Fund, in private enterprise, and in civil society—to seize the opportunities identified in this report. Now, united, the world can initiate and facilitate the global investments in health that can transform the lives and livelihoods of the world's poor.

Notes

1. The classifications are those used by the Development Assistance Committee of the OECD. There are five categories: least-developed countries, or LDCs, the 48 lowest-development countries as categorized by the United Nations; other low-income countries or OLICs (countries with less than $755 GNP per capita in 1999 that are not LDCs); lower middle-income countries; upper middle income countries; and high-income countries. In the costing exercise we refer to the countries in Table A2.B.

2. United Nations Development Program, Table 8, p. 169.

3. Operational research involves the investigation of health interventions in practice, including issues of patient adherence, toxicity, dosing, and modes and costs of delivery. The goal is to optimize the treatment regimen to local conditions, and to identify how best to integrate the regimen into existing services. The issue of operational research is typically neglected in country programs. We might distinguish two kinds of operational research. Clinical research involves the questions of treatment regimens, such as dosage and toxicity. Nonclinical operational research involves questions of logistics, financial management, cultural aspects of treatment regimens, and other nonclinical dimensions of health-service delivery.

4. One part of surveillance is real-time monitoring of epidemics, which now takes place through the WHO Global Outbreak Alert and Response Network, which interlinks 72 existing networks. Yet the absence of requisite laboratory and epidemiological capacity in many low-income countries is a weakness that requires prompt solution.

5. Donors have called upon low-income countries to prepare a Poverty Reduction Strategy Paper (PRSP),

which is the basis for a sustained and comprehensive attack on poverty supported by donor funding and debt cancellation.

6. Millions more deaths per year would be averted by a dramatic reduction in cigarette smoking as well.

7. Per capita income in the low-income countries is currently around $410 per person per year in 1999. With growth of per capita income equal to 2 percent per annum, this would be $563 per year in 2015. 330 million DALYs would therefore result in a gain of $186 billion. There are good reasons to value each DALY at a multiple of per capita income, however, so that the direct benefits could be twice or more $186 billion. These calculations do not, furthermore, take into account the effects of better health on faster economic growth.

8. Many have asked the Commission what to do if the donor money is not made available—in essence, how to triage with less money. We are asked to prioritize millions of readily preventable deaths per year, since we have already narrowed our focus to a small number of conditions that have an enormous social burden and that have low-cost interventions that are at least partially effective. Not only is this kind of triaging ethically and politically beyond our capacity, but it is also exceedingly hard to do in sensible way. Those who hope for a simple answer, for example to focus on the cheap interventions (immunizations) while putting off the expensive interventions (higher-cost prevention programs and antiretroviral therapy needed to fight AIDS) to a later date, misjudge the practical choices we face. The AIDS pandemic will destroy African economic development unless controlled; to fight measles but not AIDS will not begin to meet Africa's human and economic needs. It would be wrong to go to the other extreme as well, and let the legitimate need to fight AIDS end up starving the cheaper interventions, so we advocate *both.* Moreover, the infrastructure developed to fight AIDS will support the infrastructure needed to fight measles, especially if strengthening such complementarities is explicitly built into the AIDS control effort. It is vastly more fruitful to design and finance a comprehensive program that addresses many critical health needs than to pick and choose the apparently inexpensive items.

9. *Differential pricing* refers to charging different prices in different markets, which are kept separate by physical and regulatory barriers. In this case, differential pricing would involve charging the lowest viable commercial price in the low-income markets, and at the same time charging higher (often patent-protected) prices in the high-income markets.

The Risk of Livelihood Conflicts and the Nature of Policy Measures Required

Leif Ohlsson
University of Goteborg

Poverty increasingly is caused by environmental scarcities of arable land and water, resulting in loss of livelihoods. A common denominator for causes of conflict in many recent internal wars is the loss of livelihoods resulting in young men being unable to reach the positions in life earlier generations of men could expect. Policy attempts to break the vicious path to conflict need to address both poverty and environmental issues. Reconstruction of exhausted environmental resources will work towards both these ends. Strategies for accomplishing this, however, crucially need to take a human rights framework as their point of departure.

This piece is built on the—perhaps self-evident—observation that the common denominator for many, if not most, of the internal wars and conflict plaguing Africa, South Asia, and Latin America during the last decade, is poverty as a result of *loss of livelihoods*, in turn often caused or exacerbated by environmental degradation.

Empirically, it has been difficult to establish that either poverty *or* environmental factors, in and by themselves, are strong determinants of conflict. I will argue that loss of livelihood constitutes an often missing link in explanations of current conflict patterns, and that an exposition of this link will bring out the full salience of both poverty *and* environment. (The elimination of poverty, and environmental reconstruction, needless to say, remain first-order goals *per se*, not requiring further grounds for policy action.)

While poverty may be a near-endemic condition in certain societies, loss of livelihood marks a rapid transition from a previously stable condition of relative welfare into a condition of poverty or destitution. It is this *rapid process of change*, resulting in a sudden and unexpected fall into poverty, more than the endemic condition of poverty, which creates the potential for what here will be termed *livelihood conflicts*.

A common feature of many such contemporary livelihood conflicts is that the rank and file of most atrocious militias around the world are filled by large cohorts of young men, who have been subjected to a rapid devaluation of their expectations as a result of loss of family livelihoods. These young men have been forced to accept a much more lowly position in society than the dominant ideology of their culture has led them to take for granted that they were entitled to by their gender.

Young women form a much smaller, if any, part of these militias. As a consequence of loss of family livelihoods they instead commonly first have to forgo their school in order to help out at home; later they take on the role of family providers themselves in subsistence agriculture. Loss of livelihoods in subsistence agriculture predominantly undermines the social security of women and their dependants, children and ageing family members. In livelihood conflicts women regularly become the first victims, and the first to lose their livelihoods.

Contemporary losses of livelihoods in the world have many causes, some of them amenable to immediate policy changes, while others are not. These latter cases have to be met by addressing the challenges they pose. Developing countries are particularly severly challenged by the social consequences resulting from a scarcity of job opportunities in relation to the number required (as a result of the unavoidable part of the population increase to come).

Failures to meet these challenges create opportunities for extremely vile political forces. In Kosovo, both the KLA and Slobodan Milosevic managed to mobilize popular support at a rate they would never otherwise have been able to, if poverty, unemployment, and environmental degradation had not spread at such a rapid rate during the decades preceding the open conflict.

The losses of livelihood resulting from environmental scarcities of arable land and water form a special case of increasing importance. Although now, at the turn of the century, roughly half the human population are living in cities, agriculture is still by far the largest single source of livelihoods and income. Losses of those livelihoods as a result of environmental scarcities of arable land and water demonstratively was one of the major factors enabling the *genocidaires* of Rwanda to mobilize a large part of the population as perpetrators in the first fullblown genocide after the Holocaust, and environmental scarcities remain a driving force for mobilizing the foot-soldiers of many, if not most, of the on-going livelihood conflicts.

Agriculture forms the economic and material base for livelihoods also in cities, as well as for the larger part of present poverty elimination policies. A basic productive resource for agriculture, water and competition for scarce water resources has been portrayed as a source of international conflict. Nations, however, and the international system have learned to manage this threat. There is now a growing consensus that water scarcity will not create wars between nations—but there is also a growing certitude that water scarcity may work in a direction to exacerbate the basic conditions that fuel livelihood conflicts, particularly as countries go through the crucial transition period between dependence on agriculture and a modern society, based on economic growth in cities.

The argument put forward in what follows is that a great and increasing scarcity of healthy, productive eco-systems in the world today seems to run parallel to an equally great and unused asset made up by all those women and men who have suffered losses of livelihood due to environmental destruction or unsustainable agriculture. Juxtaposing these two glaring facets of poverty and environment offers a potential for conflict prevention, poverty elimination *and* environmental reconstruction.

Policy measures to accomplish these ends, however, often run counter to mainstream economic logics, and therefore have to be grounded in a welfare-state logic and a human-rights framework. If this appears overly idealistic, we would do well to remember that welfarism and human rights is what underpins the entire work of the U.N., and of most of the work done by international aid and development cooperation agencies.

The Environment-Poverty-Conflict-Hunger Nexus

A delimitation of the field to be treated in the following pages would start with the classical Malthusian concern of whether the food-producing capacity of the agricultural system on the planet will suffice to feed still growing populations, who are getting—or, hopefully, will get—better lives, thereby requiring more food, as well as better food. The last factor—increased dependence on animal protein—weighs particularly heavy in this threefold increase of pressure on agricultural systems.

Although the food-producing sector of global agricultural systems has made fantastic progress during the last decades—managing to provide a doubling population with more to eat per capita on average—yields and production are no longer increasing at previous rates. Estimates of how much global food production has to increase by 2030 in order to give everybody sufficient nourishment vary between 50 percent and 100 percent, i.e., possibly another doubling. The jury is still out on whether this is at all possible, as well as on whether it will in fact happen.

More interesting though, the issue of potential supply constraints is quickly superseded by a more immediate bottle-neck, namely the question of whether social systems will be able to provide growing populations with adequate food under conditions of rapid social change. Here, the verdict is fairly clear and unambiguous: Close to 800 million people are not getting enough food, or the right kind of food, even to sustain minimum requirements for healthy growth.

There is an increasing consensus that the number of hungry people in the world does not, taken by itself, indicate a failure of the production system, i.e., supply-side constraints. It should rather be undstood as reflecting a demand deficiency. To put it simply, the farmers of this world have never grown food in order to demonstrate how much is possible to produce. They grow to satisfy a current economic demand. Eight hundred million hungry people go hungry in the world because they are indeed invisible to the economic system; they are too poor to buy the food that the agricultural system might—or might not—be able to produce.

This is the link between hunger and poverty, which also forms the rationale of the present focus on poverty deprivation within all international agencies. Here, the goal was set five years ago by two large families of international organizations, the FAO family dealing with agricultural production, and the UNDP family, dealing with poverty issues. The objective agreed upon was that the number of hungry people, as well as the number of utterly poor people were to be halved by 2015. This was the firm commitment of the world's governments in 1996.

Today, five years later, it is evident that we are simply not doing it. The number of hungry people is diminishing, but not quickly enought to meet the goal set in 1996. At the present rate of decrease, the number of hungry people in the world will be halved by 2030, at the earliest, and the main reason why the number of hungry people is not decreasing fast enough is that work to reach the concommittant goal of reducing poverty is progressing at an excruciatingly slow rate.

Scholars studying the grounds and reasons for this failure quickly find themselves returning to constraints within the agricultural sector, albeit in a more roundabout way. There is a growing consensus that a significant portion of the failure to reduce poverty (and thereby hunger) is caused by loss of, or failures to create and sustain, livelihoods within the agricultural sector (not least among smallholders).

Causal explanations for this, in turn, are sought for within three large fields. The two first reflect the supply-demand dichotomy, namely constraints of environmental nature, and dysfunctions in the macro-economic system of trading agricultural products. The third field contains the most malignant cause of loss of livelihoods, namely internal conflicts now devastating an increasing number of developing countries.

Environmental constraints include serious scarcities of arable land and water, climate change threatening agricultural productivity, depletion of soils due to unsustainable practices (both in large-scale industrial and smallholders subsistence farming), and loss of biodiversity as a result of all these factors combined.

Trade-related problems belong squarely within the sector of social system failure, and is reflected in the vociferous debate on WTO agreements and the consequences of neoliberal globalization, from Seattle and onwards.

Conflicts, finally, clearly account for the most visible signs of loss of livelihoods as a cause of poverty and hunger. In war-torn countries like Angola, Afghanistan, Congo, Sierra Leone, parts of Nigeria, and Ethiopia/Eritrea, people become displaced to the tune of millions in a single country, cut off from their sources of livelihoods by marauding militias or wide-spread minefields, become unable to support themselves and increasingly turn dependent on international aid—if and when such aid is able to get through.

The insidious part of these "new kinds of conflicts," however, is that they not only result in loss of livelihoods, but also to a significant part are caused by losses of livelihoods, which, in turn, are caused by environmental scarcities. In what follows, this particular causal path, and some of its intricacies, will be traced, starting from a short exposition of what is known about environmental factors as a cause of conflict.

Beyond the Poverty-Environment Controversy

The quest for explanatory clarity sometimes creates unwarranted and counterproductive controversies, such as, for example, whether poverty *or* environmental degradation is *the* major source of conflict. Such disputes, I believe, arise from a misunderstanding of what the scientific need of studying a limited number of variables at a time entails.

If two studies, each pursuing explanations of conflicts and the causal mechanisms leading up to them from different independent variables (e.g., "poverty" or "environment"), are poised against each other, the resulting controversy may become extremely counterproductive, on at least three grounds: i) explanatory pathways departing from "poverty" and "environment," respectively, are best viewed as complementary rather than contesting; ii) further studies may very likely reveal that poverty as well as environmental degradation work together in common or parallell causal mechanisms; iii) if so, the needs of policy-making for a rich variety of explanations are ill served by poising the two sets of explanations and causal pathways against each other.

For explanations on a higher level, which would bring two independent, already exhaustively studied, variables, such as "poverty" and "environment," together in a new explanatory pathway, other sets of intervening variables may have to be explored in equal depth. Choosing those variables customarily requires the researcher to step back and take a broader, as yet not fully substantiated, view.

In that sense, this study is very much exploratory. It builds on the reasonable, yet so far unsubstantiated, supposition that there are important causal mechanisms linking *both* poverty and environmental factors to conflict. The study promotes, as an hypothesis, that "livelihoods" would be a hitherto missing link in formulating such mechanisms.

The main argument is constructed on the concept *environmental scarcity*, and the rich amount of research emerging from it (Homer-Dixon 1999). Environmental scarcity denotes the social effects of the combined impacts of i) *environmental degradation* shrinking the total size of an imagined environmental "resource pie," e.g., arable land or an aquifer; ii) *population increase* shrinking the size of the equitably alloted "slices" of the resource pie; and iii) *unequal resource access* allowing powerful segments of the population to access inequitably large amounts of resource slices in a process of "resource capture," resulting in ecological marginalization and loss of livelihoods for large and relatively powerless groups of the population.

The end results of this vicious circle entailed by growing environmental scarcities are vastly increased social inequalities, a rapid increase of economically marginalized people, and, as a consequence of threatened livelihoods, the involuntary need of those marginalized from that point and onwards to utilize resources unsustainably. The conflict mechanisms put in motion by this process include relative deprivation and the strengthening of bonds along ethnic, linguistic, national or regional fault lines prevalent in almost all societies, but not gaining full salience until livelihoods are threatened in rapid, and sometimes dramatic, processes of change.

The concept "environmental scarcity" is uniquely applicable for linking poverty and environmental factors in causal pathways leading to conflict, since it comprises economic, environmental and social factors. It is also well suited from a policy-making point of view, since the causal mechanisms leading to conflict predicted by the environmental-scarcity model posit that the state, and, more precisely, state legitimacy, will be the first target of frustrations created by loss of livelihoods caused by environmental scarcities.

The Economic Logic of Militia Livelihoods

In the late nineties the search for the causal mechanisms behind internal wars was extended to include frustrated expectations, among excluded élites as well as marginalized segments of the population. In a seminal article, "The Economic Functions of Violence in Civil Wars," David Keen (1998) maintains that internal wars, pervasive to many parts of the developing world, ought not to be understood as inherently "irrational." Instead, the chaos created by internal wars is readily exploited for economic purposes by segments of the élite whose aspirations to climb to a powerful position in society have been stymied by competing élites.

Wars, according to Keen, constitute more than the commonly understood breakdown of the social order. Wars are also a means for creating new systems for profits, power, and even security of a kind. In areas controlled by warlords new kinds of war economies are brought into existence, each with its own particular logic.

This view offers an explanation to the persistence and longevity of internal wars, since winning, in fact, may not be a goal of any of the respective combatants. The objective of wars, such as they have become transformed during the later part of the last century, may be exactly to attain legitimacy for actions that in peacetime would be considered as crimes. In other words: Fuelling internal wars has become a means to the end of outright criminal activities.

This analysis also throws some light on the immense difficulties facing the international community in bringing these devastating conflicts to an end. A tacit and common understanding underpinning such attempts is that both parties to an internal war supposedly share an interest in ending their strife. Keen's argument is that the warring parties instead may have a strong common interest in keeping the war going.

This, however, does not preclude meaningful attempts of international peace-making. The war objectives of the parties to the conflict may turn out to be remarkably similar: survival, power, a life filled with more excitement than a peaceful existence might offer, and, perhaps more important than all of the above, economic advantages. The key to peace-making is to build societies where such common goals may be attained by peace rather than by war. Easier said than done, it nevertheless puts the focus squarely on livelihoods, and peace-time sources for livelihoods.

Keen's analysis would seem to be amply born out by an analysis of the role of diamonds in the internal wars of Angola, Sierra Leone and Liberia; the role of narcotics in countries as far apart as Afghanistan and Colombia; and the role of mineral wealth in the "seven-nation war" in DR Congo. Although none of this at first sight would seem to have any bearing whatsoever on environmental scarcities of renewable resources—rather the opposite, since the internal wars in developing countries, if anything, seem to be about non-renewable resources—there is a common important link which does not become visible until loss of livelihoods is brought into the picture.

The missing link is found by looking for the factors which make it possible to mobilize such large numbers of foot-soldiers in the militias of the warlords of this world. No presumptive warlord, however charismatic or ruthless, could ever hope to gain a substantive following of the necessary number of foot-soldiers, unless there already exists in society a sufficiently large number of not only poor, but in addition fairly recently deprived, young men. There is no larger single source of such deprivation in the world today, than scarcities of arable land, forcing young men to migrate to cities in search of livelihoods.

Unemployed young men, in cities as well as in rural areas, become easy targets for hate-propaganda directed at easily identifiable ethnic, linguistic, national or regional cleavages in their particular society. From there it is but a short step to accept the promise of a salary—and the prospective of looting—held out by joining one or another militia under a powerful emerging leader. In Rwanda, employment in the state administration, in the army, or—at the end—in the murderous militias was virtually the only way for a young man to attain his expectations. The prize he had to pay was undivided loyalty to the instigators of genocide. Similarly, in the Westbank and Gaza, fully a quarter of the available jobs are provided by the Palestinian authority, and half of those are in the security or police forces.

Young women may be equally susceptible to hate propaganda; their gendered role, however, rather prescribes for them to abandon all expectations of even getting started towards bettering their lives. As an example, in the West Bank and Gaza employment rates are a low 66 percent for men, but an excruciatingly low—even for the region—12 percent for women.

In rural areas, young women are the first to be forced out of school when the livelihood of families requires that they help out at home, carrying water, chopping wood or tilling the soil. Very soon, they will find themselves in charge of providing not only for a husband who has migrated to the nearest city, but also a growing number of children, in addition to ageing parents and in-laws. When conflict breaks out, they will be the first to find themselves robbed of the fruit of their toil, frequently abused and abducted, and finally forced to find refuge for themselves and their dependants in the camps of a growing number of internally displaced persons.

Against this backdrop, there would seem to be few more pressing issues than finding the means to stem this vicious circle of conflict and violence by attempts to safeguard as much as possible of peace-time livelihoods, and the environmental resources on which they build, in poor countries with still high population increases. There is no such source more important than agriculture, crucially dependent on healthy ecosystems and undepleted environmental resources of arable land and water.

Livelihood Conflicts Created by Agricultural Failure

The link between loss of peace-time livelihoods and conflict is presented by de Soysa & Gleditsch et al. in their (1999) article, "To Cultivate Peace: Agriculture in a World of Conflict." Reviewing the research on links between environment and conflict, they arrive at a common denominator for the intra-state wars of the 90s:

> Most of the armed conflicts, whether domestic or international, are concentrated in regions heavily dependent on agriculture, such as South Asia, Central Africa, and parts of Latin America. In countries that have a low dependence on agriculture [...], we find only a handful of conflicts. Indeed, only five out of sixty-three states who exhibit a low dependence on agriculture have suffered armed conflict after the Cold War.
>
> —(de Soysa & Gleditsch et al. 1999, p. 17)

The authors cite several cases in Africa, South Asia, South and Central America, the Middle East and elsewhere, where a conflict analysis reveals clear connections between issues related to agriculture and the origin of an armed conflict. In spite of such sometimes clear links, the authors are very careful not to infer an overall causal link between heavy dependence on agriculture and the incidence of armed conflict.

Instead they argue strongly for the missing link being *poverty*, defined as "the lack of physical, human, and social capital." The lack of these factors generates conditions which are unfavorable for development, and hence for peace:

> The conflict-producing conditions that may emanate from acricultural and rural issues, such as land tenure conflcts, are manifestations of the incapacity of social and political systems to handle such crises. Moreover, capricious politics are likely to create conditions of underdevelopment such as low economic growth and simultaneously cause the extreme grievances that drive individuals and groups to take up arms. (ibid. p. 18)

I would argue that the authors have indeed found a missing link, but that the missing link connecting poverty to conflicts is best captured, not by simply designating it as poverty *per se*, but by a slightly more elaborated approach aimed at capturing certain aspects of the large processes of change going on in the world. A three-step delineation of such a "livelihood conflicts" approach might look like this:

1) Departing from the de Soysa & Gleditsch et al., the hypothesis would be that poverty indeed is an important conflict-generating factor; not however as much the *state* of poverty, as the *rapid falling into poverty*.

   Rapid processes of pauperization, in turn, may be identified in the widely acknowledged trend of rapidly *increasing inequalities*, both within and between countries. For analytical purposes this trend may be distinguished into i) an unprecedented and welcome gain in welfare for larger groups of people than ever, but also ii) equally rapid and deleterious processes of *deprivation* and *marginalization*.

   Building on this, conflict-generating mechanisms therefore should be sought for in processes that i) *rapidly make* people poor; and/or ii) results in *increased inequality* in a society or community.

2) The overall and almost self-evident reason *why* people are pauperized at an unprecedented rate is that they lose or are unable to attain *livelihoods.*

   In order to understand the magnitude and character of the challenges for policy-making, the research effort arguably therefore ought to be directed at describing in detail the major *reasons* why so many people are losing or find themselves unable to attain livelihoods.

3) Agriculture traditionally has been the *single largest source of livelihoods.* The present difficulties of agriculture to sustain this role therefore should be described and researched. Two levels of investigation may be identified:

   i) The failure of agriculture as an economic sector to *absorb still growing populations*, who instead increasingly have to search for livelihoods in urban areas; and the social consequences of that failure, including risks of conflict.

   ii) The part of the reasons why agriculture no longer can fulfill its traditional role that stems from *environmental factors*, such as degeneration of arable land and ecosystems in general as a result of unsustainable practices; and the social consequences of those practices.

The concept *livelihood conflicts* thus would include, although not be restricted to, what has previously been investigated as "environmental conflicts" (environmental conflicts, in fact, could be regarded as a special case of livelihood conflicts).

The core concept of this approach is *livelihoods*; the process in focus is *loss of livelihoods*; the delimitation is to study loss of livelihoods in *agriculture* (with specialized studies carried out with a further sub-limitation, namely the loss of livelihoods in agriculture due to *environmental factors*); and the final goal of the approach is to identify and describe the *mechanisms* whereby loss of livelihoods in agriculture could lead to *livelihood conflicts*, as demonstrated by past or present cases.

From a policy point of view a particular task would be to identify, from such research and other sources of knowledge, the role that the *reconstruction of environmental assets* could play in *creating and sustaining livelihoods*, in order to avoid the vicious circle of loss of livelihoods, poverty, environmental degradation, and the ensuing risks of livelihood conflicts.

Much of the rationale for a livelihood conflicts approach is well captured by de Soysa & Gleditsch et al. Compare for their description of the conflicts in West Africa:

> The wars in Liberia and Sierra Leone, for example, can be viewed as emanating from subsistence crises. Indeed, many of the state failures emanate from the inability of these weak states to provide the basic needs of people. High numbers of unemployed youth [*sic!*] in the cities and the countryside are ready combatants within various criminal insurgency groups that form to battle over the control of resources and whatever state power is left intact. (ibid. p. 19)

Here, a remark is necessary—the ungendered identification of unemployed "youth" as the main culprits is seriously misleading. Young women and girls are not found in "high numbers" among the "various criminal insurgency groups." Those that are found, generally have been brought there by abduction, and they are forced to accept roles as carriers, cooks, servants for militias, and sex-slaves for militia commanders.

The "ready combatants" that "battle over the control of resources and whatever state power is left intact" are first and foremost young men and boys, some of which tragically also has been abducted and forced to join the growing ranks of child soldiers in the world, but others having joined readily at the promise of looting and plundering, as a direct result of loss of livelihoods:

> The new conflicts may be traced to the loss of livelihood, the hopelessness of surviving at the margins, and the alternative life of crime and banditry. The bulk of the rural population seems to be non-participant victims rather than the active and passive supporters of utopian revolution.[...] Ironically, the foot soldiers of much of the armed violence today might just be trying to stay alive. (ibid. p 19)

Here, the authors, without making the connection explicit, in fact provide material salient to the controversy touched upon earlier, whether the apparent focus in many on-going livelihood conflicts on non-renewable resources, such as gold and diamonds, and illegal activities, such as drug-trading, does not in fact constitute a refutation of the hypothesis that renewable resources and environmental factors play an important role in conflict-creating mechanisms. This controversy is sometimes captioned "need or greed": Is the main reason for the present pattern of conflict destitution and poverty, or is it the opportunity to enrich oneself by, e.g., illegal diamond trading?

In a livelihood-conflicts approach the apparent contradiction between the two parts of the question would be possible to transcend. Young men do not (at least not in significant numbers) regularly seek immediate rewards in illegal activities and looting, as long as the society they live in can provide livelihoods (usually based on agriculture, renewable resources, and depending on healthy ecosystems) and a social position which they have been culturally taught to expect as men in that society.

When such expectations are frustrated, however, young men *in particular* (since their gendered roles have taught them to expect more of life as their birthright) become easy targets for the attempts by political forces serving their own purposes to mobilize them also for extremely violent actions, in pursuit of easy gains (often based on control over and exploitation of non-renewable resources and illegal trade).

Young women, on the other hand, most often long before that have had their expectations of a better life stymied from the start, by having had to leave school early (or not attending at all) as a result of having to assist in sustaining family livelihood, or by a culturally prescribed role as providers (in subsistence agriculture), not only of their own new and growing family, but also of a husband who may have migrated to the nearest city, as well as of elderly dependants. As a consequence, they are particularly vulnerable to environmental effects degrading their main source of livelihood, agriculture.

The authors cite many cases of present or past conflicts (e.g., Somalia, Uganda, DR Congo, Malawi, Republic of Kongo, and others), which would merit to be fleshed out in full-blown case-studies according to a livelihood-conflicts approach. In addition, one or several null cases (where large-scale open conflict has not yet broken out, despite widespread loss of livelihoods and/or ravaging environmental degradation) would be needed for methodological stringency.

The case of India would seem to be such a case. It is commonly noted that in India poverty for a long time seems to have been compatible with relative stability. India therefore is often discussed as an example of culture's mitigating role; the social ability of creating a culture of "spreading poverty equally" (although this "equal spreading" of course never applied to the extremely rich in India).

The crucial test for the validity of the approach in the case of India would be to apply it to developments in the immediate decade to come, when successful economic growth is creating a whole new prosperous middle class—and inequalities thus increase rapidly—while environmental destruction still is rampant.

According to the livelihood conflicts approach, the critical factor would not necessarily be increased inequalities as such, but the point when increased inequalities and/or environmental degradation lead to the further marginalization of large segments of populations, whether this is caused by marginal groups losing their present livelihoods, or by new generations never managing to attain livelihoods in the first place. If the Indian society manages to avoid this pitfall, the conflict potential, according to the presented hypothesis, might still be kept within bounds. If, however, further rapid marginalization occurs, the conflict potential would increase.

Below, three further sketches are provided of how livelihood conflicts could be portrayed. The order is chosen to form a progression from loss of livelihoods making ethnic cleavages more salient (Kosovo); over scarcity of agricultural land creating conditions that ultimately facilitated genocide (Rwanda); to the imperative of creating jobs in cities experienced by water-scarce societies (Egypt).

The Case of Kosovo—Loss of Livelihoods Fueling Extremism

In 1976 the per-capita income in the province of Kosovo was 86 percent of Jugoslavia's average, with a positive trend. Even the most out-of-reach villages were connected to the power-grid and enjoyed piped water. Ninety-five percent of children in Kosovo were enrolled in elementary schools. Life expectancy had gone up to sixty-eight years, due mainly to the number of doctors having increased to one per 2,009 people, up from one per 8,527 in 1952. (All data from Kaufmann 1999.)

The rapid population increase, which is to be expected from such a benign development, in addition to an overly large dependence on heavy industry, and in combination with increasing land scarcity, and land degradation, led to a very rapidly increasing unemployment. The unemployment rate rose from 19 percent in 1971 to 28 percent in 1981, 56 percent in 1989, and 70 percent in 1995.

In 1999 there were two million people in Kosovo, a doubling since 1960. The rate of annual population increase was 2.1 percent, which exceeded economic growth. It is also a higher rate than in many developing countries.

The biological productivity of Kosovo's 10,000 square kilometers previously has been much higher than it is today. Forests have been cut down as a result of land scarcity. Cities have great problems with waste management. A large part of the persistent environmental problems have their origin in the out-dated heavy industrial infrastructure. (The closure of the Mitrovica smelter for environmental reasons by the UNMIK forces is a good example here.)

Kaufmann (1999) argues that the environmental destruction in Kosovo was utilized by the Kosovo-Albanians as an argument against Jugoslav rule (although other parts of Jugoslavia were equally polluted). In other aspects as well, Kaufmann's main argument runs parallel to the livelihood conflict approach.

The discontent that finally led to open conflict in Kosovo was created by poverty, in turn caused by unemployment due to industrial decline. Other sources of fresh livelihoods were limited by land scarcity and degradation, in turn creating conflicts over land-rights. The discontent caused by poverty led to increased politicization of relations between the two main ethnic groups. This, in turn, enabled both KLA and Slobodan Milosevic to mobilize support for their extreme policies to a degree they would otherwise never have been able to.

In traditional analyses, the ethnic aspect of conflicts is often highlighted. Conveniently forgotten here is the fact the two or more ethnic groups may lead perfectly harmonious lives together for long periods—as long as society is able to satisfy the welfare demands of all citizens. When this no longer was feasible in Kosovo, traditional analyses concentrate on the "apartheid" system of job redistribution created by the Serbs. Conveniently forgotten then, is the fact that internal population increase was responsible for the greater part of unemployment.

A livelihood-conflict approach thus would highlight the causal contributions of demographic, as well as environmental degradation and resource scarcities. Conventional analyses tend to shirk from these issues—understandably so, since the challenges posed by these large and rapid processes of change are very difficult to deal with on a policy level. And yet, there is no getting away from them, in the Balkans, or in the rest of the world.

The Case of Rwanda—Environmental Scarcity Enabling Genocide

Nowhere were these pressures greater than in Rwanda at the beginning of the nineties. And no person may have been better placed at the time to judge the severity of the situation than James Gasana, minister of agriculture, livestock and environment (1990-92), and minister of defense (1992-93) in the Rwandan government at the time.[1]

The case of Rwanda is crucial to the validity of a livelihood conflicts approach, both since it constitutes the first full-blown genocide after the Holocaust, and since Rwanda was exhibiting widespread poverty and loss of livelihoods as a result of, among other hardships, environmental scarcity.

Gasana (2002) demonstrates how environmental scarcities became acute in the eighties as an effect of soil degradation, continuing high population pressures, and inequitable land distribution (i.e., the textbook definition of environmental scarcity, as defined by Homer-Dixon 1999). The resulting scarcity of arable land led to a high rate of rural unemployment, leading to dissatisfaction among the poor peasantry, mostly in the southern region.

The socio-economic crisis converged with power rivalries between different segments of the élite and strengthened the opportunity for internal opposition, threatening the regime's legitimacy. In a series of linked events, the author notes, "environmental scarcities not only influenced the strategies and tactics of political and military actors but also [...] amplified the political violence."

Here is the sequence of events identifed by Gasana:

1) Following a ravaging famine in 1988-89, regime legitimacy was severly weakened by the dissatisfaction of the peasantry of southern Rwanda with the weak government response.
2) The regime failed to inform the nation on the seriousness of environmental scarcity in general, and on the famine in the south in particular. Lack of free debate on appropriate responses further alienated the southern élite.

3) The mounting political dissension distilled into organizations of dissatisfied peasantry. (As Gasana remarks, environmental scarcities thus in fact hastened the move to increased political pluralism, which is one of the peculiarities of this case.)
4) Rebelling forces of exiled Rwandans in the Ugandan armed forces created the RPF, and seized the opportunity created by the dissatisfaction of the peasantry and by the regime's decreased legitimacy to launch an invasion of Rwanda.
5) The tyrannical reaction of the regime to war further reduced its legitimacy and strengthened the opposition.
6) War in the north against the invading RPF forces caused displacement of up to one million inhabitants, inducing additional resource demand and reducing supply, thus causing sharp grievances and strong anti-rebellion sentiment among the Rwandan people.

These were the conditions that created a situation ripe for ruthless exploitation by segments of the élite. Against the backdrop of extreme poverty and rapid pauperization, due to loss of livelihoods for a long time caused by environmental scarcity, and acutely aggravated by a large part of the population being turned into internal refugees as a result of civil war, the existing ethnic cleavages and historical animosities between groups were opened for exploitation by extremist forces in order to mobilize a very large part of the majority group of the population as perpetrators against the minority group in the first full-blown genocide since the Holocaust.

Gasana is at great pains, however, to underline that at no time was this outcome *determined* by growing environmentals scarcities. Scarcities, by way of loss of livelihoods, merely provided an *opportunity* for opportunistic political forces to mobilize people made vulnerable by poverty into atrocious acts. The lesson to remember here is that losses of livelihood continue to create such opportunities in a growing part of the world at present.

In the policy sphere, Gasana authoritatively concludes that conserving the environment is essential for long-term poverty reduction, in order to break the vicious circle entailed by environmental scarcitites.

The Case of Water—The Imperative of Livelihoods in Cities

If a single river, and a single country, were to be chosen to epitomize the challenges posed by and the conflict risks ensuing from water scarcity, the Nile and Egypt certainly comes to mind first. Here, for thousands of years civilizations have bloomed along the banks of the Nile, providing sustainable livelihoods for hundreds of generations.

Then, in a time-span of just about a single generation, from 1970 to 1990, Egypt as a country regressed from complete self-reliance in food production, to a 40 percent import dependence. Three factors mainly account for this momentous change:

1) The limiting factor for food production in Egypt is not arable land as such, but the area which can be sustainably irrigated by the necessarily limited amount of water flowing into the country through the Nile. No other major renewable source of water exists, since there are virtually no rains.
2) The limiting factor of productivity increases on the severly restricted agricultural land along the Nile is water. Although the period 1970-90 coincided with the great era of increased agricultural productivity through the Green Revolution, the full benefits of these techniques could not be reaped in Egypt, due to the fact that all available water in the Nile was already utilized.
3) When, in a situation like this, the demands of a still rapidly growing population exceed the productive capacity of the agricultural sector, rapid import dependence will follow, since all population additions from then on will have

> to be fed by imports. Legitimate development expectations from the total population will add further to the pressure for imports.

Evolving scenarios of this kind have given rise to regularly voiced fears of "water wars" (in the case of Egypt most likely with Ethiopia, who provides 80 percent of the water that is carried into Egypt by the Nile) in many parts of the world, mainly the Middle East (Israel against several neighboring countries; Turkey against downstream states Syria and Iraq), but also the Indian sub-continent, and Southeast Asia.

No such water wars have materialized, in spite of acutely growing water scarcity, and it now appears unlikely that they will. Nations, prompted both by the necessity to cooperate over shared water resources, and by international efforts to promote such cooperation, have learned to negotiate their way out of open conflict about water. A major reason for this success may be that it is very difficult to imagine how such a water war would be waged. It is not that easy to conquer water resources, or to get control over their usage.

Instead, awareness is growing that the most insidious conflict risks connected to water scarcity is not the risk of first-order conflicts about water itself, but the risk of *second-order conflicts*, caused by the inability of a society to deal with the social consequences of not being able to aquire a sufficient amount of water for the needs of the agricultural sector in that country. (For a more detailed discussion of the concept of first- and second-order conflicts over water, see Ohlsson 1999, chapter 5.)

The focus on agriculture here is important, since this sector is the greatest water consumer by far of any society. On a global average, some two-thirds of all water diverted from rivers or aquifers go to agriculture. In countries or regions heavily dependent on agriculture this proportion may be as high as 90 percent of the total amount of diverted water (whether in desert but still industrialized California, or in a dry-region developing country).

The inability to allocate a sufficient amount of water to agriculture, however, does not necessarily imply food scarcity. Egypt has managed very well, albeit at a high cost to their foreign currency reserve, to compensate by importing food. What it does imply, is immediate problems with livelihoods. New generations in the rural areas of Egypt no longer can expect to make a living out of agriculture as previous generations, way back to the Pharaoes, have become used to.

Instead, the big cities of Egypt are swelling, as are all cities in developing countries. Kairo and Alexandria are bursting under the pressure of new arrivals from rural areas, unable to find a livelihood in agriculture, and hoping to find one in the city. On the success of the Egyptian state to create the necessary number of new jobs in the cities depends the political stability, not only of Egypt, but of the entire region, since unemployed workers regularly move between countries in the region in search of jobs.

Finding jobs for this rapidly growing potential workforce is a formidable challenge, and requires an exceptionally strong and rapid economic growth. As an example the economy of Egypt would have to grow at an annual rate of 7 percent for at least five years if the employment rate is to increase. Similar figures are required for all countries with still young and growing populations.

These problems are creating social turmoil, including conflicts, in all countries in the Middle East. Recently, frustrated Egyptian workers created the worst social turmoil in the history of Kuwait. In such a relatively prosperous country as Jordania the unemployment rate is around 25 percent, and 300,000 illegal immigrants are competing with the indigenous workforce for largely non-existent jobs (*Middle East Economic Survey*, Vol. XLII, No. 46, Nov. 1999).

Thus, in the political hot-beds of big cities, unemployed young men today already are forming the potential armies of future livelihood conflicts, all too ready to be mobilized by political extremist leaders. Whether such conflicts will materialize to an even greater extent than they already have (Algeria would be a particularly apt case in comparison to Egypt), crucially depends on the capacity of societies to adapt to the challenges posed by the risk of second-order livelihood conflicts.

Other Illustrative Cases

Ever since the return of civilan rule at the end of the nineties, the most populous nation of Africa, Nigeria, increasingly has been afflicted by violent conflicts between different national, ethnic and religious sections of society. In one flagrant instance of these diverse conflicts, the links to livelihoods is particularly evident.

In October 2001 federal Nigerian troops were deployed in the central region to end a continuing bloody feud between the Tivs and the Jukuns, two of the many ethnic minorities in that vast and diverse country. The two groups have engaged in intermittent fighting for decades, mostly over land. The most recent outbreak took a very serious turn, since advocates of the Tiv identifed government troops as allied to the Jukuns and killed nineteen captivated soldiers.

Tiv organizations openly threatened a war which, in their own words would be "vicious, bloody, and [...] fought with a ferocity that it may produce consequences worse than, or at least, similar to the horrible spectacles seen in disasters of Bosnia, the Democratic Republic of Congo and even Rwanda." The ensuing reprisal attacks from federal forces resulted in halv a million internally displaced people in the central region, and tensions persist (IRIN 011024, 011107).

This case would seem to be in urgent need to understand not only from the point of view of ethnic and national cleavages, but from a livelihood-conflicts perspective.

Such a perspective would go a long way to understand the root causes also of other conflicts in Nigeria. Muslims and Christians have previously been able to live together peacefully in both northern (predominantly Muslim) and southern (predominantly Christian) Nigeria. The potential for conflict inherent in religious, ethnic and national cleavages seldom come to the fore until justifiable expectations for better lives remain unfillfilled. When livelihoods are threatened, however, by the inexorable forces entailed by environmental scarcities these cleavages become very salient and the ugly mechanism of blaming "the other" for difficulties experienced by your own group come to the fore.

The same mechanisms are quite evident in one of the many hot-spots today, Pakistan. Here, the inability of the agricultural sector, dependent on limited and increasingly scarce water resources, to absorb still large yearly increases of population, and the corresponding ability of a dysfunctional state to create livelihoods in cities at the appropriate rate has led to a large outmigration of people (not only the well-off and educated, see IRIN 010618). Internally, the danger of extremist movements pulling the country apart is used by a self-imposed milititary regime as an argument to remain in power, thus further increasing tensions. Meanwhile, the proximity to Afghanistan and historic animosities with India have contributed in creating one of the most volatile areas on the planet.

Even more volatile is the Middle East area proper, where it seems almost presumptuous to point out the acuteness of the livelihoods factor in the Israel-Palestine conflict. As already noted, fully a quarter of all livelihood opportunities on the Palestinian side are provided by the Palestinian Authority itself, and half of those opportunities are within the police and security services.

The legitimacy of the Palestinian Authority critically depends on its ability to create livelihood opportunities for a population which still increases at one of the highest rates on the planet. Agriculture still remains the main strategy for absorbing all these new people that are coming on board in the next decades, although scarcities of water, one of the critical resources for growing in the area—let alone for increasing the agricultural sector—are among the most acute on the planet and already a source of sometimes violent contention.

The social outcome of lack of livelihoods in Palestine has already created extremist movements which have proved to be among the most willing of any region or country to deploy suicide bombers. Two Intifadas have demonstrated the salience of frustrated young men as a triggering factor for unpredictable conflicts and outbreaks of violence. Demonstrations with virtually all-male attendance on the streets of Palestinian, Pakistani, Egyptian, Indonesian and cities of many other countries continue to underline this salience globally.

Livelihoods and the Need to Liberate Social Resources

By the livelihood-conflicts approach employed so far I hope to have demonstrated, first of all, the crucial importance of generating and sustaining livelihoods for avoiding conflicts. Secondly, the importance of maintaining environmental resources above critical sustainability levels, in order to facitilitate the task of sustaining livelihoods, has been stressed. The third and last point to emphasize is that even the necessity of creating livelihoods in cities have to be underpinned by healthy ecosystems, both for the immediate and day-to-day survival of populations, and in order to reduce the pressure on creating jobs in cities. Individuals who can maintain a life in rural areas will not become foot-soldiers in the potential armies of the unemployed fomenting in cities.

Against that backdrop, the annual report from the World Wildlife Fund on the state of the world's ecosystems raises serious alarm. The report (WWF 2000) states that the productivity and resilience of ecosystems have deteriorated by at least 30 percent during the last 30 years. During the same span of time human pressure on the environment (the "ecological footprint" of human societies) has increased by some 50 percent. The report further concludes that sustainability levels of ecosystems as a whole in facts were transgressed already at some time during the seventies.

Further alarming news comes from the UN Environmental Program (UNEP), who in a recent report (UNEP 2001) concludes that harvests of some of the world's most important food crops could fall by as much as a third in some crucial parts of the planet as a result of climate change. Rising temperatures could damage the ability of vital crops such as rice, maize and wheat to flower and set seed. Key cash crops such as coffee and tea in some of the major growing regions will also be vulnerable over the coming decades to global warming.

What these reports imply is that at the exact period of time when environmental resources would be most needed in order to provide livelihoods, they are depleted below their regenerating ability—ironically to a large degree as a result of the imperative to maintain and create livelihoods. In the future, larger populations will not even have access to the same amounts of environmental services previous generations enjoyed, but less. On a per-capita level environmental services, of course, will be far less.

The world at present thus seems to abound with one great scarcity, namely that of renewable resources and healthy ecosystems, forming the base for livelihoods; and one potential great affluence, namely the productive capacity of all those women and men rendered powerless and poor by their inability to find livelihood opportunities. Fortunately, the combination of these two facets also offer a potential for overcoming the glaring discrepancy posed by them.

A new study by the WorldWatch Institute reports that creating an environmentally sustainable economy already has generated an estimated fourteen million jobs world-wide, with the promise of millions more in the century ahead of us. The often voiced fear of a contradiction between jobs and environmental protection is, according to the report, in fact fiction. "Jobs are more likely to be at risk where environmental standards are low and where innovation in favor of cleaner technologies is lagging," says author Michael Renner (2000).

Environmental job creation today may be largest in developed countries (e.g., in the wind-power generating sector), while job creation is particularly important in the developing world, where almost all of the global growth in population will take place in the coming decades. "The trouble is that human labor appears too expensive, while energy and raw material inputs appear dirt cheap," says Renner. "Businesses have long sought to compete by economizing on their use of labor. To build a sustainable economy, we need to economize on the use of energy and materials instead."

Here lies the greatest challenge ahead. Protecting and regenerating ecosystems and environmental resources to as much as possible of their former wealth will take enormous amounts of the ultimate resource available to humans, namely *social resources*; the capacity to adapt successfully to a changing environment and to new challenges.[2] Fortunately, this ultimate resource is not scarce, but abundant. What it takes to liberate it is insight in the mechanisms that may lead to further deterioration, the will to break away from that path, and the persistence of agencies to change their policies accordingly.

Effective policy measures must be far-reaching if conflict already has set in. In these cases, the international community very likely will have to resort to the full gamut of measures increasingly necessitated by the growing number of man-made complex humanitarian emergencies. If, contrastively, development cooperation is targeted towards the overriding goal of maintaining existing and creating new livelihoods, the vicious path to conflict may be broken. Some general features for policies required to reach that goal could be outlined.

Social undertakings which require manpower, rather than scarce natural resources or activities which undermine or pollute the resource base, should, in the present difficult era, be regarded as beneficial from a livelihood conflicts perspective. Almost all tendencies prevalent in the workings of the global economic system, however, seem to go against the grains of this tenet. The relevant policy question therefore is: What kind of overarching political principles could make a dent in the almost universally applied conventional economic wisdom?

Today, efforts to promote women's status and power as autonomous political and economic agents is acknowledged as a goal in its own right (at least by international agencies and many governments). In large, and possibly growing, parts of the world, however, such strivings all too often are translated into a zero-sum game of livelihood opportunities, where women, from a vastly disadvantaged position, compete with men. Accordingly, a cardinal policy question therefore is: What kind of overarching political principles could make recalcitrant men accept that they would have to lose some of their hitherto unquestioned male prerogatives, in order to make room for women?

While some of the general policy goals thus would seem to be almost universally acknowledged, there is less general agreement on, and far less discussion about, the nature of the specific policies required to achieve them.

Human Rights—The Bottom Line

Nobel peace prize laureate and U.N. Secretary General, Kofi Annan, repeatedly has stressed that a globalization which does not serve to uplift the poorest parts of the global population is to no avail. Co-recipients of the peace prize, other U.N. agencies, work every day in different ways to realize that insight. The interesting part is what they use as leverage.

When the World Food Program (headed by Catherine Bertini) keeps a nation like North Korea—which has virtually plunged into a social black hole—afloat (to the extent of feeding every third North Korean), it does so with no more power than the argument that it is the universal right of the humans thus afflicted to eat a daily minimum of calories and nutrients. The very same argument underwrites the demands—largely met—on the more affluent countries of the world to sustain eighty-three million desperately hungry people, fully one tenth of all those going hungry on the planet.

The benefits of this program do not stop with the food, however—although that would have been quite sufficient in anyone's book. In disaster areas food is not just distributed to the needy—meaningful jobs are offered and work demanded in return for the food. Such food-for-work programs may include the rehabilitation of dykes or terracing to stop erosion. In an ambitious school-feeding program, food is offered on equal basis to boys and girls, as groups, which translates into a powerful incentive for parents to send also their daughters to school, not just the oldest son.

When the U.N. Children's Fund (UNICEF, headed by Carol Bellamy) and the World Health Organization (headed by Gro Harlem Brundtland) send personnel with doses of polio vaccine in cooling bags over their shoulders into a war-torn Congo, or even into an Afghanistan under international bombardment, they do so because the struggle to rid future generations of this crippling disease is so close to success, that the risks are deemed worth taking. A possible gain for future generations are deemed more important than even personal security.

When the UNAIDS (headed by Peter Piot) really get down to the task of combatting the terrible pandemic of HIV/AIDS they focus on men and men's behavior as a risk not only to themselves but to women in general and young women and girls in particular. Here, UNAIDS is clearly informed by lessons learned by women's and human rights organizations.

Similarly, when the special adviser to the Sectretary General on gender issues, Angela King, travels to refugee camps, she takes the fact that women still are donning the burqa in Peshawar, or are subjected to rape or genital mutilation in Tanzania, as a challenge to the workings of the U.N. system. Albeit excruciatingly slowly, policies are hammered out aimed at transforming women from victims of war and persecution, to independent political actors and peace-builders in their own right.

In some of these cases, main-stream economic incentives may prove to be useful tools. But these incentives are never applied—much less regarded—as a magical "silver bullet" in their own right. On the contrary, for economic incentives to be useful in humanitarian work and livelihoods-creating efforts, the neo-liberal tenet of the blessings of the "invisible hand" always has to be tempered and guided by a welfare-state perspective, where politics has the upper hand.

If the U.N. system, and its multifacetted goals, is understood as a token of that kind of politics, representing the highest and noblest aspirations of men and women striving to be just that, then it should also be recognized that the workings of this system build entirely on the recognition of the human-rights framework as a *bona fide* force for change in the world.

It may not always seem to be winning the day. But it is a bottom line which will make every policy attempt, built on it and informed by it, a more powerful, long-lasting and successful one.

Notes

1. Gasana went into exile shortly before the genocide. His analysis of environmental scarcities as a cause of conflict and how it enabled the instigators of genocide in their extreme pursuits will be published in a 2002 IUCN book on environment and conflict. For this very brief condensation I rely on the author's manuscript. Researchers eager to get in contact with the author will find his email address in the References.

To my mind, this is without doubt the best and most reliable treatise on the role of environmental scarcities in Rwanda. It is far superior to e.g., Percival & Homer-Dixon's early study. Gratifyingly, Gasana's analysis fully corroborates my own attempt (Ohlsson 1999, chapter 4), built on far less privileged access to knowledge.

2. The concept "social resources", as necessitated by growing environmental scarcities, is introduced more fully in Ohlsson (1999). The concept is roughly comparable to what now is vigourously discussed as "social capital" by the World Bank and other multilateral organizations.

References

Gasana, James K., 2002, "Natural Resource Scarcity and Violence in Rwanda" [in a IUCN volume of case studies on environment and conflict; author's email: jgasana@intercoop.ch].

Homer-Dixon, Thomas F., 1999, *Environment, Scarcity, and Violence*, Princeton, NJ: Princeton University Press.

IRIN, Integrated Regional Information Network (the UN humanitarian news agency).[Available at: http://www.irinnews.org]

Kaufmann, K. H., 1999, "The role of demographics and resource-stress in the Kosovo conflict". [Available at: http://www.igc.org/desip/StressInKosovo.html].

Keen, David, 1998, *The Economic Functions of Violence in Civil Wars*, Adelphi Paper 320, London: International Institute for Strategic Studies.

Ohlsson, Leif, 1999, *Environment, Scarcity, and Conflict—A study of Malthusian concerns*, Department of Peace and Development Research, University of Göteborg. [Available as pdf-files at http://www.padrigu.gu.se/ohlsson/files/ESC.html]

Percival, Valerie & Thomas Homer-Dixon, 1995, *Environmental Scarcity and Violent Conflict: The Case of Rwanda*, University of Toronto: Occasional Paper for the Project on Environment, Population, and Security.

Renner, Michael, 2000, *Working for the Environment: A Growing Source of Jobs*, WorldWatch Paper no. 152, WorldWatch Institute.

de Soysa, Indra & Nils Petter Gleditsch (with Michael Gibson & Margareta Sollenberg), 1999, "To Cultivate Peace: Agriculture in a World of Conflict," The Woodrow Wilson Center. *Environmental Change & Security Project Report*, Issue 5 (Summer 1999), pp. 15-25. [Available as a pdf-file at http://ecsp.si.edu/pdf/Report5-Sect1.pdf]

UNEP (UN Environmental Programme), 2001, "Climate Change: Billions Across The Tropics Face Hunger And Starvation As Big Drop In Crop Yields Forecast." [Availale at: www.unep.org/Documents/Default.asp?DocumentID=225&ArticleID=2952]

WWF (World Wildlife Fund), 2000, *The Living Planet Report 2000*. [Available at: http://panda.org/livingplanet/lpr00/]

Overcoming Deprivation, Hunger and Poverty

Michael N. Dobkowski
Hobart and William Smith College

Why should affluent societies in Europe or the Americas care about the population explosion in the developing world, ecological disasters in the Mediterranean basin, and the spread of mass poverty and disease in the far-flung corners of the world? What practical concern is it for a banker in Tokyo, a businessman in Copenhagen, a farmer in Iowa, or a housewife in Alberta—who are busy trying to live their lives—that there are famine and civil war in Somalia, floods in Bangladesh, and genocide in Rwanda, Bosnia, or East Timor? There always have been enormous gaps between the rich and the poor nations. People in the developed world should realize that it is in their self-interest to limit the exponential growth in population and resource depletion.

The demographic imbalance between rich and poor societies is producing a migratory flow from the poor to the rich societies. This is challenging the ability of the rich societies to absorb the poor without devastating conflict. Historically, it is clear that people have inflicted damage upon their environment. Human beings have cut down, burned, over-grazed, and polluted their habitats since ancient times. Yet, the environmental crisis we now confront is quantitatively and qualitatively different from anything we have faced before. So much damage has been inflicted on the world's ecosystem during the last century that the system as a whole—not simply its parts—may be in danger. The result is world population growth, increasing rates of resource depletion, ecological damage, and the widening disparities of income and resource use between developing and developed nations. All of these tendencies strain the capacities of the world's ecosystem to sustain itself into the next century without regional or global disasters. In the past, modernization and industrialization have confronted us with many great problems. Millions have been forced into deprivation, poverty, wars, and premature death. Yet, solutions seemed attainable in the past—more land could be cultivated, additional water and energy could be found, and environmental limits were seldom reached. Not today nor in the near future when we will experience a temporal conjunction of four sizable bottlenecks: population, land for food production, energy, and environmental carrying capacity. All are intricately related. They form a complex system whose very balance has never been so delicate and yet so important to our survival. That constellation of factors and suggested remedies is the focus of the following essay.

Population Growth

Industrialization has been associated with significant population growth. The world's population roughly doubled from 1750 to 1900 and again from 1900 to 1950. In 1800 it still took far more than a hundred years for the world population to double. Today it takes only thirty-eight years. Approximately 1.7 billion people inhabited this planet by 1900. In 1990 it was 5.3 billion, 6 billion in 1999, and in the year 2025 we shall have between 8.5 and 9 billion. The world population is growing at the rate of 80 million people a year, as compared to 47 million in 1955. Only about one-fifth of the world's population lives in the fully transformed and industrialized part of the world, including Eastern Europe. About two-fifths alone live in India and China, giving China a slightly larger population than India. Sixty percent of the world's population lives in Asia, about 9 percent in Latin America, and about 12 percent in Africa. The reasons for the increasing population growth are well known. Although birthrates have tended to decline, they have not decreased fast enough to compensate for the gains of lower infant mortality and the general increase in life expectancy. These gains have been made possible not by high-tech medicine, but by relatively simple techniques, such as an improved diet, better control over bacterial environments (general hygiene, water supply, food storage, and antibiotics), and by vaccinations against various contagious and other diseases. The worldwide knowledge of these techniques, the possibility for their widespread deployment at a low cost, world information on social and medical problems, political pressure, the need for social control, and human compassion have been major causes for the ever accelerating population growth. At this time, it is not expected that AIDS or diseases such as cholera or tuberculosis, although growing, will significantly alter the rate of population growth in the near future.

One of the correlates of modernization has been that birthrates decrease with increased urbanization and a higher standard of living. Experience in the fully transformed industrial countries generally has shown that population growth tends to stabilize at a low positive rate and that some countries even have slightly negative growth rates. This leads to the notion that, once the rest of the world will be transformed into more fully industrialized and economically developed economies, the world population too will stabilize in its growth. The crucial assumption made by this assessment is that it is possible to provide the world with the standard of living of industrial countries, irrespective of the economic systems—particularly capitalism, which chronically tends toward overproduction and crisis—and it pays little attention to the negative ecological effects of modernization.

It is true that the increase in the rate of world population has slowed in recent decades, because overall fertility rates are decreasing in some countries. Even among today's fast-expanding populations in the developing world, demographers expect average family sizes to decrease in the future, as these "modernizing" factors begin to take effect. These are gradual changes that are decades away, even if the predictions are accurate, and it may not be until 2045-50 before we reach population stability or even negative population growth.

Experience shows that most campaigns to more swiftly reduce the birthrate are successful only in societies with a sufficiently high standard of living. However, they can also be successful in relatively poor societies with a low standard of living if, and only if, social and economic justice is simultaneously given a high priority. The more vulnerable people become economically, and the more they are threatened by modernization and industrialization, the more they are inclined to adhere to birthrates that enhance population growth. This pattern is often seen as an example of irrational behavior. Allegedly, it prevents families from accumulating the human, social, and financial capital needed for the family's economic improvement, and it is said to annul all productivity gains made on the macrolevel to improve the standard of living. However, it is a proven fact that, when people must live at the margins of existence, they tend to *minimize risks and not to maximize profits and accumulation.* By adhering to higher birthrates, they aim to spread severe existential risks to more people, which from their point of view is a reasonable thing to do.

However, it is also true that women often give birth to more children than they desire, and that the children are required for the family's survival and future succession. Because this condition is usually induced by gender inequality, it follows that birthrates can also be reduced in part by strengthening the position of women in society. In sum, without sufficient equality on the micro and macro levels, there is little hope to more quickly reduce the birthrate sufficiently for population growth to level off.

The question is, do we have the time to wait for these developments? Can a global, modern, industrial civilization sustain four or five decades of growth without destroying itself or greatly endangering the well-being of future generations? How can we support growing populations in the developing world and increasing affluence in the developed world without destroying the earth and undermining global industrial civilization? In fact, between now and 2025 around 95 percent of all global population growth will take place in the developing countries. In the poorest and the fastest-growing continent of all, Africa, which now contains almost 700 million people, the total is forecast to increase almost threefold, to 1.6 billion by 2025. Elsewhere in the developing world, the likely increases are almost as large. China's total may rise from today's 1.2 billion to about 1.5 billion in 2025, whereas the faster growing population of India may increase from 885 million to between 1.5 and 2 billion. The point is that the struggle to feed exploding populations and improve living standards throughout the world may only be accelerating the global destruction of the environment.

Migration and Employment

Because the transformation occasioned by modernization reduces the percentage of the population employed in agriculture, and because insufficient alternative employment is available in rural areas, people have migrated to cities. The nineteenth-century transformation of agricultural society channeled migrants into industrial work—if they found employment. The tertiary, mostly service, sector was developed later. Today, just the opposite is true. The formal economy favors the expansion of services. In addition, the huge informal economic activity belongs itself more to the tertiary than to the secondary sector. This pattern seems to confirm the notion that we are far from growing into a true world industrial society. Once displaced from agricultural occupations, people end up with few perspectives and no vision that can make them feel part of a new era, involving such things as the creation of nation-states, industrial production, and mobility, which were characteristic of the nineteenth century.

The growing levels of mass poverty in the cities is a major concern because cities will experience a significant percentage of the world population growth. A few examples will suffice. Today about 1.5 billion people are living in the urban areas of developing countries. That will rise to a daunting 4.1 billion in 2025. By that time Latin America will be the most urbanized region in the world, with nearly 85 percent of its population living in cities followed by Africa with around 58 percent and Asia at about 53 percent. As we entered the twenty-first century, there were twenty megacities with populations of eleven million or more, of which seventeen were in the developing world. Leading that list is Mexico City at around 24 million, followed by Sao Paulo (23 million), Calcutta (16 million), Bombay (15 million), and Shanghai (14 million). We can easily imagine the stresses that these populations will place on the infrastructures of such cities' already overtaxed housing, sanitation, transportation, public safety, health, food distribution, employment opportunities and general quality of life.

Energy and Other Resources

Thus far, all industrialization and urbanization have been associated with an increased use of energy, directly and indirectly replacing the human and animal energy used in production and distribution, expanding the sphere of unnecessary consumption, and allowing for world markets and their corollary, the world division of labor. This expansion of world trade and the world division of labor is, of course, again a precondition for world industrialization.

World energy consumption, although increasing, remained relatively low until 1950. From 1950 to 1990, however, the use of energy increased sevenfold, far outpacing the population, which approximately doubled during the same period. Most of this increase came from the use of fossil fuels, of which oil and gas constituted the largest share. The contribution of atomic and hydroelectric power to the world's energy supply is only about 15 percent.

As the gross national product (GNP) per capita grows, so does the use of energy. Therefore, one-fifth of the world's population uses about four-fifths of the world's energy, most of it as industrial fuels. Traditional fuels (wood, peat, and dung) supply about 5 percent of the world's energy and are almost entirely (85 percent) used in peripheral countries. At the present rate of use, it is estimated that the world has oil for another 40-60 years, gas for another 60-80, and coal for another 660 years. Coal supplies about a third of today's energy.

It is not possible here to address the future supply of all resources such as minerals and water. It is important, however, to mention that the arable land available for the production of food and fibers tends to shrink. Any expansion will be possible only at the expense of forests or grasslands, jeopardizing other resources, particularly water and topsoil. Any increases in the agricultural output would, therefore, have to come from different growing techniques, pest controls, irrigation, the use of fertilizers and plant breeding.

Bottleneck: A Historically Unique Constellation

Impending bottlenecks center in population growth, land resources, energy, and environmental constraints. What is most crucial is that we have never found ourselves in a situation in which all four factors are so closely linked. Sure, we have had a growing population and population pressures before, but there has always been more land to be cultivated. Sure, we have had large populations to care for before, but more energy-intensive agricultural production and improvements in plant breeding have always been possible. Sure, we have had the need for more energy before, but there has always been some new oil field just a few feet below the ground. Sure, we have had all these pressures before. But have we experienced them as impenetrable limits, as absolute deficiencies of land and energy? Have we experienced them all at the same time and as impenetrable limits? Have we ever simultaneously experienced such severe land and energy limits and also faced the real danger of an ecological collapse? Have we ever experienced such divergence between the have and yet to have nations of the world? Certainly not.

On the one hand, global economic integration, known as globalization, is contributing to spectacular wealth for the 20 percent who live in the developed world, but, on the other hand, it is creating massive poverty, social unrest and the conditions for massive violence and conflict for the 80 percent who live in the developing world. Between 1960 and 2000, rather than shrinking, the income gap between the rich and poor actually grew. The richest 20 percent of the world earned thirty times as much income as the poorest 20 percent in 1960, sixty times as much income in 1990 and seventy-four times as much income by 1997. The richest 20 percent of the world consumes 86 percent of the world gross domestic product, and the poorest 20 percent consumes just one percent of the GNP. Instead of trickling down, the developing world is falling farther and farther behind. The same is true for resources.

Today, the planet counts some 6 billion people. In 2025, it will contain 8.5 billion. Beyond 2025, we do not know how much the population will grow. Current opinion tends to assume that, as a result of economic development, the birthrate will "automatically" fall to about two children per family before 2050, a level now observed for transformed countries. This assumption is very unrealistic. But even if the assumption should prove correct, the population is expected to reach 9.5 billion in 2050 and to level off at about 10 billion in 2075. If we are to feed this population, we will need to increase agricultural production three to four times and increase energy consumption six to eight times. However, by then, we shall also have exhausted the presently known oil reserves, or about 30 percent of today's energy supply, or (together with oil) about one-half of today's energy supply, although owing to population growth, we shall also have reduced the per capita energy consumption by about 40 percent.

The energy crunch is made worse by environmental limits. The degree to which we have been using fossil fuels is changing our ecosystem and the human, animal, and plant reproduction and survival patterns that have for centuries been built around it.

Since the birth of the modern industrial world, we have witnessed accelerating air and water pollution; destruction of farmland, forests, and fisheries; depletion of nonrenewable natural resources; and loss of biodiversity. Lester Brown warns in *State of the World* (1995) that eroding soils, shrinking forests, deteriorating rangelands, expanding deserts, acid rain, stratospheric ozone depletion, the buildup of greenhouse gases, and air pollution threaten global food production and future economic growth. Given the complexity of the biosphere and of the countless interactions between the earth's air, sea and land, there is still some scientific uncertainty on what is actually happening to the environment. The consensus of opinion, however, strongly points to the probability that human economic activities are creating a dangerous "greenhouse effect" of global warming with consequences for the earth's entire ecosystem and way of life, for rich and poor nations alike. If substantial global warming occurs because of rising CO_2 levels then the earth's sea levels could rise simply because a warmer liquid has more volume that a cold liquid. A warmer earth would also mean a melting of the ice mass in the Antarctic. Even a relatively small rise would be significant because it would cause significant coastal flooding. It is estimated that 30 percent of the world's population lives in a thirty-mile-wide coastal strip and is concentrated in Asia and Europe. Millions of people would have to be relocated as environmental refugees, their lives would be threatened by floods and tidal waves, more fertile arable land would be lost, and the erosion inland would be more severe owing to increased rains.

As a result, many of the most important environmental organizations urge a 30 percent reduction of carbon dioxide levels by 2005, a 50 percent reduction by 2020, and an 80 percent reduction by 2050. These reductions would indeed necessitate a drastic change in our present energy-use patterns and amount to a drastic absolute cut in the amount of energy used—all this in times of significant population growth.

Finally, the tremendous food pressures must be reiterated. We can cultivate the land more intensively and turn our lawns into vegetable gardens, but how many millions more can be fed by such measures? We may resort to the oceans for protein, but oceans are already overfished. We may turn away from animal protein to feed more people with the same amount of grain, but this reserve applies only to the transformed world and becomes increasingly insignificant as the Third World population grows. We may resort to ocean farming, greenhouse and hydroponic production, but can we compensate for the destruction of agricultural lands because of overuse and overexposure to wind and water? Can we compensate for the loss in land because of urbanization and the increased demand for housing? Can we compensate for the loss in plant growth and crop yield because of increased ultraviolet radiation? It does not appear likely that these challenges will be met without bottlenecks that may cost the lives of millions.

It seems evident now that there will be a temporal conjunction of four sizable bottlenecks: population, land, energy, and environmental carrying capacity. All of them are so intricately related that they form a system complexity whose very balance has never been so delicate yet so important to our survival. Therefore, we must also distinguish between bottlenecks that present continuous but stable challenges and the ones that represent discontinuous and unstable challenges. Population growth, for example, is a challenge with great continuity. However, as we approach the question of energy and land, particularly if environmental pressures are included, we can increasingly expect challenges characterized by discontinuity. Even though energy resources may not be depleted, the supply of energy could for technological, political, or economic reasons become highly discontinuous. Agricultural land may increasingly go out of commission in a discontinuous way, be it because of events such as droughts, floods, erosion, or drastic overuse. As the system reaches an ever greater complexity, any jolt to the system is bound to make survival more immediately a matter of life and death.

Furthermore, the jolts emitted by the economic system are also of importance, since production factors such as population, land, energy, as well as many environmental constraints are mediated and coordinated by markets. Markets, however, are also known to have a great deal of discontinuity owing to the anonymous number of their participants and the unforeseeable outcome produced by their myriad market interactions. Thus, the capitalist market, the *very* technique chosen to *manage* survival, is itself a *threat* to survival, as is exemplified by speculation, recessions, and depressions, booms and busts. Market dynamics themselves upset the delicate balance among land, energy, population, and the environment, and thereby directly determine survival and death rates.

Additionally, techniques to *ensure* continuity in a world of random but significant disturbances may break down. Already insurance companies suspect that a number of weather-related events may have ceased to be sufficiently random or insignificant or both to be insured. The private market insurance system may soon prove unable to insure against certain ecosystem risks. The instability would thereby increase, leaving politics as the last potential guarantor of continuity and stability, as is already the case with atomic power plants, where no private insurer is willing to cover the entire risk, *nor could such risk be covered.* However, how many big risks, should the event and the scarcity associated with them occur, can the political system handle before solidarity breaks down, instability increases, conflicts grow, and massive death results?

In times of growth and system expansion, potential conflicts can more likely be ignored, for their resolution is relatively easy. The going gets much tougher, though, and more lives are at stake, when conflicts await resolution during system contraction, increased scarcity, and shrinking surpluses. First, the number and severity of conflicts tend to increase and more of them tend to be intrastate conflicts. Intrastate conflict is understood as violence between or among one or more advantaged or disadvantaged groups within a state in order to gain a greater share of limited resources or to secure control or autonomy over the state. Violence may take on tribal, ethnonationalist, or religious dynamics. Much of this violence within states has been aggravated by economic deprivation and scarcity. In societies from the former Soviet Union, former Yugoslavia, Rwanda, Liberia, the Congo, Ethiopia, Sudan, Indonesia, East Timor and currently in Afghanistan, increased pressure on scarce resources and the struggle to achieve some semblance of equity has led to bloody civil wars and unrest. Scarcity, although not the only factor, when aggravated by inequality, has contributed to the disintegration of these societies and to the internal polarization between those who "have" and those who "want". Second, conflict potentials can no longer be as easily ignored, for, should they erupt, the disturbance would only augment the scarcity and make any resolution increasingly and unnecessarily more difficult. Third, resolutions to conflicts are politically and economically much *harder* to find in times of general scarcity and contraction.

Presently, our world still relies on expansion as a solution to conflict. Capitalism, which is now the world's dominant political and economic system, thrives on market expansion. However, how compatible is capitalism with the long-term zero— negative growth environment of the future? It is incompatible! Not only does capitalism have great difficulty in handling such conditions, economically and politically, but it also has, for the same reasons, difficulty in preparing for them. Thus, markets, if left to themselves, cannot factor in long-term scarcity. Has the price of oil, for example, signaled that oil will soon be very scarce? On the contrary, oil markets have, if anything, signaled an ever growing supply of oil. The same could be said for land, lumber, and many other natural resources in limited supply.

The ability of the capitalist market system to guide us through the next decades of increasing scarcity and downscaling of industrial production is very limited indeed, and if lives are to be preserved, the primacy of politics over markets will have to be introduced again, as was the case for practically all of human history, except its bourgeois phase.

We may be entering a "new cold war" or North-South resource war directed against the developing world, replacing the ideological East-West cold war of old. The only way to win this war is to resolve the global crises of overpopulation, poverty, scarcity, resource depletion and chronic underdevelopment.

Solutions to Be Contemplated

To enter an age of scarcity and downscaling is to enter an age of increased conflicts that contain a great potential for mass death and even genocide. More global conflicts in the twenty-first century will be rooted in the convergence of overpopulation, resource scarcity and environmental depletion. Scarcity intensifies human degradation and exacerbates ethnopolitical and religious hatreds. What can be done to avoid these catastrophes? We must first clearly identify the problem and its causes. Before there can be meaningful action, the problem must be fully understood. We must warn the general public of impending bottlenecks and thus make them a legitimate focus of public discourse. We must maximize the use of alternative technologies that minimize the use of resources. We must develop as much self-sufficiency as we reasonably can at the national level, the regional level and the household level. Regional self-sufficiency, if coupled with democratic access to the means of production, can help inhibit migration, and possibly decrease the birthrate. We should do everything we can to promote small-scale, highly self-sufficient local economies. We should learn to live with less. We must identify the kind and level of industrial production and modern cultural and social life that must be retained to effectively and efficiently downscale while simultaneously meeting growing needs. We must define national security in more humane terms so that the protection of political and economic human rights are the priorities. State security must be understood in more global terms. Survival is indivisible. Prosperity for some and misery for the majority guarantees an inherently unstable world. Relative equity and prosperity for all is the only real security.

The Enlightenment of the eighteenth century bore two different and opposing conceptions of the human being. Hobbes argued that left to their own devices, people would descend to the level of the animal, so that without the proper ordering of society and civilization, human beings would be ruled by the law of the jungle. The contrary position is that of Rousseau, who argued that people are inherently good but society was the corrupting influence. Modernist faith has largely followed Rousseau's position: the self was thought of as ultimately good. What was needed was a societal revolution that allowed the natural goodness of the individual to emerge and flourish.

We are highly skeptical of the belief in the inherent goodness of the self. Enlightenment, education, culture, and science will not necessarily produce individuals who will do what is right. The genocides of the twentieth century, spilling over into the twenty-first, have unveiled the true heart of humanity. At our center lies an ability to commit evil of an almost unimagined degree. We have seen the nature of human beings and found that the most ordinary among us can transport millions to their death, can fill the earth and sky with the victims of killing fields. The theory of the inherent goodness of the human being was daily disproved in Nazi Germany and in the other state-sponsored genocides and massacres. Therefore, if Rousseau's argument was shown to be naïve, then so has Hobbes's been proved wrong.

As time passes, the genocides of the twentieth century will recede into memory. From this moment on, however, fundamental assumptions about human behavior and about civilization can no longer stand unchallenged, for though the occurrence is past, the phenomenon remains, as well as the causes exacerbated by the political, social, and economic bottlenecks outlined above. The unthinkable has already happened; the potential for future catastrophes is therefore not unthinkable.

Global interdependence in the twenty-first century means that the crises of hunger, environmental degradation, population growth and resource depletion cannot be confined within natural borders and ignored. No individual, group or nation can remain indifferent. Collective interests must replace narrow, selfish interests. Unless the survival of the few leads to the survival of all, the safety and prosperity of all are called into question. The future portends immense challenges. If it is to be met successfully, it must first be confronted honestly and with an informed citizenry. That citizenry should support policies that further the goals of sustainable development, environmental stewardship, equitable and limited resource consumption, stable population growth and the amelioration of poverty. The future survival of society as we know it demands radical and immediate changes in how we think and act.

References

Blumberg, Paul. 1980. *Inequality in an Age of Decline.* New York: Oxford University Press.

Brown, Lester, Christopher Flavin, and Sandra Postel. 1991. *Saving the Planet: How to Shape an Environmentally Sustainable Economy.* New York: W.W. Norton.

Brown, Lester, eds. 1995. *Nature's Limits. In the State of the World.* 1995, 3-20. New York: W.W. Norton.

Brown, Lester, and Hal Kane. 1980. *Building a Sustainable Society.* New York: W.W. Norton.

Dobkowski, Michael N., and Isidor Wallimann, Editors. 1998. *The Coming Age of Scarcity: Preventing Mass Death and Genocide in the Twenty-First Century.* Syracuse: Syracuse University Press.

Dobkowski, Michael N., and Isidor Wallimann, Editors. 2002. *On the Edge of Scarcity.* Syracuse: Syracuse University Press.

Ehrlich, Paul R., and Ann H. Ehrlich. 1990. *The Population Explosion.* New York: Touchstone.

Friedman, Thomas L. 2000. *The Lexus and the Olive Tree.* Rev. ed. New York: Anchor Books.

Gore, Al. 1992. *The Earth in Balance: Ecology and the Human Spirit.* Boston: Houghton Mifflin.

Human Rights Watch. 1995. *Slaughter Among Neighbors: The Political Origins of Communal Violence.* New Haven: Yale University Press.

Kaplan, Robert D. 1994. "The Coming Anarchy". *Atlantic Monthly* (Feb.): 44-76.

Kaplan, Robert D. 2000. *The Coming Anarchy.* New York: Random House.

Kennedy, Paul. 1993. *Preparing for the Twenty-First Century.* New York: Random House.

Morales, Waltraud Q. 1998."Intrastate Conflict and Sustainable Development," in *The Coming Age of Scarcity*, edited by Michael Dobkowski and Isidor Wallimann, 245-68. Syracuse: Syracuse University Press.

United Nations Development Program. 1995. "Redefining Security: The Human Dimension". *Current History* 94, no.592 (May): 229-36.

Deprivations and Their Cures

Nazli Choucri
Massachusetts Institute of Technology

Making globalization work for the 'have-nots' is an issue that raises critical questions about the nature of globalization, the meaning of 'have-not' and the implications thereof for individuals, groups, states, and non-state actors at both local and global levels. More fundamentally, this essay is about changing structures and processes in world politics, about new tensions and new responsibilities for state and society, and about creative venues for enhancing prospects of well being for humans and for their environments.

The presumption driving this essay is this: prospects for peace are undermined by poverty and economic deprivation that threaten human well being; unrelenting globalization and high opportunity costs exacerbate these threats, thus undermining prospects for peace. It is rather unlikely that anyone, anywhere, can successfully engage in efforts to reduce these threats on philanthropic grounds alone. It would be far more realistic to address the social costs of persistent deprivation, and then consider specific actions needed as well as appropriate incentives and institutional supports.

This chapter begins with the fundamentals of globalization and its definitions, and then reviews the dimensions of deprivation and its implications. This will allow us to address the potentials for mitigation given institutional mandates and capabilities *already in place.*

What is the current understanding about the nature of the fundamentals: What is *globalization*? What is *deprivation*? And to the extent that they are connected, what can be done to *reduce human misery* given contemporary patterns of globalization? We are less concerned with unraveling the 'causal connections' (i.e. what is it that creates deprivation?) or addressing its corollary (namely, to what extent is deprivation a function of globalization), than we are about what can be done to enable and empower the have-nots under the dual conditions of globalization and deprivation.

The burden of our argument is this: Any efforts to reduce pressures on the have-nots created or exacerbated by globalization processes must be accompanied by concerted policies supporting localization. Central to such prospects are (a) the possibility of 'leapfrogging' inherent in wise uses of connectivity (electronic 'wiring' and social networking) coupled with ways in which new technologies can be used to support strategies for improving the lot of the 'have-nots', and (b) the possibility of reducing the globalization sources of deprivation by forging adaptive policies that empower the have-nots without undermining the foundations of social cohesion, and economic performance all around.

Globalization Debates & Dilemmas

In the course of many centuries, a major "architectural" alteration of the international system occurred as populations expanded their activities and political entities broadened their reach. By the close of the 1980s, it was already clear that economic activities in the world were undergoing an unprecedented transformation, a fundamental shift, perhaps even the beginning of a new economic order. The ongoing "globalization" may well constitute the greatest challenge to world populations since the end of Western European feudalism, which led to the Congress of Westphalia and the establishment of the 'state' system as the most authoritative mode of governance.

Confusion and Contention

Today, almost everyone agrees that the planet is rapidly "globalizing", but fundamental differences still exist regarding the meaning of this term, and its attendant implications. However, it is not always easy to determine which is growing faster: globalization itself or the globalization debates. But the fact remains that both are rapidly developing and are becoming increasingly mutually interdependent, which confounds most efforts to untangle 'causes' and 'effects'. The extent of the interdependency is less important than the domain over which interdependence takes place, the issues, and the stakes involved.

Prevailing contentions on matters of meaning and implications of globalization are highlighted by *The End of the Nation State*[1] on the one hand, and *When Corporations Ruled the World*[2], on the other. Both were written early in the politicization of globalization, and none of the debates have been resolved since. The former stresses the emergence of the Information Age coupled with the creation of regions without 'borders', such as Silicon Valley in California. The latter highlights the creation of international institutions and non-governmental agencies; these are new institutional forms that cut across the boundaries of national sovereignty.

Transcending this polarity are more fundamental issues pertaining to definitions and underlying assumptions. In general, the more modernized sectors of the global economy assume that globalization yields common gains for everyone, however uneven these might be. The less modern segments argue that large fractions of the world's population are being left behind, as actors and agencies compete for the gains of globalization. It goes without saying that 'what one sees' depends on 'how one looks at it'. By the same token, what 'counts' depends on 'who' is counting and what is being counted.

If we turn to broader scholarly debates, we can identify two dominant views of 'globalization': the traditional one that focuses largely on *economics and economic transactions* and the emergent one that stresses the *complexity* of globalization and the interdependence among its multiple critical dimensions.

The traditional view defines globalization as the *increased integration of national economies* in terms of input, factor, and final product markets. Much of the related scholarship focuses on *within-state* impacts and state-based responses, including matters such as policy coordination, divergence and convergence. This economy-centric view is clearly important, of course, but it appears rather restrictive in today's global context, obscuring many of the more pervasive *system-transforming* features of globalization. It also impedes full appreciation of the extent to which globalization impinges on matters of governance induced by transformations of socio-political and economic processes.

Complexity of Globalization

The emergent perspective seeks to understand the complexities engendered by interactions among dimensions of globalization, which are driven by significant flows of populations, goods and services, effluence and influences, etc., across state boundaries. This view examines impacts of these flows along a feedback-type of "causal" chain: from flows to impacts on national structure; from structural changes to the impacts of international processes; and from process-effects to the consequences for international structure.

Some features of globalization complexity are illustrated in Table 1, which covers economic, demographic, strategic, communication, and environmental factors—as well as indigenously shaped institutional responses. Conceptual ambiguities invariably plague efforts to render precision to any significant degree. (Earlier literatures would have addressed the elements in Table 1 in the idiom of "interdependence"; however, the condition of increasing integration of input and final products markets *as well as* activities and processes highlighted in Table 1, and their interconnections, generate a qualitatively different reality than characterized by "interdependence".) While "interdependence" highlights conditions of mutual sensitivity and vulnerability (asymmetrical as these might be), complex globalization focuses our attention on the *system transforming* properties of interdependence, the invariably overlapping policy domains, and the necessity for creating and shaping new policy spaces, both literally and figuratively.

Limited in elegance, this table nonetheless serves as a reminder of the domains at issue. Even from the narrower perspective of the traditional view, it is not difficult to see the "other" effects that can be engendered by patterns of production, investments, trade, or consumption. Nor is it difficult to recognize the potentially globalizing effects of "other" dimensions (such as those listed above). It can also be used as corrective against undue emphasis on one or another of these dimensions. Implied in Table 1, clearly, are matters of scale and scope—for each of these issue areas as well as for their interaction. The emergent institutional challenge thus centers on the formation of common and overlapping *policy spaces* for shared institutional responses on a global scale.

Emergent Institutional Imperatives

It is reasonable to ask: When globalization 'happens' in terms of one or more of these basic dimensions, how much of this change is reversible? If we consider reversibility in terms of "undoing" some process, then none of the dynamics implied in Table 1 can be "undone"—even in theory alone. If we consider reversibility in terms of a return to initial structural (or system-wide) conditions, then even this sense of the term is beyond the realm of reasonable conjecture.

Complex globalization highlights the contextual and structural factors engendered by economic activity (for example, the economics of the petroleum industry in any region of the world) and then draws attention to the emergent processes (which can literally be traced to the evolution of the consequences, such as trade in oil and attendant financial flows). The value-added of recognizing complexity is that it avoids artificial boundary conditions of the economics-only view and enables the tracing of the empirical disturbances that shape globalization conditions, arising directly, indirectly, or in part, *not but exclusively*, from the underlying economics.

The fundamental imperative in Table 1 is to draw attention to the emergent pressures for globalization. And the core feature thereof is the necessity for coordinated action across national jurisdictions, across domains of activity, and across interests both public and private. This feature refers to the *endogenization* of new organizational mechanisms designed to manage the changes that are taking place. Matters of reversibility and complexity point to the emergent structures and processes that require joint attention in decision-making and public policy contexts.

As a result, new policy contingencies invariably arise, shaped by the relative scale and scope of variables as those in Table 1. It goes without saying that such processes are also accompanied by the consolidation of new actors, collectivities, and interests.[3]

We can consider the entire contents of Table 1 in terms of the cleavage between the "have's" and the 'have-nots', which enables us to fathom the salient inequalities within and across each of these dimensions.

Dimensions of Deprivation

Who are the 'have-nots' and what is it that they do not have? Clear as this question might seem, it nonetheless obscures the basic fact that who 'has' is often in the luxurious position of defining what it is that the have-nots do not have. It goes without saying that we are accustomed to hearing the voices of those that *have* rather than those that *have-not*. It is commonly noted, the 'rich get richer and the poor get poorer'—a cliché perhaps but certainly one with a strong kernel of truth. It is generally believed that roughly 80 percent of if the world's population remains 'poor'.

In this chapter we consider three dimensions of deprivation that jointly best define 'have-not'. This term refers to people lacking: (a) assurances

Table 1: Illustrating the Complexity of Globalization
Highlighting Dimensions and Drivers of Emergent Institutionalization

- *Economic Dimensions—**Creating Livelihoods & Well-being***
  - Nature of production processes
  - Types of capital transfers & trade
  - Modes of investments, transactions & finance
  - Patterns of consumption & import shifts
- *Demographic Dimension—**Shaping Identity & Ethnicity***
  - Population Attributes
  - Characteristics of labor markets
  - Types of voluntary vs. induced migration
  - Implications of demographic composition
- *Strategic Dimensions—**Affecting Security & Stability***
  - Security of the state
  - Regime & governance security
  - Global & environmental security
  - Security as survival
- *Communication & Connectivity—**Creating Actors & Networks***
  - Physical, Virtual, & Social Networks
  - Type & Value
  - Extent of reach
  - Scale & scope
- *Environmental Dimensions—**Influencing 'Nature' & its Assets***
  - Atmospheric dislocations
  - Terrestrial damages
  - Water degradation
  - Transmission of damages
  - 'Traveling traumas'

of basic survival; (b) access to opportunity; and (c) prospects for political participation. Of these the first is most essential; for without survival matters of opportunity and participation are of limited relevance.

Basic Survival

One common statistic sums the survival situation: About 1.2 billion people live on one dollar a day. Yet it masks some stark realities about daily life. According to the United Nations, life expectancy at birth for the least developed countries is 50.5 years, in contrast to 76.9 in North America or 73.3 in Europe. Infant mortality among the least developed countries is 99 per live 1000 births; in North America it is 7 per 1000, and in Europe 12 per 1000. These figures are for 1995-2000.[4]

Some would argue that despite such statistics, things are better today than they have ever been. Others would disagree. Still others would claim that we now know more about these conditions than we knew in the past. And yet others might say that stark statistics such as these reflect more on the improved state of our own understanding than on the nature of the human condition itself. However, it is likely that no one would dispute the reality of the basic message about the pervasiveness of deprivation.

More to the point is that these figures represent basic survival under 'normal' conditions. They do not take into account the miseries created by war, famine, drought, refugeeism, environmental damage, natural disasters etc.—all of which may have only tangential connections to globalization, as cause or effect, but whose impacts invariably exacerbate human miseries.

Access to Opportunity

It is generally believed that opportunity is closely linked to education as well as to prevailing economic conditions. And often it is the disconnect between proverbial supply and demand in labor markets that creates its own closed doors for opportunity. Among the least developed countries, the existence of a market already endowed with some modern properties must be presumed before we can effectively talk about facilitating labor participation (formally, informally, or marginally as the case may be).

Few simple statistics shed light on the predicament of the have-nots or on the presumed remedy —depending on one's perspective. Over the past 20 years, we have seen a 10-fold growth in flows of foreign investments from industrial countries to less developed countries, the total today estimated as exceeding $200 billion. Is this good news or bad news?

While we recognize the differentials in recipients by country, sector, industry, and investment type, the fact remains that we have only rough indications of the potential impact of these investments on the more disadvantaged segments of society. Indeed, many would argue that the current problems of the have-nots cannot be traced solely (or even mainly) to the presence or to the absence of foreign investments, nor to the dearth of private sector funds flowing the developing (and to some limited extent, to least developing) regions.

The standard *investor* view is that prevailing institutional and other such barriers severely impede incentives for investment. The solution, it follows, lies in the removal of barriers, and this solution is usually viewed as being the responsibility of the state. The standard *state* view is that the government is doing the best it can and is moving as fast as it can, and the solution lies in more accommodating investors. And the standard *have-not* view is that investors and governments seldom, if ever, consider the well-being of the least advantaged sectors of society.

In sum, without trivializing the legitimacy of each position, or the salience of the attendant issues, such a situation begins to approximate what is commonly referred to as a 'dialogue among the deaf'.

Prospects for Participation

If there is one common set of considerations found in all discussions of globalization, it surely must be 'who gets what, when, and how'—the standard definition of politics in all societies at all times. This simple phrase forces us to consider the implications of each of the individual terms. *Who* refers to those counted as relevant in the situation at hand. *Gets* refers to rights and entitlements as well as access to things of value. *What* points to the stakes, gains, or 'utilities' in question. *When* is a matter of timing. And *how* refers to the process that takes place and, more importantly, the nature of the process.

Much of this boils down to *whose* views matter. In other words, participation in the political process is a necessary prerequisite for shaping the policy spaces through which the stakes are determined and apportioned. Not only is this a matter of who participates, more importantly, it is one of *legitimate* participation. In these terms, the 'have-nots' cannot be said to participate nor is the necessity of their participation regarded as an essential feature of national politics. So, even assuming some basic survival conditions as well as some minimal access to opportunity, if prospects of participation are dim, then this will inevitably undermine any potentiality for further improvements in either basic survival or access to opportunities.

Positioning for Practice

Unless all three factors are addressed head on—survivability, opportunity and participation—then any effort to improve the conditions of the 'have-nots'—rooted in or exacerbated by globalization—will invariably fail. Ironically, in order to improve prevailing miseries, the logic that begins with basic survival, then addresses access to opportunities followed by prospects for participation must be turned on its head.

This means that it is the potential for participation—coupled with the reality of involvement in the political process—that is a necessary requisite for enabling opportunities and enhancing conditions of basic survival. The aforementioned backwards logic is empowered by one of the most significant features of globalization, namely the technological advances that have led to nearly worldwide electronic connectivity. It is through connectivity that voices can be heard, and it is when voices are heard that the first step toward effective participation is taken.

In sum: when the have-nots' voices cannot be heard, their presence does not become a political reality. Without such reality there can be no participation. Participation is a necessary requisite for empowerment. Without empowerment, there can be no viable social position and no effective demand for good practice. Without such demand local conditions remain hostage to global realities. However, when there *are* 'voicing' possibilities, global realities may begin to respond to the imperatives of local conditions. Hence, when there is participation, local conditions become salient for global actors.

Connectivity as Conduit for Voices that 'Have-Not'

If there is one robust indicator of globalization—as both 'cause' and 'consequence' thereof of systemic transformation—it is the rapid growth of electronic connectivity along with the attendant diffusion of uses and users worldwide. The Internet is opening new venues for everyone, and the full implications of this remain unclear for both rich and poor.

Disparities aside, the fact remains that widespread access to electronic communication along with increased reliance on advanced technology for generating, storing, and diffusing information has become a fact of life in industrial countries, and is in the process of shaping new frontiers in developing societies. We can anticipate a continued extension of this technology and capability to all parts of the world. This expectation is based on a review of major networking national initiatives such as those supported by the United Nations Development

Programme (UNDP), among others. And it is this expectation that provides the foundations for the expression of the voices of the have-nots.

One cliché that most aptly characterizes the competitive features of the world economy today concerns the "global race for knowledge."[5] Thus, if we acknowledge that 'knowledge is power', then the global economy as we enter the twenty-first century is becoming increasingly reliant on the use of cyberspace for fuelling its performance and for accelerating transformation of knowledge into power for everyone. This is true for the haves as well as the have-nots.

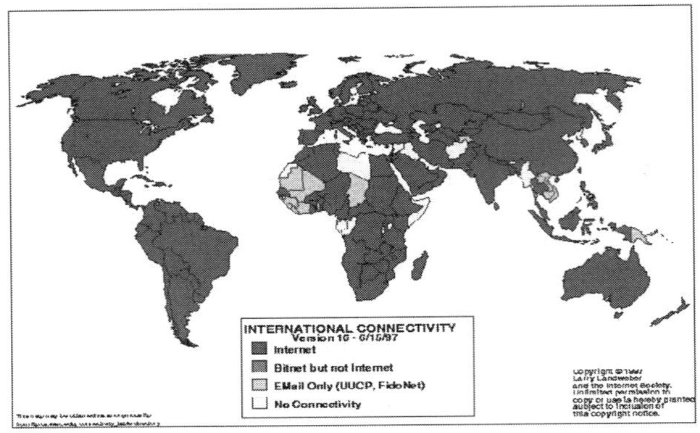

Figure 1

The Connectivity Explosion

Until the mid 1990s, the worldwide web had been largely "open-space" for the individual users. A system that had originally been created by the US Department of Defense as a means of retaining operations for its computer networks in case of nuclear attack was gradually evolving into a network for governments and universities. It was not until the close of the past century that the full implications of the worldwide commercial 'net-explosion' became realized.

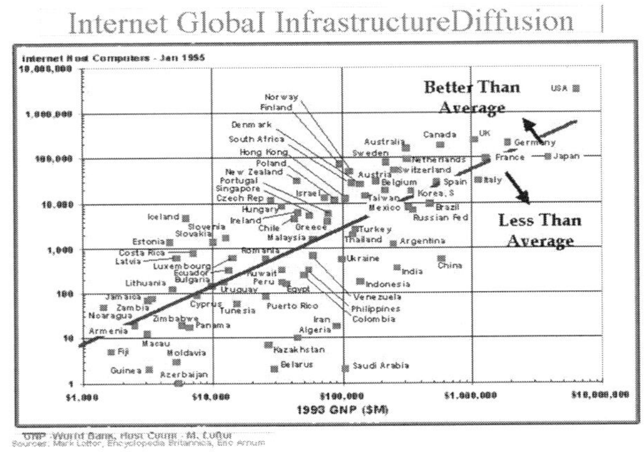

Figure 2

Figure 1 shows the scale and scope of worldwide connectivity in 1997. At that time, every country in the world was 'wired' electronically, in some form or another. By then, the nascent multidimensionality of the Internet and of the worldwide web interactions and exchanges had 'taken off'.[6] But an understanding of the economics of cyberspace had yet to be developed. The explosion of use had not yet led to the explosion of profit from electronic exchanges that subsequently became apparent.

By 1998 it was estimated that there were over 150 million users of the Internet worldwide, a figure that was expected to increase to 700 million by the year 2001[7]. At that time about 50% of cyberspace use was within the US, but it was anticipated that within a year or two, over 80% would be outside the US. No one was prepared for the speed of diffusion.

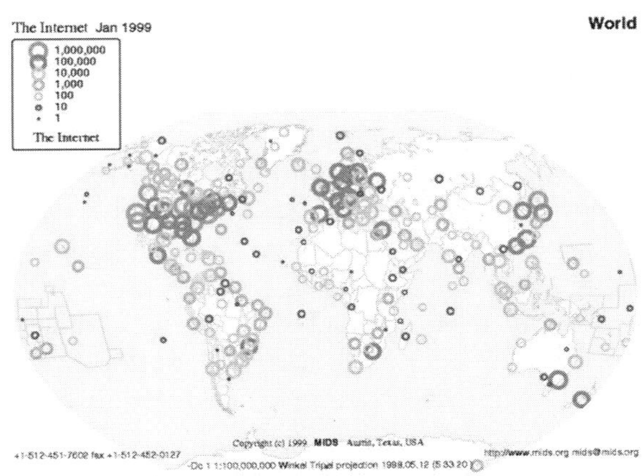

Figure 3

Compared to earlier innovations—the radio, the

personal computer, television, for example—the Internet is the fastest growing information mechanism in human history. And despite significant disparities in cost structures, everywhere around the world transmission of documents through the Internet is significantly cheaper than through other mechanisms.

At this writing, we now have a situation of enhanced globalization in the domain of electronic communication and networking. Invariably, this has increased the intensity of prevailing debates about the effects of globalization in cyberspace, as well as the impacts of cyberspace use on globalization.

Figure 2 visually depicts the extent of global electronic connectivity, revealing the densities as well as the paucities of linkages. A global reality as well as a regional perspective is revealed in Figure 3, which shows Internet users as a 'global enclave'.[8]

It goes without saying that there remain profound parameters of inequality surrounding effective access to cyberspace.

Parameters of e-Inequality

Differential access to the Internet has heightened everyone's awareness of worldwide socioeconomic gaps along with the implications of infrastructure constraints and the fundamental reality of English as the prevailing language that generates linguistic obstacles to the diffusion of knowledge. If we to Figure 3, we find that when viewed in cross-regional contexts, the stark discrepancy between total population, on the one hand, and percent Internet use, on the other, amply document the critical distributional parameters.

Today, the "United States spends 10 to 12 percent of its economy on computer hardware and software…[and] spends about $3000 per person per year on computers. Bangladesh spends $3 per person".[9] At issue here are the reflected implications of prevailing inequalities worldwide. It is not that Bangladesh wishes to spend only $3 on computer related services, rather it is able to do only that. This case illustrates both the constraints and the opportunities inherent in current developments in information technology. Inequalities are real and deeply rooted in the parameters of the global system.

Based on this alone, it is tempting to draw the conclusion that the have-nots are also being marginalized in the cyber domain, that they are outside the pale of modern communication highways. However, the empirical record is substantially more complicated. Perhaps the only robust generalization is this: despite worldwide disparities in the amount of access to information technologies, everyone, everywhere, is being ratcheted into a participatory Internet-based culture. Indeed, the whole issue of 'leapfrogging' implies not only the possibility of such manipulation but also the desirability of shaping new parameters and new opportunities that rely on applications of information technology and its attendant infrastructure.

Connectivity, content, and capacity are the minimally required interacting processes that jointly serve as necessary conditions for participation in the Internet culture. We have characterized these as "3C's" since they are essential prerequisites for sustaining Internet access and uses.[10]

Connectivity refers to the infrastructure needed for a viable presence in cyberspace, covering basic telephone lines, telecommunication systems, satellite connections etc, as well as including all related managerial and operational requisites. *Content* is strictly a matter of quality and quantity of information and knowledge-bearing materials accessible or available, with the value determined by users and their needs. *Capacity* is an empowerment notion referring to the skills required of individuals before they can utilize physical connectivity and then make effective use of the knowledge-content transmitted—in any market, context, or jurisdiction of relevance.

Invariably, countries differ markedly along each of the 3C's, as to the way they differ in terms of venues for the voicing of the views of the have-nots.

Venues for Voicing Views of the 'Have-nots"

According to the United Nations Development Program (UNDP), the Internet "runs along the fault lines of national societies, dividing educated from illiterate, men from women, rich from poor, young from old, urban from rural".[11] As sweeping as this generalization may be, it remains that the Internet *reduces* nation-wide marginalization and provides the foundations for empowerment—in social, political, and commercial terms. And it is when governments move toward an 'Internet-push' strategy that the stark divides along national fault lines begin to erode.

As we show further along, creative ways of communicating knowledge, sharing new ideas, and forging new research strategies provide means to bypass some key impediments to access and to thrive under less-than-optimal conditions. The development of *community-based* modes of organization for access, as opposed to continued reliance on individual use, is a common yet significant element found in almost all known cases. Services that are provided in Cyber-cafes, which are widespread in more developed countries, appear now to have a wide range of counterparts in the developing world. International institutions have generally heralded such initiatives as supporting of individual and community creativity—accurate, but singularly incomplete if not misleading—because far more important are the implications for reducing barriers to knowledge.

This inference can be derived from UNDP data. Egypt, Estonia, and India, for example, have adopted different communication and cyber-strategies, which enable even the most peripheral communities to become connected and link to the mainstream. In Egypt the pilot for a national strategy of Technology Access Centers provides services associated with connectivity and capacity-building. Estonia's strategy is to push Internet access for all citizens. In India, the M.S. Swaminathan Research Foundation targets the most remote villages with supporting services to enable group-based access. (We will turn to another Indian case later on.)

These examples show how people can be enabled to express their views, derive information, shape preferences, and so forth—all of which are essential for 'voicing'. For illustrative purposes, we now turn to four venues or trajectories for potential voicing—within the virtual state, in urban conglomerations, for 'citizenship' purposes at a global level, and for imperatives of global governance.

Voicing in the Virtual State

The first trajectory is characterized by the title of R. Rosecrance's book, *The Rise of the Virtual State* (1999).[12] The essence of the 'virtual state' lies in its ability to garner the power of finance and of ideas, and to transform ideas into sources of global influence. Seemingly simple in its conception, the implications of this presumption are pervasive in that they call into question the fundamentals of traditional politics among nations and their competition for territory, trade, and military prowess. These implications also suggest the replacement of traditional sources of performance by new parameters tied to educational capability, levels of skills, modes of managing ideas, and all related facets of processing the powers of the brain.

Once today's cyber-realities are fully recognized, then the implications for how we think about politics, nationally and internationally, will be revolutionary indeed. This, of course, is if we presume that we can render credibility to the 'virtual state' and to the substitution of skills and ideas for the traditional bases of economic power, namely physical goods and manufactured products. A fully-recognized cyber reality also means that any policies for improving the conditions of the have-nots must include enabling potentials for participating in the virtual state.

The prescriptive nature of this argument is straightforward: investment in education is the fundamental source of individual and social effectiveness. Knowledge is power. But even if one were to acknowledge the limits of full substitution, the fact remains that in almost all societies, access to knowledge—and putting in place the infrastructure that enables this access—ranks high in national priorities. None of this presumes commensurate performance, however, it does presume intent and anticipation of new opportunities for all—most importantly for the 'have nots'.

Voicing in Urban Concentrations

The second trajectory for have-not voicing is within urban contexts—characterized by both the new 'mega-city' which stresses the size of urban conglomerations, as well as by the more traditional concept of 'city-state' which highlights the old and familiar. These are sub-national agglomerations, and both remind us that: Internet services are invariably more developed in urban centers; that the city populations are more familiar with cyber-explorations; and that the density of communication is by definition far greater in urban contexts.

Because the world's population is increasingly urban, the convergence of population density and cyber-communication creates a virtual reality that parallels the demographic realities. Both realities carry their own components of 'have-nots', and provide contexts within which mitigation policies can be framed. But the important point is this: However interesting such aggregate, macro-characterizations might be, they are rooted in their enabling of cyber-connections at the individual level—the micro-unit of social systems. When enabling takes place, voices are raised and demands become articulated.

'Have-Nots' as Global Citizens

The third trajectory pertains to the reach of individual connectivity and its implications for the state and for the global community. Most commonly, the term 'global citizen' is used to connote individual responsibility in, and to, the world at large. In less than a decade, and without undermining the state-bound legal foundations of the term citizen, Internet use has made it possible for individuals to express demands, make claims, articulate political preferences, assume postures, and argue positions. It has empowered people in ways that are truly unprecedented, in scale and scope.

Do these trends translate into greater, and more effective, 'voicing' for participation on a global scale?

On the 'demand' side, the mere existence of a growing number of Internet sites that address one facet of democratization or other, suggests that cyberspace is being used as a conduit for expressing positions, making claims, and, to the extent possible, calling for 'action'. All of this illustrates the increasing robustness of the demand side.

The trends on the 'supply' side are neither as stark nor as seemingly unambiguous in salience and content as those on the demand side. There is some evidence of the provision of government services through the Internet, as well as of the use of cyber-facilities by candidates during electoral competitions. And there is a clear 'push' by international institutions to try and show evidence of effective economic performance. But none of this can be considered sufficiently indicative of the 'supply' side.

Overall, it seems reasonable to conclude—however tentatively—that the demand side of the Internet-based participation (or democratization) process is far more developed than is the supply side in terms of reliable and effective supportive electronics and services. Voices can be and are raised; claims can be and are made; and groups are organizing—nationally and internationally.

While on the supply side more information is being offered or provided, at least in principle, there is little to suggest that the nature of the response is commensurate with the demands being made. At a minimum, the two sides of the democratization process are "moving" but they are not converging; there is insufficient basis to infer the reduction of the gap between 'supply' and 'demand'. Nonetheless, the overall impacts are far from neutral—in national or international contexts.

Voicing for Global Governance

Since Internet access generates new possibilities

for the empowerment of individuals, by necessity it also opens up new venues for governance. It provides new modes for interaction across levels of authority, both formal and informal. Therein may be found another cyber-created paradox. On the one hand, Internet use can legitimately be characterized as chaotic and as reinforcing global 'anarchy'. No 'one' is in control. On the other, the voicing potentials may push toward governance patterns (in terms of structures and processes) that bypass the constraints of state-based territorial sovereignty, as they are conventionally understood.

Several UN agencies have actively embarked on initiatives that would expand Internet usage in order to help countries support nascent initiatives in the direction of global governance. For example, while carefully avoiding any implication of undermining state sovereignty, *Agenda 21* devotes an entire chapter to information needs for institutional development. Moreover, follow-up activities on both *Agenda 21* and two key global conventions—the United Nations Convention on Climate Change and the Convention on Biological Diversity—stress the importance of developing electronic modes of national reporting in order to make it easier for countries to comply with their international commitments.

Clearly, compliance *per se* does not translate into global governance, however, ensuring compliance is indeed a major step toward institutionalization of new global regimes. Developing protocols for tracking the impacts of networking on modes of governance as well as on the management of multiple voices that have previously not been heard, is a major challenge for research and for policy.

Specific Examples of Emergent Voice

At first glance, it does not seem unreasonable to argue that the have-nots are so deprived that the last thing they would wish for is access to electronic communication technologies. The conjunction of illiteracy, poor health conditions, and pervasive poverty makes it impossible, so the argument goes, to draw on such technologies for purposes of improving human conditions. It would be better to wait until the have-nots are actually less wanting and then consider technology strategy.

Reasonable as this view might sound, it is profoundly misleading as it harbors a self-reinforcing tautology. It is this: the have-nots cannot improve their circumstances because they have not; they must have something before they can improve their lot; but having something requires a shift in perspective to enable access to new technologies; this access can be used to improve their conditions; but they cannot have such access until they have something, and so goes the circular logic.

We now address this argument head on by showing two cases in which 'voicing' can be—and is in fact—directed toward improving the conditions of the have-nots. In these case examples, the very dimension of globalization that serves as an accelerator of the process (i.e. via electronic connectivity), also serves as a mechanism for drawing the have-nots out of the vicious cycle of not-having, and therefore of being, and remaining, have-nots.

The first case is an ongoing initiative in rural Indian communities that uses information technologies as a means of creating self-sustaining income generation, as well as improving individual and community well being. This is a case of gains due to 'local connectivity'. The second case involves state-of-the-art global knowledge networking, which is dedicated to reducing the digital divide while, at the same time increasing the knowledge base and the value of knowledge for all participants. This is a case of 'globalization for localization.'

Our purpose below is only to introduce these two examples—as they are operational and not theoretical in nature—not to discuss them in any great detail.

Internet-Enabled Rural Development

Internet-enabled development in rural areas seeks to establish a process of self-sustaining empowerment for the poor. For example, in rural India, all of the participants are 'have-nots'. The strategy in question is driven by the paradox that "despite the existence of vast and real human needs, there is little actual demand; although a huge capacity exists to generate products, yet there is no supply."[13] Although the Indian government estimates that over 50 percent of the national income comes from rural areas, there do not exist commensurate efforts to tap market potentials. In response, the *TARAhaat Information and Marketing* Services has been established by private citizens as a rural-based e-business. The goal, states the Tarahaat Business Plan, is to "bootstrap the village economy and leapfrog even the most remote and forgotten communities directly from the 19th century into the 21st"[14]

Closely coupled with, and inspired by, India's *Development Alternatives Groups* (a grassroots non-governmental set of institutions which focuses on technology and innovation in a wide range of forms, including but not limited to e-business), *TARAhaat.com* seeks to reduce two critical bottlenecks in rural areas—the death of jobs and the lack of information—through judicious and context-specific applications of Internet technologies. A new type of e-business venture, the operation combines a mother portal, *TARAhaat.com*, which is supported by franchised networks of village cybercafes as well as delivery systems, and provides a full range of services directly relevant to, and required by, its clients.

Nearly completing its prototype phase, *TARAhaat.com's* revenues come from payments received for services, commissions on sales, fees for advertising and entertainment, royalties and other such sources of earnings. The financial structure of *TARAhaat.com* breaks new ground in that it provides for equity shareholder value and societal stakeholder wealth simultaneously, in ways that maximize both. The model relies on domiciling parts of its shares in a non-profit foundation, which aims to support civil society and community-based action that will benefit local communities, while at the same time supporting national objectives.

Local-Global Knowledge Networking

Knowledge networking is a matter of devising and implementing operational ways of reducing the 'digital divide'—i.e., the proverbial e-gap between rich and poor, and between North and South—through the use of 'state-of-the-art' technology and management strategies.

Internet-based knowledge networking is one of the rapidly growing strategies for harnessing the power of knowledge, however, still latent are working initiatives for transforming this power into sources of value-added. The barriers to applications in the globalization domain include: (i) complexity of the concept itself; (ii) explosion of information; (iii) dominance of English in the non-English world; (iv) difficulties of access in developing countries; (v) dominance of Internet users from industrial countries; and (vi) infrastructure costs, financial bases, and price structure.

In response, the partnership strategy of the *Global System for Sustainable Development* (GSSD) is: (i) to provide a conceptual framework for mapping the domains and dimensions of sustainability; (ii) to implement specialized search and browser functions on quality controlled web-based materials selected from resources from over 250 institutions worldwide; (iii) to introduce multilingual capacity (Chinese, Arabic, French, and shortly Spanish and Japanese); (iv) to establish mirror sites (exact replicas) of the MIT system in different parts of the world for distributed knowledge provision, management and sharing; and (v) to develop and implement guidelines for provision of local knowledge in developing region including remote areas.[15]

Barriers to Internet access created by prevailing costs and prices are generally managed by the GSSD partners. These are almost entirely dependent on national policy and international practice. Further, local operating costs are presently borne by the partners, and development and system upgrade costs are borne largely by the loosely organized

Consortium on Global Accord for Sustainable Development.

What makes the GSSD partnership distinctive is its new institutional approach, which is grounded in the principle of *distributed knowledge-networking* on a global scale. According to this approach, a knowledge network is defined as:

> "A computer-assisted, organized system of discrete actors with (a) knowledge-producing capacity, (b) combined through common organizing principles such that (c) actors retain their individual autonomy (d), the network enhances the value of knowledge to the actors, and (d) enhanced knowledge value generates greater investment in, and value for, new knowledge."[16]

This mechanism supports decentralized and lateral quality-controlled forms of routinized knowledge management. It generates, captures, shares and distributes knowledge generated by different people in different parts of the world, as well as cuts across cultural, linguistic, economic, and other 'fault lines'.

Recognizing Conflicting Realities

These two cases ultimately suggest that reality is confusing, as it is accompanied by conflicting premises and paradoxes. It is true that the disadvantaged populations of the world cannot be expected to accommodate readily to technological advances nor can they be expected to accept the speed of such innovations. But it is also true that waiting until they no longer have-not may simply be unacceptable, due to the costs of the wait in individual, social, national and international terms.

Such a logic forces us to consider 'leapfrogging' strategies, which would involve devising ways of reaping potential gains of exposure to advanced technologies while concurrently minimizing the 'waiting time' inherent in the overall development process itself. This is not an argument in support of the proverbial technological fix; it is instead one that seeks to mobilize the enabling features of technological developments in ways that accommodate local conditions, customs, and practices.

The case of Internet-enabled rural development shows that 'leapfrogging' in information technology can actually help reduce barriers to the development process. The case of global knowledge networking shows the potentials for effective partnering across large income and cultural divides.

Localization Given Globalization

One obvious set of conclusions we can draw from the foregoing is that (a) globalization will not go away; (b) the have-nots are embedded in local conditions; and (c) therefore localization strategies for distributing the connectivity gains due to localization might be strategically beneficial for all involved.

The term 'localization' refers to the adaptation of existing information and infrastructures (i.e. those already in place) for use in local environments, making sure not to impose undue constraints on either the operational or strategic contexts, given the reality that the have-nots are such because they actually do not have. The above examples are powerful illustrations of potential ways of generating localization gains, without undermining globalization benefits.

Given conflicting realities and attendant contingencies—what can now be done about making globalization work for the have-nots?

What Must Be Done?

Coping Contexts & Conditions

For most countries, the challenge of "coping" is all-pervasive; it is difficult to untangle those policies targeted specifically at economic globalization from those aimed at the management of complexity which would reduce the vulnerabilities associated with concurrent dimensions and domains of globalization. Economies in the developing regions are usually dominated by the public sector, where governmental authority is presumed to be extensive. In practice, however, the informal economy can often be largely relative to a system that is subject to official recognition and accounting procedures, thereby eluding the reach of government authorities.

As we can see from Table 1, for example, public policies targeting the labor market are intimately tied to the country's economic conditions and to its prevailing strategic situations. By the same token, policies designed to enhance investments are generally framed within the context of employment, migration, and labor-related contingencies. To a large extent, even the narrowly defined "input, factor and final product markets" are seldom insulated from contextual or strategic elements. Seemingly 'isolated' strategies such as environmental responses, after taking into account the logic of Table 1, enable us to appreciate that such isolation is more a figment of theory than of reality.

Paradoxically, while the informal sector is generally quite large, the formally designated private sector is relatively small. Hence, it is believed that the reach of private development strategies is highly limited—even when addressing its intended targets. This belief is misleading, however, because under globalization conditions, the term 'private' typically means 'foreign' enterprises. These enterprises then remain 'private' in preference and priority even when the 'public' itself is a sizeable market for their activities and investments.

Reasons such as these force us to customize proposed coping strategies to fit the capabilities of actors and agents at hand—or on the ground, as the case may be.

Coping Strategies

The strategies we propose begin with actions of the corporate community, followed by some suggested reconfiguration of national governmental responsibilities. We then turn to actions of international institutions, and finally to specific moves that can be made by non-governmental organizations. However, it is not so much the sequence of moves that is important, but rather their content, the identification of responsibilities, and delineation of expected outcomes.

Corporate Community—More Profitability with Responsibility

The global corporate community is ideally placed to improve the lot of the have-nots without having to assume any considerable added burdens of such actions. Three rather simple things can be done to help offset negative impacts of globalization while at the same time reinforcing its contributions.

The first would be to draw on corporate public relations in order to account for (or redirect) expenses toward social supports at the local level—in the form of health, education, or infrastructure provision—in those areas where actual investments are taking place.

Second would be to use the supply chain—a necessary feature of any complex system—as a conduit for transmitting skill-enhancing programs to grass root communities. This will probably amount to a miniscule investment over and above those already accounted for, but may create considerable value-added, in terms of enhancing skills and hence potentials for opportunity.

And third would be to incorporate 'helping-the-have-nots' as an explicit clause in the corporate responsibility initiatives. Already we see significant moves in the direction of enhanced responsibility, but actual commitments to date appear limited, and somewhat devoid of effective action. By conceiving of such moves as 'good business' rather than simply 'helping the poor', corporations may be able to gain approval for such moves from both stockholders and stakeholders at little or no added real cost.

National Governments—Better Provision of Public Goods

It is unfortunate that the globalization debates have

increased the prospects for the 'end of the nation state', and by extension include the premise that national governments can no longer control domestic developments. While true that globalization affects governments, more important is the fact that globalization causes domestic changes that force governments to reconsider their roles and to reshape their responsibilities. For example, the provision of public goods becomes an even more central governmental responsibility.[17] It is essential that the 'have-nots' be incorporated within the scope of delivery.

If globalization is expected to *push* the engine of growth in national economies from the top, so to speak, it behooves governments to support *pull* measures from the bottom, by focusing priorities for the provision of public goods on the have-nots. In other words, if the power of the market is deemed to be enhanced through globalization, then national governments must concentrate on improving the lot of those whose marginality places them outside the bounds of the market.

The related presumption here is that the public good provision would also serve as a transitional mechanism supporting moves-to-market, not only as an end in its own right, i.e. on a 'stand-alone' basis. The responsibility of national governments can now be modified and realigned given the expected contributions of the globalization process. The resulting relevant modifications, of course, would be to stress the distributive dimensions of public policies, in conjunction with those that enable individual performance, namely education, training, etc.

International Institutions—Less Redundancy

The single most important move that international institutions can make on behalf of the have-nots is to streamline their own delivery programs—by reducing overlap, minimizing redundancy, and controlling institutional overhead. Any financial gains from such moves could legitimately be turned into direct grants for alleviating poverty or, at minimum, for improving prospects for basic survival.

The foregoing is relevant for all international institutions—at the global or regional level. It is especially relevant to operations at the grassroots level where it is not unusual for multiple institutions to support often overlapping, if not potentially conflicting, development programs.

Non-governmental organizations—More Accountability

What can (or must) non-governmental organizations do? Compelling as this question is, it assumes a reliability in the operations of the NGO's. It also assumes that they are immune to pressures of bureaucratic rationality and remain driven entirely by altruistic motives. (It is essential to distinguish between 'private-not-for-profit' and 'private-philanthropic'. Both are non-state in essence, but goals and criteria of success may differ significantly.) To be effective as an agent for 'coping', NGOs must inject a strong element of accountability into their operations. While in principle the state and its government are accountable to the population as the ultimate constituency, and mechanisms are thought to be in place to ensure or at least facilitate accountability; this is generally not the case for NGOs. And even when NGOs are held responsible, it often only applies regarding the deployment of funds, rather than to overall accountability.

So, if the NGOs are to be truly effective players in their efforts to help the 'have-nots', it is imperative that their operations be carefully assessed, considering the imperatives of complex globalization. NGOs are one of the few institutional forms operating in the global playing field whose accountability is not as fully developed as are national governments and international institutions. The very lack of accountability that provides NGOs flexibility in the short term, may itself undermine their effectiveness in the longer term.

Conclusion

Despite evidence of unrelenting globalization, the reality of global politics—and its legal underpinnings or lack thereof—is that only states are enfranchised to act on behalf of individuals. Only states represent populations; only governments represent constituencies with legal standing. Individuals *per se* do not yet possess any formal mechanism of representation other than the state—whether they 'have' or 'have-not'.

A corollary reality is that globalization processes have empowered a set of actors and agents other than the state. And, while there is some movement toward recognition of alternative 'voices' in international forums, only the state is recognized as a legitimate 'voter'. And within states, it is only those that are more powerful or more participant that are usually heard.

Thus, designing specific policies to facilitate the empowerment of the have-nots is one of the most important challenges of the 21st century. And establishing mechanisms enabling 'voicing' is necessary—but far from sufficient—for improving the conditions of the 'have-nots' under conditions of unrelenting globalization.

Notes

1. Kenichi Ohmae, *The End of the Nation State: The Rise of Regional Economics.* New York: The Free Press, 1995.

2. David C. Korten, *When Corporations Rule the World. Conn.*: West Hartford: Kumarian Press, 1995; and 2001.

3. See, for example, Joseph S. Nye and John D. Donahue (eds). *Governance in a Globalizing World.* Washington, D.C. Brookings Institution Press, 2000.

4. United Nations, Population Division. *Population, Gender and Development*, New York, 2000, pp 16-19.

5. United Nations Development Report, *Human Development Report*, UNDP, 1999, p. 57

6. Anecdotally, it is illustrative of trends and timing that the Person of the Year for *Time* is the chief of Amazon.com, with the cover page note of "E-commerce is changing the way the world shops". December 27, 1999.

7. United Nations Development Report 1999, *Human Development Report*, UNDP, 1999, p. 58

8. United Nations Development Report, *Human Development Report*, UNDP, 1999, p. 63.

9. Michael Dertouzos, Director of MIT's Computer Sciences Laboratory, as quoted in *Boston*, December 1999, p. 142.

10. Nazli Choucri, "Introduction: CyberPolitics in International Relations". *International Political Science Review.* 2000. Vol. 21, No. 3, pp. 243-264.

11. United Nations Development Report, *Human Development Report*, UNDP, 1999, p. 62.

12. Richard Rosecrance, *The Rise of the Virtual State: Wealth and Power in the Coming Century.* New York: Basic Books, 1999.

13. TARAhaat.com, Business Plan, 2000, p. 5

14. TARAhaat.com, Business Plan, 2000, p. 5

15. See http://gssd.mit.edu/.

16. Nazli Choucri, "Connectivity for Sustainability: New Opportunities for Value-Added—Local and Global" Prepared for Dialogue on the *World Development Report 2003 on Sustainable Development with a Dynamic Economy*, German Development Policy Forum in collaboration with the World Bank and the German Ministry of Economic Cooperation Berlin, 2001, p. 9 ms.

17. Philip G. Cerny. "Globalization and the Changing Logic of Collective Action." *International Organization* 1995. Vol. 49 (4): 595-625.

Globalization: Evening the Odds

P.J. Simmons
Carnegie Endowment for International Peace

Globalization's promise is large—freer, faster flows of capital, commerce, technology, and knowledge that spread opportunity and prosperity is in their wake. Actual performance, however, has been mixed at best. In a world of increasingly porous borders, disease, pollution and desperate refugees can move almost as easily as investment, and investment itself often tends to be volatile, hunting short-term profits rather than patient gains. Even trade seems to bring the greatest rewards to those with the deepest pockets. Against that setting, many critics argue that globalization is worsening the lot of the poor, deepening North-South inequalities, promoting exploitation of people and natural resources and impeding sustainable development.[1]

Whether or not the persistence of poverty can be blamed on the rise of world-wide markets and the revolution in communications linking financial and political decision-makers, the widening gap between the affluent and the indigent is undeniable. "The income ratio between the fifth of the world's people in the richest countries and the fifth in the poorest was 30 to 1 in 1960, and 60 to 1 in 1990; by 1997 it had grown to 74 to 1."[2] Not only did the wealthiest fifth control most of global GDP in the late 1990s, that same top layer of the planet's population profited from 68 percent of all foreign direct investment (FDI). The poorest nations, by contrast, accounted for just one percent of GDP and received only one percent of FDI.[3] As developing countries' share of global trade dropped over the last two decades from 0.8 to 0.4 percent, moreover, per capita incomes also fell in the last decade in more than 80 countries.[4]

The benefits of globalization, it is obvious, have been unevenly apportioned. Less certain is the proposition advanced by the passionate protesters outside of recent meetings of the World Bank, the International Monetary Fund and the World Trade Organization, that trade liberalization and international lending actively harm poor countries and poor people. If autarchy worked to promote growth and prosperity, North Korea and Albania would be the envy of the developing world. The abiding misery of the have-nots may well reflect not the inherent evil of a global economic system that exploits them but their relative exclusion from that system. If they are too weak to be successful participants in the global game, the most promising remedy lies not in shutting down the game but in insuring that its rules are fair and that the poor gain the strength to take a place at the table.

This chapter makes the case for a number of remedial actions. Important as they are, they will not come easily. Nevertheless, some ingredients in the new international mix can and should be made to serve the cause of globalization with a human face. The strongest therapeutic forces are also the newest: the vigorous non-governmental organizations (NGOs) that have come into being at all levels of society in almost all countries to advance causes ranging from banning land mines to protecting endangered species. This civic activism, an expression and a beneficiary of the information revolution, has already produced remarkable advances, rewarding private actors with influential roles at international conclaves where they used to be only spectators. Their presence and their pressure have helped turn once-controversial concepts—micro credit, the empowerment of women, sustainability—into conventional wisdom in the area of development assistance. Their expertise, sometimes put to the service of developing nations, has strengthened the negotiating hand of states whose own, few technocrats are spread far too thin.

The speed and reach of information can be additional levers for change in favor of the poor. The ability to share knowledge can translate into movements or moments that capture the public imagination, forcing responses from governments and international institutions. The AIDS crisis in Africa, for instance, generated sufficient global sympathy to constrain pharmaceutical companies to lower their prices for patent-protected medicines. Earlier, the drumbeat of popular and expert concern over environmental degradation compelled reluctant governments to accept (though not yet to implement) broad, concerted measures to preserve biodiversity and control climate change.

Those international agreements are products of a third characteristic of a globalizing world: the habit of cooperation. In the last half of the last century, what had been a rarity among sovereign states became routine as negotiations defined global regimes of governance in trade, finance, communications, fisheries, arms control, labor rights, the global commons and other areas. Few, if any, of those agreements are perfect; none are self-implementing. Still, the collective effort to set norms of international conduct and to devise mechanisms for their application represents a remarkable advance in human history and sets the stage for a new push to make developing nations partners in the enterprise of globalization.

That's the good news. The flip side of these three developments is not so encouraging. The proliferation of private actors—NGOs, business groups, foundations and international organizations—may assure more effective advocacy for the have-nots, but it also makes their voices harder to hear in the general, international multilogue. Similarly, as information expands in a seeming geometrical progression, the competition for attention can become cannibalistic. To make their case heard, the poor may need celebrity spokesmen and women, a sophisticated sense of timing and even a large measure of good luck. Finally, the international agenda is increasingly crowded. The global to-do list is endless, and Third World poverty does not automatically take priority.

An examination of the history of globalization in recent decades, however, strongly suggests that the leadership of a powerful nation or group of nations is usually the essential catalyst for international collaboration. In light of that abiding reality, the recommendations that follow stress the responsibility of the rich powers—the United States, in particular—to the poor. As the primary engines of the globalizing dynamo, the developed countries have a moral obligation to insure that the benefits of their policies are widely shared. They also have a profound self-interest in avoiding the perils of a house, or a planet, divided. U.S. Treasury Secretary Robert Morgenthau, an architect of the post-war financial system that is the foundation of subsequent globalization, once observed that prosperity is a remarkable commodity in that it expands the more widely it is shared. That understanding should be the basis of a renewed, determined effort to overcome poverty and steer development toward a globalization that is genuinely global.

No single formula for development has proved to be universally successful. This chapter advocates an approach rather than a set of guidelines. Its premise, however, is consistent: development should transform societies that are now incapable of benefiting from globalization into full participants in the process. The challenge is to build capacity where human and natural resources are depleted and government is inept or corrupt. Globalization can contribute to that endeavor. Retreating from engagement with the developed world, on the other hand, can only produce new failures.

Urgent Repairs

The agenda for action is a long one. Most of the issues on it are familiar. Some, though, are pressing, and this section highlights trade terms, the negotiating power of the developing states, levels of assistance, and U.S. climate policy not only as global concerns that deserve priority but also as issues where prompt responses can generate relatively rapid, positive change.

Fix unfair trade rules on low-tech manufacturing, agriculture and patents

Some of the rules for admission into the world economy are stacked against developing countries. Most notably, according to economist Dani Rodrik, international trade "agreements on anti-dumping, subsidies and countervailing measures, agriculture, textiles, and trade-related intellectual property rights lack any economic rationale besides the mercantilist interests of a narrow set of powerful groups in advanced industrial countries."[5] At the November 2001 World Trade Organization summit in Doha Qatar, developing countries asserted their relatively newfound influence in international trade by refusing to allow rich countries to move WTO negotiations forward into new areas (the so-called "Singapore issues" including investment, environment, competition policy, finance and other issues)—unless they promised to do better on fulfilling 1994 Uruguay Round commitments to open markets to developing countries' products.

That concession has been long—too long—in coming. Freeing trade to include the developing countries, while not a panacea, is indispensable to the have-nots' hopes of strengthening their own economies. Yet despite their high-minded rhetoric about the benefits of free trade for all, Northern industrialized countries have combined insurmountable tariff walls with the use of subsidies, import quotas and anti-dumping laws to protect their own workers from developing-country competition. One area is textiles, the biggest low-tech manufacturing sector in developing countries. "For manufactured goods (including food products), which now account for almost three-quarters of developing country exports, tariffs facing developing countries exports to high-income countries are, on average, four times those facing industrial country exports to the same market."[6] The terms of some bilateral agreements are even worse. The African Growth and Opportunity Act of 2000 grants African countries more access to the American market, but only if African apparel manufacturers use U.S.-produced fabric and yarns.[7] In Japan and the EU, "fully processed food products face tariffs twice as high as those on products in the first stage of processing. In Canada the ratio is even higher, with tariffs on fully processed food products twelve times those on products in the first stage. This can discourage industrialization efforts in developing countries."[8] To make matters worse, the United States uses import quotas and anti-dumping laws to block low-wage manufacturing competition from poorer countries. As Sebastian Mallaby put it, the situation is "imposed by Westerners who supposedly rejoice in a swashbuckling pro-success culture. If Sam Walton sells a lot, he's an American hero. If a Pakistani shirt factory sells a lot, then naturally that's illegal."[9]

The same pattern holds true for agricultural goods, including meat, sugar and dairy products. European Union countries and Japan protect their farmers with high tariffs, tight quotas and export subsidies. Rich country tariffs on agricultural goods are almost five times those on manufactures;

the EU's tariffs on meat products, for example, "peak at 826 percent."[10] The United States discriminates against poor countries trying to trade by lavishing subsidies on its own farmers—six times as much money, in fact, as its entire development assistance budget to poor countries.[11] Sebastian Mallaby describes the cycle whereby subsidized farmers "...grow more food than they would otherwise, which pushes down world prices and punishes Third World producers. Overproduction by European wheat farmers, who derive fully half their income from subsidies, cripples the export prospects of rivals such as Argentina, a country that is about to default on its debt because it can't export enough to keep its repayment schedule."[12] According to the World Bank, high-income countries' tariffs and subsidies on agricultural goods alone are estimated to impose annual welfare losses of almost $20 billion on developing countries—"equivalent to about 40 percent of the official development assistance given to developing countries in 1998."[13]

Meanwhile, agreements on intellectual property (heavily influenced by American corporations) contain wildly unrealistic deadlines for implementation and compliance by developing countries. The regulations can even prevent developing countries from pursuing the very policies that worked for rich countries in the past. Intellectual property laws help countries when they have enough money to buy existing inventions and want to give firms incentives to keep inventing, but harm poor countries that cannot afford existing technology.[14] The imbalance, however, may be changing. Developing countries won a major concession on intellectual property rights in 2001: an agreement at the Doha trade summit—albeit a non-binding one—to allow developing countries to break patent laws in order to obtain medicines at reasonable cost to treat victims of AIDS and other diseases. But critics say the situation generally is part of an overall pattern in international trade whereby successful countries are "pulling up the ladder after they had climbed it."[15]

Other thorny issues in intellectual property have barely even scratched the surface of global debates. Poor countries and their advocates find several trends worrisome. One is that research and knowledge that was until 1987 primarily generated by public entities (and thus freely accessible) is now predominantly coming from private companies—mainly in industrial countries, which hold 97 percent of the world's patents.[16] A great deal of this research involves genetics and biotechnology, fields that promise to deliver substantial benefits for poverty alleviation, health, nutrition and agricultural yields. These scientific advances, however, have thus far been out of reach for developing countries, even though they often involve genetic material and knowledge originating in developing countries. According to the World Bank, the ownership of such research "raises a concern that a system of property rights designed to protect industrial machinery may not be able to cope fairly and effectively with the complexities of genetically manipulated organisms."[17] Major debates are ahead over trade rules, the scientific, safety and ethical issues connected to genetic research, and how to ensure that genetic advances do not bypass the interests of the poor. One constructive proposal is to create an international scientific advisory group on biotechnology along the lines of the Intergovernmental Panel on Climate Change; the group "could bring together a wide spectrum of scientific and medical opinion and seek a consensus that would inform debate among policy-makers."[18]

Overall, the arena of international trade is one where decisive battles will be fought between protectionist interests in the North and the struggling economies of the South. A victory for the have-nots should not be seen as a loss for the developed countries. On the contrary, measures that expand participation in global markets will benefit all parties. Such agreements cannot come too soon.

Improve developing country analytical and negotiating capacity—especially on economic matters

Despite the multiplication of state and non-state

actors in global problem-solving, the rich countries still dominate most negotiations on rules that impinge on state sovereignty. The IMF and World Bank, for example, employ discriminatory voting procedures that give disproportionate power over key decisions to the biggest capital contributors. Even seemingly more equitable formal arrangements can mask an imbalance against the have-nots. Decision-making by consensus in the World Trade Organization (WTO), for example, does improve the bargaining position of weaker parties. Nonetheless, developing-country negotiators are at a serious disadvantage when it comes to tracking, analyzing and commenting on the myriad trade issues constantly under discussion at the approximately 45 meetings a week in Geneva.[19] The need is not unique to international economic issues, but also present in other global negotiations that require developing countries to weigh knowledgeably the commitments and sacrifices that potential agreements entail.

Since 1995, membership in the WTO has grown from 76 to 142 member countries, about three-quarters of which were developing countries.[20] But according to John Audley and Ann Florini, their numerical dominance "has not translated into influence, or even regular participation."[21] The World Bank reports that only two-thirds of developing countries "even have offices in Geneva, including only 12 of the 29 least developed WTO members."[22] And development scholar Melanie Grindle notes that whereas industrialized countries "had an average of 6.8 people monitoring events at the WTO in 1997; developing countries had an average of 3.5 people to accomplish the same mission. Twenty African countries sent no representatives at all, and thirteen had three or fewer representatives."[23] Without adequate ability to decipher, never mind to shape, the labyrinthine issues under constant discussion, formal power is meaningless.

Efforts are already underway to close the gap. The WTO Secretariat, for example, works with the IMF, UN Development Program, the World Bank and other international organizations to offer seminars that "assist developing country government officials in designing development strategies consistent with international trade disciplines."[24] But these efforts are still widely seen as too little, too late. The situation is aggravated in part by the shortfall between the WTO staff and budget and the need for technical support. Since 1995, the WTO's budget has grown only 18 percent and its staff increased only by 6 percent—despite the 87 percent increase in WTO membership and concomitant demands for help.[25]

Some recommend more bilateral aid from the United States to train economists and government officials of the countries most in need of help—especially on negotiating market access for their goods and agreements that would affect economic reforms and priorities at home. Others urge the creation of a "global participation fund" that would be "self-administered by developing countries, to support the fair involvement of all in global arrangements."[26] Such a fund "would expand on the work of the United Nations Conference on Trade and Development in supporting developing countries."[27] A supplementary idea is to set up self-administered arrangements at the regional level, "such as aid funds and regional versions of the IMF."[28] Still others suggest a "unit in Washington to help developing countries prepare positions on issues coming to the Boards of the international financial institutions," and provide "more focused legal help to developing countries in WTO negotiations and disputes."[29]

Additional models are available in the history of negotiations in global forums on technical matters where similar expertise gaps have occurred—for example in the Law of the Sea talks and various arms control negotiations. To bridge such divides, international organizations have helped by assembling specialized information, serving as central reference points and providing technical assistance to one and all. For example, the International Panel on Climate Change (IPCC), set up under the auspices of UNEP and the World Meteorological Organization (WMO), brought together experts and scientists from both North and South. It was instrumental in identifying the problem of global warming and in creating a common frame of reference with respect to the problem.[30] NGOs are helping too. They have played a major role, for example, in helping 40 small island nations prepare for and negotiate at global talks on climate change—beginning in 1992 at the international negotiations in Rio de Janeiro on the Framework Convention on Climate Change.[31]

The initial form that objective, accessible, technical support takes is probably less important than the commitment to give all countries the same tools with which to design global arrangements and the common future.

Increase development assistance contributions by the U.S. and other advanced industrial economies from 0.1 percent to at least 0.7 percent of GDP

More equitable trade rules are a necessary—but not sufficient—condition to ensure that globalization does not leave poor countries and the have-nots behind. The prevalent consensus among economists holds that if developing countries are to grow their economies, alleviate poverty, and protect themselves from financial contagion, they must adhere to a policy agenda that is, according to Melanie Grindle, "long, expensive, and interdependent."[32] Among other things, developing countries are expected to undertake economic reforms to spur growth and maintain macroeconomic stability, diversify dependence on exports of primary commodities, build institutional capacity to make, regulate and enforce laws, educate citizens, invest in health care, build physical infrastructure, enhance agricultural and industrial productivity, provide social safety nets, create capacity for indigenous science and technology, and more.[33]

The poorest countries cannot possibly be expected to make headway on such a daunting list without help. Recognizing a practical imperative to help poor countries help themselves by removing key impediments to progress, developed countries in recent years have announced various goals to be advanced through bilateral and multilateral assistance. Among these ambitious commitments are those to reduce extreme poverty (those living on less than $1 a day) by half by 2015 and infant and child mortality rates by two-thirds by 2015. Other campaigns seek to enroll all children in primary school by 2015 and, to provide access for all who need reproductive health services by 2015. Some undertakings pledge to reduce the incidence of HIV/AIDS, eliminate hunger, prevent treatable deaths, provide access to safe water, prevent environmental devastation, prevent deadly conflict, reduce technical and digital divides, and more.[34]

Unfortunately, as such goals proliferate, the prospect of reaching them recedes.[35] A staggering 3 billion people still live on less than $2 a day (the poorest to be found throughout Africa, parts of the Andean region, the Gangetic valley of India, and central Asia). One and a half billion individuals lack safe drinking water. Thirty-four million (and the number is rising) people are dying of AIDS with 20 million already dead. And the going is not likely to get any easier, with the world expecting 2 billion more babies to be born—mainly in the developing world—before 2025 and another 2 billion by 2050.[36] Despite pledging themselves to the lofty goals itemized above, most developed countries have withheld the assistance in funds and in kind required to honor their promises and meet the needs of development.

As the world's richest nation, the United States holds the key that can unlock the coffers of other developed countries and release a flow of contributions proportionate to their means and equal to global needs. Yet among all the advanced industrial democracies, the United States is ranked dead last in its per capita foreign assistance allocations—around 0.1 percent of GDP. Since the end of the Cold War U.S. foreign aid has dropped from an average $42 per American in 1993 to $32 in 1998.[37] Nearly a third of the total goes to Egypt and Israel. Only about one-sixth is spent on the 600 million poorest people in the least developed parts of the world.[38] Aid has also declined "in many European countries with the budgetary belt-tightening that accompanied the creation of the monetary union."[39] And "only five rich countries (Denmark, Sweden, Norway, Luxembourg and the Netherlands) meet a United Nations target of spending 0.7 percent of their GNP on aid."[40]

Doing better is not just a moral imperative determined by the need to alleviate human suffering. It is also mandatory if the developed countries want to make progress on a range of global issues they care about—from cracking down on terrorists and transnational criminal networks, curbing proliferation of weapons of mass destruction, reducing corruption, saving the global environment, preventing the spread of infectious disease, and so on. Many weaker and younger states' governments lack the administrative, legal, judicial and enforcement capacity to carry out the costly and complicated measures required by various multilateral pacts. Or they lack the expertise to draft effective implementing legislation, the administrative institutions and human resources to put new rules into practice and the enforcement power to control troublesome private conduct. In the environmental field, at least, outside assistance has helped states comply with treaties regarding trade in endangered species, ozone depletion and the protection of World Heritage Sites. But other areas–international anti-crime efforts, for example—have not been closely tied to development aid. Many states that voice support for the anti-money laundering regime, for example, have little or no capacity to oversee and regulate their banking sectors.[41]

Experience over the last half century with development aid shows that while amounts matter so—crucially—do the uses to which money is put and the setting in which it is spent. More aid must also be matched by better aid. Many long-familiar hurdles remain—among them, problems associated with poor coordination, donor competition, project fragmentation, redundancy of effort, and the improper use of conditionality. Still, past successes and failures have taught many lessons that have, according to Catherine Gwin, "led to the embrace, at least rhetorically, of two new overarching approaches to aid."[42]

The first is the use of a "performance-based" approach that bases allocation decisions not on promises from recipients but on demonstrated actions.[43] Success requires that donors and recipients agree on clear objectives, benchmarks for measuring progress, and good monitoring and evaluation procedures. This methodology departs from past practices described by William Easterly, who argues that donors rarely enforced conditions on assistance and continued lending "even when recipient government actions destroyed any hope of economic growth."[44] Today, as the *Economist* reports, donors are "getting better at monitoring how their aid is used, and stopping it when misuse is suspected, as in Kenya, Zimbabwe, [and] Malawi. As with debt relief for the poorest, donors try to make sure that poor-country governments do not cut back their own spending on things like health and education just because foreign money goes there too."[45]

The second approach—an acknowledgment that solutions and reforms cannot be imposed from the outside[46]—is to give aid recipients far more control over the process, thus generating the kind of "ownership" and incentives that lead to results.[47] Development assistance strategies reflecting only donors' interests have a poor track record compared to those that emerge from local priorities and those that delegate responsibility for implementation and accountability for results to local groups and institutions.[48] This borrower-knows-best attitude draws on a critical lesson from past failures showing that "one country's experience is at best an imperfect guide for any other."[49] For instance, since educating women has produced significant returns around the world, aid money to educate girls in rural Pakistan sounds like a sure thing. Local families, however, often expect girls to carry water from distant wells for eight hours a day. Accordingly, building a piped water system may be a prerequisite for basic schooling.

To be sure, aid has its limitations. As Carol Lancaster observes, the "problems of African development, for example, are deep-seated, poorly understood in their fundamentals, and often location-specific. Solving them will require African efforts primarily, over a period of time. We must not fool ourselves that development mantras such as ownership and participation or even the establishment of democracy will solve these problems, even though each of them is useful in its own right."[50] Still, well spent money—and enough of it over a sustained period of time—can reduce poverty, spur economic growth, and create the opportunities that give poorer countries' governments and citizens the strength to help themselves.

Shutting off aid or disbursing it in meager and dwindling amounts only invites failure. As a prime beneficiary of globalization, the United States has a huge stake in seeing the process expand to the poorest countries. It has both an obligation and an opportunity to lead by example in boosting its flow of aid and credit, beckoning others to follow.

Reverse do-nothing U.S. climate change policy

The distinguished scientists on the International Panel on Climate Change (IPCC) have sent a clear message to governments: the evidence is conclusive that human activities are causing atmospheric warming; the pace of climate change this century will drive dramatic changes in weather patterns and rising sea levels which, in turn, threaten to destroy ecosystems, reduce safe water supplies, reduce agricultural productivity, drown coastal areas and small island nations, destroy homes and infrastructure, spread disease, and harm human lives in other ways. The IPCC warns that developing countries and the poor will be hardest hit.[51]

There are already, according to the environmental research consortium Climate Hot Map, signs of climatic changes in Africa, including "spreading disease...warming temperatures in drought-prone areas, and sea-level rise and coral bleaching along the coastlines."[52] The first-ever outbreak of malaria in the Kenyan highland in summer 1997, for instance, killed hundreds. According to the Consultative Group on International Agricultural Research, countries' ability to cope will depend heavily on economic resources and access to technology. Even a "modest warming," they report, will cause losses:

> In the tropics and subtropics...[agricultural] yields are likely to decrease with even small increases in atmospheric temperature. Overall agricultural productivity in Africa and Latin America could decrease during the next century, leading to hunger and malnutrition in vulnerable areas, especially in drought-prone regions of Africa....More frequent and longer droughts will have a potentially adverse effect on agriculture, particularly in developing countries located in arid and semiarid areas. Moreover, changing patterns of rainfall and runoff, coupled with population growth, will lead to huge pressures on water supplies. At present, 1.7 billion people live in areas where water resources are scarce. This number is expected to increase to about 5.4 billion over the next 25 years.[53]

The rich countries will certainly be hit, too,—and likely in unpredictable ways that scientists cannot yet anticipate—but they have far better means of coping. Residents off the coast of England could move inland; flooded businesses in Manhattan would be able to recoup losses from insurance companies and disaster relief; Canadians can obtain anti-malarial drugs if mosquitoes travel too far North. But in the meantime, developed countries that are the primary source of warming and that created the polluting technologies increasingly being used in developing countries have a responsibility to act.

The United States—which emits 25 percent of the world's greenhouse gases with less than five percent of the world's population—has alternated between the roles of quarterback and sideline spectator in global efforts to address the problem. America helped shape the 1992 International Framework Convention on Climate Change to reduce carbon dioxide emissions and other "greenhouse gases" by voluntary means. When that non-binding approach failed, the U.S. joined other countries to design a binding framework—the 1997 Kyoto Protocol—to mandate specific emissions reductions and deadlines. But after years of promising to act first with other industrialized countries before expecting developing countries to undertake commitments, the United States changed its tune. In 1997 the U.S. Senate announced almost unanimously that it would not ratify the treaty unless the U.S. negotiators reversed course and won the consent of developing countries to undertake their own commitments under the Protocol.

After more years of fits and starts in global negotiations, President George W. Bush in March 2001 announced that America would abandon the Kyoto framework without offering an alternative plan. Infuriated, the rest of the world decided to go ahead without America, hoping that it would rejoin the global effort in due course. Without U.S. participation, the fate of the Kyoto Protocol—itself only a minor step in the right direction—is substantially less assured. Still, the best course for America now would not be to sign onto a Protocol with which it cannot comply, nor try to renegotiate the agreement's terms and potentially delay the rest of the industrialized world from constructively moving ahead. Instead, the United States should focus on cleaning up its own act and activities.

The Senate has begun to consider a range of bipartisan proposals to improve matters—from a national system to "cap and trade" emissions, to better emissions standards for cars and trucks, tax incentives and funding for research and development of cleaner energy sources, including fuel cells. The September 11, 2001, terrorist attack understandably diverted attention from these initiatives and the climate issue more generally. But having assembled an international coalition against terrorism, America will need to take into account its partners' other priorities—global environmental issues not least among them—to maintain it.

The U.S. message on climate change thus far has been like a reprise of the early Reagan administration's wear-hats-and-sunglasses answer to the threat of ozone depletion. Fortunately, that administration reversed itself, and America led the international effort that produced the timely 1987 Montreal Protocol. Getting back on the right path on climate change—and doing it soon—matters. The problem of global climate change is as real as the potential at least to slow it. The right incentives, for instance, could boost the transfer of environmentally less-harmful technologies to developing countries like China and India, where over 2 billion people will otherwise merely stumble down the same emissions path taken by the industrialized North.

The longer that potential goes unexplored, the more expensive remedial action and the consequences of inaction will be. In the years ahead when climate change becomes more than an abstraction, the world will ask, "What did the world's most powerful nation do to prevent this?" If current behavior is any guide, the answer is not one any American will be proud to give.

Priority Upgrades

The "urgent repairs" discussed above tend to emphasize the responsibility of the rich states, especially the United States, to bolster their poor neighbors on an increasingly crowded planet. States must lead, but international institutions must also reshape some of their conduct to advance the shared goal: strengthening the developing nations as masters of their own house and as partners in global affairs. This section highlights three areas for collective enterprise.

Fix, don't dismantle, the IMF, World Bank and WTO

The financial and currency crises of 1997-1998 in Southeast Asia and Russia exposed every country's vulnerability—especially emerging market economies—to severe shocks in a hyper-connected, turbulent global economy. That crisis also fueled the ire of many critics of many international institutions—especially the IMF, World Bank and the WTO—in which confidence was already steadily eroding. Since then, protesters have become a familiar presence at global economic gatherings, many accusing the IMF and World Bank of doing more harm than good and criticizing rulemaking in the WTO as insufficiently democratic and accountable.

Most advocates of change find common ground in acknowledging the need for more humility, flexibility and humanity in global economic institutions and rules. Beyond that, they agree on very little. Recommendations for improvement are all over the map. Some want to slow down the pace of globalization by tossing some "sand in the gears of the system"[54]—for instance, by taxing certain currency transactions, encouraging governments to impose limited capital controls, limiting the amount of money banks can lend, or allowing poor countries to use protectionist trade practices as the rich countries did while developing their economies.[55] Where a few want to dismantle the Bank and IMF altogether, others instead advocate trimming their mandates and returning to "core competencies"—for example, requiring that the Bank lend only to projects that raise per capita income, that the IMF only lend to countries with payments and liquidity problems.[56] Some would do away with the practice of tying conditions to loans, assistance and debt relief, while others want more conditions with better enforcement. A different school pushes for new international bodies—including a supranational authority to regulate financial institutions; an international bankruptcy court or more formal global procedures to allow countries temporarily to suspend their debt payments during negotiations with creditors; and a new, permanent financial facility to help fund expenditures on global public goods and help finance debt relief. These ideas are only representative of the diversity of views.

Given the intense disagreements and lack of expert consensus on how best to proceed, radical views—such as tearing down the international financial institutions, overhauling voting rules, or replacing them with new supranational authorities—are not likely to win favor over the next decade. Instead, we are likely to keep learning as we go. That being the case, it is all the more important to improve the process of debate and decision-making within global forums with great influence on the world economy. In particular, the institutions need to provide far more information and offer more opportunities for poor countries, affected citizens and their advocates to be heard.

Such an opening is mandatory—both to improve effectiveness and legitimacy—especially as the missions and activities of international economic institutions expand and reach deeper into countries. For instance, Ngaire Woods reports that both the IMF and World Bank "are now engaging governments in negotiations which cover virtually all issues in economic policy-making—and beyond, with 'good governance' extending into areas such as the rule of law, judicial reform, corporate governance and so forth. This new, wide-ranging domain of advice and conditionality directly affects a broader swath of policies, people, groups and organizations within countries."[57] Yet many developing countries find themselves "far removed from the workings of the representative body (the Executive Board), which in turn exerts too little control over the staff and management of the institutions for its role to be described as an exercise of vertical accountability."[58]

The good news is that all three major institutions under attack—the Bank, IMF and WTO—are now publishing considerably more information about their analyses, activities and deliberations, including on their websites. The Bank and IMF are also "pressing governments to permit greater disclosure and publication of policies and agreements made with governments…"[59] And going "even further, [they] in some cases now require governments to consult more and to be more actively accountable to their own people."[60] Both institutions are also "requiring governments wanting enhanced debt relief under the Heavily Indebted Poor Countries initiative (HIPC) to produce plans setting out how they intend to reduce poverty. [Plans] must be 'nationally owned' and produced in consultation with 'civil society.' Uganda and Mauritania were the first to qualify for enhanced debt relief under this programme [both had pre-existing plans]."[61] In dealing with civil society, the Bank does more than provide a sounding board mechanism for selected NGOs to air their views; it now disseminates more detailed information about its decisions and activities so outside groups can weigh in. And it uses a variety of techniques to elicit feedback and track NGO expertise—including surveys, advisory groups, public meetings, and private meetings with staff. Consequently, the bank is more apt to consult and partner with the right groups when designing and implementing specific projects.[62]

And to improve accountability of the World Bank and IMF, important mechanisms have been established. The World Bank has an Inspection Panel, created in 1993, that hears complaints from groups that might be adversely affected by Bank projects or those who legitimately represent them. And in 1999, an Office of Compliance Advisor/Ombudsman (CAC) of the IFC and Multilateral Investment Guarantee Agency (MIGA) was created "after consultations with shareholders, NGOs and members of the business community aimed at finding a workable and constructive approach to dealing with environmental and social concerns and complaints of people directly affected by IMF and MIGA financed projects."[63] Significantly, the responsibility for selecting the head of the office was assigned to an external search committee with NGO and business representatives.[64]

More needs to be done, and a range of proposals have been put forward to keep moving the IFIs towards constructive reform. Possible actions include publishing Board minutes, letters of intent, country assistance strategies, and internal evaluations unless there are overriding market reasons not to; setting up right-to-know procedures with an appeal mechanism; increasing the number of developing country seats on Boards.[65] Such steps would help improve assessments of these institutions' performance.

The WTO has also undertaken major changes in its disclosure practices. According to John Audley and Ann Florini, the Secretariat has "made significant progress toward document availability" and increased "the flow of information publicly available about their plans, policies, and proceedings." It has also "organize[d] public meetings and consultations, as well as engage[d] in a series of regular conferences and workshops designed to encourage interaction between the WTO Secretariat and the public." Yet too often, write Audley and Florini, interaction between governments, international organizations and the public is "sporadic, and is often based on late or leaked documents and occasional WTO-organized symposia." Citizens "still lack access to the information that would enable them to comment on trade policy as it is being considered or to present their views in any meaningful way." In addition, the dispute settlement lacks sufficient mechanisms for public input—which is especially important because it has become the "de facto policy-setting organ" in the absence of resolution of policy tensions on thorny issues, including trade and environment.[66]

It is understandable that many governments—especially those of developing countries—oppose more transparency and citizen participation in the international financial institutions and the WTO. Weak governments have a hard enough time asserting their own interests in these global bodies. And richer Northern civil society groups tend to exert greater influence because they employ more money and experience than their Southern counterparts. Still, as Audley and Florini argue on the WTO, "NGOs have proven their value as sources of ideas and as educators of the public on a wide range of international issues...[and] civil society demands have become so strong, effective, and globally connected that efforts to fend them off will only result in damage to the WTO." "Ultimately," they argue, "the threat to the global trading system is not just violence in the street, but a backlash against the

WTO and a much-reduced chance for further trade liberalization."[67] The same is true for other international bodies.

Reform the G-7/8 and G-20 processes

Two serious problems plague annual gatherings of heads of state and financial ministers from some of the world's most powerful countries. The first, involving the G-7 (now G-8 to include Russia) annual meetings of representatives of the leading advanced industrial democracies, is that the meetings no longer do what they were designed to do—that is, as former U.S. Secretary of State Henry Kissinger points out, to be a forum for states to "face up to their political as well as economic challenges." Instead, they have "degenerated into a cumbersome, almost exclusively public relations exercise" that should be "restored into a forum for deliberate discussion and decision to deal with the long-term challenges of the industrial world"—including, he argues, the concerns of developing countries.[68] A number of procedural changes could help. Gordon Smith and Moises Naim recommend, for example, "that leaders assemble in small groups for several hours of real discussion about the real problems they share...problems of urbanization or education, transnational crime or ethnic reconciliation, development or environment." Government officials should "dispense with dull texts, [be] spared pseudo-negotiations over prewritten and unread communiques, [and] engage in the real work of governance in a complicated world."[69]

But getting the rich countries' leaders to talk with each other more openly and effectively is only part of the battle. The other crying need is to give greater voice to those governments excluded from the club and its discussions. As Gordon Smith argues, the tradition "of closed consultations among the participants is now a liability...[and more] needs to be done to include others in the preparatory process, to change the perception that other views are not listened to."[70] The creation of the G-20 in 1999 for ongoing discussions on preventing and managing systemic financial crises helped in part; it includes seven developing countries (Argentina, Brazil, China, India, the Republic of Korea, Mexico, and South Africa).[71] However, the arrangement "lacks formal provisions for including any of the poorest or smallest countries, which, though not yet integrated enough into the global economy to present a risk of starting systemic crises, can certainly be affected by them."[72] Meanwhile, the G-8 remains the locus of discussion for many other pressing issues in globalization—issues that deserve wider discussion. As Gordon Smith has noted, "some proposals—for example on debt, or transparency and accountability of the IFIs—may have a better chance of winning wider support if they are prepared in the G20 rather than the G7/8."[73]

As government leaders think through improvement, they should look to other models in global issues problem-solving. A good one is the Global Environment Facility (GEF), which helps poorer countries fund projects that benefit them and the global environment but would not be financed without outside help. The GEF—half of whose members are from developing countries—boasts an innovative decision-making system. The sixteen representatives from developing countries represent not individual countries but constituency groups, i.e. countries that get funding—six from Africa, six from the Asia-Pacific region, four for Latin America and the Caribbean, and two for Central and East Europe and the former Soviet Union. If consensus is not reached, the GEF uses a double-weighted voting system: decisions are made when there is a 60 percent simple majority *plus* 60 percent of votes based on levels of contributions. Other instructive models might be systems that try to incorporate the views of diverse and numerous civil society groups. For example, the International Fund for Agricultural Development uses a highly respected system to consult with NGOs. In between its major biannual meetings, it conducts extensive work to build consensus among groups in preparing the agenda, position papers and more.[74]

Expand cooperation across the full range of global issues, recognizing connectivity

This recommendation is by far the most general, but also perhaps the most important. The preceding discussion has focused on a number of areas where governments could do better—but it is by no means comprehensive. Beyond development to build capacity among the have-nots, many other issues on the global agenda need consistent attention if globalization is to turn out well for all. Examples are the need to strengthen mechanisms to curb the proliferation of nuclear, biological and chemical weapons; to prevent terrorism; to save rapidly dying species; to monitor and prevent the spread of infectious disease; to head off and end armed conflicts; to narrow technological divides; to curb crime and corruption; to promote democracy; and to safeguard basic human and labor rights. Each of these challenges could stand alone, but none can really be resolved without an awareness of the way they are connected one to the other. The linkages may not always be immediately apparent, but unless their existence is recognized and holistic policies developed to deal with them, setbacks will be more frequent than sustained progress.

In the years ahead, it will be essential for decision-makers and advocates alike to recognize the spreading tendency of issues to overlap with one another, requiring problem solvers to identify and analyze both positive and negative connections. Development is the cause of the ecologically harmful use of natural resources. Or it is the cure. Or both. Making environment and development part of the same equation for many national and international policymakers is at least a crucial step toward a coherent approach. Creating vaccines for malaria does no good if one cannot deliver the medication because corrupt governments divert it or inept ones fail to build and maintain a health care infrastructure. Building schools for girls is wasted effort if their parents refuse to forego the girls' work in fields where laborsaving agricultural technology has made no inroads. Rural electrification can be a failed investment if bribes are required to obtain a connection or even if the irrigation pumps water land the title to which is contested in inaccessible, corrupt courts. Child immunizations are worthless if children become sick in polluted workplaces with ignored labor violations. Rising GDP today buys little for children tomorrow if bulldozers destroy forests and land that provide the basis to sustain future generations. As Tony Blair, Wim Kok, Goran Persson and Gerhard Schoder argued, "The key for development is to establish a virtuous circle between laudable aims that too often are pursued in isolation—debt relief, conflict prevention, trade promotion, educational and health investment, environmental enhancement."[75]

Despite the need for integrated approaches, however, compartmentalized thinking in analyses and policy responses remains commonplace. This is understandable, for simplicity is bound to be elusive in dealing with issues that are not only complex in and of themselves—development assistance, refugee relief and nuclear non-proliferation, for example—but that put on layers of difficulty as they intertwine with other issues. Issue experts can barely keep track of the amount of knowledge required to be effective within their own fields, never mind understanding how issues affect each other.

In response, Inge Kaul, Isabelle Grunberg, and Marc Stern have proposed a "more formal process for identifying and ranking global public goods [that] would allow states to explore potential trade-offs of mutual support that could bring gains to all sides."[76] They advance several innovative ideas along these lines worthy of continued debate. Among them is a call for governments to start labeling overseas development assistance (ODA) and expenditures in ways that track whether money is going to (1) country allocations to assist poor states in their national endeavors; and/or to (2) allocations that help to create global public goods (clean air, a stable climate, fresh water, ocean fisheries, technological and scientific knowledge, sustainable agriculture, creation of vaccines, supporting developing countries' capacity to participate in global trade and finance, and more).[77]

Such clarity about means and ends would at least be a beginning. As with the proverbial journey of a thousand miles, it is vital to take a first step.

In the Meantime

Although it is up to governments to implement the measures presented above, problems of such a scale have, to date, generated tardy and usually cramped responses. In too many cases, by the time multilateral groupings of states move out of first gear, their agreements only formalize or legitimate procedures that have been informally in place long enough to be standard practice. Even trail-blazing international accords—particularly dealing with environmental threats—often do not go far enough in establishing goals and obligations. Negotiating the Kyoto Protocol was a feat in itself, but it was also only a hesitant, partial step in the right direction. Full compliance, if attained, would only slow the pace of advancing climate change. The increasingly common fallback on soft law and non-binding commitments will prove little more than camouflage for inaction until the parties move beyond annual meetings and calls for patience to action on multiple fronts that formalizes demanding commitments and motivates real behavioral change over time.

We need to demand more. But in the meantime, business leaders, citizen activists and NGOs, governmental elites, and international organizations can launch supplementary rule-making and problem-solving actions—alone and in partnerships that transcend national boundaries and sectoral lines. Already, these policy entrepreneurs have moved into the civic space left open by ineffective government-led action or designs. Activist networks selectively target and change the behavior of influential public and private players in ways that others follow. NGOs, private foundations and businesses—beyond serving merely as contract agents for states and international organizations—increasingly provide services and money and normative values. And under pressure from civil society and shareholders, self-selected coalitions of businesses monitor and enforce their own negotiated rules.[78]

Empowered to a large degree by the processes that propel globalization itself, these private actors are also among the agents able to steer its course. Some have already made a serious dent in global problem-solving and, thanks to imaginative experiments in governance, some are developing interesting, practical approaches to other problems. Such supplementary approaches offer genuine promise as new levers of intergovernmental cooperation. They hold special appeal in areas where the only international agreements that exist are non-binding ones and where traditional state-based approaches make little headway against private conduct that gives rise to or exacerbates particular problems. The more cutting-edge initiatives—some of them described below—are helping to force a re-conceptualization about who does what in governance and how.[79]

Power of Partnerships

The activities of NGOs and corporations are taking on a fairly new dimension as private actors team up with governments and international organizations to form what Wolfgang Reinicke calls "global public policy networks" or "cross-sectoral networks." These partnerships undertake direct palliative and preventative action on domestic problems that contribute seriously to global ones or that are major symptoms of global problems. Such networks can be seen as offspring of the information revolution that puts individuals and organizations with matching concerns in touch with one another and with the know-how they share or seek.[80]

International organizations are often indispensable catalysts and pivots for partnerships. In the interest of alleviating global poverty and improving health care, for example, the United Nations has helped to recruit major corporations, foundations, and others into a Health InterNetwork. Its goal is to establish 10,000 on-line sites connecting hospitals and clinics in developing countries with up-to-date medical information.[81] The UN is also working with the Swedish communications firm Ericsson, the Red Cross and others to provide mobile phones and microwave links for humanitarian relief workers in areas affected by natural disasters and emergencies.[82]

Some partnerships fill gaps or provide more rapid intervention than older institutions can and sometimes push innovative actions that more conventional international bureaucracies might simply study to death. The Medicines for Malaria Venture (MMV), for example, "was launched to solve the problem of private-sector underinvestment in vaccine research and production and thus to respond to a steady decrease in private involvement in malaria prevention and control since the 1960s." Joining philanthropic entities, the pharmaceutical industry and the public sector, it "seeks to create incentives for the development of new drugs and vaccines and thus to spur the development of new medicines that would otherwise never be brought to market. Its goal is "to secure the registration (every five years, on average) of one new anti-malarial drug affordable to the worst-hit populations and capable of countering the growing resistance to existing vaccines."[83]

Moving into a vacuum left by conventional banking institutions, micro-credit networks provide small loans to the poor and enlist NGOs, domestic and international donors and even some commercial lenders to support financing that builds both economic strength and local self-governance. Bangladesh's Grameen Bank, supported in part by Western donors, holds the intellectual patent on such initiatives, but its model has been widely emulated by the various chapters of India's Self-Employed Women's Association, for instance. In the Bangladesh countryside, Grameen provides not just micro-credit but communications infrastructure—cellular telephones that put globalizing technology into the hands of have-nots.

Information as Power

Transparency has also become a powerful tool in the hands of citizen activists, allowing them to shape business and government behavior even in the absence of interstate agreements. Widely used in local and national settings to target particular governments' or firms' behavior, it can also be applied transnationally. At its most powerful, it can deter bad behavior in ways that eliminate the need for formal regulation. It can draw attention to problems that have been too long ignored, prompting meaningful action. More often, it steers actors towards desired behavior until formal regulatory accords are in place.[84]

Transparency International's use of its Corruption Perception Index (CPI) has been held up as a model by transparency advocates. Many credit the threat that investors will pull out of corruption-ridden countries at the bottom of the list with helping to deter governments from demanding bribes as a matter of routine. Less known are TI's national survey instruments that help expose domestic publics to the extent of corruption in their countries and uncover specific problem areas. Some TI chapters conduct "service delivery surveys" of consumers of public services and then publish "report cards" that rate individual government agencies based on "the incidence and magnitude of bribes typically demanded and paid."[85] Among other techniques, TI also developed "Big Mac Indexes" that "reveal unexplainable cost discrepancies within a country for similar commodities (such as school lunches, aspirins in a hospital, etc.)." A Big Mac survey conducted by TI/Argentina "revealed that a school lunch in Buenos Aires cost the equivalent of U.S. $5. A comparable lunch in Mendoza, which had been implementing anticorruption measures, cost the equivalent of $0.80. Within days of publication of the survey's result, the cost of a school lunch in Buenos Aires was more than halved."[86]

The use of transparency generates its share of fears and criticisms—especially when employed by non-state actors who are "unelected and unaccountable, and sometimes less transparent than the institutions they monitor."[87] The biggest fear, perhaps, is that information can be misused or misrepresented, for as Ann Florini put it, "transparency reveals behavior, not intent." Information taken out of context, or not grounded in good analysis, can lead to mistaken conclusions. Simply posting information about companies' toxic releases on the Internet, for example, without explaining how much of a toxic chemical causes harm to humans or ecosystems, might spark undeserved criticism or lead well-intentioned citizen groups to spend precious energy, time and money fighting battles of marginal significance.[88]

Targeting influential companies

Multinational corporations that are regularly demonized by the opponents of globalization exercise great power, but no longer unrestricted or immune to pressure from other sources of private influence. Beginning with environmental concerns and spreading to other issues, activists of different stripes have begun to shape corporate policy. What started as picket lines, though, has moved into partnerships. NGOs, international organizations, individual governments and other forces have lobbied or made common cause with top corporations, aiming for those that set industry norms. Individual NGOs, albeit predominantly U.S.-based, are forming strategic partnerships with business to help develop more environmentally friendly technologies and production processes—Conservation International with Starbucks, Environmental Defense with McDonalds, The Natural Step with Home Depot, and on and on.

A remarkable and far-reaching recent demonstration of business sensitivity to pressure occurred in early March 2001, when the drug conglomerate Merck reversed its determined opposition and announced it would dramatically cut the price of AIDS drugs to developing countries to one-tenth the level charged in developed countries. A week later, Bristol-Myers Squibb, the third largest U.S. drug company, did the same, with strong indications that many others would follow. The decisions to use differential pricing—consistent with the TRIPS agreement and supported by WHO, the European Commission, and the WTO—came in the wake of enormous pressure from critics who charged that by protecting drug patents, the industry was reaping enormous profits at the expense of poor, desperately sick people. The precedent is unlikely to be limited to AIDS medications or even to drugs.[89]

As participants in campaigns of capacity-building for developing states, multinationals may be moved by the desire to be good citizens in the jurisdictions where they do business. BP, for instance, provides solar-powered refrigerators in Zambia to store anti-malarial vaccines.[90] Primarily, though, the bottom line is most likely to influence their decisions, and outsiders seeking to direct corporate conduct into less exploitative paths will need to offer imaginative incentives—rather than sporadic protests. Formal certification and consumer labeling schemes offer one such avenue of setting rules that reward complying businesses. The Forest Stewardship Council, for example, issues a consumer label to wood products if it finds that they came from forests managed in an environmentally sustainable way.[91]

To influence the behavior of firms and governments confronting corruption in different localities in developing countries, the transnational anti-corruption movement pioneered the innovative use of "islands of integrity"—mini-governance arrangements with built-in incentives and sanctions that cover large contracts, industry segments or entire cities. Industry participants promise to comply with rules that require disclosure of payments to third parties and allow monitoring; government participants must publicize criteria and evaluation data for bids. If bidders cheat, governments remove them from consideration for future contracts and other parties may attempt to invoke arbitration proceedings.[92]

The examples above suggest both the potential

of private actors to influence the course of development and the gap between their achievements and the challenge. Globalization has intensified old problems—grave disparities of power and well-being between the haves and the have-nots—but it is also bringing forth imaginative initiatives and novel partnerships to confront those problems.

The Challenge Ahead

In between the extremes of complacency and despair, rational analysts can find hope that, even as their numbers grow, Earth's inhabitants will see the global threats to their well-being shrink. Old habits are changing. New agents of change are gaining strength. In the positive forces that globalization feeds and in the experiments being developed and launched in global diplomacy, there is good reason for optimism.

It should be premised on the considerable, often untapped, ability of the poor to help themselves if the help directed their way not only increases significantly but also increases their ability to compete successfully in global markets where many of the odds are still stacked against them. For the have-nots to profit from globalization, fair play must govern its commerce, and trade liberalization must open roads to the developed countries not just accelerate the flow of goods and services from North to South. In such an environment, developing countries can actually develop, not stagnate. Mauritius has. So has China. Others can follow similar paths.

The people of the developing world are their own strongest resource. If their governments provide the right policy setting, the right tools and the right incentives, ordinary men and women have a fair chance of becoming effective global citizens. Not easily and not overnight. But investments in basic education for both men and women, in primary health care, in elementary sanitation including the provision of clean drinking water lay the foundation for individual and societal development. People who demand those services—and often become the agents for delivering them to their communities—take the first and crucial step toward freeing themselves from poverty.

Outsiders who want to assist in that liberation need to recognize the endeavor as a partnership, an expression in practical terms of one of the clearest lessons from the history of global problem-solving. Whether pushing an issue to prominence or getting results on international promises, that history confirms that combining forces and techniques is a far more promising and frequently a more productive course than trying to rely on a single lever or formulation. Silver bullet solutions are a recipe for losing ground. Building coalitions and mixing options is a slow and often frustrating way to make a difference, but in many global situations, it can be the only profitable way.[93]

When it comes to debates over how to help the have-nots, the jury is still out on the best means to apply. No one set of recommendations—including those in this chapter—provide a sure road-map to success, largely because there is still so much to be learned. Differences will persist and mistakes will dog the well-intentioned. Given the complex mix of challenges, however, it is certain that no narrow, inflexible, or ideological theories and no cookie-cutter approaches will bring enduring success.

If, however, adaptation to globalization is used as a primary yardstick of development and collaborative effort is taken as the most promising instrument over time, a range of pragmatic interventions become not just possible but desirable. In other areas of global governance, no single form or formula for action has proved to be best. Sometimes effectiveness has come from a few powerful states acting first—not 189 trying to march in step. Other times it has meant a network of several governments working alongside business and civil society leaders to forge new means to address an issue. In some instances, a transnational advocacy group by publicizing an issue has prompted changes in behavior absent any formal undertakings. Some issues can only be successfully addressed via global frameworks and mechanisms; others may be best approached at regional, national or local levels.[94]

It is often tempting to call for entirely new institutions and regimes when problem-solving is not working particularly well. But new institutions may do little to overcome fundamental obstacles. And so much political capital can go into the fight to win individual victories that the larger battle—requiring attention on multiple fronts—is lost. While it is worth debating proposals for new institutions such as, for example, an Economic Security Council, the clearest, steadiest focus should be on the practices that now sideline the poorest states and on realistic measures to address them.

Leadership—not just who can or will exercise it but how nations and their peoples can be led when risks rise from many quarters—is and will remain a crucial concern for global governance generally and development assistance more narrowly. As this chapter has argued, the United States holds special leadership responsibility given its extraordinary wealth and power—and the fact that it holds keys to many solutions and is the architect of many of the barriers to breakthroughs. But given America's deep tradition of selectivity and exceptionalism in foreign policy, it would be a mistake to pin all hopes or focus all advocacy efforts on changing U.S. policy.

Making the world better for the have-nots—sooner rather than later—will require leadership from other governments in developed and developing countries. Without such leaders, there is too much of a risk for extremists and opportunists to distort facts, inflame passions, provoke misunderstandings, sharpen divisions, and keep fueling unproductive cycles of blame that lead to stalemates. As Moises Naim and Gordon Smith observed: "There is no time now for the sanctimonious hectoring that passes for policy when North lectures South. And there is no time left for the self-righteous victimism of the South, where too many bad governments have made excuses for their own bad mistakes [and corrupt practices]. What is needed… is first of all straight talk."[95]

With civil society groups increasingly acting as intermediaries and catalysts for experiment, policy-making leadership will almost certainly be diffuse and may, ironically, be more effective because it is less concentrated in any one country or institution. To traditionalists, that trend may spell anarchy. In a globalized world, though, such diversity is the order of the day and potentially the architecture of tomorrow.

Recommended Reading

Audley, John and Ann M. Florini. "Overhauling the WTO: Opportunity at Doha and Beyond." *Policy Brief.* Washington, DC: Carnegie Endowment, 2001.

Birdsall, Nancy. "A Step in the Wrong Direction," *Financial Times.* April 10, 2000.

Birdsall, Nancy and Augusto De La Torre. *Washington Contentious.* Washington, DC: Carnegie Endowment for International Peace and Inter-American Dialogue, 2001.

Birdsall, Nancy. "The World Bank of the Future: Victim, Villain, Global Credit Union?" *Policy Brief.* Washington, DC: Carnegie Endowment, 2001.

Boli, John and Frank Lechner, eds. *The Globalization Reader.* Malden, MA: Blackwell, 1999.

Braithwaite, John, and Peter Drahos. *Global Business Regulation.* Cambridge: Cambridge University Press, 2000.

Cairn, Barry and Gordon S. Smith, eds. "Rethinking Governance' Handbook: An Inventory of Ideas to Enhance Accountability, Participation, and Transparency." Victoria: The University of Victoria's Center for Global Studies, 2001.

Carnegie Commission on Preventing Deadly Conflict. *Preventing Deadly Conflict.* New York: Carnegie Corporation of New York, 1997.

Commission on Global Governance. *Our Global Neighborhood.* Oxford, UK: Oxford University Press, 1995.

Edwards, Michael. Future Positive: International Co-operation in the 21st Century. London: Earthscan, 1999.

Friedman, Thomas L. *The Lexus and the Olive Tree: Understanding Globalization.* New York: Anchor Books, 2000.

Graham, Kennedy. "Development: Introduction." In Kennedy Graham, ed., *Planetary Interest.* New Jersey: Rutgers University Press, 1999.

Grindle, Merilee S. "Ready or Not: The Developing World and Globalization," in Nye, Joseph S., Jr. and John D. Donahue, Eds., *Governance in a Globalizing World.* Washington, DC: Brookings Institution Press, 2000.

Held, David et al. *Global Transformations: Politics, Economics and Culture.* Cambridge UK: Polity Press, 1999.

Kaul, Inge, Isabelle Grunberg, and Marc A. Stern, eds. *Global Public Goods: International Cooperation in the 21st Century.* Oxford, UK: Oxford University Press, 1999.

Karns, Margaret P. and Karen A. Mingst. "The United States as 'Deadbeat'? US Policy and the UN Financial Crisis," in Stewart Patrick and Shepard Foreman, eds. *Multilateralism and U.S. Foreign Policy.* Boulder, Colorado: Lynne Rienner, 2001.

Keohane, Robert O. and Joseph S. Nye, "Introduction," in Joseph S. Nye and John D. Donahue, eds., *Governance in a Globalizing World.* Washington: DC: Brookings Institution, 2000.

Kissinger, Henry. *Does America Need a Foreign Policy?* New York: Simon & Schuster, 2001.

Lancaster, Carol. "Developing Countries: Winners or Losers?" In Richard L. Kugler and Ellen L. Frost, eds. *The Global Century: Globalization and National Security.* Washington, DC: National Defense University Press, 2001.

Patrick, Stewart, and Shepard Foreman, eds. *Multilateralism and U.S. Foreign Policy.* Boulder, Colorado: Lynne Rienner, 2001.

Pleskovic, Boris and Nicholas Stern, eds. *The Annual World Bank Conference on Development Economics 2000.* Washington DC: The World Bank, 2001.

Reimagining the Future: Toward Democratic Governance. Victoria: The Department of Politics, La Trobe University, 2000.

Reinicke, Wolfgang, and Francis Deng. *Critical Choices: The United Nations, Networks, and the Future of Global Governance.* Ottawa: International Development Research Centre, 2000.

Rodrik, Dani. "Trading in Illusions," *Foreign Policy.* March/April, 2001.

Sachs, Jeffrey. "Keynote Address: A New Global Consensus on Helping the Poorest of the Poor." In Boris Pleskovic and Nicholas Stern, *The Annual World Bank Conference on Development Economics 2000.* Washington DC: The World Bank, 2001

Scott, Bruce R. "The Great Divide in the Global Village." *Foreign Affairs.* January/February, 2001.

Simmons, P.J. and Chantal de Jonge Oudraat, eds., *Managing Global Issues: Lessons Learned.* Washington, DC: Carnegie Press, 2001.

Smith, Gordon and Moises Naim. *Altered States: Globalization, Sovereignty, and Governance.* Ottawa: International Development Research Centre, 2000.

Stiglitz, Joseph E. "Keynote Address: Development Thinking at the Millennium." In Boris Pleskovic and Nicholas Stern, eds., *The Annual World Bank Conference on Development Economics 2000.* Washington DC: The World Bank, 2001.

UN Development Programme. *Human Development Report* (annual).

The World Bank. *Building Institutions for Markets.* Washington, DC: World Bank, 2001.

The World Bank. *Global Development Finance: Building Coalitions for Effective Development Finance.* Washington, DC: The World Bank, 2001.

The World Bank. *World Development Report 2000-2001: Attacking Poverty* (and other annual editions) New York: Oxford University Press, 2001.

Woods, Ngaire. "Making the IMF and the World Bank More Accountable," *International Affairs,* 77:1: 83-100, 2001.

Notes

1. This chapter draws in part on findings from P.J. Simmons and Chantal de Jonge Oudraat, eds., *Manag-*

ing Global Issues: Lessons Learned (Washington: Carnegie Endowment for International Peace, 2001).

2. Gordon Smith and Moises Naim. *Altered States: Globalization, Sovereignty, and Governance* (Ottawa: International Development Research Centre, 2000), p. 8.

3. Merilee S. Grindle (citing the 1999 UN Human Development Report) in "Ready or Not: The Developing World and Globalization," in Joseph S. Nye, Jr. and John D. Donahue, eds., *Governance in a Globalizing World* (Washington, DC: Brookings Institution Press, 2000), p. 187.

4. Mats Karlsson, "Opening Address," in Boris Pleskovic and Nicholas Stern, eds. *The Annual World Bank Conference on Development Economics 2000.* Washington DC: The World Bank, 2001; and Smith and Naim, page 8.

5. Dani Rodrik, "Trading in Illusions," *Foreign Policy*, March/April 2001, p. 58.

6. The World Bank. *World Development Report 2000-2001: Attacking Poverty* (New York: Oxford University Press, 2001), p 180.

7. Rodrik, p. 58.

8. World Bank, Attacking Poverty, p. 180.

9. Sebastian Mallaby, "Helping the Rich, Harming the Poor," *Washington Post*, November 5, 2001.

10. World Bank, *Attacking Poverty*, p. 180.

11. Mallaby, "Helping the Rich, Harming the Poor."

12. *Ibid.*

13. World Bank, *Attacking Poverty*, p. 180.

14. Mallaby, "Helping the Rich, Harming the Poor."

15. Gordon Smith. Rapporteur's Report: 2020 Global Architecture Conference (Unpublished, Victoria: August 29-31, 2001).

16. World Bank, *Attacking Poverty*, pp. 184-5.

17. *Ibid*, p. 185.

18. Gordon Smith. Rapporteur's Report: 2020 Global Architecture Conference (Unpublished, Victoria: August 29-31, 2001).

19. World Bank, *Attacking Poverty*, p. 186.

20. Audley, John and Ann M. Florini, "Overhauling the WTO: Opportunity at Doha and Beyond," *Policy Brief*, (Washington, DC: Carnegie Endowment, 2001), p. 3.

21. *Ibid*, p. 3.

22. World Bank, *Attacking Poverty*, p. 186.

23. Grindle, "Ready or Not: The Developing World and Globalization," p. 190.

24. Audley and Florini, pp. 3-4.

25. *Ibid*, p. 4.

26. Executive Summary of Inge Kaul, Isabelle Grunberg, and Marc A. Stern, eds., *Global Public Goods: International Cooperation in the 21st Century* (Oxford, UK: Oxford University Press, 1999), p. 21.

27. *Ibid.*

28. *Ibid.*

29. Gordon Smith. Rapporteur's Report: 2020 Global Architecture Conference (Unpublished, Victoria: August 29-31, 2001).

30. P.J. Simmons and Chantal de Jonge Oudraat, *Managing Global Issues* (Washington: Carnegie Endowment for International Peace, 2001), p. 683.

31. Simmons and de Jonge Oudraat, p. 675.

32. Grindle, p 193.

33. *Ibid.* And Jeffrey Sachs, "Keynote Address: A New Global Consensus on Helping the Poorest of the Poor," in Boris Pleskovic, and Nicholas Stern, eds. *The Annual World Bank Conference on Development Economics 2000* (Washington DC: The World Bank, 2001), p. 43.

34. World Bank, *Attacking Poverty*, p. 5.

35. *Ibid.*

36. Karlsson, p. 8-9; and Sachs, p. 43.

37. Joseph Kahn, "The World's Bankers Try Giving Money, Not Lessons," *New York Times*, October 1, 2000.

38. Sachs, p 39. Judy Mann, "No Time to Be Shortchanging Foreign Aid," *Washington Post*, November 14, 2001, C-12.

39. Kahn, "The World's Bankers Try Giving Money, Not Lessons."

40. "Enough Talk," *Economist*, Nov 22, 2001.

41. Simmons and de Jonge Oudraat, pp. 699-701.

42. Catherine Gwin, "Development Assistance," in Simmons and de Jonge Oudraat, p. 190.

43. *Ibid.*

44. William Easterly, "The Failure of Development," *Financial Times*, September 7, 2001.

45. "Enough Talk," *Economist*, Nov 22, 2001.

46. Stiglitz, p. 31.

47. Gwin, "Development Assistance," p. 190.

48. Gwin, "Development Assistance," p. 183-4.

49. Gwin, "Development Assistance," p. 155.

50. Carol Lancaster, "Developing Countries: Winners or Losers?", in Richard L. Kugler and Ellen L. Frost, eds.

The Global Century: Globalization and National Security (Washington, DC: National Defense University Press, 2001), p. 663.

51. See http://www.ipcc.ch/

52. See http://www.climatehotmap.org/africa.html

53. See: http://www.cgiar.org/research/res_climate.html

54. Thomas L. Friedman, *The Lexus and the Olive Tree: Understanding Globalization*, (New York: Anchor Books, 2000), p. 459.

55. Ibid. And Rodrik, pp. 55-62.

56. For a review and analysis of various recommendations for World Bank reform, see Nancy Birdsall, "The World Bank of the Future: Victim, Villain, Global Credit Union?" *Policy Brief*, (Washington, DC: Carnegie Endowment, 2001).

57. Ngaire Woods, "Making the IMF and the World Bank More Accountable," *International Affairs*, 77:1: 2001, p. 89.

58. Woods, p. 84.

59. Woods, p. 90.

60. Woods, p. 91.

61. Woods, p. 91.

62. P.J. Simmons, "Learning to Live with NGOs," *Foreign Policy*, Fall 1998, p. 93.

63. Woods, p. 94.

64. Gordon Smith. Rapporteur's Report: 2020 Global Architecture Conference (Unpublished, Victoria: August 29-31, 2001).

65. See, for example, John J. Gershman, "Globalization and the Challenge of Governance: Reform of International Financial Institutions for Sustainable Human Development," *Monograph #16*, (Wayne, NJ: Center for UN Reform Education, September 2000).

66. Audley and Florini, pp. 5-6.

67. Audley and Florini, pp. 5-6.

68. Henry Kissinger, *Does America Need a Foreign Policy?*, (New York: Simon & Schuster, 2001), p. 232.

69. Smith and Naim, p. 65.

70. Gordon Smith. Rapporteur's Report: 2020 Global Architecture Conference (Unpublished, Victoria: August 29-31, 2001).

71. World Bank, *Attacking Poverty*, pp. 186-7.

72. *Ibid.*

73. Gordon Smith. Rapporteur's Report: 2020 Global Architecture Conference (Unpublished, Victoria: August 29-31, 2001).

74. See Barry Cairn and Gordon S. Smith, eds., "Rethinking Governance' Handbook: An Inventory of Ideas to Enhance Accountability, Participation, and Transparency," (Victoria: The University of Victoria's Center for Global Studies, 2001).

75. Tony Blair, Wim Kok, Goran Persson and Gerhard Schroder, "Progressive Equation: Globalization and Welfare," *International Herald Tribune*, September 7, 2000.

76. Inge Kaul et al., pp. 22-23.

77. *Ibid*, pp. 20-22.

78. P.J. Simmons and de Jonge Oudraat, pp. 710-1.

79. *Ibid*, p 711.

80. *Ibid*, p. 717 citing Reinicke and Deng, *Critical Choices*, p. 47. The Consultative Group on International Agricultural Research (CGIAR) is one of the oldest examples, set up in 1971. An alliance of 58 donor states and organizations and co-sponsored by FAO, UNDP, UNEP and the World Bank, CGIAR works in partnership with research institutions in developed and developing countries to share scientific knowledge on feeding the hungry in developing countries.

81. *Ibid*, p. 718 citing See http://www.un.org/millennium/media/health_kit.htm.

82. *Ibid*, p. 718.

83. *Ibid*, p. 718 citing Reinicke and Deng, *Critical Choices*, pp. 54-55.

84. *Ibid*, p. 716.

85. Peter Richardson, "Corruption," in Simmons and de Jonge Oudraat, pp. 93-4.

86. *Ibid.* And Simmons and de Jonge Oudraat, p. 716.

87. *Ibid*, p. 717 citing Ann M Florini, "The End of Secrecy," *Foreign Policy*, no. 111 (Summer 1998), pp. 60-1.

88. *Ibid*, p. 717.

89. *Ibid*, pp. 713-4.

90. *Ibid*, p. 717.

91. *Ibid*, p. 714.

92. *Ibid*, p. 715.

93. *Ibid*, p. 719.

94. *Ibid*, pp. 13-14.

95. Smith and Naim, p. 63.

Making Globalization Work

James H. Mittelman
American University

As the indomitable Margaret Thatcher once remarked about neoliberal globalization: "There is no alternative."[1] Known as TINA, this slogan means that globalization is here to stay. Globalization is inevitable. Globalization is a juggernaut. Right?

Not at all. To understand why not, let's look beyond immediate events, however compelling they may be, and adopt a perspective that the French historian Fernand Braudel called the *longue durée.* The focus should be on a long-time horizon that extends to the future of globalization—alternatives to its current constitution.

Indeed, globalization can be politically disempowering if one regards it as a juggernaut, that is, a totalizing or inevitable force governing history. Two factors tend to sublimate the politics of globalization. First, there is the rush to implement a series of neoliberal policies—namely, liberalization, deregulation, and privatization—that promotes market integration. Second, there is a preoccupation with market growth rather than balanced development or equity. What, then, are the possibilities for recapturing politics and the prospects for making it work for the world's majority?

In answering this question, I want to argue that globalization has opened spaces, expanding the boundaries associated with political life. Of course, one cannot predict the future from a set of structural disjunctures. History is fundamentally propelled by human will, albeit subject to evolving global forces; it is an open-ended process. But if globalization was made by humankind, then it can be unmade or remade by political agency. As with slavery, feudalism, and mercantile capitalism, there is no reason to believe that neoliberal globalization is eternal.

Myths

To explore how globalization could be made to work in the interests of social equity, the first task is to identify traps and confusions about this set of processes. Especially important here are categories of analysis and language—the very vocabulary used to discuss globalization, which bears directly on thought patterns that are implicated in the exercise of power.

Integral to the debates over globalization are categories of analysis that predate the contemporary globalization period. Without reflection on this matter, it is generally assumed that old categories can be carried over and applied to the current phase of globalization. However, globalizing processes, such as the criminalization of the state in some parts of the world and the privatization of erstwhile public functions, blur precursor categories—for example, state and non-state actors, and legal and illegal activities—deeply ingrained in social thought and represented in the media. Strikingly, many of them are binary oppositions rendered obsolete by globalization. If so, globalization cries out for intellectual innovation and new ways of understanding. In addition, the pedagogical implications are far-reaching (and threatening to the education establishment). The question is: In an era of globalization, can students at the university and pre-university levels be taught as ever before? If not, what types of curricular changes and teaching materials are needed?

Insofar as the power of globalization is addressed by the schools and in public, the coverage embraces a number of myths. One is the notion of a "global village." This pithy phrase helps to direct attention to the compression of time and space, facilitated by new technologies, but is misleading in that it clouds increasing discrepancies between the winners and losers in contemporary restructuring. It is not that everyone is coming together in a single world-wide community, but certain zones, especially much of Africa and enclaves elsewhere, some of them in the wealthiest countries, are marginalized from the central mechanisms of political and economic globalization. These zones and enclaves have been excluded from the so-called global village. There are also heightened global conflicts dividing the supposed single world community, most dramatically seen in the September 11 terrorist attacks on the Pentagon and World Trade Center. What is more, globalizing processes are destroying scores of villages. Increasingly, villagers are being drawn into a globalizing economy—for instance, in export-processing zones in their home countries and by opportunities for work overseas—a development that tears at indigenous social structures, is associated with the spread of AIDS, and wipes out the most productive segments of the population in many villages. In fact, some of the villages in Uganda where, several years ago, as a student at Makerere University, Kampala, I stayed are now ghost towns. The social structures are no longer intact, and the dwellers are only the elderly and young children, many of them orphans—a phenomenon practically unknown in the days when the extended family was expected to, and could, provide a safety net.

Another myth, then, is that globalization homogenizes conditions throughout the world. True, there is a large amount of standardization, as with consumer products. Some of them are world products like automobiles, reflecting cross-border mergers and the parceling out of production processes, as well as design and assembly, to different countries. At the same time, greater diversity is emerging in the form of new hybrids of the global and the local. Take the English language, often considered as a key agent in the spread of globalization. Actually, actors in various locales are appropriating English and creating novel forms of speech, as with Singlish in Singapore.

By the same token, it is wrong to subscribe to the myth that globalization and Americanization are one and the same. Yes, the United States has probably benefited more from globalization than any other country. Globalization is surely heavily American. But not all global products are American forms. Consider reggae music, the croissant, and Japanese animation. How many young Americans, Europeans, and Asians of different nationalities are growing up watching not Bugs Bunny or Mickey Mouse, but Japanese cartoons from Doraemon to Dragon Ball and Crayon Shinchan? Also, like other parts of the world, mid-America is experiencing the shocks of globalization, as formerly tightly knit neighborhoods absorb new waves of immigration and the job market changes, to a certain degree prompted by plant closings in favor of cheap labor overseas.

These patterns should not be construed as what the mythology presents as a move toward a "borderless world." Although European countries have established a European passport and facilitated the movement of citizens across borders, it is the state that grants citizenship and restrains or eases migration. Even if certain global flows, such as knowledge and information on the Internet, easily transcend national borders, the principle of territoriality still matters. Territorially based sovereignty has not disappeared, but must be seen in conjunction with other principles of social organization. They coexist in an emergent multilevel word order, subject to increasing contestation.

Contrary to what is frequently alleged, globalization is not irresistible. There is no juggernaut of expanding markets and technological forces powering history to a forgone conclusion. History is not foreordained. There is no finality. The resistance apparent in Seattle and other venues of protest over globalization is emblematic of fledgling efforts to reshape neoliberal globalization.

The idiom "antiglobalization," which has become commonplace in the media and popular writing, warrants scrutiny, for it is vague and used promiscuously. This idiom is most often applied to head-on confrontations—notably, the 1999 "Battle of Seattle" over World Trade Organization (WTO) policy, followed in 2000 by protests in Washington and Prague at the annual conference of the International Monetary Fund (IMF) and the World Bank, demonstrations in Melbourne at a gathering of the World Economic Forum (WEF), clashes in Seoul surrounding the Asia-Europe Meeting, and collective action at the 2001 Quebec City Summit of the Americas and the Group of Eight meeting at Genoa, which culminated in violent encounters with police and the death of a protestor.

By slotting a wide variety of stances on globalization in two boxes—for and against—this idiom obscures the varied complaints about globalizing trends that have emerged from different points on the political spectrum. What becomes obscure are the diverse attempts to engage—not evade—globalization. In fact, most of the resistance is *against* neoliberalism and *for* globalization such that it should serve social ends. In this sense, the resistance is not *anti-* but *pro*globalization. Moreover, the label "antiglobalization" fails to capture crucial distinctions along the continuum between reformist and nonreformist positions. Some protestors have advanced proposals for institutional adjustments, while others (not only on the left, but also proponents of free trade) have advocated abolishing the institutions themselves. There have been efforts to change the direction and content of policy, and intentions to transform the underlying structures. Indeed, it is important to distinguish along a spectrum between those against globalization but not capitalism, and those against capitalism itself, with globalization deemed to be the current phase.

My point is that the prevalent imagery of "antiglobalization" is problematic since it defines a phenomenon solely as a negation. It impoverishes social criticism by mystifying what may be learned from the debates over globalization. At the venues where public protests against neoliberal globalization have taken place, varied social movements have raised important issues about the dark side of globalization, including increasing market power relative to political authority, a matter that worries not only groups within civil society but also the holders of state power.

For example, when the Asian economic crisis struck Malaysia in 1997 and, within a few weeks, resulted in a forty percent drop in the value of the ringgitt, equivalent to the economic gains of forty years of political independence, Prime Minister Mahathir Mohamad complained loudly about currency speculators, but found that there was no international body empowered to act on his grievances. His main adversary in this script, financier George Soros, also cautioned that markets, when left to their own devices, do not tend toward equilibrium. Markets, he held, are unstable, and the global system urgently requires a new form of regulation. Similarly frustrated by the inability to harness globalizing processes, President Fernando Henrique Cardoso candidly stated that he does not rule Brazil, because globalization is swallowing national states. He lamented that the "increase in inequality and exclusion that globalization fuels is intricate and difficult to counter" (as quoted in Leite 1996, 25).

Neoliberal Globalization as Utopia

Sponsors of globalization seek to create a global market in which the peoples of the world increasingly relate to each other only as individuals. Putting it baldly, Margaret Thatcher declared, "There is no such thing as society, only individual men and women and their families." If so, neoliberalism thus undermines society, subordinating it to the market. From this perspective, globalization is an attempt to achieve the utopia of freeing the market from social and political control. It is a utopia in the sense that this condition has never existed.

Not only is the utopia of a free market comprised of individual actors ahistorical, but also, in Karl Polanyi's memorable phrase, "*Laissez-faire* was planned; planning was not" (Polanyi 1957: 141). In an earlier century, concerted action by a liberal state in Great Britain spawned a supposedly self-regulating economy, yet the pressure for ensuing anti-*laissez-faire* legislation beginning in 1860 started in a spontaneous manner and picked up gradually. Notwithstanding a variety of such enactments, the opening of the so-called free market fomented an "economic earthquake": a socially disruptive and polarizing process amid periods of apparent economic improvement. Polanyi traced the trajectory from social control over the market to a disembedding of market activities. The market gained autonomy, leading to the subordination of society to market forces; in turn, this subordination provoked a protectionist countermovement from social forces, particularly the English working-class.

In his challenge to the myth of a self-running market, Polanyi not only unmasked economic liberalism by providing an account of the dystopia of market society, but also pointed to the need to *re-embed* market forces in society. What must be explicated, however, is the meaning of and strategies for this re-embedding—actually making globalization work, as will be discussed.

Globalization in Flux

Globalization calls into question the ability of the existing interstate system to cope with certain fundamental transnational problems. After all, the Westphalian model of states is a relic of the seventeenth century, established in the West and grafted on to other parts of the world. Strains on this system include the properties of new technologies—interconnectivity and lightning speed—as well as massive concentrations of private economic power that dwarf the resources of many national units and challenge state sovereignty.

Of course, the state does not remain idle. Those who hold the reins of power try to adjust by accommodating global flows and turning them to national and local advantage. Not all states suffer to the same extent from power deflation. So, too, it would be a mistake to portray global processes and the state as locked into a zero-sum relationship. With globalization, some elements within the state gain power while others lose. Among the winners are the economic portfolios and administrative agencies dealing with the external realm. Meanwhile, the offices charged with responsibility for social policy are reduced in scope. Nevertheless, to varying degrees, all states are losing autonomy in the emerging multilevel system. Quite clearly, they operate in a rapidly changing context. The interstate system is durable, but despite its persistence, when are states free to act independently of market constraints? Increasingly, market power disciplines the state, for example, via IMF conditionalities and currency speculation.

Against this backdrop, the state is reconstituting itself, attempting to be proactive in order to harness globalizing processes. However, the capacities of various states to tame these processes differ markedly. The general pattern is the reduction of regulatory activity, the easing of borders, and the lowering of barriers. The restructuring of the state means that it is becoming more of a facilitator of globalizing activities, insofar as they are localized within the domain of a sovereign entity (Cox 1987,

253-65; and for an opposing point of view, see Weiss 1998).

To aggregate their power, states have established a highly institutionalized system. Not only has there been a proliferation of international organizations in recent decades, but also, when faced with new problems of globalization such as transnational cybercrime, the holders of state power seek a higher level of institutionalization and more effective coordination in the interstate system. Hence, there are many rounds of summitry in forums such as the Group of Eight for the most powerful countries, and the Group of Fifteen in the developing world. Another formula, increasingly evident, is informal attempts at policy coordination, for example, in the WEF, an annual gathering usually in Davos, Switzerland, which brings together CEOs of the 1,000 largest corporations in the world, central bankers, presidents, prime ministers, journalists, and scholars. Another informal mode of governance is the Trilateral Commission, which consists of corporate, political, and intellectual leaders from the advanced capitalist countries. In addition, privatized forms of governance are becoming more prominent. The structural power wielded by legal and financial services firms (Sassen 1996) and credit-rating agencies, such as Moody's and Standard and Poor's, is based on evaluations of national economies that enable borrowers to raise money, or prevent them from doing so, and influences the terms of loans (Sinclair 1994a; 1994b). This power can make or break certain developing economies.

The nub of the problem is that the interstate system relies on national institutional forms at a level that does not correspond to an increasing portion of the world's political and economic activities. This incongruity between the cage of the nation-state and actual global flows is an invitation to use more fully the political imagination. Globalization, at bottom, involves a quest for an appropriate temporal and spatial scale for governance (Jessop 1997). But in this quest, what are the alternatives? The alternatives, I believe, are constituted not by well-meaning proposals that wish away the problems of power and conflict of interests, but by countervailing power, which, today, means a multiplicity of resistances to neoliberal globalization.

Resistances

Although Margaret Thatcher's argument about TINA is correct insofar as neoliberalism is predominant and may not have run its course, there are grounds for questioning the triumphalism reflected in her contention. This point is evident in South Africa, where, as the poet Dennis Brutus put it, there is a struggle between TINA and THEMBA, which in the Zulu language, stands for "There must be an alternative," or, in short, "hope" (Bond 1995, 3, 7). To be sure, it is important to ask whether the neoliberal way of ordering the world will stay or wane. Like prior forms of capitalism, neoliberalism has a history, and histories have their beginnings and ends. Certainly, neoliberalism will not simply peter out of its own accord. Rather, faced with myriad discontents and counterpressure, neoliberalism is being challenged by various forces that are incipient, but, arguably, mounting. Especially noteworthy is the drive, rapidly gaining momentum, toward *reregulation*, particularly apparent in Latin America and evident elsewhere as well. Among the reasons for this trend were ways in which the 1997-98 Asian economic crisis deeply affected other regions and the buildup of social problems linked to neoliberal policies.

In different contexts, resistance has emerged not only in the public sphere, but also in the private, more personal, and even intimate realm. The resistance is not necessarily loudly voiced by the state or civil society; it may be quietly expressed in the lifeways of individuals. In other words, resistance to globalization may not be openly declared, but is often latent, local, and uncongealed. Also, resistance is not merely against an imposing structure, but may contain positive and affirmative elements.

At the venues where public protests against globalization took place, collective action by varied social movements drew attention to the drawbacks to globalization, especially world inequality, a lack of transparency with regard to heightened market power relative to political authority, and, in some cases, the erosion of, or affronts to, cultural dignity. The "Battle of Seattle" has thus become a galvanizing metaphor signaling a new dynamic in globalization: increasing political intervention by a coalition of heterogeneous citizens groups in the global economy.

Yet, some countries, Japan being one of them, have not experienced such events in the streets dramatizing the harms of globalization. During the 1990s and into the new millennium, a period of heightened market integration when Japan's bubble burst, the steep decline of the economy has been accompanied by the buying up of many of its financial institutions and other assets by foreign capital, the breakdown of certain protectionist barriers, and marked social dislocation of various sorts, such as a rise in homelessness, said to be unavoidable in the teeth of sharp global competition. While it is striking that public protests against market integration have not occurred in Japan, it would be short-sighted to overlook the points of resistance to market and state power that have emerged in the private and intimate realms of life.

Taking a close look, there is resistance to genetically modified foods by the Consumers Union of Japan and dairy farmers, not stridently sounded but softly spoken (elicited in interviews by student researchers at Ritsumeikan University in Kyoto). So, too, Japanese rice growers are tactfully challenging a key tenet of globalization—liberalization—because they do not want to face international competition. Opening to the global market is perceived as a threat to their identity, connections to nature, and cultural and spiritual heritage, of which rice is a principal part. Another palpable issue is global flows that directly affect women, including the transnational sex industry and child prostitution in locales such as Osaka Prefecture. Each of these matters surrounding food and gender pertains to the vital forces of the human body, the site where the philosopher Michel Foucault examined the capillaries of power and resistance.

Picking up on the Japanese case, there is considerable micro-resistance to globalization, a pattern freighted with macro significance. The challenge is to mediate micro-resistance and macro-resistance. The distinctive features of the Japanese experience also suggest that there is no one best world-wide strategy for making globalization work. It would be facile to search for a single solution to a vast range of complex problems that manifest differently in various locales with distinctive histories, cultures, and resource endowments. There is no realizable alternative of a kind good for all times and places. But are there prototypes, diverse patterns from which alternatives can be derived?

Alternative Scenarios

The evidence points to a range of efforts to imagine alternatives and convert them into practice. They fall into three basic groups. The first involves modifications in neoliberal globalization without challenging its underlying structures, and the second and third call for the destruction of this paradigm, entailing an attack on the ideas and type of policies that form the bedrock of neoliberalsim.

The first group takes as axiomatic the proposition that within the globalization matrix itself, there are real choices. Notwithstanding structural constraints, especially the rise of hyper-competition and the trend toward the "Washington consensus" (the wave of deregulation that began in the United States in the 1970s, accompanied by major reductions in social spending), the choice is essentially a political one. It is held that the market can benefit society while to some extent being kept at bay by innovative state policies.

In the vortex of enormous pressure to globalize more, France exemplifies a resistant state, one that maintains much regulation, generous welfare provisions (in schooling, health care, vacations, retirement, and unemployment entitlements), and a large government-run infrastructure such as its reliable subways and rail networks. Its critics point to a high unemployment rate far exceeding that of the United States; a mounting government deficit; frequent strikes and demonstrations impeding daily life, if not rendering it chaotic; and labyrinthine labor legislation, banking codes, and an educational system that discourages innovation. Faced with the Anglo-American model of neoliberalism, and urged to adopt "the American solution," President Jacques Chirac responded that his country has a global sense of itself and will fight to maintain a way of life: "France," he said, "intends to remain France" (as quoted in Truehart 1997). In the face of unpopular changes to meet intensifying global economic pressures, a nationalist backlash is thus emerging not only from the disadvantaged segments of society but also from some states themselves. France's resistance, of course, is atypical, far different from the courtesan role played by the some states in serving interests embodied in neoliberal globalization.

There are several modes of adaptation to globalization, and no dearth of proposals for institutional reform. In the domestic arena, important adjustments in administrative agencies and legal procedures—say, in the field of immigration—can alleviate some of the problems brought by globalization. In the realm of finance, proposed national reforms include tougher bank standards, curbs on hedge funds, an "exit tax," which would penalize investors for quickly withdrawing their money from a country, and other forms of re-regulation. Crucially, social policy may blunt the sharp edges of the market, especially the global trend toward increased income inequality (Teeple 1995). Advocates of safety nets and social clauses are pushing in this direction, but skeptics contend that they may serve as public relations devices deflecting attention from more fundamental issues. To be sure, there is debate about the proper role of the state in the provision of public goods: specifically, in eliminating absolute poverty, dispensing piped water as well as electricity and modern sanitation for all citizens, protecting the environment, supporting the family as a unit, alleviating congested cities, curbing escalating crime, stopping corruption and cronyism, and promoting the equality of women and the rights of children. If there is a political will for such measures, then the appropriate scale for these interventions may be transnational as well.

Globally, calls for reform include some of the basic conditions on which the IMF insists, notably transparency and greater accountability by government, aspects of structural adjustment that even the fund's critics find laudable. (However, some of them add that the IMF practices double standards by maintaining secrecy in its operations and that the fund should take its own prescription). In practice, adopting the formula of transparency and accountability requires that regimes confront the political economy of domination, often the very basis of their political support. Hence, many leaders, as was the case in Suharto's Indonesia, have found themselves in the dilemma of desperately needing foreign capital and yet reluctant or unwilling to commit political suicide by dismantling the structures of dominance that sustain the state.

Another proposal for international reform is the Tobin tax, which would place a small charge on cross-border capital flows in order to discourage the rapid transfers by speculators that upset vulnerable economies. Suggestions also include the creation of an "early warning system," alerting the world to approaching economic trends, a global central bank, and semi-fixed exchange rates among leading currencies. There can be little doubt about the need for institutional reform, but for the foreseeable future, it is difficult to conceive of heads of state galvanized to agree on and implement a new architecture for global governance, let alone wield the wherewithal to rein in corporate power, which, after all, is transnationally constituted and thus largely escapes the jurisdiction of sovereign entities. More fundamentally, these alternatives cannot work if they fail to come to grips with the power relations inscribed in globalization. At bottom, a really "new international financial architecture" would entail, or require, a new political architecture.

The second order of alternatives calls for structural change, and seeks to rewrite the script of globalization. On the right of the political spectrum, activists and intellectuals have sought to reassert identities based on membership in religious, racial, ethnic, or linguistic communities subject to globalizing forces, often personified by the immigrant, a representation of the other. Movements based in religion have reacted sharply to the convulsive processes of globalization, partly recognition of the ways in which globalizing tendencies are undermining the values of community and ripping the social fabric. Inasmuch as neoliberal globalization facilitates cross-boundary flows, challenges national culture, and tolerates immigration, right-wing movements, especially in Europe and the United States, have opposed major elements in this structure, though not market society per se. Not only have xenophobic groups invoked a sense of nativism, but also there has been opposition to regional schemes, such as the North American Free Trade Agreement and the attempt to expand it beyond Mexico into Chile and throughout South America, on the grounds that they weaken sovereignty and are a precursor to world government. The right's political project embraces the principle of sovereignty, and would build a fortress around territorially bound notions of the state, thereby implicitly calling for the downfall of globalization.

In the search for alternatives, there is a third, also structural, yet even more embryonic project that similarly poses the question, Is globalization indefinitely sustainable? The torchbearers involved in this effort represent a broad constellation of social forces, generally the victims of globalization, elements in civil society, some politicians, and organic intellectuals. They do not advocate a status quo ante; there is no going back to pre-globalization conditions, and the Keynesian welfare state of bygone decades is not the solution. Unlike the right, this group would promote the relaxation of sovereignty in favor of identities at other levels, which would involve redrawing the boundaries of political economy. This project affirms the importance of engaging yet localizing the global and of bottom-up processes. If anything, the latter entails a greater diffusion of power. It includes new venues for experimentation and reinventing the relations among the market, state, and society. It is an effort to redefine politics, to expand the space for nonstate politics. It calls for participatory democratic control of market forces, which ultimately is a matter of political agency. It is also a matter of asserting, relative to globalizing forces, greater *autonomy*, a political and moral precept used by ancient Greek writers, in a somewhat different sense by social contract theorists, and in Kantian ethics.

The core of autonomy is self-determination—a tenet that resonates with contemporary liberalism, as illustrated by aspects of John Rawls's theory of justice (1993). The principle of autonomy implies that agents have the capacity for critical reflection and, notwithstanding structural pressures, the right to choose among options. Exercising this right requires some control over conditions and actions. The principle of autonomy thus means political and economic self-governance by the majority, and allows for freedom and equality in pursuit of the "common good" (Held 1995, 146-47; and on the coupling of globalization and democratic theory, Rosow 1999). Building autonomy from below should not be confused with fencing off and attempting to erect a fortress against the world, actions that could disable civil-society responses to globalization, which in fact often gain strength from their transnational elements. And an assertion of autonomy from below eventually requires topping up: initiatives within the arena of state politics to bring about greater accountability. After all, the netherworld below the state can be a perilous place, usually marked by fragmentation, and sometimes by intolerance and authoritarian forms of identity politics at odds with democratic life. In the face of the drive by neoliberalism to limit the scope of the state (both its activities and budget) and enforce market discipline, a strong state permitting broad access to power and a vibrant civil society pressing for democratic politics, as exemplified by the new environmental and feminist movements, stand to strengthen one another and possibly serve as a counterpoint to globalization from above (Walzer 1999). Although there is no reason to believe that the nation-state is eternal, at present the state and civil society, with their many joint members, seem to need each other in the quest for *democratic globalization.*

A Normative Way Forward?

One response to neoliberal globalization is to pose the question, Is it ethically sustainable? Morally and politically, is it possible to maintain a global system in which, at present, the world's 225 richest people have a combined wealth equal to the annual income of 2.5 billion people, the poorest forty-seven percent of the world's population? In which the three richest people have assets that exceed the combined gross domestic product of the forty-eight least developed countries (United Nations Development Program 1998, 30)? Is it ethically defensible to claim that this is the price paid for the gains that accompany expanding market forces? Or would it be better to attempt to reduce the cost by searching for a democratic solution, which, is, above all, a normative preference? Surely this would not be a panacea; there are different versions of democratic theory, and normative preferences cannot be realized without countervailing power. Within the scope of this chapter, I can offer only points for further consideration, not a full-blown analysis. These points are principles, not policies, for the latter must be devised for different conditions, which, as noted, is to say that the principles may not converge on one best answer for all times and places.

To clear the path for examining the nexus between globalization and democratization, it is important to assess the argument that economic globalization is an emancipatory political force. This thesis is "out there"—being discussed—in scholarly forums and now and again appears in the popular press (e.g., Friedman 1997, 1999). According to this contention, globalization emanates from neither above nor below, but from beyond. In this view, globalization—a lateral movement crossing state borders in the form of capital, technologies, tourism, information, and knowledge—spreads norms and values that penetrate the state. China and some other states have tried to block these forces, but have found that the values accompanying global flows are unstoppable. It is therefore argued that economic globalization brings democracy: "Global markets today are demanding, in return for their investments, the rule of law, transparency, predictability, cooperation and pluralism in financial affairs" (Friedman 1997).

Yet, the correlation of neoliberalism and liberal democracy is more varied and problematic than this interpretation suggests. While free market reforms and liberal democracy have taken root in some Latin American countries, such as Paraguay, there are also signs, overwhelmingly reflected in polls, that people are discontent with the impact of this combination: basic failings in the banking system and a major drop in the value of the currency, accompanied by large increases in unemployment, crime, poverty, and income inequality. Indeed, the argument that market liberalism fosters liberal democracy fails to allow for reverses and nondemocratic change: the erosion or downfall of democracy brought on, at least in good part, by economic reforms. For example, in 1997, a time of great economic tribulation, Bolivians returned their former dictator to the country's highest office. In Africa, there is wide variation: diverse patterns of economic reform and very different types of democratization reflecting distinctive conjunctions of precolonial, colonial, and postcolonial systems as they encounter globalizing forces. Clearly, the conjecture that economic globalization is a source of democratic politics does not account for Africa's collapsed states, which, after incorporation into the Westphalian system and long contact with world markets, have taken a nondemocratic course.

More basically, the problem with the claim that economic globalization generates democracy is that it misses the point that economic markets themselves lack accountability. It also misspecifies the linkage between wealth and power. Markets exercise structural power, including the power to punish the state if it strays too far from the neoliberal path. This often entails coercion, as with the implementation of the structural adjustment programs that have triggered IMF riots in several countries. Adhering to the logic of a market system, the economically powerful, after all, seek to maximize profits and beat their competitors. Although liberal democracy may prove convenient or preferable to other methods of governance, the beneficiaries of globalization have no inherent interest in promoting democracy. The logics of markets and democracy clash over the issue of liberty versus equality, depending on the meaning attributed to these constructs. Then, too, there is the question of the caliber of different versions of democracy.

Democracy in its several variations revolves around the notion of accountability. The Western liberal variant of democracy separates accountability in politics, economics, and society, each sphere subject to different forms of governance. Emphasis in the Western variant is accorded to institutional forms, especially electoral mechanisms. Equity among social strata—reducing inequality in the economic realm—is not the priority in a system whose cardinal feature is a rotation of political power among those who usually represent the interests of the privileged segments of society. Hence the tension between globalization and democratization. How then can democracy be an antidote for a form of globalization that has spun out of control to the extent that its discontents are expressed by holders of state power, financiers, preeminent neoliberal economists, and the marginalized alike? In other words, how can the contents of globalization be revised so as to maintain its many important achievements and relieve the discontents?

To approach this compelling question, if only in a preliminary and schematic manner, one must grasp what democratic control in the context of globalization would mean. Put briefly, democracy is a contested concept; different and competing forms are appropriate for varied social and historical structures, though accountability remains a central criterion of democratic rule. Additionally, democracy is not a final state of affairs but unfolds with changing dynamics. Democracy heretofore has been framed for territorially bounded states that purportedly can contain the movement of people, ideas, and technologies. However, many states, especially the ones with large concentrations of diasporic populations and citizens employed by firms based in other regions, are now subject to deterritorialization and denationalization. To make globalization work, democracy must be *reterritorialized*—strengthened both within and across state borders—as a method of governance for regions and, indeed, for solving global problems.

Democracy is by no means a panacea. In fact, democratization is fraught with catches. Nonetheless, by building democratic procedures for resolving conflicts, the ordinary person can help to achieve world peace. In conjunction with these efforts, institutional reforms designed to restrain unfettered forces in the global market become increasingly important. These initiatives, especially antitrust measures that mitigate corporate power, must transcend the national state.

At the same time, there are signs that in an intersubjective sense and in objective ways as well, the national state is becoming a *transnational state*. In a transnational state, citizens imagine their identities in terms of more than one state—as is the case with some diasporic populations—and actively participate in the politics of two or more countries, which is permitted by the laws and voting procedures in certain contexts (Glick Schiller 1999). The challenge then is to rethink the concept of national democracy and bring it in line with a form of politics in which boundaries are not eradicated but blurred or complicated by trans-border arrangements, some of them authored by the state, and others rooted in economy and culture and either sanctioned by a reluctant state or not at all legitimated by the state.

A transition to democratic globalization is about both good governance and global governance. Good governance in the national realm is a key to reshaping globalization, even if the state is not the exclusive, or even an optimal, unit for managing this process. As Polanyi suggested, the task is to re-embed political and economic power in society, its rules and institutions. In both the countryside and the towns, this is a matter of civil-society empowerment, which includes the advancement of women. There is also the issue of establishing channels to power for the poor and most vulnerable strata, who have had little role in making decisions about the allocation of resources. Moreover, an appropriate legal framework includes not only the rule of law and the constitutional guarantee of human rights, but also free and vibrant media. These core values underpinning good governance are promoted by building viable linkages between civil society and the state, as well as to global governance.

In this transformation, a vital issue is the matter of access. How can global governance be recast so that civil society may participate meaningfully in the steering mechanisms and economic processes of a powerful structure, globalization, that has the potential to deliver to the many—not merely the few—aggregate economic gains (including a cornucopia of consumer goods), technological advances, greater information, new knowledge, and an escape from long-established forms of social control? There cannot be much assurance of the eventual outcome of an open-ended, historical process, but making clear the dynamics, knowing the constraints, and imagining the possibilities, if only a glimmer of the prospects, mark the direction likely to make globalization work.

Globalization after September 11

Did the terrorist attacks on the Pentagon and World Trade Center, icons of U.S. power and global capitalism, change this direction? Have the September 11 terrorists killed hopes for making globalization work?

It would be a grave error to confuse the acute pain inflicted on September 11 and a chronic condition. The terrorist attacks did not demolish the durable structures of globalization. While homeland security tops the policy agenda in the United States and elsewhere, the basic trends marking globalization, especially global market integration and the expansion of regional processes, endure. Surely the underlying issues have not gone away.

Global terrorism and globalization are closely intertwined. Both are trans-border phenomena that challenge the territorial basis of state sovereignty. Both rely on modern technologies and worldwide financial networks. And both feed on marginalization.

Some of the poor and disenfranchised, especially in countries with repressive and corrupt governments, have sought to escape debilitating conditions, including unemployment rates of around 60 percent for young males. In societies in which fatalism—as in the expression *In sha Allah*, or "Whatever God wills"—is commonplace, and where *madrassas* (Muslim religious schools) have radicalized youth, it is not difficult to enlist marginalized men in suicide missions. These marginals believe that their deadly acts provide a ticket to paradise. Although their leaders are drawn from the middle classes and are bankrolled by Osama bin Laden's wealth, festering discontent fills a pool of on-the-spot losers in the globalization scenario, some of whom can be recruited into terrorist activities.

Global terrorists and globalizers alike propagate what they regard as universal truths. On the one side, terrorists and those who abet them use the idiom of religious values to control behavior—of women, children, and all those labeled "nonbelievers." On the other side, the beneficiaries of globalization also attempt to disseminate a value system—the freedom of markets, competition, efficiency, consumerism, and individualism—to promote a different vision of the way in which society should be ordered.

These competing visions are in no sense morally equivalent, but the rhetoric of the protagonists,

Osama bin Laden and President George Bush, converges: a *jihad*, or holy war, pitting believers against "infidels" versus a "crusade" led by the U.S. government, also the torchbearer of globalization, against "evildoers."

Put in perspective, the globalization of terrorism is one in a series of crises in globalization. The first crisis was the defeat of the Multilateral Agreement on Investment, a treaty introduced by the United States in the Organization for Economic Cooperation and Development in 1995. Far-reaching in scope, its objectives were to remove barriers on foreign trade and extend capital markets. Ultimately, a coalition of citizens' groups pressured their governments to withdraw from the negotiations.

Second, the 1997-98 Asian financial crisis was not really Asian, but global, for it rippled to Brazil, South Africa, Russia, and elsewhere. It was about the risks of globalization. Directing his strident rhetoric at George Soros and other currency speculators, Malaysian Prime Minister Mahathir Mohamed, a leader in the mainstream Islamic world, found his country—indeed the entire region and beyond—in a dilemma: No one really governs globalization.

Third, the 1999 "Battle of Seattle" not only buffeted the WTO, but more generally signaled resistance to economic globalization. Plainly, the "Battle of Seattle" and subsequent street demonstrations in world cities on five continents represent rage over the underside of contemporary globalization.

Then, on September 11, 2001, the resistance perpetrated by a global network reached a crescendo that took the form of atrocities. The terrorism crisis is a globalization crisis. The root issue is the same set of heavily American values deemed loathsome by not only the terrorists but also several global justice movements (which, nonetheless, do not endorse the grotesque September 11 tactics).

To come to grips with the implications of September 11 for globalization, it is worth recalling Adlai Stevenson's admonition. As U.S. ambassador to the United Nations, he quipped that the modern technology that Americans most need is a hearing aid. What must be heard today, above all, are messages about different value systems. This is not to suggest that all values are morally equivalent or right. Rather, making globalization work requires recognition that insistence on absolute values will not solve the chronic problem: a world order with unconscionable numbers of marginalized peoples living in sheer misery. It is well to remember that the Abrahamic faiths hold in common a belief in social justice.

Note

1. Neoliberal globalization refers to the complex of ideas and policies centered on increasing integration in the world market. This chapter draws from, and extends, my previous work on alternative globalization: *The Future of Globalization* (Bangi, Malaysia: Penerbit Universiti Kebangsaan Malaysia [National University of Malaysia Press], 1999); *The Globalization Syndrome: Transformation and Resistance* (Princeton: Princeton University Press, 2000); and "Alternative Globalization," in Richard Sandbrook, ed., *Civilizing Globalization* (Albany: State University of New York, forthcoming).

References

Bond, Patrick. 1995. "Under the Microscope: The ANC in Power." *Southern Africa Report* (Toronto) 10, no. 3: 3-7.

Cox, Robert W. 1987. *Production, Power, and World Order: Social Forces in the Making of History*. New York: Columbia University Press.

Friedman, Thomas L. 1997. "Berlin Wall, Part 2: Asia's New Route to Democracy." *New York Times*, 6 May.

———. 1999. *The Lexus and the Olive Tree*. New York: Farrar, Straus and Giroux.

Glick Schiller, Nina. 1999. "Citizens in Transnational Nation-States: The Asian Experience." In *Globalization and the Asia Pacific: Contested Territories*, ed. Kris Olds, Peter Dicken, Philip Kelly, Lily Kong, and Henry Wai-chung Yeung, 202-18. London: Routledge.

Held, David. 1995. *Democracy and the Global Order: From the Modern State to Cosmopolitan Governance.* Cambridge: Polity Press.

Jessop, Bob. 1997. Comments at the workshop on "The Logic(s) of Globalization." Singapore: National University of Singapore, December.

Leite, Paulo Moreira. 1996. "Males Globalizados." Trans. Lillian Duarte. *Veja*, 29, no. 9 (28 February): 24-25.

Mittelman, James H. 1999. *The Future of Globalization.* Bangi, Malaysia: Penerbit Universiti Kebangsaan Malaysia [National University of Malaysia Press].

———. 2000. *The Globalization Syndrome: Transformation and Resistance.* Princeton: Princeton University Press.

———. Forthcoming. Alternative Globalization. In *Civilizing Globalization*, ed. Richard Sandbrook. Albany: State University of New York Press.

Polanyi, Karl. 1957. *The Great Transformation: The Political and Economic Origins of Our Times.* Boston: Beacon Press.

Rawls, John. 1993. *Political Liberalism.* New York: Columbia University Press.

Rosow, Stephen J. 1999. "Globalization/Democratic Theory: The Politics of Representation of Post-Cold War Political Space." Paper presented to the annual meeting of the International Studies Association, Washington, DC, February.

Sassen, Saskia. 1996. *Losing Control? Sovereignty in an Age of Globalization.* New York: Columbia University Press.

Sinclair, Timothy J. 1994a. "Between State and Market: Hegemony and Institutions of Collective Action under Conditions of International Capital Mobility." *Policy Sciences* 27, no. 4: 447-66.

———. 1994b. "Passing Judgment: Credit Rating Processes as Regulatory Mechanisms of Governance in the Emerging World Order." *Review of International Political Economy* 1, no. 1 (Spring 1994): 133-59.

Teeple, Gary. 1995. *Globalization and the Decline of Social Reform.* Atlantic Highlands, NJ: Humanities Press International.

Truehart, Charles. 1997. "French Hold Proudly Fast to Benevolent Central Rule." *Washington Post*, 14 July.

United Nations Development Program. 1998. *Human Development Report.* New York: Oxford University Press.

Walzer, Michael. 1999. "Rescuing Civil Society." *Dissent* (Winter): 62-67.

Weiss, Linda. 1998. *The Myth of the Powerless State.* Ithaca, NY: Cornell University Press.

Sufi 12, a hand colored dry point engraving from the Sufi series.

Provided courtesy of Zeki Findikoglu.

Part Six

Confronting the Universal Quest for Identity:

Family, Religion, and Culture

Tribeless, homeless, lawless
is he, who loves horrid
civil war

—Homer (8th century B.C.)

PART SIX OFFERS A MORE INTIMATE PERSPECTIVE of the causes of conflicts and war within countries, thus touching on one of the book's principal tenets: that modern conflicts are more often waged intra-nationally rather than internationally. Essential to this argument is the notion of identity and self-determination and how competing interests within the state are able to co-exist peaceably. Through works by Jean Bethke Elshtain, and Huston Smith, we examine those identifying elements of family, language and religion that ultimately serve to define man.

Within this analytical framework, authors John Roth and Richard Falk question how governments are to deal with pluralistic and competing interests within their given societies. What does it take to maintain peace between conflictual groupings? And how have the shared histories of these groups prepared them today for war or peace? To that end, how do individuals with multiple identities and loyalties within the state structure react to conflict and peace?

Philosophic Reflections on the Family at Century's Unfolding

Jean Bethke Elshtain
University of Chicago

By education and training, I am a political and civil philosopher. This means that I tend to what is happening to the social and political fabric of my own society in particular, and other societies more generally. Although my focus for this paper, as far as the data is concerned, will be on trends manifest in the United States, I will move back and forth between contemporary concerns and historical and philosophical claims in order to make my case.

The evidence from the streets, the neighborhoods, the schools, the churches, and our homes: the eloquent and often terrifying testimony of events—violence suffered and perpetrated; children unhappy, ignored, home alone; teen mothers, isolated and hovering in drug-ridden dangerous places; teachers afraid of their students; students afraid of other students; civic leaders gazing at a precipitous decline in involvement and participation in all community activities at all levels: this is one face of America today. The evidence is overwhelming, based on hundreds of studies by reputable scholars from dozens of disciplines: indeed, none but the individual committed to the status quo can cast his or her eyes over this encroaching wasteland and say, "This is good. Let's have more of it." It is, of course, all too easy to work oneself up into a lather about teen pregnancies, deadbeat dads, violent youth, and children in poverty. We do that in North America all the time. But we tend to overlook a common denominator that lies beneath or behind so many of these phenomena—the spreading collapse of marriage. With each passing year, an ever smaller percentage of citizens in the United States is married. An even larger percentage of the nation's children live in households absent a parent—most often the father: this figure now stands at about one-third of American children overall. Mind you, I, for one, have no desire to "marry everyone off." I recognize that many people choose not to marry and that they live rich and interesting lives and contribute to their communities in a variety of ways. No, my concern is with how difficult it is to grow up in America. Because, where children are concerned, regularity in human relationships is vital and such relations go by the names "marriage" and "family."

What do we see when we look around? We see that more and more children are growing up with little or no experience of married life, hence no living examples of what it means for two people to commit themselves to one another over time. More American children everyday are growing up with little or no confidence that they could be, or even want to be, in an enduring marital relationship, as the *Marriage Report of the Council on Families in*

Jean Bethe Elshtain, "Reflections on the Family at Century's Unfolding." Reprinted with permission of Professors World Peace Academy from *The Family in Global Transition*, © 1997.

America argues. (New York: Institute for American Values, March, 1995.) Over the past three or four decades, the message American children receive from the wider culture is one that is high on romance and sex but hostile or, at best, indifferent to marriage. It does not seem at all farfetched to say that we, as a society, are failing in the task of social reproduction or, in more econometric terms, there is a strong failure in social capital formation. All this means, in laymen and women's terms, is that we are not imparting to the next generation a set of fundamental norms and beliefs about the meaning and purposes, responsibilities and freedom, of marriage and family life. This, in turn, has a debilitating effect on civic life overall. Democratic civic life relies on persons who have been formed in such a way that they are capable of commitment; understand and accept responsibility; share a sense of stewardship about their communities; appreciate the fact that the creation of decent and relatively stable relationships and societies is a complex and fragile task, not an automatic outcome when human beings share a territorial space or even a bedroom. Perhaps a few bits of dismal data are in order. In the decades 1960-1990, the percentage of out-of-wedlock births skyrocketed from 5.3 percent to 30 percent. If the children from such single-parent units were doing just fine, perhaps there would be no problem. But they are not: they are at far greater risk than children from two-parent households. As well, in those same decades, the divorce rate doubled or tripled, depending upon how it is calculated. As a result, the percentage of children living apart from their biological fathers rose from 17 percent to 36 percent and rising. Juvenile violent crime has also increased in the past three decades. Reports of child neglect and abuse have quintupled since 1976. The teen suicide rate has tripled. As reported recently in the *New York Times,* children from broken homes have two to three times more behavioral and psychological problems than do children from intact homes. (Susan Chira, "Struggling to Find Stability When Divorce is a Pattern." The *New York Times,* March 19, 1995, pp. 1, 17.) Finally, the poverty rate of young children stands at 25 percent, the highest since 1969, and family formation, or the failure to form families, has been indicted as a central causal factor in the growth in childhood poverty. (The *Marriage Report* summarizes this data.)

Because all societies have a stake in the creation and sustaining of norms surrounding sexuality, child-rearing, and other vital human activities tied to our complex social and embodied identities, all societies have attempted to regularize these activities in some way. No society has ever declared any of this to be a matter of indifference. There are many possible arrangements, of course, some more restrictive; some less. But sometimes, it seems, "less" can become "more." That is, as a general laissez-faire attitude toward social arrangements spread, it fuels many different varieties of social troubles. Or so our recent history suggests. Ironically, the growth in "self-expression" and "individualism" appears to go hand-in-hand with a growth in fearfulness, destructive forms of dependency, and even greater social conformism as the primary reference group for the young becomes an age-specific cohort, with adults scarcely in the picture.

There are big conceptual and historical issues here. There are also simple, humble truths. The humble truth is that every child needs and deserves the love and provision of caring adults in a relationship that perdures. The committed, two-married-parent family is the best environment we know anything about in which to rear children. Because it is the main teacher of the next generation, and a protector and defender of our love of, and commitment to, pluralism, it is also an irreplaceable foundation for long-term civic vitality, endurance, and flexibility. A British observer, summarizing the data for his own society, reports that: "...every form of psychosocial disorder among young people—crime, suicide, depression, eating problems, vandalism, alcohol and drug abuse—can be linked to the modern-day cult of juvenile freedom, to their spending power, their moral and social independence from their parents, and their entire lifestyle of music, clothes, sex and whatever. In short, the problem is a colossal and chronic breakdown in parenting. By no means does this only apply to Britain." (Clifford

Longley, "Valuing the Family," *The Tablet*, 10 June, 1995, p. 735.)

What we seem to have lost along the way is an earlier conceptual richness that recognized, as the *Marriage in America Report* argues, that marriage contained, or encompassed, at least five basic dimensions. It was viewed as, in some sense, a natural institution, flowing from basic bodily imperatives. It was a sacramental institution, surrounded by rituals and sacral norms. It was an economic institution, an arena of both production and consumption; of human fabrication and laboring. It was a social institution, helping to create cultural forms that encouraged certain kinds of behavior and discouraged others. It was a legal entity, protected and regulated by a complex body of public and private law. In each of these arenas, the family has sustained a series of body blows that have had the effect, over time, not so much of transforming the family with each of these five interlocked imperatives in mind—but deinstitutionalizing the family by removing many previous imperatives and norms and putting nothing in their place. Let me reiterate: *If* what we were currently seeing was a growth in child well-being, there would be little reason to raise the alarm. But that is not what we see. It is arguably also the case that seductive but elusive chimera, "adult happiness," has not been well served either, but that is not my primary concern. Let's take a brief look, in the form of a review and overview, of how scholars of the family themselves have played a role, for some unwitting, for others quite knowing, in these developments. The dominant conceptual framework within which the family was studied in the American academy, at least from mid-century on, was a school of sociology called functionalism. For the functionalist, the family is a structure that performs certain functions. To be sure, the family is a universal institution. No society has yet been discovered in which an entity which could be either identified or labeled 'family' did not exist. For the functionalist, the important question is what functions the family performs for the wider society. But there were serious drawbacks to this approach. For one thing, it tended to promote an ahistorical approach to the family. For another, functionalists were (and are!) rather flatfooted when it comes to consideration of the sacramental and the biological, or embodied, dimensions of human life, focusing almost exclusively on "socialization" and on "systems maintenance." This meant, as well, that the family's role in civic life-in the creation of citizens was also ignored, as functionalists viewed men and women in and through the language of roles almost exclusively.

The central claim of functionalists was that: "Whenever a country becomes modern, industrial, urban, family organization shifts from large kinship groups to a more isolated nuclear or conjugal pattern." (Arlene Skolnick, "Families Can Be Unhealthy for Children and Other Living Things," *Psychology Today*, vol. 5, no. 3, August, 1971, p. 20.) This assumption received its most elaboration theoretical formulation in the works of Talcott Parsons. Parsons claimed that the nuclear family was a product of the economic and social forces of the past several hundred years. He posited an alteration in family structure along with changes in family function and viewed this alteration as the ineluctable result of forces impinging on the family from the outside. The assumption was that the basic nuclear family configuration (mother, father, children) did not exist before the forces of modernization brought it into being. (See Talcott Parsons, "The Family in Urban Industrial America," in *Sociology of the Family*, ed. Michael Anderson. Baltimore, Maryland: Penguin Books, 1971, pp. 43-62.)

The functionalist model held that the extended family was the ideal typical family prior to industrialization. In this schema, the extended family placed undue restraint on many things, including the creation of a mobile labor force. Because a mobile labor force is necessary to the maintenance and stability of modern society, family structure altered to meet the new demands of the "macro-order." The picture of a tidy fit between industrialization and the nuclear family became nigh irresistible. Notice that there is no room in this model for families to resist change, or to serve as catalysts for change. Families were seen as entities shedding one "function" after another as the macro-order mutated. The family, having lost many functions, was then forced to become "a more specialized agency." In Parsons' terms: indeed, he claimed that it was "important that socializing agents should not themselves be too completely immersed in family ties," as a too strong commitment to the family would handicap such persons in their ability to "fit" with the needs and demands of a mobile, opportunistic society. (Parsons, p. 59) Women got assigned an "expressive" role; men, an "instrumental-adaptive role."

Having construed the family within functionalist terms, scholars deprived themselves of any normative stance from which to evaluate what was, in fact, happening to and with families. So long as the abstract "needs" of the overall social order were served, then all must be well (more or less) with families. The importance of parenting to the well-being of real flesh and blood children—rather than the abstract needs of an abstractly construed "social order"—was slighted or ignored altogether. It was easy to accept any changes that appeared in family norms, including the rise in divorce, as just the latest variation in the family's endless mutability given the demands of social life. Mothers and fathers fell out of the picture as role players came to dominate. This led, in turn, to the notion that so long as a "role" was being served, it scarcely mattered who occupied the role. Indeed, I heard one family sociologist (at a feminist conference in mid-1970s), argue that "antibiotics and birth control made mothering unnecessary." She advocated the total replacement of mothers by professional childrearers in order that women, too, could be part of the mobile labor force required by industrial capitalism.

Because the functionalist schema extended to internal family relations as well, and because it tended to celebrate greater "role differentiation" as an inevitable thing (and inevitability within functionalism tends, implicitly, to be equated with "what is good"), academic scholars tended to be unabashed celebrants of the "role divergence" that comes with a rapidly changing social order. The story went like this: The family performs pared down functions. It turns out that many other institutions could perform these functions as well. It further happens that we don't really need "mothers" and "fathers" so long as various persons or institutions are assigned "nurturant" and "socialization" tasks. This no doubt overstates, but not by much.

To be sure, there were critics, including the so-called Cambridge School of historic demographers, who challenged the abstractedness of the functionalist formula. They argued that, in fact, the basic mother-father-children configuration had always been the pattern, certainly in Western societies, with variations on that mode. The so-called "nuclear family" was not a recent invention, coming into being only with industrialization. (Peter Laslett, "The Comparative History of Household and Family," *Journal of Social History,* vol. 4, no. 1, Fall, 1970, pp. 74-87.) The demographic evidence indicated that a basic nuclear or conjugal household had long pertained and that, even in pre-industrial epochs, marriage meant the formation of a new household, often with members of the couple's households of origin figuring as central or adjunct members, so to speak.

Of course, calling into question the dominant functionalist model means one is obliged to offer another set of categories and explanatory features, especially if one hopes to make the case that the family is in trouble; that what we are witnessing is, in fact, family decline. How do we know? Here the focus must shift to the well-being of children and on that score, as I have already indicated, things do not look good. There are ways in which a wider order may be served, particularly in its current consumption-driven, expressivist forms in the United States, even as individuals are ill served and the overall society itself, over time, reels from the changes that are taking place, although it may come to realize that too late. My claim is that our societal experiment in loosening the ties that bind has failed: that it has failed our children, first and foremost, but that also, in ways we are only just beginning to recognize, it has failed adults understood as moral agents and responsible citizens, not just as a "mobile labor force."

This is the harsh truth of the matter: Americans,

at the end of the twentieth century, suffer from the effects of a dramatic decline in the formation of social bonds, networks, and trust coupled with a diminution in investment in children. Children have borne the brunt of decades of negative social trends whose results are just now coming into clear focus; standing out in harsh relief. Family breakdown, in turn, generates unparented children who attend schools that increasingly resemble detention homes rather than centers of enduring training, discipline, and education and contributes to out-of-wedlock births and adolescent violence that, so far as we know is now at unprecedented levels.

Here a reminder from the perspective of political and civil philosophy is in order as a way to reaffirm the *civic dimensions* of this question. Democratic theorists historically have either taken for granted a backdrop of vibrant, informal and formal civic associations, or they have articulated explicitly the relationship between democracy and the everyday actions and spirit of a people, most famously de Tocqueville in *Democracy in America.* Democracy requires laws, constitutions, and authoritative institutions, as I argue in my book, *Democracy on Trial* (Basic Books, 1995), but it also requires what might be called democratic dispositions. These include a preparedness to work with others for shared ends; a combination of often strong convictions coupled with a readiness to compromise in the recognition that one can't always get everything one wants; a sense of individuality and a commitment to civic goods that are not the possession of one person or of one small group alone. The world that nourished and sustained such democratic dispositions was a thickly interwoven social fabric—a web of mediating institutions, of which the family was one. (Note the very different model implied here: rather than the family as a sub-system playing functions for a wider system—a series of boxes with connecting lines, with some dominating over others—the implied picture is one of a web of interlaced *institutions, a social ecology.)*

Now, in his great book, Tocqueville warned of a world different from the democracy he surveyed. He urged Americans to take to heart a possible corruption of their way of life. In his worst fears, narrowly self involved individualists, disarticulated from the saving constraints and nurture of the overlapping associations of social life, would require, even come to demand, more control from above to muffle at least somewhat the disintegrative effects of what he called a bad form of "egoism." Only small scale civic bodies enabled citizens to cultivate the democratic virtues and to play an active role in the democratic community.

But the tale I am telling argues that the deinstitutionalization of the family is part and parcel of a wider unraveling of the institutions of civil society tied, in turn, to a dramatic upsurge in all forms of social mistrust, generalized fearfulness, and cynicism. Recent studies show that Americans, without regard for race, cite very similar social problems: fear of crime, concern about poor education, the decline of home and family. Indeed, if anything, African-Americans are more insistent that their society faces a crisis in values, beginning with the family.

What, then, is to be done? The sociologist, Robert Bellah, reports that Americans today brighten to tales of community, especially if the talk is soothing and doesn't appear to demand very much. Yet when discussion turns to institutions, and the need to sustain and to support authoritative civic institutions, attention withers and a certain sourness arises. This bodes ill for liberal democratic society, a political regime that requires robust yet resilient institutions that embody and reflect, the urgencies of democratic passions and interests. As our mediating institutions, from the Parent Teachers Association to political parties, disappear or are stripped of legitimacy, a political wilderness spreads. People roam the prairie fixing on objects or policies or persons to excoriate or to celebrate, at least for a time, until some other enthusiasm or scandal sweeps over them. If we have loss of the sturdiness and patience necessary to sustain civil society over the long haul, liberal democracy is in trouble.

This is why the family matters. This is why conformist insouciance concerning what is happening to the family rings increasingly hollow. This is why the functionalist perspective is not up to the conceptual task, given its inability to account for change as anything other than a kind of lock-step transmutation of certain structures to keep up with functions they are either deprived of, or new job descriptions they are assigned, by the "macro-order." What we require here at century's end is a way to reweave the threads of community; to restore our faltering faith in cultural forms themselves. The speed and glitz of late modernity—at least in the consumerist West—helps to stoke the fires of great impatience. Americans are especially known for being an impatient people. We want things to happen right away. We want problems to be solved overnight. But that isn't going to happen, not when we are faced with problems of such social, economic, sacramental, legal, political and, yes, embodied power and force. Late twentieth century moderns are dealing with the wreckage that mounted because, in the words of Vaclav Havel of the Czech Republic, we have forgotten that we are not God.

Although the family is the locus of private life, it is also critical to public life, to the life of the community and to civic associations. Here the testimony of parents and experts converges. When parents are asked to tell their own version of our current discontents, they lament the fact that it is harder to do a decent job raising children in a culture that is unfriendly to families and family attachments. The overwhelming majority of Americans, between 80-85 percent, believe that being a parent is much more difficult than it used to be. Pessimism about the decline of family norms is on the rise among all groups, especially among women and African-American and Hispanic citizens.

The family of which I speak is not an isolated unit but very much a social institution, nested in a wider surround, that either helps to sustain parental commitment and accomplishment or puts negative pressure on mothers and fathers. That pressure obviously takes many forms. I have articulated just a few. Being a parent is more than playing a role. Being a parent is more than a "life-style choice." It is an ethical vocation. We, as a society, and this I would urge on all societies more generally, should, insofar as this is possible, lighten the burdens and smooth the paths for parents in order that the complex joys of family life might rise to the surface and in order that the undeniable burdens of family responsibility might be more openheartedly borne.

Children lost to society in increasing numbers may be a growing phenomenon, but it is one we must name for what it is: a loss, a crying shame. Protecting, preserving, and strengthening family autonomy and the well-being of mothers and fathers is a way of affirming our commitment to the individual and to democratic social life. We have, it appears, lost the recognition that the rights of persons are fundamentally social. What is at stake in the family debate, and in our response to it as we near century's end, is nothing less than our capacity for human sociality and community.

Here are a few concluding questions for further consideration; indeed, they are inexorable questions given my analysis:

- What are the root causes of family disintegration? What are the effects of this deinstitutionalization?
- Why is concern with the family a civic and ethical issue?
- What does the family (mothers and fathers; brothers and sisters; grandparents; uncles, aunts, cousins; etc.) do that no other human institution can?
- What is the role or responsibility of individuals, communities, business, and government in dealing with family issues?
- How can we move to stem the tide of out of wedlock births, teenage violence, family breakdown without enhancing the avowedly coercive apparatuses of states?

This is a tall order. If we are not up to the task, the twenty-first century will be a tale of further coarsening of social life and deepening pressure on democratic society to enhance its coercive powers in order to save us from ourselves. If we hope to forestall this unhappy prospect, we must tend to our social ecology before it is too late. The family belongs on the list of endangered species.

Family, Religion, and Globalization: The Implications for World Peace

William R. Garrett
Saint Michael's College

Several mega-trends, including the transformation of family systems both with respect to their structural and functional dimensions, the growth of religious fundamentalism and terrorism, as well as the take-off of globalization processes, are examined in this essay using a sociological frame of reference as the central interpretive backdrop. The implications of each of these substantive changes is then assessed in relation to the likelihood of the attainment of a genuine peace in the post-Cold War age.

The essential thesis proposed herein contends that the family as a social institution both contributes to the conflicts likely to emerge in the contemporary context and this institution also brings to current hostilities some resources for promoting their resolution. In a similar fashion, religion has now clearly manifested both benign and malevolent capabilities, depending on the sort of use to which religious sentiments are devoted. And finally, globalization processes—understood as a broader movement than the economistic accounts most often propounded by journalists or anti-capitalistic activists—have ushered in a new set of contemporary circumstances for contextualizing current social movements. Whether these changes taken in concert will promote more peaceful social relations in late modernity remains a problematic matter.

Introduction: The Times They are a Changing

"The times they are a changing" was a song lyric of the sixties which aptly summed up the tumultuous events of that decade, but the line now seems even more appropriate for the opening decade of the twenty-first century. Several sociological trends of overwhelming importance will be reviewed in this brief essay, including the transformation of family structures and processes, the heightened public importance of religious movements (Casanova, 1994; Juergensmeyer, 2000), and the emergence of globalization processes wherein the "world" as we know it is being substantively restructured. All of these trends hold both promise and peril for human well-being in the near future. The ultimate question with which this essay will be concerned, however, pertains to whether the family or religion *qua* social institutions can help promote the prospects for peaceful social relations under the conditions of globality. In the process of attending to this issue, we shall also explore the limitations enjoined on familial and religious life in the endeavor of seeking peaceful social relations among members of the human community.

Given the grand scale of the empirical materials to be covered in this writing, the sociological trends—which form the backdrop to the interpretive thesis being developed herein—will necessarily have to be sketched with very broad strokes. Nonetheless, the argument will be developed below that the familial institution can through its socialization processes facilitate the internationalization of attitudes and behaviors supportive of peaceful social relations. And conversely, family socialization can legitimate attitudes and behaviors whose outcome fosters aggression in violent support of individual, ethnic, religious, or national interests. In both instances, however, normative patterns established during primary socialization in the family are subject to revision and transformation as a self moves into interaction with other references groups in later life. The ability of the family—or the religious community—to control the outcome of maturing selves is strictly circumscribed and, in many instances, it may not even be the most important factor in shaping aggressive or peaceful behaviors among its adult members. One cannot sanguinely assume, therefore, that proper socialization in the nuclear family will automatically translate into more peaceful social conditions in society at large.

A Theory of Globalization

Since the interpretations of the familial and religious institutions are couched within the framework of a globalization theory, it makes sense to expound that theory before attending to the institutional analyses. Several theories of globalization are available for this interpretive account. The oldest and perhaps the best known is the world systems theory of Immanuel Wallerstein (1974; 1980; 1989). The central theme of this account is that world capitalist expansion since the sixteenth century is the integrating factor which is uniting the globe into a singular system. Even those outside the capitalist system are integrated by virtue of being outsiders. An alternative approach is provided by John Meyer (1980; and Meyer and Hannan, 1979) under the rubric of world polity theory. This approach stresses the political underpinnings to global integration through such political instruments as treaties, non-governmental organizations, international law, systems of nation–states—like NAFTA, NATO, the U.N., the E.U., and the like. Meyer and his colleagues are not contending that a one–world government is emerging, but that the nations of this planet are being linked into a global polity which has a critical impact on the way in which nation–states and systems of nation–states relate to one another.

A third alternative—and the one utilized in this analysis—is the globalization theory developed by Roland Robertson (1992) and his associates (see, Robertson and Garrett, 1991; Garrett, 2000; Simpson, 1989; Lechner, 1989; and Beyer, 1994). A central claim of this paradigmatic stance is that the world is being compressed, so that more and more citizens of the planet are coming to see the globe as "one place." The major factors responsible for this compression include the integrating function of information, transportation, economic, educational, religious, legal, athletic, and political systems. In other words, globality is a consequence of a combination of economic, political, and cultural forces.

The global field or the "global human condition" can be expressed with reference to four salient components, namely, selves, nation-states, systems of nation-states, and humanity (Robertson, 1992: 27). Changes related to each of the component units warrants a brief summary.

Selves. The central claim here holds that selves are becoming increasingly conscious of their responsibility for defining who they are and constructing their own biographies. Ascriptive roles based on inherited characteristics such as gender, race, ethnicity, social class, and so forth, are giving way to achieved roles which are selected by discrete selves. Hence, the range of discretionary behaviors is being decidedly increased, with the result that contemporary actors are afforded a wider latitude of opportunities insofar as the framing of their lifestyles and personalities are concerned. Under conditions of globality, therefore, the expectation becomes more widely diffused that selves will take firmer control over their own identity declarations.

Nation-states. Alongside the cultivation of individualism there is a simultaneous upsurge in nationalism—or the consciousness of one's affiliation with and commitment to a given nation–state. Prior to the late nineteenth century, affairs of state were largely a function of the nobility and elite classes—often including the Church in the West. Common folk identified with their village or region much more than with the national regime that held formal jurisdiction over them. The rise of the middle–class in Western societies resulted in demands for greater opportunities for political participation as well as a burgeoning sense of attachment on the part of citizens to the central regime. For its part, the nation-state also appropriated an "interventionist" stance, predicated on the claim that the nation-state alone could "...raise the living standards of the population, educate them, unify them, give them a sense of pride and well-being, and administer public affairs in a 'rational' and calculative manner" (Smith, 1983:231-232). Moreover, since one's "place" in the world could only be defined in reference to one's position within a specific nation-state, globalization dynamics actively impelled an upsurge in nationalism. World citizenship thus presupposed a firm sense of national citizenship.

Individualism and nationalism constitute a reflexive and mutually reinforcing relationship, with both driven by the emergent forces of globalization.

Systems of Nation-States. The emergence of the nation-state coincided with the development of systems of nation-states in the late nineteenth century, and inter-societal organizations have experienced exponential growth in the last half century. Prominent examples of systems of nation-states include: the United Nations, NATO, OPEC, NAFTA, the European Union, as well as more *ad hoc* organizations such as the coalition of nation-states who participated in the Gulf War and the coalition for the Afghan conflict against terrorism. Entry into organizations comprised of nation-states has the ironic consequence of relativizing the status of nation-state members, for participation requires the relinquishing of some measure of nation-state sovereignty. When Poland joined the NATO alliance, for example, she would have been hard-pressed not to send troops into Bosnia as a part of NATO's peacekeeping efforts had such a request been extended by the organization's leaders. Moreover, some Arab nations were reluctant partners in the Gulf War coalition, since their contributions seemed to be legitimizing the effort to contain the Muslim nation of Iraq by a largely Western military force. In both instances, leaders of national regimes felt confined in pursuing an independent foreign policy by virtue of the membership in interstate organization. Thus, under contemporary conditions of globality with the number of systems of nation-states sharply on the rise, the nation-state as such is simultaneously and paradoxically experiencing an increase in its importance, along with a relativization of its sovereignty.

Humanity. The claim with respect to this final category is that persons around the world are becoming increasingly conscious of their interdependence as global citizens. Identification as a part of humanity cuts across ethnic, national, gender, class, and economic divisions. Evidence of this common humanity was clearly visible in the response of millions of observers to the terrorist attacks on the World Trade Center, wherein persons around the globe swiftly pointed out that this was not just an assault on the United States, but an attack on the world. This was not just a recognition that citizens of other countries perished in the assault on the Twin Towers, but a forceful expression of the outrage and repugnance to the inhumane character of the violence, which was apparently unleashed under the guise of religious motivations.

The meaning to be assigned to the construct of humanity has been defined most definitively in the various human-rights instruments enacted by both nation-states and the *Universal Declaration of Human Rights,* embraced by the United Nations in 1948 and the subsequent covenants and documents pertaining to the rights of children, women, ethnic groups, linguistic communities, refuge groups, and the like. All of these instruments add practical signification to the concept of humanity, even though not all national regimes are willing to accept the ramifications of specific human-rights principles. There is, in fact, an ongoing dialogue among diplomats, scholars, and religious leaders with respect to working out specifically problematic aspects of these various human-rights instruments (see, Twiss, 1998).

One consequence of the rising salience of the construct of humanity in human consciousness around the globe has been to further relativize the nation-state as well as some systems of nation-states. And this has resulted in the calling into question claims by some leaders of nation-states, mostly notably, by the People's Republic of China and North Korea, that what actions regimes take with respect to their own citizens is exclusively their own business and that action cannot be legitimately impugned by persons beyond their borders. This stance has been soundly rejected by such groups as Amnesty International, Doctors Without Borders, and Human Rights Watch, as well as individual nation-states or systems of nation-states, like the EU or NATO. The result has been a burgeoning criticism against China, for example, for its harsh repression of students in Tiananmen Square, the practice of female genital mutilation in societies like the Sudan, the repression of women under the Taliban rule in Afghanistan, the treatment of Muslim and Sikh minorities in India, the zealous recourse to the use of capital punishment in the United States, and the list could be extended almost indefinitely. The common theme in all these crucial situations is that violence against any one of the groups cited above constituted an act of violence against the whole of humanity, since these people share with us a common destiny and a common identification with other members of humanity. Thus, violent actions by governmental regimes against their own citizens are now regarded as violence directed against all of us, because the "us" now embraces the whole of humankind. And this definition of the situation gives persons around the globe with the "right" to critique the action of any government which acts in a repressive or hostile manner toward even members of its own societal community.

A similar sentiment extends to matters related to the ecological condition of the world. The rain forests, the whales, the coral reefs, the oceans, the growth of carbon dioxide gasses in the air, and other environmental issues, all have their specific influence on the quality-of-life for human beings as a species. Thus, in the name of humanity, we can readily condemn the harvesting of whales, the destruction of the rain forest, the increased sale of energy-inefficient and polluting SUVs, and the dumping of garbage in the oceans as a threat to the commonweal, indeed, the very survival, of humanity as a whole. While there may not be a basis in international law to sustain the claims of humanity with respect to these several issues, there certainly is emerging a political culture world-wide which views the violation of these concerns extremely problematic. We may discover, in fact, that political pressure may be more effective in the long run than legal sanctions in fostering compliance to expectations developed in the larger framework of humanity (Waters, 1995:102-103).

In light of the schematic presentation of the globalization paradigm above, several caveats are in order to curtail any confusion that may arise from this discourse. The first caveat is that globalization is not regarded as a new period in Western social history. Although Martin Albrow (1996) has argued that we are now entering a "global age," most theorists regard globalization as a process—which has had antecedents in other historical eras (see, in this connection, Robertson and Garrett, 1991; Giddens, 1990)—but its dynamics have been greatly intensified in late or high modernity, that is, in the last fifty years or so. Another caveat pertains to the homogenization of cultures and political orders that are frequently assumed to be a part of the globalization process. The fact of the matter is that globalization requires each nation-state to carve out its own unique niche within the larger context of the community of nations. Indeed, under the conditions of globality, nation-states are inclined toward the "invention of tradition," if they lack a requisite narrative history to undergird their own peculiar form of nationalism (see, Hobsbawn and Ranger, 1983). And finally, the distinction needs to be firmly drawn between describing a phenomenon like globalization and extending approbation to such a social process. The aim of the globalization theory described above is to provide a theoretical paradigm for understanding ongoing empirical processes. Certainly, Robertson and his colleagues have made quite clear that globalization may unleash destabilization in interstate relations and create trouble spots around the globe of such intensity that we may look back on the Cold War as the "good old days," that is, a time when the superpowers of the East and West were able to contain in large measure the divisive forces that had the potential to subvert peaceful social relations around the globe. Thus, the emergence of the conditions of globality portrayed in this analytical model constitute an effort to describe what "is" and not necessarily what "ought" to be. Whether globalization is a desirable state of affairs is an altogether separate matter to be analyzed and evaluated independently of the effort to provide a descriptive account of changes currently transforming the social reality in which we all participate.

It is against the background afforded by this particular paradigm of globalization theory that a consideration of changes within the familial and religious systems of societies around the world is being developed in the present context, with special attention being directed toward the implications of these changes for securing more peaceful relations in the world. The conventional assumption, of course, is that both families and religious bodies are benign communities whose influence is conducive to the development of peaceful relations among fellow human beings. On the basis of historical and recent empirical evidence, however, such a view is no longer tenable and may even be characterized as naïve in a variety of instances. In the case of murder, for example, the first suspects investigated by police units are usually close family members, since crimes of violence are more often committed by relatives than complete strangers. And more and more around the globe, violent clashes are motivated by religious sentiments rather than simply devolving from political or class interests (see, Huntington, 1996). To put the issue quite pointedly, then, as agencies of socialization, families and religious groups are as capable of inculcating propensities toward violence as they are of instilling commitments to peaceful social relations. The eventual outcomes of socialization dynamics undertaken by these two institutions derives from both the belief systems and the interest structures operative among the members of familial and religious groups.

Clearly, family and religion are not the only agencies implicated in socialization processes, but they are unquestionably pivotal at crucial stages in the course of character formation and the molding of behaviors. In the analysis which follows, both familial changes as well as modifications in the outlooks of religious communities—along with their public functions—will be explored. The aim animating this effort is not to provide an exhaustive summary of basic modifications occurring in these two institutions, but to call attention to those changes in each one that have aided or frustrated relations of peaceful coexistence in the contemporary global circumstance.

Recent Transformations in the Modern Family

The modern family is a phenomenon of remarkably recent vintage, since its appearance in Europe can be dated from approximately the 1850s (Shorter, 1977), although it emerged somewhat earlier in America (Garrett, 1998). Indeed, Shorter has proposed that the modern family supplanted the family of the "bad old days" of later medieval times. The medieval family was characterized by arranged marriages overseen by parents whose mate selection for their children was defined almost exclusively by economic considerations, little intimacy prevailed in husband-wife relations, family members enjoyed little privacy and were constantly subjected to community surveillance, high death rates were normal for infants—largely produced by parental neglect, a high birth rate was necessitated by the high infant mortality rate, the divorce rate was low because marriages were arranged and divorce could impact the economic status of the family negatively, family life was adult centered—interests and needs of children received low priority in family decision-making, life expectancy for adults was short and life was hard, the economy was dominated by agrarian activities, and social life was village-oriented. On balance, then, medieval family life was stifling and love was absent from spousal or parental relations.

The coming of the modern family introduced sweeping changes in familial relations. Since marriages were no longer arranged, then courtship emerged under couple controls, romantic attachment became the basis for mate selection, intimacy became the norm for wife-husband relations, family members attained privacy from community surveillance—especially since the work-place was separated from the home, the death rate for infants sharply decreased—largely as a function of greater parental concern for their offspring, the birth rate declined, family life became child-centered—in the sense that parents came to take the needs and interests of their children into consideration when making family decisions, life expectancy increased as well as the standard of living, the economy was dominated by industrialization set within an urbanized social environment (see, Garrett, 1982:43).

The early modern family has subsequently experienced a variety of additional changes—Shorter (1977) has argued that these modifications signal the emergence of the post-modern family, but the adequacy of that term is still being debated among family sociologists. Certainly, it can be agreed that since the 1960s we have witnessed these alterations in family life: Courtship is now strongly influenced by the peer group, husband-wife relationships are less stable with the divorce rate now attaining 50 percent, children gain a greater freedom from parental controls by moving into the peer group at an earlier age, relations with extended kin decline, the birth rate decreases with the result of smaller family size, family life is oriented more toward personal fulfillment—whether the person is adult or child, women enter the labor force in larger numbers, so that family affluence increases, more family income is devoted to leisure activities, and the economy is more geared toward higher professional occupations and service sectors jobs (see in this connection, Skolnick, 1991; Stacey, 1991; 1996).

The initial, almost knee-jerk, reaction to these major changes was the announcement by many social scientists that the Western family was in a state of rapid decline. I (1997) have argued elsewhere that the decline-of-the-Western-family thesis was premature and that family systems in modernized societies were, in fact, experiencing a transformation, becoming more pluralistic, and more egalitarian. For example, the participation of women in the paid labor-force outside the home (Davis and Robinson, 1991; Casper, McLanahan, and Garfinkel, 1994) has been correlated with a heightened divorce rate in some studies (South and Lloyd, 1995), while other scholars have challenged this interpretation of the data (Voydanoff, 1987). What does seem clear is that women's economic participation elevates their decision-making power within the nuclear family unit and may also increase their value insofar as their spouse is concerned. Women who are no longer totally dependent on their husband's earning power have the option to terminate unhappy marriages and go it on their own, while husbands who have wives who are making significant contributions to the overall family income may make greater efforts to keep their wives happy and satisfied rather than forego the benefits derived from elevated family earnings (see, Cherlin, 1981: 65-68).

Quite apart from the enhanced self-esteem many women experience from developing a career outside the home, the additional benefit accruing to working women is their elevated status within the nuclear-family unit itself in relation to their husbands. Thus, for many women, pursuing a career or finding employment outside the home is not simply an economic necessity in order to maintain or attain a particular standard of living, it is also a means for promoting egalitarian relations within the household—a goal of considerable significance given the emphasis of equality in the American value-system.

Moreover, data related to recent trends for women in the paid, rather than domestic, labor force reveal more optimistic signs of gender equality than previously detected. That is to say, women are now more disproportionately represented in all levels of higher education as well as graduate and professional schools, signaling the likelihood that they will soon occupy higher positions in the job market than was previously the case. Women can now expect to spend at least 30 years in the paid labor-force, even if they take some time off for child-birth. Forty percent of white college educated women now earn as much or more than their husbands. Women employed outside the home are now spending considerably less time in child-care and performing household tasks than was true thirty years ago, while husbands who are employed are spending more time with children and engaged in household responsibilities. And, although employed women still devote more time to family activities, experts are now predicting that the rate of decline for women in these responsibilities is so dramatic that there will be a convergence between men and women in the next twenty years or so (Barnett and Hyde, 2001). All of this suggests, then, that the domestic and familial workloads between husbands and wives are beginning to even out with a more equal division of household labor and participation in the paid labor-force outside the family.

Of all the alterations in family life among modernized social orders over the last half century, perhaps the most far-reaching in its consequences is the emergence of the ideal of a companionate relationship between husband and wife. By the early 1960s, Blood and Wolfe (1965) documented that companionship had become the most valued aspect of marriage, outpacing such other desirable features as love, sex, children, social-class standing, and the like. Companionship implied love, but also much more. It included such features as being your mate's best friend, your confidant, the person to whom one turned for sympathy, moral support, the person with whom one built up a common biography so that memories could be replayed and savored. For companionship to develop, couples needed not only a great deal of time for the relationship to develop, but quality time spent with one another in joint activities, conversation, and the sharing of feelings. For a companion is a person with whom one could share one's hopes and fears, one's dreams and aspirations, as well as one's deepest hurts and failures. Moreover, a true companion is one who is always ready to take your side when the rest of the world is competitive, harsh, critical, and unsympathetic. A companionate relationship, therefore, provides a "haven in a heartless world," a person to whom one can turn for ready acceptance and solace, and, therefore, the most intimate and important relationship into which persons nowadays enter.

While companionship is regarded almost universally as a boon for marriage partners and for the institution of marriage generally—because it promotes love, loyalty, equality, commitment, fulfillment, and psychological balance between spouses—a latent consequence of the ideal of companionship has been to help elevate the overall divorce rate. Many divorces, of course, are the result of drug addition, alcohol abuse, violence against children or a marriage partner, or infidelity, an increasing number of divorces are a function of the failure to achieve a companionate relationship, at least in the United States. Evidence in support of this interpretation can be gleaned from the relatively high remarriage rate that has paralleled the upward spiral of the divorce rate over the last several decades—a pattern not only present in the United States, but also in other industrialized nations (Goode, 1993:36-40). Cherlin (1981:28) has pointed out that five out of six men and three out of four women remarry after divorce. The inference to be drawn from these statistics is that persons who divorce have not given up on marriage; they simply have given up on the particular partner to whom they were married. Or, in the view of Spanier and Thompson (1987:17): "Divorce is a response to a failing marriage, not a failing institution. The family system can remain strong while divorce rates remain high."

Put somewhat differently, the divorce rate can be viewed as in part a response to the American commitment to a high-quality marriage. That is to say, persons now appear to be much less willing to settle for an inferior marriage that does not attain the level of companionship which they regard as optimum. Accordingly, more and more spouses are prepared to go through the trauma of divorce in order to reenter the marriage market and try again to find a mate with whom they can achieve a companionate relationship. This situation presents, then, a curious irony: If Americans would be willing to settle for a less satisfying marriage, then the divorce rate would probably go down. But an unwillingness to accept a less than companionate ideal has functioned—and will probably continue to function—it elevate the divorce rate in American society.

The question can properly be raised: Is a high divorce rate problematic? Does it reflect deep underlying problems in the marriage system that could impair the functioning of the familial institution as a whole? Perhaps the best response to these questions has been phrased by Mary Jo Bane (1976:3) who observed that "Worry about the family is mostly worry about the next generation. Falling birthrates, rising divorce rates, increasing numbers of working mothers, and other indicators of the alleged decline of the family would probably seem much less alarming if adults alone were affected by the making and dissolving of families." Bane is undoubtedly correct that the concern over the divorce rate is primarily a concern for the children of divorced parents. Will they be properly socialized and will they grow to maturity with psychological stability, able to cope with life's problems? Bane's initial answer is that more children are now in intact families than in earlier generations in American life. Previously, children grew up with only one parent because of the high mortality rate. As the mortality rate of parents has decreased, the divorce rate has increased, so that children today are in single-parent families for a different reason than earlier generations.

The overarching question, however, of whether children suffer from growing up in single-parent families cannot be answered definitively. Some social scientists insist that being raised in a single-parent family is inherently damaging to children (Council on Families in America, 1995). Others suggest, however, that growing up in a family where there is parental strife can be more damaging to young children than growing up in a single-parent family. They contend that the level of conflict within the nuclear-family unit is far more important than family structure for understanding children's psychological well-being or their propensity to engage later in deviant behavior (Demo, 1992).

What may well impact children of divorce more significantly than the psychological issues associated with a fragmented nuclear family is the decline in economic resources available to children after divorce. Leonore Weitzman (1985:323) argues, for example, that in the first year after divorce men experience a significant increase in their standard of living, while women experience a significant decline. She attributes this to the fact that women, in ninety percent of divorce settlements with children, receive physical custody of a couple's offspring and must then find the material resources to support that child (or children) largely on her own. Shortly after the introduction of the no-fault divorce system, therefore, social scientists began to describe what they labeled the "feminization of poverty" (Weitzman (1985:350). Indeed, Arendel (1986) concludes that economic deprivation after divorce may well be more devastating than the absence of a parent and Coontz (1992:206) recommends that we should not try to force bad marriages to continue "for the sake of the children," but we should devise more equitable "exit rules" from marriage so that women and children are not so frequently thrust into poverty.

Concern over the impoverishment of single mothers and their children pertains fundamentally to the matter of whether a lack of economic resources will impact negatively on the ability to socialize and nurture children properly. A major responsibility associated with parenthood is the social training provided through this role to cultivate civic virtue, promote well-being, and mold behavior within children which allows them to become responsible and productive adult members of society. It is largely for this reason that the family is typically regarded as the "seedbed" institution for constructing a harmonious, civil, and cooperative social order. That parents share this view and take their responsibilities seriously has been confirmed in a study related to the changing value attached to children. Zelizer (1985) reports that there has been a dramatic increase in the social value accorded children over the last century—so that children are now regarded as priceless, unique, and individually irreplaceable. Moreover, this attitude is shared by parents of all economic levels, including those who are trapped in poverty. While there are, of course, some parents who continue to abuse or neglect their offspring, the evidence seems to suggest quite strongly that parenting is being taken more seriously now than ever before, even though the fiscal resources required for adequate nurturing are not always available.

If parental love and commitment toward children appears to be increasing within the family systems of modernized societies (LaRossa, 1986: 98-106), then should we expect a corresponding upturn in amity and civility among generations currently moving through the primary socialization process? Unfortunately, this question cannot be answered in the affirmative without a qualification of rather substantial proportions. For the fact is that there is no one-to-one correspondence between parental socialization processes and adult outcomes relative to peaceful aims. Intervening in the process are other references groups—and especially the youth peer group—whose norms, values, and legitimated behaviors may well be quite different from those espoused by the nuclear family (see, Garrett, 2000). Conservative interpreters of family dynamics, in particular, are more likely to overlook the loss of hegemony by parents to alternate reference groups whose influence may overwhelm the initial socialization instilled by parental leaders. Certainly, with respect to drug experimentation, premarital sexual activity, cohabitation, and various forms of violence, the youth peer group, in particular, may resocialize youth into patterns of behavior which parents vehemently oppose. Yet, on a more positive note, the youth peer group did sustain commitments to equality, racial justice, fairness in class relations, and a host of other patterns that promoted greater human dignity, especially during the sixties and thereafter. The best that can be said, then, is that sometimes the family stood in corrective opposition to patterns of behavior that were clearly destructive and yet supported by the youth peer group, while on other occasions the peer group promoted attitudes and behaviors which were more inspiring and humanitarian than those promulgated by a significant number of nuclear families. Moral virtue or turpitude cannot be clearly assigned to family or peer group in a sweeping sort of affirmation; it can only be assigned on the basis of considering one issue after another in a moral calculus which takes into account the complexity of the contemporary situation.

This singular point can be underscored with one dramatic illustration drawn into the public spotlight by recent events in the global arena, namely, the attack by terrorists both in Israel and in America on September 11. In a chilling article by Joseph Lelyveld (2001) in the *New York Times Magazine*, exploring the issue of suicide bombings by Arab extremists, the author interviewed a mother whose eldest son had just blown himself up in a suicide assault against the Israelis. When asked how she felt when she heard her son had killed himself in an attack that also killed two Israeli soldiers, she replied, "I was very happy when I heard....To be a martyr, that's something. Very few people can do it. I prayed to thank God. In the Koran it's said that a martyr does not die. I know my son is very close to me. It is our belief." Also, in the course of the interview, she bluntly stated: "I hope my other children do the same."

This episode may be extreme, but it is not altogether unique. Moreover, it also underscores the fact that families are not always agencies promoting peaceful social relations. In an age of ascending religious fundamentalism, families can often be a formidable obstacle to promoting social relations oriented toward harmony and pacification. Within the context of globalization dynamics, fundamentalism can also be understood as rejection of a modernized world-view deemed antithetical to one's own religious aspirations and ethnic/national interests—although this is not the only cogent interpretation of fundamentalism in relation to globalization processes, as we shall see below. The issue to be underscored here, however, is that the familial institution, just like the religious institution, can be directed toward goals that are harmful to humanity, almost as readily as this institution can be oriented toward aims related to the promotion of civility and the edification of humankind.

Recent Transformations in the Religious Institution

One of the more hotly contested issues among social scientists over the last several decades has been concept of secularization and its continued relevance for understanding the role of religion in the contemporary world order (Swatos and Olson, 2000). Classical theorists in the discipline of sociology—Comte, Spencer, Marx, Durkheim, Weber, Troeltsch, and Simmel—all predicted that the corrosive effects of modernity would be to differentiate religious influence into public and private spheres, while simultaneously marginalizing the influence of the religious institution in the public arena and driving it into the recesses of privatized personal experience. The overall result would be a precipitous and steady decline in religious influence insofar as the masses of citizens located in industrializing social orders were concerned.

The data for much of Western Europe reveal a pattern similar to that which earlier theorists anticipated, but secularization has not manifested itself so dramatically in the United States and, certainly, the pattern of Western Europe has not been replicated in the rest of the world in recent decades. Globally, there has been a resurgence of religious vitality in much of Africa, the Middle East, Latin America, Asia, and even Eastern Europe, replete with a vigorous presence of religion in the public sphere. Secularization theories have not so much been proven wrong by recent events as much as they have been shown to be misplaced in their focus and less adequately nuanced in their empirical assessments than would have been conducive to an illuminating understanding of religious influence in the various regions of the world today (see Demerath, 2001:228-230).

The features of religion of most interest for this discussion concern the rise of religious terrorism and fundamentalism in recent years as well as the upsurge in militant religious groups oriented toward the peaceful resolution of turbulent conflicts, since these two separate but related forms of religious activism relate directly to the prospects for the cultivation of peaceful social relations in the years ahead. Extremists driven toward acts of religious violence, often of horrific proportions, among virtually every major religious community have captured global attention of late (see, Lawrence, ([1989] 1995; Juergensmeyer, 2000; Kepel, 1994; and Kaplan, 1992), but less attention has been directed toward those militant religionists committed with corresponding fervor and dedication to peacemaking (Appleby, 2000). Each camp subscribes to a quite different conception of religious beliefs and an alternative definition of the world, a definition which directs one cluster of movements toward violent conflict and the other toward willful reconciliation. Both orientations warrant brief explication.

The fundamentalism project overseen by Martin Marty and R. Scott Appleby (1991, 1993a, 1993b, 1994, and 1995) compiled what is undoubtedly the largest single collection of research on this particular form of religious resurgence. The central thesis of this project held that fundamentalism in all the major world-religions was essentially a negative response to at least certain aspects of the processes of modernization which they perceived as a threat to the cogency of their religious tradition (Marty and Appleby, 1991:824-833). Like Bruce Lawrence ([1989] 1995), Marty and Appleby acknowledged that the fundamentalist revolt against the modern age was decidedly selective in its approach, since modern technology was appropriated quite readily, even as the central ideational structure of modern-thought forms was rejected. Not all fundamentalists, of course, took the additional step of moving into the ranks of terrorists and violent extremists, who were prepared to launch campaigns of aggression against those putative enemies of their particular religious persuasion.

The distinguishing feature of terrorist activists among the ranks of fundamentalists appears to be the conviction that the world is differentiated into two categories, namely, infidels and believers, saints and sinners, the righteous and the evil-doers—with the latter concept appropriated and given common currency by President George W. Bush. The central thrust of fundamentalists committed to a violent and terrorist agenda has been to foist on human consciousness a socially constructed vision of the world wherein we are all embroiled in a cosmic war between the forces of good and evil, a warfare wherein there can be no thought of compromise or mediation given the ultimate consequences of those stakes at risk in the controversy. When terrorist acts were the work of political ideologues, they could be addressed more readily by threats of harsh sanctions or even rational dialogue. The introduction of the religious factor, however, creates a more troublesome set of circumstances, since compromise can now be equated with apostasy or bad faith—whatever the religious tradition.

Mark Juergensmeyer (2000) cogently argues that the terrorist contingents of fundamentalist movements embrace violence with the firm conviction that they are enacting what is "in the mind of God." Terror is a dramatic mechanism for prompting others—friends and foes alike—to confront the exigencies of a world gone awry. Most often, the reasons enumerated for the current corruption of the world include the triumph of the modern, secular state over a religiously grounded regime wherein a fusion of church and state prevails, a decline in moral standards fostered in part by the mass media, a devaluation of family relations exhibited in feminist liberation and rising rates of abortion, and secularization whereby religious sentiments are displaced by materialism, political ideology, and libertine life-styles. To one holding such a perception of reality, the fact appears palpable that humanity is already engrossed in a cosmic war so vivid and horrifying that the only appropriate response entails attacks of escalating violence whose very scale cannot be perceived as anything but Armegeddon.

The lethal danger such an approach poses, of course, is that opponents among governmental regimes or other adversaries such as systems of nations will succumb to the temptation to respond in like manner by employing the rhetoric of cosmic warfare and, thereby, acquiesce to the definition of the situation advanced by terrorist activists. Once this symbolic concession has been accomplished, terrorists have achieved one of their central goals, namely, to control the framing of apprehended reality in such a manner so as to make their actions appear to be rational rather than misguided or psychotic/pathological.

Warriors embarked on a course delineated by a cosmic battle plan, Juergensmeyer (2000:122-126) continues, are less driven by political motivations or concerns relative to transformations of public policy than they are with demonstrating the reality of cosmic conflict through what he labels "performance violence." By this construct, Juergensmeyer denotes a situation wherein actors, using a kind of peculiar internal logic, are intent on making a symbolic statement whose importance extends beyond the immediate target of, say, the World Trade Center, a nerve-gas attack on the Tokyo subway, or killing physicians on their way to an abortion clinic. Performance violence, then, strives to effect a dramatic illustration, a theatrical public ritual, that may have some vague and distant long-range benefit, but whose more immediate purpose lies in creating cataclysmic spectacles that transform taken-for-granted understandings of the world.

Accordingly, many of the victims of the violence of religious terrorism are unknown to the perpetrators and pose no immediate danger to the religious interests of the terrorists. Persons who fall prey to terrorist attacks are deemed less important in the grand scheme of things than the message delivered through the medium of the violence. The stage on which these acts are played out is now global, since the ever presence of the media affords the opportunity to transmit images of the event around the world almost instantaneously. The acts of September 11, for example, were not only replayed time and again on television in the United States, but it was carried live over CNN and other networks to virtually every nation-state on earth. Moreover, horrific events like those of September 11 are "... sometimes more than symbolic: by demonstrating the vulnerability of governmental power, to some degree it weakens that power. Because power is largely a matter of perception, symbolic statements can lead to real results" (Juergensmeyer, 2000:132). Certainly, the frequent statements after September 11 that citizens of the United States had lost their innocence, that the world after that date had been permanently changed, would seem to confirm Juergensmeyer's contention that symbolic acts can possess authentic transformative power.

Finally, Juergensmeyer (2000:159-163) proposes that symbols become deadly and are likely to be characterized as a cosmic war under several conditions, including: (1) when "(t)he struggle is perceived as a defense of basic identity and dignity;" (2) when "(l)osing the struggle would be unthinkable;" and (3) when "(t)he struggle is blocked and cannot be won in real time and in real terms." All these conditions would seem to have been met with respect to Osama bin Laden and the Al Qaeda network in relation to the World Trade Center and Pentagon attacks of September11. Those terrorists who commandeered airliners were drawn from the ranks of persons from middle-class backgrounds—not the slums of Cairo or the refugee camps of Gaza—and they apparently concluded that their dignity was impugned and their religious identity threatened by the expansion of secularity which they alleged emanated from the West, and more particularly from the United States. Confronting the United States in a conventional military fashion was obviously not a strategy with any hope of success and, thus, the struggle had to be elevated to a sacred domain where righteous terror could be subject to God's deliverance. Similar calculations were undoubtedly at play in the first attack on the World Trade Center in 1993; in Timothy McVeigh's bombing of the Federal Building in Oklahoma City; in the Aum Shinrikyo release of Sarin gas on a Tokyo subway train; in the murder of a physician and his escort on his way to an abortion clinic in Pensacola, Florida, by the Reverend Paul Hill (Presbyterian) as well as the bombing of abortion clinics by the Reverend Michael Bray (Lutheran); in the massacre of Palestinian Arabs in the shrine at the Tomb of the Patriarchs in Hebron by the Israeli terrorist, Baruch Goldstein; and in numerous other incidents of Hindus against Sikhs, Protestants and Catholics in Northern Ireland, Serbs against Bosnians, and the list of atrocities could be readily extended to a whole succession of virulent conflicts around the globe.

At the risk of obscuring the nuanced complexities operative in each of these discrete episodes, it does seem possible to suggest that the religious motivations undergirding these violent actions have had the effect of intensifying the ferocious character of the plots against putative enemies of the perpetrators. For many secularists, the rise of religious violence has simply underscored in their minds the conviction that religion has always been a source of persecution, pogroms, inquisitions, crusades, and the like. The other side of the coin, however, is that religious sentiments and movements both have been and are a source of peacemaking. Although the headlines of late have gone to the religious terrorists, other religious actors have been just as militant in promoting harmony and reconciliation among conflicting parties. The activities of this cortege of dedicated and often courageous folk have not garnered the attention properly warranted by their achievements, but their influence may well be equal if not more impressive than those of warriors acting in God's name.

All the world's religions have accentuated the goal of realizing peace in human relations as a fundamental precept in their theological symbol systems. Indeed, the fact that peace has figured so prominently in their intellectual/ethical deliberations is one index of the fact that violence has historically figured very prominently in the interrelations of religious traditions within the world community. The yearning for concord and harmony has been accentuated by the global recognition of our common participation as members of humanity and many within the world community have taken this identification quite seriously, so that they are prepared to devote the whole of their energies and intellectual resources toward the end of contesting religious extremism. Militants for peace, by in large, have arrived at the conclusion that violence as a means of fostering religious ends is a debilitating strategy which more often than not plants the seeds for its own destruction through provoking retaliatory counter-violence either from members of the religious community who are not in agreement with the violent militants or from stiff repression by the state (Appleby, 2000:121-122).

Militant nonviolent actors and movements are as varied in their theological stances and strategies as their violent counterparts. Some follow the leadership of a charismatic activist, such as Samdeck P. Maha Ghosananda, a Buddhist monk from Cambodia (Appleby, 2000:122-132); Martin Luther King, Jr.; or Gandhi (Lefebure, 2000:23-24 (1); others are inspired by intellectuals such as Madjid and Wahid in Indonesia, who are attempting to make peace between Islamic traditionalism and neo-modernist, thought-forms (Saeed, 1997; Barton, 1997); and still others are inspired by religious organizations such as the Mennonite Central Committee, the World Council on Religion and Peace, an NGO affiliated with the United Nations, the Buddhist Peace Fellowship, Catholic Relief Services, and numerous other international and regional religious non-governmental organizations (Appleby, 2000). Many of these groups integrate their religious convictions with a passionate pursuit of human rights in areas of the world where human-rights violations are rampant.

The human-rights connection is a potent and crucial component for agencies striving to promote peacemaking. Not only has human rights become a salient issue under the conditions of globality, but they also possess a critical linkage to world religious communities, since a religious anthropology derived from each of the world religions affords a basic building-block on which concepts of the rights redounding to selves is predicated (Stackhouse, 1984; Little, Kelsay, and Sachedina, 1988; De Bary and Tu, 1998). Moreover, reaching a consensus on the signification attending specific human rights precepts can ameliorate real and potential conflicts among religious actors or communities and thereby foster peaceful relations in a subtle yet efficacious fashion. The human rights traditions also possesses at its core a concern for tolerance, both religious and secular. Religious tolerance promotes a respect for pluralism, even as it also dampens the likelihood that actors will embrace the practices of persecution and repression.

The success of militant, nonviolent religious

activists and agencies remains difficult to calculate with any degree of certainty. Some members of activist groups prefer to operate incognito insofar as their religious affiliations are concerned, while others enjoy high visibility as a function of their preeminent roles as heads of large international religious organizations—such as Pope John Paul II. High visibility can in certain situations function to enhance the influence of the peacemaking initiatives, but it may also have counterproductive consequences, especially when a process open to public surveillance fails miserably and leaves frustration as well as disappointment in its wake. More subtle efforts at conflict resolution avoid this pitfall, but they just as assuredly lack the sort of social pressure inherent in public campaigns to bring contending parties into more harmonious, consensual relations.

The overriding question remains as to whether nonviolent militant responses will prove sufficient to quell recruitment to and operations of terrorist campaigns motivated by deeply held religious sentiments. There can be little doubt that the casuistry that leads from religious principles to violent actions can just as readily—and perhaps more convincingly—be transformed into a casuistry that leads toward nonviolent solutions as well. For this to occur, participants in religious conflicts must refrain from defining humanity in exclusivistic terms which relate only to their own ethnic, national, or civilizational groups, so that all "others" are defined as outside the realm of humanity and, therefore, expendable in that cosmic warfare unilaterally declared by terrorists as currently underway. This would make innocent citizens fair game as victims of violent assaults without any sense of guilt or remorse on the part of terrorist activists who regard their actions as religiously justified.

Conclusion: Family, Religion, and the Global Enterprise of Peacemaking

The central theme of this brief analysis of family and religion and their implications for promoting peace under the conditions of globality can be summarized in these terms: although neither family nor religion are intrinsically benign or malevolent institutions, each can contribute to violent or nonviolent actions, depending on the sort of ideological motivations animating actors and the definition of the situation which actors conceive as their environmental arena. From a functional point of view, the religious and familial institutions accomplish quite distinctly different ends; that is to say, religion is a value-generating institution, while the family is a value-transmitting institution. The religious institution is capable of generating values because it has this central advantage over other social institutions, namely, it has access to the sacred as a legitimating force capable of imposing authority on a particular configuration of value constructs. The family, by contrast, internalizes values in its neonate members through its socialization processes. The sociological processes of value legitimation (the religious function) and socialization (the familial function) are morally neutral. The cultural content and social situation combine to determine whether the outcome will be ennobling of the human spirit or demonic.

The familial institution within the contemporary global circumstance is undergoing systemic change both with respect to families in modernized social orders and families on the cusp of entering modernizing social processes. There is considerable debate over whether family life is improving for persons in modernizing societies, although it does appear that one can make a strong case that family life is not in a steep rate of decline. Moreover, for women, family relations certainly appear to be changing for the better quite significantly. The companionate relationship with marriage and the improved status of working women suggest that domestic relations are becoming more egalitarian and more satisfying for many women in industrialized social orders. The increased participation of men in the expression dimensions of family life also portends more satisfying social relations in what many regard as life's most gratifying institution.

Women in third-world nations lack many of the opportunities and benefits accruing to women in modernized societies, but, for many, the quality of family life is improving under the conditions of globality. Partly, this is due to the fact that an international women's movement is attempting to address the many forms of discrimination and repression against women that have developed historically in patriarchal and traditional societies (Sassen, 1998). The greater freedom and equality women experience in family settings can only enhance the ability of women to promote tolerance and peaceful social relations among clan, tribal, ethnic, and national communities in the larger social order. A transition from local to global peacemaking will not be automatic, of course, yet the movements afoot relative to international women's issues proffers some promise for enhancing the chances for more harmonious cooperation on peacemaking efforts in the future.

Another major area of concern pertains to the relationships between parents and children. Despite journalistic accounts of latchkey children and more time spent by children in day-care facilities for children in industrially advanced societies, the current data indicate a greater concern on the part of parents relative to the outcome of their children and an increasing concern over the quality of interaction parents devote to children as well as the parental investment of time in the socialization of children. As we noted above, however, parents are not the only agencies of socialization who impact their children's adult outcomes. There are, in addition, the youth peer group—perhaps the most significant socializing agency apart from parents nowadays—the community, the extended family, the church (or some other religious community), and the primary group in the labor force. Thus, the nuclear family of orientation (that is, of socialization) can no longer be held exclusively accountable for the decisions youth make on their way to becoming full adults in contemporary society.

This latter point needs to be underscored. For the fact of the matter is that, when youth go astray, it is commonplace to place the blame on parents—and especially the mother—when the outcome of children is deviant. Yet, in point of fact, it is almost always parents who least want their children to get involved in drugs, become pregnant out of wedlock, enter into cohabiting relationships, or embrace other behavior patterns which deviate from current societal norms. And, it should also be noted, that it is parents who are most willing to attempt to come to the aid of their children when their behaviors lead them into situations which threaten their quality-of-life in the immediate and distant future. Indeed, parents are often caught on the horns of a dilemma in part generated by globalization dynamics; that is to say, parents want their children to develop as independent and authentic selves, even as they stand ready to serve as a support network when experimentation in selfhood goes awry.

What, then, can we say about the ability of the family institution to promote peaceful social relations in the near future? A facile answer can be easily articulated, but a more nuanced response is more appropriate, although it can be less conclusively formulated. Certainly, it can be affirmed that the Palestinian mother cited above who declared that she would be happy if all her children became suicide bombers is atypical of mothers globally. Few parents from third-to first-world countries are so callous about the death of their children, even if they have a putative religious ideology to justify their sacrifice. Indeed, to the contrary notwithstanding, the empowerment of women would seem to augur well for extending the hopes of developing more peaceful relations among the various conflicting communities around the globe. Certainly, in Northern Ireland, mothers have had an enormous impact of challenging the violence that has visited that nation-state in recent decades.

Peace in the world cannot rely on mothers alone, however, since many conflicts require the acquiescence of male members of the community as well. If women gain more power within the nuclear family unit, then they will certainly be in a better position to coerce or otherwise convince male family members to strive for peace rather than violent resolutions to conflicts. Thus, the global feminist movement may have a great deal to offer in terms of promoting international cooperation and global initiatives with respect to the institutionalization of peaceful human relations, especially insofar as such efforts are integrated with a meaningful extension of human rights inclusive of women. Moreover, as Paul Kennedy (1993:340-343) has so ably argued, enhancing the educational opportunities for women has been inextricably related to the position in both developing and developed societies, so that improving the literacy rate may well both elevate the status of women and accord them more social power to influence public policies related to reconciliation and peacebuilding.

The religious institution may exercise considerably more authority and power in the global enterprise of peacemaking than the family, whose influence will almost certainly be more effective at the micro-level of social relations and more covert in its operations. Historically, however, religious communities have manifested a remarkable propensity to legitimate holy wars, pogroms, and other acts of violence against their enemies or competitors (see in this connection, Johnson, 1997). And certainly, Huntington's (1996) contention conveys an implicit warning that, after the collapse of the Cold War, the new fault lines of international conflict will fall along civilizational boundaries, and the secular values of civilizations are intractably predicated on precepts drawn from one the world's major religions. The global circumstance may well play a central role in the sort of religious terrorism and violence prominently featured in newscasts around the world nowadays.

Yet, the pessimism attending this perspective can be overdrawn. There are also an abundant number of counter examples of religious leaders and communities striving toward the reconciliation of warring factions and the mediation of hostile relations. The fact that the notion of peace figures saliently in the symbol systems of all the world religions augurs well their function as a vital resource in the search for pacification strategies worldwide. For such strategies to be effective, however, leaders of specific religious communities must exercise considerably more diligent oversight with respect to the factions of their own faith who would distort religious precepts into ideologies legitimating violence and outright warfare. Especially for Islam, which lacks a central religious authority even within its major branches, exercising some means of social control over dissident groups will undoubtedly prove extraordinarily difficult (Esposito, 1991; 1992:204-212). Moreover, when religious nationalism is factored into the equation, the opportunities for demonizing one's opposition and exonerating those who employ violent techniques are sharply heightened.

Yet, as Mark Juergensmeyer (2001:79) astutely points out: "In a strange way, the point of all this terrorism and violence is peace. Or rather, it is a view of a peaceful world that will come into being when the cosmic war is over, and when the vision of righteous order held by militant religious nationalists triumphs." From this perspective, then, what separates secularists from religious nationalists, pacifists from terrorists, is not so much a disagreement over the absolute goal, namely, peace, but the tactics which can legitimately be employed on the way toward the achievement of this absolute aim. And as we have seen of late, the issue of tactics is no superficial matter.

What the various religious communities bring to this current situation are ethical assets that can serve as a basis for critiquing strategies oriented toward peaceful outcomes in some distant, perhaps mythical, future. One does not need to be highly skilled in moral calculations or even the finer points of ethical casuistry to point out, for example, that there is a fundamental contradiction in the effort to stop abortions—because that entails killing babies—by murdering physicians who are engaged in providing that medical service in a legal manner. This and other indiscriminate uses of lethal force, even against innocent men, women, and children, in campaigns undertaken by religious terrorists effectively demonstrates that there are no universal moral rules common to all religious traditions which are regarded as binding on all participants. If radical elements within all the world religions are to be effectively contained and their violent actions curtailed, then moral leadership by high-placed representatives of these religions must act with courage and determination.

The dynamics of nonviolent religious militants constitute a source of encouragement that personnel among worldwide religious communities are, in fact, committed to quelling the upsurge in extremism that has emerged on the global scene, especially during the last couple of decades. Perhaps the most important contribution these actors can effect is the control over the definition of the situation or, put differently, the conceptions of reality that delineate what behaviors and policy choices are likely to be most efficacious. For, if terrorists are afforded the license to frame conceptions of the world, then the consequence will be an ever expanding circle of escalating violence. The most serious outcome would be to fall into the trap that parties in the conflict are all now engaged in a cosmic war—whether that cosmic war is a product of Islamic, Christian, Jewish, Buddhism, or Hindu reasoning.

By the same token, secular states must also avoid the temptation of accepting the conflict model perpetuated by religious extremists. To couch the response to terrorists attacks in the language symbolic of a cosmic war essentially acquiesces to precisely what the terrorists want, namely, a legitimation that their conception of the world possesses validity. No institution has greater power in defusing this interpretation than religion. The question remains, however, whether religious leadership and lay folk in the larger faith communities will rise to the task of forging relationships of reconciliation necessary to restrain the advocates of religious extremism. The failure to do so could result in an almost endless exposure to religious terrorism and the innocent loss of life.

The prospects for global peace in the immediate future are, at best, mixed. Both the family and the religious institution can contribute positively to the processes of peacemaking, but one cannot naively assume that the resources of these two fundamental institutions will be brought to bear on the problems confronting the world community with proficiency and effectiveness. The family can work most effectively at the micro-level of interpersonal relations, while the religious institution has access to macro-level structures and processes as well as micro-level interactions. Perhaps the seriousness of the contemporary global situation will inspire both family members and believers to rededicate their efforts to ushering in the sort of peaceful social environment everyone desires—both the terrorists and the pacifists. On this hope rests the future of the world as we know it.

References

Albrow, Martin. 1996. *The Global Age.* Stanford, CA: Stanford University Press.

Appleby, R. Scott. 2000. *The Ambivalence of the Sacred: Religion, Violence, and Reconciliation.* Lanham, MD: Rowman & Littlefield Publishers.

Arendell, Terry. 1986. *Mothers and Divorce.* Berkeley, CA: University of California Press.

Bane, Mary Jo. 1976. *Here To Stay: American Families in the Twentieth Century.* New York: Basic Books.

Barnett, Rosalind Chait, and Janet Shibley Hyde. 2001. "Women, Men, Work, and Family: An Expansionist Theory." *American Psychologist.* 56:10:781-796.

Barton, Greg. 1997. "Indonesia's Nurcholish Madjid and Abdurrahman Wahid as Intellectual *Ulama:* The Meeting of Islamic Traditionalism and Modernism in Neo-Modernist Thought." *Islam and Christian-Muslim Relations.* 8:3:323-350.

Berger, Brigitte, and Peter Berger. 1983. *The War Over the Family.* Garden City, NY: Doubleday.

Beyer, Peter. 1994. *Religion and Globalization.* London: Sage Publications.

Blood, Robert O. Jr., and Donald M. Wolfe. 1965. *Hus-*

band and Wives: The Dynamics of Married Living. New York: Free Press.

Casanova, Jose. 1994. *Public Religions in the Modern World.* Chicago: University of Chicago Press.

Casper, Lynne M., Sara S. McLanahan, and Irwin Garfinkle. 1994. "The Gender-Poverty Gap: What We Can Learn From Other Countries." *American Sociological Review.* 59:4:594-605.

Cherlin, Andrew J. 1981. *Marriage, Divorce, Remarriage.* Cambridge, MA: Harvard University Press.

Coontz, Stephanie. 1992. *The Way We Never Were: American Families and the Nostalgia Trip.* New York: Basic Books.

Council on Families in America. 1995. *Marriage in America: A Report to the Nation.* New York: Institute For American Values.

Davis, Nancy J., and Robert V. Robinson. 1991. "Men's and Women's Consciousness of Gender Inequality in Austria, West Germany, Great Britain, and the United States." *American Sociological Review.* 56:1: 72-84.

De Bary, Wm. Theodore, and Tu Weiming, eds. 1998. *Confucianism and Human Rights.* New York: Columbia University Press.

Demerath, N. J., III. 2001. *Crossing the Gods: World Religions and Worldly Politics.* New Brunswick, NJ: Rutgers University Press.

Demo, David H. 1992. "Parent-Child Relations: Assessing Recent Changes." *Journal of Marriage and the Family.* 54:1.

Esposito, John L. 1991. *Islam and Politics.* 3rd ed. Syracuse, NY: Syracuse University Press.

————, 1992. *The Islamic Threat: Myth or Reality?* New York: Oxford University Press.

Garrett, William R. 1982. *Seasons of Marriage and Family Life.* New York: Holt, Rinehart, and Winston.

————, 1997. "The Decline of the Western Family Thesis: A Critique and Appraisal." pp. 323-355 in Gordon L. Anderson, ed., *The Family in Global Transition.* St. Paul, MN: A PWPA Book.

————, 1998. "The Protestant Ethic and the Spirit of the Modern Family." *Journal for the Scientific Study of Religion.* 37:2:222-233.

————, 2000. "The Youth Peer Culture and the Cultural Revolution of the 'Sixties': Implications for Identity and Character Formation." pp. 407-438 in Morton A. Kaplan, ed., *Character & Identity: The Sociological Foundations of Literary and Historical Perspectives.* St. Paul, MN: A PWPA Book.

Giddens, Anthony. 1990. *The Consequences of Modernity.* Stanford, CA: Stanford University Press.

Goode, William J. 1993. *World Changes in Divorce Patterns.* New Haven, CT: Yale University Press.

Hobsbawm, E. and Ranger, T., eds. 1983. *The Invention of Tradition.* Cambridge: Cambridge University Press.

Huntington, Samuel P. 1996. *The Clash of Civilizations and the Remaking of World Order.* New York: Simon and Schuster.

Johnson, James Turner. 1997. *The Holy War Idea in Western and Islamic Traditions.* University Park, PA: The Pennsylvania State University Press.

Juergensmeyer, Mark. 2000. *Terror in the Mind of God: The Global Rise of Religious Violence.* Berkeley: University of California Press.

————, 2001. "The Global Rise of Religious Nationalism." pp. 66-83 in Dwight N. Hopkins, Lois Ann Lorentzen, Eduardo Mendieta, and David Batstone, eds. *Religions/Globalizations: Theories and Cases.* Durham, NC: Duke University Press.

Kaplan, Lawrence, ed. 1992. *Fundamentalism in Comparative Perspective.* Amherst, MA: University of Massachusetts Press.

Kepel, Gilles. 1994. *The Revenge of God: The Resurgence of Islam, Christianity, and Judaism in the Modern World.* University Park, PA: Pennsylvania State University Press.

Kennedy, Paul. 1993. *Preparing for the Twenty-First Century.* New York: Random House.

LaRossa, Ralph L. 1986. *Becoming a Parent.* Beverly Hills, CA: Sage Publications.

Lawrence, Bruce. B. [1989] 1995. *Defenders of God: The Fundamentalist Revolt Against the Modern Age.* Columbia, SC: University of South Carolina Press.

Lechner, Frank J. 1989. "Cultural Aspects of the Modern World-System." pp. 11-27 in William H. Swatos, Jr., ed., *Religious Politics in Global and Comparative Perspective.* Westport, CT: Greenwood Press.

Lefebure, Leo D. 2000 *Revelation, The Religions, and Violence.* Maryknoll, NY: Orbis Books.

Lelyveld, Joseph. 2001. "All Suicide Bombers Are Not Alike." *New York Times Magazine.* Oct. 28, pp. 48ff.

Little, David, John Kelsay, and Abdulaziz Sachedina. 1988. *Human Rights and the Conflicts of Culture: Western and Islamic Perspectives on Religious Liberty.* Columbia, SC: University of South Carolina Press.

Marty, Martin E., and R. Scott Appleby, eds. 1991. *Fundamentalisms Observed.* Chicago: University of Chicago Press.

———, 1993a. *Fundamentalisms and Society.* Chicago: University of Chicago Press.

———, 1993b. *Fundamentalisms and the State.* Chicago: University of Chicago Press.

———, 1994. *Accounting for Fundamentalisms.* Chicago: University of Chicago Press.

———, 1995. *Fundamentalisms Comprehended.* Chicago: University of Chicago Press.

Meyer, John W. 1980. "The World Polity and the Authority of the Nation State," pp. 109-137 in Albert Bergesen, ed., *Studies of a Modern World System.* New York: Academic Press.

Meyer, John W., and M. T. Hannan, eds., *National Development and the World System: Educational, Economic, and Political Change, 1950-1979.* Chicago: The University of Chicago Press.

Robertson, Roland. 1992. *Globalization: Social Theory and Global Culture.* London: Sage Publications.

Robertson, Roland, and William R. Garrett, eds., 1991. *Religion and Global Order.* New York: Paragon House.

Saeed, Abdullah. 1997. "*Ijtihad* and Innovation in Neo-Modernist Thought in Indonesia." *Islam and Christian-Muslim Relations.* 8:3:279-295.

Sassen, Saskia. 1998. *Globalization and Its Discontents.* New York: The New Press.

Shorter, Edward. 1977. *The Making of the Modern Family.* New York: Harper.

Simpson, John H. 1989. "Globalization, the Active Self, and Religion: A Theory Sketch," pp. 29-38 in William H. Swatos, Jr., ed , *Religious Politics in Global and Comparative Perspective.* Westport, CT: Greenwood Press.

Skolnick, Arlene. 1991. *Embattled Paradise: The American Family in an Age of Uncertainty.* New York: Basic Books.

Smith, Anthony D. 1983. *Theories of Nationalism.* London: Duckworth.

South, Scott J., and Kim M. Lloyd. 1995. "Spousal Alternatives and Marital Dissolution." *American Sociological Review.* 60:1:21-35.

Spanier, Graham B., and Linda Thompson. 1987. *Parting: The Aftermath of Separation and Divorce.* Updated Version. Newbury Park, CA: Sage Publications.

Stacey, Judith. 1991. *Brave New Families.* New York: Basic Books.

————. 1996. *In The Name of the Family: Rethinking Family Values in the Postmodern Age.* New York: Basic Books.

Stackhouse, Max L. 1984. *Creeds, Society, and Human Rights.* Grand Rapids, MI: William B. Eerdmans Publishing Company.

Swatos, William H., Jr., and Daniel V. A. Olson. 2000. *The Secularization Debate.* Lanham, MD: Rowman & Littlefield Publishers, Inc.

Twiss, Sumner B. 1998. "A Constructive Framework for Discussing Confucianism and Human Rights," pp. 27-53 in Wm. Theodore de Bary and Tu Weiming, eds. *Confucianism and Human Rights.* New York: Columbia University Press.

Voydanoff, Patricia. 1987. *Work and Family Life.* Newbury Park, CA: Sage Publications.

Wallerstein, Immanuel. 1974. *The Modern World System I.* New York: Academic Press.

————, 1980. *The Modern World System II.* New York: Academic Press.

————, 1989. *The Modern World System III.* New York: Academic Press.

Waters, Malcolm. 1995. *Globalization.* London: Routledge.

Weitzman, Leonore J. 1985. *The Divorce Revolution.* New York: Free Press.

Zelizer, Viviana A. 1985. *Pricing the Priceless Child: The Changing Social Value of Children.* New York: Basic Books.

The Worldwide Impact of Religion on Contemporary Society

Huston Smith
University of California, Berkeley

Religion is about power quite as much as is politics. Archaeologists have found no ancient city which does not have a ceremonial center as its oldest layer—an altar, a megalith, whatever. It is as if a divine intrusion into history was required to provide the energy—in this case a centripetal, focusing energy—for pastoral and agrarian societies to gather and concentrate themselves in urban centers. Within the full light of history, we have the instance of Islam. The Qur'an's incursion into history occasioned the greatest political explosion the world has ever seen, one that produced in a century an empire that stretched from the shores of the Atlantic to the confines of China. We tend to associate religion with the invisible, but it would be a mistake to think the invisible is impotent. If we can trust what the physicists tell us, it makes more sense to link it with power. A thimbleful of vacuum, that shows us nothing at all, contains more energy than do all the atoms in our visible, thirteen billion lightyear universe.

Initially, religion's power was all-embracing, blanketing society as a whole. Nowhere in the primitive world was there a meaningful distinction between the political and the religious. Civilization could not have gotten off the ground without priest-kings whose temporal power derived from sacred sanction. Without the Mandate of Heaven, the Chinese emperors were no more than commoners, while Islam's most effective political years were those in which the caliphate, an office in which sacred and secular were combined, was a reality. In Europe, once the doctrine of the Divine Right of Kings was abandoned, kingship was no longer taken seriously. This permeation of the secular by the sacred was not (in early times) restricted to heads of state. Not just secular societies but secular components *of* society are recent developments. At their start, the great historical religions looked more like civilizations than like religions as currently conceived; they were prescriptions for ordering the entire range of human affairs: economics, politics, ethics, law, philosophy, art, and diet. There was a time when, in a large sector of the world, everything from the smallest drinking cup to the most impressive Mamluk or Mogul palaces carried the stamp of Islam, a point which holds for the other great religio-civilizations as well.

Today, of course, only tribes provide us with examples of religion-saturated societies. In civilizations, the passing of centuries brings complexity and role differentiation. Religion ceases to blanket the whole of life, and takes its place as one of life's compartments. The interface between religion as one of life's compartments and politics as another compartment—both compartments concerned

Huston Smith, "The Worldwide Impact of Religion on Contemporary Society." Reprinted by permission of Paragon House Publishers from *Spirit Matters: The Worldwide Impact of Religion on Contemporary Politics*, © 1985.

with power, let us not forget—is the focus of this book, so to that interface I now turn.

Personal Religion

Religion affects politics at two levels: an individual or personal level, and a collective or institutional level. The second is the more visible of the two, being where religion can become a lobbying force, so to speak; and as it is also the guise most related to the object of this book, I shall give it most of my attention. But I have already suggested that invisible does not necessarily mean unimportant, and here is a case in point. Before turning to institutionalized religion, we need to take a sharp, if brief, look at the way individual or personal religion impacts politics.

By personal religion, I mean it to be what I think Whitehead had in mind when he defined religion as "what an individual does with his own solitariness." In religion at this level, we are not concerned with institutional affiliation—whether the individual in question belongs to a church or engages in collective rites and observances. Our eye is on the unique and radically private dimension of his existence. To help us get a grip on that dimension we might imagine him in moments when he is most alone. Perhaps he is involved in a period of soul-searching and has driven off for a day by himself. Or he may be lying on his deathbed, engaged in his final withdrawal from his social identity. What goes on in the deepest interior of a self at such moments—moments when, as it were, an individual steps into life's voting booth, closes the curtains behind him, and casts his ballot: for his egoistic interests only or for those of others as well; for resentment or gratitude as his response to life; for hope or despair as his stance towards the future? I shall not answer that question. All I need say is that what does go on is what I mean by "personal" in the phrase "personal religion." The drama takes place in every moment of our lives, but for the most part subliminally. Institutions and history itself are but aggregates of the micro, capillary responses which, moment by moment, are enacted in the personal dimensions of our lives. Which is why this intimate dimension of religion, obscure though it is, cannot be omitted, even when the focus, as in this book, is on religion's most visible consequences, in politics. The word "religion" in "personal religion" indicates the direction in which the individual's decisions move. *Morally,* religion stands for love of neighbor; *aspirationally,* for hope over despair; and *conceptually,* for the conviction that goodness is more deeply rooted in reality than is evil. Personal religion is that within the deepest recesses of the self which, in difficult situations, enables it to decide and act in these religious directions.

The definition of religion just given is normative, for at this basic, personal level it seems difficult to finesse the question of religion's worth. The problem with defining religion normatively, of course, arises from the discrepancy between profession and practice; it could be protested that the foregoing definition may accurately describe what religions preach, but what about their actual behavior? Almost invariably, the behavior the objectors have in mind here are public, collective ones like the Inquisition or Crusades. I shall speak to these when, after the present section, I proceed to institutional expressions of religion.... Here these institutional aspects of religion must take their place alongside its private, personal yield. Religion would hardly have persisted, as perpetual as play, as universal as song, had it not, on balance, served some important human need. Even scientists who admit to having no religious beliefs of their own concede that, in the long run, religion is "probably adaptive"; that is, life furthering,[1] and the fact that no society has been found without it seems to support that point. Human life requires more meaning than it routinely perceives, and more altruism than is built into its genes. From an evolutionary standpoint, religion has the look of a supplementary diet that compensates for these deficiencies.

The bearing of this on politics is not far to seek. Governments require of their constituents what they cannot themselves provide: meaning and motivation, including motivation that is directed toward the public good. It used to be taken for granted that religion was an important custodian of such motivation; John Locke's *Essay on Toleration* is one of the most powerful defenses of that virtue ever penned, but he thought it would be a mistake to tolerate atheists because, as he said, they could not be counted on to keep their word. What has become evident, though, is that, since the disestablishment of religion, the West has been unable to come up with a convincing theory of political responsibility. Many versions of utilitarianism have been proposed, but they have not gained wide acceptance. This is not surprising, for no merely utilitarian definition of civic loyalty is going to persuade anyone that it makes sense for him to die for his country or even report his taxable income honestly. For over a century now, social critics have been warning us that the West is living off the accumulated moral capital of traditional religion and traditional moral philosophy. These critics were never popular because, as Irving Kristol points out, "the educated classes...simply could not bring themselves to believe that religion or philosophy was that important to polity." "Well," he continues, "I think it is becoming clear that religion and a moral philosophy associated with religion, is far more important politically than the philosophy of liberal individualism [under which we currently operate] admits."[2] Philip Rieff likens faith to the glue that holds communities together, adding that Dostoevsky's question, "Can civilized men believe?" has become," Can unbelieving men be civilized?"[3]

We do not have to try to determine here how far our moral capital has been depleted. Rising crime and suicide rates are not reassuring,[4] and social critics, on the whole, tend to be pessimistic. Solzhenitsyn describes the West as being in a state of "spiritual exhaustion,"[5] and in his important recent book, significantly titled, *After Virtue*, Alasdaire MacIntyre concludes that "morality has to some large degree disappeared."[6] Our object here is not to diagnose, but rather to register an abiding point. Politicians tend to regard religion as a nuisance, an annoyance that must be dealt with, but in its micro, personal workings it eases their tasks enormously. On this underside of the tapestry where, like happiness, religion has no history, it strengthens the meaning, the motivation, and the altruism that collective life requires. And it provides an alternative to demands which, if they were directed entirely to the public sector, would create discontents which governments would have difficulty handling. In all societies, the overwhelming majority of people lead lives of considerable frustration. Religion provides two resources for coping with this frustration: hope that it can have an end, and assurance that it provides the prod for spiritual growth. No amount of harping on the way these can be turned into instruments for exploitation—Marx's belief that religion is the "opiate of the masses"—will cause another, more basic, fact to go away: Remove religion's two internal ways of coping with frustration, and what is left is an external way that asks society to relieve it. One consequence of the decline of faith and growing skepticism about "the consolations of religion" has been that the demands placed on society and government in the name of temporal happiness have become ever more insistent and ever more unreasonable. So modernity, having spiritually expropriated the masses of its citizenry, finds their demands for material compensations becoming as infinite as the ontological religious Infinity that has been denied them. A regime which has to pacify a populace that is seeking fulfillment in the wrong place, will find its problems insuperable.

Institutional and Communal Religion

In personal religion, I was concerned with a generic phenomenon: namely religion as source and custodian of virtues that are so important that even avowedly secular regimes spawn civil religions to nurture them. When we move on to religious organizations, we are obviously in a world that is different in being pluralistic from the start. There may be something corresponding to "religion" in the singular, but religious institutions and communities are perforce multiple.

Of the two, institutions are more palpable than communities. They consist of buildings, texts, rites, officiants, and beliefs that are relatively easy to identify. Religious communities derive from religious institutions, but are broader in scope and less tangible; in ways they are like shadows that institutions cast. One can belong to a religious community in this extended sense (we could equally say to a religious culture) without belonging to its institutions or even subscribing to its tenets—the secular Jew is an obvious example. All that is required are certain "habits of the heart," as De Tocqueville called them, that bind us to those who share those habits, while making persons who don't, seem foreign. The habits may have been acquired through family rituals and other shared practices of childhood, or simply assimilated (as naturally as the air we breathe) from our primary culture, that "artificial, secondary environment" consisting of language, habits, ideas, beliefs, customs, artifacts, and values that human beings superimpose on the natural world. Considered sociologically, religion, in Tillich' s aphorism, is the substance of culture, culture the form of religion.

It is through its communities and institutions that religion's impact on politics becomes visible, so the rest of this introduction will deal with it in these twin guises. The safest generalization that can be made about institutional and communal religion is that they are at once inevitable and morally ambiguous. The second of these inevitabilities leads many to reject organized religion wile granting it a place in private life; kept to oneself it can be useful, these privatists argue, but institutionalized religion is a scourge and an abomination. The position is understandable—Cardinal Newman's "O how we hate one another for the love of God" carries us to its point immediately—but as a considered stand it fails because institutions are the primary channels by which ideas take hold in history. Institutionalization counters death and demise; without it ideas and essences evaporate. So we must accept the inevitability of religion's becoming institutionalized, and the equal inevitability of the ambiguities and compromises that attend this move. Nowhere are religion and politics more alike than in these twin inevitabilities, which is why emperors and popes understand each other so well. Samuel resists the Israelites' demands for a king, foreseeing with uncanny prescience the evils that will follow: "You will cry out because of your king, whom you have chosen for yourselves" (I Sam. 8:18). In the end, though, he yields. The human condition being what it is—"It is not you [Samuel] they have rejected, but they have rejected me [God] from being king over them" (I Sam. 8:7).

As for the ambiguities that plague institutionalized religion, they all derive from the fact that we live in what Arthur Koestler calls a holarchic universe that is made up of a hierarchy of holons. Everything is a "holon" or whole in its own right, a stable integrated structure, equipped with self-regulatory devices and enjoying a considerable degree of autonomy or self-government; thus cells, muscles, nerves and organs all have their intrinsic rhythms and patterns of activity. At the same time, each is part of a larger whole. So holons are Janus-faced. Each turns upward, towards the higher levels on which it depends; concomitantly, it faces downwards, towards its own constituents, in which respect it is a whole of remarkable stability.

It is easy to place our individual selves in this holistic framework. Each of us is a holon that needs to discover and maintain its identity while, at the same time, participate deeply and meaningfully in communities in which we are embedded and without which we could not live. And communities are comparably Janus-faced. They, too, have their consolidating needs; their need to keep their boundaries intact—keep their fences mended—to maintain their self-definition: here, issues of orthodoxy and heresy, loyalty and treason, inevitably arise. But communities also have outgoing impulses. They not only need, but want to traffic with the world, through diplomatic missions and embassies to be sure, but also in ways that are intrinsically ecumenical. Balancing the adage that "good fences make good neighbors," are ones that proclaim an open door policy: "Don't fence me in," and "something there is that doesn't love a wall."

Religion lies on the cusp of these centripetal/centrifugal, self/other propensities. In both individuals and communities, it provides a reference for self-definition and identity, while at the same time pressing towards deep reaches of consciousness where our selfhood opens onto our shared humanity and we find our lives by losing them.

The ambiguities that attend religious institutions derive directly from these opposing, self/other pulls which all life must accommodate and learn to live with. Four of these ambiguities are relevant for the present study.

1. The group identity that religious institutions generate is both good and bad. It is good in binding members into larger holons or wholes, inspiring in each community a healthy self-image and group morale. But the dark side of this virtue is the exclusion that identity requires. Things are defined as much by their edges as their contents; as much by what they differ from as by what they positively present.

2. The preceding point—that there can be no group without edges that prompt both in-group and out-group feelings—leads into a second ambiguity. The feelings that are directed towards outsiders can be either positive or negative. From the fact that religion is a major force for in-group cohesion (and, by the same token, for out-group exclusion), it would be wrong to conclude that it only (or even mostly) builds walls. It levels them as well. The Buddha renounced caste; Jonah enlarged "Yahweh's" horizons to include an enemy, Assyria; and Christ's parable of the Good Samaritan changed the definition of "neighbor." In *The Two Sources of Morality and Religion,* Bergson makes the tension between religion's constricting and expanding propensities the focus of his entire study. Max Weber does something of the same when he argues that "shattering the fetters of the sib" was the great achievement of ethical religions. These religions established the superior community of faith and a common ethical way of life in opposition to the community of blood; in extreme circumstances they even sanction opposition to the family. Again we encounter ambiguity. Religion pulls in opposite directions. Either impulse can carry the day and, historically, according to time and place, has done so.

3. The ambiguities continue if we narrow our focus to the role religious institutions play in their own societies and cultures. They can become ingrown, centering their energies on institutional preservation and self-aggrandizement, or they can look beyond themselves to the needs of others.

4. Finally, on the conserving—innovating continuum, religion again works both sides of the street: it has both priestly and prophetic roles. Clifford Geertz sees religion as essentially pattern-maintenance, but Dean Inge was fond of claiming that Mary's *Magnificat* contains more social dynamite than the *Communist Manifesto.* Religion is a conservative force, and it is profoundly subversive; it is opiate *and* catalyst. It creates enclaves and levels social barriers. Too often we find it raising church budgets, but it has also raised the oppressed. It makes peace with iniquity, and, to the extent that the world can be redeemed, it redeems the world.

A recent exchange may help to illustrate the points this section has outlined abstractly. I had been asked to lecture on religion in a history course entitled *The Middle East Today,* and in the discussion that followed, it became evident that the students were puzzled. They had hoped to find, in the teachings of Judaism, Christianity and Islam differences that were commensurate with the political differences that have made the region a combat zone for centuries; ethical or doctrinal differences which, if they did not justify the reigning antagonisms, would at least explain them. It became my task to argue that if it was causes of conflict they were looking for, it would be unwise to expect much from a religious historian. As far as teachings go, Jesus considered himself a Jew to the end, and it surprised Muhammad that the Jews did not recognize him as a true successor to Abraham. To be sure, the differences in the way the two men were perceived by their contemporaries quickly produced distinct communities that elongated into different religions. But once their separate identities were in place, the religions became, in their historical interactions, primarily touchstones for social identity. The hurts that each collectivity suffered at the hands of the others were plastered onto the originating revelations until (again, if it is historical interplay our eye is on) the differences in revelational content scarcely mattered, only the overlay being visible. Even if the differences in content were visible, would they matter: would spirit matter? Yes, but in political confrontations between religious communities, not much. That brothers were raised not only in the same religion but in the same family doesn't keep them from going to court if they have a falling out over their inheritance.

Politics And Religion: Regional Differences

The West tries to separate the two terms, church and state, and accord rights to each. Once the separation is effected, there is the question of their relationship. A modicum of tension between Caesar and God is built into the arrangement, and periodically it erupts into open conflict. Still each basically respects the other, even while at times opposing it.

Almost the opposite situation pertains in the Soviet Bloc. For more than half a century, Communism has sought to abolish the religion-politics polarity by removing its religious term. But as man is by nature *homo religiosus*[7]—his religion element cannot be completely repressed—so, too, in Marxism we find it surfacing, though in disguise. The phenomenological parallels between Christianity and Communism were visible almost from the start, with the historical process doubling for God, *Das Kapital* and *The Communist Manifesto* for Bible and Creed, the Communist Party for the Church, Marxist orthodoxy for Christian theology, revisionism for heresy, purges for Inquisitions, and the classless society for the Second Coming. It is a truism that Communism cannot be understood apart from its religious zeal, its messianic consciousness, and its salvific claims. But if phenomenologically, in appearance, Communism looks in many ways like a religion, ontologically, in its vision of reality, it remains relentlessly atheistic, despising the theism of the Orthodox Church. For fifty years this Church has been politically helpless, but we have noted Malcolm Muggeridge's contention that the inability of the Soviets to stamp it out is the most revealing historical lesson of our century.

If, according to Marxist Leninism, religion shouldn't interface with politics because there should be no religion, the opposite pertains in Islam: there should be no secular state. The rationale for this is that the Quran orders collective life—its social, legal, economic and political structures—as much as it regulates private devotion. This orthodox view of the matter, though, is theoretical rather than actual. Not since the death of Ali, Muhammad's nephew, has the Caliphate managed to provide an inclusive political umbrella for Islam. As a consequence, Islamic history presents a picture not radically different from that of Europe up to the Enlightenment. It is a picture of constantly shifting patterns of partnership, confrontation, and compromise between political leaders and the *ulema* (Doctors of the Law) in a relationship that is basically symbiotic. There is an important difference, though, in the way the two great branches of Islam Sunni and Shiite, envision the relationship. The Shiites, who represent 15% of Islam and are concentrated in Iran and Iraq, hold that political leaders should be descendants of Muhammad who carry spiritual as well as political endowments, almost in their genes, we might say; whereas the Sunnis have always held that rule should be lodged with the most capable political leader as determined by representatives of constituent groups. This difference makes Shiites more suspicious of secularized political, military and administrative power than are Sunnis. Western political analysts who were not aware of this difference or who doubted that spirit could "matter" decisively in an economically prosperous Iran governed by a Westernized Shah who was backed by an immense army, paid the price of their ignorance.

In China, religion and politics are interacting in a way that presents yet a different pattern. No more than in Soviet Communism is there room for either supernaturalism or religious institutions that might challenge the state's absolute sway, and the two communisms are also alike in the way politics assumes the trappings of a civil religion. What is different is the degree to which Chinese-Communism has been, and is continuing to be, shaped by China's cultural, specifically Confucian, past. If we consider traditional Chinese culture to be religious, as in a profoundly humanistic way we should, the impact of religion on politics in contemporary China is the impact of the past upon the present; Confucius characterized himself as "a lover of the ancients," and Mao could almost have done the same—that harsh things he *said* about the ancients are beside the point here. China's this-worldly emphasis and preoccupation with the social problem made her receptive to Marxism in the first place, as did her yin/yang dialectic into which Marx's dialectic slipped as to hand into glove. The Confucian virtues of filial piety, loyalty, respect for authority, and self-discipline were ready-made for Mao. As Robert Lifton observed, "the Chinese became filial Communists." Langdon Gilkey states the general point here in words I cannot improve on:

> The embeddedness of the in individual in and her responsibility to the community, the ineradicability and value of relationships and their obligations, the priority, therefore, of community obligations over obligations to the self, the absolute importance of the category of the "common good" as a balance to that of the person—all of these communal emphases are peculiarly oriental, as the Confucian tradition in both China and Japan witnesses. They reappear in modern, progressive, and creative form in Maoist thought and in the reality of the new life in China: in the principles of the Mass Line, of the polarity of elite and peasant, in the emphasis on the social origin and character of knowing and theory, and in the identity of the substance of China with the whole *People* of China.[8]

We see the hand of religion—in the Chinese configuration, to repeat, religion appears in the presentness of her past—in the subordination of technology to the embracing of ideology, the subordination of the expert and technician to the political and moral goals of society, and the insistence that theory be reinterpreted through praxis. These are not just the politization of life and absolutizing of an ideology, as Gilkey rightly remarks. They represent the continuing impact of a tradition that was, and remains, importantly religious in ways we are still trying to clearly discern.

More than anywhere else, South America is the place where the principles of liberation theology are currently being explicitly worked out and tested, so this is where religion faces politics in a posture most directly challenging and confrontational; I refer not to South America as a whole, but to what, for our purposes, are its most important pockets. As that continent is treated extensively elsewhere in this book, I shall pass over it to my last characterization, which is of India.

Such a fascinating, bewildering, paradoxical complex of currents and cultures! Who can presume to speak of India? Yet there she is: *a propos* our topic, the most overtly religious country in the world and, at the same time, its largest working democracy. It is enough here to point out the obvious: the distinctive element India introduces into the study of politics and religion is caste. There is no hope of understanding the interface between those two forces in South Asia without understanding caste, and that is a task which (despite the best effort to date, namely, Louis Dumont's *Homo Hierarchicus*) has yet to be accomplished, if indeed the Indians understand caste themselves. If in the West, the church is viewed as the sacred social structure, and in the Soviet Bloc, the Communist Party in ways fills that role, in India, caste is the social institution by which spirituality takes on social form. Political, economic, educational, cultural, and legal functions are determined by it quite as much as are religious ones. Today almost no one outside India says a good word about caste, and in India, parliament, drawing heavily on its British inheritance, has moved concertedly against it. But at the village level, where most Indians still live, it remains the order of the day. At that level, elder representatives of the various castes and sub-castes continue to meet and adjudicate in India's age-old *panchiat* tradition. And in many respects, the delegates to modern parliamentary bodies continue to represent castes or coalitions of castes in that ancient "council of five" tradition.

So, religion and politics are arrayed in six distinguishable patterns in the world today. In the West, they are *partners.* The Soviet Bloc tries to *deny religion,* while orthodox Islam tries to *deny the secular state.* In China, religion (without the name) enters politics through her *present-informing past.* In test points in South America, church *confronts* the state. In India, religion, through caste, *sets conditions* through which democratic processes work.

Clearly, it is time to move to the specifics in these several arrangements.

Notes

1. Alex Comfort, *That (New "biblio") p. 69, I.* The full statement reads: "Religious behaviors are...probably adaptive; [their] dialog with "nature"...is an important integrator of [man's] whole self view in relation to world and to activity."

2. *Two Cheers for Capitalism* (New York: Basic Books, 1978), p. 66.

3. *The Triumph of the Therapeutic* (New York Harper & Row, 1968), p. 4.

4. In *New Rules,* Paul Yankelovich notes that the suicide rate among teenagers in the United States has risen 200% in the last thirty years (Toronto: Bantam Books, 1982), p. 184.

5. Alexander Solzhenitsyn, *A World Split Apart* (New York: Harper & Row, 1978), p. 35.

6. Notre Dame: University of Notre Dame Press, 1980, p. 21.

7. Even sociobiologists, who as a group seem not overly pleased by the finding, tend to concede that religion probably has a genetic base. Edward O. Wilson says that the religious impulse in humans is Ain all probability ineradicable." (*On Human Nature* [New York: Basic Books, 1978], p. 176).

8. *Society and the Sacred* (New York: Crossroad Books, 1982), p. 145.

The Price of Peace: Religion and Politics in Western Europe

John K. Roth
Claremont McKenna College

In recent years, Western Europe, no less than the United States, has witnessed mass protests against nuclear weapons. It is reliably estimated, for instance, that just prior to the International Public Hearing on Nuclear Weapons and Disarmament, held November 23-27, 1981 in Amsterdam by the World Council of Churches, some 400,000 persons gathered in that Dutch city to dissent against the nuclear arms, race and to advocate disarmament.[1] Before the autumn and early winter of 1981 had ended, some two million Western Europeans had participated in similar demonstrations. Though Western Europe's states remain diverse, where certain aspects of nuclear politics are concerned, a sufficient consensus exists to warrant speaking about a Western European Peace Movement. This paper describes and analyzes some of the religious elements that influence it. Because space will not permit an in-depth account of the situation in every country, instead, the goals will be: (1) to suggest what the Western European Peace Movement is like overall as far as its religious components are concerned; (2) to focus some specific practical problems that the religious elements in the Peace Movement bring out; (3) to reflect on some of the broader philosophical questions raised by the religious orientation of the Peace Movement; and (4) to summarize some public policy considerations that merit attention as one puts together the first three pieces of this puzzle.

I do not approach this four-part goal without some fundamental assumptions. Indeed my introductory remarks imply them, even as I hope those opening comments suggest that these assumptions are not unexamined, but, instead, are rooted in actual experiences about which I have thought a good deal. Although the list is not exhaustive—no enumeration of one's own assumptions in an inquiry ever can be—here are some of the most important.

Even if it is a truism to say that nobody wants nuclear war per se, Hiroshima introduced a nuclear age that entails two things: first, we may not survive with nuclear arms, but, second, we are not going to live without them either.

As the predicament of Third World and recently developing regions indicates, there are conditions that could trigger nuclear war—limited or total—and those conditions have everything to do with an irreducible fact, namely, that the world has too many people competing for too few resources.

If Middle Eastern dilemmas are any indication, we occupy a world in which national interests, far from receding in favor of international harmony, are intensifying and thus creating mistrust that will be hard-pressed to resist temptations to break into violence, unless there is a balance of power that can

John K. Roth, "The Price of Peace: Religion and Politics in Western Europe." Reprinted by permission of Paragon House Publishers from *Spirit Matters: The Worldwide Impact of Religion on Contemporary Politics*, © 1985.

maintain stability.

Although Western Europe is a far more secular society than it once was, religion, specifically Protestant and Catholic Christianity, is anything but moribund. Its influence bears watching as we consider the prices of peace in the late twentieth century.

As far as its religious ingredients are concerned, how should the Western European Peace Movement be characterized? At least four traits stand out. First, from a religious perspective this Peace Movement is both substantial in its impact and yet varied in its intensity, the latter factor correlating largely with national boundaries. Next, the religious input within the Western European Peace Movement is not naive; instead it is well-informed by current research in political science, economics, military strategy, and the technologies of thermonuclear warfare. Third, if the religious voices in the Peace Movement at times advocate unilateral steps toward a nuclear freeze or other disarmament strategies, that stance is not held by all of them at all times. More generally pervasive, however, is the effort of each religious group to put pressure on the regime currently in power in its own state. Finally, the motivation behind the religious activism in the Peace Movement is based on humanistic-spiritual values that few people in the West would be likely, at least in principle, to question let alone to reject. This fact makes it difficult to criticize the religious thrust of the Peace Movement without running the risk of being portrayed as insensitive, intransigent, inhumane, or worse.

* * *

Most Western Europeans feel caught between a rock and a hard place. For many, however, fear of Soviet domination does take second place now to concerns about the potential nuclear battlefield in which they live. That tradeoff emerges from some complex factors. During much of the I 970s, for example, Western Europeans tolerated a policy of deterrence crafted by NATO and Soviet policies together. It was called "mutually assured destruction"—MAD for short. This strategy did indeed seem to produce a balance of terror, but one of the cunning ironies of nuclear competition is that it reinstates the threats of conventional warfare. That prospect kept the military strategists at work. The NATO perception has been that if the conventional forces of the Soviet Union and the Warsaw Pact, which are judged to be superior to NATO's, were mobilized against Western Europe, the line of defense could not be an all-out nuclear attack but would need to be a more controlled one. Hence the concept of limited or even isolated use of nuclear weapons asserted itself. This prospect seems literally "mad" to many Western Europeans. They see little assurance that such use of nuclear devices would not trigger all-out nuclear war. Furthermore, the very concept of a controlled, limited use of nuclear weaponry appears unconvincing because any use of these weapons will unleash aftereffects that continue to kill long after the detonation. One result of Chernobyl is the reinforcement of these antinuclear convictions. Especially in Europe, people seem to equate the peril of nuclear accidents with the deadly potential of nuclear weapons. Some experts, moreover, had argued that accidents such as the one at Chernobyl could virtually never happen. The falsification of that argument will not make it easier to convince Europeans that their hopes for peace are best grounded in strengthened nuclear arsenals.

* * *

By the autumn of 1981, for example, the German Evangelical Church, largest and most powerful of the Christian churches in West Germany, had adopted many of the positions taken earlier by the Dutch Council.[2] One result was a huge rally in Bonn (October 10, 1981), where the speakers included a wide range of political and religious leaders. if they were predominantly left-of-center, it is important to note that none of the most important were Communists, let alone the Kremlin's agents.

Nor, it must be added, were many of the Bonn demonstrators purely pacifists or advocates of unilateral antinuclear initiatives. They did wish, however, not to replicate the political passivity that characterized the German populace under Nazi government. Thus, these dissenters have worked to create an environment in which political decision-makers must reckon with their desires. Those aims include: "(1) resistance to the introduction of new nuclear weapons in Europe; (2) withdrawal of NATO support for the decision to deploy new medium-range missiles; (3) a decrease in the number of nuclear weapons in both Western and Eastern Europe, with the aim of arriving at a multilateral and global disarmament process; (4) a Europe in which nuclear weapons are neither manufactured, stored nor used; and (5) initiatives taken by European governments toward effective disarmament negotiations."[3] These goals are not simply those of the religious in West Germany. They are shared by a Peace Movement encompassing an array of political opinion, much of it non- or even anti-religious. Yet the Peace Movement in West Germany and in the Netherlands could never enjoy the power and the respectability it possesses without the infusion of a religious spirit that is "more attracted to nonviolence, more broadly based, less marked by intergenerational hostility and more inclusive of the working class" than were any of the social protest movements of the 1960s.

* * *

The Western European Peace Movement, especially in its religious dimensions, is not emanating from a lunatic fringe but from society's mainstream. Equally significant, this movement is not naive, at least not if one equates 'naive' with 'ill-informed.' Twice devastated by war in this century alone, Western Europe contains a historical consciousness that understands mass violence all too well. As both the United States and the Soviet Union carry on their military competition to become or to remain "Number One," that scenario seems increasingly absurd, and the sanity of striving instead for a reduction of arms in both Western and Eastern Europe appears increasingly sensible. Since the Western European nations have greater clout with the United States than with the Soviet Union, it is also understandable that they work in that direction to get the first steps toward limitation and reduction under way.

In Western European religious communities, however, more than a historical consciousness produces current antinuclear moods. For instance, well organized centers for peace studies and antinuclear strategies—the Stockholm International Peace Research Institute is one of the better known—are becoming commonplace. They have religious support. Headquartered in Western Europe, the World Council of Churches actively promotes similar activities, to date the most dramatic of which was the aforementioned International Public Hearing on Nuclear Weapons and Disarmament held in Amsterdam.[4] It attracted a distinguished group of politicians and scientists, as well as religious figures, and gave a considerable boost to delegitimizing human attitudes that place trust in the further development and stockpiling of nuclear devices. The sophisticated nature of the research done within the Peace Movement has vastly complicated the entire picture. Those who take exception to its positions can no longer afford to do so merely on grounds that the peace advocates have not done their homework. They have done and are continuing to do it. One outcome is that decisions about policy in these matters can no longer be regarded simply as a matter of lining up facts and making decisions based on what the facts clearly and obviously mean. For the facts no longer speak for themselves, if they ever did. They are so many and so liable to diverse interpretations that what we must contend with, at least as much as anything else, are some very basic and prior assumptions about people and politics. More about those assumptions shortly, but the point to underscore here is that it remains debatable whether the religiously motivated Peace Movement advocates or those who are skeptical of their aims are the greater realists.

Already noted, the specific policies that various religious groups advance in the Western European Peace Movement are essentially of two kinds, both aimed at reduction of arms in the short run and at total nuclear disarmament in Europe as the long range objective. Representative examples are provided by the Dutch and the Germans, although it would be incorrect to infer that opinion is undivided in either place. Dutch voices, especially within the ICK, urge Western European countries to commit themselves at least "to some unilateral initiatives in the field of arms reduction or arms control or in the political field."[5] Wearied by a strategy of arms control negotiations predicated on the principle of bargaining always from a position of strength, which seems to entail the paradox of arming in order to disarm, plus a refusal to disturb the balance of power, this perspective banks instead on the premise that "only carefully designed unilateral steps can stop the arms race and turn it around."[6] Negotiation is not to be tossed out as fruitless, but it will be carried out in a context where one side has broken a previous deadlock by acting concretely to reduce its nuclear forces, thus creating pressure, if not good will, to make the other side "put up or shut up" where its professed claims for and peace are concerned.

* * *

The ethical reflection and religious rhetoric undergirding the Peace Movement emphasize the need, as one representative statement has it, to accept "the risk of change that could reduce tensions, overcome inequities between peoples, and establish the basis for reconciliation that is grounded in justice."[7] Everything does depend on the risks one is willing to take, but without much question, such aims are noble. The Peace Movement doubtlessly has real advantages in this debate because it can more easily speak the language of religious faith and of moral idealism than can those who see the best chances for peace existing in the maintenance of strong military force that depends upon continued nuclear weaponry. The issue here is not to judge whether one perspective is right and the other wrong. It is to hold that public policy debates on such matters are not going to occur in a religious and moral vacuum. Those who contact the religious and moral sensitivities of men and women by using authentically the language that moves them possess a persuasive power whose potential influence can hardly be overestimated. A return to these points will make additional sense once the prices of peace are considered more concretely.

A Practical Dilemma

As the editors of *Christianity and Crisis* have asserted, two salient historical facts merit consideration. First, since the atomic bombing of Nagasaki on August 9, 1945, no nation has used nuclear weapons in a war. Second, although the world has witnessed scores of wars since that time, none has been on the scales of World Wars I and II. "We have not seen another Hiroshima," remind these writers, "neither have we experienced another Stalingrad or Dresden." It does not follow, they acknowledge, that an umbrella of nuclear terror has sheltered us from World War III or that a continuation of nuclear threats will go on to provide an admittedly fragile and precariously balanced protection. Moreover, they continue, the costs of these present arrangements are huge; the resources spent on nuclear defense could do boundless good elsewhere if it were feasible to redirect them. Still, if "Armageddon has not happened…yet; and there is some connection between that reality and the very awfulness of the Bomb," so far it remains a fact, too, that "the only system we have for preserving a peace is a balance of terror."[8]

At this juncture the Peace Movement joins the issue. Here also lurks the most crucial practical dilemma that confronts any assessment of the prices of peace, and the case of Western Europe and her religiously sensitive peace proponents heightens the tension as well as any example that can be found.

Those proponents' assumption is that there has to be, must be, a better way to make peace. Nearly everyone would share that premise as a hope, but opinion splinters over acting upon that supposition and well it should. Faced by what they see as a tremendously unstable situation, the religious leaders of the Western European Peace Movement want not merely to alter those circumstances, but to take what they acknowledge are considerable risks to do so. In short, to stabilize an unstable situation they are advocating policies that will destabilize things even further, at least in the short run, in the expectation that a more genuine stability will emerge over the longer haul. The issue that looms large is this: in a world and particularly in a European environment that are clearly in a precariously peaceful situation, how much and what kinds of stress are tolerable before a breakdown ensues that will lead to things worse than we have now?

* * *

At the other end of a spectrum could be a situation in which the Western European Peace Movement, sparked by its religious components, is substantially successful in getting its policy implementation under way. As things stand today, that success would include not only bilateral negotiations but also a series of unilateral actions, the effect of which would be to weaken, for however short a time, the nuclear striking capacity of NATO. These advocates would assume that this momentary weakening of strength is a means to the end of a vastly more stable peace. The question is whether that outcome is the one most probable. Answers depend on how one analyzes the intentions of East and West, but history offers a record full of inconvenient facts for those who would take a sanguine view of Soviet goodwill. Soviet communism may not be the evil that Western demonology has made it out to be, but that system has slaughtered millions of its own citizens, and the world has witnessed what happened in Hungary, Czechoslovakia, and Poland. Hardly any Western Europeans would deny that they would feel much safer if the Soviets had no nuclear-armed missiles to point in their direction. Of course they do have such missiles in abundance, and the fact remains that even if a freeze on or the removal of some NATO counter forces were to occur, especially if those steps were to be taken unilaterally, there would still be more incentive than disincentive for the Soviets to keep their fire power in place as far as possible. To see why, it is important to remember two dimensions of the present nuclear dilemma.

* * *

Strength need not become the euphemism for superiority that some would want it to be. The lesser of evils in our circumstances, where there are so few goods that are within reach, is a situation in which terror indeed is balanced so that neither side can afford to take the risk of striking first. As long as that balance exists, Western Europeans have a relative safety from nuclear devastation, which is as much as any person can be guaranteed in this world. In addition, they also have a degree of freedom and prosperity that few persons under Soviet domination enjoy. The prices of peace are always high. The dilemma that faces the Western European Peace Movement is how much to pay for what kind of peace. Those who advocate destabilizing an already instable situation by taking stands that make a moral statement—unilateral freezes or disarmament steps would be the best and most dangerous examples—may be correct in saying that conventional policies of nuclear deterrence are mad. But in a world with as many dark sides as this one, theirs might be even more so. Mistrust spawned the nuclear arms race initially. If mistrust is what makes it so hard to stop such competition, that same factor also ought to make us quiz very hard whether the most deep-seated yearnings to disarm are coming too fast and too trustingly. Trust and mistrust—those realities point to another issue, a broader one standing at the heart of these matters and specifically at the core of the religious motivations behind the Western European Peace Movement.

In God We Trust?

One who testified at the 1981 World Council of Churches hearing in Amsterdam was the distinguished Dutch Catholic theologian, Edward Schillebeeckx. His remarks contain a helpful sample of views that continue to form the most fundamental issue raised by the religious proponents in the Western European Peace Movement. Following up his assertion that "the need for unilateral nuclear disarmament forces itself upon us," Professor Schillebeeckx went on to say:

> If we consider that private citizens cannot exercise any direct influence on the decisions of other countries, but on the other hand do have some influence on the decisions of authorities in their own country, I would, taking everything into account, venture to maintain that the strategic slogan "Free the world of nuclear weapons, and first of all our own country," implies a responsible historical decision, which is closer than any other to the demands of the Gospel, it becomes the social-political content of Christian hope in terms of a historical practice. In this light there are solid grounds on which also the Christian churches, in view of their prophetic task with regard to universal peace as work of global justice, can base a *theologically responsible decision* to back the first risky step of starting with unilateral nuclear disarmament, without any naivete, but not without *the theological hope* against all hope.[9]

Two concepts are of particular interest in this statement, which is rather typical of the religious language that guides the Peace Movement in Western Europe and in the United States as well. They are the ideas of *theological hope* and of *theological responsibility.*

If the meanings of those concepts are unpacked, they include some basic convictions about the nature of reality itself. Prominent among them would be: (1) faith that God exists; (2) conviction that God's power (whether omnipotent or limited) favors what is good, thus falsifying in the long if not the short run the proposition that human might alone makes right; and (3) belief that in contemporary life the policies formulated by the Peace Movement are at least in their general orientation, if not in their precise detail, so consonant with God's will that, if they are pursued, not only is theological responsibility carried out but also there is good reason to hope that they will prevail. Usually words of caution are added to such statements to alert people that smug presumption about the righteousness of a particular set of plans must be avoided, for God's ways are not necessarily those of any one human community. Nor does this outlook suggest that there is some cosmic insurance policy to guarantee that the projects of peacemaking will win out. Schillebeeckx, for one, speaks forthrightly about the risks involved. Yet the outlook described here does affirm that reality ultimately contains a moral component. Power itself is finally governed by a transcendent goodness. Divine Providence, to use an older theological category, is real and cannot be challenged with impunity. The religiously responsible person tries to the ways of that Providence, lets his or her life be defined by them as far as possible, and strives to advance those ways by using human energies in their service.

* * *

Whatever its ends may be and however noble they are, the existence of a state depends on its ability to use and to control violence. Political leaders, cautions Weber, lose sight of that reality at everyone's peril, which is to say that political leaders who bank too much on any version of Divine Providence will not be acting responsibly, at least not in terms of their political function, which cannot be divorced from the recognition that political leaders are at once to direct and serve the state. To make his or her state survive and flourish is the political leader's calling as political leader; to do anything that compromises those aims is to betray politics as a vocation.

Some Conclusions about Public Policy

These reflections on the prices of peace began with an excerpt from Reinhold Niebuhr. Constantly tugged and pulled between Christian idealism and political realism, Niebuhr once said of himself: "I persevere in the effort to combine the ethic of Jesus with what might be called Greek caution…I might claim for such a strategy the full authority of the gospel except that it seems to me more likely to avoid dishonesty if one admits that the principle of love is not qualified in the gospel and that it must be qualified in other than the most intimate human associations. When one deals with the affairs of a civilization, one is trying to make the principle of love effective as far as possible, but one cannot escape the conclusion that society as such is brutal, and that the Christian principle may never be more than a leaven in it."[10] Niebuhr's poignant statement provides a framework in which to sum up three of the most important public policy considerations that this study of the Western European Peace Movement suggests.

* * *

One way to interpret the buildup of nuclear arms is to say that it is a symptom of the fact that we live in the time of "the death of God." At least functionally speaking, nuclear warheads and their ballistic delivery systems make the statement that human beings are all-too-tragically in charge of their own destiny. We might wish it were otherwise, and religious voices claiming it is otherwise are far from silent. No doubt that situation will also remain. Hence things will be more complicated than they might be if everyone concurred that human power in history is what is ultimate, or if everyone agreed that there is an ultimate power transcending human existence and that it is a moral force which will ensure, in some sense, history's redemption. But if such matters are not to be settled, it does not follow that it is unimportant to bring them up. On the contrary, disagreements are rarely more dangerous than when they remain latent, undiscussed, and ill-understood. As a matter of public policy, then, every interested party, but especially those who hold political power and those who actively seek to change it, could do far worse than to meet each other not only to debate specific practical proposals about nuclear arms, but also to probe their beliefs about what is ultimate and their reasons for thinking as they do. Then we might at least grasp why we are better in the dilemmas that confront us, and we might find ways to accommodate each other that have gone undetected because we have failed to look for them.

* * *

Strength and resolve can secure enough stability in this unstable world to keep democratic freedom alive. The prices for peace of that kind are going to be high, too, but those who make public policy will not be doing their jobs as well as possible if they fail to argue as persuasively as they can that a stability based on strength is still the most trustworthy basis for peace that presently exists. Such a plan need not be non- or anti-religious. No less than others that have unfurled religious banners, this approach can affirm unapologetically that its stance is based on an ethic that takes the wasting of human life as its enemy. A divinely inspired respect for human life can and ought to be the end which its means try to serve, insofar as the realities and possibilities of our life together responsibly permit. Reasonable prices of peace require aiming, as Reinhold Niebuhr said, "at some stable equilibrium between moral adventure and necessary caution." To seek that equilibrium is indeed fundamental for religion and politics in Western Europe, and in every part of the world as well.

Notes

1. James E. Will, "European Peace and American Churches," *The Christian Century* (March 24, 1982), p. 330.

2. See Marjorie Hope and James Young, "The Renaissance of the European Peace Movement," *The Christian Century* (November 4, 1981), p. 1132.

3. *Ibid.*, p. 1133.

4. See, for example, Bruce Best, "War That Passes All Understanding," *One World*, No. 73 (January-February 1982), pp. 9-11. *One World*, published in Geneva, Switzerland, is a monthly magazine of the World Council of Churches.

5. ter Veer, p. 389.

6. *Ibid.*, p. 390.

7. Robert F. Smylie, "Things That Make for Peace," a special double issue of *Church & Society* (November-December 1980–January-February 1981), Introduction, pp. 3-4.

8. "Give Ear to These Voices," *Christianity and Crisis* (January 18, 1982), pp. 370-71.

9. Edward Schillebeeckx, "A Time for Prophecy," *Christianity and Crisis* (January 18, 1982), p. 373. The italics are mine.

10. Niebuhr, pp. 196–97. The passage was written in 1928.

The Many Faces of Islamic Revivalism

Edward Azar
Scholar and Teacher (1908-1991) and

A. Chung-in Moon
Yonsei University, Korea

Islam is a very big sea, but which star should one choose to steer by?[1]

"Muslims are coming! Muslims are coming!" Lately such cries have resounded across the Western world. Indeed, together with the Russians, the recent resurgence of Islamic activism seems to be regarded as the largest potential threat to the Western world's interests, order, and stability. From the remote corners of the Saharan Desert across the strategic crescent straddling the crossroads of three continents, and to the southern tier of the Pacific Ocean (Indonesia and Malaysia), the visibility and influence of Islamic activism with a revivalist orientation is growing sharply. Efforts to rediscover Islam's spiritual roots and to reassert its political, economic, and social power in a collective or individual manner have been manifested in various forms of activism which range from successful revolutionary crystallization in Iran, to violent underground resistance in Egypt and Syria, and the unique Afghan armed struggle against the Soviet Occupation Army. Its list of enemies includes a range that runs from corrupt individual Muslims to atheists, capitalists and finally, repressive political rulers who are regarded as not sufficiently God-fearing.

Why is Islam suddenly blossoming in a highly politicized form? As a prominent Orientalist, H. A. R. Gibb, observed quite some time ago, did not Islam erode as a value system and as a political force long ago?[2] To borrow a bit of 1960s modernist jargon, did not Islam wither away like the "shattering of glasses"[3] in the face of a high tide of modernization which swept Muslim societies? Or as optimistically projected, was not Islam doomed to be progressively incorporated into a dialectical synthesis of "a secular humanism-pragmatism" in the deterministic manner?[4] Contrary to all these earlier projections, Islam is far from dying. Perhaps we are even witnessing a vehement return of its spirit rising from the depth of Islam's past glory. In the last several years, Islam has proven beyond a doubt that it is still alive, vigorous, and full of spirit. It moves, transforms, and overturns individuals, societies, and even the world. It provides Muslims with a *modus operandi,* a normative buttress, strategies, an ideology, and higher goals to strive for. Islam has not yet eroded; nor has it "shattered away." Islam is not yet doomed to be incorporated into a secular humanism-pragmatism. Rather, Islam is reasserting its vital functions as an ethical system, a mode of conduct, and most importantly, as a revitalized political power.

Why have earlier theoretical conjectures proven incorrect? What is the nature and structure of the

Edward Azar and A. Chung-in Moon, "The Many Faces of Islamic Revivalism." Reprinted by permission of the Paragon House Publishers from *Spirit Matters: The Worldwide Impact of Religion on Contemporary Politics* © 1987.

recent resurgence of Islamic activism? How does Islamic revivalism fit into the political spectrum in the contemporary world? What messages do Western audiences receive from these revivalist trends? What impact will this revivalist movement have on the broadly perceived order and stability of the international system? These are the questions to be raised and discussed in this paper. It is our desire and intention that candid discussions of the issue will reduce the cognitive gap between Muslims and non-Muslim Westerners by augmenting the general body of knowledge about Islam.

The Western Perception of Islamic Revivalism: A Critical Overview

For the last several years, we have experienced a series of drastic events in the Islamic part of the world. These include the collapse of the Shah's regime and the emergence of Ayatollah Khomeini (1979), the Mecca Incident in Saudi Arabia (late 1979), the Soviet invasion of Afghanistan and the subsequent Mujahideen resistance (1979–present), and the dramatic assassination of Anwar Sadat in Egypt (1981). These events are sufficient to trigger mass-media enthusiasm and academic interest. The Western mass media has intensively covered the rising tide of Islamic revivalism, and scholars in the Western hemisphere—notably Americans—have now paid greater attention to this new syndrome. As a result, an extensive literature has accumulated on the topic.

The recently burgeoning literature offers five major explanations for Islamic Revivalism.[5] The first interprets the revitalization as a return to the fundamentals of the faith: the original teachings of the Quran and the Sunnah are to be restored, and the society of the early Caliphate revived in all its aspects. Hence, it envisions Islamic Revivalism as the total reconstruction of the society and polity in the Islamic manner. Ultimately, such a reconstruction takes the form of a transformative political movement.

The second theme or explanation, which often appears in the literature, is an emphasis on the distorted impacts of modernization or secularization on the Islamic movement. It argues that the galloping, uncoordinated pace of modernization has reaped bitter fruits, one of which is Islamic Revivalism. This theme is an extension of the idea that tension between traditionalism and modernization inevitably emerges in all developing countries and that the rise of Islamic Revivalism is just another manifestation of this ever-present tension.

Another important common theme is the tendency to identify Islamic Revivalism as a militant opposition movement. However, the moderate and legitimizing aspects of this revivalist movement are seldom noted. This may be related to a positive semantic association between the term *Jihad* (Holy War) and the movement. While it is indisputably central to the movement, the term *Jihad* has multiple subtle meanings. When it is discussed in conjunction with Islamic Revivalism, however, it is seen as violent, aggressive, brutal, and oppositional. The worst example is the effort to link nuclear industrial development in some Islamic countries to a so-called "Islamic bomb," which implies an atom bomb.[6]

The fourth important common theme in the literature is an emphasis on what is termed as a regressive return to the past. This is best illustrated by quoting Wilfred C. Smith:

> The fundamental malaise of modern Islam is a sense that something has gone wrong with Islamic history. The fundamental problem of modern Muslims is how to rehabilitate that history; to get it going again in full vigour, so that Islamic society may once again flourish, as a divinely guided society should and must.[7]

In other words, most recent analysts who focus on the Islamic movement tend to view the revivalist trend as a product of a cognitive dissonance between Islam's glorious historical past and its presently perceived status. This line of reasoning is preoccupied with the historical nature of the

Islamic identity in which the restoration of past glory and idealism constitutes the core of the revivalist movement. Proponents of this idea confine themselves to the idea of Islamic history and tend to overlook other important elements of the current situation.

The last common dimension is an inclination to reject a paradigmatic approach or an aggregate comparative analysis to explain Islamic Revivalism in general. In fact, the only way to understand Islamic Revivalism is through contextual analysis. Neither universal claims nor subsequent application to particulars are acceptable, because, as in the words of Edward Said, "Islam varies from place to place, subject to both history and geography."[8]

The five common themes outlined above can be combined in the following definition of Islamic Revivalism: *a militant and fundamentalist revitalization of core Islamic values in the form of historical regression, occurring as a reactionary protest to the modernization process, which can be explained by particularistic, contextual analysis.* To a very limited extent, this conventional interpretation of Islamic Revivalism is acceptable; it has some validity and predictive power. Yet, we do not fully support this definition to the approach to the problem because it entails a narrow perspective, which is fraught with methodological imbalance.

The first noticeable shortcoming is the identification of revivalism with fundamentalism. According to the *Oxford Dictionary*, "revival" is the "act of reviving after decline or discontinuity." Hence the revival of Islam from partial discontinuity and forced decline can have many different forms and dimensions. It may have a fundamentalist character *à la* early wahabbism or the Iranian revival. But Islamic revival need not be exclusively fundamentalist. Modernist-reformist trends may constitute the central part of revivalist movements, as in the cases of Jamal al-Din Afghani, Mohammad Abdu, Mohammad Iqbal, etc. Thus, it is fallacious and unfair to fully equate revivalism with fundamentalism. Rather, today's revivalism is a broader, more comprehensive trend, of which fundamentalism is only one part.

Second, contrary to assertions made by Western scholars and journalists, Islamic revivalism does not necessarily require or connote militant violence, and opposition movements are not the only ones, which are inspired by it. Islamic revivalism is wide in its choice of activistic instrumentality. It can be militant, violent, and massively transformative. Yet it may also appear in forms of moderate bargaining, accommodation, and incremental protests. Here again the militancy of revivalism is not the only approach available to current Islamic resurgence movements. The leaders of each movement have a wide array of choices in this regard, and the choice of tactics and instruments is a function of various factors. These factors include the context in which the movements are located, leadership style, intensity and pervasiveness of repression and injustice, and ruling regimes' responses. Furthermore opposition groups do not have a monopoly on revivalist elements of Islam. These elements are also widely utilized and manipulated by the ruling regimes as effective legitimization tools. Thus it is risky and fallacious to label recent revivalist movements as militant, violent, and exclusively tools of opposition groups.

Third, conventional interpretations of Islamic revivalist movements are far too preoccupied with the role of history and the dichotomy of modernization and traditionalism. It is correct to point to the rapid pace of modernization as the primary cause of Islamic revivalism. It is equally valid to argue that history has become an idealized source of future direction in Muslim societies. However, this approach overlooks the fact that the rate of modernization is less important than its overall direction and outcome. If the direction and outcome of modernization disturb the core values of Islam, create social and political inequalities, and require the victimization of the masses in Muslim societies, they are certainly central to understanding the rise of Islamic revivalist movements. But it is quite fallacious to assert that traditional Islam opposes any and all modernization efforts, or that the Islamic revivalist movement demands an unconditional, blind regression to the past. In Islam, progress that remains within the boundaries of the *Quran* and the *Sunnah* is most valued, and encouraged. This concept of progress inspires Muslims to incorporate modernization creatively and to recapture or advance the declined glory of Islam. The excessive emphasis on history, which is so prevalent in the current literature, can hinder more than enhance a correct understanding of Islamic revivalism.

Finally, the insistence on understanding each separate revivalist movement within its particular context undermines a systemic conceptualization of this transnational phenomenon. While particulars are important for analysis, the universal characteristics in the rising tide of Islam cannot be ignored. Without a firm grasp of these universal characteristics and attributes, it is impossible to comprehend the particulars or to measure relative distances between different revivalist movements. Without such measurement of relative distances, any projection of the global implications of the movement will be a difficult task. Thus our key methodological assertion is such that we can and must formulate a universal framework through which we can understand numerous particulars in a coherent and systematic manner. It follows that aggregate data analysis is a useful tool for understanding this transnational revivalist phenomenon.

The Causal Structure of Islamic Revivalism

Why is Islam reviving? And why do different types of revivalist movements exist? Why does Islamic Revivalism possess a dynamic nature, characterized by changes from one kind of movement to another, rather than a static nature? These important questions must be examined in order to grasp the overall nature of revivalism. Nazih Aybui, an Egyptian sociologist, makes an interesting remark regarding these questions: "If resistance is taking more of an Islamic form in such countries, it is partially because Islam represents one of the most entrenched (and therefore least alien) cultural traits in the society. More practically, however, revolt takes an Islamic expression because quite often there are no other outlets left in society for channeling political demands."[9] Although we disagree with his claim that Islam is used simply as an outlet of last resort, we agree that Islam is the most entrenched cultural trait and that Islamic resistance is a result of the discontent of masses who happen to be Muslims.

We will attempt to show that Islamic Revivalism can be explained by the gap between the ideals shaped by the Islamic socialization process and the reality faced by masses of Muslims. In order to understand this gap, we employ two major concepts of social psychology: those of cognitive dissonance, and those of relative deprivation.[10] Cognitive dissonance refers to the level and degree of incongruence between the internalized images of the socio-economic-political world and the world that actually exists. Relative deprivation describes the discrepancies between the perceived 'ought', and the perceived 'is', of collective value satisfaction. Using these two methodological concepts, we may be able to explain the causal structure of Islamic revivalism cogently.

Islam does not distinguish between immanence and transcendence, church and politics, religion and economics, secularism and divinity, and so on. Islam is a unified way of life. Islam, as a social totality, plays important socioeconomic and political roles in the socialization process of Muslims. It determines their mode of conduct and ethical systems. It shapes their conception of political and economic reality. And it provides a sense of group solidarity.[11] Thus, Islam powerfully contributes to the formation of internalized collective images of the ideal society in the process of socialization. The internalized images of the ideal society are directly or indirectly linked to the basic principles of Islam revealed in the *Quran* and *Sunnah,* and to their concrete crystallization in the period of the Prophet and early Caliphates. The internally socialized images of ideal society include the following dictates:

1. The political community should be fully legitimate by securing the service of God through *shura* (consultation) and the other democratic elements. No repression, dictatorship, or domination is allowed. People are prevented from exploiting each other, the individual freedoms are protected, and law and order prevail. And the *ijma* (consensus) of the *Umma* (community) becomes the very basis by which governance is to be executed. Since sovereignty belongs to God alone by the principle of *tawhid*, all people are equal in the *Shariah*, the law of God. And political leadership is subject to the choice of the *jama'a* (the group), being the *ahl al-'aqd wal-hall* (those with power to bind and to loosen), as representative of whole political community.[12]
2. In the economic realm, social justice and the promotion of public goods are the basis of the Muslim society or *Umma*. By the same principle of *tawhid*, God alone is the owner of all the bounties of the earth, and people share the resources and materials provided by God equally. As a manifestation of God's sovereignty, everyone in the *Umma* is entitled to all those things provided by God, and all its members have legitimate claims on equal shares in it. It is by this principle that basic human needs should be given priority. Thus, in principle, Islam does not tolerate monopolies, inequitable income and wealth distribution or any type of exploitation of the economically helpless. Islamic institutions, such as *Zakat* (alms-giving), *Sadaqa* (voluntary alms), prohibition of interest *(riba)* and so on, are some good examples of implementing economic justice in the Islamic system. And the leadership of an Islamic system has the obligation to regulate these individual rights and to protect the community from excess. In the ideal Islamic regime, there are no class distinctions or handicaps attached to social status or occupation, and thus complete equality of opportunity for all believers is preserved and guaranteed.[13]
3. In the social, historical, and cultural realms, Islam has pursued independent and glorious ideals and practices of its own. Islam does not permit any form of mass alienation or social atomization, characteristics of modernized society's pathological dimension. It rejects any factors, which would reduce mankind to moral degradation or personal frustration. In a true Islamic *Umma*, moral integrity and virtues prevail and individual souls blossom to their fullest. Communal and familial solidarity among Muslims is firm and therefore there is no chance for Muslims to go astray or become alienated. Islam is an autonomous ethical and social system that does not need any exogenous sources to rely on.[14]

In addition, the historical legacy of Islam fortifies Muslims with pride in its glorious past. The light of Islam glowed from Granada to Delhi. Less than a hundred years after the death of Muhammad, his followers had burst out of the Arabian desert to conquer and create an empire whose glories were to shine for a thousand years. They defeated the Byzantines, conquered the Persian Empire, and spread the faith through North Africa into Spain, to the Indus River, Malaysia, Indonesia, and the Black tribes of Africa.

To this historical expansion, there is also a cultural pride in past history. While darkness prevailed in Europe, Islamic culture and civilization were the bridges between Hellenistic heritage and Europe's modern renaissance. On top of this, Saladin's victory over the Crusaders, the cultural preservation of Islam even under the Mongol conquest, and the creation of a new Islamic empire under the umbrella of Ottoman rule are all indicative of past glory. Furthermore, the role of Islam in resisting Western imperialists in the late 19th and 20th centuries made a firm impression on the minds of Muslims. Overall, Islam has been a religion of victory and noble pride, rather than one of exodus and cruxiflcation.[15]

In sum, the ideals inherent in Islam have induced or compelled Muslims to cultivate and socialize a collective vision of an ideal society in which a legitimate and consultative polity exists, a just and equitable economic system is set in motion, social harmony and moral integrity prevails, and the past glory of victory and independence is restored. What, however, does the present reality have to offer? Political repression and domination, economic injustice and social atomization, injured pride over past glory, and systematic penetration of the values and economic domination...these are the foundations of the current reality. Our conjecture is that the incongruence between the perceived 'ought', created by the socialized ideals of Islam and the perceived 'is', manifested in today's reality of collective value satisfaction, is the core force which triggers, shapes, and conditions the direction of Islamic revivalist movements. Since the structure of Islamic ideals are outlined above, the best way to trace and explain the causes of revivalism would be to analyze the present situation which confronts Islamic countries.

What are the present circumstances in Islamic countries? According to an official account of the World Muslim League and the Organization of Islamic Conferences, in all [total] there are forty-four Islamic countries, which have gained independence since the Second World War. The present political, economic, and socio-historical conditions in these countries fall quite short of the ideals and visions set by Islam. Despite the recent surge of oil wealth in some of these countries, the overall socio-political-economic conditions are desperate, helpless, chaotic, and fragmentary. Political repression, worsening living conditions, social atomization and withdrawal, and injured historical pride constitute the daily bread in these countries. Within these general conditions, Islamic revivalism easily spreads firm roots. Alienation, poverty, anger, and misery translate into collective cognitive dissonance and deprivation, which eventually burst into various forms of Islamic revivalism. Thus, Islamic revivalism is not a purely "religious" phenomenon. It is in this fact that a collective expression of indignant protests over the perceived reality which falls far short of the ideals and visions of Islam that have been so deeply engraved in Muslim minds throughout the socialization process. Thus, in order to describe and explain Islamic revivalism, we must first carefully examine the social, political, and economic roots of this trend.

Socio-Historical Reality: Pathology of Defeatism

In an ideal Islamic society, political soundness and economic prosperity and justice should be complemented by moral integrity and consolidation of the Islamic historical identity. Islam is conceived to be a religion with a perfect ethical system, a religion of victory and glory. Muslims believe that Islam provides them with the necessary and sufficient conditions for the formation and preservation of moral integrity, which leaves nothing to be borrowed from other exogenous ethical systems. At the same time, Muslims become excited whenever they hear of the battles like that of *Badr,* in which the Prophet fought and won. And they take great pride in Islamic civilization and culture. In addition, they are fascinated by historical episodes, which describe the expansion of the Islamic empire and the Muslim defeat of the Crusaders. Islam, as a self-sufficient ethical system and as a source of a glorious past, shapes and locates the present locus of the pathological dilemma of socio-historical reality of Islamic countries.

Contrary to this ideal vision of moral integrity and historical pride, Muslims of Islamic countries today are tainted with moral confusion and injured historical pride. With the massive influx of Western influence, either through colonial legacy or through the massive modernization process, the authentic Islamic value system has been endangered. This derives not from the superiority between the two, but from the social destructiveness accompanied by this influx. Massive urbanization has led to social atomization, alienation, and mental frustrations among the Muslim masses. The immense penetration of

Western values with its decadent nature, as revealed in liberalized sexual life styles, pervasive prostitution, and other negative values, through global networks of the mass media, has eroded the authentic and desirable values of Islam. Most importantly, Westernization has entailed a Hobbesian version of egoistic atomized individualism in these societies, which is threatening the Islamic notion of family and *Urnma,* so central to the ethical and social system of the Islamic world.

In addition to this Western-inspired moral degradation, Islam is facing another crucial historical crisis: a feeling of defeatism prevails, with respect to exogenous forces. This defeatism has culminated in consecutive military defeats with Israel, and the loss of Jerusalem and the Al-Aqsa mosque.[16] The Soviet invasion of Afghanistan revealed this defeat all too clearly: Islamic countries were helpless, despite their condemnation of the invasion. On a much broader level, this defeatism can be found in the deepening of economic, cultural, military, and political dependency on the West. In other words, even after the attainment of formal independence from the colonizers, these Islamic countries are bound by the power and influence of the dominant actors in the international system, not only in the realm of international politics and military relationships but also in economic and cultural spheres. If it is not the actuality, there has been at least a *common feeling* among the Muslim masses that modernization paths pursued by the Muslim world has meant Westernization and a drifting away from Islamic moral values, and that political leaders of Islamic states have been totally dependent upon foreign forces such as communism and Western capitalism combined with Zionism.[17] In particular, the existence of a subtle form of patron-client linkage between corrupt or authoritarian rulers and dominant international actors (i.e., U.S.A. and Soviet Union) has further aggravated a collective image of self-defeatism among the Muslim masses.

In sum, it has been argued that Islamic revivalism is caused and conditioned by the cognitive dissonance of the Muslim masses between ideal visions of Islamic society and actual performance. This cognitive dissonance syndrome has been salient and pervasive in the Islamic countries in terms of the political legitimacy crisis, economic structural victimization, and socio-historical defeatism. However, it is important to keep in mind the fact that, as there are many different levels of these political, economic, and socio-historical malaises, there are correspondingly different types of revivalism. Depending upon the intensity and depth of political, economic, and socio-historical conditions, the rate, direction and means of Islamic revivalism can differ, revolving around those eight dimensional coordinates. The relationship between the causes and the resultant patterns of revivalism is, therefore, multiple rather than single. And, the study of these multiple relationships will be reserved for another time. To be more specific, for example, if the overall performance level in legitimacy, structural victimization, and socio-historical defeatism is high, the direction of Islamic revivalism is likely to move from the militant, social and total transformative efforts to the moderate, individual and partial dimension. On the other hand, if the degree of incongruence is large (i.e., performance level is low), the reverse trend is likely to emerge in the revivalist movements.[18]

Political Implications of Islamic Revivalism

So far, we have discussed major causal factors leading to the rise of revivalist phenomenon and the resultant types of revivalist movements. Given the multiplicity of types and causes of the revivalist phenomenon, however, it is quite difficult to delineate a discernible commonality of political implications universally applicable to all the cases. Political ideologies, formation of major political actors, political issue context, and tactical and organizational character of each revivalist movement may not be subject to cogent generalization. This is mainly so because all the political factors listed above are contingent upon dynamic changes in the causal structure and the subsequent patterns of revivalist movements.

For example, a revivalist movement in the line of Eclectic Modernism is likely to be less politicized with moderate political ideology. Thus, the overall political implication of this line of revivalist movement may be less visible or significant in relation to the existing socio-political mood of a given country. On the other hand, Orthodox Fundamentalist and Partialist Radical revivalist movements pose visible and significant political impacts on the existing socio-political structure. In the latter case, political ideologies are much more politicized, formation of political actors sympathetic with, or actually involved is well articulated, and the level of political protests and organizational capability are quite sufficient to threaten the existing regimes.

For all the dynamicity and multiplicity of the revivalist phenomenon, however, it is not impossible to diagnose the present status and project future trends of these revivalist movements in a general and/or comparative sense. A careful examination of the causal variables in the comparative perspective sheds some light on the proper diagnosis and projection of the overall political contents of the revivalist movements. Put differently, a comparative data analysis of legitimacy crisis, structural victimization, and socio-historical defeatism, briefly discussed above, helps us capture the overall direction of the revivalist movements.[19] With this in mind, the following section attempts to discuss the various political implications entailed by recent Islamic revivalist movements, with specific focus on the domestic and international dimension.

Domestic Dimension

In the domestic realm, Islamic revivalism is showing at least the three important political characteristics. These are the pervasiveness of the followers, gradual intensification in the form of political protests, and the dual politicization of revivalist sentiments. First, compared with past historical records, Islamic revivalist sentiment, albeit differences in the types of revivalist ideology, is becoming pervasive among the masses in Islamic countries. Islam no longer remains as a bureaucratic religion left to administrative domain of the court or the ministries of Awqaf and religious affairs, or as petrified traditional religion monopolized by *ulama* and other traditional actors. As *Time* magazine has recently reported, Islam is becoming the religion favored by the youth, women, and the masses themselves.[20] A number of people attending the Friday prayer, observing fasting during the month of Ramadan, and participating in informal religious meetings have rapidly increased. Young women are voluntarily wearing veils in public, and Islamic student organizations have become the dominant student organizations in many parts of Islamic countries. Briefly, the mass level efforts to search for Islamic identity and consciousness have grown spontaneously. This could be a reflection of the overall worsening conditions of causal factors leading to the rise of Islamic revivalism. That is to say, enduring legitimacy crisis, deepening structural victimization, and the accumulation of socio-historical defeatism are responsible for this pervasive nature of Islamic revivalism.

Second, this expanded basis of popular sector mobilization in terms of Islamic revivalism is becoming coupled with a further intensification of the militant nature of revivalism. In other words, there is a growing tendency in various revivalist movements to move from the moderate, individual, and partial transformative dimension, to the militant, social, and total transformative dimension. The Iranian revolution, the assassination of Anwar Sadat, the Mecca Incident, growing militancy of Islamic student organizations in Egypt, Algeria, Syria, Malaysia, Turkey, and Indonesia, etc., are good indicators of such a trend. It is important here to keep in mind that these violent and militant movements have gained substantial popular support. The massive popular support for the Iranian Revolution in its initial stage, the surprisingly low level of people's condolence shown on the violent death of Sadat, and the chain effects of the Mecca Incident in other regions of Saudi Arabia and its neighbors indicate that there is a direct relationship between the expanding base of revivalist sentiment among the masses and the high level of intensity and frequency of political violence in the revivalist movements. This tendency in turn implies a high probability of socio-political instability in many Islamic countries. It is particularly so, given the possibility that militant oriented revivalist movements may have strong spillover effects on the followers of other moderate and eclectic revivalist movements. As a matter of fact, this possibility is becoming much more plausible in the sense that the success of the Iranian Revolution has implanted a high aspiration among militant revivalists with specific lessons of the tactics, strategy, organization, and ideology of struggle.[21]

The third important political content of Islamic revivalism is the dual politicization of Islamic revivalist sentiments. While opposition groups, in particular, and the masses, in general, have attempted to delegitimize the incumbent ruling regimes, the ruling regimes, in turn, have recently tried to enhance their legitimacy base and consolidate power by utilizing Islam. At the crossroad of the exhaustion of exogenous ideologies and subsequently weakened legitimacy, it would be quite a natural choice for political elites to mobilize Islam as a counterveiling instrument to the mounting opposition from the various revivalist groups. A telling example would be the case of Pakistan under Zia ul-Haq. Zia has witnessed the consecutive failure of two exogenous ideologies: that of capitalism under Ayub Khan and of socialism under Zulfiqer Bhutto. Thus, Islam was a logical choice for him. Immediately after the seizure of power, he proclaimed the comprehensive introduction of the Islamic system *(Nazim-i-Islami)*, by which the *Sharia* benches are supposed to be established, *hudud* (Islamic punishment of drinking, adultery, theft, and false testimonies) are implemented, and the gradual actualization of the Islamic welfare system is promised.[22] Zia's choice is fundamentalistic and orthodox, to the extent that it has gone beyond original expectations of Islamic opposition groups such as the Jamaat-i-Islami. Nonetheless, there is no sign of reduction of political opposition. Rather, opposition has intensely grown, and the political climate in Pakistan has become more precarious. The reason behind this stalemate is that Zia attempts to realize Islamic goals by violating other essential elements of Islamic political principles, such as consent, consensus, and consultation with Islamic community. Surely military autocratic rule of the present regime will not provide him with the Islamic legitimacy that he is desperate to obtain.

The dual politicization of Islamic revivalism in terms of antagonistic conflict between legitimation and delegitimation is not unique to the case of Pakistan. Immediately following the Mecca Incident, the ruling regime in Saudi Arabia had pursued a tighter implementation of the *Sharia* in all aspects of society. This was not only in response to a specific event, such as the Mecca Incident, but also a part of the overall attempts to re-enhance the weakened political legitimacy of the ruling regime in the process of rapid modernization. However, oppositional sentiments are prevalent among *ulama*, young Muslim fundamentalists, and some traditional actors.[23] Qadhafi's adherence to Islam,[24] Sadat's advocacy of Islam in the eclectic modernist line,[25] Bathist regimes' appeasement policy to Islamic opposition groups in Syria and Iraq,[26] and Mahathir's accommodative approach to Islamic fundamentalists in Malaysia,[27] and so on, are good examples of utilizing Islamic revivalist sentiments to legitimize their regimes and consolidate political power from broader segments of society. For all the political concessions and goodwill gestures on the basis of incremental, eclectic, modernist revivalist sentiments, however, the ruling regimes seem to face continuing political difficulties. Surely, the future pattern of political violence, and hence the dynamics of political change in Islamic countries, are likely conditioned and affected by the levels and degrees of the gaps between these two extreme poles of politicization of Islamic revivalism. And the narrowing of such gaps and the increased coping capability of the ruling regimes may be achieved if, and only if, they are able to solve the current structural pathological problems as manifested in terms of legitimacy crisis, structural victimization, and sociohistorical defeatism.

International Dimension

Political impacts of Islamic resurgent movements are not limited to the domestic political arena. Rather it has become a transnational phenomenon with actual and/or potential impacts on the order and stability in the international system. Some salients of its international political implications may be summarized by looking into the four major issue-areas: transnational linkage, international Muslim solidarity, strategic impacts, and anti-Western sentiment. During the last decade, first, one of the most noticeable attributes of Islamic revivalism seems to be a growing network of transnational linkages among various revivalist movements. Revivalism has not been confined to a specific region or countries. It permeates national borders, not only among Muslim majority Islamic countries, but also among Muslim minority countries. The nature of the linkage network, through which revivalist sentiments, ideologies and tactics are spread all over the world, is by no means a systematic nor elaborate one. It is rather random and spontaneous. Yet, its intensity and pervasiveness have been quite impressive. The Iranian Revolution has incurred a series of intense chain effects not only to neighboring Gulf States, but also to Egypt, Morocco, Algeria, and down to Malaysia and Indonesia. The agents of transmission of revivalist messages are not clearly delineable. But they are eventually disseminated to the grass roots level masses of Islamic countries. A more amazing aspect of this transnational linkage is its visible impacts on Muslim minority countries. As a good example we may cite the case of China. Throughout the 1970s and particularly in the early 1980s there has been a series of serious Muslim revolts in the Western provinces of China, particularly Yunan and Xinjiang. These revolts have ended up with quite a number of casualties highlighting the political significance of Muslim minorities in the western provinces of China. The surprising fact is that the rebellions led by Muslim youths were encouraged by the worldwide resurgence of Islamic sentiments, eventually linking defense of Islam with local political autonomy. Since then, the central government of China has shown remarkable appeasement policies to Muslim ethnic groups.[28] This linkage phenomenon is becoming more pervasive, encompassing the Soviet Union,[29] India, Sub-Saharian African countries,[30] and Southeast Asian countries including the case of Mindanao in the Philippines.

As some observers point out, however, this recent global politicization of Islamic revivalism may not generate significant collective power bases of Islamic countries, despite the aforementioned global diffusion and linkage.[31] Diversified pluralism, fragmentation, and political divisiveness may be responsible for the weakened power base of worldwide Islamic community. As a matter of fact, bitter Sunni vs Shi'a division, growing socioeconomic stratification and the overall rank differentials, and a considerable heterogeneity in political ideologies and regime types are the central part of today's reality of the Islamic world. Surely, the basis of unity and solidarity among Islamic countries have eroded in the long historical process and the idea of Pan-Islamism, as proposed and advocated by al-Afghani, *Ikwhans,* and King Faisal, has been overshadowed by pan-Arabism and other variants of local nationalism and socialism.

For all its heterogeneity and fragmentation, however, there was, until the Iran-Iraq war, a growing epicentric structure of international Islamic solidarity and unity. The success of OPEC and OAPEC collective actions generated political, psychological and economic leverages, which could lead to further cohesiveness among Islamic countries. The recent politicization of the Organization of Islamic Conferences, systematic utilization of the Islamic Development Bank attached to it, and the ever-increasing bilateral economic assistance between capital-rich Islamic countries and poor ones provided world Islamic community with a strong sense of Islamic identity and solidarity. While the past efforts to spread pan-Islamism ended up with failures mainly due to empty promises and resolutions, this pattern of cooperations and consultations was concrete and practical enough to induce the voluntary feelings of unity and solidarity. Apart from these formal economic and political organizations, there have been equally growing voices from international Islamic missionary groups. The World Muslim League *(Rabitat al-A lam al-Islami)*, the central religious organ encompassing all the global Islamic organizations, has played a more efficient and powerful role in coordinating and orchestrating divergent interests and opinions of Muslim organizations. *Dar ul Ifta* of Saudi Arabia, the Islamic Call Society of Libya, and the World Assembly of Muslim Youth supported by the Saudi government have engaged in the global dissemination of revivalist sentiments. They have sent out thousands of *D'ai* (missionary workers) all over the world, particularly developing Islamic and Muslim minority countries, and have been involved in publishing Islamic booklets, organizing international conferences, and supporting Muslim revivalist organizations financially and spiritually. Other than these organizational efforts to promote unity and solidarity on the global plane, the annual gathering of Muslims at Haji,[32] educational activities at the major international Islamic universities, such as al-Medina Islamic university and al-Azhar university have created an intangible international infrastructure of Islamic revivalist movements through which new ideologies are spread, the network of personnel connections is instituted and maintained, and finally a homogenized feeling of unity and solidarity becomes prevalent, particularly among non-governmental actors, which are the major part of revivalist movements.

This growing unity and solidarity can be related to the expanding zone of Islamic influence in the global political scene. As a matter of fact, according to a recent report, the Organization of Islamic Conferences is carefully studying the feasibility of collective actions among Islamic countries in a much more concerted way.[33] Among others, economic integration scheme, formation of producers' cartel in major primary commodities, and the creation of a systemic body of economic cooperation among Islamic countries are seriously being considered. And although they may end up with symbolic exercises, the resolutions and agreements made at the recent Taif Summit meeting of the Organization of Islamic Conferences have revealed a growing consensus in political agenda among Islamic countries and their commitment to solving impending political problems through collective actions. The OIC's ever increasing influences over the Arab League, Non-Aligned Movement, and various fora of the United Nations have been remarkably visible. One of the underlying forces affecting the degree of unity and solidarity among Muslims and their governments may be a currently prevailing disenchantment and disillusion with the external powers, particularly the two superpowers. In other words, Islamic revivalist movements in a high tide are pressurizing the discard of both capitalist and socialist lines of political ideologies and the search for an Islamic alternative.[34] Even if there is very little chance of doing so in the domestic arena of Islamic countries, there is likely to be a high plausibility of such a choice in their external behaviors.

To be more specific, the upsurge of Islamic revivalist movements and Islamic countries' accommodative attitudes to the demands of oppositional revivalist movements may lead to a strategic consensus among them in such a manner that they refute strategic dependency on the Soviet Union and the United States. This potentiality seems to generate substantial impacts on the broadly perceived order and stability in the present international system. Strategically, the Islamic zone (so called Green Belt) is located along the buffer zone between the West (USA) and the East (USSR), spreading from the Straits of Malacca (Malaysia) to the Indian Ocean, Persian Gulf, and to the sensitive part of the Mediterranean Sea. Given the present status of power vacuum with the collapse of the Baghdad Pact, any changes in this sensitive zone of superpower rivalry may affect the existing balance of power system significantly by shaping the different patterns of strategic calculations by the United States and the Soviet Union.

The last important implication of recent Islamic revivalism is its tendency to negate the West, particularly the United States. Disenchantment with the West is not a new syndrome among Islamic countries. It has been a historical pattern originated by a strong common feeling of the past historical reality manifested in terms of bitter memory of the Crusades, colonial experiences, and the persistent cultural penetration. But recent recurrence of such feelings can be differentiated from the former in the sense that the latter has a much more specific target, that of the United States. In fact, the central part of revivalist hostility has been intense and violent anti-American sentiment. The scenes generated by the Iranian hostage crisis, popular attacks on American embassies in Libya and Pakistan, and most recently, the mass boycott movements of American goods in Malaysia well illustrate such sentiments prevalent in many Islamic countries.[35] This phenomenon can be interpreted as an inevitable consequence of American foreign policy behaviors. The inseparable connection between the United States and Israel, and the loss of Jerusalem and al-Aqsa mosque, the U.S.'s explicit and implicit alliance with oppressive and exploitive regimes of the Islamic world in particular, and of the Third World in general, and the nature of mass-culture stemming from the U.S. are directly or indirectly responsible for this anti-American sentiment. Of course, this is an unavoidable cost to be paid for the maintenance of hegemonic power in the international system. Nonetheless, the cost is likely to be prohibitively high in the future.

Concluding Remarks

The primary objective of this study has been to identify different types of Islamic revivalism, to trace its causal structure among them and to measure political impacts derived by revivalist movements. Our findings (or assertions) are such that: (1) Islamic revivalism cannot be confined to one type, i.e., Militant, Fundamentalist, and Orthodox revivalism type. Depending upon the object, rate and amount, and types of tactical means chosen, Islamic revivalism can be classified into at least eight different types. (2) The causal structure of Islamic revivalism cannot be attributed to one sole factor, such as the failure of modernization, an historical factor, or political incompetence of ruling regimes. It is, rather, a function of three clusters of causal variables, that is, the level of political legitimacy crisis, the extent of structural victimization, and the depth of socio-historical defeatism. (3) The types of revivalist movements are mainly determined by the relative distance between Islamic ideals socialized in the minds of Muslims and the actual reality of these three causal factors. And (4), political impacts of Islamic revivalism can be characterized by growing politization of Islam, affecting order and stability of the existing political systems, both internally and externally. The research efforts rendered in this paper are the initial part of an ongoing massive comparative research enterprise. The next step to be followed includes the elaboration of analytical schemes, generation of rich hypotheses, and the empirical testing of such hypotheses on the basis of additional aggregate data.

Notes

We have benefited from the comments of Cesar A. Majul and the editorial and research assistances of Erica Andes, Kate Shnayerson and Hedayatollah Tahbaz.

1. Mohammed Heikal, *Iran: The Untold Story, An Insider's Account of America's Iranian Adventure and Its*

Consequences for the Future (New York: Pantheon Books, 1981), p. 129.

2. H.A.R. Gibb, *Mohammedanism* (New York: Oxford University Press, 1962), pp. 190–192.

3. M. Halpern, *The Politics of Social Change in the Middle East and North Africa* (Princeton: Princeton University Press, 1963), Chapter 7.

4. Donald Smith, *Religion and Political Development* (Boston: Little, Brown and Co., 1970), p. 244.

5. For exemplary works in this line of reasoning, refer to the following books: Mohamed Ayoob, *The Politics of Islamic Reassertion* (New York, St. Martin Press, 1981); Hillal A. Dessouki (ed), *Islamic Resurgence in the Arab World* (New York: Praeger, 1982); J. Esposito (ed), *Islam and Development* (Syracuse, NY: Syracuse University Press, 1980); M. Curtis (ed), *Religion and Politics in the Middle East* (Boulder, CO: Westview, 1981); Yvonne Y. Haddad (ed), *Contemporary Islam and the Challenge of History* (Albany, NY: CUNY Press, 1982); P. Stoddard, D. Cuthell, and M. Sullivan (eds), *Change and the Muslim World* (Syracuse, NY: Syracuse University Press, 1981).

6. The Western media and some scholars have linked the nuclearization efforts of Pakistan, Iraq, and Libya to the formation of militant Islamic power in the international system. To put it differently, they tend to perceive the nuclearization of some Islamic countries in terms of potential sources of nuclear terrorism backed by militant Islamic revivalism.

7. Wilfred C. Smith, *Islam in Modern History* (Princeton: Princeton University Press, *1957),* p. 18.

8. Quoted from interview with Edward Said, in *Time:* "Special Report on World Islam" (April 16, 1979), p. 54. Also refer to his *Orientalism* (New York: Vintage Books, 1979).

9. Nazih N. M. Ayubi, "Political Revival of Islam: The Case of Egypt," *International Journal of Middle East Studies,* 12 (1980), p. 487.

10. For these social-psychological notions, refer to Ted Gurr, *Why Men Rebel* (Princeton: Princeton University Press, 1970); and R. Clark, Jr., *Development and Instability: Political Change in the Non-Western World* (Hinsdale, IL: Dryden Press, 1974).

11. For a good discussion of political values in Islam, refer to R. S. Humphreys, "Islam and Political Values in Saudi Arabia, Egypt, and Syria," *Middle East Journal.*

12. Regarding this matter, consult the following Quranic injunctions: "Blessed be He in whose hands is dominion, and He over all things has power" (Sura 67:1); "O you who believe! Obey God, and obey the Messengers (of God) and those charged with authority among you. If you differ in anything among yourselves, refer it to God and His Messenger, if you do believe in God and the Last Day. That is best, and most suitable for final determination" (Sura 4:59). Also on the evolution of political thought in Islam, refer to Hamid Enayat, *Modern Islamic Political Thought* (Houston, TX: University of Texas Press, 1982).

13. On the matters of economic justice, refer to the following two excerpts from the *Quran:* "O you who believe! Stand firmly for justice, as witnesses to fair dealings, and let not the hatred of others to you make you swerve to wrong and depart from justice. Be just: that is most close to piety, and mind God for God is well-acquainted with all that you do" (Sura 5:9); "And the Firmament has He raised high, and He has set up the Balance (of Justice) in order that you may not transgress (due) balance. So establish weight with justice and fall not short in the balance" (Sura 55:7-9). For a comprehensive understanding of economic aspects of Islam, refer to Kharshid Ahmad, ed., *Studies in Islamic Economics* (Leicester: The Islamic Foundation, 1980), and to J. Cummings, H. Askari, and A. Mustafa, "Islam amid Modern Economic Change," in Esposito, ed., *Islam and Development,* pp. 25-48.

14. H. Abdalati, *Islam in Focus,* pp. 123-125.

15. For a good introduction to the cultural and historical legacy of Islam, consult Abul Hassan Ali Nadwi, *Islam and the World* (Beirut: the Holy Quran Publication House, 1977); M. Lombard, *The Golden Age of Islam* (New York: American Elsevir Publishing Co., 1975).

16. On the linkage between military defeatism and the rise of popular Islamic movements, refer to Nazih Ayubi, *Political Revival;* and to S.E. Ibrahim, *Anatomy of Islamic Groups.*

17. The designation of capitalism, communism and Zionism as the ultimate enemies of Islam has been the most common theme of Islamic revivalist movements regardless of types and national origin.

18. Using the three clusters of causal factors as inde-

pendent variables and the eight different types of revivalist movements as dependent variables, we may be able to generate many interesting hypotheses to be tested. For the sake of brevity, however, an in-depth study of multiple relationships between the causal factors and the types of movement will be reserved for future research agenda.

19. We are in the process of collecting massive comparative aggregate data on these three variables on the longitudinal time series base encompassing all the Islamic countries and some important Muslim minority countries such as India, China, and the Soviet Union.

20. "Special Report on the World of Islam," *Time* (April 16, 1979).

21. The success of the Iranian Revolution has greatly affected militant Islamic revivalist movements in Egypt, Malaysia, Algeria, and some Gulf States including Saudi Arabia. The most important thing regarding this matter is the fact that Islamic cause and actors could be successful in overthrowing the existing political regimes. Thus, symbolic as well as practical implications derived from the case of the Iranian Revolution can be evaluated as being substantial.

22. Mohammad Zia ul-Haq, *Introduction of the Islamic System in Pakistan* (Islamabad: Government of Pakistan, 1979).

23. It has been said that a growing number of students at the Mecca Sharia College of the King Abdul Aziz University and at al-Medina Islamic University have shown a feeling of disenchantment with the conservative and accommodative line of Sheikh Abdul Aziz Bin Baz, the ultimate authority in Islamic matters in the Kingdom. And it is also reported that there have been quite a substantial number of sympathizers with the rebels of the Mecca Incident.

24. Ann Mayer, "Islamic Resurgence" in Dessouki, *Islamic Resurgence.*

25. Saad Eddin Ibrahim, *Anatomy of Islamic Groups.* Also refer to Daniel Crecelius, "The Course of Secularization in Modern Egypt," in Esposito, (ed.), *Islam and Development*, pp. 49-70.

26. For example, in a recent debate on the constitutional role of Sharia in the Syrian state system, the Syrian government has given concessions to Islamic groups by retreating from its initial insistence on the secular, Baathism-based nature of the new constitution. Iraq also has pursued an appeasement policy to Shia opposition groups centered around the Shia holy cities of Najaf and Kerbela. Consult R.A. Hinnebusch, "The Islamic Movement in Syria," in Au Dessouki, ed., *Islamic Resurgence*, Chap. 7. Also M. Hudson, "Islam and Political Development," in Esposito, ed., *Islam and Development.*

27. Mahathir has been successful in co-opting Anwar Ibrahim, president of ABIM, the most fundamentalist opposition group, into a part of his regime. It was known that Ibrahim's participation in the ruling regime was made possible as a result of Mahathir's consent that religious matters remain the domain of Ibrahim. In fact, Ibrahim was appointed as deputy minister in charge of religious affairs in the prime minister's office and the recent development in Malaysia indicates that Mahathir government pursues very accommodative policies on the demands of the fundamentalist groups.

28. Lillian C. Harris, "China's Islamic Connection," a paper presented to annual convention of Association for Asian Studies, (March 1981) Toronto; Raphael Israeli, "The Muslim Minority in Traditional China," *Asian and African Studies* 10:2 (1975).

29. G. Jukes, "The Soviet Union," in Ayubi, (ed.), *The Politics of Islamic,* Chap. 13. A. Bennigsen, "Official Islam and Sufi Brotherhood in the Soviet Union Today," in A. Cudsi and A. Dessouki, (eds.), *Islam and Power in the Contemporary Muslim World* (Baltimore: Johns Hopkins University Press, 1981).

30. Sulayman S. Nyang, "Sub-Saharan Africa: Islamic Interpretation," in Stoddard, Cuthell, and Sullivan, (eds.), *Changes and the Muslim World,* pp. 145-150.

31. This point was asserted by Faud Ajami, *Arab Predicament* (New York: Cambridge University Press, 1981).

32. For a good description of tile socio-political aspect of *Hajj,* refer to David Long, *The Hajj Today* (Albany, NY: State University of New York Press, 1979).

33. Organization of Islamic Conference, *Areas of Economic Cooperation Among Islamic Countries* (Ankara: Statistical, Economic and Social Research and Training Center for Islamic Countries, 1980).

34. According to a recent report, Iraqi prisoners of

war detained in Iran are forced to recite the following phrase every day: "*La Sharqiun La Gharbiun Jumhurial Islamiun* (Neither West, not East, but Islamic Republic)." This episode can be interpreted as an effort to search for Islamic alternative.

35. As a result of the Israeli invasion of Lebanon, the Malaysian Muslim Youth Movement, in cooperation with student organizations, waged a nationwide boycott movement of American goods, with the accusation that the United States, by its constant support of Israel, was responsible for the Lebanese tragedy.

The Religious Foundations of a More Peaceful World

Marc Gopin
Tufts University

The Dual Nature of Religion

The most constructive way in which religion can contribute to a peaceful world at the present time is for those who are committed to religion's value to acquire a sober view of its dual nature. The religions of the world have all contributed at one time or another to the creation and perpetuation of ethical values and behaviors that are indispensable to peace and civil society. It is equally within the capacity of the world's religions to generate, justify, and even exult in the most cruel and barbaric behavior that human beings are capable of experiencing. Religions go through periods of history in which one or the other of these two alternatives will dominate, and it is also invariably the case that there are always individual members, at any time of history, who devoutly embrace one or the other of these alternatives.

How and when the pendulum shifts between these alternatives is governed by a broad range of external factors, which influence the internal dynamics of a religion's leadership and the predominant interpretations of myths, symbols, texts, laws and customary practices. These external factors include, the level of inequity or equity felt by the populations in question, levels of security and insecurity, levels of fulfillment in terms of structures of meaning and community, levels of injury from war, and many other factors too extensive to enter into here.[1]

Rage, Clerical Power, and the Search for Peace

Historically speaking, the world's most salient examples of mass violence have almost always included two major factors: a generalized rage of the public in search of an outlet, and leaders who know how to manage their ideological constructs in such a way that uses that rage to further their aims and their power. Religion is no different. There is an uncanny power to religious leaders when they stand behind the presence of generalized rage in search for an outlet. Some clerics will shrink from followers who demand greater radicalism, and greater militarism in their world-view. But others will seize the opportunity to further their own militarized view of their religion and its aims. Much of this in recent times is also mediated by the degree to which a clerical class is socialized to modern constructs of the state, and coexistence with other religions and secular institutions. Many of the world's great religious leaders and clerics have made their peace with a religious vision that is not one of hegemony and domination. While others are deeply offended by modern arrangements.

The reasons why populations may be enraged are largely due to external factors in the world that create a prison of their existence. Militarized religion and accompanying constructed identities appear to them to be a way out. But they would not and could not move the religion hermeneutically in the direction of ultimate violence if it were not for a class of clerics hungry to achieve leadership and power in this way. In rare instances, it is not about local clerical needs for empowerment, it is about fantasies of global cataclysm and ultimate domination.

Scopes of Inclusion/Exclusion in Mythic and Ethical Constructs

There are two aspects of religion that are most relevant to our subject: 1. The power of religion in terms of world-view, myth, and ritual; and 2. The power of religion as an architect of ethical constructs of the human mind, in addition to its effect on the character of community.

Both of these aspects tend to augment the power of violence *and* the power of peace. Religious zeal is an enhancer and catalyst of basic human tendencies. Mythic religion can create new and better realities, coexist with and enhance already good elements of society, or destroy society. Ethical values can be creative or destructive depending upon the degree to which pro-social values are extended to others who are different. In other words, the scope of inclusion in one's ethical universe is the core determinant of the constructive/destructive ratio, not the beauty or exaltedness of the ethical idea. This scope can be very broad, though nuanced, such as special care for family and co-religionists alongside universal commitments to justice, compassion, or, at the very least, limitations on aggression. Or the scope can be extremely narrow such that only true believers who are men have rights and are deserving of dignity and respect.

Superordinate Educational Goals and Values

We live in a world where too many members of liberal religious elites around the globe have been so busy articulating the most beautiful and exalted visions of inclusive ethics emanating out of their traditions, that they have been completely unprepared for the power of rage, and its corrupting influence on religious leadership. Furthermore, they have been unprepared to guarantee the most basic outer limitations on religious behavior, such as what is beyond the pale of any legitimate religious behavior. The most salient example is the killing of noncombatants. By this stage of history, and after a hundred years of beautiful multi-faith international gatherings, there should have been a realistic set of agreed upon taboos that are not only articulated by famous religious personalities at the United Nations, *but taught in every religious school on the globe.* This should have been done by multi-faith international treaties long ago. In other words there should have been a move from political statements to educational policy. But this has not been done for even the most rudimentary taboos, such as the deliberate targeting of civilians. I know of no religious curriculum coming out of one religious community that teaches at a young age something akin to, "all the major religions of the world have agreed that it is right to aid the poor, wrong to kill noncombatants in war, right to welcome strangers, etc." If and when they teach such values, it is in the name of their own religion, generally in a chauvinist fashion that suggests that only their religion contains the best expression of these values.

The best asset, however, of religious communities and their leaders is that they are fabulously gifted in the promotion of myths that give meaning, structure, and a desire to be good. Nothing is more indispensable to building a global culture of peace and justice. This theme will be revisited shortly.

Rights Merging with Duties

A major clash afoot between the world of religion and the secular construct of states that must be addressed in the future is the dichotomy of rights and duties, where the liberal state is constructed upon rights, and religion's main claims, especially in monotheism, are constructed upon duties. Forward-thinking people, who want to avoid a global clash between organized religion and the state, should more creatively investigate and articulate integrated constructs of the modern state that give honor to both rights and duties, with due acknowledgement that we are not always in agreement on the specifics of those duties. For example, we know that the world over, in countless cultures and religions, there could be a commitment to a duty to protect human life. But we know that there are disagreements about whether a fetus is included in that duty, or, in other words, whether a fetus is human life. We could still construct international sets of duties, however, with full acknowledgement of where we agree to disagree. It is the overarching sets of moral duties, the superordinate values and goals, in addition to superordinate rights, that will strengthen the modern state, while giving due honor to cultures and religions, but without allowing any religion to tyrannize the public order or the life of the individual.

In general we must think of what religion's assets are in the construction of a vibrant, sustainable, peaceful human civilization at the same time that we acknowledge and protect ourselves from the dangers.

It is useful to focus on one example at this point of a region and a set of religions, which desperately need the constructive and creative side of religion to be injected into war prevention and the search for peace. Let us then explore the Middle Eastern conflict and, in particular, the Arab-Israeli conflict.

The Abrahamic Myth as a Fateful Bond

Relatives, such as father, mother, brother, sister, and cousin, seem to be pervasive as metaphors the world over for deep, collective human entities and their relationships. In the Middle East, in particular, the use of the metaphor of family, specifically the family of the Biblical Abraham, to describe the cultural and religious origins of people, is remarkably pervasive. In this metaphor of Abrahamic family identities are established. In this metaphor old wounds are expressed. Ancient competitions and conflicts are given a quality of cosmic significance. In this metaphor victory over the forces of ignorance and idolatry is celebrated, and those forces are seamlessly conflated with whoever is an enemy of the Abrahamic tribe.

The Abrahamic tribe is also held to strict standards of devotion to a single God whose betrayal has harsh and violent consequences. But in this metaphor there also resides some profound possibilities of a nonviolent future, which we will explore shortly.

What is possibly even more remarkable is that this family of Abraham is truly mythic, in the sense that there never has been and probably never will be any evidence—independent of the Bible and the Qur'an—for the existence of Abraham or his family. The Bible, even by traditional counting, was written many centuries after Abraham's existence. In recent times, centuries of scholars have doubted that the book of Genesis was written earlier than at least a thousand years later than when Abraham would have lived.

The Abrahamic family myth lives and breathes an independent reality, nevertheless, in the minds and hearts of hundreds of millions of Jews, Christians and Muslims. It is a critical means of organizing the world and making sense of one's history, one's origins, and even one's future. However, it is a story mediated through different lenses, depending on the religious group, with innumerable variations, based on the sub-groupings and individual predilections of millions of interpreters.

Yet the unifying power of the metaphor is unmistakable. The persistence the Abrahamic myth has over millennia becomes a metaphor, in and of itself, of an abiding connectivity that monotheistic peoples feel toward each other, even though that connectivity has often expressed itself as jealousy, competition, disappointment, and brutalizing murder. In a word, monotheists often act as relatives in an intense but troubled and murderous family.

I am using "myth" in the sense of a story that contains some ultimate and enduring truth, and a way of making sense of amorphous reality, for those who believe in it. Whether the myth is believed to be literal history, approximate history, or simply didactic legend, depends on the believer.

But myth means something much deeper and more important for conflict and peacemaking. Myth that is shared has a way of bringing infinitely complex problems into a manageable cognitive structure of reality. This allows problems of dizzying proportions to be understood by the human mind and absorbed by the human heart. This, in turn, is a perfect tool for motivating large groups of people to violence—or to peace.

Myth is not static, despite fundamentalist facades, and this is the most essential point. Myth has always been characterized by development through repetition, communication and interpretation. It has allowed communication to proceed by means of the myth itself expanding and developing, or extending itself, to contemporary, "real time" constructs that often elude rationalistic methods of negotiation and diplomacy. And the less education in rationalistic constructs of the religion the more prone people are to the expansion of myth.

This is how millions become motivated to hatred by the manipulation of symbols. But this also creates possibilities, rarely utilized by liberal elites, in the pro-social development of human relations. Mythical possibility is the midwife of cultural conflict-resolution and peacemaking.[2] It provides the dramatic construct for thinking about and treating enemies in a fundamentally new way—which at the same time becomes embedded in familiar myth.

Let us outline the parameters of the Abrahamic myth by stating at the outset that the mediation of this myth by all three traditions is extremely varied, and that, roughly speaking, the mediated interpretations of the myth generally serve the interests of each respective corporate religious entity. Islamic versions will confirm the centrality and importance of Arabian ancestry in Abraham and the confirmation of Abraham and Ishmael as the first believers and servants of Allah. Jewish mediations of the story will centralize the importance of Isaac and Israel as the inheritors of God's favor. Christian retellings of the story are much more rare but generally emphasize Abraham as the first man of faith in one God.[3] All will claim the special favor of God proven through their telling and re-telling of the story.

Let us begin with the Hebrew Biblical myth. Abraham was a man who discovered a monotheistic world-view in the midst of an idolatrous culture. In particular, he developed a relationship with a God who promised that Abraham would be the father of many peoples, *av hamon goyim*.[4] Abraham and his wife Sarah were unable to have children until a very old age, but Abraham had a child, Ishmael, with Sarah's maidservant, Hagar. Abraham was promised another son, and Sarah gave birth to Isaac.

Abrahamic Family Tragedies

The Hebrew Biblical tradition is clearly focused on the fate of Isaac as the ancestor of the Jewish people. In fact, Sarah, resenting or suspecting the influence of Ishmael on her son, insists that the maidservant and son be thrown out of the house, which Abraham does. Thus, in addition to being willing to sacrifice his son, Isaac, Abraham is also willing to send his other son and wife to the desert, both times with the approval or command of a divine voice. This is the first in a series of subtle presentations of family tragedies in the Genesis stories, which will have consequences for inter-group relations later.

In Jewish rabbinic interpretation, Isaac is the key

to Jewish lineage, Ishmael to Arab and Islamic lineage, and Esau, Jacob's brother, is the key symbol for Roman/European/Christian lineage. The separation of these three relatives—and their animosity—is the key to the rabbinic mythical account of later history and later tragedies.[5]

That Abraham expelled Hagar and Ishmael is mediated somewhat by some later rabbinic myths that Abraham went seeking after Ishmael, concerned with his welfare and who he would marry.[6] On the whole, however, the moral problematic of this expulsion is not confronted in most rabbinic literature.[7] On the contrary, the expulsion is seen as a necessary way to protect Isaac from Ishmael, and to prepare Isaac to be God's chosen, the patriarch of God's people.[8]

Sarah clearly instigates the expulsion of Hagar and Ishmael (Gen. 21:10), and it seems to be based on some actions of Ishmael involving the verb, *metsahek*, a difficult word to translate. She sees Ishmael "making sport," or perhaps it means ridicule. We really do not know from the Biblical text, which is why rabbinic literature elaborates and interprets. Rabbi Akiva claims that Sarah saw Ishmael bringing idolatry into Abraham's house. Rabbi Simeon ben Yohai is very telling. He claims that the "ridicule" was motivated by all the attention being given to Isaac as the son of Abraham who will inherit a double portion. But Ishmael says that he is, in fact, the eldest, and by right (Deuteronomy 21:17) should inherit the double portion.

We have right here in the rabbinic literature the essence of the tragic relationship of brothers—and competing monotheistic religions. They compete over who is idolatrous and who is authentic, and they compete for the love of the father, embodied in the double portion of inheritance.

Contemporary Reverberations

Rabbinic defensiveness over the expulsion of Ishmael and Hagar betrays ambivalence over this historic relationship, and this defensiveness is further confirmed as we read some modern interpreters. Aviva Zornberg, for example, a modern Orthodox Jewish Bible interpreter who resides in Israel, sees Sarah's insistence on expulsion as a necessary response to the dangers for her son. She emphasizes Ishmael as a mortal danger to Isaac.[9] Furthermore, in a progressive reversal of traditionalist rabbinic gender typologies, Zornberg portrays Sarah as the embodiment of incisive analysis and calculation of danger, versus Abraham who is "too entangled in emotions" (a characterization generally reserved in Jewish and Western culture for women) to make the tough, analytical decision for expulsion. Ironically, however, this embrace of the Jewish Sarah as a strong model of female analytic capacity is coupled in Zornberg's interpretation with an uncritical embrace of the expulsion of a woman and her child without any protection! This is a feminist position for Jewish wives only but not for gentile maidservants.

The mortal fears of Jews from Ishmael that is Arabs, in the Israeli context must be seen as part of the interpretive emphases and hermeneutic choices of contemporary interpreters such as Zornberg. When she concludes that the brothers seem to be playing together but that they cannot coexist "for there is murder in the wind," this sounds like a strong echo of one contemporary attitude on Arab-Israeli coexistence. The latter reverberates in both Jewish and Arab circles, always accompanied, of course, with partial and selective evidence.[10] Interpretation of myths is often an unconscious way to structure predictable reality and repeat all the tragedies of the past. Self-fulfilling prophecy in enemy systems is comforting at a deep existential level even if it is self-destructive in reality.

Hated Brother Myths Revisited

As stated, there is a tendency in ancient Jewish rabbinic culture to justify the expulsion, and to paint both Isaac as well as Jacob as vulnerable to the wildness or simple evil of their respective brothers,

Ishmael and Esau. But the Hebrew Bible has a subtle and complicated relationship to both brothers. Ishmael is, in fact, blessed. Esau is later embodied in Edom, and there is a specific prohibition against hating Edom in the Bible.[11] Furthermore, despite the tendency to see Ishmael as utterly other in rabbinic Judaism, there are some curious issues, such as the fact that Ishmael, through the voice of Rabbi Simeon ben Yohai, cited above, does make a good Biblical case for why Ishmael, not Isaac, should inherit the double portion. This is enormously telling, in terms of the dramatic and tragic tension between these two monotheistic people, concerning who is the one that is favored by God, or who has the purest faith. In the Jewish sources the emphasis is on who is favored and loved. In the Islamic case it tends to be described as who has the purest faith, the true Islam.

Another interesting point in the Hebrew Bible complicates the relationship to Ishmael. When the Bible records the death of Ishmael, it uses a classic ethnic/national metaphor of death that is usually seen as a deeply unique place of Jewish reunion. It says Ishmael was "gathered unto his people,"[12] a phrase generally reserved for the most important figures of Jewish life![13] Who could Ishmael have been gathered into other than the family of Abraham? And if so, what does it say about the nature of this family? Is there consciously or unconsciously embedded in ancient Jewish tradition, a Jewish family, a family of Adam or humanity, and then some in-between family? An Abrahamic family perhaps that includes both Jews and gentiles, or at least all Semites? If so, why has this been left undeveloped in Jewish theology? We will leave this open for now, except to point out the rich texture of hermeneutic possibility, the curious way in which this subject has been repressed or ignored, and the way in which hermeneutical observation is intimately related to the believer's horizon and psychological context.[14]

Islam's Abrahamic Family

Arab culture and Islam share the belief that Abraham existed, was the founder or restorer of monotheism, and that Hagar and Ishmael are the key ancestors of the Arabian peoples. But whom God has chosen is a different matter. The Biblical account of the expulsion of Hagar and Ishmael is accepted in Islam in a certain way. It is elaborated upon later, however, in critical ways. According to Al-Baizawi, Abraham does expel them, due to Sarah's jealousy.[15] According to one tradition, Abraham accompanies them, but then leaves them in Mecca. According to another tradition, Abraham takes them to Mecca, leaves them with a bag of dates, and then prepares to leave. Hagar beseeches him to stay, and asks if God commanded him to do this, and he says, "yes." And she says that God will cause no harm to come to her. Then later Abraham prayed for them that others may be kind to them.[16]

The spring that God provided for Hagar's survival, according to Islamic traditions, is seen to be in Mecca. This spring or well is called Zamzam and it sprang miraculously from beneath the foot of Ishmael. The hills that are critical to this myth are Safa and Marwah, and to run between them is a rite of pilgrimage to this day. Ishmael and Hagar are believed to be buried in *hijir ismail*, an enclosure right next to the *ka'abh.*[17] Hagar and Ishmael are critical to the mythic interactions of every pilgrim to Mecca, now and throughout all these past centuries.

Mythic Re-reading and Reconciliation

Is there room here for a hermeneutic re-reading of both traditions, Arabic and Jewish, in terms of mothers and sons, the pain of mothers in the threats of violence to their sons, but also the violence that mothers may encourage toward other or rival sons and mothers? Is this not a mythic backdrop for all violence and war where the sons must be sacrificed for the sake of the survival of the family? Are there not in every culture unique ways in which both mothers and fathers, in different venues, are simultaneously and paradoxically engaged in the nurturing and even exaltation of their sons, only to sacrifice them to violence and abandonment on the field of battle? Which eighteen year-old dying on the field of battle does not cry out for his mother? Who cannot see the essential mythos and pathos of sacrifice in the movie *Born on the Fourth of July*, where Tom Cruise, in one of his best performances to date, embodies the favored son born to be abandoned and sacrificed? This movie is a must-see for a classic contemporary rendering of the Abrahamic sacrifice stories.

We have here an historic opportunity for inter-cultural engagement on these fateful matters. Especially in the circumstances of the Israeli-Arab conflict, where several generations of mothers and fathers have now sacrificed their children to this battle, such discussion in familiar cultural terms may open a gateway for communication. Furthermore there may be an opportunity for a kind of cultural/psychological process of reconciliation and mourning in which Abraham, Isaac, Ishmael and Hagar become the central mythic actors. This family's chronological distance, which is paradoxically combined with their cosmic significance in both communities, may provide the basis for a dramatic evolution of their relationship.

Let me digress with eyewitness testimony and evidence. I have seen mythic re-reading and evolution in action. I have watched courageous rabbis stand before their fundamentalist students engaged in deep study of Abraham and his family, weaving seamlessly a tale of Isaac's chosenness together with reconciliation between Isaac and Ishmael as the true will of God. I have seen an heroic Muslim Palestinian sheikh risk his life to show his love for Jews, even as he cries at night in his search to understand the continued violence, asking himself again and again, "why do the children of Abraham continue to harm each other?" Such people are often alone and unsupported, but only because the world has yet to understand the critical role of these extraordinary human beings for the future of peace on this planet.

Abrahamic Paths to Social Change

The key to the future is the strengthening of mythic readings and re-readings of coexistence by using the best moral and spiritual practices of religious traditions. There is one fundamental advantage to cultural processes of human social change, and one fundamental advantage to religious processes of change. The former expresses itself in an unabashed embrace of and dependence upon non-rational ritual and formalism as a way of transforming outer behavior as well as internal states of being. The latter expresses itself in an unabashed commitment to and dependence upon ethics and morality as a motivation of human behavior that has specific sanction by the highest sacred authorities, both human and divine. Cultures and religions affected by the Palestinian/Israeli conflict share both of these characterizations.

Both of these phenomena have been completely neglected by elite diplomacy and conflict resolution efforts in the Palestinian/Israeli conflict, but only on a conscious level, I would argue. There is no doubt in my mind that one can find ritualistic and symbolic processes at work in the both the successes and failures of secular, high-level negotiations. But they are rarely admitted to, and thus lose their usefulness in terms of replicability and expansion to larger populations. While I applaud high-level processes, they are always vulnerable to rejectionist terrorism precisely because they *dis-empower* rather than empower, they exclude rather than include. Thus, the religious terrorist knows that he has to go a relatively short distance in order to overwhelm the public consciousness with fear of and revulsion at peace with the enemy other.

Our goal is to magnify a passion for peacemaking as broadly and as deeply as possible. Here is where culture and religion can be so helpful, and where elite processes must develop more humility. A major effort must be made to mine the depths of the ethical traditions of each monotheistic tradition, and elicit specific ethical principles that will give sanction to conflict resolution practices, as well as give expression to those practices in new ways that specifically reflect the cultures involved. But in monotheistic traditions (perhaps in all traditions) the religious/ethical prescriptions are inextricably tied to cultural habits and inter-personal expectations that elicit feelings of warmth and devotion, when adhered to, and elicit feelings of alienation and anger when violated.

Now these religious and cultural habits express themselves in two distinct kinds of human engagements: 1. informal, and 2. formal or ritualistic. Both are vital for the future of conflict resolution. Various religious actors globally place different emphases on these two human engagements. For example, high-level relationship building between religious leadership, conducted by the World Conference on Religion and Peace, or by the Vatican, emphasizes formal contacts and conversations between key leaders, although this does not exhaust the range of their work. The origins of Moral Re-Armament (now called Initiatives of Change) in a Protestant, evangelical style, by contrast, has tended to emphasize the slow growth of inter-personal relationships over time between key figures of enemy groups, as well as some very direct appeals to emotions, sometimes in a rather anti-intellectual fashion. MRA members also have formal gatherings and interactions, but one of their great strengths has been the model of informal networking and relationship building. The latter has important theological roots for them, for it is in the "surprises" of human connections and chance meetings that they see the Divine Hand guiding human beings towards reconciliation with others and with God. As such, they have filled a void in many conflicts wherein fruitless, formal negotiations are endlessly engaged and disengaged, but deep human connection between enemies is missing entirely, off the radar screen of "pragmatic" priorities. The failures of so many formal negotiations due to the utter incapacity to bring populations along in peace processes makes one question who in this debate of methods is more devoted to pragmatism. Religious peace actors may sometimes be accused of an excessive faith in the transformative power of emotions to the point of impracticality, but elite representatives may be accused of excessive fear of emotions to the point of impracticality.

Deep Engagement with the Enemy

It has become clear to me over time that many of the same actors who stand for peace and peacemaking, and who commit themselves to difficult compromises, against the wishes of their own community, have little or no contact with enemies, and sometimes do not want any. In fact they often have little contact with their own community, as well as that of the enemy, confining themselves to their own group of fellow believers. The latter group, while well-intentioned, has not been challenged by peace processes to really know the enemy other in a deep way, the enemies on all sides. But without this emotional ability and/or ethical directive, the deepest impasses of negotiations are not overcome.

It is time for the world to learn that the non-rational interaction is the grease for the wheels of "rational" negotiations. For some, like those in MRA, there is a theological-teleological function of informal relationship building, bringing God into people's lives, by bringing reconciliation. For others, such as Jewish religious peacemakers in Jerusalem, the relationship building acts are simple *mitsvot*, good deeds that represent an end in themselves, a very difficult act whose fulfillment represents a courageous offering to God. Of course, they too, have a teleological agenda of religious vision. But their actions are felt to be deontological, to borrow from Kantian thought, a religious end in itself that fulfills a religious mandate which binds them to (and creates?) the Torah's path of peace, something they believe in and create by their way of life. In either case, the point is that we must trace the vital role of both formalistic and ritualistic actions, on the one hand, and, on the other, subtle, informal, non-rational processes of interaction whose value to peacemaking is insufficiently appreciated. In fact, it is the hidden cornerstone upon which all courageous social change depends, secular or religious.

Symbol in the Ethical Encounter

Let us now delve into the specific significance of the inter-religious encounter, and the power of symbol and metaphor. We will begin the investigation of this kind of encounter at its most elemental level. Let us talk about the human face, a rich topic for social psychology, phenomenology, cultural studies, and, less well known, for monotheistic ethics.

It cannot be overestimated how important the human face is to the success or failure of human encounters. This has not been studied sufficiently in terms of conflict resolution, because the interaction between communications theory, social psychology, and conflict resolution theory, is spotty, dependent on the scholarly background of various theoreticians. Obviously, those with a background in communications and social psychology have the "permission" professionally, in terms of their home departments, to highlight the importance of these phenomena. No one in the academic study of conflict, however, has the permission or the background to examine the effect of religious and ethical sanctions on the experience of inter-human and face-to-face encounter. At best this is studied in terms of taboo, but the power of religious ethics to impact the effect of the use of the face on peacemaking goes unrecognized and unappreciated.

In terms of monotheism, the face and the eyes become a crucial test of love or hate, the beginning or end of relationship. Charisma, a critical characteristic of the Biblical figure Joseph, and the evidence of his chosenness by God, is expressed by way of those who "find favor [*hen*] (charisma, sweetness, compassion?) in his eyes." Many other examples abound.[18] The point is that the pro-social relations begin with the eyes and with the look. Clearly there are powerful effects of eyes on human behavior in the social/psychological orientation of the Bible. There is a level of concreteness of love or care in this view that does not allow it to be abstract. The face embodies one's emotions and also one's ethics.

The nightmare converse of peacemaking in this regard is the strange way in which murderous people in any number of circumstances seem to go berserk when looked in the eye. Looking in the eye is regarded as a dangerous challenge, and this appears to be the case among various primates as well.[19] If this is the impact negatively of the eyes and face, it stands to reason that this is an untapped resource for the emotions and ethics of pro-social engagement.

Monotheism understood this well. Thus, in addition to the uses of facial imagery in a descriptive fashion in the narrative Biblical portions, like the Joseph stories, it naturally occurs in the prescriptive, legal portions of the Bible. One is commanded to honor or beautify the face of the elder in one's community,[20] but not to honor faces with partiality in terms of legal judgments, in other words to let justice take its course, without allowing charisma or anything else to sway a judge towards one party's face.

There is also the notion of a hardness to the face which, in rabbinic Judaism is one of the quintessential sins.[21] The alternatives of a kind face, based on *hen*, or a hard, murderous face, is rooted in the alternative presentations of Divine imagery in the Bible.[22] There are Biblical precedents for withholding the kind Divine face from certain groups of people.[23]

Here is the most important point. The foundations and sanctions in all three monotheisms for the compassionate use of the face should be seized upon as basic to the peacemaking meeting, to training in peacemaking, to the evocation of peacemaking as a religiously sanctioned discipline. No cross-religious, cross-cultural training should neglect to problematize the ways to greet and engage the face of the other. This has immense potential to help change the engagement of enemies in formal and especially informal encounters, and to hurt those same encounters in which this vital cultural phenomenon is neglected.

The Centrality of Shame and its Antidote, Honor

In Judaism, there are specific commandments to prohibit the whitening of the face, in other words humiliation which, in rabbinic metaphor, leads to a loss of blood to the face. The rabbis seize on this as akin to murder, the shedding of blood. This moves us toward another key cultural/religious issue, honor and shame, one of the single most important issues in Middle Eastern conflicts, but truly a universal characteristic of most long-standing conflicts.

Honor and shame are central moral and spiritual categories in monotheistic ethics, particularly in Judaism and Islam. The bestowal of honor and dignity are critical to any listing of classic moral categories of Islam.[24] The same is true in Judaism.[25] It is something so fundamental to proper human relations, and to adhering to the personality paradigm of either the Prophet, in Islam, God, in Judaism, or Jesus in Christianity, that it seeps into the style and character of countless classical texts.

Honor and the prevention of shame are not only ethical precepts. They embody a way of being, a critical component of a metaphysical intentionality to the universe that has placed the human being in an exalted and responsible role of a caretaker. Therefore, the violation of human dignity is felt to be not only an ethical failure and an immense personal injury, it is also an affront to God and the Divine plan. Furthermore, because these traditions have such deep communal roots in the Biblical corpus, a personal affront to one human being is often seen as an affront to the Umma, in Islam, or Islam itself. In Judaism, an assault on the dignity of a Jew is an assault on a member of God's own people, and on the image of God that every human being reflects.

One of the subtle differences in the lived tradition and experience of the enemy groups in Israel and Palestine is that, at least for European Jewry, the interpretation of 'assault' as a generalized assault on God and goodness seems to be particularly activated when Jews suffer actual physical injury from gentiles, especially when they are singled out as Jews. This is what seems to activate for Jews the metaphorical drama of the victimized righteous of God, a drama that was etched in stone millennia ago by the exquisitely sensitive writing of the Psalmist, the essential book of Jewish prayer.

It is with injury and death, particularly of women and children, that so many religious Jews retreat to the safe space of historical prayers, where the righteous will survive, and enemies of God will be subdued and crushed by God someday. This is when feelings of honor, shame, and dignity betrayed, seem to reach fever pitch, with the Holocaust being the ultimate magnification of this dramatic tragedy and permanent fixture of God's strange and inscrutable, but ultimately just, universe. Much of this metaphorical drama is also played out in Christian literature, only now applied to the truly chosen lambs of God, the True Israel, the followers of Jesus.

This is not quite the same in the fusion of Arab culture and Islamic religion. In the lived experience of this culture and religion, particularly when it applies to this century of Palestinian/Israeli conflict, the dynamics of honor, dignity and shame, work themselves through this conflict in ways that are *sui generis*. This is a sensitive, difficult subject, and, in a certain way, the only proper response to this issue is to listen carefully to those involved, and let *them* determine and describe what has happened and how it has affected them.

What all this means is that, as Jews and Arabs gather, and begin to attempt peacemaking in a more lasting way than mere political negotiation, they had better expect that their response to issues of honor and shame are different but equally sensitive. But they should also anticipate that the active effort to make the recovery of honor a central axis of peacemaking will yield some powerful results, if they do this carefully, listening to each other, and accepting the humble processes of trial and error.

What will it take to restore lost dignity? What will it take for rejectionists in the Jewish camp to feel that it is not only by the gun that the value and dignity of a Jewish life can be restored in this world? What will it take for a Palestinian family and clan to recover dignity in the wake of the humiliations and hardships of forced displacement, persecution, and merciless poverty? What about those who have good resources and education now, but incessant memories of lost property and a lost sense of place that just will not dissipate? And I speak here of both Palestinians and Jews, the latter having lost this in a different location. What will it take for those who have nothing in a refugee camp, and how much will the latter depend on the honest integration of cultural dignity and economic rights? What will restore honor?

How do you factor into this the complex way in which the deepest and most destructive humiliations of Jews, in many cases utterly indescribable in their horror, are embedded into most family memories from events that occurred elsewhere, in Europe? Yes, at the hands of non-Jews, gentiles who wanted them dead, but not the Palestinians. But now, in the Palestinian/Israeli war, how do these Jews distinguish between a non-Jew who wanted them dead fifty years ago for one set of reasons and a Palestinian who might want to kill them now for a very different set of reasons? Some can make the rational distinction, but can they distinguish the emotional response when the images of mangled, destroyed bodies of loved ones and kin are the same? How does one cope with this triangulation of humiliation and living nightmares?

There is only one answer that I know of to emotional damage, and that is the intentional reversal of that damage, humiliation being healed by sorrow and mourning, but ultimately, and more constructively, by honor.

That is the short answer. The long answer, and the humble answer, is that these are questions that should be posed to all people on both sides about themselves *and* about the enemy other. Of course, in the actual dialogic moment it would be obscene to tell the other side what it needs and does not need for dignity. That is not the intention. Rather, it is the empathetic psychology that needs to be stimulated. The exercise of anticipating the other's dignity and shame is not an effort to supplant the moment of encounter, but rather an act of preparation for it.

Deeds More Than Words

The most important point is that conversations about honor and shame may have some beneficial results, but nothing can compare to carefully crafted gestures and symbols of honor, ways in which enemies convey honor to the humiliated other. This is at the heart of peacemaking, and it is often completely overlooked by formal processes of peacemaking, except for the perfunctory requirements of diplomacy. Rarely have I seen a conflict in which both sides, no matter how many security or economic imbalances there may be, do not need and indeed crave gestures of honor from the other side.

As wounded and paranoid victims of war, we crave evidence of a safe, new world. We look for actions that speak volumes, and pious deeds more than pious words. We wait to see if there will be a new universe in which we can bind our wounds, or whether we must continue the battle with the ubiquitous enemy other.

In sum, religion must become the great ally in the process of peacemaking and diplomacy on a global scale. Ritual and legally sanctioned ethical action are cornerstones of religious traditions. No diplomatic discourse of negotiation for peace should proceed without a course of moral action and penitent gestures. In this way mind and heart are both engaged and challenged in a process of profound social change. The power of myth, symbol, and parallel courses of meaningful ethical actions must become the glue that holds together an emerging global social contract. We can no longer afford elite processes of global or state civil society building that do not enter into the hearts and minds of billions of believers, that does not enter into the texts and structures of their education. But if we work harder at an integration of these processes, thus undercutting the more unscrupulous leanings of power-hungry clerics, we can struggle together, religious and secular, rich and poor, to create a global civilization of rights and duties that speaks to the hearts and minds of most, if not all, residents of the globe.

Notes

1. See Marc Gopin, *Between Eden and Armageddon: The Future of World Religions, Violence, and Peacemaking* (New York: Oxford University Press, 2001). The arguments of this article are more fully developed in my *Holy War, Holy Peace: How Religion Can Bring Peace to the Middle East* (New York: Oxford University Press, 2002).

2. I use these last two terms separately because conflict resolution, while appropriate to certain circumstances, has a rather limited usefulness in cultural contexts. Many cultures, for example, may have poor precedents for resolution of a problem between enemies, but may be more likely to have mythical constructs that maintain relationships in family and society, despite underlying differences. They also may be rich in common symbols and dreams that provide a nonviolent glue to the society, while at the same time not necessarily expressing this as a resolution of a conflict.

3. Based on a particular Christian interpretation of Genesis 15:6, Abraham is seen as the "knight of faith" who is "justified" by that act of faith. This becomes an important justification of the Pauline move to emphasize faith over works and cast Abraham as the first true follower of the Pauline Jesus. See Letters to the Hebrews 11:8-12, 17-19; Galatians 3:6-9, 15-18. But see James 2: 20-24 which suggests a different perspective in which Abraham is justified by both faith and works, the latter being much closer to the original Jewish position on Abraham.

4. Genesis 17:5

5. Esau is also called Edom (Gen. 25:30; 36). The enmity between the nation of Edom and Israel is apparent in many places in the Bible and parallels mythically the Jacob/Esau competition and struggle. In later history, especially when Roman persecution of Jews became intense, Esau and Edom became identified with Rome (*Talmud Yerushalmi Ta'anit* 4:8, 68d; *Genesis Rabbah* 65: 21, for example). When the Roman Empire became the Christian Roman Empire, and the persecutions took on religious zeal and significance in the Church, Esau and Edom came to symbolize in Judaism everything that is evil about the persecution and the persecutors. As far as isolated positive statements about Esau in rabbinic literature, some rabbis admired his capacity for honor of father, while others believed that he expressed authentic compassion, and even repented of his cruelties (*Genesis Rabbah* 65:16; 66:13). Furthermore there is a sense from some rabbis that the Jewish people paid a price for the suffering incurred by Esau when his birthright was taken by Jacob, that his cries are paid for by Jewish cries in later history (*Genesis Rabbah* 67:4). We have here at least some hermeneutic basis for remorse over the past relationship, and a perception of some good in the ancient fraternal enemy. It is a minority view in the classical Jewish sources, but new historical contexts and new relationships often become the basis hermeneutically for turning something minor culturally into something major and vice versa. That is the whole assumption of my work. As far as Ishmael is concerned, his identification with Islam is confirmed by Islam's own stories that clearly have an effect on Jewish sources. See next note.

6. *Pirkei de Rabbi Eliezer* 30; *Midrash ha-Gadol* Genesis: 339-340. For a translation, see *The Book of Legends*, eds. Hayim Bialik and Yehoshua Ravnitzky, trans. William Braude (New York: Schocken, 1992), 39: 43. Ishmael's two wives are identified in the rabbinic story as Ayesha and Fatima, who are Mohammed's two wives in the Qur'an! The influence of one on the other is obvious but not clearly understood historically or causally. Furthermore, the rabbinic story of Abraham's instigation of Ishmael's divorce from his first wife also appears in Islamic sources, though I have been unable to verify this for certain in Islamic sources. See H.A.R. Gibb and J.H. Kramers, *Shorter Encyclopedia of Islam* (Leiden and New York: E.J. Brill, 1991), 179. Extra-Qur'anic sources are very hard to verify. Despite many negative evaluations, and support of Sarah's decision to banish Hagar and Ishmael, there are some positive evaluations of Ishmael

by the rabbis. A man who sees Ishmael in a dream will be blessed *(T. Berakhot* 56b). Most importantly, Ishmael is seen to have repented completely at the end of his father's lifetime (*T. Baba Bathra* 16b). Here, too, there is an interpretive basis for nuancing the complicated relationship between these brothers on a Jewish spiritual level. Of course, the notion is a common one in the Abrahamic monotheisms of seeing the alienated other as *good to the degree to which*, through story and allegory, the other repents of his ways. The potential and the peril of this theological move is, once again, made clear through hermeneutics. If, on the one hand, such repentance stories signify mainly the potential for change and for goodness even in enemies then they are constructive for peace making and coexistence. If, on the other hand, the repentance stories about nonbelievers are meant to signify a conversion story then they are destructive for peacemaking and coexistence. In this form they only signify the absorption of the enemy other into the self, not an acceptance of the other's existence, and certainly not a love of the other, in any normal sense of that term. Thus, repentance stories about Jews in Christian and Islamic literature that are interpreted to mean or literally say that the end result is conversion hardly can be included in the hermeneutics of reconciliation. Of course in the Islamic case it is somewhat easier because how one defines the acceptance of Islam or the true worship of Allah is a subject of debate that is open to discussion. Liberal Muslims could conceivably read such stories not as conversion stories—*if they wish to*—but rather stories in which Jews in the time of Muhammad purified their own practice and worship *as Jews* as a result of contact with Mohammed. It would be impossible for Christians to read or re-read a story about a Jew who finds Jesus Christ as anything but a conversion story, although I should not preempt creative interpretation in any tradition.

7. In almost none of the literature of any of the faiths is the tragedy and mistreatment of Hagar truly confronted. The Bible clearly shows God's care for Hagar, but not a true confrontation with Abraham's actions regarding this maidservant. No one, in any faith, seems to take Abraham to task for his decision. I presume that part of the reason for this is God's instruction to Abraham, according to the Bible, to listen to Sarah and expel Hagar and Ishmael. I am convinced, however, that the Deuteronomy text (21:17), cited interpretively by Ishmael himself, concerning the proper and improper treatment of multiple wives and eldest sons, seems to me to be an inner biblical exegetical repudiation of Abraham's choice—and God's own command in the Genesis story! The later, and authoritative, Jewish legal source on inheritance actually sides with Ishmael! What does this mean? How is a traditional Jew supposed to integrate the Deuteronomic instruction on inheritance and God's support in Genesis for the opposite? It seems to beg interpretation, more hermeneutic development, and perhaps opens the door for a contemporary revisitation of the larger Abrahamic family as a religious entity.

8. *Genesis Rabbah* 53:11. For a translation, see *The Book of Legends*, 39: 41.

9. Avivah Zornberg, *Genesis: The Beginning of Desire* (Philadelphia: Jewish Publication Society, 1995), 134-136.

10. Note the opposite Jewish modern hermeneutic trend about Arab-Jewish relations that can be found in Waskow's midrashic readings, as I have analyzed them elsewhere.

11. Deuteronomy 23:8

12. Genesis 25:17. I thank Yaacov Travis for pointing out this text and its significance.

13. Just nine verses before Ishmael is "gathered unto his people", the Bible records this of Abraham in Genesis 25:8. On Isaac: Genesis 25:39; on Jacob, Genesis 49:33; on Aaron, Numbers 20:24; on Moses, Deuteronomy 32: 50.

14. I use Gadamerian concepts throughout my work. See Hans Gadamer, *Truth and Method*, 2d rev. ed., trans. Joel Weinsheimer and Donald G. Marshall (New York: Crossroad, 1989).

15. *Tafsiru 'l-Baizawi*, p. 424.

16. See, for example, Thomas Hughes, *A Dictionary of Islam* (London, W.H. Allen: 1895), 216-220.

17. Cyril Glassé, *The Concise Encyclopedia of Islam* (San Francisco: Harper and Row, 1989), 193.

18. Genesis 6:8; 34:11; Exodus 11:3; Esther 2:17. On charisma or grace as the most valued human asset, see Proverbs 22:1. It is a difficult word to translate but includes the meanings of grace, benevolence and favor, but

with a special attachment to the facial metaphor. On the relationship of *hen*, and pity or compassion, *tahanunim*, see Zechariah 12:10. Zechariah has a vision of God who brings destruction on other peoples who are near Jerusalem, but who, at the same time, fills the House of David and the inhabitants of Jerusalem with a spirit of *hen ve'tahanunim*, grace and compassion, as they lament over the dead of the *other* peoples, as if the dead were their own children, their own favored son or first born. This suggests a powerful prophetic precedent for the extension of *hen* to enemies, especially in the context of Jerusalem.

19. See Stuart Altmann, "The Structure of Primate Communication," in Stuart Altmann, ed., *Social Communication Among Primates* (Chicago: University of Chicago Press, 1967), pp. 325-62; N.G. Blurton Jones, "An Ethological Study of Some Aspects of Social Behaviour of Children in Nursery School," in Desmond Morris, ed., *Primate Ethology* (Chicago: Aldine, 1967), pp. 347-68. See generally under "eye contact," in *The Nonverbal Dictionary of Gestures, Signs, and Body Language Cues* (2000), by David B. Givens, at *http://members.aol.com/nonverbal3/refs.htm*, visited 11/17/00.

20. Leviticus 19:32; 19:15; Exodus 23:3

21. See Deuteronomy 28:50 and Daniel 8:23 as characterizations of evil empires and rulers in terms of this characteristic; *T.B. Ta'anit* 7b; *Otsar Midrashim* Messiah 3;

22. See Psalms 34:17 on the face of God and the destruction of the wicked, but Psalms 42:3 on the desire to see the face of God. On beseeching the face of God and prayer, see I Kings 13:6; II Kings 13:4. On the face of God and destruction, see also Jeremiah 3:12; Ezekiel 15:17. Psalms 27:8 suggests a powerful reconciliation through the metaphor of the face. "On Your behalf has my heart said, 'seek My face' Your Face will I seek."

23. Deuteronomy 7:2

24. See in general Majid Fakhry, *Ethical Theories in Islam* (Leiden and New York: E.J. Brill, 1994). Being honored is a coveted experience, but is dependent, according to the Qur'an, on righteousness, Surah 49:13; 95:4. Entering into another's home is a particular point of interaction that is either respectful or not. It is vital in Islamic ethics that this be done with honor and respect. See Surah 24:27-29. This relates strongly in context to sexual morality, but it is clear from the text that it also involves basic dignity issues regarding the home. Note also *Malik's Muwatta*, Book 49, Number 49.3.4.

Yahya related to me from Malik from Yahya ibn Said that Said ibn al-Musayyub said, "Ibrahim, may Allah bless him and grant him peace, was the first to give hospitality to the guest and the first person to be circumcised and the first person to trim the moustache and the first person to see gray hair. He said, 'O Lord! What is this?' Allah the Blessed, the Exalted, said, 'It is dignity, Ibrahim.' He said, 'Lord, increase me in dignity!'"

On honor as an Arab value predating Islam, see Reuven Firestone, *Jihad: The Origin of Holy War in Islam* (New York: Oxford University Press, 1999), 30-31.

25. The most famous quote is "Ben Zoma said, 'Who is honored? He who honors all God's creatures.'" *M. Avot* 4:1. Note also, for example, *Midrash Shohar Tov* 17, "Rabbi Joshua ben Levi said, 'When a human being walks down the street a coterie of angels go before him, proclaiming and announcing: Make way for the image of God (based on Genesis 5:1)!'"

The Clash of Civilizations

Samuel P. Huntington
Harvard University

The Next Pattern of Conflict

...It is my hypothesis that the fundamental source of conflict in this new world will not be primarily ideological or primarily economic. The great divisions among humankind and the dominating source of conflict will be cultural. Nation states will remain the most powerful actors in world affairs, but the principal conflicts of global politics will occur between nations and groups of different civilizations. The clash of civilizations will dominate global politics. The fault lines between civilizations will be the battle lines of the future.

Conflict between civilizations will be the latest phase in the evolution of conflict in the modern world. For a century and a half after the emergence of the modern international system with the Peace of Westphalia, the conflicts of the Western world were largely among princes—emperors, absolute monarchs and constitutional monarchs attempting to expand their bureaucracies, their armies, their mercantilist economic strength and, most important, the territory they ruled. In the process they created nation states, and beginning with the French Revolution the principal lines of conflict were between nations rather than princes.... This nineteenth-century pattern lasted until the end of World War I. Then, as a result of the Russian Revolution and the reaction against it, the conflict of nations yielded to the conflict of ideologies, first among communism, fascism-Nazism and liberal democracy, and then between communism and liberal democracy. During the Cold War, this latter conflict became embodied in the struggle between the two superpowers, neither of which was a nation state in the classical European sense and each of which defined its identity in terms of its ideology.

These conflicts between princes, nation states and ideologies were primarily conflicts within Western civilization.... With the end of the Cold War, international politics moves out of its Western phase, and its centerpiece becomes the interaction between the West and non-Western civilizations and among non-Western civilizations. In the politics of civilizations, the peoples and governments of non-Western civilizations no longer remain the objects of history as targets of Western colonialism but join the West as movers and shapers of history.

The Nature of Civilizations

During the cold war the world was divided into the First, Second and Third Worlds. Those divisions are no longer relevant. It is far more meaningful now to group countries not in terms of their political

Samuel P. Huntington, "The Clash of Civilizations." Reprinted by permission of *Foreign Affairs*, Vol. 72, No. 3, (Summer 1993).

or economic systems or in terms of their level of economic development but rather in terms of their culture and civilization.

What do we mean when we talk of a civilization? A civilization is a cultural entity. Villages, regions, ethnic groups, nationalities, religious groups, all have distinct cultures at different levels of cultural heterogeneity.... A civilization is thus the highest cultural grouping of people and the broadest level of cultural identity people have short of that which distinguishes humans from other species. It is defined both by common objective elements, such as language, history, religion, customs, institutions, and by the subjective self-identification of people.... People can and do redefine their identities and, as a result, the composition and boundaries of civilizations change.

Civilizations may involve a large number of people...or a very small number of people.... A civilization may include several nation states...or only one.... Civilizations obviously blend and overlap, and may include subcivilizations.... Civilizations are nonetheless meaningful entities, and while the lines between them are seldom sharp, they are real. Civilizations are dynamic; they rise and fall; they divide and merge. And, as any student of history knows, civilizations disappear and are buried in the sands of time.

Westerners tend to think of nation states as the principal actors in global affairs. They have been that, however, for only a few centuries. The broader reaches of human history have been the history of civilizations. In *A Study of History*, Arnold Toynbee identified 21 major civilizations; only six of them exist in the contemporary world.

Why Civilizations will Clash

Civilization identity will be increasingly important in the future, and the world will be shaped in large measure by the interactions among seven or eight major civilizations. These include Western, Confucian, Japanese, Islamic, Hindu, Slavic-Orthodox, Latin American and possibly African civilization. The most important conflicts of the future will occur along the cultural fault lines separating these civilizations from one another.

Why will this be the case?

First, differences among civilizations are not only real; they are basic. Civilizations are differentiated from each other by history, language, culture, tradition and, most important, religion. The people of different civilizations have different views on the relations between God and man, the individual and the group, the citizen and the state, parents and children, husband and wife, as well as differing views of the relative importance of rights and responsibilities, liberty and authority, equality and hierarchy. These differences are the product of centuries....

Second, the world is becoming a smaller place. The interactions between peoples of different civilizations are increasing; these increasing interactions intensify civilization consciousness and awareness of differences between civilizations and commonalities within civilizations....

Third, the processes of economic modernization and social change throughout the world are separating people from longstanding local identities. They also weaken the nation state as a source of identity.... The revival of religion, "la revanche de Dieu," as Gilles Kepel labeled it, provides a basis for identity and commitment that transcends national boundaries and unites civilizations.

Fourth, the growth of civilization-consciousness is enhanced by the dual role of the West.... A West at the peak of its power confronts non-Wests that increasingly have the desire, the will and the resources to shape the world in non-Western ways.

...A de-Westernization and indigenization of elites is occurring in many non-Western countries at the same time that Western, usually American, cultures, styles and habits become more popular among the mass of the people.

Fifth, cultural characteristics and differences are less mutable and hence less easily compromised and resolved than political and economic ones. In the former Soviet Union, communists can become democrats, the rich can become poor and the poor rich, but Russians cannot become Estonians and Azeris cannot become Armenians. In class and ideological conflicts, the key question was "Which side are you on?" and people could and did choose sides and change sides. In conflicts between civilizations, the question is "What are you?"...

Finally, economic regionalism is increasing.... The importance of regional economic blocs is likely to continue to increase in the future. On the one hand, successful economic regionalism will reinforce civilization-consciousness. On the other hand, economic regionalism may succeed only when it is rooted in a common civilization.

***

Culture and religion also form the basis of the Economic Cooperation Organization, which brings together ten non-Arab Muslim countries: Iran, Pakistan, Turkey, Azerbaijan, Kazakhstan, Kyrgyzstan, Turkmenistan, Tajikistan, Uzbekistan and Afghanistan. One impetus to the revival and expansion of this organization, founded originally in the 1960 by Turkey, Pakistan and Iran, is the realization by the leaders of several of these countries that they had no chance of admission to the European Community....

As people define their identity in ethnic and religious terms, they are likely to see an "us" versus "them" relation existing between themselves and people of different ethnicity or religion.... Most important, the efforts of the West to promote its values of democracy and liberalism as universal values, to maintain its military predominance and to advance its economic interests engender countering responses from other civilizations. Decreasingly able to mobilize support and form coalitions on the basis of ideology, governments and groups will increasingly attempt to mobilize support by appealing to common religion and civilization identity.

The clash of civilizations thus occurs at two levels. At the micro-level, adjacent groups along the fault lines between civilizations struggle, often violently, over the control of territory and each other. At the macro-level, states from different civilizations compete for relative military and economic power, struggle over the control of international institutions and third parties, and competitively promote their particular political and religious values.

The Fault Lines Between Civilizations

The fault lines between civilizations are replacing the political and ideological boundaries of the Cold War as the flash points for crisis and bloodshed.... As the ideological division of Europe has disappeared, the cultural division of Europe between Western Christianity, on the one hand, and Orthodox Christianity and Islam, on the other, has reemerged. The most significant dividing line in Europe, as William Wallace has suggested, may well be the eastern boundary of Western Christianity in the year 1500. This line runs along what are now the boundaries between Finland and Russia and between the Baltic states and Russia, cuts through Belarus and Ukraine separating the more Catholic western Ukraine from Orthodox eastern Ukraine, swings westward separating Transylvania from the rest of Romania, and then goes through Yugoslavia almost exactly along the line now separating Croatia and Slovenia from the rest of Yugoslavia. In the Balkans this line, of course, coincides with the historic boundary between the Hapsburg and Ottoman empires.

***

Conflict along the fault line between Western and Islamic civilizations has been going on for 1,300 years. After the founding of Islam, the Arab and Moorish surge west and north only ended at Tours in 732. From the eleventh to the thirteenth century the Crusaders attempted with temporary success to bring Christianity and Christian rule to the Holy

Land. From the fourteenth to the seventeenth century, the Ottoman Turks reversed the balance, extended their sway over the Middle East and the Balkans, captured Constantinople, and twice laid siege to Vienna. In the nineteenth and early twentieth centuries as Ottoman power declined Britain, France, and Italy established Western control over most of North Africa and the Middle East.

After World War II, the West, in turn, began to retreat; the colonial empires disappeared; first Arab nationalism and then Islamic fundamentalism manifested themselves.... This warfare between Arabs and the West culminated in 1990, when the United States sent a massive army to the Persian Gulf to defend some Arab countries against aggression by another. In its aftermath NATO planning is increasingly directed to potential threats and instability along its "southern tier."

This centuries-old military interaction between the West and Islam is unlikely to decline. It could become more virulent. The Gulf War left some Arabs feeling proud that Saddam Hussein had attacked Israel and stood up to the West. It also left many feeling humiliated and resentful of the West's military presence in the Persian Gulf, the West's overwhelming military dominance, and their apparent inability to shape their own destiny. Many Arab countries, in addition to the oil exporters, are reaching levels of economic and social development where autocratic forms of government become inappropriate and efforts to introduce democracy become stronger. Some openings in Arab political systems have already occurred. The principal beneficiaries of these openings have been Islamist movements. In the Arab world, in short, Western democracy strengthens anti-Western political forces. This may be a passing phenomenon, but it surely complicates relations between Islamic countries and the West.

***

Historically, the other great antagonistic interaction of Arab Islamic civilization has been with the pagan, animist, and now increasingly Christian black peoples to the south. In the past, this antagonism was epitomized in the image of Arab slave dealers and black slaves. It has been reflected in the on-going civil war in the Sudan between Arabs and blacks....

On the northern border of Islam, conflict has increasingly erupted between Orthodox and Muslim peoples, including the carnage of Bosnia and Sarajevo; the simmering violence between Serb and Albanian.... Religion reinforces the rev[i]val of ethnic identities and restimulates Russian fears about the security of their southern borders. This concern is well captured by Archie Roosevelt:

> Much of Russian history concerns the struggle between the Slavs and the Turkic peoples on their borders, which dates back to the foundation of the Russian state more than a thousand years ago. In the Slavs' millennium-long confrontation with their eastern neighbors lies the key to an understanding not only of Russian history, but Russian character.[1]

The conflict of civilizations is deeply rooted elsewhere in Asia. The historic clash between Muslim and Hindu in the subcontinent manifests itself now not only in the rivalry between Pakistan and India but also in intensifying religious strife within India between increasingly militant Hindu groups and India's substantial Muslim minority.... With the Cold War over, the underlying differences between China and the United States have reasserted themselves in areas such as human rights, trade and weapons proliferation. These differences are unlikely to moderate. A "new cold war," Deng Xaioping reportedly asserted in 1991, is under way between China and America.

***

The interactions between civilizations vary greatly in the extent to which they are likely to be characterized by violence. Economic competition clearly predominates between the American and European subcivilizations of the West and between both of them and Japan. On the Eurasian continent, however, the proliferation of ethnic conflict, epitomized at the extreme in "ethnic cleansing," has not been totally random. It has been most frequent and most violent between groups belonging to different civilizations....

Civilizational Rallying: The Kin-Country Syndrome

Groups or states belonging to one civilization that become involved in war with people from a different civilization naturally try to rally support from other members of their own civilization. As the post-Cold War world evolves, civilization commonality, what H. D. S. Greenway has termed the "kin-country" syndrome, is replacing political ideology and traditional balance of power considerations as the principal basis for cooperation and coalitions....

First, in the Gulf War one Arab state invaded another and then fought a coalition of Arab, Western and other states. While only a few Muslim governments overtly supported Saddam Hussein, many Arab elites privately cheered him on, and he was highly popular among large sections of the Arab publics....

***

Muslims contrasted Western actions against Iraq with the West's failure to protect Bosnians against Serbs and to impose sanctions on Israel for violating U.N. resolutions. The West, they alleged, was using a double standard. A world of clashing civilizations, however, is inevitably a world of double standards: people apply one standard to their kin-countries and a different standard to others.

Second, the kin-country syndrome also appeared in conflicts in the former Soviet Union. Armenian military successes in 1992 and 1993 stimulated Turkey to become increasingly supportive of its religious, ethnic and linguistic brethren in Azerbaijan.... With the end of the Soviet Union, however, political considerations gave way to religious ones. Russian troops fought on the side of the Armenians, and Azerbaijan accused the "Russian government of turning 180 degrees" toward support for Christian Armenia.

Third, with respect to the fighting in the former Yugoslavia, Western publics manifested sympathy and support for the Bosnian Muslims and the horrors they suffered at the hands of the Serbs. Relatively little concern was expressed, however, over Croatian attacks on Muslims and participation in the dismemberment of Bosnia-Herzegovina. In the early stages of the Yugoslav breakup, Germany, in an unusual display of diplomatic initiative and muscle, induced the other 11 members of the European Community to follow its lead in recognizing Slovenia and Croatia. As a result of the pope's determination to provide strong backing to the two Catholic countries, the Vatican extended recognition even before the Community did. The United States followed the European lead. Thus the leading actors in Western civilization rallied behind their coreligionists. Subsequently Croatia was reported to be receiving substantial quantities of arms from Central European and other Western countries. Boris Yeltsin's government, on the other hand, attempted to pursue a middle course that would be sympathetic to the Orthodox Serbs but not alienate Russia from the West. Russian conservative and nationalist groups, however, including many legislators, attacked the government for not being more forthcoming in its support for the Serbs. By early 1993 several hundred Russians apparently were serving with the Serbian forces, and reports circulated of Russian arms being supplied to Serbia.

***

In the 1930s the Spanish Civil War provoked intervention from countries that politically were fascist, communist and democratic. In the 1990s the Yugoslav conflict is provoking intervention from countries that are Muslim, Orthodox and Western Christian. The parallel has not gone unnoticed. "The war in Bosnia-Herzegovina has become the emotional equivalent of the fight against fascism in the Spanish Civil War," one Saudi editor observed. "Those who died there are regarded as martyrs who tried to save their fellow Muslims."

Conflicts and violence will also occur between states and groups within the same civilization. Such conflicts, however, are likely to be less intense and less likely to expand than conflicts between civilizations. Common membership in a civilization reduces the probability of violence in situations where it might otherwise occur. In 1991 and 1992 many people were alarmed by the possibility of violent conflict between Russia and Ukraine over territory, particularly Crimea, the Black Sea fleet, nuclear weapons and economic issues. If civilization is what counts, however, the likelihood of violence between Ukrainians and Russians should be low....

Civilization rallying to date has been limited, but it has been growing, and it clearly has the potential to spread much further. As the conflicts in the Persian Gulf, the Caucasus and Bosnia continued, the positions of nations and the cleavages between them increasingly were along civilizational lines. Populist politicians, religious leaders and the media have found it a potent means of arousing mass support and of pressuring hesitant governments....

The West Versus the Rest

The west in now at an extraordinary peak of power in relation to other civilizations. Its superpower opponent has disappeared from the map. Military conflict among Western states is unthinkable, and Western military power is unrivaled. Apart from Japan, the West faces no economic challenge. It dominates international political and security institutions and with Japan international economic institutions. Global political and security issues are effectively settled by a directorate of the United States, Britain and France, world economic issues by a directorate of the United States, Germany and Japan, all of which maintain extraordinarily close relations with each other to the exclusion of lesser and largely non-Western countries. Decisions made at the U.N. Security Council or in the International Monetary Fund that reflect the interests of the West are presented to the world as reflecting the desires of the world community.

***

That at least is the way in which non-Westerners see the new world, and there is a significant element of truth in their view. Differences in power and struggles for military, economic and institutional power are thus one source of conflict between the West and other civilizations. Differences in culture, that is basic values and beliefs, are a second source of conflict. V. S. Naipaul has argued that Western civilization is the "universal civilization" that "fits all men." At a superficial level much of Western culture has indeed permeated the rest of the world. At a more basic level, however, Western concepts differ fundamentally from those prevalent in other civilizations. Western ideas of individualism, liberalism, constitutionalism, human rights, equality, liberty, the rule of law, democracy, free markets, the separation of church and state, often have little resonance in Islamic, Confucian, Japanese, Hindu, Buddhist or Orthodox cultures. Western efforts to propagate such ideas produce instead a reaction against "human rights imperialism" and a reaffirmation of indigenous values, as can be seen in the support for religious fundamentalism by the younger generation in non-Western cultures. The very notion that there could be a "universal civilization" is a Western idea, directly at odds with the particularism of most Asian societies and their emphasis on what distinguishes one people from another....

The central axis of world politics in the future is likely to be, in Kishore Mahbubani's phrase, the conflict between "the West and the Rest" and the responses of non-Western civilizations to Western power and values.[2] Those responses generally take one or a combination of three forms. At one extreme, non-Western states can, like Burma and North Korea, attempt to pursue a course of isolation, to insulate their societies from penetration or "corruption" by the West, and, in effect, to opt out of participation in the Western-dominated global community. The costs of this course, however, are high, and few states have pursued it exclusively. A second alternative, the equivalent of "band-wagoning" in international relations theory, is to attempt to join the West and accept its values and institutions. The third alternative is to attempt to "balance" the West by developing economic and military power and cooperating with other non-Western societies against the West, while preserving indigenous values and institutions; in short, to modernize but not to Westernize.

The Torn Countries

In the future, as people differentiate themselves by civilization, countries with large numbers of peoples of different civilizations, such as the Soviet Union and Yugoslavia, are candidates for dismemberment. Some other countries have a fair degree of cultural homogeneity but are divided over whether their society belongs to one civilization or another. These are torn countries.... The most obvious and prototypical torn country is Turkey. The late twentieth-century leaders of Turkey have followed in the Attaturk tradition and defined Turkey as a modern, secular, Western nation state. They allied Turkey with the West in NATO and in the Gulf War; they applied for membership in the European Community. At the same time, however, elements in Turkish society have supported an Islamic revival and have argued that Turkey is basically a Middle Eastern Muslim society....

During the past decade Mexico has assumed a position somewhat similar to that of Turkey. Just as Turkey abandoned its historic opposition to Europe and attempted to join Europe, Mexico has stopped defining itself by its opposition to the United States and is instead attempting to imitate the United States and to join it in the North American Free Trade Area....

...Globally the most important torn country is Russia. The question of whether Russia is part of the West or the leader of a distinct Slavic-Orthodox civilization has been a recurring one in Russian history. That issue was obscured by the communist victory in Russia, which imported a Western ideology, adapted it to Russian conditions and then challenged the West in the name of that ideology. The dominance of communism shut off the historic debate over Westernization versus Russification. With communism discredited Russians once again face that question.

***

To redefine its civilization identity, a torn country must meet three requirements. First, its political and economic elite has to be generally supportive of and enthusiastic about this move. Second, its public has to be willing to acquiesce in the redefinition. Third, the dominant groups in the recipient civilization have to be willing to embrace the convert. All three requirements in large part exist with respect to Mexico. The first two in large part exist with respect to Turkey. It is not clear that any of them exist with respect to Russia's joining the West....

The Confucian-Islamic Connection

The obstacles to non-Western countries joining the West vary considerably. They are least for Latin American and East European countries. They are greater for the Orthodox countries of the former Soviet Union. They are still greater for Muslim, Confucian, Hindu and Buddhist societies. Japan has established a unique position for itself as an associate member of the West: it is in the West in some respects but clearly not of the West in important dimensions. Those countries that for reason of culture and power do not wish to, or cannot, join the West compete with the West by developing their own economic, military and political power. They do this by promoting their internal development and by cooperating with other non-Western countries. The most prominent form of this cooperation is the Confucian-Islamic connection that has emerged to challenge Western interests, values and power.

***

The conflict between the West and the Confucian-Islamic states focuses largely, although not exclusively, on nuclear, chemical and biological weapons, ballistic missiles and other sophisticated means for delivering them, and the guidance, intelligence and other electronic capabilities for achieving that goal. The West promotes nonproliferation as a universal norm and nonproliferation treaties and inspections as means of realizing that norm....

The non-Western nations, on the other hand, assert their right to acquire and to deploy whatever weapons they think necessary for their security. They also have absorbed, to the full, the truth of the response of the Indian defense minister when asked what lesson he learned from the Gulf War: "Don't fight the United States unless you have nuclear weapons."

***

A Confucian-Islamic military connection has thus come into being, designed to promote acquisition by its members of the weapons and weapons technologies needed to counter the military power of the West. It may or may not last. At present, however, it is, as Dave McCurdy has said, "a renegades' mutual support pact, run by the proliferators and their backers." A new form of arms competition is thus occurring between Islamic-Confucian states and the West....

Implications for the West

This article does not argue that civilization identities will replace all other identities, that nation states will disappear, that each civilization will become a single coherent political entity, that groups within a civilization will not conflict with and even fight each other. This paper does set forth the hypotheses that differences between civilizations are real and important; civilization-consciousness is increasing; conflict between civilizations will supplant ideological and other forms of conflict as the dominant global form of conflict; international relations, historically a game played out within Western civilization, will increasingly be de-Westernized and become a game in which non-Western civilizations are actors and not simply objects; successful political, security and economic international institutions are more likely to develop within civilizations than across civilizations; conflicts between groups in different civilizations will be more frequent, more sustained and more violent than conflicts between groups in the same civilization; violent conflicts between groups in different civilizations are the most likely and most dangerous source of escalation that could lead to global wars; the paramount axis of world politics will be the relations between "the West and the Rest"; the elites in some torn non-Western countries will try to make their countries part of the West, but in most cases face major obstacles to accomplishing this; a central focus of conflict for the immediate future will be between the West and several Islamic-Confucian states.

This is not to advocate the desirability of conflicts between civilizations. It is to set forth descriptive hypotheses as to what the future may be like. If these are plausible hypotheses, however, it is necessary to consider their implications for Western policy. These implications should be divided between short-term advantage and long-term accommodation. In the short term it is clearly in the interest of the West to promote greater cooperation and unity within its own civilization, particularly between its European and North American components; to incorporate into the West societies in Eastern Europe and Latin America whose cultures are close to those of the West; to promote and maintain cooperative relations with Russia and Japan; to prevent escalation of local inter-civilization conflicts into major inter-civilization wars; to limit the expansion of the military strength of Confucian and Islamic states; to moderate the reduction of Western military capabilities and maintain military superiority in East and Southwest Asia; to exploit differences and conflicts among Confucian and Islamic states; to support in other civilizations groups sympathetic to Western values and interests; to strengthen international institutions that reflect and legitimate Western interests and values and to promote the involvement of non-Western states in those institutions.

In the longer term other measures would be called for. Western civilization is both Western and modern. Non-Western civilizations have attempted to become modern without becoming Western. To date only Japan has fully succeeded in this quest. Non-Western civilizations will continue to attempt to acquire the wealth, technology, skills, machines and weapons that are part of being modern. They will also attempt to reconcile this modernity with their traditional culture and values. Their economic and military strength relative to the West will increase. Hence the West will increasingly have to accommodate these non-Western modern civilizations whose power approaches that of the West but whose values and interests differ significantly from those of the West. This will require the West to maintain the economic and military power necessary to protect its interests in relation to these civilizations. It will also, however, require the West to develop a more profound understanding of the basic religious and philosophical assumptions underlying other civilizations and the ways in which people in those civilizations see their interests. It will require an effort to identify elements of commonality between Western and other civilizations. For the relevant future, there will be no universal civilization, but instead a world of different civilizations, each of which will have to learn to coexist with the others.

Notes

1. Archie Roosevelt, *For Lust of Knowing,* Boston: Little, Brown, 1988, PP 332-333.

2. Kishore Mahbubani, "The West and the Rest," *The National Interest,* Summer 1992, pp. 3-13.

Religion and Global Governance: Harmony or Clash?

Richard Falk
Princeton University

Even before the September 11 attacks, the relevance of religion to global governance was a subject of controversy and confusion. After the Cold War, it was the energies of Islam that mounted the greatest threat to the sort of world order that the West was championing, which rested on a domestic governance model of constitutionalism and a strong private-sector economy. The role of global institutions was mainly a facilitative one, especially with respect to the smooth operations of the world economy. This vision of a future based on liberal values of moderate states and robust markets was widely promoted as the best path to progress and prosperity, especially as underpinned by a growing willingness of governments to acknowledge the authority of human rights. Such a vision was no longer challenged ideologically by Marxist/Leninist thinking or geopolitically by a block of states under the dominion of a nuclear superpower. Indeed, the collapse of the Soviet Union, the embrace of the liberal model by the successor states, and the incredible rate of capitalist growth achieved by Communist China in the 1990s seemed to confirm the historical weight of such trends in global politics.

In retrospect, it is evident that such an outlook was a mixture of wishful thinking and blinkered perception. There were clear indications even before the end of the Cold War that this Western model of the future for states and world society was not universally acceptable, especially in the countries of the South. The Iranian Revolution in 1978-79 against the Shah's White Revolution was one sign of trouble. The emergence on the world-stage of Ayatollah Khomeini suggested the potency of another way of envisioning governance and human destiny that rested on traditional values and the primacy of religious leaders and institutions in shaping the life of society. Beyond this, Khomeini enunciated what amounted to a declaration of war against the United States and its world-view, calling America "the Great Satan." What was most significant about this challenge was that it mobilized Iranian society to rise en masse and overthrow a leader who had previously been regarded as strong and secure. Khomeini's message seemed also to resonate powerfully with "the Islamic street," the peoples of the Islamic world, even as it frightened their secular leaders. When Islamic radicals seized the American embassy in Tehran in late 1979, and held the diplomatic community hostage it intensified the impression that political Islam conceived of America as its enemy.

The Iranian Revolution had these two faces: to base governance on Islam and to define the historical situation by reference to a post-colonial struggle against American-led globalization. Both of these faces found varying parallel expressions in other circumstances. The rise of Hindu nationalism in India was directed, above all, against an abandonment of tradition so as to achieve the benefits of economic globalization. Even authoritarian China seemed most challenged from within by the religious movement known as the Fulan Gong. And in the West, especially the United States, the political leverage of the religious-right was more strongly felt than ever before in the central citadels of governance. Elsewhere, the fear of American cultural and economic primacy was paramount as in much of Asia where globalization was being uncritically pursued, at least until the roadblocks of the Asian Financial Crisis of 1997, and resistance was mounted by invoking "Asian values." Shortly thereafter, first at the Seattle meetings of the World Trade Organization, an anti-globalization movement took shape that challenged the market-driven view of global policy.

Against such a background it is not surprising that the Huntington thesis of "a clash of civilizations" caused a stir when it first appeared in 1992, provoking a strong counter-tendency in ensuing years beneath the banner of "a dialogue of civilizations." The clash thesis seemed dangerous and simplistic, drawing ethnic and religious battle-lines that anticipated a new epoch of cultural wars based on inter-civilizational enmity, culminating in the slogan "the West against the rest." Such an outlook was at odds with the globalization thesis as well as with the liberal idea that the American model of state and global governance could and should be exported to non-Western countries. By emphasizing civilizational identities, the clash thesis also rejected the economic determinism of the globalization model that seemed to make markets the new driving force of history, thereby perversely adopting the basic Marxist hypothesis of materialism at the very moment when Marxism was disappearing as an ideological weapon. To counterpoise culture to economics, created an opening for religion that had seemed closed by reference to either economistic or highly rationalistic worldviews that were essential features of modernity as shaped by the West. And finally, by asserting "civilizations" as the unit of primary relevance to the future, Huntington encouraged the view that the long period of dominance exercised by territorial sovereign states was in the process of being superseded, which put into question traditional state-centric forms of global governance.

It is against this complex background that the events of September 11 and their aftermath must be taken into account. The character of the attack, its inspiration deriving from Osama Bin Laden extremist views of Islamic faith and his genocidal hostility directed against Americans, Jews, and "Crusaders," gave this experience of apocalyptic terrorism religious overtones. These were reinforced due to the identity of the hijackers as militant foot soldiers of Islam fully prepared to engage in suicidal missions of mega-terrorism. In fashioning a response, the U.S. Government has been generally careful to designate the enemy as "terrorism," and not Islam, and to emphasize that Arab-Americans, and adherents of Islam, should not be singled out for discrimination. At the same time, the wider sympathies evoked by the Bin Laden outlook, especially its castigation of the United States for its policies toward Palestinians, its maintenance of sanctions against Iraq a decade after the Gulf War ceasefire, and its general military encroachment close to the most sacred Islamic sites, suggest that the risk of provoking a civilization war cannot be ignored, nor can the relevance of religion to the encounter be ignored. It is not surprising that in this setting there have been contentions made that the September 11 attacks prove that Huntington was, after all, correct, even a prophet.[1] Equally disturbing are civilizational readouts that suggest that Osama Bin Laden was emboldened to act because the United States was squeamish about the use of force in response to prior terrorist attacks and instances where its troops experienced resistance that produced casualties, most notably in Somalia during 1993 peacekeeping operations.[2]

What is unfortunate about the current world-setting is that it tends to polarize views about the relevance of religion to humane forms of global governance. There are those who view religion as disposed toward extremism, even terrorism, as soon as it abandons its modernist role as a matter of private faith and belief that should be not intrude upon governance. Their opponents argue the opposite thesis, which contends that without rooting governance in the dictates of religious doctrine, the result is decadence and impotence. This essay seeks to advance a different view of the relevance of religion. It argues that all great religions have two broad tendencies within their traditions: the first is to be universalistic and tolerant toward those who hold other convictions and identities; the second is to be exclusivist and insistent that there is only one true path to salvation, which if not taken results in evil. From such a standpoint, the first orientation of religion is constructive, useful, and essential if the world is to find its way to humane global governance in the decades ahead, while the second is regressive and carries with it a genuine danger of a new cycle of religious warfare carried out on a civilizational scale. The hope of the future is to give prominence and support to this universalizing influence of religion and, at the same time, to marginalize religious extremism based on an alleged dualism between good and evil.

It should also be noted that secular views that hold the line against their perception of religion also can adopt fundamentalist canons of belief, and view those who seek to center their identity on religious affiliation as intrinsically evil. Such secular intolerance is as unwelcome with respect to informing patterns of global governance as its religious counterpart. Both religionists and secularists can only contribute to the emergence of humane forms of global governance if they adhere to an ethos of tolerance.

The issue of governance is central at this historical moment. The transnationalization of social, cultural, political, and economic relations is overwhelming the capacities of territorial states to provide secure patterns of governance for their citizenry. Whether the issue is crime prevention, the control of immigration, the flows of arms and drugs, the elusiveness of money, business practices, environmental protection, or trade and investment, the limits of state regulatory authority are apparent. What international institutions exist, some of which make major contributions to global governance, especially with respect to economic interactions and in relation to certain regional settings (particularly Europe), are also criticized as exhibiting "a global democratic deficit" and as being non-representative of non-Western peoples and their religious/cultural perspectives.

While establishing the present context of religious relevance is necessary, it is also essential to take into account antecedent conditions and longer-term trends. At this point it is difficult to assess the degree to which the revived preoccupation with "security," along with its accompanying recourse to global war by the leading country to address "terrorism," will bend these trends in enduring ways. It is currently impossible to discern the scope and disorienting effects of the war on global terror, partly because its goals have not been clearly defined and partly because the degree and success of terrorist counter-moves has not been established. The remainder of this essay proceeds on the assumption that global normalcy will reemerge within next year or so, and with it, a renewed preoccupation with global governance in an era of globalization, almost as if September 11 had not occurred. Possibly, the traumazing impact of this unanticipated war experience will even make leaders and social forces more attentive to the reconciliation of markets and human well-being, the greatest challenge of world-wide significance before September 11.

Narrating the Interplay of Religion and Politics: The Emergence of Modernity

The religious dimension of human experience has

been generally excluded from the serious study and practice of governance for several centuries, especially in the West. The exclusion is definitely a consequence of the European Enlightenment and its endorsement of autonomous reason as the only reliable guide for human affairs, as well as its general tendency to ground politics upon a secular ethos, a principal feature of which is the separation of church and state. Of course, as with many questionable moves in history, this development had positive aspects and was rooted in a particular set of historical circumstances in Europe at the time of the formation of the modern state system, a process whose origin is difficult to locate with precision but is often, although somewhat arbitrarily, dated to coincide with the Peace of Westphalia in 1648.

Without entering into this complex story in any detail, the justification for the exclusion of religion had to do with the perception that religious institutions were inimical to the rise of science and material progress in human affairs and the undeniable reality that the split in Christendom had contributed to a series of terrible wars. The exclusion of religion always had certain normative costs, including the realization that religious attachments are so strong in society that religion, excluded from entering the front door of political life, will find other entrances, including concealed trap-doors. The effects of this reassertion of religious relevance may be to obstruct an understanding of how public policies are actually being shaped.

So in an important sense, historically, it is necessary to understand that the exclusion of religion from political life was seen as a vital step in the ongoing struggle to establish humane governance, that is governance based on reason, religious and ethnic tolerance, gender equality, and the dignity of the individual human being. In many respects Hugo Grotius, a typical Renaissance figure, was generally regarded as the founder of modern international law and an intellectual figure who sensitively embodied the passing of Medieval Europe to the new Europe of independent, sovereign, territorial states. Grotius was a witness to the Thirty Years War that ravaged Europe and represented a struggle that was fought along the geographical and ideological fault line that separated Catholicism from Protestantism. Grotius was, in one sense, seeking to restore the religious possibility for human life by removing it from the violent rivalries of the political realm. In his vivid, often-quoted words, "Throughout the Christian world I observed a lack of restraint in relation to war, such as even barbarous races should be ashamed of; I observed that men rush to arms for slight causes, or no cause at all, and that when arms have once been taken up there is no longer any respect for law, divine or human; it is as if, in accordance with a general decree, frenzy had openly been let loose for the committing of all crimes."[3]

In adopting this critical stance Grotius combined two of the defining characteristics of modernity, a claim of moral superiority associated with the specific identity of "the Christian world" that should inform political life wherever possible and an implicit deprecation of non-Christian societies as the vast domain of "barbarous races."[4] The first impulse led to the idea that the relations among states are to some extent governed by law, while the second gave a sort of underpinning to the Eurocentric conceptions of world order and hierarchical relations between Western and non-Western peoples that came to flourish in the colonial age. Such liberal rationalizations for the politics and structures of domination were later produced by the most admired Enlightenment figures: Hegel, Kant, and John Stuart Mill, among others. Neither led to humane governance for the peoples of the world: International law was too weak to contain the passions of nationalism or dreams of empire, and the validation of colonial rule amounted to little more than a rationalization for the exploitation and domination of non-Western peoples and generated in many instances deep patterns of resentment and frustration that surfaced in the form of intense intrasocietal violence in post-colonial settings.

There have been attempts in the recent past to associate this normative orientation toward political reality with an emergent and evolving world order that had within it the potentiality to achieve humane governance for the entire world. Hedley Bull, an influential Oxford professor of international law, depicted an international society of states that sustained a balance between sovereign rule within territorial limits and a kind of prudent moderation, safeguarded by the benevolence of leading military powers, in the relations among states, a type of world order described as an "anarchic society."[5] Myres McDougal, the founder of the New Haven School of Jurisprudence and International Law, together with a group of collaborators depicted the spread of Enlightenment values through the commitment to democratic types of public order systems as an evolving foundation for a humane intercivilizational pattern of governance that had the capacity to produce, by stages, peaceful and equitable governance structures of benefit to the entire world.[6]

Both of these normative approaches to the future were premised on the persistence of the states system as the basis of world order, the role of power in managing relations among states, and were in these resepcts rooted in the anti-utopian traditions of political realism.[7] Additionally, building on the heritage of Woodrow Wilson and the experiments in world organization represented by the League of Nations and the United Nations, there emerged a more utopian strain of secular thought that fundamentally believed that the only secure and legitimate form of world order depended upon the establishment of world government, a body of thought that came to be associated with world federalism and is probably still best represented by the work of Grenville Clark and Louis B. Sohn in the form of *World Peace through World Law*.[8]

Even the World order Models Project (WOMP), with its explicit undertaking to consider the diverse world order perspectives representative of the leading regions and ideologies active in the world, failed to include in any serious or systematic manner the relevance of religion, although it did acknowledge that world order values, widely shared on an intercivilizational basis, provided the normative framing of any successful project to establish, or even to envisage, humane global governance.[9]

Although the perspectives arising from the work of Bull and McDougal remain useful as moderating guides with normative foundations for operations within the existing framework of world order, their regulative capabilities and potentialities seem far too modest to address the deficiencies of international political life that arise from the persistence of war and militarism, from the pervasiveness of poverty and economic deprivation, from the circumstances of political oppression and religious extremism, from the disregard of environmental decay and danger, and from the neglect of the spiritual sides of human nature and aspiration. The advocacy of world government as a normative project seems strangely discordant with the current weakening of support for even the feeble efforts to sustain existing world political organizations.[10] Such weakening is epitomized by the recent travails of the United Nations, and although there is an increasingly frequent framing of political life in relation to the metaphor of a "global village," it is seen primarily as an expression of the potency of economic globalization, intense preoccupations with transnational terrorism, criminality, and drug trafficing, and as expressive of the new borderless cyberworld of the internet.[11] In effect, the best of secular thinking falls short of providing either a plausible path to travel in pursuit of humane global governance or a sufficiently inspiring vision of its elements that would mobilize a popular grassroots movement for drastic global reform.[12]

This failure is partially due to the exclusion of religious and spiritual dimensions of human experience from the shaping of the vision and practices associated with the quest for global humane governance. This essay intends an overview: first, a section on dominant world order trends and tendencies with respect to global governance; then some consideration of the extent to which these recent world order trends, which are shaping the historical situation at the start of the third millennium, are also creating new, unexpected openings for religious and spiritual energies, a development that also, as with the secularist era of exclusion, has deeply disturbing, as well as encouraging, aspects. This religious resurgence is discussed as part of the double-edged relevance of religion for the kind of global governance most likely to emerge. The final section argues for the inclusion of emancipatory religious and spiritual perspectives in world order thinking and practice, along with an enumeration of their potential contributions.[13]

Current World order Trends, or Pathways to Inhumane Governance

Without entering into a detailed inquiry, it seems evident that there are several dominant world order trends that are converging in such a way as to generate a more integrated form of governance at the global level, but in a form that undermines several critical world order values to a significant degree and thus qualifies the emergent new world order as a variant of "inhumane governance." Such an indictment is not meant to be a total condemnation. There are aspects of these globalizing developments that represent normative improvements on prior conditions (for instance, a reduction in the prospect for large-scale nuclear war, a diminishing likelihood of traditional warfare among states in general, and the alleviation of poverty and economic deprivation for hundreds of millions of people, particularly those living in several of the most populous, and previously some of the most severely and hopelessly impoverished, countries of the Pacific Rim), but the overall impact has been to fracture the peoples of the world, to neglect the plight of those who are most deprived and vulnerable, to place nonsustainable burdens on the environment that seem likely to diminish the life quality of future generations, to deepen over time the disparities between rich and poor, and to engender an ethos of consumerism that forecloses the most fulfilling forms of individual and social self-realization.[14] As such, despite this mixed picture, it seems appropriate to describe the resultant arrangements of global governance as cumulatively contributing to "global inhumane governance." This assessment is reinforced by the severity of the terrorist backlash, which in turn has produced an unprecedented tansnational war on global terror pitting an American-led coalition of states against a multi-state and transnational al Qaeda network with operations in as many as sixty states world-wide, each which is targeted for cooperative law enforcement activity, and possibly military intervention as needed.

The Dynamics of Economic Globalization

There is no doubt that the greater mobility of capital is facilitating a more materially efficient use of resources, if the benchmarks are the return on capital (profitability), economic growth, and the expansion of world-trade. This pattern of global economic development is fostered, as well, by a global media that is one aspect of globalization, and is notable for its shameless promotion of a consumerist conception of human happiness and fulfillment in a societal setting of increasing inequality, persisting massive poverty, and growing anxiety. The interdependence of economic activity, as well as the extraordinary complexity arising from spectacular technological innovations, are creating a growing and manifest need for effective regional and global governance in the form of policy coordination and institutionalized regimes of control. The strength of global-market forces is now such that existing governance structures at the level of the sovereign state are losing their political independence and autonomy; the discipline of global capital is becoming an iron-cage constraining policy choice.[15] This pattern is most evident in relation to the heavily indebted countries of the Global South, especially in the form of intrusions by the World Bank and IMF into the policy-making spheres of government. But the process is almost as evident in the affluent countries of the Global North that make seemingly spontaneous adjustments in their policy options to reflect the priorities of global capital and governing elites, encouraging fiscal austerity and subordinating societal claims on resources.[16]

The governance consequences are two-fold: (1) the creation of formal and informal arenas for the coordination of global economic policy according to the priorities of capital, and (2) the creation of institutional arrangements that can give behavioral effect to such priorities. In the first category one can mention the Annual Economic Summit of Industrial Countries, originally the so-called G-7, now the G-8 with the addition of Russia, in which the heads of state of these leading countries gather each year in one of their member countries for several days of discussion and photo opportunity. These G-8 meetings are far less significant in relation to their substantive achievements than in signaling to the world the ascendancy of dominant economistic forces within the global setting. The attention given to these economic summits far outweighs the participation of these leaders in the activities of the United Nations where it is rare indeed for any leader, if he or she shows up at all, to remain in attendance for more than a few hours, if at all. An informal arena along the same lines, although operating in a more obscure fashion, is the annual World Economic Forum held in Davos, Switzerland, in which the main participants are business leaders. Eligibility depends on representing a company or financial institution that has sales of more than $700 million per year. It is at Davos, and less well-publicized similar occasions, that the priorities of global capital are articulated in relation to changing market conditions.

With respect to institutionalization, the main effort has been to liberalize global trade, reducing the significance of national frontiers and national economic policy. Successive cycles of complex trade and tariff negotiations have tried to establish a liberalizing dynamic, selectively negotiating away protectionist policies and prerogatives and pushing toward an integrated single market for the world, but in a manner that reflects the leverage of the North. A big step in the process of carrying this vision forward involved the establishment in Geneva of the World Trade Organization (WTO), which has an expanding mandate to override national efforts to place burdens on most internationally traded goods and services, but in a manner that has in the past been accused of worsening the terms of trade for many poor countries in the South and of shaping the agreed framework in an oligarchical fashion controlled by the North. The admission of China to membership in 2001 is a big victory for market inclusiveness, enjoying a priority over ideological and normative concerns (China's poor record on human rights).

The global governance framework that is emerging is seeking to implement a conception of the future that is responsive to the geopolitically managed logic of market forces.[17] Territorial states are contributing to this process to the extent that their political elites have been globalized to view their role as primarily one of carrying out the policies decreed by adherents of the economistic world picture.[18] Such a cumulative trend is not without resistance within leadership circles. The more geopolitically oriented elites, often associated with the more militarized sections of government bureaucracies and the armaments industry, continue to favor a conception of world order that emphasizes rivalry among leading states (and their allies); the importance of such traditional ideas as containment, deterrence, and balance of power as well as the closely related academic fixation, especially in the United States, on "grand strategy."[19] This tension between the economistic and geopolitical world pictures is currently being worked out by the United States primarily with respect to its relationship with China, and to a lesser extent in relation to Europe, Japan, and Russia in the post-cold war absence of ideological tension.[20] In these settings, there is a renewed sense that despite globalization, territorially-oriented bases of political and military power remain crucial in working out the future of world order, but only on the basis of a dialectical interaction with economic considerations that are of a predominantly nonterritorial character. In an important sense this stress on non-territoriality has been reinforced by the advent of the war on terrorism, with its trans-national locus of war-fighting that lacks clear spatial dimension as the enemy is concealed, and the selection of targets indirect. It should also be noted that non-state actors as of September 11 demonstrated the vulnerability of strong states, as well as their own capacity to inflict significant harm.

Briefly, the effects of this rising economistic view of global governance are: (1) Heavy investments in situations where the conditions are such that rapid and large returns on capital can be expected. (These investments have favored economic situations in which skilled labor exists but where workers do not have high expectations in terms of wages or unionized operations.); (2) Very impressive economic growth rates for an expanding number of countries in the Asia/Pacific area. However, these rates are subject to turbulent reversals, as revealed by the Asian financial crisis of 1997 and the years following, as well as the more fundamental travails of Japan and Indonesia. Economic growth has led to impressive alleviations of poverty, but also to predatory forms of labor abuse, a promiscuous disregard of environmental harm and disruptive social effects, and the emergence of new patterns of mass impoverishment; (3) A refusal to invest in those settings where the returns on capital were not positive, either because of political instability, an unskilled labor force, or high degrees of regulatory interference, factors that on balance have led to the disregard of most of sub-Saharan Africa and the Caribbean, as well as to selective deindustrialization in parts of the Global North; (4) As a consequence of the market-ization of government policy, there has been a cumulative downward pressure on the provision of public goods (welfare, higher education, the arts, environmental protection) outside the area of military defense, which means that even when a national economy and its leading companies are doing extremely well, as exhibited by record profits and share prices on stock exchanges, there are few benefits for ordinary citizens, even those in the broad middle classes. Economic growth continues impressively, but the quality-of-life declines as people are increasingly squeezed in struggles to sustain their living standards and societal circumstances; (5) This atmosphere of diminished support for public goods is accentuated by a shift in fiscal orientation away from Keynesian ideas about deficit financing and demand creation and toward balanced budgets, deficit reduction, and monetarist approaches to economic policy; (6) In this atmosphere political support for *global* public goods (protection of the global commons, the United Nations, economic assistance for the South) falls away with adverse consequences, given the absence of either a supportive constituency or any significant perceived contribution by such public goods to the short-term prospects of economic globalization; (7) The domestic political climate in the United States, the unquestioned global leader in this period, has taken a conservative turn that accentuates these tendencies adverse to social justice; (8) The burst bubble of the Silicon Valley boom that had inflated stock prices to astronomical height and has been followed by world-wide recession is raising new concerns about the self-regulating character of the world economy.

The Ideological Climate

These various tendencies, which are associated with the imprecise and slippery, yet indispensable, term globalization, have been accentuated by certain developments associated with the historical circumstances that existed in these closing years of the second millennium. The ending of the Cold War provided a convenient occasion to discredit socialist and so-called "socialistic" ideological alternatives to capitalism. Indeed, the virtual disappearance of any serious socialist challenge has encouraged the architects of economic policy to believe that it is not politically necessary any longer to make concessions to the "dangerous classes."[21] This ideological circumstance is reinforced by two additional factors: (1) the post-industrial decline of the political leverage exerted by organized labor on government policy of democratic states and the convergent national electoral strategies of mainstream political parties, and (2) the widespread disillusionment of publics in the democracies of the Global North with an activist state, as well as criticisms of the excesses of the welfare state and a growing skepticism about the problem-solving capabilities of political leaders of states. At least temporarily, the reemergence of the strong security state has reversed this earlier impression of a withering away of the state, but whether this reaction to the global terrorist challenge is a temporary phenomenon or something more basic cannot be discerned at present. In the background, as well, are the complementary attitudes associated with "netizens," the new militant political identities arising out of close affiliation with the Internet; political sensibilities that gravitate toward the ethos of self-adjusting systems; and a libertarian resistance to governmental regulation in any form. In relation to governance, the prevalence of such attitudes works against exhibitions of compassion for victims of globalization. Such exhibitions of social concern are resisted because they would seem to validate activist interventions by government to protect those who are being painfully marginalized by globalization. It is also hard to know whether the revival of statist claims in the security sphere will spillover into a renewed effort to engage the state in social concerns such as poverty reduction and jobs programs at home and abroad.

Normative Results from the Perspective of Global Governance, or Why "Inhumane"?

To some extent, the preceding paragraphs explain why economic globalization, while clearly improving the material and social conditions of life for many millions, is still properly viewed as responsible for a dangerous momentum that is leading in the direction of "inhumane global governance." Four adverse normative effects will be stressed here, although there are others:

(1) Polarization and global apartheid: It is undeniable that globalization has fostered widening income and skill gaps, whether these are measured by class, region, gender, or race.[22] A crucial dimension of polarization is what some call the "digital divide," a term used to identify those who acquire the Internet skills needed for gainful access to the information age. This digital divide tends to accentuate the other, more familiar, dimensions of polarization. The contrast between the economic conditions, work skills, and political supremacy of Euro-American whites in the Global North and sub-Saharan African blacks in the Global South as situated at the two ends of the poles gives plausibility to the allegation that world order as now constituted bears a significant resemblance to apartheid as it functioned in South Africa during its period of racist governance, although there are some important differences as well. This inflammatory contention of global apartheid also pertains to the flows of refugees and migrants, drugs, nuclear and other ultra-hazardous wastes, and weapons, with the white Global North being ever more vigilant gatekeepers while the darker portions of the Global South become more and more looked upon as dumping grounds for whatever is unwanted by or dangerous for those who are prospering. It should also be noted that the affluence of the Euro-American North has not succeeded in diminishing either absolute or relative poverty.[23]

(2) Neglect of human suffering: This dynamic of polarization, even if separated from its racial and civilizational implications, is also destructive to an ethos of human solidarity and community, as it rationalizes the distinction between winners and losers, treating the range of outcomes as justifiable results of market operations and not occasions for remedial action. To the extent that the state becomes implicated in this outlook, there is a shift by stages from

the compassionate to the cruel state, a social circumstance that recalls the earliest phases of the Industrial Revolution, when market logic reigned supreme and worker abuse was rampant, early nineteenth century conditions influentially depicted in Marx's critique of capitalism and also in the novels of such writers as Charles Dickens and Emile Zola. By neglecting vulnerable sectors of national, regional, and global society, globalization has the unintended side effect of creating forms of governance that are minimally motivated to act for the relief of human suffering. Of course, this trend should not be exaggerated. Government spending on social services, especially in Western Europe, remains close to historic highs. Actually, it is a change of mood and outlook—that is, of ideas—rather than a shift of resources that best captures the essence of the link between government and social well-being.[24]

(3) Decline of the global public good: Globalization, as accompanied by neoliberal economic outlooks, relies on private sector initiatives to uphold the claims of the public good. Such an orientation operates in various ways, including the social disempowerment of the state, by constraining its capacity to mobilize resources and by undermining public confidence in the willingness of political leaders to engage in disinterested action for the public good of their own citizenry. One expression of this disposition is the current effort to "downsize" the United Nations, while making sure that the organization does not challenge the priorities of global capital. In this regard, to the extent that portions of the U.N. system earlier became oriented in favor of an ethos of global equalization, the right to development, and overall democratization, the organization was widely perceived in the North as an antagonist of globalization. Such a perception seemed confirmed by the tenor of U.N.-sponsored conferences on large global issues during the early 1990s, when transnational social forces (womens groups, human rights and environmental NGOs, peoples coalitions against Third-World debt) challenged the market/statist coalition with ideas about governance that were premised on human solidarity, empathy with the marginalized, and a commitment to upholding the public good of all peoples in the world. The U.N. Social Summit of 1995, held in Copenhagen, tried in its way to place the social claims of people on the global agenda, thereby seeming to reject the economistic world picture as the wave of the future.[25]

Such events engendered a series of negative reactions within the United Nations led by its dominant members, giving rise to reforms that would remove or drastically downgrade U.N. activities regarded as hostile to market forces. "Downsizing" was less about money than about this restructuring of the organization to satisfy the demands of the guardians of globalization and to ensure that the United Nations operates primarily as a vehicle for neoliberal ideas and relies mainly on the market-oriented Bretton Woods institutions (that is, the World Bank and IMF) when it comes to the economic matters. Significantly, given that the World Trade Organization was deliberately located outside the formal organizational network comprising the U.N. system. In part, this was a concession to the anti-U.N. mood prevailing in the U.S. Congress. Beyond this the United Nations is seen as selectively and potentially useful to implement global security in situations of the sort vividly prefigured in the Gulf War of 1991. Later developments, starting with Somalia (1993) and culminating in the NATO War over Kosovo (1999), cast doubt on the future of the United Nations even with respect to peacekeeping. This marginalization of the UN is also evident in the current setting of the response to September 11, with the U.N. role up through 2001 being confined, as in Kosovo, to post-conflict reconstruction efforts. Such an allocation of functions leaves global security firmly in the hands of geopolitical forces with only minimal deference to the standards of limitation embedded in international law.

What has been said about the United Nations also extends to the efforts to protect the global commons. Already, at the Earth Summit in Rio (1992), there was an effort to subordinate the environmental movement to the guiding role of the market. Maurice Strong made a thinly disguised move to give business effective control over the way in which environmental standards were to be implemented and articulated and even nurtured the grand illusion that business could be trusted to heed market signals in a sufficiently timely fashion to provide adequate environmental protection with only the most minimal reliance on institutional governance.[26] During the late 1990s, the U.N. Secretary General, Kofi Annan, made a series of well-publicized overtures to the leaders of corporate globalization. His basic proposal culminating in the Global Compact of 2000 was to induce multinational corporations to make a voluntary commitment to uphold international standards in relation to human rights, environment, and labor practices as an independent responsibility, that is, even if the territorial government did not itself impose such standards. These undertakings, dubbed by critics as "blue washing" while not yet fairly tested, did distract overall attention from this determined shift of emphasis in relation to global problem-solving from reliance on public sector initiative to encouragement of private sector solution. The voluntary character of Kofi Annan's approach to the implementation of international standards can be understood in this light as deference to private sector primacy in this era of economic globalization.

In effect, the social forces aligned to globalization were acting to ensure that governance structures responsive to the public good were contained if not rolled back. This required challenging certain democratizing tendencies that were moving the United Nations in an opposite direction and were giving the United Nations and other governance structures a stronger identity as agents of the global public-good. This visionary undertaking was primarily delimited by transnational activist initiatives on behalf of the peoples of the world.[27] Such a confrontation can also be schematically simplified as an encounter between globalization from above (transnational corporations/banks/states) and globalization from below (transnational civic initiatives/women/indigenous peoples/human rights/environmental activists).[28]

(4) Looming technological horizons: Another complicating aspect of the current era is the emergent prospect of technologies with radical implications for human existence and the meaning of life. The human genome project, biotechnology, super-intelligent machines, and menacing robots are all on the horizon and are being developed in response to private-sector priorities. The capacity to clone or fashion human genotypes, to identify "weak" and "strong" genetic traits, to construct "thinking" computers with super-human capabilities and sensitivities seems likely to confer upon technological innovators a role that far exceeds their regulative wisdom, posing great challenges to human survival and civilizational identity. In this sense, the problematic adjustment to nuclear weaponry within the public sector, where profits don't drive behavior to nearly the extent they do in the private sector, is a small foretaste of the challenges likely to face the next few generations.[29]

A Summary Assessment

These negative developments confront us with the likelihood that the third millennium will witness the fashioning of a durable form of inhumane governance that will pose severe risks of ecological and social catastrophe. Such an outcome is the latest, purest, and most ambitious phase of the fundamental application of the Enlightenment Project to human affairs: The continuous stream of technological innovations adapt to secularized political space in order to achieve the greatest material advantage for the owners of capital goods. To be sure, there are important contradictory tendencies evident and progressive varieties of resistance, described by the rubric globalization from below, but the political leverage of such forces is likely to remain limited to local battlegrounds and has the nuisance value of global gadfly unless such dispositions are strengthened by religious commitments and by support from important sectors of the organized religious community. It is this possibility of a religiously grounded transnational movement for a just world order that in the end alone gives hope that humane global governance can become a reality, or at least an alternative future, sometime early in the twenty-first century. This hope is, of course, currently clouded over by the perceived dangers to minimum order and stability associated with religious extremism in all its forms. In the West this situation encourages efforts to put religion back in the box constructed by secularism over the centuries, thereby confusing religious extremism with religion generally, and failing to recognize that religion generates both intolerance and an ethos of human solidarity.

Why Religion? Openings and Regressions

Among the surprises of the last several decades has been a multifaceted world-wide resurgence of religion as a potent force in human affairs, suggesting a relevance to the concerns of the public as well as the private sphere. From the perspective of humane governance, this religious resurgence has a double-coded message: portending the hopeful possibility and necessity of transcending the constraints of economistic secularism, which has become the signature of a disturbing interface between late modernity and a nihilistic postmodernity, but also simultaneously disclosing a range of regressions in the form of extreme variants of inhumane governance that arguably, in certain instances, make the repudiation of secularism a terrifying descent into political extremism as a prelude to repression and violence. On the negative side, I have in mind the regressive politics that religion has brought to such countries as Iran, Afghanistan, Algeria, and, to some extent, India and Sudan in recent years, but also the tragic and gruesome behavior of religious cults such as Heaven's Gate and Aum Shinriky, which have been seemingly incubated in the midst of secularized contemporary modernity.[30] And most of all, of course, the credible emergence of the al Qaeda network headed by Osama Bin Laden as an opponent of the established order that has the will and capability to shake the foundation of existing structures of world order. Historically, then, it would appear that the outer limits of secularism are giving rise both to transformative possibilities that lead in the direction of humane governance and to regressive potentialities that mix in various ways the most severe deficiencies of premodernity with the most frightening sequels to modernity.

It is, of course, difficult to give an account of this religious resurgence that adequately situates it within the framework of the present, but this resurgence seems closely related to an exhaustion of the creative capacity of the secular sensibility, especially as it is embodied in the political domain. It is within this domain, of course, that modernity has been so closely associated with the preeminence of the territorial sovereign state.[31] Such a preeminence has been virtually unchallenged in this century with respect to the organization of governance in international society and is powerfully, if imperfectly, reinforced by nationalism, by far the strongest ideology of modern times.[32] Even the innovations associated with the establishment of the League of Nations and the United Nations were deeply rooted in a statist system of world order, and mainly represented extensions of statism that perpetuated the allocation of governance capabilities to territorial sovereigns, with the management of the whole entrusted to geopolitical arrangements that reflected the special governance role of leading states, what political scientists have called "hegemonic actors." In other words, a statist world order, although claiming to respect sovereign equality, was always based on a series of hierarchies, especially strong against weak, center versus periphery, Western or Eurocentric versus non-Western, and, most recently, North versus South.[33] It also presupposed the availability of war as a geopolitical instrument of dominant sovereign states, despite a certain lip-service given to legal and moral restraints on the use of force in recent decades.

But although this statist world order validated many patterns of abuse, either by way of immunizing domestic political order from scrutiny or through the interventionary and exploitative behavior of dominant states, it also gave rise to important normative ideas: limitations on the legitimate use of force, human rights, humanitarian intervention, asylum, criminal accountability of leaders. These normative ideas have been often subordinated to geopolitical manipulations of various sorts, but they provided some encouragement for liberal perspectives, which were imbued with the idea of progress in human affairs, and anticipated a gradual evolution of this statist world in the direction of peace and harmony. This approach to humane global governance is associated with the "democratic peace" hypothesis, which asserts that the spread of constitutional democracy brings an assurance of peaceful relations among democratic states, and thus if the whole world could be made to consist of nothing but democracies, then it would be a peaceful world, and if buttressed by an effective international law of human rights, it would fulfill the requirements of humane governance for the planet without requiring either disarmament or the centralization of political authority in international institutions.[34]

The world order difficulty with this approach to humane governance is that it neglects the social impact of economic globalization as enacted in an ideological climate shaped by neoliberalism. As earlier discussed, the overall cumulative impact of economic globalization, despite its positive aspects, is to predispose world order toward third millennium forms of inhumane global governance. And what is more, the influence of the economistic world picture upon governing political elites and the mainstream media is such as to condition and constrain the social roles of states. States, as now oriented, lack the will and capacity to safeguard their own autonomy, much less to fashion the ingredients of a just and peaceful world order. In this regard, it is notable that it is political elites that are most enthusiastic about institutionalizing the economistic worldview at regional and global levels as seen, for instance, in the political controversies associated with the World Trade Organization, North American Free Trade Agreement (NAFTA), and European Union, despite the fact that such advocacy means that significant governance responsibilities are transferred from the level of the state to incipient supranational actors. The European developments are the most dramatic in this respect, especially the remarkable relinquishment by European governments of their national currencies, long a central symbol of social and political identity and distinct statehood. The establishment of a Euro zone, together with the suspension of border controls for intra-European travel, does move a long way toward creating a European identity as supplemental to the identity associated with citizenship in a particular state. Of course, for repressed and dissatisfied minorities, the prospect of a regional identity may offer a partial escape route from statist entrapment.

Expressing this interpretation in the context of my wider argument, then, is a matter of understanding that the secular imagination is dependent upon the problem-solving capacities of the state, and that these have increasingly deferred to the main arenas of economistic authority (that is, World Economic Forum, G-7, WTO, etc.). One possible development, with relevance, is the degree of territorial backlash and revived security agenda,that might conceivably reverse this political energy and restore the role of the state as an autonomous source of authority, thereby rendering it potentially capable of creating a new social equilibrium between human needs/public goods and the logic of the market.[35] In the nineteenth century a kind of social equilibrium emerged out of societal reactions to market-led industrialization, partly as an effort by elites to co-opt, or at least moderate, working-class discontent. It was essentially a secular reaction that had its most influential expression in the Communist revolutionary movement spearheaded by Marxism/Leninism/Maoism, which was avowedly atheistic and aggressively antireligious, partly attributing acquiescence to an unjust social order to the otherworldliness of religious teaching and doctrine. Of course, there was an important insight in the assault on the role of religion, as religious institutions were generally aligned with ruling elites, and even otherwise radical religious leaders (e.g., Luther, Calvin) were at the same time characteristically hostile to the claims of the poor and of underclasses generally. But beneath this social line of criticism was the more fundamental spirit of modernity, with its search for truth in the realms of secular knowledge, illustrated here by the insistence of Marxists that their interpretations were based exclusively on social laws and that the resulting normative outlook was one of "*scientific* socialism," as contrasted with the visionary gropings of "utopian socialism," which were scorned as lacking in political relevance. That is, the acute social tensions of the early industrial revolution were addressed within the frame of modernity and secularism, treating religion as either irrelevant or as a mind-pacifying obstacle to social progress and the improvement of the human condition.

In the present setting, the revisioning of governance is by way of the market, and, to some extent, is reinforced by the self-organizing, globalist ethos of the digitized sensibility that shapes the Internet world picture. It is generally opposed to the social functions of government, to public goods, and to any deliberate effort to achieve humane governance. In opposition is the diverse transnational array of networks, coalitions, associations, and initiatives that has been earlier labeled here as "globalization from below."[36] It is my contention that this early effort to construct a democratic global civil society is informed by religious and spiritual inspiration, and if it is to move from the margins of political reality to challenge entrenched constellations of power in a more serious way, it will have to acquire some of the characteristics and concerns of a religious movement, including building positive connections with the emancipatory aspects of the great world religions.[37] Without religious identity, prospects for global humane governance appear to lack a credible social or political foundation, and, more important, miss the spiritual character that can mobilize and motivate on a basis that is potentially more powerful than what the market, secular reason, and varieties of nationalism have to offer.

What is meant by "religion" here requires considerable clarification in the course of constructing a global civil society and recasting the meaning of citizenship and democratic practice.[38] It is evident that religion cannot be reduced to any single religious tradition, although it can draw strength from the collaborative support of the various traditions, and that some aspects of certain religious traditions are antithetical, especially claims of being "the chosen people" or the exclusive or superior instruments of a divine or sacred design or of the enactment of some apocalyptic scenario for ascent to a higher or purer forms of existence, especially as achieved by way of holy war or *jihad* involving struggle to crush the infidels and non-believers. Such aspects of the overall religious heritage may authentically engage the lives and sensibilities of persons of genuine faith, but they offer nothing constructive in relation to the struggle to create patterns of humane global governance for all the peoples on earth. As the global terror of al Qaeda exemplifies, such initiatives pose a great threat to all efforts to move history forward, and are particularly damaging to the potential contributions of religion.

Religious Pillars of Humane Global Governance

Having identified forms of religious expression inimical to the quest for humane governance, it is appropriate to consider the potentially helpful contributions of religion. In setting forth these contributions, it is necessary that we allow considerable cultural space for a wide spectrum of interpretations of specific religiously based undertaking. It is also important to acknowledge that humanist styles of thought are also capable of reaching parallel points of ethical and political reference but lack the deep historical foundations and universal roots of religion in the collective memories and experiences of peoples of varied backgrounds and identities, that such an appeal without borders is needed to arouse widespread adherence. The relevance of religion cannot be separated from its persistence in human consciousness and its role throughout history in the social construction of human nature. Religion is understood here as encompassing both the teachings and beliefs of organized religion and all spiritual outlooks that interpret the meaning of life by reference to faith in and commitment to that which cannot be explained by empirical science or sensory observation and is usually associated with an acceptance of the reality of the divine, the sacred, the transcendent, the mysterious, the ultimate. In these respects, religion encompasses belief in God or gods, but does not depend on such convictions.

The introduction to the complex matter of religious relevance offered here is intended only to be suggestive and is designed mainly to stimulate discussion, reflection, and dialogue on the positive roles of religion in the context of a global democratic movement for humane governance. A series of domains associated with religion and its practice can be identified and listed, without elaboration at this point, and absent of any appraisal of intercivilizational and intracivilizational variations:

- An appreciation of suffering: The religious impulse is strongly associated with a Gandhian acknowledgment of the "last man" (or woman), of the lowliest class, caste, race, and with a central commitment to lift up those who suffer acutely, a dedication to those most acutely victimized. It was Gandhi's insistence that politics be practiced so as, above all, to lift up persons at the bottom of the social, economic, and political hierarchy in society.
- Civilizational resonance: Whereas secular transformative thought tends to appeal mainly to intellectuals not strongly bonded with existing structures of governance, religious revolutionary language and utopian aspirations enjoy a sense of legitimacy in popular culture and possess great mobilizing potential, despite modernity, if activated at certain historical moments by charismatic individuals.
- An ethos of solidarity: Closely related is the unitive feature of religious consciousness, the oneness of the human family that gives rise to an ethos of human solidarity, the unity of all creation, and, with it, the sense of both the wholeness of human experience and the dignity of the individual. Such solidarity is a sign of religious inclusiveness and celebration of religious diversity, contrasting with the narrow paths of intolerance traveled by exclusivist religiosity.
- Normative horizons: A compassionate response to suffering and affirmation of human solidarity imply a belief in normative horizons that define human potentialities in an affirming and hopeful manner that contradicts and transcends present conditions, including the market ethos, which neglects many forms of acute human suffering. This ethos tends to elevate the claims of the part or the fragment over those of the whole, of winners over that of losers, and is fraught with the sort of consumerist and materialist preoccupations nurtured by mass advertising and franchise capitalism. Religiously oriented normative horizons embody and converge in many respects with the secularly defined priorities of a human-rights

culture, especially with regard to economic and social needs of the most materially disadvantaged or impoverished individuals and peoples.

- Faith and power: A belief in the transformative capacities of an idea that is sustained by spiritual energy lends itself to nonviolent forms of struggle and sacrifice, thereby challenging most secular views of human history as shaped primarily by governing elites, warfare, and a command over innovative military technology. Especially in the disillusioning aftermath of Marxist experiments in governance, the secular imagination is suspicious of any advocacy of utopian solutions, whereas the religious consciousness is not so constrained.
- Limits: Religion contributes profound humility in relation to human thought and action that is sensitive to human fallibility, if not sin and evil, and appreciates the limited capacity of the inquiring mind to grasp the fullness of reality or to claim the truthfulness and correctness of any particular interpretation of what needs to be done in the world. This allows persons to remain open at all stages to dialogue with strangers and apparent adversaries, which can serve to correct mistakes and insensitivities, and to experience a sense of awe in face of the divine, which can protect humanity from idolatry.
- Identity: Identity can emerge from many sources and is existentially being reshaped by overlapping appeals to aspects of human nature, the shifting boundaries of community, and the scientific validation of an enhanced concept of human consciousness and genuine experience. As well, the era of exclusive subjection to the expectations of loyalty to the sovereign state are being superseded in many settings by both various modes of reexperiencing the deepening reality of the whole and by the increasing sense of the yet-unfulfilled future, an emphasis that can be highlighted and explored by replacing the idea of "citizen" with that of "citizen pilgrim." This distinctly religious understanding of essential political identity by reference to a spiritual journey that is unseen and unlikely to be completed within the span of this lifetime but the value of which is an object of intense faith and dedication that extends beyond prescribed and instinctive loyalties to nation and state. It embraces temporal loyalties to a future that brings justice and peace to the entire human family.
- Reconciliation: Diverse ways of knowing are alternative respected means of coping with the effects of human finitude and the impingement of limits, thereby diminishing the obstacles to a needed and desirable reconciliation of science, reason, and spirituality. Whether this reconciling process occurs within the domain of formal religion or without, or in both, is of secondary significance.

These positive features of inclusive religious outlooks provide an inter-civilizational grounding for transnational efforts to improve the normative and institutional governance of human affairs. Patterns of governance are situated at all levels of social interaction from the extremely local efforts to challenge the siting of high dams and nuclear power plants to planetary concerns about global warming and human cloning. Religious dialogue can facilitate understanding and the development of the sort of ethically sensitive consensus that engages popular participation in way that cannot be achieved by inter-governmental diplomacy and treatymaking.

Religion and Humane Global Governance: Concluding Observations

The perspective proposed is that a religious/spiritual orientation needs to inform of the energies of globalization from below if it is to have any serious prospect of launching a political project that offers an alternative to that being foreshadowed and actualized by the largely economistic forces associated with globalization from above. It is not a matter of repudiating state or market but of insisting that these organizing arenas of authority and influence be spiritualized in accordance with the generalized attributes of religion. But it is also not expecting a miraculous rescue from above *(deus ex machina)*, whether in the form of a sudden embrace of world government or the emergence of regional institutions and the United Nations as political actors no longer constrained by geopolitics and the reigning neoliberal world picture.

Humane global governance will only occur as the outcome of human struggle, and in this sense is similar to past efforts to overcome slavery, colonialism, and apartheid. Each of these struggles was substantially inspired by direct and indirect religious thought as embodied in the lives and works of devout adherents. Each undertaking seemed "impossible" at its point of origin given the array of social forces, fixed beliefs, and institutional supports affirmed by the conventional wisdom of the day to validate and uphold inhumane practices. In the recent past we have witnessed successful struggles against oppression carried on by the peoples of Eastern Europe and the Soviet Union, of many countries in Asia, and of the victims of apartheid in South Africa. They have enjoyed limited or overall success against great historical odds, although following through with humane patterns of reconstruction has not proved easy.

We do not now know enough to conclude pessimistically that humane global governance is an impossibility. We do know enough to understand that such an outcome, if it occurs, will not come about spontaneously or without anguishing struggles, and that given the historical ascendancy of market forces and the widespread acceptance of the economistic world picture an alternative orientation can only hope to emerge if nurtured and guided by inclusive religious energies creatively adapted to the specific problems and concerns that exist at all levels of social reality.

The complexity and precariousness of a globalizing world is bringing into being an unprecedented degree of global governance. The forms of this governance cannot be understood by reference to the United Nations but are related above all to the efforts by market forces to coordinate and stabilize their operations on a regional and global basis. The extension of this type of global governance is threatening to human well-being and to the quality of social and political life at the level of the state. The religious challenge is to infuse the struggles of the peoples of the world for democracy, equity, and sustainability with a vision of human existence that is human-centered yet conscious of the relevance of the sacred and of mysteries beyond the grasp of reason and machines.

The complexity of this undertaking is heightened by September 11 and its aftermath, both diverting energies and resources from the policy agenda associated with alternative patterns of globalization and by reviving a paralyzing preoccupation with the dynamics of war. Such a preoccupation freezes the structural character of global governance, and leads to an underestimation of threats to stability and justice that fall outside the domain of the war effort. Such observations seem particularly true with respect to the war against global terror, which lacks a clear definition of goals and whose limits cannot be geographically specified. The territorial base of terrorist activities is fluid, and can be situated even within the country leading the anti-terrorist campaign. A further difficulty relating to the inquiry of this essay is the linkage, real and projected, between al Qaeda terrorism and religious commitment. Osama Bin Laden's mobilization of support and rationale for political extremism and the commission of crimes against humanity is premised on his interpretation of Islam. What separates this interpretation from dismissal as the ravings of a demented mind is that it evokes a wide and potent resonance in the Islamic world, especially with respect to its animating message of anti-Americanism.

This ambiguous reality provides ammunition for those who would generalize the response to September 11 by taking on the entire Islamic world, especially its Arab sectors, and use this context as an occasion to confront religion as the enemy of modernity and democracy. From such a vantage point Turkey is celebrated for its secularism, and the distinction is abandoned between the positive and negative dispositions of religion.

In this setting the most sinister renderings of the implications of September 11 attain a quality of plausibility. The erudite and influential Middle East specialist, Bernard Lewis, has put forward the idea that Osama Bin Laden's challenge has been mounted so formidably because he was encouraged by the reluctance of the United States to use its military power to crush opposition to its interests. Without a word of criticism of the U.S. role in relation to either the Israel/Palestine conflict or the maintenance of indiscriminate sanctions against Iraq, Lewis encourages maximal policies associated with extending anti-terrorist war making to the Middle East, specifically Iraq and Iran. Lewis writes "...it is difficult for Middle Easterners to resist the idea that this refusal to implicate Saddam Hussein is due less to a concern for legality than to a fear of confronting him."[39] Such an assertion is made as part of an indictment of American "squeamishness" with respect to the use of force against its challengers, which according to Lewis, pushes Islam into the arms of the Bin Laden worldview, and thus ends up with a mighty clash of civilizations. Such thinking argues that the two alternatives prefigured by September 11 are either an expansive war now against hostile forces in the Islamic world or a massive religious war later.

This sort of counter-apocalyptic reading of September 11 is dangerous and unnecessary. The al Qaeda attack needs to be addressed by an effective response that includes war-making in Afghanistan and intense law enforcement wherever else the network operates. It also should be extended to peacemaking with the wider Islamic world, which will depend on a fair solution for the Palestinian ordeal, the internationalization of Jerusalem, the elimination of all weapons of mass destruction from the military arsenals of all countries, and a credible effort to make globalization operate in a manner that is more equitable and protective of the most vulnerable peoples in the world. Lifting the gaze beyond the battlefield will also enable a recovery of the degree to which Islam, and religion generally, is part of the solution, and not only the problem. With consideration of these more distant horizons, the challenge of establishing humane global governance takes on the importance it deserves, as well as contributes to our understanding that defeating terrorism in the world is associated with justice as well as with the weaponry of counter-terrorism and war.

Notes

1. Robert D. Kaplan, "Looking the World in the Eye," *The Atlantic Monthly*, December 2001, 68-82; see also Andrew Sullivan, "This is a Religious War," *NY Times Magazine*, October 7, 2001, 44-47, 52-53.

2. Bernard Lewis, "The Revolt of Islam," *The New Yorker*, November 19, 2001, 50-63, esp. 60-63.

3. Hugo Grotius, "Prolegomena," in *On the Law of War and Peace* (New York: Bobbs Merrill, 1925), p. 20.

4 . For general assessments of the Grotian impact, especially as a facilitator of the transition to modernity by way of the passage from religious to secular authority see Hedley Bull, Benedict Kingsbury, and Adam Roberts, eds., *Hugo Grotius and International Relations* (Oxford University Press, 1990); also Yasuaki Onuma, ed., *A Normative Approach to International Relations: Peace, War, and Justice in Hugo Grotius* (Oxford University Press, 1993).

5. Hedley Bull, *The Anarchic Society: A Study of Order in World Politics* (New York: Columbia University Press, 1977).

6. See Myres McDougal and associates, *Studies in World Public Order* (New Haven, CT: Yale University Press, 1960); McDougal and Harold D. Lasswell, *Jurisprudence for a Free Society*, 2 vols. (New Haven, CT: New Haven Publishers, 1992); see esp. vol. 2.

7. The anti-utopian outlook was, perhaps, best artic-

ulated in response to the peace settlement of World War I by E. H. Carr, *The Twenty Years' Crisis, 1919-1939.* (New York: Harper & Row reprint of 1946 2nd ed., 1964).

8. Grenville Clark and Louis B. Sohn, *World Peace through World Law*, 3rd ed. (Cambridge, MA: Harvard University Press, 1966).

9. For representative works from WOMP over the period of its existence see Saul H. Mendlovitz, ed., *On the Creation of a Just World Order* (New York: Free Press, 1975); R. B. J. Walker, *One World/Many Worlds: Struggles for a Just World Peace* (Boulder, CO: Lynne Rienner, 1988); Richard Falk, *On Humane Governance: Toward a New Global Politics* (University Park, PA: Penn State University Press, 1995); and Ali Mazrui, *A World Federation of Cultures* (New York: Free Press, 1976).

10. For one assessment of this U.N. weakness, especially relative to the strength of international financial institutions and European regionalism see Richard Falk, "Meeting the Challenge of Multilateralism," in Thomas H. Hendriksen, ed., *Foreign Policy for America in the Twenty-first Century: Alternative Perspectives* (Standford, CA: Hoover Institution Press, 2001) 33-48.

11. But see articulate argument in favor of world government in David Ray Griffin, "Global Government: Objections Considered," in *Toward Genuine Global Governance: Critical Reactions to Our Global Neighborhood*, edited by Errol E. Harris and James A. Yunker (Westport, CT: Praeger, 1999), pp. 57-68.

12. A more obscure secular theme focuses on the European regional experience as a prelude to a "world of regions." Such an image, while more promising than world government, remains a dim and remote prospect at present.

13. The emphasis on "emancipatory religious and spiritual perspectives" is premised on a distinction between "inclusive" and "exclusive" interpretations of the meaning of human existence. Inclusive interpretations are nondogmatic, allowing moral and political space for alternative interpretations and worldviews. Exclusive interpretations are insistent that there is only one true path and that the embrace of alternatives is inherently false, immoral, and worthy of destruction.

14. For negative assessments of globalization see John Gray, *False Dawn: The Delusions of Global Capitalism* (New York: New Press, 1998); and Richard Falk, *Predatory Globalization: A Critique* (University Park, PA: Penn State University Press, 1999).

15. Whether this constraint is objective or "constructed" is beside the point. For helpful discussion see Grahame Thompson and Paul Hirst, *The Myth of Globalization* (Cambridge, UK: Polity, 1996). Also George de Martino, *Global Economy, Global Justice: Theoretical Objections and Polity Alternatives to Neoliberalism* (New York: Routledge, 2000).

16. The regulative mechanisms are subtle and elusive: the logic of competitiveness that exerts pressure on production costs, especially labor; the neoliberal orientation of elites; and the veto power exercised by financial and business sectors due to the mobility of capital. For further discussion see Paul Krugman, *Peddling Prosperity: Economic Sense and Nonsense in the Age of Diminished Expectations* (New York: Norton, 1994). For helpful study of variable state adaptations to the challenges of globalization, see David Held, Anthony McGrew, David Goldblatt, and Jonathan Perraton, *Global Transformation: Politics, Economics and Culture* (Cambridge, UK: Polity, 1999).

17. By "geopolitically managed logic" is meant the impact of political and economic power on terms of trade. Thus agriculture is protected in many developed, rich countries that preserve their cultural identity and political balance, but in a manner that distorts trade flows and hurts the agricultural exports of economically disadvantaged countries.

18. For helpful discussions, see contributions to "The Globalization of Liberalism?", a special issue of *Millennium* 24 (1995): 377-576. Also Yoshikazu Sakamoto, ed., *Global Transformation: Challenges to the State System* (Tokyo: UNU Press, 1994).

19. See Barry R. Posen and Andrew L. Ross, "Competing Visions for U.S. Grand Strategy," *International Security* 21 (1996/1997): 5-53.

20. The ebb and flow of U.S./China relations is partly expressive of a tug-of-war between the economistic worldview (the "new geopolitics") of the treasury department and the balance-of-power, statist world-view of the Pentagon. Of course, this is an oversimplification of perspectives, a stereotyping of bureaucratic outlooks

that neglects intrabureaucratic nuances and tensions. It also overlooks the Chinese role in shaping U.S. perceptions of threat and opportunity.

21. See Immanuel Wallerstein, *After Liberalism* (New York: New Press, 1995).

22. For documentation see United Nations Development Program, *Human Development Reports* (New York: Oxford University Press, 1990-1999).

23. See John Williams, "Look, Child Poverty in the Wealthy Countries Isn't Necessary," *International Herald Tribune*, 12 July 2000, p. 8.

24. See Vito Tanzi and Ludger Schuknecht, *Public Spending in the 20th Century* (Cambridge, UK: Cambridge University Press, 2000); see also interpretation of findings in Martin Wolfe, "The Golden Age of Government," *Financial Times*, 12 July 2000, p. 17.

25. For a valuable review of the ideals and undertakings of the Copenhagen Social Summit, see the volume reporting on the "Copenhagen Seminars for Social Progress." *Building a World Community: Globalisation and the Common Good* (Copenhagen, Denmark: Royal Danish Ministry of Foreign Affairs, 2000).

26. Stephan Schmidheiny and the Business Council for Sustainable Development, *Changing Course: A Global Business Perspective on Development and the Environment* (Cambridge, MA: MIT Press, 1992); also Richard Falk, "Environmental Protection in an Era of Globalization," *Yearbook of International Environmental Law* (Oxford: Oxford University Press, 1996), pp. 3-25.

27. See Daniel Archibugi and David Held, eds., *Cosmopolitan Democracy* (Cambridge, UK: Polity, 1995); David Held, *Democracy and Global Governance* (Stanford, CA: Stanford University Press, 1995).

28. This encounter is a major theme of Falk, *Predatory Globalization*, n. 9, pp. 127-36.

29. For eye-opening discussions see P. Kurzweil, The *Age of Spiritual Machines* (New York: Viking, 1999); see an essay by a founder of Sun Microsystems, Bill Joy, "Why the Future Doesn't Need Us," *WIRED* 8, no. 4 (April 2000): pp. 238-47.

30. Robert Jay Lifton, *Destroying the World to Save It: Aum Shinrikyú, Apocalyptic Violence, and the New Global Terrorism* (New York: Metropolitan Books, 1999); Mark Juergensmeyer, *Terror in the Mind of God: The Global Rise of Religious Violence* (Berkeley, CA: University of California Press, 2000).

31. See Stephen Toulmin, *Cosmopolis: The Hidden Agenda of Modernity* (New York: Free Press, 1990); R. B. J. Walker, *Inside/Outside: International Relations as Political Theory* (Cambridge, UK: Cambridge University Press, 1993); Hendrick Spruyt, *The Sovereign State and Its Competitors* (Princeton, NJ: Princeton University Press, 1994).

32. "Imperfectly" to the extent that national identities do not necessarily correspond with state boundaries.

33. See Immanuel Wallerstein, *The Modern World-System*, 3 vols. (New York: Academic Press, 1974-1989); Samir Amin, *Eurocentrism* (New York: Monthly Review, 1989); Samir Amin, *Rereading the Postwar Period: An Intellectual Itinerary* (New York: Monthly Review, 1994).

34. For example, see Bruce Russett, *Controlling the Sword: the Democratic Governance of National Security* (Cambridge, MA: Harvard University Press, 1990), esp. pp. 119-145; Bruce Russett, *Grasping the Democratic Peace for a Post-Cold War World* (Princeton, NJ: Princeton University Press, 1993); for critical view see Joanne S. Gowa, *Ballots and Bullets: The Elusive Democratic Peace* (Princeton, NJ: Princeton University Press, 1999).

35. This argument is developed in Richard Falk, "Siege of State: Will Globalization Win Out?" *International Affairs* 73, no. 1 (January 1997): 123-136.

36. For further clarification see Paul Wapner, *Environmental Activism and World Civic Politics* (Albany, NY: SUNY Press, 1996); Ronnie D. Lipschutz, *Global Civil Society and Global Environmental Governance* (Albany, NY: SUNY Press, 1996); Richard Falk, *Explorations at the Edge of Time: The Prospects for World Order* (Philadelphia, PA: Temple University Press, 1992).

37. The work of Hans Küng has moved in this direction in recent years. See Hans Küng, *Global Responsibility: In Search of a New World Ethic* (New York: Crossroads, 1991).

38. For a closely comparable revisioning of religious consciousness, see the important book by Charlene Spretnak, *The Resurgence of the Real: Body, Nature, and Place in a Hypermodern World* (Reading, PA: Addison-Wesley, 1997).

39. Lewis, note 2, at 63.

Contemporary Israeli Bumper Sticker, 2001.

Courtesy of Dafna Margolin.

"Please Let's Make a Private Peace,
I with You, and You with Me
We will not Shout, nor will we Quarrel
But We will Speak, and will also Listen,
Thus a Little to Peace, We All May Contribute."

Part Seven

Pluralism and Its Discontents:

Harmonizing Domestic and Global Diversity

...no man who can imagine the unimaginable possibilities of the next war, can advocate war out of irritability or frustration or impatience.

—John F. Kennedy (1960)

The number of purely white people in the World is proportionably very small. All Africa is black or tawny. Asia is chiefly tawny. America (exclusive of the new Comers) wholly so.... Perhaps I am partial to the Complexion of my Country, for such Kind of Partiality is natural to Mankind.

—Benjamin Franklin (1751)

CONTINUING WITH ONE OF THIS COLLECTION'S central themes which asserts that domestic conflicts currently outpace international wars and that "abuse of power" has been the scourge of pluralistic societies, Part Seven further explores the need to better address the effects of growing pluralism in society. With pluralism reflecting a growing diversity in populations it has been viewed as accounting for divisiveness and for distinct and conflicting loyalties. It is argued in this part that the so-called nation-state is a misnomer, since with the breakdown of strict borders in many states are made up not of a homogenous people, but of diverse ethnic, religious, cultural or linguistic communities. How is harmony and peace to be maintained in such diverse communities and how are formerly "pure" societies reacting to the change? Ted Robert Gurr, a renowned expert in the arena of civil conflicts and wars offers readers his Five Principles. A most compelling example of a multiethnic and multicultural state's progress in harmonizing conflicting communal interests is later described by South Africa's Albert Venter. How does a nation avoid what America's Federalist founders termed "a tyranny of the majority"?

Some see pluralism as primarily a growing national phenomena, with countries such as Germany and the United Kingdom losing their homogeneity due to the influx of foreign workers. Yet growing pluralism also raises new questions on the international peace agenda.

Pluralism has always existed globally and it has served as the spark to innumerable human conflicts. Wars in the name of religion, ethnicity or political ideology have long been fought under the flags of nations. Today, as citizen groups advance their single agendas they also break ranks with the nation-state by attempting to promote their agendas on an international level. As ethnic Chechnyans exert their claims for a free and pure state, they have also taken their fight to an international level.

Today, local conflicts in Northern Ireland, Kashmir and Palestine capture international attention as a result of the pluralistic fervor they incite. So as leaders grapple with the competing interests within their own society, they should remain cognizant of the global issues they may be raising.

Beyond Sovereignty

Arnold Brecht
Political Theorist (1884-1977)

What is the foremost, or the ultimate, cause of wars between sovereign countries? Is it merely bad will, wantonness, envy and stupidity? Is it population pressure and economic necessity? Is it escape from domestic failures or from financial collapse? Shortcomings in the peace treaty that happens to be the last one? Inherent pugnacity, competitive militarism and armament? Capitalism, communism, fascism? Instability of democratic policy? The progress of technology and invention? The missteps of poor diplomacy? Certainly none of these factors can claim first rank above all others as a cause of war. Each of them needs careful study. For each of them, separately, there might be found some remedy or antidote. But there is a cause of wars between sovereign states that stands above all others—the fact that there *are* sovereign states, and a very great many of them.

It is not only for logical reasons that this fact should be emphasized. Of all the conditions contributing to war, those that appear to be the most insuperable are necessary implications of the principle of state sovereignty—the principle that supreme legal power is strictly separated along state lines. And yet this principle is neither ordained by God nor found nature: it is man-made. It was not always recognized in the past, it may not always be recognized in the future. Only in modern times have three notions been coordinated which are different in their historic and philosophical origins: the notion of the political-economic unit (state), of supreme legal power (sovereignty), and of homogeneity (nation). These notions do not cover identical fields and therefore their coordination has proved pernicious.

I

If the world is to be divided into political units there must be some yardstick (at least in theory) by which to determine the optimum size of these units. And indeed, despite the great varieties in the realm of facts, there have always been ideas on what the optimum size would be. To Aristotle it was the city, to Rousseau it was the Swiss canton, to contemporary thought it is the nation (whatever that may mean), with some allowance for the ideas of "natural boundaries," historical derivations and domination over backward peoples. The transition from city-state to nation-state was made in a roundabout way through the idea of a universal realm of supreme power. Before proceeding to contemporary problems it would be well to recall the reasons why this intermediate step was profoundly logical, why it could last so long and what it was that finally brought it to an end.

After Macedon subjected Athens (338 B.C.), after Rome subjected Macedon (146 B.C.), and Greece finally became a Roman province (27 B.C.), it was no longer possible for any city or neighborhood to continue as an independent unit. It was very natural then for people to espouse the idea that supreme power should pass from the city, not to a neighboring city or tribe, but to civilized mankind. There was less humiliation in being a city in a universal empire than in being merely a member in the realm of another tribe. This natural trend of feeling, which brought the interests of defeated cities and other units in line with the selfish interests of the rising Roman empire, was strongly supported by an other idea prominent in classical and medieval thought: the idea of a universal natural law, above all the governmental actions of separate entities. If there was such a universal law it was logical to have a universal power to administer it and protect peace according to it. These arguments were finally strengthened by the rise of Christianity. If all Christendom was one brotherhood before God, equal before God, equal in ultimate purposes, ruled by one divine law, no implication was more natural than that also in temporal affairs all Christendom should rally to one universal standard.

So strong were these arguments that the idea of the universality of supreme power held sway in philosophical and political thinking from the time of Augustus, the anniversary of whose two thousandth birthday has recently been celebrated, to the seventeenth century, with the possible exception of some three or four hundred years in the Dark Ages. It was so deeply rooted that it was seized upon again and again, and was carried on and on, regardless of the poor realization it had found, regardless of the shortcomings which make students of our age laugh at the Holy Roman Empire and wonder that it was maintained at all instead of making them consider why the idea was so cherished by popular feeling, even under its strange disguises.

No idea of nationality or racial homogeneity opposed the rising Holy Roman Empire when, a thousand years ago, the German King Otto I had himself crowned emperor. Nationalities and races had too evidently blended in many parts of Europe, especially in Italy, and had done so rather recently. The Romans and the north Italian peoples had always belonged to different stocks. The migrations of the Goths and Lombards had added to the entanglement of racial crossings. Magyars and Arabs had devastated Italy. Hugo, king of Italy, had been neither a Roman nor a Lombard but a prince of Burgundy, and his successor, Berengar, a prince of the northwestern Alpine region. When finally he was displaced by Otto there could hardly be any objection on the grounds of race or nationality. Nor was there, for a long time, any other counter-idea that could vie in force with the idea of the universality of supreme power. Not before the end of the Middle Ages did such counter-ideas arise.

By that time events had gone far in overcoming the factual significance of the empire. Its long dispute with the rivaling church, the practical nonrecognition of the empire by outside forces, and gradual corrosion from the inside by former vassals who forged their way to independence, had fatally weakened it. For a long time, however, these historical shortcoming were merely factual; the ideal as such was not questioned or shaken. Similarly rooted in the realm of facts rather than ideas was the influence which economic changes and the rising mercantilist practices exercised on the trend for separation. Only very late did *ideas* arise that ran counter to the ideal of universality.

The religious reformation, of course, played a great role in this development because it destroyed the universality of the Roman Catholic creed (that is, of the divine law) and at the same time aligned the Protestant princes against the Catholic emperor. As an idea, however, the religious reformation was not antagonistic to universality. Certainly the reformation, unable to replace the old by a new universality, made for secession and separation. Yet this was again a matter of fact rather than a counter-idea. The doctrine which later emerged that prince and people should have the same religion might be called an antiuniversalist idea, excluding as it did the recognition of one universal lord. This transient doctrine has long since been superseded, however, by the principle of religious toleration, and therefore it would not stand in the way of universality today.

Another counter-move which was more accurately in the realm of ideas and was much more tenacious, prevailing up to the present day, was the legal and political doctrine of sovereignty. In the fight of the separate territories against the universalist claims of both empire and church the jurists, in developing this doctrine, passed the princes their most successful weapon. Sovereignty, so they announced, is the supreme legal power over citizens and subjects, *unrestrained by law.* This power is creator of law but is not itself bound by law. The sovereign state cannot legally be bound by any force.

This way of thinking was profoundly repugnant to the idea of universal law and all medieval thought. It was advanced with slight hesitations and contradictions by Jean Bodin (who had a few precursors but was the first to use the term sovereignty in the new sense) and carried to its most relentless consistency by Thomas Hobbes—within the short period from the end of the sixteenth to the middle of the seventeenth century. The term sovereignty became unpopular for a while in England, because Hobbes had used his one hundred per cent version of the doctrine as a buttress for his radical thesis of monarchical absolutism—so unpopular that the term does not occur a single time in Locke's *Two Treatises of Government*—but the substance of the doctrine prevailed. When Rousseau combined the rigid concept of sovereignty with the idea of absolute power not of the king but of the people (as Roger Williams in America had done unnoticed a hundred years earlier) the resultant doctrine of "sovereignty of the people" freed the legal concept from popular disrepute and made it capable of carrying an ambiguous freight. Once more the jurists took hold of the notion and used it to reject any universal, supernational law beyond the positive law given by the sovereign. In John Austin, in the middle of the nineteenth century, they found the master of inexorable formulation, and his school with but little modification dominates to this day the foreign offices of all countries, democratic, fascist and communist.

Meanwhile many a scholarly warrior, it is true, has fought a valiant theoretical battle against the orthodox doctrine of sovereignty—Leon Duguit, Hans Kelsen, Hugo Krabbe, Harold Laski and many others. But none of them has ever occupied the foreign office of his country, none ever influenced the official language and actions of any country on that point. To this day the actual practice of the foreign offices, at least as far as their own countries are concerned, follows the classical theory of sovereignty, as presented by the juristic theory of the state and the analytical school of jurisprudence, as a rule the only definite "concession" being that treaty obligations, at least those that are voluntary, and *approved* international usages are held mandatory upon states despite their sovereignty.

The great effect exercised by the rise of the theory of sovereignty, which indeed marks the juncture between the Middle Ages and modern times in politics, has as a rule been described with a view to the center of power—princes or parliaments—or to the relation between domestic and foreign centers of power. It may even better be described with a view to the periphery of power, the territorial boundaries. In the Roman and medieval empires boundaries between territories had a relatively restricted, a "soft" meaning. In the Roman period they marked off mere provinces or administrative districts, and in medieval times they marked imperial fiefs, crown lands, free cities and their subdivisions. Boundaries within the empires had no final meaning to the freeman. Transcending any such boundary were the imperial, the divine and the natural laws, the imperial administration of justice allowing appeal from territorial justice to the emperor's courts, at least in the most important cases. The emperor could intervene as an arbiter or avenger, as the sword of the church or as the ultimate guardian of peace.

With the change in theory the meaning of boundaries also changed. The greater vassals had already succeeded in limiting the emperor's intervention and had thereby tightened the meaning of boundaries, but not until the doctrine of sovereignty was invented was this movement led into its ultimate channels. Every prince wanted then to be a sovereign. In this mood the Westphalian peace of 1648 applied the new ideas to the territories of the former imperial vassals in Germany. Thereafter the concept of sovereignty began to make boundaries mean what they mean today. Within a country's boundaries no law counts other than that issued by the sovereign, be it prince, parliament or people—no higher law, no imperial law, no divine law, no natural law. There is no appeal to any higher court, no arbiter, avenger or ultimate guardian of peace and justice.

Thus it was that the boundary line grew stronger and gradually became the formidable wall both in fact and in idea that it is today.

II

After the victory of the doctrine of sovereignty, just as after the construction of the tower of Babel when God scattered mankind, people found themselves more separate from others than they had formerly been. In both the Roman and the Holy Roman empires everyone had been accustomed to be affiliated with everyone, with peoples of all races and languages, in the same ultimate entity, that is, in the universal empire, the universal Christian brotherhood. This was no longer the case. People now felt themselves surrounded by narrower and higher walls.

There they lived in one of three situations. Some groups were constituted of one race, homogeneous from of old, with no memory of ever having blended with other races. So it was with Sweden, Denmark and a great many of the smaller German territories, of which there were more than a thousand in the eighteenth century. Others, though obviously not of homogeneous origin but sprung from multifarious intermixtures, had nevertheless attained a great degree of homogeneity because wholesale admixtures had ceased some six hundred years earlier and, since that time, inbreeding had generated a new and characteristic race, even though broadly diversified. This was the case with England, where wholesale immigration had ceased with William the Conqueror, and with France, where the many contributions from Latin, Phoenician, Arabian, Germanic and Celtic races had been absorbed over an even longer period. After so many centuries of intermarriage the typical Englishman, the typical Frenchman, began to emerge. Indeed, six hundred years were sufficient to make every Englishman related to almost every Englishman, every Frenchman to almost every Frenchman.[1] Even in the various states of Italy the melting pot had produced an average type by the end of the eighteenth century.

But a third group of the new sovereign countries was in quite a different situation, having two or more distinct populations living together without blending. So it was with Austria, Turkey, parts of Prussia, Saxony, the Kingdom of the Netherlands and others. The new and rigid meaning of boundaries brought the existence of such mixtures more and more to popular attention. Hence the idea of nationality, which had already played some part in many previous movements, crystallized into a conscious idea and became a ready yardstick for the optimum size of sovereign states. This new trend of thinking was but strengthened when conquerors continued to add distinct races to their territories, as did Russia, Prussia and Austria with the three partitions of Poland, and England with the consolidation of Ireland, and in particular Napoleon with the annexation of great parts of Germany, the Netherlands and other territories.

Thus the idea of nationality was being added to the idea of sovereignty, where it had not preceded it, as a forceful concomitant in the ideological fight against universality. This idea, as has often been observed, has two logical implications, one liberalistic or separative, the other imperialistic or expansive: state boundaries ought not to include many subjects of another nationality, nor should they sever citizens from people of the same stock. Both sides of the idea reached high triumphs in the nineteenth and twentieth centuries. The new yardstick of nationality superseded all others. Factors such as size of area, number of inhabitants and economic basis were almost completely disregarded. This becomes the more obvious the farther one climbs down the ladder from the larger to the smaller countries.

Numerically at the top in the present line-up of states are China, with more than four hundred million inhabitants, the Soviet Union, with more than one hundred and fifty, and the United States, with more than one hundred and thirty million. They are followed at some distance by Germany and Japan with some seventy million inhabitants each (Japan without Korea), and by the four countries in the forty millions: Great Britain (without colonies), France, Italy and Brazil. Poland is the only country in the thirty millions (disregarding Manchukuo), Spain the only one in the twenties. They constitute the transition to the ten states having between ten and twenty million each, three of them in Europe (Rumania, Jugoslavia, Czechoslovakia), three in the Americas (Mexico, Argentina, Canada), three in Asia (Turkey, Iran and Siam) and Egypt in Africa. All the remaining sovereign states have less than ten million inhabitants apiece. Thus almost three fourths of the thirty-odd European states have fewer than the eight million inhabitants that live in the city of Greater New York; nevertheless they are enclosed by the boundaries of sovereign states. All but three of the Central and South American countries have less than that figure, as does also the whole continent of Australia. Almost half of all European and American countries fail to reach even half that amount.

The idea of nationality came to a climax at the conclusion of the World War, when at least nine new nation-states were created in the jammed space of Europe: one of more than thirty million (Poland), one between ten and twenty (Czechoslovakia), two between five and ten (Hungary and Austria) and five much smaller ones (Finland, Lithuania, Latvia, Estonia, Danzig, in addition to Memelland). This meant the creation of seven thousand miles of new boundaries in the heart of Europe, boundaries in the rigid sense imputed to them by the doctrine of sovereignty.

Even if we overlook the imperfections and perversions in the way that the yardstick of nationality has been applied (which it has recently been tried to correct to a certain degree), it is obvious that homogeneity of population does not always, or even generally, square with political and economic requirements. This discrepancy is given an explosive character by the element of sovereignty.

III

The meaning imparted to boundaries by the principle of sovereignty is of such a kind that human wit can hardly find a solution that does not lead to war. In the domestic field this principle implies the legal freedom of every sovereign country in the regulation of its own domestic affairs. This, at first, sounds reassuring and liberal. Thank God, mine is a sovereign country. There is no outside power entitled to give us orders. We are free to settle our own affairs according to our own ideas.

But even if this were the whole story it would be far from satisfactory. Free of any limitations, of any minimum standards whatever, domestic sovereignty not only relieves each country, in theory, from the legitimate interference of another power but also deprives its people of any legitimate appeal to a higher power. Inside the sovereign country, might makes right. Courts and public servants have to apply the laws given by those who exercise sovereignty. After a change of regime they may, during a very short stage of transition, question the legitimacy of usurpers, but with the modern device of "sliding" revolution, that is, a transformation observing the forms of legitimacy, even this right is all but illusory. Once sovereign power has been firmly established the courts are not entitled to apply any higher law against its legal commands. The individual judges are not to be blamed for such submission to the positive legal order of the land. It is what is required of them by their professional ethics according to the doctrines of sovereignty and legal positivism, to which the official and legal authorities pay homage in all countries. Judges may retire and starve—but if they stay they have to apply the positive law as it is handed down to them by the sovereign power. It is true that three hundred years in early Stuart England, Sir Edward Coke placed common law above the positive law. But his famous Dr. Bonham's case has long since been overruled in theory (Blackstone) and practice even in England: whenever the positive law is clear and distinct it is the only law that counts.

Boundaries are appeal-proof. Except in the case of treaty obligations there is no appeal to any higher judge. No other country is entitled to interfere except on invitation by the government (whatever that may mean). The slightest violation of an international obligation may be made a just cause for international interference (the non-delivery of a few cubic feet of wood and coal was made a cause for the occupation of the German *Ruhrgebtete* by France in 1923); but in the fact that there are appalling occurrences within the sovereign country or that it violates basic standards of justice and civilization there is no sufficient cause for official steps by other countries or even for an attempt to require a clear investigation of the facts.

Another implication is that each country is free to push its armament and other military preparation to what degree it likes, except in excess of treaty obligations. All this leads to a policy of mutual *laissez faire* which is likely to result, and actually does result, in a complete lack of confidence and in a frenzied race of armaments.

Even these first implications of the doctrine of sovereignty show it to be hardly compatible in the long run with international peace. Unfortunate as they are, certain arguments have nevertheless been advanced in their favor. Suppressed people, it is said, may make a revolution of their own. Intervention in the domestic affairs of another country involves by nature a kind of aggression, and even when undertaken for the sake of civilization has so often been abused for selfish purposes and reactionary measures that non-intervention has come to be looked upon as the superior principle for the maintenance of peace. Doubt can be cast on the final wisdom of this view; it seems to be a result of previous guilt and bad conscience rather than of intrinsic logic. To be sure, it is not advisable and is rather odious to prescribe to other countries their system of government, their organization and, unilaterally, their armament. But it is possible to imagine a system of minimum standards and of international information and publicity which would make for more justice, more confidence and more peace, for fewer rumors and more truth. This, however, would be contrary to the doctrine of sovereignty unless agreed to voluntarily.

But these domestic implications of sovereignty reveal only one side of the story. Another side, very different in character, is of still greater, and more conclusive, significance in reference to peace and war. The doctrine that in every sovereign country there is no law other than that approved by the sovereign power and that courts and public servants have to apply such law in full and nothing else—this principle reaches far beyond the country's own citizens. It makes insecure any alien within its boundaries and it makes the country's natural resources its monopolistic asset and privilege, which it may exploit at pleasure for its own benefit to the exclusion of any other country unless voluntary treaties limit this arbitrary power.

With respect to aliens, a sovereign country can restrict their immigration at pleasure, using whatever arbitrary principle it pleases, even to complete exclusion. If they are admitted, their establishment in trade or business or professions may be restricted, as may be also their acquisition of land titles or of shares in corporate property. Intermarriage with aliens, or with certain aliens, may be prohibited. The sovereign country may even expel any alien at any time for political reasons.

Among the natural resources which a country may reserve for its own use there is a greater variety than is generally seen. Gold and silver, iron, copper and tin, coal and oil, wheat, meat and fruit, fat and fodder, rubber and water power—these are part, but not all. There may be virgin soil. There may be a particularly healthful and pleasant climate, outstanding landscape and beauty. There may be especially high manpower. If there are not treaty limitations the sovereign country may raise barriers around such natural resources at any time, as high as it likes, the barriers ranging from mere taxation of foreign exploiters to their non-admittance, from export duties to a full embargo on export to all or certain countries. A sovereign country's consumptive power is also an important asset, and the country may strike at pleasure at any other country's trade by measures that range from slight financial tariffs through highly protective tariffs to import quotas and complete import prohibitions. The sovereign country may make its bills legal tender in its own territory and restrict exchange with other currencies to any extent for any reason. All this can be done under the doctrine of sovereignty. Most of it has been done, here or there or everywhere.

Certainly many countries will not resort to some of these measures, even over a long period, either because of an established public opinion—as prewar England refrained from protective tariffs for two generations because she believed that for her free trade was the best policy—or because of mutual treaties or fear of retaliation. As a result it seemed for a while that it might be possible to break down the frontiers, making the civilized world a great community with at least a minimum standard of rights, a minimum certainty of intercourse. But this did not happen, or at least it did not last. For one thing, no country has ever abandoned all its natural resources to others without discrimination, accepted foreign currency as legal tender, or admitted all foreign commodities duty free, and rarely has any country allowed all aliens to enter into free competition with its own residents. But this may be passed over. The real calamity is that there is no guarantee that public opinion will remain what it was, and no guarantee that treaties will be concluded, and renewed after they expire, that notice will not be served at the next date allowed for withdrawal. As long as there is sovereignty so long will there be this right to reject the conclusion of treaties and their renewal, not to speak of the retaliation that may be meanwhile resorted to for alleged violations of treaties.

Therefore no favorable public opinion and no temporary contractual arrangement between sovereign states, not even between neighboring ones, can give security to a country that is not self-supporting, for its needs in a future war. This is the cross through the *t* and the dot over the *i* of the word *frontier.* No country can be sure that it will get what it needs from other sovereign countries under continuous and stable conditions, or that it will get it at all when its need is greatest. Therefore no necessitous country can cease to be afraid that in a period of war it will starve for lack of food or be vanquished for lack of raw material, even if for the time being trade treaties look very satisfactory.

From this there follows a conclusion which is as, unpleasant as it is incontrovertible: it is *desirable* for any major sovereign power to cover so much territory as to make it self-sufficient within its own boundaries, or within the boundaries of dependencies with which mutual communication is safe in peace and war. That is to say, it is desirable for any major sovereign country to expand until it reaches a high degree of self-sufficiency in peace and war. Today such expansion is (except for the scientific development of substitutes for various products) the only way for a country to make itself, in regard to its own necessities for life, independent of the will, the pleasure, the whim and the currency of other countries.

This implication is crystal clear. In the social sciences conclusions as definite as this are seldom possible. There is no argument against it. Science has the duty to push aside all misty and flowery concealments of this basic truth and has to denounce all soft and talkative peace organizations that do take account of it at the outset.

There are limitations, to be sure. Acquisition of resources with which the country is already saturated may be of little advantage Abandonment of more defendable boundaries for less defendable ones may offset the advantage of expansion. Annexing additional people that would not keep domestic peace or would be disloyal in war may weaken rather than strengthen power. The cost of expansion, or of developing a substitute, may make the grapes hang too high. Such limitations are sure to have their influence on practical politics. But they do not controvert the truth that, for any major county that is not self-sufficient, the expansion of boundaries or acquisition of dependencies is highly desirable for times of peace, and may be vital for times of war. And war is a realistic potentiality for every country, no alliance or isolation, no cleverness or good behavior being a guarantee against it.

For this logical thrust toward expansion, deterrents are the only palliative we have invented these four hundred years since the victory of the doctrine of sovereignty. There is only the mutual play of threat against threat, of fear against fear, yielding for fear against abstaining for fear. Peace is today, at best, a balance of fears.

IV

The combination of the doctrines of state, nation and sovereignty has led us into an impasse. We have to retrace our steps and follow other signs if we are to advance beyond this fatal point. Only a change in our way of thinking in terms of these three doctrines, or at least of their present procrustean combination, can lead us to any reliable progress in solving the problem of peace and war.

Easily as this is stated in critical analysis, it is actually very difficult to disentangle the three fields in a satisfactory way. For, at the time being, there *is* this established sovereignty of the multitude of states, and according to its first principle it cannot be changed without their individual consent, unless it be by force. Whatever international attempts have been made to overcome the evils without the application of force have so far evaded the issue. They have bowed to the principle of domestic sovereignty and, in addition, to the principle of the status quo. In other words, they have tended to maintain the motley map of the world, if with a few minor corrections, and to retain the principle of sovereignty as the best concomitant of the national state. They have vaguely trusted that love of justice and goodwill would assert themselves, not recognizing that *love of justice and goodwill cannot do the job alone without a constructive correction of the three principles that underlie the problem.*

It is a popular idea that all warfare could be immediately prevented if an energetic League of Nations would apply sanctions of an economic and if need be a military kind against any aggressor. This dream has been dreamt. There is little chance that it will come true. The explosive force of sovereignties can scarcely be met in this way. In many indirect ways, as we know now, aggression can be avoided and yet war be carried on. The members of the League are not always at one. Not all nations are members; none can be forced to be a member or can be prevented from withdrawing. Also, this plan does not cope with any of the real causes of tension. For countries that are not self-sufficient it does not remove any of those complaints that follow from the impossibility of reaching security on a contractual basis. Nor does it envisage a justifiable interference in the troubled domestic affairs of any country, not even for the purpose of reorganization in a civil war like that in Spain. It merely adds a more or less effective threat to other more or less effective threats. It may precipitate war as prevent it.

Thus it is clear that the ultimate remedy, to be reliable, include a new understanding of the meaning of boundaries around nationalities would be maintained but they would be given a softer, less rigid meaning. Larger entities would be set up for the satisfactory regulation of economic needs and for the guarantee of minimum standards in the administration of justice.

How can we ever proceed to such a New Age when individual consent is required for any change? Can any man in his senses declare himself for such a program, such a utopia? Certainly he would not be in his senses if he expected immediate realization. But thinking for the future is not to be scorned. Every realization of ideas contradictory to established ruts of thought needs long and thoughtful preparation. New principles and awareness of the need for them must be firmly established in man's exchange of thought until they gradually assume reality, fortified with the invincible power of logic that has been understood.

Today, while the scholar may decry sovereignty, the practical politician shrinks from even mentioning this term in condemnatory sense. People still cling to the magic of the old conception. The politician rightly feels that he must act under a positive rather than a negative program. Nevertheless, his positive program must imply an infringement of sovereignty if it is to be more than a palliative.

This is not the place to formulate the lines of a practical program. In such an undertaking a great many changing factors have to be taken into account. Any practical program would include several steps. Possibly one of them would be an attempt at sensible progress toward self-sufficiency for combinations of nations that separately lack it—combinations such as those that have been attained to such a large degree in the British Empire, the United States and the Soviet Union. For such combinations to be effected it would be necessary, in the territories concerned, to modify the meaning of boundaries by the formation of unions or federations, or of combinations on the pattern of the British Commonwealth, or by allowing a major power to make neighboring or overseas countries into practical dependencies, or by new constructive devices. In such territories the rigid equation of sovereignty, nationality and state would be abandoned or mitigated. Practical policy is likely to lead on this road anyway, with or without the help of theory.

Another step might be to induce the major countries or combinations of the world to lower their walls voluntarily, at least after a better balance of self-sufficiency has been reached—for before that has been achieved they are not likely to give in.

In connection with such plans it might be feasible to set up minimum standards and to use available sanctions against governments that do not comply with such standards or that refuse to give information and evidence if an international investigation is undertaken.

Evolution from the present status of hyper-archaic nationalism and an-archaic internationalism, of high-tension law within and lawlessness without, to comprehensive combinations and to some minimum level of universal law and its guarantee, cannot be expected to materialize from analytical discussion alone. But without careful analysis of the situation that confronts us we cannot hope for any definite progress. We are not justified in completely dismissing the hope that the present cramped convulsions of multiple territorial sovereignties will not be final. They may be regarded as the product of insufficient and treacherous solutions, and it may be that to a later generation they will appear as the travails of a new and better order, with less rigid boundaries, and more peace.

Note

1. In order to understand this fully one must realize that, reckoning thirty years for each generation, a present-day Englishman would have had a billion ancestors at the time of the Conqueror, and even a quintillion at the Roman period, had they not continually intermarried with their own relatives, mostly without knowing that they were relatives. How much they must have done so obvious from a comparison of the small number of people that lived in England in those periods, or came in later, with the astronomic figures that would have been necessary to produce a single present-day English man without intermarriage of relatives.

Attaining Peace in Divided Societies: Five Principles of Emerging International Doctrine[1]

Ted Robert Gurr
University of Maryland

An extraordinary shift has taken place in the last decade in strategies for the transformation of what I call ethnopolitical conflicts—conflicts in which cultural, racial, and religious minorities seek equal rights and political participation, and national peoples demand self-determination. Consider a few examples:

> Apartheid South Africa at the beginning of the 1990s was transformed into a African-dominated multiracial democracy—not through bloody race war, as many observers predicted, but by a largely peaceful process of political and constitutional change.
>
> After Indonesia's transition toward democracy in 1998, the new government grudgingly accepted a referendum on Timor's secession and opened negotiations with representatives of the secessionist Free Aceh movement. Ethnopolitical violence continues in Aceh, in Iriyan Jaya, and elsewhere, but what was unthinkable under Suharto's authoritarian regime has now become the acceptable practice of seeking accommodation with rebels rather than relying exclusively on force.
>
> The German government, after decades in which citizenship was defined exclusively by descent, began in the late 1990s to lower in a meaningful way the barriers used to deny citizenship to the vast majority of Turkish and other non-German immigrants.
>
> Virtually every news analysis and essay on the future of Afghanistan written since September 2001 has stressed that the country's future stability depends on establishing a power-sharing coalition among leaders of its Pashtun, Tajik, Uzbek, and Hazara communities. This is in marked contrast to the discourse of the 1980s and early 1990s, in which outside observers saw only the conflict between mujahedeen rebels and a communist regime in Kabul, and ignored the ethnic rivalries that have driven Afghan politics for centuries.

These transformations are hardly isolated. Instead they bespeak a new global doctrine for managing conflicts in heterogeneous societies. It is based on premises that communal contention about access to the state's power and resources should be restrained by recognizing minority rights and negotiating power-sharing arrangements; that threats to divide a country should be managed by the devolution of state power; and that the international community has proactive responsibility for promoting these outcomes. Once-common strategies of forced assimilation, racial separation, and ethnic cleansing—the phrase is new, the practice ancient—have been tossed into the dustbin of history, adding a new layer to the moldering relics of colonial conquest and imperial rule. The older strategies still have local defenders and practitioners, but the most influential international actors now assert the normative and practical superiority of pluralism, power-sharing, and regional autonomy within existing states.

The impact of the new doctrine is somewhat obscured by the brutality of recent ethnopolitical conflicts in Central and West Africa, in Kosovo and Chechnya, in Timor and Myanmar, and the messiness or absence of international responses to them. But the trends are unmistakable, as I show below. Among them are a long-run and near-global improvement in the status of minorities, a sharp decline in new ethnic wars, the settlement of many protracted wars, and proactive efforts by states and international organizations to recognize group rights and channel ethnic disputes into conventional politics.

International Principles for Managing Conflict in Heterogenous Societies

The norms and practices of international responsibility for racial, ethnic, and cultural conflict evolved rapidly during the 1990s. Protection of human rights and redress for past discrimination against minorities were more actively promoted within and among countries. Norms prescribing international responsibility for managing violent ethnic conflicts were asserted more forcefully. And international actors did in fact engage more frequently and directly in preventive diplomacy, negotiated settlements of ethnic wars, and collective peacekeeping, peace enforcement, and humanitarian intervention

In my view these norms and practices constitute the elements of a new international doctrine. The doctrine incorporates five principles about how to promote peace and mitigate violent conflict in divided societies, principles that can be expected to drive international policy during the early decades of the twenty-first century following precedents established during the 1990s.

(1) The Human Rights Regime: International Norms about Individual and Group Rights: The first principle of the emerging doctrine is recognition and active protection of the rights of racial, cultural, and religious minorities. This means freedom from discrimination based on race, national origin, language, or religion, complemented by institutional means to protect and promote their collective interests.

Western democracies have been most consistent in articulating, promoting, and implementing such policies. After World War II a human rights regime evolved in the Atlantic democracies that emphasized the protection of individual rights.[2] During the early 1990s the emphasis of many Western advocates shifted from individual rights to protection of collective rights of national minorities. The effect of standard-setting texts adopted in 1990–95 by the Organisation for Security and Cooperation in Europe and the Council of Europe was to establish what Preece calls "an international regime for protection of national minorities in Europe—however limited." The texts embody several principles. One is prohibition against forced assimilation and population transfer; another is endorsement of autonomy for minority communities within existing states; a third is recognition that national minority questions are "once more legitimate subjects of international relations both at the United Nations and within European regional organizations."[3]

These texts are not binding, but they provide the legal basis for a political program that includes advocacy of individual and group rights by states, regional organizations, NGOs, and politically organized minority groups themselves. The texts are worded so as to endorse the rights of individual members of ethnic and religious minorities and do not specify that groups as such have rights. Nonetheless it is a widely-recognized corollary of this package that the right to organize and act politically implies the rights of minorities to pursue collective interests, including the exercise of some degree of autonomy over their own affairs. That is, it follows that if minority peoples who constitute a majority in one region of a heterogeneous state have the right to protect and promote their collective interests, they also have a claim right to local or regional self-governance within existing international boundaries.

Virtually all European democracies have implemented these principles, sometimes from the top down but usually in response to pressures from politically-organized minorities. In the first stage of democratization in post-communist Europe, at the beginning of the 1990s, some ethnonational leaders manipulated the democratic process to serve nationalist interests at the expense of national minorities such as Russians in the Baltic states, Hungarians in Slovakia and Romania, and Serbs in Croatia. In most of these countries a combination of diplomatic engagement by European institutions and the democratic process led to a reversal of discriminatory policies by the end of the decade.

We have detailed evidence on the extent to which these principles have been implemented in Europe and elsewhere. The Minorities at Risk project has tracked the status and collective actions of nearly 300 politically significant national and minorities throughout the world across the last half-century. This includes annually-coded information on each group's experience of political and economic discrimination. Group members are subject to *political discrimination* to the extent that their members are or have been systematically limited in the exercise of political rights or access to political positions by comparison with other groups in their society. *Economic discrimination* consists of systematic limits on group members' access to desirable economic goods, conditions, or positions that are open to others in their society. We distinguish four patterns of discrimination, from least to most severe:[4]

Remedial (coded 1): Substantial under-representation or poverty due to historical marginality, neglect, or restrictions. Current public policies aim to substantially improve the group's status.

Neglect (coded 2): Substantial under-representation or poverty due to historical marginality, neglect, or restrictions. No social practice of deliberate exclusion. No formal exclusion. Protective or remedial public policies, if any, provide limited gains.

Social discrimination (coded 3): Substantial under-representation or poverty due to prevailing social practice by dominant groups. Public policies are neutral or, if positive, inadequate to offset active and widespread social practices of discrimination.

Official discrimination (coded 4): Public policies (formal exclusion or recurring repression or both) substantially restrict group members' political participation or economic opportunities in contrast with other groups.

Fifty-year trends in the severity of political discrimination are traced in the accompanying figures. On average, political discrimination has declined in severity since the 1950s by about one category on the five-category scale (above), with the greatest gains occurring in the 1990s (see the middle line in Figure 1). This despite an increase during much of this period in numbers of groups subject to the most severe type of discrimination—the top line in Figure 1. The increase was driven by government responses to the rash of ethnic wars that began from the 1960s through the 1980s. Regimes facing ethnopolitical rebellions usually ratcheted up political restrictions and repression against the challenging groups. The bottom line in the figure shows the positive consequences of the human rights regime. Despite increased discrimination against rebellious groups, there was a steady half-century-long increase in numbers of minorities benefiting from substantial public efforts to compensate for discriminatory inequalities. The three indicators, taken together, are clear evidence that the principles of minority rights promoted by Western NGOs and governments had a global impact in the 1990s.[5]

The timing and extent of improvement in minority status have varied widely among world re-

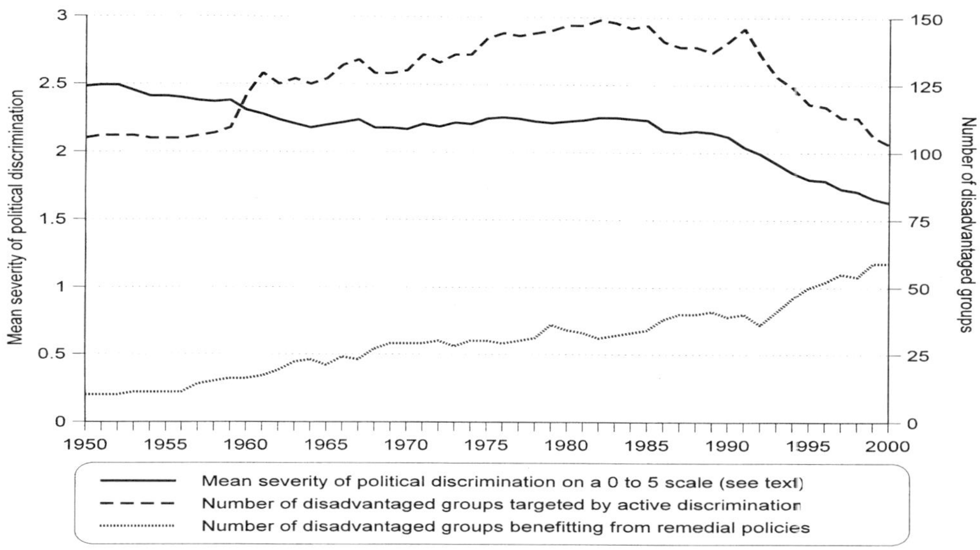

Figure 1. Political Discrimination against Minorities, 1950-2000

Note: Annual numbers of politicized minorities in all independent states with greater than 500,000 population; actual numbers vary from 182 in 1950 to 303 in 2000.

gions, as shown in Figures 2 and 3. The rights of minorities in Western democracies improved most substantially, beginning in the 1960s (Figure 2). Latin American countries, which historically have excluded or marginalized most indigenous and African-American peoples, imposed more political restrictions on minorities than Western democracies in the 1950s but improved significantly nonetheless. The Soviet and communist East European regimes promoted equal treatment for most minorities and national peoples as a matter of ideological principle, though informal discrimination weighed heavily on some groups—the Roma, for example, and Turks in Bulgaria. Thus the mean scores of political discrimination in this region were low and invariant until the late 1980s. After a slight upward spike at the end of the Cold War—signaling the initial impact of militant nationalism in the Baltics and the Balkans—the political rights of minorities increased markedly during the 1990s to the lowest mean level observed in any world region. This suggests just how widely Western principles of minority rights have been accepted and implemented by the post-communist states.

The human rights regime has had less impact on the status of minorities in the global South (Figure 3). Political discrimination in North Africa and the Middle East is directed mainly at religious minorities such as Copts in Egypt, Hindus in Bangladesh, Ahmadis in Pakistan, and Shi'a almost everywhere. The trend is essentially flat—no significant overall improvement in half a century. Political discrimination against minorities in Asian countries intensified before 1975—mainly because of political repression against rebellious minorities in Burma, Indonesia, India, and elsewhere—but then gradually subsided to its 1950 level. Sub-Saharan Africa is the only region in the Third World with a recent decline in political discrimination comparable to the pattern in Western democracies. This is due only in part to political change in Southern Africa. The longer-run pattern in African societies since decolonization was a slight increase in political discrimination—targeted at communal contenders and rebels—giving way to a significant decline as civil wars were settled and power-sharing arrangements

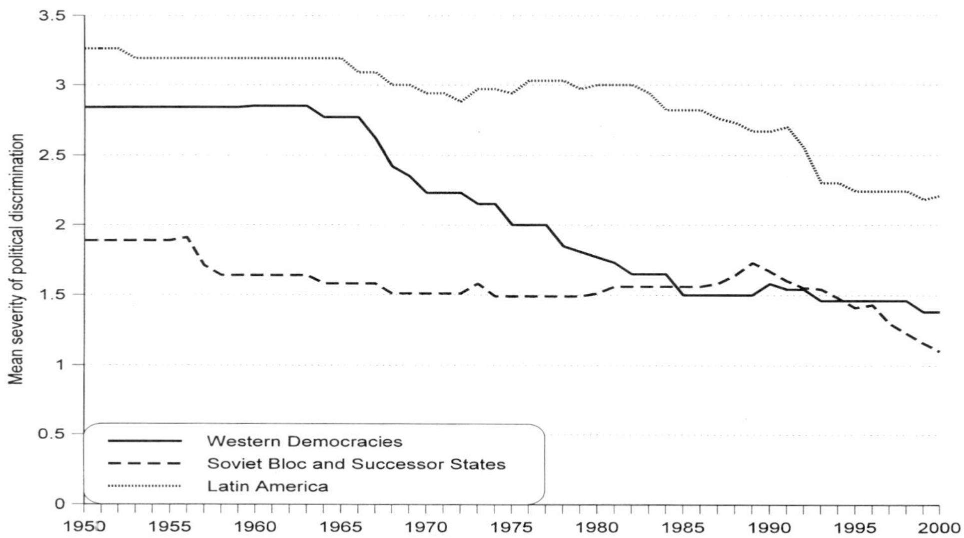

Figure 2. Political Discrimination against Minorities in Europe and Latin America 1950-2000

were more widely implemented. The improvement was more pronounced than is indicated by the average shown in Figure 3. From 1985 to 2000 there was a forty-three to nineteen decline in the number of African communal groups subject to active political discrimination and a doubling, from nine to eighteen, in groups benefiting from substantial remedial policies.

(2) Democratization: Promoting Institutions for Pluralism and Power Sharing: If recognition and protection of minority rights is the first principle of contemporary doctrine for managing ethnic conflict, then democratization is the second. Democratic institutions are the preferred domestic means for guaranteeing group rights in heterogeneous societies and for pursuing political programs to redress inequalities that have resulted from discrimination. Within the context of democratic institutions, mutual accommodation is the optimal strategy for managing conflicts between challenging groups and states, rather than suppression or forced assimilation of groups that claim separate identities and interests. There are other institutional mechanisms for the protection of communal groups' interests, for example, the hegemonic exchange system (the term is Donald Rothchild's) found in many non-democratic African states. Nonetheless democracy, in one of its European variants, is widely regarded as the most reliable guarantee of minority rights. It is inherent in the logic of democratic politics that all peoples in heterogeneous societies should have equal civil and political rights. Democratic governance also implies acceptance of peaceful means for resolving civil conflicts.

These preferences have normative and practical force. Normatively, the leading states in the international community operate on democratic principles and strongly support the establishment and continuation of democratic institutions elsewhere.[6] The declining trend in group discrimination, documented above, is paralleled by the better-known global shift from autocratic to democratic governance traced in Figure 4. As recently as 1978, autocracies outnumbered democracies by more than two to one (counting only countries with populations greater than 500,000). By 1994 the ratio was

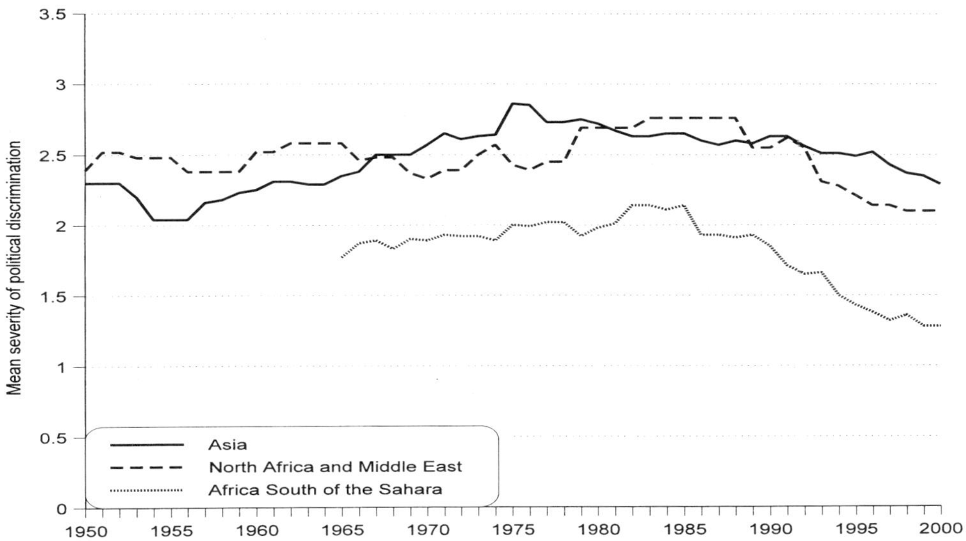

Figure 3. Political Discrimination against Minorities in the Global South 1950-2000

Note: Figures for Africa south of the Sahara before 1965 are not internally consistent due to decolonization and are not reported here.

reversed, with eighty democracies compared to less than forty autocracies plus another forty transitional regimes that incorporated elements of both democracy and autocracy.[7]

The new democratic states established during this period have a strong record of acknowledging and promoting minority rights. In a global analysis I found that about three out of ten groups subject to political discrimination in 1990-91 had more political rights and greater access by 1998 (60 of 211), and that about two out of ten groups subject to economic discrimination gained over the same period (41 of 179). Minorities were especially likely to gain in new democracies and transitional regimes. Restrictions on minorities also eased in some autocracies. Ironically, minority status was least likely to change during the 1990s in the long-established democracies, for several reasons. First, levels of political discrimination were already relatively low in the old democracies at the beginning of the 1990s (see Figure 2). Second was the onset of conservative social resistance to remedial policies, such as affirmative action in the United States—that had been enacted in previous decades. Third, we know that economic discrimination is resistant to change: it is easier for governments to give minorities better access to political institutions than to remedy economic disadvantages that are historically derived and structurally rooted.[8]

Democratization also tends to change the nature of ethnopolitical conflict. It has long been recognized that the "democratic peace" among democracies is paralleled by a similar "democratic peace" within such states. In particular, democracies are likely to have less ethnic rebellion (but more ethnic protest) than other kinds of regimes. Consistent with this principle is our evidence that Latin American, Asian, and African countries which had successful democratic transitions between 1980 and 1995 were likely to experience a decline in ethnopolitical rebellion. The counterpart of this principle is that democratization also prompted an increase in ethnopolitical protest. Groups that heretofore had been either quiescent or rebellious took advantage of democratic openings to pursue their interests by peaceful means. There is one important set of

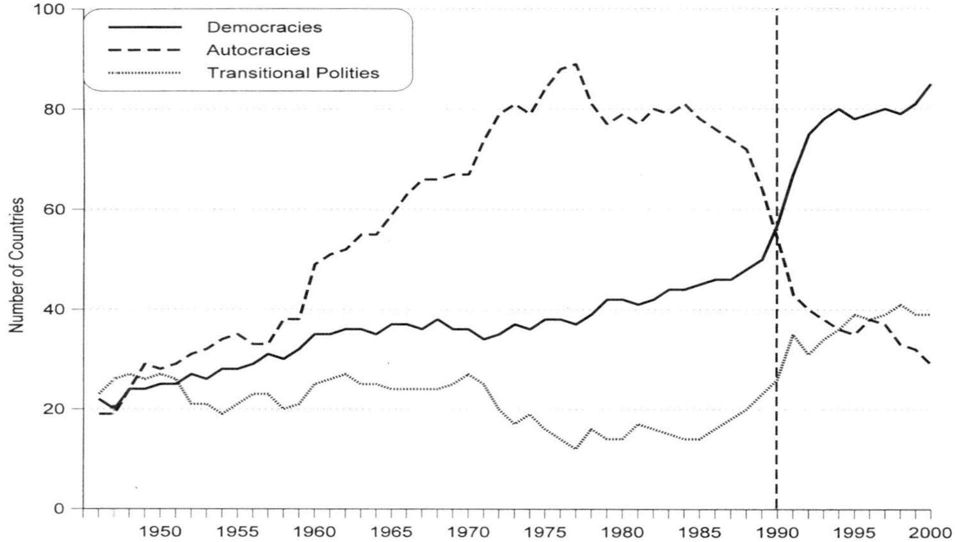

Figure 4. Global Trends in Democratic, Autocratic, and Transitional Regimes 1946-2000

exceptions to these generalizations. Democratic transitions in the Soviet and Yugoslav successor states were likely to precipitate both new ethnic rebellions and increased protest. The pacifying effects of democratization in these states were longer in coming, and in some instances democratization was killed in its cradle by ethnic contention.

This observation points to a crucial qualification of the democracy principle. In practice democracy and power-sharing are not a one-size-fits-all solution to the political tensions of heterogenous states. In poor states with a history of protracted communal conflict, such as Burundi and Rwanda in the early to mid 1990s, external pressures for power-sharing may contribute to political disasters.[9] The weight of evidence favors democratic approaches to ethnic conflicts rather than authoritarian rule or partition. Whether it is appropriate in specific circumstances is best determined by careful weighing of alternatives.

(3) Autonomy Solutions for Self-Determination Disputes: Demands of national peoples for independent statehood challenge the paramount importance that governing elites usually give to preserving the integrity of the state and its territory. Most ethnic wars of the last half-century have been fought over these issues. A recent survey shows that sixty-eight territorially concentrated ethnic groups fought armed separatist between the 1950s and 2000. More than a third of them continue to fight for greater self-determination in 2001; for example some Somalis and Oromo in Ethiopia, Tamils in Sri Lanka, and Chechens in Russia. We also have identified fifty-four other territorially concentrated groups in 2001 that sought greater self-determination by non-violent political means.

Many observers have feared that contemporary self-determination movements will continue the process of state breakdown signaled by the breakup of the Soviet Union and the Yugoslav Federation at the beginning of the 1990s. In fact only four internationally recognized states were born in armed separatist conflicts during the last 40 years. They are Bangladesh (1971), Slovenia (1991), Croatia (1991), and Eritrea (1993). One can expand this list by citing several de facto states established by

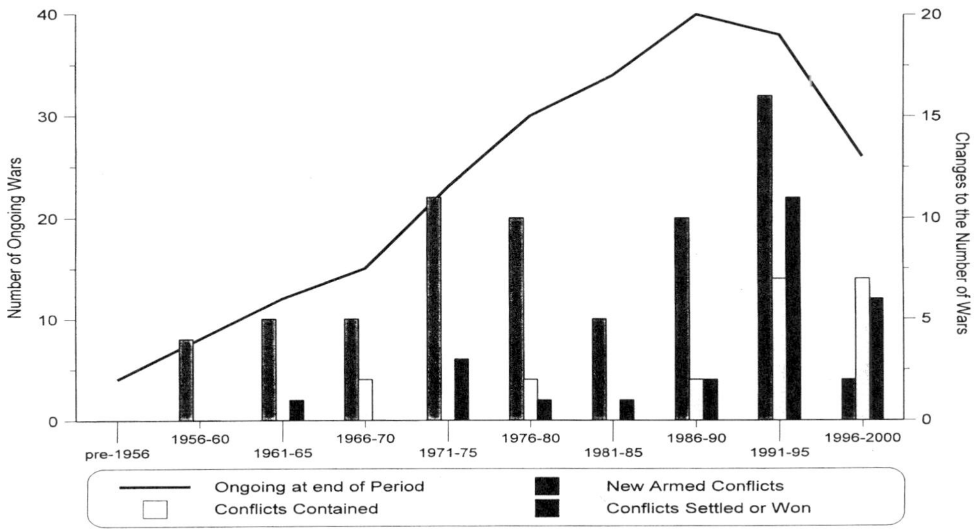

Figure 5. Global Trends in Armed Conflicts for Self-Determination 1956-2000

separatist movements, political entities which are not recognized as such by the international community.[10] These exceptions aside, *the most common outcome of self-determination conflicts is a negotiated settlement between a government and group representatives that acknowledges collective rights and provides institutional means for attaining them.* Sometimes a group gains better access to decision-making in the central government, often it gains regional autonomy, and of course some settlements include both kinds of reforms. Thus the outcome of self-determination movements seldom is a redrawing of international boundaries, but rather devolution of central power and redrawing of boundaries within existing states. Autonomy agreements are sometimes feared as a prelude to all-out war for independence. This is an unlikely outcome. The more common scenario is that most people accept and work within the framework for autonomy while a few spoilers continue to fight in hopes of greater concessions. The greatest risk in autonomy agreements is not the eventual breakup of the state, rather it is that spoilers may block full implementation, thereby dragging out the conflict and wasting resources that might otherwise be used to strengthen autonomous institutions.[11]

The use of negotiated autonomy agreements to manage self-determination disputes was strikingly effective during the waning years of the twentieth century. Armed conflicts over self-determination spiked sharply upwards at the end of the Cold War, but only after they had been building in frequency since the late 1950s, and doubling between 1970 and the early 1980s. Figure 5 summarizes the evidence. From five ongoing secessionist wars in the 1950s their numbers reached a maximum of 47 in 1991. But then they declined even more precipitously, to a low of twenty-six ongoing wars at the beginning of 2001, a smaller number than at any time in a quarter-century. Moreover about half of these were de-escalating at the end of 2000. The only new armed secessionist conflict of 2001 was initiated by Albanians in Macedonia.

The immediate reason for the decline has been a pronounced increase in local, regional, and international efforts to contain and settle self-determination conflicts, usually through autonomy agreements. During the Cold War a half-dozen were contained, usually when the rebels were defeated militarily, and another nine were settled or, in the case of Bangladesh, led to independence. Three of the negotiated settlements were in India, two of which—with Nagas (1963) and Tripuras (1972)—led to second-generation wars. During the 1990s an additional fourteen wars were contained, often as a result of internationally backed negotiations and peacekeeping, and another seventeen were settled by negotiated agreements or—in Slovenia, Croatia, and Eritrea—by internationally recognized independence for rebel nationalists. The guerrilla war of Albanians in Macedonia followed a familiar trajectory. By the end of 2001 it had been contained by an agreement negotiated under heavy international pressure. *More than two-thirds of all terminations of separatist wars during the last half-century—32 of 47—have occurred since 1990.*[12]

It is noteworthy that democracies did substantially better than authoritarian regimes in reaching negotiated settlements of self-determination wars. Twenty of the twenty-six settlements achieved between 1956 and 2001 were negotiated by democratic governments—often after new leaders came to power during transitions from autocracy to democracy.[13]

Self-determination wars are easiest to settle in their early years. Between 1988 and 1994 eleven began in the USSR, Yugoslavia, and their successor states. By 2000 all had been contained or settled except in Chechnya, after an average of three years of fighting. During the same seven years, from 1988 to 1994, another thirteen self-determination wars began in Africa and Asia. By 2000 five of the six new African wars were over and four of seven Asian wars, after an average of about seven years of fighting. International engagement helped end most of the separatist wars in the post-communist states, which helps account for their short durations. Asian and African separatist wars usually were contained or settled without international mediation or peacekeeping, which helps explain the fact that they persisted more than twice as long as those in post-communist states. By contrast, the longer self-determination wars drag on, the more resistant they are to either containment or settlement. The average duration of the twenty-six armed conflicts being fought at the end of 2001 was twenty-three years and their median duration eighteen years. Two-thirds are being fought in Asia, most of the others in Africa.

Less visible than the recent shift toward settlement of wars of self-determination is a parallel trend toward accommodation of self-determination conflicts that have not yet escalated to protracted rebellion. An example from the early 1990s was the sequence of political shifts and negotiations that preempted an ethnic rebellion by the Gagauz in Moldova. One remarkable and little-noticed achievement of democratic Russia has been the successful negotiation of sub-state autonomy agreements with Tatarstan, Bashkiria, and some forty other regions in the Russian Federation.[14] These agreements provide models that could and should have been employed to head off ethnic wars in Chechnya and Kosovo. Accommodation failed in these two instances because of the intransigence of one or both parties to the disputes and, in the case of Kosovo, international mismanagement.[15]

(4) International Engagement in Containing Ethnic Conflict: International support for group rights, democratization, and autonomy agreements have had some negative, as well as positive, consequences. Not least, international policies have encouraged some putative national groups to assert their ethnonational identities and demand self-determination. International engagement is usually necessary, though rarely sufficient, to induce contenders in ethnonational conflicts to give up demands for total independence and to persuade state elites to extend some form of sub-state autonomy.

The emergent norm is that international and regional organizations, and individual states, have responsibilities to engage in such conflicts and to engage, using force if necessary, to check gross violations of human rights. As a practical consequence the protagonists in self-determination conflicts are very likely to face multilateral and bilateral pressures to reach negotiated settlements. Some such efforts are highly publicized, not necessarily to good effect, while others take less visible diplomatic forms. The best-known models for sub-state autonomy agreements have been reached through negotiated settlements of ethnonational rebellions. Such rebellions usually begin with demands for complete independence—and usually end with negotiated or de facto autonomy for the ethnonationalists. What can be discerned is a growing disposition of parties to these conflicts to work toward accommodation in early stages rather than after prolonged warfare. Serbia became the pariah state and bombing range of Europe in 1999 precisely because militant Serb nationalists blatantly violated principles about group rights and autonomy in Kosovo that elsewhere have become widely accepted.

The United Nations Security Council has authorized fifty-two peacekeeping operations during the past half-century, fifteen of which were in place in early 2001. Most of them aimed at containing armed conflicts within states.[16] Current debates within and about the U.N. responsibility for internal conflicts focus on two issues, first improving the capacity of the U.N. to anticipate and respond proactively to emerging crises and second, improving the effectiveness of U.N. peace operations. Improving peace operations is the objective of the "Brahimi Report," named for Lakhdar Brahimi, the Algerian diplomat who chaired the panel that prepared it. This report to the U.N. Secretary General in late 2000 recommended comprehensive reforms including long-term strategies for conflict prevention; better Secretariat capacity for strategic analysis, planning, and support of peace operations; the need for bigger, better equipped peacekeeping forces with robust rules of engagement; and means to support more rapid and effective deployment, preferably within thirty days of a Security Council resolution authorizing an operation. This ambitious set of proposals illustrates the current evolution of the doctrine of international engagement. Its acceptability was signaled when the Security Council adopted a resolution that endorsed the report's key recommendations (U.N. Security Council Resolution 1327, 13 November 2000).

The U.N. has often suggested that regional organizations take more responsibility for conflict management. Some have done so with Security Council authorization and some have not—most recently and notably NATO's 1999 intervention in Kosovo. In general there is great variability in the willingness and ability of regional organizations to engage in societal conflicts. European organizations—the European Union and the OSCE—have been proactive in identifying and reacting to potential as well as current conflicts, for example in Macedonia in 2001. The Organization of American States and, especially since the early 1990s, the Organisation of African Unity also have sought to prevent and mitigate armed conflicts. No such regional efforts are evident in Asia. Also at issue is the role of individual states in peacekeeping operations. The U.S. and Russia have engaged in unilateral peacekeeping operations, Nigeria and South Africa have done so through the guise of sub-regional organizations. The criticism inevitably leveled at such operations is that, whatever their rationale, they aim at advancing the initiating countries' national interests. Nonetheless they can be expected to recur whenever the U.N. and regional organizations fail to act.

Another issue is the fact that some regional powers, like India and China, cannot initiate preventive or peacekeeping measures without raising profound suspicions among neighbors about their motives. Russia, China, and India also are examples of regional powers whose policies toward domestic challengers are all but impervious to international engagement. There is little chance that international cavalry will ride to the rescue of rebellious Chechens, Uighers, or Kashmiris. The examples in this and the previous paragraph suggest that application of the principle of international engagement is and will continue to be constrained by realist considerations.

(5) International Use of Force to Contain Armed Conflicts: Threats of international use of force and military presence have a critical and expanding role in the process of engagement. Jentleson argues vigorously for what he calls *coercive prevention*, saying that "while coercion rarely is sufficient for prevention, it often is necessary" and that without it, "we will continue to do too little too late to prevent ethnic wars and other deadly conflicts."[17] The doctrine of coercive prevention means the use of credible threats of military action to deter fighting and gross human rights violations, as well as to compel an end to them once underway. Coercive prevention may include preventive deployment of military forces, as was done in Macedonia in 1993 and, as Jentleson points out, should have been done in East Timor before or immediately after the August 30, 1999, independence referendum there.

When preventive means fail to deter conflicts that pose serious threats to regional security or cause gross violations of human rights, the U.N. and some regional organizations have come to accept the obligation to respond with military sanctions and peace enforcement operations. Historically most U.N.-authorized peacekeeping forces were used to ensure implementation of agreements that had largely ended hostilities. Peace enforcement refers to the evolving doctrine and strategies by which force is used proactively to contain ongoing conflict even in the absence of agreement by the contenders. A recurring criticism of the U.N. Security Council during the 1990s was that it authorized peacekeeping missions in situations where missions should have been authorized, manned, and equipped for robust peace enforcement operations, for example in Bosnia (UNPRFOR, 1992-95), Rwanda (UNAMIR, 1993-96), Sierra Leone (UNOMSIL, 1998-99), and most recently in eastern Congo.[18]

One further step in the evolution of international doctrine of engagement is acceptance of the principle that, when authority and security have collapsed, multilateral force can be used to maintain international protectorates while civil governance is reestablished. In effect this has happened in Kosovo and East Timor but it is too soon to suggest that the precedents establish a general principle. The U.N. and the United States initially suggested that a similar policy should be followed in Afghanistan following the collapse of the Taliban regime late in 2001.

Proactive international engagement in societal conflicts implies long-term responsibilities. Once settlements have been brokered and civil order reestablished, outside actors have an obligation to provide the material assistance and political guarantees needed to ensure that peace is sustained. A case can be made that if international actors use political and military means to contain internal conflict, they have a normative obligation to help pick up the pieces afterward. As a practical matter, early withdrawal risks losing all the gains achieved by intervention. In fact political and military engagement has been sustained, more often than not, in most internationalized civil conflicts of the 1990s. The United States' long-term support of peace processes in Northern Ireland and the Middle East is one kind of example. The continued presence of peacekeepers and civilian advisors in Bosnia, Kosovo, and East Timor is another. But there also are counter-examples. One was the 1994 withdrawal of U.N. forces from Somalia, after the deaths of 100 peacekeepers (including 18 U.S. Rangers). Outside parties also gave up on implementation of peace accords in Angola in late 1998; peacekeepers were pulled out and diplomatic efforts suspended in view of overwhelming evidence that both UNITA and the Luanda government wanted to fight on.

Conditionalities

Five principles for managing conflict in heterogeneous societies have taken firm hold in international norms and practice during the last decade. I have referred to them collectively as a new regime, a doctrine, or simply a set of "good practices." In prescriptive form they read as follows:

- The individual and collective rights of racial,

ethnic, and religious minorities require international recognition and protection

- Democratic institutions are the preferred domestic means for guaranteeing group rights in heterogeneous societies and for pursuing political programs to redress inequalities
- Conflicts over self-determination are best settled through negotiations that provide regional autonomy and institutional means for pursuing collective interests within existing states
- International and regional organizations have responsibilities for protecting and promoting minority rights, anticipating and deterring the onset of ethnic wars, and promoting and enforcing negotiated settlements in wars once they are underway
- When preventive means fail to deter ethnic and other conflicts that threaten regional security or gross violations of human rights, the U.N. and individual states acting with international authorization have the right and obligation to respond with military sanctions and peace enforcement operations.

These principles are not uncontroversial. Some liberals contend that individual rights, but not collective rights, deserve international protection. Leaders of new states fear that autonomy arrangements will weaken national identity and contribute to political fragmentation. Many in the global South question the right of international actors to judge and intervene in their domestic affairs. Nonetheless the principles are widely asserted and acted on. They are invoked by the United Nations, by major powers, by European and some other regional organizations, by non-governmental organizations, and by members of civil society in countries divided by political and ethnic cleavages. And, as the evidence suggests, application of the principles has contributed to a substantial improvement in the status of minorities in most parts of the world and a steady diminution of deadly ethnic conflict.

International doctrine and practice for managing conflict in heterogeneous societies remain a work in progress. They have evolved in a trial-and-error process that will continue for the foreseeable future. Each democratic transition in a divided society, each new diplomatic offensive aimed at a crisis situation, each new peace enforcement operation is in part a political experiment whose success or failure shapes and constrains future engagement. These are some of the big lessons learned thus far.

- Promoting democratic transitions and power-sharing in heterogeneous societies is risky business. The poorer the country and the deeper its divisions, the less likely are new institutions to take root. If they are to have a chance, they require sustained political and material nurturing by outside actors.
- The most effective strategies of conflict management are usually those applied early, before the onset of armed conflict or gross violations of human rights, not late. Prevention by political and diplomatic means is less costly than the costs of coercive intervention and reconstruction. The point is widely recognized by policy makers, observers, and scholars but not yet consistently acted upon. The problem is two-fold. One is the lack of reliable and convincing risk assessments about crises that lie more than a year or two over the horizon. The second is that policy-makers in the U.N. and the major powers focus most of their limited political and material resources on containment of immediate crises.[19]
- The most effective kinds of engagement are both multilateral and multidimensional. The multilateral principle is well established with regard to peacekeeping and peace enforcement operations. Less widely recognized is the principle that effective engagement in any crisis situation requires collaborative planning among interested states and the U.N. to design strategies that integrate diplomatic, political, economic, and military moves.
- Strategies should be designed with fall-back objectives. The first objective is to forestall

violent conflict in high-risk situations. When prevention fails (or is not attempted), the second-best objective is to induce the warring parties to negotiate an end to conflict. If efforts to induce settlement fail, plan three should be to contain spillovers from armed conflict into neighboring states. Plan four is a peace enforcement mission, worth consideration where humanitarian costs and security threats are high. Successful peace enforcement missions, as suggested at several points above, presuppose a high degree of resolve (or political will) on the part of states that lead such missions and a long-term commitment of resources.

- Military options should always be on the table, not as separate strategies but as part of the meta-strategy of engagement. The options range from coercive deterrence, to rescue and training missions, to peacekeeping and peace enforcement, to air and ground warfare. Any threat or use of these actions in specific conflict situations should be integrated vertically with the larger political strategy designed to deal with the conflict, and horizontally across all participating states and international organizations.
- There are no fixed scenarios of political and military engagement. A Sierra Leone requires different strategies than Kosovo or Iraqi Kurdistan or Afghanistan. It is possible to profile high-risk situations, identifying countries and regions at high risk of humanitarian crises and ethnic wars with reasonable accuracy.[20] It is much more difficult to design optimum responses except in the context of a given region, country, and conflict situation. There is always the risk that policy-makers will learn the wrong lessons from a particular success or failure, using it as a simple guide about what (not) to do next time. "Next time" in fact is likely to differ significantly from "last time."

Moreover it is important to recognize that the five principles for peace-building in divided societies cannot be expected to contain all internal wars, for reasons suggested at various points above. Intense and protracted ethnic wars like those in Sudan, Sri Lanka, and Chechnya have a momentum that is very difficult to check. Antagonists may not want their conflicts settled; rather some are determined to win. Others do not accept the basic principles of power-sharing and democratic governance that are essential to most negotiated settlements.

Despite the best efforts of international actors to shore up weak states, failed states will continue to provide both incentives and opportunities for future wars. The Democratic Republic of Congo is an example. Like Somalia and Sierra Leone it is not even a "state," rather it has become a political arena in which a multiplicity of local and foreign contenders are fighting for control of resources and local power.

It also is the case that some parts of the world are off-limits to the operation of the five principles because regional hegemony like India, Russia, and China reject intervention in their spheres of influence. This does not mean that engagement is irrelevant in these regions. On the contrary, quiet but persistent diplomatic and political initiatives should be pursued, not because they are likely to succeed in the short run, but because they increase the long-run prospects for proactive peacemaking in places like Kashmir and Tibet, if and when a regime change or regional crisis provides a political opening.

The Challenge of Afghanistan

The evolution of international doctrine and practice for promoting peace in heterogeneous societies was one of the signal accomplishments of the international community during the post-Cold War era. It inspired many sustained and creative efforts to contain and settle serious conflicts that once were thought to be intractable. And it has many successes to its credit including recognition of minority rights by new democratic regimes in

East Central Europe and Asia, internal wars ended in southern Africa and Central America, humanitarian crises checked in Timor and Kosovo, serious ethnic conflicts deflected in the Baltic states. These successes should be enough to offset skepticism induced by failures to end warlord rule in Somalia, or halt genocide in Rwanda, or dissuade Pakistan and India from fighting a proxy war in Kashmir.

Let me conclude by asking whether the U.S.-led assault on the Taliban regime in Afghanistan in late 2001 challenges the emerging doctrine sketched here. I think not. Intractable though the Afghan conflict has seemed, it was the focus of international efforts at negotiated settlement throughout the 1990s. In recent years three parallel peace-tracks sought to end fighting between the Taliban and the Northern Alliance and to establish a multi-ethnic coalition government in Kabul. The U.S. was party to the "six-plus-two group"—the six states bordering Afghanistan plus Russia and the U.S.—that issued the Tashkent Declaration in July 2000 which aimed at this objective. The U.N., the Organization of the Islamic Conference, and supporters of Zahir Shah, the former king of Afghanistan, worked toward the same end.

The new U.S. strategy for eliminating Osama bin Laden's base of support is, in the language used above, "both multilateral and multidimensional." Intensive diplomatic effort has been given to building a supportive international coalition. A serious effort has been made to articulate the military campaign with a political strategy to lay the groundwork for a post-Taliban coalition government—a strategy that involves the parties and invokes the principles of previous peace efforts. The U.S. and its allies have encouraged Pashtun leaders to defect from the Taliban and at the outset held back military support for the Northern Alliance, to further the political objective of establishing a broadly based successor government. Observers and policy-makers recognize that Afghanistan is a humanitarian and economic disaster area and that major efforts will be needed for economic as well as political reconstruction of a post-Taliban Afghanistan. A multinational peacekeeping and police force are being deployed. The U.N. Development Program and the World Bank plan a long-term reconstruction effort. In short, the U.S.-led approach to Afghanistan may be driven by the desire to retaliate against massive terrorism, but it is guided by many of the principles and lessons learned during the 1990s about how best to build peace in divided societies.

Notes

1. This chapter incorporates arguments developed in the author's *Peoples versus States: Minorities at Risk in the New Century* (Washington, DC: United States Institute of Peace Press, 2000), chap. 8, and his chapter "Containing Internal War in the Twenty-First Century," in Fen Osler Hampson and David M. Malone (eds.), *From Reaction to Conflict Prevention: Opportunities for the UN System* (Boulder, CO and London: Lynne Rienner, 2002), pp. 41-62. It also makes use of evidence reported in Ted Robert Gurr, Monty G. Marshall, and Deepa Khosla, *Peace and Conflict 2001: A Global Survey of Armed Conflicts, Self-Determination Movements, and Democracy* (College Park, MD: Center for International Development and Conflict Management, 2001). Monty G. Marshall analyzed the trends in group discrimination and democratization reported here.

2. See, for example, Hugh Miall, (ed.), *Minority Rights in Europe: Prospects for a Transnational Regime* (New York: Council on Foreign Relations Press, 1994); and Jennifer Jackson Preece, "National Minority Rights vs. State Sovereignty in Europe: Changing Norms in International Relations?" *Nations and Nationalism* 3, no. 3 (1997), pp. 345-364.

3. Preece, "National Minority Rights vs. State Sovereignty," pp. 357-360, quotations from pp. 345-346, 359.

4. Note that this approach uses an intra-societal standard of comparison rather than attempting to assess the implementation of universal norms. The approach is explained in Ted Robert Gurr and James R. Scarritt, "Minorities Rights at Risk: A Global Survey," *Human Rights Quarterly* 11 (1989), pp. 375-405. For detailed ex-

amples and a survey of global evidence in the late 1990s see Gurr, *Peoples versus States* (note 1), chap. 4. Annual information on group discrimination from 1950 to 2000 was recoded in 2001 by research teams of the Minorities at Risk (MAR) project headed by Victor Assal and Randi Mack, analyzed by Monty G. Marshall, and is summarized here. For more information on the MAR project see its web site at www.bsos.umd.edu/cidcm/mar.

5. Data on economic discrimination trace the same global and regional trends but change more gradually over time.

6. Leading NGOs in North American and Europe promote these principles, notably the National Endowment for Democracy in the United States and the International Institute for Democracy and Electoral Assistance in Sweden. A good statement of the norms and practices alluded to in the text is Peter Harris and Ben Reilly (eds.), *Democracy and Deep-Rooted Conflict: Options for Negotiators* (Stockholm: International IDEA, 1998).

7. Procedures used to distinguish democratic, autocratic, and transitional regimes are summarized in Gurr, Marshall, and Khosla, *Peace and Conflict 2001* (note 1), pp. 19-20 and, in more detail, by Keith Jaggers and Ted Robert Gurr, "Tracking Democracy's Third Wave with the Polity III Data," *Journal of Peace Research*, 31, no. 4 (1995), pp. 469-482. Annual codes for all independent countries from 1800 to 2000 are available at www.bsos.umd.edu/cidcm/inscr/polity.

8. The evidence is summarized in Gurr, *Peoples versus States* (note 1), pp.163-177.

9. On Burundi see Michael Lund, Barnett R. Rubin, and Fabienne Hara, "Learning from Burundi's Filed Democratic Transition, 1993-1996: Did International Initiatives Match the Problem?" in Barnett R. Rubin (ed.), *Cases and Strategies for Preventive Action* (New York: Century Press for the Center for Preventive Action, 1998), pp. 47-92.

10. Examples include the Turkish Cypriot Republic, the TransDniester Republic in Moldova, Abkhazia in Georgia, and Somaliland and Puntland in Somalia.

11. A recent comparative analysis is John Darby, *The Effects of Violence on Peace Processes* (Washington, DC: United States Institute of Peace Press, 2001). My survey of the outcomes of self-determination movements, completed in late 2000, identified eleven "contested agreements"—conflicts in which an interim or final agreement had been negotiated, but was rejected and actively opposed by parties within the group or government, or both. See Gurr, Marshall, and Khosla, *Peace and Conflict 2001* (note 1), pp. 4-5.

12. The survey and assessment of self-determination movements is reported in Gurr, Marshall, and Khosla, *Peace and Conflict 2001* (note 1), pp. 14-21 and 29-32.

13. Based on global comparisons using the Minorities at Risk dataset, summarized in *Peoples versus States* (note 1), pp. 163-174 and 204-206, and in Gurr, Marshall, and Khosla, *Peace and Conflict 2001* (note 1), pp. 20-21.

14. Only some of these forty regions were potentially secessionist. An account of Russia's successful management of regional conflicts is Daniel S. Treisman, *After the Deluge: Regional Crises and Political Consolidation in Russia* (Ann Arbor, MI: University of Michigan Press, 1999). However, Graeme P. Herd contends that after August 1998 the centrifugal tendencies accelerated and that Russia's federal system of governance "is disintegrating not by design but by default" in "Russia: Systemic Transformation or Federal Collapse?" *Journal of Peace Research* 36 (May 1999): 259–269, quote from p. 259.

15. See Steven L. Burg, "Nationalism and Civic Identity: Ethnic Models for Macedonia and Kosovo," in *Cases and Strategies for Preventive Action*, vol. 2, *Preventive Action Reports*, (ed.), Barnett R. Rubin (New York: Century Foundation Press, 1998), chap. 2, for a study of preventive strategies for Kosovo and Macedonia, written before conflicts intensified. Studies that document the descent into war and repression after the fact include Mohammed Sahnoun's first-hand account, *Somalia: The Missed Opportunities* (Washington, DC: United States Institute of Peace Press, 1994) and Valerie Tishkov's analysis of the origins of the Chechen war, "Ambition and the Arrogance of Power," in his *Ethnicity, Nationalism, and Conflict in and after the Soviet Union: The Mind Aflame* (London: Sage Publications for the International Peace Research Institute, Oslo, 1997), chaps. 9, 10.

16. There was a flood of writings during the 1990s and early 2000s on the normative and legal bases of forceful international intervention in societal conflicts.

See, for example, Barbara Harff, "Rescuing Endangered Peoples: Missed Opportunities" and other contributions to the Spring 1995 special issue of Social Research, vol. 62 (Spring 1995); Thomas G. Weiss and Cindy Collins, Humanitarian Challenges and Intervention, 2d ed. (Boulder, CO: Westview Press, 2000); and, for a comprehensive review, The Responsibility to Protect: Research, Bibliography, Background: Supplementary Volume to the Report of the International Commission on Intervention and State Sovereignty (Ottawa: International Development Research Centre, 2001).

17. Bruce W. Jentleson, *Coercive Prevention: Normative, Political, and Policy Dilemmas,* Peaceworks No. 35 (Washington, DC: United States Institute of Peace, October 2000), p. 5.

18. Many factors, political as well as military, internal as well as international, contribute to the failures of UN-authorized peacekeeping missions. See for example Dennis C. Jett, *Why Peacekeeping Fails* (New York: St. Martin's Press, 1999).

19. European institutions are something of an exception to this generalization. They have been relatively effective in anticipating and heading off potentially serious ethnic conflicts in the post-Communist states of East and Central Europe. See P. Terrence Hoppman, *Building Security in Post-Cold War Eurasia: The OSCE and U.S. Foreign Policy* (Washington, DC: United States Institute of Peace Press, 1999) and Bruce W. Jentleson (ed.), *Opportunities Missed, Opportunities Seized* (Lanham, MD.: Rowman & Littlefield, 2000).

20. Social scientists have a growing capacity to provide empirically based assessments of the risks and stages of ethnic and political conflict that complement the more conventional expert-based assessments used by foreign policy-makers. See the approaches and evidence in John L. Davies and Ted Robert Gurr (eds.), *Preventive Measures: Building Risk Assessment and Crisis Early Warning Systems* (Lanham, MD: Rowman & Littlefield, 1998) and Hayward R. Alker, Ted Robert Gurr, and Kumar Rupesinghe (eds.), *Journeys Through Conflict: Narratives and Lessons* (Lanham, MD: Rowman & Littlefield, 2001).

The Myth of Ethnic Warfare: Understanding Conflict in the Post-Cold War World

Charles King
Georgetown University

The deadly clashes that erupted between Russians and ethnic Tatars in the early 1990s were utterly predictable, According to Stuart J. Kaufman's *Modern Hatreds: The Symbolic Politics of Ethnic War* (2001). Having invaded the Russian steppes alongside the Mongols in the thirteenth century, the Tatars were seen by medieval Russian chroniclers as the epitome of Oriental barbarism. Although the power of the Tatars eventually waned, the Russians did not forget their misery at the hands of these Muslim invaders. In the sixteenth century, Ivan the Terrible razed the Tatar capital. Two centuries later, Tatar nomads were brutally driven as far as China. And during the Second World War, Stalin deported thousands of Tatar families to Central Asia. Once the Soviet Union began to falter, Tatars in several regions began to call for greater rights and eventual independence. Those demands set off a spiral of fear and loathing that drew fuel from the memory of bloodshed on both sides.

The only problem with this story is that there were no such deadly clashes in the 1990s. Russia devolved sovereignty to Tatarstan, one of the federation's constituent republics, without any violence. So successful was the process, in fact, that the "Tatar model" is now touted as a template for how Russia's relations with its other ethnic minorities should work.

Had modern Tatar autonomy not come about so painlessly, it would have been easy to read the bloodshed as yet another case of the inevitable clash of civilizations. Just such an impulse explains why Russia's ongoing war against Chechnya still sends observers scrambling for their Lermontov and Tolstoy: to search for historical allusions to Moscow's long-standing entanglement in the same zone. But as Stuart J. Kaufman shows in his ambitious new book, *Modern Hatreds,* explaining contemporary wars with reference to ancient troubles is not only a terrible cliché—it is also fundamentally wrong.

The Seeds of Conflict

In years to come, what looks today like a disconnected string of small, brutish wars across southeastern Europe and Eurasia—five in the former Yugoslavia and six in the former Soviet Union—is more likely to be considered by historians to be part of one process: the wars of communist succession. Most of these battles pitted newly independent governments against territorial separatists, but all sprang from a range of disparate causes: the collapse of federations, the end of authoritarianism, the reemergence of old quarrels, the meddling of outside powers, political demagoguery, and—a major catalyst of organized violence everywhere—plain old thuggery.

The puzzle is not why there were so many recent wars in this region, but why there were not more. Given the fact that every ethnic group in the area has been hard done by at some point in its history, why have only some of the aggrieved become aggressors? Kaufman assays four possible explanations. One is the ancient hatreds view, the idea that some of these ethnic groups have been at each other's throats for centuries and thus conflicts between them are likely to continue. A second answer is based on the power of unscrupulous and manipulative politicians who profit from communal rivalries. A third looks to economics, arguing that contests over resources can quickly turn poor communities against perceived exploiters and rich ones against freeloaders. And a fourth answer is based on what scholars call a security dilemma. With no overarching institutions left in the region to ensure law and order, survival became a self-help game. But one group's effort to increase its own security—by stockpiling Kalashnikovs, say—automatically reduces the security of its rivals, thereby setting off a spiral toward war.

Yet as Kaufman shows, each of these explanations for why war occurred is insufficient on its own. People do feel strongly about their ethnicity, but very few convinced nationalists actually go so far as to exterminate their neighbors. Maniacal leaders clearly play an important role in civil wars, but simply saying so does not explain why some end up as powerful demagogues while others simply rant in obscurity. Economic grievances and security dilemmas can also push groups toward violence, but such explanations predict far more conflict than actually occurs in the world.

Kaufman's solution to this conundrum is to focus on what he calls the "symbolic politics" of conflicts—that is, how existing beliefs about neighboring ethnic groups are used to justify violence, and how these beliefs then seem to be confirmed once violence breaks out. Kaufman focuses on several wars that broke out during the collapse of communism: in the Dniester region of Moldova, in Georgia's South Ossetia and Abkhazia, in the Nagorno-Karabakh enclave inside Azerbaijan, and in the former Yugoslavia. These conflicts all raged from the early to the mid-1990s and left hundreds of thousands dead and millions displaced.

In a series of lucidly written case studies, Kaufman argues that each of these wars displayed three conditions essential for communal violence. First, in each case politicians used a preexisting reservoir of myths about rival ethnic populations to mobilize the public along cultural lines. Second, in every instance particular ethnic groups feared being swamped—economically, politically, and demographically—by other groups. And third, in each of these wars the communities involved had plenty of time to mobilize and shore up their own security before their neighbors got the upper hand. Without any one of these ingredients, Kaufman says, these postcommunist conflicts would never have occurred.

Imagined Communities

It is difficult to argue with any of Kaufman's claims. He is certainly right that each of the individual explanations for conflict he describes is, on its own, inadequate. And no one would deny that all civil conflicts have a volatile mix at their core: myths that can be mustered into service, politicians willing to use those myths, and a state apparatus too weak to ensure basic civil order.

The problem with Kaufman's explanation, however, is determining whether a thing called "ethnic war" even exists. Of course, there are such things as ethnic groups, and they do occasionally come into conflict—although as Kaufman rightly points out, they do so far less often than we normally think. But it is worth asking whether talking about a distinct category of violence called "ethnic war" is as useful as Kaufman (and many others) think.

How we label an armed conflict often has very little to do with anything intrinsic to the conflict itself. Think, for example, about how rare it is today to hear anyone talk of "insurgencies." Yet this term was once the standard way of referring to many civil wars around the world, especially those in which the so-called insurgents were supported by the Soviet Union. The idea of "ethnic war" may be similarly contingent, the product of a particular time and place—the time being the end of the Cold War and the place being Europe. After all, the upsurge in writing on ethnicity and violence in the last decade is a direct result of the fact that the wars in the Balkans interested Western policy-makers. That does not necessarily mean, however, that communal violence is a new phenomenon, or that there is more of it now than in the past (in fact, there is less), or that the types of conflicts that arose in the 1990s are significantly different from those that have long raged in many other parts of the world. Indeed, on the scale of human misery, the postcommunist wars barely register: they involved relatively few deaths, they lasted for only a short time, and crucially, they attracted the attention of the great powers, in particular the United States.

The "ethnic conflict" label is fine as an easy shorthand for wars in which the belligerents define themselves, in part, along cultural lines. But viewing such conflicts as essentially different from any other instances of large-scale violence within a single state can be misleading, in two senses. First, hatred does not need much scaffolding. In some cases, the cultural myths that Kaufman identifies as essential to violence are long-standing—as between Armenians and Azerbaijani "Turks," for example. But in plenty of others the myths were manufactured in relatively short order, and usually after violence had already started. There was little in Georgian or Abkhaz national mythology to explain the depth of hatred that arose during the conflict there. And in Moldova, one would have had to be very creative to forge a coherent narrative of oppression on either side. Most civil wars—whether involving ethnic groups, ideological factions, or any other social category—have a way of manufacturing their own inevitability.

Second, the "ethnic conflict" label can encourage analysts and potential peacemakers to conflate two distinct issues—the pathologies of individual belief and the rational motivations for group mobilization—or, in other words, to mistake the causes of hatred for the causes of violence. The former is about precisely the "symbolic politics" that Kaufman identifies, the narratives of national suffering that can be useful in whipping up the masses. The latter is about getting armies into the field, and for that no amount of symbol manipulating will get anywhere without a leadership and a state bureaucracy intent on perpetrating violence. Why people hate each other ought to concern psychologists and marriage counselors. Why they kill en masse is the purview of social scientists and statesmen.

Kaufman courageously offers what he calls "a systematic general theory" of ethnic conflict: myths of oppression and revenge create dividing lines between social groups; real fears for communal survival create an incentive for mobilization; a faltering state, a strong leader, or an outside power provides the spark that ignites all-out violence. Take away any one of the three elements and the violence fizzles. It is easy enough to do this kind of analysis after a conflict has already broken out, as Kaufman has done. But probably the best that pundits or theorists can do is point out what countries and peoples are most at risk. We cannot know for certain why large-scale violence, of whatever type, breaks out. Even if we could, the factors involved would probably be disappointingly banal: clashing economic interests, politicians' attempts to oust opponents, lots of young men with nothing to do and easy access to guns. The rest is, to use a technical term, history.

All this is particularly relevant to the post-Soviet cases on which Kaufman bases his argument. After reading this book, one might come away with the idea that Georgia, Moldova, and Azerbaijan remain embroiled in internal disputes largely because of the myths, fears, and opportunities that originally sparked the wars. But in all these cases, the issues that first brought the various sides to blows are very different from the dynamics that have perpetuated the quarrels.

In each of these regions, a tense cease-fire has been in place since the mid-1990s, but no progress has been made toward a final peace accord. Today, much of these states' territories is controlled by unrecognized but fully functional quasi states: the so-called republics of Abkhazia and South Ossetia (in Georgia), the Dniester Moldavian republic (in Moldova), and the republic of Nagorno-Karabakh (in Azerbaijan). None of these statelets has a seat at the United Nations. None is recognized by any sovereign country. But each possesses the basic desiderata of statehood—a population, a territory, a government, an army, an economy—and functions about as well as (and in some cases, better than) the flaccid countries of which each is still supposedly a part.

The Organization for Security and Cooperation in Europe and the U.N. have spent the better part of a decade "mediating" these various disputes, and the organizations' main strategy has been to address precisely those beliefs and insecurities that Kaufman identifies. That approach has led nowhere, however, and for one simple reason: Ethnic myths and fears have become largely irrelevant to most of the actors in these dramas. In fact, the current status quo—no fighting but no final peace accord, either—suits most folks just fine. The separatists get a de facto country. Corrupt officials in the central governments get a transit route for illegal commerce. Foreign governments get relative peace and, therefore, no Christiane Amanpour on the scene to raise concerns at home. International organizations get multiple rounds of "negotiations" and willing recipients for their good offices.

In the long run, however, everyone ends up a loser. The unresolved disputes have had cancerous effects on the regions where they occurred, feeding corruption, weakening governance, and gnawing away at what little democracy exists in Georgia, Moldova, and Azerbaijan. They have created havens for international criminals and conduits for the smuggling of drugs, weapons, and people into Europe and beyond. None of that, incidentally, has much to do with ethnicity.

The Way to War

What does all of this mean for policy? Kaufman rightly calls on outside powers to pay greater attention to potential conflict areas before war erupts. Some of his recommendations are supremely reasonable: to focus on pre-crisis peacebuilding rather than post-crisis peacekeeping, to encourage historians to write less tendentiously, to name and shame politicians who trot out ethnic stereotypes in political campaigns. Others—such as the idea that national epics glorifying war should be "banned" (by whom? on whose reading?)—cannot possibly be meant seriously. And no form of outside intervention, however early, can guarantee success. After all, it would be difficult to find a more concerted recent effort at peacebuilding than occurred in Macedonia, a case that Kaufman cites approvingly. (The book was published too early to take full account of the recent violence there between the government and Albanian guerrillas.) Long before the shooting started, school curricula were reformed under the eyes of the U.N. and major nongovernmental organizations. Internationally mediated talks were held. There was even a Macedonian version of *Sesame Street,* created and funded by foreigners, that featured cast members from all of Macedonia's ethnic groups living in harmony. The show became wildly popular with local children. But as for the results, consult CNN.

The real lesson to be learned from the postcommunist conflicts, including the latest one in Macedonia, is probably different from the one Kaufman intended. Myths, fears, and opportunities might be a good recipe for a pogrom, but they rarely lead to large-scale, sustained violence. For that, you need the same kinds of forces that sustain any war, whether "ethnic" or otherwise: entrepreneurs who benefit from the violence, arms supplied by foreign powers, charismatic leadership, and plenty of bored young men. And these are the same factors that external governments and international organizations are most useful at counteracting—that is, in the rare instances when they have both the will and the wherewithal to get involved. Outsiders can, as Kaufman recommends, try to ban books, shut down radio transmissions, rewrite school curricula, and enforce an internationally acceptable standard of ethnic correctness on historians and teachers. But silencing every bigot in the world would require a monumental effort—one for which afflicted states do not have the cash, nor Western governments the fortitude.

Besides, the attempt would probably yield only spotty results and violate the principle of state sovereignty in the process. Kaufman's symbolic politics account offers an intriguing analysis of communal violence, but the policy recommendations that flow from it are, to say the least, disconcerting.

Still, Kaufman's chief insight is that the obstacles to violence are usually pretty high. Hence the large number of disputes across the postcommunist world that could have descended into war but never did: between Romanians and Hungarians, Estonians and Russians, Bulgarians and Turks, even Russians and Tatars. Being mad as hell at one's neighbor is rarely enough to make people take up arms. When they do, it is usually only to defend something they stand to lose (their home) rather than to gamble on getting something they lack (their ancient homeland). *Modern Hatreds* presents a powerful critique of some of the currently popular but simplistic modes of understanding how conflicts start and describes how, in some rare cases, the obstacles to war were overcome with devastating results. This is a useful contribution to a larger process: trying to figure out why some chauvinists become Miloseviæ while others are content to write bad poetry.

Justice for Minorities

Hurst Hannum
Tufts University

In the same resolution that proclaimed the Universal Declaration of Human Rights on December 10, 1948, the General Assembly confessed its inability to agree even on general principles that would define and protect the rights of minority populations in independent countries. "It was difficult to adopt a uniform solution for this complex and delicate question [of minorities], which had special aspects in each State in which it arose."[1] While this did not mean that the United Nations ignored issues related to minorities in succeeding years, it did underscore the sensitivity with which the issue was viewed.

This sensitivity was due, in part, to abuses of the concept of minority rights by the Nazi regime in Germany, as well as to the Western-led push to recognize individual human rights for all, not just special rights for groups with powerful and interested neighbors. The United Nations and human rights advocates believed that the norms of equality and non-discrimination—combined, eventually, with the norm of self-determination in the form of decolonization—would suffice to protect the interests of groups in preserving their culture.[2] At the same time, most states (whether new or old) assumed that assimilation into the dominant culture would eventually decrease or even eliminate the need for special minority protections.

The United Nations did create a Sub-Commission on Prevention of Discrimination and Protection of Minorities, but its parent bodies soon made it clear that they preferred that the Sub-Commission focus on the first aspect of its mandate. The Sub-Commission eventually expanded its work to the whole range of human rights issues (to the occasional displeasure of the Commission on Human Rights), but it never regained its initial focus on discrimination and minority issues.

In its early years, the United Nations also addressed several specific situations in which minority issues were at the heart of political conflicts. These included Trieste, the Italian South Tyrol, the Croat and Slovene minorities in Austria, and Eritrea.[3] However, attention to such politically sensitive situations was more reminiscent of the selective attention to minority rights paid by the League of Nations than of the "universal" human rights proclaimed by the United Nations.

Finally, the adoption of the 1948 Genocide Convention is additional evidence of the United Nation's awareness of the potentially devastating consequences of unchecked violations of minority rights.

As human rights standard-setting expanded during the 1960s, several international texts were adopted that addressed aspects of minority rights.

The UNESCO Convention Against Discrimination in Education recognized, inter alia, the right of members of minorities to engage in their own educational activities, although these remained subject to the educational policy of each state.[4] The International Convention on the Elimination of All Forms of Racial Discrimination contained a broad definition of racial discrimination that incorporates discrimination against many minorities, i.e., any distinction "based on race, colour, descent, or national or ethnic origin."[5] Article 27 of the International Covenant on Civil and Political Rights addressed minority religious, linguistic, and cultural rights.[6]

In the mid-1970s, the Sub-Commission on Prevention of Discrimination and Protection of Minorities finally began to address minority issues in greater detail. In a well-received study, Special Rapporteur Francesco Capotorti outlined many of the problems facing minorities around the world and proposed what has remained perhaps the most widely accepted definition of a minority:

> [a] group numerically inferior to the rest of the population of a State, in a non-dominant position, whose members—being nationals of the State—possess ethnic, religious or linguistic characteristics differing from those of the rest of the population and show, if only implicitly, a sense of solidarity, directed towards preserving their culture, traditions, religion or language."[7]

Partially in response to the Capotorti report, in 1979 Yugoslavia introduced a draft declaration on minority rights to the UN Commission on Human Rights; thirteen years later (and, ironically, at about the same time that Yugoslavia itself disintegrated), the General Assembly finally adopted a Declaration on the Rights of Persons belonging to National or Ethnic, Religious or Linguistic Minorities ("Minorities Declaration").[8] In 1981, the General Assembly adopted a Declaration on the Elimination of All Forms of Intolerance and of Discrimination Based on Religion or Belief.[9]

None of the major regional human rights instruments adopted prior to the 1990s specifically refers to minority rights, with the exception of a rather vague reference to protecting "national minorities" that is found in the 1975 Helsinki Final Act of the Conference on Security and Cooperation in Europe.

Thus, even up to the early 1980s, minorities had received little formal recognition in international law. The minimalist rights recognized in the Civil and Political Covenant and the general non-discrimination rights in the Racial Discrimination Convention added very little to the scope of human rights applicable to all individuals, whether or not they also were members of a minority community. While the Helsinki Final Act inspired a resurgence of human rights activity in Eastern Europe and the Soviet Union, little attention was paid to minority issues per se.

Of course, members of minorities were frequently the victims of violations of "ordinary" human rights, such as those related to free expression, freedom of religion, freedom of association, and the right to engage in political activities. Complaints of discrimination were raised in UN and regional fora by groups as varied as Catholics in Northern Ireland, Kurds, Tamils in Sri Lanka, Tibetans, Bretons, German-speakers in Italy, Blacks in the United States, Fijian Indians, Ugandan Asians, Roma in various European countries, and politically marginalized tribes in many countries in Africa. Well before the end of the Cold War and the contemporary preoccupation with "ethnic conflicts," violent, ethnically charged conflicts erupted in Congo-Kinshasa, Nigeria, Pakistan, India, Sri Lanka, Turkey, Iraq, Lebanon, Cyprus, and Spain, and unfulfilled demands for "minority" rights often led to the assertion of rights to self-determination and secession.

Periodic reports submitted by states to the Human Rights Committee and the Committee on the Elimination of All Forms of Racial Discrimination tend to recite domestic legal provisions regarding minorities, but they rarely concede that members of minorities suffer any adverse consequences because of their minority status.[10]

Under the First Optional Protocol to the Civil and Political Covenant and article 14 to the Racial Discrimination Convention, individuals may file communications with the respective committees, alleging the violation of rights guaranteed under the treaties. Although the process tends to be long and relies purely on written evidence, some individuals have been able to receive redress under these procedures.

In interpreting article 27 of the Covenant, for example, the Human Rights Committee found that withdrawing the right of a woman to reside on an Indian reserve because of her marriage to a non-Indian violated her right, "in community with the other members of [her] group, to enjoy [her] own culture."[11] The Committee also has addressed whether or not various governmental acts interfere with the rights of ethnic Saami to engage in reindeer herding, an integral part of Saami culture.[12] The Committee determined that the reference in article 27 to minorities "within...States" does not include the English-speaking minority in the province of Quebec,[13] but a subsequent case held that freedom of expression under article 19 of the Covenant includes the right to express oneself in the language of one's choice outside the spheres of public life in which use of an official language may be required.[14]

The Committee on the Elimination of All Forms of Racial Discrimination has considered very few cases under article 14, and none of its first five cases dealt with minority rights per se.

New procedures to implement human rights norms created in the United Nations in the 1970s and 1980s largely responded to gross violations of civil and political rights rather than to the problems of vulnerable groups. The so-called "thematic mechanisms" of the Commission on Human Rights, for example, initially addressed violations of personal security and integrity, such as disappearances, arbitrary executions and detention, and torture (although a Rapporteur on religious intolerance was appointed by the Commission in 1986 and on racism and xenophobia in 1993). Nongovernmental organizations frequently voiced concerns over the situation of minorities in many states during statements to the Commission on Human Rights and Sub-Commission on Prevention of Discrimination and Protection of Minorities, but they were forced to couch their complaints in terms of traditional human rights. There was little acceptance of any affirmative obligation on the part of states to protect and promote minority cultures.[15]

Although many long-standing conflicts fueled by the East-West rivalry began to wind down in the 1980s, the political uncertainty and economic insecurity that followed the withdrawal of the Soviet Union from central and eastern Europe and, soon thereafter, the dissolution of the Soviet Union itself, brought new and widely publicized instances in which minority groups seemed to be the targets of persecution. Just as newly independent states in the 1960s often sacrificed pluralism and diversity on the altar of "nation building," those states freed from Soviet domination appeared to be more interested in consolidating their often ethnically-defined states than in tolerance.

The normative response to this new situation was surprisingly rapid. In 1990, the Copenhagen meeting of the Conference on the Human Dimension of the Conference on Security and Cooperation in Europe (CSCE) adopted a Final Document by consensus.[16] This remarkable document (which also contains detailed provisions relating to democracy, the rule of law, and other human rights issues) was drafted and agreed to in only six weeks, and it represents the first detailed articulation of minority rights by governments since the post-World War I minorities treaties. Its provisions went well beyond existing guarantees in article 27 of the Civil and Political Covenant, addressing, in particular, language use, education, and political participation.

Not to be outdone, the Council of Europe adopted and opened for ratification in 1992 a Charter on the Protection of Minority and Regional Languages.[17] Modeled after the European Social Charter, the 1992 Charter offers a wide range of obligations from among which States may choose the provisions they are willing to accept. In the following years, the Parliamentary Assembly of the Council of Europe recommended that a protocol on minority rights be added to the European Convention on Human Rights, although that suggestion has not yet been acted upon.[18] A more ambitious Framework Convention for the Protection of National Minorities was adopted in 1995.[19]

The Declaration on the Rights of Persons belonging to National or Ethnic, Religious or Linguistic Minorities was finally completed and adopted by the UN General Assembly in 1992.[20] While it continues the individualistic orientation of article 27 of the Covenant on Civil and Political Rights by referring to "the rights of persons" belonging to minorities, the Declaration does expand on existing provisions and contains progressive language related to minority participation in the political and economic life of the State. In addition, the Preamble recognizes that protecting minority rights will "contribute to the political and social stability of States in which they live" and, in turn, "contribute to the strengthening of friendship and co-operation among peoples and States."

The UN Declaration is the only universally applicable instrument on minority rights and was adopted by the General Assembly without a dissenting vote. Among the more noteworthy provisions of this relatively short declaration are the following paragraphs:

Article 1

1. States shall protect the existence and the national or ethnic, cultural, religious and linguistic identity of minorities within their respective territories, and shall encourage conditions for the promotion of that identity.

2. States shall adopt appropriate legislative and other measures to achieve these ends.

Article 2

2. Persons belonging to minorities have the right to participate effectively in cultural, religious, social, economic and public life.

3. Persons belonging to minorities have the right to participate effectively in decisions on the national and, where appropriate, regional level concerning the minority to which they belong or the regions in which they live, in a manner not incompatible with national legislation....

5. Persons belonging to minorities have the right to establish and maintain, without any discrimination, free and peaceful contacts with other members of their group and with persons belonging to other minorities, as well as contacts across frontiers with citizens of other States to whom they are related by national or ethnic, religious or linguistic ties....

Article 4

2. States shall take measures to create favourable conditions to enable persons belonging to minorities to express their characteristics and to develop their culture, language, religion, traditions and customs, except where specific practices are in violation of national law and contrary to international standards.

3. States should take appropriate measures so that, wherever possible, persons belonging to minorities have adequate opportunities to learn their mother tongue or to have instruction in their mother tongue....

5. States should consider appropriate measures so that persons belonging to minorities may participate fully in the economic progress and development in their country.

Article 5

1. National policies and programmes shall be planned and implemented with due regard for the legitimate interests of persons belonging to minorities.

Perhaps in an attempt to breathe more meaning into the narrow language of article 27 of the Civil and Political Covenant, the Human Rights Committee, after much debate, issued a General Comment on minority rights in 1994. The Committee observed in a cursory manner that "it is not relevant to determine the degree of permanence that the term 'exist' connotes" and then went on to express the view that article 27 applies to everyone belonging to one of the named categories of minorities and present within a country, including "migrant workers or even visitors."[21]

The Committee does not refer to the relevant legislative history to support its conclusions, and the General Comment is perhaps best interpreted as representing the personal views of Committee members rather than an authoritative interpretation of the text of the Covenant.[22] At the same time, however, the expansive reading is generally consistent with the more detailed principles set forth in the 1992 General Assembly Declaration.

Thus, by the fiftieth anniversary of the Universal Declaration, the international community had agreed on a fairly substantial set of norms concerned directly with the rights of minorities. While these norms remain largely undefined beyond the texts of the various instruments, they certainly go a considerable distance to offering the "uniform solution for this complex and delicate question" that eluded the drafters of the Universal Declaration of Human Rights in 1948.

Of course, members of minority groups who are victims of violations of either "new" minority rights defined since 1990 or the more traditional rights of non-discrimination and equality need procedures to enforce the rights that are guaranteed on paper. In addition to the activities of the Human Rights Committee and the Committee on the Elimination of All Forms of Racial Discrimination, referred to earlier…there are two additional mechanisms specifically concerned with minority rights that deserve attention.

Two years after adopting the Copenhagen Document, the CSCE (now known as the Organization on Security and Cooperation in Europe [OSCE]) created the position of High Commissioner on National Minorities, in order to provide "'early warning' and, as appropriate, 'early action' at the earliest possible stage in regard to tensions involving national minority issues that have the potential to develop into a conflict within the CSCE area, affecting peace, stability, or relations between participating States."[23] Although the high Commissioner's mandate is to prevent conflict rather than to protect minority rights per se, his interventions thus far appear to have contributed to both objectives.

The work of the High Commissioner is theoretically confidential, but the OSCE has authorized publication of most of his formal communications with governments. Primarily through quiet diplomacy, the High Commissioner (the position has been held by former Dutch Foreign Minister Max van der Stoel since its inception) has consulted with governments, NGOs, and others regarding the situations of, in particular, minorities in a number of newly independent states that were formerly part of the Soviet Union.[24] Although the High Commissioner cannot formally address violations of the rights of individuals, his office should certainly be viewed as a focal point to which aggrieved minorities within the geographic scope of the OSCE should appeal.

Following approval of the 1992 Minorities Declaration by the General Assembly, the UN Sub-Commission adopted a report on "the possible ways and means of facilitating the peaceful and constructive solution of problems involving minorities."[25] It was not until 1995 that the Commission on Human Rights agreed to create a mechanism to monitor observance of the Minorities Declaration, when it authorized the Sub-Commission to establish a five-member working group to "[r]eview the promotion and practical realization" of the Declaration, "[e]xamine possible solutions to problems involving minorities…[and recommend] further measures, as appropriate, for the promotion and protection of the rights of persons belonging to national or ethnic, religious and linguistic minorities."[26]

This Sub-Commission working group, which meets annually in Geneva for a one-week session, usually in May, is likely to become the major forum for discussion of minority-specific issues within the UN system. Its mandate was extended indefinitely by the Commission on Human Rights in 1998, in a resolution that "[r]eaffirm[ed] the obligation of States to ensure" implementation of the rights in the Minorities Declaration.[27] As is true of the OSCE High Commissioner, the working group cannot consider individual complaints of violations. Nonetheless, it provides a means whereby minority grievances can be inserted into the UN system in an informal way. Perhaps more importantly, the working group also provides an international setting in which dialogue between minorities and governments can be initiated, to address both positive and negative aspects of minority-majority relations.

Another task of the working group will be to articulate in greater detail what is meant by the Declaration's various provisions. Phrases such as "appropriate measures," "adequate opportunities," and "participate effectively" can only be given content in the context of specific situations, and it is hoped that the working group will develop expertise in the comparative law of minorities so that it may contribute to resolving or preventing conflicts in situations in which tensions between minority and majority are increasing.

Minority rights remains a particularly sensitive issue for many governments, and international activity in this area often is made more difficult because of concerns over the rights of the majority, the political and territorial integrity of states, and the right of every people to determine its own form of government. Creating a meaningful national identity is a legitimate goal of any state, even though such an identity may be perceived by some as conflicting with pre-existing identities based on regionalism, ethnicity, or culture.

At the same time, members of minorities are concerned that they will lose their identity as an inevitable result of the social pressures of modern society and the modern state. Increasing global communication and homogenization—particularly economic and social—may only reflect the timeless tension between change and the status quo, but it also has contributed to a cultural resurgence among ethnic and linguistic groups around the world that feel threatened. Economically weaker regions inhabited primarily by minorities may feel isolated from centralized decision makers, and minorities may view economic and political marginalization as resulting from discrimination rather than simply reflecting inevitable regional disparities.

Minority rights can only be understood within the broader context of international human rights law, which has developed considerably since the adoption of the Universal Declaration in 1948. Formerly, the treatment of minorities fell within the domestic jurisdiction of the state; unless there were broader geopolitical reasons to be concerned about their fate, they would be left wholly to the mercy of the majority. Today, however, members of minorities are protected by the same umbrella of human rights that protects all other persons within a state's jurisdiction.

In many cases, victims of violations of minority rights are also victims of other human rights violations, and it is with the latter violations that any attempt at redress must begin. For example, among the "minority" rights identified in the various instruments referred to...are the rights to physical integrity and existence, including protection against forced assimilation; non-discrimination; freedom of religion; the right to enjoy one's own culture; the right to establish one's own associations; and the right to use one's language. These rights are already guaranteed in international instruments and are widely accepted by states.

Of course, there are other rights more directly related to the needs of minority groups and individuals, such as the right of minorities to participate effectively in political, economic, and cultural life, including participation in decisions which directly affect them; the right to use one's language in various public ways, such as before administrative authorities or to identify local place names; and the right to establish one's own schools and to be educated in one's mother tongue. These rights may be more difficult to articulate with precision, and their protection may require greater modification of internal constitutional structures or governmental institutions than is generally required to protect other human rights.

At the same time, it must be borne in mind that the protection of minority rights does not require the artificial conservation of every existing culture, without change. Individuals and groups should remain free to encourage either assimilation or greater distinctiveness, so long as these choices are available without undue pressure to conform—to either the minority or majority culture.

The challenge of protecting the rights of persons belonging to minorities is to balance the legitimate concerns of majority and minority communities, so that broader political and economic decisions may be reached in an atmosphere of full equality and respect for human rights. The international community has made significant strides in articulating this balance in only a few years. As with other human rights, however, the task now is to ensure that the political and legal commitments accepted by states are monitored and implemented in good faith.

Now that meaningful minority rights are becoming more widely accepted, it may be possible to prevent future victimization through preemptive dialogue about government structures, devolution, and power-sharing. Such a dialogue is possible only in a country in which human rights and the rule of law are respected. Only in such a context can the will of the majority to govern successfully accommodate the rights of the minority to exist and prosper.

Notes

1. G.A. Res. 217C (III) (1948).

2. Articles 1 (3) and 55 of the UN Charter refer, for example, to human rights "for all without distinction to race, sex, language, or religion."

3. For a brief discussion of these situations, see Hurst Hannum, *Autonomy, Sovereignty, and Self-Determination: The Accommodation of Conflicting Rights* (2d ed. 1996), at 57-58, 337-41, 400-06,432-40.

4. Adopted 14 Dec. 1960, entered into force 22 May 1962, 429 U.N.T.S. 93, arts. 5, 6.

5. Adopted 21 Dec. 1965, entered into force 4 Jan. 1969, 660 U.N.T.S. 195. See generally Natan Lerner, *Group Rights and Discrimination in International Law* (1991), at 45-74.

6. Adopted 16 Dec. 1996, entered into force 23 Mar. 1976, 999 U.N.T.S. 171. Article 27 reads in its entirety: "In those States in which ethnic, religious or linguistic minorities exist, persons belonging to such minorities shall not be denied the right, in community with the other members of their group, to enjoy their own culture, to profess and practise their own religion, or to use their own language."

7. Study on the rights of persons belonging to ethnic, religious and linguistic minorities (1979), reissued as UN Sales No. E.91.XIV.2 (1991), at 96.

8. G.A. Res. 47/135 (1992). See discussion *infra* at 6-7.

9. G.A. Res. 36/55 (1981).

10. Surveys of some of these country reports may be found in Hannum, *supra* note 3, at 64-69; Theodor Meron, *Human Rights Law-Making in the United Nations* (1986), at 36-44; Sia Spiliopoulou, "Protection of Minorities under Article 27 of the International Covenant on Civil and Political Rights and the Reporting System [under] the Human Rights Committee," in Frank Horn, ed., *Writings in Human and Minority Rights* (1994), at 57-99; and Patrick Thronberry, *International Law and the Rights of Minorities* (1991), at 272-80.

11. *Lovelace v. Canada*, Communication No. 24/1977, reported in the Human Rights Committee's Annual Report, UN Doc. A/36/40 (1991), at 166.

12. See, e.g., *Kitokv. Sweden*, Communication No. 197/1985 (27 July 1988); *Sara et al. v. Finland*, communication No. 431/1990 (23 Mar. 1994); *Länsman et al. v. Finland*, Communication No. 671/1995 (14 Mar. 1996).

13. *Ballantyne et al. v. Canada*, Communication No. 359/1989 (31 Mar. 1993).

14. *Singer v. Canada*, Communication No. 455/1991

(26 July 1994).

15. Article 2 of the Racial Discrimination Convention does require that state parties take, in appropriate circumstances, "special and concrete measures to ensure the adequate development and protection of certain racial groups or individuals belonging to them, for the purpose of guaranteeing them the full and equal enjoyment of human rights and fundamental freedoms." However, this provision does not set forth additional minority rights, per se; it merely addresses the issue of equality. In addition, the measures to be taken should be temporary, which may not be sufficient to protect legitimate minority interests in the long term.

16. Document of the Copenhagen Meeting of the Conference on the Human Dimension of the CSCE, adopted 29 June 1990, reprinted in *United Nations, A Compilation of International Instruments,* vol. II, Regional Instruments, UN Sales No. E.97.XIV. 1, at 389-405.

17. "European Charter for Regional or Minority Languages, signed 5 Nov. 1992, entered into force 1 Mar. 1998. Europe. T.S. No. 148.

18. Parliamentary Assembly of the Council of Europe, Recommendation 1201 (1993), 44th Sess., 22nd Sitting, 1 Feb. 1993.

19. Framework Convention for the Protection of National Minorities, signed 1 Feb. 1995, entered into force 1 Feb. 1998, Europe. T.S. No. 157, reprinted in UN compilation, *supra* note 16, at 286-95. The convention had been ratified by twenty states as of spring 1998.

20. *Supra* note 8.

21. General Comment No. 23(5), para. 5.2 (1994).

22. Compare, for example, the Annotations on the text of the draft International Covenants on Human Rights, prepared by the Secretary-General for the General Assembly in 1955: "It was agreed that the article should cover only separate or distinct groups, well-defined and long-established on the territory of a State." UN Doc. A/2929 (1955), para. 184. Other references may be found in M. Bossuyt, Guide to the "*Travaux Préparatoires*" of the International Covenant on Civil and Political Rights, Dordrecht, Martinus Nijhoff, 1987, pp. 493-499. Citing, inter alia, the Capotorti study, *supra* note 7, a more recent commentator concluded (prior to the adoption of the Committee's General Comment) that "aliens are *prima facie* excluded" from the scope of article 27. Thornberry, *supra* note 10, at 171.

23. Conference on Security and Cooperation in Europe, Helsinki Document 1992, Decisions, Sec. II, reprinted in UN Compilation, *supra* note 16 at 430, 431-37.

24. A useful summary of the High Commissioner's work is *Foundation on Inter-Ethnic Relations, The Role of the High Commissioner on National Minorities in OSCE Conflict Prevention: An Introduction* (1997).

25. The final report, by Sub-Commission member Asbjørn Eide, is found in UN Doc. E/CN.4/Sub.211993/34 and Adds. 1-4 (1993).

26. Commission on Human Rights Res. 1995/24 (3 Mar. 1995), para. 9.

27. Commission on Human Rights Res. 1998/19 (9 Apr. 1998), para. 2. The resolution also calls upon the human rights treaty bodies, special rapporteurs, the High Commissioner for Human Rights, and others to give particular attention to issues within their competence that affect minorities.

Faith-Based Initiatives: Can Islam Bring Democracy to the Middle East?

Ray Takeyh
Washington Institute for Near East Policy

The televised footage of an airliner crashing into the World Trade Center is now the prevailing image of Islam. Media pundits decry anti-Muslim bigotry and hasten to remind the public that Islam is a religion of peace and tolerance, notwithstanding the actions of an extremist minority. But in the same breath many of those pundits warn of a clash of civilizations—a war that pits the secular, modernized West against a region mired in ancient hatreds and fundamentalist rage.

This simplistic choice between "Islam" and "modernity" ignores a third option that is emerging throughout the Middle East. Lost amidst the din of cultural saber-rattling are the voices calling for an Islamic reformation: A new generation of theological thinkers, led by figures such as Iranian President Muhammad Khatami and Tunisian activist Rached Ghannouchi, is reconsidering the orthodoxies of Islamic politics. In the process, such leaders are demonstrating that the region may be capable of generating a genuinely democratic order, one based on indigenous values. For the Middle East today, moderate Islam may be democracy's last hope. For the West, it might represent one of the best long-term solutions to "winning" the war against Middle East terrorism.

Militant Islam continues to tempt those on the margins of society (and guides anachronistic forces such as Afghanistan's Taliban and Palestine's Islamic Jihad), but its moment has passed. In Iran, the Grand Ayatollah's autocratic order degenerated into corruption and economic stagnation. Elsewhere, the Islamic radicals' campaign of terror—such as Gamma al-Islamiyya in Egypt and Hezbollah in Lebanon—failed to produce any political change, as their violence could not overcome the brutality of the states they encountered. The militants' incendiary rhetoric and terrorism only triggered public revulsion, not revolutions and mass uprisings. Indeed, the Arab populace may have returned to religion over the last two decades, but they turned to a religion that was tolerant and progressive, not one that called for a violent displacement of the existing order with utopias.

Political Islam as a viable reform movement might have petered out were it not for one minor detail: The rest of the world was changing. The collapse of the Soviet Union and the emergence of democratic regimes in Eastern Europe, Latin America, and East Asia electrified the Arab populace. Their demands were simple but profound. As one Egyptian university student explained in 1993, "I want what they have in Poland, Czechoslovakia. Freedom of thought and freedom of speech." In lecture halls, street cafes, and mosques, long dormant ideas of representation, identity, authenticity, and

Ray Takeyh, "Faith-Based Initiatives." Reproduced with permission from *FOREIGN POLICY* #127 (November/December 2001).

pluralism began to arise.

The task of addressing the population's demand for a pluralistic society consistent with traditional values was left to a new generation of Islamist thinkers, who have sought to legitimize democratic concepts through the reinterpretation of Islamic texts and traditions. Tunisia's Ghannouchi captures this spirit of innovation by stressing; "Islam did not come with a specific program concerning life. It is our duty to formulate this program through interaction between Islamic precepts and modernity." Under these progressive readings, the well-delineated Islamic concept of *shura* (consultation) compels a ruler to consider popular opinion and establishes the foundation for an accountable government. In a modern context, such consultation can be implemented through the standard tools of democracy: elections, plebiscites, and referendums. The Islamic notion of *ijma* (consensus) has been similarly accommodated to serve as a theological basis for majoritarian rule. For Muslim reformers, Prophet Mohammed's injunction that "differences of opinion within my community is a sign of God's mercy" denotes prophetic approbation of diversity of thought and freedom of speech.

The new generation of Islamists has quickly embraced the benefits wrought by modernization and globalization in order to forge links between Islamist groups and thinkers in the various states of the Middle East. Through mosques, Islamists easily distribute pamphlets, tracts, and cassettes of Islamic thinkers and writers. In today's Middle East, one can easily find the Egyptian Brotherhood's magazine *Al-Dawa* in bookstores in the Persian Gulf while the Jordanian Islamist daily *Al-Sabil* enjoys wide circulation throughout the Levant. The advent of the Internet has intensified such cross-pollination, as most Islamist journals, lectures, and conference proceedings are posted on the Web. The writings of Iranian philosopher Abdol Karim Soroush today appear in Islamic curricula across the region, and Egypt's Islamist liberal Hassan Hanafi commands an important audience in Iran's seminaries.

In the future such Islamists will likely vie to succeed the region's discredited military rulers and lifetime presidents. But what will a prospective Islamic democracy look like? Undoubtedly, Islamic democracy will differ in important ways from the model that evolved in post-Reformation Europe. Western systems elevated the primacy of the individual above the community and thus changed the role of religion from that of the public conveyor of community values to a private guide for individual conscience. In contrast, an Islamic democracy's attempt to balance its emphasis on reverence with the popular desire for self-expression will impose certain limits on individual choice. An Islamic polity will support fundamental tenets of democracy—namely, regular elections, separation of powers, an independent judiciary, and institutional opposition—but it is unlikely to be a libertarian paradise.

The question of gender rights is an excellent example or the strengths—and limits—of an Islamic democracy. The Islamists who rely on women's votes, grass-roots activism, and participation in labor markets cannot remain deaf to women's demands for equality. Increasingly, Islamic reformers suggest the cause of women's failure to achieve equality is not religion but custom. The idea of black-clad women passively accepting the dictates of superior males is the province of Western caricatures. Iran's parliament, cabinet, and universities are populated with women, as are the candidate lists for Islamic opposition parties in Egypt and Turkey. But while an Islamic democracy will not impede women's integration into public affairs, it will impose restrictions on them, particularly in the realm of family law and dress codes. In such an order, women can make significant progress, yet in important ways they may still lag behind their Western counterparts.

Moderate Islamists are likely to be most liberal in the realm of economic policy. The failure of command economies in the Middle East and the centrality of global markets to the region's economic rehabilitation have made minimal government intervention appealing to Islamist theoreticians.

Moreover, a privatized economy is consistent with classical Islamic economic theory and its well-established protection of market and commerce. The Islamist parties have been among the most persistent critics of state restrictions on trade and measures that obstruct opportunities for middle-class entrepreneurs.

The international implications of the emergence of Islamic democracies are also momentous. While revolutionary Islam could not easily coexist with the international system, moderate Islam can serve is a bridge between civilizations. The coming to power of moderate Islamists throughout the Middle East might lead to a lessening of tensions both within the region and between it and other parts of the world. Today, security experts talk of the need to "drain the swamps" and deprive terrorists of the state sponsorship that provides the protection and funding to carry out their war against the West. Within a more open and democratic system, dictatorial regimes would enjoy less freedom to support terrorism or engage in military buildups without any regard for economic consequences.

Ultimately, however, the integration of an Islamic democracy into global democratic society would depend on the willingness of the West to accept an Islamic variant on liberal democracy. Islamist moderates, while conceding that there are in fact certain "universal" democratic values, maintain that different civilizations must be able to express these values in context that is acceptable and appropriate to their particular region. Moderate Islamists, therefore, will continue to struggle against any form of U.S. hegemony, whether in political or cultural terms, and are much more comfortable with a multipolar, multi-"civilizational" international system. Khatami's call for a "dialogue of civilizations" presupposes that there is no single universal standard judging the effectiveness of democracy and human rights.

Certainly, the West should resist totalitarian states who use the rhetoric of democracy while rejecting its essence through false claims of cultural authenticity. But even though an Islamic democracy will resist certain elements of post-Enlightenment liberalism, it will still be a system that features regular elections, accepts dissent and opposition parties, and condones a free press and division of power between branches of state. As such, any fair reading of Islamic democracy will reveal that it is a genuine effort to conceive a system of government responsive to popular will. And this effort is worthy of Western acclaim.

Mediating Racial, Ethnic, and Cultural Conflicts: The Lessons of South Africa

Albert Venter
Rand Afrikaans University

> The brief seconds when the majority of honourable members quietly assented to the new basic law of the land have captured, in a fleeting moment, the centuries of history that the South African people have endured in a search for a better future. As one, you, the representatives of the overwhelming majority of South Africans have given voice to the yearnings of millions. And so it has come to pass that today South Africa undergoes her rebirth, cleansed of a horrible past, matured from a tentative beginning and reaching to the future with confidence.
>
> —President Nelson Mandela, Parliament, 8 May 1996

This very brief quote from Nelson Mandela's speech at the adoption of the final version of the South African democratic constitution marked the formal culmination of South Africa's transition form an authoritarian state to a democratic one. And it must count as one of the major success stories of transitions in racially and ethnically deeply divided societies. After the 1994 founding elections South Africa's political leadership adopted an interim constitution, which came into effect on 27 April 1994. Following this election, South Africa's first representative Constitutional Assembly had exactly two years, from May 1994, to draft a new Constitution which would replace the Interim Constitution (Act No. 200 of 1993).

Despite the desertion by the Inkatha Freedom Party the Constitutional Assembly displayed a remarkable political will to finish the task at hand within the two-year, time-constraint imposed by the Interim Constitution. Written into the political will to finish the constitutional text on time were two disparate narratives: the one a history of domination; the other a history of striving for liberation.

The last-minute negotiations about contentious issues, such as the education, property and right to strike clauses in the Bill of Rights and the burning issue of the powers of the provinces raised fears that a popular referendum would be unavoidable as these conflicts seemed to be intractable. The parties finally succeeded in addressing many of the outstanding questions and contentious clauses in a marathon negotiating session lasting well into the weary hours of the morning of 8 May 1996.

Attendance at the National Assembly chamber was almost 100 percent when the Constitutional Assembly adopted the draft constitutional text on 8 May 1996. The constitution was adopted by 421 votes, well in excess of the two-thirds requirement of 327 votes. Following the adoption of the draft text the Constitutional Assembly referred it to the Constitutional Court for certification. During the period July to September 1996 the Court held ten days of hearings to consider argument on the short-comings of the draft, and delivered its verdict. The chapter on local government and eight other sections were referred back to the Constitutional Assembly. On 11 October 1996 the Assembly agreed to amendments made to the clauses identified by the Court, and the document was sent back to the Constitutional Court for certification. On 10 December 1996 President Nelson Mandela signed the constitution into law at a ceremony in Sharpeville, and on 4 February 1997 the new Constitution (Act No. 108 of 1996) entered into force.

This is the big success story of South Africa's transition to democracy. But South Africa remains racially divided; the new political order has not changed that. The main argument of this text is that South African society has been successful in rearranging its political order into sharing a common space, but that the greater challenge will be to develop a shared sense of history (time). The first seven years of democracy has not solved this challenge. It is to this problematic that I now turn.

The Major Failure: Continued Racial Divisions in South African Society

It is common knowledge that South African society is marked by racial divisions, and that these were strengthened and reinforced by the history of segregation and later on, of apartheid in South Africa. The recent post-apartheid political history of South African society, despite the above-mentioned constitutional successes, reflects a major failure—the deracialisation of society. While it is official ANC-government policy to "build a non-racial" society, the practical implementation of its affirmative action and black empowerment policies, unintentionally is leading to the reracialisation of society.

In 1999 and in 2000 the South African Human Rights Commission report regarding racism in the public media highlighted these divisions. Moreover, the deeply resented experience of ongoing racism by black South Africans from their white compatriots were clear in the International Conference on Racism in South Africa held in Sandton in August of 2000. Far from eradicating racism, the political changes since 1994 has enabled black South Africans to put the issue on the public agenda and to insist that steps to eradicate racism from South African society be undertaken by government intervention. This provoked a response from white-led opposition parties that among other things, the government's laws regarding affirmative action were leading to a new from of racial division in South Africa: whites that have to stand back in competing for jobs in South Africa merely on the grounds of skin colour. This is not the place to offer solutions for the problem, but to alert readers to the fact that South Africa's racial divisions are far from solved. One significant point to take into account when reflecting on this problem is that the various race groups have different conceptual frameworks when dealing with the problem of racism. These frameworks are difficult to reconcile and often lead to misunderstanding and conflict. Racial differences in South Africa, as well as pervasive racist attitudes in many sectors of society, point towards potential serious conflicts in society.

White South Africans lament about reverse discrimination against them in the workplace, some mourn a lost past and others withdraw into apathy and estrangement from mainline society. Current President Mbeki is unhelpful in his persistent notion that South Africa consists of two nations: one black and poor and the other white and rich. This is superficial stereotyping that might have been valid fifteen years ago. Black South African elites have been significant beneficiaries of economic empowerment the last fifteen years and white South Africans have been the major losers in this economic restructuring.[1] Mbeki's talk provides fodder for continued racial attitudes and undermines the necessary feeling of social unity amongst South Africans of different racial groups.

The New Challenge: Developing a South African Patriotism

The purpose of this essay[2] is to reflect on the problem of building a national political identity or common patriotism for South Africans by peaceful means. National identity refers to the characteristics that subjectively define membership in a particular political community (Citrin *et al* 1990: 1128). In many states national identity is founded on a common language, religion, ethnic heritage and historic legacy. This is quite obviously not the case in South Africa. There may be a formal and legalistic reply to the question: *"Who is a South African?" = A citizen of the Republic of South Africa.* My concern however is that the usual cultural-ethnic criterion as defining principle of South African national identity is extremely problematic in South Africa. Are there, or can there indeed be, South Africans in the sense that there are "Japanese", "Koreans", "Swedes", "Germans" or "Dutch"?[3]

A linked question that concerns me in this essay is whether a South African national identity can be engineered by state intervention—in other words, can a nation be "built" or "engineered" by state intervention? Alternatively, the question is whether it could develop over time by "natural" means, in contrast to a purposefully designed nation through the agency of state institutions. Could/should a national identity be left to "market forces" of free cultural enterprise? What are the obstacles to either an officially sanctioned creation of a national identity, "state nation building"?

The essay is based on the theoretical claims of what could be named "symbolic politics." This perspective asserts that an individual's politically relevant orientations are unusually persistent and powerful. Predispositions based on symbolic politics are established early in life, they are reinforced by later learning, their objects are invested with emotional meaning and they are central to people's self-conceptions. National, racial, religious and linguistic group identifications are potent symbolic predispositions. The theory of symbolic politics holds that the position one adopts is likely to be rooted in the emotional defence of one's prior cultural identifications (cf. Citrin 1990, Horowitz 1985). Moreover this essay is premised on the idea of S.P. Huntington that civilizational differences can lead to an inter-civilizational clash in a deeply divided society such as South Africa. In other words I take the point of view that the subjective sense of national identity is decisively shaped by the civilizational context within which such a person is born, educated and socialised. The civilizational context is the deepest or ultimate predisposition that forms a person's sense of political/national identity (cf. Huntington 1996, Von Laue 1987). The personal sense of political identity of a person that is part of the Islamic civilization will be decisively influenced by Islamic civilizational norms. In the same vein a Westerner's worldviews will be influenced by Western civilization and so on. It stands to reason that many other factors will also influence a person's sense of identity. However, for the purposes of this essay I shall concern myself with the national political identity of people in South Africa and how this is shaped by civilizational norms. I therefore go beyond the customary wisdom that South Africa is a racially and culturally deeply divided society—its divisions go deeper than this, two major civilizations confront each other in South Africa. I challenge the view that a South African nation with a common identity can be shaped by state imposed political-social engineering. Instead I argue that a defensible project in creating a South African national/political identity would be to nurture a form of constitutional patriotism, rather than creating an artificial "South African nation."

Furthermore, I shall advance the view that South Africa after apartheid lacks a generally accepted "Creed of South Africa." Nominally, the outlines of such a Creed can be found in the Constitution. The Preamble suggests that the Constitution is intended to "lay the foundations for a democratic and open society in which government is based on the will of the people and every citizen is equally protected by law." Section 1 of the Constitutions professes that the South African state is founded on the values of human dignity, achievement of equality, advancement of human rights and freedoms, non-racialism and non-sexism. The Constitution recognises eleven official languages (section 60) and guarantees everyone the right to freely engage in their religion (section 15) and to enjoy their culture, use their language and to form cultural religious and linguistic associations (section 31). However it is the operationalisation of these values that need to be addressed in South Africa. To date, in my judgment, such social consensus on how these values are to be lived is lacking in South Africa.

This lack of a common creed is a general dilemma facing governments in newly democratised, deeply divided, multicultural societies: could or should governments engineer a common national identity and impose it various ways on their citizens? I take it as common knowledge and given that the apartheid as well as white colonial legacies of South Africa's previous political order did nothing to encourage a common South African national political identity. Indeed quite the opposite is true: apartheid was a typically modernist system of social engineering that enforced an ethnic identity and nationality on Africans and black people in South Africa, dictated to them what professions they could enter into, what universities to go to, what towns and villages to move to, who they could marry; it repressed freedom of religion and freedom of speech. In modernist fashion, apartheid as an ideology posited an unquestionable truth, which had to be enforced if necessary, on unwilling victims. The historic record of this social engineering is well known and is not repeated in this paper. The problem is that after centuries of white domination and four decades of legalised apartheid, how does one forge a national creed for South Africans?

In order to promote my argument, some demographic features of South African society are presented next.

Some Demographic Features of South Africa

The problem confronting South Africans after apartheid is apparent: There are no South Africans in the sense that there are Swedes, Germans, Portuguese, and Japanese. The name of the country, *South Africa,* is a mere geographic expression: it does not signify any ethno-cultural entity such as Sweden or Japan would. In cultural-ethnic terms the dilemma can easily be demonstrated by a simple demographic survey of the population. The major population groups of South Africa in linguistic-ethnic-cultural terms are estimated to be as follows: (South Africa Yearbook 1999: 1).

Non-African "White"		
Afrikaners		3 million
Anglo-English		2 million
Recent immigrants: Portuguese, Italian, Greek, Polish, German	ca.	500 thousand
Non-African "Black"		
Asians of Indian descent		1 million
Cape "Coloureds"		3.5 million
Africans		
Sotho-Tswana		9 million
Swazi		1 million
Tsonga		1 million
Venda		1 million
Zulu		8.5 million
Xhosa		6.5 million
"Other African"		3 million
Total population	ca.	40 million

In terms of the new Constitution of South Africa, eleven official languages are provided for. In practice English is the commercial and administrative language of most of South Africa—despite the fact that it is the first language of only about two million South Africans, of mostly, but not exclusively, British-Anglo descent. The identity problem is further illustrated by the multiplication of religious affiliations.

Religious Affiliation

African independent churches	7 million
NG (Dutch Reformed) Church Family	3 million
Roman Catholic	2.6 million
Methodist	2 million
Anglican	1 million
Lutheran	800,000
Presbyterian	470,000
Apostolic faith Mission	423,000
Congregational	404,000
Nederduitsch Hervormde	280,000
Baptists	262,000
Full Gospel	213,000
Gereformeerde Kerke	168,000
Assemblies of God	160,000
Seventh day Adventist	88,000
Greek Orthodox	27,000
Other Christian	1.3 million
Total Christians	**21 million**
Non-Christian Religions	
Hindu	410,000
Muslim	1 million
Judaist	70,000
Buddhist	3,000
Other	25,000

African Traditional Religions: Unknown, but according to some commentators have many millions of adherents, since it is not an institutionalised religious affiliation. Mdende (1997: 41), a well-known commentator and scholar of African traditional religions, given to rather strong language, writes: "Most black Christians are Christians on Sunday, but African Traditional Religion from Monday to Saturday." Others place the affiliation at 18 percent of the population, around 6 million people (Kotzé 1997:13). It is clear from this brief demographic survey that a single South African national identity could not be defined in religious, ethnic or linguistic terms. In order to reflect on the problematic of a South African national creed, one other point of departure needs to be clarified, to wit the Kuhnian concept of a paradigm.

Paradigms

For the sake of convenience I will follow the argument of Thomas Kuhn by using his conception of paradigms to depict the different civilizational forces at play in South Africa. The notions of Western civilization, African civilization, Afrikaner nationalism and African nationalism will be portrayed as intellectual constructs within which a particular *Weltanschauung* is held. *Paradigm* is shorthand to conceptualise the difference and similarities between these world-views. One can also understand these worldviews as conceptual frameworks in terms of which the world is understood. Such frameworks are the spectacles through which the world is recognised, but they have their limitations. Although a conceptual framework is useful and unavoidable for human beings to get a grip on the complexities of reality, it can also stifle innovation, lead to intellectual "blindness" and an inability to perceive other aspects of reality. Moreover, quite often conceptual frameworks and paradigms are incommensurable. A paradigm is not necessarily falsified by "facts" or empirical testing and observation. Facts or reality are interpreted in terms of a given paradigm. The process of accommodating contending paradigms is more often than not a *gestalt* switch rather than the facts speaking for themselves. I do however, accept that paradigms can change, quite often by piecemeal processes rather than through dramatic and sudden revolutions.[4]

A Civilizational Perspective

Following the work of S.P. Huntington, I define a civilization as a cultural entity that refers to the overall way of life of a people; a civilization is a culture writ large. It involves values, norms, institutions and modes of thinking to which successive generations in a given society have attached a primary importance. It is a kind of moral milieu encompassing a certain number of nations, each national culture being a particular form of the whole. A civilization may have a common "bloodline" or racial attribute, a religion, way of life. To a large degree the major civilizations of human history have been closely identified with the world's great religions. Civilization and race are not necessarily identical, although a significant correspondence exists between the division of people by cultural characteristics into civilizations and their divisions by physical characteristics into races (Huntington 1996: 42).

Civilizations are comprehensive: A civilization is a totality. Their constituent units cannot be fully understood without reference to their civilizational context: regions, states, ethnic groups within civilizations differ at the lower level. But at higher levels they share common traits: the culture of a village in East Anglia may differ noticeably from a village in Northumbria, but both will share a common English culture. Likewise English culture may differ from French and German culture, but they are part of the Western civilization. They share common traits, which distinguish them from Chinese, Hindu or Arab communities. According to Huntington 1996: 43, a civilization is the highest cultural grouping of people and the broadest level of cultural identity people have, short of that which distinguishes humans from other species. It is defined both by common objective elements such a language, history, religion, customs, institutions, and by subjective self-identification. Civilization is the biggest "we" within which humans feel culturally at home as distinguished from all other people. Civilizations have no clear-cut boundaries and no precise beginnings or endings. People can and do redefine their identities and as a result the shape and composition of civilizations change over time. Civilizations are mortal, but usually long-lived. Their unique and particular essence is their long historical continuity. Political systems are transient expedients on the surface of civilization (Bozeman 1976: 26). While civilizations endure they also evolve. They are dynamic, rise and fall merge and divide, they disappear. Civilizations are cultural entities; therefore they do not maintain order as political entities or do other things that governments do. A civilization may contain many political units. Sometimes a civilization and a state do coincide, like Japan. Western civilization is not represented by a single state but by a wide-ranging group of societies. Religion is central to defining the characteristics of a civilization. Of Weber's five world religions, four—Christianity, Islam, Hinduism and Confucianism are associated with major civilizations (Huntington 1996: 43,44). For the purposes of this essay I shall propose that two civilizational paradigms confront each other in South Africa: the Western and the African. Hence a brief exposition of the two civilizational paradigms follows.[5]

The African Civilizational Paradigm

In South Africa, through the forces and legacy of history, two major civilizational paradigms have come to exist side by side, i.e., the African and the Western. Islamic and Hindu civilizations are represented by a numeric minority of people, around 1.2 million people out of a total of 40 million. To avoid misunderstanding, a few words on the utility of the term "African" in the context of this paper is necessary. Africa is a continent of many different tribes, ethnic groups, states and civilizations. For our purposes North Africa represents a part of the Islamic civilization and is predominantly a Mediterranean-Arabic region of that civilization. Africa refers to Africa south of the Sahara, mostly but not exclusively "tropical Africa," mainly inhabited by Africans.[6] At the peril of stereotyping, these inhabitants often refer to themselves, as "black Africans." Much of the following conception of the "African world-view" is drawn from the work of Themba Sono, a well-known, if somewhat controversial, black intellectual in South Africa. Again, depicting a complexity such as an African civilizational view in a short paper must of necessity be brutal and brief. But it serves the purpose to illustrate the problem confronting South African national identity.

According to Sono (1994: xvi), the African civilizational world-view can be conceptualised as being "traditional." The African world-view is oriented more towards the glorious, perfect, primordial state of the past than towards an unknown and uncertain future. The world of the ancestors is always the best, closer to the perfect origin and has more potency than the present or the future. The best in life lies in the past. That which has been passed down by the ancestor's culture, religion, and technology must be maintained and passed on to the next generation

(Y Turaki 1991: 134,135 in Du Toit 1997: 127).

A past-oriented culture venerates the primordial and pristine values of its tradition. It craves continuity rather than change. It is unwilling to experiment and or recreate ideas, harmony and unity are cherished, uniformity worshipped and community venerated. It is anti-intellectual since intellectualism dispenses with tradition and throws overboard the past. In African culture there is no separation between the profane and the sacred. Time in Africa is diffused, an unlimited commodity, profusely in abundance (Sono 1994: xviii).

The role of the group in African consciousness is pervasive. This group mentality is stronger on spiritual belief than reason, on sameness than difference. Rationality is overwhelmed by emotional identity, conformity. To agree is more important than to disagree, tradition is venerated, continuity revered, change feared, difference shunned. It is a civilization of consent. This group consciousness tends to demand consensus and is inclined to become coercive, since refusal to agree can lead to punishment. African culture is intolerant of heresy or difference and is potentially totalitarian (Sono 1994: 2-5).

African-thought proceeds not dialectically, but communally. It strives for the protection of the community. The individual is nothing without the community and the community allegedly survives without the input of the individual qua individual. One has no choice but to belong to a community; to break away is to define you as an alien. Those who remain in a community are those that conform remain silent and keep within the confines of the hierarchy. According to Bozeman the merger of thought with emotion, behaviour, social structure and the synthetic approach to all knowledge and experience have combined to foster a metaphysical world view that requires the confounding of all phenomena. The natural world is thus not perceived as separate from the supernatural realms, animals and men exist in symbioses unimaginable in literate thought contexts, masks are treated as persons, shadows are real, the dead are presumed alive and the living can interchange identities and destinies (Bozeman 1976: 29). The status of blood relationship is the cornerstone of the traditional African political way of life. This phenomenon is closely associated with the oral tradition, which emphasises a personal experiential relationship through an oral tradition. The consequence is that the group is constantly emphasised at the expense of the individual. The difference between the tribe and the nation is that the tribe conceptualises relationship in terms of the bloodline, while the nation conceptualises itself in terms of space.

As Bozeman puts it:

> The great African societies were neither territorial states nor nation states in the occidental sense of the term. The normative principle that presided over their inception, survival and decline was the personality of the king or paramount chief, who might not represent a dynasty or lineage. In fact the states did not even have names until the Arabs began identifying them by their ruler's titles or places of residence. (1976: 131).

Tribal politics thus has certain specific characteristics, which follows the fact that it is a process of emphasising continuity; it is a process that is determined by status rather than contract. The tribesperson is such by virtue of birth, not by virtue of self-determination or naturalisation. Past and present, subject and object, nature and culture are seen as one whole, no difference is made between secular and sacred, the ordinary and the magical. The symbolic and reality are seen as the same (Louw 1979: 72).

For Africa the dominant conception of reality is one of a symbolic circle: it symbolises the longing to be part of one cosmic whole. All contradictions are reconciled within this greater whole—a seamless totality of past, present and future, an interconnect-edness of all things (Es'kia Mpahlele in Sono 1994:8, 9). The symbolic portrayal of reality emerges in the natural rhythms of the sun, the moon, planets and stars, birth, life and death, destruction and regeneration. This cyclical conception of time is strongly represented in funeral rituals: the dead is reunited with mother earth from which they came, a reunification that leads to new life. From this follows the conception of the life of the forebears: those that are dead are virtually still present with the living. The symbol of the circle helps Africans to understand the great mysteries of life: no state of suffering lasts forever: after death there will be new life, spring follows the deadly winter, after crop failure success, and so on. It has its downside: fatalism that the great forces of life simply have to be accepted, nothing can be done to stop or circumvent misfortune—it has to be born stoically. In social affairs the danger can be that destruction is seen as the precursor to renaissance: destroy all that is unacceptable before the renewal can start. In revolutions in Africa this has obvious nefarious effects, for example burning of schools in the South African township revolts (1976-91), the Mau-Mau terror in Kenya (1956-60), the prophecies of Nonquase in the Transkei (East coast of South Africa) in the middle of the nineteenth century and so. The further downside is: The good also leads to the bad. Advance inevitably must lead to regression. The consequence of such symbolism stifles innovation, renewal, reform and criticism. In the words of Scripture: all is a chasing of the winds (Van Niekerk 1996: 2-15, Sono 1994: 8,9).

In resolving conflict, the African way is to get a solution that will accommodate the forces which are at the root of disharmony: the passage of life requires that a balance be struck between good and evil. A clear decision on guilt is almost always avoided, or is not deemed desirable. In African conceptions of justice, the guilty and the innocent are not clear-cut. Space is left for manoeuvring in order to allow harmony between conflicting parties to be re-established. Concepts like causality, innocence and guilt acquire new and different meanings in the African conception in contrast to the Roman law traditions of the West. Unknown forces of which the "guilty party" may not even be aware may cause evil. In adjudication, space has to be left for settlement, a compromise which would give everyone a place: both the guilty as well as the aggrieved. Rituals may need to be performed to exorcise evil from society and individuals. There is little or no concept of personal guilt and responsibility: the origin of evil is outside the individual and rites must restore harmony. Quite often collective responsibility is accepted for misdeeds so that no individual need be blamed or named (Van Niekerk 1996: 26).

K.C. Anyanwu writes:

> The unity of self and world, mind and matter, is something magical because it defies any rational understanding. We can only say that the self and the world interpenetrate each other in such a way that we do not know where the self begins and the world end.... The West seeks rational causality in all things. What happens if nature is alive, if spirit permeates the whole universe, if consciousness cannot grasp the factors of causality? Effects would then be interpreted as magical. Magic raises up the question of causality...the whole truth about cause is magical, that is it belongs to the non-material world" (Quoted in van Niekerk 1996: 57).

Traditional African culture can be summarised as the primary or mythological experience of the cosmos—of an earth below, of the heaven and celestial bodies and their movements above, of seasonal changes, of fertility rhythms of plants and animal life, of human birth and death. It is a cosmos full of spirits (gods and ancestral). It is an order imposed on the world by spirits who hold back the forces of chaos. The cosmic order is one of uncertain truths of existence and come into existence as a reassuring symbolism against the fear of disorder. World and being are not yet differentiated: humans live in this cosmological order in a charmed circle in which everything encountered has power, will and feeling: plants, animals and kings could be gods and spirits. In this cosmological order the creation of a political authority is an enterprise of world ordering. The creation of the polity is a cosmion, a little cosmos, and an analogical repetition of the cosmos. Cosmos and cosmion are supplementary; the chief protects the cosmion, the gods the cosmos. Society is a microcosmos of reality. When society decays, for some mysterious and inexplicable reason, the cosmos cannot serve as a source of order for the cosmion and humans have to seek an alternative source of order (cf. Voegelin 1952: 52,53).

The Essence of the Western Civilizational Paradigm

The Western civilization paradigm can obviously not be sketched in a short article such as the present one. I follow Huntington's exposition. In a similar fashion, von Laue 1987 has written on the precepts of civilization. Following Huntington 1996: 69,70 the following foundations are offered as the essence of what can be termed "Western Civilization." For a full treatment the reader is referred to Huntington's work.

- **The classical legacy.** The West inherited much from the classic civilizations of Rome and Greece. These legacies include Greek philosophy and rationalism, Roman conceptions of law, the Latin and Greek languages and Christianity.
- **Catholicism and Protestantism.** Western Christianity is deeply influenced by Catholicism and Protestantism. Indeed the single most important characteristic of the West is its historic legacy of Christianity. Christianity brings with it a conception of the dignity of the individual, the idea of individual responsibility for one's life: salvation is an individual experience. It also provides Westerners with the experience of historical time as linear, in which God, in an unrepeatable act, creates the world at the beginning of time; consequently there will be a final end to historical time.
- **European languages.** The West differs from most major civilizations in its multiplicity of languages. In general the Western languages share a common Indo-European ancestry and are heavily influenced by Greek and Latin. The languages of the West are grouped loosely into the Romance and Germanic languages.
- **Separation of spiritual and temporal authority.** The West distinguishes between temporal and spiritual authority: but did not do so in its entire history. Bitter struggles between church and state for temporal power took place some five hundred years ago. In general it is accepted in Western civilization at present that church and state should have separate spheres of influence and power. This separation contributed to the conception of political and social freedom in the West—which is protected by the state.
- **Rule of law.** The rule of law is a central concept in Western governance. The rule of law is deemed to be a corrective on the power of the state and the ruler. In mediaeval times the philosophers held the conception of natural law to be a corrective in terms of which rulers exercised their powers. The idea that an external law restrains human power is the basis of constitutionalism in the West, including the protection of human rights, property rights, and the constraint on the arbitrary exercise of executive power.
- **Social-pluralism.** The West is distinguished by the idea that diverse and autonomous groups have the right of existence in civil society. Historically these found expression in guilds, the aristocracy, the church, and in modern times a wide variety of interest groups, political parties, professional associations and so on.
- **Representative bodies.** The West has a thousand-year history of representative bodies to represent the stakes of diverse interest groups in society. These include parliaments, estates general, bodies in which the clergy could participate in political decision making (e.g., the English House of Lords). This representation is also effected at the local level: villages, towns and cities have enjoyed autonomous govern-

ment in the West for a long time.

- **Individualism.** Individualism is probably the strongest contemporary cultural trait of the West. The idea of the autonomous individual who is competent to exercise choices on an individual level regarding marriage partners (or the right to remain single), whether to convert to Christianity or any other religion, the right to chose a career and the right to exercise free political association. On top of this, is the notion of formal individual equality of people. All humans are equal qua humans on a formal level in the West. Which entails an equal right to vote and equal treatment before the law.

These worldviews can schematically be represented as follows (Sono 1994: xvii)

Western	**African**
Individuality	Groupness
Uniqueness	Sameness
Competition	Co-operation
Separateness	Collective responsibility
Survival of the fittest	Survival of the tribe
Control over nature	Unity with nature

The two civilizational paradigms can be contrasted as opposites: (Sono 1994: xvii)

- Western culture is experimental and innovative, African culture is deferential and hierarchical.
- Western culture is contentious, African culture values harmony and consensus.
- Western culture is assertive of individual rights; African culture observes group obligations.
- Western culture values liberty, African culture esteems fraternity.
- Western culture values individualism, African culture values solidarity.
- Western culture cherishes impartial and impersonal application of rules, African culture values sensitivity to personal needs of others.
- Africans reach decisions through discussion rather than application of rules.
- The West venerates change, African culture embraces tradition and authority.
- Western culture is future oriented; African culture is past oriented.
- Western culture seeks gender equality; African culture venerates and elevates the status of men.
- The West promotes trial and error; Africa likes the tried and tested.

A Civilizational Clash?

Caveat Lector

The above exposition of a clash of civilizational values should not be construed or interpreted by the reader as though I conceptualise one of the two civilizations as superior or better than the other. The concepts are used as tools of analysis to get to grips with the problematic of the quest for a national sense of patriotism in South Africa.

From the above exposition it is clear that there are many potential areas of conflict between representatives of the two major civilizations in South Africa. In many important respects, African and Western civilizations hold diametrically opposed worldviews or paradigms. Calls from African and Black Consciousness intellectuals that South Africa should reflect the hegemony of Africans, in my view will have serious repercussions for fostering a South African identity.[7] A South African identity should accommodate the variety of linguistic, cultural, religious and civilizational diversity in the country. Consider the above exposition: Africa values group solidarity, the West values individuality, the West values uniqueness, African treasures sameness, the West welcomes and solicits competition, Africa cooperation, the West treasures separateness, Africa collectiveness, for the West survival of the fittest is the economic dogma, for Africa survival of the tribe. The West strives for control over nature; Africa seeks unity with nature. And so on. Africanising

South Africa would not lead to a common identification of everyone with the state and its national symbols: it would lead to violent clashes, especially from Westerners that would feel marginalised and threatened. I argue that the apartheid project was one in which Western civilizational hegemony was enforced on the African people of South Africa by all manner of means, including violent repression, cultural engineering through schools and job reservation.[8] The apartheid project in a sense tried to keep Africans from enjoying Western rights and forced them into small nonviable territories, where they could live out an "African identity" on terms dictated by the South African white dominated polity. The violence and bloodshed that followed this project is common knowledge. The apartheid policies also held that the two civilizational paradigms were unbridgeable. The solution to the problem of state-sponsored social engineering was however normatively indefensible in terms of the basic precept of the equality of human beings. The question is how these major differences can be accommodated in post-apartheid South Africa? In my view replacing white (Western) hegemony with African hegemony is indefensible and unworkable.

Moreover, the group solidarity and past orientation of African civilization is incommensurable with capitalism and free enterprise. "Africanisation" of South Africa's public values would lead to an economic disaster of the first magnitude—these values do not fit a free enterprise system. A form of state *dirigisme* would be more compatible with African civilizational values. It is taken as given and common knowledge, for the purposes of this essay that Marxist-socialist oriented economic policies have failed decisively in Africa, Latin America as well as in Central Europe and the USSR. On the failure of socialism, with apology to the words of the epitaph of Sir Christopher Wren, if you want to see socialist failures, look around you. The human cost of such an enterprise would be staggering.

Besides, a civilizational conflict could well be internationalised. So-called fault-line wars have been fought all over the globe during recent times. In Bosnia, Israel, Chechnya, the Sudan, Kashmir and other places on the globe civilizational clashes in the form of civilizational fault-line wars have been internationalised (cf. Huntington 1996: 266-298). This means that kindred civilizational groups take the side of the civilization involved in the conflict. For example in Bosnia the Russians support the Serbs, the Germans the Croats, Islamic states the Muslims. In Israel in the final instance, the West supports Israel, Islamic states the Palestinians, in Africa in the Sudan a clash between Muslims and African Christians has shown a similar pattern of civilizational support (Huntington 1996: 267). Such internationalising inevitably ups the ante in these conflicts, lengthening their resolution. One can well imagine the cost of a civilizational clash in South Africa being considerable in terms of bloodshed as well as economic deprivation of ordinary people.

It would in my view therefore not make sense, from a civilizational point of view, to engineer an "African" nation from such a wide-ranging set of differences between the people of South Africa. It would not encourage a common South African identity. Moreover, when using state power to impose an identity on citizens of South Africa, an African majority could easily be tempted to define African identity as the pure and exemplary identity of South Africanness, while making the Western (often called Eurocentrist identity) into an evil to be eradicated. The Western identity could become the site against which the African identity is expressed (cf. Connolly 1991: x). A state engineered national political identity would, in my view, lead to civilizationally based ethnic nationalist clashes. A brief excursus on ethnic nationalism in South Africa is therefore necessary.

Ethnic Nationalism: Death Knell for South Africa?

Ethnicity and ethnic consciousness, contrary to the expectation of many liberal theorists of nation-building, is reviving and rampant on a world-wide scale. The list of ethnic conflicts is seemingly endless, and not only confined to "backward" Third World ethnically divided states. Globally "ethnic genies" are surging out of their enchanted lamps. Belgium, Canada, France, Britain, Australia, Switzerland, Spain, Czechoslovakia, Yugoslavia, (Bosnia), the old USSR, India, Bangladesh, Sri-Lanka, Nigeria, Somalia, Burundi, Indonesia, Malaysia, Iraq, Syria and Turkey. One can even have the place names alliterate Biafra, Bangladesh, Burundi, Brussels, Beirut and Belfast.

In post-Second World War ethnically divided societies, ethnic conflict has been exacerbated by the role of the state in society. The actions of the state have been used to condition ethnic groups into responses of ethnic mobilisation. In ethnically divided societies the state has neither been a non-autonomous executive committee of the capitalist classes, nor the neutral arbiter in service of society espoused by early liberal political theorists. In post-colonial, ethnically divided states, a single ethnic group took control of the state and used its powers to exercise hegemony over other ethnic groups. It is true to say that in many instances the state was the executive committee of the dominant ethnic group. Numerous states have found it useful to recruit their armies, police, judiciary and civil servants predominantly or disproportionately from one ethnic community. In states with coherent and organised ethnic groups, dominant ethnic classes have been able to enhance and preserve their dominance through state power. Malaysia, Sri Lanka, the Serbs of Yugoslavia, the Tutsi dominated state of Burundi, and Zaire under Mobutu, as well as the National Party governments of South Africa between 1948-94 are classic examples.[9] In essence this means that the national identity of such societies was engineered around the identity of the dominant ethnic group.

Where does this leave South Africa and its future as a non-racial society? The Afrikaans community is a classic example of one where state policies, from the 1910 Botha and Smuts governments onwards, aided ethnic mobilisation and the eventual capture of state power by the Afrikaner nationalists. After 1948 the state was used to advance the material as well as symbolic interests of Afrikaners and to manipulate black ethnic identity. This exercise started to unravel by 1978 and eventually led to a transfer of state power to a dominant and numerically superior race group: black Africans.

In South Africa the Africans are divided among ethnic lines, although these are at present neither salient nor being exploited politically. What is interesting here is that the winning party in this group is ideologically committed to some form of ethnically neutral, but racially representative state. The ANC conspicuously avoids the beating of ethnic tribal drums. Its official ideology is progressivist and developmentalist: to it tribalism and parochialism are anathema. Moreover, in the April 1994 and June 1999 national elections as well as the November 1995 and December 2000 local polls, black voters from all black ethnic groups universally supported the ANC. It garnered overwhelming majorities among all black ethnic groups except the Zulus. In black politics, the ANC is a truly transethnic party.

What has to be decided in the post-apartheid era of a black dominated government and political order, is whether the ANC can maintain its stance of an ethnically neutral state.[10] Some elements in South African society—the Zulu-based Inkatha Freedom Party, the Afrikaans rightwing *Volkstaters*—already perceive a threat to their ethnic identity in the new political order. Should it become clearer in time that in effect the supposedly ethnically neutral state is but a Xhosa and African dominated state, a reactionary ethnic response is likely. Support for the ANC could be transformed by ethnic entrepreneurs into mobilisation of the various African and black subcultures against the ANC. Some evidence of such mobilisation is emerging in the Western Cape where the ANC is facing continuous problems of reconciling the material interests of the "Coloureds" and Africans in their constituency. Indeed, this is immobilising the ANC in that province, with the National Party capitalising on the ANC's impotence regarding the contradictions in its support base in this province.

Mutatis mutandis a white radical response is possible if the ethnically neutral state is perceived and experienced as an exclusivist Africanist hegemonic, dominated and manipulated state. Calls for a separate white (Western) state could well turn into a bloody Northern Ireland or Bosnian style of white separatist struggle. The challenge to the governing ANC is to remain true to their ideal of a non-racial state with which all ethnic communities can identify. The debate and struggle for control of the Jacobin faction in the ANC versus the old time liberal pluralists will be crucial in deciding the ethnic neutrality of the state, in contrast to an ethnically dominated central state.

While the leaders of the ANC in the new-order go out of their way to downplay ethnicism and tribalism in South Africa, the struggle for a unique black African identity of the South African State has by no means ceased. In May of 1997 the ANC as governing party in South Africa held a special caucus meeting to debate the "national question" in South Africa. The caucus was held in response to calls by Africans in the ANC that black people were underrepresented in parliament, cabinet and other government structures. The consensus that emerged from this meeting was that black people have to play a leading role in South Africa after apartheid, but that there is a place for minorities in South Africa. The caucus decided that a balance had to be found between a narrow black-based leadership and a meaningless non-racism on the other. However, the liberation of black people was a particular focus of the freedom struggle, according to the caucus.[11] In addition, African people, according to Wally Serote, black intellectual and Member of Parliament, are the indigenous people of South Africa and there should be a special positioning for them in the liberation process and in the solution to the "national question" (*Beeld*, 26 May 1997).

The Desirability of the State Engineering a National Identity in South Africa

The official policy of the majority party in government in South Africa, the African National Congress, is to "build a nation" and forge a national identity in South Africa by means of state intervention. This mode of thought pervades almost all major policy documents, be it educational, economic redevelopment or the Truth and Reconciliation Commission—which unearthed the history of the struggle for freedom the last 30 years.[12] The ideal is also part of the preamble to the constitution of South Africa "to build a united and democratic South Africa." It forms part of a constitutional chapter: Chapter 3, section 41, reads inter alia: "All spheres of government...must preserve the national unity and indivisibility of the Republic."

However, the idea of "building a nation" is fraught with conceptual, ideological and practical difficulties. Nation building as a policy, moreover, needs some normative framework as a basis from which to formulate public policy. Therefore an analysis of the term nation building and its desirability as a public policy must be undertaken. First a short discussion on the term "nation" is necessary. Etymologically, nation is derived from the Latin word *natio*: a being born, from *natus*, past participle of *nasci*: to be born. According to *Webster's Dictionary* its primary meaning is "a people connected by supposed blood ties, generally manifested by community of language, religion, customs and so on..." The *Penguin Dictionary of Politics* notes the difficulty of the definition: A nation is a body of people at who least see part of their similarity in terms a single communal identity with some considerable historical continuity of union, with major elements of a common culture, and with some sense of geographical location, at least for a good part of those who make up the nation (*Penguin Dictionary of Politics:* 223). The difficulty is that all of these criteria may be false in any set of examples. Is there such an entity as the Belgian, British or United States "nations"? In terms of people connected by common blood ties, South Africa will hardly qualify as having a "nation." And therein lies the "rub"—if there is no such thing as a South African nation, what sort of national identity does a South African have, or should s/he have?

Furthermore one can note in passing that nation-building exercises in ethnically deeply divided societies have for the most part been singularly unsuccessful during the last 50 years of decolonisation of such societies. Moreover, in my judgement, the former Soviet Union and Yugoslavia are further examples of spectacular failures in nation-building exercises by government fiat or official utopian constitutional engineering (cf. Horowitz 1985: 567).

It is clear that some further conceptual clarification is needed. To start with, a distinction should be made between a nation and an ethnic group. An ethnic group or *ethnie* refers to the complex combination of racial, cultural and historic characteristics by which societies are sometimes divided. At a simple level the idea is exemplified by racial groupings in which skin colour is the separating characteristic: e.g., "whites" in South Africa. At a more refined level, an ethnic group would consist of people of the same skin colour or race, a common language, a shared religion, sometimes a shared political ideology. But this is also difficult: Jews the world over have the same religion, but not a common language or skin colour, nor for that matter a common history—except for the idea of the Diaspora and recent Israeli history.

One way to escape the difficulty of getting a conceptual grip on the terms ethnicity, ethnie and nation, is to view these as social constructs and not as empirical and primordial phenomena akin to natural science phenomena which and can be defined in universal terms, verified by scientific experiment and so on. Following Degenaar 1994: 24, one can conceptualise *ethnicity* as a social construct, which consists of a group of people of common descent (race and skin colour), culture and language. "Cultural nation" refers to a group of people organised and legitimised on the basis of a congruence of culture and power. When the congruence of culture and power concerns a homogeneous communal culture, organic terms such as birth and growth of a nation are used as metaphors to describe the nation, expressing its sovereignty in a nation state. In the case of a state using its power to impose a common culture on a plurality of people cultures in a multi-cultural society, the metaphor of nation building is used and a "state-nation" can be said to have been engineered. Tamarkin likewise distinguishes between a state-nation and a nation-state. "The concept of a state-nation, as distinguishable from a nation-state, acquired academic credence and legitimacy and currency. The notion of a state-nation assumes that Leviathan (the state) can, and is morally entitled to, forge a national identity out of diverse ethnic groups. For him this notion is as deterministic as it is dangerously Jacobin. It is deterministic because it assumes that the end result of the endeavour of the state-nation is bound to be the nation-state. It is dangerously Jacobin because it assumes that there is a national 'general will' which entitles the wielders of power to coerce and to destroy identities which groups of people voluntary assume" (Tamarkin 1992: 18,19).

Moreover the idea of social engineering on the scale that would be necessary to build a South African "nation" has been decisively criticised by Karl Popper (1966). Such a project would of necessity be a utopian project premised on the basis of some final solution or final state of goodness, i.e. "*The Nation*". In Popperian terms, to forge "*The Nation*", the state would need to make use of utopian social engineering. In essence the power of the state would be used to make people behave in a pre-ordained fashion. The idea of a "thought police" regarding nation building immediately springs to mind. Instead of a pluralistic conception of a South African national identity, the state would decide on that identity and enforce it through means of state power and institutions. The problem is furthermore that the different civilization paradigms in South Africa have different interpretations of morality. Forging a South African identity on the grounds of the Africanness of the majority of the people in South Africa would lead to a single morality—the African—becoming hegemonic. This will most likely be unacceptable to the majority of Westerners. Mutatis mutandis a Western hegemony would be unacceptable to the African majority. If it is accepted that the constitution of 1996 is a type of social contract between the different civilizational identities, the content of this contract will through time need to be reinterpreted. This interpretation is always fraught with difficulty. The Western civilizational identity would, in my view, tend to interpret the Constitution in terms of positive law, while the African civilizational identity would have a predilection to interpret the Constitution in terms of natural law. Should one of the identities wish to have their interpretation enforced on South African society, that would lead to serious clashes. In my view a majoritarian, state engineered South African identity is indefensible, dangerous and undesirable.[13]

Against the Engineering of a State Nation

In the debate regarding nation building in post-apartheid South Africa, the Stellenbosch philosopher Johan Degenaar argues against the sentiment of a nation state as well as a state nation. In his view both conceptions negate individuality and plurality. The use of nationalist terminology is dangerous since it feeds on the myth of a collective personality and creates nefarious expectations in the minds of citizens. Nationalism makes use of nineteenth century terminology; it is a modernist discourse in a post-modern age. It is modernist by positing the nation as the sole source of truth and existential being, while the post-modernist paradigm rejects this as authoritarian and anti-pluralistic. In essence it goes against the core of democratic values in which the individual worth of the person is held in highest esteem (Degenaar 1994: 24).

Degenaar rejects the Stalinist conception of the nation as being possible in South Africa. The type of cultural nation which is defined as: an historically evolved stable community arising on the basis of a common language, territory, economic life and psychological make-up manifested in a community of culture (Degenaar 1992: 9). This type of nation entails the congruence of power, culture and language and state. During the apartheid years the National Party tried to give this conception pragmatic reality by creating black nation states. The project failed because the incipient African nations could not be confined to specific territories and resulted in racial discrimination inside "white South Africa," which in any case was a racist and not a cultural entity. Degenaar conceptualises an alternative idea of the nation in which the nation is constituted by a common loyalty to a transcendent factor: the democratic constitution. This conception comes close, in my view, to the United States conception of nationhood.

Furthermore the ideal of "building a nation" is compounded by the history of the struggle for political power by the indigenous African people of South Africa. The African National Congress, founded as the South African Native National Congress in 1912, was strongly ideologically based. It could not be otherwise, since there was no common ethnic or national background to its founding. From its inception the ANC followed a non-racial ideology which was inclusive of all national groups of South Africa. In the absence of a common language, culture or religion it had to base its politics of resistance on the ideology of struggling on behalf of the repressed class of African workers. The enemy was not the colonial power, as in much of the rest of Africa, but the white ruling class. An identity based on the classical precepts of language, culture and religion was impossible since the African people themselves were deeply divided on these issues. The common factor was the experience of repression by the white dominated political order, therefore against whom the struggle for freedom was aimed was more important than what it tried to achieve. There was and is no alternative African

South African nation in the ethno-national sense of the term, with a myth of common descent and a distinctive language and culture. The only sense of identity that African freedom movements have been able to impose on their newly found independent political entities was that of a type of territorial identity: Zambia, Zimbabwe, Namibia and so on. The "national self" is determined by geography. The dominant mass party in power takes it upon itself to determine who the nation is. This can lead to dangerous Jacobinism: where people are forced to assume a particular identity.

Moreover economic modernisation will not necessarily lead to a common culture or civilizational paradigm in South Africa. The Japanese for instance, have undergone a historically rapid transition economically—a civilization of 1500 years old was economically modernised in less than 100 years—yet retain their basic Japanese identity. There is little reason to believe, in my judgement, that the African civilizational paradigm will become westernised simply through economic modernisation. There may be an elite acceptance of some sense of Westernisation, but that will hardly turn around the millions of ordinary Africans in South Africa into becoming "Western." Especially in the light and context of an elite-led resurgence of African self-confidence in South Africa. Having captured state power and being part of a majority of Africans on the continent of Africa, Africans in South Africa are looking to a renaissance of their African identity, not to becoming black Westerners in Africa.[14] India's post colonial experience and the experience of Hong Kong since its reintegration into China suggests that civilizational norms are particularly obdurate to rapid change (cf. Huntington 1986: 56-72).

A South African nation engineered in terms of an African nationalistic paradigm would inevitably hegemonic of some dominant group. According to Degenaar 1992 it would have the following characteristics:

- It would operate on an ideology of primordialism, assuming the nation as a natural given, and culminate in slogans of one nation, one state, one culture. It would invite demagoguery,
- It would enforce one homogeneous culture, which would have to be manufactured by a state ideology,
- It would need the myth of a chosen people and would use such a myth to legitimate unjust actions,
- Such a nation would not be able to accommodate minority cultures and minority rights. It would by definition follow a policy of elimination, repression or segregation,
- The right of the individual would be subsumed under the rights of the collectivity, the state,
- It would reduce the differentiation between state and civil society making the state a paramount entity, and,
- It would tend to ignore the precepts of the balance of power. The sovereignty of the people would be invoked against the powers of the courts and other balancing institutions in society (Cf. Degenaar 1992: 11,12).

Degenaar's comments point to the problematic of the vision of engineering a nation in South Africa. There is no commonly accepted Creed in terms of which such a nation could be engineered/or "built." In the liberal "melting pot" vision of society, a common creed is a necessary condition towards forging a nation. The sufficient conditions would include that differing groups can exist comfortably with each other and tolerate modest differences. No one is allowed to distort or radically change the core national identity or common creed. Liberal individual rights form the basis of such a melting pot vision of society. The foregoing analysis has clearly demonstrated that such a vision has not been accommodated in South Africa.

South African Identity Through the Constitution?

South Africa should in my view follow the example of the United States in any attempt to encourage a sense of national identity. The "nation" of the United States, according to leading scholars such as Kohn, Huntington, Gleason and Harrington, is a political and ideological concept, based on shared space (Citrin 1990: 1128). Whatever one's background, to be an American one has to accept the national creed defined in its constitution and live in America (Citrin 1990: 1129). Citrin summarises this basic American value system as follows: democracy (republicanism, popular sovereignty), liberty, equality of opportunity, individual achievement and self-reliance. The sense of American identity refers to the emotional attachment Americans have to these political symbols. Furthermore there seems general acceptance that American identity is enshrined in the idea of popular political participation, economic individualism, and egalitarian social manners. In a study conducted in California, Citrin *et al.* found a high consensus on the constituent elements of "American" identity: such as treating all people irrespective of race alike and voting in elections (civic responsibility). Not surprisingly, English as the dominant language of America is widely accepted; 76 percent of respondents in the survey thought that it was important that true Americans speak English. Belief in God was only very important for 40 percent of respondents (Citrin 1990: 1128, 1129).

The outlines of a constitutionalist-based South Africanness is to be found in the new South African constitution. The Constitution of 1996 is a truly basic law, following the continental German custom of a *Grundgesetz.* The ensuing values pervade the new constitution: The unity of the South African state and its territory, a common South African citizenship, a common national anthem, a flag, a recognition of eleven official languages, a Bill of Rights that is classically liberal and permissive, but including a strong commitment to equality and third generation rights such as the right to a clean environment. Important for the purposes of cultivating a South African constitutional-based identity is the guarantee of freedom of association and freedom of religion, belief and opinion.[15] It would be unconstitutional, in my view, to try and engineer a South African nation that would reflect African hegemonic values. The Bill of Rights guarantees individuals the right to use the language and participate in the culture of their choice. Moreover, cultural, religious and linguistic communities are guaranteed the right to enjoy their culture as well as to form religious and cultural associations. I would therefore argue that the common denominator for the development of a sense of South Africanness would be to encourage and develop a common allegiance to the land (space) and constitution (basic rules of conduct). Whatever one's origin one should endorse this basic creed to be identified as a South African. A national identity can no more be engineered by government action than people can be converted to Christianity or any other religion for that matter, by the exercise of political power. The turn-around (*periagogè*) necessary to acquire such an identity comes from an inner conversion: it cannot be enforced.

Constitutional Patriotism

In my view building a *national identity* (not an artificial "nation") should entail cultivating patriotism based on a shared constitution. The role of the state should be minimal, and the actions of individuals and civil society maximal in encouraging such a sense of national identity. The German term "*Verfassungspatriotismus,*" constitutional patriotism, can serve as a useful marker of South African identity. This could lead to acceptance and mutual strengthening of common values enshrined in the constitution. The overwhelming majority of South Africans support the Constitution of 1996. The South African constitution was the end product of a process of mutual accommodation of political, social and economic values, which took four years to produce. It was uniquely popularised by receiving more than a million submissions, and after its acceptance was distributed to almost every household in South Africa. It was legitimised by a Constitutional Assembly freely elected on a proportional list system that gave the tiniest political minorities say in its genesis. It is in the process of being institutionalised through actions in the Constitutional Court. The Constitution reflects to a large extent, the consensus reached in our society after decades of armed struggle,centuries of white domination and four years of hard negotiation. A constitution cannot fabricate a consensus, but it can maintain and enhance a consensus already reached. However, the governing majority, which will be tend to be black African dominated in the future, would have to tread a careful path in maintaining the integrity of the Constitution and fostering a sense of constitutional patriotism. An ethnic minority, which believes and experiences the constitution as being irrelevant in protecting their human rights as a distinct group, will have little reason to support it. The constitutional consensus reached in 1996 will not be a self-perpetuating one: it will need constant nurture. An exclusively African majoritarian reading of its contents will almost certainly lead to its failure as a source of patriotism. Conversion to a South African *Verfassungspatriotismus* must of necessity be consistent with the principles of a free and open society.

In addition, using pluralistic symbols, such as the "rainbow nation," could add to the sense of plurality which South Africans should be encouraged to share with one another. In practical terms, sport teams and heroes could also serve as binding factors. However such patriotism is short-lived: national identity built on sports teams tend to wax and wane with the success of such teams. Moreover, due to historic reasons, sports teams in South Africa are racially fragmented: rugby and cricket are "white" sports, soccer is the most popular sport among Africans and so on. In my view, national teams which foster a sense of national identity are a bonus, but cannot serve as the point of departure for the building of such an identity.

In short, what is needed is to understand the process of developing and fostering a national identity for South Africans is that a societal dialectic is needed. A dialectical process which the two incommensurable civilizational paradigms are synthesised into a common national identity. The various civilizational entities in South Africa, while partly incommensurable, are human systems, subject to change and adaptation. Civilizations are not entities cast in granite and immutable. As Huntington has written, while civilizations endure they also evolve. They are dynamic, rise and fall merge and divide, they disappear. Civilizations are cultural entities, therefore they cannot have supra human characteristics such as eternal immutability. Over time, a uniquely South African civilizational identity may appear, but not through utopian social engineering.

Moreover, the constitutional patriotism argued for in this essay would entail that individuals will have to interpret the constitution into their own sense of national identity. One can then expect a post-modernist, rich texture of a sense of national identity, rather than one definable "legislated or engineered" national identity. In a post-modern, world-order, arguments for cultural or civilizational hegemonies where the freedom of the individual is threatened are simply indefensible. Pluralism and tolerance are what is needed to encourage constitutional patriotism, not unity and hegemony.

Conclusion

In this essay I have argued for the development and fostering of a post-apartheid national patriotism in South Africa based on its Constitution. I have challenged the notion that a national identity could be engineered by means of state manipulation. Drawing on the notion of the serious consequences of a conflict based on deeply held civilizational values, I argued that the divided nature of South African society mitigates against trying to forge a national identity: such a project would inevitably boil down to a zero sum game. In such a game, the minority—the Westerners—would have to give in to the majority, the Africans.

For those South Africans who dream of a homogeneous, African-dominated society the lack of a fusion of cultures and people through a socially engineered crucible, this vision is surely problematic. For practical people, a "South African nation" is but a metaphor, and a tenuous one at that. However, this does not mean that there can be no social solidarity in a multicultural society. Peace and unity does not require uniformity, but social coherence. What South Africa does need is an acceptance of differences between cultures, linguistic communities, civilizations, races and religions. Mutual respect for each other will maintain and reinforce peace. To foster that respect, constitutional patriotism is a step in the direction of a national creed that could cultivate greater unity.

Instead of a state-enforced civilizationally based ethno-cultural identity—which would reflect the civilizational view of the African majority—South Africans should strive for a spatial identity, as has been the case with the United States. Constitutional patriotism is defended as the least conflictual and most practical way of constructing and promoting a common South African national identity. The challenge for a national creed in a multicultural society is to reconcile the shared space (the land, the state) with a shared vision or experience of historical time. The two major civilizations in South Africa have accepted the sharing of the common space. The greater problem will be to develop a shared sense of history (time).

References

Adam, H. 2001. *Minorities and Globalisation: Locating Afrikaners*, unpublished paper delivered at the *Group of 63 Conference*, 25 August 2001, Kempton Park, South Africa.

ANC 1997, July. *Building on the foundation for a better life: draft strategy and tactics of the African National Congress.*

ANC 1997, July. *Character of the National Democratic Revolution.*

Bozeman, A.B. 1976. *Conflict in Africa*, Princeton: Princeton University Press.

Brown, D. 1989. "Ethnic revival: perspectives on state and society", *Third World Quarterly*, October.

Citrin, J. and Reingold, B. 1990. American identity and the politics of ethnic change, *Journal of Politics*, vol. 52 no. 4 November.

Connolly W.E. 1991. *Identity/Difference*, Ithaca: Cornell University Press.

Constitution of South Africa, Act 108 of 1996, Pretoria: Government Printer

Degenaar J.J. 1992. *Nations and nationalism: The myth of a South African nation*, Cape Town: Idasa.

Du Toit, C. 1997. "The quest for African identity and the concept of nation-building as motives in the reconstruction of South African society," *Dialogue and Alliance*, vol. 11 no. 1 Spring/ Summer.

Faure, A.M. 1981. Karl Popper, *Open Societies* en Suid Afrika, in *Politikon* vol. 8 no.1 June.

Giliomee, H. 1991. "Building a new nation: alternative approaches, in Cloete," F. 1991. *Policy options for a new South Africa*, Pretoria: HSRC Press.

Horowitz, D. 1985. *Ethnic groups in conflict*, Berkeley: University of California Press.

Huntington, S.P. 1996. *The clash of civilizations and the remaking of world order*, New York: Simon and Schuster.

Kaplan M.A. 1984. *Science, language and the human condition*, New York: Paragon House.

Kotzè, H.J. 1997. *Culture, ethnicity and religion: South African perceptions of social identity*, Johannesburg: Konrad-Adenauer-Stiftung.

Kuhn, T.S. 1970. *The Structure of Scientific revolutions*, Chicago: Chicago University Press.

Lötter, H.P.P. 1997. "Personal identity in multicultural democracies," RAU: Unpublished paper.

Louw, A. du P. 1979. "Swart politiek in Suid-Afrika," *Politikon*, vol. 6 no. 1 June.

Mazrui, A. A. 1986. *The Africans: a triple heritage*, London: BBC publications.

Popper, K.R. 1966. *The Open Society and its Enemies*, London: Routledge.

Popper, K.R. 1970. "Normal science and its dangers," in Lakatos, I. and Musgrave, A. (editors). 1970. *Criticism and the growth of knowledge*, Cambridge University Press.

Robertson, D. 1986. *The Penguin Dictionary of Politics*, Penguin: Harmondsworth.

Sono, T. 1994. *Dilemmas of black intellectuals in South Africa*, Pretoria: Unisa Press.

Tamarkin, M. 1992. *Nationalism, nation building and society in Africa: fateful connections*, Cape Town: Centre for African Studies.

Teffo, L.J. and Ramose, M.B. 1993. "Steve Biko and the interpreters of black consciousness: a response to Lötter," in *Acta Academica*, vol. 25, no. 2 & 3 December.

Turaki, Y. 1991. "Culture and modernisation in Africa: a methodological approach," in *Culture and diversity in Africa: Embarrassment or opportunity?*, PU for CHE Publication, Institute for Reformational Studies, no. 40.

Van Niekerk, A. 1997. *Anderkant die Reënboog*, Kaapstad: Tafelberg.

Voegelin, E. 1952. *The new Science of Politics*, Chicago: University of Chicago Press.

Von Laue, T. 1987. *The world revolution of Westernisation*, Oxford: Oxford University Press.

Webster's New Collegiate Dictionary. 1960. London: Bell and Sons.

Notes

1. The income of black people in the high-income group in South Africa has increased form a share of 13 percent in 1996 to 23.7percent of GDP in 2001. A very significant increase in five years (*Beeld* 20 February 2001: 6).

2. This "paper" is an essay in the sense of "a composition, analytical or interpretative, dealing with its subject from a more or less limited or personal standpoint" (Webster's New Collegiate Dictionary, 1960).

3. These references are to nations in which the state-nation and the nation-state, tend to correlate almost perfectly in terms of ethnic and cultural identities: one would be surprised to find a Swede with the physical and cultural characteristics of a Chinese person, or a blonde Norwegian speaking, "native Korean" in Korea. The point is, in South Africa one can find a blonde African-speaking South African, a "brown" English-speaking South African and an African person of Xhosa descent who is a South African.

4. Karl Popper, in *Normal science and its dangers* (1970), has argued that Kuhn's view of the incommensurability of paradigms makes us prisoners of intellectual frameworks. My position is that competing paradigms are difficult to translate, but not impossible to change or adapt. Cf. also M.A Kaplan, 1984 *Science language and the human condition.*

5. The two civilizational paradigms are sketched rather starkly and without too much nuance. This is done to illustrate the utter reality of the difference between the two civilizations, as well as for reasons of all essays: space is limited. Many Africans have accepted some of the tenets of the Western paradigm, inter alia its emphasis on rational and reasoned discourse, a scientific worldview and so on. On the other hand, Huntington suggests that when the lines are drawn, civilizational conflict tends to fall back on its most basic levels of belief. That makes the incommensurability thesis all the more compelling and an enforced fusion of the two civilizations undesirable.

6. This conception of Africa may be contestable, cf. Ali Mazrui 1986, chapter 3. However many black intellectuals in South Africa, including Themba Sono and the late Steve Biko share this interpretation of "Africa." Cf.

Themba Sono 1994. Much of it may be romanticising of a bygone era.

7. According to apologists of the exclusivist Africanist view of the South African liberation struggle, the struggle for national emancipation, and the regaining of all things lost as a result of the white conquest of Africa, is the cornerstone of Africa's struggle for liberation. The Africanists accept the battle cry "Africa for the Africans". Another example of this exclusivism is to be found in the maxim: African people are the pivot of the new nation with their main allies the so-called coloured and Indians in South Africa. The concept of the nation in this view is closely linked to black culture. This exclusionary view of a South African nation has been decisively defeated by the ANC in the 1994 founding elections, but the sentiments, especially among black intellectuals, have not been expiated form South African body politic (Cf. Degenaar 1992: 6).

8. Note the following comment on apartheid by African scholars in South Africa: "...The undying white belief that people with black skin colour are naturally incapable of growing into mentally mature human beings, and that, consequently they are unable to take responsibility for themselves..." (Teffo and Ramose: 1993: 3.)

9. Cf. David Brown, "Ethnic revival: perspectives on state and society", *Third World Quarterly*, October 1989.

10. The whole question of ethnicity and ethnic consciousness has not suddenly evaporated in post-apartheid South Africa. In a comprehensive survey of contemporary ethnic consciousness and attitudes in South Africa, Kotzè, 1997 has come to the conclusion that: "ethnicity is a reality in South Africa, and this would seem to be true of the overwhelming majority of South Africans. In addition. ethnic identification appears to have *increased, especially among Blacks (my emphasis)* since the 1994 elections" (Kotzè 1997:14). Importantly Kotzè has also found, and this is extremely important in the context of the argument of this essay, that "all the respondents from the specific racial groups claim to have the most in common with their own race, language or cultural group" (p. 11). In personal conversations, Kotzè has confirmed that his latest research shows these attitudes have not changed materially in the last four years.

11. It is rumoured in the press that Cheryl Carolus, a woman of "Cape Coloured" origins and acting Secretary General of the ANC, decided against standing for election as the full-time Secretary General in the December 1997 Congress of the Party. An ANC Party source, Rhoda Kadalie, claims that Carolus did not want to fight an exhaustive battle against African candidates, who would be the favourite to fill the post. In the African National Congress, apparently it would not do that a Coloured woman should fill the top Party post, in spite of the ANC's commitment to non-racism and gender equity. This is known as the principle of African leadership, in essence that in all important respects the institutional face of society should reflect the majoritarian position of Africans in our society". Cf. *Femina*, August 1997.

12. Cf. a recent statement by the ANC on National Identity: "Critical to nation-building is the de-racialisation of South African society. It means creating a society in which the position that individuals occupy in political, social and other areas of endeavour is not defined on the basis of race, ethnicity, and language, religious, cultural or other such considerations. It means integrating communities in residential areas, at the work place and within the trade union movement, in sports and other areas. It also means a considered programme of affirmative action to eradicate the disparities created by apartheid. The ANC recognises that individuals within such a nation will have multiple identities, on the basis of their physiological make-up, cultural life and social upbringing. Such distinctive features will not disappear in the melting pot of broad South Africanism.... But it is critical that the overarching identity of being South African is promoted among all those who are indeed South African, as part of a process of building an African nation on the southern tip of the content. The affirmation of our Africanness as a nation has nothing to do with the domination of one culture or language by another—it is a recognition of a geographic reality and the awakening of a consciousness which colonialism suppressed" (ANC July 1997). The ANC further takes the position: "The main thrust of the National Democratic Revolution (NDR) is not to promote fractured identities, but to encourage the emergence of a common South African identity... The main content of the NDR is the liberation of the Black peoples in general and Africans in particu-

lar...(The question of) the identity of the South African nation in the making (is) whether it should truly be an African nation on the African continent, or a clone, for example, of the U.S. and U.K. in outlook; in the style of and content of its media, in its cultural expression, in the language and accents of its children.... Hence what is required is a continuing battle to assert African hegemony in the context of a multi-cultural and non-racial society" (July 1997).

13. For a fuller treatment of this problem, cf. Faure, 1981: 100 and Louw, 1979: 72

14. Cf. President Thabo Mbeki's address to the Corporate Council Summit, Chantilly, VA, USA, April 1997.

15. The relevant sections in the Constitution are: Section 9: the right to equal treatment by the state, specifically "the state may not unfairly discriminate directly or indirectly against anyone on one or more grounds including race, religion, culture language or birth." Section 15: everyone has the right to freedom of conscience, religion, thought, belief and opinion. Section 30: everyone has the right to use the language and to participate in the cultural life of their choice. Section 31: persons belonging to a cultural, religious or linguistic community may not be denied the right with other members of that community to enjoy their culture, practice their religion or use their language, and to form, join and maintain cultural, religious and linguistic associations and other organs of civil society. The constitution includes a qualification that these rights may not be exercised in a manner inconsistent with any provisions of the Bill of Rights. The general tenor of the Constitution is that limitations on rights and the exercise of these rights must be "reasonable and justifiable in an open and democratic society based on human dignity, equality and freedom" (Section 36).

Courtesy of the author.

Nueva Democracia by David Alfaro Siqueiros. Central mural – Piroxilina, Palacio de Bellas Artes.

Part Eight

Arts, Science and Technology in the Service of Peace

The social function of science vis-à-vis *ideologies is first to understand them—what they are, how they work, and what gives rise to them—and second to criticize them, to force them to come to terms with (but not necessarily to surrender to) reality.*

—Clifford Geertz (1964)

The guns and the bombs, the rockets and the warships, are all symbols of human failure.

—Lyndon Baines Johnson (1965)

Author Deepak Lal perhaps best summarizes the problems raised by putting science and technology to the service of peace when he asks "Does modernization require Westernization?" The question of what science can contribute to the cause of peace has occupied man since the onset of the industrial revolution. Man's growing resort to technology in the conduct of war has made him a more dangerous and destructive warrior. With the awesome power of the instruments of war having increased exponentially in the twentieth century, what can technology offer us now in the promotion of peace?

As Daniel Bradlow deftly illustrates, the promotion of massive projects intended to augment a nation's technical capacity can often be viewed as forcing technologies onto an unwilling or uncomprehending people. The displacement of entire populations by dams, roads, pipelines and other "development" schemes, all in the name of progress, have quite often resulted in even greater discontent regarding the state or the institution that promoted the project. To be sure, the application of technology has created new issues in the battle for peace and the equality of opportunity. But at what point does technology cease to be a tool of the rich and the powerful and begin to be an equalizer?

Culture, Literature and Arts in the Service of Peace

Ada Aharoni

International Forum for the Culture and Literature of Peace (IFLAC)

Creating a New Peace Culture

> *Ours is a world of nuclear giants and ethical infants! We know more about war than we do about peace. We know more about killing than we do about living.... It is not the magnitude of the problem that is the great obstacle. It is our colossal indifference to it.*
>
> —General Omar Bradley

At the dawn of the third millennium, due to high technology and globalization, societies are in a constant state of dynamic transformation, be these cultural, economical, or political. We need a world at peace so that it can function and flourish securely, and one of the basic requirements for attaining security and an effective and sustainable development of the world, is the creation of a global and regional "Culture of Peace System," as well as an objective, balanced and ethical media. Leaders should build this new peace culture system in such a way that it could counteract and replace the often prevalent culture of violence in our global village. Its major aims should be:

1. To address cultural and ethical root-causes of violence, conflicts, terror and war.
2. To build harmonious bridges of culture, understanding, and respect among people and nations.
3. To spread a culture of peace climate nationally and globally, and to make "peace news" and "peace culture" developments newsworthy.

A powerful and influential new peace culture system, with the aid of a peace media, could diffuse required peace values, ideas and ethics, through arts, literature and education, which would reach the various sectors of society and the masses. What people watch, hear, and read, and the kind of culture, films, literature, and art they are exposed to and absorb, influence their thoughts, feelings and ethics. It is therefore of crucial importance that those communications and stories we watch on television and in films, and which we listen to on the radio, should be forwarded by programs that create and build and do not destroy.

Culture is a powerful constituent and vehicle at the core of possible transformations, given that it mediates and transfers ideas, values and intellectual refinement between generations and between civilizations. It is both a preserving and a reproductive force, by transmitting the cultural patterns of the past and the present to the future, and an important innovative influence, by its power to inculcate new attitudes, thoughts, values and norms. The major idea exposed in this essay is that culture is a key factor in promoting genuine peace. If a peace culture system instills recognition of the "other," respect for its identity and culture, as well as commitment to solving conflicts and differences by peaceful means, then the chances for peace will be greatly enhanced. By contrast, if the cultural and educational system instill self-centeredness, rejection and hatred of the "other," of its identity and of its culture, and calls for and justifies the resort to violence to solve conflict—then peace will be endangered.

If leaders succeed in building the needed reformed "peace culture and communications system," it can make it possible for the creative voices of the many lands around the globe yearning for peace to be heard and to be listened to. The writers, filmmakers, dramatists and poets, encouraged by a culture of peace, would give voice to the craving of the preponderant majority of the global community to build a world beyond war, terror, and violence. There is, therefore, a crucial need for reform at an international scale, concerning culture, literature and the arts, which can replace the culture of violence and crime, which is often a major mode nowadays.

What is the exact definition of "culture?" According to the *Webster Dictionary* "culture" is defined as: "The development, improvement and refinement of the mind, emotions, interests, manners, tastes, as well as the arts, ideas, customs and skills of a given people in a given period." The *Oxford English Dictionary* adds to this definition, that culture is: "The intellectual side of civilization." Culture can therefore be perceived as the essence of personal and national identity. The definition of "culture" used in this essay is based on all the above.

And what precisely is meant by the term "peace," in the expression "a culture of peace"? The *Webster Dictionary* defines "peace" as: "freedom from war, public security, freedom from disagreement or quarrels, harmony, concord, serenity." The definition of "peace" in this essay conforms to all the above; however, in the context of a "peace culture," it includes in addition, a more active mode and meaning of "peace." It considers peace not merely as the absence of violence and war, but furthermore, as a dynamic and continuing creative process.

An important step forward toward the goal of creating a new peace culture system took place when the year 2000 was proclaimed by the United Nations General Assembly as the Year of the Culture of Peace. As a follow-up to this crucial initial stage, the United Nations, together with decision-makers all over the world, could implement a period of, say, five years for the establishment of the "Cinquenial Peace Culture System," in which a powerful network of peace culture could be widely established and developed, with the help of governments and peace culture organizations all over the world. This new needed global "culture of peace system" could be empowered to implement the vast and dynamic changes and reforms needed for the peaceful sustenance of the world.

In the present essay the possibility, significance and impact of the creation of a new and effective regional and global "culture of peace system," and communications network, relying on arts and literature in the pursuit of peace, will be explored, analyzed, defined and discussed. In addition, recommendations as to how to create and effectively implement such a system will be offered.

What Does a New Peace Culture Consist of?

> Dear Descartes, I Create therefore I am, and not merely, I think therefore I am!

The process of initiating and building an innovative peace culture system, by global and national leaders, can be related to ongoing initiatives of educational institutions affiliated to the United Nations and other establishments. The proposed "culture of peace system" should have intra-state as well as inter-regional dimensions, and it should be established on the basis of solid and thorough research at various levels. Recent research studies have pointed to the need for the building and promotion of a culture of peace, for example Adams D's study *"From A Culture of War and Violence to A Culture of Peace and Non-Violence,"* sponsored by the "Year for the Culture of Peace."

What should be the structure of this new peace culture system, and who should be in charge of establishing and developing it? Until now, NGOs (non-governmental organizations), in several countries took it upon themselves to promote the culture of peace. However, the various NGOs, staffed by underpaid or mostly unpaid volunteers, do not have the means or the power to build such an elaborate system. Neither do they have the amenities to compete with the flood of hate propaganda from extremists, fundamentalists, and fanatical political groups.

Anti-peace organizations are usually well funded and staffed by professionals. They have their own television and radio stations and all the amenities to spread their violent hate propaganda. Therefore, to counteract fanatical and violent hatred, an effective and powerful "peace culture system" should be urgently established and it should aim at the utmost level of professionalism and expertise. After the horrendous terrorist attack on the Trade Center in New York (September 11, 2001), it has become obvious that it is urgent to build a powerful and effective peace culture system and network at the governmental level.

Hence, the following measures are recommended at the national and international levels:

1. Leaders, decision-makers and governmental bodies should consider establishing ministries of "Peace Culture and Communications," with appropriate budgets that can accomplish the huge task of changing the often rampant global and national culture of violence and terror to one of harmony and peace.
2. Leaders, decision-makers and municipalities should build a multi-layered structure and framework for the establishment and propagating of the innovative culture of peace system and communications network and media, which will need to be minutely planned and designed.
3. Literature and the arts, in the service of peace, should be widely developed and promoted by decision-makers and cultural institutions, and peace education and peace studies at all levels should be initiated and established, including global Peace Satellites, Television and Radio.
4. NGO's: Non-governmental peace organizations in the various countries should be involved in the creation of the new peace culture system and network, and leaders and decision-makers should widely promote and sponsor them, to enable them to operate effectively and in an interconnected fashion for the building of a peace culture system based on literature and the arts in the service of peace.

NGOs could also help in the collection of the various pluralistic cultural contributions of peace literature, poetry and the arts, from the best that is available, thus reflecting the many "Voices of the Earth" for a peaceful world without violence or terror. This new vital and pluralistic peace culture should be promoted by governments, as part of the needed peace culture system. These multicultural works of art and literature based on peace values could promote powerful components of BCMs: "Building Confidence Measures," among people and nations, including the values of understanding, appreciation and respect for the culture of "the other." The specific discipline and research of multicultural "peace culture," based mainly on literature and the arts, has to be more developed and propagated. It is mainly NGOs that have developed the ideology and conception of the culture of peace. The International Peace Research Association (IPRA) has been a pioneer in propagating this required new discipline, as well as The International Forum for the Literature and Culture of Peace (IFLAC).

Governments today should invest in developing the culture of peace and save in armaments. The creation, developing and spreading of a culture of peace system could be the best investment for defense. As in "preventive medicine," a systematic promotion of the culture of peace can prevent the dangerous influence on society caused by a widespread violent culture and rise of terror and hatred that lead to conflicts and wars. The culture of peace system should be implemented at all levels of education, from kindergardens to universities, where it should be made a regular subject of teaching in schools, as for instance, reading and mathematics.

In addition, a wide program of peace education should be implemented regionally and globally, through popular universities, based on peace arts and literature. Furthermore, radio, television, and satellite networks, spreading programs and films initiated by the new culture of peace system, should be promoted by every nation.

In a conflict or war situation, there are several benefits to be reaped from the development of a culture of peace system. These can be grouped in three major stages: before, during, and after the occurrence of a conflict or a war.

Before: In a tense situation, peace culture can function as a preventive remedy. After coming into contact with the culture of "the other" and listening to his side of the "story" or the conflict, an acceptable agreement by both sides becomes easier and he ceases to be a threat. There is a popular saying: "An enemy is someone to whose story we have not listened to."

During: An open, pluralistic culture of peace, based on values of tolerance and moderation, can help in arriving to a solution. Even when conditions for a settlement may have developed, attainment of peace can be delayed by the mistrust created by the conflict situation. The building of bridges of understanding of the "other's" view, and respect for the other's culture and identity, can help by building confidence measures.

After: A well-organized culture of peace system can also help in building renewed trust between people and nations after the conflict or war is over. During a war, not only are buildings destroyed, but also the image of the enemy, who is usually portrayed as a "demon" by each of the sides. Deep residues of fear, hatred, and mistrust linger in the hearts of former opponents. These sentiments cannot be overcome only by the signing of a peace treaty by leaders, but require also a thorough re-construction of a positive image of each other, by the people themselves, and by acquiring knowledge, understanding, and respect of each other's identity, ethnicity and culture.

A suitable vehicle for this required "reconstruction," are the arts: literature and poetry, for they are vehicles of feelings, and as such they have the ability to reach the deeply emotional layers of mistrust and hatred built over the years in the hearts of enemies, and they have the power to dissipate them.

Another possible innovative aspect of the building of a new global peace culture system, which leaders and municipalities could consider, is the founding of "peace museums." This innovative development has recently been established in various countries to help propagate the peace culture heritage of nations, and to make it accessible to the whole of humankind. Peace museums have been founded in various countries, including Japan, England, Samarkand and other countries. Japan is a leading figure in this new trend, and it has already founded more than sixty peace museums. They demonstrate the great yearning of the Japanese people for a peace culture, after having suffered the atrocities of the atomic bombs on Hiroshima and Nagasaki.

Peace museums can be a great aid in promoting and presenting national and global cultures of peace. They represent a new conception of what a museum should be, they are "alive" and full of vital activity, and are becoming increasingly popular. Schoolchildren and students regularly visit them, and use their materials for their works and research on the culture of peace. In addition, public lectures, exhibitions of arts, peace literature and poetry, are organized and presented to the wide public. Ideally, peace museums should become a "must" in every major city and town in our global village. Such a huge task as the building of peace museums globally and regionally can only be accomplished by a well-financed governmental or municipal budget.

Where will the money for building this required new peace culture system come from? It is a question of prerogatives and choices. The U.S. for instance, spends an estimated $50 billion on maintaining the fifth fleet in the Persian Gulf and the American presence in Saudi Arabia. All the aid to all peace NGOs in the region together, from private as well as government sources, would barely amount to $100 million. There is no "Culture of Peace" radio or television station in the Middle East. The efforts to uproot violence and hatred and to build confidence measures and understanding between Arab/Palestinians and Israelis, for instance, could be greatly facilitated by a peace network of satellite, television and radio stations, as well as Internet programs. Leaders and decisionmakers should take this important and urgent task as a major and most crucial one, and implement it as soon as possible.

This innovative network could use peace research works and peace literature, as well as multicultural peace art and conflict resolution programs, which could promote the implementation of the new culture of peace system. A resourceful culture of peace system could also establish a "Peace Culture Internet Network," which would include technical help for Internet facilities and the building of peace websites for organizations and individuals all over the world.

The struggle for the creation of a peace culture system must be waged on a large scale, comparable to the efforts for obtaining petroleum, and with as much perseverance and tenacity. This huge endeavor could perhaps gain momentum by involving the World Bank, and the private financial sectors, that would gain in investing in such a venture, as they would be protecting themselves from possible violence and terror.

The Dangers of a Culture of Violence on Television

He playfully showed with a smile and a wink, and a Teddy Bear hug—it could be the beginning of a honey-laden decade in a brave new world—by wisely trading guns for Teddy Bears

A. Aharoni—You and I Can Change the World

Television and other electronic media often provide a vicious and distorted mirror of life and humankind, which has a harmful influence on society. The films and programs based on violence that are continuously aired often condone and prepare the atmosphere for violence and war, and they present distorted models of human relations that endanger society. The mirror they hold up to their audiences is that we live in a horrible jungle, where no one deserves to be trusted.

Satellite and television have become the major cultural and educational influence around the world. To build a culture of peace, therefore, it is necessary to examine the contents of culture and entertainment presented on national and global networks. It has been observed that many films and programs, presented daily on television and other electronic media, are mainly homicide, murder and crime films. The films on these violent themes have reached such dimensions that it seems sometimes they are advertising crime. They are inflated by sensation and "rating-seeking" producers and markets that disregard their bad influence on society.

It is often difficult nowadays to find non-violent films on television, as most of them show men shooting guns and killing people. In the past, some psychologists maintained that violence on television caused no harm, and that on the contrary, it had a beneficial "catharsis" influence on viewers. However, recent research has shown that its violent influence far from being beneficial is destructive and dangerous to society. Today, the major consensus among specialists, and viewers, is that the continuously growing crime-films industry presents a serious threat to human well-being and to the healthy and sustainable development of our global village, and a drastic reform is crucially required.

Pennell AE and Browne KD, in their research on: "*Film Violence and Young Offenders' Aggression and Violent Behavior on Television,*" maintain that viewing violent material influences children, adolescents and adults, who commit violent acts, and heavy exposure to television violence in childhood is associated with violent crime as an adult. Ways in which screen violence can effect behavior includes: 1) imitation of violent roles and acts of aggression, 2) triggering aggressive impulses in predisposed individuals, 3) desensitizing feelings of sympathy towards victims, 4) creating an indifference to the use of violence, and 5) creating a frame of mind that sees violent acts as socially acceptable responses.

Zann M, in "*Children, Television and Violence,*" reports that several studies, mainly conducted in North America, have found a correlation between television violence viewing and aggressive behavior. In additional research, Singer MI, in "*Contributors to Violent Behavior Among Elementary and Middle School Children,*" reports: a significant association was also demonstrated linking violence exposure and television-viewing habits with violent behavior. Much the same findings were reported in a review of the literature on "*Violent Games and Aggression,*" conducted by Griffiths M. The study showed that most video games feature aggressive and violent elements, and that they have a detrimental effect on individuals and children who play such games. Even seemingly innocent cartoon films were shown they could be destructive and induce violence and aggression. All the above findings clearly support the need of a reform in the culture of violence on television, films, and in the video industry.

Responsible institutions should replace the culture of violence by a culture of peace, based on arts and literature in the pursuit of peace: exciting, constructive and creative films, drama and programs, that profoundly delineate problems of human life and society. Scriptwriters and program directors of television, cinema and videos, could also explore new visions of a better present and future, and present constructive and imaginative new horizons on how to resolve our real existential problems and conflicts.

A television and electronic media based on reality, should not only condemn and provide knowledge about the atrocities of war, such as in the films on the Holocaust, "Shoa", produced by Lanzman, and "Schindler's List," by Spielberg, as well as some of the moving films produced in protest of the Viet-Nam War—but there should also be programs and exciting imaginative films produced about what a world at peace could be. For instance, in the book *Peace Flower* (A. Aharoni), two youngsters bravely face the danger of "Nuki the Nuclear Dragon" who wants to destroy humanity, by flying into space to "Esperia: the Land of the Future," to find the Flower of Peace, and to bring it from the future to our present and to our own reality. This book is used in peace education programs, and it has been translated into several languages. A television film based on it could promote its message and enhance the culture of peace. Unfortunately, unlike *Peace Flower*, most of the futuristic films which we have been exposed to are about a future full of unspeakable horrors, wars, terror and violence.

We are often told that viewers enjoy violent films and that is why television gives them what they want. However, the research in this field has proved that this view is inaccurate. It seems that the films that were the most successful from the point of view of sales in Hollywood were not violent films, but rather, the peaceful family and love films based on Jane Austen's novels.

One of the successful projects of "IFLAC: The International Forum for the Culture and Literature of Peace," termed: "*Turn Off Murder on TV,*" encourages viewers who are offended by violent films on television and deem them to be bad for society, to shut down the violent and offensive television program, and to write to the sponsors and directors along the following lines: "You have lost your money, for we stopped watching your violent film, as it can cause great harm. If you want us to watch, give us good and exciting films that create and build, and that show us how to repair our planet and our lives." This project is gaining momentum, it is not costly and is easy to implement, and it could serve as a model to other organizations and institutions. It is recommended that decision-makers and various cultural and educational institutions adopt this effective project and sponsor and spread it regionally and globally. In general, viewers are delighted to voluntarily take part in the "Turn Off Murder on TV Project."

Thus, the production and marketing of violent films, television programs and video games, including pornographic films, should shift to the production and marketing of constructive and realistically harmonious films and videos. These suggestions have to be organized and implemented through an influential global network, directed and coordinated with other countries, possibly under the auspices of the U.N., the World Bank, private financial concerns and other related institutions. A successful spreading of the culture of peace could make a change in the markets, induced by the populations, who would refuse to watch violent films, and cause the markets to shift to the producing and selling of constructive and beneficial films and video games.

Those kinds of projects are especially crucial in the light that violence has grown not only in cities, towns and schools all over the world, but even in the midst of the family. Drugs, rape, and domestic wife-beating violence and killing of wives and girlfriends, are unfortunately on the increase, regionally and globally. The electronic media, including violent videos and advertisements, are often one of the influences indirectly responsible for that increase. If channeled toward the building of a peace culture, they could contribute a great deal to correct that, and to being instrumental in bringing about the ethical and cultural changes that are so much needed.

It is therefore obvious that satellite and television can play an important role in developing and propagating the necessary new philosophy, values and attitudes concerning the solving of conflicts and differences by peaceful means. A television that would promote the ushering of a new responsible era built on a solid "culture of peace system," would greatly enhance the global and national chances of global peace.

The Necessity of a Peace Media in an Era of Globalization

The same stream of life that runs through my veins day and night runs through the world.

—Rabindranath Tagore

The media, like satellite and television, has a great responsibility in shaping perceptions and opinions of people, and in building the regional and global cultural climate. The global developments that have recently taken place have increased consciousness concerning the notion of the oneness of humanity. The electronic media—satellite, television, radio, and the Internet—can have a great impact in promoting this consciousness, as they ensure fast movement of information, and reach global multitudes simultaneously. Links in cyberspace is an added dimension for the formation of partnerships and they render possible a wide expansion of contacts.

Hence, there is today, a possibility to create and develop a "peace media system" which would be part and parcel of a "culture of peace network." The efficient and successful "Peace Radio," linked to the U.N. University based in Puerto Rico, can be considered as a first step of the peace media system. The main goals would be to develop and promote the various aspects of a culture of peace and make them available to the wide masses around the world.

The media and telecommunications play an important role of interconnection between people and nations, and are a key factor in the process of the globalization of culture. Until recently, people in each society mainly read news concerning their own society and watched their own local media. The growing global telecommunications system promotes the interconnection of different societies and facilitates their attempts to reach each other, and to open up to other realms than just their own. In doing so, the global media can breal up stereotypes and bring about the required openness and changes in the consciousness of individuals and in society. Hence, the modern electronic communications can play a key role in the creation and the promotion of the required culture of peace system.

The spreading by high technology communications and the media of a new ethical peace culture built on meritorious literature and arts can play a major role in counteracting violent cultures. It also has the power to impart pluralism and peace values and to convey the vision of the possibility of creating a peaceful world beyond war, terror and violence.

Decision makers and people responsible for communications should strive to reform them in such a way that they can become reliable vehicles for the promotion and diffusion of the culture of peace. In addition, the people in each country who usually have an impact on popular consciousness concerning issues of war and peace—culture researchers, writers and journalists—should be personally involved and motivated to contribute the best of their talents toward the development and promotion of the culture of peace system.

The media should often confer with peace culture researchers, and their ideas and views should be exposed and made available to all. In addition, they should be given ample opportunity to launch and expose their creations and research.

Another main challenge facing telecommunications and the media at the dawn of the twenty-first century is to consider contributions to peace "newsworthy." There should be a balanced coverage of peace news, and not merely a focusing on the sensational reporting of violence and crime, that often presents an inflated negative view of society, and is a deformation of reality and normalcy. The media should cover the aspects of society and culture that are positive and constructive, such as peace literature, poetry and drama, and expose writers, poets, playwrights and artists.

In our era of globalization, there is a new wave of global culture spreading all over the world, parallel to the spread of global international relations, markets, information and technology. However, unfortunately, at this stage, the emerging globalized culture is more influenced by the predominance of violence than by peace and harmony. The media also powerfully influences the political atmosphere, and it can create the necessary climate that enables governments to reach peace agreements more easily.

In his "Ethical Code of the Media," Sergio Tripi, editor of *GNA: The Good News Agency* (Rome, Italy), discusses the effect of the media on various aspects of life, and emphasizes the responsibility of people in this field: "The building of a just and peaceful world is man's duty, just as man could determine its destruction." A functional and effective "Ethical Code of the Media," as part of the framework of a general system of peace culture, can have the power to strengthen the sense of cultural kinship between individuals and toward the whole of humanity.

The awareness of the oneness of humanity and the consciousness of common values and norms in all cultures, can promote the new identity of the "global citizen," in addition to an identity according to a particular culture. There is a dynamic balance and a symbiotic enrichment of both levels when they come in contact with each other. In confronting the universal quest for identity, telecommunications and the media can indeed promote the advancement towards global identification and unity within diversity.

Thus, the electronic media has to aim at healing our planet of the violent characteristics, terror and wars, which are infesting it in many parts of the world, where violence is often erroneously equated to strength. A conscientious, balanced and responsible media, based on a culture of peace system and network, can help to change all that.

The Role of Peace Literature

I am the enemy you killed, my friend!
—*Strange Meeting*, Wilfred Owen

Culture, literature, and the arts, are an important part of our lives, and they also constitute the building blocks of the required culture of peace system—however, we do not give their contents and impact enough attention. The major components of literature: novels, fiction, poetry, and drama, are often made into films and television scripts. As various studies have shown, viewed fiction can often influence more than facts.

Johan Galtung, in his enlightening article "Not A Question of When, but How—Some Roads to Cultural Integration for Peace," asks a relevant question: How to create and spread the needed culture of peace? The answer to this question is obviously to build and develop a powerful and influential peace culture system, that would include satellite, television and radio. These would spread the culture of peace at all levels, through the establishment of popular universities, and present programs on peace literature, art, and films, at the regional and global levels.

Both classical and modern peace creations collected from multi-cultural resources around the world should be used as models for building the needed peace culture. Outgoing, open and pluralistic works of literature and art should characterize the opening of the new millennium. A positive and harmonious global culture, based on the cooperation of national cultures, can play a significant role in enriching our global village, and in abating conflicts and wars.

There should be a thorough examination of what has already been achieved globally and in national cultures that can help the building of a climate of peace. Despite the fact that our global village has been affected by cultural upheavals and splits caused by conflicts, wars, and differences in development and standards of living levels, peace culture treasures exist in all civilizations. They have been developed at different periods of history, and in different regions, and they should now be collected and used in the present, for reinforcing the common cultural themes of humankind, and the new global citizen consciousness. Those multicultural collected peace works can furthermore constitute important stepping stones toward new peace culture developments.

The manifold benefits of literature and the arts in the pursuit of peace should be made available to the wide public all over our global village. Various valuable classical literary peace sources that have stood the test of time, such as Rabindranath Tagore's philosophical poems, Wilfred Owen's peace poetry, Jubran Khalil Jubran's *The Prophet,* and Leo Tolstoy's *War and Peace,* and many other valuable creative works should be widely presented to audiences around the world, through satellite and television, and utilized as entertainment and in education at all levels. Peace culture research studies of world literature could also highlight new angles of peace themes in great classical drama, as for instance the condemnation of violence and war in the works of Shakespeare, as in: *Romeo and Juliet, Hamlet* and *Othello.*

Peace literature should also be intensively researched in contemporary culture and literature, and new peace books, like for instance, the historical novel: *From the Nile to the Jordan* (A. Aharoni), on peace in the Middle East, and the biography of the peace heroine Thea Wolf, in: *Not in Vain: An Extraordinary Life* (A. Aharoni), should be explored and used. The latter book describes the cooperation of Jews and Arabs in Egypt, in saving refugees from Nazi Europe during the Second World War. This cooperation in the past should be made known, as it gives hope for a cooperation in the present between Israelis and Palestinians.

We find involvement and words of peace in all cultures and in all religions. In the Holy Bible we can find: "How beautiful upon the mountains are the feet of the messenger of good tidings that announces peace!" (Isaiah 52), and in the Koran: "He who walks with peace—walk with him!" (Sura 48), and in our own times, Pope John Paul II admonishes: "War is a defeat for humanity. Only in peace and through peace can respect for human dignity and its inalienable rights be guaranteed."

Governments, relevant institutions, NGOs, and the large public, should be made aware of the power of arts and culture in the pursuit of peace, to 1) render the world a safer place to live in 2) to enrich the intellectual and ethical standard of living and to improve and "repair the world," while retaining and promoting its democratic structure and freedom.

This view of a constructive, ethical, and harmonious culture does not imply an escapist or unrealistic attitude. On the contrary, the underlying sources and grievances of people and nations should be thoroughly investigated and addressed, not only socially and politically, but also through the projection of effective cultural programs: films, art, literature, and drama, about the real lives, experience and problems of real people.

In his influential book *Education Through Art*, the English poet and critic Herbert Read, a pioneer in the development of the concept of peace culture, presents a view of human nature as capable of cooperative activity, mutual respect, and close communal relationships. His premises are that literature and the arts are the best tools for developing personal relations, values, and moral virtue. A function of literature and the arts in society and education, Read explains, is to expand human responsibility, ethical values, capacities and potentialities. He criticizes the over-emphasis and over-grading of science and technology on mainly abstract thinking, at the expense of rational "emotive wisdom," or what is termed today EQ (Emotional Quotient), versus IQ (Intelligence Quotient). According to Read, thoughts, emotions, imagination and vision that can be expressed and acquired through literature and the arts are more important than abstract ideas, for they involve not only the mind but also the heart.

For Read, cultural and aesthetic education properly conceived is also a philosophical, ethical and moral education. Throughout his work the ethical and aesthetical are intimately linked. He considers culture as the means by which the deepest levels of the mind combine with the deepest levels of the heart and soul, when they are expressed through great works of literature and art. He strongly believes that the moral function of art and of literary education is to unite all humanity in a common bond and common ideals. Read's theory and conception of a strong global bond of all humankind through literature and the arts, are especially valuable and pertinent today, and they should be at the basis of the new peace culture system needed for a sustainable global development.

To create this bond between nations, as well as a vibrant multicultural literature of peace, it is important to translate the works of peace writers, poets, and playwrights, so that they can become accessible to neighboring people and countries, and to all the global village. This is especially important in the case of former enemies, as the access to the culture and literature of the "other" can overcome mistrust and fears, and open doors, minds and hearts, in a radical way. When conflicting parties or former opponents have the chance to understand each other, and share their literature and culture together, they succeed to come in contact and touch a deep level of their identities which gives them better chances of creating bridges of reconciliation, common interests and comprehension.

Translation of literary works can play an important role by allowing former opponents to penetrate windows of different realities, views, and conceptions. Conflicts always include two stories, and the presentation and sharing of each others' stories is a great step forward toward a full reconciliation, which is a higher phase than peacemaking. Translation of great literature and poetry, and making it globally available, can moreover demonstrate the basic oneness and similarity of humankind.

Therefore, it is important that institutes for translation of peace works should be founded nationally and globally.

Involved Writers

Could I have but a line a century hence, crediting a contribution to the advance of peace, I would gladly yield every honor which has been accorded me in war.

—General Douglas MacArthur

Writers are often termed the "consciousness of the people" as in T.S. Eliot's words, and they usually honestly express their own deepest thoughts and feelings and their views on life, society and the world, in various kinds of literature and art. However, there is sometimes a certain irrational reticence among writers and publishers of what is thought to be "artistic didacticism." Some writers are afraid to be called "engaged" writers and they therefore shy away from involvement. However, "engaged' does not mean that the writer has been commissioned by some authority other than himself. His engagement and involvement come from his own consciousness and his will to contribute of his creative skills to better the world.

The strong yearning for peace around the world is so much an integral part of peoples' lives that it should also become a basic and major theme in literature and art. If writers, artists, dramatists and poets, refrain from expressing their own real inner aspirations, feelings and thoughts in relation to their life experience, and to major subjects involving society, like war and peace, they become escapists, and thus fail to produce great and important works of art.

At the commencement of the third millennium, writers and intellectuals, as well as philosophers and scientists, should be encouraged to courageously confront critical issues and needed national and international amendments of modern society and the world. They should become the arrowheads of those urgently needed reforms, for they have the power to enlighten the people, and "when people move, leaders will follow." Writers should be encouraged to tackle the great problems of sustained existence, through a free and democratic atmosphere. Attention to the creative building of peace culture could be promoted by peace prizes, grants and competitions on peace themes in the various creative arts.

Writers, dramatists and poets, living at insecure periods threatened by the evils of conflicts, terror and war, cannot for instance, write about love without feeling and expressing their haunting fears for the beloved. They would be untrue to themselves, to their experience of life, their emotions and their psychological predicament, if they did. If, under these circumstances, they decide to be uninvolved and disengaged, and to toe the line and follow the dictate to write only for "art's sake," and not for humanity's sake, their art is diminished in importance and in artistic value.

A responsible and committed attitude towards humanity and the real problems of our lives and times, can increase the greatness of art and its influence on society. Culture in general is a basic determinant of how people envisage and interpret their lives and world, and it should contain all the shades of life, including both bright and dark colors, and all the shades in between. That is, cultural and artistic means should also be used to celebrate the beauty of the world, and to describe the joy of life, and not only the problems and tragedies we encounter in life. Their power should be used both for abating and overcoming conflicts, and also for maintaining a realistic optimism and openness to life, in the present and for the future.

New Directions Needed in the Arts

The Power of creation seems to favor human beings who love life unconditionally, and I am certainly one who does!

—Arturo Rubinstein

The plastic arts and music can fulfill a special role in the creation and promotion of a peace culture, and artists should be made aware of their possible contribution. The human ability to perform artistic creative works that display form, beauty, and keen perceptions, should not be denuded of responsibility toward society and the world.

Art often entails an artistic and graphic representation of what is present and available in the "here and now" mediated by what might or should be, as well as what "should not be." The resulting tension between the actual and the hoped for, or the "not hoped for," is what produces many of the central dilemmas that lie at the heart of great art. Unfortunately, sometimes, instead of the kind of art and portrayal with which we can identify and be moved by, we sometimes get empty canvases often showing only one color, or non-comprehensible scribbling or twisted insignificant forms.

What is at times erroneously termed "modern," often designates a tendency to hide the shallowness and emptiness of pseudo works of art. To preserve real art from charlatanism and the "King's New Clothes" situation, a consistent critical view of the role of art in modern times is in place. Decision-makers, promoters and judges of artistic exhibitions and competitions, as well as curators of museums, should have criteria that designate real and important works of art that touch not only the eye, but also the heart and mind. Such an approach could raise the plastic arts to the peaks they deserve, and to their important role as an expression of human aspirations, and their function as part of the creators of the needed new culture of peace so much yearned for by the people of our global village.

Various studies of the link between art, music and emotions, have recently been undertaken, and it was noticed that not all sectors cultivate art and music that are beneficial to the development of humankind. Some kind of music nowadays does not try to be either harmonious or peaceful; it is often too loud, and it sometimes invokes nervousness and even aggressiveness. A civilization that wants to preserve itself from violence has to be wary of what kind of art or music it wants to produce, promote and spread. Furthermore, recent research has shown that loud music impedes on hearing and it often leads to physical problems and sometimes even to deafness, especially among young people who are often exposed for long hours to loud music in discotheques.

Leaders should take into account that a similar kind of reform that is needed in literature and the media, is also required in the plastic arts and musical tendencies and approaches. Not only paintings and sculptures, but also music and dance that inspire, move, and lend harmony and inspiration to human beings to perfect our world, could greatly help in the building of a climate and culture of peace.

Peace Culture Education

I'm sure that someday children in schools will study the history of the men who made war as you study an absurdity. They'll be shocked, just as today we're shocked with cannibalism.

—Golda Meir

Education provides an important channel for the creation of an influential and effective peace culture. It is desirable to give appropriate attention to the teaching of peace education, which can include contacts with people of various cultures, conflict resolution through non-violent means,and concern for the local and global environments.

The growing boom and expanding dimensions of communication technology offers various new opportunities and directions for the promotion of peace education. International co-operation and cross-disciplinary research, promoted by electronic technology and information services, can significantly enrich peace education. Recognizing the importance of this new trend, UNESCO convened a conference on "The Impact of Information and Communication Technologies on Teaching and Teachers," (Khvilon, Patru, 1997) in order to strengthen international co-operation in the pursuit of peace and international understanding. More conferences of this kind should be convened, nationally and globally.

Literature and the arts are important educational factors as a means of fostering consciousness and sensitivity to lacks and deficiencies in the world around us. They have the ability, as well, to promote willingness to take creative action to build a better world. The subject of peace in general, has received relatively little attention in education, and no serious research has been conducted on the role that literature and the arts can play in peace education. Ministries of education globally and regionally should correct this, and should include peace studies and peace culture as required subjects at all levels of schooling.

Schools and colleges are suitable forums where culture, values, ideals and identity, as well as world views, are formed. Curricula should pay attention to the central events that mark our era, such as wars and terror, and address the necessity of the building of a peace culture to counteract them. Peace educators need to carry out programs that would give young people and children, as well as adults, a vision of what could be, a future view that would draw on their imaginations to create new visionary dimensions of a world beyond war and poverty.

Peace culture should be considered as a central focus and should inspire and influence all aspects of education. Violence in most cases arises from the mistaken notion that force is the only way that can solve conflicts. The study of peace culture would demonstrate that it is otherwise, and it should be applied to all subjects. In the teaching of history, for example, attention should be given to the policies that lead to the successful conclusion of peace treaties, and not concentrate mainly on the waging of the wars, as is often the mode in the present. The two sides of the conflicts should be presented in a lively and convincing way, and historical novels, such as *From the Nile to the Jordan* (A. Aharoni), are a good means to present this.

In the study of literature, furthermore, lives of heroines and heroes who have advanced the cause of peace, like Thea Wolf in *Not In Vain: An Extraordinary Life,* should be extensively studied, and presented as models, both in educational curricula, and to the wider public. Anthologies of the Culture of Peace should be used as textbooks to teach conflict resolution through culture and the arts. The IFLAC Anthologies: *New Waves: In Memory of Yitzhak Rabin,* and *The Culture of Peace Anthology,* are used in schools and universities for the teaching of peace studies, as well as *A Song to Life and to World Peace* (ed. A. Aharoni).

The attitude towards peace in education programs in various parts of the world often reflects the tension between preservation of traditional values and the need for change. Established ideological and religious influences, attempting to maintain their leading positions, are not always for peace, or the teaching of peace, and prefer to assert their extremist national identity and exclusive roles. Universities in some parts of the world are unfortunately ideal recruiting grounds for fundamentalism and extremists. However, if colleges and universities become open to other cultures and attuned to developing and adopting a "Peace Culture" curriculum, fundamentalist influences and violent trends could be abated, and in time would disappear.

The attitude towards education has an important effect on society as a whole, for the dilemmas that confront the education system are a microcosm of the contradictions and struggles of the whole of society. The promotion of a Culture of Peace through education is therefore of central importance in trying to establish the dynamics that mark the interplay between society and peace.

Educational institutions should establish departments of "Literary Peace Studies," nationally and internationally, and they should be empowered to function as initiators of cultural bridges among nations. They could also promote the publication of periodicals and journals, including Electronic Peace Journals. One of the electronic journals that is widely used by schools, colleges and universities for peace education is: IPRA's *Horizon Pave Peace,* and the *IFLAC_USA* website (yahoo).

Leaders and decision-makers should initiate and found Peace Prizes for peace culture research in education, and the encouragement of the writing of peace literature, film-scripts, and plays. The organizing of competitions, awards, and prizes, among youths could have an advantageous and high payoff. Books, cassettes, and videos displaying various educational aspects of entertainment based on peace literature and the arts should be produced. These should present in an attractive manner the various themes and aspects of the peace culture system, as well as its advantages.

Women Building a World Beyond War and Violence

As a woman, my country is the whole world...
—Virginia Woolf

There is a close link between peace and gender. Women give life and are on the side of life, and they believe in the possibility of creating a world beyond war more than men do. Women have expressed themselves accordingly throughout history. Jehan Sadat, wife of President Sadat of Egypt, wrote in her letter to "The Bridge: Jewish and Arab Women for Peace in the Middle East" published in *Women Creating A World Beyond War and Violence:* "I firmly believe that woman, as a mother, a wife, a daughter and a sister, can play an active role in protecting humanity from the horrors, dangers and damages of war. I do wish that the word 'War' would be cancelled from the dictionary of human relations."

In our globalized era, when there are profound cultural shifts and new social relations, the necessity for women to be equal partners in the building of a world beyond war is becoming more obvious and urgent. The Russian writer Tatyana Mamonova writes: "Women give life and appreciate life...they are organically against war, and they can really save the world if they are permitted to play an equally active part in government."

Women also have the ability to regard themselves as citizens of the world, and they mourn for every child who is killed in wars. In this context, the Palestinian Sai'da Nusseibeh writes about the Palestinian Israeli Conflict: "What price is peace? How many more must be killed, before the two nations wake up to look at their blood-soaked hands? There is so much anger, hatred and fear, and the wall between the two nations (the Palestinians and the Israelis), is getting higher—both sides are getting away from reality, and closing their ears, eyes and heart to the suffering of the 'other.' We should look into ways to bring down the wall of fear, brick by brick, "*for all the mosques, synagogues and churches in the world—are not worth the blood of one killed child.*" If the men leaders too, like Saida Nusseibeh, would think and feel like her, and understand the sanctity of life is above all, there would be better chances for peace in the Middle East and in the world.

The question of women and peace, and the meaning of peace for women, cannot be separated from the broader question of relationships between women and men in all spheres of life, including in the family. Discriminatory practices and negative attitudes towards women should be eliminated, and traditional gender norms changed to enhance women's participation in building the new culture of peace system, and in full participation in the governance of the world.

Abusive practices against women are still rampant in our world—as those against the women in Afghanistan by the oppressive Taliban—who have fortunately been recently overthrown. These discriminatory practices are justified in the context of cultural norms, religious beliefs and unfounded theories and assumptions. Whatever its political or religious system, a society patterned on dominance inevitably gives rise to such distortions of power as violence against women. The building and promotion of a culture of peace can help in overcoming such dominance, discrimination and violence against women.

Women can be a tremendous force, for they are half the citizens of the world. If the women of the world unite, together with all the democratic men who yearn for a world beyond war, peace would have a better chance. If they can succeed in reaching peak positions in relation to their fates, and hold equal key positions in governments, municipalities, educational institutions, the violence against them would disappear. Their contribution to the culture of peace through their creative power would then freely flourish and be a benefit to the whole of humanity.

Women are good allies for promoting peace through their creative efforts. A book describing women's contribution to peace, especially in the Middle East, titled *Women Creating A World Beyond War and Violence* (A. Aharoni), has recently been published, and is used in peace education programs, and in women studies departments. It depicts several important aspects of women's struggle for peace through their organizations, activities, research, articles, poems, stories, letters and pictures. This book shows the power of women to creatively build a world beyond war, and that there is no greater challenge in the world today than that of living in peace, respect, and harmony with one's neighbors.

Some of the questions posed and examined are: At a time when the world is still caught up in the clutches of wars, terror and violence, will humankind know how to "listen to women for a change?" Can the women of the world unite and throw the thwarted belief that wars can solve conflicts, into the anachronistic dustbin of history where it belongs? War is not democratic, as most of the people of the world do not want wars. Will women, who are the majority of the citizens of the world—together with all the men who also yearn for a world beyond war—succeed in achieving their democratic right to live in peace?

Among the various subjects covered by this new book is also a description of a quarter of a century of peace activity by: "IFLAC-LENA (formerly called The Bridge): Jewish and Arab/Palestinian Women for Peace in the Middle-East," the first movement of its kind in Israel. It also includes, among other important documents, a correspondence with Mrs. Jehan Sadat, wife of the late President of Egypt, Anwar Sadat, as well as a section on: "The Four Mothers" organization, and their successful campaign: "Leave Lebanon In Peace." Thanks to this women's organization, the Israeli soldiers retreated from Lebanon after twenty years. The young soldiers were delighted that the "Four Mothers" had freed them. The *Poems from Lebanon*, in "Women," are inspired by moving letters that protest against war, written by Israeli soldiers while they were still in Lebanon.

Women's organizations all over the world, such as LENA-BRIDGE, UNIFEM, and WILPF, are struggling for their basic women's right to live in peace, and to attain fully equal rights in society. Will women succeed to be at the summit of their fate? Will the media, worldwide, give women's struggle for peace and equality, the backing, coverage, and credit they deserve? With determination, vision and united action, it could indeed become possible. If global leaders and decision-makers take it upon themselves to help the women of the world to unite, under the umbrella of a resourceful and effective "culture of peace system and network"—which would have its special women's branch—the vision of a world beyond war could indeed become a reality.

How Can Leaders Facilitate the Culture of Peace?

I want to kill you war, and I do not know how, and I do not know why, all the people of the world don't join hands to kill you war—you the greatest killer of all!

—You and I Can Change the World

The Roman saying, "*If you want peace—prepare for war*" should be replaced today by: "*If you want peace—prepare for peace.*" There is not enough preparation for peace in the world today, and for the banning of the whole conception and practice of war. The opening of the third millenium is an appropriate opportunity for leaders and decision-makers to take it upon themselves to globally and nationally "prepare for peace," by facilitating the creation of a culture and communications peace system and network, which would be instrumental for banning the very essence of wars and violence. The new pluralistic peace culture system delineated in this present essay can be a suitable umbrella for the preparation for banishing war. It could spread into various new directions and it could generate a climate of peace that would have a preventive influence on impending dangers of conflicts and wars.

The following concluding recommendations are suggested to leaders and decision-makers to help facilitate a culture of peace and to "repair" the world:

1. *To Establish A New Peace Culture System.* The foundation and organization of a powerful, influential and resourceful global and national "Peace Culture System," as delineated above, would constitute an important step toward the building of a world beyond war.

2. *To Build An Innovative Telecommunications Peace Culture Network.* This innovative system assisted by a global and national peace media network would initiate and organize popular universities on the air, and would develop and spread entertainment based on literature and the arts in the service of peace.

3. *To Promote Peace Education and Peace Studies.* Leaders should promote peace education and peace studies, based on literature and the arts, at all levels, from kindergarden to university, including the founding of a global and national satellite system for peace education and peace studies. Peace culture should be made a required subject in schools and colleges, just as the teaching of reading and mathematics.

4. *The Funding And Promotion of Literature and the Arts.* This would include programs on peace literature, poetry, drama, and the plastics arts, as well as music and dance, as basic determinants of how we interpret a better present and future for our world. It would also include the organization of courses on creative peace writing and art. "Paving of Peace," Literature, Stories, Poetry, Drama and Movie Script Contests, should be established, to enhance the writing, producing and publishing of films, stories, poetry, legends, and myths on the various themes of peace. There should also be the awarding of prestigious Peace Prizes for outstanding achievements in all literary and artistic fields, including special awards for peace programmers and directors of electronic communications. Futhermore an additional Nobel Prize for "Peace Literature" should be established.

5. *Establishing A Peace Internet and Network of Peace Websites.* Leaders should establish a global interconnected Peace Internet Network that would make the building of websites and discussion groups for peace available and influential, and it would diffuse national and global peace developments and information.

6. *Conflict Resolution.* The organizing of "Conflict Resolution through Culture" programs, symposia, and international conferences. These would help to disseminate a conflict resolution view of life, and the belief that a positive and open view of "the other", and of humankind, can help in solving conflicts. They would also help to dissipate and discourage the ethos of despair, cynicism, selfishness, and the ego.

7. *Women and the Culture of Peace.* Institutes of peace culture creativity for women should be widely established, as well as centers for the promotion of women as equal partners in running the world and join the creation of a world beyond war. "Eliminating Violence Against Women" films, video productions, books, and works of arts, should be widely produced and propagated.

8. *Translation Institutes and Foundations.* It is recommended to establish "International Translation Institutes, Centres and Foundations," for the promotion of the translation of multi-cultural works of literature and art. The awarding

of International and National Peace Prizes for outstanding works of translation should be allocated to translators and publishers.

9. *Outstanding "Literature for Peace" prizes and Awards.* To encourage the outstanding " Peace Voices of the Earth" so that they may be better heard, listened to, and enjoyed, prestigious Global and National Peace Prizes and Awards, should be allocated to outstanding writers, poets, playwrights, dramatists, as well as to media producers, directors and journalists.
10. *Peace Museums.* The global establishment of a wide network of Peace Museums would facilitate the culture of peace and encourage peace developments. It can be a functional platform for the presentation of peace art and literature, with lively activities for school children and adults. It could include peace films and peace videos and games; it would be established in major towns and cities, globally and regionally, and made freely accessible to people.
11. *Establishing A Peace Culture Economy.* Economies and markets for peace culture should be developed. The production and marketing of violent films, television programs and videos should be researched and discouraged. Leaders should encourage a significant shift to the production and marketing of constructive and peaceful films and videos. After the attack on the Twin Towers in New York, many Americans do not want to see violent films anymore; this trend should be encouraged globally, and it could change the whole market as it is sensitive to ratings.
12. *Organize Globally the "Turn Off Violence on TV Project."* The organizing and spreading, nationally and internationally, of the "Turn Off Violence on TV Project," discourages sponsors, directors, and editors from producing violent films and programs.
13. *Support of NGO's for Peace.* Significant support of NGOs working for peace would augment their power to facilitate the culture of peace and to promote peace literature and the arts, as well as to convince governments to invest in the building of the required culture of peace system.
14. *Terror and Suicide Bombers.* Leaders and governments could help in counteracting terror and suicide bombers, not only by defending ourselves against them, but furthermore, by propagating the culture of peace. The horrific tragedy of the terrorist attack, on the Twin Towers in New York City and the Pentagon, was a tantalizing warning that the war of cultures is underway. The whole phenomenon of having young men whose minds have been fed on fanatic fundamentalism by extreme Islamic terrorist groups, ready to sacrifice their lives in abominable suicide attacks, should be thoroughly uprooted. Possible preventive methods and solutions in the framework of a peace culture system should likewise be explored and implemented. The solution to the phenomenon of suicide bombers probably lies in getting to the minds of the suicidal volunteers, with powerful and influential contents of a culture of peace, before their minds are poisoned.

Concluding Remarks: Innovative Lights

War is a terrible thing and must be abolished at all costs.

—Albert Einstein

The wave of terror and suicide bombers that has recently infested our world shows that the colossal task of building a new global "Culture of Peace System and Network", by leaders, decision-makers, and governmental institutions, should be considered one of the major goals of humankind today. Our major challenge at the beginning of this new millennium is to search out new strategies and adopt fresh models capable of eliminating terror, violence and wars as a means of solving conflicts, and encourage a more peaceful and democratic society. The building by leaders of an effective "Culture of Peace System and Network," using literature and the arts, can facilitate these important goals. It can create bridges of understanding and respect, among people and nations, and moreover, it could function as the antidote to violence, conflicts, terror and war, regionally and globally.

The role of leaders and governmental institutions in developing this needed new system is primordial. Decision-makers and governmental bodies and institutions should take urgent steps to curb the growing violent culture and terror in our global village, and to replace it with a powerful, substantial and influential peace culture system. There should be a thorough rethinking and reform of governance and financial support of culture, literature and the arts, and of NGOs promoting the culture of peace, as well as of women's organizations for peace, regionally and globally.

The creation of a regional and global culture of peace that would create an atmosphere conducive to peacemaking and to promote a world beyond war, is yearned for by the majority of the people in our global village. A comprehensive innovative peace culture system, that includes: literature, art, philosophy, and the media, which involve both regional and global scopes and implications, should be the number one order of the day in national and international agendas of governments and responsible institutions all over the world.

Modern telecommunications and technologies such as satellite, television, radio and the Internet, can facilitate harmonious inter-cultural relations, as well as the bond and dialogue between people, nations, and civilizations. These modern technologies can also promote the consciousness of a new global citizenship, based on a shared peace culture. With commitment, determination and vision, and with the aid of the media, it is indeed possible to create and promote a resourceful, effective and influential new ethical culture of peace, both regionally and globally.

The creation and promotion of a global and national peace culture system based on literature and the arts in the service of peace, should be urgently carried out as a defensive measure of the very existence and sustainability of life on earth.

Keywords

Peace culture, literature, arts, music, cultural and literary research, peace media, peace culture system, sustainability, ethics, cultural values and norms, education, violence on television, film effects, telecommunications, media, Internet, NGOs: non governmental organizations, women and peace, equality, globalization, global citizen, global governance, governmental budgets, peace museums, United Nations, war, conflict, terror, suicide bombers, environment.

The Global Environmental Challenges of the 21st Century

John D. Shilling
World Bank and

James H. Beall
St. John's College

Throughout the world, energy use is the engine of growth and development. It is also the main cause of human-related greenhouse emissions. The good news is that as economies advance, improved technologies help bring about lower energy use per unit of output. The bad news is that growth has proceeded faster than the efficiency gains, and total energy use and greenhouse gas emissions are still increasing.

The developed world (one billion people), representing about one-sixth of the world's population, is the largest producer of greenhouse gases, accounting for about two-thirds of all emissions. Within this group, there is tremendous variation between countries. For example, the United States produces about half again as much CO_2 per unit of output as Europe and twice that of Japan. For these countries, simply stabilizing greenhouse gas production is viewed as a major effort, but possible.

The next third of the world's population (two billion) lives passably well on per capita incomes of roughly $1000 to $8000. These countries are entering the phase of development characterized by major accumulations of physical capital, productive capacity, and consumer durables (e.g., refrigerators, air conditioners, and cars). They often lack the concomitant investment needed to yield energy efficiency gains and pollution control. Even with increased efficiency, they will undoubtedly contribute to a major increase in energy consumption and greenhouse gas emissions because of these transitions.

The remaining half of the world's population lives on less than $2 per day, and energy consumption is miniscule per capita, though substantial overall. If we achieve stated goals of improving the standard of living of this segment of the global population, their energy consumption will increase substantially. If this occurs, another 3 billion people (5-6 billion by 2050) will achieve the standard of living of a present-day Mexico. This implies the development of a substantial infrastructure, including hundreds of millions of additional cars, hundreds of thousands of miles of roads, and the energy to power these economies. It is an open question whether it is possible for the two lower per capita energy-consuming groups of nations to avoid most of the negative environmental impacts of their predecessors by adopting the latest energy efficient and non-polluting technologies and practices.

It is a significant challenge to use models to determine how fast and how long the increasing rates of greenhouse gas emissions will continue. It is not unreasonable to suppose that lower rates of CO_2 accumulations in the atmosphere would produce lower risks of severe climate changes, and provide more

John D. Shilling and James H. Beall, "The Global Environmental Challenges of the 21st Century." Reprinted by permission of the *COSMOS 2001 Journal.*

flexibility and options for future generations. But slowing down the rate of greenhouse gas emissions will require stepped-up research efforts in energy efficiency technologies, and shifting demand in developed countries to lower energy use patterns. The latter will have benefits both for its direct effect and for its utility as an example to billions who want to emulate a modern lifestyle. Technology transfer to developing countries could be accelerated to spread use of the most efficient technologies as quickly as possible, although this may have implications for export control policies that apply to technologies that can be used for military purposes.

Population Dynamics

Population growth will have a tremendous impact on any attempts to project energy use and greenhouse gas emissions. A great concern of the 20th century was the global population explosion, which saw the world grow from 2 billion to 6 billion people—the greatest expansion in the history of the human race. Economic progress, improved nutrition, and better health management all contributed to the population expansion, especially where poorer nations were able to improve diet, health, and life spans in the latter half of the century.

As the increase in population became manifest, Malthus' doctrine on the carrying capacity of the land gained new currency, prompting renewed efforts in population planning. A combination of population planning, improved economic welfare, and other related factors have brought many industrialized nations to a level at or near zero population growth. However, during the 20th century, the populations of developing nations have continued to expand exponentially, raising demand for water, energy, and other natural resources.

These demographic trends have widespread implications for the global economy and for climate change models. In the industrialized nations, for example, the demographic shifts resulting from low or zero population growth rates suggest that the aging populations will not be able to provide the amounts and types of labor needed to sustain these economies. This scenario already is evident in Europe and Japan. In America, the dynamism of the economy in recent decades can be explained partly by the contributions of immigrants, but there are growing concerns about the ability of our society to support the growing numbers of retirees. Cultural and social conditions could present either remarkable opportunities or severe challenges if the developed countries try to meet their labor needs with surplus labor from the poorer countries.

The demographic evidence suggests that this type of population "bust" trend may emerge in some of the larger developing countries by mid-century. We have begun to examine in the Soirées the possible impacts of an aging population. With more retirees, it seems plausible that there could be greater demand for leisure activities, some of which are energy intensive (e.g., travel), and greater demand for personal services. To the extent a younger population is more dynamic and innovative, the rate of technological change may slow as the population ages. But an aging population could create more demand for innovations, particularly in medicine. Since many of the implications have different potential impacts on carbon emissions and climate change, this will be a major topic in future discussions.

Any population models, however, are sensitive to advances in medicine and the virulence of disease vectors that would alter demographic patterns. In developed countries, infectious diseases have been drastically reduced as a cause of death, and this will continue, absent a pandemic of a new killer like Ebola or a particularly deadly flu strain. Medical advances and the promises of biogenetic research are not only increasing life expectancy, but may extend the ultimate possible life spans so more people can live and remain active longer. This has many implications for economic, social, and political activities.

In developing countries, however, infectious diseases are still the most important killers, and this will only change as medical services and general welfare increase. It may be unrealistic to hope that pharmaceutical companies will direct greater efforts toward solving some of the world's age-old medical needs. Malaria, for instance, kills millions every year, but more money has been spent in recent years producing and marketing Viagra than on malaria control.

New dangers lurk in the shadows with the potential to affect all populations, in both richer and poorer nations. New infectious diseases can emerge and travel quickly to all corners of the Earth. HIV/AIDS has both spread worldwide and is devastating the poorest parts of the world. Other, as yet unknown, viruses may emerge. Deteriorating health practices, both in other countries and in the industrialized world, can lead to the resurgence of treatment-resistant diseases, such as tuberculosis, which can be carried to other industrialized countries no longer prepared to treat them on a large scale. Overuse of antibiotics in animal feed can create resistant strains of bacteria that attack both man and animals. Animals, too, have become global travelers, as the recent European crises with hoof-and-mouth disease and bovine spongeiform encephalitis (BSE) attest. BSE also was discovered recently in Japan.

Providing Adequate Welfare

For the first time in human history, there are no accessible land frontiers that growing populations can use to feed, clothe, and house themselves. Nearly one billion people exist with inadequate nutrition, a figure that has remained roughly constant for several decades. UN Food and Agriculture Organization studies indicate that the world probably will have enough capacity to feed the expected population in 2030, based on reasonable assumptions about productivity growth, irrigation intensification, and some expansion of cultivation into land currently in other use. This latter change in land use is partly to make up for the expansion of urban and suburban areas as the global urban population grows to exceed the rural population in about another decade. The ease of feeding everyone would depend in part on preferences: high-meat diets require more land than low-meat diets to generate the same number of calories.

More important, perhaps, will be the policies concerning the distribution of food. Abundant surpluses are expected in the affluent temperate zones (North America, Europe, Australia, and Argentina), even absent the possible beneficial effects of global warming. The demands for food in excess of production will be among the poor living in the tropical zones, where global climate change is likely to have the most adverse effects. Economic, structural, and political issues related to the distribution of food will have to be addressed in order to prevent widespread malnutrition and suffering in these areas. Such regions are fertile grounds for strife.

Water Resources

While global warming may help boost agricultural production in developed (and well-fed) countries, this hopeful prediction of adequate food supplies depends on a number of factors, including abundant water resources. Currently, 40 percent of the world's population lives in areas facing water stress. That proportion is expected to increase, bringing new pressures on water resources, and new disputes over water rights. Any possible climate changes associated with global warming will likely mean sharp declines in surface water availability in many areas, and it is unclear whether changes in rainfall patterns will help the situation in other areas. Access to clean water is also vital for improving health.

The outcomes in these areas will depend far more on policy—both national and international—than on technology. Most important will be proper pricing and other allocation methods to reduce inefficient and wasteful use of water and improve the technology for distribution and use (e.g., drip irrigation and covered aqueducts). The results of these decisions, in terms of political stability and conflict levels, will have a major impact on how much progress can be made in other areas. If water needs can be met peaceably and with a reasonable degree of equity, prospects for adequate food production and access to clean water and sanitation will increase.

The Role of Technology

The degree to which technological innovation can be relied upon to provide solutions to some of these global problems is one of the most difficult aspects discussed at the Cosmos Club Soirées. Information technology clearly has a number of effects on society. Telecommuting and video-conferencing, for example, can reduce demands on the transportation sector and potentially lower $C0_2$ emissions, but only if there is a sophisticated and flexible infrastructure already in place. This includes acceptance of such practices in the workplace, as well as the investment in fiberoptic cables to link telecommuters and teleconferencers.

Perhaps the most critical aspect of public policy in support of technological revolutions is the significant and continued investment in basic research and technology development. The microelectronics revolution began not simply with the invention of the transistor (deriving from basic research), but with strategic investments in integrated circuitry by the Defense Advanced Research Projects Agency in the 1970s and 1980s. These investments were targeted because of a prescient understanding of the role they could play in military equipment, but they were readily adapted for use by the commercial sector.

The reformation that has resulted has extended to every aspect of life in a technological society, from the home office to the factory floor. Just-in-time production and transport now replaces the storage of large inventories that once were required to keep factory output at peak levels. This is only one of thousands of examples of the effects of the microelectronics revolution on modern life. It is not an exaggeration to say that the beginnings of this reformation can be traced to a strategic investment by a single government agency. In this epoch, one of the most promising areas of research should focus on improving energy efficiency and reducing the carbon emissions of energy production. Energy itself is not the problem; it is the byproducts that result from energy production that are problematic. To catalyze the next round of innovations, we need similar strategic investments based on credible and farsighted public policy.

World Scientists' Warning To Humanity

Union of Concerned Scientists

November 1992

Human beings and the natural world are on a collision course. Human activities inflict harsh and often irreversible damage on the environment and on critical resources. If not checked, many of our current practices put at serious risk the future that we wish for human society and the plant and animal kingdoms, and may so alter the living world that it will be unable to sustain life in the manner that we know. Fundamental changes are urgent if we are to avoid the collision our present course will bring about.

The Environment

The environment is suffering critical stress:

The Atmosphere

Stratospheric ozone depletion threatens us with enhanced ultraviolet radiation at the earth's surface, which can be damaging or lethal to many life forms. Air pollution near ground level, and acid precipitation, are already causing widespread injury to humans, forests and crops.

Water Resources

Heedless exploitation of depletable ground water supplies endangers food production and other essential human systems. Heavy demands on the world's surface waters have resulted in serious shortages in some 80 countries, containing 40 percent of the world's population. Pollution of rivers, lakes and ground water further limits the supply.

Oceans

Destructive pressure on the oceans is severe, particularly in the coastal regions which produce most of the world's food fish. The total marine catch is now at or above the estimated maximum sustainable yield. Some fisheries have already shown signs of collapse. Rivers carrying heavy burdens of eroded soil into the seas also carry industrial, municipal, agricultural, and livestock waste—some of it toxic.

Soil

Loss of soil productivity, which is causing extensive Land abandonment, is a widespread byproduct of current practices in agriculture and animal husbandry. Since 1945, 11 percent of the earth's vegetated surface has been degraded—an area larger

Union of Concerned Scientists, "World Scientists Warning to Humanity." Warning was issued in November, 1992. Reprinted with permission of the Union of Concerned Scientists from http://deoxy.org/sciwarn.htm, December 3, 2001.

than India and China combined—and per capita food production in many parts of the world is decreasing.

Forests

Tropical rain forests, as well as tropical and temperate dry forests, are being destroyed rapidly. At present rates, some critical forest types will be gone in a few years and most of the tropical rain forest will be gone before the end of the next century. With them will go large numbers of plant and animal species.

Living Species

The irreversible loss of species, which by 2100 may reach one third of all species now living, is especially serious. We are losing the potential they hold for providing medicinal and other benefits, and the contribution that genetic diversity of life forms gives to the robustness of the world's biological systems and to the astonishing beauty of the earth itself.

Much of this damage is irreversible on a scale of centuries or permanent. Other processes appear to pose additional threats. Increasing levels of gases in the atmosphere from human activities, including carbon dioxide released from fossil fuel burning and from deforestation, may alter climate on a global scale. Predictions of global warming are still uncertain—with projected effects ranging from tolerable to very severe—but the potential risks are very great.

Our massive tampering with the world's interdependent web of life—coupled with the environmental damage inflicted by deforestation, species loss, and climate change—could trigger widespread adverse effects, including unpredictable collapses of critical biological systems whose interactions and dynamics we only imperfectly understand.

Uncertainty over the extent of these effects cannot excuse complacency or delay in facing the threat.

Population

The earth is finite. Its ability to absorb wastes and destructive effluent is finite. Its ability to provide food and energy is finite. Its ability to provide for growing numbers of people is finite. And we are fast approaching many of the earth's limits. Current economic practices which damage the environment, in both developed and underdeveloped nations, cannot be continued without the risk that vital global systems will be damaged beyond repair. Pressures resulting from unrestrained population growth put demands on the natural world that can overwhelm any efforts to achieve a sustainable future. If we are to halt the destruction of our environment, we must accept limits to that growth. A World Bank estimate indicates that world population will not stabilize at less than 12.4 billion, while the United Nations concludes that the eventual total could reach 14 billion, a near tripling of today's 5.4 billion. But, even at this moment, one person in five lives in absolute poverty without enough to eat, and one in ten suffers serious malnutrition. No more than one or a few decades remain before the chance to avert the threats we now confront will be lost and the prospects for humanity immeasurably diminished.

Warning

We the undersigned, senior members of the world's scientific community, hereby warn all humanity of what lies ahead. A great change in our stewardship of the earth and the life on it, is required, if vast human misery is to be avoided and our global home on this planet is not to be irretrievably mutilated.

What We Must Do

Five inextricably linked areas must be addressed *simultaneously*:

1. We must bring environmentally damaging activities under control to restore and protect the integrity of the earth's systems we depend on. We

must, for example, move away from fossil fuels to more benign, inexhaustible energy sources to cut greenhouse gas emissions and the pollution of our air and water. Priority must be given to the development of energy sources matched to third world needs—small scale and relatively easy to implement. We must halt deforestation, injury to and loss of agricultural land, and the loss of terrestrial and marine plant and animal species.

2. We must manage resources crucial to human welfare more effectively. We must give high priority to efficient use of energy, water, and other materials, including expansion of conservation and recycling.

3. We must stabilize population. This will be possible only if all nations recognize that it requires improved social and economic conditions, and the adoption of effective, voluntary family planning.

4. We must reduce and eventually eliminate poverty.

5. We must ensure sexual equality, and guarantee women control over their own reproductive decisions.

The developed nations are the largest polluters in the world today. They must greatly reduce their over-consumption, if we are to reduce pressures on resources and the global environment. The developed nations have the obligation to provide aid and support to developing nations, because only the developed nations have the financial resources and the technical skills for these tasks.

Acting on this recognition is not altruism, but enlightened self-interest: whether industrialized or not, we all have but one lifeboat. No nation can escape from injury when global biological systems are damaged. No nation can escape from conflicts over increasingly scarce resources. In addition, environmental and economic instabilities will cause mass migrations with incalculable consequences for developed and undeveloped nations alike. Developing nations must realize that environmental damage is one of the gravest threats they face, and that attempts to blunt it will be overwhelmed if their populations go unchecked. The greatest peril is to become trapped in spirals of environmental decline, poverty, and unrest, leading to social, economic and environmental collapse.

Success in this global endeavor will require a great reduction in violence and war. Resources now devoted to the preparation and conduct of war—amounting to over \$1 trillion annually—will be badly needed in the new tasks and should be diverted to the new challenges.

A new ethic is required—a new attitude towards discharging our responsibility for caring for ourselves and for the earth. We must recognize the earth's limited capacity to provide for us. We must recognize its fragility. We must no longer allow it to be ravaged. This ethic must motivate a great movement, convince reluctant leaders and reluctant governments and reluctant peoples themselves to effect the needed changes. The scientists issuing this warning hope that our message will reach and affect people everywhere. We need the help of many.

We require the help of the world community of scientists—natural, social, economic, political;

We require the help of the world's business and industrial leaders;

We require the help of the worlds religious leaders; and We require the help of the world's peoples.

We call on all to join us in this task.

Prominent Individuals Among More Than 1,500 Signatories

Philip Anderson, Nobel laureate, Physics; USA
Christian Anfinsen, Nobel laureate, Chemistry; USA
Werner Arber, Nobel laureate, Medicine; Switzerland
Julius Axelrod, Nobel laureate, Medicine; USA
David Baltimore, Nobel laureate, Medicine; USA
Baruj Benacerraf, Nobel laureate, Medicine; USA
Georg Bednorz, Nobel laureate, Physics; Switzerland
Sune Bergstrom, Nobel laureate, Medicine; Sweden
Hans Bethe, Nobel laureate, Physics; USA
Michael Bishop, Nobel laureate, Medicine; USA
Konrad Bloch, Nobel laureate, Medicine; USA

Nicholaas Bloembergen, Nobel laureate, Physics; USA
Norman Borlaug, Agricultural Scientist, Nobel laureate, Peace; USA and Mexico
Adolph Butenandt, Nobel laureate, Chemistry; Fmr. President, Max Planck Institute, Germany
Georges Charpak, Nobel laureate, Physics; France
Stanley N. Cohen, Geneticist, Wolf Prize in Medicine, USA
E.J. Corey, Nobel laureate, Chemistry, USA
John Cornforth, Nobel laureate, Chemistry; Great Britain
Gerard Debreu, Nobel laureate, Economics; USA
Pierre-Gilles de Gennes, Nobel laureate, Physics; France
Johann Deisenhofer, Nobel laureate, Chemistry; Germany and USA
Renato Dulbecco, Nobel laureate, Medicine; USA
Manfred Eigen, Nobel laureate, Chemistry; Germany
Gertrude Elion, Nobel laureate, Medicine; USA
Richard Ernst, Nobel laureate, Chemistry; Switzerland
Val Fitch, Nobel laureate, Chemistry; USA
William Fowler, Nobel laureate, Physics; USA
Jerome Friedman, Nobel laureate, Physics; USA
Kenichi Fukui, Nobel laureate, Chemistry; Japan
Carleton Gajdusek, Nobel laureate, Medicine; USA
Murray Gell-Mann, Nobel laureate, Physics; USA
Donald Glaser, Nobel laureate, Physics; USA
Sheldon Glashow, Nobel laureate, Physics; USA
Roger Guillemin, Nobel laureate, Medicine; USA
Herbert Hauptman, Nobel laureate, Chemistry; USA
Dudley Herschbach, Nobel laureate, Chemistry, USA
Gerhard Herzberg, Nobel laureate, Chemistry; Canada
Antony Hewish, Nobel laureate, Physics; Great Britain
George Hitchings, Nobel laureate, Medicine; USA
Dorothy Crowfoot Hodgkin, Nobel laureate, Chemistry; Great Britain
Roald Hoffman, Nobel laureate, Chemistry; USA
Robert Holley, Nobel laureate, Medicine; USA
Nigeria Francois Jacob, Nobel laureate, Medicine; France
Jerome Karle, Nobel laureate, Physics; USA
Henry Kendall, Nobel laureate, Physics; Chairman, Union of Concerned Scientists; USA
John Kendrew, Nobel laureate, Chemistry; Great Britain
Klaus von Klitzing, Nobel laureate, Physics; Germany
Aaron Klug, Nobel laureate, Chemistry, Great Britain
Leon Lederman, Nobel laureate, Physics; Chairman, American Association of Advanced Science; USA
Yuan T. Lee, Nobel laureate, Chemistry; USA
Jean Marie Lehn, Nobel laureate, Chemistry; France
Wassily Leontief, Nobel laureate, Economics; USA
William Lipscomb, Nobel laureate, Physics; USA
James Meade, Nobel laureate, Economics; Great Britain
Hartmut Michel, Nobel laureate, Chemistry; Germany
Cesar Milstein, Nobel laureate, Medicine; Argentina and Great Britain
Franco Modigliani, Nobel laureate, Economics; USA
Nevill Mott, Nobel laureate, Physics; Great Britain
Joseph Murray, Nobel laureate, Medicine; USA
Louis Neel, Nobel laureate, Physics; France
Erwin Neher, Nobel laureate, Medicine; Germany
Marshall Nirenberg, Biochemist; Nobel laureate, Medicine; USA
George Palade, Nobel laureate, Physics; USA
Linus Pauling, Nobel laureate, Chemistry and Peace, USA
John Polanyi, Nobel laureate, Chemistry; Canada
George Porter, Nobel laureate, Chemistry; Great Britain
Ilya Prigogine, Nobel laureate, Chemistry; Belgium
Edward Purcell, Nobel laureate, Physics; USA
Tadeus Reichstein, Nobel laureate, Medicine; Switzerland
Burton Richter, Nobel laureate, Physics; USA
Frederick Robbins, Nobel laureate, Medicine; USA
Carlo Rubbia, Nobel laureate, Physics, Italy and Switzerland
Abdus Salam, Nobel laureate, Physics; President, Third World Academy of Sciences, Pakistan and Italy
Frederick Sanger, Nobel laureate, Chemistry; Great Britain
Melvin Schwartz, Nobel laureate, Physics; USA
Julian Schwinger, Nobel laureate, Physics; USA
Glenn Seaborg, Nobel laureate, Physics; USA
Kai Siegbahn, Nobel laureate, Physics; Sweden
Herbert Simon, Nobel laureate, Economics; USA
George Snell, Nobel laureate, Medicine; USA
Roger Sperry, Nobel laureate, Medicine; USA
Jack Steinberger, Nobel laureate, Physics; USA and Switzerland
Donnall Thomas, Nobel laureate, Medicine; USA
Jan Tinbergen, Nobel laureate, Economics; Netherlands
Samuel C.C. Ting, Nobel laureate, Physics; USA
James Tobin, Nobel laureate, Economics; USA
Alexander Todd, Nobel laureate, Chemistry; Great Britain
Susumu Tonegawa, Nobel laureate, Medicine; Japan and USA
Simon van der Meer, Nobel laureate, Physics; Netherlands and Switzerland
John Vane, Nobel laureate, Medicine; Great Britain
Harold Varmus, Nobel laureate, Medicine; USA
George Wald, Nobel laureate, Medicine; USA
E.T.S. Walton, Nobel laureate, Physics, Ireland
James Watson, Nobel laureate, Medicine; USA
Thomas Weller, Nobel laureate, Medicine; USA
Torsten Wiesel, Nobel laureate, Medicine; USA
Maurice Wilkins, Nobel laureate, Medicine; Great Britain
Geoffrey Wilkinson, Nobel laureate, Chemistry; Great Britain

Over 1,500 members of national, regional, and international science academies have signed the Warning. Sixty-nine nations from all parts of Earth are represented, including each of the twelve most populous nations and the nineteen largest economic powers. The full list includes a majority of the Nobel laureates in the sciences.

Making Science Serve Peace

Tor Ragnar Gerholm
Physics Department, University of Stockholm

Why War?

What—if anything—can science do to prevent war? To a question like this a scientist's immediate response is likely to be: what is or are the cause or causes of war? Rightly or wrongly scientists tend to believe that the one and only way to avoid the effect (war) is to alter its cause. Only then do we have, at least potentially, the means to change the course of events by deliberate action such that what was bound to happen will not occur.

Laymen often argue in a similar way but less rigorously. War can be prevented if the proper socio-political actions are taken. The problem is, of course, the notorious lack of agreement on what constitutes these "proper socio-political actions."

On the other hand, it is obvious that the causes of war cannot be studied by rigorous scientific methods. People wage wars for a bewildering number of reasons. They fight each other for borderlines, for agricultural land and access to fresh water, for possessions of raw materials, for minority rights and feelings of inferiority or superiority, for revenge or fear or frustration and, last but not least, for religious reasons. In fact, the number of wars, and armed conflicts within countries, with a religious component has been increasing ever since the end of World War II.

It is difficult to identify a common denominator except one: wars between sovereign nations ultimately rest on the state's monopoly on violence. But, alas, during the last century more people were killed, or rather murdered, in peace by their own governments than by foreign soldiers in wars. For the protection of life, peace is necessary but unfortunately not sufficient.

It is instructive to pose the complementary question: why peace? It is certainly true that most people, given a choice, prefer to live in peace. But not at all costs. Wars are being fought almost invariably with popular consent. Obviously it is not peace as such people aspire but a certain *quality* of peaceful coexistence. Which quality?

A reasonable hypothesis may be that when most citizens feel free to pursue their own individual pathways to happiness, whatever that means to them, they are not inclined to accept state-sanctioned actions of violence directed against themselves or against their fellow citizens. Under such civic circumstances the quality of peaceful coexistence prevails. But it is nevertheless always threatened and may have to be defended.

A lesson learned from the Vietnam War and the present War on Terrorism is that people in Western democracies strongly dislike military violence, however "collateral," when directed against what appears to be innocent people.

But this dislike is not necessarily felt in less favored countries, where the poverty of people breeds political oppression, racial discrimination, religious fanaticism, civil disorder and criminality which eventually leads to totalitarianism. These feelings represent a serious threat to the quality of peaceful coexistence as the horrible acts of terrorism on September 11, 2001 have effectively demonstrated.

We must not forget, however, that there are overt expressions of distress even in mature democracies in particular at times of economic slowdowns and rising unemployment. Political parties, with an anti-immigration platform, have met with success in general elections. Immigrants are perceived by many as threatening the indigenous peoples' hard-earned welfare and cultural inheritance. This is not merely disgusting, it is dangerous, as we have learned, or at least should have, from the European disaster in the 1930s and 40s.

When the quality of peaceful coexistence seems threatened or when people feel deprived of their own and individual means for the pursuit of happiness, they are inclined to join forces with others, similarly motivated, to achieve *collectively* what they cannot obtain as individuals. Political solidarity can no doubt work miracles to create or restore freedom and welfare, providing dignified lives for peace-loving people. Political work within democratic institutions for conflict resolutions is necessary for upholding a civic framework conducive to peace. But far too often we have seen social progress blocked by power-hungry politicians and corrupt leadership or simply by *lack of resources.* And, as von Clausewitz said: "War is nothing more than the continuation of politics by other means."

Science can do little to prevent the misuse of political power by unscrupulous leaders except to expose them and their mischiefs. But science can do what probably is more important at least in the long run. In an expanding economy, science and technology can create the resources necessary for a sustainable development defined in the Brundtland Commission's report *Our Common Future* as "meeting the needs of the present without compromising the ability of future generations to meet their own needs." In essence it is a development that ensures a better quality of life for everyone, now and for generations to come. It is a dynamic rather than a static concept, which serves to prevent war and armed conflicts within nations by removing one of the major threats to peace: lack of resources required to maintain and improve the standard of living (at least in a material sense).

Creating Resources

The idea that natural resources literally can be *created* seems incredible to many. On the contrary, according to a widespread notion economic growth is a zero sum game such that one's gains equal somebody else's losses. Consequently the material wealth in the rich countries is possible only at the expense of poverty in less fortunate parts of the world, and for that matter also of future generation's in their own countries. Limited resources are "consumed." The world is simply too small to allow everybody to share the standard of living enjoyed by today's rich people. This would require two more planets like our own and even then these lifestyles would be unsustainable.

It is further argued that this is the *real* cause of war and of terrorism. The rich world must share in a more equitable way what is still left of natural resources.

If this notion were correct, humanity would face a bleak future indeed. But fortunately it is not.

A single example suffices to illustrate the point. In the table the ten most important industrial metals are listed. Taken together, they account for more than 80 percent of the value of the whole world's production of all kinds of metals. The metals listed in the table are therefore a necessary, but far from sufficient, precondition for life in an industrial society.

Half of these metals *did not even have a name* in

Table 1

Important metals	Science Discovery	Technology Production breakthroughs
Iron	—	Bessemer process 1855 Martin process 1865 Electrosteel process 1900s High frequency heating 1930s
Aluminium	Örsted 1825	Electrolytic prod. 1880s
Copper	—	Chemical prod. from ore Copper-bessemer process Cementation and electrolysis Refining
Lead	—	Calcination—reduction Hunting-Heberlein Dwight-Lloyd
Zinc	—	Carbon reduction (>1000°C) Electric evaporation
Manganese	Gahn 1774	Goldschmidt's method
Chromium	Vaugelin 1797	Goldschmidt's method
Nickel	Cronstedt 1751	Oxford (Bessemer) process Mond process Hybinette process Electrolytic refining
Magnesium	Bussy 1880	Electrolytic production
Tin	—	Carbon reduction in furnace Reduction from melt ore

the pre-industrial society. They were discovered in the industrialized Europe. In addition, and more to the point, what have made the listed metals industrially important are the technical breakthroughs in production, purification and utilization. These innovations have all been done in the Western world during its process of industrialization and economic growth.

Far from consuming natural resources, the industrial society has indeed created the necessary means. And the industrial metals are produced from ores in the developed countries, not in the Third World.

Produced but not "consumed," since they cannot be destroyed they remain and are available. In an expanding economy they make up a growing inventory from which they can, and indeed are, recovered by recirculation, as is currently being done with used aluminium cans and scrapped iron from worn-out automobiles.

But What About Energy?

Strictly speaking, energy is always conserved. It can neither be "produced" nor "consumed." Like for metals usage implies *conversion* rather than consumption. The conversion takes place from qualities of pure or high concentration to more diluted ones of lower quality.

All of the goods and services produced by the use of energy by necessity involve some degree of degradation towards the lowest form of energy quality: low temperature heat.

On the global level, fossil fuels currently account for more than 80 percent of the current supplies of high quality energy. These resources are indeed consumed. It may therefore reasonably be argued the "energy has been used in an unsustainable manner."

However, due to continuous exploration activities and technical development, the supplies of fossil fuels are more abundant now than ever before in the history of mankind. The common notion that energy raw materials are finite and hence not sustainable is misleading.

But even if the use of energy, so far, has met the criterion of sustainability, as defined above, it may still be said that in a business-as-usual regime this is not likely to apply in the long-range future. It is argued that, so far, energy use has developed "haphazardly" and in a "random manner." "The substantial changes required will not be achieved by market pressure alone...governments need to make it an explicit goal of their policies for energy pricing to consumers." "It is clear that a low energy path is the best way towards a sustainable future."

The quotes in the preceding paragraph all come from the Brundtland report *Our Common Future* where it is argued that, "The period ahead must be regarded as transitional from an era in which energy has been used in an unsustainable manner. A generally acceptable pathway to a safe and sustainable energy future has not yet been found."

But the non-renewable fuels—coal, oil and natural gas—are not extracted for the sake of their material constituents, coal and hydrogen, but for *energy* they contain, energy which is released in the process of burning. Therefore, if energy of equivalent or higher quality can be obtained from virtually unlimited non-fossil fuels or from renewable sources of energy there is no obvious limit to energy's future use.

It is quite clear that this is the case. Nuclear and solar energy are—with current technology—available at competitive, or nearly competitive, prices ready to called upon when the era of fossil fuels is completed be it for lack of resources or for environmental protection or both.

In short: there are no *natural* resources, there are only *human* resources. But will they be sufficient?

The Future

Will progress in science and technology allow for a sustainable future and in addition create the necessary means for upgrading poor peoples' standards of living? This is in essence what science is called upon to deliver if future wars and terrorism are to be prevented.

By combining projections from different disciplines one can arrive at conclusions about the needs in the future conclusions that seem to be both robust and reliable and yet astonishing almost beyond belief.

By far most the important question when contemplating the future fate of mankind is, of course: how many of us will there be?

Seen as a biological species, man has been remarkably successful. We have grown in number by a factor of 1,000 since 10000 B.C. and increased life expectancy at birth from what has been estimated to some 20 years to the current global average of 55.

But the doubling time has been reduced from a reassuring 8000 years to an alarming 40. This is clearly not sustainable. Are we heading towards a Malthusian catastrophe in the near future? Prophets of doom tell us that drastic measures have to be taken now lest we face disaster.

But we have reasons to hope for something better. Population growth has already *passed the inflection point.* It has turned from acceleration to deceleration. We are now in the process of slowing down and heading for a stabilization, which in fact may not be so far away.

This levelling off is highly significant for two different reasons. First, it means that people, and in particular women, will be relieved from part of the burden they have had to shoulder in caring for their too many children. Second it implies relatively more people within the productive age brackets.

In other words: more workers and more time per worker to spend on production for today's customers, rather than on an excessive reproduction of future consumers bound to spend their lives on a subsistence level outside the realm of the monetary economy.

But population growth there will be in particular in the developing countries. The magnitude of the expected growth staggers imagination. We are, no doubt, entering a new era of human relations. Boding signs are visible now but rarely recognized as such.

Demographers have another important message to convey: *urbanization.*

In the early nineteenth century only 3 percent of the people in the Western world lived in cities. In the developed countries urbanization is now an almost completed process. In the West, 80 percent are urbanized.

Not so in the developing world where most people still live in rural areas. But in spite of this there are already more big cities and more urbanized people in the developing world than in the OECD region.

And this is just the beginning. The expected urbanization is colossal and it will almost entirely take place in the developing world.

Expressed in numbers the current 2.2 billion people now living in urban agglomerations will multiply to some 5.2 billion 30 years from now. Urban areas will take care of—or rather will *have to* take care of—almost all of the expected population increase, about 3.2 billion people.

How much is 3 billion urbanized people? One way to measure is to say that it represents 300 new megacities of a population of 10 million each of which there are only 12 today. Only three of these are in the OECD region.

We are not going to see hundreds of megacities mushrooming out of sheer wilderness. We will rather see massive growth of already existing urban centres. This process already is very much with us from Seoul and Kuala Lumpur in the east to São Paulo in the west.

Traditional nation states can hardly cope with such monstrous social creatures. Today's feverish attempts to recapture political control by fusing nations into super national entities, such as the European Union, can at best serve as a transitional stage. The megacities are bound to break loose and assume their own economic, cultural and political identity, more or less like the medieval cities, which often challenged their feudal landlords by establishing their own autonomy.

What about their economic prospects? What can the future inhabitants of urban conglomerates afford to buy?

Here we are in for another big surprise: the colossal growth of wealth. During the next 30 years billions of people will rise out of poverty, to middle income standards.

Since GDP, apart from savings, corresponds to the gross domestic consumption an increase in GDP per capita represents a corresponding increase in purchasing power.

It is well known that annual growth rates in developing countries tend to be significantly higher than the corresponding rates in the developed countries. But this superior performance has generally failed to impress us since it has been matched by a parallel and almost equally large population growth. Thus the GDP per capita has not increased or increased very slowly. The peoples' purchasing power has remained pathetically small in spite of their nations' often quite impressive economic performance.

But this will change. As soon as the population growth slows down the GDP per capita will rise. And an increase in wealth, however modest, spurs motivation. Nothing succeeds like success. We will see many more "tigers" and not only in booming Asia but also in Latin America, perhaps even in Africa.

This may seem too optimistic. But it is based on historical data, robust projections and sheer arithmetic. It is much more likely to happen than not.

In the next 25 years the world GDP is projected to reach about 55 x 10^{12} USD (1950). Half of the growth will take place in the developing countries. By the year 2020 the average GDP per capita will then be about 3900 USD (1990) corresponding to what is today defined as upper middle income standard. Needless to say there will be great differences between different countries and different social strata.

From then on, after 2025, the developing world will overtake the OECD region in absolute growth and the current distinction between "developed" and "developing" will eventually cease to apply.

The people in the developing countries will need:

- food and housing
- water and sanitation
- electricity and motor fuel
- schools and hospitals
- banks, insurance, police
- restaurants and entertainment
- sports facilities and recreation areas
- cultural centers for art and music
- central administration

All of this and much more. And a lot of it.

Is this a far too optimistic scenario? Will it ever

materialize? We do not seem to have the resources, and even if we had we will never accomplish this feat. It takes superhuman managerial skills.

Will we have the resources? I think the answer is a cautious yes.

Food supply should not be a problem but distribution might. Over the last 30 years *per capita* food production has increased by nearly 20 percent in a more or less regular fashion in spite of the sizable population increase. Even more encouraging: food prices have declined to some 60 percent, in real terms, of what they used to be.

Poor people will starve no matter how much food there is on the market. But poor people are getting richer and food is getting cheaper.

It is not overly optimistic to believe that the world's farmers and the agricultural industry will manage to feed the people, in particular since there is still plenty of room for gains in area productivity.

Public debate has focused on the supply of potable water, already now a serious problem in many parts of the world. But it also acknowledged that even where water is scarce it is very inefficiently used. The main reason is that it is treated as a free commodity available at no cost, if available at all. The spillage and spoiling of fresh water is a textbook example of what is known as the "tragedy of the commons." Nobody owns it and nobody cares. But even if they did, water shortage is not a problem, readily dismissed. Large-scale desalination of seawater, like in Saudi Arabia today, may become a necessity in many parts of the world.

Theoretically it takes only 0.7 kWh to produce one cubic meter of desalinated water. The cost of this energy input is a trifle of what people in water-rich countries, such as Sweden, pay today per cubic meter of water. But they do not pay for the water as such. They pay for the operation, maintenance and depreciation of their pumping, purification and storage systems, their distribution and sewage networks and for their wastewater treatment.

People are not poor because they have no water. They have no water because they are poor.

We are not going to run out of raw materials, metals and minerals. Reserves and resources are more abundant today than ever before. The Commodity price index is half of what it used to be in the early 80s when the Club of Rome sounded the alarm with its dreary report: *Limits to Growth.*

Speaking as a natural scientist I can see no reason why the optimistic scenario *must* fail.

But fail it may for *social* reasons. Are these huge urban conglomerates really manageable? Can 10 billion people live healthily and happily in a galaxy of mega cities scattered all over the globe? Can human ingenuity meet the managerial challenge? Are we, the genetic heirs of hunting and gathering ancestors, morally equipped to urban life, locked in and crowded?

Perhaps. Humans have proven to be flexible and able to adjust. Our cities have changed from the sheltered markets and military camps of the Roman empire, to autonomous centres for religious might in medieval times, and further to become the cradles for industrial revolution, focal points for innovation, and for economic and political power.

These transformations were truly dramatic. They were not foreseen, not intended and never planned. They simply took place, as it were. But people kept up with the change and eventually learned to like it.

The emergence of a global galaxy of mega cities is a new, unique, and unprecedented social metamorphosis. Today's information technology, instantaneous data processing, and all the rest of current technology provide the means. The unsmogging of London and the resurgence of New York may be omens. Hopefully, people will make it.

Certainly some of these mega cities will turn out more successful than others. Urban success will not be measured only, and probably not primarily, in monetary terms. But economic growth will for long remain a necessary, but not sufficient, condition for social progress.

The mega cities of the world will be very different, just as New York and London, Hong Kong and Buenos Aires are today. They will take advantage of their differences to attract whatever they need of capital and labor, managers, scientists, engineers, innovators, artists, musicians and priests. They will be in hard competition to meet their inhabitants' needs not merely in terms of goods and services available at the market place. People have other needs, too.

In Conclusion

Science and technology can provide some of the means necessary to prevent war. But not alone. It takes a proper social framework for the means to be useful. It takes stable institutions for democratic conflict resolution, with laws and law enforcement. Property right must be defended. Banks and insurance companies must be available for venture capital and for providing social security. It takes infrastructure and transportation systems. It takes ample supplies of fresh water and food. Above all it takes healthy, happy and well-educated people with access to hospitals and sanitary systems, schools and universities.

If all this is made available when required, as I believe it can, we will have peace. If not there will be wars, armed conflicts and terrorism.

Does Modernization Require Westernization?

Deepak Lal
University of California, Los Angeles

For the purposes of this essay, three types of liberty need to be distinguished: political, civil, and economic. Although it has become common, especially in America, to conflate the three, F.A. Hayek, among others, clearly distinguished them. As a development economist I am particularly concerned with the roles of these distinct types of liberty in promoting economic development.

For economic performance, economic and civil liberty are important because they underwrite the sanctity of private property. Moreover, the rule of law is fundamental in upholding both, as Hayek argued so eloquently in *The Constitution of Liberty.* But various political forms—including democracy, oligarchy, and autocracy—are compatible with maintaining the rule of law, as the example of Hong Kong attests. Indeed, hereditary monarchy, not democracy, delivered the Industrial Revolution. As the triumph of the market over central planning has demonstrated, economic liberty is essential for prosperity; but political liberty as embodied in majoritarian democracy is not—a point on which I concur with David Hume, Alexis de Tocqueville, and Hayek.

As defined by Hayek in *The Constitution of Liberty,* liberty or freedom is "that condition of men in which coercion of some by others is reduced as much as is possible in society" (11). This conception of individual liberty is closely related to the notion of individualism, a distinctly Western concept to which most other civilizations have not subscribed. But growing individualism, along with other elements of what the historian of Chinese science Joseph Needham called "a packet of change," was responsible for the "European miracle" of modern economic growth.

To promote in the rest of the world the material prosperity that this miracle has brought to the West, does the unique Western value system also need to be transferred, and if so, how? As a venerable debate in development studies has framed the question: Does modernization require Westernization? Hayek clearly seemed to think it did. He maintained that the market economy requires cultural underpinnings in the form of a set of "modern" values based on individualism (see the epilogue of his *Law Legislation and Liberty).* He even argued that a form of cultural evolution had, in an unplanned way, led from a Stone Age culture with its sense of communal bonds to a modern culture with respect for abstract rules, such as the rule of law, and a "detachment from communal, co-operative ends" (168). For him the process of cultural evolution involved forms of "group selection"—can idea currently scorned by sociobiologists—with the more

Deepak Lal, "Does Modernization Require Westernization?" This chapter is reprinted with permission of the publisher from *The Independent Review: A Journal of Political Economy* (Summer 2000, vol V, no. 1).

successful cultural practices "winning out." In this view it would seem that, even though the culture of liberty arose in the West, because of its success it should naturally spread across the world. A similar implicit belief underlies the current Western moral crusade around the world, in which a combination of the market and good governance (a euphemism for democracy) is increasingly offered as a panacea for poverty and war.

In my view, matters are not so simple. It was not some process of cultural evolution á la Hayek but contingent events linked to the actions of the medieval Western Christian Church that led to the rise of the West. Although individualism was an essential aspect of the West's subsequent trajectory, it is not essential—or inevitable, as Hayek's cultural evolutionary view would suggest—for the "Rest" to adopt this particular Western value in order to reproduce the West's economic success. As I argue in support of the foregoing positions, I will also discuss related issues involved in continuing debates about whether democracy is necessary for development, about the role of so-called Asian values in the success of East Asia, and about whether "Asian" values—or, more specifically, Confucianism—are compatible with "human rights."

Culture and Social Equilibria

The role of culture remains at the center of these debates, but culture remains a murky concept. I have found particularly useful a definition adopted by ecologists (Colinvaux 1983). They emphasize that, unlike other animals, the human one is unique because its intelligence gives it the ability to change its environment by learning. It does not have to mutate into a new species to adapt to the changed environment. It learns new ways of surviving in the new environment and then fixes those ways by social customs. These form the culture of the relevant group and are transmitted to new members (mainly children) who then do not have to invent the "new" ways *de novo* for themselves.

This conception of culture fits in well with the economists' notion of equilibrium. Frank Hahn (1973) describes an equilibrium state as one in which self-seeking agents learn nothing new, so that their behavior is routinized. It represents an adaptation by agents to the economic environment in which the economy "generates messages which do not cause agents to change the theories which they hold or the policies which they pursue" (59). Such routinized behavior closely resembles the ecologists' notion of social custom, which creates a particular human niche. In this view, the equilibrium will be disturbed if the environment changes, and therefore in the subsequent process of adjustment the human agents will have to abandon their past theories, which come to be systematically falsified. To survive, they must learn to adapt to their new environment through a process of trial and error. There will then arise a new social equilibrium: a state of society and economy in which "agents have adapted themselves to their economic environment and where their expectations in the widest sense are in the proper meaning not falsified" (61).

This equilibrium need not be unique or optimal, given the environmental parameters. But once a particular socioeconomic order is established and proves to be an adequate adaptation to the new environment, it is likely to be stable, because the human agents have no reason to alter it in any fundamental manner unless and until the environmental parameters change. Nor is this social order likely to be the result of a deliberate rationalist plan. We have known since Adam Smith's time that an unplanned but coherent and seemingly planned social system can emerge from the independent actions of many individuals pursuing their different ends, and in that system the final outcomes can differ greatly from those intended.

It is useful to distinguish two major sorts of beliefs about the environment: the *material* and the *cosmological* beliefs of a particular culture. The former relate to ways of making a living and encompass beliefs about the material world, particularly about the economy. The latter are related to understanding mankind's place in the world; they determine how people view the purpose and meaning of their lives and their relationship to others. There is considerable cross-cultural evidence that material beliefs are more malleable than cosmological ones. Material beliefs can change rapidly with changes in the material environment. There is greater hysteresis of cosmological beliefs, that is, of ideas about how, in Plato's words, "one should live." Moreover, the cross-cultural evidence shows that these worldviews correlate more closely with language groups (and thus with cultural origins) than with environments (Hallpike 1986).

The distinction between material and cosmological beliefs is important for economic performance because it translates into two distinct types of transactions costs that are important in explaining not only market failure but also government or bureaucratic failure (Lal 1997). Broadly speaking, transactions costs can be usefully categorized as those associated with making exchanges and those associated with policing opportunistic behavior by economic agents. The former relate to the costs of finding potential trading partners and determining their supply-demand offers, the latter to enforcing the execution of promises and agreements. These two aspects of transactions need to be kept distinct. The economic historian Douglass C. North and the industrial organization theorist Oliver Williamson have evoked transactions costs to explain various institutional arrangements relevant for economic performance. These analysts are concerned primarily with the cost of opportunistic behavior, which for North is associated with the more anonymous, nonrepeated transactions that accompany the widening of the market and, for Williamson, with the asymmetric information of principals and agents, a situation that allows crucial characteristics of the agent relevant for measuring performance to be concealed from the principal.

To appreciate the relevance of the distinction in beliefs and the related kinds of transactions costs for economic performance, it is useful to briefly delineate the broad changes of material and cosmological beliefs since the Stone Age in Eurasia.

Changing Material and Cosmological Beliefs

Evolutionary anthropologists and psychologists maintain that human nature was set during the period of evolution ending with the Stone Age. Since then the time lapse has been insufficient for any further evolution. This human nature appears darker than Rousseau's characterizations of it and brighter than those of Hobbes. It is closer to Hume's view that "there is some benevolence, however small... some particle of the dove kneaded into our frame, along with the elements of the wolf and serpent" (Hume [1750] 1975, 271). Even in the hunter-gatherer Stone Age environment the supremely egotistical human animal would have found some form of what evolutionary biologists term "reciprocal altruism" to be useful. Cooperation with one's fellows in various hunter-gatherer tasks yields benefits for the selfish human that can be further increased if he can cheat and be a free-rider. In the repeated interactions between the selfish humans composing the tribe, people could mitigate such cheating by playing the game of "tit for tat." Evolutionary biologists claim that the resulting reciprocal altruism would be part of our basic Stone Age human nature.

Archaeologists have also established that the instinct to "truck and barter," the trading instinct based on what John Hicks (1979) called the "economic principle"—"people would act *economically;* when an opportunity of an advantage was presented to them they would take it" (43)—is also of Stone Age vintage, and part of our basic human nature.

With the rise of settled agriculture and the related ancient civilizations, as well as the stratification this involved between men wielding the sword, the pen, and the plow, most of the Stone Age basic instincts that constitute our human nature became dysfunctional. As interactions multiplied between human beings in agrarian civilizations, many of the transactions took place among anonymous strangers who might never see one another again. The "reciprocal altruism" of the Stone Age, which depended on repetition of transactions, was no longer sufficient to curtail opportunistic behavior.

Put differently, the tit-for-tat strategy for playing the repeated prisoners' dilemma game among a band of hunter-gatherers in the Stone Age would not suffice, given the increased number of one-shot prisoners' dilemma games that arose with settled agricultural civilization and its widening of the market. To prevent the resulting dissipation of the mutual gains from cooperation, agrarian civilizations internalized restraints on such "antisocial" action through moral codes embedded in their "religions." But those belief systems were more ways of life than true religions, inasmuch as they did not necessarily depend on a belief in God.

The universal moral emotions of shame and guilt are the means by which the moral codes embedded in cultural traditions are internalized through the socialization process during infancy. Shame was the major instrument of this internalization in the great agrarian civilizations. Their resulting cosmological beliefs can be described as communalist.

The basic human instinct to trade would have been disruptive for settled agriculture, for traders are motivated by instrumental rationality to maximize economic advantage. Such behavior would threaten the communal bonds that all agrarian civilizations have tried to foster. Not surprisingly, most such civilizations have looked upon merchants and markets as necessary evils and sought to restrict them. Thus, the material beliefs of the agrarian civilizations were not conducive to modern economic growth.

Communalism versus Individualism

The ethic of the two remaining great agrarian civilizations, the Sinic and the Hindu, was distinctly communalist rather than individualist. But there were important differences in the cosmological beliefs of these two ancient civilizations.

The Hindu civilization, unlike the Sinic, did have a role for a form of individualism reminiscent of that found among the Greek Stoics. The anthropologist Louis Dumont has labeled this individualism "out-worldly" in contrast to the "in-worldly" individualism that is the hallmark of the "modern" individual. Hinduism allows the person who renounces the world and becomes an ascetic to pursue his own personal salvation without any concern for the social world. Like the Greek Stoic, this Hindu "renouncer is self-sufficient, concerned only with himself. His thought is similar to that of the modern individual, but for one basic difference: we live in the social world, he lives outside it" (Dumont 1986, 26).

For a Hindu who has not renounced the social world, Western individualism is impossible, as Ernest Gellner (1988) tellingly illustrates by imagining a Hindu Robinson Crusoe, a polyglot called Robinson Chatterjee. "A Hindu Crusoe," he notes, "would be a contradiction. He would be destined for perpetual pollution: if a priest, then his isolation and forced self-sufficiency would oblige him to perform demeaning and polluting acts. If not a priest, he would be doomed through his inability to perform the obligatory rituals" (121).

The Sinic civilization did not even have this "out-worldly" individualism of the Hindus and the Greeks. Its central cosmological beliefs have been summarized as optimism, familialism, and bureaucratic authoritarianism (Hallpike 1986; Jenner 1992). The strategic custom or institution is "ancestor worship and its social and political correlates involving hierarchy, ritual deference, obedience and reciprocity" (Keightley 1990, 45). There is little room for even the out-worldly individualism of the Hindus or Greeks in these cosmological views, which have been labeled Confucianism despite continuing controversy over whether the ancient sage should be implicated as originator of the distinctive features of Chinese civilization.

More recently, provoked in part by the events at Tiananmen Square, there has been an attempt to reconcile Confucianism with Western notions of human rights (de Bary 1988; de Bary and Tu 1998). The notion of rights is murky even within the Western philosophical tradition, but, as Henry Rosernont rightly points out, within the Confucian framework

> rights-talk was not spoken, and within [that framework] I am not a free, autonomous individual. I am a son, husband, father, grandfather, neighbor, colleague, student, teacher, citizen, and friend. I have a very large number of relational obligations and responsibilities, which severely constrain what I do. These responsibilities occasionally frustrate or annoy, they more often are satisfying: and they are always binding.... And my individuality, if anyone wishes to keep the concept, will come from the specific actions I take in meeting my relational responsibilities. (1998, 63)

As Rosemont notes, the attempt to reconcile a different "way to live" with the universal claims of Christianity has been a constant factor in the West's encounter with China. Those who found the Chinese way incompatible with universal Christian beliefs sought to convert the Chinese, while others of a less imperialist bent tried to find ways of making Chinese beliefs fit the universal Christian ethic.

Christianity and the Rise of the West

In this context it is worth noting the important difference between the cosmological beliefs of what became the Christian West and those of the other ancient agrarian civilizations of Eurasia. Christianity has a number of distinctive features, shared with its Semitic cousin Islam but not entirely with its parent Judaism, that are not found in any of the other great Eurasian religions. The most important is its universality. Neither the Jews, the Hindus, nor the members of the Sinic civilizations had religions claiming to be universal. You could not choose to be a Hindu, a Chinese, or a Jew; you were born as one. Hence, unlike Christianity and Islam, those religions did not proselytize. In addition, only the Semitic religions, being monotheistic, have been egalitarian. Nearly all the other Eurasian religions endorsed some form of hierarchical social order. By contrast, alone among the Eurasian civilizations, the Semitic ones (though least so the Jewish) emphasized the equality of men's souls in the eyes of their monotheistic deities. Dumont has characterized the resulting profound divide between the societies as one between *Homo aequalis,* which believe all men are born equal (as the *philosophes* and the American Declaration of Independence proclaimed), and *Homo hierarchicus,* which believe no such thing.

Thus Christianity, as we shall see, is and remains at the heart of the West's beliefs and at the heart of that "clash of civilizations" posited by Samuel Huntington. There can be little doubt that neither the Hindu nor the Sinic civilization has adhered to the Western notions of liberty and equality based on individualism.

But, for a long time, neither did the West. For although Christianity came inadvertently to promote the "in-worldly" individualism that is a hallmark of Western civilization, in its basic teachings it did not differ from the communalism found in the other great ethical beliefs systems of the ancient world. Like the Greeks and the Hindus, Christianity did provide a place for "out-worldly" individualism. As Dumont notes, "there is no doubt about the fundamental conception of man that flowed from the teaching of Christ...man is *an individual in-relation-to God*...this means that man is in essence an out-worldly individual" (1986, 27). So, how did the "in-worldly" individual arise in the West?

The rise of the West was mediated by the Catholic Church, from the time of Pope Gregory I (the Great) in the sixth century to the time of Pope Gregory VII in eleventh century, through its promotion of individualism, first in family affairs and later in economic relationships. Church actions included the introduction of all the legal and institutional requirements of a market economy as a result of Gregory VII's papal revolution in the eleventh century (Berman 1983).

The twin papal revolutions arose because of the unintended consequences of the Church's search for bequests, a trait that marked it from its earliest days. From its inception the Church had grown as a temporal power through gifts and donations, particularly from rich widows. So much wealth had the Church acquired in this way that in July 370 the Emperor Valentinian addressed a ruling to the Pope that male clerics and unmarried ascetics should not hang around the houses of women and widows and try to worm themselves and their churches into the women's bequests at the expense of the women's families and blood relations. The early Church's extolling of virginity and its discouragement of second marriages helped it to increase the number of single women who would leave bequests to the Church.

This process of inhibiting a family from retaining its property and promoting its alienation accelerated with the answers that Pope Gregory I gave to some questions posed in 597 A.D. by Augustine, the first Archbishop of Canterbury, concerning his new charges. Four of these nine questions concerned sex and marriage. Gregory's answers overturned the traditional Mediterranean and Middle Eastern patterns of legal and customary practices in the domestic domain. The traditional system was concerned with the provision of an heir to inherit family property. It allowed marriage to close kin, marriages to close affines or widows of close kin, the transfer of children by adoption, and concubinage, a form of secondary union. Amazingly, Gregory banned all four practices. In consequence, for instance, the adoption of children was not allowed in England until the nineteenth century. There was no basis for these injunctions in Scripture, Roman law, or the existing customs of the Christianized areas (Goody 1983).

This papal family revolution made the Church immensely rich. Demographers have estimated that the net effect of the Church's prohibitions of traditional methods of dealing with childlessness was to leave 40 per cent of families with no immediate male heirs. The Church became the chief beneficiary of the resulting bequests, accumulating vast wealth. Thus, for instance, in France one-third of the productive land was in ecclesiastical hands by the end of the seventh century.

But this accumulation also drew predators who worked from within and without to deprive the Church of its acquired property. To deal with this predation, Pope Gregory VII instigated his papal revolution in 1075 by putting the claims of God, enforced by the spiritual weapon of excommunication, above those of Caesar. As the Church projected itself boldly into the world, the new Church-state created all the administrative and legal infrastructure we associate with a modern polity—the essential institutional infrastructure for the Western dynamic that in time led to Promethean growth. Gregory VII's papal revolution lifted the lid on the basic human instinct to "truck and barter" and in time led to a change in the traditional Eurasian pattern of material beliefs with its suspicion of markets and merchants. The ultimate result was modern economic growth.

But the first papal revolution also led to a change in traditional Eurasian family patterns, which were based on various forms of joint families and related family values, and thereby released other opportunistic basic instincts that the shame-based moral codes of Eurasia had held in check. To counter the potential threat this release posed to its way of making a living—settled agriculture—the Church created a fierce guilt culture in which Original Sin was paramount and morality was underwritten by the belief in the Christian God (Delumeau 1990).

The Course of Western Individualism

Although the course of individualism in the West has been complicated, the importance of St. Augustine's "City of God" must be noted. The West has been haunted by its cosmology. From the Enlightenment to Marxism to Freudianism to Eco-fundamentalism, Augustine's vision of the Heavenly City has had a tenacious hold on the Western mind. The same narrative, with a Garden of Eden, a Fall leading to Original Sin, and a Day of Judgment for the

Elect and Hell for the Damned, keeps recurring.

Thus, the *philosophes* displaced the Garden of Eden by classical Greece and Rome, and God became an abstract cause—the Divine Watchmaker. The Christian centuries were the Fall, and the Christian revelations a fraud, as God expressed his purpose through his laws recorded in the Great Book of Nature. The Enlightened were the elect, and the Christian paradise was replaced by Posterity (Becker 1932). By this updating of the Christian narrative, the eighteenth-century philosophers of the Enlightenment thought they had salvaged a basis for morality and social order in the world of the Divine Watchmaker. But when, in the wake of Darwin, the Watchmaker was understood to be blind, then, as Nietzsche proclaimed from the housetops at the end of the nineteenth century, God was dead, and the moral foundations of the West thereafter lay in ruins.

Subsequent attempts to found a morality based on reason are vulnerable to Nietzsche's fatal objection in his aphorism about utilitarianism: "Moral sensibilities are nowadays at such cross purposes that to one man a morality is proved by its utility, while to another its utility refutes it" (Nietzsche [1881] 1982, 220).[1] Nietzsche's greatness lies in his clear vision of the moral abyss that the death of its God had created for the West. Kant's attempt to ground a rational morality on his principle of universalizability—harking back to the biblical injunction "therefore all things whatsoever ye would that men should do to you, do even so to them"—founders on Hegel's two objections: it is merely a principle of logical consistency without any specific moral content, and, worse, it is as a result powerless to prevent any immoral conduct that captures our fancy. The ink subsequently spilt by moral philosophers has merely clothed their particular prejudices in rational form.

The death of the Christian God did not, however, put an end to variations on the theme of Augustine's "City," which proceeded through two further mutations in the form of Marxism and Freudianism and a more recent and bizarre mutation in the form of Eco-fundamentalism.[2]

Marxism, like the old faith, looks to the past and the future. There is a Garden of Eden—before "property" relations corrupted "natural man." Then comes the Fall as "commodification" gives rise to class societies and a continuing but impersonal conflict of material forces, which leads in turn to the Day of Judgment with the Revolution and the millennial paradise of communism. This movement toward earthly salvation would be mediated not as the Enlightenment sages had claimed, through learning and the preaching of goodwill, but by the inexorable forces of historical materialism. Another secular "city of God" had been created.

Eco-fundamentalism is the latest of these secular mutations of Augustine's "City of God" (Lal 1995). It carries the Christian notion of *contemptus mundi* to its logical conclusion. Humankind is evil, and only by living in harmony with a deified Nature can it be saved.

The West's current cosmological beliefs, inadequately summarized by the word *liberty*, are thus, at present, incoherent. As the philosopher Alasdair MacIntyre (1990) has powerfully argued, the current Western notion of self has three contradictory elements. The first, derived from the Enlightenment, is a view of individuals as being able to stand apart from the social influences that undoubtedly mold them and able to shape themselves in accordance with their own true preferences. The second component of the Western self concerns the evaluation by others of oneself. Here the standards are increasingly those of acquisitive and competitive success, in a bureaucratized and individualist market economy. The third clement of the Western self derives from its remaining religious and moral norms, and is open to various "invocations of values as various as those which inform the public rhetoric of politics on the one hand and the success of *Habits of the Heart* on the other" (MacIntyre 1990, 492). This aspect of the self harks back to the Christian conception of the soul and its transcendental salvation.

These three elements constituting the Western

conception of self are not only mutually incompatible; they are incommensurable and lead to incoherence, because there are no shared standards by which the inevitable conflicts between them can be resolved.

> So rights-based claims, utility-based claims, contractarian claims, and claims based upon this or that ideal conception of the good will be advanced in different contexts, with relatively little discomfort at the incoherence involved. For unacknowledged incoherence is the hallmark of this contemporary developing American self, a self whose public voice oscillates between phases not merely of toleration, but admiration for ruthlessly self-serving behavior and phases of high moral dudgeon and indignation at exactly the same behavior. (Maclntyre 1990, 492)

The Family

As we have seen, the family revolution instigated by Gregory the Great is largely responsible for the individualism that characterizes the West, and a major manifestation of the divergence in cosmological beliefs between the West and the Rest may be found in the domestic domain. Will a process of cultural evolution—as postulated by Hayek, for instance—entail that as the Rest embraces the market it will also find itself being Westernized in the domestic domain?

From about the late sixth century, the Western Christian world, particularly in its northwestern region, deviated from what had been the traditional family pattern in Eurasia (Macfarlane 1986). The Church came to support the independence of the young in choosing marriage partners, setting up their households, and entering into contractual rather than affective relationships with the old. The Church promoted love marriages rather than the arranged marriages common in Eurasia. Friar Lawrence in *Romeo and Juliet*, egging on the young lovers against their families' wishes, is emblematic of this trend. But why did the Church promote love marriages?

It has been thought that romantic love, far from being a universal emotion, was a Western social construct of the age of chivalry in the Middle Ages. Recent anthropological and psychological research, however, confirms that this belief is erroneous: romantic love is a universal emotion (Jankowiak 1995; Fisher 1992). Moreover, it has a biological basis. Neuropsychologists have shown that it is associated with increased levels of phenylethylamine, an amphetamine-related compound. Interestingly, the same distinct biochemicals are also to be found in other animal species, such as birds, that also evince this emotion. However, it appears that the emotion is ephemeral. After a period of attachment, the brain's receptor sites for the essential neurochemicals become desensitized or overloaded, and the infatuation ends, setting up both the body and brain for separation or divorce. The period of infatuation has been shown to last for about three years. A cross-cultural study of divorce patterns in sixty-two societies between 1947 and 1989 found that divorces tend to occur around the fourth year of marriage.

A universal emotion with a biological basis calls for an explanation. Sociobiologists maintain that in the primordial environment it was vital for males and females to be attracted to each other to have sex and reproduce and also for the males to be attached enough to the females to look after their young until they were old enough to move into a peer group and be looked after by the hunting-gathering band. The traditional period between successive human births is four years, which is also the modal duration of marriages that end in divorce today. Darwin strikes again! The biochemistry of love, it seems, evolved as an "inclusive fitness" strategy of our species.

The capacity to love may be universal, but its public expression is culturally controlled. As everyone's personal experience will confirm, it is an explosive emotion. Given its relatively rapid decay, with settled agriculture the evolved instinct for mates to stay together for about four years and then move on to new partners to conceive and rear new young would have been dysfunctional. Settled agriculture required settled households. If households were in permanent flux, there could not be settled households on particular parcels of lands. Not surprisingly, most agrarian civilizations have sought to curb the explosive primordial emotion that would have destroyed their way of making a living. They have used cultural constraints to curb this dangerous hominid tendency by relying on arranged marriages, infant betrothal, and the like, restricting romantic passion to relationships outside marriage. The West stands alone in using this dangerous biological universal as the bastion of its marriages, as reflected in the popular song lyric "Love and marriage go together like a horse and carriage."

The reason for this Western exceptionalism goes back to the earliest period of the Christian Church, as we have seen. But the Church also had to find a way to prevent the social chaos that would have ensued if the romantic passion its greed had unleashed as the basis for marriage had been allowed to run its course in what remained a settled agrarian civilization. First it separated love and sex; then it created a fierce guilt culture based on Original Sin. Its pervasive teaching against sex and the associated guilt it engendered provided the necessary check on the "animal passions" that otherwise would have been unleashed by the Church's self-interested overthrow of the traditional Eurasian system of marriage.

Once the Christian God had died in the scientific and Darwinian revolutions, however, the restraints built on Original Sin were loosened and, in the 1960s sexual revolution, finally removed. The family as most civilizations have known it became sick in the West as people reverted to the "family" practices of their hunter-gatherer ancestors.

Karl Marx and Friedrich Engels promoted with some success the view that as modernization proceeds, the traditional extended family identified with preindustrial societies is doomed. Modern families will become more and more like Western families, characterized by love marriages, nuclear family units, and a cold-hearted attitude toward the old. Others maintain that, because the Western-style family seems to go back at least to the Middle Ages in Northern Europe, this modern family pattern must be not merely the consequence but the cause of the Western Industrial Revolution. Research by the Cambridge anthropologist Jack Goody (1990) casts serious doubts on both these positions.

First, the historical evidence shows that the Western family revolution predated the Industrial Revolution; therefore, the latter could not have caused the former. Second, as Goody shows at length, the purported advantages of the Western system, leading to a greater control of fertility, were also inherent in many other Eurasian family systems, but those systems did not deliver the Industrial Revolution.

Western cosmologies contained, however, a different way to deal with the death of the Christian God, which did not rely on still another secular variation on Augustine's "City" to provide the moral cement of its society. These views sprang from the Scottish Enlightenment, in particular from its most eminent sages, David Hume and Adam Smith.

Hume, unlike the *philosophes*, saw clearly that Reason could not provide an adequate grounding for morality. He was also clear about the role of morality in maintaining the social cement of society and understood that morality depended on a society's traditions and forms of socialization. Neither God nor Reason need be (or can be) evoked to justify these conditioned and necessary habits. This view of ethics resembles that of the older non-Semitic Eurasian civilizations whose socialization processes are based on shame.

However, as this account shows, there is no reason whatsoever for the rest of the world to follow the peculiar and particular Western trajectory. It is not modernization but the unintended consequences of Pope Gregory I's family revolution that have led to the death in the West of the Eurasian family values that the Rest rightly continue to cherish. The Rest do not have to embrace this cosmology. Even their Westernized elites can heal their fractured souls by embracing the Scottish sages: Hume's morality based on tradition and Smith's material beliefs based on the market. This classical liberalism provides a means of modernizing without succumbing to the moral emptiness of the current Western cosmology.

Democracy and Development

Is there any necessary link between democracy and development? A number of cross-sectional statistical studies claim to have found such a relationship. But the statistical proxies used for the political variables in these studies do not inspire much confidence, and the studies are further plagued by the econometric problem of identification. In our recent book, Hla Myint and I found no relationship between the form of government and economic performance during the thirty-year economic histories of the twenty-five developing countries that we studied (Lal and Myint 1996). Rather than the polity, the initial resource endowment, in particular the availability or lack of natural resources, was a major determinant of policies that impinged on the efficiency of investment and thereby the rate of growth. This effect was basically due to the inevitable politicization of the rents that natural resources yield, with concomitant damage to growth performance. By contrast, resource-poor countries, irrespective of the nature of their government, were forced to develop their only resource, their human subjects. Thus, the economic performance of resource-poor countries such as the Far Eastern Gang of Four (South Korea, Singapore, Hong Kong, and Taiwan) tended to be much better on average than that of countries with abundant natural resources, such as Brazil and Mexico. Countries such as India and China, whose factor endowments fall between these extremes, swerved between following the policies of their resource-abundant and their resource-poor cousins, with a resultant intermediate economic performance. The difference in performance was further explained by the other major determinant of growth, the volume of investment. For example, although the efficiency of investment in India and China during both their dirigiste and their more economically liberal periods was about the same, China's investment rate has been about twice India's, resulting in a growth rate also about twice as high.

If differences in the polity cannot explain differences in economic performance, is there any reason to prefer one type of polity over another, in particular, to prefer democracy over some authoritarian alternative? As usual, Alexis de Tocqueville was both succinct and prescient. In his *Ancien Regime* he wrote:

> It is true that in the long run liberty always leads those who know how to keep it to comfort, well-being, often to riches: but there are times when it impedes the attainment of such goods; and other times when despotism alone can momentarily guarantee their enjoyment. Men who take up liberty for its material rewards, then, have never kept it for long...what in all times has attracted some men to liberty has been itself alone, its own particular charm, independent of the benefits it brings; the pleasure of being able to speak, act, and breathe without constraint, under no other rule but that of God and law. Who seeks in liberty something other than itself is born to be a slave.

Democracy, then, is to be preferred as a form of government not because of its instrumental value in promoting prosperity, for at times it may not do so, but because it promotes the different but equally valuable end of liberty. However, as the experience of many countries—not all of them in the Third World—attests, democracy is a frail flower. India is unique in having successfully nurtured it in such a vast, diverse, and poor country. The assault on democracy during the Emergency only showed how deeply rooted it had become in the Indian soil.

Whether such success will be achieved depends upon the political habits of different cultures, which have been formed as much by the geography of the territory where the relevant culture was formed as by any ideology. Thus, China, originating in the relatively compact Yellow River valley, constantly threatened by the nomadic barbarians from the steppes to its north, developed a tightly controlled bureaucratic authoritarianism as its distinctive polity which has continued for millennia to our day. By contrast, Hindu civilization developed in the vast Indo-Gangetic plain, protected to a greater extent by the Himalayas from the predation of barbarians to the north. This geographical feature (together with the need to tie the then-scarce labor to the land) accounts for the traditional Indian polity, which was notable for its endemic political instability among numerous feuding monarchies and for its distinctive social system embodied in the institution of caste (Lal 1988). The latter, by making war the work of professionals, saved the mass of the population from induction into the deadly disputes of its changing rulers. The tradition in which a certain customary share of the village output was remitted to the current overlord discouraged any victor from disturbing the daily business of his newly acquired subjects.

The democratic practices gradually introduced by the British have fit these ancient habits like a glove. The ballot box has replaced the battlefield for the hurly-burly of continuing "aristocratic" conflict, and the populace accepts with weary resignation that its rulers will through various forms of rent-seeking take a certain share of output to feather their own nests.

Given the differences among countries in their historically determined political habits, it is by no means certain that democracy will be viable in many climes. But because democracy is not necessary for prosperity, countries can prosper by allowing economic freedom while maintaining their ancient habits, favoring various modes of maintaining social order over political systems based on individual political liberty.

Asian Values and Economic Performance

What role did Asian values play in the East Asian economic miracle? The conventional economic explanation maintains that this success arose entirely from very high rates of savings and from investment deployed efficiently, most importantly by making use of the gains from the international division of labor.[3]

Moreover, the factor-endowment story about the political economy of countries where labor is abundant and land is scarce (briefly outlined in the preceding section) can explain why those countries adopted outward-oriented policies. Nothing about authoritarianism or democracy per se can be adduced as necessary for development. This interpretation leaves us to consider the role of familial values, in particular those of the overseas Chinese and their family-based networks *guanxi*, in explaining East Asia's success.

As regards the success of the overseas Chinese and these purportedly neo-Confucian societies, W.J.F. Jenner (1992) is surely right in stating that their success has little to do with China's past but owes much to "European economics, commercial law, science and technology" (172). It was the interaction of these Western institutions with some inherited Asian values that brought about successful development. In the absence of the

> dynamic, alien, Western institutions and forms of economic organization...that have transformed these other countries the familistic values [of the mainland] are more likely to impede than to support change and development. In particular, China is still under the rule of a thinly disguised, premodern imperial bureaucracy, unlike those former colonies. (172-73)

A similar explanation and prognosis for different parts of the Chinese world is provided by L.W. Pye (1985). For Japan, M. Morishima (1982) argues that, in large part, *deviations* from Japan's Confucian past explain its extraordinary economic success.

Finally, E.F. Vogel's (1991) argument that the meritocratic bureaucratic tradition of China, based on entrance exams, has been an important contributor to East Asia's success can be countered by two examples. India and the United Kingdom established modern meritocratic bureaucracies, with considerable social cachet in the late nineteenth century. They compare favorably on every dimension with those of East Asia. But the mandarins certified by those examinations have not been able to improve the economic prospects of their respective countries.

The most heated debates surround the role of the Chinese family as the agent of a distinctive and productive familial capitalism in the Sinic world. As M.K. Whyte notes in an excellent survey of the literature on the role of the Chinese family (1996), there has been a complete reversal of views. The traditional view, associated with Max Weber and various modernization theorists, held that the Chinese family acted as a major brake on economic progress because its nepotism, initiative-sapping patriarchy, and personal rather than universalistic value system would make enterprises based on it inefficient. Now, by contrast, the same Chinese family is being hailed as the engine of growth in the Sinic world, based on the undoubted success of the family-based businesses of Hong Kong and Taiwan and the growth of family-based industry in the private sector in China. Many of these arguments in favor of familialism, for instance, that the form of cronyism known as *guanxi* is efficient, are just not persuasive, particularly in a broad comparative framework (Greif 1994). The argument that Chinese families have always been entrepreneurial but have been "cabin'd cribb'd and confin'd" by predatory states, has more merit. The most important reason for taking the optimistic view of the role of the Chinese family in development is the undoubted success of the family mode of production in the Sinic world. This needs an explanation.

Whyte argues that as the Chinese family has changed over the last century, many aspects of it—for example, the strict patriarchy—have altered. At the same time, particular features of the Chinese family have proved valuable in the emerging world division of labor as the nature of production relations in that economy has changed. In particular, small-scale family-based enterprises enjoy an advantage because of the flexibility with which they can switch seamlessly from one activity to another.

Whyte's argument can be put into a wider perspective. John Hicks (1969) characterized the major feature of the Industrial Revolution as the substitution of fixed for circulating capital, as epitomized by the replacement of the "putting-out system" by the "factory system." The putting-out system, of course, involved mainly household enterprises. Today, we witness a substitution of human for fixed capital in many aspects of industrial production.

Unlike heavy industry, much of the industry supplying consumer goods is becoming almost bespoke. Instead of mass-producing consumer goods on large production lines—called "Fordism" by some in recognition of the revolution in standardized mass production of consumer durables achieved by Henry Ford—the current tendency is to produce differentiated versions of the same good more closely tailored to differing individual tastes. Variety rather than standardization is the objective in this "designer" world of commodities in the affluent West. Shifts in its variegated tastes are increasingly reflected in differentiation of products to meet the volatile demand. Such demand conditions have created the need for highly flexible production enterprises that can quickly shift from producing one type or variety of the good to another. Because scale economies have less importance in manufacturing such goods than in the production of the old standbys of Fordist consumerism, small-scale enterprises that can react flexibly to shifts in tastes (designs) are not only not at a disadvantage but are likely to have a comparative advantage over more traditional and bureaucratically organized firms.

Into this emerging economic niche the Sinic family-based enterprises in both mainland China and its smaller outposts in Southeast Asia have moved. In this modern version of the putting-out system, the design capacity, which is human-capital intensive, is located in the rich countries. Enterprises establish "virtual factories," with their production bases spread across the world, and use modern telecommunications to convert the designs into the differentiated custom-made goods increasingly demanded by consumers in the West. The design centers are not a monopoly of the West. Witness the transformation of Hong Kong from a manufacturing to a service economy that mediates this fickle affluent-consumer economy between the designers in the West and the flexible production lines based on family-type enterprises in southern China. This is an ideal environment in which to unleash the entrepreneurship of the familial business, and the Sinic family has taken advantage of it in a spectacular manner. But without modern communications and modern legal and commercial codes, it would come to nought.

The importance of Hong Kong for the development of southern China lies as much in its colonial institutional and legal system, which has allowed this late-twentieth-century division of labor to be adopted, as in its traditional role as an entrepôt and financial center. Thus, as Whyte emphasizes, the particular conjunction of economic, technological, and institutional circumstances at the end of the millennium, not any essential Confucian attributes of the Chinese family, has made it an engine of growth today that it was not in the past.

Cultural factors may have played a part in the processes of socialization using shame to inculcate Sinic cosmological beliefs. These have provided the cement of their societies, and to the extent that they are based on the ancient veneration of the family in Chinese culture, they can also explain the widespread prevalence of "delayed gratification" that has led to extraordinarily high rates of saving (and thus investment) in these countries. The more dynastic family interests govern individual choices, the lower is likely to be the private rate of time preference and hence the higher the saving rate. Although the same argument should apply to the joint-family-based society of India, that country's saving rate has been about half of its Far Eastern neighbor's, although this situation seems to have changed with the recent acceleration in growth rates associated with the 1991 liberalization. More important perhaps is that, as Lee Kwan Yew has noted, the family-based societies can still rely on the social safety nets of the family rather than having to create welfare states like those in the West, which, paradoxically, have been both a symptom and an indirect cause of the accelerating erosion of the cement of societies in the West.

Conclusion

Gregory VII's eleventh-century papal revolution played a crucial role in propagating the material beliefs that promoted the institutional changes required for the growth of the market economy. By now these beliefs have been embraced around the world. However, to promote the modernization sought worldwide, there is no need for the non-Western world to accept the cosmological beliefs promoted by Gregory the Great's papal revolution of the sixth century. Societies can modernize without Westernizing. Rather than heed the continuing Western moral crusade in pursuit of its "habits of the heart"—which, far from being universal, remain the culture-specific, proselytizing, and egalitarian ethic of what is still, at heart, Western Christendom—the non-Western world, observing the social decay that the West's cosmology has caused, might well invoke the ancient biblical injunction, "Physician heal thyself."

References

Becker, C.L. 1932. *The Heavenly City of the Eighteenth-Century Philosophers.* New Haven: Yale University Press.

Berman, H.J. 1983. *Law and Revolution.* Cambridge, MA: Harvard University Press. Colinvaux, P. 1983.

The Fates of Nations. London: Penguin.

De Bary, W.T. 1998. *Asian Values and Human Rights.* Cambridge, MA: Harvard University Press.

De Bary, W.T., and Tu Weiming, eds. 1998. *Confucianism and Human Rights.* New York: Columbia University Press.

Delumeau, J. 1990. *Sin and Fear: The Emergence of a Western Guilt Culture, Thirteenth to Eighteenth Centuries.* New York: St. Martin's.

Dumont, L. 1970. *Homo Hierarchicus.* London: Weidenfeld and Nicholson.

_______. 1986. *Essays on Individualism.* Chicago: University of Chicago Press.

Fisher, H. 1992. *Anatomy of Love.* New York: Norton.

_______. Gellner, E. 1988. *Plough, Book and Sword.* London: Collins Harvill.

_______. 1993. *The Psychoanalytic Movement: The Cunning of Unreason.* Evanston, IL: Northwestern University Press.

Goody, J. 1983. *The Development of the Family and Marriage in Europe.* Cambridge, England: Cambridge University Press.

_______. 1990. *The Oriental, the Ancient and the Primitive.* Cambridge, England: Cambridge University Press.

Greif, A. 1994. "Cultural Beliefs and the Organization of Society: A Historical and Theoretical Reflection on Collectivist and Individualist Societies." *Journal of Political Economy* 102: 912-50.

Hahn, F. 1973. *On the Notion of Equilibrium in Economics.* Cambridge, England: Cambridge University Press.

Hallpike, C.R. 1986. *The Principles of Social Evolution.* Oxford: Clarendon.

Hayek, F.A. 1960. *The Constitution of Liberty.* London: Routledge.

_______. 1979. *Law, Legislation and Liberty.* Chicago: University of Chicago Press.

Hicks, J.R. 1969. *A Theory of Economic History.* Oxford: Oxford University Press.

_______. 1979. *Causality in Economics.* Oxford: Blackwell.

Hume, D. [1750] 1975. *An Enquiry Concerning the Principles of Morals.* London: Oxford University Press.

Jankowiak, W., ed. 1995. *Romantic Passion.* New York: Columbia University Press.

Jenner, W.J.F. 1992. *The Tyranny of History: The Roots of China's Crisis.* London: Penguin.

Keightley, D.N. 1990. "Early Civilization in China: Reflections on How It Became Chinese." In *Heritage of China,* edited by P.S. Ropp. Berkeley: University of California Press.

Lal, D. 1988. *The Hindu Equilibrium.* 2 vols. Oxford: Clarendon.

_______. 1995. Eco-Fundamentalism. *International Affairs* 71: 515-28.

_______. 1997. "The Communications Revolution and Economic Performance." Paper prepared for Nemetria's sixth conference on Ethics and Economics, Foligno, Italy.

_______. 1998. *Unintended Consequences: The Impact of Factor Endowments, Culture, and Politics on Long-Run Economic Performance.* Cambridge, MA: MIT Press.

_______. 1999. *Unfinished Business.* New Delhi: Oxford University Press.

Lal, D., and H. Myint. 1996. *The Political Economy of Poverty, Equity and Growth.* Oxford: Clarendon.

Macfarlane, A. 1986. *Marriage and Love in England.* Oxford: Blackwell.

MacIntyre, A. 1990. "Individual and Social Morality in Japan and the United States: Rival Conceptions of the Self." *Philosophy East and West* 40: 489-97.

Morishima, M. 1982. *Why Has Japan Succeeded?* Cambridge, England: Cambridge University Press.

Nietzsche, F. [1881] 1982. *Daybreak: Thoughts on the Prejudices of Morality.* Cambridge, England: Cambridge University Press.

North, D.C. 1990. *Institutions, Institutional Change and Economic Performance.* Cambridge, England: Cambridge University Press.

Pye, L.W. 1985. *Asian Power and Politics: The Cultural Dimensions of Authority.* Cambridge, MA: Harvard University Press.

Rosemont, H., Jr. 1998. "Human Rights: A Bill of Worries." In *Confucianism and Human Rights,* edited by W. T. de Bary and Tu Weiming. New York: Cambridge University Press.

Sen, A.K., and B. Williams, eds. 1982. *Utilitarianism, For and Against.* Cambridge, England: Cambridge University Press.

Vogel, E.F. 1991. *The Four Little Dragons.* Cambridge, MA: Harvard University Press.

Webster, R. 1995. *Why Freud Was Wrong.* London: Harper Collins.

Whyte, M.K. 1996. "The Chinese Family and Economic Development: Obstacle or Engine?" *Economic Development and Cultural Change* 45: 1-30.

Williamson, O.E. 1985. *The Economic Institutions of Capitalism.* New York: Free Press.

Acknowledgments

An earlier version of this article was presented at the regional meeting of the Mont Pelerin Society, Bali, July 8-11, 1999. The article draws heavily on Lal 1997 and Lal 1998.

Deepak Lal is the James S. Coleman Professor of International Development Studies at the University of California, Los Angeles.

The Independent Review, v. V, n. 1, Summer 2000, ISSN 1086-1653, Copyright © 2000, pp. 5-24.

Notes

1. A point only reinforced by the contributions to Sen and Williams 1982.

2. That Freudianism follows the same narrative is argued by Gellner 1993 and Webster 1995.

3. See Lal and Myint 1996 and Lal 1998 for details and references.

Building a Scientific Basis for a Global Culture of Peace

Walter L. Wallace
Princeton University

In addition to everything that historians, journalists, and forecasters (as producers of information about the actual past, the actual present, and the likely future, respectively) want to know, scientists also want to know what still unrealized *potentialities* are latent in the world. Physical scientists, for example, want to know how new kinds of materials can be synthesized, even if those materials have never yet existed and would probably never exist without informed intervention.

Similarly, social scientists want to know if a world without war, and without poverty, illiteracy, autocracy, and gender, ethnic, "racial," or nationality discrimination of any kind, is realistically possible—even though such a world has never yet existed. And we would also like to know, if such a world *is* possible, how to make it a reality—and, if it is *not* possible (as many people nowadays seem to think), how to adapt both culturally and social structurally to that impossibility.

Science's way of seeking answers to questions of this sort is to collect empirical information about the way the world actually has worked in the past and is working in the present; compile this information into time trends; project these trends into the future via hypothetical scenarios in which different conditions prevail; and, finally, select for real-life trials those scenarios that show high probability of working in desired directions.

Accordingly, this paper will offer highly condensed answers to two questions: (1) What long-term trend information does modern science—including the social, biological, and physical sciences—offer that would support a global culture of peace?; (2) What hypothetical information about the future does modern science offer that might motivate such a culture and light our way to it?[1]

What Long-Term Trend Information Does Science Offer in Support of a Global Culture of Peace?

The relevant long-term trend information that modern science offers may be summarized under the headings of four extended stages that our species, *Homo sapiens*, has experienced so far—namely, species origin, species dispersion, species diversification, and species contact. These will serve as the four major points on the trend-line to be developed here from which we shall project a tentative future.

Species Origin

There now seems to be a clear consensus among paleoanthropologists and geneticists that *Homo sapiens* (latest product of the 2.5 million year-old evolution of the genus *Homo*), evolved perhaps 200 thousand years ago, somewhere in the southern limb of the Great Rift Valley that stretches 1500 miles through eastern Africa from the Afar triangle at the southern end of the Red Sea deep into present-day Tanzania (see Klein 1999:146, 257, 511-514; Ayala 1995:1935; Tattersall 1995:243-246; Marks 1995:17; Fagan 1989:81–120; 1990:15, 20; Wilford 1995; compare Wolpoff, Zhi, and Thorpe 1984:464–467; Norris 1999).

Homo sapiens seems to have spent the first three-quarters of its entire lifetime so far eking out a precarious but mostly peaceful existence in small and scattered, nomadic, food-foraging bands that were slowly growing in size and dispersing locally—that is, up and down the African Rift Valley—and coexisting there with several other hominid species that have not survived (see Tattersall 2000).

Species Dispersion

Then, about 50 thousand years ago (see Klein 1999: 494; Stringer and McKie 1996:143-169)—probably under pressure of competition from more powerful bands that were also present in the territory—some bands of *Homo sapiens* began foraging beyond the valley itself. In so doing, these bands took the first steps in what would turn out to be a two-thousand-generations-long, leapfrog, push-me-pull-you, journey to the ends of the Earth. In the course of this journey, many bands would die out for one reason or another but others would survive to establish themselves on all the major landmasses of the Earth except Antarctica (and since the International Geophysical Year 1957-1958 research bases have been set up and maintained even there). Perhaps the first to be colonized were Arabia and India, then north Africa and the Middle East, Eurasia both east and west, then on to Australia and Polynesia, Siberia, the Arctic, the Americas, and, a scant two thousand years ago, New Zealand (see Fagan 1990:234; Molnar 1992:190; Quintana-Murci et al. 1999).

Species Diversification

To the degree and duration of their separation from the parent population and from each other, the descendants of each band that left the African Rift Valley homeland, and that survived, would eventually have grown so different from the descendants of other bands and from those remaining in the homeland as to become new hominid species. It had happened before. Indeed, the Origin-to-Dispersion-to-Diversification-to-*Speciation* hypothesis is central to Darwin's entire theory of how all the more than two million existing species of life as a whole came to be: "I think all the grand leading facts of geographical distribution [of life forms] are explicable on the theory of migration...together with subsequent modification and the multiplication of new forms....The varieties, or incipient species, thus produced ultimately become converted...into new and distinct species" (Darwin 1968 [1859]:393, 397; see Ridley 1993:444 for a more modern formulation).

The most important of all facts about our species' history so far, however, is simply that we have *not* stuck to this typical Darwinian track. A lucky combination of things switched us onto another (atypical, but still basically Darwinian[2]) track about five thousand years ago. This track has certainly been less traveled by, and it has made all the difference.

Species Contact

After the crucial Paleolithic technological inventions—namely, the stone hand-axe, controlled fire, the spear, and counting records (on the latter, see Barrow 1992:31-32), all of which originated in sub-Saharan east Africa earlier than thirty thousand years ago—came the Neolithic ones: domestication of plants and animals, significant tool improvements, the beginnings of metallurgy, and sedentism (see McCorriston and Hole 1991; Sherrat 1997; Diamond 1997:119-153).

Then, combining all these inventions and inconceivable without them, there came the most consequential invention of all—namely, intensive large-scale agriculture (contrast this evaluation with Diamond 1987). This invention appeared first about five thousand years ago in two ecologically special territories: the naturally fertile valleys of the Tigris and Euphrates, and of the Nile, rivers—the two such valleys nearest to *Homo sapiens*' place of origin. Then, somewhat later, the same invention was made in the more distant but similarly fertile valleys of the Huang He river (five thousand years ago), and the Indus river (four to five thousand years ago), and still later in the Peruvian Andes (the latter also dependent on the ready availability of fresh water, but an availability that accompanied the emergence of the El Niño/Southern Oscillation rainfall pattern one to two thousand years ago [see Hecht 1999a; also McCorriston and Hole 1991]).

The sharp escalations in population size and in food stores and other wealth to which large-scale agriculture gave rise encouraged the populations practicing it to expand the territory under their control, to enlarge and functionally diversify the labor-force at work there, and so to increase their economic wealth, their political power, their empirical knowledge and technical know-how, and the honor/prestige/blessing they could count on receiving both in this world and in the next (see McNeill 1985:15; Wallace 1994:47-72). In this way, the first, ancient, "empires" were constructed—mainly through force of arms—an event whose significance for the Diversification-to-Contact transition is apparent in the very definition of empires as states having "a great extent of territory and *a great variety of peoples under one rule*."[3]

The invention of intensive large-scale agriculture, then, seems clearly the mechanism that switched *Homo sapiens* off the contact-*breaking*, speciation-bound, track (on which it had been slowly creeping for its first 195 thousand years) onto the contact-*making* track on which it has been rolling, rocking, occasionally stalling, occasionally backing, but generally accelerating, for these last five thousand years.

And heeding that cue, let us pause for a moment to highlight the basic (though unavoidably ballpark) numbers we are dealing with here: 200 thousand years ago, the beginning of the species; fifty thousand years ago, the beginnings of species dispersion and of species diversification; five thousand years ago, the beginning of large-scale species contact. So if someone asks, "Why haven't we achieved world peace by now?" the numbers alert us to the Rome-wasn't-built-in-a-day possibility that a mere five thousand years of contact is just not enough to overcome forty-five thousand years of spatial separation compounded by many cross-cutting ethnic and "racial"othernesses. The real wonder may be that it has taken only five thousand years to get as close as we are. Indeed, if we keep to the present speed with which our many populations are coming together worldwide, another thousand years will surely see our descendants maintaining global peace no less comfortably than Americans today maintain peace between our former Confederate and Union states.

* * *

Now, having briefly described the four main points on *Homo sapiens*' trend-line so far, it hardly needs saying that there is more to science than *describing* events. Scientists also want to *explain* events. Knowing *why* things happen can make a huge difference in how we project their trends into the future. For example, we make very different predictions about where a projectile will land depending on whether its past and present motion has been due to some instantaneous shock (like a bullet) or to some ongoing and variable thrust (like a jet plane).

In what follows, our explanations focus on the *transitions* from one stage to the next—from Origin to Dispersion, from Dispersion to Diversification, and from Diversification to Contact—as marking the most obviously fundamental turning-points in our species' history so far.

Explaining the Origin-to-Dispersion Transition

The change covered by this first transition saw Homo sapiens spread out from a highly localized and relatively homogeneous habitat where it was vulnerable to localized catastrophes of many kinds, to a global and highly heterogeneous habitat where it was, by definition, not liable to destruction from any single local cause. This change, then, represented a decided increase in the species' survival chances.

Territorial Climate Fluctuations and Resource Competition

The original dispersion of *Homo sapiens* from the African Rift Valley seems likely to have occurred not in a steady migratory stream but in many pulses of varying sizes and durations (Stringer and McKie 1996:153). The mechanisms driving these pulses almost surely varied in detail, but one recurrent mechanism seems to have been closely related to the local territory in which *Homo sapiens* originated—that is to say, the topography, geology, and ecology of the land there, climate fluctuations there, and the resultant fluctuations in the quantity and quality of available drinking water, food, and shelter (see Fagan 1990:18-19, 230; Turner 1984:199; Gamble 1993:89). Thus, Sherratt says "[Climatic] cycles, tempting human populations to expand and then lowering the ceiling, were typical of the Pleistocene" (1997:281), and such ceiling-lowerings would have led to periods of increased competition between and within bands of *Homo sapiens*—with the losers being either wiped out or driven out (see Tattersall 1995:241).

Explaining the Dispersion-to-Diversification Transition

With its dispersion from the African Rift Valley, Homo sapiens not only multiplied its external habitats but its internal organizational structures. In particular, it evolved from a species that had once shared a single sociocultural, ethnic, and "racial" identification to a species diversified into many different sociocultural, ethnic, and "racial" parcels. This change, too, represented an improvement in the species' survival chances inasmuch as it generated a large repertory of survival-adapted ways of life that might, eventually, become compiled into a single, broadly comprehensive, toolbox of adaptations available for use as needed.[4]

Separation, Founder Effect, Drift, and Territorial Luck

A combination of four mechanisms seems to have propelled the diversification of the various bands that migrated out of the African Rift Valley locale of origin. The first three mechanisms were spatial separation, founder effect, and drift (see Wilson 1992: 81-82; Crick 1982:114; Molnar 1992:80-81, 203). Spatial separation was fundamental insofar as it at least attenuated, if it did not rupture completely, all interchange among the groups in question. To this, founder effect adds that any two or more populations (especially small ones) that separate from a given parent population are very likely to differ initially (through various selection and self-selection mechanisms) from each other and from the parent population, and that such initial differences are apt to be passed on to the descendant populations (Molnar 1992:203 cites some historical examples).

Enter the drift mechanism, saying that no human population can long remain stable—whether genotypically, phenotypically, or socioculturally—because of the many random and nonrandom shocks ("Giddy Fortune's furious fickle wheel," Shakespeare says) to which that population and its members are always susceptible. So any populations that separate from each other are almost sure to diverge from each other—and the longer and more completely they remain separated, the greater their divergences will be.

But neither the separation, founder effect, nor

drift mechanism says anything at all about the directions or the speeds that diversification is likely to take. A fourth mechanism, which it seems appropriate to call "the luck of the territorial draw," speaks to these questions.[5]

This mechanism's "territorial" component says the land on which any given migrating population happened to settle would have imposed its own particular environmental conditions to which that population simply had to adapt or die—or move on to some other territory where it would face the same alternatives all over again (see Molnar 1992:214-253). Moreover, the territories where populations did settle would drive diversification still further: Some territories would foster development in one direction and at one speed, while other territories would foster development in other directions and at other speeds (see Diamond 1997: 53-66, 386, 397). And, almost needless to say, the term "territorial" here includes not only the state of a particular territory at a particular time, but changes in that territory over time. "The largest example," says Sherrat, "is the changing Sahara desert, successively sucking in human occupants and then expelling them—what I have called the 'Saharan pump'...which was an important factor in propelling successive hominid populations out of Africa." In addition, he says, "temporary climatic deterioration may well have forced populations to cultivate artificially the calorie-providing species normally collected from the wild, at places where their production could be expanded. When conditions ameliorated, the way of life so created was able to expand. It was the cyclical nature of the process (carrot/stick/carrot) which provided the stimulus" (1997:281, 278; see also Sandweiss, et al. 1999:500; Wilford 1996).

In sum, the "territorial" component of the "luck of the territorial draw" claims that the main determinant of a given human population's history has been not *who* its members were—because, despite founder effect and drift, every population's members remained (and have remained, ever since) equally Homo sapiens—but *where* they were, because territorial locations vary greatly across the continents and climate zones of Earth (see Molnar 1992:188, 203; Lewis and Berry 1988:10-12; McNulty 1977:36-40; Vaughn 1977:22; Fage 1995:32).[6]

The "luck" component says two things: First is the plain impossibility that any Paleolithic human population could have spotted more than a few on-the-ground, slightly above-ground, or slightly below-ground, technologically accessible and immediately usable, resources of the territory in which it settled. Whether a given migrant population (or the parent population that did not migrate) found itself occupying a territory—say, one harboring deeply subterranean deposits of, say, coal, iron, copper, oil, gold, diamonds, uranium—that turned out, many hundreds of generations later and with vastly more technological know-how, to be "richer" than other territories could only have been a matter of blind luck. Second, the first population to settle in a given territory thereby took up a strong position to prevent any other population from settling on that particular territory. Here the emphasis is on "luck of the *draw*," and the analogy is to the card player who, by drawing a particular card from a fair deck, automatically prevents all other players from playing that card—barring fight, trade, or gift (see Simmel 1955:115-116; Schwartz 1975).

Now let us decompose the notion of diversification and consider the way a succession of different diversifications builds up over time in spatially separated populations. This will help us appreciate the immense inertial resistance that any mechanisms working to bring such populations into lasting, peaceful, contact with each other would face—and, to this day, still face.

Sociocultural, Ethnic, and "Racial" Diversifications

The first type of diversification to weigh-in among dispersing bands of humans would have been sociocultural, as each group began—probably even before it actually pushed off—to develop its own social structure and its own culture (see Sherif and

Sherif 1953:248-270).

The second type of diversification (whose weight was added to the first one without replacing it) would have been *ethnic* as, over many generations of relative isolation, each population lost track of its species-common ancestors and came to think of itself as having descended from its own unique ancestors—the latter typically portrayed as possessing supernatural powers and as having specially created the population's members from scratch.

The third and by far the most recent, "*racial*," type of diversification (Klein says "it seems increasingly likely that the modern races formed mainly...after 12-10 [thousand years] ago" [1999: 502]) would have been added to the others as still more generations of isolation and population in-breeding passed, and some easily visible and genetically heritable anatomical features became stabilized in each already doubly diversified population.

Now let us examine the latter two types of diversifications—namely, ethnic and "racial"—first together, because they share an important factor in common, and then separately, to see what distinguishes them from one another.

Ethnicity and "Race"

Weber defines ethnic populations as "groups that entertain a *subjective belief* in [members'] *common descent*,"[7] and then, by way of emphasizing the subjectivity point, he adds that "*it does not matter whether an objective blood relationship exists.* Ethnic membership differs from the kinship group precisely by being a *presumed* identity" (1978:389, italics added). Then, alluding to the role of religion in such beliefs, he adds that "behind all ethnic diversities there is somehow naturally the notion of the '*chosen* people'" (Weber 1978:391, italics added; see also Smith 1992).

Weber takes much the same view of "race" identification as he does of ethnic identification. Thus, after noting that "race" identification refers to "common inherited and inheritable traits that actually derive from common descent," he emphasizes the subjectivity of that identification: "Race creates a 'group,'" he says, "only when it is *subjectively perceived* as a common trait" (1978:385, 389; italics added). And, although Weber himself does not say so, it seems abundantly clear that behind all "racial" differences, too, there lies "the notion of the 'chosen people'" (see Wood 1970:1; Dower 1986:8, 9).

Two points here merit special attention. First, Weber's distinction between a subjectively cultural, and an objectively genetic,[8] meaning of "racial" identification allows us to recognize that the boundary between different subjective identifications of "race" (as well as ethnicity) may vary from place to place within the same society as well as from one society to another, and that any such identification of a given individual may change during her/his lifetime.[9] It is these subjective variabilities—not the few and minor objective and invariant differences that geneticists have found to be related to the concept of objective race (see Angier 2000)—that come into play when different groups of people meet. In Venter's taut phrase, "'Race is a social concept, not a scientific one'" (quoted in Angier 2000), and to symbolize this point the words "race" and "racial" are enclosed in quotation marks throughout this paper.

The second point is that the content of "racial" as well as ethnic boundaries refers to the belief of individuals on either side that they share a *common descent.* Descent from common ancestors seems almost universally regarded as the epitome of a 'naturally' close-knit coalition. Thus, popular shibboleth has it that "blood is thicker than water;" that "birds of a feather flock together;" and, combining these two ideas, the slogan of the Nazi Anschluss into Austria: "*Blut will zu Blut.*" The special coalition-binding power of common-descent beliefs, indeed, is probably why Weber says such beliefs arise "particularly in the political sphere" (1978:389)—which is to say, in the sphere of decision-making-and-enforcement concerning how a given population should behave toward its competitors either inside or outside its borders (see Weber 1978:910-911).

So much for the element that ethnic and "racial"

identifications have in common—namely, a subjective belief in their members' common descent. What, then, distinguishes ethnic from "racial" identifications? It seems reasonable to say this distinction rests on the two identifications' reliance on different *indicators* of common descent (see Banton 1996:103-104). In the case of ethnicity, the indicators are selected *behavioral* characteristics (that is, things that people do, and the mental thoughts and emotional feelings those actions are taken to express). In the case of "race," the indicators are selected *anatomical* features—in a word, not what people do, but how they look (see Geertz 1996:43; Dikötter 1996; Fenton 1999:3). Indicators of the "ethnic" sort include people's speech and song, the way they dress and dance, the things they like and dislike, the physical distance they maintain when conversing with others (see Hall 1969:131-164), their food and how they prepare and eat it (see Hicks 1997:10), their gods and how they worship them, and so forth (see Weber 1978:387; compare Nash 1996:25, 26 and Fishman 1996:64). Indicators of the "racial" sort include people's skin-color, eye-color, hair-color and texture, nose, lip, eye, and head shape and size, body type and stature, and so on.

Both types of indicators serve exactly the same function as far as relations between groups are concerned—the same function, indeed, as do the uniforms and other insignia worn by soldiers in time of war, and the passports carried by border-crossing travelers in time of peace. That is, they serve as rough-and-ready, naked-eye, identifiers of 'us' and 'them,' which is to say, friend and foe. They "make recognition at a distance, or in a fleeting instance, possible" [Nash 1996:25]) in the sometimes deadly struggles over the resources of the good life and, indeed, of any life at all.

Note also that both ethnic and "racial" indicators are culturally *selected* indicators. It seems clear that a very large number of *objectively* heritable anatomical differences (see Sherratt 1997:282), and of *objectively* learnable behavior differences, among human populations would have evolved during the 45 thousand years covered by the Dispersion and Diversification stages. However, the naked-eye distinctions that a given group drew between 'us' and 'them' could only be arrived at when that group made contact with some other group with which it could compare itself. Then both sides could select some subset of those distinctions as its own particular indicators of ingroup or outgroup membership (see Molnar 1992:5; Eriksen 1996:29; Fenton 1999:6-7). As Nash says, "what is relevant for social differentiation is not given in the body form of persons but in the cultural attention and stipulation of aspects of that body form" (1996:26; see also Fenton 1999:5). And insofar as that attention and stipulation arise from inter-population contact and comparison, "ethnicity is less of an identity among 'us' than a relation with 'them'" (Frank and Gills 1995:391; see also Armstrong 1994). Note also that the culturally selected heritable anatomical differences between, say, Scandinavian Europeans and Mediterranean Europeans, between Chinese and Japanese, between Ainu and Honshu Japanese, and between Hutu and Tutsi Rwandans, are no less "racial" in type than culturally selected heritable anatomical differences between Africans, Asians, and Europeans as larger wholes.

It also follows from their subjective nature that "Ethnic [and 'racial'] identities are...subject to change, redefinition and contestation....[Therefore, we] should understand ethnicity [and "race"] as a *social process*, as the moving boundaries and identities which people, collectively and individually, draw around themselves in their social lives" (Fenton 1999:10; also see Yetman 1985:8; Marger 1991:410; Gossett 1997:3-4; Lind 1998). Such boundaries express what Weber calls "the familiar tendency to monopolistic closure" of the group to outsiders (1978:386)—a closure that finds its major focus in endogamy and its group-monopolistic restrictions on the inheritance of wealth, power, knowledge/know-how, and honor.

By building up these successive types of diversification, then, the many spatially separated human populations would have been heading straight for the speciation that Darwin predicted—where at least some of these populations would have become so inbred as to be unable to cross-breed and produce fertile offspring with any other population.[10]

As already mentioned, however, this eventuality did not occur. The next transition along our trend-line turned out to be the track-switch that literally made history.

Explaining the Diversification-to-Contact Transition

Territory Again

When starting to explain the Diversification-to-Contact transition, the first thing to do is zoom out far enough to see our home planet as located squarely in the narrow zone where Sol's radiation gives life, rather than in the vastly larger zone where life is denied. (What bigger bit of territorial luck can one imagine?) After this, come two other characteristics: First, Earth's gravitation has been strong enough to ensure that every moment of Homo sapiens' drama to date (except for a very few, very short-term, explorer-tourists) has been played out in what has been an effectively closed space. Second, less than 30 percent of that closed space is land, and the principal continents of this land surface have been spread out but physically connected, or nearly so, throughout the entire drama. (It cannot be overemphasized that none of these things had to be. Once it came together, Pangaea could have stayed together, or it could have broken up differently than it did—say, with hundreds of miles of deep ocean all around the continent of *Homo sapiens'* origin. Any such difference would have had radically different effects on *Homo sapiens'* history, if, indeed, there had been a *Homo sapiens.*)

The relevance of these facts for the Diversification-to-Contact transition is this: Together, the closedness of Earth, and the connectedness of its relatively small land surface, made it nearly inevitable that all the dispersing and growing human populations would eventually make contact with each other (and eventually, I argue, re-join each other).[11]

Now let us zoom back in to continue our closer look at how the transition in question has unfolded.

Among the spatially separated and diversifying populations, a few were lucky enough to settle on much more fertile lands than others, and these lucky populations developed advanced techniques of stone tool-making, plant and animal domestication (see Diamond 1997:104-156; Keegan 1993: 123-125), irrigation, and crucially, food-production, more rapidly than others.

"The impact of food-production on the development of any society," Lamphear says, "is tremendous. A food-producing population, especially one engaged in agriculture, has to become more sedentary than a food-gathering population, so that farmers can tend their fields. As agricultural technology develops and production intensifies, farmers often begin to produce more food than their own families can consume. This surplus not only brings about...population explosions, but also enables some of the population to become involved in non-food-producing activities. Such people can devote their energies exclusively to religious, political, or military activities, or they can become full-time artisans, craftsmen, or traders" (1977: 86–87; see also McNeill 1963:10, 11; Molnar 1992:295-296; Curtin et al. 1978:7; Campbell 1985:397; Desmond 1975:21–23; Keegan 1993:126-136).

Then, to Lamphear's emphasis on how food-production influenced the size and internal complexity of human societies, Carneiro adds the idea—a central one for explaining the Diversification-to-Contact transition—that "As population density increases, and arable land comes into short supply, fighting over land ensues. Villages vanquished in war, having nowhere to flee, are forced to remain in place and to be subjugated by the victors" (1981:64; see also Leakey and Lewin 1992:xviii, 233; Spencer 1961:176; Pinney 1972:13, 15; Ekholm and Friedman 1995; Diamond 1997:386).[12]

Thus, McNeill tells us that "Sumerian and Egyptian civilizations, the earliest on record, both began with *conquest*" (1985:7–8, italics added; see also Childe 1942:88, 141–143, 154–155; McNeill 1978: 3-19), with the result that "by the time they enter the historical record, perhaps half a million inhabitants of southern Mesopotamia were part of a single civilization.... They may have spoken the same language. Their few professional scribes wrote in a common script" (Mann 1986:90; see also Adams 1966:153). A little later, and for the same reasons, contact-making began to take off among the diverse populations that had settled in the eastern end of Eurasia: "China's size and ecological diversity initially spawned many separate local cultures. In the fourth millennium B.C. those local cultures expanded geographically and began to interact, compete with each other, and coalesce.... [F]ierce competitions between warring chiefdoms drove the formation of ever larger and more centralized states.... China's political unification [came] under the Chin dynasty in 221 B.C. China's cultural unification accelerated during that same period" (Diamond 1996:83–84).

In addition to the valleys of the Nile and of the Tigris and Euphrates themselves, settlers in the natural passageway that connects these valleys found themselves enjoying their own luck of the territorial draw. Starting at the northern end of the Red Sea, running up through the Dead Sea, the Jordan River, the Sea of Galilee, the Phoenician coastal plain and the Bekaa valley, and so on north and east to Mesopotamia, this territory was lucky not only in its ecological contents (archaeological digs in the area have yielded the earliest-known evidences of domesticated plants; see Sherratt 1997) but also in its strategic location: "viewing the Old World as a whole, the Middle East occupies a 'crossroads' position; movement of ideas or techniques between eastern Asia, western Europe, and the African continent would very likely pass through this area. Given this and the fact that most of what is called invention rests on combining two or more preceding ideas or techniques, the peoples of the Middle East occupied a unique position. They were most likely to obtain the greatest number of new ideas and techniques before other areas" (Munson 1977: 72). In short, the Middle East crossroads became a smaller focus of inter-ethnic and inter-"racial" contact inside a larger region that stretched from the southernmost reach of Egypt to the northernmost reach of Mesopotamia, and from there east to India and China.[13]

Thus, largely because of the natural fertility of the territories on which some of its dispersing populations were lucky enough to settle, humankind was able to build its first empires—its first nations[14]—and to begin there what would soon become a world-wide turnaround from contact-lost to contact-regained. Locke and Stern summarize the long-term significance of this turnaround as follows: "Cultures may develop complexity through certain internal development and variation, but by far the main source of cultural growth and development seems always to have been through the forces of external contact.... Civilization is largely the accumulative product and residue of this ever-widening process of culture contact, interchange and fusion" (1946:7; see also Childe 1951b:173; McNeill 1978:12; Sherratt 1997:282).

Two mechanisms—both of them characteristic of empire- and nation-building—have been driving this turnaround for the last five thousand years up to and including the present. The mechanisms are *intersocietal people-migration*, and *intersocietal coalition-formation*. And largely as a result of technological advances, both of these mechanisms have grown enormously in their reach and grasp over the last five thousand years.

Intersocietal People-Migration

People that migrate from one society to another fall into four broad categories (some migrants may be placed in two or more categories, and some may change from one category to another). The categories are: *invaders*—people who voluntarily go out from one society to conquer or otherwise profit without permission from another society (Keegan says "charioteers were the first great aggressors in human history" [1993:139]); *slaves* and other bondspersons—conquered, purchased, or debt-bound members of one society who are shipped from that society to another society and compelled to live and work there; *refugees*—people compelled by threats of extermination, enslavement, incarceration, disease, and/or natural disaster to move from one society to another society which accepts them, usually involuntarily; and *emigrants/immigrants*—people, including settlers, sojourners, traders, and tourists who move voluntarily from one society to another society in which they are also accepted voluntarily (see, for example, Kane 1995:132).

Summing up the contact-making achievements of recent times (in which numerical relations among the four listed types of migrants has shifted from the predominance of invaders and slaves to that of refugees and emigrants/immigrants—although all types remain present), Pan reminds us that "A thousand years ago there were no Irishmen in Australia; no Thais in Bangkok; no white, nor black, Americans in America. Migration is the great travel saga of all time" (1994:375, see also 43-83; also Weiner 1995:21-25; Daniels 1990:11-16; Brooks 1977:120–124; Fage 1995:244–291). In our own time, *Homo sapiens* is even more on the move. The Population Reference Bureau says "International migration is at an all-time high. About 145 million people lived outside their native countries in the mid-1990s, and the number is increasing by anywhere from two million to four million each year" (1999). And French tells us that that the number of tourists crossing some international border grew from sixty-nine thousand per day in 1950 to two million per day in 1998; adding that "today, the total number of refugees worldwide—including internally displaced persons, asylum seekers, and people living in refugee-like situations—tops fifty-six million" (2000:6-7; see also Weiner 1995:2).

Huntington notes that "in Germany, Turkish foreign residents numbered 1,675,000 in 1990, with Yugoslavia, Italy, and Greece providing the next largest contingents.... By the mid-1990s, approximately four million Muslims lived in France and up to thirteen million in Western Europe overall. In the 1950s two-thirds of the immigrants to the United States came from Europe and Canada; in the 1980s roughly 35 percent of the much larger number of immigrants came from Asia, 45 percent from Latin America, and less than 15 percent from Europe and Canada" (1996:199–200). And to this, Kane adds that "about 2.5 million Mexicans live in the United States. Some 400,000 South Africans and Middle Easterners were living in Kuwait before they fled the war in 1991, and some 1.2 million foreign workers were in Saudi Arabia at the same time" (1995:143). Ahmed and Donnan tell us that "Muslim society...totals something like one billion people living in about 50 countries with significantly some ten to fifteen million living in the USA and Europe," and that "the bulk of Muslim migrant labor has settled abroad on a permanent basis.... Muslim doctors and engineers live as American or British citizens," and, Ahmed and Donnan add, "their children have no intention of going back to their place of origin" (1994:2, 5).

Responding to changes in patterns of economic opportunity, of transportation and communication technologies, and of culture (including the fitful spread of religious tolerance and non-discriminatory immigration and emigration laws which, in turn, both reflected and influenced changes in intersocietal coalition-formation; see Huntington 1996:198–199; Weiner 1995:11, 25, 212), people-migrations have swelled in size and multiplied in directions. They "now function on larger scales, as men and women from villages in India think not just of moving to Poona or Madras, but of moving to Dubai and Houston, and refugees from Sri Lanka find themselves in South India as well as in Canada, just as the Hmong are driven to London as well as to Philadelphia" (Appadurai 1990:297). Not surprisingly, then, Rudolph reports that "over the last twenty years or so Oklahoma City has acquired five mosques, four Hindu temples, one Sikh gurudwara, and three Buddhist temples.... There may be as many as seventy mosques in the Chicago metropolitan area and fifty temples in the Midwest

Buddhist Association. Muslims outnumber Episcopalians in the United States by two to one, and are likely to outnumber Jews in the near future" (1996: 26).

Weiner concludes that "More than ever before, individuals have become aware of the opportunities for employment and income [and, one should add, also for improvements in their political power, empirical knowledge/know-how, and in the respect accorded them] in other countries.... The declining cost of travel, moreover, is making it easier for migrants and refugees to go longer distances" (1995:221). Portes notes how the process builds momentum and inertia: "Migration...develops an increasingly dense web of contacts between places of origin and destination. Once established, such networks allow the migration process to become self-sustaining and impervious to short-term changes in economic incentives" (1995:22).

Intersocietal Coalition-Formation

Coalitions are formed between societies whenever, and to the extent that, they pool their economic wealth, their political power, their empirical knowledge/know-how, and/or their honor—including pooling the human populations that produce and carry such resources. One expects that coalitions will be occasioned by at least one partner's perception (whether true or false) of some threat or opportunity that it can better address with outside help than without that help.

In principle, coalitions can be formed, maintained, and/or terminated without migration of people between the coalition-partners; the communication of messages and the hand-to-hand transportation of goods may suffice. Similarly, migrations of people can occur without intersocietal coalition. Explorers (classifiable as invaders, or as tourists, depending on how they are received) and traders, for example, have migrated to and from societies that were entirely unaware of each other's existence. Between such extremes of independence, however, intersocietal coalitions do seem to facilitate migrations of people between their partner societies (witness the recent migration impact of the reunification of Germany), and vice-versa (witness the stronger coalitional ties of present-day New World societies to Western Europe than to Eastern Europe, Asia, or Africa).

The magnitude of intersocietal coalition-formation and its contribution to the currently developing Species Contact stage of human history rests largely on the invention, made first in the ancient empires of Sumer and Egypt, of what was then a new kind of shared subjective identification of persons. This identification, and the sociocultural entities it has sustained, have been serving as vital intermediate steps between a species that once consisted of many ethnically and "racially" diverse local populations and a species that is now rapidly becoming consolidated into a single global society.

The entities I have in mind are *nations;* their unifying subjective identification is *nationality;* and Simon's watchmaker analogy is helpful in grasping just why their role is so vital. One watchmaker, Simon says, tried to assemble a watch from its thousand elements in one go. But if this watchmaker "had [a watch] partly assembled and had to put it down—to answer the phone say—it immediately fell to pieces and had to be reassembled." By contrast, the other watchmaker first "put together subassemblies of about ten elements each. Ten of these subassemblies, again, could be put together into a larger subassembly; and a system of ten of the latter subassemblies constituted the whole watch. Hence, when [the second watchmaker] had to put down a partly assembled watch in order to answer the phone, he lost only a small part of his work and he assembled his watches in only a fraction of the man-hours it took [the first watchmaker]" (1965: 65-66).

To this, one needs only add Robertson's acute observation that "Much of world history can be fruitfully considered as sequences of 'miniglobalization,' in the sense that, for example, historic empire formation [and, let us add, the formation of those mini-empires called nations] involved the unification of previously sequestered territories and social entities" (1992:54; see also Tibi 1996:29; Jennings 1993:309; Smith 1995).

Nations as Coalitions of Ethnic and "Racial" Groups

Two obvious things about nations are that they are territorially based, and that they have almost always come into being as coalitions of ethnically and "racially" diverse populations that had either long been settled on separate but contiguous land areas inside that territory, or (as in the cases of the United States, Canada and Israel) that had recently invaded such a territory and forcefully made refugees of its inhabitants.

Now in every such set of neighboring groups it is a statistical near-certainty that one of them will be somewhat wealthier, politically stronger, more empirically and technologically knowledgeable, and accorded more prestige, than the rest. Typically, leaders of this top population would take the lead in forming a coalition (that is, a nation) with surrounding populations—the better to compete both with unallied populations in the area and with similar coalitions near and far that were striving to grow in the same way.

Gellner claims the formation of such a nation-coalition depended, in part, on "the general imposition of a high culture on society, where previously low cultures had taken up the lives of the majority...of the population. [This imposition involved] the generalized diffusion of a school-mediated, academy-supervised idiom, codified for the requirements of reasonably precise bureaucratic and technological communication" (1994 [1983]: 65). And when we ask what would be the unifying ideological content of this "high culture," Weber asserts that "above all, national solidarity may be linked to...[belief in] a *common political destiny*"; that "The earliest and most energetic manifestations of the idea [of a nation]...have contained the legend of a providential '*mission*'" (1978:923, 925; italics added); and that the nation concept contains "a specific belief in responsibility toward *succeeding generations*" (1946:173; italics added).

So it seems fair to conclude that whereas ethnic and "racial" group identifications center on members' beliefs in their common *past descent*, nationality identification center on members' beliefs in their common *future destiny*[15]—as seems well expressed in the U.S. President John Quincy Adams' injunction that immigrants to the new American nation should "look forward to their posterity rather than backward to their ancestors" (quoted in Gordon 1964:94).

Because of its emphasis on the future rather than the past, the principle of nationality identification can be mapped over the principle of descent-based ethnic and "racial" identifications, leaving individual citizens free to accept both sorts of identifications without experiencing any intolerable conflict of interest. The result is that, as Huntington points out, "almost all countries are heterogeneous in that they include two or more ethnic, racial, and religious groups" (1996:137; see also Connor 1996:71; Weber 1978:923).

Many examples of the inter-ethnic and inter-"racial" nature of the coalitions that constitute modern nations come to mind: The present "Chinese" nation includes Han, Kazakhs, Mongols, Uygurs, Koreans, plus some fifty other ethnic groups. The "French" nation includes Basques, Bretons, Burgundians, Normans, Franks, Provençales, Moroccans, Algerians, Côte d'Ivoirans, and other groups. The "German" nation includes Saxons, Thuringians, Bavarians, Frisians, Sorbs, Alemmani, Prussians, Turks, and other groups. The "English" nation includes Celts, Angles, Saxons, Jutes, Scots, Welsh, Danes, Normans, Indians, Pakistanis, Nigerians, Jamaicans, and many others. The "Nigerian" nation includes Hausa, Yoruba, Ibo, Ibibio, Nupe, Mumuye, Chamba, Tiv, Idoma, Ogoni, Urhobo, Eket, Mama, Ekoi, Fulani, and several score of others. As many of us have recently learned, the nation of "Afghanistan" includes some twenty ethnic groups among which the Pashtuns, Tajiks, Hazara, Turkmen, and Uzbeks are prominent; and the "Pakistan" nation includes Punjabis, Sindhis, Pashtuns, and Baluchis, among others. The "American" nation (largely for reasons of territorial location and geology-ecology) probably includes individuals who trace their ancestries to all the above groups and many more besides.

What *sort* of "destiny" or "providential mission" does nationality foretell and advocate? Weber, again, provides the basic insight when he answers: "the glory of power over other communities" (1978:911; see also 923, 925)—but it seems essential to include, along with the glory of superior power, the glory of superior wealth, the glory of superior empirical knowledge/know-how, and, indeed, the glory of superior glory—that is, honor or prestige—because nations never rest with being narrowly political entities but strive to become complete societies equipped with full complements of the basic societal institutions.

Relations Between National Coalitions: War and Peace

Thus, although the most decisive means that any nation can use in pursuing all these superiorities are the military and police forces of its political (power-producing, power-distributing, and power-wielding) institution (see Weber 1978:54-56, 980-982), every clash between different nations' armed-forces tests not only the nations' political strengths but also the strengths of their economies, of their scientific-technological-educational institutions, and of their religious institutions. And underpinning all these strengths is, of course, "national unity"—that is, unity among the nation's ethnic, "racial," and other-nationality constituencies (see Gellner 1994 [1983]:65; Hobsbawm 1994 [1983]:76-82; Smith 1994 [1989]:150-151).

As a result of the often huge accumulations of resources that have been staked on the outcome of wars and rebellions, such contests have had (until very recently) a winner-take-all character—as is clear from the aptly-named *sackings* that have so long, and so universally, marked human history (see Lattimore 1962:13; Diamond 1997:53-66). For this reason, national leaders have urged the ordinary citizens of their nation to embrace the supreme altruism—to risk "death in the group interest," as Weber puts it—and to do so with enthusiasm, even. To the extent that this altruism is distributed more or less evenly among the nation's constituent ethnic and "racial" groups, Weber continues, "War makes for an unconditionally devoted and sacrificial community [whose] feelings break down all the naturally given barriers of association" (1946:335; see also Tilly 1975a:42, 73–76; 1975b:623; Arnold 1991: 10; Bennet 1997; Braudel 1988:373-375; McNeill 1985:47-48).[16] Moreover, every nation's "community of political destiny...[in the] struggle of life and death, has given rise to groups with joint memories which often have a deeper impact than the ties of merely cultural, linguistic, or ethnic community. It is this 'community of memories' which...constitutes the ultimately decisive element of 'national consciousness'" (Weber 1978:903).

In this way, nearly all survivors of a nation's wars, whatever their ethnic and/or "racial" identifications, are fashioned into *nationalists*—that is to say, into patriots—who feel indebted to those "who gave the last full measure of devotion," a debt that can only be repaid with the survivors' own devotion ("that from these honored dead we take increased devotion"). It follows that the more dead, the greater the debt, the greater the debt, the greater the devotion, and the greater the devotion the more secure the nation. Consequently, Grossman says, "Nations celebrate their costliest battles, even losing ones—the Alamo, Pickett's charge, Dunkerque, Wake Island, and Leningrad are examples—due to the bravery and nobility of the sacrifices involved" (1995:206). No wonder that in Mussolini's view, "It matters little who wins. To make a people great it is necessary to send them to battle even if you have to kick them in the pants" (1955:926).

At the same time that all this is going on, leaders of nations typically seek to augment their citizenry's common-destiny consciousness with a common-descent consciousness (see Alba 1990: 311-312). Balibar puts it this way: "As social formations are nationalized, the populations included within them, divided up among them or dominated by them are ethnicized—that is, represented in the past or in the future *as if* they formed a natural community, possessing of itself an identity of *origins*" (1996:164, italics changed). Thus the common descent implications of nationalist terms like "Motherland," "Fatherland," "founding fathers," "patriotism" (and matriotism?) as well as slogans implying that the nation is divinely descended and divinely honored: "Pro Deo et Patria"; "For England and St. George"; "God Save the Queen"; "God Bless America," "In God We Trust." This deliberately "invented tradition" (Hobsbawm 1994 [1983]) of common-descent beliefs may eventually (and almost surely unintentionally) strengthen the similarly common-descent beliefs of the ethnic and "racial" groups to which the nation's citizens also belong. The latter groups may then come to feel themselves strong enough to compete with the nation for their shared members' loyalty (see Enloe 1981; Carmichael and Hamilton 1967:44-56; Nagel and Olzak 1982). Du Bois 1961:15-22 expresses African Americans' reaction of ambivalence ("twoness") to this competition, and Dippel (1996:xxii-xxiii) gives an account of Jewish Germans' similar reaction in a similar situation.

But inculcating both common-destiny and common-descent loyalties and actions among their own citizens (and undermining them among rival nations' citizens) are not the only competition strategies that the leaders of nations adopt. Another strategy is to form cooperative *coalitions*—federations, confederations, councils, alliances, ententes, axes, leagues, unions—with some nations against other nations.

For example, World War I was fought out between two European coalitions formed for the purpose (the Allies, originally consisting of three nations, versus the Central Powers, originally consisting of two nations), and this war gave birth to the League of Nations—a far more global peacetime coalition (originally including forty-two Asian, African, European, and New World nations). World War II was carried on by one coalition called the Allies (consisting of fifty European, New World, Asian, and African nations) and another called the Axis (consisting of nine European and Asian nations), and this war gave birth to the United Nations, a still more globally inclusive peacetime coalition whose charter was originally signed by fifty nations and is currently subscribed to by some 185 nations around the world.

Now from even this brief recitation one begins to suspect that war-making and coalition-formation (more generally, competition and cooperation) complement each other as two sides of a single self-enhancing interactive process. Moreover, one suspects that this same process may operate at *all* levels of life, from that of competitive single-cell animals, each with its own internally cooperating organelles, up to the whole competing-cooperating web of terrestrial life (see Margulis and Sagan 1986; Spencer 1898,I:464-469).[17]

Relations Between Coalitions: The Interaction of Competition and Cooperation

In other words, it seems that whenever three or more groups (or, for that matter, three or more individuals) compete with each other for some scarce resource, each competitor is likely to seek a cooperative coalition with at least one other competitor against the remaining competitors (see Simmel 1950:154-162; Caplow 1968).[18] (Note that the cooperation in question need not be voluntary; one competitor may compel others to cooperate with it—conquest followed by enslavement is an obvious case, but there are others in which the threat of conquest is sufficient). Then, in their own defense, all competitors that are left out of the first coalition will feel pressured either to join it or to form their own coalition against it (see Huntington 1996:231), and this process will continue until only coalitions of this sort are left in the arena. Then, as competition develops among them, these new coalitions are apt to form coalitions-of-coalitions which eventually become the only competitors in the arena—and so it goes, as the system bootstraps itself up toward the cooperative integration of more and more competitors (see Simmel 1950:154-162; Vansina 1990: 252-253; Gomes-Casseres 1996:1; Bleeke and Ernst 1993:1; Huntington 1996:185; Pohl 1997).[19]

Now if what we said above about the same competition-cooperation process operating at all levels is true, when we shift our focus from what goes on *between* coalitions to processes that go on, at the same time, *within* coalitions, that similarity should be borne out.

Relations Within Coalitions: The Interaction of Cooperation and Competition

Although a coalition's partners will (by definition) cooperate in their competition with outsiders, they are also likely to compete against each other for smaller shares of the costs of the coalition and for larger shares of the coalition's benefits (see Axelrod 1984). In this competition each partner will employ the same two-fold, offensive-defensive, strategy that may be found in all Homo sapiens' competitions whenever and wherever they occur—as follows.

In the first kind of strategy, all competitors, regardless of their relative strength or weakness, strive to influence their own, and each other's, *psychological* behaviors. The principal forms this strategy takes are disseminating (1) cognitive stereotypes of themselves and each other, (2) affective prejudices toward themselves and each other, and (3) normative dispositions to behave, physically, in discriminatory ways toward themselves and each other (see Sherif and Sherif 1953; Stephan and Rosenfield 1982; Merton 1976; Bodenhausen, Macrae, and Garst 1998).

In the second kind of strategy, all competitors strive to influence their own, and each other's, *physical* behaviors—that is to say, the things they actually do to themselves and to each other. This class of strategies includes the use of physical force—military, police, and/or vigilante—to prevent outgroup members from engaging in the particular behaviors, and enjoying the particular rewards, that ingroup members would monopolize for themselves (see Bonacich 1972; Sowell 1981: 137, 139; Nagel and Olzak 1982; Castles and Miller 1982:177-178, 188, 194; Alba and Moore 1982:378; Gans 1972; Caplovitz 1963; Coleman 1992:213; Massey and Denton 1993; Portes and Rumbaut 1996:21; Portes 1995:27-29; Wilson 1978, 1987; Tilly 1998:149-169).

Almost needless to say, competitors' psychological strategies are positive (at the extreme, superhumanizing) toward themselves, and negative (at the extreme, dehumanizing) toward each other (see Lifton 1986; Dower 1986:8-9). Similarly, competitors' physical strategies are helpful (at the extreme, monopolizing of resources and rewards) toward themselves, and harmful (at the extreme, exterminative) toward each other (see Staub 1989:8; Mazian 1990; Fonseca 1995:253-277). And again needless to say, the two types of competition strategies—psychological, and physical—reinforce each other and are readily institutionalized as a single weapon wielded, whether strongly or weakly, by each side in the contest.[20]

Nevertheless, as mentioned above, relations between partners inside a given coalition are never exclusively competitive. By definition, coalition partners cooperate against a common enemy and, in addition, each of them almost always seeks cooperative alliances with one or more of their partners against other partners inside the coalition (see Merton 1957:377-379). We should therefore expect to see the following two consequences of such cooperative relations when they occur in the context of some more inclusive competitive relations.

First, coalition-formation introduces an element of *subjective equality* among the partners inside the coalition that would not be available to them were they outside it. Initially, this element is merely the partners' awareness of being in the same coalition, as opposed to some being in and the others out. In the course of continued cooperation against the common enemy, however, that awareness tends to undermine the stereotypes (especially the outgroup homogeneity hypothesis; see Jones 1990:77-111) held by each partner in regard to all the others. Greider seems to have this process and its consequence for ethnicity, "race," and nationality exactly right: "The process of globalization is visibly dismantling enduring stereotypes of race and culture, ancient assumptions of supremacy," and "this transformation," he says, "will someday be understood as the most radical dimension of the [globalization] revolution" (1997:20).

Second, every coalition's cooperation introduces an element of *objective equality* among its partners. For one thing, as Simmel points out (1950:154-162), a potential partner in a given coalition who is the weakest of all in resources may nevertheless have great "pivotal power" (the term is Kahan and Rapoport's; see 1984:217-218) in the sense that the others who have already joined may perceive the weak one's cooperation as a prize whose attainment will tip the scales in favor of the whole coalition. As a result, strong partners may be willing to pay the weak one a premium in "sidepayments" (Kahan and Rapoport 1984:28-30) in order to gain its cooperation in the coalition, and such payments tend to equalize the partners' resources (see Takaki 1998:20-21).

Similarly, strong partners' continuing efforts to protect themselves by strengthening their weak partners against the probings of the coalition's opponents also tend objectively to equalize the partners. Then, when we take into account that the coalition's enemies include not only competitor coalitions but innumerable other debilitating shocks that can come from inside as well as outside itself, it becomes apparent that Greider has gotten this one right, too: "For the first time in human history...a fateful connection is emerging between the first and the last. One end of the ladder (or seesaw) cannot defend its own general prosperity without attending to human conditions at the other end" (1997:43).

Now clearly, if mechanisms that enhance objective as well as subjective equalization among coalition partners (coupled with the expectation that that competition will extend the scope of coalition-formation, and therefore of both kinds of equalization, up toward globality) were actually working in the modern world, there should be some empirical evidence to that effect. Such evidence does exist, and at the bedrock level of *individuals*, indeed.

Signs of the Global Equalization of Individuals

Regarding the equalization of individuals with respect to their political *power*, Karatnycky points out that "Today, 3.1 billion persons out of a world population of 5.7 billion live under democratically elected governments. While not yet a universal standard, democracy has deepening and widening roots in all parts of the world" (1996:5). Similarly, Fisher and Onishi tell us that "In 1975, only three heads of state [in Africa] were chosen through elections. Last year, thirty-two of fifty-four leaders were elected" (2000:A10; see also Anonymous A 1999). These are no small accomplishments. No such statements—even admitting wide variability in the operational meanings of "democratic" and "election"—could have been made before in all the five thousand years of human history, not to mention the 195 thousand years of prehistory.

Regarding equalization in the realm of *empirical knowledge/know-how*, UNESCO reports the percent illiterate in the world's population aged fifteen years and older declined from 30.5 percent in 1980 to 22.6 percent in 1990 (see UNESCO 1996: 2-9; Anonymous B 1999). This figure, though progressing far more slowly than one would like, is still undoubtedly the lowest it has ever been at any time since writing was first invented, and that seems another epochal accomplishment. Moreover, French tells us that "Between 1960 and 1998, the number of lines linking non-cellular telephones directly to the global phone network grew eightfold, from 89 million to 838 million. In developing countries, the number of phone connections per 100 people jumped [sic] from only one in 1975 and two in 1985 to six in 1998." French also reports that "Since 1995, the internet has grown by roughly 50 percent each year, following fifteen years of more than doubling in size annually. In 1998...an estimated 147 million people [were wired] to the internet. Today, one in every 40 people has access" (2000:7; also see Inkeles 1998:13-15)—although none of these various connections has yet come even close to equal distribution across ethnic, "racial," and nationality groups.

Regarding the equalization of individuals' secular *honor* (i.e., their "human-rights"), the Charter of the United Nations stands as an historically unique declaration of determination "to reaffirm faith in fundamental human rights, in the dignity and worth of the human person, in the equal rights of men and women and of nations large and small" (Vincent 1976:191; see also United Nations 1994: 1, 2; Renner 1999:157-158), and Zolberg notes "the dissemination of liberal norms regarding persons, expressed in the remarkable emergence of a widely shared notion of universal human rights, as well as of an unprecedented sense of "'species' consciousness in the face of common dangers" (1995:37). (We shall come back to this idea of " 'species' consciousness in the face of common dangers" in the section following this one.)

Regarding the variety of honor, prestige, approval, or "blessing" that is regarded as divinely conferred—and conferred differentially on believers and non-believers of a given faith—Dogan reports its decline and, by implication, some degree of equalization in this respect: "Religion, nationalism and authority were the traditional pillars of the old state-societies of Western Europe. Three generations ago it was still a sacrilege to criticize them.... During the last four decades these traditional values have declined simultaneously, at different speeds, in all Western European countries, without a single exception" (1998:77; see also Inglehart, Basañez, and Moreno 1998).

The various religious fundamentalisms, however, cast themselves as sworn enemies of the worldwide equalization of divine—and also secular—honor (see Lechner 1989:25-26; Simpson 1989:31, 37-38; Swatos 1989:62-63). Thus, a spokesperson for the Christian fundamentalist Bob Jones University declares that, "At the Tower of Babel, God used language to disrupt man's plans for a one-world government. As a result of this disruption, the people were scattered and the races were polarized. One thing is clear: God wanted a divided world, not a federalized world." Not unexpectedly, the same fundamentalist spokesperson disparages non-fundamentalists in his own faith: "We love the practising Catholic and earnestly desire to see him...leave the false system that has enslaved his soul" (Anonynous B 2000; see also Balmer 1999). Referring to another variety of fundamentalism—namely, the Islamic one—Lechner says it is "based on absolute dedication to maintenance of a particular value pattern.... After a successful Islamic revolution, the globe is intended to become a common religious civilization" (1989:25-26; see also Marty and Appleby 1993:640-641).

It seems reasonable, however, to look upon all such fundamentalist refusals to grant equal honor (divine and/or secular) to all human individuals as understandably panicked responses to the Diversification-to-Contact transition. McNeill provides the clue here: "Population growth on the one hand and new forms of communication on the other brought disruption to local use and wont on a massive scale, creating personal uncertainty, isolation, and disappointment more often than not. Resulting distress can and often does find expression in fundamentalist movements that counteract uncertainty by emphatic affirmation of eternal truths, and counteract isolation and disappointment by forming supportive communities of fellow believers" (1993:561). So it seems reasonable to expect that such fundamentalist denials of honor equalization will decline as the transitional disruptions to which McNeill refers are completed, and as the several other equalizations (in wealth, power, and knowledge/know-how) discussed here continue their advances.

However, when we come to consider the possibility of a trend toward the global equalization of individuals with respect to *wealth*, we confront another area of high resistance. In fact, the following summary statement is nearly devastating: "the ratio between income in the richest one-fifth of countries and the poorest one fifth has widened from thirty to one in 1960 to sixty-one to one in 1991" (Brown 1996:3-4; see also Falk 1992). But then one notices other statements that mitigate this one. Firebaugh, for example, argues that although per capita income ratios between countries *are* diverging, the divergence is due to differential population growth rather than economic dependence or differential economic growth (see 1999:1622). And regarding differential population growth, one finds that (1) rates in the less-developed regions of the world have been declining since 1965-70 (although they remain at considerably higher levels than in the more developed regions) and are expected to continue declining at least to 2020-2025 (United Nations 1991:20), and (2) there is good reason to think exposure to mass media messages significantly lowers fertility rates in poorer nations (Westoff and Bankole 1997).

Firebaugh also tells us that "the centuries-old trend of increasing intercountry income inequality has *stalled* at least since 1960" (1999:1621, italics added; see also United Nations 1998:2; and see Kahn 2001; Kahn and Flanders 2001; and Weinstein 2001); French (2000:6-7) reports that capital flows to developing countries grew eighteen-fold, from $21 billion in 1970 to $227 billion in 1998 (while foreign investment in general grew fifteen-fold, from $44 billion to $644 billion); and *The Economist* reports that a computer simulation of future global economic developments suggests that "the past few decades [may] represent a turning-point... in a centuries-long process by which the economic advances of the industrial revolution were spread right around the globe" (Anonymous A 2000).

It seems fair to say, then, that although none of the above institutionally specific equalizations—whether in power, knowledge/know-how, honor, or wealth—is anywhere near being fully achieved, none is a lost cause and all are making some progress.

Signs of Global Intersocietal Coalition-Formation

Boli and Thomas tell us that "for a century and more, the world has constituted a single polity. By this we mean that the world has been conceptualized as a unitary social system, increasingly integrated by networks of exchange, competition, and cooperation, such that actors have found it 'natural' to view the whole world as their arena of action and discourse" (see also Wilkinson 1995: 232 quoted earlier here). In addition, the number of international *non*-governmental organizations (INGOs) of private individuals has been increasing since World War II: "By 1947 over 90 organizations a year were being founded, a pace that was maintained and even surpassed through the 1960s [and into the 1970s]" (Boli and Thomas 1997:172, 177; see also Sheets and Maurer 1999:iii), and French adds that the number of international non-governmental organizations grew from 985 in 1956 to twenty-three thousand in 1998—a rate of not ninety but more than 500 foundings per year (see 2000: 7). Renner proposes the conclusion, consistent with the present argument, that "added to the old spectacle of alliances of nation states there is now the new phenomenon of mixed coalitions that, on an issue-by-issue basis, bring together like-minded governments and civil-society organizations.... We no longer live in a state-centric world.... The meaning of national borders is inevitably changed in an age when such boundaries can and are traversed with ever greater ease" (1999:167).

Bornstein reports specifically on the growth of non-governmental coalitions in developing countries: "Twenty years ago social activists could identify only one independent organization working to protect the environment in Indonesia. Today there are more than 2,000, an environmental network based in Jakarta reports. Citizen organizations have been similarly emerging across much of the world. In Slovakia, there were a handful of such organizations active in the 1980s; now there are more than 10,000. In the Philippines, registered nonprofit organizations grew from 18,000 to 58,000 between 1989 and 1996," and also cite "the defeat of apartheid in South Africa; the end of the dictatorship in Chile; the political transformation in the Philippines; the overthrow of Communist regimes in Central Europe; the creation of an international treaty prohibiting land mines; the establishment of an international criminal court" (1999:B7) as recent events in which non-government organizations were major players.

* * *

In summary, then, on the first big question addressed by this paper—namely, What long-term trend information does science offer in support of a global culture of peace?—it seems clear that both the trends themselves and their likely explanations indicate that such a culture is a definite potentiality. In this connection, it seems significant that a leading specialist historian, not of peace but of warfare, sees "grounds for believing that at last, after five thousand years of recorded warmaking, cultural and material changes may be working to inhibit man's proclivity to take up arms" (Keegan 1993:56).

We turn now to the second big question of this paper, in order to inquire further into the chances of that potentiality becoming a reality.

What Hypothetical Information About the Future Does Modern Science Offer That Might Serve a Global Culture of Peace?

Science has two kinds of hypothetical information to offer about the human future: (1) trend-line projections showing the shape of things likely to come if past and present conditions continue, and (2) trend-line projections showing how potential changes in those conditions might affect that shape—and how those changes might be deliberately influenced, if we choose to try.

We focus first on projections concerning two kinds of future dangers to humankind—dangers that come from outside our species, and dangers that come from inside.

Dangers from Outside the Species

D.H. Henderson, a scientist who led the near-eradication of smallpox, is quoted to the effect that "there is a growing belief that mankind's well-being, and perhaps even our survival as a species, will depend on our ability to detect emerging diseases.... Where would we be today if HIV were to become an airborne pathogen? And what is there to say that a comparable infection might not do so in the future?" Henderson therefore urges a program for global preparedness and asks, "Can we afford to invest in such a program? A better question is whether we can afford *not* to invest in a program that could be a determinant in our own survival as a species" (Garrett 1994:602, 604–605; see also 619–620). Garrett herself concludes that "rapid globalization of human niches requires that human beings everywhere on the planet go beyond viewing their neighborhoods, provinces, countries, or hemispheres as the [limits] of their personal ecospheres. Microbes, and their vectors, recognize none of the artificial boundaries erected by human beings" (1994:618). Similarly, Goldberg points out that the "biological national-security of the United States is threatened by the unchecked spread of infectious disease in Africa; therefore, Africa's health is very much our problem" (1999:22).

We have also been warned, recently, that "The earth has entered a period of climatic change that is likely to cause widespread economic, social and environmental dislocation over the next century if emissions of heat-trapping gases are not reduced" (Stevens 1995:A1). Thus begins a report which goes on to cite some "possible early effects" of global warming—including a rise in average sea levels around the world; an "increase in extremes of temperature, dryness and precipitation in some regions" leading to more droughts, heat waves, floods, and woodland fires; a "retreat of mountain glaciers," leading to diminished river and stream flows in some regions. In some regions, there would be milder winters and faster crop growth, but other regions, "especially sub-Saharan Africa, South and Southeast Asia and tropical Latin America—could suffer loses in their harvests. Deserts are expected to expand, and the heartlands of continents to become drier" (Stevens 1995:A1; see also Stone 1995). Frank, Hironaka, and Schofer underscore the emergence of global attempts at solutions to such environmental problems: "Driven first by a rising conception of nature as a life-sustaining global ecosystem and second by a general structuration of the world policy, global blueprints for natural environmental protection have proliferated rapidly over the twentieth century" (2000a:100; also see French 2000:162-178).

Finally, one notes Broad's claim that nowadays "the Chicken Little crowd, which once drew smiles by suggesting that Earth could be devastated by killer rocks from outer space, is suddenly finding its warnings and agenda taken seriously now that Jupiter has taken a beating [from comet Shoemaker-Levy] in recorded history's biggest show of cosmic violence.... Astronomers already know of more than one hundred [major comets or asteroids] whose paths occasionally cross Earth's orbit and estimate as many as 2,000 may be speeding through space on such paths and are big enough to do global damage" (1994; see also Matthews 1992; Ferris 1997:49; Hecht 1999b; compare the reduced estimations by Izevic et al. 2001).

Dangers from Inside the Species

To set a context for considering dangers to our species that originate inside it, let us begin with Comte's view that "Institutions good at one period may be and frequently are bad at another and vice versa. Thus, for example, slavery, which is now a monstrosity, was certainly at its origin an admirable institution, designed to prevent the strong from destroying the weak, constituting an unavoidable transition in the general development of civilization" (1975:48).

As long as the costs and rewards of competition were themselves fixed (that is, by the sedentism mentioned earlier here—including the high place-fixity of wealth in land; of power in fortified towns and strongholds; of knowledge/know-how in libraries; and of the conferral and refurbishment of honor in temples), and as long as weapons systems were short-ranged, the fixity of ethnic, "racial," and nationality labels increased *Homo sapiens*' survival chances.[21] But under present and likely future conditions of increasingly mobile, global, and rapidly evolving varieties of wealth, power, knowledge/know-how, and honor, the fixity of ethnic, "racial," and nationality identifications has turned against these chances by inhibiting or preventing more flexible and inclusive coalitions—as well as suppressing universalistic competition and creativity between individuals inside those coalitions.

The trouble that identification-fixity, though useful in the past, brings with it into the present and future world does not stop there, however, because it implies that individuals who carry a given fixed identification should never permit themselves to be influenced by the arguments of individuals carrying some other, competing, fixed identification. Those who do permit themselves to be so influenced risk dishonoring themselves and being declared traitorous by others on both sides.[22] Under such circumstances, each side tends to be limited to two alternatives: either to break off contact with the other side or to kill the other side off when they become engaged in some zero-sum competition. Greenfield and Chirot put it this way: "In ethnic [and let us add, inter-ethnic and inter-'racial'] nationalisms...the borderline between 'us' and 'them' is *impermeable*.... The tendency to 'demonize' the enemy population...is built-in to ethnic nationalism" (1994:87, italics added; see also Tilly 1998:72). And between impermeable borders and ineradicable demonization on the one hand, and extermination on the other, there has long been only the shortest and slipperiest of slopes.

By contrast, when identifications are flexibly subject to one's changing current life experiences and life achievement (see Linton 1936:115-116; Parsons 1951a:117, 1951b:207-208), persuasively *converting* rather than *killing* the people on the other side can become the normatively preferred strategy.[23] Indeed, it is the belief that people can be honorably converted that most sustains the peaceful transfer of political power in democracies. The party that loses one election can rationally and realistically believe it may win the next, not by killing off, imprisoning, disenfranchising, or exiling its opposition—and thereby weakening the entire society over which it seeks to rule—but by persuading members of the opposition to come over to its side.

For this reason, the key institutions of political democracy are not assassins and jailers, whether legally authorized or not. Instead, they are the aptly named 'parliaments' and peer-juries, plus some part of the mass media (but see Thompson 1994), and virtually all of the scholarly media. Similarly, belief in conversion as an honorable human possibility sustains the peaceful efforts of subordinate ethnic, "racial," and nationality groups to achieve equality with superordinate groups—as expressed in Martin Luther King, Jr.'s "I have a dream that one day...the sons of former slaves and the sons of former slaveowners will be able to sit down together at the table of brotherhood."

When, to the centrality of fixed ethnic, "racial," and nationality boundaries in our now global sociocultural system, we add that nuclear, microbiological, and chemical weapons stockpiles, together with their global rapid-delivery systems, all stand poised to defend those boundaries, the result is a species holding a loaded gun to its own head (see Schell 1982).[24] But even more than that, it is now the *combination* of species-inside and species-outside threats to the continued survival of *Homo sapiens* that provides perhaps the strongest and most widely acceptable motivation for a global culture of peace and equality among all human individuals.

But motivation aside, is such a culture *feasible*, or is it a foolish waste of time to even think about it?

Just a Few Practical Problems

How, for one thing, can we possibly achieve and sustain an equality-fostering global economy of abundance unless the world provides itself with some new, cheap, virtually inexhaustible energy supplies—because we know that fossil-fuel supplies will be finished, for good, in the next few hundred years (see Kerr 1998; Perutz 1989; Starr, Searl, and Alpert 1992; Asimov 1979:315; Criswell, 1985:52, 60–75; Jones and Finney, 1985:91; Brown 1996:15)? How can new energy supplies be accessed in time to avoid rewinding human-history back to the age of stone tools (see Asimov 1979:315)?

And that is not all.

Even with the proliferation of democratic *national* governments that Karatnycky points to, how can the world construct a democratically organized *international* government (see Glossop 1993: 225-226) that will guarantee equal rights of participation in the production and administration of political power to people everywhere, and that will enable the world's citizens to come and go across all present national (not to mention ethnic and "racial") boundaries as freely, and causing as little sociocultural disruption, as Americans now come and go across the former Mason and Dixon line, and as Japanese, Italians, and Germans on the one hand, and British, French, Chinese, and Americans now almost commute back and forth across our several national borders. Can we do this in time—before one or another sovereign nation's (or sovereign religion's) leaders ignites a truly global firefight?

And, thinking even beyond universal functional literacy (for which we still have a long way to go), what about a globally consolidated scientific-technological-educational institution that can implement Weinberg's anticipation of "the day when science can no longer be identified with the West but is seen as the shared possession of humankind" (1992:190; see also Hin and Subramaniam 1999)? How can we assure that every member of Homo sapiens can become truly *knowing*—that is, not merely literate, but comprehending and participatory regarding empirical knowledge and know-how of the way things work—while it can still make a difference?

And what on Earth would it take, in practical terms, to transcend all our religious differences and construct a globally consolidated, universally voluntary and egalitarian, religious community—perhaps one such as Lukas Vischer, then director of the Secretariat of the Commission on Faith and the Constitution of the World Council of Churches, has envisioned: "a community of questioning and searching, a community of fundamental agreement and, in many respects, also of fundamental uncertainty" (1979:105; see also Durkheim 1965:493; Spencer 1961:161; Wuthnow 1991:36)?

All such questions seem absolutely crucial from the standpoint of the continued survival of *Homo sapiens.* Solving them therefore presents an essential qualification to which every social policy everywhere should verifiably contribute.

But how are we to verify, and judge among, alternative policies? At present we rely heavily on hand-waving, horse-trading, backslapping, baby-kissing, and money-and-muscle-flexing (all fitted out with full deniability), plus some "gut feelings" and variously "experienced" and "sophisticated" (but inevitably selective and forgetful) guesses. None of us can yet rigorously, replicably, and therefore convincingly, demonstrate how the probabilities of success and failure are distributed among alternative policies—some of which may directly affect the continued survival not only of this or that nation, "race," or ethnic group, but of *Homo sapiens* itself.

Now it should be understood that no one asks for, or expects, social policies to approach the reliability levels that the applied physical sciences routinely achieve, but we could certainly use a significant increase above present levels of the former. In a word, we could use much better foresight of the consequences of alternative policies so that our choices among them could be more *informed.*

A New Informational Contribution to the Human Future from Science

The earliest automobiles had no headlights at all, but headlights are now standard, and legally required equipment, especially for night-driving. In driving through the policy-night ahead of us, we need an analogue of headlights—namely, more and better data-storing and data-processing power than the human brain alone is capable of, and more and better power in these respects than current state-of-the-art computers are capable of.

And here we run smack into some good news: Fortunately for our descendants if not for ourselves, this power is already being developed.

I refer to the foresight-enhancing power of the experimenting microsimulation of complex, interactive, and dynamic human sociocultural processes. This is the scientific 'implementation' of a global culture of peace to which the second main question addressed in this paper refers.

Two recent observers report that "developments in the world of microsimulation in the past five years" have been "fast" (Kapur and Gupta 2000:1; compare Orcutt and Nakamura 2000:ix), and two others report that "microsimulation models have now become very popular, as much for the design and evaluation of policy measures, as for the empirical implementation of theoretical research" (Decoster and Van Camp 2000:15). So it seems fair to say that this baby is well and growing toward making its eventually indispensable mature contribution to *Homo sapiens'* future.

Orcutt originally described microsimulation as follows: "The most distinctive feature of this new type of model is the key role played by actual decision-making units of the real world such as the individual, the household, and the firm. In each time period, some types of behavior of each individual unit are conceived of as being determined by one or more random drawings from one or more discrete probability distributions. The probabilities associated with alternative behaviors or responses are treated as dependent on conditions or events prior to the behavior. Thus, these probabilities vary over time as the system develops or as external conditions change, and the model presented is a recursive type which progresses by short, but discrete, steps. Solutions of models...will involve extensive calculations, and it is only the advent of very powerful computing facilities that makes this kind of model an exciting possibility" (1957:117; see also Citro and Hanushek 1991; Mitton et al. 2000).

The views of Epstein and Axtell help to put microsimulation in perspective vis-à-vis the social sciences (and indeed all the sciences) when they argue that the social sciences are "the 'hard' [that is, difficult] sciences" for several reasons. First, "many crucially important social processes are complex. They are not neatly decomposable into separate subprocesses—economic, demographic, cultural, spatial—whose isolated analyses can be aggregated to give an adequate analysis of the social process as a whole" but "there is no natural methodology for studying these processes together, as they coevolve." Second, "the social science are also hard because certain kinds of controlled experimentation are hard...[and it is therefore hard to answer the question] How does the heterogeneous micro-world of individual behaviors generate the global macroscopic regularities of the society?" Third, "it is standard practice in the social sciences to suppress real-world agent heterogeneity in model-building [as often expressed in the assumption that all social actors are rational in the same way] but there has been no natural methodology for systematically studying highly heterogeneous populations." Finally, "there has been no natural methodology for studying nonequilibrium dynamics in social systems" (1996:1-2). Epstein and Axtell conclude that microsimulation[25] represents the "natural methodology" that is needed to address all these shortcomings of social science.

Now, of course, the problems of microsimulating a global human population of over 6.1 billion divided into 185 named countries and areas (United Nations 2001) are gigantic, but improvements in computer hardware and in software techniques of sampling and aggregating individual-based data should not be dismissed either. In his pioneering article, Orcutt dreamed of "a large electronic machine, such as the IBM 704 or the UNIVAC II, or some improved successor to these powerful giants" (1957:119) as the microsimulation instrument of choice. But just forty-four years later Kapur and Gupta point to "developments in computer technology [which] have meant that models can be transferred to or implemented on desk-top machines with faster run and elapsed time for additional simulations" (2000:5). Who can tell what another 44 years will bring (see Chang 2001)?

At any rate, it seems reasonable to count on further developments in computer hardware and software being driven by global economic competition. But it also seems reasonable to predict that the application of those developments to the microsimulation of global sociocultural processes would get a much needed, and much-deserved, boost from being publicly (and fiscally) targeted as an urgent goal in the continuing efforts of our species, permanently endangered from within and from without, to survive.

Finally, consider one more science-based thought: Astronomers now know of some 100 billion galaxies in the visible universe, each containing roughly 100 billion stars. Moreover, at least a dozen stars in our own immediate neighborhood have in recent years been found to have planetary systems. All this leads one to speculate that planetary systems more or less like our own may be strewn, however thinly, across the entire universe and that ours may not be the only intelligent, dexterous, mobile, and social lifeform struggling to make it. So if we (or any one of the others) don't make it, it may not be that big of a deal. Most seeds that hit the ground never make it to mature planthood.

But some may. And if any do, then evolution has at least a chance at the next step-whatever that may be. Primate curiosity says it's worth a try.

Notes

*My thanks to Sarane Boocock, Tom Espenshade, Wardell Haywood, Eric Kaufmann, Samir and Roseanne Khalaf, John Kitsuse, Marty Morand, Koji Shibahara, Jerry Stamler, Randy Yang, and Howie Zinn, all of whom have, in various ways, and whether they know it or not, helped me think one or more of the ideas I have tried to set down here.

1. "Culture" is here defined as any set of interpersonally shared psychological behaviors—including cognitive existence beliefs, affective preferences, and conative behavior-dispositions. The informational contributions of science pertain primarily to the cognitive (knowledge) component, and secondarily to the conative (know-how) component of culture. This paper will not address the affective (value-judgement) component, on the ground that "an empirical science cannot tell anyone what he *should* do—but rather what he *can* do" (Weber 1949:54; see also 1946:144). However, it should be noted that the specifically future-oriented last part of this paper implicitly takes as its guiding value the continued survival of our species, *Homo sapiens.* It does so on the ground that this value is a precondition for the achievement of many other values and so may be widely acceptable. Note that a global *culture* of peace does not, by itself, guarantee global peace. A global *social structure* (i.e., interpersonally shared *physical* behaviors) of peace, equipped with a global *technology* directed toward peace, is also required for that, but the culture helps would be an indispensable support to them both.

2. See Ridley 1993:412–413.

3. See, especially for Mesopotamia, Postgate 1992; for Egypt, Caminos 1997; and for both, Childe 1951a:114-142; 1951b:136-160; Keegan 1993:128-136; Mark 1997.

4. For just one peace-related example, Keegan, noting that "The world community needs...skilful and disciplined warriors who are ready to put themselves at the service of its authority," stresses that "The style in which [these warriors] fight for civisation—against ethnic bigots, regional warlords, ideological intransigents, common pillagers and organised international criminals—cannot derive from the western model of warmaking alone. Future peacekeepers and peacemakers have much to learn from alternative military cultures, not only that of the Orient but of the primitive world [sic] also. There is a wisdom in the principles of intellectual restraint and even of symbolic ritual that needs to be rediscovered" (1993:391-392).

5. Although Darwin had no particular term for what is here called "the luck of the territorial draw," the idea seems unmistakably implicit in his attribution of the origin of species to "migration...together with subsequent modification and the multiplication of new forms" (quoted above). For discussion of the impact of territory (and especially climatic changes therein) on hominid evolution, see Tattersall 1995:197-198, 233-235, 241-242; Diamond 1992:236, 237; 1996:84; Blaut 1993:182.

6. See Ross and Nisbett's discussion of "the fundamental attribution error" (1991:4, also 140-141; see also Jones 1990:96).

7. This element is present in many other definitions as well: see Schermerhorn 1970:12; Smith 1986:24; Nash 1996:25; Fishman 1996:64; Balibar 1996:167; Hutchinson and Smith 1996:6-7; Fenton 1999:4, 6-8, 10.

8. On the latter, see Molnar 1992:21-31, 188-194; Swedlund 1993:16, 52-60; Eriksen 1996:29; Fenton 1999:5.

9. Regarding societal differences in classification, and individuals changing their personal identifications, see Stuckert 1976; Simpson and Yinger 1985:298; Marger 1991:410; Williamson 1980:100-101; Griffin 1977; Gans 1979:7-8; Nagel 1954:154-156.

10. It has been pointed out that neighboring populations were likely to keep in touch with each other in one way or another. But as distance along any such chain of populations increased (particularly when broken into by deserts, oceans, and mountain ranges) that touch would have dwindled virtually to zero.

11. Note, however, that in certain areas of the world some dispersed populations remained isolated well into modern times (see Diamond 1992:229, 232).

12. At first glance, Keeley may seem to take issue with this assessment of war: "There is simply no proof that warfare in small-scale societies was a rarer or less serious undertaking than among civilized societies. In general, warfare in prestate societies was both frequent and important" (1996:39). But when Keeley compares the warfares of these two types of societies, he finds a difference that supports the view taken here: "In general," Keeley says, "nonstate groups preserved the lives of cap-

tives only when some material benefit would accrue; this approach generally limited the persons spared to women and children. States, by contrast, often have a strong material interest in preserving the lives of defeated enemies—even adult males—because they can become tax- and tribute-paying subjects, serfs, or slaves.... Economically, the state is usually best served by the submission of its enemies, not by genocide" (1996:39, 87; see also 3-4).

13. Regarding the African continent's topography, climate, and ecology—and its bearing on human history there—see Wallace 1997:50-54.

14. These ancient societies are included here under the term "nations" (see also Silverman 1997:22-23, 32-35). I thereby depart radically from those who argue that "Historically, the nation and nationalism were *Western* concepts and *Western* formations. The first steps...towards nationhood, were also *Western*" (Smith 1986:144, italics added); that "The nation-state is a construction specific to the *modern* era" (McNeely 1995:149, italics added); and that "The first nation was *England*, which became one in the sixteenth century" (Greenfield and Chirot 1994:79, italics added). Instead, I share the spirit of Tilly's view, that "nationalism has existed as long as states have existed" and "states have existed somewhere in the world...[for] over 10,000 years" (1994a:133), except that I believe "over 5,000 years" is a likelier estimate—especially if one distinguishes a "state" from a "nation" (as I do).

15. To my knowledge, the present theory (see also Wallace 1997; 2000) is the only one (including Weber's) that singles out shared destiny-orientation as the distinctive feature of nationality identification, but this orientation plays some role in many views that do not make it central or even, sometimes, explicit (see Renan 1994: 17; Geertz 1994:30; Gellner 1994:55; Hutchinson 1994: 123, 128, 129, 131; Seton-Watson 1994:136-137; Reynolds 1994:137; Armstrong 1994: 141; Nairn 1994:72, 75; Brass 1994:85; Tilly 1994b:18; Bauman 1990:154).

16. It should be clear by now that I reject the view that ethnic and "racial" diversities are "primordial" (see Geertz 1996:40-45) or "naturally given" (Weber 1978: 335). I look upon both these diversities as *socioculturally constructed*, and therefore take that construction as something to be explained rather than taken for granted.

17. One is reminded of fractals, and of Jonathan Swift's fractal aphorism: "So, naturalists observe, a flea / Hath smaller fleas that on him prey; / And these have smaller still to bite 'em; / And so proceed ad infinitum."

18. Going-it-alone (i.e., refusing to join any coalition at all) is a strategy likely to be followed only (1) by a competitor that believes its own power is superior to that of any coalition that might form against it; or (2) by a competitor that believes its going-it-alone is supported by a sufficiently powerful coalition of other competitors—as, for example, in the case of the individual rights guaranteed by the Constitution of the United States, and by the Declaration of Human Rights (United Nations 1994:1, 2). A weak competitor's going-it-alone because it regards a coalition with a powerful competitor as merely tying its hands until that competitor finds it convenient to crush it outright (see Machiavelli 1940:84; Carmichael and Hamilton 1967:80–81; Caplow 1968: 152) seems likely to be quickly abandoned if it finds one or more partners with which it can form a coalition for mutual defense.

19. To this, we must add that close interdependences among similar institutions belonging to different human societies (for example, among the scientific-technological-educational institutions, or among the religious institutions) make it likely that ascending coalitional steps in one of them will be accompanied (with variable time-lags) by similarly ascending steps in all the others. For example, Chase-Dunn et al. claim that "Economic globalization creates a great demand for political globalization because markets are unable to resolve the problems of distributive justice and uneven development that they create" (2000:93).

20. As Merton points out, these two strategies are logically independent insofar as "Prejudicial attitudes *need not* coincide with discriminatory behavior" (1976: 192, italics added) and vice-versa. Nevertheless, the mutually reinforcing nature of psychological behavior ("attitudes") and physical "behavior" makes it very likely that the coincidence to which Merton refers will *actually* emerge unless specifically hindered from doing so. Thus Merton himself describes "the prejudiced non-discriminator" as refraining from discriminatory behavior for fear of "*sanctions* that might otherwise be visited upon him" (1976:196, italics added).

21. By the "fixity" of identifications like ethnicity, and "race" (and to a lesser degree, nationality) I mean they are labels applied to individuals at or before birth, and they tend to stick, unchanged, throughout the lifetimes of those individuals. Kallen illustrates this basic idea (if one can overlook his 1915 sexism) as follows: "Men may change their clothes, their politics, their wives, their religions, their philosophies...[but] they cannot change their grandfathers" (quoted in Gordon 1964:145; see also Barth 1996:75-82). And this reference to "grandfathers" indicates that the identifications in question tend to be not only fixed across the lifespan of the person to whom they are applied; they are also fixedly heritable from one generation to the next. With this combination, such identifications tend to become *permanently* fixed. Note, however, that the strong *tendency* toward fixity of ethnic and "racial" identifications being emphasized here is not meant to deny the atypical, but significant (because fixity-weakening), changes in such identifications that were mentioned in note 9.

22. In a word, under these conditions of identification-fixity, accepting a compromise tends to be equated with being compromised.

23. Note, however, that the changeable (achieved) statuses of today tend to become the fixed (ascribed) statuses of tomorrow. In particular, the achieved statuses of parents tend to be passed on to their children as ascribed statuses. As a result, ascribed identifications do not appear readily susceptible to any once-and-for-all solution but probably yield only to recurrent resettings to zero. The principle of such resetting, of course, is already familiar: It underlies the imposition of term limits on elected office-holding, and it also underlies inheritance taxes, and entrance (including driver's) examinations of all sorts. Simmel suggests "the drawing of positions by lot" (1950:295). On George Washington's extraordinary insight into the social dysfunctions of kin-inherited ascriptive status, see Dalzell and Dalzell 1998:216-222.

24. At the same time, however, Goldstein tells us that although "wars are becoming more severe—annual fatalities during war increasing more than a hundred-fold over the five centuries," it is also true that "the incidence of great power war is declining...[and] the great power wars are becoming shorter" (1985:432). Renner, too, notes a change in war participants: "with the end of the Cold War...violence between sovereign states, though not unthinkable, has become less likely and far less frequent, whereas violence within societies has become depressingly commonplace" (1999:156). See also Chase-Dunn, who argues that to avoid future wars "The peace movement...must realize that a world-state is necessary and must strongly support its creation" [1995:422, 438]).

25. Epstein and Axtell's term for microsimulation is "agent-based computer modelling" (1996:2).

References

Adams, Robert McC. 1966. *The Evolution of Urban Society.* Chicago: Aldine.

Ahmed, Akbar S., and Hastings Donnan. 1994. "Islam in the Age of Post-modernity." In Akbar S. Ahmed and Hastings Donnan (eds.), *Islam, Globalization and Post-modernity.* London, England: Routledge, pp. 1–20.

Alba, Richard D. 1990. *Ethnic Identity: The Transformation of White America.* New Haven, CT: Yale University Press.

Alba, Richard D., and Gwen Moore. 1982. "Ethnicity in the American Elite." *American Sociological Review* 47 (June): 373–383.

Angier, Natalie. 2000. "Do Races Differ? Not Really, Genes Show." *New York Times,* August 22: F1, F6.

Anonymous A. 1999. "Democracy? Freedom? Justice? Law? What's All This?' *The Economist* (December 31): 27-29.

Anonymous B. 1999. The Great Learning." *The Economist* (December 31): 73-74.

Armstrong, John. 1994. "Nations Before Nationalism," in John Hutchinson and Anthony D. Smith (eds.), *Nationalism.* New York: Oxford University Press, pp. 140-147.

Barrow, John D. 1992. *Pi In the Sky: Counting, Thinking, and Being.* Boston: Little Brown.

Barth, Fredrik. 1996. "Ethnic Groups and Boundaries,"

in John Hutchinson and Anthony D. Smith (eds.), *Ethnicity.* New York: Oxford University Press, pp. 75-82.

Boli, John and George M. Thomas. 1993. "World Culture in the World Polity: A Century of International Non-Governmental Organization." *American Sociological Review* 62 (April): 171-190.

Chang, Kenneth. 2001. "Nanowires May Lead to Superfast Computer Chips." *New York Times,* November 9:A24.

Chase-Dunn, Christopher. 1995. "World-state Formation: Historical Processes and Emergent Necessity," in Christopher Chase-Dunn (editor), *The Historical Evolution of the International Political Economy,* Vol. II. Brookfield, VT: Edward Elgar, pp. 421-443.

Citro, Constance F. and Eric A. Hanushek. 1991. "Summary." In Constance F.Citro and Eric A. Hanushek (eds.), *Improving Information for Social Policy Decisions.* Washington DC: National Academy Press, pp. 1-20.

Coleman, David. 1992. "Ethnic Intermarriage." In A. H. Bittles and D. F. Roberts (eds.), *Minority Populations: Genetics, Demography and Health.* Hampshire, England: Macmillan, pp. 208–240.

________. 1994. "Trends in Fertility and Intermarriage Among Immigrant Populations in Western Europe as Measures of Integration." *Journal of Biosocial Science* 26:107-136.

Comte, Auguste. 1975. *Auguste Comte and Positivism: The Essential Writings.* New York: Harper.

Connor, Walker. 1996. "Beyond Reason: The Nature of the Ethnonational Bond," in John Hutchinson and Anthony D. Smith (eds.), *Ethnicity.* New York: Oxford University Press, pp. 69-75.

Crick, Francis. 1982. *Life Itself: Its Origin and Nature.* New York: Simon & Schuster.

Criswell, David R. 1985. "Solar System Industrialization: Implications for Interstellar Migrations." In Ben R. Finney and Eric M. Jones (eds.), *Interstellar Migration and the Human Experience.* Berkeley, CA:University of California Press, pp. 50–87.

Curtin, P., S. Feierman, L. Thompson, and J. Vansina. 1978. *African History.* Boston: Little, Brown.

Dalzell, Robert F., Jr. and Lee Baldwin Dalzell. 1998. *George Washington's Mount Vernon: At Home in Revolutionary America.* New York: Oxford.

Daniels, Roger. 1990. *Coming to America.* New York: Harper.

Darwin, Charles. 1968 [1859]. *The Origin of Species.* New York: Penguin.

Decoster, André and Guy Van Camp. 2000. "The Unit of Analysis in Microsimulation Models for Personal Income Taxes: Fiscal Unit or Household?" In Lavinia Mitton, Holly Sutherland, and Melvyn Weeks, editors, *Microsimulation Modelling for Policy Analysis.* Cambridge, England: Cambridge University Press, pp. 15-41.

Desmond, Annabelle. 1975. "How Many People Have Ever Lived on Earth?" In Kenneth C. W. Kammeyer (ed.), *Population Studies: Selected Essays and Research.* Chicago: Rand McNally, pp. 18–32.

Diamond, Jared. 1987. "The Worst Mistake in the History of the Human Race." *Discovery* 8 (May): 64-66.

________. 1992. *The Third Chimpanzee.* New York: HarperCollins.

________. 1996. "Empire of Uniformity." *Discover* 17 (March): 78–85.

________. 1997. *Guns, Germs, and Steel.* New York: Norton.

Dikötter, Frank. 1996. "The Idea of 'Race' in Modern China," in John Hutchinson and Anthony D. Smith (eds.), *Ethnicity.* New York: Oxford University Press, pp. 245-254.

Dippel, John V.H. 1996. *Bound Upon a Wheel of Fire.* New York: Basic Books.

Dogan, Mattei. 1998. "The Decline of Traditional Values in Western Europe: Religion, Nationalism, Authority," *International Journal of Comparative Sociology,* XXXIX, 1:77-90.

Dower, John W. 1986. *War Without Mercy.* New York: Pantheon.

Du Bois, W. E. Burghardt. 1961. *The Souls of Black Folk.* New York:

Fawcett. Durkheim, Emile. 1965. *The Elementary Forms of the Religious Life.* Glencoe, IL: The Free Press.

Eckholm, Kajsa, and Jonathan Friedman. 1995. "'Capital' Imperialism and Exploitation in Ancient World-Systems," in Christopher Case-Dunn (editor), *The Historical Evolution of the International Political Economy,* vol. I. Brookfield, VT: Edward Elgar, pp. 209-231.

Enloe, Cynthia. 1981. "The Growth of the State and Ethnic Mobilization: The American Experience," *Ethnic and Racial Studies.* Vol. 4, No. 2 (April), pp. 123-136.

Epstein, Joshua M. 1998. "Zones of Cooperation in Demographic Prisoner's Dilemma." *Complexity* 4 (November-December): 36-48.

Epstein, Joshua M. and Robert Axtell. 1996. *Growing Artificial Societies.* Washington D.C.: Brookings Institution Press.

Eriksen, Thomas H. 1996. "Ethnicity, Race, Class and Nation," in John Hutchinson and Anthony D. Smith (eds.), *Ethnicity.* New York: Oxford University Press, pp. 28-34.

Fagan, Brian M. 1989. *People of the Earth: An Introduction to World Prehistory.* 6th ed. Glenview, IL: Scott, Foresman.

_______. 1990. *The Journey from Eden.* London: Thames and Hudson.

Fage, J. D. 1995. *A History of Africa.* 3rd ed. New York: Routledge.

Falk, Richard. 1992. *Economic Aspects of Global Civilization.* Princeton, NJ: Princeton University Press.

Fenton, Steve. 1999. *Ethnicity: Racism, Class and Culture.* Lanham: Rowman & Littlefield.

Ferris, Timothy. 1997. "Is This the End?" *The New Yorker.* January 27:44–55.

Firebaugh, Glenn. 1999. "The Empirics of World Income Inequality," *American Journal of Sociology,* Vol. 104, No. 6 (May), pp. 1597-1630.

Fisher, Ian and Norimitsu Onishi. 2000. "Many Armies Ravage Rich Land in the 'First World War' of Africa." *New York Times* (February 6), pp. A1, A10.

Fishman, Joshua. 1996. "Ethnicity and Being, Doing, Knowing," in *Ethnicity,* John Hutchinson and Anthony D. Smith (editors). New York: Oxford University Press, pp. 63-69.

Fonseca, Isabel. 1995. *Bury Me Standing.* New York: Random House.

Frank, Andre Gunder, and Barry K. Gills. 1995. "The Five Thousand Year World System: An Interdisciplinary Introduction," in Christopher Chase-Dunn (editor), *The Historical Evolution of the International Political Economy,* Vol. I. Brookfield, VT: Edward Elgar, pp. 334-412.

Frank, David John, Ann Hironaka, and Evan Schofer. 2000a. "The Nation-State and the Natural Environment Over the Twentieth Century." *American Sociological Review,* Vol. 65, No. 1 (February): 96-116.

_______. 2000b. "Environmentalism as a Global Institution: Reply to Buttel." *American Sociological Review,* Vol. 65, No. 1 (February): 122-127.

French, Hilary. 2000. *Vanishing Borders.* New York: Norton.

Freud, Sigmund. 1961. *Civilization and Its Discontents.* New York: Norton.

Fu, Xuanning and Tim B. Heaton. 1997. *Interracial Marriage in Hawaii, 1983-1994.* Lewiston NY: Edwin Mellen Press.

Gamble, Clive. 1993. *Timewalkers: The Prehistory of Global Colonization.* Phoenix Mill, United Kingdom: Alan Sutton.

Gans, H. J. 1972. "The Positive Functions of Poverty." *American Journal of Sociology* 78: 275–289.

_______. 1979. "Symbolic Ethnicity: The Future of Ethnic Groups and Cultures in America." *Ethnic and Racial Studies* 2, no. 1 (January): 1–20.

Garrett, Laurie. 1994. *The Coming Plague.* New York: Farrar, Straus and Giroux.

Geertz, Clifford. 1994. "Primordial and Civic Ties," in

John Hutchinson and Anthony D. Smith (eds.), *Nationalism.* New York: Oxford University Press, pp. 29-34.

________. 1996. "Primordial Ties," in John Hutchinson and Anthony D. Smith (eds.), *Ethnicity.* New York: Oxford University Press, pp. 40-45.

Gellner, Ernest. 1994 [1983]. "Nationalism and Modernization," in John Hutchinson and Anthony D. Smith (eds.), *Nationalism.* New York: Oxford University Press, pp. 55-63.

Glossop, Ronald J. 1993. *World Federation? A Critical Analysis of Federal World Government.* Jefferson, NC: McFarland.

Goldberg, Jeffrey. 1999. "Microbes on the Move," *New York Times Magazine,* October 10, pp. 21-22.

Goldstein, Joshua R. 1995. "American Kinship Networks that Cross Racial Lines: The Exception or the Rule?" Paper presented at the Annual Meeting of the American Sociological Association, August 20, 1990.

Goldstein, Joshua S. 1985. "Kondratieff Waves as War Cycles," *International Studies Quarterly,* Volume 29, Number 4 (December), pp. 411-444.

Gomes-Casseres, Benjamin. 1996. *The Alliance Revolution.* Cambridge, MA: Harvard University Press.

Gordon, Milton M. 1964. *Assimilation in American Life.* New York: Oxford University Press.

Gossett, Thomas F. 1997. Race: *The History of an Idea in America.* New York: Oxford University Press.

Greenfield, Liah, and Daniel Chirot. 1994. "Nationalism and Aggression," *Theory and Society* 23 (February): 79-130.

Greider, William. 1997. *One World, Ready or Not.* New York: Simon & Schuster.

Griffin, John Howard. 1977. *Black Like Me.* New York: Houghton Mifflin.

Grossman, Dave, Lieutenant Colonel. 1995. *On Killing: The Psychological Cost of Learning to Kill in War and Society.* Boston: Little, Brown.

Hall, Edward T. 1966. *The Hidden Dimension.* New York: Doubleday.

Hecht, Jeff. 1999a. "Born in a Storm." *New Scientist.* 22 May, pp. 38-41.

______. 1999b. "Playing the Cosmic Lottery." *New Scientist.* 12 June, p. 17.

Hicks, George. 1997. *Japan's Hidden Apartheid.* England: Ashgate.

Hin, Leo Tan Wee, and R. Subramaniam. 1999. "Scientific Societies Build Better Nations," *Nature.* 399 (17 June), p. 633.

Hobsbawm, Eric. 1994 [1983]. "The Nation as Invented Tradition," in John Hutchinson and Anthony D. Smith (eds.), *Nationalism.* New York: Oxford University Press, pp. 76-83.

Huntington, Samuel P. 1996. *The Clash of Civilizations and the Remaking of World Order.* New York: Simon & Schuster.

Hutchinson, John. 1994. "Cultural Nationalism and Moral Regeneration," in John Hutchinson and Anthony D. Smith (eds.), *Nationalism.* New York: Oxford University Press, pp. 122-131.

Hutchinson, John and Anthony D. Smith. 1996. "Introduction," in John Hutchinson and Anthony D. Smith (editors). *Ethnicity.* New York: Oxford University Press, pp. 3-14.

Inglehart, Ronald, Miguel Basañez, and Alejandro Moreno. 1998. *Human Values and Beliefs: A Cross-Cultural Sourcebook.* Ann Arbor MI: University of Michigan Press.

Inkeles, Alex. 1998. *One World Emerging? Convergence and Divergence in Industrial Societies.* New York: Westview Press.

Izevic, Željko, et al. 2001. "Solar System Objects Observed in the Sloan Digital Sky Survey Commission Data." *The Astronomical Journal.* Vol. 122, No. 5 (November): 2749-2784.

Jennings, Francis. 1993: *The Founders of America.* New York: Norton.

Jones, E. E. 1990. *Interpersonal Perception.* New York: Freeman.

Jones, Eric M., and Ben R. Finney. 1985. "Fastships and

Nomads: Two Roads to the Stars." In Ben R. Finney and Eric M. Jones (eds.), *Interstellar Migration and the Human Experience.* Berkeley: University of California Press, pp. 88–103.

Kahan, James P. and Amnon Rapoport. 1984. *Theories of Coalition Formation.* Hillside, NJ.: Lawrence Erlbaum.

Kahn, Joseph. "Nations Back Freer Trade, Hoping to Aid Global Growth." *New York Times.* November 15:A12.

Kahn, Joseph and Stephanie Flanders. "U.S. and 21 Other Nations Vow to Spend Billions on Afghanistan." *New York Times.* November 21: B1, B5.

Kane, Hal. 1995. "Leaving Home." Worldwatch Institute, *State of the World 1995.* New York: Norton, pp. 132–149, 231–235.

Kane, Thomas T. 1989. *Streams of Change.* New York: Garland.

Kapur, Vishnu and Anil Gupta. 2000. "Introduction and Overview." In Anil Gupta and Vishnu Kapur, editors, *Microsimulation in Government Policy and Forecasting.* Amsterdam, The Netherlands: Elsevier, pp. 1-26.

Karatnycky, Adrian. 1998. "The Comparative Survey of Freedom 1997–1998; Freedom in the 'Democratic Age.'" in *Freedom in the World.* Freedom House Survey Team. New Brunswick NJ: Transaction, pp 3-16.

Keegan, John. 1993. *A History of Warfare.* New York: Viking.

Keeley, Lawrence H. 1996. *War Before Civilization.* New York: Oxford.

Kerr, Richard A. 1998. "The Next Oil Crisis Looms Large—and Perhaps Close," *Science,* Vol. 281, 21 August: 1128-1131.

Kim, Yoon Shin. 1985."Marriage Pattern of the Korean Population in Japan." *Journal of Biosocial Science.* (17): 445–450.

Klein, Richard G. 1999. *The Human Career* (second edition). Chicago: University of Chicago Press.

Lamphear, John. 1977. "Two Basic Themes in African History: Migration and State Formation." In Phyllis M. Martin and Patrick O'Meara (eds.), *Africa.* Bloomington: Indiana University Press, pp. 83–97.

Lattimore, Richard. 1962. "Introduction," *The Iliad of Homer.* Chicago: University of Chicago Press.

Leakey, Richard, and Roger Lewin. 1992. *Origins Reconsidered.* New York: Doubleday.

Lechner, Frank J. 1989. "Cultural Aspects of the Modern World-System." In William H. Swatos, Jr. (ed.) *Religious Politics in Global Perspective.* New York: Greenwood, pp. 11-27.

Lewis, L. A., and L. Berry. 1988. *African Environments and Resources.* Boston: Unwin Hyman.

Lieberson, Stanley and Mary C. Waters. 1988. *From Many Strands.* New York: Russell Sage Foundation.

Lifton, Robert Jay. 1986. *The Nazi Doctors: Medical Killing and the Psychology of Genocide.* New York: Basic Books.

Lind, Michael. 1998. "The Beige and the Black." *The New York Times Magazine,* August 16:38-39.

Linton, Ralph. 1936. *The Study of Man.* New York: Appleton-Century.

Locke, Alain, and Bernhard J. Stern. 1946. "In the Setting of World Culture." In Alain Locke and Bernhard J. Stern (eds.) *When Peoples Meet: A Study of Race and Culture Contacts.* Revised. New York: Hinds, Hayden & Eldredge, pp. 3-11.

Machiavelli, Niccolo. 1940. *The Prince and The Discourses.* New York: Modern Library.

Mann, Michael. 1986. *The Sources of Social Power.* Vol. I. Cambridge: Cambridge University Press.

Marger, Martin. 1991. *Race and Ethnic Relations: American and Global Perspectives.* 2nd edition. Belmont CA: Wadsworth.

Margulis, Lynn and Dorion Sagan. 1986. *Microcosmos.* New York: Summit.

Mark, Samuel. 1997. *From Egypt to Mesopotamia.* College Station TX: Texas A&M University Press.

Marks, Jonathan. 1995. *Human Biodiversity: Genes, Race, and History.* Hawthorne, NY: Aldine de Gruyter.

Marty, Martin E. and R. Scott Appleby. 1993. "Conclusion: Remaking the State: the Limits of the Fundamentalist Imagination," in *Fundamentalisms and the State,* Martin E. Marty and R. Scott Appleby (editors), Chicago: University of Chicago Press, pp. 620-644.

Massey, Douglas S., and Nancy A. Denton. 1993. *American Apartheid.* Cambridge, MA: Harvard University Press.

Matthews, Robert. 1992. "A Rocky Watch for Earthbound Asteroids." *Science* 255 (6 March): 1204–1205.

Mazian, Florence. 1990. *Why Genocide?* Ames: Iowa State University Press.

McCorriston, Joy, and Frank Hole. 1991. "The Ecology of Seasonal Stress and the Origins of Agriculture in the Near East," *American Anthropologist,* 93, No. 1 (March): 46-69.

McNeely, Connie L. 1995. *Constructing the Nation-State.* Westport, CT: Greenwood.

McNeill, William H. 1963. *The Rise of the West.* Chicago: University of Chicago Press.

________.1978. "Human Migration: A Historical Overview." In William H. McNeill and Ruth S. Adams (eds.), *Human Migration: Patterns and Policies.* Bloomington: University of Indiana Press, pp. 3–19.

________.1985. *Polyethnicity and National Unity in World History.* Toronto: University of Toronto Press.

______. 1993. "Fundamentalism and the World of the 1990s." In Martin Marty and R. Scott Appleby (eds.), *Fundamentalisms and Society.* Chicago: University of Chicago Press. Pp. 558-573.

McNulty, Michael L. 1977. "The Contemporary Map of Africa." In Phyllis M. Martin and Patrick O'Meara (eds.), *Africa.* Bloomington: Indiana University Press, pp. 24–49.

Merton, Robert K. 1957. *Social Theory and Social Structure.* Revised and enlarged. Glencoe, IL: Free Press.

________. 1976. *Sociological Ambivalence.* New York: Free Press. Molnar, Stephen. 1992. Human Variation. 3rd ed. Englewood Cliffs, NJ: Prentice-Hall.

Munson, Patrik J. 1977. "Africa's Prehistoric Past." In Phyllis M. Martin and Patrick O'Meara (eds.), *Africa.* Bloomington, IN: University Press, pp. 62–82.

Mussolini, Benito. 1955. *Familiar Quotations by John Bartlett.* Boston: Little, Brown, p. 925.

Nagel, Joane. 1994. "Constructing Ethnicity: Creating and Recreating Ethnic Identity and Culture." *Social Problems* 41, February 152–176.

Nagel, J., and S. Olzak. "Ethnic Mobilization in New and Old States: An Extension of the Competition Model." *Social Problems* 30, December: 127–143.

Nairn, Tom. 1994. "The Maladies of Development," in John Hutchinson and Anthony D. Smith (eds.), *Nationalism.* New York: Oxford University Press, pp. 70-76.

Nash, Manning. 1996. "The Core Elements of Ethnicity." In John Hutchinson and Anthony D. Smith (eds.). *Ethnicity.* New York: Oxford University Press, pp. 24-28.

Norris, Scott. 1999. "Family Secrets." *New Scientist* (19 June):42-46.

Orcutt, Guy H. 1957. "A New Type of Socio-Economic System." *The Review of Economics and Statistics,* Vol. 39, No. 2 (May):116-123.

Orcutt, Guy H. and Alice Orcutt Nakamura. 2000. "Foreword," in Anil Gupta and Vishnu Kapur, editors, *Microsimulation in Government Policy and Forecasting.* Amsterdam, The Netherlands: Elsevier, pp. ix-x.

Pan, Lynn. 1994. Sons of the Yellow Emperor. New York: Kodansha. Parsons, Talcott. 1951a. *The Social System.* Glencoe, IL: Free Press.

________.1951b. *Toward a General Theory of Action.* Glencoe, IL: Free Press.

Perutz, Max F. 1989. *Is Science Necessary?* New York: Dutton.

Pinney, Roy. 1972. *Slavery: Past and Present.* New York: Thomas Nelson.

Pohl, Hans. 1997. Introduction, in Hans Pohl, editor,

Competition and Cooperation of Enterprises on National and International Markets (19th–20th Century). Stuttgart, Germany: Franz Steiner Verlag, pp. 7-11.

Popper, Karl R. 1961. *The Logic of Scientific Discovery.* New York: Science Editions.

Population Reference Bureau. 1999. *World Population: More Than Just Numbers.* Washington, D.C.

Portes, Alejandro. 1995."Economic Sociology and the Sociology of Immigration: A Conceptual Overview." In Alejandro Portes (ed.), *The Economic Sociology of Immigration.* New York: Russell Sage Foundation, pp. 1–41.

Portes, Alejandro, and Ruben G. Rumbaut. 1996. *Immigrant America.* 2nd ed. Berkeley, CA: University of California Press.

Postgate, J.N. 1992. *Early Mesopotamia: Society and Economy at the Dawn of History.* London: Routledge.

Quintana-Murci, Lluis, et al. "Genetic Evidence of an Early Exit of Homo sapiens sapiens From Africa Through Eastern Africa," *Nature Genetics,* Vol. 23, No. 4 (December):437-441.

Renan, Ernest. 1994. "Qu'est-ce qu'une nation?" in John Hutchinson and Anthony D. Smith (eds.), *Nationalism.* New York: Oxford University Press, pp. 17-18.

Renner, Michael. 1999. "Ending Violent Conflict." Pp. 151-168 in *State of the World,* edited by Lester R. Brown, Christopher Flavin, Hilary F. French, and Linda Starke. New York: Norton.

Reynolds, Susan. 1994. "Regnal Sentiments and Medieval Communities," in John Hutchinson and Anthony D. Smith (eds.), *Nationalism.* New York: Oxford University Press, pp. 137-140.

Ridley, Mark. 1993. *Evolution.* Boston: Blackwell.

Robertson, Roland. 1992. *Globalization: Social Theory and Global Culture.* Newbury Park, CA: Sage.

Ross, Lee, and Richard E. Nisbett. 1991. *The Person and the Situation.* Philadelphia: Temple University Press.

Rudolph, Susanne Hoeber. 1996. "Transnational Religion and Fading States." *Items* 50 (June-September): 25–30.

Sandweiss, Daniel H., Kirk A. Maasch, David G. Anderson. 1999. "Transitions in the Mid-Holocene," *Science,* Vol. 283, 22 January: 499-500.

Schwartz, Barry. 1975. *Queuing and Waiting: Studies in the Social Organization of Access and Delay.* Chicago: University of Chicago Press.

Schell, Jonathan. 1982. *The Fate of the Earth.* New York: Knopf.

Schermerhorn, R. A. 1970. *Comparative Ethnic Relations.* Chicago: University of Chicago Press.

Seton-Watson, Hugh. 1994. "Old and New Nations," in John Hutchinson and Anthony D. Smith (eds.), *Nationalism.* New York: Oxford University Press, pp. 134-137.

Sheets, Tara E., and Christine Maurer (eds.). 1999. *Encyclopedia of Associations: International Organizations.* 34th Edition, Part I. Detroit: Gale.

Sherif, Muzafer, and Carolyn W. Sherif. 1953. *Groups in Harmony and Tension.* New York: Harper.

Sherratt, Andrew. 1997. "Climatic Cycles and Behavioural Revolutions: the Emergence of Modern Humans and the Beginnings of Farming," *Antiquity,* 71, No. 272 (June):271-287.

Shuzhang, Yang, and Liu Weijiang. 1992. "Ethnic Population: A Macro Analysis of Population Growth of China's Ethnic Groups in the 1980s," *China Population Today* 9, no. 3:9–11.

Silverman, David P. 1997. *Ancient Egypt.* New York: Oxford University Press.

Simmel, Georg. 1950. *The Sociology of Georg Simmel.* Glencoe IL: Free Press.

______. 1955. *Conflict & The Web of Group Affiliations.* Glencoe IL: Free Press.

Simon, Herbert A. 1965. "The Architecture of Complexity." General Systems: *Yearbook of the Society for General Systems Research,* Vol. X, pp. 63-76.

Simpson, John H. 1989. "Globalization, the Active Self, and Religion: A Theory Sketch." In William H. Swatos, Jr. (ed.) *Religious Politics in Global Perspective.* New York: Greenwood, pp. 29-38.

Simpson, George Eaton, and J. Milton Yinger. 1985. *Racial and Cultural Minorities.* New York: Plenum.

Smith, Anthony D. 1986. *The Ethnic Origin of Nations.* Oxford: Blackwell.

_______.1992. "Chosen Peoples: Why Ethnic Groups Survive," *Ethnic and Racial Studies,* (15), 3, pp. 440-449.

_______.1994 [1989]. "The Origin of Nations," in John Hutchinson and Anthony D. Smith (eds.), *Nationalism.* New York: Oxford University Press, pp. 147-154.

Smith, H.W. 1995. *The Myth of Japanese Homogeneity.* Commack NY: Nova Science.

Smolowe, Jill. 1993. "Intermarried...With Children." *Time* 142, no. 21 (Special Issue, Fall):64–65.

Sowell, Thomas. 1981. *Ethnic America.* New York: Basic.

_____. 1996. Migrations and Cultures. New York: Basic.

Spencer, Herbert. 1961. *The Study of Sociology.* Ann Arbor, MI: University of Michigan Press.

Starr, Chauncey, Milton F. Searl, and Sy Alpert. 1992. "Energy Sources: A Realistic Outlook." *Science* 265 (15 May): 981–987.

Staub, Ervin. 1989. *The Roots of Evil.* New York: Cambridge University Press.

Stephan, W. G., and D. Rosenfield. 1982. "Racial and Ethnic Stereotypes." in *In the Eye of the Beholder,* edited by A. G. Miller. New York: Praeger, pp. 92-136 .

Stevens, William K. 1995. "Scientists Say Earth's Warming Could Set Off Wide Disruptions." *New York Times,* September 18, pp. A1, A8.

Stone, Richard. 1995. "If the Mercury Soars, So May Health Hazards." *Science* 267 (17 February): 957–958.

Stringer, Chris and Robin McKie. 1996. *African Exodus.* London: Jonathan Cape.

Stuckert, Robert P. 1976. "Race Mixture: The Black Ancestry of White Americans" in *Physical Anthropology and Archaeology,* edited by Peter B. Hammon. New York: Macmillan, pp. 135-139.

Swatos, William H., Jr. 1989. "Ultimate Values in Politics: Problems and Prospects for World Society." In William H. Swatos, Jr. (ed.) *Religious Politics in Global Perspective.* New York: Greenwood, pp. 55-73.

Swedlund, Alan. 1993. "Human Races." Chicago: *World Book Encyclopedia,* Vol. 16, pp. 52-60.

Takaki, Ronald. 1998. *A Larger Memory: A History of Our Diversity,* with Voices. Boston: Little, Brown.

Tattersall, Ian. 1995. *The Fossil Trail.* New York: Oxford.

_________. 2000. "Once We Were Not Alone," *Scientific American,* Vol. 282, No. 1 January:56-62.

Thompson, Mark. 1994. "Forging War: The Media in Serbia, Croatia and Bosnia-Herzegovina." No place given: Article 19; International Centre Against Censorship.

Tibi, Bassam. 1996. "Old Tribes and Imposed Nation-States in the Middle East," in John Hutchinson and Anthony D. Smith (eds.), *Ethnicity.* New York: Oxford University Press, pp. 174-179.

Tilly, Charles. 1975a. "Reflections on the History of European State-Making." In Charles Tilly (ed.), *The Formation of National States in Western Europe.* Princeton, NJ: Princeton University Press, pp. 3–83.

_______.1975b. "Western State-Making and Theories of Political Transformation." In Charles Tilly (ed.), *The Formation of National States in Western Europe.* Princeton, NJ: Princeton University Press, pp. 601–638.

_______. 1994a. "States and Nationalism in Europe 1492-1992," *Theory and Society* 23 (February):131-146).

_______.1994b. "A Bridge Halfway: Responding to Brubaker," *Contention,* Vol. 4, No. 1, Fall, pp. 15–19.

_______.1998. *Durable Inequality.* Berkeley, CA: University of California Press.

Turner, Alan. 1984. "Hominids and Fellow-Travellers: Human Migration Into High Latitudes as Part of Large Mammal Community." In Robert Foley (ed.), *Hominid Evolution and Community Ecology.* New

York: Academic, pp. 193–218.

UNESCO. *1996 Statistical Yearbook* 1996. Paris: United Nations Educational, Scientific, and Cultural Organization.

United Nations. 1991. Population Studies Number 120: *World Population Prospects 1990.* New York: United Nations.

_______. 1994. *Human Rights: A Compilation of International Instruments.* Vol. I (1st part). New York: United Nations.

_______. 1998. *World Economic and Social Survey 1998: Trends and Policies in the World Economy.* New York: United Nations.

_______. 2001. *World Population Prospects, The 2000 Revision: Highlights.* New York: United Nations.

U.S. Bureau of the Census. 1990. Statistical Abstract. Washington, DC: U. S. Government Printing Office.

Vansina, Jan. 1990. *Paths in the Rainforests.* Madison, WI: University of Wisconsin Press.

Vaughan, James H. 1977. "Environment, Population, and Traditional Society." In Phyllis M. Martin and Patrick O'Meara (eds.), *Africa.* Bloomington: Indiana University Press, pp. 9–23.

Vincent, Jack E. 1976. *A Handbook of the United Nations.* Revised. Woodbury, NY: Barron's Educational Series.

Vischer, Lukas. 1979. "An Ecumenical Creed?" In Hans Kung and Jurgen Moltmann (eds.), *An Ecumenical Confession of Faith?* New York: Seabury, pp. 103–117.

Wallace, Walter L. 1994. *A Weberian Theory of Human Society: Structure and Evolution.* New Brunswick, NJ: Rutgers University Press.

_______.1997. *The Future of Ethnicity, Race, and Nationality.* Westport CN: Praeger.

_______. 2000. "A Darwinian Theory of Ethnicity, 'Race,' and Nationality." *International Journal of Comparative Sociology.* Vol. XLI, No. 2 (Spring): 147-201.

Weber, Max. 1946. *From Max Weber: Essays in Sociology.* Edited by H. H. Gerth and C. Wright Mills. New York: Oxford University Press.

_______. 1949. *The Methodology of the Social Sciences.* Glencoe, IL: Free Press.

_______.1978. *Economy and Society.* 2 vols. Edited and translated by Guenther Roth and Claus Wittich. Berkeley, CA: University of California Press.

Weinberg, Steven. 1992. *Dreams of a Final Theory.* New York: Knopf.

Weiner, Myron. 1995. *The Global Migration Crisis.* New York: HarperCollins.

Weinstein, Michael M. "A Better Chance for Free Trade." *New York Times.* November 21:a19.

Westoff, Charles F. and Akinrinola Bankole. 1997. *Mass Media and Reproductive Behavior in Africa.* DHS Analytical Reports No. 2. Calverton, MD: Macro International Inc.

Wilford, John Noble. 1995. "Believers in African Eve Think They Have Found Adam(s)." *New York Times,* May 26, p. A16.

_________. 1996. "Geologists Link Black Sea Deluge to Farming's Rise." *New York Times,* December 17, pp. C1, C10.

Wilkinson, David. 1995. "Central Civilization," in Christopher Chase-Dunn (editor), *The Historical Evolution of the International Political Economy,* Vol. I. Brookfield, VT: Edward Elgar, pp. 232-260.

Williamson, Joel. 1980. *New People.* New York: Free Press.

Wilson, Edward O. 1975. *Sociobiology.* Cambridge, MA: Harvard University Press.

_______.1992. *The Diversity of Life.* Cambridge, MA: Harvard University Press.

Wilson, William Julius. 1978. *The Declining Significance of Race.* Chicago: University of Chicago Press.

_______. 1987. *The Truly Disadvantaged.* Chicago: University of Chicago Press.

Wolpoff, Milford H., Wu Xin Zhi, and Alan G. Thorpe. 1984. "Modern Homo sapiens Origins: A General

Theory of Hominid Evolution Involving the Fossil Evidence from Eastern Africa." In Fred H. Smith and Frank Spencer (eds.), *The Origins of Modern Humans: A World Survey of the Fossil Evidence.* New York: Alan R. Liss, pp. 411–483.

Wood, Forrest G. 1970. *Black Scare: The Racist Response to Emancipation and Reconstruction.* Berkeley, CA: University of California Press.

Wuthnow, Robert. 1991. "International Realities: Bringing the Global Picture into Focus" in *World Order and Religion,* edited by Wade Clark Roof. Albany, NY: State University of New York Press, pp. 19-37.

Yetman, Norman R. 1985. "Introduction: Definitions and Perspectives." In Norman R. Yetman (ed.), *Majority and Minority: The Dynamics of Race and Ethnicity in American Life.* Fourth edition. Boston: Allyn and Bacon, pp. 1-20.

Zolberg, Aristide R. 1995. "Response: Working-Class Dissolution." *International and Working-Class History* no. 4 (Spring):28–38.

Mediating the Traumas of Techno-Economic Change: A Case Study in Popular Input

Daniel Bradlow
American University

Over the past quarter century, conflicts over large dam projects[1] have become more frequent, widespread, and acrimonious. The intensity of the conflicts between the proponents and the opponents of large dam projects has complicated water and energy management in many countries. The World Commission on Dams was established to try to find a resolution to this problem. Its task was to study the impacts and costs and benefits of existing large dams and to see if it could develop "recommendations, policies, standards, [and] guidelines"[2] that could assist in reducing the conflict generated by future decisions relating to large dam projects.

The opponents of dams argue that governments decide to build dams without paying adequate attention to their associated social and environmental costs, thereby causing them to be understated and externalized. They also argue that the proponents of dams are too eager to find reasons to build dams and thus under-value other ways of meeting society's water and energy needs. In addition, they contend that the sponsors of dam projects make decisions about the projects in ways that are not very transparent and do not offer all those who the proposed dam projects will affect an opportunity to participate in the decision-making.

The proponents of dams believe that dams are an efficient and effective way to manage the water and energy needs of human society. They argue that their opponents over-estimate the capacity of alternatives to dams to meet the growing water and energy needs of human societies. They also contend that their opponents under-estimate the benefits of dams and the costs of more transparent, participatory, and publicly accountable decision-making processes. Moreover, they argue that there is a risk that these costs could be so high that they effectively make it impossible to build dams. Many proponents also believe that decisions about the broader social and environmental effects of dams are political decisions that should be resolved through the political process and not through the specific project's decision-making process.

This brief description suggests that the underlying conflict between the proponents and opponents of dams is not so much about dams *per se* as it is about governance and perceptions of the appropriate way in which societies should make decisions about water and energy projects. At the intellectual heart of this debate is a disagreement about what constitutes desirable "development decision-making." By "development decision-making," I mean the way in which individuals, groups, and institutions decide to adopt and then implement policies, programs, and projects that affect the evolution of either their own and/or other's social and physical environments. The issue of development decision-making is applicable to all societies regardless of their level of development; and it applies to decision-making at the local, national, and international level in both the public and private sectors.

Thirty or forty years ago, all interested parties shared a common view of appropriate development decision-making. They premised this view on a clear distinction between political and social issues and technical and economic issues. They agreed to address decisions about environmental and social issues through the political process, while addressing technical and economic issues in a project or program specific decision-making process.

Today, this general agreement has broken down, and we are now involved in a complicated process of trying to develop a new model of development decision-making that is generally acceptable to all stakeholders. While the various participants in the debates about development decision-making all have their own views on the subject, their views tend to cluster around two idealized visions of development decision-making. The first vision is the original view, which in this paper is referred to as the "traditional" view of decision-making for development. The second vision is a new, still evolving view, which in this paper is called the "modern" vision of development decision-making. Since these are both idealized visions, they are not necessarily an accurate description of the views of any particular group.

This debate about development decision-making is occurring in other contexts besides dams. This debate is being waged in many decision-making structures at the local, national, and international level. These include the controversies that have surrounded natural resource and physical infrastructure projects in many countries,[3] the conflicts surrounding corporate relocation decisions,[4] and the protests against the World Trade Organization ("WTO") in Seattle in 1999 and against the International Monetary Fund ("IMF") and World Bank in Prague in 2000. The protests against the various aspects of structural adjustment policies that have taken place in many countries around the world implicate the same issue.

The participants in all these protests are motivated by a broad range of often inconsistent and incompatible social, economic, environmental, cultural, and political concerns. However, these protestors all share a common concern with other stakeholders in development decision-making. In particular, like the opponents of dams, they seek to broaden the range of issues that decision-makers consider, and expand the range of actors who can participate in development decision-making at the local, national, and international level. Furthermore, they aim to ensure that people and governments hold key decision-makers accountable for the decisions they make and their consequences. Their opponents, like the supporters of dams, are relatively satisfied with the current approach to development decision-making. The similarities in the view of the protagonists in the dams and these other debates suggest that the WCD's proposals for decision-making are relevant to this broader debate about development decision-making as well as to dams.

This paper explores the relevance of the WCD's proposed decision-making framework to the broader debate over development decision-making. The first section of the paper will describe the two idealized views of decision-making for development. This section will also discuss the implications of each vision for their proponents' understanding of development; the role that participation, accountability, and democracy play in each vision; and the implications of the vision for sovereignty. The second section will focus on the WCD's report and its proposal for decision-making in the case of dams. The third section will discuss the relevance of the WCD report to the broader debate on development decision-making. The final section will discuss some unresolved issues that arise from the WCD proposal and that are also relevant to the broader debate over development decision-making. It will also contain some comments on the contributions that law and lawyers can make to the resolution of this debate.

The Competing Visions of Development and the WCD

The descriptions of the traditional and modern views of development suggest that, in general, opponents of dams, opponents of other large development projects, and those who protest against the WTO, the World Bank, and the IMF all propound some version of the modern vision of development decision-making. These descriptions also suggest that, in general, the supporters of dams, multinational corporations, international economic organizations, and governments advocate a view of development decision-making that is closer to the traditional vision. The similarities in the position of the protagonists of the dams debate and the competing participants in other debates about development projects and policies and about governance suggest that the WCD report can offer some interesting lessons for the broader debate about development decision-making.

The following description of the findings and proposals of the WCD will clarify the relevance of the WCD Report to this broader debate. It will be followed by a discussion of the lessons that the WCD offers to the protagonists in the broader debate about development decision-making.

A. The WCD Report

The WCD's assignment was to study the issue of dams and to recommend criteria, guidelines, and standards that could be used in future proposed dam projects. The twelve member WCD, in order to produce its report, developed a knowledge base that consisted of: eight dam case studies, country studies of India and China, a briefing paper on Russia and the newly independent states, a cross-check study of one hundred twenty-five dams, seventeen thematic reviews, one hundred thirty technical papers, nine hundred forty-seven written submissions, and four regional consultations in which fourteen hundred people from fifty-nine countries participated.

1. The Findings of the WCD

Today, there are approximately 45,000 large dams in 145 countries.[5] Approximately 40,000 of these large dams were constructed in the second half of the twentieth century.[6] About eighty percent of these large dams are in five countries: China (22,000), the United States (6,390), India (over 4,000), Spain and Japan (1,000-1,200 each).[7] While the rate of construction has decreased, 1,700 large dams are currently under construction.[8] This means, given that the average construction period for a large dam is 5-10 years, between 160-320 new dams become operational each year.[9]

These dams have profoundly impacted the world as "large dams have fragmented and transformed...rivers."[10] Forty-six percent of the world's primary watersheds have at least one dam.[11] Dams supply water to thirty to forty percent of the two hundred sixty-eight million hectare of irrigated land in the world and, as a consequence, contribute to "at most" twelve to sixteen percent of world food production.[12] They produce nineteen percent of the world's electricity supply.[13] In about one-third of the world's countries, however, hydropower generates over fifty percent of the available electricity.[14] About thirteen percent of all large dams play an important role in managing floods, which affect the lives of more people than any other type of disaster including war, drought, and famine.[15]

The WCD found that governments have often over-estimated the benefits that these dams would produce, while simultaneously underestimating the costs.[16] This is due both to poor estimations of costs and benefits and to the failure to incorporate all the costs into the planning of the project. Most significantly, project planners have tended to pay inadequate attention to the social and environmental costs associated with dams.

The social costs of dams have nevertheless been substantial. Dams have displaced people, disrupted the lives of the communities into which the displaced people have moved, and deprived riverine communities, particularly those downstream from dams of their livelihoods.[17] In some cases, the reservoirs or rivers transformed by dams have deprived whole societies of their access to natural resources and of their cultural heritages.[18]

No one is sure how many people dam projects have adversely affected. However, experts have estimated that the construction of large dams has displaced between forty to eighty million people worldwide.[19] This estimate only refers to those whom dams have displaced directly. It does not include people displaced by other aspects of dam projects such as canals, powerhouses, roads, and compensatory measures such as biological reserves.[20] Commonly, the definition of "affected persons" governments have used in determining who to compensate excludes downstream communities and landless and indigenous people.[21] The result is that often only those with legal title to land receive compensation. Consequently, many adversely affected people have not been adequately compensated for their losses.

Dams have also involved significant environmental costs. For example, dams are the main physical threat to riverine ecosystems.[22] The reason is that dams fragment the river thereby transforming both aquatic and terrestrial ecosystems.[23] This has contributed to the extinction or endangerment of at least twenty percent of all fresh water fish species in recent years.[24] This, in turn, has adverse consequences for the one billion people for whom fish is a critical source of protein.[25] The fragmented rivers also impair the ability of watersheds to perform their many ecosystem functions, including nutrient recycling, water purification, soil replenishment, and flood control. It has also adversely impacted estuaries leading to loss of mangrove swamps, wetlands, and salt intrusion.[26] Interestingly, the WCD found that dams, because of the rotting vegetation left in their reservoirs, are net emitters of greenhouse gases, thereby challenging the conventional wisdom that dams are a clean source of energy.[27]

The financial costs of dams are also significant. Economists estimate that the world has invested two trillion United States dollars in large dams.[28] During the 1990s, the world spent approximately thirty-two to forty-six billion United States dollars annually on large dams, eight percent of which was spent by developing countries.[29] The public sector directly financed about eighty percent of the twenty-two to thirty billion dollars spent annually in developing countries.[30] The WCD found that many dams have not met their financial and economic projections.[31]

2. The WCD's Proposal: A New Framework for Decision-Making

The WCD proposes a new framework for decision-making about water and energy management that is based on the United Nations Charter, the Universal Declaration of Human Rights, the United Nations Declaration on the Right to Development and the Rio Declaration on Environment and Development.[32] The first two documents establish the principle that all human beings have human rights by virtue of their humanity and that any policy or law "must contain the intention to respect the rights and entitlements of all."[33] These two documents, together with the Declaration on the Right to Development, establish the indivisibility of civil, political, economic, social, and cultural rights. A rights-based approach to development therefore includes "rights to life, health care, education, shelter, food, water, remedy, security, subsistence, and livelihood"[34] as well as rights of free speech and association, due process, religion, and culture.[35] These documents also place on each state the responsibility to use its legal system and legislative process to give expression to and establish institutional mechanisms for upholding these rights. Therefore, the WCD argues that, "a rights based approach...provides a principled basis for mediating development choices among competing interests."[36]

The Rio principles, while recognizing the right to development, insist that it must be met in a way that equitably balances the rights of both the present and future generations.[37] Principle 10 of the Rio Declaration imposes on all human beings the obligation to involve themselves in environmental issues and to participate in decisions relating to the environment.[38] Principle 22 elaborates on this by recognizing the vital role of indigenous people and other local communities in environmental management and development.[39]

The WCD uses these documents to develop a decision-making framework based on the following five "core values and shared understandings:" equity, efficiency, participatory decision-making, sustainabil-ity and accountability.[40] Based on these principles, it derives a principle for decision-making that aims to assess both the rights affected by the proposed decision and the associated risks it creates. Its approach assumes that no party's rights will extinguish any other party's rights and that, where different people's rights come into conflict or competition, "negotiations conducted in good faith offer the only process through which various interests can be legitimately reconciled."[41] These negotiations should take place "within a legal and procedural framework, including arbitration, recourse and appeal mechanisms to ensure equitable adjudication in cases where negotiated settlements are not achievable or are contested."[42]

The WCD offers seven strategic priorities and policy principles to effectuate its assessing rights and risk approach to negotiated decision-making. The WCD has twenty-six guidelines that further develop these seven strategic priorities. These strategic priorities and guidelines together help define a participatory decision-making process for both water and energy policy making and project design, implementation and operation.

These seven strategic priorities are:

Gaining Public Acceptance: First, this requires a process for identifying the stakeholders in each decision, policy or project that is based on "recognizing rights, addressing risks, and safeguarding the entitlements of all groups of affected people, particularly indigenous and tribal peoples, women and other vulnerable groups."[43] Second, it requires decision-making procedures that allow for informed participation by all stakeholders in the decision and that result in demonstrated public acceptance of key decisions.[44] This means that all stakeholders must negotiate key decisions regarding water and energy resources. This includes the need for the prior, informed consent of indigenous peoples for all actions that affect their interests.[45]

Comprehensive Options Assessment: First, this means that governments and international development organizations must base the choice of water and energy policy and project options on a "comprehensive and participatory assessment of the full range of [available] policy, institutional, and technical options."[46] Thus, governments and development organizations should undertake impact studies at both a strategic level before making water and energy policy and at the project level. Second, this means that the impact studies must address environmental, social, health, and cultural heritage issues. Third, "in the assessment process, social and environmental aspects [must] have the same significance as economic and financial factors."[47]

Addressing Existing Dams: This priority recognizes that the context within which dams operate can change. Changes take place in priorities in water use, land use, technology, and policy. It therefore imposes on societies the responsibility to review and, if necessary, alter the operations of reservoirs to optimize the benefits of existing dams. This includes ensuring that dam operating rules and procedures adequately address all social and environmental issues.[48]

Sustaining Rivers and Livelihoods: The WCD premises this priority on the importance of rivers and their watersheds to life and the livelihood of local communities.[49] It underscores the need for decision-makers to prioritize the "avoidance of impacts, followed by the minimization and mitigation of harm to the health and integrity of...river system[s]."[50] To do this, it is important that those contemplating dam projects undertake baseline ecosystem surveys before beginning the decision-making process.

Recognizing Entitlements and Sharing Benefits: This priority is intended to ensure that all stakeholders share in the benefits of the project and that dam project sponsors not deprive them of their entitlements. It requires governments or others sponsoring a dam to identify all those whose rights the proposed project affects and ensure that they are able to participate in the planning, design, construction, and operation of the dam. In other words, policy and project sponsors need to ensure that they understand the risks to baseline social conditions before making any decisions. Further, it requires that all people whose rights may be at risk are able to conclude mutually agreed and legally enforceable mitigation, resettlement, and development entitlements with the other relevant stakeholders in the project. Dam project sponsors must pay particular attention in this regard to ensure that adversely affected people are "first among the beneficiaries of the project."[51]

Ensuring Compliance:[52] Public confidence in the project will only exist if governments, developers, regulators, and operators all comply with their obligations.[53] This suggests that the plans for each project should include a compliance plan. This plan should spell out how those planning and building the dam will achieve compliance and how the parties will enforce the compliance plan. Possible mechanisms for ensuring compliance with all project-related commitments include independent review panels for social and environmental matters, and performance bonds and trust funds to support compliance with project-related social and environmental commitments.

Sharing Rivers for Peace, Development, and Security: Transboundary rivers can be a source of tension between countries. This priority suggests that one way to overcome this problem is for the affected states to shift their focus "from the narrow approach of allocating a finite resource to the sharing of rivers and their associated benefits."[54] This approach is also consistent with the principles of equitable and reasonable use, no significant harm, and the prior sharing of information that are embodied in recent international water law instruments.[55]

Combined, these principles offer a new approach to decision-making that is dramatically different from the traditional approach in water and energy management. This new approach seeks to have decisions regarding dams emerge from a bottom-up process as opposed to the top-down process traditionally utilized in dam building. It also seeks to treat dams holistically and to incorporate all elements of the project within the decision-making process. The traditional approach, on the other hand, seeks to limit decision-making criteria to technical, economic, and financial issues.

* * *

Some Key Unresolved Issues Arising from the WCD Report that are Relevant to the Debate over Development Decision-Making

It's Great to Know the Ideal, but What Is the Minimum Acceptable Standard?

The WCD's proposed new framework for decision-making has achieved two important things. First, it demonstrates that it is possible to design an operationally useful decision-making process, consistent with the contention that the social, environmental, cultural, and political aspects of development are so completely intertwined with the economic aspects that decision-makers must treat them holistically. Second, it indicates that it is possible for the various different stakeholders in a contentious development debate to agree on what principles should underlie a tenable approach to development decision-making.

This suggests that the next task is the challenge of implementation. The WCD's proposal, in fact, is a description of an ideal decision-making framework. It does not address many of the concrete problems that decision-makers are likely to face in implementing this proposal. For example, it does not discuss how decision-makers can decide what is enough consultation, especially if there are some recalcitrant stakeholders who refuse to compromise or to accept third-party dispute settlement. It also does not discuss how decision-makers can know if they are allocating an acceptable proportion of their budget and human resources to these consultations. The WCD also does not give any guidance for determining what constitutes an adequate budgetary allocation for either strategic or project level options assessments, particularly in relation to the overall budget for the proposed sector or project level activity.

This suggests that there is an urgent need to conduct research on these issues and to empirically test different methods for implementing the proposal. One of the most pressing issues is developing the minimum acceptable standards for development decision-making. To put it another way: how much deviation from the WCD ideal is acceptable, or what constitutes "substantial compliance" with its guidelines and criteria? These minimum standards are needed to guide the empirical testing that must take place if we are to learn how to make the WCD proposal operational. They are also necessary to guide the transition process that must be undertaken if we are to move from the current problematic state of development decision-making to a decision-making process that will lead to socially and environmentally sustainable development.

The WCD report seems to suggest that the "floor" in its approach is that no acceptable decision-making process should allow projects to take place if they would result in uncompensated losses to some people or in the violation of other human rights.

What About the Victims?

According to the WCD, dam construction has forced between forty to eighty million people to resettle. This estimate does not include those who have suffered losses because of dam-related structures, such as power houses, access roads or canals, nor those who live upstream or downstream from the dam and have suffered losses due to changes in the river flow. Many of these people have never received appropriate compensation for the loss of their property, livelihoods, or cultural heritage or for the environmental, social, and health injuries they have suffered. In many cases, these people are suffering on-going injuries. Currently, dams "in the pipeline" threaten many others with similar injuries.

The WCD's new framework for decision-making implicitly highlights the failure of past decision-makers to adequately protect these people's rights in their development decisions. It also raises the issue of whether those who decided to build dams owe these victims compensation for the injuries they have suffered. The importance of this issue is likely to grow as these people and their advocates learn about the opportunities that are now available to protect their interests. Similarly, the debate will grow as the victims of dam projects realize that current dam project sponsors are providing those adversely affected by new projects with greater compensation and more opportunities for protections than past decision-makers offered or delivered. In fact, the demands from these victims for reparations are already beginning.[56]

The case for compensating these victims is morally very strong. However, it is legally problematic. In many cases, it is unclear who exactly caused the injury and should be held legally liable. In other cases, no obvious forum exists in which to bring the action. The victims' advocates will need to conduct legal research to resolve these issues so that the problem of compensating the victims in a fair and balanced manner is fairly resolved. If this does not happen, it is likely the issue will continue to grow as a political problem that states, international financial institutions, and corporations may be forced to address on an ad hoc basis.

The significance of this issue should not be underestimated. The problems of victims of dams are conceptually the same as the problems of people who have suffered injuries from other infrastructure, mining and natural resource projects, and large commercial ventures of all sorts. There is no reason to assume that these victims will be any less determined to press their claims once they see how their counterparts are treated under new decision-making frameworks.

How Do We Reform Institutions?

We have seen that the modern version of development decision-making and the WCD approach are both based on participatory and bottom-up decision-making. These methods of decision-making are applicable to all development decision-makers. Thus, they apply to corporations, international organizations, governments, and to large non-governmental organizations. The current structures and operating principles of many of these institutions are not conducive to these new ways of decision-making. This suggests that a key issue for the future will be reforming these institutions to make their structures and operating principles more compatible with the new approach to development decision-making.

What Role for Lawyers?

Both the modern view of decision-making for development and the WCD proposal pose important challenges to lawyers. For these ideas to become operational and for the lessons learned from the WCD to be usefully applied, lawyers will be needed for a number of tasks. These include:

- Skilled legal negotiators and drafters will be needed to conclude negotiated agreements between development decision-makers and the other stakeholders in their decisions;
- The issue of victim compensation will require lawyers to identify forums and develop legal theories that these claimants can utilize to get relief;
- The issue of developing minimally acceptable standards of compliance with the proposed decision-making framework will require legal research and analysis of international human rights and environmental law, as well as skilled legal drafters; and
- The reform of institutions raises interesting issues of corporate governance, administrative procedure, and international law. These issues will need to be researched and proposals for reform will need to be analyzed for consistency with applicable legal principles.

Conclusion

The rapid changes that the world has undergone over the past few decades have destroyed confidence in the traditional approach to decision-making for development and rendered it non-viable. So far, the international community has been unable to agree upon a new approach to development decision-making. The WCD's proposed new framework for decision-making for water and energy management establishes an important precedent for this broader debate. It suggests that it is possible to develop a new framework for development decision-making that is acceptable, at least in principle, to most stakeholders in the development decision-making debate. It also demonstrates that this new framework must incorporate many of the insights of the modern view of development decision-making. Finally, the WCD proposal challenges all interested parties, including lawyers, to work to overcome the problems involved in implementing the WCD's proposed new framework for decision-making and to adapt its lessons to the design of a new framework for all development decision-making.

Notes

1. The World Commission on Dams ("WCD") defined a "large dam" as a dam with a height of at least 15 m from the foundation or a dam that is between 5-15 m high and has a reservoir volume of more than 3 million m3. This is the definition used by International Commission on Large Dams ("ICOLD"). See *World Commission On Dams, Dams And Development: A New Framework For Decision Making* 11, Box 1.2 (Earthscan 2000) [hereinafter *WCD Report*].

2. *Large Dams: Learning from the Past, Looking at* the *Future: Workshop Proceedings*, Gland, Switzerland, IUCN and the World Bank (1997), at 10.

3. See *generally*, Ariadne K. Sacharoff, *Multinationals in Host Countries: Can They Be Held Liable Under the Alien Tort Claims Act for Humans Rights Violations?*, 23 *Brook. J. Int'l L.* 927, 958-60 (noting the conflict over the environmental impact of Shell Oil operations in Nigeria); "Chilean, Bolivian Presidents Meet in Brasilia," *Xinhua Eng. Newswire*, Sept. 1, 2000, *available at* 2000 WL 25639192 (discussing a road project designed to link Bolivia, Brazil, Paraguay, and Chile); "Rio Believes it Can Weather Slowdown," *Times* (London), Apr. 13, 2001 *available at* 2001 WL 4891452 (discussing opposition to a uranium mining project in northern Australia); *Japan: Airport Projects Take Wing, Travel Trade Gazette Asia*, May 19, 2000 *available at* 2000 WL 15017781 (describing airport construction in Japan); World Bank, *Project Information, at* http://www4.worldbank.org/sprojects/project.asp?pid=P048202 (last modified June 5, 2001) (describing a pipeline project in Chad-Cameroon); *Indonesian Court Opens Environmental Suit Against Freeport*, Agence Fr.-Presse, Mar. 8, 2001 *available at* 2001 WL 2357429 (detailing a lawsuit filed by an environmental group against Freeport Indonesia for its mining activities that have degraded the environment).

4. See Janice R. Bellace, *The European Works Council Directive: Transnational Formation and Consultation in the European Union*, 18 *Comp. Lab. L.J.* 325, 346-349 (1997) (discussing a controversial Vredeling draft directive in 1980 by the European Commission that sought to oblige employers to disclose information to employees and consult with them on certain corporate decisions). See generally Roger Blanpain, *The Badger Case and the OECD Guidelines for Multinational Enterprises* (Kluwer 1977) (analyzing industrial relations between large multinational enterprises and local societies of smaller nations where they locate business operations); *Barry Bluestone & Bennett Harrison, The Deindustrial-ization of America* (1982) (examining plant closings and their relation to the problem of private industrial development in the United States).

5. See *supra* note 1 (providing a definition of "large dams").

6. See *WCD Report, supra* note 1, fig. 1.5, at 8 (showing distribution of large dams at end of 20th century).

7. See *id.* at 9.

8. See *id.* at 10 (explaining that currently, the largest dam builders are India (695 to 960 dams under construction), China (280), Turkey (209), South Korea (132), and Japan (90)). The number of dams under construction in India is a matter of debate and the number depends on the source consulted. See *id.*

9. See *id.* at 10 (discussing world average of dams constructed annually).

10. See *id.* at l5.

11. See *id.* (noting that the world has 106 primary watersheds).

12. See *WCD Report, supra* note 1, at 13 (analyzing the considerable variation between countries). For example, dams account for 100 percent of irrigated land in Egypt but only 1 percent in Bangladesh and Nepal. See *id.*

13. See *id.* at 14 (stating that hydropower is used in over 150 countries).

14. See *id.* (expressing the fact that in 24 countries, over 90 percent of power is provided by hydropower, and, in another 63 countries, over 50 percent of electricity is provided by hydropower).

15. See *id.* at 14–15 (revealing that floods affected the lives of 65 million people between 1972–1996, and that during this period, an estimated 3.3 million people were left homeless each year by floods).

16. See *id.* at 37-71 (examining the technical, finan-

cial, and economic performance of large dams).

17. See *WCD Report, supra* note 1, at 16 (evaluating the negative impacts of large dams on populations).

18. See *id.* (describing the losses caused by dams).

19. See *id.* at 104 (analyzing the level of global displacement). Experts estimate that between 1986–1993, an average of 300 dams starting construction each year displaced four million people annually. See *id.* at 17 (citing *World Bank, Resettlement and Development: The Bankwide Review of Projects Involving Involuntary Resettlement* 77 (1996)).

20. See *id.* at 104 (noting the limitations of the figures, and emphasizing that the figures only refer to physical displacement).

21. See *id.* at 105 (stating that WCD case studies show that communities situated downstream from the dam, those without land or legal title, indigenous people, and those affected by project infrastructure were not considered as affected people at the time of the dam design and so were not included in any planned compensation schemes).

22. See *WCD Report, supra* note 1, at 16 (citing dams as one of the many factors leading to the degradation of ecosystems).

23. See *id.* (noting that the ecosystems are transformed with a range of effects varying in duration and degree of reversibility).

24. See *id.* at 16 (noting that the world has over 9,000 fresh water fish [species]).

25. See *id.* (stating that 40 percent of the world's fish inhabit watersheds).

26. See *id.* (noting that ecosystem transformations also close the mouths of major rivers).

27. See *id.* at 75 (estimating that emissions from reservoirs may account for 1-28 percent of greenhouse gases).

28. See *WCD Report, supra* note 1, at 11 (explaining that dams are promoted as an important means of satisfying water and energy needs).

29. See *id.* (estimating annual large dam expenditures).

30. See *id.* at 11 (describing the public sector's investment in dams in developing countries).

31. See *id.* at 39-42 (stating that the average cost overrun of dam projects surveyed was 56 percent).

32. See *id.* at 197-211 (discussing the foundations of the globally accepted framework for establishing universal goals and norms).

33. See *id.* at 200.

34. See *WCD Report, supra* note 1, at 200

35. See *id.* (noting the expression of rights and entitlements in law).

36. See *id.*

37. See *Report of U.N. Conf. on Environment and Development: Rio Declaration on Environment and Development,* U.N. GAOR 47th Sess., Annex 1, Agenda Item 21, at 8, U.N. Doc. A/Conf. 151/26 (Vol. 1) (1992) (declaring how the right to development must be fulfilled).

38. See *id.* at 10 (declaring that each person shall have access to environmental information and the opportunity to be a part of the decision-making process).

39. See *id.* at 12 (declaring that indigenous people and local communities have a vital role due to their knowledge and customs, and that the state should encourage their participation).

40. See *WCD Report, supra* note 1, at 202.

41. See *id.* at 206.

42. See *id.* at 206-7.

43. See *id.* at 215.

44. See *id.* (describing the kinds of decision-making processes and mechanisms utilized).

45. See I.L.O. Convention Concerning Indigenous and Tribal Peoples in Independent Countries, June 27, 1989, art. 16, 28 I.L.M. 1382, 1387-88 (stating that where informed consent is not possible, appropriate procedures established by national law and regulation, providing the opportunity for representation of those concerned apply).

46. See *WCD Report, supra* note 1, at 221.

47. *Id.*

48. See *id.* at 225-233 (insisting that opportunities to improve the environment and social performance of dams be taken).

49. See *id.* at 234 (referring to rivers and watersheds as "the biological engines of the planet").

50. See *id.*

51. See *id.* at 240.

52. See *WCD Report, supra* note 1, at 244 (requiring

commitments for the planning, implementation, and operation of dams to be met).

53. See *id.*

54. *Id.* at 251.

55. See, *e.g.*, Convention on Non-Navigable Uses of International Watercourses, Apr. 11, 1997, arts. 5-9, *at* 1997 WL 434401 (declaring that watercourses shall be used to attain optimal utilization; States shall participate in use and protection of watercourses; riparian states can make reasonable and equitable use of international watercourses; appropriate measures shall be taken to prevent significant harm to other watercourse States; and watercourse States shall regularly exchange information on the condition of the watercourse); Helsinki Rules on the Uses of Waters of International Rivers, August 1966, ch. 2, *at* http://www.international waterlaw.org/IntlDocs/Helsinki_Rules.htm (listing the factors to be considered in determining what is a reasonable and equitable use of watercourses).

56. Demands have come from victims in Guatemala, Panama, and Chile. See "Chixoy Dam Affected People Seek Reparations" *IRN Update* (Int'l Rivers Network, Berkeley, CA), Mar. 14, 2001 *at* http://www.irn.org/dayofaction/2001/010314.chixoydoa.html (reporting that victims in Guatemala are demanding reparations); "Princeton Report on World Bank: Chixoy Dam/Rio Negro Massacres Reparations Campaigns," *Dam Update* (Rights Action, Guatemala), Mar. 2, 2001, *at* http://www.rightsaction.org/urgent_com/c010301a.htm (reviewing conflicting claims against World Bank for human rights violations in regard to the Chixoy Dam); *see also* Monti Aguirre,"Indigenous People Demand Reparations from Panama," 16 *World Rivers Rev.* 7 (2001) (reporting that victims from Panama are demanding reparations) (Mar. 1, 2001); Email from Barbara Rose Johnston, AAA Ombudsman to Meg Taylor, IFC Ombudsman on WCD (Feb. 7, 2001) (on file with author) (discussing the WCD and Chilean victims' demands for reparations).

Photograph courtesy of the Franklin D. Roosevelt Library.

Eleanor Roosevelt holding the Universal Declaration of Human Rights.

Part Nine

Building Legitimate Governance

Transparency, Human Rights, Democracy, and Accountability

Strait is the gate and narrow is the way that leads to liberty,
and few nations, if any, have found it.

—John Adams (1821)

Our country has been engaged in numerous wars,
against democracies as well as oligarchies.

* * *

But, I would not hesitate to maintain that I think it better
that all Greeks should be our enemies under democracy
than our friends under oligarchy.

—Demostenes of Athens (384-322 B.C.)

In Part Nine we put the nation-state under a magnifying glass and seek to understand the causes of conflicts between a government and its citizens. Rummel's preeminent text opens by submitting his findings that democide, the killing of people by their own government, accounted for more loss of life in the twentieth century than all international conflict.

From this finding is drawn a further conclusion that democratic governments are less likely to engage in international wars against each other. Ann Florini builds upon this to advance her argument in favor of democratic governance, as one which allows for a transparent system of accountability, a regard for the rights of minorities, and a person's greater freedom to move both into and within one's country.

Paul Williams and Michael Scharf take a different route to the process of reconciliation governments and their people must undertake. In the last decade of the twentieth century, the world was witness to horrific wars of democide in Yugoslavia, Burundi and Rwanda, in which millions lost their lives. Today, tribunals have been established and reconciliation committees created to heal the wounds of old animosity and to lay the groundwork for a compatible future. Perhaps through these new organs of justice, those formerly disenfranchised will be able to reconnect to the fabric of society. But is a government by the people and for the people really the main tool for fostering peace?

Abuse of Power: War Isn't the Biggest Killer

R.J. Rummel
University of Hawaii

Our century is noted for its absolute and bloody wars. World War I saw nine million people killed in battle, an incredible record that was far surpassed within a few decades by the 15 million battle deaths of World War II. Even the number killed in twentieth century revolutions and civil wars have set historical records. In total, this century's battle killed in all its international and domestic wars, revolutions, and violent conflicts is so far about 35,654,000.

Yet, even more unbelievable than these vast numbers killed in war during the lifetime of some still living, and largely unknown, is this shocking fact. This century's total killed by absolutist governments already far exceeds that for all wars, domestic and international. Indeed, this number already approximates the number that might be killed in a nuclear war. Table 1 provides the relevant totals and classifies these by type of government (following Freedom House's definitions) and war. By government killed is meant any direct or indirect killing by government officials, or government acquiescence in the killing by others, of more than 1,000 people, except execution for what are conventionally considered criminal acts (murder, rape, spying, treason, and the like). This killing is apart from the pursuit of any ongoing military action or campaign, or as part of any conflict event. For example, the Jews that Hitler slaughtered during World War II would be counted, since their merciless and systematic killing was unrelated to and actually conflicted with Hitler's pursuit of the war.

The totals in the Table are based on a nation-by-nation assessment and are absolute minimal figures that may under estimate the true total by ten percent or more. Moreover, these figures do not even include the 1921-1922 and 1958-1961 famines in the Soviet Union and China causing about 4 million and 27 million dead, respectably. The former famine was mainly due to the imposition of a command agricultural economy, forced requisitions of food by the Soviets, and the liquidation campaigns of the Cheka; the latter was wholly caused by Mao's agriculturally destructive Great Leap Forward and collectivization. However, Table 1 (following page) does include the Soviet government's planned and administered starvation of the Ukraine begun in 1932 as a way of breaking peasant opposition to collectivization and destroying Ukrainian nationalism. As many as ten million may have been starved to death or succumbed to famine related diseases; I estimate eight million died. Had these people all been shot, the Soviet government's moral responsibility could be no greater. The Table lists 831 thousand people killed by free—democratic—governments, which should startle most readers. This

R.J. Rummel, "War Isn't the 20th Century's Biggest Killer." Reprinted by permission of the author from the website http://www.hawaii.edu/powerkills.

Table 1

Twentieth Century Killed or Dead by Cause[s]

Cause	Totals (000)	Averages per 10,000 Population
Government	119,394	349
Non-Free	115,423	494
Communist	95,154	477
Other Non-Free	20,270	495
Partially Free	3,140	48
Free	831	22
War	35,654	22
International	29,683	17
Civil	5,970	26

a. All figures in the table are rounded; therefore the totals of subcategories may be slightly off.

figure involves the French massacres in Algeria before and during the Algerian war (36,000 killed, at a minimum), and those killed by the Soviets after being forcibly repatriated to them by the Allied Democracies during and after World War II. It is outrageous that in line with and even often surpassing in zeal the letter of the Yalta Agreement signed by Stalin, Churchill, and Roosevelt, the Allied Democracies, particularly Great Britain and the United States, turned over to Soviet authorities more than 2,250,000 Soviet citizens, prisoners of war, and Russian exiles (who were not Soviet citizens) found in the Allied zones of occupation in Europe. Most of these people were terrified of the consequences of repatriation and refused to cooperate in their repatriation; often whole families preferred suicide. Of those the Allied Democracies repatriation, an estimated 795,000 were executed, or died in slave-labor camps or in transit to them.

If a government is to be held responsible for those prisoners who die in freight cars or in their camps from privation, surely those democratic governments that turned helpless people over to totalitarian rulers with foreknowledge of their peril, also should be held responsible.

Concerning now the overall mortality statistics shown in the table, it is sad that hundreds of thousands of people can be killed by governments with hardly an international murmur, while a war killing several thousand people can cause an immediate world outcry and global reaction. Simply contrast the international focus on the relatively minor Falkland Islands War of Britain and Argentina with the widescale lack of interest in Burundi's killing or acquiescence in such killing of about 100,000 Hutu in 1972, of Indonesia slaughtering a likely 600,000 "communists" in 1965, and of Pakistan, in an initially well planned massacre, eventually killing from one to three million Bengalis in 1971. A most noteworthy and still sensitive example of this double standard is the Vietnam War. The international community was outraged at the American attempt to militarily prevent North Vietnam from taking over South Vietnam and ultimately Laos and Cambodia. "Stop the killing" was the cry, and eventually, the pressure of foreign and domestic opposition forced an American withdrawal. The overall number killed in the Vietnam War on all sides was about 1,216,000 people. With the United States subsequently refusing them even modest military aid, South Vietnam was militarily defeated by the North and completely swallowed; and Cambodia was taken over by the communist Khmer Rouge, who in trying to recreate a primitive communist agricultural society slaughtered from one to three million Cambodians. If we take a middle two-million as the best estimate, then in four years the government of this small nation of seven million alone killed 64 percent more people than died in the ten-year Vietnam War. Overall, the best estimate of those killed after the Vietnam War by the victorious communists in Vietnam, Laos, and Cambodia is 2,270,000. Now totaling almost twice as many as died in the Vietnam War, this communist killing still continues.

To view this double standard from another perspective, both World Wars cost twenty-four million battle deaths. But from 1918 to 1953, the Soviet government executed, slaughtered, starved, beat or tortured to death, or otherwise killed 39,500,000 of its own people (my best estimate among figures ranging from a minimum of twenty million killed by Stalin to a total over the whole communist period of eighty-three million). For China under Mao Tse-tung, the communist government eliminated, as an average figure between estimates, 45,000,000 Chinese. The number killed for just these two nations is about 84,500,000 human beings, or a lethality of 252 percent more than both World Wars together. Yet, have the world community and intellectuals generally shown anything like the same horror, the same outrage, the same out pouring of anti-killing literature, over these Soviet and Chinese megakillings as has been directed at the much less deadly World Wars?

As can be seen from Table 1, communist governments are overall almost four times more lethal to their citizens than non-communist ones, and in per capita terms nearly twice as lethal (even considering the huge populations of the USSR and China).

However, as large as the per capita killed is for communist governments, it is nearly the same as for other non-free governments. This is due to the massacres and widescale killing in the very small country of East Timor, where since 1975 Indonesia has eliminated (aside from the guerrilla war and associated violence) an estimated 100 thousand Timorese out of a population of 600 thousand. Omitting this country alone would reduce the average killed by noncommunist, nonfree governments to 397 per 10,000, or significantly less than the 477 per 10,000 for communist countries.

In any case, we can still see from the table that the more freedom in a nation, the fewer people killed by government. Freedom acts to break the use of a governing elite's power over life and death to pursue their policies and ensure their rule.

This principle appeared to be violated in two aforementioned special cases. One was the French government carrying out mass killing in the colony of Algeria, where compared to Frenchmen the Algerians were second-class citizens, without the right to vote in French elections. In the other case the Allied Democracies acted during and just after wartime, under strict secrecy, to turn over foreigners to a communist government. These foreigners, of course, had no rights as citizens that would protect them in the democracies. In no case have I found a democratic government carrying out massacres, genocide, and mass executions of its own citizens; nor have I found a case where such a government's policies have knowingly and directly resulted in the large scale deaths of its people though privation, torture, beatings, and the like. Absolutism is not only many times deadlier than war, but itself is the major factor causing war and other forms of violent conflict. It is a major cause of militarism. Indeed, absolutism, not war, is mankind's deadliest scourge of all. In light of all this, the peaceful, nonviolent, pursuit and fostering of civil liberties and political rights must be made mankind's highest humanitarian goal. Not simply to give the greatest number the greatest happiness, not simply to obey the moral imperative of individual rights, not simply to further the efficiency and productivity of a free society, but also and mainly because freedom preserves peace and life.

Note

Published in the *Wall Street Journal* (July 7, 1986). This was based on a pilot survey of possible sources of democide data. As a result of this study I applied for a grant from the United States Institute of Peace to do a much more methodical survey of democide, which eventuated in my Death by Government and Statistics of Democide. This pilot study underestimated these final totals by about 42 percent.

Further data regarding aviations of peace (by means of starvation, genocide and democide) by governments throughout recent history are provided by tables 2-5 that follow.

Table 2

The World at War: International and Domestic Conflicts (1950-2000)**

• Indicates an international as contrasted with an intrastate or domestic war or conflict

Recent and Pending Conflicts

Afghanistan Civil War 1989 -->
Algeria FIS / GIA Struggle 1992 -->
Angola Second War with UNITA 1992 -->
Burma Insurgency 1950 --->
Burundi Civil Conflict 1993 --->
China Spratly Islands 1988 -->
Colombia FARC & ELN Insurgencies 1970s -->
Congo (Congo-Brazzaville) Civil Conflict 1997-->
Congo (Zaire) Congo War 1998 -->
Ethiopia Eritrea War 1998-->
Georgia Civil War 1991-->
India Kashmiri Uprising 1970s -->
India Naxalite Uprising 1967 -->
Indonesia Aceh 1986 --->
Indonesia East Timor 1974-1999
Indonesia Kalimantan 1983 --->
Israeli-Palestinian Conflict 1999–>
Indonesia Papua / West Irian 1963 --->
• Korea Korea Confrontation 1953 -->
Mexico Zapatista Uprising 1996 -->
Namibia Caprivi Strip Secession 1966--->
Nigeria Civil Disturbances 1997 -
Peru Shining Path Rebellion 1970s -->
Philippines Moro Uprising 1970s--->
Russia Chechen Uprising 1992 --->
Rwanda Civil War and Genocide 1991 -
Senegal Casamance 1982 -->
Sierra Leone Civil War 1990-1999?
Solomon Islands Civil Disturbance 1999 --->
Somalia Civil War 1991-->
Spain Basque Uprising 1970s -->
Sri Lanka Tamil Uprising 1980s -->
Sudan Second Civil War 1983 -->
Turkey Conflict with Kurds 1984 -->
Uganda Civil Conflict 1980 --->
United States-Taliban War 2001 --->

Concluded Conflicts

Afghanistan Soviet Invasion 1979-1989
Albania Civil War 1997
Algeria War of National Liberation 1954-1962
Angola War of National Liberation 1961-1974
Angola First War with UNITA 1975-1992
Argentina Dirty War 1960s-1970s
• Argentina Falklands/Malvinas War 1982
Azerbaijan Nagorno-Karabakh Conflict 1990s
BoliviaRevolution 1952
Bosnia Civil War 1992-1995
BougainvilleIndependence 1990s
Brazil Generals' Coup 1964
Burkina Faso Ankara Coup 1980s
Burundi Ethnic Strife 1970-1974
Burundi Ethnic Strife 1984-1989
Burundi Ethnic Strife 1990-1994
• Cambodia U.S. Invasion 1970
Cambodia Civil War 1970s
Canada Quebec Separatism 1960s-1970s
Central African Republic Coup and Civil War 1980s-1990s
Chad Civil Wars 1960s-1990s
Chile Coup Against Allende 1973
China Civil War 1940s
• China Invasion of Tibet 1950
China Quemoy and Matsu 1954-1958
China Border War with India 1962
China Sino-Soviet Border Clashes 1969-1978
• China Invasion of Vietnam 1979
China Tiananmen Violence 1989
ComorosCoups 1980s
Congo (Zaire) Post-Independence War 1960-1965
Congo (Zaire) Kabila Uprising 1996-1997
• Croatia War with Serbia 1991-1995
Cuba Communist Revolution 1950s
Cuba Bay Of Pigs 1961

Cuba Missile Crisis 1962
Cyprus Civil and Turkish Invasion 1970s
CzechoslovakiaCoup 1948
• Czechoslovakia Soviet Invasion 1968
Dominican Republic Coup and U.S. Invasion 1965
• Ecuador Border Dispute with Peru 1947-1999
• Egypt War with Britain 1951
Egypt War of Attrition 1967-1970
• El Salvador Soccer War with Honduras 1969
El Salvador Civil War 1970s-1980s
Eritrea War for Independence 1958-1991
EthiopiaRevolution 1974-1978
• Ethiopia First War with Somalia 1977-1978
• Ethiopia Second War with Somalia 1998-1999
Ethiopia Civil War 1978-1991
Fiji Ethnic Conflict / Coup 1980s
Georgia 1990-1994
Germany Berlin Crises 1948 & 1958-62
Germany East German Uprising 1953
Ghana Rawlings Coup 1978
Greece Civil War 1944-1949
Grenada U.S. Invasion 1982
Guatemala Coup Against Arbenz 1954
Guatemala Civil War 1965-1969
Guatemala Civil War 1970-1974
Guatemala Civil War 1975-1979
Guinea-Bissau (Portugal) Independence 1960s-1974
Guyana Ethnic Conflict 1970s-1980s
Haiti Civil War 1990s
• Hungary Soviet Invasion 1956
India Post-Independence 1940s
• India Invasion Of Goa 1961
• India War with Pakistan 1965
• India Bangladeshi Independence War 1971
India Sikh Uprising 1980s
IndonesiaIndependence 1940s
Indonesia Suharto Coup 1965
Iran 1970-1974
Iran Islamic Revolution 1979
• Iran Iran-Iraq War1980-1989
Iraq Revolution and Coups 1958-1968
Iraq Kurdish Rebellions 1960s-1990s
• Iraq Iran-Iraq War 1980-1989
• Iraq Gulf War 1990-1991
Ireland (Britain) Religious Conflict 1969-1999
• Israel War of Independence 1948-1949
Israel Palestinian Struggle 1948-
• Israel Sinai War 1956
• Israel Six-Day War 1967
• Israel Yom Kippur War 1973
• Israel Attack on Iraqi Nuclear Reactor 1981
Israel Terrorist Attacks 1960s-1980s
• Israel Invasion of Lebanon 1978, 1982-2000
Italy Anti-Mafia 1980s-1990s
Jordan British Intervention 1961
Jordan Civil War 1970
Kenya Mau Mau Uprising 1952-1956
Korea Korean War 1950-1953
Laos Pathet Lao Uprising 1960s-1970s
Lebanon Civil Conflict 1958
Lebanon Civil War 1975-1990
Liberia Doe Coup 1980
Liberia Civil War 1989-1997
Libya Qaddafi Coup 1969
Libya U.S. Air Attacks 1980s
Libya War with Chad 1986-1987
Macedonia Ethnic Conflict 1990s
• Madagascar Independence Struggle 1950s-1960s
Malaysia Communist Uprising 1940s
Mexico Student Massacre 1968
Morocco Polisario-Moroccan War 1975-1979
Mozambique War of Independence 1964-1974
Mozambique Renamo War 1970s-1992
Myanmar/Burma 1965-1969
Myanmar/Burma 1980-1984
Myanmar SLORC Coup 1980s
• Namibia War of National Liberation 1966-1990
• New Caledonia Independence Struggle 1980s-1990s
NicaraguaRevolution 1970s
Nicaragua Contra War 1980s
Niger Coups
Nigeria Biafra Civil War 1966-1969

NigeriaCoups 1980s-1990s
North Korea Seizure of the Pueblo 1968
Pakistan Coups and Internal Conflicts 1960s-1980s
Palestine Intifada 1987-1992
• Panama U.S. Invasion 1989
Peru 1980-1984
Philippines Huk Rebellion 1948-1953
Philippines 1970-1974
Puerto Rico Independence Terrorist Actions 1950s
Russia Chechnya Uprising 1994-1996
• Russia Moldova 1994 -->
Rwanda 1960-1964
Rwanda 1990-1994
Serbia Kosovo Secessionist Movement 1990-1999
Somalia 1980-1984
Somalia 1984-1989
South Africa Anti-Apartheid Struggle 1948-1994
• Soviet Union Conflict with Iran over Azerbaijan 1945-1946
• Soviet Union Conflict with Turkey 1945-1953
Sri Lanka 1970-1974
Sri Lanka 1980-1984
Sudan First Civil War 1955-1972
Tajikistan Civil War 1992-1997
TogoCoups 1963-1990
Uganda 1965-1969
Uganda Anti-Amin Struggle 1971-1979
Uganda 1980-1984
Uruguay Tupamaros Uprising 1960s-1970s
• Vietnam First Indochina War 1946-1954
• Vietnam Second Indochina War 1964-1973
• Vietnam Third Indochina War 1978-1981
• Western Sahara Polisario-Moroccan War 1975-1991
Yemen Civil War 1960s-1980s
Yemen 1990-1994
Yemen AR 1960-1964
Yemen PR 1984-1989
YugoslaviaDisintegration 1990s
Zimbabwe Struggle for Majority Rule 1965-1980

**The World at WarFAS | Military Analysis | DOD 101 | US Ops |||| Index | Search | Join FAS

List originally created by John Pike
http://www.fas.org/man/dod-101/ops/war/

TABLE 3

Twentieth-Century Democide ***
Democide (000) a

Regimes	Year	Total
Megamurderers	1900-87	51,491
Dekamegamurderers	1900-87	128,168
USSR	1917-87	61,911
China (PRC)	1949-87	35,236
Germany	1933-45	20,946
China (KMT)	1928-49	10,075
Lesser Megamurderers	1900-87	19,178
Japan	1936-45	5,964
China (Mao Soviets)	1923-49	3,466
Cambodia	1975-79	2,035
Turkey	1909-18	1,883
Vietnam	1945-87	1,678
Poland	1945-48	1,585
Pakistan	1958-87	1,503
Yugoslavia (Tito)	1944-87	1,072
Suspected Megamurderers	1900-87	4,145
North Korea	1948-87	1,663
Mexico	1900-20	1,417
Russia	1900-17	1,066
Centi-Kilemurderers	1900-87	14,918
Top 5	1900-87	4,074
China (warlords)	1917-49	910
Turkey (Atatürk)	1919-23	878
United Kingdom	1900-87	816
Portugal (dictatorship)	1926-82	741
Indonesia	1965-87	729
Lesser Murderers	1900-87	2,792
WORLD TOTAL	1900-87	169,202

A Includes genocide, politicide, and mass murder; excludes war dead. These are most probable mid-estimates in low to high ranges. Figures may not sum due to rounding.

*** Modified from R.J. Rummel, *Death by Government* (London: Transaction Publishers, 1994).

TABLE 4

Fifteen Most Lethal Regimes ***

Regime	Years	Duration (years)	Type	Domestic Democide (000)
Cambodia (Khmer Rouge)	1975-79	3.83	C	2,000
Turkey (Atatürk)	1919-23	4.08	A	703
Yugoslavia (Croatia)	1941-45	4.17	A	655
Poland (Post-World War II)	1945-48	3.33	A	1,585
Turkey (Young Turks)	1909-18	9.17	A	1,752
Czechoslovakia (Post-World War II)	1945-48	2.83	A	197
Mexico	1900-20	21.00	A	1,417
USSR	1917-87	71.00	C	54,769
Cambodia (Samrin)	1979-87	8.92	C	230
Uganda (Amin)	1971-79	8.33	A	300
Angola	1975-87	12.17	C	125
Rumania (Carol/Michael)	1938-48	10.08	A	484
Korea, North	1948-87	39.33	C	1,293
Uganda (Post-Amin)	1979-87	8.75	A	255
Mongolia	1926-87	61.17	C	100
World	1900-87	17.46 [a]	C	129,909 [b]

Key: A = authoritarian; C = communist
a. Average
b. Total

*** Modified from R.J. Rummel, *Death by Government* (London: Transaction Publishers, 1994).

TABLE 5

20th Century's Bloodiest Megamurderers ***

Dictator	Ideology	Country	Years	Murdered (000)[a]
Joseph Stalin	C	USSR	1929-53	42,672 [b]
Mao Tse-tung	C	China	1923-76	37,828 [c]
Adolf Hitler	F	Germany	1933-45	20,946
Chiang Kai-shek	M/F	China	1921-48	10,214 [d]
Vladimir Illich Lenin	C	USSR	1917-24	4,017 [e]
Tojo Hideki	M/F	Japan	1941-45	3,990 [f]
Pol Pot	C	Cambodia	1968-87	2,397 [c]
Yahya Khan	M	Pakistan	1971	1,500
Josip Broz Tito	C	Yugoslavia	1941-87	1,172 [c]

Key:

C = communist; F = fascist; M/F = militarist/fascist; M = militarist

a These are the most probable estimates from a low to high range. Estimates are from or based on Rummel 1990, 1991, 1992 and *Statistics of Democide.*
b Citizens only.
c Includes his guerrilla period.
d Includes his warlord period.
e Includes one-third the democide for the NEP period 1923—28.
f Estimated as one-half the 1937—45 democide in China plus the World War II democide

*** Modified from R.J. Rummel, *Death by Government* (London: Transaction Publishers, 1994).

Increasing Transparency in Government

Ann Florini
Carnegie Endowment for International Peace

Information is the lifeblood of both democracies and markets. Without information, citizens have no basis upon which to evaluate their representatives or voice their opinions, and both elections and the very process of representation become a meaningless sham. Without information, the financial markets upon which modern economies depend become irrational exercises in guesswork, and governmental regulators cannot hope to carry out their responsibilities. The key to good governance is thus to make governments and markets transparent. And as the world becomes more tightly integrated, a compelling need is arising to ensure that people in one part of the globe have access to information about what is going on elsewhere, so that they can have voice in far-away matters that now affect them directly. Only such open flows of information can ensure that governments and economic systems will enjoy the long-term stability and widespread legitimacy upon which peace and prosperity depend.

That is a daunting task. The world has too few mechanisms for collecting and distributing information, and the people who have information often have incentives not to share it. But it is by no means undoable.

Transparency is one end of a long continuum of behavior. At one extreme, nothing is hidden. All government files are open to inspection by anyone wanting to see them, and meetings are always public. At the other, secrecy reigns supreme, and no one outside the narrow circles of government is permitted to know anything. No country actually functions at either extreme, but some come close. Sweden first enshrined the ideal of public access to information in its basic law in 1766 and now is among the world's most effective practioners and promoters of transparency. Countries like Iraq fall closer to the other end of the spectrum. The task is thus to move global society closer to the transparency end of the spectrum.

Such movement is possible because the degree of transparency that prevails is the result of deliberate choices. Governments must choose to release information. Sometimes those choices are governed by specific laws or constitutional requirements, and sometimes they are individual initiatives on an ad hoc basis. But files do not open themselves. Increasing transparency requires that someone, somewhere, decides to hand over information.

The stakes are high. Those choices now lie at the heart of the debate over democracy, governance, the international economy, and the fate of an increasingly globalized world. Everyone, from leaders of international organizations to protestors on the street, is demanding that others turn over information. But at the same time, powerful forces are fighting back, arguing that information can be misused by corporate competitors, other governments, even terrorists. The outcome of the battle between transparency and secrecy will do much to determine whether the twenty-first century sees endless conflict, or long-term peace and prosperity.

This chapter will address several specific matters. First, it investigates how transparency is related directly to achieving and maintaining international peace, by transforming the security relationship between countries. Second, it examines transparency's indirect role in contributing to legitimate and effective governance. Third, it explores the trends in transparency in national politics, international organizations, and environmental management.

Global Security Through Transparency

Over the past five decades, a new idea has grown deep roots: that states can pursue security not through the threat or use of force, but by actively persuading others that they have nothing to fear. That persuasion takes the form of detailed disclosures about military practices and capabilities. Transparency both constrains a state's ability to undertake successful aggression and, increasingly, provides a powerful signal of benign intentions. Today, the world's major military powers have enmeshed themselves in a web of confidence-building measures and arms-control treaty verification provisions that, taken together, require an extraordinary level of disclosure. Those transparency measures range from relatively painless steps, such as refraining from concealing activities from surveillance satellites, to more difficult measures such as providing detailed data disclosures, up to the point of requiring countries to host highly intrusive inspections of sensitive military and civilian installations.

The extent of transparency in the security field is particularly striking in view of how rapidly countries have scaled that ladder of increasingly intrusive transparency measures, starting from attitudes less than a century ago that found the whole idea of transparency an intolerable invasion of national sovereignty. The first significant proposals in the early part of the twenty-first century met a chilly response. The Treaty of Versailles, at the insistence of the French, contained provisions for regular and detailed inspections of Germany. Those provisions were not, of course, "voluntary" for Germany, and it is hardly surprising that German's compliance was limited. The more difficult reaction to explain was that of the United States and Britain. The British and Americans seemed far more concerned with upholding norms of sovereignty over the often-incompatible requirements of disclosure. The Americans argued that a Peace Treaty that returned sovereignty to Germany could not simultaneously undermine that sovereignty with disclosure requirements.[1] The British objected on pragmatic grounds that intrusive requirements such as inspections would more likely provoke conflict than bolster the cause of peace.[2] The end result was a compromise between the French desire for a permanent monitoring commission and the British and American preference for reliance solely on the reports of their military attaches regarding Germany's compliance with its disarmament obligations. Under Articles 203 and 204 of the Treaty of Versailles, three Inter-Allied Control Commissions were established to monitor German compliance, and Article 205 gave the Commissions the authority to inspect any site in German territory at any time.[3]

The system did not last long largely because the concept of expecting transparency from a sovereign state remained anathema to so many. By 1922, Germany was openly defying the obligatory inspections. Despite strident French protests, German intransigence went unpunished, and in January 1927 the last of the Control Commissions was dissolved, even though the Allies recognized that German non-compliance with its disarmament obligations remained significant.[4]

Arms-control treaties of the time similarly indicated little support for notions of transparency.

The most important of the interwar security agreements, the three multilateral treaties on naval arms control generally referred to as the Washington Treaty system, generally relied for verification solely on the traditional method of reporting by military attachés. The disarmament efforts of the League of Nations, in a series of meetings beginning in 1925, found themselves most deeply divided over the issue of what, if any, verification measures should apply to any convention. The United States, Britain, Chile, Sweden, and Italy favored reliance on the good faith of nations, while Belgium, Czechoslovakia, Finland, France, Poland, Romania and Yugoslavia wanted a permanent supervisory agent.[5] By the first session of the World Disarmament Conference in July 1932, the United States had shifted to a vague call for adequate measures of supervision and control, probably in response to public pressures stemming from the lack of adequate information on the Japanese invasion of Manchuria.[6] When Franklin Roosevelt, who had long supported greater transparency to verify arms control compliance, became president, progress on transparency for the first time began to seem possible.[7] But by 1934 the negotiations had collapsed for other reasons, and the evolution of transparency in the security field had to wait decades for a more propitious climate.

After World War II, the United States took on France's previous role as the leading promoter of transparency in the security field, in a generally futile effort to elicit information about its highly secretive adversary in the emerging Cold War. From the beginning, U.S. early proposals for nuclear-arms control included highly intrusive inspection provisions.[8] The most dramatic move came with President Dwight D. Eisenhower's 1955 "Open Skies" proposal to allow the United States and the USSR to overfly each other as a means of building confidence that no untoward or threatening activities were going on below.[9] Although discussions continued for several years, they proved inconclusive, and Open Skies faded away once the advent of spy satellites rendered the need for aerial overflights less pressing. In talks about general and complete disarmament, the U.S. and the USSR used rhetoric endorsing unprecedented transparency measures, none of which led to concrete agreements.

In the 1960s, both superpowers began spy satellite programs that introduced a substantial degree of involuntary transparency, but they refrained from making efforts to shoot down one another's satellites, a kind of tacit acceptance of the resulting disclosures of information.[10] Such national technical means enabled the two superpowers to finesse the whole problem of information disclosure in the first major nuclear-arms control accord, the 1963 Limited Test Ban Treaty.[11] In the SALT I interim agreement limiting deployments of strategic nuclear-launch vehicles and in the Anti-Ballistic Misile (ABM) Treaty curtailing development and deployment of strategic defenses, both in 1972, the two sides made that tacit acceptance explicit, promising not to interfere with or use deliberate concealment measures against each other's national technical means of verification.[12] In other bilateral nuclear arms control treaties negotiated in the 1970s, the superpowers agreed to add some (unverified) data exchanges to the arsenal of transparency provisions.[13] One, which did not come into force until the 1990s, would have allowed mutual on-site inspections under restricted conditions, a real breakthrough in transparency for the time.[14]

In 1968, the adoption of the Non-Proliferation Treaty (NPT) expanded the application of significant transparency measures to a wide range of countries.[15] The Treaty required signatories that were not already recognized as possessing nuclear weapons to allow the International Atomic Energy Agency to monitor all of its nuclear facilities and materials to determine whether they were being diverted for use in a weapons program.

On the conventional-weapons front, progress toward transparency was slow until well into the 1980s. The 1976 Helsinki accord among member-nations of NATO and the Warsaw Pact and other European countries introduced some basic transparency provisions such as advance notification of planned large military maneuvers, largely at the insistence of the neutral and non-aligned states.[16]

But as it turned out, all these relatively minor steps cumulatively laid the groundwork for what would become a major transformation in the 1980s. Some of this was superpower politicking—various members of the Reagan administration, which came to power in 1982, made sweeping transparency proposals either because they believed such transparency was essential to deter what they saw as inevitable Soviet cheating, or because they abhorred arms control altogether and found such proposals a politically expedient means of deflecting pressure for serious negotiations. But when Mikhail Gorbachev came to power, things changed. Virtually the first move that the new Soviet leadership made to demonstrate its new international attitude was to agree to accept mandatory foreign inspection of much of its territory to demonstrate that their military maneuvers did not exceed various restrictions.[17] Over the next few years, transparency-related proposals flew fast and furious between the two sides. By 1991, they had signed a Treaty on Intermediate-Range Nuclear Forces in Europe; an agreement to reduce, not just limit, their strategic nuclear delivery vehicles; and a Treaty on Conventional Forces in Europe, all requiring very detailed exchanges of data and numerous and intrusive on-site inspections of military facilities. They even managed to sign, at long last, an Open Skies accord among all the members of NATO and the by then former Warsaw Pact, permitting overflights of one another's territory, although that treaty has never come into effect.[18]

By the early 1990s, in other words, a norm of transparency had become thoroughly entrenched in the security area among the former adversaries of the Cold War. Two decades ago they were prepared to send one another into oblivion. Now, they think nothing of providing one another with detailed listings of all military holdings and inviting one another's military commanders to check out their latest equipment.

In the 1990s, security-related transparency began to reach well beyond the European context. The Gulf War, and especially the subsequent revelations about Iraq's broad-brush efforts to develop weapons of mass destruction on the sly, led to several major multilateral agreements. It showed the limits of effectiveness of the multilateral transparency instruments then in use, such as the inspection of nuclear facilities mandated by NPT. The experience of the inspections system imposed on Iraq as part of the cease-fire terms indicated just how intrusive transparency might have to be to address proliferation threats.

Following the Gulf War, revelations about Iraq's nuclear, chemical, and biological weapons program led to U.N. Security Council resolutions requiring Iraq to dismantle those programs, subject to sweepingly intrusive monitoring by the IAEA and a United Nations Special Commission (UNSCOM). Perhaps the most striking evidence of the degree to which transparency is now seen as normal in international relations was the unanimity with which the international community agreed to impose the most stringent monitoring conditions possible, not only on the Iraqi disarmament process, but on Iraq for the foreseeable future. To verify that Iraq's ability to make weapons of mass destruction was eliminated, the United Nations Security Council imposed extraordinarily intrusive transparency measures.[19] To carry out these measures, the U.N. created UNSCOM, with virtually unlimited authority to go anywhere and see anything in Iraq to uncover and dismantle Iraq's biological, chemical, and ballistic missile programs. Security Council Resolution 687 also extended to the International Atomic Energy Agency an enhanced inspection and monitoring mandate. Both the IAEA and UNSCOM were charged with ensuring that existing systems and production facilities were destroyed and with establishing and implementing a long-term monitoring plan to guard against any revival of the programs.

UNSCOM and the IAEA inspectors began their work with the premise that Iraq had accepted the terms of the resolution and that their work would be much like that of verifiers of arms-control treaties, who must be alert for cheating but generally expect to find compliance. As any reader of headlines in the 1990s knows, they were sorely disappointed. Iraq made innumerable efforts to delay handing over information, providing incomplete or blatantly falsified documents, interfering with and intimidating UNSCOM and IAEA inspectors, and in general evading the letter and the intent of its legal obligation under Resolution 687.[20] Although the international community has been badly divided over how strongly to deal with Iraq, it is striking that Iraqi complaints that the inspections constitute an affront to its national sovereignty have fallen on deaf ears, in sharp contrast to the post-Versailles experience of Germany. Then, as described above, some members of the victorious coalition publicly and privately expressed their sympathy with Germany's sense of forced disclosure as an affront. Now, some of the victors may be more interested in pursuing their vested economic interests in Iraq than in ensuring that Iraq cannot bring its weapons programs back. But with the exception of China, which has consistently abstained from U.N. votes regarding Iraqi inspections, no country has objected to the idea of enforced monitoring.

One of the most important effects of the Iraqi revelations was to spur multilateral agreement on a highly intrusive treaty to ban possession and production of chemical weapons. As of 1999, the Chemical Weapons Convention (CWC), which entered into force in 1997, had 170 signatories (of whom 126 had ratified the treaty). The treaty itself is less than 50 pages long, but the Verification Annex is more than twice that length. And the scrutiny to which they subject non-governmental actors, the provisions go beyond any other international agreement. The same chemicals that have revolutionized agriculture and medicine over the past century can be used to make chemical weapons. Because these substances are so widespread and so thoroughly integrated into the fabric of the international economy, with a few exceptions they cannot simply be banned. Instead, the verification net must be cast both wide and deep, covering an enormous range of chemicals and imposing stringent verification requirements. These include routine and very-short-notice surprise inspections of a vast array of often privately-owned chemical facilities. The Organization for the Production of Chemical Weapons (OPCW), established by the terms of the CWC to carry out implementation, has carried out more than 500 such inspections in some 30 countries. In addition, parties are required to provide detailed declarations about which facilities on their territories produce or consume certain chemicals (above "threshold" amounts). All parties have access to the declarations of all other parties.

Despite its high aspirations for transparency, the implementation record has been mixed. On the positive side, in 1996 the U.S. Department of Defense not only disclosed information required by the CWC but also declassified a multitude of details about the U.S. chemical-weapons stockpile.[21] Britain makes all of its declarations publicly available.[22] In July 1997, India, after years of denying that it had any weapons of mass destruction, openly declared its possession of stocks of chemical weapons, even though Pakistan had not yet ratified the CWC and even though India's chemical weapons program had not previously been publicly revealed.

Unsurprisingly, the transparency provisions of the CWC have not been enthusiastically embraced by all parties. Many are failing to disclose all the information required by the CWC. More than a quarter have not even filed the mandatory initial declarations covering chemical weapons, weapons facilities, and portions of the commercial chemical industry. The United States has awarded itself the right to veto challenge inspections of U.S. facilities if the president so decides.[23] Yet compared to the information previously available to the public and to most governments, the CWC represents a striking advance.

In addition to this web of formal transparency commitments, there is a large number of voluntary transparency arrangements and treaties that have not entered into force—and may never do so—but that incorporate stringent transparency procedures. One such is the Comprehensive Test Ban Treaty, which prohibits all nuclear explosions. It was signed by more than 70 countries in September 1996 but is unlikely to enter into force because of the refusal of India to adhere and the recent rejection of the treaty by the United States Senate. The Treaty establishes an International Monitoring System (IMS) of 321 stations around the world, an International Data Center, a communications system, and on-site inspections to monitor compliance, and the Preparatory Commission of what is intended to become the Comprehensive Nuclear Test Ban Treaty Organization (CTBTO) is establishing the global verification system. It has to date exchanged more than 40 letters of agreement with 31 states hosting monitoring facilities to enable work to proceed, pending the conclusion of formal bilateral agreements, and has concluded such formal arrangements with Canada and New Zealand.

The United Nations Register on Conventional Arms was established in response to the shock of the Gulf War, when members of the coalition against Iraq sometimes found themselves fighting weapons they themselves had originally supplied. The political impetus behind efforts to increase transparency in international conventional arms transfers came initially from Japan and Britain, with strong support from France and Germany. Negotiations over the establishment of the Register were heated. Developed countries proposed a Register in which countries would report only on transfers of finished conventional weapons. Pakistan argued that ignoring stockpiles and indigenous production of weapons would provide a very incomplete picture of arms. Egypt objected strongly to the exclusion of weapons of mass destruction, saying that by omitting these the Register could not provide an adequate basis for reasonable national security calculations. Brazil and Argentina, among others, questioned the focus on finished weapons systems, noting that transfers of dual-use technology mattered just as much as transfers of completed weapons systems.[24] In the end, these objections were met largely by promises to consider them later, promises that have largely gone unfulfilled.

Nonetheless, since the Register started in 1992, more than 90 reports have been filed every year, with 80 countries providing reports just about every year and many others participating more sporadically.[25] These reports cover transfers of seven categories of major conventional weapons: battle tanks, armored combat vehicles, large-caliber artillery, combat aircraft, attack helicopters, warships, and missiles and missile launchers. Because the United Nations provided few definitions about what constitutes a transfer (When a sale is agreed on? When the importer actually receives the weapons?), substantial discrepancies sometimes arise between the reports of exporters and importers.

There are enormous regional discrepancies in participation rates. OECD states, countries of the former Soviet Union, the larger states of the Americas, and much of Asia regularly file reports. China participated until 1998, when it withdrew in protest over the inclusion of exports to Taiwan in the U.S. submission, arguing that "arms transfers from the U.S. to Taiwan are neither legitimate nor transfers between sovereign states."[26] In the Middle East and North Africa, only Israel and Iran regularly report, while members of the Arab League have refused to participate in a Register that does not encompass weapons of mass destruction. Few sub-Saharan countries take part.

A variety of transparency-related security measures also exist at the regional level, beyond the European ones described above. Argentina and Brazil began a program of mutual inspections of each other's nuclear facilities in the late 1980s.[27] In 1999, the Organization of American States adopted an Inter-American Convention on Transparency in Conventional Arms Acquisitions.[28] The Middle East has seen its share of transparency measures too, particularly in the form of mutually-agreed aerial monitoring of cease-fire zones.

Overall, the idea of transparency as a contributor to rather than a threat to security is well established. It has become so widespread that it can no longer be seen as merely the result of a few states' calculation of immediate national self-interest. Rather, it reflects a wholesale shift in thinking: a change in norms as to what behavior is appropriate and desirable for states. A new standard of behavior now enables states to signal their non-aggressive, cooperative intentions.

One major question-mark for the future is China. China has taken some significant steps toward greater transparency, accepting the verification provisions of the CWC, participating until recently in the UN Register, and taking part in military exchanges with the United States. But the key issue is not so much China's reaction to specific transparency proposals as China's acceptance or rejection of the broader normative structure within which transparency is embedded. China is still reluctant to embrace that normative structure, as its refusal to support international inspections of Iraq indicates. But that reluctance is not outright rejection.

The other major, and as yet unanswerable, question is what consequences the September 11, 2001 attacks will have on global attitudes toward transparency. This question takes us beyond the security realm and will be addressed at the end of this chapter.

Why Transparency is Essential to Legitimate and Effective Governance

In the security field, transparency has emerged for purely pragmatic reasons: It works. But the debate over transparency's broader role in governance is normative as well as practical. The justification for demanding greater transparency gets down to fundamental issues of the moral basis for governance.

Both governments and corporations suffer from what social scientists call the "principal-agent problem." Governments are not supposed to be independent actors doing whatever suits their own interests. They are supposed to be agents, acting on behalf of their "principals," the citizens. Similarly, corporate managers are supposed to be the agents of corporate stockholders, and increasingly of other stakeholders such as local communities. But agents often have interests that differ from those of their principals. The academic school-of-thought known as public choice theory points out that governmental officials face incentives to increase their budgets and bureaucratic fiefdoms, actions that do not necessarily serve the public interest. Similarly, corporate managers often act to increase their personal incomes rather than the incomes of the shareholders they ostensibly serve.

Overcoming the principal-agent problem is thus one of the basic conundrums of governance, whether corporate or governmental. One of the basic solutions is to increase the transparency of the agent's behavior, making it possible for the principals to monitor what is going on. The informational asymmetry always favors the agents (agents inherently know what they are doing, while principals have to come up with ways of finding out what the agents are up to), but transparency can go far to reduce that asymmetry and thus reduce the power the agents have over the principals. And it is a fundamental tenet of democratic theory that the accountability made possible by transparency leads to better results. Without transparency, there is no way to know whether institutions are pursuing their goals efficiently and effectively, or even whether they are pursuing the right goals.

The principal-agent framework provides a powerful answer to the normative questions about the value of transparency. If agents are employed to serve the interests of the principals, the prevailing presumption should be in favor of agent transparency. Agents have no inherent rights to withhold information from principals.

That leaves unanswered the pragmatic questions about how and when to promote transparency. After all, under some conditions secrecy is necessary to enable agents to serve the interests of the principals. Transparency is not always a good thing. It can be neutral, or even harmful. It merely enables people to acquire information. It does not by itself enable people to do anything with that information. Nor does it convey any understanding of the meaning of the information. It does little good if no one cares to do anything with the information. And sometimes the sheer cost of amassing information far outweighs the public benefit that would accrue from its disclosure.

The list of situations in which disclosure can do more harm than good is fairly obvious: national security, individual privacy, and corporate-trade secrets all need protection. The same military information that reassures other countries that your military forces are not massing for attack can enable others to locate and attack your forces. There is no public right to know the details of other people's private lives. Corporations depend on their trade secrets to stay in business.

Moreover, in the absence of universally shared, or at least mutually compatible, norms, transparency can aggravate conflict. It may simply remove the ambiguity that can otherwise conceal conflicts or soften disagreements. For example, the world is arguably better off politely ignoring Israel's well-known but undeclared nuclear capability than demanding that Israel own up to it. Although the principle of nuclear non-proliferation is well established among most other countries, few expect that Israel can be made to accept it. The costs to the nonproliferation regime of forcing the issue may well be higher than the benefits.

And information can easily be misused or misinterpreted. Transparency reveals behavior, but does not always give accurate clues about the meaning of that behavior. What someone is doing may be less important than why they are doing it. Americans do not worry about the British building nuclear weapons because Americans believe that Britain harbors no hostile intent. But they remain anxious about the possibility of a nuclear Iraq.

But while there are legitimate grounds for secrecy and concerns about transparency, they are easily taken too far. Protection of national security, for example, easily becomes an excuse for cover-ups of government incompetence or venality. And the costs of secrecy need to be kept in mind, even in these cases. When agents withhold information, they engender suspicion and hostility. They also are far more likely to make mistakes, even if their intentions are good. The complexity of many problems is simply too great for government managers to handle alone. They require feedback mechanisms so that new information is constantly incorporated. How can and should societies strike the appropriate balance?

A Brief History of Transparency

To answer that question, we start by looking at how the balance has varied over time. Demands for open flows of information have a long history in both politics and economics. One of the framers of the American Constitution, James Madison, wrote compellingly on the importance of information in a democracy:

> A popular Government, without popular information, or the means of acquiring it, is but prologue to a farce or a tragedy; or perhaps both. Knowledge will forever govern ignorance; and a people who mean to be their own governors must arm themselves with the power which knowledge gives.

In the economic sphere, corporations have found themselves facing demands for disclosure of financial data for almost as long as publicly-held corporations have existed. Great Britain experimented with disclosure laws starting in the mid-1800s.[29] In America, starting early in the 1900s, large numbers of small investors proved able to put substantial political pressure on the government to institute corporate disclosure standards that would protect them from deceit and insider dealings. The first organized body of professional accountants was not formed in the United States until 1886 and until the turn of the century corporate disclosure was not a public issue.

In the early part of the twentieth century, however, as in Great Britain, the extent of corporate disclosure gradually began to rise. That increase reflected significant changes in the nature of American business and investing, as some firms became too large to avoid scrutiny and, as in Britain, the number of small investors increased substantially. Those small investors proved willing to seek government action to reform commercial practices, accompanied by increasing criticism of management accounting and reporting practices by critics of big business and leaders of the public accounting profession. During the 1920s, the Investment Bankers Association of America tried to promote voluntary financial disclosure in order to protect legitimate investment bankers from the growing public resentment against the sellers of fraudulent securities and to forestall governmental regulation. In 1926, the New York Stock Exchange (NYSE) officially recommended that all listed companies publish quarterly reports containing some minimal disclosure of financial information.[30] At the same time, the American Institute of Accountants, the leading association of accountants, began to promote the development of standards of auditing and accounting, and encouraged the Stock Exchange to move further in this direction. In 1933, the NYSE announced that henceforth it would require independent audits of companies seeking a listing on the exchange, a practice already voluntarily followed by 90 percent of listed industrial companies.[31]

These moves proved insufficient to fend off the enactment of federal legislation. Spurred by the 1930s backlash against unregulated capitalism, the 1934 Security Exchange Act authorized the creation of a regulatory agency, the Securities and Exchange Commission (SEC), that would oversee a variety of new mandatory corporate disclosure practices. Companies whose securities were listed on national securities exchanges were thenceforth required to file periodic reports whose form and content would be determined by the SEC.[32] In subsequent years, the SEC worked with the American Institute of Accountants to establish the new standards, principles and practices of accounting and auditing.[33]

After World War II, the Universal Declaration of Human Rights (Article 19) explicitly recognized the right to "freedom of opinion and expression: this right includes freedom to hold opinions without interference *and to seek, receive, and impart information and ideas through any media and regardless of frontiers*" (emphasis added). But with the expansion of governmental bureaucracies in many countries and with the emergence of multinational corporations and large inter-governmental organizations came new concentrations of power able to withhold information from people whose lives they affected. At the same time, the Cold War led to the rise of a highly secretive national security complex in the traditional bastion of transparency, the United States.

Counter-pressures to all this were limited, although there were some. One notable victory for transparency came in the form of the U.S. Freedom of Information Act, first passed in 1966 and strengthened in 1974. In the 1980s, transnational networks of civil society activists launched campaigns demanding information from inter-governmental organizations, particularly the World Bank. East and West negotiated some arms control agreements that included verification provisions that made the security establishments of the two sides increasing transparent to each other.

But the real explosion of global demands for transparency came in the 1990s. At that time, the end of the Cold War eliminated one significant rationale for extreme secrecy. The spread of democratic norms, the increasing strength of civil society organizations, and the rise of increasingly independent media around the world have intensified pressures on governments to release information to their citizens. At the same time, global economic integration has led international investors (and the governments of capital-rich countries) to demand disclosures on corporate and national accounts in emerging economies, especially in the wake of the Asian crisis, which many blamed on the excessive secrecy of the Asian corporations and governments. International financial institutions, which are major promoters of economic integration, are demanding information from governments and then posting that information on web sites. Those international institutions themselves face intense pressure from activists around the world to open up their analyses and processes of decision making. All these demands are facilitated by information technology, which is making information ever easier to locate and share.

Now a broad struggle is underway between the forces of secrecy and the promoters of transparency. Freedom of Information laws and constitutional provisions are popping up in countries from the United Kingdom to South Africa to Thailand to Japan, but many are weak or are not being fully implemented. Intergovernmental organizations of all types are debating new or revised disclosure policies. Environmental management is entering a third wave, based not on centralized regulation or market-based incentives but instead on what might be called "regulation by revelation." The backlash against transparency has been strengthened, though not caused, by the horrific events of September 11, 2001. Below we will see where the struggle stands.

National Governments

The world is awash in proposals to require national governments to increase public access to information about them. Some of these demands are occurring in countries that have recently made, or are trying to make, a transition from autocracy to democracy, but many are taking place in countries long seen as well-established democracies that are good at holding free elections but not necessarily so good at keeping their citizens informed. Some of the constitutions of newly democratic or democratizing states contain provisions requiring governments to provide information to their citizens. In other cases, countries are enacting Freedom of Information Acts (FOIA) that lay out how citizens can get information from their governments, and restricting the conditions under which governments are allowed to refuse those requests.

Sweden claims pride of place as the first country to adopt a law, its press freedom act, requiring access to governmental information, in 1766. Finland was also an early adopter of formal legislation, with its Publicity of Documents Act adopted in 1951.[34] The United States followed with the Freedom of Information Act in 1966, although it was not until the Act was strengthened in 1974 in response to the Watergate scandal that meaningful implementation began. The momentum then picked up, with five additional countries adopting FOIAs in the 1970s, and six in the 1980s. By the 1990s, a wave of countries began debating the desirability of increasing government transparency, with 12 countries enacting FOIAs. South Africa has powerful transparency provisions written into its 1996 constitution.[35] Also in the 1990s, the United States passed an Electronic Freedom of Information Act to extend FOIA provisions to cover information not available in print. Following a report by a bipartisan national Commission on Government Secrecy headed by Senator Daniel Patrick Moynihan that was highly critical of governmental secrecy, the U.S. Congress began debating new legislation that would reduce the propensity of the governmental bureaucracy to classify everything in sight.[36] More recently, Bosnia, the United Kingdom, and Bulgaria adopted legislation. Laws are under discussion in India, Fiji, Botswana, Lithuania, Moldova, and Nigeria.[37]

Although this adds up to an impressive-looking flurry of activity, the devil is, as always, in the details. For many of these laws, the details raise serious questions about just how far the laws contribute to the transparency of governments. The proposed legislation in Zimbabwe and Belarus, for example, arguably constitute something closer to official secrets acts than to means of shifting governments closer to the transparency end of the continuum.

Even in countries with strong Freedom of Information laws, bureaucrats who want to withhold information find many ways to hold on to secrets. In the U.S. case, for example, implementation continues to fall far short of expectations. Part of the problem is sheer shortage of funding and personnel to respond to the 600,000 requests for information made under the law each year. FOIA offices within agencies are chronically under-funded and short-staffed, so it is unsurprising that most U.S. FOIA offices are backlogged—that is, they are not in compliance with the law's demand that FOIA requests receive a response within twenty days. Some agencies, like the CIA, the Federal Bureau of Investigation, and the Departments of Energy and State, take a year or two on average to respond. And often the responses themselves consist of heavily blanked-out documents. Even worse is compliance with the 1996 Electronic Freedom of Information Act, requiring government agencies to make computer databases, electronic documents, word processing documents, and even mail accessible to the public, to create "electronic reading rooms" that would contain substantial information, and to publish an annual report on their FOIA activities. Although many agencies have created the required web sites, many are hard to find and woefully incomplete, and compliance with requests for electronic information suffer all the problems seen with requests for paper documents.

The problems with implementation are partly normal bureaucratic matters, but they also reflect competing conceptions within the United States of what information should be freely available. The political parties have been feuding for decades over what constitutes compliance with the 1966 Freedom of Information Act. The feud takes particularly visible form in the competing memos issued by successive Attorneys General. Whenever a new administration of a different party from the preceding administration takes office, the Attorney General sends a memorandum to the heads of all federal departments and agencies laying out the standard the Department of Justice will use in deciding whether to defend agency decisions on FOIA matters when those decisions are challenged in court. The first was issued in May 1977 by Attorney General Griffin B. Bell when the Carter administration took office. The second was issued in May 1981 by the Reagan Administration's new Attorney General, William French Smith. None came from the first Bush Administration. Attorney General Janet Reno, who served under President Clinton, issued the third in October 1993, and the fourth came from Attorney General John Ashcroft on October 12, 2001.

A comparison of the two most recent memos illustrates how great the differences in implementation of transparency laws can be.

The Reno memo pushes agencies to

> ensure that the principle of openness in government is applied in each and every disclosure and nondisclosure decision that is required under the Act." It therefore "rescind[s] the Department of Justice's 1981 guidelines for the defense of agency action in Freedom of Information Act litigation. The Department will no longer defend an agency's withholding of information merely because there is a "substantial legal basis" for doing so. Rather, in determining whether or not to defend a nondisclosure decision, we will apply a presumption of disclosure.... In short, it shall be the policy of the U.S. Department of Justice to defend the assertion of a FOIA exemption only in those cases where the agency reasonably foresees that disclosure would be harmful to an interest protected by that exemption. Where an item of information might technically or arguably fall within an exemption, it ought not to be withheld from a FOIA requester unless it need be.[38]

The Ashcroft memo, after a quick genuflection in honor of governmental accountability, makes clear that it intends to strike rather a different balance than the previous administration. It says:

> The Department of Justice and this Administration are equally committed to protecting other fundamental values that are held by our society. Among them are safeguarding our national security, enhancing the effectiveness of our law enforcement agencies, protecting sensitive business information, and, not least, preserving personal privacy.... I encourage your agency to carefully consider the protection of all such values and interests when making disclosure determinations

> under the FOIA. Any discretionary decision by your agency to disclose information protected under the FOIA should be made only after full and deliberate consideration of the institutional, commercial, and personal privacy interests that could be implicated by disclosure of the information.... When you carefully consider FOIA requests and decide to withhold records, in whole or in part, you can be assured that the Department of Justice will defend your decisions unless they lack a sound legal basis...[39]

In other words, during the Clinton administration government agencies would have to demonstrate harm to justify withholding information requested under FOIA, or the Department of Justice would not defend them in court. During the second Bush administration, agency heads can rest easy if they have any legal justification for withholding information, and they receive no encouragement to release information.

The United States is not the only democracy where conflicting opinions on transparency are evident. Britain is in the midst of a major struggle over implementation of its new freedom of information law, enacted in November 2000. Prime Minister Tony Blair wanted to delay implementation until all 50,000 government bodies were prepared to adopt its provisions. Others in the government, including the lord chancellor Lord Irvine who is responsible for overseeing implementation, wanted to phase the law in gradually over three years. The prime minister won. As a result, the Act will not come into effect until January 2005, more than four years after parliament passed it.[40] And as we will see below, the September 11, 2001 attacks have led Canada to attempt to crack down on its Access to Information Act provisions.

International Organizations

As the world becomes increasingly tightly integrated, international organizations are becoming important actors in the transparency debate. They are particularly interesting actors, because they are on both sides simultaneously: demanding greater transparency from others but often resisting the application of transparency's principles to themselves.

For several years, the World Bank and especially the International Monetary Fund have pressed their member governments to make public information on a range of governmental economic and financial data. They argue that such transparency is necessary if countries are to attract foreign investment. Since 1996, the IMF has had a Special Data Dissemination Standard in place for countries that have or are seeking access to international capital markets.[41] (Countries not yet trying to integrate themselves into the global economy are expected to follow a less demanding General Data Dissemination Standard.) Scores of countries that subscribe to the Special Data Dissemination Standard list information on the Fund's Dissemination Standard Bulleting Board. The IMF has also adopted a Code of Good Practices on Fiscal Transparency and has released a Manual on Fiscal Transparency.

But the battle to open up governmental economic information is far from won. Particularly when it comes to national budgets, governmental officials face strong incentives to muddy the waters. After all, if citizens know exactly how much money is being spent on what, they might object to the choices being made and demand changes in the policies—or in the officials. Governments thus resort to all sorts of tricks that enable them to hide taxes, overemphasize the benefits of spending, and conceal government liabilities. They present highly optimistic projections of growth and tax revenues, and then express surprise at later deficits. They keep some items off-budget or postpone major changes to late years.[42]

In addition to their role as proponents of national transparency, international organizations are targets of calls for greater disclosure. No international organization has faced more vociferous demands to open up than the World Bank. Beginning in the early 1980s, a wide range of NGOs began pressuring the Bank to be more forthcoming about its plans and policies, arguing that "if development bank project planning and design were open and transparent...fewer disastrous projects would be approved and a greater opportunity to promote development alternatives would exist."[43] Three different transnational civil society networks—on poverty, environment, and structural adjustment—have coalesced around opposition to World Bank projects and procedures.[44]

The proponents of World Bank transparency are right. In the days when the Bank remained cloaked in secrecy, too often government officials in both borrowing and donor countries were less concerned with the quality of the projects being funded than with such considerations as the political imperatives of channeling funds to particular governments or the opportunities for personal enrichment or political power. Although at least some of the actors now demanding transparency from the Bank undoubtedly have their own agendas, if the Bank becomes truly transparent all agendas will have to be contested openly.

These pressures for transparency have had an impact, in part because the argument has resonated so effectively with U.S. policymakers. Members of Congress proved willing to hold funding for the Bank hostage to the establishment of new Bank disclosure policies.[45] Under the disclosure policy established over a decade ago, the Bank releases a project information document on every project. Also available are final staff appraisal reports, environmental impact statements, and other documents.

Since then, there has been much rhetoric from the Bank promoting a more participatory model of development. Bank President James Wolfensohn began emphasizing the importance of "inclusive decision-making" processes. Bank publications began stressing the importance of "empowerment" in reducing poverty. Because access to information is a necessary (though not sufficient) condition for such participatory development, expectations were high when the disclosure policy came up for revision in 2000. But the revision of the disclosure policy turned out to entail a considerable fight, one that usefully illustrates the ongoing political struggle over transparency throughout the world.

The Bank staff who drafted the revisions found themselves facing competing pressures. Although the Bank already releases enough information to allow for after-the-fact accountability, its disclosures do not enable citizens to participate in policy debates before decisions are made. On one side were civil-society groups from all parts of the world, along with the governments of a few wealthy countries, who called for much more disclosure of Bank documents. This side argued that information disclosure is essential to foster informed public debate and constructive engagement between society and government, a crucial if often missing piece of the development puzzle. Moreover, the pervasive fears of Bank and Fund interference with national sovereignty can only be assuaged if the public, including the legislature and other representative institutions, are informed about what decisions are actually being made and by whom. Disclosure of what the Bank is doing and what agreements it is signing with governments is necessary if the Bank is to deliver on promises to include new voices in the deliberative process.

On the other side were many governments, particularly from the larger developing countries. (Smaller countries have already essentially been forced by the world's wealthiest nations to disclose documents that richer developing countries are still permitted to keep secret.) They argued that it is up to them, not to the Bank, to determine what information ought to be released at what time and to whom. Information needs to be restricted to prevent market upheavals and to "protect the deliberative process." When pushed, off-the-record some said that what they most objected to was the possibility that their political opposition at home would use information from Bank documents in political fights against them—exactly what political oppositions are supposed to do in democracies.

In the end, anti-transparency forces largely won.

The Bank's revised disclosure policy makes only minor improvements, and most significantly does not release project appraisals or country assistance strategies before the Bank's Board takes action on them. In other words, the policy continues to permit only after-the-fact accountability, not informed participation during the planning and decision-making processes.

Even the existing disclosures often do not measure up to expectations. Whether meaningful transparency has been achieved—or can be achieved—at the World Bank remains unclear. As is virtually always the case, policies from above to promote transparency within an institution provide only a starting point. Whether project information documents actually contain information that make it possible for outsiders to comment meaningfully on projects in the early stages of planning will depend on the incentives World Bank staff face. If staffers are rewarded primarily for getting large projects through the pipeline quickly, they will have every incentive to make those documents as bland and meaningless as possible, in order to ward off objections to their projects. If, however, Bank staff are held accountable for the ultimate success of projects, they will have every incentive to permit widespread participation in the planning and preparation of projects in order to be able to anticipate problems and ensure that stakeholders in the borrowing countries support rather than oppose those projects. In short, the disclosure policy by itself means little. It can be just another bureaucratic hurdle, or it can be a useful and welcome tool.

Beyond this question of the utility of transparency as a means of helping the Bank do its job better lies the moral issue discussed above. The Bank is not an end in itself. It exists to provide certain services. It was constituted by national governments, but its avowed goal is to help the world's poor. In other words the Bank is an agent, but it answers to two quite different principals: those affected by the projects it helps to finance and the governments of its member states. Governments are in turn supposed to be agents for their citizens. When governments use Bank funds in ways that are not in the interests of their citizens and those citizens complain to the Bank about those uses, should the Bank withhold information from affected citizens on the grounds that only their governments—their supposed agents—are entitled to see that information?

The World Trade Organization is now undergoing a similar debate over what information it should make public. As the disciplines of the global-trading system have grown more effective, they have alarmed many people now demonstrating their concerns both on the streets and in repeated demands for greater transparency. Many governments, especially from developing countries, object strongly to calls for greater citizen participation, arguing that public input should take place only at the national level and that both negotiations and dispute settlement are properly handled exclusively by governments, who will decide for themselves what information to release to their citizens. In part, their objections stem from the North-South imbalance. Northern civil society groups, including trade associations, generally have the resources to engage the WTO. Many Southern governments fear that allowing greater civil-society participation will further turn the odds against them. It is understandable that these new WTO members are reluctant to dilute the benefits of their membership to this once-exclusive "club." But civil society demands have become so strong, effective, and globally connected that efforts to fend them off will only result in damage to the WTO as a whole. If the WTO wishes to recapture widespread public legitimacy, it needs to undertake a systematic effort to address the widespread public perception that the international trade regime is largely closed to public scrutiny and participation.

The WTO's relationship with the outside world has already begun to change. The increasing impact of trade rules on other policy areas has compelled the WTO to engage in regular interaction with a wider range of multilateral organizations, especially the United Nations Environment and Development Programs (UNEP and UNDP, respectively).

Growing public interest in its work has compelled the WTO to organize public meetings and consultations, as well as engage in a series of regional conferences and workshops designed to encourage interaction between the Secretariat and the public. The WTO Secretariat has also made significant progress toward document availability. Its 1996 derestriction policy, informal but regularized meetings with the public, and the Internet now enable more people around the world to review its material.

Nevertheless, citizens still lack access to information that would enable them to comment on policy as it is being considered or present their views in any meaningful way. Citizens must be empowered to participate in the formation of trade policy before decisions are made, not after. While public participation is seldom efficient, democratic governments must earn public support by engaging in a degree of open discussion, sharing information, and subjecting their decisions to public scrutiny. The WTO has yet to satisfy civil-society groups on these counts.

Other intergovernmental organizations have done better. Indeed, efforts to remain opaque are swimming against a powerful tide of greater citizen participation in global institutions. The United Nations and many of its agencies routinely involve NGOs in their deliberations, with standard procedures in place for accreditation. In intergovernmental treaty negotiations on many issues, non-governmental organizations have become constructive players with full access to information. They are routinely incorporated into negotiations on environmental issues, receiving country position-papers and draft treaties as a matter of course.

Saving the Environment Through Transparency

The issue area where transparency has as of yet contributed the most is environment. The story begins in the United States over fifteen years ago. In 1986, in response to the Bhopal catastrophe in India, the U.S. Congress enacted the Emergency Planning and Community Right-to-Know Act. This Act requires companies to disclose what amounts of a few hundred specified toxic chemicals they release into the air or the water or onto the land (above certain threshold levels). The companies must send the information to the U.S. Environmental Protection Agency (EPA), which uses it to compile a Toxics Release Inventory that is then made public. The act itself puts no limits on emissions of these toxic chemicals. It merely requires companies to own up publicly about what they are emitting. But that has proved sufficient to bring about an enormous change in behavior. Emissions of the indexed chemicals at facilities covered by the law fell 44 percent between 1988 and 1994, even though production of those chemicals rose 18 percent. No environmentalist would have dared dream of getting a 44 percent reduction mandated by the usual types of environmental regulations. It turns out that regulation by revelation can work much better than the more traditional regulation by governmental dictate.

The success of this new approach has drawn the most sincere form of flattery—imitation. Indonesia in recent years adopted a similar, but simpler, approach, publicly grading facilities by color according to how well they meet existing regulations. According to the World Bank, the program is significantly increasing compliance with environmental regulations. Its success, due to the pressure of both local public opinion and the business community's desire to market to environmentally sensitive foreign consumers, has spurred further imitation. In 1997, the Philippines announced the introduction of a public-information program called Ecowatch. Mexico's environmental agency recently announced that it will begin to publish information on the environmental performance of 3,000 industries to provide incentives for them to clean up their act.

Governments are not the only ones attempting to use information to improve the state of the environment. A major U.S. environmental group called

Environmental Defense has launched a website called "Scorecard" (www.scorecard.org) that makes TRI and other data accessible to anyone with an Internet connection. The site is very user-friendly. An American types in his or her postal code, and up pops a map that displays local schools, major roads, and TRI facilities. Included is information on the relative toxicity of specific compounds and rankings of which facilities pose the biggest health threats. The site has been the topic of stories in the national television news and national news magazines. And it is heavily used, with over 11 million hits in its first year of operation.

An Indian non-governmental organization, the Centre for Science and Environment (CSE), is also pursuing the transparency approach to environmental regulation, publishing ratings that compare companies within a given industry on their environmental performance. Since the Indian government does not require companies to provide public information about environmental records, the CSE decided to ask the companies directly. To induce companies to provide information, the CSE adopted a carrot and stick policy. The stick was that any company that failed to provide information would automatically be ranked at the bottom. The carrot was that if companies could prove they were trying to improve their environmental performance, their efforts would be reflected in the rankings.

With funding from the United Nations Development Programme (funneled through the Indian government), CSE set out to rank companies in the pulp-and-paper industry, a renowned polluter. Much to the surprise of CSE, by the time the ratings were released, every company in the industry had provided the requested information, apparently convinced that the harm to their reputations of refusing to comply—and thus being ranked last—outweighed any possible harm from complying with the survey. Although the rankings were released only this summer, CSE claims already to have had an impact, primarily by raising the profile of environmental concerns to the highest levels within the companies.

Responses to September 11, 2001

In short, while transparency is highly desirable, it is by no means inevitable. Many of the responses to the horrific events of September 11, 2001 provide powerful evidence of governmental ability and willingness to fight back against transparency. Although the national struggles described above are part of the long-term seesaw between opponents and proponents of transparency, particularly in the United States September 11 spurred substantial backsliding from previous progress toward greater transparency.

Most notable is the newly popular practice of "scrubbing" websites, i.e., removing information that someone believes might aid terrorists in planning attacks. Ironically, the Government Secrecy Project at the Federation of American Scientists, one of the leading NGO proponents of governmental transparency, removed information from its own web site, primarily concerning the location of secure intelligence facilities on the grounds that such information was not publicly available elsewhere.[46] Other scrubs raised more serious concerns about the appropriate balance between protecting legitimate secrets and ensuring that citizens have the information necessary to protect themselves.

The Environmental Protection Agency, for example, has removed a database with information on chemicals used at 15,000 industrial sites in the United States.[47] The database was the result of a Congressional requirement several years ago, after the Bhopal disaster in India, that companies submit information about potential toxic waste spills so that local emergency services and residents could make appropriate plans to deal with worst-case scenarios.[48] But now, the EPA apparently feels that the danger of providing terrorists with ready access to such information outweighs the public's right to know whether their children's day-care centers are located next to potentially dangerous chemical sites.

Other government agencies, including many at the state level, are pursuing a similar course of action. The Nuclear Regulatory Commission temporarily closed down its web site altogether, and when it reopened the web site restored only "select content." The Internal Revenue Service now prohibits unescorted public access to the reading rooms Congress required it to establish, ostensibly out of concern for employee safety. The state of Pennsylvania has removed some environmental information from its website, and the state of Florida is withholding public access to information on crop dusters.[49]

Since there are other easy ways for terrorists to locate significant targets, not least by looking in the phone book, it is at least debatable whether such removal of information actually serves the interests of the American public. The greatest danger is not that information about vulnerable facilities might be misused. The danger is that making it difficult for citizens to find out about vulnerable facilities makes it far less likely that the vulnerabilities will be corrected or that sensible precautionary planning to deal with potential attacks will take place.

The United States is not alone in its concerns over transparency in an age of terrorism. The Canadian government introduced legislation in October 2001 that would entitle the Minister of Justice to issue certificates suspending applications of Canada's Access to Information Act. Department of Justice officials claimed that terrorist groups had used the Act to try to obtain sensitive information, although they admitted that no sensitive information was actually released.[50] The Justice Minister argued that the change was necessary to maintain information-sharing agreements with Canada's allies.[51]

The Future of Transparency

The struggle to create a broad global culture of transparency still clearly has far to go. The cliché about information being power has much truth to it, and holders of such power are rarely willing to share it in the absence of compelling incentives. But the opponents of greater transparency are not merely the vested interests. Secrecy is a deep-rooted habit of thought in many circles. Overcoming all this will take long-term, consistent effort, with a healthy respect for the relatively narrow sets of circumstances in which secrecy is truly more appropriate.

Fortunately, the promoters of transparency have some powerful weapons on their side as well. First, the broad trend toward greater democracy brings with it a normative shift more accepting of transparency principles. When governments are seen as entities whose purpose it is to serve the public interest, governmental rights to keep secrets from the public face a higher standard of justification. Second, in issue areas from security to economics to environment, many parts of the world have enjoyed much success with transparency, providing powerful models of how disclosure can serve broad public interests.

To ensure that these positive trends continue will require concerted action on the part of many people. The broad trend toward appropriate national legislation needs to be strengthened. International organizations need to commit themselves to serious disclosure policies. The wide array of civil society groups and others working to promote transparency need to collaborate across issue areas and national and organizational boundaries. The various rationales for continued secrecy (and particularly the new justifications based on anti-terrorism efforts) need to be fully and publicly evaluated. The fight will not be easy, and it will probably never be fully won. But the progress made in recent decades provides good reason to believe that further progress is possible.

Notes

1. Richard Dean Burns and Donald Urquidi, *Disarmament in Perspective: An Analysis of Selected Arms Control and Disarmament Agreements Between the Two World Wars, 1919-1939* (California State College at Los Angeles Foundation, 1968), vol. 1, p. 44.

2. *Ibid.*

3. Treaty of Versailles, in Charles I. Bevans, compiler *Treaties and Other International Agreements of the United States of America, 1776-1949* (Washington, DC: United States Government Printing Office, 1969), vol. II, pp. 130-131.

4. Burns and Urquidi 1968, vol. I, p. 179; Neal H. Peterson, "The Versailles Treaty: Imposed Disarmament," in Richard Dean Burns, ed., *Encyclopedia of Arms Control and Disarmament* (New York: Charles Scribner's Sons, 1993), p. 630.

5. Richard Dean Burns, "International Arms Inspection Policies Between World Wars, 1919-1934," *The Historian: A Journal of History,* vol. 31, no. 4 (August 1969), pp. 589-600.

6. Richard Dean Burns, "Origins of the United States' Inspection Policy, 1926-1946," *Disarmament and Arms Control,* Spring 1964, p. 163.

7. Davis 1993, pp. I-A-26, I-A-27.

8. Walter La Feber, *America, Russia, and the Cold War: 1945-1971* (New York: John Wiley and Sons, second edition, 1972), p. 34; "The Baruch Plan: Statement by the United States Representative (Baruch) to the United Nations Atomic Energy Commission, June 14, 1946," in United States Department of State, *Documents on Disarmament 1945-1959,* vol. 1, (Washington, DC: United States Government Printing Office, 1960), p. 11.

9. "Statement by President Eisenhower at the Geneva Conference of Heads of Government: Aerial Inspection and Exchange of Military Blueprints, July 21, 1955," in *Documents on Disarmament 1945-1959,* 1, pp. 486-487.

10. John Lewis Gaddis, "The Evolution of a Reconnaissance Satellite Regime," in Alexander L. George, Philip J. Farley, and Alexander Dallin, eds., *U.S.-Soviet Security Cooperation: Achievement, Failures, Lessons* (New York: Oxford University Press, 1987), pp. 353-372.

11. "Treaty Banning Nuclear Weapons Tests in the Atmosphere, in Outer Space, and Under Water, August 5, 1963" in *Documents on Disarmament 1963,* pp. 291-293.

12. Article XII of the Treaty Between the United States of America and the Union of Soviet Socialist Republics on the Limitation of Anti-Ballistic Missile Systems, 26 May 1972; Article V of the Interim Agreement Between the United States of America and the Union of Soviet Socialist Republics on Certain Measures with Respect to the Limitations of Strategic Offensive Arms, reprinted in Roger P. Labrie, ed., *SALT Hand Book: Key Documents and Issues 1972-1979,* (Washington, DC: American Enterprise Institute, 1979) pp. 18, 21.

13. "SALT II, Protocol to the Treaty Between the United States of America and the Union of Soviet Socialist Republics on the Limitation of Underground Nuclear Weapons Tests, July 3, 1979," in *Documents on Disarmament 1974,* pp. 228-9.

14. Treaty Between the United States of America and the Union of Soviet Socialist Republics on Underground Nuclear Explosions for Peaceful Purposes, May 28, 1976, in *Documents on Disarmament 1976,* pp. 328-332.

15. Treaty on the Non-Proliferation of Nuclear Weapons, in *Documents on Disarmament 1968,* pp. 461-465.

16. Document on Confidence-Building Measures and Certain Aspects of Security and Disarmament, Conference on Security and Cooperation in Europe, Final Act, 1975; John J. Maresca, *To Helsinki: The Conference on Security and Cooperation in Europe, 1973-1975* (Duke University Press, 1985).

17. Document of the Stockholm Conference on Confidence and Security-Building Measures and Disarmament in Europe, convened in accordance with the relevant provisions of the concluding Document of the Madrid meeting of the Conference on Security and Cooperation in Europe, paragraph 65.

18. "Treaty Between the United States of America and the Union of Soviet Socialist Republics on the Elimination of the Intermediate-Range and Shorter-Range Missiles," in Stockholm International Peace Research Institute, *SIPRI Yearbook 1988: World Armaments and Disarmament* (Oxford: Oxford University Press, 1988), pp. 395-485; Treaty on Conventional Armed Forces in Europe; *Vienna Document 1990* of the Vienna Negotiations on Confidence- and Security-Building Measures Convened in Accordance with the Relevant Provisions of the Concluding Document of the Vienna Meeting of the Conference on Security and Co-Operation in Europe, Official Text (Washington, DC: United States Arms Control and Disarmament Agency, 1990); "Treaty Between the United States of America and the Union of Soviet Socialist Republics on the Reduction and Limitation of

Strategic Offensive Arms," *Arms Control and Disarmament Agreements* (Washington, DC: United States Arms Control and Disarmament Agency, 1991.

19. Security Council Resolution 687 (1991), "Iraq-Kuwait," section C.

20. See, e.g., Tim Trevan, "UNSCOM Faces Entirely New Verification Challenges in Iraq," *Arms Control Today* vol. 23, no. 3 (April 1993), p. 11.

21. "CWC Implementation Factoids," Chemical and Biological Weapons Nonproliferation Project, Stimson Center, www.stimson.org/cwc/factoids.htm.

22. *Ibid.*

23. http://wwv.armscontrol.org/ACT/aprmay99/jgam99.htm.

24. Michael Moodie, "Transparency in Armaments: A New Item for the New Security Agenda,": *Washington Quarterly,* vol. 15, no. 3 (Summer 1992).

25. "Developing Arms Transparency," 1997, www.acronym.org.uk/35armreg.htm.

26. www.acronym.org.uk/35armreg.htm.

27. http://www.stimson.org/cbm/la/lachron.htm

28. Organization of American States, "Convention on Transparency in Weapons Acquisitions Adopted," Press release, www.oas.org/juridico/english/releases/htm.

29. The Britain Joint Stock Companies Act became law in 1844, requiring joint stock companies to keep books of account; to present a 'full and fair' balance sheet at each meeting of shareholders; to file a balance sheet with the Registrar of Companies; and to appoint auditors who were entitled to examine the books and question officers of the company. The Companies Act of 1856, however, erased the 1844 act, and companies remained nearly completely free in accounting matters until the twentieth century. Since 1900, Britain has gradually increased the regulation of financial statements and audits through various Companies Acts. The 1900 Companies Act, for example, once again made annual audits compulsory for joint stock companies. The 1948 Companies Act required the disclosure of a profit and loss account. T.A. Lee and R.H. Parker, eds., *The Evolution of Corporate Financial Reporting.* Garland Publishing, Inc.: NY, 1984, p. 194. The reason for the shift in favor of transparency was a growing recognition that a stock market could not function efficiently over time without it. As the British Government's Greene Committee noted in 1926 "Small shareholders are becoming more numerous and more intelligent; investors and their advisors are increasingly guided by precise information rather than by private tips or market rumor; public policy and economic necessity are gradually changing our conceptions of how much the shareholders and the public ought to know." Quoted in Nissim Aranya, "The Influence of Pressure Groups on Financial Statements in Britain," in Lee and Parker, p. 268.

30. David F. Hawkins, "The Development of Modern Financial Reporting Practices among American Manufacturing Corporations," in J.R. Edwards, ed., *Studies of Company Records, 1830-1974,* Garland Publishing, Inc., NY, pp. 261-294.

31. John Carey, "The Origins of Modern Financial Reporting," in Lee and Parker, pp. 241-264.

32. George Cochrane, "The Auditor's Report," in Lee and Parker, p. 176.

33. George J. Benston, "Public (U.S.) Compared to Private (U.K.) Regulation of Corporate Financial Disclosure," in Gary John Previts, ed., *The Development of SEC Accounting.* Reading, MA: Addison-Wesley Publishing Company, 1981, pp. 275-290. The essential difference between British and American practices of corporate disclosure remains today that Great Britain has no regulatory agency like the SEC. Instead, the British Companies Acts stand on their own because the nature of the disclosure required is described specifically in the Acts. The British Department of Trade has the power to investigate failures to conform to the requirements of the Acts, but mainly it serves as a repository for the statements filed and it is rather private regulatory agencies, such as the London Stock Exchange and associations of investment bankers, that investigate disclosures. Unlike the SEC, however, these private British groups have no power to add regulations to the law. As a result, the United States system of financial disclosure regulations and monitoring is more extensive and costly than the British one.

34. http://web.missouri.edu/~foiwww/intlfoi.html.

35. For examples of FOIAs in the 1990s, on the Irish law, see http://indigo.ie/~pwatch/foi.htm. On the Japanese law, see Jon Choy, "New Law Provides Ax to Fell Bureaucracy's Bamboo Veil," *JEI Report,* no. 20, vol.

1999, May 21, 1999; Sonni Efron, "Right-to-know Law Changing Shape of Japan," *Los Angeles Times*, May 11, 1999, p. A1.

36. *Report of the Commission on Protecting and Reducing Government Secrecy*, Pursuant to Public Law 236, 103rd Congress (Washington, DC: Government Printing Office, 1997).

37. On the United Kingdom's debate, see, for example, the Freedom of Information Bill, available at http://www.publications.parliament.uk/pa/cm199900/cmbills/005/2000005.htm; the Freedom of Information Consultation on Draft Documents, available at http://www.homeoffice.gov.uk/foi/dfoibill.htm; and the House of Commons Committee on Public Administration report on the government white-paper on freedom of information, July 1998, available at http://www.parliament.the-stationery-office.co.uk/pa/cm199798/cmselect/cmpubadm/398-vol1/39802.htm. On the Indian debate, see Vikram Khub Chand, "Legislating Freedom of Information: India in Comparative Perspective," Paper prepared for the Right to Information Workshop hosted by the Commonwealth Human Rights Initiative at Dhaka, Bangladesh, July 5-7, 1999.

38. www.id.doe.gov/doeid/foia/memo.htm.

39. www.usdoj.gov/oip/foiapost/2001foiapost19.htm.

40. David Hencke and Rob Evans, *The Guardian*, October 30, 2001.

41. International Monetary Fund, "IMF Launches the Dissemination Standards Bulletin Board on the Internet," Press Release 96/47, 1996.

42. Alberto Alesina and Robert Perotti, *Budget Deficits and Budget Institutions* (Washington, DC: International Monetary Fund, 1996).

43. Lori Udall, "The World Bank and Public Accountability: Has Anything Changed?" In Jonathan A. Fox and L. D. Brown, eds., *The Struggle for Accountability: The World Bank, NGOs, and Grassroots Movements* (Cambridge, MA: MIT Press, 1998), p. 391.

44. Paul Nelson, "Internationalizing Economic and Environmental Policy: Transnational NGO Networks and the World Bank's Expanding influence," *Millennium: Journal of International Studies* 25 (3): 605-33, 1996.

45. Udall op. cit.

46. Lou Dolinar, "Access Denied," *Newsday.com*, October 24, 2001.

47. Robin Toner, "A Nation Challenged," *New York Times*, October 27, 2001

48. The Risk Management Plan information was collected under Section 112 of the Clean Air Act. See "The Post-September 11 Environment: Access to Government Information," www.ombwatch.org/info/2001/access.html; Dolinar op cit.

49. See OMBWatch, "The Post-September 11 Environment."

50. "Open Government Canada Calls proposed Bill C-36 Amendments 'Inadequate,' Press Release, Toronto, November 20, 2001, www.opengovernmentcanada.org.

51. Ian Jack, "Drop Plan to Let Minister Shield Data, MPs Advise," *National Post Online*, November 1, 2001. www.national.post.com/news/national/politics/story.html?f=/stories/20011101/765132.html

International Human Rights as Instruments for Justice and Peace

Eleanor Roosevelt
First Chair, United Nations Human Rights Commission

The Wisdom of Eleanor Roosevelt

One of the most important things for our young people to learn is the difficult art of being at home in the world. Ahead of them lies the gigantic, but infinitely rewarding, task of learning to know and understand other peoples, and the equally difficult task of helping other peoples to know and understand them.... The greatest and most inspiring adventure of all time probably will be carried out in the next fifty years, the adventure of building a new world. As our young people come to have a closer and deeper understanding of that world and its peoples, they will learn that there is not one civilization, from the oldest to the very newest, from which we cannot learn.

The Universal Declaration of Human Rights: Rights, Peace, and...Words[1]

I will take the first three Articles [of the Universal Declaration of Human Rights] and tell you a little about them. In [our] Committee [on Political and Civil Rights] there [were] quite a number of women who sit as delegates. I imagine that you know that that is a good committee on which to put women! In the first place, they are naturally interested in humanitarian questions, but in addition, I think some of the members of our delegations believe, we might not do so well if we were put in the political committees or legal committees....

Right away they saw something in our document that we brought to them which we had not given much thought to. As we presented the document, it was perhaps a little too Anglo-Saxon, a little too much like the American Declaration. It said "all men" in the beginning of a great many paragraphs; the final Article reads, "All human beings are born free and equal in dignity and rights. They are endowed with reason and conscience and should act towards one another in a spirit of brotherhood."

After I got home I received a letter from a gentleman who said, "How could you as the United States Delegate vote for Article I of the Universal Declaration when it is not like our Declaration?"

* * *

Perhaps one of the things that some of us learned was that in an international document you must try to find words that can be accepted by the greatest number of people. Not the words you would choose as the perfect words, but the words that most people can say and that will accomplish the

Eleanor Roosevelt, "International Human Rights as Instruments for Justice and Peace." Originally titled "Reflections of a Peace Worker: International Human Rights as Instruments for Justice and Peace," 1938. From http://newdeal.feri.org/er/er35.htm, December 20, 2001 ends you desire, and will be acceptable to practically everyone sitting round the table, no matter what their background, no matter what their beliefs may be. So that's what happened to us....

There is one other word that I want to tell you about because it cost us a great deal of time, and it illustrates one of the difficulties of writing a document of this kind. It is in Article II which reads:

> Everyone is entitled to all the rights and freedoms set forth in this Declaration, without distinction of any kind, such as race, colour, sex, language, religion, political or other opinion, national or social origin, property, birth or other status.
>
> Furthermore, no distinction shall be made on the basis of the political, jurisdictional or international status of the country or territory to which a person belongs, whether it be independent, trust, non self-governing, or under any other limitation of sovereignty.

Now, the word we had so much difficulty about was the word "birth" in the first paragraph. Our Russian colleague was making a speech, stating something he wished to have included in the Article, but he and the translator had a different opinion as to the way his idea was translated, and he stopped and said "That translation is wrong. It does not say what I mean." So he was finally asked if he would explain what he wanted to express. And he said that he wanted to say in French the word "etat"; in English the word "estate".... I said: "Well, I don't think the word 'estate' would mean a great deal to people in the English-speaking countries."

So, our Russian colleague said he would accept the word "class," and that I didn't like very much. I said: "I think in many countries we're getting away from the use of that word, and it would be a mistake to write it in a universal document." So, finally, after long discussion we settled on the word "birth" as a translation that our Russian colleague would accept and I thought that was all settled. But then our China colleague, who, perhaps, is more interested in the English language even than we who call it our mother tongue, Dr. P.C. Chang of China, decided that since we were going to put the word "birth" it should come after the word "race" and should read: "without distinction of any kind such as race, birth, colour, sex," etc.

Our Russian colleague would have none of it; that was not the right place. We argued for a long while, and finally it was put after "property." Then for a reason that I have never been able to understand, our Russian colleague sat back apparently feeling that he had gained a complete victory—that it now meant something that it had not meant before, and was perfectly satisfied and voted for that Article. Of course, in the end he abstained on the whole Declaration.

Conceptions of Freedom

The interesting thing is that...many of the peoples...don't know the meaning of freedom as we know it. In Japan, for instance, freedom only means license. There was no character in the Japanese language which meant freedom as we understand it, so that when we tried to explain what freedom meant, they had to evolve a new character, because when they speak of a child who acted with complete irresponsibility and complete license, they said he was acting with freedom....

[W]hen you argue with [the USSR representative] Mr. Vishinsky, he will say there is no such thing as absolute freedom, and of course you and I know that is true. All freedom is conditioned by the freedom of other people, but nevertheless there is for human beings something very precious, which we know as freedom, the freedom to help govern ourselves, the freedom to help develop the future. These are very important things for us, more important perhaps than the actual assurance by the state of certain economic and social rights.

Now I am going to read you just one Article, because it will explain to you why it was impossible for the U.S.S.R. to vote in favor of this document, and it will show you the cleavage in thought which somehow, some day, we have to bridge. We are not going to bridge it right away. It is going to take time, but the understanding of it is necessary before we can begin to decide how we can work. The Article is one of freedom of movement. It reads:

> Everyone has the right to freedom of movement and residence within the borders of each State. Everyone has the right to leave any country, including his own, and return to his country.

The amendment they wanted to that was:

> Everyone has the right to leave any country, including his own, and to return to his country according to the laws of his country.

That would have meant that the law said you couldn't leave your country without permission of the government.

Naturally, in discussion it was brought out that many countries have regulations. I have to pay my income tax; I have to take the little piece of paper from my doctor saying when I was vaccinated. I must have been vaccinated within the last three years or I can't come back. But when that is done, I can leave and come back, and I can move anywhere within my own country and can do it when I wish, and I can settle where I wish.

After defeat of the amendment, I went over to talk to Mr. Pavlov, and I said: "Mr. Pavlov," (I should say that he speaks French very well) "do you see no difference between the regulations which my country puts on freedom of movement, and the regulations of the U.S.S.R. which forbid a citizen to leave without permission from his government, and to give no permission?" He looked at me and he said: "All regulations are the same." Now that is a very interesting thing because that is a good illustration of where we think differently....

I have thought a great deal, of course, about our first and most important difficulty, which is the U.S.S.R. I suppose you read what their delegates say to us. They say: "Perhaps in the military and economic sense you have the upper hand." (They never say, "We have..." they say "perhaps.") "But time is on our side. We can afford to wait, because our ideas are much stronger than yours; our ideas, our belief in communism, are going to gain the world. It makes a great appeal because we believe in basic human rights. We believe that all races, all people are equal; we believe that men and women are equal."

The International Covenant on Human Rights: Systematic Denial of Basic Human Rights Lie at the Root of Our Troubles[2]

Three years ago, when the General Assembly met in Paris, the chairman of the United States delegation, Secretary Marshall, said that the "systematic and deliberate denials of basic human rights lie at the root of most of our troubles and threaten the work of the United Nations...." In this Assembly, Secretary Acheson made clear that these words are even more pertinent today than they were in 1948.

It is a tragic commentary on the status of civilization in the middle of the twentieth century that the systematic and deliberate denials of human rights by some governments are so widespread in certain areas of the world that they are almost taken for granted. The kind of callous brutality which would have shocked the conscience of mankind a century ago is now unfortunately a commonplace occurrence in those areas.

All members of the United Nations have a responsibility, individually and collectively, to see that the lights of freedom are not further extinguished throughout the world.

Every member has a responsibility to see that the rights of men are safeguarded, for no country is perfect in protecting the individual rights of its citizens.

Three years ago...the General Assembly proclaimed the Universal Declaration of Human Rights. That Declaration has already become the yardstick by which all can measure the conduct of governments. The language of that Declaration has been written into the constitution of a number of states. The United Nations must now move ahead to develop new methods for advancing human liberty and for translating human rights and fundamental freedoms into action. One of these methods is the Draft International Covenant on Human Rights.

The task of drafting the Covenant, of putting human rights into treaty form, is not an easy one. We have been working in the United Nations on this draft Covenant since 1947.

I would like in particular to discuss the matter of economic, social, and cultural rights.

When the General Assembly last year called on the Commission on Human Rights to include economic, social, and cultural provisions in the Covenant on Human Rights, the United States fully cooperated in the 5-weeks' session of the Commission this spring in Geneva in drafting these provisions. The United States delegation voted last year in the General Assembly against the inclusion of economic, social, and cultural rights in the same Covenant with civil and political rights. At no time, however, did my delegation to the Commission on Human Rights question the responsibility of the Commission to prepare a draft with these provisions for the consideration of the General Assembly. The United States delegation to the Commission felt that, as a member of a technical commission, we should cooperate in doing that which the General Assembly had asked us to do at that time.

We did vote at the end of the Commission session for a resolution introduced by the delegate of India requesting a reconsideration by the General Assembly of the question of including economic, social, and cultural rights in the same Covenant with civil and political rights. This resolution did not, however, interrupt the technical work of the Commission. This Indian resolution pointed out that economic, social, and cultural rights, though equally fundamental and therefore important, formed a separate category of rights from that of the civil and political rights in that they were not justifiable rights and their method of implementation was different.

At this session of the General Assembly we have before us a resolution of the Economic and Social Council inviting the General Assembly to reconsider its decision of last year. It is entirely appropriate for us in the General Assembly this year to reconsider this matter. In view of the importance of the Covenant on Human Rights, we must be willing to study and restudy the basic problems involved in the drafting of this document. There may be differences of opinion in this Committee on the question of whether there should be one covenant or two covenants, but at no time should anyone argue that this Committee should avoid a further consideration of this very important question.

Principal Provisions of the ECOSOC Resolution

The resolution of the Economic and Social Council points out that there are certain differences between the provisions on civil and political rights and the provisions on economic, social, and cultural rights and that these differences warrant a consideration of two covenants rather than a single covenant. The Council resolution also refers to the difficulties which may flow from embodying in one covenant two different kinds of rights and obligations.

Let us examine these differences which have been recognized by the Commission in a number of ways in drafting the provisions of the Covenant.

In the first place, article 19 of the draft Covenant recognizes that the economic, social, and cultural provisions are objectives to be achieved "progressively." This obligation is to be distinguished from the obligation applicable to the civil and political rights in the Covenant. In the case of civil and political rights, states ratifying the Covenant will be under an obligation to take necessary steps fairly quickly to give effect to these rights. A much longer period of time is clearly contemplated under the Covenant for the achievement of the economic, social, and cultural provisions. This is obvious and is, of course, to be expected....

A second difference between the civil and political provisions and the economic, social, and cultural provisions is the manner in which the obligation is expected to be performed. In the case of the civil and political rights, they can in general be achieved by the enactment of appropriate legislation, enforced under effective administrative machinery. On the other hand, it is recognized that economic, social, and cultural progress and development cannot be achieved simply by the enactment of legislation and its enforcement. Private as well as public action is necessary. The Commission on Human Rights repeatedly rejected the proposal by two members of the Commission to limit the achievement of economic, social, and cultural rights solely through state action. The Commission fully recognized the importance of private as well as governmental action for the achievement of these rights.

A third difference between the civil and political provisions and the economic, social, and cultural provisions relates to the difference in the implementation contemplated. Initially the Commission on Human Rights drafted provisions for the establishment of a Human Rights Committee to which complaints by one state against another state may be filed. The Commission did not then have time at its session this spring to decide whether this machinery should also be applicable to the economic, social, and cultural provisions, but there actually was general sentiment in the Commission that this complaint machinery should be limited to the civil and political provisions of the Covenant. It was felt by those with whom I discussed this matter in the Commission that this machinery is not appropriate for the economic, social, and cultural provisions of the Covenant, since these rights are to be achieved progressively and since the obligations of states with respect to these rights were not as precise as those with respect to the civil and political rights. These members of the Commission thought that it would be preferable, with respect to the economic, social, and cultural rights, to stress the importance of assisting states to achieve economic, social, and cultural progress rather than to stress the filing of complaints against states in this field....

A fourth difference between the civil and political rights and the economic, social, and cultural rights relates to the drafting of these rights. The economic, social, and cultural provisions were necessarily drafted in broad language as contrasted to the civil and political provisions. For example, article 22 simply provides that "The States Parties to the Covenant recognize the right of everyone to social security." It was thought in the Commission that since economic, social, and cultural provisions were being stated in terms of broad objectives, general language would be adequate.

It seems...that these four basic differences between the civil and political rights and the economic, social, and cultural rights warrant the separation of the present provisions of the Covenant into two covenants, one covenant on civil and political rights and another covenant on economic, social, and cultural rights. By a separation of these rights into two separate covenants we would avoid a great deal of confusion that is naturally inherent in a combination of all these different provisions in one covenant.

Equality of Importance in the Two Groups of Rights

Of course, I realize that some members of this Committee argue for a single covenant to include all the provisions now before us. The principal argument urged by those pressing this view is that there should be no differentiations in importance between civil and political rights and economic, social, and cultural rights. In the proposal that I wish to make to the Committee there is no question raised with respect to the importance of one group of rights as against another group of rights. I consider each group of rights of equal importance. My proposal would maintain this equality of importance.

My delegation proposes that two covenants of equal importance be completed in the United

Nations simultaneously and be opened for signature and ratification at the same time. Neither one nor the other covenant would be called the first or the second covenant. Each of the two covenants would be on human rights, one setting forth the civil and political rights, and the other setting forth the economic, social, and cultural rights....

I Was Denied a Visa to Red China[3]

Winchester, Va.—One of [the] newspapers (the *New York Post*) has asked me if I would be willing to go to Communist China and try to interview some of the people in the government there. I had long wanted to go to China, just as my husband always wanted to go there.

Hoping that the State Department was ready to relax its rules and allow for communication between our countries through the press, I made application for a visa and was told that, as yet, no newsman was permitted by our government to visit Communist China.

I still hope that the State Department may find it possible to allow all correspondents who wish to gather news from this area of the world to go there if the Chinese will allow them to enter....

All of my life, it seems to me, I have been interested in China—even before I knew of my husband's interest in it. My Grandmother Hall had cherished some beautiful old blue and white china that came from her ancestors who either had bought it from Chinese traders or themselves had gone to China.

Neither my husband nor I ever traveled to China, however, and the possibility became more remote as the situation there grew more and more serious.

I have been saddened by the final results brought about by what undoubtedly was a bad government. Reforms which should have been made never seemed possible, and finally Communism became the answer.

The establishment of this new regime seems to have cost 800,000 lives, according to the admission of the present government. This does not seem to be a happy way to inaugurate reform....

Above all else, the peoples of the world desire to live without war. We must feel secure from attack, but in the long run just building up military strength is not the way to find out how to live together in the new world we face.

"Tomorrow Is Now," 1963

While it is essential for us to cope at once with the social revolution in this country we must, at the same time, learn to adjust to the social revolutions in other parts of the world. This is not only a matter of common decency, it is a matter of common sense.... We can no longer oversimplify. We can no longer build lazy and false stereotypes: Americans are like this, Russians are like that, a Jew behaves in such a way, a Negro thinks in a different way. The lazy generalities—'You know how women are.... Isn't that just like a man?' The world cannot be understood from a single point of view.... This is the inevitable growth in our thinking as a nation—the practical application of democratic principles. No one today would dare refer to the mass of people, as Alexander Hamilton once did, as 'that great beast.' And that, perhaps, is a minor victory in the long battle for human rights.

Notes

1. Originally published in Phi Delta Kappan 31 (September 1949): 23–33. Speech to the Second National Conference on UNESCO, Cleveland, Ohio, April 1, 1949.

2. Originally published in Department of State Bulletin, December 31, 1951, pp. 1059, 1064–1066.

3. My Day, June 25, 1957

Human Rights Confront Globalization

Adamantia Pollis
New School University

The eighteenth and nineteenth century liberal political philosophers, in the context of the industrial revolution, conceived of man as autonomous and possessed of innate, inalienable individual rights. But it was not until the aftermath of World War II with the adoption by the General Assembly of the U.N. of the Universal Declaration of Human Rights in December, 1948, that human rights entered the international agenda. The subsequent decades, however, were characterized by competing paradigms as to the essence of human rights both at the political level and in scholarship. Intellectual thought in any historical period is the outcome of a dialectical relationship with social reality. At times it is explanatory, or justificatory, and at times critical. Often, reflective of ideological and geo-political considerations, human-rights scholars have articulated contradictory theories of rights which have competed for hegemony.

The most intense debate among human-rights scholars in recent decades has been the dichotomy between universalists and cultural relativists. Just as development or modernization theories presumed a "transition" from traditional to industrial society, it was (and is) frequently assumed by universalists that non-Western cultures will gradually evolve so that the universalist doctrine of human rights will prevail. Such a deterministic approach to universality was bound to fail as it has in development theory. Cultural relativists in turn are frequently equally deterministic, assuming the fixity and unchangeability of communally based traditional culture.

Another dichotomy, that between the primacy of civil/political over economic/social rights, is no longer as salient as it was during the decades of the Cold War. While the preeminence of individual civil- and political-rights remain foremost in the Western political agenda, overall, human-rights scholars have come to recognize the interdependence of these two sets of rights. A more recent dichotomy is that between individual versus minority or communal rights. Largely ignored in the immediate post-World War II decades,[1] which emphasized individual rights, it has emerged as a controversial issue in liberal thought but more acutely in the discourse on ethnicity and nationalism and its political ramifications.

Equally vexing are the relatively new, so-called third-generation rights; issues of self-determination and environmental rights. Both are collective rights and can not be realized through action by individual states. Environmental rights, despite the Kyoto accords, are neither protected by international law nor do global implementation mechanisms exist, yet they have a profound impact on the daily lives of peoples throughout the globe. The right to self-determination was initially conceived of by the United Nations as providing legitimacy for the independence of colonial territories. In its present usage it has provoked major debates particularly with regard to what constitutes "a people" entitled to secceed from an established state. Furthermore, the rights of indigenous peoples do not neatly fit into any category, but analytically they are closest to the right of self-determination. More recently a new socio-economic issue with profound implications for human rights has come to the fore. As economic globalization spreads and intensifies it impacts the entire complex of human rights transcending the dichotomies that have characterized human-rights scholarship.

Historical Background

Before embarking on an analysis of the impact of globalization on human rights it is instructive to review the evolution of human-rights scholarship in the context of the post-World War II world-order. Advocates of the doctrine of universal human-rights, contend that certain rights inhere in all individuals regardless of cultural context. Grounded in liberal political philosophy, universalism presupposes the individual as the basic social unit, whose inalienable individual rights are civil and political, inclusive of the right to private property. Until the extension of the franchise in the course of the nineteenth century in England, only white men with property were viewed as possessing reason and hence entitled to rights. Despite efforts by feminists in the aftermath of the French revolution to argue for equal rights,[2] women and non-white males were not possessors of these fundamental individual rights: they were perceived as lacking reason. Only gradually, and through partially successful social struggles for inclusion, have individual rights been extended to women and peoples of color. Recently, the demand for homosexual rights has come to the fore as a further extension of persons entitled to individual rights.

The historical epoch during the eighteenth century in which the liberal doctrine of human rights emerged was a time of massive socioeconomic change in western Europe precipitated by the rise of capitalism. Mercantilism, an early stage of globalization, which served the interests of kings by extracting wealth and precious metals from the world to fill their coffers and build their military, was overthrown, as technology progressed, by domestic manufacturing and the industrial revolution. A new patriarchal industrial class, taking advantage of scientific/technological advances, was anxious to remove the fetters on competition and private property imposed by the monarchical state. Individual civil-and political-rights became instrumental in its drive for political power. Classical economists and liberal political philosophers provided the intellectual rationale for the emerging new capitalist social order thereby endowing it with legitimacy. The social contract theories of modern liberal political philosophers, such as John Locke, set the political framework for the emergence of representative government and later for democracy. Classical economists, such as Adam Smith and David Ricardo, provided the additional rationale of the "invisible" hand of the market, and hence capitalism.

Over the centuries, in particular since the end of World War II, when human rights became part of the international political agenda, this universalist doctrine of human rights became increasingly disconnected from its earlier cultural and socioeconomic moorings.

Theorists such as Maurice Cranston[3] most forcefully, but also Ronald Dworkin,[4] and John Rawls[5] assert that individual civil and political rights are fundamental; they are entitlements for all. But they have been conceptualized as abstract legal rights thereby ascribing a meaning to equality devoid of consideration of the necessary preconditions for their accessibility, either institutionally or in terms of the socioeconomic requisites for their realization. Economic and social rights were dismissed during the Cold War era by Western scholars and political leaders as Soviet rhetoric. Community, the crux of the cultural relativists' model, was nowhere to be found in the universalist human-rights paradigm. In fact, communalism is often seen as oppressive and a denial of the true nature of man. In summary, it can be argued that the universalists have decontextualized civil- and political-rights which are left swirling in their own sphere, as the theorists debate the niceties of their reasoning, which are often cloaked in moral imperatives.

Cultural relativists by contrast, contend that fundamental values are culturally specific and that the communal group, whatever that might be—tribe, village or kinship—is the basic social unit.[6] A person's identity is prescriptive, dependent on membership within the group and his/her status and role in this community. The language of rights—a modern Western construct—is largely non-existent. Interpersonal relations are governed by a mutuality of unequal rights and obligations, which are diverse, as are their underlying values and behavioral expectations. However, what is common is that notions, such as the autonomous individual, individualism, freedom of choice or legal equality are alien, often meaningless concepts. The person is subsumed within the communal group whose well-being and welfare has primacy, albeit the particulars of what constitutes the community good varies. Building on Clifford Geertz's[7] pioneering studies of what he labelled primordial cultures, western theorists formulated the doctrine of cultural relativism as a powerful challenge to universalism.[8] It is noteworthy that it was Westerners who articulated this doctrine and in so doing they employed a Western cognitive framework; both a Western ontology and a Western epistemology. Inevitably, non-translatable concepts have been ignored even though they may convey significant concepts, values and behavioral expectations.[9] Furthermore, some cultural relativists reify "traditional" cultures and ascribe a static quality to them neglecting the dynamic of social change through historical time.

The cultural relativist argument, while initially espoused by anthropologists, has permeated all the social sciences. It should be noted that some Muslim states, such as Saudi Arabia, repudiated the UDHR by abstaining, claiming that Islamic theology embodied human rights. Unfortunately however this doctrine has been exploited in recent years, most forcefully by east Asian states, to justify their repressive regimes.[10] Under the rubric of "Asian values" Singapore, China and Malaysia, among others, have argued that they have a distinctive historical and cultural legacy and as a consequence their values diverge from western notions of democracy and human rights.[11] Efforts to "impose" Western values or to claim their moral superiority are denounced as cultural imperialism and a sign of disrespect for their civilizations and heritage. Ignored in this argument is the empirical reality that non-Western countries, whether through colonialism or their own reconstitution, have adopted the Western social organization of the nation-state and the ubiquitous goal of modernization and economic development. Neither the Asian elites, nor most scholars, take into account or analyze the impact of these transformations on "traditional" cultural values. This is not to argue that values and notions of human rights are in fact universal, it is to argue that contemporary Asian, African and Middle Eastern societies and cultures must be probed in greater depth to ascertain the reconstructed cultural configurations that have emerged as a result of social change.[12]

In recent years the dichotomy between universalists and cultural relativists has been challenged. Universalists have come to recognize that cultural diversity is a reality.[13] Despite this, the presumption of the moral superiority of the Western human-rights doctrine persists, particularly in U.S. foreign policy. In addressing the issue of cultural diversity, some universalist theorists argue that "modernization" will be accompanied by the incorporation of the western rights concepts, often pointing to the rise of a middle-class in Asian countries as the precipitating factor in their democratization. But, as will be discussed below, economic globalization challenges both the universalist and cultural relativist paradigms. On a scholarly level, analysts such as Renteln,[14] search for equivalences in non-Western philosophies and cultures. Others, An-Na'im[15] in particular, have embarked on a process of cross-cultural dialogue and internal cultural discourse. Through these processes An-Na'im believes that non-Western cultures will move closer to the west.

The dialogue between universalism and cultural relativism has been hampered by its neglect of an important analytic dimension. For most human-rights scholars Western ontology sets the conceptual framework for understanding the world. This is the case not only for Western analysts but for many scholars from non-Western societies who have internalized Western thought. Hence the portrayal of social reality and the evidence that is amassed to validate it is filtered through the lens of this framework and its attendant paradigm. Albeit an abstraction, the construction of social reality by social theorists is inevitably selective. It attends only to those aspects and that evidence deemed significant and consonant with its paradigm. Concepts or data external to the prevailing paradigm are frequently overlooked. A theoretical consequence of this cognitive framework is that western ontology becomes the referent whereby non-Western cultures and societies are understood and acquire meaning. Using a Western referent has led inevitably to the dichotomization between universalists and cultural relativists. In order to move beyond this impasse a recasting, free of ethnocentrism, is essential whereby elements from the theories of both universalists and cultural relativists can be merged and synthesized into a new reconstructed universalism, or more accurately global human-rights.

In addition to the cultural relativist/universalist debate, there has been much ferment and fluidity recently in several other areas of human-rights scholarship. A significant shift, heralded by Henry Shue's study of basic rights,[16] is a growing consensus among human-rights scholars (with some exceptions) on the interdependence of civil/political and economic/social rights.[17] But even then, and despite the Vienna Declaration of Human Rights' repeated assertion of this interdependence, in practice, economic and social rights are viewed in the west as secondary. The United States, for example, remains unwilling to ratify the U.N.'s Convention on Economic, Social and Cultural Rights.[18] For many Western liberal states issues such as starvation remain primarily a humanitarian matter while sweatshops and gross infringements of labor rights are not seen as violations of fundamental rights but as the unfortunate consequences of economic realities or policy. In other words, economic and social rights remain a second-order priority, particularly for doctrinaire universalists and Western policy-makers.

As stated earlier, several relatively new theoretical issues have entered the human-rights discourse: minority rights, women's rights, homosexual rights and environmental rights. Despite the efforts of Will Kymlicka,[19] liberal theorists face the paradox of advocating minority rights as policy but are unable to ground them in liberalism's central tenet of individualism. Presuming freedom-of-choice, Kymlicka argues that individuals in liberal societies should be free to choose their societal culture. But his argument revolves around the assumption of the "individual" and choice, ignoring the fact that in many cultures neither psychologically nor culturally is he/she free to choose.[20] Cultural relativists, on the other hand, have not concerned themselves with the issue of minorities within communal groups implicitly presuming that by definition they do not exist, or are so marginal as to be inconsequential.[21] By contrast, issues such as women's rights and homosexual rights are not group rights but demands for individual rights by the excluded. Hence they are an extension and application of liberal human-rights doctrine. For rigid cultural relativists women's rights are a non-issue since the ostensible subordinate position of women is one aspect of "traditional" culture. Like women's rights, homosexual rights philosophically are easily incorporated within liberal thought while cultural relativists have nothing to say on this matter.

So-called third-generation rights, such as the environment, are external to the cultural relativist-universalist dichotomy since they are collective rights that transcend the person however she/he is conceptualized, and extend beyond political borders. Only recently, with the realization that the absence of clean air and clean water are threats to the very right-to-life, has the environment as a human-rights issue become of concern to scholars.[22] Moreover, another issue, external to the dichotomies that have characterized human-rights scholarship, in need of scrutiny and analysis is the global human-rights consequences of economic globalization.

Embedded Assumptions and Presuppositions

The "international bill of human rights" is hailed as reflecting a world-wide consensus on the nature and substance of human rights. It is a deceptively false consensus Ratification of the various convenants and conventions, frequently with exceptions, is an assertion of membership in the world community and not a commitment to the implementation of these rights or to their legitimacy. A dramatic example is the decision by the People's Republic of China in 1998 to sign the Covenant on Civil and Political Rights at the same time as it was imprisoning more dissidents and forcing others to flee the country. The absence of a genuine consensus on human rights necessitates rethinking and a search for new foundations for the construction of a reconstituted human rights theory. A crucial initial step towards a reconstructed universalism, towards a global theory of human rights, is a probing of the assumptions imbedded both in the universalist and the cultural relativist doctrines of human rights. Upon reflection it becomes apparent that advocates of Western liberalism while recognizing the historical origins of their human-rights doctrine overlook the implicit assumptions underlying their contemporary theory. Prior to the industrial revolution western Europe itself was a communal society. Varying forms of feudalism prevailed while states were ruled by monarchies of differing degrees of absolutism. The feudal system itself was communal and in areas where feudalism was weak, such as Great Britain, villages constituted a community. Although loyalty to the monarch was demanded of his/her subjects, rights and obligations were largely interpersonal and unequal; they were contingent on one's position in the hierarchical structure, both at the local and state levels.

The socioeconomic transformations accompanying the industrial revolution and the rise of capitalism, characterized by a new social structure including a new class formation, private ownership of the means of production, wage labor, urbanization, did not obliterate community. Rather, it was transformed, and recast. More or less simultaneous with the rise and consolidation of capitalism was the reconstitution of states into nation-states. By contrast to the monarchical state, the nation-state ideally is a community of those sharing a national identity. It provides the sovereign state with legitimacy, not grounded on the rights of kings, as with monarchies, but on the principle of nationality. As with capitalism, the nation-state evolved gradually. Symbolically, it was consolidated at the time of the French Revolution, with the clarion call of the Declaration of the Rights of Man and Citizen, rights which were to be implemented within the new community.

Frequently overlooked by human-rights scholars in their discussions of freedom, democracy and the primacy of individual rights are the constraints to individual liberties inherent in nation-state citizenship. Regardless of its underlying ideological principles, the nation-state constitutes a political community to which all citizens owe loyalty and obligations. National interest, the interest of all, their survival and well-being, can transcend and preempt individual freedoms and the pursuit of individual interest even in liberal societies. Universalists do not incorporate in their paradigm the restrictions on individual civil and political rights which stem from the primacy of the state (community interests).[23] National emergencies—wars, external or internal threats—are frequently occasions for further restrictions on individual rights.

The nation-state was not the only newly formed community. Within the borders of the nation-state a new political community was constructed. Although a basic element in the thought of the modern political philosophers was the belief that the atomized individual in the state of nature possessed certain inalienable rights,[24] this individual was an analytic construct, not a description of social reality. Whether primitive communism, sedentary or nomadic tribes, societies have been governed by a mutuality of interpersonal relations and customs. "Individuals" in the state of nature, according to the liberal philosophers, would come together and through a social contract form a political community. The social compact envisaged the construction of a community in which individuals, at least men, would come together to determine the rules and regulations governing their society—in other words their community. While inalienable individual civil- and political-rights were the foundational principles of the emerging social and political order, they were imbedded in the socioeconomic particularities of their societies and constrained by the rights of others, the rules governing behavior and the national interest. No man was unfettered to freely pursue his self-interest to the detriment of his fellow men, community or the state.[25]

It should be noted furthermore, that even during the early heyday of rampant capitalism society felt a moral obligation to provide for the "unfortunate", the destitute. Provision was made, through voluntary philanthropic associations, for those in the community who failed in the competitive struggle, thus mitigating the Hobbesian vision. Economic and social rights, considered of little importance in liberal thought, were thus partially fulfilled by non-state actors. By the mid-twentieth century, political pressure and concerns about the unemployed, the poor, the disabled and the elderly, who did not enjoy the benefits of capitalist development, led to the rise of the welfare state. Unfortunately, with the ascendancy of market economies, neo-liberalism and the global economy in the last decade of the twentieth century, the welfare state is being eviscerated, public services privatized and aid to the needy is once again reverting to voluntary associations, all in the name of the general welfare.

Only since the end of World War II have human rights been universalized, decontextualized and deemed to be applicable throughout the globe regardless of their consonance with socio-economic reality and with cultural imperatives. As argued above, probing the doctrines of the eighteenth and nineteenth century liberal political philosophers reveals that the exercise of individual rights was expected to be within the context of their reconstructed political communities. John Stuart Mill spoke not only of individual rights but of the mutuality of obligations between the individual and society.[26] It is contemporary universalists who have recast individual rights into abstract legalities thus theoretically disassociating them from community and from other norms and values governing society.[27] While their conceptualization of individual rights excludes communal rights, as noted earlier, there are implicit inarticulated givens in the universalist paradigm. Underlying principles, structures, institutions, ideals and goals may differ dramatically in liberal states from "traditional" communalism but not the existence of community. Whether decisions are taken by tribal chiefs, legislative bodies or authoritarian, repressive rulers, they are all justified in the name of the common good. Non-Western societies manifest enormous diversity among themselves in their historical trajectories and in their cultural systems. Empires, theocracies and tribes had been dominant until the end of World War II. During the late-nineteenth and early twentieth centuries, imperialism, in the form of colonialism, arbitrarily divided up much of the world's territory at times under the ideological rubric of a "civilizing mission." Civilization did not include conveying democracy or recognition of human rights but did succeed in causing the massive disruption of tradition. It was at this time that modern-state structures were imposed on the non-Western world.

Overall cultural relativists contend that the culture, values and norms of non-Western societies,[28] however much they differ among themselves, are devoid of conceptions of the individual, individualism, individual autonomy, freedom-of-choice and equal rights. Yet, leaving aside the issue of social change for the moment, just as the universalists ignore community as the context within which individual rights are realized, relativists have ignored spheres of personal autonomy and freedom of choice extant within communal societies. The person is subsumed within the communal group while her/his identity is ascribed by his/her status and role within the group. Obligations to others and to the group are paramount. Furthermore, relativists often tend to reify "traditional" cultures and view them as static and unchanging thereby neglecting the evolutionary aspects of all societies and cultures. A more in-depth probing of communal societies would reveal that spheres of personal autonomy have existed. Personality differences, even within the confines of communalism, often result in struggles to excel, as a housewife, a hunter, a warrior or a statesman. Moreover, behavior and activities which are outside the parameters of the communal definition of self and the requisite roles and obligations, are permissible and do not violate sacred norms. Artistic talents, aptitudes and skills are given free reign for personal expression. The cultural artifacts of a society, including music, dance and art, on the whole, are the creative products of individual persons. The art of the Chinese Empires, music and art in Castro's Cuba, the woodcarvings of Africa, and folklore throughout the globe, were neither communal products nor mandated by one's role in a group.

Another cultural relativist assumption which needs to be rethought is the presumption of the absence of personal choice. Despite rigid stratification and the submersion of the person into the communal group, empirical evidence exists of a modicum of socioeconomic mobility in some cultures. The market women of West Africa, (particularly Ghana, the Ivory Coast and Nigeria)[29] and the meritocratic recruitment for the bureaucracy in the Chinese Empire[30] challenge elements of the cultural relativist paradigm. Research, which divests itself of Western ethnocentric bias, is needed to investigate thoroughly the scope and spheres of freedom-of-choice and the particular constellation of prescribed versus ascribed roles in communal societies. Undoubtedly, much variation will be found from one culture to another. Critical for facilitating this analysis is a probing of concepts and values which do not have equivalences in the west, and are not translatable into western languages, but which may have a significant impact on values and behavior.

Social scientists studying communally based or non-Western societies in which roles are prescriptive, presume the subordination of women. Patriarchy prevails whereby women are subject to domination by men while their labor is demeaned. However, at least in some cases, this could be a transposition backward from western patriarchy to "traditional" cultures. Further research is needed on the position and roles of women in non-western societies. In addition to the market women in West Africa mentioned earlier, who retained their earnings while they dominated and controlled the market structure, women in many, "traditional" societies both in Africa and some Asian villages were the agriculturists.[31] In pre-capitalist societies such a productive activity was the core of their subsistence economy. The facile assumption of the subordination of women in all non-western societies needs to be critically reexamined. The particular cultural configuration, gender relations and roles need to be revisited. Subordination of women in one sphere, sex for example, does not necessarily extend to all spheres of life. Patriarchy has characterized western societies and it has been presumed as a given for non-Western societies, which, after all, are underdeveloped. Significantly, it has been well documented that the failure of bilateral and United Nations aid programs designed to assist agricultural development and modernization was often the consequence of their being targeted to men even though it was the women who engaged in farming.[32]

As noted, the language of rights, a Western construct, has been non-existent in traditional societies. For many cultural relativists this is conflated into an absence of rights, a position reinforced by ethnographic studies. Yet a closer look reveals that in many traditional societies that which in rights vocabulary is labeled socio-economic rights, are obligations of the community towards all its members.[33] Obligations are the reverse side of rights. Thus, if the community must insure food, shelter, care for the aged, the disabled, in fact for all its members, in essence all group members possess equal-rights entitlements. Such a conception of obligations/rights differs radically from the Western notion of legal rights. In both there is a concept of equality but its meaning is substantively different. In "traditional" communities entitlements stemming from power, authority and privileges, are differential, dependent on one's status within the communal group, but economic and social rights are equal entitlements for all members. Conversely, in Western liberal societies, individual civil and political rights are equal entitlements, but economic and social rights are differential.

A basic tenet of liberalism is political participation. In addition to separation of powers, democratic theory espouses representation of the electorate through which the popular will is articulated. Non-Western societies, it is argued, have been ruled, as Max Weber would say, by traditional authority. A rethinking of this argument is in order. Is rule by a tribal chief in Africa, in consultation with the Council of Elders, any less representative than nineteenth century Great Britain with its restricted franchise? And is the power to destool a tribal chief-functionally different from elections which change rulers in a liberal society or from impeachment of elected officials in the United States?

By contrast to the plethora of historical studies of Western societies which document and analyze their ideological and socioeconomic transition to modernity, there has been little analysis of the effects of social change on traditional values and norms in non-western societies either historically or in the contemporary era. This is not to argue that no histories exist, but that, with some exceptions, their focus has not been on changing culture, values and norms. Many studies trace the geographic spread of various religions and/or regime changes through conquest or revolution, but in-depth analysis of what, if any, transformative impact these events may have had on traditional culture is sparse. This is not to argue that such an investigation would reveal a trajectory similar to that of the west. It is to argue that a historical cultural analysis would yield understanding and insight into the reconfiguration of values and norms which would challenge reification and the presumption of unchangeability.

In non-Western societies, to the extent that industrialization, capitalism and a democratic polity has emerged, (dubious at best), they have not been indigenous developments. In fact, the evolutionary processes of change that all cultures and societies undergo were brutally rendered asunder in Asia, Africa and the Middle East, by the imposition of external power during the era of western imperialism. Subsistence, but self-reliant economies were demolished. The transformations in non-western societies that took place were the result of the African slave trade, colonialism, "state building," commodification, modernization and forceful integration into a dependent position within the world economy. All of this brought about massive disruptions of indigenous societies and economies. To understand and evaluate the impact of these externally imposed institutions, forms of governance, economic policies and goals, a thorough investigation of the resulting reconfiguration of values and norms is necessary. Colonial policies such as the imposition of Western legal systems, modern state structures, and a market economy inevitably profoundly affected "traditional" tribal and village structures, land-ownership systems, communalism, village autonomy and prevailing norms. In addition to a historical analysis, research is needed on the effects in the post-independence era of non-Western state domestic policies and global developments, inclusive of the so-called Asian miracle, on values and norms. Of great significance is the impact of globalization and the financial crisis of the 1990s on traditional communal solidarity, particularly as it has affected Asia and Latin America.

Minority rights, a burning contemporary issue in Western liberal states, are demands for group rights, be it ethnicity, language, culture or religion. An analysis of their cultural context, in particular their values and conceptions of rights, necessitates research along the same lines as those proposed for communally based non-western cultures. Vital is a probing of the impact of living in an individually based society and the linkage of minorities to the dominant culture. What reconfiguration of traditional values takes place as a consequence of the penetration of the dominant culture and of the minorities' interaction with the new culture and society?

More vexing is the issue of ethnonational states. Their ideology equates ethnic with national identity which, in turn, is embodied in the state. This inexorably results in violations of both individual and minority rights.[34] Communalism, endemic to non-Western societies, has been transposed and equated with the boundaries of the modern state. A democratic ethnonational state can protect individual rights but not if their exercise challenges the givens of ethnic identity. Nor does it implement or protect the rights of "the other". Furthermore, in part a reaction to globalization, fragmentation into ethnically exclusive groups poses a serious threat to an evolution towards a reconstructed univeralism. Conceptually and ideologically an ethnonational state denies rights to all who are not ethnically pure but live within the borders of a state.

Towards a New Paradigm

The human species shares biological features and physical needs. Yet each person is distinctive in his/her appearance, specific biological and genetic makeup, and may satisfy physical needs in different ways. An analogy can be drawn to social life. Although a multitude of world views, belief systems, social structures, cultural patterns, institutions, theologies, values and norms exist, their permutations can not be infinite since we are constrained by the limitations of human intelligence, creativity and needs. In addition to physical and biological needs, equally fundamental are psychological and social/communal needs which can be fulfilled in a multiplicity of ways. Scholars, by divesting themselves of ethnocentric biases and the dominant cognitive frameworks, may unearth hitherto unsuspected commonalities in social existence which transcend the multitudinous social and cultural diversity.

At present, human-rights scholarship is in what Thomas Kuhn calls a pre-paradigmatic state, a condition which characterizes social science theory as a whole. The previous section raises issues and points to directions for further research which may lead to a reconstructed universal, or more accurately global, human rights paradigm. Probing unstated givens in both the universalist and cultural relativist doctrines yields points of contact. It is postulated that in both cases their implicit assumptions speak, at least partially, to the articulated, visible conceptions of their opposite. In other words, the presupposition of community in universalism is the core of cultural relativism while the imbedded assumption of spheres of individual autonomy among relativists speaks to the individualism of the universalists. Further research is needed to probe the extent to which and the ways in which the Western doctrine of individual civil and political rights is embedded in its community structures.[35] And further research is essential to probe the extent to which and the mechanisms through which personal autonomy and freedom of choice exist in communally based societies. One possible outcome of this endeavor would be a synthesis of fundamental shared elements of both human rights doctrines incorporating community and individual autonomy. Cultural forms and structures would continue to differ, among non-Western societies, between Western and non-Western societies and within the West itself, but a consensus may emerge on elements of a reconstructed minimal global paradigm.

Nevertheless, probing the unstated givens in both human-rights paradigms is insufficient in itself to lead to a new universalism. An in-depth analysis must be made of the extent to which disparate religions and philosophies share values and principles. In this endeavor certain cross-cultural similarities immediately come to mind. No philosophic/cultural system sanctions arbitrary killings, disappearances, or torture.[36] The right to life is sacrosanct, at least for the members of one's community, be it the nation-state or the tribe. This is not to say that the right to life is not violated in practice, in western as well as in non-Western societies. Ruthless tyrants have ruled in "traditional" societies, and in ancient Empires, and are frequently overthrown. And in Western liberal societies, dictatorships, ferocious tyrants, and repressive regimes which have violated the right to life, have not been uncommon as witnessed in Nazi Germany, fascist Italy and military regimes. Although in liberal societies, such as Israel and the United States, the death penalty is imposed after due process of law,[37] it remains a denial of the right to life. Nevertheless, the right to life was and remains a universal principle.

Moving beyond the bedrock principle of the right to life, abstract concepts such as justice, respect, human dignity and humaneness are ubiquitous. They are manifest in Christianity, Buddhism, Confucianism, Islam, Judaism, liberalism and "traditional" or animistic cultural norms. Consensus on abstract principles does not translate into shared notions on the meaning and content ascribed to these values. In fact contradictory behavior and actions may fulfill the same abstract value. What constitutes justice in liberal thought is not the same as justice in Buddhism. Human dignity entails different behavior and social expectations in Islam and Christianity. A veiled woman has dignity in Islam while in the west it is a mark of inferiority. Humaneness necessitates different actions in these diverse cultural/philosophic systems. Similarly, treating persons with respect is culturally specific and can not be generalized. But the question remains. Are there interactive processes through which overlapping core elements can be distilled whereby a common grounding can evolve?

The task of probing for shared core elements in diverse cultures and philosophies would be facilitated by a recognition of the multiple strains of thought in each philosophic, religious or intellectual tradition. Linkages may exist across civilizational lines but not necessarily with the dominant strain at any point in time. No dominant philosophic or cultural principles should be reified as representing the Islamic or the liberal dogma. Norms and values are in continuous contention and in flux both in the West and the non-West. Which strain emerges triumphant, Mencius or Confucious,[38] John Locke or David Hume,[39] is the outcome of a myriad of interacting social forces in a particular historical epoch. One need only look at Christianity to realize that beyond a belief in God and Jesus Christ, Christian dogma is often contradictory. Or one can look at the competing interpretations of Islamic thought.

Minimal evidence exists of the incorporation of elements of eastern philosophy into Western thought. Despite its emphasis on obedience, Buddhism's conception of the transcendental unity of nature and man is reflected in the environmental movement that has spread in western liberal societies.[40] The underlying holistic principles of Buddhism are open-ended and amenable to incorporating new experiences and new realities. There is no absolute truth, just a spiritual unity. The absence of philosophic rigidity and absolutism in such an ontology facilitates reinterpretation while its holistic ontology can be a corrective to the west's fragmented intellectual thought.

An initial step in the reinterpretation of cultural values and beliefs has been undertaken by An-Na'im.[41] He proposes an internal cultural discourse and an intra-cultural dialogue as processes whereby rights may be universalized. His call for dialogue however is somewhat one-sided in that he expects changes to take place primarily in non-western cultures. An-Na'im's approach should be extended. The liberal doctrine of human rights should also be subjected to discourse and dialogue. Such an undertaking can be facilitated by recognizing the absence of a single overriding verity in each philosophic tradition, particularly as it pertains to a person and her/his rights. By not engaging primarily or necessarily with the official dogmas and accepting potential alternative strains within each tradition, shared values may be ascertainable. Some Islamic theologians are currently challenging the traditional interpretation of the subordination of women and are doing so within the theological parameters of Islam.[42] By modifying An-Na'im's approach through an interpenetration between the universalist and cultural relativist doctrines both can be reconstructed leading to a minimal common ground.

Theories of human rights are amiss in neglecting the impact of social change on historic values and norms and on conceptions of human rights—an issue that is particularly salient at the present time. Globalization has brought about massive changes, but the extensive literature on globalization does not on the whole address its impact on rights,[43] and on prevailing concepts. Whether one speaks of culture, technology, information, finance, or consumption and production, globalization is a multi-faceted, multi-dimensional phenomenon. Structures and institutions have been adapted, sometimes created, to accommodate these changes. Questions have been raised regarding the changing role of the state, if not its loss of sovereignty, as a consequence of the transnational power exercised by a global financial and economic oligarchy.[44] What is embryonic are analyses of the impact of these transformations on values and notions of rights.

Illustrative of the far-ranging impact of socio-economic change is Japan. In the post-World War II decades it had successfully blended traditional values with the requisites of a modern industrial society, in itself a reconfiguration of traditional values and behavior. Today Japan is confronting the disintegration of its unique system. Lifetime employment in a firm, to which the traditional community had been transposed, has ended, while unemployment is increasing, as is homelessness. Deeply embedded values, such as solidarity, community and economic and social rights, have been shattered by economic realities. Faced with massive transformations as a result of the financial crisis and the decline in the Japanese economy, its ideological/cultural premises and their public and private institutionalization have disintegrated. Other than structural changes in finance, banking and production, what impact is globalization and its attendant crisis having on Japanese values? Similar questions can be raised about Thailand, Indonesia, Malaysia, South Korea and the Middle East countries.

Are There Global Human Rights?

"The International Bill of Human Rights" and the Vienna Declaration of Human Rights (1993) have been largely unenforceable rhetoric and subject to multiple interpretations. The world-order embodied in the U.N. extols the primacy of state sovereignty, while states, the principal violators of rights, are concurrently expected to be the foremost implementers of rights. Recently however, there is growing evidence of an emerging global recognition and acceptance, cutting across religions, ideologies and cultures, of one fundamental human right—the right to life.[45] In this one realm of physical survival global human-rights are being consolidated.

Several recent developments, in fact, portend the establishment of mechanisms geared towards implementing basic human-rights and prosecuting individual violators. Universal jurisdiction is becoming a viable principle,[46] thus validating the claim made in the earlier section regarding the distilling of a consensus from diverse philosophies on minimal values which incorporate notions of the right to life. The formation of the war crimes tribunals in Arusha, Tanzania, in 1994 and the Hague Tribunal in 1993 to prosecute individuals charged with genocide, torture or crimes against humanity,[47] in Rwanda and the territory of former Yugoslavia, constitute significant steps in the institutionalization of global human-rights. In marked contrast to any actions taken by the U.N. which necessitate individual state concurrence, and even though these tribunals were established by the Security Council, they are autonomous and are not subject to state sovereignty or state veto. While not resoundingly successful they have tried and convicted numerous persons, Tutsis, Hutus, Serbs, Croats, and Bosnians. Most dramatic is the indictment of Slobodan Milosevic, ousted president of Yugoslavia, in the Hague in 1999, whose trial on multiple charges, including genocide, is under way. This prosecution signals that heads of state will no longer be immune and can be extradited to courts outside their own state. Moreover, domestic state courts are increasingly bringing charges against individuals regardless of the place these crimes were committed or the nationality of the offender. The charges of genocide and crimes against humanity brought against Augusto Pinochet, the former dictator of Chile, in Spain and those against two Rwandan nuns in Belgium, among others, attest to the extent to which one category of rights—those revolving around the right to life—is acquiring international legal and normative recognition.

Of great potential significance moreover is the signing in Rome in July 1998 of the treaty establishing the International Criminal Court with an independent prosecutor empowered to prosecute individuals accused of genocide and crimes against humanity. Such action can not be vetoed or rejected by any state and is binding on all states after the necessary ratifications, hence the autonomy of the court is assured. Sixty ratifications are needed for the ICC to come into force. As of August 2001 there were thirty-seven ratifications and several were pending. It should be noted that while ex-President Clinton reluctantly signed the treaty in December 2000, President Bush has categorically rejected it. Clinton's hesitancy and Bush's adamant opposition is largely on the grounds that it infringes on state sovereignty.[48] Notwithstanding the United States' stance, a consensus is emerging on the universality of basic, fundamental human-rights and they are gradually becoming globalized, through the increasing application of human-rights law in domestic courts and the establishment of regional or global courts mandated to prosecute violators. It is to be hoped that one can look forward to a future when the globalization of human rights extends beyond the right to life, a process that could be facilitated, as discussed earlier, by a synthesis of the shared values between the universalist and the cultural relativist doctrines.

Economic Globalization and Human Rights

Ironically the emerging philosophic consensus on human rights and their institutionalization may be furthered by the global impact of economic globalization which challenges both the universalist and the cultural relativist paradigms. The controversies surrounding the substance of human rights—civil/political vs. economic/social and universalism vs. cultural relativism—have been overshadowed in recent decades, by the devastating negative impact of economic globalization on the entire complex of rights. Communalism, the bedrock of cultural relativism, has been torn asunder by the deleterious consequences of economic globalization.[49] Millions of people throughout the globe, both in Western industrial societies and in non-Western ones, are experiencing deprivation of the entire complex of rights. With the collapse of community in non-western societies, individuals have become atomized since the community can longer fulfill its obligations to provide for economic and social needs. Much of the scholarly discourse on human rights has become somewhat distanced from social reality. Although globalization may facilitate the development of a single normative human rights doctrine its deleterious effects pose a threat to the implementation of all human rights.

Globalization has been evolving over many centuries but in its contemporary form it exhibits distinctive features. A multi-layered, multi-faceted phenomena, fueled by modern technology, it consists of free trade on a global scale, transnational investments, currency flows, instantaneous financial markets and information services. Overall these cross-border transactions are not regulated by the state,[50] thereby limiting a state's ability to set standards or to implement human rights. The process of globalization has spawned the emergence of a new capitalist class,[51] which constructs its own rules, adopts its own policies and is not accountable. There is a loss of state sovereignty and in fact states, proponents of neo-liberalism, have become facilitators of economic globalization. Trans-national investments, particularly in non-Western states, frequently involving the shifting of productive facilities throughout the globe in search of cheap labor or the exploitation of oil and gas resources leaves the local population destitute. It has resulted in gross violations of labor rights, child labor and the erosion of economic and social rights which communal societies had enjoyed, and often civil and political rights. Furthermore, as will be shown below it is not only non-Western societies that have experienced the deleterious effects of economic globalization but also the industrialized states.

Statistics are revealing of the scope and breadth of the negative impact of globalization on rights.[52] According to the U.N. 1.3 billion people lived on less than $1 per day in 1997 and 2.8 billion on less than $2 per day in 1998. Furthermore, the income gap between the richest fifth of the world's people and the poorest fifth increased from 34 to one in 1970 to 70 to one in 1997, while in 1993 the richest 1 percent of the world's people received as much income as the poorest 57 percent. Unemployment, below subsistence wages, poverty, lack of sanitation and absence of medical care, are on the rise

Clearly the less developed countries have suffered the most from globalization. To cite a few examples: In Indonesia from 1989–1994, 8 percent were below the national poverty line but between 1984–1999, 27.1 percent were below this poverty line, whereas in the Philippines between 1984 and 1999, 36.8 percent were below the national poverty line. In Malaysia interestingly between 1989-1994, 15 percent were below the national poverty line and between 1984–1999 it continued to be 15 percent. Reliable data for Africa is scarce as it is for China. But it is estimated that in Nigeria in the period 1984–1999, 34.1 percent were below the national poverty line, whereas in Uganda for the same period it was 44.1 percent. Significantly there is no data for Singapore which had prided itself that its regime had succeeded in withstanding the Asian financial crisis of 1997 although recently it too is experiencing an economic downturn. It must be stated that the gross abuse of economic and social rights inexorably results in the violation of civil and political rights, even in democratic states. Exploited workers, often held in semi-slavery have no recourse. There are no civil rights for redressing their grievances and no political rights, such as freedom of expression and freedom of assembly.

Although awareness of the deleterious effects of globalization on human rights in many less developed regions of the world is growing, little attention has been paid to its severe repercussions in highly developed industrialized countries. Prior to September 11 and its economic consequences, and prior to the recent global recession, economic globalization had marginalized thousands and thousands of people in the United States, western Europe and Japan. It is noteworthy that the United States, with 14 percent, was among the three countries, the others being the United Kingdom and Australia, with the highest percentage of people living below the poverty line.[53] At a time when profits of corporations were soaring, 22 percent in 1998, as were the salaries of CEOs, the situation of the marginalized worsened dramatically. Over the last twenty years low-income families in the United States lost 10 percent of their income while at the top there was a 25 percent increase and the middle-class remained stagnant. The income gap between the top 20 percent of families and the bottom 20 percent grew between the 1980s and the late 1990s.[54] Gobalization processes such as downsizing, outsourcing and contract labor has resulted in the loss of fringe benefits and a shift of employment to unskilled work, primarily in the service sector. Furthermore, many firms, faced with threats of unionization and enticed by low labor-costs have been shifting production overseas. It is particularly astonishing that sweatshops, eliminated decades ago have returned, while violations of labor rights, usually associated with less developed countries are rampant in the United States.[55]

Conclusion

The post-World War II decades were noted for a tripartite division regarding the substance of human rights. The West considered individual civil and political rights as fundamental, and the Soviet Union and communist countries viewed individual economic and social rights as basic, while non-Western countries were rooted in communalism. These divisions in turn were manifest in the scholarly discourse on human rights. Two dichotomies dominated; civil/political vs. economic/social and universalism vs. cultural relativism. The civil/political vs. economic/social controversy has largely abated in part because of the collapse of the Soviet Union but more fundamentally because of an increasing political and scholarly recognition of the interdependence of the two sets of rights. Simultaneously, in recent years, scholars have embarked on the task of probing the multiple philosophies, religions and cultures in order to distill commonalities among them regarding rights while simultaneously preserving cultural diversity. In one sphere, the right to life, a growing consensus is emerging, a consensus moreover, that is reflected in an evolving institutionalization and enforcement of human rights. Probing the presuppositions of the prevailing doctrines of human rights, in-depth analysis of points of contact in differing philosophic systems, cross-fertilization and dialogue among different cultures, the transformations resulting from social change, in particular globalization, will set the foundations for the globalization of human rights. A future expansion of global; human rights would eliminate or at least minimize one area of world conflict.

Unfortunately, the prospects for an expanding globalization of human rights and the establishment of mechanisms for their enforcement and the prosecution of violators is seriously endangered by the dire consequences of globalization. Millions throughout the world are experiencing severe deprivation; poverty, unemployment, homelessness, lack of clean air and water and lack of health care, while they have no recourse to civil or political rights with which to express their grievances and obtain redress. Worsening the situation of those deprived of rights is the destruction of the communal foundations of non-Western societies, which in the past had insured shelter and food. The hopeful prospects for greater justice through an emerging consensus on human rights has been severely jeopardized because of the dire consequences of globalization. Only the political will of the international community to establish global agencies which regulate the global economy, which establishes standards of behavior, including human rights and which holds its principal actors accountable, can lead to a more peaceful, just and secure world.

Notes

1. By contrast, after World War I, with the redrawing of the map of Europe and the collapse of the Hapsburg and Ottoman Empires, numerous treaties provided for the protection of minority rights. But these pertained only to minorities living in states whose home country was another European state.

2. Mary Wolloncraft *The Vindication of the Rights of Women*, 1792.

3. Maurice Cranston *What Are Human Rights?* Basic Books, New York, 1963

4. Ronald Dworkin *Taking Rights Seriously*, Harvard University Press, Camgridge, MA, 1978.

5. John Rawls *Theory of Justice*, Harvard University Press, Cambridge, MA, 1971; Influenced by analytic philosophy, despite his concern with justice, he does not deal with class position, institutional context or with the socioeconomic context.

6. In ancient Athenian democracy, a person was an integral member of several concentric groups, with the polis at the apex.

7. Clifford Geertz *Old Societies and New States*, Free Press, Glencoe, 1963.

8. Among the earliest cultural relativist volumes are Adamantia Pollis and Peter Schwab (eds.) *Human Rights: Cultural and Ideological Perspectives*, Praeger Publishers, 1979 and Peter Schwab and Adamantia Pollis (eds.) *Toward a Human Rights Framework*, Prager Publishers, 1982; Michael Ignatieff in a recent article "The Attack on Human Rights" *Foreign Affairs*, November–December, 2001, argues that the attack on universal human-rights comes from three sources; the Islamic, the Asian and domestically from cultural relativists.

9. A classic study by a social psychologist, Harry Triandis, highlights the difficulties in cross-cultural research when a culture's dominant concepts do not exist cross culturally. For example, while he recognizes the centrality of the Greek value of philotimo in behavior and attitudes, he admits it can not be translated into English and attempts, unsuccessfully to circumvent it, *The Analysis of Subjective Culture*, Wiley, Inter-Science, New York, 1972.

10. See Adamantia Pollis "Cultural Relativism Revisited: Through a State Prism" *Human Rights Quarterly*," Vol. 18., No. 2, My, 1995 316–344.

11. See in particular the Bangkok Declaration, April, 1993, preparatory to the Vienna Conference on Human Rights; Extracts appear in *The UNESCO Courier*, United Nations, New York, Vol. 40, March 1994; see also Sangwon Suh "No Easy Answers" *Fortune*, May, 1997 which reports the Malaysian Prime Minister Mahathir Mohamad's call for a review of the 1948 UDHR on the grounds that it was "formulated by superpowers who did not understand the needs of poor countries"

12. Interestingly, little has been heard of Asian values since the 1998 financial crisis and the more recent economic downturn, an understandable political retreat given that a principal rationale for repression—for maintaining "social order" and the denial of individual liberties—was the east Asian countries success in bringing about development and prosperity.

13. In a recent article Jerome J. Shestack, revealing his strong ethnocentric bias, states "cultural relativism as a concept to justify departures from human rights standards in international law on cultural grounds has scant claim to moral validity" "The Philosophic Foundations of Human Rights" *Human Rights Quarterly*, Vol. 20, No. 2, May, 1998.

14. Allison Dundes Renteln *International Human Rights: Universalism vs. Relativism*, Sage Publications, Newbury Park, CA, 1990.

15. Abdullahi Ahmed An-Na'im "Toward a Cross-Cultural Approach of Defining International Standards of Human Rights: The Meaning of Cruel, Inhuman or Degrading Treatment or Punishment" An-Nai'm (ed.) *Human Rights in Cross-Cultural Perspectives*, University of Pennsylvania Press, Philadelphia, 1992, 19–43.

16. Henry Shue *Basic Rights: Subsistence, Affluence and U.S. Foreign Policy*, Princeton University Press, Princeton, 1980.

17. Jack Donnelly *Universal Human Rights in Theory and Practice*, Cornell University Press, Ithaca, NY, 1989 34–37; in this volume the author, a foremost advocate of the primacy of civil/political rights, has come to recognize the interdependence of rights and develops his own complex of rights derived from several sources.

18. It is noteworthy that the United States did not ratify the Convention on Civil and Political Rights until 1993.

19. Will Kymlicka *Multi-Cultural Citizenship: A Liberal Theory of Minority Rights*, Oxford Clarendon Press, 1995

20. An interesting and significant edited volume dealing with minority rights from numerous perspectives is Will Kymlicka (ed.) *The Rights of Minoritieis*, Oxford University Press, 1995.

21. Nor do cultural relativists deal with minorities

within the borders of a modern state or with internal minorities in minority groups. For an exception see Leslie Green "Internal Minorities and their Rights" in Kymlicka op.cit.

22. See Barbara Rose Johnston "Human Environmental Rights" Adamantia Pollis and Peter Schwab (eds.) *Human Rights: New Perspectives, New Realities,* Lynne Rienner Publishers, 2000, Chapter 5.

23. The United States Constitution says little about emergency powers and which branch of government can exercise them. The restrictions of individual liberties during the McCarthy era, including the rights to travel, are well known but it is significant to note that as far back as the civil war the writ of habeas corpus was suspended. See Leonard D. Levy *Encyclopedia of the United States Constitution,* Collier Macmillan, London, 1986 for a compilation of cases involving national emergencies and restrictions on rights; President George W. Bush's executive orders in November, 2002 establishing military courts and restricting the rights of foreigners is beyond the scope of this study; Article 15 of the European Convention for the Protection of Human Rights and Fundamental Freedoms allows for the derogation of some, but not all rights under conditions of national emergency.

24. John Locke in *Two Treatises of Government* in Peter Laslett (ed.) 2nd edition, Cambridge University Press, Cambridge, 1970, reflecting continuity with the previous era, argued that the laws of nature were God given and were ascertainable to man through the use of reason.

25. In addition to the nation-state and the political community individuals are members of a multiplicity of other groups to which they owe loyalty and obligations, be it the family or voluntary associations.

26. John Stuart Mill *Essays on Politics and Society,* University of Toronto Press, Toronto, 1977.

27. A striking consequence of this conceptualization is found in Cranston, op.cit., Chapt. VIII, in which he vehemently rejects economic and social rights, both politically and philosophically; only that which is justiciable can be a human right.

28. I use the term non-western as more accurate than third world or post colonial in referring to those societies that historically did not share the legacy of the Enlightenment.

29. See Gracia Clark *Onions are My Husband,* University of Chicago Press, Chicago, 1994.

30. For a discussion of the civil service examination system during the various Chinese dynasties and its connection to Confucian philosophy see Harold Hakwon Sunoo *China of Confucius: A Critical Interpretation,* Heritage Research House, Virginia Beach, VA, 1985, 103–109.

31. See Esther Boserup *Women's Role in Economic Development,* Allen and Unwin, London, 1970; Chapter 1 for a discussion of female farming systems in Africa and Chapter 3 for women's loss of status under colonial rule.

32. For an excellent volume on male bias in all areas of development, see Diane Elson (ed.) *Male Bias in the Development Process,* Manchester University Press, Manchester, 1995.

33. Kate Crehan *The Fractured Community: Landscapes of Power and and Gender in Rural Zambia,* University of California Press, Berkeley, 1997. Throughout this study there are references to the kinships groups' obligations to all its members.

34. See Adamantia Pollis "Are There Human Rights in Ethnonational States?" Roger Clark, Ferdinand Feldbrugge & Stanislaw Pomorske (eds.) *International and National Law in Russia and Eastern Europe,* Kluwer Law International, The Hague, 2001.

35. In the case of a country such as Rwanda its constitution makes no reference to rights, individual or collective. The successor states to Yugoslavia, while in principle bound by the Dayton accord which provide for individual and minority rights, in practice they are of little relevance.

36. Clearly there are differences in what constitutes torture among cultures including in the west; recently rape, as a political tool, has been added to the list of gross violations comparable to torture.

37. It must be noted that in the occupied territories of the West Bank, Palestinians under Israeli control have had no entitlement to the western concept of due process.

38. See Du Gangjjan and Song Gang "Relating Human Rights to Chinese Culture: The Four Paths of the Confucian Analects and the Four Principles of a New

Theory of Benevolence" Michael C. Davis (ed.) *Human Rights and Chinese Values,* Oxford University Press, New York, 1995, 35–56; The authors attempt to analyze strains in traditional Confucian thought which are consistent with modern notions of human rights. Nevertheless, even for his time, Confucius was an authoritarian whereas Mencius was more concerned with justice, with doing right by others and with humanirty.

39. A generation later that John Locke, David Hume was quite vehement in his rejection of the philosophic notion of a social (original) contract as the foundation for legitimate government. See Sir Ernst Barker *Social Contract: Locke, Hume and Rousseau,* Oxford University Press, New York, 1957.

40. In fact an American philosopher Murray Bookchin in *The Ecology of Freedom,* Black Rose Books, New York, 1991 is probably unconsciously closer to Buddhism than the environmental movement which is frequently fragmented into single issue activities. Bookchin argues for a holistic social ecology which joins the environment with socioeconomic and political life.

41. An-Na'im, op.cit.

42. See Zehra Arat, in Pollis and Schwab, 2000, 69-93.

43. Recently the realization of the impact of globalization on economic and social rights has become widespread. A forerunner is a noteworthy study by David Apter *Rethinking Development,* Sage Publications, New York, 1987; Chapter I. While the author does not address globalization per se, but economic development of states, he argues that one consequence of modernization is the emergence of marginals, that is strata who do not benefit and who are characterized by unemployment, poverty and low wages; see also Tariq Banuri "Development and the Politics of Knowledge; A Critical Interpretation of the Social Role of Development in the Third World" Stephen A. Marglin and Fredengue Appfel Marglin (eds.) *Dominating Knowledge,* Clarendon Press, New York, 1990.

44. Among the earliest works on the loss of sovereignty is Saskia Sassen *Losing Control: Sovereignty in an Age of Globalization.* Columbia University Press, New York, 1996.

45. In the past few years there has been a proliferation of studies on international justice—theoretical and case studies. Among these see Yves Beigbeder *Judging War Criminals: The Politics of International Justice,* St. Martins Press, New York, 1999.

46. For a comprehensive review of universal jurisdiction whereby "a state is entitled or even required to bring proceedings in respect of certain serious crimes, irrespective of the location of the crime, and irrespective of the nationality of the perpetrator or victim" see Menno T. Kamminga "Lessons Learned from the Exercise of Universal Jurisdiction in Respect to Gross Human Rights Offenses" *Human Rights Quarterly,* Vol. 23, No. 4, November, 2001.

47. See Margaret McAuliffe deGuzman "The Road from Rome: The Developing Law of Crimes Against Humanity" *Human Rights Quarterly,* vol. 22, no. 2, May, 2000 in which she elaborates on the meaning and substance of crimes against humanity.

48. The United States did much in the Rome negotiations to emasculate the treaty. It argued for Security Council approval before the prosecutor could act, inapplicability to those states who did not ratify the treaty and expressed its fear that American soldiers on peacekeeping missions could be tried by the ICC for crimes against humanity. For the United States' official position see the statement by David J. Sheffer, U.S. Department of State "Deterrence of War Crimes in the 21st Century" given in Honolulu, Hawaii, February 23, 1999 (Obtained from Coalition on the International Criminal Court, Home Page). For a sardonic parody on the United States position see Roger S. Clark "The ICC Statute Protecting the Sovereign Rights of Non-Parties", paper presented at Notre Dame Law School Conference on the Permanent International Criminal Court, March 19–20, 1999.

49. An earlier study discussing the interrelationship between globalization and economic and social rights is Peter Schwab and Adamantia Pollis "Globalization's Impact on Human Rights" Adamantia Pollis and Peter Schwab (eds.) *Human Rights: New Perspectives, New Realities,* Lynne Rienner Publishers, 2000.

50. For an early study on the state's loss of sovereignty see Saskia Sassen *Losing Control, Sovereignty in an Age of Globalization,* Columbia University Press, 1996.

51. William I. Robinson and Jerry Harris "Towards a

Global Ruling Class? Globalization and the Transnational Capitalist" *Science and Society*, Spring, 2000.

52. All the data following pertaining to the world economy and to individual states in the non-western world are taken from United Nations Development Program, *Human Development Report, 2000 & 2001*, Oxford University Press, 2000 & 2001.

53. UNDP, *Human Development Report, 2001*, p. 152.

54. "State Income Inequality Continued to Grow in Most States in the 1990s, Despite Economic Growth and Tight Labor Markets" Economic Policy Institute and Center on Budget and Policy Priority, January 18, 2000, available at http//www.chpp.org/1-18-00sfp.htm.

55. Human Rights Watch *Unfair Advantage: Workers Freedom of Association in the United States under International and Human Rights Standards*, August 2000 http://www.hrw/org/reports/2000/uslabor/USLBROO8-02.htm.

Globalization of Insecurity: The Democratic Imperative

Joseph A. Camilleri
La Trobe University

The word *global* has become a cliché. So have such terms as *global village*, *global economy* and *global culture*. We are often told that we live in an era of globalization. In the words of Roland Robertson, the world is fast becoming a 'single place' (1992). Others speak of a 'global condition' or of an emerging global consciousness. Yet, fashionable though globalization may now be a subject of discussion among scholars, policy-makers and citizens alike, there is no consensus on its meaning, its origins, or even its long-term implications. This is hardly surprising given that the term is used to describe and explain an elusive phenomenon which brings into play competing interests and perspectives, and assumes a different complexion in differing settings.

Globalization is in some ways as old as capitalism itself, yet it points to a new historical phase (Higgott and Payne, 2000). The contemporary world is one in which a number of seemingly distinct processes are occurring more or less simultaneously, and acquiring a global reach often in highly interconnected fashion. To cite one example: the impact of global financial flows, the role of hedge funds, the onset of the East Asian financial crisis, the fall of the Suharto regime in Indonesia, and UN intervention were all part of the complex sequence of events which culminated in self-determination for East Timor.

Yet global events and relationships do not all conform to the same logic or produce everywhere the same outcomes. Nowhere are the contradictory effects of globalization more strikingly evident than in their impact on 'human security'. In a rapidly globalizing world 'high consequence risks' (e.g., financial crises, nuclear accidents, oil spills, ozone depletion, global warming) have become integral to the functioning of society (Beck, 1992). The global condition is now one of heightened vulnerability as much for states as for groups and individuals. As the terrorist attacks on New York and Washington have demonstrated, wealth, power and nuclear arsenals offer little guarantee of protection.

If this reading of events is at all accurate, then a number of difficult questions suggest themselves: What are we to make of the *globalization of insecurity*? What are the challenges it poses to the theory and practice of governance? And what might be appropriate normative and institutional responses? Before turning to these questions, it may be useful to probe a little more deeply into the dynamic of globalization.

Global Social Change

One of the most important features of contemporary social change is its global character. The last three centuries are perhaps best described in terms of the closely interconnected transformations associated with secularization, industrialization, urbanization, the geographical extension of market relations, and, paradoxically enough, nationalism and bureaucratization. All these trends have now assumed global dimensions.

In what sense is social change global? First and most obviously in the space it occupies. Boundaries, whether underpinned by law, culture, or physical force, have not withstood the tidal flow of change. National and other boundaries may persist, but they are increasingly porous. Territorially based authority has become increasingly problematic (Prakash and Hart, 1999, p. 172). Indeed, globalization is best understood as a codeword for the internationalization or even transnationalization of economic practice (technical innovation, production, trade, finance), security practice (understood in its hard or conventional sense as military or physical security), and cultural practice (understood primarily as transnational flows of people, ideas, images and messages).

Second, social change is global by virtue of the norms or principles (e.g., free trade, comparative advantage, modernization, economic growth, universal human-rights, global commons, collective security, humanitarian intervention) that states and non-state actors invoke to explain or justify their conduct. Third, the function of social change has been to create a global architecture of power, in which production, distribution, and communication are increasingly structured by international networks and strategies. Fourth, many of the agents of social change, including transnational corporations, professional associations, and diverse cultural and political movements, have developed objectives, structures, policies, and patterns of socialization that are international in scope and ethos.

Of the many actors that have contributed to globalization, it is perhaps the transnational corporation (TNC) that has played the most conspicuous role. By 1998 close to 70 percent of global trade was controlled by just 500 TNCs, one-fifth of all foreign-owned assets in the world were in the hands of 100 TNCs, while a mere 1 percent of TNCs accounted for half of the total foreign direct investment (FDI) in the world. Of the 100 largest economic actors in the world, only half were states; the rest were TNCs. UNCTAD's *World Investment Report 2000* estimated that the number of TNCs in 1999 had risen to 63,000 parent firms with approximately 690,000 foreign affiliates. Though the huge global conglomerates are comparable in scale to national economies, most TNCs are much smaller, concentrating on one or two production lines or a small cluster of related products.

Notwithstanding the diversity of transnational economic actors, two generalizations are possible. First, the transnationalization of business is accompanied and sustained by the technological revolution, especially in transportation and communication. Freed by technology from territorial constraints, capital can move to wherever wage levels, rents, taxes, and government regulations and incentives offer the prospect of higher profits. Secondly, within the global architecture of power and wealth the decisions of governments and inter-governmental organizations depend more and more on the resources, expertise and ideas of corporations, especially those with high levels of transnational organization. A striking example of this trend is the rising influence of the World Economic Forum which annually brings together senior figures of the corporate world, political leaders and a sprinkling of international civil servants, economists and other experts.

The Rise of Transnational Issues

States, even relatively powerful ones, have found it increasingly difficult to perform the various functions on which their legitimacy ultimately depends, namely to deliver security and economic well-being to their citizens. They seem less and less able to manage the competing pressures to which they are exposed within the confines of national boundaries and the limitations of national resources. Because of these difficulties states have, since 1945 and particularly since the early 1970s, found it necessary to shed at least partial functions to a range of subnational, supranational, international, and transnational organizations. Nowhere is the contemporary predicament of the state more strikingly evident than in the areas of financial and environmental policy. The predicament becomes acute in circumstances where the state confronts ecological disorders that have their origins outside its domain (e.g., transboundary pollution); or where it is compelled to navigate powerful economic forces over which it has at best limited control (e.g., developing states beset by high and rising levels of foreign debt). Two cases may help to illustrate the general trend.

In April 1985, in the Ukraine near Kiev, the Chernobyl nuclear reactor caught fire. As the fire raged, and then smouldered, over some ten days vast quantities of radioactive gases swept across Scandinavia, then spread southwards over other parts of Europe, moving on to contaminate parts of England, eventually dispersing over an even wider area causing significant increases in radiation levels as far afield as Japan. A number of governments were forced to introduce emergency measures—from monitoring radiation levels to withdrawing certain foodstuffs from the market or advising communities to change their diet. The number of deaths that will ultimately result from the accident remains the subject of scientific debate, but is likely to be in the tens, if not hundreds, of thousands. What the accident tells us is that national governments may build nuclear stations, equip them with complex safety systems, and lay down elaborate regulations to make their operation safer, but the actual risks involved extend beyond the control of any one state. Economic activity has, it seems, integrated our physical environment with human technology on a scale which exceeds the problem-solving capacities of individual states. To this extent at least, it is arguable that our economic and political institutions have developed largely in the context of national polities and decision-making processes poorly suited to cope with the challenges of globalization.

The growth of international debt generally, and Third World debt in particular, offers another graphic illustration of the limited freedom of action available to national governments. Consider Brazil, where the destruction of the Amazonian rainforest has been proceeding at an alarming pace. Almost half of the world's rainforest has been felled or burnt, endangering or eliminating countless species and annually releasing billions of tons of carbon dioxide into the atmosphere. Deforestation in Brazil alone accounts for an estimated 20 percent of all carbon released from deforestation globally. These far-reaching environmental effects, which are global in scope, are closely connected to economic processes which have themselves assumed global proportions. During the 1980s Brazil, which laboured under a large and chronic foreign debt (estimated at $115 billion in 1987), was obliged to adopt the structural adjustment policies of the International Monetary Fund (IMF), to increase exports and reduce public spending. This meant in practice forcing peasants off their traditional land to make it available for cash crops, and extend agricultural and industrial activity into the rainforest. The net effect was to accentuate the already wide inequalities of wealth and income and to reduce a growing fraction of the population to abject poverty. Malnourishment bordering on hunger afflicted close to 35 million people living in the northeast of Brazil, which includes much of the Amazonian forest. Notwithstanding the rhetoric of sovereignty, the range of options available to any Brazilian government committed to servicing the country's debt appeared severely constrained by existing institutional arrangements.

What these two examples point to is the increasing interconnectedness of the international system. Over time, national and territorial boundaries, though they still give rise to periodic conflicts, can no longer be considered the central ordering principle in the organization of human affairs. The two examples we have just considered, the repercussions of nuclear power development and Third World debt, are but two manifestations of a wider and more complex trend.

Environmental degradation in its various forms, the overt and covert proliferation of weapons of mass destruction and of the materials used in their manufacture, the licit and illicit international arms trade, the increasingly dangerous spread of light weapons, drug trafficking, piracy, large and often unforeseen population movements, including refugees, internally displaced people, guest workers and legal and illegal immigrants, all these are an integral part of the emerging 'macropolitical agenda' (Camilleri and Falk, 1992: 148–151). They have one common characteristic: they all in different ways and to different degrees exceed the institutional capacities and resources of states. They call into question the usefulness of the traditional notions of *national interest* and *national security* in making sense of the contemporary human condition.

The Economic Engine Driving Globalization

While the environmental, political, cultural, and intellectual dimensions of globalization are critically important, it is the rapidly accelerating trade, investment, finance and technology flows across national boundaries that constitute the driving engine (Malhotra, 1997). International economic activity is increasingly shaped by transnational strategies geared to production for world markets (Camilleri, 1994, 1997). The aim is to shift capital, technology and labour in ways which maximize profitability, and that means achieving the most advantageous combination of factors, including the cost of labour, the cost of land, taxation rates, environmental and other forms of regulation, interest rates and exchange rates. For production to be organized in this way, it becomes necessary to remove obstacles to the free movement of money (financial deregulation), capital (investment liberalization), goods and services (trade liberalization) and labour (industrial deregulation). The name of the game is mobility and speed.

Characteristic of this period has been the rise of the neo-liberal project, sometimes referred to as 'economic rationalism' and the corresponding decline of Keynesian demand management in most parts of the Western world. Though the obsession with the virtues of deregulation has been most conspicuous in the Anglophone world, nowhere has economic policy been left unscathed by the affliction. The trend has become truly global, extending—courtesy of several international institutions, notably the IMF and the World Bank—to numerous African and Latin American countries, and more recently to the former Soviet Union and much of Eastern Europe.

The hallmarks of the new OECD orthodoxy have been reduced public spending, a fall in real wages, the slow but steady erosion of the welfare system, and various forms of deregulation, especially of the financial and labour sectors. Much of this has been done and justified by national governments of varying political complexion in the name of greater international competitiveness, normally translated in terms of improved export performance. In the process a rapidly shifting international division of labour has emerged, which has meant, among other things, a substantial shift of manufacturing capacity from advanced industrial to newly industrializing economies, initially to the four East Asian tigers and a handful of Latin American countries, but increasingly to a number of other developing economies, including Malaysia, Thailand and most dramatically China.

Another distinguishing feature of this period has been the emergence of a new 'production structure', which, by virtue of the accelerating rate of technical change, now means continuous product innovation (and obsolescence), that is, the introduction of new products and services and new systems of information gathering, storage, and dissemination. The compressed time scale of the productive cycle and the associated costs of research, development, and production require higher profits than those likely to be derived solely from local or national markets; hence, the shift to global markets and the adoption of global production strategies. In the process, the state, regardless of the size or structure of the economy or the complexion of its political institutions, has little option but to accept the competitive logic of the world market. To this rule, the supposedly strong states of East Asia are no exception, as evidenced by the 1997 financial crisis. All states must negotiate with the international and transnational institutions which exercise decisive leverage in shaping the balance of costs and benefits, or risks and opportunities within the world economy. That leverage flows from their command of technology, their ready access to global markets and global sources of capital, and their ability to play off one sovereign jurisdiction against another.

The emergence of 'global factories', 'global offices', and 'global labs' suggests that national governments, as much in developing as in industrialized countries, have come to operate within a global production system that substantially shapes the strategic options as well as policy instruments at their disposal. Compounding and in some ways reshaping this trend over the last twenty years has been the globalization of financial markets. The revolution in computing and information technology coupled with the deregulation of national banking and finance has led to massive flows of investment and speculative capital, which have rapidly assumed even greater importance than international trade. The daily turnover of currency transactions in 1986 was estimated at $188 billion, but by 1995 the volume was close to $1.2 trillion, or 85 percent of the total currency reserves (not including gold) held by the world's governments (Singh, 1998). The same trend is evident in the expansion of total private capital flows to developing countries from $62.1 billion in 1991 to $299.8 billion in 1997 (World Bank, 2001). The ebb and flow of national regulation is itself now subject to external factors, or, to be more precise, to pressures generated by an increasingly integrated, geographically unrestricted system of transnational finance.

There now exists a global social structure of production that penetrates national economies and the policy-making structures of national governments. As Robert Cox has observed, 'there is a transnational process of consensus formation among the official caretakers of the global economy' involving unofficial forums like the Trilateral Commission and the World Economic Forum and official bodies like the Organization for Economic Cooperation and Development (OECD), the International Monetary Fund (IMF), and the G7 (Cox, 1996, p. 301). Significantly, the most powerful ministries and agencies of government are those that are most closely connected with the global economy and its institutions. This may help to explain why, despite wide national variations in political traditions and institutions, so many advanced capitalist states have, since the late 1970s, abandoned the strategy of Keynesian demand management and substantially lowered the expectations associated with the welfare state, all of this in the name of greater international competitiveness. In the process, it is the state itself that is both internationalized and denationalised, with global integration creating and feeding upon differential rates of productivity, technical innovation, economic growth, and income within, as much as between, national societies (Gill and Mittelman, 1997).

Faced with these contradictory pressures, the state may pursue one of two strategies: delegation, or reassertion of authority. The first strategy involves the formal or informal transfer of powers to a range of supranational or international (regional or global) institutions charged with developing mechanisms of consultation, co-operation, and coordination. The World Bank, the IMF, the General Agreement on Tariffs and Trade (GATT), and its successor, the World Trade Organization (WTO), the OECD, the Western Economic Summits (the G7–Group of Seven), the International Atomic Energy Agency (IAEA), the Bank for International Settlements, the Standing Committee on Banking Regulations and Supervisory Practices (the Cooke Committee), and a burgeoning web of macroregional organizations—the European Union, the North American Free Trade Agreement, the Association of Southeast Asian Nations (ASEAN), and now APEC—all these are part of the institutional infrastructure that has been created to provide a degree of regulation in the wake of the state's diminishing capacity for economic management. These institutions have assumed expanded functions and resources, enabling them to operate as 'transgovernmental coalitions' connected to a web of bureaucratic structures within each of the member states. By setting agendas and defining policy options, they help to establish the consensual framework that underpins the state apparatus. Though deviant behaviour remains possible, it is effectively discouraged by virtue of the penalties that such behaviour invariably attracts.

The state may choose an altogether different strategy. It may reassert its own perception of the *national* interest and *national* authority by a degree of financial reregulation or by providing local industry with various forms of protection. By itself, however, such a strategy is unlikely to restore national control over the instruments of economic policy, much less over economic outcomes. It may provide one or more states with temporary leverage in an intensified competitive struggle, but it is unlikely to change the underlying transnational structure and may even have the effect of extending and deepening the internationalization of production and finance. Neither the individual state, viewed as a single structure or agency, nor the international system of states taken as a whole, can be expected to function independently of the institutional framework of a rapidly integrating world economy.

Implications for Human Security

The foregoing analysis makes it clear that globalization, as it has unfolded in recent decades, poses a serious challenge to the capacity of states and governments to manage the national economy. The erosion of local and national autonomy—a trend whose far-reaching implications needs careful scrutiny—is not, however, the only troubling facet of globalization. It is now reasonably clear that the dominant neo-liberal growth paradigm, championed by the managerial classes, G7 governments and such international institutions as the IMF, World Bank and WTO, has not achieved sustainable and human social development for most developing economies or even for the world as a whole. Indeed, very few societies, regardless of their technological sophistication or size of their economies, are able to deliver to the vast majority of their members choices and opportunities that lead to a long healthy, creative life and the enjoyment of an adequate standard of living, freedom, self-esteem and the respect of others.

Disparities between rich and poor have grown starker as much within as between countries. In 1997, the wealthiest 20 percent of the world's population accounted for 86 percent of world GDP, 82 percent of world exports, 68 percent of FDI, and 93 percent of Internet use. The poorest 20 percent accounted for a mere 1 percent of world GDP, 1 percent of world exports, 1 percent of FDI, and 0.2 percent of Internet use (Human Development Report, 1999, p. 2). During the 1990s the concentration of income, resources and wealth has become more pronounced both within nations and the corporate sector. The world's 200 richest people had more than doubled their net worth in the four years to 1998, to more than $1 trillion. The assets of the leading three billionaires exceeded the combined GDP of all least developed countries with a population of some 600 million. By 1998, following a wave of mergers and acquisitions, the top ten companies in pesticides controlled 85 percent of the global market (estimated at $31 billion). The corresponding share of the top ten companies in the telecommunications industry was 86 percent of a $262 billion market (Human Development Report, 1999, p. 3).

Technological optimists have consistently argued that innovative technologies hold the key to progress. Technological breakthroughs have undoubtedly contributed to significant advances in human development. Vaccines and antibiotics have been instrumental in the substantial decline in mortality rates over the last 60 years in many part of Asia. Technical innovations in plant breeding, fertilizers and pesticides have been credited with a marked reduction in chronic malnourishment in much of South Asia (from around 40 percent in the 1970s to 23 percent in 1997). Yet these aggregate figures tell only part of the story. They do not reveal the substantial disparities in health-care available to different sections of society, nor do they indicate the negative environmental consequences of the green revolution, the medium- and long-term pollution effects of heavy reliance on fertilizers and pesticides, or the widening income gap between landowners who have the purchasing power or credit worthiness to be able to apply new agricultural techniques and poor peasants who do not. As of the late 1990s some 93 countries with 62 percent of the world's population were still struggling to reduce infant mortality rates, and as many as 70 countries had little prospect of substantially reducing income poverty.

Even if one accepts the proposition that technology has the capacity to deliver solutions to a range of problems associated with food production, education, transportation or health-care, it does not follow that all societies or, to be more accurate, all sections of society will be in a position to take advantage of these technological possibilities. The UNDP's 2001 *Human Development Report* calculated that in 1998 the 29 OECD countries with 19 percent of the world's population "spent $250 billion on research and development—more than the combined economic output of the world's 30 poorest countries." Of the 347,000 new patents issued in 1998, 91 percent were accounted for by the OECD, and most of that research and development activity was conducted by the private sector. By contrast developing countries had miniscule access to the latest technical know-how, and little capacity to mobilize technological resources to meet the needs of the poor. Of the $70 billion devoted to global spending on health, only $300 million was allocated to vaccines for HIV/AIDS and about $100 million to malaria research. These global disparities mirror and reinforce domestic inequalities. Whereas India was home to a world-class technology hub in Bangalore, illiteracy in that country stood at 44 percent, with only 28 telephones for every 1,000 people (*Human Development Report*, 2001, p. 3).

The picture we have painted is well known and the subject of extensive documentation (Dent and Peters, 1999; Bello, 1999; Chossudovsky, 1997; Oxfam, 1995). Economic insecurity is the condition of a very large fraction of humanity. Such insecurity, however, is not confined to the so called least developed economies. As the financial crises that afflicted Mexico, Russia, South Korea, Malaysia, Indonesia and Thailand during the 1990s have graphically illustrated, transitional, industrializing, and even industrialized economies can fall victim to the ravages of financial volatility. The very high levels of capital flow to South Korea, Malaysia, the Philippines and Thailand during the first half of the 1990s (estimated at $93 billion in 1996) were reversed almost overnight: an inflow of $96 billion in 1996 was followed by an outflow of $12 billion in 1997. The reversal of short-term capital flow was followed by a succession of bankruptcies and bank closures, widespread shedding of jobs, sharp falls in real wages, and drastic cuts in health and education budgets.

Economic insecurity is in most countries inseparable from social insecurity. Its' most obvious manifestations include job and income insecurity, including the casualization of labour, the dismantling or curtailing of welfare provisions, the failure of the health system to deliver essential medical services and supplies, the inability to adopt effective preventive strategies to deal with the HIV/AIDS pandemic (almost 6 million new infections in 1998). The cumulative effect of these pressures on everyday life is to reduce life prospects and opportunities not only in a material sense, but just as importantly to stunt the development of human energies, intellectual creativity, and emotional fulfilment. Before long the insecurity assumes a cultural dimension. Indigenous cultures themselves become stifled as they are increasingly deprived of the material and social conditions necessary for self-expression. All the more so as one of the dominant features of a rapidly globalizing world has been the sustained one-way flow of images, symbols, and cultural practices from the hegemonic centre (the rich West, especially the United States) to the periphery (the vast majority of societies in Asia, Africa and Latin America). Global media networks and communications technologies have become the conduit for the transmission of imported tastes, fashions, and standards encompassing every facet of everyday life. The intrusiveness of Coca-Cola, Nike, McDonald's and Hollywood is but the outward expression of a much deeper cultural malaise and insecurity that afflicts economically and technologically dependent societies.

There are, of course, other dimensions to insecurity. For reasons of space we can do no more than highlight three of these: environmental, personal, and political. Reference has already been made to the subtle but profound interconnections between economic and environmental impoverishment (Camilleri, 1996). Chronic environmental degradation as of now undercuts the livelihood of hundreds of millions of people, whether through desertification, deforestation, the exhaustion of fisheries, acid rain, and environmentally induced diseases. Global warming is looming as a major threat to the economic viability of several low-lying coastal regions, including many of the small islands that dot the Pacific Ocean. Conversely, grinding poverty leaves many little choice but to engage in food gathering, agricultural and other practices that put added pressure on the environment. A significant factor in recent population flows, both in Africa and Asia, is the economic imperative, which is itself closely connected to the diminishing capacity of land to sustain a given population (Renner, 1996, 35–75).

Personal insecurity assumes a multitude of forms, depending on cultural and economic context. Here we simply draw attention to the fears and anxieties that are the inevitable by-product of the illicit trade in drugs, women, weapons and laundered money. The deregulation of capital markets, advances in information and communications technology, and cheaper transport have to varying degrees stimulated or given added momentum to the traffic in women and girls for sexual exploitation, people smuggling in its various guises, and the trade in light weapons. Transnationally organized networks sustain rising levels of criminal and pathological behaviour which enmesh not only its primary victims but ever expanding layers of society, including highly placed elements in government, police and the judiciary. Closely related to all these forms of insecurity are the tensions and rivalries which set one community against another. Personal, social and economic insecurity sets the stage for political polarization, based on race, ethnicity or religion. It is worth noting that of the 61 major armed conflicts between 1989 and 1998, 58 were intra-state conflicts. The phenomenon, sometimes inappropriately referred to as "failed" or "collapsed" states, points precisely to the increasing incidence and intensity of human insecurity and the inability of fragile local and national institutions to cope with the ensuing pressures. The much greater frequency and scope of U.N. and other forms of multilateral intervention in intra-state conflicts are the inescapable consequence of this trend.

Insecurity in its various dimensions is not the preserve of the South. Industrial restructuring and financial deregulation have resulted in severe social and economic dislocation in many parts of the North. Responding to the pressures of global competition, governments and corporations have pressed for the deregulation of the system of industrial relations, including more flexible employment policies that have translated into less secure jobs, substantial retrenchments, and a relaxation of occupational health and safety standards. Despite sustained attempts by European governments and the European Union to maintain acceptable levels of economic growth, unemployment in Europe stands at 35 million. It is hardly surprising that in times of social and economic anxiety, and in the face of rising numbers of guest workers, refugees and asylum seekers, racism and xenophobia should have become increasingly visible in the streets and politics of many European countries. If to this should be added the mounting fears of environmental degradation, terrorist attack, and the losing battle against rising levels of drug abuse, the heightened and seemingly pervasive experience of individual and collective anxiety becomes readily understandable.

We may safely conclude that human insecurity is deeply troubling, not in the sense that it is a novel phenomenon but that it poses a normative and institutional challenge of critical proportions. As a submission to the UN's Independent Commission on Human Security so aptly put it:

> The insecurity generated by the globalization of the political economy has two sides, it is increasing the demand for security and decreasing the availability of supply in the public goods indispensable for the satisfaction of human needs, indispensable for their basic security (Open Letter forwarded in September 2001 by Professor Kinhide Mushakoji on behalf of 40 leading international scholars).

The emphasis here on insecurity is deliberate, for it reminds us that security is primarily not a physical but a psycho-social experience. After all, fear of physical attack is itself a psycho-social phenomenon. Analytically, what is critical to human security is not sustainable development, human rights and fundamental freedoms, the quality of the environment, or social equity *per se.* These are all highly desirable outcomes, and no doubt integral to human well-being, but their relationship to security is more complex. What is critical to security is the maintenance of a social order, which has enough pattern and regularity to it to inspire confidence in the future. By contrast, insecurity relates to the experience of social disruption, the fragility of social relationships, the absence of cognitive control over, or affective empathy with, various forms of human intercourse. In that sense psycho-social insecurity is the perceived disruption—actual or potential—of the social order. We may speak of a cleavage or dissonance in the patterns of mutual knowledge and in the fabric of common norms and shared loyalties. To grapple at all effectively with the problem of insecurity it becomes necessary to construct and sustain a "legitimated social order," one which sufficiently resonates with the deeper needs and aspirations of its members to inspire confidence in the future.

Recent Approaches and Proposals

Reflecting the urgency and multifaceted character of the contemporary predicament, numerous solutions have been offered by practising and retired policy-makers, scholars, experts of various kinds, think-tanks and independent commissions. Some have addressed specific problems or areas of policy, whether to do with peace and security, development, human rights, or environment (Bird, 1996; Evans, 1993; Homer-Dixon, 1991; Independent Commission on Security and Disarmament Issues, 1989). Others have dealt with larger questions of social and political organization, focusing on national, regional or international organizations (Knight, 2000; Cox, 1997; Childers and Urquhart, 1992).

The proliferation of these reform-oriented studies over the last decade, though of uneven intellectual rigour and imagination, has certainly advanced our understanding of the challenges posed by globalization. It is neither possible nor necessary to outline here the enormous range of ideas and recommendations which they have brought to the attention of theorists and practitioners alike. It is enough for our purposes to draw on two contributions: the Report of the Commission on Global Governance published in 1995, and the annual reports and publications of the United Nations Development Programme of the last ten years. These two have been selected because each in different ways gives due consideration to the values that should guide the reform agenda and to the interconnections between different areas of policy. Moreover, in line with our analysis of human security, they both attempt a holistic approach to social and political change.

The UNDP's *Human Development Reports* of the last decade have put forward a series of policy initiatives, to be introduced either at the national or international level, which have contributed to what may be loosely referred to as a new paradigm of 'sustainable human development.'[1] Among the globally oriented proposals, four are worth highlighting:

a) the *20:20 initiative* (1992) which envisages every developing country allocating 20 percent of its domestic budget, and every donor country 20 percent of its official development assistance, to basic health-care, basic education, access to safe water and sanitation, and basic family-planning packages for all couples;

b) the creation of a *global human security fund* (1994) to deal with drug trafficking, international terrorism, communicable diseases, nuclear proliferation, natural disasters, ethnic conflicts, population movements and environmental degradation—the fund of $250 billion a year would be financed from a range of sources, including reduced global military spending, a tax on speculative international capital movements, a global energy tax, and official development assistance;

c) a *new global architecture* (1994), which would see the establishment of economic security council, a world central bank, an international investment trust, and a world anti-monopoly authority to monitor the activities of international corporations;

d) a timetable to eliminate legal gender discrimination (1995), setting the year 2005 as the date by which the legal equality of men and women would be universally recognized, using as the framework the 1979 Convention on the Elimination of All Forms of Discrimination Against women (CEDAW).

National proposals, premissed on a human-centric notion of development and a more active role for local communities and civil society more generally, have included:

a) *restructuring social expenditures* (1991) so as to shift the focus from military spending to social spending;

b) enhancing women's representation (1995) with the specific aim of giving women at least 30 percent representation in all decision-making processes—locally and nationally;

c) agenda for poverty eradication (1997)—a six-point agenda aimed at giving individuals, households and communities greater control over their lives and resources, and promoting a higher level of state activism geared specifically to the eradication of poverty.

Whereas the UNDP's recommendations understandably focused on human development and the elimination of poverty, primarily in a Third World context, the Commission for Global governance offered a more encompassing set of recommendations. Animated by a global civic ethic and pointing to the emergence of a global civil society, *Our Global Neighbourhood* posited a set of common rights and responsibilities for the whole of humanity, including active participation in governance. It formulated broad principles of security policy (e.g., right of all peoples and states to a secure existence, illegitimacy of weapons of mass destruction as instruments of national defence), economic policy (e.g., need for a framework of rules and order for global economic competition, urgency of radical debt reduction, especially for heavily indebted low-income countries), U.N. reform (e.g., reorganization of Security Council membership, revitalization of General Assembly), and rule of law (e.g., acceptance of the compulsory jurisdiction of the International Court of Justice, establishment of international criminal court). Other more specific proposals called for the development of a U.N. Rapid Reaction Force, the integration of peacekeeping into the U.N.'s annual budget, and an enhanced role for the IMF. The Report also recommended that the Trusteeship Council should be given a new mandate over the global commons; that an annual Forum of Civil Society Organizations should be created; that the U.N. Secretary-General should be empowered to seek the advice of the International Court of Justice, particularly in the early stages of emerging disputes; and that the International Law Commission should be authorized to explore how international law-making could be expedited.

The multiple ideas and recommendations emanating from the UNDP and the Commission for Global Governance have cumulatively enriched the discussion of current trends and future options. Each in its own way identifies with considerable analytical insight the inadequacies of existing policies and institutional arrangements, and offers imaginative proposals seeking to bridge the gap between actuality and the preferred future. Yet both fall short of the mark. To be viable the reform agenda requires a sharper analysis of globalization and a set of policy prescriptions that are simultaneously more radical yet more attuned to emerging geopolitical, economic and socio-cultural trends.

The analytical framework elaborated in the first part of this essay specifically addressed the first requirement. It identified the following as the distinguishing characteristics of globalization: the global character of contemporary social change; the rise of transnational issues which exceed the problem-solving capacities of national states; the current ascendancy of the neo-liberal project with its emphasis on the unfettered movement of goods and services, capital, technology, money and labour; and the emergence of a global production structure whose inner logic is far removed from the human security paradigm. The end result is best described as the *globalization of insecurity*. Turning to the second requirement, the notion of "global cosmopolitan democracy" offers us perhaps the beginnings of an answer. The notion itself and the practices which it suggests cannot be viewed as set in concrete. On the contrary, they must be painstakingly refined and negotiated against a backdrop of a rapidly changing geopolitical, economic and cultural landscape. It is to this task that we now turn our attention.

The Democratic Imperative

The ideas presented here have been developed largely through the *Global Governance Reform Project* jointly sponsored by the School of Social Sciences (La Trobe University, Melbourne), Focus on the Global South (Bangkok), and the Toda Institute for Global Peace and Policy Research (Tokyo and Honolulu). The central concern of this five-year project has been to 'rethink the puzzle of global governance by placing it squarely within the context of a globalizing economy' (Camilleri, Malhotra and Tehranian, 2000, xvii). The key question it addresses is disarmingly simple yet extraordinarily complex: Is it possible to devise responses to the challenges of globalization which are consistent with the principles of human security outlined above? Expressed a little differently, the question becomes: Can the emerging system of global governance be made legitimate in the eyes of all its principal constituencies: states, peoples, and the international community generally? (Falk 1995, 105-133). If the answer is to be in the affirmative, then, as previously indicated, the global social order has to be legitimated. It has to resonate with its constituencies—with their needs, anxieties and aspirations—sufficiently to inspire confidence in the future.

The key argument advanced here is that all facets of globalization—economic as much as political and cultural—must be subjected to the test of democratic legitimacy. Such democratisation must breathe life into the decision-making processes and institutions, not just of the international community but of local, national and regional communities. Needless to say, a great number of structural impediments stand in the way of such transformative change. The most obvious of these is what Richard Falk has labelled "geopolitical closure" (Falk, 1999, 113), an arrangement institutionalized by the Security Council, whereby any one of five permanent members has the power to block any initiative to which it is opposed. There are, however, other more fundamental obstacles, implicit in our earlier analysis, of which three are especially troubling. The first has to do with the state-centric ethos governing the U.N. system and most multilateral organizations. The second relates to the dominant ideology of globalization shaped by transnational corporations, financial markets and the institutional guardians of the global economy, notably unofficial bodies like the world Economic Forum and official bodies like the OECD, the G7, and the IMF. The third refers to the geopolitical, military, economic and cultural hegemony exercised by the United States. The combined impact of these three tendencies is to concentrate decision-making in relatively few hands, to exclude the most critical issues of human security from the global agenda, except in peripheral or tokenistic ways, and to entrench Western dominance, in particular forms of discourse and practice which are at best culturally insensitive and at worst likely to create unprecedented levels of global polarization.

There are nevertheless a number of countervailing tendencies, two of which are perhaps critical to the success of the democratic project, namely the emergence of a new kind of universalism, and the slow, at times erratic but unmistakable diffusion of power. Contributing to the first tendency is the increasing universality of the U.N. system, as measured not only or even primarily by the number of member states, but by the increasing participation of a wide range of non-state actors, the widening scope of consultation, and the U.N.'s steadily expanding agenda and forms and techniques of intervention. Increasingly, the world's global and regional institutions are in practice, if not in theory, rethinking the centrality of the principle of sovereignty. Mirroring and reinforcing that tendency is the embryonic development of a global civil society which is giving rise to new processes of global communication. This new universalism coincides with the growth of tensions and contradictions which place severe limits on the exercise of hegemonic power. At face value the post-Cold War period has given rise to a unipolar system based on U.S. military and economic preponderance. In reality, subtler but more enduring trends point to a multipolar system in which Europe, Japan, China, Russia, India, and possibly an Islamic coalition are likely to play an increasingly important role in defining the priorities of the international agenda. The increasing tensions that mark the North-South divide, whether on issues of trade, debt or environment, the growth of regional formations, and the development of a more balanced triangular relationship between state, market and civil society, are all likely to influence the future architecture of the world economy and international political order.

How, then, might the democratic project be pursued to take account of structural impediments and countervailing opportunities as part of a wider strategy directed to the advancement of human security? First, the various levels of governance—local, microregional (or provincial), national, macroregional and global—must be complementary and mutually constitutive. Institutions at each level remain autonomous and act within their own sphere of competence, but democratization at one level connects with and reinforces democratization at other levels (Held, 1995, 232). Secondly, a civic culture must flourish in all three arenas: state, market and civil society, with participation in each arena drawing inspiration from and sustaining participation in the other two. Thirdly, high priority must be given to maximizing and equalizing access to educational opportunities and to ending highly concentrated control of scientific and technological innovation. The formation of public opinion and expression of the democratic will must rest on the free and balanced flow of knowledge, ideas and argument.

The proposals that follow, though they are primarily directed to the global level of governance, are designed to give shape and content to this multifaceted notion of cosmopolitan democracy, to endow institutions at all levels with renewed legitimacy. Using the existing U.N. system purely as point of departure, they point to a programme of radical yet feasible transformation. The proposed restructuring has five interconnected objectives: a) to reduce the dominance of the major centres of power and wealth in the ordering of human affairs; b) to enable states to participate fully in regional and global decision-making; c) to enhance the role of the U.N. system as the centrepiece of regional and global organizations entrusted with security and economic functions; d) to open up regional and global institutions to the voices of civil society, that is to a range of non-state actors and to world public opinion generally; and f) to make all levels of governance more attuned to the interconnected challenges posed by the search for human security in a rapidly globalizing world.

United Nations' General Assembly. A revitalized General Assembly has become critical to a more secure world. At its annual meeting the General

Assembly should be presented with reports by the Security Council and a newly formed Economic and Social Security Council (as outlined below). Using these reports as the basis of its deliberations, the Assembly would formulate guidelines for global security and economic policy in the coming year, which would provide the broad direction for the programme of action and decisions of the two Councils.

Where the General Assembly deems that either Council has not acted in the spirit of those guidelines, it would have the power to request the Council to review its decisions in the light of the advice given by the Assembly. Although the Assembly would not have the power to override the two Councils, the proposed strengthening of its authority would enable all members states to have greater input into security and economic policy-making at the global level and, at the same time, to make such policy more open to international scrutiny and debate.

People's Assembly. The General Assembly can only represent the governments of member states, many of which have poor democratic credentials and questionable legitimacy. There is, therefore, a strong case for a second chamber, a People's Assembly, which would provide a forum for a much wider range of views. The People's Assembly would not have legislative powers, but would function as a house of debate and review over all aspects of U.N. activity.

Members would be elected by their constituencies by universal suffrage, a secret ballot, one vote one value. The boundaries of each constituency (of about 6 million people) would be determined by a U.N. electoral commission. The elections would be preceded by widespread public debate and widely accessible media coverage, and organized by the relevant national government, but closely monitored by a U.N. inspection team to ensure proper procedure. Each country's membership of the General Assembly would be conditional on meeting these electoral requirements. These arrangements would have a democratizing effect on the political processes of many countries, including liberal democracies, improve the international image of the United Nations, and encourage a better informed world public opinion.

Consultative Assembly. The overarching goal of the United Nations is to improve global conditions conducive to human security. To put it differently, the environment, population movements, food and energy security, marine resources, trade and financial flows, human rights, transnational crime and much else are integral elements of the global governance agenda. It makes good sense therefore that organizations that have a close involvement with, or acknowledged expertise in, these matters should contribute to the U.N.'s consideration of these issues, and to its decision-making processes.

A third chamber, the Consultative Assembly, would consist of representatives drawn from three sectors: the corporate sector (represented through international and regional umbrella organizations); the trade union and professional sector (also through their umbrella organizations), and the 'third sector' including a wide range of educational, scientific, cultural, religious and public-interest organizations involved in issues of human security. The General Assembly would determine the membership of the Consultative Assembly on the recommendation of the U.N. Secretariat.

United Nations' Security Council. To enhance its legitimacy, the Security Council must be opened up to broader membership and wider input into its discussions and decision-making processes. The veto rights of the five permanent members must be qualified and gradually phased out, over perhaps fifteen to twenty years. Initially, permanent members might retain the veto, but limitations could be placed on the frequency with which it is used or the manner in which it is exercised.

Great powers would retain permanent membership, but such membership would be reviewed, perhaps every ten years, to ensure it reflects global power realities.

To ensure greater representation, the membership of the Security Council should be expanded from the current fifteen to between twenty-three and twenty-five. Permanent members could be expanded from five to between seven and nine—Germany, Japan, India and, perhaps, Brazil might be suitable candidates for permanent membership. Depending on the progress of European integration, it may be appropriate at the end of the first ten-year period for Germany, France and Britain to relinquish their permanent membership in favour of the European Union.

The Security Council's membership could be expanded along regional lines. The world could be divided into regions, one possible classification being: Western Europe, Eastern Europe and Russia, Africa, the Middle East and West and Central Asia, South Asia, East Asia and Oceania, North and Central America, and South America); each of these eight regions could elect two representatives to the Council, each member serving a three-year term.

To pave the way for this long-term change in the composition of the Security Council, a short- to medium-term solution not requiring Charter amendment might be to give a number of states (major regional powers such as Germany, Japan, Brazil, India, Indonesia) 'semi-permanent' status. These members would be elected more frequently than other rotating members, which might also help to familiarize them with the processes and responsibilities associated with Security Council membership.

Economic and Social Security Council. The centrepiece of a global 'human security' policy must be the creation of a new, broadly based Economic and Social Security Council as a principal entity of the UN, replacing the current Economic and Social Council (ECOSOC) and accountable to the General Assembly.

The Economic and Social Security Council, without veto power, should in the longer term take on key decision-making roles in the areas of its mandate, similar to those of the reformed Security Council. Both the IMF and the World Bank would be brought under its direct scrutiny. The World Bank would be required to coordinate with other U.N. agencies and funds a concerted poverty reduction programme based on human security principles. The IMF would be expected to implement a universal surveillance role, with particular emphasis on surveillance of international capital flows, the operations of hedge funds, and major financial markets generally. The Economic and Social Security Council would assume primary responsibility for establishing a coherent, consistent and comprehensive world financial framework, which respects the principle of subsidiarity and encompasses institutions and arrangements at the national, regional and global levels. In the long run, this framework should be further formalized and a *World Financial Authority* (WFA) created to function as the overall regulator of finance at the global level, but accountable to the Council.

The Economic and Social Security Council would also oversee the introduction of a Currency Transactions Tax on international foreign exchange transactions, to be implemented nationally, but within the framework of an international co-operation agreement. A supranational body, an *International Taxation Organization*, with participating member states as its Board of Governors and accountable to the Council would take responsibility for the allocation of revenues. Similarly, an *International Independent Debt Arbitration Mechanism* would be created to remedy the presently unsustainable situation, particularly in the case of heavily indebted low-income countries, where creditors are currently the final arbiters of international debt relief.

Secretary-General and Secretariat. The success of any reform programme will, to a considerable degree, depend on the stature, authority, and administrative and financial resources of the Secretary-General and his/her staff.

The role of the Secretary-General must be defined more clearly. First, the Secretary-General, while acting in accordance with the decisions of the U.N.'s principal deliberative organs, must be empowered to use greater initiative particularly when dealing with crises. In addition to preparing detailed reports for the consideration of the Security Council and the Assemblies, the Secretary-General should also be able to submit detailed proposals and recommendations to them on a regular basis.

Second, the independence of the office being paramount, the Secretariat must be protected from any appearance of bias. The process of appointment must be transparent and the result of a much more inclusive consultative process than at present.

Third, part of the Secretary-General's role must be to articulate a vision for the U.N. system that is faithful to its principles and at the same time sensitive to changing world conditions. Fourth, the Secretary-General must engage systematically with all key players in world affairs—paying particular attention to the voices of civil society. Fifth, the Secretary-General, with the assistance of the various departments under his/her authority, must more effectively coordinate all the organs and activities that comprise the U.N. system. For this purpose, an inter-departmental/inter-agency committee should be set up—with the Secretary-General as its Chairperson and with overall responsibility for its agenda—which would function as a Cabinet for the entire U.N. system.

United Nations' Reform Commission. To consider the changes proposed here and elsewhere, the U.N. General Assembly should establish a U.N. Reform Commission composed of distinguished representatives from government, business, and civil society to study and report on the matter within a year.

Financial arrangements. The General Assembly should establish a new high-level independent Financial Advisory Committee. Its aim would be to provide the U.N., over the next ten years, with greater and more reliable access to financial resources, in ways that do not compromise but rather enhance its independence. The Committee should re-examine several proposals/initiatives that have been advanced in recent years (e.g., a Peacekeeping Reserve Fund and a Revolving Credit Fund). Particular attention should be given to the introduction of an international tax—to be applied, for example, to financial transactions, air travel or arms transfers.

As a broad objective, the total amount derived from national assessments for the U.N.'s general budget and for its peace operations budget should be increased by an annual 10 percent over the next ten years. Over the same ten-year period, a new structure of assessments should be arrived at, such that no member state contributes more than 10 percent to the total amount, provided that no additional burden is placed on developing economies. Any reduction in the contribution of the United States should be made up by other OECD countries and the more affluent among the newly industrialized countries.

If a member state fails to pay its dues on time for reasons other than acute financial hardship, penalties should be imposed (including fines and possible forfeiture of some of its voting rights). It should forfeit all its voting rights if it continues to default for two or more years in succession. Financial contributions from non-government sources should be accepted, but only under strict conditions of transparency and accountability to the General Assembly.

Regional Organizations. Regionalism appears to be growing rapidly (Mansfield and Milner 1999). The Secretary-General should initiate a periodic review of existing regional organizations, with a view to improving consultative arrangements with the U.N., and increasing their capacity to collaborate with the U.N. on all aspects of human security.

At the regional level several initiatives should be considered depending on regional needs and circumstances: a) regional peacekeeping centres, which might oversee the preparation and development of training programmes; b) crisis centres, which could enhance early-warning and early-response capabilities; and c) more effective liaison between regional organizations and regional arms of the U.N. system (e.g., the UN Regional Centre for Peace and Disarmament in Kathmandu).

Where it is proposed to delegate operational peacekeeping or peace enforcement tasks to a regional organization, the U.N. should conclude a formal agreement with the regional organization, setting out the specific functions delegated to it. Any such peace operation would still require the explicit authorization of the U.N. Security Council, as would its continued functioning and eventual termination. If a regional organization is to play a key role in a U.N. peace operation, it must have a high degree of legitimacy in the region, an established infrastructure, a charter totally consistent with U.N. principles, and personnel trained to the required U.N. standards. It must comply with accepted U.N. procedures.

In the light of recent financial upheavals, there is a strong case for considering the creation of regional, or where appropriate, sub-regional monetary institutions or arrangements (e.g., the East Asian Monetary Fund). The objective would be both to have institutions that are more responsive to regional and country-specific needs anc circumstances, and to encourage greater competition and pluralism.

Peacebuilding. Institutional innovation of the kind outlined here has one overriding objective: to enhance the framework of global governance in ways that take account of the challenges posed by globalization yet are consistent with human security principles. Central to this purpose is the development of a more systematic peacebuilding strategy. Peacebuilding should be made an integral part of all U.N. peace missions, and an inter-departmental peacebuilding unit established with direct access to the Secretary-General.

Equally important is the development of a multi-track conflict prevention strategy which would integrate inter-governmental (first-track) diplomacy with unofficial (second-track) forums and mechanisms; economic diplomacy, including aid packages designed to sustain peace agreements; mediatory and other third-party interventions by civil society organizations; communications diplomacy, with media-generated information and analysis helping to mobilize public opinion and mould the perceptions of policy-makers: other forms of citizen diplomacy, including the establishment of peace zones, peace corridors, and co-operation zones; peace education programmes addressing the root causes of conflict and promoting a culture of peace; creative diplomacy centred on the contribution of well known artists and entertainers (e.g., Live Aid, Band Aid, Comic Relief).

A comprehensive light-weapons control program should be established, whose functions would be to: a) destroy all illicit weapons after they are seized; b) incorporate mandatory and public destruction of weapons and ammunition; c) provide international regulation of all arms exports (using codes of conduct developed and applied by regional organizations and arms control regimes but with regional practices registered with and monitored by U.N.); d) mark weapons at the points of manufacture and import; and e) improve the keeping of records.

This necessarily brief and selective outline of the reform agenda has sought to place the democratic idea at the core of global governance. It advocates the construction of a democratic legal framework in which the functions, powers and resources normally assigned to the state are devolved across different but interacting and mutually reinforcing levels of governance—from the local to the global. A new culture of participation, however, if it is to flourish and animate every level of decision-making, must also incorporate the insights and aspirations of civil society. It is only by drawing on the diverse agencies and networks that comprise civil society that the multi-tiered system of governance can give meaning and content to the idea of human security. Conversely, it is only through the democratisation of political institutions that civil society can most effectively help to set the standards of humane governance, and critically monitor the application and enforcement of those standards.

A Concluding Note: Prospects for Civilization Dialogue

Globalization, as we have noted, is an elusive, confusing and contradictory phenomenon. With the collapse of communism no credible alternative to global capitalism is in sight. There is as of now no international agency or political movement which can exercise effective leadership in interpreting, much less guiding, economic and political change. There is no simple or single solution to this predicament.

Yet, for all the uncertainties and complexities of the present conjuncture, the notion of human emancipation continues to provide an essential ethical and political compass for the journey ahead. We have already considered in some detail the implications of that emancipatory response in the context of human security and democratic governance. There is, however, one other dimension which merits close attention. The struggle for human emancipation is now by definition global and cannot therefore be confined within the boundaries of locality, nation, or region. In dealing with this complex question we have thus far argued that in a rapidly globalizing world the democratization of global governance holds the key to any project committed to satisfying human needs and upholding human dignity. But that key may not by itself open all doors. Civilizational dialogue offers another valuable key.

Any project aimed at forging a new concept of international legitimacy will inevitably entail prolonged and dynamic interaction between cultures. Such a project needs to appreciate the specificity of each culture, while contributing to an evolutionary process which builds on commonality but, more importantly, strives for synthesis. Here we can draw a useful lesson from the evolution of the human rights agenda over the last fifty years. Beginning with the U.N. Charter and the Universal Declaration, a succession of U.N. resolutions, declarations, covenants, conventions and protocols has given rise, despite differences of emphasis and interpretation, to a wide-ranging normative consensus, which incorporates civil and political as well as social, economic and cultural rights, individual as well as collective rights. The contribution of different civilizational influences has been critically important to the success of this project.

The contribution which a civilizational dialogue might continue to make is multi-faceted, but five dimensions merit special attention. First, it can provide a richer and more varied conception of political community and humane governance by establishing a closer connection between human rights and the range of human needs, not least those of the disadvantaged (hence the emphasis on social and economic justice). Second, it can offer a more holistic understanding of the human condition by establishing a closer connection between rights and responsibilities and between the individual and the community. Third, it can help to situate human rights within a larger social context so that their application is not confined to individuals as disaggregated atoms but as members of larger collectivities, and of the international community as a whole, hence the emphasis on the rights of peoples—not only the right to self-determination but the right to a healthy environment, the right to peace, the right to food security, the right to share in the common heritage of humanity.

The other two dimensions flow from the preceding three but have an importance of their own. The first involves a rejection of Western domination that is, a rejection of the view that the West enjoys a monopoly on the definition of human needs and good governance. The Western liberal model—and the particular view of progress on which it rests—cannot apply universally across time and space. Human-rights and governance standards may be universal in scope at any one time, but how these standards are defined and applied is likely to change over time. This brings us to the last aspect of inter-civilizational discourse, namely the emphasis on respectful communication and interaction. If this is an important criterion of legitimate governance within a society, then presumably the same criterion ought to apply when the arena shifts from national to international governance. It follows that the development of a global civil society must proceed by way of negotiation and involve all of the parties concerned.

To put it simply, inter-religious and inter-cultural dialogue can help articulate a new internationalism, an internationalism that goes beyond mere economic or technological interdependence, and subjects economic and political orthodoxy to ethical scrutiny. What important principles might underpin the search for a new internationalism?

The first principle is the one that animates this entire essay: globalization must be democratized.

There is a need for a global *perestroika*—for providing local, national and regional communities with a say over key decisions, not least economic decisions. Much serious thinking and open discussion will be needed to develop institutions and processes that are both democratic and culturally sensitive.

Secondly, if economic globalization is to continue, the present vicious circle must be transformed into a virtuous one, occurring hand in hand with an enriched public sphere, improved human rights, full employment, better working conditions and more extensive public services. On all these fronts, the objective must be progress in the South, rather than regression in the North. Such a programme will in practice require a web of regional and international governmental and civil society coalitions O'Brien, Goetz, Scholte, Williams, 2000, 1–24).

Thirdly, while science, technology and economic activity will no doubt continue to operate transnationally, this need not be at the expense of autonomy for either local or national communities. Greater self-reliance should mean, among other things, a capacity to meet basic needs—clothing, shelter and food—by using as far as possible one's own resources. This in turn means a greater effort to ensure that the economy generally, and our energy systems in particular, function in accordance with the principles of ecological sustainability. Such a project must by definition be international in scope and inspiration.

Contributing to the new internationalism must be a new regionalism. This will need to take several forms. It must operate at least as much at the non-government as at the governmental level, providing effective political space not only for business enterprises but for a range of religious, cultural and social movements. The new regionalism will need to be simultaneously issue-based, concerning itself with such issues as poverty reduction, women's rights, industrial rights, environmental protection, or conflict resolution, and constituency-based, involving, among others, the professions, trade unions, religious and cultural associations, and public interest organizations.

The new internationalism and the new regionalism should dovetail with a new, outward-looking multiculturalism and, it cannot be stressed enough, with a revised and expanded notion of democracy. These principles will need to underpin the reorganization of national as much as international institutions. The global economy must be subjected to the discipline of democratic practice at all levels of governance, and its workings made consistent with the principles of human security. The urgent task before us is to identify, support and connect the numerous but diverse constituencies that are ready to reimagine the future and so transform the present.

References

Aksu, Eşref and Joseph A. Camilleri, *Democratizing Global Governance*, London: Palgrave (forthcoming).

Beck, Ulrich, *Risk Society: Toward a New Modernity*, London: Sage, 1992.

Bello, Walden with Shea Cunningham and Bill Rau, *Dark Victory: the United States and Global Poverty*, Oakland, CA: Food First Books, 1999.

Bird, Graham, "The International Monetary Fund and Developing Countries: A Review of the Evidence and Policy Options," *International Organization*, 50 (3), Summer 1996, pp. 477– 511.

Camilleri, Joseph A. and Jim Falk, *The End of Sovereignty? Politics in a Shrinking and Fragmenting World*, Aldershot: Edward Elgar, 1992

Camilleri, Joseph, "Music of the Sphere," *Arena Magazine*, 13, October/November 1994, pp. 33–37.

Camilleri, Joseph A., "Human Rights, Cultural Diversity and Conflict Resolution: the Asia Pacific Context," *Pacifica Review*, Vol. 6, No. 2, 1994, pp.17-41.

Camilleri, Joseph A., "Impoverishment and the Nation State," in F.O. Hampson and J. Reppy (eds), *Earthly Goods: Environmental Change and Social Justice*, Ithaca: Cornell University Press, 1996, pp. 122-153.

Camilleri, Joseph, "What is Globalisation?" in Ken Coghill (ed), *Globalisation and Local Democracy*,

Melbourne: Montech for Monash University, 1997, pp. 13–18.

Camilleri, Joseph A., Kamal Malhotra and Majid Tehranian, *Reimagining the Future: Towards Democratic Governance*, Melbourne: Department of Politics, La Trobe University, 2000.

Childers, Erskine and Brian Urquhart, *Towards a More Effective United Nations*, Uppsala: Dag Hammarskjöld Foundation, 1992.

Chossudovsky, Michel, *The Globalisation of Poverty: Impacts of IMF and World Bank Reforms*, London: Zed Books, 1997.

Commission on Global Governance, *Our Global Neighbourhood*, Oxford: Oxford University Press, 1995.

Cousens, Elizabeth M. and Chetan Kumar, with Karen Wermester (eds), *Peacebuilding as Politics: Cultivating Peace in Fragile Societies*, Boulder, CO: Lynne Rienner, 2001.

Cox, Robert W., *Approaches to World Order* Cambridge: Cambridge University Press, 1996.

Dent, Martin and Bill Peters, *The Crisis of Poverty and Debt in the Third World*, Aldershot: Ashgate, 1999.

Evans, Gareth, *Cooperating for Peace*, Sydney: Allen & Unwin, 1993.

Falk, Richard, *On Humane Governance: Towards a New Global Politics*, London: Polity, 1995.

Falk, Richard, *Predatory Globalization: A Critique*, London: Polity, 1999.

Gill, Stephen and James H. Mittelman (eds), *Innovation and Transformation in International Studies*, Cambridge: Cambridge University Press, 1997.

Held, David, *Democracy and the Global Order: From the Modern State to Cosmopolitan Governance*, Cambridge: Polity Press, 1995.

Higgott, Richard and Anthony Payne (eds), *The New Political Economy of Globalisation*, Cheltenham: Edward Elgar, 2000.

Malhotra, Kamal, "Globalisation: Where it is leading us and do we want to go there?" *Focus Files*, November 1997.

Mansfield, Edward D. and Helen V. Milner, "The New Wave of Regionalism," *International Organization*, 53 (3), Summer 1999, pp. 589–627.

O'Brien Robert, Anne Marie Goetz, Jan Aart Scholte, Marc Williams, *Contesting Global Governance: Multilateral Economic Institutions and Global Social Movements*, Cambridge: Cambridge University Press, 2000.

Prakash, Aseem and Jeffrey A. Hart (eds), *Globalization and Governance*, London: Routledge, 1999.

Renner, Michael, *Fighting for Survival: Environmental Decline, Social Conflict and the New Age of Insecurity*, New York: W.W. Norton & Company, 1996.

Robertson, Roland, *Globalization: Social Theory and Global Culture*, London: Sage Publications, 1992.

Singh, K., *A Citizen Guide to the Globalization of Finance*, Delhi: Madhyam Books, 1998.

Watkins, Kevin, *The Oxfam Poverty Report*, Oxford: Oxfam, 1995.

World Bank, *Global Development Finance*, 2001.

Note

The author is indebted to Muhammad Yunus, "Ten Years of Human Development" (http://www.undp.org/hrdo/10year.html, sighted 13 November 2001).

Can European Democracy Survive Globalization?

Ralf Dahrendorf
House of Lords, United Kingdom

Democracy today is under serious pressure, not least in Europe. The pressure, notably on representative or parliamentary democracy, is such that we will have to rethink the very constitution of liberty. This pressure comes moreover from two sides at the same time. Within countries, several developments conspire to set in motion a kind of creeping authoritarianism. These internal developments are reinforced by what is crudely called globalization, that is, the emigration of important decisions to spaces for which democratic processes and institutions do not exist.

Americans recognize some of these problems, but for a number of reasons the American position is different. Like Larry Siedentop in his influential book, *Democracy in Europe,* my concern focuses on the countries of Europe and with the European Union since 1989.[1] Many of us still remember with joy those months twelve years ago when country after country east of the crumbling Iron Curtain emerged from *nomenklatura* rule to the first halting steps toward democracy. As a Popperian I never subscribed to the view that threats to liberty were forever dispelled and that Hegel's (or Kojève's) final synthesis had arrived. At the same time I did not anticipate that within little more than a decade the risks to democracy would become so powerful.

This spring, two of the major countries of Europe, Italy and the United Kingdom, underwent—and survived—national election campaigns. In both cases, these campaigns were an expression of what might be called anti-politics. This was especially evident in Italy. The winning candidate used all his experience with—as well as ownership of—the media to project the image of a leader who is different: a star, a celebrity, an entrepreneur who knows what his customers want. It is also worth remembering what happened on the other side of the Italian political spectrum. A prime minister who by common consent did his job exceptionally well, Giuliano Amato, was considered insufficiently telegenic to lead the center-left into the election. Someone more attractive to viewers was found in the person of Francesco Rutelli. In the event, Rutelli turned out to be a very serious candidate, but the reasons for his choice tell the relevant story.

Some would argue that something similar happened in Britain, because the "real" prime minister is the Chancellor of the Exchequer, Gordon Brown, whereas Tony Blair, who likes to surround himself with stars from anywhere but politics, is needed to get the votes. However that may be, Blair is a leader who likes to bypass political institutions like party and parliament and turn directly to the people, or, better still, to "focus groups" selected as representatives of the people.

Ralf Dahrendorf, "Can Democracy Survive Globalization?" Reprinted by permission of the German Historical Institute and the *National Interest.*

Celebrity politics tends toward snapshot politics. Somehow, continuity has gone out of the democratic process. What counts is the view of the moment—and this is highly volatile. A week after the election, the voters are just as likely to turn against their choices. The chosen leader (if that is the word) for his part is happy to abandon his projects if what he regards as the people want something different. Throwaway politics is another notion that comes to mind: like tins of Coca-Cola, indeed like cameras and radio sets and soon mobile phones, policies are chosen, used and discarded for their short-term utility. What has gone out of our democracies is extended debate and the patient pursuit of objectives through periods of popular support as well as those of popular doubt.

Institutionally speaking, what has gone is the pivotal role of parliament. Mr. Blair's first act after his election in 1997 was to reduce "Prime Minister's Questions" in the House of Commons from two days to one—a symbolic yet significant act. Perhaps the British Parliament has always been more malleable than those of countries with a clearer separation of powers, but the tendency to strengthen the executive and weaken parliament is widespread. I am a member of a committee of the Upper House whose task it is to scrutinize bills in order to prevent government from using legislation to delegate powers to the executive. In recent years there has been a massive increase in such attempts. Elsewhere in Europe, and especially in the European Union, secondary legislation remains largely outside parliamentary control. Government by what we call "Henry VIII clauses"—that is, provisions in primary legislation that enable the executive to alter the very purpose of an act or even revoke it—is widespread.

There is also another side to the picture. While turnout in elections is still high in Europe, at least compared to the United States, observers nevertheless find widespread apathy, if not cynicism, with regard to politics. People do not care, and while they do not trust anyone in power, they cannot be bothered to do anything about it. This is how the authoritarian syndrome emerges. Contrary to totalitarianism, authoritarianism is founded not on the permanent mobilization of all subjects, but on their disinterest. People—citizens indeed!—can do what they want as long as they do not interfere with the smooth exercise of power. This power, in turn, is more and more concentrated in the executive.

Now, such creeping authoritarianism does not always prevail. In France there is a well-established tradition of 100,000 teachers or farmers or nurses descending on Paris and forcing the government to mend its ways. Last year, a number of European countries reacted to blockades by lorry drivers demanding lower taxes on petrol. But none of this is democracy as James Madison or John Stuart Mill envisaged it. "Strengthening Parliament", to quote the title of a recent report by British Conservatives, has become an uphill task.

This is all the more so in view of the other half of the somewhat somber picture before us—globalization. Democracy means three things: change is possible without violence; there are checks and balances to the exercise of power; the people have a decisive say in the process. Representative or parliamentary democracy links these elements through the election of representatives who in and through parliament can change policies and, if necessary, government, as well as scrutinize and control the exercise of power. Such institutions were historically developed in the nation-state, and, indeed, in many cases alongside the formation of nation-states. Both Madison and Mill (and many others) offered important reflections on the size and the nature—or rather, the culture—of the communities in which democratic institutions work; Madison speaks of a space in which there are "chords of allegiance", Mill of "nationality."

However we define or describe the traditional political space for democratic institutions, from a European perspective at least, it is rapidly losing relevance for important decisions. Whether and when interest rates are changed is decided by an unaccountable European Central Bank. Attack from the air on Kosovo is planned and initiated by

NATO. Whether Russia receives further help from the international community, despite the halting repayment of its debt, is a matter for the International Monetary Fund. While in these cases one can at least point to institutions, other decisions of great significance issue from less defined agencies, as when a Japanese company decides to invest in Wales rather than in Normandy or an American speculator grabs an auspicious moment to drive the pound sterling out of the European Monetary System and, by so doing, puts billions of dollars into his own accounts. Sometimes it is just wholly anonymous "markets" that seem to call the tune.

So what happens to democracy? Change without violence? This is hard to bring about if one does not even know who does what, when and how. It could be argued that all international agencies should apply an equivalent of the Twenty-second Amendment to the U.S. Constitution and impose strict limits on the terms of office of their leaders. That might solve one problem. Checks and balances? This is arguably the area on which we should concentrate in years to come. There are ways of controlling the exercise of power in a globalized environment. In part they are judicial in the widest sense of the term, including regulators and arbitrators. In part, and at an earlier stage in the process, auditing international decision-makers is a prerequisite of control. Information technology helps bring to light relevant facts and figures. In some cases, national parliaments could gear themselves up to scrutinize international decisions without jeopardizing the advantages of global spaces in the process.

This is a list of items on the agenda for a democratic response to the emigration of decisions from traditional political spaces, but it fails to address the remaining and fundamental issue: How can the people have a say in processes for which there are no appropriate institutions? The large, and at times violent, demonstrations in Seattle and Washington and Prague and Genoa are clearly not the answer, though they do underline the question. They show that people want a say, that they resent the removal of important decisions from their grasp. This conclusion is derived not so much from the slogans of demonstators convened over the Internet, but from the quiet support that they get from many who would not dream of setting cars on fire or smashing shop windows, though they enjoy reading the anticapitalist diatribes of Viviane Forrester and others. As a result the "politics of cultural despair" is once again with us, and with it the political dangers that led Fritz Stern to write a book of this title about antimodernism in Imperial Germany.[2]

It is hard to escape the conclusion that democracy and the nation-state are tied to each other. The weakening of the nation-state by a process of internationalization is by the same token a weakening of democracy. So far we have not been able to apply the principles of democracy to political spaces beyond the nation-state. What, then, may be said about the European Union? Is it not an example, even a successful example, of democracy beyond the nation-state?

It is true that recent years have seen a shift in the arguments advanced for Europe to form an ever-closer union. Few now argue that the motive force should be to prevent war, or even to keep Germany under control. Some think that the main purpose of European integration today is to enable Europe to hold its own *vis-à-vis* the United States. At times, an anti-American sentiment creeps into such views, but it is animated more often by a belief that a "European model", notably of economic and social policy, is worth defending. Many of a more liberal persuasion, however, see the institutional Europe as a step toward coping with globalization by democratic means. If we cannot have global democracy just yet, we can at least begin the journey to that goal by creating a large world region, Europe, along democratic principles.

One may appreciate the intention, but is far from the reality of the European Union. The Union has now laid down very serious tests of democratic virtue for so called accession countries. If, however, it applied these tests to itself, the Union, the result would be dismal. It is not just a joke to say that if the EU itself applied for accession to the EU it could not be admitted because it is insufficiently democratic. The Union was, of course, set up as a Common Market, later extended by its greatest leader so far, Jacques Delors, into the Single Market. For this purpose the very French—indeed Cartesian—construction of its institutions may well have been appropriate. The right to propose rests with a Commission constructed to embody the common European interest; the right to dispose, to decide, remains with a Council of Ministers that assembles the various national interests. A Court of Justice makes sure that both institutions remain on the straight and narrow.

And democracy? I am convinced that the European Assembly (as it was then called) was an afterthought when the Treaty of Rome was drafted in 1956. It had no real function, and since that time has only gradually acquired further rights, though even now these do not include the right to determine its own seat, or to raise funds for its own budget, or indeed to pass legislation as the sovereign representation of the people of the Union. It is directly elected, but sovereignty remains elsewhere—in nation-states, in the executives, in elusive spaces beyond the grasp of the people.

In any case, what people are we talking about? There is now a lively debate on such issues among both speech-making politicians and puzzled academics. But the key is this: There is no such thing as a European *demos* on which to build a European democracy. Public opinion, even published opinion, is fragmented into national segments at best (and often into regional enclaves within the countries). European elections leave most voters uninterested; turnout in many countries is below 50 percent. Those who vote in fact vote on national issues, notably on the popularity of their own government at the time. The resulting parliamentary assembly is similarly fragmented. More than fifty of its members never turn up. Those who do are frequently people who failed to get into national parliaments, or have retired from more important national positions.

As a result, the decision-making process of the European Union is an insult to democracy. This is all the more important at a time when the Union is trying to venture out of the constraints of the Single Market into all kinds of new areas, notably in foreign and security policy and in the justice and home affairs field. (At the same time, it is useful to remember that, in budgetary terms, "Europe" remains a rather minor power, disposing as it does of less than 1.2 percent of the GDP of countries which themselves give their parliaments and governments control over 40 percent and more of their GDP.) It would be possible, and perhaps rewarding, to look in more detail at the decision—making processes of the European Union, but such a closer look would not dispel the conclusion that Europe's institutions fail the democracy test. Far from being a successful step in the direction of applying democracy beyond the nation-state, Europe proves that this is all but impossible to achieve.

Having spread almost unmitigated gloom on the subject, it is time to look for encouragement. This is not so simple, but one can point to three sets of ideas, of hints, about the future of democracy from a European perspective.

First, it is important to remember that the nation-state is still the single most important political space at the beginning of the twenty-first century. It may have lost some of its strength, but it remains the relevant inclusive community for most people. For those who have just escaped from imperial domination, like the formerly Soviet-ruled countries of central and eastern Europe, the nation-state embodies not just sovereignty, but freedom. Everywhere in Europe, key social policies are decided by national parliaments. The varieties of economic and political culture bear witness to the strength of nation-states.

This means that parliamentary democracy is not a spent force. It has to be, and it can be, defended against all pressures. Within countries, the main danger today is, on the one hand, the creeping authoritarianism noted above, and, on the other, a new regionalism. While this regionalism often appears in the name of self-determination, it is a very dubious contribution to democracy. Beyond countries, another dubious trend must be resisted: the use of "globalization" as a pretext for decisions that have nothing to do with such trends. Rural post offices do not have to be closed for reasons of globalization. Thus there are plenty of themes for the vigorous defense of parliaments and representative democracy generally.

Secondly, as we move beyond the nation-state, we must beware the pretense of democracy when, in truth, the voice of the people does not reach decision-makers in any regular and constitutional way. It is quite likely that this central feature of true democracy will for some time be lacking in international political spaces all the way from the European Union through NATO to the U.N. and its agencies, including as well the IMF, the WTO and the World Bank. This means that, for the time being, we have to concentrate on setting up effective and transparent checks and balances. There are many ways of going about this task. I have alluded to the Twenty-second Amendment, and also to judicial and auditing institutions. Publicity itself is an instrument of controlling those in power.

This still leaves the third and most difficult task unresolved, which is giving people a voice in matters that are decided beyond the nation-state. Unfortunately, this will have to remain unresolved. For some time to come, we shall live with a confused and rather uncomfortable mix of highly imperfect attempts to democratize global decision-making. One may with good reason speak unkindly of the European Parliament but, of course, it documents at least good intentions, as do the Parliamentary Assembly of the Council of Europe, the North Atlantic Assembly, and other similar institutions. There is also the array of non-governmental organizations (NGOs). At times they aspire to be more governmental than is good for them; at other times, they are more anti-governmental than is good for the rest of us. But in their chaotic way, they express the views of many people. The same is true in an even more diffuse fashion for the "Internet debates" that are going on everywhere. And soon we are back to Seattle and all that—inchoate expressions of frustration by people who have a right to be heard, but cannot find a way to give voice to their views. For the moment, there is no way to give true democratic shape to this cacophony.

Except for one final point, perhaps. Germany's Weimar Republic has been well described as a democracy without democrats. This was one of the reasons why Weimar democracy could not last. However, the opposite condition offers more hope. If we cannot have world or even European democracy, at least we can have democrats: people who are conscious of their rights as citizens, and take seriously the responsibility actively to defend them. Citizens do not just let things happen. They speak up, and even if they are not always heard, their voices still matter. They use all non-violent means to check the untrammeled exercise of power. They support visible initiatives, such as the counter-World Forum at Porto Alegre earlier this year [Fall 2001]. They form an invisible network of defenders of freedom that, in principle, spreads all over the world. Democrats without democracy offer a more hopeful prospect than the reverse. Perhaps this was the secret of postwar Germany: there were democrats, like Gerd Bucerius, who were prepared to practice what they believed, and thus created a working democracy.[3] For all we know, something of this kind may one day be achieved beyond the nation-state.

Notes

1. Siedentop, *Democracy in Europe* (New York: Columbia University Press, 2001)

2. Stern, *The Politics of Cultural Despair: A Study in the Rise of the Germanic Ideology* (Berkeley, CA: University of California Press, 1961).

3. Gerd Bucerius was the founder of *Die Zeit* and a Christian-Democratic member of the first Bundestag. See my *Liberal und unabhangig: Gerd Bucerius und seine Zeit* (Munich: C.H. Beck, 2000).

Democracy and War Involvement

Erich Weede
University of Cologne, Germany

Most quantitative researchers had agreed that regime type and war involvement are not significantly related to each other until Rummel recently challenged this consensus. According to Rummel, libertarian or democratic states are less intensively involved in foreign conflict and tend to participate in wars less often than do other states. Rummel's assertion is disputed in this article. Relying on various definitions of war and compilations of data for the 1960s and 1970s, it is demonstrated that democracy and war involvement are not consistently and significantly correlated with each other. Only in the late seventies did democracies succeed in avoiding involvement in wars. Unfortunately, this period seems rather exceptional.

Whether a nation enjoys democratic rule or suffers from dictatorship, the risk of getting involved in war is the same. This has been one of the findings in Weede (1971: 380). Nor was this an isolated finding. Indeed, my work was heavily indebted to, Rummel's (1968) pathbreaking study and, as far as the democracy-war involvement relationship is concerned, merely replicated Rummel's (1968: 191, 207) earlier results. Relying on a much larger war data base, Small and Singer (1976) also found that democracy and war involvement are unrelated. With the exception of some dissenting voices (like Haas, 1965),[1] surveys of the literature (McGowan and Shapiro, 1973: 94, and Zinnes, 1980) or textbooks (Russett and Starr, 1981: 204) also claimed that regime type does not affect foreign violence or war. Until recently there was an overwhelming consensus on this point.

But the consensus has been broken by one of its founding fathers, Rummel:(1979: 292-293; 1983a). Reading Rummel's (1979) *War, Power, Peace* was not too disturbing at first. His joint freedom proposition claims that libertarian (democratic) states do not go to war against one another. Even if this were true the joint freedom proposition says little about war involvement of democratic states. It refers to the regime of their opponents rather than to their own frequency of resorting to arms. But Rummel (1979: 292) added a freedom proposition which claims that "freedom in inhibits violence." Rummel's elaboration of the freedom proposition, however, poses some problems of interpretation. On the one hand Rummel (1979: 292) argues: "The more libertarian a state, the less it tends to be involved in violence." On the other hand, he argues on the very same page: "I do not expect that there will be a correlation between libertarianism and the frequency of involvement in war or violence." This latter quote sounds as if Rummel were still part of the consensus he helped to create 15 years ago.

Erich Weede, "Democracy in World Involvement." From Erich Weede, *Journal of Conflict Resolution* (Vol. 28, No. 4), pp. 649-664,

Whatever Rummel's message was in 1979, in 1983 it is as clear as it was back in 1968, but it differs radically in substance. Now Rummel (1983a: 55) writes that "we also would expect that the more libertarian states are, the less they have wars. The data support this, significantly." If true, this would constitute good news about the otherwise often dismal field of politics. If the freedom proposition were true, then a nation may reduce the risk of getting involved in war by becoming more libertarian or democratic. For once, desirable means would serve desirable ends. But there remain two kinds of doubts. First, how compelling is the evidence that libertarian or democratic regimes are involved in war less often than other regimes? Second, how convincing is the underlying theoretical argument?...

Theoretically, I always found the argument fairly convincing that democratic governments are more concerned with the avoidance of war than are other governments. Such concern, however, may contribute little to peace. Although the disinclination of the citizenry to pay for war with money, life, and limb puts pressure on democratic governments to avoid war involvement, such pressure need not succeed. First, the very same citizenry that objects to military action may on occasion simultaneously object to the concessions required for maintaining peace. Second, even if citizen pressure on democratic government is devoid of such internal contradictions of peace-loving peoples and democratic governments may try a policy of appeasement, thereby projecting an image of weakness and indecision that invites exploitation by more ruthless decision makers abroad and therefore possibly increasing the risk of war. Among contemporaries, Podhoretz (1980, 1983) is an important spokesman for such worries. Moreover, Rummel's (1976; 1979: 22) criticism of détente seems to be very close to Podhoretz's:

Our foreign and defense policies were the opposite of that which would preserve nuclear peace with freedom...the results showed the foreign policy of detente to be based on false premises about international relations and conflict; and that this policy and associated military trends were in fact increasing the likelihood of war. And time then seemed critical and still does.

Rummel's (1983a: 55) recent empirical findings assert that libertarianism reduces violence and that democracies are less likely to become involved in war. Yet Rummel (1976, 1979) worries about détente increasing the risk of war, although détente commanded considerable support among Western democracies for quite some time and still does in many of them. How can the democratic penchant for dangerous policies and the expectation of happy results be reconciled? In my view, the most elegant way to overcome the contradiction between Rummel's (1968, 1983a) old and new findings, between Rummel's (1979: 293) and other readings of the evidence (McGowan and Shapiro, 1973: 94; Russett and Starr, 1981: 204; Zinnes, 1980), and between Rummel's (1983a) recent findings and his harsh criticism of policies that have been popular in many democracies and still are in some of them, is simply to demonstrate that Rummel's (1983a) recent findings constitute nothing more than an aberration from the close-to-zero relationship between democracy and war involvement.

Research Design and Data Analysis

My period of observation is 1960-1980. Why this period? I do not want to include the, late fifties; both Rummel (1968) and I (Weede, 1971) had already found that regime type and war involvement are unrelated to each other, thereby biasing my results in favor of replicating earlier findings. But I do want to include the late seventies, on which Rummel (1983a) recently relied, in order to demonstrate either that the late seventies constitute an exceptional period or that the essentially zero relationship between democracy and war involvement holds even there....

In Rummel's (1983a) view, a regime is more libertarian, with stronger civil liberties and political rights and wider economic freedom. Given that economic freedom is usually not part of definitions of democracy and that Rummel's (1983a) results (according to his own account) do not depend on the inclusion of economic freedom, I do not consider the issue of the impact of economic freedom on war involvement.

An ideal measure of democracy for the purposes at hand should refer to civil liberties and to political rights, and it should cover the globe for the entire period of war observation. I am not aware of the existence of such a measure. But Bollen's (1980: 387-388) widely used political democracy index comes close. According to it, a nation gets a higher democratic score if there is press freedom and toleration of group opposition; if the government rarely, if ever, resorts to negative sanctions; if executive and legislative branches of government are elected; and if elections are fair. Scores are provided from 124 nations two points in time 1960 and 1965....

Before correlating various indicators of democracy and war involvement, one might wish to know whether democracy or libertarianism and war involvement are stable characteristics of nations....

Table 1: Correlations Between Democracy and War Involvement

	1960-1980	*1960-1974*	*1975-1980*
Butterworth war	—	-0.16 (0.03)	—
Singer and Small interstate war	-0.09 (0.09)	+0.01 (0.24)	-0.28 (0.002)
Singer and Small interstate or extrasystemic war	-(0.14 (0.04)	+0.01 (0.24)	-0.32 (0.00.1)
Kende war	-0.02 **(0.22)**	+0.06 **(0.14)**	-0.21 **(0.01)**

NOTE: All coefficients are product-moment correlations. One-tailed significance levels are given in parentheses. N varies between 97 and 100.

The first task is to find out whether democracy and (war involvement are correlated for the entire 1900-1980 period. Bollen's (1980) index for 1965 is the only index of democracy; but there is a variety of measures of war involvement. The first column of Table 1 provides the results. The sign consistently favors the opinion that more democratic states are less frequently involved in war, but little else does. The numerical size of the correlation coefficients, and to a lesser degree the fact that the 5 percent significance level is passed only once[2] out of three times, seems to justify the conclusion: More democratic states were about as frequently involved in war as other states were in the sixties and seventies. This is the most important finding of this analysis. It holds irrespective of the operationalization of war. It agrees with Rummel's (1968) earlier findings and a lot of other evidence, but it contradicts Rummel's (1983a) most recent findings. Although the only significant correlation for the 1960-1974 subperiod (column 2 of Table 1) supports Rummel's expectations, it is again very small in size. But results in column 3 of Table 1 demonstrate that more democratic states were less frequently involved in war during the 1975-1980 subperiod. The relationship is highly significant, although it explains only about 10 percent of the variance in war involvement. My ability to replicate Rummel's findings for the late seventies is particularly gratifying, as it implies that choosing a narrow definition of freedom or democracy instead of a wider one or looking at war frequencies instead of foreign conflict intensities matters little, as Rummel (1983a: 55) himself had pointed out before. But the period of observation matters.

Conclusion

Rummel's (1983a) finding that democracies tend to be involved in war less often than other states is entirely due to his period of observation. In the post-World War II period, Americans, British, French, Belgians, Israelis, and Indians wee fairly often in interstate or extrasystemic or colonial wars, while simultaneously enjoying reasonably good democratic performance. In the late seventies, however, all of these democracies succeeded in avoiding involvement in interstate wars, surpassing the Singer and Small (1972, 1982) casualty threshold, and most of them also succeeded in avoiding involvement in lesser military conflicts. Although there are periods of observation where libertarianism or democratic performance is negatively correlated with war involvement, such periods have been short in duration.

Notes

I. It may be disputed, however, whether Haas's (1965) data really support his interpretation.

2. There is a minor contradiction between Chan's (1984) and my own findings. According to Chan, the "freedom promotes peace" proposition receives less support if we include extrasystemic wars. Here the proposition is significantly supported for the entire 1960-1980 periods only if extrasystemic wars are included. Of course, Chan's finding rests on a war database that extends much father back (to 1816) than my own (to 1960).

References

Bollen, K.A. (1980) "Issues in the comparative measurement of political democracy." *Amer. Soc. Rev. 45* (June): 370-390.

Butterworth, R.L. (1976). *Managing Interstate Conflict, 1945-1974.* Pittsburgh: University Center for International Studies.

Haas, M. (1965). "Societal approaches to the study of war." *Journal of Peace Research* 2, 4: 307-323.

Kende, I. (1982) *Über die Kriege seit 1945.* Bonn: Deutsche Gesellschaft für Friedens und Konflikforschung.

McGowan, P.J. and H.B. Shapiro. (1973). *The Comparative Study of Foreign Policy.* Beverly Hills, CA: Sage.

Podhoretz, N. (1983). "Appeasement by any other name." *Commentary* 76 (July): 25-38.

Podhoretz, N. (1980). *The Present Danger.* New York: Simon & Schuster.

Rummel, R.J. (1983a). "Libertarianism and international violence." *Journal of Conflict Resolution* 27 (March): 27-71

Rummel, R.J. (1983b). "Wiberg's review essay on Rummel: a reply." *Journal of Peace Research* 20, 3: 279-280.

Rummel, R.J. (1979). *Understanding Conflict and War, Vol. 4: War, Power, Peace.* Beverly Hills, CA: Sage.

Rummel, R.J. (1976). *Peace Endangered.* Beverly Hills, CA: Sage.

Rummel, R.J. (1968). "The relationship between national attributes and foreign policy behavior." pp. 186-214 in J.D. Singer, ed., *Quantitative International Politics.* New York: Free Press.

Russet, B.M. and H. Starr. (1981). *World Politics: The Menu for Choice.* San Francisco: Freeman.

Russett, B.M., J.D. Singer, and M. Small. (1968). "National political units in the twentieth century: a standardized list." *American Political Science Review LXII* (September): 932-951.

Singer, J.D. and M. Small. (1972). *The Wages of War: A Statistical Handbook.* New York: John Wiley.

Small M., and J.D. Singer. (1982). *Resort to Arms: International and Civil Wars, 1816-1980.* Beverly Hills, CA: Sage.

Small M., and J.D. Singer. (1976). "The war-proneness of democratic regimes, 1816-1965. *Jerusalem Journal of International Relations* 1 (Summer): 50-69.

Taylor, C.L., and D.A. Jodice. (1983). *World Handbook of Political and Social Indicators* (2 vols.). New Haven, CT: Yale University Press.

Weede, E. (1971). "Charakteristika von Nationen als Erklärungsgrundlage für das internationale Konflictverhalten." Sozialwissenschaftliches Jahrbuch für Politik 2: 327-401.

Wiberg, H. (1982). "Review essay: Rudolph J. Rummel: *Understanding Conflict and War, Vols. 1-5.*" *Journal of Peace Research 19,* 4: 369-386.

Zinnes, D.A. (1980). "Why war? Evidence on the outbreak of international conflict," pp. 331-360 in T.R. Gurr, ed., *Handbook of Political Conflict.* New York: Free Press.

Responding to Claims for Self-Determination

Hurst Hannum
Tufts University

The first rush of post-cold-war secessions may be over, but there is little doubt that conflicts within states (many, but not all, based on ethnicity or cultural differences) will continue to proliferate in the foreseeable future. 'Ethnic conflict' has replaced the Cold War as the primary interest of political and military theorists, and even conflicts which may be primarily political or economic in nature are frequently given an ethnic cast both by those directly involved and by outsiders.

Of course, whether the violence that frequently accompanies these conflicts is characterized as ethnic or 'civilizational', the threats to international peace and human life are substantial. Ignoring such threats seems to be impossible—although little enough attention has been paid by the international community to ethnic strife in Sri Lanka, India, pre-1994 Rwanda and Burundi, Sudan, Nagorno-Karabakh, and elsewhere. Increasingly, however, governments and international organizations are being called upon to influence, intervene in, or broker solutions to these very difficult conflicts.

Ethnic wars of secession highlight the inherent tension between 'self-determination', on one hand, and 'sovereignty' or 'territorial integrity', on the other. However, one of the major impediments to developing coherent responses to such conflicts is the vagueness of these terms. Self-determination in the context of decolonization meant immediate independence, but there is continuing disagreement over its applicability to non-colonial situations. Obeisance is also routinely paid to territorial integrity, but the shattering of the Soviet Union, Yugoslavia, Czechoslovakia, and Ethiopia within the past decade is a precedent not lost on many 'nations' that would be states.

Of course, neither sovereignty nor self-determination is an absolute right; each is limited by other rights and international obligations. Sovereignty is limited not only by the rights of other states and the innumerable political and economic ties which bind states to one another, but by legitimate international interest in human rights, protection of the environment, and other issues formerly considered to be wholly within a state's domestic jurisdiction. Outside of the classic context of European decolonization, the free exercise of self-determination has been constrained by great power rivalry, questions about the potential economic and political viability of new states, and the overarching goal of maintaining order and stability by preserving existing territorial arrangements wherever possible.

Insofar as international law has attempted to balance these two principles of self-determination and territorial integrity, it has taken a generally conservative position. Despite continuing assertions of a 'right' of secession from groups in Asia, Africa, Europe, and the former Soviet Union, no such right has yet been recognized by the international community. The diplomatic and military support given by NATO to ethnic Albanians in Kosovo and Macedonia in 1999-2001 deliberately excluded any statements or actions that might be interpreted as supporting secession, despite the clear wishes of the population of Kosovo for just such an outcome. Of course, international law does not prohibit secession, whether it is voluntary or violent, but it neither recognizes a right to secede nor has it identified even tentatively the conditions which might give rise to such a right in the future.

***

Recent experience in former Yugoslavia, Ethiopia, Sudan, and elsewhere has made clear the limits of international intervention in support of secessionist groups, no matter how great the human rights violations or war crimes committed by the government. Most civil wars continue to be viewed as internal matters, and outside forces are appropriately reluctant to attempt to impose solutions to internal struggles over borders or political power. As demonstrated in Chechnya, the Kurdish regions of Turkey and Iraq, Kashmir, Sudan, and Sri Lanka, international condemnation of the means of warfare is almost never accompanied by support for the goal of secession....

If the international community feels compelled to insert itself into the extraordinarily difficult process through which people accept or reject national identity, it must agree on criteria for intervention which go beyond simple political preference for one side or the other....

But if territorial claims should not justify foreign intervention, does this mean that self-determination claims should be totally ignored? Such silence is often politically impossible and, in some cases, might even be morally objectionable. We must therefore try to define the appropriate scope of legitimate foreign involvement in claims for self-determination, under an almost infinite variety of circumstances.

I suggest that there are two historically acceptable and morally justifiable purposes that are served by contemporary forms of 'self-determination' and thus deserve international support. These purposes are, first, to protect individual and group identity and, second, to facilitate effective participation in government. The former purpose is today reflected in large part, although not entirely, by human rights norms that have developed since 1945, including those concerned with minority and indigenous rights. The latter aspect, sometimes referred to as 'internal' self-determination, implies identifying appropriate levels of democratic self-government so that effective participation by all citizens in the economic and political life of the country is guaranteed.

***

One need not engage in a detailed review of the history of human rights since 1945 or the expansion of minority rights in the past decade in order to observe that the United Nations, the Organization on Security and Cooperation in Europe, the Council of Europe, and many individual states have become increasingly willing to criticize central governments on minority rights issues. It is no longer sufficient for such governments merely to label sub-state self-determination movements as 'terrorists' or 'rebels' and to ignore regional or ethnic differences. Indeed, diplomats and non-governmental organizations frequently urge states with ethnically diverse populations to adopt more flexible constitutional arrangements, in order to accommodate desires for local self-government and cultural protection and to decrease the likelihood of violent conflict. In Europe, at least, this attention has been codified in the Framework Convention for the Protection of National Minorities,[1] to which 34 states were parties as of late 2001.

This new interest in minority rights and, by necessary implication, internal constitutional arrangements raises difficult questions concerning the distinction between issues that fall wholly or primarily within a state's domestic jurisdiction and issues which are the legitimate concern of the international community. Even the most ardent world federalists or human rights advocates are not ready to dictate the appropriate form of government for each of the world's nearly 200 independent states. At the same time, however, one needs to translate international norms protecting identity and participation into domestic reality.[2] This task can only be achieved by recognizing the essential role of democracy (as articulated through international standards related to freedom of expression and association, free elections, and related 'political' rights) and the rule of law in guaranteeing that minority rights are protected, in addition to their more traditional role in safeguarding 'individual' rights.

***

The discussion thus far leads to several conclusions that, if not entirely unobjectionable, would at least seem to fall readily within the positions currently maintained by most countries with respect to human rights, self-determination, and related issues.

First, neither self-determination nor territorial integrity is absolute, and each principle must be interpreted in light of other rights. Although there is no international right to secession, there may be circumstances in which the division of a state may be the best solution.

Second, self-determination should be concerned primarily with people rather than territory. The primary purposes of self-determination are to protect identity and facilitate democracy, not to resolve often questionable historical claims over territory that has been disputed for centuries. Nearly every state in the world was founded directly or indirectly on conquest, and 'self-determination' cannot provide a meaningful standard against which to overturn acts that were generally considered lawful at the time they were committed. (One might parenthetically note that those who claim a right to independence based on historical arguments tend to choose that historical period which would give them the greatest amount of territory, i.e., the period in which they themselves were successful conquerors.)

Third, both minorities and majorities have widely recognized human rights that must be protected under all circumstances. As is true of other human rights, implementation is not easy, but such difficulties do not detract from the legitimacy of the underlying rights.

***

The following principles are therefore proposed as an alternative to the present *ad hoc* approach of states and international organizations to claims for self-determination. They are not be sufficiently detailed to be applied in a formulaic manner, but it is hoped that they will help to achieve progress towards achieving the goals that self-determination and human rights are ultimately designed to further.

1. Protecting basic human rights should be the foremost goal that policy-makers seek to achieve when responding to self-determination claims.

Self-determination itself is a human right.... A basic factor in formulating responses to self-determination claims therefore should be whether or not a particular action is likely to promote the rights of all of the people concerned, not whether it is consistent with abstract notions of sovereignty or fictitious claims of national destiny.

Cultural, linguistic and religious rights must be respected, and neither minority nor majority should seek to impose its values on the day-to-day lives of the other.... As recognized under international instruments, achieving equality in fact may require recognition of special rights for minority groups and individuals, such as affirmative action, government representation, devolution of powers, or support for cultural activities[3]

2. We must reject the notion that every ethnically or culturally distinct people, nation, or group has an automatic right to its own state or that ethnically homogeneous states are inherently desirable.

Even in an environment in which human rights are respected, it is clear that a system of states based primarily on ethnicity and/or historical claims is impossible to achieve on a global basis. Except in the smallest or most isolated environments, some minorities will be 'trapped' no matter how carefully boundaries are drawn. The existence of minorities serves as a constant reminder that ethnically based states are inherently self-selected and unfair; they do not emerge inexorably from any moral or political principle that can be easily identified or justified.

***

To some extent, such state building (at least with respect to language) may be necessary to develop the administrative and economic ties that bind a community together. Thus, those who find themselves part of a cultural or ethnic minority in a particular territory must accept that status and not expect that their beliefs and customs will be reflected at the national level to the same extent as those of the majority population. This does not mean, however, that a minority need submit to a majority which seeks not merely to mandate conformity to necessary state-wide standards, but rather to destroy cultures which deviate from the dominant model.

3. Maintain as a firm principle that there is no legal right of secession, although division of a state by agreement is permissible.

Clear enunciation of this principle will shift the terms of debate from the conclusory, 'We are a nation, therefore we have the right to a state,' and require a fuller and more logical explanation from 'nationalists' as to why they deserve the political power that accompanies statehood....

On the other side, central governments should be required to demonstrate why devolution of power should not be granted when it is demanded by significant groups. They should be willing to explain how minority rights are being effectively protected in fact, rather than allowed to hide behind the facade of national unity.

***

First, a demand for secession may ripen into a right deserving of international support where massive human rights violations, approaching the scale of genocide, are perpetrated against a group or region on a discriminatory basis. Under such circumstances, where there is no likelihood of a change in the attitude of the central government (or where the majority population supports the repression), secession may be the only effective remedy for the besieged group....

A second exception might accept a right to secession and independence if reasonable demands for local self-government or minority rights have been arbitrarily rejected by a central government, even without accompanying large-scale violence. However, this exception would come into play only when minimal demands are rejected; it does not mean that the United Nations or a group of states (such as the EU or OSCE) should substitute its judgment of what is fair or politically reasonable for that of the parties involved.

4. Without exalting the present territorial division of the world into sovereign states as being immutable, the settlement of self-determination claims by solutions short of secession should be encouraged.

Statehood is not necessary to guarantee the legitimate human rights of groups and individuals to protect and promote their own culture, language, and traditions. The fulfillment of other goals, such as increased political and economic power, is more legitimately sought through the normal political processes available in a democratic state.

***

Respecting the rights of both minority-national-regional groups and the majority-state-central population need not mean transferring as much power as possible from the center to the region or minority group. Rather, the challenge is to identify the level at which needs are best addressed and to locate powers accordingly (perhaps along the lines of the EU concept of 'subsidiarity')....

Acceptance of this principle does not imply opposition to division or secession in every situation, so long as there is persuasive evidence that such a solution is desired by a substantial segment of the population. At the same time, the international community must reaffirm that adopting federal or other power-sharing structures does not make a state's territorial integrity any less secure on the international plane; this reassurance can only be achieved by rejecting any general right to secession, as proposed here.

5. Where a new state is created based largely on ethnic or linguistic claims, the 'new minorities' trapped in such a state should enjoy the same right of secession or self-determination that was asserted by the seceding population.

Legitimate self-determination should only be exercised on the basis of the consent of *all* involved parties, not just those who wish to separate. If neither international law nor international politics offers a mechanism through which minorities trapped within a new ethnic state may rejoin their former state or, at least, create an autonomous region within their new home, rejection of the new borders by force may be the only alternative.

***

The impossibility of such a moral choice is nowhere more apparent than when new states created out of the dissolution of older states are themselves immediately endowed with the immutable borders based on the principle of territorial integrity that, by definition, they rejected when the same principle was advanced by their former sovereign. If our concern is with peoples rather than territories, then there is no reason to regard existing administrative or even 'republic' boundaries within states as sacrosanct.

This principle is formulated to treat groups equally, but it also serves to remind those who desire their own state that such a decision is not without consequence....

6. Finally, when armed conflict occurs, we must clearly distinguish responsibility for war crimes and crimes against humanity from the underlying political agendas of all sides.

A principled response to self-determination claims prior to the outbreak of armed conflict cannot depend on whether war crimes are committed after the conflict begins. It may be possible to influence the conduct of a civil war by making it clear that the international community will not support any party that condones war crimes or similar human rights violations, no matter how strong the appeal of that party's political demands. However, an overly rigid position may render impossible a compromise solution under which each side could obtain what it views as vital, e.g., the possibility of post-conflict border changes or a comprehensive territorial settlement prior to recognition of any new state(s).

The principles outlined above will not necessarily deter highly motivated groups (or power-hungry individuals) from seeking independence, whether for honest or ulterior motives. However, the present lack of both normative and moral clarity may be responsible for at least some of the increased separatist violence that has occurred thus far in the post-cold-war years. Emboldened by the international community's acceptance of the disintegration of Yugoslavia, dissatisfied groups in all parts of the world have decided that wars of national liberation are more likely to obtain meaningful outside support than lower-keyed appeals for minority rights or autonomy. A more clearly formulated set of international norms, such as those suggested here, may discourage at least some questionable claims and the ready resort to violence that often accompanies them.

The human cost of misplaced faith in fuzzy principles of self-determination and the likelihood of foreign support—despite the fact that *no* current secessionist movement is publicly supported by even a small number of states—is staggering. Adopting the nuanced approach suggested here will return the focus of the debate to the purported objects of the exercise of self-determination: the people themselves. At the same time, public recognition of the fact that national unity is not inviolable under all circumstances may encourage repressive states to move, however slowly, towards allowing greater participation for all groups and meaningful respect for human rights within their societies. Such a position is consistent not only with the values espoused by the United Nations and international law, but with long-term interests in stability and peace.

Balance among competing rights and interests is never easy to achieve. It does not lend itself to ringing slogans extolling the virtues of yesterday's 'national' identity or today's modern state. However, recognizing and accommodating conflicting rights is the only way in which the world and the states within it can respond to diametrically opposed appeals in a politically and morally principled manner.

Notes

1. Signed 1 Feb. 1995, Europe. T.S. No. 157, reprinted in 34 *Int'l Legal Mat.* 351 (1995).

2. Under the auspices of the OSCE High Commissioner on National Minorities, the Foundation on Inter-Ethnic Relations attempted to do just this in a series of expert meetings designed to amplify the scope of relevant minority rights. The Foundation's efforts led to three interesting sets of recommendations, which are available on the High Commissioner's website: the Hague Recommendations Regarding the Education Rights of National Minorities (1996), the Oslo Recommendations Regarding the Linguistic Rights of National Minorities (1998), and the Lund Recommendations on the Effective Participation of National Minorities in Public Life.

3. *See* e.g., International Convention on the Elimination of All Forms of Racial Discrimination, adopted 21 Dec. 1965, entered into force 4 Jan. 1969, 660 U.N.T.S. 195, art. 2; Declaration on the Rights of Persons Belonging to National or Ethnic, Religious or Linguistic Minorities, UN Gen. Assembly Res. 47/135 (18 Dec. 1992), art. 4; Framework Convention for the Protection of National Minorities, signed 1 Feb. 1995, Europe. T.S. No. 157, reprinted in 34 *Int'l Legal Mat.* 351 (1995), arts. 4, 5.

An Illusory Fork in the Road to Peace: Justice vs. Accommodation

Paul R. Williams[1]
American University and

Michael Scharf[2]
New England School of Law

During the process of peace building a number of norms and approaches may play an important role in bringing an end to the conflict and creating the foundation for a meaningful and lasting peace. The most relevant norms and approaches tend to be justice, accommodation, economic inducement and the use of force. The case of the dissolution of the former Yugoslavia will be used in this chapter as a case study to identify and discuss the relationship between these norms and approaches during the peace building process and to argue for a greater, yet clearly defined, role for justice.

When appropriately applied the relevant norms and approaches serve valuable roles during the peace building process. At times, however, the over reliance on a particular norm, or a lack of understanding of the risks associated with its application to the exclusion of others may undermine the peace building effort. Moreover, there is an unfortunate tradition of conflict between the norm of justice and the approach of accommodation, and the Yugoslav crisis proved no exception to this history. To promote lasting peace, it will be necessary for foreign policy makers and scholars to understand the mutually supportive roles that may be played by the various approaches, and how best to integrate them into the process of peace building.

This chapter will now define what is meant by the norm of justice and articulate its functions. The chapter will then briefly describe the approaches of accommodation, economic inducement and use of force, and examine the traditional conflict between accountability and accommodation—noting that this conflict proved central to the policy debates over the Yugoslav peace process. The chapter will conclude with a discussion of the need for heightened efforts to apply a hybrid mix of normative approaches. As noted by the former Prosecutor for the Yugoslav Tribunal, "One must not expect too much from justice, for justice is merely one aspect of a many-faceted approach needed to secure enduring peace in a transitional society."[3]

I. Defining Justice

The word "norm" refers to collectively established guides for action; it originates from a Greek word referring to a carpenter's square. When the norm of justice is applied to the peace building process, it operates as a carpenter's square in that it constrains the actions of state and sub-state parties to the dispute, including the actions of third party actors. The norm of justice also guides and in some cases dictates the actions to be taken by the parties, and may in some instances dictate specific terms to be included in a peace agreement or actions to be undertaken to aid the peace building process. The sides of the carpenter's square of justice are comprised of truth, fairness, rectitude, and retribution/requital.

As important as understanding the definition of justice, is to understand the nature of certain acts which undermine the effectiveness of the norm of justice, or acts which may be deemed to constitute the norm of anti-justice. These would be intentional falsehoods and propaganda, perpetual impartiality and moral equivalence, the active erosion of the moral imperative to take action, and impunity and de facto or de jure immunity.

A. The Essence of Justice

In the context of peace building, truth relates to an accurate understanding and recording of the causes of a conflict, as well as which parties are responsible for which actions, and which parties, including individuals, may be characterized as the victims or the aggressors/violators (including the possibility that both parties are the aggressors). Truth also requires an understanding and articulation of the objectives of the various parties, including those of third parties, and an assessment of those interests in light of generally accepted rules of international behavior—in particular those set forth in the U.N. Charter and other legal instruments.[4]

An example of the use of truth to influence the peace process is the report of the War Crimes Commission created by the United Nations in 1993 to assess the nature of the conflict in Yugoslavia and the extent to which the various parties were responsible for war crimes. This report, consisting of over 3,000 pages, paints a fairly accurate portrayal of the nature and extent of the crimes committed by all the parties, finding that although representatives of each party had committed crimes, warranting the creation of an international tribunal, it was clear that the Serbian forces were acting as aggressors and that they had committed the vast majority of crimes.[5] This may be contrasted with what the authors were told were efforts of David Owen, the Co-Chair of the U.N./E.U. Peace Process, to persuade the Chairman of the War Crimes Commission to find that all three of the parties had committed a roughly equal number of crimes and all were therefore equally culpable.

Fairness relates to an initial approach of impartiality—which can and must be adjusted in light of the truth about the conflict. Thus, while fairness requires that at the initiation of the conflict third parties approach peace building in an impartial manner, it also requires that once elements of truth are ascertained, they not be misrepresented in order to maintain artificial impartiality, but rather that they be incorporated into the decision making process and that policy be adjusted accordingly. An example of the use of fairness to guide the peace process is the State Department's attempts in the spring of 1999 to provide extensive detail to the public as to the nature of the crimes being committed by the Serbian regime in Kosovo, even to the extent of naming names of suspected war criminals.[6]

Fairness also requires that third parties do not seek to apply undue pressure on the victims of a conflict in order to achieve an expedient political objective. This act is best exemplified by the United States efforts at the Rambouillet Paris negotiations to openly acknowledged the victim status of the Kosovars. Thus, although the United States sought to persuade the Kosovar delegation to accept major concessions sought by the Serbian side, it did not initially seek to exploit their victim status. This can be contrasted with the approach of the United States four years earlier in the Dayton negotiations, where the United States threatened to close the talks and blame their failure on the Bosnian delegation if the Bosnians failed to agree to a number of concessions, which the Bosnians thought might undermine any serious effort to build peace—knowing that if the Bosnians were blamed for the failure of the negotiations, this would erode international support for protecting them from the continued campaign of genocide.

Rectitude encompasses a sense of moral virtue, integrity and righteousness, requiring the parties to "do the right thing" based in part on their assessment of the truth and the application of fairness, but also including the legitimate interests of the third party states and institutions—the legitimacy of which is defined by principles of international law and generally accepted norms of state behavior. Although rectitude may seem subjective, in matters of armed conflict involving ethnic aggression and crimes against humanity it is usually possible to draw certain boundaries around the behavior of state and sub-state actors.

A peace process influenced by rectitude, for example would likely find states reluctant to substantially accommodate or appease those responsible for orchestrating crimes against humanity as this legitimizes those actors and their methods, while also providing an opportunity for them to ratify at the negotiating table the fruits of their crimes. Moreover, the likelihood of building a meaningful peace on the promises and commitments of individuals and institutions responsible for crimes against humanity is greatly diminished, as evidenced by the multitude of failed cease-fires negotiated by various UNPROFOR Generals with Serbian leaders Mladic and Karadzic, who were indicted by the Yugoslav Tribunal for genocide.[7]

The guide of rectitude may also lead third parties to adopt appropriate policy responses to the conflict. For instance, in the Bosnian conflict and the early stages of the Kosovo conflict, the United States and its allies sought a negotiated settlement with those directly responsible for orchestrating the ethnic aggression. Failing to heed the guide of rectitude resulted in five atrocity-filled years of conflict, and a peace settlement in Bosnia that many critics believe ratifies the gains of ethnic cleansing, widespread war crimes and crimes against humanity. In contrast, when in the case of Kosovo the United States and its allies ascertained that negotiations with the perpetrators would no longer suffice as a viable policy, they embarked on the use of force to defeat the Serbian military forces operating in Kosovo. As a result, the gains of ethnic cleansing were reversed, and there appears to be a greater likelihood for a meaningful peace in Kosovo.

Retribution/requital comprises notions of compensation for victims, punishment of aggressors, recompense for physical damage, delegitimization of responsible institutions, and reimposition of the rule of law. It does not encompass notions of revenge, retaliation or reprisals. Institutions frequently associated with this norm include war crimes tribunals and truth commissions. Retribution/requital is particularly important in peace building as according to one notable commentator, "in the fragile political climate that exists following a settlement, the temptation for retribution and revenge are considerable." Retribution/requital and associated institutions "bring an element of impartiality that is necessary to restore faith in the judicial process and in the rule of law," something the parties and their domestic institutions are unlikely to accomplish on their own.[8]

An example of the influence of retribution/requital on the peace process is the establishment of the Yugoslav Tribunal to try those responsible for war crimes within the territory of the former Yugoslavia. Other examples include the case against the FRY brought in the World Court by Bosnia and a similar case pending by Croatia, the Dayton Accords' creation of a property restitution commission, and discussions about a possible Bosnian Truth Commission.

B. The Essence of Anti-Justice

The antithesis of truth is falsehoods perpetrated through propaganda. For example, as detailed in U.S. Department of State cables, and a number of more recent publications, Slobodan Milosevic relied upon a highly capable propaganda machine to at first stir the nationalist feelings of the Serbian population into support for his objective of an ethnically pure greater Serbia and to promote recruitment into the paramilitary forces responsible for many of the brutal acts of ethnic cleansing.[9]

As noted by Ambassador Zimmermann, through a barrage of propaganda via the State-owned media,[10] Milosevic played on Serb fears and feelings of victimization, going back to their defeat by the Ottomans at Kosovo in 1389, and emphasizing their treatment at the hands of the Ustasha during World War II. "The virus of television," Ambassador Zimmermann recounts, "spread ethnic hatred like an epidemic."[11]

Slobodan Milosevic then turned his propaganda enterprise toward the international community and successfully imbued western foreign policy makers with notions such as the war was caused by the bubbling over of "ancient ethnic hatreds," all the parties were in effect "warring factions," equally responsible for the commission of atrocities, the conflict was a "civil war" not involving Serbia, and the Bosnian government was prone to killing its own civilians in order to garner international sympathy and intervention.[12] The adoption of these falsehoods greatly undercut the influence of the norm of justice.[13]

While the U.S. Embassy in Belgrade accurately reported on the efforts of the Serbian regime to use propaganda to influence the international community,[14] a number of foreign policy makers succumbed to these efforts.[15] In particular, David Owen readily adopted the notion of warring factions equally responsible for atrocities as it promoted his objective of a negotiated settlement of the conflict without the complicated involvement of the norm of justice. Similarly, Secretary of State Warren Christopher adopted Milosevic's notion of ancient ethnic hatreds along with the notion of warring factions,[16] to create the impression that the conflict was inevitable and that the American government could therefore not be faulted for failing to prevent the conflict or the continuing atrocities.[17] And the propensity for UNPROFOR commander General Janvier to "believe Serb propaganda" according to his aides was in part responsible for his rejection of Close Air Support to defend the U.N. declared safe area of Srebrenica, and the subsequent massacre of 7,000 civilians.[18]

Not all those involved in seeking a resolution of the conflict fell victim to Milosevic's propaganda ploys, as illustrated by General Clark's assessment that "above all, I recognized that fundamentally, quarrels in the region were not really about age old religious differences but rather the result of many unscrupulous and manipulative leaders seeking their own power and wealth at the expense of ordinary people in their countries."[19]

The antithesis of fairness is artificial impartiality and moral equivalence. An example of moral equivalence created through falsehoods would be when immediately after the Sarajevo market was struck by an artillery shell in 1995 killing 68 Bosnians, General Michael Rose threatened that unless the Bosnian government signed up to yet another cease-fire, the General would disclose to the media that the Bosnian government had killed its own people in an attempt to gain international sympathy. General Rose's threat was made with the full knowledge that a U.N. investigation had indicated the shell had in fact been fired by Serbian forces, and that the U.S. Embassy in Belgrade had reported that the conspiracy theory of Bosnian government responsibility had in fact originated in Belgrade as part of its propaganda effort.[20]

The antithesis of rectitude is behavior intended to erode the moral imperative to take action. For example, Secretary Christopher sought to erode the moral imperative to use force or take other aggressive action, when he testified to the U.S. Congress in the spring of 1993 that all parties to the conflict were equally responsible for the atrocities, and that the atrocities did not amount to a campaign of genocide. At the time internal CIA and State Department reports—subsequently leaked to the *New York Times*—indicated that over 90 percent of the atrocities were being committed by Serbian forces, and that the campaign very likely constituted attempted genocide.

The antithesis of retribution/requital is political legitimization and de facto or de jure immunity. Political legitimization occurs when individuals responsible for war crimes are embraced by the international mediators or others as "partners in peace," and essential to the peace process. For instance, David Owen repeatedly legitimized Radovan Karadzic by embracing him as a legitimate partner in the ICFY negotiations in Geneva, despite Karadzic's clear culpability at the time for attempted genocide. Similarly, Holbrooke's now famous quote just before the negotiation of the Dayton Accords, "you can't make peace without President Milosevic,"[21] re-established Milosevic as a legitimate partner-in-peace despite his orchestration of genocide against non-Serbs. De facto immunity is best represented by NATO's initial reluctance to apprehend indicted war criminals at large in Bosnia and what may be perceived as Slobodan Milosevic's immunity until the spring of 1999 for his international crimes.

II. Articulating The Functions of Justice

Within the context of creating stable, peaceful societies out of war-torn states, the norms and institutions of justice may serve several functions. These include establishing individual responsibility and denying collective guilt, dismantling and discrediting institutions and leaders responsible for the commission of atrocities, establishing an accurate historical record, providing victim catharsis, and promoting deterrence.

A. Establishing Individual Responsibility and Denying Collective Guilt

The first function of justice is to expose the individuals responsible for atrocities and to avoid assigning guilt to an entire people. As illustrated by the above quote, if foreign policy makers fail to grasp the notion of individual responsibility, they are likely to assign collective responsibility to an entire population. Not only is such an assignation of guilt inappropriate and unfair, but it will likely skew the policy options under consideration for managing the crisis.

Importantly, by assigning guilt to specific perpetrators on all sides, the Tribunal was designed to avoid the assignment of collective guilt which had characterized the years following World War II and in part laid the foundation for the commission of atrocities during the 1990s Balkan conflict. "Far from being a vehicle for revenge" the President of the Yugoslav Tribunal, Antonio Cassese explains, by individualizing guilt in hate-mongering leaders and by disabusing people of the myth that adversary ethnic groups bear collective responsibility for the crimes, "the Yugoslav Tribunal is an instrument for reconciliation."[22]

The assignment of individual guilt to government leaders would also serve the purpose of providing the justification for any use of force to prevent the continued commission of atrocities. As noted by Michael Walzer, "the assignment of responsibility is the critical test of the argument for justice.... If there are recognizable war crimes, there must be recognizable criminals.... The theory of justice should point us to the men and women from whom we can rightly demand an accounting, and it should shape and control the judgments we make of the excuses they offer (or that are offered on their behalf).... There can be no justice in war if there are not, ultimately, responsible men and women."[23]

While this function requires prosecution of responsible leaders, where the norms and institutions do not attach individual liability to a significant number of the individuals responsible for the commission of war crimes, they run the risk that they will be unable to perform the function of denying collective guilt, as many victims and observers will still believe that large or important sections of the group associated with the atrocities are still at large and will thus tend to blame the entire group rather than risk inadvertent impunity. Moreover, those persons who escape individual responsibility will feel emboldened by their impunity and more likely to commit future crimes or interfere with the peace building process in other ways. This risk is particularly acute in the former Yugoslavia where the Office of the Prosecutor has publicly indicted under 100 individuals, and has obtained custody of half that number, while the parties to the conflict estimate there are anywhere between 8,000 and 12,000 who are directly responsible for the commission of war crimes.

B. Dismantling Institutions and Discrediting Leaders Responsible for Atrocities

The second function of justice is to provide a foundation for dismantling institutions and discrediting leaders and their ideology that have promoted the commission of humanitarian crimes. When a government pursues policies of ethnic cleansing or systematically denies human rights, it is often done through legal structures. South Africa's apartheid government used its constitution to oppress, and special government forces to torture and murder, members of black opposition groups. The South African Truth and Reconciliation Commission was later given the task of documenting the full extent of government involvement in racial killings and incidents of torture to help remove the stigma of past wrongs from new governmental institutions. In Yugoslavia, too, government leaders and government forces were a driving force behind much of the ethnic killing.

Through the work of various justice based institutions, in particular the Tribunal, it becomes possible to promote the dismantling of the institutions and a discrediting of the leaders that encouraged, enabled, and carried out the commission of humanitarian crimes. Drawing on his experience as the head of South Africa's Goldstone Commission (a predecessor to the South African Truth and Reconciliation Commission), Justice Goldstone observes that "exposure of the nature and extent of human rights violations frequently will reveal a systematic and institutional pattern of gross human rights violations. It will assist in the identification and dismantling of institutions responsible [for these crimes] and deter future recurrences."[24]

In the case of Serbia, there is particular benefit to laying bare to Serbs unscathed in Belgrade the consequences of nationalistic rhetoric.[25] Even for those who continue to support Bosnian Serb leader Radovan Karadzic and former Serb President Slobodan Milosevic, "it will be much more difficult to dismiss live testimony given under oath than simple newspaper reports," the Tribunal's Deputy Prosecutor, Graham Blewitt points out. "The testimony will send a reminder in a very dramatic way that these crimes were horrendous,"[26] and presumably aid in the continued democratic transformation of Serbia. A notable effect to date of the norm of justice has been to discredit the concept that it is permissible to commit atrocities in the effort to create a greater Serbia. For instance, the Serbian Orthodox Patriarch Pavle, speaking in Kosovo in June 1999 declared, "if the only way to create a greater Serbia is by crime, then I do not accept that, and let that Serbia disappear. And also if a lesser Serbia can only survive by crime, let it also disappear. And if all the Serbs had to die and only I remained and I could live only by crime, then I would not accept that, it would be better to die."[27]

By failing to make sufficient information available about the individuals, institutions, and ideologies associated with the commission of atrocities, there is a significant risk that these individuals, institutions and ideas may in fact attain some degree of *de facto* legitimization. For instance, the Office of the Prosecutor's prolonged failure to publicly indict the leaders of the Serbian political and military regime responsible for the atrocities in Bosnia and the United States failure to consistently identify certain political leaders as suspected war criminals—and in fact publicly rehabilitating them—served the purpose of legitimizing the Serbian regime, which then committed nearly identical atrocities in Kosovo. Moreover, the failure to indict Slobodan Milosevic prior to the Dayton negotiations enabled him not only to substantially influence the institutional structure of post-war Bosnia in a manner which furthered his objectives, but also legitimized him as a partner in peace.

The need for the mechanisms of justice to

delegitimize the perpetrators of international crimes is all the more crucial given the propensity of international peace negotiators to either avoid assigning responsibility for such crimes, or to actually praise the behavior and personal characteristics of war criminals. A telling example is a previously classified State Department demarche to Radovan Karadzic in April of 1994 concerning the commission of war crimes in Banja Luka and the U.N. safe area of Gorazde, which declares: "Those responsible for committing these crimes should be apprehended and punished. We expect you to do so."[28] As noted in the Tribunal's indictment of Karadzic for genocide, he was in fact the individual known to be responsible for orchestrating these crimes. More damaging to the peace process and the operation of the norm of justice may be frequent accolades, such as Lord Owen's description of Radovan Karadzic (later indicted for genocide) as a "gracious host," with "excellent English." Other examples of this include Warren Christopher's characterization of Slobodan Milosevic (later indicted for crimes against humanity) as "though unscrupulous and suspected of war crimes, Milosevic has a rough charm and he appealed to some Western European leaders as a bulwark against an Islamic tide."[29] Richard Holbrooke similarly characterized Milosevic as willing to walk the extra mile for peace in Dayton. One of the more vivid journalistic accounts, according to Carol Hodge, was a Milosevic-friendly BBC program aired during the Kosovo air campaign titled "In the Mind of Milosevic," which portrayed him as a man who "talks, laughs, is a good singer, and likes a drink occasionally, and, unlike President Clinton, does not cheat on his wife."[30] Finally, British Army officer characterized General Mladic (indicted for genocide) in the following terms: "he has presence, and when he had power he wielded it ruthlessly. That brought him some grudging respect, if not admiration."[31]

C. Establishing an Accurate Historical Record

The third function served by justice is to establish an accurate accounting of the actions of all parties and to create an accurate historical record. If, to paraphrase George Santayana, a society is condemned to repeat its mistakes if it has not learned the lessons of the past, then a reliable record of those mistakes must be established if we wish to prevent their recurrence. Michael Ignatieff recognizes that the "great virtue of legal proceedings… [is] that their evidentiary rules confer legitimacy on otherwise contestable facts. In this sense, war crimes trials make it more difficult for societies to take refuge in denial—the trials do assist the process of uncovering the truth."[32] The Chief Prosecutor at Nuremberg, Supreme Court Justice Robert Jackson, underscored the logic of this proposition when he reported to President Truman that one of the most important legacies of the Nuremberg trials following World War II was that they documented the Nazi atrocities "with such authenticity and in such detail that there can be no responsible denial of these crimes in the future and no tradition of martyrdom of the Nazi leaders can arise among informed people."[33]

In both Guatemala and El Salvador, truth commissions were established to resolve disputes between the former combatants as to who was responsible for which atrocities. In each case an objective historical record has led to the establishment of credible judicial systems that can then help to sustain peace.[34] The problems of accurately assessing blame for war crimes in the former Yugoslavia is especially acute. In Richard Goldstone's words, "It doesn't take hours after human rights violations for the denials to begin.… Justice plays a vital role in stopping that fabrication, in stopping that cover-up, which is inevitable."[35]

The need for the establishment for an accurate accounting of the conflict is all the more compelling in the case of the former Yugoslavia as according to Natasha Kandic, head of the Humanitarian Law Fund in Belgrade, "when I tried to talk about what I had seen and experienced [concerning atrocities in Kosovo], people would get impatient and change the subject. It's as if people here simply don't want to know the truth about what happened in Kosovo. Even the intellectuals are under the influence of official propaganda."[36]

If the institution of the Yugoslav Tribunal operates as designed, the Tribunal should generate a comprehensive record of the nature and extent of crimes against humanity and genocide in the Balkans, how they were planned and executed, the fate of individual victims, who gave the orders and who carried them out. By carefully proving these facts one witness at a time in the face of vigilant cross-examination by distinguished defense counsel, the international trials would produce a definitive account that can pierce the distortions generated by official propaganda, endure the test of time, and resist the forces of revisionism.

Failure to create a comprehensive records will undermine many, if not all, of the benefits associated with creating an accurate record. This risk is heightened when only one institution of justice is employed, or where others are minimized. For instance, although the Yugoslav Tribunal is capable of creating a lengthy record for cases on its docket, there is no official process for summarizing findings, and no process for including facts not relevant to the specific cases before the Tribunal. In addition, where a defendant is not present before the Tribunal the indictment and Rule 61 hearing provide only a minimal basis for assessing the truth of the alleged actions. In other cases, the death of defendants prior to judgment led to a dismissal of their case, thereby erasing the official history of atrocities.

D. Victim Catharsis

The fourth function of justice is to acknowledge the victims of crimes—an often overlooked but equally important element to the success of any peace process as is punishing the offenders. Offering victims an opportunity to state their injuries publicly can "provide victims with a sense of justice and catharsis—a sense that their grievances have been addressed and can more easily be put to rest, rather than smoldering in anticipation of the next round of conflict."[37]

In South Africa, the Truth Commission heard tearful testimony from thousands of victims as well as the confessions of many who played a role in brutal killings for the apartheid regime. Although some of this testimony was offered in exchange for amnesty, the overall effect was to purge the national consciousness of past racial killings so that the society may be rebuilt. In Yugoslavia there is no mechanism for forgiving crimes, yet the same logic was used in the International Criminal Tribunal's creation. According to the Yugoslav Tribunal's first President, Antonio Cassese, the pursuit of justice "is essential to the restoration of peaceful and normal relations especially for people who have had to live under a reign of terror [because] [it breaks the cycle of violence, hatred, and extra judicial retribution."[38]

As Richard Goldstone noted, "the Nuremberg Trials played an important role in enabling the victims of the Holocaust to obtain official acknowledgement of what befell them."[39] Such acknowledgement constitutes a partial remedy for their suffering and a powerful catharsis that can discourage acts of retaliation. According to Antonio Cassese, the "only civilized alternative to this desire for revenge is to render justice" for otherwise "feelings of hatred and resentment seething below the surface will, sooner or later, erupt and lead to renewed violence."[40] As confirmed by Munira Subasic, who lost two sons in the Srebrenica massacre, "if we are deprived of the right to justice, then we shall seek the right to revenge."[41]

If the norm of justice is employed, but not effectively, it can have the disadvantage of raising the expectations of victims, and then causing them additional psychological trauma as they come to perceive themselves as abandoned, or worse, used by the international community to clear its own conscience. As Justice Goldstone noted in response to the persistent failure of the international community to arrest indicted war criminals Radovan Karadzic and Ratko Mladic, "imagine [the victim's] disappointment at the failure of the international community to follow through with the arrest of those indicted. If this situation is not corrected, the establishment of the Yugoslav Tribunal will have caused more harm than good to the persons it was intended to benefit."[42]

E. Deterrence

Finally, in the case of criminal prosecutions, the execution of justice ideally acts as a deterrent against future humanitarian crimes, or at least sets a precedent for accountability. As observed by David Scheffer, the U.S. Ambassador at Large for War Crimes Issues, "we know from experience in Bosnia that local authorities—camp commanders and temporary local officials—sometimes do what they can to improve the circumstances of those under their care once they know that the international community will investigate and punish those who fail to respect human rights standards."[43] Richard Goldstone adds that the existence of the Tribunal may have deterred widespread human rights violations during the Croatian army offensive against Serb rebels in August 1995. "Fear of prosecution in the Hague," he said, "prompted Croat authorities to issue orders to their soldiers to protect Serb civilian rights when Croatia took control of the Krajina and Western Slavonia regions of the country."[44]

Unfortunately, as the Tribunal was not at the time perceived to be a meaningful threat, these "orders" were generally ignored with the consequence that the Serbian population was subject to numerous atrocities. Goldstone has also argued that by broadcasting televised highlights of the trials throughout Bosnia and Serbia, that message can get through directly to the citizenry: "People don't relate to statistics, to generalizations. People can only relate and feel when they hear somebody that they can identify with telling what happened to them. That's why the public broadcasts of the Tribunal's cases can have a strong deterrent effect."[45]

Moreover, the international prosecution of responsible individuals can become an instrument through which respect for the rule of law is instilled into the popular consciousness.[46] As Judge Gabrielle Kirk McDonald, who presided over the Yugoslav Tribunal's first trial, succinctly put it: "We are here to tell people that the rule of law has to be respected."[47] The establishment of the rule of law is particularly important since a dominant characteristic of the post-Cold War era in international affairs is that conflicts occur among peoples of different ethnic and religious backgrounds *within* states, not between them. In war-torn societies, one of the most basic obstacles to reconciliation is a lack of trust on the part of citizens to each other and to their government. And one of the most effective ways to institutionalize that trust is to establish a stable legal system, or the rule of law.[48]

Although the punishment of crimes committed in the Balkans would send the message, both to potential aggressors and vulnerable minorities, that the international community will not allow atrocities to be committed with impunity, if a Tribunal is established and fails to indict those responsible for orchestrating the campaign of terror—as the case with the Office of the Prosecutor's initial failure to indict Mr. Milosevic for war crimes in Bosnia, then it may in fact encourage them to feel free to commit atrocities in future conflict—as in Kosovo, believing they possess some degree of *de facto* immunity.

In many cases, however, the nature of injustice and internal pressures militate toward the establishment of a truth commission often accompanied by grants of amnesty to bring the dark practices of civil violence into the light without necessarily prosecuting the guilty.[49] A version of this system has been practiced particularly in South Africa, El Salvador, Chile and Argentina, where the calculation was made that the benefits of healing wounds through the establishment of the truth outweighed the benefits of retributive justice.[50] But the particular circumstance of the crimes committed in the former Yugoslavia required the formation of an ad hoc criminal tribunal for both moral and practical reasons. First, the genocide, rape and torture that occurred was of a nature and scale so horrific that nothing short of full accountability for those responsible would provide justice.[51] Second, the domestic legal systems in some of the republics of the former Yugoslavia had been so thoroughly corrupted that they were not competent to conduct a fair trial of the war's perpetrators, some of whom are still in power.

Given that the norm of justice is based upon near universally accepted principles and serves a variety of policy relevant functions ranging from deterrence to victim catharsis, one might expect that it would play a central if not determinative role in the peace building process. The norm of justice must, however, compete for influence with other highly relevant and practicable approaches such as accommodation, economic inducement and the use of force, which are based on equally compelling principles, and which have a longer history of use by peace builders. To establish the necessary background to understand the relationship between the norm of justice and these other approaches in the Yugoslav peace process, the next section will define these normative approaches and discuss their traditional relationship to the justice-based approach of accountability.

III. Defining the Approaches of Accommodation, Economic Inducements and the Use of Force

A. Accommodation

The approach of accommodation seeks to reduce conflict by accommodating the interests of adversarial states or parties. In most instances, the approach of accommodation instructs a negotiator to seek to end the conflict by meeting as many of the objectives of each party as possible—thereby accommodating their interests and satiating their appetite for more conflict. If applied appropriately, the norm can lead to the creation of win-win gaming situations where each party is able to attain its objectives without unduly prejudicing the interests of the other party—this is most probable in a prisoners' dilemma and related situations, and least possible in deadlock situations. If applied recklessly or forced on a deadlock situation, the norm can ratify illegitimate actions of a party and enhance its appetite for similar gains through further conflict.

Institutions most frequently associated with the approach of accommodation include Foreign Ministries; special envoys such as Yasushi Akashi and Richard Holbrooke; and ad hoc diplomatic institutions such as the International Conference for the Former Yugoslavia created by the United Nations and the European Union and co-chaired at various times by Lord Carrington, Cyrus Vance, David Owen, Carl Bildt, and Thorvald Stoltenberg. Accommodation is frequently the approach of choice because it is the approach around which it is the easiest to build political will, and it is the approach most likely to lead to a formal agreement among the parties.

The brokering of the Washington Agreement between Croatia and Bosnia represents an example of the appropriate utilization of the accommodation norm in that it was used to craft a relationship between Bosnia and Croatia which sought to meet the needs, as far as possible, of both parties while creating a system of democratic government capable of preserving those interests. Unfortunately the system has in practice proven difficult to implement, and may have represented too much of an accommodation of minority interests.

One of the more committed applications of the accommodation norm was the proposed Vance/Owen Peace Plan which intended to bring peace by essentially partitioning Bosnia into ethnically based cantons and de facto permitting the Serbian cantons to confederate with Serbia proper—thus ratifying the aims of the campaign of ethnic cleansing and legitimizing the anti-multicultural nationalism propagated by the Serbian and Croatian combatants. In fact, earlier David Owen had proposed that as EU mediator he actively engage the parties in redrawing their territorial boundaries. When this was rejected by eleven of the EU states he believed "[t]he refusal to make these borders negotiable greatly hampered the EC's attempt at crisis management in July and August 1991 and subsequently put all peacemaking from September 1991 onwards within a straitjacket that greatly inhibited compromises between the parties in dispute."[52]

As it was, the Vance/Owen Peace Plan was widely perceived as the catalyst for the conflict between Bosnian Croats and the Bosnian government as the Bosnian Croats sought to capture land "promised" them under the Peace Plan.[53] Similarly, with the aim of peace, the peace negotiators embarked on an approach until 1995 of continually redrafting peace plans to offer more and more favorable terms to the Serbian party when they rejected earlier "take it or leave it" offers by the Contact Group.[54] Some critics have even argued that UNPROFOR commander General Janvier deliberately denied Close Air Support to the U.N. Dutch defenders of Srebrenica in order to make a negotiated settlement more feasible,[55] and because the French government had promised General Mladic it would seek to block air strikes in exchange for the release of two French pilots and several hundred UNPROFOR peacekeepers held hostage by Bosnian Serb forces.[56]

The perspective of those supporting unfettered accommodation when faced with the criticism that the approach of accommodation might reward the use of force and ethnic cleansing, is typified by Canadian General Lewis MacKenzie, the former head of the U.N. forces in Bosnia when he testified before the U.S. Congress that "[n]ow obviously the critics will say this rewards force and sets a bad example. I can only say to them, read your history. Force has been rewarded since the first caveman picked up a club, occupied his neighbor's cave, and ran off with his wife."[57] According to the U.N. report on Srebrenica, as a result of views like those held by General MacKenzie, "[Serb] leaders engaged in high-level negotiations with representatives of the international community while their forces on the ground, executed and buried thousands of men and boys within a matter of days.... At various points during the war, these negotiations amounted to appeasement."[58]

The over reliance on the approach of accommodation can create situations where once diplomacy alone has failed, policy makers are reluctant to move onto or incorporate other norms, creating even more intractable conflicts. As noted by Former British Defense Minister Sir John Nott in 1994, "[w]e will not bring about a diplomatic solution. Even if there is peace obtained, it cannot hold. We have given these diplomats, these committees...two and a half years to bring about peace, and they have failed...I would remove the arms embargo [on the Bosnian Government] straight away because it is only a military balance now in that part of the world that can restore stability."[59] Similarly, Ed Vulliamy, the *Guardian* correspondent during the Bosnian conflict, has argued that an early use of force against Serb military targets designed to neutralize their artillery and destroy their communications system would have brought them to the negotiating table, and then "the Serbs would have been required to dismount the sieges and to accept international supervision in a complete reversal of ethnic cleansing. This would have been infinitely easier in 1992 than the imposition of the Dayton plan—with its pledge to return all refugees—is now."[60] This assessment was supported by Manfred Worner, the then NATO Secretary General.[61]

In the end, the primary risk associated with the approach of accommodation is that it can become one of appeasement, and possibly even coercive appeasement. While accommodation may be a useful and valuable tool, appeasement is characterized by an artificial moral equivalence, neutrality in the face of aggression, active efforts to erode moral imperative to become involved, and total exclusion of the use of force and the norm of justice, with the effect of often encouraging further violence and atrocities.

The approach of coercive appeasement is more nuanced and entails appeasement within the context of the perceived use of force and the perceived incorporation of the norm of justice. Coercive appeasement is characterized first by a general diplomatic deficit which entails the failure to create the conditions for effective leadership or the articulation of a clear policy objective coupled with the inability to structure a coordinated or capable diplomatic process for peace building, and a failure to adequately undergo institutional and personal "learning" during the peace building process. Often the diplomatic deficit encompasses the unintentional misuse of diplomatic signaling, and the readily transparent articulation of intentions and available means by the peace builders. Coercive appeasement is also characterized by aggressive accommodation, which entails the pursuit of actions designed to meet the needs and interests of the aggressor, coupled with intentional or unintentional obfuscation of the aggressor's true objectives.

Moral duplicity is also an element of coercive appeasement, consisting of the application of pressure on the victims designed to compel their acquiescence to the primary demands of the aggressor, coupled with intentional and unintentional actions designed to create division within the political representation of the victim. Moral duplicity also frequently entails declarations and actions designed to create the perception of moral equivalence among the parties, thereby eroding the distinction between aggressor and victim and spreading culpability among all parties. Frequently these official pronouncements are designed to actively erode the moral and strategic imperative to adopt approaches other than that of accommodation. Finally, coercive appeasements characterized by constrained use of force (which entails activities designed to constrain and minimize the use of legitimate force), and marginalized justice, (which entails actions designed to minimize and obfuscate the role of justice, including the political resurrection of culpable partners in peace).

B. Economic Inducement

The approach of economic inducement entails the notion that it is legitimate to seek a modification of a party's behavior through the employment of both financial incentives and financial disincentives. The economic inducement approach assumes that states are neither obligated to engage in economic transactions with another state, nor are they prohibited from offering financial incentives to modify a state or sub-state actors' behavior, and in fact may, with the appropriate international legal approval—such as a Chapter VII U.N. Security Council Resolution—seek to forbid other actors from engaging in economic relations with a state.

Institutions generally associated with the approach of economic inducement include the United Nations Security Council, which has the authority to impose economic sanctions, the European Union, and the International Financial Institutions, which although mandated to operate in a non-political manner can provide or deny assistance and membership in order to effect state behavior. Other relevant institutions include state Export-Import Banks and Overseas Development Funds.

Economic incentives may take the form of direct financial assistance, preferential trade practices, and financial rewards for certain actions—such as the apprehension of indicted war criminals. Economic disincentives include a spectrum of sanctions ranging from the denial of air travel and trade preferences, to the imposition of a full scale economic embargo prohibiting any type of trade, investment or financial transactions other than those necessary for humanitarian purposes. In the Yugoslav conflict, for instance, in 1992, the U.N. and EU enacted a wide range of sanctions against all of the parties to the Yugoslav conflict, but most particularly toward Serbia. While Milosevic's regime undertook a concerted effort to bypass the sanctions, to some degree they did limit his capacity to pursue the conflict in Croatia and Bosnia. As the nature of the conflict became more apparent, the U.N. and EU suspended their economic sanctions against all the parties except the FRY, and began to provide financial assistance to Croatia and Bosnia. They did, however, continue to maintain an arms embargo against all the parties. Subsequently, economic inducements in the form of hundreds of millions of dollars in conditional aid prompted Croatia to turn dozens of indicted citizens over to the Yugoslav Tribunal, and ultimately compelled Serbia to surrender Slobodan Milosevic for trial at The Hague.

C. Use of Force

The use of force approach provides that in certain narrowly defined circumstances such as individual and collective self-defense, humanitarian intervention to prevent crimes against humanity, or where authorized by the U.N. Security Council as a necessary act to promote peace and security, states and regional organizations may use military force to affect the behavior of another state or sub-state entity.[62] According to some scholars, force may be used to punish an aggressor state in order to deter further aggression or to protect a civilian population from massive human rights abuses.[63] The use of force approach also embodies principles of necessity, proportionality, and respect for the laws and customs of war.

The institutions associated with the use of force approach include each state's Ministry of Defense, regional military alliances such as NATO, and the United Nations Security Council, which has the authority to authorize the "use of all necessary means" to resolve a dispute and to deploy U.N. peacekeepers if made available by member states.

Examples of the appropriate application of the use of force approach in the former Yugoslavia include NATO air strikes in August of 1995 to prevent further Serbian aggression against Bosnia; the deployment of an International Force (IFOR) on the territory of Bosnia following the Dayton Peace negotiations for the purpose of implementing the Accords; the spring 1999 air campaign conducted against Serbian forces in Kosovo and Serbia proper in order to deter Serbian aggression in Kosovo;[64] and the deployment of Kosovo Force (KFOR) to provide security during the implementation of U.N. Security Council Resolution 1244 providing for the interim international management of Kosovo.

There exist a number of counter examples where the use of force approach was either misapplied, such as in 1993-1995 when NATO was limited to striking only those specific military assets which had fired on civilian targets, rather than any asset in the unit engaged in the attack; or where it was not applied at all, as in the case where UNPROFOR commanders failed to act upon the request for Close Air Support by UNPROFOR forces defending the safe areas of Srebrenica and Zepa, the citizens of which were subsequently ethnically cleansed or massacred.[65] The norm was also distorted when the United Nations maintained an arms embargo against Bosnia even though it was being subjected to territorial aggression and genocide,[66] on the basis that this would help prevent an escalation of the conflict.

In many instances the use of force approach is misapplied as key actors fail to understand the role of "diplomacy backed by force" (as enunciated by Secretary of State Madeline Albright) or misconstrue the extent of force that must be used to accomplish an objective. For instance, at the height of the atrocities in Bosnia when Senate Majority Leader Bob Dole and House Speaker Newt Gingrich were calling for the withdrawal of UNPROFOR, the arming and training of Bosnian Government forces, and extensive air strikes against the Bosnian Serbs if they continued to commit atrocities, President Clinton ruled out "a military solution," and Secretary of State Warren Christopher labeled the plan a "war strategy," and argued that the only two options for the United States in Bosnia were either to stick to diplomacy alone or to send in more than a hundred thousand U.S. ground troops.[67] It subsequently required only a meaningful ground offensive by combined Croat/Bosnian forces and NATO air strikes to compel the Serbian forces to end their attacks and negotiate the Dayton Accords.

As confirmed by a complex time-series statistical analysis conducted by Joshua Goldstein and Jon Pevehouse, the threat or actual use of force by NATO produced compliance and cooperation by Serbian forces. The research further demonstrated that "Serb forces were more responsive to American actions than European ones."[68] According to the authors, "the results thus support the assumptions of the aggressor-victim school of thought that the international use of force could induce Serbian cooperation in this regional conflict." Importantly, the authors also note, "by contrast, the warring-factions school of thought, with its preferred policy of using international cooperation to elicit Serbian cooperation toward Bosnia, receives little support."[69] As put concisely in lay terms by Serbian Human Rights Lawyer Srdja Popovic, "from the very beginning, I thought that only a military defeat could put an end to Slobodan Milosevic's regime. As far as I am concerned, what happened in Kosovo actually confirms that. Until Milosevic was militarily defeated, there was no chance to remove him."[70]

The lack of an understanding of the parameters of the use of force approach and the capabilities of military institutions has led to contradictory outcomes, such as when the United States only agreed to use force to support the withdrawal of UNPROFOR troops, but not to protect civilians subjected to atrocities. As proclaimed by Richard Hass, "I don't know if it's tragic or ironic or both that the only time we're now considering to use meaningful force in Bosnia is for the purpose of a pull-out."[71]

In other instances the use of force approach can be complicated when two or more institutions are responsible for the employment of the norm. In Bosnia, for instance, UNPROFOR officials exercised control over U.N. troops on the ground, while NATO exercised control over air assets. When the safe area of Bihac was under attack, NATO sought to respond with extensive air strikes, while UNPROFOR objected, arguing that such strikes would provoke the Serbs into killing UNPROFOR troops.[72] Thus, UNPROFOR commanders limited the NATO strike against the strategic Udbina airfield in Serb-held Croatia to inflict only cosmetic damage to the runway—in fact the planes responsible for attacks on the safe area were specifically exempted from attack. UNPROFOR even later criticized the independent action of NATO in destroying Serbian anti-aircraft installations after British warplanes were fired upon near Banja Luka, and subsequently denied permission to NATO to attack other Serbian anti-aircraft installations, which NATO officials said had to be destroyed before any meaningful action could be taken to defend Bihac from the air.

IV. Forcing a False Choice between Justice and Accommodation

A. The Tradition of Conflict Between Justice and Accommodation

Traditionally, many foreign policy practitioners and scholars have perceived of justice and peace in conflicting terms. The choices are often cast in terms of either working toward peace and ignoring justice, or seeking justice at the price of jeopardizing any chance for peace. Proponents of peace are typically characterized as "more aware, more worldly," while those in favor of justice are characterized as "living in an unreal world, shall we say, a metaphysical or idealistic realm."[73]

The traditional dichotomy between justice and accommodation is best summed up by a quote from Ed Vulliamy, a correspondent for *The Guardian,* who argues that "Justice being done, and being seen to be done, is the difference between a lasting peace and an interval between hostilities,"[74] and an anonymous U.N. official who argues that "The 'peace-makers' primary responsibility is to end the war—but not to call for justice."[75]

While this distinction is overly artificial, historically, amnesty or *de facto* immunity from prosecution has often been the price for peace. The Turks, who many considered responsible for the genocidal massacre of over one million Armenians during World War I were given amnesty in the 1923 Treaty of Lausanne;[76] the French and Algerians responsible for the slaughter of thousands of civilians during the Algerian war were given amnesty in the Evian Agreement of 1962; and Bangladesh gave amnesty in 1973 to Pakistanis charged with genocide in exchange for political recognition by Pakistan.[77]

During the 1980s, the governments of Argentina, Chile, El Salvador, Guatemala, and Uruguay each granted amnesty to members of the former regime who commanded death squads that tortured and killed thousands of civilians within their respective countries in order to facilitate a transition to democracy.[78] To this list must be added the modern practice of the United Nations, which in the early 1990s worked to block mention of prosecuting former Khmer Rouge leaders for their atrocities from inclusion in the Cambodia peace accords, pushed the Mandela government to accept an amnesty for crimes committed by the apartheid regime in South Africa, and helped negotiate, and later endorsed, a broad amnesty for the Haitian military regime in order to induce them to relinquish power.[79]

Even the Nuremberg experience eventually involved the bartering away of accountability as the cost for German support of the Western alliance during the beginning of the cold war. Within ten years of the conclusion of the Nuremberg Tribunal and Control Council Law Number 10 trials, all 150 of the convicted German war criminals (including several who were serving life sentences and a few who were sentenced to death) were released from Landsberg prison pursuant to a controversial clemency program.[80] While this program removed a "diplomatic pebble...from the State Department's shoes," it had the effect of undermining the purpose of the Nuremberg Trials. In a nation-wide survey conducted by the U.S. State Department, West Germans overwhelmingly indicated their belief that the reason for American leniency was that "they realize the injustice of the trials."[81]

As explained by an anonymous U.N. official, the quest for "justice and retribution" is traditionally believed to hamper the search for peace, which in turn prolongs the conflict, enables the continuation of atrocities, and increases human suffering. The U.N. official also asserts that the intrusion of fact-finding missions seeking to investigate crimes committed by one side may complicate the task of peace negotiations to the point where they become prolonged or impossible.[82]

Efforts to build peace in the former Yugoslavia were not exempt from the conflict between justice and accommodation.[83] According to Payam Akhvan of the Office of the Prosecutor of the Tribunal: "From its very inception in 1993, the International Criminal Tribunal for the former Yugoslavia was surrounded by the so-called 'peace versus accountability' controversy.... It was argued that indicting political and military leaders such as Radovan Karadzic and Ratko Mladic would undermine the prospects of a peace settlement because they were indispensable to on-going negotiations, and because they would have no incentive to put an end to the fighting without assurances of immunity or amnesty."[84] In fact, during his tenure as Co-Chairman of the Yugoslav Peace Conference, David Owen expressly opposed the prosecution of Serbian officials engaged in the peace negotiations on the basis that this would undermine his efforts to craft a settlement.[85]

Even after the massacres in Srebrenica and the clear pattern of genocide, policy makers doubted the compatibility of justice and accommodation. As noted by Richard Goldstone, "particularly at the time of the negotiations at Dayton, Ohio, in September, 1995, there were many astute politicians and political commentators who suggested that, in fact, peace and justice were in opposition, and that the work of the Yugoslav Tribunal was retarding the peace process in the Balkans."[86] Some commentators even noted that with Radovan Karadzic's alleged approval rating among Bosnian Serbs of 79 percent, any NATO efforts to capture him would undermine the implementation of the Dayton Peace Accord and foster the Serbian people's belief that they were subject to perpetual injustice and persecution.[87] Goldstone rightly expressed surprise at this view, especially in light of the atrocities which had been committed over four years, and the clear view of the Security Council when it established the Tribunal in May, 1993.[88]

In some cases, the existence of a mechanism of justice, such as a tribunal, may be used to further the efforts of those pursing an approach of accommodation by indicating that the norm of justice plays a role outside the peace process and that questions of culpability belong solely with that mechanism. For instance, in February 1994, when Secretary of State Warren Christopher was under pressure by the media to identify those responsible for the commission of war crimes in Bosnia—which would have limited his ability to accommodate the interests of those individuals—his standard press guidance was "I would like to emphasize that no conclusion can or should be drawn at this stage as to the culpability of particular individuals. This is a question that should be reserved for the War Crimes Tribunal or other court, where the question of culpability will be considered on a case-by-case basis."[89]

Still others, like Richard Holbrooke, asserted that in order to achieve the aims of justice, it was necessary to negotiate with and if necessary accommodate/appease those who were responsible for the commission of atrocities.[90] As such, the insistence on a role for justice is characterized as something which undermines the effectiveness of the negotiator. When asked by Senator Smith during his confirmation hearing why he had systematically declined to ever indicate Milosevic's guilt for the war and atrocities in the former Yugoslavia, Holbrooke responded, "This is tough slogging, and my job was not to make moral judgments. I leave that to moralists and political pundits and columnists, most of whom think they're moralists anyway.... I was well aware of the fact that I might have to continue to be engaged on other issues. And the highest goal here was to avoid war, bring peace."[91]

Many peace builders also assert that the conflict between accommodation and justice reflects the perspectives of those on the ground trying to save lives vs. those more distant from the conflict. For instance, during his confirmation testimony, Ambassador Holbrooke responded to criticisms of his persistent failure to acknowledge Milosevic's culpability as made "by people who haven't been there, who haven't tried to end wars and prevent wars."[92] Similar statement were made by numerous generals serving in UNPROFOR, who also invoked the mantra of "saving lives" over pursuing justice.[93] In fact, as reported by Cambridge Historian, Brendan Simms, many of the actual on the ground in the Safe Areas, and particularly SAS troops were keenly aware of the failings of accommodation and urged for a stronger use of force.[94]

The "saving lives" rational, while encapsulated in only two words, is a powerful tool used by the negotiators to undermine the influence of the norm of justice. By characterizing accomodation/appeasment of war criminals in the cloak of "saving lives," it automatically infers that those interested in justice are not interested in saving lives, or at least are willing to permit more killing in order to accomplish an idealistic objective. This view is succinctly stated by an anonymous U.N. official who criticized the then Yugoslav Tribunal Prosecutor and its President at the time for their public pressure on the Dayton negotiators. The U.N. official argues that "their 'ill-considered statements' could have led to a breakdown of delicate negotiations in Dayton.... Everyone who was at the Dayton proximity talks knew that if this issue [mandatory cooperation with the Tribunal] were pressed it could have ruined the talks."[95] He declares that they were acting "irresponsibly" and asks "in the name of what moral principle would one be able to defend those [further] deaths?"[96] As evidenced by the subsequent conflict in Kosovo, it was in fact the act of accommodation at Dayton that resulted in further deaths, and that only the use of force, coupled with the indictment of Milosevic, brought an end to ethnic cleansing perpetrated by Serbian forces.

Some scholarly commentators assert that the tension between justice and accommodation is inherent in that "the need to establish power sharing structures that accommodate rival factions and interests may well clash with the desire to punish perpetrators of human-rights abuses...[and] the need to reform the police and the military may be at odds with the practical need to bring those powerful groups into the peace process."[97] In their eyes, the inherent tension "prompt[s] the question of which model works best in a given situation, the power-sharing conflict manager's model, or the democratizer's political justice model? Empirical evidence suggests that a concern for justice must be tempered by the realities of negotiation and by the parties' interests in reaching a political settlement."[98]

In response, defenders of the justice norm have argued, "in short, there is a grudging but emerging widespread acceptance—even among the so-called 'realists'—that regional peace and stability, democratization and multiethnic coexistence in Bosnia-Herzegovina are at best precarious without the arrest and prosecution of indicted persons," and that "the [Yugoslav Tribunal] demonstrates that far from being irreconcilable, peace and accountability, realities and ideals, are inextricably interlinked."[99] According to Richard Goldstone, "if one is talking about short term cease-fires, short term cessation of hostilities, it could be that the investigation of war crimes is a nuisance. But if one is concerned with real peace, enduring and effective peace, if one is talking about proper reconciliation, then, in my respectful opinion, there is and can be no contradiction between peace and justice."[100]

Despite the tradition of an apparent overwhelming preference for accommodation over justice, there is no clear evidence that this approach has promoted peace building.[101] In fact, the opposite may be the case. For example, history records that the international amnesty given to the Turkish officials responsible for the massacre of the Armenians during World War I encouraged Adolf Hitler some twenty years later to conclude that Germany could pursue his genocidal policies with impunity.[102] In 1939, in relation to the acts of genocide and aggression committed by German forces, Hitler remarked, "Who after all is today speaking about the destruction of the Armenians?"[103] As David Matas, a Canadian expert on international law, observed: "Nothing emboldens a criminal so much as the knowledge he can get away with a crime. That was the message the failure to prosecute for the Armenian massacre gave to the Nazis. We ignore the lesson of the Holocaust at our peril."[104]

Richard Goldstone has declared that in the case of the former Yugoslavia the failure of the international community to prosecute Pol Pot (Cambodia), Idi Amin (Uganda), Saddam Hussein (Iraq) and Mohammed Aidid (Somalia), among others, encouraged the Serbs to launch their policy of ethnic cleansing with the expectation that they would not be held accountable for their international crimes.[105] When the international community encourages or endorses an amnesty for human rights abuses, it sends a signal to other rogue regimes that they have nothing to lose by instituting repressive measures; if things start going badly, they can always bargain away their crimes by agreeing to peace. The apprehension of Slobodan Milosevic in the spring of 2001 may be the first step in reversing this impact.

Given the poor track record for accommodation, there has been increasing demand for an inclusion of the norm of justice in peace building since the end of the Cold War.[106] For example, since 1989, some level of justice, in the form of international tribunals and truth commissions, has been pursued in Argentina, Cambodia, Chile, East Timor, El Salvador, Ethiopia, Guatemala, Honduras, Rwanda, Sierra Leone, and South Africa, as well as the former Yugoslavia. As discussed in the next section, there is a role for each of the approaches of accountability, accommodation, economic inducement and use of force in the peace building process.

V. Getting the Right Mix of Approaches

Individual peace building approaches generally are not capable of building a lasting peace in isolation from other peace building approaches. Moreover, when peace building approaches operate, they generally do so in relation to other peace building approaches. The task of foreign policy practitioners is to ascertain the proper role for each approach and to apply an appropriate mix. As noted by General Nash, "the reality is, that all the world is a compromise of many, many issues and as you try to go towards an objective state; an objective goal, you've got to work things in stages and you have to balance things."[107]

While some diplomats contend that the approach of accommodation may be sufficient in and of itself, most commentators would agree with the assessment that "the military and security components of peace building are a critical part of the peacemaking process," and that "peacekeeping remains essential to international efforts to prevent the renewed outbreak of violence or military hostilities in a country."[108] Furthermore, the prompt deployment of competent and capable peacekeepers may promote confidence in the peace building process.

In the case of Bosnia for instance, most observers would acknowledge that "the final factor smoothing the path to Dayton was the international community's new willingness to use force, especially air power, as a partner to diplomacy."[109] Observers would also readily acknowledge that the application of economic sanctions on the FRY were insufficient in and of themselves to deter Serbia's aggression against neighboring states. As will be discussed below, however, the employment of economic inducements against Croatia and later Serbia to turn over indicted war criminals to The Hague for trial, and thus neutralize their ability to inhibit the peace building process, and the use of economic inducements to prompt the handover of Slobodan Milosevic, were highly effective.

Unfortunately, foreign policy makers frequently underestimate the need to adequately employ all relevant approaches, and thus in the Bosnia case, they were slow to utilize the approach of the use of force. According to Elizabeth Cousens, despite the fact that very clear legal justification existed for the use of force, "various explanations account for the under-use of armed force to respond to the Yugoslav wars, from the nationally parochial through the bureaucratically predisposed and militarily arcane, to the ontologically confused."[110] This failure to grasp the utility of the use of force is all the more difficult to understand as key foreign policy makers often set forth compelling rationales for the use of force to protect human rights. For instance, in a now declassified memorandum from Assistant Secretary of State John Shattuck to Secretary Christopher on July 19, 1995, Mr. Shattuck argues:

> We know from these recent and past events what will happen if the Bosnian Serbs' 'ethnic cleansing' campaign is not stopped. And, we know that the ever-growing refugee problem poses both a humanitarian catastrophe and a security problem as population flows disrupt the delicate balance in the Bosnian Federation and neighboring countries. On human rights and humanitarian grounds alone, the disaster of Srebrenica demands that the international community use the authority it has to protect the remaining safe areas, including through the use of military force.[111]

Regrettably, on frequent occasion, foreign policy makers may in artfully mix the employment of most or all of the approaches, resulting in the creation of a set of circumstances where the approaches work at cross-purposes and are inconducive to the establishment of peace. For instance, in the Bosnia conflict the U.N. deployed lightly armed peacekeepers which provided some protection to civilians, but did not act decisively when confronted with large-scale ethnic cleansing and genocide against Bosnian Muslims. During the same period, policymakers enacted, but initially failed to enforce a no-fly zone over Bosnia; established safe areas without protecting them; and authorized, but never employed, force to deliver humanitarian aid.

When EU policymakers sought to address the initial conditions of conflict in Bosnia, and Serbs and Croats escalated their behavior, the prevailing guide to action for the EU lay in accommodation and tightly calibrated displays of force, rather than the meaningful use of force. The contradictory employment of the various approaches came to a head when in the summer of 1995 NATO forces were prohibited from using force to protect the U.N. designated safe areas of Srebrenica and Zepa because of the risk of Serb retaliation against lightly armed peacekeepers stationed in those safe areas.[112]

In large part because of the failure of the international peace builders to settle on a proper and effective mix of approaches, Yugoslavia slid into a decade of war marked by crimes against humanity and acts of genocide. The task for future peace builders is to ensure they attain the proper mix of justice, accommodation, economic inducement and use of force to establish a meaningful and lasting peace.

Notes

1. Assistant Professor of Law and International Relations, American University.

2. Professor of Law, New England School of Law.

3. Richard J. Goldstone, "Justice as a Tool for Peace-Making." *N.Y.U. Journal of International Law & Policy* 28: 485, 486.

4. See Goldstone, "Justice as a Tool for Peace-Making," 486.

5. U.N. War Crimes Commission, "Final Report." U.N. Doc. S/1994/674, 27 May 1994.

6. U.S. Department of State, "Erasing History: Ethnic Cleansing in Kosovo." See also, Rubin, "Responsibility of Individual Yugoslav Army and Ministry of Internal Affairs Commanders"; Rubin, "Press Briefing on Massacre of Kosovar Albanians"; Scheffer, "On-the Record Briefing on Atrocities in Kosovo;" U.S. Department of State, "The Ethnic Cleansing in Kosovo."

7. "Karadzic and Mladic Indictment," IT-95-5, 24. "Bosnia and Herzegovina," Initial indictment, 13 February 1995.

8. Fen Osler Hampson, "Can Peace Building Work?" *Cornell International Law Journal* 30: 714.

9. For a concise summary of the Milosevic propaganda campaign, see Georgie Anne Geyer, "How the Conscience of the West Was Lost." In *The Conceit of Innocence Losing the Conscience of the West in the War Against Bosnia,* ed. Stjepan G. Meštovi*f*. College Station: Texas A&M University Press, 1997: 91-95.

10. For a review of the use of media by all three parties, see Mark Thompson, *Forging War: The Media in Serbia, Croatia and Bosnia-Herzegovina.* London: University of Luton, 1994: 271.

11. Warren Zimmermann, *Origins of a Catastrophe: Yugoslavia and its Destroyers—America's Last Ambassador Tells What Happened and Why.* New York: Crown Publishing Group, 1996: 120. According to Ambassador Zimmerman, "Those who argue that ancient Balkan hostilities account for the violence that overtook and destroyed Yugoslavia ignore the power of television in the service of officially provoked racism."

12. For a comprehensive refutation of the myth of the "bubbling over of ancient ethnic hatreds," see Robert Donia and John Fine, *Bosnia-Herzegovina: A Tradition Betrayed.* London: Phoenix House, 1994. For a more concise refutation, see Geyer, "How the Conscience of the West Was Lost," 91-95.

13. For example, according to Carol Hodge, in 1991, Robert Wareing, a member of the House of Commons Select Committee on Foreign Affairs publicly informed the House of Commons that the 1992 bread line massacre in Sarajevo, which killed 20 Muslim civilians, was carried out by Muslims to gain sympathy from the world community and increase antipathy toward Serbia. Carol Hodge, "The Serb Lobby in the United Kingdom." *12 Donald W. Treadgold Papers, Russian, East European, & Central Asian Studies.* September 1999: 13.

14. For examples of State Department reporting on Serbian propaganda, see Department of State Cable number Belgrade 01209 151953, 15 February 1994 (declassified 31 March 1997); Department of State Cable number Belgrade 01232 162107Z, 16 February1994 (declassified 31 March 1997); Department of State Cable number Belgrade 05955 071806, October 1994 (declassified 17 February 1998).

15. For a dense, but useful, assessment of the extent to which Serbian misrepresentations found there way into the political decision-making process, see David Campbell, *National Deconstruction: Violence, Identity and Justice in Bosnia.* Minneapolis, MN: University of Minnesota Press, 1998. See also, Paolo Rumiz, *Maschere per un Massacro: Quello che non Abbiamo Voluto Sapere della Guerra in Jugoslavia.* Rome: Editori Riuniti, 1998: 166; see Kjell Arild Nilsen, *Europas Svik: Et Oppgjor med*

Vestlig Unnfallenhet I Bosnia. Oslo: Spartacus, 1996. A typical example of the absorption of Serbian propaganda by government officials is former U.S. Secretary of State Lawrence Eagleburger's statement in July 1995 just after the Srebrenica massacre that, "they have been killing each other with a certain amount of glee in that part of the world for some time now." Televised interview with Charlie Rose, 13 July 1995, Charlie Rose Transcript #1420, 1995 Thirteen/WNET, cited in Michael Sells, *The Bridge Betrayed: Religion and Genocide in Bosnia.* Berkeley: University of California Press, 1996: 124.

16. See for example, Secretary of State Warren Christopher at the opening statement at a news conference on 10 February 1993 entitled "New Steps Toward Conflict Resolution In the Former Yugoslavia" where he proclaimed, "Those circumstances have deep roots. The death of [Yugoslav] President Tito and the end of communist domination of the former Yugoslavia raised the lid on the cauldron of ancient ethnic hatreds. This is a land where at least three religions and a half-dozen ethnic groups have vied across the centuries. It was the birthplace of World War I. It has long been a cradle of European conflict, [and] it remains so today." See also Interview of Secretary of State Warren Christopher by Mr. Roger Mudd, "MacNeil/Lehrer Newshour," 11 August 1993, where he declared, "In Bosnia, there are such ancient hatreds that evidently the ethnic groups want to try to divide it and be in separate enclaves. That will be a decision that they will have to make, and it's very hard to dictate that from a distance;" And, Remarks by U.S. Secretary of State Warren Christopher at the Conference on Security and Cooperation in Europe Plenary Session on 30 November 1993, where he proclaimed, "We call upon all warring parties to stop their unconscionable conduct that blocks the delivery of critically needed supplies through [Tuzla airport]. We also call upon the warring parties to live up to their recently signed agreements to permit secure land access for relief convoys. The warring parties must see that this is in their best interests. Full access will serve the vital needs of all Bosnia's factions." Even President Clinton found himself adopting the notions of warring factions and civil war in an exchange with reporters, where he declared, "But there will not be—the killing is a function of a political fight between three factions. Until they agree to quit doing it, it's going to continue. I don't think that the international community has the capacity to stop people within the nation from their civil war until they decide to do it. "Exchange with Reporters, 24 January 1994," *Public Papers of the Presidents of the United States,* William J. Clinton 1993, Book I, 122.

17. See Geyer, "How the Conscience of the West Was Lost," 91.

18. According to David Rohde, "A key element in Janvier's thinking was an apparent belief that he could do business with the Bosnian Serbs. Janvier may have turned down the crucial request for Close Air Support on the night before the town fell because he sincerely believed General Tolimir's promise the Serb attack had stopped. Janvier was quick to believe Serb propaganda and Mladic's complaints about Muslim provocations, according to aides. Janvier argued in the 9 June meeting in Split that the Serbs would no longer defy the U.N. if they were treated with respect." David Rohde, *Endgame: The Betrayal and Fall of Srebrenica, Europe's Worst Massacre Since World War II.* Boulder, CO: Westview Press, 1997: 367.

19. Wesley K. Clark, *Waging Modern War: Bosnia, Kosovo, and the Future of Combat.* Reading, MA: Oxford: Perseus, 2001: 68.

20. Department of State Cable number Belgrade 01232 162107Z, 16 February 1994 (declassified 31 March 1997).

21. Jurek Martin, "Holbrooke Sees 'Tough Slog' to Peace in Bosnia," *Financial Times,* 2 November 1995.

22. President of the Yugoslav Tribunal, "First Annual Report of the International Criminal Tribunal for the Former Yugoslavia," para 16.

23. Michael Walzer, *Just and Unjust Wars.* New York: Basic Books, 1979: 287-288.

24. Goldstone, "Justice as a Tool for Peace-Making," 490.

25. For an important discussion of how the citizens of Serbia have managed to psychologically shield themselves from the atrocities committed in their name, see Peter Morgan, *A Barrel of Stones: In Search of Serbia.* Aberystwyth: Planet Books, 1997.

26. Graham Blewitt, Deputy Prosecutor of the Inter-

national Criminal Tribunal for the Former Yugoslavia, Interview by Michael Scharf, The Hague, Netherlands, 25 July 1996.

27. Carlotta Gall, "Crisis in the Balkans: The Church," *New York Times*, 29 June 1999.

28. Department of State Cable number State 092092 080354z, April 94 (declassified 23 December 1996).

29. Warren Christopher, *In the Stream of History: Shaping Foreign Policy for a New Era.* Stanford, CA: Stanford University Press, 1998: 352.

30. See Hodge, "The Serb Lobby in the United Kingdom," 32.

31. Unnamed British UNPROFOR officer, *Reuters* 10 November 1996. Not every military officer shared this view. As noted by General Clark in his memoirs, "[Mladic] carried a reputation among the U.N. forces for cunning and forcefulness, I found him coarse and boastful. He knows far less than he thought about NATO, airpower, and the capabilities of the United States." Clark, *Waging Modern War*, 58.

32. Michael Ignatieff, *Articles of Faith, Index on Censorship.* September/October 1996 (reprinted in 294 *Harper's*, 15 March 1997).

33. Report to the President from Justice Robert H. Jackson, (7 June 1945).

34. See Neil Kritz, *The Rule of Law in the Postconflict Phase, Managing Global Chaos.* Chester A. Crocker, Fenn Osler Hamson, & Pamela Aal, ed. Washington, DC: U.S. Institute of Peace Press, 1996: 598-99.

35. Justice Richard Goldstone, *Healing Wounded People* (Speech by at the United States Holocaust Memorial Museum, 27 January 1997).

36. "Serbs Shun Discussion of Atrocities," *Washington Post*, 24 June 1999, A1.

37. Ambassador David Scheffer, Address at Dartmouth University, 23 October 1998.

38. Yugoslav Tribunal, Press Release, 24 November 1995.

39. Richard Goldstone, "Fifty Years after Nuremberg: A New International Criminal Tribunal for Human Rights Criminals." *Contemporary Genocides: Causes, Cases, Consequences.* Albert J. Jongman ed. Leiden: PIOMM, 1996: 215.

40. President of the Tribunal, "First Annual Report of the International Criminal Tribunal for the Former Yugoslavia," para 15.

41. BBC Broadcast, "Survivors Condemn 'Lenient' Verdict," 2 August 2001, 20:11 GMT 21:11 UK

42. Goldstone, "Justice as a Tool for Peace-Making," 499.

43. Scheffer, "International Judicial Intervention," 34.

44. "War Crimes Prosecutor Says Tribunal May Have Deterred Violations," *Deutsche Presse-Agentur*, 26 January 1996.

45. Justice Richard Goldstone, Interview in Brussels, Belgium, by Michael Scharf, 20 July 1996.

46. See Payam Akhavan, *Justice in The Hague, Peace in the Former Yugoslavia? An Essay on the United Nations War Crimes Tribunal*, 1997: 9.

47. William Horne, "The Real Trial of the Century." *American Lawyer* (Sept. 1995): 5.

48. By rule of law, one generally assumes the presence of an independent judiciary that is transparent, predictable, and impartial to the parties involved. The rule of law also relies upon a legitimate, representative government to enforce the judiciary's decisions. This should be distinguished from rule by law, through which authoritarian governments often use the legal system to legitimate their oppression. See Kritz, *The Rule of Law in the Postconflict Phase.*

49. In the cases of Chile and Argentina, for example, "the prospect of trials for the gross violations of human rights perpetrated under the old regime provoked bald threats of military intervention." Kritz, *The Rule of Law in the Postconflict Phase*, 595.

50. The South African Truth Commission is the most successful example of this type of justice. Established with a two-year mandate, the Commission has strict criteria for whether or not applicants qualify for indemnity in return for their testimony. There has to have been a political motive for the applicant to have committed human rights violations and there must be some degree of proportionality between that motive and the offenses committed. At the time of this writing over 4,500 applications for indemnity had been received by the Commission. See Goldstone, "Justice as a Tool for Peace-Making."

51. For a detailed accounting of "Serbian rape war-

fare" constructed from interviews with victims of mass rape, see Seada Vranic, *Breaking the Wall of Silence: The Voices of Raped Bosnia.* Zagreb: Izdanja Antibarbarus, 1996. See also, Alexandra Stiglmayer, ed., *Mass Rape: The War Against Women in Bosnia and Herzegovina.* Lincoln, NE: London: University of Nebraska Press, 1994; Maria Von Welser, *Am Ende Wunschst du dir nur Noch den Tod: Die Massenvergewaltigungen im Drieg auf dem Balkan.* Munich: 1993; and Beverly Allen, *Rape Warfare: The Hidden Genocide in Bosnia-Herzegovina and Croatia.* Minneapolis, MN: University of Minnesota, 1996.

52. David Owen, *Balkan Odyssey.* New York: Harcourt Brace, 1995: 33.

53. See Yves Heller, *Des Brasiers mal Éteints: un reporter dans les Guerres Yougoslaves 1991-1995.* Paris: *Le Monde,* 1997. For a first hand account by a British Officer of the conflict resulting from the Vance Owen Peace Plan, see Stewart, Colonel Bob *Broken Lives: A Personal View of the Bosnian Conflict.* New York: London: Harper Collins, 1994.

54. See "Week in Review October 17-23," *Balkan Watch,* 24 October 1994.

55. According to David Rohde, "The series of statements and proposals made by Janvier before, during and after Srebrenica's fall indicate he may have intentionally allowed the safe area to fall." Rohde, *Endgame,* 364. Rohde acknowledges though that "Taking the extraordinary step of deciding to sacrifice a U.N. safe area on his own without the permission of his superiors does not fit into Janvier's character, according to supporters and detractors. 'This was a man who should've been selling roasted chestnuts on the streets of Paris,' said one former UNPROFOR official. 'Not making these kinds of decisions.'" Rohde, *Endgame,* 368. Rohde also noted that "Suspicions about what U.S. intelligence knew about the attack on Srebrenica and subsequent executions have been high. The CIA, the theory goes, knew of the pending attack and knew the town would fall. The United States then stood by as Srebrenica fell and an enclave that didn't fit into Anthony Lake's endgame strategy was eliminated. Aerial photos of suspected mass graves, according to the theory, were suppressed until after the executions were well over to avoid embarrassment and the United States being called on to stop the killing." Rohde, *Endgame,* 368-69.

56. Chuck Sudetic, "Why is France Protecting Indicted War Criminals." *Atlantic Monthly* (April 2000).

57. General Lewis MacKenzie "Testimony Before the U.S. House Armed Services Committee," Washington, DC, 26 May 1993.

58. "Secretary-General, "Report Pursuant to General Assembly Resolution 53/35," *Srebrenica Report.*

59. Sir John Nott, Former British Defense Minister, 26 November 1994 *Reuters*; "Week in Review November 21-27," *Balkan Watch,* 28 November 1994.

60. Ed Vulliamy, *Bosnia: The Crime of Appeasement,* 81.

61. Geyer, "How the Conscience of the West Was Lost," 82-83.

62. For a detailed accounting of the constraints involved in the use of force, see Clark, *Waging Modern War.*

63. Walzer, *Just and Unjust Wars,* 62.

64. See generally Clark, *Waging Modern War.*

65. For a critical Secretary-General's U.N. report on the failure of UNPROFOR to prevent the Srebrenica Massacre, see Secretary-General, "Report Pursuant to General Assembly Resolution 53/35," *Srebrenica Report.* For an edited diary recounting the activities of the UNPROFOR mission in Srebrenica, see Herman Veenhof (ed.), *Srebrenica.*

66. For a comprehensive critique of the arguments in favor of the arms embargo see Norman Cigar, *The Right to Defence: Thoughts on the Bosnian Arms Embargo.* London: Alliance Publishers, Ltd., 1995.

67. "Week in Review November 28-December 4," *Balkan Watch* 1, no. 13 (5 December 1994).

68. Joshua Goldstein and Jon Pevehouse, "Reciprocity, Bullying, and International Cooperation." *American Political Science Review* 91 No. 3 (September 1997) 527.

69. Goldstein and Pevehouse, "Reciprocity, Bullying, and International Cooperation," 527.

70. Radio Free Europe, South Slavic Report 8 February 2001, Volume 3, Number 5, "Only The Bombing Got Rid Of Milosevic. Part I."

71. Bill Nichols, "For Clinton, Bosnia Offer Risky Move," *USA Today,* 9 December 1994; "Week in Review December 5-11," *Balkan Watch* 1, no. 14 (12 December

1994). For a discussion of the contradiction between the moralistic impulse and a lack of collective will to use (some) force on the part of the international community which led to the Srebrenica massacre, see Honig, Jan Willem and Norbert Both. *Srebrenica: Record of a War Crime.* London: Viking Penguin, 1996.

72. For a first-hand account of the siege of Bihac see Brendan O'Shea, *Crisis at Bihaf: Bosnia's Bloody Battlefield.* Stroud: Sutton, 1998.

73. Keith Doubt, "We Had to Jump Over the Moral Bridge: Bosnia and the Pathetic Hegemony of Facework." *The Conceit of Innocence Losing the Conscience of the West in the War Against Bosnia,* ed. Stjepan G. Meštovif. College Station, TX: Texas A&M University Press, 1997: 121.

74. Vulliamy, *The Crime of Appeasement,* 89 (quoting Justice Goldstone).

75. Anonymous, *Human Rights in Peace Negotiations,* 255.

76. See Vahakn Dadrian, "The Historical and Legal Interconnections Between the Armenian Genocide and the Jewish Holocaust." *Yale Journal of International Law* 23 (1998): 503. Initially, the Allies Powers sought the prosecution of those responsible for the massacres. The Treaty of Sevres, which was signed on 10 August 1920, would have required the Turkish Government to hand over those responsible to the Allied Powers for trial. See "Treaty of Peace between the Allied Powers and Turkey (Treaty of Sevres), 10 August 1920," reprinted in *American Journal of International Law* 15, no. 179 (Supp 1921). The Treaty of Sevres was, however, not ratified and did not come into force. It was replaced by the Treaty of Lausanne, which not only did not contain provisions respecting the punishment of war crimes, but was accompanied by a "Declaration of Amnesty" of all offenses committed between 1914 and 1922. See "Treaty of Peace between the Allied Powers and Turkey (Treaty of Lausanne), 24 July 1923, League of Nations Treaty Series 11," reprinted in *American Journal of International Law* 18, no. 1 (Supp. 1924).

77. See M. Cherif Bassiouni, *Crimes Against Humanity in International Criminal Law.* The Hague: Boston: Kluwer Academic Publisher, 1987: 228-230. During the war of Bangladesh's independence, West Pakistan troops killed approximately one million East Pakistanis who supported efforts to establish the independent nation of Bangladesh. India and Bangladesh initially agreed to bring charges of genocide and crimes against humanity against 195 of the 10,000 Pakistani troops who had been captured by India. Meanwhile, Pakistan filed a case before the International Court of Justice to compel India to repatriate the Pakistani troops. Ultimately, political considerations prevailed and in 1973 Bangladesh and India agreed not to prosecute the Pakistani prisoners in exchange for political recognition of Bangladesh by Pakistan and the withdrawal of Pakistan's case against India before the International Court of Justice. See Bassiouni, *Crimes Against Humanity,* 228-230.

78. See Naomi Roht-Arriaza, "State Responsibility to Investigate and Prosecute Grave Human Rights Violations in International Law." *California Law Review* 451 (1990) 458-461, 484.

79. See Naomi Roht-Arriaza, *Conclusion: Combating Impunity, and Human Rights.* New York: Oxford University Press, 1995: 299-300.

80. See Adalbert Rückerl, *The Investigation of Nazi War Crimes.* Hamden, CT: Archon Books, 1980: 135 n. 6. The Nuremberg Trials include the trial of the major Nazis before the International Military Tribunal and the twelve subsequent trials at Nuremberg (August 1946-April 1949) under the authority of Allied Control Council Law No. 10.

81. Peter Harlan Maguire, *Law and War: An American Story.* New York: Columbia University Press, 2000.

82. Anonymous, *Human Rights in Peace Negotiations,* 256.

83. See Jean E. Manas, "The Impossible Trade-off: 'Peace' versus 'Justice'." *The World and Yugoslavia's Wars,* ed. Richard H. Ullman. New York: Council on Foreign Relations, 1996.

84. Akhvan, "Justice in The Hague," 1-2.

85. Application of the Realist and Liberal Perspectives to the Implementation of War Crimes Trials: Case Studies of Nuremberg and Bosnia." *UCLA Journal of International Law & Foreign Affairs* 2: 154 (citing Mirko Klarin, "The Moral Case for a War Crimes Tribunal," *Wall Street Journal Europe,* 17 March 1994).

86. Goldstone, "Justice as a Tool for Peace-Making," 488.

87. See. Charles G. Boyd, "Making Bosnia Work." *Foreign Affairs* 77 (Jan/Feb 1998).

88. Goldstone, "Justice as a Tool for Peace-Making," 488. See also Floyd Abrams and Diane F. Orentlicher, "In Cambodia, as in Bosnia, Issue Is Punish or Pardon," *Los Angeles Times*, 15 September 1996, 1M.

89. Department of State "Final Genocide q/a," Press Guidance, drafted 25 October 1993. (Released 13 December 1998).

90. See Holbrooke, Richard. *To End a War.* Ontario, Canada: Random House Inc., 1998: 367.

91. Holbrooke, "Hearing of the Senate Foreign Relations Committee Subject: Nomination of Richard Holbrooke as U.S. Ambassador to the United Nations," 24 June 1999.

92. Holbrooke, "Hearing of the Senate Foreign Relations Committee Subject: Nomination of Richard Holbrooke as U.S. Ambassador to the United Nations," 24 June 1999.

93. Brendan Simms, *Unfinest Hour. Britain and the Bosnian War.* London: Allen Lane, 2001. For a more detailed discussion of the approach of "saving lives" and the "man on the ground" argument, see chapter 5 entitled "The Men on the Ground."

94. Simms, *Unfinest Hour.*

95. Anonymous, *Human Rights in Peace Negotiations,* 256.

96. Anonymous, *Human Rights in Peace Negotiations,* 257.

97. Hampson, "Can Peace Work?," 712.

98. Hampson, "Can Peace Work?," 712. (citing generally William Zartman, ed. *Elusive Peace: Negotiating an End to Civil War.* Washington, DC: Brookings Institution, 1995; Donald K. Horowitz, *Ethnic Groups in Conflict.* Berkeley: University of California Press, 1985; Timothy D. Sisk, *Power Sharing and International Mediation in Ethnic Conflicts.* New York: Carnegie Corporation, 1996; David A. Lake and Donald Rothchild, "Containing Fear: The Origins and Management of Ethnic Conflict." *Internatinal Security* (Fall 1996): 41; Neil J Kritz, ed., *Transitional Justice: How Emerging Democracies Reckon with Former Regimes.* Washington, DC: US Institute of Peace Press, 1995: 82-103, 292-334, 375-438. Timothy D. Mak, "The Case Against an International War Crimes Tribunal for Former Yugoslavia." *International Organization* 48 (Spring 1994): 536.

99. Akhavan, "Justice in The Hague," 3-4.

100. Richard J. Goldstone, "The United Nations' War Crimes Tribunals: Am Assessment." *Connecticut Journal of International Law* 12: 233-4.

101. For a review of the failings of amnesties, See Aryeh Neier, *War Crimes: Brutality, Genocide, Terror, and the Struggle for Justice.* New York: Times Books, 1998: 96-107.

102. See Vahakn N. Dadrian, "The Historical and Legal Interconnections Between the Armenian Genocide and the Jewish Holocaust: From Impunity to Retributive Justice." *Yale Journal of International Law* 23 (1998): 532.

103. Adolf Hitler, "Speech to Chief Commanders and Commanding Generals," 22 August 1939, quoted in M. Cherif Bassiouni, *Crimes Against Humanity in International Criminal Law.* The Hague: Boston: Kluwer Law International, 1992: 176, n. 96.

104. David Matas, "Prosecuting Crimes Against Humanity: The Lessons Learned of World War I." *Fordham International Law Journal* 13 (1989-1990): 104.

105. See Michael Scharf, "The Case for a Permanent International Truth Commission." *Duke Journal of Comparative and International Law* 398 (1997): n. 128.

106. For more on the increased demand for, and ability to provide, justice to those that have become victims of international war crimes, See David Scheffer, "International Judicial Intervention." *Foreign Policy* 102 (1996): 34-51.

107. Interview with General William Nash, by Michael Scharf, Cambridge, MA, 29 September 1998.

108. Hampson, "Can Peace Building Work?," 705.

109. Elizabeth Cousens, "Making Peace in Bosnia Work." *Cornell International Law Journal* 30: 796.

110. Cousens, "Making Peace in Bosnia Work," 796.

111. Department of State, Information Memorandum "Defense of the Safe Areas in Bosnia," 19 July 1995 (declassified 17 February 1998).

112. For a more detailed description of the manner in which various norms operated at cross-purposes, See Cousens, "Making Peace in Bosnia Work," 793.

Choir, oil pastel on paper, Tommy Motswai, 1987

Photograph courtesy of Gavin Younge. Painting courtesy of Tommy Motswai.

Part Ten

Humanitarian Intervention and Nation-Building

Nations, like individuals, are subject to punishments and chastisements in this world

—Abraham Lincoln (1863)

Nations are changed by time; they flourish and decay; by turn command and obey.

—Ovid (c.2 B.C.)

It must be a peace without victory...and a common participation [by all parties] in a common benefit.

—Woodrow Wilson, Address to United States Senate (1917)

NO TOPICS IN THE CONTEMPORARY AND CONSTANTLY EVOLVING ARENA of peace studies and conflict resolution have received more attention in the past two decades than humanitarian intervention and nation-building. The first of these topics has come up most frequently in the ever-increasing instances of *internal* violence and warfare—where countries or organizations external to a conflict believed it necessary (albeit with the consent of a requesting status) to intercede or intervene, in order to prevent or interrupt indiscriminate violence or other massive domestic violations of human rights. Nation-building, on the other hand has been mostly used to describe non-military activities by foreign countries or international organizations in an effort to stabilize the governance of war ravaged nations.

Although in recent years the term humanitarian intervention has been used primarily to describe various forms of military interference in the domestic affairs of foreign states, and often against the territorial sovereignty of those states. The earlier history of the practice discloses many varied and less invasive examples. The efforts of the American Jewry to have the United States government intercede with Russia's Czarist government on behalf of a threatened religious or ethnic minority clearly illustrate the early and strong reluctance of governments to intervene in the domestic affairs of other sovereign nations. The chronology of the Vatican's humanitarian efforts—or lack thereof—during World War II further points to the complexities and perceived hazards inherent in humanitarian intercessions. With the contemporary shrinking of the traditional concept of sovereignty, more and more calls have been heard in recent years not only for moral and economic pressures but also for actual participation by foreign or international armed forces in the prevention of bloodshed and the restoration of order in countries at risk. Yet neither the justifications for nor the efficacy of humanitarian intervention have been objectively reviewed and determined to date.

"Nation-building" has likewise been a much frequently discussed topic at the end of the twentieth and the commencement of the twenty-first century. The term is usually used to describe the role of the international community or the members there of in the structuring or restructuring of governmental institutions and operations in war-torn nations. Nation-building describes primarily the establishment or reform of governmental infrastructures as a means for restoring peace and the role of law in countries rocked by domestic dissensions and violence. Called for particularly in the instance of multi-religious or multi-ethnic countries, often carved out arbitrarily by the former colonial rulers, the uncertainties and hazards of nation-building efforts by external participants have been much debated in recent years.

The formulation of clear and objective standards which will serve to justify and specify measures of humanitarian intervention, as well as the articulation of the types of nation-building opportunities which are deemed to be effective and therefore encouraged, are particularly important tasks for the international community of nations and in a world less insistent on the rights of sovereignty.

SHALL THE UNITED STATES INTERVENE IN CUBA?

A Corrupt Election—Revolution or Intervention in Prospect

Herbert J. Spinden
Anthropologist (1879-1967)

The United States is confronted with the question whether or not it shall again intervene in Cuba. This question is raised now because in the election held on November 1, 1920, it is so generally believed that Dr. Alfredo Zayas, the candidate of the League, a coalition about 90 per cent Conservative, won by fraud. Cubans are not gaining faith in the possibility of changing from one administration to another by the constitutional method of an election and are feeling more confirmed in the necessity of reverting to revolution as a method of changing the party in power.

The Cuban people have held six elections since they were freed from Spain. Two of these were held under American supervision, and these two were fair elections quietly held. One of the four elections held under purely Cuban auspices was accepted as a fair election. The other three were not so accepted. A revolution followed one which necessitated American intervention. An unsuccessful revolution (in 1917) followed another and at present a revolution is not an improbable consequence of the third. The record of the Cuban people on this prime requisite of self-government—the ability to hold an honest election and abide by its results—is 75 percent bad.

Self-government in Cuba has not shown that the Cubans have the political ability to hold elections instead of revolutions. As I shall show by documents and incidents, there is cause for revolution in Cuba now, a possibility that it will occur, and a moral obligation on the United States to prevent chaos.

By the terms of the Platt Amendment, incorporated in the Cuban constitution, Cuba bound itself to continue, among other things, the sanitary administration begun under the American occupation and agreed to the right of the United States to intervene. The provision was as follows:

That the Government of Cuba consents that the United States may exercise the right, to intervene for the protection of Cuban independence, the maintenance of a government adequate for the protection of life, property, and individual liberty, and for discharging the obligations with respect to Cuba imposed by the treaty of Paris on the United States, now to be assumed and undertaken by the Government of Cuba.

Under this provision, if there occurs a breakdown in constitutional government, the United States is in duty bound to intervene. Added to this general obligation is another more specific.

The Liberal Party leaders at the end of August voted to withdraw from the elections, being convinced that they would not be given a fair deal. This was, of course, an act of coercion on their part,

From World's Work magazine, p. 465-483, 1921.

since such a decision was notice that, they would start a revolution unless guarantees of fair dealing, which they believed in, were forthcoming. In this crisis President Menocal was prevailed upon to issue a manifesto declaring that the election would be free and honorable. To make this declaration more effective the American Legation issued a note on August 30, 1920, stating that, while the United States Government did not join either party, it did favor a legal election held under the safeguards of the electoral law freshly prepared by the Cubans. Notice was also given in this note that the United States Government, while it would not undertake to supervise, would have its own observers located in the different provinces of Cuba, from whom impartial accounts could be secured.

Now, if under these conditions an election has been stolen and a revolution threatens in consequence, the moral obligation of the United States is particularly pointed.

The Cuban elections were held on November 1, 1920, one day before those of the United States, and while official returns indicate that Dr. Alfredo Zayas, the candidate of the National League (chiefly Conservative), won over the Liberals by a narrow margin in five out of six provinces, yet the courts throughout the island are jammed with legal cases protesting the count of votes in entire municipalities. There are also numerous criminal cases dealing with infractions of the electoral law by members of the army who should have preserved order.

As a result of the disturbed condition, General Crowder was sent to Cuba by President Wilson on January 3rd under instructions to make a special study of the situation in all its aspects and to confer with President Menocal regarding the remedies to be applied. General Crowder was active in framing the new electoral law of Cuba and in organizing the census of 1919, and, therefore, has a real and deep interest in this mission. It was his hope that the grave abuses of previous elections could be avoided by a law blocking the old evil practices and by a freshly certified register of voters. But the paper barrier proved no protection to the Cuban people against the active leaders fighting for the spoils of office, and it remains to be seen whether a stimulation of legal action will accomplish permanent good.

The fact that nearly every type of evil in the Cuban elections can be matched in some city in the United States should make us lenient in our judgments. At least it should make us realize that the political morality of a social group cannot be applied as a personal reproach to the individual members of that group. Cubans have many admirable qualities, but the ability to operate the kind of self-government which Americans have evolved as suited to themselves and which we passed on to the Cubans, is not one of the virtues. At least so the record seems to show.

This article is written in the belief that the light of truth is the best disinfectant.

And now for the story of the election which has brought on this crisis in Cuban affairs.

When Lord Bryce wrote his report on the German atrocities in Belgium, he carefully excluded all cases where it did not appear that the deeds complained of were the result of orders. Similarly, as regards intimidations and other abuses that occurred during the period of the Cuban elections, we can afford to leave out of consideration all cases of merely personal or local quarrels and examine only those where the trail leads to high officers of the Government or of the political parties. Indeed, we may even go so far as to waive all strictly party activities, and rest a case against the fairness and legality of the elections upon the evidence of a governmental conspiracy. By a governmental conspiracy is not meant a mere political activity of officeholders fighting for reelection. What is meant by this phrase is a collusion among the highest officers of the state including the President, various members of his cabinet, and certain congressmen, etc., to defeat the popular will through the deliberate abuse of their governmental powers.

Also, it would not be fair to be too critical if the evils of the Cuban elections in 1920 were the result of momentary passions. The question is, was there a cynical conspiracy against public morality, developed over a period of several months and participated in by the highest authorities? Were the instigators men holding such high offices in the state as practically to be above effective correction and punishment in courts of justice? Did the men in power use the machinery of government not to govern but to reelect themselves to office?

The record shows that they did. And as long as the men in office do this, the men out of office have but one method of getting in—namely, by revolution.

Theoretically there is [a] remedy for correcting an election that has been fraudulent, besides revolution or American intervention—due process of law. But the Cuban people are not convinced of its effectiveness. Their recent experiences give some explanation of this.

***

The revolution of 1917 began four months and ten days after the election and was made necessary, according to Cuban psychology, by the failure of the courts to give effective correction. In view of the tremendous amount of fraudulent voting on both sides during that election, it must be admitted that the courts had a large job before them. The registers in 1916 contained well over a million names and about 800,000 votes were cast, according to the official counts. Yet when the new census was taken in 1919, less than 500,000 qualified voters were found in all Cuba. The fraud was on both sides, and the courts were given the problem of arriving at the real truth, stripped of all fictions and devices.

Moreover, what we do will not affect Cuba alone. The fact that we gave Cuba her independence has been one of the chief arguments not only for the independence of the Philippines but also for more independence for all peoples held in government tutelage, such as the people of India, of Egypt, and of many other countries. Have we done better by Cuba or by Porto Rico?

If we are to make Cuba an example, it must be a good example of independence. If it is not a good example, we cannot continue to use it as a precedent.

We have tried to give Cuba a form of government that we regard as successful among ourselves—or successful with that eternal vigilance which is the price of liberty. We naïvely think of the problems of Cuba in terms of our own life and national psychology, forgetting that these take very different forms in a Latin-American community.

The racial make-up of the Cuban population is Southern European and African. There is an impression among many persons that the proportion of Negroes in Cuba is much larger than it really is.

THE SOCIAL MAKE-UP OF CUBA

In the old slave days, between 1817 and 1861, the Negroes amounted to from 55 to 58 percent of the total population. But slavery came to an end in 1878 and the proportion of Negroes, mulattoes, etc. has been falling off markedly since that time. According to the recent Cuban census there were 2,088,047 whites and 800,957 colored persons, the latter number including about 11,000 Orientals. There are still several thousand Negroes who give Africa as their birthplace. The attitude of persons of white blood is much more tolerant toward the Negroes in Cuba than in our own Southern states and no suggestion is made of excluding them from the suffrage. The proportion of Negro soldiers in the Cuban armies of independence was high and the national hero, Maceo, was a black man.

***

It is quite possible that with education this Old World society will disappear in a truly New World democracy. Until it does, however, it is not fair to the Cuban people to bring a general indictment of misgovernment against them. But at least they have not been able to keep up the government we gave them.

Since the World War, American public opinion

is more than ever opposed to any military intervention. After the discussions of self-determination as an American principle at the peace table, Americans would particularly like to escape from exercising any control in Cuba. Since a free and independent Cuba has been one of the chief arguments of our disinterestedness in our relations with Latin-America any form of intervention is unwelcome. Moreover. Cuba as a self-governing country on a successful basis has been one of our proudest achievements on which we have delighted to dwell in speech and writing. A State Department that recognized the facts in Cuba today and acted upon our responsibilities under the Platt Amendment would have to go counter to an enormous popular prejudice. This pride and prejudice would be much more difficult to overcome than the actual conditions in Cuba.

If some form of intervention is necessary it is not necessarily a military intervention. One such man as General Wood whose reputation is today higher in Cuba as a fair and successful administrator than any other man, American or Cuban, could go as Governor-General, and with practically no other Americans in office make the Government of Cuba work as it did under his administration before.

If intervention should take no more stringent form than the acceptance by the Cuban Government of a commission of high-minded American citizens who in advisory capacity should oversee expenditures and be responsible before the public opinion of the world for good; sanitation, good banking regulation, good transportation and port facilities, and, most of all, good schools in Cuba, the gain would be immediate and tremendous. Evil things curl up and die under the clear light of publicity.

The United States Intercedes with the Czarist Government: Theodore Roosevelt, and Russian Jewry

Isidore Singer
Managing Editor, The Jewish Encyclopedia (1859-1939)

The details of the 1903 United States intercession are recorded in the address and documents below.

The massacre of the nearly two hundred Jews in the Russian city of Kishinev in 1903 appalled the American Jewish community. On June 15, 1903 representatives of the executive committee of B'nai B'rith, the oldest Jewish fraternal organization in the United States, called on President Theodore Roosevelt in connection with the disturbing reports. Theodore Roosevelt refused to respond to their requests for diplomatic intercession calling upon the Russian government to stop the abuse of that country's Jews, on the ground of Russian sovereign rights. The President this time supported his Secretary in the position that an official diplomatic protest was out of the question, but Roosevelt offered to forward to Russia a petition signed by American citizens. Secretary of State John Hay, however, counseled delay to see if Russia would accept such a petition. Count Cassini, the Czarist ambassador, in his communication of such, made it clear his country would not accept the petition. Roosevelt, irritated, wished to send the petition immediately but was prevailed upon to wait by Hay. On July 16, a State Department communiqué, containing the controversial petition, was sent to J. W. Riddle, American Charge d' Affaires of the embassy at St. Petersburg, and, as expected, was refused by the Russian government. Roosevelt had however satisfied the Jewish feelings in the United States.

1. Address by the President of the United States to the Visiting Jewish Delegation

(June 15, 1903)

GENTLEMEN: I need not dwell upon the fact so patent as the widespread indignation with which the American people heard of the dreadful outrages upon the Jews in Kishinev. I have never in my experience in this country known of a more immediate or a deeper expression of sympathy for the victims and of horror over the appalling calamity that has occurred.

***

I have been visited by the Russian Ambassador on his own initiative, and in addition to what has been said to Secretary Hay, the Russian Ambassador has notified me personally, without an inquiry upon my part, that the Governor of Kishinev has been removed; that between three and four hundred of the participants in the outrages have been arrested: and he voluntarily stated that those men would be

Russia at the Bar of the American People, A Memorial of Kishinef, Records and documents collected and edited by Isidore Singer, Ph.D. Published by Funk and Wagnalls Company, New York and London, 1904.

punished to the utmost that the law would permit.

I will consider most carefully the suggestions that you have submitted to me, and whether the now existing conditions are such that any further official expression would be of advantage to the unfortunate survivors, with whom we sympathize so deeply. Nothing that has occurred recently has had my more constant thought, and nothing will have my more constant thought than this subject.

In any proper way by which beneficial action may be taken, it will be taken, to show the sincerity of the historic American position of treating each man on his merits without the least reference to his creed, his race, or his birthplace.

2. On June 25th, 1903 Leo N. Levi [the National President of the Independent order of B'nai B'rith] received from Secretary of State Hay the following letter:

Department of State
Washington, June 24, 1903

Dear Sir:

The President has concluded to transmit to the Russian government the petition of which you presented to him a draft on the fifteenth of this month. The matter which he had to consider most seriously was whether or not such a proceeding would be to the advantage of your persecuted and outraged coreligiousists in Russia. On this point he has decided to accept your opinion, and that of the numerous and intelligent groups of American citizens of the Jewish faith whom you represent. He requests that you will send him the petition in due form at your earliest convenience.

Of course, you will understand that the President cannot tell you what reception your petition will meet with at the hands of the Russian government. I am, sir,

Faithfully yours,
John Hay

3. On July 15, 1903, the following dispatch was cabled to the American Chargé d'Affaires at St. Petersburg:

Department of State
Washington, July 15, 1903
Riddle, St. Petersburg

You are instructed to ask an audience of the minister of foreign affairs and to make him the following communication:

"Excellency—The Secretary of State instructs me to inform you that the President has received from a large number of citizens of the United States of all religious affiliations, and occupying the highest positions in both public and private life, a respectful petition, addressed to his Majesty the Emperor, relating to the condition of the Jews in Russia, and running as follows:

> To his Imperial Majesty, the Emperor of Russia:
>
> The cruel outrages perpetrated at Kishinev during Easter of 1903 have excited horror and reprobation throughout the world. Until your Majesty gave special and personal directions, the local authorities failed to maintain order or suppress the rioting.
>
> The victims were Jews, and the assault was the result of race and religious prejudice.
>
> The rioters violated the laws of Russia.
>
> The local officials were derelict in the performance of their duty.
>
> The Jews were the victims of indefensible lawlessness. These facts are made plain by the official reports of, and by the official acts following the riot.
>
> Under ordinary conditions, the awful calamity would be deplored without undue fear of a recurrence. But such is not the case in the present instance. Your petitioners are advised that millions of Jews—Russian subjects—dwelling in southwestern Russia are in constant dread of fresh outbreaks. They feel that ignorance, superstition, and bigotry, as exemplified by the rioters, are ever ready to persecute them; that the local officials,

unless thereunto specially admonished, cannot be relied on as strenuous protectors of their peace and security; that a public sentiment of hostility has been engendered against them and hangs over them as a continuing menace.

Even if it be conceded that these fears are to some extent exaggerated, it is unquestionably true that they exist, that they are not groundless, and that they produce effects of great importance.

The westward migration of Russian Jews, which has proceeded for over twenty years, is being stimulated by these fears, and already that movement has become so great as to overshadow in magnitude the expulsion of the Jews from Spain and to rank with the exodus from Egypt.

No estimate is possible of the misery suffered by the hapless Jews who feel driven to forsake their native land, to sever the most sacred ties and to wander forth to strange countries. Neither is it possible to estimate the misery suffered by those who are unwilling or unable to leave the land of their birth; who must part from friends and relatives who emigrate; who remain in never-ending terror.

Religions persecution is more sinful and more fatuous even than war. War is sometimes necessary, honorable, and just; religious persecution is never defensible.

The sinfulness and folly which give impulse to unnecessary war received their greatest check when your Majesty's initiative resulted in an international court of peace.

With such an example before it, the civilized world cherishes the hope that upon the same initiative there shall be fixed in the early days of the twentieth century the enduring principle religious liberty; that by a gracious and convincing expression your Majesty will proclaim, not only for the government of your own subjects, but also for the guidance of all civilized men, that none shall suffer in person, property, liberty, honor, or life because of his religious belief; that the humblest subject or citizen may worship according to the dictates of his own conscience, and that government, whatever its form or agencies, must safeguard these rights and immunities by the exercise of all its powers.

Far removed from your Majesty's dominions, living under different conditions and owing allegiance to another government, your petitioners yet venture, in the name of civilization, to plead for religious liberty and tolerance; to plead that he who led his own people and all others to the shrine of peace will add new luster to his reign and fame by leading a new movement that shall commit the whole world in opposition to religious persecution.'

I am instructed to ask whether the petition will be received by your Excellency, to be submitted to the gracious consideration of his Majesty. In that case the petition will be at once forwarded to St. Petersburg.

I avail myself, etc.

You will report at the earliest possible moment your execution of this instruction.

Hay

4. The response of the Russian government was set forth in the following letter from Secretary Hay to Mr. Leo N. Levi: [National President, the Independent Order of B'nai B'rith]

Department of State
Washington, July 17, 1903

Sir:

I am directed by the President to acquaint you that this department is informed by the American Embassy in St. Petersburg that the Imperial Government of Russia has declined to receive or consider the petition in relation to the condition of the Jews in Russia, which was addressed to his Majesty, the Emperor, by a large number of citizens of the United States, and which this department, by direction of the President and at your request, undertook to transmit to its high destination.

I am, sir,
Very respectfully yours,
John Hay

5. To the Hay letter the following reply was made:

July 20, 1903

Hon. John Hay
Secretary of State
Washington, D. C.

Sir:

I am just in receipt of your esteemed favor of July 17, 1903, wherein, by direction of the President, you acquaint me with the fact that the Imperial Government of Russia has declined to receive or consider the petition in relation to the condition of the Jews in Russia, and which your department, by direction of the President, and at the request of the Executive Committee of the Independent Order of B'nai B'rith, undertook to transmit to the Emperor of Russia.

Acknowledging receipt of your courteous note, I take occasion again, in behalf of my associates and myself, to express our deep sense of obligation to you and the President for the cordial and effective support extended to us.

***

I am, sir,
Very respectfully yours,
Leo N. Levi
[National] President Independent
Order of B'nai B'rith

6. After the refusal of the Russian government to receive the petition, the President of the Executive Committee was requested by the Associated Press and many newspapers to make a statement of the resulting situation, in response to which he gave out the following:

Statement of Leo N. Levi
President of the I. 0. B. B.

The answer made, by Russia to Secretary Hay's note is no surprise to me. While, of course, it was within the range of possibility that the Czar and his Ministers would be moved by considerations of humanity and expediency courteously to receive a petition from the American people, it was well understood that the probabilities were all the other way. The movement, however, has had all the good effects that were in contemplation, and even more. It has enabled the American people and the government to make an enduring record of their views on the Kishinev horror. It has brought the emphatic expression of those views home, not only to the people of Russia, but to the Russian Emperor and his Ministers. They have become acquainted with the contents of the petition, not only by seeing it in the press, but also because its full text was communicated in the note which asked if the original would be received.

The petition, being now an official document, will be preserved in the archives of the United States, and will forever testify to the lofty humanity of the people which is so splendidly represented by the signers, and of the President and his official advisers.

There, too, it will remain as a witness that the friendship of Russia for the United States was not strong enough to permit a respectful appeal for religious liberty, made by citizens of this country.

I am convinced, too, that the influence in Russia of the petition, and of the agitation which preceded it, has been powerful and good.

The number [nearly 13,000] and character of the signatures [twenty-two Governors of States, eight ex-Governors, seven United States Senators, sixteen Chief Justices, thirty United States Congressmen, three Archbishops, seven Bishops, etc.] to the petition stamp it as a convincing expression of the religious tolerance and sympathy of the American people. It is doubtful if there has ever been in this country such a representative written expression of opinion. The people, without regard to racial, religious, or political affiliations, have stood behind the President in his manly and humane activity.

***

It now remains to get in all the petitions which are in circulation, bind them up, and deposit the bound volumes in the State Department.

***

7. The petition was delivered October 31st by Simon Wolf to Secretary Hay, with the following letter from the President of the I. 0. B. B.:

October 5, 1903

Hon. John Hay
Secretary of State
Washington, D.C.

Sir:

On July 14, 1903, by direction of the President, the loose sheets of the so-called "Kishinev Petition" were delivered to him, to be transmitted to St. Petersburg or placed among the archives of our own State Department, as subsequent developments might determine.

***

For all time to come, it will testify to the love of Justice, Humanity, and Liberty which moved the President to give it countenance and its signers to father it. It stands as the verdict of the whole people condemning the denial of religious liberty, and upholding the President in asserting that condemnation. If it be without precedent, it is the more precious for becoming one. Civilization made a distinct and notable advance when a great nation of eighty millions of people, speaking not only through its official head, but also through its most representative citizens in their individual capacities, served notice on the world that those who are made to suffer martyrdom for conscience's sake, wherever they may abide, have friends and sympathizers in this country. Such an example will not be lost. The oppressor will hereafter pause before he strikes, and his victim will be saved from utter despair by the consciousness that the voice of humanity will be raised in his behalf.

In this view, the services rendered by the President, his advisers, and the people generally are not to be measured by the benefits conferred upon the Jews alone. This is one of the oft-recurring cases in which the Jews, by their misfortunes, have led the world to a just appreciation of the truths of which they are the devoted missionaries.

***

In delivering the petition into your hands, we avail ourselves of the opportunity to make this record of our profoundly grateful appreciation.

I am, sir,
Very respectfully yours,
Leo N. Levi

8. Secretary Hay replied to Mr. Levi's letter as follows:

Department of State
Washington, D.C.
October 31, 1903

Leo N Levi, Esq.,
President of the Executive Committee of
the Independent Order of B'nai B'rith
New York, N.Y.

Dear Sir:

***

Although this copy of your petition did not reach the high destination for which it was intended, its words have attained world-wide publicity, and have found a lodgment in many thousands of minds. This petition will be always memorable, not only for what it contains, but also for the number and weight of the signatures attached to it, embracing some of the most prominent names of our generation—men renowned for intelligence, philanthropy, and public spirit.

In future when the students of history come to peruse this document they will wonder how the petitioners, moved to profound indignation by intolerable wrongs perpetrated on the innocent and helpless, should have expressed themselves in language so earnest and eloquent and yet so dignified, so moderate, and so decorous. It is a valuable addition to public literature, and will be sacredly cherished among the treasures of this department.

I am, sir,
Very respectfully yours,
John Hay

9. In the subsequent period of 1903-1909 a total of some 50,000 Russian Jews were massacred in anti-semitic pogroms.

Pope Pius XII and Nazi Germany: A Controversial Role

A. Chronology of Events[1]

Carol Rittner
The Richard Stockton College of New Jersey and

John K. Roth
Claremont McKenna College

1849 — The future Pope Pius XII's grandfather, Marcantonio Pacelli, founds the Holy See's official newspaper, *L'Osservatore Romano.*

1876
March 2 — Eugenio Maria Giuseppe Giovanni Pacelli, the future Pope Pius XII, is born in Rome.

1894
November — Pacelli begins studies for the Roman Catholic priesthood. For health reasons Pacelli is granted in 1896 extraordinary permission by Pope Leo XIII to continue as a day student only at the Capranica College.

1899
March 2 — Pacelli is ordained a Roman Catholic priest

1901 — Father Pacelli is offered a position in the Vatican Foreign Office by Cardinal Mariano Rampolla, Vatican Secretary of State.

***

1917
April — Pacelli is appointed apostolic nuncio to Bavaria (Germany).

May 13 — Pacelli is Consecrated an archbishop by Pope Benedict XV.

May 20 — Pacelli leaves Rome for his new post in Munich, carrying Pope Benedict XV's peace plan to end World War I.

June 29 — Meeting with Kaiser Wilhelm II to discuss the papal peace plan, he fails to secure the Kaiser's agreement to peace talks.

***

1920
June 30 — Archbishop Pacelli is appointed the Vatican's first apostolic nuncio to Germany.

***

1929 — Nuncio Pacelli confronts "an intruding gun-toting Communist revolutionary" in his Munich residence, during an attempted armed Communist takeover of the Bavarian government.

February 11 — The Vatican and Italy sign the Lateran Pact, giving the pope sovereignty over

[1] Excerpts from Carol Rittner and John K. Roth, *Pope Pius XII and the Holocaust* (London: Leicester University Press, 2002)

Vatican City (109 acres located within the city of Rome).

December 16 Pacelli named a cardinal of the Roman Catholic Church by Pius XI.

1930

February 7 Cardinal Pacelli named Vatican Secretary of State by Pius XI.

1933

January 30 Adolf Hitler assumes the office of Chancellor of Germany.

March 20 The Dachau concentration camp is established some ten miles northwest of Munich.

April 1 Nazi-organized boycott of Jewish businesses in Germany.

May 10 The public burning of books by Jewish and non-Jewish authors opposed to Nazism.

***

July 20 A Vatican concordat with Nazi Germany, negotiated by Pius XI's Secretary of State, Cardinal Pacelli, is signed. The concordat protects key Church rights. It also requires the withdrawal of the Catholic Church from German politics, and enhances Hitler's legitimacy.

1936

October Cardinal Pacelli, the first Vatican Secretary of State (and future pope) to do so, arrives in America for a whirlwind tour. He refuses to meet with President Franklin Roosevelt until after the November presidential elections.

October 25 A treaty forming the Rome—Berlin Axis is signed by Hitler and Mussolini.

1937

March 14 Pope Pius XI releases his encyclical *Mit brennender Sorge* (With Deep Anxiety), drafted in large part by Pacelli. Although vigorously condemning racism, it does not mention Hitler or Nazism by name.

1938

March 13 The Anschluss: Nazi Germany annexes Austria.

June 22 John LaFarge, an American Jesuit priest, and two other Jesuits, Gustave Desbuquois and Gustav Gundlach, are asked by Pius XI to draft an encyclical letter denouncing racism and antisemitism. The letter, *Humani Generis Unitas* (The Unity of the Human Race), it is not published.

***

1939

January 30 The German Reichsfag is told by Hitler that a world war will mean "the annihilation of the Jewish race in Europe."

February 10 Pope Pius XI dies.

March 2 Cardinal Eugenio Pacelli is elected pope and takes the name Pius XII.

***

October

November

214 Catholic priests are executed and over 1000 Catholic clergymen are imprisoned by the Nazi occupation forces in Poland. (Overall, about 2600, or 20 percent, of all Polish clergy died at the hands of the Nazis.)

***

December 25 Pope Pius XII delivers the first of his "Christmas addresses." He attacks the "premeditated aggression against a small, hard-working and peaceful nation." He deplores the "disregard for dignity, freedom, and human life that has brought about acts that cry to heaven for vengeance."

1940

***

April 27 Himmler orders the establishment of a concentration camp near Oswiecim (Auschwitz), Poland. It will become the largest center in the entire Nazi system of concentration and death camps.

May 10 Germany invades France, Belgium, and the Netherlands. *L'Osservatore Romano* condemns the invasion. Mussolini confiscates and burns all copies of the paper.

Late May The Vatican transfers more than $7.5 million worth of gold bars for safe deposit in the United States.

June 10 Italy declares war on France and Britain. Vatican Secretary of State Maglione instantly asks Britain for a guarantee that the RAF will not bomb Rome.

***

1941

March 30 Hitler tells his military leaders that the forthcoming war against the Soviet Union will be one of "extermination."

June 22 Operation Barbarossa: Germany attacks Russia. The Axis powers label the attack a "Holy War." All of Poland falls under German domination. The Einsatzgruppen engage in mass killings.

July 31 Hermann Goering signs orders giving Reinhard Heydrich authority to commence "the final solution of the Jewish question."

***

September 29-30 More than 33,000 Jews from the Ukrainian city of Kiev are murdered by Einsatzgruppen 4a at the Babi Yar ravine. Msgr. Burzio, chargé d affaires in Slovakia, reports to the Vatican about vast numbers of Jews being shot by Germans.

October 10 Angelo Roncalli, Apostolic Nuncio to Turkey, has an audience with Pope Pius XII. Roncalli writes in his diary concerning that audience, "He [the pope] asked me if his silence regarding Nazism was not judged badly."

November 12 Vatican Secretary of State Maglione, in a note to Charles Sidor, Slovak minister to the Holy See, intercedes on behalf of baptized Jews and the rights of the Roman Catholic Church in Slovakia. The note is unanswered.

November 21 Father Pirro Scavizzi, who frequently travels through Poland on trips between Italy and the Russian front, delivers a report containing the complaints of the Catholic Poles about the failure of the pope to intervene.

***

1942

March 1 The Nazis begin construction of a new death camp at Sobibór.

***

August Croatian rabbi Miroslav Shalom Freiberger writes to Pope Pius XII asking for his help to save Jews in Croatia. Abbot Giuseppe Ramiro Marcone is instructed by the Holy See to thank him for his letter but to do so prudently and tactfully.

Summer Belgium's Cardinal Josef-Ernest Van Roey, Archbishop of Malines, tells the Vatican that the persecution of the Jews is provoking a feeling of revolt among the population of Belgium.

***

December 6 Pius XII formally requests the Italian Fascist government to withdraw from Rome, along with their German advisors.

***

December 24 In his annual Christmas message, the pope deplores the bloodshed of war but fails to denounce the Nazis. In a veiled reference to Jews, Pope Pius XII laments the "hundreds of thousands who, through no fault of their own...have been consigned to death or slow decline."

The New York Times praises the pope for his devotion to peace.

December 30 Pope Pius XII tells an American representative that he regards the atrocity stories about Jews as an exaggeration "for the purposes of propaganda."

1943

January 2 In a letter from London, the Polish president Wladislas Raczkiewicz reminds Pius XII of statements made by his predecessors on Poland's behalf. He begs the pope to break his silence.

January 17 Berlin Bishop Konrad Graf von Preysing, the German Catholic prelate who opposes the German government's Jewish policies, tells Pope Pius XII that he will resign unless the Nazi collaborative behavior of the other German bishops with the Nazis ceases.

March 6 Bishop Preysing writes to Pius XII about the round-up of Berlin's Jews. Preysing asks the pope to speak out against it.

***

April 19 The Vatican writes to the government of Slovakia expressing concern at the rumors that it is about to expel "the Jews who live in Slovakia without discrimination for women and children and without excepting even those who have entered the Catholic religion."

***

June 29 Pius XII issues his encyclical, *Mystici Corporis Christi* (On the Supernatural Nature of Christ s Body).

***

July 19 Allied aircraft, intending to hit the railways in Rome, mistakenly bomb and badly damage the Basilica of San Lorenzo.

July 20 Pius XII sends an angry message to President Roosevelt, writing, "As Bishop of this sacred City we have constantly tried to save our beloved Rome from devastation... But this reasonable hope has, alas, been frustrated."

***

September 19 Pius XII officially receives Field Marshal Kesselring, the commander of German forces in Rome, at the Vatican.

***

September 30 Pius XII issues the encyclical, *Divine Afflante Spiritu* (On the Promotion of Biblical Studies), which condemns the scriptural exegesis of the modernists.

***

October 17 German ambassador to the Vatican Ernst von Weizsäcker reports to the German Foreign Ministry that the College of Cardinals has been "particularly dismayed" since the round-up of Jews in Rome is occurring below the "very windows of the Pope." Still, the pope continues to do all he can "not to burden relations with the German government and German agencies in Rome."

***

1944

March 12 Pius XII appears in public, to an overflowing crowd in St. Peter's Square, for the first time since the German occupation. He pleads with the world to protect Rome from the horrors of warfare.

***

June 4 The American Fifth Army liberates Rome. Pius XII praises the preservation of Rome.

June 6 D-Day: Allied forces land at Normandy.

June 25 Pope Pius XII sends Admiral Miklós Horthy of Hungary a telegram asking him to stop the deportation of Hungarians "to an unknown destination" because of their race. He does not use the word "Jew" in his message.

June 25 Pope Pius XII's "Open" telegram to Admiral Horthy reads as follows: "We are being beseeched in various quarters to do everything in our power in order that, in your noble and chivalrous nation, the sufferings, already so heavy, endured by a large number of unfortunate people, because of their nationality or race, may not be extended and aggravated."

***

October 28 By this date, nearly 430,000 Jews have been deported from Hungary to the German concentration and killing camps.

1945

January 27 Soldiers of the Red Army liberate Auschwitz.

April 28 Italian dictator Benito Mussolini is executed.

April 30 Adolf Hitler and Eva Braun commit suicide in Hitler's Berlin bunker.

May 5 The presiding Bishop of the German Catholic bishops' conference instructs his priests to say Mass in Hitler's memory.

December 25 Pius XII, in his Christmas address, warns against the growing power of Communism in Europe.

***

1947

November 20 Pius XII issues an encyclical, *Mediator Dei* (On the Sacred Liturgy), which defines the participation of the laity in the Holy Sacrifice of the Mass.

1948 Pope Pius XII requests mercy for all Nazi war criminals condemned to death by the Nuremberg Tribunal. His appeal is turned down by Deputy Military Governor General Lucius Clay.

May 14 Britain's mandate to govern Palestine expires. Palestine is divided into the State of Israel and the Kingdom of Jordan. The Jewish National Council proclaims the independent State of Israel.

1950

November 1 Pius XII issues his encyclical, *Munificentissimus Deus* (The Most Bountiful God), in which he solemnly declares the dogma of Mary's Assumption into heaven.

***

1958

October 9 Pope Pius XII dies.

***

1978

August 6 Pope Pius VI dies.

***

September 28 Pope John Paul I dies.

October 16 Cardinal Karol Wojityla of Poland is elected pope. He takes the name of John Paul II.

***

1986

April Pope John Paul II visits the Great Synagogue in Rome, the first pope to do so.

1993 After 16 years of existence, the Vatican recognizes the State of Israel and exchanges ambassadors with Israel.

B. The Priests of Dachau

William J. O'Malley, S.J.

For five years, Konzentrationslager Dachau, a short bicycle ride across the sodden moors northwest of Munich, was the site of the largest religious community in the world. Because many records were hurriedly burned as the American tanks approached in April 1945, the best estimate, based on clandestine lists kept by priest-prisoners in the work offices, is that 2,771 clergymen were interned at KZ Dachau—of whom at least 1,034 died in the camp. The 2,579 Catholic priests, lay brothers and seminarians came from 38 nations, from 134 dioceses and 29 religious orders and congregations. Their community included 109 Protestant, 30 Orthodox and two Moslem clergymen.

That figure, surprising as it might be, does not include the clergy or nuns shot or beheaded or tortured to death in squares and alleys and jails all over Europe. In the first 16 months of the war, 700 Polish priests died at the hands of the Nazis and 3,000 more were sent to concentration camps; more than half did not return. In Dachau, 868 Polish priests perished—300 of them in medical experiments or by torture in the prison showers. In France, too, by February 1944, the Gestapo had arrested 162 priests, of whom 123 were shot or decapitated before ever reaching any camp. According to the International Tribunal at Nuremberg, 780 priests died of exhaustion at Mauthausen and 300 at Sachsenhausen, and there were hundreds of other camps and satellites in the network. Nor does the total figure of 2,771 take into consideration that one-quarter to one-third of those shipped to any camp often arrived dead.

The Polish clergy in Dachau (1,780) far outnumbered the others. They arrived first, and most of the 830 who survived did so, unbelievably, for five years. As for the Czech and Slovak priests (109) and the Yugoslavs (50), the reason for incarceration was, as with the Jews, racial. Hitler believed Slavs were ordained by Providence to be slaves to the Aryan race, a fact their very name "proved." Any Slav who had achieved an education had, by that fact, flown in the face of his own nature. Moreover, these priests were not only educated Slavs but apostles of a church that Hitler had vowed to "crush like a toad" when final victory arrived.

The German and Austrian clergy at Dachau (447) were for the most part men who realized that being a good Christian and a good Nazi were as irreconcilable as compassion and sadism. These men, being celibate, were freer than family men to take risks. They had run underground presses and underground railways to rescue retarded children from the euthanasia laws and Jews from deportation. Any priest was free to defy the Pulpit Law and speak out against the racism and paganism of the Third Reich, but except for the redoubtable Bishop Von Galen of Muenster it would be his final public word. German priests and pastors were exiled to Dachau for preaching love of neighbor, for insisting that Jesus was a Jew, for warning S.S. men that they could not abjure their faith to achieve promotion, for offering requiem Masses even for relatives of Communists. German religious were interned on trumped-up-charges of spiriting funds out of the country to their headquarters in Rome and, in much publicized cases, for seducing boys and girls. Two old priests were sent to Dachau for failing to give the Hitler salute when Hermann Goering and his entourage entered a Berlin restaurant. All the Gestapo needed was to present a paper to any priest: "Evidence confirmed by the State police shows that by his behavior he is endangering the stability and security of the State."

The 156 French, 63 Dutch, and 46 Belgians were primarily interned for their work in the Underground. If that were a crime, such men as Michel Riquet, S.J., surely had little defense; he was in contact with most of the leaders of the French Resistance and was their chaplain, writing forthright editorials for the underground press, sequestering Jews, POW's, downed Allied airmen, feeding and clothing them, providing them with counterfeit pa-

Reprinted from http://www.catholicleague.org/piusxii_and_the_holocaust.

pers and spiriting them into Spain and North Africa. Henry Zwaans, a Jesuit secondary school teacher in The Hague, was arrested for distributing copies of Bishop Von Galen's homilies and died in Dachau of dropsy and dysentery. Jacques Magnee punished a boy for bringing anti-British propaganda into the Jesuit secondary school at Charleroi in Belgium; Leo DeConinck went to Dachau for instructing the Belgian clergy in retreat conferences to resist the Nazis. Parish priests were arrested for quoting Pius XI's anti-Nazi encyclical, *Mit Brennender Sorge*, or for publicly condemning the anti-Semitic film, "The Jew Seuss", or for providing Jews with false baptismal certificates. Some French priests at Dachau disguised themselves as workers to minister to young Frenchmen shanghaied into service in German heavy industry and had been caught doing what they had been ordained to do.

There is little need to rehearse the conditions of their lives in the camp. It was a hell before which Dante would stand mute. A good day was one on which you'd been beaten to your knees only once or twice; one small wad of bread and a cup of watery soup; 12 hours of hard labor, dragging the corpses to the roll call each morning and evening; warehoused at night in tiers, sleeping three to each lice-infested bunk; lugging one's soul from place to place in the fellowship of zombies; the cold, the filth, the endless degrading "hazing", the typhus, the inhuman joy when your best friend was beaten senseless and you were ignored. For some, hell lasted five years of days.

In 1940, it seemed a diplomatic coup that the German bishops and the Vatican had persuaded Heinrich Himmler to concentrate all priests from the network of European camps into one camp, to house them in separate blocks together, with lighter work and a chapel. In early December 1940, priests already interned in Dachau were put into Barracks 26, 28 and 30 at the end of the west side of the long camp street, "Liberty St.". Within two weeks they were joined by 800-900 more from Buchenwald, Mauthausen, Auschwitz and other camps, a Babel of haggard strangers. With the conquest of Western Europe, arrests of priests increased so that, now concentrated into two barracks instead of three, despite the deaths, they were rarely fewer than 1,500 men in beds and toilet facilities built for 360. Hardly any priests remained in the other camps.

Priests from Dachau worked in the "Plantation" and in the enormous S.S. industrial complex immediately to the west of the camp. In February 1942, two groups of younger Polish priests and scholastics were chosen for work as carpenters' apprentices, but they had actually been chosen (at the express order of Heinrich Himmler) to be injected with pus to study gangrene or to have their body temperature lowered to 27 degrees Centigrade in order to study resuscitation of German fliers downed in the North Atlantic. The Rev. Andreas Reiser, a German, was crowned with barbed wire and a group of Jewish prisoners was forced to hail him as their king, and the Rev. Stanislaus Bednarski, a Pole, was hanged on a cross.

Although a few priests did throw themselves in despair on the electrified wire and a few did sink into the affectless, zombie Nirvana the prisoners called "going Muslim," most clung to a faith that kept them plodding on. They had been schooled to a charity that was often strained, even with their fellow clergy, by national and ethnic differences. They could communicate at least in Latin across language barriers that divided other prisoners. They were educated men used to using their wits and to taking charge. In early 1943, when the tide of the war began to turn against Germany, and the need to get all the labor possible out of the slaves became clear to the camp commander, the S.S. saw that it was better to have disciplined, educated secretaries and managers. This allowed priests into offices where they could manipulate labor schedules, into the hospital where they could minister to the sick, especially during the two horrifying typhus winters, into the package depot where they made sure that packages (now allowed to ease the food shortage) got to the most needy, especially the Russians who obviously had no packages at all, and into the munitions factories where they could work minor sabotage, particularly with the planned gas oven at Dachau—which never became functional due, at least in part, to their efforts.

But most important to them, they had their chapel. At first, it was a single empty room with two tables shoved together for an altar and the contents of two army chaplains' Mass kits for vestments and vessels. In five years they managed to jerry-rig, "liberate" and sneak in through the Plantation roadstand the elements of a quite creditable chapel. It was to focus their minds and raise their spirits. And when eight months after the chapel opened, the Polish priests were moved to another barrack and forbidden entrance, hosts and wine were spirited to them; from both barracks, the Eucharist spread throughout the camp in tins that had held aspirin and zinc ointment and tobacco. Their greatest triumph, in December of 1944, was the ordination as priest of a young deacon of the diocese of Muenster, Karl Leisner, by his fellow-prisoner, Bishop Gabriel Piquet of Clermont-Ferrand—with full vestments made from material "liberated" from the stores, even a biretta for the ordained, a miter and red shoes for the bishop and a ring and pectoral cross made by a Communist inmate in the Messerschmitt works at Allach—and the S.S. never found out.

The most admirable priest-rogue was a Jesuit former master of novices named Otto Pies. Released from Dachau in the Spring of 1945 as the Americans were advancing, he disguised himself as an S.S. officer and came back to the camp with a truckload of food—rousted God knows where in those bitterly foodless days. He drove into the camp, into the priests' wired-off compound, and then drove off with 30 of the priests hidden in the back. Two days later, when 5,400 prisoners—88 of them priests—were led off into the Alps to be lost in the snow, Otto Pies came back in the same uniform and truck and picked up more.

Humanitarian Assistance

Allan Gerson
George Washington University and

Nat Colletta
George Washington University

Sovereignty is no longer a guarantee of unqualified membership within the international community. As Mark Duffield has noted, there has in the last decade been an opening up of "humanitarian space." Kosovo and East Timor are the most recent examples of the fact that time-worn conceptions of sovereignty will no longer be allowed to stand in the way of protecting lives put at risk by the excesses of government.[1]

In these circumstances, particularly where warring factions disregard fundamental humanitarian principles and put a civilian population at grave risk of displacement, starvation and death, humanitarian agencies have sought to provide four basic types of assistance:

(1) Save lives by meeting food, shelter and other basic survival needs;

(2) Promote a social welfare safety net in the wake of weakened traditional support systems;

(3) Protect human rights; and

(4) Enable rehabilitation and livelihood development. In the latter case, humanitarian agencies have now stretched their mandate to venture into reconstruction and development, or what are now called "gray zone activities."

In places like Rwanda, UNHCR now finds itself not simply repatriating refugees but engaged in shelter and income-generating and resettlement activities. These are tasks it is ill-equipped to handle. But in the absence of others coming in to do the job, it has assumed these additional responsibilities. The result, unfortunately is to often inadvertently plant the seeds of further conflict. In Afghanistan, the ICRC now finds itself managing and financing the operation and maintenance of hospitals and clinics, although it started by simply providing emergency medical supplies. The UN World Food Program now often finds itself supplying seeds and planting tools along with food. Development aid is surely needed in this gap between relief and development. But without a legitimate governmental authority or well-equipped institutional partner, measures like those of UN HCR and the UN World Food Program are severely handicapped. Traditional development performance standards are not utilized nor conditionalities made to prompt the collapsed state entities to recovery.

Operating under these conditions, humanitarian agencies have been vulnerable to a range of setbacks. Most prominently is the difficulty in maintaining core values of neutrality and humanity as they are subjected to increasing manipulation and politicization. For example, in the UN's Operation Lifeline Sudan (OLS), access is continually negotiated with both government and rebel sides with the result that agencies have been directly or indirectly assisting different warring factions.[2]

Margaret Buchanan-Smith[3] summarized several important ways in which relief can be manipulated. These include management of access to relief, use of malnourished populations to attract humanitarian resources, siphoning off of goods and services to support armed fighters or personal ales, taxation of relief goods, monopolizing procurement, and contracting for the transportation of illicit as well as licit goods and services. The unintended consequences of relief when it becomes politicized are great. This is especially true with regard to distortions which humanitarian relief, despite all its good intentions, can create in a local economy.

Humanitarian assistance has become big business. The OECD recorded a growth in expenditure on emergency relief from $600 million in 1985 to over $6 billion in 1995. That marks a growth of over 1,000% in less than a decade. The relief industry has grown to such proportions that there are now annual trade fairs marketing the wares and services of a multitude of private firms ranging from mine removal equipment to packaged foods, mini portable water purification facilities to instant tent cities and solar driven communication equipment. Such trade fairs, moving between Geneva and New York, reflect an entire industry. The World Aid directory lists more than 2,000 commercial suppliers and over 500 aid agencies that exhibited at the UNOPS-organized international Aid and Trade Conference held in New York May 31-June 1, 2000. With the emergence of a global contract culture in pursuit of the spoils of humanitarian relief, it is understandable that relief agencies have been accused of perpetuating greed and fueling conflict in the name of altruism and peace. Bilateral donors have joined the bandwagon of advertising their largesse, anxious to demonstrate that they are responsive to CNN images of starving children. In so doing they also seek to portray themselves as having "legitimately" intervened in a "humanitarian" crisis, thus enabling relief to emerge as a subtle but important arm of foreign policy.

Robin Davies brilliantly captures the unintended distortions that humanitarian assistance, in concert with a large contingent of peace-keepers and international civil servants, can have on a local economy. He notes the purely inflationary impact wrought by the injection of such massive amounts of capital, from Cambodia to Mozambique and most recently the Balkans and East Timor.[4] With foreign money surging into the local economy, the local currency quickly becomes depreciated due to inflation in local prices for goods and services. Those sectors of the population living off the local economy are faced with exorbitant prices and the necessity to retreat into subsistence agriculture to survive, unless they are one of the few fortunate nationals to land a job in the UN administered economy. In terms of macro economic policy, the increase in the money supply without a proportional increase in products and services offered leads not only to runaway inflation, but also to rendering ineffective the traditional methods of controlling the money supply (i.e., by buying and selling government bonds). In the medium to long term, the power of the domestic government to maintain GDP growth with low inflation can be severely crippled.

Inevitably massive distortions occur, affecting wages and the local labor market. Suddenly, teachers in the Balkans traditionally making $30 per month in the classroom are abandoning their students to take up jobs as drivers and office clerks of the various relief and peacekeeping bodies at $300 per month. This internal brain drain has the additional negative effect of diverting much needed scarce local capacity away from the necessary task of reconstructing the public sector. Of course, the consequence of not hiring local labor is also problematic, as it gives many in the indigenous population the status of "aid recipient." The result can often be to subtly create an "entitlement" welfare-oriented mentality which is difficult to overcome when the aid is no longer there, turning to bitter resentment against the hand that fed. Compounding the difficulty of transition to a self-reliant, sustainable economy are the following ubiquitous factors: a) the external brain drain faced by fledgling states, b) the reduction in the labor force due to refugee streams, and c) the illusion of a sustainable economic boost that humanitarian assistance often creates before being burst upon withdrawal.

There are more often than not long-term budgetary and human capacity implications of such short-term relief assistance. First, successful implementation of many projects requires long-term funding and capacity, most of which must be undertaken by local actors. Thus the entire issue of sustainability is left up in the air, as neither the capability to raise revenues for continued financing nor the human capacity has been transferred or put in place locally to sustain institutions and operations.

***

Because humanitarian assistance is often fungible, especially budgetary support through structural adjustment operations, it can, if placed in the wrong hands, fuel conflict as well as support reconstruction and development. Humanitarian relief in Goma (Rwanda) ended up feeding an army in training, the Intrahamwe; while aid to the treasury in Rwanda freed up local resources to support armed struggle in the Democratic Republic of the Congo. These problems call for greater accountability and transparency. They also call for a review of budgeting and planning procedures for relief and development work.

Trade, too, can be linked to conflict. As Neil Cooper explains: "Conflict goods are non-military materials, knowledge, animals or humans whose trade, taxation or protection is exploited to finance or otherwise maintain the war economies of contemporary conflicts...."[5]

Notes

1. See Mark Duffield, "Complex Emergencies and the Crisis of Developmentalism," IDS Bulletin 25:37–45, 1994; also see Mark Duffield, "Aid Policy and Post-Modern Conflict: A Critical Review," Occasional Paper 19, The School of Public Policy, University of Birmingham, 1998.
2. Karim, A., et al., "Operation Lifeline Sudan: A Review," Report, 1996, UNICEF.
3. Margaret Buchanan-Smith, "Humanitarian Aid in the Political Economy of Collapsed States: Changes, Dilemmas and Unintended Consequences," paper presented at Conference on State Collapse and Reconstruction: Lessons and Strategies, ICRC/PSIS, Geneva, December 2000, pp. 1–13.
4. Robin Davies, "The Dynamics of Large-Scale Humanitarian Assistance," paper presented at the World Social Summit, Geneva, July 2000, pp. 1–16.
5. Neil Cooper, "The Role of Conflict Goods in State Collapse and Reconstruction," paper for conference on State Collapse and Reconstruction, ICRS/PSIS, Geneva, December 6-10, 2000.

Humanitarian Interventions in a New Era

Thomas G. Weiss
The City University of New York

In the aftermath of the Cold War, struggles for decolonization and self-determination have disintegrated into ethnic, religious, and political fragmentation. The results—egregious violence, life-threatening suffering, and human rights abuses—are more routinely becoming accepted as legitimate international concerns. We are moving in fits and starts away from the idea that state sovereignty serves as an all-purpose rationalization for narrowly defined *raisons d'etat,* and lurching toward a world in which states and armed insurgents, as well as other nonstate entities, are challenging conventional notions of territorial sovereignty and insisting upon greater accountability.

More particularly, since Operation Provide Comfort—the April 1991 relief campaign that established a "safe zone" in northern Iraq for more than a million Kurds displaced during the Persian Gulf War and provided food, shelter, and clothing for them—a growing number of analysts, as well as institutional members of the international community, are beginning to argue that there is a right to international intervention for humanitarian purposes. The significant precedent set in northern Iraq, along with actions in Somalia and Bosnia-Herzegovina, moved the international community to begin developing tenets in stark contrast to the conventional wisdom of the past, which held that sovereignty overrides all other principles of international behavior.

Intervention was never unlawful in itself, but nonintervention, once considered the logical corollary of territorial sovereignty, was the conceptual basis of interstate relations and the U.N. Charter. In reality, this fiction of sorts—meant to protect weaker states from the powerful—instead frequently served as a last line of defense for autocratic governments to fend off outside criticism and interference in their domestic repression. With the international community increasingly willing to recognize and act against human rights abuses, we stand at the brink of a new era, one in which, in the words of Adam Roberts, "Humanitarian war is an oxymoron which may yet become a reality."[1]

The Phenomena of Intervention

Intervention is not a single phenomenon.[2] Loosely and commonly understood as the spectrum of possible actions intended to alter internal affairs elsewhere, intervention is perhaps synonymous with the practice of international relations, which by definition consists of efforts by governments to influence the behavior of other states. Intervention, as such, is inevitable; great powers have throughout history exerted influence of varying degrees of intensity—from telephone calls of a foreign ministry to intelligence gathering to the actual dispatch of troops—within their spheres of influence and elsewhere when they have perceived their national interests to be at stake.

In efforts to pressure nations to improve their domestic affairs, intergovernmental organizations are also active, as when the World Bank or International Monetary Fund imposes economic conditions that limit policy options by governments borrowing resources for structural adjustment. Many nongovernmental organizations also seek to wield influence, as when Human Rights Watch or Amnesty International calls for conditioning outside finances on improved human rights performances by recipient governments. All such actions constitute interventions.

Weak states are generally unable to resist outside pressures, sometimes even from nonstates in the humanitarian arena. Numerous cross-border operations by emergency relief institutions have reached threatened populations in areas not controlled by a central government. For example, recent efforts on behalf of civilian populations in Eritrea and Tigray and for the Afghan *mujahidin* were mounted mainly by private humanitarian agencies from a neighboring country's territory and specifically against the wishes of the constituted government.

When local political authorities are able to resist, the international community has the option of using diplomatic pressure before considering direct physical coercion. This amounts to twisting arms diplomatically before attempting to break them through economic or military sanctions. A well-documented success story of international arm-twisting was Operation Lifeline Sudan in 1989, when as a result of pressure from donors, both the Khartoum authorities and the armed rebels in the south agreed to respect "corridors of tranquility." Such a quasi-voluntary change in policy is certainly preferable to nonconsensual intervention, both because the expensive deployment of the military is avoided, and, more important, because outside relief organizations can operate within a better climate for cooperation and dialogue with belligerents about humanitarian operations.

When various forms of subtle pressure do not work, economic sanctions are a first interventionary step, despite little agreement about their utility and much debate about their devastating consequences for vulnerable populations. When these sanctions do not work or the international community becomes impatient, however, coercion can he ratcheted up through the most dramatic form of enforcement, or intervention: the physical breaking of arms by outside military forces. Both economic and military sanctions can be either approved by or, in the case of military sanctions, put under the control of the United Nations pursuant to the authority of Chapter VII of the U.N. Charter.

Major governments, including the United States as the remaining superpower, are looking to the United Nations as the sole global institution that can legitimize or undertake intervention. To the extent possible within the limits of the existing balance-of-power politics, reducing unilateral decisions about intervention and increasing the international monitoring of actions by the major powers is desirable. The need for an international system of oversight and restraints is clear, particularly for U.N. interventions based upon a human rights or humanitarian rationale. Blatant rationalization and manipulation by states have historically characterized such interventions—as epitomized by Japan's 1931 invasion of Manchuria and Germany's 1938 invasion of Czechoslovakia, both undertaken in the name of humanitarianism.

Grumblings about big-power manipulation and lack of international control were especially conspicuous in the decision to use military force against Iraq. However, the emphatic decisions in 1990 by the Security Council to reverse Iraqi aggression against Kuwait and in 1991 to dictate the terms of the peace suggest the extent to which the United Nations has become the center for decision-making about international intervention. This was even more evident in the precedent-setting decision to create havens for Kurds in northern Iraq.

Subsequently, in late 1992, the Security Council approved intervention in Somalia by military forces led by the United States to ensure humanitarian access. This set the stage, beginning in May 1993, for the first Chapter VII military operation unambiguously under the direct command and control of the U.N. secretary general to ensure humanitarian access and disarm warlords.

In Bosnia-Herzegovina, Chapter VII was invoked to authorize "all measures necessary" to protect humanitarian personnel and to coordinate life-saving assistance. Following on what some argued was an illicit interpretation of resolutions about Iraq, the Security Council specifically approved the enforcement by NATO fighter planes of comparable no-fly zones in Bosnia-Herzegovina. Authorization for the use of air strikes against Serbian forces besieging Muslim enclaves in Bosnia in order to protect U.N. forces there followed.

These are unequivocal precedents that provide teeth for international decisions when there is sufficient will in the community of states to bite and not just sneer.

The Case against Humanitarian Intervention

Two main dissenting groups are less than enthusiastic about the potentially incongruous concept of "military humanitarianism." First, many developing countries exhibit considerable reticence or even outright hostility toward U.N. intervention. Many, fearing that interveners are only the most powerful, cling to the idea that state sovereignty does not permit outside intervention. Sovereignty is their only protection against bullying by major powers. They also claim, and perhaps rightfully so, that intervention is messy—it is easier to get in than to get out.

Finally, they argue that the Security Council's definition of "international peace and security" is expanding to cover virtually any situation. It is a truism that changing world politics circumscribe when and where it is possible to intervene, and aggression across borders and opprobrious violence against populations do nor always trigger international outrage and response. The situation in Somalia did prompt an international response, while that in neighboring

Sudan, whose suffering in 1992 was just as acute, did not. Yet whatever one's views about the evolution of the right to interfere, or about whether there is a *de jure* right to intervene on humanitarian or human rights grounds, there is a *defacto* one once the Security Council labels events as aggression or a threat to international peace and security. When ratifying the U.N. Charter, member states agreed to acquiesce in the Security Council's own interpretation of its functions. Thus, claims of domestic jurisdiction are irrelevant once the Council weighs in; its imprimatur determines what is justifiable versus unjustifiable intervention. Hence, threats to international peace and security do effectively constitute what Stanley Hoffmann has called an "all-purpose parachute."

Developing countries understandably avoid publicizing Thucydides' Melian dialogue—the strong will do what they can and the weak will do what they must. But we should not be surprised by geopolitical calculations. The Security Council makes decisions to intervene, not according to objective criteria, but rather according to what the international political traffic will bear. The inclusion in the last few years of humanitarian access as a basis for intervention is a logical extension of past practice.

Developing countries themselves secured an expansive reading of Chapter VII, and a corresponding reduction in domestic jurisdiction, against white-minority governments in Rhodesia and South Africa. Their human rights policies were not just an affront to civilization but also a threat to international peace and security when the Security Council acted against egregious racism within these states. The expansion of the Council's jurisdiction began with collective actions in southern Africa and continued with decisions for northern

Iraq and Somalia.

The other group wary of more robust U.N. intervention is led mainly by many civilian humanitarians—including some of the very people working in the trenches on the front lines to alleviate suffering. They believe that "humanitarian intervention" is indeed a contradiction in terms. Moreover, they are quite likely to support the view of critics who see the new American dominance of multilateral military efforts as a continuation of past U.S. hegemony—that is, as rarely, if ever, producing salutary results.

These perspectives go beyond the concerns of some humanitarian institutions—for example, Quakers and Mennonites—that reflect religious and philosophical traditions eschewing violence. These dissenters argue that humanitarian initiatives are by their nature strictly consensual. Protected by the international law of armed conflicts of which the International Committee of the Red Cross is the custodian,[3] political authorities in armed conflicts must be persuaded to meet their commitments for access to and respect of civilians.

Since humanitarian intervention not only raises the levels of violence in the short run, but also makes reconciliation more difficult in the longer term, further objections emanate from those who argue that the *sine qua non* of emergency relief is strengthening civilian institutions within countries suffering from wars. The involvement of outside military forces for humanitarian intervention makes the task of the country's own civilian authorities—both inside and outside of government—more problematic. From this point of view, abandoning the norm of nonintervention produces further instability and weakens democratic institutions within war-affected countries.

Granted, humanitarian intervention may be uncomfortable for some and could be counterproductive to the long-range task of democratization. But to halt genocide, massive abuse of human rights, and starvation—in a world with one in every 130 people forced into flight from war[4]—it is absolutely essential. Otherwise, the United Nations is condemned to the fate of the League of Nations. The United Nations was supposed to be different from its defunct predecessor because of military might to back up international decisions to counteract aggression and atrocities in such a setting as Bosnia. Yet the characterization of the U.N. Protection Force for the former Yugoslavia (UNPROFOR) now circulating in its Zagreb headquarters—"eunuchs at the orgy"—suggests the extent to which the League of Nations "model" has reemerged.

Too many pleas for consistency or against inevitable selectivity amount to arguing that the United Nations should not intervene anywhere unless it can intervene everywhere there are analogous conditions. These objections constitute either *naïveté* or sophistry, but both justify inaction. However imperfect, the dangers of big-power abuse are actually reduced by relying on a practical system for intervention under U.N. auspices. Moving toward a U.N. monopoly in this area should help deter both the abuse of populations by political authorities and the resort to unilateral intervention by major powers.

Changes in rhetoric and some of the actual military efforts in northern Iraq and Somalia have therefore brought the international community to the brink of a new era. Yet while these U.N. actions exemplify the readiness and ability to intervene on the basis of humanitarian concerns, the situations in Somalia and Bosnia-Herzegovina have been increasingly problematic. The operational inadequacies of the United Nations and the evident unwillingness in Western capitals, particularly Washington, to enforce the peace pose a significant barrier against moving briskly forward, and may signal a move backward.

Remaining on the Brink

Until early in 1993, the dominant perception of humanitarian intervention was largely positive. The dramatic life-saving activities by the U.S.–led coalitions in Operation Provide Comfort in northern

Iraq and Operation Restore Hope in Somalia had led to high hopes. In spite of the lack of resolve in Bosnia, it seemed possible that we were entering an era when governments and insurgents would no longer be allowed to abuse their citizens with impunity. Analysts even pointed to an ill-informed and perhaps dangerous breed of humanitarians, "the new interventionists."[5]

During the past year, this euphoria has been tempered by the realities of the U.N. operations in Somalia and the former Yugoslavia. What are the military lessons that emerge from these humanitarian interventions?

There is a growing requirement to employ military might to help quell ethnic violence, create humanitarian space, and protect fundamental human rights. But the first lesson is that *international military intervention in support of humane values should be timely and robust or shunned altogether.*

While Western citizens, legislatures, and governments seek to avoid commitments, poignant media coverage sometimes elicits halfway measures. When massive and egregious abuses of civilians as well as widespread violence and starvation become unpalatable, the "CNN factor" often provokes action. But it also encourages much wishful thinking, underestimates long-term realities, and overlooks crises where journalists do not find convincing copy or footage for their editors.

The military efforts in northern Iraq were sufficient to maintain access; and the determination to stay the course was, and still is, present. The initial deployment of crack troops from the United States, Britain, France, and the Netherlands was backed by NATO air cover. When the soldiers withdrew, aircraft based in Turkey continually remained an effective threat because bombing sorties were authorized along with sanctions and other punitive measures.

The Iraqi Kurds have thus fared better than their Somali or Bosnian counterparts. The ineptness of the first U.N. Operation in Somalia (UNOSOM) was followed by the narrowness of the mandate for the U.S.-led Unified Task Force (UNITAF), also known as Operation Restore Hope, in Somalia. Because of American unwillingness to remove heavy arms from warring factions and to remain firmly in place until a semblance of a government was functioning, the second U.N. operation in Somalia was doomed to fail. Chapter VII was invoked. For the first time, the U.N. secretary general was in charge of such an operation. Also for the first time, the United Nations intervened in the domestic affairs of a member state even though that state did not present a military threat to its neighbors. But the initial U.S.-led intervention was not long enough or ambitious enough to ensure the preconditions for a successful U.N. takeover.

For Bosnia-Herzegovina, governments switched their rhetoric from the tone of peaceful settlement of Chapter VI to the shrill enforcement of Chapter VII, albeit in the context of the protection of personnel. However, this remained only rhetoric and lacked an accompanying military commitment to implement the U.N. mandate. The U.N. condemned its forces to "wandering in the void" between peacekeeping and enforcement.[6]

Shortly before resigning in January 1994 from a soldier's nightmare as the U.N. commander in the area, Lieutenant General Francis Briquemont lamented the disparity between rhetoric and reality: "There is a fantastic gap between the resolutions of the Security Council, the will to execute those resolutions and the means available to commanders in the field."[7] "All measures necessary" is quintessential double-speak; U.N. troops have not fought a single battle with the numerous factions in Bosnia who routinely disrupt relief convoys.

Moreover, the United States and its Western allies have failed to provide for a systematic contribution to U.N. operations in places such as Somalia and Bosnia-Herzegovina. The result is that these governments are "particularly prone to crisis induced reactions chosen for their symbolic value and ease of execution rather than their decisive effect."[8] The visceral reaction is to seek magical "quick fixes" and respond incrementally, hoping that warring parties will somehow come to their senses. This potentially counterproductive strategy is hardly the basis for a workable military policy.

The second lesson is that *the U.N. secretary general's command and control has serious problems, and these shortcomings are unlikely to improve.* U.N. military professionalism has not kept pace with dramatically increased demand. The capacity to plan, support, and command peacekeeping—let alone peace enforcement—is scarcely greater now than during the Cold War—which is to say, barely functional. The improvisation that was a necessity in earlier years should not continue to be made into a virtue either at headquarters or in the field.

Deficiencies in U.N. command and control have traditionally reflected three shortcomings. On the purely technical side, communications have been notoriously difficult because of multiple languages, procedures, and equipment. The lack of common training for individual contingents and staff structures with redundant quotas to reflect all troop contributors exacerbated matters further. Second, operations have suffered from multiple chains of command within a theater, and between the military and the civilian sides of the U.N. secretariat. Third, the normal tendency for contingents to seek guidance from their own capitals customarily has intensified with complexity and danger.

U.N. military operations in Somalia and the former Yugoslavia have thus reflected multiple strains that did riot exist in northern Iraq, where NATO procedures clearly determined command and control and where the governments participating in the coalition's efforts operated under American orchestration. Casualties and dissension among troop contributors in Somalia started with the tragic attack in June 1993 on the Pakistani contingent in Mogadishu. The United Nations has been unable to exercise effective command and control over UNOSOM II. The announced withdrawal of all Western soldiers by the end of March 1994 began immediately to detract from the already mediocre morale and performance of the U.N. operation.

The unusually dispersed command structure of UNPROFOR actually consists of three distinct operations. The headquarters for the Bosnia-Herzegovina command is at Kiseljak, near Sarajevo, and includes a kind of subcontract with the Northern Army Group of NATO; the four sectors of the U.N. Protected Areas report separately to Zagreb; and the Macedonia command's headquarters is in Skopje. The dangerous situation on the ground in Bosnia-Herzegovina has exacerbated the usual tendency for contingents to emphasize a national rather than a U.N. *modus operandi.* This ultimately detracts even further from military cohesion and effectiveness throughout the UNPROFOR theater of operations.

The growing number of multilateral military undertakings has given rise to a veritable cottage industry of analyses about peacekeeping, to which even U.N. secretary general Boutros Boutros-Ghali has contributed his *Agenda for Peace.* New thinking in many staff colleges and defense ministries has shown the beginnings of a debate about the merits of international versus national command and control. But these developments have yet to lead to significant operational improvements within the United Nations. Militaries of major or middle powers simply do not feel at ease about placing the United Nations in charge of serious combat missions in Somalia, the Balkans, or elsewhere.

Symptomatic of this reality was the contentious interagency debate that erupted in mid-1993 within the Clinton administration, when a draft presidential decision directive about the wisdom of placing U.S. combat troops under U.N. command in Somalia was leaked to the media. The same tension surfaced in September, as heavy American casualties were experienced in Mogadishu. Furthermore, the minority report of the U.S. Commission on Improving the Effectiveness of the United Nations[9] and the Defense Department's 1993 *Bottom Up Review* called into question the feasibility of multilateral military efforts in general, and in particular the Pentagon questioned the wisdom of sending troops to Haiti as part of U.N. efforts to implement the Governors Island Accord.

American forces ought to remain under U.S.

or NATO command and control. The Pentagon should cede them to the U.N. secretary general only for safer and smaller operations, such as the one in Macedonia. Specifically, NATO should maintain command and control in the unlikely event that a new force materializes soon for Bosnia-Herzegovina. The troops from NATO countries already in UNPROFOR should be integrated into the new NATO command rather than vice versa.

But in spite of considerable rhetoric to the contrary, the third lesson is that *regional organizations are not really a viable alternative to the United Nations.* Advocates of greater reliance on regional institutions find them attractive for three reasons. Their member states are supposedly ready to act because they suffer most from the destabilizing consequences of war and have the greatest stake in the management arid resolution of conflicts in their locales. Regional actors also understand the dynamics of strife and cultures more intimately than outsiders, and thus they are ostensibly in a better position to mediate. Finally, the argument goes, issues relating to local conflict are more likely to be given full and urgent consideration in regional forums than in global ones, where there are broader agendas, competing priorities, and distractions.

These advantages, however, exist more in theory than in practice.[10] In the first place, most regional institutions have virtually no collective military experience or resources—with the sole exception of NATO, which in fact is not a "regional arrangement," but an "alliance," thus avoiding any implications of possible subservience to the Security Council. Moreover, regional organizations normally contain dominant states whose presence makes legitimate intervention problematic. Syria's occupation of Lebanon under the auspices of the Arab League, or Nigeria's occupation of Liberia under those of the Economic Community of West African States, illustrate the prevalent reality. Recent overtures by Russia for a U.N. blessing of its arbitration of disputes in the former Soviet Union, for instance, amount to dressing up traditional Russian hegemony in the guise of Commonwealth of Independent States peacekeeping.

Regional groupings of essentially small countries—for example, the Contadora Group and the Association of Southeast Asian Nations—are less threatening and can sometimes be helpful on the diplomatic front. In military terms, however, the interests of geopolitically important neighbors normally disqualify these groupings from objective mediation and enforcement. C.W. Maynes' "benign realpolitik" straightforwardly recognizes the revival of spheres of influence—albeit with U.N. oversight. It is thus not so much regional institutions but regional powers that count.

In fact, ill-founded reliance on Europe's panoply of regional institutions for the conundrum of the former Yugoslavia provides what some social scientists might even call the "best case." Even well-endowed regional organizations failed the test: the European Community (now Union) and the Conference on Security and Cooperation in Europe were unable to develop a common foreign policy about recognizing independence with guarantees for minorities; and member governments dithered about possible military action within NATO and the Western European Union. A military response to either the international aggression or the continued civil war in the former Yugoslavia would hardly have been an "out of area" operation. Yet European diplomacy slowed down and sometimes impeded the one entity mandated to authorize outside military intervention, the U.N. Security Council.

In addition to the glaring operational inadequacies of U.N. operations, there is another explanation for remaining on the brink of, or even retreating from—rather than moving into—the new era. This is the growing reluctance in the capitals of the West, especially Washington, to tackle militarily the ever-burgeoning number of complex emergencies. As a result, the debacle of humanitarian interventions in Somalia and the pain from the halfhearted efforts in Bosnia have caused a case of collective amnesia in the West about the real difference made—and continuing to be made—in northern Iraq.

In Somalia, Washington raced ahead without

understanding what was necessary in order to enforce the peace. In particular, UNITAF forged ahead with the laudable motive of stopping starvation, but never considered the implications if other necessary steps—disarmament and trusteeship—were not also in the mission's mandate. In Bosnia-Herzegovina, the United Nations provided a convenient forum for governments to appear to be doing something without really doing anything substantial to thwart aggression, genocide, and forced movements of people. David Owen himself aptly described his performance as the EC mediator as "masterly inactivity"—doing nothing with flair.

In the United States, the consequence of these failures is clear: weakened popular support for military participation in U.N. operations to deal with humanitarian crises; an inability to face up to the situation in Haiti; and diminished trust by the United Nations and other member states in the ability of the United States to stay the course in the most trying circumstances. Whether this damage is irreparable remains to be seen. But the Pentagon's *Bottom Lip Review* is discouraging in its recommendation that the United States only participate in multilateral military operations under conditions that very few, if any, U.N. operations will ever meet.

The resigned attitude of the secretary general now reflects this new reality. Barely one year after the Publication of his relatively bullish *Agenda for Peace,* Boutros-Ghali confesses: "History is accelerating. The pace is alarming. The direction is not entirely clear."[12] Upon his return from a visit to the U.N. operation in Somalia in October 1993, in an appearance before the Security Council, the world organization's CEO added to the confusion: "The United Nations cannot impose peace; the role of the United Nations is to maintain the peace."[13]

The United Nations is apparently no longer in the peace-enforcement business, in spite of mandates overriding the respective sovereignties of Iraq, Somalia, Haiti, and the former Yugoslavia. The square brackets around Chapter VII—that is, warring parties need to consent to U.N. military and humanitarian efforts as during the Cold War—should reduce considerably the problem of overstretch. But then the United Nations would be largely absent from the most urgent moral and operational challenges of our turbulent times.

No Alternative

The shortcomings of recent efforts by the United Nations in the military and humanitarian arenas are substantial, and the political climate for an expansion of multilateral operations is unpropitious, to say the least. Political measures from almost every direction now point to what many critics of intervention seem to prefer, namely, paring back the U.S. military and stopping those U.N. military efforts intended to alleviate suffering. But what is the alternative to international intervention in order to halt atrocities in Bosnia, to give civil society a chance to take root in Somalia, or to restore an elected government in Haiti?

The fatalism arid isolationism that flow from most objections to humanitarian intervention are as distressing as the political situations in countries suffering from ethnic conflict where such action is required. Critics who are worried about sovereignty and the need for consent, or about overstretch, join Richard Falk in concluding that it is "nearly impossible to carry an intervention to political completion" in light of "the limits of military power in the post-colonial world."[14]

A purely noninterventionist position amounts to abstention from the foreign policy debate. In today's world, U.N. decision-making is the only available and sensible way to coordinate global responses to genocidal misery and massive human rights abuse in war zones around the world. Only through such a world organization will the major powers subject themselves to some standard of international law and oversight. And whatever one's view about the fairness of the preponderant role (some would say leadership) of the permanent members of the Security Council, a decision to intervene against governments and insurgents that resist the expressed international will is legitimate now when the Council authorizes it.

While many lament the absence of an independent U.N. military, the reality of the present balance of forces means that there can be no effective international enforcement for the foreseeable future without a dominant role for American armed forces, In the future, preventive measures could forestall the spread of chaos. In the long term, economic and social development may mitigate conflict, but the use of military forces, too, is essential. Effective prevention today and tomorrow necessarily entails the physical deployment of well-armed troops. These soldiers require contingency plans and reserve firepower for immediate retaliation, amounting to an advance authorization for Chapter VII measures.

Skyrocketing demand for military intervention and humanitarian action is unsettling and calls for some tough decisions in light of a serious lack of available resources. "Compassion fatigue" and "donor distraction" are often facile and unacceptable excuses to avoid responsibilities. Yet domestic recessionary and budgetary requirements are in conflict with the need for outside help in numerous crises around the world. Four years after the official end of the Cold War, a survey of elite and popular opinion in the United States indicated that when asked to identify the most urgent foreign policy priority, most Americans named a domestic issue, with a particular emphasis on the economy.[15]

What this means is that *triage*, the French term to describe the wrenching and repugnant process of selection, will soon be making a comeback. As does the surgeon on the battlefield, decisions must be made about categories: those who need no help; those who cannot be helped; and those who can and must be helped.

While much remains to be done to get more from existing military and humanitarian machinery, policymakers and citizens nonetheless cannot avoid painful ethical dilemmas. Is it desirable to channel resources to those who can be saved, rather than spreading them inadequately to as many suffering souls as possible? Does it make more sense to use resources to ease the suffering of civilians who are likely to be killed subsequently by shellings, or to help those in areas where belligerents have agreed to cease-fires?

While we are likely to retreat from the brink rather than move into the new era, we cannot ignore the costs of inaction. The disasters looming behind ethnic conflict in much of the Third World and the former Soviet Union demand immediate policy decisions in Washington. The United States must improve not only its capacity for humanitarian interventions, but also the ability of the United Nations to oversee them. And other countries must be compelled to contribute their fair share. Improving American capacities will not in itself suffice, because the United States cannot afford to go it alone, and the American people would not tolerate this. But Washington also cannot limit it itself simply to improving the capabilities of the United Nations.

As has become obvious in Somalia, Bosnia, and Haiti, if the United States does not participate in the toughest assignments, no one else will either.

Notes

The author wishes to thank the Naval War College for the opportunity to have developed this argument for a conference in February 1994. An expanded version will appear in *Beyond Traditional Peacekeeping*, edited by Don Daniel (London: Macmillan, 1995).

1. Adam Roberts, "Humanitarian War: Military Intervention and Human Rights," *International Affairs* 69 (1993), p. 429.

2. For further discussions of intervention and ethical issues, see Thomas G. Weiss, "Intervention: Whither the United Nations?" *Washington Quarterly 17* (Winter 1994), pp. 109-28; and "U.N. Responses in the Former Yugoslavia: Moral and Operational Choices," *Ethics & International Affairs* 8 (1994), pp. 1-22.

3. *The Geneva Convention of August 12, 1949, and Protocols Additional to the Geneva Conventions of 12 August 1949* (Geneva: International Committee of the Red Cross, 1989).

4. For this and other gruesome statistics, see Sadako Ogata, *The State of the World's Refugees: The Challenge of Protection* (New York: Penguin, 1993).

5. Stephen John Stedman, "The New Interventionists," *Foreign Affairs* 72 (1993), pp. 1-16.

6. John Gerard Ruggie, "Wandering in the Void," *Foreign Affairs* 72 (November/December 1993), pp. 26-31.

7. "U.N. Commander Wants More Troops, Fewer Resolutions," *New York Times*, December 31, 1993, p. A3.

8. John Steinbruner, "Memorandum: Civil Violence as an International Security Problem," reproduced as Annex C in Francis M. Deng, *Protecting the Dispossessed: A Challenge for the International Community* (Washington, DC: Brookings Institution, 1993), p. 155.

9. *Defining Purpose: The U.N. and the Health of Nations* (Washington, DC: United States Commission on Improving the Effectiveness of the United Nations, 1993).

10. See S. Neil MacFarlane and Thomas G. Weiss, "Regional Organizations and Regional Security," *Security Studies 2* (Fall/Winter 1992-93), pp. 6-37; and "The United Nations, Regional Organizations, and Human Security: Building Theory in Central America," *Third World Quarterly* 15 (April 1994).

11. Charles William Maynes, "A Workable Clinton Doctrine," *Foreign Policy,* no. 93 (Winter 1993-94), pp. 3-20.

12. Boutros Boutros-Ghali, "An Agenda for Peace: One Year Later," *Orbis* 37 (Summer 1993), p. 332.

13. As quoted by Julia Preston, "U.N. Officials Scale Back Peacemaking Ambitions," *Washington Post,* October 28, 1993, p. A40. For a further discussion of conceptual fuzziness, see Thomas G. Weiss, "New Challenges for U.N. Military Operations: Implementing an Agenda for Peace," *Washington Quarterly* 16 (Winter 1993), pp. 51-66.

14. Richard Falk, "Intervention and Resistance," *Boston Review* 18 (December/January 1993-94), p. 11.

15. Times Mirror Center for The People & The Press, *America's Place in the New World: An Investigation of the Attitudes of American Opinion Leaders and the American Public about International Affairs* (Washington, DC: Times Mirror Center, November 1993).

Doing It Right: The Future of Humanitarian Intervention

Michael E. O'Hanlon
Brookings Institution

Using military force to save lives is difficult, dangerous, rarely politically rewarding—and yet somehow here to stay. American presidents, UN Security Councils, and western publics will almost always want to do something when thousands or tens of thousands of innocent people are dying as a result of war. But dozens of civil wars are being waged around the world at any given time; demands being made on the U.S. armed forces already verge on being excessive; and conducting successful interventions is difficult. American policymakers must be judicious in deciding when and how to use force to save lives in conflicts that do not involve vital, strategic U.S. interests.

Each such decision requires answering three crucial questions. When and where should we intervene? How should we do so? And who should do the intervening? By answering these questions carefully—and by trying to develop more global capacity for conducting peace and humanitarian operations—the international community can significantly reduce violence around the world in the years ahead.

When and Where to Intervene?

Given the many conflicts in the world today, how can we possibly decide which ones to try to resolve by force? The answer is to focus on those where the scale of death and suffering is greatest, where intervention is unlikely to create great-power conflicts, and where a mission can be designed that promises many lives saved at low cost to intervening soldiers.

But aren't civil and ethnic conflicts spinning out of control to the point that the problem is intractable? The short answer is no. Yahya Sadowski argued convincingly in a 1998 Brookings book that contrary to what doomsayers have been prophesying for years, the prevalence and intensity of civil conflict are not increasing as a result of the end of the Cold War, globalization, or anything else. Of the many civil wars around the world, most are not especially violent. Their per capita death rates, for example, are not notably worse than murder rates in U.S. cities. That is not to say we should ignore these conflicts—only that the blunt, dangerous, and expensive instrument of forcible military intervention should not be applied in most instances. As Steve Solarz and I have argued, the United States and like-minded countries cannot be expected to try to make the rest of the world safer than U.S. society.

In the 1990s, ten conflicts were extremely lethal: those in Sudan, Rwanda, Angola, Somalia, Burundi, Liberia, Iraq, Sierra Leone, Bosnia, and Chechnya.

Michael E. O'Hanlon, "Doing It Right: The Future of Humanitarian Intervention," from the *Brookings Review*, Winter 2002. Reprinted with permission by the Brookings Institution Press.

These should have been the prime candidates for humanitarian intervention, as should any future conflicts of comparable severity (Kosovo and Haiti were not on this list, but the Clinton administration's wise decisions to intervene in those places reflected the presence of strategic stakes alongside humanitarian concerns). But it would not have been wise to intervene in all ten, which brings us to the second criterion for intervention—that a mission not risk major-power war costing far more lives than could possibly be saved. Notably, intervening in Chechnya was and is simply out of the question, given Russia's size and nuclear weapons capability. (In North Korea, where not war but severe repression and misgovernment, joined with starvation, caused at least hundreds of thousands of deaths last decade, intervention was also impractical given the North's ability to retaliate and cause at least tens of thousands of casualties in South Korea. Likewise, a hypothetical intervention in Kashmir would be unthinkable without the permission of India and Pakistan. And similar considerations rule out any forceful military mission to protect Tibet from Chinese oppression.)

What about the other nine terrible wars of the 1990s? How could outside powers have used force to save lives without making the problems worse than they already were and costing many lives of intervening troops in the process? That is probably the hardest question of all.

How to Intervene?

Simply deciding to intervene is not enough. Using force the wrong way can exacerbate some conflicts and get a lot of people, including U.S. troops, killed as well.

For this reason, it is often said that the United States needs an exit strategy before choosing to intervene. That is generally good advice—as long as the exit strategy is sound. Sometimes, however, as in Kosovo, insisting on a precise itinerary of intervention and a concrete political end-state for the region before becoming involved would be counterproductive. We do not, and probably cannot, know in advance how long outside forces might be needed; setting arbitrary deadlines risks creating unrealistic expectations at home and undesirable doubts abroad as to our commitment. Trying to determine now whether Kosovo will remain part of Yugoslavia, become independent, or be divided into two parts would do more to reignite the Serb-Albanian conflict than to resolve it.

But at a minimum, the international community needs some sense of how it will apply military force before intervening. Should it simply do enough to feed starving people, should it create safe havens for individuals or groups at risk, should it impose a ceasefire line between warring parties—or might it even help one side to win a conflict?

It all depends. Where tens of thousands are at risk from war-related famine, disease, or exposure, simply setting up protected humanitarian zones may make sense. That is particularly the case when, as in Somalia in the early 1990s, the conflict that has produced the problem seems severe and intractable.

Imposing ceasefire lines, or even permanently partitioning countries into two or more parts, can work well in some ethnic conflicts. We need not always create multiethnic, inclusive societies; sometimes saving lives is accomplishment enough. The international community's long-term goal in Bosnia remains recreating a multiethnic state, but in the short term, at least, allowing separate entities with separate armies is sound policy and represents a huge improvement over the state of war that prevailed there five years ago. In Sudan, if the war-related famine again becomes severe, dividing the country into an Arab north and a Christian south may save the vast majority of threatened Sudanese lives at the lowest cost in dollars—and in the blood of intervening troops.

Finally, we should even be willing to take sides when one party to a conflict is clearly the better choice for its own country and when taking sides is likely to end a conflict. For example, the Bush administration was right to overthrow Manuel

Noriega in Panama, clearing the way for a democratically elected successor; the Clinton administration was right to threaten to depose the Cedras regime in Haiti to allow the Aristide regime to take charge. Had the global community been willing to step up its involvement in Rwanda in 1994, it would have been wisest to ally with the Tutsi-led Rwandan Patriotic Front against the Hutu-led armed forces that, in league with various militia groups, ultimately carried out that country's terrible genocide.

What about the future?

The world's most severe wars today include those in Sierra Leone, Congo, Angola, Algeria, Colombia, and Sri Lanka. Intervention in the last three would pit outside forces against battle-toughened, dedicated, and rather large insurgencies fighting on terrain advantageous for guerrilla-like warfare. Those are the situations U.S. and other outside forces should generally avoid, since they are likely to inflict substantial casualties on intervening troops. But the other conflicts in Africa, particularly the brutal war in small Sierra Leone, may be easier to contain. Any intervention there should take the side of the government against Liberia-financed mercenary rebels. It has been no credit to the international community that it did not address this conflict seriously; instead hoping for the best while poorly armed peacekeepers interposed themselves in a civil war they were not able to contain. Things may be changing for the better, however, as of this writing.

The war in Angola involves larger indigenous fighting forces over a much wider area. The government—the lesser of two evils in this case—has recently been making inroads against the rebel forces of former U.S. client Jonas Savimbi. Were outside countries to try to stop this extremely bloody, long, and pointless war, they would be wise to side with the government and help it win a decisive victory. But it could take many thousands of international troops—and most likely dozens of fatalities to them-to do so. Finally, in the huge country of Congo, the global community should be willing to deploy a force at least 10 times larger than the 5,500-person UN monitoring operation now proposed if a true ceasefire ever is accepted. The larger force would deploy along a ceasefire line running north-south through the center of the country, forcibly keeping hostile armies apart and denying sanctuary to the Hutu extremists who fled to Congo from Rwanda several years ago. But muscular interventions in wars like those in Angola and Congo will probably not happen until more countries develop the military capabilities for such operations, which brings us to the final question.

Who Should Intervene?

How much of the work in forcible humanitarian interventions should the United States be expected to do? It seems unreasonable—not to mention politically unsustainable—for U.S. troops to do most everything. Saving lives is not a uniquely American interest. And the United States, alone among the major western powers, already maintains high military vigilance in the Persian Gulf and the Korean peninsula.

Unfortunately, other countries in general have neither the forcible entry capabilities nor the sustainable logistics to intervene in distant lands to save lives. Australia has done most of the work in East Timor, and our European allies have provided the vast majority of troops in Bosnia and Kosovo, of late. But U.S. capabilities are generally needed, at least initially, in the face of armed opposition. And the United States will need to contribute troops to postwar missions in places like the Balkans if it wishes to influence their conduct.

Although the United States need not create a specialized armed force for peace operations, it should modify its military force structure to lessen the strain of various types of limited missions around the world. Primary U.S. military attention must remain focused on those parts of the world where our economic interests are greatest, allies are at risk, and dangerous military competition could break out if local parties are not reassured or deterred. That means a continued emphasis on Europe, the Persian Gulf, and East Asia. But some military units—including special forces with particular language and political skills, military police, and support units that provide water, food, and medical care—should be beefed up for peace operations. Some of these special units, many now in the reserve force structure because they do not require constant training and drilling to do their jobs in war, are being overused. Placing more of them in the active-duty force structure would allow them to be deployed without excessively disrupting the lives of reservists, many of whom do not expect such duty short of a national crisis. Some 10,000 to 20,000 specialized troops should be added—at a cost of about $1 billion a year, less than half of 1 percent of the defense budget. That is not too high a price to pay.

Other countries have much more work to do. The European allies, Canada, and even Japan should improve their ability to move troops to distant combat zones. The United States should overcome its ambivalence about its allies strengthening their military capabilities and enthusiastically endorse most any steps they take toward greater military burden-sharing.

Among the major western European nations, the model for improving peace operations and forcible intervention capabilities is clear. In a word, it is Britain. Its military is smaller than that of France or Germany but much more useful beyond its own borders. It can deploy perhaps 50,000 combat troops, with air support, well beyond its territory within three to four months and sustain them there for months. Britain is also planning to acquire more sealift and airlift to move its forces fairly rapidly. Smaller European countries cannot use Britain as an exact model, of course, but they can scale their efforts to some extent proportionately or band together in subgroups, with each country developing certain specialties. Because the European Union cannot be expected in the near term to act as a single entity in matters of war and peace, the most realistic alternative is for several countries or subgroups of countries each to have the capacity for meaningful military action abroad on their own or as coalitions of the willing.

What of budget constraints? Most European countries do not need to spend more—they need to spend differently. Large force structures are no longer needed, as Britain has already recognized and as Germany appears to be concluding as well. By cutting troops and buying lift and mobile logistics, NATO European countries can do far more than they do now with the $170 billion a year they spend on defense.

Were Germany and Japan to follow the above prescriptions, their neighbors might be highly agitated, worrying about their capacity for autonomous power projection. The simplest way to defuse—or at least contain—such concerns is to begin with modest military ambitions for those two cases. Deploying troops only under multilateral, and preferably UN, auspices would further reassure nervous neighbors.

What about non-Western countries? Expensive hardware such as airlift capabilities, helicopters, and fighter aircraft, especially in large numbers, will generally be beyond their means. It is more realistic to ask these countries to develop well-trained soldiers, proficient in basic combat and peacekeeping skills, and equipped with serviceable small arms, body armor, vehicles for transport, and logistics and communications support for sustained operations abroad. Even if such countries cannot be expected to lead forcible interventions, they can provide valuable combat forces that enable peacekeeping missions to uphold ceasefires and peace accords under challenge. As the world witnessed in Angola in the early 1990s, some of the worst and most deadly conflicts erupt in countries where peace accords are reached, but later disintegrate. The breakdown of the Sierra Leone peace accord in 2000 that left many African troops held hostage is another reminder of the need for better-prepared peacekeeping troops, particularly from regions such as Africa, where conflicts are most common.

The United States and other western countries can do a great deal to help in this regard by providing modest sums—perhaps a couple hundred million dollars a year in all—for improved training, equipment, and other basic military needs. Programs like the African Crisis Response Initiative (ACRI), created by the Clinton administration, should not only be continued, but expanded dramatically. At present the ACRI funds only occasional training rotations for a few thousand regional troops, to the tune of about $20 million annually.

Again, the focus should be on improving individual countries' military capacities, so that they can deploy as ad hoc coalitions, rather than depending on unanimous participation from all members of regional security groups to carry out missions. Regional institutions are useful for negotiating peace accords and politically legitimating interventions, but not for owning or maintaining actual military forces—at least not yet.

This agenda is not particularly demanding for the United States. It involves small changes in the U.S. armed forces, limited aid to certain poorer countries, and diplomatic efforts to promote the plan. But the actions outlined here can make a big difference in preparing the world to handle peace operations in war-ravaged lands like Angola and Congo—lands whose forsaken people are now being often forgotten.

NATO and Humanitarian Intervention

Clara Portela
Consultant to Berlin Information-center for Transatlantic Security

'Reviving' the Notion of Humanitarian Intervention

Some within NATO claimed that military intervention in another state can be justified in cases of overwhelming necessity. While all leaders clearly put the emphasis on the humanitarian distress, reference to the theory of humanitarian intervention was sometimes made more explicitly than others. NATO Secretary-General Solana repeatedly stressed that the campaign's objective was to "avoid a humanitarian disaster". In the above-mentioned letter explaining the Allies' approval of the activation order, he mentioned, "the very stringent report of the Secretary-General of the United Nations pursuant to both resolutions, (which) warned inter alia of the danger of a humanitarian disaster in Kosovo". He further referred to "the continuation of a humanitarian catastrophe, because no concrete measures towards a peaceful solution of the crisis have been taken by the FRY."[1] The risk of the conflict spilling-over the Yugoslav borders took a secondary place:

> Our objective is to prevent more human suffering and more repression and violence against the civilian population of Kosovo. We must also act to prevent instability spreading in the region...must stop violence and bring an end to the humanitarian catastrophe now taking place in Kosovo. We have a moral duty to do so. The responsibility is on our shoulders and we have to fulfil it.[2]

Among NATO leaders, British Prime Minister Tony Blair most vigorously intended to conceptualise the moral rationale of the intervention, even formulating a 'doctrine of the international community':

> I believe that a real sense of moral purpose is also motivating NATO. We either allow ethnic cleansing to succeed, or we say that the world community has an obligation to stop this most violent form of nationalism. Our job is to go in there and reverse it and defeat it.[3]

While the validity of the two first mentioned justifications—UN Security Council resolutions and international treaties—was easily dismissed, the question of the humanitarian intervention is more complicated. Could the doctrine of humanitarian intervention confer some legitimacy to the Kosovo operation?

In order to give an answer to this question, the first issue to be clarified is whether the humanitarian intervention actually exists as an institution.

Humanitarian intervention "encompasses any use of armed force by a State against another State for the purpose of protecting the life and liberty of the citizens of the latter State unwilling or unable to do so itself."[4] Although a majority of writers supported the idea of a lawful humanitarian intervention during the era previous to the signing of the UN Charter, it is debatable whether it was clearly established under the customary international law of that time. In any case, it is clear that even if that right had existed prior to 1945, it had not survived the adoption of the Charter; although no explicit reference is made in the Charter to humanitarian intervention, it is in conflict with the prohibition of the threat or used of force in Art. 2 (4).

Only a minority of jurists maintained in the period after 1945 that the institution of humanitarian intervention is permitted under customary international law, a recognised source of international law. They argued that the principles of non-violence and the protection of human rights must be balanced against each other in any particular case, with the result that in extreme situations involving seriously inhumane treatment, the latter principle should override the former. It was often adduced that humanitarian interventions were not precluded by Art. 2 (4) of the UN Charter since it only banned the use of force when directed "against the territorial integrity or political independence" of the target state, and not at the protection of its population.[5] This argument is based on a wrong understanding of the terms in question, which were not added to the text in order to restrict its scope, but in the spirit of specifying the prohibition. Furthermore, it has been generally rejected as incompatible with the system of the Charter, since its framers had attributed a predominant role to individual non-violence. The recognition of humanitarian intervention as an exemption from this prohibition of Art. 2 (4) was deliberately abnegated in order to prevent a confrontation of the two power blocks.[6]

Some of these specialists have voiced the need for reappraisal of this question in view of a number of events taking place after the end of the Cold War. They contend that notions of legitimacy are changing, with humanitarian reasons emerging as a third option for justified military intervention in a sovereign state.[7]

Two constitutive elements define the existence of an international custom: *diuturnitas,* i.e. a consistent international practice and *opiniojuri.c,* i.e. acceptance of this custom by states.[8] In order to determine the existence of the institution of humanitarian intervention, it should be demonstrated that both elements are present. Advocates of this notion point to recent UN and state practice and codified and non-codified signs of growing acceptance of this institution. In the following, these arguments will be examined.

Assessing the Practice

The argument based on state practice Greenwood defends that states' practice allows for the consideration of this institution as established under customary international law. He contends that enough precedents of humanitarian interventions justify the claim that most states accept them as legal.[9] For him, the emergence of "at least a limited right of intervention" is best exemplified by the allied intervention in northern Iraq in 1991 on behalf of the Kurds and the imposition of a no-fly zone it southern Iraq on behalf of the Shiites some months later. As further examples, he cites the cases of India's invasion of Bangladesh (1971), Tanzania's invasion of Uganda (1979) and ECOWAS' intervention in Liberia (1990). In Greenwood's words,

> It seems that the law on humanitarian intervention has changed both for the UN and for individual states. It is no longer tenable to assert that whenever a government massacres its own people or a state collapses into anarchy international law forbids military intervention altogether.[10]

Greenwood cites cases in which there was no state authority to request or allow outside intervention, or when in civil strives, foreign help met with the consent of all parties to the conflict. These examples cannot bear precedential character for cases when a state authority existed.[11] This leaves the enforcement of a no-fly zone in Iraq as the only case of non-UN authorised state intervention that would qualify as a humanitarian intervention.[12]

The UK justified its participation on this basis, stating that it intervened "in exercise of the customary international principle of humanitarian intervention"[13], thus invoking this institution by name. Former British Foreign Secretary Douglas Hurd declared:

> government or a French government takes has to be underwritten by a specific provision of a UN resolution provided we comply with international law. International law recognises extreme humanitarian need.... We are on strong legal as well as humanitarian ground on setting up this "no fly" zone.[14]

Nevertheless, non-compliance with UN-imposed requirements does not authorise states to use force. An enforcement provision is still required. One should not be mislead by official statements: Interventions conducted outside the UN umbrella are illegal. The enforcement of a no-fly zone in Iraq falls within this category.

Very few interventions both in the pre-Charter period and after 1945 often cited as precedents can be described as humanitarian without serious difficulties.[15] Greenwood himself acknowledges that the circumstances under which the intervention in Iraq took place are rather unique and unlikely to be repeated.[16] One author has written that "the first respectful piece of practice supporting the doctrine of humanitarian intervention is represented by the NATO air campaign against the FRY."[17]

In this particular instance, trends from UN authorised and non-authorised practise seem to converge: NATO, which had acted previously as a "UN subcontractor", emancipated itself from UN Security Council's authorisation to take action and placed itself outside legality, while claiming to aim at achieving compliance with UNSC Resolutions.

The Argument Based on UN Practice

Some commentators contend that the UN Security Council has established a practice legitimising humanitarian grounded interventions so that they can now be considered part of customary law. This argument suggests that increased UN involvement in civil war situations can be regarded as evidence that international obligations and problems of humanitarianism may rank alongside the defence of national interests.[18] As precedents, reference is made to Resolution 699 of 5 April 1991 on Iraq, Resolution 770 of 13 August 1992 on Bosnia-Herzegovina, Resolution 794 of 3 December 1992 on Somalia, Resolution 929 of 22 June 1994 on Zaire and Rwanda, Resolution 940 of 31 July 1994 on Haiti and resolution 1101 of 28 March 1997 on Albania. According to this analysis, NATO's strikes on FRY would be legal.

Indeed, cited developments evidence a notable shift underway in terms of the principle and practice of humanitarian intervention over the past ten years, suggesting that the protection of human rights in situations of extreme deprivation and suffering is sometimes given pre-eminence over the sovereignty principle.[19] In order to correctly assess the existence of an international custom, though, Security Council and non-authorised practice require a separate analysis. This is so because, as explained above, military action taken by the Security Council is one of the legal exceptions provided for in the Charter, while state practice without authorisation is not.

In recent years, the UN Security Council has clearly become more active and more assertive in the field of security. This quantitative evolution was accompanied by a qualitative one in two senses:

First, in the early nineties, the UN Security Council conducted a considerable number of forcible interventions, or "peacekeeping of third generation."

During the Cold War, peacekeeping interventions were governed by the strict principles of consent of the parties on the deployment of the forces, impartiality and non-use of force, with the peacekeeping tasks being restricted to the interposition between the contending parties and the monitoring of the cease-fires. Towards the end of the 1980s, peacekeeping began to turn multifunctional, including new tasks such as election monitoring, national reconciliation or demining. Namibia, El Salvador and Cambodia are examples of the so-called peacekeeping operations of second generation. In this period it became the practice of the Security Council to allow for military action to conduct humanitarian relief or rescue operations; most examples mentioned by Guicherd correspond to this tendency. Nevertheless, the basic principles mentioned above continued to be respected.

At a third stage, the UN increasingly authorised operations conducted by regional organisations such as OSCE's Kosovo Verification Mission, NATO-led IFOR and SFOR in Bosnia-Herzegovina, CIS' in the Trans-Caucasian area and international coalitions such as the Italian-led coalition in Operation Alba. The UN also authorised an individual state, the US, to act in Haiti, as permitted under Art. 52 of the UN Charter. Some of these operations, notably Somalia, Rwanda, and IFOR/SFOR in Bosnia have been characterised differently from previous peacekeeping operations. They present characteristics such as the emergence of a coercive dimension beyond the right to self-defence[20] and the delegation of the use of force to national (or coalition) forces.

While some observers have denominated these interventions "peacekeeping of third generation", others prefer to call them 'peace-enforcement operations', as a type separated from peacekeeping. This type has been subject to more acute criticism than the peacekeeping of first and second generation.[21]

Second, the UN Security Council has shown an increasing willingness to conduct this kind of forcible interventions in cases of purely domestic humanitarian distress.

Beyond its more active role in humanitarian aid operations,[22] the Security Council is increasingly willing to characterise the plight of the people of a state as a threat to international peace and security, and to authorise interventions resting merely 'on humanitarian ground.[23] This constitutes a substantial restriction of the scope of Art. 2 (7) of the Charter, which reads:

> Nothing contained in the present Charter shall authorise the United Nations to intervene in matters which are essentially within the domestic jurisdiction of any state or shall require the Members to submit such matters to settlement under the present Charter; but this principle shall not prejudice the application of enforcement measures under Chapter VII.

This trend suggests that the rationale of non-intervention in internal affairs enshrined here is being replaced by the principle that massive or widespread violations of human rights or humanitarian law arising from governmental acts or internal conflicts and the magnitude of human suffering that they engender can constitute a threat to international peace and security. In those circumstances, the Security Council can take appropriate measures, including the use of force for the protection of humanitarian relief operations. This was especially evident in the case of Somalia, where the threat to neighbouring states was relatively small and arguably receding by the time Resolution 794 was adopted.

In this light, it becomes clear that important difficulties remain with the argument that the Security Council has been authorising a number of "humanitarian interventions".

First, there seems to be confusion in the understanding of the term 'humanitarian intervention'. Guicherd's analysis overlooks an important fact: with the sole exception of Resolution 940, all cited Security Council Resolutions authorised the use of force to protect humanitarian relief and rescue operations, but not to conduct operations effectively intervening in the conflict and aimed at influencing its outcome. NATO's intervention in Kosovo would not fall into this category. 'Humanitarian' operations are designed to provide food, shelter, and medicine directly to victims of conflicts, or to protect relief workers who furnish these goods and services, and are not meant to influence the political incentives of the actors in a conflict. They should be distinguished from 'peace enforcement' operations, which can imply the use of force against one of the parties to enforce an end to hostilities.

The above-mentioned analysis also fails to recognise that when resolutions provided for forcible implementation without the consent of the government of the target country, they did so in situations when there was effectively no government that could authorise such an operation.[24]

Finally, a further problem remains. While the practice shows a lesser degree of respect towards the sovereignty principle than in the Cold-War era, it is debatable whether developments taking place within a codified legal system such as the UN Charter can serve as a basis for justifying actions outside the UN umbrella.[25]

Assessing the Acceptance by States

What about the *opinio furls?* Legal doctrine attaches more importance to the psychological element than to the material one, noting that practice needs to be accompanied by a manifestation by states bringing it home that they view their behaviour as legal. In fact, it is the conviction that the act is legal what differentiates law from mere courtesy.

Since the entry into force of the UN Charter, most states taking forcible action abroad have tended to reject the notion that their actions were humanitarian interventions. Even in cases where there appeared to be a clear humanitarian rationale such as in India's intervention in East Bengal in 1971 or the Vietnamese intervention in Cambodia in 1978, states did not make any reference to humanitarianism, what is still interpreted as an indication that they were willing to uphold the non-interventionist regime.[26]

Do developments following the Kosovo events add something new to this state of affairs? Several authors contend that now a majority of states regard humanitarian interventions as legal, pointing out that the voting on two UN Security Council resolutions can be seen as granting post-facto legitimisation to the Kosovo operation:

A draft resolution tabled by Russia two days after the commencement of the NATO strikes against FRY calling for the cessation of the use of force against the FRY was defeated by twelve votes to three—those of Russia, China and Namibia.[27] Further, resolution 1244 of 10 June 1999 authorising "Member States and relevant international organisations to establish the international security presence in Kosovo", adopted with the abstention of China, can be regarded as sanctioning NATO's presence in Yugoslav territory.[28]

It is actually striking that most Third World countries, which have traditionally displayed firm opposition to humanitarian interventions, were supportive of the resolution. However, it should be kept in mind that opposition by states is enough to prevent the formation of a custom. A "majority of states" would not be enough. With the consistent expressions of disapproval by a number of states, in particular coming from countries such as Russia and China, no international custom binding upon them could be set up.

As a further sign of a growing international acceptance of humanitarian-grounded interventions, some commentators adduce that a principle recognising that populations in danger of starvation, massacre or other forms of massive suffering have the right to receive assistance was set out by General Assembly Resolution 43/131 of 8 December 1988.[29]

However, it is important to make clear that the resolution merely invites countries to contribute and to facilitate the provision of humanitarian assistance 'in natural disasters and similar situations'. GA resolutions fall short of furnishing a legal basis, since they are not legally binding. At best, they can be considered to reflect a change in general attitudes of the international community. Only a wide interpretation of the resolutions allows for a recognition of the right of endangered populations to humanitarian assistance. Furthermore, the wording 'right to humanitarian assistance' can be found nowhere in the text of Resolution 43/131.[30]

The existence of this principle could not be claimed without later Security Council availing itself of a right of humanitarian intervention in a number of Resolutions, still necessary to legitimise the action. Not even the combined right of victims to assistance and the right of the Security Council to authorise humanitarian interventions with military means do amount to a right to humanitarian intervention by states.[31]

The case against the existence of this institution, represented by the overwhelming legal opinion, is quite conclusive: Both constitutive elements of the international custom, *diutumitas* and *opinio furls* are lacking. Neither is there a consistent state practice nor the general agreement of the community of states required to establish an international custom is given. Therefore, it is clear that the institution of humanitarian intervention does not exist under customary international law.

Notes

1. Letter from Secretary-General Javier Solana, addressed to the permanent representatives to the North Atlantic Council dated 9 October 1998.

2. Press statement by Javier Solana on 23 March 1999 at 23:00.

3. Hoagland, Jim: Blair on NATO: We must defend human values, *The Washington Post,* 19 April 1999

4. Beyerlin, Ulrich: Humanitarian intervention, in: R. Bernhardt (ed.), *Encyclopaedia of Public International Law,* Vol. I (1992), p. 926. The use of armed force for the protection of its own nationals will not be considered here.

5. This claim was voiced once again with regard to the war against Yugoslavia. See Guicherd 1999, p. 23.

6. Beyond the teleological explanation, Deiseroth has drawn attention to the unacceptability of the notion that military intervention does not affect the territorial integrity of a state: "Die Anwendung von militllrischer Waffengewalt gegen das Territorium und die Bevölkerung eines Staates...stellt durch die Beeinträchtigung und die Zerstorung der angegriffenen Ziele einen massiven Obergriff auf das Staatsgebiet dar, und zwar unabhängig davon, ob die Gewaltanwendung subjektiv auf die Eroberung des Gebietes abzielt oder nicht." Deiseroth, Dieter: Humanitäre Intervention' und Völkerrecht, *Neue Juistische Wochenschrift,* Heft 42, 1999, p. 3086.

7. See for instance Greenwood, C.: "Legal Limitations of the Prohibitions of Use of Force" in: Souchon, Lennard (Hrsg.): *Völkerrecht tend Sicherheit,* Herford 1994.

8. This is defined in Art. 38 (1) b of the Statute of the International Court of Justice. See for instance: Fernández Flores, J.L.: "Fuentes del derecho internacional ptlblico", in: Fundación Tomás Moro: *Diccionario Juridico Espasa,* Madrid 1991, p. 443, Shaw, M.: *International Law,* Cambridge 1997, pp. 58-59, Simma, B: "Das Volkergewohnheitsrecht", p. 39 in Neuhold, H.: *Osterreichisches Handbuch des Völkerrechts,* Wien 1997, Hillier, T.: *Principles of Public International Law,* Cambridge 1999, p. 19.

9. Quoted in "War with Milosevic", *The Economist,* 3rd April 1999, p. 18.

10. Greenwood, Christopher: Is there a right of humanitarian intervention? *The World Today,* 49(2), February 1993, p. 40

11. As were respectively the cases of Somalia and Liberia. The intervention of ECOWAS in Liberia in 1990 was carried out without a mandate, but was given post-facto legitimacy by Security Council Resolution 788. In contrast to the above-mentioned interventions of the seventies (India in East Bengal in 1971, Tanzania in Uganda and Vietnam into Kampuchea in 1979), a declaration issued by the ECOWAS Heads of State and Government made clear that the peacekeeping force was sent with a humanitarian rationale, see UN Doc. S/ 21485, 9 August 1990. The Liberian case is a doubtful example since ECOWAS encountered the consent of all factions.

12. The US and British governments justify their unilateral campaign on the basis of the determination of a threat to international peace and security by the Security Council in a resolution. They indicated that they do not consider a UN mandate indispensable for the international military action, claiming that they still comply

with international, law.

13. See *British Year Book of International Law*, vol. 63, 1992, p. 827.

14. 37 Interview on *BBC Radio* 4, 19 August 1991.

15. The he interventions in Belgian Congo (1964) and in the Dominican Republic (1965) can either be more appropriately classified as interventions to protect nationals abroad, while the incursions of Vietnam into Kampuchea and Tanzania into Uganda (1979) were aimed primarily at other political ends. See Beyerlin in: Bernhardt (ed.) 1992, p. 926.

16. The scale of Iraq's violations of human rights had been extensively documented, the scope and purpose of the intervention were limited and the situation had been internationalised by the war to liberate Kuwait. See Greenwood 1993, p. 40. See also Beverlin in: Bernhardt (ed.) 1992, p. 931: "The circumstances under which the intervention took place were rather unique; thus, this isolated relief action cannot furnish evidence that humanitarian intervention may henceforth be considered as allowed under customary international law".

17. Ronzitti 1999, p. 52.

18. Guicherd 1999. For other adepts of this view, see Mayall, James: *The New interventionism 1991-1994: United Nations experience in Cambodia, Former Yugoslavia and Somalia,* Cambridge 1996, p. 1; Ipsen Knut: *Der Kosovo-Einsatz-Illegal? Gerechtfertigt? Entschuldbar?, Die Friedens-Warte,* 74 (1999) 1-2, p. 22 and Tomuschat, Christian: *Völkerrechthche Aspekte des Kosovo-Konflikts, Die Friedens-Warie,* 74 (1999) 1-2, p. 34.

19. For a comprehensive survey see: Abiew, Francis K.: Assessing humanitarian intervention in the post-Cold War period, *International Relations,* XIV (2), August 1998.

20. In the case of operations under UN command, the use of force is often not stipulated in original resolutions, but authorised later by supplementary mandates for the protection of humanitarian convoys and the civil population (rules of engagement).

21. Bouchet-Saulnier writes: "Cette troisième génération du maintien de la paix a jeté un lourd discredit sur l'ONU, et marqué un coup d'arrét au lancement d'interventions en faveur de la paix." Bouchet-Saulnier, Françoise: Maintien de la paix, in: *Dictionnaire pratique du droit humanitaire,* Paris 1998, p. 242.

22. Examples abound: Bettati lists 65 resolutions of the Security Council between April 1991 and December 1995 insisting that warring states should allow access to humanitarian organisations, urging parties to a conflict to refrain from obstructing humanitarian relief and demanding at times that they facilitate such relief. See Bettati Mario: *La droit d'ingerence,* Paris 1996, p. 329-340.

23. As Damrosch has noted, recent resolutions 'evidence a newly emerging consensus that the Security Council's enforcement powers may be invoked in purely domestic situations in Damrosch: *Changing conceptions of intervention in international law,* in: Reed and Kaysen (eds.): *Emerging Norms of Justified Intervention,* Cambridge, 1993, p. 105.

24. According to declarations of UN Secretary-General Boutros Ghali at the time when Resolution 794 was adopted, "no government exists in Somalia that could request and allow such use of force". (See UN Doc. S/24868). For its part, Resolution 770 was adopted several months after the Arbitration Commission established by the Peace Conference on Yugoslavia had determined that the Socialist Federal Republic of Yugoslavia (SFRY) was in the process of dissolution (Opinion n. 1 of the Badinter Commission, *International Law Reports* 162). See also Greenwood 1993, p. 38: "Although the conflict in what was the SFRY was originally perceived as a conflict within a state, the break-up of the SFRY meant that the conflict later became an international one. From that moment at least, the legal basis for outside intervention, whether by individual states or by the United Nations, no longer needed to rest on any theory of humanitarian intervention."

25. In principle, this argument tries once again to extract a norm from a non-codified practice, and if put to the test, it would hardly qualify as such. Further, it overlooks the fact that the codification of international concern for situations of extreme humanitarian distress either in the form of the Declaration of Human Rights, the Geneva Conventions or the Convention on Genocide or other international treaties, did not include any enforcement provisions. Simma indicates that international concern for these situations is not contrary to the respect for the Charter because the international

community can make use of countermeasures allowed for in the Charter in such cases. See Simma 1999, p. 1.

26. This argument is even used to support the idea that the non-interventions principle is based on customary law. See Ipsen, Knut: *Völkerrecht,* München 1999, p. 956.

27. See "War with Milosevic", *The Economist* 3rd April 1999, p. 18. Nevertheless, the rejection of the Resolution does not mean that the air raids received an 'implicit authorisation', as has been argued, since Russia and China explicitly opposed the war.

28. Ronzitti insinuates that a parallel could be drawn with the Tanzanian invasion of Uganda, which was condoned by the international community. See Ronzitti 1999, p. 51.

29. This resolution was later reaffirmed by another General Assembly Resolution 45/100 of 14 December 1990.

30. In contrast, the "Declaration on the Inadmissibility of Intervention in the Domestic Affairs of States and the Protection of their Independence and Sovereignty", General Assembly Resolution 2131 of 21 December 1965, although much older, displays a much more assertive language against the right of humanitarian intervention.

31. Bettati characterises this as an "hypocrisy" within international law: while the right of victims to assistance is recognised as part of customary international law, it is not possible to derive a right of states to bring this assistance by all means, including military force. See: Bettati 1996, p. 171.

International Political Entanglements and the Building of Political Institutions[1]

Llewellyn D. Howell
University of Hawaii, Manoa

George W. Bush has committed himself as a nation and institution builder. He campaigned in the Presidential election of 2000 as someone dead set against "nation building" as he saw it in Clinton and Gore terms. He regarded the use of US troops in Bosnia and Kosovo as being inappropriate for soldiers who are trained to fight, not place themselves in danger (and debt) simply to keep combatants apart while political institutions were being constructed. Institutions, in someone else's homeland, were someone else's responsibility.

As with many other policies after September 11, President Bush has made a 175 degree turn. It is the master challenge that he has undertaken in Afghanistan, trying to determine how to take tribes and factions that have fought and killed each other for centuries and make them into some Western leaning alternative to the Taliban. This is not simply rebuilding an institution but instead will be creating a particular democratic institution nearly from scratch.

But why not start with the most difficult? If the US is successful in Afghanistan, then others will be easy. And there are others. So many, in fact, that choosing *where* to expend resources on institution building rather than *whether* to expend them is the real issue.

With the Pol Pot government in Cambodia of the 1970s and early 1980s, the realist strategy of choosing the enemy of your enemy as your friend came back to bite us when Pol Pot slaughtered millions of his own countrymen while the US kept his seat warm at the United Nations—simply because he opposed the Vietnamese, our former enemy. So it has been with the Taliban. The US strongly supported the tribalist and fundamentalist factions fighting the Soviet army in Afghanistan in the 1980s. That support of radical and violent movements has now been turned on its head, with that training being used against the Afghan's former ally, the US.

The US government obviously still hasn't learned this lesson. Drawn from classic international politics (read Henry Kissinger for the modern version) the enemies of enemies friends equation directs itself at only the immediate and critical. The long term is set aside. We have made this same mistake again and again. Expediency has been the substitute for strategy, common ideology, and compatible culture in choosing our allies and in condoning their behavior. Beyond Pol Pot and the Mujahideen, we can recall readily, in the historical context, governments of Iran, Guatemala, Nicaragua, South Vietnam, Zaire, and many others that have fallen as a result of their own internal contradictions, despite strong US support (including 58,000 dead in

Vietnam), and America's reputation has fallen with them.

But now George Bush has a chance, in his new nation-building mode, to put all that right. He can easily see the handwriting on the wall that stems from where the US is today and change direction—not to accommodate the immediate but to repair the US position for the future. Before the situation becomes cataclysmic, the fundamentals of democratic political institutions can be joggled into place, more cheaply and with many fewer lives lost than with the repair function approach that the US has employed in the past.

Here are some nation building and institution building efforts President Bush should consider doing. These are not necessarily in order but recent events dictate some priorities.

Palestine: By all reckoning except that of the Israelis, there needs to be a Palestinian state. Despite other challenges to the existence of Israel that will almost inevitably come later, nothing can be settled in the Middle East until the Palestinians have a country of their own, with a sense of sovereignty that doesn't exist in a West Bank entity full of Israeli settlements. While Israel clearly has a right to exist, that right doesn't extend to an expanding list of settlements in the West Bank and Gaza. The US should throw its full weight behind ensuring the existence of Palestine and demanding that it be a democracy in the fullest sense. One of these won't work without the other.

Saudi Arabia: Many questions have been raised about how the Saudis have played the terrorist game and how they have funded the Wahabi version of Islam to groups that turned Islam against American interests. Except for our fear that Osama bin Laden's nation building effort in Saudi Arabia might result in an even more intolerant and abusive regime, any twenty-first century look at this government should tell us that it is incompatible with just about every notion of democratic, humanitarian, and integrationist behavior that we can count as necessary parts of a globalized society and economy. From one realist view it may be necessary to support them as a lesser evil but from another future-oriented realist view it may be time to shift away from upholding governments in the hands of families and individuals. In this age, how can an individual or a family own a country? Let's also take another look at the governments of Oman, Brunei and other sultanates that are anachronisms left over from the seventeenth, not the twentieth century. While temporary allies they may be, in the long run the lack of democratic institutions makes them all breeding grounds for resentment and far reaching violence.

Sub-Saharan Africa (name a country): Exactly why was it that the US didn't intervene in the slaughter in Rwanda but did intervene in Kosovo (on behalf of a Muslim but European population)? Since no chain is stronger than its weakest link, the global economy can't succeed until African turmoil is ended. That turmoil is based on the prevalence of tribal political systems and the absence of strong support for democratic institutions and governments. The US needs to be far more involved in what is happening in Africa than it ever has been. Given American history, no excuse for not being on the ground on that continent will get past charges of racism that have plagued the US since the beginning of the Cold War.

International Institutions: After September 11, George Bush decided that he needed the UN. After September 11, George Bush decided that international treaties on germ and chemical warfare are important enough for the US to at least be present in discussions of their pursuit. After September 11, George Bush decided that nuclear non-proliferation was important enough to back away from the reactionary positions of conservatives in Congress and begin to look for means of cooperation with the growing number of states who are similarly concerned but are in weak bargaining positions individually. After September 11, George Bush still needs to discover what interdependence means and to learn that negotiation involves give and take (and it's not they give and we take). Only under a system of global institutions will the roughly 200 nation-states contribute to international and domestic stability in a way that a US-dominated hierarchy cannot possibly command. To lead, the US should be shaping the nature and environment of global institutions rather than surreptitiously laying minefields before the inexorable movement toward international organization. This is where international leadership has meaning, not in commanding military might against rogue subcultures.

There is a reason for both national and international political structures that will serve as means of distribution and as a means of securing rights and protection in an increasingly crowded world. Some structures are better than others. Democracy does work and it's in our own interest to propagate it, with our deeds and not just our words…with our money, our peace keeping as well as fighting soldiers, our Peace Corps Volunteers, our diplomats, our investors, and our government's interest in proactively fixing—what we can—of what's wrong in the world.

Nothing will have been learned from the World Trade Center and Pentagon attacks unless we understand that past American behavior—and non-behavior in many cases—has set events in motion that have resulted in the position of the US today in having to deal with global terrorism without the whole-hearted support of many, and maybe most, countries. Helping to build nations and institutions instead of having to destroy them will be just as expensive as routing out terrorism but none of the costs will be as great as having to clean up in the aftermath of a nuclear explosive in the American homeland.

Note

1. This chapter is adapted and expanded from Llewellyn D. Howell, "Nation Building II," *USA Today Magazine*, Vol. 130, No. 2680, January 2002, p.29.

Nation-Building or Nation-Destroying?

Walker Connor
Middlebury College

Scholars associated with theories of "nation-building" have tended either to ignore the question of ethnic diversity or to treat the matter of ethnic identity superficially as merely one of a number of minor impediments to effective state-integration. To the degree that ethnic identity is given recognition, it is apt to be as a somewhat unimportant and ephemeral nuisance that will unquestionably give way to a common identity uniting all inhabitants of the state, regardless of ethnic heritage, as modern communication and transportation networks link the state's various parts more closely. Both tendencies are at sharp variance with the facts, and have contributed to the undue optimism that has characterized so much of the literature on "nation-building."

It is not difficult to substantiate the charge that the leading theoreticians of "nation-building" have tended to slight if not totally ignore, problems associated with ethnic diversity.... In order to be justified, such omissions must be occasioned either by the fact that most states are ethnically homogeneous or that ethnic diversity poses no serious problems to integration.

The former possibility is readily eliminated by reference to the actual ethnic composition of contemporary states. The remarkable lack of coincidence that exists between ethnic and political borders is indicated by the following statistics. Of a total of 132 contemporary states, only 12 (9.1 percent) can be described as essentially homogeneous from an ethnic viewpoint. An additional 25 states (18.9 percent of the sample) contain an ethnic group accounting for more than 90 per cent of the state's total population, and in still another 25 states the largest element accounts for between 75 and 89 percent of the population. But in 31 states (23.5 percent of the total), the largest ethnic element represents only 50 to 74 percent of the population, and in 39 cases (29.5 percent of all states) the largest group fails to account for even half of the state's population. Moreover, this portrait of ethnic diversity becomes more vivid when the number of distinct ethnic groups within states is considered. In some instances, the number of groups within a state runs into the hundreds, and in 53 states (40.2 percent of the total), the population is divided into more than five significant groups.[1] Clearly, then, the problem of ethnic diversity is far too ubiquitous to be ignored by the serious scholar of "nation-building," unless he subscribes to the position that ethnic diversity is not a matter for serious concern.

The validity of this position apparently also rests upon one of two propositions. Either loyalty to the ethnic group is self-evidently compatible with loyalty to the state, or, as mentioned earlier, ethnic identification will prove to be of short duration, withering away as modernization progresses. More consideration will be later given to the matter of the two loyalties (i.e., to the ethnic group and to the state), but clearly the two are naturally harmonious....

If the processes that comprise modernization led to a lessening of ethnic consciousness in favor of identification with the state, then the number of states troubled by ethnic disharmony would be on the decrease. To the contrary, however, a global survey illustrates that ethnic consciousness is definitely in the ascendency as a political force, and that state borders, as presently delimited, are being increasingly challenged by this trend.[2] And, what is of greater significance, multiethnic states at all levels of modernity have been afflicted. Particularly instructive in this regard is the large proportion of states within the technologically and economically advanced region of Western Europe that have recently been troubled by ethnic unrest. Examples include (1) the problems of Spain with the anti-Castilian activities of the Basques, the Catalans, and on a lesser level, the Galicians; (2) the animosity indicated by the Swiss toward foreign migrant workers, and the demands of the French-speaking peoples of Berne for political separation from the German-speaking element; (3) the South Tyroleans' dissatisfaction with Italian rule, currently muffled by recent concessions on the part of the Italian Government; (4) evidence of Breton unhappiness with continued French rule; (5) the resurgence of Scottish and Welsh nationalism, the conflict in Northern Ireland, and the wide-scale popularity of anti-immigrant sentiments epitomized in the figure of Enoch Powell—all within the United Kingdom; and (6) the bitter rivalry of the Walloon and Flemish peoples within Belgium. Outside of Europe, the challenge to the concept of a single Canada represented by the Franco-Canadian movements, and the existence of black separatist movements within the United States also bear testimony that even the combination of a lengthy history as a state and a high degree of technological and economic integration does not guarantee immunity against ethnic particularism.

That social mobilization need not lead to a transfer of primary allegiance from the ethnic group to the state is therefore clear. Can we go beyond this to posit an inverse correlation between modernization and the level of ethnic dissonance within multiethnic states? Admittedly, there is a danger of countering the assumption that the processes of modernization lead to cultural assimilation with an opposing iron law of political disintegration which contends that modernization results, of necessity, in increasing demands for ethnic separation. We still do not have sufficient data to justify such an unequivocal contention. Nonetheless, the substantial body of data which is available supports the proposition that material increases in what Deutsch termed social communication and mobilization *tend* to increase cultural awareness and to exacerbate interethnic conflict. Again, the large and growing number of ethnic separatist movements can be cited for substantiation.

There are many statesmen and scholars, however, who would protest this macroanalytical, approach because the data cited for support contain a number of former colonies. The inclusion of former dependencies in a list purporting to substantiate a correlation between modernization and ethnicity is improper, they would contend, because ethnic consciousness was deliberately kept alive and encouraged by the colonial overseers as an element in a policy of divide-and-rule. The prevalence of ethnic consciousness and antagonism in these territories is therefore held to be the product of the artificial stimuli of colonial policy. Otherwise, ethnicity would not constitute a serious problem for the new states....

Perhaps an even more important factor in explaining the recent upsurge of militant ethnic consciousness in advanced as well as less advanced states involves not the nature or density of the communications media, but the message. Although the expression "self-determination of nations" can be traced to 1865,[3] it did not receive great attention until its endorsement by a number of world-renowned statesmen during the World War I era. Not until after World War II was the doctrine officially endorsed by an organization aspiring to global jurisdiction.[4] It is therefore of very recent vintage. But despite its short history, it has been widely publicized and elevated to the status of a self-evident truth.

Still another element contributing to the upsurge in ethnic consciousness is the evident change in the global political environment, which makes it much more unlikely that a militarily weak polity will be annexed by a larger power. …

A summary of our findings thus far would consist of the following points. The preponderant number of states are multiethnic. Ethnic consciousness has been definitely increasing, not decreasing, in recent years. No particular classification of multiethnic states has proven immune to the fissiparous impact of ethnicity: authoritarian and democratic; federative and unitary; Asian, African, American, and European states have all been afflicted. Form of government and geography have clearly not been determinative. Nor has the level of economic development. But the accompaniments of economic development—increased social mobilization and communication—appear to have increased ethnic tensions and to be conducive to separatist demands. Despite all this, leading theoreticians of "nation-building" have tended to ignore or slight the problems associated with ethnicity.

If we turn to an analysis of the reasons for this wide gap between theory and reality, twelve overlapping and interrelated possibilities offer themselves.

(1) Confusing Interutilization of the Key Terms, Nation and State:

It may appear whimsical to *begin* with the often picayune matter of semantics. It is very doubtful however, that any discipline has been more plagued by the improper utilization of its key terms than has international relations. Anthropologists often bemoan the nebulosity underlying the concept of race—an ambiguity which has been reflected in many unscientific theories, which, in turn, have required time-consuming repudiations. But, though the concept of race is a matter of great significance to anthropology, it is not the key concept, that being *man*. By contrast, the concept of the state and of man's relationship to the state are at the heart of international relations. Yet, despite their key roles, both of these concepts are shrouded in ambiguity because of careless use of terms.

Consider first the concept of the state and the manner in which it is commonly treated as synonymous with the vastly different concept of the nation. The League of Nations, the United Nations, and, indeed, the expression *international relations* are but a few of the many available illustrations of the fact that statesmen and scholars are inclined to the indiscriminate interuse of the two concepts.[5] Why this confusion in terminology has been perpetuated is difficult to explain, for authorities are certainly well aware of the distinctions between the state and the nation. Thus, a dictionary designed for the student of global politics defines the state as "a legal concept describing a social group that occupies a defined territory and is organized under common political institutions and an effective government."[6] By contrast, a nation is defined as "a social group which shares a common ideology, common institutions and customs, and a sense of homogeneity." It carefully adds: "A nation may comprise part of a state, be coterminous with a state, or extend beyond the borders of a single state." Writers of textbooks and monographs in international relations generally also detail these same distinctions between state and nation. Unfortunately, however, these same writers are then apt to revert to the indiscriminate interutilization of the two terms.[7]

It is probable that the tendency to equate the two expressions developed as alternative shorthand substitutes for the hyphenate, *nation-state*. This term is also supposed to have a precise meaning, referring to a situation in which the borders of the nation approximate those of the state. We have noted that, technically speaking, less than 10 per cent of all states would qualify as essentially homogeneous. But authorities nevertheless tend to refer to all states as nation-states[8].

The definitions of state and nation quoted above make clear that what we have thus far been calling self-differentiating ethnic groups are in fact nations. Loyalty to the ethnic group, therefore, should logically be called nationalism. But nationalism, as commonly employed, refers to loyalty to the state (or to the word *nation,* when the latter has been incorrectly substituted for state).[9] Thus, the same dictionary whose precise definitions of state and nation we have just cited defines *nationalism* as a mass emotion that "makes the *state* the ultimate focus of the individual's loyalty." (Emphasis added.) With the term *nationalism* thus preempted, scholars have felt compelled to offer a substitute to describe loyalty to the nation. Regionalism, parochialism, primordialism, communalism, ethnic complementarity, and tribalism are among those that have been advanced. Unfortunately, however, the perpetuation of the improper use of the word *nationalism* to refer to devotion to the state, while using other terms with different roots and with fundamentally different connotations to denote devotion to the nation, is hardly conducive to dissolving the confusion surrounding the two loyalties.[10] On the contrary, it is conducive to dangerously underestimating the magnetism and the staying power of ethnic identity, for those terms simply do not convey the aura of deeply felt, emotional commitment that *nationalism* does. Every schoolboy is made aware, for example, that the German and Celtic tribes of antiquity became obliterated in a higher identity; that regionalism within the United States or Germany has steadily receded in significance. By contrast with these vanquished forces, the schoolboy learns that nationalism is a vibrant force that has largely shaped the direction of global politics for the past two hundred years. But since *nationalism* is equated with loyalty to the state, the student has been preconditioned to perceive the state as the certain ultimate victor in any test of loyalties with these lower-form anachronisms that have been proven to be ephemeral.

If the nation-state were in fact the universal form of polity, the confusion would not be important. In those cases in which, the nation and the state essentially coincide, the two loyalties mesh rather than compete. A common pitfall of scholarship, however, has been to equate the resulting emotional attachment to a nation-state with loyalty to the state alone. The study of nationalism in the late twentieth century has been heavily influenced by the experiences of Germany and Japan, perceived as illustrations of the extreme dedication that nationalism is able to evoke. The implication is that other states have the potential for evoking the same type of mass response, though, it is to be hoped, in a less fanatical form. Largely ignored is the fact that these two states are among the very few that are ethnically homogeneous.[11] As such, *Deutschland* and *Nippon)* have been something far more profound to their populations than mere territorial-political units called states; they have been ethno-psychological inclinations called nations. To perceive German or Japanese, nationalism as loyalty to the state is to miss the mark badly. It is also to distort beyond recognition the power to evoke loyalty to the to the state in the absence of a linking of state and nation in the popular psyche. With that linkage, the leaders can voice their appeals in terms of the state *(Deutschland)* or the nation *(volksdeutsch, Volkstum, Volksgenosse),* because the two trigger the same associations. The same is true for members of the politically dominant group in some multiethnic states. Thus, the Han Chinese are apt to view the state of China as the state of their particular nation, and are therefore susceptible to appeals in the name of China or in the name of the Han Chinese people. But the notion of *China* evokes quite different associations, and therefore quite different response, from Tibetans, Mongols, Uighurs, and other non-Han people. The confusing use of terminology has diverted scholars for some time from asking the key question: How many examples come to mind of a strong "state-nationalism" being manifested among a people who perceive their state and their nation as distinct entities?

The likelihood of contemporary scholars being diverted from the posing of this question would have been greatly reduced had the misnomer, "nation-building," not been adopted. Since most of the less developed states contain a number of nations, and since the transfer of primary allegiance from these nations to the state is generally considered the *sine qua non* of successful integration, the true goal is not "nation-building" but "nation-destroying." Would scholars have been less sanguine concerning the chances of success if proper terminology had been employed?...

(2) A Misunderstanding of the Nature of Ethnic Nationalism and a Resulting Tendency to Underrate Its Emotional Power:

In its broadest implications, this reason for the failure of authorities to pay proper heed to ethnicity is the end product of all other reasons. If so understood, it is a statement of the problem rather than an explanation. However, as used here, it is intended to point to the tendency of scholars to perceive ethnic nationalism in terms of its overt manifestations rather than in terms of its essence. The essence of the nation is not tangible. It is psychological, a matter of attitude rather than of fact....

Because the essence of the nation is a matter of attitude, the tangible manifestations of cultural distinctiveness are significant only to the degree that they contribute to the *sense* of uniqueness. Indeed, a sense of vital uniqueness can come about even in the absence of important, tangible cultural characteristics of a distinctive nature, as evidenced by the ethnopsychological experience of the American colonists, the Afrikaners, and the Taiwanese with regard to their former British, Dutch, and Han Chinese identities. Conversely, the concept of a single nation can transcend tangible cultural distinctions, such as the Catholic-Lutheran division within the German nation[12]....

The abstract essence of ethnic nationalism is often not perceived by the observer. There is an understandable propensity, when investigating a case of ethnic discord, to perceive the struggle in terms of its more readily discernible features. Thus, Ukrainian unrest is popularly reported as an attempt to preserve the Ukrainian language against Russian inroads; Belgium's major problem is also viewed as essentially linguistic; the Ethiopian-Eritrean, as well as the Northern Ireland conflict, is seen as religious; the Czecho-Slovak, the West Pakistani-Bengali, and the Serbo-Croatian disputes are characterized as essentially matters of economic differentiation. Linguistic, religious, and economic distinctions between peoples are all easily discerned and, what is of at least equal moment, are easily conveyed to one's audience....

As a result of the tendency for both participant and reporter to describe ethnopsychological phenomena in terms of tangible considerations, the true nature and power of ethnic feelings are not probed. Indeed, in many cases analysts fail to realize they are dealing with ethnic nationalism. Northern Ireland offers a contemporary case in point....

Unfortunately, the survey failed to correlate national identity with the religion of the respondents, but it is safe to assume, on the basis of the ethnic and religious histories of the island, that there exists a close correlation between self-identification as Irish and adherents to Catholicism.[13] The important distinction, however, lies between those who consider themselves Irish, and those who either do not so consider themselves or are not so considered by the bulk of the Irish element. That the religious issue is largely extraneous helps to account for the fact that the consistent urging of tolerance by all but a handful of religious leaders has gone unheeded.[14] Indeed, with at least as much accuracy, the conflict could be described as one of surnames rather than religions. Despite some intermarriage, the family name remains a relatively reliable index to Irish heritage, as compared to English or Scottish.[15] It is for this reason that a surname is apt to trigger either a negative or positive response. One tragic manifestation of this phenomenon has been the tendency of militant Irishmen (described as Catholics) to be particularly aggressive toward Scottish units of the British forces sent from the island of Great Britain, because of the preponderance of Scottish names among Northern Ireland's non-Irish population.[16] In popular Irish perception, their local enemies and the Scottish troops are linked in their common foreignness and Scottishness....

In summary, ethnic strife is too often superficially discerned as principally predicated upon language, religion, customs, economic inequity, or some other tangible element. But what is fundamentally involved in such a conflict is that divergence of basic identity which manifests itself in the "us—them" syndrome. And the ultimate answer to the question of whether a person is one of us, or one of them, seldom hinges on adherence to overt aspects of culture....

(3) An Unwarranted Exaggeration of the Influence of Materialism upon Human Affairs:

A number of authorities have noted a propensity on the part of American statesmen and scholars of the post-World War II era to assume that economic considerations represent the determining force in human affairs. Programs of foreign assistance, for example, have been promoted and defended on the ground that the economic status of a state correlates directly with its form of government, political stability, and aggressiveness.[17] Policy-makers in the United States have also attempted to defuse a number of highly charged interstate (and interethnic) conflicts by making cooperation between the adversaries a condition of material recompense (for example, the Jordan, Indus, and Mekong River projects). The Marshall Plan, Point Four, the Eisenhower Doctrine, and the Alliance for Progress could all be interpreted as attempts to alter attitudes by appealing to material self-interest.

This presumption—that economic considerations constitute the primary force which shapes the basic ideas and attitudes of man—has had an evident impact upon much of the literature concerned with political integration. An ethnic minority, it is implicitly or explicitly held, will not secede from a state if its living standards are improving, both in real terms and relative to other segments of the state's population.[18] Such a prognosis again underestimates the power of ethnic feelings and ignores contrary evidence: With regard to the matter of economic inequity among groups, for example, there are a number of cases in which the ethnic consciousness of a minority and its animosity toward the dominant element became accentuated although the income gap between the group and the dominant element was being rapidly closed.... But economic factors are likely to come in a poor second when competing with the emotionalism of ethnic nationalism. Numerous colonial ties were severed irrespective of whether or not they were economically beneficial to the colonial people. Separatists (whether Anguillan, Eritrean, Naga, or Welsh) are not apt to be dissuaded by the assertion that the nation is too small to comprise an economically viable unit. There is a simple, yet profound message of the broadest applicability in the slogan, "Better a government run like hell by Filipinos than one run like heaven by Americans."

(4) Unquestioned Acceptance of the Assumption that Greater Contacts Among Groups Lead to Greater Awareness of What Groups have in Common, Rather than of What Makes them Distinct:

A number of authorities have also noted that American foreign policy is heavily influenced by an optimistic view of human affairs in which man is seen as essentially rational and possessed of good will, and therefore preordained to find reasonable answers to problems.[19] As applied to ethnicity, this optimism is manifest in the conviction that misunderstandings among nations are due to lack of knowledge concerning each other. Greater contacts, it would follow, should lead to greater understanding and harmony. One manifestation of this belief is the person-to-person diplomacy that forms the rationale of the Peace Corps and official sanctioning of massive cultural and educational exchange programs. It is also evident in the lack of official concern that the presence of large numbers of Americans in a foreign state is apt to trigger a xenophobic response.[20] This view also probably helps to account for the slighting of ethnicity in works dealing with political integration. If greater contacts, brought about by more intensive communication and transportation networks, promote harmony, ethnic heterogeneity is not a matter worthy of serious consideration....

(5) Improper Analogizing from the Experience of the United States:

Many works on political integration contain direct reference to the successful assimilationist history of the United States as evidence that the basic identity of people can be rather easily transferred from the ethnic group to a larger grouping coterminous with the state.[21] It is probable, moreover, that the "melting pot" idea has had an unarticulated influence upon much larger numbers. If broad-scale assimilation could occur within the United States, practically without design, why not elsewhere? If an extremely diverse ethnic hodgepodge became quite naturally a single American nation, one may well expect the same process to occur quite naturally elsewhere. The analogy is a dangerous one, however....

In sum, then, analogies drawn from the experience of the United States are apt to be specious. A proportionately small number of people who have voluntarily left their cultural milieu to enter an alien politico-cultural environment in which cultural assimilation is perceived positively as indispensable to success is one thing; a situation characterized by two or more large groups, each ensconced in a territory it considers its traditional homeland and cultural preserve is something quite different. The second situation characterizes the overwhelming number of ethnic struggles.

(6) Improper Analogizing from the Fact that Increases in Communications and Transportation Help to Dissolve Cultural Distinctions Among Regions within what is Fundamentally a One-culture State, to the Conclusion that the Same Process Will Occur in Situations Involving Two or More Distinct Cultures:

...If one is dealing not with variations of a single culture-group, but with distinct and self-differentiating culture groups, then increased contacts, as we have noted, tend to produce disharmony rather than harmony. Discord between the Basques and Castilians, the Czechs and Slovaks, the Russians and Ukrainians, the Walloons and Flemish, the Welsh and English, the French-speaking and English-speaking Canadians, and the Serbs and Croats has increased with increased contacts. The same development has been noted in the case of Thailand and of Ethiopia. Increased contacts tend to have one impact in a one-culture situation, and quite a different impact in a variegated culture area.[22]

(7) The Assumption that Assimilation is a One-directional Process:

If assimilation is assumed to be irreversible, then any evidence of a move toward assimilation becomes an irrevocable gain and a basis for optimism. Thus, because the Scottish and Welsh people had undergone generations of acculturation, including almost total linguistic assimilation, and because the concept of a British national identity did indeed possess an important measure of meaning to the preponderant numbers of Scots and Welshmen, authorities were for years almost unanimous in their conviction that homogeneity of identity had once and for all been achieved.[23] The sudden upsurge in Scottish and Welsh nationalism during the 1960's illustrates, however, that assimilation may indeed be reversed so long as some glimmer of a separate ethnic identity persists.

(8) Interpretation of the Absence of Ethnic Strife as Evidence of the Presence of a Single Nation:

The existence of a single national consciousness that is shared by all segments of the population of a state *cannot* be deduced simply from the absence of overt ethnic conflict. Such a conclusion is always dangerous, for, just as the fervor with which ethnic nationalism is embraced and the form in which it is manifested can vary substantially among individuals, so too, can it fluctuate widely within a particular nation over time. Few would contend that German nationalism is dead, although it is obviously more subdued, and following different channels, than was the case in the 1930's. Periods in which nationalism takes on more passive forms may be followed by periods of militant nationalism and vice versa. In addition, the bilateral relations between ethnic groups, just as those between states, vary greatly. They may range along a continuum from a genocidal relationship to a symbiotic one....

The error of misconstruing the absence of strife between ethnic groups as indicative of national unity has not been restricted to peaceful situations. Another common pitfall has been to impute a single national consciousness to militant movements whose ranks include members of different ethnic groups. Ethnic consciousness is not an automatic bar to cooperative, nor even to coordinated or integrated, activities against a mutually perceived enemy or in pursuit of a mutually desired goal....

The tendency to see ethnic unity in the absence of overt ethnic discord has had an important impact upon theories of "nation-building."...A second outgrowth of this tendency is to view outbreaks of ethnic nationalism on an *ad hoc* basis rather than as only one contemporary manifestation of a more enduring global phenomenon. An outbreak of ethnic hostilities in Malaysia, in Jamaica, in Burundi, in Spain, or in Canada is viewed as an isolated phenomenon, soon forgotten by most outside observers after a more peaceful relationship has been reinstituted. The ubiquity and significance of ethnic nationalism are therefore not fully appreciated.

(9) Improper Regard for the Factor of Chronological Time and Intervening Events When Analogizing from Assimilationist Experiences Prior to "The Age of Nationalism":

In emphasizing the manner in which the nations of Western Europe and Eastern Asia were created from rather disparate ethnic materials, authorities have failed to consider that the fact that the models predate the nineteenth century may obviate their pertinence to the current scene. No examples of significant assimilation are offered which have taken place since the advent of the age of nationalism and the propagation of the principle of self-determination of nations.

By and large, those peoples who, prior to the nineteenth century, were seduced by the blandishments of another culture—those who became "them"—were not aware of belonging to a separate culture-group with its own proud traditions and myths. There was no keen competition for group allegiance. By contrast, peoples today are everywhere much more apt to be cognizant of their membership in a group with its own mythical genesis, its own customs and beliefs, and perhaps its own language, which *in toto* differentiate the group from all others and permit the typical individual to answer intuitively and unequivocally the question, "What are you?" The spontaneous response, "I am Luo" rather than Kenyan, or "Bengali" rather than Pakistani, does not bode well for the architect of a nation-state.

As we have noted, there are numerous reasons for this increase in ethnic consciousness since the early nineteenth century, among them the great increase in the frequency, scope, and type of interethnic and intraethnic group contacts. At least in terms of "assimilationist time" (the time required to produce full assimilation), the radio, telephone, train, motor vehicle, and aircraft are recent innovations, postdating the advent of the age of nationalism and its standard of ethnicity as the basis of political legitimacy....

(10) Improper Regard for Durative Time by Failing to Consider that Attempts to Telescope "Assimilationist Time," by Increasing the Frequency and Scope of Contacts, may Produce a Negative Response:

If the matter of chronological time could be overcome, there would remain the matter of durative time. As indicated by the resurgence of Scottish nationalism, the total assimilation of a large people predominating in a particular territory requires a period of long duration extending over several generations. To be successful, the process of assimilation must be a very gradual one, one that progresses almost without visibility and awareness.[24] Since the essence of national identity is psychological and involves self-acceptance, a greater intensity of contacts, whether by accident or design, will conceivably not only fail to speed up the process, but will prove to be counterproductive....

This relationship of assimilation to durative time casts serious doubt on whether the process of assimilation is subjectable to social engineering. Planning is more geared to action than to inaction, and more to a time span of one generation or less than to a multigenerational period. More important, however, is the fact that modernization largely dictates its own timetable. There is an inbuilt accelerator in the technological advances and other forces that causes a continuous "shrinking of the world" and the shrinking of its states as presently defined. The frequency and pervasiveness of intergroup contacts appear, therefore, to be fated to increase exponentially, regardless of the desire of the planner.

(11) Confusing Symptoms with Causes:

Most of the theoretic writings on political integration, as noted earlier, have been characterized by an unwarranted degree of optimism. But as the newly formed states proved less cohesive than had been anticipated, explanations for their political disintegration have become increasingly common. Many of these explanations, however, confuse some of the symptoms and minor contributing elements of political decay with its primary cause....

The prime cause of political disunity is the absence of a single psychological focus shared by all segments of the population. Admittedly, ethnic homogeneity is not in itself sufficient to guarantee such a consensus. The intraethnic Vietnamese struggle illustrates this point. But in the case of the multiethnic state, we have noted that, for most of the inhabitants, primary identity will not extend beyond the ethnic group. And all but a handful of the new states are multiethnic....

It bears repeating that ethnic homogeneity is not by itself sufficient to guarantee a bond of unity so infrangible that it can withstand any and all fissiparous forces. The impact of institutions, economic opportunities, geography, literacy, urbanization, and a host of other factors may therefore be very germane to the study of the components of an efficacious identity. But the experience of multiethnic states, past and present, strongly suggests that the ethnic nation may well constitute the outer limits of that identity. If there are means of transferring primary identification and allegiance from the nation to the state, or if there are ways of satisfying national aspirations within a multiethnic state, these possibilities should certainly be explored. But the potent fissiparous force of ethnic particularism should not be obscured by ascribing its role of prime mover to its symptoms.

(12) The Predispositions of the Analyst:

The last in this list of possible contributing factors to the broadscale underassessment of the ramifications of ethnic nationalism is the most difficult to document: it involves the influence that the ideals of the analyst exert upon his perception. Given the multitude of overt manifestations of ethnic nationalism throughout Africa and Asia (as well as elsewhere), it is difficult to reconcile its total absence or cursory treatment in so many studies on development....

*This article is an expanded version of a paper presented at the Seventh World Congress of the International Sociological Association, held at Varna, Bulgaria, in September 1970.

Notes

1. The 132 units include all entities that were generally considered to be states as of January 1, 1971, with the exception of a few microunits such as Nauru and Western Samoa. However, East and West Germany, North and South Korea, and North and South Vietnam were treated as single entities in the belief that such treatment would minimize their distorting effects. It should not be assumed that the inclusion of all microunits would substantially alter the statistics in favor of homogencity. In the case of Nauru, for example, despite a population of only 6,500 the largest ethnic element fails to constitute a majority.

2. For a treatment of this trend as a global phenomenon, see Connor, "Self-Determination: The New Phase," *World Politics,* xx (October 1967), 30-53.

3. The expression appeared as part of the Proclamation on the Polish Question, endorsed by the London Conference of the First International. The Proclamation noted "the need for annulling Russian influence in Europe, through enforcing the right of self-determination, and through the reconstituting of Poland upon democratic and social foundations." Cited in G. Stelkioff, *History of the First International* (New York 1968), 85. For a reference to a still earlier use of the expression by Karl Marx in his *Herr Vogt* (1860), see Stefan Possony, "Nationalism and the Ethnic Factor," *Orbis,* x (Winter 1967), 1218.

4. United Nations Charter, art. I, par. 2.

5 *The Worldmark Encyclopedia of the Nations,* 3d ed., I (New York 1967), 254-57, lists fifty intergovernmental organizations whose names begin with *International.* Not one of them has anything to do with nations.

6. Jack C. Piano and Roy Olton, *The International Relations Dictionary* (New York 1969).

7. See, for example, A.F.K. Organski, *World Politics* (2d rev. ed., New York 1968), 12: "The story we are about to tell is a tale of nations. Nations are the major characters, and it is with their actions, their goals and plans, their power, their possessions, and their relations with each other that we shall be concerned." See also Deutsch (fn. 14), where, despite defining the word nation to mean a people (i.e., an ethnic group) in charge of a state (p. 19), the author refers to the multiethnic populations of Spain (p. 13), and of Belgium (p. 70), as nations. See, too, the concluding paragraph of Dankwart Rustow, *A World of Nations* (Washington 1967) in which he notes that "more than 130 nations, real or so-called, will each make its contribution to the history of the late twentieth century." The author had earlier (e.g., p. 36) differentiated between state and nation. For evidence that studies dealing specifically with the problems that ethnic diversity poses for state integration are also not necessarily immune from improper interuse of terminology, see Donald Rothchild, "Ethnicity and Conflict Resolution," *World Politics,* xxii (Tuly 1970), particularly 597-98. "First, in spite of the oft-used distinction between a fairly coercive domestic order and a fairly noncoercive international order, the jockeying for power of ethnic groups within states corresponds markedly to that of *nation* and *nation*.... New and more productive 'decades of development,' with their presumed attempts at re-allocation, may be as indispensable to the comity among ethnic groups within the state as they are among the *nations* of the world." (Emphasis added.) Examples abound of this tendency to use key terms improperly, so the authorities who are singled out in this and the following footnotes are *not* selected because they have been unusually uncircumspect in their terminology. On the contrary, they have been selected, in part, because they are acknowledged scholars.

8. See for example Norman J. Paddleford and George A. Lincoln, *The Dynamics of International Politics* (2d ed., New York 1967), 7: "The actors in the international political system are the independent nation-states." Or Louis J. Halle, *Civilization and Foreign Policy* (New York 1952), 10: "A prime fact about the world is that it is largely composed of nation-states." And Elton Atwater and others, *World Tensions: Conflict and Accommodation* (New York 1967), 16: "Since there are some 120 different nation-states in the world..." Karl Deutsch also regularly

refers to all states as nation-states. See, for example, *Nationalism and Its Alternatives* (fn. 14), 61, 125, and 176. For his description of the multiethnic states of Czechoslovakia, Rumania, and Yugoslavia as nation-states, see 62-63.

9. Meanwhile, expressions such as *statism* or *étatisme*, which should refer to loyalty to the state, have been assigned still other meanings that have little to do with loyalty of any sort.

10. See, for example, the section in Edward Shils, *Political Development in the New States* (The Hague 1968), entitled "Parochialism, Nationality, and Nationalism," 32-33. As used therein, parochialism refers to loyalty to the ethnic group, and nationality and nationalism refer to identity with, and loyalty to, the state.

11. One manifestation has been the grouping of the *nationalism* of Japan and Germany during the 1930's and early 1940's with that of Italy and of multiethnic Argentina and Spain under the single rubric of Fascism, a doctrine positing the superiority of the corporate state.

12. Since the concept of the nation does not preclude significant internal divisions, it actually embodies two important levels of attitudes. Relative to *intranational* distinctions and similarities, the stress, when need be, is upon those traits that unite; relative to distinctions and similarities among nations, the ultimate stress is upon those that divide.

13. The religious composition is 35 percent Catholic, 29 per cent Presbyterian (Church of Scotland), 24 percent Episcopal (Church of England), 10 per cent other Protestant, and 2 per cent other. *Ibid.*, 13.

14. See the *New York Times*, January 24, 1971, for an account of a protest demonstration by Belfast women before a Catholic Bishop's house because he had given a sermon advising Catholics not to have anything to do with the outlawed Irish Republican Army.

Evidence that the basic driving force of Irish militancy has been not simply the desire for civil reform is offered by the fact that reforms promoted by the moderate government of Chichester-Clark were followed by greater militancy on the part of the Irish element.

15. "A notable exception is Terrence O'Neill, the former, moderate Prime Minister. An awareness within Northern Ireland's political community that strong emotions are often associated with surnames caused his colleagues to presume that his name would prove a real asset in gaining the respect and trust of the Irish minority.

16. See the *New York Times*, April 30, 1970. See also the *New York Times* of two days earlier, where it was reported that order was restored in Belfast only after Scottish troops were replaced by English troops.

As is evident from the above-mentioned survey on national identification, the term Scotch-Irish is a misleading ethnic description. It simply refers to people whose Scottish ancestors emigrated to Ireland, but it need not indicate any Irish ancestry

17. For descriptions of this tendency, see Hans Morgenthau, "The American Tradition in Foreign Policy," in Roy C. Macridis, ed., *Foreign Policy in World Politics* (3d ed., Englewood Cliffs 1967), 254, and Stanley Hoffman, *Gulliver's Troubles in the Setting of American Foreign Policy* (New York 1968), 120-21.

18. As noted earlier, Karl Deutsch explicitly held this opinion in 1961.

19. Particularly significant for the present discussion is the comment of Gabriel Almond: "This overt optimism is so compulsive an element in the American culture that factors which threaten it, such as failure... are pressed from the focus of attention and handled in perfunctory ways." *The American People and Foreign Policy* (New York 1961), 50-51. See also Frederick Hartman, *The New Age of American Foreign Policy* (New York 1970), 58.

20. Contrast, for example, the American practice of encouraging huge numbers of American troops to furlough in Bangkok, to the Soviet practice of minimizing the Russian presence in such states as the United Arab Republic. For a discussion of the impact of a foreign presence upon a guerrilla struggle, and the sharp contrast in awareness of this impact between the United States on the one hand, and China, the Soviet Union, and North Vietnam on the other, see Connor (fn. 25), 51-86

21. See, for example, Karl Deutsch's comment, cited above on p. 322.

22. This inverse relationship causes the use of the term *regionalism* to be a particularly dangerous and inappropriate substitute for *ethnic nationalism.*

23. Richard Rose is among those authorities. In 1964 he observed that "today politics in the United Kingdom is greatly simplified by the absence of major cleavages along the lines of ethnic groups, Language, or religion.... The solidarity of the United Kingdom today may be due to fortuitous historical circumstances; it is nonetheless real and important." *Politics in England* (Boston 1964), 10 and 11. But by 1970, the situation had changed so drastically that Professor Rose entitled a work *The United Kingdom as a Multi-National State* (fn. 41). On page 1, Rose lists L.S. Amery, Samuel Beers, Harry Eckstein, Jean Blondel, and S.E. Finer as recent Writers who have failed to detect the potential significance of ethnic divisions within the United Kingdom. These men were hardly unique in their failure to anticipate the great change in attitude about to manifest itself in Scotland and Wales. See, for example, Connor (fn. 20), 39n., in which this author acknowledged but underestimated the imminent power of the Scottish nationalist idea. See, also, J.D. Mackie, A *History of Scotland* (Baltimore 1964), 367-70, in which a scholar also fails to appreciate the submerged but emerging power of Scottishness among his own people.

24. This statement presupposes that the government is not prepared to take such extreme measures as coercive population transfers and forced intermarriages.

Revisiting "Nation-Building"

Allan Gerson
George Washington University and

Nat J. Colletta
George Washington University

Writing in the *New York Times* on February 13, 2001, syndicated columnist Tom Friedman put in perspective what has become increasingly clear to many policymakers: "Nation-building—helping others restructure their economies and put in place decent non-corrupt governments"—must, he contended, be a cornerstone of US foreign policy. To be sure, there is still little bipartisan consensus on the issue. However there is little doubt that the concept's vitality has been resurrected since the debacle in Somalia.

Much of the current thinking on "nation building" and the role of international organizations stems from the 1992 *Agenda for Peace,*[1] the landmark study by former UN Secretary-General Boutros Boutros-Ghali. The *Agenda* contends that the United Nations needs to transform itself—to go beyond the traditional missions of peace enforcement and peace-keeping. State failures, characterized by crumbling or abandoned democratic structures and the regression of economic self-sufficiency, have, according to the *Agenda,* been compounded by ethnic and tribal war. "Nation-building" is propounded to meet the underlying grievances that propel civil conflict. Despite its recent bad name in U.S. policy debates, the aim of nation-building is unassailable: to stop the unrest, and then to promote the rule of law and good governance. So too is the conclusion that nation-building may not be possible without the restoration of security through international peace enforcement, more heavily armed than traditional peacekeepers and authorized to use force in cases where "[c]ease fires have...been agreed to but not complied with."[2]

In advocating expansion of the UN's security role, the *Agenda for Peace* was treading on soil entirely new to the UN experience. Though peace enforcement is the only military role explicitly authorized by its 1945 Charter, the UN's role first expanded to encompass a complex form of peacekeeping in response to the 1962 Congo crisis, an intervention supported by the United States. Despite Soviet objections, the right of the UN to perform this function was endorsed by the International Court of Justice in the *Certain Expenses of the United Nations* case.[3] Peacekeeping—even where a force is authorized by the General Assembly, rather than the Security Council—was justified as a legitimate UN activity insofar as it was tied to the Charter goal of maintaining international peace and security. In the view of the Court, the Security Council retained a *primary* but not exclusive responsibility in that area.

By contrast, "nation-building" has never received similar judicial endorsement. To be sure, various UN agencies like UNDP and UNICEF have always operated in the nebulous zone between humanitarian assistance and development, working to assist movements toward democracy and good governance. This is a part of "nation-building." But as contemplated by Boutros-Ghali, "nation-building" encompasses the deployment of international troops to support national transformations. The disastrous results of the UN intervention in Somalia in 1993 led, however, to American disillusionment and then hostility to the concept. The subsequent failure, at enormous cost, of UN nation-building efforts in Cambodia further shook the confidence of key states at the United Nations. Rather suddenly, the very term "nation-building" took on a somewhat odious air, and Boutros Boutros-Ghali, as its chief proponent, became the object of a concerted campaign by the United States and others to defeat his bid for reappointment.

Yet, at about the same time, and with far less fanfare, "nation-building" was gaining a more receptive welcome at the World Bank. Although criticism of local governance had been considered off limits for the Bank over the years, as a consequence of internal legal opinions reading its mandate as reaching only purely economic matters, increasingly the Bank came to realize that it could ill afford to take such a narrow view. It seemed myopic to ignore the political context when lending monies or engaging in project support in war-torn regions. Failure to promote good governance, in situations where the opportunity presented itself, seemed at odds with poverty alleviation. Accordingly, the Bank's December 2000 policy on Development Cooperation and Conflict stipulates: "The Bank recognizes that economic and social stability and human security are preconditions for sustainable development." The military security concerns of peacekeeping are now giving way to a broader definition of security, that is, "human security," which (more sympathetic to "nation-building") includes the protection of human rights and economic well-being as well as physical well-being. It also includes environmental security, justice under the rule of law, and development through its focus on poverty alleviation as an instrument of conflict prevention.

In 1992, the opportunity for readjustment of institutional inhibitions arose in two important areas—demilitarization in Africa, and peacemaking in Central America. The World Bank's entry into demilitarization, although outwardly responding to public expenditure concerns, particularly the imbalance in defense expenditure vis-à-vis social and productive investments, was based on a political calculation beyond its traditional reliance on purely macroeconomic factors. Understanding that idle standing forces in countries prone to war may serve to provide additional spurs for war, the World Bank—operating through its Africa Bureau, rather than any centralized initiative—undertook the difficult and novel task of devising incentives for demobilization in Uganda. Uganda's leadership had to be convinced to accept demobilization, fearing that it would be destabilizing to leave thousands of former soldiers restless and unemployed, ready to join anti-government militias. Demobilization required that the Bank promote the reintegration of ex-combatants through retraining and provision of land and employment opportunities. The initiative was successful, and a harbinger of others to come with full World Bank approval.[4]

Yet earlier the Bank did not innovate as well in its other "political" engagement of 1992, the implementation of the El Salvador Peace Accords. The Accords called for joint UN-World Bank efforts aimed at far-reaching political, social and economic reforms, including a rigorous economic stabilization and structural adjustment program, and demilitarization and reintegration of ex-combatants. Despite its formal collaboration with the United Nations, the World Bank in fact took no part in demilitarization efforts and restricted its efforts to purely macroeconomic matters. The results, as characterized by two distinguished commentators, "was as if a patient lay on the operating table with the left and right sides of his body separated by a curtain and unrelated surgery being performed on each side."[5] Still, it would plant the seeds for the Bank's more successful cooperation with the UN half a decade later in Bosnia, Kosovo and East Timor.

In 1995 James Wolfensohn ascended to the presidency of the World Bank, and with that came a strong new voice for engagement in the "political" arena. A small but significant outpost, the Post Conflict Unit, was established under the leadership of the former head of Africa War-to-Peace Transition Team, Nat J. Colletta and assigned to handle overall coordination of World Bank engagement in war-to-peace transitions. The search for "partnering" with various United Nations agencies began. Kofi Annan on behalf of the United Nations and James Wolfensohn on behalf of the World Bank realized they would be better positioned to deliver a stabilizing "peace dividend" to leaders opting for settlement of their armed conflicts if they worked together. As described by Secretary-General Kofi Annan in his Millennium Report, this new-found joint commitment means that "[c]onflict prevention, post conflict peace building, humanitarian assistance and development policies need to become more effectively integrated."[6] Provision of employment and economic opportunities thus came to be viewed as pivotal to peacemaking, and active participation by private enterprise as its indispensable component.[7]

Notes

1. *An Agenda for Peace: Preventive Diplomacy, Peacemaking and Peacekeeping,* U.N. Doc. A/47/277 and S/24111 (Jun. 17, 1992), para. 22.

2. *Ibid.,* para. 44. On continuing implications for international organizations of Boutros-Ghali's pioneering suggestions, see J. Stremlau & F. Sagasti, *supra* note 25, ch. 1.1 ("Boutros-Ghali's readiness to acknowledge that the problems of governance are also a general and legitimate concern of the UN marked a significant departure for an intergovernmental organization. The nature and policy implications of this challenge for the UN and other international institutions—including the World Bank—will be difficult to delineate and address.") For a critique of the concept of nation-building and its expansion into a norm of humanitarian intervention, see E. Luttwak, "Kofi's Rule—Humanitarian Intervention and Neocolonialism," 58 *The National Interest* 57 (Winter 1999–2000).

3. [1962] I.C.J. 150.

4. See generally Nat J. Colletta, Markus Kostner & Ingo Wiederhofer, *The Transition from War to Peace in Sub-Saharan Africa* (World Bank 1996), *excerpts obtainable from* http://www.worldbank.org/html/extpb/warpeace/ transit.htm.

5. Alvaro de Soto and Graciana del Castillo, "Obstacles to Peace Building," 94 *Foreign Policy* 69 (Spring 1994).

6. Kofi Annan, *We The Peoples: The Role of the United Nations in the 21st Century,* U.N. Doc. A/54/2000* (Mar. 27, 2000), para. 48, *also obtainable from* http://www.un.org/millennium/sg/report!full.htm. Integration of functions becomes critical "to transfer the momentum of crisis response to recovery, rehabilitation and development activities," United Nations Development Programme, *Bridging The Gap: A Report on Behalf of the Inter-Agency Standing Committee (IASC) Reference Group on Post-Conflict Integration,* August 1999, at 2, *obtainable from* http://www.reliefweb.int/ iasc/Documents/wg38_2.doc.

7. *See* Secretary-General Proposes Global Compact On Human Rights, Labour, Environment, In Address To World Economic Forum In Davos, U.N. Press Release SG/SM/6881/Rev.1 (Feb. 1, 1999), *obtainable from* http://www.un.org/ews/Press/docs/1999/19990201.sgsm6881.r1.html>; *see also* Report of the Secretary-General on the Work of the Organization, U.N. Doc.A/54/1 (Aug. 31, 1999), paras. 136-139, *obtainable from* http://www.un.org/Docs/SG/Report99 /toc.htm>.

The Sad Lessons of Nation-Building

Nicholas D. Kristof
New York Times Columnist

Black Hawk Down is, regrettably, a pretty good movie.

It puts you in the heart of the Mogadishu gun battle in 1993 between Somali paramilitary forces and American Army Rangers, and you leave the theater, heart pounding, wanting to pull out a machine gun and mow down crowds of Somalis. But the real problem is that the film powerfully reinforces the two main lessons that America absorbed from the Somalia debacle—and both lessons are wrong and have already hurt the struggle against terrorism.

They are:

1. Nation-building is bloody, costly and futile. So if people in piddling third-world countries want to tear each other apart, let 'em.
2. Casualties are completely unacceptable in American military operations. At the first sign of blood, politicians abandon missions and generals are retired.

These phobias were counterproductive and ultimately helped produce more terrorism and more casualties. They meant that in the 1990's we stayed away in droves from places like Afghanistan, Sudan and Somalia, allowing a chaos that breeds terrorism.

Even now President Bush continues to stiff Afghanistan's caped hero, Hamid Karzai, as he pleads for American troops to help secure all of Afghanistan.

There is nothing Afghanistan needs more desperately. At the moment, every time you drive between cities in Afghanistan you look nervously out the windows for signs of bandits who shoot up cars (or even cut off travelers' noses and ears). But we refuse to contribute to the international security force because of our dread of another Somalia scenario.

It is not even necessary to wrestle with the humanitarian argument for helping tottering countries. Afghanistan, Serbia and Somalia all demonstrate the realpolitik merit of solving messes as they happen: if we leave countries to rot, eventually the rot spreads and comes back to infect us.

No one is in favor of American casualties; the question is simply how best to minimize them in the long run. And many diplomats and military officers alike agree—although they are reluctant to say so out loud, because they remember the Vietnam-era slogans about old men dreaming up battles for young men to die in—that the zero-casualty standard of recent years has been counterproductive. It creates more American casualties in the long run by showing weakness and by turning nations into petri dishes for terrorists.

"Bin Laden learned lessons from Somalia, too," said Ken Menkhaus, a Somalia expert at Davidson College in North Carolina. "He learned that you go kill a few Americans and they go away."

To his credit, Mr. Bush has reversed his initial hostility to nation-building and ended up in favor of what one senior administration official impishly calls "nation-building lite" in Afghanistan. Mr. Bush has also tried to drum in the truth that in military action, body bags are inevitable as well as tragic.

The United States need not dispatch troops in every direction. But we should lead an international order that confronts the problem of failed states. It's difficult but not hopeless. Even Somalia might, with better policy and luck, have made gradual progress—rather like its once equally hapless neighbors Ethiopia and Eritrea.

"It was a mishandling of the situation by the U.S. and the U.N., rather than any innate hatred among the Somalis for us" that led to disaster, says Robert B. Oakley, a former ambassador to Somalia and Pakistan. Likewise, an American who watched the fighting involving American troops in Somalia from a rooftop in Mogadishu, where he then worked for the United Nations, said: "The mission was not fated to fail. It failed because of U.N. and U.S. blundering."

Nation-building is a blunder-prone business, but it can succeed. In 1992 Mozambique was forlorn and war-ravaged, but with military and civilian help from the United Nations it has since become one of the faster-growing economies in the world.

Likewise, Uganda was one of the world's horror stories in the 1970's, and now (after a push by Tanzanian troops in 1979 to evict Idi Amin) it's among the stars of Africa. I have a special warmth for Uganda because I was on a small plane that crash-landed there five years ago; with its fire trucks and unflappable immigration officials, Uganda makes an outstanding country in which to crash.

And now, with luck, Afghanistan will again prove that helping war-torn third-world countries is a smarter policy than running away from them.

The Only Acceptable Purpose of War is to Restore More Durable Peace

Richard Falk
Princeton University

This is my third attempt to assess the military component of the response to September 11. The first stable element in this assessment has been the underlying conviction that the attacks were of a character as to make recourse to war, rather than an exclusive reliance on law enforcement, politically inevitable and morally/legally justifiable. The second stable element has been my view that unless this necessary military element is kept subordinate to the nonmilitary dimensions of response, the war against global terror will be lost in the end. The unstable aspects of my response have involved changing perceptions of the proportionality of means and ends as it related to the use of force in Afghanistan.

Early on, I was overly persuaded by the language used by President Bush and other leaders that they understood that force must be used sparingly and with great sensitivity in relation to civilian innocence. As the military campaign in Afghanistan deepened, with America once again seeming to confine its battlefield role to high-altitude bombing and Vietnam-era tactics, I felt unable to endorse any longer the justice of the means. Now, given the unexpectedly rapid collapse of the Taliban regime and the obvious impact on the operational nexus of Al Qaeda, there seems, at least temporarily, to be a restored sense of proportionality between means and ends.

Should military force subsequently be used excessively or vindictively in Afghanistan, this judgment could again be reversed. The prospect of such a further reversal is heightened by the late November massacre of hundreds of surrendered Taliban fighters locked into the prison fortress at Mazar-i-Sharif. It was clearly a joint Northern Alliance/US operation, combining US airstrikes at close range with Northern Alliance ground operations in a setting where the more objective journalists reported that US military advisers were "running the show." Such blatant criminality seemed an indirect outcome of Defense Secretary Donald Rumsfeld's expressions of indifference with respect to Northern Alliance behavior, especially with respect to the execution rather than capture of Al Qaeda and Taliban soldiers. These are deeply troubling portents of what the future holds in store.

As troubling has been Bush's expansive definition of terrorism and the goals of war, which appear increasingly to contemplate extending the military undertaking beyond the borders of Afghanistan, and specifically to renew full-scale warfare against Iraq. Increasingly, Bush relies on an inflated conception of the 9/11 threat that appears to express a commitment to wage war against nonstate political violence around the world even if it has no

Reprinted with permission from the December 24, 2001 issue of *The Nation*. From "In Defense of 'Just War' Thinking," by Richard A. Falk.

relevance to the specifically apocalyptic terrorism associated with the bin Laden vision. And most recently, Bush went so far as to associate "terrorism" with the possession of weapons of mass destruction that might fall into the hands of terrorists, presumably to explain why Iraq is now fair game. Given the likely domestic source of the anthrax incidents, such a policy, if scrupulously carried out, would imply waging an auto-war against America!

Against this background, a central challenge of September 11 for progressives and conservatives alike is to identify the shape and limits of a proper response. The starting point for such an understanding is appreciation of the security-shattering character of the attacks combined with their implicit and credible threat of future attacks of comparable or even greater magnitude. In such circumstances, any government must mobilize its capabilities to achieve a maximally effective response and generate the widest possible popular support. Such imperatives are even stronger in the case of the United States, given its leadership in world society, as well as its linchpin role with respect to global security, however flawed its execution has been in several past instances (including Vietnam, the Israel/Palestine conflict, the post-cold war abandonment of Afghanistan and the follow-up to the Gulf War).

The Bush presidency has performed reasonably well so far in meeting the crucial elements of this challenge. It recognized the challenge with clarity and mobilized society for a necessary and prolonged struggle. It warned against expectations of a quick or easy fix, it defined the mission in relation to terrorism rather than Islam and it made a serious effort to reassure the Muslim minority in America that their rights would be protected. Beyond this, the White House developed a multilevel response that combined the diplomatic mobilization of an international coalition, a comprehensive effort to disrupt Al Qaeda's funding sources, a global coordination of national police and law enforcement efforts to find and prosecute members of Al Qaeda cells dispersed in as many as sixty countries, and made at least nominal recourse to the UN Security Council to obtain a unanimous endorsement of such initiatives.

More controversial, of course, was the military component of the response, and its focus on destroying the Taliban regime as well as mounting search and destroy missions against Osama bin Laden and the overall Al Qaeda presence in Afghanistan. The tactics relied upon, especially carpet-bombing B-52s, cluster bombs and 15,000-pound "Daisy Cutters," created a sense of revulsion and distrust, as if the lessons of Vietnam had not been learned and we here in America would be in for a long and savage military campaign that would inflict great suffering on the Afghan people. But at this point, in view of the unexpectedly rapid collapse of the Taliban, the overall undertaking appears reasonable, having been sufficiently related to weakening those who staged September 11 and declared war against the civilian population of America, if not the entire Judeo-Christian West. Provided the Afghanistan phase of the response seeks the restoration of governmental normalcy under difficult circumstances, humanitarian catastrophe associated with famine is minimized and the elimination of the Al Qaeda presence in the country is achieved, it will be possible to conclude that the Bush Administration deserves credit for reaching its preliminary international goals.

Its domestic record, with respect to civil liberties, is far more problematic and does create the possibility that as the war against Al Qaeda is being pursued effectively, the political war at home to sustain security without jeopardizing liberty is being lost. Such an assessment is made without relying on a normative framework of appraisal, which is a great temptation given the unprecedented nature of the attack and threat. But it is a temptation that should be resisted, at least in part. It is the case that the nonstate source of this global terror, and its grandiose agenda of civilizational war, overwhelms the most authoritative frameworks: international law and the UN. Both are anchored too directly in a world of sovereign states to be really useful in shaping an overall response, at least with respect to its most controversial aspect, the role of force. Besides this, the UN as currently constituted cannot manage a central security challenge directed at a leading state, an acknowledgment implied even in 1945 by vesting veto power in each of the five permanent members of the Security Council. At the same time, to avoid the impression that recourse to war remains a discretionary matter for such states, and to set limits on how war should be conducted, there is an urgent need for some normative framework of limitation that enjoys widespread support. Such a framework is also needed to draw a bright line between the violence of the terrorists and the violence of their victims.

The "just war" doctrine provides the most flexible and relevant normative framework. It has roots in the ethics of all the great world religions, it is a vital source of modern international law governing the use of force and it focuses attention on the causes, means and ends of war. Just-war thinking does have limitations. The abstractness of its main principles allows too much room for interpretation in specific instances, thereby making it of rather little use in providing belligerents with a code of conduct. What just-war thinking allows, and indeed demands, is that contested policy provide justifications, essentially by providing convincing reasons to overcome a general and significant bias against those who rely on war to solve problems and resolve conflicts. Analysis along these lines must address recourse to war, the means by which it is conducted and the ends pursued. Each dimension deserves brief discussion in the context of the evolving response to the September 11 attacks.

On recourse to war in Afghanistan, the just-war grounds seem persuasively related to the threat, at least at this stage of military operations. The attacks on the World Trade Center and Pentagon were of a magnitude that engaged the right of self-defense, although not in an international-law sense, as the attacker was not a state. Only the just-war approach has the flexibility to expand the scope of self-defense to encompass the sort of global terrorist entity embodied in Al Qaeda. The just-war test of recourse to war is thus related to whether the action taken by the US-led coalition was proportionate to the harm inflicted and the threat posed. Although the assessment seemed in doubt during the early weeks of bombing, the collapse of the Taliban regime and the apparent disabling of Al Qaeda operations from Afghanistan now permits, even mandates, a provisional endorsement of recourse to war.

This endorsement is made in the face of an unfortunate reliance by the United States on legally dubious weaponry and tactics, but is offset to a degree by the rapidity of battlefield success and the beneficial side effect of liberating the people of Afghanistan from the oppressive brutality of the Taliban regime. Although I earlier overestimated the combat capabilities of the Taliban, it would be a further error to now overstate their collapse. The hard-core Taliban are quite capable of regrouping and shifting tactics to mount a guerrilla war. The future holds many additional uncertainties as to whether governmental normalcy can be achieved in Afghanistan and whether the war-makers in Washington will now devote sufficient energy and resources to the political and economic reconstruction of the country. Such reconstruction can best be handled by the UN, but only if it is provided with a clear mandate and sufficient capabilities; the UN must be careful, as the organization cannot afford a repetition of the Bosnian experience, where its "safe havens" were turned into slaughterhouses.

What gives the just-war approach its current significance is less its appraisal of the past and present response than relevance to the future of the response, and specifically its appraisal of any attempt to rely on war in the aftermath of Afghanistan. Such a prospect has been debated in the media with respect to Iraq. Prudential reasons can be mounted on either side of the argument, although there are persuasive reasons not to go to war against Iraq: breaking the coalition, generating dissent in America, sidelining Israel/Palestine peace efforts, destabilizing several governments in the Middle East, undertaking a difficult and costly military campaign. The normative argument reinforces this prudential assessment: Just-war thinking requires that the side initiating war maintain a burden of persuasion. While Afghanistan was integral to the September 11 operations, Iraqi connections are at most marginal, and quite possibly nonexistent. While Al Qaeda with its suicidal enactment of jihad is undeterrable, Baghdad behaves in a horrible manner but acts to sustain its survival, bargains for advantages and can be contained and deterred by threats and capabilities. There is thus neither justification in relation to the Al Qaeda threat nor necessity with regard to addressing the deformed character of the Iraqi regime. Whether a case exists for humanitarian intervention of a nonmilitary character is another matter, but not one that validates the call to wage war against Iraq.

Just-war thinking makes two important contributions to our understanding of the military side of the September 11 response:

(see) it provides a provisional and limited endorsement of the Afghanistan war;

(see) it reinforces the prudential arguments against military extension of the war on global terror to other settings, most relevantly Iraq.

Such clarity allows us to think more clearly about what should be done post-Afghanistan. From the perspective of coercive diplomacy, what needs to be done is to move forward as efficiently as possible with the nonmilitary aspects of the campaign against global terror, relying on law enforcement techniques and intergovernmental cooperation. The legitimate role of large-scale military operations is thus confined to Afghanistan.

Ever since just-war thinking emerged, initially and most notably in the writings of St. Augustine, there has been an emphasis on the just goals or ends of war, as well as on its just causes and just means. In this regard, there is a consensus among just-war thinkers that the only acceptable purpose of war is to restore peace on a more durable basis. What does such a requirement suggest in the current context? It is here that the broader issues of the US role in the Islamic world should be subject to reappraisal, not to reward the terrorists but to take an opportunity to correct past mistakes of policy and judgment. Solving the Israel/Palestine conflict so as to provide both peoples with independent and secure states with equality of sovereign rights is the first priority. Such a challenge is formidable given the questionable leadership on both sides. But it is time for the international community, along with the United States, to take a more active role in shaping a fair solution and exerting great influence on both sides to accept such an outcome. What this means concretely is that international humanitarian law must govern Israel's occupation and any resumed peace process, and cannot be deferred until negotiations are completed. In this setting, international law provides a framework for discerning fairness, while a contrary deference to "facts on the ground" reinforces the geopolitical disparity between the sides. The current impasse is tragic for both Palestinians and Israelis, implying a dismal future, as well as contributing to regional instability and a deepening of a widely diff-used anti-Americanism.

If modernity is to be made to work successfully in the Islamic world it will need to be accompanied by respect for robust traditional cultural and religious identities, as well as the dedication of energies and resources to economic growth. The Iranian revolution led by Ayatollah Khomeini should have taught the West such a lesson. Let's hope that the crimes against humanity committed on September 11 are the last such learning experience that Americans are made to undergo. We can fashion out of these experiences an approach to the Islamic world that both promotes our values and serves our interests.

On the Merits of Nation-Building

Saibal Mitra
University of Tulsa

With the defeat of the Taliban government in Afghanistan, it is appropriate to go back and revisit some of the promises made by George W Bush in his September 20, 2001, speech to Congress. He made two major points. First, terrorism is a "global threat" and the United States is going to go after the terrorists and "those who harbor them." Second, the war against terrorism will be won when there are no more terrorist incidents in the world.

It is clear that this bombing/shooting war will be considered only a partial success if it results in the capture of Osama bin Laden, dead or alive. The chances are that this will require a prolonged effort, resulting in more civilian casualties. Great loss of civilian life would, at best, deny the United States the moral high ground and, at worst, sow the seeds of a deeper conflict. However, by Bush's own standard, the capture of bin Laden isn't the yardstick by which to judge Bush's policy on global terrorism. Success will be achieved only if global terrorism is completely stamped out. Herein lies the rub. Terrorism is a chronic disease that may be controlled but probably never eliminated. Thus, military victory over the Taliban and bin Laden will prove illusory.

The growth and spread of terrorism depends on myriad conditions including poverty, hopelessness, lack of secular education, and, above all, frustration at the inability of citizens to control their own destiny. After all, participatory democracy provides ownership in government, which, in my opinion, is key to a deep sense of personal dignity. That is an effective antidote for terrorism.

So how do we get from here to there? Though the answer isn't straightforward, it is clear that this journey would demand visionary leadership from Bush. But it is in the "vision" area that Bush has yet to prove himself. For starters, I would like to see him declare war on the root causes of terrorism.

The signs are not encouraging. Bush, despite his stirring speech to Congress, misdiagnosed the causes of terrorism and hence his solutions are likely to be ineffective. The cause of terrorism isn't jealousy of our freedoms, as Bush implied in his speech to Congress, but rather a deep sense of frustration at the lack of freedom in other societies. There is a deep sense of alienation on the Arab street in relation to the United States and its policies. Right or wrong, many think the United States has a sorry track record of supporting oppressive kings, emirs, and dictators. They blame the United States for "oppressive" policies—like the sanctions against Iraq which have resulted in the deaths of half a million children. They argue that, like Saddam Hussein, the United States has made Iraqi

Reprinted by permission of *The Humanist* article, "Winning the Real War on Terrorism," January/February 2002 and the author.

children the pawn of international politics. Hussein, most acknowledge, is a monster. What's the United States' excuse, they ask?

Bush has shown considerable disdain for the concept of nation building. Yet, the Marshall Plan, which rebuilt Europe both physically and psychologically after World War II, was all about nation building. The task ahead is even more difficult. We have to win the battle of ideas. And our approach should be built around two principles. First, we should work toward political and economic freedom in these countries. Nations like Saudi Arabia should be encouraged, even pressured; to open up their political process and let the people have a voice in their own governance. Second, we should encourage the growth of secular education in these societies. In the fundamentalist circles of Islam, not many are aware of the poems of Omar Khayyam or Rumi. Nor are they aware of the contribution of Islamic scholars in the area of mathematics, science, and arts, and so on.

If the rest of the world can help these ideas take root, we would be pleasantly surprised at the quality of artists, doctors, lawyers, and investment bankers that come out of countries like Afghanistan within a generation or two. Then, we will have finally won the war on global terrorism...

Center panel of *Rainbow Shabbat* from the *Holocaust Project,* © Judy Chicago 1992, stained glass, 4' 6" x 16'. Fabricated by Bob Gomez, hand-painted by Dorothy Maddy from Judy Chicago's cartoon.

Collection: the artist and Through the Flower Corporation. Photo credit © Donald Woodman.

Part Eleven

Mobilizing for Peace:

The Public Sector and Civil Society

Since wars begin in the minds of men, it is in the minds of men that the defense of peace must be constructed.

—Constitution of UNESCO (1946)

World War I ushered in a new era in the pursuit of "world federalism." The idea that institutions should be established to check the unchallenged power of nation-states was born out of the desire to avoid future conflicts of increasing destructive power. At the dawn of the twenty-first century, institutions created in the pursuit of global cooperation are searching for a new role and a new agenda in the international system. The works of Bruce Russett and Chantal de Jonge Oudraat endeavor to take account of the strengths and shortcomings of our existing international institutions in maintaining peace. Why have they been unable to temper the tide of warfare, and what changes can be made to improve their effectiveness? How would this increased internationalism affect the work of sovereign governments and the lives of the governed?

A differing grassroots approach is also offered as a complimentary means of promoting peace. John Prendergast with Emily Plumb and Benazir Bhutto argue that the empowerment of citizens at the local level will ultimately set society on a more just and egalitarian footing, thereby mitigating the causes of conflict.

A third school urges that what is needed, at both local and international levels, is a concerted peace movement centered around the notion of peace education. As this volume has attempted to denote, peace studies, peace education and peace research have been a long neglected academic discipline on college campuses and in research organizations. While subjects like "dispute resolution" have come into fashion among theorists and grant-makers, that concept has focused too narrowly on the concept of "negative peace," which is to say, the absence of war. A new wave of peace activists urge that peace can and should embody the concepts of contentment, stability, empowerment and cooperation. Alan Gilbert presents innovative approaches to the subject of implementing peace. In Part One Sigmund Freud sought to answer the question, "Why war?" Perhaps the time has come when man should be asking "Why not peace?"

The United Nations and Three Great Forces for Peace

Bruce Russett
Yale University

There are three great forces for peace in the world: democratic government, economic interdependence, and international organizations. These are the same three elements of a peaceful world identified by Immanuel Kant more than 200 years ago. The difference from Kant's era is that we now have solid evidence of the power of these three elements. That evidence is in [the] book…: Bruce Russett and John R. Oneal, *Triangulating Peace: Democracy, Interdependence, and International Organizations.* It scrutinizes the full record of states' behavior in international relations since 1885: who fought whom, in wars or other violent but more minor engagements; who threatened to fight whom; and which states did not fight or threaten each other. In other words, we now can establish the conditions which put certain kinds of states at risk of fighting each other, and the conditions under which international violence is rare and non-violent means of conflict resolution are the norm.

The three Kantian conditions operate as follows:

1) Democracies generally live in peace with other democracies. They even are somewhat more peaceful in general than are dictatorships. Leaders chosen in regular, free, and competitive elections cannot pursue aggressive foreign policies designed to line their own pockets or benefit only a small circle of their supporters. If they do, they risk being thrown out of office by the majority, which suffers, rather than gains from war.

2) Economically interdependent states are more constrained in their resort to the use of force with each other than are states whose economic ties are minimal. A strong network of commercial exchange creates powerful incentives to maintain the peaceful relations on which economic interest depends.

3) Thick networks of international organizations provide their member states with a range of means of conflict avoidance and nonviolent conflict resolution that are not available to nonmembers. A great variety of organizations—regional and global, of narrow purpose or broad and multi-faceted like the U.N.—together provide these conflict-resolving capabilities.

Between states identified by these Kantian characteristics, relations are governed by principles of negotiation, compromise, reciprocity, and mediation, and the threat or use of force is usually absent. Violent conflict may sometimes occur anyway, but it is rare. The stronger the Kantian characteristics

Bruce Russett, "The United Nations and Three Great Forces for Peace." From *Renewing the United Nations and Building a Culture of Peace*, NY: Interreligious and International Federation for World Peace (IIFWP), 2000. Reprinted by permission.

are—the more democratic the states, the greater their interdependence, the more numerous their international organization ties—the less likely is violence. States strongly sharing these ties have been, over more than a century of experience, less than 30 percent as likely to fight or threaten each other as have merely "average" states. *No* two states sharing all three characteristics waged war against each other during that time. This is no coincidence—the three characteristics are why they haven't fought each other. In addition, democracy, interdependence, international organizations, and peace all strengthen one another.

It is the absence of strong Kantian linkages, not a "clash of civilizations," that has brought war. This insight pervades the three great documents produced by Boutros Boutros-Ghali when he was Secretary-General of the UN: his *Agenda for Peace, Agenda for Development,* and *Agenda for Democratization.* It also appears in Kofi Annan's statements, notably *We the Peoples.* He calls for good governance, comprising "the rule of law, effective state institutions, transparency and accountability in the management of public affairs, respect for human rights, and the participation of all citizens in the decisions that affect their lives" (p. 22—this sounds like democracy to me). He calls for economic growth to reduce poverty and inequality, saying, "The surest route to growth is through successfully engaging in the global economy" (p. 23). And he proclaims the U.N.'s purpose as "transforming relations among states, and the methods by which the world's affairs are managed" (p. 6). Peace depends upon maintaining and deepening the Kantian constraints.

Relations between states that do not share these constraints are different. A non-Kantian state may if possible practice negotiation and compromise, seek reciprocity, or get mediation, but its threat to use force remains ever-present. Because a non-Kantian state may resort to force, in dealing with it a Kantian state may have to use force to protect its interests. When the interests of non-Kantian states collide with others, peace depends primarily on the traditional instruments of deterrence: national power and collective power as manifested in alliances.

Not all states can be neatly divided between Kantian and non-Kantian ones. Some may be in transition between the two conditions or lie on the margins, neither fully integrated into the Kantian system nor one of the few isolates which clearly stand outside of it. In relations with these states, neither pure non-violent conflict resolution nor pure threat of force is satisfactory. Some mixture must be employed. Means must be found to increase or solidify the marginal states' incorporation into the Kantian system of relationships. If non-Kantian states come to share the three Kantian characteristics—by learning from the example of Kantian states' success in peaceful interactions—the Kantian community can be expanded and deepened.

During the cold war the superpowers managed—perhaps with a great deal of luck—to avoid a world war. But there were plenty of smaller international wars in the world. From 1950 to 1989 the world experienced almost eight wars (major conflicts, at least 1,000 battle deaths) per decade. With the end of the cold war, the 1990s saw some improvement, with no more than five additional international ones. It is also a fact—not widely recognized—that the number of civil wars dropped sharply after peaking in 1992. While some civil wars arose out of the collapse of previously Soviet-supported regimes, many conflicts once sustained by superpower meddling collapsed as the patrons lost interest or capability. More conflicts were settled than erupted. In these settlements, the United Nations often played a crucial role. The U.N. did not always try, and did not always succeed where it did try, but many violent conflicts importantly owe their end to the Urn's efforts. It is not just a peacekeeper, but a peace-builder in facilitating the emergence of democracy, in encouraging trade and development, and in mediating conflicts and promoting basic human rights.

This does not mean that large-scale violence is

a phenomenon of the past. Many ethnic potential tinderboxes remain. So-called rogue states and terrorists can make life hazardous. But it does mean that the post-cold war era so far has certainly not been more violent, and probably less so, than the era which preceded it. The prospect of any war between two great powers in the next couple of decades or so is miniscule. How many other times during past centuries could one have said that? And why can one say it now?

One very big reason is, of course, that while the international system contains several states which can reasonably be characterized as great powers, there is only one really great power. The United States maintains by far the largest and strongest military establishment in the world. By itself it outspends for defense all the rest of NATO, and spends 75 percent more than all of its more or less plausible adversaries combined. No state or combination of states can endanger its existence or sovereignty.

Some observers characterize the United States as hegemonic. It also has non-military means of exerting influence. Its ideological principles of democracy and free enterprise govern much of the global polity and economy. Those—whether apologists for authoritarianism, religious fundamentalists, or post-modernists—who reject one or both of those great organizing principles do so in tone more of defensiveness than of confidence. The United States also has great potential economic leverage. The North American Free Trade Area contains the world's largest market, bigger even than the European Union. Other states must export to that market. When it so wishes, America has enormous power to influence trade practices, combat financial and copyright offenses, and enforce environmental standards.

The United States does not always get its way. Who does, anywhere? With its self-imposed fiscal restraints the American government is hampered in mobilizing the enormous wealth of its economy. Its people are properly reluctant to carry on sustained or costly wars, or to impose new forms of government on others. Yet democracy and the other Kantian conditions can be enhanced by a range of economic and political assistance to states and peoples that are willing to liberalize their political and economic systems. The most important contribution to peace would be to help democratizing states reach a high level of democracy smoothly and rapidly.

Hegemony is not a long-term prescription for success. A hegemon perceived as prevailing by force will in time provoke the emergence of countervailing force by those who see that hegemony as unjust. The current dominance of the United States and its allies will give way to a more diffused distribution of global power. Military deterrence will remain an essential tool for preventing or rebuffing some aggressive challenges. It cannot be wished away. But it cannot be the exclusive tool, nor even the primary one. Deterrence—especially nuclear deterrence—is a miserable way of avoiding war, and a miserable way to live.

A different kind of world can be nurtured, one in which most conflicts of interests are not managed primarily by the threat of violence. That world is emerging, as for the first time in world history more than half of states' governments are democratic, economic interdependence is at its all-time peak, and international organizations are incrementally strengthened. Multilateralism—the cooperative exercise of power with states sharing similar though not identical goals—is a key. In the long term, influence depends on shared beliefs and perceptions about legitimate action. Though the world lacks a formal system of rule substantially limiting states' sovereignty, normative principles are emerging to govern action in the international interest.

These principles and their binding power remain unsettled. Nevertheless, they are continually brought to bear in debates, as applied to particular interventions (e.g., Iraq, Somalia, Haiti, Bosnia, Kosovo) and to discussions about the proper composition and procedures of the UN Security Council. Even the most powerful states take great risks when they ignore those principles.

Many people might like to have it otherwise.

Isolationists prefer to avoid international actions and entanglements—but they are not always ready to live with the consequences of inaction. Unilateralists are prepared to exercise military power in pursuit of vital national interests without great concern for the niceties of international consent. This strain is evident among those who would expand military budgets while simultaneously cutting support for international institutions. But no country can control the world by unilateral military action. It needs not just the approval, but also the active support of many allies.

The United States does not always reflect this understanding. It has failed to ratify a long list of multilateral treaties. They cover just about the full spectrum of international issues, and include the Comprehensive Test Ban Treaty, the Land Mines Convention, the Law of the Sea Convention, the International Convention on Women, the International Convention on the Rights of the Child, the treaty to establish a permanent International Criminal Court, and the Kyoto Protocol on global warming. None of these agreements is flawless, and they should be improved, but most countries have ratified them or will do so. U.S. leaders are still grudging about fulfilling their legal obligations to pay U.N. dues, threaten to abrogate the Anti-Ballistic Missile Treaty, and move ever more overtly to making nuclear threats to deter the use of biological and chemical weapons in violation of pledges given in support of the Nuclear Non-Proliferation Treaty.

International institutions like the U.N. need to be enhanced, not gutted. All countries—not just a few—must be able to see those institutions as serving their interests. Claims of interest have to be bolstered by credible claims to legitimacy. Multilateralists, while acting on their own interests, understand the need to act within a generally acceptable normative framework. All states have the opportunity to build a peace based not only on military force but on Kantian principles. Kant would say there is a moral imperative to do so. It's not "idealism"; it's just a prudent way to live.

The Role of the United Nations in International Peace and Security

Chantal de Jonge Oudraat[1]
Johns Hopkins University

On December 10, 2001, the Norwegian Nobel Committee awarded the Nobel Peace Prize to the United Nations (UN) and its Secretary-General, Kofi Annan. Although UN programs and related activities had received the Nobel peace prizes on previous occasions, this was the first time that the United Nations, as such, was awarded the prize.[2] In its citation, the Committee praised the work of the world organization to build "a better organized and more peaceful world." According to the Nobel Committee, "the only negotiable route to global peace and cooperation goes by way of the United Nations."

Since its creation in 1945, the United Nations has been the hub of international efforts to deal with problems posed by international peace and security. Although the United Nations' ability to handle peace and security problems was severely constrained during—and by—the Cold War, it has been a more active participant in international peace and security issues since the end of the Cold War. The United Nations has focused much of its energies on internal conflicts, recognizing that internal conflicts are one of the major peace and security problems with which the international community has to contend. Internal conflicts almost always involve neighboring states, and they pose serious threats to regional security. Internal conflicts almost always cause great suffering to civilian populations, and they ravage the economic and social structures of the countries and regions in question. Ethnic cleansing and genocide pose grave moral questions. Unfortunately, states did not always react in the morally appropriate fashion during the 1990s. The 1994 genocide in Rwanda stands out as a staggering humanitarian and moral failure of the international community.

In the aftermath of the September 2001 attacks on the World Trade Center and the Pentagon, states have begun to understand that internal conflicts are also fertile breeding grounds for international terrorists. An international consensus is emerging: these conflicts cannot be left simmering. States—the United States, in particular—recognized now more than ever that the United Nations has a critical role to play in dealing with these threats. The centennial Nobel peace prize was seen by many, including Annan, as a timely boost for the United Nations.

At the end of 2001 the United Nations was engaged in nation-building activities in Bosnia, Kosovo, and East Timor, and it was embarking on a major operation in Afghanistan. At the same time, conflicts in Africa—such as those in Sierra Leone, Congo, and Burundi—required international attention, but were in danger of being neglected as international attention focused on the war against terrorism. Similarly, the fight against HIV/AIDS and the fight against poverty were in danger of being neglected, despite urgent appeals by the UN Secretary General.[3]

Whether the United Nations will succeed in responding in an effective manner to these demanding problems will depend on the commitment of its members. Indeed, it is a mistake to think of the United Nations as an independent political actor with respect to peace and security issues: it is more accurate to think of the United Nations as a policy instrument of the organization's member states. Except for limited actions undertaken by the Secretary-General (such as fact-finding and mediation efforts) member states—in particular, the permanent members of the Security Council (the P-5)—determine the shape and content of major UN operations in the peace and security field.

The role of the United States is particularly important in this respect. Throughout the 1990s, U.S. support for the United Nations waxed and waned and became hostage to domestic U.S. politics. The administration of George W. Bush was initially infused with strong unilateralist impulses. The United Nations was not on its list of priorities. However, in the wake of the September 11 attacks, the President and senior Administration officials started calling for a broad international coalition to fight terrorism. President Bush stated that "the defeat of terror requires an international coalition of unprecedented scope and cooperation." The United States sought and received support at the United Nations, where resolutions condemned the attacks and mobilized support for retaliatory action. In addition, President Bush has acknowledged that the United Nations has an important role to play in rebuilding war-torn Afghanistan. The Bush administration now recognizes that multilateral coalitions and institutions are necessary if the United States is to achieve its international goals. It acknowledges that "if done right a commitment to multilateralism need not constrain U.S. options but expand them."[4] It stresses that, for multilateralism to succeed, it should not be limited to counter terrorism.[5]

In this chapter I will briefly review UN efforts in the 1990s to deal with major international peace and security problems, focusing on the central issue of internal conflict. First, I will analyze the track record. Second, I will examine the legal conundrums of UN intervention in internal conflicts, highlighting progress made regarding individual international criminal responsibility. Third, I will examine the operational and political conundrums of UN intervention in the 1990s. Finally, I will examine the United States-United Nations relationship.

The Track Record

The United Nations was established to ensure and develop peaceful and friendly relations between states. The UN Security Council—the UN body with primary responsibility for the maintenance of international peace and security—is empowered by the UN Charter and member states to act in response to any "threat to the peace, breach of the peace, or act of aggression." To enable the Council to take effective action, each member of the United Nations was to make national armed forces available to the Council. This was one of the keys to the system of collective security and enforcement envisioned in the UN Charter.

For most of the Cold War, however, this system was crippled by two problems. First, Security Council decisions had to be supported by all five permanent members of the Council—China, France, the Soviet Union, the United Kingdom, and the United States—and these five states rarely reached a consensus on international peace and security issues. Conflicts abounded, but rarely could they agree on a joint course of action.[6] Second, effective action was impaired because armed forces were never made available to the Council in the way envisioned in the Charter. The Council thus remained totally dependent on the inclinations of individual states to make forces available on a case-by-case basis. Enforcement actions by the

United Nations as foreseen in the Charter were consequently undercut.

That said, member states recognized that regional conflicts could escalate into all-out war. This led to the development of peacekeeping operations. These types of operations were not provided for in the UN Charter, but developed over time as crisis control instruments that could keep regional conflicts from escalating into U.S.-Soviet confrontations. They consisted of military forces positioned between two or more warring parties. Deployed with the consent of relevant local parties, the United Nations' main mission was to monitor agreed-upon cease-fires. UN troops did not take sides. The use of force was restricted to self-defense. Peacekeeping operations helped major powers to disengage from potentially volatile and violent situations, without losing face. Countries such as Canada, Norway, Sweden, Denmark and the Netherlands—that is, small or neutral countries—contributed disproportionately to such operations.

With the end of the Cold War, the need to avoid great power confrontation has greatly diminished. In the early 1990s, many thought that the United Nations would at last become an effective guarantor of international peace and security. Many hoped that the United Nations would at last bring into play the full range of enforcement measures provided for in Chapter VII of the UN Charter.

Many new peacekeeping operations were launched in the late 1980s and early 1990s. Many of these operations were remarkably ambitious, dealing with conflicts that continued to rage. Initial successes in Namibia encouraged the UN to push forward with efforts in Angola and Central America. The 1991 Gulf war gave an additional boost to international confidence: many believed that war and terror could be defeated collectively. In the Gulf war's wake, UN operations were launched in El Salvador, Western Sahara, Cambodia, the former Yugoslavia, Somalia, Mozambique, and Rwanda. These were followed by operations in Georgia, Liberia, and Haiti. Many of these operations were launched because of humanitarian concerns.

Unfortunately, setbacks in a number of these operations as well as violent attacks on international peacekeepers in Somalia and Bosnia greatly tempered enthusiasm for these types of operations. The deaths of 18 American soldiers in Somalia had a particularly profound impact on U.S. attitudes toward peacekeeping operations.[7] Television footage showing dead U.S. Marines being dragged through the streets of Mogadishu led to intense congressional pressure to withdraw U.S. forces from Somalia. Three days later U.S. President Bill Clinton announced that all troops would be withdrawn from the country within six months. By late 1993 retreat was in the air.[8] This message was not lost on the military junta in Haiti or the *genocidaires* in Rwanda. In both cases, local parties managed to scare great powers that were more preoccupied with domestic public opinion polls than with questions of peace and justice. Thugs got the upper hand.[9] This had disastrous consequences: over 800,000 people were slaughtered in Rwanda in just one hundred days in the spring and summer of 1994.[10]

Communual strive is difficult to ignore in an increasingly interdependent and globalized world. Images of gross human rights abuses create pressures on outside powers to intervene. Developments in Kosovo throughout the summer and autumn of 1998 created such pressures and in March 1999 the United States and its North Atlantic Treaty Organization (NATO) allies decided to intervene militarily, without having been authorized to do so by the UN Security Council. Afraid of being accused of applying double standards Western powers agreed on the launching of new UN operations in East Timor and Sierra Leone in 1999.[11]

Legal Conundrums

The Kosovo crisis and the subsequent U.S./NATO intervention unleashed a recurring debate in international policy circles over humanitarian intervention. In September 1999, Annan took this debate to the UN General Assembly and urged states to develop criteria to permit humanitarian interventions in the absence of a consensus in the Security Council. In setting the stage for the debate, Annan asked those countries who had vehemently opposed the U.S./NATO intervention—for example, Algeria, China and India—what they would have done if, in the case of Rwanda, a coalition of states had been prepared to act in defense of the Tutsi population, but did not receive prompt Security Council authorization. "Should such a coalition have stood aside," he asked, and "allowed the horror to unfold?" Similarly, he asked the U.S. and its West European allies what type of precedent their action had set. To what extent had that intervention undermined the prohibition on the use of force and the system created after World War II to deal with security threats?[12]

The debate revealed major tensions amongst UN member states. At the heart of the legal debate on humanitarian intervention lies the question whether force can be lawfully used in situations other than those foreseen by the UN Charter.[13]

The debate features two schools of thought. One school argues that the UN Charter contains a general prohibition on the use of force as contained in Article 2(4) of the Charter:

> All members shall refrain in their international relations from the threat or use of force against the territorial integrity or political independence of any state, or in any other manner inconsistent with the Purposes of the United Nations.

They argue that the Charter allows for only two exceptions to this rule: (1) in response to an armed attack (Article 51);[14] and (2) when the use of force is authorized by the Security Council in order to maintain or restore international peace and security (Article 42).[15]

The other school of thought argues that Article 2 (4) does not contain a general and comprehensive prohibition on the use of force and asserts that it merely regulates the conditions under which force is prohibited. They contend that the Charter leaves room for exceptions—only two of which are mentioned in the Charter (Articles 51 and 42). They defend the notion that the Charter permits the use of force in other circumstances.

State practice seems to concur with the latter view, even though declaratory policies of states often adhere to the first school of thought. Over the years governments and legal scholars have argued that force can be lawfully used to protect and rescue one's national abroad; free people from colonial domination; fight terrorism; or protect people from gross violations of human rights; or to combat the spread of weapons of mass destruction.[16] At the same time, states take great pains to situate their international actions within the framework of the UN Charter. For example, when defending the Kosovo intervention, the United States argued that previous UN Security Council resolution gave it authority to act.[17] Similarly, even before it took military action against the Al-Qaeda and the Taliban the United States informed the Security Council and told it that it would take action under authority of UN Charter Article 51.

Parallel to the debate about military intervention by outside powers in situations where gross human rights violations take place, the 1990s saw a debate on individual international criminal responsibility. The idea of individual international criminal prosecution has been regularly discussed in the UN General Assembly and the UN International Law Commission since 1946. The possibility of establishing an international criminal court was also anticipated in the 1948 Genocide Convention. Apart from the Nuremberg (1945-1946) and the Tokyo (1946-1948) tribunals, however, no international bodies were set up to try crimes under international law.

The failure to establish an international criminal tribunal may be attributed to Cold War politics and the profound aversion of states to allowing a foreign body to adjudicate with respect to acts committed on their territories, and to seeing their citizens called before a jurisdiction other than their own. The end of the Cold War eliminated one of these obstacles, but it was the genocidal slaughter in the former Yugoslavia and Rwanda that prompted action. In 1993 and 1994, the UN Security Council created two ad hoc international criminal tribunals—one for the former Yugoslavia and one for Rwanda.[18] The tribunals were created under Chapter VII of the UN Charter. That is, the UN Security Council recognized that the widespread and egregious violations of human rights were a "threat to international peace and security." The tribunals were given three main tasks: to prosecute and try persons responsible for serious violations of international humanitarian law; to deter further crimes; and to contribute to the restoration and maintenance of peace.

The Yugoslav tribunal is authorized to adjudicate: grave breaches of the 1949 Geneva conventions; violations of the laws and customs of war; genocide; and crimes against humanity. The Rwandan tribunal is authorized to adjudicate violations of humanitarian international law in the latter two cases as well as violations of article 3 of the 1949 Geneva Conventions that pertains to internal, as opposed to international, conflicts. Both tribunals, particularly the Rwandan tribunal, got off to slow starts and have been hampered by resource constraints. They have also been handicapped by the unwillingness of many states, including those contributing international peacekeeping forces in parts of the former Yugoslavia, to arrest indicted war criminals. Even so, some war criminals have been brought to the Hague and Arusha—the seats of the two tribunals—and in most cases the political careers of indicted war criminals have been curtailed. Moreover, the two ad hoc courts have contributed to the development of international humanitarian law. For the first time, mass rape has been recognized not only as a war crime, but also as a crime against humanity. Finally, the creation of the two ad hoc tribunals gave renewed impetus to the negotiations over an International Criminal Court (ICC). Negotiations over the ICC statute were concluded in 1998 in Rome.[19] The Court will have authority to adjudicate genocide, war crimes, and crimes against humanity, such as widespread or systematic extermination of civilians, rape, sexual slavery, enforced disappearances, and the crime of apartheid.[20]

Support for individual criminal responsibility also got a boost in 1999. Acting on a warrant issued by a Spanish judge, the British police arrested Augusto Pinochet, the Chilean general responsible for the coup d'etat in Chile in 1973 and accused of crimes against humanity. The British House of Lords subsequently upheld the extradition request. As Lord Phillips of Worth Matravers concluded:

> There are some categories of crime of such gravity that they shock the consciousness of mankind and cannot be tolerated by the international community. Any individual who commits such a crime offends against international law (...) it is desirable that jurisdiction should exist to prosecute individuals for such conduct outside the territory in which such conduct occurs.[21]

While great progress has been made in making individuals accountable for criminal behavior, complacency is not in order. The ICC has not yet entered into force, and U.S. ratification is not expected soon. Human rights are still trampled upon daily in many countries around the world. International organizations tasked with monitoring and verifying compliance have seen dramatic increases in their workloads, but funding has not kept up. In short, problems persist, and international remedies are still inadequate.

In sum, the increased emphasis on internal conflicts during the 1990s challenged long-established legal principles, such as non-interference in the domestic affairs of states and state sovereignty. Many developing countries were deeply concerned about increasing UN involvement in internal conflicts. Yet, by the end of the 1990s, the idea that the UN Security Council can and should intervene militarily to stop genocide or gross violations of human rights was widely accepted. Similarly, the idea of individual international criminal responsibility had gained greater acceptance. Progress has been made. Increasingly the Council deemed internal conflicts and gross violations of human rights to be threats to international peace and security and thus legitimate reasons for international action. The war against terrorism launched at the end of 2001 relegated debates about humanitarian intervention to the background. Yet, intra-state, not interstate, conflicts continued, and will continue to dominate the agenda of the UN Security Council. Moreover, the emphasis on terrorism underscored the importance of individual international criminal responsibility.

Operational and Political Conundrums

The results of Security Council actions in the 1990s were mixed. The new peacekeeping operations of the 1990s were different from previous peacekeeping operations. The nature of the situations in which peacekeepers were deployed—warring factions were often still fighting—meant that these operations were often very risky. The nature of the tasks peacekeepers were asked to carry out—including the demobilization of armed forces, the training of local police, the organization of elections and more generally, helping to promote the economic recovery and development of the country in question—were more ambitious and involved a wide range of military and civilian personnel. The growing scope and complexity of these multifunctional peacekeeping operations created more room for organizational and administrative mishaps. Finally, the participation of the P-5 created new problems and affected the political dynamics of these operations. UN interventions in internal conflicts have posed major challenges to the international community. Four problems stand out.

First, the involvement of the permanent members of the UN Security Council—particularly France, the United States and the United Kingdom, and to a lesser extent Russia and China—changed the nature of UN interventions and the political dynamics of UN operations. During the Cold War, UN military interventions—that is, peacekeeping operations—had as their primary aim the prevention of great power confrontation. Consequently, the P-5 were usually not involved or present with troops on the ground. Canada and Northern European countries were preferred troop contributors. Monitoring of cease-fires with the consent of local parties and keeping Moscow and Washington at arms length was what traditional peacekeeping operations were all about. With the end of the Cold War, the risks of great power confrontation diminished. At the same time, the persistent and violent nature of many internal conflicts and hence the need for substantial resources to deal with these conflicts required direct great power involvement. Permanent members of the UN Security Council—particularly France, the United Kingdom and the United States—began to assume a leading role in many peacekeeping operations.

The involvement of the great powers is, however, a double-edged sword. It raises not only the profile of UN interventions, but also the expectations people have of them locally and internationally. Intervention by the great powers does not guarantee success, nor is it a risk-free proposition. The involvement of one of the P-5 may increase the odds of operations becoming more violent. Local parties may try to get one of the great powers on their side and have it actively intervene on their behalf. Local parties have not been shy in using such tactics—that is, tactics that make the other party look bad and to invite outside intervention. Such tactics have been abundantly used, most notably in Bosnia and Kosovo. Veton Surroi, a member of the Kosovar delegation at the 1999 failed peace conference in Rambouillet, France, and publisher of the Kosovar newspaper *Koha Ditore*, publicly acknowledged as much when he wrote in the *New York Times*, that one of the lessons he had learned from Bosnia was that

> ...a problem is a problem only when it becomes an armed one. Only when the first guns were heard from the Kosovar side did the leaders of the West's democracies react.[22]

Great powers became aware of these risks and gradually became more hesitant to intervene.

Moreover, they realized that once they intervened they had better succeed. Intervention engaged not just their military resources, but also their political prestige and credibility. Failed interventions could have far reaching national and international consequences incommensurate with the initial stakes or interests involved.

By 2000, most of the great powers were no longer engaged militarily in UN-peacekeeping operations. Top troop contributing countries all came from the developing world. Great powers were involved in the Balkans, but there troops fell under NATO command. The disengagement of the great and rich industrialized powers posed new challenges for the United Nations.

Second, the sheer number of internal conflicts and limited international resources confronted members of the Security Council with difficult choices about when and where to intervene and with what objectives. Since many internal conflicts did not engage major interests of the P-5, intervention decisions were often based on muddled political and humanitarian considerations and lowest political common denominators. Indeed, despite the end of the Cold War, UN Security Council members continued to have divergent interests and wanted to pursue different objectives in the international arena. Absent an agreement on political objectives, conflict containment and the delivery of humanitarian aid became primary objectives of UN operations.

Not recognizing the political nature of humanitarian assistance in conflict situations was responsible for many of the failures of post-Cold War peace operations. The most important error policymakers made was thinking that humanitarian assistance could be dispensed in a neutral and impartial manner and that providing humanitarian assistance could shield them from tackling the political causes of humanitarian emergencies. Because UN Security Council members often failed to appreciate the political ramifications of humanitarian assistance and because they failed to recognize that local actors did not always see humanitarian assistance as benign, they often also failed to appreciate that operational environments were not as benign as they appeared. Under-estimation of risks and dangers was common and highly problematic.

Third, in addition to confusion about the objectives of many new UN operations, member states had very different ideas about the use of force in UN operations. These doctrinal differences created many problems. The principles of traditional peacekeeping operations—consent, neutrality, impartiality, and use of force only in self-defense—proved to be ineffective when dealing with internal conflicts. It made no sense to request warring parties for permission to intervene when such was justified for humanitarian reasons—that is, to stop ethnic cleansing, forced deportation, or genocide. In addition, a stance of neutrality and impartiality—*de rigueur* in traditional peacekeeping operations—was hard to defend when faced with such heinous crimes.

Traditional peacekeeping principles and operational procedures were also unhelpful when it came to implementing or enforcing peace deals. In Angola, Bosnia, Cambodia, East Timor, Rwanda, or Kosovo, the international community was formally invited to implement a negotiated agreement. However, this initial local consent was often fragile and hard to maintain. Groups involved in these conflicts had weak and fractured lines of authority. Moreover, local parties often signed peace agreements for tactical purposes, with no intention to honor the provisions of the agreements. In addition, peace processes often created spoilers—that is, leaders and factions that had not achieved their war aims. Such parties often used violence to undermine negotiated settlements or peace processes.[23] Only coercive measures—such as the threat or use of military force—could prevent the breakdown of these peace processes. As one Albanian Kosovar has put it "political arrangements (to stop internal conflicts) require war, both as the igniting and driving forces, and as the action that seals them."[24] International actors were, however, hesitant to embark on such routes. It entailed waging war on local parties and thus the risk of casualties.

Impartiality and neutrality—principles that worked well in traditional peacekeeping operations—proved to be unhelpful in internal conflict situations. Indeed, they undermined the effectiveness and credibility of international forces. In Bosnia and elsewhere, UN peacekeepers became hostages of warring factions. UN member states, however, hesitated confronting warring factions head on. The domestic political fall-outs of possible casualties weighed heavily on the minds of policymakers. UN peacekeepers thus became the victims of hesitant policies by UN member states and domestic politics.

Fourth, UN peacekeeping operations throughout the 1990s suffered from chronic resource problems. The single most telling indicator in this respect was the number of troops made available to UN operations. Operations in Bosnia, Somalia, Haiti or Sierra Leone were chronically understaffed. One explanation for these mismatches between mandates and resources is that the United Nations Security Council is responsible for defining mission mandates, but is not directly responsible for implementing its decisions. For implementation, the Security Council is dependent on the good will of individual member states. This lack of direct accountability makes it possible for the states in the Security Council to define ambitious tasks for UN peacekeepers, without providing the peacekeepers with the necessary means to carry out these tasks.

As was observed by the American UN Association's International Task Force on the Enforcement of UN Security Council Resolutions:

> It (was) as if nation states to some extent relinquish(ed) their sense of individual responsibility—and the press and public cease(d) to hold them accountable—once the baton ha(d) been passed to the United Nations as the collective vehicle for enforcement.[25]

Indeed, the United Nations became an easy scapegoat for faulty policies at the national level. The UN—instead of Washington, Paris or London—was unjustly blamed for the failures of international operations in Bosnia, Somalia or Sierra Leone. The real responsibility for these policy failures belonged to the members of the Security Council—the P-5 in particular—that failed to back up their tough talk with real action.

This explains why the UN secretariat, in the mid-1990s, became wedded to the idea that enforcement operations should be carried out by coalitions of the willing, and not by UN troops.[26] The international panel appointed by the UN Secretary-General in March 2000 to review UN peace operations reaffirmed "that the United Nations does not wage war" and considered that enforcement actions needed to be entrusted to "coalitions of willing states"[27] At the same time it recommended that the Secretariat take a tougher stance when dealing with UN Security Council members. It suggested:

> The Secretariat must tell the Security Council what it needs to know, not what it wants to hear, when recommending force and other resource levels for a new mission, and it must set those levels according to realistic scenarios that take into account likely challenges to implementation.[28]

In sum, when assessing efforts by the United Nations in the 1990s, it should be stressed that Council members often did not have major interests in the conflict situations they tried to address. They failed to correctly assess local situations and define clear political objectives for intervention. Hubris and wishful thinking led to a lack of resources and more generally to an under-estimation of risks and dangers. Local parties, on the other hand, saw great power intervention as either a chance or challenge that could make or break their cases. They had major interests—survival—at stake. When the going got tough, the great powers would most often retreat. The UN Secretariat and UN peacekeepers would frequently find themselves caught in untenable situations. Innocent civilians paid the price for these policy failures.

In the aftermath of September 11, 2001, many internal conflicts will now be assessed in terms of the war against terrorism, rather than humanitarian considerations. This may not be a bad thing for local populations subject to long-raging wars, particularly if the United States and other major powers realize that solutions to these problems require long-term international responses. Unfortunately, if current history is a guide, local populations should not be too optimistic—international attention is often short term. Hence they should work for local solutions to their problems, and not pin their hopes on international actions.

The United States and the United Nations

U.S.-UN relations have long been rocky. This uneasy relationship predated the end of the Cold War, but the arrival of the Clinton Administration in 1992, with its talk of "assertive multilateralism," held out the promise that U.S.-UN relations would ameliorate. Instead, the 1990s saw a worsening of relations between the United Nations and the United States. Because the White House was preoccupied with domestic issues, relations between the UN and the United States were defined elsewhere, most notably in the U.S. Senate. Republican Senator Jesse Helms, in particular, became deeply involved in U.S. policies towards the United Nations.

Several issues tarnished U.S.-UN relations. First, and overshadowing everything was the UN dues question. The fact that for most of the 1990s the largest economy in the world had a debt equaling almost twice the annual budget of the United Nations was incomprehensible to many outside the United States.[29] It signaled a clear disrespect of international legal obligations and encouraged others to engage in similar behavior.[30] The argument that this sorry state of affairs was due to a regressive and conservative U.S. Congress was unconvincing to those outside the United States.

U.S.-UN contribution problems can be traced to 1981, when the Kemp-Moynihan amendment denied U.S. funding for UN programs involving the Palestine Liberation Organization (PLO) and the South West Africa's People Organization (SWAPO). It was the first time that U.S. funding was made contingent upon programmatic demands. It was followed in 1985 by the Kassebaum amendment, which called for a withholding of 20 percent of assessments in case the UN General Assembly failed to institute weighted voting on budgetary issues. During the 1990s, U.S. contributions to the UN were made conditional on management reform and eradicating so-called bureaucratic waste.

Many of Washington's demands for reform would be met. Yet, it was not enough. In 1994 the U.S. Congress decreed that the United States could not pay more than 25 percent of the UN peacekeeping budget. Moreover, payment of accumulated U.S. arrears became hostage to the U.S. abortion debate.[31] In November 1999, faced with the possibility that the United States—because of its arrears—would lose its right to vote in the UN General Assembly, some progress was made when the U.S. Congress finally voted on the Helms-Biden agreement. This agreement authorized payment of arrears over a period of three years.[32] However, in 2000 and 2001 several Senate and House actions upheld payment of both arrears, and part of UN peacekeeping funds.[33] This happened even though the UN General Assembly adopted reductions of U.S. assessments for the UN regular budget from 25 percent to 22 percent and for peacekeeping from 30 percent to 26.5 percent in 2003.

It was only in the aftermath of the September 2001 terrorist attacks that House representatives dropped their conditions and adopted a bill allowing for the payment of both regular dues and arrears.[34] On September 14, 2001, John Negroponte, the designated U.S. Ambassador to the United Nations, was quickly confirmed by the U.S. Senate. The release of funds and the confirmation of Negroponte lifted a major irritant in U.S.-UN relations.

The second question that clouded U.S.-UN relations, and more generally U.S. relations with many UN members states, had to do with the issue of burden sharing. U.S. policy-makers often argue that the United States pays an extraordinary amount for peacekeeping operations and humanitarian programs around the world and contributes far more than others do. In January 2000, Senator Helms in an address to the UN Security Council argued that "The UN lives and breathes on the hard-earned money of American taxpayers," and he resented the "lack of gratitude" shown to the United States. According to Senator Helms, the United States contributed $10.2 billion to the work of the United Nations in 1999—$1.4 billion in the form of assessments and voluntary contributions and $8.8 billion in the form of U.S. military assistance.[35]

However, many UN delegates pointed out that Senator Helms was mixing apples and oranges. Indeed, the quoted $1.4 billion lumped together 1998 assessment for the regular budget and specialized agencies such as the World Health Organizations and the International Labor Organization ($653 million); arrears payment ($187 million); U.S. contributions to peacekeeping operations and the international criminal tribunals for Yugoslavia and Rwanda ($257 million); voluntary contributions to UN programs such as the UN Development Program, UNICEF or the World Food Program ($295 million); and monies disbursed for voluntary peacekeeping ($75 million).

The $8.8 billion was composed of monies spend by the U.S. Department for Defense (DOD) for operations the United Nations had not authorized. Some $5.6 billion was for an operation—Kosovo—for which the United States had failed to obtain a UN Security Council authorization. Moreover, the Bosnia operation was, upon United States insistence, NATO—not UN—led.[36] Finally, the $1.5 billion spent for operations in Iraq were hotly contested within the UN Security Council, even among Washington's closest allies.

Senator Helms' figures thus greatly distorted the truth. In fact U.S. contributions to the United Nations are modest, particularly when calculated in relative terms. Japan, for example, contributes over 20 percent to the UN budget even though it has half the U.S.'s GDP and population.[37] Similarly, the European Union contributes over 36 percent to UN budgets. Germany, France, Italy, the Netherlands and the UK alone contribute almost as much to the United Nations in absolute terms as the United States—$910 million versus $920 million for the United States.[38] Given that their combined GDP represents 21 percent of the world total, as opposed to 30 percent for the United States, it is hard to argue that U.S. allies are not carrying their fair share of the burden.[39]

If peace and stability in the world is defined in broader terms—as it should—and includes development assistance, European countries quickly surpass the United States not just in relative terms, but even in absolute terms. The E.U. disburses over $26 billion in Official Development Assistance (ODA)—that is, 40 percent more than the United States. France, with little over 20 percent of the U.S. population and less than 16 percent of its GDP, spends almost as much as the United States in absolute terms on ODA. If ODA and UN contributions are combined, Japan disburses $2 billion more in absolute terms than the United States. France and the Netherlands, with a combined population less than 28 percent of the United States and a GDP less than 20 percent of the United States, also outdistance the United States with more than $2 billion. Seen in this context, it is not surprising that U.S. complaints over burden sharing are considered ill-placed in Japan and Europe.[40]

Even in terms of troop commitments, U.S. burden-sharing complaints sound hollow. In the 15 UN missions active in October 2001 and amongst the 38,100 UN peacekeepers deployed in the field, the United Sates contributed one military officer; he was engaged in East Timor. Bangladesh with 5,788 troops was the UN biggest troop contributor followed by Pakistan, with over 5,103 troops; Nigeria had fielded 3,303 troops; India had 2,175 troops deployed; Kenya 1,966 troops; Ghana 1,912 troops; Jordan 1,864 troops; Ukraine 1,279 troops; Australia 1,221 troops; and Portugal 933 troops.[41] When comparing troop contributions in NATO-led operations we see similar trends. In August 2000, the Stabilization Force in Bosnia (SFOR) had 20,800 troops deployed, including 2,200 troops from non-NATO countries. The United States contributed some 4,300 troops to the operation in Bosnia.[42]

The NATO force in Kosovo had 43,600 troops deployed in August 2000, 7,900 of which were from non-NATO countries. The United States had some 5,500 troops deployed, plus an additional 670 in Macedonia to operate a staging base for U.S. troops entering and departing Kosovo. France, Germany, Italy and the United Kingdom provided three times as many troops, with France, Germany and Italy each providing over 4,500 troops. Non-NATO countries provided 18 percent of the total; the United States, 13 percent. In sum, U.S. allies—not the United States—provided the lion's share of the troops for NATO operations in the Balkans.

The third irritant in U.S.-UN relations is the former's hesitant and often unilateralist stance. U.S. hesitation and inaction—even in the face of humanitarian crises—has tainted America's image in the United Nations. In addition, blaming the UN for obvious U.S. policy shortcomings—which happened in Bosnia, Somalia and Rwanda—is unworthy of the world's only remaining superpower. Openly flouting the UN Security Council arms embargo on the former republics of Yugoslavia sent a message that UN Security Council edicts can be violated. Blaming the UN for the unfortunate deaths of the U.S. soldiers in Somalia was simply shameless! It distorted the truth. Standing by and obstructing outside intervention in Rwanda in 1994 was unworthy of policy-makers around the world, but the United States, the world's most powerful country, bears more political and moral responsibility than others.

UN member states often look to the United States for leadership. Ironically, the end of the Cold War saw a steady decline in U.S. interest in multilateral efforts. The United States has been a hesitant and reluctant participant in UN peacekeeping operations. It took the lead in Bosnia only after agonizing for three years about whether and how to get involved. In Somalia, Washington took the lead for four months, but then it distanced itself from the operation and eventually pulled out all together. In Haiti, the United States agreed to go along with an international intervention, only in 1994. The multinational force authorized by the UN Security Council in November 1996 to stave off starvation for hundreds of thousands Hutu refugees in Zaire and to create humanitarian corridors to lead them back into Rwanda, while nominally headed by Canada, could only get off the ground if the U.S. and France were willing to participate in the operation. Since Washington and Paris refused to join in, this relief effort never got under way. Canada could not carry out such an undertaking on its own.

The United States often failed to play an effective leadership role. More specifically, it often failed to identify a clear and compelling course of action, articulate its position to others, and get other states to participate in joint efforts. Many states resented Washington's imperial attitude and its willingness to push multilateral organizations—including the United Nations—aside when these organizations could not agree on a course of action that was to the liking of the United States. Being a leader does not mean bullying others into submission. As Ronald Steel has pointed out,

> The more the United States, because it is so powerful, arrogates the right to act alone without regard to the wishes of other nations, or even in defense of them, the more it loses the legitimacy to act in their name.[43]

And the more it loses the support of others for joint international undertakings.

It may well be true that most internal conflicts around the world will not engage U.S. or other great power interests. However, as great powers, the United States and the other permanent members of the Security Council have special responsibilities for safeguarding regional and international security. They should take these responsibilities seriously. Declarations cannot substitute for engagement on the ground.

The arrival of the Bush administration in January 2001 had many people around the world worried. The unilateral impulses of the Administration were strong. Many commentators, even American conservatives such as Robert Kagan, worried that the new Bush administration was likely to "neglect its responsibilities" as the world's dominant power. Kagan argued that there was a danger that this administration would "allow the international order that it [the US] created and sustains to collapse."[44]

September 11 marked a new beginning for UN-U.S. relations. With U.S. payment of both its dues and its arrears, major irritants have been removed from U.S.-UN relations. U.S. leaders have called on other states to join in an international campaign against terrorism. States around the globe have responded favorably to this appeal. In his inaugural address to the United Nations General Assembly, President Bush thanked these states for their support and for the swift condemnations of the terrorist attacks by both the UN General Assembly and the UN Security Council.[45] The President also acknowledged that the United Nations had an important role to play in rebuilding war-torn Afghanistan.

Whether President Bush will seize this opportunity and forge a broad-based, long-term and durable international foundation for peace and security, remains to be seen. Washington would do well, however, to learn the lessons of its rocky relations with the United Nations. The United States cannot champion international cooperation when it is convenient for Washington to do so, and slight it the rest of the time. Many global peace and security threats can only be overcome if states work together on a host of issues. International cooperation cannot be turned on and off again. Building international patterns of cooperation requires constant attention and takes steady and sustained engagement. It should also be based on mutual respect. Most importantly, though, international cooperation needs a strong institutional foundation.

The United Nations is the only organization with near-universal membership and a broad mandate for the maintenance of international peace and security. It is the best available platform for the formation and maintenance of international coalitions to combat global security threats. A strong United Nations is therefore in the interest of all states, including the United States.

Notes

1. Chantal de Jonge Oudraat is a Robert Bosch Foundation Research Scholar at the American Institute for Contemporary German Studies (AICGS), John Hopkins University.

2. UN peacekeepers received the Nobel prize in 1988. The Office of the United Nations High Commissioner for Refugees (UNHCR) received the prize twice, in 1954 and 1981. The United Nations Children's Fund (UNICEF) received the prize in 1965. The International Labor Organization (ILO) received the prize in 1969. Dag Hammerskjöld, the second UN Secretary-General who perished in a plane crash in the Congo in 1961, was awarded the prize posthumously in that same year.

3. See, for example, Kofi Annan, "No Letting Up on AIDS," *Washington Post*, November 29, 2001, p. A33.

4. See the speech by Richard Haass, Head of Policy Planning, (U.S. State Department) at the Carnegie Endowment on November 14, 2001, www.ceip.org.

5. *Ibid.*

6. What constitutes a "threat to the peace, breach of the peace, or act of aggression" is not defined in the Charter because the great powers, particularly the United States and the Soviet Union, wanted to maintain control over UN decisions in this area on a case by case basis: precise, formal definitions would have impinged on the P-5's political control of the organization.

7. The U.S. soldiers were killed October 3, 1993, while attempting to capture the Somali warlord Mohamed Aideed.

8. By that time the final touches were put on U.S. Presidential Decision Directive 25 (PDD-25), a public summary of which was released in May 1994. It outlined U.S. policy towards UN peace operations. See Ivo H. Daalder, "The United States and Military Intervention

in Internal Conflict," in Michael E. Brown, *The International Dimensions of Internal Conflict* (Cambridge, MA: MIT Press, 1996), pp. 480-482.

9. In Haiti, on October 11, 1993, supporters of the junta staged an unfriendly reception for UN (mostly American) peacekeepers in the harbor of Port Prince. With the debacle of Somalia fresh in the minds of policymakers in Washington President Clinton ordered the ship to return to the United States. Disembarking the peacekeepers was believed too great of a risk. That said, the image of a U.S. warship fleeing from a bunch of unorganized thugs was to haunt the Clinton administration—it made Clinton and the U.S. appear weak and local parties elsewhere took notes.

10. Attempts by Bosnian Serbs in the spring of 1995 to scare off Western powers by taking UN peacekeepers hostage had less result in this regard. Western powers, albeit hesitantly (it took the massacre of seven thousand Muslim boys and men in Srebrenica), would force Bosnian Serbs in the summer of 1995 to retreat and accept a negotiated peace agreement, that would subsequently be enforced and guaranteed by NATO forces.

11. Peace talks in other parts of Africa were also given renewed attention in 1999 and early 2000. In addition, the UN Security Council recognized HIV/AIDS as a serious security threat.

12. See "Secretary-General Presents His Annual Report to the General Assembly," United Nations Press Release, SG/SM/136 and GA/9596, September 20, 1999.

13. For more on this debate see Chantal de Jonge Oudraat, *Intervention in Internal Conflicts: Legal and Political Conundrums* (Washington, D.C.: Carnegie Endowment for international Peace, Working Paper, No. 15, August, 2000).

14. Article 51 of the UN Charter reads as follows: "Nothing in the present Charter shall impair the inherent right of individual and collective self-defence if an armed attack occurs against a Member of the United Nations, until the Security Council has taken measures necessary to maintain international peace and security. Measures taken by members in the exercise of this right of self-defence shall be immediately reported to the Security Council and shall not in any way affect the authority and responsibility of the Security Council under the present Charter to take at any time such action as it deems necessary in order to maintain or restore international peace or security."

15. Article 42 of the UN Charter reads as follows: "Should the Security Council consider that measures provided for in Article 41 [that is measures not involving the use of armed force] would be inadequate or have proved to be inadequate, it may take such action by air, sea, or land forces as may be necessary to maintain or restore international peace and security. Such action may include demonstrations, blockade and other operations by air, sea, or land forces of Members of the United Nations."

16. Post-September 11 declarations of the Bush administration have emphasized this latter point.

17. U.S. and UK legal justifications were contested by many states and legal experts. The U.S. and its European allies made weak legal cases when defending their intervention in Kosovo and Serbia and did not exhaust all legal avenues. For example they failed to invoke the "Uniting for Peace" resolution of 1950. By this resolution the UN General Assembly gave itself the right to vote on the use of force to restore or maintain international peace and security in case the Security Council was logjammed. For the legal debates see, for example, Catherine Guicherd, "International Law and the War in Kosovo," *Survival*, Vol. 41, No. 2 (Summer 1999), pp. 19-34; and Serge Sur, "Les aspects juridiques de l'intervention des pays membres de l'OTAN au Kosovo," *Revue de Defense Nationale*, December 1999, pp. 44-62. See also Anthony Clark Arend and Robert J. Beck, *International Law and the Use of Force* (London/New York: Routledge, 1993).

18. In 2000, the Security Council requested the UN Secretary-General to enter into negotiations with the Sierra Leonean government to establish an international court to prosecute those responsible for atrocities in Sierra Leone. Unlike the Yugoslav and the Rwandan court, this court will be established by a treaty between Sierra Leone and the United Nations. The composition of the court is mixed: the two trial chambers will have two international judges and one Sierra Leonean judge; the appeals chamber will have three international judges and one from Sierra Leone. In addition, jurisdiction of the court extends to certain domestic laws. The court will

be based in Sierra Leone. However, like the Yugoslav and Rwandan courts, funding for this court will come from assessed UN member states contributions. In January 2001 Cambodia's national assembly approved guidelines to set up an international court to try the leaders of the Khmer Rouge. The Court was to be composed of international and Cambodian judges. However, in February 2002 the UN broke off negotiations with Cambodia—it could not guarantee the independence, impartiality and objectivity of the proposed court.

19. The statute will enter into force once 60 states have ratified the agreement. As of March 6, 2002, the statute had 139 signatures and 53 ratifications. Among the permanent members of the UN Security Council, France and the United Kingdom had signed and ratified the treaty, Russia, and the United States have signed, but not ratified the statute. The United States signed the statute in the last days of the Clinton administration; ratification is highly unlikely in the near term. China has neither signed nor ratified the statute.

20. Crimes of aggression, terrorism, and drug trafficking might be considered at future review conferences.

21. Cited in Shirley Williams, "Human Rights in Europe," in Samantha Power and Graham Allison, eds., *Realizing Human Rights: Moving from Inspiration to Impact* (New York: St. Martin's Press, 2000), p.105.

22. Veton Surroi, "In Kosovo, War is Peace," *New York Times*, March 26, 1999, p. A23.

23. See Stephen John Stedman, "Spoiler Problems in Peace Processes," *International Security*, Vol. 22, No. 2, (Fall 1997), pp. 5-53.

24. Veton Surroi, "In Kosovo, War is Peace," *New York Times*, March 26, 1999, p. A23.

25. International Task Force on the Enforcement of UN Security Council Resolutions, *Words to Deeds: Strengthening the UN's Enforcement Capabilities: Final Report* (New York: United Nations Association-USA, December 1997), p. 6.

26. See, for example, *Supplement to an Agenda for Peace: Position Paper of the Secretary-General on the Occasion of the Fiftieth Anniversary of the United Nations*, A/50/60, or S/1995/1, January 3, 1995, and the *Report of the Panel on United Nations Peace Operations* (New York: United Nations, A/55/305 or S/2000/809, August 21, 2000) (Hereafter: *The Brahimi Report*).

27. *The Brahimi Report*, p. 10, para 53.

28. *The Brahimi Report*, p. x.

29. The regular United Nations budget is generally around the $1 billion mark. The peacekeeping budget fluctuates. Peacekeeping costs for 2000-2001 were estimated at some $2 billion. To put things in perspective, the budget for the UN's core functions—with Secretariats in New York, Geneva, Nairobi, Vienna and five Regional Commissions—is about 4 percent of New York City's annual budget and $3.7 billion less than the annual budget of New York State University System. The United States Defense Budget for 2001 exceeded $310 billion dollars. United States debts to the United Nations for the 1990s were less than the cost of one B-2 bomber—that is, $2.1 billion.

30. In 1999, the Japanese Diet was considering legislation that would limit Japanese assessments for the UN regular budget. See Eric Schmitt, "U.S. Delegate sees UN Dues Cut as Unlikely," *New York Times*, January 22, 2000, p. A8.

31. Republican pro-life representatives led by Representative Chris Smith attached unrelated family planning language to any legislation that had to do with payment of the UN arrears.

32. The Helms-Biden agreement had been held up for almost three years by Representative Chris Smith.

33. In the Senate Judd Gregg, Chairman of the Senate Appropriations Subcommittee refused to release funds for payment of the arrears pending the resolution of issues he would like to see happen in Sierra Leone, East Timor, Congo and Kosovo. In the House Representative Harold Rogers withheld funds destined for UN peacekeeping operations. He wanted assurances that the United States would not spend more than $500 million for peacekeeping in 2000 and that money appropriated by Congress for peacekeeping in Kosovo would not be diverted. See Judd Gregg, "A Graveyard Peace," *Washington Post*, May 9, 2000, p. A31, and Tim Weiner, "Solitary Republican Senator Blocks Peacekeeping Funds," *New York Times*, May 20, 2000, p. 1A. See also Tim Weiner, "G.O.P. Senator Frees Millions for UN Mission in Sierra Leone," *New York Times*, June 7, 2000, p. A10, and Colum Lynch, "Gregg Drops "hold" on Money for UN,"

Washington Post, June 7, 2000, p. A5. In 2001 the release of arrears was held up by Republican Tom DeLay, the House Majority Whip. He insisted that the Bush Administration accept linkage of the "American Servicemembers' Protection Act." Under this legislation U.S. military personnel had to be immunized from the International Criminal Court's (ICC) jurisdiction before the U.S. participates in any UN peacekeeping operation, and no U.S. military assistance could be extended to any country that had ratified the treaty establishing the ICC, with the exception of major U.S. allies.

34. An attempt in the U.S. Senate to have the Administration pay its dues on time—that is, each January instead of each October—by authorizing a double appropriation for the regular UN budget did unfortunately not receive the needed support in the U.S. Congress. (It would have meant appropriating $1.1 billion). The House would probably have voted against it, moreover the State Department apparently did not consider this to be a high priority. For more on the budget issues see Washington Reports at www.unausa.org.

35. See the address before the United Nations Security Council by Senator Jesse Helms, Chairman U.S. Senate Committee on Foreign Relations, January 20, 2000.

36. According to one calculation this insistence of having NATO lead means that U.S. taxpayers have to disburse roughly $2 billion per year. A UN-led operation in Bosnia would have brought the costs for the United States down to roughly half. See Jeffrey Laurenti and Tobi Trister Gati, *America At Risk from Weakening International Institutions,* (New York: United Nations Association of the USA, 1999, www.unausa.org)

37. The fact that Japan's share of the assessed UN budget is approximately 7 percent larger than the total shares of the four other permanent members of the UN Security Council is in this regards a particular thorn in Japanese eyes.

38. The U.S. share of the UN budget for 1998 was $298 million—the equivalent of $1.11 per American. San Marino, for example, paid $4.26 per citizen to the United Nations. See Emergency Coalition to Fund the UN, www.clw.org/ecun/mythreality.html.

39. Germany, France, Italy, the Netherlands, and the UK have combined a population of 273 million.

40. See, for example, the speech of the French Ambassador M. Dejammet to the UN Security Council, January 20, 2000, or the statement of the Japanese permanent representative to the UN, Mr. Yukio Satoh, at the 54th session of the UN General Assembly, Fifth Committee, March 23, 2000 http://www.un.int/japan/sa0323_0.htm. In terms of disbursements for humanitarian and post conflict reconstruction efforts the Europeans also outdistance the United States by a large measure. For example, at the first donor conference for Kosovo in July 1999 EC and EU member states pledged $1.139 billion as opposed to $557 million for the United States. Overall assistance to Kosovo's neighboring states in 1999 amounted to 733 million Euros (approximately $733 million). Between 1991 and 1999 the EC assistance amounted to 7.5 billion Euros. See European Union, *Fact Sheet European Union's Contribution to the Balkans,* New, No. 54/99, August 1999.

41. The U.S. did a little better in the civilian police department. It came in second with 761 police officers, most of them were deployed in Bosnia and Kosovo. In October 2001 Jordan was the top police contributor with 827 policemen; then came the U.S. with 761; India with 642; Germany with 454; Pakistan with 385; Ghana with 342; the UK with 228; Ukraine with 219; Portugal with 217; and Bangladesh with 196 police officers.

42. U.S. troops in Bosnia, as part of the NATO-led force, have steadily declined from about 18,000 in February 1996 to 6,900 in October 1998 and to about 4,300 in April 2000.

43. See Ronald Steel, "Lonely at the Top," *New York Times,* 1 March 1998, p. 15. See also Ronald Steel, *Temptations of a Superpower: America's Foreign Policy After the Cold War* (Cambridge, MA: Harvard University Press, 1995), p. 109.

44. Robert Kagan, "The World and President Bush," *Survival,* Vol. 43, No. 1, Spring 2001, p. 7. Kagan is a Republican and Co-Editor with William Kristol of the conservative news magazine, *Weekly Standard.*

45. See the speech by President Bush to the UN General Assembly on November 10, 2001.

Civil Society as a Facilitator of Peace

John Prendergast
International Crisis Group and

Emily Plumb
National Aeronautic and Space Administration

Civil society plays an essential role in facilitating peace. Where civil society is left out of the peace-making or peace-implementation equation, war often continues. This chapter will describe the innovative techniques that domestic civil society organizations (CSOs) use to promote peace. A strong civil society not only fosters communication and reconciliation within divided societies and across battle lines, but it can also mediate conflicts, encourage buy-in for peace agreements and support justice initiatives. Civil society also can play a pivotal role in post-conflict reconstruction, by providing education, resettlement and health services, and by boosting economic and political opportunities, thus ensuring that peace is so attractive, to return to conflict would be unlikely.

Civil society involvement is not a panacea. There are certain services and functions that civil society cannot provide, and it would be irresponsible to expect these from upon civil society actors. For instance, first track diplomacy and demobilization programs are best left to national governments or international organizations, such as the United Nations. In most cases, CSOs do not have the experience, capacity or finances to support large-scale efforts. On the other hand, CSOs are often better equipped than international, regional and national actors to understand the needs of the people. Excluding civil society could preclude grassroots buy-in, which is fundamental in building a constituency for peace and making a peace agreement successful.

Civil Society as a Facilitator

Although the composition of civil society varies from place to place, it is generally defined as a group of individuals, larger than the family and excluding the government or military, that is working towards a common goal. Common examples of CSOs include non-profit organizations, student associations, religious, traditional and business leaders, unions, women's groups, agricultural collectives and commercial actors.

In some locales there is a tradition or history of separation between civil society and the state; in others, they operate much more closely. It should be noted that CSOs are not neutral actors; they most likely have political biases, and some actors may have provocative agendas, going so far as to exacerbate conflicts, rather than resolve them. One also must distinguish between international nongovernmental organizations (INGOs) and domestic civil society. This paper tries in most places to focus on the role of domestic civil society in the first instance, while looking at how international agencies can support the involvement and participation of domestic CSOs.

Around the world, civil society is participating in activities to promote peace: early warning detection and conflict prevention, mediation, dialogue, justice and post-conflict reconciliation and reconstruction initiatives. This paper will argue that while CSOs should not be the only actors engaged in these activities, at times they are the most effective vehicles and thus deserve deliberate, sustained international support.

Civil society involves itself in peacebuilding for obvious reasons. These endeavors, which are often dangerous and rarely lucrative, are undertaken by groups and individuals that are usually personally affected by the conflict. A recent survey of CSO participation in peace-building in East Africa clearly demonstrated this phenomenon. Of the forty civil society actors interviewed, thirty-seven of them said that they formed or joined their peacebuilding organization because they were personally affected by the situation. Many also added that they felt compelled to work for a solution because not only could they provide unique insight and understanding, but also they believed that the dominant approach was ineffective.[1]

In other words, CSOs take up peace-building to resolve conflicts in their own back-yard, conflicts they have a vested interest in seeing resolved. Their understandings of the issues involved, their sensitivity to cultural norms and their passion to the cause of peace-building often give CSOs advantages that their international counterparts or track-one diplomacy do not possess. Outside actors may rely on a more ad hoc approach, achieving less success. Similarly, the need to put in place complex systems of early warning indicators becomes less vital when grassroots organizations are involved. When a strong network of effective CSOs exists, they keep each other informed of developments on the ground and alert diplomats and donors to pressing needs. Finally, CSOs are in a unique position to help build intercommunal links, which are critical to reconciliation.

Roles and Methods

It is a widely accepted theory in the mediation field that a conflict must be "ripe" in order to be successfully resolved through third-party mediation. In other words, certain preconditions must exist in order for parties to be open to the idea of a ceasefire and any subsequent peace agreement.[2] This concept of "ripeness" also applies to the effectiveness of CSOs as peacebuilders.

This section discusses the avenues by which CSOs may participate in conflict prevention, mediation, dialogue, justice and post-conflict reconciliation and reconstruction. Timing, in addition to expertise, plays a key role in determining on which activity a CSO should focus. While grassroots reconciliation initiatives might not be effective during a high level of violence in the conflict cycle, another method may prove valuable, such as keeping open channels of communication, or using the media to minimize negative stereotypes and perceptions across lines of division. Thus there is a need for CSOs with a variety of skills and expertise as well as a need for these CSOs to be flexible in adapting their programs to fit the stage of the conflict. As the techniques below suggest, CSOs have developed a wealth of resources for facilitating peacebuilding activities.

Mediation, Post-Conflict Reconstruction and Psycho-Social Trauma Initiatives

State or multi-lateral actors, not CSOs, usually undertake conflict mediation. Third-party mediators are usually higher-profile government officials, bilateral teams or international organizations. CSOs usually do not have the political clout to be effective mediators. They may lack neutrality and financial resources as well as an ability to leverage warring parties to remain at the table. However, mediation may take different forms, usually less direct than getting the leaders of warring parties around a table. CSOs often have a comparative advantage at the sub-national level, where violent conflict often goes unattended or unresolved. With close links to groups on the ground, CSOs can build trust and links across lines that are crucial to dispute resolution.

An example of such CSO mediation is the New Sudan Council of Churches' (NSCC) efforts to mediate sub-national conflicts between ethnic groups in southern Sudan. Divisions between Nuer and Dinka communities tore Sudan apart in the 1990s, as a war-within-a-war erupted, partly because of a successful government policy of divide-and-rule. The NSCC undertook an initiative to bring together chiefs and other community leaders for a series of meetings culminating in a major peace conference in mid-1999, resulting in a peace agreement that helped end large-scale aggression between Nuer and Dinka communities. Other meetings have followed, expanding to other areas of southern Sudan affected by inter-communal fighting.[3]

Another illustrative example is the Nairobi Peace Initiative's (NPI) behind-the-scenes work in Kenya, Ghana and Burundi. NPI's approach involves assembling local and mid-level leaders whose buy-in to a peace agreement is seen as essential and then mediating the disputes between each other.[4] With NPI and other CSOs, mediators are often chosen for their neutrality and for being seen as someone far removed from the conflict, but there are occasions in which a mediator's familiarity with the conflict is seen as an asset. At times, the presence of outsiders in resolving a conflict is seen as intrusive and inappropriate. Homegrown solutions for local problems may be more appealing to combatants.

Civil society's most important contribution to mediation efforts may be their willingness to step in and address problems that are being neglected by national leaders and international organizations. "[In Kenya,] it is a problem of poor governance," says Dr. Peter Bisem of the National Council of Churches of Kenya (NCCK). "Civil society needs to be proactive and intervene, sometimes in volatile areas, to undertake mechanisms of conflict resolution. We must take ownership for our problems instead of waiting for the government to intervene."[5]

CSOs can perhaps be more effective taking on mediation activities on a smaller scale, and local conflict should not be overlooked as a vital concern. As Tecla Wanjala, Coordinator of the Peace and Development Network (Peace Net), a Kenyan CSO states, "In East Africa, more and more, conflicts are taking place at the community level. Regular people need to learn conflict-transformation skills." Her organization's peace committees, teams of between nine and fifteen people trained by Peace Net in conflict transformation skills, repeatedly mediate cattle rustling conflicts in the Eldoret region of Kenya. The peace committee assembles tribal elders to open a dialogue. They also recover the stolen cows; and if someone has been murdered or if property has been damaged, the committee negotiates the compensation.[6] Similarly, Chem Chemi, a Kenyan grassroots organization specializing in active nonviolence as an approach to conflict, trains volunteers to intervene in community-level disputes. ChemChemi was able to successfully interpose at a high school that experienced riots after one student accused a student from another tribe of raping her. The conflict took on political dimensions as students chose sides based on tribal affiliations. ChemChemi mediated between the affected parties and led the rest of the school in an open dialogue about the incident while offering suggestions on how to solve conflicts nonviolently. By the end of the third day, the fighting had stopped and students voluntarily took pens and wrote on their T-shirts "I am for peace."[7]

Post-conflict reconstruction is an essential aspect of peace-building and one to which CSOs are particularly well-equipped to contribute. The sustainability of a peace effort is directly linked to the effectiveness of reconstruction efforts. The United States' war on terrorism in Afghanistan provides an excellent example by which to present CSO reconstruction potential. As the United States, its bilateral partners, the United Nations and international NGOs pave the way for a post-war government, they must be equally concerned with nurturing civil society.

First, CSOs can promote peace agreement buy-in. By lauding a peace settlement as just and equitable and by supporting a new government or transitional authority, CSOs are able to convince their constituents that returning to war is not a worthwhile cause. Second, by developing civil society, a rich selection of educational, economic and political opportunities are created for people, further conditioning them not to return to war. In Afghanistan, for example, CSOs will need funding and guidance to establish programs that support women who are keen to find jobs and continue their education which was interrupted in 1994. Skills training should be made available to former combatants who are unlikely to return to school but will still need jobs. Local human-rights organizations need international support so that they may ensure that justice filters down to the community level.

One of the most important elements of CSO involvement in reconstruction is the inclusion of civic education. CSOs frequently cite the public's ignorance of their own rights as a root cause of conflict. When individuals are unaware of their rights, they can be easily manipulated. According to Edith Awino of the Amani's People Theatre, a CSO in Kenya, the poor and disenfranchised are easily manipulated by politicians who want to exploit citizen anger for political gain.[8] Too often, politicians are able to incite one ethnic group to attack another by convincing them that their adversaries have stolen community resources, such as land, property or livestock. When citizens are aware of their rights, this sort of manipulation becomes less likely. Likewise, the military and police also require training in the area of civil and human rights.

Thus, the development of civil society makes the transition to peace more comprehensive. A holistic approach is needed. The building of civil society should be done simultaneously with humanitarian assistance, economic development, refugee and internally displaced person (IDP) resettlement, human rights and justice, institution building and restoration of the rule of law.

It is well documented that war may leave psychological scars on combatants as well as on civilian bystanders. International NGOs, often working with domestic CSOs, routinely incorporate programs aimed at healing those who suffer from chronic trauma or Post-Traumatic Stress Disorder (PTSD). PTSD occurs when the victim, often a child, experiences a variety of symptoms that hinder his ability to develop or cope emotionally. As a crucial contribution to peacebuilding and reconciliation, CSOs can play important roles in restoring individual and community mental health.

Gulu Support the Children Organization (GUSCO) is a grassroots NGO in northern Uganda that runs a reception center for recently returned child soldiers who fought in the war in southern Sudan, or conducted attacks in northern Uganda. Their specialty is devising counseling programs for children suffering from PTSD. These counseling sessions may take place in group or one-on-one settings. The children's therapy also includes sports as a way to increase socialization as well as skills trainings in carpentry, sewing and bricklaying to compensate for the school-time lost while the children fought in the bush. In addition, GUSCO sees to it that no child is returned to his or her family or village without first having attended a community sensitization program. Often, the community is resentful of the child who may have been forced to attack his own village by his commanding officers. GUSCO explains to the community that the child was forcibly conscripted and encourages forgiveness.[9]

CSOs can act as a guide or facilitator in helping the community expand and develop indigenous recovery strategies. Culturally sensitive programs will enable former child soldiers or victims of war to more freely and constructively process their trauma and incorporate their emotions into their worldview. Assisting communities in devising strategies to help protect children from the effects of war is an important role for aid agencies that can help members of the community (teachers, parents, social workers, police) better understand aggressive behavior displayed by children suffering from chronic trauma and how a parent's reaction can influence a child's behavior. The establishment of daily routines and stable structures by teachers and parents can also help former child combatant's work through their emotions in a more acceptable manner. Political and social reality dictates that program initiatives should be placed in a broader social context if the programs are to be beneficial to the community.

Peace Animators, Peace Media, and Peace Conferences and Committees

Peace animators are individuals who are trained in conflict resolution and reconciliation techniques, and then sent out into the community to train more individuals, mediate conflicts and promote forgiveness. Peace animators can play an important role in detecting early warning symptoms of future conflicts. They may also serve as community educators, keeping people informed of current developments related to the peace and explaining civil rights. GUSCO's peace animators, with the help of Save the Children Denmark, one of their international donors, sensitize the Ugandan army about the proper way to treat returning child soldiers who suffer from PTSD.[10] In Rwanda, peace animators have been able to foster reconciliation in communities where people who lost loved ones and property during the war and genocide still distrust their neighbors. Oswald Uwanyirigira, a peace animator for a Catholic diocese in Rwanda, regularly settles such disputes among his neighbors whom an overburdened justice system has overlooked.[11] In southern Sudan, the NSCC is training peace educators to undertake dispute resolution at the community level.

Reaching large numbers of people in war-effected environments is most efficiently done through the media. It is estimated that there are over fifty million radios spread throughout the developing world, including millions in areas currently or formerly controlled by rebel or government forces in which propaganda has been the main source of information. Diplomats and aid officials are paying increased attention to the potential role of media, and how to influence it positively in favor of peace efforts. For example, there is increasing recognition of the impact which radio programming can have on education, as well as on reconciliation processes. Debates are intensifying about the roles of international NGOs and domestic CSOs in promoting reconciliation through media outlets. Increasing legitimacy is being lent to ideas such as training journalists in sensitivity to conflict issues; providing airtime to local peacemakers, rather than just the combatants; and highlighting the economic benefits of peace through the media. This all parallels a debate within the journalism community about whether reporting is meant to reflect or change society.[12] In Cambodia after the peace agreement was signed, the U.N. worked with CSOs to initiate radio broadcasts designed to counter rumors and inaccurate information. By many accounts this lowered tensions and suspicions.[13] Radio programming geared toward peace is a low-cost intervention that can—if necessary—be undertaken from a great distance. Countering hate radio, for example, is critical for providing alternative points of view in highly charged societies.

The Amani People's Theatre (APT) employs a participatory multi-arts approach, which integrates education, research and entertainment in exploring context-specific issues of peace and reconciliation in East and Central Africa. Rather than focusing on dialogue or teaching, APT expects its audience to use theatre, dance and storytelling to recreate everyday incidents of conflict and subsequently act out possible solutions. A more advanced, three- to four-day workshop builds on those ideas by introducing participants to conflict-resolution theories, and a "graduate program" asks participants to apply lessons learned in the previous workshops to conflicts with which they are unfamiliar. According to Edith Awino, an APT member, the objectivity of the facilitators is extremely important to their methods. "We are only catalysts and facilitators. We ask the people to brainstorm the solutions. We don't act anything out; we just ask people to relive their experiences. Otherwise we would be leading them too much and offering a prescription." She adds that there are no costumes in APT productions. "Costumes are false identities, and they could hinder people from participating, opening up and being honest."[14]

LIPRODOR, a Rwandan human rights NGO, also utilizes peace theatre. Rather than focus on a participatory approach such as the APT does, they use a traveling theatre troupe to perform morality plays, depicting everyday conflict situations and proposing solutions.[15] Besides radio and theatre, television has also been employed as a mode of transmission for ideas of tolerance. An example of the latter is Search for Common Ground's programming in South Africa.

Peace conferences and peace committees are ways in which grassroots actors can influence a peace agreement or promote reconciliation. Peace conferences may consist of trained volunteers or elected community representatives who meet to propose peaceful solutions to a conflict or to consolidate an existing peace agreement. *Kacoke Madit* is a citizen-peace assembly organized by a group from the northern Ugandan Diaspora. At one major gathering in 2000, they included tribal, religious and other civil society leaders, representatives of the Governments of Sudan and Uganda, as well as members of the international community who had expressed commitment to resolving the conflict. The diaspora also raised funds so that two students and two teachers from each affected high school could attend the event. The first day of the conference was dedicated to the accomplishments and concerns of CSOs in the region.[16] Although Kacoke Madit did not directly bring an end to the fighting in northern Uganda and southern Sudan, it is seen by participants as an important forum for information sharing as well as an idea-generating and networking tool and it helped support other higher level efforts aimed at ending the Sudan-supported insurgency in northern Uganda. The international meetings keep the conflict in the public eye, both at home and abroad, and serve as a morale booster for those who are dedicated to peace in the region.

Peace commissions and committees are another strategy for bringing together mid-level actors in a conflict or post-conflict situation. The Central American peace agreement, signed by all five countries in the region, called for the creation of National Peace Commissions in each country. In Nicaragua, regional and local commissions were established as well, including one composed of mid-level religious leaders for the conflict between the Sandanista government and the Yamata umbrella group for the East Coast opposition. John Paul Lederach notes that this was a model example of an insider-partial approach to peace-building, in which intermediaries come directly from all sides of the conflict setting.[17]

Similarly, regional and local peace committees were formed in South Africa after the National Peace Accord. The successes of the South African commissions are not well advertised, but in many cases they have contained potential violence. For example, after the assassination of African National Congress official Chris Hani in April 1993, peace commission personnel worked successfully to restrain revenge-seeking individuals and groups. The number of casualties would have been far higher than 200 in the absence of the commissions.[18]

Unless attached to some broader post-conflict reconciliation process, peace conferences are limited by the small numbers of people attending the conferences themselves and the usual lack of follow-up. Diplomats all too often don't see the relevance of such second-track initiatives and thus do not bring them into a broader strategy of peace-building.

Cross-Line Aid Programming, Peace Advocacy, Peace Festivals and Indigenous Methods

Once the proper analytical framework has been constructed, there are situations in which reconciliation initiatives have much clearer chances of success. For example, in Angola before the reignition of the war in 1998, some analysts contended that feelings of revenge and hatred were strongest among the leadership of the two warring parties, while these emotions were much less strong at local levels. Even at the leadership level there was great variation from province to province. Many Angolan families were divided on both sides of the ceasefire line, and desires for family reunification provided a strong impetus for reconciliation.[19] Nevertheless, there was a dearth of creative activities aimed at bridging divisions at the local level. The devastation caused by the war left a legacy of distrust and division, and these "circles of revenge" helped undermine the Lusaka peace agreement.

CSOs have begun to address this grassroots bridge-building in order to increase contacts across government/rebel lines. Globally, INGOs and CSOs are examining new approaches to the provision of aid and community development that help build economic and social links between communities.[20]

CSO involvement in advocacy is key. CSOs are increasingly equipping themselves to recognize what the bottlenecks are to the consolidation of peace through their unique windows and working to keep the implementing authorities accountable. Aside from directly pushing for peace, advocacy could be undertaken for the free movement of people and goods, refugee return and equity in service provision.

In Angola, one of the most significant barriers to reconciliation before the breakdown of the Lusaka Accords was that almost no travel was allowed across lines of division by the warring parties. Cross-line contact among communities formerly in conflict is an essential means of promoting reconciliation. This would involve advocacy and engagement with the formerly warring parties in Angola and elsewhere. Angolan CSOs are increasingly important for both kinds of peace advocacy. CSOs have launched a peace campaign, which has softened the ground for the future possibility of a peaceful resolution of the long-running civil war. CSOs are also key in promoting free movement of people across lines of division. In the war between Ethiopia and Eritrea, religious leaders from both sides worked together to promote a peaceful resolution between the two governments.

Some CSOs have focused efforts on events celebrating the strengths of communities and emphasizing the kinds of activities people enjoy most, and connected them to peace-building initiatives. In Rwanda, youth committees, groups of elected youth leaders from the national level down to the village level, organize Peace Days. These celebrations include peace essay-writing contests, skits and sports competitions with the goal of fostering better community relations.[21] Peace Net in Kenya has held several peace festivals that also target youth. The program may include conflict resolution trainings, AIDS educational sessions or a football "Peace Cup." "We have no problems with attendance," explained Tecla Wanjala, Coordinator of Peace Net. "Usually it is (the youth's) initiative."[22]

In many cultures, indigenous peace-building tools have been lost or forgotten over time. Similarly, modernization, colonization or occupation by foreign entities may have also eroded traditional leadership structures, such as the African chiefs or the church, which would have historically held the responsibility for peacebuilding and reconciliation. In these cases, relying solely on indigenous methods may not be an adequate option. However, in a supporting role and at the local level, indigenous conflict resolution techniques can be very effective tools, particularly in the area of reconciliation. In northern Uganda, GUSCO encourages relatives to perform "cleansing ceremonies" when a former child soldier is reunited with his family. Tradition holds that by following a ritual, which includes sacrificing an animal, pouring water on the roof of a house and stepping over eggs in the doorway, an offender will be cleansed of his sins and embraced by his family and neighbors.[23]

Indigenous methods may also be appropriate for justice initiatives. In Rwanda, authorities are reviving the *gacaca* system, the traditional community system for resolving legal problems. Since the national legal system is backlogged with cases related to the 1994 genocide, it is argued that *gacaca* will help relieve the Rwandan judicial system of some of its caseload burden. As in the case of *gacaca*, international organizations can play an important role in reviving these traditions and strengthening their contribution to peace-building.

Of course, it is sometimes difficult to separate modern techniques from traditional ones. A common civil society method is to facilitate dialogue between alienated groups. This may parallel contemporary approaches, but in Africa, elders have a long tradition of meeting to discuss conflicts. "It is important to involve the tribal elders. In many places, they still command respect—more than the police, for instance," said Wanjala.[24] Similarly, psycho-social initiatives and trauma counseling do not seem like such foreign concepts if one considers the fact that talking through problems is a familiar idea in many cultures. In the end, peacebuilding initiatives should only be about best practice. The methods to use are the ones that work—regardless of whether or not they are indigenous to a community.

Challenges of CSOs

Given their small size, the stressful environment in which they work, limited resources and the constant search for funding, CSOs encounter continuous challenges. One of the most obvious challenges is the attitude of authorities toward independent activity often perceived as innately political. CSOs in Asia, Africa, Latin America and parts of Europe are often harassed, intimidated, restricted, undermined or worse in the context of state crackdowns on possible sources of opposition. This will only be exacerbated in the aftermath of the September 11 terrorist attacks and domestic crackdowns in the name of counter-terrorism. Another frequently cited challenge for CSOs is the inability to form effective networks of those engaged in peacebuilding activity. Small numbers of staff and constrained funding mean that it is particularly crucial for CSOs to pool their resources. Networks also minimize the opportunity for duplicating services and are more powerful vehicles for advocacy. CSOs may try to form formal networks through regular meetings; there is a tendency, however, for these gathering to be so large and inclusive that they are unproductive. Rather, CSOs should form networks to keep each other informed of their activities and then meet in smaller groups for more relevant information sharing. "We have the knowledge, but we are not good at sharing it with people doing similar work. We are also bad at documenting our work," said Paul Helsoot, technical advisor for the Community Peace Building Development Project (CPBD) of the National Council of Churches in Kenya (NCCK). Helsoot also recommends exchange visits that would allow civil society actors to visit another organization's projects that interest them and pertain to their own work.[25] These visits would also provide an opportunity to ask detailed questions that are inappropriate in large meetings.

The Kenya-based Peace and Development Network (Peace Net) is one example of a successful network of CSOs. The organization not only boasts 300 members from independent CSOs but also has established ten peace committees around the country, which are the implementing arm of Peace Net's community peace work. Through membership dues, Peace Net has been able to train 500 community workers in conflict transformation skills. A quarterly "peace journal," or newsletter, aids members in information sharing. It also links communities to various international NGOs.[26]

Evaluating Progress

It is impossible to overstate the difficulty most CSOs have in finding funding. Part of this problem is inevitable, resulting from a limited pool of resources in a sea of seemingly unending needs. However, the other side of the funding issue is directly tied to the question of a donor's need to evaluate a recipient and its peacebuilding efforts. Not surprisingly, donors want to evaluate a CSO's progress in order to judge if the peacebuilding activities are an effective use of funding.

Evaluation can be a complicated process, particularly for a small organization overwhelmed by operational requirements. CSOs are the first to admit that it is difficult to measure progress since successful peacebuilding means a change in attitudes has occurred. This is a difficult phenomenon to quantify. Indicators are not necessarily obvious. Moreover, such attitude changes may take place slowly, manifesting themselves years later. And while a decrease in violent incidents is certainly a quantifiable benchmark, community success stories are often clouded by continuing violence on a national or international level, or even by state crackdowns in response to local successes.

Further complicating the picture is the idea that peacebuilding activities should be only one piece of a larger puzzle. CSO activities such as those described above should be coupled with such macroeconomic or structural initiatives such as economic reconstruction, free elections and institution building. Thus it would be difficult to isolate which factors are most responsible for fostering a sustainable peace. Lastly, multiple peacebuilding activities by different groups may blur the evaluation process. According to Helsoot, "The bad thing about donors insisting on assessment is that we will never know if the results achieved can be credited to us. Maybe it was a charismatic minister somewhere who was responsible for reconciling two warring groups. You can't trace the sources of changes. How can you show it was your action that brought this (particular) result?"[27]

Evaluation assessments have become a necessary evil. CSOs complain of spending limited time and resources documenting their perceived successes at the insistence of donors. Donor governments and organizations often have onerous reporting requirements, involving indicators that are difficult to quantify. Some admit to putting on unnecessary workshops because they are under the impression that donors will only be impressed by large numbers of activities, rather than by the quality of a smaller number of initiatives. These criticisms are not meant to suggest that there should be no means of accountability. In fact, the opposite is true. However, donors must be more sensitive to the concerns of CSOs, and allow their time and resources to be spent undertaking peace-building activities.

To be fair, ineffectiveness abounds; many CSOs are neither well-equipped nor dedicated enough to produce worthwhile activities. A CSO in Uganda with the objective of reintegrating former soldiers into post-conflict life boasted having 230 members but also admitted to having accomplished little because of a lack of funding. Survival of the fittest also applies to civil society. It is not the responsibility of international donors to prop up failing or ineffective organizations. Ideally, once these organizations have proven themselves, a less rigid evaluatory system, which is agreed on by both donor and recipient, should be put into place. At the same time, donors must stay current of the recipient's progress in less intrusive ways; maintaining regular communication, for example, is one basic method.

The National Council of Churches in Kenya (NCCK) has developed a sophisticated system for evaluating its work. First, NCCK makes a distinction between output and impact indicators and examines both forces. Output indicators include recording the number and kind of different activities offered (e.g., four legislator/parliamentary workshops, six good neighborliness seminars and 100 youth-club meetings). On the other hand, impact indicators often require more research. In addition to tracking the number of workshop participants, NCCK employees ask a series of questions: which ethnic/religious groups were represented?; were the participants first-time or regular attendees?; what degree of interaction amongst participants of different backgrounds accompanied the workshop? They also evaluate societal interactions as a whole: are people participating in joint trade and economic ventures? Are community members sharing community resources, such as water and land, peacefully? In addition, NCCK tracks more traditional indicators such as the number incidents of ethnic violence as well as interruptions to resettlement work.[28]

Finally, just as CSOs should look for conflict warning signs, they also should look for widespread behavioral changes as signs that peace and reconciliation are taking hold. Such signs might include the return of children to schools, vendors to a marketplace, or worshippers their places of worship; the level of inclusion in the media; and the degree of economic cooperation among divided communities. And CSOs should do follow-up work on all of their programs. Trauma counselors, for example, should locate children who received counseling and interview those children, as well as their friends and family, to ascertain if the counseling services were effective. Such follow-up work is the only way to judge if current methods are useful or if they need to be revised.

Conclusion

Civil society plays an essential role in creating a favorable environment for the conclusion and implementation of negotiated settlements. International donors should take advantage of these actors' expertise and dedication to solving conflicts by providing resources and by supporting the capacity for grassroots peacebuilding.

If international actors exclusively work with government and/or rebel leaders during a conflict, their accomplishments will be limited. Involving CSOs allows for contacts throughout society, especially with key non-governmental, opinion-shapers. These people and groups are key in building constituencies for peace in divided societies. It is especially important to nurture these relationships in regions where corruption is rampant and leaders are encouraging people to continue waging war.

CSOs can play important roles in facilitating peace. Their effectiveness is increased if their facilitative role is part of a larger peace strategy developed by those responsible for negotiating or implementing peace agreements. A holistic approach to peacemaking and peace-building requires the bottom-up contacts and environment for reconciliation that CSOs are best positioned to provide. There are numerous examples of how CSOs have been employed in successful peacebuilding initiatives. By studying these examples and by sharing them with the parties involved, the future effectiveness of CSOs in facilitating peace can only increase.

Notes

1. Field research conducted by Emily Plumb in East Africa, June-December 2000.

2. Chet Crocker, Fen Osler Hampson, Pamela Aall, Herding Cats, (Washington, DC, U.S. Institute of Peace Press, 1999), p. 21-28.

3. International Crisis Group, "God, Oil and Country: Changing the Logic of War in Sudan," ICG: Brussels, 2002.

4. Interview with George Wachira, Nairobi Peace Initiative, Nairobi, Kenya, 11/17/00.

5. "Case for Kenya: An Agenda for Peace" conference, lecture by Dr. Peter Bisem, National Council of Churches of Kenya, Nairobi, Kenya, 12/07/00.

6. Interview with Tecla Wanjala, Peace and Development Network, Nairobi, Kenya, 11/16/00.

7. Interview with Otieno Ombok, ChemChemi, Nairobi, Kenya, 11/16/00.

8. Interview with Michael Owiso and Edith Awino, Amani's People Theatre, Nairobi, Kenya, 11/16/00.

9. Interview with George Omona, Gulu Support the Children Organization, Gulu, Uganda, 07/18/00.

10. Omono, 07/08/00.

11. Interview with Oswald Nwanyirigira, Peace Animator, Catholic Diocese of Guitarama, 09/21/00.

12. Clare Pointon, "Small Wars and Smart Relief," Crosslines Global Report, July 1996, p. 33-34.

13. Mary Anderson, *Do No Harm: How Aid Can Support Peace or War,* (Boulder: Lynne Rienner, 1999), p. 40-41.

14. Owiso, Awino, 11/16/00.

15. Interview with Théobald Rutihumza, Rwandan

League for the Promotion of the Defense of Human Rights (LIPRODOR), Kigali, Rwanda, 10/05/00.

16. Kacoke Madit Citizen Peace Assembly, Nairobi, Kenya, 11/26/00.

17. John Paul Lederach, *Building Peace: Sustainable Reconciliation in Divided Societies* (Washington, DC: USIP, 1997), p. 26.

18. Michael Lund and John Prendergast, *Preventing and Mitigating Violent Conflict: A Guide for Practioners,* (Washington, DC: Creative Associates International, 1997), p. B22-24.

19. David Smock and John Prendergast wrote two "Special Reports" for the U.S. Institute of Peace on Angola exploring these themes. See:http://www.usip.org.

20. John Prendergast, *Frontline Diplomacy,* Boulder: Lynne Rienner, 1997.

21. Interview with John Rusimbi, National Youth Council, Kigali, Rwanda, 9/20/00.

22. Wanjala, 11/16/00.

23. Interview with Chief David Onen Acana, Gulu, Uganda, 07/20/00.

24. Wanjala, 11/16/00.

25. Interview with Paul Helsoot, Community Peace Building Development Project, National Council of Churches of Kenya, 11/17/00.

26. Wanjala, 11/16/00.

27. Helsoot, 11/17/00.

28. Helsoot, 11/17/00.

International Economic Organizations: Working Globally for Material Well-Being and Peace

Doug Bandow
CATO Institute

The United Nations faces challenges on many fronts. Perhaps nowhere does it veer closer to obsolescence than in dealing with the international economy. Whereas the UN, assorted specialized agencies and allied organizations once played a significant role in shaping the global economic system and aiding underdeveloped states, today rampant globalization has largely passed by the UN.

Huge private capital flows dwarf official aid levels. Market reforms have swept away *dirigiste* economic planning. Mobile transnational corporations have reduced the importance of international borders. Ever-accelerating entrepreneurial and technological change have marginalized government regulation.

The UN and other international organizations should promote rather than combat such trends. The advance of economic freedom will ultimately benefit most people around the globe, helping to free them from financial poverty and political repression. The UN's most important duty is to first do no harm by impeding such liberating forces. Second, it should encourage freer and more open markets wherever possible.

The 20th Century was the bloodiest and most brutal period in human history. Although its many conflicts led to untold human misery, they also settled some basic issues. People prefer freedom to slavery. Capitalism enriches while socialism impoverishes. Liberty is inseparable: economic and political freedoms build upon and promote each other. The importance of economic liberty was a particularly important lesson for Third World states.

History of Development Theory

Extensive government economic intervention has long existed around the world, including the West, for political as well as philosophical reasons. Such policies have been especially evident throughout the 1900s. In particular, the vast majority of Third World states traveled the socialist path as decolonization proceeded after World War II. Their decision was in part nationalistic; many new countries believed that true independence required indigenous control of economic resources. Ghana's Kwame Nkrumah, for instance, explained that his nation's "socialist transformation would eradicate completely the colonial structure" of the economy. Statism also tended to benefit, both economically and politically, the elites that gained power after independence.

But there was also a genuine belief that the government had to guide the development process.

Said Nkrumah, "only a socialist form of society can assure Ghana of a rapid rate of economic progress without destroying that social justice, that freedom and equality, which are a central feature of our traditional way of life."

This *dirigiste* philosophy was not, however, based on local tradition. Indeed, in countries like Ghana the very concept of development was an alien idea, introduced by the West. Observed Columbia University's Robert Rothstein, "Imported doctrines of rapid growth and industrialization, and simplistic exhortations about the ease with which the conditions of underdevelopment could be overcome, also ensured that the developing countries would become increasingly involved with a complex international environment—and for this, the Western governments and Western experts must share some part of the responsibilities." In short, it was outsiders who most encouraged ambitious leaders of poor lands to attempt to drag their people into the industrial age as quickly as possible.

Having helped ordain the goal of rapid industrialization, Western politicians and economists also played a major role in developing the statist strategies that many Third World nationalists were to call their own.[1] Of the many foreigners who have acted as the sirens in Homer's *Odyssey,* luring Third World economies, instead of wandering seafarers, upon the rocks, perhaps the most important was Lenin. While Marx, ironically, viewed the colonial experience as a progressive force in the undeveloped world (lauding the potential of capitalism to transform such societies in *The Communist Manifesto),* it was Lenin, in *Imperialism: The Highest Stage of Capitalism,* who specifically applied socialist principles to underdeveloped states. Lenin's arguments had enormous influence throughout the Third World, providing ruling elites with both a program for political action and an excuse for economic failure.

The British Fabian socialists argued for a more gradual collectivist transformation. According to Indian economist Jagdish Bhagwati, this approach exercised "a powerful impact through the large numbers of the Indian elite that were processed through the English educational institutions prior to Indian independence in 1947." Other developing countries, too—especially other former British colonies—looked to Fabian principles as they structured their economies to be dominated by the public sector.

Along with the philosophy came practical economic controls. The policies promoted by the London School of Economics eventually suffused the British Colonial Office. Many officials in London as well as colonial governors, writes P.T. Bauer, "took for granted the case for the most diverse forms of state economic intervention." Business licensing, trade restraints, agricultural marketing boards, and more were part of the administrative apparatus handed over to many new governments upon independence.

Western development economists, who advised both underdeveloped states and Western aid agencies, generally leaned towards the so-called "structuralist school." It treated developing economies as inflexible and unresponsive to market forces. Changes in factors such as prices, taxes, and regulations were thought to have little effect on economic progress.

So pervasive was the anti-capitalist bias in terms of Third World development that even economists who recognized an important role for the private sector in advanced economies viewed developing states differently. Wrote Robert Heilbroner, "In the great transformation of the underdeveloped areas, the market mechanism is apt to play a much smaller role than in the comparable transformation of the West during the industrial revolution."[2] Heilbroner saw the need for more than just active public sector management: "Powerful, even ruthless, government may be needed:" He saw communism "as a technique for attempting to bring about the deep-seated changes required for rapid modernization."[3]

Most fundamental to traditional development dogma of all collectivist stripes was the need for central planning. Indeed, for years the only question was how extensive the state control should be.

Development specialists like Gunnar Myrdal advocated a ubiquitous public sector: "One of the most serious shortcomings of policy in the countries in which comprehensive planning has been undertaken is the failure to plan more ambitiously and on a larger scale," contended Myrdal.

Finally, even some Western economists who did not advocate full government economic planning nevertheless endorsed the sort of micromanagement that has been increasingly recognized as a failure in the industrialized nations. Expansive fiscal and monetary policies, for instance, were a Keynesian norm. Equally persistent was pressure on developing countries to increase taxes.

International Financial Organizations and Development

Alas, Western economists did not only write about such theories. They also used international institutions to push their views. There are exceptions, such as the General Agreement on Trade and Tariffs (GATT), more recent World Trade Organization (WTO), and regional trade forums, such as the Asia-Pacific Economic Cooperation (APEC). But the organizations with money behind them largely pushed a more statist agenda.

Consider the World Bank, mistakenly criticized by left-wing demonstrators as a tool of global capitalism. Although today the Bank at least theoretically endorses market-oriented reform, it did not always do so. Since shortly after its creation, the Bank backed statist development strategies. "By the time the World Bank made its first loan outside Europe in 1948:" write Bank staffers Warren Baum and Stokes Tolbert, "it found many developing countries committed to or already engaged in some form of centralized economic planning." But the bank did little to try to change those strategies.

Why should it have done so, however? Most of its staff seemed to believe in the "structuralist" theory of development, which assumed that Third World peoples could do little to advance their own lives but had to have a development program imposed from above by a strong central regime. Consider Stanley Please, a senior manager at the Bank. As he prepared to retire in 1983, Please wrote that he was "a committed socialist" when he arrived at the Bank, but: "I was surprised and shocked by the emphasis which the Bank at the time gave to the public sector in general and to the government in particular. Here was an institution which has the reputation of being ultra free enterprise and market-oriented, yet had more confidence in the rationality, morality and competence of governments than I ever had."[4]

Given that orientation of the Bank's management, one that intensified as Robert McNamara, appointed president in 1968, doubled and redoubled Bank lending, it is perhaps not surprising that for years the Bank lent to public entities, underwrote all manner of state development activities, and refused even to suggest alternative strategies. Yet despite left-wing attacks on the Reagan administration for allegedly pressing the Bank to support capitalism, in 1987 Bank President Conable, a de facto Reagan administration appointee, stated, "Obviously, while I have some prejudice in favor of market resolution of difficulties, an institution like the World Bank cannot take a rigid position on such things."[5]

Thus, in the same year the Bank lent Ethiopia \$39 million for, *inter alia,* augmenting its Ministry of Agriculture—the very bureau to blame for exacerbating the ongoing famine. Other beneficiaries of Bank financing that year included Ghana's agricultural bureaucracy, China's Ministry of Chemical Industry, Guinea-Bissau's Ministry of Rural Development and Fisheries, Tunisia's Agency for Energy Conservation, and Zaire's economic planning agencies. And Bank lending continues to flow to government departments that direct large segments of the borrowers' economies.

The fundamental problem is that the Bank itself is a public institution and tends to favor its own kind. One senior Reagan administration official complained, "It's hard to expect a government-owned multilateral body not to be primarily responsive to other governments and take the view that government-sponsored, government-owned, government-guaranteed projects are the best thing going. Because there is that bias, you have to fight to develop a private sector."

No different is the International Monetary Fund. It, too, has been criticized for its supposed commitment to free markets. Yet economist John Williamson has defended the IMF against the criticism that it is too market-oriented:

> It has also been charged that the Fund is biased against socialism. That the Fund welcomes those governments that are willing to work with market forces cannot be doubted. At the same time, the Fund clearly does not have an evangelical zeal for spreading "the magic of the market" parallel to that of, say, the Reagan administration. Its attitude, it would claim, is nonideological: it seeks to promote economic rationality, and it just happens that under a wide range of circumstances the readiest means to that end involves harnessing, instead of fighting, market forces.
>
> What is surely true is that the Fund does not refuse to provide financial assistance to members with left-wing governments. On the contrary, [in late 1989] some 16.5 percent of IMF credit was directed to the six communist member countries (China, Kampuchea, Laos, Romania, Vietnam, and Yugoslavia)...and Michael Manley's Jamaica was at one stage the heaviest per capita borrower from the Fund.... Moreover, the Fund continued to give the Allende government the benefit of the doubt in drawing from the compensatory financing facility.[6]

The IMF similarly disclaims a bias against collectivist systems: "The Fund has had programs in all types of economies and has worked with their authorities, identifying the best way to achieve external balance or exercising its function of surveillance over the payments and exchange system.... In many instances, Fund-supported programs have accommodated such nonmarket devices as production controls, administered prices, and subsidies."[7] It is hard to take seriously an organization's claim to be "pro-development" when it regularly pours large sums of money into the worst economic systems on earth.

In an assessment of lending to communist states, for example, Valerie Assetto writes, "Romania's economic reforms were superficial and actually worked to increase the power of the state. The ensuing economic crisis quickly eclipsed the 'reform' movement, and it quietly expired. Fund and Bank support of the Romanian development effort continued throughout this period."

Similarly, she found that the "Yugoslav authorities actually retreated slightly from the market orientation of the 1960s" despite generous assistance in following years. As late as 1990 Camdessus lauded the fact that the IMF remained engaged in that country, supporting "a comprehensive and bold program to stop inflation in its tracks and to reform the economy over the medium term." Yet economists Jeffrey Sachs and David Lipton blame the Fund's conditions—particularly its commitment to continued devaluations—as helping to "cause Yugoslavia to drift from high inflation into hyperinflation."

At times it would appear that the more perverse the policies the more generous the IMF. The problem is not just the one-time Soviet bloc, but the many Third World regimes that followed statist economic policies for decades. For instance, India collected more money than any other developing state from the IMF which acted more as a lender of first rather than last resort, during its first 40 years. Yet while India was borrowing prodigiously from the IMF (and other multilateral institutions) it was pursuing a Soviet-style industrialization program. Observes Catherine Gwin of the Carnegie Endowment of International Peace:

> India's economy is continental in scope; highly industrialized and extremely poor; centrally planned—some would say overly planned; administratively encumbered and rampant with corruption; caste-bound and socialist-inspired; determinedly self-reliant; and, though guided by principles of social democracy, protective of the interests of politically powerful, propertied groups.

The Mexican government was destroying its economy in the 1970s even as it was a regular IMF customer. When Mexico's threatened default on its vast international obligations essentially set off the debt crisis in 1982, the IMF helped come to the rescue. Yet the loans did little to improve Mexico's economic performance; that nation did not begin making major market-oriented reforms until the end of the decade after squandering billions more of foreign money on counterproductive state-led development schemes.

In 1974 the IMF negotiated a loan to Tanzania, which agreed to adopt a package "of compromises that might be called socialist realism," in the words of one observer. But the government, which had ruined the economy through such policies as forced agricultural collectivization (the Ujamaa program), refused to cut spending and the IMF terminated the program, having done no more than further subsidize the leading example of "African socialism:" In 1983 Reginald Herbold Green, of the Institute of Development Studies, concluded, "IMF influence on Tanzanian action has, to date, been fairly modest. Direct impact since 1976 has, arguably, been negative. Indirect effects are hard to assess."

The experiences of the regional multilateral lending institutions—the African, Asian, and Inter-American Development Banks and the European Bank for Reconstruction and Development (EBRD)—are much the same. The former three have boasted remarkably statist lending policies; the African Development Bank's experience was particularly disastrous. Largely because it was created later, after the importance of markets was more widely accepted, with an institutional requirement to support private as well as government projects has the EBRD performed better.

United Nations Organizations and the World Economy

The multilateral lending institutions have obviously played the most important economic role. However, other international agencies, many more firmly within the UN system, also have influenced economic events. And for years their impact was largely malign.

Throughout the 1970s and early 1980s a host of UN organizations, including official (UNCTAD, UNITAR) and autonomous (UNESCO, WHO) promoted what was then known as the New International Economic Order (NIEO). Kenneth Adelman, a Reagan administration official, noted that without the UN system there would have been no "institutional, concrete locale" that gave "substance to what might otherwise be merely an abstract wish."

The conglomeration of UN-related agencies also provided money and staff to promote a highly statist and redistributionist economic agenda. Professional staffs of a myriad UN agencies, wrote economist P.T. Bauer and journalist John O'Sullivan, "have discarded even the appearance of neutrality to become, in effect, union organizers for the Third World," most notably the Group of 77 voting block.

The NIEO was a hydra-headed program of international economic intervention. It included placing natural resources under UN control (e.g., the seabed through the Law of the Sea Treaty, or LOST), fixing prices for commodities (LOST, UNCTAD), establishing commercial preferences for developing countries (UNCTAD), mandating technology transfers (LOST, UNCTAD, United Nations Industrial Development Organization, or UNIDO), imposing global taxes and increasing foreign aid (LOST, UNIDO, UNCTAD, UNITAR, UNDP), undermining intellectual property rights (UNCTAD, UNIDO, World Intellectual Property Organization), regulating international commerce (LOST, UNIDO, UNCTAD, WHO, Center for Transnational Corporations, International Labor Organization), and even controlling the international media (UNESCO).[8]

However well-intentioned this approach in theory, it turned out to be enormously wrong-headed in practice. Although such redistribution offered short-term rewards to incumbent governments, over the long-term such attacks on private entrepreneurship, investment, and business guaranteed that underdeveloped states would languish in poverty, it came as no surprise when, in 1996, the United Nations reported that 70 countries were poorer than they were in 1980; 43 were worse off than they were in 1970.[9]

Indeed, by 1989 history had clearly rendered its judgment on collectivism, with the consequent collapse of communism, implosion of numerous authoritarian Third World regimes, and conversion of many others from statism to free markets. The obvious lesson of this experience has received increasing acceptance: without reliance on relatively open markets, there is little that can be done to foster development and progress.

What Causes Development?

The West's dramatic escape from poverty has always been a good place to start in attempting to understand development. The rapid economic and social progress of Europe, during which people first rose out of the dismal poverty that characterized most of human history, was largely limited to a specific kind of regime—classical liberalism. The resulting systems generally allowed markets to operate, respected the rule of law, protected private property, and permitted competition. Historian Ralph Raico explains that the "European Miracle" developed because of greater market autonomy, which was possible only through "the inhibition of the predator-state." Obviously, individual national experiences varied, but the grand sweep of history presents powerful evidence that the West's development was not accidental. Observes the late economist David Osterfeld in his well-documented book, *Prosperity Versus Planning:*

Aggregate data, as unreliable as they may be, still show two things quite conclusively: (1) The nations of the Western or First World are far more productive and wealthier than those in either the Second or Third Worlds. This was not always so. Just a few hundred years ago all areas of the world were poor. In fact, the West was probably poorer and less advanced than most other areas at that time, especially China. (2) The West, over the past few hundred years, has traditionally been far more market oriented than the other areas of the world. The likely relationship between the West's economic institutions and its economic growth and development cannot be ignored.[10]

This experience has been repeated rather more quickly and spectacularly in East Asia, where it has taken but a generation or two for desperately poor nations to turn into some of the world's most successful economies. (This is not to say that that the British or German, let alone the Japanese or South Korean, experiences were *laissez faire.* Rather, all broadly relied on market forces, despite varying degrees of government economic involvement.) What makes the East Asian experience so important is that it is more recent, reflected a conscious break with the reigning collectivist consensus, and succeeded so spectacularly. As a result, writes economist Deepak Lal, "The West had succeeded, in a fairly short period of time, in erecting a second great liberal economic order."

What was true of Great Britain, the U.S., Japan, and South Korea is also true of today's successful developing states. Perhaps the best broad-based study of economic policies over the last two decades is *Economic Freedom of the World: 1975-1995* (updated annually), by economists James Gwartney, Robert Lawson, and Robert Block.[11] They created an index of 17 component parts to measure economic freedom, as well as three alternative summary indexes. Ranked highest were Hong Kong, Singapore, the U.S. and New Zealand. At the bottom came numerous Latin American and African countries. Most improved between 1975 and 1990 were Chile, Iceland, Jamaica, Malaysia, and Pakistan.

Obviously, the results for individual countries may be affected by many factors. But the overall result is compelling. Explain the authors: "No country with a persistently high economic freedom rating during the two decades failed to achieve a high level of income. In contrast, no country with a persistently low rating was able to achieve even middle income status."

Second, changes in economic policy affect national growth rates. According to the study, the 17 nations with the greatest increases in economic freedom enjoyed an average growth rate of 2.7 percent in per capita GDP from 1980 to 1990, and 3.1 percent from 1985 to 1994. All 17 grew, while 11 of the 16 nations with the largest drops in economic freedom suffered a decline in per capita GDP Collectively they suffered an average drop of 6 percent in real per capita GDP.

Similar are the results of the *1996 Index of Economic Freedom* (also updated every year), written by Heritage Foundation analysts Bryan Johnson and Thomas Sheehy.[12] Although their study offers somewhat less systematic international comparisons, they reach the same conclusions. Johnson and Sheehy explain that their analysis "demonstrates that economic freedom is the single most important factor in creating the conditions for economic growth and prosperity." Their data also show that countries that place the greatest reliance on open markets consistently have the highest growth rates.

Studies by other analysts and organizations yield the same general results. Researchers at Cornell University and the OECD have used a computable general equilibrium (CGE) economic model in an attempt to measure the impact of different policy measures. Market-oriented reforms in exchange rate, fiscal, and monetary policies all improve economic growth rates. Benefits tend to flow to poorer, rural residents; urban elites who were enriched through political manipulation of the economy are usually the biggest losers.

A decade ago economists E. Dwight Phaup and Bradley Lewis surveyed a dozen "winners" (with average annual growth rates exceeding six percent) and a score of "losers" (average growth rates below 2.2 percent a year). Phaup and Lewis concluded: "It would appear that whether LDCs are winners or losers is determined mainly by their domestic economic policies. Resource endowment, lucky circumstances, former colonial status, and other similar factors make little difference in the speed with which countries grow economically. The results of domestic policy choices pervade every economic area."

The late Mancur Olson, Jr., of the Center for Institutional Reform and the Informal Sector at the University of Maryland (College Park), came to much the same conclusion. He reported that such factors as access to knowledge and capital couldn't explain the relative income differences between nations. "The only remaining plausible explanation is that the great differences in the wealth of nations are mainly due to differences in the quality of their institutions and economic policies," he explained. He found that poorer nations with the best economic policies consistently grow the fastest.

Phaup and Lewis relied in part on a detailed World Bank study, published as part of the 1983 *World Development Report.* The Bank assessed the relative economic distortions in 31 primarily developing nations and found that countries with the least interference with the marketplace had annual growth rates twice as fast as those of nations with the most inefficient policies. The more market-oriented countries also enjoyed far greater domestic savings, additional output per unit of investment, and increases in both agricultural and manufacturing output. Explained the study: developing nations that introduced fewer "distortions" into their economies—particularly price controls, import restrictions, interest rate limits, and similar policies—did better, while "those countries with the worst distortions experienced significantly lower domestic saving and lower output per unit of investment, thus leading to slower growth." The Bank estimated that inefficient intervention could cut annual GDP growth by as much as two percent.

The larger legal and political systems also matter. For example, David Osterfeld reviewed the economic impact of a range of variables: corruption, food, foreign aid, migration, multinationals, population, and resources. His conclusion was that development occurred most quickly in an "enabling environment" in which the rule of law was stable, property was protected, political power was decentralized, and most of the economy was private.

The Bank has focused particular attention on protectionism. In 1987 the institution devoted much of its annual *World Development Report* to trade. It concluded: "The economic performance of the outward-oriented economies has been broadly superior to that of the inward-oriented economies in almost all respects:" The former enjoyed twice the rate of real GDP growth between 1963 and 1973, and more than three times the growth rate between 1973 and 1985. Countries with less restrictive trade policies also benefited from much higher increases in per capita income and domestic savings, and slightly lower inflation. Moreover, outward-oriented economies industrialized more quickly. Four years later the Bank published additional research yielding the same result.

America's Agency for International Development has reached similar conclusions. According to U.S. AID: "recent academic and policy experience has shown a linkage between international trade policy and overall economic progress." Particularly important, in its view were open trade policies—more outwardly oriented countries grew by upwards of four times as fast as more protectionist states. U.S. AID also pointed to the friendliness of the investment climate to domestic and foreign business alike. The difference in average annual per capita growth between the most open economies and least open economies was seven percentage points.

These sort of general assessments are reinforced by the results of narrower studies of different regions and nations. The East Asian economic powerhouses of today—Hong Kong, Japan, Singapore, South Korea, and Taiwan—were much poorer than such Latin American countries as Argentina after World War II. Of the many differences between them, the most important is the economic road taken. Latin America firmly embraced the *dirigiste* model. East Asia chose various forms of capitalism. The nations of Africa, the poorest on the globe, followed Latin America over the abyss of collectivist development strategies.

Policy Implications for International Organizations

Every nation's economic environment is made up of a complex aggregation of individual laws and regulations. All governments, including those in the industrialized West, do stupid things—sometimes out of ignorance, sometimes in response to interest group pressure, and sometimes in an attempt to achieve non-economic ends. The basic question is whether economic stupidity is the exception or the rule.

To the extent that international organizations have a role in the world economy, it should be to reduce economic stupidity. There is good reason to doubt that any government-to-government assistance program can do much good: the records of both the World Bank and IMF suggest that their rhetoric on behalf of free markets has been undercut by continued lending to irresponsible borrowers, resulting in little practical impact.[13] Moreover, as Alan Carter of London's Heythrop College has warned, "Aid primarily serves to prop up regimes that are complicit in the exploitation of their people and the destruction of their environment."[14]

Of course, almost everyone in the policy community today acknowledges that good domestic policies (outward-oriented, market-friendly) are the fundamental determinant of growth. Aid officials have tried arguing that they can induce countries to move to market, but foreign transfers more often subsidize economic failure—witness Russia. In fact, World Bank economists Craig Burnside and David Dollar have concluded: "We find no systematic influence of aid on our index of fiscal, monetary, and trade policies." For each case where one can argue assistance advanced reform, they report, "there is a Zambia, in which policy deteriorated continuously from 1970 until 1993, while aid receipts rose continuously."[15]

Even less should be expected from formal UN agencies. Although the NIEO has long faded from public view, the politics of relatively autonomous international staffs backed by poorer voting majorities spending the money of a few wealthier states tends to push global institutions towards intervention. Other than trade organizations, which have the *raison d'être* of encouraging international commerce, no UN body is likely to lead a crusade for freer markets against the usual special interests more interested in subsidies, redistribution, and privilege. The Law of the Sea Treaty is a case in point. Although the treaty has been renegotiated to eliminate several of its most counterproductive provisions, it remains inimical to free development of the seabed.[16]

Nevertheless, international organizations concerned about the plight of the world's poor—the wealthy require no global guardians—have an opportunity to explain the importance of creating national and international conditions conducive to competitive, entrepreneurial capitalism and reducing barriers to international exchange. Global agencies should first explain that real capitalism requires free markets with free entry, in contrast to the special interest, crony kleptocracies that have often been passed off as variants of capitalism. To promote genuine capitalism, multilateral organizations need not provide subsidies, loans, and grants, since international capital will flow to countries with positive investment climates. Rather, multinational agencies should help educate governments about what works.

Ill-considered state intervention in the economies of developing nations has taken four general forms. The first involves the size of the public sector and the number of goods and services directly produced by it. Many countries have a host of state enterprises that, either on a competitive or monopoly basis, participate in nearly every aspect of business activity, including production of electricity, oil and gas, steel, pharmaceuticals, and textiles. The vast majority of these entities lose money, draining valuable capital and personnel away from more productive economic sectors.

Restrictions on prices and production, which skew the incentives of suppliers and the demand of consumers, are a second type of self-inflicted economic wound. Some Third World countries prop up their exchange rates, overvaluing their exports and making imports artificially inexpensive. High tariffs and import licensing programs are often used to protect selected domestic industries, raising costs to other indigenous enterprises, including exporters. Many countries favor their urban populations by subsidizing the prices of food, utilities, and other goods and services; some use state marketing boards to hold down the prices paid to farmers. Such policies discourage private production and innovation, inflate demand, and exacerbate national budget deficits.

Third, many governments have adopted perverse credit, fiscal, and monetary policies. Expansionary money growth, exceptionally high marginal income tax rates and heavy overall tax burdens, large budget deficits, strict interest rate limits, and other disruptive credit controls have all contributed to widespread economic instability and stagnation.

Finally, developing countries often discourage investment, particularly by foreign enterprises. A host of burdensome rules have been imposed on multinational corporations, including: limits on repatriation of profits and ownership of shares in local operations; hiring preferences and quotas for local labor; business disclosure requirements; patent and trademark abridgments; detailed business regulations, including private and supplier controls; and technology transfer mandates. These many investment disincentives are compounded by the difficulty of dealing with often grossly inefficient and corrupt bureaucracies, the risk of nationalization, and a prohibition of outside investment in certain economic sectors. Negative investment climates discourage domestic entrepreneurship as well.

Obviously, one may argue about which of the forgoing policies are the most important, and which might be justified as promoting other important social goals. But, in general, the fewer such policies implemented by Third World governments, the more likely their economies are to grow, and grow fast.

Other Issues

As critical as are the right economic policies in promoting development, economic growth is obviously not the only element of development. Moreover, most people and governments are concerned about the distribution as well as creation of wealth. But wealth creation is the only sensible starting point, the necessary if not sufficient condition for ensuring that the starving are fed, the ill are healed, and the poor have an opportunity to prosper. Without wealth creation there is nothing to distribute, and without market-oriented policies (which, as noted earlier, means competitive rather than crony capitalism) governments will be unable to generate the prosperity that offers the only hope to better the lot of the poor.

This is, in fact, the practical lesson of Third World development. In a detailed study for U.S. AID, economist Elliot Berg reported, "To the extent that reforming countries enjoy faster growth, which now seems to be happening in countries of [Africa and Latin America], their poor are on the road to becoming clearly better off."[17] Pranab Bardhan of the University of California (Berkeley) reached a similar conclusion: "In the last two decades of poverty research there is clearly a better appreciation of the fact that policies fostering economic growth need not be inconsistent with poverty reduction. In fact in many countries (for example, in east and southeast Asia) growth promoting policies have brought about substantial reductions in mass poverty."[18]

Similarly, Bank economists Lionel Demery and Lyn Squire, though defending the importance of well-targeted social spending, emphasize that policy reform brings economic growth, and hence poverty reduction; better reforms reduce poverty the most.[19] In its *World Development Report 1990*, which was devoted to international poverty, the Bank compared social and economic indicators of a number of poorer states. Its succinct conclusion, even after acknowledging the difficulty of making transnational comparisons: "growth reduces poverty."[20] The data presented therein demonstrated that social advance generally followed economic gains, though disputes over the appropriate level of social spending remain.

Growth Versus Poverty

In a thorough report on international poverty, the World Bank provided a detailed, multinational analysis. It found that "economic growth reduces poverty" and that "there is no evident relationship between growth and income inequality."[21] In many cases policy reform and economic growth have actually reduced income inequality, though the exact results vary dramatically by country. Using the Gini coefficient, for instance, the Bank concluded that outward-oriented economic policies tend to widen the distribution of income.[22]

Even where growth has not diminished income inequality, it has, according to economists Michael Lipton and Martin Ravallion, nevertheless tended to reduce poverty.[23] In their view, "The benefits of growth are typically felt well below the poverty line." (That is, one can reduce absolute poverty even if relative differences between incomes are growing. Write Demery and Squire, "The poor as a whole may benefit from growth despite worsening inequality,"[24] though they also believe it is possible in some cases for some of the poorest to simultaneously end up worse off.) Related Bank research, detailed in *World Development Report 1995*, demonstrates how economic gains benefit workers. Explained the Bank:

> Economic growth is good for workers. Low and middle-income countries cannot sustain the growth they need without making the best use of

> their working-age populations. Sustained growth with rising labor demand has been achieved by countries that have relied on markets—domestic and international—to guide the process of development, whereas inward-looking and centrally planned strategies have generally failed to bring sustainable gains to all workers.[25]

In fact, the impact of globalization demonstrates the truth of this argument. In the 1980s, advanced economies grew at an average of 2.4 percent a year, compared to 1.9 percent for developing states. During the 1990s, when globalization accelerated, average annual per capita output for industrialized nations dropped to 1.8 percent, but that in poorer nations accelerated, to 3.6 percent.

Conclusion

Ultimately, people in developing states control their own destinies. Their most important responsibility is to get their governments' policies right. In their effort to do so, international organizations might have a positive role to play. Most obviously, they should end foreign aid, which inevitably subsidizes incumbent regimes and *dirigiste* economic policies. Multilateral institutions should promote market-oriented reforms in rich and poor economies alike. Perhaps most important, they should combat protectionism in industrialized states, which economist Michael Finger of the World Bank figures costs the Third World twice as much as those same countries provide in aid. There is perhaps no greater tragedy today than the failed societies which dot the globe. But more than a half century of experience with the UN and a plethora of international agencies demonstrates that they can offer no panacea for promoting economic development. All they can do is help remove the many artificial and unnecessary barriers to the world's peoples more fully participating in the international economy.

Notes

1. For a more detailed discussion of this issue, see Doug Bandow, "The First World's Misbegotten Economic Legacy to the Third World" in James A. Dorn, et al., eds., *The Revolution in Development Economics* (Washington, DC: Cato Institute, 1998), pp. 207-28.

2. Robert Heilbroner. *The Economic Problem* (Englewood Cliffs, NJ: Prentice Hall, 1968), p. 616.

3. *Ibid,* pp. 619, 622. Gunnar Myrdal, too, was quite forthright in justifying state coercion. Development in East Asia, he wrote, would require "much more social discipline than the prevailing interpretation of democracy in the region permits." Gunnar Myrdal, *Asian Drama: An inquiry into the Poverty of Nations* (London: Allen Lane, 1968), p. 67.

4. Stanley Please, "A Candid Look at Yesterday, "*The Bank's World,* September 1983, p. 7.

5. Quoted in James Bovard, "The World Bank vs. The World's Poor," Cato Institute Policy Analysis No. 92, September 28, 1987, p. 21.

6. John Williamson, "The Lending Policies of the International Monetary Fund," in John Williamson, ed., *IMP Conditionality* (Washington, DC: Institute for International Economics, 1983), p. 653.

7. International Monetary Fund, *Ten Common Misconceptions About the IMF* (Washington, DC International Monetary Fund, 1989), p. 8.

8. Doug Bandow, "Totalitarian Global Management: The UN's War on the Liberal International Economic Order," *Cato Institute Policy Analysis No. 61,* October 25, 1985. See also Burton Yale Pines, ed., *A World Without a U.N.* (Washington, DC: Heritage Foundation, 1984); Burton Yale Pines, ed., Report on the U.S. and the U.N.: A Balance Sheet (Washington, DC: Heritage Foundation, 1984).

9. United Nations Development Program, *Human Development Report 1996* (New York: Oxford University Press, 1996), p. 1.

10. David Osterfeld, *Prosperity Versus Planning: How Government Stifles Economic Growth* (New York: Oxford University Press, 1992), p. 17.

11. James Gwartney, et al., *Economic Freedom of the World: 1975-1995* (Vancouver: Fraser Institute, 1996).

12. Bryan Johnson and Thomas Sheehy, *1996 Index of Economic Freedom* (Washington, DC: Heritage Foundation, 1996).

13. See, e.g., Doug Bandow and Ian Vásquez, eds., *Perpetuating Poverty: The World Bank, the IMF and the Developing World* (Washington, DC: Cato Institute, 1994); Doug Bandow, *The Politics of Envy: Statism as Theology* (New Brunswick, NJ: Transaction, 1994), pp. 131-74.

14. Alan Carter, "The Nation-State and Underdevelopment," 16 *Third World Quarterly* 4 (1995), p. 615.

15. Craig Burnside and David Dollar, "Aid, Policies and Growth," World Bank draft paper, November 1996, pp. 3-4.

16. Doug Bandow, "Faulty Repairs: The Law of the Sea Treaty Is Still Unacceptable," Cato Institute Foreign Policy Briefing No. 32, September 12, 1994.

17. Elliot Berg, et al., "Poverty and Structural Adjustment in the 1980s: Trends in Welfare Indicators in Latin America and Africa," Development Alternatives, Inc., September 1994, p. i.

18. Pranab Bardhan, "Research on Poverty and Development Twenty Years after Redistribution with Growth," Presented to World Bank Conference on Development Economics, May 1-2, 1996, Washington, DC, p. 5.

19. Lionel Demery and Lyn Squire, "Macroeconomic Adjustment and Poverty in Africa: An Emerging Picture," *The World Bank Research Observer* 1 (February 1996), p. 40.

20. World Bank, *World Development Report 1990* (New York: Oxford University Press, 1990), p. 47.

21. World Bank, *Poverty Reduction and the World Bank: Progress and Challenges in the 1990s* (Washington, DC: The World Bank, 1996), pp. 34, 35.

22. *Poverty Reduction and the World Bank,* p. 87.

23. Michael Lipton and Martin Ravallion, "Poverty and Policy," in J. Behrman and T.N. Srinivasan, eds., *Handbook of Development Economics,* Vol. III (Elsevier Science Publishers B.V., 1994), p. 2606.

24. Demery and Squire, p. 43.

25. World Bank, *World Development Report 1995* (New York: Oxford University Press, 1995), p. 16.

Women's Rights, Human Rights: Peace in the New Century

Benazir Bhutto
Former Prime Minister of Pakistan

It is impossible to separate women's rights from human rights, just as it is impossible to separate economic justice from political liberty. In the modern era, these issues are the essential elements of morality, of civility, of a just society. In the long term, the universalization of human rights may be the underpinning of internal stability within nation states, and peaceful relations between national states.

I address this issue from a unique double focus. On one level, as the target of human rights violations today and in the past, and on another level as someone who has had the extraordinary opportunity to address human and women's rights in my own country. I wear the scars, on my body and my soul, of the abuse of basic human rights, and thus I view oppression through the eyes of the victim. I also can attest to the price of world peace that is paid when insistence on human rights is not integral to the foreign policy goals of the major democratic players in international affairs—Europe, the Americas and Japan.

We do not live in a perfect world, and even amongst the rapidly expanding democratic community there often seems coldness, indifference, hypocrisy and lingering prejudice. Unfortunately, heaven did not appear on earth with the crumbling of the Berlin Wall. The world may be far more united, but the cause of justice for women and other traditionally discriminated people is far from complete. Inequality and injustice fuel frustration and anger, which when exploited and manipulated by evil people, can have the most tragic consequences. In the words of the American poet Langston Hughes, a "dream deferred" can very well explode.

Unfortunately we do not always view the world—its people, its cultures, and its religions—with a single moral standard. And clearly the West may be the primary culprit of this selective morality. The West applies human rights standards when political expedient, not as a central and universal principle of policy. Democracy, women's rights, human rights, press freedom are allcritical—sometimes. Violations of these principles lead to international sanctions—sometimes.

The world is not yet a fair or just place, and will not be so until each and every human being on our planet is treated equally. That will not occur until the nations of the world insist upon it, not just in their own countries but also everywhere on the planet where women and men are still oppressed.

Liberty is the most enduring and powerful personal and political value on earth. We recognize that it was not the ideology of mass movements, but the aspirations of individuals, that turned the tide in the historic political revolutions during the period 1988 to 1990. Communism was not defeated by capitalism or by the forces of NATO; it was defeated by humanism. Vaclav Havel has so accurately noted that "communism was not defeated by military force, but by the human spirits, by conscience, by the resistance of man to manipulation. It was defeated by a revolt of human individuality."

Democracy is the first step toward humanity's liberation. But it is not an end in itself. Liberty and freedom depend on social and economic justice, and above all on the universal, non-selective application of human rights to all citizens of the world. Economic development and political development are surely linked, but both are predicated on guaranteed human rights. And the cause of human rights must begin within us, within our individual communities and within our own nations. We cannot proselytize justice abroad if we do not fight for it in our own homes, and in our own homelands. This was stated so eloquently by Eleanor Roosevelt, who asked in 1958, "Where, after all, do universal human rights begin? In small places, close to home—so close and so small that they cannot be seen on any map of the world. Yet they are the world of the individual person: the neighborhood he lives in; the school or college he attends; the factory, farm or office where he works. Such are the places where every man, woman and child seeks equal justice, equal opportunity, equal dignity without discrimination. Unless these rights have meaning there, they have little meaning anywhere. Without concerted citizen action to uphold them close to home, we shall look in vain for progress in the larger world."

And there is no human right more fundamental, and more universal, than equal rights for women in the new century. As the first woman ever elected to head an Islamic nation, I feel a strong responsibility about issues that relate to women. Central to the issue of religion in modern society is the treatment of women. I am afraid in the post September 11 environment, the true nature of Islam has been so distorted by those who would exploit religion for political purposes, that Islam has become something not only foreign to the rest of the world, but also something feared. This is dangerous and destructive. If human rights are to triumph in the new millennium, tolerance and pluralism must flourish. Racial discrimination, gender discrimination, ethnic discrimination and religious discrimination are the central underpinnings of an inhumane society. Inhumane societies are, by definition, unstable societies. For the sake of universal human rights and for the sake of peace in the modern era, we must learn about each other before we can respect each other and live with each other in a global civil society.

This is a very sad time for me, as it is for most of the civilized people on earth. I write this monograph at a wonderful confluence of the holidays of the three great Abrahamic religions on earth. Simultaneously, the Moslem world celebrates Eid, as Jews celebrate Hanukah and the Christian world begins the celebration of Christmas. Three great religions and three great peoples should be rejoicing. But December 2001 is not like any December that preceded it. The joy of the season is muted and the sound of laughter is missing. We cannot forget that thousands of our innocent sisters and brothers—of all faiths, of all religions, of all races—lie buried and entombed under the ground zero that marks the site of the bloody attack that struck New York and struck all of humanity on September 11, 2001. It is just for this reason that this essay and this book become even more important. Without tolerance, without justice, without human rights and without peace we cannot survive. It is a lesson I learned long ago but it was brought home again to me as I watched in disbelief those great towers—and those innocent people—disintegrating under the weight of hate. It is to them that I dedicate the words of this monograph.

There is a special reason that I feel America's pain. Four of the happiest years of my life were spent at Harvard where I learned of—and flourished in—America's freedom, tolerance, pluralism, openness, and equal opportunity for all of your citizens. The values of freedom and liberty that are enshrined in the United States Constitution are beacons of hope for all women and men across the world. In a real sense there is logic that America was the prime target of the terrorists' wrath. The pluralism of America, in a very real sense, is the extremists' and the fanatics' worst nightmare. The microcosm of America that was destroyed on September 11—people of all races, ethnicities and religions—is everything the extremists abhor: men and women, working side by side as equals; blue collar busboys and window-washers earning money to send their children to college so they can have a better life than their parents; Muslims, Christians, Jews, and Hindus—together and indistinguishable—building worldwide trade and communication and cooperation.

Let me address the issue of human rights in their relationship to some of the current forces working against their universalization, to provide context to the discussion. The West frequently provides monitors to elections in the transitional democratic world. The evaluations of what is "free and fair" are often structured to the political importance of the incumbent governments whose elections are being evaluated. In 1999 and 2000 several of the Republics of the former Soviet Union in Central Asia had parliamentary and presidential elections, which were harshly criticized by the United States and the OSCE. In the current environment of basis in Central Asia being critical to the coalition war effort against Al Queda and the Taliban, such electoral criticism would be tempered if not completely disappear. Western observers often evaluate elections in Gulf countries as "steps toward democracy" even though women are excluded from participating. The press and NGOs are all but decimated in my home country of Pakistan and the judiciary has been politicized and intimidated, but because of General Musharraf's cooperation with the effort in Afghanistan, these human rights violations are seldom mentioned. Certainly the principle of self-determination is given strong verbal endorsement by nations committed to basic principles of human rights, but violations of self-determination in Kashmir or on the West Bank are not generally criticized because of the political importance of India and Israel. Sanctions are rightfully imposed of the military junta in Burma that overturned a freely and democratically elected woman, yet military dictators in Pakistan are praised. Democracy is demanded in small and non-strategic countries, but violations are overlooked in obvious strategic giants. This is the context of selective application of human rights standards that weaken the cause of human rights, women's rights and democracy all over the world.

Hypocrisy is not only within the pervue of the West. Surely within the Islamic world, selective applications of human rights standards and perverted interpretations of religion to justify acts of aggression are relatively commonplace. At this time of crisis, the people of the world must understand that those who would use violence and terror in the name of Islam are hypocrites, criminals, not clerics. Their actions are antithetical to the teachings of the Holy Book, to the teachings of the Holy Prophet. Their goal is to establish linked and intertwined theocracies of ignorance that they can control and manipulate for their own political ends. They are not just the enemies of western values; they are the enemies of all humanity.

Terrorism and fanaticism will not succeed unless we fall into the psychopaths' trap. Professor Samuel Huntington of Harvard has written of an inevitable clash of civilization between the West and the Islamic world. I argue that this clash is not inevitable, unless we make it so. There is nothing in the precepts of Islam that make it inconsistent with Judeo-Christian values. In the Holy Book, Abraham is our father, just as Moses and Jesus are our prophets. There will only be a clash of civilizations if we allow ignorance and fanaticism to take control, to shape the agenda and to shape the debate. Osama and his cohorts use commercial airliners as bombs against cities to provoke the clash of cultures under which they will thrive.

There is nothing noble in their actions. They want the people of America, and indeed people all over this world, to actually believe that this is a *jihad*, a holy war between Islam and the west. And those in the West, who would target and beat innocent Muslims and burn and desecrate Mosques as a response to Osama, are merely swallowing the fanatics' poisonous bait, advancing the fanatics' perverted dreams.

I am not unfamiliar with the criminals of Al Qaeda. I know them well; I know how they operate, how they think and I know what they want. As Prime Minister of Pakistan, I stood up to them. I battled with many of these same criminals, including Osama Bin Laden himself. I took them on, and often paid a price. During the Afghan-Soviet war, my country became the breeding ground for their political religious manipulation and exploitation. Hiding under the cloak of religion, they preached a message that would enslave not liberate, teach children not to write but rather to hate, keep people hopeless and desperate, bitter, xenophobic and paranoid.

I closed their so-called universities. I disarmed their Madrassas, their sham primary schools that do not teach children literature, science or mathematics but rather turn children into fanatics and criminals. I tried to restore law and order to our cities under incessant assault from terrorist attack. My government extradited the terrorists, like Ramzi Youseff, who had exported death and destruction to New York in the 1990s. They struck back at my allies and me. They destroyed the Egyptian Embassy in Islamabad. They burned our National Assembly, hijacked school buses, gunned down diplomats and businessmen in the streets of Karachi and Lahore, and organized and financed schemes to topple my government. As a woman, I was their enemy. As a democrat, I was their antithesis. But above all, as someone who offered hope to our people—education, jobs, communication and modernity—I was a dangerous obstacle to the forces of hate. I took them on with my eyes open. I knew they would strike back, just as we expect that these fanatics will strike again in America. Despite the personal and political price I paid over the years, my only regret is that we were unable to eliminate them completely, before they rained terror on America. Peace is often difficult to achieve, and even more difficult to maintain. The words on the Korean War Memorial on Washington's great mall never have rung more true—"freedom is not free." Hatred and fanaticism, if not contained, spreads quickly and consumes all around it.

The fanatics' greatest fear is the spread of information, social equality and democracy. These three principles choke off the oxygen of terrorism. These three goals guided my years as prime minister. Maybe this could explain the two assassination attempts against me by Al Qaeda. We heralded the information age by introducing fax machines, digital pagers, optic fiber communications, cellular telephones, satellite dishes, computers, Internet, e-mail and even CNN, into Pakistan. Under my government Pakistan integrated into the global economy that which the fanatics so fear, and we became one of the ten emerging capital markets of the world, attracting over 20 billion dollars in foreign investment, particularly in power generation. We eradicated polio in our country. We dramatically reduced infant mortality.

Despite the constraints of a political system that was rigged against democrats, and a social system that was biased against women, when I became Prime Minister of Pakistan I used my office to try to reverse centuries of discrimination against women. My tenure was a textbook affirmative-action program against gender discrimination. We increased literacy by one-third, even more dramatically among girls. We built over 30,000 primary and secondary schools, targeting rural Pakistan. Our education program targeting girls and rural areas has been dismantled by the military junta. We brought down the population growth rate by establishing women's health clinics in thousands of communities across our Nation. We outlawed domestic violence and established special women's police forces to protect and defend the women of Pakistan. We appointed women judges to our nation's benches for the first time in our history. We instituted a new program of hiring women police officers to investigate crimes of domestic violence against the women of Pakistan. The special police force has been dismantled. I systematically appointed women judges to the courts of the land. The affirmative action program for women in the judiciary has been dismantled. I condemned the honor killing, by members of their own families, of women. The military junta is now silent to these abominations.

I encourage women's and girl's participation in sports, both nationally and internationally, by lifting the ban imposed on their participation. I refused attempts by reactionary forces within my country to turn Pakistan into a theocracy by declaring the chief executive a spiritual leader in the mould of the Taliban leader Mullah Omar. I created a special Women's Development Bank to guarantee small-business loans to women entrepreneurs, because I firmly believed that economic justice would build political justice.

Case by case, issue-by-issue, policy-by-policy, the military junta that rules Pakistan with the strength of armed force has reversed policies aimed at ameliorating the role and rights of women in Pakistani society. The women of Pakistan cannot be expected to struggle alone against the forces of discrimination, exploitation and manipulation. I recall the words of Dante who reminded us that "the hottest place in Hell is reserved for those who remain neutral in times of moral crisis."

To the fanatics and the extremists, we became the enemy, the threat, and the obstacle. To Islam at the crossroads, a modern Pakistan was one fork in the road, fanaticism and ignorance the other.

Our religion is not only committed to tolerance and equality, but it is committed to the principles of democracy. The Holy Book says that Islamic society is contingent on—and I quote—"mutual advise through mutual discussions on an equal footing." Rest assured the Taliban skip this section when they brainwash children in Madrassas all across Pakistan. In Islam, dictatorship is never condoned, nor is cruelty. Beating, torturing and humiliating women is unIslamic. Denying education to girls violates the very first word of the Holy Book: "Read." According to our religion, those who commit cruel acts are condemned to destruction. Sometimes tragedy can lead to resurrection of hope and spirit.

As America and the international community plan an effective response to the most monstrous terrorist attack in history, we must remember the lessons of history and not repeat the mistakes of the past. Osama Bin Laden did not emerge like whole cloth from a nightmare. His depravity was long in the making, and there were errors—of omission and commission—that must never be repeated.

Afghanistan is a tragic case in point of how retreating from the principles of human rights and democracy can have the most tragic unanticipated consequences. In the closing days of the Soviet occupation of Afghanistan, during a State Visit to America I cautioned that U.S. policy to defeat the Soviets had empowered and emboldened the most fanatical, extremist elements of the Afghan seven-faction Mujahadeen at the expense of the moderates, creating a "Frankenstein" that could come back to haunt us in the future. The overall policy of standing against Soviet aggression in Afghanistan was right. Indeed it was noble. Yet the early decisions by the U.S. Administration working with its Pakistani counterpart to arm, train, supply and legitimize the most extreme fanatics sowed the seeds for the twenty-first century terrorism that is now swirling around us. In America and Pakistan's combined and admirable zeal to end the Soviet occupation, we did not plan or work for a post-war Afghanistan built on democratic and Islamic principles of coalition, consensus, and cooperation. The fundamental mistake, which contributed to a long-term historical calamity, was that we were not consistently committed to the values of freedom, democracy, social equality and self-determination that ultimately undermine and belie the basic tenets of terrorism. Short-term battlefield strategy is often myopic, as the anarchy, civil war, and Taliban terror in Afghanistan so painfully proves.

Just as democracies do not make war,

democracies also do not sponsor international terrorism. The goal of the international community's foreign policy agenda must always be to simultaneously promote stability and to strengthen democratic values, not selectively but universally, not when it is convenient but rather because it is right. General Musharraf has made the correct decision to stand with America at this moment of crisis. But the United States and the rest of the world must remember that Pakistan has an extra-constitutional military government with no democratic legitimacy. Elections in Pakistan are scheduled in October 2002 and the United States and its allies must insure that these elections not only take place, but that they are free, fair, and open to all parties and candidates. A democratic Pakistan is America's best guarantee of the triumph of moderation and modernity among 1 billion Muslims at the crossroads of our history. The alternative of a long-term, nuclear-armed Pakistani dictatorship has consequences that could make September 11 look like a mere prelude to an even more horrific future for the civilized world.

This is not the simple world we dreamed of with the end of the Cold War. And mine is not the simple life I dreamed of growing up in Pakistan and going to school at Harvard and Oxford. The gauntlet of leadership was thrown down before me. I had no choice but to pick it up. But it has often been very difficult, often very sad. Leadership is not easy. It is never meant to be easy. It is born of a passion, and it is a commitment—a commitment to an idea, to principles, to fundamental human values.

It has not always been an easy life for me, or for my family. But this is nothing new, really. Women have always had to make difficult choices, often choices that men have not been forced to make. And we must live with the consequences, for better or worse. Those of us in positions of responsibility understand this special, unique, and extraordinary moment in history. We fight for all the women who came before us who gave us this opportunity. And most of all, we do it for all woman who will come after us—the baby girls yet unborn!

As a child of my age, in the late sixties, I was influenced by the social ferment around me. The worldwide students movement, from Rawalpindi, to France, to Washington, were important factors in my youth. The fight against apartheid shaped the ferocity of my commitment to stand up for principle. The burgeoning movement for women's rights empowered and emboldened me.

As an Asian at Harvard, I bitterly resented the war in Vietnam and joined up with American students to protest a war that they thought was unjust and did not want to fight. These important steps helped shape my outlook on life, helped me focus on fighting injustice, promoting freedom and safeguarding the rights of the weak and dispossessed. But above all, in America during the Vietnam War I saw the awesome power of the people to change policies, change leaders, and change history.

From Harvard I went to Oxford, where Enoch Powell was threatening to throw all Asians into the sea. While I was at Oxford, the Conservative party chose a woman, Margaret Thatcher, as the Leader of Opposition and the idea of the first female British Prime Minister became a hot topic for student discussions. At Oxford, I was the first female foreigner to be elected as President of the Oxford Union. The Oxford Union reflects the British House of Commons. It was there that I learned to debate, slowly gaining confidence before an audience. I had been told that as a foreigner, I could not win the Presidency and should not run. I had been told that as a woman, I could not win, and should not run. But I did run and did win and overcame my fear of losing. I learned to overcome fear and to take risks. I learned never to give in when the task seemed formidable or impossible.

What has always been clear to me is that the extraordinary educational opportunities given to me have given me a range of life and career options denied to most women, and certainly almost all women of the developing world. My own experiences at Harvard and Oxford have made it clear to me that only educational opportunity promotes empowerment for women. If women are truly to be defined by themselves and their own accomplishments and abilities, they must have the level of education that empowers them. Education leads to the kind of financial independence that causes women to break the shackles of being only a man's daughter or a man's wife.

As the Prime Minister of Pakistan I appeared before an historic Joint Session of the United States Congress in 1989. In that address, the most meaningful line to me was my simple message to the woman of America, my message to the women of the world. Three simple, powerful words: YES YOU CAN! I urged women all over the world not to accept the status quo, not to accept "no" for an answer. It is critical that women—whether in London or Kabul—refuse to accept traditional roles and traditional constraints if they wish otherwise. Acquiesce to a tradition dictated by men—a tradition of subjugation of mothers and daughters—can no longer be accepted. And it is not just the Taliban that has perpetuated this kind of human rights injustice. The West has not been immune, although the discrimination has been more benign, more refined. But in this new era, we must reject the psychological constraints just as we reject the Fundamentalists' dictates. In the West and in the East we must stand up and reject the notion that leadership and femininity are contradictory. That is a nonsensical myth.

I recall the words of Lady Margaret Thatcher. "When a woman is strong, she is pushy. But when a man is strong…ah…he is a great leader!" We've made progress; we've smashed many glass ceilings. But there are thousands left to break, many battles left to fight. The greatest obstacles to progress for women in the third millennium is the bigotry of men, and nowhere is that bigotry more venal than in the Taliban and the fanatics that have declared war on democracy. We fight not against terrorism, but the bigotry and intolerance that will confine and constrain and victimize in the generations ahead. Victimization of significant elements of society and the concept of long-term peace are mutually exclusive. The denial of human rights is a bomb that will ultimately explode.

These are difficult times. Freedom is under assault. Democracy is under assault. Criminal terrorists hijack my religion just as they hijack America's planes. The solutions will not be quick or simple. But if we maintain our commitment to the principles that define us—the principles of racial, gender, and religious equality, the principles of political pluralism and tolerance, and the principle of peaceful change through democracy—we shall prevail in the end.

In addressing the new exigencies of the new century, we must translate dynamic religion into a living reality. We must live by the true spirit of Islam, not only by its rituals. Those who are ignorant of Islam must cast aside their preconceptions about the role of women in our religion. Contrary to what many believe, Islam embraces a rich variety of political, social, and cultural traditions. The fundamental ethos of Islam is tolerance, dialogue and democracy.

Just as in Christianity, Judaism, and other religions, we must always be on guard for those who will exploit and manipulate the message of religion for their own narrow political ends, who will distort the essence of pluralism and tolerance for their own extremist agendas. These manipulators exist all over the world, but nowhere were they more dangerous than the last years of the Taliban era in Afghanistan. And most central to the Taliban bigotry was its concept and treatment of women. For the Taliban, and other extremists throughout the Moslem world, refute that the central ethos of Islam is equality, especially equality between the sexes. There is no religion on earth that, in its writings, is more respectful of the role of women in society than Islam. It is this tradition of Islam that has empowered me, has strengthened me, and has emboldened me. It is this tradition of Islam that has allowed me to battle for political and human rights, and strengthens me today in this hour of crisis for my family, my nation and myself.

Islam denounces inequality as the greatest form of injustice. It enjoins its followers to combat oppression and tyranny. It enshrines piety as the sole criteria for judging humankind. It shuns race, color, and gender as the basis of distinction in society.

When the human spirit was immersed in the darkness of the Middle Ages in Europe, Islam proclaimed equality between men and women. When women were viewed as inferior members of the human family, Islam gave them right to divorce, child custody and inheritance. When women were treated as chattel, Islam said that humans, men and women, were equal in the eyes of God. Sadly, tragically, the teachings of Islam about women have been ignored for political purposes. But based on the teachings of my religion, I believe that traditional men and traditional societies deny women the fundamental rights that Islam gives them.

Today in Pakistan, the cause of women's rights is set back as women's issues take a back seat. The cause of human rights is also being set back decades. But the cause of women's rights, I am sad to say, is being set back a century. My immediate successor's attempt to turn back the clock on women's rights, on pluralistic democracy focused on me, on destroying me politically at home and destroying my reputation abroad. We have become accustomed to all and every attempt to use the politics of personal destruction to turn back the course of democracy, human rights and women's rights in our homeland. It didn't work then and it will not work now.

The Musharraf regime reluctantly supported the international war against terrorism. It feared the consequences of taking any other path. That is different than taking path from conviction and principles. Many within its folds continue to harbor secret sympathy with the Taliban. The intensity of this sympathy led to Pakistan being the last country to recognize the Taliban. Even after the fall of Kabul, Islamabad was reluctant to break ties with the Taliban.

As a front-line state in the war against terrorism and given its influence in its neighborhood, Islamabad could have been the engine that brought an end to the Taliban regime. But it was the Afghan General in the North, General Dostum, rather than General Musharaf in the South, who became the catalyst of change that drove the Taliban out of the North and into their stronghold in the South.

The Pakistani democratic forces gave unconditional support to the Musharaf military regime at the time of the war against terrorism. Given the support of the democratic forces in Pakistan, the demonstrations called for by the religious parties in support of the Taliban failed. General Musharaf and his military regime owe much to the democratic forces for having weathered the religious storm that was threatening to topple his regime as it sided with the International Coalition.

Yet General Musharaf has done little to acknowledge the support given by the democratic forces. His continued persecution of popular leaders through trumped up politically motivated charges, in special courts monitored by colonels and through special laws, denies fundamental rights even as it sows the seeds of political instability.

Pakistan is situated in a volatile region of the world. It borders both Afghanistan, home to the Taliban, and Iran, home to the Ayotullah-driven Iranian revolution. The rise of Sunni and Shia Islamic revolutions on its borders has repercussions on Pakistan itself.

As Pakistan enters the twenty-first century with politically motivated religious battles swirling in its neighborhood, stability becomes important to the region and the wider world community. In my view the West must avoid making in Pakistan the mistake it made in Iran under the Shah of Iran.

Under the Shah of Iran, the people of Iran had two choices. They could choose between a Western-backed dictator or a clerical-backed dictator. The people of Iran finally chose to throw in their lot with the unknown dictatorship rather than accept the oppression of the incumbent dictatorship.

I would like to see the people of Pakistan have a third choice between a Western-backed dictatorship and a clerical-backed dictatorship. That third choice is the democratic choice for, as we learned in the twentieth century, the forces of freedom cannot be denied.

The military junta in Pakistan is attempting to crush the moderate political parties, exile their leaders, prevent their leading members from contesting elections, tame the judiciary through removals of independent judges, and intimidate the press by beating up journalists that ask awkward questions. They do this to concentrate power in themselves but in so doing they make change possible through non-parliamentary means. The strong forces able to lead extra parliamentary forces are either the armed private militias in the country or the officers of the military. As such, the steps to crush the moderate political parties and silence any debate creates a vacuum which the theocratic forces are more ably positioned to fill.

The continuation of military dictatorship would be dangerous for the future political direction of Pakistan and with it of the South Asia region. The South Asian region comprises two nuclear capable states: India and Pakistan. These two countries have already fought three wars. They nearly went to war in 1998 in the icy peaks of an area called Kargil. It was the intervention of the United States which prevented the Kargil crisis from erupting into a full scale, possibly nuclear, war.

The stability of Pakistan is therefore important to the South Asian region, as well as the larger world community.

The world is presently focused on the destruction of the Al Qaeda network. It is grateful to the Pakistani military regime for having joined the international coalition irrespective of the reasons that led Pakistan to join. But gratitude for General Musharaf making the decision to join the international coalition should not blind the international community to the larger goal of carrying the 140 million people of Pakistan as well as ensuring a stable Pakistan.

The rights of women in Pakistan are fundamentally tied up with the political dispensation in Pakistan. In fact, all fundamental rights are tied up to the road Pakistan takes in the future, either as a democratic Nation or a dictatorship. These include the causes of women's rights, human rights, press freedom, and democracy.

Even as Pakistan enters a period of peril where it must choose between dictatorship and democracy, the women of Afghanistan emerge from the veil of repression. With the end of the Taliban regime, women can finally make free choices for themselves. They can decide whether they wish to work, what they want to wear and what they want to do with their lives. Women from sixty nations, including from my home country of Pakistan, united world-wide on December 1, 2001, to plead the cause of Afghan women. Even though the military regime arrested and harassed some women activists, women members of my Party demonstrated in front of the United Nations office to demand the inclusion of women as the Bonn talks took place in Germany. As a result of the struggle of the Afghan women in exile, as well as the international community, the voice of women world-wide was heard. The new Afghan interim government has within it two leading women members as deputy prime minister and as health minister. This is an achievement for Afghan women but it is also an achievement for women all over the world.

Today in this world, in the fight for the liberation of women, there can be no neutrality. And the world's outrage at violence and discrimination directed at women cannot be selective. We cannot turn our backs on the women of Islam, if our words are to carry any moral weight or political force. We cannot turn our backs on dictatorship in Asia, just as we did not turn our backs on dictatorship and oppression in Yugoslavia. Hate, bigotry, and violence have no international borders. Every shamed, abused girl, wherever she lives, is a mute witness for all women, everywhere in the world.

I see great progress looming as the forces that shape the new century and the new millennium come together around the world. It is a confluence of energy committed to universal social, economic and political values—this triad definition of comprehensive human rights for the future. It is a confluence of ideology that must shape a world free from exploitation and maltreatment of women, a world in which women have opportunities to rise to the highest level in politics, business, diplomacy, and other spheres of life. The new century must, for once and for all, exclude even the notion of battered women. It must be an era where honor and dignity are protected in peace, and in war, where women have economic freedom and independence, where women are not defined by their fathers or husbands, but by their own achievements, where they are equal partners in peace and development.

And even as we catalogue, organize and hopefully attain our goals, step by step by step, all of those around the world who are committed to the common, interlinked causes of human rights, women's rights and peace, must be vigilant. Like in Pakistan today, repressive forces always will stand ready to exploit the moment and push us back into the past. It seems that the words of Goethe continue to resonate: "freedom has be re-made and re-earned in every generation."

Thus none of us will be free until democracy is returned to Pakistan and to other places like Burma where the will of the people is denied. In the new global community none of us can be free if some of us are enslaved. The world will not be free until human rights are restored everywhere. We cannot be a free planet until women are no longer abused, exploited and persecuted in Pakistan and Afghanistan, and all across Asia, Africa, Europe, and the Americas. We are not free if girls cannot read, for a girl who cannot read has no future; and a girl with no future has no human rights.

In the time it took to read this book chapter, over 1,000 children have starved to death on this planet. As long as these basic violations of human rights are allowed to continue, none of us—regardless of where we live, regardless of how elegant or civilized our life-styles, regardless of our own personal circumstances and comforts—are free.

My father, Prime Minister Zulfiqar Ali Bhutto, was toppled and ultimately murdered by the forces of dictatorship and fundamentalism two decades ago. I recall vividly those dark and tragic days, with my father languishing in a dark prison, living in the most inhumane conditions, with the world helpless to stop his murder. But he remained courageous to the end, and he remained optimistic even in the hours before his death. I want to end this monograph with the words that he used to end his last letter to me, quoting Robert F. Kennedy, himself a victim of assassination, commenting on the poetry of Alfred Lord Tennyson. Despite the crisis under which we live today, I believe these words set the tone for a new and brighter future.

In 1979, from the horror of my death cell, my father wrote: "Every generation has a central concern, whether to end war, erase racial injustice, or improve the conditions of working people. They demand a government that speaks directly and honestly to its citizens. The possibilities are too great, the stakes too high, to bequeath to the coming generation only the prophetic lament of Tennyson—"Ah, what shall I be at fifty…if I find the world so bitter at twenty-five."

Overcoming America's Estrangement: The Role of Education and Media

Sanford J. Ungar
President, Goucher College

Seventeen years ago, as a senior associate at the Carnegie Endowment for International Peace, I organized and edited a collection of essays evaluating the position of the United States in the international community. Published as Estrangement: America and the World, *on the occasion of the Endowment's seventy-fifth anniversary in 1985, the volume presented the views of historians, political scientists, economists, and journalists on the emerging predicament of a seemingly lonely superpower. One theme that ran throughout was that, even as there were new dreams of a shrinking, less contentious world community where everyone had common interests, America seemed ever more distant and removed from other actors on the international stage. Much has happened in the intervening period, most notably the end of the Cold War and the collapse of Communism in Europe—not to mention profound political upheavals in South Africa and other parts of the world and the emergence of "globalization" as a hotly contested phenomenon—and yet my introduction to the collection seems eerily relevant today, in the midst of a crisis over terrorism that once again raises major questions about the position of the United States in the larger world. I present it here with only minor revisions:*

Certain events in the life of a nation and a people are almost impossible to forget; they embody hopes and fears and other intense emotions, and eventually they become symbols of a mood or a moment in history.

Asked to identify such events from the 1940s, Americans would surely choose Pearl Harbor and Hiroshima, the Berlin airlift, and perhaps the founding of the United Nations. From the 1950s, they might select President Harry S. Truman's decision to intervene in Korea, the Supreme Court's judgment outlawing school segregation, or the Soviet launch of the first Sputnik satellite. From the 1960s, they would certainly remember the assassination of President John F. Kennedy and could draw from a long list of other dramatic events: the Cuban missile crisis; the construction of the Berlin Wall; the Tonkin Gulf Resolution, the Tet offensive, and other dramatic incidents during the American involvement in Vietnam; the civil rights marches on Washington and from Selma to Montgomery, Alabama; the assassinations of Martin Luther King, Jr., and Robert F. Kennedy; and the chaos of the Democratic National Convention of 1968 in Chicago, the music festival at Woodstock, or some other stirring of the peace movement and the counterculture.

From the 1970s, the Watergate scandal and the resignation of President Richard M. Nixon dominate the national (and to some extent even the international) memory, but there are other developments from that decade—not unrelated to each other—which compete for recollection: the clash between the federal government and the news media, especially over publication of the "top secret" Pentagon Papers; the dramatic American opening to China; the OPEC oil embargo; the fall of Saigon; and the first Camp David peace accords between

Israel and Egypt.

There is still another event from the 1970s— from the very end of the decade—that may have been, in retrospect, the most important and far-reaching of all: the hostage crisis at the U.S. embassy in Tehran in which at first sixty-six, and ultimately fifty-two, Americans were held by militant Islamic fundamentalists as a protest against Washington's long-standing support for the Shah of Iran. That it began one year to the day before the U.S. presidential election of 1980 and ended just as Ronald Reagan was being sworn into office on January 20, 1981, makes it all the easier to mark the hostage crisis as a watershed event in recent American history. It touched raw nerves and provoked a frantic overreaction. In the end, it was the ultimate notification to the United States that its standing overseas had changed dramatically and might never be the same again. Perhaps even more than the American disaster in Vietnam, the Iran hostage crisis represented the end of a post-World War II era of illusion for the United States; it remains a symbol of America's bewilderment and incapacitation.

The fall of the Shah earlier in 1979, following the return to Iran of the exiled Ayatollah Ruhollah Khomeini, was an event whose importance was at first overlooked and ignored by many Americans. But the connection with the Shah was the thickest and most complicated relationship the United States ever had in the Third World; it engaged major corporations, universities, foundations, the media, and other key American institutions. The Shah was the ultimate American client. His dynastic pretensions were indulged and his authoritarian habits overlooked, all in the name of friendship and strategic calculation. Despite clear signals of human rights violations and the suppression of dissent in Iran, President Jimmy Carter, during the Shah's visit to Washington in November 1977, said that Iran had "blossomed forth under enlightened leadership" and had become "a very stabilizing force in the world at large." The next month, spending New Year's Eve in Tehran, Carter proclaimed Iran "an island of stability in a turbulent corner of the world." In October 1978, after the Shah's regime had begun to crumble, Carter told Crown Prince Reza, the Shah's son, during a photo session in the Oval Office, that "our friendship and alliance with Iran is one of the important bases on which our entire foreign policy depends."[1] Although some of the Shah's behavior was not particularly loyal to the United States—he was, for example, a leader of the "price hawks" in OPEC who drastically raised the cost of energy to America and to many more vulnerable nations around the world—he seemed to carry American prestige with him.

Even so, had the Shah gone quietly, only to be replaced by another willing U.S. surrogate, many Americans would hardly have noticed. But his fundamentalist Islamic successors were determined not to let that happen. And once the American hostages had been taken, the ghastly vision of hundreds of thousands of anti-American demonstrators, some flailing themselves with chains as they marched past the embassy and denounced "the Great Satan," became a disturbing and unforgettable image, fixed in the American psyche. It was literally a nightmare, brought by the miracle of technology into American living rooms every evening just in time to disturb the nation's sleep. (Indeed, ABC's *Nightline,* a popular television news broadcast, is one of the enduring legacies of the hostage crisis; it grew out of that network's nightly special reports on the events in Iran, entitled "America Held Hostage.") If television coverage of Vietnam had converted the American people into temporary pacifists, the video images from Iran turned them into a pack of snarling wolves, and not so temporarily.

The Iranian militants took advantage of satellite linkups to protest the evils of American-inspired modernization. They cut immediately to the quick of America's national ego. The hostage crisis—crude and random episode that it seemed to be—sparked an extraordinary surge of American patriotism and xenophobia, reminiscent of the reaction when the battleship *Maine* was blown up in Havana harbor in 1898 and the United States went straight to war with Spain. Politicians demanded revenge against Iran, and an angry public took its own feeble steps—reacting to their country's humiliation in songs, on T-shirts and bumper stickers, and, in scattered ugly incidents, by attacking Iranian students and others from the unfathomable Third World. The drama in Tehran quickly became the preeminent symbol of a world gone awry, where nothing seemed to be the way it used to be, or (more accurately) the way Americans had come, since World War II, to expect it to be. Precisely because there was no way, place, or method to go to war or otherwise obtain vengeance without disastrous side effects, the nation felt all the more frustrated and betrayed.

Once the Iran hostage crisis had begun, it was easy enough to indulge in a retroactive blaming process, to go back and reinterpret many events and trends since World War II as signs that the world was going bad, if not mad. Ho Chi Minh, Charles de Gaulle, Leonid Brezhnev, Fidel Castro, Indira Gandhi, Muammar al-Qaddafi—they and a cast of a thousand others could now be seen as co-conspirators in the effort to make the earth a precarious place for the United States and its well-intentioned leaders to live. Suddenly, America had to fend for itself and could count on no one else. It was bad enough that the United Nations, the very epitome of postwar American idealism, had turned into what one U.S. representative…, Daniel Patrick Moynihan, called "a dangerous place."[2] But worse, the allies acted unreliably, the beneficiaries of American largesse seemed ungrateful, and even adversaries did not behave predictably. Everywhere the American people turned, they found new evidence not only of grave problems but also of Washington's apparent inability to solve them.

If events were examined closely and calmly, outside the climate of hysteria that was so prevalent in Washington at the time, it was possible to see that America's changing circumstances were part of a general shift in international relationships. Other nations and people, some of them having only recently emerged from the experience of colonialism, were asserting more than symbolic independence and deploying whatever power they could muster to seek greater control over their own lives and national destinies. But that was not how things looked and felt from the perspective of an embattled, weary America. And so in many instances, when other actors on the international scene discovered the dramatic effect their rhetoric could have on the United States—the severe aggravation they could cause with simple gestures—they merely escalated it. The greater the tendency of Americans, including presidents and secretaries of state, to interpret an evolving world as a deteriorating world, the more the United States seemed to be losing control and influence. There was an element of self-fulfilling prophecy to it all.

When the Soviet Union invaded Afghanistan less than two months after the hostages had been taken in Tehran, Carter tried a smorgasbord of sanctions, not a single one of which was effective. Indeed, Carter's ultimate means of expressing his distaste for Soviet actions, the American-led boycott of the Moscow Olympics in 1980 (on which the United States spent an enormous amount of diplomatic and political capital), did more harm to the U.S. image than it did to Soviet prestige. As almost anyone could have predicted at the time, it produced a Soviet-led counter-boycott of the Los Angeles Olympics four years later. In the end, the United States found itself blamed, perhaps not unreasonably, for politicizing international sports.

West Europeans seemed incapable of sharing American outrage over Soviet behavior, or of being persuaded to fall into line. They refused to institute severe sanctions over the Afghanistan affair or, even later, over the declaration of martial law in Poland. On the contrary; in the midst of this critical chain of events, the Europeans signed a contract with the Soviet Union to construct a natural-gas pipeline and granted Moscow credit for the project on favorable terms.

In Lebanon during the early 1980s, the United States proved utterly unable to provide anything but targets for terrorists. The Reagan administration's brief foray into on-the-ground Middle East peacekeeping there turned into a disaster, costing the lives of hundreds of American servicemen but in no way advancing the cause of local or regional reconciliation. In Nicaragua, the Central Intelligence Agency and its "contras" were incapable of overthrowing the Marxist government of the Sandinistas, or even, in the president's own inelegant term, of making them "cry uncle." And in the case of the tiny Caribbean island of Grenada, where the Pentagon did manage to oust a small Cuban garrison and the radical fragment of a left-wing regime—scoring what passed, at least among most Grenadians and Americans, for a great success—the State Department could not find many friends or allies to pat America on the back. The vote in the U.N. General Assembly in favor of a resolution "deeply deploring" the American move into Grenada was 108 to 9, with 27 abstentions. The only supportive votes came from a few other Caribbean states, El Salvador, and Israel. Many countries regarded as stalwart supporters of America voted to condemn the invasion, and the best the United States could get from Britain, West Germany, Japan, and Canada was an agreement to withhold their votes altogether.

It was hard to imagine what other insults might be devised to wound the American ego, but a usually compliant Pacific ally, New Zealand, found one early in 1985. The newly elected Labor party government there declared that it would not permit a U.S. Navy destroyer to make a port call unless it received assurances that the ship was not carrying nuclear weapons. Such assurances being against long-standing American military policy and practice, the Reagan administration fell into an unseemly public quarrel with a nation that had sent troops to fight alongside Americans not only in World War II but also in Korea and Vietnam. It would not have been an easy dilemma for even the most skillful negotiators to solve, but the Reagan administration made matters worse by overreacting to the heartfelt fears of New Zealanders, who had had their atmosphere poisoned over the years by the fallout from French nuclear tests in the South Pacific and thus felt a more than routine abhorrence of nuclear weapons. Hinting at trade sanctions, the United States came off looking like a bully frustrated by his inability to get everyone else to play his game by his own rules. What might have remained a minor incident was blown far out of proportion, because it touched another sensitive nerve among Americans. Before long, rather than searching quietly for a compromise, Washington virtually nullified ANZUS, the mutual security pact the United States had signed with Australia and New Zealand in 1951. A mouse had roared, and the startled American lion characteristically responded by trying to punish it for disturbing the peace.

* * *

The United States emerged from World War II with a unique position and an unusual role in the world. Rarely in modern history had a single nation enjoyed so much prerogative and influence. Alone among the major actors on the international scene, America had survived a nearly global conflict intact and, as a result, perceived itself to be capable of enjoying political and economic ascendancy over its allies and adversaries alike. There was no immediate evidence that this kind of domination would not be sustainable. The American public demanded peace and power, and the country's leadership, regardless of party, felt confident that it could provide both without straining the domestic political system or the new world structure that the United States had guided into existence.

Indeed, U.S. foreign policy in the postwar period was conducted on the basis of a simple vision of the world and of the American role in it. The self-image of the United States was that of a keeper of world peace. As the primary sponsor of the new international order drawn up in San Francisco (the United Nations) and at Bretton Woods (the World Bank and International Monetary Fund), the American government believed that its role in the allied victory in Europe and the Pacific brought with it broad responsibilities for the indefinite future and assurances of cooperation from every quarter.

Whether in the context of the United Nations, the North Atlantic Treaty Organization, or on its own, the United States wanted to put out brushfires that threatened international calm. Because the assignment seemingly had universal endorsement, carrying it out was not expected to provoke serious dispute at home or dissatisfaction abroad.

One way that America initially sought to keep the peace was as leader of a broad new Western alliance and, more ambitiously, of an entire "free world" arrayed against communism and other menacing forces. The credentials for membership in this free world were sometimes confused and often required stretching the language to accommodate dictators and tyrants. Moreover, the United fates; self-confident and cocksure, saw no necessity for occasional reviews of its performance as leader; in the beginning, at least, few other countries were in a position to criticize or complain.

America's confidence was based in part on the assumption that it could be the dominant party in the new but quickly expanding rivalry between the postwar superpowers. This competition was aggressive, sometimes openly angry and highly dangerous, but the United States believed—and, again, saw little convincing evidence to the contrary—that it enjoyed a technical and, even more important, a moral superiority over the Soviet Union. From the perspective of the late 1940s, with the American nuclear monopoly intact, these assumptions seemed entirely reasonable. Many U.S. and European policymakers and analysts even regarded the emerging superpower standoff as an ultimately stabilizing element in world affairs. With the globe neatly divided into two camps and no one trying to occupy a confusing middle ground, it would be clear where everyone stood. The United States would face no surprises, and it could manage any new crises that did arise. Or so it seemed.

The America of the late 1940s also saw itself as a role model—a political, philosophical, economic, and cultural hero to the developing societies that would soon become autonomous, sovereign countries. By all available evidence and, the West believed, by any rational process of reasoning, these societies would be inspired not by Marxism but by Franklin D. Roosevelt's emblematic Four Freedoms and the vision of equality contained in the Atlantic Charter. The concept of a "Third World" with pretensions of going its own way was almost impossible to imagine, especially for the United States, a country whose example now seemed to have something approaching a divine force behind it.

Consistent with a commitment that went back to the early years of the nineteenth century, the United States intended to act more than ever in the postwar period as the protector and defender of the Western Hemisphere from incursions by outside forces and ideas. There had been occasional upheavals in Latin America before World War II (Augusto Sandino's uprising in Nicaragua, for example), but Washington had usually been able to restore order by marching right in. With the new levels of American power and influence, it seemed as if this would be easier than ever to do. The *Pax Americana* would be extended elsewhere, too—notably in Vietnam and the Persian Gulf—but circumstances in its own hemisphere often had a profound effect on America's policy and behavior in other parts of the world. The rise of Fidel Castro in Cuba and his affiliation with the Soviet Union, a subversive event that took place only ninety miles from the tip of Florida, thus intensified the American determination to prevent similar unsettling developments elsewhere, near or far.

It is by now a commonplace that the comfortable, or at least familiar, post-World War II world is in its twilight, but the implications of the change are still unfolding and only beginning to be understood. The contrariness of a former wartime partner, Charles de Gaulle, in the 1960s sent the Western alliance into a process of disintegration. Misunderstanding became the order of the day, and although the United States and the other European allies managed to coordinate on military matters without France, their political relations were often full of recrimination. There were quarrels over trade and other elements of international economic policy. Certainly the Europeans, having belatedly learned the lessons of nationalism, could not understand what the United States was trying to do in Vietnam; later they refused to defer to Washington even in Central America. In one crisis after another, the United States saw itself as the solution, but in nearly every case a significant number of other nations and their leaders began to see the United States as part of the problem. The term *free world* virtually lost its meaning, to the point of becoming an object of mockery and derision, and America's capacity to lead what was left of that world was called seriously into question.

The assumption that the U.S.-Soviet rivalry imposed a kind of stability on an unruly world withered quickly. The Soviet Union proved unwilling from the start to play its assigned role of junior partner in the postwar superpower competition. Once it had its own nuclear arsenal, there was no reason for it to do so. For a time American rhetoric seemed more believable, and U.S. nuclear power more benign, than their Soviet counterparts; but even America's moral edge—its special claim to credibility—faded over the years, especially in the view of the growing bloc of "nonaligned" countries, which blamed both sides for the world's parlous state but still found some attraction in the Communists' anti-colonial rhetoric. The concept of mutual deterrence, an important element in the postwar balance of power, became less reassuring and reliable, and ever more fragile. Increasingly, the U.S.-Soviet contest looked like a destructive, rather than a constructive, organizing force; it demanded a vast share of both societies' resources and left much of the rest of the world quivering at the prospect of nuclear catastrophe. Meanwhile, the recurring issue of whether America could retain, or reestablish, the superiority it had enjoyed in the immediate postwar period provoked a caustic domestic political debate in the United States and often contorted not only superpower relations but also the rest of U.S. foreign policy.

Far from fulfilling America's naive hopes and dreams and looking to its leadership, the Third World became a caldron of unrest and despair. The United States often experienced the shock of being regarded as an ally and extension of colonialism, rather than as a society that offered inspiration for future development. In the United Nations and other international forums, American diplomats came gradually to be subjected to a torrent of abuse and accusations that tried the nation's patience and provoked its temper. Overseas they were frequently threatened by acts of terror and violence, and some lived with a daily fear of assassination.

The most painful events were those closest to home. In Latin America, once Castro had come to power, the tide seemed to run inevitably against perceived American interests, and credible surrogates—not to mention simple friends—became ever harder to find. Instead of the just and intrepid "Good Neighbor," the United States was increasingly portrayed as a grotesque caricature, the evil purveyor of "*Yanqui* imperialism."

There and elsewhere, American policymakers tried to promote the ideal of stable change managed by moderate forces. But rarely did that work, and when the extremes clashed, the United States generally found itself, wittingly or unwittingly, in alliance with conservative, often repressive forces opposed to change. The persistent tendency by American administrations of both parties to cling to symbolic leaders on their way out—the Shah, Anastasio Somoza in Nicaragua, Haile Selassie in Ethiopia, and Ferdinand Marcos in the Philippines, to name a few—reinforced the impression. In a great range of circumstances, from Vietnam in the 1960s to southern Africa in the 1980s, the United States became the object of vilification and mistrust by the majority of the people. The great nation that wanted to be a peacemaker somehow seemed more a party to than a preventer of conflict. And conflict was becoming more likely, in more places, all the time. As the proliferation of nuclear-weapons-making capability went virtually unchecked, notwithstanding American moral appeals and the Nuclear Non-proliferation Treaty, the gravity of potential conflicts grew, and the prospect of disorder deepened.

American politics and U.S. foreign policy adapted awkwardly to the breakdown of the world the United States had tried to create and lead. For a brief period John F. Kennedy seemed to offer America and the rest of the world fulfillment of the frayed postwar vision after all, but beginning with Lyndon B. Johnson, the succession of men who came into the White House were treated as objects of international puzzlement rather than admiration. Courses in American Studies overseas became a combination of psychohistory and sociogeography. The impasse in Vietnam, the U.S. domestic upheaval growing out of it, and the civil rights movement, combined later with the extraordinary collection of events known as Watergate, led many Americans to cease their perennial lectures to the people of other countries about consensus or corruption. Other Americans kept lecturing, but few people in the intended audience were listening. Peace and political legitimacy were becoming hard enough to attain at home; America hardly had the moral qualifications or the physical capacity to establish peace and project its power around the world anymore.

With the U.S. economy threatened by its own decline in productivity, the growing assertiveness of oil producers, and competition from other rapidly expanding industrial economies, the American success story became a less obvious model to admire or emulate. Indeed, German chancellors and French presidents who knew something about economics were baffled by American presidents who apparently did not. Meanwhile, much of the domestic discussion of international issues deteriorated into an examination and dissection of the "post-Vietnam syndrome," as if some failure of will had not only constituted a stab in the back in Southeast Asia but had also induced a crippling caution that now prevented the United States from taking effective action anywhere. Some people began to search for another place—perhaps Central America—where a new group of tough American leaders could "do it right." Nearly everyone craved simplicity in foreign affairs. It was as if a cascade of unhappy events—the climax being the prolonged hostage crisis in Iran—had sent the United States back into a parochial, unsophisticated pre-World War II attitude toward an ever more complex world.

* * *

The United States is estranged from that complex world—separate, aloof, more alone than even the most cynical or pessimistic observers might have predicted in the heyday of American postwar power. The symptoms are obvious everywhere: in trade friction with Japan; in the antinuclear, anti-American sentiment infusing European political movements; in some countries in Central America, where only the most conservative, most narrow-based, elements will align themselves openly with U.S. policy; and in South Africa, where recognized black leaders have become cautious about meeting with even liberal Americans who agree with them and support their cause. Although it often emerges in the form of bravado or contempt for others, the unease is also deeply felt inside the United States. It is a phenomenon that extends across party and ideological lines.

Part of what makes today's world so uncomfortable for Americans is the perfectly understandable tendency to reject a new reality, especially strong in a society where self-confidence is part of the national ideology. "Americans feel unqualifiedly that this is the best country in the world," the pollster Daniel Yankelovich has observed. They are taught to believe that from their earliest days in school, and any politician who disputes this fundamental truth (as Jimmy Carter seemed to do toward the end of his term in the White House, when he worried aloud about the American "malaise") is severely punished for his heresy. "The dark side of this attitude is that we don't believe we can be wrong," Yankelovich went on; "we're not looking at the world from anybody else's point of view."[3]

The United States has provided frequent reminders in recent years that it sees the world through its own unique, self-interested prism, often profoundly influenced by domestic political considerations that outsiders find difficult to comprehend. On three issues that became international symbols, America's isolation was particularly stark: In May 1981, at a meeting of the World Health Organization in Geneva, the Reagan administration cast the sole dissenting vote against the adoption of an international code of ethics curtailing the promotion of baby formula. (The issue had arisen because of concern that the aggressive marketing of formula in Third World countries, where it was often mixed with contaminated water and fed in unsterilized bottles, was causing an increase in infant deaths.) In April 1982 the American delegation to the U.N. Law-of-the-Sea Conference cast one of only four votes against a draft treaty, because of objections to the provision establishing a global authority to regulate seabed mining. At the end of 1984, although 138 other nations and 21 international organizations had already signed, the United States (influencing Britain, West Germany, and nine other countries, with varying degrees of reluctance, to go along), let the deadline for signatures pass, effectively eliminating itself from any role in the cooperative international management of ocean resources. At the U.N.-sponsored International Conference on Population in Mexico City in August 1984, the United States found itself virtually alone against the rest of the world in arguing for the adoption of a fundamentalist anti-abortion policy and in attempting to insert language promoting free-enterprise economic policies into resolutions that came before the conference.

There was a time, in the early post-World War II period, when a preoccupation with America's well-being was not necessarily regarded as inconsistent with a genuine concern for and generous interest in the rest of the world. Christoph Bertram, political editor of the West German weekly *Die Zeit* and former director of the International Institute for Strategic Studies in London, recalls an era "when the United States was a superpower in the true sense: confident not only in its strength but also in its ability to build, together with others, a world of shared duties and rights, and to be ready to carry the major burden in this enterprise."

That was an era when Marshall McLuhan's vision of the "global village" was just dawning, when it was still reasonable to dream of a world community in which geographical and social distances were rendered meaningless by methods of communication that promoted understanding—restoring, McLuhan believed, something of our species' original sense of being part of a village or tribal unit. The importance of physical distances, and of some of the social ones, has been reduced even further in recent decades, but the concept of a global village now seems naive and the notion of the United States taking responsibility for it, in the current domestic and international political climate, nothing short of ridiculous. "America has given up the traditions it established after World War II," says Bertram, "without regrets but with a sigh of relief." Rather than promoting a new "international order that promises cooperation and stability for the 1990s, America prefers to pursue its own interests alone," he says. Bertram concludes that "we are now back in [a world] where the strong do what they want and the weak suffer what they must, where superpower, once again, is a measure of military strength alone."[4]

There are many competing diagnoses of the problem, of course. Conservatives tend to blame America's lack of resolve. For Jeane J. Kirkpatrick, U.S. ambassador to the United Nations during the first Reagan administration and a leading proponent of the new American assertiveness, the critical change occurred during the late 1960s and the 1970s, when the United States suffered from "an attitude of defeatism, self-doubt, self-denigration, and self-delusion." One of Kirkpatrick's predecessors, Moynihan, pointed to a pervasive American sense of guilt and "a failure of nerve" within the U.S. foreign policy elite. "Inhibitions had arisen in the American polity," Moynihan observed, "which prevented us from responding to ideological conflict." Michael Ledeen, once an aide to Reagan's first secretary of state, Alexander M. Haig, Jr., complains that in recent years American leaders "have tended to adopt moralistic abstractions instead of realistic appraisals of the world, and we have rarely suited our diplomatic, economic, and military means to our national objectives." The problem is compounded, according to Ledeen, by the fact that "fashionably correct positions on many issues are defined by a group of journalists who are themselves ignorant of the dynamics of international affairs and who are themselves explicitly engaged in political activity with strong professional investments in certain outcomes."[5]

Many liberals, on the other hand, think America has closed its eyes and ears to certain developments in the postwar world. Jonathan Kwitny, who has traveled the globe for the *Wall Street Journal*, believes that in the Third World

> we continue to press not our system, which encourages free choice, but some convoluted notion of our system, which imposes *our* choice. We insist on imposing solutions to particular problems involving foreign people: They are asked to live by our choices, when they often don't want or even understand them.

U.S. foreign policy is above all simplistic, according to T. D. Allman: "The most intractable myth of American nationalism is that there are intrinsically good guys and bad guys." And three analysts of the American foreign policy process—I. M. Destler, Leslie H. Gelb, and Anthony Lake—contend that the United States has

> lost a coherent sense…of national interests, the enduring purposes of policy that flow from values, geography, and our place in the hierarchy of world power. In almost all other nations, it takes a revolution to redefine these basic purposes. For the last two decades in the United States, it has required only a Presidential election or the prospect of one.

For Fouad Ajami, a scholar of the Third World who was born in Lebanon and now teaches in the United States, the issues are more complex, involving the export of ideas by the United States that are somehow unrecognizable when they are espoused by others. "America has formed so many of its rivals," Ajami has written.

> The images we do not like in distant societies are often reflections of ourselves. America has held up before older societies a revolutionary message of social change and political equality; every now and then we ride into storms that we helped stir up. When we understand this, we will no longer imagine "others" as men of dark sensibilities in thrall to frightening forces. We will also begin to understand the deep roots of America's presence, as well as the ambivalence with which it is greeted by men who hector us in metaphors at once familiar and threatening, in places that invite us in and then reject us.[7]

Indeed, however it is analyzed and explained, there is in America's estrangement an implication of prior attachment and affection, a sense that at some other moment in the recent past the United States and the rest of the world had more in common or understood each other better. It is as if a once very popular member of a family suddenly found himself at odds with all his relatives; after such a relationship has begun to sour, it is difficult to stop the downward spiral. And it is virtually impossible to be estranged from someone unknown or little known; only because of an established familiarity is a complex relationship vulnerable to deterioration.

But an argument over familiarity—or a lack thereof—lies at the heart of America's uncomfortable estrangement. The leaders and the intellectuals of many other countries believe that they have been asked to appreciate American processes and points of view, and even to imitate them, without an equivalent effort being made in the opposite direction. The result is an astonishing asymmetry: the minutiae of American politics and society are followed compulsively by others as a critical component of life in the real world, while the U.S.

government and individual American citizens seem to show an ever declining knowledge of and interest in anyone else. Whether out of discomfort, indifference, or contempt, Americans—even those holding high positions—often laugh at the hard-to-pronounce names of foreign capitals or statesmen while expecting others to treat American place and family names with reverence. But is Ouagadougou (the capital of Burkina Faso, formerly Upper Volta, in West Africa) really any more exotic a name than Massachusetts or Tallahassee? And is it any more eccentric for people from Spanish cultures to put their mother's maiden name after their surname than for Americans to insist on using middle initials?

The ignorance of Americans about international affairs is legendary, and it has been growing worse. Even on matters of current controversy—issues that are theoretically decisive in U.S. presidential and congressional elections—the public is remarkably unaware. Asked merely to tell the location of El Salvador in a survey sponsored by CBS News and the *New York Times,* only 25 percent of the sample got it right. When ABC and the *Washington Post* asked people to say which two nations had been involved in the SALT (Strategic Arms Limitations Treaty) talks, only 37 percent answered correctly; 13 percent gave a wrong answer, and 50 percent said they had no idea. In response to other questions, fewer than half of the people surveyed knew whether it was the United States or the Soviet Union that belonged to the NATO alliance or which countries had participated in the Camp David peace talks sponsored by the United States.[8]

Schoolchildren show little promise of improving on their parents' records. One study published in the late 1970s showed that more than 40 percent of American high school seniors surveyed could not locate Egypt on a map, and more than 20 percent had no idea where to find France or China. The President's Commission on Foreign Language and International Studies, reporting in November 1979, found a striking decline in the study of languages at the high school, college, and graduate levels. It warned that the network of institutions and special programs in international studies, "built by foundations, the government, and the universities themselves in a period of great scholarly advances after World War II," was now "in danger of imminent collapse."[9] The commission recommended a major effort to increase federal support and other funding for such centers, but since then the Reagan administration has proposed, in several successive fiscal years, reducing that item in the Department of Education's budget to zero. (Congress repeatedly resisted that proposal and insisted on funding regional centers for language and area studies, but education organizations fear that congressional resistance will soon disappear.)

The American government is notorious for sending diplomats overseas with little or no knowledge of the cultures, let alone the languages, of the countries where they will serve; among the U.S. embassy staff in Iran who became hostages, for example, only a handful were fluent in Farsi, the country's most important language. Political appointees are often selected for certain ambassadorial posts, especially in Europe and Africa, without any regard for the nominees' qualifications.

Given these educational trends and federal policies, it is little wonder that, as political scientist Howard J. Wiarda has noted, at the root of U.S. foreign policy dilemmas in the Third World lie "a deeply ingrained American ethnocentrism, an inability to understand the Third World on its own terms, an insistence on viewing it through the lenses of our own Western experience, and the condescending and patronizing attitudes that such ethnocentrism implies."[10] Such neglect and narrowness is bound to have lasting consequences for America.

* * *

Still, America's estrangement is not without its paradoxes.

Even as U.S. political and economic influence comes in for growing criticism and often virulent attack, American cultural symbols seem to flourish almost everywhere. For years, Americans traveling to the Soviet Union were advised to take along blue jeans, chewing gum, and ballpoint pens if they really wanted to have doors opened to them. European leftists sitting in cafes and complaining about the United States are as likely as not to be drinking Coca-Cola, and even in the tensest moments of Nicaraguan-American relations—when U.S.-supported "contras" are attacking, the Sandinistas' press censorship is at its peak, and the government is sounding alarms about an imminent U.S. invasion—movie theaters in Managua are likely to be featuring a festival of American films. McDonald's and other American-franchised fast-food outlets have become a permanent feature of life in Japan, as have other aspects of U.S. popular culture. Indeed, after World War II, during the American occupation of Japan, General Douglas MacArthur succeeded in shaping various aspects of public and private life there (including, for example, television networks) according to the American model; there have been frequent complaints about the loss of Japanese traditions, but few serious efforts to do anything about it.

Jazz is virtually a lingua franca in the Third World; and in many places, if the "Voice of America" has taken hold, it is substantially because of its broadcasts of American popular music. American television serials such as "Dallas" or, in their time, "Gunsmoke" and "Kojak" have been dubbed and subtitled in so many languages and sent around the world so many times as to inspire local fan clubs and imitations. Professionals and intellectuals in many developing countries where the local press is tightly controlled wait every week for the arrival of American news magazines, so they can learn about developments on the international scene (and even in their own nations), and in other places where those magazines cannot be sold openly, copies fetch high prices on the black market. For much of the twentieth century, Americans and Americanophiles had dreamed of the "Americanization" of the world,[11] but by the 1960s and 1970s the dream had, in certain respects, become a reality. And the Soviet system, for all of the American warnings about its spread, had offered no alternative, attractive models.

So thorough is the saturation of some parts of the developing world with American culture that truly revolutionary forces—as distinct from mainstream political opponents of a regime in power—often find they must attack symbols of that culture before they can be taken seriously. Thus, when the Shining Path guerrillas in Peru wanted to take their antigovernment campaign from the countryside to the capital city of Lima, one of their first targets was a chain of Kentucky Fried Chicken outlets.

Another paradox is that the American example of a good life achieved through financial prosperity, material consumption, and technological progress, while initially admired and envied, has ultimately led to alienation rather than appreciation. It was long assumed by U.S. officials, business interests, and journalists that modernization was the dream of the poor and the oppressed around the world. It was as if they expected the American dream to take hold so thoroughly that before long people everywhere would aspire to live in suburban homes with modern conveniences—to act out the lives they glimpsed in American television series or in advertisements for American products in American publications. But that, of course, was far from the truth. Most of the citizens of developing societies were, in the first place, concerned with far more basic problems, such as feeding, clothing, and sheltering themselves and keeping their children alive from one season to the next. And for those few members of the elite who did have access to Western ways and advanced education, the preservation of traditional values often became a more important consideration than many outside experts or aid donors imagined.

As Wiarda pointed out, the United States has been a prime sufferer from Eurocentrism, a "belief that the developmental experience of Western Europe and North America can be repeated, even imitated (albeit belatedly) in the Third World." Thus, Americans have expected economic, political; and social change to follow the Euro-American model, especially in countries of particular interest to the West, and they may be baffled when Islamic, Confucian, Buddhist and other traditions or sensibilities assert themselves. Iran is the classic example of a client state where American expectations dissolved as the domestic political situation went haywire. There the encounter with Western culture did not at all lead to an American-style pluralistic and secular society, but rather to a harsh, theocratic, ultimately totalitarian regime.[12] And the establishment of that regime was greatly facilitated by the easy access of ordinary people to high-tech implements. The Ayatollah Khomeini's subversive speeches against the Shah received their widest circulation on cassette tapes that were smuggled into the country and then heard on miniature tape players (manufactured in Japan, perhaps, but inspired by American habits).

Probably the most striking paradox—and the one that may allow Americans to overlook or dismiss their country's estrangement from the rest of the world—is that while the United States is often the target of international criticism, it nonetheless remains a mecca for immigrants. In fiscal year 1984 alone, some 544,000 people emigrated legally from their home countries to America, and the Immigration and Naturalization Service apprehended more than 1.2 million others who had come illegally. It is indisputable that however unpopular the United States may be on the international political scene, a vast percentage of humanity still regards America as the promised land where economic opportunity and a liberal political system make it possible to dream of a better life.[13] This overwhelming attraction fortifies the self-congratulatory impulse of many Americans and helps them reject national introspection and self-criticism in favor of defiance, anger, and a new nationalism.

There is a natural temptation, especially during difficult periods in their nation's life, for Americans to try to withdraw, literally or figuratively, from international involvement—to rely on their country's geographical isolation and self-sufficiency and try to live apart from the world's turmoil, as it once seemed possible to do. But it is no longer feasible to reach for such an alternative. Georgi A. Arbatov, director of the Institute of U.S. and Canadian Studies in Moscow, has observed that

> the situation has changed, and America finds herself not only at a rough parity with the USSR militarily but absolutely equal with other countries in terms of her own vulnerability to a holocaust should a war break out. This is a new situation for Americans. It is undoubtedly not easy to get used to it, not easy to get along with it.[14]

Indeed, separation—one possible and logical result of any process of estrangement—is not an option in today's world, especially not for an open and influential society like America, still preoccupied with peace and power. An isolated, backward nation like Albania can, for quite some time, withdraw into itself and keep foreign influences from crossing its borders. A xenophobic culture like Burma can restrict visitors to short stays. Even the world's most populous country, China, could undergo a "cultural revolution," turning into itself at the expense of impoverishing itself further and delaying its entry into modern life. What America must do now is uniquely complex and difficult: It must rethink its role in the world, and it must begin by recognizing that old myths of invulnerability and invincibility are no longer sustainable. As Ronald Steel has written, "the United States is still incontestably the richest and strongest nation in the world.... It can do many awesome things: move mountains, topple governments, confer riches, and inflict horrors." But that power is now finite and greatly circumscribed. "The reason that [America] cannot always call the tune is to be found not in the decline of American will," Steel observes, "but in the recovery of the world, a recovery we did so much to make possible. Now we have to learn to live with that recovery."[15]

* * *

The events of September 11, 2001, with their cruel

and random outcome, constituted a horrifying reaffirmation of America's estrangement. The first reaction to the terrorist attacks, of course, amidst fears and prayers and tears, was a mostly healthy display of patriotism. But the crisis also became an occasion for self-examination, for calculation of policy and strategy, a confusing interlude that boggled the mind and challenged Americans' collective national and international imagination. Every institution suddenly found itself considering how to chart a course through a drastically changed global landscape.

One thing was surely clear: the United States, however unique a nation it might somehow claim to be, could no longer invoke the right, through a combination of moral superiority and geopolitical influence, to stand apart from all other countries. Looking back, the 1980s and 1990s were notable as a time when vast numbers of Americans told the pollsters that they had simply "lost interest" in the rest of the world.

Lost interest indeed. In a trend that only accelerated with the end of the Cold War, Congress had actually cut the foreign affairs budget. U.S. consulates and other posts in far-flung corners of the globe were shut down. America's commercial and marketing influence actually grew further; but the American libraries and cultural centers that had once served as a resource for people to learn about a great, diverse country came to be regarded as too expensive to maintain. Over a period of time, the Voice of America, an agency that I later had the privilege to lead for two years, was virtually starved of resources—making it almost impossible for it to fulfill its congressional mandate to report comprehensively for the rest of the world on what was happening across the United States.

Overall, the media exacerbated this new isolation. In the 1980s and the 1990s, coverage of international news for an American audience practically disappeared, especially from the commercial broadcast networks that had become such an important and routine source of information. (CNN has been the exception, but it attracts a large audience only in times of crisis.) Foreign bureaus were closed. One network proudly proclaimed the virtue of its drastic cuts in costly overseas reporting; no one was watching, said the decision-makers. Entertainment squeezed out substance; sound bites and factoids replaced thoughtful analysis. Whole continents actually went unmentioned on the nightly news for a year or two, while the lowest common denominator flourished. Who wanted to learn about, say, a fundamentalist Islamic regime that was taking hold in Afghanistan with American-supplied weapons, if the alternative was to watch our neighbors compete to become millionaires by answering questions about the most trivial of things?

Somehow and somewhere along the way, apparently, the United States became unpopular among many people around the world, and Americans barely noticed. Was it really not enough for politicians to keep telling them they had the greatest country on earth? Could it be that—waves of immigrants notwithstanding—not everyone wanted to live like Americans after all? Were Americans so self-satisfied that they had no idea terrorists were establishing themselves and hatching their schemes in their very midst? Was it rational to suppose that having tried and failed once to blow up the World Trade Center in New York, the perpetrators would not come back and try again, with a more effective method?

In the aftermath of the attacks, Congressman Henry Hyde of Illinois, the chair of the House International Relations Committee, wondered aloud on Capitol Hill, "How is it that the country that invented Hollywood and Madison Avenue has such trouble promoting a positive image of itself overseas?" But with just a few days' perspective, most observers realized that it might take more than unleashing the geniuses of the movie industry and the advertising world to make things right—to make America popular again, the object of admiration rather than hate.

Of course America does have a great story to tell, but it must be told with subtlety and sophistication, and just perhaps a dose of modesty and reserve. Americans can also pay much closer attention to how others are seeing them—how they feel, for example, if, for presumed geopolitical reasons, the United States supports repressive regimes in their countries. Instead of bragging about their own allegedly perfect democracy—which everyone can agree functioned less than perfectly at the time of the 2000 presidential election—Americans must seek to understand more about other systems and cultures. And they should consider the seemingly radical notion that others may have ideas to offer them—that distant, perhaps even quite small, nations may have found intriguing solutions to housing, clothing, and feeding people, transporting them from one place to another, immunizing them against diseases, and promoting literacy. Another Illinoisan, the great Adlai Stevenson, once said that the modern technology Americans most need to employ is the hearing aid. As in any educational enterprise, Americans must learn to observe and to listen. They may soon realize that they do not have a world exclusive on the definition and practice of "family values."

Educational institutions and the media have a particular role to play in changing American attitudes and practices. They need to inculcate the idea that citizens can lead full and fascinating—and yes, prosperous—lives that are enriched by a global consciousness. Along the way, it should become clear that international awareness is not a luxury, but a necessity.

Notes

1. Barry Rubin, *Paved with Good Intentions: The American Experience and Iran* (New York: Oxford University Press, 1980), pp. 200-201; and Gary Sick, *All Fall Down: America's Tragic Encounter with Iran* (New York: Random House, 1985), pp. 30 and ff.

2. See Daniel Patrick Moynihan (with Suzanne Weaver), *A Dangerous Place* (Boston: Atlantic-Little, Brown, 1978).

3. "American Values: Change and Stability," a conversation with Daniel Yankelovich, *Public Opinion*, December/January 1984, p. 5.

4. Christoph Bertram, "When America was a Superpower," *Washington Post*, November 25, 1984, p. C-7. For McLuhan on the global village, see *War and Peace in the Global Village*, written with Quentin Fiore (New York: McGraw-Hill, 1968).

5. Jeane J. Kirkpatrick, *The Reagan Phenomenon—and Other Speeches on Foreign Policy* (Washington, DC: American Enterprise Institute for Public Policy Research, 1983), p. 30; Moynihan, op. cit., p. 256; and Michael Ledeen, *Grave New World* (New York: Oxford University Press, 1985), pp. 25 and 29.

6. Jonathan Kwitny. *Endless Enemies: The Making of an Unfriendly World* (New York: Congdon & Weed, 1984), p. 394; T.D. Allman, *Unmanifest Destiny* (New York: Doubleday, 1984), p. 376; and I.M. Destler, Leslie H. Gelb, and Anthony Lake, *Our Own Worst Enemy: The Unmaking of American Foreign Policy* (New York: Simon & Schuster, 1984), p. 12.

7. Fouad Ajami, "The End of the Affair: An American Tragedy in the Arab World," *Harper's*, June 1984, p. 63.

8. Barry Sussman, "El Salvador is Not in Louisiana," *Washington Post*, January 2, 1983, p. B-5.

9. *Strength through Wisdom: A Critique of U.S. Capability, A Report to the President from the President's Commission on Foreign, Language and International Studies* (Washington, DC: U.S. Government Printing Office, November 1979), pp. 7-8 ff. See also Paul Simon, *The Tongue-Tied American: Confronting the Foreign Language Crisis* (New York: Continuum, 1980).

10. Howard J. Wiarda, *Ethnocentrism in Foreign Policy: Can We Understand the Third World?* (Washington, DC: American Enterprise Institute for Public Policy Research, 1985), p. 1.

11. See, for example, W. T. Stead, *The Americanization of the World, or The Trend of the Twentieth Century* (New York and London: Horace Markley, 1901).

12. Wiarda, op. cit., pp. 4 and 29.

13. For this author's more extensive thoughts on immigration, see Sanford J. Ungar, *Fresh Blood: The New American Immigrants* (New York: Simon & Schuster, 1995; revised edition, Urbana: University of Illinois Press, 1997).

14. Georgi A. Arbatov, "Relations Between the United States and the Soviet Union—Accuracy of U.S. Perceptions," in *Toward Nuclear Disarmament and Global Security: A Search for Alternatives*, Burns H. Weston, ed. (Boulder, CO: Westview Press, 1984), p. 280.

15. Ronald Steel, "Behaving Like a Great Power," *Vanity Fair*, February 1984, pp. 36-37. See also Ronald Steel, *Pax Americana* (New York: Viking, 1967).

Privatizing Peace: From Conflict to Security

Allan Gerson
George Washington University and

Nat J. Colletta
George Washington University

There may be another way out of the current scourge of recurrent armed civil conflict with its attendant toll of millions of wasted human lives and vast stretches of squandered economic opportunity. We have seen no evidence of it. The path herein proposed (which is, of course, only a partial solution) is an integrated unified field approach, centered around the privatization of many peace-related functions. The alternative—the retention of old methodologies—is fragmentation. It would continue what has been described as a pattern of international organizations acting as "stove pipes" (reaching upward or downward but without hands across to touch other actors), and NGOs as "food chains" (competing with one another for scarce resources and unable to integrate their efforts).

A unified field approach offers a new vision, one centered on partnering as a three-dimensional quest. It focuses immediately and directly on the intended beneficiaries, the people on the ground most in need of help. And it also looks to a new relationship among the "benefactors": NGOs, governments and multilateral institutions which have often been at loggerheads with each other, suspicious of one another's motives and unable to bridge the divide of insular institutional cultures. Here it seeks partnering and involvement of the private sector in keeping with the spirit of our times, the zeitgeist of globalization.

Globalization can be a force for peace, not merely for enhanced commerce. Success hinges on whether a new architecture can be developed for not allowing the new energy it unleashes to be harnessed rather than allowed to dissipate. Privatization of many peace-related functions carried out in union with civil society and the public sector, both national and supranational, can be its fundamental building block. With commitment to such an undertaking, the gnawing sense of futility that underlies so much of today's armed conflicts can give way to the promise of a better tomorrow.

The idea that governments and multilateral institutions are alone capable of peacemaking and peacebuilding is already recognized as an anachronism. In the age of globalization the open dissemination of knowledge, information and culture goes hand in hand with openness of markets and the enterprise of producers, rewarding whomever can deliver goods or services most efficiently.

Surely, peace is the supreme good which precedes all others. Economic growth and opportunity cannot be divorced from peacebuilding any more than it can be denied that the private sector is the engine of growth in our time. But there must be incentives of an economic and non-economic kind to induce adequate and responsible private sector engagement. There must also be adequate regulation—some self-imposed, some by treaties and conventions—to curb excesses and provide for transparency and accountability.

A proposed new institutional structure, a Peace Transitions Council (PTC), would allow for the evolution of a three-dimensional partnership—encompassing the United Nations and the World Bank, governments and civil society, and the private sector—cooperating on a global scale with regional nodes. It needs not be any more of a fantasy than the idea that the vacuum tube technology of the 1950s would one day be replaced by the integrated circuit boards of today.

The Changing Face of Armed Conflict

The twentieth century idea of curbing the scourge of war through supranational institutions—an initiative which led to the creation of the United Nations, and, to a lesser but no less important degree, the Bretton Woods Institutions (the World Bank and International Monetary Fund)—had run out of steam by the year 2000. The thinking which had preoccupied the statesmen and humanitarians who were the progenitors of this idea focused on interstate war, on aggression across recognized state frontiers. But as fighting between states ebbed toward the end of the century, intrastate war—conflict within sovereign or less-than-sovereign borders—picked up with a vengeance. The end of the Cold War precipitated this transformation. In the Cold War's wake, 101 civil wars erupted between 1989 and 1998. And according to the authoritative research of Peter Wallensteen and Margareta Sollenberg at the Department of Peace and Conflict Research of Sweden's Uppsala University, there were by contrast, only seven interstate wars during that period.[1] Although, as demonstrated by the University of Maryland's Center for International Development and Conflict Management, a downward trend occurred in the incidence of civil conflicts, from a high of 55 in 1992 to a low of 34 in 1997, by 1998 that trend reversed itself: there were 36 active civil-type conflicts in 1998, and no significant abatement since.[2]

Many of these internal wars reflect deeply rooted ethnic and identity-related conflicts independent of Cold War factors. But their true nature has often been masked by the ideological overlay of the Cold War, where war by proxies became the rule. Other internal conflicts have had, and continue to have, less to do with ethnicity and identity than with greed and power. Here, conflict has often swirled over control of new systems of patronage centered around abundant natural resources and their potential for huge profits.[3] Lauri Nathan, of the Center for Conflict Resolution of the University of Cape Town, South Africa, has identified four basic structural conditions which spawn almost all of the ongoing civil conflicts in Africa: authoritarian rule; the exclusion of minorities from governance; socio-economic deprivation combined with inequity; and weak states that lack the institutional capacity to manage normal conflict associated with social and economic transformation.[4] Ruha Auvinen and Wayne Nafziger at the World Institute for Development Economics Research (WIDER) reached a similar conclusion in their study on the causes of complex humanitarian emergencies. On the basis of a comparative study covering 124 countries between 1980 to 1995, they found that that civil conflict is virtually always related to five factors: stagnation and decline in real GDP, a high ratio of military expenditure to national income, a tradition of violent conflict, high income inequality, and slow growth in average food production. More often than not, they concluded, "relative deprivation explains political conflict."[5]

Regardless, however, of the causes of intrastate wars, humanitarian emergencies inevitably follow. Usually they are identifiable by the presence of "the four horseman of apocalypse": death, displacement, hunger, and disease. It is thus hardly surprising that civil wars tend to start in, and to especially scar, the world's poorest countries. In the last decade they have left a terrible legacy: more than five million dead, millions more driven from their homes, physical resources destroyed, and institutions and social cohesion weakened to the breaking point. Today, over 22 million displaced persons and refugees, compared to a fraction of that number prior to 1990, burden the responsibilities of the United Nations High Commission for Refugees. Its staff has risen from 33 with a budget of $300,000 and operations exclusively in Europe in 1951, to in 1999 a staff of around 5,000 and a budget of over $1 billion with operations in over 120 countries.[6]

Today, the scourge of civil wars challenges conventional wisdom about the nature of wars, the means for deterrence, and the handling of their aftermath. Traditionally, states have waged war against one another with professional armies. The majority of the casualties were combatants. A military victory signaled the end of hostilities. The subsequent peace, usually accompanied by a formal agreement, allowed each side to rebuild roads, bridges, houses, schools, and livelihoods. Over time, they would come to terms with the wounds of war. At the very least, there would be some form of peaceful coexistence. By contrast, the intrastate armed violent conflicts now plaguing the world are waged largely by youthful combatants with little formal military training. Civilians are increasingly targeted, and often left displaced, maimed, or dead. Stalemate rather than victory is the typical end. Resolved inconclusively, they stand ready to flare up again at the slightest provocation. Formal peace agreements have become rare; their full implementation even rarer. And "post-conflict" periods are rarely "post" at all, as small-scale violence often continues to torment war-torn areas, leaving them in a state of neither war nor peace.

In many instances, war continues by other means. Diplomatic means and economic tools gain currency as those of the battlefield are discredited. What persists is the will to weaken if not destroy one's adversary. With little trust and only fleeting reconciliation, former belligerents remain enemies; live ammunition may be foregone, but no reinvigorated desire to live together peaceably replaces it. Billions of dollars in aid and thousands of peace-keepers (e.g., Bosnia and Kosovo) offer no guarantee of an end to this state of affairs. Nor can reintegration and reconciliation of ex-belligerents be legislated by any number of UN Security Council resolutions.[7]

Neither the United Nations nor the Bretton Woods Institutions, alone or in tandem, can control or prevent such wars. Indeed the institutional mandates and methodologies of these supranational organizations are often part of the problem. Any workable solution demands more comprehensive planning and a radical readjustment of insular institutional cultures. Others, the private sector, as well as non-governmental organizations and civil society generally must become engaged. A new partnership for sustainable peace must arise if efforts at political, economic and social peacebuilding are not to fail.[8]

The Peace Transitions Council: Steps Toward a New Global Architecture of Peace

A Peace Transitions Council would work to close a number of gaps in the present system through meaningful partnering among key players in peacebuilding. It would aim at better coordination of functions and synergistic gains, taking advantage of what the private sector can contribute to central system-wide strategy, reconciliation of contending institutional principles and mandates, and coordination through integration of information systems to avoid redundancies in effort. Soliciting and recommending apportionment of public and private capital would be among its other useful functions.

It would build on efforts that have taken place within the UN system itself for better coordination of functions in post conflict scenarios. The UN Inter-Agency Steering Committee (IASC) on Post-Conflict Integration found a number of "planning mechanism failures" within the UN system, and between the UN system and the World Bank. Five critical planning elements were cited as missing:

- failure to bring in all relevant actors at the outset of the planning period;
- cumbersome nature of the planning instruments;
- disconnects between agreed strategies arising out of the instruments and individual
- agencies' programs and appeals;
- no mechanism for effective regional and sub regional (transborder) planning; and
- inadequate linkages between peace agreements and measures to ensure that "gaps" are closed.

Each of these missing elements could be filled through active private sector engagement in a PTC at global, national and local levels.[9]

Framework for Engagement: Legal and Operational Aspects of a Peace Transitions Council

Equality among PTC partners in sharing burdens and responsibilities along agreed divisions of labor is critical to its success. The private sector and NGO community would not be limited to an advisory function. The private sector could take the lead in encouraging foreign and local investment. It could, for example, plan training and the development of human capital in line with new technologies to create an attractive and disciplined workforce, retraining workers from inefficient enterprises to match entrepreneurial needs, and encouraging short-term worker training by use of new computerized, Internet-based distance learning technologies. The NGO community could focus on bridging relief, development, and good governance. In making recommendations pertinent to overall strategy, each partner would speak with an equal voice.

Although the actual modalities for PTC operations would necessarily evolve through negotiations and trial and error, the principles listed below are suggested as guidelines.

At the global level, the PTC would consist of 20 representatives, coming from and appointed by the respective entities of the United Nations, the World Bank, the NGO community, and the international business community, with 5 seats allocated to each. Terms of appointment should be for two years, subject to renewal. Representatives of the United Nations and World Bank would serve ex officio, concurrent with their existing positions. Private sector and NGO representatives would be expected to serve independently of their other affiliations. A President of the PTC would be elected by majority vote of the representatives. Such a representative mix of actors would be reflected in similar organizations at the regional, national and local levels.

Global PTC headquarters could be located in Washington D.C., giving it proximity to the World Bank and to the ambassadorial and NGO communities. It would have a Secretariat and Executive Director. Operating expenses would be covered by joint assessments for all representative sectors. Private sector funding should come from as wide a base as possible, enlisting all segments of the business community. The focus should be on multinational corporate and global NGO engagement. The PTC would be convened on a regular basis to review peacebuilding efforts worldwide, and on an exceptional basis at the request of any of the parties or its President.

The PTC would establish links with regional organizations and development banks to share information and resources pertaining to common interests in peacebuilding missions and the avoidance of redundant efforts.

The PTC would seek to contribute to ongoing efforts at avoiding bureaucratic logjams and streamlining operations, including elimination of needless layers of bureaucracy in international organizations and crisis response architecture.[10]

The PTC would be directly answerable to no other authority, thus assuring its complete independence as an advisory body. It would encourage centralized decision making with regard to overall strategy and planning, but not act as a decision making entity with regard to functions normally assumed by the United Nations or the World Bank.

The PTC would initiate a data system, communications system, and control center that can integrate the pertinent data, on a real-time basis, of all of its constituent entities.

The PTC would be global in scope and focus on globalization as a potentially inclusive mechanism for rapid growth and development.

The PTC would aim to overcome differences between NGOs and private enterprise through demonstrating that joint participation advances common interest in peacebuilding. NGO autonomy would not be infringed upon insofar as all associations and implementation of recommendations would be voluntarily assumed.

In this way, the PTC would operate on two levels: (1) encouraging foreign investment and (2) providing advice and recommendations along a wide plane of issues affecting regional peace and stability. Composed of distinguished individuals noted for their objectivity and expertise, the PTC's recommendations would be hard to ignore. The private sector could contribute its expertise in the identification of realistic investment opportunities, management, provision of products and services, creation of new industries, and development of infrastructure. But by regularly interacting with multilateral institutions and civil society, the private sector would also become an integral part of international peacebuilding efforts.

It would thus enable coherence of approach through provision of multiple perspectives, better relate costs to means, and assess levels of commitment and commensurate goals. Country action plans could be developed that pay greater attention to labor market institutions, including necessary education and training, capital market institutions, including banking and development funds, and the development of legal institutions conducive to private sector entry. The PTC could bolster these efforts by promoting legislative and other measures aimed at further reducing the risk of foreign investment in troubled areas, such as enhanced political risk insurance to reward early entrants. Moreover, the PTC could serve as a model of cooperation for international organizations, NGOs and businesses in the field.

The PTC is, of course, only a working model. Issues to still be worked out include: Who will appoint representatives? Which industries, NGOs, and divisions of the World Bank and UN will be present? How will local governments and agencies be included? Will regional and national offices be created? Will specialized crisis management teams emerge? How will military forces factor into decision-making? Yet despite the necessary fine-tuning, the PTC model is ripe for implementation, enabling non-traditional actors to play an unprecedented role in conflict mitigation and resolution. Perhaps the best starting point is to pilot a PTC model in a few select post-conflict regions before moving on to the establishment of a global PTC.

Undertaking Projects

Applying the aforementioned guidelines, among the projects the PTC could undertake are the following:

1. Centralize targeted data collection. Even in the best of circumstances, private sector entry into war-to-peace transition countries will be realistic in only a relatively narrow class of cases. Those cases need to be identified, if only to persuade businesses that they should delve further. To date, there is no comprehensive data source available on such entry. A common data bank should be established, analyzing three different types of situations: (1) high-profile and politically prominent cases where resources are available—i.e., South Africa, West Bank/Gaza, Angola, Congo, Bosnia, and the Balkans; (2) low-profile conflicts, where resources are scant—i.e., Rwanda, Burundi and Somalia;

and (3) partial-conflict nations—i.e., Colombia, Indonesia, and Sri Lanka. This data would also permit firmer conclusions about what conditions have induced economic entry, and what enhancements are necessary or desirable to induce further entry.

2. Improve "atmospherics" of UN, IMF and World Bank relations with the business community and civil society. The business community must be convinced that the World Bank and the United Nations are open to its concerns. One important measure is a demonstration of commitment to reducing the nature and amount of economic and personal risk presented in investment in transitional societies. Another is greater transparency in UN budgetary measures, to facilitate complementary planning. The PTC could also boost private sector confidence by allaying fears that certain UN efforts, such as aspects of *Agenda 21* adopted at the 1992 Rio Conference on the Environment and Development (UNCED), are intended to lead to the mandatory transfer of corporate resources and know-how at less than market rates.[11] While the PTC certainly cannot rewrite the Rio Agenda or any other international agreement, it can influence the way these documents are interpreted, and help assure that they are not misconstrued to create needless roadblocks to effective interaction.

3. Place emphasis on early-stage entry. Without early-stage entrants in significant numbers, there is little springboard for subsequent entry. A critical mass of private business activity may have to be generated to invigorate the political/economic environment, and provide a counterweight against the continued influence of nationalist political parties or other conflict-prone actors. Building this "expeditionary" business community must begin with enhanced awareness in the corporate sector of profit opportunities in still anarchic stages—including the delivery of emergency humanitarian relief such as housing, food, medicine, and the provision of security—and in other areas such as the development of basic infrastructure.

   In early entry where the security situation has stabilized, two questions are central to business: (1) Is there an opportunity to get enhanced returns because of market misapprehension of the degree of risk? (2) Is there an opportunity to establish a market position ahead of other future competitors?

   By engaging in commercial activity in a region that others consider too risky, businesses can lay the groundwork for future long-term profits despite short-term risk. Early-entry businesses can establish a loyal consumer base, customize infrastructure for their own purposes, enact favorable deals and regulations with local government and already-existing businesses, and secure concessionary rights to land, water, and other resources that will sustain future profits.

   The World Bank and the United Nations can create and advertise private opportunities for establishing a secure market position ahead of the competition, making use of their presence in the field and good working relations with the local government. They can open doors, in much the way that national governments do in developed markets. They can observe and facilitate the interaction between the private sector and the post conflict governments. Early private sector entrants interested in economic reform can then help to shape the economy to their liking, serving as benchmarkers in the region to ensure that forthcoming investors meet previously negotiated standards of operation. Thus, the business-government climate can be positively influenced for years to come, and the private sector can avoid being saddled with the corrupt or inefficient framework of a vestigial regime which a new government might otherwise be inclined to continue.

4. Court existing as well as potential business entrants. Much of the international private

sector's awareness of opportunities in transitional countries is shaped by discussions with local private sector entities which have survived the years of conflict. The World Bank and the United Nations must pay greater attention to improved relations with these local companies. Often, local businesses will express resentment and uncertainty about the future, after dealing with the conflict-prone prior regime. World Bank discussion with new governments can help local business communities overcome these fears, which might otherwise deter international entrants. In a number of countries, including Liberia and Nicaragua, World Bank representatives have been working with the new governments to assure the honoring of contracts undertaken during prior regimes, so that the grievances of an earlier era would not be perpetuated.

5. Make political risk insurance comprehensive and affordable. Private sector entry is necessarily tied to a reduction of risk and assurance against the acute types of "political" risks inherent in transitional war-to-peace societies. Currently, some insurance is provided by the Multilateral Investment Guarantee Agency (MIGA). Private industry cannot compete with MIGA rates. However, MIGA provides only limited project insurance. For example, in Gaza, where the average proposed project is valued at $25 million, MIGA provided a maximum of $5 million insurance in 1999. In areas with ongoing armed conflicts or susceptible to renewed fighting, MIGA will not provide any insurance at all.

   Post-conflict countries would benefit from the provision of privately-based primary political risk insurance, supported by MIGA reinsurance. American and international insurance companies may be willing to provide services under such an arrangement, which also has the advantage of employing private sector networks and capacities to launch effective advertising campaigns. Dialogue between the private sector and MIGA should be encouraged to assure the most effective allocation of resources—i.e., to balance the problem of too much risk (and therefore no investment) against too little risk (and resulting moral hazard). It would seem reasonable that the highest risk be allocated to MIGA, and that the private sector be permitted to take the next level of risks.

6. Build bridges between the NGO, civil society and business communities. Economic development by itself cannot rebuild a fractured society. Hence, the NGOs must be full PTC partners. NGOs are on the ground in conflict areas, know the local players, and are key in transitions from relief to development. NGOs have become a primary vehicle for the delivery of relief, and will continue to play a role in post conflict development.[12] Care should be taken to build bridges and develop common aims between the private sector and the NGO community in post-conflict societies. If the business community represents economic development, the NGOs can help to represent the voice of the local community and the "public interest." Private sector engagement with NGOs and other civil society actors can be facilitated through a PTC framework, to visibly demonstrate the benefit that business brings to economic development, reconstruction and social stability. This in turn can serve as a model for interaction at the field level. Social responsibility and economic development have too often suffered as a result of the mutual suspicion and distrust that have too often, and unnecessarily, characterized relations between the business sector and NGO community.[13]

7. Assist in popular advocacy and marketing and develop a strategy for an international response. In an important policy paper, "Recovering From Conflict: Strategy for an International Response," Shepard Forman, Stewart Patrick and Dirk Salomons have proposed a more coordinated approach to bilateral and multilateral aid for countries emerging from

civil war.[14] They recommend the establishment of "a full-fledged Strategic Recovery Facility to facilitate timely and effective action."[15] Like a PTC, but without private sector participation, the Strategic Recovery Facility would encompass the United Nations, the World Bank and the IMF, regional organizations, governments and NGOs. As aid is the first step to recovery and provides the stage for private sector entry, the PTC should work closely with such a Facility toward a truly integrated approach. Indeed, functions of the proposed Facility might better be served by being merged or subsumed under the broader agenda and wider base of the PTC. This would, among other advantages, enhance opportunities for achieving common objectives through popular advocacy and marketing in support of post conflict initiatives by both donor governments and private sources. It would also recognize that, as in the case of Bosnia, even coordinated international aid is not enough to stimulate the foreign investment necessary to repair war-torn countries.[16] Rather, what is needed is a broad-based strategy where the strength of market economies, operating under the aegis of the rule of law, helps to guide postwar reconstruction.

8. Assist in combating corruption. The business community has an enormous stake in combating corruption. While individual firms may prosper in a corrupt atmosphere, private foreign investment on a larger scale is stifled by the absence of open market economies. In Bosnia, for example, McDonald's refused to set up operations after demands by officials for bribes, and large Italian and German construction companies pulled out after heavy losses.[17] Self-policing through industry-wide standards, however, can provide an effective mode of regulation even where others have failed. A PTC would have the authority and reach to implement such codes of conduct, making a pariah of any business entity that engages in corrupt practices beyond the reach of the Foreign Corrupt Practices Act and other international standards.[18]

9. Assist in privatization of "governmental" functions. Partnership with the private sector should facilitate the privatization of functions that are not efficiently handled by governments or international institutions. Such activities may span the gamut from provision of humanitarian relief to infrastructure reconstruction as part of peacebuilding. It could even include the provision of security services.[19] Control is not wrested from governments or institutions, but structured and regulated, so that operational responsibility is allocated to the sector most capable of efficiently providing needed services. Establishing the right mix of private-public responsibility is a task ideally suited for PTC engagement, and indeed probably could not be established in the absence of such an arrangement.

10. Support exchange of research and knowledge of best practices. Research would be based on expressed needs from the bottom up and endeavor to help shape legislation and policies of governments. It would fill critical information and knowledge gaps among the many actors, ensuring a level playing field and full public accountability. Such free flows and access would help dispel rumors, give voice to those typically marginalized, provide a source of inclusion and preemptive action, and generally build the institutions for democratic dialogue and the mediation of differences before they become sources of grievance and violence. Meaningful partnering arrangements—between the United Nations, the World Bank, and the private sector, along with the NGO community—are a necessary and welcome development. Regional disorder and civil conflicts have replaced aggression as the world's number one security concern. No longer impeded by superpower rivalries, and empowered by the advent of globalization and innovative leadership at the United Nations and the World Bank,

effective partnering among all the major stakeholders in building and sustaining peace is an idea whose time has come.

Today, private sector flows have begun to outpace public sector flows to developing countries. The challenge lies in encouraging capital to enter countries and regions torn by war, and in using partnership arrangements to support the evolution of civil societies based on market-driven economies and girded by the protection of human and property rights. To accomplish this, the private sector must be given a greater stake in shaping the outcomes of war-to-peace transitions.

Formation of a Peace Transitions Council would allow a unified approach in formulating and implementing strategy for recovery. Of course, the success of a PTC in meeting the demands of peacebuilding are not assured. As always in partnerships, questions of costs and benefits will arise. Adding another layer of bureaucracy often appears to be an invariable consequence of creating new fora for shared decision-making. Similarly, additional delay sometimes results when consultation with a broader group of stakeholders is encouraged. Yet, with active private sector and NGO engagement in strategic planning and management, these costs can be minimized and easily outweighed by the benefits. Fortunately, the boldness of new ideas, coupled with a greater readiness for shared responsibility by the United Nations, the World Bank, the private sector, and the NGO community, bodes well for transforming peace through partnering, from concept to reality, through a new institutional framework for collaboration.[20]

Notes

1. Peter Wallensteen and Margareta Sollenberg, "The End of International War? Armed Conflict, 1989–1995" in *The Journal of Peace Research*, Vol. 33, No. 3, 1996, pp. 353–370. Also see Margareta Sollenberg (ed.), States in Armed Conflict 1998, Department of Peace and Conflict Research, Uppsala University: Sweden, Report No. 54, pp. 1–28.

2. See Ted Robert Gurr's recent work with Monty Marshall and Deepa Khosla, *Peace and Conflict 2001: A Global Survey of Armed Conflicts, Self-Determination Movements, and Democracy*, Center for International Development and Conflict Management, University of Maryland, January 2001. Also see Gurr's earlier work, *Peoples Versus States: Minorities at Risk in the New Century*, United States Institute of Peace Press: Washington, DC Gurr surveys the behavior of some 275 politically active ethnic groups during the 1990s and pinpoints factors that encourage the assertion of ethnic identities. He identifies some ninety groups as being at significant risk of conflict and repression in the early 21st century.

3. See Paul Collier's work *On the Economic Causes of Civil War*, Oxford Economic Papers 50 (4), 1998; and Nat J. Colletta and Markus Kostner, "Reforming Development Cooperation: From Reconstruction to Prevention," in *Forum: Special Issue on War, Money and Survival*, ICRC, February 2000, pp. 96–99.

4. Laurie Nathan, "The Four Horsemen of Apocalypse: The Structural Causes of Crisis and Violence in Africa," p. 26. Originally presented at Consultation on the Nexus between Economic Management and the Restoration of Social Capital, World Bank and the Center for Conflict Resolution, Cape Town, October 11–13, 1999.

5. Auvinen, Ruha and Wayne Nafziger, "The Sources of Humanitarian Emergencies," *Journal of Conflict Resolution*, Vol. 43, No. 3, June 1999, pp. 267–290.

6. *The State of the World's Refugees: Fifty Years of Humanitarian Action*. Geneva: The UNHCR and Oxford University Press, 2000.

7. See Nat J. Colletta and Taies Nezam, "From Reconstruction to Reconciliation: The Nature of War Determines the Nature of Peace," in *Development Outreach*, Vol. I, No. 2, Fall 1999

8. See I. Elbadawi, "Civil Wars and Poverty: The Role of External Interventions, Political Rights and Economic Growth," presented at the World Bank's Development Economic Research Group Conference on Civil Conflicts, Crime and Violence, World Bank, Washington DC, Feb. 22–23, 1999, obtainable from http://www.worldbank.org/research/conflict/papers/war000.pdf (study of 138 conflicts since World War II,

linking civil wars and poverty and demonstrating that "poverty...influences the probability of a civil war."). See also Paul Collier, *Economic Causes of Civil Conflict and Their Implications for Policy* (World Bank, 2000), obtainable from http://www.worldbank.org/ research/conflict/ papers/civilconflict.pdf.

9. "Symposium: State Reconstruction After Civil Conflict."

10. For example, the confusion of international agencies in the Bosnia reconstruction effort has been notorious, allowing opponents of the peace process to attempt to set one against the other, and permitting continued prosecution of ethnic war by other means.

11. *Agenda 21,* the framework for action adopted at the Rio Conference, called for limitation of greenhouse gas emissions through the decreased use of fossil fuels and coal. See *Agenda 21,* United Nations Conference on Environment and Development, U.N. Doc. A/CONF. 151/26 (1992), obtainable from http://www.un.org/esa/sustdev/ agenda21text.htm or http://www.igc.org/habitat/ agenda21/. Toward this end, the United Nations Environment Program is authorized to facilitate "the transfer of environmentally sound technologies to the developing countries and assist" in their effective application. *Agenda 21,* supra, paras. 38.21–38.23; United Nations Framework Convention on Climate Change, May 9, 1992, adopted May 9, 1992, S. Treaty Doc. No. 102–38 (1992), 31 I.L.M. 849 (1992), Art. 4, para. 5. The transfer provision has been interpreted by some UN officials as including privately-owned technologies. Although the transfer is to be accomplished on a voluntary basis, the U.S. coal industry has raised concerns that the "transfer" provision will be used to demand the sale of technology at less than market rates. See R. Reinstein, "See, generally, for earlier formulation of many of the ideas present in this chapter, A. Gerson, "The Private Sector's Role" in 95 *Am. J. Int'l L.* 102 (2001), special issue "Understanding the Global Decisionmaker," 17(1) Coal Voice 23 (Winter 1994).

12. On the growing power and prominence of NGOs in advancing peace processes, see P. Aall, "Non-Governmental Organizations and Peacemaking," in *Managing Global Chaos: Sources and Responses to International Conflict* (C. Crocker, F. Hampson and P. Aall, eds., 1996); L. Gordenker and T. Weiss, "Devolving Responsibilities: A Framework for Analyzing NGOs and Services," in *Beyond Subcontracting: Task-Sharing with Regional Security Arrangements and Service-Providing NGOs* (T. Weiss, ed., 1998); and R. Wedgwood, "Legal Personality and the Role of Non-Governmental Organizations and Non-State Political Entities in the United Nations System," in Rainer Hofmann, ed., *Non-State Actors as New Subjects of International Law,* Kiel Walthur-Shucking Institute of International Law (Duncker & Humblot, Berlin, 1998).

13. See Nicanor Perlas, *Shaping Globalization: Civil Society, Cultural Power and Threefolding 1* (2000) (contending that: "[C]ivil society emerged from the Battle of Seattle as a third global force. It took its place beside business and government as one of the key global institutions that must now determine the quality and direction of globalization. The emergence of global civil society changes the world from a uni-polar to bi-polar world to one that is tri-polar."). Be that as it may, the scars between business and the NGO community from the "Battle of Seattle" during the 1999 World Trade Organization (WTO) summit have yet to be healed.

14. Shepard Forman, Stewart Patrick and Dirk Salomons, *Recovering From Conflict: Strategy for An International Response* (Center on International Cooperation, New York University 2000) obtainable from http://www.nyu.edu/pages/cic/pubs/PayingEssentials02.11.html. See also their companion volume, *Good Intentions: Pledges for Postconflict Recovery* (Shepard Forman and Stewart Patrick, eds.), supra note 162, especially, J. Boyce, *Beyond Good Intentions: External Assistance and Peacebuilding.* On the urgent need for "far better coordination and discipline" among aid agencies, see also C. Lancaster, "Redesigning Foreign Aid," 79 *Foreign Affairs* 74, 80 (Sept.–Oct. 2000)

15. S. Forman, S. Patrick and D. Salomons, ibid., p. 11.

16. See B. Stein & S. Woodward, supra note 165

17. See Chris Hedges, "Leaders in Bosnia Are Said to Steal Up To $1 Billion," supra note 165

18. Current international initiatives against corruption include the OECD standards denying the tax

19. Deductibility of bribes and calling on member countries to criminalize international bribes, and the

Inter-American Convention on Illicit Payments.

20. The problem of local security has been addressed only through the advisory functions of the UN Civil Police Administration. But CivPol has limited effect when local police agencies are corrupt or are committed to nationalist conflict. The High Commissioner for Refugees has faced the dilemma of the intermingling of armed nationalist militias with civilians in refugee camps, in conflict areas such as East and West Timor, and the African Great Lakes, without any Security Council mandate for UN peacekeepers to provide an alternative source of order in the camps. The privatization of security services in the pursuit of civil peace need not, however, be limited to developed economies. Nor should the experience of well-known private security firms like Executive Outcomes and Sandline operating in Africa be considered indicative of the prospects for successful deployment of privatized guard and security services operating under UN auspices in a regulated framework.

Innovative Approaches to the Advancement of Democracy and Peace

Alan Gilbert
University of Denver

Will the Sole Great Power Work for Peace and the Rule of Law?[1]

With the death of the Soviet Union and termination of the Cold War, the United States became the lone great power—or empire—in the world. Its officials purport to stand for "markets," "democracy" and "human rights." Yet, during and after the Cold War, the American government has often overthrown parliamentary regimes and harmed civilians abroad. Domestically, it has built up a vast military-industrial apparatus at the expense of projects to benefit most citizens and of their freedom to debate government policies.

A decade into this new era, will the American regime adhere to the moral integrity of its rhetoric: pursue peace, the rule of international law, fair trade and the gradual phasing out of major war, as well as more democratic practices and a deliberated common good at home? The United States could strongly benefit from international example and urging. It could also, however, do more to further peace and democratic institutions internationally, and to build a coalition for these changes, than any other power. Correspondingly, peaceful resolution of global crises and the inauguration of fair trade might lead to a reduction of violence in domestic conflict.[2]

Or will America pursue the uneasy security of a uniquely powerful, outlaw state? Will it refuse to sign or violate common good-sustaining international agreements? Will it station its troops all over the world, and war on civilians in poorer nations on behalf of repressive elites? Will it attempt to root out its genuine enemies and states that support them by war or boycott largely against civilians? Will it extend "free trade" at the cost of impoverishing nearly half the world's population? Will it ignore or silence criticism at home? This second course engenders the hatred of many ordinary people in less developed countries, and, as an outlier, the terrorism of a few. Under Presidents Clinton and Bush, the United States has already squandered opportunities to pursue the first course. In a new century, however, the chances for a world of peace, more democratic institutions and comparatively fair commerce are real.

The following essay will contrast these two paths. The second section briefly sketches the necessity of robust citizen democracy across borders, often against the policy of their own states, in international politics (*democratic internationalism*). It also underlines some broad characteristics of the U.S. military-industrial empire. The third highlights three common good sustaining treaties which might further the cause of a just peace. The fourth focuses on the horror of September 11. It questions the War in Afghanistan (and quite possibly in Iraq and beyond) as a response. This section will also suggest a fourth international accord. Part five traces the anti-democratic feedback of the War on domestic politics, undercutting the liberties and public discussion of citizens and consolidating the military-industrial complex. Section six centers on the mass impoverishment which has accompanied globalization and the currently harmful role of global economic institutions. The seventh stresses the emergence of an international democratic movement from below. Despite repression and media distortion, this movement demands "fair trade" through mass, nonviolent protest. This section will lay out several further international and American reforms. In contrast to today's U.S. government, the eighth will emphasize greater toleration of civil disobedience as the measure of a decent, democratic regime.

Citizen-based Democracy from Below

My recent book, *Must Global Politics Constrain Democracy?*, offers an internal, democratic internationalist critique of the leading theory of foreign policies, *great power realism*. To sketch this debate, the first, basic premise of realists is that global competition among states, conceived only as "powers," shapes national interests, largely independent of domestic politics. Granting this premise for the sake of argument, I pose a novel, *internal* question: what effect would such a world of power-rivalry have on democracy at home? As in the case of the Alien and Sedition Acts of 1798, Woodrow Wilson's Palmer Raids against radicals just after the Russian Revolution, and Truman-McCarthyism, the answer is, for ordinary Americans, a devastating one. Leaders can stigmatize common good-sustaining reforms as a plot by a "foreign conspiracy," and denounce opponents as agents of, or soft on, an "enemy." For instance, in 1798, President John Adams and Alexander Hamilton tried to kill a fledgling second party led by Jefferson and Madison. They denounced the latter as "Gallomen" (followers of the French Revolution) and "wild Irish." In 1798, the Irish had risen up against the British Empire. Forgetting the American Revolution, Adams' supporter, Congressman Harrison Gray Otis, stigmatized Irish immigrants fleeing English imperialism as "*democratic disorganizers*." The administration jailed Scottish and Irish editors of Republican newspapers. As Thomas Jefferson strikingly argued, "The friendless alien has been selected as the safest subject of a first experiment; but the citizen will soon follow, or rather, has already followed, for already has a sedition act marked him for its prey."[3]

As we will see, this example foreshadows the combination of secret military tribunals for terrorists that the Bush administration has hastily created, and the undercutting of liberties already in process for citizens. In today's international relations theory, such instances also break down the rigid division between global politics—the study of uniform "powers"—and the study of specific, domestic governments. I name this effect the *anti-democratic feedback* of great power rivalry.

Drawing on the paradigm of Woodrow Wilson's "crusading democracy," the punitive Treaty of Versailles, and the rise of Nazism, realists also stress a misguided, second thesis. As George Kennan puts it, a state should always undertake "professional diplomacy" and deter "popular diplomacy." But once again, realists consider only external threats—the extreme punishment of Germany at Versailles engendering Nazism and World War II. They neglect, however, Wilson's Palmer Raids, his smashing of the Industrial Workers of the World (IWW) and his attempt to break militant unionism (the great steel strike of 1919 uniting workers who spoke 12 different languages, the Seattle General Strike). They disregard the legal lynching of Joe Hill, the fomenting of eugenics against immigrants and the attempt to divide immigrant from citizen.[4] They ignore Wilson's showing of "Birth of a Nation" at the White House and praise of the Ku Klux Klan, and the subsequent forging of a racist, "Nordic" American identity in the Immigration Act of 1924. Here is a common kind of equation among political leaders: external phobias, repression of a democratic public life.

Thus, in contrast even to sophisticated realisms, democratic internationalism stresses the harmful effects of global politics on democracy at home (*anti-democratic feedback*). It offers a competing second thesis: in every inegalitarian society, leaders will have a political and psychological incentive to conjure "enemies," often turning differences into enmity. They cast the world, in George Bush's phrase toward the Taliban (whom the United States created, a decade and a half ago, to fight the Soviet Union), in terms of "good" and "crusaders" (us) versus "evil." In this recent case, the American cause is just. On September 11, 2001, terrorists horrifically slaughtered about 3,500 innocents. But is the War in Afghanistan—and this way of fighting it—a just response? Will even swift victory reduce the threat of terrorism or further, in a new century, the rule of international law?

I then offer a third thesis: leaders can stigmatize domestic critics as foreign "agents" or those who are unwittingly soft on dangerous enemies. They can limit reform, and undermine a common good (the needs and interests of ordinary people). I call this *the constraint of political options, public corruption thesis.* Correspondingly, ordinary citizens often have common interests against important policies of their state(s), which sometimes result in movements from below. Such interests are aligned with those of citizens abroad (*democratic internationalism).*[5]

Every version of great power realism, modified in this democratic internationalist way, also challenges today's popular, democratic peace hypothesis: that parliamentary regimes will not go to war with one another. During and after the Cold War, the U.S. government has overthrown many elected regimes, for instance, those of Guatemala (1954), Iran (1954), Brazil (1965), Chile (1973), Indonesia (1965), Guyana (1965) and Haiti (1991). Yet for spurious "methodological reasons,"[6] the proponents of democratic peace deny this pattern of aggression. Following the misguided doctrine of operationalism, they categorically distinguish between an "intervention" (all these cases do not involve, on the American side, a loss of 1000 soldiers) and a "war." They dismiss aggressions against (nonwhite, radical-led) democracies as "interventions." By this methodological sleight of hand, they offer a stunningly apologetic version of ostensible "democratic peace." By this standard, since the Taliban have so far killed only one American, the U.S. government is not waging war in Afghanistan.

The arguments this essay will make about American institutions will apply, with modifications to deal with important differences, to other parliamentary regimes. I will focus on common good-sustaining treaties and institutions internationally. I will also stress, however, some new domestic democratic practices and institutions.[7] For democratic institutions, responsive to the needs and interests of most citizens, contrast sharply with today's oligarchies with parliamentary forms.[8] In the latter, even on great issues, the electoral process does not lead to public debate. Within them, only democratic, often transnational, movements from below, after time, effort and suffering, can bring about limited change.

Further, the unique scope of American power results in a *stealth bellicosity*, which accentuates the need for democratic counter-movements from below. Today, there exists but one empire in the world. The United States is now analogous in its dominion only to the Roman Empire. It has no great power rival.[9]

Only one power today stations 250,000 troops abroad. No others, unilaterally, have substantial forces on foreign soil.[10] Only one has troops supplied with the most advanced weapons, including nuclear ones, at 61 major bases, in 19 countries. Only one has military "representatives" at over 800 foreign "installations."[11] Only one power's special forces secretly train repressive militaries, from Turkey to Columbia, against their own peoples. *Only one power's military-industrial establishment produces a quarter of its Gross Domestic Product.*

Only one power relies primarily on bombing to wage war and tolerates, itself, but a tiny number of casualties. Only one thus frequently intervenes massively and harmfully, in so-called "collateral damage," toward civilians. Such policies nurture enmity toward the United States among ordinary people abroad. Among an outlying group, they create a continuing threat of terrorism toward American civilians and soldiers, which Chalmers Johnson calls *blowback.*[12] Borrowed from the CIA, Johnson's term refers to "*the unintended consequences of [aggressive, imperial] policies that were kept secret from the American people.*"[13] For instance, in 1985, Ronald Reagan welcomed the turbaned, bearded leaders of the Mujahadeen (today the Taliban) to the White House. In the War against the U.S.S.R., he likened them to "our founding fathers." Osama Bin Laden learned terror from the CIA. Today, President Bush and the mainstream media erase this heritage. The War on Terror, however, has already exerted, as we will see in section 4, dramatic negative effects on the liberties of and knowledge available to most Americans. Thus, blowback creates the *restriction of public options* for candidates, policies and even discussion among citizens—the intimidation of dissidents—which my argument highlights.

For instance, Johnson discusses the resentment produced by American troops stationed in Okinawa. A range of one-third to one-half the young women report that American soldiers have accosted them "on the way to school or back home."[14] In 1995, a gang-rape of a 12-year-old girl infuriated the Japanese:

> A few weeks later, from his headquarters at Pearl Harbor, Hawaii, the commander of all U.S. forces in the Pacific, Admiral Richard C. Macke, remarked to the press, 'I think that [the rape] was absolutely stupid. For the price they paid to rent the car, they could have had a girl.' Although Macke was permitted to retire following this lighthearted [sic] comment, there was no Congressional or official inquiry into his leadership of the Pacific Command and no review of why a decade after the end of the Cold War, the United States still had 100,000 troops based in Japan and South Korea. There was only endless public relations spin about how the gang-rape of a child was a singular "tragedy," not a consequence of U.S. basing policy, and how East Asia "needs" American peacekeepers.[15]

Quartering large numbers of American troops, often on prized land, would, at any time, stir friction with civilians. But in the post-Cold War era, no plausible pretext for foreign troops exists. Further, national governments cave in to U.S. power without public discussion. In such cases, friction becomes fury.

In her book on the prostitution of Korean women for the American military, Katharine Moon limns the environment surrounding miles-long, sequestered bases:

> They are like stage sets, in a sense, for the U.S. military presence in South Korea, characterized by dimly lit alleys blinking with neon-lit bars boasting names like Lucky Club, Top Gun, or King Club. The alleys rock with loud country-western or disco music, drunken brawls, and American soldiers in fatigues and heavily made-up Korean women walking closely together with hands on each other's buttocks.[16]

In February 1998, near the ski resort of Cavalese, Italy, an illegally low-flying American military jet cut a ski-lift cable. Twenty people plunged to their death. Subsequently, at Camp Lejeune, North Carolina, a military "court" exonerated those responsible for "a training accident." President Clinton offered, but Congress—Senator Jesse Helms in the lead—refused to pay damages to the families.

For the U.S. government will not let soldiers accused of crimes be tried in a local court. In addition, as an outlaw state, the American government, alone among major parliamentary democracies, also refused, at Rome, to sign off on an International Criminal Court. It fears that American soldiers will be prosecuted for either war crimes or "extra-curricular" ones.[17] I leave aside the case of Henry Kissinger whose massive, deliberate crimes against innocent people deserve to be tried before an international court.[18] But the Criminal Court Treaty establishes a seven-year grace period during which officials and soldiers of the signees will be held innocent. France had feared prosecution for its officers' role in training the Hutu in the massacres in Rwanda in 1993 and 1994. Yet it, too, signed.[19] But even with all these protections for past American crimes, the U.S. government still will not sign.

Further, even where the U.S. stations fewer troops, its activities harm civilians and undercut democracy. For instance, through Joint Combined Exchange Training (JCET), the military trains repressive regimes in "special operations" against popular movements, such as that of Turkey against the Kurds.[20] A vast military-industrial complex, combined with what Morgenthau named an "academic-political complex," sustains this Cold War apparatus in a new era.[21] The media, mainstream politicians who are "bipartisan" about foreign policy, and as we will see below, much of the educational establishment tolerate no public discussion about whether stationing 250,000 troops on foreign soil today fosters international peace or benefits most Americans. A democracy would debate so important an issue. America—an oligarchy with parliamentary forms—does not.

Three International and Domestic Reforms for Peace

As one step toward peace, the U.S. government should withdraw its troops from foreign territory. Further, as a major global reform, it should sign *a new international treaty to bar the stationing of troops by any power on foreign soil, except by multilateral, United Nations (not NATO) agreement for cases of humanitarian emergency.* Such an international convention would follow from outlawing aggression—the primary aspect of unjust war—and conquest.[22] Thus, the only U.S. troops abroad would serve in multilateral, peace-keeping missions.

Second, an international treaty—and domestic legislation—should bar arms sales abroad. Governments and corporations may mandate the production of weapons for defense within a territory, but are not to profit from stirring up conflict between states or arming them against their own peoples. War is the most lucrative and least competitive commerce. Yet the mainstream American press also does not discuss this issue. I will briefly clarify the nature and magnitude of this complex.

As I have noted, *military expenditures account for nearly 25 percent of annual U.S. gross domestic product.* The government employs approximately 6,500 people to coordinate its arms sales program in conjunction with senior Embassy officials—actually, weapons salespersons—world-wide. From 1990-96, Pentagon foreign military, construction, and commercial sales totaled roughly $80 billion dollars. In addition, the government spent $18 billion to subsidize arms purchases by foreign governments. This artificial procuring of sales abroad, and the use of Embassy personnel and Defense Department staff as salespersons, is an even more belligerent and publicly undiscussed waste of taxpayer dollars than ordinary military expenditure.

According to the Stockholm International Peace Research Institute (SIPRI), in 1997, *the U.S. spent two-thirds of the world total on military research and development: $37 billion out of a total of $58 billion.* U.S. research expenditures exceeded second-place France's 7 times. In 1997, the Pentagon's Quadrennial Defense Review projected indefinitely military budgets in the $250-260 billion dollar range. For the year 2000, the military spent $267 billion, with a supplement for bombing Kosovo. In 1995, the U.S. doubled the expenditures of Russia, China, Iraq, Syria, Iran, North Korea, Libya and Cuba combined. Focusing only on Pentagon-labelled "rogue states," the U.S. outspent Iraq, Syria, Iran, North Korea, Libya and Cuba 22 to 1.[23]

Stirring global conflicts, the U.S. has armed opponents in Iran and Iraq; Greece and Turkey; Saudi

Arabia, Egypt and Israel; and China and Taiwan.[24] It provided Saddam Hussein with anthrax for missiles in Iraq's War against Iran.[25] Saddam was America's leading arms customer of the 1980s, before becoming a public enemy in the Gulf War, and, as we will see, quite probably in today's "War against Terrorism." Thus, the simplest explanation for why the U.S. has chosen the second course—to bomb Afghanistan and overturn its government—is the sheer, unrelenting power of the military-industrial complex. It is there; it shapes what the U.S. government can do; it must be used.[26]

The military-industrial complex would find a ban on arm sales abroad far harder to swallow than withdrawing troops. Thus, to enact this treaty, democratic internationalist movements from below—here and abroad—would be a necessity. But in a new century, citizens need to phase out such complexes, and move toward what liberals like Montesquieu two and a half centuries ago named: *peaceful commerce*.[27]

As a third reform, international treaties (and domestic legislation) should bar "covert actions" by the secret police or military forces of any power in another country. Within the United States, a democratic movement needs to force Congress to convert the vast U.S. "intelligence" apparatuses solely to knowledge-gathering and assessment, not to overthrowing or undermining other regimes, especially elected ones. For covert action nurtures the military-industrial complex. Its abolition would leave intact the power of the United States, publicly, after political deliberations, to make war on other regimes. War would thus require public justification in contrast to bipartisan licensing of secret subversion beneath the radar of democratic accountability.[28]

After September 11, the need for competent information-gathering is glaring. In contrast, Cold War covert actions abroad have also never, from a democratic point of view, been effective. To the dishonor of American democracy, they have only instituted or strengthened reactionary regimes[29] and slaughtered (or tortured) vast numbers of innocents.

A Just Cause, a Largely Unjust (and Expanding) War

On September 11, 19 Islamic terrorists struck with stolen American commercial planes at the World Trade Center and the Pentagon. Though damaging American power, they also murdered some 3,500 innocent Americans. They produced the largest, non-intra-American, casualty toll on U.S. soil in modern history. They slaughtered individuals of 89 nationalities. Any of us could have been on those planes. Many of us knew people swept away. This crime inspires a keen desire for justice.

But 19 killers committed suicide in the attack. The Osama Bin Laden network (Al-Qaeda) previously bombed American troops at the El-Khobar Towers in Saudi Arabia.[30] Al-Qaeda also killed some 5,000 civilians in bombing the U.S. Embassy in Kenya. It is, however, as yet, unclear that Bin Laden is responsible for this atrocity.

As part of the first course recommended above, the U.S. could strive to unite governments to root out Al-Qaeda cells, gather information with its immense "intelligence" apparatuses and those of its allies, use special forces to capture (or kill) Bin Laden and other leaders, bring prisoners before an International Criminal Court (*if* it signed off on the Treaty), and uphold *the rule of law*. Governments have immense power, while individuals do not. To protect individuals from torture, "disappearance" or frame-up, the *rule of law* mandates public charges and hearings with the possibility of bail, except for unusual circumstances, for prisoners (*habeas corpus*), the right to counsel, the right to privacy of client-attorney communications, public trials, the use of direct rather than hearsay evidence, the right to cross-examine witnesses, the right to trial by jury, and the right of appeal. It requires an *independent judiciary*. These cornerstones of equal liberty contrast with tyranny and Inquisition.[31]

But the Bush administration has hastily proclaimed secret military tribunals, with no due process, and judges under hierarchical, executive command, for suspected terrorists:

> Pentagon officials...are considering the possibility of trials on ships at sea or on United States installations like the naval base in Guantanamo Bay, Cuba. The proceedings promise to be swift and largely secret, with one military officer saying that the release of information might be limited to the barest facts, like the defendant's name and sentence. Transcripts of the proceedings, this officer said, could be kept from public view for years, perhaps decades...the provisions alter some basic principles of the American judicial system—like the right to a jury trial, the privacy of the attorney-client relationship and strong protections against the use of preventive detention.[32]

As ostensible justifications, Bush wishes to prevent Bin Laden from speaking and to protect sources. Bin Laden might embarrass the U.S. about the Iraq boycott and the plight of Palestinians.[33] Anne-Marie Slaughter, a Harvard professor of international law, names the hypocrisy:

> Imagine how this looks to the rest of the world: Timothy McVeigh killed 168 of his fellow citizens. Yet he was entitled to all the constitutional protections and safeguards of a federal criminal trial—held in the United States, in public. Now when the defendants are foreigners, most likely Muslims, the administration of justice is left to an ad hoc military tribunal.

To diminish mass support in Muslim countries for the terrorism of a few, the United States needs to act justly. It cannot merely bully and murder civilians and kill (if it can find them) its enemies. Slaughter continues:

> But if the public relations war is as important as the military war, as our allies and the Administration insist, such trials would give the enemy a victory of enormous proportions. President Mohammed Khatami of Iran denounced the Sept. 11 attacks, but said he needed evidence that Osama Bin Laden was responsible. Presenting evidence in secret will convince no one and will only fortify Mr. Bin Laden's propaganda. And military executions of terrorists after such trials will create a new generation of martyrs.[34]

Former Deputy Attorney General, Phillip Heymann, supports most Bush abridgments of liberty ostensibly to achieve security. Yet of secret military tribunals, he says: "I think it's the most reckless, unpatriotic indifference to a source of American pride that I can imagine."[35] That pride is in free, fair, public trials. Military tribunals, Senator Patrick Leahy suggests, "send a message to the world that, when confronted with a serious challenge, we lack confidence in the very institutions we are fighting for."[36]

Spanish Judge Balthazar Garzon has arrested a terrorist cell. Yet Spain will not extradite because of "the use of hearsay evidence, which would be allowed in such tribunals under Mr. Bush's order...'In Europe, we're very suspicious of special courts,' said Marie Elisabeth Cartier, a professor of criminal justice at the University of Paris. 'Everybody stands behind the U.S. and we understand that these events are exceptional. But we'd rather have normal procedure, one that is not military.'"[37] *As a fourth reform, the United States should affirm the International Criminal Court, and endorse the public trial of suspected terrorists.*

Instead, following the second course, the U.S. government has opted to "do something, do anything"—because, given the military-industrial complex, it can—and invaded Afghanistan. It spent the first five weeks bombing often poorly selected targets from 35,000 feet. It destroyed the headquarters of a U.N.-sponsored mine removal unit and killed four Pakistanis (the U.S. also alone refuses to sign the international Treaty against Land Mines).[38] It blasted Red Cross headquarters not once—they then painted an even bigger red cross on it—but twice. It aided its previous "enemies" in the barbarous Northern Alliance to rout its even more barbarous former clients, the Taliban. At Qala Jangi fort, rebellious Taliban prisoners killed a C.I.A. agent. American forces then participated in General Dostum's massacre of every last prisoner. (According to the U.N., in 1997, Dostum's forces "threw Taliban prisoners down wells and tossed in grenades to finish them off."[39]) From a sophisticated great power realist standpoint, in a murderous cycle, the U.S. government relentlessly intervenes to clean up the "blowback" of its earlier, relentless intervention.

On October 25, the *New York Times* celebrated a conference of 700 scholars, politicians, and former guerillas who were all pro-American, would-be post-Taliban leaders. Three paragraphs down in the story, however, the reporter notes that *each* opposes the bombing: "Though the very opportunity to topple the Taliban is owed to the recent American military attacks, each orator urged the United States to stop the air raids. '*What happened on Sept. 11 was a tragedy,' said Maulvi Samullah Najabi*, the fifth man to the podium…'*But now what was done to their people they are doing to our people.*"[40] Murdering Afghani innocents is as criminal as murdering American innocents. So long as the United States follows only the second course, the cycle of terror will continue.[41]

The Taliban's repressiveness and weakness, however, made well-targeted bombing effective. The Northern Alliance overran Kabul and penetrated the South. On one level, the American regime is very lucky. Since the Taliban fled to the mountains, it can now diminish the bombing. But more deeply, stirring American "hubris," this "luck" may lead to yet another invasion, urged by Secretary of Defense Donald Rumsfeld, Paul Wolfowitz, and others in the Bush administration, to "finish off" Saddam.[42] Bush's ultimatum to Saddam about permitting U.N. weapons inspectors in Iraq parallels his demand to the Taliban for Bin Laden.[43]

Whether the Taliban is so weak, without the American, Pakistani, and Saudi support that gave it victory against the U.S.S.R., that this War is nearly over, or whether a long struggle with guerillas in the Southern mountains will occur is still unclear. Yet, even if the U.S. kills Bin Laden and entirely roots out this enormously repressive regime, it is unclear that the American government can fashion something substantially better—except for women[44] and the preservation of sacred objects[45]—on a few weeks notice.

Moreover, as Middle East historian Rashid Khalidi aptly put it:

> To the discomfort of American policy-makers as well as critics of American policy, these radical extremists [Al-Qaeda] espouse—whether genuinely or out of opportunism—causes that are popular throughout the Arab and Islamic worlds, as well as unpopular radical-Islamic nostrums for the ills of Middle Eastern societies. The popular causes include Palestinian self-determination,[46] an end to the sanctions imposed on Iraq since the Gulf War, the removal of American bases from Saudi Arabia, and opposition to autocratic, corrupt regimes that dominate most countries of the region [largely sustained by U.S. military aid and training].[47] This is problematic for policy-makers who claim that the United States acts in the name of freedom, for if the freely expressed views of people in these countries were known, most would very likely be opposed to U.S. policy on all of these issues.[48]

Pursuing the second course, the U.S. government may, very likely, make Bin Laden a martyr to millions, rather than, as he is, a mass murderer.

But this is the best case. The U.S. and Northern Alliance ground troops may run into the difficulties in the mountains of their British and Soviet predecessors. A long bloody war, with no definitive resolution, may ensue. Bin Laden, like Saddam Hussain, may escape.

Anti-Democratic Feedback from the Afghanistan War

In addition, over the next 10 years, this war is likely to provoke zealous, sectarian forms of Islam in more powerful states. For example, contrary to a Pakistan and U.S. agreement, the Northern Alliance—which at best represents only a few tribes—took over Kabul and penetrated the South. Despite negotiations in Germany, it has the forces on the ground. But this American "victory" strengthens Islamic allies of the

Taliban in Pakistan, especially among the Pashtuns. The Musharraf dictatorship is already unpopular. If it falls, Pakistan has nuclear weapons.

As another example, in Saudi Arabia, *wahhabism*, the austere Islam of Bin Laden, is the religion. Children are taught in schools that the West and America are evil. With U.S. money acquired for oil, the princes thus support an atmosphere which breeds terror. But how long will the princes last?

The Saudi elite spreads the story (told to mislead "the gringos," as it were) that Bin Laden has been thrown out by the "family" (do his many brothers now shun Bin Laden?). Fifteen years ago, Bin Laden went, he said, to Afghanistan because the King and his family chose him. Listen to the acute sense of kinship in Bin-Laden's words:

> To confront the Russian atheists, the Saudis chose me as their representative in Afghanistan. They had decided to participate actively in the Islamic resistance and turned to the Bin Laden family, my family, that had close ties with the throne. *And my family chose me.*[49]

Since 1994, Saudi Arabia has formally declared Bin Laden *persona non grata*, but his version of radical Islam could win out there. Is the United States government prepared to deal with the medium run consequences—"blowback"—of its policies?

Great power realism and democratic internationalism have long been skeptical of *crusading* interventions. "Crusade" was Bush's word of choice, before those in his administration more conscious of the term's horror for Muslims—the onetime target of Christian Crusades—persuaded him to drop it. Ironically, Bush campaigned to avoid such murky involvements. As if a song of wisdom plays weakly in the background, the administration hesitates to commit to allout American bombing or massive use of ground troops. Yet the hubris of its policy, particularly its threat of indefinitely expanding wars, is evident.

Now the U.S. has also bombed Afghanistan with food supplies—a good thing. But this winter, 25 percent of Afghanis, by Red Cross and Oxfam estimates, may starve. In its zeal to destroy the Soviets, the U.S. contributed greatly to the Taliban's rule. Yet its role in today's horrors was indirect. In the damage to Afghani infrastructure and the disruption of food supplies, however, the U.S. has made itself directly responsible for forthcoming famine. Given military victory, perhaps it can now massively provide food. But rampant warlordism and chaos in the North prevent deliveries.[50] If many starve this winter, will the policy have produced, even in this respect, a mitigated threat of terrorism?

In addition, in a devastating example of *anti-democratic feedback*, liberties crumble daily in the United States. Avoiding Congressional approval or even consultation, President Bush has mandated, as I noted above, secret military tribunals for suspected terrorists. He has also given permission to bug lawyer-client conversations in prison. The government has detained some 1200 Arab immigrants indefinitely, without charges. Securing information from University authorities, the FBI sweepingly investigates foreign students.

But abandonment of civil liberties for immigrants leads, as Jefferson suggested, to the same process for citizens. For instance, in Denver, on September 28, the police charged a nonviolent march of 1000 people, beating and arresting nine demonstrators dressed in black. A Provost-sponsored "Teach-in" at the University of Denver invited no critic of the War to speak.[51] At New York University, some Trustees attacked faculty members who, horrified by September 11, nonetheless also criticized the War at a Teach-in. The mainstream press did not cover these professors' speeches or responses. Expert knowledge, when accompanied by doubts about War, was not welcome. As I have noted, the American elite—an oligarchy with parliamentary forms—is too frail to allow a real discussion of policies, an answer to dissidents, and thus, a potential connection, in Morgenthau's idiom, of truth with power: democratic deliberations. Instead, truth and power, sadly, go their separate ways. But that separation is against the interests of ordinary Americans. In Morgenthau's phrase, the United States still chases not the *substance* of democratic power—the first course sketched above—but its illusory, imperialist *shadow*.[52]

Some abridgements of liberty, for example, tightened airport surveillance, are plainly necessary to the physical and moral security of individuals. Unusual response to any *immediate* threat of terrorism is also needed. But the forms of repression I have described are not.

In addition, the taxes of ordinary citizens sustain the "military-industrial apparatus," including troops abroad, at Cold War levels. *As another democratic reform, the government could, instead, direct such funds to repair American cities, improve schools and retrain employees in the war industries, provide affordable medical care for all, and offer humanitarian aid abroad. In a democratic regime, one which permitted (quasi-fair) public debate, such a "peace dividend" might have been realized a decade ago.* Pursuit of the second course, with its attendant harms to most Americans, exemplifies *anti-democratic feedback.*

Poverty, "Globalization" and American Power

The post-Cold War triumph of capitalism has brought about an era of "globalization" of commerce accompanied by mass poverty. In the year 2000, the World Bank published, in three volumes, a participatory survey of 60,000 poor people, *The Voices of the Poor*. In Brazil, a father names poverty: "to come home and see your children hungry and not have anything to give them."

> Often she has to decide who will eat, she or her son.
>
> —Ukraine, 1996

> Your hunger is never satiated, your thirst is never quenched; you can never sleep until you are no longer tired.
>
> –Senegal 1995

> The poor person has to exist so he can serve the great one, the rich. God made things like that.
>
> —Brazil 1995

> Poverty is lack of freedom, enslaved by crushing daily burdens, by depression and fear of what the future will bring.
>
> —Georgia 1997

> When one is poor, she has no say in public and feels inferior. She has no food, so there is famine in her house, no clothing and no progress in her family.
>
> —Uganda 1998

> Absence of latrines forces women to use the bush before dawn and after dusk, exposing them to snake bites, sexual harassment, and attacks.
>
> —Pakistan 1993

> Take the death of this small boy this morning, for example. The boy died of measles. We all know he could have been cured at the hospital. But the parents had no money and so the boy died a slow and painful death, not of measles, but of poverty.
>
> —Ghana, 1995

> When I leave for school in the mornings I don't have any breakfast. At noon there is no lunch, in the evening I get a little supper, and that is not enough. So when I see another child eating, I watch him, and if he doesn't give me something I think I'm going to die of hunger.
>
> —a 10-year old child, Gabon 1997[53]

The World Bank estimates that 1.4 billion people live on an income of less than $1 per day. Nearly half the world's people, 2.8 billion, live on an income of less than $2 per day. The Bank also sponsored Amartya Sen's lectures, which he has since published as *Development as Freedom.* Among other striking policy suggestions, Sen stresses the role of increasing female literacy and providing microcredits for (cooperatives of) women in producing a declining birth-rate, a diminution of deaths of children under five, and increased equality. He invokes particularly the Grameen Bank in Bangladesh, which has provided credit to women and has an extraordinarily high repayment rate. He also stresses the experience of Kerala, a province of 30 million people in India.[54] There, decent education and medical care dramatically improved the "capabilities" of ordinary people. Shockingly, men and women in Kerala, and even in Sri Lanka, Jamaica and Costa Rica, have longer life expectancies than comparatively high income, U.S. Afro-American men and women.[55] Thus, Sen stresses a service-led, as opposed to an increasing income-led, approach to securing a longer, healthier life.

Historically, however, the World Bank and the International Monetary Fund (IMF), connected to the economic interests and counsel of the American government, have forced structural adjustment programs on borrowing countries. Such adjustment cuts away common good-sustaining programs—health care and education—in order to bolster the military (often through purchasing American weapons and training), repay foreign debt and throw open the economy to U.S. business. In the Indonesian crisis of 1997, for example, IMF-mandated programs, Chalmers Johnson reports, resulted in the impoverishment of half the population: 100 million people. In addition, the state fomented programs toward Indonesians of Chinese origin: "By the time the IMF was finished with Indonesia, over a thousand shopkeepers were dead (most of them Chinese), 20 percent of the population was unemployed, and a hundred million people—half the population—were living on less than one dollar a day. William Pfaff characterized the IMF's actions as 'an episode in a reckless attempt to remake the world economy with destructive cultural and social consequences that could prove as momentous as those of nineteenth century colonialism.'"[56]

Moreover, American corporations hastily bought up Indonesian companies "for a song."[57] As Johnson rightly suggests, this sort of "international regime" breeds mass resentment. Short of economic and perhaps military coercion, such countries will not rely on United States leadership in the future, but choose some Asian leader, probably Japan. Worse yet, the crisis has revived Islamic militancy: "'Because of the economic crisis, we are seeing more people joining militant groups,' said Dien Samsyudin, an official of the Indonesian Ulema's Council, a coalition of moderate Islamic clerics. 'The emergence of Islamic militancy is influenced by social, economic and political injustices.'"[58] Yet erasing history, American newspapers cover these events as if they reveal the dangers of Indonesian democracy rather than the blowback of IMF/World Bank/U.S. government policy.

In *Must Global Politics Constrain Democracy?*, I stress the anti-democratic feedback of such *international economic regimes*. When, for example, a European democratic socialist government introduces common good-sustaining reforms in health care or education, or limits income inequality, investors flee the country (permitted by international financial regimes), an economic downturn occurs, the government retreats, its popular support wanes, and a rightwing campaign discredits "socialist" measures. Similarly, IMF or World Bank-promoted structural adjustment removes control of economic policies from elected governments. It harms most citizens in the less developed counties. These institutions and, as we will see, the World Trade Organization (WTO), all present a sharp target for a new democratic internationalist movement from below.

In 1994, the Clinton administration campaigned for a WTO, a body to strike down "obstacles" to international commerce, and to be advised only by "trade experts." As a result, before the Seattle protests in 1999, the Organization had overturned as "trade restrictive" *every* domestic—democratically-mandated—law to defend the environment, provide inexpensive medical care, protect human rights or maintain sustainable farming that came before it.[59] An environmental organization which wished to defend the U.S. law barring harm to dolphins while fishing for tuna would have to enlist the

U.S. government, improbable even before the Bush era, to make its views heard before the WTO. But the WTO welcomes "commerce experts."

For instance, South Africa seeks to provide inexpensive, generic AIDS medicine to the 10 percent of its population who have now tested HIV-positive. Representing the large pharmaceutical companies, Al Gore launched a WTO suit against Nelson Mandela. For domestic politics, pluralist theory imagines that other forces, such as unions, can balance the power of the rich and achieve a common good. But according to pluralist theory, in international politics, no comparable, counterbalancing forces to business exist. As a matter of conscience, Gore could have refused corporate requests, but, as pluralism, extended internationally, suggests, he chose, instead, to represent the lone powerful interest in the field.[60]

Pluralism, however, neglects how the consciences and interests of citizens in other countries align with those of ordinary people in South Africa. Protests emerged by South African workers, Doctors without Borders, Act Up members disrupting several Gore Presidential rallies, the European Medical Commission, and the like.[61] As a result of publicity and demonstrations, Gore stepped aside. Pharmaceutical companies, first Merck and Yale University (co-owner of Merck), and then the others, dropped the suit: a victory for democratic internationalism. But consider the secretive *oligarchic* structure which could have launched such a suit, and the nature of the WTO, which, unreformed, expedites such suits, requires such remedies.

Democratic Internationalism from Below

Since the late 1990s, an international democratic movement has emerged demanding: 1) forgiveness of Third World debt (possibly in exchange for government programs that help most citizens and particularly the poor), and 2) fair trade. Fair trade is, among other things, the idea that a modest, Tobin Tax of 0.25 percent should be levied on international currency exchanges and a fund created to benefit the poor in the less developed countries. As War on Want puts it, "2 trillion dollars a day is exchanged on world financial markets. 95 percent is speculative. When markets crashed in East Asia in 1998, ten million people [sic—an underestimate] were thrown into poverty. A Tobin Tax of 0.25 percent would make most transactions unprofitable and thus calm markets. It would also generate a revenue of $250 billion which could be used to eradicate world poverty."[62]

Debt-forgiveness and the Tobin Tax are two more international measures which could reduce the misery of half the world's population. In addition, the U.S. government could launch a major program of international aid, not to sustain repressive regimes or bolster foreign purchases of American weapons, but to help the poor. Such programs would redirect globalization in the direction of fairness rather than mass impoverishment, cultural desolation, and American empire. Such additional measures would also minimize terrorism-breeding resentment toward the U.S. But unlike France, which endorses the Tobin Tax, or the English parliament, which discusses it, the American government opposes it. James Tobin teaches economics at Yale and has won a Nobel Prize. Yet the press is silent.[63]

Through demonstrations in Birmingham, Cologne, Seattle, Washington, Millau, Prague, Davos, Porto Alegre, Quebec, Gothenburg and Genoa, an internationalist movement has challenged the G-8, the World Bank (meeting recently in Doah, Qatar, as far away from the protestors as it can get), the WTO, and the like. In 1997 and 1998, large demonstrations demanding debt-relief for poor countries at the G-8 meetings in Birmingham and Cologne were not attacked by the police.

In Seattle, however, under President Clinton and Mayor Paul Allen, American politicians, in this case Democrats, launched a reign of state terror against protestors, accompanied by a media drumbeat about how demonstrators had no specific demands, were "flat-earth," "antitrade" people, and, because a handful broke store windows, "violent." I should note: harm to property, though misguided and (venially) criminal, is not violence. *Massive police attack on nonviolent demonstrators is violence.*

On November 30, 1999, at ten in the morning, the police marched against 50,000 peaceful demonstrators. In defiance of causality, the "violence" the media emphasized from the "Black Bloc" occurred in the afternoon, five or six hours later. Yet CBS news anchor Dan Rather opined: "The meeting of the World Trade Organization was thrown into turmoil by violent demonstrations that went on into last night. That brought on today's crackdown." (12/1/99) Or, in CNN's fantasy, "as tens of thousands marched through downtown Seattle, [a] small group of self-described anarchists smashed windows and vandalized stores. Police responded with rubber bullets and pepper gas."(12/1/99)[64]

Over the Internet, Matt Guyen, a nonviolence trainer, reported more accurately:

> In one scene I witnessed this morning (at 8th Avenue and Seneca), police who had been standing behind a blockade line began marching in lockstep toward the line, swinging their batons forward, and when they reached the line they began striking the (nonviolent, seated) protestors repeatedly in the back. They ripped off the protestors' gas masks, and sprayed pepper spray at point-blank range into their eyes repeatedly. After spraying, they rubbed the protestors' eyes and pushed their fingers around on their lips to aggravate the effect of the spray. And after all THIS, they began striking them with batons.... The police then were able to break up the line, and the protestors retreated to the steps of a nearby church for medical assistance.[65]

No criticism of police brutality appeared in the mainstream "media." A front page *Los Angeles Times* story featured a subhead "Police Commended for Restraint," which invoked a lone source: Seattle police chief Norm Stampler.[66]

Many people who have thought and written about as well as acted against international economic oppression engage in these demonstrations, such as Vandana Shiva, Jose Bové, Walden Bello, Susan George, and Ignacio Ramonet. The American news media, including the *New York Times*, cannot be bothered to interview any of them. Instead, columnists like Thomas Friedman fulminate against "knaves like Pat Buchanan [Buchanan played no role in the protests]" who ostensibly "duped a Noah's Ark of flat-earth advocates, protectionist trade unions and yuppies looking for their 1960s fix."[67]

But the protestors were not "antitrade" nor did they advocate specific, national tariffs for one country's products against another's. Instead, envisioning "globalization from below," they demand a Tobin Tax on currency transactions and a fund to aid the world's poor: "fair trade." If one wants honest debate about globalization, one must turn to *Le Monde Diplomatique*, whose editor, Ignacio Ramonet, is a founder of ATTAC (the French organization for the Tobin Tax). Neither that distinguished journal (also published in English), nor Ramonet, nor even French Prime Minister Lionel Jospin who endorsed the Tobin Tax on August 29, is, however, worthy of reporting in the mainstream American press.[68]

In "How We Really Shut Down the WTO," a nonviolent activist from the San Francisco Bay Area, Starhawk, wrote eloquently about the problems the protesters' democracy and decentralization caused for hierarchical, pseudo-democratic Seattle and police power:

> When authoritarians think about leadership, the picture in their minds is of one person, usually a guy, or a small group standing up and telling other people what to do. Power is centralized and requires obedience.
>
> In contrast, our model of power was decentralized and leadership was invested in the group as a whole. People were empowered to make their own decisions, and the centralized structures were for coordination, not control.... The participants in the action were organized into small groups called Affinity Groups. Each group was empowered to

> make its own decisions around how it would participate in the blockade…
>
> Affinity groups were organized into clusters. The area around the Convention Center was broken down into thirteen sections, and affinity groups and clusters committed to hold particular sections. As well, some groups were 'flying groups'—free to move to wherever they were most needed. All of this was coordinated at spokescouncil meetings, where Affinity Groups each sent a representative who was empowered to speak for the group…
>
> When faced with tear gas, pepper spray, rubber bullets and horses, groups and individuals could assess their own ability to withstand the brutality. As a result, blockade lines held in the face of incredible police violence.… No centralized leader could have coordinated the scene in the midst of the chaos, and none was needed—the organic, autonomous organization we had proved far more powerful and effective…
>
> The affinity groups, clusters, spokescouncil and working groups involved with DAN [Direct Action Network] made decisions by consensus—a process that allows every voice to be heard and that stresses respect for minority opinions. Consensus was part of the nonviolence and jail trainings and we made a small attempt to also offer some special training in meeting facilitation. We did not interpret consensus to mean unanimity. The only mandatory agreement was to act within the nonviolent guidelines. Beyond that, the DAN organizers set a tone that valued autonomy and freedom over conformity, and stressed coordination rather than pressure to conform.
>
> The action included art, dance, celebration, song, ritual and magic. It was more than a protest; it was an uprising of a vision of true abundance, a celebration of life and creativity and connection, that remained joyful in the face of brutality and brought alive the creative forces that can truly counter those of injustice and control."[69]

Both the organizing process and the nonviolent action itself were public.[70] The American press could read the material or interview the people. Large corporations controlled by a few—the AP, the UP, the *New York Times*, Fox Television, and the like—do not. An announcement of Disney/ABC's Seattle affiliate strikingly reveals the ideology of elite-appointed editors: "KOMO 4 News is taking a stand on giving some protest groups the publicity they want.… So if you see us doing a story on a disruption, but we don't name the group or the cause, you'll know why." Unwittingly revealing the influence of business over democracy, news director Joe Barnes described civil disobedience as "*illegally disrupting the commerce of the city*."[71]

Yet despite repression and media distortion, the protests have grown more massive over time. In Genoa, in summer 2001, some 250,000 people turned out against the G-8. Sealed behind massive police barricades in a luxury hotel, English Prime Minister Tony Blair, in a cliché of antidemocratic ideology,[72] denounced the "self-appointed" masses of people. The police murdered one and wounded six hundred.

Democratic Toleration of Civil Disobedience

Today's elections in oligarchies with parliamentary forms display a "deliberative deficit."[73] They are mainly personality contests, characterized by negative campaigning and the irrelevance of, or dishonesty about, issues. Further, given inequalities of wealth and corporate influence on government, voting alone has not altered large-scale injustices: slavery, denial by group or sex of the right to vote, aggressive wars such as Vietnam, homelessness, the oppression of poor children and the feminization of poverty, and the like. As another way of putting it, the democratic deliberations on which the American regime prides itself—those leading to abolition, women's suffrage, unions, unemployment insurance and social security, civil rights, and the like—stemmed mainly from nonparliamentary protest from below, not from electoral activity.[74]

Thus, as a further reform, *any democratic regime, here and now, would look to augmented civil disobedience as a vehicle to raise comparable issues.* It would consider obstruction—temporary violations of property rights such as Daniel and Phillip Berrigan's pouring of blood on draft files during Vietnam—tax resistance or even the breaking of windows, as in Seattle, far less weighty than the patterned violations of civil rights, impositions of suffering domestically and internationally, and war, characteristic of mainstream American politics.[75] It would bar police riots against civil disobedients demanding fair trade who protested the WTO, the G-8, the World Bank and IMF from Seattle to Genoa. Further, lengthy sentences for damage to property during Vietnam,[76] a democrat might say, highlight a regime where "property" has rights, and people do not. In this context, disobedience becomes an instigator of deliberative democracy.

In John Rawls' dialectical idiom, for a "nearly just" regime, civil disobedience resists a particular unjust law within the context of overall "fidelity to law."[77] Such disobedience also illustrates Dennis Thompson's and Amy Gutmann's criterion of *civic magnanimity*. For although militantly opposing unjust policies, disobedience respects not only the capacity for moral personality, but the souls of the powerful. It seeks to generate a comparable reflectiveness in the rich,[78] to *civilize* American and international politics.

In a frequent, fierce response to civil disobedience, however, *hubris*, as Thucydides and Reinhold Niebuhr suggest, preys on the seemingly weak, and highlights the *incivility* of injustice: consider Bull Connor's police dogs in Birmingham or police violence from Seattle to Genoa. Disobedients must expect a price.

This conception of civil disobedience, however, extends the First Amendment to the U.S. Constitution. To instigate *public* debate, it underlines a deliberative justification—beyond respect for individual conscience—for participation in and government toleration of civil disobedience. For a vibrant democracy allows issues to be raised and discussed, with mutual regard among participants. In contrast, state violence toward and media lying about mass demonstrations against international financial organizations or recent anti-Afghanistan War protests hardly fulfills democratic criteria.

In this essay, I have suggested eleven international and domestic reforms which would further peace, democracy, the rule of law, fair trade, and the decline of terrorism:

1. an international treaty to abolish the stationing of troops on foreign soil by any power, except in multilateral humanitarian interventions under United Nations' command.
2. a treaty barring arms sales abroad, and thus, weakening military-industrial establishments.
3. a treaty barring "covert actions" to overturn the governments of or destablize foreign countries.
4. a treaty mandating an International Criminal Court to hear charges against individuals of crimes against humanity.
5. a Tobin Tax on international currency transactions.
6. debt relief by the IMF, the World Bank, and the main creditor states to poor countries (in exchange for programs targeted at the poor).
7. a massive, U.S. aid program targeted at the poor.
8. in less developed countries, governments should specially fund literacy programs for women (Sen).
9. parallel to the Grameen Bank in Bangladesh, financial institutions should specially provide micro-credits for women in small businesses and cooperatives.
10. in democratic politics, the state should tolerate civil disobedience. It should bar official violence, and exaggerated sentences not tied to the nature of the "crime."[79] Trespassing or temporary disruptions by peaceful demonstrators should often not—or should minimally—be punished.

11. the use of funds released from the military-industrial complex—the previously illusory, "peace dividend"—to repair cities, fund education including retraining for arms workers, provide affordable medical care for all, create jobs, and the like.

To be fully effective, such measures depend on one another.[80] Spurred by democratic movements from below, they offer a hope, in the new century, for a dramatically different world.

Notes

1. I am grateful to Paula Bard for helpful conversations about these issues.

2. See George Kennan on the likely domestic benefits of moving to nonviolent, citizen noncooperation to withstand aggression in Europe: "Foreward to Gene Sharp, *Making Europe Unconquerable*," p. xvi: "'With effort, risks, and cost, it is possible for Europeans—and all peoples—to make themselves politically indigestible to would be tyrants.' Perhaps these words overstate the case; but if so, not greatly. One ends the reading of the book wondering whether, if this change of political philosophy were to take place, it might not have wider effects than just those that relate to the concepts of national security—whether many other things might not also change and, in the main, usefully so." Gilbert, *Must Global Politics Constrain Democracy?* (Princeton: Princeton University Press, 1999), pp. 108-09.

3. Jefferson, *Writings*, ed. Merrill D. Peterson. New York: Library of America, 1984, pp. 453-55. Gilbert, 1999, p. 30.

4. Eugenics legitimized the Palmer Raids—jailing and deportation—against "Slavs" and "Jews" ostensibly connected to the Russian Revolution. Gilbert, *Democratic Individuality* (Cambridge: Cambridge University Press, 1990), ch. 11.

5. For a full account of this debate, see Gilbert, 1999, introduction, ch. 1.

6. Ibid, pp. 10-11.

7. For extensive suggestions about democratic institutions which might align government policy ordinarily with a common good for citizens, see Gilbert, ibid, ch. 5, and 1990, ch. 8.

8. Gilbert, 1999, pp. 186, 265 n. 7-11.

9. Stanley Hoffmann, "Why Don't They Like Us: How America has become the Object of Much of the Planet's Genuine Grievances—and Displaced Discontents," *The American Prospect*, November 19, 2001, p. 19.

10. Despite legalities, one might consider Russian troops in Chechnya an important exception, however.

11. Chalmers Johnson, *Blowback: The Costs and Consequences of American Empire* (New York: Henry Holt, 2000), p. 4.

12. See the prescient report of the bipartisan Hart-Rudman commission on National Security/21st Century to the President *(www.nssg.com)* on the danger of terrorism 2 years before Sept. 11 (September 15, 1999), which the media ignored.

13. Johnson, 2000, p. 8.

14. "Ben Takara, an Okinawan poet and chemistry teacher at Futenma Senior High School told *Newsweek*, 'The rape case...was just the tip of the iceberg. I must say that the Japan-U.S. security treaty has not protected the safety of Okinawans.'" Johnson, 2000, p. 44.

15. Johnson, 2000, p. 35.

16. Katharine H.S. Moon, *Sex among Allies: Military Prostitution in U.S.-Korea Relations* (New York: Columbia University Press, 1997), p. 7. Johnson, 2000, p. 35

17. Johnson, 1999, p. 66. Gilbert, 1999, p. 212. Only China, Israel, Qatar (an isolated place, as we have recently seen, for the World Trade Organization to hide from democratic protest), and Yemen voted against such a court. Though a democracy, the Isreali government is trapped in a murderous, neocolonial war against Palestinians (see note 44 below). It too fears an international criminal court.

18. Christopher Hitchens, *The Trial of Henry Kissinger*. London: Verso, 2000.

19. Johnson, 1999, p. 67.

20. In 1998, the U.S. conducted such operations in 19 Latin American and 9 Caribbean countries, in addition to Rwanda, Equatorial Guinea, Sri Lanka, Pakistan and Papua New Guinea. These operations violated U.S. human rights policies, and sometimes directed Presidential

(in the case of Colombia) or Congressional prohibitions. Johnson, 2000, p. 73.

21. Many international relations specialists and other professors would summon Morgenthau to their offices and say how much they disagreed with the Vietnam War, but let him go out alone, to speak against it. In Morgenthau's words, "As the integrity and independence of the government have been subverted by the 'military-industrial complex,' so the integrity and independence of the educational community have been impaired by the academic-political complex. The educational community has in large measure become *the handmaiden of government*, while maintaining its pretence to independence." Hans J. Morgenthau, *Truth and Power* (New York: Frederick Praegar, 1970), pp. 54, 434.

22. Michael L. Walzer, *Just and Unjust Wars* (New York: Basic Books, 1977). John Rawls makes this his central criterion for the justice of "peoples" in *The Law of Peoples* (Cambridge, MA: Harvard University Press, 1999).

23. I draw these figures from Johnson, 2000, pp. 86-87.

24. Johnson, 2000, p. 89.

25. Francis Boyle, author of the "U.S. Anti-Biological Weapons Terrorism Act," cited in Gilbert, 1999, p. 275, n. 161.

26. Morgenthau, *Politics among Nations*, 5th ed., pp. 7-8.

27. Montesquieu, *De l'esprit des lois* (Paris: Garnier, 1961). Bk. xx.

28. For CIA crimes against democracy and human rights, abroad and at home, see Gilbert, 1999, pp. 197-200, 226, 269 n. 74. Morgenthau, "How Totalitarianism Starts" in 1970, p. 52.

29. Walzer, 1977, ch. 6, stresses the need—echoed by sophisticated realists—for democratic and radical movements to proceed by "self-help." Gilbert, 1999, p. 198.

30. If the American government had not sent troops into the Muslim Holy Land in the Gulf War and, with ignorance and contempt, continued to station them there afterwards, Bin Laden, previously working with the CIA, might not have turned against the U.S.

31. Montesquieu, 1961, book xi.

32. Matthew Purdy, "Bush's New Rules to Fight Terror Transform the Legal Landscape," *New York Times*, November 25, 2001, pp. A1-B4.

33. The U.S./U.N. won the Gulf War. But United Nations reports recount the horrors visited on civilians of the contining boycott. By 1995, according to the Food and Agricultural Organization, since the U.N. imposed sanctions, a million civilians—including 567,000 children—died. Contrasted to the period before the boycott, infant mortality doubled. The number of children who die before the age of 5 multiplied by six. Phillippe Heffinck, a UNICEF representative, estimated that from hunger or disease, 4,500 children perish each month: "it is the singular characteristic of warfare in our time that children suffer most." Gilbert, 1999, pp. 213-14, 274-75, n. 153-54. Yet no public discussion of maintaining the boycott has occurred in the U.S.

34. Anne-Marie Slaughter, "Al Qaeda Should Be Tried Before the World," *New York Times*, November 17, 2001, p. A29.

35. Cited in Pam Belluck, "Civil Liberties: Hue and Murmur over Curbed Rights," ibid, p. B8. William Safire has also spoken out against these violations of the rule of law.

36. George Lardner Jr., "Justice Official Defends Tribunals: No need to tell Congress, he says," *Denver Post*, November 29, 2001, p. A20.

37. "The Legal Front: Spain Says It Won't Extradite 8 Terror Suspects to Face Tribunals in the U.S.," *New York Times*, November 24, 2001, p. B4.

38. Gilbert, 1999, p. 208.

39. Burt Herman, "Details of Prison Fight Buried with Victims: Alliance's account of uprising differs from eyewitnesses,'" *Denver Post*, November 29, 2001, p. A18.

40. Barry Bearak, "Postwar Plans: Leaders of the Old Afghanistan Prepare for the New," *New York Times*, October 25, 2001.

41. Abdul Haq, "US Bombs are Boosting the Taliban: Days before the Kabul regime killed him, Afghan leader Abdul Haq argued against the American raids," *Guardian of London*, Friday, November 2, 2001.

42. William Safire, "Big Mo," *New York Times*, November 19, 2001, p. A23 bays for war: "If Dr. [Condoleeza] Rice reflects the president's mindset, Phase II in the war on terror is only a matter of time."

43. Elisabeth Bumiller, "Readmit Inspectors, President Tells Iraq; 'Or Else' is Unstated," *New York Times*, November 27, 2001, p. A1. In 1998, a U.N. inspector, Richard Zalinskas, contended on National Public Radio that the U.N. teams had investigated "all reasonable weapons sites" and "destroyed whatever potential existed." Gilbert, 1999, pp. 213-16, and n. 175.

44. The Taliban forbade women, who comprised 70% of teachers, jobs and beat them horribly for going outside the house without a man. Amy Waldman, "Behind the Burka: Women Subtly Fought the Taliban," *New York Times*, November 19, 2001, p. A1. The pro-Soviet regime had fostered the advance of women. Elisabeth Bumiller, "The Politics of Plight and the Gender Gap," ibid, p. B2. The new emphasis of Laura Bush—and the administration—on a prominent role for emancipated women in a new Afghanistan is an unrelieved improvement in American policy.

45. The Taliban horribly destroyed giant, ancient statues of Buddha.

46. The occupation of the West Bank and Gaza—and settlements—have been a disaster for Israeli citizens and a cause of decadence among Israeli soldiers. A recent article by former *New York Times* Middle East Bureau chief, Chris Hedges, "A Gaza Diary," *Harper's*, October 2001, p. 64, depicts luxurious Israeli settlements, like Southern California suburbs, guarded by soldiers next to the Palestinian slums at Khan Younis. Children, hopeless, see nothing to do but die as martyrs. Israeli soldiers horribly taunt them, and then murder them with silencers. In exchange for treating Palestinians as "barbarians" and killing them at a rate of nearly 7 for each Israeli who dies through Palestianian attacks (as of December 1, 2001, 778 Palestianians have died; 118 Israelis), a vengeful terrorism has grown against Israel. In response, the government targets (suspected) terrorist leaders in Palestine. The result is not peace. As the stronger powers, Israel and the United States need to work for a two state accord and the Israeli relinquishing of settlements in the occupied territories.

47. For instance, in 1954, the U.S. overthrew the democratically elected Mossadegh regime in Iran and installed the Shah. Subsequently, it trained the Shah's secret police (the Savak) and sold Iran the latest weapons.

48. Rashid Khalidi, "American Anointed: How the United States Sowed the Whirlwind," *American Prospect*, November 19, 2001, p. 16.

49. Interview in *Le Soir* (Paris), August 27, 1998. My translation. I am grateful to Doug Vaughn for this insight.

50. Trent Seibert, "Chaos Hinders Relief Efforts: Jalalabad's looters take vital supplies from aid agencies," *Denver Post*, November 29, 2001, p. A1. Jonathan S. Luby, "Lawlessness Takes Over in Countryside," ibid, p. A18.

51. As a well-regarded professor at that University who suggested a "teach in," I am, unfortunately, a witness to the process. More precisely, a committee invited Edward Said, who could not come, but asked no American critic of the War.

52. Morgenthau, "The Shadow and Substance of Power," in *Vietnam and the United States*, Washington, DC: Public Affairs Press, 1965.

53. Deepa Narayan et al, eds., *Voices of the Poor: Can Anyone Hear Us?* (New York: Oxford University Press for the World Bank, 2000), pp. 35-45.

54. Amartya Sen, *Development as Freedom* (New York: Anchor Books, 1999), p. 201.

55. Sen, 1999, pp. 21-4.

56. Johnson, 2000, pp. 211-12. Walden Bello, *Dark Victory: the United States and Global Poverty* (London: Pluto Press, 1994).

57. Johnson, ibid, p. 227.

58. Slobodan Lekic, "Indonesian Militancy on the Rise: Muslim Extremism Worries U.S. Officials," *Denver Post*, November 26, 2001, p. A17.

59. Lori Wallich and Michelle Sforza, *Whose Trade Organization?: Corporate Globalization and the Erosion of Democracy* (Washington, DC: Public Citizen, 1999). Vandana Shiva, *Stolen Harvest: the Hijacking of the Global Food Supply* (Cambridge, MA: South End Press, 2000).

60. I contrast pluralism with democratic internationalism thoroughly in 1999, ch. 5.

61. Though I teach about these issues, I couldn't figure out what the protesters were concerned about from the mainstream press, and learned only through reading Wallich and Sforza, 1999, pp. 121, 123

62. War on Want, "Fighting Global Poverty" at

www.tobintax.org.uk. I am grateful to Jim Cole for calling my attention to this site.

63. I also learned about the Tobin Tax only on the Internet.

64. Seth Ackerman, "Prattle in Seattle: Media Coverage Misrepresented Protests" in Danaher and Burbach, eds., *Globalize This! The Battle against the World Trade Organization and Corporate Rule,* (Monroe, ME: Common Courage Press, 2000), p. 63.

65. Ackerman, 2000, p. 64.

66. Ackerman, 2000, p. 64-5.

67. *New York Times,* December 1, 1999. Ackerman, 2000, p. 62.

68. As Michael Albert notes, due to pressure from grassroots media and the like, coverage of Washington on April 16, 2000 was somewhat better. Albert, "Assessing A16," in Danaher, ed., 2000, pp. 63-64. But the quality of mainstream coverage has, again, deteriorated for subsequent demonstrations, notably Genoa, outside the U.S.

69. Starhawk, "How We Really Shut Down the WTO" in Kevin Danaher and Roger Burbach, eds., 2000, pp. 36-39. These demonstrations created an international *democratic feedback* (a feedback of democratic example). But in another illustration of anti-democratic feedback, the U.S. government sent Starhawk's picture to the Canadian police to prevent her—one of thousands of Americans so coerced in violation of their basic rights—from demonstrating in Quebec.

70. See also the poet Denise Levertov's account of the Clamshell Alliance in *Light Up the Cave* (New York: New Directions, 1981). Gilbert, "Exquisite Balances." *Denver Quarterly,* spring, 1992.

71. Ackerman, 2000, p. 65.

72. By antidemocratic ideology, I refer to antiradical or anticommunist ideology discussed in Gilbert, 1999, introduction, ch. 1. In contrast, French conservative Jacques Chirac, like New York Mayor Giuliani after September 11, exhibited sensitivity and honesty: "there are 200,000 people out there; we had better listen to them."

73. Dennis Thompson and Amy Gutmann, *Democracy and Disagreement* (Cambridge, MA: Harvard University Press, 1996), p. 12.

74. Richard Cloward and Frances Fox Piven, *Poor People's Movements* (New York: Pantheon, 1977). Richard W. Miller, *Analyzing Marx* (Princeton: Princeton University Press, 1983).

75. John Rawls, *A Theory of Justice* (Cambridge, MA: Harvard University Press, 1971), sections 53-59. Gilbert, 1990, ch. 1. Hannah Arendt, "Civil Disobedience," part III in *Crises of the Republic* (Harmondsworth, Middlesex: Penguin, 1973). In an oligarchy with parliamentary forms, Thoreau's stand against slavery is a paradigm of such resistance.

76. In 1996, as a result of civil disobedience against the "training" of Central and Latin American officers at Fort Benning, Georgia, the courts sentenced Father Roy Bourgeois and others to six months in prison. A manual of the Institute of the Americas in Panama—a similar, U.S. training center—in Spanish, withdrawn only in 1991 because of public protest, detailed ways of "neutralizing" (murdering) dissidents. Gilbert, 1999, p. 151.

77. John Rawls, *A Theory of Justice* (Cambridge, MA: Harvard University Press, 1971), sections 53-59. Since no existing democracy is "nearly just," civil disobedience must often have broader goals.

78. Mohandas Gandhi, *Essential Writings of Mahatma Gandhi,* ed. Raghavan Iyer (Oxford: Oxford University Press, 1994) p. 310.

79. Montesquieu, 1961, book xi.

80. For a discussion of domestic democratic reforms, see Gilbert, 1999, ch. 5.

Mohandas K. Gandhi

Photograph courtesy of Mahatma Gandhi Foundation, India; www.mahatmagandhi.org.in.

Part Twelve

Building a Culture of Peace:

Education, Democracy, Conflict Resolution, Economics, Ethics and Law

We have it in our power to begin the world all over again.

—Thomas Paine, *Common Sense* (January 1776)

Tzu-Kung asked about government.
The Master said, "Give them enough food, give them enough arms, and the common People will trust in you."

Tzu-Kung said, "If one had to give up one of these…which should you give up first?"

"Give up arms."

—Confucius (550-479 B.C.)

Just what is a "culture of peace?" What are its components and how is it to be achieved? The search for peace is as old as human existence and yet periods of uninterrupted peace are so few as to be discouraging. The Roman notion that one must prepare for war in order to be assured of peace seems to belie the notion that a culture of peace can ever exist. And yet, this volume has presented ways that such culture can come about: through dialogue, democracy, education, empowerment, equality and socio-economic justice. The question that must be asked, however, is when will these components of peace be given priority over the militarism, arms races and deterrence theories that have laid the groundwork for war?

Spencer Weart and Minxin Pei assert that democratic states and institutions can and are laying a basis for peace in this new century. But as Harold Saunders maintains, until citizens and their governments begin to put a greater value on the need for peace, through a process of sustained dialogue addressing man's many discontents, the prospects for peace remain dim.

One more approach to mitigating conflict and promoting a genuine culture of peace is advanced by William Schabas who urges that the laws which govern the daily lives of man can be applied more effectively to govern the conduct of states. Where an eighteenth century trade dispute between two nations may have resulted in all out war, today organizations like the WTO provide a forum for dispute resolution. Tribunals like the European Court of Human Rights, moreover, are empowering citizens to seek legal redress against their own governments. Could this system also not be promoted globally to give citizens and their governments an alternative to conflict?

Nonviolence as a Strategy for Change

April Carter
Somerville College

The history of how people have tried to change society is often presented as the history of wars and violent revolutions. But there is a significant if less visible tradition of nonviolent resistance. Religious believers have upheld and practised their faith despite state suppression and at the cost of martyrdom—this was true of the early Christians and of persecuted Christians since. Conquered nations like the Poles have kept alive over long periods their language, culture, history and hope of political independence. The campaign to extend democratic rights has often depended on illegal pamphleteering, meetings and mass demonstrations, while the labour movement has won many victories through strikes and boycotts. Even revolutions have often begun with popular demonstrations, strikes and appeals to the military to defect, as in February 1917 in Russia.

Nonviolence, like violence, can be interpreted narrowly or given a much wider meaning. Violence may simply mean inflicting physical hurt or damage, but is often extended to cover inflicting psychological hurt and to denote repressive social institutions and practices. When Franz Fanon, a theorist of the Algerian revolution against the French, denounced colonialism as an expression of violence he meant a system of oppression and racial denigration which denied dignity and autonomy to colonized peoples, as well as a system which resorted to torture and killing of those who dared to rebel against it.[1] Similarly, nonviolence must at minimum imply refraining from taking up arms or killing or wounding people. When people adopt nonviolent methods of protest or resistance for purely tactical reasons this may be all that nonviolence means to them. But belief in nonviolence in principle does involve rejection of any use of physical violence on moral grounds and also includes a commitment to try to persuade or convert an opponent to see the justice of one's cause. The aim of a nonviolent struggle based on a philosophy of nonviolence is not victory over the other side, but mutual gain through realizing an intrinsically good end. Nonviolence may also be understood as a basis for social organization: a nonviolent society would avoid social hierarchies and discrimination, political and economic oppression and war. Finally, it can be embraced as a personal way of life.

Nonviolence as a strategy for change was developed most fully by Mahatma Gandhi in his campaigns centred on the goal of independence from Britain.[2] Gandhi's campaign involved large numbers in noncooperation and civil disobedience, but also stressed the need for nonviolent discipline and seeking a settlement recognized as just by all concerned. Gandhi was prepared to call off a campaign

April Carter, "Nonviolence as a Strategy for Change." Reprinted by permission of the editors from *A Reader in Peace Studies*, edited by Paul Smoker, Ruth Davies, and Barbara Munske. Published in UK by Pergamon Press, plc.

that turned violent and to make compromises with his opponents. The Gandhian strategy included a strong emphasis on a constructive commitment to develop economic independence for India, symbolized by spinning and weaving their own cloth, and promoting a vision of democracy based on local autonomy. Gandhi campaigned to end the injustices inherent within Indian society, in particular the caste discrimination of Hinduism and the plight of the untouchables, and the growing divisions between Hindus and Muslims. He also believed in the power of example and practised an ascetic and spiritual mode of life based on his own nonviolent community.

Gandhi fused religious values and practices, for example fasting, with political goals and a shrewd political strategy. Much of his inspiration for adopting nonviolence stemmed from religious traditions. Nonviolent principles can be found in Buddhism and in the Christian gospels, and the latter have promoted a tradition of nonviolence, first among the early Christians and later among various sects that rebelled against established churches and tried to live by Christ' s teaching in the gospels. Many of these groups created before or during the Reformation withdrew as far as possible from all involvement in the state, the law and politics, not only refusing to bear arms but to hold any public office, and concentrating on spiritual salvation. But there has been a more activist and political strand of Christian pacifism, represented for example by the Quakers, which found expression in the manifesto of a small group of Americans, who came together in 1838 to found the New England Non-Resistance Society and urge active but nonviolent opposition to war and all preparations for war.[3]

The writings of Adin Ballou elaborating on the concept of non-resistance influenced Leo Tolstoy, who in later life was passionately opposed to the organized violence of the state, expressed in floggings, hangings and war and to the economic oppression resulting from a few owning large tracts of land and major industrial enterprises on which the majority of peasants and workers depended.[4] Tolstoy called for a return to the pure precepts of the gospels and argued that if the exploited peoples refused to cooperate with their political and economic masters' tyranny, colonialism and other government hierarchies would collapse and that mass refusal to serve in the armed forces would prevent further wars. Tolstoy's political essays were read by Gandhi when he was beginning to develop his own concept of nonviolent resistance and to blend a strategy of political noncooperation and challenging disobedience with a nonviolent philosophy he found in the Hindu religion, in particular the *Bhagavad-Gita.*

Gandhi's examples and ideas had a considerable influence on other movements. Nonviolent methods of noncooperation and civil disobedience were taken up by some African parties campaigning for independence from the British, by the Civil Rights Movement in the Deep South of the USA in the late 1950s and by Western peace movements to protest against military policies, in particular nuclear weapons testing and nuclear bases. Martin Luther King, Jr. was inspired by the Gandhian philosophy of nonviolence and in the civil rights campaigns he led combined nonviolent tactics with a strong emphasis on Christian values of love and forgiveness towards white racists.[5] But most of those who were directly or indirectly influenced by Gandhi's strategy focused on the possibilities of nonviolent resistance as a method of struggle.

Western theorists of nonviolent resistance have set out to translate Gandhian ideas into a more acceptable vocabulary. Gandhi used Hindu terms for his key concepts—for example *satyagraha,* literally 'holding on to truth', for his technique of nonviolent resistance—which made his thought culturally alien and could make it seem irrelevant. Western writers also related Gandhian ideas to Western psychology and Western political thought, as well as linking the method of nonviolent struggle to wider historical examples of nonviolent resistance, for example the Hungarians' struggle through noncooperation to win independence from Austria in the nineteenth century. Finally, theorists of nonviolent resistance often saw it not only as an effective and creative means of opposing social evils or foreign rule, but as a moral and political alternative to war. These themes were taken up by Richard Gregg in a now classic work *The Power of Nonviolence,* first published in 1935.[6] Gregg laid particular stress on the 'moral jiu-jitsu' achieved by nonviolent resisters who accepted imprisonment or physical injury without retaliating and demonstrated courage and willingness to suffer voluntarily for their cause, and on how nonviolent resistance could sap the morale of the opposite side and work through its persuasive power.

Gene Sharp, best known contemporary theorist of nonviolent action, has laid most emphasis on the power of noncooperation, noting how a ruler's power depends on the obedience of his subjects, and that even a regime relying largely on enforced obedience through terror relies on the willing obedience of the police and armed forces.[7] There are indeed examples of nonviolent resistance under the most repressive regimes, for example the strikes in the Vorkuta labour camps in the Soviet Union where prisoners demanded abolition of the camps very soon after the death of Stalin in 1953. Some of the most impressive examples of mass noncooperation and nonviolent resistance come from Nazi-occupied Europe during World War Two, especially the successful opposition by Norwegian teachers and other professionals to the imposition of a fascist state, and the cooperation by the Danes to save the lives of the Danish Jews. Examples of national resistance to colonial occupation, to German occupation in World War Two and to Soviet armed force in eastern Europe—in particular the initial Czechoslovak refusal to surrender the gains of the Prague Spring in the face of Soviet occupation in August 1968—have encouraged research into the possibility of a nation deterring occupation by systematic preparations for nonviolent resistance. Although defence through nonviolent methods was first proposed in the 1930s, this idea has gained in urgency and persuasiveness since the invention of nuclear weapons.[8]

There is a good deal of evidence, both from spontaneous examples of nonviolent action and from consciously nonviolent campaigns, that nonviolent resistance can be effective. There are also persuasive arguments why nonviolent methods of struggle are preferable to violent ones, both morally and politically. But there are important questions and problems to be raised about the effectiveness of nonviolent methods, their applicability in all situations, and the realism of nonviolent prescriptions.

One common objection is that nonviolence may work against a moderate opponent like the British, in a context where there was explicit support for Indian independence freely expressed within Britain itself, but it will not work against a ruthless and dictatorial regime. Civilian resistance to German occupation in the Second World War is not a wholly convincing rebuttal of this argument, since the major examples occurred in countries where Nazi rule was mildest and in a context of hope for liberation by the Allied powers. But sustained nonviolent resistance to dictatorship—especially the kind of open defiance embodied in Gandhian nonviolence—may require quite impossible levels of heroism.

It follows from this objection that nonviolent resistance may sometimes be impossible, even though in theory noncooperation could topple the regime or undermine a system of racial or economic oppression. Doubts as to whether nonviolence can necessarily overthrow foreign occupation also raises questions about the validity of a defence policy based purely on nonviolent resistance. There are other difficulties too about this particular application of nonviolent methods of struggle—defence policy is intended to deter a wide range of threats to national security and actual occupation may be a remote danger.

Proponents of nonviolence can legitimately respond that violent resistance too is often ineffective. Indeed a well-armed and ruthless regime may find it easier to quell some forms of guerrilla warfare or violent uprising than a major strike or mass noncooperation, the reprisals are often even more savage, and repression of violence is easier to justify, internally and externally, if any justification is required. The case for nonviolence rests heavily on the destruction and suffering caused by resort to violence, in particular in modern warfare. If defence of people's lives and way of life depends on weapons which could, if used, result in total destruction of that society, and if humane and civilized values are to be defended by inhumane weapons of mass destruction, there is a total disjunction between the declared ends and the means.

One central tenet in the theory of nonviolence is that there must be congruence between ends and means. Means that are ignoble or destructive, and that generate hatred, ruthlessness or intolerance among those who resort to them, will corrupt the ends. So if national independence is won by violent struggle there will be a temptation for groups who lose out politically in the new state to resort again to the gun. Or if a struggle for freedom is waged by a military organization requiring strict hierarchy and military obedience, those principles may be carried over into the organization of the independent country and there will be a temptation to crush political opponents and forget the true meaning of freedom. The belief that a just society could only be attained by good means was at the heart of Gandhi's philosophy and is maintained by later theorists of nonviolent struggle. The argument may be over-simplified (certainly use of violence or nonviolence may not be the only relevant factor affecting the outcome of a struggle and the subsequent nature of that society), but it does have considerable force.

There is however a rather different objection that can be raised, and that is the difficulty of ensuring any major campaign remains nonviolent. The historical evidence indicates that this is a real difficulty. Although a particular demonstration may remain totally nonviolent, any prolonged strike, boycott or other form of noncooperation is likely to be marked by sporadic violence if not actual riots. It must also involve psychological coercion, if not outright violence and intimidation, against blacklegs or those who refuse to join in the resistance and demonstrate solidarity in the struggle. There is also a tendency for a campaign which begins with nonviolent action to escalate into violence over time, because nonviolence is seen to be ineffective, or because even though it has gained some success it seems insufficiently radical. For example, the African National Congress in South Africa moved from nonviolent protest in the 1950s to guerrilla warfare, and the U.S. Civil Rights Movement, despite gains in breaking down segregation in the South, gave way to the Black Power movement of the later 1960s that looked to guerrilla warfare, not to Gandhi, as a model.

There are psychological reasons for the tendency to resort to violence, which is often a natural response to anger and frustration and a way of reacting to and denying fear. There is also a deep-seated identification of the image of the warrior with courage, pride and assertiveness, and indeed with true masculinity, in Western and many other cultures. This image encourages romanticization of violent action and of the bearing of arms, and promotes distrust and dislike of nonviolence, often quite falsely characterized as 'passive' or acquiescent.

The advocate of nonviolence can respond that the incidental violence which may arise out of mass noncooperation is different in kind from deliberate resort to guerrilla warfare and does not invalidate the value of effectiveness of the method itself—though if popular violence turns into sustained rioting there may be a case for trying to end the campaign temporarily. One possible approach is to try to train people for nonviolent action so that they retain a nonviolent discipline, but this is only possible for small numbers who might undertake exemplary civil disobedience or be assigned to lead local protests. As for the continuing psychological attractions of violence, it is the aim of nonviolent action to translate courage, dignity and assertiveness into an effective form of struggle, and Gandhi stressed that nonviolence should require more, not less, bravery than violence. Now that television transmits to us directly examples of popular nonviolent resistance, for example the overthrow of President Marcos in part by demonstrations of 'people's power' in the Philippines, the image of nonviolent action may become more positive. Warlike attitudes, soldierly virtues and indeed definitions of masculinity itself are also being challenged by both peace movements and by feminism.

One final criticism of nonviolent struggle that we should note briefly here is that because it implies moderation and compromise it does not pose a radical challenge to vested economic or political interests. This is a criticism often made by Marxists. It may also be linked to specific criticisms of Gandhi—for example his acceptance of support from big businessmen—or of Martin Luther King, Jr. for trying to work through the Democratic Party and the political establishment in the USA. Since nonviolence depends in part on persuasion of opponents and does not aim at their total destruction it is less likely to achieve rapid social change than a successful violent revolution, but may avoid too the danger of creating a new form of repression.

The issues of what kind of social policies are promoted by nonviolent campaigns raises the question of what is meant by a nonviolent society. This concept does imply repudiating armed forces for external defence and reliance on a police force and repressive punishment to maintain internal order, and is also closely associated with the idea of decentralizing political and economic power. The goal of a nonviolent society is therefore closely associated with pacificist anarchism—Tolstoy represents this link between nonviolence and anarchism. But there is no consensus on whether a nonviolent society would be strictly anarchist, whether it would be rigorously egalitarian, how the means of production should be owned, and whether it would be compatible with modern technology or, as Gandhi suggested, implies emphasis on a simple and small-scale technology. The method of nonviolent struggle has been much more rigorously conceptualized than the goal of nonviolent society.

Notes

1. Fanon, Franz. *The Wretched of the Earth.* Translated by C. Farrington. London: MacGibbon and Kee, 1965.
2. Bondurant, Joan. *Conquest of Violence: The Gandhian Philosophy of Conflict.* Princeton, NJ: Princeton University Press, 1958.
3. The Society's statement of principles and Adin Ballou's definition of 'non-resistance' can be found in Peter Mayer (ed.), *The Pacifist Conscience.* Harmondsworth: Penguin, 1966.
4. Tolstoy's views were set out in a number of essays and letters. Two of the best-known are "Letter to a Non-commissioned Officer" and "Letter to a Hindu," which can be found in Peter Mayer, op. cit.
5. See King, Martin Luther. *Stride Toward Freedom.* London: Gollancz, 1959.
6. Gregg, Richard B. *The Power of Nonviolence.* London: James Clarke, 1960.
7. Sharp, Gene. *The Politics of Nonviolent Action.* Boston, MA: Porter Sargent, 1973.
8. See King-Hall. Sir Stephen. *Defence in the Nuclear Age.* London: Gollancz, 1958; and Roberts, Adam (ed.). *Civil Resistance as a National Defence Policy.* Harmondsworth: Penguin, 1969.

Gandhi: The Prophet of Nonviolence

Rodrigo Carazo
President of Costa Rica (1978-1982)

Mahatma Gandhi is, from our perspective, the clear symbol of what he practiced and preached: the local and the universal—to the India of his time, Gandhi had a local meaning. For the rest of the world, he has a universal spiritual meaning.

For India, as a local figure, he was able to communicate to his own people the concepts of freedom, independence, techniques to improve development, self-sufficiency under conditions of extreme poverty, protection of the distinctive social values of his people, and the need to breach the enormous gap between the wealthy nations and his country.

Gandhi showed an undeniable capacity to strengthen his ideas with actions. This enlightened his country about fundamental truths which were necessary to enhance, against the external pressures represented by British colonialism. Thus, salt, the spinning wheel, and the rejection of foreign clothes, symbolized autonomy and the usage of spare time to obtain non-dependency and the identity of his nation.

Emancipation was achieved through non-violence, a concept practiced by Gandhi, conceived as the only viable means to liberate a numerous and disarmed nation, which was confronting one of the mightiest military powers of history. The spinning wheel represented the ability and will of a nation painfully affected by unemployment. The image of Gandhi at the spinning wheel personified not only an effort against dependence on foreign nations, but also the proof that labour is basically a service which is necessary not only for the worker but also for the community.

Productivity is not an essential factor, nor of direct immediate value, when the maximum effort is directed towards political independence, perceived as something fundamental before aspiring to achieve the social development of a populous nation living in abject poverty. Those who look for economic principles in Gandhi's actions will only find themselves in a never ending labyrinth and in an apparent web of contradictions. This is because Gandhi locally pertained to India, he was India itself: a distant and unknown factor for those whom ignore the reality and identity of his people.

To depend on what is local and to abandon illusory benefits of what is foreign was fundamental to Gandhi's India. He was able to prove this with unique intelligence using the image and the worth Gandhi sought to illustrate with his spinning wheel and his march to the salt, the possibility of rural self-reliance as opposed to the subduing urban dominance, and the economic independence of a poor nation in the face of colossal dominance by financial centers. These, as well as local control over a nation's own natural resources, were fundamental goals.

Gandhi gave a clear definition of India's identity through his spirituality and simplicity. But at the same time he was also a universal figure; although, the symbols he used to communicate with his people were local, the principles he inspired have permanent application for every nation of the planet.

His ideas light the path that poor nations must travel if they really desire to overcome the gap that separates them from the industrialized world, a gap which originates from the exploitation caused by the prevailing relationships between countries.

As long as development is measured exclusively by the prevailing statistical systems of the rich nations; as long as progress continues to be expected only from abroad; as long as natural resources are given away to be exploited by foreigners; as long as self-sufficiency is not strengthened, there is no possibility of overcoming obstacles which impede the self-improvement and the true development of the poor nations.

Thus, Gandhi's principles, which cannot be applied to all nations in the way he illustrated them for India, remain standing to be applied by the leaders of our nations, adapting them to each particular case. Those principles become universal guidelines to the governments of the Third World countries, inasmuch as their leaders truly aspire to orient their actions, as Gandhi proposed, on behalf of the impoverished majorities, those overwhelming and miserable majorities. With the certainty that the great differences between rich and poor countries can only be diminished when the needs of the poor are taken into consideration.

Gandhi was able to demonstrate the power of the majority, and India became independent and free as the result of a singularly peaceful revolution. However, we should not forget that the movement led by Gandhi was in fact a revolution which, as all revolutions, occur when governments forget their primary responsibilities.

Gandhi left an enduring message to the rich nations: there can be no peace if you cannot walk the path of truth. Truth itself is justice and, we must emphasize this fact, there can be no peace without justice.

The wealth of the planet has to be utilized to cultivate happiness for the people...for all people of all nations. The rich countries cannot live in peace if they do not practice justice. The inexorable march of millions of human beings from the poor countries to the rich countries in search of shelter is dramatic evidence of this. An endless army of unarmed people invade today's rich nations, in spite of immigration laws and in spite of police security...it is an action of "nonviolence" as opposed to the violence that has prevailed for centuries because of injustice...millions upon millions of human beings are following the path through which, their country's wealth previously passed...and there is only one way to end this avalanche...through an integral development of the planet, so that all human beings may live contentedly in the land that saw them come to life. Peace through unity in diversity.

Gandhi's ideas were not perceived by the wealthy nations until their own technological achievements produced weapons, from the effects of which no one can be saved. If there is an atomic conflict, there will be neither winners nor losers; the risk of extinction is shared by all of humanity. The generalization of fear has driven the rich nations towards a desperate search for a superior force, superior to the weapons its technology has created. Many have already found it: non-violence.

But, what is non-violence? How is it practiced? What is the inspiration behind it? People who are unaware of the origin of non-violence seem to be surprised to find behind this concept a small, simple, poor and thin figure, symbol of a country that is often regarded as backward by rich nations; a figure that sharply contrasts with all that contemporary power represents.

Gandhi is the symbol of non-violence and at the same time his image is beginning to reveal, for many, something the media has never reported; a sense of authenticity, justice, and self-reliance, of the true independence of nations, and of non-violence understood not only as opposed to weapons that kill by explosion, but above all those lethal weapons represented by abuse, exploitation and ignorance.

Today, more than ever, the world is being nurtured by Gandhi's thoughts. The Third World sees him as an inspiration, and the First World is finding that history is written not only by itself, but that, the matrix of the destiny of nations seems to have been moving since the end of the Second World War, towards those continents, unknown and enigmatic, which hold eighty percent of the earth's inhabitants. At the beginning of the Twentieth First Century, these people, until recently spectators, are swiftly becoming the protagonists, aspiring to achieve justice and to share in the wealth of Creation.

Mankind today lives the reality of decolonization internecine wars, rebellions and disconformity. Hunger impels the peoples of the world towards any action to overcome injustice.

Truly, Gandhi is the man that changed the course of history by leading his country to an indisputable victory, with the indestructible weapon of non-violence. Likewise, Gandhi has changed the course of history by showing that the poor nations can utilize non-violence as well as showing the rich nations and their leaders that it is never too late to implement justice.

Like a resurrection of the prophets of all times, like a remembrance of the teachings of Jesus Christ, from behind a spinning wheel, there appears to our contemporary civilization that figure, rising from the dust of India and the misery of the people: the image of Mahatma Gandhi changing the course of history.

All revolutions occur when men who have in their hands the destiny of the people forget their essential responsibilities...Mahatma Gandhi's local endeavor is expanding over time, to become a universal philosophy for humankind.

Educational Policies and the Peace Process: Not Just the Absence of War

Shlomo Avineri
Hebrew University, Israel

In 1979, following the signing of the Israeli-Egyptian peace treaty, I was a member of the Israeli delegation that negotiated the cultural, scientific, and educational agreement between our two countries.

This was in the halcyon days of what was then perceived as the new era of peace, initiated by Egyptian president Anwar Sadat's visit to Jerusalem in November 1977. We all hoped not only for the end of war, but also for the beginning of a process of reconciliation between Jews and Arabs in the region.

It was in this spirit that our delegation suggested to our Egyptian counterparts to set up a joint commission on history textbooks.

We took a leaf out of the Franco-German experience, where such a commission, made up of educators and scholars, did much to replace the traditional nationalist narratives on both sides by a more moderate and less confrontational approach. We thought that our Egyptian colleagues would welcome such an initiative.

We were totally unprepared for the Egyptian response. The head of the Egyptian delegation, a deputy minister, virtually went through the roof: "This is totally unacceptable. You want to dictate to us what will be in our textbooks? This is part of our sovereignty."

All our entreaties—bringing the German-French reconciliation as an example between, after all, two sovereign nations—were to no avail. Such a commission was never set up.

I have been haunted by this experience, though at the time we all tended—naively, it now appears—to play it down: what does it matter what is in the schoolbooks, so long as people are not killed on the border and our nations are at peace and not at war?

But more than 20 years later, and in the current global crisis, something can be learned from our exercises in well-intentioned futility.

Egyptian textbooks were not changed regarding Israel, which continues to be depicted to Egyptian schoolchildren as a Nazi-type country, much as it was when our countries were at war. The image of the United States, and the West in general, has not been changed either from the times of president Gamal Abdel Nasser, and the old anti-Western rhetoric is still dominant. And this has consequences for the current stand of the Egyptian government when it comes to the global war against terrorism.

How can President Hosni Mubarak really mobilize his people—and not only the government—on the side of the war against terrorism when in his own schools, day in and day out, America and the West are depicted as imperialist, colonialist and war-mongering?

Jerusalem Post, "Peace is not Just the Absence of War," November 23, 2001. Reprinted by permission of the *Jerusalem Post* and the author.

Where would Egyptian schoolchildren learn about the democratic values of equality, liberty, rule of law, freedom of speech—if their schoolbooks do not teach them these values? How should he or she know that the West is also about emancipation, not only about imperialism, if this is never mentioned in school? Or if World War II and the victory over Nazism is never really discussed? It is in this context that American support for Israelis also presented in the Egyptian and Arab narrative as another example of the West's imperial designs on the Arab world.

The reason for this convoluted educational policy—recently repeated in newly minted Palestinian textbooks—is obvious: it is an easy, and cheap way of diverting criticism from the democratic deficit so glaringly obvious in the Arab world, and in Egypt itself.

The absurd allegations against one of Egypt's foremost intellectuals, Sa'ad Eddin Ibrahim...sentenced to jail by an Egyptian State Security Court, is another example of this total alienation of the Egyptian regime from western, democratic values.

But the Egyptian government has been riding a tiger: by continuing to demonize Israel, it has created the anti-Israeli atmosphere in the Egyptian media and universities that has soured for many Israelis the meaning of peace. And by nurturing anti-Americanism as a defensive strategy, Mubarak's regime has created the sea in which bin Laden's fish can so easily swim. Mohammed Atta first learned to hate the US in Egyptian schools and from Egypt's state-controlled media.

When the US next negotiates strategy with Egypt, not only bases, intelligence-sharing and arms deliveries should be mentioned, but also school textbooks. And when Israel next negotiates—with the PLO, or with Syria—it should look not only at strategic hilltops, but also at textbooks—not as we did in 1979.

A peace that is not anchored in people's hearts and minds is not peace, and it collapses with the first wind. The US has been as generous financially to Egypt as it has been to Israel in the last 20 years: it is now reaping a whirlwind of hatred and is faced by an Egyptian government which is hemmed-in by the consequences of its own educational and ideological anti-Western policies.

Winning the war means that this has also to change, and the burden is on the Egyptian government. Everyone understands the sensitivities involved. But just as there was no compromise about Nazism, there can be no compromise about the ideological underpinnings of the murderous ideology responsible for September 11, 2001. As President Bush said, "You are either with us or against us."

Educating for Peace: The Partnership of Home, School and Community

Tony Devine
International Education Foundation and

Josephine Hauer
Bridgeport Hope School

Through all the daily transactions of family, school and neighborhood, young people [should] encounter a unified consensus of core values.
—William Damon

The home, school and community are central forces for the cultivation of heart and character. Together, they form a powerful partnership. The perspective of three life goals—1) personal maturity, 2) loving relationships and family, and 3) contribution to society—speaks to the nature of this partnership and how it fosters the education of the whole person. When schools implement a life goals approach, they are naturally strengthening the relationship between these three strong influences and helping them to send a consistent moral message.

The first life goal is supported by schools' commitment to character development. The second life goal is cultivated by recognition of and facilitation of parental involvement in character and academic objectives. The third life goal is modeled by community service activities and creative school projects in conjunction with business, government, the media and community agencies. Thus, the three life goals framework pulls together the three crucial elements of comprehensive character education—the home, school and community.

Toward the First Life Goal: School-Wide Character Education

School-wide character education means to intentionally provide opportunities for character development as an integral aspect of school life. When all members of the school community—faculty, staff, and students—share the commitment to character education, it leads to the creation of an ethos conducive to respectful and caring actions. For example, how respectfully and politely the students line up and take their food in the cafeteria, how they clean up after themselves, how they show respect for the cafeteria workers and how the cafeteria workers show respect for the students are all opportunities for training in character. In such ways, students have a consistent experience of moral concern throughout the school day, in and out of class.

Fostering the First Life Goal – School-Wide Character Ethos

- Planning and leadership for the character education initiative
- Public commitment to character
- Observable standards

- Balance between character goals and academic performance
- School-wide culture of character
- Time for moral learning

Planning and Leadership for the Character Education Initiative

School-wide character education begins with the process of planning where all stakeholders—including parents and representatives of the community—are involved and their concerns addressed. Sanford McDonnell and Esther Schaeffer, chairman and executive director of the Character Education Partnership, sent out a letter in early 2000 to all state governors and legislators across the country, offering suggestions on ways to ensure that character education is both effective and comprehensive. Among other guidelines, these character leaders emphasized influencing both school culture and academic curriculum. They also affirmed that planning should address "transformations of the school environment and classroom culture, revised curriculum, new teaching strategies, discipline, school procedures and evaluation of all grade levels."[1]

Leadership, professionalism, staff training, clear program expectations, communication and assessment are commonly affirmed as hallmarks of an effective character education initiative. David Wangaard, Director of the School for Ethical Education in Bridgeport, Connecticut, helps schools to begin the character education process, encouraging school leaders to consider a five-component model:[2]

1. *Partnership Mission Statement and Role Modeling:* Develop a mission statement that clearly states goals for all those involved in moral education and keeps the ultimate outcome constantly in focus. It may include specific behavioral and/or attitudinal goals for students.
2. *Teacher and Staff Training:* Schedule time for teacher and staff training in character education methodologies and techniques. Teachers also need a basic grounding in the moral developmental needs of children and training in cooperative learning and behavior management skills.
3. *Curriculum and Project Activities:* Provide students with consistent exposure and opportunities to learn, reflect upon and practice ethical values.
4. *Assessment:* Include assessment in regard to implementation as well as its impact on students and faculty. Character education efforts are best designed with evaluation and assessment in mind. Assessment may include both formal and informal activities—review of the school's baseline statistics, parent meetings, questionnaires, impromptu meetings, general observations, community service activities, and empirically based evaluations.
5. *Principal Leadership:* Leadership from the school principal is essential. Supportive principals publicly demonstrate commitment to the school's character efforts and recognize worthy efforts of faculty, parents and community helpers.

Public Commitment to Character

Many educators agree that a school's commitment to character should be intentional and public. This may take the form of a mission statement posted in the classrooms, hallways, and in printed materials. One reason for this is to counteract the negative effects of the "hidden curriculum." Daphne Paxton, principal of Cross Roads School from Georgia warns: "In many southern communities, the school is thought to exist so the inhabitants have athletic teams to support nights. The hidden curriculum then becomes one that produces winning teams. Character and academic development often get lost in the compelling pursuit of getting a winning team."[3] Every school has some sort of ethos, for better or for worse. Public commitment to character allows educators to gain control of this ethos and direct it to educative purposes.

In a growing number of schools throughout the country, character traits are posted in classrooms, on bulletin boards in the hallways, and in the cafeteria. Elementary schools have incentive plans to recognize students displaying model behavior: posting their pictures in the cafeteria, treating them to lunch at a local restaurant, or having students read the morning announcements over the intercom. Motivational speakers reinforce the importance of good character. Brookside Elementary School in Binghamton, New York, has monthly assemblies promoting a particular virtue. The principal may read a story; students present skits, join in cheers or recite a pledge. "My kids are always talking about the assemblies," says one parent.[4]

Buck Lodge Middle School of Prince George's County, Maryland, offers a daily closed-circuit television broadcast featuring "Dr. Character," who tends to the ethical questions common to adolescents. Questions are posed to the puppet character who becomes a focal point for peer discussions about a multitude of behavioral and attitudinal issues. Situations that arise when applying virtues are dealt with in a compelling way that gets the students talking and gives the teachers a point of reference to discuss virtue throughout the day.[5]

Observable Standards

When values are expressed in terms of concrete behavior, the entire school is more likely to be held accountable. Telling students and faculty to show respect means little if it is not explained in terms of actions. Explaining precisely to students how to greet elders or school administrators overcomes the ambiguity and variety of interpretations that can accompany and even obfuscate the norm of respect. When good character is modeled, it can be learned.

At the front door of Douglass Academy in Harlem, rules are laid down the instant students step inside. In the alcove are nine mirrors and several benches where students adjust ties, skirts and shirts and change from street sneakers into regulation black dress shoes. "At the front door, you set the tone for the entire school day," says Principal Hodge, who makes no apologies for his role as fashion cop. Appearance, he believes, means self-respect.[6]

The Character Plus program in St. Louis uses consensus building to identify good traits and behaviors. Parents, teachers, administrators, bus drivers, custodians, librarians, etc. come together for a series of meetings to decide on a manageable number of character traits, to prioritize them, define them and clarify the behaviors that exhibit them. Then they incorporate these into the mission statement and policies of the school and guidelines for each grade level.[7] The Traut Core Knowledge School, an alternative public school in Fort Collins, Colorado, uses a "Door to Door Handbook of Character Education" to describe for adults what student embodiment of the core values looks like, from the time of leaving home in the morning to arriving back in the afternoon.[8]

Character Balanced with Performance

Academic achievement is a primary means of character building. The Camden, New York, Middle School instituted an "I Can" program in which students set a goal to improve their grades in one or more courses and sign a pledge that is co-signed by a parent. In addition to the academic benefits, the experience of setting a goal and accomplishing it is a valuable character lesson.

Nevertheless, assessment, tracking and other aspects of academic evaluation need review in light of the ethos they support. Are effort and improvement recognized, or only the number of correct answers? Is constructive risk-taking rewarded or punished? Are good grades trumpeted more than good character? A balance in emphasis can go a long way towards discouraging cheating and cutthroat competitiveness.

To make this character emphasis, the school leaders have to be careful to avoid an excessive focus on external achievements such as test scores. This is no easy task when teachers too often feel their main job is to get the students to pass the next round of state examinations. The subtle pressures for teachers to "teach for results" on standardized achievement tests often undermines the more important character and social development of students in the classroom. Yet a character focus can improve academic results. "We get more done because we have fewer disciplinary problems," says Camden Middle School principal Vicki Mace.[9]

School-Wide Culture of Character

A teacher can best foster character growth in her classroom by promoting a caring environment and at the same time requiring that her students be morally accountable. This principle applies throughout the school. Any disparity between the warm feeling of a favored teacher's classroom and coldness or downright hostility in the rest of the building is not lost on students, especially adolescents. The young readily revert to selfishness when the environment seems to demand it. This is a special challenge in large institutions, which tend to be impersonal.

Consistency of standards applies throughout the whole school community. "The character of the adult community" is the third of three pillars of the character education Responsive Classroom™ project of the Northeast Foundation for Children, after curriculum and the school climate. Co-founder Chip Wood describes the challenge: "This issue is probably the crux of the matter. As in most professions, we in education have been focused largely on a 'client-centered' approach.... We have done all this without really looking closely in the mirror. What is it like in the teachers' room?"[10]

In families, the relationship between parents greatly influences the spirit of the home. In the same way, the most confronting reality for administration and faculty is not what the students do, but how the adults treat each other. Educator Roland Barth remarks, "Four years of public schooling, and ten years as a principal, convince me that the nature of the relationships among adults who inhabit a school has more to do with a school's quality and character, with the professionalism of its teachers, than any other factor." Barth noticed that when staff improved their interaction, they tended to be more caring toward students. He found that after establishing a character initiative, staff no longer left office equipment broken without reporting it. Even staff members who did not like each other began to treat each other with respect.[11]

Creating a consistent, school-wide culture of character requires attention to the typically unsupervised and unstructured areas where the worst demonstrations of anti-social behavior are too often the norm. These areas include the school bus, hallways, study halls, bathrooms, playground and cafeteria. When standards of propriety are brought into these outside-the-classroom areas, they enhance a positive school ethos that is supportive of character. The fundamental objective is to cultivate within students the essence of Lord Macaulay's comment that "the measure of a man's real character is what he would do if he knew he would never be found out." Otherwise, these areas often become negative pockets of fear and abuse. A classroom reminder that "The pen is mightier than the sword" can be neutralized by a lunch table experience that asserts that "Might makes right."

In Tonawanda, New York, the bus drivers in the district formed a committee to implement a values education program. They posted signs on the buses stating that these were "positive buses," and some of the drivers began teaching bus safety and conduct in the primary classrooms. Mindful of the need to recognize all members of the school community, the bus drivers organized a "Caring Day." They gave out pieces of green ribbon to all the students and asked them to give the ribbon to an adult in the building who showed them care and concern. Students gave the ribbons to secretaries, cafeteria workers, guidance counselors and teachers, who wore them proudly.[12]

Time Dedicated to Character

Weaving moral discussion into daily life is an invaluable part of character education. Yet there is also merit in devoting some time for exclusive exploration into morality, ethics and meaning. In the realm of formal education, besides that which arises in religion classes at parochial schools, some schools choose to dedicate periods of time or specific courses to character education.

The Kimberley Academy in Montclair, New Jersey, has a general morality and ethics course in each grade. Students learn about ethical traditions and are coached in moral reasoning skills. Allotting time for such courses is more common in China, Russia and other countries where what once were ideological political indoctrination classes on all grade levels are now yearlong character education classes, and new character education curricula have been developed for them.

Many schools allow a short time daily for reflection, often at the start of the day. It is commonly focused on a specific theme or character trait. Principal, teachers, and students may address the entire school through the public announcement system. In this way, the Buck Lodge Middle School introduces a virtue on Mondays and explores positive and negative experiences related to the virtue on Tuesdays. A community guest comes in to discuss its practical application on Wednesdays, while Thursdays bring narrations about historical role models. On Fridays, students present projects showing an understanding and application of the virtue.

Toward the Second Life Goal: Home and School Partnership

The school and the home are natural partners in character education, since these contexts dominate a young person's most formative years. Attitudes and discipline gained in the home affect success at school, while the demands of school influence home life. Over 90 percent of Americans believe that public schools should share with families in the responsibility of teaching universally held values such as respect and responsibility.[13] When teachers are asked what single most important improvement could be made in education, they invariably cite greater parental involvement and cooperation.[14] The National Association of Elementary School Principals NAESP "strongly urges the formation of 'home-school partnership programs'."

Researcher Michael Rutter found that good schools resemble good homes.[15] In particular, a comprehensive character-building environment in a school holds some similar features to a home with a strong moral ethos. In those cases where the home is not working well, the school ethos provides a measure of compensation, showing what a positive and caring atmosphere looks like.

Fostering the Second Life Goal—Home and School Partnership

- Respectful and frequent communication between teachers and parents
- Parent collaboration in the school's character education program
- Parent engagement in character lessons in school and at home
- Cooperation against destructive influences
- Family activities at schools
- Parent cohort groups
- Parenting education seminars at schools

Communication

Respectful and frequent communication between teachers and parents helps to foster mutual trust and good will. Some teachers take the time to call parents in early September, thus starting the year positively. Susan Pelis of Greenfield Center School in Greenfield, Massachusetts, engages parents at the start of the year with "book bags." These bags hold the student's storybook that is read in class by day and is finished with the parent at night. This simple device strengthens the bond between school and home.[16] Teachers in School No. 2 in Kamenka, Russia, pass along information through a notebook, which includes comments and scores on behavior, attitude and grades. If a disciplinary problem arises, the teacher has a greater chance of winning the sympathy of parents if a dialogue as already been established.

The Internet is providing new ways for families and teachers to communicate with one another. America Online's Family Education Network is a service that allows teachers and students to create their own secure websites. Through this medium, teachers involve parents in the daily life of their class by posting homework assignments, class activities, academic goals and even student grades. Teachers and parents exchange comments and ideas daily by e-mail.

One of the most striking examples of home and school cooperation is the Jefferson Junior High School in Washington, D.C., located in a district beset with teenage pregnancy, violence crime and drugs. It was able to turn things around with an award-winning character education initiative, the key to which was setting high expectations for parents. Parents are required to come to school for Back-to-School Night and to parent-teacher conferences during the year. Parents are also asked to volunteer twenty hours of service to the school each year.

Collaboration in Planning and Implementation of School Programs

Schools can encourage direct parental involvement in the planning and implementation of character efforts. The Character Plus program brings parents into the planning process from the very beginning—to meet, reflect, develop goals, define desirable character traits, and develop school policies. This process typically takes a year or more, but the wide consensus it builds makes it worthwhile.

"It is not top-down management, but truly a collaborative process. As a result, teachers, parents and neighbors of the school feel like stake-holders; they have ownership," said B.R. Rhoads, Principal of Bristol Elementary School in Connecticut. "We learned that it has a lot to do with compromise. Our communities include right-wing groups, liberals and people who find themselves somewhere on the continuum between these two poles."[17]

The Benjamin Franklin Charter School in Franklin, Massachusetts, has parental involvement as one of its four pillars.[18] A parents' committee actively helps plan and troubleshoot their character education efforts. In addition, teachers send home a curriculum description for all grades with suggestions as to where parents may be helpful, such as teaching a section, providing background information or sharing experiences from different cultures. The school also sends home Family Readings Suggestions, a list of books to complement that month's character focus, as well as Family Service Suggestions—ideas for the practice of virtue at home and in the neighborhood.[19]

One of the benefits of a solid character building effort is the greater willingness of parents to volunteer at school. At Kennedy Middle School in Eugene, Oregon, parents were reluctant to volunteer for lunchroom monitoring or much of anything else due to serious student discipline problems. After three years of a character focus, parent participation became so high that one parent serves almost as a full-time volunteer to coordinate it all.[20]

Parental Engagement in Character Lessons

A character education program can increase parental involvement through engaging them in their children's lessons. English teachers might assign students to ask their parents what person has had the greatest impact on their lives and why. Students may write a short essay on a parent's hero, or ask a parent to share about a challenge they faced and overcame. This idea is popular with parents, as it facilitates meaningful conversation and offers occasions for passing on important values to their children. In homes where a parent asserting his values only provokes emotionally charged conflicts, it provides a neutral context in which children can learn their parents' point of view and engage in reasoned reflection.[21]

When Jeff's ninth-grade economics teacher assigned the class to interview their grandparents about life during the Great Depression, Jeff discovered that his grandparents, who now owned a mansion and a golf-range on their extensive property, had suffered greatly, sometimes going without food. This was quite a surprise for the teenager. When he interviewed his grandmother, she could barely speak about it without sobbing. "Hard times. Hard times," she said, and went on to describe daily life. Now a graduate student, Jeff recalls this assignment as one of his most memorable ones.[22]

An innovative approach in School No. 10 in Novotalitsa, Russia, invites parents into classrooms to observe and participate in moral lessons.[23] Larisa Schmakova, a seventh-grade teacher, asked both the students and their parents to write down the names of each family member and list things that they were learning from and teaching to that person. When parents and children compared their lists, it generated both humor and insight. Parents were surprised by the youngsters' views and experiences. Students learned something new by hearing their parents' images of responsibility. The exercise promoted perspective taking and generated meaningful conversations between students and parents.

Cooperation against Destructive Influences

Parental guidance regarding use of alcohol, tobacco and other substances is one of the critical factors in helping youth avoid destructive habits. School counselors provide invaluable support by coaching parents in how to discuss sensitive topics with their children.

Parents often appreciate school support in controlling and limiting television viewing. Some schools have participated in a national "Turn It Off" or "Pull the Plug" week where families voluntarily give up television for a week. In general, the response is positive. One mother said that during that week without television her son developed a lasting interest in reading. Another mother commented that without the anesthetizing effect of television, her children fought more, but they fought more fairly. Some families reported not missing television at all and became busy with other interests. Many families reported a heightened awareness of how television watching had taken an excessive toll on their family life.

Family Activities at School

Schools also might sponsor appealing parent and family initiatives. Brookside Elementary School invites families to come to the school for PTA-planned games and crafts once a month.[24] On a recent Valentine's Day the school sponsored a father-daughter dance night. This was one of its most popular events, where fathers and daughters had an unusual opportunity to connect in a positive way.

Hazelwood Elementary School of Louisville, Kentucky, sponsors evenings that bring families together to participate in enjoyable, interactive activities. On Family Science night, parents do hands-on science activities with their children. On Family Reading night, parents and children read together in small groups, and on Family Arts and Crafts Night, parents and children work together on a craft.[25]

At Kennedy Middle School, parents are encouraged to stop in and have lunch with their children whenever possible. "One father arranged his work schedule so he could eat lunch here every Thursday," says Kay Mehas, director of school services. She emphasizes to parents that their presence is needed in middle school even more than when the children were younger. "Students are figuring out where they fit into society. When they see you at school, it sends them a message about your priorities."[26]

Many schools have designated a Grandparents Day, which is an opportunity for older family and community members to share their wisdom and to experience the school and community's respect and appreciation.[27] "Grandparents and Books" is a national program that brings seniors to children in the library. Don and Rosemarie Sparling are among the many senior volunteers who host young visitors to the school library after school, sitting and reading a book together. "Most of these children have no money, they have no place to be after school and they need to know that someone really cares about them," says Rosemarie. "I feel like she's really my grandma," says Sean Cortez, 7.[28]

Parent Peer Groups and Parenting Education

Certain schools have formed parent peer groups which meet periodically either in the school or in parents' homes. This is a response to the reality that many parents find little time to socialize with other parents and may have never met the parents of their children's friends. When they meet in organized peer groups, they often compare notes with each other and determine mutual standards on such matters as bedtimes, permissible movies and television programs, and dating. Parents work together to plan events for the school and community, and support each other by reinforcing their commitment to good values.[29] The schools participating in the Child Development Project in California have parent groups that help families implement the same character goals affirmed in the classroom.[30]

Some schools offer parenting programs to help parents improve their discipline and communication skills. Others offer workshops about the parents' role in building up their child's character. The Los Angeles Parent Institute for Quality Education offers a nine-week course, taught in both the morning and evening to accommodate working parents.[31] The Easterling Primary School in Marion, South Carolina, provides a variety of workshops for parents on topics ranging from discipline to the content and methodology of their character education program.[32] The school has a parent resource center with books and tapes on child development and character education that is open to all families. The school also makes house calls that strengthen the home-school liaison.

The Mt. Lebanon School District in Pittsburgh, Pennsylvania developed the Parent Education Action Plan. In the fall, they present a six-part series devoted to several elements of character education, such as the stages of moral development, and skills and strategies for helping children recognize and adopt core values. They also dispense parenting advice. During the spring term, a series of single topics extend the subjects introduced earlier. These include the father's role in moral development, media literacy, the acquisition of virtues and discipline.[33]

Through such education, parents can gain valuable insights and skills. They become aware of their strengths and weaknesses, and as a result strive to better themselves for their own sake as well as that of their child. They can also learn to have higher ethical expectations of their children. Hearing teachers tell about how fifth grade children gave up a Saturday to clean out a trash-laden river, or that a group of high school students are volunteering to tutor the learning disabled encourages parents to believe in their child's moral potential.

Toward the Third Life Goal: Community Partnership

Aristotle taught that people become virtuous by participating in the life of a moral community. Likewise, communities become moral through the cultivation of virtuous individuals. Schools and communities nurture each other's moral ethos in a variety of ways. Schools fulfill their primary obligation to society through supporting student's individual moral growth into worthy citizens. Likewise, schools can harness community involvement in support of its moral education goals. Drug abuse prevention and community health experts,[34] social workers, family therapists[35] and character educators[36]all agree that promoting prosocial behavior among the young requires community modeling and multifaceted learning opportunities in the community.

Schools enhance the promotion of character when they recruit the help of local community groups—businesses, youth organizations, service organizations, social organizations, local government, and the media.[37] Likewise, the community supports character efforts of the school by promoting service opportunities, values in the workplace, civics and environmental conservation.

Partnership between School and Business

In 1994, Walter Segaloff of Newport News, Virginia, decided that businesspeople needed to help the schools, government and churches with the job of education. He established the award-winning An Achievable Dream Academy, a public school for at risk children, which partners with businesses and non-profit organizations in a program called "job shadowing."[38] For two weeks in the summer, seventh and eighth-grade students volunteer to help in local workplaces. The work connects the youngsters—most of whom have only one parent or guardian—to mentors in local hospitals, colleges and universities, in law firms and science laboratories. Though the practical benefits are apparent, "the primary purpose of this program is to develop the relationship between students and mentors," says Richard Coleman, principal.[39]

Business representatives perform a helpful service when they speak in schools about how ethical practices pay off in greater productivity and personal advancement at work. This is regular feature at the James E. McDade Classical School in Chicago, which emphasizes using real life to reinforce good values.[40] Easterling Primary School invites business leaders to serve as role models and tutors to their students.

Media Involvement

Schools have recruited local news media to publicize its core values and promote examples of character in daily life. In collaboration with St. Louis's citywide character education effort, the local CBS affiliate television station produces a Saturday morning program on storytelling for young children, emphasizing good character traits. In that same city, the local newspaper in conjunction with the local police department joined with Character Plus in a project called "Do the Right Thing." This program recognizes young children who are setting an example of service in their community.

The local newspaper in Binghamton, New York, features a "Character Corner" that highlights the Brookside Elementary School's designated virtue of the month. Senior citizens look forward to the feature and express their support. Once a week a community television station airs a student-written "Character Minute" on the evening news.[41]

Local Government Participation

The Utah Project, a statewide character education initiative, gives children practice in participating in public forums. They learn the rules of decorum and respectful debate and gain practice in good citizenship. This initiative has also fostered partnerships between schools and local governments.[42]

At the An Achievable Dream Academy, soldiers from nearby Fort Eustis actively mentor youngsters. After leading the 90-minute morning ceremonies for third through fifth graders, the soldiers spend time in classrooms helping with teaching, disciplining or simply listening and offering advice.[43] The Yu Ying Middle School in Beijing, China partners with the army in a preventative approach to discipline that helps set the tone for courteous relations among teachers and peers. During the first week of the academic year, seventh and tenth-grade students train and drill with the soldiers. They learn proper bearing and manners. In the process, they come to appreciate and make friends with their mentors in uniform, who also perform many functions in the community. Parents attend the event at the end of the week for a report and celebration.

"We are a community of character" is emblazoned on the police cars of Lombard, Illinois, reflecting the training officers have received.[44] Reflecting the character education initiative in local schools, a police department in Wake County,

North Carolina, developed a program that employed police and community members as role models for youth. The result was a halving of the juvenile court referrals after just two years. The county park and recreation department integrated virtues into their summer program so that all 5000 youngsters participating received similar messages, ones that echoed what they heard in schools.[45]

In these and myriad other ways, the basic human aspirations for personal maturity, thriving families and a healthy society are served when young people's characters are formed through the concerted efforts of home, school and community. Yet these three life goals also frame a variety of educational methodologies employed in the character-building classroom and school-wide efforts....

Notes

1. "CEP Urges States to Carefully Consider Character Education Mandates," *Character Educator* 8/3 (Spring 2000).

2. David Wangaard, "Character Education Program Components in a Public Elementary School: A Case Study," Ed.D. dissertation, University of Northern Colorado.

3. Gordon Vessels, *Character and Community Development: A School Planning and Teacher Training Handbook* (Westport, CT: Praeger, 1998).

4. Philip Fitch Vincent, ed., *Promising Practices in Character Education* (Chapel Hill, NC: Character Development Group, 1966), p. 7.

5. Vincent, *Promising Practices,* pp. 2-3.

6. Andrea Billups, "Academy in Harlem Enforces Strict Rules," *The Washington Times,* March 27, 2000.

7. Vincent, *Promising Practices,* pp. 12-14.

8. "1999 National Schools of Character: Best Practices and New Perspectives," McGraw-Hill Companies and Character Education Partnership, 1999, p. 23.

9. Ibid., p. 16.

10. Vincent, *Promising Practices,* pp. 57-58.

11. Remarks given at the *Business Week* Schools of Character Awards Dinner, New York, April 27, 1998.

12. Vincent, *Promising Practices,* p. 33.

13. "Character Education—A Growing National Movement," *Character Educator* 7 (Spring 1999), p. 1.

14. William J. Bennett, *The De-valuing of America: The Fight for Our Children and Our Culture* (New York: Simon & Schuster, 1994), p. 53.

15. Michael Rutter, B. Maughan, P. Mortimore, J. Ouston and A. Smith, *Fifteen Thousand Hours* (Cambridge: Harvard University Press, 1979).

16. Susan Pelis, "Book Bags: One Simple Way to Bridge School and Home," *Responsive Classroom: A Newsletter for Teachers* (Summer 1999), p. 5.

17. Vincent, *Promising Practices,* p. 13.

18. "Schools of Character: Reclaiming America's Values for Tomorrow's Workplace," McGraw-Hill Companies and Character Education Partnership, 1998, pp. 2-3.

19. "1999 National Schools of Character," pp. 2-3.

20. "Schools of Character: Reclaiming America's Values," p. 38.

21. Lawrence J. Walker and John H. Taylor, "Family Interaction and the Development of Moral Reasoning," *Child Development* 62 (1991), pp. 264-83.

22. Joseph W. Gauld, *Character First: The Hyde School Difference.* (Rocklin, CA: Prima, 1995).

23. Josephine Hauer, "Class Teachers in Russia: Lifelong Mentors and Partners in Moral Education," paper presented at the Moral and Social Interdisciplinary Colloquium, University of Utrecht, Netherlands, July, 1999.

24. "Schools of Character: Reclaiming America's Values," p. 5.

25. Ibid., p. 10.

26. "1999 National Schools of Character," p. 40.

27. "The Child Development Project: A Brief Summary of the Project and Findings from Three Evaluation Studies," Oakland, California: Developmental Studies Center, September 1998.

28. Elizabeth Shepard, "How You Can Help a Child," *Parade,* September 1998, p. 6.

29. Thomas Lickona, *Educating for Character* (New York: Bantam Books, 1991), pp. 35-36.

30. Ibid., p. 402.

31. Cindy J. Christopher, *Building Parent-Teacher Communication—An Educator's Guide* (Lancaster, PA: Technomic, 1996), p. 33.

32. "Schools of Character: Reclaiming America's Values," p. 9.

33. Henry A. Huffman, *Developing a Character Education Program—One School District's Experience* (Alexandria, VA: ASCD, 1994), pp. 64-70.

34. D. A. Johnson, et al., "Relative Effectiveness of Comprehensive Community Programming for Drug Abuse Prevention with High Risk and Low-Risk Adolescents," *Journal of Consulting and Clinical Psychology* 58 (April 1990), pp. 447-56; R. C. Lefebrere, T. M. Lassater, R. A. Carleton, and G. Peterson, "Theory and Delivery of Health Programming in the Community: The Pawtucket Heart Health Program," *Preventive Medicine* 16 (1990), pp. 80-95.

35. I. Goldenberg and H. Goldenberg, *Family Therapy: An Overview* (Pacific Grove, CA: Brooks/Cole, 1991).

36. Lickona, *Educating for Character;* Wangaard, "Character Education Program Components."

37. B. Moody and Linda McKay, "CHARACTER PLUS—A Process, Not a Recipe," *Educational Leadership* 51(1993), pp. 28-30; C. E. Carlson, "HIIP: A Comprehensive School-Based Substance Abuse Program with Cooperative Community Involvement," *Journal of Primary Prevention* 10 (April 1990), pp. 289-301.

38. "1999 National Schools of Character," p. 34

39. Ibid., p. 37.

40. "Schools of Character: Reclaiming America's Values," p. 12.

41. Ibid., p. 5.

42. "Utah Project," http://www.usoe.k12.ut.us/curr/char_ed/.

43. "1999 National Schools of Character," p. 35.

44. Report by Gary M. Smith at the Cooperating School Districts conference, "For Home, School, Community and World," St. Louis, MO, July 8–10, 1999.

45. "1999 National Schools of Character," p. 52.

Toward a Global Initiative on Education

Gene B. Sperling
Brookings Institution

At the April 2000 World Education Forum in Dakar, Senegal, 180 countries including the United States committed themselves to a simple yet profound goal: providing quality education for all the world's children by 2015. Part of the aim of the Dakar conference was to assess the steps taken since 1990, when most of the same participants had met in Jomtien, Thailand, and promised that all poor children would have access to quality primary education within a decade. So the Dakar declaration was simultaneously an admission of failure and a pledge to try again—a triumph, as Dr. Johnson once said about second marriages, of hope over experience.

The jury is still out on whether the Dakar pledge will join the Jomtien compact in the crowded graveyard of overly ambitious development goals. It is true that countries and international institutions have exhibited a great deal of energy and continued commitment on the education front. The United Nations Children's Fund (UNICEF) recently launched a Girl's Education Initiative with high-level political backing from Kofi Annan, Nelson Mandela, and Graça Machel, Mandela's wife and a prominent activist for children's rights, education, and development. World Bank President James Wolfensohn has declared that no country with a viable plan for achieving universal education should be allowed to fail for lack of resources, even though World Bank lending for education has declined over the past two years. And the U.N. Educational, Scientific, and Cultural Organization (UNESCO) has continued the Education for All (EFA) initiative renewed at Dakar with follow-up meetings at the national and global levels.

This activity has been spurred by a growing body of research showing that investment in education—particularly for girls—in the world's poorest countries produces impressive health benefits and high economic returns. Education boosts family income, and female education in particular leads to smaller, healthier families by lowering infant and maternal mortality and improving child nutrition. In Africa, a child born to an uneducated mother faces a 20 percent chance of dying before the age of five, whereas the risk for a child whose mother has attended at least five years of school drops to 12 percent. In Brazil, illiterate women have, on average, six children each; literate mothers average between two and three. Indeed, a 1995 study of 72 countries found that "the expansion of female secondary education may be the single best lever for achieving substantial reductions in fertility." Recent research on AIDS prevention in the urban areas of Zambia suggested that teenagers between the ages of 15 and 19 who had received at least a medium level

Gene B. Sperling, "Toward a Global Initiative on Education." Originally a speech given to the Washington Foreign Law Society on February 26, 2002. Reprinted with permission of author.

of education had a lower incidence of the AIDS virus than did their less-educated counterparts. And schools provide an important vehicle for delivering vaccines, medicines, vitamins, and meals.

Studies suggest that every additional year of schooling can increase the wages of workers in poor nations by 10 to 20 percent. In this way, completing basic education can produce significant gains in income. But as ambitious as it seems to shoot for universal primary education, basic education should really be seen as a starting point rather than an end goal. The need to eventually provide secondary and higher education to the world's children is only heightened by recent research on globalization's impact on wages in Latin America. Studies suggest that the wage premium from globalization going to workers who have received secondary and higher education has risen dramatically relative to that for workers with only primary schooling.

No matter how well intentioned, however, current efforts will not be sufficient to fulfill even the Dakar goals. The scope of the problem is simply too large to be addressed fully by scattered, piecemeal projects. According to Oxfam, 130 million children between the ages of 6 and 11 are currently not in school, and another 150 million drop out before completing four years of basic education and gender disparity continues to depress enrollment rates, leaving girls behind.

The only solution is a global initiative that will leverage systemic reform in developing nations. Major national reform will carry significant political and economic costs. If the developed countries want the leaders of developing nations to bear these costs, they will have to offer substantially more aid. Mobilizing the necessary resources will require a new global compact on education, one with a compelling framework that clearly sets out the roles and responsibilities of key stakeholders. This framework must bring together the dispersed multilateral education efforts, build confidence among advanced nations that any additional resources they contribute will be used effectively, and persuade developing countries that aid will deliver concrete benefits without imposing intrusive conditions or generating more international bureaucracy.

The Global Education Contract

Ideally, development efforts should rest on a mutually beneficial social contract. Such an understanding currently underlies international cooperation on poverty reduction: poor countries understand that aid can help them reduce poverty, and rich countries and international civil society understand that the aid they give can promote international economic growth, foster certain foreign policy goals, and make the world more equitable.

If either side begins to doubt the benefits of the partnership and questions this implicit social contract, however, the process can grind to a halt. Several different tensions can disrupt the contract and prevent it from achieving development goals. Donors, for example, sometimes worry that their contributions are not being used for the intended purposes. This fear is commonly reflected in arguments that aid-receiving nations lack the "absorptive capacity" and efficiency to channel resources effectively, or that corruption or politics diverts aid to unintended beneficiaries. Donors are also concerned about burden-sharing—each country being reluctant to provide more aid than it considers its appropriate share. Recipients, meanwhile, sometimes fear that the conditions accompanying aid will force them to undertake unpleasant reforms and accept infringements on their sovereignty.

Donors and recipients can thus end up at odds with one another. Externally imposed performance requirements can sometimes actually help developing-country governments and nongovernmental organizations (NGOs) overcome resistance to reform among entrenched domestic interests. Still, tension over such conditions lies at the heart of many major development debates today. The more rich countries seek to improve outcomes through rigorous performance monitoring, the more poor nations fear being subjected to the stipulations of international donors. This tension can be finessed but can never be entirely alleviated.

Debt relief is one area that has seen significant success in mitigating the tensions enough to sustain the contract among rich and poor nations. The Heavily Indebted Poor Countries (HIPC) Debt Initiative—proposed by the World Bank and the International Monetary Fund (IMF) and agreed to by international governments in 1996—worked through the burden-sharing concern by laying out the exact obligations of each donor country and it reduced fears about aid's effectiveness by requiring recipient countries to develop explicit strategies for channeling freed-up resources toward poverty reduction. On the other hand, it also mitigated fears of excessive outside intrusion by making poor countries the authors of their own strategies.

The success of the debt relief initiative can be instructive for reaching other development goals. The most likely way to achieve universal education by 2015 is through a clear framework for collective action that outlines appropriate and realistic roles and responsibilities for donor countries, recipient countries, and multilateral institutions. Such a global alliance on basic education (GABE) could raise resources for poor countries with good education plans by combining multilateral, bilateral, and NGO assistance into a pooled lending structure. Ideally, this global fund would disburse resources through a single lending and grant-making instrument. But rather than let the best be the enemy of the good, it might start by simply coordinating the existing aid instruments.

Like the HIPC example, the Dakar declaration called on recipient countries to devise plans showing how they might actually meet their stated education goals. But the EFA structure that was set up to realize the goals set at Dakar has no means for assessing these national plans, and even if it can decide that a nation has come up with a satisfactory strategy, it provides no assurance that that country will actually receive aid to help implement its plan. Without a global effort espousing well-defined roles and responsibilities, the Dakar initiative is likely to fail because donors will have little confidence that resources will be well spent, and recipients will have little incentive to undertake painful reforms. Reform can succeed if the political will to support it exists—Ugandan President Yoweri Museveni's promotion of education, for instance, has led to a dramatic expansion of primary-school enrollment in his country. But such willingness to undertake reform will be partly contingent on assurances that international assistance will be available to make ambitious reform plans financially viable.

***

Any viable global education initiative must also find ways of ensuring that every dollar of international aid actually adds up to a full dollar of spending for its intended purpose—in other words, that international aid does not simply free up recipient governments to divert their own spending to other issues. This will require a sufficiently specific and transparent budgetary process to determine "baselines" from which to judge what amount of spending would have occurred without aid. It will also require the ability to track and monitor the flow of aid once it has been disbursed.

As the Dakar goals move education development assistance from the level of individual projects to the level of systemic reforms, questions of how to classify and track specific budgetary expenditures will become more important. It is easier to monitor whether funds have been diverted, for example, when aid goes to capital projects—a new airport or a new bridge—than when it is directed at something as elusive and broad as education reform. Monitoring the performance of education initiatives will depend on clear and transparent budgeting procedures, which many developing nations have not yet adopted. Fortunately, the process of helping HIPCs has already initiated budget reform and improvements in expenditure tracking. A joint World Bank-IMF report has found that, although comprehensive budget reform will require considerable effort, temporary, short-term steps can be taken to track spending on education and other social issues. For example, Uganda has created a poverty action fund that serves this purpose, and Guyana has made significant headway in tagging portions of its budget that are used for poverty reduction.

Spotlight on Education

In poor nations as in rich countries, education creates a foundation for economic growth, higher standards of living, better health, and a more informed citizenry. Curiously, however, the cause of universal basic education has captured very little public attention compared to other important development issues such as debt relief and fighting AIDS. Given the synergies between education, health, and economic growth, tackling the crisis in education should be recognized as a key to unlocking other development goals.

Unlike some of the world's other important problems, moreover, limited access to education in poor nations is not a disease without a cure. Where there has been true high-level commitment to expanding education—as in Uganda, Malawi, and the Indian state of Kerala—significant progress has been achieved. Without a coordinated global effort that can channel resources and create publicly defined obligations for the major global actors, however, progress in this area is likely to be slow and sporadic. Today 130 million of the world's children are without schooling and hundreds of millions more will be equally deprived in years to come. They all deserve better.

Making the World Safe Through Democracy: A Historical Survey

Spencer Weart
American Institute of Physics

When the French overthrew their monarchy, people who longed passionately for liberty in their own lands set out for Paris. In 1790 France's newly elected National Assembly welcomed representatives at a ceremonial session. Spaniards, Poles, Greeks and Turks in exotic costumes took turns declaiming that the French example was inspiring their people to throw off their chains. The French agreed that a new democratic age was coming—an age of universal peace. Everywhere tyrannies would collapse, undermined by their own vices. Of course it might be necessary to give them a little push.[1]

What could better satisfy the Revolution's ideals, and distress its enemies, than helping foreign peoples to revolt against their oppressors? The ambition was so enormous that for an appropriate term the French leaders had to hark far back in history. They announced that their nation would sponsor "a crusade for universal liberty."[2] A fantastic project, yet not unique. It was only one instance of a tendency that has been so common we could almost call it a historical law: Republican regimes commonly seek to create their own kind of regime where it does not exist.

Why go to the trouble? We shall see that the motives were partly idealistic. A belief that equality in liberty is the birthright of every person necessarily leads to a conviction that tyranny should be put down wherever it is found. But usually the most obvious motive was pragmatic. In any struggle against a tyrant, fellow democrats would be a reliable ally, simply because they shared the fear and hatred of tyranny. Beyond that was a vision embodied in a banner put up by the democratic faction in Venice after French Revolutionary troops entered the city: "ESTABLISHED LIBERTY LEADS TO UNIVERSAL PEACE."[3]

This was not fantasy. As I have argued elsewhere, well-established democracies do not make war on fellow democracies. The democratization of all nations is thus by far the most promising path to a durable world peace.[4] But leaving aside the reasons that have been proposed for attempts to foster democracy in foreign nations, the attempts themselves are widespread and important enough to merit close study.

This essay provides the only existing survey of such attempts throughout history.[5] We shall see that the tendency turned up in a suprising number of settings over 25 centuries. We shall find that the goals always included not just liberation but also peace, and that the means towards these goals have been markedly improved in the past half-century.

Greek, Italian and German City-States

By the early fifth century B.C.E. the elites in many Greek cities had thrown off their monarchs or tyrants and created republican regimes. Ambitious autocrats threatened to conquer or subvert these regimes, and the free men became convinced that they must help one another to defend their liberties. They looked for allies not only at home but abroad. The new belief in equality of political rights (at any rate for the well-born and educated male elite) made it reasonable to seek common cause with men in other republics. A neighboring city might be only a day's walk away, and in the political struggles of the time exiles from the neighbor often came to live in your own city. Men driven into exile by a tyrant would seek your help to restore republican government in their homeland. By supporting the exiles now you would be better placed if someday you needed help to restore your own liberties.

The situation grew more complicated when Athens and other cities extended voting rights to the masses in a sort of democracy, while Sparta and others kept their old oligarchic forms. Leadership and policies in both types of regime were determined by free voting—these were all republics, not autocracies—but in the oligarchies only a small minority of the men (typically less than 10 percent) held these political rights. Democrats and oligarchic elites feared one another, and in many cities regime types alternated in cycles of revolt, suppression and exile. Often in such struggles the democratic faction got material help from foreign democracies. Oligarchic regimes replied in kind.

Towards the end of the century, the Peloponnesian wars brought an almost complete split between the two types of regime. To pick at random among many examples, we hear how an Athenian army marched through Thessaly "setting up democracy and arming the serfs against their masters." Aristotle later put the matter in a nutshell: "The Athenians used to suppress oligarchies everywhere, and the Spartans democracies."[6] So far as we can tell from the fragments of evidence that survive, these policies were not a *cause* of the wars but a *consequence*—a weapon devised in the heat of a struggle among cities for predominance or survival.

There was nothing subtle in the methods: a foreign state was conquered through invasion or subverted in a coup, and a democratic regime was installed by force. Usually the opposing leaders were driven into exile or executed. Once the like-minded regime was installed, the state was often left to govern itself, for its democratic allies trusted it to remain a reliable friend. Treaties carved in stone and recovered by archeologists from the dirt reveal democracies sealing an alliance not with another state as such but with its "demos"—the democratic masses—each pledging not only to defend the other against foreign enemies but also to maintain democracy in their own states. Here little distinction was made between a state's own citizens and foreign democrats.[7]

The Athenian orator Demosthenes said baldly, "Our hostility toward oligarchies, purely on the grounds of principle, is stronger than our hostility toward democracies on any grounds whatsoever." He held that it would be better for Athens to have all other Greeks as formal enemies but under democratic regimes than to have them as allies but under oligarchic (or worse, autocratic) rule. For the Athenians would easily make peace with fellow democracies, "but with an oligarchic state I do not believe that friendly relations can be permanent."[8] The surviving evidence, which is extremely sketchy, suggests that a zone of peace may indeed have been maintained among the Greek democracies. If so, it vanished when they were overwhelmed by the Roman legions.

The same tendencies reappeared a dozen centuries later, as soon as republican government reappeared in Italy and Germany. These were not democratic regimes but oligarchic city-republics. A rudimentary ideal of mutual support among such regimes coalesced during the fourteenth century when republics joined against emperors and popes and dukes, sometimes swearing alliance against any tyrant whatsoever. For example, from the 1370s an alliance with other republics became the backbone of Florence's foreign policy. In the council chambers, speakers rose to declare that Florence's liberty depended on sustaining liberty in every neighboring republic. Florentines began working not only to preserve fellow republics but even to convert cities from autocratic rule into republics. As Florence's army marched to aid insurgents, they held aloft a banner of a kind the world had never seen. Instead of the lily, traditional heraldic symbol of their city, they carried a red cloth with seven huge white letters: *LIBERTÀ*. This army fought in the name of a universal ideal.[9]

When Florentines promised to defend republican government in the neighboring city of Lucca, they explained that it was in their interest to surround Florence with a ring of free cities in alliance against threatening autocrats. More, they promised to treat any Luccan on Florentine territory as if he were himself a Florentine. The ideal of freedom and equality among citizens had stretched across the frontier.[10] As hoped, the policy fostered not only liberty but peace. Florence never did have a serious war with Lucca or other neighbors so long as both sides were free republics.

Around this same time Swiss regimes began to act in a similar fashion. A half-dozen backwoods cantons could loosely be called democratic. When they conquered a neighboring region they tended to set up democratic peasant assemblies modelled on their own. The practice first appeared around 1405 when the canton of Appenzell took up arms against neighboring lords, burning their castles and liberating their peasants. One of their enemies exclaimed in disgust that the Appenzellers "accept everyone as a citizen...even the serfs!" They were not liberating serfs purely out of altruism, but also because they hoped to surround themselves with free communities in permanent alliance against lords; the policy worked splendidly.

Meanwhile oligarchic city-republics elsewhere in Switzerland, and scores of German ones in the Hanseatic League, established and defended oligarchic republican governments in their neighbors.[11] They counted on this policy to forge durable friendships, and they were not disappointed. As in ancient Greece, oligarchic and democratic regimes warred on one another and on autocrats. But the democratic cantons never, and the oligarchic cities almost never, fought their own kind of regime. The remarkable zone of nearly perfect peace among many dozens of independent city-republics endured for centuries, until they were swamped by the rise of monarchical nation-states.

As in ancient Greece, the Italian, Swiss and German efforts were mainly exercises in force. Where a regime was converted to a republic it was generally through military conquest or a coup. The losing party, those who survived, were forced into exile.

At the simplest level the proclivity for propagating one's own type of regime seems chiefly to reflect a desire to create a solid ally. All these republics foresaw that states they converted to their own kind of regime would stick with them against tyrants, kings, emperors or dukes. There are many such cases in more modern times. For example, Britain sponsored independent democracies in Canada and Australia, counting on them to be faithful allies, and the hope was amply fulfilled in both World Wars.

It is not only republics that wish to reproduce their own form of government. Feudal lords worked to weaken city councils and peasant assemblies in favor of feudal lordship. The princes of nineteenth century Europe likewise created princely states, for example in Bulgaria when it was liberated from Ottoman rule. Even Joseph Stalin, whose only principle of government was paranoid absolutism, sponsored little Stalins from East Germany to North Korea. Authoritarian states, however, had far less success in creating reliable allies. For example, the Communist Vietnamese helped to install a Communist government in Cambodia, but soon found it so disagreeable that they invaded and overthrew it. Authoritarian regimes cannot reliably keep peace with a similar regime even when it is their own creation. In any case, autocrats have most commonly followed their hierarchical principles by fighting to extend their own personal rule over others rather than by fostering external autocracies. It is republics, with their doctrine of natural rights extending to worthy people everywhere, that have worked most fervently and effectively to create independent regimes like their own.

The Corrupted Crusade of the French Revolution

The scarcely articulated ideals of ancient and early modern republicans were developed in depth by audacious thinkers of the Enlightenment. They maintained that "the Cause of Liberty...is ONE COMMON CAUSE." The radicals who seized power in France had been taught that men in any nation who loved democracy were their natural allies. But initially they hardly thought to take action abroad, expecting the decadent aristocracies would collapse in their own corruption once their subjects learned and copied the French example. When France got into a war with neighboring monarchies it seemed a matter of old-fashioned territorial rivalries and domestic tensions. Then the pressure of combat itself pushed more extreme ideas to the fore.[12]

Wherever French armies thrust into neighboring regions, native radicals leaped up to demand help in overthrowing their rulers, and exiles in Paris rushed to support the idea. Clearly it would be to France's military advantage to encourage rebellion in enemy lands, but the mood of French leaders flew beyond pragmatism. In 1793 that ardent revolutionary Maximilien Robespierre pushed through a new official ideology, persuading the French National Assembly to proclaim that whoever denied rights to people anywhere was the enemy of everyone. All peoples should help one another against every despot, Robespierre declared, exactly as if they were "citizens of a single state."[13]

The crusade advanced with stunning success. Armies of peasants, propelled by revolutionary fervor, scattered monarchical troops from the Netherlands to Naples. The French set up freely elected assemblies: a Batavian Republic for the Dutch, a Roman and a Cisalpine Republic for the Italians and so forth. Old oligarchies too were swept aside. In Venice, commoners welcomed their liberation with speeches and dancing in the Piazza San Marco.

Many Venetians, however, watched the ceremony in sullen discontent. In every conquered region not only elites but also the majority of peasants and laborers, confused and troubled, longed for the return of their familiar priests and princes. The revolutionary creed that ordinary people will automatically take to democracy was a fatal error. The new governments were only miniature factions of urban radicals who had to be protected from their own populace by a fence of French bayonets.

So far it looked much like the strictly military efforts of the ancient Greeks and early modern Italians and Swiss. But the deep thinkers of the Enlightenment had created a more sophisticated understanding of political life. The radical democrats understood that to survive they must reshape the entire political culture of their nations. To inculcate republican ideas, ceremonies with speeches and banners were only a beginning. The new regimes worked tirelessly to transform education, suppress the reactionary influence of the clergy, and foster an outspoken free press. Most important, they destroyed forever the web of feudal privileges that had enmeshed everyday life in hierarchy.

Republican ideals were not taken up so easily. The radical leaders themselves, unaccustomed to tolerance of dissent, would not submit to elections. Each of the new regimes split into factions that displaced one another by lawless coups. Suspicions of fellow citizens burgeoned; after all, aristocrats were plotting to restore the old order, and in wartime any whiff of subversion was intolerable. The French government, terrified of secret agents, arrested thousands of citizens and foreigners. The newborn republics all around France likewise stamped upon suspected counter–revolutionaries.

The government in Paris also used force to control the client regimes. As the wars dragged on

French armies took to looting the regions they occupied, bursting into houses and seizing everything down to the silverware. Was it not the right of the Revolution to have whatever it needed to defeat the monarchies? Actually France was now ruled by the authoritarian Directory and far from democracy, but the regime's crimes discredited democratic ideology in many eyes. Eventually the neighboring peoples all turned against France and helped defeat it.

The failures of the French democratic crusade should not conceal its successes. For a little while revolutionary France did surround itself with devoted allies, and over the long term their destruction of feudal regimes proved irreversible. The policy only faltered when the leaders themselves abandoned toleration and legality.

The French had followed a path already trod by ancient Athens. In the fifth century B.C.E. the grand alliance that defeated the invading King of Persia gave rise to the Delian League, a confederacy of republics scattered around the shores of the Aegean. Unfortunately Athens, the strongest member by far, gradually took full command. The Athenians' overbearing insistence on control was normal at this early point when ideas about equal rights were scarcely born. When Athens went to war against Sparta, oligarchic factions in some allied states forced a break with Athens. The Athenians' failure to leave the League states with equal rights contributed to a disastrous defeat.[14] Like France two millenia later, Athens had been tempted to domineer because it was far stronger than the others; like France, it had justified its control by claiming that as the chief defender of democracy it should gather the strength of the others and have its way. This unhappy pattern of a great republic bossing its neighbors would reappear, as we shall see, in modern North America.

What brought the French, like the Athenians, to exploit their neighbors was a desperate war. The immense expenses of armament, and the wartime fears of subversion, drove France and its client republics to use coercion within their own territories. When a crusade for liberty descends into war it may defeat itself, undermining liberty even at home.

The shabby collapse of French democracy did not destroy the ideal of international republican solidarity. A new generation of romantic radicals arose, recognizing no frontiers, throwing themselves into doomed conspiracies. That republicans everywhere were allies was increasingly taken for granted. As a British diplomat remarked in 1832, "people are much more liberals or the reverse than they are Frenchmen or Germans or Italians."[15]

When that division brought on the revolutions of 1848, wherever radicals won influence they called for a universal crusade against despots. Once again exiles swarmed into Paris, armed themselves and launched raids into their homelands. This time, however, the fragile new French republic declined to support the exile bands. French republicans had learned something from history, and feared that foreign wars would open the way for authoritarian reaction (their president, Louis-Napoleon Bonaparte, showed they were right by using a war against the Romans to consolidate autocratic power).[16] In other lands the revolutionaries were still more uncertain, and they had little energy to spare as they contended with the tradition-minded domestic peasant majority. Although radicals did want to support their foreign counterparts, 1848 saw no organized international democratic crusade. Soon aristocratic forces thrust down republicans across the continent, and the survivors despaired of any grand international movement.

The idea hung on precariously where republican government survived, above all in Great Britain. Throughout the nineteenth century the British discreetly promoted in foreign regimes what they called "constitutional" government, meaning civil rights and the rule of law. Some British ministers applied diplomatic pressure, issuing warnings and deploying an occasional warship. By the century's end they could claim to have helped increase liberty, or at least stave off despotism, in nations including Spain, Greece, Belgium and Turkey. The effort was sporadic, for British cabinets usually put imperial strategy well ahead of civil rights in other nations. Conservatives feared anything that smelled of democracy, while liberals distrusted any expansion of governmental power and were the first to oppose any use of military force.

The history of nineteenth century Europe thus repeats the lessons of the French Revolution and ancient Athens. First, that wherever there are people who hold republican ideals they will profess a solidarity with like-minded people everywhere, and some will indeed work energetically to foster republican government abroad. Second, that these aspirations have little room for maneuver between visions of universal democracy and a nation's practical needs, between too much zeal and too little.

The United States, Beacon and Bully

The problems raised by democratic crusading were nowhere so persistent as in the policies of the United States. When the nation won its independence it had little scope for action abroad. The only foreign land within reach was Canada, and when ardent bands attempted to rouse Canadians against the British king they were dumbfounded by the lack of support. Through the next century the United States had neither a strong desire to transform other regimes nor the means to do so. Most Americans felt that it was up to foreign peoples to free themselves when they were ready.

Meanwhile the United States would be guided by strategic and commercial interests, for the nation's first responsibility was to survive and flourish. Its historic mission would be to inspire the world by showing how well democratic governance could work. The strategy had considerable success, for countless democrats abroad have indeed taken the United States as a model, even to copying phrases from the Declaration of Independence and the Constitution.

Americans offered a tainted example, however, so long as many of them owned slaves. Northerners had often heard that criticism from foreigners, and some said they must fight Southern slavery to set a better example for the world. Yet when the Civil War began only a dedicated minority aimed to put a quick end to slavery. It was the terrible pressures of warfare that made Northerners grudgingly accept Lincoln's proclamation of emancipation—as a weapon to weaken the South. People also began to realize that blacks escaping to the protection of Northern armies could never be driven back into slavery, especially after tens of thousands put on the blue uniform and fought heroically. As the toll of war mounted so did a crusading spirit, a conviction that only some great transforming good could justify the tragic sacrifices. By 1864 the North had accepted the abolition of slavery as a sacred war aim.[17]

After the South's defeat, Northern Republicans determined to effect a total change in its politics—a Reconstruction. Their first step was to give Southern blacks the vote under the protection of troops. Former slaves eagerly took up politics, striking alliances with democratically inclined Southern whites and winning high offices. The North had forced through nothing less than a democratic revolution.[18]

Some Northern radicals hoped to go farther, breaking the planter class with land reform in order to transform the entire political culture. However, most Americans rejected such an infringement on property rights. Some thought it sufficed to have national civil rights laws. Others argued for stimulating industry so that rising prosperity would reconcile blacks and whites. Still others pinned their faith on building public schools.

These policies would take a long time to work if they were valid at all, and Southern whites moved faster. With naked terrorism they barred blacks from the polls and politics. Whites who supported black rights were likewise silenced or slain. Only Northern troops could suppress the Ku Klux Klan. But the North was increasingly dominated by industrialists who, with an eye on their own restive workers, denounced any thought of government intervention on behalf of common folk. Nor were liberals comfortable with the prospect of endless rule by bayonet over the South against the will of the majority (that is, whites). Racism added its poison, for many believed that the failure of blacks to maintain their rights proved their congenital inferiority. By 1880 the North had left the South to its own devices under the rule of a minority of wealthy whites.

The remarkable fact about the attempt to impose democracy on the South is not that it failed, but that it was attempted at all. Once again the fires of war had ignited a crusading spirit. Once again the enterprise was defeated largely because the political culture in the conquered regions was too deeply rooted in coercion and inequality. And once again, what made failure certain was a weakness in the egalitarian convictions of the conquering leaders themselves. Not only in the South but around the world, the spirit of democratic crusade was stifled under racist and imperialist ideology.

The spirit revived with shocking force in 1917. Yet again a dire war was forcing people back upon fundamental ideals. It seemed like a God-sent opportunity to President Woodrow Wilson, whose polestar was equal rights under law. Wilson launched his vision into history on April 4, 1917, when he addressed the United States Congress to ask for a declaration of war upon Germany. In somber tones Wilson held the crowded hall spellbound as he declared that the peaceful reign of equal rights that prevailed among the individual citizens of a democracy should likewise prevail among the nations of the world. To achieve such harmony it was only necessary to thrust down the militarist ruling elites—it was these that had always been the cause of wars. The grand aim of going to war, the president explained, was to "make the world safe for democracy." Wilson slid past the phrase without special emphasis, but the audience caught its import: the hall detonated in applause.[19]

Wilson's vision might have made little headway amid the imperialist struggle for survival and dominion, but help came from an enemy. The Bolsheviks who seized Russia that November also believed in world-wide egalitarian liberation, and their thunderous denunciations of oppression aroused subject peoples around the world. Meanwhile French and British leaders desperately required support from every quarter—from neutrals, from Americans, from their own common people—and they appealed to everyone by announcing that the war was a battle for universal self-determination.

"Self-determination" was not as plain as it seemed. "The phrase is simply loaded with dynamite," Wilson's Secretary of State warned him confidentially. "It will, I fear, cost thousands of lives." Millions would have been closer to the mark.

Self-determination had two meanings for Wilson. First was a nation's internal freedom from domination by a militarist aristocracy. That could not be done short of full democracy, and Wilson did not mean to impose his ideal on others. His second meaning of self-determination was freedom from coercion by external powers. It would suffice to pull down the militarists and let people choose their own government; surely they would eventually settle down in democracy and peace. Events at the end of the war seemed to confirm this vision, for the Germans rose and chased the Kaiser into exile, and other nations too spontaneously elected their first democratic parliaments. There was no need for Reconstruction-style military occupation.[20]

A weakness in self-determination soon appeared. One must define the people who will do the self-determining, the body of citizens whose majority is sovereign. To define such a body one must draw boundaries, and that can awaken demons. Amid the social wreckage of fallen empires, many people found community and security by clinging together within a group boundary, exalting their collective rights as Hungarians or whatever. The new regimes, still pervaded by authoritarian political culture, scarcely knew how to maintain individual rights against these group passions. One by one most of the newborn democracies fell to nationalist dictators.

Although Wilson's crusade for democracy failed in the short run, over the long run he won his point. Entire peoples had been freed from the Russian, German, Austro-Hungarian and Ottoman empires to go their own way. Wilson's rhetoric, oddly teamed up with Communist propaganda, also fired resistance among peoples still held subject. From Ireland to the Philippines came demands for the self-determination that the democratic nations themselves proclaimed. Wilson wanted only a gradual emancipation of "backward" colonial peoples under the tutelage of their masters. But Americans and Soviets had accepted, and swayed much of the world to adopt, a new principle: foreign rule was illegitimate except insofar as it would foster self-government.

Meanwhile there was one region where the president hoped to sponsor democracy more directly. The little nations of the Caribbean had languished for generations in cycles of despotism, corruption and insurrection, and progressives in the United States believed they had the power to correct that. They had already tried out the idea following the Spanish-American War, when the United States felt a responsiblity to set up democracy in liberated Cuba. Shiploads of managers and engineers were sent to improve everything from schooling to sanitation and to organize elections (taking care to exclude candidates hostile to the United States). For the first time since the French Revolution, a nation had actively planted a democracy upon foreign soil. Unfortunately the flower did not flourish in Cuba, with its tradition of shameless manipulation of ballot boxes.[21]

Wilson and other presidents ordered many more such interventions. U.S. Marines tramped ashore with some local support to regulate elections in Panama, the Dominican Republic, Haiti and Nicaragua. Uninvited, the United States invaded Mexico (twice) and Honduras. United States governments also worked to undermine despotism in nations as distant as Chile through economic sanctions. The first example came in 1917 when a dictator seized power in Costa Rica and Wilson refused to grant diplomatic recognition, making commerce so difficult that the dictator had to step down.

Historians argue over the motives behind these interventions. How much were elites in the United States aiming to advance private business interests—how much were they working to prevent European powers from gaining a dangerous military foothold—how much were they driven by ideology to spread democracy? Few progressives at the time would have seen much difference among these motives. In their view, what Latin America needed above all was plain political stability. That would remove the pretexts that European imperialists had often used to intervene, and at the same time provide the right climate for economic development and public education, with democracy to follow in due course. The idea was to build democratic political culture from the bottom up with paved roads, good schools and honest officials.[22]

The results were not encouraging. In Puerto Rico and the Philippines the United States did create democracies, but they had limitations and even that took half a century of economic privileges and paternalistic supervision. Elsewhere the fine plans scarcely got started. Progressives supposed that fair elections would bring stability by conferring legitimacy on those elected. But to many Caribbean leaders, if an election was worth anything it was to show which faction actually held effective power; holding an election without fraud would be as pointless as holding a war without battles. Sometimes the United States sent in soldiers to keep down the cheating, but foreign supervision scarcely encouraged self-government. The losing factions would go back to plotting coups, howling that the Yankees had connived to install their opponents. Sometimes these accusations were correct. In Nicaragua, for example, United States envoys backed up by Marines frankly dictated who could run for office. Such elections discredited the idea of democratic intervention.[23]

As these problems became clear the United States tried another approach. The incessant coups and caudillos in the Caribbean all came from the military establishments, so these should be replaced with police forces trained in constitutional law.

Such constabularies were set up under Yankee tutelage in Cuba, Haiti, the Dominican Republic and Nicaragua, and they did put an end to civil wars and regional insurrections. But consolidating territorial states was not sufficient. In each country the constabularies themselves took to politics and started their own cycles of coups and dictatorships.

In the 1930s the United States gave up trying to impose its democratic ideals on the Caribbean. In agrarian societies where nearly all the land was owned by a handful of families, establishing full democracy would mean overturning the whole social and economic system. If that were possible at all (which many doubted for such "backward" peasants), it would be intolerably costly, and would violate liberal ideals of property rights and self-determination.

Everywhere the crusade for democracy seemed exhausted. World economic depression accelerated the rout of democratic governments from Argentina to Japan, and many people decided that the future belonged to more brutally "efficient" forms of rule. The only thing that could restore the democratic crusading spirit would be another terrible war.

Replacing Fascist Political Cultures

In 1944 some British scholars and civil servants were given time off from the war against fascism to read school books. They sat down to stacks of German texts by the hundred, diligently working through the pages. What they read struck them with dismay. Scarcely any of these books seemed suitable to place in the hands of children. Even books written well before the Nazis took power reeked of chauvinism, militarism and racism. The true enemy of democracy was not just the madman Hitler but an entire political culture.[24]

Many people in Britain and the United States thought that after the First World War the effort to promote democracy had stopped too soon. They thought it obvious that if, this time, the defeated nations could be turned into solid democracies, that would automatically keep them from starting yet another war. But how to establish lasting democracy?[25]

Once victory was won the defeated nations must have new leaders. But to impose a government would flout ideals of self-determination, making more enemies than friends. The solution was to clear the ground so that democrats could rise by themselves. American officers and their allies ruling as Occupation authorities in Germany, Japan and other conquered nations devoted their chief effort to purging dedicated fascists from positions of authority. Hundreds of thousands were removed.

Germany, Japan, Austria and Italy had all had some practice at democracy in the 1920s, and many citizens remembered how it should work. In the space cleared by the purges, with fascism itself discredited by shattering military defeat, democratically inclined men and women took their stand. Thousands of them came straight from jail. Protected from the violence of their old foes by Occupation authorities, they formed political parties and founded governments.

If the democrats were to hold out after the foreign troops withdrew, they must have a foundation to stand on. Americans and the British therefore designed a hugely ambitious plan: they would transform entire political cultures. In the words of Japan's new viceroy, General Douglas MacArthur, the defeated nation would become "the world's great laboratory for an experiment" whose aim was nothing less than a "reshaping of national and individual character."[26] It was a heroic assumption that such a transformation was possible—but that very assumption was central to democratic belief. To be a democrat is to believe that appropriate conditions can make a good citizen out of practically anyone.

In pursuit of their grand goal, authorities did not scruple to set aside civil rights for a time. They purged every teacher and journalist who could be accused of fascism, in some places well over half the total, and strictly censored fascist thought in every medium from storybooks to movies. Meanwhile a new generation of teachers was trained by imported democratic instructors, or sent abroad themselves to interact with teachers familiar with democracy. Entire newspapers and radio companies were confiscated from right-wing owners and turned over to liberals. Occupation authorities also directly pressured educators and the media to celebrate democracy. The most important thing about the censorship and pressures, however, was that they were weak. Schoolteachers, writers and film-makers, released from the iron cage of fascist thought control, were glad to try their wings.

The most forceful measures were taken in Japan, where hierarchical traditions were most deeply entrenched. Americans decided the Japanese political and social and economic systems must all be radically changed. The Occupation authorities began by writing an entire new constitution and forcing it upon the Japanese. Next came wholesale land reform (many of the Americans were New Dealers who believed that helping common people could take priority over property rights). MacArthur and his crew also sponsored free trade unions, emancipated women, and imposed other revolutionary changes.

In both Germany and Japan, the construction of democratic civil society was aided by many private American organizations. Labor unions, women's leagues, 4-H Clubs and so forth each worked to reproduce its kind by sending missions abroad and by bringing foreigners back to watch democracy at work.

These efforts were intense, but brief. The Occupation forces kept control for only a few years, far too little to uproot all the fascists and their beliefs, before attention turned to the Cold War. From the outset the aim had never been revolutionary democratization in the fashion of the Swiss or French who had roused peasant mobs to drive lords from their manors. The Occupation authorities even discouraged attempts to mobilize workers in the name of radical change, which smelled to them of Communism. Instead they relied on the old elites, not only the moderates but often conservatives. As the Cold War took hold even former fascists were sometimes accepted as allies against Communism. This limited approach to changing society was a main reason there was no authoritarian reaction after the troops sailed home.[27]

Democracy did take root, profoundly changing the political cultures of Germany and Japan (Italy had never been so deeply fascist). Many who had doubted that democracy could ever work in their nation changed their minds when they saw how well it served. Others who had always hoped for democracy now found a chance to stake their careers upon it. Polls showed that citizens gradually took to democratic ways of thinking, while leaders settled into practices of tolerating dissent and negotiating compromises.[28] To the surprise of many, the experiment produced exactly what it aimed for. As predicted, all these nations gave up their former predilection for wanton aggression abroad. And as predicted, they all became steadfast allies of the other democracies.

One reason for success was that the combative spirit did not fade away after a few years but was reinvigorated by the Cold War. After China fell to Communism and Stalin imposed his rule upon Eastern Europe, democrats responded with furious activity to preserve their liberty.

The most crucial battleground was Italy, where many predicted that the Communists would be voted into power in the 1948 elections and then impose a Stalinist dictatorship. The American government secretly channeled large sums of money to the Christian Democrats. American experts advised Italians on political organization, corporations helped out by financing propaganda, and private groups from Italian-American clubs to the American Catholic church threw in their support. Probably the Christian Democrats would have won the election in any case, but the outside help boosted them to a decisive majority. Through the 1950s the U.S. Central Intelligence Agency continued to give Italian democratic parties massive secret aid.[29]

Americans similarly aided democratic parties all across Western Europe through the postwar decades, and as each European democracy grew strong it added its own forces to the work. European governments withheld economic cooperation in order to weaken dictators and military juntas, for example in Spain and Greece, and actively assisted nascent democratic groups by every nonviolent method they could think of. Many private organizations joined in the effort. The deliberate aim was not only to secure reliable allies against the Soviet Union, but also to end the long tale of warfare in Western Europe with a stable peace. And that did happen. The patient campaign for democracy in Europe turned out to be one of the most successful foreign policies in all history.

The Destruction of Colonial Political Cultures

To see a different route toward democracy let us visit one more locale. The very thought of democracy was unknown in the wretched fishing village called Calcutta when the British purchased it, inhabitants and all, from its owners. Included in the deal was a malarial swamp which in time became a parkland with gardens and tree-lined promenades. Overlooking the park to this day is a statue of William Bentinck, the Governor-General of India in the 1830s, a progressive gentleman who established a uniform and honest administration for the subcontinent. As the epitaph on his pedestal truly declares, he was among those "Who infused into oriental despotism the spirit of British freedom."[30]

In such colonial possessions republics had their best chance to fulfill the vision of replacing despotism with freedom. Holding supreme power for generations, it might seem that they could have built whatever political culture they chose. But in fact imperialism stubbornly impeded democracy.

From the nineteenth century on, many people in republics assumed that their colonies would eventually become some sort of republics themselves. As evidence there were Britain's "white dominions" from Canada to Australia, which the British yielded up to the inhabitants in an unprecedented gamble. However, everyone assumed that countries with more alien cultures, immemorially ruled by hereditary power and cruelty, could not govern themselves democratically except in a remote future. Perhaps after centuries of economic progress and education the colonies could mature into social and political duplicates of the mother countries.

This complacent program was shaken by the preachings of Wilson and Lenin, and still more by the rise of native associations in the subject lands. Once natives had been educated in equal rights and the methods of public contestation, they demanded independence without delay. During the Second World War, when the United States government insisted it was fighting to end imperial rule everywhere, imperialists began to realize that they would not be granted centuries to uplift their colonies.[31]

If there was barely a single generation to work in, it seemed urgent to give indigenous leaders a democratic political culture. British colonial administrators set up local councils to offer experience in self-government. They hoped to gradually transfer power to an educated elite which would follow British ways down to the powdered wigs worn by judges. French leaders cherished a still grander vision: the Greater French Republic. The natives would be educated into virtual Frenchmen and absorbed into a world-wide federation, voting as the equals of citizens back in France.

These romantic plans ran afoul of the political cultures within the colonies themselves—and not only the cultures of the indigenous peoples. European colonial officials, trained in military and administrative rule, had little more experience than the natives in managing affairs through a democratic council. It seemed only natural to go on governing by passing commands down through the traditional tribal chiefs, sheiks or sultans. European colonials had a hard time imagining that natives with deep-rooted traditions of despotic rule, ignorant people with outlandish ways and dark skins, could ever be capable of democratic self-government. Such doubts redoubled in territories where groups striving for independence organized themselves into secret societies, terrorist organizations, and entire guerrilla armies under authoritarian leaders. Those were immediately scorned as "bandit" gangs, or painted in the demonic red of international Communism.

Here we see how flaws in a nation's own democracy can get in the way of fostering democracy elsewhere. Racial prejudice and political stereotyping made it hard to recognize that some native leaders might be cultivated as suitable negotiating partners. Hierarchical sub-cultures were allowed to pursue their authoritarian ways. Most colonial officials fought the independence movements tooth and nail. When natives who sought to organize peacefully for self-government were obstructed, they sometimes saw no way to reach their goals except by forming violent illegal bands. Democratic governments automatically battled these as criminal enemies, closing a vicious circle.

The independence movements grew irrepressibly, and European governments found that attempts to keep a grip on colonies not only drained money but disgusted democratic voters at home. By the latter 1950s most people everywhere found the denial of self-government incompatible with ideals of equal rights. In many countries the imperial powers pulled out abruptly, abandoning their half-hearted plans for eventually building democracy. Often they left behind a faction-ridden society that had known only hierarchical governance. Elections were held, but for lack of any tradition of civil rights, leaders often used the democratic "majority principle" to justify mobilizing ethnic groups to grab everything for themselves. Minority cliques fought back with coups. The fraction of the world's independent nations that were democratic fell back below the level of the 1920s.[32]

Nevertheless on balance European colonial rule did advance world democracy. Deliberately or not it had undermined traditional authoritarian structures, and when the colonial officials pulled out, whatever hierarchy remained was drained of prestige and power. The mutilated societies might fall into despotism or pure anocratic chaos, but they were also free, for the first time ever, to seek a new configuration. Here and there the colonists had left behind some democratic ideals and institutions—occasionally well entrenched, although often only sparks smoldering in the wreckage. Yet in dozens of new nations democracy was stamped out only to flare up again with indestructible vigor.

Centuries of tutelage were not necessary after all to create democratic government. A variety of societies already had their own traditions of the rule of law (or solid community custom), holding rulers publicly accountable for their policies, toleration of dissent and the protection of minority rights. Applied within institutions modelled on Europe's, these traditions could suffice to sustain democracy. Even impoverished tribal lands like Botswana and Papua New Guinea proved they could govern themselves in a generally democratic fashion.

Most impressive of all was the almost ungovernable conglomeration of India, which found indigenous roots for the principles of nonviolent public contestation. Mohandas Gandhi combined that with tactics such as the hunger strike and boycott, developed especially by the Irish as they wrested their freedom from Britain while retaining democracy. Gandhi's brilliant contribution was a more spiritual force: He would alter the political culture of the oppressors themselves. The methods that others had used to raise up democracy—furious insurrections, crusading armies, foreign troops guarding the polls, sweeping purges, generations of paternalistic tutelage—none of that was necessary. A tolerant politics could be cultivated as part of the liberation struggle itself. This nonviolent route to freedom was one of the greatest discoveries of the twentieth century.

Stumbling Toward a Democratic World

At the close of the Second World War many nations lacked freedom—not just colonial dominions but most of the rest from Latin America to Eastern

Europe. In all these the United States hoped to nurture democracy. As the world's predominant power it felt more certain than ever that its way of life was best. Foreigners would surely want to "Americanize" themselves, and it was simple morality to help them.

One method would be military intervention. On the occasions when this was tried, however, it generally brought more blame than praise. When the troops came home they might leave behind an approximately democratic regime as in the Dominican Republic, or a ravaged police state as in Vietnam. In either case it was arguable that the intervention had done more to impede democratic development than to promote it.

Diplomatic pressure was less risky. The United States and its allies pressed insistently for free elections everywhere from Poland to Brazil, reinforcing their words by granting or withholding trade preferences and military aid. The results were mixed. Some regimes indignantly rejected the pressure, some held elections yet wound up with new authoritarian governments anyway, but some did move toward democracy.

This was no crusade, for American presidents gave more attention to a tough realpolitik that aimed to advance the material position of the United States and restrict the Communist powers. The United States freely bestowed economic and military aid upon authoritarian regimes in hopes of improving regional stability and free-market economies; democracy could follow in its own good time. Besides, the only alternative to a dictator or junta was usually an opposition that sought power with its own secrecy and violence—promptly branded as Communist conspiracy.

Unfortunately, in many lands economic aid only increased the dominance of wealthy elites, while military aid only increased the power of militarists. Democracy spread less quickly than slums and torture. Supporting dictatorships did not even win stability. Just as coercive methods cannot bring permanent peace to a set of nations, so apparently are they liable to bring bitter struggles within a given nation.[33]

By the late 1950s some American leaders saw that the policy was faulty and began experimenting with other approaches. President John F. Kennedy's "Alliance for Progress" aspired to send young idealists and government money to reform the entire social and economic structure of Latin America, making it more receptive to democracy. In the 1970s the United States Congress and President Jimmy Carter focussed on demands that foreign nations respect human rights, putting pressure on undemocratic regimes from Chile to South Africa by reducing military, economic and diplomatic support. In some nations these policies did help bring greater democracy. But in others, most notoriously Iran, the fall of an autocrat led only to worse repression.[34]

When Ronald Reagan became president he proclaimed a global "crusade for freedom," partly because he felt more democracy would promote world peace. The means would be to foster "the infrastructure of democracy, the system of a free press, unions, political parties, universities."[35] Although in fact the Reagan administration gave short shrift to unions and universities, and supported some unsavory governments in the name of anti-Communism, it did work to train democratically-inclined cadres in political skills. Washington put diplomatic and economic pressure on authoritarian leaders, meanwhile reassuring them that a safe way could be found for them through a transition to democracy. These efforts significantly aided the indigenous groups that forced through free elections in the Philippines, El Salvador, South Korea and elsewhere. Above all with the Soviet Union, the Reagan administration combined tough pressure with affable reassurance in a deliberate effort to help leaders and dissidents in their repudiation of authoritarian rule.[36]

And democracy increased. In 1974 the Portuguese liberated themselves; Spain established democracy two years later; in the following decade the movement swept through Latin America, replacing an entire corps of uniformed tyrants with democratic presidents. The movement continued around the world, perhaps most unexpectedly in South Africa. No less surprising, these transitions were mostly without bloodshed, for Gandhi's discovery had become common knowledge. Lech Walesa made the point plainly on his way from rebel workman to elected president of Poland: Through all the arrests and beatings, he boasted, "We did not smash a single windowpane." A wary restraint from punishing former rulers often proved essential for the stability of the new regimes. Where toleration and the search for consensus were genuine, even despots and torturers could safely relinquish power.[37]

Historians will long argue over how much influence the older democracies had in causing these changes. Certainly nothing would have happened but for the intrinsic weaknesses of the juntas and totalitarian parties, and the supreme courage of their domestic opponents. Yet democratic governments had sustained a tireless pressure of diplomatic criticism, reliable information broadcast by the Voice of America and the BBC, and overt economic warfare that cut off nations like South Africa and the Soviet Union from vital markets and technologies. Meanwhile there was the beckoning example of free societies. By now nearly all of the world's wealthiest and most culturally creative nations were democratic.

As a further inducement, most democrats held that international relations would improve precisely insofar as governments became democratic. For example, in 1991 the American Secretary of State warned nations emerging from the ruins of the former Soviet Union that the support the United States gave them would depend on their degree of democracy. A chief reason for backing democracy, he said, was that it would make for peace in the region. The new Russian foreign minister went farther, declaring that "the United States and other Western democracies are as natural friends and eventual allies of the democratic Russia as they were foes of the totalitarian USSR." President George H.W. Bush agreed that "Democrats in the Kremlin can assure our security in a way nuclear missiles never could." After all, as Bush's rival Bill Clinton would declare in his 1994 State of the Union address, "Democracies don't attack each other."[38]

A Few Lessons

Scholars who have studied modern efforts to promote democracy are beginning to draw general lessons.[39] They admit that direct military intervention can succeed, as in Germany and Japan. But the cost is horrendous and the results uncertain. Crusades to impose democracy, from Athenians in the Aegean to Americans in the Caribbean, usually made more enemies than friends. Entrenched elites were not easily cast out, least of all by people who respected civil rights, while intruding foreigners could be so domineering that they discredited democracy itself. Tearing down a government by force also undermines the highly desirable goal of fostering an international political culture of the "republican" sort, where problems are resolved in nonviolent public contestation. These arguments for international restraint mirror the advice that experts offer to groups striving for reform within a nation. Studies of recent attempts to construct democracy show that nonviolent pressure, negotiation and mutual concessions have been far more successful than bloody coups or rebellions.[40]

More than direct military force, republics have tried economic sanctions to push other nations to change. Trade embargoes have been common since the days of the Hanseatic League, but the results have often been ambiguous. A regime under economic pressure may become more authoritarian, or fall to a rebellion that only puts a new dictator in charge. One survey of 120 modern cases of trade sanctions, imposed for a variety of purposes, estimated that only about a third achieved their goals.[41] Still that is something, and a boycott is usually less costly and cruel than an invasion.

A still cheaper, more humane, and more effective method is to foster a free civil society. The idea of helping local efforts in this direction has been developed since 1945 into an arsenal of tools for modifying political culture. It appears that national transformations can be promoted with expenditures trivial by comparison with military budgets. Moral and material support can nourish public-interest groups and publications, training can improve the work of officials from legislative staffs down to neighborhood policemen, poll-watchers can discourage corrupt elections, and so forth. Much of the funds and personnel for this enterprise can be mobilized from private organizations, which rouse less suspicion than national governments. Many such programs are now underway and a great deal more could be done.[42]

Meanwhile at the governmental level democratic leaders need to strike a careful balance of advice, assistance and pressure. Pulling down a dictator may only open the way for a new tyranny; an abrupt lunge toward majority rule may only create conditions for ethnic strife. Outsiders need to help the parties to negotiate revisions in the distribution of power by piecemeal and cautious steps. An outside nation can also offer to guarantee minority rights. None of that will ensure success. Much depends on luck, timing, and the emergence of national leaders blessed with political skill, democratic commitment and true moral quality. Where such leaders can be found, working with them offers democracies high rewards for little risk and expense.[43]

Where conditions are not so propitious we must be cautious. With our ignorance of foreign cultures and our tendency to confuse self-interest with altruism, we can end up doing more harm than good. Besides, people have legitimate purposes in areas remote from civil rights. We are not called upon to press democracy urgently upon a nation that is preoccupied with avoiding economic catastrophe or a collapse into genocidal strife. It might even increase the risk of war to change a somnolent autocracy into an insecure and volatile proto-democracy (especially if neighboring autocracies find democratization a threat).[44] Anyway, for a long time to come many nations will be ruled by dictators and juntas. To keep the peace we must temper the push for democracy while employing more short-term methods of avoiding war, not excluding alliances with despots and the other tools of realpolitik.

Prudently or not, existing democracies will surely keep striving to reproduce their own kind, as so often in the past. The historical record also gives every reason to expect that each new democracy will establish peaceful relationships with the others. As practical consequences, nations within the democratic zone of peace can devote more of their energies to economic expansion, while combining their military efforts on confronting authoritarian regimes.

Nothing in this allows us to sit back and await an automatic triumph. In important nations from Egypt to China it is hard to imagine full democracy any time soon. And as rising populations crash against the barriers of finite ecosystems, entire regions now precariously democratic could fall back into despotism or chaos. Further, new information and behavioral technologies may push even the most stable democracies toward different forms of governance, as yet unsuspected and perhaps unwelcome. If democracy is to survive and expand, many people must devote lifetimes, many must give their very lives, as millions before us have done. The goal is worth the effort. We may already be near a critical point where the preponderance of democracies transforms the entire world system of international relations, eliminating outright war among nations.[45]

Notes

1. Most of the text of this essay is drawn from Spencer Weart, *Never at War: Why Democracies Will Not Fight One Another* (New Haven: Yale University Press, 1998), especially Chapter 15. The book's notes contain more extensive documentation and references. French Assembly: Thomas Carlyle, *The French Revolution* (1837), part 2, book 1, ch. 10.

2. Albert Mathiez, *La Révolution et les étrangers* (Paris: Renaissance, 1918), esp. ch. 6, "crusade" (Brissot, 1791), quoted p. 61; Jacques Godechot, *La Grande nation: L'expansion révolutionnaire de la France dans le monde*

1789-1799 (Paris: Aubier, 1956), 2 vols., esp. vol. 1, chs. 3, 4.

3. John Julius Norwich, *A History of Venice* (New York: Random House, 1989), 2 vols., vol. 2, p. 616-634.

4. Weart, *Never at War.*

5. Inattention even to the American efforts is discussed by Tony Smith, *America's Mission: The United States and the Wordwide Struggle for Democracy in the Twentieth Century* (Princeton, NJ: Princeton University Press, 1994), Appendix, esp. p. 346-348.

6. Thessaly: Xenophon, *A History of My Times (Hellenica),* trans. Rex Warner (New York: Penguin, 1966) 2.3.36. Aristotle, *Politics,* trans. Benjamin Jowett (New York: Random House Modern Library, 1943), 1307b.

7. Treaties: Donald Kagan, *The Outbreak of the Peloponnesian War* (Ithaca, NY: Cornell University Press, 1969), p. 118; Jack Cargill, *The Second Athenian League: Empire or Free Alliance?* (Berkeley: University of California Press, 1981), p. 44, 64-66, 190-191, 263.

8. Demosthenes, *On Organization,* 8-9, in Demosthenes, *Orations and Letters,* Loeb Classical Library, ed. J.H. Vince and A.T. Murray (New York: G.P. Putnam's Sons, 1926-1949).

9. Giovanni Villani, *Cronica di Giovanni Villani* (Florence: Magheri, 1823) 11.48-50, p. 95-100; Matteo Villani, *Cronica di Matteo Villani* (Florence, 1825), 1.77, vol. 1, p. 129-130; Gene A. Brucker, *Florentine Politics and Society 1343-1378* (Princeton: Princeton University Press, 1962), p. 268, 351.

10. Christine Meek, *Lucca, 1369-1404: Politics and Society in an Early Renaissance City-State* (Oxford: Oxford University Press, 1978), p. 140-141.

11. Emile Dürr, *La politique des Confédérés au 14e et au 15e siècle,* vol. 4 of *Histoire Militaire de la Suisse. Part I. 1315-1515. De Morgarten à Marignan* (Berne: Commissariat central des guerres, 1935), ch. 8, "accept everyone" quoted p. 157; Johann Caspar Zellweger, *Geschichte des Appenzellischen Volkes* (St. Gallen: Scheitlin und Zollikosen, 1842), 3 vols., vol. 1, p. 332 ff. See *Klingenberger Chronik,* ed. Anton Henne von Sargans (Gotha: Perthes, 1861) for 1407.

12. "Common cause" London newspaper quoted by Pauline Maier, *From Resistance to Revolution: Colonial Radicals and the Development of American Opposition to Britain, 1765-1776,* (New York: Knopf, 1972), p. 198. Robert R. Palmer, *The Age of the Democratic Revolution: A Political History of Europe and America, 1760-1800,* 2 vols. (Princeton: Princeton University Press, 1964).

13. Speech of 24 April 1793, Maximilien Robespierre, *Oeuvres* (Paris: Presses Universitaires de France, 1910) vol. 9, p. 469. Simon Schama, *Citizens: A Chronicle of the French Revolution* (New York: Knopf, 1989), p. 586-597.

14. Russell Meiggs, *The Athenian Empire* (Oxford: Clarendon, 1972); G.E.M. de Ste. Croix, "Character of the Athenian Empire," *Historia* 3 (1954): 1-41.

15. Lamb quoted Charles K. Webster, "Palmerston and the Liberal Movement, 1830-1841," *Politica* 3 (1938): 299-323, p. 299-300. William L. Langer, *Political and Social Upheaval, 1832-1852* (New York: Harper and Row, 1969), esp. ch. 3.

16. Lawrence C. Jennings, *France and Europe in 1848: A Study of French Foreign Affairs in Time of Crisis* (Oxford: Clarendon, 1973).

17. James M. McPherson, *Abraham Lincoln and the Second American Revolution* (New York: Oxford University Press, 1991), chs. 2, 4; Randall C. Jimerson, *The Private Civil War: Popular Thought During the Sectional Conflict* (Baton Rouge: Louisiana State University Press, 1988), p. 38-49.

18. William Gillette, *Retreat From Reconstruction 1869-1879* (Baton Rouge: Louisiana State University Press, 1979); Eric Foner, *Reconstruction: America's Unfinished Revolution, 1863-1877* (New York: Harper & Row, 1988).

19. Arthur S. Link, *Woodrow Wilson: Revolution, War and Peace* (Arlington Heights, IL: AHM, 1979); Frederick S. Calhoun, *Power and Principle: Armed Intervention in Wilsonian Foreign Policy* (Kent, OH: Kent State University Press, 1986), esp. chs. 4, 5. Speech: Robert H. Ferrell, *Woodrow Wilson and World War I, 1917-1921* (New York: Harper & Row, 1985), p. 1-3.

20. Gordon N. Levin, Jr., *Woodrow Wilson and World Politics. America's Response to War and Revolution* (New York: Oxford University Press, 1968), esp. ch. 7, "dynamite" quoted p. 248.

21. David Healy, *Drive to Hegemony: The United States in the Caribbean, 1898-1917* (Madison: University of Wisconsin Press, 1988); Lester D. Langley, *America*

and the Americas: The United States in the Western Hemisphere (Athens: University of Georgia Press, 1989); Walter LaFeber, *The American Age: United States Foreign Policy at Home and Abroad since 1750* (New York: W.W. Norton, 1989).

22. Richard V. Salisbury, "Good Neighbors? The United States and Latin America in the Twentieth Century," in *American Foreign Relations. A Historiographical Review.*, ed. Gerald K. Haines and J. Samuel Walker (Westport, CT: Greenwood, 1981), p. 311-333.

23. Theodore Paul Wright, Jr., *American Support of Free Elections Abroad* (Washington DC: Public Affairs Press, 1964).

24. Arthur Hearnden, ed., *The British in Germany: Educational Reconstruction after 1945* (London: Hamish Hamilton, 1978), p. 77, 101, 108-130.

25. Joshua Muravchik, *Exporting Democracy: Fulfilling America's Destiny* (Washington, DC: American Enterprise Institute, 1991), esp. ch. 8; Edward N. Peterson, *The American Occupation of Germany: Retreat to Victory* (Detroit: Wayne State University Press, 1977); Richard B. Finn, *Winners in Peace: MacArthur, Yoshida and Postwar Japan* (Berkeley: University of California Press, 1992).

26. MacArthur quoted in Toshio Nishi, *Unconditional Democracy, Education and Politics in Occupied Japan, 1945-1952* (Stanford: Hoover Institution, 1982), p. 193 and Muravchik, *Exporting Democracy*, p. 100.

27. Hermann-Josef Rupieper, *Der Wurzeln der westdeutschen Nachkriegsdemocratie: Der amerikanische Beitrag 1945-1952* (Opladen: Westdeutscher, 1993); Jeffrey M. Diefendorf, Axel Frohm and Herman-Josef Rupierer, *American Policy and the Reconstruction of the West* (Washington, DC: German Historical Institute, 1993).

28. David P. Conradt, "Changing German Political Culture," in *The Civic Culture Revisited*, ed. Gabriel A. Almond and Sidney Verba (Boston: Little, Brown, 1980), p. 212-272; Kendall Barker, Russell Dalton and Kai Hildebrandt, *Germany Transformed. Political Culture and the New Politics* (Cambridge, MA: Harvard University Press, 1981).

29. Paul Ginsborg, *A History of Contemporary Italy. Society and Politics, 1943-1988* (New York: Penguin, 1990), p. 64-70, 115-118 and chs. 2, 3; Antonio Gambino, *Storia del dopoguerra. Dalla Liberazione al potere DC* (Rome-Bari: Laterza, 1975), esp. 446-457.

30. James Morris, *Heaven's Command. An Imperial Progress* (San Diego: Harcourt Brace Jovanovich, 1973), p. 278.

31. Phillip Darby, *Three Faces of Imperialism. British and American Approaches to Asia and Africa, 1870-1970* (New Haven, CT: Yale University Press, 1987); Kenneth Robinson, *The Dilemmas of Trusteeship: Aspects of British Colonial Policy Between the Wars* (London: Oxford University Press, 1965).

32. Prosser Gifford and William Roger Lewis, ed., *Decolonization and African Independence: The Transfers of Power, 1960-1980* (New Haven: Yale University Press, 1988); Henri Grimal, *Decolonization: The British, French, Dutch and Belgian Empires, 1919-1963*, trans. Stephen De Vos (Boulder, CO: Westview, 1978); Donald L. Horowitz, *Ethnic Groups in Conflict* (Berkeley: University of California Press, 1985), ch. 11 and p. 186-194; Samuel P. Huntington, *The Third Wave: Democratization in the Late Twentieth Century* (Norman: University of Oklahoma Press, 1991), ch. 1.

33. For pioneering exploration of this and related issues see R.J. Rummel, "Freedom, Democracy, Peace; Power, Democide, and War," http://www.hawaii.edu/powerkills.

34. Stephen G. Rabe, *Eisenhower and Latin America: The Foreign Policy of Anticommunism* (Chapel Hill: University of North Carolina Press, 1988), chs. 6, 8; Joshua Muravchik, *The Uncertain Crusade: Jimmy Carter and the Dilemmas of Human Rights Policy* (Lanham, MD: Hamilton, 1986); Smith, *America's Mission*, esp. chs. 8-9; Gaddis Smith, *Morality, Reason, and Power: American Diplomacy in the Carter Years* (New York: Hill and Wang, 1986).

35. "Crusade": 8 June 1982, in U.S. Dept. of State, *American Foreign Policy. Current Documents* (Washington, DC: U.S. Govt. Printing Office, 1982), p. 14-20.

36. Thomas Carothers, *In the Name of Democracy: U.S. Policy Toward Latin America in the Reagan Years* (Berkeley: University of California Press, 1991); Abraham F. Lowenthal, ed., *Exporting Democracy: The United States and Latin America* (Baltimore: Johns Hopkins University Press, 1991).

37. Walesa quoted by Daniel Patrick Moynihan, *On*

the Law of Nations (Cambridge, MA: Harvard University Press, 1990), p. 125.

38. "Natural friends:" Andrei Kozyrev (1991) quoted in his "The Lagging Partnership," *Foreign Affairs* 73 (1994): 59-71, p. 59. "Assure our security:" Bush quoted by James A. Baker 3rd, *New York Times*, 5 Aug. 1992. Clinton: *New York Times*, 26 Jan. 1994. See also Bruce Russett, *Grasping the Democratic Peace: Principles for a Post-Cold War World* (Princeton, NJ: Princeton University Press, 1993), p. 128-129.

39. Lowenthal, ed., *Exporting Democracy*; Muravchik, *Exporting Democracy*; Giuseppe Di Palma, *To Craft Democracies: An Essay on Democratic Transitions* (Berkeley: University of California Press, 1990); National Research Council. Commission on Behavioral and Social Sciences and Education, *The Transition to Democracy: Proceedings of a Workshop* (Washington, DC: National Academy Press, 1991); Guillermo O'Donnell, Phillippe C. Schmitter and Laurence Whitehead, eds., *Transitions from Authoritarian Rule: Prospects for Democracy* (Baltimore: Johns Hopkins University Press, 1986), Part IV.

40. Huntington, *Third Wave*, p. 192-207 and chs. 3, 4.

41. Gary Clyde Hufbauer, Jeffery J. Schott and Kimberly Ann Elliot, *Economic Sanctions Reconsidered: History and Current Policy*, 2nd ed. (Washington, DC: Institute for Economic Relations, 1990).

42. Muravchik, *Exporting Democracy*; Larry Diamond, "Promoting Democracy," *Foreign Policy* no. 87 (Summer 1992): 25-46.

43. Huntington, *Third Wave*; Stanley Kober, "Idealpolitik," *Foreign Policy* 79 (1990): 3-24; Horowitz, *Ethnic Groups*, esp. p. 570-571, 681-684; Douglas J. Macdonald, *Adventures in Chaos: American Intervention for Reform in the Third World* (Cambridge, MA: Harvard University Press, 1992), esp. p. 277-282.

44. Edward D. Mansfield and Jack Snyder, "Democratization and the Danger of War," *International Security* 20, no. 1 (Summer 1995): 5-38, and Reinhard Wolf et al., "Correspondence: Democratization and the Danger of War," *International Security* 20, no. 4 (Spring 1996): 176-207.

45. George Modelski and Gardner Perry III, "Democratization in Long Perspective," *Technological Forecasting and Social Change* 39 (1991): 23-34; Russett, *Grasping the Democratic Peace*, esp. p. 132-138; Huntington, *Third Wave*, ch. 6.

Implementing the Institutions of Democracy: A Blessing or Threat?

Minxin Pei
Carnegie Endowment for International Peace

The most important political development in the last quarter of the twentieth century has been, without doubt, the global movement toward democratic rule. Termed the "third wave" of democratization by the eminent political scientist Samuel Huntington, this great transition began in the early 1970s in Southern Europe, swept to Latin America and East Asia in the 1980s, and culminated in the collapse of the Soviet empire and the births of numerous democratic states in Eastern Europe and parts of the former Soviet Union in the early 1990s.[1] Although the momentum of the "third wave" appeared to have since slowed down considerably as fewer countries made the transition toward democracy, the global movement toward democratic rule, coinciding with the acceleration of economic globalization after the Cold War, was beginning to reach regions where conditions for the emergence of democratic institutions had long thought to be inhospitable.[2]

Many factors contributed to the democratic surge in the last three decades.[3] Of course, different factors played varying roles in the democratic transitions of different countries. For instance, economic success might have contributed to the emergence of democratic regimes in South Korea, Taiwan, Thailand, and Chile while economic failures helped undermine the legitimacy of many autocracies (such as in the Philippines, the former Soviet bloc, most parts of Latin America and Africa). Generally speaking, however, democratic transition is most likely to occur as a result of three factors:

Table 1: Electoral Democracies in the World

	Total Countries	Democracies	Democracies as a Percentage of Total
1974	145	39	26.9
1990	165	76	46.1
2000	192	120	62.5

Source: Freedom House, *Freedom in the World*, Various Years

1. Economic and Social Development

Closely identified with modernization theory, the idea that economic and social development may lead to the emergence of democracy has influenced generations of scholars and policy-makers. Central to this idea is the belief, supposed by historical examples and empirical evidence, that rising levels of economic well-being would create the conditions conducive to democratic governance.[4] Although the mechanisms through which economic development may contribute to democracy remain a subject of debate, scholars have identified the impact of economic modernization on class structure as the key link. Most importantly, the rise of a middle-class as a result of economic development is considered the most crucial social requisite for democracy.[5] Additionally, economic development may enhance the autonomy and power of civil society by creating the material resources necessary for social pluralism and widespread accessibility of information.[6]

However, the modernization theory can explain, at best, only a relatively small group of countries that underwent democratic transition in the late twentieth century. For the most part, these countries are located in East Asia and, until hit by the East Asian financial crisis in 1997, experienced sustained high economic growth.[7] A closer look shows that even the East Asian story is mixed: while the transition to democracy in Thailand, Taiwan, and South Korea took place after successful economic development in these countries created most of the social and economic conditions favorable to democratic rule, the same transition occurred in the Philippines and Indonesia largely as a result of the failure of the autocratic regime to develop.[8] Indeed, the majority of democratic transitions in the third wave elsewhere in the world appeared to be the result of development failures, rather than development success. For example, the regime transitions in Latin America occurred mostly because the military dictatorships were proved incapable of dealing with the debt crisis in the 1980s. In turn, the countries in the region suffered a decade of economic stagnation.

2. Elite Decision

The poor applicability of the modernization theory to the third-wave transitions led to the rise of theories that held elite decision-making and elite preferences as the key factor in regime transition.[9] The core idea is that the decisions made by the authoritarian rulers play the most fundamental role in a democratic transition process. Such decisions are unlikely to be influenced by structural conditions, such as the level of development or the size of the middle-class. Rather, factors such as the division within the ruling elite, the dynamics of the initial political opening, and the prospects of post-transition stability weigh heavily on the minds of the ruling elite. Thus, some scholars have proposed the argument that democratic transition is determined by elite decision, while the durability of democracy may depend on economic conditions.[10]

3. Foreign Intervention

Democracies may also be installed through foreign intervention. Historically, foreign (military) intervention played the dominant role in ousting dictatorial regimes and establishing democracies (the best examples are Japan, Germany, and Italy following the defeat of the fascist regimes in the Second World War). During the third wave, military intervention became only one of the forms of foreign intervention in fostering democracy in developing countries, as in the case of Panama and Haiti. However, other forms of foreign intervention have gained importance in recent years. During the transition stage, foreign financial assistance helped opposition forces to gain power (for example, in Portugal, Serbia and Nicaragua); American withdrawal of support for the autocratic rulers at the eleventh hour also dealt a death blow to the old regime and sealed its fate (as in the case of the Philippines). The importance of foreign intervention becomes more critical in the consolidation phase, as new democracies struggle to establish functioning political institutions, such as an effective legal system.

Democracy, Peace, and Good Governance

The international community's support for democracies in developing countries is based on many considerations. For instance, geopolitics played a role in the West's support for democracies in certain parts of the world during the Cold War when supporting democracy was compatible with the West's strategy of containing the Soviet Union. Unfortunately, the same set of strategic concerns also led the West to a policy of inconsistency in the support of democracies. In the post-Cold War era, supporting democracies has gained greater importance as the collapse of the Soviet Union removed the Soviet threat and allowed the West to focus greater efforts on democratic promotion. Two theories underlie the West's strategy of democratic promotion. First, the establishment of democracies around the world is considered conducive to world peace because liberal democracies do not wage war with each other. Second, democracies are thought to have the more effective political institutions for economic development and good governance.

1. The Democratic Peace Theory

To be sure, the idea that democratic institutions established within the borders of sovereign countries may ensure peace between countries with similar institutions is not new. At the end of the eighteenth century, Kant speculated that nations would naturally develop into liberal states as they struggle to achieve security. In turn, trade, cultural interaction, and the disincentives of warfare would provide an impetus for the creation of a mutually beneficial "pacific union."[11] But the crystallization of this seminal idea into a theory of international relations did not take place until the 1980s. Michael Doyle's influential work on the subject inspired new research aimed at understanding how democratic institutions actually promote peace.[12] According to Doyle, historical evidence suggests that democratic states enjoy peace among themselves but have demonstrated a willingness to fight against autocratic states in defense of liberal values. Building upon Doyle's work, Bruce Russett proposes that liberalism develops and institutionalizes norms that are conducive to peaceful relations among nations. Based on historical case studies, Russett identified the end of the nineteenth century in general, and the "special relationship" between Britain and the United States in particular, as the beginning of the consolidation of such norms in international affairs. However, Russett's work modifies Doyle's "democratic peace" claim. If interstate war is defined as conflict resulting in more than 1,000 casualties, Russett's research finds that democracies rarely engage in *large-scale* warfare with one another.[13]

The "democratic peace" theory has also met its own skeptics. Some scholars question the methodologies with which the theory was developed.[14] Others dispute the direct linkage between democratic institutions and peaceful norms assumed by the proponents of the theory. National interest is found to be a more reliable predicator of a democratic nation's willingness to wage war.[15] Still others suggest that "democratic peace" may be a historical accident—one created by balance of power rather than ascendance of liberal values. Henry Farber and Joanne Gowa note that, although the probability of disputes is lower between democratic states in the twentieth century, democracies fought more often than autocracies before 1914. "Democratic peace" did not prevail until after 1945. This was primarily a shift in national interests that made it useful for the Western nations to ignore their differences and ally against the Soviet Union.[16]

Despite academic disputes regarding the validity of the "democratic peace" theory, expanding democracies around the world became one of the top foreign policy priorities of the West, especially the United States in the 1990s. Indeed, top U.S. government foreign policy-makers in the Clinton administration explicitly linked the promotion of democracies in developing countries with vital American national interest. In their justification of this strategic change in American foreign policy, U.S. policy-makers provided a detailed argument as to why the spread of democratic regimes around the world would advance key American interests in the protection of human rights, economic development, and international peace.[17] The "enlargement of democracy" strategy was viewed as the centerpiece of the "Clinton doctrine."[18]

2. Democracy and Good Governance

The establishment of democratic institutions may also produce practical benefits for the countries that adopt them. Such benefits may come in various forms, such as less corruption in government, better protection of human rights, and greater economic prosperity. The work by Amartya Sen has made a powerful case that political rights protected under democratic institutions can drastically improve the well-being of average citizens.[19] The argument that democratic governance, which fosters political competition and public participation in the political process, should help contain corruption seems quite persuasive. The world's most corrupt regimes in recent years, which include Marcos in the Philippines, the Duvaliers in Haiti, Mobutu regime in the former Zaire, and Suharto in Indonesia, were all dictatorships that had degenerated into kleptocracies. Theory and evidence both support the view that democracies, which have by definition real opposition forces, organized civil society groups, and a watchful press, are unlikely to allow such predatory regimes to survive for so long and plunder their countries so thoroughly. Researchers who have used extensive data to analyze various factors that may contribute or curb corruption conclude that civil liberties and their institutional manifestations (such as a free press and vigorous civil society) play an important role in explaining the variations in the degree of corruption across nations: countries with higher degrees of civil liberties are found to have less corrupt government.[20] Of course, there are significant variations in the level of good governance achieved by democracies across countries. Generally speaking, however, established democratic regimes are perceived to be less corrupt than newly democratized ones.[21]

The argument that democracy promotes development rests on the central idea that the political institutions critical to economic development are more likely to exist and function effectively under democratic rule. These institutions include the rule of law, which protects property rights; individual liberties that foster creativity and entrepreneurship; freedom of expression, which ensures the production and unimpeded flow of information; and institutional checks and balance that prevent the massive theft of public wealth often observed in autocracies.[22] One statistical study of growth data for 115 countries from 1960 to 1980 claims that countries with high degrees of political openness achieved an average annual real per capita growth rate of 2.53 percent, compared with 1.41 percent in more closed political systems. This implies that democratic countries grow 80 percent faster than less democratic ones.[23] Other statistical studies, however, have yielded more ambiguous conclusions.[24]

Implementing Democratic Institutions: Risks, Failures, and Unfulfilled Promises

Although few would deny the long-term benefits of democratic institutions, many are justifiably concerned with both the short-term risks involved in regime transition and the difficulties in making democracy work in countries where democratic institutions, such as electoral systems, political parties, rule of law, mechanisms of accountability, checks and balances, and civil society groups, remain relatively weak and will need a long period of time to consolidate. No doubt, a small group of countries is able to achieve such consolidation within less than a decade and has begun to reap the substantial rewards from democratization, such as improvement in human rights, greater accountability of government, better governance, membership in the world's democratic community, increasing attractiveness to foreign investors, and domestic political stability. Among the Eastern European countries that made the transition following the collapse of the Soviet Empire, Hungary, Poland, and the Czech Republic are the success stories. In Latin America, Brazil and Chile are the shining examples of the democratic triumph. East Asia, South Korea, Thailand, Taiwan and, to a slightly lesser extent, the Philippines, have made tremendous progress toward consolidating democratic institutions since their transitions in the 1980s.

However, the story of implementing democratic institutions around the world is not one of unambiguous triumph. Instead, the record is decidedly mixed. Whereas successful democratic transition and consolidation may vindicate the strategy that democracy promotion serves the long-term interests of Western democracies, transitional breakdowns, failures of democratic consolidation, and perversion of democratic institutions in transition regimes should argue for a more cautious and selective approach to the expansion of democracy around the world.

1. Democratization and Interstate Conflict

The process of regime change—the fundamental restructuring of power relations between the state and society as well as within the state itself—is itself often destabilizing and likely increases the danger of war. Consequently, democratic transition is fraught with risks of instability and conflict.[25] Democracy may bring peace among nations, but democratization could cause war, both among and within nations. Edward Mansfield and Jack Snyder argue that democratizing states are unstable and therefore have a greater propensity for external war. The risks of war may be low during the initial stages of regime change; but the likelihood of warfare increases over the next decade after transition.[26] Historically, cases of democratizing states that initiated major wars included Weimar Germany and Taisho Japan. More recently, wars among some of the former Soviet republics (Armenia against Azerbaijan; Russia against Chechnya), and among former Yugoslav republics (Croatia against Serbia, for instance) may also count as examples. The statistical analysis performed by Mansfield and Snyder suggests that the probability of interstate war may increase by 50 to 135 percent when an autocracy undergoes a regime transition to democracy. In addition to interstate war, democratization may also lead to civil war, most often ethnic conflict. According to Mansfield and Snyder, the probability of any type of warfare during a regime transition from autocracy to democracy can increases by 35 to 105 percent.[27] The case of East Timor, where a democratizing Indonesia failed to prevent a brutal suppression of the East Timorese independence movement by the Indonesian armed forces and their proxies in East Timor, is a sad but apt example.

Mansfield and Snyder identify two principal causes that make the process of democratization a dangerous period for war. First, the ruling elites of the autocratic regimes whose survival is in doubt resort to nationalist appeals in order to gain public support.[28] Thus, foreign policy (and in many cases, domestic policies toward ethnic minorities) is hijacked by these elites to serve their narrow political interests. Although it is unlikely that the surviving elites of the autocratic regime are initially bent on war, because war is a high risk undertaking and a defeat could spell the end of the regime, the politics of nationalism is often so volatile that, once the ruling elites' initial appeal succeeds in gaining mass support, a vicious cycle may set in and lead to a course of events completely unanticipated and uncontrollable by the same elites.

Second, the weakness of political institutions in democratizing regimes may also contribute to the outbreak of violence. Ruling elites often succeed in exploiting such weaknesses to acquire political power, enhance their legitimacy, and implement policies that make war more likely.[29] In established democracies, the effectiveness of checks and balances, vigilance of opposition parties, an independent and skeptical press, and dissenting voices from civil society groups are likely to form a powerful countervailing force against nationalist demagogues. However, in a democratizing regime, the likelihood of institutional failure can be high, especially when a populist leader skillfully manages to use public opinion to overcome institutional resistance to his belligerent policies. Thus, those mechanisms designed and established to curb the power of the government (particularly the executive branch) frequently fail to do so during transition, often with disastrous consequences for peace.

2. Democratization and Internal Conflicts

In addition to the increasing likelihood of interstate conflict during democratic transition, internal conflicts may also erupt in a regime transition process. In the post-Cold War era, the declining appeal of political ideologies has made traditional armed clashes between the left and the right quite rare. Indeed, with the exceptions of Colombia and Nepal, insurgency movements based on Marxist ideologies have become almost extinct in the developing world. However, replacing class-based political ideologies is an equally powerful ideology centered on ethnic or national identities, commonly labeled as ethno-nationalism. In many cases, such ethno-nationalism is also colored by religious beliefs, a combination that makes its appeal doubly potent. As a result, the most common form of conflict in democratizing states in recent years is ethnic strife.[30]

Ethnic conflicts are more likely to occur in a democratizing state for several reasons. The repressive policies pursued by the departing autocratic regimes against ethnic minorities have often created a legacy of inter-ethnic hostility and an environment conducive to the emergence of radical ethno-nationalist movements. Ethnic divisions were merely frozen, rather than erased, under autocratic rule. The removal of autocratic governments may help release long-simmering ethnic resentments in multi-ethnic societies.[31] During democratic transition, such hostility tends to find violent expression in the form of ethnic conflict. Under autocratic rule, few ethnic minorities have access to the political process or are permitted to articulate and advance their interests through legitimate channels. Therefore, the democratization process becomes a rare opportunity for such minorities to break away from a polity in which their rights and interests are unprotected. During the initial stages of democratic transition, ethnic minorities that have long suffered socio-economic hardship and institutionalized discrimination are usually receptive to nationalistic/ethnic sentiment. Ethno-nationalist elite then typically attempt to manipulate ethnic identity (often through the newly liberalized media) to mobilize support and resources. At the same time, however, semi-open political process and elite-imposed restrictions do not allow genuine democratic participation that would have provided an outlet of ethnic frustrations. This manufactured nationalism may spill over into outright ethnic conflict.[32]

In most cases, states undergoing democratic transition lack the institutional mechanisms to produce political accommodations acceptable to all sides. Additional complications arise when ethnic secessionist movements have armed insurgency organizations regarded as "terrorists" by the dominant ethnic majorities (as in the case of Yugoslavia's Kosovo and Indonesia's East Timor and Aceh). The failure of peaceful separation results in outbreak of intense ethnic conflict. Lastly, democratic transition may occur as a result of the collapse of the autocratic regime. Under these circumstances, state failure is most likely (the most illustrative example is the collapse of the Mubuto regime in Zaire). One tragic consequence of state failure is the eruption of large-scale violence as ethnic groups compete for power.[33]

3. The "Quality" Issue for New Democracies

One of the most vexing issues in democratic consolidation is the "quality" of new democratic governance. Transitions to democracy in developing countries do not necessarily lead to measurable improvement in governance. Indeed, ruling elites in newly democratized states often pervert democratic institutions in order to protect their parochial interests and shield their power from the scrutiny of the public and constitutional constraints. Therefore, the third wave of democratization has led to the rise of "illiberal democracies" or "delegative democracies"—political systems that have flawed elections, populist leaders unaccountable to legislatures, a weak rule of law, and poor protection of civil liberties.[34] One prominent political analyst claimed that about one-third of all democracies in the early 1990s should be considered "illiberal."[35]

The emergence of illiberal or delegative democracies poses a serious problem to the international community. While such democratic regimes may enjoy some form of popular legitimacy through relatively free elections, their institutional practices do not qualify them as full democracies for the following three reasons.

First, most such democracies lack what the political scientist Guillermo O'Donnell called "horizontal accountability"—a system of institutional checks and balances that hold the executive branch not only accountable to the voters, but also to the legislature, the courts, and the media.[36] The lack of horizontal accountability may stem both from institutional and leadership failures. Institutionally, new democracies have only vague boundaries defining the powers of various branches of the government. In most cases, even when such power may be defined clearly on paper, the actual mechanisms of enforcement do not exist, allowing opportunistic political leaders to trespass on the prerogatives of other institutions. Poorly defined institutional boundaries also make it difficult for various branches of the government to hold each other accountable since the source of their power to do so remains unclear and thus questionable. Weak opposition parties further reduce the incentives for ruling parties to be accountable. For example, in the case of Uganda, the country's new political system was, effectively, a "no-party democracy" that granted its democratically elected president unimpeded power.[37] Leadership failures are thus closely linked to institutional failures because flawed institutions create incentives for politicians to violate democratic procedures with immunity. A frequent political outcome of low horizontal accountability is a strong presidency. In many cases, strong presidents, such as Boris Yeltsin in Russia, Alberto Fujimori in Peru, Hugo Chavez in Venezuela, and their counterparts in the former Soviet republics in Central Asia, routinely bypass or even ride roughshod over their legislatures. Abuses of constitutional power are more likely in president-dominated systems than in parliamentary ones. A large number of "third-wave" transition states, such as Belarus, Peru, Ukraine, and nearly all Central Asian republics, have degenerated into semi-authoritarian regimes principally because presidents in these countries misused their lightly constrained constitutional powers in undermining the democratic process, persecuting the opposition, and maintaining a network of corrupt political supporters inside the government.

Second, illiberal democracies have a poor record in protecting human rights. According to Zakaria, a hallmark of illiberal democracies is that, in the Freedom House freedom index, such countries score better on "political rights" (which typically means electoral rights) than on "civil liberties."[38] In practical terms, press freedom, rights of free association, religious freedom, and rights of ethnic minorities are inadequately protected. For example, president Vladimir Putin of Russia used the strong arm of the state to prosecute the owners of independent Russian media establishments in order to consolidate his hold on power, and managed to eliminate all the independently owned television networks in Russia by the end of 2001. Russia's war in Chechnya also resulted in the deaths of thousands of innocent civilians. Similar repression of press freedom also occurred in Ukraine under President Leonid Kuchma. In some countries, rulers of illiberal democracies directly resorted to political violence in order to vanquish their opposition, as was observed in Kenya in the mid-1990s. Such practices effectively turn these regimes into "dictablandars"—authoritarian regimes that, in the view of Philippe Schimitter, "introduce democratic mechanisms into their polities in order to placate international forces demanding democratization."[39]

Finally, the introduction of political participation in new democracies does not always automatically bring about the empowerment of ordinary people, especially those social groups that occupy disadvantaged and marginal positions in the political system. More specifically, in new democracies, elected leaders usually lack the political power to introduce meaningful social and economic reforms in order to remedy the socio-economic inequities in their societies. At a deeper level, the existence and institutionalization of such inequities mean that newly enfranchised citizens do not possess the economic resources to be full members of the political community. On the other hand, social elites, such as large landowners and family-controlled industrial and commercial conglomerates enjoy special access to the new democratic ruling elite (mainly through their political donations and other favors). As a result, such democracies risk becoming effective oligarchies.[40]

Implementing Democratic Institutions: Examples and Lessons from the Recent Past

The recent historical record of implementing democratic institutions in various parts of the world is decidedly mixed. There have been cases where the process of democratic transition unfolded peacefully and consolidation of democratic rule was achieved within a decade, such as Spain, Portugal, South Korea, Taiwan, Thailand, Chile, Brazil, Argentina, the Czech Republic, Poland, and Hungary. Democratic transition also has failed spectacularly, most notably in Haiti and Albania. In between lies a large number of ambiguous cases where the emerging democratic rule is marred by institutional and leadership failures.

1. Success: Democratic Transition and Consolidation in Taiwan

Taiwan's transformation from an authoritarian regime to a democratic one has spawned a large number of studies.[41] Taiwan's democratic transition began in the late 1970s, with an informal opposition group winning one-third of the vote in the 1977 elections of provincial assemblymen and city councilors. Despite a brief crackdown on the opposition movement in 1979, the ruling Kuomintang Party continued to permit the informal opposition group to compete in national and local election. The breakthrough in Taiwan's transition occurred in 1986 when the Democratic Progressive Party (DPP) was founded despite the government's ban on political parties and participated in elections to the national legislature at the end of that year as a formal opposition party. The establishment of the DPP and, significantly, the KMT's decision not to suppress it, marked a new chapter in Taiwan's political development. In the following year, martial law and a ban on political parties were lifted. The pace of transition accelerated in the 1990s. In December 1991 a competitive election created a new National Assembly. The transition to democratic rule entered the consolidation phase in April-May 1992 after the National Assembly passed key amendments to the constitution, paving the way for many important institutional reforms.

The consolidation phase in Taiwan began in the early 1990s with several rounds of constitutional reform and increase in party competition.[42] These constitutional reforms produced a mixed presidential-parliamentary system and strengthened the role of the judiciary. The most significant process in consolidation, however, occurred in the arena of inter-party competition. During the 1990s, the long-dominant ruling KMT party rapidly lost political strength, while the island's main opposition party, the DPP, gained political support on a broad front, measured in terms of both the share of popular votes captured in various elections and the number administrative and legislative positions won in each round of elections. Eventually, the ruling KMT split—three times. The self-destruction of the ruling party, which in retrospect appeared to be engineered in no small part by its own top leader, Lee Teng-hui, greatly aided the rise of the DPP as a credible alternative to the KMT. Thus, in the presidential election of 2000, the DPP's candidate won a three-way race. In the parliamentary elections in 2001, the DPP claimed the largest number of seats in the legislature (although it failed to win an outright majority). The replacement of the KMT by the DPP in both the executive and legislative branches marked the completion of the consolidation of democracy in Taiwan.[43]

Taiwan's democratic transition and consolidation, when compared with the experience of many other countries, stands out as a success story mainly because this process was characterized by stability and gradualism. Moderation prevailed both in the ruling and opposition parties, party competition gradually rose, civil society grew, legal institutions improved, and human rights were protected. In the meantime, Taiwan managed to maintain an impressive economic performance record (until the global slow-down of 2001).

Four factors greatly contributed to Taiwan's success in implementing democratic institutions.

Favorable socio-economic factors that resulted from Taiwan's sustained rapid economic development since the 1950s: The economic and social transformation of Taiwan produced a large middle-class, distributed economic wealth to autonomous sectors of society, enhanced the influence of an increasingly independent mass media, and fostered the growth of a civil society.[44]

Political factors: Unlike the Chinese Communist Party (CCP) on the mainland, the KMT in Taiwan was not ideologically opposed to democracy. Its official ideology, the "Three Principles of the People," defined democracy as a goal of the regime.[45] The absence of ideological constraints gave the KMT more flexibility to pursue political opening. In addition, Taiwan's authoritarian system contained a few semi-democratic institutional enclaves, such as local self-government and elections. The most important of these was the institution of semi-competitive local elections established in the late 1950s. The KMT's initial motivation for holding such elections originated from its dire need to establish a basis of popular legitimacy on an island where its early policy failures and brutal rule had thoroughly alienated the native Taiwanese population. However, even limited electoral institutions produced an important long-term impact. Semi-open elections allowed ambitious elements—within the KMT and outside it—a legally sanctioned channel to compete for power, which gradually resulted in the weakening of the KMT and the rise of independent politicians. The practice of local elections also eventually forced the KMT to open up national political institutions (such as the Legislative Yuan) to elections. Electoral processes provided Taiwan's incipient opposition movement with a valuable mechanism to gain popular support, acquire campaign experience, and fine-tune their message. Semi-open elections gave the ruling regime both short-term benefits (a limited degree of legitimacy) and a sense of security: as the KMT learned how to use the electoral mechanism to control and contain political opposition, it less frequently resorted to more brutal means of repression and gradually became a soft-authoritarian regime.[46]

Convergence of democratic yearnings and ethnic tensions: A unique characteristic of the democratic transition in Taiwan is its ethnic dimension. Ethnic tensions both within the regime and between the regime and the opposition were an important factor in Taiwan's transition. In many ways, the democratic yearnings of Taiwanese society coincided with the rise of Taiwanese ethnic identity and the demand to seize power from the mainlander-dominated KMT regime.[47] Ironically, the KMT's own program of "Taiwanization" (the co-optation of native-born elites), which was implemented in the 1970s, greatly contributed to the convergence of ethnic identity and political mobilization, and eventually enabled many Taiwanese elites to be well positioned to challenge the mainlanders inside the KMT during the transition. Native Taiwanese elites constituted the opposition DPP in 1989.[48] The strong Taiwanese identity of the opposition movement provided a rare cohesive force to the fledgling DPP and helped it to meet its initial challenges. At the same time, the rising Taiwanese elite within the KMT deftly capitalized on the strong sentiments of Taiwanese identity among the population to defeat the more conservative mainlanders inside the

KMT. This two-pronged attack on the old KMT power structure quickly led to the unchallenged dominance of Taiwanese elites in the top echelons of power.[49]

External factors: Taiwan's transition seems to have benefited from both worldwide and regional trends of democratization that began in the mid-1970s in Southern Europe and later spread to Latin America and East Asia. In the case of Taiwan, the opposition movement received direct and indirect support from the U.S. Congress and Taiwanese immigrant communities in the United States. Fear of loss of American support also constrained the ruling KMT's hand in dealing with the opposition. In a geopolitical sense, Taiwan's leaders seemed to believe that a democratizing Taiwan would be more likely to gain international, especially American, support in its rivalry with the undemocratic and increasingly powerful mainland. Indeed, Taiwan reaped enormous security and political benefits (such as procurement of high-tech weapons systems from the United States and France and American Congressional support for Taiwan's security) from its democratic transition.

2. Failure: Democratic Transition in Haiti

The American-led international efforts to build democracy in Haiti in the mid-1990s must be considered the West's most ambitious undertaking to implement democratic institutions in a society where socio-economic and political conditions are highly inhospitable to such efforts. One of the most impoverished nations in the Western Hemisphere, Haiti's per capita GDP was $250 a year, and about three quarters of its population (over 7 million) were illiterate. Decades of misrule under the Duvalier family dictatorship left the island with little industrial development and a subsistence-based agrarian economy. Unemployment typically hovered around 75 to 80 percent.[50] The basic political infrastructure of the state, such as the courts, the bureaucracy, and public service delivery systems, were either decrepit or non-existent.

Additionally, the democratic transition in Haiti began under the most inauspicious circumstances. In theory, transitions from authoritarian rule are more likely to succeed where state-society power is more balanced, the authority of the state is preserved during transition, and moderates within and outside the regime prevail over hard-line conservatives and radicals.[51] Unfortunately, these favorable conditions did not exist in Haiti. The long-ruling Duvalier regime collapsed suddenly in February 1986; the transition from authoritarian rule thus began in a political vacuum. This allowed both hard-liners within the regime, as represented by the military, and the radicals opposing the old regime, to seize the political agenda. Haitian politics became polarized toward the end of the 1980s while signs of instability were abundant (for example, Haiti had five different governments from 1986 to 1990). Thus, even the decisive electoral victory by Jean-Betrand Aristide in the presidential election of December 1990 failed to resolve the political impasse. Barely eight months into his term, Aristide was ousted by a military junta supported by the Haitian business and social elites who were fearful of Aristide's leftist ideological rhetoric.

The military coup in Haiti, which took place amid the high tide of the third wave of global democratization, was viewed as totally unacceptable by the international community. Further compounding the issue was the flood of Haitian refugees who were forced to flee the country for the United States because of the repressive policies of the ruling junta and the paramilitary groups it had unleashed on the Haitian society. The refugee crisis, Haiti's worsening political situation and increasing domestic political pressure from human rights groups and African-American leaders forced U.S. President Bill Clinton to intervene militarily to restore Aristide back to power (despite the widespread anti-intervention sentiments among the American public). In September 1994, three years after he was forced into exile from Haiti, Aristide returned to Haiti's presidential palace with the help of 20,000 U.S. soldiers. Following the American

Table 2: Political Rights and Civil Liberties in Haiti: 1994-2000

	Political Rights	Civil Liberties	Status
1994	7	7	NF
1995	5	5	PF
1996	5	5	PF
1997	4	5	PF
1998	4	5	PF
1999	5	5	PF
2000	5	5	PF

NF = Not free; PF = Partly free

Source: Freedom House, *Freedom in the World*, various years

military intervention, the international community poured more than $2 billion in economic, humanitarian, and political development aid into Haiti ($50 million alone in support to hold elections).

The Haitian experience in democratic consolidation since the return of Aristide is generally regarded as a failure.[52] Several indicators support this bleak assessment. First, although Haiti is no longer a society ruled by armed thugs, the conditions of political rights and civil liberties have improved only modestly since the return of American-imposed democracy in 1994. According to the rankings by the Freedom House, Haiti belongs to the "partly free" category. Toward the end of the 1990s, Haiti's political rights (which measure mostly the integrity of the electoral process and openness of the political process) actually deteriorated.

Second, Haiti's new ruling elites have failed to demonstrate their commitment to democratic rule and process. Consequently, democratic institution-building (which entails the development of checks and balances, the rule of law, and a system of facilitating compromises among various interest groups) has been neglected. Politics were centered on one personality, President Aristide, who manipulated the political process to ensure his tight hold on power. As a result, the immature Haitian democratic institutions, severely flawed to begin with, were further perverted. The quality of democracy deteriorated significantly. For example, vote-turnout rate remained extremely low in both presidential and parliamentary elections (ranging from 5 to 25 percent in the legislative and presidential elections conducted since 1994). Such low-level of popular participation revealed, on the one hand, the lack of credibility of the post-1994 system in the eyes of average voters (a poll found only a minority of Haitians believed that elections in Haiti were honest).[53] It also put into question the legitimacy of Haiti's "elected" government on the other. Haiti's new ruling party Lavalas headed by Aristide also undermined its own legitimacy by trying to steal the legislative and local elections in 2000. In response the international community isolated the Aristide government and froze aid, while the Haitian opposition parties refused to cooperate with the government controlled by Aristide loyalists and boycotted the presidential election of November 2002 (which Aristide won unopposed). Haitian's democracy was effectively eviscerated.

Third, Haitian's new rulers wasted valuable opportunities to implement the right economic policies and pursue reforms shortly after the international community helped to restore Aristide's government in Haiti and was willing to invest considerable resources to help the poverty-stricken country to develop. Pro-market policies such as privatization were abandoned by the Aristide government; international aid was used on temporary job-creation programs with no long-term positive effects on the Haitian economy. Corruption and patronage was rife. The paralyzed Haitian politics also deterred potential foreign investors. Consequently, economic growth stagnated through the late 1990s, disappointing both the Haitian public and the international donor community.

On balance, the international community's intervention in Haiti achieved only its short-term objective: ousting a brutal illegitimate military junta, restoring a democratically elected leader to power, and averting a horrific refugee crisis. Its long-term goal—building viable democratic institutions—remains unfulfilled. Two important lessons emerge from the Haitian experience. The first lesson is that, for democratic institutions to take root in an inhospitable environment such as Haiti, the international community must remain firmly committed for the long haul. Unfortunately, the intervention in Haiti appeared to be driven largely by the domestic concerns of the Clinton administration and was not based on a long-term strategy. The international community was simply sucked into the Haitian political vortex both by the American pressure and by the prospect of a humanitarian disaster in the country. The short-term considerations of the Clinton administration meant that as soon as the specter of political chaos and refugee crisis in Haiti receded, it would no longer treat Haiti as a foreign policy top priority. International support for sustainable democratic institution-building would dwindle over time. Without the long-term commitment of the international community, democracy-building in places like Haiti is impossible. The second lesson is that democracy-building must have "local owners." In other words, the local elites must recognize and accept democratic rules and procedures as the fundamental principles of politics. In Haiti, such basic commitments to democracy turned out to be questionable among its post-1994 elites. The lack of local ownership of democratic institutions created a vicious cycle: local elites would use opportunities to undermine the democratic process for their parochial and short-term interests even at the risk of jeopardizing their relations with the international community. A disillusioned international community would react with bitterness, termination of aid, and withdrawal, a move sure to give the local elites an even freer hand to subvert democratic institutions.

3. Mixed Story: Implementing Democratic Institutions in Russia

Few transitions to democracy have as great an impact on international peace as that in the Russian Federation of the former Soviet Union. While the collapse of the former Soviet Union effectively ended the Cold War, sustained peace in the huge land mass of the former Soviet Union would remain questionable without the consolidation of democratic institutions in Russia, which inherited most of the military might, diplomatic influence, and economic power of the former Soviet Union. Recognizing the crucial importance of implementing democratic institutions in Russia, the international community has committed considerable economic and political resources to the assistance of its economic reform and political transition. The results, however, remain mixed.

On the positive side, the fact that Russia has retained, at least on surface, the rudimentary institutions of an emerging democracy and repeatedly defeated the attempted comeback of unreconstructed Communists should be considered as a positive step forward. Survey data also suggest that Russians widely support the "general norms" of democracy, despite their reservations about the actual practice of democracy at home. In addition, despite an overwhelming displeasure with the existing system, support for a return to an un-reformed Soviet model remains low in today's Russia.[54] These developments, both institutional and psychological, also ensured that Russia would be able to play an international role more compatible with the interests of the West. The decisive turn toward the West made by the Putin government following the terrorist attacks on the United States on September 11, 2001, appears to have vindicated this view.

However, the Russian transition has a very mixed record, both economically and politically. The sad story of post-Soviet economic reform in Russia is well-known and needs no repeating here. More important is the uneven development of democratic institutions in post-Soviet Russia. Although the dreaded reversion to authoritarian rule did not occur, Russia's transition to a full-fledged democracy has barely begun. Indeed, one of the most prominent American analysts on Russia argues that the initial two attempts to forge democratic institutions, respectively by Mikhail Gorbachev and Boris Yeltsin, failed miserably. It was only in the second half of the Yeltsin administration that some progress was beginning to be made in real democratic transition.[55]

However, Russia's new political institutions resemble those of an illiberal democracy more than a liberal one. Indeed, most observers of Russian politics believe that three factors have severely degraded the "quality" democracy in the post-Soviet Russia.

First, the existence of an excessively strong executive branch centered on the Kremlin has resulted in a weak and servile legislature (especially after the parliamentary elections in December 1999 and the 2000 presidential election). This situation has led to what Shevtsova describes as a "presidential pyramid"—a system of "strong executive power" buttressed by political appointments that weakens accountability and hinders democratic development. When combined with a frequent resort to presidential decree, and the "virtual impossibility" of impeaching the president, the system allows the executive to gain the power to act "unchecked." Although this system may make economic reforms easier initially, it may prove brittle in the face of future demands for substantive reform.[56] The combination of a top-down reform decision-making process, imbalance of power among various branches of the government, personalistic top leadership, and politics of co-optation may have created "bureaucratic quasi-authoritarianism" rather than democracy.[57]

Second, a half-reformed economic system and a government structure centered on the executive branch can breed a virulent form of crony capitalism that benefits a few well-connected business interests while excluding the majority of other groups. Russia's experience under Yeltsin typified the pitfalls of such a combination. Valuable state assets were practically given away to a small group of so-called "oligarchs" who then funneled funds into the coffers of Yeltsin's political machines to keep him in power. Russia's political system thus effectively became "a mixture of arbitrariness, kleptocracy, and democracy." The victims of this hybrid system are mostly politically weak groups (workers in formerly state-owned factories whose assets were stripped away by the oligarchs). In addition, this system rendered the institutions of the state, such as the courts, the civil service, and law-enforcement agencies, either ineffective or fragmentary (a situation Yeltsin's successor Putin was apparently trying to remedy).[58]

Finally, civil society remains weak and protection of democratic rights is uncertain under the current regime. In part, this is due to the Russian ruling elites' own ambivalence toward the fundamental rights guaranteed under democracy and toward independent centers of power potentially capable of challenging the state. Such ambivalence may have become even more pronounced since the rise of the Putin presidency, a regime that barely conceals its own preference for economic reform over democratic consolidation. Most threatened is Russia's nascent independent media. After Putin took office, the Russian government launched a well-planned assault on independent media outlets, especially the television networks. The resulting atmosphere of intimidation restricted press freedom and led to the practice of self-censorship by journalists.[59]

Implementing Democratic Institutions in the Twenty-first Century

This survey of the theoretical literature on democratic transition and the brief analysis of three cases suggest that although the effects of democratization in different countries have been diverse and uneven, there is sufficient evidence to support the proposition that, generally speaking, the implementation of democratic institutions contributes to international peace and helps improve the conditions of human rights in those societies that have started the transition toward democracy. Even in Haiti, it is hard to deny that the removal of a repressive military junta by the U.S.-led forces produced an immediate improvement in human rights conditions in the misery-stricken nation. In Russia, the economic sufferings and the flaws in the post-Soviet political system may disappoint those who harbored higher expectations, but the overall level of well-being for Russian citizens (including, most importantly, freedom from fear) has improved enormously when compared with the era of communist rule. Of course, when democratic transition and consolidation occurs in a society where conditions are most conducive to democratic rule (as in Taiwan), the implementation of democratic institutions represents an unambiguous step forward.

The real challenge for the international community in the twenty-first century, however, is not only the prevention of violent conflicts in countries undergoing democratic transition, but the promotion of democratic institutions in societies where violent conflicts have been averted but effective democratic governance remains elusive. During the third wave of democratization, the international community committed more resources to the initial transition from authoritarian rule to democracy than to the building of viable and effective democratic institutions. Such a strategy might have served the strategic interests of the United States well (especially given its overriding objective of winning the Cold War), but it needs to be revised for the twenty-first century.

For the United States, it must assume the leadership of democracy-promotion. In the past, Washington has pursued its policy of democratic enlargement hesitantly, opportunistically, and inconsistently. As a result, its policies have been heavily influenced by domestic political considerations, military security needs, and commercial interests. Such lack of consistency makes the U.S. democracy-promotion rhetoric hollow, if not hypocritical, and its policies lacking in credibility. In the new century, the U.S. must pursue a multi-pronged approach to democracy-promotion that uses its own moral authority and exemplary behavior at home to demonstrate democratic society's superiority to skeptics abroad. Its foreign policy must also be centered on a multilateral approach so as to build an international order favorable to democracy. In particular, the U.S. must significantly increase its assistance to the developing countries (now less than one-tenth of a percentage of the U.S. GDP) so that its rhetoric is backed by substantive deeds. The U.S. political establishment must also adopt a long-term and patient approach to democracy-promotion abroad. Such an approach must focus on the development of the critical infrastructures required by a democratic political process, such as political parties, a legal system, civil society groups, independent press, and a professional and apolitical military. Most critically, American political leaders must recognize that such efforts serve the long-term interests of the U.S. and must not be derided as futile projects of "nation-building." Failed states are more likely to emerge from failed authoritarianism and aborted democratic transition. These states can be the breeding ground of ethnic radicals, religious extremists, and international terrorism, as demonstrated by the Taliban-controlled Afghanistan. They not only inflict unspeakable sufferings on their own people, but threaten the peace and stability of the entire international community.[60]

Adjustments are also required in the strategy and tactics of democracy-promotion. The most authoritative study on democracy-promotion in the late twentieth century recommends a strategy of flexibility and "local ownership" as the most cost-effective and viable approach to implementing democratic institutions in developing countries. Such a strategy would avoid several mistakes made in the past efforts of democracy-promotion, such as over-reliance on a "core strategy" based on an idealized American model of socio-economic development, ignorance of local conditions and power relations, wasteful use of aid on projects that have no chance of long-term success, and an simple-minded emphasis on elections as sign of healthy democracy, rather than a starting point.[61] Most important, the new strategy must involve a paradigm shift in building democratic institutions in developing societies. In the recent past, democracy-promotion has been mostly supply-driven: Western democracies were the principal force pressing for the establishment of democratic institutions in countries lacking such institutions. In the future, democracy-promotion will succeed only when it is driven by indigenous demand.[62] Such a strategy helps build not only viable democracies, but also lasting peace.

Notes

1. Samuel P. Huntington, *The Third Wave: Democratization in the Late Twentieth Century* (Norman: University of Oklahoma Press, 1991). Also see Larry Diamond and Marc Plattner, eds., *The Global Resurgence of Democracy* (Baltimore: Johns Hopkins University Press, 1997).

2. For example, democratic transitions occurred in parts of Africa (South Africa, Nigeria and several other countries) in the 1990s; Indonesia saw its 30-year old dictatorship collapse in 1998.

3. Huntington provides a comprehensive analysis of the causes of the democratic surge in the *Third Wave*, pp. 31-108.

4. The seminal article on this theory is Seymour Martin Lipset, "Some Social Requisites of Democracy: Economic Development and Political Legitimacy," *American Political Science Review*, vol. 53, no. 1, (March 1959), pp. 69-105.

5. Two important works linking class structure and democracy are Barrington Moore, *Social Origins of Dictatorship and Democracy: Lord and Peasant in the Making of the Modern World* (Boston: Beacon Press, 1966), and Dietrich Rueschemeyer, Evelyne Huber Stephens, and John Stephens, *Capitalist Development and Democracy* (Chicago: University of Chicago Press, 1992).

6. See Robert Dahl, *Polyarchy: Participation and Opposition* (New Haven: Yale University Press, 1971).

7. The World Bank, *The East Asian Miracle* (New York: Oxford University Press, 1993).

8. In the Philippines, the Marcos regime looted the nation. In Indonesia, despite 30 years of developmental success, the Suharto regime became so predatory that it fatally undermined the financial system of the country and became a victim of the financial crisis of 1997.

9. The classic work is Guillermo O'Donnell and Philippe Schmitter, *Transitions from Authoritarian Rule: Tentative Conclusions about Uncertain Democracies* (Baltimore: Johns Hopkins University Press, 1986).

10. See Adam Przeworski, Michael Alvarez, Jose Antonio Cheibub, and Fernando Limongi, *Democracy and Development: Political Institutions and Well-Beijing in the World, 1950-1990* (New York: Cambridge University Press, 2000).

11. Immanuel Kant, *Perpetual Peace*, Lewis White Beck, tns., (New York: Bobbs-Merrill, 1957).

12. See Michael W. Doyle, "Kant, Liberal Legacies, and Foreign Affairs," *Philosophy and Public Affairs*, vol. 12, no. 3 and 4 (Summer and Fall 1983), pp. 205-35, 323-53, and "Liberalism and World Politics," *American Political Science Review*, vol. 80, no. 4 (December 1986), pp. 1151-1169.

13. Bruce Russett, *Grasping the Democratic Peace* (Princeton: Princeton University Press, 1993). Also see David Lake, "Powerful Pacifists: Democratic States and War," *American Political Science Review*, vol. 86, no. 1 (March 1992), pp. 23-37.

14. William R. Thompson and Richard Tucker, "A Tale of Two Democratic Peace Critiques," *Journal of Conflict Resolution*, vol. 41, no. 3 (June 1997), pp. 428-454.

15. Christopher Layne, "Kant or Cant: The Myth of the Democratic Peace," *International Security*, vol. 19, no. 2 (Fall 1994), pp. 5-49.

16. Henry S. Farber and Joanne Gowa, "Polities and Peace," *International Security*, vol. 21, no. 2 (Fall 1995), pp. 183-96.

17. See Strobe Talbott, "Democracy and the National Interest," *Foreign Affairs*, vol. 75, no. 6 (November/December 1996), pp. 47-63.

18. Douglas Brinkley, "Democratic Enlargement: The Clinton Doctrine," *Foreign Policy*, no. 106 (Spring 1997), pp. 111-127.

19. For a summary of his argument, see Amartya Sen, "Freedoms and Needs: An Argument for the Primacy of Political Rights," *The New Republic* (January 10, 1994), pp. 34-37.

20. Daniel Kaufmann, "Corruption: The Facts," *Foreign Policy*, no. 107 (Summer 1997), pp. 114-131.

21. This is based on the data on public perception of corruption compiled by Transparency International. For a detailed analysis of the difference between established and new democracies, see Minxin Pei, "Political Institutions, Democracy, and Development," in Farrukh Iqbal

and Jong-il You, eds., *Democracy, Market Economics and Development: An Asian Perspective* (Washington, DC: World Bank, 2001), pp. 25-47.

22. See Gerald Scully, "The Institutional Framework and Economic Development", *Journal of Political Economy*, vol. 96, no. 3 (June 1988), pp. 652-662; Mancur Olson, "Dictatorship, Democracy, and Development", *American Political Science Review*, vol. 87, no. 3 (September 1993), 567-576; Barry Weingast, "The Political Foundations of Democracy and the Rule of Law," *American Political Science Review*, vol. 91, no. 2 (June 1997), pp. 245-263.

23. Scully, p. 657.

24. These results were reported in Przeworski and Limongi, "Political Regimes and Economic Growth", *Journal of Economic Perspectives*, vol. 7, no. 3 (Summer 1993), pp. 51-69.

25. William R. Thompson and Richard Tucker, "A Tale of Two Democratic Peace Critiques," *Journal of Conflict Resolution*, vol. 4, no. 3 (June 1997), pp. 428-454.

26. Edward Mansfield and Jack Snyder, "Democratization and War," *Foreign Affairs*, vol. 74, no. 3 (May/June 1995), pp. 79-97.

27. This is in comparison to a state that remains an autocracy. Mansfield and Snyder, "Democratization and the Danger of War," in Michael Brown et. al., eds., *Debating Democratic Peace* (Cambridge: MIT Press, 1996), p. 313.

28. Mansfield and Snyder, "Democratization and the Danger of War," pp. 315-316.

29. Ibid.

30. Larry Diamond and Marc Plattner, eds., *Nationalism, Ethnic Conflict, and Democracy* (Baltimore: Johns Hopkins University, 1994).

31. Daniel Byman and Stephen Van Evera, "Hypotheses on the Causes of Contemporary Deadly Conflict," *Security Studies*, vol. 7, no. 3 (Spring 1998), pp. 1-50.

32. Jack Snyder, *From Voting to Violence: Democratization and Nationalist Conflict* (New York: W.W. Norton, 2000).

33. Jeffrey Herbst, "Responding to State Failure in Africa," *International Security*, vol. 21, no. 3 (Winter 1996/97), pp. 120-144.

34. Guillermo O'Donnell, "Delegative Democracy," *Journal of Democracy*, vol. 5, no. 1 (January 1994), pp. 55-69.

35. See Fareed Zakaria, "The Rise of Illiberal Democracies," *Foreign Affairs*, vol. 76, no. 6 (November/December 1997), pp. 22-43.

36. Guillermo O'Donnell, "Illusions About Consolidation," *Journal of Democracy*, vol. 7, no. 2 (April 1996), pp. 15-33.

37. Nelson Kasfir, "No-Party Democracy in Uganda," *Journal of Democracy*, vol. 9, no. 2 (April 1998), pp. 47-63.

38. Zakaria, "The Rise of Illiberal Democracies."

39. Richard Joseph, "Africa, 1990-1997: From Abertura to Closure," *Journal of Democracy*, vol. 9, no. 2 (April 1998), pp. 3-17; Philippe Schmitter, "Dangers and Dilemmas of Democracy," in Larry Diamond and Marc Plattner, eds., *The Global Resurgence of Democracy* (Baltimore: Johns Hopkins University, 1996), p. 79.

40. For a detailed discussion on the need for socio-economic reform under new democracies, see Larry Diamond, *Developing Democracy: Toward Consolidation* (Baltimore: Johns Hopkins University Press, 1999), pp. 64-116.

41. See Tun-Jen Cheng, "Democratizing the Quasi-Leninist Regime in Taiwan," *World Politics*, vol. 41, no. 4 (July 1989), pp. 461-499; Yun-han Chu, *Crafting Democracy in Taiwan* (Taipei; Institute for National Policy Research, 1992); Tun-jen Cheng and Stephan Haggard, eds., *Political Change in Taiwan* (Boulder: Lynne Rienner, 1992); Jaushieh Joseph Wu, *Taiwan's Democratization: Forces Behind the New Momentum* (Hong Kong: Oxford University Press, 1995). This section is based on part of Minxin Pei's "Democratization in Greater China," *Access Asia Review*, vol. 1, no. 2 (July 1998), pp. 5-40.

42. See Hung-mao Tien and Yun-han Chu, "Building Democracy in Taiwan," *The China Quarterly*, no. 148 (December 1996), pp. 1141-1170.

43. See Shelley Rigger, *From Opposition to Power: Taiwan's Democratic Progressive Party* (Boulder: Lynne Reinner, 2001).

44. See Jaushieh Joseph Wu, *Taiwan's Democratization*, pp. 33-72, for detailed analyses of the role of Taiwan's socio-economic conditions in its transitions.

45. Andrew J. Nathan and Yangsun Chou made this observation in "Democratizing Transition in Taiwan" in

Andrew J. Nathan, ed., *China's Crisis: Dilemmas of Reform and Prospects for Democracy* (New York: Colombia University Press, 1990), pp. 129-152.

46. Edwin Winckler, "Institutionalization and Participation on Taiwan: From Hard to Soft Authoritarianism," *The China Quarterly*, no. 99 (September 1984), pp. 481-499.

47. See Shelley Rigger, *Politics in Taiwan* (London: Routledge, 1999).

48. Jaushieh Joseph Wu, *Taiwan's Democratization*, p. 114.

49. See Michael Ying-mao Kau, "The Power Structure in Taiwan's Political Economy," *Asian Survey*, vol. 36, no. 3 (March 1996), pp. 287-305.

50. For two studies of the West's experience in Haiti, see James Morrell, Rachel Neild, and Hugh Byrne, "Haiti and the Limits to Nation-Building," *Current History* (March 1999), pp. 127-132; John Sweeney, "Stuck in Haiti," *Foreign Policy*, no. 102 (Spring 1996), pp. 143-151.

51. See O'Donnell and Schmitter, *Transitions from Authoritarian Rule.*

52. See Jean-Germain Gros, "Haiti's Flagging Transition," *Journal of Democracy*, vol. 8, no. 4 (October 1997), pp. 94-119.

53. Mark Falcoff, "What "Operation Restore Democracy" restored," *Commentary* (May 1996), p. 46.

54. Timothy J. Colton and Michael McFaul, "Are Russians Undemocratic?," *Carnegie Working Paper*, no. 20, (June 2001).

55. Michael McFaul, *Russia's Unfinished Revolution: Political Change from Gorbachev to Putin* (Ithaca: Cornell University Press, 2001).

56. Lilia Shevtsova, "The Problem of Executive Power in Russia," *Journal of Democracy*, vol. 11, no. 1 (January 2000), pp. 32-39.

57. Lilia Shevtsova, "Russia's Hybrid Regime," *Journal of Democracy*, vol. 12, no. 4 (October 2001), pp. 65-70.

58. Archie Brown, "From Democratization to 'Guided Democracy'," *Journal of Democracy*, vol. 12, no. 4 (October 2001), pp. 35-41.

59. Michael McFaul, "One Step Forward, Two Steps Back," *Journal of Democracy*, vol. 11, no. 3 (July 2000), pp. 19-33; "Putin in Power," *Current History*, (October 2000), pp. 307-314.

60. Graham T. Allison and Robert P. Beschel, "Can the United States Promote Democracy?" *Political Science Quarterly*, vol. 107, no. 1 (1992), pp. 81-98.

61. Thomas Carothers, *Aiding Democracy Abroad: The Learning Curve* (Washington, DC: CEIP Press, 1999).

62. Marina Ottaway and Theresa Chung, "Toward a New Paradigm," *Journal of Democracy*, vol. 10, no. 4 (October 1999), pp. 99-113.

Peace and Security: Conceptual Notes

Nigel Dower
University of Aberdeen, Scotland

In the U.N. Charter and other international documents, 'peace and security' tend to go together, indeed so close is their union that one suspects they would be lost without each other. Whatever increases international security makes the world more peaceful, and conversely whatever leads to peace provides security.

And yet they are in many ways very different from one another. I want to consider two ways in which they may be viewed as different. The first is to work the idealist/realist distinction in a certain way, the second is to recognize that whilst they can both be used in idealist and in realist contexts, their fundamentally different logics point to different, even if complementary, features both of the human condition and of human values.

Military Security Contrasted to Peace as s Positive Ideal

Given the typical contexts in which discussions of security take place, it is easy to think of security as the state of a country in which in virtue of its military defence posture it is, and perceives itself to be, reasonably free from military attack from another country or group of countries. How this is achieved is of secondary importance: it might be, as traditionally, by being sufficiently well armed and/or protected by military alliances, or by devising international institutions so as to deliver 'common security'. The point is that it is based on the goal of removing or minimizing the risk of being attacked and upon the means of using armed forces, coupled with the apparatus of alliances and international law. Much international effort, both within and outside the U.N. system, in the last fifty years has been to achieve this goal, by strengthening the relative role of law, agreement and cooperation and lessening the role of, and hence the need for large units of, military power itself. But the framework is still military/arms related.

For many thinkers the pursuit of security so thought of as synonymous with the pursuit of peace in the modem world. But for many others such an account of peace will seem very tame and inadequate. Peace, it may be said, is not just the absence of war, maintained by adequate security arrangements, it is, or should be seen as, something positive, a set of relationships or harmony.[1] Nor should peace be seen as something applicable only to the relations of states. Peace exists, or can exist, at all levels—social relationships, family relationships, and, as perhaps the source of real peace at all other levels, the inner quality of peace within any individual. On this view peace is better contrasted with

Nigel Dower, "Peace and Security: Conceptual Notes." Reprinted with permission from the editors of *Essays on Peace: Paradigms for Global Order* edited by Michael Salla, Walter Tenetto, & Enrique Martínez.

something more general like violence (including structural violence) or conflict, than with war, and the pursuit of peace is going to be more complex and far reaching than the avoidance of war between states,[2] which is what the maintenance of security is generally taken to be.

Such an account of peace will no doubt be seen as more 'idealistic' than more modest or 'realist' accounts of it as the avoidance of war,[3] and this may be accepted both by its advocates and by its critics. The critics may want to dismiss such ideas of peace as unrealistic in the world of international relations and therefore either irrelevant or dangerous vis-à-vis the pursuit of what is possible in the world. The idealist will claim that only if more far-reaching goals and values are adopted, and if we stop seeing international relations as a separate or special domain, cut off from wider issues of social and interpersonal relationships, will we make real progress in making a more peaceful world. What however, may well be agreed, by advocate and critic alike, is that peace so thought of is more far-reaching than the modest ideas of international security. That is, the conceptual gap between peace and security is created by restricting security to a realist/pragmatic sense and allowing peace to be given a more idealistic interpretation.

There may however be rather different reasons for wanting to disconnect the ideas of peace and security, reasons which acknowledge that there is more to be said for the idea of security than is implied by the above account. Security also can be given a more extensive, even idealistic sense—one that it would be good for us to promote—but one which can be significantly contrasted to the idea of peace more idealistically understood.

Some Conceptual Points About Security

Security comes from a Latin root meaning 'lack of care'–care in the sense of concern or anxiety about something. Now whilst etymology is no obvious guide to present meaning (it certainly is not vis-à-vis 'peace'), it does help here to throw light on the root idea involved. This is the idea that a person is secure in something if that thing is (a) something he/she values, (b) he/she currently has it (c) he/she will continue to have it into the future, (as long as he/she values having it) (d) and he/she is confident that he/she will continue to have it and does not feel anxiety over the possible loss of it.

The first thing to notice is that security is relative to some value system. The agent must value something—e.g. not being attacked, nationality, a job, food, affection, spouse, the pursuit of learning—for him/her to be said to be secure in anything. The second thing to notice is that there is both a subjective and an objective level to security. A person may actually be secure in relation to some future good—that is he/she will continue to have it—but lack the confidence that this is so.

Thus, if he/she feels insecure with regard to this—and feels fear, anxiety, lack of hope etc. vis-à-vis it—then he/she would lack security in the fullest sense. Conversely, if he/she was quite confident that the good in question exists or will continue, but in fact it does not or will not, then notwithstanding feeling secure, he/she would not in a full sense be secure in it. Various further points need to be made.

First, it is of course possible to talk of security as such, not in respect of some particular good. A person may be generally secure or have security in his/her life, if overall he/she is, or believes him/herself to be secure in respect of most things in his/her life. Obviously how a person copes with the pattern of things which are secure or are not secure in his/her life, makes a big difference to the way he/she sees the world.

Second, implied in the above is the recognition that complete security is in fact impossible. There is no way that one can guarantee that what one values will continue. All that one can accept as a goal is the pursuit of a reasonable level of security. What 'reasonable' means is a matter of great importance, and has of course great relevance to its application to international relations. 'Reasonable' is also a concept, the application of which, as I note later, presupposes a set of moral values, to do with fairness, relative importance in the hierarchy of values etc.

Third, we tend to concentrate on those aspects of what we value in life which, we see as liable to be lost, whether through natural processes (such as ageing), competitive interactions with others, or deliberate attacks on our goods by others. If the continuation of what we value is not seen as vulnerable, we may not think about it in 'security' terms. This may be justifiable if it really is not vulnerable, but it may not be, if our assumptions are not right, ie, some good may in fact not be secure though we continue to think of it as secure (or rather do not think of it as secure because it is not thought of at all). A case in point are the various environmental goods, such as clean air and water, which can no longer be taken for granted.

The measures we take to achieve a reasonable level of security in respect to goods we see as possibly under threat reflect the level of care or concern we show towards them, but by the same token are intended to remove the source of care in the sense of anxiety, insecurity and other negative feelings.

Conversely a person may indeed be secure in some good without realizing it and it be an important part of their hierarchy of values. Evidence of this would be the fact that if it were to be threatened or lost they would feel such negative feelings as fear, anxiety or insecurity. A child may be secure in the affection and care given to them by their parents, without thinking of it as something it is important to be secure in.

Two limitations on the pursuit of security are important: first, we need to ensure that the measures we take to ensure a level of security are such as not to undermine other people's (group's or countries') attempts to achieve a like level of security. This is one of the 'moral' limitations on the idea of reasonableness mentioned earlier. Clearly the traditional pursuit of military superiority often does not conform to this principle. Second, the pursuit of security in one domain needs to be consistent with pursuit of it in respect to all other domains in which one's goods are, or could come to be, under threat. Thus if for example massive commitment to military technology seriously aggravates our environmental condition, then the pursuit of military security (assuming that that were all right) might come into conflict with environmental security.

New Ideas of Security

The example of environmental security serves two purposes here. First, it is an example of how one form of security may be undermined by the pursuit of another kind of security. Second, perhaps more importantly, it provides a model of how security needs to be achieved which runs counter to traditional ways of thinking about military security. Transboundary pollution and common global effects, such as global warming from CO^2 emissions, may negatively affect a country in ways which it cannot stop. No amount of defensive barriers along frontiers will stop it. The only way to achieve environmental security in these respects is to have a situation in which the polluting country stops polluting or countries generally reduce CO^2 emissions, i.e. cooperation is needed and compliance to agreed norms.

Similarly with resources—a key to both environmental and economic security—safeguarding future resources on a global scale cannot be secured without general cooperation by all or nearly all countries. The search for 'common security' in the military sphere is, of course, somewhat similar in that it recognizes that real security cannot be achieved by pointing more and more weapons at other countries, but by creating a global political environment in which countries are not motivated or perceived to be motivated, to attack one another. (In a multi-polar world there can be no reasonable security via superiority in arms or adequate capacity to inflict unacceptable damage to an aggressor, given that any combination of countries could form alliances against any one country.)

Security has recently become quite fashionable, and for good reason, with discussion not only of environmental security, but also of things like food security, water security, economic security. An example may be given from Sara Parkin's *Green Futures,* where she speaks of redefining security, and of thinking, for example, of it in terms of 'the number of communities able to satisfy their needs near to where they live'.[4] Continuing in this vein, I suggest that it may well be useful to think of 'development' (for any country or community) in terms of security, i.e. in terms of the spread of the goods in which people wish to be secure, and in such a manner as to be consistent with the like security interests of others elsewhere and in the future.

The Relation Between Peace and Security

How then does peace relate to security? The idea I wish to develop is as follows. Peace is, on the one hand, one of the things which people wish to be secure in, i.e. it is one of the objects of security, and as such it may be both valued in its own right as an end or valued as a means to other things wanted. On the other hand, peace is also one of the ways or means by which security is pursued, promoted or maintained.

As the former, that is as an object of security, peace is best thought of in the negative sense, viz. the absence of war, violence, conflict—because in the hierarchy of human interests, the absence of these conditions is generally of such importance. As the latter, namely as the means to security, peace is much better understood in the 'positive' sense, as the presence of certain positive characteristics which enable security to be achieved. Harmony and cooperation are clearly important here, but what is, perhaps, of more importance are the moral values and commitments which underpin and make possible such harmony and cooperation.

Peace as an Object of Security Interest

Peace then is one of the things which we seek to be secure in but it is not the only thing, and this points to one of the reasons why peace and security are conceptually distinct. As I indicated earlier, we can seek security in respect of anything which we value and feel afraid may be taken away but which we can take measures to protect. Just as we can seek security in respect of a clean environment, adequate food or an interesting retirement, so we can seek security in respect of not being attacked in our person, whether by lawless thugs or gunmen, by the arm of the state or by foreign soldiers. Such security interests, expressed for instance by Shue as basic security rights,[5] are an important part of what makes peace a value in its own right.

But of course peace is not, in this sense of freedom from attack, primarily valued as an end. It is primarily valued as a means—viz. the means towards the successful achievement of one's goals, whatever they may be. This simply expresses the truism that without order and stability, people cannot pursue properly the goals they want to pursue,[6] and is reflected in the recognition that real development is impossible in any country which is at war (especially with itself). In a parallel way having enough to eat and the other basic necessities of life is very much something of value in its own right but it is also important as a precondition for the pursuit of all the other goals which an agent may wish to pursue.

I noted earlier that peace as an object of security should be thought of primarily as negative peace. There is, of course, no logical necessity for peace as the object of security to be so thought of. A person could easily think of, and no doubt some do think of, peace as what they wish to be secure in as some state of social harmony or inner personal peace. But characteristically, such values are seen as aspirations or desiderata, what a person would like to see in society or like to achieve in their own personal life, rather than states which if removed or threatened or not yet achieved would give rise to fear, anxiety or the like, i.e. feelings of insecurity.

Furthermore, even if these were states of affairs which did meet the criteria of things one wished to be secure in, they would necessarily be states of less practical importance compared with the primary concerns for freedom from attack and violence, proper economic well-being, basic social order, etc. Whilst there is a sense in which ends are more important than the means to them, there is another sense in which, practically speaking, the securing of the means is what matters, and most security interests tend, for this reason, to be focused on questions of the means.

Peace as a Means to Security

How then is security to be achieved—that is, security in respect of the range of things which are generally seen as practically important for people—the threat to which or the absence of which would lead to a sense of insecurity and practical efforts to remove the source of insecurity? A complete answer to this question is not attempted here, even in outline. All I want to point out is that, in an important sense, the commitment to the 'way of peace' is precisely the means, or at least the most important means, to achieving such security.

The point here is that peace as a means is peace as a commitment to action, something which agents as agents do to promote or sustain peace. Here there is a contrast to the sense indicated earlier in which peace may be a value one wishes to be secure in because it is a means or necessary condition for the pursuit of one's goals in life. In this sense peace is valued by someone qua recipient not qua agent. It is the peace which exists because of what everyone around one is, or has been, doing, or not doing.

The Moral Basis of Commitment to Harmony and Cooperation

One of the key features of peace as a means is the role of moral principles and action informed by them in creating and sustaining the structures of peace. Harmony and cooperation do not usually just happen. They require commitment most of the time by most people to moral values.[7] Some of these moral values have nothing directly to do with peace, such as respect for others, truthfulness and sincerity, justice and fairness (though they may well be seen as part of the fullest account of peace). Other values are directly to do with peace itself, like commitment to non-violence and pacifism, or alternatively, commitments to finding and using a range of non-violent ways of tackling conflicts before using violence as a last resort. It is worth noting in passing that even Hobbes, whose willingness to endorse the 'helpes of warre', especially in international relations, is notorious, did stress the obligation to 'endeavoure peace' wherever it is possible.[8]

Clearly there can be many different levels and forms of harmony and cooperation both within countries and between them. In some ways, the distinction between positive and negative definitions of peace has to be seen as overdrawn—perhaps a heuristic device only—since even peace, as merely the continued absence of war and violence, is unlikely to be achieved without certain kinds of levels of cooperation which cannot exist without moral commitments of various kinds. Peace as the absence of conflict and, thus, the object of security interests is less likely to be maintained, the less firm and deeply established are the structures of commitment to peace in the richer sense.

But there are, as I noted, levels of cooperation and obviously different levels of 'endeavour' for peace and of the forms which this can take. What a person takes themselves to be morally committed to by way of sustaining or promoting the structures of peace will vary considerably from person to person. Two issues arise, one as to the levels and kinds of personal commitment to rules of respect, truthfulness, fairness, non-violence etc. and the other as to how far, in an imperfect world, one should work for, or promote, peace (justice, human rights, truth) beyond one's own moral integrity. (There is an immense difference between acting justly or peacefully and promoting justice and peace, and it must be noted that the possibility of taking moral shortcuts with the former for the sake of the latter can always arise.) Here is not the occasion to go into the normative issue of just what form of moral commitment are appropriate to the pursuit of peace, except to note that one of the key dividing points hinges on the issues of how far one's own obligation is a function of the level of general commitment already in existence. Pacifism represents one pole in this respect ('no'), hard-nosed realism the other ('yes'), but there are various other positions between them. That is, established reciprocity and mutual compliance are a necessary condition for one to have an obligation to take positive or further steps?

Conclusion: Complementary but Distinct Concepts

Various bits of the logical geography of peace and security have been offered, and much more, of course, needs to be added. But I hope I have said enough, in a somewhat sketchy way, to suggest that, in certain respects, the close coupling of peace and security may be misleading, but that the sharp contrast between positive and negative conceptions of peace may also be misleading.

Security is a set of relations and a set of perceptions of those relations between a subject and the things which people value but sees to be liable to be under threat. Seeking security occurs when someone seeks to have those relations to things which they value which they either lack, or find, under threat.

Peace, on the other hand, is one of the things which is generally valued both for its own sake and as a precondition of many other things valued, and is thus one of the objects of security interest. But it is also a form of social harmony or cooperation which is seen as an object of moral commitment, the means whereby security in a wide range of human goods may be achieved.

Notes

1. See e.g. A. Curie, *True Justice,* and J. MacQuarrie, *The Concept of Peace.*

2. See I. Jenkins, "The Conditions of Peace," Monist, 1973, for a useful discussion of this and related points.

3. See e.g. 1. Hobbes, *Leviathan,* (London: Everyman's Library, 1979) chapter 13.

4. S. Parkin, *Green Futures* (Harper Collins, 1991) p. 61.

5. H. Shue, *Basic Rights: Subsistence, Affluence and US Foreign Policy* (Princeton University Press, 1980) chapter 1.

6. Order and stability are, in Rawls' sense, primary goods (though assumed in the background of a well ordered society rather than asserted in Rawls' own account) see J. Rawls, *A Theory of Justice* (Harvard University Press, 1971).

7. On the importance of moral principles underlying peace see R.M. Hare, "Peace," *Applications of Moral Philosophy.*

8. Hobbes, *op. cit.,* chapter 14.

The Peace Process: Sustained Dialogue to Transform Deep-Rooted Human Conflicts

Harold H. Saunders
Kettering Foundation

The conflicts that will dominate the stage in the twenty-first century will increasingly be triggered by citizens outside government. I call them "deep-rooted human conflicts." Many of them will be fueled by ethnic and racial tensions. Many will be sparked by citizens' alienation from the social, political, and economic mainstream. They will be fed by feelings of hopelessness and powerlessness—lack of meaningful work, a political voice, and human dignity. Although governments will continue to be critical to solutions in many cases, other conflicts will result from the failure of states.

I have called this "The Citizens' Century"—for better or for worse. While citizens outside government may trigger conflict, they also hold the key to peace, economic progress, and the solution to the world's most intractable problems.

These causes of tension and conflict are not new, but they burst upon the world dramatically with the end of the Cold War. They moved to the top of the world's agenda with the attacks in New York and Washington on September 11, 2001. Practices for dealing with such conflicts that were carefully developed and tested in the latter decades of the last century must now move to center stage.

We will not have a powerful approach to the prevention and resolution of such conflict until we change our conceptual lenses and strengthen these new practices. People ask me as a practitioner why I speak about concepts. Experience over the past forty years in working with five presidents of the United States and other world leaders convinced me that the conceptual lenses that leaders use to bring the world into focus and give meaning to events will determine how they act. This is just as true of citizens outside government as it is of those who govern. If we are going to deal with these "new" conflicts, we need to see the world through different lenses. That is why I begin this chapter with a few pages on the conceptual transformation that is essential to developing and practicing widely the new approaches to conflict that are required.

Whole Bodies Politic

This change of lenses begins with broadening our conceptual framework. Traditionally, political theory and theories of conflict have focused on states, their governments, and other institutions. They have focused on the traditional instruments of statecraft—mediation, negotiation, diplomacy, use of force, economic sanctions. States and governments will remain the principal organizing units in the world for the foreseeable future, but by themselves they will not be sufficient to meet the world's challenges.

Experience in the late twentieth century confirmed that there are some things only constituted governments can do. These include negotiating binding agreements, funding programs to meet the needs of society, organizing relations with other state units, enforcing order, and providing for the common defense. Governments must be helped to meet these obligations with increasing effectiveness. The causes of some of the "new" conflicts are the insensitivity of governments to real human needs and their failure to meet those needs effectively.

At the same time, there are some things that only citizens outside government can do. These include transforming conflictual human relationships, changing political culture, and modifying human behavior. Governments can sign peace agreements; only people can make peace. Governments can develop the apparatus of democracy; only citizens claiming responsibility for their own futures can create a culture of democracy; governments can interdict some drug traffick; only citizens can overcome addiction.

Both government—citizens inside government—and citizens outside government are essential to a healthy body politic. Both are parts of whole bodies politic. We need a conceptual framework broad enough to embrace both.

To speak in terms of a whole body politic is to restore the democratic equation. There have been two threads in Western democratic thought—not just one. We need a conceptual framework that brings them together again.

The first of those threads has focused on the machinery of democratic governance: one person/one vote, basic civil-rights for each citizen, representative government, independent judiciaries, separation of powers, written constitutions, free media, and a rule of law. Many people in the twentieth century found how precious these are when they lived under or observed totalitarian or authoritarian systems in Nazi Germany, the Communist bloc, and military dictatorships around the world. When millions of people emerged from under those systems in the late 1980s, they naturally turned to the machinery of democracy with great joy and expectation.

The second thread in Western democratic thought focuses on the citizen as a political actor and on the associations that citizens form together to do their work, often without reference to government. The great eye-opening revelation of the 1990s was the realization that democratically elected and installed governments could not by themselves solve the problems of the polities they governed. Looking back, citizens realized what important roles they had played in such places as Wenceslas Square and in such movements as the "vote no" campaign against Chilean dictator, Agusto Pinochet. They also realized that, after democratic elections, those citizens had left the political arena to pursue their own interests rather than staying in the political arena to help pursue the public interest.

In short, democracy—in whatever historical or cultural tradition it forms itself—cannot work until these two threads are brought together. We need a conceptual framework large enough to focus on whole bodies politic—citizens inside and outside government working together for the public good.

A study and practice of politics focused on government alone is not adequate. A conceptual framework that embraces both citizens in and out of government makes available a tremendous reservoir of human energy and talent in the service of the common good. We learned in the twentieth century how citizens under totalitarian regimes were beaten into looking only to government for the solution of problems. We saw those economies stagnate one by one. Citizens must invest their energies in a dramatic build-up of public capital.

Another way of putting this point is to state that governments face more and more problems both within countries and across borders that no one government can deal with alone. Within countries, they need new cooperation with their own citizens to deal with addictions, crime, and HIV/AIDS because they can be dealt with only when citizens change their behavior. Across borders, problems such as terrorism, global warming, drug trafficking, disease, and environmental degradation require intergovernmental collaboration and the collaboration of international non-governmental groups. As a corollary, people outside government increasingly influence the course and policies of their own governments and the interaction between bodies politic.

The challenge is to find new ways of conducting relationships within bodies politic and between whole bodies politic globally. The challenge is to develop and sustain the relationships needed to deal with problems that no one group, government, or country can deal with alone and to work to overcome differences that would undercut their efforts. Even polities like those of the United States and some in Western Europe have yet to tap fully the resources latent in whole bodies politic.

Whole Human Beings in Whole Bodies Politic

The second enlargement of our conceptual framework requires focusing on *whole human beings.* I use the word *whole* to distinguish my point from the political scientist's, the economist's, the sociologist's, or the psychologist's slice of a human being or of a body politic. I am writing of the whole persons in all of their complexities who inhabit whole bodies politic. I am writing about the whole individuals who have within them the capacity to commit the noblest acts and the most horrible atrocities—sometimes rational and calculating, sometimes far-seeing and compassionate, sometimes self-centered, irrational, or bestial. I am writing both about whole human beings within the structures of government and power and whole human beings outside those structures.

We are suffering a crisis in the conduct of relationships. Neither government nor civil society is strong in its own right because human beings in and out of government are not conducting their relationships in productive ways. Relationships involve whole human beings. It is time to integrate the human dimension—whole human beings—into the study of whole bodies politic and the practice of politics.

Ever since the Western Enlightenment, we in the West have tended to rate the rational side of human beings more highly than the emotional or intuitive side. Gradually toward the end of the twentieth century, we have begun to think more of both sides of ourselves as essential to the whole. Eastern philosophies have, by and large, not suffered this separation; they have a fuller sense of the whole. Unfortunately in the West, this disaggregation of a whole into its parts is reflected in the academic tendency throughout the twentieth century to turn the study of human beings in their various activities into "sciences" where the focus is on what can be measured. To measure, they had to reduce complex phenomena to narrowly defined components. That required separating those who, for instance, focused on interests defined in terms of wealth as the economists do from those who studied interests defined in terms of power as the political scientists do. One task of the new century is to find ways of breaking down these barriers between academic disciplines. They are an obstacle to seeing the world through conceptual lenses wide-angled enough to free us to meet the immense challenges we face.

If we could do that, we would shift our lenses so as to focus on *whole human beings in whole bodies politic* rather than on government and citizens on different sides of a wall. We would focus on whole human beings with needs for survival and dignity, personal fulfillment and spiritual life, meaningful work and a voice in shaping their futures, multiple identities and allegiances.

If we took this conceptual leap, we would first see in a body politic a political process of continuous interaction among shifting complexes of citizens, in and out of government, across permeable borders—not just a static collection of institutions and not just citizens as measurable voters or consumers. The emphasis would be not just on action and reaction between formal institutions but on *inter*action among human beings in a multitude of associations. This shift in lenses requires nothing less than a revolution in our thinking about how the political world works.

Picture citizens as whole human beings interacting around common concerns. Each values a number of personal, professional, identity, religious, cultural, economic, and other interests. Each brings those interests into different interactions with others sharing them. Each citizen's life involves a complex of clustered interactions—some overlapping, some not. These clusters interact with other clusters in numberless ways. Picture clusters, groups, associations of citizens in and out of government thinking, talking, acting together because they are concerned about particular problems. Suspend your inclination to define those clusters in terms of their structures and instead see the permeable boundaries of each group defined only by the pattern created by their interactions—not by constitutions and by-laws. Think of the body politic as the kaleidoscope in which these continuously changing groups interact.

Even government can be thought of in this way. Anyone who has served even in a big government knows that it, too, breaks down into groups reaching across bureau, department, and agency boundaries to focus on particular problems. These often interact informally with groups outside government sharing the same interests and concerned about the same problems. So while the roles of citizens may be different, the gulf between citizens in and out of government is not always so wide as some assume.[1]

If one has moved this far in first bringing the two threads of Western democratic thought together under the conceptual umbrella of "whole bodies politic" and, second in bringing the two lines—rational and emotional—of thinking about human beings together as "whole human beings," one is ready to think about a new political paradigm.

A Political Paradigm for the Twenty-First Century

I have repeatedly in writing and speaking offered a new paradigm and a concept for organizing the analysis and practice of political life: *Politics is a cumulative, multilevel, and open-ended process of continuous interaction over time engaging significant clusters of citizens in whole bodies politic across permeable borders, either within or between countries.* This focus on a *multilevel process of continuous interaction* contrasts to focus on a linear sequence of actions and reactions among institutions as in a chess game. Continuing *inter*actions are the essence of that process. What is important are the interplay and the interpenetration between entities, not just the action by one on another. Of course, some of these entities are highly structured institutions with unique cultures and character, while others are loosely formed associations; all are brought to life by the human beings who inhabit them.

To give hands and voice to that paradigm, I have defined the *concept of relationship.* The concept of relationship provides the analytical and operational framework through which the new paradigm reveals itself, may be studied, and is put into practice. The mantra of scholars trying to turn the study of politics into a science has been: "Politics is about power." My response to the political scientists is: "Politics is about relationship." Power is, of course, an element of relationship—but only one of several.

The concept of relationship is a diagnostic tool because it permits one to organize the elements of complex interactions for analysis. It is an operational tool because the practitioner can get inside each element of relationship to change it.

For the sake of analytical precision and operational use, I have defined relationship in terms of five components—five arenas of interaction in constantly changing combinations within and between the parties interacting: (1) *identity,* defined in human as well as in physical characteristics—the life experience that has brought a person or group to the present; (2) *interests,* both concrete and psychological—what people care about—that bring people into the same space and into a sense of their dependence on one another—*interdependence*—to achieve their goals; (3) *power,* defined not only as control over superior resources and the actions of others but as the capacity of citizens acting together to influence the course of events without great material resources; (4) *perceptions, misperceptions, and stereotypes;* and (5) the *patterns of interaction*—distant and close—among those involved, including respect for certain *limits on behavior* in dealing with others.

Power is, of course, an important component of a relationship, but much of the time other components are more likely to determine how a person or group acts or to shape the character of an interaction. Power must be defined much more broadly than it has been. Instead of defining it as control, I define it as the capacity to influence the course of events. This capacity is most often seen when citizens act in concert with others.

To repeat, the concept of relationship can be both a diagnostic and an operational tool. One can analyze a relationship through this prism, and then one can actually get inside any of these components to enhance understanding or to change an interaction. In dialogue, identity can be understood and can grow. A person can be humanized as misperceptions and stereotypes give way to realistic pictures. Common interests can be discovered. In that light, patterns of interaction can change from confrontational to cooperative. As respect for another's identity grows, individuals impose limits on themselves to reflect that respect. Those changes also introduce new elements into the equation of power. As one understands that dynamic process of continuous interaction, one learns that power in part may emerge from careful and sensitive conduct of the process, rather than only from wielding material resources.

Relationships can be good or bad, constructive or destructive, mature or regressive, argumentative or cooperative, close or distant. They pervade our lives; the question is how to conduct and develop them constructively. Thinking in terms of relationship changes how we act. It enriches our capacity to conduct interactions productively and enlarges our resources for conducting and changing them without resort to violence.

I call my paradigm "the relational paradigm" in contrast to "the realist paradigm." For years, scholars of international relations have operated from a paradigm that can be captured in a sentence like this: leaders of nation-states amass economic and military power to pursue objectively defined interests in zero-sum contests of power against other nation-states. They have defined power as the ability of one party to force another to do what it does not want to do. Political scientists writing about politics within states have said simply, as noted earlier: "Politics is about power." The "relational paradigm" is intended for both the international and the intranational arenas.

The relational paradigm and the concept of relationship are designed to bring the human dimension into the study and practice of political life. That does not reject the importance of states, governments, and other institutions. I spent twenty-five years in the United States Government and am proud of many of our accomplishments in those years, but I also learned what governments cannot do. The relational paradigm is intended to broaden our focus to include whole bodies politic—citizens both inside and outside government.

Engaging Whole Bodies Politic

One way to draw these remarks together is to say that the challenges of our troubled world require broadly political—not just technical—responses. The global project of the twenty-first century is to engage citizens in and out of government—whole bodies politic—in growing a culture of democracy that both builds on traditions and meets needs. In the words of Czech President Vaclav Havel: "It is not that we should simply seek new and better ways of managing society, the economy, and the world. The point is that we should fundamentally change how we behave."[2] Only by engaging the resources of whole bodies politic can we respond to our challenges.

A courageous World Bank study titled *Voices of the Poor: Can Anyone Hear Us?* is introduced with these words: "What is it that the poor reply when asked what might make the greatest difference in their lives? They say, organizations of their own so that they may negotiate with government, with traders, and with nongovernmental organizations. Direct assistance through community-driven programs so that they may shape their own destinies. Local ownership of funds, so that they may put a stop to corruption. They want nongovernmental organizations and governments to be accountable to them.... These are strong voices, voices of dignity."[3] They are the voices of citizens outside normal power structures reaching for political engagement. Bodies politic that exclude much of their populations are not whole; nor are they engaging the full range of resources they need to meet the challenges of this new century.

We are taxing the earth beyond its ability to sustain us, and we lack political capacity to come together to right the balance. Our countries are at odds. Our societies are increasingly fragmented, crime-ridden, and violent. Some see the new century as a crossroads for humankind. Engaging whole bodies politic is both a moral and a practical imperative. I write for all those who feel the necessity of engaging in this project—beginning in their own communities.[4]

If citizens are to engage in meeting their challenges, they must have tools comparable to those of government. We will not discard valuable tools developed through centuries of trial but we must enlarge our toolkit.

The Genesis of Sustained Dialogue

One of those tools is what I call sustained dialogue. It has been developed and tested over more than twenty years in thousands of hours of dialogue among citizens outside government.

Pioneers in developing systematic non-official dialogue such as John Burton, Herbert Kelman, and Vamik Volkan worked in the 1960s and 1970s to develop and refine ways of bringing enemies together in dialogue. Their purposes were to understand the dynamics of conflict and to create spaces in which the parties to conflict might come to understand the grievances and pain of their adversaries more fully.

Beginning in 1960, American and Soviet citizens came together in the "Dartmouth Conference"—named because the first meeting took place at Dartmouth College in Hanover, New Hampshire. It has become the longest continuing bilateral dialogue among American and Soviet, now Russian, citizens. In 1981, the plenary group established task forces in two areas to probe more fully the Soviet-U.S. interactions that had led to the demise of détente in the 1970s.

In 1982, I became co-chair of the Dartmouth Conference Regional Conflicts Task Force along with my Soviet colleague, Evgeny Primakov, who later became Foreign Minister and Prime Minister of Russia. Meeting on an average of every six months, this task force afforded the first opportunity of a citizens' dialogue group to experiment with the experience of regular meetings over extended periods of time involving a core of the same people to focus with increasing depth on a conflictual relationship—in this case, the relationship between the two superpowers. By the end of 2001, the task force had met thirty-six times.

As one meeting followed another, the co-chairs felt the pressure of getting more out of each successive meeting. Primakov said after one meeting, "Let's begin the next meeting where this one ended." As we followed that practice, we learned that a group sustained over years could build a cumulative agenda, could develop a growing shared body of knowledge which participants could test from individual experience between meetings, and could learn to think, talk, and even work differently together.

By the end of the 1980s, I recognized that the capacities of a group like this develop through a progression of stages. I began to characterize each of these stages and to conceptualize a five-stage process. In 1993, my Russian co-chair and I wrote an article, "A Public Peace Process,"[5] which he translated into Russian. In 1999, I published *A Public Peace Process: Sustained Dialogue to Transform Racial and Ethnic Conflicts.*[6]

In 1993, six participants in the Dartmouth Regional Conflicts Task Force launched a dialogue among factions from the civil war in the former Soviet republic of Tajikistan—a dialogue which participants came to call "the Inter-Tajik Dialogue within the Framework of the Dartmouth Conference." As of the end of 2001, this group had held thirty-two meetings and had formed their own non-governmental organization, the Public Committee for Promoting Democratic Processes in Tajikistan.

Sustained Dialogue in Practice

Sustained dialogue among citizens outside government can be a point of entry into the relationships among the groups with which they identify. I have laid this process out as developing through these five stages:

- *Stage One:* Either people on different sides of a conflict decide to reach out to each other, or a third party creates a space for dialogue and invites conflicting parties to come together there. People decide to engage in dialogue—often with great difficulty—because they feel a compelling need to build or change a relationship to resolve problems that hurt or could hurt their interests intolerably. These participants are themselves a microcosm of their communities.
- *Stage Two*: They come together to talk—to map and name the elements of those problems and the relationships responsible for creating and dealing with them. In early meetings, they vent their grievances and anger with each other in a scattershot way. This venting provides both the ingredients for an ultimate agenda and an opportunity for moderators to analyze and "map" the interactions—to understand the dynamics of the relationships. This stage ends—at least for a time—when someone says: "What we really need to focus on is...."
- *Stage Three:* In much more disciplined exchanges, they probe specific problems to uncover the dynamics of underlying relationships with these aims: (1) to define the most pressing problems; (2) to probe the dynamics of the relationships underlying these problems; (3) to lay out broadly possible ways into those relationships to change them; (4) to weigh those choices and to come to a sense of direction to guide next steps; (5) to weigh the consequences of moving in that direction against the consequences of doing nothing; and (6) to decide whether to try designing such change.
- *Stage Four:* Together, they design a scenario of interacting steps to be taken in the political arena to change troublesome relationships and to precipitate practical steps. They ask four questions: What are the obstacles to moving in the direction we have chosen? What steps could overcome those obstacles? Who could take those steps? How could we sequence those steps so that they interact—one building on another—to generate momentum behind the plan for acting?
- *Stage Five:* They devise ways to put that scenario into the hands of those who can act on it.

These five stages are not rigid; the process is anything but neat and orderly. One stage does not fully end before the next begins. Participants move back and forth across the stages often when they need to update a changed situation, rethink an earlier judgment, or tackle a new problem. Or their minds may be all over the place when they are groping for focus. When they do go back, it is at a deeper level because they are continuously deepening their experience with their relationships through the course of the dialogue. The real purpose of the five-stage framework suggested is to give moderators and participants some touchstones for judging what has been accomplished and for defining the work that needs to be done at a particular moment if the dialogue is to have a rigorous sense of purpose and direction and if it is to produce fundamental change in conflictual relationships.

In short, sustained dialogue can create a microcosm of the relationships between whole groups and an experience in analyzing and changing those relationships. In the 1990s, the process was tested and refined by the Kettering Foundation in dialogues among Americans and Soviets, now Russians, and Americans and Chinese. It has been used extensively by American and Russian colleagues working together in conflicts that broke out on the territory of the former Soviet Union. It is now being taught by the Kettering Foundation to community organizations in North America who are working to reduce ethnic and racial tensions in their cities. Perhaps the best way to illustrate this process is to recount briefly the story of the Inter-Tajik Dialogue.

In 1992 after the Soviet Union dissolved, members of the Dartmouth Conference Regional Conflicts Task Force decided that they would together attempt to apply the process of dialogue that they had learned together to one of the conflicts in the new Commonwealth of Independent States. They chose Tajikistan.

Beginning *Stage One* of the process, two Russian colleagues went to Tajikistan and talked with more than one hundred possible participants in a dialogue among factions of the civil war. They were looking for individuals at the second or third levels of their organizations—not the highly visible leaders. The thought was that such individuals could speak with authenticity about the perspectives of their groups and would be listened to when they returned from the dialogue, but they would not be as bound as leaders might be to posture or defend fixed positions. Participants also need to be willing to listen with minds open to some degree, a primary requirement in dialogue. They need to recognize their own interest in reaching out to the other side to try to end violence. The two Russians also briefed government leaders on what we were trying to do. They chose nine individuals to come to an exploratory meeting in Moscow in March 1993.

A reflection by these two Russian colleagues underscored the importance of the convener in such dialogues: "Although we felt we were trusted because of previous academic associations, we do not believe participants would have accepted an invitation unless Americans were to be present. They might not even have accepted an invitation from Americans and Russians. They could accept an invitation from what they called an 'international movement'—the Dartmouth Conference." This point was underscored a year later when participants wrote their first joint memorandum and called themselves "the Inter-Tajik Dialogue within the Framework of the Dartmouth Conference."

Most of the main groups in the political life of Tajikistan were reflected in the composition of the group, but not all. For instance, it was extremely difficult for some time to include an appropriate Islamic voice in the group. Then as the situation in the country unfolded, it became necessary at periodic intervals to add further voices to the group. So the work of Stage One remains continuously under review. Although some early participants dropped away and others were added, others have been remarkably continuous in their involvement.

Stage Two began when the group sat down in that exploratory meeting in Moscow. Participants could barely look at each other. They poured out their grievances and their anger. At one point in the meeting, one of the co-moderators was able to point out that everyone in the room had voiced what it felt like to be excluded in one way or another from the political life of the country. The interactions among participants gradually enabled the American and Russian members of the management team to begin to understand the dynamics of the conflict. It was not just a battle between two sides but a battle among groups with complex roots and motives. It was a contest for power based in clans and regions; it was a battle over ideological differences involving former Communists, new democrats, moderate and militant Islamists, and cultural nationalists, to name a few.

This downloading of intense feeling generated by the hostilities of the civil war continued over most of two further three-day meetings in June and then in August. Through all of this, they were beginning to recognize that their adversaries were serious people with legitimate feelings and differences of view.

Finally, on the second day of the third meeting, someone in the group said: "What we really need to work on is starting a negotiation between government and opposition about creating conditions for the return of refugees to their homes. Nothing can happen in our country until the one out of seven people who have fled are home again. We cannot write a new constitution, hold elections, disarm illegal armed elements, or begin economic rehabilitation until that happens." Others agreed.

With that statement, the group began its *transition to Stage Three*. The quality of the dialogue began to change because members of the group were now focusing on a problem that all agreed affected the interests of all.

At the same time, this experience illustrated what happens in a group when it takes steps to a deeper level of dialogue. Although they had identified a problem, they could go no further in working on it at that meeting. A co-moderator asked everyone to write two paragraphs—one a paragraph from the government inviting the opposition to negotiations and the other, the opposition response. Each required offering some assurance of safety to the other side. No one in the group could come to the point of writing those assurances at that time. They could not overcome the negative feelings about reaching out to the other side. This experience illustrates the usefulness of thinking about stages in the unfolding of relationships; the transition to a deeper level often leaves participants momentarily fearful of moving closer to the enemy and knowing that can help everyone identify the obstacle to moving forward.

The period between that third meeting and the fourth also illustrated the importance of the time between meetings in a sustained dialogue. Not only did participants have time to absorb the implications of the step to which they had agreed; events in the world around them also affected their thinking. In this case, the situation within Tajikistan further deteriorated, and Russian President Boris Yeltsin shelled the Russian White House the week before the fourth meeting.

That fourth meeting showed the group clearly in *Stage Three*, ready to focus on the problem they had identified and to probe it in depth. The question was *how* to begin a negotiation between government and opposition. One of the main problems they identified was the fact that the opposition included many factions that were geographically dispersed and ideologically diffuse. "Who from the opposition would come to a negotiation? Where would we find opposition representatives? How would we get in touch with them?" asked pro-government participants. Another question was whether leaders who were obviously responsible for atrocities would participate. Although participants did not resolve all of these questions, they clearly identified obstacles that needed to be removed.

The next development illustrates the difficulty in assessing the degree to which a dialogue group such as this can be given credit for an outcome. Leaders of the opposition factions gathered in Tehran, Iran, a month later, wrote a common platform, and created an opposition coordinating committee in Moscow. Two Dialogue participants signed that platform, and four became members of the coordinating group's steering committee. That sequence of events suggests some credit for the creation of the United Tajik Opposition (UTO) to represent opposition forces in negotiation, but presumably there were numerous other inputs to the decision.

Opposition participants came to the fifth

meeting in early January 1994 prepared to explain the new platform in detail. Pro-government participants questioned them steadily over two days. Members of the management team wrote down the answers of opposition members, who presented their views clearly and tactfully. Pro-government participants left the meeting saying: "We believe the basis for negotiation now exists. We will report these exchanges to our government."

Through these months a representative of the United Nations Secretary-General had been pressing government and opposition forces to come together in a U.N.-mediated negotiation. Within six weeks of the Dialogue meeting, the government accepted that invitation. Again, is it possible to claim credit for the Dialogue in precipitating that decision? No, not completely, but a key government official involved in the decision told us later that the work of the Dialogue helped create a more positive environment for that decision because no one could argue any longer that it was impossible to talk with the opposition. April was set for the beginning of negotiations.

In the sixth meeting in March, participants in the Dialogue were able to write their first joint memorandum, "Memorandum on a Negotiating Process for Tajikistan." At this point, they entered *Stage Four*, actually designing a course of action to be followed by the negotiating teams. Their memorandum reflected an imaginative political philosophy. They not only noted that the negotiations would now take place between a government delegation and a delegation from the newly formed United Tajik Opposition. They proposed that the negotiating teams establish four working groups under their authority. These groups would deal with return of refugees, constitutional and political change, disarmament, and economic development. Their idea was that each of these groups would include both participants from all relevant government units and participation by non-governmental groups who had to be involved. In other words, the necessary work of these groups was to provide a context—a process of continuous interaction—within which opposing groups could begin to rebuild their relationships.

When the negotiations were convened, three members of the Dialogue were delegates—one on the government side and two on the opposition side. In that context, they were able to put their design for the negotiations into the hands of those with capacity to put them into action. Those participants were acting in *Stage Five.*

I will not recount in detail the experience of the next three years. The negotiators eventually in June 1997 produced a peace agreement that was signed in Moscow. It included four ideas that the Dialogue had put forward in subsequent memoranda. One of those ideas may have originated in the Dialogue; others were ideas in the air that they put in context in their joint memoranda.

One of the most important of those ideas—included in a memorandum in June 1996—was the idea of establishing a National Reconciliation Commission *under* the authority of the negotiating teams. The opposition had proposed such a body as a supra-governmental organization—a proposal that aroused government fear that the opposition was seeking to supersede the government. The creation of the National Reconciliation Commission by the peace agreement was an imaginative step. Although the government had refused to create a coalition government involving the opposition, it agreed to a fifty-fifty allocation of positions in the National Reconciliation Commission and agreed that the Commission would be headed by the leader of the opposition with the President of Tajikistan as his opposite number.

That Commission and its four sub-commissions provided a space where issues such as the allocation of government positions that could not be decided in negotiation were worked out one case at a time. It also provided oversight for the complex problem of disarming opposition elements and incorporating them into the armed forces of Tajikistan. Through a third sub-commission it provided a context within which a new constitution and political laws for the country could be written. When the Commission was convened, five members of the Dialogue were members. Other members subsequently joined the Dialogue.

When the work of the Commission formally ended with a series of elections in late 1999 and early 2000, members of the Dialogue, reaching out to other prominent Tajikistani citizens, formed their own non-governmental organization—the Public Committee for Promoting Democratic Processes in Tajikistan. Chaired by one of the veteran members of the Dialogue, the Public Committee embarked on work that illustrated the way in which sustained dialogue can not only play a role in resolving conflict but can then play a role in what the Tajiks called the "post-accord phase" in developing the sinews of a peaceful society.

Sustained dialogue and kindred approaches have advanced the field of conflict resolution by one significant step in providing space for those in conflict who are not ready for formal mediation and negotiation to come together to talk about the conflict and how to end it. Many of the conflicts which seize our attention in the twenty-first century are not ready for formal mediation and negotiation because people do not negotiate about their historic grievances, their loss of dignity, their fears, their identities, and their stereotypes, but they can come together to talk about them. Such dialogue can pave the way ultimately for formal mediation and negotiation.

The second step beyond the traditional field of conflict resolution was taken when theorists began to recognize what happens during a civil war: The sinews of a peaceful society which permit people to work across the normal divisions of society are torn asunder. A mediator may come in and work out a cease-fire or even a more basic peace agreement. Then normally the mediator goes home, and no one stays around to help reconnect those sinews. That is the work of what former U.N. Secretary General Boutros Boutros-Ghali called "post-conflict peace-building." The Public Committee for Promoting Democratic Processes focused on that agenda.

Since mid-2000, the Public Committee has been working along four tracks: First, they have developed a series of day-long "mini-dialogues" beginning with a series of six in Dushanbe, the capital city, and then in August 2001 establishing comparable dialogues in four other regions of the country. Participants in these mini-dialogues began by dealing with the sensitive subject, "the state, religion, and politics." Tajikistan is the only country in Central Asia that has a legitimized Islamic party. Participants in the Inter-Tajik Dialogue have pointed out that Muslims throughout the Islamic world are engaged in a major debate on the relationship between Islam and modernization and Islam and democracy. These Tajikistanis are bringing this broad debate down into their own communities in sustained dialogue. In February 2002, they trained moderators for these regional dialogue groups and will try to connect them in an "all-national dialogue."

Second, they have established Economic Development Committees (EDCs) in three communities especially devastated by the civil war to focus on putting those communities on their feet economically. As one Tajikistani colleague said: "The government has neither the competence nor the resources to help put all communities in Tajikistan on a sound economic footing. If anyone is going to do that, it will be the citizens themselves." This is a project with far-reaching implications. Its foundation lies in the interactions of diverse groups within a community who begin forming the civic infrastructure in the community essential to sustainable economic development. Economists and funding institutions such as the World Bank call this building "social capital." The process underlying the civic development in these communities is what we have called the "citizens' political process," a framework much like the five stages of sustained dialogue that recognizes how relationships unfold as people in a conflictual setting come together to define common problems, to lay out possible approaches to those problems, to weigh their choices among those approaches, to design action, and finally to implement a course of action.[7]

Third, complementary to the work of those Economic Development Committees, a group working on a parallel track has framed issues for public deliberation in all regions of Tajikistan around issues such as poverty, education, and drugs. The purpose of these public forums is to give citizens an experience in the process of deliberation—a process of weighing choices in a dialogue in communities where relationships among people are such as to permit them to sit down together and address common problems. It is designed to move citizens slowly toward thinking that they do not have to wait for government to solve their problems—that they are capable of thinking about their choices and actually deciding to do something about them themselves.

Fourth, under an agreement between the Public Committee and the Ministry of Education, a project has begun engaging professors from eight universities in developing programs and courses in resolving conflict and building a peaceful society. U.S. foundations are supporting the participation of some of the best American scholars and practitioners in resolving conflict to work with the Tajikistanis in this project.

In short, a sustained dialogue over nine years has worked its way through the heat of a civil war, a process for its gradual resolution, and activities through which citizens can become engaged in the political and social life of their country.

A Multilevel Peace Process

One more word about the larger conceptual framework for this overall approach to peace-making and peace-building is essential. If one works from the concept of whole bodies politic, one must recognize that peacemaking is a process that must engage citizens at all levels of the body politic and in all walks of life.

In early 1974, the phrase "peace process" was—in the eyes of those of us who participated—born during the diplomatic shuttle flights of U.S. Secretary of State Henry Kissinger after the October 1973 Arab-Israeli war. We began by calling what we were doing "the negotiating process." We did so because the explicitly stated strategy was to build one mediated agreement on top of another to generate momentum in changing the relationships between belligerent countries and to make it possible to negotiate in a succeeding agreement what was not possible in a previous agreement. As we proceeded, we gradually recognized that the agreements mediated were actually changing the larger political environment and slowly opening in the eyes of citizens the possibility of peace. So we came to call what we were doing "the peace process."

In the fall of 1996 in the Inter-Tajik Dialogue, we began broadening that phrase to refer to the "multilevel peace process." One Dialogue member had participated in a joint commission of government and opposition members to work out a cease-fire in a particularly sensitive area of the country where fighting severed communications on a key road linking the eastern and western parts of that mountainous country. His story was gripping because some of the members of the commission had been held hostage and their lives threatened, but the outcome became a model for similar agreements around the country. When he had finished telling his story, another Dialogue participant said: "The reason cease-fires have not been held in this country is that they have been negotiated by the president of the country and the leader of the opposition without any reference to fighting forces and civilian authorities on the ground with their own interests and with their guns. What we need in this country is a multilevel peace process that links the official negotiations with the local combatants."

The concept of the multilevel peace process permits us to acknowledge that, of course, official negotiations are often essential parts of peacemaking, assuming that official bodies are directly involved in violent conflict. A second level in the peace process involves groups such as the Inter-Tajik Dialogue with participants from what one might call policy-influencing communities. These groups not only provide a link between influential citizens outside government and the official level of the peace process, but they also reach down into those local communities and associations where citizens outside government pursue their own important interests. The third level, then, involves those in the larger body politic—both citizens outside government and those who may be in local governments as well.

I introduce the idea of the multilevel peace process not because any one person or group will be able to manage that process but because it is important for those heavily engaged in transforming conflictual relationships to recognize the complementarities of action that may be taken at differing levels in the peace process. As stated at the beginning of this chapter, there are some things that only governments can do and some things that only citizens outside governments can do. It is essential to recognize those differences and the possibilities of complementary action. The concept of the multilevel peace process provides a framework for doing that. It provides the practical framework within which the relational paradigm and the relationships among whole human beings in whole bodies politic play themselves out.

Notes

1. These ideas were first expressed in the author's article, "Whole Human Beings in Whole Bodies Politic," *Kettering Review*, Fall 1998, pp. 69-70.

2. Vlclav Havel, "The End of the Modern Era," *New York Times* (March 1, 1992), p. E15, quoted in David Mathews, *Politics for People* (Urbana and Chicago: University of Illinois Press, 1994), p. 163.

3. James D. Wolfensohn, President, the World Bank Group, Address to the Annual Meeting of the Board of Governors, September 28, 1999, in words used to introduce Deepa Narayan with Raj Patel, Kai Schafft, Anne Rademacher, Sarah Koch-Schulte, *Voices of the Poor: Can Anyone Hear Us?* (Oxford: Oxford University Press for the World Bank, 2000), before the title page.

4. The three foregoing paragraphs are from the manuscript of my forthcoming book, *Politics Is about Relationship: A Relational Paradigm for the Citizens' Century.*

5. Gennady I. Chufrin and Harold H. Saunders, "A Public Peace Process," *Negotiation Journal* (vol. 9, no. 2, April 1993), pp. 155-177.

6. Harold H. Saunders, *A Public Peace Process: Sustained Dialogue to Transform Racial and Ethnic Conflicts* (New York: St. Martin's Press, 1999; PALGRAVE paperback edition, 2001).

7. Ramón Daubón and Harold H. Saunders, "Deconstruction of Social Capital: A Strategy to Enhance Communities' Capacity to Concert," *International Studies Perspectives*, May 2002.

The Cause and Resolution of Conflicts

June Saunders
International Educational Foundation

In the wake of the shootings at Columbine High School in April of 1999, popular opinion about protecting students from conflict includes support for such measures as installing metal detectors in schools. Yet most of the conflicts that affect youth—and which affect youth all over the world—take place under far more ordinary circumstances. Children and teenagers suffer from quarrels between their parents, discord within their neighborhoods, and clashes with schoolmates indirectly, children suffer from the workplace disagreements their parents cannot leave behind as well as marital quarrels; these drain parents of the energy and aplomb needed to optimally care for their children. These conflicts take their psychological and emotional toll on young people, affecting them deeply, cumulatively, and often permanently.

Understanding the causes of conflict and the means of resolving it are ways to lessen this psychological toll and help children grow into maturity with secure inner working models for forging good relationships even in the midst of the inevitable tensions they will face.

The Value of Resolving Conflict

Conflict is a fact of life. Under ordinary circumstances, conflict is neither good nor bad in and of itself. It is the way people respond to conflict and handle it that determines its outcome. If conflict is feared and regarded as negative, it has little growth-promoting potential. Conflict, like all adversity, is best looked upon as an opportunity for character growth—a chance for individuals to call upon and refine their inner resources—to challenge themselves to new frontiers of empathy and relationship skills.

Conflict is a symptom and sign that the emotional subtext of a relationship needs correction and improvement. Tensions may even be welcomed as a herald of potential to deepen a relationship. Many a couple feels closer and more intimately connected to each other after a dispute has been resolved. Friendships are often strengthened by successful resolution of a disagreement. New bonds have been forged in the fires of conflict in all types of relationships.

Unfortunately, many people respond to the presence of conflict by seeking to terminate the situation where they find it. They quit jobs, leave schools, divorce, sever friendships, never go into a certain store again or stop speaking to a relative. These avoidance methods bring temporary relief, but in fact, unresolved conflicts inevitably return to haunt the person. They often reappear in a new form or with new people, continuing to resurface until resolved. Conflict cannot be compartmentalized. Until the problem is healed on the deepest levels of the human heart, it inevitably permeates a person's interactions with others.

Dawn, a mother of three, had an altercation with a neighbor over her children playing in the back of his parked truck. He strongly urged her to ground her children for the offense. Dawn remembered, however, that he often let the children play in the truck when he was in a good mood. How could he be so inconsistent? Dawn was angry with the neighbor and decided not to punish her children. Yet when her husband and children came home, she found herself yelling at them over every minor offense. Dawn realized her unresolved anger over the incident with the neighbor was causing her to lash out at her family.

Resolving conflict is desirable for many reasons. The cessation of tensions removes the paralyzing impasse that leaves both sides feeling isolated and stagnant. It opens the doors to forgiveness and reconciliation, which in turn free up time and energy for creativity and progress. The amount of emotional energy lost in maintaining friction—the defensive moves and retaliations—could be more efficiently directed toward living a full and productive life and promoting more gratifying relationships.

Peter from New Haven recalls the sense of renewal and resurgent relationship upon resolving a difficulty as a child. "When I was a small boy I used to play every afternoon with my best friend. Our favorite game was setting up our army of tin soldiers. I was especially proud of a little army truck my father had given me. I even marked it in a special way. Then one day, the truck disappeared. What was worse, I discovered that my friend had taken it. Because of the little mark I had made, there was no doubt in my mind that this was my truck. I said nothing and my friend said nothing, but our happy little world lay in ruins. I knew that he took it, and he knew that I knew that he took it. We could not face each other. We could not play together. Then, in a day or two he came up to me and said, 'I'm sorry. I took your truck. Please forgive me.' There was a moment of silence. 'Oh, forget about it,' I answered. 'What do I care?' Suddenly all the world around us was bright and happy again."

A person is able to make his or her world of relationships better by seeking the means to resolve conflict. Part of this resolution involves understanding that there are often deep underlying emotional and psychological needs beneath the surface of disputes.

Causes of Conflict

Among school children, disputes arise over personal possessions and school resources, cliques, differing ideas and opinions, cheating, bullying, and such abusive moves as shoving for a better place in line, using put-downs and name calling. Many schools have conflict resolution programs in place to deal with such everyday issues,[1] but schools with character education programs are already teaching their students the basics of respect, courtesy, manners and the treatment of all people as equal and worthy, proactively addressing the issues that underlie much conflict. Such preventative efforts keep clashes from arising in the first place.

In the home, disagreements occur over such common issues as discipline and obedience, parenting styles, money, sibling rivalry, homework and grades, children's possessions and teenagers' desire for independence. Conflicts tend to escalate when self-control, patience, forbearance, long-sightedness and other virtues are deficient. Thus, building healthy marriages and giving children the foundation of good parenting reduce conflicts.

Conflicts in families are exacerbated and amplified by substance or alcohol abuse. In addition, certain destructive patterns such as schizophrenia and alcoholism tend to run in families, producing strife. Negative patterns of family interaction—violence, insults and sarcasm, among others—tend to be imitated from generation to generation until one member of the family has enough perspective and courage to change it in his or her generation. People who have interrupted the negative cycles of neglect and abuse in their personal histories to become loving, respected parents to their own children sometimes feel they are literally altering fate, breaking up the bad "karma" of their family line.[2]

Tensions with a History

Individuals and families in neighborhoods and communities are often affected by hostilities stemming from actions, past and present, by or against their ethnic, racial, religious or national group. Sometimes crimes were committed against a certain group as part of a national mindset or policy. The result is that succeeding generations inherit a legacy of racial and ethnic resentments and prejudice. Such tensions fuel fires that can escalate simple interpersonal conflicts into community conflagrations.

One such incident happened on a sunny summer day in New York, when eleven-year-old Steven pushed ten-year-old Joey to the ground and kicked him hard in the ribs during a dispute over a game. When Joey's mother went outside, she found him on the ground, in pain and gasping for air. Fortunately, Joey's asthma medicine restored his breathing, and a doctor's visit showed that he had a bruised rib, not a broken one. That, however, was not the end of the incident.

Steven's family had come to the United States from Puerto Rico, and the only housing that had been available to them when they first came was in a ghetto area where Steven had quickly learned to defend himself and his brothers. He and his family already felt that white people were against them, and that feeling was exacerbated when neighbors grew cold after the incident with Joey. For their part, the white neighbors feared Steven's ferocity and viewed him and his growing brothers with suspicion, wondering about a future Puerto Rican gang, as they'd read about in the newspapers. The ethnic mistrust that permeates American society hardened the families' attitudes toward one another, reinforcing old prejudices and leading to catcalls, rudeness and minor scuffles whenever paths crossed. Thus, due to racial prejudice, a simple playground fight polarized a whole neighborhood.

Recurring Effect of Unresolved Conflict

Tensions over racial inequities is a prime example of how an issue of conflict will resurface repeatedly until it is finally resolved. Although the United States was founded upon the highest ideals of democracy and freedom translating these ideals into practical reality has been a continuous challenge throughout its history.

The issue of slavery was never dealt with during the founding of America. Thomas Jefferson said slavery kept him awake like an alarm bell in the night foreboding the death of the Union.[3] George Washington predicted that this unfinished business would someday divide the nation. His guilt and uneasiness over slavery led him to free his own slaves upon his wife s death and to work for the education of all slaves. "I clearly foresee that nothing but the rooting out of slavery can perpetuate the existence of our union," he said,[4] and vowed that if the nation ever divided on the issue he would fight on the side against slavery. Yet Washington's efforts to better the lots of slaves in Virginia were fruitless. The unresolved issue raised its head again as these presidents predicted it would several generations later. The Civil War was fought over the issue of slavery at the cost of half a million lives.

Abraham Lincoln vowed to fight slavery to the end, even "until every drop of blood drawn with the lash shall be paid by another drawn with the sword."[5] He believed that the war was payment for long unresolved injustices. But even though the Civil War was consciously fought to right an historical wrong, the issue of inequality between races was not settled and was left to another generation to resolve on a deeper level—the level of the heart.

One hundred years after the Civil War, Martin Luther King, Jr. and others worked to establish civil rights and equality for all races. King's soaring oratory and his courage through a campaign of non-violent demonstrations called America to her conscience on race relations. Many whites experienced a genuine change of heart. Legislation was passed, and as they had in the Civil War, federal troops were called in to defend blacks' rights to participate in democracy. African-Americans entered mainstream national life in unprecedented numbers and ways. Although race relations are far from what they should be, King and others catapulted race relations forward through the peaceable resolution of conflict, bringing the ideal of human equality closer to actuality.

If social problems and crises are not dealt with thoroughly and well, they will inevitably resurface in the future until they are properly resolved. There have been many cases where one side won a war only to be re-engaged in battle years later because the original animosities never were addressed. Physical force may stop an aggressor in the moment, but it does not stop the enmity and resentment that caused the aggression in the first place. Defeating an enemy does not answer his or her grievances or end hatred. Unless the defeated one's desire for vengeance is abated by kindness and fairness, sooner or later the urge for revenge will rise again, often in an even more destructive form. This is why history often appears to repeat itself. Until the deep, underlying factors are resolved, the conflicts will arise again and again.

Conflict needs to be dealt with on the deep, causal emotional level before peace can be well and fully established—whether it is peace between nations, races, societies, communities, students, families or within an individual. The heart of the problem is the human heart.

Conflict and the Human Heart

When people feel their human dignity has been violated, the reflex is to strike back. According to psychologist Steven Stosny, anger and the desire for vengeance stem from a sense of diminishment of self. The person feels disempowered and belittled. Therefore, he seeks to re-empower himself. Too often, such empowerment is attempted through counter-productive means.[6]

A nation may feel stung by actions that threaten its sovereignty, impugn its motives, or threaten to harm its well-being through interdiction of goods and services. That nation may go to war. On the community level, some individuals feel disenfranchised by the system. They feel left out, deprived, treated unequally. Such individuals may resort to crime and become even further marginalized.

After the Columbine massacre, fellow students reported that Columbine killers Eric Harris and Dylan Klebold had been the victims of brutal teasing. They were badgered, shoved up against lockers, bashed into walls, and people cut in front of them in line, acting as if they did not exist.[7] Erik Veik, a friend of the pair, reported that Klebold and Harris said they wanted to get revenge for the constant hazing. "They were tired of those who were insulting them, harassing them. They weren't going to take this anymore, and they wanted to stop it. Unfortunately, that's what they did."[8]

Police psychologists Marisa Pynchon and Robert Fein interviewed other students now in jail for school shootings and found that they, too, were often the victims of harsh teasing. Luke Woodham, convicted for shooting his girlfriend in school in 1997, stated, "They'd call me stupid or fat or whatever. Kids would sometimes throw rocks at me and push and kick me and hit me." These psychologists emphasize the need for adults to understand the intensity of teasing and similar conflicts between students at school.[9]

People who are marginalized or disrespected naturally seek to reassert their importance and value. While nothing can justify the actions of these students, it is possible that an atmosphere dedicated to the resolution of conflict and respectful treatment of others could have encouraged them to seek the help they so desperately needed instead of resorting to their horrendous actions.

Authentic empowerment comes from accessing the intrinsically good and most fundamental part of the self: the heart. Others' careless and thoughtless words do not—indeed cannot—diminish this core value of a human being. As Eleanor Roosevelt once said, "No one can make you feel small without your cooperation." Difficult circumstances may tarnish the "shine" from a person's heart but ultimately cannot destroy its potential to love and relate in a healthy way.

Stosny teaches children this concept with a coloring book that depicts "My Good Heart" and helps children get in touch with their best selves through drawings and questions. When asked, "What happens when people are not in touch with their good hearts?" children invariably draw pictures of people hitting each other, yelling at each other and committing acts of violence—scenes of escalated conflict.

Yet accessing the heart is not always easy. Without proper cultivation, the heart remains buried and often tangled in conflicting desires. Martin Luther King, Jr., commented on such intrapersonal tensions—tensions within the person himself: "Each of us is something of a schizophrenic personality, tragically divided against ourselves. A persistent civil war rages within all of our lives."[10] This inner divisiveness between the individual's best impulses and his worst ones is the root of conflict. This has been described and dramatized in countless ways throughout history.

Plato described the human personality as a charioteer with two willful horses pulling in opposite directions. Psychology depicts it as a battle between the socialized self and the infantile self. Some cultures have characterized it as a battle between the animal self and the human self. Poets, artists, philosophers and the religious have often seen it as a war between metaphysical forces of good and evil. However it is viewed, this inner struggle is inevitably reflected in quarrels with others, whether within the family, in the school, or in the community. When people are not at peace with themselves, it is easy to clash with others. The quarrels between spouses, strife between groups, and hostilities among nations are all reflections of the conflict within each individual.

One way to access the heart is to affirm such universal values as respect and the interrelatedness and common humanity of all people. Indeed, universal values lie at the core of peacemaking and rebuilding a sense of connection and community. Kay Pranis of the Minnesota Department of Corrections said, "Communities are value-laden structures. Resilient, sustainable communities are built on respect, caring, taking responsibility, fulfilling obligations, a sense of shared fate."[11] Any attempts to arrive at peace that are not value-driven are usually ineffective.

Universal values include the notion that every person is worthy of respect. This respect extends to the one who is considered the offender in the conflict too. The offender, even in the wrong, is a human being responding to pain—a person in need of correction, but in need of support and help as well. To bring the offender back into good standing with the others he or she has affected is the goal. This means healing the rift rather than just meting out punishment. Ideally, it means restoring the relationship on the level of the heart.

Steps to Resolving Conflict

Mohandas K. Gandhi, the great peacemaker of India, discovered in his early law practice that everyone benefited if his motivation was to bring the parties together rather than to "win" his cases. Indeed, if restoring the warring parties into a good relationship is the basic motivation of conflict resolution, the problem is already well on its way to being solved. There are three distinct phases or steps that characterize all good conflict resolution efforts:

Step One: Reflection and Reorientation. This step involves getting in touch with the heart and higher motives as well as considering the ways in which one might have been at fault.

Step Two: *Reversal and Restitution* is the step of acting upon these better impulses to ameliorate some of the injury and separation.

Step Three: Reconciliation and Renewal is the experience of coming together again and making a fresh start.

Whether consciously or not, conflict resolution goes through these steps naturally. People clash and separate. After they cool off and calm down, they often find themselves having regrets and even charitable feelings toward the other party. These sentiments gently prod them to renew the relationship. They approach the other person with an apology or other expression of sorrow over the incident. Then the two parties begin to restore some degree of harmony and good feeling.

Step 1 — Reflection and Reorientation

Upon reflection, those who have been involved in a conflict may realize how their own conduct contributed to the problem in some way big or small. Rueful second thoughts about their own words or behavior—or the motivation behind them—are often part of this process. So is clarifying why the other person or group affected them in such a way. Parents and educators can guide students to consider such questions as: "What could I have done differently? What is the real problem here? What do I really want and need? Where do I need to change myself? How did I contribute to the problem?"

Students usually need special help with this process. When emotions are running high, a teacher can encourage reflection by first helping the parties cool down and think. The Falk Laboratory School at the University of Pittsburgh in Pennsylvania has developed a creative program called Conflict and Resolution Education (CARE) that helps students to think things through by use of a traffic light image. The red light reminds students to stop and "Cool Down" and recall the "Ground Rules." "Tell Your Side" and "Listen" are labels for the yellow light. The green light exhorts them to "Brainstorm Ideas" for solving the problem.

At the end of the first year, teachers reported that conflict resolution had taken on a collaborative problem-solving dimension. One primary grade teacher found that students were applying techniques taught and practiced in classrooms at home. One insightful seven-year-old student urged his parents to use the conflict-resolution traffic light because "it works in school."[12]

Another technique to encourage reflection and reorientation is taught by Volunteers of America. It is called "Have a SODA." Students at odds are given a picture of a large ice cream soda and asked to sit down and reflect on the meaning of the acronym. S means "Stop." O means consider the "Options"—"If I do this, this will result, and if I do that, that will result." D stands for "Decide" which option to take, and A stands for "Act" according to a good decision.

Step 1: Reflection and Reorientation

- Identify one's contribution to the problem
- Recognize how it affected the other's feelings
- Evaluate one's attitude and behavior in light of universal values
- Consider how one might have better dealt with the problem
- Decide to take responsibility for one's contribution to the problem
- Plan how to make amends

Thinking about Values and Outcomes

The reflection phase also includes thinking about values: Do I believe in fighting? Are angry words, harsh gestures and unforgiving attitudes conducive to good human relationships? Are all people inherently worthy of respect and fair treatment—even my so-called enemy of the moment? Am I worthy inside, no matter what the other person has said or done? Such reflection can often calm a person down and motivate him or her to take responsibility to heal the conflict.

In the upper grades at New Hope School in Bridgeport, Connecticut, behavior journals function as a method to cool off, gain perspective and process negative feelings about a situation that made a student angry or agitated. When teens are overwhelmed by feelings of unfairness, frustration, impotence or anger, their ability to reflect on goals and values is greatly compromised. In their journals students describe their view of what happened, the variety of emotions surrounding the experience, and to consider the implications if "everybody responded that way." Then they identify a value or action that will help resolve the conflict.

This technique worked well for one student, Steve. During the stressful time of his parents' divorce, he yelled a racial slur at the school janitor, and later defended his action by claiming that the janitor had previously called him names and spread rumors about him. Steve's teacher did a lot of work to help him get to the heart of the matter—his own pain and frustration—and to see the value of practicing respect even though he might not feel adults always deserve it. After begrudgingly writing an apology to the janitor, Steve began to feel true remorse and decided to apologize face to face.

Reflection also means to clarify the desired outcome of the conflict and to consider means to bring this about. In a thoughtful moment, a person may realize that some types of vengeful actions or expressions of anger will not bring about the results they really desire and might even have an opposite effect.

For instance, Patricia, a mother of two elementary school children, was enraged when her nine-year-old son came home from school saying that his teacher had accused him of lying, in front of the class. The boy had expressed confusion and concern at home about test scoring, and when his father had called the school to inquire, the teacher had become defensive and thought the boy had gone home with tall tales about unfair test scoring practices.

Patricia and her husband were angered on behalf of their son, but they reflected upon what they wanted to come out of the ensuing parent-teacher conference. What they really wanted, they decided, was for their son to receive a sincere apology in front of the students who had heard the accusation and for the teacher to be more charitable toward him (and other students) in the future. They did not want to take him out of school in the middle of the academic year. They decided to work toward these ends.

Upon reflection and discussion with the principal, the teacher decided that she had been in the wrong. She adopted the policy that when an issue came up with a parent, she would first discuss the issue thoroughly with the parent and the principal before confronting a child. She reoriented herself toward giving children the benefit of the doubt.

The Role of a Mediator

A mediator may be needed in the case when the parties involved need help in getting the process started. A mediator is a neutral and mutually trusted figure who is not personally involved in the conflict. The mediator helps the disputing sides find a common basis—points of agreement—for constructive interaction. Thus the mediator encourages both sides to take the first two steps of restoring peace and find their way towards reconciliation and renewal.

An effective mediator affirms the value of both parties and thus helps each to affirm the other's value. The goal of the mediator-although it is not easy—is to achieve a collaborative, win-win outcome where both sides can feel satisfied. The mediator helps the parties find possibilities for cooperation and mutual benefit.

School mediation is typically led either by teachers or peers. Six basic steps of successful teacher-led mediation are as follows:

1. Initiate mediation: Approach the conflict and make a statement, stop aggressive behavior, neutralize any object of conflict by holding it (i.e., a disputed piece of sports equipment will be appropriated by the teacher).
2. Gather information about the victim's feelings and aggressor's wants and assure the disputants that each will be heard.
3. Define the problem in terms satisfactory to both sides by paraphrasing their feelings and concerns.

4. Generate alternative solutions by encouraging suggestions from disputants and observers and allowing ample time for them to come up with ideas on their own.
5. Agree on a solution: paraphrase it and spell out how the solution will be implemented.
6. Follow through by arranging someone to monitor the implementation and announce its success when this has occurred.[13]

Some schools have success with peer mediation programs for older students. The Mediation for Kids training program[14] trains young mediators how to see both sides, remain impartial and not react to the excesses of emotion involved in the disagreement, and assert values over vengeance. It provides an activity format to guide students through the mediation process.

Properly trained, peers can be understanding and helpful mediators, though they need the support of the administration, teachers and other adults to be effective. Peer mediators are uniquely placed to find and understand the underlying emotional and psychological needs operating in their peers and to help them "save face" and survive in the school environment.

Step 2 — Reversal and Restitution

Reversal and restitution is the substantial attempt to right the wrong that was done to the other party and to reverse whatever caused him or her to feel hurt or violated. It is a sincere effort to soothe the sorrow and pain that was caused. It is an admission of wrong and a gesture of good will which strives to make amends and reconnect with the other person by whatever means are necessary to make an opening to renew the relationship. In the case of Patricia's son, the teacher issued an apology to the boy in front of the class and from that time on treated him with more kindness.

Often, the motivation to restore a damaged relationship and forgive cannot be awakened without an actual gesture showing sorrow or compunction. Such a gesture serves as payment or indemnity for losses incurred. In common incidents, it is a peace offering: the enraged heart of a neighbor is assuaged when the boy who put a ball through his window offers to pay for it; the wife who is angry at her husband's neglect is mollified by a huge bouquet of roses.

This concept of making concrete reparations, called "restorative justice," is enjoying increasing popularity in the criminal justice system.[15] Some offenders are being held financially liable to their victims for the losses and damages they caused. In other cases, the offender not only pays compensation in the form of service to the community or in fines or incarceration, but also he or she meets with the victim and their representatives and listens to their story of how the offense affected their lives. In many cases, this leads to greater understanding between the two and reduces recidivism as the offender is schooled in empathy. The victims also feel relief at having been heard.

Restitution may take the form of lesser compensation, such as an apology or an act of kindness in a relationship that is basically sound. On the other hand, there are situations where "equal" restitution is necessary. If property is damaged, it may have to be repaired or replaced for the full value of what it was worth before it was damaged. In some cases, the restitution required may be greater than the original injury.

A $50 debt that is left unpaid may be increased to $60 to cover the delay and frustration of the creditor. Someone who has made a hurtful remark to someone they do not know well may have to make many gestures of sincerity before the person is able to trust them. Insincerity or failure to fulfill an earlier promise may increase the time and amount of restitution required. This is one reason why it is desirable to resolve conflict when it first crops up.

Step 2. Reversal and Restitution

- Reverse whatever caused the other to feel violated
- Make restitution to correct injustice and repair

damage done

- Be open to receive restitution

A Change in Attitude

Sometimes a reversal in a person's attitude and behavior is the key to restoring harmony. Certain attitudes provoke friction. Arrogance is one of them, and practicing humility reverses it. Humility involves being able to admit to not always having the superior or correct view and being receptive to learning from others. Often, a stubborn insistence on being right hinders people from seeing events from another person's point of view. A person with humility defers to the common humanity of all people, recognizing that everyone, including herself, has shortcomings and can improve.

"I hadn't talked to my brother Piet for a year after we had a big blow-up in a restaurant over his claiming to be out of money again and asking me to pay," recalls, Joan, a middle-aged illustrator. "I went ballistic after all the money I've lent him that he still hasn't paid back. When he finally called me up and apologized for that, I found myself admitting to myself that I once owed Dad quite a bit of money, too. Somehow I could let it go and enjoy talking to Piet." Thus does humility often beget more humility. If a person can bring him or herself to humbly admit to wrongdoing or a bad attitude, the other person is much more inclined to forgive—or even to sheepishly admit to his or her own weakness or role in the problem.

Generosity reverses greed. An episode on a popular television series showed how a woman had undercut a talented friend in order to take center stage and become a star. When confronted with her greed, the star generously allowed her friend to go on stage in her place, giving her a moment in the spotlight. She also helped her friend's daughter succeed in a stage career. In this way, she reversed and made up for her self-centered and hurtful actions.

Feeling themselves superior to others, people sometimes treat one another in cruel or unjust ways, spawning resentment, anger and a desire for retaliation. An attitude of service reverses the pain caused by such actions and attitudes. A hospital orderly on the West coast tells of one episode of service removing resentment. "The doctors sometimes march around like little kings and never even notice you. But I'll never forget the first time a doctor remembered my name, thanked me, and even gave me a present later for my new baby. I was stunned. I felt different after that."

Anger is reversed by compassion. A program for New York City bus drivers designed to help them cope with stresses and frustrations on their jobs helped them develop compassion toward their passengers through changing their frame of reference. The bus drivers were shown a film clip of a woman getting onto a bus very slowly and holding up all the other passengers, as well as traffic. The bus drivers found this maddening. Couldn't the woman understand the pressures of traffic and route timing that the drivers were under? Why was she deliberately moving so slowly? Then it was explained to the drivers that the woman had a disability which was not visible but which caused her to walk slowly and with much pain. Back on the job after such training in compassion, the bus drivers all reported a decrease in tension, anger and conflict. Some of them even felt sorry about the way they had treated customers in the past and began to deal with their customers with more empathy and understanding.[16]

Two Sides to Every Story

Taking responsibility for restitution is not the sole burden of the offender. Often it is not even easy to determine who is the offender and who the offended. In most clashes, both parties wind up hurting each other, or the present offender might think that he or she is only evening up the score from a previous injury committed by the other party. Sometimes, too, the apparent offender lacks the maturity or clarity of mind to make any gestures of reparation, and if the relationship is valued enough—as between family members—the offended may need to make the first move if any restoration of the relationship is going to occur. "Realistically, I knew my mother was bullheaded and proud and she wouldn't budge even if it killed her," says Matt, 38, a stock analyst in Canada. "Not coming to my wedding just tops a long list of insults. But she is my mom and I want my kids to have a grandma, so I've made overtures and even apologies so she can be part of our lives without admitting she did wrong." It is wise for both sides of a conflict to think in terms of how each may take responsibility to rectify the problem; however, in the end it may well be that whoever has the heart to do so has to initiate efforts to repair the relationship.

Consciously applying the strategy of Reversal and Restitution shows people what to do when they are feeling stymied by conflict. Though they may not feel inclined to do so, once they have made a gesture of restitution, they are likely to experience a great release of good feeling and a strong sense of renewed relationship. This is the transition to Step Three of conflict resolution—Reconciliation and Renewal.

Step 3 — Reconciliation and Renewal

In the case of Patricia mentioned above, although the teacher had apologized for the miscommunications that had led to the altercation over test scoring, this mother still felt distant from the school and brooded over whether she should keep her child there. She realized upon reflection, however, that she had been feeling distant from the school for a long time before the incident and had not been cultivating a relationship with her child's teacher as much as she should have. At the next opportunity, she went up to the teacher after school and sincerely apologized for her part in the conflict, presenting a small gift. The teacher was a conscientious woman who had deeply regretted the incident, and when Patricia apologized to her, she had a hard time holding back her emotions. Mother and teacher promised to work more closely together in the future. Patricia felt a rebound of loyalty and affection for the school and began to think of ways she could contribute as a volunteer.

This third step in peacemaking is a result of the work done in the first two steps. It is a transitioning from broken relationships to restored ones: reconciliation. Often, the restored relationship is stronger than it was before the conflict happened. Based on reconciliation, there may be renewal. Once the parties understand each other better, new avenues of friendship and relationship open. Having had an emotional experience together, people who have successfully resolved a conflict may feel closer and more bonded than ever before. Reconciliation means people have had to take a closer look at one another and at themselves; it is often a spur to new levels of understanding and sympathy.

Step 3: Reconciliation and Renewal

- Give up claim to retaliation
- Forgive and be open to forgiveness
- Support the other's reform
- Foster good will

The Element of Forgiveness

Forgiveness is an essential aspect of reconciliation to bring tensions to an end. Forgiveness means to give up the claim to retaliation and to allow positive energy to flow in the relationship again. Forgiveness does not excuse the wrongful or hurtful actions; nor does it mean that repetition of such actions is acceptable. However, forgiveness means that the actions no longer stand in the way of relating. The blockage is at least partially removed.

It is also well to note that forgiving is as beneficial to the one who forgives as to the one who is forgiven. Forgiveness brings relief. Letting go of the resentment, ill will, residual desires for revenge and negative expectations of the other brings a new sense of freedom.

"I'll never forget the feelings I had when the airplane started to shake and dip," said Toby, a woman in her late twenties, who was flying from California to New York at the time. "I gripped the seat handles and thought, 'What if I die?' Then the next thought that came was, 'Who haven't I forgiven?' I realized I hadn't forgiven Jesse, who had jilted me after a year's engagement. He'd approached me several times afterward, trying to be friends, but I'd just spurned him. In those moments before I thought we were going to go down, I thought, 'Jesse, I forgive you. I let you go.' Well, the plane didn't crash, but after that I found that whenever thoughts of Jesse occurred—less and less as time went by—I felt peace in my heart. I've heard he's married now, and I wish him well."

Forgiving is not easy. It requires the individual to find a certain amount of trust that he or she will not lose by forgiving. Forgiveness is easier if the second step of Reversal and Restitution has been done sincerely and well. Yet, even without these steps, the forgiving person is the one who finds the greater peace within and more gratifying relationships with people in general.

It is easier to reconcile when one person is able to see the other as a vulnerable fellow human being. Reconciliation and renewal are humanizing processes. The other person may be operating from a base of fear or pain or deprivation, and once this is understood, it is easier to forgive. As Henry Wadsworth Longfellow wrote, "If we could read the secret history of our enemies, we should find in each man's life of sorrow and suffering enough to disarm all hostility."[17]

A woman in her sixties had been shaken upon discovering a homeless man who had broken into her basement and lived there for three days. The sight of the man and the mess he had made of her basement had terrified her. When she saw him again, this time in court, however, she felt sorry for him. The man had gone through a rehabilitation program and now humbly apologized, telling her he understood her feelings of fear and violation. The woman suddenly saw him as a person like herself, not a threatening figure at all. She realized that his crime against her property had been more a result of his own confusion and helplessness rather than an attack upon her. She said, "I saw him as another human soul trying to put sense into life. I see that person as myself in many ways, that frightened, sometimes beaten soul."[18]

The heart is where conflicts become embedded, and they will proliferate and rise again until truly resolved on this profound level. Conflict need not be feared or avoided, but rather seen as an opportunity for deeper relatedness. After proceeding through three discrete steps, conflict resolution can welcome people firmly back into the camp of human belonging, resulting in hope and resurgent relationships.

Notes

1. Gordon G. Vessels, *Character and Community Development: A School Planning and Teacher Training Handbook* (Westport, CT: Praeger, 1998), pp. 136-138.

2. Judith S. Wallerstein and Sandra Blakeslee, *The Good Marriage* (New York: Warner, 1996), p. 93.

3. In spite of his own usage of slaves, Jefferson's early drafts of the Declaration of Independence denounced slavery. Bruce Lancaster and H. Plumb, *The American Heritage Book of the Revolution* (New York: Dell, 1958) p. 147.

4. James Thomas Flexner, *Washington: The Indispensable Man* (New York: Little, Brown and Company, 1974) p. 386.

5. John Grafton, ed., *Abraham Lincoln, Great Speeches* (New York: Dover, 1991), p. 107.

6. Steven Stosny, *The Miracle of Empowered Love,* unpublished, 1997.

7. Peter Forsbrig, Columbine student, speaking on "Talking It Out" with John Donovan, *ABC News,* April 23, 1999.

8. Jonathan Dube, "High School Hell," *ABC News,* April 28, 1999.

9. *60 Minutes,* March 13,2000.

10. Martin Luther King, Jr., *Strength to Love* (Philadelphia: Fortress, 1963), p. 49.

11. Kay Pranis, "Moral Education in Restorative Practices," conference of the Association for Moral Education, University of Minnesota, November 18-21, 1999.

12. Marian L. Voilmer, Ellen B. Drook, and Patricia J. Hamet, "Partnering Character Education and Conflict Resolution," *Kappa Delta Pi Record* (Spring 1999), pp. 122-25.

13. S. Dinwiddie, "The Saga of Sally, Sammy and the Red Pen: Facilitating Children's Social Problem Solving," *Young Children,* July 13-19, 1994.

14. F. Schmidt, A. Freidman, and J. Marvel, *Mediation for Kids: Kids in Dispute Settlement* (Miami Beach, FL: Grace Contrino Abrams Peace Education Foundation, 1992).

15. Howard Zehr and Harry Mika, "Fundamental Concepts of Restorative Justice," Mennonite Central Committee publication, 1997.

16. Carol Tavris, "Anger Defused," *Perspectives on Marriage, A Reader,* Kieran Scott and Michael Warren, eds. (New York: Oxford University Press, 1993), p. 231.

17. Quoted in Harville Hendrix and Helen Hunt, *The Couples Companion: Meditations and Exercises for Getting the Love You Want* (New York: Pocket Books, 1994), p. 331.

18. Kay Pranis, "Victims in the Peacemaking Circle Process," *The Crime Victim Report* (September—October 1999), p. 63.

Cross-Cultural Conflict Resolution

Abdul Aziz Said
American University and

Nathan C. Funk
American University and

Lynn M. Kunkle
American University

Islam, like all religions, is not only a theological affirmation but also a living historical process with multiple syntheses and expressions that must be taken into account.

***

To transform relations between Islam and the West, we need a new framework for cross-cultural conflict resolution that underscores the role of faith in peacemaking. By affirming the role of faith, we can create space for authentic communication in the midst of conflict—communication from which a new narrative of cooperation may yet emerge.

Many Paths to Peace

At the turn of the twenty-first century, the rising prominence of protracted ethnic and religious conflicts, combined with emergent fears of so-called "civilizational" clashes, have convinced many scholars and commentators that dominant models of human and social development may be incomplete, insofar as they understate the power of the religious impulse and cultural particularity while searching for material but not spiritual common denominators. Clearly, the cultural and religious aspects of conflict and its resolution must be taken seriously. While the conditions for broad-based dialogue—and hence for full actualization of the role of faith in conflict resolution—have yet to be met, an emerging literature on religion, conflict resolution, and peace has contributed significantly to prospects for new forms of ecumenical dialogue and collaborative effort in the domain of faith-based peacemaking.

Ideals of peace span across all religions and cultures, incorporating such values as security and harmony as well as justice and human dignity. Every major system of faith and belief, whether religious or secular in character, has in some way or another promised peace as an outcome of the implementation of its precepts. While the character and content of ideals has differed, conceptions of peace nonetheless recur in the most diverse philosophical and religious systems—in the *Republic* by Plato, the scholasticism of Abrahamic traditions, the humanism of the Enlightenment, the *Arthashashtra* by Kautilya, and the *realpolitik* of modern international relations theory. While peace is sometimes construed narrowly, to denote a simple absence of war, the word carries deeper resonances and broader significations, suggesting a presence of human dignity or social, ecological, and spiritual harmony. While scholars and activists have only just begun to identify cultural pluralism as a potential *resource* for a dynamic and sustainable world order, some have attempted to promote a truly cross-cultural research agenda.[2]

Each living religious and philosophical tradition possesses a repertoire of peace-related precepts and practices that is in some sense both universal in significance and uniquely particular in form. Even where ideals converge within a single tradition, praxeological styles often diverge, leading to manifold ways of relating essential precepts and values to daily practices. For example, Christians who share belief in the redemptive love of God through Christ have differed over the proper means of aspiring to create the peaceful "City of God." Historically, some have viewed imperial power and centralized authority as an appropriate means to the sought-after ends; others have favored an approach centered on the witness of small communities of faith, and still others have underscored individual conscience and social renewal through the reform of institutions.

When we speak of the role of faith in cross-cultural conflict resolution, our challenge is to honor the diversity of the world's humanistic and spiritual traditions while seeking common ground among them. What is needed, in other words, is an agenda for research, dialogue, and activism that is global in conception, and responsive to common challenges of peacemaking and coexistence within and among the world's many traditions. It is no longer sufficient for transnational agendas for the advancement of peace to be defined primarily by the cultural experiences and perceived security threats of a particular nation or culture. We need new frameworks for thinking about religion, culture, and spirituality—frameworks that recognize the powerful role that faith and belief play in conflict and conflict resolution, and that do not privilege one culture as "normal" and label another as "exceptional."

***

From an experiential perspective, religion may be defined as a path of ultimate transformation, comprising a "system of symbols [upholding] deep-seated attitudes and motivations, providing a complete system of values for human life."[3] As an interconnected system of symbols, religion provides a basis for what Galtung calls "deep culture," a comprehensive and coherent ethical system, with patterned, idealized courses of action for handling conflict to achieve harmony. Distinctive patterns of conflict resolution testify to successfully established cosmologies from which adherents may take for granted shared normative frames of reference for interpreting the rightness or wrongness of events.

The ways that religion informs a collective cosmology[4] are profound but often subtle. Cosmology includes the unstated expectations, the subconscious or "common-knowledge" framework and measure by which behaviors, gestures, and responses are all given meaning. These patterned expectations arrive from religious and other social experiences, and are so deeply ingrained that they do not always surface consciously. They are surfaced and most pronounced in conflict situations, however, where expectations of *what should be* are violated and new circumstances must be evaluated and responded to. In these instances, collective cosmologies become manifest in the conflict dynamic though the choice of language, invoked imagery, and appeal to certain values and goals regarding the "intended order." Appeals to shared values regarding justice and the intended social order are especially important for addressing and resolving conflicts where pronounced power asymmetries exist between parties. Likewise, recurring violations of *what should be* can lead to a larger crisis of meaning. In this way, resolving "horizontal" conflicts between participants play an important role in upholding a larger, "vertical" sacred order.

By encompassing a broad repertoire of models or precedents of desirable behavior in conflicted circumstances while admonishing others, religion implicitly influences the desirability and likelihood of certain courses of action over others. In turn, strategic responses to conflict tend to be rationalized in a manner that is not injurious to religious value systems, but which will tend to reaffirm core beliefs. As they attempt to justify responses to a conflict situation, members of an identity group may go to considerable lengths to filter and select information about adversaries. Commitment to a particular enemy image, then, can be fundamental to preserving a moral self-image and avoiding cognitive dissonance, even if a more sober and painful assessment of self and other would be more true to a more deeply rooted the religious impulse.

In many societies, religion provides a powerful framework of social identification, a framework within which the authenticity and validity of ideas and social practices are evaluated. Religion is thus an important element in the fabric of group and individual identity, and in some societies, particularly Muslim societies, a shared religious identity is understood to underpin that fabric. The "deep" presuppositions of religions—collective, cultural vehicles for human faith—operate both explicitly and implicitly at the group and individual levels, and are personally validated and socially reinforced over time. Understanding these highest values and fundamental beliefs regarding human nature and establishment of right relation to the divine is essential for comprehending different cultures' conceptions of the conditions that both characterize and cultivate peace.

***

...Significantly, Christianity is the most unequivocal of the monotheist traditions in encouraging unilateral, personalized methods for resolving conflict, based on such principles as confession, repentance, and forgiveness accompanied by personal transcendence and beginning "anew." In both Islam and Judaism, reciprocal or other social arrangements are strongly emphasized which may weigh social considerations over or as much as the strictly personal, and which view the continuity of community tradition more heavily than "clean breaks" from the past. Whereas Christianity conceives of forgiveness as a moral and religious imperative, Islam affirms forgiveness as a noble course of action, as a social good, and as a source of heavenly reward, but places less emphasis on its redemptive, psychological significance for the individual and society.

***

Activation of religious and cultural resources for conflict resolution supports empowerment at both practical and motivational levels. At the level of practice, a thorough accounting of methods and strategies can be made; at the level of motivation, it is worth noting that local conflict resolution approaches speak directly to the highest aims and moral values of a particular religious culture. Precisely because conflict can rend at the fabric of a community and create rupture in the lives of individuals, societies evolve resolution styles and norms celebrating norms that can help to control escalation and, ideally, restore a sense of harmony or wholeness.

***

Affirming Collective Religious Beliefs and Personal Spirituality: A Faith-Based Approach to Conflict Resolution

As they respond to conflict events, parties to conflict struggle to avoid the experience of rupture and fragmentation in their lives and values—indeed, in their relationship to the divine. In a far from insignificant way, religious narratives themselves are tales of struggle to approximate an ideal amidst the tensions of life, to achieve resolution or become an agent of divine will. It is no wonder then, that religious elements may be found both within conflict dynamics and in efforts to transcend them, and that even mediators who express indifference to religion as conventionally practiced often profess an interest in matters of spirituality and faith.

By invoking the sacred, religion brings forth ideas of wholeness, ultimate meaning, existential security, and transformation that are particularly relevant to, and sought after by, parties in conflict.

Religious beliefs, then, can influence preferred conflict resolution approaches directly, by presenting idealized actions and guidelines for moral conduct, as well as implicitly, through emotional memory and religiously based principles and values. Most importantly, religious cosmologies provide coping mechanisms for handling conflict, stress and trauma. In this way, parties to conflict can achieve healing and the transformations necessary for renewal and a return to wholeness.

Through a process of conflict resolution that is sensitive to religious and spiritual concerns, participants are afforded the possibility of restoring and renewing their social relations. Faith-based conflict resolution, then, offers prospects for individuals to be redeemed in terms of their own conscience, their spiritual relation with the divine, and their highest ideals. It affirms deeper needs and ideals that are conducive to personal empowerment and humanization of the "other," and helps to separate that which is essential in a personal or communal identity structure from that which is more superficial. It encourages participants to look to the guidelines and moral exemplars of their own cultural or religious tradition, while also drawing forth their own personal spirituality as they seek to recognize legitimate claims, to take responsibility for a share of the conflict situation, and, if and when they feel it necessary, to reconsider fundamental assumptions about self and other. By attending to communal beliefs and values while creating a space that affirms the personal potentially transcultural character of spirituality, a faith-based approach to conflict resolution accounts for important cultural differences and resonates with the experience of conflict and reconciliation at a deep, existential level. In situations where belief systems differ, particularistic doctrines are recognized and incorporated but not absolutized, and parties to conflict are provided with opportunities to "stretch" the limitations of their prior understandings and to identify exemplars of ecumenical concern within their own tradition.

Attempts to divorce the spiritual from conflict resolution practices deny an essential component of healing and social restoration that permits conflicts to be *experienced* as resolved. This is in part because conflict resolution processes that do not address spiritual transformation processes are prone to a sense of incompleteness or mere suspension of conflict, lacking in restoration, wholeness or healing. The existential ruptures that occur in conflict situations often require symbolic redress, or meaningful exchange of human acknowledgement within the frameworks offered by collective cosmologies. By advancing a vision of social harmony and the role of the individual within it, faith-based practices elucidate what resolution and peace will require, so that a deeply embedded system of meaning and appropriate coping mechanisms are engaged for healing and transformation.

***

While there are many debates regarding the most fitting and proper manner to interpret and apply *shari'a* in the modern world, the principal concern of *shari'a* is the maintenance of proper, harmonious relationships on and across all levels—between the individual and God, within the individual, within the family and community, among Muslims, between religions, and ultimately with all of humanity and creation. Law is expected to support and promote the fulfillment of lasting, deeply rooted human needs and discourage the pursuit of false satisfiers. Religious tolerance is built into Islamic precepts, which confer to the "People of the Book" a protected status. From the standpoint of Islamic universalism, particularly as it has been articulated by those who have contemplated the Qur'anic passage, "*To every people (was sent) a Messenger*" (10: 47), humankind is ultimately one community; comparative evaluation of prophets is discouraged, for all are deemed messengers of one God.[5]

A striking feature of Qur'anic discourse is the emphasis on people's use of their innate intelligence in comprehending the revealed guidance, which is accessible both in the Holy Book and in the Book of Nature. Time and again the *Qur'an* exhorts its hearers to ponder, reflect, think, and understand. Religion is armed with arguments designed to persuade through force of logic, emotional appeal, appeals to universal cosmic order and Divine providential purpose, and, failing these, promises of eschatological rewards or punishments. Above all, it is recognized that people cannot be dissuaded from pursuing the wrong course in this life through force or violence: "*There is no compulsion in faith!*" asserts the *Qur'an* (2:256).

***

Islam and the West: A Search for Common Ground

Discussions of Islamic conceptions of peace and conflict resolution lead quite naturally to the question of Islamic political activism. Contemporary Islamic activism is not a backward-looking rejection of the modern world, but rather a deeply felt expression of cultural identity and a critique of domestic as well as international political orders.[6] Islam provides its adherents with a language that addresses all aspects of life, and Islamic activism equips Muslims with a vocabulary through which they may affirm their identity and project themselves politically.

***

All too often, differences between Islamic and Western concepts and values are either over-represented or under-represented. When they are over-represented, the result is the "incompatibility" story mentioned at the beginning of this essay, in which dialogue between the West and Islam is portrayed as an exercise in futility. In large part to counteract this story, a second story—the story of compatibility—has also been told, identifying genuine similarities but sometimes seeking to subsume Islamic precepts within a Western framework. A third story—a story of intercultural complementarity and reconciliation, we hope—has yet to be written….

***

Because Islamic traditions provide a set of powerful political precepts and practices with universal implications, Islam can make important contributions to an integrated world order—one that affirms the unique value of all cultural traditions. In particular, Islam prescribes a strong sense of community and solidarity of people; it postulates a collaborative concept of freedom; and it demystifies the Western myth of triumphant material progress and development. Moreover, Islamic precepts offer strongly affirmative statements on the subject of cultural pluralism.

Societies have so often been repressive that a strong Western tradition has emerged that sees the elimination of repression and want as the chief goal of society. Though Muslim societies might benefit from careful study of Western individualism, they need not embrace the West's dichotomy between the individual and the community, in which the individual is seen as serving the individual. It is true that cultural systems, like political, economic and social ones, have usually contained much to impede human development: forces such as prejudice, chauvinism, competitiveness, racism, sexism, and so on. This does not change the fact that the cultural community is where most human realization must take place. Thus, the cultural community needs to be served by political, economic and social systems, rather than the reverse.

There are many roads to humanistic cultural pluralism, many potential systems of communitarian, free, creative life, and many potential languages, arts, music, dramas, and literatures that are compatible with humanistic ethics. No doubt, every community needs some "cultural revolution" to remove those things that dehumanize society or inhibit human development. But only as the primacy of the cultural community is made clear will creativity have a chance to replace conformity, with cooperation replacing competition.

***

...We live in an era of transition, one whose scope and depth goes beyond anything yet witnessed in human history. We live in the midst of suffering and hope, between tragedy and efforts to make new beginnings. We either face the choice of moving in the direction of creativity or becoming even less so than we are today.

***

Where do we go from here...? In a world of collapsing boundaries, cultures need to experience their commonality. This is necessary if the suffering that Americans and Westerners are undergoing in the face of scourges like terrorism is to find its counterpoint in the suffering of those who turn to militant belief systems or are unable to prevent their companions from doing so.

In other words, divergent worlds of perception—Islam and the West, the South and the North—must move from isolation toward unity. To do so, we need to stimulate reflection, find meaning in common tragedies, and share our most sacred values, including our conceptions of peace. Such activities permit a search for meaning and commonality. The discovery of commonality, in turn, makes reconciliation possible, through the re-identification and reaffirmation of the core spiritual precepts upon which our religious narratives, images, and values have been built. In the process, we may also derive common responses to shared human suffering.

***

Throughout history, though admittedly for limited periods, various civilizations have demonstrated how spiritual values can engender social progress. At the same time, we would hasten to acknowledge that these same values have just as often been corrupted and manipulated to justify actions that represent their antithesis. This in itself, however, should not prevent an appreciation of the historic association between the emergence of a truly moral social order and widespread commitment to spiritual values.

While we in no way wish to denigrate traditional religious commitments, we believe that, at the present juncture of human development, it is useful to make a distinction between spirituality and religion, even though the terms are often used interchangeably because both refer to matters of faith. The term *religion* refers to an institutional framework within which a specific theology is pursued, usually among a community of like-minded believers. *Spirituality*, on the other hand, transcends the boundaries of religion, suggesting broader human involvement that comes from the inner essence of a person. At the level of the individual, it refers to action borne of a commitment that is not necessarily informed by allegiance to a particular religion.

Just as we find the naïve materialism of the post-Renaissance centuries is no longer working, changes have begun in the direction of a more inclusive epistemology. As we enter the twenty-first century, we are recognizing that the deeper we delve into the fundamentals of science, the closer we are to the fundamentals of many of the traditional mysticisms. We are now coming to recognize the reality of "the sacred," which we define as any process that explicitly links us to the largest possible context to which we belong....

***

A new ethic must allow humanity to experience itself as complete, as we already are. It must value acceptance of the self as a whole, embracing the unconscious as well as conscious. The integration of the personality at the individual level becomes a metaphor for the integration of humanity at the species level.

***

Religious traditions and spirituality, however, must be reborn if they are to respond to contemporary spiritual needs and permit intercultural reconciliation. Though most religious and ethical systems promote reciprocity and goodwill, their institutions and outlooks are too frequently identified with just those aspects of the past that contribute to current division and conflict. Put very simply, spiritual values for the present and future cannot be partisan; they must speak to the universal human need for transcendence, unity, and justice.

In conclusion, we affirm that achieving a unifying global consensus as the basis for a humane, ecologically viable, new global system is possible. The essence of such a vision must be felt as well as rationally argued, because it involves both the head and the heart. From this perspective, a new global system requires new political and social arrangements, a new (or renewed) vision of humankind's existential reality and purpose, and an unrelenting effort to make the former truly reflect the latter. This is an agenda for conflict resolution that is worthy of the best in human nature and experience.

Notes

1. Some of the material in this chapter is appearing in the Spring, 2002 issue of *Peace and Conflict Studies.*

2. See, for example, Leslie E. Sponsel and Thomas Gregor, eds., *The Anthropology of Peace and Nonviolence* (Boulder, CO: Lynne Rienner, 1994); Kevin Avruch, *Culture and Conflict Resolution* (Washington, DC: United States Institute of Peace Press, 1998).

3. Ludwig, Theodore. (1994) *The Sacred Paths of the West.* MacMillan College Publishing Co. NY: 5.

4. Cosmologies are the basis of the "shared cultural universes" which are essential to the identification of both "conflict" and the legitimate means by which to resolve major disputes. As Galtung has emphasized, conflict is a matter of group consciousness: "each party [to a conflict] interprets the same phenomenon within its own framework," Galtung, Johann (1997) "Conflict Life Cycles in Occident and Orient." In *Cultural Variation in Conflict Resolution: Alternatives to Violence,* Douglas P. Fry and Kaj Bjorkqvist, eds, Lawrence Erlbaum Associates, Mahwah, NJ.: 49.

5. *Qur'an* (2:136).

6. Richard Falk, "False Universalism and the Geopolitics of Exclusion: The Case of Islam" (*Third World Quarterly,* vol. 18, no. 1, 1997, pp. 7-23). Falk unequivocally defends the right of Muslims to equitable participation *as Muslims* in the contemporary world order, and suggests that contemporary Islamic movements manifest resistance to cultural as well as political marginalization. Michael Salla, "Political Islam and the West: A New Cold War or Convergence?," (*Third World Quarterly,* vol. 18, no. 4, 1997, pp. 729-742) has advanced a similar argument. Salla suggests that there is a need to move beyond both stereotypical "essentializations" and fragmentary models based on historical contingency, toward representations of Islam as a discourse that critiques the dominant liberal democratic paradigm in a manner similar to many other religious discourses.

Competition vs. Monopoly in the Development of Peaceful Societies

Gordon L. Anderson
Professors World Peace Academy

> Everyone, without exception, is struggling to gain happiness.... Every person feels happy when his desire is fulfilled.[1] —*Divine Principle*

> And God blessed them, and God said unto them, "Be fruitful, and multiply, and replenish the earth, and subdue it: and have dominion over the fish of the sea, and over the fowl of the air, and over every living thing that moveth upon the earth."
> —*Genesis* 1:28

> And therefore if any two men desire the same thing, which nevertheless they cannot both enjoy, they become enemies...and sometimes...endeavor to destroy or subdue one another.[2] —*Leviathan*

Competition is Natural

In the pursuit of happiness, each human being tries to obtain as much power, wealth, and resources possible in order to have an easier, more pleasant, and more secure life. The attempt to expand one's sphere of influence and control inevitably leads to conflict with others who are attempting to do the same. We live together on one planet with finite resources and finite land area. This competition for resources is a natural feature of our existence.

Ironically, if we compete to make things better for others we enrich ourselves and the world becomes more prosperous, but if we seek to gain for ourselves at another's expense we may have a personal temporary gain but an unhappy end. In this paper, I hope to show clearly how this process works.

Unrestrained Competition Leads to War, Poverty, and Human Misery

Thomas Hobbes, the founder of modern political science, argued that this state of nature is a state of war.[3] Without physical or moral restraint, human beings will resort to any methods possible to gain for themselves at the expense of others. Primitive hunting societies warred with one another over hunting territory. Agricultural societies fought over farmland. The same is true with respect to the other natural resources, such as trees or minerals, and money. A situation of unrestrained competition is called anarchy, or more popularly "the law of the jungle."

In "the jungle" the most powerful prevail and the weak suffer. The powerful will gradually accumulate all of the land, political control, or money until they obtain monopoly power. They often use the weak as slaves, or drive them out into the wilderness. They establish societies based on tyranny and oppression. Thus, while anarchy is the initial condition of unrestrained competition, it is quickly followed by consolidation and eventually monopoly. We can use the example of the anarchy which followed the collapse of communism in Russia in 1991, followed by the consolidation of economic power by a mafia. Unless competition is somehow restrained, this will inevitably be the result of anarchy.

Those that have monopoly power are not at peace, for they must always be on guard for others seeking to usurp their power, conquer their land, and plunder their wealth. Their domination through force always generates resentment as others are unable to pursue happiness on their own. As St. Augustine said in *The City of God,* "Even while waging a war every man wants peace, it is merely to fashion a new peace nearer to the heart's desire; it is not because they dislike peace as such. It is not that they love peace less, but that they love their kind of peace more." Rule by force is never a true peace, a true peace is one in which all people are able to pursue their own happiness, and not a situation where the majority are forced to live for the ends of the few.

Much of human history is a record of the succession of rules by force. When peace exists based on love and human sharing, it is not recorded. As Mohandas Gandhi stated in *Non-violent Resistance*:

> The fact that there are so many men still alive in the world shows that it is based not on the force of arms but on the force of truth or love. Therefore the greatest and most unimpeachable evidence of the success of this force is to be found in the fact that, in spite of the wars of the world, it still lives on.... History is really a record of interruption of the even working of the force of love or of the soul.[4]

Even though we have witnessed so much fighting, conquering, and monopoly rule in history, we have hope because human beings have also been given a social nature. We want to be loved, to raise families, have friends and live in communities that are secure. Therefore many societies and civilizations have arisen based on religious teachings, law and freedom; societies in which citizens who pay taxes and obey laws receive the freedom to pursue their own livelihood and happiness. In such societies, those who rule also feel bound by the laws which allow citizens freedom to pursue their ends as long as they do not damage others or pose a threat to social order.

Monopoly Power Eliminates Competition

Monopoly power can exist in any social institution, such as politics, economics, religion, and the family. The United States Founding Fathers were primarily concerned with political power when they framed the U.S. Constitution. However, they were also quite well aware of the stifling effects that religious monopolies can have on societies. They seemed less aware of the problems of economic monopoly, and they lived in traditional families where the male head of the household often exercised a form of monopoly power.

In any institution where monopoly power exists, competition is eliminated. Any other power which would gain access to similar resources would immediately be perceived as a threat to the monopoly, and would be seized or acquired at an unfair price. When an institution has monopoly power, the highest priority is to preserve the monopoly. This is because the head of a monopoly has authority, wealth, or control by virtue of his position. In that position, everyone must acquire a share from him on his own terms. If he loses monopoly control, he must compete with others for his power or income. This is harder work, and as social conditions change it requires constant adaptation.

An institution with monopoly power will inevitably serve the interests of the heads of the monopoly. There is no built-in incentive to deliver goods or services in a manner more appropriate to the desires of the people who would need these services.

Those people are dependent on the monopoly and are forced to follow its rules, even if they are viewed as unjust and inefficient. In the view of those who do not control the monopoly, such an institution is illegitimate. The average person has only two ways to gain access to the goods or services. One is to meet the demands of the powerful, or to earn their favor, often in demeaning ways. The other is to mount an opposition and attempt to wrest control of the resources through some form of rebellion.

Traditional fairy tales which have descended from medieval life portray the only hope for a young peasant girl to become rich was to marry a prince. In other words, please the person with power and wealth. In the Catholic Church a theologian could only rise to a position of authority when he was viewed as defending the doctrines of the Pope. Competition of ideas was not allowed. Those that did not conform to the views of the Church hierarchy were considered heresy; and religious heretics are treated like political traitors. Under communism, Russian philosophers had to quote Marx or Lenin at the beginning of every treatise. When monopoly control exists, one is either defending the monopoly power or is considered against it. Good and evil actions are often viewed in the context of which side one supports. Those outside the power channels view the monopoly as being evil. Those with monopoly power view those who disagree as evil.

Peace upheld by force, the peace of a monopoly power, is a false peace. There is always disgruntlement and disillusion under the surface of such a peace. Such institutions are characterized by extortion, corruption, tyranny, oppression. True peace occurs when each person is allowed to pursue his or her ends. True peace is when all people have an opportunity to be happy and fulfilled. This is true of every human institution; the family, the community, religion, the economy, and the state.

Competition in the Political Realm

The United States Founding Fathers knew that monopoly power, when invested in a political ruler (i.e., the King) led to corruption, oppression, and inefficiency. They devised a system of government with a system of checks and balances that limited such power (though perhaps not perfectly). Thomas Jefferson argued that "a bill of rights are what people are entitled to against every government on earth, general or particular."[5]

To eliminate monopoly control of political power, a system of representative government was devised whereby the people could elect representatives for a term of office and remove them the next election if they did not serve satisfactorily. The election process fosters competition. People have to compete with their ideas, plans and promises about how they will serve the interests of the voters. Thus this system of elective government forces leaders to serve the people, to live for the sake of others, or they will not prosper. This system is the opposite of a king who selects deputies and ministers based on how well they support *his* interests.

The tripartite system of government was designed to allow the legislature to control the tax money of their constitutents, the president to lead where decisive action was necessary, and the judicial system that would guarantee freedoms and the continuation of the constitutional setup. The Senators, who were seasoned statesmen, would represent interests of the states, and Representatives would more directly represent interests of voters. For a bill to pass the entire congress it would therefore have to be in the interests of both the society as a whole and the individuals who make it up.

The government of the United States is the longest surviving government and is admired throughout the world. It is not without flaws, but it has allowed its citizens to pursue happiness with minimal government interference. While elected officials do not always serve the interests of their electorate, they can be replaced without violence.

Further, the United States has been able to expand to include women, slaves and minorities in the process of government. As such, there is not a wide boiling cauldron of unrest under the surface, as in monopoly governments that control by force.

Internally, the United States established a system of government that instituted checks and balances on power, allowing freedom and prosperity to develop. Ironically this very success is both its bane and its glory, for while the freedom, prosperity, and justice *within* the United States are envied by much of the world, the power of the United States, unchecked in the world at large, is the root of great fear, a fear that can fuel the rhetoric of a terrorist like Osama bin Laden.

It is my argument that it is because of competition in the United States, it has become more prosperous and powerful than those governments that rule by monopoly power. So such regimes must either attack the more successful nation or fall by the wayside. It is quite well known that the Soviet regime needed to make the United States its enemy to retain the loyalty of its citizens. It's the only way to retain some aura of legitimacy in the face of Western prosperity. Today we see something similar going on in the Islamic world and other places where political monopolies rule.

Finally, it has been well documented that modern representative democracies rarely initiate wars. One reason is that it is much easier for a king to send his subjects' sons to war than for the mothers and fathers of a democracy to send their own sons to fight. Further, at least in modern global society, money is more important than land. Ruling other people in this day and age becomes more of a burden, because machines are more productive than slave labor and they don't complain. I will cite the conclusion of R.J. Rummel, the foremost authority on democracy and war:

> With two possible exceptions, since the Napoleonic Wars there is no historical record of a war between democratic states. Moreover, there is virtually no record of violence between democracies. These facts are so important that I should underline them in a different way: historically, democracies between themselves have formed oases of nonviolence, while around them hundreds of wars and violent engagements have been fought in the last 160 years.[6]

Competition in the Economic Realm

The main difference between an authoritarian government and a totalitarian government is that an authoritarian regime often allows freedom in areas of society outside the political—such as economics and religion—while a totalitarian regime tries to exert total control over the people under its power. The Soviet Union was totalitarian in that it attempted to centrally control the economy, while China has moved to an authoritarian system of political power with much more economic freedom.

Great civilizations and empires of the past often arose when competition in the economic realm flourished, even though the political system was ruled by emperors or kings. Governments succeed or fail based on the degree to which they are viewed as legitimate, and they are viewed as legitimate to the extent they enable their citizens to pursue their own ends. The Babylonian Empire under Hammurabi and the Roman Empire before it became too corrupt are good examples. In both cases, during periods ruled by dependable laws and when taxes were not overbearing, people were free to pursue their ends with minimal interference of the government.

However, economic power, when unrestricted, is like the jungle. It will begin with the appearance of free enterprise and competition and end up as monopoly, with the strongest in control. While in free enterprise, producers and sellers must compete to serve the desires of the consumer, the monopolist tells the consumer what a product or service will cost, and delivers it with little enthusiasm, courtesy, or efficiency. The economic monopoly can prey on the vulnerabilities of those that require the product or service it provides.

This was not a big concern for the United States Founding Fathers. When most of the economy was based on family-owned farms and storefront businesses, there was a measure equality of power and a lot of fair competition. The farmer who grew the best food would have the most sales, the blacksmith who offered the best steel for the lowest price would get the business, etc. In such an environment "the invisible hand" in the economic theories of Adam Smith would appear to work. But the "invisible hand" is really not totally invisible, it works only when there is fair competition and a possibility for all people to provide goods and services.

The rise of industrialization in Europe and later in America led to critiques by Karl Marx and others. Actually, Marx missed the point in *das Capital* when he blamed unemployment on capitalism. The real culprit was monopoly. And the solution to the problem was not, as Marx hypothesized, another form of monopoly (state monopoly) to displace the one that already existed, but a market economy in which fair competition could exist. The United States addressed the problem of economic monopoly through anti-trust laws and government regulation of some industries, for example utilities. However, as we witness the rise of global conglomerates, billion-dollar acquisitions and mergers, and other forms of economic consolidation today, we can see that the problem of economic monopoly has not been sufficiently addressed.

I'd like to illustrate the problem using the example of recent developments in the telecommunications industry. In the United States in the 1970s, the telephone system monopoly by Bell Telephone was a very stagnant and uncreative system. Sometimes people would have to wait months for phones to be installed. Much of the communications infrastructure was based on antiquated technology from the 1930s. Service became so bad that the government intervened and broke the monopoly up into seven smaller companies we called "baby bells." This led to more fair competition in the industry by the baby bells and allowed new companies to enter this business sector. Real competition began to provide the best service possible. The company that provided the best phone service, or the phone service with the most creative technologies, got the most customers. This competition stimulated the development and deployment of fiber-optic cable, cable television, wireless telephone systems, internet service providers, DSL, and a host of other options with which companies could attract customers. It also led to one of the longest economic-boom periods in United States history. However, this situation did not last. Today, there is speculation that the recent re-accumulation of near monopoly power by the descendants of the "baby bells" was in part responsible to the collapse of several technology companies and the NASDAQ in 2000.[7]

The present health care system in the United States, which is based on third-party payers and large health management companies with near monopoly power, is another example of economic inefficiency and frustration for consumers. It has reached the point where the managers of these large companies dictate the health care, rather than compete to make their customers happy.

The President and Board of Directors of a monopoly will resist the breakup of their company, yet history proves that natural competition to create a better society through providing superior service to others makes people happier and more prosperous.

In the economic realm, as well as the political, fair competition leads to the necessity of serving others rather than exploiting them.

Single-party states often suffer the same fate as corporate monopolies. They are destined to fall behind in their ability to serve their citizens. In many cases those people who suffer economically today live under the rule of governments that exercise monopoly power. It is ironic that, although republican Theodore Roosevelt fought economic monopolies with anti-trust legislation, in the contemporary United States the Republican Party, which prides itself on the principles of the Founding Fathers and political freedom, turns a blind eye toward, or is bought off by, economic monopoly. It shows an intellectual and moral weakness that creeps in when an economy is doing reasonably well.

Competition among the Religions

In the case of religion, monopoly power (e.g., a state church) leads to the same phenomenon as in politics and economics. It is no accident that in the United States, where freedom of religion exists, there is greater religiosity and church attendance than in Europe where state churches have monopoly power. In the United States religious leaders have to say believable things that help people in their daily and moral life or the consumer goes elsewhere.

People have philosophical questions about life and social needs that require the teaching of virtue, sacraments of marriage, birth and death, etc. But people do not enjoy being forced to believe something simply because a leader says it is true. Religious monopoly is well known in history. One of the most notorious examples was the Roman papacy's refusal to accept the earth was round for three hundred years after it had been proved round by scientists. Many of the problems with Islam today stem from its monopoly power as a state religion, rather than the basic teachings of Mohammed. These problems are similar to the Catholic Church during the time of the Holy Roman Empire, or even with Lutheranism in Sweden or Finland today. In Europe, new religions are theoretically allowed, but state taxes go to support official churches, and the hierarchy of those official churches fight tooth and nail to prevent new religions from proselytizing.

In a religious monopoly, there is no real incentive to care for souls, and every incentive for a religious leader to devote his time trying to win the favor of his leaders, so he can be the bishop or cardinal of the only official religion. There is often a threat to citizens that their souls will be damned if they don't give their tithes for a project the church leaders have planned. They will be damned if they speak out against the official doctrines of the church. Such religion is stifling and of little service to the spiritual life of people.

Competition in the Family

The family is the smallest and most basic social institution, but monopoly power can play a negative role there as well. A marriage should be a partnership, but often, the physical strength (monopoly) of the husband has determined who serves who. So the history of male chauvinism can also be linked to monopoly power. In the post-industrial society, where physical strength is less important to economic income, women and men compete for money on a more level playing field. Women capable of financial independence are able to demand more genuine love from the men that court them and establishes competition among men to become better husbands.

Competition in International Affairs

Some of the disparity in the world today, especially as it relates to international debt, is the result of the UN General Assembly, which in 1949 passed legislation that guaranteed that all technical assistance from international organizations (i.e., the World Bank, etc.) had to be given to official heads of state. Since the General Assembly is made up of representatives of heads of state, it was in all of their interests to control international money and aid aimed at solving poverty in their nations. There were no checks and balances in the charter of the United Nations to prevent this. This legislation, which designated monopoly control of international aid to a single player, led to the history of corruption of regimes we witnessed in the past fifty years. People would kill and exterminate leaders and tribes to gain access to those funds. Corrupt generals would borrow international funds, put them in Swiss bank accounts, declare democracy, retire to Europe and let the people try to pay off the debt. Under the masquerade of "national sovereignty" (another slogan for political monopoly) much of the mischief of the twentieth century was accomplished.

However, if loans would have been given to private entrepreneurs, as is now happening with great success in Bangladesh and elsewhere, there would have been no incentive for anyone to squirrel off funds and flee the country. Private entrepreneurs, using their loans to provide competitive goods and services to their communities, are more accountable, traceable, and motivated to succeed.

Conclusion

In all institutions of society there is the possibility of monopoly rule by force or competitive living of human beings under some form of social contract with laws that limit monopoly power and treat all human beings as having equal opportunity.

When there is monopoly power, there are a few on the top and the rest are forced to push and shove one another for the scraps that remain. When fair competition exists the people who do the best are those who provide the most for others. Monopoly power results from and breeds selfishness, while fair competition forces people to become unselfish and think of the needs of others.

Our job should be to help people understand these basic principles, to educate people how to compete without fighting, how to grow prosperous without exploiting. This means giving people the tools of productivity, service, and ingenuity in educational programs. It also means designing social systems that provide each person maximum freedom in all areas of life, but denying them the right to infringe on the rights of others.

Our job should be to avoid monopoly power whenever possible.

Notes

1. *Divine Principle,* attributed to Sun Myung Moon (NY: HSA-UWC, 1973), p. 1.

2 Thomas Hobbes, *Leviathan,* ed. Michael Oakeshott (NY: Macmillan, 1962), pp. 98-99.

3. Ibid., pp. 98-100.

4. M.K. Gandhi, Non-violent Resistance (NY: Schocken Books, 1974, p. 16.

5. Letter to James Madison, 19 December 1787. From *The Papers of Thomas Jefferson,* edited by Julian P. Boyd (NJ: Princeton University Press, 1958), vol. 12, p. 440.

6. R.J. Rummel, "On Fostering a Just Peace," *International Journal on World Peace,* vol. 1, no. 1, Autumn 1984, p. 10.

7. Karen Kornbluh, "Disconnect: How Bush and Michael Powell are killing the New Economy, and how to turn it around." First Appeared: *The Washington Monthly,* October 1, 2001, http://www.newamerica.net/frames/fr_econ_2k.html.

The Need for a New World Ethic

Hans Küng
University of Tübingen

No World Peace without Religious Peace

I. The Two Faces of Religion

Around a quarter of century ago—to be more precise, in April 1967—the centenary was being celebrated of what was then the most significant academic institution in the Near East, the American University in Beirut. Muslim and Christian theologians were invited to give festival lectures: from the Christian side Dr Visser't Hooft, the then General Secretary of the World Council of Churches; Cardinal Johannes Willebrands, later President of the Vatican Secretariat for Unity; and myself, as a theological Benjamin. Beirut, the city at the point of intersection between Christianity and Islam: what an opportunity for the encounter of religions, what a unique opportunity to experience Muslim theologians directly as conversation partners! However, things turned out differently.

1. Religions at War

(a) The case of Lebanon

A remarkable thing happened: Muslim theologians were nowhere to be seen when we appeared, and none of us Christian theologians had a chance to meet them. Why not? Because in accordance with the programme they had all already spoken a week before us. When I personally asked Charles Malik, the President of the Congress, at that time Lebanese Foreign Minister and President of the United Nations General Assembly, why now—after the Second Vatican Council with its pioneering declarations on religious freedom and the attitude of church to Judaism and Islam—Christian and Muslim theologians had not been invited together, his answer was: 'Cher Professeur, c'est trop tot!' 'It's too early!" In 1967—too early!

At that time Lebanon was still regarded as the 'Switzerland of the Near East', a peaceful island in the midst of regions and religions which were being fiercely fought over. But already at that time whispers could be heard in Lebanon that the situation was explosive, that the political balance between Christians and Muslims was fluid, that the Christian predominance was endangered by the growth in the Muslim population, and that the present constitution could not be maintained in the long term. However, would things turn out so badly for this rich-poor land? No one could really suspect so at the time.

I have not forgotten this Beirut experience. Now—after one of the longest and most fearful civil wars in history—I can put it in. context. For

I have come to the conclusion—and Lebanese have endorsed this insight—that had a serious religious dialogue between Christians and Muslims in Lebanon been sought twenty-five years ago, and had this been supported by the religious communities, Lebanon would not have slithered into a catastrophe of this dimension. A religious understanding could have served as a basis for a reasonable and just political solution. A fanaticism of violence, murder and destruction fed by the religions could thus have been mitigated. In the spirit of a Christian renunciation of power, already in the early 1970s Christians would voluntarily have been able to make those concessions to the Muslims which were subsequently wrung from the Gemayel government by force of arms in the 1980s and which then could no longer pacify the land. In short, the civil war and immeasurable bloodshed could have been avoided. Instead of gruesome chaos, Lebanon would now have stood as a model of ecumenical understanding. And I am convinced—I shall put this in a single sentence: Like Lebanon, so too the state of Israel and the city of Jerusalem can find peace and continued existence only through religious and political dialogue between Jews and Muslims, Israelis and Palestinians, and not through a sixth, seventh and eighth war. Is all that an illusion?

(b) Negative consequences

Of course the question may rightly be asked: can religions contribute so much? There is no disputing that in negative, destructive terms they have made and still make an enormous contribution. So much struggle, bloody conflicts, indeed 'religious wars' are to be held to their account; so many economic, political and military conflicts have been partly started, partly coloured, inspired and legitimated by religions and this also goes for the two world wars.

Many massacres and wars not only in the Near East between Maronite Christians, Sunni and Shi'ite Muslims, between Syrians, Palestinians, Druse and Israelis, but also between Iran and Iraq, between Indians and Pakistanis, Hindus and Sikhs, Singhalese Buddhists and Tamil Hindus, and earlier also between Buddhist monks and the Catholic regime in Vietnam, as also today between Catholics and Protestants in Northern Ireland, were or are so indescribably fanatical, bloody and inexorable because they have a religious foundation. And what is the logic? If God himself is 'with us', with our religion, confession, nation, our party, then anything is allowed against the other party, which in that case must logically be of the devil. In that case even unrestrained violation, burning, destruction and murder is permissible in the name of God.

However, there are examples to the contrary.

2. Religions at Peace

(a) Germany, France, Poland as opposite examples

Religions can also contribute an infinite amount in a positive sense, towards building up, and have done so. They can intervene through individuals, religious groups or whole religious communities in a tenacious way for peace, social justice, non-violence and love of neighbour in the world. They can propagate and activate basic attitudes like readiness for peace, renunciation of power and tolerance. Here are just two political examples.

1. For centuries France and Germany were regarded as arch enemies. In the nineteenth and twentieth centuries they waged three great wars in a nationalistic spirit, two of which developed into world wars. The world owes the fact that after the Second World War the old resentment did not revive and a politics of revenge no longer dominated to men like Charles de Gaulle, Konrad Adenauer, Maurice Schuman, Jean Monnet and Alcide de Gasperi. As great politicians they did not think primarily in bureaucratic and technocratic terms along Brussels lines, but because of their fearful experiences they pursued (quite realistically in political terms) a vision with an ethical and religious foundation. That put an end, once and for all, to these wars between European nations. A united Europe on a Western, Christian foundation, bound together economically and politically in defence is

the best guarantee that in future the nations will live together in peace. And to make it clear that the reconciliation of France and Germany after so much anti-Christian devilry came from a Christian spirit, de Gaulle and Adenauer sealed this reconciliation before the world at the cathedral in Rheims, where the French kings were crowned.

2. After the Second World War, the ideological fronts between the Federal Republic of Germany and the states of the Warsaw Pact were fully hardened. How—after the unprecedented atrocities of Germans in the East and the expulsion of millions of Germans from their ancestral homes—could there be mutual forgiveness? Already at the end of the 1950s Julius Döpfner, then Bishop of Berlin and later Cardinal of Munich, took a first step towards reconciliation with a bold appeal. But he was quickly silenced by a storm of indignation. It was the Evangelical Church in Germany which ventured a new attempt in 1965. Through a theologically well-argued and politically well-balanced memorandum it prepared for reconciliation between Germans on the one hand and Poles, Czechs and Russians on the other. This made possible years later not least that policy of treaties with the East which, even if one might criticize it in details, in fact proved to be a tolerable basis for a provisional political normalization until the great revolution finally came in 1989.

(b) No world peace without religious peace

Examples can be multiplied: I could have mentioned the Civil Rights Movement in the United States in the 1960s, which was started by a black pastor, Martin Luther King, and was supported by many pastors, priests and nuns. I could have mentioned the peace movement of the 1980s and 1990s, which is headed by people with religious motivations—above all Christians and Buddhists—from the USA to Japan, from Northern Ireland and Eastern Europe to South Africa. I could continue, but instead of this I shall ask, with a view to the future:

What would it mean for tomorrow's world if the religious leaders of all religions, great and indeed small, decided today to give resolute expression to their responsibility for peace, love of neighbour and non-violence, for reconciliation and forgiveness? If from Washington to Moscow, from Jerusalem to Mecca, from Belfast to Teheran, from Amritsar to Kuala Lumpur, instead of helping to foment conflicts they were to help in resolving them? All the religions of the world today have to recognize their share in responsibility for world peace. And therefore one cannot repeat often enough the thesis for which I have found growing acceptance all over the world: there can be no peace among the nations without peace among the religions. In short, there can be no world peace without religious peace.

Constructive engagement with the other religions of this world for the sake of peace in the world is vitally important for survival. In the third millennium—following the example of Europe—we shall have either a quite different peaceful 'ecumene' or we shall have no 'ecumene', no 'inhabited earth' at all. In 1988 computer photographs were published of the part of the Milky Way most remote from our cosmos (4C41.17); it is fifteen billion light years away from us. No, in view of the immense size of the universe and our own boundless human overestimation of ourselves, a God of creation and evolution is truly not dependent on our little planet, which flies along on the periphery of galaxies which go into hundreds of millions. Conversely, this planet is desperately in need of a God of creation and evolution. This insight compels us to perceive our responsibility for one another and to abandon our dogged stubbornness in dealings with one another. And this applies centrally to what is perhaps the most disputed question in religion, the question of truth.

C. No Religious Peace Without Religious Dialogue: Prolegomena to an analysis of the religious situation of our time.

* * *

IV. An Ecumenical Theology for Peace

In view of the differences and contradictoriness of

religious ideas and practices, an accumulation of encyclopaedic knowledge is not enough. That can be found in any the numerous collections of sources—not to mention the flood of specialist literature. In connection with religion, too, we suffer more than ever from an excess of information: the problem is not the collection of material, but the way in which it is assimilated and interpreted. Here—and for me in this respect Max Weber, the founder of the sociology of religion, is the model[1]—to achieve our task what we need is the power of an integral view, an eye to the essentials and a differentiated judgment. Often we need not so much a mirror, which reflects everything, as a magnifying glass, which can concentrate our gaze.

1. Understanding and Collaboration

(a) No unitary religion

Here the aim of a Christian theologian's research will certainly not just be better information for Christian colleagues, however much this is always necessary. Nor will it just be more thorough discussion with Jewish and Muslim partners in faith who have already deliberately put the same invitation to themselves. No, in addition to information and discussion there is a need to strive for a transformation, for religious understanding and collaboration, to the degree that such collaboration is necessary for peace among the religions and thus also peace among the nations. It should be stressed once again that here the postulate is not a unitary or universal religion of the kind that was already called for in before Toynbee by the American philosopher William E. Hocking,[2] from the Indian side by Swami Vivekananda at the Parliament of Religions in Chicago in 1893,[3] and later by Sarvepalli Radhakrishnan (India's first state president).[4] But there is a need for a contribution to peace between the religions, particularly between the prophetic religions Judaism, Christianity and Islam, which have so long been at enmity.

(b) A creative and concrete theology of peace

A theology for peace between Christians, Jews and Muslims should therefore first be worked out: to avoid not only any hot or cold wars (in the Near East and elsewhere), but also any pernicious self-righteousness, intolerance and rivalry. But this theology of peace must be convincing by its concreteness. For what is the use of an abstract, appellative theology of peace of the kind that is so often preached in Rome and Geneva (and sometimes also in Jerusalem)? It costs nothing because it makes all too general appeals for a readiness for understanding and a willingness for peace, and requires nothing of its own church, party or nation; so it remains voluntary, harmless and inefficient. That is no help to a creative and concrete theology of peace which

- does not shirk the labour of investigating theological foundations;
- analyses the structures of thought and conduct which have crept in;
- picks up the central differences in the religions and between the religions;
- calls for self-criticism and self-correction on all sides.

This may be thought to be an ambitious programme, and yet it is a realistic one: it is no sheer support of the *status quo* in society, state and church, no helpless admonition to show loyalty to tradition, to march on well-trodden paths, to display museum pieces. But on the other hand it is no convenient flight into a religious utopia, no completely illusory recipe, no set of impracticable suggestions or useless experiments.

So in such a research project there must be a course between the extremes, on which one neither drifts into a random pluralism nor isolates oneself with a claim to absoluteness. What I said in principle in part B of this programmatic book is now being applied here in practice: a random pluralism which accepts all religions on the same footing and presupposes that the ecumenical understanding which lies so far in the future has already achieved perfect realization, instead of working intensively for it, cannot be the goal of a realistic theology of peace. Far less, however, can the endorsement of a claim to absoluteness of Jewish, Christian or Muslim provenance, which lays absolute claim to its own truth, detached from the truth of the others, for its own religion alone. All three religions are concerned with truth, justice and salvation.

(c) The ecumenical horizon

The aim can only be a critical or self-critical differentiation which measures any religion critically by its own origin and by a humane ethic, without claiming it for itself. We do not arrive at peace through syncretism but through reform of ourselves; we arrive at renewal through harmony, and at self-criticism through toleration. So what is being fought for here is a theology of peace which finds the way to peace not by bracketing off the question of truth but by incorporating it and responding to it, and which above all discloses and helps to work out those conflicts and points of unrest in the world of which the religions themselves are the cause.

Such a theology for peace calls for a truly ecumenical theology which is strictly pertinent and politically and ethically relevant, and thus at the same time directed towards the future. Such an ecumenical theology claims the role neither of a self-righteous and moralizing high priest nor of an allegedly neutral supreme judge. It is as remote from any church court theology as from any uncommitted academic university theology. Despite any criticism from the church and authentic scholarship it will always primarily concerned with the fate of those individuals and communities of faith which are affected, indeed with the future of our divided and exploited world. Theologians should not be brake-blocks, but pioneers on the way to the future.

2. Prospect

(a) The programme

World religions are primeval and contemporary, are supra-individual, international and transcultural systems, which one has to understand if one is to understand our world. Only a global, world-historical and world-wide approach will do justice to them, one which at the same time strives for two things:

- Analyzes of the religious forces of the past, both the great names and the social movements, which are still effective in the present after millennia of history. That means a historical and systematic anamnesis and diagnosis;
- Forecasts from the analysis of the present of the different religious options which are relevant for the future, both spiritually and intellectually, and socially and politically. That means a practical-ecumenical therapy and prognosis.

So for Judaism, Christianity and Islam it has to be demonstrated that:

> Only if we know why it has come about ('the paradigm of the past'), can we understand our position ('the demands of the present'), and can we conjecture where everything is going ('the possibilities of the future').

So we have the past which is still present, the transitory present, and the future which is already present: the whence continues to determine the where, and the where the whither.

(b) A differentiated global survey

If the difficult task of a basic orientation of the religious situation of humankind is to succeed, I hope that:

- We shall gain a differentiated global view of the situation of religion at the threshold of a new millennium, despite all the differences between nations, regions of the world and world religions;

- We shall be able to recognize a convergence that is to be encouraged, despite the powerful and many much-splintered entities that the world religions are, extending over several thousand years, and despite the differences which are all too manifest;
- We shall see at least some fundamental and persistent constants in doctrine, practice and spirituality, despite all the striking variables in any religion: permanent factors which determine this religion through all the centuries over lands, cultures and continents, and through all paradigm changes. I hope that we shall see the same as it were eternal stars (*stellae*) by which we orientate ourselves to the present day, but which form constantly new epoch-making 'constellations'.

* * *

V. Imperatives for Inter-Religious Dialogue in the Postmodern Period

It has become clear from beginning to end that a new post-colonial, post-imperialistic, postmodern world constellation is in the making, and thus a polycentric world which is being bound ever closer together by new communication technologies. But at the same time this polycentric world must be a transcultural and multireligious world. In this polycentric, transcultural and multireligious world ecumenical dialogue between the world religions takes on quite new importance; for the sake of its peace this postmodern world needs more than ever the global religious understanding without which a political understanding will in the last resort no longer be possible. The slogan of the hour is therefore, 'We must begin on global religious understanding here and now!' We must advance inter-religious understanding energetically in the local, regional, national and international spheres. We must seek ecumenical understanding with all groups and at all levels. As we saw, the 'postmodern' paradigm can be described in religious terms as an ecumenical paradigm. In connection with this I would like to sketch out the specific requirements in the form of some brief ecumenical imperatives.

1. Inter-Religious Dialogue with All Groups

The decisive problems for the future with other religions are not just distant problems but problems in our midst. There are hardly any countries now without significant religious minorities (almost two million Muslims in Germany; a million Muslims and half a million of both Hindus and Sikhs in Great Britain). A new religious overview is called for; we need to seek new viable ways and strive for a new inter-religious openness, encounter and bond.... I began from major political questions: the civil war in Lebanon; relations between Germany on the one hand and France and Poland on the other. From this macro-level, to end with I shall come to the meso- and micro-levels and also address specific groups. Therefore:

(a) Politicians, businessmen, scientists

- We need people in all continents who make themselves better informed and orientated about the people of other lands and cultures, who take up the impulses of other religions and at the same time deepen the understanding and practice of their own religion.
- In particular we need men and women in politics who do not just see the problems of world politics which have newly arisen from the perspective of strategic supreme commanders or of the world market, but try to realize the conception of international peace, into which the longings of people in Europe and the world for reconciliation and peace, fed by religion, can be taken up.
- In addition we need men and women in business who do not just exploit the people of other lands and cultures—at home or abroad—as those who provide services, or use them in a

purely economic function as trade partners, but rather attempt to go beyond their narrow economic sector and see their partners whole, as people, becoming sympathetic to the other human histories, cultures and human religions with which they have to do.

- In short, we need politicians, diplomats, business people, officials and also academics, not just with ever more quantitative statistical background knowledge but with deep historical, ethical and religious knowledge. The communication of knowledge without criteria of value leads people astray.

(b) Churches, theology, religious education

We need churches which despite all present tendencies towards conservatism (in the Roman Catholic, Protestant and Eastern Orthodox spheres) do not react to new spiritual and religious challenges in a hierarchical and bureaucratic way, but internally and externally act close to the grassroots and are aware of problems. They should be not centralized but organized pluralistically; not dogmatic, but attuned to dialogue; not turned in on themselves in a self-satisfied way, but in all the doubts of faith approaching the questions of the future self-critically and in an innovative way. In practice we need:

- a theology and theological literature which advances inter-religious dialogue spiritually and intellectually in the interest of peace;
- religious education, teachers and books which serve the communication of knowledge between the religions and which understand this work of enlightenment as practical education for peace.

(c) The different religions

We need religions which after all the hot and cold wars, after all the co-existence which has been more divisive than peaceful, involve themselves in constructive pro-existence and cooperation, leading to peace in local and regional conflicts. We need a closely interwoven network of inter-religious information, communication and co-operations. In practice all religions, as companions with equal rights, need:

- more mutual information;
- more reciprocal challenge;
- more transformation on all sides in the common quest for the greater truth, for the mystery of the one and true God, which will only be fully revealed, if God so wills, at the end of history.

2. Inter-Religious Dialogue at All Levels

I am not calling for an inter-religious dialogue at all levels and in all forms for its own sake, as an end in itself, but for the sake of individuals, churches and religions, for their reconciliation, as this was convincingly worked out by the Harvard specialist in religions, Diana L. Eck, in her report for the World Council of Churches in Potsdam in 1986.[5] Therefore:

(a) Unofficial and official dialogues

- We need not only religious conferences and gatherings on the model of the 'World Conference of the Religions for Peace', but also the most intensive institutional contacts and bilateral relationships (World Council of Churches, Vatican Council for Inter-religious Dialogue, national church organizations, international Jewish, Muslim and Buddhist associations).
- Even more, we need local and regional inter-religious base groups and working parties which discuss and remove problems where they arise, and investigate and realize possibilities for practical collaboration.

(b) Scientific and spiritual dialogue

- We need a more intensive philosophical and theological dialogue of theologians and specialists in religion which takes religious plurality seriously in theological terms, accepts the challenge of the other religions, and investigates their significance for each person's own religion (Christian-Jewish and Christian-Buddhist dialogue are models for this).

- But at the same time we need the spiritual dialogue of religious communities, of monks, nuns and laity, who are silent, meditate and reflect together and are concerned with a deepening of the spiritual life, and the questions of a spirituality for our time.

(c) Everyday dialogue

Even more, we need everyday dialogue of all the people of different religions who meet and discuss daily and hourly all over the world on all possible occasions: in mixed marriages and shared social projects, on religious festivals or in political initiatives, all over the place, where in questions great and small the religions constantly interact in a quite practical way. So in quite specific terms we need:

- external dialogue of those who live in the same street or in the same village, work in the same factory or study at the same university;
- internal dialogue, the discussion that goes on in ourselves, in our heads and hearts, whenever we encounter strangers, a person or a book, whenever for example Christians hear something from the Qur'an or Muslims something from the Gospels.[6]

The implication of the many levels of interreligious dialogue is that not only are good will and an open attitude necessary at all Levels, but—on each level—also solid knowledge. But this is still often lacking—not least at the scholarly and theological level, where the problems of foundations in particular are still worked on all too little. Therefore the programme which guides us and which comes together as one may be summed up once again in three basic statements:

- no human life together without a world ethic for the nations;
- no peace among the nations without peace among the religions;
- no peace among the religions without dialogue among the religions.

Notes

1. Cf. M. Weber, *Gesammelte Aufsätze zur Religionsoziologie*, Vols I-III, Tübingen 1920.

2. Cf. W.E. Hocking, *Living Religions and a World Faith*, New York 1940.

3. For Vivekananda the eternal principle (*sanatana dharma*) of the Hindu tradition, as distinct from the social principle (*svadharmana*) as expressed in the caste tradition, stands over all creeds and religions: 'Do not care for doctrines, do not care for dogmas, or sects, or churches, or temples: they count for little compared with the essence of existence in each man which is spirituality' (*Speeches and Writings of Swami Vivekananda*, Madras nd, 31); quoted in J.M. Kitigawa, *The 1893 World's Parliament of Religions and its Legacy*, Chicago 1983.

4. S. Radhakrishnan, *Eastern Religions and Western Thought*, London 1939; cf. DGE GI2, 'All equally true?'.

5. See the report of the working party of the sub-unit 'Dialogue with People of Other Religions' of the World Council of Churches for the Potsdam conference of 13-20 July 1986, Diana L. Eck, 'Interreligöser Dialog—was ist damit germeint? Ein Überblick über die verschiedennen Formen des interreligiösen Dialogs', *Una Sancta* 43, 198, 189-200.

6. With the focus of 'Christianity and Islam' religion as a factor of education for peace was the theme of the third Nuremberg Forum. Cf. the numerous contributions in J. Lähnemann (ed.), *Weltreligion und Friedenserzeihung. Wege zur Toleranz*, Hamburg 1989. The volume edited by U. Schmidt from an educational perspective, with particular reference to the Third World, *Kulturelle Identität und Universalität. Interkulturelles Lernen als Buildungsprincip*, Frankfurt 1986, takes a similar line (see especially the articles by P.V. Dias, A. Imfeld and G. Flaig).

International Law as a Deterrent of the Ravages of War

William A. Schabas
Irish Center for Human Rights

International law, as we now think of it, is often said to have arisen with the Peace of Westphalia, in the mid-seventeenth century. The term apparently owes its origin to Bentham, and has prevailed since then over the more ancient expression "law of nations" or *jus gentium*.[1] But one of the great and pioneering writers on the subject, Hugo Grotius, looked to the classical Greeks for guidance and precedent as to the norms of behaviour of human communities. If some areas of modern international law only make sense in the contemporary context of nation states, problems of war and peace, of both *jus in bello* and *jus ad bellum*, seem to be of more ancient origin. In this latter category, it may sometimes seem as if little has really changed over the centuries.

In an historical sense, apparently, the first efforts to govern matters of war and peace by law rested on the concept of "self-help." Where the primitive equivalent of nations or states breached applicable norms, the other could and often did attempt to enforce the law by means of reprisal. Sophisticated techniques of settling international judicial disputes might not have been present, but this was without a doubt the application of legal rules and principles. Their breach by one of the parties to the dispute, nevertheless, was "adjudicated" more or less unilaterally by the other. With reprisal or self-help the victim of the breach affirmed that there was a price to pay for lawlessness. The obvious purpose of such action was deterrence, a utilitarian concept aimed at preventing future violations, whether by the initial perpetrator or by others.

Over time, the law has become infinitely more robust, especially in the area of enforcement, where a range of political and judicial mechanisms operate to ensure that states behave according to recognised rules of conduct. And yet the concept of self-help or reprisal is still very much present in international conflict. The reaction to the terrorist attacks of 11 September 2001 confirms this observation. It was said, again and again, that military response was required as "retaliation" for the destruction of the World Trade Center, or that the "assets" of terrorists and those who harboured them, such as the Taliban regime in Afghanistan, would be "degraded" if they did not conform to standards of civilised behaviour. In debates about the appropriate way to deal with terrorism, many who argued for reliance on existing judicial mechanisms, drawn essentially from the growing *armamentarium* of international criminal law, were accused of being unrealistic and naïve.

Despite this resort to self-help or reprisal, the *Charter of the United Nations* seems to leave no room for the doctrine as a means of enforcement of international law. The applicable reference is Article 51 of the *Charter*, a mysterious and ambiguous provision: "Nothing in the present Charter shall impair the inherent right of individual or collective self-defence if an armed attack occurs against a Member of the United Nations, until the Security Council has taken measures necessary to maintain international peace and security." Much like the justification of self-defense as it is known in ordinary criminal law (where it is invoked to by every scoundrel and villain, yet rather rarely believed by judge and jury), individual or collective self-defence of states has been regularly, indeed systematically, pleaded in virtually every case of the unilateral resort to force in international affairs. Often, perhaps usually, self-defense in the context of ordinary criminal law is confused with reprisal. Courts regularly explain to defendants, as they are being convicted and sentenced, that victims of attack are not entitled to "retaliate," and that as a general rule self-defense is confined to immediate, necessary and proportionate measures of self-protection until such time as law enforcement agents can intervene.

This seems why the parallel between self-defence in the ordinary criminal law context and self defence as it is meant in international law appears to break down. The individual victim of assault is expected to summon the police for protection, because society has its recognised organs for the implementation and enforcement of law. The uncertain reaction of the Security Council, whose judgments and decisions are motivated by a political rather than a judicial or moral agenda, can hardly be compared with that of the forces of order in a society founded upon the Rule of Law. The inherent right of self defence of the individual who is a victim of attack is limited and restrained because that individual is entitled to rely upon the state for protection. This duty has been affirmed again and again by international human-rights tribunals.[2]

We are not so demanding upon the state that is the victim of assault. Apparently the state may not only take the initiative but hold onto it, all in the name of this "inherent" right to self defence that even the *Charter of the United Nations* cannot have usurped. Thus, the tension between the primitive enforcement technique of self-help and the more "civilised" approach to law, of political and ultimately judicial settlement, continues to pervade contemporary international relations. We are forced to concede the legitimacy of self-help or reprisal precisely because of the weakness and inadequacy of the enforcement mechanisms available to international law. Indeed, this seems an inevitable interpretation of the *Charter* itself, with its two-pronged vision of response to aggression and breach of the peace, one rooted in "inherent" self defence, the other in international control and prevention under the aegis of the Security Council.

Peace and War: Two Dimensions of Public International law

A century ago, international law conceived of war as the ultimate and quite legitimate exercise of the attributes of State sovereignty. Public international law textbooks presented themselves as a tandem: the law of war and the law of peace.[3] Little wonder, then, that a reformer like Alfred Nobel would conceive of awarding a prize for peace. Some notions from this earlier age when the resort to force was still legitimate—the declaration of war, for example—remain to this day a part of popular conceptions of the applicable norms, although they have been long abandoned in fact.

Because there was no general prohibition on the use of force, states wove a complex web of treaties, so as to protect themselves against aggression. Many of these pacts, *ententes* and covenants were secret; some of them were accompanied by full-blown military alliances and contractual obligations to intervene if allies were attacked by a third party. Woodrow Wilson expressed the growing disaffection with the system in his fourteen points. But when the victorious allies, gathered in Paris, proposed criminal prosecution of Kaiser Wilhelm

II, his alleged crime was not making war as such but rather breach of international agreement. Article 227 of the *Treaty of Versailles* dictated that he be tried for "for a supreme offence against international morality and the sanctity of treaties."[4]

International law was transformed in the interwar years. By the Kellogg-Briand Pact or Pact of Paris of 27 August 1928, sixty-three states condemned "recourse to war for the solution of international controversies" and renounced it as an instrument of national policy. Its breach became the core of the convictions at Nuremberg of Nazi leaders for "crimes against peace." The Nuremberg judgment of 30 September–1 October 1946 stated: "To initiate a war of aggression, therefore, is not only an international crime; it is the supreme international crime differing only from other war crimes in that it contains within itself the accumulated evil of the whole." According to the International Military Tribunal, "War is essentially an evil thing. Its consequences are not confined to the belligerent states alone, but affect the whole world." The Tribunal said that it was not strictly necessary for it to consider at what point the waging of aggressive war had become prohibited by international law, given that the crime was defined in the London Charter of 8 August 1945, which was the legal framework for the activity of the Tribunal. Nevertheless, in order to stifle critics who claimed this was an exercise in retroactive prosecution, the judges examined the question in some detail, demonstrating that from the adoption of the Kellogg-Briand Pact "resort to a war of aggression is not merely illegal, but is criminal."

Thus, the Nuremberg judgment confirmed the customary legal nature of a fundamental norm of international relations set out in article 2(4) of the *Charter of the United Nations*, adopted at San Francisco in June 1945: "All Members shall refrain in their international relations from the threat or use of force against the territorial integrity or political independence of any state, or in any other manner inconsistent with the Purposes of the United Nations." Article 2(4) reformulated and reaffirmed articles 1 and 2 of the Kellogg-Briand Pact of 1928. The *Charter of the United Nations* admits two exceptions to this principle: self-defence, and collective action under the Security Council pursuant to Chapter VII. In theory, the Security Council's intervention is confined to matters of international peace and security, a mandate that appears to eliminate its involvement in internal conflict as a general rule. In any event, the fragile balance of the five permanent members resulted in a power that was rarely used, at least until the end of the Cold War provided a temporary lull in great power tension. The fall of the Berlin Wall and the breakup of the Soviet Union opened a window of opportunity for an expansive view of the Council's mandate. By the early 1990s, intervention under Chapter VII was being conducted in the name of the protection of human rights in countries where the threat to *international* peace and security was more virtual than real.

Parallel to this new legal regime prohibiting the use of force was the growth of international human-rights law. Human rights language can be found throughout the *Charter*, although the 1945 San Francisco Conference stopped short of including a detailed declaration setting out the substance of such standards. That task was undertaken a few years later with the adoption of the *Universal Declaration of Human Rights*, a document whose guiding light was the American stateswoman Eleanor Roosevelt. The *Declaration*'s preamble described it as a "common standard of achievement."[5] At the time, it was barely thinkable that the United Nations might one day express opinions and actually condemn human rights violations occurring within the borders of sovereign states. Indeed, in the early years of the United Nations, when individuals from various parts of the world complained to the Secretary General that their rights were being violated, he simply forwarded the complaint to the accused government with an accompanying note explaining that such matters were none of his business. But over time, this conservatism and reticence dissolved. Relatively secondary United Nations organs, principally the Commission on Human Rights, took the lead during this initial phase. In time, human rights percolated up to the General Assembly and, ultimately the Security Council.

But there was a counterweight to these developments, its spirit crystallized in Article 2(7) of the *Charter*, which cautioned that nothing would "authorize the United Nations to intervene in matters which are essentially within the domestic jurisdiction of any state." The message of respect for state sovereignty is also transmitted in Article 1's reference to the self-determination of peoples. All of this seemed unequivocal enough in 1945 when the *Charter* was adopted. Slightly more than half a century later, a glance at the agenda of the Commission on Human Rights, or for that matter of the General Assembly, shows how much this once strict protection of state sovereignty is now transformed. To be sure, it is obviously far too soon to speak of the end of sovereignty. Nevertheless, the wall that international law once erected and maintained around states, in effect ensuring that what transpires within their own borders is immune to international scrutiny and involvement, has been irrevocably breached.

Humanitarian Intervention

The concept of humanitarian intervention has relatively ancient origins. In the nineteenth century, some world powers affirmed a right and even, in certain cases, a duty to intervene in the interests of conflict prevention, the promotion of democratic ideals and securing the rights of minorities. The most frequently cited example is that of France in Lebanon during the 1860s, but the paradigm is large enough to include the Monroe doctrine. The intervention was unilateral and it was politically colorable, due to the presence of a rather clear correspondence between the right to intervene and a concept of spheres of influence of major powers.

By the 1950s and 1960s, "intervention" had become a dirty word and "sovereignty" a sacred and intangible value, but towards the end of the century the pendulum was to swing back in the other direction. Fundamentally, it was the growth of the human rights discourse that authorized the international community to claim the right to involve itself in areas that had been beyond its reach in the past. Although the United Nations provided perhaps the most important forum for these developments, the role of regional organizations must not be overlooked. For example, by the early 1960s, the Inter-American Commission on Human Rights was studying the question of human rights within Cuba, needless to say without the express or implied consent of the Cuban government. Basket Three of the Conference on Security and Cooperation in Europe opened the door to Western involvement in human rights-type issues within the Soviet bloc. It did much to prepare and promote the fall of the socialist regimes at the end of the 1980s.[6] Yet, as in the *Charter of the United Nations*, the modest human rights language of the 1975 *Helsinki Final Act* was couched in the classic references to self-determination and the sanctity of international borders.

Throughout this gestation period, much of the debate centered on the racist regime in South Africa and, to a somewhat lesser extent, in Southern Rhodesia (now Zimbabwe). The new states of the so-called "third world" were the most nervous and uncomfortable with any suggestion of a right to intervene. Yet they pushed forward the agenda in the case of *apartheid*, treating it as a special and exceptional case. *Apartheid* was, of course, an egregious violation of fundamental rights. United Nations resolutions and treaties would call such racist domination of the majority a crime against humanity. In any event, intervention in the case of *apartheid* was confined to relatively modest proportions, principally in the area of trade, and cultural and athletic exchanges. Nevertheless, the fact that *apartheid* was a subject of international concern set a precedent whose implications might be enormous. Once the principle was recognized, there were other serious violations of human rights that could warrant comparable international efforts.

United Nations peacekeeping is another dimension in the evolving doctrine of humanitarian intervention. The *Charter* had contemplated the raising of United Nations forces within the context of Chapter VII and it even provided for the creation of a Military Staff Committee. But the major peace-keeping operations—Suez, Cyprus, Kashmir—relied on Chapter VI, and would never have taken place without the consent of the parties. Peacekeeping troops facilitated conflict resolution, but essentially in situations where willing parties needed a neutral international umpire to help them move the process along. Where this will was lacking, Chapter VII could be the only vehicle. But as long as the Security Council was dominated by power struggles between two great superpowers, both intensely (and not unreasonably) suspicious of the other, it could rarely agree upon implementing Chapter VII.

The defining moment in these developments was the Gulf War. When Iraq invaded Kuwait in mid-1990, asserting territorial grievances dating to the time of colonization, the Security Council responded with an ultimatum to withdraw and, when that failed, robust military intervention. Yet "Operation Desert Storm" was grounded in uncontroversial premises, the inherent right of Kuwait to self-defense and the unchallengeable role of the Security Council in the case of aggression, in accordance with Article 51 of the *Charter*. The precedent here was United Nations' involvement in the Korean War, in the earliest days of the organization. Thus, from a legal standpoint, the ability of the Security Council to authorize intervention had existed since 1945. But from a practical standpoint, the Soviet veto and superpower rivalry had made this impossible in the past. Indeed, during the Korean War, a deadlocked Security Council was bypassed in favor of the General Assembly, by means of the "Uniting for Peace" resolution whose authorship is credited to Dean Atcheson. Forty years later, however, the major powers had lost any enthusiasm for such a role being exercised by a General Assembly whose overwhelming majority now lay in the southern half of the planet.

When Iraq withdrew from Kuwait, the *raison d'être* of the intervention evaporated. The Security Council then turned to a radically new dimension within its Chapter VII powers, authorizing ongoing intervention including the creation of "no-fly zones" in the name of the protection of ethnic and religious minorities within Iraq itself. Resolution 688, adopted in April 1991, provided the legal framework for military attack as well as economic embargo of Iraq that would continue through to the end of the decade. The precedent it established rapidly led to a range of initiatives, previously considered unthinkable, in various parts of the world: Somalia, Rwanda, Haiti, Bosnia, Kosovo, East Timor.

What was so radically different about these interventions was the difficult and tenuous link with the Security Council's remit. By what stretch of the imagination did the persecution of minorities within Iraq fall within the ambit of aggression, or a breach of the peace? Essentially, the Council took the view that internal developments could threaten international peace. The link, though welcomed by human rights advocates, was often unconvincing. A frequent argument was that the refugee flows that usually accompany internal strife have devastating consequences on neighboring states, thereby threatening the peace. But as the 1990s progressed, these rationalizations became less and less important. Massive human rights violations, in and of themselves, were deemed sufficient to trigger the provisions of Chapter VII.

The collapse of the Soviet Union had provided the window of opportunity for Security Council-mandated intervention. Though the agenda during this period was generally set by the three western permanent members, this was not always the case. In April and May 1994, it was the elected members, particularly New Zealand, Spain and the Czech Republic, who urged intervention in the Rwandan genocide while the permanent members dawdled.[7] That international intervention in an internal conflict could be justified without the imprimatur of the Security Council still remained beyond the pale of international law, however.

The argument that international law provided a basis for humanitarian intervention irrespective of the provisions of the *Charter*, or even in conflict with them, had been supported by some scholars in the United States since the 1970s, although the weight of international opinion considered any such initiatives to be illegal.[8] Views rapidly evolved in late 1998 as the United States started mooting the possibility of military intervention in the Federal Republic of Yugoslavia so as to protect the persecuted Kosovar Albanian minority from "ethnic cleansing." A Soviet veto of any Security Council mandate for the use of force seemed inevitable, and in the end the matter was never even tested with a vote. The North Atlantic Treaty Organization (NATO) proceeded to attack Yugoslavia on its own and without Council authorization.

The legality of the bombing of Yugoslav military targets by NATO aircraft and missiles remains uncertain at best. The broad participation of a major regional organization combined with the lack of condemnation by major international forums, such as the General Assembly of the United Nations, has led some to suggest the permissibility of such practice. They have cited Chapter VIII of the *Charter*, which allows regional arrangements for enforcement action, although the relevant provisions explicitly insist upon Security Council approval. On the other hand, the silence of the *Charter* and the lack of any other "black letter" law on the subject leaves the parameters of such humanitarian intervention vague. Subsequent statements by some of the NATO participants even suggest a profound reluctance to claim Kosovo as a precedent that can be cited to justify similar initiatives in the future.

Some treaties have been invoked as a basis for humanitarian intervention in the absence of any Security Council authorization. The reasoning is that by accepting certain conventional norms, states have voluntarily recognized the prospect of intervention and furthermore have committed themselves to participate as required by circumstances. The 1948 *Convention for the Prevention and Punishment of the Crime of Genocide* creates an obligation to both "punish" and "prevent" what has been called the "crime of crimes."[9] But while the *Convention* spells out in some detail its punitive dimension, its preventive side remains enigmatic. In 1994, as genocide raged in Rwanda, uncertainty about the scope of the obligation to prevent genocide influenced some states to eschew use of the "g-word." There was a fear that a direct reference to genocide in a Security Council resolution might generate a legal obligation to intervene, one that some members of the Council were not prepared to assume.[10]

A similar argument can be made based on common Article 1 to the four *Geneva Conventions* of 1949, in its requirement that states both "respect and ensure respect" for the other provisions in those humanitarian-law treaties. It seems somewhat contradictory that treaties whose purpose is to humanize the worst abuses of armed conflict and protect non-combatants would also encourage the use of force. However, there are historic roots for such a concept in the notion of belligerent reprisals, by which violations of the laws of war may be tolerated to the extent they are imposed in order to compel the other side's respect of such laws.

The Flourishing of International Courts

In the final international armed conflict of the twentieth century, as bombs fell upon Belgrade and other Yugoslav towns and cities, both sides in the war found themselves being taken to court. Serb leader Slobodan Milosevic was the first off the mark, suing ten NATO countries for aggression and genocide before the International Court of Justice. An application for a provisional order against his enemies was dismissed by the Court. But tension and uncertainty instilled by his arguments, which cut deeply among some NATO members who were profoundly troubled with the legality of their efforts, may well have altered dynamics within the alliance. A few weeks later, Prosecutor Louise Arbour of the International Criminal Tribunal for the Former Yugoslavia announced that Milosevic himself had been charged with crimes against humanity, that an international warrant had been issued against him and that any foreign assets of his would be seized.

For the first time in history, then, a parallel international conflict was being waged in the courtrooms of The Hague while a shooting war raged a thousand miles away. Did international litigation simply continue armed conflict but by other means, to paraphrase von Clausewitz, or was an innovative and promising response to conflict resolution emerging, albeit in a still primitive and imperfect form? In any event, to the extent that legal rules and their implementation by the courts were being injected into a complex international crisis, there was an additional element of unpredictability. While this may represent some degree of triumph of principle over pragmatism, it is certainly arguable that the insistence that conflicts be conducted and resolved in accordance with international law makes their settlement easier and more likely. Indeed, the contrary may well be the case, as some have charged. Debates about "fundamental rights," particularly with respect to sovereignty and minority rights issues, often muddle the search for common ground.[11] Sometimes, states may agree upon terms of a settlement that actually conflict with rules of international law of a peremptory character. They might, for example, agree to grant amnesty for perpetrators of war crimes and crimes against humanity. Those who seek peace at all costs will accept such concessions, while those who stick to other principles of international law, including a growing insistence in human rights law on resisting impunity, will argue that such settlements are improper and, ultimately, invalid.

The relationship between international responses to conflict and judicial mechanisms dates back more than a century, to the Hague Conference of 1899. That meeting took a number of initiatives in the direction of the regulation of armed conflict as well as its prevention, and devised the Permanent Court of Arbitration in order to provide states with a judicial institution where disputes could be settled. Previously, arbitration had been undertaken on an *ad hoc* basis, often designating a monarch or other head of state as a neutral arbiter.

But the Permanent Court of Arbitration was really only the forerunner of moves to establish an international court, a body created in the aftermath of the First World War. Named the Permanent Court of International Justice, it operated until the end of the Second World War, when it was reconstituted into the International Court of Justice. The International Court of Justice has its seat in The Hague. The *Statute* of the Court is an annex to the *Charter of the United Nations.* However, while all states have some involvement in the Court because it is a United Nations organ, contentious cases can only come before the Court that involve states that have accepted its jurisdiction, and these are still a minority.

During the inter-war years, the Permanent Court of International Justice developed a body of jurisprudence in the realm of minority rights, applying and interpreting the web of treaties and declarations governing post-Versailles eastern Europe. The Court's rulings did much to define the rights of minorities. Although the practical significance of the minority rights treaties should not be exaggerated, there is evidence that some of Hitler's anti-Semitic policies were checked temporarily because of special guarantees contained in the applicable instruments.[12]

After the Second World War, the work of the International Court of Justice resumed at only a modest pace. The Soviet Union and its allies stayed well clear of its jurisdiction during the Cold War context. African and other third world countries became quickly disenchanted after observing the Court's reticence to get involved in a series of Namibia cases. But in the mid 1980s, the Court's stock rose considerably in these quarters after it condemned the United States for supporting attempts of the *contras* to destabilize the Sandinista regime in Nicaragua. The United States, which had successfully challenged Iran in the Court over the Tehran Embassy occupation a few years earlier, actually refused to participate in the Nicaragua proceedings, arguing that the Court was not entitled to exercise jurisdiction. Impressed that the Court could tackle and ultimately condemn a superpower like the United States, many states recognized the Court's jurisdiction or withdrew reservations to its jurisdiction that had been attached to relevant international treaties. Suddenly a Court whose docket had never contained more than a couple of cases, and whose judges worked at the most leisurely of paces, found itself overwhelmed with litigation, some of it dealing with ongoing conflicts and requiring it to navigate through intensely political waters.[13]

In late-March 1993, as war raged in the disintegrating Yugoslavia, the newly created State of Bosnia and Herzegovina filed an application directed against Belgrade based on a number of specific treaties, including the old minority treaty adopted in the aftermath of the First World War and the 1948 *Genocide Convention.*[14] The application charged the Milosevic regime with fomenting genocide through its policy of "ethnic cleansing," which it said was carried out on Bosnian territory by armed groups taking direction from Belgrade. Bosnia coupled its application with a request for provisional measures. It asked the Court to issue an immediate order to Yugoslavia to cease a detailed list of hostile and aggressive acts.

Representations were made by both sides within a matter of days. The Court granted Bosnia's request for such an interim order. By its very nature, a provisional order avoids detailed study of the merits of a case. Nevertheless, the Court will not issue one unless there is a serious basis for a claim. But Bosnia's victory in Court had little or no practical significance on the ground. It was, nevertheless, a useful propaganda tool. Note was taken of the Court order in a variety of international documents, including a Security Council resolution. Bosnia returned some months later for a second order, whose real consequences were similarly symbolic. It also threatened to sue the United Kingdom for its failure to prevent genocide, but cooler heads in the Bosnian foreign ministry eventually prevailed.

Since then, Bosnia's case against Yugoslavia has returned periodically to the Court's docket as a variety of preliminary matters have been addressed pending a full hearing on the Bosnia claim. There were rumors that the case would be dropped as part of the Dayton Agreement. While this did not happen, the political compromise made at Dayton has made further progress in the case problematic. In effect, the Republika Srpska, an "entity" of Bosnia and Herzegovina, has not shown any enthusiasm for the case, for obvious reasons. But its unlikely accord seems necessary if the matter is to go to trial.

There were other interesting attempts to influence the war in the former Yugoslavia through judicial means. In September 1991, faced with the imminent breakup of Yugoslavia as well as of the Soviet Union, the European Commission issued a declaration setting out its conditions for recognition of any new states that might be created. The European standards included evidence of a democratic manifestation of a desire for any new State, and commitments to protect human rights, particularly those of ethnic minorities. In order to assess compliance with these terms, the European Commission established a form of tribunal, chaired by French constitutional judge Robert Badinter.

The "Badinter Commission" promptly ruled that the European Commission's terms for recognition were fulfilled in Slovenia and Macedonia. In the case of Croatia, it was not satisfied with the human rights and national minority issues. With respect to Bosnia and Herzegovina, the Badinter Commission considered that an adequate referendum had not taken place. The results were chaotic and, arguably, provocative. Despite the clean bill of health, Macedonia was not recognized for years, the consequence of political concerns with Greek objections. Although Badinter had frowned on Croatian recognition, Germany broke ranks and recognized the new state just before the end of 1991. And Bosnia, in order to comply with the ruling, plunged into a referendum campaign that arguably incited the outbreak of armed conflict.

The Badinter Commission applied international law, drawing on precedents of the International Court of Justice and similar bodies, and interpreting documents derived from the United Nations and the Conference on Security and Cooperation in Europe. One of the more intriguing and controversial conclusions of the Commission was that the possibility of creation of new states was not unlimited. Making an analogy with the decolonization in South America and Africa, the Badinter Commission said new states could only be created along pre-existing administrative boundaries (*uti posseditis juris*), effectively ruling out attempts by Bosnian Serbs to join a "Greater Serbia." The same principle would return years later to rule out initiatives for an independent Kosovo or a "greater Albania."[15]

The European Commission's attempt to govern the process of recognition of new states with rigorous legal norms and judicial institutions appealed to the jurist but shocked many politicians and diplomats. Clearly, it limited the options of negotiators at a time when the utmost flexibility was required. Here, then, judicial intervention is vulnerable to the charge that it may have aggravated conflict and inhibited efforts at peaceful settlement. Yet in the result, political leaders seem to have followed the judicial precedents of the Badinter Commission only when these corresponded to their own intuitions and strategies, suggesting that international law is disposable, a comfortable support when it confirms political judgments but little more than a minor annoyance when it does not.

International human rights courts also have their role to play in dealing with inter-state conflict. The *European Convention on Human Rights* and the *American Convention on Human Rights*, as well as the *International Covenant on Civil and Political Rights*, all permit inter-state complaints. States have proven themselves reluctant to use such mechanisms and, in practice, there have been only a handful, all of them in the European system. One of the first cases before the European Commission on Human Rights, back in the 1950s, was filed by Greece against the United Kingdom and concerned alleged abuses during the independence struggle in Cyprus. Cyprus has lodged a series of applications against Turkey before the European Commission and the European Court of Human Rights, all dealing with the 1974 invasion and its aftermath. In the mid-1970s, Ireland successfully sued the United Kingdom about conditions in detention camps in Northern Ireland.

But the most interesting petitions have come, surprisingly, from individuals. In 1996, the European Court of Human Rights ruled in favor of an application from a Greek Cypriot who claimed her right to enjoyment of property had been violated by the Turkish invasion. Two years later, the Court awarded her damages of approximately $1 million.[16] If other Cypriots file similar claims, judgment debts could extend into the billions of dollars. So far, Turkey has refused to honor the judgment, and has even threatened to withdraw from the Council of Europe. But a hostile posture on human rights may irreparably compromise its application to join the European Union. Thus, although this was not its overt purpose, an individual litigant's claim may help advance the peaceful settlement of one of Europe's most long-standing disputes.

Issues arising from the war in Yugoslavia are also being litigated before the European Court of Human Rights. Although Yugoslavia is not yet a member of the Council of Europe or a party to the *European Convention on Human Rights*, several of the NATO States that bombed it in 1999 are. Relying upon the precedent set in a claim against Turkey for its acts in occupied Cyprus, families of journalists who were killed during the attack on the Yugoslav television station have filed suit claiming a violation of Article 2 of the *Convention*, which enshrines the right to life. If the case is ruled admissible, the Court may have to resolve questions arising from tension between two related but distinct bodies of international law, the law of human rights and the law of armed conflict. It is conceivable that the bombing of Yugoslavia in 1999 could be judged contrary to European human rights standards, even if in another forum applying another body of law it might be considered both compatible with the laws of war (*jus in bello*) and an acceptable exception to the prohibition on the use of force (*jus ad bellum*).

Criminal Prosecution of Leaders of a Belligerent Party

A very different tack on judicial involvement in the wars of the former Yugoslavia emerged in late 1992 and early 1993 following investigations into atrocities by a United Nations fact-finding commission. The call for an international war crimes tribunal was picked up quickly. The Security Council, whose resolution 827 of May 1993 actually established the International Criminal Tribunal for the Former Yugoslavia (ICTY),[17] was able to build on work then ongoing within the United Nations International Law Commission aimed at creating a permanent international criminal court. The international criminal court project had been around since 1948 but became obscured during the Cold War and had only been revived in 1989.

Unlike the International Court of Justice, whose litigants were sovereign States, the ICTY was to judge individuals for war crimes, crimes against humanity and genocide. The precedent, of course, was the Nuremberg trial of 1945-1946. But there were some important distinctions: The conflict was ongoing and the tribunal itself had been established not by victors but by an ostensibly impartial international community. And while Nuremberg's philosophical underpinning had been retribution imposed upon the leaders of a defeated regime, the ICTY was focused on deterring future atrocities. Also unlike Nuremberg, the ICTY was plagued with the problem of bringing the main suspects into custody.

The initial indictments were filed against relatively minor players in the conflict. Indeed, there was much speculation that prosecutions of the leaders in the conflict were being stymied by political pressure. How could a peace process be launched and negotiations proceed if the spokespersons for the parties were on the Tribunal's most wanted list? In political circles, concern was expressed publicly that prosecution would abort a negotiated settlement. Then, in mid-1995, in the days following the summary executions at Srebrenica of thousands of civilian non-combatants, Prosecutor Richard Goldstone announced that charges had been laid against Bosnian Serb leaders Radovan Karadzic and Ratko Mladic. The immediate result was not, as some had feared, to sabotage the peace process. In fact, within weeks encouraging negotiations were underway at Dayton, but those indicted refused to come.[18] Goldstone's indictment had marginalized Karadzic politically, and he would never really recover. Stigmatization of the Karadzic-Mladic leadership, later confirmed in a preliminary hearing on the overall sufficiency of the charges, had been accomplished.

Justice Goldstone's 1995 indictment of Karadzic was only the dress-rehearsal. In May 1999, as NATO bombs rained down on Serbia, Prosecutor Louise Arbour indicted Slobodan Milosevic for crimes against humanity. Weeks earlier she had stood on the border of Kosovo and warned him of the consequences, and critics will surely point to this as a failure of the Tribunal's deterrent function. The timing of the indictments left Justice Arbour open to charges of political interference, but she was in fact criticized on all sides. Possibly the most troublesome element in the exercise of prosecutorial discretion was the suggestion that her decision to charge Milosevic had been dependent on obtaining high-level communications intercepts from NATO intelligence services. To the extent NATO controlled the evidence, it also helped to set the agenda for the Tribunal's prosecutor.

Short of obtaining the diaries of Milosevic's confidantes, it will never be possible to establish with any precision the role that the ICTY indictment played in bringing an end to the Kosovo conflict. There were some very immediate and practical consequences of the Tribunal's initiative, including an order freezing assets of Milosevic that might be located outside Yugoslavia. In announcing the indictment, Justice Arbour also claimed that Milosevic, as an indicted war criminal, could no longer participate legitimately in negotiations. This was a questionable assertion, because until a final judgment is issued he remains entitled to the presumption of innocence. But on a political level, this was also a dangerous and troubling claim. Ruling out a negotiated peace because a leader has been indicted is rather like the judicial equivalent of saying "take no prisoners." It seems destined to prolong a conflict, not shorten it.

Meanwhile, Milosevic was up to some judicial mischief of his own. In late April 1999 he filed an application with the International Court of Justice, borrowing a page from his Bosnian adversaries, whose lawsuit against Yugoslavia launched in 1993 is still pending. Yugoslavia charged ten NATO countries with a breach of the peace, contrary to the *Charter of the United Nations*, and genocide, in violation of the 1948 *Genocide Convention*. An order for provisional measures was sought aimed at an injunction to the NATO states to stop bombing. While hostilities continued, lawyers for both sides debated the matter in The Hague. At the very least, Milosevic had an arguable case in his claim that the *Charter* had been violated, because the use of force by NATO had been conducted without authorization by the Security Council. But Yugoslavia had only accepted the jurisdiction of the Court a few days before filing suit, a cynical move that discredited its suit. This was only one of several obstacles to the admissibility of the application. Ultimately, the Court refused to grant its request for an interim order against the NATO states, although the case itself is proceeding and may still be heard on the merits. Milosevic's lawsuit was not likely to unbalance the more steadfast members of the Alliance, but it seems probable that this very visible and credible challenge to the legality of the campaign may well have contributed to wavering among NATO's less determined members.

The International Criminal Court

The idea of a permanent international criminal court has been studied seriously within international organizations since before the Second World War. The United Nations War Crimes Commission, established by the Allies in 1943 in order to prepare prosecutions of Nazi war criminals, drafted a statute for a permanent international court. But while the prosecutorial efforts that followed the War were bold and innovative in many respects, the international community balked at creating a permanent institution. Further study of the matter was requested of the General Assembly's International Law Commission. With Cold War tensions, the matter fell off its agenda and was only reactivated in 1989. Intense work and negotiations culminated in a diplomatic conference in June-July 1998, and adoption of the Rome Statute of the International Criminal Court. The Court will actually be created when sixty states have ratified the Statute, a development that is expected during the year 2002.[19]

The International Criminal Court is arguably the most significant new international organization to be created since the United Nations. It sits squarely within the three themes that have been addressed throughout this essay: the decline in State sovereignty, humanitarian intervention, and the enhanced protection of human rights. Yet because the Court is created by treaty, it is consensual in nature. Participation by states in the Court system is not a denial of sovereignty but rather its assertion.

The Court will have jurisdiction over the "most serious crimes of international concern." Four categories of crime are listed, of which the first three, genocide, crimes against humanity and war crimes, echo the terms of the *ad hoc* tribunals for the former Yugoslavia and Rwanda. The final category of crime is aggression, but here the work of the drafters is unfinished. The Diplomatic Conference was unable to agree on the subject, and left the reference to aggression in the *Statute* as a kind of place-holder, all the while providing that there could be no prosecutions for aggression until the States parties to the *Statute* agreed upon a definition and other issues.

The "aggression" issue highlights the problems that arise when an international criminal court attempts to contribute to furthering international responses to conflict. It is argued that Article 39 of the *Charter of the United Nations* reserves to the Security Council the authority to determine whether an act of aggression has been committed. To allow another international body to address the same question might lead to inconsistency and conflict. But the alternative, by which prosecution for aggression would be dependant upon a Security Council ruling that the crime had actually taken place, is extremely problematic because it denies a defendant the forum to contest the basic material elements of the crime.

The consequences for international conflict of an International Criminal Court with jurisdiction over the crime of aggression are potentially enormous. The other key international crimes may or may not be committed in the context of international armed conflict. They were alleged during the Kosovo war of 1999, with both sides being accused of crimes against humanity or genocide, as has already been discussed. However, charges of aggression during international armed conflict would seem almost unavoidable. In some future reprise of the Kosovo conflict, a frustrated Milosevic or even an independent prosecutor on his or her own initiative might threaten criminal prosecution of NATO leaders.

Alongside the question of jurisdiction over aggression is the broader issue of the relationship between the International Criminal Court and the Security Council. The initial draft of the Court's *Statute*, prepared by the International Law Commission in 1994, stated: "No prosecution may be commenced under this Statute arising from a situation which is being dealt with by the Security Council as a threat to or breach of the peace or an act of aggression under Chapter VII of the Charter, unless the Security Council otherwise decides." In effect, then, matters being considered by the Council were simply off limits as far as the Court was concerned, unless the Council ruled otherwise. But the provision provoked great controversy as the drafting proceeded. Resentment about the composition of the Council, and particularly the veto power of its five permanent members, helped drive efforts to whittle down any role it might have in controlling the prosecutorial agenda. The final result still allows the Council to block prosecutions, but this must be done by a positive resolution valid for only one year, a far more demanding standard than the initial draft's requirement that the matter be a "situation being dealt with."

It seems easy to imagine circumstances where the Court and the Security Council might be at cross purposes. The Council could consider that threatened prosecution for aggression or any of the other three crimes risks complicating delicate political negotiations, possibly involving a formal or informal grant of amnesty or some other inherently political decision. As for the Court, it might refuse to bow to decisions of the Council on the grounds that they are *ultra vires* the powers of that body pursuant to Chapter VII of the *Charter*, which are confined to matters of international peace and security.

In the vote at the conclusion of the Rome Conference in July 1998, the Court's *Statute* was adopted by 120 to 7, with twenty-one abstentions. The handful of opponents included the United States, China and Israel. The United States has been a keen supporter of international criminal justice, dating from the Nuremberg and Tokyo trials in the 1940s to the more recent *ad hoc* tribunals for the Former Yugoslavia and Rwanda. However, it is uncomfortable with a number of aspects of the *Rome Statute*, including the power granted to the Court's Prosecutor to initiate prosecution unilaterally and the limitations on the Security Council's right to suspend or defer cases. The most important difficulty for the United States is the enlargement of the Court's jurisdiction to cover persons committing crimes within the territory of a state that has ratified the *Statute*. The United States considers that jurisdiction should only extend to nationals of a state that has ratified the *Statute*. The principal concern, it seems, is with the threat of prosecution of United States military personnel when engaged in activities beyond its borders. In reply, defenders of the Court argue that the *Statute* would not allow it to assume jurisdiction to the extent that the United States shows its willingness to prosecute its own soldiers for war crimes. During the Vietnam War, American servicemen, such as those involved in the My Lai atrocity, were prosecuted for war crimes, to much international publicity. There is no reason to believe that military prosecutors would behave differently in future conflicts, should the situation arise.[20]

Transitional Justice: Prosecute or Forgive?

Historically, conflict resolution has often involved some form of forgiving and forgetting. In this spirit, the Geneva Convention on prisoners of war dictated prompt repatriation at the end of the conflict. In 1977, when the Geneva Conventions were expanded with a protocol addressing non-international armed conflict, it too called for "the broadest possible amnesty to persons who have participated in the armed conflict." The conventional wisdom reflected in these provisions was that peace could be purchased in exchange for a promise that the past would be forgotten. But self-proclaimed amnesties by repressive rulers in South America during the 1980s gave the concept of amnesty a sour taint. By the 1990s, in an ironic shift, even non-governmental organizations like Amnesty International were condemning amnesties as being incompatible with human rights. Accordingly, the Rome Statute of the International Criminal Court leaves little room for amnesty or any alternative approaches to accountability.

This complicates conflict resolution by insisting upon an almost inexorable judicial dimension. The logic of releasing prisoners of war at the end of the conflict was that this promise of fair and humane treatment would encourage them to surrender and therefore shorten the period of hostilities. This same wisdom has been applied with favorable effect in Haiti, where a pledge of asylum elsewhere prompted putschist Raoul Cedras to relinquish power, and in South Africa, where the farsighted truth and reconciliation commission of Nelson Mandela and Desmond Tutu avoided a predictably bloody day of reckoning between the proponents of apartheid and its adversaries, but one whose outcome would be uncertain. These options now seem to be largely foreclosed by the new and rather intransigent insistence upon accountability before criminal courts, be they national or international.

The wisdom of a rigorously judicial approach remains unproven.[21] The drafters of the *Rome Statute* searched vainly for a formulation that would enable them to distinguish between the amnesties granted by Mandela, which most found acceptable, and those by Pinochet, which most found repulsive. Ultimately, the matter now seems to rest with the discretion of the Prosecutor, a profoundly unsatisfactory situation reflecting the continuing inadequacy of our understanding of this problem. The Prosecutor may refuse to proceed with a case, even when submitted by a State party or by the Security Council, when "[t]aking into account the gravity of the crime and the interests of victims, there are nonetheless substantial reasons to believe that an investigation would not serve the interests of justice." The *Statute* also allows the Court itself to decline jurisdiction in matters which are "not of sufficient gravity to justify further action." International judges might well be inclined to include here cases where alternative methods of accountability, such as truth commissions, had functioned in a genuine and sincere fashion. But then again, they might not.

Conclusion

International and non-international conflict is being increasingly judiciarized. This is due in part to a proliferation of international legal norms that simply did not exist a century ago, in particular those belonging to the relatively new field of human rights. It was not until after the First World War that international law abandoned the idea that states could go to war legally, as long as they did not violate applicable bilateral or multilateral non-aggression pacts, as well as the idea that states go basically do as they pleased as long as they did it within their own borders and to their own nationals. Now, a much broader range of state behavior is actually contemplated by international law. Moreover, a variety of new forums have been created where this law can be litigated, the principal bodies being the International Court of Justice, the international criminal tribunals and international human rights courts.

Examples of successful dispute settlement through essentially legal mechanisms abound, but these mainly concern boundary disputes and the like. In the early 1980s, Canada and the United States went before the International Court of Justice to have a line drawn in the Gulf of Maine along a previously disputed border. The suggestion they would otherwise have gone to war is preposterous. But some cases get closer to the line between peaceful, judicial settlement of disputes and resort to force. In the past, Chad and Libya have crossed swords on a boundary issue. Later, they agreed to submit the matter to the International Court of Justice in The Hague. When the Court ruled in Chad's favor, border guards on both sides are said to have had a farewell party before the Libyans politely retreated to the new line. These are clear success stories, but some of the examples discussed in this article—Yugoslavia, Cyprus, South Africa—leave many questions unanswered.

Proving the law's effectiveness, in any context, is a formidable challenge. Criminal codes prohibit serious crimes against the person and against property, and yet murder, rape and theft are not infrequent occurrences. Does this demonstrate the law's failure to influence the behavior of individuals? It is widely believed that punishment deters crime, but we can never prove this because it is impossible to document and quantify the uncommitted crimes. Transposed to an international law context, how can we know whether conflict is prevented, calmed and perhaps, in some cases, incited, by law's participation?

This resort to international law and to international courts seems to add a degree of rigidity into conflict resolution that may appear counter-productive in some cases. For example, it may in effect veto amnesties and similar compromises that are the price for peace and transition, or forbid parlay and negotiation with those condemned or even charged as war criminals. While it will be wise to be watchful for such deformations, current practice does not suggest that the injection of law and litigation into crises unduly complicates the work of mediators. On balance, international law's contribution would appear to be generally quite helpful. How else can we explain the almost universal enthusiasm for the creation of new judicial mechanisms like the International Criminal Court. The gamble, of course, is that increased reliance upon and adherence to a law that prohibits aggressive war and the persecution of vulnerable minorities or individuals will ultimately enhance chances for peace and reduce conflict.

Notes

1. Alain Pellet, Patrick Daillier, *Droit international public*, 6th ed., Paris: L.G.D.J., p. 37.

2. *Streletz, Kessler and Krenz* v. *Germany*, European Court of Human Rights, 22 March 2001.

3. For example: H. Lauterpacht, ed., *Oppenheim's International Law*, London, New York: Longmans, Green, 1944.

4. The Kaiser had sought refuge in The Netherlands, a neutral country at the time, and was never extradited to stand trial. He died there shortly after the outbreak of the Second World War. See: M. Cherif Bassiouni, "From Versailles to Rwanda in Seventy-Five Years: The Need to Establish a Permanent International Criminal Court," 10 *Harvard Human Rights Journal* 11-62 (1997). These pro-

visions of the *Treaty of Versailles* were regularly cited as precedent during the debate surrounding claims of immunity for former Chilean president Augusto Pinochet during 1998 and 1999.

5. On the development of the international law of human rights, see: Louis Henkin, *The Age of Rights*, New York: Columbia University Press, 1990.

6. Gérard Cohen-Jonathan, Jean-Paul Jacqué, "Obligations Assumed by the Helsinki Signatories," in Thomas Buergenthal, ed., *Human Rights, International Law and the Helsinki Accord*, Montclair, NJ: Allenheld, Osman, 1975, pp. 43-70.

7. See: Linda Melvern, "Genocide Behind the Thin Blue Line," (1997) 28 *Security Dialogue* 333, p. 341. Also: Boutros Boutros-Ghali, *Unvanquished, A U.S.-U.N. Saga*, New York, Random House, 1999, pp. 129-140

8. For the position favourable to a right of humanitarian intervention, see: W. Michael Reisman, M.S. McDougal, "Humanitarian Intervention to Protect the Ibos," in R.B. Lillich, ed., *Humanitarian Intervention and the United Nations*, Charlottesville: University of Virginia Press, 1973, pp. 178-183; Bartram S. Brown, "Humanitarian Intervention at a Crossroads," (2000) 41 *William & Mary Law Review* 1683. For a recent review concluding that the *Charter of the United Nations* leaves no room for humanitarian intervention, see: Djamchid Momtaz, "NATO's 'humanitarian intervention' in Kosovo and the prohibition of the use of force," (2000) 837 *International Review of the Red Cross* 89. Also: Albrecht Randelzhofer, "Article 2(4)," in Bruno Simma, ed., *The Charter of the United Nations*, Oxford: Oxford University Press, 1995, pp. 106-128, at pp. 123-124

9. *Prosecutor* v. *Kambanda*, (Case no. ICTR-97-23-S), Judgment and Sentence, Sept. 4, 1998, para. 16.

10. William A. Schabas, *Genocide in International Law*, Cambridge: Cambridge University Press, 2000.

11. See for example: Melanie C. Greenberg and John H. Barton, "Lessons of the Case Studies," in Melanie C. Greenberg and John H. Barton, eds., *Words Over War: Mediation and Arbitration to Prevent Deadly Conflict*, New York: Carnegie Commission on Preventing Deadly Conflict, 2000, pp. 343-369, especially at pp. 357-360.

12. In Upper Silesia, for example, the Nazis delayed introduction of racist laws because this would have violated the applicable minorities treaty norms. Jews in the region, protected by a bilateral treaty between Poland and Germany, were sheltered from the Nuremberg laws and continued to enjoy equal rights, at least until the convention's expiry in 1937. See: Jacob Robinson, *And the Crooked Shall be Made Straight*, New York: MacMillan, 1965, pp. 72-73.

13. The current president of the International Court of Justice, Gilbert Guillaume, has penned a lively account of the relationship between litigation before the Court and ongoing international crises: Gilbert Guillaume, *Les grandes crises internationals et le droit*, Paris: Editions du Seuil, 1994.

14. Much has already been written on the early stages of the case: Peter H.F. Bekker, Paul C. Szasz, "Casenote: Application of the Convention on the Prevention and Punishment of the Crime of Genocide," (1997) 91 *American Journal of International Law* 121; Ben Gaffikin, "The International Court of Justice and the Crisis in the Balkans: Application of the Convention on the Prevention and Punishment of the Crime of Genocide (*Bosnia and Herzegovina v. Yugoslavia*)," (1995) 17 *Sydney Law Review* 458; Thomas D. Grant, "Territorial Status, Recognition, and Statehood: Some Aspects of the Genocide Case *(Bosnia and Herzegovina v. Yugoslavia)*," (1997) 33 *Stanford Journal of International Law* 305; Christine Gray, "Application of the Convention on the Prevention and Punishment of the Crime of Genocide (*Bosnia and Herzegovina v. Yugoslavia* (Serbia and Montenegro))," (1994) 43 *International & Comparative Law Quarterly* 704; William L. Hurlock, "The International Court of Justice: Effectively Providing a Long Overdue Remedy for Engaging State-Sponsored Genocide *(Bosnia and Herzegovina v. Yugoslavia)*," (1997) 12 *American University Journal of International Law & Policy* 299.

15. Marc Weller, "The International Response to the Dissolution of the Socialist Federal Republic of Yugoslavia," (1992) 86 *American Journal of International Law* 569, Alain Pellet, "L'activité de la Commission d'arbitrage de la Conférence européenne pour la paix en Yougoslavie," (1992) 38 *Annuaire français de droit international* 220.

16. *Loizidou* v. *Turkey (Article 50)*, Judgment, July 28, 1998.

17. On the ICTY, see: M. Cherif Bassiouni, Peter Manikas, *The Law of the International Criminal Tribunal for the Former Yugoslavia*, Irvington-on-Hudson, New York: Transnational Publishers, 1996; Virginia Morris, Michael P. Scharf, *An Insider's Guide to the International Criminal Tribunal for the Former Yugoslavia: A Documentary History and Analysis*, New York: Transnational Publishers, 1995.

18. See: John R.W.D. Jones, "The Implications of the Peace Agreement for the International Criminal Tribunal for the Former Yugoslavia," (1996) 7 *European Journal of International Law* 226.

19. Roy S. Lee, *The International Criminal Court, The Making of the Rome Statute*, The Hague/London/Boston: Kluwer Law International, 1999; Otto Triffterer, ed., *Commentary on the Rome Statute of the International Criminal Court, Observers' Notes, Article by Article*, Baden-Baden: Nomos, 1999; Flavia Lattanzi, William A. Schabas, eds., *Essays on the Rome Statute of the ICC*, Rome: Editrice il Sirente, 2000; William A. Schabas, *Introduction to the International Criminal Court*, Cambridge: Cambridge University Press, 2001.

20. David J. Scheffer, "The United States and the International Criminal Court," (1999) 93 *American Journal of International Law* 12.

21. For the authoritative work on forms of accountability, including a range of non-judicial mechanisms, see: Neil J. Kritz, ed., *Transitional Justice, How Emerging Democracies Reckon with Former Regimes*, Washington: United States Institute of Peace, 1995.

Courtesy of Fenimore Art Museum, Cooperstown, New York. Photo of painting courtesy of Richard Walker.

Peaceable Kingdom, ca. 1830-1835, by Edward Hicks, oil on canvas

Part Thirteen

Visions of the Peaceable Kingdom

The most disadvantageous peace is better than the most just war.

—Erasmus (1466–1536)

Everlasting peace is a dream, and not even a beautiful one.

—Helmuth von Moltke (1880)

It is madness for a sheep to make peace with a wolf.

—Thomas Fuller (1732)

. . . reason condemns war and makes peace an absolute duty. . . .

—Immanuel Kant, Perpetual Peace (1795)

What do we mean by a peaceful society? Is this to be confused with a utopian society? We end this volume with lofty hopes that through the processes, techniques and institutions of peace our contributors have laid out, a more peaceful global society might evolve. But what will this society look like and how will it be governed? Some theorists have offered that the only way to achieve a truly global peace would be to surrender authority to a world federalist body. Is this possible or desirable? Could we expect a world body to be responsive to the discontents of a local citizenry?

Perhaps a less ambitious agenda would be the creation of a global consultative body. That organ would help set an agenda for peace through research and education. What is suggested in one of the final essays is a Council of the Earth, set up to harmonize issues of global concern.

One may not be able to tell humanity's next steps in the pursuit of peace. But violence, war, democide and genocide have in recent years reached epidemic dimensions. Alvin and Heidi Toffler assert in their closing essay that man and society have evolved greatly in the course of human civilization. Where should we have this evolution take us?

World Peace Index 2000

Kim Kyong-Dong
Seoul National University, Korea
and Committee For the Culture of Peace,
Peace Forum, the Munhwa Ilbo Daily

Declaration of Peace

The number of human[s] [in] our global community [will] reach ten billion in this new millennium for the first time since the creation of the earth four billion years ago. The planet named earth is facing an absolute shortage of space, forests, water and energy to the extent that humankind has never experienced. A great transformation in human culture has taken place. The change in the living conditions including the aging of the population, urbanization, traffic, refugees, and immigration is now being experienced at the global level. Environmental issues including pollution of the earth, the water, the ocean and the sky, and the wastes, and the climate changes are becoming global as well. We believe that it is our historic mission, for the survival of mankind, to carry on [this] project of creating peace.

***

Background

Human civilization has witnessed historic transformations in the past century. Epoch-making development in scientific discoveries and technological innovations enabled humanity to improve conditions of economic life and the quality of cultural life. On the other hand, however, the twentieth century will be recorded as an era of violent revolutions and warfare. Looking to the newly unfolding twenty-first century, the global community is facing a need to design an entirely new paradigm of civilization around a new set of central values. The utmost values we are to pursue in the future may be summed up in "peace for the entire humanity" and "happiness for the individual human being." This requires a paradigm shift from that of "rich nation, strong army" to that of peace. This new age calls for a peace paradigm. It is time to pursue peace and mutual understanding instead of war and conflict. In place of conflict and confrontation, war and violence, we must actively seek reconciliation and peace if we are to create a new society in the changing world order.

***

It is against this background that we propose a peace movement through the construction of a World Culture of Peace Index (WCPI) with a view to promote peace, harmony, and prosperity for the entire human race.

***

Reprinted by permission of the Peace Forum, the *Munhwa Ilbo Daily,* World Culture of Peace Index 2000, December 29, 2000 from website www.wpf.or.kr/english/publications

The Concept of Peace

Because the conceptual meaning of peace can be so varied, it is difficult to offer a simple definition.

***

Currently, there are three major directions of research that peace studies [would] ordinarily pursue. The first tends to focus on reduction, prevention, and resolution of conflicts through inter-group conflict studies. The second is leaning towards the resolution of economic conflict along class lines. And finally, the third emphasizes peace education in order to help change human consciousness and to encourage more peace-friendly mind. In short, the continuation of research in the field of peace would encompass not only political and military realms, but also economic, social, and cultural elements.

The diversity of peace studies demonstrates that the usage of the term, peace, is not uniform. The definition depends upon whether it is viewed as a negative or positive concept. Peace as a negative concept simply connotes an absence of war and a state of nonintervention of sovereignty. Viewed as a positive concept, on the other hand, peace is supposed to guarantee quality of life in terms of liberty, equality, justice, ecological safety, prosperity, and the like. When approaching peace as a positive concept, it is not easy to delineate its substantive contents. One could only say that it is not maintained through physical strength, but that it is obtained by eradicating the source of structural violence found in society. It is then necessary to identify the key factors behind structural violence. In this sense, the essence of positive peace is to establish democracy and expand human rights and justice by eliminating authoritarianism and economic injustice.

In the international society, the preservation of human rights and justice, the elimination of poverty, and the protection of the environment are all prerequisites for peace. Furthermore, building a truly global community is a common destiny that all societies share. Every nation and individual can overcome ecological and nuclear crises by forming international solidarity within a cooperative framework. This research adopts the positive approach to the peace concept rather than the negative one, for it is believed that such an approach broadens our view of peace and eventually would contribute to the promotion of peace not only for Korea, but also throughout the world.

In order to handle such elements of peace concept, we are proposing to define peace as follows:

> Peace is defined as the state of affairs where people's right to survival and development is not threatened by either overt or potential violence. In such a state, national societies enjoy security and individuals enjoy safety. To be more specific, a national society is said to be in a peaceful state if it is not in violent conflict with one or more of other societies, if the society's internal conflict of interests is resolved through non-violent means, and if it is devoid of any institutionalized restraints, including political oppression, on individual member's opportunity for self-development and quality life.

Obviously, no society would enjoy perfect peace specified by the above definition. We do believe, however, that the level of peace varies substantially across nations and over time, and its measurement would be both empirically and practically meaningful. Thus, we conceptualize the peace index of a national society in a particular period of time as the level of peace that the member individuals of the society enjoy on average.

***

Concepts and Procedures

In [this] project, peace is defined as the state of affairs where people's right to survival and development is not threatened by either overt or potential violence. In such a state, national societies enjoy security and individuals enjoy safety. To be more specific, a national society is said to be in a peaceful state, if it is not in violent conflict with one or more of other societies, if the society's internal conflict of interests is resolved in non-violent manners, and if it is devoid of any institutionalized restraints, including political oppression, on individual member's opportunity for self-development and quality life.

While such a state of affairs would be a utopia and no society would enjoy perfect peace so defined, the level of peace varies across nations and over time, and its measurement would be both empirically and practically meaningful. The WCPI measures the level of peace that the member individuals of a national society enjoy at the particular period of time on average.

In WCPI, peace is conceived along two substantive dimensions, i.e., politico-military (PM) and socio-economic (SE), and two modes of expressions, i.e., structural and behavioral. Together, measurement of peace in four broad dimensions is conducted: (A) structural aspect of peace in politico-military dimension (PM-S, or A); (B) behavioral aspect of peace in politico-military dimension (PM-B, or B); (C) structural aspect of socio-economic dimension (SES, or C); and (D) behavioral aspect of socio-economic dimension (SE-B, or D).

Eight elements that are deemed to either reflect or affect the level of peace in PM-S are identified and measured numerically: (1) history of international relations, (2) geo-political condition, (3) militarization of the society, (4) ongoing interstate conflict, (5) history of domestic political relations, (6) democracy, (7) structure and history of ethnic conflict, and (8) ongoing domestic political conflict. Note that (1) through (4) are international, and (5) through (8) are domestic. Measurement is done in two generic categories in PM-B: (1) events of interstate conflict and reconciliation, and (2) events of domestic political conflict and reconciliation.

Five elements in SE-S are identified and measured: (1) ecological-social safety, (2) social and psychological (in) stability, (3) structuralized economic (in) stability, (4) level of social welfare, and (5) inequality and want. Measurement for SE-B is done for (1) events of social conflict, and (2) events of economic (in) stability.

A number of observable indicators are identified and measured in each of the above 17 categories. Measures in each category are standardized and then weighted. Weighting scale is obtained through international internet survey of experts. Finally, the scores are rescaled to 0 to 100 scale.

Using statistical data as well as media sources, the measurement is conducted for 74 countries for the overall composite index, and 140 countries for politicomilitary dimension. Exclusion of some countries is due to availability and reliability of the data sources.

Results and Findings

Out of 74 countries that are measured for the composite WCPI, Denmark is ranked 1st (WCPI=84.4) and Russia is ranked the last (WCPI=39.8). The world average is 69.9. The Republic of Korea is ranked 44th (WCPI=70.3); the United State of America 51st (WCPI=67.2); China 55th (WCPI=64.6); and Japan 29th (WCPI=75.1).

The World Level of Peace: The world average of 69.9 may mean that in 2000 the world's national societies on average have enjoyed about 70 percent of the peace that can be possibly obtained. If one pits this against the perfect score of one hundred, one may conclude that the world peace in this year is fair, or not too bad. But such a conclusion is both hasty and overly optimistic for two reasons. First, since countries with large populations score low in general, the level of peace that the individual members of the global community enjoy is much lower. In fact, the world average weighted by the size of population is only 59.7. Second, this average is for only 74 countries, or less than half the countries in the world, which have been excluded from the calculation due to the lack of information and statistics. If one accepts the proposition that availability of statistics reflects the capacity of government that could also be a good indicator of peace, one could conclude that the level of peace for the excluded countries could be much lower, so as to lower the world average far lower than the calculated value of 69.9 or even the weighted average of 59.7. The majority of people on the planet earth are suffering from a lack of peace.

Peace in Politico-Military and Socio-Economic Dimensions: It is found that the countries, which are highly ranked in the overall WCPI, are also ranked in both politico-military and socio-economic dimensions. This implies a certain causal relationship between the two dimensions (r=0.72). A closer examination yields that in today's world, many of the people in the world are suffering more from the lack of peace in socio-economic dimension than that in politicomilitary dimension.

Regional Patterns: Europe turns out to be the most peaceful. Although its average value is lowered due to low scores in former socialist countries and Commonwealth of Independent States, its average score (73.8) is higher than that of the second region (the Americas, WCPI=69.7) by more than four. Furthermore, nine out of the top ten countries in WCPI are Western European countries. The finding is both ironical and revealing. It is ironical that Western European countries, which had been the most warring countries in the world throughout the most of the modern era, are enjoying such a high level of peace. It is also revealing in that the history of enduring feuds and conflicts are not necessarily insurmountable.

The Cost of Great Powers: An odd finding is that all of the Permanent Members of the United Nations Security Council are ranked low in WCPI (France, 50th; USA, 51st; China, 55th; UK, 59th; and Russia, 74th). While they are paying the costs for their intrinsic characteristics such as big size, history, and early industrialization, they are also paying the cost for the roles that the international society is asking them to pay.

***

Conclusions

Analysis of the WCPI scores yields two general, albeit tentative, conclusions.

First, the inhabitants of the planet earth are suffering from the lack of peace, not just in terms of overt, physical violence (freedom from fear), but also in terms of covert, but more profound structural violence (freedom from want). An intriguing finding is that the two dimensions of peace tend to move together proposing a potential causal links between the two. Peace researchers are called for to pay a closer attention to the causal link.

Second, being a Great Power internationally does not guarantee peace for the individual members of its society. Even though someone might argue that the world average level of peace is maintained by the roles played by the Great Powers, we nonetheless claim that being big and great on the international basis, a typical symptom of the paradigm of "rich nation, strong army," does not necessarily bring peace for their individual members. Wider recognition of and calling for the paradigm of peace would prove valuable in the twenty-first century.

***

Results

The Overall Patterns

[Our Table 1] presents the rank orders and scores of WCPI for seventy-four countries in the world. While this report includes 140 countries altogether, the overall WCPI is calculated for only 74 countries due to the [in] availability and [un] reliability of source data in socio-economic dimensions. We report WCPI in politico-military dimensions for the remaining 66 countries.

Table 2, reports the limited WCPI rankings, by income, throughout the world.

Table 3 reports the limited rankings, by politico-military criteria, throughout the world.

Table 4 reports the limited WCPI rankings, by socio-economic criteria, throughout the world.

Table 5 presents a world map with colored rankings.

Table 1. World Culture of Peace Index 2000

Rank	Nation	WCPI2000	Politico-Military Peace Index	International PMPI	Domestic PMPI	Socio-Economic Peace Index	Structural Peace Index	Behavioral Peace Index
	Mean World of Nations	69.9	72.4	72.4	72.4	67.0	70.7	69.1
1	Denmark	84.4	85.6	80.3	90.5	83.1	86.7	82.2
2	Netherlands	84.4	85.1	79.1	90.5	82.7	86.5	81.5
3	Portugal	83.3	84.7	80.2	88.4	81.6	82.4	84.1
4	Sweden	82.9	84.9	82.0	87.4	80.5	85.5	80.3
5	Ireland	82.5	81.8	75.5	87.4	83.3	81.0	84.0
6	Finland	82.1	84.6	79.2	89.4	79.2	83.6	80.5
7	Norway	81.4	82.7	77.4	87.4	79.9	84.5	78.4
8	Belgium	81.3	80.6	75.8	85.5	82.0	83.9	78.7
9	Chile	81.1	80.5	79.8	80.9	81.8	74.5	87.5
10	Austria	80.9	82.9	76.4	89.1	78.6	86.2	75.7
11	New Zealand	80.7	84.6	84.9	84.4	76.3	81.0	80.4
12	Swiss	80.4	85.2	82.8	87.4	74.9	82.4	78.4
13	Mauritius	80.0	83.8	81.0	86.5	75.6	79.1	80.8
14	Canada	79.6	82.3	80.2	84.4	76.6	82.2	77.1
15	Australia	79.6	80.7	73.2	87.4	78.3	81.0	78.1
16	Panama	79.0	82.3	79.0	85.1	75.2	78.8	79.2
17	Costa Rica	78.9	84.2	83.4	85.1	72.9	83.1	74.9
18	Luxemburg	78.8	84.3	80.9	87.4	72.5	80.5	77.1
19	Uruguay	78.7	83.3	80.5	85.8	73.5	76.2	81.1
20	Singapore	78.7	81.8	84.3	79.7	75.0	74.4	82.8
21	Germany	78.5	80.6	81.5	79.8	76.2	80.3	76.8
22	Lithuania	78.4	83.3	74.8	91.3	72.8	72.4	84.3
23	Trinidad and Tobago	78.2	84.3	87.3	82.1	71.2	75.8	80.5
24	Czech Republic	77.4	79.3	76.3	81.7	75.3	80.0	75.0
25	Greece	77.4	82.4	76.2	87.2	71.7	77.8	76.9
26	Slovenia	77.0	81.6	76.2	86.5	71.8	74.6	79.4
27	Belarus	76.5	78.3	79.1	77.8	74.5	70.9	82.0
28	El Salvador	75.4	77.6	79.8	75.9	72.9	69.6	81.0
29	Japan	75.1	84.0	70.0	88.5	64.9	81.6	68.7
30	Hungary	74.6	81.8	74.0	88.8	66.4	76.8	72.4
31	Argentina	73.2	80.5	77.9	82.5	64.8	73.5	72.9
32	South Africa	72.8	79.6	82.0	77.8	65.0	71.8	73.7
33	Bolivia	72.5	72.9	76.2	69.2	72.0	71.9	73.0
34	Tunisia	72.5	77.5	76.4	78.8	66.9	72.5	72.5
35	Morocco	72.2	75.0	69.9	79.7	68.9	67.8	76.4
36	Jamaica	71.5	85.1	85.1	85.5	56.1	78.2	65.0
37	Poland	71.1	69.8	77.4	60.8	72.5	76.2	66.2
38	Italy	71.1	77.8	77.3	78.4	63.5	76.8	65.6
39	Kazakstan	71.1	75.2	81.7	69.6	66.4	59.2	82.7
40	Bulgaria	71.0	80.9	77.0	84.5	59.3	73.2	68.8
41	Ecuador	70.8	71.6	78.2	66.2	69.3	67.5	73.9
42	Albania	70.6	77.6	77.7	77.7	62.7	68.3	72.8
43	Croatia	70.4	74.7	74.0	75.6	65.5	65.2	75.4
44	Korea, Rep. Of	70.3	77.7	65.4	88.5	61.3	73.3	67.4
45	Syria	69.5	64.2	58.7	69.1	75.5	58.9	79.7
46	Ukraine	69.3	76.4	79.9	73.6	61.2	66.1	72.5
47	Jordan	69.3	74.7	69.5	79.6	63.1	64.0	74.5
48	Romania	69.1	78.7	75.0	82.1	58.3	71.9	66.5
49	Brazil	69.0	74.6	76.4	72.4	62.7	70.2	67.9
50	France	67.9	72.6	69.3	75.2	62.4	79.3	56.7
51	United States	67.2	68.7	58.1	78.7	65.6	70.4	64.2
52	Turkey	66.6	73.7	78.4	68.8	58.5	57.5	75.5
53.	Thailand	66.1	73.4	76.3	70.4	57.8	73.7	58.7
54	Spain	65.2	63.8	77.0	51.9	66.8	70.9	59.7
55	China	64.6	61.7	64.2	59.0	68.0	56.0	73.0
56	Peru	62.8	65.0	71.3	59.1	60.3	62.7	62.9
57	Malaysia	62.5	57.2	58.4	56.6	68.6	57.7	67.2
58	Kenya	62.2	65.8	63.2	69.7	58.1	63.3	61.1
59	United Kingdom	61.9	54.1	70.9	37.6	70.7	64.8	59.0
60	Mexico	61.7	62.0	79.3	46.7	61.3	60.6	62.7
61	Bangladesh	61.6	57.9	34.5	81.0	65.9	61.8	61.4
62	Israel	61.4	54.9	34.1	74.7	68.9	66.3	56.7
63	Egypt	61.2	66.8	62.4	71.7	54.9	64.9	57.6
64	Nicaragua	59.1	58.7	61.4	55.9	59.6	63.3	55.0
65	Venezuela	57.2	63.8	66.8	61.9	49.7	57.9	56.6
66	Zimbabwe	56.2	59.0	58.7	61.1	53.0	57.5	55.0
67	Philippines	53.8	52.8	59.0	48.0	54.9	59.9	47.7
68	Sri Lanka	49.5	44.7	81.1	10.8	55.0	55.1	44.1
69	Colombia	47.5	42.3	72.6	13.9	53.3	51.2	43.8
70	Pakistan	47.5	42.8	28.7	57.7	52.9	50.1	45.0
71	Algeria	47.0	47.3	72.9	21.9	46.7	52.5	41.6
72	India	44.9	40.1	31.3	49.3	50.4	50.3	39..7
73	Indonesia	41.9	46.4	57.4	36.6	36.7	52.5	31.5
74	Russia	39.8	37.0	57.2	17.7	42.9	48.9	30.9

Table 2. World Culture of Peace Index 2000 by National Income

	Nation	WCPI2000	Politico-Military PI	International PMPI	Domestic PMPI	Socio-Economic
High Income Nations	Denmark	84.4	85.6	80.3	90.5	83.1
	Netherlands	84.0	85.1	79.1	90.5	82.7
	Portugal	83.3	84.7	80.2	88.4	81.6
	Sweden	82.9	84.9	82.0	87.4	80.5
	Ireland	82.5	81.8	75.5	87.4	83.3
	Finland	82.1	84.6	79.2	89.4	79.2
	Norway	81.4	82.7	77.4	87.4	79.9
	Belgium	81.3	80.6	75.8	85.5	82.0
	Austria	80.9	82.9	76.4	89.1	78.6
	New Zealand	80.7	84.6	84.9	84.4	76.3
	Swiss	80.4	85.2	82.8	87.4	74.9
	Canada	79.6	82.3	80.2	84.4	76.6
	Australia	79.6	80.7	73.2	87.4	78.3
	Luxemburg	78.8	84.3	80.9	87.4	72.5
	Singapore	78.7	81.8	84.3	79.7	75.0
	Germany	78.5	80.6	81.5	79.8	76.2
	Greece	77.4	82.4	76.2	87.2	71.7
	Slovenia	77.0	81.6	76.2	86.5	71.8
	Japan	75.1	84.0	70.0	88.5	64.9
	Italy	71.1	77.8	77.3	78.4	63.5
	Korea, Rep. Of	70.3	77.7	65.4	88.5	61.8
	France	67.9	72.6	69.3	75.2	62.4
	United States	67.2	68.7	58.1	78.7	65.6
	Spain	65.2	63.8	77.0	51.9	66.8
	United Kingdom	61.9	54.1	70.9	37.6	70.7
	Israel	61.4	54.9	34.1	74.7	68.9
High Income Nations Average		76.7	78.8	75.3	82.1	74.2
Middle Income Nations	Chile	81.1	80.5	79.8	80.9	81.8
	Mauritius	80.0	83.8	81.0	86.5	75.6
	Panama	79.0	82.3	79.0	85.1	75.2
	Costa Rica	78.9	84.2	83.4	85.1	72.9
	Uruguay	78.7	83.3	80.5	85.8	73.5
	Lithuania	78.4	83.3	74.8	91.3	72.8
	Trinidad and Tobago	78.2	84.3	87.3	82.1	71.2
	Czech Republic	77.4	79.3	76.3	81.7	75.3
	Belarus	76.5	78.3	79.1	77.8	74.5
	El Salvador	75.4	77.6	79.8	75.9	72.9
	Hungary	74.6	81.8	74.0	88.8	66.4
	Argentina	73.2	80.5	77.9	82.5	64.8
	South Africa	72.8	79.6	82.0	77.8	65.0
	Bolivia	72.5	72.9	76.2	69.2	72.0
	Tunisia	72.5	77.5	76.4	78.8	66.9
	Morocco	72.2	75.0	69.9	79.7	68.9
	Jamaica	71.5	85.1	85.1	85.5	56.1
	Poland	71.1	69.8	77.4	60.8	72.6
	Kazakstan	71.1	75.2	81.7	69.6	66.4
	Bulgaria	71.0	80.9	77.0	84.5	59.6
	Ecuador	70.8	71.6	78.2	66.2	69.8
	Albania	70.6	77.6	77.7	77.7	62.7
	Croatia	70.4	74.7	74.0	75.6	65.5
	Syria	69.5	64.2	58.7	69.1	75.5
	Ukraine	69.3	76.4	79.9	73.6	61.2
	Jordan	69.3	74.7	69.5	79.6	63.1
	Romania	69.1	78.7	75.0	82.1	58.3
	Brazil	69.0	74.6	76.4	72.4	62.7
	Turkey	66.6	73.7	78.4	68.8	58.5
	Thailand	66.1	73.4	76.3	70.4	57.8
	Peru	62.8	65.0	71.3	59.1	60.3
	Malaysia	62.5	57.2	58.4	56.6	68.6
	Mexico	61.7	62.0	79.3	46.7	61.3
	Egypt	61.2	66.8	62.4	71.7	54.9
	Venezuela	57.2	63.8	66.8	61.9	49.7
	Philippines	53.8	52.8	59.0	48.0	54.9
	Sri Lanka	49.5	44.7	81.1	10.8	55.0
	Colombia	47.5	42.3	72.6	13.9	53.3
	Algeria	47.0	47.3	72.9	21.9	46.7
	Russia	39.8	37.0	57.2	17.7	42.9
Middle Income Nations Average		68.5	71.8	75.1	68.8	64.7
Low Income Nations	China	64.6	61.7	64.2	59.0	68.0
	Kenya	62.2	65.8	63.2	69.7	58.1
	Bangladesh	61.6	57.9	34.5	81.0	65.9
	Nicaragua	59.1	58.7	61.4	55.9	59.6
	Zimbabwe	56.2	59.0	58.7	61.1	53.0
	Pakistan	47.5	42.8	28.7	57.7	52.9
	India	44.9	40.1	31.3	49.3	50.4
	Indonesia	41.9	46.4	57.4	36.6	36.7
Low Income Nations Average		54.8	54.1	49.9	58.8	55.6

Table 3. Politico-Military Peace Index

Rank	Nation	Politico-Military PI	PM-Structural Index	PM-Behavioral Index	International PMPI	Domestic PMPI
World Average		69.7	69.8	69.6	70.8	68.9
1	Bahamas	86.2	95.4	77.8	85.2	87.4
2	Malta	85.9	97.3	75.6	81.2	90.5
3	Denmark	85.6	94.3	77.8	80.3	90.5
4	Swiss	85.2	91	80	82.8	87.4
5	Netherlands	85.1	93.2	77.8	79.1	90.5
6	Jamaica	85.1	93.1	77.8	85.1	85.5
7	Sweden	84.9	90.3	80	82	87.4
8	Portugal	84.7	87.5	82.2	80.2	88.4
9	Finland	84.6	92.2	77.8	78	90.5
10	New Zealand	84.6	92.1	77.8	79.2	89.4
11	Iceland	84.6	89.6	80	84.9	84.4
12	Luxemburg	84.3	91.4	77.8	80.9	87.4
13	Trinidad and Tobago	84.3	89.1	80	87.3	82.1
14	Costa Rica	84.2	88.9	80	83.4	85.1
15	Japan	84	90.8	77.8	79	88.5
16	Mauritius	83.8	90.3	77.8	81	86.5
17	Estonia	83.6	87.5	80	80.3	86.5
18	Dominican Republic	83.4	87.2	80	84.7	82.5
19	Uruguay	83.3	86.9	80	80.5	85.8
20	Lithuania	83.3	84.5	82.3	74.8	91.3
21	Latvia	83	86.4	80	79.1	86.5
22	Mongolia	83	86.3	80	81.3	84.5
23	Austria	82.9	93.3	73.4	76.4	89.1
24	Norway	82.7	88.1	77.8	77.4	87.4
25	Greece	82.4	80.1	84.4	76.2	87.2
26	Canada	82.3	87.2	77.8	80.2	84.4
27	Panama	82.3	84.8	80	79	85.1
28	Malawi	82	84.1	80	80.2	83.6
29	Ireland	81.8	88.6	75.6	74	88.8
30	Singapore	81.8	86.2	77.8	75.5	87.4
31	Hungary	81.8	81.4	82.2	84.3	79.7
32	Ghana	81.7	86.1	77.8	80	83.6
33	Slovenia	81.6	85.8	77.8	76.2	86.5
34	Bulgaria	80.9	84.3	77.8	77	84.5
35	Australia	80.7	86.3	75.6	73.2	87.4
36	Belgium	80.6	88.6	73.4	75.8	85.5
37	Germany	80.6	78.7	82.2	81.5	79.8
38	Chile	80.5	78.5	82.2	79.8	80.9
39	Argentina	80.5	78.5	82.2	77.9	82.5
40	Mali	80.5	78.5	82.2	84.6	77
41	South Africa	79.6	79.1	80	82	77.8
42	Czech Republic	79.3	85.9	73.3	76.3	81.7
43	Papua New Guinea	79	85.3	73.4	73.4	84.5
44	Romania	78.7	79.6	77.8	75	82.1
45	Central Africa	78.6	79.4	77.8	77.8	79.6
46	Guinea	78.5	76.7	80	78.3	78.8
47	Namibia	78.5	69.5	86.6	79.7	77
48	Belarus	78.3	76.4	80	79.1	77.8
49	Italy	77.8	77.7	77.8	78.2	77.8
50	Gambia	77.8	75.4	80	77.3	78.4
51	Korea. Rep, of	77.7	80.1	75.6	65.4	88.5
52	El Salvador	77.6	74.9	80	79.8	75.9
53	Albania	77.6	74.9	80	77.7	77.7
54	Tunisia	77.5	77.1	77.8	76.4	78.8
55	Guatemala	76.9	76	77.8	77.5	76.9
56	Ukraine	76,4	70.1	82.2	79.9	73.6
57	Nepal	76.2	79.4	73.4	71.2	81.3
58	Slovakia	76.2	74.4	77.8	75.2	77.4
59	Arab Emirates	75.9	73.8	77.8	72.9	78.8
60	Botswana	75.5	77.8	73.4	65.6	84.5
61	Kazakstan	75.2	65	84.4	81.7	69.6
62	Cameroon	75.1	69.7	80	78.9	72.3
63	Morocco	75	72	77.8	69.9	79.7
64	Mauritania	75	69.4	80	78.1	72.6
65	Croatia	74.7	73.7	75.6	69.5	79.6
66	Jordan	74.7	71.2	77.8	74	75.6
67	Brazil	74.6	78.6	71.1	76.4	72.4
68	Honduras	74.3	68.1	80	64.2	82.9
69	Fiji	74.2	70.2	77.8	84.2	66.3
70	Niger	74.2	67.9	80	74.6	74.2
71	Tanzania	73.9	69.6	77.8	77.6	71.3
72	Turkey	73.7	69.2	77.8	74	73.9
73	Mozambique	73.7	54.5	91	78.4	68.8
74	Thailand	73.4	78.4	68.9	76.3	70.4
75	Bolivia	72.9	82.4	64.4	76.2	69.2
76	Lybia	72.9	67.4	77.8	67.4	77.8

Rank	Nation	Politico-Military PI	PM-Structural Index	PM-Behavioral Index	International PMPI	Domestic PMPI
77	Qatar	72.9	65.1	80	72.8	73.2
78	Zambia	72.7	81.8	64.6	65.3	80.7
79	France	72.6	81.6	64.4	69.3	75.2
80	Cambodia	72.6	64.5	80	71.5	73.8
81	Oman	72.4	66.4	77.8	66.3	77.8
82	Laos	72.3	71.1	73.3	77.8	67.7
83	Ecuador	71.6	69.7	73.3	78.2	66.2
84	Yemen	70.4	62.1	77.8	70	71.1
85	Taiwan	69.9	80.7	60.1	58.3	80.7
86	Poland	69.8	88.3	53.2	77.4	60.8
87	Uzbekistan	69.8	58.6	80	80	61.6
88	Bahrain	69.7	65.6	73.4	67.4	72.4
89	Toga	69.7	60.8	77.8	78.1	63.2
90	Vietnam	69.6	58.2	80	69.7	69.8
91	United States	68.7	68.3	69	58.1	78.7
92	Senegal	68.6	73.3	64.4	77.7	60.1
93	Nigeria	68.1	55	80	74.6	62.9
94	Cuba	68	64.5	71.2	65.6	71.1
95	Paraguay	67.9	71.9	64.4	79.8	57.1
96	Egypt	66.8	64.3	69	62.4	71.7
97	Korea DPR	66.7	59.3	73.4	53	78.9
98	Kenya	65.8	67.2	64.6	63.2	69.7
99	Peru	65	80.6	50.9	77.7	52
100	Gabon	65	68.2	62.2	71.3	59.1
101	Kyrgyzstan	64.6	55	73.3	78.6	52
102	Syria	64.2	49.2	77.8	58.7	69.1
103	Armenia	64.1	58.8	68.9	66.5	61.5
104	Tajikistan	63.9	53.6	73.3	71.9	56.4
105	Spain	63.8	63.2	64.4	77	51.9
106	Venezuela	63.8	60.5	66.7	66.8	61.9
107	'Kuwait	62.9	46.5	77.8	52.9	71.7
108	Saudi Arabia	62.1	39.8	82.2	67.3	57.7
109	Mexico	62	59.3	64.4	79.3	46.7
110	China	61.7	53.7	68.9	64.2	59
111	Zimbabwe	59	52.9	64.6	58.7	61.1
112	Nicaragua	58.7	67.1	51.1	61.4	55.9
113	Bangladesh	57.9	72.4	44.7	34.5	81
114	Uganda	57.6	40.2	73.4	61.3	55.5
115	Ma(Malaysia	57.2	54	60	58.4	56.6
116	Georgia	56.4	52.4	60	62	52.2
117	Chad	55.4	45.3	64.6	56.3	56.5
118	Israel	54.9	54	55.7	34.1	74.7
119	United Kingdom	54.1	55.2	53.2	70.9	37.6
120	Iran	53.6	46.4	60	58.5	49.9
121	Philippines	52.8	54.6	51.1	59	48
122	Sierra Leone	49.5	62.7	37.5	77.8	22.2
123	Ethiopia	49	49	49	39.6	58.3
124	Algeria	47.3	55.6	39.7	72.9	21.9
125	Moldova	46.8	57.1	37.5	71.6	22.4
126	Indonesia	46.4	48.6	44.4	57.4	36.6
127	Sri Lanka	44.7	52.7	37.5	81.1	10.8
128	Angola	44.1	26.7	59.8	66.3	22.3
129	Myanmar	43.7	40.7	46.5	71.1	18.2
130	Lebanon	43.2	46.4	40.3	22.2	64.9
131	Pakistan	42.8	43.3	42.4	28.7	57.7
132	Colombia	42.3	42.7	42	72.6	13.9
133	Azerbijan	40.9	39.4	42.3	43.8	39.9
134	India	40.1	45	35.7	31.3	49.3
135	Burundi	39.8	42.2	37.5	76	6
136	Russia	37	38.9	35.4	57.2	17.7
137	Rwanda	31.7	34.9	28.8	45.6	19.1
138	Iraq	30.5	27.1	33.5	18.7	43.4
139	Congo, Dem Rep. of the	29	34	24.5	37	22.7
140	Sudan	28	31.8	24.5	35.9	21.7

Table 4. Socio-Economic Peace Index

Rank	Nation	WCPI 2000	Socio-Economic Peace Index	SE-Structural Index	SE-Behavioral Index
World Average		69.9	67.0	66.8	67.3
1	Ireland	82.5	83.3	75.5	91.6
2	Denmark	84.4	83.1	78.7	87.7
3	Netherlands	84.0	82.7	79.8	86.0
4	Belgium	81.3	82.0	79.0	85.2
5	Chile	81.1	81.8	70.3	94.1
6	Portugal	83.3	81.6	77.0	86.4
7	Sweden	82.9	80.5	80.4	80.6
8	Norway	81.4	79.9	80.7	79.1
9	Finland	82.1	79.2	74.7	83.9
10	Austria	80.9	78.8	78.8	78.5
11	Australia	79.8	78.3	75.5	81.3
12	Canada	79.6	76.6	77.0	76.2
13	New Zealand	80.7	76.3	72.0	80.8
14	Germany	78.5	76.2	81.9	70.1
15	Mauritius	80.0	75.8	87.2	84.5
16	Syria	69.5	75.5	69.2	82.2
17	Czech Republic	77.4	75.3	73.8	77.0
18	Panama	79.0	75.2	72.5	78.1
19	Singapore	78.7	75.0	67.0	83.6
20	Swiss	80.4	74.9	73.4	78.5
21	Belarus	76.5	74.5	65.1	84.4
22	Uruguay	78.7	73.5	65.0	82.5
23	Costa Rica	78.9	72.9	77.0	68.5
24	El Salvador	75.4	72.9	64.2	82.2
25	Lithuania	78.4	72.8	59.7	86.8
26	Poland	71.1	72.6	63.8	82.3
27	Luxemburg	78.8	72.5	69.0	76.2
28	Bolivia	72.5	72.0	60.9	83.8
29	Slovenia	77.0	71.8	62.9	81.3
30	Greece	77.4	71.7	75.5	67.6
31	Trinidad and Tobago	78.2	71.2	61.8	81.1
32	United Kingdom	61.9	70.7	75.0	66.3
33	Ecuador	70.8	69.8	65.2	74.7
34	Morocco	72.2	68.9	63.4	74.7
35	Israel	61.4	68.9	79.3	57.9
36	Malaysia	62.5	68.6	61.7	76.0
37	China	64.6	68.0	58.4	78.2
38	Tunisia	72.5	66.9	67.7	66.0
39	Spain	65.2	68.8	79.0	53.8
40	Hungary	74.6	66.4	64.5	68.5
41	Kazakstan	71.1	66.4	53.1	80.6
42	Bangladesh	61.6	65.9	50.5	82.2
43	United States	67.2	65.6	72.5	58.2
44	Croatia	70.4	65.5	58.8	72.5
45	South Africa	72.8	65.0	64.1	65.9
46	Japan	75.1	64.9	12.0	57.4
47	Argentina	73.2	64.8	68.2	61.2
48	Italy	71.1	63.5	78.3	47.7
49	Jordan	69.3	63.1	53.8	73.0
50	Albania	70.6	62.7	61.5	63.9
51	Brazil	69.0	62.7	61.3	64.1
52	France	67.9	62.4	76.8	47.1
53	Korea, Rep of	70.3	61.8	66.1	57.1
54	Mexico	61.7	61.3	82.0	60.6
55	Ukraine	69.3	61.2	62.0	60.6
56	Peru	62.8	60.3	56.9	63.9
57	Bulgaria	71.0	59.6	61.5	57.6
58	Nicaragua	59.1	59.6	59.3	59.9
59	Turkey	66.6	58.5	60.5	56.3
60	Romania	69.1	58.3	63.3	52.4
61	Kenya	62.2	58.1	59.3	56.9
62	Thailand	66.1	57.8	68.7	46.2
63	Jamaica	71.5	56.1	62.5	49.2
64	Sri Lanka	49.5	55.0	57.6	52.3
65	Egypt	61.2	54.9	65.6	43.4
66	Philippines	53.8	54.9	65.5	43.5
67	Colombia	47.5	53.3	60.1	46.1
68	Zimbabwe	56.2	53.0	62.3	43.1
69	Pakistan	47.5	52.9	57.3	48.1
70	India	44.9	50.4	55.8	44.6
71	Venezuela	57.2	49.7	55.1	44.0
72	Algeria	47.0	46.7	49.3	44.0
73	Russia	39.8	42.9	59.4	25.3
74	Indonesia	41.9	36.7	56.7	15.5

Table 5. State of Peace Around the World

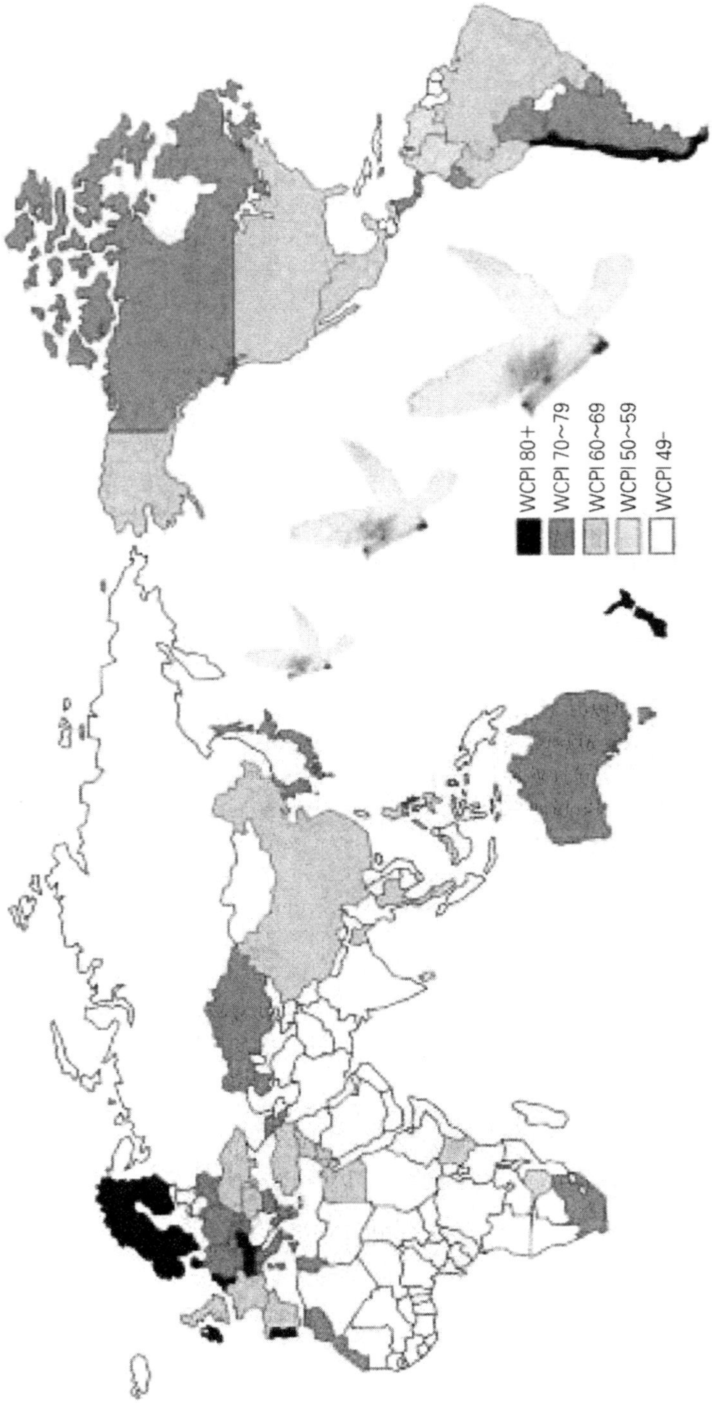

Peace Search: From the Secular to the Christic

Bernard Swan[1]
University of New England

This century has been extraordinarily rich in promise and in opportunities for good. Nonetheless, the signs of unpeacefulness have also seemed unending, more visible and ominous than ever before: wars, conflicts, enmities and hatreds, violence, injustice, greed, hunger and poverty, gross violations of human life, power struggles, arms build-ups, the mushroom-cloud, the unremitting degradation of the planet's life-support systems. All these and analyses, which say that the world is in severe crisis[2] and that peace is the impossible dream, throw many into profound pessimism for peace on earth. Yet everywhere people cry 'Peace!' and live in the hope of peace as they construe it. In its quest, some are more diligent than others. Some are more vocal. The majority are circumspect in its pursuit. They dance around it, sing songs extolling peace but hesitate to approach it, through fear that peace might be more than they bargain for, that too much might be required of them if they accept its embrace.

At the individual level peace is widely regarded as well-being interior and exterior calm, pleasant satisfying relationships, access to desired goods and services, security, a minimum of trouble and misfortune and good health and long life to enjoy it all. Collectivities share somewhat similar views although scales are different the number of those included in the circle whose well-being is desired and sought varies from one collectivity to another. The family, the interest group, the company, the conglomerate, the sub-nationality, the state, the alliance, all have differing perspectives of peace.

For centuries, religion was regarded as affording the richest insights into peace, but these duly conflicted with the views of the temporal ruler, today typified by the secular sovereign state and its government which claimed, as they still do, responsibility for peace in the earthly realm, attempting both to confine the jurisdiction of religion to the spiritual realm as defined by the secular sovereign, and to induce religious authorities to endorse their policies. The separation was rationalised and intensified by theories of temporal power which accorded the ruler the right and duty to pursue the interests of state untrammelled by moral considerations: theories and doctrines which held religion to be a private matter; that it was the duty of the subject to obey the ruler whether right or wrong. The problems arising from the privatisation of religion and concomitant pervasive moral ambivalence have persisted ever since.

The Study of Peace

The rise of the peace movement, rainbow in composition and pluralistic in its aims and methods, but avowedly pursuing peace, was followed by the

Bernard Swan, "Peace Search: From the Secular to the Christic." Reprinted with permission from the editors of *Essays on Peace: Paradigms for Global Order* edited by Michael Salla, Walter Tenetto, & Enrique Martínez.

emergence in academia of Peace Studies, undertaken by those who saw the need for researching peace and what militated against it, and for disseminating their findings and ideas through educational processes. Peace research, undertaken shortly after the detonation of the atom bomb, gathered momentum as its scope widened in response to the Cold War, the nuclear arms race and the problems of development encountered by nations that had emerged following the break up of political empires, particularly after the Second World War.

On account of the horrors of modern warfare, early peace research was based on the assumption that peace should be narrowly defined as the absence of war, to which was tagged later the idea that peace was the absence of distributive injustice. These definitions did not sit comfortably together because it was thought by some researchers that only through violence could injustice be effectively combated. Today, peace has more positive connotations as well: the building of a better, more humane world respectful of ecological imperatives and needs. Not only is the past dwelt upon for empirical studies of peace and conflict, and the present critically appraised so as to understand the causes of unpeacefulness and to help resolve conflict, but in the interests of peace for the morrow, peace strategies are designed and optional futures explored as well.[3]

Peace, as identified by those who study it, may be understood better if placed in different categories which may be arranged in tiers.

State peace: negative peace type (i)

At the base of the tiers of peace considered is the peace acknowledged by the state and the general public: peace born of law and order in the realm; peace as the absence of war between states and of violence within the state, or against it, on the part of those living within it. Such peace has to be kept. Peace, however, is not the uppermost of the state's priorities. More important are its own integrity, security and well-being, held to be the national interest. War itself, as demonstrated repeatedly through history, may be engaged in when 'necessary': the legitimate means of 'last resort', not only in the face of aggression by another state, but also for the resolution of seemingly intractable problems or for satisfying needs that other means might take longer to achieve, if at all. Especially noteworthy is the pragmatism and a morality of the state, which forbids violence and killing by its citizens but condones it and, indeed, demands it in defence of the national interest.

As a general precept, peace is to be defended by means of diplomacy, trade, economic progress; by weapons to deter aggression and by arms control to curb arms races which such deterrence might serve to stimulate. Because of the importance to the state of goods and services and in countries where the state itself does not monopolise these, it is expedient for the state to uphold the interests of those who produce or deliver them. A symbiotic relationship tends to develop between the state and big business. The former endeavours to safeguard the latter, through direct or indirect action. Prince and Merchant work hand-in-glove, with the Citizen required to support both.[4]

This concept of peace finds acceptance in many academic and applied sciences, such as political, international, strategic and military studies, or where Peace Studies itself is beholden to sponsorship by the state or big business. Offshoots of this philosophy of peace, in vogue even within Peace Studies conducted in tertiary institutions, include conflict limitation, conflict resolution and mediation research: for the necessary and commendable skills to induce contending parties to talk to one another, often through the offices of a neutral third party, to defuse tension, to duly arrive at a compromise and a settlement of their differences, and thereby to dispense with the 'need' for direct violence.

Negative peace type (ii)

Through analysing the world system, those aspects of it which militate against peace and those which are conducive to peace, Peace Studies may question the thinking of the state, of entrepreneurs and fellow travellers, and find these wanting. Through its analysis of peace and through identifying its requisites, Peace Studies points to the need for going beyond the limits of the conventional wisdom so that peace, and what facilitates its realisation, may duly supersede whatever works against it.

State peace values and strategies are transcended when Peace Studies argues for other means for alternative defence, such as disarmament, mutual confidence-building measures and non-military and even non-violent means of defence, culminating in the abolition of war itself.[5] Where there is insistence on this elementary transcendence, Peace Studies risks incurring the suspicion and opprobrium of the state and of those who believe that in military methods and organised violence lie the ultimate source of power to defend, protect, safeguard and recover that which is worthy, even the very things of God.

Oppositional peace

Transcendent thinking is heightened when it is recognised that the abolition of international war is no guarantee of peace; that the deeper-seated causes of unpeacefulness must be addressed as well. These are regarded as stemming from the silent violence and oppression perpetuated by the privileged and the powerful upon the underprivileged and the weak, through systems of social, cultural, economic and political organisation and control. Such indirect violence, which marginalises, impoverishes and often eventually kills (usually from a distance through deprivation of basic requirements of life), needs to be identified, confronted and eliminated along with direct violence, argue exponents of oppositional peace, if meaningful peace is to be achieved between and within nations.[6]

Insistence that there can be no peace worthy of the name without transcending indirect violence encounters resistance from the state and from those committed to maintaining the *status quo*. It comes also from those peace researchers who prefer to concentrate on *peace as the absence of war*.[7] In the contestation of indirect violence, not all agree over how to do so. Some argue according to the logic of Karl Marx, which subsumes the logic of the state, that in pursuing desired ends, whatever means are necessary may be adopted. They point out that both Prince and Merchant form a resolute and unyielding duo in the defence of sectoral wealth, power and privilege, and can only be overthrown by force. Yet others declare that where the yoke of oppression cannot be cast aside by other means, the Just War clause of last resort might be invoked to justify recourse to direct violence. However, there exists also a class of peace researchers and educators who maintain that violence of any kind begets further violence, and warn that exchanging tyrannies is not the way to peace.[8] These advocate non-violent methods for overcoming oppression and injustice.[9]

Positive peace

Positive Peace constitutes the topmost of the tiers familiar to Peace Studies. It is usually seen as resting on the second (peace through opposing the status quo) upon which it builds towards humane development, liberation and fulfilment. It is sometimes placed directly upon the bottom tier (peace as the absence of war) by those who wish to by-pass some of the more confrontational aspects of the second tier, in the hope that the problems which the struggle against injustice and oppression would radically deal with would duly dissolve in the harmonious milieu of positive peace. For, not only is war rejected as an instrument of policy for peace and deliverance from oppression and injustice and the structures of violence that support them rejected also, but peace-making is accepted as a positive dynamic. It is the building of a better world: the fruit of education for peace, of justice, respect for human rights and human dignity, and the quest for development that is humane and ecologically sustainable, a development that is qualitative rather than quantitative. The debate that develops here is over what constitutes humane development, and how to achieve it.

Peace Studies: a Critique

Peace Studies is comparatively young. It has been widely treated with reserve and cynicism in academia on grounds that it is not a discipline, that it is emotive, normative and prejudiced against the status quo. Such allegations themselves are often flimsy, and themselves are illustrative of the bias, the norms and the subjectivity of those who make them in the name of dispassionate objectivity.

Peace Studies is not without shortcomings. These are attributable to the pressures upon it to concentrate upon issues of war, conflict and violence. They are also due to the academic and cultural values and assumptions of those who undertake or teach them, often with backgrounds in other disciplines. Peace Studies originated as a Western reaction to problems generated largely by the West and by those who take their cue from the West. Western values permeate Peace Studies, as do Western ways of thinking, seeing and doing: emphasis is on problem-solving and the pragmatic attainment of goals. There is considerable attention to, indeed exhaustive analysis, of conflicts and of the signs and the consequences of unpeacefulness at meso- and macro-scales of societal being. There is awareness of much of what Peace Studies should help lead away from (e-duco). There is less confidence over what such studies should lead to (ad-duco), excepting that it should be to peace, and if possible, in peace. The concept of peace itself is in need of further exploration and fuller development.

Today, there is growing acceptance of the idea that peace is indivisible, a seamless garment. This points to the need for a genuinely holistic approach to the subject, which would only be possible if peace researchers and educators are liberated from cultural shackles which constrain them, but which many are oblivious of. One such limiting factor is the commitment on the part of Peace Studies to research conducted in the secular mode: so very noticeable in the academic journals on peace. Little heed is paid to the lessons of metaphysics, theology and religion on peace, and a vast body of literature and thought on the subject is left untapped or barely so: an attitude quite inconsistent with the holistic ideal which urges lateral thinking and integration instead of tunnel vision. There appears to be subscription to the notion that metaphysics, theology and religion afford insights that are less amenable to proof and that, as such, they are removed from realpolitik, practicality and even credibility.

This is, in part, attributable to the academic training of many peace researchers and educators, in which reason and the scientific method and its social-science variant have long been upheld as the appropriate and reliable means of seeking objective truth and achieving credibility in the intellectual circles.

This tradition, which claims to be value-free, rejects as subjective, untestable and therefore unreliable or invalid, those activities of the brain thought to be associated with right-lobe functions: intuition, feeling, spiritual and mystical cognisance, the sense of compassion, mercy, justice and the like. This 'cerebral' approach accepts mind knowledge, but not heart knowledge, as a means of understanding reality and is only quasi-cerebral. It is not holistic or value free or wholly objective for it supports a hidden agenda (Figure 1[10]).

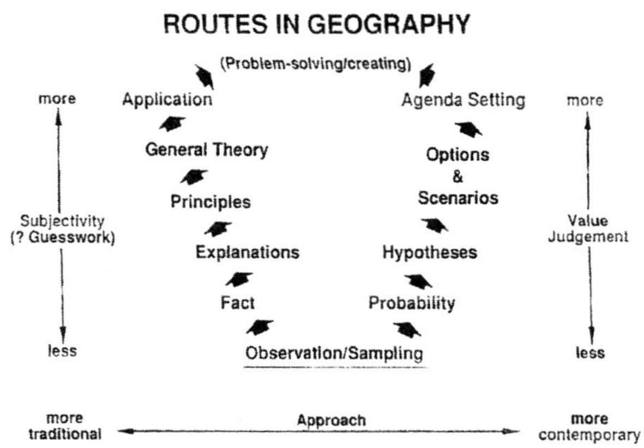

Figure 1

Despite its normative emphases,[11] peace studies tends also to positivism, in that peace is regarded as a goal to be achieved through analysis, appropriate methodology, effort and perseverance, with peace itself construed in social, economic and political terms. There is occasional reference to, and commendation of, spiritual values, but these are seen primarily as aids to empowerment and the attainment of objectives, rather than as themselves worthy of fuller investigation and adoption in relation to peace.

Toward Balanced Enquiry

Peace researchers and educators espouse certain values which are seeds of potential transformation, for widening and deepening the subject. Some emphasise the desirability of 'heart-based' learning (experiential and normative) to complement purely cerebral knowledge. In order to balance learning and knowing and render these more fully human, left-lobe and right-lobe functions of the brain should both be exercised and respected by academics and realists. Without sacrificing the obligation to think rationally and logically, it should be accepted that in the study of peace both mind and heart must have a place; with this should come the admission that knowledge based on scientific and rational means alone is incomplete and therefore narrowly true at best.[12]

A co-idea emphasises the importance of holistic search if peace is to be better understood. This too calls to question the capability and adequacy of positivist-reductionist methods of seeking truth and generating light about peace. It also challenges the peace researcher to ask how holistic the holism espoused in the process really is. It goes further to recognise that peace enquiry is not to be regarded merely as a lens through which the world 'out there' is to be examined and found wanting, but also as a mirror which signals the need for self-appraisal and, perhaps, for fuller conversion on the part of the enquirer. None of this exempts the student of peace from rational thought. Rather, it should deepen commitment to it. However, holistic search demonstrates that reason itself has its limits. It can carry its user to the threshold of greater knowing and urge that this be crossed for the sake of that knowledge and truth. The realm beyond is of faith and religion.[13]

Imaging the Future

Although negative, oppositional and positive peace are the principal categories recognised in Peace Studies, with ecopeace (greenpeace) impinging upon all three, the entire subject of peace may be approached from either of two ways. One is pragmatic. The other is principled and explicitly or implicitly religious (Figure 2[14]).

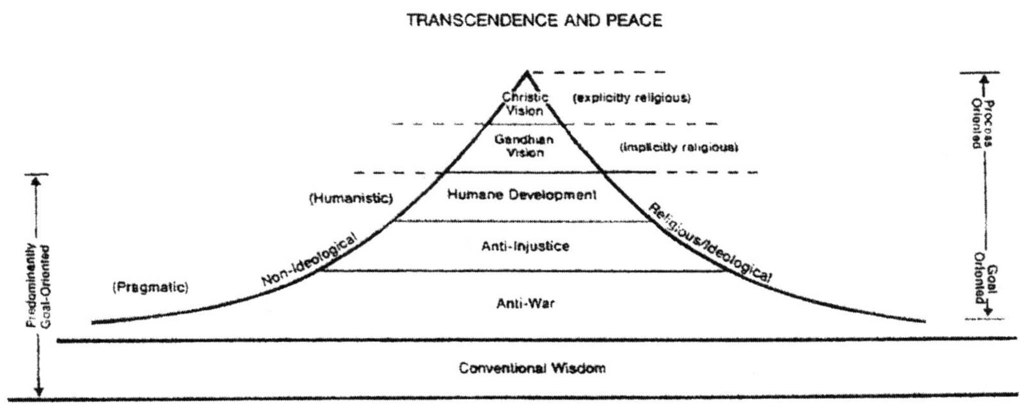

Figure 2

In the first instance, peace, however construed, is a goal which clear analysis and understanding and appropriate strategies could lead to. The prime need is to get suitable policies in place, envisage alternative scenarios and have contingency plans ready in the event of the unexpected occurring. In this endeavour, reality, the empirical world, is seen not as an absolute to be accounted for, but one among several worlds, which might become our tomorrow depending on the choices we make today. To the peace researcher the future could be one of many possibilities: the outcome of inertia; the outcome of positivism which attempts to mould the future, or the outcome of inexorable determinism. There is belief, however, that peace education itself could have a decisive, beneficial impact on the future. On the other hand there is the religious alternative which, to many, is more hopeful and empowering. Here, the future may be regarded as the function of the time ahead, of present action and inaction, the legacy of the past and the hand of Divine Providence. Some difficulty in accepting the notion of Providence may be experienced by those steeped in secular intellectualism and in the worlds of commercialism and advanced technologic discovery. Among them confidence in human ability to be the effective arbiter of its destiny is matched only by despair over the futility of such an enormous enterprise as the quest for peace on earth (Table 1).

Peace and Religion

Discussion of the relevance of religion to peace, raises the question as to what religion is. At one level it could be regarded as that which leads to an experiential encounter with the mystical, where the term mystical is construed as that which evokes devotion, that which is profoundly moving and revitalising. Quasi-religion is rooted in nature or the human spirit. "Religious" experience and fervour could be generated through a social encounter, a political speech, a sporting event, a panorama, an opera or music, a humanitarian action. It might even be induced chemically or sexually. At this level, virtually anything could become the object of adulation or the catalyst in the experience. The encounter may be moving but does not necessarily effect commitment or change on the part of the 'worshipper'. On the other hand, it may result in this, even leading to political or social altruism. It could work or draw upon the best in human nature with 'faith' expressed in life and deed.

Religion may also be seen as "...a social and individual relationship, vitally realised in a tradition and community, with something that transcends or encompasses man and his world; with something always to be understood as the utterly final true reality (the Absolute, God, Nirvana)...religion is concerned at once with a message of salvation and

TABLE 1: Possibilities for Peace through the Secular Mode

A. School of high hopes		**B. School of despondency**	
The human potential virtually unlimited		The human	: weak, foolish, flawed
The human	: its own light, semi-divine		: selfish, aggressive
	: can solve its problems		: a crisis animal, reacts to short-term problems rather than long-term needs
	: can build peace		: impaled upon its weaknesses
Requisites	: ideals, vision, goals, strategies, effort	Requisites	:disaster and crisis management, conflict management, conflict resolution if possible
"Peace is possible"		**"Peace, an utopian, unrealistic ideal"**	

the way to salvation". In this case the something that transcends or encompasses man and his world may be a philosophy, a moral code, the response to which results in self-change, the burgeoning of virtue and self-lessness: the way of Tao and of Buddhism.[15] Or, that which is seen to transcend or encompass man and his world may be identified in ecological or cosmic terms rooted in nature or universal energy and universal relationships, then deified in a Gaia sense,[16] where the principles and precepts, the language and the 'deity' are humanly derived and constructed. Yet others cross the threshold of faith to enter a realm of reality and possibility where the human engages in a relationship with Some One: a dynamic that is consuming, sustaining, exhilarating, inspiring, worshipful, reverent, prayerful, reconciling, healing, loving, trusting and empowering.

For those who take religion seriously, peace becomes increasingly a journey rather than a destination, a concomitant of a process that must be enjoined for an even greater reason. Expediency and the primacy of achieving goals are rejected. The quest for peace is integrated into the quest for integrity, honesty and truth. However, where religion does not include God or the supernatural but emphasises principles, a moral code or ethic, inconsistencies and contradictions may arise.

Matters of Morality

Unpeacefulness signals that all is not well with the human condition, that something better is necessary. What that something is requires the exercise of moral judgement which assumes a moral sense and ability to distinguish between justice and injustice, honesty and deceit, right and wrong, good and evil. There is required on the part of the peace researcher and educator, continual moral evaluation of situations and actions and options for tomorrow. This poses a question often left unanswered. It is whether morality is relative and grounded in expediency and appropriateness to situations, or whether in its application there should be consistency. This begets another question which asks whether an exclusively secular view of the world can accommodate or generate a moral sense that is anything other than relative and reflecting only the mores and cultures of the times.

In turn, this raises the question as to whether there could be any morality, other than that which is relative and socially engineered, if the human were no more than a chance phenomenon destined for oblivion, and whose material substance would be duly re-cycled through the ecosystem. Were that the case, the honestly secular rational view should be that human morals are illusory, though perhaps useful social constructs, and that there is no call for moral indignation in the event of the re-cycling process alluded to above being expedited through acts of volition, violence or neglect: these may be uncomfortable for the recipients but would be neither right nor wrong of themselves. It is just as difficult to discover logic or internal consistency in the notion of morals without religion as in that of religion without morals.

It is here believed that moral sense would only have validity if there is a spiritual principle in the human, a principle that transcends the limitations of re-cyclable matter: one which is non-material and therefore not subject to the consequences of bodily death and break-down. Moreover, morality implies not an inanimate something or a value which is impugned and insulted through non-moral behaviour, but Some One, exterior to and beyond the human and to whom the human is accountable. Accountability and its consequential implications cannot be with reference to an automaton or an abstraction, but to Who Is.

Moral Violence

In this context violence, and non-violence too acquire new meaning. Firstly, the notion of violence may be expanded. Johan Galtung along with many others has stated that the opposite of peace is violence. In his paper on 'Cultural Violence'[17] he refers to the violence triangle which consists of direct violence, structural violence and cultural violence. The first is overt. The second institutionalises indirect violence, which thus becomes intrinsic to the socio-economic and political system. The third colours the values of people rendering the other types of violence morally justifiable, or at least morally neutral. However, in the opinion expressed here, there needs to be recognised a fourth category of violence which underlies other classes of violence, making the violence triangle a violence tetrahedron. This is moral violence, the ethic of ethical inconsistency. It is violence that originates in the belief that the human is its own point of reference and the sole arbiter and judge of what is right and wrong, reducing morality to personal or social preference and need. Morality is then seen as relative. Moral violence manipulates and neutralises notions of right and wrong or changes their moral colour, as is the case with Galtung's cultural violence. It is the subterfuge which substitutes, often in the name of expediency and even of good, the spurious for the genuine, the inferior for the superior, the shadow for the substance, the creature for the Creator. Moral violence confuses and culminates in societies where the blind believe that they see, and lead the blind. It militates against peace, for it may infect and indeed, poison nations, societies, organisations, groups and individuals, whether secular or religious, and even those who would speak for peace.

Non-violence too is seen as potentially dualistic.[18] Not all, but much so-called non-violence is planned or practiced with coercive intent: as a tactic used against another to attain an objective, to force submission to one's will. As such it could be intrinsically violent. It becomes a device used to secure a goal, often all that is left to the weak in confronting the strong. Such non-violence is usually pragmatic. Its use depends on the degree of success it is likely to meet with. On the other hand there is principled non-violence which is practiced with, rather than against an opponent, in the hope of achieving not just a specified goal but also higher truth, mutual growth and conversion for all parties to the encounter. Principled non-violence is humble, courageous and merciful, equates means with ends, indeed values means more than ends and is seen not in strategic terms but as a way of life to be practiced consistently, and if necessary, unilaterally. Its essence is recognition of the inviolable dignity of the other, always cognisant of the divine (however hidden and suppressed) in the other, of the other as a child of God. There is also willingness to risk suffering and apparent failure in being faithful to the quest for truth and justice.

The conclusion reached in this discussion, is that, if it is admitted that there are moral and spiritual dimensions to the human and also to peace, ignoring or glossing over these in the study of peace would be irresponsible. To admit of these is to recognise that the study of peace necessarily requires entry into the realm of religion, belief and action.

Toward Christic Peace

Of the many who regard peace as a supreme human value, some have no particular religious affiliation and may not believe in the supernatural or in an after-life. Others take religion seriously. Both groups subscribe to ideals and values that are grounded in religious faith. Both groups see in religious values and ideals principled and humane means for political struggle and the resolution of conflict and extol these. Their inspiration comes from people of faith who confronted imperialism, oppression and injustice without compromising their integrity and their religion, with Mohandas Karamchand Gandhi and Martin Luther King among the models taken. Non-violence and commitment to truth are the fundamental values embraced, and with them concomitant virtues, such as readiness to engage in dialogue with and to forgive adversaries, courage and willingness to suffer in the cause of right.

Nonetheless, there is a difference in the concept of peace where religious belief is explicit, where faith is not in principle, ethic or idea but is a relationship, a total trusting commitment to Some

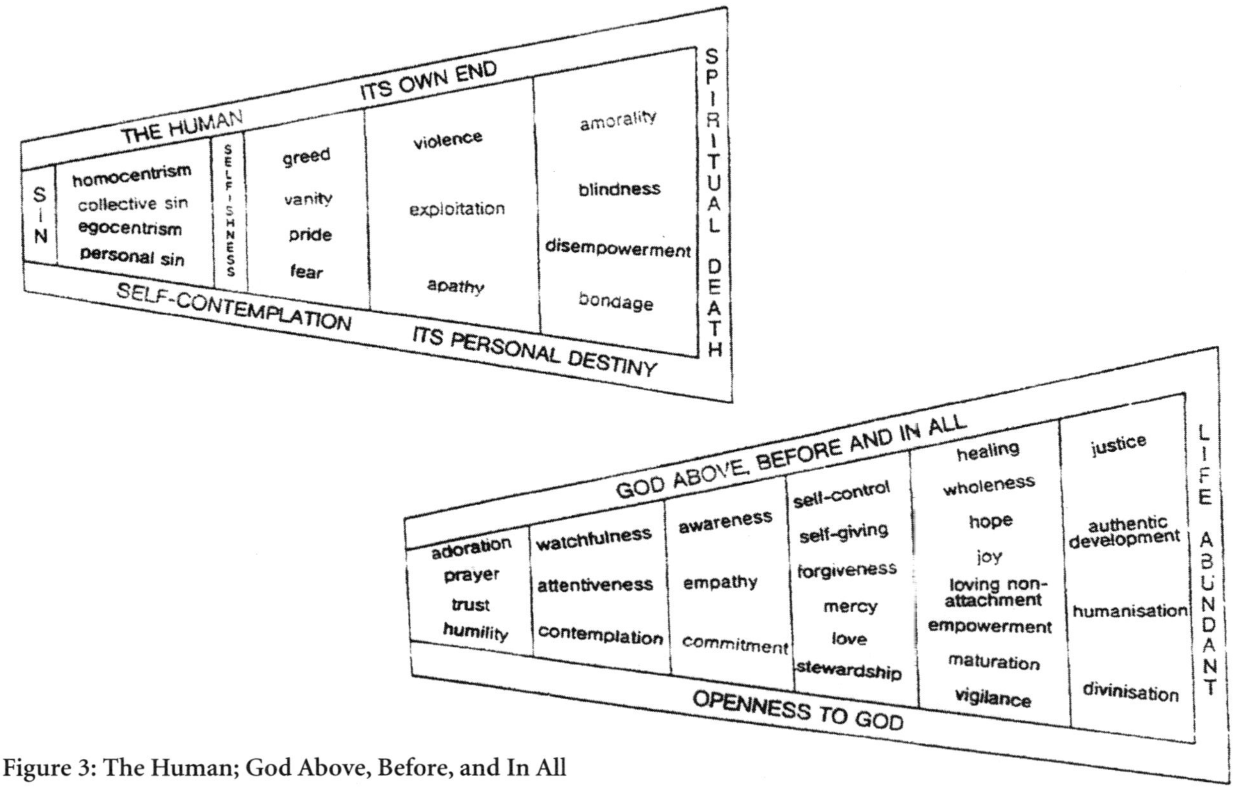

Figure 3: The Human; God Above, Before, and In All

One, an unequivocal 'Yes' to God. Peace emerges as individual and or society become that assent which places God above and before all else. This is here termed Christic Peace, because it was wholly exemplified in the life, death, person and teaching of Jesus Christ. It is also the quintessence of theistic scriptures (e.g. the Bhagavad Gita, the Torah, Bible and Koran) of Gandhi's vision, and is paralleled in its ideals in the Dhammapada of Buddhism. By the same criterion, the opposite of peace is not war or violence, as some peace researchers maintain, but the human refusal to become that 'Amen'. It is where in the pursuit of what promises to satisfy or be good, even peace itself, primacy is accorded the created, usually self in its personal or collective form, in preference to the Creator. This is sin, the opposite of peace, which may be the result of deliberate choice, or the consequence of pseudo-innocence which is the fruit of the human refusal to seek, to learn and to grow, and leads in a different direction (Figure 3[19]).

Christic peace is entry into a dynamic spiritual identity to which all are invited. The expression of that peace is 'Shalom', holistic peace which includes health, healing transformations and relations,[20] where micro-peace begets macro-peace and macro-peace supports micro-peace. Christic Peace bestows what other types of peace cannot. Not only does it liberate (starting from within) from all that enslaves and dehumanises, but it vests even the darkest darkness with light, bringing hope and meaning to areas and situations that often occasion bitterness, despair or hurt silence, as where there is pain and suffering, privation, neglect, abandonment, failure and death. It brings vision, expectancy, strength, endurance and courage. It shuns all retaliation and recourse to strategies of power. Instead, it offers forgiveness, love, even unilateral love of enemy, and through these, healing and healed relationships. Its concomitants are integrity, wholeness and holiness.

All this is possible, because Christic Peace is not self-generated. It is a gift inspired, upheld and transformed by the prayer of mind, of heart and of life. As such, its potential for renewal lies not in the intelligence, fitness, organisational skills and general capability of recipients, but in their willingness to seek integrity through acting justly, loving tenderly and walking humbly with their God. The way of Christic Peace exacts a price: the cross of selflessness, of self-giving which seeks no reward other than God, doing God's will and loving all creation. From this flow empowerment and dedication to peace. Clearly, this is the realm of grace (Table 2).

Discussion and Conclusions

Although it sometimes seems so in the literature, Peace Studies is not the same as contemporary politics, international studies, conflict studies or development studies. It includes aspects of these but is more. For long, peace studies have been pre-occupied with the 'e-duco' aspect of peace education: to 'lead away' from war, violence and destructive conflict, peace *sensu constricto*. It has yet to explore more fully the 'ad-duco' aspects of peace education that 'lead towards' peace *sensu lato*. During the height of the nuclear threat to humankind, peace-researchers advised proponents of nuclear deterrence, to get away from the thinking that maintained "If you want peace, prepare for war" and to shift instead to the idea that "If you want peace, prepare for peace". If this commendable advice is taken seriously by those who seek peace today, it would impel them to face up to the challenges of peace, which point to the highest levels of transcendence. These have responsible following across the world, including those who believe that Jesus Christ's Sermon on the Mount offers the soundest constructive political realism for the modem age.[21]

Christic Peace and paths to it, illumine and increasingly call to peace at all other levels. It invites to peace and salutes the divine in all people, especially those of goodwill. It contributes to Gandhian peace, reinforcing its principles and values, highlighting its religious basis. It renders explicit the idea

TABLE 2

CHARTING PEACE

← GOAL ______ PEACE AS ______ PROCESS →

STATE PEACE	NEGATIVE PEACE	OPPOSITIONAL PEACE	POSITIVE PEACE		TRANSCENDENT PEACE	
peace as fulfilment of personal, sub-national & national ambitions	peace as absence of war	peace as absence of all forms of violence & oppression	peace as distributive justice & economic development	peace as social justice & humane, ecologically responsible development	peace as integrity forgiveness, reconciliation & loving kindness	peace as a divine-human dynamic
pressure, skill, mastery; physical & indirect force as power	economic development, diplomacy & basic deterrence as power	non-violent techniques as power	law, policy and non-violent suasion as power	suasion based on respect, reflection & responsibility	self-giving & voluntary abandonment of power as empowerment	joyous trusting "Yes!" to God immanent & transcendent
(inertia)	(war prevention)	(subversion)	(conversion i)		(conversion ii)	(conversion iii)

← CONVENTIONAL WISDOM ______ PEACE THROUGH ______ TRANSCENDENCE →

(strategy) (grace)

that truth as an abstract concept and non-violence as a virtue make sense only where there is acknowledgment, even if only *de facto* of a Supreme Reality and the spiritual principle in the human. The contribution to positive peace is, *inter alia,* the Christic enrichment of the principles for humane development. The intrinsic dignity of men and women is underlined. Each human being is seen as a beloved child of God, hence the validity of notions of a human family, each member of which is vested with inviolable dignity and inalienable rights. For those who insist on secular vision, it offers the recognition that the human is the fruit of billions of years of cosmic evolution, that being in whom earth and universe attain reflexive consciousness.[22]

Christic vision sees human dignity compromised and sullied and people reified wherever governments, commerce, industry, research bodies and people's organisations define progress and development primarily in quantitative, materialistic, technological, consumerist and temporal terms; wherever goods and services, and hedonism and licence are offered as the substance of happiness and freedom. The Christic peace paradigm, rejects such interpretations of development, pointing out that these dazzle, disorient and de-humanise as they become false gods set up by the values of the day, gods which people are urged to venerate, serve and defend.[23] It recognises that it is more important for people to be more, rather than, to have more. It also perceives that men and women need to mature and grow in order to receive and make use of goods and services, if they are not to be overwhelmed by them; that the problem of the provision and distribution of goods and services is secondary to the problem of preparing people for them: a matter ignored by most experts on development. The paradigm emphasises essential development needs, enhancement goods of a qualitative and spiritual order, and the need for personal and collective integrity through commitment to a consistent ethic of life, in the place of double standards and pragmatism, as the *sine qua non* of development.[24] For those who concentrate on oppositional peace, the confrontation of injustice and inequity, Christic Peace challenges all selfishness and greed that seeks well-being and prosperity at the expense of others. There is no hesitation to proclaim that no one, no country, is entitled to keep for exclusive use what is not needed, when others lack necessities. Not only should the superfluous wealth of rich countries be placed at the service of poor nations, but no country may claim to keep its wealth for itself alone.[25]

Peace is seen as justice, as development, an indivisible trinity, which demands radical innovations and transformations. Yet, when justice is defined in Christic terms, these are neither legalistic nor in the language of distributive economics alone. While justice is the rejection of exploitation and imperialisms of all kinds, it is inseparable from love, mercy, forgiveness and reconciliation. A Christic theology of liberation seeks not only the liberation of the materially poor and the socio-politically downtrodden, but also liberation from the multitude of poverties that keep people in chains, including those of their own making.[26] Deliverance is offered even for the affluent[27] and those afflicted by insidious bankruptcies of the spirit.

For those who address issues of war, defence and direct violence for the sake of peace, Christic vision calls away from casuistry, retaliation and the use of power even in the name of good. Even more, it teaches the unity of life; that ends and means adopted for their attainment should be consistent. This leaves no place for the dualism of privatised religion which encourages worship of God at one level of being, while at another condones the substitution of Caesar or mammon for God.[28]

To some the Christic concept of peace may seem unrealistic, naive and have a fundamentalistic ring about it. To others such vision is fundamental if peace that is authentic is wanted. The Christic vision emphasises the wholeness of peace, which needs to be understood as such, and not as discrete entities to be sought only at either the macro- or the micro-scale. It recognises that even in a world without war and want, where people have access to all the goods and services they may desire and where the environment is kept wholesome and healthy, peace may not be present. In such a world there could be decadence, discontent and despair among those sated or dissatisfied in their abundance. Pain and anguish would still exist. For there to be peace the deepest needs and yearnings of the human heart and mind would also need to be addressed by those who speak for peace. These are spiritual needs. Centuries ago, St. Augustine expressed the problem this way, "Lord, you have made us for yourself and our hearts are restless until they rest in you."

Kenneth Boulding[29] once said that "A 'peace which surpasseth all understanding' is perhaps, hard to do research on", urging concentration upon the task of striving for peace as the absence of war. Such notions, that regard the secular and religious as distinct spheres, and that never the twain should meet in the quest for peace on earth, need revision. Christic peace calls to faith which is absolute, beyond all human calculations and which opens up new possibilities, empowers, and thereby gives ground for rational hope for peace on earth. It draws attention not only to the symptoms of unpeacefulness but to their deep-seated causes. Above all, it maps the way of peace itself.

Notes

1. My thanks are expressed to the Administrative Assistants of the Department of Geography and Planning for typing the manuscript, and to Mr. Graham Fry of the same department for finalising the diagrams.

2. E.g., R.J. Johnston & P.J. Taylor, eds. *A World in Crisis: Geographical Perspectives* (Oxford: Blackwell, 1989).

3. See also J. Galtung, "Twenty five years of peace research," *Journal of Peace Research* 22:2 (1985): p. 153.

4. M. Friberg & B. Hettne, "Social mobilization and world system politics," *International Social Science Journal* 117 (1988): p. 344.

5. E.g., G. Sharp, "Making the abolition of war a realistic goal," *Essay* (New York: Institute for World Order, 1980).

6. J. Galtung, "A structural theory of imperialism," *Journal of Peace Research* 13:2 (1971): pp. 81-94.

7. E.g., K. Boulding, *Stable Peace* (Austin: University of Texas, 1978).

8. N. Young, "Non-violence and social change," *A Reader in Peace Studies*, eds. P. Smoker, R. Davies & B. Munske (Oxford: Pergamon, 1990) pp. 217-220.

9. T. Weber & R. Burrows, "Non-Violence: An Introduction," *Peace Dossier* 27 (Melbourne: Victorian Association for Peace Studies, 1991).

10. The scientific approach to knowledge emphasises the importance of observation and fact-finding, and where the entire population cannot be measured or observed, to recourse to sampling and statistical analysis. Geography, an example familiar to the writer, adopts methodologies of science. Laudable though this may be, neither subjectivity nor value-judgement is eliminated. The figure above demonstrates what happens to the results obtained by such methods and illustrates the limitations of what is usually regarded as scientific truth. Such "truth" needs to be treated with respect, and also with reserve.

11. E.g., R.C. Slye and S.H. Mendlovitz, "World order," *World Encyclopaedia of Peace*, 1986, vol. 2, p. 570.

12. M. Fox, *The Coming of the Cosmic Christ* (Melbourne: Collins-Dove, Melbourne, 1988); and B. Swan, "An ethical appraisal of Australian defence policy," *Australian Journal of Politics and History* 34:1(1990): pp. 73-92.

13. R. Panikkar, *The Unknown Christ of Hinduism* (London: Darton, Longman & Todd, 1968); and R.L. Franklin, "New Horizons: Reflections on the Future of Religion and Science," *Occasional Paper* 43 (University of Tasmania, 1986).

14. The search for peace calls to transcendence of the conventional wisdom and its values, whether the search is conducted along secular or religious, or non-ideological or ideological lines. Movement from the more conventional to the more religious levels requires change in perception and in method. From being predominately goal-oriented, peace becomes increasingly, and then completely, a process. See B. Swan, "Peace Studies and Transcendence," *Interdisciplinary Peace Research* 4:1 (1992): pp. 76-88.

15. H. Küng, *Christianity and World Religions* (London: William Collins, 1987).

16. F. Barnaby, ed. *The Gaia Peace Atlas* (London: Gaia Books, 1988) p. 10.

17. J. Galtung, "Cultural violence," *Journal of Peace Research* 27(1990): pp. 291-305.

18. C. Ostergaard, "Duality in non-violence," *Peace News* (July 1977).

19. A Christic interpretation of the bases of anti-peace and peace and their concomitants. Contrasting approaches to life, with contrasting implications for peace that is Christic, and which world religions whose terminologies may differ but whose underlying vision is similar (vide the Judaeo-Christian-Islamic, Hindu and Buddhist traditions), are ever cognisant of.

20. B. Häring, *The Healing Power of Peace and Non-Violence* (Slough: St. Paul Publications, 1986) pp. 7-16.

21. F. Alt, *Peace is Possible: The Politics of the Sermon on the Mount* (New York: Schocken, 1985).

22. T. Berry, "Twelve principles for understanding the universe and the role of the human in the universe process," *Riverdale Papers on the Earth Community* (New York: Riverdale Centre for Religious Research, 1980).

23. B. Swan, "An ethical appraisal of Australian defence policy."

24. L.J. Lebret, in D. Goulet, *A New Moral Order* (Maryknoll, NY: Orbis, 1974).

25. E.g., Paul VI, "Populorum Progressio," *Papal Encyclical* (Rome: Vatican, 1967) section 23.

26. R. Tagore, *Gitanjali* (1913; Delhi: Macmillan, 1984).

27. T. Balasuriya, *Liberation of the Affluent,* ed. Diana Santleben, (Sydney: Action for World Development, 1989).

28. Swan, "An ethical appraisal of Australian defence policy."

29. Boulding, *Stable Peace,* p.6.

Vision of a Non-violent Society: What Should Be Society's Aims?

Ralph Summy[1]
University of Queensland, Australia

Before outlining my vision of a nonviolent society, let me make a few general remarks about social/political visions *per se*. Firstly, visions are not goals; they are not attainable specifics. As I have indicated in the sub-topic of this article, I am writing about *aims*. What can we aim or strive for? While we should always have before ourselves a clear notion of the *general direction* in which we are heading (that is, our aim should be spelled out), we should not expect to reach some well defined end or be able to reify our ideal. The pursuit—the chase (and how we conduct it)—represents the reality of the exercise.

Think of the dog that likes to chase cars. What would the dog do if it ever caught a car? Eat it…or take it back to its kennel to display as a trophy! A lot of reformers and revolutionaries in the past have not practiced what the dog instinctively knows. They have confused ideal or vision with attainable reality and consequently have not only themselves become bitterly disillusioned eventually, but in the process often wrought untold misery on their fellow citizens. Tolstoy called this 'the dreadful superstition'[2]—to think it is possible to foresee the actual future shape of society. Since the totality of truth cannot be known, the hope for living nonviolently—as Gandhi so clearly understood—was to focus on the quest rather than the perfectibility of humankind.[3]

Which brings me to my second point if the vision cannot be converted into a specifically defined end point, then the means become all important. They become a series of 'ends' in the making to be guided by the vision we have adumbrated. The means converge into ends which in turn become means for the next ends and so on *ad infinitum*—all in pursuit of an unattainable vision. As Gandhi says: "If we take care of the means we are bound to reach the end sooner or later."[4] To engage in fixed-end thinking, ignores the fact that ends are hypotheses constantly needing to be formed and reformed by logic, experiment and experience. What is required, in other words, is more concentration on creative means to resolve conflict. Let the means become end-creating.

My third point is that simply because we are unable to realize the nonviolent society does not mean the struggle is futile. Far from it! Not only do I believe that we can move closer to the ideal of our vision, but unless we make this effort, society will surely move in the opposite direction, toward an increase in violence. Meeting, moreover, the very challenge itself can be a life enhancing exercise, making our lives worth living. The struggle for nonviolence should be, and can be fun. An exhilarating experience of everlasting toil! You may remember the Greek myth of Sisyphus. Despite his

Ralph Summy, "Vision of a Non-Violent Society: What Should Be Society's Aims?" Reprinted with permission from the editors of *Essays on Peace: Paradigms for Global Order*, edited by Michael Salla, Walter Tenetto and Enrique Martinez.

fate of having to roll a heavy boulder up a mountain, only to have it plummet back at the summit, he revelled in the perpetual challenge which heightened his consciousness. Thus the struggle has intrinsic merit and joy.[5]

The fourth and final point relates to struggle. Struggle means conflict. We are inclined to think of struggle solely in terms of negative conflict. However, conflict can range over a spectrum from the extremely violent, destructive, undesirable, and socially disintegrative to the constructive, desirable, socially functional, and peace creating. Our task, as human beings with a degree of control over our destiny, is to move conflict out of the realm of the negative (in the utilitarian sense) and into that of the positive. Morton Deutsch, a social-psychologist, attributes three main personal and social benefits to conflict:

a) It prevents stagnation; it is the generator of progress; it is the medium through which problems can he aired and solutions arrived at the root of personal and social change.

b) Conflict stimulates interest and curiosity—makes life worth living. Through conflict, we test and assess ourselves; this can be highly enjoyable as one experiences the pleasure of the full and active use of one's capacities.

c) Conflict also demarcates groups from one another and thus helps to establish group and personal identities. Conflict directed against outside groups need not dehumanize the 'out' members in order to foster an internal cohesiveness of one's own group.

Having made these extensive preliminary remarks, let me proceed quickly to the main question of this article: What should be society's aims? The aims of society should be, in my view, to strive to create the conditions where everyone's universal 'basic needs' can be met, and to do this, we must engage in 'positive peace'. It is through positive peace, directed at the realisation of people's basic needs, that we break the cycle of violence usually embedded in negative conflict resolution. Positive peace is the only way to prevent the constant recrudescence of violence, and to shift conflict along the continuum to its more creative forms.

Human Needs

As I have indicated, two terms feature in my vision of the society worth struggling for: human needs and positive peace. These terms represent the cornerstones of a nonviolent society. Both require detailed explanation. First, human needs: they are, in my opinion, what must be fulfilled in order to eliminate the direct and the structural violence in the world. This thinking parallels the approach of John Burton, who is featured later in this book.[6] He asserts:

> There are certain human needs concerned with development, as well as survival, which are ontological and universal. Their frustration is a sufficient explanation for political and social instabilities. Policies of intervention and attempts at resolving conflicts fail unless this is taken into account. The current return to the individual as the unit of concern is not because of some vague notion of natural justice; it is a concern that there are needs that must be satisfied if the individual within the social system is to be supportive of it. In the tension between human needs and institutions, it is change in institutions that is required.

Burton strongly refutes the commonly accepted view, that the social malleability of human behaviour has no limits.[7] "This convenient construct," he avers, "presupposes that the person has no needs to be satisfied that are inherent or human."

An increasing number or social scientists and philosophers "have focussed on the importance of the concept of human needs in understanding human behaviour."[8] Whilst the explicit list of needs varies from one social scientist to the next, it includes categories fairly similar to those of Johan Galtung.[9] He depicts four categories of needs and indicates how each can be thwarted by either 'direct violence' or 'structural violence':

Needs	Direct Violence	Structural Violence
1. survival	killing	exploitation A (reduced life span)
2. well-being (morbidity its antonym)	maiming	exploitation B (inequity)
3. identity (alienation)	desocialisation (take culture away) resocialisation secondary citizen.	penetration (look at life from top dog point of view) segmentation (each party only knows its area)
4. freedom (repression)	torture detention expulsion	marginalisation (everyone defined as secondary citizen) fragmentation (parts have freedom, but are cut off from each other and whole)

As I have been suggesting, failure to satisfy these universal human needs is 'a sufficient explanation of dissidence and of deviant behaviour'. Further, no society can function harmoniously or survive indefinitely, unless it proceeds to satisfy these needs. There must at least be the expectation that they will be satisfied. If they are not eventually met by society, the individual degenerates into "a malfunctioning unit, finally destroying the total system."[10]

Western social thought and practice, have been largely based on the premise that the anti-social violent behaviour of individuals can be controlled by external socialisation, and, if this fails, then threats and coercion. To some extent this is true, but it breaks down eventually when societies attempt to project their malleability policies into the arena of basic human survival and development needs. What happens when these needs are left unattended is that violence festers or erupts in many forms: it can take the form of revolution against the state and its ruling power elite; it can be reflected in rising crime statistics; it can appear in interpersonal relationships in acts such as wife beating and psychological debasement; it can turn inward and be manifested in the self destruction of drug abuse or suicide; and it can simmer in the 'quiet desperation' that afflicts the lives of so many of the world's powerless. The pain of this last group perpetually hovers on the threshold of arousal, waiting for some self proclaimed messiah, perhaps the next 'Fuhrer' to redirect vicariously their pain on to some other group of unfortunates.

To prevent these various manifestations of social disintegration (revolutionary violence, crime, inter-personal breakdown, self-inflicted violence, and rampant exclusionary nationalism), the centrality of the individual's human needs must command our primary attention. To repeat what Burton has said: "In the tension between human needs and institutions, it is change in institutions that is required."[11] He might also have added that norms and values (though they shape the precise way in which our basic needs are expressed) must likewise be altered and no longer treated as an independent variable. Thus, as many social scientists besides Burton are now proclaiming (e.g., Johan Galtung, Victoria Rader, Mary Clark, Paul Sites, Paul Smoker, et al), no matter how sophisticated the social control mechanisms might become, human malleability has a stretching, cut off limit. A point is eventually reached where no amount or juridical rulings, ecclesiastical pronouncements, exercise of coercive political power, pulling of economic levers and the like will contain the individual. Unless the individual's survival and development needs are acknowledged, and the structures and social environment tailored to serve those needs—instead of vice versa (the structures attempting to determine people's needs)—violence in one form or another will remain endemic to the society and possibly even escalate to the point of societal collapse.

'Positive Peace'

Positive peace prevails when there is neither overt violence nor the more subtle phenomenon of structural violence. Instead, there exists the creation of a just, sustainable world a way of life that nurtures life itself. The direction is towards wholeness and harmony within oneself and also amongst individuals, within the community, and amongst nations. When problems arise, their solution is sought in a cooperative, non divisive spirit. The focus is on finding win/win rather than win/lose outcomes. Another term for positive peace is social justice. It characterises the creation of the nonviolent society.

Almost everyone, it seems, abhors violence and wants at least negative peace (the absence of direct or personal violence). The only obvious exceptions to such goodwill are a handful of ideological psychopaths and a larger body of unfulfilled malcontents who use violence (especially when legitimated as in war) to escape the tedium of their pedestrian lives. But the overwhelming majority of people are genuinely for peace: they seek a 'gentler society'. Why then don't we have it? The answer (if there is one) is complex; there are multiple reasons why people's interests and values clash in violence, but of overriding significance, in my view, is the fact that most people fail to make the distinction between negative peace and positive peace. And if they do, they reject a commitment to the latter. Again, one can ask why!

Let me suggest two major obstacles to positive peace. The first features the word 'distrust'. If individuals or societies do not protect themselves with violence or the threat of violence, the other party will gain the advantage and subject them to exploitation. One of the West's most influential and brilliant political theorists to espouse this view was Thomas Hobbes. He depicted the nature of human beings as "solitary, poor, nasty, brutish and short." Life was a constant state of war: all against one and one against all. Humans behaved like 'wolves' to each other.

Our basic 'Hobbesian distrust' of one another means we attempt to secure peace with violence, because it is generally believed that when all else fails in the conflict resolution process, superior physical force will be called upon. It is the ultimate sanction. Such a view is encapsulated in the famous Roman maxim, "*Si vis pacem para bellum*" (If you want peace, prepare for war). This fundamental premise of our society, which operates at both the domestic and international levels, is like a self-fulfilling prophecy. We defend ourselves with violence or its threat which, in turn, provokes the distrust which justified our use of violence in the first place. We are walking an endless treadmill that ensures most of our conflict—if it is resolved at all—will be done so at the minus end of the conflict spectrum. The peace that is secured will not be a genuine peace but an absence of direct violence. There may be no violence which can clearly be attributed to a particular party, but all kinds of structural violence will continue unabated. The so-called peace prevailing in this situation is, or course, what Galtung meant by 'negative peace'.[12] It may, for a limited period, suppress open violence, but it usually also serves as a breeding ground for the next round of violence. To get out of the cycle of violence, it is necessary to engage in positive peace.

The credibility of positive peace depends initially on refuting the presupposition that human beings are phylogenetically programmed to be violent and therefore cannot be trusted or expected to be cooperative. There is extensive literature on this subject, most of it now critical of the biological argument—for example, the important Seville Statement on Violence.[13] However, despite an overwhelming number of social and life scientists denying the thesis of our species' innate violence, politics continues to be conducted from the perspective of negative peace. Keeping a cap on the violence that will erupt at any time is the standard governmental approach! The general public, according to survey findings, also endorses this view. As a result, little effort is made to explore the avenues of positive peace. The answer as to why government leaders and the public refuse to recognise the scientific evidence and hold on to the shibboleth of innate violence and depravity, is even more complicated than the original question about the state of human nature. One explanation would stress vested interest. The fact that we say violence is in our genes (inevitably) means we need strong controls or government to make life secure and tolerable. With this need for controls we prop up economic privilege, but we then 'civilise' the system with the minimum controls of a safety net for the powerless. The myth of our unruly nature, moreover, justifies a lot of jobs for sycophantic administrators. It also justifies strong military defences and the need to go to war occasionally (since war must be expected as part of our natural behaviour). Such a deterministic outlook on the cause of violence absolves the individual of taking any responsible counter action for peace. Therefore, a major task of peacemakers, in my view, is to confront head-on the prevailing assumption of violence as an integral part of our nature.

The credibility of positive peace is also undermined by a second, equally dubious, assumption. Like the distrust, fostered by the prevailing view of human nature, it represents a major obstacle to peace. It concerns our understanding of nonviolence. A key component of positive peace (namely nonviolent action), is generally seen as only effective up to a certain point, when vital interests and values are not at stake and when one is dealing with a relatively benign or reasonable opponent. Like most people in society, government officials adhere to the position that in conflict situations when all else fails, the *ultima ratio* (the final argument) is violence.[14] Whilst I think it is unlikely that state leaders (as such) can be persuaded of the efficacy of nonviolent action over a violent response (the difficulty can be traced to the fact they are committed to an institution, that defines itself on the basis of possessing superior physical force over the society's other sections), individual government officials and the citizenry are open to the proof of argument and demonstration. If we are going to work towards a 'gentler society', we must convince others of the viability of a nonviolent response to conflict.

Nonviolent political action can be divided into two basic categories: it can be seen as either a method or a principle—that is, a way of life. In my opinion we are not going to attract people to nonviolence as a way of life until they are first convinced of its efficacy as a political instrument. We are a highly pragmatic society. We value something for its practical consequences. Thus, we must begin with nonviolent action by pointing out a number of conventional fallacies surrounding it—for example, that it is passive resistance, that it requires martyrdom, that it is unnatural, that it is ineffective against an extremely ruthless opponent, that its record of successes is limited, and so forth. People must be prepared to explore its theoretical foundation—namely, that initiative lies with the ruled. No powerholder can maintain his/her position without the acquiescence of large segments of the society.[15] At the disposal of the subjects, are countless techniques of nonviolent resistance, as well as guidelines for understanding how they can be integrated into an effective strategy.[16]

In Conclusion

Moving toward positive peace entails more than conceptualising from a starting point of human needs and overcoming the twin obstacles of distrust and ignorance about nonviolence that I have stressed. Indeed, our task extends well beyond the absorption of a few key concepts. Not only are there more concepts to intellectualise, but there is learning to exchange through direct experience and role modelling. This applies to all the building blocks of positive peace; they all involve a daily, constant commitment in our personal lives.

My vision of a nonviolent society incorporates a commitment to the universal satisfaction of human needs and to the creation of positive peace. These two aspects are indivisible. Moreover, just as there are four basic needs that can be singled out, there are four major components to highlight in the achieving of positive peace. Besides nonviolent action, these constitute ecological wholeness (the recognition or our integrated role in the functioning of the biosphere, and becoming aware that we seek to dominate it at the risk of our extinction); also economic well being for the entire human race (as the welfare or one becomes the welfare or all); and finally, and most importantly the commitment itself, which involves our personal transformation. Despite all our human foibles, we can at least attempt to make our personal lives a microcosm of the world we envision. Providing we retain the necessary humility, the evidence of our personal lives can be the most powerful argument.

Notes

1. This article is a revised version of an address delivered at the annual conference of the Mental Health Association of Queensland in November 1991.

2. Leo Tolstoy, "The Law of Love and the Law of Violence," A *Confession and Other Writings* (Ringwood, Victoria: Penguin Books, 1987) p. 216.

3. S. Malik, Gandhian Satyagraha and Contemporary World (Rohtak: Manthan Publications, 1985) p. 4.

4. Mohandas Gandhi, *Satyagraha* (Ahmedabad: Navajivan Publishing House, 1951) p. 42.

5. Albert Camus, *The Myth of Sisyphus and Other Essays* (London: Hamish Hamilton, 1955) pp. 96-97.

6. John Burton, *Global Conflict: The Domestic Sources of International Crisis* (Brighton: Wheatsheaf Books, 1984) pp. ix-x & 20.

7. John Burton, *Conflict Resolution and Prevention* (London: Macmillan, 1990) p. 31.

8. R.A. Coates and J.A. Rosati, eds. *The Power of Human Needs in World Society* (Boulder: Lynne Riener Publishers, 1988) p. 3.

9. "Cultural Violence," *Journal of Peace Research* 27: 3 (1990).

10. John Burton, *Deviance, Terrorism and War: The Process of Solving Unsolved Social and Political Problems* (Canberra: Australian National University Press, 1979) pp. 58-59.

11. *Global Conflict,* p. 20.

12. JohanGaltung, "Violence, Peace and Peace Research," *Journal of Peace Research* 6 (1969) pp. 188-91.

13. The Seville Statement on Violence, *Alternatives* 12:2 (1987) pp. 271-74.

14. Ralph Summy, "Some Dynamics of Nonviolent Political Action," *World Review* 2:4 (1987).

15. See Gene Sharp, *The Politics of Nonviolent Action* (Boston: Porter Sargent, 1973) pp. 7-62.

16. *Ibid.*

Creating Spaces for Peace: A Comparative Overview of Zones of Peace

Majid Tehranian[1]
University of Hawaii

The stunning events of 1989-91 have inaugurated a new era in international relations. From the Malta Summit of 1945 to the Yalta Summit of 1989 the world was dominated by the Cold War. Since Malta, a new order has been emerging.[2] This order is, however, very fragile. It can easily break down as it already has in many places, including the Persian Gulf, former Soviet Union and Yugoslavia. Other protracted conflict areas such as the Korean Peninsula and the Indian-Pakistani border are also at risk. The Cold War was characterised by a balance of nuclear terror between the super powers leading to a precarious peace. The universalist ideological pretensions of the Cold War have now been replaced by rising ethnic, religious, and nationalist conflicts. With the increasing proliferation of nuclear, biological, and chemical weapons into the hands of smaller states, the threats to international peace and security may have in fact increased rather than decreased. The new cold wars between North and South Korea, India and Pakistan, the Arabs and Israelis (to name just a few) can erupt into full-scale wars of incalculable costs.

To usher in a period of durable peace, therefore, the new world order requires a new paradigm to understand an increasingly interdependent and vulnerable world system.[3] The emerging paradigm calls for planetary consciousness, global responsibility, and world citizenship. In place of the outmoded ideologies of capitalism, communism, and non-alignment which divided the world into first, second, and third worlds, the new paradigm must recognise at least the following three conditions: (1) the essential unity of the world when confronted by nuclear or ecological disasters such as the Three-Mile Island, Chernobyl, Exxon-Valdez, the burning of over 600 Kuwaiti oil wells, and the greenhouse effect; (2) the mounting divisions of the world between the centres and peripheries of power as reflected in the gender, religious, ethnic, and nationalist conflicts; and (3) the urgent need for new principles and methods of human organisation towards pacific settlement of disputes and cooperation for social and economic progress.

The idea of zones of peace (ZOP) offers one such opportunity for restructuring the world system from confrontation to cooperation. It is an idea whose time has come. In fact, it promises to turn into a grassroots movements in which governments will have to respect the demands of their citizens for new peace zones. According to Elise Boulding, the number of nuclear weapons free zones (NWFZ) has increased from 250 in 1982 to some 5,000 in 1991.[4] There are already 24 countries in the world which have unilaterally declared themselves as NWFZs. There are also 5 formal NWFZ treaties

Majid Tehranian, "Creating Spaces for Peace: Zones of Peace." Reprinted with permission from the editors of *Essays on Peace: Paradigms for Global Order* edited by Michael Salla, Walter Tenetto, and Enrique Martínez.

signed among governments.

Broadly speaking, a ZOP may be defined as (1) a well defined territory or region in which the parties at dispute commit themselves to non violent and pacific settlement of their conflicts by total or partial disarmament and through binding adjudication, arbitration, or mediation procedures, (2) with a governing authority, consisting of the governments or parties at dispute, over that territory under the supervision of the United Nations Trusteeship Council, (3) with a land authority for the development of a free economic zone among the members and other interested parties acquiring "peace bonds" with commercial rates of return, and (4) in instances of protracted ethnic conflict, with a culturally homogeneous majority guaranteeing however, the civil and human rights of the ethnic or religious minorities residing in the zone.

This essay will provide a brief introduction to the history of the idea, its philosophical underpinnings, and some policy issues facing its development and implementation. However, the richness and diversity of the concept and its varieties of actual and potential practice require more research and longer expositions.

History

Zones of peace are as old as history itself. Religious sanctuaries and secular zones of neutrality have historically provided some respite from the brutality and intensity of violence. In modern times, some countries such as Switzerland, Austria, and Costa Rica also have declared their neutrality in regional or world conflicts. It is remarkable that these protestations of neutrality by relatively small powers, have been in some special instances respected by the great powers leading, in effect, to the creation of new peace zones. ZOPs may thus serve very practical purposes for all parties at conflict, including sanctuary as well as a haven for spies, banking services for the rich, and prosperity for the hosts.

In the post-war period, the idea has found its greatest advocates among those powers with the greatest to lose from protracted conflict. The nonaligned movement, launched by Nehru, Sukarno, Nasser, Chou En-lai, and Tito at the Bandung Conference of 1955, sought to avoid the costs of entanglement with the Cold War through a doctrine of neutrality and peaceful co-existence. The moral authority of this movement as well as the worldwide peace movement, however, came from the practice of nonviolent resistance led by such figures as Gandhi, Martin Luther King, and Bishop Tutu. Although ZOPs need not be fully committed to nonviolence, many proponents of the idea believe in the Gandhian principles of Satyagraha and nonviolent resistance against any form of oppression.

In more recent years, the idea of peace zones has been proposed by a number of scholars and activists, including Johan Galtung, Bishop Antonio Fortich, Edna Fuerth Lemle, Cheju International Council in Korea and Dalai Lama. Johan Galtung has proposed it for Palestine. Bishop Fortich and his co-workers have, in fact, successfully established a number, of peace zones in The Philippines. The Filipino zones of peace are civilian initiated demilitarised areas created to allow noncombatants to establish homes and economic bases without the fear of becoming caught in the cross fire between the military and the rebels. The communities define geographic areas where neither rebels nor government forces may enter. Inhabitants practice strict nonviolence, maintain their infrastructure of roads, bridges and schools, and form peacekeeping that monitor the presence of strangers. Edna Lemle has pursued this idea with the British and Argentine governments for a peaceful settlement of the Falkland/Malvinas Islands conflict. The Cheju International Council is proposing to turn the island into a zone of peace for the reconciliation of North and South Korea. Most recently, Dalai Lama has called for the establishment of a zone of peace based on nonviolence in Tibet within the sovereign territory of the People's Republic of China. In these two latter cases, the issue of sovereignty assumes an importance secondary to the practice of nonviolence and cooperation.

The idea and practice of ZOPs has historically gone through four stages, from sanctuaries to specific purpose, general purpose, and empowering peace zones. In the first stage, religious sanctions predominated. The ancient Polynesians had a practice of 'puuhonua' or place of refuge, where wrong doers were forgiven.[5] The ancient Israelites had cities of refuge and Sabbaths. The Christian world in the Middle Ages knew about the 'Truce of God' and the 'Peace of God.' Islam divides the world into a zone of peace (Dar al-Islam) and a zone of war (Dar al-Harb); it also considers the mosque as a zone of peace to which the combatants could take refuge.

In the second stage of their development, ZOPs have evolved into secular and functionally specific territories of peace. In modern history, diplomatic missions (embassies and consular offices) have served as the territorial extensions of the guest in the host country with a zone of peace immunity. Moreover, the Red Cross headquarters and vehicles in the midst of combat, the countries declaring themselves neutral in times of wars, and the nuclear weapons free zones (NWFZ) all have one feature in common. For specific times, places, and functions, certain designated territories might be considered as inviolable by the combatants or contestants. In the case of NWFZs, a ban is imposed on one particular weapon of mass destruction. The six NWFZ treaties encompass Antarctica, Outer Space, Latin America, International Seabed, South Pacific and Indian Ocean.[6]

The third stage of development of ZOPs is of more recent origin. The general purpose zones of peace are often the result of years of peaceful social, economic, cultural, and political cooperation and integration, declared or undeclared. Since the War of 1812, for instance, the US-Canadian border has been a general purpose ZOP. Since 1945, The European Community (EC) also has become one such zone. Since its establishment in 1967, ASEAN has similarly provided a general-purpose framework for peace, security, and cooperation among, its member states in Southeast Asia.[7] With the world-wide movement toward regional cooperation and security arrangements, as exemplified by the Conference on Security and Cooperation in Europe (CSCE) and Asia Pacific Economic Cooperation (APEC), prospects for general purpose ZOPs look encouraging.

The fourth stage of development of ZOPs, however, is of even greater promise. It indicates a deepening and broadening of the concept beyond the often-limited acts of governments and towards citizen action and participation in the building of peace zones. That is why it may be called a citizen *empowering* phase of the development of the concept. This phase ultimately points to a time that no one would show up to fight when and if governments declare war. This parallels the citizens' initiatives in many parts of Japan (1500 communities), the United States (168 such declarations of which 87 are legally binding), Canada (178) and Europe (nearly 2000) in unilateral declarations of their localities as nuclear weapons free zones. Twenty-four countries also have explicitly or implicitly prohibited nuclear weapons by national law, policy or constitution.[8] In this respect, the story of Palau is most instructive. As of 1991, after 7 rounds of voting, the people of Palau have refused to give in to US pressures for a change in their constitution which calls for a nuclear free zone in that Pacific island country.

Philosophy

Zones of peace philosophically depend on the doctrine of peace with peaceful means rather than peace through military strength. Although this doctrine has its roots in the great religious traditions, it has come into its own by the great non-violent struggles of this century. It has also achieved credibility and practical possibility by a distinct paradigm shift in international relations. World order has historically evolved from *repressive,* to *hegemonic,* to what may now be called *communitarian.*[9] All the imperial systems of the past, from the Persian to Greek, Roman,

Arab, Mongol, Ottoman, Spanish, French, German, Japanese, British; and American empires have been more or less repressive. They subjugated by *force* vast numbers of peoples in the peripheries to the will of a dominant centre.

Eventually, imperial rivalries among the great powers led to two devastating world wars in the twentieth century. With the invention of weapons of mass destruction, war itself seemed to be an outmoded instrument of foreign policy. A new world order had to be invented. Under the League of Nations and its successor, the United Nations, the principle of collective security became the cornerstone of this new order. Another principle, that of unanimity among the Great Powers to act as the world policemen, became the guarantor of collective security. A third principle, pacific settlement of disputes, set forth the preferred method of conflict resolution except in cases of grave violations of international peace and security.

A *hegemonic* world had been thus born. Under the League and the U.N., the new world order recommended both force and persuasion, collective security arrangements as well as ideological debates and legal wranglings. This new order, however, proved still born. Without the participation of the United States, the League did not enjoy much credibility. The invasion of Ethiopia by Mussolini, in 1935, and the failure of the League of Nations to act collectively against the aggressor, put the last nail on the coffin of that order. Similarly, the Cold War between the two superpowers following World War II, left little opportunity for the U.N. Security Council to play its role as the world policeman.

With the demise of the Cold War, what are the chances for a peaceful new world order? Despite the disappointments of the post Cold War and post Gulf War, there is a new world consensus on the requirements for an enduring international peace and security. That consensus recognises that enduring peace can come only out of a sense of community. Hence, the emerging world order may be called *communitarian.* Three elements seem essential to the construction of an effective world community, including common interests, norms, and laws. ZOPs are perhaps the most effective method of achieving a sense of community underwritten by common interests, norms and laws. The development of regional common markets is taking on a new lease on life in 1992 when the European Community enters a new phase of monetary and political union. Other regions of the world also are following suit. The Association of South East Asian Nations (ASEAN) has set the pace for the developing countries, a North American Free Trade Area (NAFTA) was launched in 1993, and an Asia Pacific Economic Community (APEC) has been meeting to develop a Pacific community analogous to an Atlantic community.

There is a risk, of course, that these budding regional blocs would turn into intense economic competition and possible political and military confrontation rather than cooperation. However, an emerging consensus recognises the global political, economic, and ecological interdependence. The emerging norms emphasise the need for the global protection of the environment, use of technology, trade, and development policies to overcome the gaps between the rich and the poor, universal application of human rights, and collective denunciation of the use of violence in national and international conflicts.[10] The world community ultimately depends on a fragile moral community. Without solidifying these norms, it will be torn apart. ZOPs in all of their varieties can build these norms and networks more effectively than any other community of common interests, norms, and laws.

Policy

There is no general agreement on how to define ZOPs. Nevertheless, issues of *sovereignty, governance,* and *surveillance* are the main policy problems facing them all. Sovereignty is perhaps the thorniest issue. The United Nations Charter recognises the indivisible sovereignty of its member states and forbids any direct interference in their internal affairs. However, the traditional notions of indivisible national sovereignty have been chipped away on both global and local fronts. On the global front, the rights of the international community to intervene in the internal affairs of a sovereign state on humanitarian or collective security grounds have now been established in international law.[11] The U.N. Security Council was willing to directly intervene in the internal affairs of post war Iraq in the name of humanitarian interventions to save the Kurds and the Shiites from persecution. It also intervened on grounds of collective security to dismantle Iraq's nuclear weapons and rearmament plans. On the local front, the rights of municipal governments to determine by popular referenda their own defence policies have received increasing popular recognition. Many municipalities in the United States and Europe have unilaterally declared themselves nuclear weapons free zones; some in the U.S. have even established their own Office of Municipal Foreign Policy. The U.S. Federal Government, however, considers decisions dealing with defence and foreign policy within its own jurisdiction. It does not generally recognise any authority for municipal or even state governments in such matters.

National sovereignty has been further undermined both practically and theoretically by other developments. Practically, some new telecommunication technologies such as global satellite surveillance, direct broadcast satellites (DBS), electronic cash transfers, and transborder data flows have effectively limited national government control of national borders.[12] Theoretically, notions of transnational as opposed to national sovereignty had provided the basis for the U.N. Trusteeship over former colonial territories. As I have argued elsewhere,[13] the concept of trusteeship can be now extended in order to establish ZOPs in situations of protracted conflict such as Kurdistan, Palestine, Kashmir, or Bosnia. In these cases, a ZOP may be defined as (1) a transnational entity whose sovereignty resides in a U.N. or any other appropriate internationally sponsored Board of Trustees consisting of the governments or parties at dispute over a territory, (2) a global land authority for the development of a free economic zone among the members and other interested parties acquiring 'peace bonds' with commercial rates of return, and (3) to the extent possible, culturally homogeneous zones for the ethnically disenfranchised majorities but with strict guarantees of human rights for the ethnic or religious minorities residing in the zone.

The above political, economic, and cultural requirements leave considerable room for the negotiation of details in order to achieve positive rather than negative or zero sum games for the parties at conflict. The plan aims at making peace profitable to all sides. By resolving protracted conflicts in a peaceful way, clearly all parties win more security. By entering into a common market or establishing a free trade zone, the participating governments and populations win in economic prosperity. By giving autonomy and status to disenfranchised ethnic groups, the entire world wins in the achievement of greater human rights and international harmony. In the case of Kurdistan, for instance, none of the states presently controlling the Kurdish population is willing to grant independence. All of them should be willing, however, to recognise the cultural autonomy of the Kurds under a plan that puts them in control (as members of the U.N. Board of Trustees) while attracting millions of dollars for cooperative development of the region.

Even if the issue of sovereignty is resolved satisfactorily, the problem of governance of peace zones presents the next most important policy dilemma of how to give *de facto* powers sufficient incentive in the governance of ZOPs in order to elicit their recognition of the *de jure* status of ZOPs as zones of partial or general disarmament? The answer to this question depends on the functional and spatial scopes of ZOPs.

Table I provides a typology of ZOPs based on their spatial scope (local, provincial, national, regional, or global) and functional parameters (sanctuaries, specific purpose, general purpose, and empowering). As demonstrated by the examples, the governance problems of each of these types is uniquely different. Holy sites and diplomatic missions (consular offices and embassies) have been historically treated as inviolable zones of peace. One of the latest examples of this was when General Noriega took refuge in the Vatican Embassy in Panama and could not be captured until he negotiated his surrender to the U.S. authorities.

Table I. A Typology of Zones of Peace: Matrix of Spatial and Functional Scopes

Functional Scope	Spatial Scope				
	Local	Provincial	National	Regional	Global
Sanctuaries	Holy sites Embassies	Holy sites Embassies	Holy sites Embassies	Holy sites Embassies	Holy sites Embassies
Specific Purpose ZOPs	NWFZ Counties & City	NWFZ Provinces	NWFZ Countries	NWFZ Oceans, World region	NWFZ Earth Outer Space
General-Purpose ZOPs		Cheju Falkland/ Maldive Border	US-Canada Border	ASEAN EU	
Empowering ZOPs		Areas of conflict reconciliation, eg. Kurdistan, Palestine			

The NWFZs have been declared either unilaterally or negotiated into treaty agreements among a number of states. The general-purpose ZOPs are best represented by those world regions such as the European Union (EU) and ASEAN which have achieved durable peace and security through long-term social, economic, cultural, and political cooperation. The empowering ZOPs are essentially of two kinds, top-down or bottom-up. The top-down variety is best represented by the postwar U.N. trusteeship system in which the former colonial powers were put in charge of a territory for the purpose of preparing it for self-government. The bottom-up variety is best represented by citizens' initiatives in North America, Europe, Japan, and Asia-Pacific for the establishment of NWFZs in their own localities. The initiatives by the Cheju Islanders or Falkland Islanders represent yet another popular effort to turn their land into zones of peace for reconciliation between the parties at conflict, namely North and South Korea and Argentina and Britain.

The ultimate success of a peace zone largely depends on the degree of mutual trust it generates and the extent of mutual benefits it bestows. Problems of surveillance and inspection are central to both outcomes. Open flows of information and communication so that the parties to the agreement can, in fact, monitor the progress of the situation is therefore essential to the entire enterprise. Under conditions in which a high degree of trust already exists, such as democratic municipalities declaring themselves as NWFZs, internal monitoring systems suffice. But when this level of trust does not exist or mutual suspicions run high, intergovernmental or transnational monitoring agencies are essential. Ultimately, those peace zones succeed which bestow tangible benefits upon their inhabitants without providing a threat to the outside world. EU and ASEAN are the two prime examples.

Conclusion

This essay has provided a brief introduction to the evolution of and prospects for zones of peace. It also has argued that in the post Cold War era, a new *communitarian* paradigm in international relations is creating a social movement for ZOPs. The normative principles of this paradigm call for a ban on weapons of mass destruction (nuclear, biological, chemical, and high tech 'star wars'), pacific settlement of all disputes, development of economic communities, and ultimately a ban on all forms of violence from the face of the earth.

In the absence of the universalist ideological pretensions of the Cold War, however, a resurgence of ethnic, religious, and nationalist conflicts threatens the fragile foundations of the new paradigm. ZOPs provide an effective, incremental method for dealing with these threats. They build the communities of affinity needed for the development of communities of interest. To mobilise public opinion in this direction, there is a need for the establishment of a network among the 5,000 already established ZOPs spread around the world. A zone of peace network (ZOPNET) could provide channels of communication for information sharing, problem solving, and public education.

Notes

1. This is an updated version of a paper presented as a keynote address at the First International Conference of Cheju International Council, Cheju City, October 24-26, 1991. A condensed version of this essay has appeared in *The Encyclopedia of War and Ethics,* (Westport, CT: Greenwood Press, 1994). I am grateful to Elise Boulding and Ramon Lopez-Reyes, both pioneers in peace studies, for sharing with me their unpublished papers on zones of peace. Boulding, "The Zone of Peace Concept in Current Practice: Review and Evaluation," and Lopez-Reyes, "The End of the Cold War: Beyond Neutrality and Nonalignment to Zone of Peace."

2. Johan Galtung, "The emerging conflict formations," *Restructuring for Peace: Challenges for the Twenty-first Century,* eds. Katharine & Majid Tehranian (Cresskil, NJ: Hampton Press, 1992).

3. Katherine and Majid Tehranian, eds. *Restructuring for Peace.*

4. "The Zone of Peace Concept in Current Practice."

5. "The End of the Cold War."

6. For further details, see Boulding, "The Zone of Peace Concept in Current Practice," Table 2.

7. Michael Hass, "A paradigm of community for the post-Cold War world," *Restructuring for Peace,* eds. Katharine and Majid Tehranian.

8. Boulding, "The Zone of Peace of Concept in Current Practice," Table 1.

9. Majid Tehranian, "The New World Order: A Communitarian Perspective," *Peace Perspectives* 6:1 (Fall 1991).

10. Elise Boulding, *Building a Global Civic Culture: Education for an Interdependent World* (New York & London: Teachers College, Columbia University, 1988).

11. Ved Nanda, "Humanitarian Intervention," *Restructuring for Peace,* eds K. and M. Tehranian.

12. Majid Tehranian, *Technologies of Power: Information Machines and Democratic Prospects* (Norwood, NJ: Ablex, 1990).

13. Majid Tebranian, "Peace zones might settle the Kurdistan question," *Honolulu Star Bulletin* (May 17, 1991): p. A31.

Towards a Global Educative Authority: The Council of Earth

Michael Salla
American University and

Walter Tenetto
University of Queensland, Australia and

Enrique Martinez
Australian Multicultural Book Review

We begin with the assertion that the transition towards global institutions which aim to prevent war and further peace, while maintaining environmental sustainability, social justice and cultural autonomy is imperative for our planet. It follows that the concepts of 'peace' and 'security' forming as they do, the necessary focus for such institutions, should depart from the nurturing of narrow constructions, based on military defence considerations or the preservation at all costs of the prevailing socio—economic systems. As Nigel Dower argues in his examination of these two concepts, 'peace' and 'security' are often uncritically combined, thus overlooking their distinct logics and the 'different, even if complementary, features both of the human condition and of human values.'

The politics of 'peace and security', as they are presently positioned through diplomatic parlance and international treaties, reveal an uncritical combination of the concepts 'peace' and 'security', into a narrow conceptual rendering that engenders 'structural violence' in the sense of an unnecessary deprivation of basic human needs. A lack of security undermines the individual's power to stand for oneself and live an independent life; it also tends to boost an energetic, reactive approach to solving problems which affect the individual and ultimately the state.

Without first alleviating fears, attendant on a lack of security which affects individuals most directly, there is no possibility of establishing the peace which has eluded humanity since its beginnings. In this respect Goenka's contribution addresses the deep-rooted causes of fear and anxiety at the base of this feeling of insecurity and shows a way toward establishing peace as an individual experience of happiness.

The 'perpetual peace' that so exercised the minds of Enlightenment thinkers, remains a theoretical proposition devoid of any practical significance, as long as individuals, communities and states experience a lack of security.[1] This impacts upon attempts to establish effective international institutions that significantly contribute to the politics of peace and security.

I. Impediments to the emergence of effective global institutions

Contemporary efforts to develop global institutions are either already dominated by states and the inter-governmental offshoots, or states are ac-

Michael Salla, Walter Tenetto and Enrique, "Toward a Global Educative Authority: The Council of Earth." Reprinted with permission from the Editors, "*Essays on Peace*," edited by Michael Salla, Walter Tenetto and Enrique Martinez.

corded a prominent position in the projected configuration of future global institutions. Given the importance of managing a responsible development of institutions that bow to global exigencies (or aspire to do so), an assessment of the individual national efforts must be made, and of how these might dovetail with global needs, asking at the same time how much 'splicing' needs to be effected for change to occur.

Before a broadening to proper, egalitarian internationalism can occur, there needs to come into being, national organizations (both governmental and NGO) that supervise and impel national reorientation, being themselves necessarily attuned to global considerations. Part of this process will involve the depoliticisation of political or quasi-political agendas, of bending the banana backwards so that national concerns, the previous narrowness and rapacity's for national self enhancement that beset all agendas and the politics of peace and security, don't rationalise what ought to become quintessentially global processes. Without this depoliticising procedure, nationalistic and expansionist designs will continue to be imprinted on the well-intentioned effort. The reality of the present situation, however, is that most efforts invariably fall back into precedent error. One might pre-empt the objection, to carry the metaphor of fruit, a step furthe—that the banana can't be straightened out, that crookedness is its natural shape. But it is a fruit bending away from the earth after fertilisation, pointing towards the sun; or, regarded from a different angle, some countries are too warmed by historical opportunity, by pillage and subordination of militarily weaker nations, and need to move a little into the shade, allowing other things to grow beneath the sun of opportunity and socio-economic ripening.

The idea of a state's 'sovereignty' has always been subject to definitional quandaries, as indeed is the notion of 'statehood'.[2] It is nevertheless assumed here, that the behaviour of any given state is always motivated by concern for maintaining its sovereignty in terms its citizenry, territory, institutions and 'national interest'; invariably (the adversarious caps being scotched into our pates) in opposition to other states.

As long as maintaining state sovereignty commands its unequalled position as the cynosure guiding national institutions, contemporary efforts at rectifying imbalances are likely to remain fraught with considerable flaws. It will also continue to stymie resolution of conflict whenever and wherever it arises. The 'worth' of a Foreign Minister, tossed with arms waving into the national scale as he or she is from time to time by party or plebiscite, comprises one part diplomacy, two parts recalcitrance to 'foreign' interests and concerns. Chameleons, by comparison, are usually considerably less adept at changing their colours.

The way towards the establishment of global institutions which, in pursuing the wider concerns of the global community, effectively equalise national interests, is thus likely to continue to remain encumbered with difficulties of astounding complexity. Susan George has shown with enough clarity how U.S. interests, for example, remain the most important ingredient in the assessment of international conflicts. The banner of democracy is waved over the heads of weaker military forces in a show that does much to discredit the so-called democratic tradition. Examples are not lacking elsewhere in the globe. The French have also tried to maintain their lagging hegemony over Rwanda and, in doing so, have managed to enlist the support of the U.N., launching the infamous Operation Turquoise, which, as has been later confirmed, attempted to disguise an ongoing French arm-selling venture with the overthrown Hutu government. The recent example of Haiti, again provides much food for thought. The U.S. record of anti-humanitarian activity in its blockade of Cuba's international trade has been enhanced by this latest show of force, there will be few who would willingly accept the tour the force as a diplomatic victory on Haiti's unconstitutional government. Assuming even that global needs are genuinely perceived by the power-brokers of nations to be essential for equitable continuity of all often running counter to usurious investments by these syndicates in countries thus destabilised the chief difficulty likely to arise pertains to a successful transfer of the traditional responsibilities of state institutions to the jurisdiction of international establishments, i.e., leading to a decrease in state sovereignty. The transfer of state sovereignty from national bodies would even in positions of clarity, only proceed to international levels if the independence and internationalism of this highest level were not in question. A tall order indeed.

II. Contemporary Efforts to Introduce Global Institutions

Contemporary efforts to create global institutions fall into three broad categories. There are those which focus on the idea of Collective Security and envisage their models mindful of this end. The second category comprises efforts aimed at reforming the United Nations so as to create an intergovernmental organisation that might more equitably represent the interests of all its member states. The final category refers to those efforts bent on introducing international federal institutions, that is, a global federalism. While the three categories encompass wide differences, they are all ultimately controlled by states, either through the mechanisms operating in their foundation as states or through the processes expounded in their constitution.

The first category is centred on the idea of collective security and finds its historical antecedents in the Concert of Europe that arose in the aftermath of the Napoleonic wars.[3] The triumphant monarchic order in Europe, decided to act collectively in order to suppress the revolutionary fervour and any further challenge to the status quo in Europe. Similarly, the modern practice of collective security unites major states against the challenges to current political and socio-economic patterns around the globe.

Though discredited after the two World Wars, the notion of collective security has enjoyed an enthusiastic (and somewhat gung-ho and controversial) resurgence due to the end of the Cold War and the expulsion of Iraqi forces from Kuwait by an international coalition of states.[4] But politics, we have to remind ourselves, has much in common with refraction; and political expediency is a concave lens, possessing the singular trait of diffusing our understanding the closer we attempt to focus on its workings. Focusing on the Gulf War and the ill winds of Desert Storm, we might discover that what we are tutored to perceive as 'coalition' had continued dependence on bribery and fulsome ingratiation, thus being at root an enterprise with particular political agendas at work. It revealed a reluctance, for instance, to deal with the human rights' abuses of nearby Israel and its annexation of foreign territory, and an over exertion of righteousness with regimes similar to Saddam Hussein's elsewhere.

Despite reservations originating from previous disappointments over its international efficacy, the major weakness of collective security is that the institutions it creates to promote peace and security are founded on the interests of the leading states in the international community. Consequently, if one or more of the major states deems it in their national interest to frustrate the collective will or, for that matter, the interest of the remaining states in the international community, collective security is effectively rendered inoperable. That in itself would be regrettable enough, but the mechanisms of collective security usually spin on, desirous of persuading the world that the search for solutions goes on. Its infamy is thus a suggestion of activity, not an acceptance of truth, of inertia.

The second category of efforts concerns the reform of the United Nations aimed at establishing intergovernmental organizations which might promote more equitably, the interests of its entire membership. Initially representing the victorious powers of the allied forces after World War II, the UN has evolved to enjoy the participation of representatives from most of the world's states. Evidence of this is found in the General Assembly, where all member states are assigned voting rights on the democratic principle of one vote per member, and where important questions, e.g., international peace and security, are made by a two-thirds majority.[5] That many members might no longer effectively vote for their countries, or that these countries may have abrogated their own national interests through corrupt officials is another matter, and has some quarrel with the notion of democracy and the independence of nations.

Despite the putative democratic nature of the General Assembly, representation in the executive organ of the U.N., the Security Council, is currently restricted to fifteen states of which only five are permanent members: the USA, France, UK, China and Russia. This effectively accords to each of the five permanent members of the Council the right to veto policies which depart from their national interest—regardless of the desirability of the proposed reforms or the changes envisaged for the U.N. Charter. The relevant veto conferring passage in the Charter is Article 27; after stating in paragraph 2 that "decisions of the Security Council on procedural matters shall be made by an affirmative vote of nine members," paragraph 3 states that decisions "on all other matters shall be made by an affirmative vote of nine members including the concurring votes of the permanent members..." Since the body in greatest need of reform is indeed the Security Council with the disproportionate share of power it confers to its permanent members over the rest of the member states, it appears that any reformation which challenges the established procedures is unlikely to survive the rulings of the Council's veto holding members. Consequently, the predictable play of national interests erodes significantly the efficacy and impartiality of the U.N. It is possible then to conceive of the power tugs the five permanent members of the Council, must often confront and even perpetuate in order to maintain a status quo based on an inscrutable logic. If indeed the powerful are to hold on to such discriminatory power, why aren't Japan or Germany allowed to form part of the circle of honour. Are they still paying a sort of moral compensation that democracies, for the mere fact of actually carrying the name, remain exempt from. No amount of democratic spirit stopped France, the U.K. or the U.S .from sacrificing troops of both their own armies and those of the enemies in the Vietnam campaigns, the Korean war, the Gulf War, the Falklands War etc. If peace is to be given a chance, then casualties should be counted amongst enemy and allied armies alike.

The third category involves the idea of a global federation as the basic tenet for establishing international institutions. Such form of federation can be traced back to the era of European Enlightenment during which the leading thinkers hypothesised a time when 'perpetual peace' would pervade the world, e.g., Kant writes:

> ...Peace cannot be founded or secured without a compact of the Nations with each other. Hence there must be a compact of a special kind which may be called a PACIFIC FEDERATION *(foedus pacificum),* and which would be distinguished from a mere treaty or *Compact of Peace (pactum pacis)* in that the latter merely puts an end to one war whereas the former would seek to put an end to all wars for ever.[6]

Kant believed, that through the effects of the wars which progressively cause destruction and chaos amongst the states and their peoples, a global federation would emerge to ensure 'peace and security' in the world.[7] Such a global federation would comprise the world's states through a process of institutionalisation of the interactions among its members and the acknowledgment a transfer of sovereignty to these institutions from members states.

As Keith Suter points out in his article, global federalists are found today among prominent individuals, governments and intergovernmental organizations, and essentially argue for the formation of a fourth layer of government to the national, provincial or state, and local. As pointed out by Suter elsewhere, three processes can be identified for the formation of a global federation: 'drift', 'disaster' and 'design'.[8] 'Drift', describes a global process by which, through the continued interdependence and integration of the world's states, international federalist structures finally evolve; 'disaster' refers to a global procedure which is reminiscent of Kant's view that federalist institutions emerge as a consequence of the worsening effects of international conflict. The latter view is exemplified by the formation of the League of Nations and the UN after the two World Wars. For its part, 'design' suggests that international institutions of a federalist character will be formed as a result of the conscious action of individuals, groups and governments through the media of education, international conferences and assemblies.

In spite of the appeal of some features of global federal institutions, two major hurdles arise: first, in the process of bringing about the formation of these federal institutions; and second, as a *consequence* of their foundation. The first hurdle arises because state sovereignty still forms a primary concern among states which jealously guard against any attempt by international institutions at 'usurping' their traditional state responsibilities. This is exemplified in the case of the United Kingdom where in 1992-93, rebellious Tory MPs maintained a sustained campaign to derail the Maastricht treaty on the basis of its erosion of British sovereignty.

The second hurdle arises when the current power disparities among states, become institutionalised after the formation of a global federalist body, thus allowing a 'legitimate' continuation of extant imbalances among states. Consequently, even if a global federation emerges, the peace and security it augurs will still be largely determined by those states exercising most influence in the formation of the international institutions in question. The example of Cambodia, where, it was thought by some, UN activity had furnished the best result, yet is a point in case here. Pressure groups, both national and international and a long history of economically oriented international mismanagement of Cambodian affairs, of misguided empowerment of dangerous groups and tremendous miscalculations about the reactions of the native population, have decimated and continue to decimate (the land mine legacy haunts the life of Cambodians) a people at the mercy of arms bargains and political pressure play. No amount of 'banner-waving' in the name of democracy has achieved a result other than the establishment of an authority which finds it increasingly difficult to extricate itself from the pangs of armed conflict and the sore border altercation issues it has nurtured in one form or another over the last decades. The scene in Cambodia, although reversed, is reminiscent of that struggle for 'democracy and freedom' which during the Tiananmen upsurge of June 1989 in Beijing (and other major urban centres) uncovered the face of Western indoctrination in the guise of democracy; and, it will be agreed that Li Peng's massacre can never be excused, indoctrination is something the Chinese do not need more of.

The international institutions emerging from each of the three categories discussed above collective security, intergovernmental institutions and Global Federalism are subject to the roles played by the individual states. This suggests that the role of individuals and non-government organizations will be ancillary insofar as they rest largely with their capacity to lobby home governments, organise representations to foreign governments and attend international events on at best a consultative basis.[9]

As a result of the role of individual states in the formation of international institutions, 'peace and security' are likely to be interpreted in the sense which is most amenable to the national interests of individual states, a sense which is unlikely to transcend the level of the lowest common denominator, that is: maintaining the current political and economic systems. The expansion of the implementation of concepts like 'peace' and 'security' will therefore depend on the efforts of individuals and non-government organizations who, discontented with uncertainties in the official international echelon, will endeavour to create parallel international institutions to exercise some authority in international affairs.

III. Formation of Parallel International Institutions

Parallelism will become an important goal for individuals, and for non-government organizations wishing to rise beyond national interests to establish a global order based on an indusive sense of peace and security. This predicates freedom from institutional ties to national, subnational or international bodies, in order to reflect more profoundly a commitment to the interests of humanity and the globe as a whole.

Thus, at the structural level, we have come to recognise the impossibility of achieving peace and security through traditional means which have attracted most political and philosophical consideration. The debate moves, of necessity, towards an alternative proposition. Of course, the world does not lack experience in the search for alternatives: it has always been the prerogative of the individual to find a personal alternative to achieve an environment which temporarily might be deemed 'peaceful' and 'secure', bound in as he or she is to the disturbances and impositions of the outside world.

Historiography is of great help in the erection of new structures and the embellishment of rigid monuments to human deliberation. Yet, history is only serviceable inasmuch as it is able to pass on a *living* tradition, a tradition which does not remain impervious to change by the members of present societies. Tradition as an element of 'dead' history, unavoidably obstructs the transition towards a fully developed model which history itself has helped to create. There is no harm in recording the feats, the accidents, the births, the deaths and the thoughts and enterprises of individuals and nations, though there can be a loss of focus, a bypassing of saliencies. There is no delusion either in being able to perceive a common thread—perhaps not with an unmistakable evolutionary proclivity but a thread nevertheless—running through the events which shaped the lives of all nations. These are all pointers to a common purpose, and speak of meaning in a defiantly anonymous post modernist age.

IV. Need for a Global Educative Authority

Given the frailties of human nature at this present point in evolution, a significant transfer of sovereignty from national to international institutions is indeed somewhat Utopian, and could conceivably proceed from a global calamity or a supernatural agency. Since we have no way of preempting such forces, and have to regard with suspicion, the emergence of global institutions which are strongly influenced by dominant states, the desired changes would have to be prepared through parallel institutions. A parallel institution that has a global educative purpose that is genuinely global people centred rather than state centred, and unambiguously nonsectarian would be the preferred instrument for such change.

One educative focus would be to understand local issues and their relevance at national and international levels. The aim would be to calibrate individual and local needs while considering the importance of other communities and the international community at large. Another focus would be, the development of a communal and international spirit in which the worth of the individual is recognised. Individuality, nevertheless, needs to be encouraged with these communal and international structures. And another focus might be to ensure an uncensored or undistorted flow of information from among different parts of the world and, most importantly, between policy making organs and grass-roots communities.

Thus, a global educative authority, nourished by paradigms reflecting a spiritual nature that is responsive to global and humanitarian concerns, is required for preparing the crucial institutional change to become effected at the national and international levels. In large part, the work to be done concerns a transformation of governments and of human nature more generally.

While the attainment of such a body, a *Council of Earth*, would be indicative of a movement away from state dominated international institutions, and towards a significant removal of inequality at national levels and transfer of state sovereignty, it follows that such proposition should not be couched entirely as a counsel of perfection. Progress, it is everyone's experience, invariably occurs by degrees; hence a gradualist philosophy, an attempt at mastery of every step, would continue to underpin the most spirited and idealistic efforts.

With regard to the various protocols of a presumptive *Council of Earth*, this is not the place to examine what these might be, though they should clearly emanate from its sanctum, a centrally embedded authority of an educative nature, and work through a clearly defined succession of 'elders', if such be the need. The flow of policy from the present to a more distant future could be vouchsafed (*mutatis mutandis)* by the workings of a resurrected guild-system, so that successive authorities could be assured of centrally perpetuating the long-term projections of their forebears while remaining peripherally responsive to short-term adjustments and responses.

There is something potently suggestive of constructing future global policy again, on the principle of the wheel's motion, which has immovability at the hub and flashing spokes on the rim.[10] It goes without saying, that such long-term perception is rarely sensible outside the religious orbit, and would face vehement opposition from those who care not for the improvements to a world that will take effect when they are no longer around to gain its benefits. What can be said with certainty of present institutions claiming global concern, is that all without exception will need to change and refine present practices and policies as seen, for instance, in the state dominated workings of the UN Security Council.

V. Education and the Council of Earth

The *Council of Earth* would formulate a universal syllabus of education for adoption by national governments, and direct its resources towards genuine worldwide upliftment by knowledge and spiritual fealty. This syllabus would take regard of all particular cultural directions and expressions, as well as geographic difference, to propagate a unifying idiom and a range of subjects that can be readily universalised. Without the broadest possible education process, which ought not to remain in the hands of national governments, there will continue to be retrogression and continuous peril to such an ambitious undertaking.

The internationalisation of education is a prerequisite for the institution of a responsible and effective *Council of Earth.* Education in itself will be more far reaching than at present. It is not a passage that begins in late infancy, continues to high school and university, and then generally peters out. Educational ideals will have to exert a devising and (where necessary) censoring influence on current free market designs, that often have only monetary gain in sight, and are absolved by the same self seeking market processes of offering nourishment to the intellect, the mind and the spirit; instead many things are fast foods for the mind, turning in short time to poisonous concoctions. Thus, to educate the money lenders and business people, will become a major objective for the Council, as will the re-education of the intelligentsia and clerics. It goes without saying, that many of the former, and most of the latter, will profess immunity to this re-education and will continue their feckless slumber.

Difficulties, there will be many, if an international Council of the sort adumbrated, a society of 'elders' that is governed not by political, but global humanitarian objectives, should not come into being. It is the greatest difficulty of individuals to see beyond their self-interest to the interest of others, and even more difficult (and probably rationalised as unnecessary) to give regard to other species and to succeeding generations. A global educative authority will possess this singular capacity to project ahead, to see the future like Homunculus in Goethe's *Faust,* a luminous creature in a test-tube that once created, becomes immediately active and knows the thoughts of its ambience.

A major difficulty (immanent in these deliberations) arises with the possibility that larger and more influential states (often quite contrary to global concerns) may effectively veto policies which prospectively benefit an overwhelming majority of nations and peoples. There is no such difficulty, of course, for the stateless and for those without a sectarian passport.

VI. Conclusion

We are a long way off from a so-called *Council of Earth.* But even here, even now, we have to take the long view, and nourish purposive dreams. As Helder Camara is quoted earlier as saying: "when one is dreaming alone, it is only dreaming. When we are dreaming together it is the beginning of reality." Or, as Delmore Schwartz, the American poet putting the emphasis on restorative reverie affirms wide-eyed and lyrical, "in dreams begin responsibilities."

The role of international organizations is to facilitate the distribution of information through its human resources and to avoid a proliferation of new problems once action has been taken. There should be no primary concern with destroying the evil which lies latent in any society or social grouping; instead, the emphasis of the humanitarian work undertaken, should be to redress the acute problems arising in specific areas of the globe while providing help and advice towards the gradual evolution and deployment of forces which will eventually quell the rule of violence.

The Universal Declaration of Human Rights has achieved a workable consensus for the world community. It is in fact an allegiance to life in mostly general terms, to be implemented through structures which are themselves not ready, or at least not cognisant of a shift from the secular, mercantile, neo-positivistic approach of government to a holistic, generalised and decentralised one. The replacement of existing institutions by groups evolving from the organising efforts of individuals and non-government organizations seems, in spite of all this, a perplexing alternative.

We are undoubtedly in need of some central commission to approve of specific projects that might have global repercussions; however, the vast majority of global projects in need of urgent implementation can be managed by people residing in proximity to the conflict areas. Greater efficiency and abiding results are more easily achieved by people who need not gather information and knowledge prior to undertaking the task of stabilisation. Moreover, action by local people avoids any delay occasioned by mobilisation from foreign nations and the eventual task of handing back the power to local authorities.

Perhaps we do not yet, possess the proper building materials for the *Council of Earth,* constituted as it will have to be along lines of national disinterest and oriented towards authentically global concerns. This predicates an understanding of the complexity of relationships in life and presupposes as well an international press corps endowed with a much higher level of altruistic intelligence and unconnected to vested interest. Speed of information systems is of less importance here, than reliability and quality of information, and objectivity of preliminary assessments.

Part of the problem will also be an overcoming of the infantile plateau of human awareness which has from time immemorial been concerned with procreating and defending, in the course recognising its own limited reality as the sole object of paramount importance. To see life everywhere as *one,* not at the intellectual but at the actual level, implies that the *Council of Earth* will come into being once a much more knowledgeable and wiser global educative authority has been impanelled, beginning perhaps with some such structure in a country that has assumed leadership beyond economic muscularity.

When this milestone is finally reached, a duly constituted *Council of Earth* will be seen as the old jagged stepping-stone that it is; nothing more, nothing less.

Notes

1. The notion of perpetual peace is most clearly articulated in Kant's celebrated essay, "Perpetual Peace: A Philosophical Essay," *Theory of International Relations: Selected Texts from Gentili to Treitschke,* eds. M.G. Forsyth, H.M. Keens-Soper & P. Savigear (London: George Allen & Unwin, 1970) pp. 200-244.

2. For a thorough analysis of the notions of 'state' and 'sovereignty', see Alan James, *Sovereign Statehood: The Basis of International Society* (London: Allen & Unwin, 1986).

3. Cf., Bull, H. and A. Watson, eds. *The Expansion of International Society.* Oxford: Clarendon Press, 1984.

4. See Gareth Evans & Bruce Grant, *Australia's Foreign Relations: In the World of the 1990s.* Melbourne: Melbourne University Press, 1991.

5. See Article 18 of the UN Charter.

6. *op. cit.,* pp. 212-13 (second section, article ii.)

7. *ibid.,* pp.216-24 (First supplement).

8. See Keith Suter, *A New International Order: Proposals for Making a Better World* (Sydney: World Association of World Federalists (Australia), 1981).

9. This was exemplified by the role of NGO at the UN's special disarmament conferences held throughout the 1970s and 1980s.

10. The symbolism of the wheel (Lat. rota), the great symbol of good fortune of ancient civilisation, and more recently as an image of the bewildering passage of time, reaches through all religious traditions, from the wheel of dharma of the Buddhists, to the wheels of Ezekiel (1: 15-21) and Daniel (7:9) of Judaeo-Christian teachings.

Towards a Federal World Order?

Keith Suter
University of Sydney

When in 1945 [the UN] Charter was adopted in San Francisco, I was disappointed that the United Nations was merely a continuation of the association of sovereign nation states similar to the former League of Nations. Already at the time of my service in the Secretariat in the League of Nations in Geneva, I pleaded for a transformation in the League of Nations into a World Federation in the sense of a Global State. What is the difference? An association of sovereign nation states can only act with the consensus of its members. Enforcement of decisions on individuals is not possible. The League of Nations and the United Nations have no possibility to prevent wars.... There have been, up to now, over 100 wars between members of the United Nations.... Only a federative organization of mankind, a Federal World State has the means to disarm all its units and by eliminating the instrument of war, the national armies, can ensure enduring peace.[1]

Max Habicht (1899-1986) was a Swiss Quaker and a distinguished international lawyer. This quotation, from a posthumous collection of his writings on Peace and World Federalism, provides the framework for this essay. Habicht was an internationalist, in the sense that he believed international problems required international responses, and that national governments alone could not respond to these problems. He welcomed the League of Nations (1920-1946) as an improvement over the previous chaos, and he welcomed the UN (1945) as an improvement over the League. But both organizations did not (and do not) go far enough; hence his support for some sort of supra-national world federal organization.

As this essay progresses, it will become clear that there is not a set definition of 'world federalism'. I am therefore, not going to set out a specific scheme as a model one: Dr Habicht's books contain his ideas; others views of equal value will be encountered in these pages.

The federal principle is that governmental powers and responsibilities should be divided between levels of government (federal, state and local). Particular matters that cannot be handled satisfactorily on one level should be handled at another. This is also called the 'subsidiarity principle', whereby the decision is made at the political level that corresponds best to its geographical scope. Allied to this is the principle of democracy: that the individual should make as many decisions locally as possible. The standard example of a federal constitution is the US one, adopted in 1787 after four years of independence from the UK in which the new Confed-

Keith Suter, "Toward a Federal World Order?" Reprinted with permission from the editors of *Essays on Peace: Paradigms for Global Order* edited by Michael Salla, Walter Tenetto, and Enrique Martínez.

eration failed to come to grips with disputes over commerce and boundaries. Despite some problems, the 1787 Constitution remains one of the world's most visionary legal documents.

World federalism is simply adding a fourth layer of government (to national, state and local). It is not so much about world government—as about a governed world. World federalists want the same concerns about law and order within a nation's borders to be carried to the global level. A globe of increasing trade, communications, tourism and banking cannot afford to remain in a state of anarchy. There is a need for, among other things, a network of binding treaties, a system of courts to interpret the laws and adjudicate disputes, an executive backed by a police force adequate to enforce the laws, and a sourced tax revenues to finance all these activities. That is the core of world federalism. The rest of this essay provides additional insights into both its context and its content.

This essay deals with five matters. First, it looks at the renewed interest in 'world governance' in general and federalism in particular. The ending of the Cold War has created a vacuum, what is now to be the basis of the new world order? Second, it is necessary to situate world federalism within the broad spectrum of ideas on world governance. There are various approaches to it and world federalism is only one of them. Third, world federalism (and many other ideas for world governance) has grown out of an impatience (reflected in the Habicht quotation) with the League of Nations and United Nations. Consequently, it is necessary to situate the world federalist approach within the context of the two main attempts so far at world governance. Fourth, the world Federalist movement contains several strands. There is not a set 'world federalist platform'. Individuals (for example, Winston Churchill) have flirted with world federalist ideas, others have written books setting out their schemes. For the newcomer, the range of views is bewildering. Consequently, it is necessary to provide an impression of the movement's diversity. Finally, if the concept of world federalism is so appealing to its supporters, why has so little progress been made to date (especially outside Western Europe)? This essay contains, then, a list of some of the recurring issues which arise in world federalist discussions.

It is important not to end on a note of despair. The world federalist movement is campaigning for one of the biggest global changes ever attempted during the past few centuries. It cannot expect success easily or quickly. What is notable, is not that the world federalist movement has failed, but that so many people (often thinking independently of each other) have come to the same conclusion: the need for some sort of world federalism. If the idea has failed it can also be said to be durable. There is something about it which guarantees its continual existence. It is here to stay and will eventually be implemented.

World Governance

This essay deals with 'world governance' rather than 'world government'. There is a crucial difference. People are worried about 'world government'. It has the overtones of 'Big Brother' from George Orwell's novel *1984*. 'World governance', by contrast, refers to the manner or system of governing. It has no set agenda of how the globe should be managed—only that management of it cannot be left to national governments alone.

World governance (not necessarily via that phrase) is now a standard item in international relations. This section looks at four instances of this.

Revived Interest in the UN

There is revived interest in the UN. The UN had grave political problems from the outset, notably the breakdown of the World War II Grand Alliance between the US, USSR and UK, and the onset of the Cold War. The UN itself became a site for Cold War disputes. The UN Security Council, which was designed to handle threats to international peace and security, itself became redundant as the Big Five

(US, USSR, UK, France and China) each threatened to use their veto power to block any Security Council action in a dispute in which one or more of the Big Five were involved.

The end of the Cold War began in 1985, with Mr. Gorbachev becoming the Soviet leader. As part of his restructuring *(perestroika)*, Mr. Gorbachev needed to discard the futile, if not counterproductive, overseas operations initiated by his predecessors. He invited the UN Secretary General to negotiate an agreement between the warring parties in and outside Afghanistan (USSR, US and Pakistan) to enable the USSR to leave Afghanistan.

Additionally, Mr. Gorbachev reversed the negative attitude of his predecessors towards the UN. None of his predecessors had been fond of the UN and all of them had a cynical attitude towards it, seeing it partly as a place to locate spies.[2] Mr. Gorbachev, by contrast, could see how the USSR could gain from increased involvement in the UN, such as the World Bank. He also paid the USSR's back debts.

A momentum began to build up. The UN was able to negotiate peace agreements covering disputes in which the USSR was not directly involved notably Namibia, Iran-Iraq, Cambodia, Central America and Western Sahara.

After Iraq's invasion of Kuwait in August 1990 the US also began to be more interested in the UN. The US was very involved in the UN's affairs from 1945 until the 1960s, during which time its views were shared by the majority of the UN member-nations. As decolonisation gathered momentum and UN membership became dominated by the non-aligned Third World so the US became increasingly disenchanted with the UN. It began to use the phrase 'tyranny of the majority'—originally used by the USSR in the late 1940s and throughout the 1950s when the US's views were dominant.

US hostility towards the UN peaked during the Reagan Administration (1981–89) when the US refused to pay some of its contributions to the UN, resigned from UNESCO (the UN Educational Scientific and Cultural Organisation) and boycotted some UN projects (such as the law of the sea treaty).

Iraq's invasion of Kuwait meant the US suddenly had a use for the UN. There is a continuing debate as to whether the UN was used in the way that it was designed to be used.[3] American international lawyer Richard Falk wrote:

> It is certainly true that the United Nations formally authorised the United States approach.... But behind this formal mandate from the United Nations lie extremely serious questions about whether the Organisation has been true to its own Charter and to the larger purposes of peace and justice that it was established to serve. And below these concerns is the disturbing impression that the United Nations has been converted during this Gulf Crisis into a virtual tool of US foreign policy thereby compromising its credibility in the future.[4]

The UN's role in the Gulf Conflict was, in retrospect a culminating point in the trend over the preceding half decade whereby the UN has become a more important player in international politics. It has also forced people to think about the UN's structure, powers and limitations. Consequently talk of UN reform is coming from three sources.

For previous critics of the UN, the Gulf conflict suddenly provided the UN with a redeeming feature. Since August 1990, the US, for example, has undertaken to repay back debts to the UN. These critics want UN reform to ensure that their money is not going to be wasted.

For UN supporters, by contrast, the UN's role in the Gulf conflict was a disappointment: the UN was created to prevent war and not to win wars. Some of them are now calling for UN reform, so as to democratise UN decision-making and not have it controlled by the Big Five. For example, conferences have been held on how to create a more democratic UN, for example, via a second General Assembly with delegates elected directly by the general public.[5]

Finally, the Gulf crisis jolted peace groups into thinking about the UN. Previously they had tended to regard it as a remote bureaucracy isolated from their own activities. They were broadly sympathetic to it, but not greatly interested in it. The Gulf conflict has obliged them to take more interest in UN matters. The subject of UN reform has now become a campaign issue for them.

Transnational problems

Diseases, plagues, famines and financial crises are not new. But in recent decades they have acquired a greater transnational character. These problems seem to be beyond purely national control or solution. Governments are being obliged to work together not because they want to—but because they have to. Nations either work together or perish separately. Some examples will illustrate these points.

More people in First World countries are now dying from malaria, which is principally a Third World disease. The UN's World Health Organisation (WHO) has an annual research budget of only $5 million for malaria. Drug companies' estimate that a new drug would cost about $100 million to research, test and register and, since no Third World country could afford to buy it, it is not profitable to develop it. Consequently First World tourists are still using Chloroquine and Malopim on their exotic travels, and risk encountering mosquitoes which are now resistant to them. Malaria is one of the world's major problems, but gets overshadowed by diseases which are far more prevalent in First World countries (such as heart attacks). Malaria has killed more Australian soldiers this century than have been killed in action in Asian/Pacific campaigns. Now First World civilians are being exposed to it.

The biggest financial scandal in 1991 was the collapse of the Bank of Credit and Commerce International. As the UK newspaper *The Guardian* commented:

> The first lesson of the collapse of the Bank of Credit and Commerce International is the need to create an international mechanism to police the billions of footloose funds, legal and illegal, which can be shifted around the world at the press of a computer keyboard without adequate control. The 1980's gave us international deregulation, but not the international surveillance which should go with it. Owned by Arab money and run by Pakistanis, it was not only rudderless but stateless as well, with no central bank standing behind it. This does not answer the question of why a bank which had been indicted for laundering drug money and which secretly bought control of two American banks was allowed to get away with it for so long. The governor of the Bank of England observed that "innuendo is one thing, evidence quite another." That is exactly the point. If there isn't an international body to keep watch on a global fraud, there will only be innuendo until a bank becomes so financially rotten that, as with BCCI, it is in danger of dropping from the tree by itself.[6]

The next major conflict in the Middle East is as likely to be over water as over oil. Israel, for example, has a serious water problem. The water comes from three main sources: the Sea of Galilee and two aquifers (underground supplies). One runs down the coast of Israel and the second begins in the occupied territory of the West Bank, before flowing underground into Israel itself. Israeli authorities restrict Palestinian use of water so that the water can flow into Israel. The Palestinians, with their high population growth rate are even more short of water. A possible solution would involve one or two water pipes that would transfer water from Turkey's Seyhan and Ceyhan rivers across to the Middle East and provide for all the nations of the region. Unfortunately, international politics, for the moment anyway, would rub out such an obvious solution.

A final example of transnational problems comes from an instance where finance and the environment are involved. There is concern at present about both the size of the Brazilian foreign debt and the 'greenhouse effect' caused in part by the loss of forests. There is this irony that Brazil cuts down its forests, to facilitate cattle grazing to earn money to repay the foreign debt to bankers whose grandchildren will suffer from the 'greenhouse effect'.

To sum up, these few examples all illustrate the futility of relying upon national governments to settle problems which are essentially of a transnational type. Indeed, national pride may actually make the problems worse because governments prefer pride to co-operating with supposed 'enemies' (such as in the Middle East example).

The Stockholm Initiative

During the 1980s some 'independent international commissions' were established, composed mainly of former politicians, to take a broad view of what should be the world's response to Third World development, disarmament and environmental protection. Some of the participants of these bodies then turned their attention to the practical aspects of international implementation of their ideas. The Stockholm Initiative was published in April 1991.[7] This 48 page report was signed by 36 world leaders, including Willy Brandt, Norwegian Prime Minister Harlem Brundtland, then Swedish Prime Minister Ingvar Carlsson, Jimmy Carter, President Vaclav Havel, Robert McNamara and Eduard Shevardnadze.

Among the key points made in the Stockholm Initiative were the following:

- Securing peace, sustainable development and democracy requires nations, in their common interest, to create a new system of global security and governance.
- Increasing economic and ecological interdependencies have not been met by a corresponding strengthening of global co-operation and governance.
- After a decade, the greater part of which was characterised by selfishness and arrogance, we need to restore global morality. We need the vision of being one global neighbourhood. That is the idea of international solidarity, without which humankind might not survive the next century. We need a new world order, based on justice and peace, democracy and development, human rights and international law.
- We propose the elaboration of a global law enforcement arrangement, in line with the United Nations Charter, focusing on the role of sanctions and on military enforcement measures.

At the conclusion of its analysis, the Stockholm Initiative makes 28 specific proposals, the last two of which read as follows:

- That a World Summit on Global Governance be called, similar to the meetings in San Francisco and at Bretton Woods in the 1940s.
- As a matter of priority, the establishment of an Independent International Commission on Global Governance.

This report is now being considered by governments and the UN. As already indicated, it has come at an opportune time.

The European Community

Western Europe is the world's best example to date of 'regional governance': of nations working together on transnational problems. Christopher Layton, has set out five ways in which the European Community is setting an example to the rest of the world: economic growth, peace and security, reconciliation, help for the Third World and environmental protection.[8]

For Layton, Europe's example of gradual integration on a regional basis is one for other parts of the world to follow:

> Just as Europe could not be united overnight, so no substantial government is going to accept an immediate leap towards world government. Just as Europe has had to be built, gradually, by functional co-operation, so, at world level, there must be a major advance in 'functional' co-operation a new economic order, worldwide agreements on certain key environmental issues, progress on security and disarmament. At world level, as at European level, functional advances must be supported by a growing political awareness that, in the end, strong joint institutions are indispensable if the whole process is not to fall back into the desuetude that has overcome the United Nations.[9]

The European Community has not been established easily or quickly. It is still not as federated as some would like. If Western Europe alone has taken so long, it is not surprising that progress at the global level has been even slower.

The Spectrum of World Governance

How *are* nations to be united? In a standard survey of proposals for 'World Government,'[10] the two authors date the first plan in 1306. Each of the subsequent centuries has brought forth proposals; the 18th century was particularly prolific in such projects, especially the revolutionary period and the Napoleonic wars of the early 19th century. Speculation about some form of 'world government' is not, then, simply a 20th century idea.[11] But this century (especially since World War I which began in 1914) has seen increased urgency given to these ideas and two small attempts (League of Nations and UN) to implement them.

For someone coming anew to this subject, the range of proposals is bewildering.[12] There is an equally bewildering range of non-governmental organisations each campaigning for separate proposals.[13] Ron Glossop has tried to systematise the different approaches as follows:[14]

- federalist approach: the deliberative decision by national governments to transfer certain powers (such as maintaining armed forces) to a world government while retaining other powers (such as establishing laws concerning ownership of property) for themselves.
- functionalist approach: the creation of more global agencies (such as the World Health Organisation) to handle a particular function (such as health) since experts can co-operate in a less politically-charged environment and eventually the globe will be covered by a network of such agencies.[15]
- populist approach: the creation of a grassroots people's movement to establish a democratic world government directly responsible to the people of the world and in the meantime to generate ideas for world government and a groundswell in favor of it.[16]

The distinctions between the three approaches are not watertight. For example, the World Federalist Campaign (to be examined later) is an illustration of a component in the third approach working for the first approach.

More significantly there is a chicken-and-egg-dilemma. In 1947 there was a debate between the American political scientist Robert Maynard Hutchins and the theologian Reinhold Niebuhr on what should come first:

> Reinhold Niebuhr whom I greatly admire takes the view that we cannot discuss world government because we have no world community to support it.... But I am afraid that Mr. Niebuhr exaggerates the state of perfection which world community must achieve before world government can be considered.... The way to promote world community is to have world government. But since we as private citizens cannot establish a world government the next best thing we can do to promote world community is to talk about world government.... For the consideration of what is necessary to unite the world, the discussion of a common problem of overwhelming importance should lead to a growing sense of community among all peoples.[17]

Consequently internationalists (such as myself) prefer to campaign on all three approaches simultaneously.

Glossop's typology is as good as can be produced. There is as Hutchins pointed out in 1947—it still applies today, a wide diversity of ideas. Although speculation about some form of world government is at least six centuries old, the ideas have changed as global factors have themselves changed.

It is now necessary to look at how this century's two main journeys on the road to world governance—the League and the UN—have come about. They are examples of Glossop's second approach and yet have implications for the first approach: world federalism.

The League of Nations and the United Nations

World War I came as a great shock to everyone. No one expected such a large or lengthy conflict. There was widespread agreement that this should be the 'war to end all wars'.

But how was this to be accomplished? Part of the debate was derived from disagreement over who or what caused the war. Several unofficial groups and individuals (Glossop's third approach) said the fault lay with the system of competing nation states. If the system itself was at fault, there should be a new international system. On the other hand, most, but not all politicians believed that the system was basically sound but it had been destabilised by Germany, and so Germany ought both to be punished for its past deeds and to be prevented from trying to repeat them.

This basic disagreement was never resolved. A punitive peace settlement was inflicted upon Germany and it helped give rise to Adolf Hitler who rode to power in 1933 on the wave of German resentment of the Treaty of Versailles. Ironically the appeasement policy of the UK and France was initiated by well-meaning people who also believed that Germany had been too harshly treated and so should be 'appeased' (that is soothed) by being permitted some concessions.

Meanwhile the League began its operations in 1920. Its highest-ranking advocate, US President Woodrow Wilson, could not get Congressional approval for US membership of it. Indeed the US not only rejected League membership but its mood of 'isolationism' also entailed a restrictive immigration policy and the imposition of high tariff barriers.

The UK and France, the League's two most important members, were wary of it. They were not accustomed to working through international organisations. Their governments lacked the vision to use the League competently. Sir Austen Chamberlain (whose half-brother Neville went on to champion 'appeasement') won the Nobel Peace Prize for his work on Franco-German reconciliation (the 1925 Locarno Treaty). But even he had a restrained perception of the League. Lord Robert Cecil (President of the UK League of Nations Union—part of Glossop's 'third approach') recalled Chamberlain's views of the League. "He thought of it as just one cog in the diplomatic machine, to be used or not at the discretion of the Cabinet. I regarded it as the essential international organ for the maintenance of peace."[18] Thus, the UKs most distinguished Foreign Secretary of the 1920s and 1930s regarded the League as having a strong moral force, but he could not envisage it as an organisation with the power to coerce its members.

Thus the League was flawed from the outset. It was able to make useful progress in world health, care of refugees, the suppression of slavery and the drug trade, and improvements in employment. It settled, particularly in the 1920s, some international disputes. But once militarism built up in Japan, Italy and Germany, the League was powerless to stop the dictators, because the member nations were reluctant, if not downright opposed, to introduce coercive measures. Consequently, the League ceased to have much political relevance by the early 1930s.

The UN grew directly from World War II. Winston Churchill, a belated supporter of the League, told Lord Cecil that War World War II should be called the "Unnecessary War" in that it "could easily have been prevented if the League of Nations had been used with courage and loyalty by the associated nations."[19] He, therefore, had no hesitation that the League's replacement should be a far more ambitious organisation—partly modelled on the Grand Alliance he helped shape: the US, USSR and UK.

Churchill was a latent world federalist. John Colville, one of Churchill's colleagues during World War II, noted in his diary in December 1940 (at the bleakest period of the war) that Churchill was already giving consideration to Europe after Germany's defeat. Western Europe should form a 'Council of Europe', 'which would have a supreme judiciary and a Supreme Economic Council to settle currency questions etc.' An international air force would be drawn from air forces of the council's member-nations:

> Once enrolled, they would be under no national jurisdiction, but they would never be obliged to co-operate in an attack on their own country. All air forces, military and civil, would be internationalised. As regards armies, every power would be allowed its own militia, because Democracy must be based on people's army and not left to oligarchies or Secret Police. Prussia [sic] alone would, for a hundred years, be denied armaments beyond her air contingent. The Council would be unrestricted in its methods of dealing with a Power condemned by the remainder in Council.[20]

Churchill continued to promote these ambitious ideas, especially for an International Air Force, throughout the negotiations leading up to the adoption of the UN Charter in June 1945.[21]

Across the Atlantic a similar process was under way. A 'third approach' organisation was formed called the Commission for a Just and Durable Peace, headed by John Foster Dulles (the US Secretary of State in the 1950s) and composed of distinguished and influential people (including Reinhold Niebuhr). The Commission wanted the US to avoid repeating the error of not joining the League. The Federal Council of Churches also supported Dulles' work, by publishing his Six Pillars of Peace in which he called for a "more egalitarian sharing of world government."[22] The American mood had swung from isolationism to a determination to be involved in any future international organisation.

But the eventual UN Charter, though a great advance on the League of Nations Covenant, was much less than could have been expected from the initial generation of ideas. First, none of the senior people waging the war could give equal consideration to the task of preparing the peace. The urgent always takes priority over the important. Consequently, Churchill simply lacked the time and energy to, for example, insist upon the adoption of his International Air Force idea.

Second, those senior people not charged directly with waging the war had their own agendas for organising the peace. These people had little interest in vision and idealism; they were more concerned with post-war national interests. An example of the triumph of finance over vision is the fate of a post-war international currency. The UK economist Maynard Keynes was recruited in 1940 from Cambridge to the Treasury to work both on how the UK was to avoid being bankrupted by the war and to recommend the creation of a post-war economic order. During the war he produced a detailed scheme for an international 'Clearing Union' with 'Bancor' as its unit of exchange; with big initial credits; with unlimited liability in the sense, that like any banking concern, it could build up its assets without a ceiling as it went along; with substantial obligations upon creditor as well as upon debtor countries; with a leadership role for the US and UK; and with the right of any country to devalue its currency by up to 5 per cent a year without prior permission. This proposal led to the eventual establishment of the International Monetary Fund and the World Bank—the UN's financial agencies. But they are far less than Keynes envisaged:

> The Americans, with moderate but not complete foresight, saw themselves as the perpetual creditor nation. They did not therefore want heavy obligations on creditor countries; nor did they want unlimited liability; or easy devaluation; nor a special joint leadership role for Britain. 'Bancor' was no more popular, although at one stage they had a unit of their own called 'Unitas'. But essentially they thought that the dollar, linked to gold, could perform the pivotal role.[23]

In other words, nationalism undermined the vision of internationalism.

Finally, the 'third approach' advocates, though they received widespread public support, failed to convert that into public policy. They were only on the margins. They could not communicate easily and quickly with latent supporters, such as Winston Churchill, who had a war to fight. Nor were they in sufficient numbers to lobby the less senior decision makers planning the post war international order.

Additionally it has to be admitted that some latent supporters (such as John Foster Dulles) became seduced by the prospects of US national power and dropped their idealism in going for the chance of public office. By the time he came to be in a position to implement his vision John Foster Dulles (as Secretary of State) was no longer articulating his earlier ideas. He would no doubt argue in true *Yes Minister* style that where you stand, depends on where you sit and the relentless and coercive power of the US bureaucracy is such, that a politician is usually bent in the direction of his or her civil service advisers.[24] Since national bureaucrats do not want to share power with another level of government they consistently opposed any substantial increase in UN power—let alone the creation of some form of federal global authority.

A good way of changing government is usually via public pressure: Glossop's 'third approach'. It is now necessary to see why the third approach has been so unproductive on the matter of world federalism.

The World Federalist Campaign

'Federalism', according to one of its main contemporary historians, "has been a world wide intellectual movement."[25] It has been far more active in generating ideas than in creating a practical, united worldwide campaign. For a movement dedicated to uniting the world, it has had great difficulty in uniting itself. This fragmentation helps explain the paradox of world federalism: it seems at first sight so appealing and yet somehow it has not come about.

The movement is, then, a movement. Is not an organisation or a specific campaign. It should be likened to the women's movement or the peace movement—each of which consists of various organisations with differing agendas and with tendencies to compete against each other. There is not one internationally agreed plan for world federation—on the contrary there are many.[26]

This variety can be explained partly by the usual factors of geography, finance and the personalities of the main activists. These colour any popular movement. I have found that Americans are the worst for not joining existing organisations, they often prefer to create fresh ones in their own image. This may be another manifestation of the US cult of the 'rugged individualist'.

Additionally individuals may respond to the same event in similar ways at the same time. For example, in response to the rise of Hitler, Clarence Streit (of the *New York Times)* called in 1939 for a union of the democracies to oppose Nazi Germany,[27] while three young Englishmen at exactly the same time created the Federal Union organisation to campaign for a similar project.[28] Similarly, the eventual completion of the UN Charter in 1945 was seen by some people as too conservative and so various campaigns began simultaneously for a stronger UN or a complete replacement of it. The best seller of this period was done by Winston Churchill's European literary agent Emery Reves[29] who wanted a fresh organisation entirely. By contrast two distinguished US lawyers believed that the UN was correct in essence but needed extensive reform.[30]

A split occurred in 1947 when the federalist movement was divided into the European Federalists and the World Federalists. The reconciliation did not commence until 1985. The controversy was over how federation should come about: with nations forming into regional federations thereby creating a global network of regions, or a comprehensive membership of all the nations into one global federation? A network of regional federations could eventually create their own form of competition against each other, as has happened with the European Community's Common Agricultural Policy which subsidises inefficient western European farmers and excludes cheap food imports from the US and Australia. Alternatively, there was a greater hope of achieving some form of regional federation than a global one and so a united Europe could set an example to the rest of the world: half a loaf is better than none. Additionally, a UN (say) co-coordinating the actions of (say) six regions would operate more efficiently than the present UN with approximately 170 nations of equal membership rights in the General Assembly.

The European federalists[31] have had their own doctrinal problems. Should a 'United States of Europe' be a confederation (an association of independent nations, like the UN) or a federation (involving a specific surrender of control to federal organs of government, such as in the national constitutions of the US and Australia)? Non-governmental opinions were as varied as the governmental ones.

Incidentally, Winston Churchill (who was then out of power) still hoped for some form of overall European federation and was one of 700 participants at an unofficial conference at The Hague in 1948 which went on to help create the Council of Europe. It began with 10 nations and now has 23—the 12 European Community (EC) nations and the other 11 which are not in the EC.[32] It has promoted the protection of human rights in Western Europe and, more recently, commenced a dialogue with Eastern European nations with a view to bringing them into the 'European house'. But its powers are still far less than Churchill advocated in his discussions with John Colville in 1940.

Federalists have their own 'Subsidiarity' problem. This principle means that each decision should be solved at the political level that corresponds best to its geographical scope. This means that federalists are obliged to tolerate a considerable diversity in fellow federalist organisations. The federalists in 1947 could not, then, insist that the Europeans stop campaigning for a regional body. Nor can the movement lay down a set 'creed' to which all aspiring individual world federalist members should adhere. Consequently, the movement has not been able to create a set focussed international campaign. Additionally, there are some basic questions which remain in dispute. These will be examined in the Essay's final section.

The Continuing Debate

One of the byproducts of studying world federalism is that it forces a person to think more deeply about the present world order. Even if that person does not regard world federalism as the answer, at least it asks some important questions. No attempt is made here to answer the questions, to do so would make this an even longer essay.

This section lists seven questions in the various debates over federalism. They do not constitute an exclusive list nor are they necessarily in any order of priority. They complement some of the issues previously raised (such as the Hutchins/Niebuhr 'chicken and egg' debate) and reflect some of the problems yet to be resolved.

What Should Be the Basic Unit?

The present basic unit of international relations is the nation—hence the term 'inter-national': transactions between nations. Some federalist proposals are based on bringing nations together. But other proposals claim that the individual should be the basic unit. To construct a federal world upon existing boundaries would be to entrench old national rivalries within the new system. Additionally, people can be governed; governments cannot. Governments act as they see fit and are very difficult to control if they break international agreements. The more powerful a nation the greater scope it has for mischief on the world stage knowing that it stands a greater chance of getting away with illegal acts. Consequently, the individual should be the basic unit in a federal world and that all people should see themselves as world citizens.

What Should Be the Role of Public Opinion?

All proposals for world federation assume that it can only come about if there is widespread public support for it, either via governments themselves or via world citizens. Two practical problems are immediately obvious. First, how is a groundswell in favour of world federation to be generated? Nationalism is instilled through, for example, the use of symbols: slogans, anthems, flags, pledges etc. How could a similar array of symbols be generated in favour of world federation? Who would pay for them?

Second, how would 'public opinion' be assessed? Presumably this would require national referenda. Many nations have no traditions of such referenda. Others which do, have a tradition of citizens preferring to opt for the status quo rather than gamble on a change; Australia is a good example of this conservatism. Would people vote 'no' in a referendum because they feel that they are already unable to influence their own national governments and fear that a global system would be even more difficult to influence? Would they vote 'no' because they would see a world federation as a 'big brother'—rather than as a guardian of human rights?

The career of UK Foreign Secretary Sir Austen Chamberlain itself contains a paradox when it comes to assessing British public opinion towards something far less ambitious than world federation: the League of Nations. Sir Austen said, "Obligations which are universal are, in the nature of things, obligations which people are not very ready to fulfil."[33] Consequently, he believed that the British were unwilling to go to war with Japan in 1931 over its invasion of China (Manchukuo/Manchuria). With the benefit of hindsight, this was the effective beginning of World War II; when Hitler came to power in 1933 he could see that the UK was unwilling to use the League to stop aggression. But, ironically, as Sir Austen's biographer has argued, "popular support for [the League] remained strong" right up until World War II.[34] But public opinion (partly mobilized by Winston Churchill) had little impact on Sir Winston's half-brother, Neville, who refused to use the League to stop Hitler. (Sir Austen's political career was largely over by 1925 and he died in 1937).

Sir Austen's observation about "universal obligations" remains valid. Do citizens really care about what happens overseas? They may give some money to help disaster relief, but this is minute compared to what they spend on themselves. Do they really care about what their actions today may result in tomorrow? The consumer book is based partly on the reckless exploitation of the environment: what has posterity ever done for me?

What is to Be Done about Nationalism?

How is world federalism to be reconciled with nationalism? Nationalism keeps bouncing back. Balkan nationalism helped inflame nationalism elsewhere in Europe in 1914. The League was based on the assumption that a new sense of internationalism would smother nationalism and so reduce the causes of war. The dictators of the 1930 era, however, were able to mobilise nationalism in the interests of aggression.

A fresh cycle of internationalism emerged in 1945, supported by claims that the world was becoming 'global village' because of television. But in Eastern Europe (including the Balkans!), Africa, even developed countries like Canada (over Quebec) suddenly nationalism is again a potent force. Nationalism is as vibrant today as it was in 1914.

How Valid is the Nation?

But how valid is the concept of the 'nation'? 500 years ago most of today's 'nations' were pockets of land governed by tribal chieftains, barons or princes. (China and England are the world's longest lasting national identities). National boundaries are often accidents of history, not something fixed and permanent. Many of today's nations were created by foreigners—such as Africa's borders which are the byproduct of European colonialism.

Allen Dulles (later head of the US Central Intelligence Agency) was a US delegate at the 1919 World War I Peace Conference redrawing the maps of Eastern Europe. He was on the Czechoslovak Boundary Commission along with a fellow American and a Frenchman, none of them had any detailed knowledge of Eastern European history. But they meant well. They wanted to make the new nation of Czechoslovakia a geographically viable one and so, in addition to Bohemia and Moravia, they also threw in a considerable piece of German speaking territory known as the Sudetenland. The Czechs were in a minority there, but it seemed to Dulles and his two colleagues that the Sudetenland gave Bohemia and its capital Prague "a hinterland where any future German attack could be held."[35] He admitted later: "I sometimes wonder whether we weren't a little too free in drawing up the boundaries." Ironically it was over the Sudetenland that Adolf Hitler created the Munich crisis in 1938 (for Neville Chamberlain), which subsequently led to World War II. Yet people regard 'nations' as a fixed aspect of life. International politics, international law and many schemes for world federalism are all based on them.

How Valid is the US Experience of 1787?

A "miracle" reported in Catherine Drinker Bowen's book, *Miracle at Philadelphia*,[36] took place at Philadelphia in 1787. The 1776 Articles of Confederation had been (just about) sufficient to win the War of Independence but not enough to keep the new entity going once Independence was achieved in 1783. After 1783, there was chaos in the 13 states; there was not even agreement on the value of the currency. After four years of chaos, a Constitutional Convention was held in Philadelphia and, in the words of its chairman, George Washington, a "miracle" was created.

The Philadelphia story colours the thinking of US World Federalists. There is a tendency to view the UN Charter as the Articles of Confederation (a nonbinding treaty that is ignored when it is convenient to do so) and to dream for some global Constitutional Convention.[37]

But there is little evidence of governments wishing to attend a global Constitutional Convention. Governments pretend to be able to handle global problems—rather than wanting to surrender their power to an international body. Plagues and pollution are forcing them to do so, but just how bad is the earth to get before governments are obliged to attend a Constitutional Convention? Would the planet be in such a poor state that the new federal authority would be unable to redeem it?

Is there scope for another type of federation?

Most federalist proposals are based either on world federalism or a specific geographical region (notably Western Europe). Henry Usborne (a former British MP and founder in 1946 of the British Parliamentary Group for World Government) has proposed a "Minifed".[38]

"Minifed" would be a federal union of the nations of the middle-world (which are not super powers). It would enforce upon its members a basic law of weapons limitation: they would not go to war. But they would retain all their other rights. Minifed would possess an efficient federal police force, strong enough to enforce its laws upon all its citizens. And, if the union is to be disarmed in the war-making sense, it must allow the UN Security Council in particular, and the world's press in general to inspect and verify all its activities. Instead of proposing an elected federal legislature of the classical type, Minifed envisages something more like a 'Treaty of Multilateral Disarmament' in which the regulations that the 'High Authority' would be required to enforce, are all written in detail into the treaty itself.

The Minifed proposal is certainly an alternative to other world federalist proposals. But it runs into the old problem of obtaining support from governments to implement it. Despite all the political friends acquired from Mr. Usborne's half a century of distinguished public life, he has not been able to get one government to support this proposal (for which he has been campaigning for a decade).

Do Federations last forever?

No! Perhaps part of the hesitancy the UK feels about the EC is derived from its poor record on creating federations. UK-created federations have often failed; why should an EC succeed?

The Canadian and Australian federations have lasted (though there is now a problem over Quebec). But Malaysia (which lost Singapore), Pakistan (which lost Bangladesh), the Central African Federation (which was established in 1953 and dissolved in 1963), the USSR (1917-1991) and the United Arab Republic (1958-1961) are all examples of short-lived UK-created federations. The USA is more the exception, rather than the rule, in the creation of durable federations. Why should the EC last forever? What guarantee is there that a world federation would not descend into a civil war?

Conclusion

World Federalism is, then, an interesting vision but with immense problems of implementation. But if nationalism keeps bouncing back, so does the idea of world federalism. First, just because there are problems with implementing world federalism does not mean that the current world order is satisfactory. A glance at today's newspapers alone would indicate that the system of competing nations is ultimately self-destructive.

Second, federalism continues to attract attention, the conversion of the USSR into the Commonwealth of Independent States was done partly through a study of federalism, especially (ironically), examining the lessons of US federalism. Meanwhile, the world federalist movement is establishing branches in Eastern Europe.

Finally, recent events such as the ending of the Cold War, re-unification of Germany and revived interest in UN reform all demonstrate just how rapidly something considered politically unrealistic becomes practical and necessary. To conclude, in 1935 the British statesman Lord Lothian presented a challenge to peace groups and supporters of the League of Nations. If they were really serious about peace, he argued, they would have to support world federalism. Almost six decades later his advice is still a challenge to all people working for peace:

> The pacifist may lay down his life in order to refuse to kill his fellow men. He will have done little to end war. The League of Nations enthusiast may find himself in the name of collective security to take sanctions and go to war against an aggressor anywhere. He will have done little to end war. He may wage wise and better wars than national states have done, but he will wage war nonetheless and run the risk of turning every local conflict into a world war. The isolationist may hope to escape war. He will fail because every war now tends to become a world war and so imperil the security of his own state and compel him to take sides. There is no way of ending war and establishing peace and liberty on earth save by creating a true Federation (not a League) of Nations. That is the central truth which I want pacifists and realists alike to realise. Only then shall we begin to move, however slowly, towards our real goal.[39]

Notes

1. Max Habicht, *The Abolition of War* (Paris: Club Humaniste, 1987) p.38

2. For the story of the highest-ranking Soviet official ever to defect (at the time he was a UN Under-Secretary General) see: Arkady N. Shevchenko, *Breaking with Moscow,* (New York: Ballantine, 1985).

3. See Keith Suter, "The United Nations and the Gulf Conflict," *After the Gulf War: For Peace in the Middle East,* eds. St John Kettle and Stephanie Dowrick (Sydney: Pluto, 1991) pp. 65-66.

4. Richard Falk, "Questioning the UN Mandate in the Gulf," *International Foundation for Development Alternatives Newsletter* (Nyon, Switzerland) April, 1991, p.83.

5. Frank Barnaby, ed. *Building a More Democratic United Nations* (London: Frank Cass, 1991).

6. "The Bank That Got Away," *The Guardian* (London) July 8, 1991.

7. *The Stockholm Initiative on Global Security and Governance: Common Responsibility in the 1990s,* April 1991 (available from the Office of the Prime Minister, Stockholm, Sweden).

8. *Christopher Layton, One Europe: One World* (London: Federal Trust for Education and Research, 1986) pp. 5-6.

9. *Ibid.,* p.12.

10. George Lloyd and Edith Wynner, *Searchlight on Peace Plans: Choose Your Road to World Government* (New York: Dutton, 1944).

11. The best magazine reviewing current world government proposals is *World Peace News* (founded in 1970): 777 United Nations Plaza, New York, 10017.

12. See Keith Suter, *A New International Order: Proposals for Making a Better World* (Sydney: World Association of World Federalists (Australia), 1981).

13. Many North American based 'third approach' organisations are in the World Government Organisations

Coalition, 8965 Tolhurst Street, Montreal, Canada H2N 1W9.

14. Ron Glossop, *Confronting War: An Examination of Humanity's Most Pressing Problem* (Jefferson, North Carolina: McFarland, 1987) pp. 276-302.

15.The person who did most to initiate this approach was David Mitrany, see his *The Functional Theory of Politics* (London: Martin Robinson 1975).

16. Four key (and separate) organisations of world citizens are: The Association of World Citizens, 110 Sutter Street, San Francisco, CA., 94104; The World Association of World Citizens, 1012 14th Street, NW, Washington DC, 20005; Global Citizens' Association, Box 94, Stanstead, Quebec, Canada; International Registry of World Citizens, 66 Bd Vincent Auriol, 785013, Paris, France.

17. Robert Maynard Hutchins "Constitutional Foundations for World Order", *The Strategy of World Order Volume* 1, eds. Richard Falk and Saul Mendlovitz (New York: World Law Fund, 1966) pp 76-77.

18. Robert Cecil, *All the Way* (London: Macmillan, 1949) p. 190.

19. *Ibid,* p. 224.

20. John Colville, *The Fringes of Power* (London: Hodder and Stoughton, 1985) p. 313.

21. Winston Churchill, *The Second World War: Triumph and Tragedy* (London: Cassell, 1954) p. 606.

22. Leonard Mosley, *Dulles: A Biography of Eleanor, Allen and John Foster and Their Family Network* (London: Hodder & Stoughton, 1978) pp. 120, 150-154.

23. Roy Jenkins, *Nine Men of Power* (London: Hamish Hamilton, 1974) p. 23.

24. The successor to the UK League of Nations Union is the UN Association. A longstanding member of it is Mrs. Margaret Thatcher, who has paid on a personal cheque for her subscription. Ironically, Mrs. Thatcher as Prime Minister was probably the UK's prime minister most hostile to the UN!

25. Joseph Preston Baratta, "The International History of the World Federalist Movement," *Peace and Change* (October 1989) p. 374.

26. See Joseph Preston Baratta, *Strengthening the United Nations: A Bibliography on UN Reform and World Federalism* (Westport, Connecticut: Greenwood, 1987).

27. Clarence Streit, *Union Now* (New York: Harper, 1939).

28. Andrea Bosco, "Lothian, Curtis, Kimber and the Federal Union Movement (1938-40)," *Journal of Contemporary History* (London) Volume 23 (1988) pp. 465-502.

29. Emery Reves, *The Anatomy of Peace* (London: Penguin, 1947).

30. Grenville Clark and Louis B Sohn, *World Peace Through World Law* (1958; Cambridge: Harvard University Press, 1966).

31. The best European review of federalism (in English) is: *The Federalist Debate,* Via Porta Perusi 27100, Pavia, Italy. There is also a new publishing venture: The Lothian Foundation Press, 1 Whitehall Place, London, SW1A 2DA.

32. This number has recently increased (and continues to increase) due to the collapse of the Warsaw Pact and the disintegration of Yugoslavia (eds).

33. David Dutton, *Austen Chamberlain: Gentleman in Politics* (Bolton, England: Ross Anderson, 1985) p. 313.

34. *Ibid,* p. 345.

35. *Supra* note 22, p. 61.

36. (Boston: Little Brown, 1986).

37. Barbara M. Walker, ed., *The World Federalist Bicentennial Reader* (Washington DC: World Federalist Association, 1987).

38. Henry Usborne, *Prescription for Peace* (available from Minifed Promotion Group, Totterdown, The Parks, Eversham, England WR11 5JP).

39. Lord Lothian (Philip K.), *Pacifism is Not Enough* (Oxford University Press, 1935) p. 30.

The Struggle for the Soul of the 21st Century

William J. (Bill) Clinton
42nd President of the United States of America

Global interdependence is the truly dominant factor of our time. Our challenge is to make it a force for good, not evil.

We are engaged in the first great struggle for the soul of the twenty-first century. Osama bin Laden and the Taliban have one set of answers. America and all the nations rallying to our side have another. To prevail, we need to understand terrorism in the context of the modern world and do everything we can not only to prevent terrorism and protect ourselves, but to undermine the conditions and attitudes that bring foot soldiers and sympathizers to the terrorists' banner.

The fundamental fact of the twenty-first century is global interdependence. It is the single factor that runs through all the other forces that are shaping our lives and our time. We live in an interdependent world where distances have collapsed, walls have fallen, and information has become pervasive. The horrible events of September 11 were the dark side of global interdependence.

They could only have happened in a world without walls. Global interdependence has brought great bounty to Americans, but it has also created vast new opportunities for the forces of destruction to come into our lives.

What will be the dominant factor of the twenty-first century? Even before September 11, at least eight forces had emerged that might be called dominant. Four of them are positive, four negative:

Globalization. Clearly, optimists would say that globalization was the defining factor of the twentieth century and will continue to dominate the twenty-first. After all, during my time in the presidency, the global economy accounted for 22.5 million new American jobs and the lowest unemployment rates our country has known in decades. It lifted more people out of poverty in 20 years than were lifted throughout the rest of human history.

Information Age. Others would cite the Internet and the explosive growth of information technology as the dominant new factor. In 1993, there were only 50 sites on the World Wide Web. By 2001, there were 350 million. Today the Internet handles 30 times more messages every day than the postal service does, a nearly unimaginable communications leap.

Democracy and diversity. Politically minded people would argue that the defining feature of our time is the spread of democracy and the growth of diversity within democracies. At the beginning of this new century, more people lived

Bill Clinton, "The Struggle for the Soul of the 21st Century." Reprinted with the permission of *Blueprint: Ideas for a New Century*, Nov-Dec, 2001. Policy Journal of the Democratic Leadership Council.

under governments of their own choosing than ever before in human history. America had become more diverse than ever, and richer for it. The very diversity of the people who lost their lives in the World Trade Center and Pentagon attacks is testimony to that.

Science. Still others might say the crucial factor about our new century is scientific advance. The sequencing of the human genome has opened new vistas for health, medical care, and longevity. We will soon be able to generate genetic profiles of young babies before they even leave the maternity wards. Scientists are working on chips to replicate spinal nerves that may someday enable people with damaged spines to get up out of their wheelchairs and walk again. Physicists will soon understand the black holes in space. Other scientists are finding new forms of life in our deepest oceans.

Any one of those great developments could be labeled the dominant factor in the new century.

But there are negatives, too.

Environment. One of those is the fragility of our environment. Some say that environmental challenges will dominate the next 50 years and swamp all the positive developments. These include climate change, the water shortage, and the deterioration of the oceans. Nine of the hottest 11 years recorded since 1400 occurred in the last decade. If this trend continues, the Florida Everglades, several Pacific island nations, and 50 feet of Manhattan Island will disappear.

Health. Another problem, even before the anthrax attacks, was our public health crisis. Health systems are breaking down all over the world. Epidemics threaten the planet, beginning with AIDS. Today there are 36 million AIDS cases in the world; 22 million people have died already. There could be 100 million AIDS cases in the next four years. The countries with the fastest-growing infection rates are no longer in Africa, but in the former Soviet Union and in the Caribbean Basin. India and China are close behind.

Poverty. Some pessimists might even call globalization itself the most negative feature of our new century. Americans may be getting rich, but half of the world's population still lives on less than $2 per day. One billion live on less than $1 per day. And since it is predicted that the world's population will grow by 50 percent in the next five decades, mostly in the countries least able to handle it, we can predict that poverty may create a breeding ground for terrorists who prey on the dispossessed.

The new terror. There's yet another negative factor that one could cite as a defining feature of our time: the marriage of terrorism by weapons of mass destruction with the explosion of ancient racial, religious, and tribal hatreds. Seven hundred thousand people, all of them innocent, were killed in Rwanda by machete in only three months. Bosnia, a country of 6 million people, lost 250,000 to ethnic cleansing. In Kosovo, 1 million refugees were created overnight.

Finding the Common Denominator

Any one of these eight factors might be considered dominant today. The four positive ones are the global economy; the explosion of information technology; the advance of democracy and diversity; and the advances in science and medicine. The four negative ones are environmental crises; health crises; poverty; and the growth of terrorism based on ancient hatreds.

But, clearly, the single factor that all these things have in common is global interdependence. That's what makes it the truly dominant factor of our time. All the others are in fact manifestations of a breathtaking increase in global interdependence.

So the great question of the twenty-first century is whether global interdependence will be a good thing. Can we expand the forces and reach of positive interdependence and shrink the impact of negative interdependence? If so, how?

First, there is a war to fight. We must defend ourselves against the present terrorist threat and support the president and others who are leading the nation. President Bush has handled the crisis extremely well and deserves the full support of all of us, regardless of political party. It's important that we stay united behind him in the war effort and the search for terrorism.

It may give some comfort to Americans to know that during the 1990s, our government was able to track and thwart terrorists many times. We were able to foil planned attacks on the Holland Tunnel, on airplanes flying from Los Angeles to the Philippines, and on Pope John Paul II. During the millennium celebration, a dozen planned terrorist attacks were thwarted. In the wake of September 11, we have to harden our defenses. We must do a better job of using modern technology to track people who mean us harm. Second, while crushing today's terrorists, we must also think about tomorrow's. We must do more to reduce the potential pool of future terrorists. This is manifestly not about blaming America; I don't belong to that crowd. But it is about knowing our enemy, understanding the threats, and acting according to our interests and values. In many of the countries where terrorists recruit, the kids never go to school. They are indoctrinated, not educated. They know no jobs will be available when they come of age. America must continue to work to reduce global poverty and increase economic empowerment. We should support debt relief, economic development, microenterprise loans, and international education and health care programs. We can reduce the pool of potential terrorists by showing people that we will not deny them the basic opportunities we claim for ourselves.

Third, we must continue to promote democracy throughout the world. The most fertile recruitment grounds for terrorists in the world occur in countries that are not democracies. When people cannot exercise any responsibility for themselves, they are kept in a state of permanent collective immaturity. It is easy to convince them that our success is the cause of their problems.

In the Middle East, it's no accident that perhaps the most stable country is not the richest. Jordan's late King Hussein recognized several years ago that if he wished to preserve the monarchy as a relevant institution in modern times, he had to give the people of Jordan greater say over their own lives. Jordan began to have real elections where real parties could run, including militant Islamic fundamentalists who could get elected to parliament. This meant that people of highly divergent political views had to learn to reconcile their differences in a parliamentary setting to get things done so that the country could go forward. This was an important step. If frustrated people have no outlet for their fury at home and never have to take any responsibility for themselves, they never develop an awareness of how to solve their own problems, get the help they may well deserve, and make the most of it when it comes.

Finally, we have to continue our efforts to show people all over the world that America is not the enemy of any faith or any people. The last time the United States used military power was to protect the lives of poor Muslims in Bosnia and Kosovo. We led the world in the campaign for debt forgiveness. We have stood for a fair and a just peace in the Middle East, one which would have given the Palestinians their state, their equities in their religious sites, and a chance to make an economically successful partnership with the Israelis. America is not the enemy of the poor or of Islam in the Middle East or anywhere else in the world. Bin Laden and his allies think we are a feeble, greedy, selfish, materialistic people, weakened by our lack of a national religion and imposed social order. Americans have proved them wrong in every conceivable way.

In fact, the way Americans of every faith and national origin came together in mutual support after the terrorist attacks proves that we're still getting it right in America. The people who gathered outside the crisis center in lower Manhattan, holding up pictures of their missing loved ones, were from every corner of the earthhey included Indians, Pakistanis, Bangladeshis, Japanese, Chinese,

British, Germans, Mexicans, Chileans, and others. Together, they were a stunning rebuke to the terrorists' world-view.

I especially applaud President Bush for his visits to mosques and Islamic groups and his call for Americans to reach out to people who don't look like ourselves and to protect those who might come under attack just because they wear a turban or practice a certain religion. When I visited the site of the World Trade Center and the armory crisis center in New York, I met a man whose story touched me deeply. He was a huge man, a head taller than me, and he was standing there with big tears in his eyes. "Have you lost a family member?" I asked. "No, not in my family," he said. "I am an Egyptian Muslim-American. Believe it or not, I probably hate what happened more than you do. And I am so afraid that my fellow Americans will never trust me again." That, of course, is just what the terrorists want. We must not give it to them.

This great struggle is about more than what we do. It's about who we are, who they are, and what the twenty-first century is going to be about. We have radically different views about the nature of truth, the value of life, and the content of community.

In America, we believe we all do better when we work together. We believe everybody counts, everybody has a role to play, everybody deserves a chance, and no one has the whole truth. Our enemies believe a community is made up of people who are all the same, who have the same religion and practice it the same way, and whose beliefs are enforced by rigorous authority.

This doesn't mean that we are without problems. We still have hate crimes. We're still vulnerable to the things that we deplore. But our community has created a lot of good and given a lot of people everywhere a chance to live their dreams. Meanwhile, our enemies' kind of community has created 4.5 million refugees in the world. People are voting with their feet. The ultimate lesson for the interdependent world is that we can no longer deny to others what we claim for ourselves. It is not enough to stop bad things from happening. In the end, we must fulfill America's eternal mission to the world—to widen the circle of opportunity, deepen the meaning of freedom, strengthen the bonds of community, and build a better, richer, more peaceful world.

The Future of Peace

Alvin Toffler and Heidi Toffler
Authors of Future Shock *and* The Third Wave

About Peace-Forms

One of the most famous combat stories in all of Western culture is the biblical tale of David, the Israelite, and Goliath, the Philistine. In it, the underdog David slays his giant antagonist with the help of a high-tech weapon—the slingshot.

Their duel exemplifies one of the lifesaving methods introduced by primitive people to minimize the effects of violence. Instead of entire tribes or clans tearing one another to shreds, many primitive groups settled their disputes by staging single combat—the choice of one champion to represent each side.

In Homeric legend, Menelaus, for the Greeks, and Paris, for the Trojans, fight a similarly decisive duel. Anthropologists have found evidence of single combat among Tlingit tribesmen in southern Alaska, Maoris in New Zealand, and other communities from Brazil to Australia.

Another lifesaving social innovation among certain primitive tribes was exemption—for example, sparing women and children, or neutrals or messengers sent by the enemy. A third idea exempted not people but certain places (in the New Hebrides, we learn, warring tribes set aside an inviolable "path of peace"). A fourth set aside certain times when fighting must stop—time out, for example, for religious ceremonies to take place.

As First Wave civilization arose, it brought into being a characteristic peace-form to match its war-form—a new set of tools, that is, for preventing war or mitigating violence.

For instance, the First Wave revolution that raised war above the level of tribal skirmishes also changed the fate of captives. Until then, live prisoners were of no use to the victorious tribe, except perhaps as replacements for fallen warriors or women needed for reproduction. Once agriculture made it possible to create food surpluses, however, and prisoners could generate more food than required to keep themselves fed, it became more profitable to enslave than to eat or kill them. Horrible as slavery was, it was one of many First Wave innovations that had the effect of reducing the battlefield body count. It was part of the peace-form of First Wave civilization.

The same thing happened when the industrial revolution arrived: Second Wave civilization, too, created its own war-form—and a peace-form to match.

For example, industrialism, when it first arose in Western Europe, placed a heavy emphasis on contractual relationships. Contracts became a part of everyday business life. Political systems were typically justified in terms of a "social contract" between the leaders and the led. It was a natural step for Second Wave nations to sign contracts with one another. Treaties and agreements thus became key elements in the Second Wave peace-form. Some set ethical limits on the behavior of the soldier.

While "humanitarian ideas have existed for thousands of years of years...," states a report of the Department of Peace and Conflict Research at Uppsala University, in Sweden, "only in the 17th and 18th centuries did governments in Europe issue 'Articles of War' establishing certain normative standards for the treatment of belligerents."

These codes laid the basis for a patchwork of treaties, customs, and judicial decisions. In 1864 nations agreed to regard battlefield doctors and nurses as neutrals, and to care for wounded and sick troops irrespective of nationality. In 1868 nations ruled certain explosive bullets out of bounds.

In 1899 the First Peace Conference in the Hague discussed (but did not accept) a moratorium on arms. It did, however, impose restraints on weapons and methods of war, such as the use of projectiles dropped from balloons, and it set up a court for the arbitration of disputes among nations.

Since then the world has negotiated treaties, covenants, and other agreements to ban or restrict chemical and bacteriological weapons, to further humanize the treatment of POWs, to prevent genocide and limit nuclear weapons. But the industrial imprint on "peace-work" went much deeper than contractual arrangements.

The modernizers who built Second Wave societies...created completely new institutions to keep the peace. In doing so, not surprisingly, they focused their efforts on nations.

The League of Nations after World War I and the United Nations after World War II differed in many respects. But both were built around nations. Both the League and the UN recognized national sovereignty, the inviolability of each national border, and the right of independent nations (and only nations) to be fully represented in them.

The very concept of "national security," in whose name the vast military buildup of the past century took place, reflects an emphasis on peace and security at the level of nations, as distinct from peace within nations or peace at the level of religions, ethnic groups, or civilizations.

The League of Nations, hailed in its time as the hope of humanity, shriveled to insignificance in the 1930s and did little to prevent World War II. The United Nations, paralyzed by the Cold War for most of its existence, has now begun to come out of its coma at precisely at precisely the moment when its fundamental unit—the nation-state—is becoming less, not more, important in the global order. And, of course, the kind of war these institutions were primarily designed to prevent were Second Wave wars of mass destruction.

Thus, Second Wave civilization, exactly like First Wave civilization before it, invented a peace-form in step with its characteristic war-form....

The Next Peace-Form

Making peace cannot depend on the prior solution of all the world's moral, social and economic ills. Those who tell us that war is a result of poverty, injustice, corruption, overpopulation, and misery may be right, though the formula seems oversimple. But if these must be eliminated before peace is possible, then war prevention or limitation becomes a utopian exercise.

The problem is not how to promote peace in a perfect world but in the world that we actually have and the new one we are creating. In today's real world we have a new global system in the making and a brand-new way of making war, yet so far few corresponding innovations in the way we try to make peace....

Then there is the United Nations, on which so many millions around the world pin their earnest hopes for peace. To assume, as many do, that peace would be served if the UN had its own, permanent, all-purpose military arm, rather than ad hoc modular forces custom-tailored for each mission, is to apply anachronistic Second Wave thinking. The variety of wars requires a variety of anti-war forces, not a single omnipurpose unit.

It is, unfortunately, equally naive to assume that the UN, given its present structure, could douse the flames of war if only it had adequate financial support. There are too many things the UN cannot do, and could not even if it had all the money it wants.

The very fact that the UN consists exclusively of nation-states is a straitjacket in today's world. The fact that the UN may work with private nonprofit agencies in disaster zones, for example, or that it extends "consultative" status to nongovernmental organizations masks the larger reality: these NGOs or nonstate actors are still regarded by the UN as a nuisance at best, a rival source of power at worst. In Bosnia, according to National Public Radio, UN forces refused to protect a humanitarian aid convoy organized jointly by Catholic and Muslim relief organizations. The Blue Helmets explained that their mandate did not extend to the protection of private-agency efforts. Yet in a world in which nonnational forces exercise increasing power, peace cannot be made or kept without them. If the UN is to work effectively in the Bosnias or Cambodias of the future, it will have to share power at the highest level with these nongovernmental organizations, not to mention global corporations and other entities. They will have to participate fully in the formulation of UN strategies for peace.

If the UN dinosaur cannot transform itself from a Second Wave bureaucratic organization to a more flexible, Third Wave organization that represents nonstate actors along with nations, competing centers of global power will be organized—"para-UNs" made up of these various excluded groupings....

Peace, Inc.

By contrast, one might also imagine the creation, someday, of internationally chartered "Peace Corporations," each of which is assigned some region of the globe. Instead of being paid for waging war, its sole source of profit would come from war limitation in its region. Its "product" would be reduced casualty numbers as measured against some recent base-line period.

Special, internationally sanctioned rules could permit these companies wide military and moral latitude to conduct unorthodox peacekeeping operations—to do what it takes, ranging from legalized bribery to propaganda to limited military intervention, to the supply of peacemaking forces in the region. Private investors might be found to capitalize such firms if, say, the international community or regional groups agreed to pay them a fee for services plus bonanza profits in years when casualties decline. And if this doesn't work, perhaps there are other ways to seed the world with highly motivated peace-preserving institutions. Why not make peace pay off?

Such ideas sound zany, and maybe they are. But, good or bad, they lie outside the common frame of reference and they are used here only to illustrate that once we think outside the conventional Second Wave framework, we may find imaginative alternatives to paralysis.

Open Skies and Open Minds

What is glaringly absent today, even as armies begin thinking strategically about the use of knowledge, are coherent knowledge strategies for peace.

Rudimentary elements of such a strategy have been in place for a long time, although not necessarily seen in relationship to one another. For example, the concept of "transparency."

This idea—that the open availability of military information might reduce suspicion and give all sides' ample warning of threatening developments—lay behind the "Open Skies" proposal first made by President Dwight Eisenhower to Soviet premier Khrushchev at a summit meeting on July 21, 1955....

Instead of bewailing the cost of space-based surveillance technologies and sea and ground sensors, we need to see these as social expenditures vital to the preservation of peace. What are needed are agreements for widespread sharing of both the information they provide and of their cost. And where viable commercial markets are insufficient to spur their development, imaginative transnational forms, perhaps a mixture of public and private, can be created to accelerate development.

The exchange of data, information, and knowledge in a world increasingly marked by regional arms races is clearly a Third Wave tool for peace.

Tracking Technology

Not all arms races lead to war—as the biggest one in history, that between the United States and the Soviet Union—proves. Intention, rather than mere capability, matters. But runaway arms sales, erratic buildups, sudden infusions of weapons into a tense region, and surprise shifts in military balances all raise unpredictability and hence the risks of violence. In light of this, the United Nations has proposed creating an "arms register," which would officially track arms exports and imports by participating governments. Some American arms-control advocates have suggested that the United States cut off aid to countries that refuse to report arms transfers to the UN....

In trying to determine whether Iraq was building nuclear weapons, the IAEA and otherwise intelligent nuclear experts were deceived not only by Saddam Hussein and by lack of tracking data but by an embarrassingly stupid assumption. They dismissed the idea that Iraq might use calutron technology to separate Uranium 235 from Uranium 238, since far more efficient ways of making weapon-grade material were now available. But Saddam pursued his drive along multiple tracks, one of which employed precisely the technology commonly regarded as obsolete in the high-tech world....

If nothing else, the Iraqi experience should have proved that the best source of information about weapons proliferation often comes from inside. It was a defecting Iraqi who reportedly first tipped off the West to Saddam's use of calutrons.

If information increasingly lies at the heart of anti-war action, why not recognize its immense value? Why doesn't the Carnegie Foundation for International Peace, or some other foundation, or the United Nations, or, for that matter, the IAEA itself, announce to the entire world that it will give a bounty of $1 million to anyone who brings in credible evidence of nuclear smuggling or of weapons proliferation. The offer to make "instant millionaires" ought to bring in plenty of whistleblowers. A whistleblower prize might prove more effective, than some of the monitoring now supposedly protecting the world from atomic horror. If the IAEA isn't already buying such intelligence, why isn't it?

How to Start (and Not Stop) a War

European and American governments gave long lists of reasons why they would not risk either ground troops or pilots in defense of the suffering people of the Balkans, Bosnian, Croatian, and Serbian alike. But no government has yet explained why it failed to take completely safe, inexpensive measures to suffocate, or at least limit, that war.

Rather than some incomprehensible eruption of thousand-year-old hatreds among people who had lived together and intermarried in peace for generations, the war was deliberately ignited.

As Communist bosses in various parts of Yugoslavia became discredited in the post-Cold War era, they sought to hold on to power by switching from Marxist ideology to religio-tribalism. Irresponsible intellectuals, sucking up to power, provided them with theories of ethnic or religious superiority and plenty of hyper-emotional rhetorical ammunition. The media provided the artillery.

In the words of Milos Vasic, an editor of *Vreme*, the only independent magazine in Belgrade, the explosion of violence was "an artificial war, really, produced by television. All it took was a few years of fierce, reckless, chauvinist, intolerant, expansionist, warmongering propaganda to create enough hate to start the fighting. . . ."

Yet not one of the Western powers—the United States, France, Germany, Germany, England—let alone the rest of the world—gave financial or political aid to domestic opponents of a war whose bloodshed these same governments denounced daily. Nor did they or the United Nations devise anything approximating a media strategy for countering hate propaganda to moderate the violence. . . .

If U.S. psychological warfare experts in the Gulf could drop 29 million leaflets on the Iraqis, could a few thousand tiny, cheap radios, tuned to a "Peace Frequency" be dropped over the war zone so that combatants could hear something other than their own side's lies?

In the United States, Grace Aaron, cochair of the Los Angeles based Peace Action, begged for the United States Information Agency to "start offshore news broadcasting to enable citizens of all former Yugoslav republics to hear balanced, accurate news reports on the war," not just in the combat zones but in Belgrade and Zagreb as well.

Others urged Radio Free Europe or Radio Liberty to take on this task. Where was the BBC? Or CNN? Or from peace-loving Japan, where was NHK? Simple translations of their regular broadcasts could have strengthened those who wanted to end the fighting.

It took two years after the outbreak of the war for the United States finally to announce that it would launch a Radio Free Serbia—but only on short wave, it being lamely explained that medium-wave radio would need bigger transmitters near the target area. In 1920 the Marconi Company in England broadcast a concert by Dame Nellie Melba that was heard as far away as Greece, but in 1993 it was somehow impossible to reach Zagreb or Belgrade from, say, Italy or from the from the oceans nearby. There were, by this time, fully 500,000 satellite dishes in Serbia and Montenegro and another 40,000 in Croatia, but no international agency took advantage of them.

In the digital age, as we speed toward global, interactive multi-media, and giant media conglomerates race to tap future communications technologies, peace propaganda is still in the age of short-wave radio.

Clearly what is needed, not just by the United States but by the UN itself, if the UN is going to continue the pretense of peacekeeping, is a rapid reaction contingency broadcasting force that can go anywhere, set up, and beam news to those cut off from it—and not just on radio, but television as well.

According to Aaron, who has produced five cable access TV programs about war and peace for airing in the United States, Balkan groups are "unbelievably sophisticated about propaganda." She has of been given propaganda videotapes by all three sides in the war, some of the tapes clearly doctored. Some were from Serbian television programs picked up by satellite in the United States and taped for distribution by American pro-Serb activists.

Despite persecution by fanatics and governments in each of the warring regions, journalists, TV commentators, camera crews, and others struggled to speak out. Says Aaron, "The peace groups and the peace media could at least have been given some equipment—laptop computers, Sony Hi 8 cameras, video recorders, laser printers, modems, software, and subscriptions to outside world information services."

The point she makes is broader than the Balkans. "We're going to see an epidemic of regional conflicts. It will bankrupt the high-tech nations if they try to put all these down with military force. Why not use 'smart weapons' for peace?"

Why not, for example, a television miniseries that, instead of drug dealers, pimps, gang members, and corrupt cops, makes a hero out of a UN Blue Helmet—or out of the heroic individuals who stand against ethnic cleansing at the risk of their own lives?

Knowledge weapons alone, even including the use of the media, may never suffice to prevent war or to limit its spread. But the failure to develop systematic strategies for their use is inexcusable.

Transparency, surveillance, weapons monitoring, the use of information technology, intelligence, interdiction of communication services, propaganda, the transition from mass lethality to low-lethal or non-lethal weapons, training, and education are all elements of a peace-form for the future.

Although they often approach issues from diametrically opposed positions, there are times when the interests of armies and peace movements actually coincide. If there were moral and strategic reasons why the United States would have preferred stability to war in the Balkans, the military, in carrying out a knowledge strategy in pursuit of that objective, might have worked with American peace activists to support their beleaguered counterparts in the war zone. Peace organizers might have called on the military for ships on which to base broadcast transmitters or planes to help deliver communications equipment to Balkan moderates.

Indeed, there is a deeper level on which peace and peacekeeping depends on knowledge. In a paper prepared for a conference of U.S. military and intelligence experts, Dr. Elin Whitney-Smith, a director of Micro Information Systems, Inc., has argued, as we have in our own work over the years, that wide access to information and communication is a precondition for economic development. Since poverty is no friend of peace, she proposed using "our military and the power of the digital revolution to get as much information and information technology out to the rest of the world [as possible] so that people in underdeveloped nations can become part of the global community....

"In the interests of national security," she continued, "we need to use this knowledge to bring prosperity to the rest of the world before all its people become immigrants, refugees, or pensioners of the West."

Her words no doubt sounded utopian to some ears. But it will take all the Third Wave ideas we can get, along with the efforts of peace advocates and soldiers alike, for us to survive the upheavals that lie ahead as the global system trisects.

The old world order, built over the industrial centuries, already lies in fragments. We have argued throughout that the rise of a new wealth creation system and a new war-form demands a new peace-form. But unless that peace-form accurately reflects twenty-first century realities, it could prove to be not only irrelevant but dangerous.

To design a peace-form for the future, however, we need a preliminary map of the global system of the twenty-first century. That map will be traced in the few remaining pages of this book.

The Twenty-First Century Global System

Efforts to prevent, limit, end, or settle wars, whether by armies or peace activists or anyone else, require some understanding of the system within which the war is taking place. If our map of the system is obsolete, picturing it as it was yesterday, rather than as it is fast becoming, even the best strategies for peace can trigger the opposite. Twenty-first-century strategic thinking, therefore, must start with a map of the global system of tomorrow.

Blaming the End of the Cold War

Most attempts to map the system begin with the end of the Cold War, as though that were the main force changing it. The end of the Cold War is still having an impact on the global system. But it is the thesis of this book that the changes arising from the breakup of the Soviet Union are secondary, and that, in fact, the global system would be caught up in revolutionary upheaval today even if the Berlin Wall had not fallen and the Soviet Union still existed. Blaming all of today's upheavals on the end of the Cold War is a substitute for thought.

We are witnessing, instead, the sudden eruption of a new civilization on the planet, carrying with it a knowledge-intensive way of creating wealth that is trisecting and transforming the entire global system today. Everything in that system is now mutating, from its basic components...to the way they interrelate...to the speed of their interactions...to the interests over which countries contend...to the kinds of wars that may result and which need to be prevented.

The Rise of the Soft-edged State

Start with the components. For the past three centuries the basic unit of the world system has been the nation-state. But this building block of the global system is itself changing.

The startling fact is that of all the present members of the United Nations roughly a third are now threatened by significant rebel movements, dissidents, or governments-in-exile. From Myanmar, with its fleeing masses of Muslims and its armed Karen rebels, all the way to Mali, where the Tuareg tribe is demanding independence, from Azerbaijan to Zaire, existing states face prenational tribalism—even though the slogans may refer to nationhood.

In testifying before the U.S. Senate Foreign Relations Committee prior to taking office, Secretary of State Warren Christopher—surely no scaremonger—warned that "if we don't find some way that the different ethnic groups can live together in a country...we'll have 5,000 countries rather than the hundred-plus we now have." In Singapore we spoke with George Yao, the Cambridge—and Harvard-educated deputy prime minister. A thirty-seven-year-old brigadier general with a laser-like intellect, Yao imagines a future China composed of hundreds of Singapore-like city-states.

Many of today's states are going to splinter or transform, and resultant units may not be integrated nations at all, in the modern sense, but a variety of other entities from tribal federations to Third Wave city-states. The United Nations may find itself, in part, a club of ex-nations or *faux* nations—other kinds of political units merely dressed in the trappings of the nation.

But that is not the only change looming on the horizon. In the high-tech world, the economic basis of the nation is sliding out under it. There, as previously noted, national markets are becoming less important than local, regional, and global markets. On the production side, it becomes nearly impossible to tell what country a particular car or computer comes from, since its parts and software come from many different sources. The most dynamic sectors of the new economy are not national: they are either sub-, supra-, or transnational.

What's more, while poor, powerless, and "wannabe" groups demand "sovereignty," the most powerful and economically advanced states of all are losing theirs. Even the most powerful governments and their central banks can no longer control their own currency rates in a world awash in unregulated tidal waves of electronic money. They cannot even control their borders as they might have in the past. Even when they try to slam the door shut to imports or immigrants—both painfully hard to do—the high-tech states find themselves increasingly penetrated from outside by flows of money, terrorists, guns, drugs, culture, religion, pop music, ideology, information, and much else besides. In 1950, 25 million people traveled outside the borders of their own nation. By the late 1980s that number had soared to 325 million a year—plus an unknown and unknowable number of illegals. The old hard edges of the nation-state are eroding.

Thus the most basic components of the global system, as understood until now, are breaking down. There are more states in the system, and not all of them, despite their rhetoric, are nations....

Survival Needs

Third Wave "postnations" form the newest tier of the global system. Unlike agrarian states, they have no great need for additional territory. Unlike industrial states, they have no need for vast natural resources of their own. (Lacking these, Second Wave Japan seized Korea, Manchuria, and other resource-rich regions. Third Wave Japan, by contrast, has grown immeasurably richer without either colonies or raw materials of its own.)

The End of Equilibrium (Not History)

We live at a fantastic moment of human history. Hidden behind all the fashionable gloom today are several tremendously positive and humanizing changes on the planet. The spread of the Third Wave economy has galvanized all of the Asia Pacific region, introducing trade and strategic tensions, but at the same time opening the possibility of rapidly raising a billion human beings out of the pit of poverty. Massive increases in global population occurred between 1968 and 1990, but despite doomsday forecasts, per capita food supplies in the world have actually increased faster, according to the World Food Organization, and the number of chronically undernourished people has fallen by 16 percent.

Using Third Wave technologies that are less energy intensive and less polluting we can now begin to clean up the ecological havoc wrought by Second Wave industrial methods in the age of mass production. Work, until now brutalizing and mind-destroying for most of those lucky enough to hold a job, can be transformed into something fulfilling and mind-enhancing. The digital revolution that is helping to fuel the Third Wave has within it the potential for educating billions.

And despite the warnings throughout these pages about the danger of war, civil outbreaks, and even nuclear attacks, the good news is that, even though some 50,000-60,000 nuclear warheads have been produced since Hiroshima and Nagasaki, and even though there have been underground blasts and nuclear accidents, not one of those thousands of bombs has been detonated in anger. Some human survival instinct has repeatedly stayed the finger that might have pushed the button.

But to survive at the dawn of the twenty-first century will take more than instinct. For all of us, civilians and soldiers alike, it will take a profound understanding of the revolutionary new linkage between knowledge, wealth, and war. These pages will have served their purpose if they have illuminated that relationship. To make that happen, we have tried to sketch a new theory of war and anti-war. We will be gratified if we have brought one new insight to awareness or helped explode one obsolete idea that stands in the way of a more peaceful world.

We believe that the promise of the twenty-first century will swiftly evaporate if we continue using the intellectual weapons of yesterday. It will vanish even faster if we ever forget, even for a moment, those sobering words of Leon Trotsky's, quoted at the beginning of this book: "You may not be interested in war, but war is interested in you."

Sketch for Peace, by Pablo Picasso

Epilogue

Coming to Terms:

From the Dream of Peace to an Attainable Truce

Undoubtedly those who call war the primordial and natural state are right. Insofar as man is an animal, he lives by struggle, he lives at the expense of others, whom he fears and hates. Life then is war.

"Peace" is much harder to define. Peace is neither an original paradisiacal state nor a form of coexistence by mutual consent. Peace is something we do not know; we can only sense it and search for it. Peace is an ideal. It is infinitely complex, unstable and fragile-a breath can destroy it. True peace is more difficult and unusual than any other ethical or intellectual achievement…

—Hermann Hesse (1877-1962)

Coming To Terms: From the Dream of Peace to an Attainable Truce?

Nicholas N. Kittrie
American University, Washington College of Law

Those "champions of peace" meriting the Nobel Peace Prize envisioned and funded by Alfred Nobel over a century ago, were to be, according to his vision, those who contributed most significantly to enhancing the "fraternity between nations." In Nobel's late nineteenth century world, in which nationalism flourished, one could reasonably believe that if the great powers would only recognize their familial affinity, the future of world peace would be assured. For if the major powers were to conduct themselves in a fraternal manner, their smaller siblings would obviously follow suit —or so the argument went.

Yet as one examines the concluding years of the twentieth century and observes the unfolding of the twenty-first century's short but jugged history, it becomes abundantly clear that it is domestic, communal or intranational wars and violence by non-state actors, rather than international conflicts between states, which have occupied the center stage of the escalating global unrest and insecurity. Increasingly, the conflicts posing the greatest threat to the well-being, and most likely, to the very survival of world order have been between sub-national communities or groups and their perceived enemies —be they individuals, other groups, states, or the world community. What must urgently be pursued and cultivated is therefore not so much the "fraternity between nations" but the fraternity between humans, be they identified as nations, tribes, clans, groups, minorities or individuals.

The New Wars of the Twentieth Century: Non-State Belligerency

Today, more than a century after Nobel, most pundits of war and peace observing the increasingly precarious worldwide balance between order and chaos, seem still to venture forth on a specious trail. For while most of these scholars and practitioners in the United States and throughout the world continue to speculate about where the international conflicts of this and the next decade are likely to erupt, and between which nations,[1] it is almost certain that the most serious oncoming world crises will be domestic or intra-national.

More countries than ever before are already being torn asunder by internal strife and communal violence. Over one-third of the world community's member states, more than 60 out of over 180 worldwide, are currently involved in wrenching and divisive domestic contests: between citizens, communities, citizens or communities and their governments, and between governments and their own populations.

While contemporary conflicts are usually the

result of long-festering grievances, often they are provoked by new complaints, deprivations or changing aspirations. Those mounting the barricades in the current struggles usually invoke such universal slogans as "justice," "liberty;" "equality" or "self-determination." But many are urged on by different or narrower orthodoxies: religious fundamentalisms, historical entitlements, divine rights, scriptural commandments, tribalism, ethnicism, racism, totalitarianism, Marxism-Maoism, or some other conviction, ideology, belief or brand of absolutism. Whatever the rationale claimed by the protagonists, the true common denominator of the struggle is the ongoing conflict between those who possess and exercise political, military, economic, or some other power and those who challenge the legitimacy of the existing order.

Colonialism's poet laureate, Rudyard Kipling, wryly observed at the conclusion of the nineteenth century that "All the people like us are We. And everyone else is They." Throughout history the primeval struggle of "We" and "They" has raged between indigenous populations and later arrivals, kings and their subjects, empires and their vanquished, the free and the enslaved, masters and servants, the well-endowed and the disenfranchised, majorities and minorities, oppressors and the oppressed, the imposers of duties and the claimers of rights. And despite or possibly because of the twentieth century's support for national and individual self-determination and human rights, the historical struggle has greatly escalated.

Over a decade ago, political writer Stephen S. Rosenfeld reported that the United Nations Security Council has been spending most of its time, not on international belligerence but on internal conflicts and civil wars. Internal strife, whether sparked by lone and disgruntled crusaders or by the uneasiness of restless masses, whether spontaneously erupting or carefully planned, whether expressed through lawful protest and civil disobedience or through indiscriminate violence and terror, whether practiced by suicide-bombers or by governmental abuse and targeted assassinations, has sent shudders through the global political environment.

It might seem at times that those who oppose the order sought to be maintained by authority, are winning. The modern nation-state, long believed to be Western society's cornerstone of political order and stability, today finds itself increasingly beleaguered by the resurgence of sectarianism and the emergence of strong centrifugal forces. Political commentator Pranay Gupte noted the overall decline in the cohesive power of the modern state. Not only in the young postcolonial countries of Asia and Africa, but also in many long-established states, says Gupta, one is "confronted with the depressing reality" that in multiethnic and multicultural countries, the most riveting issues and loyalties "are often and increasingly communal and tribal, not national." Pulitzer Prize-winning reporter Thomas L. Friedman similarly observed a few years back the increasing incidence of "challenges to the sovereignty and sanctity of nation-states from within—from ethnic, tribal and religious groups dissatisfied with the shape or content of their nations and ready to use any sort of violence to bring about change." So prevalent has intra-national, as opposed to international, dissidence become that some commentators have provocatively inquired whether we must "say goodbye to the nation-state."

Several observers of this modern centrifugal phenomenon have bemoaned what they described as a return to tribalism and to other archaic forms of social organization. But few have offered meaningful explanations for what appears to be a worldwide malady. It is our thesis that the escalating intra-state conflicts, involving growing numbers of non-state actors, are the result of growing pluralism (simply put, communal diversity) within what might have been, or had seemed to be, homogeneous and therefore peaceful entities. This pluralism is now accompanied by greater and often more militant expectations of empowerment by the different components which make-up nation-states, federations and other broadly encompassing political entities. Centrifugal forces are now constantly being unleashed through the growing assertiveness of subnational minorities or other groups, be they the Tutsi in Rwanda, the Kurds in Iraq, the Tamil in Sri Lanka, indigenous tribes in Latin America, women in Saudi Arabia, North African immigrants in France, or reform-minded students or practitioners in China.

The growing pluralistic awareness and assertiveness, some will argue, are part of a much belated and spiraling reaction to the promises of self-determination initially advanced by the United States at the end of World War I. The assertiveness might be also an echo to the "rights" movements (ranging from the rights of citizens to the rights of immigrants, from the rights of women and children to the rights of the handicapped) that have typified post-World War II America and have increasingly affected the rest of the world. Pluralistic awareness and confrontations are being further fanned worldwide by a vigorous and aggressive contemporary media. But for good or for bad, expanding pluralistic and centrifugal realities are with us, much like the opposite forces of globalization, will continue exerting increasing pressures upon existing power structures and public order.

The diversity and divisiveness of populations, is the norm in almost all human communities throughout today's world. Tribal, religious, ethnic and linguistic rivalries all exemplify pluralistic societies. And not all societies or regimes have handled this diversity and pluralism with aplomb.

Civil and communal warfare on a scale affecting the international community is indeed not new. In *A Study of War* (1965), Quincy Wright, one of America's foremost students of warfare, listed over 308 wars, which took place worldwide in the period from 1480 to 1965. These he divided into three categories: international, imperial and civil. As "international" he classified the wars conducted between states of similar category or structure; as "imperial" the military encounters between members of different civilizations; and as "civil" the conflicts between governments and insurgent domestic groups. Of his total 308 recorded wars, Wright classified 152 as international, 70 as imperial or colonial and 68 as civil.

International wars varied greatly in magnitude, they ranged from relatively minor episodes involving two or more small countries and lasting for brief periods of time, to such monumental confrontations as the Thirty Year's War (1618-48), the Seven Years War (1756-63), the Napoleonic wars (1798-1814), and World War I and II, resulting in millions of casualties. Civil wars were at times even more destructive and costly in life. They included the French Huguenot wars of the 16th century, the British Great War of the seventeenth century, the American Civil War in the nineteenth century, and the Russian revolution as well as the Cambodian Pot Pol massacre of the twentieth century. Imperial or colonial wars, according to Wright, were historically the least costly in terms of human life because of the great disparities in military power between the warring parties.

In the twentieth century, however, colonial wars, particularly those in Algeria and the Belgian Congo, accounted for some of the most bloody of human conflicts. It is also significant that of the 15 international wars of the modern era, one third were either in consequence of or the cause for contemporaneous civil wars.

In his classical study of peace and war in Europe, spanning the fifth century B.C. to the twentieth century A.D., Pitirim Sorokin reported that during the twenty-five hundred years, the European community enjoyed an average of not more than four peaceful years for each year of violent conflict. Ted Robert Gurr disclosed further that during the past two centuries, ten of the thirteen most deadly world conflicts were not international but rather rebellions and domestic wars. Violent internal conflicts were reported in 114 out of the 121 countries surveyed in the period between 1961 and 1968. "Violent attempts to overthrow governments have been more common than national elections," Gurr concluded.

Of particular concern to the broader future of peace, in contradistinction to Alfred Nobel's primary concern for peace among nations, has been therefore not only the traditional civil wars but also another newly evolving and deadly class of domestic warfare—"democide." Democide, a term coined by Professor R. J. Rummel, consists of massacres committed by governments against their own, rather than foreign populations. In his thoroughly documented compilation.[2] Rummel lists over 130 million victims of domestic massacres carried out by governments in some 15 American, African, Asian and European countries between 1900 and 1987.

Causes of and Cures for Domestic Warfare

The domestic battles raging throughout the world are mostly between those who proclaim their individual or communal rights to greater autonomy and those who profess to speak for the state or for other established institutions of authority. This growing challenge to authority—and the escalating conflict between states and non-state actors—is evident everywhere. Yet to date it has failed to receive adequate scrutiny by most all fields of social science, religious, and military analysis.

Nearly a century and a half ago, a number of prominent philosophers, political scientists and sociologists, beginning with Karl Marx (1818-83) and Friedrich Nietzsche (1844-1900) voiced their concern over the growing challenges facing the state and its political legitimacy in the age of modernity. Legitimacy, pointed out Italian political philosopher Gaetano Mosca in 1896, is sought by ruling classes through their creation and marketing of a "political formula," a metaphysical or ideological doctrine justifying the existence and exercise of power by the rulers as the logical consequence of the people's beliefs. Quite recently, the United States Supreme Court, noted that "the Court's power lies in its legitimacy, a product of substance and perception that shows itself in the people's acceptance of the judiciary as fit to determine what the Nation's law means and to declare its demands."

A rich variety of doctrines—some proclaiming the "divine rights" of princes and kings, others putting forth the entitlements of patrimony or seniority, others claiming the duties due to the nobility and gentry, still others professing the obligations imposed by "nationalism," the "social contract," or "majoritarianism"—have long supplied the requisite political formulas to legitimate authority. Classifying legitimating doctrines, German sociologist Max Weber (1864-1920) emphasized three categories: the "patrimonial," the "rational-bureaucratic," and the "charismatic." The first legitimate authority through resort to an "eternal yesterday"—ancient scriptures or traditions endowing the priest, patriarch or prince with the right of domination. The second category seeks legitimation in legal, rational, and bureaucratic sources, such as the binding effect of existing laws and political institutions. The third and charismatic category, describes a legitimation that is founded on the extraordinary and personal gifts possessed by a leader, and the people's devotion to the leader's "revelation and heroism."

Political and philosophical literature has advanced also other formulas of legitimation. But regardless of the specific categories or formulas advanced or accepted by various nations and states in the modern era, a growing number of political philosophers have been arguing that the overall legitimacy of the state's authority has been declining. Karl Marx and Friedrich Nietzsche have been two of the earliest discussants of the decline of the modern state's legitimacy. Marx, writing in 1844, attributed legitimacy's decline to the particular structure and defects of modern capitalism, which alienate man from society and authority. Nietzsche, speaking in 1888, saw legitimacy's major problem in the "advent of nihilism."

Later, other political analysts and social critics attributed the crisis of the modern state's legitimacy to such diverse causes as over-bureaucratization and the proliferation of rules (which in the end foster a spirit of evasion), the erosion of traditionalism, the decline of general public morality and civil culture, and the expansion of the cult of individualism. Martin Lipset urged that "if at any time the status of the major conservative groups is threatened, or if access to politics is denied to emerging groups at crucial periods, the system's legitimacy will . . . [be put] in question."

Inadequately answered by critics, however, has been the question of whether the contemporary decline of legitimacy is a unique or recurring phenomenon in world history. Lipset claimed some two decades ago that the crises are a "recent historical phenomenon." Adding to Marx's and Nietzsche's warnings, Lipset suggested that crises of legitimacy, and the resultant civil disorder and violence, are in great part the outcome of growing and "sharp cleavages among groups which are able, because of mass communication, to organize around different values [and structures] than those previously considered to be the only acceptable ones." Others have complained generally about the demise of mythology and the unprecedented emphasis on the primacy of individualism—combining to undercut support for communal institutions.

Robert Kaplan, a noted contemporary journalist and commentator, has attributed the escalating worldwide chaos to a variety of material causes, including over-population, environmental abuses, and nationalistic aberrations. Meriting more thorough discussion is Samuel Huntington's contradictory claim[3] that material or economic causes are not the fundamental sources of the existing or widely expected future strife. In insisting further that the source of conflict in the new age will not be primarily ideological, but rather "culturally" and "civilizationally" based, Huntington failed to recognize the particular sociopsychological force of the concept of "legitimacy" and its unique role not only in the conflict between authority and autonomy but also in defining the very essence of culture and civilization.

In making civilizational differences the primary culprits of future strife, Huntington has not explained, however, why differing civilizations might find themselves in either more or less conflicting situations. Possibly, he wants us to deduce from his skeletal thesis that it is inherent in the nature of civilizations to expand or to otherwise seek to convert all others by all available means, whether pacific or militant. Assuming that this might be Huntington's premise, we must once more address ourselves to the substantive rather than the superficial or cosmetic issues, which divide civilizations. These issues, one could suggest, might possibly go back to the primary question of how a legitimacy of authority is perceived in different civilizations. The most critical cultural or civilizational conflicts in contemporary affairs could thus be possibly distilled into the choice between *eternal*, *natural*, or *scriptural* sources of legitimacy, and, on the other hand, the opposite articulation of legitimacy as deriving from a *democratic*, *consensual*, and *ever-changing* social contract.

Searching for the Lodestar: The Fraternity of Humans

Although the concluding decade of the twentieth century has seen the generally unexpected demise of communist totalitarianism—a monumental event contributing to a worldwide shift toward more democratic governance—the historical patterns of international and domestic conflict and warfare have not been abated. The conclusion of the Cold War has not only created new power and legitimacy vacuums but has also failed to do away with or modify other domestic and international rivalries and dissatisfactions. Speaking of the future, Robert S. McNamara, former United States secretary of defense and World Bank president, warned:

> I'm not so naïve as to believe this post-cold-war world would be without conflict. There have been 125 wars leading to 40 million deaths, largely in the third world, after World War II and before the Gulf War. These were not a function of ideological differences between East and West. They were a function of the age-old causes of war—boundary disputes, economic conflicts, ethnic tensions.

The current demands of nations, peoples, groups, and individuals around the world for the substance as well as the trappings of justice and self-rule (including the safeguard and expectations inherent in the concepts of "identity," "security," "nondiscrimination," and "prosperity") are not materially different, it should be noted, from the claims for greater justice made not long ago in America's midst by Native Americans or African Americans. Often, the new demands, in what German philosopher G.W.F. Hegel (1770-1831) has described as the "struggle for recognition," differ only in the degree or intensity from the claimants' hopes in America's domestic struggles.

Many of the lesser-developed nations of the world have indeed yet to pass through some of the birth pangs of freedom and justice experienced earlier by the countries of the Western world. Some of the emerging nations are likely today and tomorrow to be repeating England's seventeenth- and eighteenth-century civil and political rebellions or the especially agonizing struggle of brother against brother that America had to endure on its way toward greater national unity, political liberty, and socioeconomic progress. The news accounts emanating from the countries of Central America, Africa, and Southeast Asia harken back to earlier histories of the European and North American continents—replete with tribal, caste, ethnic, and economic conflicts, a seemingly endless series of coups, assassinations, civil wars, and even less fathomable outbursts of hate and violence.

Throughout the world, the Age of Revolution is not yet over. "Liberty," the foremost of America's and France's triple revolutionary goals, still remains greatly unattained by many countries and their people. The right to "property," articulated in the United States Constitution, has only recently been permitted to emerge in the former socialist camp. The goals of equality and fraternity have not even been generally defined, much less implemented, in most contemporary states. Not until the post-Civil War adoption of the Fourteenth Amendment to its Constitution did America articulate a right to equality, and both the French and Soviet revolutionary experiences regarding the implementation of equality and fraternity have been grim at best. Only now, in the aftermath of Leninism-Marxism's recent demise, might new explorations of less totalitarian formulations of socioeconomic justice be undertaken in a world increasingly proclaiming democracy. Still totally unexplored and awaiting definition and reasonable limitations is the American Declaration of Independence's guarantee of the "pursuit of happiness."

How long will the Age of Revolution continue through the world? Despite modern nationalism's assertion of self-rule as a central doctrine, it is significant that this principle was not implemented except in a few European and other select nations until the end of the nineteenth century. Most peoples had to wait for the end of the First, and more commonly the Second World War before the call for independence was sounded for them.

At the conclusion of the First World War it seemed that a new era had dawned on humanity. The victorious Allies, responding to America's President Woodrow Wilson's Fourteen Points, had agreed on the new right to self-determination, and consequently the world map was to be redrawn in an effort to realize this promise. The post-World War I promises of self-determination made by the victorious Allied nations were, however, more vigorously reiterated after the surrender of the German, Italian, and Japanese Axis at the end of World War II. In its Charter, the new United Nations asserted a commitment to "the principle of equal rights and self-determination of peoples."

The post-World War II surge toward the self-determination of peoples was expected to satisfy the yearnings of the remaining millions of non-self-governing colonial populations. The global map was to be redrawn once more—this time, to some extent, by the colonized and indigenous peoples themselves. However, the global struggle for political liberty and social justice was not about to subside. New political unrest and rebellion emerged as grievances produced by domestic oppressions and injustice (contrasting with the former complaints against foreign abuses of power) were aired within the new and old nations of Africa, Asia, and Latin America. Internal struggles, in quest of political hegemony, for greater power-sharing, and particularly for socioeconomic justice, continued to be fought within the very same countries that not too long ago had won their independence from their colonial masters.

In the resulting intranational conflicts, the Katangans were defeated in their bid for secession from the Congo, and the Biafrans lost a bloody war against Nigeria. The people of Bangladesh and of East Timor, on the other hand, won their war for independence from Pakistan and Indonesia, respectively. The non-Russian and mostly Muslim republics on the southern rim of the former Soviet Union gained their secession with surprisingly few efforts. The Slovaks similarly attained their separation from the former Czechoslovak Republic through relatively peaceful means, but Yugoslavia's Slovenes, Croats, Bosnians, and Macedonians found their separations more difficult and at times particularly violent.

To the surprise of many, three-quarters of the Scots questioned not long ago told public opinion pollsters that they wanted either greater autonomy or total independence from England. "Whoever in the past would have dreamed of Breton nationalism or a Scottish national party?" responded Sir Isaiah Berlin. He then proceeded to point out with alarm the prospect of "many small nations filled with national pride and hatred and jealousies, egged on by demagogues, marching against each other as they did in the Balkans around 1912."

Historian John Lukacs similarly raised the melancholy prospects of a proliferation of small states or statelets, perhaps "a bubbling new Levantine world, a subcivilization ruled by brigands and traders—another reversion to something that existed before the Modern Age." Joining in the lamentations was Thomas L. Hughes, Chairman of the Carnegie Endowment for International Peace: "Subnational tensions are reviving, sometimes in primitive forms.... There is something primordial about all this worldwide provincialism, chauvinism, separatism, ethnicism, and fundamentalism."

Nearly a century and a half ago the pitfalls of political fragmentation were explained by Britain's Lord Acton (1934-1908). Responding to the militant advocacy of nationalism and its fierce pursuit in Europe, Lord Acton, a prominent leader of the era of imperialism, spoke of the benefits of multiethnic and multinational governance as contrasted with the hazards of the homogeneous nation-state. A state composed of a single people, Acton feared, "overrules the rights and wishes of the inhabitants, absorbing their divergent interests in a fictitious unity; sacrifices their several inclinations and duties to the higher claim of nationality, and crushes all natural rights and all established liberties for the purpose of vindicating itself." The combination of different national and ethnic communities under the same sovereignty, argued Lord Acton, guards, on the contrary "against the servility which flourishes under the shadow of a single authority, by balancing interests, multiplying associations, and giving to the subject the restraint and support of a combined opinion.... Liberty provokes diversity, and diversity preserves liberty."

What Acton called for in 1862 is possibly taking place in these early years of the twenty-first century. Although the splintering of the old empires and cumbersome nation-states has been escalating, the new states which have emerged have all eagerly sought to be admitted into such supra-national confederations and alliances as the European Community and NATO. Even the long restless African nations have recently proclaimed their desire to create a truly continental unity for the pursuit of peace and political and economic justice. A growing likelihood appears that in the memberships of these newly created comprehensive entities and international or regional aggregates, compliance with international standards of conduct and human rights will find a fertile ground.

There is little doubt that the current worldwide suspicion of and dissatisfaction with such dated and tired political formulas as "divine rights," "scriptural entitlement," "holy war," "nation-state," "national sovereignty," and even the "social compact," "democracy," and "majority rule" is what in part fuels the ongoing challenge to authority and accounts for much of the political turmoil and strife. In many of these places, the disingenuousness particularly of the doctrines of "nation-state" and "national sovereignty" and even of "justice" is what has recently torn the countries apart. In other parts of the world, even an approximation of a nation-state is impossible. With hundreds of tribes and a multiplicity of castes, how many countries in Africa or Asia could pass the requisite tests for "minority," "peoplehood" or "nationhood"?

There is no magical cure for the inherent inconsistencies that riddle the ailing notions of "democracy," "nations," "nation-state," "people," "minorities," and "sovereignty." Moreover, in the new and intensively interdependent world, the allegedly "sovereign" state finds itself less and less immune to challenges either from within or without. In many instances, contemporary states may be too large to accommodate the diverse internal interests of the disparate communities of which they are comprised. At the same time they may be too small to withstand the external pressures—for greater justice for all those within it—coming from the community of nations and from the world media. The continued functioning of history's simplistic articulations of legitimating formulas for political authority cannot be assured. These formulas and their accompanying principles require theoretical and practical rehabilitation in order to shore up their credibility in a world that insists on new foundations of legitimacy for institutions that for very long had been accepted on faith.

Giving Peace a Chance: Necessary Prescriptions and Their Side-Effects

The conclusion of the twentieth century and the unfolding of the twenty-first have made it eminently clear that the peace hopes at the conclusion of the Cold War, so unforgettably characterized by Fukuyama's proclamation of the End of History,[4] would not be realized. The expectation that the demise of the Soviet Union and the debunking of Marxist-Stalinist Communism would bring an end not only to the seventy-year ideological war between socialism and capitalism but also to other domestic and global dialectical confrontations and conflicts did not materialize. But in the face of newly emerging religious violence, ethnic cleansings, boundary wars and terrorist attacks, mostly internal and local yet violent enough to produce severe international repercussions, an understanding of the events that have been taking place in the post-End of History era is essential before the means for dealing with them might be determined.

Some commentators attribute the growing and perilous intra-national and communal resort to violence (in the alleged pursuit of security, prosperity, identify or autonomy) to the unreasonable expectations introduced into the world community by the misguided idealism of America's World War I president, Woodrow Wilson and others who followed him. *New York Times* writer David Binder reported that at the height of that world war, when President Wilson urged that "self-determination for Europe's myriad ethnic minorities...would provide stability in the post-war environment," his secretary of state, Robert Lansing, "expressed his grave concern [and belief] that the idea might make the world more dangerous." Lansing allegedly argued that self-determination would breed discontent, disorder, and rebellion. "The phrase is simply loaded with dynamite. It will raise hopes which can never be realized. It will, I fear, cost thousands of lives. What a calamity that the phrase was ever uttered! What misery it will cause!" Lansing was reported to have claimed.

Several analysts, as we previously noted, have attributed the growing incidence of violence to the decline of the nation-state as a cohesive and unifying institution in an increasingly pluralistic and global era. Others have viewed the splintering up of what had long appeared to be unified nations and communities as a form of atavism. Well-seasoned historians warned against the prospects of "new feudalism" and "new barbaric chieftains." Frequently cited was Samuel Huntington's premise, which found the seeds of conflict to be not ideological, but sprouting particularly in the fault-line between differing and clashing civilizations. Other commentators, drawing upon Marx and Nietzsche, have sought the source of the new militance in modern man's growing alienation and in the emerging popular discontent with existing institutions of authority, be they political, economic, religious, or social. Continuing in this general vein, this author's *The War Against Authority*[5] perceived domestic and often international conflicts as primarily contests between communities, cultures, or regimes claiming adherence to differing and conflicting types of authority. *The War* dwells particularly on the growing tensions between those who attribute the legitimacy of their governance to a communal "social contract," and the others who claim to rely on authority derived from some divine, scriptural or otherwise immutable source. To further advance the hypothesis of the contemporary conflict as primarily a contest between or among differing doctrines of authority and legitimacy, *The War* derives its support also from the conclusion of Roberto Michels, the early twentieth century's Italian political scientist, that "perhaps history is nothing but a struggle between different concepts of authority or between different groups personifying different kinds and degrees of authority."

It is upon the foundations supplied by the account of the differing hypotheses on the background and nature of the escalating violence and warfare, our previous review of the causes of war and the failed twentieth century's, efforts in the pursuit of peace, and, finally, the assessment of the escalation of non-state belligerency in the twenty-first century, that this epilogue seeks to build its factual and policy conclusions and finally, its prescriptive proposals. In light of the growing intra-national character of the contemporary conflicts, it is evident that any comprehensive formula for the prevention, regulation, or resolution of conflicts and wars must be applicable to and effective not only with *nations*, which have been so much emphasized by Alfred Nobel, but particularly also with regard to the growing category of not-state belligerents. These latter belligerents are usually not parties to international treaties or conventions. Not being members of the community of nations and claiming to be ideologically, ethnically, religiously, or otherwise altruistically motivated, the non-state actors usually deny owing any duty to or being required to adhere to any international standards, customs or laws of war. If we are to be successful in our quest for the advancement of global peace, then not only nation-states but also groups or individuals such as a Saudi Arabian bin Laden, Chechniyan warriors, Palestinian and Sri Lankan rebels, Basque, Irish and Kurdish revolutionaries must be satisfied to comply with, or be compelled to be bound by, the rights as well as duties which are recognized and required by the institutions of the world community.

Addressing International Warfare

For the construction of an effective prescriptive program for peace, it is essential that we distinguish again between wars involving state belligerents and conflicts involving on one or both sides, non-state actors. In the first group one would include such contemporary or recent examples as the Ethiopian-Eritrean, the Indian-Pakistani, and the Iraqi-Kuwaiti military campaigns. The second class of conflicts might be exemplified by Congo's domestic wars, the Tamil uprising in Sri Lanka, the Cambodian democide, and the Tutsi-Hutu tribal wars in Rwanda.

Whether one subscribes to Huntington's premise of civilizational clashes, to the hypothesis that the escalating conflicts are primarily contests between competing doctrines of legitimacy, or favors some other doctrine regarding the underlying causes for war, it nevertheless remains important to identify the direct or specific causes for or the objectives of the particular resort to hostile means by one state against another. To be effective any preventive or mitigating prescriptions would most likely require adaptation to the particular causes and objectives of the given conflicts.

Surveying the previous enumeration of the wide diversity of the objectives of warfare throughout history (including wars for plunder and looting, wars for the displacement of populations, for the acquisition of colonies, wars due to religious zealotry, to nationalistic ambitions, and to security considerations (including self-defense)), it becomes readily apparent that most of these objectives are not only less likely to occur in contemporary society but are also less likely to be tolerated by the twenty-first century's community of nations. Most historical classes of war are outright prohibited by present day international law.

The most common causes for conflicts between nations, as one surveys the contemporary global scene, are likely to be hostile military buildups, the development of weapons of mass destruction capabilities, boundary disputes, disputes over natural resources, and trans-boundary incursions. Beyond these direct and specific conflict causations might loom the broader and bigger yet less definitely precise specters of civilizational, legitimacy, or hegemonial clashes. As one surveys current tensions between India and Pakistan or the United States and Cuba, the underlying causes can be attributed more to a broader civilizational, legitimacy or hegemonial category than to such more clearly defined and historically more common objectives as plunder, population displacement or colonialism. How can such contemporary international tensions and conflicts be best addressed? How best can peace be preserved in an era which aggressive war is to be altogether abolished?

Such specific conflict causations as boundary and water disputes, incursions on territorial sovereignty and the like, supposedly are already subject to resolution or containment by such existing judicial or political dispute-resolution institutions as the International Court of Justice, the United Nations Security Council, regional tribunals or agencies, and through referral to *ad hoc* arbitration and mediation. To prevent such traditional disputes from escalating into war, early and *compulsory* resort to regional or international dispute-resolution agencies and procedures must be instituted.

To reduce the hazards of premature or peremptory resort to arms by aggrieved nations, permanent early warning systems need to be established throughout the world and particularly in conflict and violence prone regions, much like fire alarms and firehouses are constructed throughout domestic communities and particularly in hazardous areas. Such warning systems will not suffice unless they serve as alerts for speedily responsive and specialized regional or international agencies, set up to offer early and fitting intercessions or interventions. The first order of war prevention must therefore be the development of permanent United Nations and regional organizational capacities for intervention in the early stages of erupting conflicts and for guarding against continuation or escalation by means of international observation teams and peacekeeping forces.

More difficult to prevent and restrain are those international disputes and conflicts which are grounded in such broader and deeper causations, ideological, civilizational, legitimacy differences or in disputes rising from hegemonial competitions. Will a Western world, committed to so-called democracy (however stripped down it might be), ever tolerate the long term existence of any other governing system founded on a contrasting system of legitimacy? Can a democracy-proclaiming America long live side-by-side with a nation ruled by dictatorial yet charismatics leaders such as Col. Muamar Khaddafi or Fidel Castro? Can secular democracies like France, Germany, and the United Kingdom, long tolerate a fundamental Islamic Iran or a totalitarian and ideologically communist North Korea?

"Democracy is not for Africa," proclaimed Zaire's President for Life Mobutu Sese Seko nearly thirty years ago. Yet this has not dampened the zeal of the United States and its allies in seeking to implement their own systems of governance, legitimacy and human rights in countries in which ancient traditions continue to prevail, in which religious fundamentalisms recognize only their own scriptural legitimacies, and where mere physical survival and economic rights are deemed to be a first priority.

Critics might contend that the United States, now admittedly the only surviving world power, has not been consistent in its own pursuits of democracy. America has often chosen to overlook authoritarian or even totalitarian rule in the pursuits of its own economic or strategic self-interests or in the interest of global or regional political stability. Yet the nationwide support for an American foreign policy which promotes democratic governance worldwide cannot be reversed. As long as the United States and its allies persist in their missionary commitment to democracy, nothing less than the world's total conversion to this form of governmental legitimacy is likely to produce, for the immediate era, the hoped for End of History.

Some believe that the abolition of hunger, poverty and other deprivations will bring a reign of peace. Others argue fiercely that in a community of nations fully dedicated to the democratic cause and its processes, international conflicts, violence and wars will perish forever. Yet the handbook on *Democracy and Deep-rooted Conflict: Options for Negotiators*, published in 1998 by Sweden's International Institute for Democracy and Electoral Assistance warns that "[i]t is important to understand that there is no single or simple model of democracy." Critics of the hypothesis of an eternal democratic peace voice their fear that in a globe where all nations have come under the mantle of "democracy," new conflicts are likely to erupt among different and conflicting claimants to the "True Model of Democracy." These doubters of the power of "democracy" to resolve all international and domestic conflicts, point to the failure of Judaism, Christianity and Islam to overcome internal dissensions and strife. The mid-Twentieth century conflict between the Soviet Union, China and Yugoslavia as to who constituted the true model of Marxism-Leninism should serve as a cautionary tale for those praying for an eternally democratic world peace.

Will such full conversion to democracy ever take place? As one scrutinizes the growth of the contemporary conflict between the forces proclaiming the "social contract" and "democracy" and those claiming adherence to "scriptural," "charismatic" or other absolutist legitimacy, one cannot fail to note the lessons of the historical experience. The bloody records of such scriptural, charismatic and absolutist leaders as Stalin, Hitler, Idi Amin, Qaddafi, Khomeini, and Saddam Hussein must foster in any sound-minded person a preference for democracy's more cooperative and consensual forms of governance. But the affairs of the world, it has been claimed, are not necessarily governed by lessons of history or by the rules of sanity. What might therefore be more relevant, and reassuring, in the face of the escalating mortal conflict between democratic and absolutist legitimacy, are the emerging new forces and realities throughout the world. In an evolving global and pluralistic world community, where social, economic, technological and mass media forces overwhelm the separatism of old, and where isolation and segregation are no longer tolerated, it is a foregone conclusion that fundamentalist or scriptural legitimacy cannot long prevail as an effective formula for the governance of countries and nations. The eventual victory of the democratic or social contract form of governance over its more absolutist adversaries must therefore be viewed as assured.

Addressing Domestic or Intra-national Conflicts

Given our forecast of democracy's ultimate victory over its opponents, what are the implications of that success to the international arena? The handbook on *Democracy and Deep-Rooted Conflict: Options for Negotiators* (Stockholm: IDEA Publishers, 1998), is dominated by the theme that "appropriate democratic political structures" play a "crucial role...in forging...enduring settlement[s] to...internal conflict[s]." Is that a valid claim? Prescribing remedies for the prevention or containment of domestic or intra-national conflicts might have seemed, until not too long ago, a much less difficult task than the offering of prescriptions for international peace. Alfred Nobel's generation obviously considered international war a greater danger and the attainment of international peace as a more difficult task than the maintenance of domestic tranquility. Yet this is probably no longer so. Increasingly, through the turbulent twentieth century in which democide and genocide flourished, more people were murdered, starved, tortured, exiled and dehumanized through civil wars and the domestic initiatives of their own governments than through international warfare.

Unfortunately, many prevailing systems of governance, through the African, Asian and South American continents remain unaccountable to their citizenries. Corruption, an absence of transparency and the denial of human rights have been commonplace in more of these countries than not. It is difficult, moreover, to maintain peace in ill-shaped and inappropriately constituted communities. The boundaries of most recently decolonialized countries fail to present a well-reasoned and coherent system. Unreasonable and inequitable tribal admixtures, inexplicable borders that separate many who need to be united, military rule, and the exploitation of minorities, have all contributed to widespread discontent through many of the over than 180 nations which constitute the world community. How can domestic tranquility be achieved or maintained when many of the so-called nation-states are increasingly under internal siege?

The legitimacy of the nation-state, long held sacrosanct, has become increasingly questionable and shaky. Observers point out that it is the very vagueness in international politics and law as to what constitutes "peoples," "minorities," "autonomy" and "self-determination" which has greatly contributed to the present unrest and discontent. The legal formulations developed international law and much under the auspices of the United Nations specify that it is only a "peoples" who are entitled to nationhood and sovereign independence. Less defined and coherent communities—clannish, tribal, ethnic, religious, or cultural—come under the designation of "minorities," a status that may protect them against such abusive state practices as democide and genocide and other extreme measures of discrimination, but does not guarantee them specific measures of self-rule.

Yet who is to decide whether a community constitutes a peoples or a mere minority? By what criteria is one to judge? And if a community falls short of peoplehood, what degree of self-rule, and human rights safeguards should it be entitled? The post-World War I era, which witnessed the demise of the Austro-Hungarian, German and Ottoman empires, saw the growth of a broad body of law regarding the collective status and rights of minorities. World War II, which gave birth to a host of new multi-tribal, multi-ethnic, multi-cultured and multi-religious states, produced also a Universal Declaration of Human Rights which is primarily individually rather than collectively oriented. As a consequence people as individuals were granted a wide array of entitlements, while the diverse communities, such as tribes, clans, ethnic and religious groups, to which all humans belong and to which they might profess strong allegiances, were greatly underestimated and overlooked.

It is evident at this time that no universal and consensual definition regarding the makeup of either peoples or minorities has developed within the world community in recent years. Who, therefore, is to tell the Basques or Bosnians, Druze or Turkish that they are not a people, and consequently, are not entitled to self-determination? And if indeed they do not constitute a people, what lesser forms of autonomy should be made available to them as minorities and sub-national communities?

Objective and universal standards for defining peoplehood and minorityhood will not be crafted soon enough. A realistic definition of these terms cannot be expected to be determined by legislative or judicial organs, national or international. A realistic definition can evolve only from historical developments. Yet at the same time the questions raised by these definitions urgently call for answers. The worldwide expectations and demands for self-determination and autonomy, or for other and lesser measures of self-rule, cannot be turned back to the pre-Wilsonian era. The contemporary challenge to authority and the ongoing quest for the legitimacy of power must, therefore, be acknowledged as existing and ever-expanding forces.

Regardless of specific causations, the unrest provided by the unfilled aspirations—just or unjust, reasonable and otherwise—of a very diverse humanity (including some 300 million indigenous people and a much larger world community of ethnic, religious or other minorities) is growing more and more intense. Throughout the world individuals as well as groups seek to protect and enhance their claims for identity, security, prosperity, and autonomy. Countries that fail to deal with the past deprivations and the present expectations of their composite populations decisively, courageously, effectively, and justly will become embroiled in unrest, internal strife, and wars of secession. Governments and states that are unsuccessful in accommodating or mitigating their diverse people's growing demands for greater autonomy and justice will be swept away.

Successful countries will inevitably be the ones capable of transforming themselves into more representative and flexible pluralistic composites. Unless they carry out such transformation, China, India and Nigeria, being among the world's last extant great multi-ethnic empires, might go the way of the earlier Soviet conglomerate. Moreover, the new Russian Federation, as well as other states composed of diverse populations must likewise guard against their further splintering by responding more effectively and justly to the needs and aspirations of their composite communities.

Innovative principles and processes of governance—that recognize the globe's growing pluralistic realities, that incorporate new forms of federalism, and consociationalism, and that enhance local autonomy and communal empowerment—are essential if states are to avoid the divisiveness and turmoil that are increasingly manifested today. Dramatic changes are required not only in the principles but also in the procedures employed by governments and their bureaucracies. The future requires the replacement of monolithic political and socioeconomic dogmas with a maximization of locally determined and pluralistic priorities and institutions.

Greater attention must also be accorded to what has been described as "procedural justice"—which "views people as more interested in issues of process than issues of outcome, and...addresses the way in which...[people's] evaluations of experiences and relationships [with others and with authority] are influenced by the form of social interactions." Emphasis must be placed on clear, fair and transparent governmental processes, and procedures that provide disputants and other interested parties high control over the process, and which are perceived by the populace, as standing for fairness and equity. Such initiatives will greatly contribute to the structuring of a better and longer-lasting balance between authority and autonomy in their ongoing and indeed eternal struggle.

Our responses to the growing climate and culture of domestic or civil unrest, violence and war cannot be piecemeal, nor can they be delayed. The masses as well as the world's elites demand a minimal economic and social safety net. They have and are learning to expect greater and more meaningful means of participatory democracy. To the extent that the belief that democracy is the best guarantor of socio-economic justice gains in the idea market places of the world, greater adherence, to that extent the demand for democratic governance will increase throughout the globe.

Yet at times, even the greatest and most sincere efforts at domestic reforms—political, economic, social, educational and religious—might not suffice to continue holding disgruntled communities within a state's fold. Years and at times decades and centuries of domestic strife, deep-rooted strife, could at times be very difficult to mitigate or overcome. In such instances no solution other than secession offers the desired peace. If no compromise is available, a peaceful divorce at the earliest time obtainable must become a political and legally acceptable solution. One should note that the urge for secession is most likely to predominate in those situations where the seceding "state" is likely to gain protection from or even eventual membership is yet a larger community of nations. When such international eventuality might appear likely, those bent on secession, like the Kurds of Iraq, will be more inclined to remain in their existing nation-state fold as long as some of their fundamental aspirations are met, usually through a decentralization or federalization of that state.

The prescriptions outlined above are not simple, pretty, readily obtainable or without adverse side effects. Neither are they expected to guarantee or even help institute eternal peace. Although conflict and war may not be innate to humankind, violence and strife, much like crime and violence, are not likely to disappear from the face of the earth. "Conflict is a normal part of any healthy society," claims the Handbook on *Democracy and Deep-Rooted Conflict: Options for Negotiators* (1998). This realization, however, should not deter those committed to improving the human condition from doing the best and the most to advance not only the cause of the "fraternity among nations" but, possibly more importantly, the "fraternity among humans."

To achieve that promised land a new culture of peace must rise from the ashes of human destruction. The primary means for building that culture will be nothing less than a total retooling of education worldwide: creating an education not for hate and destruction but for civility and neighborliness, compassion and cooperation—and thereby, peace.

An International Authority for Education for Peace must therefore promptly be established within civil society, with good will and adequate support—intellectual, spiritual, political, and financial—by private and public, non-governmental and governmental, national and international organizations. Nothing can distill the essence of a culture of peace and the required education for peace better than the ancient golden rule. Until that blessed day comes upon this earth, both the public and civil societies must at the very least learn how to better engage in conflict-management if not conflict-resolution, how at the least find the commitment and means for the maintenance of a truce, if not a true and constructive peace.

Notes

1. Harry H. Almond, *The History and Future of Warfare*, The Hague: Kluwer Law International, 1999.

2. R. J. Rummel, *Death by Government*, Transaction Publishers, 1994.

3. Samuel Huntington, "The Clash of Civilizations," *Foreign Affairs*, 1993.

4. Francis Fukuyama, *The End of History*, Avon Books, 1992.

5. Nicholas N. Kittrie, *The War Against Authority*, Johns Hopkins Press, 1995.

Peace, by Pablo Picasso

Afterwords

Multinational and Multicultural Reflections on the Architecture of Peace

Peace implies reconciliation.

—Edmund Burke (1775)

We can best separate appearance from the reality, the transient from the permanent, the significant from the episodic, by looking backward whenever we look forward. There is no great mystery why this should be:...the successive generations of men tend to face the same recurrent problems and to react to them in more or less habitual ways.

—Walter Lippmann (1943)

Since Humans First Scratched Thought on Stone

Walter Cronkite
Journalist

Since humans first scratched thought on a stone we have recorded a longing for peace. The ancient Egyptians and the Greek philosophers pondered the difficulties of achieving it, and of achieving the prerequisite charity for our fellow men.

From Plutarch's *Lives* comes the quote from Anacharsis ridiculing Solon "for imagining the dishonesty and covetousness of his countrymen could be restrained by written laws." That was around 600 B.C.E., a couple of millennia ago. Not much seems to have changed.

From the lessons of the Bible and other great religious works to modern government, humans always have recognized the need for equality and charity to free the world of war, pestilence, and want. Why is that so hard to achieve? What must we do to pierce this armor of selfishness behind which individuals and governments shirk their responsibilities to their fellow man? Seeking an answer to this age-old question, I gather, is in essence the purpose of this book.

The effort obviously is a worthy one, and I suspect that the chances of success are greater than ever before. Perhaps the time has come at last when real progress can be made toward the amelioration, or even the elimination, of the problems that already afflict too much of humanity and threaten the rest of us, who in our ignorance believe that somehow we can remain immune. My optimism is based on the almost unbelievable advancement in communication that has enabled the people of the world to share their experiences and their hopes, their expectations, and, beyond, the possible solutions to our problems.

Television and the transmission of its programs by satellite has, indeed, created the global village. Its news and documentaries, with their constant close-ups of nations, civilizations, and cultures previously unknown to one another, has created a new bond of humanity—a realization among all of us that the differences presented by race or geography are not as great as our similarities. The airplane shrank our physical world; now the Internet is shrinking our intellectual world. Villagers in the most remote areas can now have, literally at their fingertips, access to the world's knowledge, wherein may be found the guidance to bring them into the modern world—to teach them, by practical example, hygiene and birth control and crop rotation and animal husbandry and a hundred other ways to improve their lives. Our great development in communication is just one of the wonders of our past century—wonders that we must harness if we are to enjoy their great promise.

In this new century, one can only stand in awe of

the potential for human advancement. In just the latter half of the last remarkable century, we were swept into at least six simultaneous eras, any one of which, by itself, could be considered an age of man. We were present at the birth of the nuclear age, the space age, the petrochemical age, the telecommunications age, the computer age, the DNA age. Together, at their confluence, flows a great river of chance, unlike anything history has encountered before.

We call it the technological revolution—a revolution surely with more impact than the previous century's industrial revolution that forever altered the world.

Already vast economical and political changes have taken place, propelled by growth and accompanied by rising expectations. But too frequently these changes have been blocked in less-developed nations by finite resources and inadequate educational systems. Meeting these problems and satisfying the needs of the disadvantaged is the challenge of our time.

And that is just my point: The new technologies give proof of humankind's intellectual capacity. Can we really believe that we are incapable of applying that same intellectual power to solving the great problems the world faces?

If we of the so-called developed nations—the possessors of these scientific and technological tools—can't solve the problems, someone else—perhaps someone less benign—will solve them for us. Can we believe that the beleaguered peoples of the world will long be tolerant of those who possess the tools but can't make them work for the good of humankind everywhere?

There is going to be a social and political and economic evolution that will explode with such suddenness as to have the character of revolution. The revolutionary forces are already at work today and they have humanity's dreams on their side.

We don't want to be on the other side. It is up to us—the educated, the informed, the wealthy possessors of the tools—to forgo self-aggrandizement and assume leadership of that revolution and channel it in a direction that will ensure freedom's future.

After The Cold War: An Era of Unprecedented Peace and Prosperity

Jimmy Carter
39th President of the United States of America and 2002 Nobel Peace Laureate

After the cold war, many expected an era of unprecedented peace and prosperity. For most Americans, this prediction has come true. Although our military has not been idle, since 1991 our country has been largely untouched by the ravages of war. And most of us—although not all—have a roof over our heads, access to jobs, and the opportunity to live healthy; productive lives.

But when we talk about prosperity; we are excluding more than 1.3 billion people in developing nations who live on less than one dollar per day. And let's consider just the most fundamental tenet of peace—the absence of war. At the nonprofit Carter Center, which my wife, Rosalynn, and I founded after leaving the White House, we monitor all serious conflicts in the world, and the sad reality is that the number of armed conflicts within countries increased dramatically. According to one estimate, more than 150,000 people—the majority of them civilians—lost their lives in 1997 alone. But these numbers don't begin to tell the whole story. That same year, some 20 million people were forced from their homes. And untold numbers suffered the indirect consequences of conflict, such as lack of health care and education, and emotional trauma—conditions that create an environment of fear and instability.

Although this has been the most violent century known to humankind, the world community pays little attention to many of the most destructive clashes. The United States and other industrialized nations focus mostly on those conflicts that directly affect them, such as those in Iraq, Bosnia, and Serbia. For example, while the war in Kosovo waged on and dominated the world's headlines, even more destructive conflicts in developing nations were systematically ignored by the United States and other powerful nations.

One can traverse Africa, from the Red Sea in the northeast to the southwestern Atlantic coast, and never set foot on peaceful territory. Fifty thousand people have recently perished in the war between Eritrea and Ethiopia, and almost two million have died during the seventeen-year conflict in neighboring Sudan. That war has spilled over into northern Uganda, whose troops have joined those from Rwanda to fight in the Democratic Republic of Congo (formerly Zaire). The other Congo (Brazzaville) is also ravaged by a civil war, and all attempts to bring peace to Angola have failed. Although formidable commitments were made in the Balkans, where white Europeans were involved, no such concerted efforts are being made by leaders outside of Africa to resolve these and other disputes.

As long as these trends continue, there can be no peace and prosperity for a large percentage of the world's people. And while it is relatively easy to see and understand the direct impact of war on a people and a nation, it is more difficult to measure other factors that make for a peaceful and productive quality of life. At the Carter Center, we maintain that peace also includes the ability to feed one's family, the right to be free from preventable disease, the right to live without the fear of human rights abuses, and the right to determine ones own future. These are the seeds of peace.

All of these things require resources. In our travels, Rosalynn and I have witnessed the most appalling poverty and the results of religious, ethnic, and political persecution. These experiences have convinced me that the greatest challenge we face as a global community is how to reduce the growing disparity between rich and poor people.

Who are the rich? Rich people feel relatively safe in their own neighborhood, have adequate food and shelter, some education, and some expectation of gainful employment They believe that there is an equal system of justice and think they can make decisions that will have a positive impact on their lives.

It is sobering that, even in the richest nation on earth, many do not enjoy these fruits of peace. This is even more evident in the developing world. At the beginning of this century, the ratio between per capita income between the richest and poorest nations was nine to one. By 1960, it had increased to thirty to one, and today it is more than sixty to one. Although capitalism and democracy are the best ways to promote these values, these systems are far from perfect. They can promote survival of the fittest—with serious consequences to the poor—if there is little social conscience or inadequate safety nets.

There is little doubt that most people, as individuals and as a society, want to lead lives that are satisfying, productive and healthy. To make this possible, a nation or society must reach for justice. This includes providing for the basic human needs of both the rich and the poor. Until we meet this challenge as a global community, there can be no true and lasting peace.

Some of My Memories are Painful and Dark

Nadja Halilbegovich
Youth for Environmental Sanity

Sometimes I take my diary and read through its pages; its white leaves unfold as gently as soft bandages revealing a scar of memories. Some of my memories are painful and dark. Some bring back the screams sirens, and the dead bodies of innocent people on the streets. Some fill my eyes with tears and wound my soul with great pain. It hurts to read; my heart wants to leap out of my body, unwilling to experience all the horrifying things again. My diary was always far more than a notebook. It was my means to survive—to remain human and sane.

Today, by reading it, I strive to preserve the life I was surviving for. I was twelve years old when the war began. I was a cheerful and carefree girl when the bloody hands of war took my childhood away. Before the war, I lived happily with my dearest parents and brother. We were an upper-middle-class family as were many others in Sarajevo. My mother was a business manager at the National Bank of Bosnia and Herzegovina. My father was a manager at a major book company. We had a beautiful fourteenth floor apartment, a house in a village where we spent our weekends, a cottage and some land on the island of Brach on the Adriatic Sea, and two cars.

It saddens me to realize that most people know little about Bosnia. Bosnia and Herzegovina is a beautiful country located between Italy and Greece. The capital of my homeland is the beautiful city of Sarajevo. From the television news footage most people may picture my city with no electricity, water, gas, or food. Though we lived without these essentials during the war, before the war Sarajevo was as modern as any city in America. Surrounded by a gorgeous ring of mountains, Sarajevo hosted the 1984 Winter Olympics. It was truly an international place where people embraced every visitor, placing a Bosnian pie, a "Cevepi" meat roll, and a glass of pure mountain springwater in front of him. My dearest Sarajevo does not look like this today, but its spirit, its soul, and the hospitality and pride of its people have never failed. They will remain forever.

The war came quickly and suddenly. I remember the morning when I woke up and started getting ready for school. I entered our living room to find my parents' faces troubled and sad. They said I could not go to school. Groups of armed men with sock masks had placed barricades throughout the city and blocked the streets.

Through the first few weeks of chaos and confusion, I believed that the craziness would soon be over and that everything would be just as it was before. I believed that the armed men would simply disappear. None of my hopes and wishes came true.

On May 31, 1992, I was frightened as never before. That day my trembling fingers opened the covers of an old notebook and I began writing my diary. I finally let my tears, frozen for so long, fall freely onto my face. I released emotions so long clutched inside. I realized that a prisoner of a city cannot remain a prisoner of his own mind and soul. The body can hurt and starve, but the mind and soul must be nourished.

Soon, we got used to living with the war. I know now that a human being can survive unimaginable conditions, because deep in the human soul lies an eternal desire to live, to be, and to become. I got accustomed to dragging water up the stairs to the fourteenth floor. I became used to not having the food we normally ate. I even found it normal to have grenades wake me up in the morning instead of the warm voice of my dearest mother. My family strove to make our lives easier, to make the sudden change a little softer. We planted vegetables on our balcony and were happy to decorate a dish of plain rice with a piece of lettuce or a slice of tomato.

My mother went to work even though she never got paid and had to walk twelve miles every day; with every step she was in danger of being killed by bombs or snipers. Countless mornings, I watched her brush her hair and put makeup on her pretty face, horrified by the thought of her getting killed. When, through my tears, I begged her not to go, she told me she couldn't stay home because the endless days would kill her.

My father was let go from his job because of our religion, so he volunteered for the Red Cross during the war. For a long time I could not comprehend the reason he was let go, as I never judged people by their religion. My family and I are believers of Islam. We believe in God solemnly, but we always embrace our friends and neighbors who are Christian, Jews, or Orthodox. I grew up with my father's saying: "One who doesn't respect the religion of others cannot respect one's own."

Being a child of peace, I never took a moment to think about everyday things that made my life so cheerful. I never thought what it would be like to wake up one morning and find them gone. The first things I was deprived of were school and my friends. Sometimes my friends from the building and I gathered in the basement with our teacher for a lesson. In the winter, each one of us would bring a piece of wood and try to warm up the little room with an old stove. Some mornings, when I got up only because I was so anxious to go to school and see my friends, the shelling would start and school would be canceled. My desire to learn in spite of everything never faded, so I often took out my books and studied on my own. I made a daily schedule and studied Bosnian, English, French, and math. I also practiced guitar and sang.

The war mercilessly stole four years of my life. Like every child would do, I acclimated to the new conditions of my life, forgetting what I had before. Every tear that stained my pillow at night, when all I could hear were sirens and grenades, was also a tear that mourned all the innocent citizens who lost their lives. I often felt sad because the scar opened my eyes at such an early age. Even though I learned a great lesson, sometimes it hurt so bad that I wish I had never learned it. Only my dreams, so beautiful that they could resist all the ugliness of war, so invulnerable that no grenades ever harmed them, kept my head and my hopes bright and high. I realized that the soft and colorful paths of my dreams often intersected with the roads of cruel reality. That was when my dreams, my determination, and my faith were tested,

War taught me that every human being has a dark and bright side. It is our choice to fight the darker side and show our warm and beautiful feelings or to let ourselves be weak and hopeless, bitter and mean. I hope that the warm and brilliant colors of the morning dawn, the radiant light of midnight's stars on the sky of my dreams will always light up my soul with goodness and faith. I hope they will light the path of my existence with peace and righteousness.

We Still Live in a World in Which We Must Study Politics and War

Colin Powell
Secretary of State, United States of America

In 1780, during our struggle for independence from Britain, patriot and future president John Adams wrote to his wife, Abigail: "I must study politics and war that my sons may have liberty to study mathematics and philosophy."

Today, more than two hundred years later, we still live in a world in which we must study politics and war. The good news is that we don't have to study war quite as much.

The century that just ended was the bloodiest ever recorded. Enormous sacrifices were required of our youth to preserve our free way of life. But because they were willing to make those sacrifices, our survival as a nation and as a free people is no longer threatened. Democracy and private enterprise, though not without their faults, have prevailed over the collectivist ideologies that threatened us with destruction.

So the world is a safer place. Many more of our young people have liberty to study mathematics and philosophy and the other arts of peace. But liberty is not quite the same thing as opportunity; the fact that young people are free to develop their abilities and talents in constructive ways does not necessarily mean that they will do so, unless they get help and support from adults.

For that reason, I decided that my next campaign after I retired from the army would be to take up the cause of the next generation. Currently, I chair a national crusade for young people called America's Promise—The Alliance for Youth. The mission of America's Promise is to endow our young people with the character and competence they need to be successful and contributing adult members of society.

We do this by keeping five basic promises to the youth of America. Every child and teenager needs:

- An ongoing relationship with a caring adult—a parent, mentor, tutor, or coach;
- A safe place with structured activities during nonschool hours;
- A healthy start;
- A marketable skill through effective education; and
- An opportunity to give back through community service.

To keep these five promises, America's Promise is building a great national coalition of government, business, nonprofits, service groups, community activists, and people of faith. Working together, we are striving to give all our young people the opportunity to develop their full potential.

For thirty-five years of my life, I was committed to training young people for the day when they might have to risk their lives in defense of this country and the cause of freedom. Today, I am helping to train a slightly younger age group to prevail in a different struggle—a struggle against drugs, neglect, apathy, ignorance, irresponsible sex, and any other threats that might blight their lives and keep them from being all they were meant to be.

Winning the peace means more than defeating the enemies of freedom. It means seizing the great opportunity we have now to raise a generation that is strong and caring and capable enough to preserve peace and freedom in this new century.

The Roots of War and Violence Go Deep, Into the Earth Herself

Ingrid Washingawatok el-Issa
Flying Eagle Woman Fund

The roots of war and violence go deep, into the earth herself. As an indigenous woman, I wish to simply state that until we make peace with earth, there will be no peace in the human community. Please allow me to explain.

As native peoples of the hemisphere, we have historically been the victims of violence and continue to be plagued by injustice and inequality. In our history we have had to go to war to protect our lands, as peace would simply mean our enslavement and extermination. And every course of action we sought—whether accommodation or resistance— had only one outcome, the theft of our lands. All this is well known.

What is not clearly understood is that all this was ostensibly done for our good, and the good of humanity. The underlying justification for the theft of our lands has always been that we were not making proper use of them, and that these lands could be put to better use. The wilderness that we cultivated and maintained was simply going to waste. It was selfish of us to padlock our vast forests and plains and deprive millions of hungry and millions of landless from their enjoyment. It was argued that stealing our land would provide for the common good of the world and all would become better off as a result. And of course during this process, we would be lifted from our less-than-civilized state and would eventually recognize the goodwill that had been lavished upon us.

Today, most of our lands and most of the wilderness are gone and yet there are more poor people than ever, more misery, more landlessness. And today there are those who still argue that tearing down the remaining stretches of lands benefits humanity, or in today's jargon, "creates jobs."

As we look upon the increasingly despoiled planet we can only ask the question: "Has our land indeed been put to better use?" Could there have been another way?

Nor only could there have been another way, there *must* be another way. Destroying natural resources, destroying the planet's ability to provide sustenance, only aggravates the worlds misery and poverty, the injustice and discontent. This is because, like everything, ultimately, the wealth of the world comes from the earth. We may fashion this wealth and remake it to perform marvelous things, but a barren planet does not create jobs, and wars for food and water could become a terrible epitaph for the human species. As we destroy the ability of the earth to sustain us, we lose our ability to address the chronic needs of the poor, the hungry, and the landless.

The current economic order—based upon an ideology that does not recognize the wealth of the natural order, that cannot place value on anything unless it is sold in the marketplace, that enshrines greed and avarice as the engines of development—is destroying the real wealth of the planet. While it pretends to create jobs and products, in reality, it is similar to burning furniture to provide heat: every bit of flame, like many of our jobs, is actually impoverishing humanity, not enriching it. For the longest time, only Indians and other natural peoples cried out against the war against nature. Today, we are allied with many environmental groups. Yet, still, the understanding of how we must fundamentally change the way we think about the planet is only now beginning to become a subject of discussion.

There are many definitions of sustainable development, and the word has become overused and almost meaningless. Moreover, it rings hollow unless the efforts of humankind are centered toward rebuilding the planet.

Indigenous peoples have long understood sustainable development. The wilderness that we inhabit is wilderness only to those who cannot grasp the complexity of our agricultural systems, which regenerate and produce in ways that work in accordance to natural laws—not against them. For this reason, our agriculture has existed with only little impact on the earth, for hundreds, if not thousands, of years—all the while producing for the needs of our people.

Among the technologies we use to produce in harmony with this earth are products such as corn developed and cultivated in this hemisphere. Corn is truly a product of our technology: it cannot live without people, just like our people could not live without corn. For this reason it was central in our spiritual and cultural existence. It was also developed in infinite varieties that were each adapted to the particular environment where it would have to exist, so that they would best fit in with the other life. And so it was designed to feed the maximum number of people with the minimum impact on the environment, and people lived close to their corn, their way of life.

Compare this to the new, genetically engineered varieties of corn, which require the habitat to be similarly engineered, and thus require tremendous inputs of pesticides, chemical fertilizers, and other agents that so change the environment and are so mechanized that people no longer live on the land and are forced to the cities. If one measures the yield, yes, it produces more corn per acre than Indian corn, but it is not sustainable and the chemicals eventually poison the land.

The true cost of working against nature is never factored into this equation, only how much money a bushel of corn brings. But the true environmental and social costs of this process far exceed the benefits for humanity, and in the end impoverish the planet further.

Yet, so often the world believes that some technological marvel will prevail and make things right. There is little consideration that maybe it is these technical marvels that are part of the problem. Development must take the path not of mitigating its impact on the environment but of enhancing the natural environment.

Instead of environmental impact statements for development, we need environmental enhancement statements. Rather than destroying the means of sustenance that this planet brings us, we need to increase it; the poverty and hunger of much of the world demand it.

We need a peace with earth. We must have it. We cannot pretend to have long-term sustainable development without it, for the very foundation of this development *is* a peace with earth. Our philosophy of development must be guided by the natural laws that have guided all living things, not some arbitrary, man-made illusion.

We indigenous people believe that development with a different focus would enrich the planet and, in so doing, alleviate some of the discontent and anger that surfaces as war and violence.

Yet for so long, indigenous peoples from across the globe have been unable to speak, to contribute to the solutions of the problems facing humanity. Many of us are ancient peoples; indeed many of our cultures are your elders, and yet you never turn to us for our opinion, even when the issues affect us directly.

As our cultures disappear with the wilderness that sustained us, we are a vast library, a repository of knowledge, intelligence, and an understanding of the earth that is being lost to the world. But we continue to be victimized and ignored. If we seek to embark on the elusive search for peace, we must first unlock the silence of our peoples, and other peoples like us. Ultimate peace lies in all of us working together, to make things better for future generations. Unlock the silence, let us speak to the world.

My Thoughts On Peace Begin with a Story My Dad Told

Hafsat Abiola
Kudirat Initiative for Nigerian Democracy

My country, Nigeria, is home to 120 million people—one fifth of continental Africa's population—who come from more than two hundred ethnic groups. Each group has its unique way of being, of relating to others, and of contributing. My group is the Yoruba. We are generally found in western Nigeria and are famous for our arts, clothing, and music. I love being Yoruba, Nigerian, and African because I come from a rich heritage and yet, because so much needs doing in my home, I know I will be kept busy.

Of all the things that serve my growth, I love best the stories and myths told to me by my parents and the Nigerian people I meet. My thoughts on peace begin with a story my dad told when he was campaigning in Nigeria's 1993 presidential election:

> Sometimes a village is beset with problems—disease, famine, conflict, and floods. All these problems come at once and despite all the best efforts of members of the community, the problems are immune to solutions. In such a situation, the village believes they may have done something to upset the gods, so they will gather all their best possessions together to offer as gifts to the gods. They then ask one of their best sons to present the gifts on their behalf. When the gods are presented with the gifts, they may become pacified and allow peace and prosperity to reign in the land. But sometimes, they are so angry they will take the best son, as well as the gifts, after which they are pacified and allow peace and prosperity to reign.

From this story, I took the lesson that peace comes from contributing the best we have, and, often, all that we are, toward creating a world that supports everyone.

In much of precolonial Nigeria, and indeed Africa, ethnic nations organized people within communities into peer groups and trained them, from babyhood to old age, to serve their communities. When successful, this system provided all members of a community not only with a sense of belonging but also with a vehicle for helping to shape the community's direction and pace of change. In this system, people knew they were entitled to help resolve any issue that affected the community.

This sense of entitlement grows out of a series of rituals that begin the day a child is born. When a baby is born, after the first few seconds, it lets out a yelp, which announces its arrival, and which is met by expressions of joy. Among the Yoruba, the arrival is acknowledged with a naming ceremony where parents give names that express rich meaning and hopes for the baby. When I arrived, my parents named me Hafsat Olaronke, which means *the trea-*

sured one and *honor is being cared for.* For my parents, they saw in me one who would be cherished and who would bring honor to her community. Many in other parts of the world are impressed when they discover my name's meanings, but the truth is that most African names have beautiful meanings.

Mark Nepo, an American poet, narrates the story of the Khoisan, a nomadic people found in southern Africa. According to Nepo, when a Khoisan returns from a journey and meets another from his community, he raises his hand and says, "I am here," and the other replies, "I see you." These practices are more than simple greetings; they affirm our belonging to the community and our right to contribute.

Nigeria is a place beset with problems, and all its members are needed if we are to meet the challenges we face. Unfortunately, until very recently, my country was controlled by a series of military governments who denied most Nigerians the right to make their contributions. Even in the period since the military relinquished power to a democratically elected government, many exclusionary attitudes—from class to ethnic and religious divisions—as well as a general lack of trust or sense of community, have effectively denied most people the freedom to engage with their country's challenges.

And yet, despite the obstacles, both individuals and groups are constantly announcing their presence, or asking the questions, Do I belong? Can I contribute? Am I accepted? Their queries are rarely met by affirmative or empowering replies. Instead they hear jeers, or expressions of disinterest, or obnoxious interrogations: "Who asks? What community? 'What have you ever done anyway?" Nothing about this process is enlightening, just humiliating.

This is because, unlike the small community, where every person lives in the illusion of having the same ideals, beliefs, and values as everyone else, in the larger context of plural communities—be it in country, continent, or globe—we live in the illusion of absolute difference. So fearing the possibility that interaction will change us, we magnify the threat involved in engaging with that which differs from us. Change is stressful, and costly, because it requires learning to navigate the unfamiliar. In the end, you cannot work with *anyone* who is different, and problems that could be resolved if we allowed everyone to contribute the best of themselves begin to look intractable.

The Persian poet Jalaludin Rumi wrote: "Out beyond ideas of right and wrong doing there is a field. I will meet you there." If there is to be space for us to speak into, we need to learn also to listen. We are the creators of this space. We must each take responsibility for examining our values, ideals and beliefs and for learning to understand those held by others, enough so that we can help them ourselves consider new possibilities.

In the end of my dad's story, he said that poverty, violent conflict, malnutrition, and disease were all increasing across Nigeria. And he asked to be able to bear our country's gifts, in order to secure for us peace and prosperity. He won the election but served out his term in solitary confinement, incarcerated by the military, and died on the eve of his release in 1998. But here was the difference he made: across ethnic, religious, and class divides, the people said *yes!*

This search for validation is universal. It is beautiful when these inquiries meet with affirmation, because it allows a person to stride forward with all he has to give. There is a story told by the conductor of the Boston Philharmonic Orchestra, Ben Zander; a maestro conductor, after having conducted a brilliant symphony, races out of the concert hall and into a waiting car, imperiously commanding the driver, "Drive!" When the driver asks, "Where to?" the conductor boldly responds, "Anywhere! The world needs me!"

Peace comes from being able to contribute the best that we have and all that we are, toward creating a world that supports everyone. But it is also securing the space for others to contribute the best that *they* have and all that *they* are. In case you are still wondering—no, it was not a wrong turn that brought you here. You *do* belong here and there *is* a contribution uniquely yours that is needed. Welcome and good luck.

All of Us Need to Take Responsibility for the World's Violence

Mairead Corrigan Maguire
Peace People

All of us need to take responsibility for the world's violence and, like Gandhi, pledge our lives to the nonviolent transformation of the world in order to resolve these insane crises through the wisdom of nonviolence.

Gandhi taught that nonviolence does not mean passivity. No. It is the most daring, creative, and courageous way of living and it is the only hope for our world. Nonviolence is an active way of life which always rejects violence and killing, and instead applies the force of love and truth as a means to transform conflict and the root causes of conflict. Nonviolence demands creativity. It pursues dialogue, seeks reconciliation, listens to the truth in our opponents, rejects militarism, and allows God's spirit to transform us socially and politically.

Getting to the root cause of the conflict continues to be the greatest challenge facing people in Northern Ireland. We need now to build a culture of genuine nonviolence and real democracy. This can only happen through consensus politics built by the people, and courageous political leadership by the government on human rights issues.

Thirty years ago, if the Northern Ireland government had implemented civil rights instead of responding to conflict with ever increasing oppression, emergency legislation, and outright militarization, the savage violence we have known would never have erupted. Today, while we are thankful that the peace process has begun, we are deeply conscious that many of the same problems that were there in 1968 still remain awaiting a solution in an atmosphere of mistrust deepened by thirty years of unnecessary violence.

The only thing we have learned is that violence makes things worse....

To enable consensus politics to develop we need to empower people where they live. This means devolving financial resources and political power down to the community level. One of the greatest blocks to movement is fear. This fear can only be removed when people feel their voices are being heard by government and when they have a say in their own lives and communities.

But Gandhi's challenge of nonviolence is not only a necessity for ourselves and for Northern Ireland; it is a challenge placed before the whole of humanity. Fifty years after his death Gandhi challenges us to pursue a new millennium of nonviolence. This is not an impossible dream.

I have come to believe, with Gandhi, that through our own personal conversion, our own inner peace, we are sensitized to care for God, for ourselves, for each other, for the poor, and for the earth, and then we can become true servants of peace in our world. Herein lies the power of nonviolence.

As our hearts are disarmed by God of our inner violence, they become God's instruments for the disarmament of the world. Without this inner conversion we run the risk of becoming embittered, disillusioned, despairing, or simply burnt out, especially when our work for peace and justice appears to produce little or no result, or seems trifling in comparison with the injustice we see around us. With this conversion we learn to let go of *all desires,* including our destructive desire to see results.

For many people this ancient wisdom of the heart, this wisdom of nonviolence, may seem too religious and too idealistic in today's hardheaded world of politics and science. But I believe, with Gandhi, that we need to take an imaginative leap forward toward fresh and generous idealism for the sake of all humanity—that we need to renew this ancient wisdom of nonviolence, to strive for a disarmed world, and to create a culture of nonviolence.

As we enter the third millennium we need to apply this ancient wisdom of nonviolence to politics economics, and science. For many, particularly in the West, increased materialism and unprecedented consumerism have not led to inner peace and happiness. Although technology has given us many benefits, it has not helped us to distinguish between what enhances life and humanity and what destroys life and humanity. The time has come to return to the ancient wisdom of nonviolence.

The Century Marked by Unprecedented Violence and Cruelty

Mahnaz Afkhami
Women's Learning Partnership

The century just passed was marked by unprecedented violence and cruelty. Most nations suffered or contributed to war, destruction, and genocide, the most egregious of which—the two world wars and the Holocaust—began and occurred mainly in the West. Untold numbers were sacrificed at the altar of ideology, religion, or ethnicity. Innocent people were led in droves to destruction in various gulags—prisons large enough to pass for cities and cities confined enough to pass for prisons.

Women and children everywhere suffered most from violence not of their making, perpetrated against them in national wars, in ethnic animosities, in petty neighborhood fights, and at home. Many of us have lived most of our lives under the threat of total annihilation because mankind achieved the technological know-how to self-destruct. The end of the Cold War removed the immediate causes of wholesale destruction—but not the threat contained in our knowledge. We must tame this knowledge with the ideals of justice, caring, and compassion summoned from our common human spiritual and moral heritage, if we are to live in peace and serenity in the twenty-first century.

The promotion of a culture of peace requires more than an absence of war. In the past two hundred years most of the world lived directly or indirectly within a colonial system. This system reflected an increasingly divided world of haves and have-nots. The modernizing elite in the technologically and economically poor nations responded to colonialism by seizing the power of the state and using it to change their societies, hoping to achieve justice at home and economic and cultural parity abroad. The politics of changing traditional social structures and processes by using state power did not always result in social progress and economic development, but it did lead to state supremacy and autocracy. In the more extreme cases autocratic regimes were transformed to either forward-looking or reactionary totalitarianism—of socialist-Marxist, fascist, or religious-fundamentalist types. These systems clearly failed or are failing. But at the time they were adopted, to many they represented hope and a promise of economic change, distributive justice, and a better future. As we move forward in the first decades of the new millennium, economic and political globalization is likely to weaken the state. Deprived of the protection of the state, a majority of the people in the developing countries will have to fend for themselves against overwhelming global forces they cannot control. The most vulnerable groups, among them women and children, will suffer most. Clearly, any definition of a culture of peace must address the problem of achieving justice for communities and individuals who do not have the means to compete or cope without structured assistance and compassionate help.

As we move into the twenty-first century, women's status in society will become the standard by which to measure our progress toward civility and peace. The connection between women's human rights, gender equality, socioeconomic development, and peace is increasingly apparent. International political and economic organizations invariably state in their official publications that achieving sustainable development in the global South, or in less-developed areas within the industrialized countries, is unlikely without women's participation. It is essential for the development of civil society, which, in turn, encourages peaceful relationships within and between societies. In other words, women, who are a majority of the peoples of the earth, are indispensable to the accumulation of the kind of social capital that is conducive to development, peace, justice, and civility. Unless women are empowered, however, to participate in the decision-making processes—that is, unless women gain political power—it is unlikely that they will influence the economy and society toward more equitable and peaceful foundations.

Women's empowerment is intertwined with respect for human rights. But we face a dilemma. In the future, human rights will be increasingly a universal criterion for designing ethical systems. On the other hand, the "enlightened" optimism that spearheaded much of the humanism of the nineteenth and twentieth centuries is now yielding to a pessimistic view that we are losing control over our lives. We sense a growing cynicism engulfing our view of government and political authority. In the West, where modern technology is invented and domiciled, many people feel overwhelmed by the speed with which things both moral and material change around them. In non-Western societies, the inability to hold on to some constancy that in the past provided a cultural anchor and therefore a bearing on one's moral and physical position today often leads to normlessness and bewilderment. In the West or East, no one wishes to become a vessel for a technology that evolves uncontrolled by human will. On the other hand, it is becoming increasingly difficult for any one individual, institution, or government to exert its will meaningfully, that is, to ethically mold technology to human moral needs.

This seemingly uncontrollable technology, however, will be a harbinger of great promise, if we agree on the shared values contained in our major international documents of rights, and if we adopt a method of decision making that justly reflects our common values. After all, we have gained almost magical powers in science and technology. We have overcome the handicaps of time and space on our planet. We have uncovered many secrets of our universe. We can feed and clothe the peoples of our world, protect and educate our children, and provide security and hope for the poor. We can cure many of the diseases of body and mind that were deemed scourges of humanity only a few decades ago. We seem to have passed the era of absolutes, where leaders assumed the right to incarcerate, slaughter, or otherwise constrain their own people and others in the name of some imagined good. We have the ability to achieve, if we master the necessary goodwill, a common global society blessed with a shared culture of peace that is nourished by the ethnic, national, and local diversities that enrich our lives. To achieve this blessing, however, we must assess our present situation realistically, assign moral and practical responsibility to individuals, communities, and countries commensurate with their objective ability and, most importantly, we must subordinate power in all its manifestations to our shared humane values.

If You Plant a Mango Seed, You Will Get a Mango Tree

James R. Mancham

Founding President of the Republic of Seychelles (1976-1977)

On Tuesday, September 21, 1976, Seychelles was accepted by acclamation as the 145th member of the United Nations. On that occasion I was privileged to address the opening session of the 1976 General Assembly.

> ...I think the time has come when we must ask ourselves what will make the world a sane world. The answer is only sane people. What will make the world peaceful? The answer is only peaceful people. For too long the strange notion has persisted in human beings that a state of sanity and peace can somehow be produced by arms struggle and violence. That the end justifies the means is a lie which has been swallowed by almost everyone. It would be much more accurate to say that the end reveals the means.
>
> We do not have to look very far or very closely to see that there are simple and natural laws which work as surely in human affairs as they do in the rest of creation. If you sow a mango seed you get a mango tree. If you sow maize you get maize. No exception to this simple law has ever occurred or ever will. By the same token if you sow the seed of contention, violence and hatred the harvest will be more violence and more hatred. Society can only change by first changing the attitude of people who live in it and the world can only change by changing the attitude of the nations who constitute it...

Today, it is clear that the fundamental response to the prevailing world crisis must be based on a consensus of universally shared values and a unity of vision that the leaders of the world can agree upon through the collective wisdom of the world's religions, of individuals and institutions such as the Eleanor Roosevelt Institute for Justice and Peace, the Nobel Peace Prize Committee and the United Nations. Just as the founding fathers of each of the nations were committed to moral and ethical principles and ideals as a foundation for their nations, any vision of a harmonized unified world and a governance of peace must likewise bring together men and women of honesty, integrity, and a selfless commitment to individual and collective justice for humanity.

Finally, I would like to thank Dr. Nicholas N. Kittrie. KStJ, Chairman of The Eleanor Roosevelt Institute for Justice and Peace to have provided me with the opportunity and privilege of co-editing this unique, historic volume in our search for peace and security and our longing for a more loving and fraternal world.

Appendix

The Nobel Peace Prize Laureates

2002 Jimmy Carter

2001 United Nations (U.N.), Kofi Annan

2000 Kim Dae Jung

1999 Médecins Sans Frontières

1998 John Hume, David Trimble

1997 International Campaign to Ban Landmines (ICBL), Jody Williams

1996 Carlos Filipe Ximenes Belo, José Ramos-Horta

1995 Joseph Rotblat, Pugwash Conferences on Science and World Affairs

1994 Yasser Arafat, Shimon Peres, Yitzhak Rabin

1993 Nelson Mandela, Frederik Willem de Klerk

1992 Rigoberta Menchú Tum

1991 Aung San Suu Kyi

1990 Mikhail Sergeyevich Gorbachev

1989 The 14th Dalai Lama (Tenzin Gyatso)

1988 United Nations Peace-keeping Forces

1987 Oscar Arias Sanchez

1986 Elie Wiesel

1985 International Physicians for the Prevention of Nuclear War Inc.

1984 Desmond Mpilo Tutu

1983 Lech Walesa

1982 Alva Myrdal, Alfonso García Robles

1981 Office of the United Nations High Commissioner for Refugees (UNHCR)

1980 Adolfo Pérez Esquivel

1979 Mother Teresa

1978 Mohamed Anwar al-Sadat, Menachem Begin

1977 Amnesty International

1976 Betty Williams, Mairead Corrigan

1975 Andrei Dmitrievich Sakharov

1974 Seán MacBride, Eisaku Sato

1973 Henry A. Kissinger, Le Duc Tho

1972 The prize money for 1972 was allocated to the Main Fund

1971 Willy Brandt

1970 Norman E. Borlaug

1969 International Labour Organization (I.L.O.)

1968 René Cassin

1967 The prize money was with 1/3 allocated to the Main Fund and with 2/3 to the Special Fund of this prize section

1966 The prize money was allocated to the Special Fund of this prize section

1965 United Nations Children's Fund (UNICEF)

1964 Martin Luther King Jr.

1963 Comité international de la Croix Rouge (International Committee of the Red Cross), Ligue des Sociétés de la Croix-Rouge (League of Red Cross Societies)

1962 Linus Carl Pauling

1961 Dag Hjalmar Agne Carl Hammarskjöld

1960 Albert John Lutuli

1959 Philip J. Noel-Baker

1958 Georges Pire

1957 Lester Bowles Pearson

1956 The prize money was with 1/3 allocated to the Main Fund and with 2/3 to the Special Fund of this prize section

1955 The prize money was allocated to the Special Fund of this prize section

1954 Office of the United Nations High Commissioner for Refugees (UNHCR)

1953 George Catlett Marshall

1952 Albert Schweitzer

1951 Léon Jouhaux

1950 Ralph Bunche

1949 Lord (John) Boyd Orr of Brechin

1948 The prize money was with 1/3 allocated to the Main Fund and with 2/3 to the Special Fund of this prize section

1947 Friends Service Council (The Quakers), American Friends Service Committee (The Quakers)

1946 Emily Greene Balch, John Raleigh Mott

1945 Cordell Hull

1944 Comité international de la Croix Rouge (International Committee of the Red Cross)

1943 The prize money was with 1/3 allocated to the Main Fund and with 2/3 to the Special Fund of this prize section

1942 The prize money was with 1/3 allocated to the Main Fund and with 2/3 to the Special Fund of this prize section

1941 The prize money was with 1/3 allocated to the Main Fund and with 2/3 to the Special Fund of this prize section

1940 The prize money was with 1/3 allocated to the Main Fund and with 2/3 to the Special Fund of this prize section

1939 The prize money was with 1/3 allocated to the Main Fund and with 2/3 to the Special Fund of this prize section

1938 Office international Nansen pour les Réfugiés (Nansen International Office for Refugees)

1937 Cecil of Chelwood, Viscount (Lord Edgar Algernon Robert Gascoyne Cecil)

1936 Carlos Saavedra Lamas

1935 Carl von Ossietzky

1934 Arthur Henderson

1933 Sir Norman Angell (Ralph Lane)

1932 The prize money was allocated to the Special Fund of this prize section

1931 Jane Addams, Nicholas Murray Butler

1930 Lars Olof Nathan (Jonathan) Söderblom

1929 Frank Billings Kellogg

1928 The prize money was allocated to the Special Fund of this prize section

1927 Ferdinand Buisson, Ludwig Quidde

1926 Aristide Briand, Gustav Stresemann

1925 Sir Austen Chamberlain, Charles Gates Dawes

1924 The prize money was allocated to the Special Fund of this prize section

1923 The prize money was allocated to the Special Fund of this prize section

1922 Fridtjof Nansen

1921 Karl Hjalmar Branting, Christian Lous Lange

1920 Léon Victor Auguste Bourgeois

1919 Thomas Woodrow Wilson

1918 The prize money was allocated to the Special Fund of this prize section

1917 Comité international de la Croix Rouge (International Committee of the Red Cross)

1916 The prize money was allocated to the Special Fund of this prize section

1915 The prize money was allocated to the Special Fund of this prize section

1914 The prize money was allocated to the Special Fund of this prize section

1913 Henri La Fontaine

1912 Elihu Root

1911 Tobias Michael Carel Asser, Alfred Hermann Fried

1910 Bureau international permanent de la Paix (Permanent International Peace Bureau)

1909 Auguste Marie François Beernaert, Paul Henri Benjamin Balluet, Baron d'Estournelles de Constant de Rebecque

1908 Klas Pontus Arnoldson, Fredrik Bajer

1907 Ernesto Teodoro Moneta, Louis Renault

1906 Theodore Roosevelt

1905 Baroness Bertha Sophie Felicita von Suttner, née Countess Kinsky von Chinic und Tettau

1904 Institut de droit international (Institute of International Law)

1903 William Randal Cremer

1902 Élie Ducommun, Charles Albert Gobat

1901 Jean Henri Dunant, Frédéric Passy

About the Contributors

The Eleanor Roosevelt Institute for Justice and Peace

The Eleanor Roosevelt Institute for Justice and Peace, a (501)(c)(3) not-for-profit organization, commemorates the pioneering contributions of Eleanor Roosevelt to the cause of human rights—as a delegate to the United Nations General Assembly, as chair of the United Nations Human Rights Commission, as one of the drafters of the United Nations Universal Declaration of Human Rights in 1948, and as a symbol of America's dedication to pluralism and justice.

By honoring Eleanor Roosevelt, the Institute acknowledges also America's historical role as a "shining city on the hill"—a nation whose long struggle for political and civil rights has been marked with many successes, both at home and abroad. The Institute is committed to furthering this progress, by addressing the questions of groups' rights and the advancement of political, social, and economic justice worldwide.

The Eleanor Roosevelt Institute for Justice and Peace is grateful to all those who saw our vision of this endeavor and helped make it a reality.

About the Editors

Dr. Nicholas N. Kittrie, KStJ, feudal Lord of Croughton, is former dean and current Distinguished University Professor in Law at the American University in Washington, DC. Nicholas N. Kittrie is Chair of The Eleanor Roosevelt Institute for Justice and Peace, Chair of The United Nations Alliance of NGOs on Crime Prevention and Criminal Justice, and Founder of the American Society of International Law's Interest Group on the Status of Minorities. He is also a member of the Executive Boards of the Section on International Law and the Section on Law and Criminal Justice of the Association of American Law Schools. Former Counsel to the United States Senate Judiciary Committee and former President of the American Society of Criminology, he has served as consultant to governmental and public agencies throughout the world. Kittrie is author of numerous books including *Rebels With A Cause: The Minds and Morality of Political Offenders*; *The War Against Authority: From the Crisis of Legitimacy to a New Social Contract*; *The Tree of Liberty: A Documentary History of Rebellion and Political Crime in America*; and *The Uncertain Future: Gorbachev's Eastern Bloc.*

H.E. Rodrigo Carazo served as president of the Republic of Costa Rica from 1978-1982. During his term as president he reactivated the Treaty of San Jose, which set up an Inter-American Human Rights Court in the Costa Rican capital. He made Costa Rica's foreign policy more universal by establishing relations with African, Asian and Arab nations, sought Latin American solidarity and independence from world political and economic power centers, and defended Costa Rican sovereignty. He founded the international University for Peace in Ciudad Colon, and assumed its presidency after completing his term as Costa Rica's leader. President Carazo continues his role as a distinguished statesman on the world state. In April 1994, he lead a delegation of the Summit Council for World Peace to Pyongyang, North Korea, which met with the late President Kim Il Sung to discuss issues relating to peace and stability on the Korean peninsula. In recognition of his contributions to world peace, he has been honored with numerous peace awards and honorary degrees.

H.E. James R. Mancham, KBE was elected as first president of the Republic of Seychelles on June 28, 1976. Less than one year later, he was overthrown in a coup d'etat while attending the Commonwealth Heads of State Conference. Sir James Mancham is widely known for his distinguished career in the service of his native country and as a worldwide promoter of peace, reconciliation and prosperity. In addition to serving as the founder of the Democratic Party of the Seychelles, Sir James served as an elected member of the legislative assembly and as the country's first Prime Minister. In 1992, he returned to the Republic of the Seychelles where he has served as the leader of the Opposition in the National Assembly. A writer and lecturer on third World development and trade, and an active voice in the Non-aligned Movement, Sir James has received l'Ordre National Française de la Légion d'Honneur and is an Honorary Knight Commander of the Order of the British Empire. His most recent book is *War on America: Seen from the Indian Ocean.*

Foreword Contributor

H.E. Oscar Arias, born in 1941, studied law and economics in his native Costa Rica, the United States, and England. He began his political career in 1970 in the left-wing National Liberation Party and was elected president of Costa Rica in 1986. He immediately set about working for peace in Central America, bringing the leaders of Guatemala, El Salvador, Honduras, and Nicaragua together for negotiations. Arias won the 1987 Nobel Peace Prize for his continuing efforts to foster democracy and peace among his war-torn neighbors. Since leaving office in 1990, he has continued his work through the Arias Foundation for Peace and Human Progress.

Preface Contributor

Jehan Sadat was born in Upper Egypt in 1934 and at the age of sixteen married Anwar Sadat, who later became president of Egypt, received the Nobel Peace Prize, and was assassinated. During the course of their thirty-two year marriage, she earned a bachelor's degree in Arabic language as well as master's and Ph.D. degrees in literature from Cairo University. Dedicated to improving the status of women in Egypt, she established the Talla Society, which trains women in various handicrafts and pays the tuition of nearly one thousand secondary school and university students. The recipient of many public service awards, she has been a professor of international studies at the University of Maryland since 1993.

Article Contributors

Hafsat Abiola founded and runs the Kunirat Initiative for Nigerian Democracy (KIND), which is dedicated to promoting democracy and strengthening civil society in Africa.

Mahnaz Afkhami is a leading proponent of women's rights in the Islamic world. She is president of Women's Learning Partnership and executive director of the Foundation for Iranian Studies.

Ada Aharoni is a peace culture researcher, writer, poet, and lecturer. She writes in English, Hebrew, and French, and has published twenty-five books to date that have been translated into several languages. She believes that culture and literature can help in healing the urgent ailments of our global village, such as war, conflict, famine, and environment. The themes of peace and conflict resolution toward the sustainability of our fragile earth are major ones throughout her works. She taught at the Israel Institute of Technology, Haifa University, and the University of Pennsylvania.

Gordon W. Allport received his Ph.D. in psychology in 1922 from Harvard University. He did further graduate work at Cambridge, the University of Berlin, and the University of Hamburg, and went on to teach in Istanbul, Turkey, at Dartmouth College, and at Harvard as a professor of psychology.

Gordon L. Anderson is Secretary General of Professors World Peace Academy, and editor of *International Journal on World Peace.* He earned his Ph.D. in Philosophy of Religion at Claremont Graduate School. He is editor of *Worldwide State of the Family,* and coeditor of *The Family in Global Transition, Morality and Religion in Liberal Democratic Societies.* He has published numerous articles on religion and society.

Shlomo Avineri, Professor of Political Science and director of the Institute for European Studies at the Hebrew University of Jerusalem, is a visiting scholar at the Carnegie Endowment. He has published widely on comparative politics, including *The Social and Political Thought of Karl Marx*; *Hegel's Theory of the Modern State*; *Israel and the Palestinians*; and *The Making of Modern Zionism: The Intellectual Origins of the Jewish State.*

Edward Azar (1938-1991) was Professor of Government and Politics and Director of the Center for International Studies at the University of Maryland.

Doug Bandow is a Senior Fellow at the CATO Institute, a nationally-syndicated columnist with Copely News Service (USA), and the former editor of *Inquiry* magazine. He formerly served as Special Assistant to U.S. President Reagan.

David P. Barash is Professor of Psychology at the University of Washington, Seattle, and is co-founder and co-director of the Peace and Strategic Studies program there. He is a Fellow of the American Association for the Advancement of Science and of the Center for Advanced Study in the Behavioral Sciences, and has also been a Fellow at the Bellagio Study Center at Lake Como. He as written nearly 200 technical articles and 21 books, which include *Stop Nuclear War! A Handbook*—nominated for the 1982 National Book Award—and *The Caveman and the Bomb* (1985), both co-authored with J. E. Lipton. He is also author of *The Arms Race and Nuclear War* (1986), *Approaches to Peace: A Reader in Peace Studies* (2000), and *Understanding Violence* (2001). *Peace and Conflict Studies* (co-authored with Charles Webel) will be published in 2002.

Peter T. Bauer is Emeritus Professor of Economics at the London School of Economics. Lord Bauer is one of the preeminent thinkers in economic development theory and a member of the House of Lords.

Roy F. Baumeister holds the E.B. Smith Professorship in Liberal Arts at Case Western Reserve University. Since receiving his doctorate in social psychology from Princeton University, he has received numerous fellowships and awards. He has published nearly 150 scientific works and is often cited in the popular media.

James H. Beall is a professor at St. John's College in Annapolis, MD, and a senior consultant to the E.O. Hulburt Center for Space Research at the Naval Research Laboratory in Washington, D.C.

A.C.F. Beales, (1905-1974) M.A. was the leading exponent of Economic History in England. He was a historian, scholar and teacher.

Francis Beer is Professor of Political Science at the University of Colorado. He received his A.B from Harvard University and M.A. and Ph.D. from the University of California, Berkeley. Professor Beer Professor Beer centered his early work on NATO and international alliances, later turning to theory and research on more general processes involved in international violence. His major work is *Peace against War: The Ecology of International Violence.*

Joseph D. Ben-Dak is a research professor at the School of the Future, University of São Paulo. He is also chief scientist for the Xybernaut Corporation.

Berlin Information-center for Transatlantic Security (BITS) is an independent research center working on security and defense policy as well as arms-control and non-proliferation issues. See www.bits.de.

Jean de Bloch (1836-1902) was a banker, railroad tycoon, author and philanthropist. He was an ardent spokesman for controlling the arms race and urged leaders to seek a more rational international order in which to peacefully resolve conflicts. He is the author of a famous six-volume treatise, *The Future of War in its Technical, Political and Economic Relations.* De Bloch is remembered as a "spiritual father" of the First Hague Peace Conference, organizer and founder of the first International Museum of War and Peace in Lucerne and as a nominee in 1901 to the inaugural Nobel Peace Prize

Benazir Bhutto became the first woman to head the government of an Islamic state when she was sworn in as Prime Minister of Pakistan in 1988. In the previous period of political struggle, Bhutto, as leader of the then-opposition Pakistan People's Party, spent nearly six years either in prison or under house arrest.

Kenneth Boulding was Distinguished Professor of Economics, Emeritus, at the University of Colorado. His major interests include: economic theory, grants economics, conflict and peace studies, evolutionary theory, general systems and the study of human knowledge and learning.

Daniel Bradlow is Professor of Law and Director of the International Legal Studies Program at American University, Washington College of Law.

Arnold Brecht (1884-1977) represented Prussia in the German Reichsrat and was a world-recognized political theorist.

C. Delisle Burns (1879-1942) was an eminent British historian and philosopher. He authored and translated many books including *The First Europe: A Study of the Establishment of Medieval Christendom,* A.D. *400-800, Modern Civilization on Trial, Leisure in the Modern World, Political Ideals, Their Nature and Development: An Essay,* and *What to Read on Philosophy.*

John Burton was a Distinguished Jennings Randolph Fellow at the United States Institute of Peace. He was an Australian delegate to the United Nations Charter Conference in 1945, and was appointed Permanent head of the Australian Foreign Office in 1947. He is the author of many books.

George W. Bush is the forty-third President of the United States of America and former governor of the state of Texas.

Joseph A. Camilleri is Professor of International Relations at La Trobe University, Melbourne. He has written a number of important books on foreign policy, international relations theory, security studies, and the Asia-Pacific region. He has been actively involved on issues of security, disarmament and arms control and given evidence to several government inquiries.

April Carter, professor emeritus, taught politics at the University of Lancaster and at Somerville College, Oxford. Her peace movement experience includes being secretary of the Direct Action Committee Against Nuclear War from 1958-1961.

Jimmy Carter, 2002 Nobel Peace Laureate, served as the thirty-ninth President of the United States from 1977 to 1981. After leaving the White House, President Carter and his wife founded the Atlanta-based Carter Center, a nonprofit organization that works to promote peace, democracy, and human rights.

Nazli Choucri is Professor of Political Science at the Massachusetts Institute of Technology. Her major areas of interest are international politics and the global environment (with a focus on conflict among nations), and international political economy. She has worked extensively on resource and technology issues with particular reference to the world energy markets and technology exchanges and collaboration.

A. Chung-in Moon is Professor of Political Science at Yonsei University in Korea. His areas of expertise are APEC, ASEAN, East Asia and GATT/WTO.

Bill Clinton was the forty-second President of the United States and former governor of the state of Arkansas.

Richard Clutterbuck was a soldier for thirty-five years and retired as a Major General in 1972. From 1972–1983 he was a lecturer and Reader in Political Conflict at the University of Exeter. He lectures on political violence to the police, business and other audiences.

Nat Colletta was founding manager of the World Bank's post-conflict unit and senior spokesperson for the Bank on reconstruction and peace building in societies emerging from violent conflict. He is currently Co-Director of the Institute for Peacebuilding and Development, and Research Professor of International Relations, at George Washington University.

Walker Connor is Distinguished Visiting Professor of Political Science at Middlebury College, Vermont. He has held resident appointments at Harvard, Dartmouth, the Woodrow Wilson International Center for Scholars, Oxford, Cambridge, Bellagio, Warsaw, Singapore and Budapest. He has published over fifty articles and five books dealing with the comparative study of nationalism.

Mairead Corrigan Maguire co-founded Peace People, a pioneering organization in the movement to end sectarian violence in Northern Ireland. She and her co-founders shared the 1976 Nobel Peace Prize for their work.

Walter Cronkite helped start the *CBS Evening News* in 1962 and anchored its half-hour broadcast until he retired in 1981. Throughout his long career, he was regarded as an objective and moderate reporter of the divisive news made by such events as presidential politics, the Vietnam War, and Watergate.

Ralf Dahrendorf is an internationally known sociologist and politician. He was a professor in Hamburg, Tübingen, Konstanz, the University of Oxford, and the London School of Economics. Lord Dahrendorf was a member of the Bundestag and federal state parliament, parliamentary undersecretary of state in the Foreign Office, European Union commissioner in Brussels and, since 1993, a member of the House of Lords.

Daniel Deudney is Professor of Political Science at Johns Hopkins University, Maryland.

Tony Devine is Vice President of the International Educational Foundation, an organization promoting holistic character education. Holder of a Masters in Education, in the late 1980s he developed and directed international exchange programs between the former Soviet Union and the United States.

Michael Dobkowski is Professor of Religious Studies at Hobart and William Smith Colleges. He has authored several books including *The Politics of Indifference: Documentary History of Holocaust Victims in America*, and *Jewish American Voluntary Organizations*. Among the books he co-edited are *The Coming Age of Scarcity* and the forthcoming, *On the Edge of Scarcity*.

Nigel Dower was Senior Lecturer in the Department of Philosophy, Politics and International Relations in the University of Aberdeen.

Jean Bethke Elshtain is the Laura Spelman Rockefeller Professor of Social and Political Ethics at the University of Chicago. She has also taught at Vanderbilt University, Harvard, and Yale Universities, the University of Massachusetts, and Oberlin College.

H.J. Eysenck was Director of the Psychology Department at the Institute of Psychiatry, Maudsley Hospital, London.

Richard Falk was a member of the Princeton faculty from 1961 until his retirement in 2001. He was the Albert G. Milbank Professor of International Law and Practice at Princeton since 1965. He will be teaching in 2002 in the Global Studies Program at the University of California at Santa Barbara. His most recent books are *Predatory Globalization: A Critique* (1999); *Human Rights Horizons* (2000); and *Religion and Humane Global Governance* (2001). He serves on various editorial boards including that of *The Nation* and *The American Journal of International Law*.

William Felice is Professor of Political Science at Eckerd College.

Ann M. Florini is Senior Associate at the Carnegie Endowment for International Peace, where she directs the Projects on Transparency and Transnational Civil Society. She has been associated with UCLA, the Brookings Institution, the Rockefeller Brothers Fund, and the United Nations Association of the USA. She is currently completing a book on transnational governance.

Sigmund Freud (1856-1937) was a physiologist, medical doctor and psychologist. Regarded as the father of psychoanalysis, Freud not only laid the groundwork for all the multiple manifestations of psychoanalysis as it exists today, but his innovations regarding the implicit symbolic significance of human actions, dreams, and even cultural artifacts have shaped a wide variety of fields, including anthropology, semiotics, and artistic creativity and appreciation in addition to psychology.

Nathan C. Funk is Assistant Professor of International Relations at the American University School of International Service. His areas of specialization include peace and conflict resolution, Islam, and Middle Eastern politics and culture. He co-edited *Peace and Conflict Resolution in Islam: Precept and Practice*.

Johan Galtung founded both the International Peace Research Institute (Oslo) and the *Journal of Peace Research*. He is the author of six volumes *Essays in Peace* and many other works. He has held numerous professorial posts around the world. In 1987 he received the Right Livelihood Award and had been a nominee for the Nobel Peace Prize for his contribution to peace research.

William R. Garrett is Professor of Sociology and Chair at St. Michael's College in Colchester, Vermont, where he has taught since 1968. He is the author of *Seasons of Marriage and Family Life* (1982), edited *Social Consequences of Religious Belief* (1989), co-edited with Roland Robertson, *Religion and Global Order* (1991), and has written over 80 papers, book chapters and journal articles on topics ranging from religion, to social theory, family life, and globalization theory.

Tor Ragnor Gerholm is Emeritus Professor of Physics at the University of Stockholm. He has published over 80 scientific papers, reports and monographs including, *Physics and Man*, *Future Tense*, *Why Nuclear Power?*, and co-authored the World Energy Conference's Conservation Commission report, *World Energy: Looking Ahead to 2020.*

Allan Gerson is Co-Director of the Institute for Peacebuilding and Development, and Research Professor of International Relations, at George Washington University. He has taught and lectured widely on various aspects of international law and has served as a Senior Fellow for International Law and Organizations at the Council on Foreign Relations. His publications include *The Price of Terror: The History Making Struggle for Justice After Pan Am 103* and *The Kirkpatrick Mission: Diplomacy Without Apology—America at the United Nations, 1981–1985.*

Alan Gilbert is John Evans Professor at the Graduate School of International Studies of the University of Denver. He has published *Marx's Politics: Communists and Citizens* (1981), *Democratic Individuality* (1990) and *Must Global Politics Constrain Democracy? Great-power Realism, Democratic Peace and Democratic Internationalism* (1999).

Marc Gopin is a consultant and trainer in conflict resolution, with a specialty in the relationship between religion, culture, war, and conflict, particularly as it pertains to the Middle East. Gopin is a Visiting Associate Professor of International Diplomacy at the Fletcher School for Law and Diplomacy of Tufts University, and a Senior Researcher in its Institute for Human Security. He is also a Senior Associate in the Preventive Diplomacy Program of the Center for Strategic and International Studies, Washington, D.C. He is the author of *Between Eden and Armageddon: the Future of World Religions, Violence and Peacemaking* (2000), and *Holy War, Holy Peace: Moving the Abrahamic Traditions Toward Peacemaking in the Palestinian/Israeli Conflict* (2002).

Amalendu Guha is head of the Institute for Alternative Development Research in Norway. Dr. Guha's area of expertise is in the Gandhian concept of nonviolent peace, the concept of human and natural ecology and ecology-based economic development.

Ted Robert Gurr is Distinguished University Professor at the University of Maryland, College Park, where he directs the Minorities at Risk project, which tracks the political status and activities of more than 300 communal groups worldwide. He has written or edited twenty other books and monographs including the award-winning *Why Men Rebel* and, most recently co-authored, *Peace and Conflict 2001: A Global Survey of Armed Conflicts, Self-Determination Movements, and Democracy.* Professor Gurr was president of the International Studies Association, held the Swedish government's Olaf Palme Visiting Professorship at the University of Uppsala, and was senior consultant to the U.S. Government's State Failure Task Force.

Nadja Halilbegovich gained international recognition for her diaries of life in wartime Bosnia, during which time she hosted a national radio show and performed in internationally broadcast solo and choir performances. She speaks to and performs choral concerts for audiences throughout North America and Europe.

Hurst Hannum is Professor of International Law at The Fletcher School of Law and Diplomacy, Tufts University, where he has taught courses in international organizations, international human rights law, peacekeeping, and nationalism and ethnicity. He has been particularly concerned with minority rights and self-determination issues and has served as a legal consultant to the UN Office of the High Commissioner for Human Rights, the Henry Dunant Centre for Humanitarian Dialogue in negotiations between the Free Aceh Movement and the Indonesian government, and the governments of the United States and the Faroe Islands on issues of autonomy and political status. Professor Hannum is author of *Autonomy, Sovereignty, and Self Determination: The Accommodation of Conflicting Rights*, and editor of *Guide to International Human Rights Practice*.

Josephine Hauer co-founded Bridgeport Hope School in Connecticut and has been Academic Dean of a high school specializing in moral education since 1997. She has taught English, Social Studies and Ethics at the high school level. Dr. Hauer frequently consults with both public and private schools on character-based program development, teacher training and curriculum infusion both locally and abroad.

Llewellyn D. Howell is Director of International Executive MBA Programs at the University of Hawaii at Manoa and International Affairs editor for *USA Today Magazine*. He has also taught at American University, and Thunderbird—The American Graduate School of International Management. He has been employed by the Peace Corps, U.S. Department of State and the U.S. Department of Defense. He is the author/editor of four books and has written more than 100 book chapters and journal articles.

Michael H. Hunt, Everett H. Emerson Professor of History at the University of North Carolina at Chapel Hill, writes and teaches in the general field of international history. His research and teaching interests are in U.S. foreign relations, the Cold War in Asia, the Vietnam War, and the post-1945 world.

Samuel P. Huntington is the Albert J. Weatherhead III University Professor at Harvard University, where he is also the director of the John M. Olin Institute for Strategic Studies and the chairman of the Harvard Academy for International and Area Studies. He was the director of security planning for the National Security Council in the Carter administration, the founder and co-editor of *Foreign Policy*, and the president of the American Political Science Association. He has authored many books and scholarly publications, including the bestseller, *The Clash of Civilizations?*

Immanuel Kant (1724-1804) was a noted German philosopher. His most original contribution to philosophy was his "Copernian Revolution." His works included *General Natural History and Theory of the Heavens*, *Critique of Pure Reason*, *Critique of Practical Reason*, *Critique of Judgment*, and *Logic*.

Majid Khadduri is Professor and Director of Middle East Studies at Johns Hopkins University School of Advanced International Studies. His areas of expertise include the Middle East, Persian Gulf, Iran, Iraq, OPEC, and international relations.

Kim Kyong-Dong received his Ph.D. from Cornell University. He has taught at North Carolina State University, Duke University and I'Ecome des Hautes Etudes en Sciences Sociales in Paris. He is currently Professor of Sociology at SNU and Chair of the Korea Information Society Association and the Civil Society Forum. He has published in the fields of development studies and industrial sociology.

Charles King is an assistant professor in the School of Foreign Service and the Department of Government at Georgetown University, where he also holds the university's Ion Ratiu Chair of Romanian Studies.

Nicholas D. Kristof is a columnist for the *New York Times*. Previously, he was associate managing editor for the Sunday Edition. Mr. Kristof joined the *New York Times* initially to cover economics. Subsequently, he served as a business correspondent based in Los Angeles, Hong Kong bureau chief, Beijing bureau chief and Tokyo bureau chief. Mr. Kristof and his wife,

Sheryl WuDunn, jointly won a Pulitzer Prize for their coverage of the Tiananmen Square democracy movement in China.

Hans Küng, Emeritus Director of the Institute of Ecumenical Research at the University of Tübingen, is an authority on world religions and their impact on society.

Lynn M. Kunkle is getting her Ph.D in International Relations at American University with a focus on Christian-Muslim relations.

Deepak Lal is the James S. Coleman Professor of International Development Studies at the University of California, Los Angeles. He is the author of several books and numerous scholarly articles. His most recent book is *Unintended Consequences: The Impact of Factor Endowments, Culture, and Politics on Long-Run Economic Performance.*

Malvern Lumsden currently works at UNESCO. He is a former Senior Research fellow at the International Peace Research Institute in Oslo, Norway and co-editor of the *Journal of Peace Research.*

Edward N. Luttwak is Senior Fellow of Preventive Diplomacy at the Center for Strategic and International Studies. He is an internationally recognized authority on geoeconomics and strategy. Dr. Luttwak has served as a consultant to the Office of the Secretary of Defense, the National Security Council, and the U.S. Department of State.

Enrique Martínez has a Ph.D. in comparative literature from the University of Melbourne. He is an assistant editor of *Australian Multicultural Book Review* and had been published in India and Australia. His research interests include multiculturalism; Chinese, French, Spanish and English Literature. He is co-editor of *No Fences Make Better Neighbors.*

Margaret Mead (1901-1978) was one of the most famous anthropologists in the world. She believed that anthropology was a way to bring new understandings of human behavior to bear on the future. While Dr. Mead taught at several different institutions, her research base was the American Museum of Natural History in New York City. During her life, she authored and coauthored approximately forty books. She was awarded the Presidential Medal of Freedom posthumously in 1978.

Mary Midgley was a professional philosopher. Formerly Senior Lecturer in Philosophy at the University of Newcastle-on-Tyne, her books include *Beast and Man*, *Wickedness, Animals and Why They Matter* and (with Judith Hughes) *Women's Choices.*

Saibal Mitra is Assistant Professor of Physics at the University of Tulsa, Oklahoma.

James H. Mittelman is Professor in the School of International Service at American University, Washington, DC. Previously, he held the Pok Rafeah Chair in International Studies and served as Distinguished Visiting Professor at the National University of Malaysia. Mittelman's most recent books are *The Globalization Syndrome: Transformation and Resistance* (2000), and as coeditor, *Capturing Globalization* (2001).

Michael E. O'Hanlon is a Senior Fellow of Foreign Policy Studies at the Brookings Institution. His areas of expertise include Arms treaties, Asian security issues, civil warfare, European security issues, military technology, missile defense, peacekeeping operations, U.S. defense strategy and budget. His books include *Defense Policy Choices for the Bush Administration, 2001-2005, Defending America: The Case for Limited National Missile Defense, Winning Ugly: NATO's War to Save Kosovo, Technological Change and the Future of Warfare,* and *How To Be a Cheap Hawk: The 1999 and 2000 Defense Budgets.*

Leif Ohlsson is a peace and development researcher at Goteborg University, Sweden. He has done reports on the relation between environmental and social resource scarcities for the FAO and for Sida, the Swedish International Development Cooperation Agency, and is a member of the Swedish Foreign Office research forum for conflict prevention. He edits the electronic newsletter "Environment, Development and Conflict—EDC News" for Sida.

William J. O'Malley, a Catholic priest, is a member of the Society of Jesus.

Chantal de Jonge Oudraat is a Robert Bosch Fellow at the American Institute for Contemporary German Studies, John Hopkins University; Adjunct Professor at the Edmund A. Walsh School of Foreign Service, Georgetown University; and Vice President of Women in International Security (WIIS). She has written widely on arms control, economic sanctions, the use of force, peacekeeping and the United Nations. She is the co-editor of *Managing Global Issues: Lessons Learned* (Carnegie Endowment for International Peace, 2001).

Minxin Pei is currently a Senior Associate at the Carnegie Endowment for International Peace. His main interest is the development of democratic political systems, the politics of economic reform, the growth of civil society, and legal institutions. Dr. Pei was an Assistant Professor in the Department of Politics at Princeton University, where he taught East Asian politics and international relations. Dr. Pei is the author of a book on Chinese and Soviet reforms, titled *From Reform to Revolution: The Demise of Communism in China and the Soviet Union.*

Gary R. Perlstein is Professor of Administration of Justice at Portland State University. His research interests include domestic and international terrorism. He is the author of "The Mercenary as Social Bandit," in *International Journal of Offender Therapy and Comparative Criminology*, "Defining Terrorism," in *Jane's Defence Weekly*, and *Perspectives on Terrorism.*

Alexander A. Pikayev is a Co-Chair of WMD Non-Proliferation Program at the Carnegie Moscow Center and Editor-in-Chief of Nuclear Proliferation Journal. Simultaneously, he holds a position of Director of Department for Disarmament Studies at the Institute of World Economy and International Relations (IMEMO) (Moscow, Russia), and advises the Defense Committee of the Russian Duma. Pikayev is author of numerous monographs and articles, among them: *The Rise and Fall of START II*, and *Russia, the US and the Missile Technology Control Regime.*

Emily Plumb is an international programs specialist at the National Aeronautics and Space Administration (NASA). She holds a Masters in Foreign Service from the Edmund A. Walsh School of Foreign Service at Georgetown University. She was a 2000 David L. Boren National Security Education Program Graduate Fellow, studying grassroots peacebuilding techniques in Eastern Africa.

Adamantia Pollis has researched and written extensively in the fields of human rights, nationalism and ethnicity and Greece and Cyprus Among her recent publications are *Human Rights: New Perspectives, New Realities,* co-edited with Peter Schwab (2000); and "Are there Human Rights in Ethnonational States" in *International and National Law in Russia and Eastern Europe*, (2001). She is currently researching the impact of globalization on human rights and its role in ethnic conflict.

Clara Portela is an external consultant at the Berlin Information-center for Transatlantic Security (BITS). She was a trainee at the Delegation of the European Commission to the United Nations in New York and at the Assembly of Western European Union in Paris. Her areas of expertise include the European Union, in particular the Common Foreign and Security Policy (CFSP), Western European Union, NATO-Russia relations, questions of public international law relevant to security, and crisis management and prevention.

Colin Powell served as the highest-ranking African-

American military officer in the United States' history. After serving in high-level positions in three presidential administrations, to include national security advisor and Chairman of the Joint Chiefs of Staff, Powell retired from the army in 1993. He re-entered government service under George W. Bush as U.S. Secretary of State.

John Prendergast is the Co-Director of the Africa Program of the International Crisis Group (ICG). He formerly worked as the Special Advisor on African conflicts at the State Department and the Director of African Affairs at the National Security Council. Before that, he worked for a variety of NGOs on issues of peace, human rights, and humanitarian assistance in Africa. He is the author of five books on Africa, including ICG's forthcoming book on *Sudan, Sudan After 11 September: Shifting Prospects for Peace.*

Carol Rittner, R.S.M., a Sister of Mercy, is Distinguished Professor of Holocaust Studies at The Richard Stockton College of New Jersey. She is the author or editor of numerous books and essays, including *The Courage to Care: Rescuers of Jews during the Holocaust* (with Sondra Myers, 1986); *Different Voices: Women and the Holocaust* (with John K. Roth, 1993); *The Holocaust and the Christian World* (with Stephen Smith and Irena Steinfeldt, 2000); and *"Good News" after Auschwitz" Christian Faith within a Post-Holocaust* (with John K. Roth, 2001).

Eleanor Roosevelt (1884-1962) was First Lady of the United States from 1932 to 1945. She was one of the most active reformers for women's rights, education and welfare reform. Mrs. Roosevelt was very active in the Democratic Party throughout her life. She served as assistant director of the Office of Civilian Defense, was a delegate to the UN Assembly, chairperson of the UN Commission on Human Rights, where she was instrumental in drafting the UN Declaration of Human Rights, US representative to the UN General Assembly and chairperson of the American UN Association.

John K. Roth is the Russell K. Pitzer Professor of Philosophy at Claremont McKenna College. A specialist in American philosophy and religion, he has been Fulbright lecturer in American studies at the University of Innsbruck, Austria

R.J. Rummel is Professor of Political Science Emeritusat the University of Hawaii. He was nominated for the 1996 Nobel Peace Prize. His areas of expertise include the causes and conditions of collective violence and war with a view toward seeking their resolution or elimination.

Bruce M. Russett is Dean Acheson Professor of International Relations and Political Science at Yale and Director of Yale University's Program in United Nations Studies. He is also editor of *Journal of Conflict Resolution.*

Abdul Aziz Said is the Mohammed Said Farsi Professor of Islamic Peace and Director of the Center for Global Peace at American University School of International Service. Dr. Said was a member of the White House Commission on the Islamic World during the Carter Administration, served as a consultant to the U.S. Information Agency and Department of State, and played an active role in Arab-Israeli dialogues. His work, *Concepts of International Politics in Global Perspective*, is now in its fourth edition.

Michael E. Salla is a lecturer in political science at the Australian National University. His areas of expertise include peace studies, ethnic/religious conflict, nonviolence and international relations.

June Saunders is Co-founder and Vice-chair of the Bridgeport Hope School and author of *Boundless as the Sea: A Guide to Family Love.* Ms. Saunders is particularly concerned with issues of marriage, family and character, and the moral impact of literature on young readers.

Harold H. Saunders is Director of International Affairs at the Kettering Foundation, where he conducts sustained non-official dialogue among those in deep-rooted human conflict. He co-chairs the Dartmouth Conference Regional Conflicts Task Force and the Inter-Tajik Dialogue. He served for 20 years on the National Security Council staff and in the State Department, last as Assistant Secretary of State for Near Eastern and South Asian Affairs. He helped draft the Camp David accords and the Egyptian-Israeli peace treaty. He received the President's Award for Federal Civilian Service, and the State Department's Distinguished Honor Award. He is author *of The Other Walls: The Arab Israeli Peace Process in a Global Perspective* and of *A Public Peace Process: Sustained Dialogue to Transform Racial and Ethnic Conflicts.*

William A. Schabas holds the Chair in Human Rights law at the National University of Ireland, Galway, where he is director of the Irish Centre for Human Rights. He is the author of several books in the field of international human rights law, including *The Abolition of the Death Penalty in International Law* (1997), *Genocide in International Law* (2000) and *Introduction to the International Criminal Court* (2001), as well as more than 100 articles in academic journals. He frequently acts as a consultant on human rights issues for international governmental organisations and non-governmental organisations.

Michael P. Scharf is Professor of Law and Director of the Center for International Law and Policy at New England School of Law. During the Bush and Clinton Administrations, he served in the Office of the Legal Adviser of the U.S. Department of State, where he held the positions of Counsel to the Counter-Terrorism Bureau, Attorney-Adviser for Law Enforcement and Intelligence, Attorney-Adviser for United Nations Affairs, and delegate to the United Nations General Assembly and to the United Nations Human Rights Commission. Scharf's publications include *Balkan Justice* which was nominated for the Pulitzer Prize in 1998, *The International Criminal Tribunal for Rwanda*, and casebooks on *The Law of International Organizations*, and *International Criminal Law.*

John D. Shilling has worked as a professor of economic development, an advisor to governments, and as a senior official at the World Bank.

P.J. Simmons is an Associate at the Carnegie Endowment for International Peace, where he co-directs the project on Managing Global Issues. Previously, he was founding director of the Environmental Change and Security Project at the Woodrow Wilson International Center for Scholars. He worked at the National Security Council's directorate on Global Environmental Affairs and at the National Security Archives. He was a Fulbright Scholar in Yugoslavia and is a term member of the Council on Foreign Relations. His publications include *Managing Global Issues: Lessons Learned*, co-edited with de Jonge Oudraat (2001).

Isidore Singer was born in Weisskirchen, Moravia in 1859. He studied at the Universities of Vienna and Berlin, receiving his Ph.D. in 1884. In 1884-1885 he founded and published the *Allgemeine Oesterreichische Literaturzeitung.* Following his first experience in publishing, Singer became a literary secretary to Count Alexandre Foucher de Careil, French Ambassador at Vienna. Moving to Paris, Singer joined the press bureau of the French Foreign Office, and became editor-in-chief of *La Vraie* Parole in 1893-1894, a journal which he founded in order to counteract anti-Semitism. Within the pages of *La Vraie Parole* Singer staunchly defended Alfred Dreyfus. In 1895, Singer immigrated to the United States in order to publish a Jewish encyclopedia. He became the managing editor of the encyclopedia, raising money for its publication, finding a publisher, enlisting scholars to contribute articles, and serving as head of the department of modern biography. The first volume of the *Jewish Encyclopedia* was published in 1901 and the final volume appeared in 1906.

Huston Smith is Professor of Religion, Emeritus, at Syracuse University. He has also taught at the Massachusetts Institute of Technology and Washington University in St. Louis. His special field is comparative philosophy and religion.

Gene B. Sperling, President Clinton's national economic adviser and director of the National Economic Council (NEC), is a Visiting Fellow at the Brookings Institution. Mr. Sperling's areas of interest include economic and fiscal issues and universal education in the world's poorest countries, particularly Africa.

Herbert Spinden received his Ph.D. in Anthropology from Harvard University. He worked at the American Museum of Natural History and at the American Indian Art and Primitive Cultures Museum at the Brooklyn Institute. He was a lecturer at universities in Peru, Chile, and Argentina. Some of his principle writings include Ancient Civilizations of Mexico and Central America, The Reduction of Maya Dates, Origin of Civilizations in Central America and Mexico, and The Study of Maya Art: Its Subject Matter and Historical Development.

Marcelo M. Suárez-Orozco is the Victor S. Thomas Professor of Education at Harvard, and co-Director of the Harvard Immigration Projects. He is author of over eighty scholarly essays and seventeen books and edited volumes, the most recent of which are *Children of Immigration* (with C. Suárez-Orozco, 2001), *Cultures Under Siege: Collective Violence and Trauma* (co-edited with A.C.G.M. Robben, (2000), and the seven-volume opus entitled *Interdisciplinary Perspectives on the New Immigration* (co-edited with C. Suárez-Orozco and D. Qin-Hilliard (2001).

Ralph Summy is Senior Lecturer in Political Science at the University of Queensland, and co-ordinates the Peace and Conflict Studies (PACS) program. He co-founded and continues to serve on the editorial collective of *Social Alternatives.* His research interests focus on nonviolent politics and the Australian peace movement.

Sun Tzu (circa 500 B.C.) was a Chinese philosopher and general. He is the reputed author of the Chinese classic *Ping-fa* (*The Art of War*), the earliest known treatise on war and military science.

Keith Suter lectures in politics at the University of Sydney and directs an Australian-based national goals think-tank. He has held executive positions in the United Nations Association of Australia and Friends of the Earth. He holds two doctorates, one on guerilla warfare and the other on the arms race.

Bernard Swan initiated the Peace Studies program at the University of New England, and gives a course on the Geography of Peace and Conflict. His degrees are from the University of Ceylon, University of London, and the University of Sussex.

Ray Takeyh is Soref Research Fellow at the Washington Institute for Near East Policy and the author of *The Receding Shadow of the Prophet: Radical Islamic Movements in the Modern Middle East.*

Majid Tehranian has a doctorate in political economy and government from Harvard University and currently teaches international communication at the Toda Institute for Global Peace and Policy Research, University of Hawaii at Manoa.

Alvin Toffler served as a visiting scholar at the Russell Sage Foundation, a visiting professor at Cornell University, a faculty member of the New School for Social Research, a White House Correspondent, an editor of *Fortune* magazine, and a business consultant.

Heidi Toffler is on the advisory council of the Center for Global Communications in Tokyo and the scientific committee of the Piu Foundation in Italy. She holds an honorary degree in law and has been awarded the medal of the President of the Italian Republic for her contributions to social thought. Both Tofflers are Distinguished Adjunct Professors at the National Defense University in Washington.

Walter Tenetto received his Ph.D. from the University of Queensland in poetry and aesthetics. His areas of expertise include European and American literatures; new literatures in English, and exile and protest literature.

Sanford Ungar is President of Goucher College in Baltimore, Maryland. A veteran journalist, he has been a staff writer for the *Washington Post*, managing editor of *Foreign Policy* magazine, and host of "All Things Considered" on National Public Radio. He was dean of the School of Communication at American University and former director of the Voice of America. He is the author or editor of six non-fiction books, including *The Papers & the Papers: An Account of the Legal and Political Battle over the Pentagon Papers*, *FBI: An Uncensored Look behind the Walls*, and *Africa: The People and Politics of an Emerging Continent.*

Union of Concerned Scientists (UCS) is an independent non-profit alliance of 50,000 concerned citizens and scientists. UCS was founded in 1969 by faculty members and students at the Massachusetts Institute of Technology who were concerned about the misuse of science and technology in society.

Albert J. Venter is Professor in the Department of Political Studies at the Rand Afrikaans University, Johannesburg, South Africa. He is Guest Professor at The South African Defence College, The Naval Staff College, and The Foreign Service Institute, Potchefstroom University. Among his publications are: *South African Government and Politics* (1989), and *The Government and Politics of the New South Africa* (2001). He has published over eighty articles in professional journals and contributed to books on political science.

Harold J. Vetter is Professor in the Administration of Justice Department at Portland State University. His published books include *Theoretical Approaches to Personality*, *Crime and Justice in America* and *Criminology and Crime.*

Carl von Clausewitz (1780-1893) was a Prussian soldier and intellectual. His book, *On War* (in German, *Vom Kriege*) has been translated into almost every language and is the most influential work on military philosophy and strategy in the Western world. Clausewitz's theories are descriptive of the nature of human-on-human strategic problems allowing the reader to develop his own strategic judgment as it relates to the current strategic environment.

Walter L. Wallace, Professor Emeritus of Sociology, Princeton University is author of *A Darwinian Theory of Ethnicity, 'Race,' and Nationality* (2000); *The Future of Ethnicity, Race, and Nationality* (1997), among other works.

Ingrid Washinawatok el-Issa, born into the Menominee nation in Wisconsin (USA), worked with many organizations to promote indigenous people's culture and rights. As executive director of the Fund for Four Directions in New York City, she worked in particular to revitalize indigenous languages. Washinawatok was one of three Americans kidnapped and executed by rebels in the remote highlands of Colombia while she was one a mission to help the U'wa tribe set up a school system in February 1999.

Spencer Weart is the Director of the Center for History of Physics at the American Institute of Physics. His area of specialization is the history of modern physics.

Erich Weede earned his Ph.D. in political science from the University of Mannheim in 1970 and has since taught as a professor for sociology at the University of Cologne and in Bonn. His research interests include comparative analyses of economic growth, income distribution and force susceptibility, both for western industrial companies and for developing countries, as well as war prevention.

Thomas G. Weiss is Presidential Professor at The Graduate Center of The City University of New York, where he is co-director of the United Nations Intellectual History Project and an editor of *Global Governance*. He served as the Executive Director of the Academic Council on the UN System, and co-directed the Humanitarianism and War Project. His latest book is *Military-Civilian Interactions: Intervening in Humanitarian Crises.*

Paul R. Williams is Assistant Professor of Law and International Relations at the American University, where he holds a joint appointment in the School of International Service and the Washington College of Law. Williams served on the Kosovar delegation to the Rambouillet/Paris Peace Talks; the Bosnian delegation to the Dayton Peace Negotiations; advised the President of Estonia on territorial negotiations with Russia, and established a program to provide legal assistance to the International Criminal Tribunals for the Former Yugoslavia and Rwanda. He is the author of a book on the role of international law in the resolution of Central and East European trans-boundary environmental disputes.

Sheldon S. Wolin was Professor of Politics at Princeton University. He also taught at the University of California, Berkeley. His book, *Politics and Vision: Continuity and Innovation in Western Politics* influenced a great number of political theorists.

Wold Health Organization was founded in 1948. A specialized agency of the United Nations, with 191 member states, who promote technical cooperation for health among the various nations, carries out programs to control and eradicate disease and strives to improve the quality of human life.

Nigel Young has been as author, lecturer, and practitioner in peace studies for over three decades. He has been director and deputy director of peace study programs as Bradford University (UK) and Colgate (USA).

Gerardo Zampaglione (1917-1996) was with the Italian Foreign service for more than 40 years. He served as Ambassador to Kuwait, Pakistan, Switzerland, and Indonesia. A graduate in Law and Political Science at the University of Rome, he published extensively on international relations, peace studies, and European integration. His books included *Italy, The Idea of Peace in Antiquity*, and the first history of Kuwait.